THE
# WISDEN
BOOK OF
# CRICKET
# RECORDS

To the memory of
Denys Heesom
Alfred Wagg
and
Michael Fordham

# THE
# WISDEN
## BOOK OF
# CRICKET
# RECORDS

## Compiled and edited by
## BILL FRINDALL

Macdonald
Queen Anne Press

A *Queen Anne Press* BOOK

© W. H. Frindall 1986

First published in Great Britain in 1986 by
Queen Anne Press, a division of
Macdonald & Co (Publishers) Ltd
3rd Floor
Greater London House
Hampstead Road
London NW1 7QX

A BPCC plc Company

British Library Cataloguing in Publication Data

Frindall, Bill
    The Wisden book of cricket records.——2nd ed.——
    (Wisden library)
    1. Cricket——Records
    I. Title    II. Series
    796.35′8′09    GV925

    ISBN 0-356-10736-1

Phototypeset by Tradespools Limited, Frome, Somerset
Printed and bound in Great Britain by Hazell, Watson and Viney
Limited,
Member of the BPCC Group,
Aylesbury, Bucks

# CONTENTS

## INDIVIDUAL RECORDS – BATTING

## INDIVIDUAL RECORDS – BOWLING

## INDIVIDUAL RECORDS – ALL-ROUND PERFORMANCES

## INDIVIDUAL RECORDS – WICKET-KEEPING

## INDIVIDUAL RECORDS – FIELDING

## TOURING TEAM RECORDS

## TEST MATCH RECORDS 1876–77 to 1985

## TEAM RECORDS

## INDIVIDUAL RECORDS – BATTING

# INDIVIDUAL RECORDS – BOWLING

# INDIVIDUAL RECORDS – WICKET-KEEPING

## INDIVIDUAL RECORDS – FIELDING

## INDIVIDUAL RECORDS – ALL-ROUND PERFORMANCES

## INDIVIDUAL RECORDS – THE CAPTAINS

## INDIVIDUAL RECORDS – GENERAL

## INDIVIDUAL CAREER RECORDS

## UMPIRES' RECORDS

# FOREWORD

It is not by chance that in the quarter of a century since it was first published, the *Guinness Book of Records* has sold forty million copies. In that time the Bible, the best of all best-sellers, has beaten it, as has the red-covered booklet, *Quotations from the Works of Mao Tse-tung*, which for something like eight hundred million Chinese was by way of being a compulsory purchase. But the Guinness book has had a remarkable run – because, whether for the wide-eyed child or the cricketer who has played in dozens of Test matches, records have an endless fascination.

In February 1968, after Fred Titmus had been carried out of the sea in Barbados with four fewer toes than when he had entered it, I had an evening caller at my hotel room. There, putting his head round the door, was Pat Pocock. 'Do you have a *Wisden?*' he asked. 'Yes', I said, 'and I know why you want one.' It was, of course, to look up the records of all the great off-spinners in Test history. With Titmus *hors de combat*, Pocock was to play next day in his first Test match – and to bowl very well.

'You have a job I greatly covet', I was told many years ago by the Regius Professor of Greek in the University of Oxford and the author of such learned works as *The Justice of Zeus* and *Myths of the Zodiac*. Thinking that he must have mistaken me for someone else, I broke the news to him that I was merely the cricket correspondent of *The Times*. 'I know', he said. 'What a *wonderful* life.' Whereupon, having revealed his lifelong passion for cricket, he asked me his favourite conundrum, which was to name a Chinaman, a Greek and a one-eyed Norwegian who had played Test cricket. The Chinaman (Ellis Achong) was easy. So was the Greek (Xenophon Balaskas). The one-eyed Norwegian floored me – as, soon afterwards, it floored Roy Webber, the best-known of Bill Frindall's many forerunners. The answer, by the way, is 'Buster' Nupen.

Only recently a ten-year-old boy wrote to me to say that he had just thrown a cricket ball more than fifty yards. What, please, was the world record? It used to surprise me, in fact, that no one had ever surpassed the one hundred and forty yards two feet of Robert Percival on the Durham Sands Racecourse in 1884, until some of the most prodigious throwers of modern times had a go at doing so on the Sandown Park Racecourse in 1975. Not even Keith Boyce, who had always looked to me as though he could have thrown in from the Pavilion End at the Oval to the Nursery End at Lord's, got to within thirty yards of the record. Percival, it seems, was a freak.

For a host of cricket-lovers, of all types and ages, this latest book of Bill's will satisfy many a curiosity. For me, together with the Almanack, *Wisden* itself, and *The Wisden Book of Test Cricket* (another of Bill's) it will be a valuable work of reference. By its very nature it can never be up to date, which is why cricket statisticians always have something to do. Although some records are virtually impregnable, others are certainly not.

Because of the changing structure of the game I doubt whether anyone will ever again score 3000 runs in an English season, let alone approach the 3816 which Denis Compton lavished upon an adoring public in 1947. At the same time you may be fairly sure that one day we shall hear from India or Pakistan that Hanif Mohammad's individual record score of 499 has been left behind. For longer than I shall write permanently about cricket, this book will be my constant companion, offsetting what it is to cost me in excess baggage by the pleasure it provides and the purpose it serves.

**JOHN WOODCOCK**
**Hampshire, April 1981**

# PREFACE TO THE FIRST EDITION

This companion volume to *The Wisden Book of Test Cricket* contains the records of all FIRST-CLASS cricket played between 1815 and the end of the 1980 English season. A supplementary section of Test match records has also been included. This updates and expands the records section which appeared in *Test Cricket* but which will not be included in future editions of that title.

I am sorry to disappoint those many devotees of minor cricket, including the vast audiences which the one-day limited-overs competitions have captivated, by omitting the records of all but first-class matches. Any worthwhile attempt at presenting such records for all minor cricket throughout the world would have involved too much space for inclusion here. Indeed, the term 'minor' embraces all matches which do not rank as first-class, including all club, league, cup, schools and limited-overs cricket – even the recent so-called World Series tournaments – and the task of compilation would be as formidable as the magnitude of any comprehensive volume of records at this level of the game.

Since I compiled my first book of records (*The Kaye Book of Cricket Records*, Kaye & Ward 1968), cricket statisticians have organised themselves into a world-wide association with a membership which is expected to reach 1000 during 1981. The coordinated energy, skill and enthusiasm of The Association of Cricket Statisticians has already produced more than twenty notable documents and booklets, the most important of which is their *Guide to First-Class Matches Played in the British Isles 1864–1946*. Until the publication of that guide, all compilers of cricket records had to decide on their own list of first-class matches before they could produce any statistics.

It was not until 19 May, 1947, that the term 'first-class match' was officially defined. On that date the six countries represented at the Imperial Cricket Conference at Lord's (England, Australia, South Africa, West Indies, New Zealand and India), agreed that 'a match of three or more days duration between two sides of eleven players officially adjudged first-class, shall be regarded as a first-class fixture. Matches in which either team has more than eleven players or which are scheduled for less than three days shall not be regarded as first-class. The governing body in each country shall decide the status of teams.' This definition did not have retrospective effect.

The 1947 ruling gave the MCC the authority to decide the status of all matches in Britain for the first time. Although they had controlled the status of the counties since 1895, the classification of matches outside the County Championship had rested largely with the Cricket Reporting Agency, who compiled the 'first-class averages' for the leading publications of the day. Only occasionally did the agency consult the MCC. The status of matches before 1895 had been even more of a lottery and, until the ACS guide was completed, statisticians had seldom reached agreement on the status of certain counties, let alone that of matches involving other teams.

Apart from discounting any match involving teams of other than eleven men, I have accepted the guide's ranking of matches for the period from 1864 until the 1947 ruling removed all problems of classification. The date 1864 is not especially significant except for the fact that from that season the division between first-class and other matches becomes more obvious; 1864 was also the year in which 'overhand bowling' was authorised, and in which *Wisden Cricketers' Almanack* was first published.

I have extended the list back to 1815 when the end of the Napoleonic Wars heralded the rebirth of 'Great Matches' involving England, MCC and the county organisations of the day after a barren four seasons. My schoolboy interest in cricket was given an extra fillip when I first read that, when the Duchess of Richmond gave her historic ball on the eve of Waterloo, many of the officers present had arrived straight from a cricket match arranged for them on the outskirts of Brussels by the Duke, their commanding officer.

The ACS has recently published another notable guide. Entitled *A Guide to Important Cricket Matches played in the British Isles 1709–1863*, it rather surprisingly commences its lists with two matches between London and Croydon played in 1707. Although its catalogue of 'important' eighteenth century matches will provide a most valuable base for future cricket historians, I feel that playing conditions before 1800 were so far removed from the modern game as to make their inclusion in these records almost absurd. No doubt a case could be made for the inclusion of some matches prior to 1815 but that date seems more appropriate than any other, marking as it did an obvious resurgence of 'Great Matches' after twelve years of war with France. In deciding on which matches to include for the period 1815–1863, I have again followed the relevant ACS guide, but omitted all matches not involving teams of eleven players.

And so to the status of matches played overseas. Again the ACS has established lists of matches for both Australia and New Zealand by publishing guides to first-class matches in both those countries. The creation of Pakistan as an independent state coincided neatly with the 1947 ruling and the status of all matches in that country has been decided by the BCCP. I have relied heavily on the wisdom of A.H. Wagg in classifying matches played in the West Indies, India and Sri Lanka, and on that of Denys Heesom for those in Southern Africa. Sadly these two old friends are no longer with us. Foremost statisticians in their own specialised fields, they both exuded a deep and abiding love for cricket and were unfailingly generous with their help.

Apart from the status of matches and the 1970 England v Rest of the World series, nothing has provoked so much controversy amongst cricket historians as the pre-1890 County Championship. For reasons detailed in my introduction to the County Championship section, I do not regard the competition to have been officially constituted until after 1889 when the counties first agreed to a method of deciding the title. Accordingly, I have omitted any pre-1890 'titles' in compiling the list of honours for each county. Whilst this revision may not gain too many supporters in Bristol or Nottingham, I hope that it will be acceptable and will be adopted by other publications.

No work of this scope can be compiled efficiently without the generous assistance of many people at all stages of its production. Robert Brooke has proved himself to be an indispensable aid; apart from checking through the entire book at galley-proof stage, he ferreted out 311 unrecorded instances of batsmen scoring a hundred before lunch – a slight oversight on the part of some of my predecessors. Sue Bullen, a fanatical Essex supporter and occasional night sister, has devoted hundreds of hours of her time, both spare and nursing, in assisting with research, compilation, typing, checking and proof-reading. Not for the first time I have been overwhelmingly fortunate in having Queen Anne Press's managing editor, Kirsty Ennever, as chief overseer of this volume. No editor could be more encouraging, conscientious or good-humoured. Above all, though, I am indebted to Alan Smith for commissioning this edition.

The following have also contributed their time and assisted in a variety of ways in the preparation of this book; to all of them I give most grateful thanks:

Philip Bailey, Deborah Brown, Tony Cozier, Anandji Dossa, Michael Fordham, Gul Hameed Bhatti, Barry McCaully, Bapoo Mama, Richard Miller, Mike Ringham, Ray Robinson, David Roylance, David Ruck, Raj Sacranie, Geoffrey Saulez, Gordon Tratalos, Roy Wilkinson, Graeme Wright, Peter Wynne-Thomas.

**BILL FRINDALL**
**London, April 1981**

# KEY TO SYMBOLS

Throughout this volume, * denotes a 'not out' innings or an unfinished partnership, 'd' means innings declared (e.g. 305-8d), and 'c' shows that the innings was closed under the 100 overs regulation (e.g. 263-7c).

All other symbols are explained within the section in which they appear.

# PREFACE TO THE SECOND EDITION

This completely revised edition updates the records of all international first-class and Test match cricket to the end of the 1985 English season from 1815 and 1877 respectively.

The layout is unchanged, with the Test match records following those covering the game at first-class level. I am greatly indebted to Robert Brooke, much assisted by Philip Bailey, who has completely overhauled this first-class section. His painstaking research has unearthed many previously undiscovered entries and removed several bogus ones. In view of recent attempts by some members of the Association of Cricket Statisticians to upgrade pre-war matches of highly dubious status, it is important to stress that they will find no haven in these records. The most controversial and publicised of these matches involve the 1930–31 visit to Ceylon by the Mararajkumar of Vizianagram's team for which Jack Hobbs (2) and Herbert Sutcliffe scored hundreds. According to John Arlott, Hobbs himself was adamant that these fixtures should not be included in his first-class records; he considered them to be merely exhibition matches in which the two England players were 'allowed' to score hundreds so that suitably inscribed plaques recording their feats could adorn the walls of Vizzy's palace. Robert Brooke, who conceived the ACS, is equally adamant on this issue. Surely statistics should complement the history of cricket, not turn it on its head.

The Test match section has been expanded to include Sri Lanka, the newest full member of the ICC. After their heroic performance at Lord's in 1984, their first Test victory—sadly just too late for this edition—was warmly applauded throughout the cricketing world. In a mere five years 137 Test matches have been played and 133 more cricketers have been elevated to Test status.

Probably the most significant development during this period has been the increase in the number of one-day internationals staged. The decade following the first of these games (a hastily-arranged affair played on the last day of an aborted Test match at Melbourne) produced 103 such matches. The next five years have seen 241, with no fewer than 52 being played during the 1985–86 overseas season. Although space does not permit their inclusion in this volume, full scores and records of all those played to the end of the 1985 English season have been published by John Wisden in *The Wisden Book of One-Day International Cricket*, my co-compiler being the Hampshire scorer, Vic Isaacs.

Geoffrey Saulez has devoted much effort into proof-reading this edition and has provided many valuable scorebook amendments, the product of his frequent travels as official scorer to a wide variety of national teams. My thanks are also due to Jeremy Gale who has relished an opportunity to search through reams of proofs for errors compiled or added. Many other enthusiasts have given freely of their time and assistance in preparing this edition. Besides the staff of Queen Anne Press, in particular Celia Kent and Richard Beswick, I should like to thank the following:

Abid Ali Kazi, David Baggett, Philip Bailey, Trevor Beling, Debbie Brown, Tony Dobbs, Keith Edwards, R.O. Evans, David Gallagher, Gul Hameed Bhatti, Brian Heald, Michael Hill, Rajesh Kumar, Mark Leopard, R.A. Lister, Bapoo Mama, Richard Miller, Francis Payne, Mike Ringham, Darren Senior, Peter Sichel, Ross Smith, John Ward, Roy Wilkinson, and Graeme Wright.

**BILL FRINDALL**
**London 1986**

# FIRST-CLASS MATCH RECORDS 1815 TO 1985

## TEAM RECORDS

## HIGHEST INNINGS TOTALS

| | | | |
|---|---|---|---|
| 1107 | Victoria v New South Wales | Melbourne | 1926–27 |
| 1059 | Victoria v Tasmania | Melbourne | 1922–23 |
| 951-7d | Sind v Baluchistan | Karachi | 1973–74 |
| 918 | New South Wales v South Australia | Sydney | 1900–01 |
| 912-8d | Holkar v Mysore | Indore | 1945–46 |
| 910-6d | Railways v Dera Ismail Khan | Lahore | 1964–65 |
| 903-7d | England v Australia | Oval | 1938 |
| 887 | Yorkshire v Warwickshire | Birmingham | 1896 |
| 849 | England v West Indies | Kingston | 1929–30 |
| 843 | Australians v Oxford & Cambridge U. P. & P. | Portsmouth | 1893 |
| 839 | New South Wales v Tasmania | Sydney | 1898–99 |
| 826-4 | Maharashtra v Western India States | Poona | 1948–49 |
| 824 | Lahore Greens v Bahawalpur | Lahore | 1965–66 |
| 821-7d | South Australia v Queensland | Adelaide | 1939–40 |
| 815 | New South Wales v Victoria | Sydney | 1908–09 |
| 811 | Surrey v Somerset | Oval | 1899 |
| 807 | New South Wales v South Australia | Adelaide | 1899–00 |
| 805 | New South Wales v Victoria | Melbourne | 1905–06 |
| 803-4d | Kent v Essex | Brentwood | 1934 |
| 803 | Non-Smokers v Smokers | East Melbourne | 1886–87 |
| 802 | New South Wales v South Australia | Sydney | 1920–21 |
| 801 | Lancashire v Somerset | Taunton | 1895 |

## INNINGS TOTALS OF 600 AND OVER

These are listed under the respective teams for England and Australia, the highest total being given when no total of 600 has been scored.

IN ENGLAND

| | | | | | |
|---|---|---|---|---|---|
| Derbyshire | 645 | v | Hampshire | Derby | 1898 |
| Essex | 692 | v | Somerset | Taunton | 1895 |
| | 673 | v | Leicestershire | Leicester | 1899 |

| | | | | | |
|---|---|---|---|---|---|
| Essex *continued* | 616-5d | v | Surrey | Oval | 1904 |
| | 609-4d | v | Derbyshire | Leyton | 1912 |
| | 604-7d | v | Northamptonshire | Northampton | 1921 |
| Glamorgan | 587-8d | v | Derbyshire | Cardiff | 1951 |
| Gloucestershire | 653-6d | v | Glamorgan | Bristol | 1928 |
| | 643-5d | v | Nottinghamshire | Bristol | 1946 |
| | 636 | v | Nottinghamshire | Nottingham | 1904 |
| | 634 | v | Nottinghamshire | Bristol | 1898 |
| | 627-2d | v | Oxford University | Oxford | 1930 |
| | 625-6d | v | Worcestershire | Dudley | 1934 |
| | 608-7d | v | Sussex | Cheltenham | 1934 |
| | 603-6d | v | Glamorgan | Bristol | 1934 |
| Hampshire | 672-7d | v | Somerset | Taunton | 1899 |
| | 645 | v | Somerset | Southampton | 1884 |
| | 642-9d | v | Somerset | Taunton | 1901 |
| | 616-7d | v | Warwickshire | Portsmouth | 1920 |
| Kent | 803-4d | v | Essex | Brentwood | 1934 |
| | 621-6d | v | Essex | Tonbridge | 1922 |
| | 616-6d | v | Oxford University | Oxford | 1982 |
| | 615 | v | Derbyshire | Derby | 1908 |
| | 610 | v | Hampshire | Bournemouth | 1906 |
| | 607-6d | v | Gloucestershire | Cheltenham | 1910 |
| | 602-7d | v | Worcestershire | Dudley | 1938 |
| | 601-8d | v | Somerset | Taunton | 1908 |
| Lancashire | 801 | v | Somerset | Taunton | 1895 |
| | 676-7d | v | Hampshire | Manchester | 1911 |
| | 640-8d | v | Sussex | Hove | 1937 |
| | 627 | v | Nottinghamshire | Nottingham | 1905 |
| | 601-8d | v | Sussex | Hove | 1905 |
| Leicestershire | 701-4d | v | Worcestershire | Worcester | 1906 |
| | 609-8d | v | Sussex | Leicester | 1900 |
| | 603 | v | Sir J. Cahn's XI | Nottingham | 1935 |
| Middlesex | 642-3d | v | Hampshire | Southampton | 1923 |
| | 637-4d | v | Leicestershire | Leicester | 1947 |
| | 634-7d | v | Essex | Chelmsford | 1983 |
| | 632-8d | v | Sussex | Hove | 1937 |
| | 623-5d | v | Worcestershire | Worcester | 1949 |
| | 621-9d | v | Nottinghamshire | Nottingham | 1931 |
| | 612-8d | v | Nottinghamshire | Lord's | 1921 |
| | 608-7d | v | Hampshire | Lord's | 1919 |
| Northamptonshire | 557-6d | v | Sussex | Hove | 1914 |
| Nottinghamshire | 739-7d | v | Leicestershire | Nottingham | 1903 |
| | 726 | v | Sussex | Nottingham | 1895 |
| | 674 | v | Sussex | Hove | 1893 |
| | 662-8d | v | Essex | Nottingham | 1947 |
| | 661 | v | Derbyshire | Derby | 1901 |
| | 656-3d | v | Warwickshire | Coventry | 1928 |
| | 642-7d | v | Sussex | Hove | 1901 |
| | 607 | v | Gloucestershire | Bristol | 1899 |
| | 602 | v | Kent | Nottingham | 1904 |
| Somerset | 675-9d | v | Hampshire | Bath | 1924 |
| | 630 | v | Yorkshire | Leeds | 1901 |
| Surrey | 811 | v | Somerset | Oval | 1899 |
| | 742 | v | Hampshire | Oval | 1909 |
| | 706-4d | v | Nottinghamshire | Nottingham | 1947 |
| | 698 | v | Sussex | Oval | 1888 |
| | 650 | v | Hampshire | Oval | 1883 |
| | 650 | v | Oxford University | Oval | 1888 |
| | 645-9d | v | New Zealanders | Oval | 1949 |
| | 635 | v | Somerset | Oval | 1885 |
| | 634 | v | Lancashire | Oval | 1898 |
| | 634 | v | Warwickshire | Oval | 1906 |
| | 631 | v | Sussex | Oval | 1885 |
| | 619-5d | v | Northamptonshire | Northampton | 1920 |
| | 617-6d | v | Oxford University | Oval | 1928 |
| | 617 | v | Kent | Oval | 1897 |
| | 616-5d | v | Northamptonshire | Oval | 1921 |

| | | | | | |
|---|---|---|---|---|---|
| Surrey *continued* | 614 | v | Oxford University | Oval | 1889 |
| | 611-9d | v | Derbyshire | Derby | 1904 |
| | 609 | v | Warwickshire | Oval | 1898 |
| | 602 | v | Warwickshire | Oval | 1897 |
| Sussex | 705-8d | v | Surrey | Hastings | 1902 |
| | 686-8 | v | Leicestershire | Leicester | 1900 |
| | 670-9d | v | Northamptonshire | Hove | 1921 |
| | 631-4d | v | Northamptonshire | Northampton | 1938 |
| | 611 | v | Essex | Leyton | 1905 |
| | 600-7d | v | Surrey | Oval | 1903 |
| Warwickshire | 657-6d | v | Hampshire | Birmingham | 1899 |
| | 645-7d | v | Worcestershire | Dudley | 1914 |
| | 635 | v | Derbyshire | Birmingham | 1900 |
| | 614-8d | v | Essex | Birmingham | 1904 |
| | 605 | v | Leicestershire | Leicester | 1899 |
| | 603-9d | v | Worcestershire | Birmingham | 1920 |
| Worcestershire | 633 | v | Warwickshire | Worcester | 1906 |
| | 627-9d | v | Kent | Worcester | 1905 |
| Yorkshire | 887 | v | Warwickshire | Birmingham | 1896 |
| | 704 | v | Surrey | Oval | 1899 |
| | 681-5d | v | Sussex | Sheffield | 1897 |
| | 662 | v | Derbyshire | Chesterfield | 1898 |
| | 660 | v | Leicestershire | Leicester | 1896 |
| Oxford University | 651 | v | Sussex | Hove | 1895 |
| | 644-8d | v | H.D.G. Leveson Gower's XI | Eastbourne | 1921 |
| | 612 | v | Middlesex | Prince's | 1876 |
| Cambridge University | 703-9d | v | Sussex | Hove | 1890 |
| | 611 | v | Sussex | Hove | 1919 |
| | 609-8d | v | MCC | Lord's | 1913 |
| MCC | 607 | v | Cambridge University | Lord's | 1902 |
| England | 903-7d | v | Australia | Oval | 1938 |
| | 658-8d | v | Australia | Nottingham | 1938 |
| | 633-5d | v | India | Birmingham | 1979 |
| | 629 | v | India | Lord's | 1974 |
| | 627-9d | v | Australia | Manchester | 1934 |
| | 619-6d | v | West Indies | Nottingham | 1957 |
| | 611 | v | Australia | Manchester | 1964 |
| Australians | 843 | v | Oxford and Cambridge U. P. & P. | Portsmouth | 1893 |
| | 774-7d | v | Gloucestershire | Bristol | 1948 |
| | 729-6d | v | England | Lord's | 1930 |
| | 721 | v | Essex | Southend | 1948 |
| | 708-5d | v | Cambridge University | Cambridge | 1938 |
| | 708-7d | v | Hampshire | Southampton | 1921 |
| | 701 | v | England | Oval | 1934 |
| | 695 | v | England | Oval | 1930 |
| | 694-6 | v | Leicestershire | Leicester | 1956 |
| | 679-7d | v | Oxford University | Oxford | 1938 |
| | 676 | v | Kent | Canterbury | 1921 |
| | 675 | v | Nottinghamshire | Nottingham | 1921 |
| | 656-8d | v | England | Manchester | 1964 |
| | 650-8d | v | Cambridge University | Cambridge | 1919 |
| | 643 | v | Sussex | Hove | 1882 |
| | 632 | v | Surrey | Oval | 1948 |
| | 629 | v | Surrey | Oval | 1934 |
| | 625 | v | Derbyshire | Derby | 1896 |
| | 624-4d | v | Sussex | Hove | 1899 |
| | 621 | v | Northamptonshire | Northampton | 1921 |
| | 620 | v | Hampshire | Southampton | 1905 |
| | 610-5d | v | Gentlemen | Lord's | 1948 |
| | 609-4d | v | Somerset | Bath | 1905 |
| | 609-6d | v | Essex | Leyton | 1909 |
| | 609 | v | Northamptonshire | Northampton | 1905 |
| South Africans | 692 | v | Cambridge University | Cambridge | 1901 |
| | 611 | v | Nottinghamshire | Nottingham | 1904 |
| West Indians | 730-3 | v | Cambridge University | Cambridge | 1950 |
| | 687-8d | v | England | Oval | 1976 |

| West Indians *continued* | 682-2d | v | Leicestershire | Leicester | 1950 |
|---|---|---|---|---|---|
| | 665 | v | Middlesex | Lord's | 1939 |
| | 652-8d | v | England | Lord's | 1973 |
| | 606 | v | England | Birmingham | 1984 |
| New Zealanders | 546 | v | Sussex | Hove | 1937 |
| Indians | 562 | v | Warwickshire | Birmingham | 1971 |
| Pakistanis | 608-7d | v | England | Birmingham | 1971 |
| | 600-7d | v | England | Oval | 1974 |
| Gentlemen | 578 | v | Players | Oval | 1904 |
| Players | 651-7d | v | Gentlemen | Oval | 1934 |
| | 647 | v | Gentlemen | Oval | 1899 |
| | 608-8d | v | Gentlemen | Oval | 1921 |

*Other innings totals of over 600 in England:*

| 676-8d | Oxford Harlequins v West Indians | Eastbourne | 1928 |
|---|---|---|---|
| 636-7d | Free Foresters v Cambridge University | Cambridge | 1938 |
| 633 | London County v MCC | Crystal Palace | 1901 |
| 631-5d | Rest of England v Warwickshire† | Oval | 1911 |
| 603-5d | Rest of England v Middlesex† | Oval | 1920 |
| 603-8d | Rest of England v Lancashire† | Oval | 1928 |

† *Champion County.*

IN AUSTRALIA

| New South Wales | 918 | v | South Australia | Sydney | 1900–01 |
|---|---|---|---|---|---|
| | 839 | v | Tasmania | Sydney | 1898–99 |
| | 815 | v | Victoria | Sydney | 1908–09 |
| | 807 | v | South Australia | Adelaide | 1899–00 |
| | 805 | v | Victoria | Melbourne | 1905–06 |
| | 802 | v | South Australia | Sydney | 1920–21 |
| | 786 | v | South Australia | Adelaide | 1922–23 |
| | 775 | v | Victoria | Sydney | 1881–82 |
| | 770 | v | South Australia | Adelaide | 1920–21 |
| | 763 | v | Queensland | Brisbane | 1906–07 |
| | 761-8d | v | Queensland | Sydney | 1929–30 |
| | 713-6d | v | Victoria | Sydney | 1928–29 |
| | 713 | v | South Australia | Adelaide | 1908–09 |
| | 708 | v | Victoria | Sydney | 1925–26 |
| | 705 | v | Victoria | Melbourne | 1925–26 |
| | 691 | v | Queensland | Brisbane | 1905–06 |
| | 690 | v | South Australia | Adelaide | 1919–20 |
| | 686 | v | Queensland | Sydney | 1904–05 |
| | 684 | v | South Australia | Sydney | 1923–24 |
| | 681 | v | South Australia | Sydney | 1903–04 |
| | 675 | v | Victoria | Sydney | 1913–14 |
| | 672-8d | v | Victoria | Sydney | 1933–34 |
| | 661 | v | Queensland | Brisbane | 1963–64 |
| | 645 | v | Rest (except Victoria) | Sydney | 1924–25 |
| | 642 | v | South Australia | Sydney | 1925–26 |
| | 640 | v | Queensland | Sydney | 1899–00 |
| | 639 | v | Western Australia | Sydney | 1925–26 |
| | 639 | v | Queensland | Sydney | 1927–28 |
| | 629-8d | v | MCC | Sydney | 1929–30 |
| | 624 | v | South Australia | Adelaide | 1903–04 |
| | 619 | v | MCC | Sydney | 1924–25 |
| | 614-5d | v | Tasmania | Hobart | 1912–13 |
| | 614-6d | v | Queensland | Sydney | 1933–34 |
| | 614 | v | Victoria | Sydney | 1924–25 |
| | 610 | v | South Australia | Adelaide | 1930–31 |
| | 602 | v | Queensland | Brisbane | 1932–33 |
| | 601-9d | v | South Australia | Adelaide | 1964–65 |
| Queensland | 687 | v | New South Wales | Brisbane | 1930–31 |
| | 613 | v | New South Wales | Brisbane | 1963–64 |
| South Australia | 821-7d | v | Queensland | Adelaide | 1939–40 |
| | 688 | v | Tasmania | Adelaide | 1935–36 |
| | 649-9d | v | MCC | Adelaide | 1970–71 |
| | 644-7d | v | Queensland | Adelaide | 1934–35 |

| | | | | | |
|---|---|---|---|---|---|
| South Australia *continued* | 642-8d | v | Queensland | Adelaide | 1935–36 |
| | 614-8d | v | Western Australia | Adelaide | 1929–30 |
| | 612 | v | Western Australia | Adelaide | 1925–26 |
| | 610 | v | Victoria | Melbourne | 1939–40 |
| | 603 | v | New South Wales | Adelaide | 1946–47 |
| | 600-8d | v | New South Wales | Adelaide | 1938–39 |
| Tasmania | 507-9d | v | Queensland | Brisbane | 1984–85 |
| Victoria | 1107 | v | New South Wales | Melbourne | 1926–27 |
| | 1059 | v | Tasmania | Melbourne | 1922–23 |
| | 793 | v | Queensland | Melbourne | 1927–28 |
| | 724 | v | South Australia | Melbourne | 1920–21 |
| | 699 | v | South Australia | Melbourne | 1907–08 |
| | 697 | v | South Australia | Adelaide | 1945–46 |
| | 660 | v | Tasmania | Melbourne | 1909–10 |
| | 649 | v | South Australia | Melbourne | 1926–27 |
| | 647 | v | Tasmania | Melbourne | 1951–52 |
| | 646-8d | v | South Australia | Adelaide | 1927–28 |
| | 639 | v | South Australia | Adelaide | 1920–21 |
| | 637 | v | South Australia | Melbourne | 1927–28 |
| | 633-4d | v | Queensland | Melbourne | 1962–63 |
| | 626 | v | Tasmania | Launceston | 1908–09 |
| | 620 | v | South Australia | Adelaide | 1921–22 |
| | 617-6d | v | MCC | Melbourne | 1922–23 |
| | 614 | v | South Australia | Melbourne | 1910–11 |
| | 609 | v | South Australia | Melbourne | 1983–84 |
| | 605 | v | South Australia | Melbourne | 1919–20 |
| | 604 | v | South Australia | Melbourne | 1925–26 |
| | 602 | v | New Zealanders | Melbourne | 1898–99 |
| | 601-7d | v | West Indians | Melbourne | 1984–85 |
| Western Australia | 615-5d | v | Queensland | Brisbane | 1968–69 |
| MCC | 734-7d | v | New South Wales | Sydney | 1928–29 |
| | 660-8d | v | South Australia | Adelaide | 1907–08 |
| | 634-9d | v | South Australia | Adelaide | 1932–33 |
| | 633-7d | v | Australian XI | Melbourne | 1962–63 |
| | 627 | v | South Australia | Adelaide | 1920–21 |
| | 626 | v | New South Wales | Sydney | 1924–25 |
| England | 636 | v | Australia | Sydney | 1928–29 |
| Australia | 674 | v | India | Adelaide | 1947–48 |
| | 659-8d | v | England | Sydney | 1946–47 |
| | 645 | v | England | Brisbane | 1946–47 |
| | 619 | v | West Indies | Sydney | 1968–69 |
| | 604 | v | England | Melbourne | 1936–37 |
| | 601-8d | v | England | Brisbane | 1954–55 |
| | 600 | v | England | Melbourne | 1924–25 |
| South Africans | 595 | v | Australia | Adelaide | 1963–64 |
| West Indians | 616 | v | Australia | Adelaide | 1968–69 |
| New Zealanders | 459 | v | South Australia | Adelaide | 1953–54 |
| Indians | 475-7d | v | Tasmania | Launceston | 1947–48 |
| Pakistanis | 624 | v | Australia | Adelaide | 1983–84 |

*Other innings totals of over 600 in Australia:*

| | | | |
|---|---|---|---|
| 803 | Non-Smokers v Smokers | East Melbourne | 1886–87 |
| 769 | A.C. MacLaren's XI v New South Wales | Sydney | 1901–02 |
| 663 | J. Ryder's XI v W.M. Woodfull's XI | Sydney | 1929–30 |
| 648 | Australian XI v Rest of Australia | Melbourne | 1908–09 |
| 624 | A.Shrewsbury's XI v Victoria | Melbourne | 1887–88 |
| 619 | Australian XI v Rest of Australia | Melbourne | 1883–84 |
| 609 | A.E. Stoddart's XI v South Australia | Adelaide | 1894–95 |

## IN SOUTH AFRICA AND RHODESIA

| | | | |
|---|---|---|---|
| 676 | MCC v Griqualand West | Kimberley | 1938–39 |
| 664-6d | Natal v Western Province | Durban | 1936–37 |
| 663-6d | South African XI v Arosa Sri Lanka | Cape Town | 1982–83 |
| 654-5 | England v South Africa | Durban | 1938–39 |
| 622-9d | South Africa v Australia | Durban | 1969–70 |
| 620 | South Africa v Australia | Johannesburg | 1966–67 |
| 620 | Australians v Griqualand West | Kimberley | 1966–67 |

**IN SOUTH AFRICA AND RHODESIA** *continued*

| | | | |
|---|---|---|---|
| 618-4d | South Africa v Rest of South Africa | Johannesburg | 1964–65 |
| 609 | Transvaal v Orange Free State | Johannesburg | 1934–35 |
| 608-6d | Transvaal v Natal | Johannesburg | 1939–40 |
| 608 | England v South Africa | Johannesburg | 1948–49 |
| 603 | Griqualand West v Western Province | Kimberley | 1929–30 |
| 602 | Griqualand West v Rhodesia | Kimberley | 1929–30 |
| 601 | Western Province v Border | Cape Town | 1929–30 |

**IN WEST INDIES**

| | | | |
|---|---|---|---|
| 849 | England v West Indies | Kingston | 1929–30 |
| 790-3d | West Indies v Pakistan | Kingston | 1957–58 |
| 758-8d | Australia v West Indies | Kingston | 1954–55 |
| 753 | Barbados v Jamaica | Bridgetown | 1951–52 |
| 750-8d | Trinidad v British Guiana | Port-of-Spain | 1946–47 |
| 726-7d | Barbados v Trinidad | Bridgetown | 1926–27 |
| 715-9d | Barbados v British Guiana | Bridgetown | 1926–27 |
| 702-5d | Jamaica v Lord Tennyson's XI | Kingston | 1931–32 |
| 698 | Barbados v Trinidad | Bridgetown | 1948–49 |
| 692-9d | British Guiana v Barbados | Georgetown | 1951–52 |
| 686-6d | Barbados v British Guiana | Bridgetown | 1949–50 |
| 681-8d | West Indies v England | Port-of-Spain | 1953–54 |
| 673 | Barbados v Trinidad | Georgetown | 1922–23 |
| 668 | Australia v West Indies | Bridgetown | 1954–55 |
| 664 | Barbados v Jamaica | Georgetown | 1961–62 |
| 657-8d | Pakistan v West Indies | Bridgetown | 1957–58 |
| 650-3d | Barbados v Trinidad | Bridgetown | 1943–44 |
| 650-6d | Australia v West Indies | Bridgetown | 1964–65 |
| 641-6 | MCC v Berbice | Blairmont | 1959–60 |
| 641-5d | Guyana v Barbados | Georgetown | 1966–67 |
| 631-8d | West Indies v India | Kingston | 1961–62 |
| 629 | British Guiana v Barbados | Georgetown | 1937–38 |
| 627 | British Guiana v Trinidad | Georgetown | 1937–38 |
| 623-5d | Barbados v Trinidad | Bridgetown | 1919–20 |
| 619-3d | Barbados v Trinidad | Port-of-Spain | 1945–46 |
| 613-5d | Leeward Islands v Trinidad | St John's | 1983–84 |
| 610 | British Guiana v Barbados | Georgetown | 1929–30 |
| 609 | Jamaica v Hon L.H. Tennyson's XI | Kingston | 1927–28 |
| 609 | British Guiana v Jamaica | Georgetown | 1952–53 |
| 607 | MCC v British Guiana | Georgetown | 1953–54 |
| 606-7d | Barbados v Indians | Bridgetown | 1952–53 |
| 605-5d | MCC v British Guiana | Georgetown | 1929–30 |
| 601-5d | British Guiana v Jamaica | Georgetown | 1956–57 |
| 601-9d | Barbados v British Guiana | Georgetown | 1946–47 |
| 601 | MCC v Barbados | Bridgetown | 1934–35 |
| 600-9d | Australia v West Indies | Port-of-Spain | 1954–55 |

**IN NEW ZEALAND**

| | | | |
|---|---|---|---|
| 752-8d | New South Wales v Otago | Dunedin | 1923–24 |
| 693-9d | Auckland v Canterbury | Auckland | 1939–40 |
| 663 | Australians v New Zealand XI | Auckland | 1920–21 |
| 658 | Australians v Auckland | Auckland | 1913–14 |
| 653-5d | MCC v New Zealand XI | Dunedin | 1935–36 |
| 653 | Australians v Canterbury | Christchurch | 1913–14 |
| 643 | Auckland v Canterbury | Auckland | 1919–20 |
| 610-6d | Australians v New Zealand XI | Auckland | 1913–14 |
| 602-8d | Otago v Canterbury | Dunedin | 1928–29 |

**IN INDIA**

| | | | |
|---|---|---|---|
| 912-8d | Holkar v Mysore | Indore | 1945–46 |
| 826-4 | Maharashtra v Kathiawar | Poona | 1948–49 |
| 798 | Maharashtra v Northern India | Poona | 1940–41 |
| 784 | Baroda v Holkar | Baroda | 1946–47 |
| 764 | Bombay v Holkar | Bombay | 1944–45 |
| 760 | Bengal v Assam | Calcutta | 1951–52 |
| 757 | Holkar v Hyderabad | Indore | 1950–51 |

| 735 | Bombay v Maharashtra | Bombay | 1943–44 |
|---|---|---|---|
| 725-8d | Bombay v Maharashtra | Bombay | 1950–51 |
| 714-8d | Bombay v Maharashtra | Poona | 1948–49 |
| 707-8 | Delhi v Karnataka | Delhi | 1981–82 |
| 705 | Karnataka v Delhi | Delhi | 1981–82 |
| 703 | Bengal Cyclone XI v Bijapur Famine XI | Bombay | 1942–43 |
| 675 | Maharashtra v Bombay | Poona | 1940–41 |
| 673 | Bijapur Famine XI v Bengal Cyclone XI | Bombay | 1942–43 |
| 664-5d | North Zone v East Zone | Bombay | 1982–83 |
| 658-8d | Southern Punjab v Northern India | Patiala | 1945–46 |
| 657-9d | Bombay v Maharashtra | Bombay | 1956–57 |
| 654 | Cricket Club of India v C.K. Nayudu's XI | Bombay | 1944–45 |
| 652-6d | Bombay v Bengal | Bombay | 1981–82 |
| 652-7d | England v India | Madras | 1984–85 |
| 652 | Bombay v Hyderabad | Bombay | 1947–48 |
| 651 | Bombay v Maharashtra | Poona | 1948–49 |
| 650-9d | Maharashtra v Baroda | Poona | 1939–40 |
| 650 | Bombay v Maharashtra | Poona | 1940–41 |
| 645 | Bombay v Baroda | Bombay | 1945–46 |
| 644-7d | India v West Indies | Kanpur | 1978–79 |
| 644-8d | West Indies v India | Delhi | 1958–59 |
| 638-8d | Bombay v Sind | Bombay | 1947–48 |
| 635-6d | Hyderabad v Bengal | Hyderabad | 1964–65 |
| 634-9d | Bombay v Madras | Bombay | 1956–57 |
| 632-7d | Bombay v Maharashtra | Bombay | 1947–48 |
| 631 | West Indies v India | Delhi | 1948–49 |
| 629-6d | West Indies v India | Bombay | 1948–49 |
| 629 | Gujarat v Maharashtra | Kolaphur | 1951–52 |
| 628-8d | Delhi v Rest of India | Delhi | 1980–81 |
| 625 | Bombay v Delhi | Bombay | 1983–84 |
| 624-5d | Maharashtra v Rajasthan | Poona | 1970–71 |
| 623 | Bengal v Orissa | Rourkela | 1983–84 |
| 623 | South Zone v Central Zone | Dhanbad | 1983–84 |
| 620 | Bombay v Northern India | Bombay | 1944–45 |
| 620 | Bombay v Baroda | Bombay | 1948–49 |
| 618 | Holkar v Bengal | Indore | 1942–43 |
| 615-4d | Cricket Club of India v Services XI | Bombay | 1944–45 |
| 615 | Holkar v Delhi | Delhi | 1949–50 |
| 615 | Rajasthan v Vidarbha | Udaipur | 1957–58 |
| 615 | Hyderabad v Uttar Pradesh | Hyderabad | 1964–65 |
| 614-5d | West Indies v India | Calcutta | 1958–59 |
| 613-7d | Northern India v NWFP | Lahore | 1941–42 |
| 613-7d | Commonwealth XI v North Zone | Patiala | 1949–50 |
| 612-6d | India in England 1946 v Rest of India | Calcutta | 1946–47 |
| 611 | Commonwealth XI v West Zone | Poona | 1949–50 |
| 608-8d | Commonwealth XI v Indian XI | Delhi | 1949–50 |
| 606 | Freelooters v Karachi | Secunderabad | 1932–33 |
| 604-6d | West Indies v India | Bombay | 1974–75 |
| 604 | Maharashtra v Bombay | Poona | 1948–49 |
| 604 | Rajasthan v Maharashtra | Poona | 1970–71 |
| 603 | MCC v Madras | Madras | 1933–34 |
| 602-7d | Bombay v Mysore | Bombay | 1966–67 |

IN PAKISTAN

| 951-7d | Sind v Baluchistan | Karachi | 1973–74 |
|---|---|---|---|
| 910-6d | Railways v Dera Ismail Khan | Lahore | 1964–65 |
| 824 | Lahore Greens v Bahawalpur | Lahore | 1965–66 |
| 774 | Lahore v Sargodha | Lahore | 1968–69 |
| 772-7d | Karachi v Bahawalpur | Karachi | 1958–59 |
| 762 | Karachi Whites v Karachi Blues | Karachi | 1956–57 |
| 731-8d | Habib Bank v Sargodha | Faisalabad | 1977–78 |
| 724-7d | HBFC v Multan | Multan | 1976–77 |
| 723-8d | PIA v Karachi | Karachi | 1977–78 |
| 722 | Habib Bank v National Bank | Lahore | 1976–77 |
| 720 | Income Tax Dept. v Bahawalpur | Bahawalpur | 1976–77 |
| 714 | PWD v Quetta | Quetta | 1969–70 |
| 709 | Karachi Blues v E. Pakistan Greens | Karachi | 1967–68 |

IN PAKISTAN *continued*

| | | | |
|---|---|---|---|
| 702 | Punjab University v Sind University | Karachi | 1958–59 |
| 680-9d | Karachi v East Pakistan | Karachi | 1968–69 |
| 678 | PWD v Customs | Karachi | 1972–73 |
| 676 | Habib Bank v Pakistan Universities | Lahore | 1977–78 |
| 674-6 | Pakistan v India | Faisalabad | 1984–85 |
| 671 | Karachi Whites v Quetta | Karachi | 1963–64 |
| 657 | PIA v Punjab B | Karachi | 1975–76 |
| 656-5d | United Bank v Multan | Karachi | 1975–76 |
| 652 | Pakistan v India | Faisalabad | 1982–83 |
| 641 | Pakistan Universities v Bahawalpur | Lahore | 1974–75 |
| 634-4d | Karachi Blues v Hyderabad | Karachi | 1964–65 |
| 633 | Lahore v Punjab University | Lahore | 1960–61 |
| 632-8d | Karachi Blues v Bahawalpur | Karachi | 1964–65 |
| 631-6d | Sind v Pakistan Universities | Lahore | 1975–76 |
| 630-9d | Commonwealth XI v Pakistan | Lahore | 1963–64 |
| 624-9d | Punjab v Pakistan Universities | Lahore | 1972–73 |
| 617 | Australia v Pakistan | Faisalabad | 1979–80 |
| 616 | Lahore Greens v Railways | Lahore | 1964–65 |
| 611 | Karachi Blues v Lahore Greens | Lahore | 1967–68 |
| 610 | PIA v Sind | Karachi | 1976–77 |
| 609-6d | PIA v Baluchistan | Karachi | 1976–77 |
| 609 | Punjab v Sind | Karachi | 1974–75 |
| 608 | Punjab v Pakistan Universities | Lahore | 1973–74 |

## HIGHEST SECOND INNINGS TOTALS

| | | | |
|---|---|---|---|
| 770 | New South Wales v South Australia | Adelaide | 1920–21 |
| 764 | Bombay v Holkar | Bombay | 1944–45 |
| 761-8d | New South Wales v Queensland | Sydney | 1929–30 |
| 726-7d | Barbados v Trinidad | Bridgetown | 1926–27 |
| 724 | Victoria v South Australia | Melbourne | 1920–21 |
| 714-8d | Bombay v Maharashtra | Poona | 1948–49 |
| 703-9d | Cambridge University v Sussex | Hove | 1890 |

## NOTABLE HIGH SCORING

| | |
|---|---|
| 1895 | Somerset, in consecutive innings, conceded totals of 692 against Essex and 801 against Lancashire, both at Taunton. |
| 1920–21 | South Australia conceded the following totals during the season: 639 (Victoria at Adelaide), 512-5d (MCC at Adelaide), 310 & 724 (Victoria at Melbourne), 802 (NSW at Sydney), 304 & 770 (NSW at Adelaide), and 627 (MCC at Adelaide). |
| 1921 | During their tour of England the Australians scored three successive totals of over 500: 621 v Northamptonshire (Northampton), 675 v Nottinghamshire (Nottingham), and 506 v Warwickshire (Birmingham). |
| 1921 | Northamptonshire conceded the following totals in successive innings: 616-5d (Surrey at The Oval), 604-7d (Essex at Northampton), 621 (Australians at Northampton), and 545-9d (Essex at Leyton). |
| 1925–26 | New South Wales scored 554, 705, 642, 593 and 708 in consecutive innings during their four-match Sheffield Shield programme. |
| 1929–30 | Western Province scored 523-4d, 601 and 538-6d in consecutive innings. |
| 1938 | The Australians began their tour with five consecutive totals in excess of 500: 541 v Worcestershire (Worcester), 679-7d v Oxford University (Oxford), 590-5d v Leicestershire (Leicester), 708-5d v Cambridge University (Cambridge), and 502 v MCC (Lord's). |
| 1948–49 | Bombay (651 & 714-8d) and Maharashtra (407 & 604) produced the highest match aggregate on record: 2376 for 38 wickets. |
| 1977–78 | Habib Bank scored 676, 731-8d, 516-6d and 508 in successive innings in the Patron's Trophy. |

## HIGHEST FOURTH INNINGS TOTALS

| | | | | |
|---|---|---|---|---|
| 654-5 | (set 696 runs) | England v South Africa | Durban | 1938–39 |
| 604 | (lost 354 runs) | Maharashtra v Bombay | Poona | 1948–49 |
| 576-8 | (set 672 runs) | Trinidad v Barbados | Port-of-Spain | 1945–46 |

| 572 | (lost 20 runs) | New South Wales v South Australia | Sydney | 1907–08 |
|---|---|---|---|---|
| 529-9 | (set 579 runs) | Combined XI v South Africans | Perth | 1963–64 |
| 518 | (lost 234 runs) | Victoria v Queensland | Brisbane | 1926–27 |
| 507-7 | (and won) | Cambridge University v MCC | Lord's | 1896 |
| 502-6 | (and won) | Middlesex v Nottinghamshire | Nottingham | 1925 |
| 502-8 | (and won) | Players v Gentlemen | Lord's | 1900 |
| 500-7 | (and won) | SA Universities v W. Province | Stellenbosch | 1978–79 |
| 495 | (lost 145 runs) | Otago v Wellington | Dunedin | 1923–24 |
| 492 | (lost 374 runs) | Holkar v Bombay | Bombay | 1944–45 |
| 473-6 | (and won) | Canterbury v Auckland | Christchurch | 1930–31 |
| 472 | (lost 79 runs) | New South Wales v Australian XI | Sydney | 1905–06 |
| 466 | (lost 86 runs) | New South Wales v West Indians | Sydney | 1930–31 |
| 463-8 | (set 568 runs) | Hampshire v Kent | Southampton | 1911 |
| 460 | (lost 5 runs) | Surrey v MCC | Lord's | 1938 |
| 458 | (lost 276 runs) | Auckland v Wellington | Wellington | 1927–28 |
| 456 | (lost 50 runs) | Queensland v Victoria | Melbourne | 1928–29 |
| 447 | (lost 111 runs) | Orange Free State v Transvaal | Bloemfontein | 1926–27 |
| 446-6 | (and won) | New South Wales v South Australia | Adelaide | 1926–27 |
| 445 | (lost 47 runs) | India v Australia | Adelaide | 1977–78 |
| 442 | (lost 45 runs) | South Africans v New South Wales | Sydney | 1910–11 |
| 440 | (lost 38 runs) | New Zealand v England | Nottingham | 1973 |
| 435-7 | (and won) | Victoria v New South Wales | Melbourne | 1931–32 |
| 430-3 | (set 448 runs) | New South Wales v South Africans | Sydney | 1931–32 |
| 429-6 | (and won) | Sind v PIA | Hyderabad | 1973–74 |
| 429-8 | (set 438) | India v England | Oval | 1979 |
| 428-5 | (and won) | Sussex v Northamptonshire | Kettering | 1939 |
| 428-6 | (and won) | Surrey & Kent v Middlesex & Essex | Kingston | 1947 |
| 427-4 | (and won) | Cambridge University v Surrey | Oval | 1925 |
| 427-9 | (and won) | Commonwealth XI v Bengal Chief Minister's XI | Calcutta | 1964–65 |
| 425 | (lost 121 runs) | A.L. Hassett's XI v A.R. Morris's XI | Melbourne | 1953–54 |
| 424-4 | (set 508 runs) | Hampshire v Worcestershire | Worcester | 1926 |
| 424-5 | (and won) | Rest of India v Delhi | Delhi | 1982–83 |
| 423-7 | (set 451 runs) | South Africa v England | Oval | 1947 |
| 422-9 | (set 499 runs) | MCC v Victoria | Melbourne | 1907–08 |
| 422 | (lost 79 runs) | PACO v National Bank | Lahore | 1983–84 |
| 420-5 | (and won) | Free Foresters v Oxford University | Oxford | 1921 |
| 419-6 | (and won) | Nottinghamshire v Leicestershire | Nottingham | 1926 |
| 417-2 | (and won) | Warwickshire v Glamorgan | Birmingham | 1983 |
| 417 | (lost 45 runs) | England v Australia | Melbourne | 1976–77 |
| 416-6 | (and won) | Kent v Surrey | Blackheath | 1934 |
| 415 | (lost 26 runs) | Victoria v New South Wales | Sydney | 1935–36 |
| 413 | (lost 76 runs) | Australians v Transvaal | Johannesburg | 1966–67 |
| 412-4 | (and won) | I. Zingari v Gentlemen of England | Lord's | 1904 |
| 412-5 | (and won) | MCC v Oxford University | Lord's | 1923 |
| 412-7 | (set 497 runs) | Guyana v Pakistanis | Georgetown | 1976–77 |
| 412-8 | (and won) | Gentlemen v Players | Lord's | 1904 |
| 412 | (lost 84 runs) | South Australia v New South Wales | Sydney | 1912–13 |
| 412 | (lost 22 runs) | President's XI v West Indians | Nagpur | 1966–67 |
| 411 | (lost 193 runs) | England v Australia | Sydney | 1924–25 |
| 410-6 | (and won) | Hampshire v Essex | Southend | 1983 |
| 409-7 | (and won) | Victoria v South Australia | Adelaide | 1924–25 |
| 409-8 | (and won) | Rest of Australia v New South Wales | Sydney | 1933–34 |
| 408-5 | (set 836 runs) | West Indies v England | Kingston | 1929–30 |
| 406-4 | (and won) | India v West Indies | Port-of-Spain | 1975–76 |
| 406-5 | (and won) | Lahore v WAPDA | Lahore | 1984-85 |
| 406 | (lost 17 runs) | South Australia v New South Wales | Adelaide | 1921–22 |
| 404-3 | (and won) | Australia v England | Leeds | 1948 |
| 404-5 | (and won) | Lancashire v Hampshire | Southampton | 1910 |
| 404 | (lost 50 runs) | MCC v Cambridge University | Lord's | 1959 |
| 403-7 | (and won) | Oxford University v Worcestershire | Worcester | 1904 |
| 403-8 | (and won) | Lancashire v Nottinghamshire | Manchester | 1910 |
| 403 | (lost 385 runs) | South Australia v Victoria | Melbourne | 1920–21 |
| 402-9 | (set 403 runs) | D.G. Bradman's XI v A.L. Hassett's XI | Melbourne | 1948–49 |
| 402 | (lost 103 runs) | Australia v England | Manchester | 1981 |
| 401-4 | (and won) | New South Wales v Queensland | Brisbane | 1928–29 |
| 401-6 | (and won) | Gentlemen of England v Cambridge U. | Eastbourne | 1908 |

# HIGHEST FOURTH INNINGS TOTALS WITHOUT LOSS

| | | | | |
|---|---|---|---|---|
| 276-0 | (and won) | New South Wales v South Australia | Sydney | 1964–65 |
| | | *R.B. Simpson (142\*) and N.C. O'Neill (133\*) in 168 minutes* | | |
| 270-0 | (set 346) | Surrey v Kent | Oval | 1900 |
| | | *R. Abel (120\*) and W. Brockwell (132\*) in 170 minutes* | | |
| 250-0 | (set 323) | West Indies v Australia | Georgetown | 1983–84 |
| | | *C.G. Greenidge (120\*) and D.L. Haynes (103\*)* | | |
| 236-0 | (and won) | Orange Free State v Eastern Province | Port Elizabeth | 1926–27 |
| | | *S.K. Coen (132\*) and J.M.M. Commaille (99\*)* | | |
| 233-0 | (and won) | Lancashire v Sussex | Eastbourne | 1947 |
| | | *W. Place (106\*) and C. Washbrook (121\*) in 115 minutes* | | |
| 226-0 | (and won) | Canterbury v Otago | Christchurch | 1948–49 |
| | | *W.A.Hadlee (110\*) and J.G. Leggat (110\*)* | | |
| 226-0 | (and won) | Lancashire v Warwickshire | Southport | 1982 |
| | | *G. Fowler (128\*) and D. Lloyd (88\*)* | | |
| 225-0 | (and won) | New South Wales v Queensland | Sydney | 1950–51 |
| | | *A.R. Morris (78\*) and K.R. Miller (138\*) in 120 minutes* | | |
| 223-0 | (and won) | Rawalpindi v Lahore | Rawalpindi | 1982–83 |
| | | *Masood Anwar (108\*) and Azmat Jalil (107\*)* | | |
| 219-0 | (set 382) | West Indians v Nottinghamshire | Nottingham | 1923 |
| | | *G. Challenor (102\*) and P.H. Tarilton (109\*) in 150 minutes* | | |
| 215-0 | (set 337) | Nottinghamshire v Derbyshire | Worksop | 1936 |
| | | *W.W. Keeton (100\*) and C.B. Harris (107\*) in 200 minutes* | | |
| 201-0 | (and won) | Nottinghamshire v Essex | Nottingham | 1936 |
| | | *W.W. Keeton (115\*) and C.B. Harris (81\*)* | | |
| 201-0 | (and won) | Northamptonshire v Sussex | Eastbourne | 1967 |
| | | *C. Milburn (141\*) and R.M. Prideaux (51\*) in 115 minutes* | | |

# HIGHEST MATCH AGGREGATES

| Runs-Wkts | | | |
|---|---|---|---|
| 2376-37 | Bombay v Maharashtra | Poona | 1948–49 |
| 2078-40 | Bombay v Holkar | Bombay | 1944–45 |
| 1981-35 | South Africa v England | Durban | 1938–39 |
| 1929-39 | New South Wales v South Australia | Sydney | 1925–26 |
| 1911-34 | New South Wales v Victoria | Sydney | 1908–09 |
| 1905-40 | Otago v Wellington | Dunedin | 1923–24 |
| 1815-34 | West Indies v England | Kingston | 1929–30 |
| 1801-40 | A.L. Hassett's XI v A.R. Morris's XI | Melbourne | 1953–54 |
| 1764-39 | Australia v West Indies | Adelaide | 1968–69 |
| 1753-40 | Australia v England | Adelaide | 1920–21 |
| 1752-34 | New South Wales v Queensland | Sydney | 1926–27 |
| 1744-40 | New South Wales v South Africans | Sydney | 1910–11 |
| 1739-40 | New South Wales v A.E. Stoddart's XI | Sydney | 1897–98 |
| 1723-31 | England v Australia | Leeds | 1948 |
| 1716-40 | New South Wales v South Australia | Sydney | 1907–08 |
| 1704-39 | J. Ryder's XI v W.M. Woodfull's XI | Sydney | 1929–30 |
| 1683-40 | Victoria v South Australia | Melbourne | 1920–21 |
| 1677-37 | Barbados v Trinidad | Bridgetown | 1926–27 |
| 1672-39 | D.G. Bradman's XI v A.L. Hassett's XI | Melbourne | 1948–49 |
| 1661-36 | West Indies v Australia | Bridgetown | 1954–55 |
| 1647-30 | Bengal Cyclone XI v Bijapur Famine XI | Bombay | 1942–43 |
| 1646-40 | Australia v South Africa | Adelaide | 1910–11 |
| 1644-38 | Australia v West Indies | Sydney | 1968–69 |
| 1640-24 | West Indies v Australia | Bridgetown | 1964–65 |
| 1640-33 | Australia v Pakistan | Melbourne | 1972–73 |
| 1635-31 | Trinidad v Barbados | Port-of-Spain | 1945–46 |
| 1619-40 | Australia v England | Melbourne | 1924–25 |
| 1615-40 | New South Wales v Victoria | Sydney | 1907–08 |
| 1611-40 | Australia v England | Sydney | 1924–25 |
| 1611-24 | Holkar v Mysore | Indore | 1945–46 |
| 1607-22 | New South Wales v MCC | Sydney | 1929–30 |
| 1605-38 | New South Wales v Queensland | Sydney | 1927–28 |

*Runs-Wkts*

| | | | |
|---|---|---|---|
| 1601-29 | England v Australia | Lord's | 1930 |
| 1587-40 | British Guiana v Barbados | Georgetown | 1929–30 |
| 1585-31 | Pakistan v New Zealand | Karachi | 1976–77 |
| 1581-39 | South Australia v New South Wales | Adelaide | 1921–22 |
| 1573-36 | South Australia v New South Wales | Adelaide | 1926–27 |
| 1571-38 | British Guiana v Trinidad | Georgetown | 1937–38 |
| 1570-40 | New South Wales v South Australia | Sydney | 1912–13 |
| 1568-34 | South Australia v New South Wales | Adelaide | 1965–66 |
| 1567-37 | Auckland v Wellington | Auckland | 1936–37 |
| 1562-37 | Australia v England | Melbourne | 1946–47 |
| 1560-37 | New South Wales v Queensland | Sydney | 1928–29 |
| 1560-39 | Bengal Chief Minister's XI v Commonwealth XI | Calcutta | 1964–65 |
| 1558-30 | Victoria v New South Wales | Melbourne | 1926–27 |
| 1558-37 | Delhi v Holkar | Delhi | 1949–50 |
| 1555-40 | Holkar v Gujarat | Indore | 1950–51 |
| 1554-35 | Australia v England | Melbourne | 1928–29 |
| 1554-40 | Wellington v Auckland | Wellington | 1922–23 |
| 1553-33 | Australian XI v Rest of Australia | Sydney | 1898–99 |
| 1545-34 | Bombay v Holkar | Bombay | 1951–52 |
| 1541-35 | Australia v England | Sydney | 1903–04 |
| 1541-28 | New South Wales v MCC | Sydney | 1924–25 |
| 1533-33 | New South Wales v Victoria | Sydney | 1924–25 |
| 1531-39 | Wellington v Auckland | Wellington | 1923–24 |
| 1528-24 | West Indies v England | Port-of-Spain | 1953–54 |
| 1522-36 | Barbados v Trinidad | Bridgetown | 1948–49 |
| 1516-37 | Barbados v British Guiana | Bridgetown | 1949–50 |
| 1514-40 | Australia v England | Sydney | 1894–95 |
| 1513-29 | New South Wales v Victoria | Sydney | 1927–28 |
| 1510-38 | South Australia v New South Wales | Adelaide | 1920–21 |
| 1507-28 | England v West Indies | Oval | 1976 |
| 1507-39 | Western Australia v West Indians | Perth | 1975–76 |
| 1504-39 | Victoria v Tasmania | Melbourne | 1912–13 |
| 1503-37 | South Australia v Victoria | Adelaide | 1924–25 |
| 1502-40 | Queensland v New South Wales | Brisbane | 1926–27 |
| 1502-28 | MCC v New Zealanders | Lord's | 1927 |
| 1502-29 | Australia v England | Adelaide | 1946–47 |
| 1501-37 | Canterbury v Otago | Christchurch | 1931–32 |
| 1500-35 | South Australia v New South Wales | Adelaide | 1929–30 |

*Aggregates of over 1400 runs in England:*

| | | | |
|---|---|---|---|
| 1723-31 | England v Australia | Leeds | 1948 |
| 1601-29 | England v Australia | Lord's | 1930 |
| 1507-28 | England v West Indies | Oval | 1976 |
| 1502-28 | MCC v New Zealanders | Lord's | 1927 |
| 1499-31 | T.N. Pearce's XI v Australians | Scarborough | 1961 |
| 1496-24 | England v Australia | Nottingham | 1938 |
| 1494-37 | England v Australia | Oval | 1934 |
| 1492-33 | Worcestershire v Oxford University | Worcester | 1904 |
| 1477-32 | Hampshire v Oxford University | Southampton | 1913 |
| 1477-33 | England v South Africa | Oval | 1947 |
| 1475-27 | Northamptonshire v Surrey | Northampton | 1920 |
| 1469-30 | Surrey v Cambridge University | Oval | 1921 |
| 1458-31 | England v South Africa | Nottingham | 1947 |
| 1451-36 | Sussex v Kent | Hastings | 1929 |
| 1446-33 | Hampshire v Kent | Southampton | 1911 |
| 1443-34 | Middlesex v Gloucestershire | Lord's | 1938 |
| 1427-21 | Sussex v Surrey | Hastings | 1902 |
| 1426-30 | Cambridge University v Free Foresters | Cambridge | 1934 |
| 1425-16 | Worcestershire v Leicestershire | Worcester | 1906 |
| 1424-30 | Hampshire v Worcestershire | Bournemouth | 1905 |
| 1423-37 | North v South | Torquay | 1955 |
| 1422-34 | Kent v Essex | Gravesend | 1938 |
| 1422-27 | England v West Indies | Nottingham | 1957 |
| 1417-32 | North v South | Kingston | 1947 |
| 1415-21 | Somerset v Warwickshire | Taunton | 1985 |
| 1414-24 | Essex v Kent | Brentwood | 1934 |

| 1410-28 | Sussex v Oxford University | Hove | 1895 |
| 1409-25 | Surrey v Middlesex | Oval | 1919 |
| 1409-29 | Oxford University v MCC | Oxford | 1919 |
| 1406-37 | Navy & Army v Oxford & Cambridge University | Portsmouth | 1911 |
| 1405-24 | Leicestershire v Middlesex | Leicester | 1947 |
| 1402-40 | Sussex v Cambridge University | Hove | 1891 |

## LOWEST INNINGS TOTALS

| 12 | Oxford University v MCC | Oxford (i) | 1877 |
| 12 | Northamptonshire v Gloucestershire | Gloucester | 1907 |
| 13 | Auckland v Canterbury | Auckland (ii) | 1877–78 |
| 13 | Nottinghamshire v Yorkshire | Nottingham | 1901 |
| 14 | Surrey v Essex | Chelmsford | 1983 |
| 15 | MCC v Surrey | Lord's | 1839 |
| 15 | Victoria v MCC | Melbourne | 1903–04 |
| 15 | Northamptonshire v Yorkshire | Northampton (iii) | 1908 |
| 15 | Hampshire v Warwickshire | Birmingham (iv) | 1922 |
| 16 | MCC v Surrey | Lord's (v) | 1872 |
| 16 | Derbyshire v Nottinghamshire | Nottingham | 1879 |
| 16 | Surrey v Nottinghamshire | Oval | 1880 |
| 16 | Warwickshire v Kent | Tonbridge | 1913 |
| 16 | Trinidad v Barbados | Bridgetown | 1941–42 |
| 16 | Border v Natal *(1st innings)* | East London | 1959–60 |
| 17 | Gentlemen of Kent v Gentlemen of England | Lord's | 1850 |
| 17 | Gloucestershire v Australians | Cheltenham | 1896 |
| 18 | The B's v England | Lord's | 1831 |
| 18 | Kent v Sussex | Gravesend | 1867 |
| 18 | Tasmania v Victoria | Melbourne | 1868–69 |
| 18 | Australians v MCC | Lord's | 1896 |
| 18 | Border v Natal *(2nd innings)* | East London | 1959–60 |
| 19 | Sussex v Surrey | Godalming | 1830 |
| 19 | Sussex v Nottinghamshire | Hove | 1873 |
| 19 | MCC v Australians | Lord's | 1878 |
| 19 | Wellington v Nelson | Nelson | 1885–86 |

(i)    After batting one short in their first innings, the full Oxford University side was dismissed for 35 at their second attempt.
(ii)   The highest individual score was 2 and there were 8 extras.
(iii)  Northamptonshire were dismissed for 27 in their first innings.
(iv)   Hampshire followed-on, scored 521 and won the match by 155 runs.
(v)    Seven wickets fell before the first run was scored, the 8th wicket fell at 2, and the 9th wicket at 8.

### IN ENGLAND

| Derbyshire | 16 | v | Nottinghamshire | Nottingham | 1879 |
| | 20 | v | Yorkshire | Sheffield | 1939 |
| | 23 | v | Yorkshire | Hull | 1921 |
| | 26 | v | MCC | Lord's | 1880 |
| | 26 | v | Yorkshire | Derby | 1880 |
| | 30 | v | Nottinghamshire | Chesterfield | 1913 |
| Essex | 30 | v | Yorkshire | Leyton | 1901 |
| Glamorgan | 22 | v | Lancashire | Liverpool | 1924 |
| | 24 | v | Leicestershire | Leicester | 1971 |
| | 26 | v | Lancashire | Cardiff | 1958 |
| Gloucestershire | 17 | v | Australians | Cheltenham | 1896 |
| | 22 | v | Somerset | Bristol | 1920 |
| | 25 | v | Somerset | Cheltenham | 1891 |
| Hampshire | 15 | v | Warwickshire | Birmingham | 1922 |
| | 23 | v | Derbyshire | Burton upon Trent | 1958 |
| | 24 | v | MCC | Lord's | 1878 |
| | 27 | v | England | Southampton | 1842 |
| | 30 | v | Worcestershire | Worcester | 1903 |
| | 30 | v | Nottinghamshire | Southampton | 1932 |
| Kent | 18 | v | Sussex | Gravesend | 1867 |

| | | | | |
|---|---|---|---|---|
| Kent *continued* | 20 | v Surrey | Oval | 1870 |
| | 21 | v England | Lord's | 1834 |
| | 23 | v Sussex | Brighton | 1828 |
| | 23 | v England *(1st innings)* | Bromley | 1840 |
| | 23 | v Sussex | Hove | 1859 |
| | 25 | v Derbyshire | Wirksworth | 1874 |
| | 25 | v MCC | Lord's | 1879 |
| | 27 | v Sussex | Town Malling | 1836 |
| | 27 | v MCC | Lord's | 1856 |
| | 28 | v Gloucestershire | Moreton-in-Marsh | 1888 |
| | 30 | v England *(2nd innings)* | Bromley | 1840 |
| Lancashire | 25 | v Derbyshire | Manchester | 1871 |
| | 27 | v Surrey | Manchester | 1958 |
| | 28 | v Australians | Liverpool | 1896 |
| | 30 | v Yorkshire | Holbeck | 1868 |
| Leicestershire | 25 | v Kent | Leicester | 1912 |
| | 26 | v Kent | Leicester | 1911 |
| | 28 | v Australians | Leicester | 1899 |
| | 30 | v MCC | Lord's | 1899 |
| Middlesex | 20 | v MCC | Lord's | 1864 |
| | 24 | v MCC | Lord's | 1815 |
| | 25 | v Surrey | Oval | 1885 |
| | 29 | v Derbyshire | Chesterfield | 1957 |
| Northamptonshire | 12 | v Gloucestershire | Gloucester | 1907 |
| | 15 | v Yorkshire *(2nd innings)* | Northampton | 1908 |
| | 27 | v Yorkshire *(1st innings)* | Northampton | 1908 |
| | 27 | v Yorkshire | Kettering | 1933 |
| Nottinghamshire | 13 | v Yorkshire | Nottingham | 1901 |
| | 21 | v MCC | Lord's | 1891 |
| | 23 | v MCC | Nottingham | 1883 |
| | 24 | v Yorkshire | Sheffield | 1888 |
| Somerset | 25 | v Gloucestershire | Bristol | 1947 |
| | 29 | v Lancashire | Manchester | 1882 |
| Surrey | 14 | v Essex | Chelmsford | 1983 |
| | 16 | v Nottinghamshire | Oval | 1880 |
| | 26 | v Nottinghamshire | Nottingham | 1876 |
| | 27 | v Gloucestershire | Cheltenham | 1874 |
| Sussex | 19 | v Surrey | Godalming | 1830 |
| | 19 | v Nottinghamshire | Hove | 1873 |
| | 20 | v Yorkshire | Hull | 1922 |
| | 22 | v Kent | Sevenoaks | 1828 |
| | 23 | v Kent | Hawkhurst | 1826 |
| | 23 | v MCC | Lord's | 1838 |
| | 23 | v MCC | Lord's | 1856 |
| | 23 | v Warwickshire | Worthing | 1964 |
| | 24 | v Yorkshire | Hove | 1878 |
| | 24 | v Lancashire | Manchester | 1890 |
| | 25 | v MCC | Lord's | 1843 |
| | 29 | v MCC | Lord's | 1861 |
| | 29 | v Gloucestershire | Cheltenham | 1878 |
| | 29 | v Lancashire | Liverpool | 1907 |
| Warwickshire | 16 | v Kent | Tonbridge | 1913 |
| | 28 | v Derbyshire | Derby | 1937 |
| Worcestershire | 24 | v Yorkshire | Huddersfield | 1903 |
| | 25 | v Yorkshire | Hull | 1906 |
| | 25 | v Surrey | Oval | 1954 |
| | 25 | v Kent | Tunbridge Wells | 1960 |
| | 28 | v Yorkshire | Bradford | 1907 |
| Yorkshire | 23 | v Hampshire | Middlesbrough | 1965 |
| | 26 | v Surrey | Oval | 1909 |
| | 30 | v Kent | Sheffield | 1865 |
| Oxford University | 12 | v MCC | Oxford | 1877 |
| | 24 | v Leicestershire | Oxford | 1985 |
| Cambridge University | 22 | v Cambridge Town | Cambridge | 1827 |
| | 30 | v Yorkshire | Cambridge | 1928 |
| MCC | 15 | v Surrey | Lord's | 1839 |
| | 16 | v Surrey | Lord's | 1872 |

| MCC *continued* | 19 | v | Australians | Lord's | 1878 |
|---|---|---|---|---|---|
| | 24 | v | Oxford University | Lord's | 1846 |
| | 27 | v | Yorkshire | Lord's | 1902 |
| | 29 | v | The B's | Lord's | 1832 |
| | 29 | v | North | Lord's | 1848 |
| | 30 | v | Lancashire | Lord's | 1886 |

*Other totals of 30 and less in England:*

| 17 | Gentlemen of Kent v Gentlemen of England | Lord's | 1850 |
|---|---|---|---|
| 18 | The B's v England | Lord's | 1831 |
| 18 | Australians v MCC | Lord's | 1896 |
| 23 | Cambridge Town v Nottingham | Cambridge | 1834 |
| 23 | Australians v Yorkshire | Leeds | 1902 |
| 24 | Players v Gentlemen | Lord's | 1829 |
| 25 | Ireland v Scotland | Dublin | 1965 |
| 26 | Slow Bowlers v Fast Bowlers | Lord's | 1849 |
| 26 | England v MCC | Lord's | 1877 |
| 26 | England XI v Australians | Birmingham (Aston) | 1884 |
| 27 | England v Sussex | Brighton | 1827 |
| 27 | United North of England XI v All-England XI | Bolton | 1871 |
| 27 | Lord Sheffield's XI v Australians | Sheffield Park | 1890 |
| 27 | Rest v England XI | Bradford | 1950 |
| 28 | England XI v Australians | Stoke | 1888 |
| 29 | Nottingham v Sheffield | Sheffield | 1829 |
| 29 | Cambridge Town v Nottingham | Nottingham | 1834 |
| 29 | Gentlemen of Kent v Gentlemen of England | Lord's | 1849 |
| 30 | England v Sussex | Brighton | 1833 |
| 30 | England v Kent | Bromley | 1841 |
| 30 | Gentlemen of England v Gentlemen of Kent | Canterbury | 1859 |
| 30 | Cambridgeshire v Yorkshire (with Durham) | Stockton-on-Tees | 1861 |
| 30 | United North of England XI v United South of England | Northampton | 1872 |
| 30 | South Africa v England | Birmingham | 1924 |
| 30 | Ireland v New Zealanders | Dublin | 1937 |

IN AUSTRALIA

| 15 | Victoria v MCC | Melbourne | 1903–04 |
|---|---|---|---|
| 18 | Tasmania v Victoria | Melbourne | 1868–69 |
| 23 | South Australia v Victoria | Melbourne | 1882–83 |
| 25 | Tasmania v Victoria | Hobart | 1857–58 |
| 27 | South Australia v New South Wales | Sydney | 1955–56 |
| 28 | Victoria v New South Wales | Melbourne | 1855–56 |
| 31 | Victoria v New South Wales | Melbourne | 1906–07 |
| 32 | Australian XI v G.F. Vernon's XI | Sydney | 1887–88 |
| 33 | Tasmania v Victoria | Launceston | 1857–58 |
| 34 | Victoria v New South Wales | Melbourne | 1875–76 |
| 35 | Victoria v New South Wales | Melbourne | 1887–88 |
| 35 | Victoria v New South Wales | Sydney | 1926–27 |
| 36 | Tasmania v Victoria | Melbourne | 1870–71 |
| 36 | South Africa v Australia | Melbourne | 1931–32 |
| 37 | New South Wales v Victoria | Sydney | 1868–69 |
| 37 | Victoria v New South Wales | Sydney | 1875–76 |
| 38 | Victoria v New South Wales | Sydney | 1856–57 |
| 38 | Victoria v New South Wales | Sydney | 1858–59 |
| 38 | Rest of Australia v Australian XI | Sydney | 1888–89 |
| 38 | Western Australia v Victoria | Melbourne | 1892–93 |
| 39 | Tasmania v Victoria | Hobart | 1889–90 |
| 40 | Queensland v Victoria | Brisbane | 1902–03 |

IN SOUTH AFRICA AND RHODESIA

| 16 | Border v Natal *(1st innings)* | East London | 1959–60 |
|---|---|---|---|
| 18 | Border v Natal *(2nd innings)* | East London | 1959–60 |
| 23 | Border v Natal | East London | 1920–21 |
| 29 | Griqualand West v Transvaal | Johannesburg | 1950–51 |
| 30 | South Africa v England | Port Elizabeth | 1895–96 |
| 31 | Griqualand West v Natal | Johannesburg | 1906–07 |
| 34 | Griqualand West v Transvaal | Port Elizabeth | 1902–03 |

| | | | |
|---|---|---|---|
| 34 | Border v Eastern Province | East London | 1946–47 |
| 34 | Eastern Province v Natal | Port Elizabeth | 1980–81 |
| 35 | South Africa v England | Cape Town | 1898–99 |
| 36 | Eastern Province v Transvaal | Port Elizabeth | 1937–38 |
| 37 | Eastern Province v Western Province | Port Elizabeth | 1933–34 |
| 37 | Orange Free State v Transvaal | Bloemfontein | 1936–37 |
| 40 | Eastern Province v Orange Free State | Durban | 1910–11 |
| 40 | Orange Free State v Transvaal B | Johannesburg | 1960–61 |

### IN WEST INDIES

| | | | |
|---|---|---|---|
| 16 | Trinidad v Barbados | Bridgetown | 1942–43 |
| 22 | Demerara v Barbados *(1st innings)* | Bridgetown | 1864–65 |
| 33 | A. Priestley's XI v Trinidad | Port-of-Spain | 1896–97 |
| 33 | Jamaica v R.A. Bennett's XI | Kingston | 1901–02 |
| 33 | West Indian XI v R.A. Bennett's XI | Georgetown | 1901–02 |
| 35 | Trinidad v Barbados | Port-of-Spain | 1893–94 |
| 38 | Demerara v Barbados *(2nd innings)* | Bridgetown | 1864–65 |

### IN NEW ZEALAND

| | | | |
|---|---|---|---|
| 13 | Auckland v Canterbury | Auckland | 1877–78 |
| 19 | Wellington v Nelson | Nelson | 1885–86 |
| 22 | Wellington v Canterbury | Wellington | 1903–04 |
| 25 | Canterbury v Otago | Christchurch | 1866–67 |
| 26 | New Zealand v England | Auckland | 1954–55 |
| 27 | Canterbury v Otago | Dunedin | 1896–97 |
| 28 | Hawke's Bay v Auckland | Auckland | 1910–11 |
| 29 | Wellington v Nelson | Nelson | 1879–80 |
| 29 | Taranaki v Hawkes Bay *(2nd innings)* | Hawera | 1891–92 |
| 30 | Wellington v Nelson | Nelson | 1883–84 |
| 31 | Wellington v Nelson | Nelson | 1887–88 |
| 32 | Canterbury v Otago | Christchurch | 1866–67 |
| 32 | Hawke's Bay v Wellington | Wellington | 1883–84 |
| 33 | Nelson v Auckland | Nelson | 1882–83 |
| 34 | Canterbury v Otago | Dunedin | 1863–64 |
| 34 | Wellington v Canterbury | Wellington | 1886–87 |
| 34 | Otago v Wellington | Dunedin | 1956–57 |
| 35 | Wellington v Auckland | Wellington | 1873–74 |
| 35 | Otago v Auckland | Christchurch | 1884–85 |
| 35 | Taranaki v Hawkes Bay *(1st innings)* | Hawera | 1891–92 |
| 36 | Wellington v Nelson | Nelson | 1885–86 |
| 36 | Otago v New South Wales | Dunedin | 1889–90 |
| 37 | Wellington v Nelson | Nelson | 1876–77 |
| 37 | Canterbury v Southland | Invercargill | 1920–21 |
| 37 | Canterbury v Wellington | Wellington | 1925–26 |
| 38 | Canterbury v Otago | Christchurch | 1873–74 |
| 39 | Taranaki v Hawkes Bay | Napier | 1891–92 |
| 40 | Otago v Canterbury | Dunedin | 1869–70 |
| 40 | Tasmania v Otago | Dunedin | 1883–84 |

### IN INDIA

| | | | |
|---|---|---|---|
| 21 | Muslims v Europeans *(1st innings)* | Poona | 1915–16 |
| 22 | Southern Punjab v Northern India | Amritsar | 1934–35 |
| 23 | Sind v Southern Punjab | Patiala | 1938–39 |
| 23 | Jammu & Kashmir v Delhi *(1st innings)* | Srinagar | 1960–61 |
| 23 | Jammu & Kashmir v Haryana | Chandigarh | 1977–78 |
| 24 | Europeans v Parsees | Bombay | 1894–95 |
| 25 | Saurashtra v Bombay | Bombay | 1951–52 |
| 27 | Kerala v Mysore | Bangalore | 1963–64 |
| 28 | Mysore v Bombay | Bangalore | 1951–52 |
| 28 | Jammu & Kashmir v Delhi *(2nd innings)* | Srinagar | 1960–61 |
| 29 | Andhra v Tamil Nadu | Coimbatore | 1978–79 |
| 30 | Europeans v Parsees | Poona | 1895–96 |
| 31 | East Punjab v Railways | Jullundur | 1958–59 |
| 32 | Rajputana v MCC | Ajmer | 1933–34 |
| 32 | Assam v Bihar | Dhanbad | 1971–72 |
| 33 | Parsees v Europeans | Poona | 1918–19 |

IN INDIA *continued*

| | | | |
|---|---|---|---|
| 33 | Bengal Governor's XI v Maharaja of Cooch<br>Bihar's XI | Calcutta | 1917–18 |
| 33 | Railways v Services | Delhi | 1958–59 |
| 33 | Kerala v Andhra | Trivandrum | 1969–70 |
| 33 | Assam v Bengal *(2nd innings)* | Jorhat | 1974–75 |
| 35 | Orissa v Bihar | Patna | 1958–59 |
| 35 | Patiala v Services | Delhi | 1958–59 |
| 35 | Assam v Bengal *(1st innings)* | Jorhat | 1974–75 |
| 36 | Kerala v Madras | Salem | 1961–62 |
| 37 | Europeans v Parsees | Poona | 1913–14 |
| 37 | Parsees v Europeans | Poona | 1898–99 |
| 37 | Parsees v Europeans | Poona | 1909–10 |
| 37 | Delhi v United Provinces | Agra | 1934–35 |
| 37 | Baroda v Nawanagar | Jamnagar | 1937–38 |
| 37 | Jammu & Kashmir v Services | Delhi | 1959–60 |
| 37 | Bihar v Bengal | Calcutta | 1972–73 |
| 38 | Mysore v Madras | Madras | 1936–37 |
| 38 | Jammu & Kashmir v Delhi | Delhi | 1963–64 |
| 39 | Muslims v Europeans *(2nd innings)* | Poona | 1915–16 |
| 39 | Maharashtra v Nawanagar | Jamnagar | 1941–42 |
| 39 | East Zone v West Indians | Jorhat | 1958–59 |
| 40 | Europeans v Parsees | Bombay | 1904–05 |
| 40 | Delhi v NWFP | Peshawar | 1938–39 |
| 40 | Railways v Delhi | Delhi | 1961–62 |
| 40 | Kerala v Mysore | Bangalore | 1965–66 |
| 40 | Vidarbha v Rajasthan | Jaipur | 1977–78 |

IN PAKISTAN

| | | | |
|---|---|---|---|
| 27 | Dera Ismail Khan v Railways *(2nd innings)* | Lahore | 1964–65 |
| 28 | Sukkur v United Bank | Karachi | 1976–77 |
| 29 | Dacca University & Board v Dacca | Dacca | 1964–65 |
| 30 | Quetta v Karachi B | Karachi | 1957–58 |
| 32 | Dera Ismail Khan v Railways *(1st innings)* | Lahore | 1964–65 |
| 32 | Sukkur v Muslim Commercial Bank | Sukkur | 1977–78 |
| 33 | East Pakistan Whites v Services | Dacca | 1956–57 |
| 34 | East Pakistan Whites v PIA | Dacca | 1970–71 |
| 39 | Dacca University v Bahawalpur | Bahawalpur | 1957–58 |
| 39 | Dera Ismail Khan v Hazara | Rawalpindi | 1983–84 |

# NOTABLE LOW SCORING

| | |
|---|---|
| 1899 | Although totalling only 86 against Somerset (Lord's), Middlesex dismissed the visitors for 35 and 44 to win by an innings and 7 runs in about three hours' playing time. |
| 1924 | Set 58 runs to win by Lancashire at Leeds, Yorkshire were all out for 33. This is the smallest target to be set a defeated side in the County Championship. |
| 1946–47 | Set 42 runs to win by Eastern Province at East London, Border were dismissed for only 34. This is the lowest target in first-class cricket for a losing team to be set. |
| 1960–61 | After declaring at 385-3, Delhi needed only two bowlers and 105 minutes to dismiss Jammu & Kashmir twice (23 & 28) in their Ranji Trophy match at Srinagar. |
| 1964–65 | Railways declared at 910-6 and then dismissed their Ayub Zonal Trophy opponents, Dera Ismail Khan, for 32 & 27. Their victory margin of an innings and 851 runs is the record for all first-class cricket. |
| 1965 | F.S. Trueman hit 26 runs off one over from D. Shackleton in Yorkshire's first innings against Hampshire at Middlesbrough; this was three runs more than the entire Yorkshire team scored in the second innings. |

# LOWEST MATCH AGGREGATES BY ONE TEAM

| | | | | |
|---|---|---|---|---|
| 34 | (16 & 18) | Border† v Natal | East London | 1959–60 |
| 42 | (27 & 15) | Northamptonshire v Yorkshire | Northampton | 1908 |
| 47 | (12 & 35) | Oxford University v MCC | Oxford | 1877 |
| 51 | (23 & 28) | Jammu & Kashmir v Delhi | Srinagar | 1960–61 |
| 52 | (33 & 19) | MCC v Australians | Lord's | 1878 |

| 53 | (18 & 35) | The B's v England | Lord's | 1831 |
| 53 | (23 & 30) | Kent v England | Bromley | 1840 |
| 55 | (22 & 33) | Demerara v Barbados | Bridgetown | 1864–65 |
| 55 | (36 & 19) | Wellington v Nelson | Nelson | 1885–86 |
| 57 | (35 & 22) | Sussex v Kent | Sevenoaks | 1828 |
| 57 | (25 & 32) | Canterbury v Otago | Christchurch | 1866–67 |
| 59 | (35 & 24) | Sussex v Yorkshire | Hove | 1878 |
| 59 | (35 & 24) | Sussex v Lancashire | Manchester | 1890 |
| 59 | (32 & 27) | Dera Ismail Khan v Railways | Lahore | 1964–65 |

† *No Border player reached double figures in either innings. N.D. During (9) made Border's highest score and hit their only boundary of the match.*

## LOWEST MATCH AGGREGATES

**COMPLETED MATCHES (i.e. not drawn)**

*Runs-Wkts*

| 105-31 | MCC v Australians | Lord's | 1878 |
| 134-31 | Kent v Sussex | Hawkhurst | 1826 |
| 134-30 | England v The B's | Lord's | 1831 |
| 147-40 | Kent v Sussex | Sevenoaks | 1828 |
| 149-30 | England v Kent | Lord's | 1858 |
| 150-30 | Cambridge Town v MCC | Chatteris | 1832 |
| 151-30 | Canterbury v Otago | Christchurch | 1866–67 |
| 153-37 | MCC v Sussex | Lord's | 1843 |
| 153-31 | Otago v Canterbury | Dunedin | 1896–97 |
| 156-30 | Nelson v Wellington | Nelson | 1885–86 |
| 158-22 | Surrey v Worcestershire | Oval | 1954 |
| 159-31 | Nelson v Wellington | Nelson | 1887–88 |
| 165-30 | Yorkshire v Nottinghamshire | Sheffield | 1888 |
| 165-30 | Middlesex v Somerset | Lord's | 1899 |
| 171-29 | Oxford University v MCC | Oxford | 1877 |
| 173-32 | Cambridge Town v Cambridge University | Cambridge | 1852 |
| 175-35 | MCC v Surrey | Lord's | 1872 |
| 175-29 | Essex v Yorkshire | Leyton | 1901 |
| 176-32 | Otago v Tasmania | Dunedin | 1883–84 |
| 181-33 | MCC v North | Lord's | 1848 |
| 183-33 | Gentlemen of Kent v MCC | Chislehurst | 1838 |
| 183-37 | Victoria v New South Wales | Melbourne | 1855–56 |
| 183-30 | Lancashire v Derbyshire | Manchester | 1871 |
| 183-40 | Nelson v Wellington | Nelson | 1883–84 |
| 184-40 | Fast Bowlers v Slow Bowlers | Lord's | 1849 |
| 184-30 | Gentlemen of England v Gentlemen of Kent | Lord's | 1850 |
| 185-30 | Kent v England | Canterbury | 1846 |
| 187-36 | MCC v Sussex | Lord's | 1890 |
| 188-32 | England v Kent | Lord's | 1834 |
| 188-30 | Gentlemen v Players | Lord's | 1837 |
| 188-30 | MCC v Sussex | Lord's | 1838 |
| 188-32 | Orissa v Bihar | Patna | 1958–59 |
| 191-40 | Oxford University v Australians | Oxford | 1886 |
| 193-30 | Hampshire v England | Southampton | 1842 |
| 193-31 | Oxford University v MCC | Oxford | 1868 |
| 193-29 | Yorkshire v Worcestershire | Bradford | 1900 |
| 194-39 | Surrey Club v MCC | Oval | 1846 |
| 197-31 | MCC v Sussex | Lord's | 1856 |
| 198-30 | Kent v England | Bromley | 1841 |
| 198-36 | MCC v Sussex | Lord's | 1862 |
| 198-22 | Eastern Province v Transvaal | Port Elizabeth | 1937–38 |

**MATCHES IN WHICH 40 WICKETS FELL**

| 147-40 | Kent v Sussex | Sevenoaks | 1828 |
| 183-40 | Nelson v Wellington | Nelson | 1883–84 |
| 184-40 | Fast Bowlers v Slow Bowlers | Lord's | 1849 |
| 191-40 | Oxford University v Australians | Oxford | 1886 |
| 210-40 | MCC v Middlesex | Lord's | 1815 |

| 210-40 | MCC v Kent | Lord's | 1856 |
|---|---|---|---|
| 210-40 | MCC v Kent | Lord's | 1879 |
| 211-40 | Nelson v Wellington | Nelson | 1879–80 |
| 220-40 | England v Kent | Lord's | 1841 |
| 221-40 | Tasmania v Victoria | Hobart | 1857–58 |
| 223-40 | Lancashire v Yorkshire | Manchester | 1893 |
| 228-40 | Sheffield v Nottingham | Sheffield | 1829 |
| 228-40 | Otago v Canterbury | Dunedin | 1863–64 |

# LARGEST MARGINS OF VICTORY

### LARGEST INNINGS VICTORIES

| Inns & 851 runs | Railways (910-6d) v Dera Ismail Khan | Lahore | 1964–65 |
|---|---|---|---|
| Inns & 666 runs | Victoria (1059) v Tasmania | Melbourne | 1922–23 |
| Inns & 656 runs | Victoria (1107) v New South Wales | Melbourne | 1926–27 |
| Inns & 605 runs | New South Wales (918) v South Australia | Sydney | 1900–01 |
| Inns & 579 runs | England (903-7d) v Australia | Oval | 1938 |
| Inns & 575 runs | Sind (951-7d) v Baluchistan | Karachi | 1973–74 |
| Inns & 527 runs | New South Wales (713) v South Australia | Adelaide | 1908–09 |
| Inns & 517 runs | Australians (675) v Nottinghamshire | Nottingham | 1921 |
| Inns & 487 runs | New South Wales (839) v Tasmania | Sydney | 1898–99 |
| Inns & 487 runs | Australians (679-7d) v Oxford University | Oxford | 1938 |
| Inns & 485 runs | Surrey (698) v Sussex | Oval | 1888 |
| Inns & 484 runs | Australians (621) v Northamptonshire | Northampton | 1921 |
| Inns & 479 runs | Karachi (772-7d) v Bahawalpur | Karachi | 1958–59 |
| Inns & 468 runs | Surrey (742) v Hampshire | Oval | 1909 |
| Inns & 456 runs | A. Shrewsbury's XI (634) v Victoria | Melbourne | 1887–88 |

### LARGEST VICTORIES BY RUNS MARGINS

| 685 runs | New South Wales (235 & 761-8d) v Queensland | Sydney | 1929–30 |
|---|---|---|---|
| 675 runs | England (521 & 342-8d) v Australia | Brisbane | 1928–29 |
| 638 runs | New South Wales (304 & 770) v South Australia | Adelaide | 1920–21 |
| 625 runs | Sargodha (376 & 416) v Lahore M.C. | Faisalabad | 1978–79 |
| 609 runs | M.C. Bank (575 & 282-0d) v WAPDA | Hyderabad | 1977–78 |
| 571 runs | Victoria (304 & 649) v South Australia | Adelaide | 1926–27 |
| 562 runs | Australia (701 & 327) v England | Oval | 1934 |
| 550 runs | Victoria (295 & 521) v Tasmania | Launceston | 1913–14 |
| 541 runs | New South Wales (642 & 593) v South Australia | Sydney | 1925–26 |
| 540 runs | Bengal (479 & 321-9d) v Orissa | Cuttack | 1953–54 |
| 531 runs | Bombay (596 & 442-5d) v Holkar | Bombay | 1951–52 |
| 530 runs | Australia (328 & 578) v South Africa | Melbourne | 1910–11 |
| 522 runs | Leicestershire (353-6d & 361-3d) v Cambridge University | Cambridge | 1984 |
| 512 runs | Wellington (447 & 374) v Auckland | Wellington | 1925–26 |

# VICTORY WITHOUT LOSING A WICKET

| Lancashire (166-0d & 66-0) beat Leicestershire (108 & 122) | Manchester | 1956 |
|---|---|---|
| Karachi (277-0d) beat Sind (92 & 108) | Karachi | 1957–58 |
| Railways (236-0d & 16-0) beat Jammu & Kashmir (92 & 159) | Srinagar | 1960–61 |
| Karnataka (451-0d) beat Kerala (141 & 124) | Chikmagalur | 1977–78 |

# VICTORY LOSING ONLY ONE WICKET

| Middlesex (464-1d) beat Essex (173 & 235) | Leyton | 1914 |
|---|---|---|
| Yorkshire (555-1d) beat Essex (78 & 164) | Leyton | 1932 |
| Yorkshire (493-1d) beat Hampshire (174 & 190) | Sheffield | 1939 |
| Lancashire (259-1d) beat Essex (104 & 129) | Colchester | 1946 |
| Sussex (181-1d & 17-0) beat Gloucestershire (84 & 113) | Eastbourne | 1953 |
| Railways (263-1d) beat Patiala (56 & 147) | Patiala | 1958–59 |
| Railways (293-1d) beat Northern Punjab (89 & 147) | Delhi | 1961–62 |
| Yorkshire (298-1d & 22-0) beat Oxford University (139 & 178) | Oxford | 1962 |

| | | |
|---|---|---|
| Bengal (389-1d & 12-0) beat Orissa (114 & 266) | Cuttack | 1963–64 |
| Services (196-1d) beat Jammu & Kashmir (47 & 81) | Delhi | 1963–64 |
| Railways (212-1d) beat Jammu & Kashmir (61 & 89) | Delhi | 1963–64 |
| Rhodesia (549-1d) beat Orange Free State (252 & 235) | Bloemfontein | 1967–68 |
| Worcestershire (388-1d) beat Cambridge University (109 & 211) | Cambridge | 1974 |
| Warwickshire (465-1c) beat Gloucestershire (243 & 161) | Birmingham | 1974 |
| Bengal (364-1d) beat Assam (116 & 69) | Calcutta | 1975–76 |
| Karachi Whites (561-1d) beat Quetta (104 & 163) | Karachi | 1976–77 |
| Middlesex (0-0d & 142-1) beat Surrey (49 & 89) | Lord's | 1977 |
| Transvaal (325-1d) beat Northern Transvaal (97 & 173) | Pretoria | 1980–81 |
| Transvaal (362-1d) beat Arosa Sri Lanka (120 & 200) | Johannesburg | 1982–83 |
| Bengal (450-1d) beat Assam (155 & 168) | Calcutta | 1983–84 |

# VICTORY AFTER FOLLOWING-ON

A Law regarding the follow-on was introduced in 1835 and compelled a side 100 or more runs in arrears on first innings to follow its innings on. The margin was reduced to 80 runs in 1854, and raised to 120 runs in 1895. In May 1900, MCC established the present law with its deficit of 150 or more runs but made the enforcement of the follow-on by the leading side optional.

| | | |
|---|---|---|
| MCC (91 & 216) beat Surrey (197 & 101) | Oval | 1847 |
| Surrey (175 & 253) beat North (257 & 118) | Oval | 1858 |
| Kent (120 & 176) beat Cambridgeshire (206 & 74) | Maidstone | 1863 |
| Nottinghamshire (162 & 181) beat Yorkshire (243 & 94) | Nottingham | 1863 |
| Gentlemen (102 & 352) beat Players (250 & 106) | Oval | 1866 |
| Surrey (110 & 297) beat Hampshire (208 & 140) | Oval | 1866 |
| Surrey (179 & 334) beat Cambridge University (339 & 160) | Oval | 1868 |
| Gloucestershire (143 & 253) beat Sussex (244 & 92) | Clifton | 1872 |
| Cambridge University (103 & 226) beat England XI (193 & 57) | Cambridge | 1878 |
| Yorkshire (128 & 195) beat Gloucestershire (253 & 63) | Sheffield | 1879 |
| Lancashire (113 & 314) beat Surrey (226 & 141) | Oval | 1880 |
| MCC (108 & 276) beat England (219 & 113) | Lord's | 1881 |
| A. Shaw's XI (146 & 198) beat Victoria (251 & 75) | Melbourne | 1881–82 |
| Sussex (182 & 222) beat Derbyshire (283 & 118) | Hove | 1882 |
| Lancashire (206 & 238) beat Kent (309 & 65) | Manchester | 1883 |
| Derbyshire (156 & 216) beat Sussex (269 & 74) | Hove | 1883 |
| Gloucestershire (101 & 321) beat Lancashire (188 & 227) | Clifton | 1884 |
| Cambridge University (84 & 342) beat C.I. Thornton's XI (164 & 154) | Cambridge | 1886 |
| Cambridge University (74 & 230) beat Yorkshire (152 & 124) | Cambridge | 1886 |
| A. Shaw's XI (201 & 264) beat Australian XI (294 & 114) | Melbourne | 1886–87 |
| Lancashire (205 & 172) beat Oxford University (315 & 42) | Manchester | 1888 |
| Victoria (137 & 178) beat New South Wales (240 & 63) | Sydney | 1888–89 |
| Yorkshire (137 & 247) beat Surrey (293 & 76) | Oval | 1890 |
| Middlesex (139 & 311) beat Lancashire (266 & 111) | Lord's | 1890 |
| Middlesex (96 & 233) beat Nottinghamshire (196 & 84) | Lord's | 1891 |
| Cambridge University (117 & 368) beat C.I. Thornton's XI (215 & 173) | Cambridge | 1892 |
| Yorkshire (81 & 226) beat Sussex (171 & 96) | Sheffield | 1892 |
| Gloucestershire (165 & 297) beat Kent (245 & 136) | Bristol | 1892 |
| South Australia (212 & 330) beat New South Wales (337 & 148) | Adelaide | 1892–93 |
| Kent (127 & 198) beat Australians (229 & 60) | Canterbury | 1893 |
| Australians (196 & 319) beat Cambridge University (290 & 108) | Cambridge | 1893 |
| Middlesex (108 & 377) beat Surrey (287 & 119) | Lord's | 1893 |
| Somerset (110 & 230) beat Kent (220 & 83) | Taunton | 1894 |
| England (325 & 437) beat Australia (586 & 166) | Sydney | 1894–95 |
| R.S. Lucas' XI (303 & 396) beat Barbados (517 & 157) | Bridgetown | 1894–95 |
| MCC (266 & 335) beat Sussex (418 & 137) | Lord's | 1897 |
| Transvaal (122 & 288) beat Natal (254 & 79) | Cape Town | 1897–98 |
| Sussex (154 & 350) beat Kent (278 & 114) | Tonbridge | 1899 |
| South Australia (304 & 454) beat Lord Hawke's XI (553 & 108) | Adelaide | 1902–03 |
| Oxford University (116 & 358) beat Kent (287 & 137) | Oxford | 1905 |
| Somerset (205 & 340) beat Gloucestershire (399 & 78) | Bath | 1905 |
| Northamptonshire (101 & 418) beat Worcestershire (266 & 212) | Worcester | 1906 |
| South Africans (95 & 281) beat Kent (273 & 101) | Catford | 1907 |
| Cambridge University (247 & 437) beat Sussex (405 & 238) | Cambridge | 1911 |
| Leicestershire (286 & 315) beat Worcestershire (463 & 130) | Worcester | 1913 |
| Hampshire (15 & 521) beat Warwickshire (223 & 158) | Birmingham | 1922 |
| Middlesex (253 & 358) beat Nottinghamshire (462 & 122) | Nottingham | 1924 |

| | | |
|---|---|---|
| Kent (115 & 389) beat Gloucestershire (351 & 129) | Maidstone | 1925 |
| Orange Free State (163 & 298) beat W. Province (393 & 44) | Cape Town | 1926–27 |
| Barbados (175 & 726-7d) beat Trinidad (559 & 217) | Bridgetown | 1926–27 |
| Minor Counties (108 & 326) beat West Indians (289 & 103) | Exeter | 1928 |
| Glamorgan (101 & 408) beat Sussex (306 & 147) | Horsham | 1929 |
| Royal Navy & Royal Marines (113 & 382) beat MCC (333 & 139) | Chatham | 1929 |
| Natal (115 & 458) beat Transvaal (370 & 190) | Durban | 1932–33 |
| Yorkshire (77 & 269-7d) beat Somerset (234 & 62) | Sheffield | 1951 |
| Auckland (180 & 302) beat Canterbury (392 & 84) | Auckland | 1952–53 |
| Glamorgan (161 & 295) beat Nottinghamshire (354 & 75) | Nottingham | 1957 |
| Yorkshire (160 & 425) beat The Rest (384-8d & 135) | Oval | 1959 |
| Northern Districts (165 & 275) beat Otago (320-9d & 105) | Dunedin | 1961–62 |
| Transvaal B (293 & 362) beat N.E. Transvaal (468 & 87) | Johannesburg | 1962–63 |
| Auckland (69 & 303) beat Northern Districts (224 & 140) | Auckland | 1963–64 |
| New South Wales (108 & 450) beat Queensland (307 & 224) | Brisbane | 1965–66 |
| Canterbury (166 & 360) beat Auckland (351-9d & 149) | Christchurch | 1973–74 |
| Natal B (121 & 413) beat Orange Free State (319 & 196) | Bloemfontein | 1975–76 |
| Gloucestershire (79 & 372) beat Somerset (333-7c & 110) | Taunton | 1976 |
| Kent (151 & 348) beat Middlesex (305-5c & 137) | Dartford | 1976 |
| Derbyshire (139 & 352) beat Lancashire (290 & 186) | Buxton | 1976 |
| England (174 & 356) beat Australia (401-9d & 111) | Leeds | 1981 |
| Essex (114 & 374) beat Warwickshire (334 & 119) | Ilford | 1984 |
| Derbyshire (139 & 381) beat Nottinghamshire (361 & 131) | Nottingham | 1984 |

## LARGEST VARIATION IN A SIDE'S TOTALS

*Runs*
*Variation*

| | | | |
|---|---|---|---|
| 551 | Barbados (175 & 726-7d) v Trinidad | Bridgetown | 1926–27 |
| 551 | Pakistan (106 & 657-8d) v West Indies | Bridgetown | 1957–58 |
| 551 | Middlesex (83 & 634-7d) v Essex | Chelmsford | 1983 |
| 543 | Somerset (87 & 630) v Yorkshire | Leeds | 1901 |
| 531 | Free Foresters (65 & 596-8d) v Cambridge University | Cambridge | 1919 |
| 524 | Cambridge University (179 & 703-9d) v Sussex | Hove | 1890 |
| 506 | Hampshire (15 & 521) v Warwickshire | Birmingham | 1922 |
| 500 | Essex (597 & 97) v Derbyshire | Chesterfield | 1904 |

## TIED MATCHES

Before 1948 a match was considered to be tied if the scores were level after the fourth innings, even if the side batting last had wickets in hand when stumps were drawn on the final day. Law 22 was amended in 1948 by Note 4 which stated: 'A "draw" is regarded as a "tie" when the scores are equal at the conclusion of play but only if the match has been played out.' Tied matches played before 1948 but which would not have qualified as such under this amendment are marked†.

| | | |
|---|---|---|
| MCC (69 & 107) v Oxford & Cambridge Universities (115 & 61) | Lord's | 1839 |
| Surrey (112 & 160) v Kent (127 & 145) | Oval | 1847 |
| Surrey (204 & 93) v MCC (175 & 122) | Oval | 1868 |
| Surrey (93 & 186) v Middlesex (112 & 167) | Oval | 1868 |
| Wellington (63 & 118) v Nelson (111 & 70) | Wellington | 1873–74 |
| Surrey (215 & 245) v Middlesex (138 & 322) | Oval | 1876 |
| Gentlemen (235 & 149) v Players (203 & 181) | Oval | 1883 |
| Surrey (97 & 124) v Lancashire (147 & 74) | Oval | 1894 |
| Worcestershire (224 & 209) v South Africans (293 & 140) | Worcester | 1901 |
| Middlesex (272 & 225) v South Africans (287 & 210) | Lord's | 1904 |
| Surrey (125 & 161) v Kent (202 & 84) | Oval | 1905 |
| Lancashire (253 & 168-7) v England XI (193 & 228-6d)† | Blackpool | 1905 |

*Lancashire had three wickets to fall with two balls to go, but insufficient time remained for another batsman to go in.*

| | | |
|---|---|---|
| MCC (371 & 69) v Leicestershire (239 & 201) | Lord's | 1907 |
| Jamaica (173 & 222) v MCC (269 & 131) | Kingston | 1910–11 |
| Somerset (243 & 103) v Sussex (242 & 104) | Taunton | 1919 |

*The last Sussex batsman, H.J. Heygate, was not allowed to bat under Law 45.*

Orange Free State (100 & 349) v Eastern Province (225 & 224-8)†   Bloemfontein   1925–26
*Eastern Province had two wickets in hand. The match was ruled as an Eastern Province win on first innings for the Currie Cup.*
Essex (178 & 137-9) v Somerset (208 & 107)†   Chelmsford   1926
*The ninth Essex wicket fell half a minute before time, and MCC ruled that the match ranked as a tie.*
Gloucestershire (72 & 202) v Australians (157 & 117)   Bristol   1930
Victoria (327 & 177-3) v MCC (321 & 183-9d)†   Melbourne   1932–33
*The third Victorian wicket fell to the last ball of the match with one run needed for victory.*
Worcestershire (130 & 142) v Somerset (131 & 141)   Kidderminster   1939
Southern Punjab (167 & 146) v Baroda (106 & 207)   Patiala   1945–46
Essex (267 & 239) v Northamptonshire (215 & 291)   Ilford   1947
Hampshire (363 & 224-7d) v Lancashire (367-9d & 220)   Bournemouth   1947
D.G. Bradman's XI (434 & 402-9) v A.L. Hassett's XI (406 & 430)†   Melbourne   1948–49
Hampshire (180 & 152) v Kent (162 & 170)   Southampton   1950
Sussex (123 & 131) v Warwickshire (138 & 116)   Hove   1952
Essex (261 & 231) v Lancashire (266 & 226-7d)   Brentwood   1952
Northamptonshire (182 & 226) v Middlesex (96 & 312)   Peterborough   1953
Yorkshire (351-4d & 113) v Leicestershire (328 & 136)   Huddersfield   1954
Sussex (172 & 120) v Hampshire (153 & 139)   Eastbourne   1955
Victoria (244 & 197) v New South Wales (281 & 160)   Melbourne (St Kilda)   1956–57
T.N. Pearce's XI (313-7d & 258) v New Zealanders (268 & 303-8d)   Scarborough   1958
Essex (364-6d & 176-8d) v Gloucestershire (329 & 211)   Leyton   1959
Australia (505 & 232) v West Indies (453 & 284)   Brisbane   1960–61
*The only instance in Test matches.*
Bahawalpur (123 & 282) v Lahore B (127 & 278)   Bahawalpur   1961–62
Hampshire (277 & 173) v Middlesex (327-5d & 123-9d)   Portsmouth   1967
England XI (312-8d & 190-3d) v England U-25 XI (320-9d & 182)   Scarborough   1968
Yorkshire (106-9d & 207) v Middlesex (102 & 211)   Bradford   1973
Sussex (245 & 173-5d) v Essex (200-8d & 218)   Hove   1974
South Australia (431 & 171-7d) v Queensland (340-8d & 262)   Adelaide   1976–77
Central Districts (198 & 202) v England XI (296-6d & 104)   New Plymouth   1977–78
Victoria (230-5d & 245) v New Zealanders (301-9d & 174-3d)   Melbourne   1982–83
Muslim Commercial Bank (229 & 238) v Railways (149 & 318)   Sialkot   1983–84
Sussex (143 & 192) v Kent (92 & 243)   Hastings   1984
Northamptonshire (124 & 330) v Kent (250-6d & 204-5d)   Northampton   1984

# MATCHES COMPLETED ON FIRST DAY

| | | |
|---|---|---|
| The B's (18 & 35) v England (81) | Lord's | 13 June 1831 |
| Cambridge University (81 & 54-2) v MCC (70 & 64) | Cambridge | 18 May 1837 |
| MCC (125) v Oxford University (34 & 86) | Lord's | 9 July 1840 |
| MCC (54 & 81-8) v Cambridge University (70 & 64) | Lord's | 19 June 1848 |
| MCC (167 & 19-3) v Surrey Club (56 & 128) | Lord's | 17 July 1848 |
| Gents of Kent (87 & 29) v Gents of England (85 & 32-5) | Lord's | 2 July 1849 |
| Gents of Kent (59 & 17) v Gents of England (108) | Lord's | 1 July 1850 |
| North (131) v South (36 & 76) | Lord's | 15 July 1850 |
| Gents of Kent (69 & 65) v Gents of England (184) | Lord's | 4 July 1853 |
| MCC (154) v Surrey Club (60 & 47) | Lord's | 12 June 1854 |
| MCC (88 & 11-1) v Sussex (75 & 23) | Lord's | 2 June 1856 |
| Surrey (166) v Sussex (35 & 31) | Oval | 16 July 1857 |
| Kent (33 & 41) v England (73 & 2-0) | Lord's | 5 July 1858 |
| Canterbury (46 & 56) v Otago (86 & 18-1) | South Dunedin | 11 February 1868 |
| N. of Thames (73 & 56) v S. of Thames (106 & 25-1) | Lord's | 8 June 1868 |
| MCC (16 & 71) v Surrey (49 & 39-5) | Lord's | 14 May 1872 |
| Wellington (35 & 120) v Auckland (53 & 103-7) | Wellington | 29 November 1873 |
| Middlesex (61 & 47) v Oxford University (123) | Prince's | 18 June 1874 |
| North (90 & 72) v South (123 & 41-0) | Lord's | 17 May 1875 |
| Oxford University (12 & 35) v MCC (124) | Oxford | 24 May 1877 |
| MCC (33 & 19) v Australians (41 & 12-1) | Lord's | 27 May 1878 |
| Oxford University (53 & 75) v MCC (85 & 41-9) | Oxford | 28 May 1880 |
| England XI (82 & 26) v Australians (76 & 33-6) | Birmingham (Aston) | 26 May 1884 |
| MCC (30 & 92) v Lancashire (53 & 71-4) | Lord's | 18 May 1886 |
| North (99 & 46-4) v South (61 & 82) | Lord's | 30 May 1887 |
| Wellington (31 & 48) v Nelson (73 & 7-1) | Nelson | 26 December 1887 |
| Lancashire (35 & 63) v Surrey (123) | Manchester | 2 August 1888 |
| Auckland (62 & 68) v Otago (48 & 83-2) | Auckland | 26 December 1889 |

| | | |
|---|---|---|
| MCC (127) v Nottinghamshire (21 & 69) | Lord's | 1 June 1891 |
| Taranaki (70 & 39) v Hawke's Bay (103 & 7-0) | Napier | 9 January 1892 |
| Lancashire (116 & 32-2) v Somerset (88 & 58) | Manchester | 9 August 1892 |
| Auckland (93 & 102) v New South Wales (185 & 14-1) | Auckland | 20 January 1894 |
| MCC (103) v Sussex (42 & 59) | Lord's | 2 May 1894 |
| Lancashire (231) v Somerset (31 & 132) | Manchester | 17 July 1894 |
| Yorkshire (173) v Somerset (74 & 94) | Huddersfield | 19 July 1894 |
| Leicestershire (35 & 35) v Surrey (164) | Leicester | 10 June 1897 |
| Hampshire (42 & 36) v Yorkshire (157) | Southampton | 27 May 1898 |
| *Benefit match for H. Baldwin* | | |
| Middlesex (86) v Somerset (35 & 44) | Lord's | 23 May 1899 |
| *Benefit match for W. Flower and the shortest match on record. Middlesex won by an innings and 7 runs only three hours and five minutes after play began.* | | |
| Yorkshire (99) v Worcestershire (43 & 51) | Bradford | 7 May 1900 |
| MCC (150 & 10-1) v London County (72 & 87) | Lord's | 20 May 1903 |
| Transvaal (180 & 4-0) v Orange Free State (118 & 64) | Johannesburg | 30 December 1906 |
| Middlesex (92 & 24-3) v Philadelphians (58 & 55) | Lord's | 20 July 1908 |
| Gloucestershire (33 & 81) v Middlesex (145) | Bristol | 26 August 1909 |
| Eastern Province (209) v Orange Free State (57 & 121) | Port Elizabeth | 26 December 1912 |
| Kent (261-6d) v Sussex (60 & 78) | Tonbridge | 21 June 1919 |
| Lancashire (130 & 20-1) v Somerset (74 & 73) | Manchester | 21 May 1925 |
| Madras (130) v Mysore (48 & 59) | Madras | 4 November 1934 |
| Ireland (79 & 30) v New Zealanders (64 & 46-2) | Dublin | 11 September 1937 |
| Derbyshire (231) v Somerset (68 & 38) | Chesterfield | 11 June 1947 |
| Lancashire (239) v Sussex (101 & 51) | Manchester | 12 July 1950 |
| Surrey (146) v Warwickshire (45 & 52) | Oval | 16 May 1953 |
| Somerset (55 & 79) v Lancashire (158) | Bath | 6 June 1953 |
| *Benefit match for H.T.F. Buse* | | |
| Kent (187) v Worcestershire (25 & 61) | Tunbridge Wells | 15 June 1960 |

*Lancashire have beaten Somerset in a single day on four occasions: 1892, 1894, 1925 and 1953.*

# FEWEST RUNS IN A FULL DAY'S PLAY

| | | | |
|---|---|---|---|
| 95 | Australia (80) v Pakistan (15-2) | Karachi | 1956–57 |
| 104 | Pakistan (0-0 to 104-5) v Australia | Karachi | 1959–60 |
| 105 | Queensland (30-1 to 135-5) v MCC | Brisbane | 1958–59 |
| 106 | England (92-2 to 198) v Australia | Brisbane | 1958–59 |
| 107 | Pakistan XI (66-0 to 173-1) v MCC | Lahore | 1955–56 |
| 110 | Combined XI (159-2 to 260) v MCC (9-1) | Perth | 1958–59 |
| 112 | Sussex (112-7) v MCC | Lord's | 1837 |
| 112 | Australia (138-6 to 187) v Pakistan (63-1) | Karachi | 1956–57 |
| 117 | India (117-5) v Australia | Madras | 1956–57 |
| 117 | New Zealand (6-0 to 123-4) v Sri Lanka | Colombo | 1983–84 |
| 122 | England (110-9 to 110) v South Africa (122-7) | Port Elizabeth | 1956–57 |
| 122 | Australia (156-6 to 186) v England (92-2) | Brisbane | 1958–59 |
| 122 | Australia (282-6 to 306 and 9-0) v England (87) | Melbourne | 1958–59 |
| 122 | Australia (243-4 to 258) v England (107-8) | Melbourne | 1978–79 |
| 123 | England (123-2 to 191) v Pakistan (55-1) | Hyderabad | 1977–78 |
| 124 | Pakistan (74-4 to 134) v Australia (64-1) | Dacca | 1959–60 |
| 124 | India (226-6 to 291) v Australia (59-2) | Kanpur | 1959–60 |
| 127 | India (162-3 to 245) v Pakistan (44-1) | Peshawar | 1954–55 |
| 127 | West Indies (291-2 to 353) v England (65-0) | Kingston | 1959–60 |
| 128 | England (53-2 to 181-9) v West Indies | Bridgetown | 1953–54 |
| 129 | Pakistan (129-6) v India | Peshawar | 1954–55 |
| 129 | India (46-1 to 149 and 26-2) v Australia | Madras | 1959–60 |
| 130 | South Africa (200-7 to 243) v New Zealand (79 & 8-1) | Johannesburg | 1953–54 |
| 130 | India (115-5 to 148) v Pakistan (97-1) | Dacca | 1954–55 |
| 130 | West Indies (349-7 to 386) v New Zealand (93-5) | Christchurch | 1955–56 |
| 134 | England (333-1 to 439) v Pakistan (28-0) | Dacca | 1961–62 |
| 134 | Glamorgan (134-3) v Hampshire | Portsmouth | 1964 |
| 136 | South Africa (138-5 to 164) v England (110-9) | Port Elizabeth | 1956–57 |
| 138 | Australia (138-6) v Pakistan | Karachi | 1956–57 |
| 138 | South Africa (138-5) v England | Port Elizabeth | 1956–57 |
| 140 | New Zealand (8-1 to 148-6) v South Africa | Johannesburg | 1953–54 |

# SLOW SCORING IN A MATCH

| Runs | Days | | | |
|------|------|--|--|--|
| 518 | 4 | Australia v England | Brisbane | 1958–59 |
| | | *142 + 148 + 122 + 106: match completed on fifth day* | | |
| 529 | 4 | Pakistan v Australia | Karachi | 1956–57 |
| | | *95 + 184 + 138 + 112: match completed on fifth day* | | |
| 538 | 4 | South Africa v England | Port Elizabeth | 1956–57 |
| | | *138 + 136 + 122 + 142: match ended on fourth day* | | |

# MOST RUNS IN A DAY

### BY ONE TEAM

| Runs | Wkts | | | |
|------|------|--|--|--|
| 721 | 10 | Australians (721) v Essex | Southend | 1948 |
| 651 | 2 | West Indians (682-2d) v Leicestershire | Leicester | 1950 |
| 649 | 7 | New South Wales (752-8d) v Otago | Dunedin | 1923–24 |
| 645 | 4 | Surrey (742) v Hampshire | Oval | 1909 |
| 644 | 8 | Oxford University (644-8d) v | | |
| | | H.D.G. Leveson Gower's XI | Eastbourne | 1921 |
| 640 | 8 | Lancashire (640-8d) v Sussex | Hove | 1937 |
| 636 | 7 | Free Foresters (636-7d) v Cambridge University | Cambridge | 1938 |
| 625 | 6 | Gloucestershire (625-6d) v Worcestershire | Dudley | 1934 |
| 623 | 2 | Kent (803-4d) v Essex | Brentwood | 1934 |
| 623 | 5 | Middlesex (623-5d) v Worcestershire | Worcester | 1949 |
| 621 | 6 | Lancashire (676-6d) v Hampshire | Manchester | 1911 |
| 621 | 8 | Australians (658) v Auckland | Auckland | 1913–14 |
| 618 | 4 | South Africa (618-4d) v Rest of South Africa | Johannesburg | 1964–65 |
| 616 | 5 | Surrey (616-5d) v Northamptonshire | Oval | 1921 |
| 608 | 7 | Australians (675) v Nottinghamshire | Nottingham | 1921 |
| 608 | 7 | Players (651-7d) v Gentlemen | Oval | 1934 |
| 607 | 3 | Hampshire (672-7d) v Somerset | Taunton | 1899 |
| 607 | 6 | Kent (607-6d) v Gloucestershire | Cheltenham | 1910 |
| 607 | 4 | Surrey (619-5d) v Northamptonshire | Northampton | 1920 |
| 603 | 5 | Rest of England (603-5d) v Middlesex | Oval | 1920 |

### BY BOTH TEAMS

| Runs | Wkts | | | |
|------|------|--|--|--|
| 685 | 23 | North (169-8d and 255-7) v South (261-8d) | Blackpool | 1961 |
| 666 | 6 | Northamptonshire (59-2) v Surrey (607-4) | Northampton | 1920 |
| 663 | 6 | Leicestershire (160-2) v Middlesex (503-4) | Leicester | 1947 |
| 649 | 11 | Hampshire (570-8) v Somerset (79-3) | Taunton | 1901 |
| 647 | 16 | Sussex (115) v Surrey (532-6d) | Oval | 1919 |
| 639 | 11 | Hampshire (245-7 and 63-0) v Gloucestershire | | |
| | | (331-4d) | Southampton | 1919 |
| 626 | 14 | Leicestershire (291) v Nottinghamshire (335-4) | Nottingham | 1919 |
| 626 | 12 | Surrey (337-2) v Hampshire (289) | Southampton | 1919 |
| 622 | 12 | Essex (99-2) v Sussex (523) | Leyton | 1919 |
| 619 | 7 | Rest of England (603-5) v Middlesex (16-2) | Oval | 1920 |
| 616 | 16 | Transvaal (557) v Orange Free State (59-6) | Johannesburg | 1929–30 |
| 613 | 7 | Worcestershire (6-1 and 47-1) v Essex (560-5d) | Leyton | 1921 |
| 610 | 13 | Kent (548) v Essex (62-3) | Gravesend | 1938 |
| 608 | 16 | Somerset (329-6) v Oxford University (279) | Oxford | 1901 |
| 604 | 13 | Natal (553) v Orange Free State (51-3) | Bloemfontein | 1954–55 |
| 603 | 9 | Kent (532-8) v Leicestershire (71-1) | Maidstone | 1962 |
| 602 | 13 | Lancashire (408) v Essex (194-3) | Manchester | 1919 |
| 601 | 15 | Surrey (361-5) v Middlesex (240) | Oval | 1919 |

*The following instances occurred during two-day first-class matches in South Africa where the hours of play were extended:*

| Runs | Wkts | | | |
|------|------|--|--|--|
| 661 | 20 | Griqualand West (460) v Border (201) | Kimberley | 1920–21 |
| 645 | 16 | Transvaal (450-9) v Orange Free State (195-7) | Johannesburg | 1920–21 |
| 644 | 12 | Natal (587) v Eastern Province (57-2) | Durban | 1939–40 |
| 641 | 12 | Transvaal (499) v P.W. Sherwell's XI (142-2) | Johannesburg | 1913–14 |

| 628 | 19 | OFS (309) v Griqualand West (319-9) | Bloemfontein | 1920–21 |
|---|---|---|---|---|
| 606 | 9 | Griqualand West (378-5) v OFS (228-4) | Pretoria | 1923–24 |
| 605 | 15 | Transvaal (339) v Rest (266-5) | Johannesburg | 1911–12 |

## FASTEST INNINGS

The following innings were scored at a rate of at least 110 runs per 100 balls (qualification: 200 runs):

| Runs per 100 balls | | Opponents | | |
|---|---|---|---|---|
| 156 | Kent (219-2) | Gloucestershire | Dover | 1937 |
| 143 | South Australia (206-7) | Victoria | Adelaide | 1982–83 |
| 132 | Nottinghamshire (279-1) | Leicestershire | Nottingham | 1949 |
| 131 | Lancashire (214-3) | Leicestershire | Manchester | 1983 |
| 127 | Yorkshire (218-5) | Sussex | Hove | 1959 |
| 127 | Victoria (237-6) | Queensland | Brisbane | 1963–64 |
| 125 | Karachi (219-3) | Quetta | Karachi | 1962–63 |
| 123 | Hampshire (267-4d) | Essex | Bournemouth | 1919 |
| 123 | Indians (253-6) | NWFP Governor's XI | Peshawar | 1982–83 |
| 121 | Griqualand West (460) | Border | Kimberley | 1920–21 |
| 120 | Warwickshire (274-4d) | Surrey | Birmingham | 1980 |
| 119 | West Indians (313-5) | Nottinghamshire | Nottingham | 1976 |
| 119 | Australians (241-3) | Worcestershire | Worcester | 1981 |
| 119 | Bombay (213-4d) | Karnataka | Bombay | 1982–83 |
| | *Excluding 20 penalty runs added for slow over-rate.* | | | |
| 117 | Ceylon (225-5) | Madras | Madras | 1966–67 |
| 115 | South Africans (224) | T.N. Pearce's XI | Scarborough | 1965 |
| 114 | Gentlemen of South (313) | Players of South | Hastings | 1907 |
| 114 | Barbados (234-9) | Guyana | Georgetown | 1968–69 |
| 113 | Board President's XI (314-7) | Holkar XI | Indore | 1957–58 |
| 112 | Hyderabad (202-7d) | Andhra | Vijayawada | 1974–75 |
| 112 | Essex (214-6) | Middlesex | Lord's | 1984 |
| 112 | Leicestershire (203-4) | Essex | Colchester | 1982 |
| 111 | Kent (234-3) | Surrey | Oval | 1939 |
| 111 | Punjab Governor's XI (292-7) | Punjab University | Lahore | 1967–68 |
| 110 | Kent (358-5d) | Somerset | Taunton | 1906 |
| 110 | New South Wales (448) | Tasmania | Hobart | 1909–10 |
| 110 | Australian XI (500) | Tasmania | Hobart | 1960–61 |
| 110 | West Indians (554-4d) | Glamorgan | Swansea | 1976 |

## BATSMEN'S MATCHES

*Qualification: 1200 runs, average 60 per wicket*

| Av | | | | |
|---|---|---|---|---|
| 189 | Cambridge University (594-4d) v West Indians (730-3) | | Cambridge | 1950 |
| 95 | Gloucs (383-3c & 404-4d) v Warwicks (438-5c & 105-2) | | Bristol | 1979 |
| 89 | Worcestershire (380 & 344-2) v Leicestershire (701-4d) | | Worcester | 1906 |
| 81 | Maharashtra (624-5d) v Rajasthan (604) | | Poona | 1970–71 |
| 81 | Yorkshire (344-3d & 321-2d) v Gloucs (321-6c & 235-4) | | Leeds | 1976 |
| 80 | Leicestershire (609-8d) v Sussex (686-8) | | Leicester | 1900 |
| 78 | Karnataka (705) v Delhi (707-8) | | Delhi | 1981–82 |
| 75 | Gloucestershire (643-5d) v Nottinghamshire (467 & 168-2) | | Bristol | 1946 |
| 75 | Nottinghamshire (420) v West Indians (489-3d & 298-3) | | Nottingham | 1957 |
| 74 | Orange Free State (537-5d & 212-2) v Border (509) | | Bloemfontein | 1969–70 |
| 73 | Surrey (551-7) v Yorkshire (704) | | Oval | 1899 |
| 73 | NSW (629-8d & 305-3d) v MCC (469 & 204-2) | | Sydney | 1929–30 |
| 72 | NSW (349 & 364-3) v MCC (734-7d) | | Sydney | 1928–29 |
| 72 | Nottinghamshire (401 & 201-4) v Surrey (706-4d) | | Nottingham | 1947 |
| 72 | South Australia (520-7d & 101-0) v Victoria (609) | | Melbourne | 1983–84 |
| 71 | Guyana (641-5d & 244-5) v Barbados (552) | | Georgetown | 1966–67 |
| 71 | Essex (387-4d & 273-5d) v Leicestershire (319-1d & 235-7) | | Leicester | 1981 |
| 70 | British Guiana (601-5d & 60-1) v Jamaica (469) | | Georgetown | 1956–57 |
| 70 | England (611) v Australia (656-8d & 4-0) | | Manchester | 1964 |
| 69 | Pakistan (580) v Commonwealth XI (630-9d & 250-2) | | Lahore | 1963–64 |
| 69 | Victoria (555-5d & 136-3d) v Pakistanis (406-9d & 288-3) | | Melbourne | 1983–84 |
| 68 | Somerset (418-7d & 263-5d) v Cambridge U. (416-4d & 268-4) | | Taunton | 1960 |

| 67 | Sussex (705-8d & 170-4) v Surrey (552) | Hastings | 1902 |
|----|------------------------------------------|----------|------|
| 67 | Glamorgan (196 & 577-4) v Gloucestershire (505-5d) | Newport | 1939 |
| 67 | Holkar (912-8d) v Mysore (190 & 509-6) | Indore | 1945–46 |
| 67 | Nottinghamshire (191 & 519-5) v Derbyshire (496-3d) | Nottingham | 1947 |
| 67 | Somerset (566-5d & 226-5d) v Warwickshire (442-9d & 181-2) | Taunton | 1985 |
| 66 | Somerset (560-8d) v Sussex (236 & 466-1) | Taunton | 1901 |
| 66 | Orange Free State (552) v Natal (402 & 452-1) | Bloemfontein | 1926–27 |
| 66 | Surrey (475-7d & 162-2) v Australians (629) | Oval | 1934 |
| 66 | Maharashtra (675) v Bombay (650) | Poona | 1940–41 |
| 65 | England (627-9d & 123-0d) v Australia (491 & 66-1) | Manchester | 1934 |
| 65 | India (273 & 333-3) v West Indies (629-6d) | Bombay | 1948–49 |
| 65 | West Indies (573 & 242-5) v Australia (650-6d & 175-4d) | Bridgetown | 1964–65 |
| 65 | Victoria (418-5d & 294-3d) v Tasmania (450-8d & 145-4) | Melbourne | 1983–84 |
| 64 | NSW (713-6d) v Victoria (265 & 510-7) | Sydney | 1928–29 |
| 64 | Kent (580-6d & 142-3) v Essex (502) | Maidstone | 1947 |
| 63 | West Indies (681-8d & 212-4d) v England (537 & 98-3) | Port-of-Spain | 1953–54 |
| 63 | Somerset (361-5d & 272-6) v Surrey (358-4d & 273-5d) | Taunton | 1961 |
| 63 | Kent (346-6d & 258-3d) v Australians (354-8d & 252-2) | Canterbury | 1964 |
| 63 | Worcestershire (400-2c & 273-1d) v Notts (328-7c & 208-9) | Worcester | 1979 |
| 63 | Warwickshire (523-4d & 111) v Lancashire (414-6d & 226-0) | Southport | 1982 |
| 62 | Essex (453 & 242-1) v Sussex (611) | Leyton | 1905 |
| 62 | England (658-8d) v Australia (411 & 427-6) | Nottingham | 1938 |
| 62 | Hampshire (594-6d) v Gloucestershire (317 & 403-5) | Southampton | 1911 |
| 62 | Maharashtra (798) v Kathiawar (442) | Poona | 1940–41 |
| 62 | Bombay (651 & 714-8d) v Maharashtra (407 & 604) | Poona | 1948–49 |
| 62 | Hasan Mahmood's XI (499-8d & 104-1d) v | | |
| | AVM Cannon's XI (365-5d & 101-3) | Karachi | 1953–54 |
| 62 | NSW (425-1d & 262-1) v Western Australia (420 & 266) | Sydney | 1963–64 |
| 62 | E. Province (387-7d & 159-3) v Rhodesia (293-3d & 420-7d) | Port Elizabeth | 1975–76 |
| 62 | Pakistanis (358-4d & 415) v South Australia (404-6d & 125-1) | Adelaide | 1981–82 |
| 62 | Queensland (318 & 439-5d) v Victoria (463-5d & 99-1) | Melbourne | 1983–84 |
| 61 | Sussex (415-5d & 281) v South Africans (555-6d & 45-0) | Hove | 1947 |
| 61 | Queensland (613 & 27-1) v NSW (661) | Brisbane | 1963–64 |
| 61 | Glamorgan (409-6d & 289-4d) v Warwickshire (315-2d & 348) | Birmingham | 1981 |
| 60 | Cambridge University (533) v Free Foresters (636-7d & 223-6) | Cambridge | 1938 |
| 60 | South Australia (649-9d) v MCC (451-9d & 235-4) | Adelaide | 1970–71 |
| 60 | Australia (511-6d & 460-8) v New Zealand (484) | Wellington | 1973–74 |
| 60 | Pakistan (503-8d & 264-4d) v India (462-9d & 43-0) | Faisalabad | 1978–79 |

# MOST HUNDREDS IN AN INNINGS

### SIX HUNDREDS IN AN INNINGS

| Holkar (912-8d) v Mysore | Indore | 1945–46 |
|---|---|---|

    *K.V. Bhandarkar 142, C.T. Sarwate 101, M.M. Jagdale 164,*
    *C.K. Nayudu 101, B.B. Nimbalkar 172, R. Pratap Singh 100*

### FIVE HUNDREDS IN AN INNINGS

| New South Wales (918) v South Australia | Sydney | 1900–01 |
|---|---|---|

    *F.A. Iredale 118, M.A. Noble 153, S.E. Gregory 168, R.A. Duff 119,*
    *L.O.S. Poidevin 140\**

| Australia (758-8d) v West Indies | Kingston | 1954–55 |
|---|---|---|

    *C.C. McDonald 127, R.N. Harvey 204, K.R. Miller 109, R.G. Archer*
    *128, R. Benaud 121*

### FOUR HUNDREDS IN AN INNINGS

| Yorkshire (887) v Warwickshire | Birmingham | 1896 |
|---|---|---|

    *F.S. Jackson 117, E. Wainwright 126, R. Peel 210\*, Lord Hawke 166*

| Derbyshire (645) v Hampshire | Derby | 1898 |
|---|---|---|

    *L.G. Wright 134, W. Storer 100, W. Chatterton 142, G. Davidson 108*

| Lancashire (580) v Somerset | Manchester | 1904 |
|---|---|---|

    *A.C. MacLaren 151, J.T. Tyldesley 103, A.H. Hornby 114, W.R. Cuttell 101*

| MCC (660-8d) v South Australia | Sydney | 1907–08 |
|---|---|---|

    *A.O. Jones 119, J. Hardstaff, sr 135, L.C. Braund 160, J.N. Crawford 114*

| | | |
|---|---|---|
| Kent (601-8d) v Somerset | Taunton | 1908 |
| *James Seymour 129, F.E. Woolley 105, A.P. Day 118, E. Humphreys 149* | | |
| Australian XI (610-6d) v New Zealand XI | Auckland | 1913–14 |
| *E.L. Waddy 140, C.E. Dolling 104, W.W. Armstrong 110\*,* | | |
| *J.N. Crawford 134* | | |
| New South Wales (690) v South Australia | Adelaide | 1919–20 |
| *W. Bardsley 106, J. Bogle 200, T.J.E. Andrews 103, C. Kelleway 121\** | | |
| Middlesex (543-4d) v Sussex | Lord's | 1920 |
| *P.F. Warner 139, H.W. Lee 119, J.W. Hearne 116\*, N.E. Haig 131* | | |
| *The first four batsmen in the order* | | |
| New South Wales (786) v South Australia | Adelaide | 1922–23 |
| *J.M. Taylor 159, A.F. Kippax 170, H.S.T.L. Hendry 146,* | | |
| *W.A.S. Oldfield 118* | | |
| Victoria (617-6d) v MCC | Melbourne | 1922–23 |
| *H.S.B. Love 192, R.L. Park 101, V.S. Ransford 118\*, A.E. Liddicut 102* | | |
| Middlesex (642-3d) v Hampshire | Southampton | 1923 |
| *H.L. Dales 103, H.W. Lee 107, J.W. Hearne 232, E.H. Hendren 177\** | | |
| *The first four batsmen in the order* | | |
| New South Wales (645) v Rest of Australia (except Victoria) | Sydney | 1924–25 |
| *H.L. Collins 106, J.M. Taylor 111, A.F. Kippax 115, C. Kelleway 101* | | |
| Victoria (1107) v New South Wales | Melbourne | 1926–27 |
| *W.M. Woodfull 133, W.H. Ponsford 352, H.S.T.L. Hendry 100, J. Ryder* | | |
| *295 – the first four batsmen in the order* | | |
| Barbados (715-9d) v British Guiana | Bridgetown | 1926–27 |
| *P.H. Tarilton 120, G. Challenor 104, E.L.G. Hoad 115, C.A. Browne 131\** | | |
| New South Wales (571) v New Zealanders | Sydney | 1927–28 |
| *J.M. Gregory 152, T.J.E. Andrews 134, A.F. Kippax 119, A.A. Jackson* | | |
| *104* | | |
| New South Wales (533) v Victoria | Sydney | 1927–28 |
| *A.F. Kippax 134, J.G. Morgan 110, W.A.S. Oldfield 101, C.O. Nicholls 110* | | |
| Nottinghamshire (656-3d) v Warwickshire | Coventry | 1928 |
| *G. Gunn 148, W.W. Whysall 132, W. Walker 146\*, F. Barratt 139\** | | |
| MCC (502) v Tasmania | Launceston | 1932–33 |
| *H. Sutcliffe 101, Nawab of Pataudi, sr 109, L.E.G. Ames 107, E. Paynter 102* | | |
| Victoria (558) v New South Wales | Melbourne | 1934–35 |
| *L.P.J. O'Brien 126, K.E. Rigg 111, L.S. Darling 106, E.H. Bromley 102* | | |
| South Australia (644-7d) v Queensland | Adelaide | 1934–35 |
| *V.Y. Richardson 185, H.C. Nitschke 116, A.R. Lonergan 137,* | | |
| *C.L. Badcock 137 – the first four batsmen in the order* | | |
| Auckland (590) v Canterbury | Auckland | 1937–38 |
| *P.E. Whitelaw 108, A.J. Postles 103, V.J. Scott 122, A.M. Matheson 112* | | |
| Australians (708-5d) v Cambridge University | Cambridge | 1938 |
| *J.H.W. Fingleton 111, D.G. Bradman 137, C.L. Badcock 186,* | | |
| *A.L. Hassett 220\** | | |
| England (658-8d) v Australia | Nottingham | 1938 |
| *L. Hutton 100, C.J. Barnett 126, E. Paynter 216\*, D.C.S. Compton 102* | | |
| Sussex (631-4d) v Northamptonshire | Northampton | 1938 |
| *J.G. Langridge 227, J.H. Parks 106, G. Cox 101, H.T. Bartlett 101\** | | |
| MCC (676) v Griqualand West | Kimberley | 1938–39 |
| *L. Hutton 149, W.J. Edrich 109, E. Paynter 158, N.W.D. Yardley 142* | | |
| South Australia (821-7d) v Queensland | Adelaide | 1939–40 |
| *K.L. Ridings 151, D.G. Bradman 138, C.L. Badcock 236, M.G. Waite 137* | | |
| Cricket Club of India (654) v C.K. Nayudu's XI | Bombay | 1944–45 |
| *M.H. Mankad 121, V.M. Merchant 130, V.S. Hazare 168, R.S. Cooper 127\** | | |
| Bombay (645) v Baroda | Bombay | 1945–46 |
| *K.C. Ibrahim 132, V.M. Merchant 171, U.M. Merchant 136,* | | |
| *K.M. Rangnekar 113* | | |
| Indians (533-3d) v Sussex | Hove | 1946 |
| *V.M. Merchant 205, M.H. Mankad 105, Nawab of Pataudi, sr 110\*,* | | |
| *L. Amarnath 106 – the only four batsmen to go to the wicket* | | |
| Surrey (706-4d) v Nottinghamshire | Nottingham | 1947 |
| *D.G.W. Fletcher 194, H.S. Squires 154, J.F. Parker 108\*, E.R.T. Holmes 122\** | | |
| Bombay (632-7d) v Maharashtra | Bombay | 1947–48 |
| *K.C. Ibrahim 159, P.J. Dickinson 122, M.M. Dalvi 143, M.N. Raiji 130* | | |
| Australians (721) v Essex | Southend | 1948 |
| *W.A. Brown 153, D.G. Bradman 187, S.J.E. Loxton 120, R.A. Saggers 104\** | | |
| West Indies (631) v India | Delhi | 1948–49 |
| *C.L. Walcott 152, G.E. Gomez 101, E.de C. Weekes 128, R.J. Christiani 107* | | |

| | | |
|---|---|---|
| Bengal (760) v Assam | Calcutta | 1951–52 |
| *Pankaj Roy 146, S. Bose 145, A.D. Gupte 117, C.S. Nayudu 119* | | |
| British Guiana (601-5d) v Jamaica | Georgetown | 1956–57 |
| *B.H. Pairaudeau 111, R.B. Kanhai 129, B.F. Butcher 154\*, J.S. Solomon 114\** | | |
| Punjab University (702) v Sind University | Karachi | 1958–59 |
| *Saeed Ahmed 140, Khalid Aziz 106, Mohammad Yusuf 115, Zafar Altaf 111* | | |
| Australians (449-3d) v Cambridge University | Cambridge | 1961 |
| *W.M. Lawry 100, C.C. McDonald 100, B.C. Booth 113, K.D. Mackay 106\* – the first four batsmen in the order* | | |
| South Africa (618-4d) v Rest of South Africa | Johannesburg | 1964–65 |
| *A.J. Pithey 110, R.G. Pollock 123, K.C. Bland 151\*, D.T. Lindsay 107\** | | |
| Railways (910-6d) v Dera Ismail Khan | Lahore | 1964–65 |
| *Ijaz Hussain 124, Javed Baber 200, Pervez Akhtar 337\*, Mohammad Sharif 106\** | | |
| Western Australia (594-6d) v New South Wales | Sydney | 1968–69 |
| *D. Chadwick 110, R.J. Inverarity 103, J.T. Irvine 128, R. Edwards 117\** | | |
| PIA (531-5d) v Karachi Whites | Karachi | 1969–70 |
| *Hanif Mohammad 114, Mohammad Ilyas 118, Mushtaq Mohammad 100\*, Zaheer Abbas 136* | | |
| PIA (609-6d) v Baluchistan | Karachi | 1976–77 |
| *Shoaib Mohammad 113, Salahuddin 125, Ghulam Abbas 132, Shafqat Rana 105* | | |
| Karnataka (705) v Delhi | Delhi | 1981–82 |
| *R.M.H. Binny 115, B.P. Patel 124, S.M.H. Kirmani 116, R. Khanvilkar 113* | | |
| Kent (616-6d) v Oxford University | Oxford | 1982 |
| *R.A. Woolmer 126, N.R. Taylor 127, C.J. Tavaré 125, M.R. Benson 120* | | |
| Pakistan (652) v India | Faisalabad | 1982–83 |
| *Javed Miandad 126, Zaheer Abbas 168, Salim Malik 107, Imran Khan 117* | | |
| West Indies (550) v India | St John's | 1982–83 |
| *C.G. Greenidge 154, D.L. Haynes 136, P.J.L. Dujon 110, C.H. Lloyd 106* | | |

# MOST FIFTIES IN AN INNINGS

EIGHT

| | | |
|---|---|---|
| Australians (843) v Oxford & Cambridge Past & Present | Portsmouth | 1893 |
| *J.J. Lyons 51, A.C. Bannerman 133, G.H.S. Trott 61, H. Graham 83, W. Bruce 191, H. Trumble 105, C.T.B. Turner 66, W.F. Giffen 62* | | |

SEVEN

| | | |
|---|---|---|
| Warwickshire (605) v Leicestershire | Leicester | 1899 |
| *S. Kinneir 111, W. Quaife 101, W.G. Quaife 117, E.J. Diver 71, H.W. Bainbridge 51, A.C.S. Glover 51, S. Santall 64* | | |
| New South Wales (918) v South Australia | Sydney | 1900–01 |
| *F.A. Iredale 118, V.T. Trumper 70, M.A. Noble 153, S.E. Gregory 168, R.A. Duff 119, T. Howard 64, L.O.S. Poidevin 140\** | | |
| Surrey (493) v Hampshire | Portsmouth | 1908 |
| *T.W. Hayward 53, J.B. Hobbs 56, E.G. Hayes 52, A. Marshal 54, J.N. Crawford 124, F.C. Holland 65\*, W.A. Spring 53 – the first seven batsmen in the order* | | |
| England v Australia | Manchester | 1934 |
| *C.F. Walters 52, H. Sutcliffe 63, E.H. Hendren 132, M. Leyland 153, L.E.G. Ames 72, G.O.B. Allen 61, H. Verity 60\** | | |
| Australians (679-7d) v Oxford University | Oxford | 1938 |
| *J.H.W. Fingleton 124, W.A. Brown 72, D.G. Bradman 58, S.J. McCabe 110, A.G. Chipperfield 53, A.L. Hassett 146, M.G. Waite 54 – the first seven batsmen in the order* | | |
| Maharashtra (798) v Northern India | Poona | 1940–41 |
| *R.V. Bhajekar 120, S.W. Sohoni 68, V.S. Hazare 65, C.T. Sarwate 63, Y.N. Gokhale 75, D.B. Deodhar 196, K.M. Jadhav 115* | | |
| Holkar (912-8d) v Mysore | Indore | 1945–46 |
| *K.V. Bhandarkar 142, C.T. Sarwate 101, M.M. Jagdale 164, C.K. Nayudu 101, B.B. Nimbalkar 172, C.S. Nayudu 73, R. Pratap Singh 100* | | |
| MCC (641-6) v Berbice | Blairmont | 1959–60 |
| *G. Pullar 65, M.J.K. Smith 50, J.M. Parks 183, K.F. Barrington 103, R. Illingworth 100, E.R. Dexter 54, R. Subba Row 58\* – the first seven batsmen in the order* | | |

| | | | |
|---|---|---|---|
| MCC (527-6d) v New South Wales | | Sydney | 1965–66 |
| *R.W. Barber 90, W.E. Russell 93, M.C. Cowdrey 63, M.J.K. Smith 59,* | | | |
| *J.M. Parks 63, F.J. Titmus 80\*, D.A. Allen 54\** | | | |
| West Zone (509-8) v North Zone | | Poona | 1967–68 |
| *D.N. Sardesai 83, A.L. Wadekar 58, C.G. Borde 52, V.L. Manjrekar 58,* | | | |
| *R.F. Surti 104, F.M. Engineer 59, R.G. Nadkarni 61\** | | | |
| Sind (599) v PIA | | Karachi | 1972–73 |
| *Taslim Arif 54, Shiraz Dharsi 65, Aftab Baloch 81, Afzal Ahmed 86,* | | | |
| *Tehsin Javed 88, W. Mathias 122\*, Vakil Tatari 57* | | | |

# ONLY FOUR BOWLERS IN AN INNINGS OF 450

| | Opponents (Total) | | |
|---|---|---|---|
| Gloucestershire | Warwickshire (484-9d) | Birmingham | 1899 |
| Lancashire | Yorkshire (489) | Leeds | 1921 |
| Gloucestershire | Lancashire (469) | Bristol | 1927 |
| Somerset | Leicestershire (490) | Frome | 1937 |
| Warwickshire | Middlesex (452-5d) | Birmingham | 1947 |
| Essex | Lancashire (510) | Clacton | 1947 |
| New Zealand | England (482) | Oval | 1949 |
| Essex | Somerset (488) | Clacton | 1949 |
| Essex | Kent (532) | Maidstone | 1950 |
| N.E. Transvaal | Transvaal (481-6d) | Johannesburg | 1952–53 |
| Tasmania | Victoria (450) | Hobart | 1953–54 |
| Trinidad | Barbados (463) | Bridgetown | 1962–63 |
| India | Australia (528) | Adelaide | 1980–81 |
| Sri Lanka | Pakistan (500-7d) | Lahore | 1981–82 |
| Pakistan | Australia (454-6d) | Sydney | 1983–84 |
| Australia | West Indies (468-8d) | Port-of-Spain | 1983–84 |
| Australia | West Indies (498) | St John's | 1983–84 |
| Young New Zealanders | Zimbabwe (479-9d) | Harare | 1984–85 |
| Australia | England (456) | Nottingham | 1985 |

*Dera Ismail Khan used five bowlers, one of whom bowled only two overs, in Railways' innings of 910-6d at Lahore in 1964–65.*

# ELEVEN BOWLERS IN AN INNINGS

| | Opponents (Total) | | |
|---|---|---|---|
| Surrey | Middlesex (455) | Oval | 1866 |
| Gentlemen of England | Cambridge University (370) | Cambridge | 1881 |
| England | Australia (551) | Oval | 1884 |
| Kent | Sussex (464) | Hove | 1884 |
| Sussex | Surrey (698) | Oval | 1888 |
| Natal | Kimberley (445) | Kimberley | 1889–90 |
| Hampshire | Warwickshire (475) | Southampton | 1897 |
| Hampshire | Surrey (579) | Oval | 1897 |
| Lancashire | Leicestershire (310-8) | Leicester | 1900 |
| Sussex | Leicestershire (609-8d) | Leicester | 1900 |
| Derbyshire | Worcestershire (463-7) | Worcester | 1902 |
| MCC | Tasmania (259-3) | Launceston | 1903–04 |
| Surrey | Warwickshire (585-7) | Oval | 1905 |
| Nottinghamshire | Lancashire (627) | Nottingham | 1905 |
| Queensland | NSW (591) | Sydney | 1907–08 |
| Sussex | Middlesex (426-8d) | Eastbourne | 1910 |
| Warwickshire | Yorkshire (495-5d) | Huddersfield | 1922 |
| Warwickshire | Middlesex (535-6d) | Birmingham | 1922 |
| MCC | Australian XI (257-5) | Brisbane | 1924–25 |
| Gloucestershire | Warwickshire (355) | Bristol | 1933 |
| Lancashire | Somerset (385-7) | Taunton | 1936 |
| Glamorgan | Nottinghamshire (260-7) | Nottingham | 1951 |
| Derbyshire | Leicestershire (345-9) | Ashby-de-la-Zouch | 1955 |
| Sussex | Glamorgan (200-1) | Hove | 1956 |
| Somerset | Leicestershire (295-3d) | Taunton | 1957 |
| Karachi Greens | Hyderabad (300) | Karachi | 1961–62 |

|  | *Opponents (Total)* |  |  |
|---|---|---|---|
| Central Districts | Pakistanis (322-9) | New Plymouth | 1964–65 |
| Glamorgan | Gloucestershire (378-4) | Bristol | 1965 |
| East Pakistan | Karachi (225-1d) | Karachi | 1968–69 |
| Khairpur | Karachi Whites (391-5c) | Karachi | 1970–71 |
| Australia | Pakistan (382-2) | Faisalabad | 1979–80 |
| Somerset | Gloucestershire (394-5) | Taunton | 1980 |
| Middlesex | Glamorgan (478-5) | Cardiff | 1985 |

# MOST BOWLERS IN A MATCH

**TWENTY-TWO**

| A.E.R. Gilligan's XI v Australians | Hastings | 1964 |
|---|---|---|

**TWENTY-ONE**

| Maharashtra Chief Minister's XI v Maharashtra Governor's XI | Poona | 1963–64 |
|---|---|---|

**TWENTY**

| Hampshire v Warwickshire | Southampton | 1897 |
|---|---|---|
| Sussex v Yorkshire | Hove | 1910 |
| Hampshire v Kent | Southampton | 1912 |
| Worcestershire v Gloucestershire | Worcester | 1933 |
| Barbados v Trinidad | Bridgetown | 1943–44 |
| India v Australian Services | Madras | 1945–46 |
| East Punjab v Delhi | Delhi | 1951–52 |
| Fazal Mahmood's XI v Chief Commissioner's XI | Hyderabad | 1959–60 |
| ACC v Chief Minister's XI | Anantapur | 1962–63 |
| West Indies XI v Rest | Kingston | 1963–64 |
| England v South Africa | Cape Town | 1964–65 |
| Indian Starlets v Hyderabad Blues | Hyderabad | 1966–67 |
| New Zealand v Australians | Auckland | 1966–67 |
| Karachi Blues v PIA | Karachi | 1969–70 |

# MOST EXTRAS IN AN INNINGS

| Ext | B | LB | W | NB | | | |
|---|---|---|---|---|---|---|---|
| 74 | 54 | 16 | 1 | 3 | British Guiana (529) v W. Shepherd's XI | Georgetown | 1909–10 |
| 73 | 48 | 23 | 2 | — | Northamptonshire (374) v Kent | Northampton | 1955 |
| 70 | 24 | — | 46 | — | Cambridge University (287) v Oxford U. | Lord's | 1839 |
| 70 | 23 | 30 | 1 | 16 | Habib Bank (722) v National Bank | Lahore | 1976–77 |
| 68 | 57 | 6 | 5 | — | Yorkshire (539) v Cambridge University | Cambridge | 1884 |
| 68 | 29 | 11 | — | 28 | Pakistan (291) v West Indies | Bridgetown | 1976–77 |
| 67 |  |  |  |  | PIA (723-8d) v Karachi | Karachi | 1977–78 |
| 66 | 49 | — | 17 | — | MCC (197) v Cambridge University | Cambridge | 1842 |
| 64 | 44 | 15 | — | 5 | Eastern Province (529) v Orange Free State | Port Elizabeth | 1946–47 |
| 63 | 36 | — | 21 | 6 | Oxford University (200) v Cambridge U. | Lord's | 1836 |
| 63 | 34 | 26 | — | 3 | NSW (775) v Victoria | Sydney | 1881–82 |
| 62 | 45 | 11 | 3 | 3 | AIF (405) v H.K. Foster's XI | Hereford | 1919 |
| 62 | 44 | 11 | 7 | — | MCC (532) v Wales | Lord's | 1925 |
| 61 |  |  |  |  | Governor's XI (349) v Chief Minister's XI | Bombay | 1962–63 |
| 60 | 4 | 27 | 11 | 18 | England (633-5d) v India | Birmingham | 1979 |
| 59 | 46 | 13 | — | — | Army (400) v Cambridge University | Cambridge | 1920 |
| 59 | 40 | 18 | — | 1 | Lahore B (384-9) v Rawalpindi | Lahore | 1973–74 |
| 58 | 38 | 18 | — | 2 | MCC (423) v Nottinghamshire | Lord's | 1899 |
| 58 | 29 | 28 | 1 | — | Cambridge U. (343-9d) v Free Foresters | Cambridge | 1929 |
| 58 | 41 | 14 | — | 3 | Wellington (380-5) v Auckland | Wellington | 1929–30 |
| 58 |  |  |  |  | U-Foam XI (423-5d) v A.N. Ghosh's XI | Hyderabad | 1972–73 |
| 58 | 6 | 22 | — | 30 | Victoria (601-7d) v West Indians | Melbourne | 1984–85 |
| 57 | 31 | 16 | — | 10 | New Zealand (387) v England | Auckland | 1929–30 |
| 57 | 27 | 12 | 14 | 4 | England (468-7d) v Australian Services | Lord's | 1945 |
| 57 | 39 | 4 | 8 | 6 | Yorkshire (468) v Essex | Southend | 1947 |
| 57 |  |  |  |  | Uttar Pradesh (164) v Rajasthan | Kanpur | 1958–59 |
| 57 |  |  |  |  | Karachi (507) v PIA | Karachi | 1962–63 |
| 57 |  |  |  |  | Punjab (447-9d) v Services | Amritsar | 1975–76 |
| 57 | 10 | 15 | 8 | 24 | Essex (499-8c) v Worcestershire | Westcliff | 1976 |

| Ext | B | LB | W | NB | | | |
|---|---|---|---|---|---|---|---|
| 57 | 7 | 21 | 10 | 19 | England (370) v West Indies | Oval | 1980 |
| 57 | 16 | 14 | 1 | 26 | India (463) v West Indies | Bombay | 1983–84 |
| 56 | 35 | — | 21 | — | Yorkshire (296) v Norfolk | Sheffield | 1834 |
| 56 | 29 | 5 | 21 | 1 | Cambridge University (266) v Oxford U. | Lord's | 1851 |
| 56 | 34 | 14 | 8 | — | Kent (555) v Worcestershire | Stourbridge | 1909 |
| 56 | | | | | Maharashtra (798) v Northern India | Poona | 1940–41 |
| 56 | 12 | 18 | — | 26 | Glamorgan (408) v Warwickshire | Cardiff | 1981 |
| 56 | 19 | 11 | 4 | 22 | Hampshire (435-2d) v Glamorgan | Portsmouth | 1982 |
| 55 | 45 | — | 9 | 1 | Cambridge University (127) v Oxford U. | Lord's | 1836 |
| 55 | 49 | 4 | 2 | — | Gloucestershire (409) v Middlesex | Lord's | 1888 |
| 55 | 41 | 14 | — | — | Ireland (409-4) v Scotland | Glasgow | 1911 |
| 55 | | | | | Otago (428-7) v Wellington | Wellington | 1914–15 |
| 55 | | | | | Jamaica (519) v Hon L.H. Tennyson's XI | Kingston | 1926–27 |
| 55 | 46 | 2 | — | 7 | Oxford University (188) v Harlequins | Oxford | 1927 |
| 55 | | | | | Indian Universities (453-9d) v Ceylon XI | Colombo | 1935–36 |
| 55 | 11 | 26 | — | 18 | Australians (511) v Barbados | Bridgetown | 1977–78 |
| 55 | 6 | 11 | 6 | 32 | Australia (345) v England | Lord's | 1981 |
| 54 | 35 | 18 | 1 | — | Gloucestershire (448) v Somerset | Moreton-in-Marsh | 1885 |
| 54 | | | | | W. Province (409) v E. Province | Cape Town | 1890–91 |
| 54 | 45 | 5 | 3 | 1 | Victoria (411) v Western Australia | Melbourne | 1892–93 |
| 54 | 32 | 19 | 2 | 1 | Somerset (505-9d) v Middlesex | Weston-s-Mare | 1933 |
| 54 | | | | | Bengal Cyclone XI (703) v Bijapur Famine XI | Bombay | 1942–43 |
| 54 | 35 | 14 | 4 | 1 | Auckland (200-8d) v Wellington | Auckland | 1973–74 |
| 54 | 7 | 13 | — | 34 | India (566-8d) v West Indies | Delhi | 1978–79 |
| 54 | | | | | PIA (272) v National Bank | Lahore | 1979–80 |
| 53 | 37 | — | 13 | 3 | MCC (204) v Oxford University | Lord's | 1837 |
| 53 | 36 | 12 | 4 | 1 | Northamptonshire (388) v Leicestershire | Northampton | 1906 |
| 53 | 47 | 2 | — | 4 | MCC (441) v West Indian XI | Georgetown | 1912–13 |
| 53 | 32 | 6 | 8 | 7 | Yorkshire (495-5d) v Warwickshire | Huddersfield | 1922 |
| 53 | 29 | 22 | — | 2 | Essex (407) v Worcestershire | Worcester | 1923 |
| 53 | 37 | 5 | 4 | 7 | H.D.G. Leveson Gower's XI (305) v Oxford U. | Eastbourne | 1923 |
| 53 | 26 | 10 | — | 17 | Canterbury (473-6) v Auckland | Christchurch | 1930–31 |
| 53 | | | | | Bengal (354) v Delhi | Calcutta | 1979–80 |
| 53 | 20 | 8 | 4 | 21 | India (487) v England | Delhi | 1981–82 |
| 53 | 6 | 17 | 2 | 28 | West Indies (606) v England | Birmingham | 1984 |
| 53 | 12 | 8 | 5 | 28 | Essex (409) v Australians | Chelmsford | 1985 |
| 52 | 42 | 7 | 1 | 2 | Surrey (650) v Hampshire | Oval | 1883 |
| 52 | 29 | 12 | 2 | 9 | London County (578-9d) v Cambridge U. | Crystal Palace | 1901 |
| 52 | 43 | 8 | 1 | — | Lancashire (359-7d) v Middlesex | Lord's | 1901 |
| 52 | 39 | 10 | 3 | — | MCC (503-9d) v Sussex | Lord's | 1905 |
| 52 | 41 | 9 | 9 | 1 | Sussex (611) v Essex | Leyton | 1905 |
| 52 | 41 | 11 | — | — | Worcestershire (578-6d) v Warwickshire | Birmingham | 1909 |
| 52 | 38 | 14 | — | — | Kent (480) v Oxford University | Oxford | 1913 |
| 52 | 42 | 5 | 5 | — | Nottinghamshire (507-3d) v Leicestershire | Nottingham | 1913 |
| 52 | | | | | Wellington (370) v Canterbury | Christchurch | 1922–23 |
| 52 | | | | | State Bank of India (465-8d) v Mafatlal XI | Hyderabad | 1972–73 |
| 52 | 12 | 7 | — | 33 | New Zealand (468) v Pakistan | Karachi | 1976–77 |
| 52 | 19 | 13 | 10 | 10 | England (252) v West Indies | Nottingham | 1980 |
| 52 | 18 | 14 | 7 | 13 | Nottinghamshire (465) v Australians | Nottingham | 1980 |
| 52 | 8 | 8 | 1 | 35 | England (309) v Australia | Brisbane | 1982–83 |
| 52 | 7 | 16 | 7 | 22 | Leicestershire (399) v Northamptonshire | Leicester | 1983 |
| 52 | 2 | 12 | 2 | 36 | Leicestershire (454) v Australians | Leicester | 1985 |
| 52 | 7 | 16 | 5 | 24 | Derbyshire (323) v Leicestershire | Chesterfield | 1985 |
| 51 | | | | | Barbados (258) v Trinidad | Port-of-Spain | 1905–06 |
| 51 | | | | | Auckland (539) v Otago | Dunedin | 1926–27 |
| 51 | 47 | 3 | 1 | — | Lancashire (592-4d) v Worcestershire | Worcester | 1929 |
| 51 | | | | | Baroda (308) v Maharashtra | Baroda | 1942–43 |
| 51 | | | | | Services (220-6) v Rajasthan | Delhi | 1959–60 |
| 51 | | | | | United Bank (412) v Punjab B | Rawalpindi | 1976–77 |
| 51 | 10 | 20 | — | 21 | India (469-7) v West Indies | Port-of-Spain | 1982–83 |
| 50 | 37 | 10 | 3 | — | Eastern Province (403) v Griqualand West | Johannesburg | 1906–07 |
| 50 | 41 | 7 | — | 2 | Queensland (232) v NSW | Sydney | 1913–14 |
| 50 | 42 | 5 | — | 3 | Free Foresters (246) v Oxford University | Oxford | 1920 |
| 50 | 33 | 11 | 3 | 3 | Kent (480-9d) v Hampshire | Canterbury | 1923 |
| 50 | 36 | 12 | 2 | — | Scotland (464-9d) v Ireland | Greenock | 1926 |
| 50 | | | | | Otago (602-8d) v Canterbury | Dunedin | 1928–29 |

| Ext | B | LB | W | NB | | | |
|-----|-----|-----|-----|-----|-----|-----|-----|
| 50 | 37 | 8 | 1 | 4 | Australia (327) v England | Oval | 1934 |
| 50 | | | | | Western Province (443-9d) v Border | Cape Town | 1934–35 |
| 50 | 22 | 19 | 1 | 8 | England (903-7d) v Australia | Oval | 1938 |
| 50 | | | | | Baroda (253) v Gujarat | Ahmedabad | 1948–49 |
| 50 | | | | | Madhya Pradesh (274) v Vidarbha | Bersingpur | 1968–69 |
| 50 | 43 | 5 | – | 2 | Rawalpindi (407) v Multan | Lahore | 1973–74 |
| 50 | | | | | Bengal (467-6d) v Assam | Calcutta | 1980–81 |
| 50 | 13 | 24 | 2 | 11 | Wellington (356) v Canterbury | Wellington | 1981–82 |
| 50 | 11 | 8 | 2 | 29 | India (566-6d) v Sri Lanka | Madras | 1982–83 |
| 50 | 13 | 9 | — | 28 | India (393-8d) v Pakistan | Karachi | 1982–83 |
| 50 | 4 | 12 | — | 34 | Warwickshire (470-8d) v Kent | Folkestone | 1983 |
| 50 | 15 | 22 | — | 13 | Somerset (516) v Middlesex | Bath | 1984 |
| 50 | 13 | 11 | — | 26 | England (464) v Australia | Oval | 1985 |

# SIMILARITY OF DISMISSAL

Instances of the same combination of fielder and/or bowler dismissing several batsmen in the same match, with the fielding side listed first:

### HAT TRICKS

| | | | |
|---|---|---|---|
| st W.H. Brain b C.L. Townsend | Gloucestershire v Somerset | Cheltenham | 1895 |
| c G.J. Thompson b S.G. Smith | Northamptonshire v Warwickshire | Birmingham | 1914 |
| lbw b H. Fisher | Yorkshire v Somerset | Sheffield | 1932 |
| c C. White b R. Beesly | Border v Griqualand West | Queenstown | 1946–47 |
| c G.O. Dawkes b H.L. Jackson | Derbyshire v Worcestershire | Kidderminster | 1958 |
| lbw b J.A. Flavell | Worcestershire v Lancashire | Manchester | 1963 |
| lbw b M.J. Procter | Gloucestershire v Essex | Westcliff | 1972 |
| lbw b B.J. Ikin | Griqualand West v OFS     - | Kimberley | 1973–74 |
| lbw b M.J. Procter | Gloucestershire v Yorkshire | Cheltenham | 1979 |

### FIRST EIGHT WICKETS TO FALL IN AN INNINGS

| | | | |
|---|---|---|---|
| c D.E. East | Essex v Somerset | Taunton | 1985 |

### FIRST SIX WICKETS TO FALL IN AN INNINGS

| | | | |
|---|---|---|---|
| c or st D. Gamsy | Natal v Orange Free State | Pietermaritzburg | 1960–61 |
| c G.C. Becker | Western Australia v Victoria | Melbourne | 1965–66 |
| c R.W. Tolchard | Leicestershire v Yorkshire | Leeds | 1973 |

### EIGHT BATSMEN IN SUCCESSION IN AN INNINGS

| | | | |
|---|---|---|---|
| c D.E. East | Essex v Somerset | Taunton | 1985 |

### SIX BATSMEN IN SUCCESSION IN AN INNINGS

| | | | |
|---|---|---|---|
| c or st K.V. Bhandakar | Holkar v Ceylon XI | Colombo | 1947–48 |
| c A.T.W. Grout | Queensland v Western Australia | Brisbane | 1959–60 |
| c A.S. Brown | Gloucester v Nottinghamshire | Nottingham | 1966 |
| c S.E. Leary | Kent v Cambridge University | Cambridge | 1958 |
| c or st W. Farrimond | | | |
| (www.wwww) | Lancashire v Kent | Manchester | 1930 |
| c A.T.W. Grout | | | |
| (wwwwww.w) | Queensland v Western Australia | Brisbane | 1959–60 |
| c A.S. Brown (.wwwww.w) | Gloucestershire v Nottinghamshire | Nottingham | |
| c Wasim Bari | | | |
| (wwww.www) | Pakistan v New Zealand | Auckland | 1978–79 |

**SIX OUT OF SEVEN SUCCESSIVE WICKETS TO FALL, INCLUDING FIVE IN FIVE**

| | | | |
|---|---|---|---|
| c W.R. Hammond *(wwwww.w)* | Gloucestershire v Surrey | Cheltenham | 1928 |
| c or st H. Elliott *(wwwww.w)* | Derbyshire v Lancashire | Manchester | 1935 |
| c or st W.H.V. Levett *(wwwww.w)* | Kent v Glamorgan | Neath | 1939 |
| run out *(wwwww.w)* | Punjab v Delhi | Jullundur | 1969–70 |

**FIVE DISMISSALS IN ONE INNINGS (OUTSTANDING CASES)**

| | | | |
|---|---|---|---|
| st E. Pooley b J. Southerton | Surrey v Lancashire | Oval | 1868 |
| st R. Pilling b A.G. Steel | Lancashire v Nottinghamshire | Manchester | 1877 |
| c F.G.J. Ford *(only 7 wkts fell)* | Cambridge University v MCC | Lord's | 1888 |
| c or st D. Hunter b W. Rhodes *(last 5 wkts)* | Yorkshire v Surrey | Bradford | 1898 |
| c T.W. Oates b A.W. Hallam *(in 34 balls)* | Nottinghamshire v Middlesex | Nottingham | 1906 |
| st N.C. Tufnell b J.H.B. Lockhart | Cambridge University v Yorkshire | Cambridge | 1909 |
| c G. Brown b A. Jaques | Hampshire v Somerset | Bath | 1914 |
| c J.F. Sheppard b J.W. McAndrew | Queensland v NSW | Brisbane | 1914–15 |
| c J.H. Nicholson b V.W.C. Jupp | Northamptonshire v Worcestershire | Dudley | 1928 |
| c W. Farrimond b E.A. McDonald *(6 such dismissals in innings)* | Lancashire v Kent | Manchester | 1930 |
| c V.Y. Richardson *(....w.wwww)* | Australia v South Africa | Durban | 1935–36 |
| c T.N. Pierce b J.E.D. Sealy | Trinidad v Barbados | Bridgetown | 1941–42 |
| st B.A. Barnett b J.S. Manning | Commonwealth XI v England XI | Hastings | 1960 |
| c A.G.E. Ealham b D.L. Underwood | Kent v Gloucestershire | Folkestone | 1966 |

*All in the same place topographically: four off right-handed batsmen at long-off and the other at long-on off a left-hander.*

| | | | |
|---|---|---|---|
| c G.A. Greenidge *(only 7 wkts fell)* | Sussex v Glamorgan | Hove | 1975 |
| c M.C. Worrell b R.O. Estwick | Barbados v Leeward Islands | Bridgetown | 1984–85 |
| c B. Reddy b T.A.P. Sekar | Tamil Nadu v Kerala | Palghat | 1982–83 |
| c D.E. East b I.L. Pont | Essex v Somerset | Taunton | 1985 |

**TEN CATCHES IN AN INNINGS BY TEN DIFFERENT FIELDERS**

| | | |
|---|---|---|
| Leicestershire v Northamptonshire | Leicester | 1967 |

*J. Birkenshaw was the only Leicestershire fielder not to take a catch.*

# UNUSUAL DISMISSALS

Although there are ten ways in which a batsman can lose his wicket, three of them occur very rarely (handled the ball, hit the ball twice, and obstructing the field) and the tenth ('timed out', introduced in 1980) has yet to claim a dismissal at first-class level. There have been few instances of a substitute wicket-keeper making a stumping, or of a bowler running-out a non-striking batsman for backing up before the ball has been bowled, and these are listed also.

### HANDLED THE BALL

Before the introduction of Law 33b in 1899, a batsman could be dismissed 'handled the ball' for removing a ball lodged in his clothing. The instances in 1872, 1893, and 1894–95 occurred before this amendment which ruled such a ball to be 'dead'.

| | | | |
|---|---|---|---|
| J. Grundy (15) | MCC v Kent | Lord's | 1857 |
| G. Bennett (0) | Kent v Sussex | Hove | 1872 |
| W.H. Scotton (18) | Smokers v Non-Smokers | East Melbourne | 1886–87 |
| C.W. Wright (4) | Nottinghamshire v Gloucestershire | Bristol | 1893 |
| E. Jones (9) | South Australia v Victoria | Melbourne | 1894–95 |
| A.W. Nourse (1) | South Africans v Sussex | Hove | 1907 |
| E.T. Benson (29) | MCC v Auckland | Auckland | 1929–30 |
| A.W. Gilbertson (7) | Otago v Auckland | Auckland | 1952–53 |
| W.R. Endean (3) | South Africa v England | Cape Town | 1956–57 |
| P.J.P. Burge (11) | Queensland v New South Wales | Sydney | 1958–59 |
| Dildar Awan (8) | Services v Lahore | Lahore | 1959–60 |
| Mahmood-ul-Hasan (50) | Karachi University v Railways & Quetta | Karachi | 1960–61 |
| Ali Raza (52) | Karachi Greens v Hyderabad | Karachi | 1961–62 |
| Mohammad Yusuf (35) | Rawalpindi v Peshawar | Peshawar | 1962–63 |

| A. Rees (14) | Glamorgan v Middlesex | Lord's | 1965 |
|---|---|---|---|
| Pervez Akhtar (9) | Multan v Karachi Greens | Sahiwal | 1971–72 |
| Javed Mirza (21) | Railways v Punjab | Lahore | 1972–73 |
| R.G. Pollock (66) | E. Province v W. Province | Cape Town | 1973–74 |
| C.I. Dey (20) | N. Transvaal v Orange Free State | Bloemfontein | 1973–74 |
| Nasir Valika (19) | Karachi Whites v National Bank | Karachi | 1974–75 |
| Haji Yousuf (13) | National Bank v Railways | Lahore | 1974–75 |
| Masood-ul-Hasan (58) | PIA v National Bank B | Lyallpur | 1975–76 |
| D.K. Pearse (2) | Natal v W. Province | Cape Town | 1978–79 |
| A.M.J. Hilditch (29) | Australia v Pakistan | Perth | 1978–79 |
| Muslehuddin (0) | Railways v Lahore | Lahore | 1979–80 |
| Jalaluddin (17) | IDBP v Habib Bank | Bahawalpur | 1981–82 |
| Mohsin Khan (58) | Pakistan v Australia | Karachi | 1982–83 |
| K. Azad (40) | Delhi v Punjab | Amritsar | 1983–84 |
| D.L. Haynes (55) | West Indies v India | Bombay | 1983–84 |
| Athar A. Khan (6) | Allied Bank v HBFC | Sialkot | 1983–84 |
| A. Pandya (1) | Saurashtra v Baroda | Baroda | 1984–85 |

## HIT THE BALL TWICE

| H.E. Bull (29) | MCC v Oxford University | Lord's | 1864 |
|---|---|---|---|
| H.R.J. Charlwood (73) | Sussex v Surrey | Hove | 1872 |
| R.G. Barlow (20) | North v South | Lord's | 1878 |
| P.S. Wimble (0) | Transvaal v Griqualand West | Kimberley | 1892–93 |
| G.B. Nichols (10) | Somerset v Gloucestershire | Bristol | 1896 |
| A.F.A. Lilley (13) | Warwickshire v Yorkshire | Birmingham | 1897 |
| J.H. King (13) | Leicestershire v Surrey | Oval | 1906 |
| A.P. Binns (151) | Jamaica v British Guiana | Georgetown | 1956–57 |
| K. Bavanna (18) | Andhra v Mysore | Guntur | 1963–64 |
| Zaheer Abbas (0) | PIA v Karachi Blues | Karachi | 1969–70 |
| Anwar Miandad (27) | IDBP v United Bank | Lahore | 1979–80 |
| Anwar Iqbal (15) | Hyderabad v Sukkur | Hyderabad | 1983–84 |
| Iqtidar Ali (27) | Allied Bank v MCB | Lahore | 1983–84 |
| Aziz Malik (21) | Lahore Division v Faisalabad | Sialkot | 1984–85 |

## OBSTRUCTING THE FIELD

| C.A. Absolom (38) | Cambridge University v Surrey | Oval | 1868 |
|---|---|---|---|
| T. Straw (8) | Worcestershire v Warwickshire | Worcester | 1899 |
| T. Straw (3) | Worcestershire v Warwickshire | Birmingham | 1901 |
| J.P. Whiteside (0) | Leicestershire v Lancashire | Leicester | 1901 |
| L. Hutton (27) | England v South Africa | Oval | 1951 |
| J.A. Hayes (0) | Canterbury v Central Districts | Christchurch | 1954–55 |
| D.D. Deshpande (6) | Madhya Pradesh v Uttar Pradesh | Benares | 1956–57 |
| M. Mehra (52) | Railways v Delhi | Delhi | 1959–60 |
| K. Ibadulla (0) | Warwickshire v Hampshire | Coventry | 1963 |
| Qaiser Khan (3) | Dera Ismail Khan v Railways | Lahore | 1964–65 |
| Ijaz Ahmed (70) | Lahore Greens v Lahore Blues | Lahore | 1973–74 |
| Qasim Feroze (24) | Bahawalpur v Universities | Lahore | 1974–75 |
| T. Quirk (10) | Northern Transvaal v Border | East London | 1978–79 |
| Mahmood Rashid (26) | United Bank v MCB | Bahawalpur | 1981–82 |
| Arshad Ali (25) | Sukkur v Quetta | Quetta | 1983–84 |
| H. Wasu (8) | Vidarbha v Rajasthan | Akola | 1984–85 |

## RUN OUT BY THE BOWLER
While backing up before the ball had been bowled

| G. Baigent (5) by T.R. Barker | Sussex v Nottinghamshire | Nottingham | 1835 |
|---|---|---|---|
| E. Martin (10) by T.R. Barker | Hampshire v MCC | Lord's | 1843 |
| F.W. Lillywhite (4) by E. Napper | MCC v Sussex | Brighton | 1850 |

*Lillywhite, aged 58, was playing against his old county and batted number 11*

| J. Huddleston (44) by J. Kinloch | Victoria v NSW | Melbourne | 1861–62 |
|---|---|---|---|
| S.W.G. Campbell (1) by N. Thompson | Victoria v NSW | Sydney | 1866–67 |

*This was Campbell's first innings in first-class cricket*

| C.W. Wright (13) by G.P. Harrison | Cambridge U. v Yorkshire | Cambridge | 1883 |
|---|---|---|---|
| E.J. Tyler (25) by A. Hearne | Somerset v Kent | Taunton | 1894 |

**RUN OUT BY THE BOWLER**—*continued*
While backing up before the ball had been bowled

| | | | |
|---|---|---|---|
| T.W. Reese (15) by A. Downes | Canterbury v Otago | Christchurch | 1894–95 |
| J. Hardstaff, jr (2) by Khadim Hussain | Lord Tennyson's XI v Sind | Karachi | 1937–38 |
| A.G. Ram Singh (58) by N.D. Sane | Madras v CP & Berar | Nagpur | 1941–42 |
| W.A. Brown (30) by M.H. Mankad | Australian XI v Indians | Sydney | 1947–48 |
| W.A. Brown (18) by M.H. Mankad | Australia v India | Sydney | 1947–48 |
| R. Routledge (1) by J.P. Fellows-Smith | Middlesex v Oxford U. | Oxford | 1953 |
| G. Barker (33) by W. Wooller | Essex v Glamorgan | Cardiff | 1956 |
| Hanumant Singh (103) by A.K. Chaturvedi | Rajasthan v Uttar Pradesh | Udaipur | 1959–60 |
| A. Corneal (71) by C.C. Griffith | Trinidad v Barbados | Port-of-Spain | 1963–64 |
| R.A. Cohen (8) by J. Ali | Jamaica v Trinidad | Port-of-Spain | 1963–64 |
| A. Khanna (0) by R. Goel | Northern Punjab v Delhi | Delhi | 1966–67 |
| G.G. Arnold (71) by Saeed Ahmed | MCC v Central Zone | Sahiwal | 1966–67 |
| R.A. Gripper (80) by B.A. Richards | Rhodesia v Natal | Salisbury | 1968–69 |
| D.J. Morgan (13) by R.A. le Roux | OFS v S.A. Universities | Bloemfontein | 1968–69 |
| I.R. Redpath (9) by C.C. Griffith | Australia v West Indies | Adelaide | 1968–69 |
| R. Swetman (1) by R.D. Jackman | Gloucestershire v Surrey | Bristol | 1972 |
| D.W. Randall (13) by E.J. Chatfield | England v New Zealand | Christchurch | 1977–78 |
| Sikander Bakht (0) by A.G. Hurst | Australia v Pakistan | Perth | 1978–79 |
| A. Rajah (21) by R.A. Harper | Trinidad v Guyana | Pointe-à-Pierre | 1981–82 |
| R.A. Austin (118) | Jamaica v Guyana | Kingston | 1981–82 |
| C.H. Lloyd (1) by S.J. Hinds | Guyana v Windward Ils | Roseau | 1982–83 |

## STUMPED BY A SUBSTITUTE

| Batsman | Substitute | Wicket-keeper | Match† | | |
|---|---|---|---|---|---|
| S.J. Snooke | N.C. Tufnell | H. Strudwick | South Africa v England | Durban | 1909–10 |
| G.C. Drysdale‡ | N.C. Tufnell | W. Findlay | Argentine v MCC | Buenos Aires | 1911–12 |
| G.S. Boyes | F.E. Kapadia | B.E. Kapadia | MCC v Bombay | Bombay | 1926–27 |
| E.L. Grant | S.R. Nayak | A. Rangabashyam | Europeans v Indians | Madras | 1927–28 |
| J.S. Mackenzie | L.E.G. Ames | R.T. Stanyforth | British Guiana v MCC | Georgetown | 1929–30 |
| Yuvaraj of Patiala }<br>Nawab of Pataudi, sr } | L. Amarnath | Dilawar Hussain | All India v Rest | Lahore | 1931–32 |
| F.R. Brown | H.S.B. Love | W.A.S. Oldfield | MCC v NSW | Sydney | 1932–33 |
| J.A. Shea | Doherty | C.W. Walker | W. Australia v S. Australia | Adelaide | 1937–38 |
| L.R. Pierre | A.M. Taylor | C.L. Browne | Trinidad v Barbados | Port-of-Spain | 1941–42 |
| D.C.S. Compton | T.V. Parthasarathy | P. Sen | Services XI v Governor's XI | Calcutta | 1944–45 |
| N. Gordon | D. Graham | A.B.J. Reid | Transvaal v W. Province | Cape Town | 1945–46 |
| I.J.M. Lumsden | R.T. Spooner | J.T. Kendall | Scotland v Warwickshire | Birmingham | 1948 |
| M.D. Mohoni | H.W. Stephenson | A.T. Barlow | Governor's XI v Commonwealth XI | Nagpur | 1950–51 |
| T.E. Bailey | P. Rochford | D.V. Brennan | MCC v Yorkshire | Scarborough | 1951 |
| J. Grove | M.K. Fitchett | I.H. McDonald | South Australia v Victoria | Adelaide | 1952–53 |
| A. Rabani | A.C. Rajmanikam | D.L. Chakravarti | Hyderabad v Madras | Salem | 1956–57 |
| P.M. Walker | L.A. Johnson | K.V. Andrew | Glamorgan v Northamptonshire | Northampton | 1959 |
| A.M. Zuill | E. Legard | A.C. Smith | Scotland v Warwickshire | Birmingham | 1962 |
| N.B. Whittingham | N.L. Majendie | A.L. Mason | Nottinghamshire v Oxford U. | Oxford | 1963 |
| J. Cotton | D.L. Murray | D.W. Allan | MCC v West Indians | Lord's | 1963 |
| D.W.J. Brown | C.J. Saunders | Asif Ahmed | Gloucestershire v Oxford U. | Bristol | 1964 |
| Pervez Sajjad | B.E. Congdon | A.E. Dick | Pakistan v New Zealand | Lahore | 1964–65 |
| B.E. Congdon | P.J.P. Burge | B.W. Jarman | Central Districts v Australians | Palmerston North | 1966–67 |
| B.D. Julien | D.L. Murray | R.W. Tolchard | West Indians v T.N. Pearce's XI | Scarborough | 1973 |
| K.R. Gattani | S. Desai | P. Krishnamurthy | Central Zone v South Zone | Nagpur | 1978–79 |
| M.J. Weston | D. Ripley | G. Sharp | Worcestershire v Northants | Northampton | 1983 |
| A.L. Jones | D. Ripley | G. Cook | Glamorgan v Northamptonshire | Northampton | 1983 |
| A. Jayaprakash | Nandan | S.M.H. Kirmani | Orissa v Karnataka | Bangalore | 1984–85 |
| Hafeez-ur-Rahman | Rafiullah | Kamal Najamuddin | Karachi Whites v Hyderabad | Karachi | 1984–85 |
| I.T. Botham }<br>M.R. Davis } | R.B. Phillips | W.B. Phillips | Somerset v Australians | Taunton | 1985 |

† *Batting side given first*   ‡ *In both innings*

# INDIVIDUAL RECORDS – BATTING

## HIGHEST INDIVIDUAL INNINGS

| | | | |
|---|---|---|---|
| 499 | Hanif Mohammad | Karachi v Bahawalpur | Karachi | 1958–59 |
| 452* | D.G. Bradman | New South Wales v Queensland | Sydney | 1929–30 |
| 443* | B.B. Nimbalkar | Maharashtra v Kathiawar | Poona | 1948–49 |
| 437 | W.H. Ponsford | Victoria v Queensland | Melbourne | 1927–28 |
| 429 | W.H. Ponsford | Victoria v Tasmania | Melbourne | 1922–23 |
| 428 | Aftab Baloch | Sind v Baluchistan | Karachi | 1973–74 |
| 424 | A.C. MacLaren | Lancashire v Somerset | Taunton | 1895 |
| 385 | B. Sutcliffe | Otago v Canterbury | Christchurch | 1952–53 |
| 383 | D.W. Gregory | New South Wales v Queensland | Brisbane | 1906–07 |
| 369 | D.G. Bradman | South Australia v Tasmania | Adelaide | 1935–36 |
| 365* | C. Hill | South Australia v New South Wales | Adelaide | 1900–01 |
| 365* | G.St A. Sobers | West Indies v Pakistan | Kingston | 1957–58 |
| 364 | L. Hutton | England v Australia | Oval | 1938 |
| 359* | V.M. Merchant | Bombay v Maharashtra | Bombay | 1943–44 |
| 359 | R.B. Simpson | New South Wales v Queensland | Brisbane | 1963–64 |
| 357* | R. Abel | Surrey v Somerset | Oval | 1899 |
| 357 | D.G. Bradman | South Australia v Victoria | Melbourne | 1935–36 |
| 356 | B.A. Richards | South Australia v Western Australia | Perth | 1970–71 |
| 355 | B. Sutcliffe | Otago v Auckland | Dunedin | 1949–50 |
| 352 | W.H. Ponsford | Victoria v New South Wales | Melbourne | 1926–27 |
| 350 | Rashid Israr | Habib Bank v National Bank | Lahore | 1976–77 |
| 345 | C.G. Macartney | Australians v Nottinghamshire | Nottingham | 1921 |
| 344* | G.A. Headley | Jamaica v Lord Tennyson's XI | Kingston | 1931–32 |
| 344 | W.G. Grace | MCC v Kent | Canterbury | 1876 |
| 343* | P.A. Perrin | Essex v Derbyshire | Chesterfield | 1904 |
| 341 | G.H. Hirst | Yorkshire v Leicestershire | Leicester | 1905 |
| 340* | D.G. Bradman | New South Wales v Victoria | Sydney | 1928–29 |
| 340 | S.M. Gavaskar | Bombay v Bengal | Bombay | 1981–82 |
| 338* | R.C. Blunt | Otago v Canterbury | Christchurch | 1931–32 |
| 338 | W.W. Read | Surrey v Oxford University | Oval | 1888 |
| 337* | Pervez Akhtar | Railways v Dera Ismail Khan | Lahore | 1964–65 |
| 337 | Hanif Mohammad | Pakistan v West Indies | Bridgetown | 1957–58 |
| 336* | W.R. Hammond | England v New Zealand | Auckland | 1932–33 |
| 336 | W.H. Ponsford | Victoria v South Australia | Melbourne | 1927–28 |
| 334 | D.G. Bradman | Australia v England | Leeds | 1930 |
| 333 | K.S. Duleepsinhji | Sussex v Northamptonshire | Hove | 1930 |
| 332 | W.H. Ashdown | Kent v Essex | Brentwood | 1934 |
| 331* | J.D.B. Robertson | Middlesex v Worcestershire | Worcester | 1949 |
| 325* | H.S.T.L. Hendry | Victoria v New Zealanders | Melbourne | 1925–26 |
| 325 | A. Sandham | England v West Indies | Kingston | 1929–30 |
| 325 | C.L. Badcock | South Australia v Victoria | Adelaide | 1935–36 |
| 324 | J.B. Stollmeyer | Trinidad v British Guiana | Port-of-Spain | 1946–47 |
| 324 | Waheed Mirza | Karachi Whites v Quetta | Karachi | 1976–77 |
| 323 | A.L. Wadekar | Bombay v Mysore | Bombay | 1966–67 |
| 322 | E. Paynter | Lancashire v Sussex | Hove | 1937 |
| 322 | I.V.A. Richards | Somerset v Warwickshire | Taunton | 1985 |
| 321 | W.L. Murdoch | New South Wales v Victoria | Sydney | 1881–82 |
| 319 | Gul Mahomed | Baroda v Holkar | Baroda | 1946–47 |
| 318* | W.G. Grace | Gloucestershire v Yorkshire | Cheltenham | 1876 |
| 317 | W.R. Hammond | Gloucestershire v Nottinghamshire | Gloucester | 1936 |
| 316* | J.B. Hobbs | Surrey v Middlesex | Lord's | 1926 |
| 316* | V.S. Hazare | Maharashtra v Baroda | Poona | 1939–40 |
| 316 | R.H. Moore | Hampshire v Warwickshire | Bournemouth | 1937 |
| 315* | T.W. Hayward | Surrey v Lancashire | Oval | 1898 |
| 315* | P. Holmes | Yorkshire v Middlesex | Lord's | 1925 |
| 315* | A.F. Kippax | New South Wales v Queensland | Sydney | 1927–28 |
| 314* | C.L. Walcott | Barbados v Trinidad | Port-of-Spain | 1945–46 |

| 313 | H. Sutcliffe | Yorkshire v Essex | Leyton | 1932 |
|---|---|---|---|---|
| 312* | W.W. Keeton | Nottinghamshire v Middlesex | Oval | 1939 |
| 312* | J.M. Brearley | MCC U-25 XI v North Zone | Peshawar | 1966–67 |
| 311* | G.M. Turner | Worcestershire v Warwickshire | Worcester | 1982 |
| 311 | J.T. Brown | Yorkshire v Sussex | Sheffield | 1897 |
| 311 | R.B. Simpson | Australia v England | Manchester | 1964 |
| 311 | Javed Miandad | Karachi Whites v National Bank | Karachi | 1974–75 |
| 310* | J.H. Edrich | England v New Zealand | Leeds | 1965 |
| 310 | H. Gimblett | Somerset v Sussex | Eastbourne | 1948 |
| 309 | V.S. Hazare | Rest v Hindus | Bombay | 1943–44 |
| 308* | F.M.M. Worrell | Barbados v Trinidad | Bridgetown | 1943–44 |
| 307 | M.C. Cowdrey | MCC v South Australia | Adelaide | 1962–63 |
| 307 | R.M. Cowper | Australia v England | Melbourne | 1965–66 |
| 306* | A. Ducat | Surrey v Oxford University | Oval | 1919 |
| 306* | E.A.B. Rowan | Transvaal v Natal | Johannesburg | 1939–40 |
| 305* | F.E. Woolley | MCC v Tasmania | Hobart | 1911–12 |
| 305* | F.R. Foster | Warwickshire v Worcestershire | Dudley | 1914 |
| 305* | W.H. Ashdown | Kent v Derbyshire | Dover | 1935 |
| 304* | P.H. Tarilton | Barbados v Trinidad | Bridgetown | 1919–20 |
| 304* | A.W. Nourse | Natal v Transvaal | Johannesburg | 1919–20 |
| 304* | E.de C. Weekes | West Indians v Cambridge University | Cambridge | 1950 |
| 304 | R.M. Poore | Hampshire v Somerset | Taunton | 1899 |
| 304 | D.G. Bradman | Australia v England | Leeds | 1934 |
| 303* | W.W. Armstrong | Australians v Somerset | Bath | 1905 |
| 303* | Mushtaq Mohammad | Karachi Blues v Karachi University | Karachi | 1967–68 |
| 302* | P. Holmes | Yorkshire v Hampshire | Portsmouth | 1920 |
| 302* | W.R. Hammond | Gloucestershire v Glamorgan | Bristol | 1934 |
| 302 | W.R. Hammond | Gloucestershire v Glamorgan | Newport | 1939 |
| 302 | L.G. Rowe | West Indies v England | Bridgetown | 1973–74 |
| 301* | E.H. Hendren | Middlesex v Worcestershire | Dudley | 1933 |
| 301 | W.G.Grace | Gloucestershire v Sussex | Bristol | 1896 |
| 300* | V.T. Trumper | Australians v Sussex | Hove | 1899 |
| 300* | F.B. Watson | Lancashire v Surrey | Manchester | 1928 |
| 300* | Imtiaz Ahmed | Prime Minister's XI v Commonwealth | Bombay | 1950–51 |
| 300 | J.T. Brown | Yorkshire v Derbyshire | Chesterfield | 1898 |
| 300 | D.C.S. Compton | MCC v N.E. Transvaal | Benoni | 1948–49 |
| 300 | R. Subba Row | Northamptonshire v Surrey | Oval | 1958 |

# HIGHEST INDIVIDUAL INNINGS FOR AND AGAINST EACH TEAM

*Complete details of each innings over 200 can be found by reference to the list of double centuries*

| ENGLAND | For | | Against | |
|---|---|---|---|---|
| Derbyshire | 274 | G. Davidson | 343* | P.A. Perrin (Essex) |
| Essex | 343* | P.A. Perrin | 332 | W.H. Ashdown (Kent) |
| Glamorgan | 287* | D.E. Davies | 302* | W.R. Hammond (Gloucestershire) |
| Gloucestershire | 318* | W.G. Grace | 296 | A.O. Jones (Nottinghamshire) |
| Hampshire | 316 | R.H. Moore | 302* | P. Holmes (Yorkshire) |
| Kent | 332 | W.H. Ashdown | 344 | W.G. Grace (MCC) |
| Lancashire | 424 | A.C. MacLaren | 315* | T.W. Hayward (Surrey) |
| Leicestershire | 252* | S. Coe | 341 | G.H. Hirst (Yorkshire) |
| Middlesex | 331* | J.D.B. Robertson | 316* | J.B. Hobbs (Surrey) |
| Northamptonshire | 300 | R. Subba Row | 333 | K.S. Duleepsinhji (Sussex) |
| Nottinghamshire | 312* | W.W. Keeton | 345 | C.G. Macartney (Australians) |
| Somerset | 322 | I.V.A. Richards | 424 | A.C. MacLaren (Lancashire) |
| Surrey | 357* | R. Abel | 300* | F.B. Watson (Lancashire) |
| | | | 300 | R. Subba Row (Northamptonshire) |
| Sussex | 333 | K.S. Duleepsinhji | 322 | E. Paynter (Lancashire) |
| Warwickshire | 305* | F.R. Foster | 322 | I.V.A. Richards (Somerset) |
| Worcestershire | 311* | G.M. Turner | 331* | J.D.B. Robertson (Middlesex) |
| Yorkshire | 341 | G.H. Hirst | 318* | W.G. Grace (Gloucestershire) |
| MCC | 344 | W.G. Grace | 281* | W.H. Ponsford (Australians) |
| Oxford University | 281 | K.J. Key | 338 | W.W. Read (Surrey) |
| Cambridge University | 254* | K.S. Duleepsinhji | 304* | E.de C. Weekes (West Indians) |

| ENGLAND continued | For | | Against | |
|---|---|---|---|---|
| England (Tests) | 364 | L. Hutton | 334 | D.G. Bradman (Australia) |
| Australians | 345 | C.G. Macartney | 364 | L. Hutton (England) |
| South Africans | 239 | C.M.H. Hathorn | 229 | G.J. Bryan (Combined Services) |
| West Indians | 304* | E.de C. Weekes | 285* | P.B.H. May (England) |
| New Zealanders | 243 | B. Sutcliffe | 310* | J.H. Edrich (England) |
| Indians | 252* | P.R. Umrigar | 246* | G. Boycott (England) |
| Pakistanis | 274 | Zaheer Abbas | 278 | D.C.S. Compton (England) |
| Sri Lankans | 190 | S. Wettimuny | 221* | D.G. Aslett (Kent) |
| Zimbabweans | 230 | G.A. Hick | {124 | D.A. Thorne (Oxford U.) |
|  |  |  | {124 | A. Heedham (Surrey) |

## AUSTRALIA

| New South Wales | 452* | D.G. Bradman | 365* | C. Hill (South Australia) |
|---|---|---|---|---|
| Queensland | 283 | P.J.P. Burge | 452* | D.G. Bradman (New South Wales) |
| South Australia | 369 | D.G. Bradman | 336 | W.H. Ponsford (Victoria) |
| Tasmania | 274 | C.L. Badcock | 429 | W.H. Ponsford (Victoria) |
| Victoria | 437 | W.H. Ponsford | 357 | D.G. Bradman (South Australia) |
| Western Australia | 243 | C. Milburn | 356 | B.A. Richards (South Australia) |
| MCC/England | 307 | M.C. Cowdrey | 307 | R.M. Cowper (Australia) |
| Australia (Tests) | 307 | R.M. Cowper | 287 | R.E. Foster (England) |
| South Africans | 209 | E.J. Barlow | 299* | D.G. Bradman (Australia) |
| West Indians | 252 | R.B. Kanhai | 242 | K.D. Walters (Australia) |
| New Zealanders | 160 | J.R. Reid | 325* | H.S.T.L. Hendry (Victoria) |
| Indians | 228* | L. Amarnath | 213 | K.J. Hughes (Australia) |
| Pakistanis | 158 | Majid Khan | 236 | R.W. Marsh (Western Australia) |
| Sri Lankans | 74 | S. Jeganathan | 69* | T.J. Zoehrer (Western Australia) |

## SOUTH AFRICA AND RHODESIA

| Border | 222 | I.D. Harty | 261* | S.S.L. Steyn (Western Province) |
|---|---|---|---|---|
| Eastern Province | 284 | E.A.B. Rowan | 247 | W.R. Endean (Transvaal) |
| Griqualand West | 215 | K.G. Viljoen | 284 | E.A.B. Rowan (Eastern Province) |
| Natal | 304* | A.W. Nourse | 306* | E.A.B. Rowan (Transvaal) |
| Northern (N.E.) Transvaal | 237 | P.L. Corbett | 300 | D.C.S. Compton (MCC) |
| Orange Free State | 258 | C. Richardson | {279* | P. Holmes (MCC) |
|  |  |  | {279* | R.A. Gripper (Rhodesia) |
| Rhodesia | 279* | R.A. Gripper | 222* | A.L. Wilmot (Eastern Province) |
| Transvaal | 306* | E.A.B. Rowan | 304* | A.W. Nourse (Natal) |
| Western Province | 271* | J.E. Cheetham | 254 | M.J. Procter (Rhodesia) |
| MCC/England | 300 | D.C.S. Compton | {176* | J.W. Zulch (Transvaal) |
|  |  |  | {176 | H.W. Taylor (South Africa) |
| Australians | 243 | R.B. Simpson | 274 | R.G. Pollock (South Africa) |
| South Africa (Tests) | 274 | R.G. Pollock | 243 | E. Paynter (England) |
| New Zealanders | 203 | J.R. Reid | 147* | W.S. Farrer (South African Colts) |

## WEST INDIES

| Barbados | 314* | C.L. Walcott | 281* | W.R. Hammond (MCC) |
|---|---|---|---|---|
| Guyana (British Guiana) | 268 | H.P. Bayley | 324 | J.B. Stollmeyer (Trinidad) |
| Jamaica | 344* | G.A. Headley | 275 | W.A. Farmer (Barbados) |
| Leeward Islands | 167 | I.V.A. Richards | 238 | I.T. Shillingford (Windwards) |
| Leeward & Windward I's | 161 | J.C. Allen | 197 | C. Wiltshire (British Guiana) |
| Trinidad and Tobago | 324 | J.B. Stollmeyer | 314* | C.L. Walcott (Barbados) |
| Windward Islands | 238 | I.T. Shillingford | 158 | E.E. Lewis (Leewards) |
| English teams | 325 | A. Sandham | 344* | G.A. Headley (Jamaica) |
| Australians | 210 | W.M. Lawry | 219 | D.St E. Atkinson (West Indies) |
| West Indies (Tests) | 365* | G.St A. Sobers | 337 | Hanif Mohammad (Pakistan) |
| New Zealanders | 259 | G.M. Turner | 227 | L.G. Rowe (Jamaica) |
| Indians | 220 | S.M. Gavaskar | 253 | E.de C. Weekes (Barbados) |
| Pakistanis | 337 | Hanif Mohammad | 365* | G.St A. Sobers (West Indies) |

## NEW ZEALAND

| Auckland | 290 | W.N. Carson | 355 | B. Sutcliffe (Otago) |
|---|---|---|---|---|
| Canterbury | 226 | B.F. Hastings | 385 | B. Sutcliffe (Otago) |
| Central Districts | 202* | B.E. Congdon | 264 | B. Sutcliffe (Otago) |

| NEW ZEALAND *continued* | For | | Against | |
|---|---|---|---|---|
| Northern Districts | 195 | J.M. Parker | 296 | J.R. Reid (Wellington) |
| Otago | 385 | B. Sutcliffe | 290 | W.N. Carson (Auckland) |
| Wellington | 296 | J.R. Reid | {206 | G.T. Dowling (Canterbury) |
| | | | {206 | M.L. Page (Canterbury) |
| MCC/England | 336* | W.R. Hammond | 197 | B. Sutcliffe (Otago) |
| Australians | 293 | V.T. Trumper | 198 | W.A. Hadlee (Otago) |
| South Africans | 255* | D.J. McGlew | 165 | M.E. Chapple (Canterbury) |
| West Indians | 258 | S.M. Nurse | 147 | G.P. Howarth (New Zealand) |
| Indians | 143 | A.L. Wadekar | 239 | G.T. Dowling (New Zealand) |
| Pakistanis | 201 | Mushtaq Mohammad | 147* | G.P. Howarth (N. Districts) |
| Sri Lankans | 105 | S. Wettimuny | 109* | D.R. Hadlee (Canterbury) |

## INDIA

| | | | | |
|---|---|---|---|---|
| MCC/England | 202 | J.M. Brearley | 203* | Nawab of Pataudi, jr (India) |
| Australians | 284 | N.C. O'Neill | 161* | G.R. Viswanath (India) |
| West Indians | 256 | R.B. Kanhai | 236* | S.M. Gavaskar (India) |
| New Zealanders | 230* | B. Sutcliffe | 231 | M.H. Mankad (India) |
| Pakistanis | 222 | Hanif Mohammad | 177* | C.G. Borde (India) |
| Sri Lankans | 215 | M. Sathasivam | 203 | S.M. Gavaskar (Indian XI) |

## PAKISTAN

| | | | | |
|---|---|---|---|---|
| MCC/England | 312* | J.M. Brearley | 157 | Mushtaq Mohammad (Pakistan) |
| Australians | 235 | G.S. Chappell | 210 | Taslim Arif (Pakistan) |
| West Indians | 217 | R.B. Kanhai | 200* | Shafiq Ahmed (Patron's XI) |
| New Zealanders | 157 | B.A.G. Murray | 209 | Imtiaz Ahmed (Pakistan) |
| Indians | 165* | S.M. Gavaskar | 280* | Javed Miandad |
| Sri Lankans | 157 | S. Wettimuny | 210 | Javed Burki (Pakistan XI) |

## SRI LANKA

| | | | | |
|---|---|---|---|---|
| Sri Lanka (Tests) | 108 | R.L. Dias | 180 | J.F. Reid (New Zealand) |
| MCC/England | 177 | J.H. Edrich | 142* | R.S. Madugalle (President's XI) |
| Australians | 143* | D.W. Hookes | 96 | S. Wettimuny (Sri Lanka) |
| West Indians | 285 | F.M.M. Worrell | 135* | M. Rodrigo (Ceylon) |
| New Zealanders | 180 | J.F. Reid | 108 | R.L. Dias (Sri Lanka) |
| Indians | 149* | Hanumant Singh | 212 | C.H. Gunasekara (Ceylon) |
| Pakistanis | 170 | Nazar Mohammad | 154 | B. Warnapura (Sri Lanka U-25) |
| Zimbabweans | 77 | D.L. Houghton | 65 | S. Warnakulasuriya (Sri Lanka) |

## ZIMBABWE

| | | | | |
|---|---|---|---|---|
| England | 129 | V.P. Terry | 108 | R.D. Brown |
| Australians | 148 | D.C. Boon | 105 | A.H. Shah |
| West Indians | 114 | A.A. Lyght | 102 | R.D. Brown |
| New Zealanders | 203 | B.A. Edgar | 124* | R.D. Brown |
| Indians | 101 | R.J. Shastri | 54 | A.J. Pycroft |
| Pakistanis | 101 | Mushtaq Mohd | 133 | A.J. Pycroft |
| Sri Lankans | 85 | R.L. Dias | 128 | A.J. Pycroft |

## HIGHEST MAIDEN HUNDREDS

| | | | | |
|---|---|---|---|---|
| 337* | Pervez Akhtar | Railways v Dera Ismail Khan | Lahore | 1964–65 |
| 324 | Waheed Mirza | Karachi Whites v Quetta | Karachi | 1976–77 |
| 292* | V.T. Trumper | New South Wales v Tasmania | Sydney | 1898–99 |
| 290 | W.N. Carson | Auckland v Otago | Dunedin | 1936–37 |
| 290 | Khalid Irtiza | United Bank v Multan | Karachi | 1975–76 |
| 282 | H.L. Collins | New South Wales v Tasmania | Hobart | 1912–13 |
| 276 | Altaf Shah | HBFC v Multan | Multan | 1976–77 |
| 275 | W.A. Farmer | Barbados v Jamaica | Bridgetown | 1951–52 |
| 274 | G. Davidson | Derbyshire v Lancashire | Manchester | 1896 |

| 271 | R.I. Maddocks | Victoria v Tasmania | Melbourne | 1951–52 |
| 268 | C.R.N. Maxwell | Sir J. Cahn's XI v Leicestershire | Nottingham | 1935 |
| 268 | H.P. Bayley | British Guiana v Barbados | Georgetown | 1937–38 |
| 264 | P. Vaulkhard | Derbyshire v Nottinghamshire | Nottingham | 1946 |
| 264* | R. Flockton | New South Wales v South Australia | Sydney | 1959–60 |
| 262* | G.L. Wight | British Guiana v Barbados | Georgetown | 1951–52 |
| 261* | S.S.L. Steyn | Western Province v Border | Cape Town | 1929–30 |
| 261 | I.R. Redpath | Victoria v Queensland | Melbourne | 1962–63 |
| 253 | L.S. Birkett | Trinidad v British Guiana | Georgetown | 1929–30 |

# DOUBLE HUNDREDS

## MOST IN A SEASON

| SIX | D.G. Bradman | 1930 | 334 | 254 | 252* | 236 | 232 | 205* |
|-----|--------------|------|-----|-----|------|-----|-----|------|
| FIVE | K.S. Ranjitsinhji | 1900 | 275 | 222 | 220 | 215* | 202 | |
| | E.de C. Weekes | 1950 | 232 | 304* | 279 | 246* | 200* | |
| FOUR | C.B. Fry | 1901 | 244 | 241 | 219* | 209 | | |
| | E.H. Hendren | 1929–30 | 254* | 223* | 211* | 205* | | |
| | W.R. Hammond | 1933 | 264 | 239 | 231 | 206 | | |
| | W.R. Hammond | 1934 | 302* | 290 | 265* | 217 | | |
| | V.M. Merchant | 1944–45 | 221* | 217 | 278 | 201 | | |
| | G.M. Turner | 1971–72 | 202 | 223* | 259 | 259 | | |

## TWO IN SUCCESSIVE INNINGS

| | | | | | | |
|---|---|---|---|---|---|---|
| Arshad Pervez | | Habib Bank | 220 | 236 | 1977–78 |
| Bakewell, A.H. | | Northamptonshire | 246 | 257 | 1933 |
| Barrington, K.F. | | England/Surrey | 256 | 207 | 1964 |
| Bradman, D.G. | (4) | NSW | 226 | 219 | 1931–32 |
| | | Australia | 304 | 244 | 1934 |
| | | South Australia | 233 | 357 | 1935–36 |
| | | South Australia | 369 | 212 | 1936–37 |
| Burge, P.J.P. | | Queensland | 283 | 205* | 1963–64 |
| Fagg, A.E. | | Kent | 244 | 202* | 1938 |
| Hammond, W.R. | (3) | England | 251 | 200 | 1928–29 |
| | | England | 227 | 336* | 1932–33 |
| | | Gloucestershire | 231 | 264 | 1933 |
| Hendren, E.H. | (2) | MCC | 223* | 211* | 1929–30 |
| | | MCC | 205* | 254* | 1929–30 |
| Merchant, V.M. | (2) | Hindus | 243* | 221 | 1941–42 |
| | | Hindus/Bombay | 221* | 217 | 1944–45 |
| Modi, R.S. | | Bombay | 210 | 245* | 1944–45 |
| Pataudi, Nawab of, sr | | Worcestershire | 231* | 222 | 1933 |
| Ponsford, W.H. | (2) | Victoria | 437 | 202 | 1927–28 |
| | | Australians | 229* | 281* | 1934 |
| Ranjitsinhji, K.S. | (2) | Sussex | 222 | 215* | 1900 |
| | | Sussex | 285* | 204 | 1901 |
| Read, W.W. | | Surrey | 247 | 244* | 1887 |
| Rowe, L.G. | | Jamaica/West Indies | 227 | 214 | 1971–72 |
| Shepherd, T.F. | | Surrey | 212 | 210* | 1921 |
| Simpson, R.B. | (2) | Western Australia | 236* | 230* | 1959–60 |
| | | Combined XI/NSW | 246 | 247* | 1963–64 |
| Tarrant, F.A. | | Middlesex | 250* | 200 | 1914 |
| Turner, G.M. | (2) | New Zealand | 202 | 223* | 1971–72 |
| | | New Zealand | 259 | 259 | 1971–72 |
| Vengsarkar, D.B. | | Bombay | 210 | 203 | 1979–80 |
| Weekes, E.de C. | (3) | West Indians | 232 | 304* | 1950 |
| | | West Indians | 246* | 200* | 1950 |
| | | Barbados | 207 | 253 | 1952–53 |
| Worrell, F.M.M. | | West Indians | 241* | 261 | 1950 |

## SCORERS OF DOUBLE HUNDREDS

| | | | | | | |
|---|---|---|---|---|---|---|
| Abdul Hai | | 217* | Hyderabad v Punjab | Jullundur | 1971–72 |
| Abel, R. | (9) | 217 | Surrey v Essex | Oval | 1895 |
| | | 231 | Surrey v Essex | Oval | 1896 |

| Abel, R. *continued* | | 250 | Surrey v Warwickshire | Oval | 1897 |
|---|---|---|---|---|---|
| | | 215 | Surrey v Nottinghamshire | Oval | 1897 |
| | | 219 | Surrey v Kent | Oval | 1898 |
| | | 357* | Surrey v Somerset | Oval | 1899 |
| | | 221 | Surrey v Worcestershire | Oval | 1900 |
| | | 247 | Players v Gentlemen | Oval | 1901 |
| | | 205* | Surrey v Middlesex | Oval | 1901 |
| Abell, G.E.B. | | 210 | Northern India v Army | Lahore | 1934–35 |
| Abrahams, J. | | 201* | Lancashire v Warwickshire | Nuneaton | 1984 |
| Ackerman, H.M. | (2) | 200* | N.E. Transvaal v Western Province | Cape Town | 1966–67 |
| | | 208 | Northamptonshire v Leicestershire | Leicester | 1970 |
| Adhikari, H.R. | | 230* | Services v Rajasthan | Ajmer | 1951–52 |
| Aftab Baloch | (2) | 428 | Sind v Baluchistan | Karachi | 1973–74 |
| | | 200* | National Bank v Baluchistan | Karachi | 1974–75 |
| Akash Lal | | 209* | Delhi v Jammu & Kashmir | Srinagar | 1964–65 |
| Allen, B.O. | | 220 | Gloucestershire v Hampshire | Bournemouth | 1947 |
| Alley, W.E. | (3) | 209* | Commonwealth XI v West Zone | Poona | 1949–50 |
| | | 206* | Commonwealth XI v CC of India | Bombay | 1949–50 |
| | | 221* | Somerset v Warwickshire | Nuneaton | 1961 |
| Altaf Shah | | 276 | HBFC v Multan | Multan | 1976–77 |
| Amarnath, L. | (4) | 241 | Hindus v Rest | Bombay | 1938–39 |
| | | 262 | India in England v Rest of India | Calcutta | 1946–47 |
| | | 228* | Indians v Victoria | Melbourne | 1947–48 |
| | | 223* | North Zone v West Indians | Patiala | 1948–49 |
| Amarnath, M. | | 207 | North Zone v East Zone | Bombay | 1982–83 |
| Amarnath, S. | (3) | 200* | Punjab v Madhya Pradesh | Jullundur | 1971–72 |
| | | 202* | Punjab v Delhi | Delhi | 1972–73 |
| | | 235* | Delhi v Rest of India | Delhi | 1980–81 |
| Ames, L.E.G. | (9) | 200 | Kent v Surrey | Blackheath | 1928 |
| | | 210 | Kent v Warwickshire | Tonbridge | 1933 |
| | | 295 | Kent v Gloucestershire | Folkestone | 1933 |
| | | 201 | Players v Gentlemen | Folkestone | 1933 |
| | | 202* | Kent v Essex | Brentwood | 1934 |
| | | 201* | Kent v Worcestershire | Gillingham | 1937 |
| | | 201 | Kent v Worcestershire | Worcester | 1939 |
| | | 212* | Kent v Nottinghamshire | Gravesend | 1947 |
| | | 212 | Kent v Gloucestershire | Dover | 1948 |
| Amiss, D.L. | (3) | 262* | England v West Indies | Kingston | 1973–74 |
| | | 203 | England v West Indies | Oval | 1976 |
| | | 232* | Warwickshire v Gloucestershire | Bristol | 1979 |
| Andrews, C.W. | | 253 | Queensland v New South Wales | Sydney | 1934–35 |
| Andrews, T.J.E. | (2) | 247* | New South Wales v Victoria | Sydney | 1919–20 |
| | | 224 | New South Wales v MCC | Sydney | 1924–25 |
| Ansari, S. | | 200 | Madhya Pradesh v Uttar Pradesh | Kanpur | 1984–85 |
| Armstrong, W.W. | (7) | 200 | Victoria v Queensland | Melbourne | 1904–05 |
| | | 303* | Australians v Somerset | Bath | 1905 |
| | | 248* | Australians v Gentlemen | Lord's | 1905 |
| | | 231 | Victoria v South Australia | Melbourne | 1907–08 |
| | | 250 | Victoria v South Australia | Melbourne | 1911–12 |
| | | 202* | Victoria v Queensland | Melbourne | 1913–14 |
| | | 245 | Victoria v South Australia | Melbourne | 1920–21 |
| Arnold, E.G. | (2) | 200* | Worcestershire v Warwickshire | Birmingham | 1909 |
| | | 215 | Worcestershire v Oxford University | Oxford | 1910 |
| Arnold, J. | | 227 | Hampshire v Glamorgan | Cardiff | 1932 |
| Arshad Pervez | (4) | 251* | Habib Bank v Karachi Whites | Karachi | 1976–77 |
| | | 243 | Habib Bank v Baluchistan | Karachi | 1977–78 |
| | | 220 | Habib Bank v Income Tax Dept | Lahore | 1977–78 |
| | | 236 | Habib Bank v MCB | Lahore | 1977–78 |
| Ashdown, W.H. | (2) | 332 | Kent v Essex | Brentwood | 1934 |
| | | 305* | Kent v Derbyshire | Dover | 1935 |
| Ashton, H. | | 236* | Cambridge U. v Free Foresters | Cambridge | 1920 |
| Aslam Ali | | 236 | United Bank v Multan | Karachi | 1975–76 |
| Aslett, D.G. | | 221* | Kent v Sri Lankans | Canterbury | 1984 |
| Atkinson, D.St E. | | 219 | West Indies v Australia | Bridgetown | 1954–55 |
| Avery, A.V. | (4) | 210 | Essex v Surrey | Oval | 1946 |
| | | 214* | Essex v Worcestershire | Clacton | 1948 |
| | | 224 | Essex v Northamptonshire | Northampton | 1952 |

| | | | | | |
|---|---|---|---|---|---|
| Avery, A.V. *continued* | | 208* | Essex v Glamorgan | Westcliff | 1953 |
| Azhar Khan | (2) | 209* | Pakistan Universities v Bahawalpur | Lahore | 1974–75 |
| | | 203 | Lahore v Bahawalpur | Lahore | 1975–76 |
| Azharuddin, M. | | 226 | South Zone v Central Zone | Jamadoba | 1983–84 |
| Azmat Rana | | 206* | Punjab Greens v NWFP | Peshawar | 1977–78 |
| Bacchus, S.F.A.F. | | 250 | West Indies v India | Kanpur | 1978–79 |
| Bacher, A. | | 235 | Transvaal v Australians | Johannesburg | 1966–67 |
| Badcock, C.L. | (4) | 274 | Tasmania v Victoria | Launceston | 1933–34 |
| | | 325 | South Australia v Victoria | Adelaide | 1935–36 |
| | | 271* | South Australia v New South Wales | Adelaide | 1938–39 |
| | | 236 | South Australia v Queensland | Adelaide | 1939–40 |
| Baichan, L. | | 216* | Berbice v Demerara | Georgetown | 1973–74 |
| Baig, A.A. | (2) | 221* | Oxford University v Free Foresters | Oxford | 1959 |
| | | 224* | South Zone v North Zone | Delhi | 1966–67 |
| Bailey, T.E. | | 205 | Essex v Sussex | Eastbourne | 1947 |
| Bakewell, A.H. | (4) | 204 | Northamptonshire v Somerset | Bath | 1930 |
| | | 246 | Northamptonshire v Nottinghamshire | Northampton | 1933 |
| | | 257 | Northamptonshire v Glamorgan | Swansea | 1933 |
| | | 241* | Northamptonshire v Derbyshire | Chesterfield | 1936 |
| Balaskas, X.C. | (2) | 206 | Griqualand West v Rhodesia | Kimberley | 1929–30 |
| | | 200* | Rest of South Africa v W. Province | Cape Town | 1932–33 |
| Baldwin, C. | | 234 | Surrey v Kent | Oval | 1897 |
| Barber, W. | (2) | 248 | Yorkshire v Kent | Leeds | 1934 |
| | | 255 | Yorkshire v Surrey | Sheffield | 1935 |
| Bardsley, W. | (7) | 264 | Australian XI v Rest | Melbourne | 1908–09 |
| | | 219 | Australians v Essex | Leyton | 1909 |
| | | 211 | Australians v Gloucestershire | Bristol | 1909 |
| | | 235 | New South Wales v South Australia | Sydney | 1920–21 |
| | | 235 | New South Wales v South Australia | Adelaide | 1920–21 |
| | | 209 | Australians v Hampshire | Southampton | 1921 |
| | | 200* | New South Wales v Auckland | Auckland | 1923–24 |
| Barling, H.T. | (2) | 269 | Surrey v Hampshire | Southampton | 1933 |
| | | 233* | Surrey v Nottinghamshire | Oval | 1946 |
| Barlow, E.J. | (6) | 209 | South Africans v Combined XI | Perth | 1963–64 |
| | | 201 | South Africa v Australia | Adelaide | 1963–64 |
| | | 212 | Transvaal v Rhodesia | Johannesburg | 1966–67 |
| | | 211 | S.A. Invitation XI v D.H. Robins' XI | Johannesburg | 1973–74 |
| | | 217 | Derbyshire v Surrey | Ilkeston | 1976 |
| | | 202* | Boland v Eastern Province B | Uitenhage | 1981–82 |
| Barnes, S.G. | (2) | 200 | New South Wales v Queensland | Brisbane | 1945–46 |
| | | 234 | Australia v England | Sydney | 1946–47 |
| Barnett, C.J. | (4) | 204* | Gloucestershire v Leicestershire | Leicester | 1936 |
| | | 259 | MCC v Queensland | Brisbane | 1936–37 |
| | | 232 | Gloucestershire v Lancashire | Gloucester | 1937 |
| | | 228* | Gloucestershire v Leicestershire | Gloucester | 1947 |
| Barrett, E.I.M. | | 215 | Hampshire v Gloucestershire | Southampton | 1920 |
| Barrick, D.W. | | 211 | Northamptonshire v Essex | Northampton | 1952 |
| Barrington, K.F. | (3) | 219* | MCC v Australian XI | Melbourne | 1962–63 |
| | | 256 | England v Australia | Manchester | 1964 |
| | | 207 | Surrey v Nottinghamshire | Oval | 1964 |
| Barton, V.A. | | 205 | Hampshire v Sussex | Hove | 1900 |
| Bashir Shana | | 208 | Hyderabad v PWD | Hyderabad | 1973–74 |
| Bates, L.T.A. | (2) | 200 | Warwickshire v Worcestershire | Birmingham | 1928 |
| | | 211 | Warwickshire v Gloucestershire | Gloucester | 1932 |
| Bates, W.E. | | 200* | Glamorgan v Worcestershire | Kidderminster | 1927 |
| Bayley, H.P. | | 268 | British Guiana v Barbados | Georgetown | 1937–38 |
| Beames, P.J. | | 226* | Victoria v Tasmania | Launceston | 1938–39 |
| Begbie, D.W. | | 207* | Transvaal v Orange Free State | Johannesburg | 1937–38 |
| Bell, J.T. | (2) | 225 | Glamorgan v Worcestershire | Dudley | 1926 |
| | | 209* | Wales v MCC | Lord's | 1927 |
| Berry, G.L. | (2) | 207 | Leicestershire v Worcestershire | Ashby de la Zouch | 1928 |
| | | 232 | Leicestershire v Sussex | Leicester | 1930 |
| Bhalekar, R.B. | | 207* | Maharashtra v Saurashtra | Poona | 1981–82 |
| Bhandari, P. | (2) | 227 | Delhi v Patiala | Patiala | 1957–58 |
| | | 202* | Delhi v Punjab | Delhi | 1968–69 |
| Bhandarkar, K.V. | | 205 | Maharashtra v Kathiawar | Poona | 1948–49 |
| Bhanot, A. | | 231* | Uttar Pradesh v Bengal | Kanpur | 1980–81 |

| | | | | | |
|---|---|---|---|---|---|
| Bhosle, V.H. | | 208 | Bombay v Rajasthan | Udaipur | 1968–69 |
| Binny, R.M.H. | | 211* | Karnataka v Kerala | Chikmagalur | 1977–78 |
| Bird, M.C. | | 200 | MCC v Orange Free State | Bloemfontein | 1913–14 |
| Birkett, L.S. | | 253 | Trinidad v British Guiana | Georgetown | 1929–30 |
| Blunt, R.C. | (3) | 221 | Otago v Canterbury | Dunedin | 1928–29 |
| | | 225* | New Zealanders v Gentlemen | Eastbourne | 1931 |
| | | 338* | Otago v Canterbury | Christchurch | 1931–32 |
| Board, J.H. | | 214 | Gloucestershire v Somerset | Bristol | 1900 |
| Bogle, J. | | 200 | New South Wales v South Australia | Adelaide | 1919–20 |
| Bolus, J.B. | | 202* | Nottinghamshire v Glamorgan | Nottingham | 1963 |
| Bonitto, N. | | 207* | Jamaica v British Guiana | Georgetown | 1952–53 |
| Boon, D.C. | (2) | 227 | Tasmania v Victoria | Melbourne | 1983–84 |
| | | 206* | Australians v Northamptonshire | Northampton | 1985 |
| Booth, B.C. | | 214* | Australians v Central Districts | Palmerston North | 1966–67 |
| Booth, M.W. | | 210 | Yorkshire v Worcestershire | Worcester | 1911 |
| Borde, C.G. | (2) | 202 | Maharashtra v Baroda | Sangli | 1969–70 |
| | | 207* | Maharashtra v Bengal | Poona | 1972–73 |
| Border, A.R. | | 200 | New South Wales v Queensland | Brisbane | 1979–80 |
| Bosanquet, B.J.T. | | 214 | Rest of England v Yorkshire | Oval | 1908 |
| Botham, I.T. | (2) | 228 | Somerset v Gloucestershire | Taunton | 1980 |
| | | 208 | England v India | Oval | 1982 |
| Bowell, H.A.W. | | 204 | Hampshire v Lancashire | Bournemouth | 1914 |
| Bowley, E.H. | (4) | 228 | Sussex v Northamptonshire | Hove | 1921 |
| | | 220 | Sussex v Gloucestershire | Hove | 1927 |
| | | 280* | Sussex v Gloucestershire | Hove | 1929 |
| | | 283 | Sussex v Middlesex | Hove | 1933 |
| Bowley, F.L. | (3) | 217 | Worcestershire v Leicestershire | Stourbridge | 1905 |
| | | 201 | Worcestershire v Gloucestershire | Worcester | 1913 |
| | | 276 | Worcestershire v Hampshire | Dudley | 1914 |
| Bowring, T. | | 228 | Oxford University v Gentlemen | Oxford | 1908 |
| Boycott, G. | (10) | 246* | England v India | Leeds | 1967 |
| | | 220* | Yorkshire v Northamptonshire | Sheffield | 1967 |
| | | 243 | MCC v Barbados | Bridgetown | 1967–68 |
| | | 260* | Yorkshire v Essex | Colchester | 1970 |
| | | 233 | Yorkshire v Essex | Colchester | 1971 |
| | | 204* | Yorkshire v Leicestershire | Leicester | 1972 |
| | | 261* | MCC v President's XI | Bridgetown | 1973–74 |
| | | 201* | Yorkshire v Middlesex | Lord's | 1975 |
| | | 207* | Yorkshire v Cambridge University | Cambridge | 1976 |
| | | 214* | Yorkshire v Nottinghamshire | Worksop | 1983 |
| Bradman, D.G. | (37) | 340* | New South Wales v Victoria | Sydney | 1928–29 |
| | | 225 | W.M. Woodfull's XI v J. Ryder's XI | Sydney | 1929–30 |
| | | 452* | New South Wales v Queensland | Sydney | 1929–30 |
| | | 236 | Australians v Worcestershire | Worcester | 1930 |
| | | 252* | Australians v Surrey | Oval | 1930 |
| | | 254 | Australia v England | Lord's | 1930 |
| | | 334 | Australia v England | Leeds | 1930 |
| | | 232 | Australia v England | Oval | 1930 |
| | | 205* | Australians v Kent | Canterbury | 1930 |
| | | 258 | New South Wales v South Australia | Adelaide | 1930–31 |
| | | 223 | Australia v West Indies | Brisbane | 1930–31 |
| | | 220 | New South Wales v Victoria | Sydney | 1930–31 |
| | | 226 | Australia v South Africa | Brisbane | 1931–32 |
| | | 219 | New South Wales v South Africans | Sydney | 1931–32 |
| | | 299* | Australia v South Africa | Adelaide | 1931–32 |
| | | 238 | New South Wales v Victoria | Sydney | 1932–33 |
| | | 200 | New South Wales v Queensland | Brisbane | 1933–34 |
| | | 253 | New South Wales v Queensland | Sydney | 1933–34 |
| | | 206 | Australians v Worcestershire | Worcester | 1934 |
| | | 304 | Australia v England | Leeds | 1934 |
| | | 244 | Australia v England | Oval | 1934 |
| | | 233 | South Australia v Queensland | Adelaide | 1935–36 |
| | | 357 | South Australia v Victoria | Melbourne | 1935–36 |
| | | 369 | South Australia v Tasmania | Adelaide | 1935–36 |
| | | 212 | D.G. Bradman's XI v V.Y. Richardson's XI | Sydney | 1936–37 |
| | | 270 | Australia v England | Melbourne | 1936–37 |

| | | | | | |
|---|---|---|---|---|---|
| Bradman, D.G. *continued* | | 212 | Australia v England | Adelaide | 1936–37 |
| | | 246 | South Australia v Queensland | Adelaide | 1937–38 |
| | | 258 | Australians v Worcestershire | Worcester | 1938 |
| | | 278 | Australians v MCC | Lord's | 1938 |
| | | 202 | Australians v Somerset | Taunton | 1938 |
| | | 225 | South Australia v Queensland | Adelaide | 1938–39 |
| | | 251* | South Australia v New South Wales | Adelaide | 1939–40 |
| | | 267 | South Australia v Victoria | Melbourne | 1939–40 |
| | | 209* | South Australia v Western Australia | Perth | 1939–40 |
| | | 234 | Australia v England | Sydney | 1946–47 |
| | | 201 | Australia v India | Adelaide | 1947–48 |
| Braund, L.C. | | 257* | Somerset v Worcestershire | Worcester | 1913 |
| Brearley, J.M. | (3) | 312* | MCC U-25 XI v North Zone | Peshawar | 1966–67 |
| | | 223 | MCC U-25 XI v Pakistan U-25 XI | Dacca | 1966–67 |
| | | 202 | MCC v West Zone | Poona | 1976–77 |
| Briers, N.E. | | 201* | Leicestershire v Warwickshire | Birmingham | 1983 |
| Brockwell, W. | | 225 | Surrey v Hampshire | Oval | 1897 |
| Brookes, D. | (6) | 200 | Northamptonshire v Worcestershire | Kidderminster | 1946 |
| | | 210 | Northamptonshire v Leicestershire | Leicester | 1947 |
| | | 257 | Northamptonshire v Gloucestershire | Bristol | 1949 |
| | | 204* | Northamptonshire v Essex | Northampton | 1952 |
| | | 210* | Northamptonshire v Somerset | Northampton | 1954 |
| | | 203* | Northamptonshire v Somerset | Taunton | 1956 |
| Brown, F.R. | | 212 | Surrey v Middlesex | Oval | 1932 |
| Brown, G. | (3) | 232* | Hampshire v Yorkshire | Leeds | 1920 |
| | | 230 | Hampshire v Essex | Bournemouth | 1920 |
| | | 204 | Hampshire v Yorkshire | Portsmouth | 1927 |
| Brown, J.T. | (3) | 203 | Yorkshire v Middlesex | Lord's | 1896 |
| | | 311 | Yorkshire v Sussex | Sheffield | 1897 |
| | | 300 | Yorkshire v Derbyshire | Chesterfield | 1898 |
| Brown, R.D. | | 200* | Rhodesia B v Eastern Province B | Salisbury | 1978–79 |
| Brown, S.M. | (2) | 200 | Middlesex v Kent | Canterbury | 1949 |
| | | 232* | Middlesex v Somerset | Lord's | 1951 |
| Brown, W.A. | (5) | 205 | New South Wales v Victoria | Sydney | 1933–34 |
| | | 206* | Australia v England | Lord's | 1938 |
| | | 265* | Australians v Derbyshire | Chesterfield | 1938 |
| | | 215 | Queensland v Victoria | Brisbane | 1938–39 |
| | | 200 | Australians v Cambridge University | Cambridge | 1948 |
| Bryan, G.J. | | 229 | Combined Services v South Africans | Portsmouth | 1924 |
| Bryan, J.L. | (2) | 231 | Cambridge University v Surrey | Oval | 1921 |
| | | 236 | Kent v Hampshire | Canterbury | 1923 |
| Buckle, W.H. | | 207 | Queensland v Western Australia | Brisbane | 1964–65 |
| Burge, P.J.P. | (5) | 210 | Queensland v Victoria | Brisbane | 1956–57 |
| | | 240 | Queensland v South Australia | Adelaide | 1960–61 |
| | | 283 | Queensland v New South Wales | Brisbane | 1963–64 |
| | | 205* | Queensland v Western Australia | Brisbane | 1963–64 |
| | | 242* | Queensland v New South Wales | Sydney | 1964–65 |
| Burke, J.W. | | 220 | New South Wales v South Australia | Adelaide | 1956–57 |
| Burnup, C.J. | | 200 | Kent v Lancashire | Manchester | 1900 |
| Butcher, A.R. | | 216* | Surrey v Cambridge University | Cambridge | 1980 |
| Butcher, B.F. | (2) | 209* | West Indies v England | Nottingham | 1966 |
| | | 203* | Guyana v Barbados | Georgetown | 1969–70 |
| Byrne, J.F. | | 222 | Warwickshire v Lancashire | Birmingham | 1905 |
| Callaway, N. | | 207 | New South Wales v Queensland | Sydney | 1914–15 |
| Calthorpe, Hon F.S.G. | | 209 | Warwickshire v Hampshire | Birmingham | 1921 |
| Carlstein, P.R. | (2) | 203 | Transvaal v Western Province | Johannesburg | 1962–63 |
| | | 229 | Transvaal v Cavaliers | Johannesburg | 1962–63 |
| Carr, A.W. | (2) | 204 | Nottinghamshire v Essex | Leyton | 1921 |
| | | 206 | Nottinghamshire v Leicestershire | Leicester | 1925 |
| Carson, W.N. | | 290 | Auckland v Otago | Dunedin | 1936–37 |
| Cartwright, T.W. | | 210 | Warwickshire v Middlesex | Nuneaton | 1962 |
| Challenor, G. | (2) | 237* | Barbados v Jamaica | Bridgetown | 1924–25 |
| | | 220 | Barbados v Trinidad | Bridgetown | 1926–27 |
| Chaplin, H.P. | | 213* | Sussex v Nottinghamshire | Hove | 1914 |
| Chapman, A.P.F. | | 260 | Kent v Lancashire | Maidstone | 1927 |
| Chappell, G.S. | (4) | 247* | Australia v New Zealand | Wellington | 1973–74 |
| | | 235 | Australia v Pakistan | Faisalabad | 1979–80 |

| Chappell, G.S. *continued* | | 204 | Australia v India | Sydney | 1980–81 |
|---|---|---|---|---|---|
| | | 201 | Australia v Pakistan | Brisbane | 1981–82 |
| Chappell, I.M. | (3) | 205* | South Australia v Queensland | Brisbane | 1963–64 |
| | | 202* | Australians v Warwickshire | Birmingham | 1968 |
| | | 209 | Australians v Barbados | Bridgetown | 1972–73 |
| Charlesworth, C. | (2) | 216 | Warwickshire v Derbyshire | Blackwell | 1910 |
| | | 206 | Warwickshire v Yorkshire | Dewsbury | 1914 |
| Chauhan, C.P.S. | (3) | 203 | Maharashtra v Gujarat | Poona | 1972–73 |
| | | 207 | Maharashtra v Vidarbha | Poona | 1972–73 |
| | | 200 | Delhi v Punjab | Delhi | 1976–77 |
| Cheetham, J.E. | | 271* | Western Province v OFS | Bloemfontein | 1950–51 |
| Chowdhury, Y.M. | | 211 | Delhi v Patiala | Delhi | 1955–56 |
| Clarke, A.J. | | 206* | Border v Eastern Province | Port Elizabeth | 1925–26 |
| Coe, S. | | 252* | Leicestershire v Northamptonshire | Leicester | 1914 |
| Collins, H.L. | (3) | 282 | New South Wales v Tasmania | Hobart | 1912–13 |
| | | 235 | AIF v South African XI | Johannesburg | 1919–20 |
| | | 203 | Australia v South Africa | Johannesburg | 1921–22 |
| Compton, D.C.S. | (9) | 214* | Middlesex v Derbyshire | Lord's | 1939 |
| | | 249* | Holkar v Bombay | Bombay | 1944–45 |
| | | 202 | Middlesex v Cambridge University | Cambridge | 1946 |
| | | 235 | Middlesex v Surrey | Lord's | 1946 |
| | | 208 | England v South Africa | Lord's | 1947 |
| | | 246 | Middlesex v Rest | Oval | 1947 |
| | | 252* | Middlesex v Somerset | Lord's | 1948 |
| | | 300 | MCC v North-Eastern Transvaal | Benoni | 1948–49 |
| | | 278 | England v Pakistan | Nottingham | 1954 |
| Congdon, B.E. | | 202* | Central Districts v Otago | Nelson | 1968–69 |
| Constable, B. | | 205* | Surrey v Somerset | Oval | 1952 |
| Cook, S.J. | | 201* | Transvaal v Eastern Province | Port Elizabeth | 1982–83 |
| Cook, T.E. | (3) | 278 | Sussex v Hampshire | Hove | 1930 |
| | | 214 | Sussex v Worcestershire | Eastbourne | 1933 |
| | | 220 | Sussex v Worcestershire | Worcester | 1934 |
| Cooper, E. | | 216* | Worcestershire v Warwickshire | Dudley | 1938 |
| Corbett, P.L. | | 237 | N.E. Transvaal v Transvaal B | Johannesburg | 1962–63 |
| Cowdrey, M.C. | (3) | 204* | Kent v Cambridge University | Cambridge | 1956 |
| | | 250 | Kent v Essex | Blackheath | 1959 |
| | | 307 | MCC v South Australia | Adelaide | 1962–63 |
| Cowper, R.M. | (2) | 307 | Australia v England | Melbourne | 1965–66 |
| | | 201* | Australians v Orange Free State | Bloemfontein | 1966–67 |
| Cox, A. | | 204 | Canterbury v Otago | Christchurch | 1925–26 |
| Cox, G. | (4) | 232 | Sussex v Northamptonshire | Kettering | 1939 |
| | | 234* | Sussex v Indians | Hove | 1946 |
| | | 205* | Sussex v Glamorgan | Hove | 1947 |
| | | 212* | Sussex v Yorkshire | Leeds | 1949 |
| Craig, E.J. | | 208* | Cambridge U. v Col L.C. Stevens' XI | Eastbourne | 1961 |
| Craig, I.D. | | 213* | New South Wales v South Africans | Sydney | 1952–53 |
| Crawford, J.N. | | 232 | Surrey v Somerset | Oval | 1908 |
| Crawley, A.M. | | 204 | Oxford U. v Northamptonshire | Wellingborough | 1929 |
| Crawley, L.G. | | 222 | Essex v Glamorgan | Swansea | 1928 |
| Creese, W.L.C. | | 241 | Hampshire v Northamptonshire | Northampton | 1939 |
| Croom, A.J.W. | | 211 | Warwickshire v Worcestershire | Birmingham | 1934 |
| Cunningham, K.G. | | 203 | South Australia v Victoria | Adelaide | 1971–72 |
| Curnow, S.H. | | 224 | North v South | Cape Town | 1932–33 |
| Cutmore, J.A. | | 238* | Essex v Gloucestershire | Bristol | 1927 |
| Dacre, C.C.R. | | 223 | Gloucestershire v Worcestershire | Worcester | 1930 |
| Darling, J. | | 210 | South Australia v Queensland | Brisbane | 1898–99 |
| Das, S. | | 221* | Bihar v Assam | Jamshedpur | 1957–58 |
| Davidson, G.A. | | 274 | Derbyshire v Lancashire | Manchester | 1896 |
| Davies, D. | | 216 | Glamorgan v Somerset | Newport | 1939 |
| Davies, D.E. | (2) | 287* | Glamorgan v Gloucestershire | Newport | 1939 |
| | | 215 | Glamorgan v Essex | Brentwood | 1948 |
| Davies, P.C. | | 220 | N.E. Transvaal v Orange Free State | Bloemfontein | 1955–56 |
| Davis, P.C. | | 237 | Northamptonshire v Somerset | Northampton | 1947 |
| De Courcy, J.H. | | 204 | Australians v Combined Services | Kingston | 1953 |
| De Saram, F.C. | | 208 | Oxford University v | | |
| | | | H.D.G. Leveson Gower's XI | Reigate | 1934 |
| De Villiers, D.I. | | 200* | Orange Free State v Border | Johannesburg | 1923–24 |

| Name | | Score | Match | Venue | Year |
|---|---|---|---|---|---|
| Dempster, C.S. | (2) | 212 | New Zealanders v Essex | Leyton | 1931 |
| | | 207* | Leicestershire v Sir J. Cahn's XI | Nottingham | 1935 |
| Denton, D. | (3) | 200* | Yorkshire v Warwickshire | Birmingham | 1912 |
| | | 221 | Yorkshire v Kent | Tunbridge Wells | 1912 |
| | | 209* | Yorkshire v Worcestershire | Worcester | 1920 |
| Denton, W.H. | | 230* | Northamptonshire v Essex | Leyton | 1913 |
| Deodhar, D.B. | | 246 | Maharashtra v Bombay | Poona | 1940–41 |
| Desai, S. | | 218* | Karnataka v Kerala | Chikmagalur | 1977–78 |
| Devey, J.H.G. | | 246 | Warwickshire v Derbyshire | Birmingham | 1900 |
| Dewes, J.G. | (2) | 204* | Cambridge University v Essex | Cambridge | 1949 |
| | | 212 | Cambridge University v Sussex | Hove | 1950 |
| Dexter, E.R. | (2) | 205 | England v Pakistan | Karachi | 1961–62 |
| | | 203 | Sussex v Kent | Hastings | 1968 |
| Diamond, A. | | 210* | New South Wales v Victoria | Sydney | 1906–07 |
| Dipper, A.E. | (3) | 252* | Gloucestershire v Glamorgan | Cheltenham | 1923 |
| | | 247 | Gloucestershire v Oxford University | Bristol | 1924 |
| | | 212 | Gloucestershire v Worcestershire | Bristol | 1927 |
| Dixon, J.A. | | 268* | Nottinghamshire v Sussex | Nottingham | 1897 |
| Doggart, G.H.G. | (2) | 215* | Cambridge University v Lancashire | Cambridge | 1948 |
| | | 219* | Cambridge University v Essex | Cambridge | 1949 |
| D'Oliveira, B.L. | | 227 | Worcestershire v Yorkshire | Hull | 1974 |
| Doll, C.C.T. | | 224* | MCC v London County | Crystal Palace | 1901 |
| Dollery, H.E. | (2) | 200 | Warwickshire v Gloucestershire | Gloucester | 1949 |
| | | 212 | Warwickshire v Leicestershire | Birmingham | 1952 |
| Donnelly, M.P. | (2) | 208* | MCC v Yorkshire | Scarborough | 1948 |
| | | 206 | New Zealand v England | Lord's | 1949 |
| Douglas, J. | | 204 | Middlesex v Gloucestershire | Bristol | 1903 |
| Douglas, J.W.H.T. | | 210* | Essex v Derbyshire | Leyton | 1921 |
| Dowling, G.T. | (2) | 206 | Canterbury v Wellington | Christchurch | 1962–63 |
| | | 239 | New Zealand v India | Christchurch | 1967–68 |
| Druce, N.F. | | 227* | Cambridge U. v C.I. Thornton's XI | Cambridge | 1897 |
| Ducat, A. | (8) | 306* | Surrey v Oxford University | Oval | 1919 |
| | | 271 | Surrey v Hampshire | Southampton | 1919 |
| | | 203 | Surrey v Sussex | Oval | 1920 |
| | | 290* | Surrey v Essex | Leyton | 1921 |
| | | 204* | Surrey v Northamptonshire | Northampton | 1921 |
| | | 235 | Surrey v Leicestershire | Oval | 1926 |
| | | 208 | Surrey v Essex | Leyton | 1928 |
| | | 218 | Surrey v Nottinghamshire | Nottingham | 1930 |
| Duckfield, R. | | 280* | Glamorgan v Surrey | Oval | 1936 |
| Dudleston, B. | | 202 | Leicestershire v Derbyshire | Leicester | 1979 |
| Duff, R.A. | | 271 | New South Wales v South Australia | Sydney | 1903–04 |
| Duleepsinhji, K.S. | (4) | 254* | Cambridge University v Middlesex | Cambridge | 1927 |
| | | 202 | Sussex v Essex | Leyton | 1929 |
| | | 246 | Sussex v Kent | Hastings | 1929 |
| | | 333 | Sussex v Northamptonshire | Hove | 1930 |
| Dyson, A.H. | | 208 | Glamorgan v Surrey | Oval | 1932 |
| Dyson, J. | | 241 | New South Wales v South Australia | Adelaide | 1983–84 |
| Eastwood, K.H. | (2) | 201* | Victoria v New South Wales | Sydney | 1970–71 |
| | | 221 | Victoria v South Australia | Adelaide | 1970–71 |
| Edgar, B.A. | | 203 | Young New Zealand v Zimbabwe | Bulawayo | 1984–85 |
| Edrich, J.H. | (4) | 216 | Surrey v Nottinghamshire | Nottingham | 1962 |
| | | 205* | Surrey v Gloucestershire | Bristol | 1965 |
| | | 310* | England v New Zealand | Leeds | 1965 |
| | | 226* | Surrey v Middlesex | Oval | 1967 |
| Edrich, W.J. | (9) | 245 | Middlesex v Nottinghamshire | Lord's | 1938 |
| | | 219 | England v South Africa | Durban | 1938–39 |
| | | 222* | Middlesex v Northamptonshire | Northampton | 1946 |
| | | 225 | Middlesex v Warwickshire | Birmingham | 1947 |
| | | 257 | Middlesex v Leicestershire | Leicester | 1947 |
| | | 267* | Middlesex v Northamptonshire | Northampton | 1947 |
| | | 239 | Middlesex v Oxford University | Oxford | 1952 |
| | | 211 | Middlesex v Essex | Lord's | 1953 |
| | | 208* | Middlesex v Derbyshire | Chesterfield | 1956 |
| Eggar, J.D. | | 219 | Derbyshire v Yorkshire | Bradford | 1949 |
| Elliott, C.S. | | 215 | Derbyshire v Nottinghamshire | Nottingham | 1947 |
| Endean, W.R. | (3) | 235 | Transvaal v Orange Free State | Johannesburg | 1954–55 |

| Player | | Score | Match | Venue | Year |
|---|---|---|---|---|---|
| Endean, W.R. *continued* | | 247 | Transvaal v Eastern Province | Johannesburg | 1955–56 |
| | | 204* | Transvaal v Border | Johannesburg | 1959–60 |
| Fagg, A.E. | (6) | 257 | Kent v Hampshire | Southampton | 1936 |
| | | 244 | Kent v Essex (*1st innings*) | Colchester | 1938 |
| | | 202* | Kent v Essex (*2nd innings*) | Colchester | 1938 |
| | | 203 | Kent v Middlesex | Dover | 1948 |
| | | 221 | Kent v Nottinghamshire | Nottingham | 1951 |
| | | 269* | Kent v Nottinghamshire | Nottingham | 1953 |
| Fane, F.L. | (2) | 207 | Essex v Leicestershire | Leicester | 1899 |
| | | 217 | Essex v Surrey | Oval | 1911 |
| Farmer W.A. | | 275 | Barbados v Jamaica | Bridgetown | 1951–52 |
| Farrer, W.S. | (2) | 207 | Border v Orange Free State | Bloemfontein | 1965–66 |
| | | 211 | Border v Eastern Province | East London | 1968–69 |
| Fasihuddin, R. | | 237 | Quetta v East Pakistan | Karachi | 1962–63 |
| Faulkner, G.A. | | 204 | South Africa v Australia | Melbourne | 1910–11 |
| Fishlock, L.B. | (2) | 253 | Surrey v Leicestershire | Leicester | 1948 |
| | | 210 | Surrey v Somerset | Oval | 1949 |
| Fletcher, K.W.R. | (2) | 228* | Essex v Sussex | Hastings | 1968 |
| | | 216 | England v New Zealand | Auckland | 1974–75 |
| Flockton, R. | | 264* | New South Wales v South Australia | Sydney | 1959–60 |
| Foster, F.R. | (2) | 200 | Warwickshire v Surrey | Birmingham | 1911 |
| | | 305* | Warwickshire v Worcestershire | Dudley | 1914 |
| Foster, H.K. | (2) | 216 | Worcestershire v Somerset | Worcester | 1903 |
| | | 215 | Worcestershire v Warwickshire | Worcester | 1908 |
| Foster, M.L.C. | | 234 | Jamaica v Trinidad | Montego Bay | 1976–77 |
| Foster, R.E. | (2) | 287 | England v Australia | Sydney | 1903–04 |
| | | 246* | Worcestershire v Kent | Worcester | 1905 |
| Fowler, G. | (2) | 226 | Lancashire v Kent | Maidstone | 1984 |
| | | 201 | England v India | Madras | 1984–85 |
| Francis, B.C. | | 210 | Australians v Combined Universities | Oxford | 1972 |
| Fredericks, R.C. | (4) | 228* | Glamorgan v Northamptonshire | Swansea | 1972 |
| | | 202 | West Indians v Combined U's | Indore | 1974–75 |
| | | 250 | Guyana v Barbados | Bridgetown | 1974–75 |
| | | 217 | Guyana v Jamaica | Georgetown | 1982–83 |
| Freeman, J.R. | | 286 | Essex v Northamptonshire | Northampton | 1921 |
| Fry, C.B. | (16) | 229 | Sussex v Surrey | Hove | 1900 |
| | | 241 | Sussex v Cambridge University | Hove | 1901 |
| | | 219* | Sussex v Oxford University | Eastbourne | 1901 |
| | | 244 | Sussex v Leicestershire | Leicester | 1901 |
| | | 209 | Sussex v Yorkshire | Hove | 1901 |
| | | 234 | Sussex v Yorkshire | Bradford | 1903 |
| | | 232* | Gentlemen v Players | Lord's | 1903 |
| | | 200 | Sussex v Surrey | Hove | 1903 |
| | | 226 | Sussex v Derbyshire | Hove | 1904 |
| | | 211 | Sussex v Hampshire | Hove | 1904 |
| | | 229 | Sussex v Yorkshire | Hove | 1904 |
| | | 201* | Sussex v Nottinghamshire | Hove | 1905 |
| | | 233 | Sussex v Nottinghamshire | Nottingham | 1905 |
| | | 214 | Sussex v Worcestershire | Hove | 1908 |
| | | 258* | Hampshire v Gloucestershire | Southampton | 1911 |
| | | 203* | Hampshire v Oxford University | Southampton | 1912 |
| Gaekwad, A.D. | (3) | 203 | Baroda v Maharashtra | Baroda | 1980–81 |
| | | 225 | Baroda v Gujarat | Baroda | 1982–83 |
| | | 201 | India v Pakistan | Jullundur | 1983–84 |
| Gaekwad, D.K. | (3) | 218 | Baroda v Bombay | Sholapur | 1957–58 |
| | | 249* | Baroda v Maharashtra | Poona | 1959–60 |
| | | 201* | Baroda v Gujarat | Baroda | 1961–62 |
| Gale, R.A. | | 200 | Middlesex v Glamorgan | Newport | 1962 |
| Gardner, F.C. | | 215* | Warwickshire v Somerset | Taunton | 1950 |
| Gatting, M.W. | (3) | 216 | Middlesex v New Zealanders | Lord's | 1983 |
| | | 258 | Middlesex v Somerset | Bath | 1984 |
| | | 207 | England v India | Madras | 1984–85 |
| Gavaskar, S.M. | (10) | 220 | India v West Indies | Port-of-Spain | 1970–71 |
| | | 282 | Bombay v Bihar | Bombay | 1971–72 |
| | | 203 | India v Sri Lanka | Hyderabad | 1975–76 |
| | | 228 | West Zone v South Zone | Baroda | 1976–77 |
| | | 205 | India v West Indies | Bombay | 1978–79 |

| Gavaskar, S.M. *continued* | | 204 | Bombay v Bihar | Bombay | 1978–79 |
|---|---|---|---|---|---|
| | | 221 | India v England | Oval | 1979 |
| | | 340 | Bombay v Bengal | Bombay | 1981–82 |
| | | 236* | India v West Indies | Madras | 1983–84 |
| | | 206* | Bombay v Delhi | Bombay | 1983–84 |
| Ghulam Abbas | (2) | 240 | PIA v United Bank | Karachi | 1975–76 |
| | | 276 | PIA v Punjab B | Karachi | 1975–76 |
| Gibb, P.A. | | 204 | Cambridge U. v Free Foresters | Cambridge | 1938 |
| Gibb, P.J.M. | | 203 | Transvaal v N.E. Transvaal | Johannesburg | 1952–53 |
| Gibbons, H.H.I. | (2) | 200* | Worcestershire v West Indies | Worcester | 1928 |
| | | 212* | Worcestershire v Northamptonshire | Dudley | 1939 |
| Gibbs, G.L. | | 216 | British Guiana v Barbados | Georgetown | 1951–52 |
| Giffen, G. | (4) | 203 | South Australia v G.F. Vernon's XI | Adelaide | 1887–88 |
| | | 237 | South Australia v Victoria | Melbourne | 1890–91 |
| | | 271 | South Australia v Victoria | Adelaide | 1891–92 |
| | | 205 | South Australia v New South Wales | Adelaide | 1893–94 |
| Gilbert, W.R. | | 205* | England XI v Cambridge University | Cambridge | 1876 |
| Gilliat, R.M.C. | | 223* | Hampshire v Warwickshire | Southampton | 1969 |
| Gillingham, F.H. | | 201 | Essex v Middlesex | Lord's | 1904 |
| Gimblett, H. | (2) | 231 | Somerset v Middlesex | Taunton | 1946 |
| | | 310 | Somerset v Sussex | Eastbourne | 1948 |
| Girdhari, S.K. | | 229* | Assam v Orissa | Cuttack | 1957–58 |
| Goddard, J.D.C. | | 218* | Barbados v Trinidad | Bridgetown | 1943–44 |
| Goddard, T.L. | (2) | 200 | Natal v Rhodesia | Durban | 1959–60 |
| | | 222 | N.E. Transvaal v Western Province | Cape Town | 1966–67 |
| Gomes, H.A. | | 200* | West Indians v Queensland | Brisbane | 1981–82 |
| Gomes, S.A. | | 213 | Trinidad v Jamaica | Montego Bay | 1976–77 |
| Gomez, G.E. | (2) | 216* | Trinidad v Barbados | Port-of-Spain | 1942–43 |
| | | 213* | Trinidad v Barbados | Port-of-Spain | 1945–46 |
| Gooch, G.A. | (4) | 205 | Essex v Cambridge University | Cambridge | 1980 |
| | | 220 | Essex v Hampshire | Southampton | 1984 |
| | | 227 | Essex v Derbyshire | Chesterfield | 1984 |
| | | 202 | Essex v Nottinghamshire | Nottingham | 1985 |
| Goonesena, G. | | 211 | Cambridge U. v Oxford U. | Lord's | 1957 |
| Gopinath, C.D. | | 234 | Madras v Mysore | Coimbatore | 1958–59 |
| Gower, D.I. | (2) | 200* | England v India | Birmingham | 1979 |
| | | 215 | England v Australia | Birmingham | 1985 |
| Grace, W.G. | (13) | 224* | England v Surrey | Oval | 1866 |
| | | 215 | Gentlemen v Players | Oval | 1870 |
| | | 268 | South v North | Oval | 1871 |
| | | 217 | Gentlemen v Players | Brighton | 1871 |
| | | 344 | MCC v Kent | Canterbury | 1876 |
| | | 318* | Gloucestershire v Yorkshire | Cheltenham | 1876 |
| | | 261 | South v North | Prince's | 1877 |
| | | 221* | Gloucestershire v Middlesex | Clifton | 1885 |
| | | 215 | Gloucestershire v Sussex | Hove | 1888 |
| | | 288 | Gloucestershire v Somerset | Bristol | 1895 |
| | | 257 | Gloucestershire v Kent | Gravesend | 1895 |
| | | 243* | Gloucestershire v Sussex | Hove | 1896 |
| | | 301 | Gloucestershire v Sussex | Bristol | 1896 |
| Graveney, T.W. | (7) | 201 | Gloucestershire v Sussex | Worthing | 1950 |
| | | 201 | Gloucestershire v Oxford University | Oxford | 1951 |
| | | 211 | Gloucestershire v Kent | Gillingham | 1953 |
| | | 231 | MCC v British Guiana | Georgetown | 1953–54 |
| | | 222 | Gloucestershire v Derbyshire | Chesterfield | 1954 |
| | | 200 | Gloucestershire v Glamorgan | Newport | 1956 |
| | | 258 | England v West Indies | Nottingham | 1957 |
| Gray, J.R. | | 213* | Hampshire v Derbyshire | Portsmouth | 1962 |
| Green, D.M. | | 233 | Gloucestershire v Sussex | Hove | 1968 |
| Greenidge, C.G. | (9) | 273* | D.H. Robins' XI v Pakistanis | Eastbourne | 1974 |
| | | 259 | Hampshire v Sussex | Southampton | 1975 |
| | | 200* | Hampshire v Surrey | Guildford | 1977 |
| | | 208 | Hampshire v Yorkshire | Leeds | 1977 |
| | | 211 | Hampshire v Sussex | Hove | 1978 |
| | | 237 | Barbados v Indians | Bridgetown | 1982–83 |
| | | 214* | West Indies v England | Lord's | 1984 |
| | | 204 | West Indies v England | Manchester | 1984 |

| | | | | | |
|---|---|---|---|---|---|
| Greenidge, C.G. *continued* | | 204 | Hampshire v Warwickshire | Birmingham | 1985 |
| Greenidge, G.A. | | 205 | Barbados v Jamaica | Bridgetown | 1966–67 |
| Gregory, C.W. | | 383 | New South Wales v Queensland | Brisbane | 1906–07 |
| Gregory, R.J. | | 243 | Surrey v Somerset | Oval | 1938 |
| Gregory, S.E. | (2) | 201 | Australia v England | Sydney | 1894–95 |
| | | 201 | New South Wales v Victoria | Sydney | 1907–08 |
| Greig, A.W. | | 226 | Sussex v Warwickshire | Hastings | 1975 |
| Greig, J.G. | (2) | 249* | Hampshire v Lancashire | Liverpool | 1901 |
| | | 204 | Bombay Presidency v O.U. Authentics | Bombay | 1902–03 |
| Grewal, S.S. | | 211 | Services v Southern Punjab | Patiala | 1950–51 |
| Grieves, K.J. | (3) | 224 | Lancashire v Cambridge University | Cambridge | 1957 |
| | | 202* | Lancashire v Indians | Blackpool | 1959 |
| | | 216 | Lancashire v Cambridge University | Manchester | 1960 |
| Gripper, R.A. | | 279* | Rhodesia v Orange Free State | Bloemfontein | 1967–68 |
| Groves, B.S. | | 237 | Natal B v Orange Free State | Bloemfontein | 1967–68 |
| Gulfraz Khan | | 207 | Railways v Universities | Lahore | 1976–77 |
| Gul Mahomed | | 319 | Baroda v Holkar | Baroda | 1946–47 |
| Gunasekara, C.H. | | 212 | Ceylon v Madras | Colombo | 1958–59 |
| Gunn, G. | | 220 | Nottinghamshire v Derbyshire | Nottingham | 1923 |
| Gunn, J.R. | | 294 | Nottinghamshire v Leicestershire | Nottingham | 1903 |
| Gunn, W. | (8) | 203 | MCC v Yorkshire | Lord's | 1885 |
| | | 205* | Nottinghamshire v Sussex | Nottingham | 1887 |
| | | 228 | Players v Australians | Lord's | 1890 |
| | | 219 | Nottinghamshire v Sussex | Nottingham | 1895 |
| | | 207* | Nottinghamshire v Derbyshire | Derby | 1896 |
| | | 230 | Nottinghamshire v Derbyshire | Nottingham | 1897 |
| | | 236* | Nottinghamshire v Surrey | Oval | 1898 |
| | | 273 | Nottinghamshire v Derbyshire | Derby | 1901 |
| Gupte, M.S. | | 200 | Maharashtra v Vidarbha | Poona | 1972–73 |
| Hadlee, R.J. | | 210* | Nottinghamshire v Middlesex | Lord's | 1984 |
| Hadow, W.H. | | 217 | Middlesex v MCC | Lord's | 1871 |
| Hallam, M.R. | (4) | 200 | Leicestershire v Derbyshire | Leicester | 1959 |
| | | 210* | Leicestershire v Glamorgan | Leicester | 1959 |
| | | 203* | Leicestershire v Sussex | Worthing | 1961 |
| | | 200* | Leicestershire v Nottinghamshire | Nottingham | 1962 |
| Hallebone, J. | | 202 | Victoria v Tasmania | Melbourne | 1951–52 |
| Hallows, C. | (3) | 227 | Lancashire v Warwickshire | Manchester | 1921 |
| | | 233* | Lancashire v Hampshire | Liverpool | 1927 |
| | | 232 | Lancashire v Sussex | Manchester | 1928 |
| Hamer, A. | | 227 | Derbyshire v Nottinghamshire | Nottingham | 1955 |
| Hammond, W.R. | (36) | 250* | Gloucestershire v Lancashire | Manchester | 1925 |
| | | 238* | MCC v West Indian XI | Bridgetown | 1925–26 |
| | | 205* | Gloucestershire v Surrey | Oval | 1928 |
| | | 218* | Gloucestershire v Glamorgan | Bristol | 1928 |
| | | 244 | Gloucestershire v Essex | Chelmsford | 1928 |
| | | 225 | MCC v New South Wales | Sydney | 1928–29 |
| | | 251 | England v Australia | Sydney | 1928–29 |
| | | 200 | England v Australia | Melbourne | 1928–29 |
| | | 238* | Gloucestershire v Warwickshire | Birmingham | 1929 |
| | | 211* | Gloucestershire v Oxford U. | Oxford | 1930 |
| | | 264 | Gloucestershire v Lancashire | Liverpool | 1932 |
| | | 203 | MCC v Victoria | Melbourne | 1932–33 |
| | | 227 | England v New Zealand | Christchurch | 1932–33 |
| | | 336* | England v New Zealand | Auckland | 1932–33 |
| | | 206 | Gloucestershire v Leicestershire | Leicester | 1933 |
| | | 239 | Gloucestershire v Glamorgan | Gloucester | 1933 |
| | | 231 | Gloucestershire v Derbyshire | Cheltenham | 1933 |
| | | 264 | Gloucestershire v West Indians | Bristol | 1933 |
| | | 290 | Gloucestershire v Kent | Tunbridge Wells | 1934 |
| | | 217 | Gloucestershire v Nottinghamshire | Bristol | 1934 |
| | | 265* | Gloucestershire v Worcestershire | Dudley | 1934 |
| | | 302* | Gloucestershire v Glamorgan | Bristol | 1934 |
| | | 281* | MCC v Barbados | Bridgetown | 1934–35 |
| | | 252 | Gloucestershire v Leicestershire | Leicester | 1935 |
| | | 217 | England v India | Oval | 1936 |
| | | 317 | Gloucestershire v Nottinghamshire | Gloucester | 1936 |

| | | | | | |
|---|---|---|---|---|---|
| Hammond, W.R. *continued* | | 231* | England v Australia | Sydney | 1936–37 |
| | | 217 | Gloucestershire v Leicestershire | Gloucester | 1937 |
| | | 237 | Gloucestershire v Derbyshire | Bristol | 1938 |
| | | 240 | England v Australia | Lord's | 1938 |
| | | 271 | Gloucestershire v Lancashire | Bristol | 1938 |
| | | 302 | Gloucestershire v Glamorgan | Newport | 1939 |
| | | 207 | Gloucestershire v Essex | Westcliff | 1939 |
| | | 211* | Gloucestershire v Nottinghamshire | Bristol | 1946 |
| | | 214 | Gloucestershire v Somerset | Bristol | 1946 |
| | | 208 | MCC v Western Australia | Perth | 1946–47 |
| Hanif Mohammad | (7) | 203* | Pakistanis v Bombay | Bombay | 1952–53 |
| | | 230* | Karachi v Sind | Karachi | 1954–55 |
| | | 228 | Karachi Whites v Karachi Blues | Karachi | 1956–57 |
| | | 337 | Pakistan v West Indies | Bridgetown | 1957–58 |
| | | 499 | Karachi v Bahawalpur | Karachi | 1958–59 |
| | | 222 | Pakistanis v Combined Universities | Poona | 1960–61 |
| | | 203* | Pakistan v New Zealand | Lahore | 1964–65 |
| Hanumant Singh | (4) | 200* | Rajasthan v Uttar Pradesh | Udaipur | 1961–62 |
| | | 210 | Central Zone v South Zone | Hyderabad | 1964–65 |
| | | 213* | Rajasthan v Bombay | Bombay | 1966–67 |
| | | 211* | Rajasthan v Maharashtra | Poona | 1970–71 |
| Hardikar, M.S. | (2) | 204 | Bombay v Gujarat | Bombay | 1956–57 |
| | | 207* | Bombay v Services | Bombay | 1964–65 |
| Hardinge, H.T.W. | (4) | 207 | Kent v Surrey | Blackheath | 1921 |
| | | 249* | Kent v Leicestershire | Leicester | 1922 |
| | | 263* | Kent v Gloucestershire | Gloucester | 1928 |
| | | 205 | Kent v Warwickshire | Tunbridge Wells | 1928 |
| Hardstaff, J., sr | | 213* | Nottinghamshire v Sussex | Hove | 1914 |
| Hardstaff, J., jr | (10) | 230* | MCC v Australian XI | Sydney | 1935–36 |
| | | 214* | Nottinghamshire v Somerset | Nottingham | 1937 |
| | | 266 | Nottinghamshire v Leicestershire | Leicester | 1937 |
| | | 243 | Nottinghamshire v Middlesex | Nottingham | 1937 |
| | | 213 | Lord Tennyson's XI v Madras | Madras | 1937–38 |
| | | 205* | England v India | Lord's | 1946 |
| | | 200* | Nottinghamshire v Somerset | Nottingham | 1947 |
| | | 202 | Nottinghamshire v Worcestershire | Dudley | 1947 |
| | | 221* | Nottinghamshire v Warwickshire | Nottingham | 1947 |
| | | 247 | Nottinghamshire v Northamptonshire | Nottingham | 1951 |
| Harris, C.B. | (2) | 234 | Nottinghamshire v Middlesex | Nottingham | 1933 |
| | | 239* | Nottinghamshire v Hampshire | Nottingham | 1950 |
| Harris, M.J. | | 201* | Nottinghamshire v Glamorgan | Nottingham | 1973 |
| Hartley, A. | | 234 | Lancashire v Somerset | Manchester | 1910 |
| Harty, I.D. | | 222 | Border v Northern Transvaal | East London | 1974–75 |
| Harvey, R.N. | (7) | 205 | Australia v South Africa | Melbourne | 1952–53 |
| | | 202* | Australians v Leicestershire | Leicester | 1953 |
| | | 204 | Australia v West Indies | Kingston | 1954–55 |
| | | 225 | Australians v MCC | Lord's | 1956 |
| | | 209 | Victoria v New South Wales | Sydney | 1956–57 |
| | | 229 | New South Wales v Queensland | Sydney | 1960–61 |
| | | 231* | New South Wales v South Australia | Sydney | 1962–63 |
| Hassett, A.L. | (8) | 220* | Australians v Cambridge University | Cambridge | 1938 |
| | | 211* | Victoria v South Australia | Melbourne | 1938–39 |
| | | 200 | Victoria v Queensland | Brisbane | 1946–47 |
| | | 204 | Victoria v Queensland | Brisbane | 1947–48 |
| | | 200* | Australians v Gentlemen | Lord's | 1948 |
| | | 205 | Victoria v Queensland | Brisbane | 1948–49 |
| | | 232 | Victoria v MCC | Melbourne | 1950–51 |
| | | 229 | Victoria v South Australia | Melbourne | 1951–52 |
| Hastings, B.F. | | 226 | Canterbury v New Zealand U-23 XI | Christchurch | 1964–65 |
| Hathorn, C.M.H. | | 239 | South Africans v Cambridge U. | Cambridge | 1901 |
| Hayes, E.G. | (4) | 273* | Surrey v Derbyshire | Derby | 1904 |
| | | 218 | Surrey v Oxford University | Oval | 1906 |
| | | 202 | Surrey v Middlesex | Oval | 1907 |
| | | 276 | Surrey v Hampshire | Oval | 1909 |
| Hayward, T.W. | (8) | 229* | Surrey v Derbyshire | Derby | 1896 |
| | | 315* | Surrey v Lancashire | Oval | 1898 |
| | | 273 | Surrey v Yorkshire | Oval | 1899 |

| Hayward, T.W. *continued* | | 203 | Players v Gentlemen | Oval | 1904 |
|---|---|---|---|---|---|
| | | 219 | Surrey v Northamptonshire | Oval | 1906 |
| | | 208 | Surrey v Warwickshire | Oval | 1906 |
| | | 204* | Surrey v Warwickshire | Oval | 1909 |
| | | 202 | Surrey v Derbyshire | Oval | 1911 |
| Hazare, V.S. | (10) | 316* | Maharashtra v Baroda | Poona | 1939–40 |
| | | 264 | Bengal Cyclone XI v Bijapur Famine XI | Bombay | 1942–43 |
| | | 248 | Rest v Muslims | Bombay | 1943–44 |
| | | 309 | Rest v Hindus | Bombay | 1943–44 |
| | | 223 | India States v Rest of India | Poona | 1943–44 |
| | | 200* | Cricket Club of India v Services XI | Bombay | 1944–45 |
| | | 244* | Indians v Yorkshire | Sheffield | 1946 |
| | | 288 | Baroda v Holkar | Baroda | 1946–47 |
| | | 204* | Baroda v Gujarat | Ahmedabad | 1954–55 |
| | | 203 | Baroda v Services | Baroda | 1957–58 |
| Headley, G.A. | (9) | 211 | Jamaica v Hon L.H. Tennyson's XI | Kingston | 1927–28 |
| | | 223 | West Indies v England | Kingston | 1929–30 |
| | | 344* | Jamaica v Lord Tennyson's XI | Kingston | 1931–32 |
| | | 224* | West Indians v Somerset | Taunton | 1933 |
| | | 200* | West Indians v Derbyshire | Derby | 1933 |
| | | 270* | West Indies v England | Kingston | 1934–35 |
| | | 227 | West Indians v Middlesex | Lord's | 1939 |
| | | 234* | West Indians v Nottinghamshire | Nottingham | 1939 |
| | | 203* | Jamaica v Barbados | Kingston | 1946–47 |
| Healy, G.E. | | 218 | Victoria v Tasmania | Melbourne | 1909–10 |
| Hearne, J.W. | (11) | 234* | Middlesex v Somerset | Lord's | 1911 |
| | | 204 | Middlesex v Lancashire | Lord's | 1914 |
| | | 218* | Middlesex v Hampshire | Lord's | 1919 |
| | | 215* | Middlesex v Warwickshire | Birmingham | 1920 |
| | | 202 | Middlesex v Warwickshire | Birmingham | 1921 |
| | | 201 | Middlesex v Gloucestershire | Gloucester | 1922 |
| | | 221* | Middlesex v Warwickshire | Birmingham | 1922 |
| | | 232 | Middlesex v Hampshire | Southampton | 1923 |
| | | 245* | Middlesex v Gloucestershire | Bristol | 1927 |
| | | 223* | Middlesex v Somerset | Taunton | 1928 |
| | | 285* | Middlesex v Essex | Leyton | 1929 |
| Henderson, S.P. | | 209* | Cambridge University v Middlesex | Cambridge | 1982 |
| Hendren, E.H. | (22) | 214 | MCC v Yorkshire | Lord's | 1919 |
| | | 201 | Middlesex v Hampshire | Lord's | 1919 |
| | | 232 | Middlesex v Nottinghamshire | Lord's | 1920 |
| | | 271 | MCC v Victoria | Melbourne | 1920–21 |
| | | 277* | Middlesex v Kent | Lord's | 1922 |
| | | 200* | Middlesex v Essex | Leyton | 1923 |
| | | 234 | Middlesex v Worcestershire | Lord's | 1925 |
| | | 240 | Middlesex v Kent | Tonbridge | 1925 |
| | | 206* | Middlesex v Nottinghamshire | Nottingham | 1925 |
| | | 213 | Middlesex v Yorkshire | Lord's | 1926 |
| | | 201* | Middlesex v Essex | Leyton | 1927 |
| | | 200 | Middlesex v Hampshire | Lord's | 1928 |
| | | 209* | Middlesex v Warwickshire | Birmingham | 1928 |
| | | 223* | MCC v Barbados | Bridgetown | 1929–30 |
| | | 211* | MCC v Barbados | Bridgetown | 1929–30 |
| | | 205* | England v West Indies | Port-of-Spain | 1929–30 |
| | | 254* | MCC v British Guiana | Georgetown | 1929–30 |
| | | 232 | Middlesex v Nottinghamshire | Nottingham | 1931 |
| | | 203 | Middlesex v Northamptonshire | Lord's | 1931 |
| | | 301* | Middlesex v Worcestershire | Dudley | 1933 |
| | | 222* | Middlesex v Essex | Leyton | 1933 |
| | | 202 | MCC v Surrey | Lord's | 1936 |
| Hendry, H.S.T.L. | | 325* | Victoria v New Zealanders | Melbourne | 1925–26 |
| Hewett, H.T. | | 201 | Somerset v Yorkshire | Taunton | 1892 |
| Hibbert, P.A. | | 230 | Victoria v Pakistanis | Melbourne | 1983–84 |
| Hick, G.A. | | 230 | Zimbabweans v Oxford University | Oxford | 1985 |
| Hiddleston, J.S. | (2) | 212 | Wellington v Canterbury | Wellington | 1925–26 |
| | | 204 | Wellington v Auckland | Wellington | 1925–26 |
| Hilditch, A.M.J. | | 230 | South Australia v Victoria | Melbourne | 1983–84 |

| | | | | | |
|---|---|---|---|---|---|
| Hill, C. | (4) | 206* | South Australia v New South Wales | Sydney | 1895–96 |
| | | 200 | South Australia v A.E. Stoddart's XI | Adelaide | 1897–98 |
| | | 365* | South Australia v New South Wales | Adelaide | 1900–01 |
| | | 205 | South Australia v New South Wales | Adelaide | 1909–10 |
| Hill, N.W. | | 201* | Nottingham v Sussex | Worksop | 1961 |
| Hirst, G.H. | (4) | 214 | Yorkshire v Worcestershire | Worcester | 1901 |
| | | 341 | Yorkshire v Leicestershire | Leicester | 1905 |
| | | 232* | Yorkshire v Surrey | Oval | 1905 |
| | | 218 | Yorkshire v Sussex | Hastings | 1911 |
| Hobbs, J.B. | (16) | 205 | Surrey v Hampshire | Oval | 1909 |
| | | 215* | Surrey v Essex | Leyton | 1914 |
| | | 226 | Surrey v Nottinghamshire | Oval | 1914 |
| | | 202 | Surrey v Yorkshire | Lord's | 1914 |
| | | 205* | Surrey v AIF | Oval | 1919 |
| | | 215 | Rest v Middlesex | Oval | 1920 |
| | | 211 | England v South Africa | Lord's | 1924 |
| | | 203* | Surrey v Nottinghamshire | Nottingham | 1924 |
| | | 215 | Surrey v Warwickshire | Birmingham | 1925 |
| | | 266* | Players v Gentlemen | Scarborough | 1925 |
| | | 261 | Surrey v Oxford University | Oval | 1926 |
| | | 200 | Surrey v Hampshire | Southampton | 1926 |
| | | 316* | Surrey v Middlesex | Lord's | 1926 |
| | | 200* | Surrey v Warwickshire | Birmingham | 1928 |
| | | 204 | Surrey v Somerset | Oval | 1929 |
| | | 221 | Surrey v West Indians | Oval | 1933 |
| Holdsworth, R.L. | | 202 | Oxford U. v Free Foresters | Oxford | 1921 |
| Hole, G.B. | | 226 | South Australia v Queensland | Adelaide | 1953–54 |
| Holmes, E.R.T. | (2) | 236 | Oxford U. v Free Foresters | Oxford | 1927 |
| | | 206 | Surrey v Derbyshire | Chesterfield | 1935 |
| Holmes, P. | (12) | 302* | Yorkshire v Hampshire | Portsmouth | 1920 |
| | | 277* | Yorkshire v Northamptonshire | Harrogate | 1921 |
| | | 209 | Yorkshire v Warwickshire | Birmingham | 1922 |
| | | 220* | Yorkshire v Warwickshire | Huddersfield | 1922 |
| | | 202* | C.I. Thornton's XI v South Africans | Scarborough | 1924 |
| | | 315* | Yorkshire v Middlesex | Lord's | 1925 |
| | | 244 | MCC v Jamaica | Kingston | 1925–26 |
| | | 279* | MCC v Orange Free State | Bloemfontein | 1927–28 |
| | | 275 | Yorkshire v Warwickshire | Bradford | 1928 |
| | | 285 | Yorkshire v Nottinghamshire | Nottingham | 1929 |
| | | 250 | Yorkshire v Warwickshire | Birmingham | 1931 |
| | | 224* | Yorkshire v Essex | Leyton | 1932 |
| Hopkins, A.J.Y. | | 218 | New South Wales v South Australia | Adelaide | 1908–09 |
| Hopkins, J.A. | | 230 | Glamorgan v Worcestershire | Worcester | 1977 |
| Hopwood, J.L. | | 220 | Lancashire v Gloucestershire | Bristol | 1934 |
| Horner, N.F. | | 203* | Warwickshire v Surrey | Oval | 1960 |
| Horsfall, R. | | 206 | Essex v Kent | Blackheath | 1951 |
| Horton, M.J. | (2) | 212 | Worcestershire v Essex | Leyton | 1959 |
| | | 233 | Worcestershire v Somerset | Worcester | 1962 |
| Hosie, A.L. | | 200 | Europeans v Hindus | Bombay | 1924–25 |
| Hosken, K.N. | | 208 | Natal B v Transvaal B | Pinetown | 1975–76 |
| Hudson, R.E.H. | | 217 | Army v RAF | Oval | 1932 |
| Hughes, K.J. | | 213 | Australia v India | Adelaide | 1980–81 |
| Humpage, G.W. | (2) | 254 | Warwickshire v Lancashire | Southport | 1982 |
| | | 205 | Warwickshire v Derbyshire | Chesterfield | 1984 |
| Humphreys, E. | (2) | 208 | Kent v Gloucestershire | Catford | 1909 |
| | | 200* | Kent v Lancashire | Tunbridge Wells | 1910 |
| Hunte, C.C. | (3) | 260 | West Indies v Pakistan | Kingston | 1957–58 |
| | | 263 | Barbados v Jamaica | Georgetown | 1961–62 |
| | | 206 | West Indians v Somerset | Taunton | 1966 |
| Hutton, L. | (11) | 271* | Yorkshire v Derbyshire | Sheffield | 1937 |
| | | 364 | England v Australia | Oval | 1938 |
| | | 202 | MCC v Eastern Province | Port Elizabeth | 1938–39 |
| | | 280* | Yorkshire v Hampshire | Sheffield | 1939 |
| | | 270* | Yorkshire v Hampshire | Bournemouth | 1947 |
| | | 201 | Yorkshire v Lancashire | Manchester | 1949 |
| | | 269* | Yorkshire v Northamptonshire | Wellingborough | 1949 |
| | | 206 | England v New Zealand | Oval | 1949 |

| | | | | | |
|---|---|---|---|---|---|
| Hutton, L. *continued* | | 202* | England v West Indies | Oval | 1950 |
| | | 241 | Players v Gentlemen | Scarborough | 1953 |
| | | 205 | England v West Indies | Kingston | 1953–54 |
| Ibrahim, K.C. | (5) | 230* | Bombay v Western India States | Bombay | 1941–42 |
| | | 250 | Bijapur Famine XI v Bengal Cyclone XI | Bombay | 1942–43 |
| | | 218* | Ibrahim's XI v M.N. Raiji's XI | Bombay | 1947–48 |
| | | 234* | Ibrahim's XI v M.K. Mantri's XI | Bombay | 1947–48 |
| | | 219 | Bombay v Baroda | Bombay | 1948–49 |
| Iddon, J. | (5) | 222 | Lancashire v Leicestershire | Liverpool | 1929 |
| | | 201 | Lancashire v Sussex | Manchester | 1932 |
| | | 204* | Lancashire v Warwickshire | Birmingham | 1933 |
| | | 200* | Lancashire v Nottinghamshire | Manchester | 1934 |
| | | 217* | Lancashire v Worcestershire | Manchester | 1939 |
| Iftiqar A. Bokhari | | 203* | Lahore v Punjab University | Lahore | 1960–61 |
| Ijaz Ahmed | | 200* | National Bank v Karachi Blues | Karachi | 1975–76 |
| Ijaz Ahmed, jr | | 201* | PACO v Karachi | Karachi | 1984–85 |
| Imtiaz Ahmed | (4) | 300* | Prime Minister's XI v Commonwealth | Bombay | 1950–51 |
| | | 213* | Pakistanis v Central Zone | Nagpur | 1952–53 |
| | | 209 | Pakistan v New Zealand | Lahore | 1955–56 |
| | | 251 | Services v Karachi Blues | Karachi | 1961–62 |
| Insole, D.J. | | 219* | Essex v Yorkshire | Colchester | 1949 |
| Iqtidar Ali | | 200* | Karachi Blues v Karachi Greens | Karachi | 1983–84 |
| Iremonger, J. | (4) | 210 | Nottinghamshire v Kent | Nottingham | 1903 |
| | | 272 | Nottinghamshire v Kent | Nottingham | 1904 |
| | | 239 | Nottinghamshire v Essex | Nottingham | 1905 |
| | | 200* | Nottinghamshire v Gloucestershire | Nottingham | 1906 |
| Jabbar, A. | | 201* | Tamil Nadu v Karnataka | Bangalore | 1975–76 |
| Jaisimha, M.L. | | 259 | Hyderabad v Bengal | Hyderabad | 1964–65 |
| Jakeman, F. | | 258* | Northamptonshire v Essex | Northampton | 1951 |
| James, R. | | 210 | South Australia v Queensland | Adelaide | 1947–48 |
| Jameson, J.A. | (2) | 231 | Warwickshire v Indians | Birmingham | 1971 |
| | | 240* | Warwickshire v Gloucestershire | Birmingham | 1974 |
| Jardine, D.R. | | 214 | MCC v Tasmania | Launceston | 1928–29 |
| Javed Baber | | 200 | Railways v Dera Ismail Khan | Lahore | 1964–65 |
| Javed Burki | (3) | 202* | Lahore v Universities | Lahore | 1962–63 |
| | | 227 | Karachi Whites v Khairpur | Karachi | 1963–64 |
| | | 210 | Pakistan v Ceylon | Karachi | 1966–67 |
| Javed Masood | | 215 | East Pakistan v Hyderabad | Hyderabad | 1962–63 |
| Javed Miandad | (7) | 311 | Karachi Whites v National Bank | Karachi | 1974–75 |
| | | 206 | Pakistan v New Zealand | Karachi | 1976–77 |
| | | 200* | Glamorgan v Somerset | Taunton | 1981 |
| | | 200* | Glamorgan v Essex | Colchester | 1981 |
| | | 280* | Pakistan v India | Hyderabad | 1982–83 |
| | | 212* | Glamorgan v Leicestershire | Swansea | 1984 |
| | | 200* | Glamorgan v Australians | Neath | 1985 |
| Jayaprakasam, A. | | 208* | Orissa v Rajasthan | Rourkela | 1983–84 |
| Jeacocke, A. | | 201* | Surrey v Sussex | Oval | 1922 |
| Jephson, D.L.A. | | 213 | Surrey v Derbyshire | Oval | 1900 |
| Jessop, G.L. | (5) | 233 | Rest of England v Yorkshire | Lord's | 1901 |
| | | 286 | Gloucestershire v Sussex | Hove | 1903 |
| | | 206 | Gloucestershire v Nottinghamshire | Nottingham | 1904 |
| | | 234 | Gloucestershire v Somerset | Bristol | 1905 |
| | | 240 | Gloucestershire v Sussex | Bristol | 1907 |
| Jesty, T.E. | | 248 | Hampshire v Cambridge University | Cambridge | 1984 |
| Jones, A. | | 204* | Glamorgan v Hampshire | Basingstoke | 1980 |
| Jones, A.O. | (4) | 250 | Nottinghamshire v Gloucestershire | Bristol | 1899 |
| | | 249 | Nottinghamshire v Sussex | Hove | 1901 |
| | | 296 | Nottinghamshire v Gloucestershire | Nottingham | 1903 |
| | | 274 | Nottinghamshire v Essex | Leyton | 1905 |
| Jones, D.M. | | 243 | Victoria v Western Australia | Perth | 1984–85 |
| Jones, W.E. | (2) | 207 | Glamorgan v Kent | Gravesend | 1948 |
| | | 212* | Glamorgan v Essex | Brentwood | 1948 |
| Jupp, V.W.C. | | 217* | Sussex v Worcestershire | Worcester | 1914 |
| Kallicharran, A.I. | (6) | 235 | Warwickshire v Worcestershire | Worcester | 1982 |
| | | 210 | Warwickshire v Leicestershire | Leicester | 1982 |
| | | 230* | Warwickshire v Lancashire | Southport | 1982 |

| | | | | | |
|---|---|---|---|---|---|
| Kallicharran, A.I. *continued* | | 209* | Warwickshire v Lancashire | Birmingham | 1983 |
| | | 243* | Warwickshire v Glamorgan | Birmingham | 1983 |
| | | 200* | Warwickshire v Northamptonshire | Birmingham | 1984 |
| Kanga, H.D. | | 233 | Parsees v Europeans | Poona | 1905–06 |
| Kanhai, R.B. | (7) | 256 | West Indies v India | Calcutta | 1958–59 |
| | | 217 | West Indies v Pakistan | Lahore | 1958–59 |
| | | 252 | West Indians v Victoria | Melbourne | 1960–61 |
| | | 253 | Warwickshire v Nottinghamshire | Nottingham | 1968 |
| | | 200* | Tasmania v Victoria | Melbourne | 1969–70 |
| | | 230* | Warwickshire v Somerset | Birmingham | 1973 |
| | | 213* | Warwickshire v Gloucestershire | Birmingham | 1974 |
| Kanitkar, H.S. | | 250 | Maharashtra v Rajasthan | Poona | 1970–71 |
| Keeton, W.W. | (7) | 200* | Nottinghamshire v Cambridge U. | Cambridge | 1932 |
| | | 242 | Nottinghamshire v Glamorgan | Nottingham | 1932 |
| | | 261 | Nottinghamshire v Gloucestershire | Nottingham | 1934 |
| | | 223 | Nottinghamshire v Worcestershire | Worksop | 1934 |
| | | 312* | Nottinghamshire v Middlesex | Oval | 1939 |
| | | 210 | Nottinghamshire v Yorkshire | Sheffield | 1949 |
| | | 208 | Nottinghamshire v Glamorgan | Nottingham | 1949 |
| Kenny, R.B. | | 218 | Bombay v Madras | Bombay | 1956–57 |
| Kenyon, D. | (7) | 238* | Worcestershire v Yorkshire | Worcester | 1953 |
| | | 202* | Worcestershire v Hampshire | Portsmouth | 1954 |
| | | 253* | Worcestershire v Leicestershire | Worcester | 1954 |
| | | 259 | Worcestershire v Yorkshire | Kidderminster | 1956 |
| | | 200* | Worcestershire v Nottinghamshire | Worcester | 1957 |
| | | 229 | Worcestershire v Hampshire | Portsmouth | 1959 |
| | | 201 | Worcestershire v Glamorgan | Stourbridge | 1960 |
| Kerr, R.B. | | 201* | Queensland v Tasmania | Brisbane | 1984–85 |
| Key, K.J. | | 281 | Oxford University v Middlesex | Chiswick Park | 1887 |
| Khalid Alvi | | 219 | Karachi v Railways | Karachi | 1980–81 |
| Khalid Irtiza | (2) | 290 | United Bank v Multan | Karachi | 1975–76 |
| | | 201 | Sind v Universities | Lahore | 1975–76 |
| Khandkar, S.S. | | 261* | Uttar Pradesh v Railways | Moradabad | 1984–85 |
| Khanna, A.K. | | 218 | Services v Delhi | Delhi | 1952–53 |
| Killick, E.H. | | 200 | Sussex v Yorkshire | Hove | 1901 |
| Killick, E.T. | (3) | 200* | Cambridge University v Glamorgan | Cambridge | 1929 |
| | | 201 | Cambridge University v Essex | Cambridge | 1929 |
| | | 206 | Middlesex v Warwickshire | Lord's | 1931 |
| Kilner, N. | | 228 | Warwickshire v Worcestershire | Worcester | 1935 |
| Kilner, R. | | 206* | Yorkshire v Derbyshire | Sheffield | 1920 |
| King, J.H. | (2) | 227* | Leicestershire v Worcestershire | Coalville | 1914 |
| | | 205 | Leicestershire v Hampshire | Leicester | 1923 |
| Kinneir, S. | (2) | 215* | Warwickshire v Lancashire | Birmingham | 1901 |
| | | 268* | Warwickshire v Hampshire | Birmingham | 1911 |
| Kippax, A.F. | (7) | 248 | New South Wales v South Australia | Sydney | 1923–24 |
| | | 212* | New South Wales v Victoria | Sydney | 1924–25 |
| | | 271* | New South Wales v Victoria | Sydney | 1925–26 |
| | | 217* | New South Wales v Victoria | Sydney | 1926–27 |
| | | 315* | New South Wales v Queensland | Sydney | 1927–28 |
| | | 260* | New South Wales v Victoria | Melbourne | 1928–29 |
| | | 250 | Australians v Sussex | Hove | 1934 |
| Kirsten, P.N. | (6) | 206* | Derbyshire v Glamorgan | Chesterfield | 1978 |
| | | 209* | Derbyshire v Northamptonshire | Derby | 1980 |
| | | 213* | Derbyshire v Glamorgan | Derby | 1980 |
| | | 202* | Derbyshire v Essex | Chesterfield | 1980 |
| | | 228 | Derbyshire v Somerset | Taunton | 1981 |
| | | 204* | Derbyshire v Lancashire | Blackpool | 1981 |
| Kishenchand, G. | | 218 | North Zone v South Zone | Bombay | 1946–47 |
| Knight, A.E. | (2) | 229* | Leicestershire v Worcestershire | Worcester | 1903 |
| | | 203 | Leicestershire v MCC | Lord's | 1904 |
| Knott, C.H. | | 261* | Harlequins v West Indians | Eastbourne | 1928 |
| Koch, L.B. | | 216* | Orange Free State v Natal | Bloemfontein | 1952–53 |
| Kortlang, H.H.L. | | 214* | Wellington v Auckland | Wellington | 1925–26 |
| Kripal Singh, A.G. | | 208 | Madras v Travancore-Cochin | Ernakulam | 1954–55 |
| Kunderan, B.K. | | 205 | Railways v Jammu & Kashmir | Delhi | 1959–60 |
| Lacey, F.E. | | 211 | Hampshire v Kent | Southampton | 1884 |

| | | | | | |
|---|---|---|---|---|---|
| Lamba, R. | | 205* | Delhi v Jammu & Kashmir | Delhi | 1981–82 |
| Langridge, J.G. | (8) | 250* | Sussex v Glamorgan | Hove | 1933 |
| | | 232* | Sussex v Northamptonshire | Peterborough | 1934 |
| | | 227 | Sussex v Northamptonshire | Northampton | 1938 |
| | | 215 | Sussex v Glamorgan | Eastbourne | 1938 |
| | | 202 | Sussex v Leicestershire | Hastings | 1939 |
| | | 234* | Sussex v Derbyshire | Ilkeston | 1949 |
| | | 241 | Sussex v Somerset | Worthing | 1950 |
| | | 200* | Sussex v Derbyshire | Derby | 1951 |
| Larkins, W. | (2) | 236 | Northamptonshire v Derbyshire | Derby | 1983 |
| | | 252 | Northamptonshire v Glamorgan | Cardiff | 1983 |
| Lashley, P.D. | (2) | 200* | Barbados v British Guiana | Bridgetown | 1958–59 |
| | | 204 | Barbados v Guyana | Georgetown | 1966–67 |
| Lawry, W.M. | (4) | 266 | Victoria v New South Wales | Sydney | 1960–61 |
| | | 246 | Victoria v South Australia | Melbourne | 1964–65 |
| | | 210 | Australia v West Indies | Bridgetown | 1964–65 |
| | | 205 | Australia v West Indies | Melbourne | 1968–69 |
| Laxman Singh | | 231* | Rajasthan v Madhya Pradesh | Indore | 1974–75 |
| Lee, G.M. | | 200* | Nottinghamshire v Leicestershire | Nottingham | 1913 |
| Lee, H.W. | (4) | 221* | Middlesex v Hampshire | Southampton | 1920 |
| | | 243* | Middlesex v Nottinghamshire | Lord's | 1921 |
| | | 200 | Middlesex v Oxford University | Oxford | 1929 |
| | | 225 | Middlesex v Surrey | Oval | 1929 |
| Lee, I.S. | | 268 | Victoria v Tasmania | Melbourne | 1933–34 |
| Lewis, A.E. | | 201* | Somerset v Kent | Taunton | 1909 |
| Lewis, A.R. | | 223 | Glamorgan v Kent | Gravesend | 1966 |
| Leyland, M. | (5) | 204* | Yorkshire v Middlesex | Sheffield | 1927 |
| | | 247 | Yorkshire v Worcestershire | Worcester | 1928 |
| | | 211* | Yorkshire v Lancashire | Leeds | 1930 |
| | | 210* | Yorkshire v Kent | Dover | 1933 |
| | | 263 | Yorkshire v Essex | Hull | 1936 |
| Lindsay, D.T. | | 216 | N.E. Transvaal v Transvaal B | Johannesburg | 1966–67 |
| Livingston, L. | (4) | 201* | Northamptonshire v South Africans | Northampton | 1951 |
| | | 210 | Northamptonshire v Somerset | Weston-s-Mare | 1951 |
| | | 200 | Northamptonshire v Kent | Maidstone | 1954 |
| | | 207* | Northamptonshire v Nottinghamshire | Nottingham | 1954 |
| Livingstone, D.A. | | 200 | Hampshire v Surrey | Southampton | 1962 |
| Llewellyn, C.B. | | 216 | Hampshire v South Africans | Southampton | 1901 |
| Lloyd, C.H. | (5) | 205* | West Indians v South Island | Dunedin | 1968–69 |
| | | 201* | West Indians v Glamorgan | Swansea | 1969 |
| | | 217* | Lancashire v Warwickshire | Manchester | 1971 |
| | | 242* | West Indies v India | Bombay | 1974–75 |
| | | 201* | West Indians v Glamorgan | Swansea | 1976 |
| Lloyd, D. | | 214* | England v India | Birmingham | 1974 |
| Lloyd, T.A. | | 208* | Warwickshire v Gloucestershire | Birmingham | 1983 |
| Lockwood, E. | | 208 | Yorkshire v Kent | Gravesend | 1883 |
| Longrigg, E.F. | | 205 | Somerset v Leicestershire | Taunton | 1930 |
| Lowndes, W.G.L.F. | | 216 | Oxford University v H.D.G. Leveson Gower's XI | Eastbourne | 1921 |
| Lowson, F.A. | | 259* | Yorkshire v Worcestershire | Worcester | 1953 |
| Loxton, S.J.E. | | 232* | Victoria v Queensland | Melbourne | 1946–47 |
| Lucas, F.M. | | 215* | Sussex v Gloucestershire | Hove | 1885 |
| Lucas, J.H. | | 216* | Barbados v Trinidad | Bridgetown | 1948–49 |
| Luckhurst, B.W. | (2) | 203* | Kent v Cambridge University | Cambridge | 1970 |
| | | 215 | Kent v Derbyshire | Derby | 1973 |
| Lyon, M.D. | (2) | 219 | Somerset v Derbyshire | Burton upon Trent | 1924 |
| | | 210 | Somerset v Gloucestershire | Taunton | 1930 |
| McAlister, P.A. | | 224 | Victoria v New Zealanders | Melbourne | 1898–99 |
| Macartney, C.G. | (4) | 208 | Australians v Essex | Leyton | 1912 |
| | | 201 | New South Wales v Victoria | Sydney | 1913–14 |
| | | 345 | Australians v Nottinghamshire | Nottingham | 1921 |
| | | 221 | New South Wales v Canterbury | Christchurch | 1923–24 |
| McCabe, S.J. | (3) | 229* | New South Wales v Queensland | Brisbane | 1931–32 |
| | | 240 | Australians v Surrey | Oval | 1934 |
| | | 232 | Australia v England | Nottingham | 1938 |
| McCorkell, N.T. | | 203 | Hampshire v Gloucestershire | Gloucester | 1951 |
| McDonald, C.C. | (2) | 207 | Victoria v New SouthWales | Sydney | 1951–52 |

| | | | | | |
|---|---|---|---|---|---|
| McDonald, C.C. *continued* | | 229 | Victoria v South Australia | Adelaide | 1953–54 |
| McDonnell, P.S. | | 239 | New South Wales v Victoria | Melbourne | 1886–87 |
| McEwan, K.S. | (2) | 218 | Essex v Sussex | Chelmsford | 1977 |
| | | 208* | Essex v Warwickshire | Birmingham | 1979 |
| McGahey, C.P. | (3) | 225 | Essex v Nottinghamshire | Leyton | 1904 |
| | | 277 | Essex v Derbyshire | Leyton | 1905 |
| | | 230 | Essex v Northamptonshire | Northampton | 1908 |
| McGlew, D.J. | (2) | 255* | South Africa v New Zealand | Wellington | 1952–53 |
| | | 213* | Natal v Border | Durban | 1957–58 |
| Mackay, J.R.M. | | 203 | New South Wales v Queensland | Brisbane | 1905–06 |
| Mackay, K.D. | (2) | 223 | Queensland v Victoria | Brisbane | 1953–54 |
| | | 203 | Queensland v New South Wales | Sydney | 1955–56 |
| McKenzie, C. | | 211 | Victoria v Western Australia | Perth | 1909–10 |
| MacLaren, A.C. | (6) | 228 | A.E. Stoddart's XI v Victoria | Melbourne | 1894–95 |
| | | 424 | Lancashire v Somerset | Taunton | 1895 |
| | | 226* | Lancashire v Kent | Canterbury | 1896 |
| | | 244 | Lancashire v Kent | Canterbury | 1897 |
| | | 204 | Lancashire v Gloucestershire | Liverpool | 1903 |
| | | 200* | MCC v New Zealand XI | Wellington | 1922–23 |
| McLean, A.R. | | 213 | South Australia v Queensland | Adelaide | 1949–50 |
| McLean, R.A. | | 207 | South Africans v Worcestershire | Worcester | 1960 |
| McMorris, E.D.A.St J. | | 218 | Jamaica v Guyana | Georgetown | 1966–67 |
| Madan Lal | | 223 | Delhi v Rajasthan | Delhi | 1977–78 |
| Maddocks, R. | | 271 | Victoria v Tasmania | Melbourne | 1951–52 |
| Mahendra Kumar, B. | | 205 | Hyderabad v Uttar Pradesh | Hyderabad | 1964–65 |
| Mahmood Ahmed | | 204 | United Bank v Railways | Lahore | 1976–77 |
| Majid Khan | (5) | 241 | Lahore Greens v Bahawalpur | Lahore | 1965–66 |
| | | 200* | Punjab U. v Karachi Whites | Lahore | 1967–68 |
| | | 200 | Cambridge U. v Oxford University | Lord's | 1970 |
| | | 204 | Glamorgan v Surrey | Oval | 1972 |
| | | 213 | Punjab v Sind | Karachi | 1974–75 |
| Makepeace, J.W.H. | (2) | 203 | Lancashire v Worcestershire | Worcester | 1923 |
| | | 200* | Lancashire v Northamptonshire | Liverpool | 1923 |
| Malhotra, A. | (3) | 224* | Haryana v Jammu & Kashmir | Bhiwani | 1979–80 |
| | | 200* | Haryana v Services | Faridabad | 1981–82 |
| | | 228 | Haryana v Services | Delhi | 1982–83 |
| Manjrekar, V.L. | (3) | 204* | Indians v Oxford University | Oxford | 1959 |
| | | 283 | Vizianagram XI v Tata S.C. XI | Hyderabad | 1963–64 |
| | | 240* | Maharashtra v Saurashtra | Poona | 1967–68 |
| Mankad, A.V. | (3) | 203* | Bombay v Maharashtra | Poona | 1976–77 |
| | | 208* | Bombay v Haryana | Bombay | 1976–77 |
| | | 265 | Bombay v Delhi | Bombay | 1980–81 |
| Mankad, M.H. | (3) | 223 | India v New Zealand | Bombay | 1955–56 |
| | | 231 | India v New Zealand | Madras | 1955–56 |
| | | 221 | Rajasthan v Vidarbha | Udaipur | 1957–58 |
| Mansoor Akhtar | | 224* | Karachi Whites v Quetta | Karachi | 1976–77 |
| Mantri, M.K. | | 200 | Bombay v Maharashtra | Poona | 1948–49 |
| Marks, A.E. | | 201 | New South Wales v Queensland | Sydney | 1935–36 |
| Marsden, T. | | 227 | Sheffield & Leicester v Nottingham | Sheffield | 1826 |
| Marsh, R.W. | | 236 | Western Australia v Pakistanis | Perth | 1972–73 |
| Marshall, R.E. | (3) | 212 | Hampshire v Somerset | Bournemouth | 1961 |
| | | 228* | Hampshire v Pakistanis | Bournemouth | 1962 |
| | | 203 | Hampshire v Derbyshire | Derby | 1972 |
| Martin, F.R. | | 204* | Jamaica v Hon L.H. Tennyson's XI | Kingston | 1926–27 |
| Marx, W.F.E. | | 240 | Transvaal v Griqualand West | Johannesburg | 1920–21 |
| Massie, H.H. | | 206 | Australians v Oxford University | Oxford | 1882 |
| Mathias, W. | (2) | 228 | Karachi Blues v Hyderabad | Karachi | 1964–65 |
| | | 278* | Karachi Blues v Railway Greens | Karachi | 1965–66 |
| Mathur, A.G. | | 201* | Uttar Pradesh v Railways | Allahabad | 1982–83 |
| Matthews, T.G. | | 201 | Gloucestershire v Surrey | Clifton | 1871 |
| Maxwell, C.R.N. | | 268 | Sir J. Cahn's XI v Leicestershire | Nottingham | 1935 |
| May, P.B.H. | (5) | 227* | Cambridge University v Hampshire | Cambridge | 1950 |
| | | 211* | Surrey v Nottinghamshire | Nottingham | 1954 |
| | | 207 | Surrey v Cambridge University | Oval | 1954 |
| | | 206 | MCC v Rhodesia | Salisbury | 1956–57 |
| | | 285* | England v West Indies | Birmingham | 1957 |

| Maynard, A. | | 200* | Trinidad v MCC | Port-of-Spain | 1934–35 |
|---|---|---|---|---|---|
| Mayne, E.R. | | 209 | Victoria v Queensland | Melbourne | 1923–24 |
| Mead, C.P. | (13) | 207* | Hampshire v Warwickshire | Southampton | 1911 |
| | | 223 | Players v Gentlemen | Scarborough | 1911 |
| | | 213 | Hampshire v Yorkshire | Southampton | 1914 |
| | | 207 | Hampshire v Essex | Leyton | 1919 |
| | | 280* | Hampshire v Nottinghamshire | Southampton | 1921 |
| | | 224 | Hampshire v Sussex | Horsham | 1921 |
| | | 235 | Hampshire v Worcestershire | Worcester | 1922 |
| | | 211* | Hampshire v Warwickshire | Southampton | 1922 |
| | | 222 | Hampshire v Warwickshire | Birmingham | 1923 |
| | | 213* | Hampshire v Worcestershire | Bournemouth | 1925 |
| | | 200* | Hampshire v Essex | Southampton | 1927 |
| | | 233 | MCC Australian Tour XI v Lord Hawke's XI | Scarborough | 1929 |
| | | 227 | Hampshire v Derbyshire | Ilkeston | 1933 |
| Mendis, G.D. | (2) | 204 | Sussex v Northamptonshire | Eastbourne | 1980 |
| | | 209* | Sussex v Somerset | Hove | 1984 |
| Merchant, U.M. | | 217 | Bombay v Hyderabad | Bombay | 1947–48 |
| Merchant, V.M. | (11) | 243* | Hindus v Muslims | Bombay | 1941–42 |
| | | 221 | Hindus v Parsees | Bombay | 1941–42 |
| | | 250* | Hindus v Rest | Bombay | 1943–44 |
| | | 359* | Bombay v Maharashtra | Bombay | 1943–44 |
| | | 221* | Hindus v Parsees | Bombay | 1944–45 |
| | | 217 | Bombay v Western India States | Bombay | 1944–45 |
| | | 278 | Bombay v Holkar | Bombay | 1944–45 |
| | | 201 | Cricket Club of India v Services XI | Bombay | 1944–45 |
| | | 234* | Bombay v Sind | Bombay | 1945–46 |
| | | 242* | Indians v Lancashire | Manchester | 1946 |
| | | 205 | Indians v Sussex | Hove | 1946 |
| Meuleman, K.D. | (2) | 206 | Victoria v Tasmania | Melbourne | 1947–48 |
| | | 234* | Western Australia v South Australia | Perth | 1956–57 |
| Meyer, R.J.O. | | 202* | Somerset v Lancashire | Taunton | 1936 |
| Midlane, F.A. | | 222* | Wellington v Otago | Wellington | 1914–15 |
| Milburn, C. | (2) | 203 | Northamptonshire v Essex | Clacton | 1966 |
| | | 243 | Western Australia v Queensland | Brisbane | 1968–69 |
| Miller, K.R. | (7) | 206* | Victoria v New South Wales | Sydney | 1946–47 |
| | | 202* | Australians v Leicestershire | Leicester | 1948 |
| | | 201* | New South Wales v Queensland | Brisbane | 1950–51 |
| | | 214 | New South Wales v MCC | Sydney | 1950–51 |
| | | 220* | Australians v Worcestershire | Worcester | 1953 |
| | | 262* | Australians v Combined Services | Kingston | 1953 |
| | | 281* | Australians v Leicestershire | Leicester | 1956 |
| Minnett, R.B. | | 216* | New South Wales v Victoria | Sydney | 1911–12 |
| Mitchell, N.F. | | 220 | Victoria v Tasmania | Melbourne | 1926–27 |
| Mitchell-Innes, N.S. | | 207 | Oxford University v H.D.G. Leveson Gower's XI | Reigate | 1936 |
| Modi, R.S. | (4) | 215 | Parsees v Europeans | Bombay | 1944–45 |
| | | 210 | Bombay v Western India States | Bombay | 1944–45 |
| | | 245* | Bombay v Baroda | Baroda | 1944–45 |
| | | 203 | Indian XI v Australian Services | Madras | 1945–46 |
| Mohammad Shafiq | | 271 | Railways v Punjab | Lahore | 1975–76 |
| Mohsin Khan | (5) | 229 | Universities v Sind | Lahore | 1973–74 |
| | | 246 | Habib Bank v PIA | Karachi | 1976–77 |
| | | 220 | Habib Bank v Income Tax Dept | Lahore | 1977–78 |
| | | 203* | Pakistanis v Leicestershire | Leicester | 1982 |
| | | 200 | Pakistan v England | Lord's | 1982 |
| Moore, D.N. | | 206 | Gloucestershire v Oxford University | Oxford | 1930 |
| Moore, H.I. | | 206* | Nottinghamshire v Indians | Nottingham | 1967 |
| Moore, R.H. | | 316 | Hampshire v Warwickshire | Bournemouth | 1937 |
| Mordaunt, G.J. | | 264* | Oxford University v Sussex | Hove | 1895 |
| Morkel, D.P.B. | (2) | 208* | Western Province v Natal | Cape Town | 1929–30 |
| | | 251 | Sir J. Cahn's XI v South Americans | Nottingham | 1932 |
| Moroney, J. | | 217 | A.R. Morris' XI v A.L. Hassett's XI | Sydney | 1948–49 |
| Morris, A.R. | (4) | 290 | Australians v Gloucestershire | Bristol | 1948 |
| | | 206 | Australia v England | Adelaide | 1950–51 |
| | | 253 | New South Wales v Queensland | Brisbane | 1951–52 |

| Player | | Score | Match | Ground | Season |
|---|---|---|---|---|---|
| Morris, A.R. *continued* | | 210 | New South Wales v Victoria | Melbourne | 1951–52 |
| Morrison, J.S.F. | | 233* | Cambridge University v MCC | Cambridge | 1914 |
| Moses, H. | | 297* | New South Wales v Victoria | Sydney | 1887–88 |
| Moss, J.K. | (2) | 220 | Victoria v South Australia | Melbourne | 1978–79 |
| | | 200* | Victoria v Western Australia | Melbourne (St K) | 1981–82 |
| Mudassar Nazar | (3) | 241 | United Bank v Rawalpindi | Lahore | 1981–82 |
| | | 211* | Pakistanis v Sussex | Hove | 1982 |
| | | 231 | Pakistan v India | Hyderabad | 1982–83 |
| Murdoch, W.L. | (5) | 321 | New South Wales v Victoria | Sydney | 1881–82 |
| | | 286* | Australians v Sussex | Hove | 1882 |
| | | 279* | Australian XI v Rest | Melbourne | 1883–84 |
| | | 211 | Australia v England | Oval | 1884 |
| | | 226 | Sussex v Cambridge University | Hove | 1895 |
| Murray, B.A.G. | | 213 | Wellington v Otago | Dunedin | 1968–69 |
| Murray, D.A. | | 206* | West Indians v East Zone | Jamshedpur | 1978–79 |
| Mushtaq Ali | | 233 | Holkar v United Provinces | Indore | 1947–48 |
| Mushtaq Mohammad | (5) | 229* | Karachi Whites v East Pakistan | Karachi | 1961–62 |
| | | 281 | PIA v Railways | Lahore | 1962–63 |
| | | 303* | Karachi Blues v Karachi U's | Karachi | 1967–68 |
| | | 201 | Pakistan v New Zealand | Dunedin | 1972–73 |
| | | 204* | Northamptonshire v Hampshire | Northampton | 1976 |
| Muzzell, R.K. | | 238* | Transvaal B v Natal B | Johannesburg | 1969–70 |
| Nadeem Yousuf | | 202* | MCB v National Bank | Lahore | 1981–82 |
| Nadkarni, R.G. | (3) | 201* | Maharashtra v Saurashtra | Poona | 1957–58 |
| | | 283* | Bombay v Delhi | Bombay | 1960–61 |
| | | 219 | Bombay v Rajasthan | Jaipur | 1962–63 |
| Naik, S.S. | | 200* | Bombay v Baroda | Baroda | 1973–74 |
| Najam-ul-Haq | | 210* | Lahore v Multan | Lahore | 1973–74 |
| Nandy, P. | | 205* | Bengal v Assam | Calcutta | 1975–76 |
| Naoomal Jeoomal | | 203* | Sind v Nawanagar | Karachi | 1938–39 |
| Nayudu, C.K. | | 200 | Holkar v Baroda | Indore | 1945–46 |
| Nel, J.D. | | 217* | Western Province v Eastern Province | Port Elizabeth | 1952–53 |
| Newham, W. | | 201* | Sussex v Somerset | Hove | 1896 |
| Nichol, M. | | 262* | Worcestershire v Hampshire | Bournemouth | 1930 |
| Nicholas, M.C.J. | | 206* | Hampshire v Oxford University | Oxford | 1982 |
| Nicholls, D. | | 211 | Kent v Derbyshire | Folkestone | 1963 |
| Nicholls, R.B. | | 217 | Gloucestershire v Oxford University | Oxford | 1962 |
| Nichols, M.S. | | 205 | Essex v Hampshire | Southend | 1936 |
| Nicolson, J.F.W. | | 252* | Natal v Orange Free State | Bloemfontein | 1926–27 |
| Nimbalkar, B.B. | (2) | 443* | Maharashtra v Kathiawar | Poona | 1948–49 |
| | | 219 | Holkar v Bengal | Calcutta | 1952–53 |
| Noble, M.A. | (7) | 200 | New South Wales v South Australia | Adelaide | 1899–1900 |
| | | 284 | Australians v Sussex | Hove | 1902 |
| | | 230 | New South Wales v South Australia | Sydney | 1903–04 |
| | | 267 | Australians v Sussex | Hove | 1905 |
| | | 281 | New South Wales v Victoria | Melbourne | 1905–06 |
| | | 213 | New South Wales v South Australia | Adelaide | 1908–09 |
| | | 213 | New South Wales v Victoria | Sydney | 1908–09 |
| Norman, M.E.J.C. | | 221* | Leicestershire v Cambridge U. | Cambridge | 1967 |
| Nourse, A.D. | (6) | 231 | South Africa v Australia | Johannesburg | 1935–36 |
| | | 260* | Natal v Transvaal | Johannesburg | 1936–37 |
| | | 240 | Natal v Western Province | Durban | 1936–37 |
| | | 205* | South Africans v Warwickshire | Birmingham | 1947 |
| | | 214* | Natal v Griqualand West | Durban | 1947–48 |
| | | 208 | South Africa v England | Nottingham | 1951 |
| Nourse, A.W. | (7) | 212 | Natal v Griqualand West | Johannesburg | 1906–07 |
| | | 200* | Natal v Western Province | Cape Town | 1907–08 |
| | | 201* | South Africans v South Australia | Adelaide | 1910–11 |
| | | 213* | South Africans v Hampshire | Bournemouth | 1912 |
| | | 304* | Natal v Transvaal | Johannesburg | 1919–20 |
| | | 204 | Transvaal v Griqualand West | Johannesburg | 1925–26 |
| | | 219* | Western Province v Natal | Cape Town | 1932–33 |
| Nunes, R.K. | | 200* | Jamaica v Hon L.H. Tennyson's XI | Kingston | 1926–27 |
| Nurse, S.M. | (4) | 213 | Barbados v MCC | Bridgetown | 1959–60 |
| | | 210 | Barbados v Trinidad | Bridgetown | 1962–63 |
| | | 201 | West Indies v Australia | Bridgetown | 1964–65 |
| | | 258 | West Indies v New Zealand | Christchurch | 1968–69 |

| Oakman, A.S.M. | | 229* | Sussex v Nottinghamshire | Worksop | 1961 |
|---|---|---|---|---|---|
| O'Brien, T.C. | | 202 | Middlesex v Sussex | Hove | 1895 |
| O'Connor, J. | (2) | 237 | Essex v Somerset | Leyton | 1933 |
| | | 248 | Essex v Surrey | Brentwood | 1934 |
| Ollivierre, C.A. | | 229 | Derbyshire v Essex | Chesterfield | 1904 |
| O'Neill, N.C. | (2) | 233 | New South Wales v Victoria | Sydney | 1957–58 |
| | | 284 | Australians v President's XI | Ahmedabad | 1959–60 |
| Ontong, R.C. | | 204* | Glamorgan v Middlesex | Swansea | 1984 |
| Ormrod, J.A. | (2) | 204* | Worcestershire v Kent | Dartford | 1973 |
| | | 200* | Worcestershire v Gloucestershire | Worcester | 1982 |
| Outschoorn, L. | (2) | 215* | Worcestershire v Northamptonshire | Worcester | 1949 |
| | | 200* | Worcestershire v Scotland | Dundee | 1951 |
| Page, M.L. | | 206 | Canterbury v Wellington | Wellington | 1931–32 |
| Paine, A.I. | | 220 | Western Province v Griqualand West | Johannesburg | 1896–97 |
| Palairet, L.C.H. | (2) | 292 | Somerset v Hampshire | Southampton | 1896 |
| | | 203 | Somerset v Worcestershire | Worcester | 1904 |
| Palia, P.E. | | 216 | United Provinces v Maharashtra | Poona | 1939–40 |
| Palmer, C.H. | | 201 | Leicestershire v Northamptonshire | Northampton | 1953 |
| Pandit, P.B. | | 262* | Kerala v Andhra | Palghat | 1959–60 |
| Parfitt, P.H. | | 200* | Middlesex v Nottinghamshire | Nottingham | 1964 |
| Park, R.L. | | 228 | Victoria v South Australia | Melbourne | 1919–20 |
| Parker, G.W. | | 210 | Gloucestershire v Kent | Dover | 1937 |
| Parker, J.F. | (2) | 204* | Surrey v Derbyshire | Oval | 1947 |
| | | 255 | Surrey v New Zealanders | Oval | 1949 |
| Parker, P.W.G. | | 215 | Cambridge University v Essex | Cambridge | 1976 |
| Parkhouse, W.G.A. | | 201 | Glamorgan v Kent | Swansea | 1956 |
| Parks, H.W. | | 200* | Sussex v Essex | Chelmsford | 1931 |
| Parks, J.M. | | 205* | Sussex v Somerset | Hove | 1955 |
| Parsons, J.H. | | 225 | Warwickshire v Glamorgan | Birmingham | 1927 |
| Passailaigue, C.C. | | 261* | Jamaica v Lord Tennyson's XI | Kingston | 1931–32 |
| Pataudi, Nawab of, sr | (5) | 238* | Oxford U. v Cambridge U. | Lord's | 1931 |
| | | 224* | Worcestershire v Kent | Worcester | 1933 |
| | | 231* | Worcestershire v Essex | Worcester | 1933 |
| | | 222 | Worcestershire v Somerset | Weston-s-Mare | 1933 |
| | | 214* | Worcestershire v Glamorgan | Worcester | 1934 |
| Pataudi, Nawab of, jr | (2) | 203* | India v England | Delhi | 1963–64 |
| | | 200 | South Zone v West Zone | Bombay | 1967–68 |
| Patel, B.P. | | 216 | Karnataka v Baroda | Bangalore | 1978–79 |
| Patil, S.M. | | 210 | Bombay v Saurashtra | Bombay | 1979–80 |
| Paynter, E. | (7) | 208* | Lancashire v Northamptonshire | Northampton | 1935 |
| | | 266 | Lancashire v Essex | Manchester | 1937 |
| | | 322 | Lancashire v Sussex | Hove | 1937 |
| | | 291 | Lancashire v Hampshire | Southampton | 1938 |
| | | 216* | England v Australia | Nottingham | 1938 |
| | | 243 | England v South Africa | Durban | 1938–39 |
| | | 222 | Lancashire v Derbyshire | Manchester | 1939 |
| Peach, H.A. | | 200* | Surrey v Northamptonshire | Northampton | 1920 |
| Pearce, T.N. | | 211* | Essex v Leicestershire | Westcliff | 1948 |
| Peel, R. | | 210* | Yorkshire v Warwickshire | Birmingham | 1896 |
| Pellew, C.E. | | 271 | South Australia v Victoria | Adelaide | 1919–20 |
| Perrin, P.A. | (3) | 205 | Essex v Kent | Leyton | 1900 |
| | | 343* | Essex v Derbyshire | Chesterfield | 1904 |
| | | 245 | Essex v Derbyshire | Leyton | 1912 |
| Pervez Akhtar | | 337* | Railways v Dera Ismail Khan | Lahore | 1964–65 |
| Phadkar, D.G. | | 217 | Bombay v Maharashtra | Bombay | 1950–51 |
| Phillips, W.B. | (2) | 260 | South Australia v Queensland | Adelaide | 1981–82 |
| | | 234 | South Australia v Tasmania | Adelaide | 1983–84 |
| Place, W. | (3) | 266* | Lancashire v Oxford University | Oxford | 1947 |
| | | 200 | Lancashire v Somerset | Taunton | 1948 |
| | | 226* | Lancashire v Nottinghamshire | Nottingham | 1949 |
| Pollock, R.G. | (5) | 209* | E. Province Invitation XI v Cavaliers | Port Elizabeth | 1962–63 |
| | | 203* | South Africans v Kent | Canterbury | 1965 |
| | | 209 | South Africa v Australia | Cape Town | 1966–67 |
| | | 274 | South Africa v Australia | Durban | 1969–70 |
| | | 233 | Transvaal v Western Province | Cape Town | 1978–79 |
| Ponsford, W.H. | (13) | 429 | Victoria v Tasmania | Melbourne | 1922–23 |
| | | 248 | Victoria v Queensland | Melbourne | 1923–24 |

| Ponsford, W.H. *continued* | | 214 | Victoria v South Australia | Adelaide | 1926–27 |
|---|---|---|---|---|---|
| | | 352 | Victoria v New South Wales | Melbourne | 1926–27 |
| | | 437 | Victoria v Queensland | Melbourne | 1927–28 |
| | | 202 | Victoria v New South Wales | Melbourne | 1927–28 |
| | | 336 | Victoria v South Australia | Melbourne | 1927–28 |
| | | 275* | Victoria v South Australia | Melbourne | 1928–29 |
| | | 220* | Australians v Oxford University | Oxford | 1930 |
| | | 200 | Victoria v New South Wales | Sydney | 1932–33 |
| | | 229* | Australians v Cambridge University | Cambridge | 1934 |
| | | 281* | Australians v MCC | Lord's | 1934 |
| | | 266 | Australia v England | Oval | 1934 |
| Poole, C.J. | (2) | 222* | Nottinghamshire v Indians | Nottingham | 1952 |
| | | 219 | Nottinghamshire v Derbyshire | Ilkeston | 1952 |
| Poore, R.M. | | 304 | Hampshire v Somerset | Taunton | 1899 |
| Pope, G.H. | | 207* | Derbyshire v Hampshire | Portsmouth | 1948 |
| Potter, J. | | 221 | Victoria v New South Wales | Melbourne | 1965–66 |
| Pretty, H.C. | | 200 | Northamptonshire v Derbyshire | Chesterfield | 1906 |
| Prideaux, R.M. | | 202* | Northamptonshire v Oxford U. | Oxford | 1963 |
| Procter, M.J. | (2) | 254 | Rhodesia v Western Province | Salisbury | 1970–71 |
| | | 203 | Gloucestershire v Essex | Gloucester | 1978 |
| Punjabi, P.H. | | 224* | Gujarat v Saurashtra | Rajkot | 1959–60 |
| Qasim Omar | (3) | 203* | MCB v Railways | Lahore | 1982–83 |
| | | 210* | MCB v Lahore | Lahore | 1982–83 |
| | | 210 | Pakistan v India | Faisalabad | 1984–85 |
| Quaife, W.G. | (4) | 207* | Warwickshire v Hampshire | Birmingham | 1899 |
| | | 223* | Warwickshire v Essex | Leyton | 1900 |
| | | 200* | Warwickshire v Essex | Birmingham | 1904 |
| | | 255* | Warwickshire v Surrey | Oval | 1905 |
| Quin, S.O. | | 210 | Victoria v Tasmania | Melbourne | 1933–34 |
| Radley, C.T. | | 200 | Middlesex v Northamptonshire | Uxbridge | 1985 |
| Ram Prakash | | 209* | Northern India v Maharashtra | Poona | 1940–41 |
| Ramchand, G.S. | | 230* | Bombay v Maharashtra | Bombay | 1950–51 |
| Randall, D.W. | (2) | 204* | Nottinghamshire v Somerset | Nottingham | 1976 |
| | | 209 | Nottinghamshire v Middlesex | Nottingham | 1979 |
| Rangnekar, K.M. | (3) | 202 | Bombay v Maharashtra | Poona | 1940–41 |
| | | 200* | West Zone v East Zone | Bombay | 1946–47 |
| | | 217 | Holkar v Hyderabad | Indore | 1950–51 |
| Ranjitsinhji, K.S. | (14) | 260 | Sussex v MCC | Lord's | 1897 |
| | | 222 | Sussex v Somerset | Hove | 1900 |
| | | 215* | Sussex v Cambridge University | Cambridge | 1900 |
| | | 202 | Sussex v Middlesex | Hove | 1900 |
| | | 275 | Sussex v Leicestershire | Leicester | 1900 |
| | | 220 | Sussex v Kent | Hove | 1900 |
| | | 285* | Sussex v Somerset | Taunton | 1901 |
| | | 204 | Sussex v Lancashire | Hove | 1901 |
| | | 219 | Sussex v Essex | Hove | 1901 |
| | | 230 | Sussex v Essex | Leyton | 1902 |
| | | 234* | Sussex v Surrey | Hastings | 1902 |
| | | 204 | Sussex v Surrey | Oval | 1903 |
| | | 207* | Sussex v Lancashire | Hove | 1904 |
| | | 200 | Sussex v Surrey | Oval | 1908 |
| Raphael, J.E. | | 201 | Oxford University v Yorkshire | Oxford | 1904 |
| Rashid Israr | (3) | 211* | PWD v Hyderabad | Hyderabad | 1973–74 |
| | | 350 | Habib Bank v National Bank | Lahore | 1976–77 |
| | | 228* | PIA v Punjab | Lahore | 1978–79 |
| Ratcliffe, A. | | 201 | Cambridge U. v Oxford U. | Lord's | 1931 |
| Read, W.W. | (3) | 247 | Surrey v Lancashire | Manchester | 1887 |
| | | 244* | Surrey v Cambridge University | Oval | 1887 |
| | | 338 | Surrey v Oxford University | Oval | 1888 |
| Redpath, I.R. | (2) | 261 | Victoria v Queensland | Melbourne | 1962–63 |
| | | 202 | Australians v Western Australia | Perth | 1963–64 |
| Reid, J.R. | (4) | 283 | Wellington v Otago | Wellington | 1951–52 |
| | | 201 | Otago v Canterbury | Dunedin | 1957–58 |
| | | 203 | New Zealanders v Western Province | Cape Town | 1961–62 |
| | | 296 | Wellington v Northern Districts | Wellington | 1962–63 |
| Relf, R.R. | (3) | 210 | Sussex v Kent | Canterbury | 1907 |
| | | 272* | Sussex v Worcestershire | Eastbourne | 1909 |

| | | | | | |
|---|---|---|---|---|---|
| Relf, R.R. *continued* | | 225 | Sussex v Lancashire | Eastbourne | 1920 |
| Reynolds, G.R. | | 203* | Queensland v South Australia | Adelaide | 1957–58 |
| Rhodes, W. | (3) | 201 | Yorkshire v Somerset | Taunton | 1905 |
| | | 210 | MCC v South Australia | Adelaide | 1920–21 |
| | | 267* | Yorkshire v Leicestershire | Leeds | 1921 |
| Rice, C.E.B. | (3) | 246 | Nottinghamshire v Sussex | Hove | 1976 |
| | | 213* | Nottinghamshire v Lancashire | Nottingham | 1978 |
| | | 213 | Nottinghamshire v Glamorgan | Swansea | 1978 |
| Richards, B.A. | (6) | 206 | Hampshire v Nottinghamshire | Portsmouth | 1968 |
| | | 224 | South Australia v MCC | Adelaide | 1970–71 |
| | | 356 | South Australia v Western Australia | Perth | 1970–71 |
| | | 219 | Natal v Rhodesia | Durban | 1971–72 |
| | | 240 | Hampshire v Warwickshire | Coventry | 1973 |
| | | 225* | Hampshire v Nottinghamshire | Nottingham | 1974 |
| Richards, I.V.A. | (9) | 217* | Somerset v Yorkshire | Harrogate | 1975 |
| | | 232 | West Indies v England | Nottingham | 1976 |
| | | 291 | West Indies v England | Oval | 1976 |
| | | 241* | Somerset v Gloucestershire | Bristol | 1977 |
| | | 204 | Somerset v Sussex | Hove | 1977 |
| | | 204 | Somerset v Surrey | Weston-s-Mare | 1977 |
| | | 216 | Somerset v Leicestershire | Leicester | 1983 |
| | | 208 | West Indies v Australia | Melbourne | 1984–85 |
| | | 322 | Somerset v Warwickshire | Taunton | 1985 |
| Richardson, A.J. | (4) | 280 | South Australia v MCC | Adelaide | 1922–23 |
| | | 200* | South Australia v MCC | Adelaide | 1924–25 |
| | | 227 | South Australia v Western Australia | Adelaide | 1925–26 |
| | | 232 | South Australia v Queensland | Adelaide | 1926–27 |
| Richardson, C. | | 258 | Orange Free State v Transvaal B | Johannesburg | 1959–60 |
| Richardson, G.W. | | 204* | Victoria v Queensland | Melbourne | 1983–84 |
| Richardson, V.Y. | (2) | 231 | South Australia v MCC | Adelaide | 1928–29 |
| | | 203 | South Australia v Victoria | Adelaide | 1932–33 |
| Riches, N.V.H. | | 239* | Wales v Ireland | Belfast | 1926 |
| Roach, C.A. | | 209 | West Indies v England | Georgetown | 1929–30 |
| Robertson, J.D.B. | (4) | 229 | Middlesex v Hampshire | Lord's | 1947 |
| | | 331* | Middlesex v Worcestershire | Worcester | 1949 |
| | | 201* | Middlesex v Somerset | Taunton | 1951 |
| | | 201* | Middlesex v Essex | Lord's | 1957 |
| Robinson, R.T. | | 207 | Nottinghamshire v Warwickshire | Nottingham | 1983 |
| Rock, H.O. | | 235 | New South Wales v Victoria | Sydney | 1924–25 |
| Roller, W.E. | | 204 | Surrey v Sussex | Oval | 1885 |
| Rose, B.C. | | 205 | Somerset v Northamptonshire | Weston-s-Mare | 1977 |
| Rowan, E.A.B. | (5) | 306* | Transvaal v Natal | Johannesburg | 1939–40 |
| | | 284 | Eastern Province v Griqualand West | Port Elizabeth | 1945–46 |
| | | 277* | Transvaal v Griqualand West | Johannesburg | 1950–51 |
| | | 202* | South Africans v Northamptonshire | Northampton | 1951 |
| | | 236 | South Africa v England | Leeds | 1951 |
| Rowe, L.G. | (4) | 227 | Jamaica v New Zealanders | Kingston | 1971–72 |
| | | 214 | West Indies v New Zealand | Kingston | 1971–72 |
| | | 204 | Jamaica v Guyana | Kingston | 1973–74 |
| | | 302 | West Indies v England | Bridgetown | 1973–74 |
| Roy, Pankaj | | 202* | Bengal v Orissa | Cuttack | 1963–64 |
| Roy, Pranab | | 206* | Bengal v Assam | Calcutta | 1983–84 |
| Russell, C.A.G. | (2) | 201 | MCC v South Australia | Adelaide | 1920–21 |
| | | 273 | Essex v Northamptonshire | Leyton | 1921 |
| Rutherford, I.A. | | 222 | Otago v Central Districts | New Plymouth | 1978–79 |
| Ryder, J. | (3) | 242 | Victoria v South Australia | Melbourne | 1921–22 |
| | | 201* | Australia v England | Adelaide | 1924–25 |
| | | 295 | Victoria v New South Wales | Melbourne | 1926–27 |
| Saadat Ali | (4) | 277 | Income Tax Dept v Bahawalpur | Bahawalpur | 1976–77 |
| | | 222 | Income Tax Dept v Multan | Multan | 1977–78 |
| | | 206* | Railways v PIA | Lahore | 1982–83 |
| | | 208 | HBFC v PACO | Bahawalpur | 1983–84 |
| Sadiq Mohammad | | 203 | Gloucestershire v Sri Lankans | Bristol | 1981 |
| Saeed Ahmed | | 203* | Karachi Blues v PWD | Karachi | 1970–71 |
| Salahuddin | (2) | 201 | Karachi Blues v E. Pakistan Greens | Karachi | 1967–68 |
| | | 256 | Karachi v East Pakistan | Karachi | 1968–69 |
| Salim Pervez | | 226* | National Bank v Quetta | Karachi | 1978–79 |

| Sandham, A. | (11) | 292* | Surrey v Northamptonshire | Oval | 1921 |
|---|---|---|---|---|---|
| | | 209* | Surrey v Somerset | Oval | 1921 |
| | | 200 | Surrey v Essex | Leyton | 1923 |
| | | 230 | Surrey v Essex | Oval | 1927 |
| | | 282* | Surrey v Lancashire | Manchester | 1928 |
| | | 248* | Surrey v Glamorgan | Cardiff | 1928 |
| | | 325 | England v West Indies | Kingston | 1929–30 |
| | | 204 | Surrey v Warwickshire | Birmingham | 1930 |
| | | 215 | Surrey v Somerset | Taunton | 1932 |
| | | 219 | Surrey v Australians | Oval | 1934 |
| | | 239 | Surrey v Glamorgan | Oval | 1937 |
| Santall, F.R. | | 201* | Warwickshire v Northamptonshire | Northampton | 1933 |
| Sarabhjit Singh | | 208 | Haryana v Delhi | Rohtak | 1980–81 |
| Sardesai, D.N. | (4) | 222 | ACC XI v Indian Starlets XI | Hyderabad | 1964–65 |
| | | 200* | India v New Zealand | Bombay | 1964–65 |
| | | 217 | Bombay v Baroda | Bombay | 1968–69 |
| | | 212 | India v West Indies | Kingston | 1970–71 |
| Sarwate, C.T. | (3) | 235 | Holkar v Delhi | Delhi | 1949–50 |
| | | 246 | Holkar v Bengal | Calcutta | 1950–51 |
| | | 234 | Holkar v Gujarat | Indore | 1950–51 |
| Sathasivam, M. | | 215 | All Ceylon v South India | Madras | 1946–47 |
| Saxena, R. | | 202* | Bihar v Assam | Dhanbad | 1969–70 |
| Scott, S.W. | | 224 | Middlesex v Gloucestershire | Lord's | 1892 |
| Scott, V.J. | (2) | 204 | Auckland v Otago | Dunedin | 1947–48 |
| | | 203 | New Zealanders v Combined Services | Gillingham | 1949 |
| Sebastien, L.C. | | 219 | Windward I's v Leeward I's | Basseterre | 1978–79 |
| Sellers, A.B. | | 204 | Yorkshire v Cambridge University | Cambridge | 1936 |
| Seymour, James | (3) | 204 | Kent v Hampshire | Tonbridge | 1907 |
| | | 218* | Kent v Essex | Leyton | 1911 |
| | | 214 | Kent v Essex | Tunbridge Wells | 1914 |
| Shafiq Ahmed | (3) | 200* | Patron's XI v West Indians | Rawalpindi | 1974–75 |
| | | 217* | National Bank v M.C. Bank | Karachi | 1978–79 |
| | | 202* | National Bank v Railways | Lahore | 1979–80 |
| Shahid Mahmood | | 220 | Karachi U. v Peshawar U. | Karachi | 1958–59 |
| Shakoor Ahmed | | 280 | Lahore Greens v Railways | Lahore | 1964–65 |
| Sharma, P. | | 206 | Rest of India v Bombay | Bombay | 1977–78 |
| Sharp, A.T. | | 216 | Leicestershire v Derbyshire | Chesterfield | 1911 |
| Sharp, J. | | 211 | Lancashire v Leicestershire | Manchester | 1912 |
| Sharpe, P.J. | (3) | 202 | Minor Counties v Indians | Stoke | 1959 |
| | | 203* | Yorkshire v Cambridge University | Cambridge | 1960 |
| | | 228 | Derbyshire v Oxford University | Oxford | 1976 |
| Shastri, R.J. | | 200* | Bombay v Baroda | Bombay | 1984–85 |
| Sheahan, A.P. | | 202 | Victoria v South Australia | Melbourne | 1966–67 |
| Shepherd, B.K. | (3) | 212* | Western Australia v Queensland | Perth | 1961–62 |
| | | 219 | Western Australia v Victoria | Melbourne | 1962–63 |
| | | 215* | Western Australia v Victoria | Perth | 1964–65 |
| Shepherd, T.F. | (5) | 212 | Surrey v Lancashire | Oval | 1921 |
| | | 210* | Surrey v Kent | Blackheath | 1921 |
| | | 207* | Surrey v Kent | Blackheath | 1925 |
| | | 277* | Surrey v Gloucestershire | Oval | 1927 |
| | | 234 | Surrey v Cambridge University | Oval | 1930 |
| Sheppard, D.S. | (3) | 204 | Sussex v Glamorgan | Eastbourne | 1949 |
| | | 227 | Cambridge U. v West Indians | Cambridge | 1950 |
| | | 239* | Cambridge U. v Worcestershire | Worcester | 1952 |
| Shiell, A.B. | | 202* | South Australia v MCC | Adelaide | 1965–66 |
| Shillingford, I.T. | | 238 | Windward I's v Leeward I's | Castries | 1977–78 |
| Shipman, A.W. | | 226 | Leicestershire v Kent | Tonbridge | 1928 |
| Shodhan, R.H. | | 261 | Baroda v Maharashtra | Ahmednagar | 1957–58 |
| Shrewsbury, A. | (10) | 207 | Nottinghamshire v Surrey | Oval | 1882 |
| | | 209 | Nottinghamshire v Sussex | Hove | 1884 |
| | | 224* | Nottinghamshire v Middlesex | Lord's | 1885 |
| | | 227* | Nottinghamshire v Gloucestershire | Moreton-in-Marsh | 1886 |
| | | 236 | Non-Smokers v Smokers | East Melbourne | 1886–87 |
| | | 267 | Nottinghamshire v Middlesex | Nottingham | 1887 |
| | | 232 | Shrewsbury's XI v Victoria | Melbourne | 1887–88 |
| | | 206 | Shrewsbury's XI v Australian XI | Sydney | 1887–88 |
| | | 267 | Nottinghamshire v Sussex | Nottingham | 1890 |

| | | | | | |
|---|---|---|---|---|---|
| Shrewsbury, A. *continued* | | 212 | Nottinghamshire v Middlesex | Lord's | 1892 |
| Shukla, A. | | 242* | Bihar v Orissa | Cuttack | 1967–68 |
| Siedle, I.J. | (3) | 212* | Natal v Border | Durban | 1928–29 |
| | | 265* | Natal v Orange Free State | Durban | 1929–30 |
| | | 207 | Natal v Western Province | Durban | 1936–37 |
| Sikdar, R. | | 201 | Orissa v Assam | Rourkela | 1977–78 |
| Simpson, R.B. | (12) | 236* | Western Australia v NSW | Perth | 1959–60 |
| | | 230* | Western Australia v Queensland | Perth | 1959–60 |
| | | 221* | Western Australia v West Indians | Perth | 1960–61 |
| | | 359 | New South Wales v Queensland | Brisbane | 1963–64 |
| | | 246 | Combined XI v South Africans | Perth | 1963–64 |
| | | 247* | NSW v Western Australia | Sydney | 1963–64 |
| | | 311 | Australia v England | Manchester | 1964 |
| | | 201 | Australia v West Indies | Bridgetown | 1964–65 |
| | | 225 | Australia v England | Adelaide | 1965–66 |
| | | 243 | Australians v N.E. Transvaal | Pretoria | 1966–67 |
| | | 277 | New South Wales v Queensland | Sydney | 1967–68 |
| Simpson, R.T. | (10) | 201 | Nottinghamshire v Warwickshire | Nottingham | 1946 |
| | | 200* | Nottinghamshire v Surrey | Nottingham | 1949 |
| | | 238 | Nottinghamshire v Lancashire | Manchester | 1949 |
| | | 230* | Nottinghamshire v Glamorgan | Swansea | 1950 |
| | | 243* | Nottinghamshire v Worcestershire | Nottingham | 1950 |
| | | 259 | MCC v New South Wales | Sydney | 1950–51 |
| | | 201 | Nottinghamshire v Oxford University | Oxford | 1951 |
| | | 212 | Nottinghamshire v Essex | Clacton | 1951 |
| | | 216 | Nottinghamshire v Sussex | Nottingham | 1952 |
| | | 200 | Nottinghamshire v Warwickshire | Nottingham | 1952 |
| Sinfield, R.A. | | 209* | Gloucestershire v Glamorgan | Cardiff | 1935 |
| Slack, W.N. | (3) | 248* | Middlesex v Worcestershire | Lord's | 1981 |
| | | 203* | Middlesex v Oxford University | Oxford | 1982 |
| | | 201* | Middlesex v Australians | Lord's | 1985 |
| Smith, D. | (2) | 225 | Derbyshire v Hampshire | Chesterfield | 1935 |
| | | 202* | Derbyshire v Nottinghamshire | Nottingham | 1937 |
| Smith D.V. | | 206* | Sussex v Nottinghamshire | Nottingham | 1950 |
| Smith, M.J.K. | (3) | 201* | Oxford U. v Cambridge U. | Lord's | 1954 |
| | | 200* | Warwickshire v Worcestershire | Birmingham | 1959 |
| | | 204 | Cavaliers v Natal | Durban | 1960–61 |
| Smith, S.B. | | 263 | New South Wales v Victoria | Melbourne | 1982–83 |
| Smith, S.G. | (2) | 204 | Northamptonshire v Gloucestershire | Northampton | 1910 |
| | | 256 | Auckland v Canterbury | Auckland | 1919–20 |
| Sobers, G.St A. | (6) | 219* | West Indians v Nottinghamshire | Nottingham | 1957 |
| | | 365* | West Indies v Pakistan | Kingston | 1957–58 |
| | | 226 | West Indies v England | Bridgetown | 1959–60 |
| | | 251 | South Australia v New South Wales | Adelaide | 1961–62 |
| | | 204 | Barbados v British Guiana | Bridgetown | 1965–66 |
| | | 254 | World XI v Australia | Melbourne | 1971–72 |
| Sohoni, S.W. | | 218* | Maharashtra v Western India | Rajkot | 1940–41 |
| Solomon, J.S. | | 201* | Berbice v MCC | Blairmont | 1959–60 |
| Spooner, R.H. | (5) | 247 | Lancashire v Nottinghamshire | Nottingham | 1903 |
| | | 215 | Lancashire v Essex | Leyton | 1904 |
| | | 240 | Lancashire v Somerset | Bath | 1906 |
| | | 200* | Lancashire v Yorkshire | Manchester | 1910 |
| | | 224 | Lancashire v Surrey | Oval | 1911 |
| Squires, H.S. | (3) | 200* | Surrey v Cambridge University | Oval | 1931 |
| | | 236 | Surrey v Lancashire | Oval | 1933 |
| | | 210 | Surrey v Derbyshire | Oval | 1949 |
| Stackpole, K.R. | | 207 | Australia v England | Brisbane | 1970–71 |
| Stevens, G.B. | | 259* | South Australia v New South Wales | Sydney | 1958–59 |
| Stewart, M.J. | (2) | 200* | Surrey v Essex | Oval | 1962 |
| | | 227* | Surrey v Middlesex | Oval | 1964 |
| Steyn, S.S.L. | | 261* | Western Province v Border | Cape Town | 1929–30 |
| Stoddart, A.E. | (2) | 215* | Middlesex v Lancashire | Manchester | 1891 |
| | | 221 | Middlesex v Somerset | Lord's | 1900 |
| Stollmeyer, J.B. | (5) | 210 | Trinidad v Barbados | Bridgetown | 1943–44 |
| | | 324 | Trinidad v British Guiana | Port-of-Spain | 1946–47 |
| | | 244* | West Indians v South Zone | Madras | 1948–49 |
| | | 261 | Trinidad v Jamaica | Port-of-Spain | 1949–50 |

| | | | | |
|---|---|---|---|---|
| Stollmeyer, J.B. *continued* | 208 | Trinidad v Barbados | Bridgetown | 1950–51 |
| Storer, H. | (2) 209 | Derbyshire v Essex | Derby | 1929 |
| | 232 | Derbyshire v Essex | Derby | 1933 |
| Storer, W. | 216* | Derbyshire v Leicestershire | Chesterfield | 1899 |
| Stovold, A.W. | 212* | Gloucestershire v Northamptonshire | Northampton | 1982 |
| Strydom, S. | 234 | Orange Free State v Transvaal B | Vereeniging | 1965–66 |
| Subba Row, R. | (2) 260* | Northamptonshire v Lancashire | Northampton | 1955 |
| | 300 | Northamptonshire v Surrey | Oval | 1958 |
| Subramanya, V. | 213* | Mysore v Madras | Madras | 1966–67 |
| Sudhakar Rao, R. | 200* | Karnataka v Hyderabad | Hyderabad | 1975–76 |
| Sugg, F.H. | 220 | Lancashire v Gloucestershire | Bristol | 1896 |
| Surti, R.F. | 246* | Rajasthan v Uttar Pradesh | Udaipur | 1959–60 |
| Sutcliffe, B. | (8) 208* | North Island v South Island | Dunedin | 1947–48 |
| | 243 | New Zealanders v Essex | Southend | 1949 |
| | 355 | Otago v Auckland | Dunedin | 1949–50 |
| | 275 | Otago v Auckland | Auckland | 1950–51 |
| | 385 | Otago v Canterbury | Christchurch | 1952–53 |
| | 230* | New Zealand v India | Delhi | 1955–56 |
| | 264 | Otago v Central Districts | Dunedin | 1959–60 |
| | 201 | Otago v Northern Districts | Hamilton | 1960–61 |
| Sutcliffe, H. | (17) 232 | Yorkshire v Surrey | Oval | 1922 |
| | 213 | Yorkshire v Somerset | Dewsbury | 1924 |
| | 255* | Yorkshire v Essex | Southend | 1924 |
| | 235 | Yorkshire v Middlesex | Leeds | 1925 |
| | 206 | Yorkshire v Warwickshire | Dewsbury | 1925 |
| | 200 | Yorkshire v Leicestershire | Leicester | 1926 |
| | 227 | England XI v Rest | Bristol | 1927 |
| | 228 | Yorkshire v Sussex | Eastbourne | 1928 |
| | 230 | Yorkshire v Kent | Folkestone | 1931 |
| | 313 | Yorkshire v Essex | Leyton | 1932 |
| | 270 | Yorkshire v Sussex | Leeds | 1932 |
| | 205 | Yorkshire v Warwickshire | Birmingham | 1933 |
| | 203 | Yorkshire v Surrey | Oval | 1934 |
| | 200* | Yorkshire v Worcestershire | Sheffield | 1935 |
| | 212 | Yorkshire v Leicestershire | Leicester | 1935 |
| | 202 | Yorkshire v Middlesex | Scarborough | 1936 |
| | 234* | Yorkshire v Leicestershire | Hull | 1939 |
| Suttle, K.G. | 204* | Sussex v Kent | Tunbridge Wells | 1962 |
| Talat Ali | (2) 258 | PIA v Rawalpindi | Rawalpindi | 1975–76 |
| | 214* | PIA v Punjab | Lahore | 1978–79 |
| Tarilton, P.H. | 304* | Barbados v Trinidad | Bridgetown | 1919–20 |
| Tarrant, F.A. | (4) 206 | Victoria v New South Wales | Sydney | 1907–08 |
| | 207* | Middlesex v Yorkshire | Bradford | 1911 |
| | 250* | Middlesex v Essex | Leyton | 1914 |
| | 200 | Middlesex v Worcestershire | Lord's | 1914 |
| Taslim Arif | (2) 205 | Karachi Blues v Hyderabad | Karachi | 1971–72 |
| | 210* | Pakistan v Australia | Faisalabad | 1979–80 |
| Tate, M.W. | 203 | Sussex v Northamptonshire | Hove | 1921 |
| Tayfield, A. | 205 | Transvaal v Eastern Province | Port Elizabeth | 1961–62 |
| Taylor, H.W. | 250* | Natal v Transvaal | Johannesburg | 1912–13 |
| Taylor, K. | 203* | Yorkshire v Warwickshire | Birmingham | 1961 |
| Taylor, M.D. | 234* | Victoria v West Indians | Melbourne | 1984–85 |
| Tehsin Javed | 200 | National Bank v Sind | Lahore | 1974–75 |
| Tennyson, Hon L.H. | 217 | Hampshire v West Indians | Southampton | 1928 |
| Thomas, G. | 229 | New South Wales v Victoria | Melbourne | 1965–66 |
| Thompson, F.C. | 275* | Queensland v New South Wales | Brisbane | 1930–31 |
| Timms, J.E. | 213 | Northamptonshire v Worcestershire | Stourbridge | 1934 |
| Townsend, C.L. | (2) 224* | Gloucestershire v Essex | Clifton | 1899 |
| | 214 | Gloucestershire v Worcestershire | Cheltenham | 1906 |
| Townsend, L.F. | 233 | Derbyshire v Leicestershire | Loughborough | 1933 |
| Trimble, S.C. | (3) 252* | Queensland v New South Wales | Sydney | 1963–64 |
| | 220 | Queensland v South Australia | Adelaide | 1964–65 |
| | 213 | Australians v New Zealanders | Wellington | 1969–70 |
| Trumper, V.T. | (8) 292* | New South Wales v Tasmania | Sydney | 1898–99 |
| | 253 | New South Wales v New Zealanders | Sydney | 1898–99 |
| | 300* | Australians v Sussex | Hove | 1899 |
| | 208 | New South Wales v Queensland | Sydney | 1899–1900 |

| | | | | | |
|---|---|---|---|---|---|
| Trumper, V.T. *continued* | | 230 | New South Wales v Victoria | Sydney | 1900–01 |
| | | 214* | Australia v South Africa | Adelaide | 1910–11 |
| | | 201* | New South Wales v South Australia | Sydney | 1912–13 |
| | | 293 | Australians v Canterbury | Christchurch | 1913–14 |
| Tunnicliffe, J. | | 243 | Yorkshire v Derbyshire | Chesterfield | 1898 |
| Turnbull, M.J.L. | (3) | 205 | Glamorgan v Nottinghamshire | Cardiff | 1932 |
| | | 200* | Glamorgan v Northamptonshire | Swansea | 1933 |
| | | 233 | Glamorgan v Worcestershire | Swansea | 1937 |
| Turner, G.M. | (10) | 202 | New Zealanders v President's XI | Montego Bay | 1971–72 |
| | | 223* | New Zealand v West Indies | Kingston | 1971–72 |
| | | 259 | New Zealanders v Guyana | Georgetown | 1971–72 |
| | | 259 | New Zealand v West Indies | Georgetown | 1971–72 |
| | | 202* | Worcestershire v Cambridge U. | Cambridge | 1974 |
| | | 214* | Worcestershire v Oxford University | Worcester | 1975 |
| | | 202* | Worcestershire v Warwickshire | Birmingham | 1978 |
| | | 228* | Worcestershire v Gloucestershire | Worcester | 1980 |
| | | 239* | Worcestershire v Oxford University | Oxford | 1982 |
| | | 311* | Worcestershire v Warwickshire | Worcester | 1982 |
| Tyldesley, G.E. | (7) | 244 | Lancashire v Warwickshire | Birmingham | 1920 |
| | | 236 | Lancashire v Surrey | Oval | 1923 |
| | | 226 | Lancashire v Sussex | Manchester | 1926 |
| | | 242 | Lancashire v Leicestershire | Leicester | 1928 |
| | | 256* | Lancashire v Warwickshire | Manchester | 1930 |
| | | 225* | Lancashire v Worcestershire | Worcester | 1932 |
| | | 239 | Lancashire v Glamorgan | Cardiff | 1934 |
| Tyldesley, J.T. | (13) | 200 | Lancashire v Derbyshire | Manchester | 1898 |
| | | 249 | Lancashire v Leicestershire | Leicester | 1899 |
| | | 221 | Lancashire v Nottinghamshire | Nottingham | 1901 |
| | | 248 | Lancashire v Worcestershire | Liverpool | 1903 |
| | | 210 | Lancashire v Somerset | Bath | 1904 |
| | | 225 | Lancashire v Nottinghamshire | Nottingham | 1904 |
| | | 250 | Lancashire v Nottinghamshire | Nottingham | 1905 |
| | | 295* | Lancashire v Kent | Manchester | 1906 |
| | | 209 | Lancashire v Warwickshire | Birmingham | 1907 |
| | | 243 | Lancashire v Leicestershire | Leicester | 1908 |
| | | 210 | Lancashire v Surrey | Oval | 1913 |
| | | 253 | Lancashire v Kent | Canterbury | 1914 |
| | | 272 | Lancashire v Derbyshire | Chesterfield | 1919 |
| Umrigar, P.R. | (9) | 229* | Indians v Oxford University | Oxford | 1952 |
| | | 204 | Indians v Lancashire | Manchester | 1952 |
| | | 204 | Indians v Kent | Canterbury | 1952 |
| | | 223 | India v New Zealand | Hyderabad | 1955–56 |
| | | 245 | Bombay v Saurashtra | Poona | 1957–58 |
| | | 213 | Bombay v Gujarat | Poona | 1957–58 |
| | | 252* | Indians v Cambridge University | Cambridge | 1959 |
| | | 203 | Indians v Somerset | Taunton | 1959 |
| | | 202* | Indians v Northamptonshire | Northampton | 1959 |
| Valentine, B.H. | (2) | 242 | Kent v Leicestershire | Oakham | 1938 |
| | | 201 | Kent v Nottinghamshire | Nottingham | 1939 |
| Vaulkhard, P. | | 264 | Derbyshire v Nottinghamshire | Nottingham | 1946 |
| Vengsarkar, D.B. | (3) | 210 | Bombay v Baroda | Baroda | 1979–80 |
| | | 203 | Bombay v Bihar | Jamshedpur | 1979–80 |
| | | 200* | West Zone v England XI | Rajkot | 1984–85 |
| Versfeld, B.J. | | 201* | Natal v Transvaal | Durban | 1965–66 |
| Viljoen, K.G. | (3) | 215 | Griqualand West v Western Province | Kimberley | 1929–30 |
| | | 200* | Orange Free State v Transvaal | Bloemfontein | 1933–34 |
| | | 201 | South Africans v Sussex | Hove | 1947 |
| Vine, J. | | 202 | Sussex v Northamptonshire | Hastings | 1920 |
| Viswanath, G.R. | (4) | 230 | Mysore v Andhra | Vijayawada | 1967–68 |
| | | 200* | Karnataka v Rest of India | Ahmedabad | 1974–75 |
| | | 247 | Karnataka v Uttar Pradesh | Mohan Nagar | 1977–78 |
| | | 222 | India v England | Madras | 1981–82 |
| Wade, W.W. | | 208 | Natal v Eastern Province | Pietermaritzburg | 1939–40 |
| Wadekar, A.L. | (3) | 235 | Bombay v Rajasthan | Bombay | 1961–62 |
| | | 229 | West Zone v East Zone | Calcutta | 1964–65 |
| | | 323 | Bombay v Mysore | Bombay | 1966–67 |
| Waheed Mirza | | 324 | Karachi Whites v Quetta | Karachi | 1976–77 |

| | | | | | |
|---|---|---|---|---|---|
| Wainwright, E. | | 228 | Yorkshire v Surrey | Oval | 1899 |
| Waite, J.H.B. | | 219 | Eastern Province v Griqualand West | Kimberley | 1950–51 |
| Walcott, C.L. | (4) | 314* | Barbados v Trinidad | Port-of-Spain | 1945–46 |
| | | 211* | Barbados v British Guiana | Bridgetown | 1949–50 |
| | | 209 | Barbados v Trinidad | Bridgetown | 1950–51 |
| | | 220 | West Indies v England | Bridgetown | 1953–54 |
| Walford, M.M. | (2) | 201* | Oxford University v MCC | Lord's | 1938 |
| | | 264 | Somerset v Hampshire | Weston-s-Mare | 1947 |
| Walker, L. | | 222 | London County v MCC | Crystal Palace | 1901 |
| Wallace, W.M. | | 211 | Auckland v Canterbury | Auckland | 1939–40 |
| Walsh, D.R. | | 207 | Oxford University v Warwickshire | Oxford | 1969 |
| Walters, C.F. | | 226 | Worcestershire v Kent | Gravesend | 1933 |
| Walters, K.D. | (4) | 253 | New South Wales v South Australia | Adelaide | 1964–65 |
| | | 242 | Australia v West Indies | Sydney | 1968–69 |
| | | 201* | New South Wales v MCC | Sydney | 1970–71 |
| | | 250 | Australia v New Zealand | Christchurch | 1976–77 |
| Waqar Hassan | | 201* | AVM Cannon's XI v | | |
| | | | Hasan Mahmood's XI | Karachi | 1953–54 |
| Ward, A. | | 219 | A.E. Stoddart's XI v S. Australia | Adelaide | 1894–95 |
| Ward, W. | | 278 | MCC v Norfolk XI | Lord's | 1820 |
| Warner, P.F. | (3) | 211 | Lord Hawke's XI v Otago | Dunedin | 1902–03 |
| | | 204 | MCC v Sussex | Lord's | 1905 |
| | | 244 | Rest of England v Warwickshire | Oval | 1911 |
| Washbrook, C. | (7) | 228 | Lancashire v Oxford University | Oxford | 1935 |
| | | 219* | Lancashire v Gloucestershire | Bristol | 1938 |
| | | 204* | Lancashire v Sussex | Manchester | 1947 |
| | | 251* | Lancashire v Surrey | Manchester | 1947 |
| | | 200 | Lancashire v Hampshire | Manchester | 1948 |
| | | 209* | Lancashire v Warwickshire | Birmingham | 1951 |
| | | 211* | Lancashire v Somerset | Manchester | 1952 |
| Watson, F.B. | (4) | 223 | Lancashire v Northamptonshire | Manchester | 1928 |
| | | 300* | Lancashire v Surrey | Manchester | 1928 |
| | | 236 | Lancashire v Sussex | Hove | 1928 |
| | | 207 | Lancashire v Worcestershire | Worcester | 1929 |
| Watson, W. | (3) | 257 | MCC v British Guiana | Georgetown | 1953–54 |
| | | 214* | Yorkshire v Worcestershire | Worcester | 1955 |
| | | 217* | Leicestershire v Somerset | Taunton | 1961 |
| Watson, W.J. | | 206 | NSW v Western Australia | Perth | 1956–57 |
| Wazir Ali, S. | (2) | 268* | Indian U. Occasionals v | | |
| | | | Viceroy's XI | Calcutta | 1935–36 |
| | | 222* | Southern Punjab v Bengal | Calcutta | 1938–39 |
| Webbe, A.J. | | 243* | Middlesex v Yorkshire | Huddersfield | 1887 |
| Weekes, E.de C. | (9) | 236* | Barbados v British Guiana | Bridgetown | 1949–50 |
| | | 232 | West Indians v Surrey | Oval | 1950 |
| | | 304* | West Indians v Cambridge U. | Cambridge | 1950 |
| | | 279 | West Indians v Nottinghamshire | Nottingham | 1950 |
| | | 246* | West Indians v Hampshire | Southampton | 1950 |
| | | 200* | West Indians v Leicestershire | Leicester | 1950 |
| | | 207 | West Indies v India | Port-of-Spain | 1952–53 |
| | | 253 | Barbados v Indians | Bridgetown | 1952–53 |
| | | 206 | West Indies v England | Port-of-Spain | 1953–54 |
| Wells, Colin M. | | 203 | Sussex v Hampshire | Hove | 1984 |
| Wells, Cyril M. | | 244 | Middlesex v Nottinghamshire | Nottingham | 1899 |
| Wessels, K.C. | (3) | 254 | Sussex v Middlesex | Hove | 1980 |
| | | 220 | Queensland v Tasmania | Devonport | 1981–82 |
| | | 249 | Queensland v Victoria | Melbourne | 1982–83 |
| White, R.C. | | 205 | Transvaal B v Griqualand West | Johannesburg | 1965–66 |
| Whysall, W.W. | (3) | 209 | Nottinghamshire v Essex | Leyton | 1926 |
| | | 244 | Nottinghamshire v Gloucestershire | Nottingham | 1929 |
| | | 248 | Nottinghamshire v Northamptonshire | Nottingham | 1930 |
| Wiener, J.M. | | 221* | Victoria v Western Australia | Melbourne (St K) | 1981–82 |
| Wight, G.L. | | 262* | British Guiana v Barbados | Georgetown | 1951–52 |
| Wight, P.B. | (2) | 222* | Somerset v Kent | Taunton | 1959 |
| | | 215 | Somerset v Yorkshire | Taunton | 1962 |
| Willey, P. | | 227 | Northamptonshire v Somerset | Northampton | 1976 |
| Williams, E.S.B. | (2) | 209 | Army v Oxford University | Oxford | 1925 |
| | | 228 | Army v Royal Navy | Lord's | 1928 |

| | | | | | | |
|---|---|---|---|---|---|---|
| Wilmot, A.L. | (2) | 222* | Eastern Province v Rhodesia | Salisbury | 1965–66 |
| | | 207 | Eastern Province v Border | East London | 1968–69 |
| Wilson, B.B. | | 208 | Yorkshire v Sussex | Bradford | 1914 |
| Wilson, J.V. | (2) | 223* | Yorkshire v Scotland | Scarborough | 1951 |
| | | 230 | Yorkshire v Derbyshire | Sheffield | 1952 |
| Winrow, F.H. | | 204* | Nottinghamshire v Derbyshire | Nottingham | 1947 |
| Wood, C.J.B. | (2) | 200* | Leicestershire v Hampshire | Leicester | 1905 |
| | | 225 | Leicestershire v Worcestershire | Worcester | 1906 |
| Woodfull, W.M. | (7) | 212* | Victoria v Canterbury | Christchurch | 1924–25 |
| | | 236 | Victoria v South Australia | Melbourne | 1925–26 |
| | | 201 | Australians v Essex | Leyton | 1926 |
| | | 284 | Australians v New Zealand XI | Auckland | 1927–28 |
| | | 275* | Victoria v MCC | Melbourne | 1928–29 |
| | | 216 | Australians v Cambridge University | Cambridge | 1930 |
| | | 228* | Australians v Glamorgan | Swansea | 1934 |
| Woods, S.M.J. | | 215 | Somerset v Sussex | Hove | 1895 |
| Woolley, C.N. | | 204* | Northamptonshire v Worcestershire | Northampton | 1921 |
| Woolley, F.E. | (9) | 305* | MCC v Tasmania | Hobart | 1911–12 |
| | | 224* | Kent v Oxford University | Oxford | 1913 |
| | | 270 | Kent v Middlesex | Canterbury | 1923 |
| | | 202 | Rest of England v Yorkshire | Oval | 1924 |
| | | 215 | Kent v Somerset | Gravesend | 1925 |
| | | 217 | Kent v Northamptonshire | Northampton | 1926 |
| | | 219 | MCC v New South Wales | Sydney | 1929–30 |
| | | 224 | Kent v New Zealanders | Canterbury | 1931 |
| | | 229 | Kent v Surrey | Oval | 1935 |
| Woolmer, R.A. | | 203 | Kent v Sussex | Tunbridge Wells | 1982 |
| Worrell, F.M.M. | (7) | 308* | Barbados v Trinidad | Bridgetown | 1943–44 |
| | | 255* | Barbados v Trinidad | Port-of-Spain | 1945–46 |
| | | 223* | Commonwealth XI v Indian XI | Kanpur | 1949–50 |
| | | 241* | West Indians v Leicestershire | Leicester | 1950 |
| | | 261 | West Indies v England | Nottingham | 1950 |
| | | 285 | Commonwealth XI v Ceylon | Colombo | 1950–51 |
| | | 237 | West Indies v India | Kingston | 1952–53 |
| Worthington, T.S. | (2) | 200* | Derbyshire v Worcestershire | Chesterfield | 1933 |
| | | 238* | Derbyshire v Sussex | Derby | 1937 |
| Wyatt, R.E.S. | (2) | 232 | Warwickshire v Derbyshire | Birmingham | 1937 |
| | | 201* | Warwickshire v Lancashire | Birmingham | 1937 |
| Wynne, O.E. | | 200* | Transvaal v Border | Johannesburg | 1946–47 |
| Wynyard, E.G. | (2) | 268 | Hampshire v Yorkshire | Southampton | 1896 |
| | | 225 | Hampshire v Somerset | Taunton | 1899 |
| Yajurvindra Singh | | 214 | Saurashtra v Maharashtra | Satara | 1979–80 |
| Yallop, G.N. | (3) | 246 | Victoria v Queensland | Melbourne | 1982–83 |
| | | 220 | Victoria v Pakistanis | Melbourne | 1983–84 |
| | | 268 | Australia v Pakistan | Melbourne | 1983–84 |
| Yashpal Sharma | | 201* | Indians v Victoria | Geelong | 1980–81 |
| Young, R.A. | | 220 | Sussex v Essex | Leyton | 1905 |
| Younis Ahmed | | 221* | Worcestershire v Nottinghamshire | Nottingham | 1979 |
| Zafar Altaf | | 268 | Lahore Greens v Bahawalpur | Lahore | 1965–66 |
| Zaheer Abbas | (10) | 202 | PIA v Karachi Blues | Karachi | 1970–71 |
| | | 274 | Pakistan v England | Birmingham | 1971 |
| | | 240 | Pakistan v England | Oval | 1974 |
| | | 216* | Gloucestershire v Surrey | Oval | 1976 |
| | | 230* | Gloucestershire v Kent | Canterbury | 1976 |
| | | 205* | Gloucestershire v Sussex | Cheltenham | 1977 |
| | | 213 | Gloucestershire v Sussex | Hove | 1978 |
| | | 235* | Pakistan v India | Lahore | 1978–79 |
| | | 215* | Gloucestershire v Somerset | Bath | 1981 |
| | | 215 | Pakistan v India | Lahore | 1982–83 |
| Zakir Butt | | 290 | Railways v NWFP | Peshawar | 1972–73 |
| Ziebell, K.P. | | 212* | Queensland v Victoria | Melbourne | 1966–67 |

# HUNDREDS BY NUMBER ELEVEN BATSMEN

| | | | | |
|---|---|---|---|---|
| 163 | T.P.B. Smith | Essex v Derbyshire | Chesterfield | 1947 |
| 126 | W.C. Smith | MCC v Barbados | Bridgetown | 1912–13 |

| 121 | S.N. Banerjee | Indians v Surrey | Oval | 1946 |

*He added 249 for the last wicket with the number 10, C.T. Sarwate who made 124\* – the only instance of numbers 10 and 11 scoring centuries in the same innings.*

| 115* | G.B. Stevenson | Yorkshire v Warwickshire | Birmingham | 1982 |
| 112* | A. Fielder | Kent v Worcestershire | Stourbridge | 1909 |
| 109* | Maqsood Kundi | MCB v National Bank | Lahore | 1981–82 |
| 106* | T.J. Hastings | Victoria v South Australia | Melbourne | 1902–03 |
| 101 | A.E.R. Gilligan | Cambridge University v Sussex | Hove | 1919 |
| 100* | Ahsan-ul-Haq | Muslims v Sikhs | Lahore | 1923–24 |

# HUNDREDS BATTING WITH A RUNNER

| A. Mynn | 125* | South v North | Leicester | 1836 |

*Injured leg during pre-match practice; the injury became sufficiently serious for amputation to be considered and he was unable to play again until 1838.*

| A.D.E. Rippon | 105* | Somerset v Sussex | Bath | 1914 |
| G.E.V. Crutchley | 181 | Free Foresters v Cambridge University | Cambridge | 1919 |
| R.C.M. Kimpton | 102 | Oxford University v Lancashire | Oxford | 1936 |

*Scored in 70 minutes with 22 fours and no chances*

| Amin Ashraf | 113 | Railways & Quetta v Karachi University | Karachi | 1960–61 |

*Strained a thigh muscle in the first over of his innings*

| R. Subba Row | 137 | England v Australia | Oval | 1961 |

*Sustained a groin injury in the first innings*

| B.R. Taylor | 173 | Wellington v Otago | Dunedin | 1972–73 |

*Injured his left knee*

| B. Hassan | 106 | Nottinghamshire v Kent | Canterbury | 1977 |
| Shafiq Ahmed | 160 | National Bank v Railways | Lahore | 1978–79 |
| D.L. Amiss | 127 | Warwickshire v Derbyshire | Derby | 1981 |

*Strained a hamstring during his first innings (109)*

| G. Fowler | 126 / 128* | Lancashire v Warwickshire | Southport | 1982 |

*Strained his thigh while fielding on the first day. He also had a runner for the last 100 runs of his first innings of 126. Only instance of two hundreds in a match being scored with the aid of a runner.*

# HUNDRED ON FIRST-CLASS DEBUT

| Aamer Malik | 132* / 110 | Lahore A v Railways | Lahore | 1979–80 |
| Aftab Butt | 151 | Multan v Income Tax Department | Multan | 1977–78 |
| Allan, P.J. | 138 | Rhodesia B v Eastern Province B | Salisbury | 1978–79 |
| Allsopp, A.H. | 117 | New South Wales v MCC | Sydney | 1929–30 |
| Anwar Hussain | 120 | Assam v Orissa | Cuttack | 1965–66 |
| Asif Ahmed | 148 | Universities v East Pakistan | Karachi | 1959–60 |
| Asif Ali | 109* | WAPDA v Universities | Hyderabad | 1975–76 |
| Aslett, D.G. | 146* | Kent v Hampshire | Bournemouth | 1981 |
| Babar Basharat | 111 | HBFC v M.C. Bank | Hyderabad | 1976–77 |
| Balaji, S. | 100 | Railways v Vidarbha | Nagpur | 1976–77 |
| Balbir Singh | 102* | Southern Punjab v Northern Punjab | Ferozepur | 1967–68 |
| Banks, D.A. | 100 | Worcestershire v Oxford University | Oxford | 1983 |
| Barker, G. | 107* | Essex v Canadians | Clacton | 1954 |
| Barrass, A.E.O. | 113 | Western Australia v Victoria | Perth | 1938–39 |
| Bhandari, P.N. | 102 | Bihar v Assam | Jamshedpur | 1959–60 |
| Bilby, G.P. | 132 | Wellington v Central Districts | Wellington | 1962–63 |
| Bill, O.W. | 115 | New South Wales v Tasmania | Sydney | 1929–30 |
| Bisgood, B.L. | 116* | Somerset v Worcestershire | Worcester | 1907 |
| Bloomfield, H.O. | 107* | Surrey v Northamptonshire | Northampton | 1921 |
| Bogle, J. | 145 | New South Wales v Victoria | Sydney | 1918–19 |
| Bradman, D.G. | 118 | New South Wales v South Australia | Adelaide | 1927–28 |
| Breakey, J.C. | 123 | Transvaal B v N.E. Transvaal | Johannesburg | 1970–71 |
| Briggs, R. | 121 | New South Wales v Western Australia | Perth | 1952–53 |
| Brook-Smith, W. | 112* | Auckland v Hawke's Bay | Auckland | 1904–05 |
| Browne, C.F. | 137 | Barbados v Trinidad | Bridgetown | 1919–20 |

| | | | | |
|---|---|---|---|---|
| Bryan, G.J. | 124 | Kent v Nottinghamshire | Nottingham | 1920 |
| Burrow, K. | 106 | N. Transvaal v Griqualand West | Pretoria | 1971–72 |
| Byrne, J.F. | 100 | Warwickshire v Leicestershire | Birmingham | 1897 |
| Callaway, N. F. | 207 | New South Wales v Queensland | Sydney | 1914–15 |
| Carew, B.J. | 107 | Rhodesia v Transvaal | Salisbury | 1949–50 |
| Chadwick, D. | 129 | Western Australia v Queensland | Brisbane | 1963–64 |
| Chambers, J.L. | 122 | Victoria v Tasmania | Melbourne | 1949–50 |
| Chandrabhan, M.T. | 163 | Gujarat v Bombay | Poona | 1957–58 |
| Chapman, A.P.F. | 118 | Cambridge University v Essex | Cambridge | 1920 |
| Cheshire, F.W. | 107 | Border v Orange Free State | Johannesburg | 1923–24 |
| Chidgey, G.J. | 113 | Free Foresters v Cambridge University | Cambridge | 1962 |
| Churi, N. | 178* | Railways v Madhya Pradesh | Delhi | 1982–83 |
| Clark, E.A. | 100* | Middlesex v Cambridge University | Cambridge | 1959 |
| Clarke, J.K. | 112* | Rhodesia v Western Province | Cape Town | 1967–68 |
| Clarke, M.I.C. | 153 | Barbados v Trinidad | Port-of-Spain | 1940–41 |
| Claughton, J.A. | 112 | Oxford University v Gloucestershire | Oxford | 1976 |
| Commins, J. | 116* | SA Defence Force v Eastern Province | Port Elizabeth | 1984–85 |
| Contractor, N.J. | 152<br>102* } Gujarat v Baroda | | Baroda | 1952–53 |
| Dawson, J.M. | 138 | R.S. Lucas' XI v Barbados | Bridgetown | 1894–95 |
| Day, S.H. | 101* | Kent v Gloucestershire | Cheltenham | 1897 |
| De Lange, C.B.L. | 112 | Northern Transvaal B v Border | East London | 1981–82 |
| Desai, K.R. | 117 | Gujarat v Maharashtra | Jalgaon | 1960–61 |
| Dilawar Hussain | 112 | Muslims v Europeans | Lahore | 1924–25 |
| Dillon, E.W. | 108 | London County v Worcestershire | Crystal Palace | 1900 |
| Doggart, G.H.G. | 215* | Cambridge University v Lancashire | Cambridge | 1948 |
| Draper, R.G. | 114 | Eastern Province v Orange Free State | Port Elizabeth | 1945–46 |
| Durani, S.A. | 108 | Saurashtra v Gujarat | Ahmedabad | 1953–54 |
| Du Toit, A. | 102 | Boland v Border | Stellenbosch | 1980–81 |
| Dutta, M. | 102 | Bihar v Orissa | Patna | 1980–81 |
| Dyer, D.V. | 185 | Natal v Western Province | Durban | 1939–40 |
| Ebden, C.H.M. | 137 | Cambridge University v<br>H.D.G. Leveson Gower's XI | Cambridge | 1902 |
| Ellis, R.N. | 100 | Victoria v Tasmania | Hobart | 1927–28 |
| Fairbairn, A. | 108 | Middlesex v Somerset | Taunton | 1947 |
| Falkner, N.J. | 101* | Surrey v Cambridge University | Banstead | 1984 |
| Favell, L.E. | 164 | South Australia v New South Wales | Adelaide | 1951–52 |
| Fernley, D.L. | 106 | Eastern Province v N.E. Transvaal | Pretoria | 1954–55 |
| Fontaine, F.E. | 118 | Victoria v Tasmania | Hobart | 1930–31 |
| Forssberg, E.B. | 143 | New South Wales v Queensland | Sydney | 1920–21 |
| Francis, J.C. | 135 | Victoria v Tasmania | Launceston | 1932–33 |
| Frank, C.N. | 108 | Transvaal v AIF | Johannesburg | 1919–20 |
| Freakes, H.D. | 122* | Eastern Province v Natal | Johannesburg | 1931–32 |
| | | *Aged 17 years 10 months, he carried his bat through the innings* | | |
| Ghani, M.T. | 104 | Commerce Bank v Khairpur | Karachi | 1973–74 |
| Gill, J.R. | 106 | Ireland v MCC | Dublin | 1948 |
| Gilmour, G.J. | 122 | New South Wales v South Australia | Sydney | 1971–72 |
| Gimblett, H. | 123 | Somerset v Essex | Frome | 1935 |
| Gooden, N.L. | 102 | South Australia v Western Australia | Adelaide | 1912–13 |
| Gordon, C.S. | 121 | Victoria v New South Wales | Melbourne | 1869–70 |
| Grangel, H.H.E. | 108 | Victoria v Tasmania | Melbourne | 1935–36 |
| Gursharan Singh | 101* | India U-22 XI v England XI | Poona | 1981–82 |
| Hall, P.M. | 101 | Oxford University v Free Foresters | Oxford | 1919 |
| Hallebone, J. | 202 | Victoria v Tasmania | Melbourne | 1951–52 |
| Hamence, R.A. | 121 | South Australia v Tasmania | Adelaide | 1935–36 |
| Hammond-Chambers-<br>Borgnis, R.P. | 101 | Combined Services v New Zealanders | Portsmouth | 1937 |
| Harbottle, M.N. | 156 | Army v Oxford University | Camberley | 1938 |
| Harris, T.A. | 114* | Griqualand West v Orange Free State | Kimberley | 1933–34 |
| | | *Aged 17 years 4 months* | | |
| Harvey-Walker, A.J. | 110* | Derbyshire v Oxford University | Burton upon Trent | 1971 |
| Haysman, M.D. | 126 | South Australia v Queensland | Adelaide | 1982–83 |
| Hearn, P. | 124 | Kent v Warwickshire | Gillingham | 1947 |
| Higgs, K.A. | 101 | Sussex v Worcestershire | Hove | 1920 |
| Hilder, A.L. | 103* | Kent v Essex | Gravesend | 1924 |
| Hill, J.E. | 139* | Warwickshire v Nottinghamshire | Nottingham | 1894 |
| Hone, B.W. | 137 | South Australia v Victoria | Adelaide | 1928–29 |

| Name | Score | Match | Venue | Year |
|---|---|---|---|---|
| Howell, I.L. | 112 | Eastern Province B v Border | Port Elizabeth | 1981–82 |
| Hughes, K.J. | 119 | Western Australia v New South Wales | Perth | 1975–76 |
| Human, J.H. | 158* | Cambridge University v H.D.G. Leveson Gower's XI | Eastbourne | 1932 |
| Hyett, F.W. | 108* | Victoria v Tasmania | Melbourne | 1914–15 |
| Imran Bucha | 120 | Servis Industries v Lahore B | Lahore | 1976–77 |
| Ireland, R.N. | 152* | Natal B v Rhodesia | Salisbury | 1967–68 |
| Jahangir Khan, M | 108 | Muslims v Hindus | Lahore | 1928–29 |
| John, G. | 111 | W. Shepherd's XI v British Guiana | Georgetown | 1909–10 |
| Johnson, J.S. | 146* | Minor Counties v Indians | Wellington | 1979 |
| Jurangpathy, R.B. | 102 | Sri Lanka U-23 v Pakistan U-23 | Kandy | 1984–85 |
| Kanitkar, H.S. | 151* | Maharashtra v Saurashtra | Poona | 1963–64 |
| Kent, M.F. | 140 | Queensland v New South Wales | Brisbane | 1974–75 |
| Kerr, C. A. | 122 | Auckland v Wellington | Auckland | 1941–42 |
| Kerr, E.A.D. | 112 | Victoria v Tasmania | Launceston | 1946–47 |
| Khurshid Sheikh | 101 | Pakistanis v Central Zone | Nagpur | 1952–53 |
| Krishna, S. | 108 | Mysore v Kerala | Mysore | 1961–62 |
| Lacey, H.S. | 102 | Transvaal v Rhodesia | Salisbury | 1945–46 |
| Laheji | 144 | Saurashtra v Maharashtra | Rajkot | 1954–55 |
| Lawson, R.J. | 119 | Victoria v Tasmania | Hobart | 1930–31 |
| Lazard, T.N. | 117 | Western Province B v OFS | Bloemfontein | 1983–84 |
| Leabeater, L. | 128 | New South Wales v Tasmania | Sydney | 1929–30 |
| Leslie, C.F.H. | 111* | Oxford University v MCC | Oxford | 1881 |
| Levy, R.M. | 129 | Queensland v Victoria | Brisbane | 1928–29 |
| Lilley, A.W. | 100* | Essex v Nottinghamshire | Nottingham | 1978 |
| Lockett, A. | 154 | Minor Counties v West Indians | Exeter | 1928 |
| Loxton, J.F.C. | 100 | Queensland v Western Australia | Perth | 1966–67 |
| Loxton, S.J.E. | 232* | Victoria v Queensland | Melbourne | 1946–47 |
| Lucas, M.J. | 107 | Queensland v New South Wales | Brisbane | 1968–69 |
| Lukeman, E. | 118 | New South Wales v South Australia | Adelaide | 1946–47 |
| Lyons, R.B. | 102 | Queensland v Victoria | Brisbane | 1955–56 |
| MacLaren, A.C. | 108 | Lancashire v Sussex | Hove | 1890 |
| MacLeod, D.N. | 117 | Central Districts v Wellington | Wanganui | 1956–57 |
| McMullan, J.J.M. | 157* | Otago v Southland | Dunedin | 1917–18 |
| McPetrie, W.M. | 123 | Victoria v Tasmania | Melbourne | 1904–05 |
| Mahmood Ahmed | 170 | Lahore B v Sargodha | Lahore | 1973–74 |
| Majid Khan | 111* | Lahore B v Khairpur | Lahore | 1961–62 |
| Malcolm, B.W. | 181* | Bengal v Madras | Calcutta | 1938–39 |
| Maqsood Ahmed | 144 | Southern Punjab v Northern India | Lahore | 1944–45 |
| Marks, N. | 180 | New South Wales v South Australia | Sydney | 1958–59 |
| Marsden, T. | 227 | Sheffield & Leicester v Nottingham | Sheffield | 1826 |
| Marsh, R.W. | 104 | Western Australia v West Indians | Perth | 1968–69 |
| Marshal, H.W. | 105 | Argentina v MCC | Hurlingham | 1926–27 |
| Martin, F.C. | 145 | Western Province v Eastern Province | Cape Town | 1929–30 |
| Martin, F.R. | 195 | Jamaica v Barbados | Bridgetown | 1924–25 |
| Marx, W.F.E. | 240 | Transvaal v Griqualand West | Johannesburg | 1920–21 |
| Maynard, A. | 200* | Trinidad v MCC | Port-of-Spain | 1934–35 |
| Maynard, M.P. | 102 | Glamorgan v Yorkshire | Swansea | 1985 |
| Medlycott, K.T. | 117* | Surrey v Cambridge University | Banstead | 1984 |
| Metcalfe, A.A. | 122 | Yorkshire v Nottinghamshire | Bradford | 1983 |
| Miller, K.R. | 181 | Victoria v Tasmania | Melbourne | 1937–38 |
| Miller, N. | 124 | Surrey v Sussex | Hove | 1899 |
| Mitchell, W.J. | 127* | Northern Districts v Pakistanis | Hamilton | 1964–65 |
| Mitra, A. | 137* | Bengal v Bihar | Dhanbad | 1983–84 |
| Mitter, J. | 136 | Bengal v Bihar | Jamshedpur | 1950–51 |
| Modi, R.S. | 144 | Parsees v Europeans | Bombay | 1941–42 |
| Mohammad Akram | 111 | Khairpair v Quetta | Sukkur | 1968–69 |
| Mohammad Ishaq | 112 | Lahore v WAPDA | Lahore | 1984–85 |
| Mohinder Singh | 132 | Uttar Pradesh v Rajasthan | Udaipur | 1955–56 |
| Morris, A.R. | 148 / 111 | New South Wales v Queensland | Sydney | 1940–41 |
| Morton, H.G.S. | 135* | Queensland v Victoria | Melbourne | 1904–05 |
| Moxon, M.D. | 116 | Yorkshire v Essex | Leeds | 1981 |
| Moyes, A.G. | 104 | South Australia v Western Australia | Adelaide | 1912–13 |
| Mullarkey, D. | 130 | New South Wales v Queensland | Brisbane | 1923–24 |
| Murray-Wood, W. | 106* | Oxford University v Gloucestershire | Oxford | 1936 |
| Mustafi, S. | 101 | Bengal v United Provinces | Benares | 1941–42 |

| Nichol, M. | 104 | Worcestershire v West Indians | Worcester | 1928 |
|---|---|---|---|---|
| Nicholson, W.G. | 101 | Scotland v Ireland | Dublin | 1929 |
| Nutt, R.N. | 102 | New South Wales v South Australia | Adelaide | 1931–32 |
| O'Donnell, S.P. | 130 | Victoria v South Australia | Melbourne | 1983–84 |
| O'Halloran, J.P. | 128* | Victoria v South Australia | Melbourne | 1896–97 |
| Ongley, J.A. | 110 | Wellington v Otago | Wellington | 1938–39 |
| Pai, M.D. | 107 | Hindus v Europeans | Bombay | 1906–07 |
| Parija, L.I. | 103 | Orissa v Assam | Cuttack | 1952–53 |
| Parikh, S. | 104 | Baroda v Gujarat | Ahmedabad | 1981–82 |
| Parnaby, A.H. | 101 | Minor Counties v Oxford University | Oxford | 1939 |
| Passailaigue, C.C. | 183 | Jamaica v MCC | Kingston | 1929–30 |
| Patel, B.R. | 131* | Bombay v Western India States | Poona | 1935–36 |
| Patel, U. | 105* | East Africa v Indians | Kampala | 1966–67 |
| Patel, Y.B. | 101* | Mysore v Hyderabad | Hyderabad | 1961–62 |
| Payne, C.A.L. | 101 | MCC v Derbyshire | Lord's | 1905 |
| Penter, C.E. | 112 | Western Australia v New South Wales | Sydney | 1979–80 |
| Persaud, C.S. | 174 | British Guiana v Barbados | Georgetown | 1937–38 |
| Pervez Akhtar | 120 | Lahore B v Railways B | Lahore | 1971–72 |
| Pinch, F.B. | 138* | Glamorgan v Worcestershire | Swansea | 1921 |
| Pinkus, H.W. | 102* | Tasmania v South Australia | Hobart | 1956–57 |
| Poddar, P.C. | 141 | Bengal v Assam | Gauhati | 1960–61 |
| Pretty, H.C. | 124 | Surrey v Nottinghamshire | Oval | 1899 |
| Pye, L.W. | 166 | New South Wales v Queensland | Brisbane | 1896–97 |
| Rasikh Akhtar | 100 | Income Tax Dept v Multan | Multan | 1977–78 |
| Rehani, Z.A. | 103 | Hyderabad Ed Board v Sind U. | Hyderabad | 1964–65 |
| Reid, T.B. | 103 | Eastern Province B v OFS | Bloemfontein | 1977–78 |
| Rhys, H.R.J. | 149 | Free Foresters v Cambridge University | Cambridge | 1929 |
| Ricketts, J. | 195* | Lancashire v Surrey | Oval | 1867 |
| Rock, H.O. | 127 | New South Wales v South Australia | Sydney | 1924–25 |
| Rodrigo, M. | 135* | Ceylon v West Indians | Colombo | 1948–49 |
| Roy, Pankaj | 112* | Bengal v United Provinces | Calcutta | 1946–47 |
| Roy, Pranab | 105 | Bengal v Assam | Dibrugarh | 1978–79 |
| Sahasrabudhe, P. | 133 | Vidarbha v Madhya Pradesh | Bersingpur | 1968–69 |
| Sajid Abbasi | 113 | PWD v Sukkur | Karachi | 1974–75 |
| Sampath, C. | 123 | Trinidad v Barbados | Bridgetown | 1948–49 |
| Sampson, H.C. | 119 | Central Districts v Wellington | Wellington | 1970–71 |
| Sarfraz Khan | 107* | Punjab University v Governor's XI | Lahore | 1967–68 |
| Sathasivam, M. | 101 | The Rest v Muslims | Bombay | 1944–45 |
| Saxena, R. | 113* | Delhi v Southern Punjab | Delhi | 1960–61 |
| Scott, D.A. | 110* | Natal B v Griqualand West | Durban | 1983–84 |
| Scott, J.G.C. | 137 | Sussex v Oxford University | Eastbourne | 1907 |
| Scott, V.J. | 122 | Auckland v Canterbury | Auckland | 1937–38 |
| Seabrook, W.J.S. | 165 | New South Wales v Victoria | Melbourne | 1984–85 |
| Sengupta, A.K. | 100* | Services v West Indians | Poona | 1958–59 |
| Sergeant, L.C. | 127 | Leeward Islands v MCC | St John's | 1967–68 |
| Seth, J.N. | 179 | Delhi v Southern Punjab | Delhi | 1949–50 |
| Shamim Khawaja | 125 | United Provinces v Central India | Allahabad | 1939–40 |
| Shepherd, B.K. | 103* | Western Australia v Queensland | Perth | 1955–56 |
| Shepherd, D.R. | 108 | Gloucestershire v Oxford University | Oxford | 1965 |
| Shipperd, G. | 131* | Western Australia v Victoria | Perth | 1984–85 |
| Shoaib Mohammad | 113 | PIA v Baluchistan | Karachi | 1976–77 |
| Siedle, J.R. | 127 | Western Province v Eastern Province | Cape Town | 1955–56 |
| Slack, J.K.E. | 135 | Cambridge University v Middlesex | Cambridge | 1954 |
| Smith, K.F.H. | 141* | Wellington v Central Districts | Wellington | 1953–54 |
| Snedden, C.A. | 119 | Auckland v Hawke's Bay | Auckland | 1920–21 |
| Solomon, J.S. | 114* | British Guiana v Jamaica | Georgetown | 1956–57 |
| Stocks, F.W. | 114 | Nottinghamshire v Kent | Nottingham | 1946 |
| Stollmeyer, J.B. | 118 | R.S. Grant's XI v British Guiana | Georgetown | 1938–39 |
| Storie, A.C. | 106 | Northamptonshire v Hampshire | Northampton | 1985 |
| Talbot, R.O. | 105 | Canterbury v Otago | Dunedin | 1922–23 |
| Tasnim Abidi | 150* | Sargodha v Faisalabad | Faisalabad | 1983–84 |
| Taylor, M.D. | 107 | Victoria v Queensland | Melbourne | 1977–78 |
| Taylor, N.R. | 110 | Kent v Sri Lankans | Canterbury | 1979 |
| Tennyson, Hon L.H. | 110 | MCC v Oxford University | Lord's | 1913 |
| Thomas, M.R. | 164 | Tasmania v Australian Services | Hobart | 1945–46 |
| Tindill, E.W.T. | 106 | Wellington v Auckland | Auckland | 1932–33 |
| Tuck, G.S. | 125 | Royal Navy v New Zealanders | Portsmouth | 1927 |

| | | | | |
|---|---|---|---|---|
| Turner, J.B. | 106 | Minor Counties v Pakistanis | Jesmond | 1974 |
| Tyson, C.T. | 100* | Yorkshire v Hampshire | Southampton | 1921 |
| Van der Linden, W.J. | 122 | Transvaal B v Natal B | Johannesburg | 1974–75 |
| Venn, H. | 151 | Warwickshire v Worcestershire | Birmingham | 1919 |
| Viswanath, G.R. | 230 | Mysore v Andhra | Vijayawada | 1967–68 |
| Walker, I.D. | 102 | Middlesex v Surrey Club | Oval | 1862 |
| Watson, G. | 175 | Canterbury v Otago | Christchurch | 1880–81 |
| Watson-Smith, R. | 183* | Border v Orange Free State | Bloemfontein | 1969–70 |
| Watt, D.G. | 105 | Otago v Canterbury | Christchurch | 1943–44 |
| Weekes, K.H. | 106 | Jamaica v Oxford & Cambridge U's | Kingston | 1938–39 |
| Wellham, D.M. | 100 | New South Wales v Victoria | Melbourne | 1980–81 |
| Whitehead, R. | 131* | Lancashire v Nottinghamshire | Manchester | 1908 |
| Whitehead, T.H. | 107* | Eastern Province v Orange Free State | Port Elizabeth | 1921–22 |
| Whitehouse, J. | 173 | Warwickshire v Oxford University | Oxford | 1971 |
| Wiener, J.M. | 106 | Victoria v Queensland | Brisbane | 1977–78 |
| Williams, O. | 100 | Leeward Islands v Jamaica | Kingston | 1958–59 |
| Williams, S.I. | 127 | Leeward Islands v Windward Islands | St John's | 1979–80 |
| Wilson, E.R. | 117* | A.J. Webbe's XI v Cambridge U. | Cambridge | 1899 |
| Winslow, L. | 124 | Sussex v Gloucestershire | Hove | 1875 |
| Wood, B.B. | 108 | Canterbury v Wellington | Wellington | 1907–08 |
| Wootton, S.E. | 105 | Victoria v Tasmania | Hobart | 1923–24 |
| Zaki Ahmed | 123 | Income Tax Dept v Multan | Multan | 1975–76 |
| Zakir Butt | 101 | Lahore Greens v Punjab University | Lahore | 1967–68 |
| Zulfiqar Chandhri | 147 | Hyderabad v Sukkur | Hyderabad | 1983–84 |

## HUNDRED IN SECOND MATCH (HAVING NOT BATTED IN THEIR FIRST)

| | | | | |
|---|---|---|---|---|
| P.F. Harvey | 125* | Nottinghamshire v Derbyshire | Nottingham | 1947 |
| B. Chanda | 113 | Bengal v Madhya Pradesh | Calcutta | 1955–56 |
| N.F. Saldana | 142 | Maharashtra v Saurashtra | Nasik | 1965–66 |
| K.P. Asher | 105 | Associated Cement Co v Hyderabad | Hyderabad | 1971–72 |
| A. Mudkavi | 100* | Rajasthan v Orissa | Rourkela | 1983–84 |

## HUNDREDS IN FIRST THREE INNINGS

| | | | | |
|---|---|---|---|---|
| | 114* | British Guiana v Jamaica | Georgetown | 1956–57 |
| J.S. Solomon | 108 | British Guiana v Barbados | Georgetown | 1956–57 |
| | 121 | British Guiana v Pakistanis | Georgetown | 1957–58 |

## HUNDREDS IN FIRST TWO INNINGS

| | | | | |
|---|---|---|---|---|
| A.R. Morris | 148 / 111 | New South Wales v Queensland | Sydney | 1940–41 |
| N.J. Contractor | 152 / 102* | Gujarat v Baroda | Baroda | 1952–53 |
| N. Marks | 180 | New South Wales v South Australia | Sydney | 1958–59 |
| | 103 | New South Wales v Victoria | Melbourne | 1958–59 |
| P.C. Poddar | 141 | Bengal v Assam | Gauhati | 1960–61 |
| | 104 | Bengal v Orissa | Calcutta | 1960–61 |
| R. Watson-Smith | 183* | Border v Orange Free State | Bloemfontein | 1969–70 |
| | 125* | Border v Griqualand West | East London | 1969–70 |
| | | *He scored 310 runs in first-class cricket before being dismissed* | | |
| Aamer Malik | 132* / 110 | Lahore A v Railways | Lahore | 1979–80 |

*A. Fairbairn (Middlesex) scored 7 and 108 v Somerset at Taunton, and 15 and 110\* v Nottinghamshire at Nottingham in his first two first-class matches (1947).*
*D. Chadwick (Western Australia) scored 129 v Queensland at Brisbane, and 58 and 114 v Victoria at Melbourne in his first two first-class matches (1963–64).*
*Zaki Ahmed scored 123 (Income Tax v Multan at Multan) and 21 and 100\* (Punjab B v PIA at Karachi) in 1975–76, in his first two first-class matches. T.N. Lazard (Western Province) scored 117 and 5 v Orange Free State at Bloemfontein, and 121 and 0\* v Transvaal B at Constantia in his first two first-class matches (1983–84).*

# HIGHEST INNINGS ON DEBUT

| | | | | |
|---|---|---|---|---|
| 240 | W.F.E. Marx | Transvaal v Griqualand West | Johannesburg | 1920–21 |
| 232* | S.J.E. Loxton | Victoria v Queensland | Melbourne | 1946–47 |
| 230 | G.R. Viswanath | Mysore v Andhra | Vijayawada | 1967–68 |
| 227 | T. Marsden | Sheffield & Leicester v Nottingham | Sheffield | 1826 |
| 215* | G.H.G. Doggart | Cambridge University v Lancashire | Cambridge | 1948 |
| 207 | N. F. Callaway | New South Wales v Queensland | Sydney | 1914–15 |
| 202 | J. Hallebone | Victoria v Tasmania | Melbourne | 1951–52 |
| 200* | A. Maynard | Trinidad v MCC | Port-of-Spain | 1934–35 |

# HUNDRED IN ONLY FIRST-CLASS MATCH

| | | | | |
|---|---|---|---|---|
| N. F. Callaway | 207 | New South Wales v Queensland | Sydney | 1914–15 |
| S.E. Wootton | 105 | Victoria v Tasmania | Hobart | 1923–24 |
| H.H.E. Grangel | 108 | Victoria v Tasmania | Melbourne | 1935–36 |
| R.P. Hammond-Chambers-Borgnis | 101 | Combined Services v New Zealanders | Portsmouth | 1937 |
| M.N. Harbottle | 156 | Army v Oxford University | Camberley | 1938 |
| D.G. Watt | 105 | Otago v Canterbury | Christchurch | 1943–44 |
| J.R. Gill | 106 | Ireland v MCC | Dublin | 1948 |
| Laheji | 144 | Saurashtra v Maharashtra | Rajkot | 1954–55 |
| J.B. Turner | 106 | Minor Counties v Pakistanis | Jesmond | 1974 |
| J.S. Johnson | 146* | Minor Counties v Indians | Wellington | 1979 |

# HUNDRED IN FIRST COUNTY MATCH
Having already made first-class debut

| | | | | |
|---|---|---|---|---|
| Abercrombie, C.H. | 126 | Hampshire v Oxford University | Southampton | 1913 |
| Baldry, D.O. | 151 | Hampshire v Glamorgan | Portsmouth | 1959 |
| Bartlett, H.T. | 122 | Sussex v Cambridge University | Worthing | 1937 |
| Barton, M.R. | 124 | Surrey v MCC | Lord's | 1948 |
| Close, D.B. | 104* | Somerset v Leicestershire | Leicester | 1971 |
| Evans, A.J. | 102 | Kent v Northamptonshire | Northampton | 1921 |
| Fiddian-Green, C.A.F. | 108 | Worcestershire v Essex | Worcester | 1931 |
| Fredericks, R.C. | 145* | Glamorgan v Nottinghamshire | Nottingham | 1971 |
| Gibb, P.A. | 157* | Yorkshire v Nottinghamshire | Sheffield | 1935 |
| Hayward, R.E. | 101* | Hampshire v Sri Lankans | Bournemouth | 1981 |
| Haysman, M.D. | 102* | Leicestershire v Cambridge University | Cambridge | 1984 |
| Javed Miandad | 140* | Glamorgan v Essex | Swansea | 1980 |
| Kanhai, R.B. | 119 | Warwickshire v Cambridge University | Cambridge | 1968 |
| Marlow, F.J.W. | 144 | Sussex v MCC | Lord's | 1891 |
| Miller, K.R. | 102* | Nottinghamshire v Cambridge U. | Nottingham | 1959 |
| Moore, D.N. | 206 | Gloucestershire v Oxford University | Oxford | 1930 |
| Pougher, A.D. | 109* | Leicestershire v Essex | Leyton | 1894 |
| Ranjitsinhji, K.S. | 150 | Sussex v MCC | Lord's | 1895 |
| Sarel, W.G.M. | 103 | Sussex v Oxford University | Hove | 1919 |
| Walford, M.M. | 141* | Somerset v Indians | Taunton | 1946 |
| Wight, P.B. | 109* | Somerset v Australians | Taunton | 1953 |
| Willey, P. | 141* | Leicestershire v Cambridge University | Cambridge | 1984 |
| Younis Ahmed | 158* | Glamorgan v Oxford University | Oxford | 1984 |

# HUNDRED ON DEBUT ABROAD

**ENGLISH TEAMS AND PLAYERS**

IN AUSTRALIA

| | | | | |
|---|---|---|---|---|
| J.T. Brown | 115 | A.E. Stoddart's XI v South Australia | Adelaide | 1894–95 |
| A.C. MacLaren | 228 | A.E. Stoddart's XI v Victoria | Melbourne | 1894–95 |
| K.S. Ranjitsinhji | 189 | A.E. Stoddart's XI v South Australia | Adelaide | 1897–98 |
| G. Gunn | 119 | England v Australia | Sydney | 1907–08 |
| F.R. Foster | 158 | MCC v South Australia | Adelaide | 1911–12 |
| C.A.G. Russell | 156 | MCC v South Australia | Adelaide | 1920–21 |

**IN AUSTRALIA** continued

| | | | | |
|---|---|---|---|---|
| R. Kilner | 103 | MCC v Western Australia | Perth | 1924–25 |
| D.R. Jardine | 109 | MCC v Western Australia | Perth | 1928–29 |
| Nawab of Pataudi, sr | 166 | MCC v Western Australia | Perth | 1932–33 |
| D.B. Close | 108* | MCC v Western Australia | Perth | 1950–51 |
| R.W. Barber | 126 | MCC v Western Australia | Perth | 1965–66 |
| J.M. Parks | 107* | MCC v Western Australia | Perth | 1965–66 |
| B.L. D'Oliveira | 103* | MCC v South Australia | Adelaide | 1970–71 |
| A.J. Lamb | 117 | England XI v Queensland | Brisbane | 1982–83 |

**IN SOUTH AFRICA AND RHODESIA**

| | | | | |
|---|---|---|---|---|
| J.B. Hobbs | 114 | MCC v Western Province | Cape Town | 1909–10 |
| G.B. Legge | 120 | MCC v Orange Free State | Bloemfontein | 1927–28 |
| E. Paynter | 158 | MCC v Griqualand West | Kimberley | 1938–39 |
| N.W.D. Yardley | 142 | MCC v Griqualand West | Kimberley | 1938–39 |
| F.G. Mann | 112 | MCC v Western Province | Cape Town | 1948–49 |
| T.A. Chapman | 124* | Rhodesia v Griqualand West | Salisbury | 1952–53 |
| P.B.H. May | 162 | MCC v Western Province | Cape Town | 1956–57 |
| | | *His first four first-class innings in South Africa were 162, 108\*, 124\* and 206* | | |
| K.F. Barrington | 111 | Surrey v Rhodesia | Salisbury | 1959–60 |
| W. Watson | 100 | Commonwealth XI v Rhodesia | Kitwe | 1962–63 |
| R.W. Barber | 108 | MCC v Rhodesia | Salisbury | 1964–65 |
| M.J. Smith | 116 | D.H. Robins' XI v E. Province | Port Elizabeth | 1972–73 |
| C.T. Radley | 125 | D.H. Robins' XI v E. Province | Port Elizabeth | 1972–73 |
| D.L. Bairstow | 106 | Griqualand West v Natal B | Pietermaritzburg | 1976–77 |
| B. Dudleston | 142 | Rhodesia v W. Province | Cape Town | 1976–77 |

**IN WEST INDIES**

| | | | | |
|---|---|---|---|---|
| E.F. Wright | 123 | Demerara v Trinidad | Georgetown | 1882–83 |
| E. Humphreys | 106 | MCC v Barbados | Bridgetown | 1912–13 |
| G.E. Tyldesley | 101 | Hon L.H. Tennyson's XI v Jamaica | Kingston | 1926–27 |
| C.P. Mead | 103* | Hon L.H. Tennyson's XI v Jamaica | Kingston | 1927–28 |
| E.H. Hendren | 223* | MCC v Barbados | Bridgetown | 1929–30 |
| A. Mitchell | 101* | Yorkshire v Jamaica | Kingston | 1935–36 |
| R.C.M. Kimpton | 113 | Oxford & Cambridge U's v Jamaica | Kingston | 1938–39 |
| W. Watson | 161 | MCC v Jamaica | Kingston | 1953–54 |
| J.M. Parks | 183 | MCC v Berbice | Berbice | 1959–60 |
| B.L. D'Oliveira | 101 | Worcestershire v Jamaica | Montego Bay | 1965–66 |
| G. Boycott | 135 | MCC v President's XI | Bridgetown | 1967–68 |
| B.W. Luckhurst | 105* | Cavaliers v Jamaica | Kingston | 1969–70 |
| D.L. Amiss | 109 | MCC v President's XI | Bridgetown | 1973–74 |
| D.I. Gower | 187 | England XI v Young West Indian XI | Pointe-à-Pierre | 1980–81 |

**IN NEW ZEALAND**

| | | | | |
|---|---|---|---|---|
| A.E. Relf | 157 | Auckland v Canterbury | Christchurch | 1907–08 |
| C.H. Titchmarsh | 154 | MCC v Auckland | Auckland | 1922–23 |
| C. Washbrook | 133 | MCC v Wellington | Wellington | 1946–47 |
| N.W.D. Yardley | 126 | MCC v Otago | Dunedin | 1946–47 |
| T.W. Graveney | 101 | MCC v Canterbury | Christchurch | 1954–55 |
| K.F. Barrington | 126 | England v New Zealand | Auckland | 1962–63 |
| P.H. Parfitt | 131* | England v New Zealand | Auckland | 1962–63 |
| B.R. Knight | 125 | England v New Zealand | Auckland | 1962–63 |
| B.L. D'Oliveira | 100 | England v New Zealand | Christchurch | 1970–71 |
| A.P.E. Knott | 101 | England v New Zealand | Auckland | 1970–71 |
| M.H. Denness | 181 | England v New Zealand | Auckland | 1974–75 |
| B.C. Rose | 107 | England XI v Auckland | Auckland | 1977–78 |
| K. Sharp | 106 | D.H. Robins' XI v N. Districts | Hamilton | 1979–80 |

**IN INDIA**

| | | | | |
|---|---|---|---|---|
| C.P. Johnstone | 135 | Europeans v Indians | Madras | 1925–26 |
| C.J. Barnett | 122 | MCC v Sind | Karachi | 1933–34 |
| D.R. Jardine | 101* | MCC v Sind | Karachi | 1933–34 |
| W.J. Edrich | 140* | Lord Tennyson's XI v Sind | Karachi | 1937–38 |
| Lord Tennyson | 118 | Lord Tennyson's XI v Sind | Karachi | 1937–38 |
| G.M. Emmett | 104 | Commonwealth v Cricket Club of India | Bombay | 1950–51 |
| T.W. Graveney | 101 | MCC v Combined Universities | Bombay | 1951–52 |
| K.F. Barrington | 149* | MCC v Combined Universities | Poona | 1961–62 |

| D.L. Amiss | 109 | International XI v Indian XI | Bombay | 1967–68 |
| K.W.R. Fletcher | 107* | International XI v Indian XI | Bombay | 1967–68 |
| B. Wood | 117 | MCC v Central Zone | Indore | 1972–73 |
| J.M. Brearley | 202 | MCC v West Zone | Poona | 1976–77 |
| G.D. Barlow | 113 | MCC v Central Zone | Jaipur | 1976–77 |
| I.T. Botham | 114 | England v India | Bombay | 1979–80 |

**IN PAKISTAN**

| G.D. Mendis | 124* | International XI v Pakistan XI | Karachi | 1981–82 |
| C. Milburn | 139 | England v Pakistan | Karachi | 1968–69 |

**IN SRI LANKA**

| C.J. Barnett | 116 | MCC v Ceylon | Colombo | 1933–34 |
| J.H. Edrich | 177 | MCC v Ceylon | Colombo | 1968–69 |
| A. Jones | 112 | MCC v Ceylon | Colombo | 1969–70 |
| G.D. Barlow | 118 | MCC v Sri Lanka | Colombo | 1976–77 |
| G. Cook | 104 | England v Board President's XI | Kandy | 1981–82 |

**IN NORTH AMERICA (USA)**

| A.C. MacLaren | 149 | K.S. Ranjitsinhji's XI v Philadelphians | Philadelphia | 1899–1900 |

**IN SOUTH AMERICA (ARGENTINA)**

| L. Green | 102 | Sir J. Cahn's XI v Argentina | Belgrano | 1929–30 |
| R.E.S. Wyatt | 162 | Sir T.E.W. Brinckman's XI v Argentina | Belgrano | 1937–38 |
| H.W. Dods | 104 | Sir T.E.W. Brinckman's XI v Argentina | Belgrano | 1937–38 |

## AUSTRALIAN TEAMS AND PLAYERS

**IN ENGLAND**

| H.H. Massie | 206 | Australians v Oxford University | Oxford | 1882 |
| M.A. Noble | 116* | Australians v South of England | Crystal Palace | 1899 |
| W.M. Woodfull | 201 | Australians v Essex | Leyton | 1926 |
| D.G. Bradman | 236 | Australians v Worcestershire | Worcester | 1930 |
| A.G. Chipperfield | 175 | Australians v Essex | Chelmsford | 1934 |
| K.R. Miller | 105 | Australian Services v England XI | Lord's | 1945 |
| A.R. Morris | 138 | Australians v Worcestershire | Worcester | 1948 |
| G.B. Hole | 112 | Australians v Worcestershire | Worcester | 1953 |
| R.G. Archer | 108 | Australians v Worcestershire | Worcester | 1953 |
| A. Turner | 156 | Australians v Kent | Canterbury | 1975 |

*E.W. Freeman (Australians) scored 116 v Northamptonshire at Northampton in 1968 in his first innings in Britain after playing in two matches without batting.*

**IN SOUTH AFRICA AND RHODESIA/ZIMBABWE**

| C. Hill | 142 | Australia v South Africa | Johannesburg | 1902–03 |
| W.A. Brown | 148 | Australians v Natal | Durban | 1935–36 |
| J.H.W. Fingleton | 121 | Australians v Natal | Durban | 1935–36 |
| S.F. Hird | 130 | E. Province v Griqualand West | Kimberley | 1945–46 |
| | | *Debut for New South Wales in 1931–32* | | |
| J. Moroney | 106 | Australians v Natal | Durban | 1949–50 |
| A.R. Morris | 153 | Australians v Natal | Durban | 1949–50 |
| I.D. Craig | 113 | Australians v Rhodesia | Salisbury | 1957–58 |
| R. Benaud | 117* | Australians v Rhodesia | Salisbury | 1957–58 |
| A.K. Davidson | 100* | Australians v Rhodesia | Salisbury | 1957–58 |
| I.R. Redpath | 139* | Australians v Rhodesia | Salisbury | 1966–67 |
| | | *Carried his bat through innings of 307* | | |
| D.C. Boon | 148 | Young Australians v Zimbabwe | Harare | 1982–83 |

**IN WEST INDIES**

| A.R. Morris | 157 | Australians v Jamaica | Kingston | 1954–55 |
| R.B. Simpson | 111 | Australians v Jamaica | Kingston | 1964–65 |
| R.M. Cowper | 121 | Australians v Jamaica | Kingston | 1964–65 |
| N.C. O'Neill | 125 | Australians v Jamaica | Kingston | 1964–65 |
| G.S. Chappell | 106 | Australians v Jamaica | Kingston | 1972–73 |
| G.M. Wood | 122 | Australians v Leeward Islands | Basseterre | 1977–78 |
| S.B. Smith | 105 | Australians v Guyana | Georgetown | 1983–84 |
| K.C. Wessels | 126* | Australians v Leeward Islands | Basseterre | 1983–84 |

IN NEW ZEALAND

| | | | | |
|---|---|---|---|---|
| E.R. Mayne | 102 | Australians v Canterbury | Christchurch | 1909–10 |
| E.L. Waddy | 130 | Australians v Auckland | Auckland | 1913–14 |
| V.S. Ransford | 159 | Australians v Auckland | Auckland | 1913–14 |
| H.H.L. Kortlang | 113 | Wellington v Auckland | Wellington | 1922–23 |
| J.L. Ellis | 103 | Victoria v Otago | Dunedin | 1924–25 |
| S.G. Barnes | 107 | Australians v Auckland | Auckland | 1945–46 |
| K.R. Miller | 139 | Australians v Auckland | Auckland | 1945–46 |
| A.L. Hassett | 121 | Australians v Auckland | Auckland | 1945–46 |
| P.J.P. Burge | 105 | Australians v Canterbury | Christchurch | 1956–57 |
| B.C. Booth | 105 | Australians v Auckland | Auckland | 1959–60 |
| J.H. Shaw | 120 | Australians v Auckland | Auckland | 1959–60 |

IN INDIA

| | | | | |
|---|---|---|---|---|
| E.A. Williams | 100* | Australian Services v Prince's XI | Delhi | 1945–46 |
| R.B. Simpson | 104 | International XI v President's XI | Bombay | 1961–62 |

IN PAKISTAN

| | | | | |
|---|---|---|---|---|
| R.B. Simpson | 167 | International XI v BCCP XI | Karachi | 1961–62 |

IN SRI LANKA

| | | | | |
|---|---|---|---|---|
| O.W. Bill | 101 | Australians v Ceylon | Colombo | 1935–36 |
| H.J. Mudge | 118 | Sir J. Cahn's XI v Ceylon | Colombo | 1936–37 |
| K.R. Miller | 132 | Australian Services v Ceylon | Colombo | 1945–46 |

IN NORTH AMERICA (USA)

| | | | | |
|---|---|---|---|---|
| W. Bardsley | 117 | Australians v Philadelphians | Manheim | 1913 |

**SOUTH AFRICAN TEAMS AND PLAYERS**

IN ENGLAND

| | | | | |
|---|---|---|---|---|
| C.M.H. Hathorn | 103 | South Africans v Hampshire | Southampton | 1901 |
| H.B. Cameron | 102 | South Africans v Worcestershire | Worcester | 1929 |

IN AUSTRALIA

| | | | | |
|---|---|---|---|---|
| A.W. Nourse | 201* | South Africans v South Australia | Adelaide | 1910–11 |
| L.A. Stricker | 146 | South Africans v South Australia | Adelaide | 1910–11 |
| J.A.J. Christy | 102 | South Africans v Western Australia | Perth | 1931–32 |
| D.J. McGlew | 182 | South Africans v Western Australia | Perth | 1952–53 |
| D.T. Lindsay | 104 | South Africans v South Australia | Adelaide | 1963–64 |

IN NEW ZEALAND

| | | | | |
|---|---|---|---|---|
| B. Mitchell | 123 | South Africans v Auckland | Auckland | 1931–32 |
| H.W. Taylor | 113 | South Africans v Auckland | Auckland | 1931–32 |
| D.J. McGlew | 255* | South Africa v New Zealand | Wellington | 1952–53 |
| A.R.A. Murray | 100* | South Africans v Canterbury | Christchurch | 1952–53 |

**WEST INDIAN TEAMS AND PLAYERS**

IN ENGLAND

| | | | | |
|---|---|---|---|---|
| R.C. Fredericks | 116 | West Indians v D.H. Robins' XI | Eastbourne | 1969 |

IN AUSTRALIA

| | | | | |
|---|---|---|---|---|
| G.St A. Sobers | 119 | West Indians v Western Australia | Perth | 1960–61 |
| R.B. Kanhai | 103 | West Indians v Australian XI | Perth | 1960–61 |
| P.J.L. Dujon | 104* | West Indies v New South Wales | Sydney | 1981–82 |

IN SOUTH AFRICA AND RHODESIA/ZIMBABWE

| | | | | |
|---|---|---|---|---|
| E.H. Mathis | 106 | Young West Indies v Zimbabwe | Salisbury | 1981–82 |
| M.A. Lynch | 105 | West Indies XI v Western Province | Cape Town | 1983–84 |

IN NEW ZEALAND

| | | | | |
|---|---|---|---|---|
| R.E. Marshall | 102* | West Indians v Otago | Dunedin | 1951–52 |
| C.H. Lloyd | 205* | West Indians v South Island | Dunedin | 1968–69 |
| C.G. Greenidge | 116 | West Indians v N. Districts | Hamilton | 1979–80 |

IN INDIA

| | | | | |
|---|---|---|---|---|
| E. de C. Weekes | 172* | West Indians v North Zone | Patiala | 1948–49 |
| F.M.M. Worrell | 109 | Commonwealth XI v Indian U's | Bombay | 1949–50 |
| S.M. Nurse | 106 | E.W. Swanton's XI v Indian XI | Calcutta | 1963–64 |
| I.V.A. Richards | 102* | West Indians v West Zone | Poona | 1974–75 |
| L. Baichan | 158 | West Indians v Combined U's | Indore | 1974–75 |

IN PAKISTAN

| | | | | |
|---|---|---|---|---|
| G.M. Carew | 100 | West Indians v Sind | Karachi | 1948–49 |
| J.K. Holt | 162 | Commonwealth XI v Pakistan | Lahore | 1949–50 |
| A.I. Kallicharran | 103 | World XI v Pakistan XI | Karachi | 1973–74 |
| L. Baichan | 105* | West Indies v Pakistan | Lahore | 1974–75 |
| T.R. Etwaroo | 136 | International XI v Pakistan XI | Lahore | 1981–82 |

IN SRI LANKA

| | | | | |
|---|---|---|---|---|
| A.F. Rae | 116 ⎫ | | | |
| C.L. Walcott | 125* ⎬ West Indians v Ceylon | | Colombo | 1948–49 |
| E.de C. Weekes | 133* ⎭ | | | |
| B.F. Butcher | 152 ⎫ | | | |
| C.H. Lloyd | 138 ⎬ West Indians v Ceylon | | Colombo | 1966–67 |
| G.St A. Sobers | 115 ⎭ | | | |
| I.V.A. Richards | 151 | West Indians v Sri Lanka | Colombo | 1974–75 |
| H.A. Gomes | 108 | West Indians v Sri Lanka | Colombo | 1978–79 |

## NEW ZEALAND TEAMS AND PLAYERS

IN ENGLAND

| | | | | |
|---|---|---|---|---|
| C.C.R. Dacre | 107 | New Zealanders v MCC | Lord's | 1927 |
| T.C. Lowry | 106 | New Zealanders v MCC | Lord's | 1927 |
| M.D. Crowe | 104 | D.B. Close's XI v Pakistanis | Scarborough | 1982 |

IN AUSTRALIA

| | | | | |
|---|---|---|---|---|
| B. Sutcliffe | 142 | New Zealanders v Western Australia | Perth | 1953–54 |
| L.S.M. Miller | 142 | New Zealanders v South Australia | Adelaide | 1953–54 |

IN SOUTH AFRICA AND RHODESIA/ZIMBABWE

| | | | | |
|---|---|---|---|---|
| J.R. Reid | 111 | New Zealanders v Western Province | Cape Town | 1953–54 |
| R.J. Kasper | 122* | Natal B v Transvaal B | Pietermaritzburg | 1970–71 |
| | | *Debut for Auckland in 1966–67* | | |
| T.J. Franklin | 153* | Young New Zealand v Zimbabwe | Harare | 1984–85 |

IN WEST INDIES

| | | | | |
|---|---|---|---|---|
| B.F. Hastings | 100* | New Zealanders v Jamaica | Kingston | 1971–72 |
| M.D. Crowe | 118 | New Zealanders v Shell Award XI | Kingston | 1984–85 |

IN INDIA

| | | | | |
|---|---|---|---|---|
| B.R. Taylor | 105 | New Zealand v India | Calcutta | 1964–65 |
| M.G. Burgess | 102 | Prime Minister's XI v President's XI | Bombay | 1967–68 |
| J.M. Parker | 104 | New Zealand v India | Bombay | 1976–77 |

IN PAKISTAN

| | | | | |
|---|---|---|---|---|
| J.R. Reid | 150* | NZ v Chief Commissioner's XI | Karachi | 1955–56 |
| R.W. Anderson | 103* | NZ v NWFP Chief Minister's XI | Peshawar | 1976–77 |

IN SRI LANKA

| | | | | |
|---|---|---|---|---|
| C.S. Dempster | 112* | Sir J. Cahn's XI v Ceylon | Colombo | 1936–37 |

## INDIAN TEAMS AND PLAYERS

IN ENGLAND

| | | | | |
|---|---|---|---|---|
| S. Wazir Ali | 108* | Indians v Glamorgan | Cardiff | 1932 |
| B.P. Patel | 107 | Indians v D.H. Robins' XI | Eastbourne | 1974 |
| Kapil Dev | 102 | Indians v Northamptonshire | Northampton | 1979 |

**IN AUSTRALIA**

| | | | | |
|---|---|---|---|---|
| F.M. Engineer | 128 | Indians v Western Australia | Perth | 1967–68 |
| M.L. Jaisimha | 101 | India v Australia | Brisbane | 1967–68 |
| C.P.S. Chauhan | 157 | Indians v Victoria | Melbourne | 1977–78 |
| S.M. Patil | 116 | Indians v South Australia | Adelaide | 1980–81 |

**IN WEST INDIES**

| | | | | |
|---|---|---|---|---|
| V.S. Hazare | 153* | Indians v Trinidad | Port-of-Spain | 1952–53 |

**IN NEW ZEALAND**

| | | | | |
|---|---|---|---|---|
| A.L. Wadekar | 122 | Indians v Central Districts | New Plymouth | 1967–68 |
| K. Azad | 127* | Indians v Central Districts | Napier | 1980–81 |

**IN PAKISTAN**

| | | | | |
|---|---|---|---|---|
| V.L. Manjrekar | 138 | Hasan Mahmood's XI v AVM Canon's XI | Karachi | 1953–54 |
| S.G. Adhikari | 128 | Indian Starlets v Lahore | Lahore | 1959–60 |
| S.M. Gavaskar | 165* | Indians v Pakistan Banks | Karachi | 1978–79 |

**IN SRI LANKA**

| | | | | |
|---|---|---|---|---|
| S.V.S. Mani | 101* | Madras v Ceylon | Colombo | 1963–64 |
| M.L. Jaisimha | 117* | Hyderabad Blues v President's XI | Colombo | 1966–67 |

**IN ZIMBABWE**

| | | | | |
|---|---|---|---|---|
| R.J. Shastri | 101 | Young Indians v Zimbabwe | Harare | 1983–84 |

## PAKISTANI TEAMS AND PLAYERS

**IN ENGLAND**

| | | | | |
|---|---|---|---|---|
| Alimuddin | 142 | Pakistanis v Worcestershire | Worcester | 1954 |
| Zaheer Abbas | 110 | Pakistanis v Worcestershire | Worcester | 1971 |
| Shafiq Ahmed | 100* | Pakistanis v Leicestershire | Leicester | 1974 |

**IN AUSTRALIA**

| | | | | |
|---|---|---|---|---|
| Mohammad Ilyas | 126 | Pakistanis v Queensland | Brisbane | 1964–65 |
| Haroon Rashid | 123* | Pakistanis v Queensland | Brisbane | 1976–77 |
| Wasim Raja | 108 | Pakistanis v Queensland | Brisbane | 1976–77 |
| Mudassar Nazar | 104 | Pakistanis v Queensland | Brisbane | 1983–84 |

**IN NEW ZEALAND**

| | | | | |
|---|---|---|---|---|
| Qasim Omar | 114* | Pakistanis v Canterbury | Christchurch | 1984–85 |

**IN WEST INDIES**

| | | | | |
|---|---|---|---|---|
| Wazir Mohammad | 134 | Pakistanis v Barbados | Bridgetown | 1957–58 |
| Majid Khan | 143 | Pakistanis v Leeward Islands | St John's | 1976–77 |

**IN INDIA**

| | | | | |
|---|---|---|---|---|
| Hanif Mohammad | 121 / 109* | Pakistanis v North Zone | Amritsar | 1952–53 |
| Khurshid Sheikh | 101 | Pakistanis v Central Zone | Nagpur | 1952–53 |
| Mushtaq Mohammad | 125* | Pakistanis v Combined Universities | Poona | 1960–61 |
| W. Mathias | 103* | Pakistanis v Combined Universities | Poona | 1960–61 |
| Javed Miandad | 110* | Pakistanis v Central Zone | Jaipur | 1979–80 |

**IN SRI LANKA**

| | | | | |
|---|---|---|---|---|
| Salim Malik | 140* | Pakistan U-23 XI v Sri Lanka U-23 XI | Kandy | 1984–85 |

**IN ZIMBABWE**

| | | | | |
|---|---|---|---|---|
| Mushtaq Mohammad | 101 | PIA v Zimbabwe | Salisbury | 1981–82 |
| Asif Mohammad | 100* | PIA v Zimbabwe | Salisbury | 1981–82 |

# MOST RUNS ADDED DURING A BATSMAN'S INNINGS

The following batsmen were at the wicket whilst over 700 runs were added during an innings in a first-class match. R. Abel carried his bat through the innings when setting the record:

| | | | | |
|---|---|---|---|---|
| 811 | R. Abel (357*) | Surrey v Somerset | Oval | 1899 |
| 801 | W.H. Ponsford (429) | Victoria v Tasmania | Melbourne | 1922–23 |
| 792 | A.C. MacLaren (424) | Lancashire v Somerset | Taunton | 1895 |
| 792 | W.H. Ponsford (437) | Victoria v Queensland | Melbourne | 1927–28 |
| 772 | Hanif Mohammad (499) | Karachi v Bahawalpur | Karachi | 1958–59 |
| 770 | L. Hutton (364) | England v Australia | Oval | 1938 |
| 745 | B.B. Nimbalkar (443*) | Maharashtra v Kathiawar | Poona | 1948–49 |
| 739 | D.G. Bradman (452*) | New South Wales v Queensland | Sydney | 1929–30 |
| 720 | A. Sandham (325) | England v West Indies | Kingston | 1929–30 |
| 712 | Aftab Baloch (428) | Sind v Baluchistan | Karachi | 1973–74 |
| 702 | G.A. Headley (344*) | Jamaica v Lord Tennyson's XI | Kingston | 1931–32 |

## DOUBLE HUNDRED IN EACH INNINGS OF A MATCH

| | | | | |
|---|---|---|---|---|
| Fagg, A.E. | 244 | 202*  Kent v Essex | Colchester | 1938 |

## HUNDRED IN EACH INNINGS OF A MATCH

| | | | | | |
|---|---|---|---|---|---|
| Aamer Malik | | 132* | 110  Lahore A v Railways | Lahore | 1979–80 |
| Adhikari, H.R. | | 129 | 151*  Baroda v Nawanagar | Jamnagar | 1945–46 |
| Aftab Gul | | 137 | 117  Punjab v Sind | Lahore | 1973–74 |
| Agha Zahid | (2) | 118 | 109  Lahore B v Rawalpindi | Lahore | 1973–74 |
| | | 102 | 119  Habib Bank v Railways | Lahore | 1982–83 |
| Ali Zia | | 176 | 102*  United Bank v PACO | Lahore | 1984–85 |
| Allan, J.M. | | 121* | 105  Kent v Northamptonshire | Northampton | 1955 |
| Alley, W.E. | | 183* | 134*  Somerset v Surrey | Taunton | 1961 |
| Amarnath, L. | | 130 | 107  Indians v Essex | Brentwood | 1936 |
| Ames, L.E.G. | (3) | 132 | 145*  Kent v Northamptonshire | Dover | 1933 |
| | | 119 | 127  Kent v Surrey | Blackheath | 1937 |
| | | 112 | 119  Kent v Gloucestershire | Bristol | 1950 |
| Amiss, D.L. | (2) | 155* | 112  Warwickshire v Worcestershire | Birmingham | 1978 |
| | | 109 | 127  Warwickshire v Derbyshire | Derby | 1981 |
| | | | *With a runner part of first innings and throughout second* | | |
| Anderson, I.J. | | 147 | 103*  Ireland v Scotland | Glasgow | 1976 |
| Armstrong, W.W. | | 157* | 245  Victoria v South Australia | Melbourne | 1920–21 |
| Arnold, E.G. | | 101* | 128  Worcestershire v Cambridge U. | Cambridge | 1903 |
| Arshad Pervez | | 115 | 110  Sargodha v Rawalpindi | Lahore | 1984–85 |
| Ashdown, W.H. | | 121 | 103  Kent v Middlesex | Lord's | 1931 |
| Asif Iqbal | | 104 | 110*  PIA v Habib Bank | Lahore | 1979–80 |
| Aslett, D.G. | | 168 | 119  Kent v Derbyshire | Chesterfield | 1983 |
| Avery, A.V. | | 117 | 100  Essex v Glamorgan | Ebbw Vale | 1949 |
| Azharuddin, M. | | 121 | 105*  Hyderabad v Andhra | Machillipatnam | 1984–85 |
| Azmat Rana | | 100 | 100*  MCB v Rawalpindi | Rawalpindi | 1981–82 |
| Badcock, C.L. | | 120 | 102  South Australia v Victoria | Melbourne | 1940–41 |
| Baichan, L. | (2) | 216* | 102  Berbice v Demerara | Georgetown | 1973–74 |
| | | 132 | 101*  Berbice v Demerara | Berbice | 1982–83 |
| Bardsley, W. | | 136 | 130  Australia v England | Oval | 1909 |
| Barrington, K.F. | | 186 | 118*  Surrey v Warwickshire | Birmingham | 1959 |
| Bates, L.T.A. | | 116 | 144  Warwickshire v Kent | Coventry | 1927 |
| Bates, W.E. | | 105 | 111  Glamorgan v Essex | Leyton | 1927 |
| Benson, M.R. | | 102 | 152*  Kent v Warwickshire | Birmingham | 1983 |
| Berry, G.L. | | 165 | 111*  Leicestershire v Essex | Clacton | 1947 |
| Bolus, J.B. | | 147 | 101  Notts v Northamptonshire | Nottingham | 1969 |
| Booth, B.J. | | 109 | 104  Leicestershire v Middlesex | Lord's | 1965 |
| Border, A.R. | | 150* | 153  Australia v Pakistan | Lahore | 1979–80 |
| Bosanquet, B.J.T. | (2) | 136 | 139  Middlesex v Leicestershire | Lord's | 1900 |
| | | 103 | 100*  Middlesex v Sussex | Lord's | 1905 |
| Boycott, G. | (3) | 103 | 105  Yorkshire v Nottinghamshire | Sheffield | 1966 |
| | | 160* | 116  England XI v Rest | Worcester | 1974 |
| | | 163 | 141*  Yorkshire v Nottinghamshire | Bradford | 1983 |

| | | | | | | |
|---|---|---|---|---|---|---|
| Boyd-Moss, R.J. | (2) | 123 | 119 | Cambridge U. v Warwickshire | Cambridge | 1982 |
| | | 139 | 124 | Cambridge U. v Oxford U. | Lord's | 1983 |
| | | | | *First instance in University Match* | | |
| Bradman, D.G. | (4) | 131 | 133* | New South Wales v Queensland | Brisbane | 1928–29 |
| | | 124 | 225 | W.M. Woodfull's XI v | | |
| | | | | J. Ryder's XI | Sydney | 1929–30 |
| | | 107 | 113 | South Australia v Queensland | Brisbane | 1937–38 |
| | | 132 | 127* | Australia v India | Melbourne | 1947–48 |
| Brann, G. | | 105 | 101 | Sussex v Kent | Hove | 1892 |
| Brookes, D. | | 112 | 154* | Northamptonshire v Sussex | Eastbourne | 1946 |
| Burke, J.W. | | 138 | 125* | Australians v Somerset | Taunton | 1956 |
| Butcher, A.R. | | 117* | 114 | Surrey v Glamorgan | Oval | 1984 |
| Butcher, B.F. | | 115 | 172 | West Indians v Combined XI | Perth | 1968–69 |
| Carew, M.C. | | 164 | 101 | Trinidad v Jamaica | Port-of-Spain | 1969–70 |
| Carpenter, H. | | 127 | 104 | Essex v Kent | Leyton | 1901 |
| Carr, D.B. | | 156* | 109 | Derbyshire v Kent | Canterbury | 1959 |
| Chappell, G.S. | (4) | 129 | 156* | South Australia v Queensland | Brisbane | 1969–70 |
| | | 180 | 101 | Queensland v Victoria | Brisbane | 1973–74 |
| | | 247* | 133 | Australia v New Zealand | Wellington | 1973–74 |
| | | 123 | 109* | Australia v West Indies | Brisbane | 1975–76 |
| Chappell, I.M. | (3) | 145 | 106 | Australia v World XI | Brisbane | 1971–72 |
| | | 141* | 130 | South Australia v Victoria | Adelaide | 1973–74 |
| | | 145 | 121 | Australia v New Zealand | Wellington | 1973–74 |
| Charlesworth, C. | | 100 | 101* | Warwickshire v Surrey | Birmingham | 1913 |
| Chinnery, H.B. | | 105 | 165 | MCC v Oxford University | Oxford | 1901 |
| Christiani, R.J. | | 131* | 100* | West Indians v Middlesex | Lord's | 1950 |
| Compton, D.C.S. | (3) | 124 | 100 | Middlesex v Lancashire | Manchester | 1946 |
| | | 147 | 103* | England v Australia | Adelaide | 1946–47 |
| | | 135 | 125* | MCC South African XI v | | |
| | | | | H.D.G. Leveson Gower's XI | Scarborough | 1948 |
| Contractor, N.J. | | 152 | 102* | Gujarat v Baroda | Baroda | 1952–53 |
| Cooper, E. | | 191 | 106* | Worcestershire v Northants | Kidderminster | 1946 |
| Cowdrey, M.C. | (3) | 110 | 103 | MCC v New South Wales | Sydney | 1954–55 |
| | | 115* | 103* | Kent v Essex | Gillingham | 1955 |
| | | 149 | 121 | Kent v Australians | Canterbury | 1961 |
| Cunningham, K.G. | | 107 | 101* | S. Australia v Western Australia | Adelaide | 1966–67 |
| Dacre, C.C.R. | (2) | 127* | 101* | Auckland v Victoria | Auckland | 1924–25 |
| | | 119 | 125* | Gloucestershire v Worcestershire | Worcester | 1933 |
| Dalton, E.L. | | 157 | 116* | South Africans v Kent | Canterbury | 1929 |
| Daniell, J. | | 174* | 108 | Somerset v Essex | Taunton | 1925 |
| Dempster, C.S. | | 133 | 154* | Leicestershire v Gloucestershire | Gloucester | 1937 |
| Denning, P.W. | | 122 | 107 | Somerset v Gloucestershire | Taunton | 1977 |
| Denton, D. | (3) | 107 | 109* | Yorkshire v Nottinghamshire | Nottingham | 1906 |
| | | 133 | 121 | Yorkshire v MCC | Scarborough | 1908 |
| | | 139 | 138 | MCC v Transvaal | Johannesburg | 1909–10 |
| Deodhar, D.B. | | 105 | 141 | Maharashtra v Nawanagar | Poona | 1944–45 |
| Dewes, J.G. | | 128 | 101 | Middlesex v Sussex | Hove | 1950 |
| Dipper, A.E. | | 117 | 103 | Gloucestershire v Sussex | Horsham | 1922 |
| Doggart, G.H.G. | | 140 | 105 | Sussex v Oxford University | Oxford | 1954 |
| Draper, R.G. | | 129 | 177 | Griqualand West v Border | Kimberley | 1952–53 |
| Duleepsinhji, K.S. | (3) | 115 | 246 | Sussex v Kent | Hastings | 1929 |
| | | 116 | 102* | Sussex v Middlesex | Lord's | 1930 |
| | | 125 | 103* | Gentlemen v Players | Lord's | 1930 |
| Eady, C.J. | | 116 | 112* | Tasmania v Victoria | Hobart | 1894–95 |
| Edrich, J.H. | (4) | 112 | 124 | Surrey v Nottinghamshire | Nottingham | 1959 |
| | | 143 | 113* | Surrey v Worcestershire | Worcester | 1970 |
| | | 111 | 124 | Surrey v Warwickshire | Oval | 1971 |
| | | 140 | 115 | Surrey v Kent | Oval | 1977 |
| Edwards, A.R. | | 103 | 105 | Western Australia v Queensland | Perth | 1950–51 |
| Emmett, G.M. | (2) | 115 | 103* | Gloucestershire v Leicestershire | Leicester | 1947 |
| | | 110 | 102* | Gloucestershire v Somerset | Bristol | 1951 |
| Enthoven, H.J. | | 123 | 115 | Middlesex v Sussex | Lord's | 1930 |
| Fagg, A.E. | (2) | 244 | 202* | Kent v Essex | Colchester | 1938 |
| | | 136 | 117* | Kent v Essex | Maidstone | 1948 |
| Favell, L.E. | (2) | 112 | 114 | South Australia v NSW | Sydney | 1956–57 |
| | | 104 | 145 | S. Australia v Western Australia | Adelaide | 1958–59 |
| Featherstone, N.G. | | 127* | 100* | Middlesex v Kent | Canterbury | 1975 |

| | | | | | | |
|---|---|---|---|---|---|---|
| Fellows-Smith, J.P. | | 100* | 102* | Transvaal v Commonwealth XI | Johannesburg | 1959–60 |
| Fishlock, L.B. | (4) | 131* | 100* | Surrey v Sussex | Oval | 1936 |
| | | 113 | 105 | Surrey v Yorkshire | Oval | 1937 |
| | | 129 | 112 | Surrey v Leicestershire | Leicester | 1946 |
| | | 111 | 118 | Surrey v Nottinghamshire | Nottingham | 1949 |
| Fletcher, K.W.R. | | 111 | 102* | Essex v Nottinghamshire | Nottingham | 1976 |
| Fordham, C.B. | | 140 | 100* | Minor Counties v Oxford U. | Oxford | 1933 |
| Foster, M.K. | | 141 | 106 | Worcestershire v Hampshire | Worcester | 1926 |
| Foster, R.E. | (3) | 134 | 101* | Worcestershire v Hampshire | Worcester | 1899 |
| | | 128 | 100* | Oxford U. v A.J. Webbe's XI | Oxford | 1900 |
| | | 102* | 136 | Gentlemen v Players | Lord's | 1900 |
| Foster, W.L. | | 140 | 172* | Worcestershire v Hampshire | Worcester | 1899 |
| Fowler, G. | | 126 | 128* | Lancashire v Warwickshire | Southport | 1982 |
| | | | | *With a runner throughout most of first innings and all of second* | | |
| Fredericks, R.C. | (3) | 127 | 115 | Guyana v Barbados | Georgetown | 1966–67 |
| | | 158 | 118 | Guyana v Australians | Georgetown | 1972–73 |
| | | 112 | 105* | Guyana v MCC | Georgetown | 1973–74 |
| Fry, C.B. | (5) | 108 | 123* | Sussex v Middlesex | Hove | 1898 |
| | | 125 | 229 | Sussex v Surrey | Hove | 1900 |
| | | 138 | 101* | Sussex v Kent | Hove | 1903 |
| | | 156 | 106 | Sussex v MCC | Lord's | 1905 |
| | | 123 | 112 | Hampshire v Kent | Canterbury | 1911 |
| Gaekwad, D.K. | | 128 | 101* | Baroda v Gujarat | Baroda | 1949–50 |
| Gardner, F.C. | | 113 | 101* | Warwickshire v Essex | Ilford | 1950 |
| Gavaskar, S.M. | (3) | 124 | 220 | India v West Indies | Port-of-Spain | 1970–71 |
| | | 111 | 137 | India v Pakistan | Karachi | 1978–79 |
| | | 107 | 182* | India v West Indies | Calcutta | 1978–79 |
| Gedye, S.G. | | 104 | 101 | Auckland v Central Districts | Auckland | 1963–64 |
| Gehrs, D.R.A. | | 148* | 100* | S. Australia v Western Australia | Fremantle | 1905–06 |
| Gibbons, H.H.I. | | 111* | 100* | Worcestershire v Hampshire | Worcester | 1939 |
| Gimblett, H. | (2) | 115 | 127* | Somerset v Hampshire | Taunton | 1949 |
| | | 146 | 116 | Somerset v Derbyshire | Taunton | 1952 |
| Gomez, G.E. | | 148 | 108* | Trinidad v British Guiana | Georgetown | 1953–54 |
| Grace, W.G. | (3) | 130 | 102* | South of Thames v N. of Thames | Canterbury | 1868 |
| | | 101 | 103* | Gloucestershire v Kent | Clifton | 1887 |
| | | 148 | 153 | Gloucestershire v Yorkshire | Clifton | 1888 |
| Graveney, T.W. | (4) | 103 | 105* | Gloucestershire v Northants | Bristol | 1951 |
| | | 153 | 120 | C.G. Howard's XI v President's XI | Bombay | 1956–57 |
| | | 106 | 101* | Gloucestershire v Warwickshire | Birmingham | 1957 |
| | | 164 | 107* | Commonwealth XI v Pakistan | Lahore | 1963–64 |
| Graves, P.J. | | 119 | 137* | OFS v Border | Bloemfontein | 1976–77 |
| Greenidge, C.G. | (3) | 134 | 101 | West Indies v England | Manchester | 1976 |
| | | 136 | 120 | Hampshire v Kent | Bournemouth | 1978 |
| | | 104 | 100* | Hampshire v Lancashire | Liverpool | 1983 |
| Gregory, J.M. | | 122 | 102 | AIF v New South Wales | Sydney | 1919–20 |
| Greig, J.G. | | 115 | 130 | Hampshire v Worcestershire | Worcester | 1905 |
| Gunn, G. | (3) | 132 | 109* | Nottinghamshire v Yorkshire | Nottingham | 1913 |
| | | 169 | 185* | Nottinghamshire v Surrey | Nottingham | 1919 |
| | | 100 | 110 | Nottinghamshire v Warwickshire | Nottingham | 1927 |
| Hall, I.W. | | 101 | 101 | Derbyshire v Kent | Folkestone | 1965 |
| Hallam, M.R. | (3) | 210* | 157 | Leicestershire v Glamorgan | Leicester | 1959 |
| | | 203* | 143* | Leicestershire v Sussex | Worthing | 1961 |
| | | 107* | 149* | Leicestershire v Worcestershire | Leicester | 1965 |
| Hallows, C. | (2) | 112* | 103* | Lancashire v Leicestershire | Ashby de la·Z. | 1924 |
| | | 123 | 101* | Lancashire v Warwickshire | Birmingham | 1928 |
| Hamence, R.A. | (2) | 130 | 103* | South Australia v Victoria | Melbourne | 1940–41 |
| | | 132 | 101* | South Australia v NSW | Adelaide | 1946–47 |
| Hammond, W.R. | (7) | 108 | 128 | Gloucestershire v Surrey | Oval | 1927 |
| | | 139 | 143 | Gloucestershire v Surrey | Cheltenham | 1928 |
| | | 119* | 177 | England v Australia | Adelaide | 1928–29 |
| | | 122 | 111* | Gloucestershire v Worcestershire | Worcester | 1933 |
| | | 104 | 136 | MCC v South Australia | Adelaide | 1936–37 |
| | | 110 | 123 | Gloucestershire v Derbyshire | Burton upon T. | 1938 |
| | | 121 | 102 | England XI v Dominions XI | Lord's | 1945 |
| Hanif Mohammad | (3) | 121 | 109* | Pakistanis v North Zone | Amritsar | 1952–53 |
| | | 133 | 146 | Karachi Whites v Karachi Greens | Karachi | 1961–62 |

| Player | | | | Match | Venue | Year |
|---|---|---|---|---|---|---|
| Hanif Mohammad *continued* | | 111 | 104 | Pakistan v England | Dacca | 1961–62 |
| Hanumant Singh | | 109 | 213* | Rajasthan v Bombay | Bombay | 1966–67 |
| Harbinson, W.K. | | 130 | 109* | Cambridge U. v Glamorgan | Cambridge | 1929 |
| Hardinge, H.T.W. | (4) | 153 | 126 | Kent v Essex | Leyton | 1908 |
| | | 175 | 109 | Kent v Hampshire | Southampton | 1911 |
| | | 117 | 105* | Kent v Hampshire | Dover | 1913 |
| | | 207 | 102* | Kent v Surrey | Blackheath | 1921 |
| Hardstaff, J., sr | | 118 | 106* | Nottinghamshire v Derbyshire | Nottingham | 1911 |
| Hardstaff, J., jr | | 100* | 114* | Nottinghamshire v Northants | Nottingham | 1949 |
| Harris, M.J. | (3) | 118 | 123 | Nottinghamshire v Leicestershire | Leicester | 1971 |
| | | 107 | 131* | Nottinghamshire v Essex | Chelmsford | 1971 |
| | | 133* | 132 | Nottinghamshire v Northants | Northampton | 1979 |
| Hassett, A.L. | (2) | 122 | 122 | Victoria v New South Wales | Sydney | 1939–40 |
| | | 187 | 124* | Australian Services v Prince's XI | Delhi | 1945–46 |
| Hayward, T.W. | (3) | 106 | 112 | Surrey v Sussex | Hove | 1904 |
| | | 144* | 100 | Surrey v Nottinghamshire | Nottingham | 1906 |
| | | 143 | 125 | Surrey v Leicestershire | Leicester | 1906 |
| | | | | *Scored in successive matches* | | |
| Hazare, V.S. | (3) | 127 | 162* | Baroda v Maharashtra | Poona | 1944–45 |
| | | 116 | 145 | India v Australia | Adelaide | 1947–48 |
| | | 130 | 101 | Baroda v Holkar | Baroda | 1949–50 |
| Headley, G.A. | (2) | 114 | 112 | West Indies v England | Georgetown | 1929–30 |
| | | 106 | 107 | West Indies v England | Lord's | 1939 |
| Headley, R.G.A. | | 187 | 108 | Worcestershire v Northants | Worcester | 1971 |
| Hearne, J.W. | | 104 | 101* | Middlesex v Glamorgan | Lord's | 1931 |
| Hendren, E.H. | (4) | 119 | 102 | MCC v Kent | Folkestone | 1927 |
| | | 189 | 100* | Middlesex v Warwickshire | Birmingham | 1931 |
| | | 101 | 101 | Middlesex v Kent | Lord's | 1933 |
| | | 104 | 101 | Middlesex v Surrey | Lord's | 1936 |
| Hignell, A.J. | | 108 | 145 | Cambridge University v Surrey | Cambridge | 1978 |
| Hill, A.J.L. | | 124 | 118* | Hampshire v Somerset | Southampton | 1905 |
| Hill, N.W. | | 101 | 102 | Nottinghamshire v Lancashire | Nottingham | 1959 |
| Hirst, G.H. | | 111 | 117* | Yorkshire v Somerset | Bath | 1906 |
| Hobbs, J.B. | (6) | 160 | 100 | Surrey v Warwickshire | Birmingham | 1909 |
| | | 104 | 143* | Surrey v Cambridge University | Oval | 1925 |
| | | 101 | 101* | Surrey v Somerset | Taunton | 1925 |
| | | 112 | 104 | Surrey v Hampshire | Oval | 1927 |
| | | 137 | 111* | Surrey v Glamorgan | Oval | 1930 |
| | | 113 | 119* | Surrey v Essex | Oval | 1932 |
| Holmes, P. | | 126 | 111* | Yorkshire v Lancashire | Manchester | 1920 |
| Hookes, D.W. | (3) | 185 | 105 | South Australia v Queensland | Adelaide | 1976–77 |
| | | 135 | 156 | South Australia v NSW | Adelaide | 1976–77 |
| | | | | *Scored in successive matches* | | |
| | | 137 | 107 | South Australia v Victoria | Adelaide | 1982–83 |
| Howarth, G.P. | | 122 | 102 | New Zealand v England | Auckland | 1977–78 |
| Howell, D.H. | | 109 | 114 | Eastern Province B v OFS | Bloemfontein | 1982–83 |
| Howell, M. | | 115 | 102 | Oxford University v H.D.G. Leveson Gower's XI | Eastbourne | 1919 |
| Human, J.H. | | 110 | 122 | Cambridge University v Surrey | Oval | 1933 |
| Humpage, G.W. | | 146 | 110 | Warwickshire v Gloucestershire | Gloucester | 1981 |
| Hutchings, K.L. | | 109 | 109* | Kent v Worcestershire | Worcester | 1907 |
| Hutton, L. | (3) | 197 | 104 | Yorkshire v Essex | Southend | 1947 |
| | | 165 | 100 | Yorkshire v Sussex | Hove | 1949 |
| | | 103 | 137 | Yorkshire v MCC | Scarborough | 1952 |
| Imran Khan | | 117* | 106 | Oxford U. v Nottinghamshire | Oxford | 1974 |
| Ingle, R.A. | | 117 | 100* | Somerset v Middlesex | Taunton | 1928 |
| Insole, D.J. | | 111 | 118 | Essex v Kent | Gillingham | 1955 |
| Jackson, A. | | 131 | 122 | New South Wales v South Australia | Sydney | 1927–28 |
| Jameson, J.A. | | 110 | 111 | D.H. Robins' XI v Indians | Eastbourne | 1974 |
| Javed Burki | | 144* | 109* | Oxford University v Essex | Brentwood | 1960 |
| Javed Miandad | (4) | 100 | 118 | Habib Bank v PIA | Lahore | 1977–78 |
| | | 107 | 123 | Habib Bank v National Bank | Lahore | 1980–81 |
| | | 137* | 106 | Glamorgan v Somerset | Swansea | 1981 |
| | | 104 | 103* | Pakistan v New Zealand | Hyderabad | 1984–85 |
| Jessop, G.L. | (4) | 104 | 139 | Gloucestershire v Yorkshire | Bradford | 1900 |
| | | 143 | 133* | Gloucestershire v Somerset | Bath | 1908 |
| | | 161 | 129 | Gloucestershire v Hampshire | Bristol | 1909 |

| Player | | 1st | 2nd | Match | Venue | Year |
|---|---|---|---|---|---|---|
| Jessop, G.L. *continued* | | 153 | 123* | Gloucestershire v Hampshire | Southampton | 1911 |
| Jesty, T.E. | | 143* | 141 | Hampshire v Worcestershire | Worcester | 1984 |
| Johnson, P.R. | | 164 | 131 | Somerset v Middlesex | Taunton | 1908 |
| Johnston, A.C. | | 175 | 100* | Hampshire v Warwickshire | Coventry | 1912 |
| Jones, A. | (3) | 187* | 105* | Glamorgan v Somerset | Glastonbury | 1963 |
| | | 132 | 156* | Glamorgan v Yorkshire | Middlesbrough | 1976 |
| | | 147 | 100 | Glamorgan v Hampshire | Swansea | 1978 |
| Jones, A.O. | | 137 | 100 | Nottinghamshire v Lancashire | Nottingham | 1903 |
| Kadri, S.M. | | 105 | 114 | Bombay v Western India States | Poona | 1935–36 |
| Kallicharran, A.I. | (2) | 152 | 118* | Warwickshire v Sussex | Birmingham | 1983 |
| | | 200* | 117* | Warwickshire v Northamptonshire | Birmingham | 1984 |
| Kanhai, R.B. | | 117 | 115 | West Indies v Australia | Adelaide | 1960–61 |
| Keith, H.J. | | 111 | 113* | South Africans v Victoria | Melbourne | 1952–53 |
| Kelly, P.C. | | 119 | 108* | Western Australia v MCC | Perth | 1965–66 |
| Kenny, A. | | 164 | 100* | Victoria v Queensland | Brisbane | 1909–10 |
| Kent, R. | | 127 | 118 | Border v Orange Free State | Bloemfontein | 1978–79 |
| Kerr, R.B. | | 158 | 101 | Queensland v Western Australia | Perth | 1981–82 |
| Khanna, S.C. | | 111 | 128 | Delhi v Karnataka | Bangalore | 1978–79 |
| Kimpton, R.C.M. | | 101 | 106 | Oxford U. v Gloucestershire | Oxford | 1936 |
| King, J.H. | (2) | 104 | 109* | Players v Gentlemen | Lord's | 1904 |
| | | 111 | 100* | Leicestershire v Northamptonshire | Leicester | 1913 |
| Kinneir, S. | | 124 | 110 | Warwickshire v Sussex | Chichester | 1911 |
| Kippax, A.F. | (2) | 127 | 131 | New South Wales v Queensland | Brisbane | 1926–27 |
| | | 158 | 102* | Australians v Sussex | Hove | 1930 |
| Kirsten, P.N. | (2) | 173* | 103 | W. Province v E. Province | Cape Town | 1976–77 |
| | | 164* | 123* | Derbyshire v Surrey | Derby | 1982 |
| Knight, D.J. | | 114 | 101 | Surrey v Yorkshire | Oval | 1919 |
| Knott, A.P.E. | | 127* | 118* | Kent v Surrey | Maidstone | 1972 |
| Lambert, W. | | 107* | 157 | Sussex v Epsom | Lord's | 1817 |
| Lance, H.R. | | 101 | 122 | Transvaal v Eastern Province | Johannesburg | 1966–67 |
| Langridge, J.G. | (2) | 115 | 129 | Sussex v Lancashire | Manchester | 1949 |
| | | 146 | 146* | Sussex v Derbyshire | Worthing | 1949 |
| Lee, F.S. | | 109* | 107 | Somerset v Worcestershire | Worcester | 1938 |
| Lee, H.W. | (2) | 163 | 126 | Middlesex v Surrey | Oval | 1919 |
| | | 124 | 105* | Middlesex v Lancashire | Lord's | 1929 |
| Lester, E.I. | (2) | 126 | 142 | Yorkshire v Northamptonshire | Northampton | 1947 |
| | | 125* | 132 | Yorkshire v Lancashire | Manchester | 1948 |
| Livingstone, D.A. | | 117 | 105* | Hampshire v Kent | Canterbury | 1964 |
| Llewellyn, C.B. | (2) | 102 | 100 | Hampshire v Derbyshire | Derby | 1905 |
| | | 130 | 101* | Hampshire v Sussex | Hove | 1909 |
| Lloyd, C.H. | | 133 | 104* | Guyana v New Zealanders | Georgetown | 1971–72 |
| Lloyd, D. | | 116 | 104* | Lancashire v Worcestershire | Southport | 1979 |
| Lloyds, J.W. | | 132* | 102* | Somerset v Northamptonshire | Northampton | 1982 |
| Lonergan, A.R. | | 115 | 100 | South Australia v Victoria | Melbourne | 1933–34 |
| Luckhurst, B.W. | | 113 | 100* | Kent v Rest of the World XI | Canterbury | 1968 |
| Lyon, B.H. | | 115 | 101* | Gloucestershire v Essex | Bristol | 1930 |
| Macartney, C.G. | (2) | 119 | 126 | New South Wales v South Africans | Sydney | 1910–11 |
| | | 142 | 121 | Australians v Sussex | Hove | 1912 |
| McCabe, S.J. | | 106 | 103* | New South Wales v Victoria | Sydney | 1931–32 |
| McCosker, R.B. | (3) | 138 | 136* | NSW v Western Australia | Sydney | 1974–75 |
| | | 111 | 115 | Australians v Sussex | Hove | 1975 |
| | | 123* | 118* | NSW v Victoria | Sydney | 1981–82 |
| McEwan, K.S. | | 102 | 116 | Essex v Warwickshire | Birmingham | 1977 |
| McGahey, C.P. | | 114 | 145* | Essex v Gloucestershire | Leyton | 1901 |
| Mackay, J.R.M. | | 105 | 102* | New South Wales v South Australia | Sydney | 1905–06 |
| MacLaren, A.C. | | 142 | 100 | A.E. Stoddart's XI v NSW | Sydney | 1897–98 |
| Madan Lal | | 140 | 100 | Delhi v Railways | Delhi | 1980–81 |
| Mahmood Arshad | | 116 | 115 | National Bank v HBFC | Multan | 1976–77 |
| Majid Khan | | 101 | 128* | Lahore v United Bank | Lahore | 1982–83 |
| Mankad, A.V. | | 105 | 100* | Indian XI v President's XI | Kandy | 1973–74 |
| May, P.B.H. | (3) | 167 | 103* | Surrey v Essex | Southend | 1951 |
| | | 174 | 100* | MCC v Yorkshire | Scarborough | 1952 |
| | | 140 | 114 | MCC v Australian XI | Sydney | 1958–59 |
| Mead, C.P. | (3) | 109 | 100* | Hampshire v Leicestershire | Leicester | 1911 |
| | | 102 | 113* | Hampshire v Leicestershire | Southampton | 1913 |
| | | 113 | 224 | Hampshire v Sussex | Horsham | 1921 |
| Melville, A. | | 189 | 104* | South Africa v England | Nottingham | 1947 |

| Name | | 1st | 2nd | Match | Venue | Year |
|---|---|---|---|---|---|---|
| Mendis, G.D. | | 103* | 100* | Sussex v Lancashire | Hastings | 1985 |
| Mendis, L.R.D. | | 105 | 105 | Sri Lanka v India | Madras | 1982–83 |
| Merchant, U.M. | | 143 | 156 | Bombay v Maharashtra | Poona | 1948–49 |
| Miller, K.R. | | 100 | 101 | A.L. Hassett's XI v A.R. Morris's XI | Melbourne | 1953–54 |
| Milton, C.A. | (2) | 150 | 100* | Gloucestershire v Sussex | Eastbourne | 1961 |
| | | 110* | 102* | Gloucestershire v Kent | Bristol | 1962 |
| Mitchell, A. | | 100* | 100* | H.D.G. Leveson Gower's XI v MCC Australian XI | Scarborough | 1933 |
| Mitchell, B. | | 120 | 189* | South Africa v England | Oval | 1947 |
| Moroney, J. | | 118 | 101* | Australia v South Africa | Johannesburg | 1949–50 |
| Morris, A.R. | (2) | 148 | 111 | New South Wales v Queensland | Sydney | 1940–41 |
| | | 122 | 124* | Australia v England | Adelaide | 1946–47 |
| Mudassar Nazar | | 103 | 123 | Pakistanis v Victoria | Melbourne | 1983–84 |
| Munir-ul-Haq | | 104* | 120* | HBFC v PIA | Bahawalpur | 1984–85 |
| Mushtaq Ali | | 109 | 130 | Holkar v Bombay | Bombay | 1944–45 |
| Mushtaq Mohammad | | 128* | 123 | D.H. Robins' XI v West Indians | Eastbourne | 1969 |
| Needham, E. | | 107* | 104 | Derbyshire v Essex | Leyton | 1908 |
| Newman, J.A. | | 102 | 102* | Hampshire v Surrey | Oval | 1927 |
| Noble, M.A. | | 176 | 123 | New South Wales v Victoria | Sydney | 1907–08 |
| Nourse, A.D. | | 147 | 108* | South Africans v Surrey | Oval | 1935 |
| Nurse, S.M. | | 106 | 135* | E.W. Swanton's XI v Indian XI | Calcutta | 1963–64 |
| O'Connor, J. | | 138 | 120* | Essex v Gloucestershire | Bristol | 1930 |
| O'Connor, L.P.D. | | 103 | 143* | Queensland v New South Wales | Sydney | 1926–27 |
| O'Keefe, F.A. | | 177 | 141 | Rest v Australian XI | Sydney | 1921–22 |
| Onyons, B.A. | | 105 | 127 | Victoria v Queensland | Brisbane | 1928–29 |
| Ord, J.S. | | 107* | 101 | Warwickshire v Nottinghamshire | Nottingham | 1948 |
| Ormrod, J.A. | | 101 | 131* | Worcestershire v Somerset | Worcester | 1980 |
| Parfitt, P.H. | (2) | 105 | 101* | Middlesex v Nottinghamshire | Nottingham | 1961 |
| | | 122 | 114 | Middlesex v Pakistanis | Lord's | 1962 |
| Parker, J.M. | | 117 | 102* | Northern Dists v Central Dists | Tauranga | 1981–82 |
| Parkhouse, W.G.A. | | 121 | 148 | Glamorgan v Somerset | Cardiff | 1950 |
| Parks, H.W. | | 114* | 105* | Sussex v Essex | Leyton | 1933 |
| Parks, J.M. | | 101 | 100* | Sussex v Worcestershire | Worcester | 1957 |
| Pataudi, Nawab of, sr | | 165 | 100 | Oxford University v Surrey | Oval | 1931 |
| Pataudi, Nawab of, jr | (2) | 106 | 103* | Oxford University v Yorkshire | Oxford | 1961 |
| | | 130 | 107* | Delhi v Services | Delhi | 1964–65 |
| Paynter, E. | (2) | 125 | 113* | Lancashire v Warwickshire | Birmingham | 1938 |
| | | 117 | 100 | England v South Africa | Johannesburg | 1938–39 |
| Perrin, P.A. | (4) | 170 | 102* | Essex v Nottinghamshire | Nottingham | 1903 |
| | | 140 | 103* | Essex v Middlesex | Lord's | 1905 |
| | | 112 | 100* | Essex v Nottinghamshire | Nottingham | 1911 |
| | | 126 | 101* | Essex v Kent | Leyton | 1919 |
| Phadkar, D.G. | | 131 | 160 | Bombay v Maharashtra | Poona | 1948–49 |
| Pilling, H. | | 119* | 104* | Lancashire v Warwickshire | Manchester | 1970 |
| Pinch, C. | (2) | 110 | 100 | S. Australia v Western Australia | Perth | 1956–57 |
| | | 102 | 102 | South Australia v Victoria | Melbourne | 1957–58 |
| Place, W. | | 105 | 132* | Lancashire v Nottinghamshire | Manchester | 1947 |
| Pollock, R.G. | (2) | 103 | 167* | E. Province v D.H. Robins' XI | Port Elizabeth | 1974–75 |
| | | 134 | 120* | Eastern Province v Rhodesia | Bulawayo | 1977–78 |
| Ponsford, W.H. | | 110 | 110* | Victoria v New South Wales | Sydney | 1923–24 |
| Poore, R.M. | | 104 | 119* | Hampshire v Somerset | Portsmouth | 1899 |
| Prideaux, R.M. | (2) | 102 | 106 | Cambridge University v Somerset | Taunton | 1960 |
| | | 106 | 100 | Northants v Nottinghamshire | Nottingham | 1966 |
| Procter, M.J. | | 114 | 131 | Rhodesia v Internat. Wanderers | Salisbury | 1972–73 |
| Qaiser Hussain | | 103* | 129* | PACO v MCB | Sahiwal | 1983–84 |
| Qasim Omar | (2) | 210* | 110 | MCB v Lahore | Lahore | 1982–83 |
| | | 174 | 110* | MCB v Karachi | Karachi | 1982–83 |
| Quaife, W.G. | | 124 | 109 | Warwickshire v Surrey | Oval | 1913 |
| Rae, A.F. | | 111 | 128 | Jamaica v Barbados | Kingston | 1946–47 |
| Randall, D.W. | | 209 | 146 | Nottinghamshire v Middlesex | Nottingham | 1979 |
| Ranjitsinhji, K.S. | | 100 | 125* | Sussex v Yorkshire | Hove | 1896 |
| Ransford, V.S. | | 182 | 110 | Victoria v New South Wales | Sydney | 1908–09 |
| Ratcliffe, A. | | 130 | 104* | Cambridge University v Surrey | Oval | 1932 |
| Rege, M.R. | | 133 | 100 | Maharashtra v Bombay | Poona | 1948–49 |
| Reid, J.R. | | 101 | 118* | New Zealanders v OFS | Bloemfontein | 1961–62 |
| Reid, T.B. | | 120* | 111 | E. Province B v W. Province B | Constantia | 1984–85 |

| | | | | | | |
|---|---|---|---|---|---|---|
| Rhodes, W. | (2) | 128 | 115 | Yorkshire v MCC | Scarborough | 1911 |
| | | 119 | 109 | MCC v New South Wales | Sydney | 1911–12 |
| Rice, C.E.B. | | 131* | 114* | Nottinghamshire v Somerset | Nottingham | 1980 |
| Richards, B.A. | (2) | 130 | 104* | Hampshire v Northamptonshire | Northampton | 1968 |
| | | 159 | 108 | Hampshire v Kent | Southampton | 1976 |
| Richards, I.V.A. | | 160 | 107* | West Indians v Tasmania | Hobart | 1975–76 |
| Richardson, B.A. | | 126 | 105 | Warwickshire v Cambridge U. | Birmingham | 1967 |
| Richardson, P.E. | | 111 | 115 | Kent v Australians | Canterbury | 1964 |
| Richardson, V.Y. | | 100 | 125 | South Australia v New South Wales | Sydney | 1924–25 |
| Rigg, K.E. | | 100 | 167* | Victoria v New South Wales | Melbourne | 1936–37 |
| Rizwan-uz-Zaman | | 119 | 121* | PIA v National Bank | Karachi | 1984–85 |
| Robertson, J.D.B. | | 147 | 137 | Middlesex v Sussex | Lord's | 1948 |
| Robinson, R.T. | | 103 | 130* | Nottinghamshire v Glamorgan | Swansea | 1985 |
| Roope, G.R.J. | | 109 | 103* | Surrey v Leicestershire | Leicester | 1971 |
| Rose, B.C. | | 124 | 150* | Somerset v Worcestershire | Worcester | 1980 |
| Rosendorff, N. | | 157 | 126* | Orange Free State v Border | Bloemfontein | 1969–70 |
| Rowe, L.G. | | 214 | 100* | West Indies v New Zealand | Kingston | 1971–72 |
| | | | | *In his first Test match* | | |
| Roy, Pankaj | (2) | 170 | 143 | Bengal v Orissa | Cuttack | 1953–54 |
| | | 112 | 118 | Bengal v Hyderabad | Calcutta | 1962–63 |
| Russell, C.A.G. | (3) | 115 | 118 | Essex v Surrey | Oval | 1922 |
| | | 140 | 111 | England v South Africa | Durban | 1922–23 |
| | | 131 | 104 | Essex v Lancashire | Liverpool | 1928 |
| Saadat Ali | | 141 | 222 | Income Tax Dept v Multan | Multan | 1977–78 |
| Sadiq Mohammad | (3) | 163* | 150 | Gloucestershire v Derbyshire | Bristol | 1976 |
| | | 171 | 103 | Gloucestershire v Glamorgan | Bristol | 1979 |
| | | 109 | 115 | United Bank v Karachi | Karachi | 1982–83 |
| Saeed Ahmed | | 105 | 102 | PIA v North Zone | Lahore | 1961–62 |
| Salahuddin | | 256 | 102* | Karachi v East Pakistan | Karachi | 1968–69 |
| Salim Malik | | 103 | 107 | Habib Bank v MCB | Hyderabad | 1982–83 |
| Sandham, A. | | 137 | 104 | MCC v New South Wales | Sydney | 1924–25 |
| Seymour, James | (2) | 108 | 136* | Kent v Worcestershire | Maidstone | 1904 |
| | | 143 | 105* | Kent v Essex | Leyton | 1923 |
| Shafiq Ahmed | | 129 | 217* | National Bank v M.C. Bank | Karachi | 1978–79 |
| Shastri, P. | | 159 | 101* | Rajasthan v Railways | Kota | 1984–85 |
| Shepherd, T.F. | | 121 | 101* | Surrey v Leicestershire | Oval | 1926 |
| Sheppard, D.S. | | 143 | 126 | Cambridge University v Middlesex | Cambridge | 1951 |
| Shrewsbury, A. | | 101 | 127* | Nottinghamshire v Gloucestershire | Nottingham | 1902 |
| Sieler, A.J. | | 157 | 105 | Victoria v Queensland | Brisbane | 1973–74 |
| Simpson, R.B. | (2) | 153 | 115 | Australia v Pakistan | Karachi | 1964–65 |
| | | 121 | 142* | NSW v South Australia | Sydney | 1964–65 |
| Simpson, R.T. | | 143 | 102* | Nottinghamshire v Leicestershire | Nottingham | 1949 |
| Smedley, M.J. | | 109 | 119 | Nottinghamshire v Lancashire | Manchester | 1971 |
| Smith, A.C. | | 145 | 124 | Oxford University v Hampshire | Bournemouth | 1959 |
| Smith, C.L. | | 110 | 100 | Hampshire v Oxford University | Oxford | 1985 |
| Smith, H. | | 120 | 102* | Gloucestershire v Hampshire | Southampton | 1919 |
| Smith, S.B. | | 105 | 116 | Australians v Guyana | Georgetown | 1983–84 |
| Sobers, G.St A. | (2) | 125 | 109* | West Indies v Pakistan | Georgetown | 1957–58 |
| | | 160 | 103* | Nottinghamshire v Surrey | Oval | 1970 |
| Solomon, J.S. | | 107 | 100* | British Guiana v Trinidad | Georgetown | 1963–64 |
| Squires, H.S. | | 131 | 102 | Surrey v Oxford University | Oval | 1932 |
| Stephens, R.S. | | 108 | 181 | Victoria v Tasmania | Launceston | 1913–14 |
| Stevens, G.B. | | 164 | 111 | South Australia v New South Wales | Sydney | 1957–58 |
| Stewart, W.J. | | 155 | 125 | Warwickshire v Lancashire | Blackpool | 1959 |
| Stoddart, A.E. | | 195* | 124 | Middlesex v Nottinghamshire | Lord's | 1893 |
| Storer, H. | | 119 | 100 | Derbyshire v Sussex | Derby | 1929 |
| Storer, W. | | 100 | 100* | Derbyshire v Yorkshire | Derby | 1896 |
| Sutcliffe, B. | (4) | 197 | 128 | Otago v MCC | Dunedin | 1946–47 |
| | | 118 | 125 | Otago v Canterbury | Dunedin | 1947–48 |
| | | 141 | 135 | Auckland v Canterbury | Auckland | 1948–49 |
| | | 243 | 100* | New Zealanders v Essex | Southend | 1949 |
| Sutcliffe, H. | (4) | 176 | 127 | England v Australia | Melbourne | 1924–25 |
| | | 107 | 109* | Yorkshire v MCC | Scarborough | 1926 |
| | | 111 | 100* | Yorkshire v Nottinghamshire | Nottingham | 1928 |
| | | 104 | 109* | England v South Africa | Oval | 1929 |
| Suttle, K.G. | | 112 | 120 | Sussex v Cambridge University | Horsham | 1971 |
| Talat Ali | | 214* | 104 | PIA v Punjab | Lahore | 1978–79 |

| | | | | | |
|---|---|---|---|---|---|
| Thomson, K. | | 102 | 102* | Canterbury v Otago | Dunedin | 1966–67 |
| Timms, J.E. | | 101 | 114* | Northamptonshire v Sussex | Kettering | 1939 |
| Tompkin, M. | | 156 | 107* | Leicestershire v Middlesex | Leicester | 1952 |
| Trimble, S.C. | | 113 | 136* | Queensland v Victoria | Brisbane | 1963–64 |
| Trumper, V.T. | | 109 | 119 | Australians v Essex | Leyton | 1902 |
| Turner, G.M. | (6) | 122 | 128* | Worcestershire v Warwickshire | Birmingham | 1972 |
| | | 101 | 110* | New Zealand v Australia | Christchurch | 1973–74 |
| | | 135 | 108 | Otago v Northern Districts | Gisborne | 1974–75 |
| | | 105 | 186* | Otago v Central Districts | Dunedin | 1974–75 |
| | | 161 | 101 | Worcestershire v Northamptonshire | Stourbridge | 1981 |
| | | 147* | 139 | Worcestershire v Warwickshire | Worcester | 1981 |
| Tyldesley, G.E. | (2) | 165 | 123* | Lancashire v Essex | Leyton | 1921 |
| | | 109 | 108* | Lancashire v Glamorgan | Cardiff | 1930 |
| Tyldesley, J.T. | (3) | 106 | 100* | Lancashire v Warwickshire | Birmingham | 1897 |
| | | 121 | 100* | North v South | Hastings | 1900 |
| | | 136 | 101 | Lancashire v Hampshire | Manchester | 1910 |
| Uttley, K.F.M. | | 132 | 138 | Otago v Auckland | Auckland | 1937–38 |
| Virgin, R.T. | | 124 | 125* | Somerset v Warwickshire | Birmingham | 1965 |
| Waite, J.H.B. | | 159* | 134* | Transvaal v Natal | Durban | 1959–60 |
| Walcott, C.L. | (2) | 126 | 110 | West Indies v Australia | Port-of-Spain | 1954–55 |
| | | 155 | 110 | West Indies v Australia | Kingston | 1954–55 |
| Walters, K.D. | | 242 | 103 | Australia v West Indies | Sydney | 1968–69 |
| Warner, P.F. | | 116 | 113* | Rest v Nottinghamshire | Oval | 1907 |
| Washbrook, C. | | 176 | 121* | Lancashire v Sussex | Eastbourne | 1947 |
| Weekes, E.de C. | | 162 | 101 | West Indies v India | Calcutta | 1948–49 |
| Wharton, A. | | 129 | 108 | Leicestershire v Middlesex | Leicester | 1961 |
| Whitelaw, P.E. | | 115 | 155 | Auckland v Wellington | Auckland | 1934–35 |
| Whitfield, B.J. | | 145* | 100* | Natal B v Eastern Province B | Port Elizabeth | 1979–80 |
| Whysall, W.W. | (2) | 100 | 167* | Nottinghamshire v Gloucestershire | Nottingham | 1926 |
| | | 117 | 101* | Nottinghamshire v Hampshire | Nottingham | 1930 |
| Wilcox, D.R. | | 104 | 129 | Essex v Kent | Westcliff | 1937 |
| Williams, R.G. | | 109 | 151* | Northamptonshire v Warwickshire | Northampton | 1979 |
| Winlaw, R. de W.K. | | 108 | 109* | Cambridge U. v Glamorgan | Cardiff | 1934 |
| Wood, C.J.B. | | 107* | 117* | Leicestershire v Yorkshire | Bradford | 1911 |
| Woolley, F.E. | | 104 | 148* | Kent v Somerset | Tunbridge Wells | 1911 |
| Worthington, T.S. | | 103 | 110* | Derbyshire v Nottinghamshire | Ilkeston | 1938 |
| Wright, J.G. | | 113 | 105 | Northern Districts v Auckland | Auckland | 1981–82 |
| Wright, L.G. | | 176 | 122 | Derbyshire v Warwickshire | Birmingham | 1905 |
| Yallop, G.N. | (2) | 105 | 114* | Victoria v New South Wales | Sydney | 1977–78 |
| | | 113 | 145* | Victoria v Western Australia | Melbourne | 1983–84 |
| Yashpal Sharma | | 157 | 142 | Punjab v Uttar Pradesh | Mohan Nagar | 1977–78 |
| Young, D.M. | | 121 | 117* | Gloucestershire v Northants | Kettering | 1955 |
| Zaheer Abbas | (8) | 216* | 156* | Gloucestershire v Surrey | Oval | 1976 |
| | | 230* | 104* | Gloucestershire v Kent | Canterbury | 1976 |
| | | 205* | 108* | Gloucestershire v Sussex | Cheltenham | 1977 |
| | | 100* | 100* | PIA v Railways | Lahore | 1980–81 |
| | | 215* | 150* | Gloucestershire v Somerset | Bath | 1981 |
| | | 135* | 128 | Gloucs v Northamptonshire | Northampton | 1981 |
| | | 162* | 107 | Gloucestershire v Lancashire | Gloucester | 1982 |
| | | 125 | 101 | PIA v Karachi | Karachi | 1982–83 |
| Zaki Ahmed | | 103 | 110* | Income Tax Dept v Lahore | Multan | 1977–78 |
| Zulch, J.W. | | 185 | 125 | Transvaal v Orange Free State | Bloemfontein | 1920–21 |

**BOTH HUNDREDS ON SAME DAY**

K.S. Ranjitsinhji scored 100 and 125* for Sussex v Yorkshire at Hove on August 22nd, 1896, starting the day with his first innings overnight score at 0*.

**CARRYING BAT THROUGH COMPLETED INNINGS**

C.J.B. Wood scored 107* and 117* out of 309 and 296 respectively for Leicestershire v Yorkshire at Bradford in 1911.

**ON FIRST-CLASS DEBUT**

| | | | | | |
|---|---|---|---|---|---|
| A.R. Morris | 148 | 111 | New South Wales v Queensland | Sydney | 1940–41 |
| N.J. Contractor | 152 | 102* | Gujarat v Baroda | Baroda | 1952–53 |
| Aamer Malik | 132* | 110 | Lahore A v Railways | Lahore | 1979–80 |

**IN SUCCESSIVE MATCHES**

T.W. Hayward (Surrey) scored 144* and 100 v Nottinghamshire at Nottingham and 143 and 125 v Leicestershire at Leicester within a period of six days in 1906.
D.W. Hookes (South Australia) scored 185 and 105 v Queensland and 135 and 156 v New South Wales, all at Adelaide in 1976–77.

**THREE BATSMEN IN A MATCH**

U.M. Merchant, D.G. Phadkar and M.R. Rege; Bombay v Maharashtra (Poona) 1948–49.

**NEAR-MISSES**

C.B. Fry, who achieved the feat five times, missed by one run on three occasions for Sussex at Hove: 99 & 131 v Hampshire in 1898, 99 & 127* v Leicestershire in 1903, and 125 & 99* v Worcestershire in 1907.
A.H. Dyson scored 96 and 104* for Glamorgan v Essex at Neath in 1934. He hit his wicket in cutting the boundary which would have given him his first innings century.
G. Boycott is alone in scoring 99 and a hundred in a Test match: 99 and 112 for England v West Indies at Port-of-Spain in 1973–74.

# MOST HUNDREDS IN CONSECUTIVE INNINGS

## SIX HUNDREDS IN CONSECUTIVE INNINGS

**Bradman, D.G.** (South Australia) in 1938–39: 118 D.G. Bradman's XI v K.E. Rigg's XI (Melbourne), 143 v New South Wales (Adelaide), 225 v Queensland (Adelaide), 107 v Victoria (Melbourne), 186 v Queensland (Brisbane), 135* v New South Wales (Sydney).
**Fry, C.B.** (Sussex) in 1901: 106 v Hampshire (Portsmouth), 209 v Yorkshire (Hove), 149 v Middlesex (Hove), 105 v Surrey (Oval), 140 v Kent (Hove), 105 Rest of England v Yorkshire (Lord's).
**Procter, M.J.** (Rhodesia) in 1970–71: 119 v Natal B (Bulawayo), 129 v Transvaal B (Salisbury), 107 v Orange Free State (Bloemfontein), 174 v N.E. Transvaal (Pretoria), 106 v Griqualand West (Kimberley), 254 v W. Province (Salisbury).

## FIVE HUNDREDS IN CONSECUTIVE INNINGS

**Weekes, E.de C.** (West Indians) in 1955–56: 156 v Auckland (Auckland), 148 v Canterbury (Christchurch), 123 v New Zealand (Dunedin), 119* v Wellington (Wellington), 103 v New Zealand (Christchurch).

## FOUR HUNDREDS IN CONSECUTIVE INNINGS

**Azharuddin, M.** (Hyderabad) in 1984–85: 151 for India U.25 v England (Ahmedabad), 121 and 105* v Andhra (Machillipatnam), 110 for India v England (Calcutta).
**Border, A.R.** (Australians) in 1985: 106 v Somerset (Taunton), 135 v Worcestershire (Worcester), 125 v MCC (Lord's), 100 v Derbyshire (Derby).
**Bradman, D.G.** (New South Wales) in 1931–32: 135 for New South Wales (Sydney), 226 for Australia (Brisbane), 219 for New South Wales (Sydney), 112 for Australia (Sydney), all v South Africa.
**Bradman, D.G.** (Australians) in 1948 and 1948–49: 150 v Gentlemen of England (Lord's), 143 v South of England (Hastings), 153 v H.D.G. Leveson Gower's XI (Scarborough) *(his last three innings in England)*, and 123 D.G. Bradman's XI v A.L. Hassett's XI (Melbourne) 1948–49.
**Compton, D.C.S.** (Middlesex) in 1946–47: 124 MCC v Combined XI (Hobart), 163 MCC v Tasmania (Launceston), 147 and 103* England v Australia (Adelaide).
**Contractor, N.J.** (Gujarat) in 1957–58: 102 v Bombay (Poona), 135 v Saurashtra (Poona), 167 v Baroda (Sangli), 110 v Maharashtra (Poona).
**Duleepsinhji, K.S.** (Sussex) in 1931: 161* v Worcestershire (Dudley), 109 England v New Zealand (Oval), 103 v Middlesex (Hove), 127 v Hampshire (Hastings).
**Fry, C.B.** (Hampshire) in 1911: 123 and 112 v Kent (Canterbury), 258* v Gloucestershire (Southampton), 102* Rest of England v Warwickshire (Oval).
**Hammond, W.R.** (MCC) in 1936–37: 141 v Western Australia (Perth), 107 v Combined XI (Perth), 104 and 136 v South Australia (Adelaide).
**Hammond, W.R.** (Gloucestershire) in 1945 and 1946: 121 and 102 England XI v Dominions XI (Lord's) 1945, 132 v Oxford University (Oxford), 134 v Lancashire (Gloucester) 1946.
**Hardinge, H.T.W.** (Kent) in 1913: 154* v Leicestershire (Canterbury), 117 and 105* v Hampshire (Dover), 107 v Northamptonshire (Dover).
**Hayward, T.W.** (Surrey) in 1906: 144* and 100 v Nottinghamshire (Nottingham), 143 and 125 v Leicestershire (Leicester). *All scored within six days.*
**Hobbs, J.B.** (Surrey) in 1920: 110 v Sussex (Oval), 134 v Leicestershire (Leicester), 101 v Warwickshire (Birmingham), 112 v Yorkshire (Sheffield).

**Hobbs, J.B.** (Surrey) in 1925: 104 and 143* v Cambridge University (Oval), 111 v Somerset (Oval), 215 v Warwickshire (Birmingham). *His two previous innings were 107 and 87 v Essex (Oval).*
**Hookes, D.W.** (South Australia) in 1976–77: 185 and 105 v Queensland, 135 and 156 v New South Wales, all at Adelaide.
**Kirsten, P.N.** (Western Province) in 1976–77: 173* and 103 v Eastern Province (Cape Town), 107 South African Universities v Orange Free State (Bloemfontein), 165 v Transvaal (Johannesburg).
**Langridge, J.G.** (Sussex) in 1949: 115* v Cambridge University (Cambridge), 115 and 129 v Lancashire (Manchester), 120 v Gloucestershire (Chichester).
**Macartney, C.G.** (Australians) in 1921: 105 v Hampshire (Southampton), 193 v Northamptonshire (Northampton), 345 v Nottinghamshire (Nottingham), 115 v England (Leeds).
**McEwan, K.S.** (Essex) in 1977: 218 v Sussex (Chelmsford), 102 and 116 v Warwickshire (Birmingham), 106* v Gloucestershire (Southend).
**May, P.B.H.** (MCC) in 1956–57: 162 v Western Province (Cape Town), 118 v Eastern Province (Port Elizabeth), 124* v Rhodesia (Bulawayo), 206 v Rhodesia (Salisbury).
**Merchant, V.M.** (Bombay and India) in 1941–42: 170* Bombay v Nawanagar (Jamnagar), 243* Hindus v Rest (Bombay), 221 Hindus v Parsees (Bombay), 153* Bombay v Sind (Bombay).
**Mitchell, A.** (Yorkshire) in 1933: 150* v Worcestershire (Worcester), 107 v MCC (Scarborough), 100* and 100* H.D.G. Leveson Gower's XI v MCC Australian XI (Scarborough).
**Pataudi, Nawab of, sr** (Oxford University) in 1931: 183* v Army (Folkestone), 165 and 100 v Surrey (Oval), 138 v H.D.G. Leveson Gower's XI (Eastbourne).
**Rowe, L.G.** (Jamaica) in 1971–72: 147 v Guyana, 227 v New Zealanders, 214 and 100* West Indies v New Zealand, all at Kingston.
**Roy, Pankaj** (Bengal) in 1962–63: 178 v Bihar, 136 v Orissa, 112 and 118 v Hyderabad, all at Calcutta.
**Sadiq Mohammad** (Gloucestershire) in 1976: 108 v Somerset (Bristol), 163* and 150 v Derbyshire (Bristol), 109 v Worcestershire (Worcester).
**Saeed Ahmed** (Pakistan International Airlines) in 1961–62: 149 East Pakistan Governor's XI v Commonwealth XI (Dacca), 127* v East Zone (Dacca), 105 and 102 v North Zone (Lahore).
**Sutcliffe, H.** (Yorkshire) in 1931: 120* v Middlesex (Lord's), 107 v Hampshire (Portsmouth), 230 v Kent (Folkestone), 183 v Somerset (Dewsbury).
**Sutcliffe, H.** (Yorkshire) in 1939: 163 v Lancashire (Manchester), 116 v Hampshire (Sheffield), 234* v Leicestershire (Hull), 175 v Middlesex (Lord's).
**Tyldesley, G.E.** (Lancashire) in 1926: 131 v Surrey (Oval), 131 Players v Gentlemen (Lord's), 106 v Essex (Nelson), 126 v Somerset (Taunton).
**Whysall, W.W.** (Nottinghamshire) in 1930: 117 and 101* v Hampshire (Nottingham), 120 v Australians (Nottingham), 158 v Warwickshire (Birmingham).
**Woolley, F.E.** (Kent) in 1929: 155 v Derbyshire (Chesterfield), 108 v Somerset (Tonbridge), 131 v Yorkshire (Tonbridge), 117 v Hampshire (Folkestone).
**Zaheer Abbas** (Pakistan International Airlines) in 1970–71: 118 v East Pakistan Greens (Dacca), 196 v East Pakistan Whites (Dacca), 161 v Bahawalpur (Karachi), 111 v Punjab University (Lahore).
**Zaheer Abbas** (Pakistan) in 1982–83: 108, BCCP Patron's XI v Indians (Rawalpindi), 215 Pakistan v India (Lahore), 186 Pakistan v India (Karachi), 168 Pakistan v India (Faisalabad).

*G. Boycott (Yorkshire) scored four hundreds in consecutive innings in County Championship matches in 1968: 100 v Sussex (Bradford), 132 v Leicestershire (Leicester), 180\* v Warwickshire (Middlesbrough), 125 v Gloucestershire (Bristol). After the Leicestershire match he scored 13 and 6 for MCC v Australians at Lord's.*

## THREE HUNDREDS IN CONSECUTIVE INNINGS

**Abel, R.** (Surrey) in 1896: 138 v Warwickshire (Oval), 152 v Leicestershire (Oval), 231 v Essex (Oval).
**Agha Zahid** (Habib Bank) in 1982–83: 102 and 119 v Railways (Lahore), 175 v PIA (Lahore).
**Ames, L.E.G.** (Kent) in 1932: 130 v Middlesex (Tunbridge Wells), 149 v Northamptonshire (Tunbridge Wells), 120 v Surrey (Blackheath).
**Ames, L.E.G.** (Kent) in 1937: 125 v Worcestershire (Worcester), 119 and 127 v Surrey (Blackheath).
**Amiss, D.L.** (Warwickshire) in 1978: 155* and 112 v Worcestershire (Birmingham), 162 v Glamorgan (Cardiff).
**Arun Lal** (Bengal) in 1983–84: 103* v Bihar (Dhanbad), 103* v Assam (Calcutta), 135 v Orissa (Rourkela).
**Balaskas, X.C.** (Griqualand West) in 1929–30: 206 v Rhodesia (Kimberley), 132 v Eastern Province (Kimberley), 101 v Western Province (Kimberley).
**Bardsley, W.** (New South Wales) in 1910–11: 191* v South Australia (Sydney), 132 Australia v South Africa (Sydney), 124 v Victoria (Melbourne).
**Bardsley, W.** (Australians) in 1926: 127 v Derbyshire (Chesterfield), 193* v England (Lord's), 112 v Northamptonshire (Northampton).
**Border, A.R.** (Australians) in 1979–80: 178 v Punjab Governor's XI (Multan), 150* and 153 v Pakistan (Lahore).
**Boycott, G.** (Yorkshire) in 1978: 113 v Northamptonshire (Northampton), 103* v New Zealanders (Leeds), 118 v Glamorgan (Sheffield).

**Bradman, D.G.** (New South Wales) in 1929–30: 157 v MCC (Sydney), 124 and 225 W.M. Woodfull's XI v J. Ryder's XI (Sydney).

**Bradman, D.G.** (New South Wales) in 1933–34 and 1934: 253 v Queensland (Sydney), 128 v Victoria (Sydney) in 1933–34, 206 Australians v Worcestershire (Worcester) in 1934.

**Bradman, D.G.** (Australians) in 1934: 140 v Yorkshire (Sheffield), 304 v England (Leeds), 244 v England (Oval).

**Bradman, D.G.** (South Australia) in 1935–36: 117 v New South Wales (Adelaide), 233 v Queensland (Adelaide), 357 v Victoria (Melbourne).

**Bradman, D.G.** (Australians) in 1937–38 and 1938: 144 v Tasmania (Hobart), 102 v Western Australia (Perth) 1937–38, 258 v Worcestershire (Worcester) 1938.

**Bradman, D.G.** (South Australia) in 1946–47: 119 v Victoria (Adelaide), 187 Australia v England (Brisbane), 234 Australia v England (Sydney).

**Bradman, D.G.** (Australia) in 1947–48: 132 and 127* v India (Melbourne), 201 v India (Adelaide).

**Brown, W.A.** (Australians) in 1948: 200 v Cambridge University (Cambridge), 153 v Essex (Southend), 108 v Oxford University (Oxford).

**Burge, P.J.P.** (Queensland) in 1963–64: 283 v New South Wales, 205* v Western Australia, 129 v South Africans, all at Brisbane.

**Cameron, H.B.** (Transvaal) in 1933–34 and 1934–35: 110 v Western Province (Cape Town) 1933–34, 182 v Griqualand West (Johannesburg), 112 v Natal (Durban) 1934–35.

**Chappell, G.S.** (Queensland) in 1975–76: 123 and 109* Australia v West Indies (Brisbane), 124 v New South Wales (Sydney).

**Chappell, G.S.** (Queensland) in 1980–81: 113 v New South Wales (Brisbane), 102* v Victoria (Brisbane), 194 v Western Australia (Brisbane).

**Chappell, I.M.** (South Australia) in 1968–69: 188* Combined XI v West Indians (Perth), 123 v West Indians (Adelaide), 117 Australia v West Indies (Brisbane).

**Chappell, I.M.** (Australians) in 1973–74: 128 v Northern Districts (Hamilton), 145 and 121 v New Zealand (Wellington).

**Chinnery, H.B.** (Middlesex) in 1901: 105 and 165 MCC v Oxford University (Oxford), 100 v Gloucestershire (Lord's).

**Christy, J.A.J.** (Transvaal) in 1927–28 and 1928–29: 103 v Rhodesia (Bulawayo), 175 v Rhodesia (Salisbury) 1927–28, 141 v Natal (Durban) 1928–29.

**Compton, D.C.S.** (Middlesex) in 1947: 112 v Worcestershire (Lord's), 110 v Sussex (Lord's), 154 v South Africans (Lord's).

**Compton, D.C.S.** (MCC) in 1948–49: 121 v Cape Province (Cape Town), 150* v Griqualand West (Kimberley), 106 v Natal (Durban).

**Cox, G.** (Sussex) in 1947: 103 v Lancashire (Eastbourne), 142 v Gloucestershire (Hove), 132 v South Africans (Hove).

**Croom, A.J.W.** (Warwickshire) in 1931: 109 v Kent (Birmingham), 105 v Northamptonshire (Peterborough), 159 v Nottinghamshire (Birmingham).

**Dalton, E.L.** (South Africans) in 1929: 157 and 116* v Kent (Canterbury), 102 v Sussex (Hove). *His first three hundreds in first-class cricket.*

**Davies, D.** (Glamorgan) in 1928: 126* v Sussex (Swansea), 103 v Northamptonshire (Northampton), 165* v Sussex (Eastbourne).

**Dempster, C.S.** (Leicestershire) in 1937: 110 v Sussex (Leicester), 133 and 154* v Gloucestershire (Gloucester).

**Dempster, C.S.** (Leicestershire) in 1938: 105 v Australians (Leicester), 110 v Hampshire (Southampton), 187 v Oxford University (Oxford).

**Denton, D.** (MCC) in 1909–10: 139 and 138 v Transvaal (Johannesburg), 104 England v South Africa (Johannesburg).

**Ducat, A.** (Surrey) in 1921: 290* v Essex (Leyton), 134 v Northamptonshire (Oval), 120 v Warwickshire (Birmingham).

**Ducat, A.** (Surrey) in 1928: 119 v Lancashire (Manchester), 179* v Warwickshire (Oval), 101* v Sussex (Horsham).

**Duleepsinhji, K.S.** (Sussex) in 1932: 116 v Worcestershire (Horsham), 126 v Surrey (Hove), 128 South v North (Manchester).

**Edrich, J.H.** (Surrey) in 1965: 139 v New Zealanders (Oval), 121* v Oxford University (Oxford), 205* v Gloucestershire (Bristol).

**Fiddian-Green, C.A.F.** (Cambridge University) in 1922: 103 v Essex (Colchester), 113 v Sussex (Hove), 120 v H.D.G. Leveson Gower's XI (Eastbourne).

**Fishlock, L.B.** (Surrey) in 1937: 113 and 105 v Yorkshire (Oval), 127 v Middlesex (Lord's).

**Foster, M.L.C.** (Jamaica) in 1971–72 and 1972–73: 101* v Barbados (Bridgetown) in 1971–72, 145* v Barbados and 136 v Trinidad at Kingston in 1972–73.

**Foster, R.E.** (Oxford University) in 1900: 128 and 100* v A.J. Webbe's XI (Oxford), 169 v London County (Oxford).

**Fry, C.B.** (Sussex) in 1900: 125 and 229 v Surrey (Hove), 110 v Middlesex (Hove).

**Gavaskar, S.M.** (India) in 1978–79: 111 and 137 v Pakistan (Karachi), 205 v West Indies (Bombay).

**Grace, W.G.** in 1871: 118 Gentlemen of South v Gentlemen of North (West Brompton), 178 South v North (Lord's), 162 Gentlemen of England v Cambridge University (Cambridge).

**Grace, W.G.** (Gloucestershire) in 1872: 112 Gentlemen v Players (Lord's), 117 Gentlemen v Players (Oval), 170* England v Nottinghamshire and Yorkshire (Lord's).
**Grace, W.G.** (Gloucestershire) in 1873: 134 Gentlemen of South v Players of South (Oval), 163 Gentlemen v Players (Lord's), 158 Gentlemen v Players (Oval).
**Grace, W.G.** (Gloucestershire) in 1874: 121 Kent and Gloucestershire v England (Canterbury), 123 MCC v Kent (Canterbury), 127 v Yorkshire (Clifton).
**Grace, W.G.** (Gloucestershire) in 1876: 344 MCC v Kent (Canterbury), 177 v Nottinghamshire (Clifton), 318* v Yorkshire (Cheltenham).
**Greenidge, C.G.** (West Indies) in 1976: 134 and 101 v England (Manchester), 115 v England (Leeds).
**Greenidge, C.G.** (Hampshire) in 1978: 112 v Warwickshire, 136 and 120 v Kent, all at Bournemouth.
**Hallows, C.** (Lancashire) in 1927 and 1928: 120 v Rest of England (Oval) in 1927, 100 v Northamptonshire (Manchester), 101 v Glamorgan (Manchester) 1928.
**Hamence, R.A.** (South Australia) in 1946–47: 116 v Victoria (Adelaide), 132 and 101* v New South Wales (Adelaide).
**Hammond, W.R.** (Gloucestershire) in 1927: 135 v Yorkshire (Gloucester), 108 and 128 v Surrey (Oval).
**Hammond, W.R.** (MCC) in 1928–29: 119* and 177 England v Australia (Adelaide), 114 v Victoria (Melbourne).
**Hammond, W.R.** (Gloucestershire) in 1937: 140 England v New Zealand (Lord's), 108 v New Zealanders (Bristol), 112 v Hampshire (Bristol).
**Hammond, W.R.** (Gloucestershire) in 1938: 110 and 123 v Derbyshire (Burton upon Trent), 240 England v Australia (Lord's).
**Hanif Mohammad** (Karachi) in 1956–57 and 1957–58: 228 Karachi Whites v Karachi Blues (Karachi) 1956–57, 123 v Sind B (Karachi), 146* v Sind (Karachi) 1957–58.
**Hanif Mohammad** (Karachi) in 1958–59: 129 v Hyderabad (Hyderabad), 499 v Bahawalpur (Karachi), 130 v Services (Karachi).
**Hanif Mohammad** (Karachi Whites) in 1961–62: 133 and 146 v Karachi Greens (Karachi), 189 v Hyderabad (Karachi).
**Harris, M.J.** (Nottinghamshire) in 1971: 107 and 131* v Essex (Chelmsford), 177 v Kent (Nottingham).
**Harvey, R.N.** (Australians) in 1953: 141 v Gloucestershire (Bristol), 118 v Northamptonshire (Northampton), 122 v England (Manchester).
**Hassett, A.L.** (Australians) in 1938: 146 v Oxford University (Oxford), 148 v Leicestershire (Leicester), 220* v Cambridge University (Cambridge).
**Hassett, A.L.** (Victoria) in 1939–40: 122 and 122 v New South Wales (Sydney), 136 Rest of Australia v New South Wales (Sydney).
**Hassett, A.L.** (Australians) in 1948: 200* v Gentlemen of England (Lord's), 103 v Somerset (Taunton), 151 v South of England (Hastings).
**Hayward, T.W.** (Surrey) in 1899: 273 v Yorkshire (Oval), 137 England v Australia (Oval), 158 v Somerset (Taunton).
**Hazare, V.S.** (Baroda) in 1943–44: 309 Rest v Hindus (Bombay), 101 v Bombay (Bombay), 233 Indian States v Rest of India (Poona).
**Hazare, V.S.** (Baroda) in 1944–45: 200* Cricket Club of India v Services (Bombay), 127 and 162* v Maharashtra (Poona).
**Hazare, V.S.** (Baroda) in 1949–50 and 1950: 130 and 101 v Holkar (Baroda) 1949–50, 114 Commonwealth XI v England XI (Kingston upon Thames) 1950.
**Headley, G.A.** (West Indians) in 1939: 106 and 107 v England (Lord's), 234* v Nottinghamshire (Nottingham).
**Hendren, E.H.** (MCC) in 1929–30: 205 England v West Indies (Port-of-Spain), 254* MCC v British Guiana (Georgetown), 171 MCC v British Guiana (Georgetown).
**Hendren, E.H.** (Middlesex) in 1931: 232 v Nottinghamshire (Nottingham), 189 and 100* v Warwickshire (Birmingham).
**Hendren, E.H.** (Middlesex) in 1933: 111 v Surrey (Lord's), 101 and 101 v Kent (Lord's).
**Hendry, H.S.T.L.** (Victoria) in 1926–27: 177 v South Australia (Adelaide), 140 v Queensland (Melbourne), 100 v New South Wales (Melbourne).
**Hill, C.** (South Australia) in 1909–10: 176 v Victoria (Adelaide), 205 v New South Wales (Adelaide), 185 v Victoria (Melbourne).
**Hirst, G.H.** (Yorkshire) in 1899: 186 v Surrey (Oval), 131 v Hampshire (Bradford), 138 v Nottinghamshire (Nottingham).
**Hobbs, J.B.** (Surrey) in 1914: 122 v Kent (Blackheath), 226 v Nottinghamshire (Oval), 126 v Worcestershire (Worcester).
**Hobbs, J.B.** (Surrey) in 1926: 261 v Oxford University (Oval), 119 England v Australia (Lord's), 200 v Hampshire (Southampton).
**Hobbs, J.B.** (Surrey) in 1932: 113 and 119* v Essex (Oval), 123 v Somerset (Taunton).
**Howell, M.** (Oxford University) in 1919: 115 and 102 v H.D.G. Leveson Gower's XI (Eastbourne), 170 v Cambridge University (Lord's).
**Hutton, L.** (Yorkshire) in 1937: 136 v Kent (Tonbridge), 271* v Derbyshire (Sheffield), 153 v Leicestershire (Hull).
**Hutton, L.** (Yorkshire) in 1947: 197 and 104 v Essex (Southend), 270* v Hampshire (Bournemouth).

**Hutton, L.** (Yorkshire) in 1952: 120 v Kent (Canterbury), 103 and 137 v MCC (Scarborough).
**Inverarity, R.J.** (Western Australia) in 1968–69: 103 v New South Wales (Sydney), 108 v Queensland (Brisbane), 114 v Victoria (Melbourne).
**Iremonger, J.** (Nottinghamshire) in 1904: 189* v Middlesex (Lord's), 272 v Kent (Nottingham), 142 v Derbyshire (Chesterfield).
**Jameson, J.A.** (Warwickshire) in 1974: 110 and 111 D.H. Robins' XI v Indians (Eastbourne), 115 v Oxford University (Oxford).
**Jardine, D.R.** (Surrey) in 1927: 120 Oxford Harlequins v Oxford University (Oxford), 147 v Leicestershire (Leicester), 143 v Lancashire (Manchester).
**Jardine, D.R.** (MCC) in 1928–29: 109 v Western Australia (Perth), 104 v Victoria (Melbourne), 140 v New South Wales (Sydney).
**Javed Miandad** (Glamorgan) in 1981: 105 v Warwickshire (Cardiff), 137* and 106 v Somerset (Swansea).
**Javed Miandad** (Pakistanis) in 1983–84: 106* v Victoria (Melbourne), 131 v Australia (Adelaide), 141* v Tasmania (Hobart).
**Johnson, P.R.** (Somerset) in 1908: 164 and 131 v Middlesex (Taunton), 117 v Hampshire (Southampton).
**Kallicharran, A.I.** (Warwickshire) in 1983: 111 v Kent (Folkestone), 152 and 118* v Sussex (Birmingham).
**Keeton, W.W.** (Nottinghamshire) in 1933: 110 v Hampshire (Southampton), 168 v Middlesex (Nottingham), 110 v Yorkshire (Bradford).
**Keeton, W.W.** (Nottinghamshire) in 1949: 109* v Hampshire (Nottingham), 208 v Glamorgan (Nottingham), 134 v Lancashire (Manchester).
**Kenny, R.B.** (Bombay) in 1956–57: 139 v Maharashtra (Bombay), 132 v Uttar Pradesh (Benares), 218 v Madras (Bombay).
**Kippax, A.F.** (New South Wales) in 1925–26 and 1926–27: 271* v Victoria (Sydney) 1925–26, 127 and 131 v Queensland (Brisbane) 1926–27.
**Knight, D.J.** (Surrey) in 1919: 114 and 101 v Yorkshire (Oval), 146 v Lancashire (Manchester).
**Lee, F.S.** (Somerset) in 1938: 109* and 107 v Worcestershire (Worcester), 141 v Surrey (Taunton).
**Lester, E.I.** (Yorkshire) in 1947: 127 v Derbyshire (Scarborough), 126 and 142 v Northamptonshire (Northampton).
**Leyland, M.** (Yorkshire) in 1934: 104* v MCC (Lord's), 100 v Oxford University (Oxford), 126 v Glamorgan (Swansea).
**Macartney, C.G.** (New South Wales) in 1910–11: 119 and 126 v South Africans (Sydney), 137 Australia v South Africa (Sydney).
**Macartney, C.G.** (Australians) in 1912: 127 v Northamptonshire (Northampton), 208 v Essex (Leyton), 123 v Surrey (Oval).
**Macartney, C.G.** (New South Wales) in 1923–24: 120 v Wellington (Wellington), 120 v Otago (Dunedin), 221 v Canterbury (Christchurch).
**McCosker, R.B.** (New South Wales) in 1981–82: 146* v South Australia (Sydney), 123* and 118* v Victoria (Sydney).
**Mackay, J.R.M.** (New South Wales) in 1905–06: 194 v Victoria (Melbourne), 105 and 102* v South Australia (Sydney).
**MacLaren, A.C.** (Lancashire) in 1895: 152 v Nottinghamshire (Manchester), 108 v Middlesex (Lord's), 135 v Leicestershire (Leicester).
**MacLaren, A.C.** (A.E. Stoddart's XI) in 1897–98: 142 and 100 v New South Wales (Sydney), 109 England v Australia (Sydney).
**Mason, J.R.** (Kent) in 1904: 138 v Yorkshire (Tunbridge Wells), 126 v Somerset (Beckenham), 133 v Essex (Colchester).
**Mason, J.R.** (Kent) in 1909: 179* v Sussex (Hove), 111 v Somerset (Taunton), 152* v Surrey (Oval).
**May, P.B.H.** (Surrey) in 1952: 197 v Leicestershire (Leicester), 174 and 100* MCC v Yorkshire (Scarborough).
**May, P.B.H.** (Surrey) in 1958: 155 v Yorkshire (Oval), 101 England v New Zealand (Manchester), 112* v New Zealanders (Oval).
**Mead, C.P.** (Hampshire) in 1921: 280* v Nottinghamshire (Southampton), 113 and 224 v Sussex (Horsham).
**Mead, C.P.** (Hampshire) in 1922: 152 v Kent (Southampton), 235 v Worcestershire (Worcester), 105 v Leicestershire (Southampton).
**Mead, C.P.** (Hampshire) in 1923: 132 v Worcestershire (Worcester), 222 v Warwickshire (Birmingham), 147 v Sussex (Hove).
**Mead, C.P.** (Hampshire) in 1933: 135 v Kent (Canterbury), 152 v Nottinghamshire (Southampton), 113* v Lancashire (Manchester).
**Melville, A.** (South Africa) in 1947: 189 and 104* v England (Nottingham), 117 v England (Lord's).
**Merchant, V.M.** (Bombay) in 1943–44: 250* Hindus v Rest, 141 Bombay v Baroda, 359* Bombay v Maharashtra, all at Bombay.
**Mitchell, B.** (South Africans) in 1947: 131 v Lancashire (Manchester), 120 and 189* v England (Oval).

**Mohammad Ilyas** (Pakistan International Airlines) in 1970–71: 152* v EPSF Greens (Dacca), 107 v EPSF Whites (Dacca), 108 v Bahawalpur (Karachi).

**Mohsin Khan** (Habib Bank) in 1977–78: 125 v Universities (Lahore), 116 v Sargodha (Faisalabad), 220 v Income Tax Dept (Karachi).

**Moroney, J.** (Australians) in 1949–50: 118 and 101* v South Africa (Johannesburg), 133 v Natal (Pietermaritzberg).

**Morris, A.R.** (Australians) in 1949–50: 102* v Griqualand West (Kimberley), 157 v South Africa (Port Elizabeth), 103 v Western Province (Cape Town).

**Mudassar Nazar** (Pakistan Universities) in 1974–75: 107 v Punjab, 100 v Sind, 165 v Railways, all at Lahore.

**Mudassar Nazar** (Pakistan) in 1982–83: 231 v India (Hyderabad), 152* v India (Lahore), 152 v India (Karachi).

**Mushtaq Mohammad** (Northamptonshire) in 1972: 120 v Surrey (Northampton), 137* v Lancashire (Liverpool), 122 v Leicestershire (Leicester).

**Nichol, M.** (Worcestershire) in 1933: 116 v Hampshire (Bournemouth), 165* v Glamorgan (Worcester), 154 v Yorkshire (Worcester).

**Noble, M.A.** (New South Wales) in 1898–99: 101 v South Australia (Sydney), 100 v Victoria (Sydney), 111 Australian XI v Rest of Australia (Sydney).

**Nourse, A.D.** (South Africans) in 1935: 147 and 108* v Surrey (Oval), 148 v Oxford University (Oxford).

**Nourse, A.D.** (Natal) in 1950–51: 124 v Border (Pietermaritzburg), 121 v Orange Free State (Bloemfontein), 114 v Western Province (Durban).

**O'Connor, L.P.D.** (Queensland) in 1926–27: 196 v New South Wales (Brisbane), 103 and 143* v New South Wales (Sydney).

**O'Keefe, F.A.** (Victoria) in 1921–22: 180 v South Australia (Adelaide), 177 and 141 Rest of Australia v Australian XI (Sydney).

**Onyons, B.A.** (Victoria) in 1928–29: 131 v New South Wales (Sydney), 105 and 127 v Queensland (Brisbane).

**Pairaudeau, B.H.** (British Guiana) in 1952–53: 101 v Jamaica (Georgetown), 126 v Jamaica (Georgetown), 115 West Indies v India (Port-of-Spain).

**Parfitt, P.H.** (Middlesex) in 1962: 122 and 114 v Pakistanis (Lord's), 101* England v Pakistan (Nottingham).

**Parkhouse, W.G.A.** (Glamorgan) 1950: 121 and 148 v Somerset (Cardiff), 127 v Combined Services (Cardiff).

**Pataudi, Nawab of, jr** (Oxford University) in 1961: 106 and 103* v Yorkshire (Oxford), 144 v Middlesex (Oxford).

**Pataudi, Nawab of, jr** (Delhi) in 1964–65: 154 v Northern Punjab, 130 and 107* v Services, all at Delhi.

**Patel, B.P.** (Karnataka) in 1978–79: 100 South Zone v Central Zone (Nagpur), 100 v Kerala (Trichur), 126 v Andrha (Udupi).

**Paynter, E.** (Lancashire) in 1936: 123* v Nottinghamshire (Nottingham), 177 v Glamorgan (Manchester, 119 v Northamptonshire (Manchester).

**Perrin, P.A.** (Essex) in 1903: 170 and 102* v Nottinghamshire (Nottingham), 102* v Derbyshire (Leyton).

**Phadkar, D.G.** (Bombay) in 1948–49: 134* v Madras (Madras), 131 and 160 v Maharashtra (Poona).

**Place, W.** (Lancashire) in 1947: 171 v Essex (Clacton), 105 and 132* v Nottinghamshire (Manchester).

**Ponsford, W.H.** (Victoria) in 1921–22 and 1922–23: 162 v Tasmania (Melbourne) 1921–22, 429 v Tasmania (Melbourne), 108 v South Australia (Adelaide) 1922–23. *His third, fourth and fifth innings in first-class cricket.*

**Ponsford, W.H.** (Victoria) in 1923–24: 159 v South Australia (Melbourne), 110 and 110* v New South Wales (Sydney).

**Ponsford, W.H.** (Victoria) in 1926–27: 151 v Queensland (Melbourne), 352 v New South Wales (Melbourne), 108 v South Australia (Melbourne).

**Ponsford, W.H.** (Victoria) in 1927–28: 133 v South Australia (Adelaide), 437 v Queensland (Melbourne), 202 v New South Wales (Melbourne).

**Ponsford, W.H.** (Victoria) in 1930–31: 109* v New South Wales (Melbourne), 183 Australia v West Indies (Sydney), 109 v West Indies (Brisbane).

**Poore, R.M.** (Hampshire) in 1899: 104 and 119* v Somerset (Portsmouth), 111 v Lancashire (Southampton).

**Prideaux, R.M.** (Northamptonshire) in 1966: 135* v Cambridge University (Cambridge), 106 and 100 v Nottinghamshire (Nottingham).

**Quaife, W.G.** (Warwickshire) in 1901: 118* v Yorkshire (Birmingham), 108 London County v Cambridge University (Crystal Palace), 117* v Derbyshire (Derby).

**Quaife, W.G.** (Warwickshire) in 1913: 124 and 109 v Surrey (Oval), 107 v Northamptonshire (Birmingham).

**Rangnekar, K.M.** (Bombay) in 1940–41: 202 v Maharashtra (Poona), 117 Indian XI v Ceylon (Bombay), 135 Rest of India v Maharashtra (Bombay).

**Ranjitsinhji, K.S.** (Sussex) in 1896: 165 v Lancashire (Hove), 100 and 125* v Yorkshire (Hove).
**Ranjitsinhji, K.S.** (Sussex) in 1900: 127 v Gloucestershire (Hove), 222 v Somerset (Hove), 215* v Cambridge University (Cambridge).
**Reid, J.R.** (New Zealanders) in 1961–62: 101 and 118* v Orange Free State (Bloemfontein), 165 v South African Colts XI (East London).
**Rhodes, W.** (MCC) in 1911–12: 179 England v Australia (Melbourne), 119 and 109 v New South Wales (Sydney).
**Richards, I.V.A.** (West Indians) in 1980: 145 v England (Lord's), 100 v Glamorgan (Swansea), 103 v Somerset (Taunton).
**Richards, I.V.A.** (Somerset) in 1985: 120 v Lancashire (Manchester), 123 v Derbyshire (Derby), 112 v Sussex (Taunton).
**Richardson, P.E.** (Worcestershire) in 1956: 134 v Nottinghamshire (Worcester), 104 England v Australia (Manchester), 147 v Essex (Worcester).
**Rizwan-uz-Zaman** (PIA) in 1984–85: 104* v Karachi (Karachi), 119 and 121* v National Bank (Karachi).
**Robertson, J.D.B.** (Middlesex) in 1947: 140 v Kent (Canterbury), 127 v Surrey (Oval), 110 v Kent (Lord's).
**Robertson, J.D.B.** (Middlesex) in 1954: 123 v Glamorgan (Lord's), 101 v Northamptonshire (Northampton), 101 v Worcestershire (Worcester).
**Rowan, E.A.B.** (Transvaal) in 1952–53: 157 v Border (Johannesburg), 195 v N.E. Transvaal (Johannesburg), 102 v Griqualand West (Kimberley).
**Roy, Pankaj** (Bengal) in 1957–58: 154 v Assam (Calcutta), 114 v Orissa (Cuttack), 114 v Bihar (Patna).
**Sadiq Mohammad** (Gloucestershire) in 1979: 171 and 103 v Glamorgan (Bristol), 100 v Hampshire (Southampton).
**Sardesai, D.N.** (Bombay) in 1969–70: 153 v Baroda (Baroda), 131 v Gujarat (Surat), 154 v Mysore (Bombay).
**Shafiq Ahmed** (National Bank) in 1978–79: 141 v Karachi B (Karachi), 129 and 217* v Muslim Commercial Bank (Karachi).
**Shiraz Dharsi** (PWD) in 1972–73: 149 v Karachi Whites (Karachi), 125 v Customs (Karachi), 100 v Universities (Lahore).
**Siedle, I.J.** (Natal) in 1936–37: 105 v Border (Durban), 111 v Eastern Province (Pietermaritzburg), 207 v Western Province (Durban). *His last three innings in first-class cricket.*
**Simpson, R.T.** (Nottinghamshire) in 1959: 108* v Surrey (Oval), 132 v Sussex (Nottingham), 100 v Indians (Nottingham).
**Smith, S.B.** (New South Wales) in 1983–84: 100* v Tasmania (Devonport), 105 and 116 Australians v Guyana (Georgetown).
**Sobers, G.St A.** (West Indies) in 1957–58: 365* v Pakistan (Kingston), 125 and 109* v Pakistan (Georgetown).
**Sobers, G.St A.** (West Indies) in 1970–71: 108* v India (Georgetown), 135 Barbados v Indians (Bridgetown), 178* v India (Bridgetown).
**Solomon, J.S.** (British Guiana) in 1956–57 and 1957–58: 114* v Jamaica (Georgetown), and 108 v Barbados (Georgetown) 1956–57; 121 v Pakistanis (Georgetown) 1957–58. *His first three innings in first-class cricket.*
**Squires, H.S.** (Surrey) in 1932: 103 v Cambridge University (Oval), 131 and 102 v Oxford University (Oval).
**Stevens, G.B.** (South Australia) in 1957–58: 164 and 111 v New South Wales (Sydney), 143 v Queensland (Brisbane).
**Stewart, W.J.** (Warwickshire) in 1959: 156 v Essex (Coventry), 155 and 125 v Lancashire (Blackpool).
**Storer, W.** (Derbyshire) in 1896: 100 and 100* v Yorkshire (Derby), 142* v Leicestershire (Leicester).
**Sunderam, V.** (Delhi) in 1977–78: 130 v Haryana (Delhi), 101 v Jammu & Kashmir (Delhi), 177 Rest of India v Bombay (Bombay).
**Sutcliffe, B.** (Otago) in 1947–48: 103 v Auckland (Auckland), 118 and 135 v Canterbury (Dunedin).
**Sutcliffe, B.** (Auckland) in 1948–49: 141 and 135 v Canterbury (Auckland), 140 New Zealand XI v Rest (Christchurch).
**Sutcliffe, H.** (England) in 1924–25: 115 v Australia (Sydney), 176 and 127 v Australia (Melbourne).
**Sutcliffe, H.** (Yorkshire) in 1928: 111 v Derbyshire (Derby), 111 and 100* v Nottinghamshire (Nottingham).
**Sutcliffe, H.** (Yorkshire) in 1931: 117 England v New Zealand (Oval), 195 v Lancashire (Sheffield), 187 v Leicestershire (Leicester).
**Tate, M.W.** (Sussex) in 1927: 113 v Cambridge University (Cambridge), 122 v Worcestershire (Hove), 101 v Hampshire (Portsmouth).
**Taylor, M.D.** (Victoria) in 1983–84: 122 v South Australia (Adelaide), 101* v Pakistanis (Melbourne), 146 v Queensland (Brisbane).
**Thomas, G.** (New South Wales) in 1964–65: 131 v Queensland (Brisbane), 125 v Pakistanis (Sydney), 162 v Victoria (Melbourne).
**Turner, G.M.** (Worcestershire) in 1981, 130* v Glamorgan (Swansea), 147* and 139 v Warwickshire (Worcester).

**Tyldesley, G.E.** (Lancashire) in 1928: 159 v Kent (Manchester), 242 v Leicestershire (Leicester), 118 v Sussex (Hove).
**Tyldesley, G.E.** (Lancashire) in 1934: 239 v Glamorgan (Cardiff), 107 v Australians (Manchester), 134 v Gloucestershire (Bristol).
**Tyldesley, J.T.** (Lancashire) in 1897: 106 and 100* v Warwickshire (Birmingham), 174 v Sussex (Manchester).
**Tyldesley, J.T.** (Lancashire) in 1904: 103 v Somerset (Manchester), 225 v Nottinghamshire (Nottingham), 196 v Worcestershire (Worcester).
**Vengsarkar, D.B.** (Bombay) in 1983–84: 149 v Rajasthan (Jaipur), 104 v Haryana (Bombay), 123 v Delhi (Bombay).
**Weekes, E.de C.** (West Indians) in 1947–48 and 1948–49: 141 v England (Kingston) in 1947–48, 172* v North Zone (Patiala), 128 v India (Delhi) in 1948–49.
**Weekes, E.de C.** (West Indians) in 1950: 246* v Hampshire (Southampton), 200* v Leicestershire (Leicester), 129 v England (Nottingham).
**White, R.C.** (Transvaal) in 1965–66 and 1966–67: 205 Transvaal B v Griqualand West (Johannesburg), 117 v Western Province (Johannesburg) in 1965–66, 103 v Rhodesia (Salisbury) in 1966–67.
**Williams, R.G.** (Northamptonshire) in 1979: 120 v Indians, 109 and 151* v Warwickshire, all at Northampton.
**Wilson, J.V.** (Yorkshire) in 1955: 109* v Somerset (Taunton), 132* v Warwickshire (Birmingham), 132 v Essex (Bradford).
**Wright, L.G.** (Derbyshire) in 1905: 195 v Northamptonshire (Derby), 176 and 122 v Warwickshire (Birmingham).
**Yallop, G.N.** (Victoria) in 1983–84: 141 Australia v Pakistan (Perth), 113 and 145* v Western Australia (Melbourne).
**Zaheer Abbas** (Gloucestershire) in 1976: 153 v Essex (Cheltenham), 230* and 104* v Kent (Canterbury).
**Zaheer Abbas** (Gloucestershire) in 1977: 205* and 108* v Sussex (Cheltenham), 100* v Hampshire (Southampton).
**Zaheer Abbas** (Gloucestershire) in 1981: 135* and 128 v Northamptonshire (Northampton), 145 v Sussex (Hove).
**Zulch, J.W.** (Transvaal) in 1920–21: 124 v Eastern Province (Port Elizabeth), 185 and 125 v Orange Free State (Bloemfontein).

## FIVE HUNDREDS IN SIX CONSECUTIVE INNINGS

| | | |
|---|---|---|
| H.T.W. Hardinge | 154*-117-105*-107-3-110 | 1913 |
| J.B. Hobbs | 107-87-104-143*-111-215 | 1925 |
| G.E. Tyldesley | 144*-226-51-131-131-106 | 1926 |
| C. Hallows | 120-100-101-51*-123-101* | 1927 and 1928 |
| Nawab of Pataudi, sr | 183*-165-100-138-68-238* | 1931 |
| D.G. Bradman | 135-226-219-112-2-167 | 1931–32 |
| E.H. Hendren | 111-101-101-12-105-154 | 1933 |
| D.G. Bradman | 144-102-258-58-137-278 | 1937–38 and 1938 |
| V.M. Merchant | 109-137-12-170*-243*-221 | 1940–41 and 1941–42 |
| W.R. Hammond | 121-102-132-134-59*-143 | 1945 and 1946 |
| P.N. Kirsten | 173*-103-107-165-22-111 | 1976–77 |
| D.W. Hookes | 163-9-185-105-135-156 | 1976–77 |

## SIX HUNDREDS IN SEVEN CONSECUTIVE INNINGS

| | | |
|---|---|---|
| G.E. Tyldesley | 144*-226-51-131-131-106-126 | 1926 |
| V.M. Merchant | 109-137-12-170*-243*-221-153 | 1940–41 and 1941–42 |
| W.R. Hammond | 121-102-132-134-59*-143-104 | 1945 and 1946 |
| P.N. Kirsten | 173*-103-107-165-22-111-128 | 1976–77 |

## SEVEN HUNDREDS IN NINE CONSECUTIVE INNINGS

| | | |
|---|---|---|
| C.B. Fry | 119*-36-88-106-209-149-105-140-105 | 1901 |
| G.E. Tyldesley | 144-69-144*-226-51-131-131-106-126 | 1926 |
| D.G. Bradman | 135-226-219-112-2-167-23-167-299* | 1931–32 |
| D.G. Bradman | 144-102-258-58-137-278-2-143-145* | 1937–38 and 1938 |
| D.G. Bradman | 202-17-67-118-143-225-107-186-135* | 1938 and 1938–39 |
| D.G. Bradman | 132-127*-201-57-115-107-81-146-187 | 1947–48 and 1948 |

## EIGHT HUNDREDS IN ELEVEN CONSECUTIVE INNINGS

| | | |
|---|---|---|
| D.G. Bradman | 103-16-202-17-67-118-143-225-107-186-135* | 1938 and 1938–39 |

**EIGHT HUNDREDS IN TWELVE CONSECUTIVE INNINGS**

| | | |
|---|---|---|
| G.E. Tyldesley | 144-69-144*-226-51-131-131-106-126-81-44-139 | 1926 |
| W.H. Ponsford | 214-54-151-353-108-84-12-116-131-7-133-437 | 1926–27 and 1927–28 |
| D.G. Bradman | 140-304-244-77-19-149*-132-15-50-117-233-357 | 1934 and 1935–36 |
| D.G. Bradman | 118-143-225-107-186-135*-5-76-64-251*-90*-138 | 1938–39 and 1939–40 |
| V.M. Merchant | 140-192-4-32-88*-109-137-12-170*-243*-221-153* | 1939 to 1942 |

# MOST FIFTIES IN CONSECUTIVE INNINGS

**TEN**

| | | |
|---|---|---|
| G.E. Tyldesley | 144-69-144*-226-51-131-131-106-126-81 | 1926 |
| D.G. Bradman | 132-127*-201-57*-115-107-81-146-187-98 | 1947–48 and 1948 |

**NINE**

| | | |
|---|---|---|
| T.W. Hayward | 61*-70*-63-144*-100-143-125-54-69 | 1906 |
| W.R. Hammond | 101-75*-59-64-58-227-336*-55-51 | 1932–33 and 1933 |
| V.S. Hazare | 264-81-97-248-59-309-101-223-87 | 1942–43 and 1943–44 |
| R.B. Simpson | 98-236*-230*-79-98-161*-67-80-52 | 1959–60 |
| J.H. Edrich | 139-121*-205*-55-96-188-92-105-310* | 1965 |

**EIGHT**

| | | |
|---|---|---|
| C.B. Fry | 135-68-72-125-229-110-96-105 | 1900 |
| C.B. Fry | 88-106-209-149-105-140-105-82 | 1901 and 1902 |
| D.G. Bradman | 85-79-144-102-258-58-137-278 | 1937–38 and 1938 |
| B. Sutcliffe | 71-74-111-62*-197-128-58-75 | 1946–47 and 1947–48 |

**SEVEN**

| | | |
|---|---|---|
| G.E. Tyldesley | 96-174*-66-58-65-82-67 | 1919 |
| D.E. Pritchard | 115-55-71-85-101-61-87 | 1924–25 |
| W.W. Whysall | 54-117-101*-120-158-60-64 | 1930 |
| W.R. Hammond | 84*-54-81-100-53-75-70 | 1930–31 |
| D.G. Bradman | 67-118-143-225-107-186-135* | 1938–39 |
| S.G. Barnes | 137-132-55-185-79-51-200 | 1940–41 and 1945–46 |
| V.M. Merchant | 62-250*-141-359*-53-84-221* | 1943–44 and 1944–45 |
| R.S. Cooper | 73-58*-62-68-127*-52-104 | 1944–45 |
| W.R. Hammond | 121-102-132-134-59*-143-104 | 1945 and 1946 |
| W.J. Edrich | 57-50-54*-189-70-102-191 | 1947 |
| A.R. Morris | 60-105-62-290-51*-54-109 | 1948 |
| L. Hutton | 125-62*-134-61-78-174-83 | 1948–49 |
| R.T. Simpson | 54-143-102*-96-63*-80-54 | 1949 |
| L. Hutton | 147-52-54-101-54-75-52 | 1949 and 1950 |
| D.J. McGlew | 85-66-53-118-68-51-69 | 1955 |
| G. Pullar | 62-57*-107-51-76*-76-105 | 1959 |
| R.E. Marshall | 51-56-104-63-63-75-63 | 1959 |
| P.H. Parfitt | 63-122-114-101*-56-92-54 | 1962 |
| R.B. Simpson | 125-138-55-57-95-105*-52* | 1964 |
| D.B. Vengsarkar | 78-151*-72*-57-53*-83-76 | 1977–78 and 1978–79 |
| Sadiq Mohammad | 78-56-165-70-171-103-100 | 1979 |
| I.V.A. Richards | 89-79-127-140-96-76-74 | 1979 and 1979–80 |
| D.W. Hookes | 97-63-53-87-137-107-74 | 1981–82 and 1982–83 |
| G. Boycott | 91-82-52-122*-62-129-69 | 1982 |
| A.D. Gaekwad | 104-225-64-81*-144-135-82 | 1982–83 |
| Zaheer Abbas | 91-126-52-125-101-57-57 | 1982–83 |

*K.F. Barrington exceeded fifty in each of the ten first-class innings he played at Adelaide Oval for MCC and England: 104-52-52*-63-132* (in 1962–63), 69-51-63-60-102 (in 1965–66).*

# MOST RUNS BEFORE BEING DISMISSED

The following batsmen scored 500 runs with a sequence of 'not out' innings before being dismissed:

| | | | | |
|---|---|---|---|---|
| 709 | K.C. Ibrahim | 218*-36*-234*-77*-144 | Bombay | 1947–48 |
| 634 | V.M. Merchant | 170*-243*-221 | Hindus | 1941–42 |
| 630 | E.H. Hendren | 205*-254*-171 | MCC | 1929–30 |
| 575 | E.de C. Weekes | 246*-200*-129 | West Indians | 1950 |
| 558 | F. Jakeman | 80*-258*-176*-44 | Northamptonshire | 1951 |

| 545 | R.B. Simpson | 236*-230*-79 | Western Australia | 1959–60 |
|---|---|---|---|---|
| 517 | D.G. Bradman | 187*-77*-253 | New South Wales | 1933–34 |
| 514 | E.H. Hendren | 223*-211*-80 | MCC | 1929–30 |
| 510 | W.H. Ponsford | 229*-281*-0 | Australians | 1934 |
| 502 | F.M.M. Worrell | 241*-261 | West Indians | 1950 |

# MOST RUNS IN A MATCH

| 499 | (499) | Hanif Mohammad | Karachi v Bahawalpur | Karachi | 1958–59 |
|---|---|---|---|---|---|
| 455 | (3 and 452*) | D.G. Bradman | NSW v Queensland | Sydney | 1929–30 |
| 446 | (244 and 202*) | A.E. Fagg | Kent v Essex | Colchester | 1938 |
| 443 | (443*) | B.B. Nimbalkar | Maharashtra v Kathiawar | Poona | 1948–49 |
| 437 | (437) | W.H. Ponsford | Victoria v Queensland | Melbourne | 1927–28 |
| 429 | (429) | W.H. Ponsford | Victoria v Tasmania | Melbourne | 1922–23 |
| 428 | (428) | Aftab Baloch | Sind v Baluchistan | Karachi | 1973–74 |
| 424 | (424) | A.C. MacLaren | Lancashire v Somerset | Taunton | 1895 |
| 402 | (157* and 245) | W.W. Armstrong | Victoria v South Australia | Melbourne | 1920–21 |

*The highest match aggregate in Test cricket is 380 by G.S. Chappell (247\* and 133) for Australia v New Zealand at Wellington in 1973–74.*

# CARRYING BAT THROUGH A COMPLETED INNINGS

The following opening batsmen have batted throughout a completed innings in which all ten of their partners have been dismissed:

IN BOTH INNINGS OF A MATCH

| | Score | Total | Score | Total | | | |
|---|---|---|---|---|---|---|---|
| H. Jupp | 43* | 95 | 109* | 193 | Surrey v Yorkshire | Oval | 1874 |
| S. Kinneir | 70* | 239 | 69* | 166 | Warwicks v Leics | Leicester | 1907 |
| C.J.B. Wood | 107* | 309 | 117* | 296 | Leics v Yorkshire | Bradford | 1911 |
| V.M. Merchant | 135* | 271 | 77* | 161 | Indians v Lancashire | Liverpool | 1936 |

IN ONE INNINGS AND LAST OUT IN THE OTHER

| | Score | Total | Score | Total | | | |
|---|---|---|---|---|---|---|---|
| H. Jupp | 31 | 102 | 94* | 297 | Surrey v Hampshire | Oval | 1866 |
| H. Jupp | 53 | 102 | 51* | 113 | Surrey v Notts | Oval | 1873 |
| F.S. Lee | 109* | 196 | 107 | 205 | Somerset v Worcs | Worcester | 1938 |

LAST OUT IN BOTH INNINGS

| | Score | Total | Score | Total | | | |
|---|---|---|---|---|---|---|---|
| D.L. Haynes | 55 | 140 | 105 | 212 | West Indies v New Zealand | Dunedin | 1979–80 |

IN ONE INNINGS
R. Abel (Surrey) holds the record for the highest score by a player carrying his bat through a completed innings: 357* v Somerset at The Oval in 1899. Surrey's total of 811 on that occasion is the highest through which a player has carried his bat.

† *Denotes completed innings in which ten wickets did not fall, one or more batsmen being retired/absent hurt/ill.*

| | | Score | Total | | | |
|---|---|---|---|---|---|---|
| Aamer Mirza | | 49* | 133 | Peshawar v Lahore Division | Sialkot | 1983–84 |
| Abel, R. | (8) | 88* | 198 | Surrey v Gloucestershire | Cheltenham | 1885 |
| | | 151* | 425 | Surrey v Middlesex | Lord's | 1890 |
| | | 132* | 307 | England v Australia | Sydney | 1891–92 |
| | | 136* | 300 | Surrey v Middlesex | Oval | 1894 |
| | | 168* | 363 | Players v Gentlemen | Oval | 1894 |
| | | 357* | 811 | Surrey v Somerset | Oval | 1899 |
| | | 153* | 302 | Players v Gentlemen | Oval | 1900 |
| | | 151* | 263 | Surrey v Sussex | Oval | 1902 |
| Ackerman, H.M. | | 39* | 77 | Northamptonshire v Surrey | Kettering | 1971 |
| Adams, W.W. | | 14* | 40 | Northamptonshire v Yorkshire | Northampton | 1920 |
| Agha Zahid | | 78* | 173 | Habib Bank v Lahore | Lahore | 1980–81 |
| Akash Lal | | 104* | 186 | Delhi v Northern Punjab | Amritsar | 1967–68 |
| Alderman, A.E. | | 124* | 291 | Derbyshire v Hampshire | Portsmouth | 1934 |

|  |  | Score | Total |  |  |  |
|---|---|---|---|---|---|---|
| Amiss, D.L. | (2) | 160* | 315† | Warwickshire v West Indians | Birmingham | 1966 |
|  |  | 122* | 273 | Warwickshire v Essex | Colchester | 1978 |
| Anson, T.A. |  | 22* | 54 | MCC v North | Burton upon T. | 1840 |
| Anwar Arif |  | 37* | 102 | NWFP v Punjab | Peshawar | 1954–55 |
| Armstrong, W.W. |  | 159* | 309 | Australia v South Africa | Johannesburg | 1902–03 |
| Arshad Pervez | (2) | 140* | 240 | Habib Bank v MCB | Lahore | 1978–79 |
|  |  | 152* | 274 | Habib Bank v Lahore | Lahore | 1984–85 |
| Ashdown, W.H. | (4) | 150* | 303 | Kent v Surrey | Oval | 1926 |
|  |  | 100* | 236 | Kent v Sussex | Tunbridge Wells | 1928 |
|  |  | 83* | 223 | Kent v Gloucestershire | Maidstone | 1930 |
|  |  | 305* | 560 | Kent v Derbyshire | Dover | 1935 |
| Ashton, H. |  | 236* | 484 | Cambridge U. v Free Foresters | Cambridge | 1920 |
| Atkinson, G. |  | 46* | 94† | Somerset v Yorkshire | Hull | 1965 |
| Atkinson, G.R. |  | 30* | 73 | Yorkshire v Nottinghamshire | Bradford | 1865 |
| Atkinson, J.A. | (2) | 144* | 277 | Tasmania v Victoria | Hobart | 1927–28 |
|  |  | 104* | 173† | Tasmania v Victoria | Launceston | 1929–30 |
| Avery, A.V. | (3) | 84* | 180 | Essex v Derbyshire | Southend | 1939 |
|  |  | 83* | 165 | Essex v Gloucestershire | Brentwood | 1946 |
|  |  | 92* | 154 | Essex v Nottinghamshire | Nottingham | 1954 |
| Azhar Qureshi |  | 140* | 302 | Punjab B v Universities | Lahore | 1974–75 |
| Badcock, C.L. |  | 43* | 147 | Tasmania v MCC | Launceston | 1932–33 |
| Bagshaw, H. |  | 114* | 218 | Derbyshire v Surrey | Oval | 1897 |
| Baichan, L. | (2) | 216* | 401 | Berbice v Demerara | Georgetown | 1973–74 |
|  |  | 101* | 257 | Berbice v Demerara | Albion, Berbice | 1982–83 |
| Bailey, J. |  | 70* | 139 | Hampshire v West Indians | Bournemouth | 1939 |
| Bainbridge, H.W. |  | 65* | 113 | Warwickshire v Kent | Birmingham | 1894 |
| Baker, A. |  | 55* | 110 | Surrey v Gloucestershire | Bristol | 1905 |
| Bakewell, A.H. | (3) | 83* | 166 | Northants v New Zealanders | Peterborough | 1931 |
|  |  | 90* | 169 | Northamptonshire v Essex | Leyton | 1931 |
|  |  | 120* | 211 | Northants v Leicestershire | Leicester | 1936 |
| Bakrania, J. |  | 137* | 244 | Gujarat v Baroda | Nadiad | 1976–77 |
| Balderstone, J.C. | (3) | 114* | 246 | Leicestershire v Essex | Colchester | 1982 |
|  |  | 100* | 198 | Leicestershire v Worcestershire | Hereford | 1983 |
|  |  | 181* | 456 | Leicestershire v Gloucestershire | Leicester | 1984 |
| Bannerman, A.C. | (7) | 71* | 171 | Australians v Orleans Club | Twickenham | 1878 |
|  |  | 45* | 83 | Australian XI v A. Shrewsbury's XI | Sydney | 1887–88 |
|  |  | 93* | 319 | Australians v Cambridge U. P. & P. | Leyton | 1888 |
|  |  | 39* | 168 | Australians v England XI | Harrogate | 1888 |
|  |  | 45* | 151 | New South Wales v Victoria | Melbourne | 1890–91 |
|  |  | 7* | 60 | Australians v Kent | Canterbury | 1893 |
|  |  | 79* | 258 | Australians v Philadelphians | Philadelphia | 1893–94 |
| Bardsley, W. | (5) | 143* | 271 | Australians v S.H. Cochrane's XI | Bray | 1909 |
|  |  | 191* | 361 | New South Wales v South Australia | Sydney | 1910–11 |
|  |  | 50* | 213 | New South Wales v Victoria | Sydney | 1914–15 |
|  |  | 200* | 352 | New South Wales v Auckland | Auckland | 1923–24 |
|  |  | 193* | 383 | Australia v England | Lord's | 1926 |
| Barker, G. |  | 36* | 80 | Essex v Kent | Westcliff | 1966 |
| Barlow, G.D. | (1) | 44* | 83 | Middlesex v Essex | Chelmsford | 1983 |
| Barlow, R.G. | (11) | 26* | 116 | Lancashire v Kent | Maidstone | 1874 |
|  |  | 34* | 187 | Lancashire v Nottinghamshire | Nottingham | 1876 |
|  |  | 34* | 99 | Lancashire v MCC | Lord's | 1878 |
|  |  | 10* | 47 | Lancashire v Yorkshire | Manchester | 1880 |
|  |  | 66* | 269 | Lancashire v Australians | Manchester | 1882 |
|  |  | 5* | 69 | Lancashire v Nottinghamshire | Nottingham | 1882 |
|  |  | 44* | 93 | Lancashire v Nottinghamshire | Liverpool | 1882 |
|  |  | 58* | 240 | Lancashire v Gloucestershire | Clifton | 1882 |
|  |  | 62* | 183 | Lancashire v Gloucestershire | Clifton | 1885 |
|  |  | 51* | 215 | Lancashire v Kent | Maidstone | 1889 |
|  |  | 29* | 131 | Lancashire v Surrey | Oval | 1890 |
| Barnes, W. |  | 118* | 236 | MCC v Oxford University | Lord's | 1880 |
| Barnett, C.J. |  | 228* | 363 | Gloucestershire v Leicestershire | Gloucester | 1947 |
| Barnett, C.S. |  | 62* | 235 | Gloucestershire v Worcestershire | Cheltenham | 1913 |
| Barnett, E.P. |  | 52* | 141 | Gloucestershire v Yorkshire | Bradford | 1905 |
| Barrett, J.E. | (2) | 67* | 176 | Australia v England | Lord's | 1890 |
|  |  | 61* | 134 | Australians v C.I. Thornton's XI | Barnes | 1890 |
| Barua, M.P. |  | 87* | 148 | Assam v Bengal | Jorhat | 1966–67 |
| Bates, L.T.A. | (2) | 96* | 207 | Warwickshire v Surrey | Oval | 1921 |

| | | Score | Total | | | |
|---|---|---|---|---|---|---|
| Bates L.T.A. *continued* | | 50* | 125 | Warwickshire v Yorkshire | Huddersfield | 1922 |
| Bates, W.E. | (2) | 200* | 390 | Glamorgan v Worcestershire | Kidderminster | 1927 |
| | | 73* | 160 | Glamorgan v Northamptonshire | Swansea | 1928 |
| Bean, G. | | 145* | 264 | Sussex v Nottinghamshire | Hove | 1891 |
| Beldam, G.W. | | 12* | 51 | Middlesex v Sussex | Lord's | 1902 |
| Bell, J.T. | (2) | 72* | 164 | Glamorgan v Essex | Cardiff | 1926 |
| | | 209* | 395 | Wales v MCC | Lord's | 1927 |
| Berry, A. | | 23* | 147† | Cambridgeshire v Nottinghamshire | Nottingham | 1862 |
| Berry, G.L. | (4) | 75* | 177 | Leicestershire v Nottinghamshire | Leicester | 1932 |
| | | 58* | 126 | Leicestershire v Derbyshire | Chesterfield | 1939 |
| | | 45* | 121 | Leicestershire v South Africans | Leicester | 1947 |
| | | 109* | 236 | Leicestershire v Somerset | Leicester | 1949 |
| Bezbarua, N. | | 8* | 33† | Assam v Bengal | Jorhat | 1974–75 |
| Bhanot, A. | | 104* | 165† | Uttar Pradesh v Bombay | Bombay | 1978–79 |
| Blunt, R.C. | (2) | 137* | 336 | Canterbury v Wellington | Wellington | 1919–20 |
| | | 131* | 204 | Otago v Canterbury | Dunedin | 1926–27 |
| Bokul, M.H. | | 90* | 159 | East Pakistan v Combined U's | Karachi | 1959–60 |
| Bolus, J.B. | | 136* | 299 | Nottinghamshire v Derbyshire | Nottingham | 1963 |
| Boon, T.J. | | 75* | 163 | Leicestershire XI v Zimbabwe | Salisbury | 1980–81 |
| Booth, B.J. | | 62* | 140 | Lancashire v Derbyshire | Liverpool | 1963 |
| Bowley, E.H. | (4) | 110* | 245 | Sussex v Glamorgan | Swansea | 1922 |
| | | 93* | 188 | Sussex v Hampshire | Hove | 1923 |
| | | 71* | 119 | Sussex v Worcestershire | Hove | 1926 |
| | | 94* | 206 | Sussex v Nottinghamshire | Hastings | 1926 |
| Bowley, F.L. | | 104* | 267 | Worcestershire v Middlesex | Lord's | 1911 |
| Boycott, G. | (9) | 114* | 297 | Yorkshire v Leicestershire | Sheffield | 1968 |
| | | 53* | 119 | Yorkshire v Warwickshire | Bradford | 1969 |
| | | 182* | 320 | Yorkshire v Middlesex | Lord's | 1971 |
| | | 138* | 232 | Yorkshire v Warwickshire | Birmingham | 1971 |
| | | 175* | 360 | Yorkshire v Nottinghamshire | Worksop | 1979 |
| | | 99* | 215 | England v Australia | Perth | 1979–80 |
| | | 112* | 233 | Yorkshire v Derbyshire | Sheffield | 1983 |
| | | 55* | 183 | Yorkshire v Warwickshire | Leeds | 1984 |
| | | 55* | 131 | Yorkshire v Surrey | Sheffield | 1985 |
| Bradburn, W.P. | (2) | 45* | 87 | Northern Districts v Wellington | Wellington | 1960–61 |
| | | 37* | 57 | Northern Districts v Wellington | Hamilton | 1961–62 |
| Brand, J. | | 80* | 146 | MCC v Godalming | Lord's | 1825 |
| Braund, L.C. | (4) | 28* | 97 | Somerset v Middlesex | Lord's | 1907 |
| | | 42* | 113 | Somerset v Yorkshire | Taunton | 1907 |
| | | 67* | 226 | Somerset v Middlesex | Taunton | 1907 |
| | | 58* | 148 | Somerset v Worcestershire | Taunton | 1914 |
| Brearley, J.M. | (2) | 90* | 197 | MCC v Yorkshire | Lord's | 1965 |
| | | 128* | 275 | Middlesex v Hampshire | Lord's | 1976 |
| Brockwell, W. | | 76* | 158 | Surrey v Leicestershire | Leicester | 1898 |
| Brookes, D. | (5) | 80* | 170 | Northants v Leicestershire | Northampton | 1946 |
| | | 166* | 347 | Northamptonshire v Kent | Northampton | 1950 |
| | | 102* | 185 | Northamptonshire v Kent | Northampton | 1952 |
| | | 139* | 300 | Rest v South | Hastings | 1953 |
| | | 113* | 252 | Northamptonshire v Glamorgan | Ebbw Vale | 1958 |
| Brown, G. | (2) | 103* | 188 | Hampshire v Middlesex | Bournemouth | 1926 |
| | | 150* | 294 | Hampshire v Surrey | Oval | 1933 |
| Brown, S.M. | | 96* | 153 | Middlesex v Cambridge U. | Cambridge | 1948 |
| Brown, W.A. | (2) | 206* | 422 | Australia v England | Lord's | 1938 |
| | | 174* | 311 | Queensland v South Australia | Adelaide | 1938–39 |
| Bruce, Hon C.N. | | 64* | 120 | Oxford U. v Worcestershire | Oxford | 1907 |
| Bryan, J.L. | (2) | 82* | 157 | Kent v Yorkshire | Tunbridge Wells | 1921 |
| | | 93* | 186 | Kent v Middlesex | Lord's | 1929 |
| Bull, C.H. | | 57* | 150 | Worcestershire v Lancashire | Kidderminster | 1935 |
| Bull, D.F.E. | | 167* | 336 | Queensland v Victoria | Melbourne | 1965–66 |
| Burke, J.W. | (2) | 162* | 360 | New South Wales v Victoria | Melbourne | 1949–50 |
| | | 132* | 281 | New South Wales v Victoria | Melbourne | 1956–57 |
| Burnup, C.J. | | 103* | 209 | Kent v Surrey | Oval | 1899 |
| Bush, J.E. | | 52* | 146 | Oxford University v Surrey | Guildford | 1952 |
| Cadman, S.W.A. | (3) | 36* | 71 | Derbyshire v Hampshire | Derby | 1912 |
| | | 73* | 155 | Derbyshire v Leicestershire | Leicester | 1914 |
| | | 19* | 53 | Derbyshire v Leicestershire | Leicester | 1920 |

| | | Score | Total | | | |
|---|---|---|---|---|---|---|
| Carew, M.C. | | 65* | 135 | Trinidad v Barbados | Port-of-Spain | 1966–67 |
| Carris, H.E. | | 35* | 92 | Middlesex v Yorkshire | Bradford | 1929 |
| Chalk, F.G.H. | | 115* | 215 | Kent v Yorkshire | Dover | 1939 |
| Challenor, G. | | 155* | 305 | West Indians v Surrey | Oval | 1923 |
| Chapman, C. | | 41* | 90 | Cambridge U. v Cambridge Town | Cambridge | 1826 |
| Chatterton, W. | | 109* | 238 | MCC v Lancashire | Lord's | 1892 |
| Chauhan, C.P.S. | | 187* | 366 | Maharashtra v Bombay | Poona | 1972–73 |
| Clark, T.H. | | 81* | 135 | Surrey v Yorkshire | Oval | 1956 |
| Claxton, N.H. | | 199* | 378 | South Australia v Victoria | Melbourne | 1905–06 |
| Clinton, G.S. | | 113* | 260 | Surrey v Derbyshire | Oval | 1984 |
| Cobcroft, L.T. | | 85* | 239 | New South Wales v Wellington | Wellington | 1895–96 |
| Collins, D.C. | | 53* | 131 | Wellington v Canterbury | Christchurch | 1906–07 |
| Collins, G.C. | | 18* | 67 | Kent v Northamptonshire | Gravesend | 1924 |
| Collins, J.C. | | 128* | 187 | Fijians v Hawke's Bay | Napier | 1894–95 |
| Cook, G.G. | (2) | 36* | 74 | Queensland v Victoria | Melbourne | 1932–33 |
| | | 169* | 400 | Queensland v MCC | Brisbane | 1946–47 |
| Cook, G.W. | | 61* | 134 | Cambridge U. v Yorkshire | Cambridge | 1957 |
| Cooper, E | (2) | 104* | 273 | Worcestershire v Lancashire | Manchester | 1939 |
| | | 69* | 154 | Worcestershire v Warwickshire | Dudley | 1951 |
| Cowdrey, M.C. | | 65* | 169 | Kent v Gloucestershire | Cheltenham | 1956 |
| Croom, A.J.W. | (4) | 131* | 311 | Warwickshire v Northamptonshire | Birmingham | 1929 |
| | | 58* | 120 | Warwickshire v Gloucestershire | Cheltenham | 1930 |
| | | 102* | 204 | Warwickshire v Lancashire | Manchester | 1931 |
| | | 69* | 133 | Warwickshire v Leicestershire | Hinckley | 1936 |
| Cutmore, J.A. | | 31* | 64 | Essex v Yorkshire | Dewsbury | 1933 |
| Dadu Sattar | | 48* | 88 | East Pakistan B v Dacca U. | Dacca | 1957–58 |
| Daffen, A. | | 72* | 249 | Kent v Gloucestershire | Gloucester | 1890 |
| Daft, H.B. | | 77* | 240 | Nottinghamshire v Surrey | Oval | 1896 |
| Daft, R. | | 12* | 48 | Nottinghamshire v Lancashire | Nottingham | 1877 |
| Daniell, J. | (3) | 24* | 82 | Somerset v Kent | Gravesend | 1903 |
| | | 129* | 312 | Somerset v Hampshire | Southampton | 1911 |
| | | 174* | 318 | Somerset v Essex | Taunton | 1925 |
| Darling, W.M. | | 85* | 179 | South Australia v NSW | Adelaide | 1978–79 |
| Das, G. | | 63* | 143 | Assam v Bengal | Calcutta | 1979–80 |
| Davey, D.C. | | 62* | 106 | Natal v Griqualand West | Kimberley | 1889–90 |
| Davies, D. | | 100* | 161 | Glamorgan v Worcestershire | Worcester | 1923 |
| Davies, D.D. | | 40* | 95 | Border v Transvaal | Port Elizabeth | 1902–03 |
| Davies, D.E. | (3) | 75* | 142 | Glamorgan v South Africans | Cardiff | 1935 |
| | | 155* | 340 | Glamorgan v Somerset | Weston-s-Mare | 1935 |
| | | 107* | 180 | Over 32 v Under 32 | Hastings | 1950 |
| Davies, P.C. | | 122* | 253 | N.E. Transvaal v Griqualand W. | Pretoria | 1955–56 |
| Davis, B.A. | | 188* | 338 | N. Trinidad v S. Trinidad | Port-of-Spain | 1966–67 |
| Dawson, E.W. | | 126* | 256 | Leicestershire v Essex | Leyton | 1928 |
| Dean, J. | | 46* | 102 | Sussex v MCC | Brighton | 1850 |
| Dempster, C.S. | (2) | 167* | 345 | New Zealanders v Glamorgan | Cardiff | 1927 |
| | | 28* | 62 | Leicestershire v Yorkshire | Bradford | 1938 |
| Denness, M.H. | | 69* | 136 | Kent v Northamptonshire | Wellingborough | 1971 |
| Denton, W.H. | (2) | 230* | 476 | Northamptonshire v Essex | Leyton | 1913 |
| | | 108* | 305 | Northants v Gloucestershire | Northampton | 1914 |
| Dewes, J.G. | | 101* | 203 | Middlesex v Surrey | Oval | 1955 |
| Dilawar Hussain | | 101* | 249 | Indians v Warwickshire | Birmingham | 1936 |
| Dillon, E.W. | | 38* | 86 | Kent v Nottinghamshire | Gravesend | 1902 |
| Dipper, A.E. | (11) | 168* | 343 | Gloucestershire v Somerset | Taunton | 1914 |
| | | 37* | 104 | Gloucestershire v Lancashire | Manchester | 1919 |
| | | 99* | 185 | Gloucestershire v Worcestershire | Cheltenham | 1919 |
| | | 120* | 175 | Gloucestershire v Warwickshire | Birmingham | 1920 |
| | | 22* | 72 | Gloucestershire v Leicestershire | Ashby de la Z. | 1922 |
| | | 37* | 138 | Gloucestershire v Kent | Cheltenham | 1922 |
| | | 87* | 192 | Gloucestershire v Warwickshire | Bristol | 1923 |
| | | 126* | 211 | Gloucestershire v West Indians | Bristol | 1923 |
| | | 85* | 210 | Gloucestershire v Northants | Northampton | 1926 |
| | | 66* | 119 | Gloucestershire v Kent | Bristol | 1929 |
| | | 64* | 192 | Gloucestershire v Glamorgan | Swansea | 1930 |
| Doherty, M.J.D. | | 130* | 284 | Griqualand West v N. Transvaal | Kimberley | 1974–75 |
| Donnan, H. | | 160* | 374 | NSW v South Australia | Adelaide | 1898–99 |
| Dudleston, B. | | 101* | 178 | Leicestershire v Essex | Leyton | 1971 |

|  |  | Score | Total |  |  |  |
|---|---|---|---|---|---|---|
| Dunn, A. |  | 42* | 136 | Griqualand West v W. Province | Kimberley | 1946–47 |
| Durity, O. |  | 74* | 159 | South Trinidad v E. Trinidad | Arima | 1970–71 |
| Dyer, D.V. |  | 49* | 96 | Natal v Transvaal | Durban | 1945–46 |
| Dyson, A.H. | (5) | 75* | 156 | Glamorgan v Northamptonshire | Kettering | 1931 |
|  |  | 109* | 204 | Glamorgan v Middlesex | Cardiff | 1932 |
|  |  | 191* | 352 | Glamorgan v Lancashire | Cardiff | 1934 |
|  |  | 110* | 210 | Glamorgan v Sir J. Cahn's XI | Newport | 1938 |
|  |  | 99* | 196 | Glamorgan v Gloucestershire | Newport | 1939 |
| Edrich, J.H. | (2) | 79* | 122 | Surrey v Northamptonshire | Oval | 1963 |
|  |  | 61* | 108 | Surrey v Essex | Southend | 1978 |
| Edrich, W.J. |  | 140* | 303 | Lord Tennyson's XI v Sind | Karachi | 1937–38 |
| Elliott, C.S. |  | 51* | 126 | Derbyshire v Leicestershire | Ashby de la Z. | 1948 |
| Ellis, R.G.P. |  | 103* | 161 | Oxford University v Glamorgan | Oxford | 1983 |
| Ellis, R.T. |  | 50* | 107 | Sussex v Australians | Hove | 1880 |
| Emmett, G.M. |  | 104* | 156 | Gloucestershire v Oxford U. | Oxford | 1948 |
| Fagg, A.E. | (3) | 37* | 127 | Kent v Gloucestershire | Gillingham | 1938 |
|  |  | 117* | 230 | Kent v Essex | Maidstone | 1948 |
|  |  | 71* | 134 | Kent v Surrey | Oval | 1950 |
| Felix, N. |  | 30* | 43 | Married v Single | Lord's | 1831 |
| Fenner, F.P. |  | 51* | 88 | Cambridge Town v Cambridge U. | Cambridge | 1840 |
| Ferris, J.J. | (2) | 62* | 170 | Gentlemen v Players | Scarborough | 1892 |
|  |  | 34* | 77 | Gloucestershire v Sussex | Bristol | 1892 |
| Fiddian-Green, C.A.F. |  | 60* | 123† | Warwickshire v Hampshire | Southampton | 1922 |
| Fillary, E.W.J. |  | 28* | 146 | Kent v Yorkshire | Dover | 1964 |
| Fingleton, J.H.W. |  | 119* | 273 | New South Wales v MCC | Sydney | 1932–33 |
| Fishlock,L.B. |  | 81* | 141 | Surrey v Australians | Oval | 1948 |
| Fishwick, T.S. |  | 85* | 181 | Warwickshire v Lancashire | Manchester | 1907 |
| Fletcher, D.G.W. |  | 127* | 271 | Surrey v Yorkshire | Bradford | 1947 |
| Franklin, T.J. |  | 153* | 311 | Young New Zealand v Zimbabwe | Harare | 1984–85 |
| Freakes, H.D. |  | 122* | 190 | Eastern Province v Natal | Johannesburg | 1931–32 |
|  |  |  |  | *On debut when aged 17 years 10 months* |  |  |
| Freeman, J.R. | (2) | 67* | 206 | Essex v Lancashire | Colchester | 1922 |
|  |  | 113* | 283 | Essex v Oxford University | Chelmsford | 1926 |
| Fry, C.B. | (3) | 104* | 197 | Sussex v Middlesex | Lord's | 1898 |
|  |  | 179* | 311 | Sussex v Yorkshire | Hove | 1898 |
|  |  | 170* | 254 | Sussex v Nottinghamshire | Nottingham | 1901 |
| Gardner, F.C. | (4) | 140* | 283 | Warwickshire v Worcestershire | Birmingham | 1949 |
|  |  | 73* | 133 | Warwickshire v Glamorgan | Swansea | 1950 |
|  |  | 184* | 286 | Warwickshire v Lancashire | Liverpool | 1952 |
|  |  | 62* | 149 | Warwickshire v Glamorgan | Birmingham | 1954 |
| Gatehouse, G.H. |  | 54* | 146 | Tasmania v Otago | Dunedin | 1883–84 |
| Gavaskar, S.M. | (2) | 156* | 307 | Rest of India v Karnataka | Ahmedabad | 1974–75 |
|  |  | 127* | 286 | India v Pakistan | Faisalabad | 1982–83 |
| Gehrs, D.R.A. |  | 148* | 235 | S. Australia v Western Australia | Fremantle | 1905–06 |
| Gibb, P.A. |  | 80* | 163 | Cambridge U. v Australians | Cambridge | 1938 |
| Gibbes, W.R.L. |  | 75* | 193 | Wellington v Canterbury | Christchurch | 1911–12 |
| Gibbons, H.H.I. | (2) | 70* | 165 | Worcestershire v Warwickshire | Kidderminster | 1934 |
|  |  | 83* | 148 | Worcestershire v Lancashire | Kidderminster | 1935 |
| Gilbert, W.R. | (2) | 205* | 383 | England XI v Cambridge U. | Cambridge | 1876 |
|  |  | 40* | 110 | Gloucestershire v Lancashire | Clifton | 1885 |
| Goddard, T.L. | (2) | 56* | 99 | South Africa v Australia | Cape Town | 1957–58 |
|  |  | 85* | 157 | Natal v Western Province | Durban | 1969–70 |
| Godsell, R.T. |  | 98* | 269 | Gloucestershire v Nottinghamshire | Bristol | 1905 |
| Grace, E.M. |  | 192* | 344 | MCC v Gentlemen of Kent | Canterbury | 1862 |
| Grace, W.G. | (17) | 138* | 215 | MCC v Surrey | Oval | 1869 |
|  |  | 117* | 183 | MCC v Nottinghamshire | Lord's | 1870 |
|  |  | 189* | 310 | Single v Married | Lord's | 1871 |
|  |  | 81* | 141 | W.G. Grace's XI v Kent | Maidstone | 1871 |
|  |  | 170* | 290 | England v Notts & Yorkshire | Lord's | 1872 |
|  |  | 192* | 311 | South v North | Oval | 1873 |
|  |  | 318* | 528 | Gloucestershire v Yorkshire | Cheltenham | 1876 |
|  |  | 221* | 348 | Gloucestershire v Middlesex | Clifton | 1885 |
|  |  | 81* | 128 | MCC v Sussex | Lord's | 1887 |
|  |  | 113* | 186 | Gloucestershire v Nottinghamshire | Clifton | 1887 |
|  |  | 37* | 87 | Gloucestershire v Lancashire | Bristol | 1889 |

|  |  | Score | Total |  |  |  |
|---|---|---|---|---|---|---|
| Grace, W.G. *continued* | | 127* | 282 | Gloucestershire v Middlesex | Cheltenham | 1889 |
| | | 109* | 231 | Gloucestershire v Kent | Maidstone | 1890 |
| | | 159* | 284 | Lord Sheffield's XI v Victoria | Melbourne | 1891–92 |
| | | 61* | 105 | Gloucestershire v Surrey | Oval | 1893 |
| | | 243* | 463 | Gloucestershire v Sussex | Hove | 1896 |
| | | 102* | 238 | Gloucestershire v Lancashire | Bristol | 1896 |
| Gray, J.R. | (2) | 118* | 208 | Hampshire v Essex | Portsmouth | 1956 |
| | | 118* | 214 | Hampshire v Somerset | Bournemouth | 1964 |
| Greenidge, A.E. | | 74* | 169 | Barbados v Trinidad | Port-of-Spain | 1980–81 |
| Greenidge, C.G. | (2) | 196* | 341 | Hampshire v Yorkshire | Leeds | 1973 |
| | | 157* | 270 | Hampshire v Glamorgan | Cardiff | 1982 |
| Greenidge, G.A. | | 100* | 180 | Sussex v Hampshire | Southampton | 1973 |
| Greenwood, A. | | 78* | 151 | Yorkshire v Gloucestershire | Clifton | 1874 |
| Greig, J.G. | (3) | 79* | 170 | Europeans v Parsees | Bombay | 1894–95 |
| | | 249* | 487 | Hampshire v Lancashire | Liverpool | 1901 |
| | | 92* | 192 | Europeans v Parsees | Poona | 1907–08 |
| Griffiths, E.L. | | 24* | 123 | Gloucestershire v Nottinghamshire | Nottingham | 1885 |
| Grimshaw, I. | | 36* | 182 | Yorkshire v Kent | Maidstone | 1881 |
| Gunn, G. | (8) | 91* | 188 | Nottinghamshire v Yorkshire | Nottingham | 1909 |
| | | 52* | 146 | Nottinghamshire v Essex | Leyton | 1911 |
| | | 62* | 176 | Nottinghamshire v Yorkshire | Dewsbury | 1913 |
| | | 64* | 144 | Nottinghamshire v Middlesex | Lord's | 1913 |
| | | 117* | 283 | Nottinghamshire v Middlesex | Lord's | 1921 |
| | | 67* | 155 | Notts v Gloucestershire | Cheltenham | 1926 |
| | | 109* | 267 | Nottinghamshire v Sussex | Eastbourne | 1929 |
| | | 85* | 186 | Nottinghamshire v Kent | Nottingham | 1931 |
| Gwynne, L.H. | | 153* | 274 | Dublin U. v Leicestershire | Leicester | 1895 |
| Hall, L. | (15) | 31* | 94 | Yorkshire v Sussex | Hove | 1878 |
| | | 124* | 331 | Yorkshire v Sussex | Hove | 1883 |
| | | 128* | 285 | Yorkshire v Sussex | Sheffield | 1884 |
| | | 32* | 81 | Yorkshire v Kent | Sheffield | 1885 |
| | | 79* | 285 | Yorkshire v Surrey | Sheffield | 1885 |
| | | 37* | 96 | Yorkshire v Derbyshire | Derby | 1885 |
| | | 50* | 173 | Yorkshire v Sussex | Huddersfield | 1886 |
| | | 74* | 172 | Yorkshire v Kent | Canterbury | 1886 |
| | | 119* | 334 | Yorkshire v Gloucestershire | Dewsbury | 1887 |
| | | 82* | 218 | Yorkshire v Sussex | Hove | 1887 |
| | | 105* | 261 | North v South | Scarborough | 1887 |
| | | 34* | 104 | Yorkshire v Surrey | Oval | 1888 |
| | | 129* | 461 | Yorkshire v Gloucestershire | Clifton | 1888 |
| | | 85* | 259 | Yorkshire v Middlesex | Lord's | 1889 |
| | | 41* | 106 | Yorkshire v Nottinghamshire | Sheffield | 1891 |
| Hallam, M.R. | | 152* | 231 | Leicestershire v Gloucestershire | Leicester | 1961 |
| Hallows, C. | (6) | 109* | 230 | Lancashire v Sussex | Manchester | 1921 |
| | | 110* | 183 | Lancashire v Leicestershire | Manchester | 1921 |
| | | 179* | 393 | Lancashire v Essex | Southend | 1923 |
| | | 158* | 297 | Lancashire v Leicestershire | Leicester | 1925 |
| | | 65* | 103 | Lancashire v Derbyshire | Nelson | 1925 |
| | | 152* | 305 | Lancashire v Yorkshire | Manchester | 1929 |
| Hamer, A. | (4) | 35* | 90 | Derbyshire v Gloucestershire | Bristol | 1950 |
| | | 147* | 272 | Derbyshire v Yorkshire | Leeds | 1954 |
| | | 112* | 208 | Derbyshire v Surrey | Oval | 1957 |
| | | 57* | 105 | Derbyshire v Gloucestershire | Bristol | 1958 |
| Hamid Nagra | | 122* | 266 | Sargodha v Railways | Lyallpur | 1963–64 |
| Hamilton, L.A.H. | | 117* | 205 | Kent v Australians | Canterbury | 1890 |
| Hanif Mohammad | (2) | 147* | 252 | Bahawalpur v Sind | Bahawalpur | 1953–54 |
| | | 142* | 241 | Pakistanis v Essex | Southend | 1954 |
| Harcharan Singh | | 104* | 201 | Southern Punjab v Delhi | Patiala | 1959–60 |
| Hardie, B.R. | (2) | 88* | 254† | Essex v Australians | Chelmsford | 1975 |
| | | 59* | 172 | Essex v Leicestershire | Leicester | 1979 |
| Hardinge, H.T.W. | (11) | 113* | 220 | Rest v England XI | Lord's | 1911 |
| | | 123* | 203 | Kent v Essex | Tonbridge | 1911 |
| | | 79* | 169 | Kent v Yorkshire | Leeds | 1919 |
| | | 172* | 339 | Kent v Essex | Canterbury | 1919 |
| | | 62* | 163 | Kent v Hampshire | Canterbury | 1920 |
| | | 118* | 196 | Kent v MCC | Lord's | 1921 |

|  |  | Score | Total |  |  |  |
|---|---|---|---|---|---|---|
| Harding, H.T.W. *continued* |  | 249* | 440 | Kent v Leicestershire | Leicester | 1922 |
|  |  | 71* | 161 | Kent v Gloucestershire | Tunbridge Wells | 1923 |
|  |  | 54* | 96 | Kent v Oxford University | Oxford | 1924 |
|  |  | 30* | 55 | Kent v Somerset | Tonbridge | 1926 |
|  |  | 49* | 122 | Kent v Essex | Southend | 1930 |
| Harris, C.B. | (2) | 117* | 246 | Nottinghamshire v Yorkshire | Leeds | 1934 |
|  |  | 239* | 401 | Nottinghamshire v Hampshire | Nottingham | 1950 |
| Harris, Lord |  | 80* | 148 | Kent v Yorkshire | Gravesend | 1883 |
| Harris, L.M. |  | 41* | 65 | Otago v Tasmania | Dunedin | 1883–84 |
| Harvey, J.F. |  | 23* | 67† | Derbyshire v Surrey | Oval | 1964 |
| Hawke, Lord |  | 107* | 229 | MCC v Oxford University | Lord's | 1902 |
| Hayman, H.B. |  | 104* | 213 | Middlesex v Kent | Catford | 1898 |
| Hayward, T. |  | 86* | 161 | Cambridge Town v Cambridge U. | Cambridge | 1860 |
| Hayward, T.W. | (8) | 156* | 287 | Surrey v Philadelphians | Oval | 1903 |
|  |  | 188* | 321 | Surrey v Kent | Canterbury | 1904 |
|  |  | 129* | 286 | Surrey v Australians | Oval | 1905 |
|  |  | 144* | 225 | Surrey v Nottinghamshire | Nottingham | 1906 |
|  |  | 114* | 190 | Surrey v Lancashire | Oval | 1907 |
|  |  | 146* | 278 | Players v Gentlemen | Lord's | 1907 |
|  |  | 90* | 156 | Surrey v Somerset | Taunton | 1909 |
|  |  | 96* | 178 | Surrey v Australians | Oval | 1909 |
| Haywood, R.A. |  | 131* | 251 | Northamptonshire v Sussex | Hove | 1921 |
| Hearn, P. |  | 12* | 32 | Kent v Hampshire | Southampton | 1952 |
| Hearn, W. |  | 58* | 126 | MCC v Oxford University | Oxford | 1879 |
| Hearne, A. | (6) | 43* | 189 | Kent v Somerset | Catford | 1892 |
|  |  | 116* | 256 | Kent v Gloucestershire | Canterbury | 1892 |
|  |  | 22* | 76 | Kent v Gloucestershire | Gravesend | 1895 |
|  |  | 55* | 114 | Kent v Sussex | Tonbridge | 1899 |
|  |  | 79* | 172 | Kent v Worcestershire | Canterbury | 1903 |
|  |  | 90* | 294 | Kent v Gloucestershire | Tonbridge | 1904 |
| Hearne, J.W. |  | 152* | 390 | Middlesex v Leicestershire | Leicester | 1931 |
| Henty, E. |  | 32* | 81 | Kent v Yorkshire | Dewsbury | 1870 |
| Hill, A. |  | 48* | 127 | Derbyshire v Kent | Maidstone | 1984 |
| Hill, N.W. |  | 23* | 57 | Nottinghamshire v Sussex | Eastbourne | 1962 |
| Hobbs, J.B. | (7) | 60* | 155 | Surrey v Warwickshire | Birmingham | 1907 |
|  |  | 154* | 292 | Players v Gentlemen | Lord's | 1911 |
|  |  | 117* | 190 | MCC v Lord Londesborough's XI | Scarborough | 1911 |
|  |  | 205* | 344 | Surrey v AIF | Oval | 1919 |
|  |  | 172* | 294 | Surrey v Yorkshire | Leeds | 1921 |
|  |  | 133* | 300 | Surrey v Yorkshire | Oval | 1931 |
|  |  | 161* | 320 | Players v Gentlemen | Lord's | 1932 |
| Hofmeyr, M.B. | (2) | 95* | 247 | Oxford U. v New Zealanders | Oxford | 1949 |
|  |  | 64* | 169 | Oxford U. v Cambridge U. | Lord's | 1949 |
| Hogue, T.H. |  | 60* | 152† | Western Australia v MCC | Perth | 1907–08 |
| Holdsworth, R.L. |  | 100* | 227 | NWFP v Southern Punjab | Patiala | 1938–39 |
| Holland, J. |  | 46* | 95 | Leicestershire v Surrey | Leicester | 1894 |
| Holloway, R.A. |  | 61* | 122 | Otago v Central Districts | Nelson | 1962–63 |
| Holmes, P. | (3) | 145* | 270 | Yorkshire v Northamptonshire | Northampton | 1920 |
|  |  | 175* | 377 | Yorkshire v New Zealanders | Bradford | 1927 |
|  |  | 110* | 219 | Yorkshire v Northamptonshire | Bradford | 1929 |
| Holt, J.K. jr |  | 103* | 196 | West Indians v C.C. of India | Bombay | 1958–59 |
| Hooker, W. |  | 8* | 19 | Sussex v Surrey | Godalming | 1830 |
| Hopkins, A.J.Y. |  | 91* | 159 | Rest v Australian XI | Sydney | 1908–09 |
| Hopkins, H.O. |  | 142* | 314 | Oxford University v Army | Oxford | 1922 |
| Hopkins, J.A. |  | 109* | 240 | Glamorgan v Derbyshire | Swansea | 1983 |
| Hopwood, J.L. | (2) | 60* | 153 | Lancashire v Somerset | Nelson | 1931 |
|  |  | 73* | 128 | Lancashire v South Africans | Manchester | 1935 |
| Hornby, A.N. | (2) | 23* | 56 | Lancashire v Yorkshire | Manchester | 1876 |
|  |  | 121* | 194 | MCC v Cambridge University | Lord's | 1882 |
| Horton, M.J. |  | 53* | 91 | Worcestershire v Lancashire | Manchester | 1966 |
| Howard, C.H. |  | 77* | 168 | Western Australia v Victoria | Perth | 1921–22 |
| Howard, T.C. |  | 47* | 202 | Western Australia v S. Australia | Fremantle | 1905–06 |
| Howell, M. |  | 15* | 73 | Surrey v Kent | Blackheath | 1920 |
| Humphrey, R. |  | 30* | 60 | Surrey v Nottinghamshire | Oval | 1872 |
| Humphrey, T. |  | 43* | 95 | Surrey v Sussex | Brighton | 1867 |
| Hunte, C.C. |  | 60* | 131 | West Indies v Australia | Port-of-Spain | 1964–65 |

|  |  | Score | Total |  |  |  |
|---|---|---|---|---|---|---|
| Hutton, L. | (4) | 99* | 200 | Yorkshire v Leicestershire | Sheffield | 1948 |
|  |  | 78* | 153 | Yorkshire v Worcestershire | Sheffield | 1949 |
|  |  | 202* | 344 | England v West Indies | Oval | 1950 |
|  |  | 156* | 272 | England v Australia | Adelaide | 1950–51 |
| Ibrahim, K.C. | (2) | 218* | 380 | Ibrahim's XI v M.N. Raiji's XI | Bombay | 1947–48 |
|  |  | 234* | 398 | Ibrahim's XI v M.K. Mantri's XI | Bombay | 1947–48 |
|  |  |  |  | *In successive matches* |  |  |
| Ijaz Butt |  | 151* | 234 | North Zone v Lahore | Lahore | 1961–62 |
| Ijaz Hussain |  | 68* | 130 | National Bank v Karachi Blues | Karachi | 1970–71 |
| Ikin, J.T. | (2) | 119* | 261† | Lancashire v Middlesex | Manchester | 1949 |
|  |  | 125* | 197 | Lancashire v Surrey | Oval | 1951 |
| Imtiaz Ahmed |  | 166* | 351 | North Zone v PIA | Lahore | 1961–62 |
| Iremonger, J. |  | 189* | 377 | Nottinghamshire v Middlesex | Lord's | 1904 |
| Jackson, F.S. |  | 59* | 162 | Yorkshire v Cambridge University | Cambridge | 1897 |
| Jadeja, M.V. |  | 75* | 160 | Saurashtra v Baroda | Baroda | 1958–59 |
| Jagdale, A.M. |  | 149* | 312 | Madhya Pradesh v Uttar Pradesh | Agra | 1966–67 |
| Javed Baber |  | 114* | 239 | Railways v Karachi B | Lahore | 1962–63 |
| Jena, B. |  | 38* | 83 | Orissa v Bihar | Jamshedpur | 1961–62 |
| Johnstone, C.P. |  | 78* | 206 | MCC v Cambridge University | Lord's | 1939 |
| Jones, A. |  | 166* | 364 | Glamorgan v Nottinghamshire | Nottingham | 1967 |
| Jones, A.O. |  | 125* | 239 | Nottinghamshire v Australians | Nottingham | 1909 |
| Jones, S.P. |  | 134* | 266 | Australian XI v | | |
|  |  |  |  | A. Shrewsbury's XI | Sydney | 1887–88 |
| Jordaan, H.B. |  | 83* | 183 | N.E. Transvaal v W. Province | Cape Town | 1946–47 |
| Jupp, H. | (12) | 94* | 297 | Surrey v Hampshire | Oval | 1866 |
|  |  | 90* | 222 | Surrey v Yorkshire | Sheffield | 1868 |
|  |  | 27* | 95 | Surrey v Lancashire | Manchester | 1870 |
|  |  | 50* | 88 | Surrey v Gloucestershire | Clifton | 1870 |
|  |  | 50* | 98 | South v North | Lord's | 1873 |
|  |  | 51* | 113 | Surrey v Nottinghamshire | Oval | 1873 |
|  |  | 43* | 95 | Surrey v Yorkshire *1st inns* | Oval | 1874 |
|  |  | 109* | 193 | Surrey v Yorkshire *2nd inns* | Oval | 1874 |
|  |  | 37* | 74 | Surrey v Yorkshire | Sheffield | 1876 |
|  |  | 73* | 268 | Surrey v Kent | Oval | 1876 |
|  |  | 91* | 264 | Surrey v Kent | Oval | 1877 |
|  |  | 117* | 284 | Surrey v Yorkshire | Sheffield | 1880 |
| Kamal Najamuddin |  | 27* | 75† | Karachi v United Bank | Karachi | 1981–82 |
| Keeton, W.W. |  | 99* | 190 | Nottinghamshire v Kent | Nottingham | 1937 |
| Kelly, P.C. |  | 82* | 147 | Western Australia v S. Australia | Perth | 1964–65 |
| Kennedy, A.S. |  | 152* | 344 | Hampshire v Nottinghamshire | Nottingham | 1921 |
| Kenyon, D. |  | 103* | 215 | Worcestershire v Hampshire | Bournemouth | 1955 |
| Kerr, J. |  | 178* | 372 | Scotland v Ireland | Dublin | 1923 |
| Kerr, J.L. |  | 146* | 243 | Canterbury v MCC | Christchurch | 1935–36 |
| Kher, D.R. |  | 56* | 106 | Maharashtra v Bombay | Bombay | 1961–62 |
| Kilner, N. |  | 40* | 119 | Warwickshire v Kent | Tunbridge Wells | 1928 |
| Kinneir, S. | (3) | 70* | 239 | Warwickshire v Leics *1st inns* | Leicester | 1907 |
|  |  | 69* | 166 | Warwickshire v Leics *2nd inns* | Leicester | 1907 |
|  |  | 65* | 164 | Warwickshire v Somerset | Taunton | 1908 |
| Kitcat, S.A.P. |  | 18* | 70 | Gloucestershire v Yorkshire | Hull | 1901 |
| Kitchen, M.J. |  | 161* | 287 | Somerset v Northamptonshire | Taunton | 1968 |
| Knight, A.E. | (5) | 91* | 155† | Leicestershire v Surrey | Oval | 1903 |
|  |  | 61* | 131 | Leicestershire v Nottinghamshire | Nottingham | 1908 |
|  |  | 137* | 345 | Leicestershire v Warwickshire | Birmingham | 1909 |
|  |  | 66* | 182 | Leicestershire v Hampshire | Portsmouth | 1911 |
|  |  | 74* | 182 | Leicestershire v Surrey | Leicester | 1911 |
| Lacey, F.E. |  | 61* | 135 | Hampshire v Derbyshire | Southampton | 1885 |
| Langdon, T. |  | 78* | 151 | Gloucestershire v South Africans | Bristol | 1907 |
| Langridge, J.G. | (3) | 108* | 218 | Sussex v Nottinghamshire | Hove | 1948 |
|  |  | 48* | 101 | Sussex v Lancashire | Manchester | 1950 |
|  |  | 111* | 191 | Sussex v Somerset | Hove | 1952 |
| Langridge, R.J. |  | 137* | 222 | Sussex v Leicestershire | Leicester | 1963 |
| Larkins, W. |  | 118* | 223 | Northamptonshire v Yorkshire | Northampton | 1982 |
| Lawry, W.M. | (5) | 150* | 309 | Victoria v South Australia | Melbourne | 1961–62 |
|  |  | 49* | 107 | Australia v India | Delhi | 1969–70 |
|  |  | 60* | 116† | Australia v England | Sydney | 1970–71 |
|  |  | 116* | 262 | Victoria v Western Australia | Perth | 1971–72 |

|  |  | Score | Total |  |  |  |
| --- | --- | --- | --- | --- | --- | --- |
| Lawry, W.M. *continued* |  | 69* | 156 | Victoria v South Australia | Adelaide | 1971–72 |
| Lee, C. |  | 96* | 211 | Derbyshire v Middlesex | Chesterfield | 1956 |
| Lee, F.S. | (3) | 134* | 236 | Somerset v Sussex | Taunton | 1931 |
|  |  | 59* | 116 | Somerset v Australians | Taunton | 1934 |
|  |  | 109* | 196 | Somerset v Worcestershire | Worcester | 1938 |
| Lee, H.W. | (2) | 80* | 212 | Middlesex v Essex | Leyton | 1920 |
|  |  | 52* | 132 | Middlesex v Essex | Lord's | 1924 |
| Lee, I.S. |  | 109* | 213 | Victoria v South Australia | Adelaide | 1936–37 |
| Lee, J.W. | (2) | 135* | 352 | Somerset v Kent | Taunton | 1934 |
|  |  | 54* | 160 | Somerset v Cambridge University | Cambridge | 1935 |
| Lenham, L.J. | (2) | 66* | 147 | Sussex v Surrey | Hove | 1957 |
|  |  | 51* | 161 | Sussex v Glamorgan | Margam | 1960 |
| Le Roux, D.P. |  | 108* | 221 | Orange Free State v Boland | Stellenbosch | 1982–83 |
| Lillywhite, F.W. | (2) | 42* | 89 | Sussex v MCC | Lord's | 1839 |
|  |  | 18* | 38 | MCC v Cambridge University | Cambridge | 1845 |
| Lloyd, T.A. |  | 124* | 230 | Warwickshire v Surrey | Oval | 1983 |
| Lockwood, E. | (2) | 67* | 115 | Players v Gentlemen | Oval | 1874 |
|  |  | 68* | 121 | England XI v Cambridge U. | Cambridge | 1879 |
| Lowson, F.A. |  | 76* | 218 | Yorkshire v MCC | Lord's | 1951 |
| Lucas, A.P. | (3) | 36* | 121 | Surrey v Gloucestershire | Clifton | 1877 |
|  |  | 43* | 126 | MCC v Lancashire | Lord's | 1881 |
|  |  | 47* | 149 | Gentlemen v Players | Oval | 1883 |
| Luckhurst, B.W. | (2) | 126* | 253 | Kent v Sussex | Tunbridge Wells | 1967 |
|  |  | 46* | 96 | Kent v Hampshire | Bournemouth | 1969 |
| McGlew, D.J. | (4) | 114* | 251 | South Africans v Hampshire | Southampton | 1951 |
|  |  | 64* | 95 | South Africans v T.N. Pearce's XI | Scarborough | 1951 |
|  |  | 54* | 147 | Natal v Australians | Durban | 1957–58 |
|  |  | 127* | 292 | South Africa v New Zealand | Durban | 1961–62 |
| McKenzie, U.M. |  | 115* | 292 | British Guiana v Trinidad | Port-of-Spain | 1943–44 |
| Mackinnon, F.A. |  | 33* | 64 | Kent v Yorkshire | Bradford | 1881 |
| McMorris, E.D.A.St J. | (3) | 190* | 383 | West Indians v Middlesex | Lord's | 1963 |
|  |  | 103* | 185 | Jamaica v Cavaliers | Kingston | 1963–64 |
|  |  | 127* | 236 | Jamaica v Trinidad | Port-of-Spain | 1965–66 |
| Makepeace, J.W.H. | (4) | 39* | 88 | Lancashire v Kent | Maidstone | 1913 |
|  |  | 71* | 185 | Lancashire v Cambridge U. | Cambridge | 1921 |
|  |  | 106* | 208 | Lancashire v Nottinghamshire | Nottingham | 1923 |
|  |  | 92* | 159 | Lancashire v Nottinghamshire | Nottingham | 1926 |
| Mankad, A.V. |  | 154* | 306 | Indians v T.N. Pearce's XI | Scarborough | 1971 |
| Mantri, M.K. |  | 64* | 229 | Bombay v Gujarat | Ahmedabad | 1950–51 |
| Marlow, F.W. | (2) | 43* | 123 | Sussex v Surrey | Oval | 1891 |
|  |  | 144* | 268 | Sussex v MCC | Lord's | 1891 |
| Marshal, A. |  | 66* | 114 | Queensland v New Zealanders | Brisbane | 1913–14 |
| Maynard, E.A.J. |  | 28* | 55 | Derbyshire v Lancashire | Derby | 1882 |
| Mayne, E.R. |  | 154* | 345 | Victoria v New South Wales | Sydney | 1923–24 |
| Mead, C.P. | (3) | 88* | 223 | Hampshire v Warwickshire | Leamington | 1909 |
|  |  | 120* | 234 | Hampshire v Yorkshire | Huddersfield | 1911 |
|  |  | 117* | 221 | Hampshire v Nottinghamshire | Nottingham | 1935 |
| Mehra, V.L. |  | 87* | 206 | East Punjab v Delhi | Jullunder | 1957–58 |
| Merchant, V.M. | (4) | 135* | 271 | Indians v Lancashire *1st inns* | Liverpool | 1936 |
|  |  | 77* | 161 | Indians v Lancashire *2nd inns* | Liverpool | 1936 |
|  |  | 86* | 197 | Indians v Warwickshire | Birmingham | 1946 |
|  |  | 184* | 317 | Bombay v Commonwealth XI | Bombay | 1950–51 |
| Midlane, F.A. | (2) | 14* | 60† | Wellington v Canterbury | Christchurch | 1910–11 |
|  |  | 222* | 498 | Wellington v Otago | Wellington | 1914–15 |
| Midwinter, W.E. |  | 16* | 76 | Australians v Nottinghamshire | Nottingham | 1878 |
| Miller, L.S.M. |  | 81* | 154 | Wellington v Otago | Dunedin | 1956–57 |
| Mills, G. |  | 106* | 235 | Auckland v Wellington | Auckland | 1895–96 |
| Mills, I. |  | 88* | 156 | Auckland v Otago | Dunedin | 1893–94 |
| Milton, C.A. | (3) | 51* | 117 | Gloucestershire v Lancashire | Bristol | 1955 |
|  |  | 28* | 69 | Gloucestershire v Middlesex | Gloucester | 1956 |
|  |  | 138* | 253 | Gloucestershire v Leicestershire | Bristol | 1966 |
| Mitchell, B. |  | 103* | 198 | South Africans v MCC | Lord's | 1947 |
| Mitchell, R.A.H. |  | 125* | 204 | MCC v Kent | Canterbury | 1872 |
| Mitford, P. |  | 65* | 97 | Army v MCC | Pretoria | 1905–06 |
| Mohammad Arif, jr |  | 20* | 57 | State Bank v MCB | Lahore | 1983–84 |
|  |  |  |  | *Only five batted* |  |  |

|  |  | Score | Total |  |  |  |
|---|---|---|---|---|---|---|
| Mohiuddin Mirza |  | 63* | 141 | Jammu & Kashmir v Services | Srinagar | 1964–65 |
| Moon, L.J. |  | 62* | 136 | Middlesex v Essex | Leyton | 1903 |
| Moore, D.N. |  | 101* | 217 | South of England v MCC | Folkestone | 1930 |
| Morgan, T.R. | (4) | 22* | 68† | Glamorgan v Yorkshire | Cardiff | 1922 |
|  |  | 14* | 47 | Glamorgan v Nottinghamshire | Cardiff | 1922 |
|  |  | 13* | 42 | Glamorgan v Lancashire | Swansea | 1922 |
|  |  | 87* | 188† | Glamorgan v Leicestershire | Leicester | 1923 |
| Morley, J.D. |  | 82* | 237 | Sussex v Surrey | Hove | 1974 |
| Morris, E.B. |  | 106* | 297 | Natal v Orange Free State | Johannesburg | 1906–07 |
| Morton, A. | (2) | 28* | 62 | Derbyshire v Yorkshire | Bradford | 1910 |
|  |  | 105* | 204 | Derbyshire v Leicestershire | Derby | 1920 |
| Moulder, E.R.D. |  | 104* | 264 | West Indian XI v MCC | Georgetown | 1912–13 |
| Moxon, M.D. |  | 119* | 279 | Griqualand West v Border | Kimberley | 1982–83 |
| Mudassar Nazar |  | 152* | 323 | Pakistan v India | Lahore | 1982–83 |
| Mudie, W. |  | 54* | 114 | New England XI v New All-England XI | Oval | 1862 |
| Munir-ul-Haq | (2) | 132* | 280 | HBFC v PACO | Bahawalpur | 1983–84 |
|  |  | 104* | 234 | HBFC v PIA | Bahawalpur | 1984–85 |
| Murdoch, W.L. | (2) | 82* | 177 | NSW v Lord Harris's XI | Sydney | 1878–79 |
|  |  | 107* | 240 | Australians v Orleans Club | Twickenham | 1882 |
| Muttaqi Hasan | (2) | 72* | 153 | Hyderabad v Karachi Greens | Karachi | 1961–62 |
|  |  | 98* | 180 | Hyderabad v East Pakistan | Hyderabad | 1962–63 |
| Naushad Ali |  | 107* | 247 | East Pakistan v Railways | Lahore | 1967–68 |
| Nayyar, G. |  | 76* | 168 | Services v Punjab | Delhi | 1978–79 |
| Nazar Mohammad |  | 124* | 331 | Pakistan v India | Lucknow | 1952–53 |
| Nazir Ali, S. |  | 64* | 185 | Roshanara v Viceroy's XI | Delhi | 1932–33 |
| Needham, E. | (2) | 58* | 111 | Derbyshire v Surrey | Derby | 1908 |
|  |  | 107* | 195 | Derbyshire v Essex | Leyton | 1908 |
| Newham, W. |  | 110* | 174 | Sussex v Lancashire | Manchester | 1894 |
| Nicholls, R.B. |  | 26* | 87 | Gloucestershire v Hampshire | Bristol | 1966 |
| Nicholson, W.G. |  | 63* | 143 | Gents of South v Gents of North | Lord's | 1862 |
| Nitschke, H.C. |  | 130* | 246 | South Australia v NSW | Sydney | 1933–34 |
| North, M.K. |  | 32* | 73 | British Guiana v R.S. Lucas's XI | Georgetown | 1894–95 |
| Northway, R.P. |  | 21* | 43 | Somerset v Yorkshire | Bradford | 1930 |
| Norton, W.S. |  | 64* | 143 | Gentlemen of Kent & Sussex v Gentlemen of England | Canterbury | 1857 |
| Oakman, A.S.M. |  | 137* | 238 | Sussex v Lancashire | Hove | 1956 |
| Oliver, L. |  | 75* | 146 | Derbyshire v Warwickshire | Birmingham | 1912 |
| Ormrod, J.A. | (4) | 66* | 187 | Worcestershire v Essex | Chelmsford | 1975 |
|  |  | 36* | 73 | Worcestershire v Sussex | Worcester | 1977 |
|  |  | 126* | 219 | Worcestershire v Hampshire | Bournemouth | 1980 |
|  |  | 63* | 136 | Worcestershire v Derbyshire | Derby | 1983 |
| Oscroft, E. |  | 53* | 94 | Nottinghamshire v Surrey | Nottingham | 1865 |
| Padgett, D.E.V. |  | 115* | 230 | Yorkshire v Gloucestershire | Bristol | 1962 |
| Palairet, L.C.H. | (4) | 22* | 58 | Somerset v Lancashire | Manchester | 1892 |
|  |  | 51* | 122 | Somerset v Kent | Taunton | 1893 |
|  |  | 113* | 172 | Somerset v Middlesex | Taunton | 1895 |
|  |  | 45* | 126 | Somerset v Surrey | Taunton | 1902 |
| Parkhouse, W.G.A. |  | 60* | 152 | Glamorgan v Lancashire | Swansea | 1954 |
| Parks, H.W. | (2) | 49* | 105 | Sussex v Yorkshire | Eastbourne | 1946 |
|  |  | 119* | 221 | Sussex v Lancashire | Eastbourne | 1947 |
| Parks, J.H. | (2) | 33* | 137 | Sussex v Glamorgan | Swansea | 1936 |
|  |  | 144* | 262 | Sussex v Cambridge University | Cambridge | 1937 |
| Parsons, A.B.D. |  | 30* | 71 | Surrey v Leicestershire | Oval | 1961 |
| Parsons, J.H. |  | 161* | 347 | Warwickshire v Gloucestershire | Nuneaton | 1913 |
| Patterson, G.S. |  | 109* | 234 | Philadelphians v F. Mitchell's XI | Philadelphia | 1895–96 |
| Patterson, W.H. |  | 107* | 306 | Oxford U. v Cambridge U. | Lord's | 1881 |
| Payne, C. | (3) | 53* | 165 | Sussex v Kent | Brighton | 1865 |
|  |  | 135* | 367 | Kent v Surrey | Gravesend | 1866 |
|  |  | 37* | 79 | Sussex v Middlesex | Brighton | 1868 |
| Payton, W.E.G. |  | 33* | 84 | Combined Services v Oxford U. | Oxford | 1947 |
| Pearson, F.A. | (4) | 154* | 342 | Worcestershire v Surrey | Dudley | 1912 |
|  |  | 67* | 152 | Worcestershire v Sussex | Eastbourne | 1914 |
|  |  | 151* | 275 | Worcestershire v Warwickshire | Worcester | 1921 |
|  |  | 68* | 123 | Worcestershire v Hampshire | Southampton | 1923 |
| Phebey, A.H. | (4) | 89* | 209 | Kent v Worcestershire | Kidderminster | 1951 |

|  |  | Score | Total | | | |
|---|---|---|---|---|---|---|
| Phebey, A.H. *continued* | | 54* | 126 | Kent v Middlesex | Lord's | 1951 |
| | | 85* | 181 | Kent v Australians | Canterbury | 1953 |
| | | 50* | 127 | Kent v Northamptonshire | Northampton | 1954 |
| Pitchimuthu, D.V. | | 93* | 208 | Bihar v Orissa | Cuttack | 1959–60 |
| Picknell, G. | | 27* | 64 | Sussex v Surrey | Oval | 1850 |
| Pickerill, J.H.M. | | 143* | 325 | N.E. Transvaal v Rhodesia | Pretoria | 1951–52 |
| Pilkington, H.C. | | 77* | 169 | Oxford University v MCC | Lord's | 1899 |
| Pinch, C.J. | | 146* | 259† | South Australia v Victoria | Melbourne | 1950–51 |
| Place, W. | | 101* | 244 | Lancashire v Warwickshire | Manchester | 1950 |
| Playle, W.R. | | 89* | 139 | Auckland v Northern Districts | Auckland | 1959–60 |
| Ponniah, C.E.M. | | 98* | 206 | Cambridge U. v Leicestershire | Leicester | 1967 |
| Ponsford, W.H. | (2) | 143* | 283 | Australians v Glamorgan | Swansea | 1926 |
| | | 109* | 185 | Victoria v New South Wales | Melbourne | 1930–31 |
| Poore, R.M. | | 49* | 97 | Hampshire v Somerset | Bath | 1898 |
| Pope, D.F. | | 87* | 216 | Essex v Glamorgan | Colchester | 1930 |
| Prentice, F.T. | | 36* | 89 | Leicestershire v Worcestershire | Hinckley | 1937 |
| Qasim Omar | | 79* | 159 | Karachi Blues v National Bank | Karachi | 1974–75 |
| Quaife, B.W. | | 31* | 112 | Worcestershire v Kent | Stourbridge | 1931 |
| Quaife, W. | | 40* | 81 | Sussex v Lancashire | Manchester | 1887 |
| Quaife, W.G. | | 178* | 475† | Warwickshire v Hampshire | Southampton | 1897 |
| Quinlan, P.F. | | 40* | 131 | Western Australia v S. Australia | Perth | 1926–27 |
| Radcliffe, O.G. | (2) | 104* | 207 | Gloucestershire v Middlesex | Lord's | 1886 |
| | | 101* | 214 | Gloucestershire v Kent | Canterbury | 1889 |
| Raghunatha Rao, K. | | 68* | 169 | Kerala v Mysore | Palghat | 1958–59 |
| Ram, D. | | 31* | 79 | Kerala v Madras | Madurai | 1957–58 |
| Ramprasad, B. | | 31* | 86 | Andhra v Tamil Nadu | Vijayawada | 1975–76 |
| Rawlin, J.T. | | 122* | 290 | MCC v London County | Crystal Palace | 1902 |
| Razaullah Khan | | 25* | 67 | Khairpur v Karachi | Karachi | 1968–69 |
| Read, W.W. | (2) | 196* | 413 | Surrey v Sussex | Oval | 1892 |
| | | 142* | 368 | G.F. Vernon's XI v Victoria | Melbourne | 1887–88 |
| Redpath, I.R. | (2) | 139* | 307 | Australians v Rhodesia | Salisbury | 1966–67 |
| | | 159* | 346 | Australia v New Zealand | Auckland | 1973–74 |
| Rees, J.S. | | 21* | 54 | South Australia v W. Australia | Perth | 1905–06 |
| Relf, R.R. | | 272* | 433 | Sussex v Worcestershire | Eastbourne | 1909 |
| Reynolds, G.R. | | 125* | 281 | Queensland v Western Australia | Perth | 1958–59 |
| Rhodes, W. | (3) | 98* | 184 | Yorkshire v MCC | Lord's | 1903 |
| | | 85* | 152 | Yorkshire v Essex | Leyton | 1910 |
| | | 79* | 165 | Capped v Uncapped | Hastings | 1923 |
| Rice, R.W. | (2) | 38* | 101 | Gloucestershire v Yorkshire | Cheltenham | 1900 |
| | | 58* | 147 | Gloucestershire v Essex | Clifton | 1901 |
| Richards, B.A. | (3) | 127* | 192† | Hampshire v Northamptonshire | Bournemouth | 1969 |
| | | 225* | 344 | Hampshire v Nottinghamshire | Nottingham | 1974 |
| | | 71* | 179 | Hampshire v Middlesex | Southampton | 1975 |
| Richardson, P.E. | (2) | 91* | 155 | Worcestershire v Hampshire | Worcester | 1955 |
| | | 59* | 105 | MCC v Pakistan XI | Dacca | 1955–56 |
| Riches, N.V.H. | (2) | 177* | 347 | Glamorgan v Leicestershire | Leicester | 1921 |
| | | 85* | 161 | Glamorgan v Yorkshire | Leeds | 1922 |
| Ricketts, J. | | 195* | 429 | Lancashire v Surrey | Oval | 1867 |
| | | | | *On debut in first-class matches* | | |
| Ridley, R.M. | | 70* | 142 | Oxford U. v Nottinghamshire | Oxford | 1970 |
| Rippon, A.D.E. | | 87* | 194 | Somerset v Kent | Taunton | 1914 |
| Rippon, A.E.S. | (2) | 19* | 66† | Somerset v Sussex | Bath | 1920 |
| | | 90* | 165 | Somerset v Hampshire | Southampton | 1921 |
| Rodrigo, M. | | 135* | 318 | Ceylon v West Indies | Colombo | 1948–49 |
| Roebuck, P.M. | | 33 | 125† | Somerset v Australians | Taunton | 1985 |
| Rogers, N.H. | (5) | 32* | 68† | Hampshire v Leicestershire | Loughborough | 1953 |
| | | 56* | 126 | MCC v Surrey | Lord's | 1954 |
| | | 172* | 327 | Hampshire v Gloucestershire | Bristol | 1954 |
| | | 125* | 221 | Hampshire v Somerset | Glastonbury | 1954 |
| | | 101* | 182 | England XI v Pakistanis | Hastings | 1954 |
| Rose, B.C. | | 76* | 146 | Somerset v Northamptonshire | Northampton | 1975 |
| Rothery, J.W. | | 53* | 258 | Yorkshire v Worcestershire | Worcester | 1907 |
| Roy, A.G. | | 84* | 180 | Assam v Bengal | Calcutta | 1951–52 |
| Russell, C.A.G. | | 89* | 161 | Essex v Northamptonshire | Northampton | 1913 |
| Rutherford, K.R. | | 89* | 241 | Otago v Auckland | Dunedin | 1984–85 |

|  |  | Score | Total |  |  |  |
|---|---|---|---|---|---|---|
| Ryder, J. |  | 93* | 188 | Victoria v New South Wales | Sydney | 1914–15 |
| Saadat Ali |  | 104* | 176† | Punjab Greens v National Bank | Lahore | 1977–78 |
| Sadiq Mohammad |  | 103* | 264 | Pakistan XI v Rest | Sahiwal | 1969–70 |
| Salim Taj |  | 82* | 250 | Lahore v PIA | Lahore | 1981–82 |
| Sandham, A. | (7) | 123* | 323 | Surrey v Hampshire | Portsmouth | 1922 |
|  |  | 155* | 330 | Surrey v Somerset | Oval | 1923 |
|  |  | 96* | 158 | Surrey v Cambridge University | Oval | 1924 |
|  |  | 159* | 271 | Sir J. Cahn's XI v West Indian XI | Kingston | 1928–29 |
|  |  | 125* | 282 | Surrey v Northamptonshire | Northampton | 1930 |
|  |  | 113* | 221 | Surrey v Hampshire | Bournemouth | 1931 |
|  |  | 169* | 333 | Surrey v Hampshire | Oval | 1933 |
| Sanjeeva Rao |  | 139* | 256 | Madhya Pradesh v Rajasthan | Sagar | 1982–83 |
| Scotton, W.H. | (4) | 110* | 223 | Nottinghamshire v Surrey | Nottingham | 1886 |
|  |  | 35* | 92 | Nottinghamshire v Lancashire | Manchester | 1887 |
|  |  | 17* | 58 | Nottinghamshire v Yorkshire | Sheffield | 1888 |
|  |  | 9* | 28 | England XI v Australians | Stoke | 1888 |
| Sebastien, L. |  | 96* | 212 | Windward Islands v Barbados | Bridgetown | 1983–84 |
| Serrurier, L.R. |  | 74* | 162 | Western Province v MCC | Cape Town | 1927–28 |
| Sewell, C.O.H. |  | 88* | 127 | Gloucestershire v Yorkshire | Sheffield | 1898 |
| Seymour, C.R. |  | 77* | 154 | Hampshire v Surrey | Southampton | 1883 |
| Shafiq Ahmed |  | 92* | 226 | National Park v PIA | Lahore | 1978–79 |
| Shaw, E.D. |  | 78* | 189 | Oxford University v Australians | Oxford | 1882 |
| Shipman, A.W. |  | 100* | 212 | Leicestershire v Lancashire | Manchester | 1935 |
| Shipperd, G. |  | 131* | 280 | Western Australia v Victoria | Perth | 1984–85 |
| Shrewsbury, A. | (8) | 224* | 415 | Nottinghamshire v Middlesex | Lord's | 1885 |
|  |  | 227* | 430 | Nottinghamshire v Gloucestershire | Moreton-in-Marsh | 1886 |
|  |  | 54* | 90 | North v South | Lord's | 1890 |
|  |  | 81* | 167 | Players v Gentlemen | Lord's | 1891 |
|  |  | 151* | 345 | M. Sherwin's XI v L. Hall's XI | Bradford | 1891 |
|  |  | 111* | 226 | Nottinghamshire v Kent | Canterbury | 1892 |
|  |  | 151* | 325 | Players v Gentlemen | Oval | 1892 |
|  |  | 125* | 277 | Nottinghamshire v Gloucestershire | Nottingham | 1896 |
| Siedle, I.J. |  | 132* | 297 | South Africans v MCC | Lord's | 1935 |
| Simpson, R.B. |  | 161* | 294 | Western Australia v NSW | Sydney | 1959–60 |
| Simpson, R.T. | (2) | 119* | 237 | MCC v Natal | Durban | 1948–49 |
|  |  | 230* | 352 | Nottinghamshire v Glamorgan | Swansea | 1950 |
| Sinfield, R.A. | (5) | 161* | 374 | Gloucestershire v Oxford U. | Oxford | 1931 |
|  |  | 39* | 104 | Gloucestershire v Sussex | Cheltenham | 1931 |
|  |  | 100* | 290 | Gloucestershire v Sussex | Bristol | 1935 |
|  |  | 38* | 106 | Gloucestershire v Derbyshire | Buxton | 1937 |
|  |  | 69* | 165 | Gloucestershire v Worcestershire | Bristol | 1939 |
| Slack, W.N. |  | 72* | 195 | Middlesex v Worcestershire | Lord's | 1985 |
| Slocombe, P.A. | (2) | 93* | 210 | Somerset v Lancashire | Bath | 1978 |
|  |  | 35* | 118 | Somerset v Middlesex | Taunton | 1978 |
| Smith, C.H. |  | 47* | 129 | Sussex v Surrey | Oval | 1868 |
| Smith, D. | (2) | 140* | 265 | Derbyshire v Hampshire | Chesterfield | 1937 |
|  |  | 57* | 112 | Derbyshire v Kent | Ilkeston | 1939 |
| Smith, D.V. |  | 147* | 256 | Sussex v West Indians | Hove | 1957 |
| Smith, F.B. |  | 50* | 124 | Barbados v Demerara | Bridgetown | 1864–65 |
| Smith, H.O. |  | 124* | 204 | Tasmania v South Africans | Launceston | 1910–11 |
| Smith, K.D. | (3) | 132* | 296 | Warwickshire v Sussex | Birmingham | 1978 |
|  |  | 120* | 230 | Warwickshire v Essex | Southend | 1980 |
|  |  | 58* | 154 | Warwickshire v Middlesex | Lord's | 1981 |
| Smith, M.J.K. |  | 76* | 137 | Oxford University v Hampshire | Bournemouth | 1955 |
| Snary, H.C. |  | 124* | 291 | Leicestershire v Indians | Leicester | 1932 |
| Spooner, R.T. |  | 98* | 210 | Warwickshire v Worcestershire | Worcester | 1952 |
| Stearman, W. |  | 26* | 51 | Kent v Sussex | Brighton | 1836 |
| Stillman, W.L. |  | 88* | 211 | South Australia v Victoria | Melbourne | 1977–78 |
| Stoddart, A.E. | (2) | 216* | 372 | Middlesex v Lancashire | Manchester | 1891 |
|  |  | 195* | 327 | Middlesex v Nottinghamshire | Lord's | 1893 |
| Stollmeyer, J.B. |  | 45* | 84 | West Indians v Somerset | Taunton | 1939 |
| Stott, W.B. |  | 144* | 262 | Yorkshire v Worcestershire | Worcester | 1959 |
| Stovold, A.W. |  | 59* | 161 | Gloucestershire v Yorkshire | Scarborough | 1978 |
| Studd, G.B. |  | 106* | 187 | Cambridge U. v Lancashire | Liverpool | 1881 |
| Sutcliffe, H. | (7) | 125* | 307 | Yorkshire v Essex | Southend | 1920 |
|  |  | 104* | 170† | Yorkshire v Hampshire | Leeds | 1932 |

| | | Score | Total | | | |
|---|---|---|---|---|---|---|
| Sutcliffe, H. *continued* | | 110* | 307† | North v South | Manchester | 1932 |
| | | 114* | 202 | Yorkshire v Rest of England | Oval | 1933 |
| | | 187* | 401 | Yorkshire v Worcestershire | Bradford | 1934 |
| | | 135* | 262 | Yorkshire v Glamorgan | Neath | 1935 |
| | | 125* | 322 | Yorkshire v Oxford University | Oxford | 1939 |
| Suttle, K.G. | (2) | 97* | 166 | Sussex v Lancashire | Liverpool | 1964 |
| | | 89* | 161 | Sussex v Leicestershire | Leicester | 1966 |
| Tancred, A.B. | | 26* | 47 | South Africa v England | Cape Town | 1888–89 |
| Tancred, L.J. | | 61* | 135 | South Africans v MCC | Lord's | 1907 |
| Tarrant, F.A. | (6) | 51* | 114 | MCC v Kent | Lord's | 1907 |
| | | 48* | 162 | MCC v Oxford University | Oxford | 1908 |
| | | 55* | 145 | Middlesex v Gloucestershire | Bristol | 1909 |
| | | 140* | 262 | Middlesex v Sussex | Lord's | 1910 |
| | | 207* | 378 | Middlesex v Yorkshire | Bradford | 1911 |
| | | 81* | 159 | Middlesex v Lancashire | Liverpool | 1913 |
| Tayfield, A. | | 133* | 261 | Transvaal v Eastern Province | Port Elizabeth | 1955–56 |
| Taylor, C.H. | | 105* | 274 | Oxford University v Worcestershire | Oxford | 1925 |
| Taylor, H.W. | | 83* | 124 | Natal v MCC | Pietermaritzburg | 1913–14 |
| Taylor, K.A. | | 81* | 222 | Warwickshire v Yorkshire | Birmingham | 1948 |
| Thompson, G.J. | | 103* | 270† | Northamptonshire v Cambridge U. | Cambridge | 1906 |
| Thomson, W.K. | | 74* | 225 | Natal v Transvaal | Durban | 1904–05 |
| Timms, J.E. | | 82* | 156 | Northamptonshire v Derbyshire | Chesterfield | 1935 |
| Tindill, E.W.T. | | 47* | 111 | Wellington v Otago | Dunedin | 1946–47 |
| Todd, L.J. | | 133* | 265 | Kent v Leicestershire | Tunbridge Wells | 1946 |
| Townsend, A.F. | | 102* | 228 | Derbyshire v Lancashire | Manchester | 1948 |
| Tremlett, T.M. | | 70* | 182 | Hampshire v Leicestershire | Southampton | 1980 |
| Troup, W. | | 127* | 388 | Gloucestershire v Worcestershire | Bristol | 1902 |
| Turner, A. | | 71* | 147 | New South Wales v Queensland | Brisbane | 1969–70 |
| Turner, G.M. | (4) | 43* | 131 | New Zealand v England | Lord's | 1969 |
| | | 223* | 386 | New Zealand v West Indies | Kingston | 1971–72 |
| | | 88* | 202 | Worcestershire v Somerset | Worcester | 1972 |
| | | 141* | 169 | Worcestershire v Glamorgan | Swansea | 1977 |
| | | | | *World record – 83% of innings total* | | |
| Ulyett, G. | | 199* | 399 | Yorkshire v Derbyshire | Sheffield | 1887 |
| Van der Berg, J.H. | (2) | 55* | 188 | Eastern Province v Transvaal | Johannesburg | 1926–27 |
| | | 47* | 177 | E. Province v W. Province | Cape Town | 1929–30 |
| Varnals, G.D. | | 151* | 267 | Eastern Province v Border | East London | 1957–58 |
| Vats, R. | | 87* | 180 | Railways v Rajasthan | Delhi | 1978–79 |
| Vials, G.A.T. | | 62* | 105 | Northamptonshire v Surrey | Northampton | 1910 |
| Vine, J. | (9) | 75* | 178 | Sussex v Middlesex | Eastbourne | 1902 |
| | | 62* | 241 | Sussex v Somerset | Hove | 1906 |
| | | 80* | 218 | Sussex v Somerset | Bath | 1906 |
| | | 78* | 222 | Sussex v Middlesex | Lord's | 1907 |
| | | 67* | 186 | Sussex v Essex | Hove | 1907 |
| | | 37* | 160 | Sussex v Gloucestershire | Bristol | 1909 |
| | | 19* | 100 | Sussex v Lancashire | Liverpool | 1910 |
| | | 23* | 98 | Sussex v Kent | Tonbridge | 1910 |
| | | 72* | 153 | Sussex v Worcestershire | Hove | 1910 |
| Virgin, R.T. | (2) | 96* | 167 | Somerset v Glamorgan | Weston-s-Mare | 1964 |
| | | 77* | 139 | Northants v Gloucestershire | Northampton | 1974 |
| Walker, D.F. | | 107* | 236 | Oxford U. v Gloucestershire | Oxford | 1933 |
| Walker, I.D. | | 47* | 126 | Middlesex v Surrey | Lord's | 1884 |
| Walters, C.F. | | 53* | 100 | Worcestershire v Glamorgan | Pontypridd | 1931 |
| Ward, A. | (5) | 140* | 281 | Lancashire v Gloucestershire | Bristol | 1893 |
| | | 45* | 97 | Lancashire v Australians | Manchester | 1893 |
| | | 75* | 168 | Lancashire v Leicestershire | Manchester | 1895 |
| | | 109* | 337 | Lancashire v Hampshire | Southampton | 1899 |
| | | 83* | 262 | Lancashire v Middlesex | Lord's | 1899 |
| Warne, F.B.T. | | 43* | 153 | Worcestershire v Middlesex | Lord's | 1937 |
| Warne, T.S. | | 61* | 129 | Victoria v A.C. MacLaren's XI | Melbourne | 1901–02 |
| Warner, E.W. | (3) | 141* | 279 | OFS v Griqualand West | Kimberley | 1936–37 |
| | | 102* | 210 | Orange Free State v Border | Bethlehem | 1936–37 |
| | | 87* | 235 | OFS v Eastern Province | Bloemfontein | 1937–38 |
| Warner, P.F. | (10) | 46* | 75 | Middlesex v Gloucestershire | Lord's | 1898 |
| | | 132* | 237 | England v South Africa | Johannesburg | 1898–99 |

| | | Score | Total | | | |
|---|---|---|---|---|---|---|
| Warner, P.F. *continued* | | 197* | 400 | Middlesex v Somerset | Lord's | 1901 |
| | | 73* | 168 | Middlesex v Yorkshire | Lord's | 1901 |
| | | 65* | 130 | Middlesex v Nottinghamshire | Nottingham | 1907 |
| | | 59* | 139 | Middlesex v Nottinghamshire | Lord's | 1907 |
| | | 64* | 95 | MCC v Yorkshire | Lord's | 1908 |
| | | 64* | 124 | MCC v Kent | Lord's | 1908 |
| | | 102* | 201 | Middlesex v Surrey | Lord's | 1909 |
| | | 145* | 279 | Middlesex v Hampshire | Lord's | 1910 |
| Washbrook, C. | | 49* | 124 | Lancashire v Worcestershire | Manchester | 1935 |
| Watson, W. | | 79* | 132 | Leicestershire v Yorkshire | Leicester | 1959 |
| Webbe, A.J. | (8) | 62* | 118 | Middlesex v Yorkshire | Sheffield | 1882 |
| | | 97* | 201 | Middlesex v Nottinghamshire | Prince's | 1875 |
| | | 44* | 134 | Middlesex v Nottinghamshire | Nottingham | 1876 |
| | | 83* | 196 | Middlesex v Surrey | Oval | 1884 |
| | | 63* | 119 | Middlesex v Oxford University | Chiswick Park | 1887 |
| | | 243* | 527 | Middlesex v Yorkshire | Huddersfield | 1887 |
| | | 192* | 412 | Middlesex v Kent | Canterbury | 1887 |
| | | 37* | 82 | MCC v Kent | Lord's | 1888 |
| Wells, G. | (2) | 38* | 81 | Sussex v Kent | Brighton | 1858 |
| | | 55* | 73 | Sussex v MCC | Lord's | 1860 |
| Wessels, N.R. | | 111* | 209 | OFS v Eastern Province | Bloemfontein | 1959–60 |
| Wettimuny, S. | | 63* | 144 | Sri Lanka v New Zealand | Christchurch | 1982–83 |
| White, E.A. | | 48* | 103 | Kent v Middlesex | Islington | 1868 |
| Whitehead, H. | | 130* | 271 | Leicestershire v Lancashire | Leicester | 1907 |
| Whitelaw, P.E. | | 99* | 183 | Auckland & Wellington v MCC | Auckland | 1936–37 |
| Whitfeld, H. | | 41* | 109 | Sussex v Surrey | Oval | 1884 |
| Whittington, T.A.L. | | 115* | 318 | MCC v Jamaica | Kingston | 1910–11 |
| Whysall, W.W. | (2) | 109* | 242 | Nottinghamshire v Kent | Canterbury | 1924 |
| | | 111* | 238 | Nottinghamshire v Essex | Nottingham | 1929 |
| Wight, P.B. | | 222* | 450 | Somerset v Kent | Taunton | 1959 |
| Wilkinson, A.J.A. | | 84* | 209 | Gents of Middlesex v Gents of England | Islington | 1865 |
| Wilkinson, C.A. | | 86* | 170 | Cambridge University v MCC | Cambridge | 1835 |
| Williams, A.B. | | 126* | 280† | West Indians v Karnataka | Ahmedabad | 1978–79 |
| Wilson, H.L. | (2) | 42* | 104† | Sussex v Somerset | Taunton | 1919 |
| | | 108* | 215 | Sussex v Warwickshire | Hove | 1924 |
| Wood, A.M. | | 73* | 149 | Philadelphians v Cambridge U. | Cambridge | 1897 |
| Wood, B. | | 53* | 107 | Derbyshire v Leicestershire | Derby | 1981 |
| Wood, C.J.B. | (17) | 21* | 98 | Leicestershire v Yorkshire | Dewsbury | 1898 |
| | | 46* | 262 | Leicestershire v Sussex | Leicester | 1903 |
| | | 118* | 322 | Leicestershire v Yorkshire | Leicester | 1903 |
| | | 160* | 419 | Leicestershire v Yorkshire | Leicester | 1905 |
| | | 200* | 507 | Leicestershire v Hampshire | Leicester | 1905 |
| | | 56* | 112 | Leicestershire v Lancashire | Leicester | 1906 |
| | | 105* | 303 | Leicestershire v Essex | Southend | 1906 |
| | | 110* | 220 | Leicestershire v Northamptonshire | Northampton | 1906 |
| | | 84* | 159 | Leicestershire v Lancashire | Leicester | 1908 |
| | | 38* | 116 | Leicestershire v Derbyshire | Derby | 1910 |
| | | 78* | 270 | Leicestershire v Kent | Leicester | 1911 |
| | | 54* | 151 | Leicestershire v Northamptonshire | Leicester | 1911 |
| | | 54* | 164 | Leicestershire v Warwickshire | Hinckley | 1911 |
| | | 107* | 309 | Leicestershire v Yorks *1st inns* | Bradford | 1911 |
| | | 117* | 296 | Leicestershire v Yorks *2nd inns* | Bradford | 1911 |
| | | 38* | 179 | Leicestershire v Lancashire | Leicester | 1913 |
| | | 164* | 392 | Leicestershire v Warwickshire | Hinckley | 1913 |
| Woodfull, W.M. | (4) | 116* | 281 | Australians v England XI | Blackpool | 1926 |
| | | 30* | 66† | Australia v England | Brisbane | 1928–29 |
| | | 67* | 164 | Victoria v MCC | Melbourne | 1928–29 |
| | | 73* | 193† | Australia v England | Adelaide | 1932–33 |
| Woolley, C.N. | (3) | 62* | 113 | Northamptonshire v Sussex | Hove | 1923 |
| | | 59* | 130 | Northamptonshire v Sussex | Hastings | 1925 |
| | | 38* | 102 | Northamptonshire v Yorkshire | Bradford | 1929 |
| Worrell, F.M.M. | | 191* | 372 | West Indies v England | Nottingham | 1957 |
| Worthington, T.S. | | 156* | 376 | MCC Australian Team v Rest | Lord's | 1937 |
| Wright, H. | | 26* | 63 | Leicestershire v Hampshire | Southampton | 1914 |
| Wright, J.G. | | 141* | 259 | Derbyshire v Nottinghamshire | Chesterfield | 1982 |

|  |  | Score | Total |  |  |  |
|---|---|---|---|---|---|---|
| Wright, L.G. | (3) | 59* | 112 | Derbyshire v Essex | Leyton | 1899 |
|  |  | 58* | 136 | Derbyshire v Essex | Leyton | 1903 |
|  |  | 50* | 104 | Derbyshire v Leicestershire | Leicester | 1906 |
| Wright, R.L. |  | 96* | 201 | Northamptonshire v Lancashire | Northampton | 1923 |
| Wright, W. |  | 127* | 371 | Nottinghamshire v Gloucestershire | Nottingham | 1883 |
| Yarde, D.K. |  | 27* | 85 | Baroda v Nawanagar | Jamnagar | 1937–38 |
| Yorke, C. |  | 23* | 73 | Tobago v North Trinidad | Port-of-Spain | 1978–79 |
| Zulch, J.W. |  | 43* | 103 | South Africa v England | Cape Town | 1909–10 |

**CARRYING BAT WITH EXCEPTION OF FIRST BALL**

| S.N. McGregor | 113* | 189 | Otago v Canterbury | Christchurch | 1967–68 |
|---|---|---|---|---|---|

*Batted number 3 after opener was out first ball*

# FAST SCORING

## FASTEST FIFTIES

*Min*

| 8 | C.C. Inman (57) | Leicestershire v Nottinghamshire | Nottingham | 1965 |
|---|---|---|---|---|

*Full tosses were bowled to expedite a declaration*

| 11 | C.I.J. Smith (66) | Middlesex v Gloucestershire | Bristol | 1938 |
|---|---|---|---|---|
| 14 | S.J. Pegler (50) | South Africans v Tasmania | Launceston | 1910–11 |
| 14 | F.T. Mann (53) | Middlesex v Nottinghamshire | Lord's | 1921 |
| 14 | H.B. Cameron (56) | Transvaal v Orange Free State | Johannesburg | 1934–35 |
| 14 | C.I.J. Smith (52) | Middlesex v Kent | Maidstone | 1935 |
| 15 | G.L. Jessop (61) | Gloucestershire v Somerset | Bristol | 1904 |
| 15 | G.L. Jessop (92) | Gloucestershire v Hampshire | Cheltenham | 1907 |
| 15 | F.R. Foster (63) | Warwickshire v Middlesex | Birmingham | 1914 |
| 15 | H.R. Murrell (50) | Middlesex v Hampshire | Southampton | 1921 |
| 15 | C.C.R. Dacre (64) | New Zealanders v Gloucestershire | Cheltenham | 1927 |
| 15 | G.F. Earle (59) | Somerset v Gloucestershire | Taunton | 1929 |
| 15 | G. Cox (51) | Sussex v Cambridge University | Hove | 1934 |
| 15 | J. Hardstaff jr (77) | Nottinghamshire v Gloucestershire | Bristol | 1937 |
| 15 | R. Smith (78) | Essex v Nottinghamshire | Brentwood | 1949 |
| 15 | D.J. Shepherd (51) | Glamorgan v Australians | Swansea | 1961 |

## FASTEST HUNDREDS

*Min*

| 35 | P.G.H. Fender (113*) | Surrey v Northamptonshire | Northampton | 1920 |
|---|---|---|---|---|

*He scored 50 in 19 minutes and 113\* out of 171 in 42 minutes, sharing an unfinished sixth wicket
partnership of 171 in 42 minutes with H.A. Peach.*

| 35 | S.J. O'Shaughnessy (105) | Lancashire v Leicestershire | Manchester | 1983 |
|---|---|---|---|---|

*Occasional bowlers were used to expedite a declaration*

| 37 | C.M. Old (107) | Yorkshire v Warwickshire | Birmingham | 1977 |
|---|---|---|---|---|

*Off 72 balls; his second fifty took nine minutes.*

| 40 | G.L. Jessop (101) | Gloucestershire v Yorkshire | Harrogate | 1897 |
|---|---|---|---|---|
| 41 | N.F.M. Popplewell (143) | Somerset v Gloucestershire | Bath | 1983 |

*Occasional bowlers were used to expedite a declaration*

| 42 | G.L. Jessop (191) | Gents of South v Players of South | Hastings | 1907 |
|---|---|---|---|---|
| 43 | A.H. Hornby (106) | Lancashire v Somerset | Manchester | 1905 |
| 43 | D.W. Hookes (107) | South Australia v Victoria | Adelaide | 1982–83 |

*Off 34 balls – the fastest on record*

| 44 | R.N.S. Hobbs (100) | Essex v Australians | Chelmsford | 1975 |
|---|---|---|---|---|
| 45 | E.M. Sprot (125*) | Hampshire v Gloucestershire | Bristol | 1911 |
| 45 | W. Voce (129) | Nottinghamshire v Glamorgan | Nottingham | 1931 |
| 46 | G. Fowler (100) | Lancashire v Leicestershire | Manchester | 1983 |

*Occasional bowlers were used to expedite a declaration*

| 48 | A.W. Carr (124) | Nottinghamshire v Sussex | Hove | 1925 |
|---|---|---|---|---|
| 49 | I.T. Botham (138*) | Somerset v Warwickshire | Birmingham | 1985 |

*Off 50 balls*

| 50 | K.L. Hutchings (100) | Kent v Gloucestershire | Catford | 1909 |
|---|---|---|---|---|
| 50 | D.R.A. Gehrs (119) | South Australia v Western Australia | Adelaide | 1912–13 |
| 50 | I.T. Botham (122) | England XI v Central Zone | Indore | 1981–82 |

*Min*

| | | | | |
|---|---|---|---|---|
| 50 | P.B. Clift (100*) | Leicestershire v Sussex | Hove | 1983 |
| 51 | J. Hardstaff jr (126) | Nottinghamshire v Kent | Canterbury | 1937 |
| 52 | W. H. Fowler (139) | Somerset v MCC | Taunton | 1882 |
| 52 | L.N. Constantine (100) | West Indians v Tasmania | Launceston | 1930–31 |
| 52 | R.M. Prideaux (118) | South v North | Blackpool | 1961 |
| 52 | R.G. Pollock (101) | International Cavaliers v Barbados | Scarborough | 1969 |
| 52 | B.L. Cairns (110) | Otago v Wellington | Lower Hutt | 1979–80 |

*Off 45 balls*

| | | | | |
|---|---|---|---|---|
| 52 | I.T. Botham (131*) | Somerset v Warwickshire | Taunton | 1982 |
| 53 | G.L. Jessop (139) | Gloucestershire v Surrey | Bristol | 1911 |
| 53 | M.G. Francis (115*) | Orange Free State v Griqualand West | Bloemfontein | 1927–28 |
| 53 | R.C. Motz (103*) | Canterbury v Otago | Christchurch | 1967–68 |
| 54 | J.E. Raphael (111) | Oxford University v Worcestershire | Worcester | 1904 |
| 54 | J.N. Crawford (114) | MCC v South Australia | Adelaide | 1907–08 |
| 55 | F.G.J. Ford (112) | Middlesex v Philadelphians | Lord's | 1897 |
| 55 | G.L. Jessop (123*) | South v North | Hastings | 1900 |
| 55 | G.L. Jessop (126) | Gloucestershire v Nottinghamshire | Nottingham | 1902 |
| 55 | G.L. Jessop (119) | Gloucestershire v Sussex | Hastings | 1907 |
| 55 | A.P. Day (100*) | Kent v Hampshire | Southampton | 1911 |
| 55 | G.L. Tapscott (111) | Rest v Transvaal | Johannesburg | 1911–12 |
| 55 | G.L. Jessop (116) | Lord Londesborough's XI v Kent | Scarborough | 1913 |
| 55 | Hon L.H. Tennyson (102*) | Hampshire v Gloucestershire | Southampton | 1927 |
| 57 | G.L. Jessop (124) | Gloucestershire v Middlesex | Lord's | 1901 |
| 57 | V.T. Trumper (101) | New South Wales v Victoria | Sydney | 1905–06 |
| 57 | H.T. Bartlett (157) | Sussex v Australians | Hove | 1938 |
| 57 | M.J. Procter (105) | Gloucestershire v Northamptonshire | Bristol | 1979 |
| 58 | K.D. Boyce (113) | Essex v Leicestershire | Chelmsford | 1975 |
| 59 | G.L. Jessop (139) | Gloucestershire v Yorkshire | Bradford | 1900 |
| 60 | E.C. Streatfeild (145) | Cambridge U. P. & P. v Australians | Leyton | 1890 |
| 60 | J.J. Lyons (149) | Australians v MCC | Lord's | 1893 |
| 60 | G.L. Jessop (112*) | Rest v A.E. Stoddart's XI | Hastings | 1898 |
| 60 | G.L. Jessop (126) | Gloucestershire v Nottinghamshire | Nottingham | 1899 |
| 60 | G.L. Jessop (109) | Gloucestershire v Middlesex | Lord's | 1900 |
| 60 | G.L. Jessop (169) | MCC v Leicestershire | Lord's | 1901 |
| 60 | R.E. Foster (111) | Worcestershire v Derbyshire | Derby | 1901 |
| 60 | W.S. Lees (130) | Surrey v Hampshire | Aldershot | 1905 |
| 60 | S.J. Snooke (121) | W. Province v Griqualand West | Johannesburg | 1906–07 |
| 60 | C.C. Page (164*) | Middlesex v Somerset | Lord's | 1908 |
| 60 | G.N. Foster (101) | Oxford University v Gents of England | Eastbourne | 1908 |
| 60 | C.B. Llewellyn (101*) | Hampshire v Sussex | Hove | 1909 |
| 60 | G.L. Jessop (165) | Gloucestershire v Worcestershire | Stourbridge | 1910 |
| 60 | H.L. Simms (126) | Sussex v Nottinghamshire | Hove | 1912 |
| 60 | A.W. Carr (100*) | Nottinghamshire v Northamptonshire | Northampton | 1928 |
| 60 | L.N. Constantine (103) | West Indians v Middlesex | Lord's | 1928 |
| 60 | C.R. Browne (103) | West Indians v Kent | Canterbury | 1928 |
| 60 | E.T. Killick (200*) | Cambridge University v Glamorgan | Cambridge | 1929 |
| 60 | T.S. Worthington (108) | Derbyshire v Nottinghamshire | Ilkeston | 1933 |
| 60 | C.J. Barnett (101) | Gloucestershire v Hampshire | Southampton | 1937 |
| 60 | G. Cox (142) | Sussex v Yorkshire | Hove | 1938 |
| 60 | C.J. Poole (154*) | Nottinghamshire v Leicestershire | Nottingham | 1949 |
| 60 | P. Bhandari (111*) | Bengal v Rajasthan | Udaipur | 1959–60 |

### FASTEST 150

*Min*

| | | | | |
|---|---|---|---|---|
| 63 | G.L. Jessop (191) | Gents of South v Players of South | Hastings | 1907 |

### FASTEST DOUBLE HUNDREDS

*Min*

| | | | | |
|---|---|---|---|---|
| 113 | R.J. Shastri (200*) | Bombay v Baroda | Bombay | 1984–85 |
| 120 | G.L. Jessop (286) | Gloucestershire v Sussex | Hove | 1903 |
| 120 | C.H. Lloyd (201*) | West Indians v Glamorgan | Swansea | 1976 |
| 130 | G.L. Jessop (234) | Gloucestershire v Somerset | Bristol | 1905 |
| 131 | V.T. Trumper (293) | Australians v Canterbury | Christchurch | 1913–14 |
| 135 | S.M.J. Woods (215) | Somerset v Sussex | Hove | 1895 |

*Min*

| | | | | |
|---|---|---|---|---|
| 135 | G.L. Jessop (233) | Rest v Yorkshire | Lord's | 1901 |
| 135 | C.R.N. Maxwell (268) | Sir J. Cahn's XI v Leicestershire | Nottingham | 1935 |
| 140 | G.L. Jessop (206) | Gloucestershire v Nottinghamshire | Nottingham | 1904 |
| 144 | D.C.S. Compton (300) | MCC v N.E. Transvaal | Benoni | 1948–49 |
| 145 | J.S.F. Morrison (233*) | Cambridge University v MCC | Cambridge | 1914 |
| 145 | C.G. Macartney (345) | Australians v Nottinghamshire | Nottingham | 1921 |
| 150 | H.K. Foster (216) | Worcestershire v Somerset | Worcester | 1903 |
| 150 | M.M. Walford (201*) | Oxford University v MCC | Lord's | 1938 |

## FASTEST TRIPLE HUNDREDS

*Min*

| | | | | |
|---|---|---|---|---|
| 181 | D.C.S. Compton (300) | MCC v N.E. Transvaal | Benoni | 1948–49 |
| 205 | F.E. Woolley (305*) | MCC v Tasmania | Hobart | 1911–12 |
| 205 | C.G. Macartney (345) | Australians v Nottinghamshire | Nottingham | 1921 |
| 213 | D.G. Bradman (369) | South Australia v Tasmania | Adelaide | 1935–36 |

## FASTEST INNINGS

| Runs | Min | | | | |
|---|---|---|---|---|---|
| 30 | 5 | J.D. Inchmore | Worcestershire v Gloucestershire | Cheltenham | 1973 |
| 34 | 6 | R.M. Edwards | Governor-General's XI v West Indians | Auckland | 1968–69 |
| 45* | 12 | J. Mercer | Glamorgan v Worcestershire | Cardiff | 1939 |
| 46 | 13 | B. Sutcliffe | New Zealanders v Hampshire | Southampton | 1949 |
| 50 | 14 | S.J. Pegler | South Africans v Tasmania | Launceston | 1910–11 |
| 51 | 15 | D.J. Shepherd | Glamorgan v Australians | Swansea | 1961 |
| 66 | 18 | C.I.J. Smith | Middlesex v Gloucestershire | Bristol | 1938 |
| 67* | 20 | L.N. Constantine | West Indians v Nottinghamshire | Nottingham | 1928 |
| 69 | 20 | C.I.J. Smith | Middlesex v Sussex | Lord's | 1938 |
| 79 | 25 | J. Spencer | Sussex v Hampshire | Southampton | 1975 |
| 92 | 35 | M.J. Procter | Gloucestershire v Warwickshire | Bristol | 1979 |
| 101 | 40 | G.L. Jessop | Gloucestershire v Yorkshire | Harrogate | 1897 |
| 107 | 41 | C.M. Old | Yorkshire v Warwickshire | Birmingham | 1977 |
| 113* | 42 | P.G.H. Fender | Surrey v Northamptonshire | Northampton | 1920 |
| 122 | 55 | I.T. Botham | England XI v Central Zone | Indore | 1981–82 |
| 143 | 62 | N.F.M. Popplewell | Somerset v Gloucestershire | Bath | 1983 |
| 147* | 89 | Majid Khan | Pakistanis v Glamorgan | Swansea | 1967 |
| 189 | 90 | E.B. Alletson | Nottinghamshire v Sussex | Hove | 1911 |
| 191 | 90 | G.L. Jessop | Gents of South v Players of South | Hastings | 1907 |
| 200* | 113 | R.J. Shastri | Bombay v Baroda | Bombay | 1984–85 |
| 201* | 124 | C.H. Lloyd | West Indians v Glamorgan | Swansea | 1976 |
| 206 | 145 | G.L. Jessop | Gloucestershire v Nottinghamshire | Nottingham | 1904 |
| 215 | 150 | S.M.J. Woods | Somerset v Sussex | Hove | 1895 |
| 233 | 150 | G.L. Jessop | Rest v Yorkshire | Lord's | 1901 |
| 286 | 175 | G.L. Jessop | Gloucestershire v Sussex | Hove | 1903 |
| 293 | 180 | V.T. Trumper | Australians v Canterbury | Christchurch | 1913–14 |
| 300 | 181 | D.C.S. Compton | MCC v N.E. Transvaal | Benoni | 1948–49 |
| 305* | 210 | F.E. Woolley | MCC v Tasmania | Hobart | 1911–12 |
| 345 | 235 | C.G. Macartney | Australians v Nottinghamshire | Nottingham | 1921 |
| 369 | 253 | D.G. Bradman | South Australia v Tasmania | Adelaide | 1935–36 |
| 383 | 345 | C.W. Gregory | New South Wales v Queensland | Brisbane | 1906–07 |
| 452* | 415 | D.G. Bradman | New South Wales v Queensland | Sydney | 1929–30 |

## FASTEST PARTNERSHIPS

| Runs | Min | Wkt | | | | |
|---|---|---|---|---|---|---|
| 152 | 29 | 4th | J.D. Love, P.E. Robinson | Yorkshire v Sussex | Hove | 1985 |
| 171* | 42 | 6th | P.G.H. Fender, H.A. Peach | Surrey v Northamptonshire | Northampton | 1920 |
| 201 | 43 | 1st | G. Fowler, S.J. O'Shaughnessy | Lancashire v Leicestershire | Manchester | 1983 |
| 202* | 75 | 2nd | G.H. Hirst, W. Rhodes | Yorkshire v Somerset | Bath | 1906 |
| 204 | 83 | 6th | G.A. Parkar, R.J. Shastri | Bombay v Baroda | Bombay | 1984–85 |
| 236 | 85 | 6th | E.R.T. Holmes, R.E.C. Butterworth | Oxford U. v Free Foresters | Oxford | 1927 |
| 255 | 90 | 3rd | J.S.F. Morrison, H.G.H. Mulholland | Cambridge U. v MCC | Cambridge | 1914 |

| Runs | Min | Wkt | | | | |
|------|-----|-----|---|---|---|---|
| 267* | 99 | 5th | K.C. Bland, D.T. Lindsay | South Africa v Rest | Johannesburg | 1964–65 |
| 291 | 105 | 4th | C.G. Macartney, C.E. Pellew | Australians v Nottinghamshire | Nottingham | 1921 |
| 295 | 120 | 2nd | A. Hartley, J.T. Tyldesley | Lancashire v Somerset | Manchester | 1910 |
| 363 | 135 | 3rd | D.G. Bradman, A.F. Kippax | NSW v Queensland | Sydney | 1933–34 |
| 371 | 165 | 2nd | J.B. Hobbs, E.G. Hayes | Surrey v Hampshire | Oval | 1909 |
| 433 | 180 | 8th | V.T. Trumper, A. Sims | Australians v Canterbury | Christchurch | 1913–14 |
| 487* | 245 | 6th | G.A. Headley, C.C. Passailaigue | Jamaica v Lord Tennyson's XI | Kingston | 1931–32 |
| 574* | 335 | 4th | C.L. Walcott, F.M.M. Worrell | Barbados v Trinidad | Port-of-Spain | 1945–46 |

## FIFTY WITH FEWEST SCORING STROKES

### ELEVEN

A.E.A. Harragan (50)   West Indians v W.G. Grace's XI   Crystal Palace   1906
*With 5 sixes, 4 fours and 2 twos*

D.A. Sparks (57*)   Orange Free State v MCC   Bloemfontein   1938–39
*Scored 50\* with 6 sixes, 3 fours and 2 ones*

D.J. Shepherd (51)   Glamorgan v Australians   Swansea   1961
*Scored 51\* out of 55 with 6 sixes, 3 fours, a two and a one*

C.C. Inman (57*)   Leicestershire v Nottinghamshire   Nottingham   1965
*Scored 51\* out of 51 in 8 minutes off 13 balls with 5 sixes, 5 fours and a one off 12 slow full tosses from N.W. Hill – 440064/466664*

R.W. Marsh (53)   Western Australia v West Indians   Perth   1975–76
*Scored 50\* out of 54 off 18 balls in 20 minutes with 3 sixes, and 8 fours*

M.J. Procter (93)   Gloucestershire v Somerset   Taunton   1979

### TWELVE

C.I.J. Smith (52)   Middlesex v Kent   Maidstone   1935
*Scored 50\* in 14 minutes with 4 sixes, 6 fours and 2 ones*

C.I.J. Smith (66)   Middlesex v Gloucestershire   Bristol   1938
*Scored 50\* in 11 minutes with 6 sixes, 2 fours, 2 twos and 2 ones*

B.D. Julien (98)   Kent v Northamptonshire   Northampton   1973
*Scored 52\* with 5 sixes, 4 fours, a three, a two and a one*

J.W. Southern (51)   Hampshire v Gloucestershire   Basingstoke   1978
*Scored 51\* with 3 sixes, 8 fours and a one*

P.R. Oliver (57)   Warwickshire v West Indians   Birmingham   1980
*Scored 51\* with 3 sixes, 8 fours and a one*

B.L. Cairns (68)   New Zealanders v New South Wales   Sydney   1980–81
*Scored 50\* with 6 sixes, 2 fours, 2 twos and 2 ones*

### THIRTEEN

F.T. Mann (53)   Middlesex v Nottinghamshire   Lord's   1921
*Scored 52\* with 4 sixes, 6 fours, a two and 2 ones*

K.M. Rangnekar (102)   Maharashtra v Western India States   Poona   1939–40
*Scored 50\* off his first 17 balls with 11 fours and 2 threes*

R.G. Wilson (67)   Combined Services v Worcestershire   Worcester   1952
B. Taylor (58)   Essex v Warwickshire   Westcliff   1954
*Scored 50\* with 12 fours and a two*

D.J. Shepherd (73)   Glamorgan v Derbyshire   Cardiff   1961
*Scored 52\* out of 57 off 16 balls in 16 minutes with 6 sixes, 2 fours, 3 twos and 2 ones*

W.J. Stewart (104)   Warwickshire v Somerset   Street   1961
*Scored 51\* with 6 sixes, a four, 2 threes, a two and 3 ones*

B. Hedges (59*)   Glamorgan v Warwickshire   Birmingham   1962
*Scored 50\* with 12 fours and a two*

A.R. Windows (69)   Cambridge University v Nottinghamshire   Nottingham   1962
*Scored 50\* with 2 sixes, 9 fours and 2 ones*

C. Milburn (65)   Northamptonshire v Middlesex   Peterborough   1963
*Scored 50\* with 2 sixes, 9 fours and 2 ones*

K.F. Barrington (51*)   Surrey v Warwickshire   Oval   1963
*Scored 51\* in 25 minutes with 3 sixes, 7 fours, a three and 2 ones*

| R.G.P. Ellis (65) | Oxford U. v Gloucestershire | Oxford | 1982 |
|---|---|---|---|
| | *Scored 50\* with 12 fours and a two in 60 minutes* | | |
| D.L. Bairstow (57) | Yorkshire v Leicestershire | Harrogate | 1983 |
| | *Scored 51\* with 4 sixes, 6 fours and 3 ones* | | |

## MOST RUNS IN A DAY

| | | | Day | |
|---|---|---|---|---|
| 345 C.G. Macartney (345) | Australians v Nottinghamshire | Nottingham | 1 | 1921 |
| | *Out of 540 in 235 minutes* | | | |
| 334 W.H. Ponsford (352) | Victoria v New South Wales | Melbourne | 2 | 1926–27 |
| | *Out of 573 in 322 minutes* | | | |
| 333 K.S. Duleepsinhji (333) | Sussex v Northamptonshire | Hove | 1 | 1930 |
| | *Out of 513 in 330 minutes* | | | |
| 331 J.D.B. Robertson (331\*) | Middlesex v Worcestershire | Worcester | 1 | 1949 |
| | *Out of 623 in 390 minutes* | | | |
| 325 B.A. Richards (356) | S. Australia v W. Australia | Perth | 1 | 1970–71 |
| | *Out of 513 in 330 minutes* | | | |
| 322 E. Paynter (322) | Lancashire v Sussex | Hove | 1 | 1937 |
| | *Out of 546 in 300 minutes* | | | |
| 322 I.V.A. Richards (322) | Somerset v Warwickshire | Taunton | 1 | 1985 |
| | *Out of 507 in 294 minutes off 258 balls* | | | |
| 318 C.W. Gregory (383) | New South Wales v Queensland | Brisbane | 2 | 1906–07 |
| | *48\* to 366\* in 345 minutes* | | | |
| 316 R.H. Moore (316) | Hampshire v Warwickshire | Bournemouth | 1 | 1937 |
| | *Out of 509 in 380 minutes* | | | |
| 315 R.C. Blunt (338\*) | Otago v Canterbury | Christchurch | 3 | 1931–32 |
| | *Out of 540 in 320 minutes* | | | |
| 312 J.M. Brearley (312\*) | MCC U-25 XI v N. Zone | Peshawar | 1 | 1966–67 |
| | *Out of 514 in 330 minutes* | | | |
| 311 G.M. Turner (311\*) | Worcestershire v Warwickshire | Worcester | 1 | 1982 |
| | *Out of 501 in 342 minutes* | | | |
| 309 D.G. Bradman (334) | Australia v England | Leeds | 1 | 1930 |
| | *Out of 456 in 340 minutes* | | | |
| 307 W.H. Ashdown (332) | Kent v Essex | Brentwood | 1 | 1934 |
| | *Out of 623 in 360 minutes* | | | |
| 306 A. Ducat (306\*) | Surrey v Oxford University | Oval | 1 | 1919 |
| | *In 280 minutes* | | | |
| 305 F.R. Foster (305\*) | Warwickshire v Worcestershire | Dudley | 2 | 1914 |
| | *Out of 448 in 260 minutes* | | | |

*E. Paynter's 322 and R.H. Moore's 316 were scored on the same day: 28 July 1937.*

## MOST RUNS IN PRE-LUNCH SESSION

| 197 W.R. Endean (235) | Transvaal v Orange Free State | Johannesburg | 1 | 1954–55 |
|---|---|---|---|---|
| | *Scored 197\* in three hours* | | | |
| 180 K.S. Ranjitsinhji (234\*) | Sussex v Surrey | Hastings | 2 | 1902 |
| | *54\* to 234\* in 150 minutes* | | | |
| 180 D.C.S. Compton (300) | MCC v N.E. Transvaal | Benoni | 2 | 1948–49 |
| | *120\* to 300 in 90 minutes* | | | |
| 174 J.R. Reid (296) | Wellington v N. Districts | Wellington | 2 | 1962–63 |
| | *0\* to 174\* in 142 minutes* | | | |
| 173 F.R. Santall (201\*) | Warwickshire v Northants | Northampton | 3 | 1933 |
| | *Scored 173\* in 116 minutes* | | | |
| 167 A. Ducat (271) | Surrey v Hampshire | Southampton | 2 | 1919 |
| | *104\* to 271* | | | |
| 165 B.S. Groves (237) | Natal B v Orange Free State | Bloemfontein | 2 | 1967–68 |
| | *72\* to 237 in 115 minutes* | | | |
| 164 G.L. Jessop (234) | Gloucestershire v Somerset | Bristol | 2 | 1905 |
| | *70\* to 234* | | | |
| 164 J.L. Powell (164) | Canterbury v Otago | Christchurch | 2 | 1929–30 |
| | *Scored 164 in 130 minutes* | | | |

# HUNDRED BEFORE LUNCH

These performances have been separated into three categories, the first of which is the most cherished by batsmen and, in Test cricket, has been accomplished only four times in 1,022 matches:
1 Hundred before lunch on the first day of a match.
2 Hundred before lunch on other days, having begun innings that morning.
3 Hundred added to overnight score before lunch.
Although the pre-lunch session of play has lasted three hours in some instances, the only qualification for inclusion in these records is 100 runs during that period.

## HUNDRED BEFORE LUNCH ON THE FIRST DAY

| | | Final Score | Lunch Score | | | |
|---|---|---|---|---|---|---|
| Abel, R. | | 152 | | Surrey v Leicestershire | Oval | 1896 |
| Asif Iqbal | | 120 | 101* | Kent v Hampshire | Southampton | 1973 |
| Awasthy, B. | | 142 | 105* | Services v Jammu & Kashmir | Delhi | 1965–66 |
| Barber, R.W. | | 138 | | Warwickshire v Australians | Birmingham | 1964 |
| Barbour, B.D. | | 106 | 106* | Rhodesia v Natal | Bulawayo | 1971–72 |
| Barker, G. | | 181* | | Essex v Kent | Colchester | 1961 |
| Barlow, E.J. | | 147 | 131* | W. Province v D.H. Robins' XI | Cape Town | 1972–73 |
| | | | | *Out of 168-0 in 90 minutes* | | |
| Barnett, C.J. | (2) | 107 | 100* | Gloucestershire v Worcestershire | Worcester | 1933 |
| | | 123 | 100* | Gloucestershire v Glamorgan | Bristol | 1934 |
| Barnett, K.J. | | 120 | 103* | Derbyshire v Somerset | Taunton | 1984 |
| Bezuidenhout, S.J. | | 112 | 102* | E. Province v Transvaal | Port Elizabeth | 1974–75 |
| Bosanquet, B.J.T. | | 108 | 108 | Gentlemen v Oxford University | Oxford | 1903 |
| Bowley, F.L. | (6) | 106 | 106 | Worcestershire v Hampshire | Southampton | 1908 |
| | | 157 | | Worcestershire v Warwickshire | Worcester | 1910 |
| | | 201 | 100* | Worcestershire v Gloucestershire | Worcester | 1913 |
| | | 177 | 136* | Worcestershire v Warwickshire | Birmingham | 1913 |
| | | 276 | | Worcestershire v Hampshire | Dudley | 1914 |
| | | 131 | 125* | Worcestershire v Essex | Leyton | 1920 |
| Bradman, D.G. | (2) | 334 | 105* | Australia v England | Leeds | 1930 |
| | | 132 | | Australians v H.D.G. Leveson Gower's XI | Scarborough | 1934 |
| Broad, B.C. | | 120 | 100* | Gloucestershire v Oxford U. | Oxford | 1980 |
| | | | | *On the first day of the season* | | |
| Brockwell, W. | (3) | 107 | 107 | Surrey v Sussex | Hove | 1896 |
| | | 119 | | Surrey v Oxford University | Oval | 1898 |
| | | 102 | 102 | Surrey v Derbyshire | Oval | 1899 |
| Brown, J.T. | | 107 | 107 | Yorkshire v Nottinghamshire | Nottingham | 1896 |
| Brown, S.M. | | 118 | | Middlesex v Essex | Westcliff | 1946 |
| Burns, W.B. | | 165 | | Worcestershire v Oxford U. | Worcester | 1904 |
| Burnup, C.J. | | 108 | 108 | Kent v Nottinghamshire | Gravesend | 1897 |
| Butcher, A.R. | | 107 | 107 | Surrey v Glamorgan | Oval | 1980 |
| | | | | *Out of 142 in 131 minutes* | | |
| Catterall, R.H. | | 117 | | South Africans v Wales | Colwyn Bay | 1929 |
| Collins, H.L. | | 117 | 117 | New South Wales v Queensland | Sydney | 1919–20 |
| Cowper, R.M. | | 110 | | Australians v T.N. Pearce's XI | Scarborough | 1964 |
| Crawford, V.F.S. | | 122 | 122 | Surrey v Cambridge University | Cambridge | 1901 |
| Dacre, C.C.R. | | 108 | | Gloucestershire v Oxford U. | Oxford | 1935 |
| Davison, B.F. | | 100 | 100 | Leicestershire v Middlesex | Uxbridge | 1982 |
| Dawson, O.C. | | 139 | 117* | Border v Rhodesia | East London | 1954–55 |
| | | | | *K.N. Kirton scored 105* in the same session* | | |
| Dempsey, D.A. | | 131 | 111* | Canterbury v Otago | Christchurch | 1980–81 |
| Denton, D. | | 112 | 100* | Yorkshire v Somerset | Taunton | 1897 |
| | | | | *Out of 217-2 with F.S. Jackson 99** | | |
| De Trafford, C.E. | | 113 | 113 | Leicestershire v Lancashire | Leicester | 1896 |
| Dexter, E.R. | | 185 | | Cambridge U. v Lancashire | Cambridge | 1957 |
| Diver, E.J. | | 184 | 121* | Warwickshire v Leicestershire | Birmingham | 1899 |
| Douglas, J. | | 114 | | Middlesex v Somerset | Taunton | 1904 |
| Draper, R.G. | (4) | 122 | | E. Province v Griqualand West | Kimberley | 1947–48 |
| | | 127 | | Griqualand West v OFS | Bloemfontein | 1951–52 |
| | | 145 | | Griqualand West v Rhodesia | Salisbury | 1952–53 |
| | | 129 | | Griqualand West v Border | Kimberley | 1952–53 |
| | | | | *Last two instances in successive matches* | | |
| Ducat, A. | | 115 | 100* | Surrey v Cambridge University | Oval | 1923 |

| | | Final Score | Lunch Score | | | |
|---|---|---|---|---|---|---|
| Duleepsinhji, K.S. | (3) | 121 | 102* | Sussex v Glamorgan | Eastbourne | 1928 |
| | | | | *Out of 137 in 65 minutes* | | |
| | | 115 | 115 | Sussex v Kent | Hastings | 1929 |
| | | 126 | | Sussex v Surrey | Hove | 1932 |
| Dyson, A.H. | | 104 | | Glamorgan v Kent | Swansea | 1937 |
| | | | | *On the first day of the season* | | |
| Edrich, J.H. | | 110 | | T.N. Pearce's XI v Australians | Scarborough | 1961 |
| Edwards, R.A. | | 105 | | N.E. Transvaal v Natal | Pietermaritzburg | 1947–48 |
| Endean, W.R. | | 235 | 197* | Transvaal v Orange Free State | Johannesburg | 1954–55 |
| | | | | *In 180 minutes* | | |
| Engineer, F.M. | | 142 | 114* | West Zone v Central Zone | Bombay | 1964–65 |
| Evans, W.H.B. | | 139* | | Oxford University v MCC | Lord's | 1905 |
| Fagg, A.E. | | 244 | | Kent v Essex | Colchester | 1938 |
| | | | | *Also added 98* in 90 minutes before lunch on the third day, taking his second innings score to 202** | | |
| Fishwick, T.S. | (2) | 131 | | Warwickshire v Gloucestershire | Bristol | 1900 |
| | | 113 | | Warwickshire v Leicestershire | Leicester | 1904 |
| Foster, H.K. | | 180 | | Worcestershire v Somerset | Worcester | 1905 |
| Foster, R.E. | | 144 | | Worcestershire v Gloucestershire | Worcester | 1907 |
| Fry, C.B. | | 150 | | Sussex v Cambridge University | Hove | 1904 |
| Fullerton, I.R. | | 145 | | Transvaal v W. Province | Johannesburg | 1962–63 |
| Gibbons, H.H.I. | | 107 | | Worcestershire v Hampshire | Southampton | 1928 |
| Gimblett, H. | (3) | 106 | | Somerset v Northamptonshire | Kettering | 1936 |
| | | 114 | | Somerset v Cambridge U. | Bath | 1946 |
| | | 111 | | Commonwealth XI v Governor's XI | Nagpur | 1950–51 |
| Gooch, G.A. | (2) | 164 | 102* | Essex v Leicestershire | Leicester | 1981 |
| | | 174 | 102* | Essex v Cambridge University | Cambridge | 1983 |
| Grace, W.G. | (7) | 127 | 116* | MCC v Kent | Canterbury | 1869 |
| | | | | *The first recorded instance in first-class cricket on the first day* | | |
| | | 178 | 135* | South v North | Lord's | 1871 |
| | | 162 | 101* | Gentlemen v Cambridge U. | Cambridge | 1871 |
| | | | | *In consecutive innings during same week* | | |
| | | 170* | | England v Notts & Yorkshire | Lord's | 1872 |
| | | 134 | 106* | Gents of South v Players of South | Oval | 1873 |
| | | 158 | 102* | Gentlemen v Players | Oval | 1873 |
| | | | | *In consecutive innings* | | |
| | | 169 | 110* | Gentlemen v Players | Lord's | 1876 |
| Green, D.M. | | 121 | | Lancashire v Glamorgan | Cardiff | 1964 |
| Greenidge, C.G. | (3) | 273* | | D.H. Robins' XI v Pakistanis | Eastbourne | 1974 |
| | | 168 | 115* | Hampshire v Worcestershire | Worcester | 1975 |
| | | 123 | | West Indians v Middlesex | Lord's | 1976 |
| Gregory, J.M. | | 152 | 103* | NSW v New Zealanders | Sydney | 1927–28 |
| Hammond, W.R. | (2) | 116 | | MCC v Trinidad | Port-of-Spain | 1934–35 |
| | | 252 | | Gloucestershire v Leicestershire | Leicester | 1935 |
| Hanif Mohammad | | 222 | 107* | Pakistanis v Combined U's | Poona | 1960–61 |
| Hardinge, H.T.W. | (2) | 117 | 113* | Kent v Hampshire | Dover | 1913 |
| | | 114 | 104* | Kent v Hampshire | Dover | 1928 |
| Hayes, E.G. | (2) | 121 | 100* | Surrey v Oxford University | Oval | 1901 |
| | | 108 | 108* | Surrey v Leicestershire | Oval | 1901 |
| Hayward, T.W. | (2) | 135 | 125* | Surrey v Leicestershire | Oval | 1906 |
| | | 106 | | Surrey v Warwickshire | Oval | 1910 |
| Hewett, H.T. | | 112 | 107* | Somerset v Gloucestershire | Taunton | 1893 |
| Hiddleston, J.S. | | 212 | 103* | Wellington v Canterbury | Wellington | 1925–26 |
| Hobbs, J.B. | (13) | 125 | | Surrey v Worcestershire | Worcester | 1906 |
| | | 205 | | Surrey v Hampshire | Oval | 1909 |
| | | 119 | 115* | Surrey v Oxford University | Oval | 1910 |
| | | 113 | 113 | Surrey v Gloucestershire | Oval | 1913 |
| | | 107 | | Surrey v Gloucestershire | Bristol | 1913 |
| | | 100 | | Surrey v Yorkshire | Bradford | 1914 |
| | | 102 | | Surrey v Lancashire | Manchester | 1919 |
| | | 134 | | Surrey v Leicestershire | Leicester | 1920 |
| | | 115 | 115 | Players of South v Gents of South | Oval | 1920 |
| | | 145 | | Surrey v Leicestershire | Leicester | 1922 |
| | | 104 | | Surrey v Gloucestershire | Oval | 1925 |

| | | Final Score | Lunch Score | | | |
|---|---|---|---|---|---|---|
| Hobbs, J.B. *continued* | | 215 | | Surrey v Warwickshire | Birmingham | 1925 |
| | | 131 | 105* | Surrey v Nottinghamshire | Oval | 1927 |
| Hudson, R.E.H. | | 217 | | Army v RAF | Oval | 1932 |
| Hutton, L. | | 241 | 100* | Players v Gentlemen | Scarborough | 1953 |
| Ijaz Hussain | | 126 | 126 | Pak PWD v Quetta | Quetta | 1969–70 |
| Imtiaz Ahmed | | 103 | 103 | Pakistanis v East Zone | Jamshedpur | 1952–53 |
| Jameson, J.A. | (3) | 110 | 110 | D.H. Robins' XI v Indians | Eastbourne | 1974 |
| | | | | *Out of 147 in 100 minutes* | | |
| | | 144 | 100* | Warwickshire v Hampshire | Bournemouth | 1976 |
| | | 103 | 103 | Warwickshire v Glamorgan | Birmingham | 1976 |
| Jessop, G.L. | (4) | 169 | 131* | MCC v Leicestershire | Lord's | 1901 |
| | | 159* | | South v South Africans | Hastings | 1904 |
| | | | | *Scored at least 140\* before lunch batting no. 5* | | |
| | | 119 | 119 | Gloucestershire v Sussex | Hastings | 1907 |
| | | 164 | | Gloucestershire v Sussex | Gloucester | 1908 |
| Johnson, P.R. | | 105 | | Somerset v Sussex | Bath | 1913 |
| Jones, A.O. | (2) | 137 | 112* | Nottinghamshire v Lancashire | Nottingham | 1903 |
| | | 103 | | Nottinghamshire v Gloucs | Nottingham | 1911 |
| Kallicharran, A.I. | | 155 | 100* | Warwickshire v Glamorgan | Cardiff | 1984 |
| Keeton, W.W. | | 110 | | Nottinghamshire v Yorkshire | Bradford | 1933 |
| Kirton, K.N. | (2) | 124 | 105* | Border v Rhodesia | East London | 1954–55 |
| | | | | *O.C. Dawson scored 117\* in the same session* | | |
| | | 111 | | Border v N.E. Transvaal | Benoni | 1955–56 |
| Koch, L.B. | | 111 | | Orange Free State v W. Province | Bloemfontein | 1954–55 |
| Larkins, W. | | 252 | | Northamptonshire v Glamorgan | Cardiff | 1983 |
| Lowndes, W.G.L.F. | | 118 | | Hampshire v Kent | Portsmouth | 1935 |
| Macartney, C.G. | | 151 | 112* | Australia v England | Leeds | 1926 |
| McDonald, C.C. | | 100 | 100 | Australians v Cambridge U. | Cambridge | 1961 |
| McEwan, K.S. | (2) | 156 | 104* | Essex v Nottinghamshire | Nottingham | 1976 |
| | | 128 | 112* | Essex v Lancashire | Southport | 1978 |
| McGlew, D.J. | | 121 | | Natal v Orange Free State | Bloemfontein | 1954–55 |
| McIver, C.D. | | 134 | 117* | Essex v Hampshire | Leyton | 1913 |
| MacLaren, A.C. | (2) | 135 | 113* | Lancashire v Leicestershire | Leicester | 1895 |
| | | 104 | 104* | Lancashire v Gloucestershire | Bristol | 1900 |
| Majid Khan | (2) | 156 | 114* | Glamorgan v Worcestershire | Cardiff | 1969 |
| | | 112 | 108* | Pakistan v New Zealand | Karachi | 1976–77 |
| Mansell, P.N.F. | | 111 | | Rhodesia v Griqualand West | Kimberley | 1954–55 |
| Mansoor Akhtar | | 153 | | Pakistanis v Somerset | Taunton | 1982 |
| Marlow, F.W. | | 155 | 114* | Sussex v Somerset | Hove | 1895 |
| Marshall, R.E. | | 163 | | Hampshire v Glamorgan | Cardiff | 1964 |
| Masood Anwar | | 186 | 105* | Rawalpindi v Hazara | Rawalpindi | 1984–85 |
| Massie, H.H. | | 206 | 100* | Australians v Oxford University | Oxford | 1882 |
| Milburn, C. | (2) | 113 | | Northamptonshire v Notts | Nottingham | 1966 |
| | | 203 | | Northamptonshire v Essex | Clacton | 1966 |
| Moore, R.H. | | 316 | | Hampshire v Warwickshire | Bournemouth | 1937 |
| Morris, A.R. | | 290 | | Australians v Gloucestershire | Bristol | 1948 |
| Mulholland, H.G.H. | | 153 | | Cambridge U. v Indians | Cambridge | 1911 |
| Murray, B.A.G. | | 157 | 103* | New Zealanders v President's XI | Rawalpindi | 1969–70 |
| Mushtaq Mohammad | | 229* | | Karachi Whites v E. Pakistan | Karachi | 1961–62 |
| Needham, A. | | 124 | 124 | Surrey v Zimbabweans | Oval | 1985 |
| Needham, E. | | 159 | | Derbyshire v Leicestershire | Leicester | 1910 |
| O'Connell-Jones, D.B. | | 121 | | Rhodesia v Orange Free State | Salisbury | 1955–56 |
| Palairet, L.C.H. | (3) | 103 | 101* | Somerset v Yorkshire | Taunton | 1901 |
| | | 182 | 114* | Somerset v Lancashire | Bath | 1901 |
| | | 140 | 100* | Somerset v Surrey | Taunton | 1901 |
| | | | | *Palairet scored five hundreds in 1901 – all before lunch* | | |
| Parks, J.H. | (2) | 140 | | Sussex v Somerset | Yeovil | 1937 |
| | | 104 | | Sussex v Nottinghamshire | Hove | 1937 |
| Paynter, E. | | 322 | | Lancashire v Sussex | Hove | 1937 |
| Perring, C.A. | | 122 | | Griqualand West v OFS | Kimberley | 1968–69 |
| Pullar, G. | | 103 | | Rest of England v Yorkshire | Oval | 1959 |
| Ranjitsinhji, K.S. | | 260 | 100* | Sussex v MCC | Lord's | 1897 |
| Rashleigh, W. | | 163 | 114* | Kent v Middlesex | Tonbridge | 1896 |
| Relf, R.R. | | 111 | 111 | Sussex v Somerset | Hove | 1919 |
| Richards, B.A. | (5) | 106 | 106 | Natal v Rhodesia | Salisbury | 1969–70 |

|  |  | Final Score | Lunch Score |  |  |  |
|---|---|---|---|---|---|---|
| Richards, B.A. *continued* |  | 126 | 120* | Hampshire v Sussex | Hove | 1975 |
|  |  | 111 | 111 | Hampshire v Glamorgan | Bournemouth | 1976 |
|  |  | 136 | 112* | Hampshire v Sussex | Hove | 1976 |
|  |  | 115 | 112* | Hampshire v Derbyshire | Bournemouth | 1977 |
| Richards, I.V.A. |  | 189 | 117* | Somerset v Lancashire | Southport | 1977 |
| Richardson, A.J. |  | 280 |  | South Australia v MCC | Adelaide | 1922–23 |
| Richardson, P.E. | (2) | 116 |  | Worcestershire v Derbyshire | Derby | 1957 |
|  |  | 124 |  | Kent v Hampshire | Canterbury | 1964 |
| Roach, C.A. |  | 180 |  | West Indians v Surrey | Oval | 1933 |
| Robertson, J.D.B. | (3) | 154 |  | Middlesex v Warwickshire | Lord's | 1939 |
|  |  | 118 |  | Middlesex v Nottinghamshire | Nottingham | 1947 |
|  |  | 119 |  | Middlesex v Sussex | Lord's | 1957 |
| Rothery, J.W. |  | 118 |  | Yorkshire v Hampshire | Bournemouth | 1905 |
| Rowan, E.A.B. |  | 176 |  | Transvaal v Rhodesia | Salisbury | 1950–51 |
| Russell, C.A.G. |  | 108 | 108* | Essex v Northamptonshire | Northampton | 1921 |
| Sandham, A. | (2) | 195 |  | Surrey v Cambridge University | Oval | 1922 |
|  |  | 150 | 133* | MCC v Europeans | Rawalpindi | 1926–27 |
| Seeff, L. |  | 156 | 117* | W. Province B v Natal B | Constantia | 1978–79 |
| Seth, J.N. |  | 179 |  | Delhi v Southern Punjab | Delhi | 1949–50 |
|  |  |  |  | *On first-class debut* |  |  |
| Sewell, E.H.D. |  | 107 | 107 | Essex v Warwickshire | Birmingham | 1904 |
|  |  |  |  | *Scored out of 142 for first wicket in 80 minutes* |  |  |
| Seyfried, F.A. |  | 144 |  | N.E. Transvaal v OFS | Bloemfontein | 1955–56 |
| Simpson, R.T. | (3) | 101 |  | MCC v Yorkshire | Scarborough | 1953 |
|  |  | 125 |  | Commonwealth XI v Holkar | Indore | 1953–54 |
|  |  | 147 |  | Nottinghamshire v Somerset | Nottingham | 1954 |
| Simpson-Hayward, G.H.T. |  | 105 | 105 | Worcestershire v Oxford U. | Oxford | 1908 |
|  |  |  |  | *Scored out of 140 in 80 minutes batting no. 6* |  |  |
| Smith, E.J. |  | 134 | 121* | Warwickshire v Hampshire | Coventry | 1912 |
| Smith, M.J. |  | 107 | 100* | Middlesex v Kent | Canterbury | 1975 |
| Spooner, R.H. | (3) | 164 |  | Lancashire v Nottinghamshire | Nottingham | 1905 |
|  |  | 240 |  | Lancashire v Somerset | Bath | 1906 |
|  |  | 186 | 100* | Lancashire v Hampshire | Manchester | 1911 |
| Stewart, W.J. |  | 151 | 131* | Warwicks v Combined Services | Birmingham | 1959 |
|  |  |  |  | *Out of 180-1* |  |  |
| Stoddart, A.E. | (2) | 195* | 101* | Middlesex v Nottinghamshire | Lord's | 1893 |
|  |  | 127 | 104* | C.I. Thornton's XI v Australians | Scarborough | 1893 |
| Tate, M.W. | (2) | 133 |  | MCC v Parsees & Europeans | Bombay | 1926–27 |
|  |  | 101 | 101 | Sussex v Hampshire | Portsmouth | 1927 |
|  |  |  |  | *Scored out of 144 for first wicket in 68 minutes* |  |  |
| Townsend, C.L. |  | 214 | 130* | Gloucestershire v Worcestershire | Cheltenham | 1906 |
| Trumper, V.T. | (2) | 104 | 103* | Australia v England | Manchester | 1902 |
|  |  | 108 |  | Australians v Gloucestershire | Bristol | 1905 |
| Tufnell, N.C. |  | 102 | 102 | Cambridge U. v Gentlemen | Eastbourne | 1910 |
| Turner, G.M. | (5) | 140 | 123* | Worcestershire v Notts | Worcester | 1973 |
|  |  |  |  | *Out of 163-2 in 135 minutes* |  |  |
|  |  | 150 | 109* | Worcestershire v Surrey | Worcester | 1978 |
|  |  | 101 | 101 | Worcestershire v Warwickshire | Birmingham | 1980 |
|  |  | 161 | 126* | Worcestershire v Northants | Stourbridge | 1981 |
|  |  | 311* | 128* | Worcestershire v Warwicks | Worcester | 1982 |
|  |  |  |  | *Out of 181-0; his 100th century* |  |  |
| Tyldesley, J.T. |  | 104 | 100* | Lancashire v Derbyshire | Manchester | 1904 |
| Vernon, G.F. |  | 106 | 105* | Middlesex v Surrey | Oval | 1880 |
| Wallroth, C.A. |  | 109 | 102* | Oxford University v Middlesex | Prince's | 1873 |
| Waqar Hassan |  | 101 |  | Karachi v Bahawalpur | Bahawalpur | 1954–55 |
| Warner, P.F. |  | 149 |  | Middlesex v Surrey | Oval | 1907 |
| Washbrook, C. |  | 124 |  | Lancashire v Glamorgan | Manchester | 1938 |
| Williams, P.V. |  | 146 |  | Army v Royal Navy | Lord's | 1920 |
| Wilson, H.L. |  | 109 | 105* | Sussex v Gloucestershire | Hove | 1913 |
| Woolley, F.E. | (3) | 110 |  | Kent v Surrey | Blackheath | 1930 |
|  |  | 105 | 105 | Kent v Leicestershire | Gravesend | 1935 |
|  |  | 136 |  | Kent v Worcestershire | Tonbridge | 1938 |
| Woolmer, R.A. |  | 125 |  | Kent v Oxford University | Oxford | 1975 |
| Worrell, F.M.M. |  | 110 |  | Commonwealth XI v North Zone | Amritsar | 1953–54 |

|  |  | Final Score | Lunch Score |  |  |  |
| --- | --- | --- | --- | --- | --- | --- |
| Wrathall, H. | (2) | 136 | 105* | Gloucestershire v Worcestershire | Worcester | 1900 |
|  |  | 135 | 133* | Gloucestershire v Sussex | Hove | 1901 |
| Zulch, J.W. |  | 185 |  | Transvaal v Orange Free State | Bloemfontein | 1920–21 |

## HUNDRED BEFORE LUNCH AFTER FIRST DAY

|  |  | Final Score | Lunch Score |  |  |  | Day |
| --- | --- | --- | --- | --- | --- | --- | --- |
| Abberley, R.N. |  | 117* | 100* | Warwickshire v Essex | Birmingham | 1966 | 3 |
| Abel, R. |  | 193 | 101* | Surrey v Derbyshire | Oval | 1900 | 2 |
| Ames, L.E.G. |  | 145 | 100* | Kent v Indians | Canterbury | 1936 | 2 |
| Badcock, F.T. |  | 105 | 105 | Otago v Canterbury | Christchurch | 1931–32 | 3 |
| Bagshaw, H. |  | 115 | 115 | Derbyshire v Yorkshire | Derby | 1896 | 3 |
| Bainbridge, H.W. |  | 104* | 104* | Warwickshire v Derbyshire | Birmingham | 1895 | 3 |
| Bairstow, D.L. |  | 100* | 100* | Yorkshire v Leicestershire | Bradford | 1985 | 3 |
| Barber, R.W. |  | 104 | 104 | Lancashire v Nottinghamshire | Worksop | 1961 | 3 |
| Bates, W. | (2) | 108 | 108 | Yorkshire v Kent | Maidstone | 1881 | 2 |
|  |  | 144* | 144* | Under-30 v Over-30 | Lord's | 1882 | 2 |
| Bhandari, P. |  | 111* | 111* | Bengal v Rajasthan | Udaipur | 1961–62 | 4 |
| Board, J.H. | (2) | 124 | 124 | Gloucestershire v Warwicks | Bristol | 1896 | 3 |
|  |  | 126 | 100* | Gloucestershire v Yorkshire | Bristol | 1897 | 3 |
| Bosanquet, B.J.T. |  | 100* | 100* | Middlesex v Sussex | Lord's | 1905 | 3 |
| Braund, L.C. | (2) | 107 | 107 | Somerset v Yorkshire | Leeds | 1901 | 2 |
|  |  |  |  | *L.C.H. Palairet scored 112\* in the same session* |  |  |  |
|  |  | 132 |  | Somerset v Hampshire | Bournemouth | 1903 | 3 |
| Broadbent, R.G. |  | 108 | 108 | Worcestershire v Leicestershire | Leicester | 1952 | 3 |
| Brockwell, W. |  | 137 | 102* | Surrey v Sussex | Oval | 1896 | 3 |
| Brown, F.R. |  | 212 | 113* | Surrey v Middlesex | Oval | 1932 | 2 |
| Brown, G. |  | 120 | 120 | Hampshire v Worcestershire | Portsmouth | 1926 | 2 |
| Brown, J.T. |  | 167 | 100* | Yorkshire v Australians | Bradford | 1899 | 3 |
| Bruce, Hon C.N. |  | 103 | 103 | Middlesex v Nottinghamshire | Nottingham | 1925 | 3 |
| Bryan, G.J. |  | 124 |  | Kent v Nottinghamshire | Nottingham | 1920 | 3 |
|  |  |  |  | *On first-class debut* |  |  |  |
| Bryan, J.L. |  | 106 | 106 | Kent v Lancashire | Maidstone | 1921 | 2 |
| Buchanan, J.N. |  | 104 | 104 | Cambridge University v MCC | Lord's | 1907 | 2 |
| Carr, A.W. | (2) | 115 |  | Nottinghamshire v Surrey | Nottingham | 1926 | 3 |
|  |  | 100 | 100 | Notts v Cambridge University | Cambridge | 1929 | 3 |
| Champain, F.H.B. |  | 149 | 120*† | Gloucestershire v Surrey | Bristol | 1907 | 2 |
| Chapman, A.P.F. | (2) | 110 | 110 | Cambridge U. v Warwickshire | Birmingham | 1921 | 2 |
|  |  | 136 | 104 | Kent v Hampshire | Canterbury | 1926 | 2 |
| Cook, T.E. |  | 176 | 100*† | Sussex v Warwickshire | Birmingham | 1934 | 2 |
| Cowdrey, M.C. | (2) | 165 |  | Kent v Nottinghamshire | Nottingham | 1957 | 2 |
|  |  | 100* | 100* | Kent v Hampshire | Canterbury | 1964 | 3 |
| Cox, G. |  | 106 | 100* | Sussex v Worcestershire | Worcester | 1952 | 3 |
| Crawford, J.N. |  | 148 |  | Surrey v Gloucestershire | Bristol | 1906 | 2 |
| Crawford, V.F.S. | (2) | 159 | 150* | Surrey v Worcestershire | Oval | 1901 | 2 |
|  |  | 102* | 102* | Leicestershire v Worcestershire | Worcester | 1906 | 3 |
|  |  |  |  | *C.J.B. Wood and H. Whitehead scored 110\* and 97\* respectively before lunch on the previous day in the same innings* |  |  |  |
| Crawley, A.M. |  | 175 |  | Kent v Essex | Southend | 1930 | 2 |
| Crowe, M.D. |  | 150 | 102* | Auckland v Central Districts | New Plymouth | 1981–82 | 2 |
| Dacre, C.C.R. | (2) | 109 | 105* | Auckland v Otago | Dunedin | 1926–27 | 2 |
|  |  | 104 |  | Gloucestershire v Worcs | Dudley | 1934 | 2 |
| Davison, B.F. |  | 104 | 104 | Leicestershire v Cambridge U. | Cambridge | 1977 | 2 |
| Denton, D. | (3) | 110 | 110 | Yorkshire v Leicestershire | Sheffield | 1899 | 3 |
|  |  | 101 | 101 | Yorkshire v Cambridge U. | Cambridge | 1903 | 2 |
|  |  | 121 | 109* | Yorkshire v MCC | Scarborough | 1908 | 3 |
| Dexter, E.R. | (2) | 107 | 107 | MCC v Leeward Islands | St John's | 1959–60 | 3 |
|  |  | 133 | 133 | Sussex v Somerset | Taunton | 1960 | 3 |
| Dixon, J.A. |  | 104* | 104* | Nottinghamshire v Leics | Nottingham | 1903 | 2 |
| Dixon, J.G. |  | 108 | 101* | Essex v Gloucestershire | Leyton | 1919 | 2 |
| Ducat, A. |  | 204* | 109* | Surrey v Northamptonshire | Northampton | 1921 | 2 |
| Duckfield, R. |  | 155* | 112* | Glamorgan v Kent | Gravesend | 1933 | 3 |
| Duleepsinhji, K.S. |  | 202 | 122* | Sussex v Essex | Leyton | 1929 | 3 |
| Edrich, J.H. |  | 127* | 101* | Surrey v Middlesex | Oval | 1972 | 3 |

| | | Final Score | Lunch Score | | | Day | |
|---|---|---|---|---|---|---|---|
| Edrich, W.J. | | 128 | 104* | Gentlemen v Australians | Lord's | 1948 | 3 |
| Emmett, G.M. | (2) | 146 | 108* | Gloucs v Worcestershire | Cheltenham | 1951 | 2 |
| | | | | *Out of 163-2* | | | |
| | | 117 | 106* | Gloucestershire v Notts | Bristol | 1952 | 2 |
| Evans, A.J. | | 143 | 103* | Kent v Lancashire | Maidstone | 1927 | 3 |
| Falcon, M. | | 122 | | Cambridge University v MCC | Lord's | 1908 | 3 |
| Ford, F.G.J. | | 150 | | Middlesex v Gloucestershire | Lord's | 1897 | 3 |
| Foster, G.N. | | 129* | 129* | Worcestershire v Sussex | Worcester | 1910 | 2 |
| Foster H.K. | (3) | 121 | 121 | Oxford U. v Cambridge U. | Lord's | 1895 | 3 |
| | | 112 | 112 | Worcestershire v Derbyshire | Worcester | 1902 | 3 |
| | | 106 | 106 | Worcestershire v Somerset | Worcester | 1911 | 3 |
| Foster, R.E. | (3) | 128 | 108* | Oxford U. v A.J. Webbe's XI | Oxford | 1900 | 2 |
| | | 136 | 107* | Worcestershire v Gloucs | Worcester | 1901 | 2 |
| | | 111 | 111 | Worcestershire v Derbyshire | Derby | 1901 | 2 |
| Fredericks, R.C. | | 102 | 102 | West Indians v Sri Lanka | Colombo | 1974–75 | 3 |
| Fry, C.B. | | 126 | 101* | Gentlemen v Players | Lord's | 1901 | 2 |
| Gale, R.A. | | 106 | 106 | Middlesex v Kent | Gravesend | 1959 | 3 |
| Gilligan, A.E.R. | | 112 | 112 | Gentlemen v Players | Oval | 1924 | 3 |
| Glover, A.C.S. | | 119* | 119* | Warwickshire v Hampshire | Birmingham | 1899 | 3 |
| Grace, W.G. | (2) | 112 | 112 | Gentlemen v Players | Lord's | 1872 | 3 |
| | | 116* | 116* | MCC v Cambridge University | Lord's | 1887 | 3 |
| Greenidge, C.G. | | 120 | 120 | Hampshire v Kent | Bournemouth | 1978 | 3 |
| Grieves, K.J. | | 123 | 123 | Lancashire v West Indians | Manchester | 1963 | 3 |
| Haig, N.E. | (2) | 104* | 104* | Middlesex v Nottinghamshire | Nottingham | 1927 | 3 |
| | | 111 | 111 | H.D.G. Leveson Gower's XI v Oxford University | Eastbourne | 1928 | 2 |
| Hallam, M.R. | | 149* | | Leicestershire v Worcs | Leicester | 1965 | 3 |
| Hallows, C. | | 104 | 104 | Lancashire v Warwicks | Nelson | 1928 | 3 |
| Hammond, W.R. | (3) | 187 | 131* | Gloucs v Lancashire | Manchester | 1927 | 3 |
| | | 110 | 109* | Gloucestershire v Cambridge U. | Bristol | 1927 | 2 |
| | | 163 | | Gloucestershire v Kent | Canterbury | 1935 | 2 |
| Hardinge, H.T.W. | | 162* | 123* | Kent v Worcestershire | Tonbridge | 1921 | 2 |
| Hardstaff, J., sr | | 124* | | Notts v South Africans | Nottingham | 1907 | 2 |
| Harrison, G.C. | | 111 | 111 | Hampshire v Gloucestershire | Southampton | 1919 | 2 |
| Hayes, E.G. | (2) | 104 | 104 | Surrey v Yorkshire | Oval | 1904 | 2 |
| | | 122* | | Players v Gentlemen | Scarborough | 1906 | 3 |
| Hayward, T.W. | | 106 | 101* | Surrey v Warwickshire | Oval | 1910 | 2 |
| Henery, P.J.T. | | 138* | 101* | Gentlemen v Oxford U. | Oxford | 1888 | 3 |
| Hewett, H.T. | | 110 | 110 | A.J. Webbe's XI v Oxford U. | Oxford | 1894 | 2 |
| Hill, C. | | 104 | 102* | Australians v Surrey | Oval | 1905 | 3 |
| Hirst, G.H. | (2) | 106 | 106 | Yorkshire v Gloucestershire | Dewsbury | 1900 | 2 |
| | | 108 | | Yorkshire v Surrey | Oval | 1904 | 3 |
| Hobbs, J.B. | (2) | 155 | 137* | Surrey v Essex | Oval | 1905 | 2 |
| | | | | *The first of 197 first-class hundreds* | | | |
| | | 117* | | MCC v Lord Londesborough's XI | Scarborough | 1911 | 2 |
| Holmes, E.R.T. | | 122* | 122* | Surrey v Nottinghamshire | Nottingham | 1947 | 3 |
| | | | | *J.F. Parker scored 108\* in the same session* | | | |
| Hookes, D.W. | | 105 | 105 | S. Australia v Queensland | Adelaide | 1976–77 | 4 |
| Horner, N.F. | | 129* | | Warwickshire v Leicestershire | Birmingham | 1956 | 3 |
| | | | | *Match began on third day* | | | |
| Humphreys, E. | | 105 | 100* | Kent v Middlesex | Lord's | 1909 | 2 |
| Hutchings, K.L. | | 101 | 101 | Kent v Hampshire | Tonbridge | 1907 | 2 |
| | | | | *J. Seymour scored over 100\* in the same session* | | | |
| Ijaz Butt | | 129* | 105* | Pakistanis v Kent | Canterbury | 1962 | 3 |
| Javed Miandad | | 172 | 103* | Habib Bank v Sargodha | Faisalabad | 1977–78 | 2 |
| Jessop, G.L. | (9) | 109 | 109 | Gloucestershire v Middlesex | Lord's | 1900 | 2 |
| | | 104 | 104 | Gloucestershire v Yorkshire | Bradford | 1900 | 2 |
| | | 139 | 139 | Gloucestershire v Yorkshire | Bradford | 1900 | 3 |
| | | | | *Only instance of this feat being achieved twice in the same match* | | | |
| | | 106 | 106 | Gloucestershire v Warwicks | Bristol | 1901 | 2 |
| | | 126 | 124* | Gloucestershire v Worcs | Bristol | 1902 | 2 |
| | | 126 | | Gloucestershire v Notts | Nottingham | 1902 | 2 |
| | | 144 | 144 | Gloucestershire v Sussex | Bristol | 1907 | 2 |
| | | 133* | 133* | Gloucestershire v Somerset | Bath | 1908 | 3 |

| | | Final Score | Lunch Score | | | | Day |
|---|---|---|---|---|---|---|---|
| Jessop, G.L. contd. | | 139 | | Gloucestershire v Hampshire | Bristol | 1911 | 3 |
| Johnson, P.R. | | 117 | 100* | Somerset v Hampshire | Southampton | 1908 | 2 |
| Kallicharran, A.I. | | 149 | 124* | Warwickshire v Surrey | Birmingham | 1972 | 2 |
| Kapil Dev | | 100* | 100* | Northamptonshire v Derbyshire | Northampton | 1982 | 3 |
| Kent, M.F. | | 122* | 104* | Queensland v Pakistanis | Brisbane | 1976–77 | 3 |
| Killick, E.T. | | 200* | | Cambridge U. v Glamorgan | Cambridge | 1929 | 3 |
| King, B.P. | | 124 | | Worcestershire v Hampshire | Worcester | 1938 | 2 |
| Knox, F.P. | | 106 | 105* | Oxford University v Sussex | Hove | 1899 | 3 |
| Lenham, L.J. | | 102* | 102* | Sussex v Middlesex | Hove | 1961 | 3 |
| Ling, W.V.S. | | 187 | 125* | Griqualand West v OFS | Pretoria | 1922–23 | 2 |
| Lister, W.H.L. | | 104* | 104* | Lancashire v Middlesex | Lord's | 1936 | 3 |
| Loxton, S.J.E. | | 123 | 123 | Commonwealth XI v Bombay | Bombay | 1953–54 | 3 |
| Macartney, C.G. | | 120 | 112* | NSW v Wellington | Wellington | 1923–24 | 3 |
| McEwan, K.S. | (4) | 218 | 103* | Essex v Sussex | Chelmsford | 1977 | 2 |
| | | 185 | 120* | Essex v Derbyshire | Chelmsford | 1979 | 2 |
| | | 132 | 103* | Essex v Lancashire | Manchester | 1984 | 2 |
| | | 110 | 110 | Essex v Cambridge University | Cambridge | 1985 | 3 |
| | | | | *Last two in successive first-class matches* | | | |
| MacLaren, A.C. | (3) | 108 | 108 | Lancashire v Somerset | Liverpool | 1900 | 2 |
| | | 174 | | Lancashire v Nottinghamshire | Nottingham | 1902 | 2 |
| | | 108 | 108 | Lancashire v Sussex | Manchester | 1904 | 3 |
| | | | | *R.H. Spooner scored 102\* in the same session* | | | |
| Majid Khan | (2) | 147* | 147* | Pakistanis v Glamorgan | Swansea | 1967 | 3 |
| | | 147 | 147 | Glamorgan v West Indians | Swansea | 1969 | 3 |
| Malik, H.S. | | 106 | | Sussex v Leicestershire | Horsham | 1921 | 2 |
| Marshall, R.E. | (2) | 163 | 104* | Hampshire v Glamorgan | Portsmouth | 1957 | 2 |
| | | 106 | 106 | Hampshire v Derbyshire | Bournemouth | 1964 | 2 |
| Mead, C.P. | (2) | 207* | | Hampshire v Warwickshire | Southampton | 1911 | 3 |
| | | 180 | 100* | Hampshire v Warwickshire | Bournemouth | 1928 | 2 |
| Melville, A. | | 152 | 102* | Sussex v Indians | Hove | 1936 | 2 |
| Morris, A.R. | | 108* | 108* | NSW v Queensland | Sydney | 1948–49 | 3 |
| Mushtaq Ali | | 108 | 108 | Prince's XI v Australian Services | Delhi | 1945–46 | 2 |
| Nash, M.A. | | 130 | 119* | Glamorgan v Surrey | Oval | 1976 | 2 |
| Neale, P.A. | | 101* | 101* | Worcestershire v Warwicks | Worcester | 1979 | 3 |
| | | | | *G.M. Turner scored 107 in the same session* | | | |
| Palairet, L.C.H. | | 173 | 112* | Somerset v Yorkshire | Leeds | 1901 | 2 |
| | | | | *L.C. Braund scored 107 in the same session* | | | |
| Parker, J.F. | | 108* | 108* | Surrey v Nottinghamshire | Nottingham | 1947 | 3 |
| | | | | *E.R.T. Holmes scored 122\* in the same session* | | | |
| Parker, J.M. | (2) | 140 | 105* | Worcestershire v Essex | Worcester | 1974 | 2 |
| | | 133 | 112* | Worcestershire v Notts | Worcester | 1975 | 2 |
| Parks, J.M. | | 155 | 111* | Somerset v Kent | Maidstone | 1973 | 3 |
| Patil, S.M. | (2) | 137 | | Indians v NWFP Governor's XI | Peshawar | 1982–83 | 2 |
| | | 121* | 121* | Bombay v Karnataka | Bombay | 1982–83 | 5 |
| Pearson, F.A. | | 113 | 100* | Worcestershire v Middlesex | Worcester | 1910 | 3 |
| Poore, R.M. | | 119 | | Hampshire v Somerset | Portsmouth | 1899 | 3 |
| Powell, J.L. | | 164 | | Canterbury v Otago | Christchurch | 1929–30 | 2 |
| Pressdee, J.S. | (2) | 107* | 107* | Glamorgan v Kent | Dartford | 1959 | 3 |
| | | 115 | 102* | Glamorgan v Sussex | Cardiff | 1961 | 3 |
| Procter, M.J. | (2) | 108 | 108 | Gloucestershire v Worcs | Cheltenham | 1977 | 2 |
| | | 122 | 122 | Gloucestershire v Leics | Bristol | 1979 | 3 |
| Ranjitsinhji, K.S. | (3) | 150 | 112* | Sussex v MCC | Lord's | 1895 | 3 |
| | | 105 | 105 | Sussex v Lancashire | Manchester | 1903 | 2 |
| | | 132 | | London County v MCC | Crystal Palace | 1903 | 2 |
| Read, W.W. | | 109 | 109 | Gents of England v Australians | Lord's | 1888 | 2 |
| Reid, J.R. | | 126 | 120 | Wellington v N. Districts | Wellington | 1964–65 | 2 |
| Relf, R.R. | | 114 | | Rest v Lord Cowdray's XI | Hastings | 1924 | 2 |
| Reynolds, B.L. | | 141 | 137* | Northants v Lancashire | Manchester | 1964 | 3 |
| Rhodes, A.E.G. | | 126 | | Derbyshire v Nottinghamshire | Ilkeston | 1949 | 3 |
| Richards, I.V.A. | (2) | 204 | 100* | Somerset v Sussex | Hove | 1977 | 2 |
| | | 101 | 101 | Somerset v Warwickshire | Birmingham | 1977 | 2 |
| Rogers, N.H. | | 106 | 105* | Hampshire v West Indies | Southampton | 1950 | 3 |
| Santall, F.R. | | 201* | 173* | Warwickshire v Northants | Northampton | 1933 | 3 |

|  |  | Final Score | Lunch Score |  |  |  | Day |
|---|---|---|---|---|---|---|---|
| Sewell, E.H.D. |  | 106* | 106* | Essex v Surrey | Oval | 1904 | 2 |
| Seymour, James |  | 204 |  | Kent v Hampshire | Tonbridge | 1907 | 2 |
|  |  |  | *K.L. Hutchings scored 101 in the same session* |  |  |  |  |
| Shahzad Ahmed |  | 131 | 131 | Karachi Whites v Khairpur | Karachi | 1970–71 | 2 |
| Sharp, J. |  | 103 | 103 | Lancashire v Somerset | Manchester | 1910 | 3 |
| Shepherd, T.F. |  | 132 | 109* | Surrey v Warwickshire | Oval | 1928 | 2 |
| Simpson, R.B. |  | 125 | 125 | Australians v Somerset | Taunton | 1964 | 3 |
| Singleton, A.P. |  | 152 |  | Worcestershire v Hampshire | Southampton | 1946 | 2 |
| Smart, C.C. |  | 114* | 114* | Glamorgan v South Africans | Cardiff | 1935 | 3 |
| Smith, M.J. |  | 100 | 100* | Middlesex v Leicestershire | Leicester | 1973 | 2 |
| Snooke, S.J. |  | 157 |  | South Africans v Somerset | Bath | 1907 | 3 |
| Spooner, R.H. |  | 102* | 102* | Lancashire v Sussex | Manchester | 1904 | 3 |
|  |  |  | *A.C. MacLaren scored 108 in the same session* |  |  |  |  |
| Sprot, E.M. |  | 147 | 147 | Hampshire v Somerset | Taunton | 1901 | 2 |
| Stewart, M.J. |  | 110* | 110* | Surrey v Sussex | Guildford | 1970 | 3 |
| Stewart, W.J. | (2) | 155 | 107* | Warwicks v Lancashire | Blackpool | 1959 | 2 |
|  |  | 182* | 103* | Warwicks v Leicestershire | Hinckley | 1962 | 3 |
| Stoddart, A.E. |  | 115 |  | South v North | Lord's | 1890 | 2 |
| Sugg, W. |  | 107 | 102* | Derbyshire v Worcestershire | Derby | 1899 | 3 |
| Sutcliffe, B. |  | 100* | 100* | New Zealanders v Essex | Southend | 1949 | 3 |
| Suttle, K.G. |  | 102 | 102 | Sussex v Gloucestershire | Eastbourne | 1965 | 3 |
| Tallon, D. |  | 152 |  | Combined XI v NSW | Brisbane | 1940–41 | 3 |
| Tate, M.W. |  | 121 | 100*† | Sussex v Northamptonshire | Hastings | 1925 | 2 |
| Trumper, V.T. | (2) | 292* | 103* | NSW v Tasmania | Sydney | 1898–99 | 2 |
|  |  | 120 | 120 | Australians v S. of England | Hastings | 1902 | 3 |
| Turner, G.M. |  | 115 | 115 | Worcestershire v Lancashire | Worcester | 1982 | 3 |
|  |  |  | *Match began on third day* |  |  |  |  |
| Turner, S. |  | 102 | 102 | Essex v Kent | Chelmsford | 1979 | 2 |
| Tyldesley, J.T. |  | 100* | 100* | North v South | Hastings | 1900 | 3 |
| Ulyett, G. |  | 107 | 107 | Yorkshire v Middlesex | Sheffield | 1884 | 3 |
| Viswanath, G.R. |  | 159 | 106* | Mysore v Kerala | Hubli | 1971–72 | 2 |
| Vorrath, W.N. |  | 103 | 103 | Otago v Wellington | Dunedin | 1927–28 | 3 |
| Wallace, W.M. |  | 115 | 115 | New Zealanders v Somerset | Taunton | 1937 | 2 |
| Walton, A.C. |  | 116* | 116* | Oxford University v Sussex | Oxford | 1956 | 2 |
| Wensley, A.F. |  | 102 | 102 | Sussex v Hampshire | Portsmouth | 1928 | 3 |
| Wheldon, G.F. |  | 103 | 103 | Worcestershire v Leics | Leicester | 1904 | 2 |
| Whitelaw, P.E. |  | 155 | 102* | Auckland v Wellington | Auckland | 1934–35 | 3 |
| Woods, S.M.J. | (3) | 103 | 103 | H.T. Hewett's XI v Cambridge University | Cambridge | 1892 | 2 |
|  |  | 109 | 109 | Somerset v Middlesex | Lord's | 1895 | 3 |
|  |  | 143 | 132* | Somerset v Sussex | Eastbourne | 1898 | 3 |
| Woolmer, R.A. | (2) | 125 | 103* | Kent v Derbyshire | Chesterfield | 1975 | 2 |
|  |  | 117 | 104* | Kent v Derbyshire | Chesterfield | 1979 | 2 |
| Zaheer Abbas | (4) | 106 | 101* | Gloucestershire v Worcs | Worcester | 1976 | 2 |
|  |  | 150* | 107* | Gloucestershire v Somerset | Bath | 1981 | 3 |
|  |  | 135 |  | Gloucs v Northamptonshire | Northampton | 1981 | 2 |
|  |  | 148* |  | Pakistanis v Derbyshire | Chesterfield | 1982 | 3 |

## HUNDRED ADDED TO OVERNIGHT SCORE BEFORE LUNCH

|  |  | Final Score | Session Scores |  |  |  | Day |
|---|---|---|---|---|---|---|---|
| Abel, R. | (3) | 217 | 19*–131* | Surrey v Essex | Oval | 1895 | 2 |
|  |  | 231 | 89*–200* | Surrey v Essex | Oval | 1896 | 2 |
|  |  | 250 | 105*–205*† | Surrey v Warwickshire | Oval | 1897 | 2 |
| Alley, W.E. |  | 221* | 12*–146* | Somerset v Warwicks | Nuneaton | 1961 | 3 |
| Amar Singh, L. |  | 131* | 17*–131* | Indians v Lancashire | Liverpool | 1932 | 2 |
| Ames, L.E.G. | (4) | 133 | 32*–133 | Kent v Sussex | Hastings | 1932 | 2 |
|  |  | 295 | 103*–203* | Kent v Gloucestershire | Folkestone | 1933 | 2 |
|  |  | 148* | 25*–148* | England v South Africa | Oval | 1935 | 3 |
|  |  | 116* | 16*–116* | Commonwealth XI v Prime Minister's XI | Bombay | 1950–51 | 2 |
| Bagguley, R. |  | 110 | 5*–107* | Nottinghamshire v Sussex | Nottingham | 1895 | 2 |
| Baig, A.A. |  | 129 | 9*–121* | Hyderabad v Kerala | Hyderabad | 1968–69 | 2 |

| | | Final Score | Session Scores | | | | Day |
|---|---|---|---|---|---|---|---|
| Bailey, T.E. | | 114* | 12*–114* | Essex v Nottinghamshire | Southend | 1955 | 3 |
| | | | | D.J. Insole scored 105* in the same session | | | |
| Bakewell, A.H. | | 143 | 17*–117*† | Northants v Notts | Nottingham | 1935 | 3 |
| Baldwin, C. | | 234 | 3*–125* | Surrey v Kent | Oval | 1897 | 2 |
| Bardsley, W. | | 164 | 32*–150* | Australia v South Africa | Lord's | 1912 | 2 |
| Barrington, K.F. | | 111 | 8*–111 | Players v Gentlemen | Scarborough | 1960 | 3 |
| Bean, G. | (2) | 145* | 45*–145* | Sussex v Nottinghamshire | Hove | 1891 | 2 |
| | | 186 | 12*–127* | Sussex v Lancashire | Manchester | 1893 | 2 |
| Berry, G.L. | | 141 | 9*–115* | Leicestershire v Sussex | Hove | 1949 | 2 |
| Binny, R.M. | | 117 | 12*–117 | Karnataka v Tamil Nadu | Bangalore | 1979–80 | 2 |
| Blunt, R.C. | | 221 | 104*–210* | Otago v Canterbury | Dunedin | 1928–29 | 3 |
| Board, J.H. | | 214 | 64*–214 | Gloucs v Somerset | Bristol | 1900 | 2 |
| Booth, M.W. | | 210 | 47*–163* | Yorkshire v Worcs | Worcester | 1911 | 2 |
| Bowden, M.P. | | 189* | 6*–162*† | Surrey v Sussex | Oval | 1888 | 2 |
| Bowring, T. | | 228 | 101*–228 | Oxford U. v Gentlemen | Oxford | 1908 | 2 |
| Boycott, G. | | 141* | 14*–117* | Yorkshire v Nottinghamshire | Bradford | 1983 | 3 |
| Bradman, D.G. | (6) | 452* | 205*–310* | NSW v Queensland | Sydney | 1929–30 | 3 |
| | | 191 | 47*–150*† | Australians v Hampshire | Southampton | 1930 | 2 |
| | | 253 | 122*–253 | NSW v Queensland | Sydney | 1933–34 | 3 |
| | | 357 | 229*–338* | S. Australia v Victoria | Melbourne | 1935–36 | 2 |
| | | 369 | 127*–262* | S. Australia v Tasmania | Adelaide | 1935–36 | 2 |
| | | 133* | 25*–133* | Australians v Lancs | Manchester | 1948 | 2 |
| Brearley, J.M. | | 124* | 11*–124* | Middlesex v Glamorgan | Cardiff | 1980 | 3 |
| Briggs, J. | | 186 | 81*–186 | Lancashire v Surrey | Liverpool | 1885 | 2 |
| Brown, J.T. | (2) | 311 | 116*–233* | Yorkshire v Sussex | Sheffield | 1897 | 2 |
| | | 128 | 20*–128* | Yorkshire v Leics | Huddersfield | 1900 | 2 |
| Burke, J.W. | | 125* | 10*–125* | Australians v Somerset | Taunton | 1956 | 3 |
| Carew, M.C. | | 126* | 17*–126* | W. Indians v Combined U's | Oxford | 1969 | 3 |
| Catt, A.W. | | 162 | 0*–121* | Kent v Leicestershire | Maidstone | 1962 | 2 |
| Champain, F.H.B. | | 120 | 20*–120 | Oxford U. v Australians | Oxford | 1899 | 2 |
| Chaplin, H.P. | | 213* | 110*–213* | Sussex v Nottinghamshire | Hove | 1914 | 3 |
| Chapman, A.P.F. | | 158 | 38*–158 | Kent v Worcestershire | Folkestone | 1927 | 2 |
| Chapman, T.A. | | 124* | 5*–124* | Rhodesia v Griqualand West | Salisbury | 1952–53 | 3 |
| Chappell, I.M. | | 141 | 16*–125* | South Australia v Victoria | Adelaide | 1973–74 | 2 |
| Chappell, G.S. | | 176 | 76*–176 | Australia v New Zealand | Christchurch | 1981–82 | 2 |
| Clarke, M.I.C. | | 153 | 38*–139* | Barbados v Trinidad | Port-of-Spain | 1940–41 | 3 |
| | | | | On first-class debut | | | |
| Compton, D.C.S. | (3) | 180* | 71*–180* | Middlesex v Essex | Lord's | 1938 | 2 |
| | | 300 | 120*–300 | MCC v N.E. Transvaal | Benoni | 1948–49 | 2 |
| | | 109 | 1*–104* | Middlesex v Essex | Leyton | 1957 | 2 |
| Cooley, B.C. | | 126* | 18*–126* | S. Africans v Cambridge U. | Cambridge | 1901 | 2 |
| Cox, G. | | 234* | 72*–172* | Sussex v Indians | Hove | 1946 | 3 |
| Crawford, V.F.S. | | 129 | 13*–129 | Surrey v Somerset | Oval | 1899 | 2 |
| Crowe, J.J. | | 151 | 31*–131* | Auckland v Northern Districts | Rotorua | 1983–84 | 2 |
| Dacre, C.C.R. | (2) | 111* | 5*–111* | Gloucs v Glamorgan | Swansea | 1932 | 3 |
| | | 117 | 2*–102*† | Gloucs v Derbyshire | Gloucester | 1934 | 2 |
| Darling J. | | 210 | 101*–201* | S. Australia v Queensland | Brisbane | 1898–99 | 2 |
| Davis, W.E. | | 112 | 11*–112 | Surrey v Derbyshire | Chesterfield | 1909 | 2 |
| Davison, B.F. | (3) | 132 | 31*–132 | Leicestershire v Notts | Leicester | 1976 | 3 |
| | | 144 | 43*–144 | Leicestershire v Hants | Southampton | 1978 | 3 |
| | | 129 | 18*–118* | Rhodesia v E. Province | Port Elizabeth | 1978–79 | 3 |
| Denton, D. | (2) | 120 | 5*–120 | Yorkshire v Middlesex | Lord's | 1919 | 2 |
| | | 209* | 26*–149* | Yorkshire v Worcs | Worcester | 1920 | 2 |
| Dews, G. | | 101* | 1*–101* | Worcestershire v Hampshire | Dudley | 1950 | 3 |
| Dexter, E.R. | | 117 | 12*–117* | Sussex v Pakistanis | Hove | 1962 | 2 |
| Dixon, J.A. | | 268* | 10*–127* | Nottinghamshire v Sussex | Nottingham | 1897 | 2 |
| Donnelly, M.P. | | 142 | 29*–142 | Cambridge U. v Oxford U. | Lord's | 1946 | 2 |
| Douglas, J. | | 143 | 23*–127* | Middlesex v Lancashire | Lord's | 1901 | 2 |
| Ducat, A. | (2) | 271 | 104*–271 | Surrey v Hampshire | Southampton | 1919 | 2 |
| | | | | E.G. Hayes scored 129 in the same session | | | |
| | | 290* | 184*–290* | Surrey v Essex | Leyton | 1921 | 3 |
| Dudleston, B. | | 142 | 34*–142 | Leicestershire v Somerset | Leicester | 1979 | 3 |
| Duff, R.A. | | 183 | 75*–183 | Australians v Somerset | Taunton | 1902 | 2 |
| Duleepsinhji, K.S. | | 254* | 30*–143* | Cambridge U. v Middlesex | Cambridge | 1927 | 3 |

|  |  | Final Score | Session Scores | | | | Day |
|---|---|---|---|---|---|---|---|
| Dunning, B. | | 142 | 33*-142 | N. Dists v Central Dists | Blenheim | 1972-73 | 3 |
| Eagar, E.D.R. | | 147 | 17*-147 | Oxford U. v Minor Cos. | Oxford | 1938 | 3 |
| Elgie, M.K. | | 162* | 15*-162* | Natal v Border | East London | 1959-60 | 2 |
| Endean, W.R. | | 204* | 96*-204* | Transvaal v Border | Johannesburg | 1959-60 | 2 |
| Fagg, A.E. | | 131 | 1*-101*† | Kent v Leicestershire | Tunbridge Wells | 1939 | 3 |
| Fane, F.L. | | 195 | 26*-150*† | MCC v Cambridge U. | Lord's | 1901 | 2 |
| | | | | *G.J.V. Weigall scored 115 in the same session* | | | |
| Farrer, W.S. | | 207 | 79*-207 | Border v Orange Free State | Bloemfontein | 1965-66 | 3 |
| Favell, L.E. | | 190 | 53*-167* | Australians v GW | Kimberley | 1957-58 | 3 |
| Ford, F.G.J. | | 111* | 4*-111* | A.E. Stoddart's XI v Rest | Hastings | 1895 | 3 |
| Foster, R.E. | (2) | 127 | 8*-127* | Oxford University v Surrey | Oval | 1900 | 3 |
| | | 246* | 47*-181* | Worcestershire v Kent | Worcester | 1905 | 3 |
| Fowler, G. | (2) | 141 | 21*-136* | Lancashire v Warwickshire | Birmingham | 1981 | 3 |
| | | 126 | 26*-126 | Lancashire v Warwickshire | Southport | 1982 | 2 |
| Francis, B.C. | | 194 | 36*-145* | D.H. Robins' XI v W. Prov. | Cape Town | 1973-74 | 2 |
| Fredericks, R.C. | | 129 | 21*-129 | West Indians v Hampshire | Southampton | 1969 | 3 |
| Fry, C.B. | (2) | 219* | 36*-141* | Sussex v Oxford University | Hove | 1901 | 3 |
| | | 211 | 27*-146* | Sussex v Hampshire | Hove | 1904 | 2 |
| Garnett, H.G. | | 114 | 9*-114 | Lancashire v Middlesex | Lord's | 1901 | 2 |
| Gibbons, H.H.I. | | 140 | 0*-140 | Worcestershire v Kent | Worcester | 1928 | 3 |
| Gilliat, R.M.C. | | 130 | 3*-130 | Hampshire v Gloucs | Southampton | 1976 | 2 |
| Gillingham, F.H. | | 194 | 60*-194* | Essex v Gloucestershire | Leyton | 1908 | 2 |
| Gooch, G.A. | | 205 | 62*-162* | Essex v Cambridge U. | Cambridge | 1980 | 2 |
| Grace, W.G. | | 288 | 32*-159* | Gloucs v Somerset | Bristol | 1895 | 2 |
| Greenidge, C.G. | (2) | 156 | 19*-150* | Hampshire v Indians | Southampton | 1982 | 3 |
| | | 154 | 52*-154 | Hampshire v Surrey | Southampton | 1983 | 3 |
| Grover, J.N. | | 121 | 14*-121* | Oxford U. v Cambridge U. | Lord's | 1937 | 2 |
| Groves, B.S. | | 237 | 72*-237 | Natal B v Orange Free State | Bloemfontein | 1967-68 | 2 |
| Guillen, S.C. | | 197 | 75*-197 | Canterbury v Fiji | Christchurch | 1953-54 | 2 |
| Gunn, J.R. | (2) | 294 | 193*-294 | Notts v Leicestershire | Nottingham | 1903 | 2 |
| | | 150* | 26*-150* | Notts v Gloucs | Nottingham | 1911 | 3 |
| Haigh, S. | | 159 | 4*-104*† | Yorkshire v Notts | Sheffield | 1901 | 2 |
| Hammond, W.R. | | 336* | 41*-152* | England v New Zealand | Auckland | 1932-33 | 2 |
| Hardstaff, J., jr | | 125* | 6*-125* | Notts v Leicestershire | Leicester | 1939 | 3 |
| Hartley, C.R. | | 139 | 6*-139* | Lancashire v Gloucs | Bristol | 1900 | 3 |
| Harvey, R.N. | (2) | 180 | 20*-152* | Australians v Glamorgan | Swansea | 1953 | 2 |
| | | 140 | 11*-134* | Australians v Notts | Nottingham | 1961 | 2 |
| Hassett, A.L. | | 146 | 30*-146 | Australians v Oxford U. | Oxford | 1938 | 2 |
| Hayes, E.G. | (4) | 218 | 73*-218 | Surrey v Oxford University | Oval | 1906 | 2 |
| | | 155 | 49*-155 | Surrey v Middlesex | Lord's | 1906 | 2 |
| | | 123 | 14*-114*† | Surrey v Lancashire | Oval | 1911 | 3 |
| | | | | *J.B. Hobbs also added over 100 runs in this session* | | | |
| | | 153 | 24*-153 | Surrey v Hampshire | Southampton | 1919 | 2 |
| | | | | *A. Ducat scored 167 in the same session* | | | |
| Hayward, T.W. | (2) | 315* | 163*-267* | Surrey v Lancashire | Oval | 1898 | 2 |
| | | 188* | 84*-184* | Surrey v Kent | Canterbury | 1904 | 2 |
| Hazare, V.S. | | 309 | 125*-246* | The Rest v Hindus | Bombay | 1943-44 | 3 |
| Hearne, J.W. | (3) | 106* | 4*-106* | Middlesex v Essex | Leyton | 1914 | 2 |
| | | | | *F.A. Tarrant scored 110* in the same session* | | | |
| | | 218* | 53*-171* | Middlesex v Hampshire | Lord's | 1919 | 2 |
| | | | | *E.H. Hendren scored 139 in the same session* | | | |
| | | 221* | 102*-221* | Middlesex v Warwicks | Birmingham | 1922 | 2 |
| Hendren, E.H. | (2) | 201 | 62*-201 | Middlesex v Hampshire | Lord's | 1919 | 2 |
| | | | | *J.W. Hearne scored 118* in the same session* | | | |
| | | 174 | 42*-174 | Rest v Lancashire | Oval | 1928 | 3 |
| Hewett, H.T. | (2) | 114 | 2*-102*† | Gentlemen v Cambridge U. | Cambridge | 1890 | 2 |
| | | 201 | 42*-168* | Somerset v Yorkshire | Taunton | 1892 | 2 |
| Higgins, H.L. | | 133 | 29*-129* | Worcestershire v Essex | Leyton | 1921 | 2 |
| Hill, C. | | 142 | 22*-138* | Australia v South Africa | Johannesburg | 1902-03 | 3 |
| Hirst, G.H. | (3) | 188 | 84*-188 | Yorkshire v Surrey | Oval | 1899 | 2 |
| | | 155 | 29*-143* | Yorkshire v Notts | Scarborough | 1900 | 3 |
| | | 153 | 21*-153 | Yorkshire v Leicestershire | Dewsbury | 1903 | 2 |
| Hobbs, J.B. | (5) | 117 | 8*-108*† | Surrey v Lancashire | Oval | 1911 | 3 |
| | | | | *E.G. Hayes also added over 100 runs in this session* | | | |
| | | 183 | 34*-183 | Surrey v Warwickshire | Oval | 1914 | 2 |

| | | Final Score | Session Scores | | | Day |
|---|---|---|---|---|---|---|
| Hobbs, J.B. contd. | | 211 | 12*–114* | England v South Africa | Lord's | 1924 2 |
| | | 261 | 142*–261 | Surrey v Oxford University | Oxford | 1926 3 |
| | | 146 | 31*–146 | Surrey v New Zealanders | Oval | 1927 2 |
| Hornby, A.N. | | 144 | 38*–144* | Gentlemen v Players | Oval | 1877 3 |
| Human, J.H. | | 125 | 2*–102*† | Middlesex v Sussex | Hove | 1937 2 |
| Hutchings, K.L. | | 144 | 41*–144 | Kent v Sussex | Hastings | 1910 2 |
| Hutton, L. | | 141 | 2*–102* | Yorkshire v Somerset | Huddersfield | 1950 2 |
| Insole, D.J. | | 114 | 9*–114* | Essex v Nottinghamshire | Southend | 1955 3 |
| | | | | T.E. Bailey scored 102* in the same session | | |
| Ireland, J.F. | | 107* | 0*–107* | Cambridge U. v Surrey | Cambridge | 1910 3 |
| Jaisimha, M.L. | | 151* | 41*–151* | Hyderabad v S.B. of India | Hyderabad | 1963–64 2 |
| Javed Miandad | (2) | 172 | 70*–172 | Habib Bank v Sargodha | Sargodha | 1977–78 2 |
| | | 181 | 0*–132* | Glamorgan v Warwickshire | Birmingham | 1980 2 |
| Jessop, G.L. | | 234 | 70*–234 | Gloucs v Somerset | Bristol | 1905 2 |
| Kallicharran, A.I. | (2) | 119 | 17*–119 | Warwickshire v Somerset | Taunton | 1981 3 |
| | | 155 | 17*–132* | Warwickshire v Leicestershire | Leicester | 1984 2 |
| Kanhai, R.B. | (2) | 192* | 50*–192* | West Indians v Oxford U. | Oxford | 1966 3 |
| | | 167* | 13*–162* | Warwicks v Oxford U. | Oxford | 1972 3 |
| Kidd, E.L. | | 150 | 17*–150 | Cambridge U. v Hampshire | Southampton | 1913 2 |
| Kilner, N. | | 228 | 57*–160* | Warwickshire v Worcs | Worcester | 1935 2 |
| King, B.P. | | 145 | 34*–145 | Lancashire v Gloucs | Gloucester | 1946 3 |
| Knight, B.R. | | 165 | 16*–122* | Essex v Middlesex | Brentwood | 1962 2 |
| Lamb, A.J. | | 107 | 2*–107 | W. Province v Rhodesia | Cape Town | 1978–79 3 |
| Langdon, T. | | 140 | 0*–100*† | Gloucestershire v Sussex | Gloucester | 1913 2 |
| Langridge, J.G. | | 137* | 27*–137* | Sussex v Middlesex | Hove | 1935 2 |
| Lester, E.I. | | 127 | 2*–113* | Yorkshire v Derbyshire | Scarborough | 1947 3 |
| Leyland, M. | | 153* | 52*–153* | Yorkshire v Hampshire | Bournemouth | 1932 3 |
| Llewellyn, C.B. | | 186 | 83*–186 | Players v Gentlemen | Bournemouth | 1905 2 |
| Lloyd, D. | | 195 | 36*–147* | Lancashire v Gloucestershire | Manchester | 1973 3 |
| Lloyd, T.A. | | 120 | 10*–120 | Warwickshire v Worcestershire | Worcester | 1981 3 |
| Macartney, C.G. | | 120 | 19*–120 | New South Wales v Otago | Dunedin | 1923–24 3 |
| | | | | A.T.E. Punch scored 116* in the same session | | |
| McCabe, S.J. | | 189* | 59*–159* | Australia v South Africa | Johannesburg | 1935–36 4 |
| McEwan, K.S. | (3) | 112 | 4*–106* | Essex v Northamptonshire | Northampton | 1976 3 |
| | | 186 | 41*–141*† | Essex v Northamptonshire | Ilford | 1978 2 |
| | | 149 | 11*–149 | Western Province v Arosa Sri Lanka | Cape Town | 1982–83 2 |
| McKenzie, K.A. | | 164* | 44*–164* | Transvaal v Natal | Durban | 1982–83 3 |
| MacLaren, A.C. | (2) | 424 | 289*–404* | Lancashire v Somerset | Taunton | 1895 2 |
| | | 149 | 41*–149 | K.S. Ranjitsinhji's XI v Philadelphians | Philadelphia | 1899 2 |
| Manjrekar, V.L. | | 283 | 183*–283 | Vizianagram XI v Tata Sports Club | Hyderabad | 1963–64 2 |
| Mann, F.T. | | 135 | 27*–135 | Middlesex v Worcestershire | Lord's | 1913 2 |
| Marchant, F. | | 176 | 29*–158* | Kent v Sussex | Gravesend | 1889 2 |
| Marshal, A. | | 167 | 58*–167 | Surrey v Kent | Oval | 1908 2 |
| Marshall, R.E. | | 111 | 0*–111 | Hampshire v Leicestershire | Bournemouth | 1960 3 |
| Mason, J.R. | | 147 | 40*–147 | Kent v Surrey | Oval | 1900 3 |
| Mead, C.P. | (2) | 182* | 19*–128* | England v Australia | Oval | 1921 2 |
| | | 213* | 105*–205*† | Hampshire v Worcs | Bournemouth | 1925 3 |
| Melville, A. | | 118 | 5*–105* | Oxford U. v Yorkshire | Oxford | 1930 3 |
| Meston, S.P. | | 130 | 25*–130 | Essex v Lancashire | Leyton | 1907 2 |
| Milburn, C. | (2) | 152* | 47*–152* | Northamptonshire v Gloucs | Northampton | 1965 2 |
| | | 137 | 7*–111* | Northamptonshire v Sussex | Hove | 1966 2 |
| Miller, K.R. | | 185 | 61*–185 | Dominions XI v England XI | Lord's | 1945 3 |
| Minnett, R.B. | | 216 | c40*–c160* | NSW v Victoria | Sydney | 1911–12 3 |
| Mordaunt, G.J. | | 264* | 158*–264* | Oxford U. v Sussex | Hove | 1895 3 |
| Morrison, J.S.F. | | 168 | 49*–168 | Cambridge U. v Sussex | Hove | 1919 2 |
| Narasimha Rao, M.V. | | 105* | 2*–105* | Hyderabad v Kerala | Cochin | 1973–74 2 |
| Newham, W. | (2) | 137 | 4*–c130* | Sussex v Kent | Tonbridge | 1884 2 |
| | | 201* | 35*–167* | Sussex v Somerset | Hove | 1896 3 |
| Oakman, A.S.M. | | 177 | 10*–120* | Sussex v Nottinghamshire | Eastbourne | 1962 2 |
| Owen-Smith, H.G. | | 129 | 27*–129 | South Africa v England | Leeds | 1929 3 |
| Palairet, L.C.H. | (2) | 181 | 80*–181 | Somerset v Oxford U. | Oxford | 1894 3 |

| | | Final Score | Session Scores | | | | Day |
|---|---|---|---|---|---|---|---|
| Palairet, L.C.H. contd. | | 194 | 73*–175* | Somerset v Sussex | Taunton | 1901 | 2 |
| Parks, H.W. | | 174 | 65*–174 | Sussex v Cambridge U. | Cambridge | 1936 | 2 |
| Parks, J.M. | | 119 | 14*–119 | Sussex v Lancashire | Hove | 1966 | 3 |
| Paynter, E. | | 260* | 49*–149*† | Lancashire v Essex | Manchester | 1937 | 2 |
| Payton, W.R.D. | | 149* | 23*–149* | Nottinghamshire v Surrey | Oval | 1907 | 2 |
| Pearce, T.N. | | 111* | 4*–111* | Essex v Kent | Ilford | 1949 | 3 |
| Pellew, C.E. | | 146 | 27*–134* | Australians v Cambridge U. | Cambridge | 1921 | 2 |
| Pollock, R.G. | (2) | 209* | | E. Province Invitation XI v Cavaliers | Port Elizabeth | 1962–63 | 3 |
| | | 180* | 31*–133* | E. Province v W. Province | Cape Town | 1976–77 | 2 |
| Ponsford, W.H. | | 429 | 234*–375* | Victoria v Tasmania | Melbourne | 1922–23 | 5 |
| Poore, R.M. | | 304 | 24*–146* | Hampshire v Somerset | Taunton | 1899 | 2 |
| Pretty, H.C. | | 200 | 50*–200 | Northants v Derbyshire | Chesterfield | 1906 | 2 |
| Prideaux, R.M. | | 109 | 7*–109 | Gentlemen v Players | Lord's | 1962 | 3 |
| Procter, M.J. | | 154 | 11*–154 | Gloucestershire v Surrey | Guildford | 1978 | 2 |
| Punch, A.T.E. | | 176 | 59*–175* | New South Wales v Otago | Dunedin | 1923–24 | 3 |
| | | | | C.G. Macartney scored 101 in the same session | | | |
| Randall, D.W. | | 121 | 1*–114* | Notts v Leicestershire | Nottingham | 1979 | 3 |
| Ranjitsinhji, K.S. | (6) | 154* | 41*–154* | England v Australia | Manchester | 1896 | 3 |
| | | 100 | 0*–100 | Sussex v Yorkshire | Hove | 1896 | 3 |
| | | 275 | 70*–191* | Sussex v Leicestershire | Leicester | 1900 | 3 |
| | | 202 | 38*–157* | Sussex v Middlesex | Hove | 1900 | 3 |
| | | 285* | 29*–150* | Sussex v Somerset | Taunton | 1901 | 3 |
| | | 234* | 54*–234* | Sussex v Surrey | Hastings | 1902 | 2 |
| Reid, J.R. | (2) | 283 | 80*–180* | Wellington v Otago | Wellington | 1951–52 | 3 |
| | | 296 | 0*–174* | Wellington v N. Districts | Wellington | 1962–63 | 3 |
| Relf, A.E. | | 153 | 23*–123*† | Sussex v Leicestershire | Horsham | 1921 | 2 |
| Reynolds, B.L. | | 155 | 7*–127* | Northants v Cambridge U. | Northampton | 1961 | 3 |
| Rhodes, W. | (2) | 105 | 1*–105 | Yorkshire v MCC | Scarborough | 1901 | 2 |
| | | 201 | 97*–201 | Yorkshire v Somerset | Taunton | 1905 | 2 |
| Richards, B.A. | (4) | 153 | 40*–153* | Hampshire v Derbyshire | Chesterfield | 1970 | 2 |
| | | 116 | 3*–116* | Hampshire v Surrey | Portsmouth | 1973 | 2 |
| | | 143* | 40*–143* | Hampshire v Kent | Southampton | 1973 | 2 |
| | | 225* | 110*–225* | Hampshire v Notts | Nottingham | 1974 | 2 |
| Richards, I.V.A. | | 156 | 4*–104* | Somerset v Middlesex | Lord's | 1979 | 2 |
| Richardson, P.E. | (2) | 134 | 12*–122* | Worcestershire v Notts | Worcester | 1956 | 3 |
| | | 131 | 26*–131 | Kent v Leicestershire | Leicester | 1963 | 2 |
| Roe, W.N. | | 132 | 22*–132 | Somerset v Hampshire | Bath | 1884 | 2 |
| Rosendorff, N. | | 178 | 55*–178 | OFS v N.E. Transvaal | Pretoria | 1964–65 | 2 |
| Rowan, E.A.B. | | 306* | 128*–230* | Transvaal v Natal | Johannesburg | 1939–40 | 2 |
| Saadat Ali | | 222 | 17*–123* | Income Tax Dept. v Multan | Multan | 1977–78 | 3 |
| Sewell, J.J. | | 166 | 29*–166 | Middlesex v Surrey | Oval | 1866 | 2 |
| Sharp, J. | | 120 | 10*–120 | Lancashire v Sussex | Manchester | 1903 | 3 |
| Sherwell, P.W. | | 144 | 6*–144 | S. Africans v Tasmania | Launceston | 1910–11 | 3 |
| Smith, F.B. | | 146 | 13*–116* | Canterbury v Auckland | Auckland | 1948–49 | 3 |
| Smith, K.F.H. | | 108 | 8*–108 | Central Dists v Wellington | Wanganui | 1959–60 | 3 |
| Smith, M.J.K. | (2) | 200* | 77*–200* | Warwickshire v Worcs | Birmingham | 1959 | 3 |
| | | 182* | 12*–124* | Warwickshire v Gloucs | Stroud | 1959 | 3 |
| Spooner, R.H. | | 215 | 84*–215 | Lancashire v Essex | Leyton | 1904 | 2 |
| Stackpole, K.R. | | 154* | 35*–135* | Australians v Sussex | Hove | 1972 | 3 |
| Steel, D.Q. | | 158 | 18*–121* | Cambridge U. v Surrey | Oval | 1877 | 2 |
| Sugg, F.H. | | 220 | 60*–204* | Lancashire v Gloucs | Bristol | 1896 | 2 |
| Surti, R.F. | | 246* | 104*–204* | Rajasthan v Uttar Pradesh | Udaipur | 1959–60 | 3 |
| Sutcliffe, B. | (2) | 264 | 156*–264 | Otago v Central Dists | Dunedin | 1959–60 | 2 |
| | | 201 | 15*–115* | Otago v N. Districts | Hamilton | 1960–61 | 2 |
| Sutcliffe, W.H.H. | | 171* | 70*–171* | Yorkshire v Worcs | Worcester | 1952 | 2 |
| Tarrant, F.A. | | 250* | 140*–250* | Middlesex v Essex | Leyton | 1914 | 2 |
| | | | | J.W. Hearne scored 102* in the same session | | | |
| Todd, L.J. | | 139 | 38*–139 | Kent v Surrey | Blackheath | 1933 | 3 |
| Townsend, C.L. | (2) | 159 | 29*–142* | Gloucs v Lancashire | Gloucester | 1898 | 2 |
| | | 134 | 34*–134* | Gloucestershire v Notts | Bristol | 1898 | 2 |
| Trumper, V.T. | (2) | 128 | 27*–128 | Australians v Cambridge U. | Cambridge | 1902 | 2 |
| | | 125 | 13*–125 | Australians v Gloucs | Cheltenham | 1902 | 2 |
| Turner, G.M. | (2) | 108 | 1*–108 | Worcs v Warwickshire | Worcester | 1979 | 3 |
| | | | | P.A. Neale scored 101* in the same session | | | |

|  |  | Final Score | Session Scores |  |  |  | Day |
|---|---|---|---|---|---|---|---|
| Turner, G.M. *contd* |  | 228* | 20*–134* | Worcs v Gloucestershire | Worcester | 1980 | 3 |
| Tyldesley, J.T. | (4) | 210 | 58*–200*† | Lancashire v Somerset | Bath | 1904 | 2 |
|  |  | 128 | 22*–128 | Lancashire v Gloucs | Manchester | 1906 | 2 |
|  |  | 209 | 38*–140*† | Lancashire v Warwicks | Birmingham | 1907 | 2 |
|  |  | 272 | 158*–272 | Lancashire v Derbyshire | Chesterfield | 1919 | 2 |
| Waheed Mirza |  | 324 | 98*–200* | Karachi Whites v Quetta | Karachi | 1976–77 | 2 |
| Wainwright, E. |  | 104 | 0*–104 | Yorkshire v Sussex | Sheffield | 1892 | 2 |
| Wallace, W.M. |  | 111 | 1*–111 | New Zealanders v Sussex | Hove | 1937 | 2 |
| Walters, K.D. |  | 127 | 2*–104* | Australian XI v World XI | Melbourne | 1971–72 | 5 |
| Ward, A. |  | 162 | 54*–162 | Lancashire v Derbyshire | Derby | 1897 | 2 |
| Warner, P.F. |  | 204 | 41*–184* | MCC v Sussex | Lord's | 1905 | 2 |
| Watson, F.B. |  | 300* | 104*–205* | Lancashire v Surrey | Manchester | 1928 | 3 |
| Weigall, G.J.V. |  | 122 | 7*–122 | MCC v Cambridge U. | Lord's | 1901 | 2 |
|  |  |  |  | *F.L. Fane scored 124*† in the same session* |  |  |  |
| White, G.C. |  | 162* | 39*–162* | S. Africans v Gloucs | Bristol | 1907 | 2 |
| White, R.C. |  | 205 | 72*–172*† | Transvaal B v | Johannesburg | 1965–66 | 2 |
|  |  |  |  | Griqualand West |  |  |  |
| Whitehouse, J. |  | 173 | 20*–150* | Warwickshire v Oxford U. | Oxford | 1971 | 2 |
|  |  |  |  | *On debut in first-class matches* |  |  |  |
| Wood, A. |  | 123* | 7*–123* | Yorkshire v Worcs | Sheffield | 1935 | 2 |
| Wood, B. |  | 198 | 48*–170* | Lancashire v Glamorgan | Liverpool | 1976 | 2 |
| Wood, C.J.B. | (3) | 176 | 73*–176 | London County v MCC | Crystal Palace | 1902 | 2 |
|  |  | 123 | 22*–123 | Leicestershire v Worcs | Worcester | 1904 | 2 |
|  |  | 225 | 22*–132* | Leicestershire v Worcs | Worcester | 1906 | 2 |
|  |  |  |  | *H. Whitehead scored 97* in the same session and* |  |  |  |
|  |  |  |  | *in the same innings, V.F.S. Crawford scored 102** |  |  |  |
|  |  |  |  | *before lunch on the next day* |  |  |  |
| Woolley, F.E. | (10) | 108* | 7*–108* | Kent v Sussex | Hove | 1911 | 2 |
|  |  | 305* |  | MCC v Tasmania | Hobart | 1911–12 | 2 |
|  |  |  |  | *Added 117 to his overnight score* |  |  |  |
|  |  | 202 | 46*–146*† | The Rest v Yorkshire | Oval | 1924 | 2 |
|  |  | 172* | 65*–172* | Rest v Lancashire | Oval | 1926 | 3 |
|  |  | 141* | 7*–113* | Kent v MCC | Folkestone | 1927 | 2 |
|  |  | 198 | 52*–170* | Kent v Derbyshire | Maidstone | 1928 | 3 |
|  |  | 198 | 10*–110*† | Kent v Somerset | Tunbridge Wells | 1933 | 3 |
|  |  | 161 | 21*–131* | Kent v Derbyshire | Canterbury | 1933 | 2 |
|  |  | 132 | 19*–132* | Kent v Surrey | Blackheath | 1934 | 2 |
|  |  | 172 | 58*–158*† | Kent v Sussex | Tunbridge Wells | 1935 | 2 |
| Woolmer, R.A. |  | 143 | 26*–127* | Kent v Nottinghamshire | Nottingham | 1976 | 3 |
| Wynyard, E.G. |  | 137 | 27*–137 | Gentlemen v Players | Scarborough | 1906 | 2 |
| Zaheer Abbas | (2) | 121* | 15*–121* | Gloucs v New Zealanders | Bristol | 1978 | 3 |
|  |  | 135* | 3*–135* | Gloucestershire v Northants | Northampton | 1981 | 2 |

*Scorebooks and match reports have not always recorded individual scores at lunch. In the above list '123†' denotes a score of 'at least 123' and 'c130' one of 'about 130'.*

## HUNDREDS BY TWO BATSMEN IN A PRE-LUNCH SESSION
*Pre-lunch runs shown in brackets*

### ON FIRST DAY
| O.C. Dawson (117*) | K.N. Kirton (105*) | Border v Rhodesia | East London | 1954–55 |  |
|---|---|---|---|---|---|

### AFTER FIRST DAY
| F.L. Fane (124*†) | G.J.V. Weigall (115) | MCC v Cambridge U. | Lord's | 1901 | 2 |
|---|---|---|---|---|---|
| L.C.H. Palairet (112*) | L.C. Braund (107) | Somerset v Yorkshire | Leeds | 1901 | 2 |
| A.C. MacLaren (108) | R.H. Spooner (102*) | Lancashire v Sussex | Manchester | 1904 | 3 |
| J. Seymour (100*†) | K.L. Hutchings (101) | Kent v Hampshire | Tonbridge | 1907 | 2 |
| J.B. Hobbs (100*†) | E.G. Hayes (100*†) | Surrey v Lancashire | Oval | 1911 | 3 |
| F.A. Tarrant (110*) | J.W. Hearne (102*) | Middlesex v Essex | Leyton | 1914 | 2 |
| J.W. Hearne (118*) | E.H. Hendren (139) | Middlesex v Hampshire | Lord's | 1919 | 2 |
| A. Ducat (167) | E.G. Hayes (129) | Surrey v Hampshire | Southampton | 1919 | 2 |
| C.G. Macartney (101) | A.T.E. Punch (116*) | NSW v Otago | Dunedin | 1923–24 | 3 |
| J.F. Parker (108*) | E.R.T. Holmes (122*) | Surrey v Notts | Nottingham | 1947 | 3 |
| D.J. Insole (105*) | T.E. Bailey (102*) | Essex v Notts | Southend | 1955 | 3 |
| G.M. Turner (107) | P.A. Neale (101*) | Worcs v Warwickshire | Worcester | 1979 | 3 |

## PRE-LUNCH HUNDRED BY A BATSMAN IN BOTH INNINGS

G.L. Jessop (104 and 139)          Gloucestershire v Yorkshire          Bradford          1900
*His innings, on the second and third days, were both begun and completed before lunch*

## MOST RUNS FROM ONE BALL

TEN

| Batsman | Bowler | | | |
|---|---|---|---|---|
| A.N. Hornby | J. Street | Lancashire v Surrey | Oval | 1873 |
| S.H. Wood | C.J. Burnup | Derbyshire v MCC | Lord's | 1900 |

*Recorded under the 'net' system of scoring in trial use in 1900*

NINE

| Batsman | Bowler | | | |
|---|---|---|---|---|
| Hon F.G.B. Ponsonby | — | MCC v Cambridge University | Cambridge | 1842 |
| T.A. Raynes | — | Gents of Surrey & Sussex v | | |
| | | Gents of England | Lord's | 1856 |
| C.J.B. Marsham | — | MCC v Surrey Club | Lord's | 1859 |
| T. Hearne | — | Middlesex v Surrey | Oval | 1870 |
| R. Daft | I.D. Walker | Players v Gentlemen | Oval | 1872 |
| A.J. Webbe | — | Middlesex v Gloucestershire | Lord's | 1888 |
| | | *Five plus four overthrows* | | |
| C. Hill | T. Richardson | Australians v Surrey | Oval | 1902 |
| | | *Scored 7, 8 and 9 off three balls in two overs* | | |
| J.A. Cuffe | — | Worcs v Philadelphians | Worcester | 1903 |
| R.A. Duff | W. Brearley | Australians v Gentlemen | Crystal Palace | 1905 |
| Hon J.B. Coventry | C.W.L. Parker | Worcs v Gloucestershire | Worcester | 1923 |
| A. Ducat | J.H. Parks | Surrey v Sussex | Oval | 1929 |
| A. Staples | E.W. Clark | Nottinghamshire v Northants | Kettering | 1932 |
| J.D.B. Robertson | H.S. Squires | MCC v Surrey | Lord's | 1948 |
| W.J. Edrich | V. Broderick | Middlesex v Northamptonshire | Lord's | 1949 |

The most runs from one ball, all-run and without the benefit of overthrows or penalties under Law 41.1, are:

NINE

| Batsman | Bowler | | | |
|---|---|---|---|---|
| Hon F.G.B. Ponsonby | — | MCC v Cambridge University | Cambridge | 1842 |

SEVEN

| Batsman | Bowler | | | |
|---|---|---|---|---|
| J. Guy | — | England v Kent | Canterbury | 1842 |
| W.D. Berridge | — | Demerara v Barbados | Georgetown | 1865–66 |
| A. Ducat | A. Jaques | Surrey v Hampshire | Oval | 1914 |

SIX

| Batsman | Bowler | | | |
|---|---|---|---|---|
| E.G. Goatley | P.G.H. Fender | Surrey v Sussex | Oval | 1913 |
| P.G.H. Fender | — | Surrey v Warwickshire | Oval | 1914 |
| C.C.C. Case | P.G.H. Fender | Somerset v Surrey | Oval | 1925 |
| | | *Case scored an all-run five two balls later in the same over* | | |
| T.G. Evans | T.E. Bailey | Players v Gentlemen | Lord's | 1949 |

## MOST RUNS OFF ONE OVER

FOUR-BALL OVERS

| | | Batsman | Bowler | | |
|---|---|---|---|---|---|
| 22 | (6466) | H.J.H. Scott | S. Wade | Australians v Yorkshire | |
| | | | | Sheffield | 1886 |
| 20 | (6446) | C.I. Thornton | D. Buchanan | Cambridge U. v Gentlemen | |
| | | | | Cambridge | 1871 |
| 20 | (6446) | G.J. Bonnor | A.P. Lucas | Australians v I Zingari | |
| | | | | Scarborough | 1882 |

## FIVE-BALL OVERS

| | Batsman | Bowler | | |
|---|---|---|---|---|
| 21 { 5 4444 | E. Jones W.P. Howell | } E.R. Wilson | Australians v Cambridge U. Cambridge | 1899 |
| 21 { 6641 4 | A.E. Trott C.M. Wells | } E.J. Tyler | Middlesex v Somerset Taunton | 1899 |

## SIX-BALL OVERS

| | | Batsman | Bowler | | |
|---|---|---|---|---|---|
| 36 | (666666) | G.St A. Sobers | M.A. Nash | Notts v Glamorgan Swansea | 1968 |
| 36 | (666666) | R. J. Shastri | Tilak Raj | Bombay v Baroda Bombay | 1984–85 |
| 34 | (646666) | F.C. Hayes | M.A. Nash | Lancashire v Glamorgan Swansea | 1977 |
| 34 | (46604446) *Including two no-balls* | E.B. Alletson | E.H. Killick | Notts v Sussex Hove | 1911 |
| 32 | (664664) | C.C. Smart | G. Hill | Glamorgan v Hampshire Cardiff | 1935 |
| 32 | (466664) | C.C. Inman | N.W. Hill | Leicestershire v Notts Nottingham | 1965 |
| 32 | (666644) | I.R. Redpath | N. Rosendorf | Australians v OFS Bloemfontein | 1969–70 |
| 32 | (466646) | P.W.G. Parker | A.I. Kallicharran | Sussex v Warwickshire Birmingham | 1982 |
| 32 | (466466) | I.T. Botham | I.R. Snook | England XI v Central Districts Palmerston North | 1983–84 |
| 32 | (666662) | T.E. Jesty | R.J. Boyd-Moss | Hampshire v Northants Southampton | 1984 |
| 31 | (666661) | A.W. Wellard | F.E. Woolley | Somerset v Kent Wells | 1938 |
| 31 | { 1 66666 | M.H. Bowditch M.J. Procter | } A.A. Mallett | W. Province v Australians Cape Town | 1969–70 |
| 30 | (466464) | D.G. Bradman | A.P. Freeman | Australians v England XI Folkestone | 1934 |
| 30 | (444666) | H.B. Cameron | H. Verity | South Africans v Yorkshire Sheffield | 1935 |
| 30 | (066666) | A.W. Wellard | T.R. Armstrong | Somerset v Derbyshire Wells | 1936 |
| 30 | (446646) | P.L. Winslow | J.T. Ikin | South Africans v Lancashire Manchester | 1955 |
| 30 | (066666) | D.T. Lindsay | W.T. Greensmith | S.A. Fezela XI v Essex Chelmsford | 1961 |
| 30 | (466266) | D. Wilson | R.N.S. Hobbs | Yorkshire v MCC Scarborough | 1966 |
| 30 | (606666) | Majid Khan | R.C. Davis | Pakistanis v Glamorgan Swansea | 1967 |
| 30 | (466626) | Zaheer Abbas | D. Breakwell | Gloucs v Somerset Taunton | 1979 |
| 30 | (4466460) *(Including one no ball)* | I.T. Botham | P.A. Smith | Somerset v Warwickshire Taunton | 1982 |
| 30 | (644664) | A.J. Lamb | A.I. Kallicharran | Northants v Warwickshire Birmingham | 1982 |
| 30 | (662664) | G.A. Gooch | S.R. Gorman | Essex v Cambridge University Cambridge | 1985 |

## EIGHT-BALL OVERS

| | | Batsman | Bowler | | |
|---|---|---|---|---|---|
| 34 | (40446664) | R.M. Edwards | M.C. Carew | Governor-General's XI v West Indians Auckland | 1968–69 |
| 32 | { 41 3 66066 | D.K. Carmody I.D. Craig | } I.W. Johnson | A.R. Morris's XI v A.L. Hassett's XI Melbourne | 1953–54 |
| 31 | (62460661) | J. Mercer | R. Howorth | Glamorgan v Worcs Cardiff | 1939 |
| 31 | { | Naseer Malik Aamer Hamid | } Gulfraz Khan | National Bank v Railways Lahore | 1976–77 |

|    |            | *Batsman*          | *Bowler*          |                            |         |
|----|------------|--------------------|-------------------|----------------------------|---------|
| 30 | (06466620) | M.G. Burgess       | R.W. Anderson     | Auckland v Central Districts |         |
|    |            |                    |                   | Wanganui                   | 1977–78 |

29 $\left\{\begin{array}{l} 1 \\ 4466440 \end{array}\right.$  H.B. Jordaan   $\left.\begin{array}{l} \\ \end{array}\right\}$ J.M. Buchanan   W. Province v E. Province
P.G.V. van der Bijl    Cape Town    1937–38

*Off the last over of the match which began with 26 runs needed for victory and with eight wickets in hand*

| 29 | (60660641) | D.W. Hookes | C.G. Thwaites | S. Australia v Victoria | 1976–77 |
|----|------------|-------------|---------------|-------------------------|---------|
|    |            |             |               | Adelaide                |         |

## MOST SIXES IN AN INNINGS

Before the law was amended in 1910 the ball usually had to be hit right out of the ground and not just over the boundary for six runs to be scored.

### FIFTEEN
| J.R. Reid (296) | Wellington v Northern Districts | Wellington | 1962–63 |
|-----------------|--------------------------------|------------|---------|

### THIRTEEN
| Majid Khan (147*)    | Pakistanis v Glamorgan       | Swansea     | 1967    |
|----------------------|------------------------------|-------------|---------|
| C.G. Greenidge (273*) | D.H. Robins' XI v Pakistanis | Eastbourne  | 1974    |
| C.G. Greenidge (259) | Hampshire v Sussex           | Southampton | 1975    |
| G.W. Humpage (254)   | Warwickshire v Lancashire    | Southport   | 1982    |
| R.J. Shastri (200*)  | Bombay v Baroda              | Bombay      | 1984–85 |

### TWELVE
| Gulfraz Khan (207) | Railways v Universities   | Lahore     | 1976–77 |
|--------------------|---------------------------|------------|---------|
| I.T. Botham (138*) | Somerset v Warwickshire   | Birmingham | 1985    |

### ELEVEN
| C.K. Nayudu (153) | Hindus v MCC                  | Bombay      | 1926–27 |
|-------------------|-------------------------------|-------------|---------|
| C.J. Barnett (194) | Gloucestershire v Somerset   | Bath        | 1934    |
| R. Benaud (135)   | Australians v T.N. Pearce's XI | Scarborough | 1953    |

### TEN
| H.L. Simms (126)     | Sussex v Nottinghamshire          | Hove             | 1912    |
|----------------------|-----------------------------------|------------------|---------|
| A.M. Crawley (204)   | Oxford University v Northamptonshire | Wellingborough | 1929    |
| W.R. Hammond (336*)  | England v New Zealand             | Auckland         | 1932–33 |
| H. Sutcliffe (113)   | Yorkshire v Northamptonshire      | Kettering        | 1933    |
| W.J. Stewart (155)   | Warwickshire v Lancashire         | Blackpool        | 1959    |
| H.R. Lance (122)     | Transvaal v E. Province           | Johannesburg     | 1966–67 |
| I.T. Botham (228)    | Somerset v Gloucestershire        | Taunton          | 1980    |
| I.T. Botham (131*)   | Somerset v Warwickshire           | Taunton          | 1982    |
| G.Fowler (100)       | Lancashire v Leicestershire       | Manchester       | 1983    |
| I.V.A. Richards (186) | Somerset v Hampshire             | Taunton          | 1985    |
| I.T. Botham (134)    | Somerset v Northamptonshire       | Weston-super-Mare | 1985   |

### NINE
| C.I. Thornton (124)      | Kent v Sussex                     | Tunbridge Wells  | 1869    |
|--------------------------|-----------------------------------|------------------|---------|
| P.J. Heather (109*)      | Transvaal v Border                | Durban           | 1910–11 |
| M.C. Bird (151)          | Surrey v Sussex                   | Hove             | 1911    |
| H. Gimblett (141)        | Somerset v Hampshire              | Wells            | 1937    |
| E. Paynter (158)         | MCC v Griqualand West             | Kimberley        | 1938–39 |
| G.J. Whittaker (148)     | Surrey v Northamptonshire         | Northampton      | 1949    |
| D.V. Smith (166)         | Sussex v Gloucestershire          | Hove             | 1957    |
| M.J. Procter (155)       | Western Province v Australians    | Cape Town        | 1969–70 |
| M.A. Nash (89)           | Glamorgan v Gloucestershire       | Swansea          | 1973    |
| I.V.A. Richards (189)    | Somerset v Lancashire             | Southport        | 1977    |
| Zaheer Abbas (147)       | Gloucestershire v Somerset        | Taunton          | 1979    |
| B.L. Cairns (110)        | Otago v Wellington                | Lower Hutt       | 1979–80 |
| G.M. Turner (228*)       | Worcestershire v Gloucestershire  | Worcester        | 1980    |
| I.V.A. Richards (100)    | West Indians v Glamorgan          | Swansea          | 1980    |
| R.O. Butcher (153*)      | Middlesex v Hampshire             | Lord's           | 1980    |
| M.W. Gatting (169)       | Middlesex v Surrey                | Uxbridge         | 1981    |
| N.F.M. Popplewell (143)  | Somerset v Gloucestershire        | Bath             | 1983    |
| I.T. Botham (80)         | England XI v Central Districts    | Palmerston North | 1983–84 |
| K.C. Williams (84*)      | Trinidad v Windward Islands       | Pointe-à-Pierre  | 1984–85 |

## SIX-HITS OFF CONSECUTIVE BALLS

### SIX

| Batsman | Bowler | | | |
|---|---|---|---|---|
| G.St A. Sobers | M.A. Nash | Nottinghamshire v Glamorgan | Swansea | 1968 |
| M.J. Procter | D. Breakwell | Gloucestershire v Somerset | Taunton | 1979 |

*Scored in separate overs: 66/6666.*

| | | | | |
|---|---|---|---|---|
| R.J. Shastri | Tilak Raj | Bombay v Baroda | Bombay | 1984–85 |

### FIVE

| Batsman | Bowler | | | |
|---|---|---|---|---|
| A.W. Wellard | T.R. Armstrong | Somerset v Derbyshire | Wells | 1936 |
| A.W. Wellard | F.E. Woolley | Somerset v Kent | Wells | 1938 |
| D.T. Lindsay | W.T. Greensmith | S.A. Fezela XI v Essex | Chelmsford | 1961 |
| M.J. Procter | A.A. Mallett | W. Province v Australians | Cape Town | 1969–70 |
| T.E. Jesty | R.J. Boyd-Moss | Hampshire v Northamptonshire | Southampton | 1984 |

### FOUR

| Batsman | Bowler | | | |
|---|---|---|---|---|
| R.E. Foster | W.G. Grace | Oxford U. v London County | Oxford | 1900 |
| E.R.T. Holmes | {J.C. Masterman / I.P.F. Campbell} | Oxford U. v Free Foresters | Oxford | 1927 |
| J.H. Parsons | O.C. Scott | Warwicks v West Indians | Birmingham | 1928 |
| A. Jepson | J.H. Wardle | Nottinghamshire v Yorkshire | Bradford | 1952 |
| R. Benaud | R. Tattersall | Australians v T.N. Pearce's XI | Scarborough | 1953 |
| D.W. White | J.D. Piachaud | Hampshire v Oxford University | Oxford | 1960 |
| C.C. Inman | N.W. Hill | Leicestershire v Notts | Nottingham | 1965 |
| Majid Khan | R.C. Davis | Pakistanis v Glamorgan | Swansea | 1967 |
| B.S. Groves | K. Morris | Natal B v Orange Free State | Bloemfontein | 1967–68 |
| I.R. Redpath | N. Rosendorff | Australians v OFS | Bloemfontein | 1969–70 |
| A.W. Greig | P.J. Lewington | Sussex v Warwickshire | Hastings | 1975 |
| C.E.B. Rice | K.W.R. Fletcher | Nottinghamshire v Essex | Nottingham | 1976 |
| A.W. Greig | U.C. Joshi | MCC v West Zone | Poona | 1976–77 |
| F.C. Hayes | M.A. Nash | Lancashire v Glamorgan | Swansea | 1977 |
| M.A. Nash | D. Breakwell | Glamorgan v Somerset | Taunton | 1978 |
| Imran Khan | D.R. Parry | Presidents XI v West Indians | Rawalpindi | 1980–81 |
| D.W. Hookes | D.J. Lillie | South Australia v Queensland | Adelaide | 1981–82 |
| Yashpal Sharma | I.V.A. Richards | India v West Indies | Amritsar | 1982–83 |
| J.E. Emburey | {D.J. Brickett / R.L.S. Armitage} | W. Province v E. Province | Cape Town | 1983–84 |
| K.C. Williams | N. Phillip | Trinidad v Windward Islands | Pointe-à-Pierre | 1984–85 |

### THREE

| Batsman | Bowler | | | |
|---|---|---|---|---|
| B.E. Gordon | — | Border v E. Province | Kingwilliamstown | 1903–04 |
| C. Hill | K.M. Ollivier | Australians v New Zealand XI | Wellington | 1904–05 |
| C.P. Carter | R.W. Sievwright | South Africans v Scotland | Edinburgh | 1912 |
| E.B. Alletson | W. Rhodes | Nottinghamshire v Yorkshire | Dewsbury | 1913 |
| F. Barratt | W. Rhodes | Nottinghamshire v Yorkshire | Sheffield | 1919 |
| F.T. Mann | M.W. Tate | Middlesex v Sussex | Hove | 1920 |
| A.W. Carr | F.E. Woolley | Gentlemen v Players | Scarborough | 1922 |
| E.P. Hewetson | T.S. Jennings | Oxford University v Surrey | Oval | 1923 |
| G.F. Earle | — | MCC v Hindus | Bombay | 1926–27 |
| A.G. Liddell | R.W.V. Robins | Northants v Cambridge U. | Northampton | 1928 |
| F. Barratt | V.W.C. Jupp | Nottinghamshire v Northants | Northampton | 1928 |
| E.H. Hendren | J. Iddon | Rest v Lancashire | Oval | 1928 |
| L.N. Constantine | W.W. Whysall | West Indians v Notts | Nottingham | 1928 |
| C. Wright | R.W.V. Robins | Kent v Middlesex | Dover | 1929 |
| A.M. Crawley | V.W.C. Jupp | Oxford U. v Northamptonshire | Wellingborough | 1929 |
| J.M. Hutchinson | C.F. Root | Derbyshire v Worcestershire | Derby | 1931 |
| G.M. Lee | V.W.C. Jupp | Derbyshire v Northants | Northampton | 1931 |
| E.T. Killick | T.W.J. Goddard | Middlesex v Gloucestershire | Clifton | 1932 |
| W.R. Hammond | J. Newman | England v New Zealand | Auckland | 1932–33 |
| G.S. Pearce | E.L.G. Hoad | Sussex v West Indians | Hove | 1933 |
| H.B. Cameron | R. Howorth | South Africans v Worcs | Worcester | 1935 |
| H.B. Cameron | H. Verity | South Africans v Yorkshire | Sheffield | 1935 |

| | | | | |
|---|---|---|---|---|
| H. Larwood | G.S. Boyes | Nottinghamshire v Hampshire | Nottingham | 1935 |
| A.E. Watt | R.A. Sinfield | Kent v Gloucestershire | Gravesend | 1936 |
| W. Voce | T.W.J. Goddard | Nottinghamshire v Gloucs | Nottingham | 1936 |
| H. Gimblett | P.F. Jackson | Somerset v Worcestershire | Yeovil | 1936 |
| R.T.D. Perks | A.P. Freeman | Worcestershire v Kent | Worcester | 1936 |
| R.T.D. Perks | W. Murray-Wood | Worcestershire v Oxford U. | Oxford | 1936 |
| H.L. Hazell | H. Verity | Somerset v Yorkshire | Bath | 1936 |
| J.C. Clay | James Langridge | Glamorgan v Sussex | Hastings | 1937 |
| D.G. Bradman | S.W.L. Putman | Australian XI v Tasmania | Hobart | 1937–38 |
| T.L. Pritchard | L.T. Groves | Wellington v Otago | Dunedin | 1937–38 |
| D.A.N. McRae | C.C. Burke | Canterbury v Auckland | Auckland | 1937–38 |
| C.I.J. Smith | R.A. Sinfield | Middlesex v Gloucestershire | Bristol | 1938 |
| L.L. Wilkinson | R. Howorth | Lancashire v Worcestershire | Manchester | 1938 |
| A.E. Watt | S.H. Martin | Kent v Worcestershire | Gillingham | 1939 |
| A.W. Wellard | D.V.P. Wright | Somerset v Kent | Maidstone | 1939 |
| H.T. Bartlett | E.P. Robinson | Sussex v Yorkshire | Bradford | 1947 |
| K.R. Miller | C.J. Knott | Australians v Hampshire | Southampton | 1948 |
| R.T.D. Perks | J.M. Sims | Worcestershire v Middlesex | Lord's | 1948 |
| K.J. Grieves | G.O. Rabone | Lancashire v New Zealanders | Manchester | 1949 |
| G.J. Whittaker | V. Broderick | Surrey v Northamptonshire | Northampton | 1949 |
| A.W. Wellard | W.E. Hollies | Somerset v Warwickshire | Birmingham | 1949 |
| G.E.E. Lambert | R.O. Jenkins | Gloucestershire v Worcs | Dudley | 1949 |
| H. Gimblett | J.E. McConnon | Somerset v Glamorgan | Ebbw Vale | 1951 |
| C.J. Scott | E. Smith | Gloucestershire v Derbyshire | Buxton | 1952 |
| W.S. Surridge | J.T. Ikin | South v North | Kingston upon Thames | 1952 |
| R.T. Simpson | R. Illingworth | MCC v Yorkshire | Scarborough | 1953 |
| J.H. de Courcy | W.T. Greensmith | Australians v Essex | Southend | 1953 |
| J.V. Wilson | J.M. Allan | Yorkshire v Kent | Scarborough | 1956 |
| T.G. Evans | I.W. Johnson | T.N. Pearce's XI v Australians | Scarborough | 1956 |
| T.W. Graveney | R. Maragh | Duke of Norfolk's XI v Jamaica | Kingston | 1956–57 |
| M.H. Mankad | R.R. Shelke | Rajasthan v Vidarbha | Udaipur | 1957–58 |
| D.B. Close | T. Greenhough | Yorkshire v MCC | Lord's | 1959 |
| J.B. Mortimore | J.S. Manning | England XI v Commonwealth | Hastings | 1959 |
| D.M. Young | J.D. Piachaud | Gloucestershire v Oxford U. | Bristol | 1960 |
| L.J. Coldwell | E.A. Bedser | Worcestershire v Surrey | Oval | 1961 |
| D.J. Shepherd | E. Smith | Glamorgan v Derbyshire | Cardiff | 1961 |
| K.F. Barrington | S.A. Durani | MCC v Rajasthan | Jaipur | 1961–62 |
| B.N. Jarman | K.N. Slater | S. Australia v W. Australia | Adelaide | 1962–63 |
| R.C. White | I.J. Davison | Gloucestershire v Notts | Nottingham | 1963 |
| D. Wilson | F.J. Titmus | Yorkshire v MCC | Scarborough | 1965 |
| D. Kenyon | B.A. Langford | Worcestershire v Somerset | Kidderminster | 1965 |
| F.S. Trueman | D. Shackleton | Yorkshire v Hampshire | Middlesbrough | 1965 |
| A.S. Brown | B.A. Langford | Gloucestershire v Somerset | Taunton | 1967 |
| Shafqat Rana | Afaq Hussain | Khairpur XI v PWD | Sukkur | 1967–68 |
| A. Buss | E. Smith | Sussex v Derbyshire | Chesterfield | 1968 |
| R.M. Edwards | M.C. Carew | Governor-General's XI v WI | Auckland | 1968–69 |
| F.S. Goldstein | J. Simmons | Oxford University v Lancashire | Oxford | 1969 |
| R.W. Marsh | A.A. Mallett | W. Australia v S. Australia | Adelaide | 1972–73 |
| J.D. Inchmore | J.B. Mortimore | Worcestershire v Gloucs | Cheltenham | 1973 |
| E.E. Hemmings | Intikhab Alam | Warwickshire v Pakistanis | Birmingham | 1974 |
| J.H. Edrich | F.M. Francke | MCC v Queensland | Brisbane | 1974–75 |
| F.C. Hayes | G.A. Cope | Lancashire v Yorkshire | Leeds | 1975 |
| I.V.A. Richards | R.G. Paulsen | West Indians v W. Australia | Perth | 1975–76 |
| H.R. Moseley | P. Willey | Somerset v Northamptonshire | Northampton | 1976 |

*(Hit five consecutive sixes off Willey; the last 3 balls of one over, first two of his next)*

| | | | | |
|---|---|---|---|---|
| K.S. McEwan | M.E. Allbrook | Essex v Cambridge U. | Cambridge | 1977 |
| M.G. Burgess | R.W. Anderson | Auckland v Central Districts | Wanganui | 1977–78 |
| Ashraf Ali | Abdul Qadir | Universities v Habib Bank | Lahore | 1977–78 |
| E. Schmidt | A.H. Jordaan | OFS v Northern Transvaal | Bloemfontein | 1978–79 |
| A.J. Lamb | A.J. Traicos | Western Province v Rhodesia | Cape Town | 1978–79 |
| Imran Khan | R.G. Williams | Sussex v Northamptonshire | Northampton | 1979 |
| Zaheer Abbas | D. Breakwell | Gloucestershire v Somerset | Taunton | 1979 |
| I.T. Botham | D.A. Graveney | Somerset v Gloucestershire | Taunton | 1980 |
| S.T. Clarke | Mohammad Nazir | West Indies v Pakistan | Faisalabad | 1980–81 |
| P.W.G. Parker | A.I. Kallicharran | Sussex v Warwickshire | Birmingham | 1982 |
| G.W. Humpage | D. Lloyd | Warwickshire v Lancashire | Southport | 1982 |
| K.S. McEwan | S.P. Sutcliffe | Essex v Warwickshire | Colchester | 1982 |

| Batsman | Bowler | | | |
|---|---|---|---|---|
| I.T. Botham | S.P. Sutcliffe | Somerset v Warwickshire | Taunton | 1982 |
| (On two occasions in same innings) | | | | |
| J. Garner | C.E. Waller | Somerset v Sussex | Taunton | 1983 |
| G.B. Stevenson | {N.G. Cowley (2), J.W Southern (1)} | }Yorkshire v Hampshire | Southampton | 1983 |
| G. Fowler | J.J. Whitaker | Lancashire v Leicestershire | Manchester | 1983 |
| D.W. Hookes | J.D. Thompson | Australian XI v Leeward Is | Basseterre | 1983–84 |
| J.E. Emburey | R.L.S. Armitage | W.Province v E.Province | Cape Town | 1983–84 |
| G.S. Le Roux | M.K. Bore | Sussex v Nottinghamshire | Hove | 1984 |
| M.P. Maynard | P. Carrick | Glamorgan v Yorkshire | Swansea | 1985 |
| M.A. Lynch | J.W. Lloyds | Surrey v Gloucestershire | Oval | 1985 |

**MOST SIXES IN A MATCH**

17   W.J. Stewart          Warwickshire v Lancashire          Blackpool          1959
His innings of 155 and 125 included 10 sixes and 7 sixes respectively

**MOST SIXES IN A SEASON**

| 80 | I.T. Botham | Somerset | 1985 |
|---|---|---|---|
| 66 | A.W. Wellard | Somerset | 1935 |
| 57 | A.W. Wellard | Somerset | 1936 |
| 57 | A.W. Wellard | Somerset | 1938 |
| 51 | A.W. Wellard | Somerset | 1933 |
| 49 | J.H. Edrich | Surrey | 1965 |
| 49 | I.V.A. Richards | Somerset | 1985 |
| 48 | A.W. Carr | Nottinghamshire | 1925 |
| 46 | F. Barratt | Nottinghamshire | 1928 |
| 46 | H.T. Bartlett | Sussex | 1938 |

**MOST RUNS FROM STROKES WORTH FOUR OR MORE IN AN INNINGS**

| Runs | 6s | 5s | 4s | | | | |
|---|---|---|---|---|---|---|---|
| 272 | — | — | 68 | P.A. Perrin (343*) | Essex v Derbyshire | Chesterfield | 1904 |
| 262 | 1 | — | 64 | A.C. MacLaren (424) | Lancashire v Somerset | Taunton | 1895 |
| 256 | — | — | 64 | Hanif Mohammad (499) | Karachi v Bahawalpur | Karachi | 1958–59 |
| 238 | 5 | — | 52 | J.H. Edrich (310*) | England v New Zealand | Leeds | 1965 |
| 230 | 15 | — | 35 | J.R. Reid (296) | Wellington v N. Districts | Wellington | 1962–63 |
| 220 | — | — | 55 | C.W. Gregory (383) | New South Wales v Queensland | Brisbane | 1906–07 |
| 218 | 1 | — | 53 | G.H. Hirst (341) | Yorkshire v Leicestershire | Leicester | 1905 |
| 216 | 8 | — | 42 | I.V.A. Richards (322) | Somerset v Warwickshire | Taunton | 1985 |
| 212 | — | — | 53 | A.W. Nourse (304*) | Natal v Transvaal | Johannesburg | 1919–20 |
| 212 | 4 | — | 47 | C.G. Macartney (345) | Australians v Nottinghamshire | Nottingham | 1921 |
| 208 | 4 | — | 46 | D.G. Bradman (369) | South Australia v Tasmania | Adelaide | 1935–36 |
| 206 | 1 | — | 50 | B.B. Nimbalkar (443*) | Maharashtra v Kathiawar | Poona | 1948–49 |
| 204 | — | — | 51 | W.G. Grace (344) | MCC v Kent | Canterbury | 1876 |
| 203 | — | 3 | 47 | A. Ducat (306*) | Surrey v Oxford University | Oval | 1919 |
| 202 | 3 | — | 46 | B. Sutcliffe (385) | Otago v Canterbury | Christchurch | 1952–53 |
| 202 | 3 | — | 46 | J.M. Brearley (312*) | MCC U-25 XI v North Zone | Peshawar | 1966–67 |
| 202 | 13 | — | 31 | C.G. Greenidge (273*) | D.H. Robins' XI v Pakistanis | Eastbourne | 1974 |
| 200 | 4 | — | 44 | C.R.N. Maxwell (268) | Sir J. Cahn's XI v Leicestershire | Nottingham | 1935 |
| 198 | 5 | — | 42 | D.C.S. Compton (300) | MCC v N.E. Transvaal | Benoni | 1948–49 |
| 198 | 1 | — | 48 | B.A. Richards (356) | S. Australia v W. Australia | Perth | 1970–71 |
| 196 | — | — | 49 | P. Holmes (275) | Yorkshire v Warwickshire | Bradford | 1928 |
| 196 | — | — | 49 | D.G. Bradman (452*) | New South Wales v Queensland | Sydney | 1929–30 |
| 196 | 2 | — | 46 | S.M. Gavaskar (340) | Bombay v Bengal | Bombay | 1981–82 |
| 194 | 3 | — | 44 | V.T. Trumper (293) | Australians v Canterbury | Christchurch | 1913–14 |
| 193 | 1 | 7 | 38 | R. Abel (357*) | Surrey v Somerset | Oval | 1899 |
| 192 | — | — | 48 | J.T. Brown (300) | Yorkshire v Derbyshire | Chesterfield | 1898 |
| 192 | — | — | 48 | J. Tunnicliffe (243) | Yorkshire v Derbyshire | Chesterfield | 1898 |
| 192 | 2 | — | 45 | D.P.B. Morkel (251) | Sir J. Cahn's XI v S. Americans | Nottingham | 1932 |
| 192 | 10 | — | 33 | W.R. Hammond (336*) | England v New Zealand | Auckland | 1932–33 |
| 190 | 1 | — | 46 | P. Holmes (277*) | Yorkshire v Northamptonshire | Harrogate | 1921 |
| 190 | 3 | — | 43 | R.H. Moore (316) | Hampshire v Warwickshire | Bournemouth | 1937 |
| 189 | — | 1 | 46 | W.W. Read (338) | Surrey v Oxford University | Oval | 1888 |
| 188 | — | — | 47 | W.H. Ashdown (305*) | Kent v Derbyshire | Dover | 1935 |

| Runs | 6s | 5s | 4s | | | | |
|------|----|----|----|----|---|---|---|
| 186 | 1 | — | 45 | W.H. Ashdown (332) | Kent v Essex | Brentwood | 1934 |
| 184 | 2 | — | 43 | F.E. Woolley (305*) | MCC v Tasmania | Hobart | 1911–12 |
| 184 | — | — | 46 | D.G. Bradman (334) | Australia v England | Leeds | 1930 |
| 184 | 2 | — | 43 | D.G. Bradman (304) | Australia v England | Leeds | 1934 |
| 181 | — | 1 | 44 | F.R. Foster (305*) | Warwickshire v Worcestershire | Dudley | 1914 |
| 180 | — | — | 45 | J.T. Brown (311) | Yorkshire v Sussex | Sheffield | 1897 |
| 180 | — | — | 45 | R.M. Poore (304) | Hampshire v Somerset | Taunton | 1899 |

## HIGHEST PROPORTION OF BOUNDARIES IN AN INNINGS

| 6s | 4s | | Inns | | | | |
|----|----|------|------|----|---|---|---|
| 5 | 3 | (42) | 42 | A.E. Watt | Kent v Nottinghamshire | Nottingham | 1933 |
| 1 | 9 | (42) | 42 | H.L. Johnson | Derbyshire v Hampshire | Southampton | 1960 |
| 4 | 5 | (44) | 44 | P.T. Marner | Lancashire v Nottinghamshire | Southport | 1960 |
| — | 11 | (44) | 44 | M.J. Harris | Nottinghamshire v Yorkshire | Bradford | 1976 |
| 2 | 8 | (44) | 46 | Majid Khan | PIA v National Bank | Lahore | 1976–77 |
| — | 11 | (44) | 47 | K.S. Ranjitsinhji | Gentlemen v Players | Lord's | 1896 |
| 4 | 5 | (44) | 48 | C.C. Inman | Leicestershire v Worcs | Leicester | 1968 |
| — | 11 | (44) | 48 | Intikhab Alam | Pakistan v Australia | Melbourne | 1972–73 |
| 1 | 10 | (46) | 48* | N.J.N. Hawke | S. Australia v Queensland | Adelaide | 1965–66 |
| — | 12 | (48) | 49 | V. Telang | Vidarbha v Maharashtra | Poona | 1972–73 |
| — | 12 | (48) | 51 | F.W. Terry | Somerset v Hampshire | Southampton | 1884 |
| 6 | 3 | (48) | 51 | D.J. Shepherd | Glamorgan v Australians | Swansea | 1961 |
| 3 | 8 | (50) | 51 | J.W. Southern | Hampshire v Gloucestershire | Basingstoke | 1978 |
| 1 | 11 | (50) | 53 | Intikhab Alam | Surrey v Somerset | Oval | 1970 |
| 3 | 8 | (50) | 53 | R.W. Marsh | W. Australia v West Indians | Perth | 1975–76 |
| 1 | 11 | (50) | 54* | J.H. de Courcy | Australians v Hampshire | Southampton | 1953 |
| 5 | 5 | (50) | 54 | A.P. Wells | Sussex v Nottinghamshire | Nottingham | 1984 |
| — | 13 | (52) | 55 | V.W.C. Jupp | Northamptonshire v Notts | Nottingham | 1928 |
| — | 13 | (52) | 56 | B.A. Edgar | N. Zealanders v D.H. Robins' XI | Eastbourne | 1978 |
| 7 | 3 | (54) | 57* | D.A. Sparks | Orange Free State v MCC | Bloemfontein | 1938–39 |
| 5 | 6 | (54) | 57 | D.L. Bairstow | Yorkshire v Leicestershire | Harrogate | 1983 |
| — | 14 | (56) | 59* | B. Hedges | Glamorgan v Warwickshire | Birmingham | 1962 |
| 4 | 8 | (56) | 61 | O.W. Herman | Hampshire v Somerset | Wells | 1937 |
| 5 | 7 | (58) | 62 | D.M. Sayer | Oxford U. v Nottinghamshire | Oxford | 1959 |
| 3 | 10 | (58) | 62 | D.L. Hays | Cambridge U. v Glamorgan | Cardiff | 1966 |
| 2 | 12 | (60) | 62 | J.B. Statham | Lancashire v Leicestershire | Manchester | 1955 |
| 4 | 9 | (60) | 66 | E.J. Lewis | Glamorgan v Cambridge U. | Pontypridd | 1965 |
| 3 | 11 | (62) | 67 | A.G.E. Ealham | Kent v Warwickshire | Dartford | 1972 |
| — | 16 | (64) | 69* | J.L. Hendriks | W. Indians v Minor Counties | Stoke-on-Trent | 1969 |
| 4 | 10 | (64) | 70 | K.J. Hughes | Australians v Sussex | Hove | 1981 |
| — | 17 | (68) | 70 | T.R. Veivers | Queensland v W. Australia | Brisbane | 1965–66 |
| — | 17 | (68) | 76 | D.L. Amiss | Warwickshire v Glamorgan | Birmingham | 1980 |
| — | 17 | (68) | 77 | P.F. Warner | Middlesex v Somerset | Taunton | 1907 |
| 2 | 14 | (68) | 78* | D.P. Hughes | Lancashire v Northants | Southport | 1971 |
| 4 | 11 | (68) | 79 | T.R. Veivers | Australians v Kent | Canterbury | 1964 |
| 6 | 9 | (72) | 79 | O.G. Smith | West Indians v L.E.G. Ames's XI | Hastings | 1957 |
| 7 | 8 | (74) | 81 | C.G. Pepper | NSW v Queensland | Brisbane | 1939–40 |
| — | 19 | (76) | 82 | A.E. Wilson | Gloucestershire v Worcs | Cheltenham | 1953 |
| 2 | 16 | (76) | 84 | T.I. Barwell | Somerset v Glamorgan | Weston-s-Mare | 1965 |
| — | 19 | (76) | 85* | B.C. Rose | Somerset v Gloucestershire | Bath | 1981 |
| 5 | 12 | (78) | 86 | L.C. Eastman | Essex v Glamorgan | Westcliff | 1937 |
| 2 | 17 | (80) | 86 | R.A. Woolmer | Kent v Derbyshire | Derby | 1971 |
| — | 21 | (84) | 88 | B.R. Knight | Essex v Warwickshire | Birmingham | 1962 |
| 8 | 9 | (84) | 93 | M.J. Procter | Gloucestershire v Somerset | Taunton | 1979 |
| 2 | 18 | (84) | 95 | M.J. Procter | Gloucestershire v Derbyshire | Cheltenham | 1972 |
| — | 21 | (84) | 96 | P.J.P. Burge | Australians v Middlesex | Lord's | 1964 |
| — | 21 | (84) | 99 | E.R. Dexter | Sussex v Kent | Tunbridge Wells | 1959 |
| 7 | 12 | (90) | 100 | R.N.S. Hobbs | Essex v Australians | Chelmsford | 1975 |
| 9 | 9 | (90) | 100 | I.V.A. Richards | West Indians v Glamorgan | Swansea | 1980 |
| 5 | 15 | (90) | 102 | M.J. Procter | Gloucestershire v Surrey | Cheltenham | 1979 |
| 5 | 17 | (98) | 105 | S.J. O'Shaughnessy | Lancashire v Leicestershire | Manchester | 1983 |
| 9 | 11 | (98) | 110 | B.L. Cairns | Otago v Wellington | Lower Hutt | 1979–80 |
| 5 | 17 | (98) | 113* | P.G.H. Fender | Surrey v Northamptonshire | Northampton | 1920 |
| — | 25 | (100) | 115 | G.J. Bonnor | Australians v Yorkshire | Bradford | 1888 |

| 6s | 4s | Inns | | | | |
|----|----|------|---|---|---|---|
| 5 | 19 | (106) 118 | R.M. Prideaux | South v North | Blackpool | 1961 |
| 1 | 25 | (106) 120 | K.J. Key | H.D.G. Leveson Gower's XI v Oxford University | Oxford | 1902 |
| 7 | 16 | (106) 122 | I.T. Botham | England XI v Central Zone | Indore | 1981–82 |
| 1 | 25 | (106) 126 | K.L. Hutchings | England v Australia | Melbourne | 1907–08 |
| 10 | 12 | (108) 131* | I.T. Botham | Somerset v Warwickshire | Taunton | 1982 |
| — | 27 | (108) 135 | M.C. Cowdrey | Kent v Nottinghamshire | Tunbridge Wells | 1961 |
| 3 | 26 | (122) 137 | R.W. Hooker | Middlesex v Kent | Gravesend | 1959 |
| 12 | 13 | (124) 138* | I.T. Botham | Somerset v Warwickshire | Birmingham | 1985 |
| 5 | 24 | (126) 144 | G.S. Chappell | Australians v Glamorgan | Swansea | 1975 |
| 7 | 22 | (130) 153 | I.V.A. Richards | Somerset v Yorkshire | Sheffield | 1981 |
| 3 | 29 | (134) 160 | W.W. Read | Surrey v Kent | Maidstone | 1881 |
| 1 | 33 | (138) 167 | R.A. McLean | Natal v E. Province | Pietermaritzburg | 1963–64 |
| — | 35 | (140) 173 | J. Whitehouse | Warwickshire v Oxford U. | Oxford | 1971 |
| 7 | 26 | (146) 187 | R.B. Kanhai | Warwickshire v Derbyshire | Coventry | 1970 |
| 7 | 26 | (146) 188 | A.R. Butcher | Surrey v Sussex | Hove | 1978 |
| 3 | 32 | (146) 191 | Majid Khan | Glamorgan v Somerset | Taunton | 1972 |
| 5 | 30 | (150) 191 | G.L. Jessop | Gents of South v Players of South | Hastings | 1907 |
| — | 38 | (152) 197 | J. Whitehouse | Warwickshire v Glamorgan | Birmingham | 1980 |
| 7 | 28 | (154) 201* | C.H. Lloyd | West Indians v Glamorgan | Swansea | 1976 |
| 5 | 34 | (166) 204 | I.V.A. Richards | Somerset v Surrey | Weston-s-Mare | 1977 |
| 6 | 34 | (172) 221* | W.E. Alley | Somerset v Warwickshire | Nuneaton | 1961 |
| — | 44 | (176) 229 | P.R. Carlstein | Transvaal v Cavaliers | Johannesburg | 1962–63 |
| 4 | 38 | (176) 243 | C. Milburn | W. Australia v Queensland | Brisbane | 1968–69 |
| — | 48 | (192) 243 | J. Tunnicliffe | Yorkshire v Derbyshire | Chesterfield | 1898 |
| 4 | 44 | (200) 268 | C.R.N. Maxwell | Sir J. Cahn's XI v Leics | Nottingham | 1935 |
| 13 | 31 | (202) 273* | C.G. Greenidge | D.H. Robins' XI v Pakistanis | Eastbourne | 1974 |
| 15 | 35 | (230) 296 | J.R. Reid | Wellington v N. Districts | Wellington | 1962–63 |
| 5 | 52 | (238) 310* | J.H. Edrich | England v New Zealand | Leeds | 1965 |
| — | 68 | (272) 343* | P.A. Perrin | Essex v Derbyshire | Chesterfield | 1904 |

# SLOW SCORING

## SLOWEST FIFTIES

| Min | | | | |
|-----|---|---|---|---|
| 357 | T.E. Bailey (68) | England v Australia | Brisbane | 1958–59 |
| 350 | C.J. Tavaré (82) | England v Pakistan | Lord's | 1982 |
| 316 | C.P.S. Chauhan (61) | India v Pakistan | Kanpur | 1979–80 |
| 313 | D.J. McGlew (70) | South Africa v Australia | Johannesburg | 1957–58 |
| 310 | B.A. Edgar (55) | New Zealand v Australia | Wellington | 1981–82 |
| 306 | C.J. Tavaré (78) | England v Australia | Manchester | 1981 |
| 302 | D.N. Sardesai (60) | India v West Indies | Bridgetown | 1961–62 |
| 300 | G.S. Camacho (57) | West Indies v England | Bridgetown | 1967–68 |
| 294 | C.L. Smith (91) | England v New Zealand | Auckland | 1983–84 |
| 290 | R.G. Barlow (51) | Lancashire v Kent | Maidstone | 1889 |
| 290 | G. Boycott (63) | England v Pakistan | Lahore | 1977–78 |
| 289 | C.J. Tavaré (56) | England v India | Bombay | 1981–82 |
| 282 | E.D.A.St J. McMorris (73) | West Indies v England | Kingston | 1959–60 |
| 280 | P.E. Richardson (117) | England v South Africa | Johannesburg | 1956–57 |
| 280 | G. Boycott (77) | England v Australia | Perth | 1978–79 |
| 277 | G. Boycott (77) | England v New Zealand | Wellington | 1977–78 |
| 275 | W.M. Lawry (57) | Australia v England | Melbourne | 1962–63 |

*Ijaz Butt (Pakistan) took 367 minutes to score 58 against Australia at Karachi in 1959–60. The time for his fifty is not known.*

## SLOWEST HUNDREDS

| Min | | | | |
|-----|---|---|---|---|
| 557 | Mudassar Nazar (114) | Pakistan v England | Lahore | 1977–78 |
| 545 | D.J. McGlew (105) | South Africa v Australia | Durban | 1957–58 |
| 525 | Hanif Mohammad (142) | Pakistan XI v MCC | Lahore | 1955–56 |
| 488 | P.E. Richardson (117) | England v South Africa | Johannesburg | 1956–57 |
| 487 | C.T. Radley (158) | England v New Zealand | Auckland | 1977–78 |

*Min*

| 484 | D.J. Schonegevel (114*) | Griqualand West v N. Transvaal | Kimberley | 1972–73 |
|-----|-------------------------|-------------------------------|-----------|---------|
| 479 | A. Dunn (100) | Griqualand West v Eastern Province | Kimberley | 1947–48 |
| 468 | Hanif Mohammad (142) | Pakistan v India | Bahawalpur | 1954–55 |
| 460 | Hanif Mohammad (111) | Pakistan v England | Dacca | 1961–62 |
| 458 | K.W.R. Fletcher (122) | England v Pakistan | Oval | 1974 |
| 455 | G.P. Howarth (122) | New Zealand v England | Auckland | 1977–78 |
| 438 | G. Boycott (105) | England v India | Delhi | 1981–82 |
| 437 | D.B. Vengsarkar (146*) | India v Pakistan | Delhi | 1979–80 |
| 435 | J.W. Guy (102) | New Zealand v India | Hyderabad | 1955–56 |
| 434 | M.C. Cowdrey (154) | England v West Indies | Birmingham | 1957 |
| 428 | S.M. Gavaskar (172) | India v England | Bangalore | 1981–82 |
| 420 | W.H. Denton (102) | Northamptonshire v Derbyshire | Derby | 1914 |
| 414 | J.H.B. Waite (134) | South Africa v Australia | Durban | 1957–58 |
| 414 | A.W. Greig (103) | England v India | Calcutta | 1976–77 |
| 409 | M.L. Apte (163*) | India v West Indies | Port-of-Spain | 1952–53 |
| 406 | D.W. Randall (150) | England v Australia | Sydney | 1978–79 |

## SLOWEST DOUBLE HUNDREDS

*Min*

| 652 | A.D. Gaekwad (201) | India v Pakistan | Jullundur | 1983–84 |
|-----|--------------------|------------------|-----------|---------|
| 622 | Nawab of Pataudi jr (200) | South Zone v West Zone | Bombay | 1967–68 |
| 608 | R.B. Simpson (311) | Australia v England | Manchester | 1964 |
| 595 | G.St A. Sobers (226) | West Indies v England | Bridgetown | 1959–60 |
| 584 | Hanif Mohammad (337) | Pakistan v West Indies | Bridgetown | 1957–58 |
| 570 | S.G. Barnes (234) | Australia v England | Sydney | 1946–47 |
| 568 | G.R. Viswanath (222) | India v England | Madras | 1981–82 |
| 559 | B.J. Versfeld (201*) | Natal v Transvaal | Durban | 1965–66 |
| 555 | I.A. Rutherford (222) | Otago v Central Districts | New Plymouth | 1978–79 |
| 552 | G.M. Turner (259) | New Zealand v West Indies | Georgetown | 1971–72 |

## SLOWEST TRIPLE HUNDREDS

*Min*

| 858 | Hanif Mohammad (337) | Pakistan v West Indies | Bridgetown | 1957–58 |
|-----|----------------------|------------------------|------------|---------|
| 753 | R.B. Simpson (311) | Australia v England | Manchester | 1964 |

## SLOWEST INNINGS

| *Runs* | *Min* | | | | |
|--------|-------|---------------|------------------------------------|-------------------|---------|
| 0 | 87 | V.R. Hogg | Rhodesia B v Natal B | Pietermaritzburg | 1979–80 |
| 1* | 98 | N. Gifford | Worcestershire v Sussex | Worcester | 1979 |
| 1 | 102 | G.E. Vivian | Auckland v Canterbury | Christchurch | 1977–78 |
| 4 | 114 | P.A. Nicholls | W. Australia v S. Australia | Adelaide | 1971–72 |
| 4 | 120 | P. Corrall | Leicestershire v Cambridge University | Cambridge | 1930 |
| 4 | 121 | R.T. Hart | New Zealanders v West Indies U-23 XI | St Kitts | 1984–85 |
| 4 | 142 | B.R. Hardie | Essex v Hampshire | Chelmsford | 1974 |
| 5 | 150 | R.G. Barlow | Lancashire v Sussex | Manchester | 1876 |
| 5* | 150 | R.G. Barlow | Lancashire v Nottinghamshire | Nottingham | 1882 |
| 5 | 210 | S. Aikut | Maharaja of Cooch Behar's XI v Lord Willingdon's XI | Poona | 1918–19 |
| 17 | 215 | R.G. Barlow | Lancashire v Nottinghamshire | Manchester | 1888 |
| 19 | 217 | M.D. Crowe | New Zealand v Sri Lanka | Colombo | 1983–84 |
| 21 | 332 | Vivek S. Hazare | Rest v Hindus | Bombay | 1943–44 |
| 31 | 450 | T. Pierpoint | Sussex v Kent | Sevenoaks | 1827 |
| 68 | 458 | T.E. Bailey | England v Australia | Brisbane | 1958–59 |
| 89 | 466 | C.J. Tavaré | England v Australia | Perth | 1982–83 |
| 99 | 505 | M.L. Jaisimha | India v Pakistan | Kanpur | 1960–61 |
| 105 | 575 | D.J. McGlew | South Africa v Australia | Durban | 1957–58 |
| 114 | 591 | Mudassar Nazar | Pakistan v England | Lahore | 1977–78 |
| 142 | 630 | Hanif Mohammad | Pakistan XI v MCC | Lahore | 1955–56 |
| 158 | 648 | C.T. Radley | England v New Zealand | Auckland | 1977–78 |
| 172 | 708 | S.M. Gavaskar | India v England | Bangalore | 1981–82 |
| 259 | 704 | G.M. Turner | New Zealand v West Indies | Georgetown | 1971–72 |
| 337 | 970 | Hanif Mohammad | Pakistan v West Indies | Bridgetown | 1957–58 |

# FEWEST BOUNDARIES IN AN INNINGS

## NO BOUNDARIES

*Runs*

| | | | | |
|---|---|---|---|---|
| 112 | R. Iddison | Yorkshire v Cambridgeshire | Hunslet, Leeds | 1869 |

*He scored 15 threes.*

| | | | | |
|---|---|---|---|---|
| 104 | A.W. Ridley | Hampshire v Kent | Faversham | 1876 |

*He hit 14 threes, 15 twos and 32 ones.*

| | | | | |
|---|---|---|---|---|
| 103 | A. Hill | Orange Free State v Griqualand West | Bloemfontein | 1976–77 |
| 100 | P.A. Hibbert | Victoria v Indians | Melbourne | 1977–78 |
| 84 | W.M. Lawry | Australia v England | Brisbane | 1970–71 |
| 84* | A.V. Avery | Essex v Derbyshire | Southend | 1939 |
| 77 | G. Boycott | England v Australia | Perth | 1978–79 |
| 74* | H.A. Pawson | Oxford University v Somerset | Bath | 1948 |
| 72 | R.A. Sinfield | Gloucestershire v Sussex | Cheltenham | 1937 |
| 67 | E.A.B. Rowan | South Africa v England | Durban | 1938–39 |
| 59 | F.M. Engineer | India v England | Oval | 1971 |
| 56 | W. Bardsley | Australia v South Africa | Nottingham | 1912 |
| 51 | J.L. Hopwood | Lancashire v Gloucestershire | Gloucester | 1935 |

*G. Boycott's innings included one four but it was all-run and included two runs from an overthrow.*

## ONLY ONE BOUNDARY

*Runs*

| | | | | |
|---|---|---|---|---|
| 118 | W.M. Woodfull | Australians v Surrey | Oval | 1926 |
| 116 | H.V. Page | Gloucestershire v Somerset | Moreton-in-Marsh | 1885 |
| 102 | A.W. Shipman | Leicestershire v Essex | Leyton | 1925 |
| 97* | T.N. Pearce | Essex v Northamptonshire | Colchester | 1935 |

## ONLY TWO BOUNDARIES

*Runs*

| | | | | |
|---|---|---|---|---|
| 157 | C.P.S. Chauhan | Indians v Victoria | Melbourne | 1977–78 |
| 132 | N.W. Hill | Nottinghamshire v Lancashire | Manchester | 1967 |
| 130 | W.N. Slack | Middlesex v Warwickshire | Lord's | 1981 |
| 120 | P.A. Gibb | England v South Africa | Durban | 1938–39 |
| 116 | C.A. Milton | MCC v Victoria | Melbourne | 1958–59 |
| 115 | A.R. Morris | Australian XI v MCC | Melbourne | 1946–47 |
| 112 | G. Gunn | Nottinghamshire v Essex | Leyton | 1924 |
| 112 | G.L. Willatt | Cambridge University v Middlesex | Cambridge | 1946 |
| 100 | Mushtaq Ali | Holkar v Hyderabad | Indore | 1950–51 |

*N.W. Hill's innings included only one four in the first 100 runs.*

## AN HOUR BEFORE SCORING FIRST RUN

*Min*

| | | | | |
|---|---|---|---|---|
| 97 | T.G. Evans (10*) | England v Australia | Adelaide | 1946–47 |
| 87 | V.R. Hogg (0) | Rhodesia B v Natal B | Pietermaritzburg | 1979–80 |
| 82 | P.I. Pocock (13) | England v West Indies | Georgetown | 1967–68 |
| 81 | E.J.W. Jackson (4) | Cambridge U. v Oxford U. | Lord's | 1974 |
| 75 | J. Vine (57) | Sussex v Nottinghamshire | Hove | 1901 |
| 74 | J.T. Murray (3*) | England v Australia | Sydney | 1962–63 |
| 74 | J. Simmons (0) | Lancashire v Yorkshire | Sheffield | 1969 |
| 73 | B.J. Versfeld (201*) | Natal v Transvaal | Durban | 1965–66 |
| 73 | P.J. Stimpson (20) | Worcestershire v Leicestershire | Worcester | 1971 |
| 72 | F.H. Vigar (3*) | Essex v Hampshire | Portsmouth | 1946 |
| 71 | M. Watkinson (3) | Lancashire v Nottinghamshire | Nottingham | 1983 |
| 70 | R.G. Barlow (5*) | Lancashire v Nottinghamshire | Nottingham | 1882 |
| 70 | W.L. Murdoch (17) | Australia v England | Sydney | 1882–83 |
| 70 | W.A. Humphreys (0*) | Sussex v Kent | Hove | 1892 |
| 69 | R.M. Hogg (7*) | Australia v West Indies | Adelaide | 1984–85 |
| 68 | D. Ward (0) | Glamorgan v Gloucestershire | Newport | 1956 |
| 68 | A. Hill (31) | Derbyshire v Kent | Derby | 1977 |
| 67 | J.M. Prodger (4) | Kent v Surrey | Blackheath | 1958 |
| 67 | C.J. Tavaré (82) | England v Pakistan | Lord's | 1982 |
| 67 | J.M. Parker (3) | Northern Districts v Wellington | Wellington | 1982–83 |
| 66 | B. Wood (4) | Derbyshire v Northamptonshire | Northampton | 1980 |
| 66 | J.G. Wright (38) | New Zealand v Australia | Wellington | 1981–82 |
| 65 | R.G. Barlow (0) | A. Shrewsbury's XI v NSW | Sydney | 1886–87 |

*Min*

| | | | |
|---|---|---|---|
| 65 | Shujauddin (45) | Pakistan v Australia | Lahore | 1959–60 |
| 65 | A. Buss (5*) | Sussex v Yorkshire | Bradford | 1965 |
| 65 | K.M.A. de Costa (12) | Sri Lanka v MCC | Colombo | 1972–73 |
| 64 | R. McDonald (7) | Western Province v Natal | Pietermaritzburg | 1955–56 |
| 63 | R.W. Barber (22) | Lancashire v Kent | Gravesend | 1959 |
| 63 | G.B. Lawrence (60*) | Rhodesia v Worcestershire | Bulawayo | 1964–65 |
| 63 | C.J. Tavaré (9) | England v Australia | Perth | 1982–83 |
| 62 | D.J. McGlew (0) | Natal v Transvaal | Johannesburg | 1955–56 |
| 61 | H.D. Davies (0*) | Glamorgan v Middlesex | Lord's | 1960 |
| 61 | M.J. Harris (2) | Middlesex v Leicestershire | Loughborough | 1965 |
| 61 | R.P. Hodson (11) | Cambridge University v Surrey | Cambridge | 1973 |
| 61 | J. Roundell (0*) | Cambridge University v Surrey | Cambridge | 1973 |
| 60 | R.G. Barlow (34*) | Lancashire v Nottinghamshire | Nottingham | 1876 |
| 60 | A.C. Bannerman (14) | Australians v England XI | Harrogate | 1888 |
| 60 | J.N. Fowke (19*) | Auckland v Canterbury | Christchurch | 1893–94 |
| 60 | E. Smith (0*) | Yorkshire v Essex | Leyton | 1905 |
| 60 | S. O'Linn (11) | South Africans v Kent | Canterbury | 1960 |
| 60 | K. Howard (2) | Lancashire v Warwickshire | Manchester | 1963 |
| 60 | A.M. Beddow (39) | Lancashire v Somerset | Taunton | 1965 |
| 60 | R. Palmer (0*) | Somerset v Glamorgan | Glastonbury | 1969 |
| 60 | D. Williams (4) | Oxford University v Hampshire | Oxford | 1971 |
| 60 | R.P. Hodson (15) | Cambridge University v Sussex | Cambridge | 1972 |
| 60 | J.E. Emburey (11*) | Middlesex v Lancashire | Lord's | 1978 |
| 60 | M.J.E. Wright (0) | Northern Districts v Wellington | Lower Hutt | 1979–80 |

## AN HOUR WITHOUT ADDING TO A SCORE

*Min*

| | | | |
|---|---|---|---|
| 131 | Shoaib Mohammad (11) | Karachi Blues v Lahore City Whites | Lahore | 1983–84 |
| 93 | Mohsin Khan (97*) | Punjab v England XI | Bahawalpur | 1977–78 |
| 91 | J.J. Crowe (21) | New Zealand v West Indies | Bridgetown | 1984–85 |
| 90 | B. Mitchell (58) | South Africa v Australia | Brisbane | 1931–32 |
| 90 | C.J. Tavaré (89) | England v Australia | Perth | 1982–83 |
| 80 | R.G. Barlow (5*) | Lancashire v Nottinghamshire | Nottingham | 1882 |
| 80 | Hanif Mohammad (142) | Pakistan XI v MCC | Lahore | 1955–56 |
| 79 | T.E. Bailey (8) | England v South Africa | Leeds | 1955 |
| 77 | D.B. Close (20) | England v West Indies | Manchester | 1976 |
| 75 | J. Vine (57) | Sussex v Nottinghamshire | Hove | 1901 |
| 75 | B. Wood (6) | Lancashire v Northamptonshire | Northampton | 1973 |
| 72 | T.E. Bailey (64*) | MCC v Australians | Lord's | 1953 |
| 70 | L. Hall (12*) | Yorkshire v Kent | Canterbury | 1885 |
| 70 | A.C. Bannerman (45*) | New South Wales v Victoria | Melbourne | 1890–91 |
| 70 | D.L. Haynes (9) | West Indies v New Zealand | Auckland | 1979–80 |
| 70 | P.A. Hibbert (119) | Victoria v New South Wales | Sydney | 1979–80 |
| 67 | W.H. Scotton (34) | England v Australia | Oval | 1886 |
| 66 | G.M. Bizzell (13) | Queensland v Victoria | Melbourne | 1963–64 |
| 65 | J. Vine (4) | Sussex v Gloucestershire | Hove | 1902 |
| 65 | A.S.M. Oakman (40) | Sussex v Lancashire | Hastings | 1960 |
| 65 | W.B. Stott (22) | Yorkshire v Surrey | Sheffield | 1960 |
| 65 | Nawab of Pataudi jr (5) | India v England | Bombay | 1972–73 |
| 63 | D.R. Jardine (24) | England v Australia | Brisbane | 1932–33 |
| 63 | W.R. Endean (18) | South Africa v England | Johannesburg | 1956–57 |
| 63 | R.A. Evans (110) | Griqualand West v MCC | Kimberley | 1956–57 |
| 63 | W.R. Playle (18) | New Zealand v England | Leeds | 1958 |
| 63 | G.M. Turner (28) | Otago v Wellington | Dunedin | 1964–65 |
| 63 | P.R. Facoory (7) | Otago v Auckland | Auckland | 1978–79 |
| 63 | J.M. Brearley (48) | England v Australia | Birmingham | 1981 |
| 62 | R. Illingworth (53) | Yorkshire v Lancashire | Sheffield | 1955 |
| 62 | K.F. Barrington (137) | England v New Zealand | Birmingham | 1965 |
| 60 | A.P. Lucas (20) | Gentlemen v Players | Oval | 1882 |
| 60 | W.H. Scotton (46) | Nottinghamshire v Gloucestershire | Nottingham | 1885 |
| 60 | A.C. Bannerman (4) | Australia v England | Sydney | 1886–87 |
| 60 | L. Hall (22) | Yorkshire v Nottinghamshire | Nottingham | 1888 |
| 60 | S. Haigh (31) | Yorkshire v Leicestershire | Leicester | 1905 |
| 60 | R. Aird (26) | Hampshire v Yorkshire | Leeds | 1923 |
| 60 | B. Mitchell (73) | South Africa v England | Johannesburg | 1938–39 |

*Min*

| | | | | |
|---|---|---|---|---|
| 60 | A. Tayfield (38) | Transvaal v MCC | Johannesburg | 1956–57 |
| 60 | T.E. Bailey (80) | England v South Africa | Durban | 1956–57 |
| 60 | M.J. Horton (5*) | Worcestershire v Warwickshire | Dudley | 1957 |
| 60 | R.A.L. Massie (12*) | W. Australia v S. Australia | Perth | 1965–66 |
| 60 | B.L. Reed (5) | Hampshire v Yorkshire | Sheffield | 1970 |
| 60 | G. Barker (29) | Essex v Glamorgan | Cardiff | 1970 |
| 60 | K.W.R. Fletcher (24) | MCC v Combined U's XI | Nagpur | 1976–77 |
| 60 | I.A. Rutherford (43) | Otago v Wellington | Lower Hutt | 1978–79 |
| 60 | H.A. Gomes (5) | West Indies v England | Port-of-Spain | 1980–81 |
| 60 | C.J. Tavaré (82) | England v Pakistan | Lord's | 1982 |

*(Unique second scoreless hour in one innings—67 minutes before scoring)*

| | | | | |
|---|---|---|---|---|
| 60 | A.R. Border (9) | Australia v Pakistan | Faisalabad | 1982–83 |

# LONGEST INDIVIDUAL INNINGS

*Min  Runs*

| Min | Runs | | | | |
|---|---|---|---|---|---|
| 970 | 337 | Hanif Mohammad | Pakistan v West Indies | Bridgetown | 1957–58 |
| 797 | 364 | L. Hutton | England v Australia | Oval | 1938 |
| 762 | 311 | R.B. Simpson | Australia v England | Manchester | 1964 |
| 750 | 350 | Rashid Israr | Habib Bank v National Bank | Lahore | 1976–77 |
| 727 | 307 | R.M. Cowper | Australia v England | Melbourne | 1965–66 |
| 720 | 290 | Zakir Butt | Railways v NWFP | Peshawar | 1972–73 |
| 716 | 268 | G.N. Yallop | Australia v Pakistan | Melbourne | 1983–84 |
| 708 | 262* | G.L. Wight | British Guiana v Barbados | Georgetown | 1951–52 |
| 708 | 172 | S.M. Gavaskar | India v England | Bangalore | 1981–82 |
| 704 | 259 | G.M. Turner | New Zealand v West Indies | Georgetown | 1971–72 |
| 685 | 180 | J.F. Reid | New Zealand v Sri Lanka | Colombo | 1983–84 |
| 685 | 210 | Qasim Omar | Pakistan v India | Faisalabad | 1984–85 |
| 683 | 256 | K.F. Barrington | England v Australia | Manchester | 1964 |
| 682 | 197* | F.M.M. Worrell | West Indies v England | Bridgetown | 1959–60 |
| 680 | 209 | Imtiaz Ahmed | Pakistan v New Zealand | Lahore | 1955–56 |
| 671 | 201 | A.D. Gaekwad | India v Pakistan | Jullundur | 1983–84 |
| 648 | 158 | C.T. Radley | England v New Zealand | Auckland | 1977–78 |
| 647 | 226 | G.St A. Sobers | West Indies v England | Bridgetown | 1959–60 |
| 645 | 219 | K.C. Ibrahim | Bombay v Baroda | Bombay | 1948–49 |
| 644 | 236* | S.M. Gavaskar | India v West Indies | Madras | 1983–84 |
| 642 | 234 | S.G. Barnes | Australia v England | Sydney | 1946–47 |
| 640 | 359* | V.M. Merchant | Bombay v Maharashtra | Bombay | 1943–44 |
| 638 | 222 | G.R. Viswanath | India v England | Madras | 1981–82 |
| 636 | 190 | S. Wettimuny | Sri Lanka v England | Lord's | 1984 |
| 635 | 499 | Hanif Mohammad | Karachi v Bahawalpur | Karachi | 1958–59 |
| 630 | 297* | H. Moses | New South Wales v Victoria | Sydney | 1887–88 |
| 630 | 275* | F.C. Thompson | Queensland v New South Wales | Brisbane | 1930–31 |
| 630 | 142 | Hanif Mohammad | Pakistan XI v MCC | Lahore | 1955–56 |
| 630 | 359 | R.B. Simpson | New South Wales v Queensland | Brisbane | 1963–64 |
| 630 | 311 | Javed Miandad | Karachi Whites v National Bank | Karachi | 1974–75 |
| 629 | 191 | G. Boycott | England v Australia | Leeds | 1977 |
| | | *His hundredth first-class hundred* | | | |
| 628 | 288 | V.S. Hazare | Baroda v Holkar | Baroda | 1946–47 |
| 628 | 290 | Khalid Irtiza | United Bank v Multan | Karachi | 1975–76 |
| 627 | 231 | Mudassar Nazar | Pakistan v India | Hyderabad | 1982–83 |
| 625 | 222 | I.A. Rutherford | Otago v Central Districts | New Plymouth | 1978–79 |
| 622 | 200 | Nawab of Pataudi jr | South Zone v West Zone | Bombay | 1967–68 |
| 621 | 437 | W.H. Ponsford | Victoria v Queensland | Melbourne | 1927–28 |
| 615 | 267 | A. Shrewsbury | Nottinghamshire v Middlesex | Nottingham | 1887 |
| 614 | 365* | G.St A. Sobers | West Indies v Pakistan | Kingston | 1957–58 |
| 612 | 302 | L.G. Rowe | West Indies v England | Bridgetown | 1973–74 |
| 608 | 256 | Salahuddin | Karachi v E. Pakistan Greens | Karachi | 1968–69 |
| 606 | 280* | Javed Miandad | Pakistan v India | Hyderabad | 1982–83 |
| 605 | 166 | G. Shipperd | Western Australia v NSW | Perth | 1982–83 |
| 603 | 259 | G.M. Turner | New Zealanders v Guyana | Georgetown | 1971–72 |
| 602 | 183 | C.A. Davis | West Indies v New Zealand | Bridgetown | 1971–72 |
| 600 | 325 | A. Sandham | England v West Indies | Kingston | 1929–30 |
| 600 | 265 | A.V. Mankad | Bombay v Delhi | Bombay | 1980–81 |

*In addition to Hanif Mohammad's record innings of 970 minutes, the following have batted for over 800 minutes in a match:*

Min

| | | | | | |
|---|---|---|---|---|---|
| 893 | Hanif Mohammad | (111 and 104) | Pakistan v England | Dacca | 1961–62 |
| 810 | H. Sutcliffe | (176 and 127) | England v Australia | Melbourne | 1924–25 |
| 801 | B. Mitchell | (120 and 189*) | South Africa v England | Oval | 1947 |

# MONOPOLISING THE SCORING

## LOWEST TOTAL TO INCLUDE A FIFTY

| | | | | |
|---|---|---|---|---|
| 66 | S. Nazir Ali (52) | Indians v Yorkshire | Harrogate | 1932 |

## LOWEST TOTAL TO INCLUDE A HUNDRED

| | | | | |
|---|---|---|---|---|
| 143 | C.E.B. Rice (105*) | Nottinghamshire v Hampshire | Bournemouth | 1981 |

## LOWEST TOTAL TO INCLUDE A DOUBLE HUNDRED

| | | | | |
|---|---|---|---|---|
| 298 | T.W. Graveney (200) | Gloucestershire v Glamorgan | Newport | 1956 |

## LOWEST TOTAL TO INCLUDE A TRIPLE HUNDRED

| | | | | |
|---|---|---|---|---|
| 387 | V.S. Hazare (309) | Rest v Hindus | Bombay | 1943–44 |

## LOWEST TOTAL TO INCLUDE A QUADRUPLE HUNDRED

| | | | | |
|---|---|---|---|---|
| 793 | W.H. Ponsford (437) | Victoria v Queensland | Melbourne | 1927–28 |

*Only completed innings qualify for the above records.*

### OVER 70% OF AN INNINGS TOTAL

| % | | | | |
|---|---|---|---|---|
| 83.4 | G.M. Turner (141*) | Worcestershire (169) v Glamorgan | Swansea | 1977 |
| 79.8 | V.S. Hazare (309) | Rest (387) v Hindus | Bombay | 1943–44 |
| 79.2 | W.G. Grace (126) | United South (159) v United North | Hull | 1876 |
| 78.9 | A.N. Hornby (45) | MCC (57) v Sussex | Lord's | 1890 |
| 78.7 | C.O.H. Sewell (63*) | Gloucestershire (80) v Sussex | Hove | 1913 |
| 78.7 | S. Nazir Ali (52) | Indians (66) v Yorkshire | Harrogate | 1932 |
| 78.2 | J. Noel (18) | South Australia (23) v Victoria | Melbourne | 1882–83 |
| 78.0 | H. Kingscote (32) | Surrey (41) v Kent | Sevenoaks | 1828 |
| 77.0 | B. Sutcliffe (385) | Otago (500) v Canterbury | Christchurch | 1952–53 |
| 75.8 | G. Barker (85) | Essex (112) v Yorkshire | Sheffield | 1962 |
| 75.3 | G. Wells (55*) | Sussex (73) v MCC | Lord's | 1860 |
| 75.2 | W. Beldham (82) | Surrey (109) v England | Lord's | 1801 |
| 75.1 | W.J. Edrich (127*) | Middlesex (169) v Gloucestershire | Lord's | 1946 |
| 75.0 | F.G. Rogers (69) | Gloucestershire (92) v Hampshire | Southampton | 1924 |
| 74.3 | G.A. Gooch (84) | Essex (113) v Kent | Canterbury | 1984 |
| 74.0 | W.G. Grace (20) | Lord Sheffield's XI (27) v Australians | Sheffield Park | 1890 |
| 73.5 | A. Morton (50) | Derbyshire (68) v Yorkshire | Chesterfield | 1914 |
| 73.4 | C.E.B. Rice (105) | Nottinghamshire (143) v Hampshire | Bournemouth | 1981 |
| 73.2 | E.F. Wright (123) | Demerara (168) v Barbados | Georgetown | 1882–83 |
| 72.8 | D.C.S. Compton (150) | Middlesex (206) v Sussex | Lord's | 1955 |
| 72.2 | N. Pilch (52) | Norfolk (72) v MCC | Lord's | 1820 |
| 71.9 | C.J. Poole (87) | Notts. (121) v Gloucestershire | Bristol | 1960 |
| 71.5 | F.E. Woolley (103*) | Kent (144) v Warwickshire | Folkestone | 1931 |
| 70.9 | Vajesingh (66*) | Saurashtra (93) v Gujarat | Rajkot | 1952–53 |
| 70.8 | F.H.B. Champain (97) | Gloucestershire (137) v Lancashire | Bristol | 1897 |
| 70.8 | A.H. Bakewell (141) | Northamptonshire (199) v Worcs | Northampton | 1935 |
| 70.6 | L. Amarnath (130) | Indians (184) v Essex | Brentwood | 1936 |
| 70.5 | W.G. Grace (122) | South (173) v North | Sheffield | 1869 |
| 70.5 | W. Flowers (67*) | Nottinghamshire (95) v MCC | Lord's | 1894 |
| 70.4 | R.E.S. Wyatt (74*) | Warwickshire (105) v Leicestershire | Birmingham | 1939 |
| 70.3 | F.E. Woolley (161) | Kent (229) v Derbyshire | Canterbury | 1933 |
| 70.2 | C.E. de Trafford (92) | Leicestershire (131) v Yorkshire | Leicester | 1894 |
| 70.1 | J.R. Reid (296) | Wellington (422) v N. Districts | Wellington | 1962–63 |
| 70.0 | E. Smith (70) | Oxford University (100) v MCC | Oxford | 1891 |

## OVER 50% OF THE TOTAL IN EACH INNINGS

| Jas Broadbridge | 63 | 92 | Sussex (121, 168) v Hampshire | Petworth | 1825 |
|---|---|---|---|---|---|
| Jas Broadbridge | 20 | 14 | Sussex (35, 22) v Kent | Sevenoaks | 1828 |
| W.G. Grace | 79 | 116 | Gloucestershire (147, 217) v Notts | Nottingham | 1871 |
| Lord Harris | 80* | 79 | Kent (148, 150) v Yorkshire | Gravesend | 1883 |
| J.T. Tyldesley | 56 | 42 | Lancashire (102, 81) v Australians | Manchester | 1899 |
| C.B. Fry | 88 | 106 | Sussex (159, 212) v Hampshire | Portsmouth | 1901 |
| L.G. Wright | 176 | 122 | Derbyshire (336, 197) v Warwickshire | Birmingham | 1905 |
| C.N. Woolley | 35 | 111 | Northants (63, 205) v Derbyshire | Northampton | 1922 |
| F.S. Lee | 109* | 107 | Somerset (196, 205) v Worcestershire | Worcester | 1938 |
| L.B. Fishlock | 129 | 112 | Surrey (244, 212) v Leicestershire | Leicester | 1946 |
| P.B.H. May | 97 | 175 | Combined Services (188, 337) v Worcs | Worcester | 1949 |
| M.C. Cowdrey | 154 | 34 | Oxford University (270, 63) v Surrey | Oval | 1953 |
| Imtiaz Ahmed | 59 | 105 | Services (101, 183) v Indians | Rawalpindi | 1954–55 |
| T.W. Graveney | 100 | 67 | Gloucestershire (153, 107) v Essex | Romford | 1956 |
| D.B. Carr | 156* | 109 | Derbyshire (257, 191) v Kent | Canterbury | 1959 |
| A. Wharton | 129 | 108 | Leicestershire (247, 201) v Middlesex | Leicester | 1961 |

## MONOPOLISING THE SCORING WHILST AT THE WICKET

This section shows each batsman's innings, followed by the total number of runs added during his time at the wicket.

| 39/39 | J.N. Crawford | Surrey v Somerset | Taunton | 1919 |
|---|---|---|---|---|
| 39/39 | B.D. Wells | Nottinghamshire v Essex | Westcliff | 1961 |
| 40/41 | G.L. Jessop | Gloucestershire v Middlesex | Lord's | 1907 |
| 40/41 | H.R. Moseley | Somerset v Northamptonshire | Northampton | 1976 |
| 43/44 | A.B. Hipkin | Essex v Yorkshire | Leyton | 1929 |
| 44/45 | A.N. Hornby | Lancashire v Nottinghamshire | Nottingham | 1875 |
| 45/46 | P.S. McDonnell | Australians v A. Shaw's XI | Leeds | 1882 |
| 50/51 | E.A. McDonald | Lancashire v Gloucestershire | Manchester | 1926 |
| 51/53 | W.G. Grace | England XI v A. Shaw's XI | Harrogate | 1885 |
| 53/54 | M. Tompkin | Leicestershire v Yorkshire | Leicester | 1947 |
| 53/54 | G.C. Gill | Somerset v Hampshire | Bath | 1902 |
| 56/57 | C.I.J. Smith | Middlesex v Yorkshire | Scarborough | 1936 |
| 57*/59 | C.C. Inman | Leicestershire v Nottinghamshire | Nottingham | 1965 |
| 61*/63 | P.G.H. Fender | Surrey v Sussex | Eastbourne | 1926 |
| 63/65 | G.L. Jessop | Gloucestershire v Yorkshire | Cheltenham | 1895 |
| 66/66 | G.L. Jessop | Gloucestershire v Sussex | Bristol | 1901 |
| 68/69 | B.L. Cairns | New Zealanders v New South Wales | Sydney | 1980–81 |
| 69/70 | P.S. McDonnell | Australians v O.U. & C.U. P.&P. | Portsmouth | 1888 |
| 72/75 | V.T. Hill | Somerset v Middlesex | Lord's | 1900 |
| 73*/80 | A.W. Wellard | Somerset v Glamorgan | Cardiff | 1938 |
| 75/80 | G.L. Jessop | Gloucestershire v Nottinghamshire | Nottingham | 1908 |
| 76/82 | G.L. Jessop | Gloucestershire v Nottinghamshire | Bristol | 1901 |
| 79/85 | S.T. Clarke | Surrey v Lancashire | Manchester | 1981 |
| 82/86 | P.S. McDonnell | Australians v North of England | Manchester | 1888 |
| 84/89 | G.E. Winter | Cambridge University v Surrey | Oval | 1899 |
| 86/92 | Asif Iqbal | Kent v Leicestershire | Canterbury | 1969 |
| 93/102 | M.J. Weston | Worcestershire v Pakistanis | Worcester | 1982 |
| 93/104 | L.B. Fishlock | Surrey v Australians | Oval | 1938 |
| 93/107 | M.J. Procter | Gloucestershire v Somerset | Taunton | 1981 |
| 93/108 | E.R. Dexter | Sussex v Warwickshire | Birmingham | 1960 |
| 95/109 | W.P. Howell | NSW v A.E. Stoddart's XI | Sydney | 1897–98 |
| 96/110 | M.F. Tremlett | Somerset v Gloucestershire | Bristol | 1948 |
| 100/113 | M.D. Crowe | Auckland v Wellington | Auckland | 1982–83 |
| 103/116 | D.C.S. Compton | Rest v England | Canterbury | 1946 |
| 106/120 | G.F. Vernon | Middlesex v Surrey | Lord's | 1880 |
| 109/120 | G.L. Jessop | Gloucestershire v Middlesex | Lord's | 1900 |
| 114*/129 | K.G. Suttle | Sussex v Worcestershire | Eastbourne | 1952 |
| 122/131 | F.R. Brown | Gentlemen v Players | Lord's | 1950 |
| 130*/145 | C.K. Nayudu | Indians v Somerset | Taunton | 1932 |
| 138*/161 | I.T. Botham | Somerset v Warwickshire | Birmingham | 1985 |
| 141*/169 | G.M. Turner | Worcestershire v Glamorgan | Swansea | 1977 |
| 143/173 | S.M.J. Woods | Somerset v Sussex | Eastbourne | 1898 |
| 149/181 | J.J. Lyons | Australians v MCC | Lord's | 1893 |
| 166/185 | Imran Khan | Worcestershire v Northamptonshire | Northampton | 1976 |
| 171*/206 | G.L. Jessop | Cambridge University v Yorkshire | Cambridge | 1899 |
| 174/220 | Hon F.S.G. Calthorpe | Warwickshire v Lancashire | Birmingham | 1925 |

| 183/224 | J.B. Hobbs | Surrey v Warwickshire | Oval | 1914 |
| 189/227 | E.B. Alletson | Nottinghamshire v Sussex | Hove | 1911 |
| 192/227 | W.R. Hammond | Gloucestershire v Hampshire | Southampton | 1927 |
| 200*/256 | R.J. Shastri | Bombay v Baroda | Bombay | 1984–85 |
| 200*/258 | A.W. Nourse | Natal v Western Province | Cape Town | 1907–08 |
| 206/265 | H.H. Massie | Australians v Oxford University | Oxford | 1882 |
| 215/282 | S.M.J. Woods | Somerset v Sussex | Hove | 1895 |
| 220/293 | K.S. Ranjitsinhji | Sussex v Kent | Hove | 1900 |
| 232/300 | S.J. McCabe | Australia v England | Nottingham | 1938 |
| 239/310 | P.S. McDonnell | New South Wales v Victoria | Melbourne | 1886–87 |
| 286/355 | G.L. Jessop | Gloucestershire v Sussex | Hove | 1903 |
| 309/373 | V.S. Hazare | Rest v Hindus | Bombay | 1943–44 |
| 317/462 | W.R. Hammond | Gloucestershire v Nottinghamshire | Gloucester | 1936 |
| 322/479 | I.V.A. Richards | Somerset v Warwickshire | Taunton | 1985 |
| 336*/492 | W.R. Hammond | England v New Zealand | Auckland | 1932–33 |
| 385/500 | B. Sutcliffe | Otago v Canterbury | Christchurch | 1952–53 |
| 424/792 | A.C. MacLaren | Lancashire v Somerset | Taunton | 1895 |

MONOPOLISING A PARTNERSHIP

BQualification for inclusion in this section is as follows: 95% of a partnership adding 50 to 99 runs inclusive, 90% of one adding 100 to 149 runs, 85% of one adding 150 to 199 runs, 80% of one adding 200 to 299 runs, and 70% of one adding 300 runs or more.

| % | Runs | Wkt | Partners (Share of Partnership) | Extras | Match | | |
|---|---|---|---|---|---|---|---|
| 88.6 | 300 | 6th | Vijay S. Hazare (266), Vivek S. Hazare (21) | 13 | Rest v Hindus | Bombay | 1943–44 |
| 77.5 | 307 | 10th | A.F. Kippax (238), J.E.H. Hooker (62) | 7 | New South Wales v Victoria | Melbourne | 1928–29 |
| 74.0 | 328 | 1st | C. Milburn (243), D. Chadwick (76) | 9 | Western Australia v Queensland | Brisbane | 1968–69 |
| 93.4 | 152 | 10th | E.B. Alletson (142), W. Riley (10) | — | Nottinghamshire v Sussex | Hove | 1911 |
| 87.2 | 173 | 9th | F.A. Tarrant (151), S. Aikut (5) | 17 | Maharaja of Cooch Behar's XI v Lord Willingdon's XI | Poona | 1918–19 |
| 95.3 | 107 | 10th | H.J. Enthoven (102), W.F.F. Price (3) | 2 | Middlesex v Sussex | Lord's | 1930 |
| 94.3 | 107 | 8th | B.L. D'Oliveira (101), B.M. Brain (4) | 2 | Worcestershire v Nottinghamshire | Worcester | 1966 |
| 92.1 | 127 | 9th | Imran Khan (117), N. Gifford (10) | — | Worcestershire v Northamptonshire | Northampton | 1976 |
| 91.5 | 119* | 9th | K.G. Suttle (109), P.A. Kelland (5) | 5 | Sussex v Worcestershire | Eastbourne | 1952 |
| 91.4 | 117 | 10th | V. Subramanya (107), B.S. Chandrasekhar (10) | — | Mysore v Madras | Madras | 1966–67 |
| 91.0 | 100* | 10th | D. Tallon (91), G. Noblet (9) | — | D.G. Bradman's XI v A.L. Hassett's XI | Melbourne | 1948–49 |
| 91.0 | 100 | 2nd | S. Jayasinghe (91), B.J. Booth (9) | — | Leicestershire v Northamptonshire | Northampton | 1964 |
| 90.6 | 107 | 2nd | D. Kenyon (97), R.G.A. Headley (10) | — | Worcestershire v Sussex | Eastbourne | 1960 |
| 90.4 | 105 | 4th | J.H. Hampshire (95), P.J. Squires (10) | — | Yorkshire v Surrey | Oval | 1976 |
| 90.2 | 134 | 6th | L.E.G. Ames (121), P. Hearn (11) | 2 | Kent v Gloucestershire | Dover | 1948 |
| 100 | 75 | 10th | R.W.V. Robins (75), J.A. Young (0) | — | MCC v Yorkshire | Scarborough | 1946 |
| 100 | 57* | 7th | J.T. Murray (57), F.J. Titmus (0) | — | Middlesex v Kent | Canterbury | 1970 |
| 100 | 64 | 10th | E.F. Parker (64), V.R. Hogg (0) | — | Rhodesia B v Natal B | Pietermaritzburg | 1979–80 |
| 98.7 | 79 | 10th | D.C.S. Compton (78), L.H. Gray (1) | — | Middlesex v Essex | Lord's | 1939 |
| 98.3 | 59 | 10th | A.K. Davidson (58), D.A. Ford (0) | 1 | New South Wales v Victoria | Sydney | 1961–62 |
| 98.2 | 57 | 10th | C.I.J. Smith (56), L.H. Gray (1) | — | Middlesex v Yorkshire | Scarborough | 1936 |
| 98.0 | 50 | 10th | W.J. Edrich (49), L.H. Gray (1) | — | Middlesex v Surrey | Lord's | 1939 |
| 97.4 | 78 | 8th | K.S. Ranjitsinhji (76), C.H.G. Bland (2) | — | Sussex v Middlesex | Hove | 1900 |
| 97.4 | 79 | 10th | A.W. Greig (77), C.P. Phillipson (1) | 1 | Sussex v Hampshire | Hove | 1972 |
| 97.0 | 67 | 10th | R.W.V. Robins (65), N.F. Turner (0) | 2 | Middlesex v Yorkshire | Lord's | 1937 |
| 96.8 | 64 | 8th | M.L. Jaisimha (62), E.A.S. Prasanna (2) | — | South Zone v North Zone | Bangalore | 1965–66 |
| 96.7 | 61 | 3rd | G.S. Chappell (59), M.J. Kitchen (2) | — | Somerset v Lancashire | Taunton | 1969 |
| 96.6 | 59* | 4th | C.C. Inman (57), P.T. Marner (2) | 1 | Leicestershire v Nottinghamshire | Nottingham | 1965 |
| 96.3 | 55 | 10th | J.A. Snow (53), D.L. Bates (1) | — | Sussex v Somerset | Eastbourne | 1966 |
| 96.3 | 71 | 10th | R.W.V. Robins (68), L.H. Gray (1) | 2 | Middlesex v Essex | Chelmsford | 1937 |
| 95.5 | 67* | 8th | M.J.L. Turnbull (64), A.H. Fabian (3) | — | Cambridge University v Yorkshire | Cambridge | 1929 |
| 95.3 | 86 | 1st | P.S. McDonnell (82), A.C. Bannerman (4) | — | Australians v North of England | Manchester | 1888 |
| 95.3 | 86 | 10th | S.H. Day (82), C.D. Dewe (4) | — | Cambridge University v Sussex | Hove | 1901 |

# 3000 RUNS IN A SEASON

| | | Season | I | NO | Runs | HS | Avge | 100 |
|---|---|---|---|---|---|---|---|---|
| D.C.S. Compton | Middlesex | 1947 | 50 | 8 | 3816 | 246 | 90.85 | 18 |
| W.J. Edrich | Middlesex | 1947 | 52 | 8 | 3539 | 267* | 80.43 | 12 |
| T.W. Hayward | Surrey | 1906 | 61 | 8 | 3518 | 219 | 66.37 | 13 |
| L. Hutton | Yorkshire | 1949 | 56 | 6 | 3429 | 269* | 68.58 | 12 |
| F.E. Woolley | Kent | 1928 | 59 | 4 | 3352 | 198 | 60.94 | 12 |
| H. Sutcliffe | Yorkshire | 1932 | 52 | 7 | 3336 | 313 | 74.13 | 14 |
| W.R. Hammond | Gloucestershire | 1933 | 54 | 5 | 3323 | 264 | 67.81 | 13 |
| E.H. Hendren | Middlesex | 1928 | 54 | 7 | 3311 | 209* | 70.44 | 13 |
| R. Abel | Surrey | 1901 | 68 | 8 | 3309 | 247 | 55.15 | 7 |
| W.R. Hammond | Gloucestershire | 1937 | 55 | 5 | 3252 | 217 | 65.04 | 13 |
| M.J.K. Smith | Warwickshire | 1959 | 67 | 11 | 3245 | 200* | 57.94 | 8 |
| E.H. Hendren | Middlesex | 1933 | 65 | 9 | 3186 | 301* | 56.89 | 11 |
| C.P. Mead | Hampshire | 1921 | 52 | 6 | 3179 | 280* | 69.10 | 10 |
| T.W. Hayward | Surrey | 1904 | 63 | 5 | 3170 | 203 | 54.65 | 11 |
| K.S. Ranjitsinhji | Sussex | 1899 | 58 | 8 | 3159 | 197 | 63.18 | 8 |
| C.B. Fry | Sussex | 1901 | 43 | 3 | 3147 | 244 | 78.67 | 13 |
| K.S. Ranjitsinhji | Sussex | 1900 | 40 | 5 | 3065 | 275 | 87.57 | 11 |
| L.E.G. Ames | Kent | 1933 | 57 | 5 | 3058 | 295 | 58.80 | 9 |
| J.T. Tyldesley | Lancashire | 1901 | 60 | 5 | 3041 | 221 | 55.29 | 9 |
| C.P. Mead | Hampshire | 1928 | 50 | 10 | 3027 | 180 | 75.67 | 13 |
| J.B. Hobbs | Surrey | 1925 | 48 | 5 | 3024 | 266* | 70.32 | 16 |
| G.E. Tyldesley | Lancashire | 1928 | 48 | 10 | 3024 | 242 | 79.57 | 10 |
| W.E. Alley | Somerset | 1961 | 64 | 11 | 3019 | 221* | 56.96 | 11 |
| W.R. Hammond | Gloucestershire | 1938 | 42 | 2 | 3011 | 271 | 75.27 | 15 |
| E.H. Hendren | Middlesex | 1923 | 51 | 12 | 3010 | 200* | 77.17 | 13 |
| H. Sutcliffe | Yorkshire | 1931 | 42 | 11 | 3006 | 230 | 96.96 | 13 |
| J.H. Parks | Sussex | 1937 | 63 | 4 | 3003 | 168 | 50.89 | 11 |
| H. Sutcliffe | Yorkshire | 1928 | 44 | 5 | 3002 | 228 | 76.97 | 13 |

# 2000 RUNS IN AN ENGLISH SEASON

W.G. Grace (2739 runs in 1871) was the first batsman to score 2000 runs in first-class matches in an English season. This aggregate was attained in every season, war years excepted, from 1895 to 1973 inclusive. No one reached this total in 1974, 1975, 1979 or 1980.

| | | | Season | I | NO | Runs | HS | Avge | 100 |
|---|---|---|---|---|---|---|---|---|---|
| Abel, R. | Surrey | (8) | 1895 | 50 | 4 | 2057 | 217 | 44.71 | 5 |
| | | | 1896 | 55 | 3 | 2218 | 231 | 42.65 | 5 |
| | | | 1897 | 50 | 3 | 2099 | 250 | 44.65 | 6 |
| | | | 1898 | 45 | 3 | 2053 | 219 | 48.88 | 7 |
| | | | 1899 | 53 | 3 | 2685 | 357* | 53.70 | 7 |
| | | | 1900 | 49 | 3 | 2592 | 221 | 56.34 | 12 |
| | | | 1901 | 68 | 8 | 3309 | 247 | 55.15 | 7 |
| | | | 1902 | 64 | 8 | 2299 | 179 | 41.05 | 7 |
| Alley, W.E. | Somerset | | 1961 | 64 | 11 | 3019 | 221* | 56.96 | 11 |
| Ames, L.E.G. | Kent | (6) | 1932 | 50 | 7 | 2482 | 180 | 57.72 | 9 |
| | | | 1933 | 57 | 5 | 3058 | 295 | 58.80 | 9 |
| | | | 1934 | 43 | 6 | 2113 | 202* | 57.10 | 5 |
| | | | 1937 | 52 | 4 | 2347 | 201* | 48.89 | 7 |
| | | | 1947 | 42 | 7 | 2272 | 212* | 64.91 | 7 |
| | | | 1949 | 47 | 2 | 2125 | 160 | 47.22 | 7 |
| Amiss, D.L. | Warwickshire | (3) | 1976 | 38 | 6 | 2110 | 203 | 65.93 | 8 |
| | | | 1978 | 41 | 3 | 2030 | 162 | 53.42 | 3 |
| | | | 1984 | 50 | 10 | 2239 | 122 | 55.97 | 6 |
| Armstrong, N.F. | Leicestershire | | 1933 | 54 | 5 | 2113 | 164 | 43.12 | 4 |
| Arnold, J. | Hampshire | | 1934 | 52 | 5 | 2261 | 160 | 48.10 | 7 |
| Ashdown, W.H. | Kent | (2) | 1928 | 55 | 3 | 2247 | 178 | 43.21 | 3 |
| | | | 1934 | 51 | 2 | 2030 | 332 | 41.42 | 6 |
| Atkinson, G. | Somerset | (2) | 1961 | 57 | 1 | 2078 | 146 | 37.10 | 3 |
| | | | 1962 | 63 | 5 | 2075 | 133 | 35.77 | 4 |
| Bailey, T.E. | Essex | | 1959 | 55 | 12 | 2011 | 146 | 46.76 | 6 |
| Bakewell, A.H. | Northamptonshire | | 1933 | 47 | 1 | 2149 | 257 | 46.71 | 7 |
| Barber, W. | Yorkshire | | 1935 | 55 | 4 | 2147 | 255 | 42.09 | 4 |

| | | | Season | I | NO | Runs | HS | Avge | 100 |
|---|---|---|---|---|---|---|---|---|---|
| Bardsley, W. | Australians | (3) | 1909 | 49 | 4 | 2072 | 219 | 46.04 | 6 |
| | | | 1912 | 52 | 6 | 2365 | 184* | 51.41 | 8 |
| | | | 1921 | 41 | 4 | 2005 | 209 | 54.18 | 8 |
| Barling, H.T. | Surrey | | 1946 | 52 | 6 | 2014 | 233* | 43.78 | 6 |
| Barnett, C.J. | Gloucestershire | (4) | 1933 | 59 | 3 | 2280 | 154 | 40.71 | 6 |
| | | | 1934 | 58 | 4 | 2348 | 194 | 43.48 | 6 |
| | | | 1936 | 58 | 3 | 2098 | 204* | 38.14 | 6 |
| | | | 1937 | 65 | 3 | 2489 | 232 | 40.14 | 5 |
| Barrington, K.F. | Surrey | (3) | 1959 | 52 | 6 | 2499 | 186 | 54.32 | 6 |
| | | | 1961 | 42 | 7 | 2070 | 163 | 59.14 | 4 |
| | | | 1967 | 40 | 10 | 2059 | 158* | 68.63 | 6 |
| Berry, G.L. | Leicestershire | | 1937 | 51 | 4 | 2446 | 184* | 52.04 | 7 |
| Bolus, J.B. | Nottinghamshire | (2) | 1963 | 57 | 4 | 2190 | 202* | 41.32 | 5 |
| | | | 1970 | 53 | 9 | 2143 | 147* | 48.70 | 2 |
| Bond, J.D. | Lancashire | | 1962 | 67 | 8 | 2125 | 157 | 36.01 | 5 |
| Bowley, E.H. | Sussex | (4) | 1923 | 66 | 5 | 2180 | 120 | 35.73 | 2 |
| | | | 1927 | 41 | 3 | 2062 | 220 | 54.26 | 4 |
| | | | 1928 | 53 | 1 | 2359 | 188 | 45.36 | 6 |
| | | | 1929 | 57 | 3 | 2360 | 280* | 43.70 | 5 |
| Boycott, G. | Yorkshire | (3) | 1964 | 44 | 4 | 2110 | 177 | 52.75 | 6 |
| | | | 1970 | 42 | 5 | 2051 | 260* | 55.43 | 4 |
| | | | 1971 | 30 | 5 | 2503 | 233 | 100.12 | 13 |
| Bradman, D.G. | Australians | (4) | 1930 | 36 | 6 | 2960 | 334 | 98.66 | 10 |
| | | | 1934 | 27 | 3 | 2020 | 304 | 84.16 | 7 |
| | | | 1938 | 26 | 5 | 2429 | 278 | 115.66 | 13 |
| | | | 1948 | 31 | 4 | 2428 | 187 | 89.92 | 11 |
| Brearley, J.M. | Middlesex | | 1964 | 54 | 5 | 2178 | 169 | 44.44 | 5 |
| Brookes, D. | Northamptonshire | (6) | 1946 | 48 | 5 | 2191 | 200 | 50.95 | 7 |
| | | | 1947 | 55 | 2 | 2217 | 210 | 41.83 | 6 |
| | | | 1949 | 54 | 5 | 2163 | 257 | 44.14 | 7 |
| | | | 1950 | 45 | 6 | 2000 | 171 | 51.28 | 5 |
| | | | 1952 | 54 | 7 | 2229 | 204* | 47.42 | 6 |
| | | | 1955 | 58 | 5 | 2012 | 177 | 37.96 | 3 |
| Brown, G. | Hampshire | | 1926 | 53 | 2 | 2040 | 146 | 40.00 | 6 |
| Brown, S.M. | Middlesex | | 1947 | 60 | 5 | 2078 | 155 | 37.78 | 4 |
| Burnup, C.J. | Kent | | 1902 | 55 | 3 | 2048 | 161 | 39.38 | 6 |
| Carr, A.W. | Nottinghamshire | | 1925 | 49 | 4 | 2338 | 206 | 51.95 | 8 |
| Carr, D.B. | Derbyshire | | 1959 | 60 | 8 | 2292 | 156* | 44.07 | 5 |
| Compton, D.C.S. | Middlesex | (6) | 1939 | 50 | 6 | 2468 | 214* | 56.09 | 8 |
| | | | 1946 | 45 | 6 | 2403 | 235 | 61.61 | 10 |
| | | | 1947 | 50 | 8 | 3816 | 246* | 90.85 | 18 |
| | | | 1948 | 47 | 7 | 2451 | 252* | 61.27 | 9 |
| | | | 1949 | 56 | 4 | 2530 | 182 | 48.65 | 9 |
| | | | 1951 | 40 | 6 | 2193 | 172 | 64.50 | 8 |
| Cook, T.E.R. | Sussex | | 1934 | 45 | 6 | 2132 | 220 | 54.66 | 4 |
| Cowdrey, M.C. | Kent | (2) | 1959 | 44 | 4 | 2008 | 250 | 50.20 | 6 |
| | | | 1965 | 43 | 10 | 2093 | 196* | 63.42 | 5 |
| Cox, G. | Sussex | (2) | 1947 | 56 | 2 | 2032 | 205* | 37.62 | 8 |
| | | | 1950 | 55 | 7 | 2369 | 165* | 49.35 | 6 |
| Crapp, J.F. | Gloucestershire | | 1949 | 48 | 4 | 2014 | 140 | 45.77 | 7 |
| Davies, D.E. | Glamorgan | | 1937 | 52 | 2 | 2012 | 140 | 40.24 | 3 |
| Denton, D. | Yorkshire | (5) | 1904 | 55 | 3 | 2088 | 119 | 40.15 | 3 |
| | | | 1905 | 60 | 3 | 2405 | 172 | 42.19 | 8 |
| | | | 1906 | 60 | 4 | 2287 | 157* | 40.83 | 7 |
| | | | 1911 | 57 | 4 | 2232 | 137* | 42.11 | 6 |
| | | | 1912 | 54 | 4 | 2127 | 211 | 42.54 | 6 |
| Dewes, J.G. | Middlesex | | 1950 | 45 | 4 | 2432 | 212 | 59.31 | 9 |
| Dexter, E.R. | Sussex | (3) | 1959 | 53 | 8 | 2055 | 127 | 45.66 | 7 |
| | | | 1960 | 53 | 2 | 2217 | 157 | 43.47 | 7 |
| | | | 1962 | 47 | 7 | 2148 | 172 | 53.70 | 5 |
| Dipper, A.E. | Gloucestershire | (5) | 1923 | 57 | 6 | 2048 | 252* | 40.15 | 3 |
| | | | 1926 | 63 | 6 | 2147 | 135 | 37.66 | 2 |
| | | | 1927 | 53 | 8 | 2246 | 212 | 49.91 | 7 |
| | | | 1928 | 49 | 6 | 2365 | 188 | 55.00 | 7 |
| | | | 1929 | 50 | 3 | 2218 | 153 | 47.19 | 3 |
| Dodds, T.C. | Essex | | 1947 | 58 | 2 | 2147 | 157 | 38.33 | 1 |

| | | | Season | I | NO | Runs | HS | Avge | 100 |
|---|---|---|---|---|---|---|---|---|---|
| Doggart, G.H.G. | Sussex | | 1949 | 51 | 6 | 2063 | 219* | 45.84 | 5 |
| Dollery, H.E. | Warwickshire | (2) | 1949 | 48 | 4 | 2084 | 200 | 47.36 | 6 |
| | | | 1952 | 51 | 2 | 2073 | 212 | 42.30 | 4 |
| Donnelly, M.P. | New Zealanders | | 1949 | 45 | 8 | 2287 | 206 | 61.81 | 5 |
| Ducat, A. | Surrey | | 1930 | 48 | 6 | 2067 | 218 | 49.21 | 5 |
| Duleepsinhji, K.S. | Sussex | (3) | 1929 | 51 | 3 | 2545 | 246 | 53.02 | 8 |
| | | | 1930 | 48 | 3 | 2562 | 333 | 56.93 | 9 |
| | | | 1931 | 51 | 2 | 2684 | 162 | 54.79 | 12 |
| Edrich, G.A. | Lancashire | | 1952 | 53 | 3 | 2067 | 162 | 41.34 | 4 |
| Edrich, J.H. | Surrey | (6) | 1962 | 55 | 7 | 2482 | 216 | 51.70 | 7 |
| | | | 1965 | 44 | 7 | 2319 | 310* | 62.67 | 8 |
| | | | 1967 | 47 | 5 | 2077 | 226* | 49.45 | 5 |
| | | | 1968 | 50 | 5 | 2009 | 164 | 44.64 | 5 |
| | | | 1969 | 39 | 7 | 2238 | 181 | 69.93 | 8 |
| | | | 1971 | 44 | 1 | 2031 | 195* | 47.23 | 6 |
| Edrich, W.J. | Middlesex | (9) | 1937 | 53 | 5 | 2154 | 175 | 44.87 | 3 |
| | | | 1938 | 51 | 6 | 2378 | 245 | 52.84 | 6 |
| | | | 1939 | 45 | 1 | 2186 | 161 | 49.68 | 7 |
| | | | 1947 | 52 | 8 | 3539 | 267* | 80.43 | 12 |
| | | | 1948 | 55 | 6 | 2428 | 168* | 49.55 | 9 |
| | | | 1949 | 62 | 5 | 2253 | 182 | 39.52 | 5 |
| | | | 1951 | 58 | 4 | 2086 | 118 | 38.62 | 2 |
| | | | 1952 | 63 | 4 | 2281 | 239 | 38.66 | 6 |
| | | | 1953 | 60 | 2 | 2557 | 211 | 47.35 | 5 |
| Emmett, G.M. | Gloucestershire | (3) | 1949 | 51 | 2 | 2005 | 116 | 40.91 | 3 |
| | | | 1951 | 56 | 5 | 2019 | 146 | 39.58 | 3 |
| | | | 1953 | 62 | 2 | 2115 | 141 | 35.25 | 4 |
| Fagg, A.E. | Kent | (5) | 1938 | 53 | 6 | 2456 | 244 | 52.25 | 9 |
| | | | 1947 | 56 | 5 | 2203 | 184 | 43.19 | 5 |
| | | | 1948 | 48 | 3 | 2423 | 203 | 53.84 | 8 |
| | | | 1950 | 54 | 3 | 2034 | 156 | 39.88 | 6 |
| | | | 1951 | 51 | 1 | 2081 | 221 | 41.62 | 6 |
| Fishlock, L.B. | Surrey | (6) | 1936 | 53 | 13 | 2129 | 133* | 53.22 | 5 |
| | | | 1938 | 53 | 1 | 2121 | 165 | 40.78 | 4 |
| | | | 1946 | 46 | 2 | 2221 | 172 | 50.47 | 5 |
| | | | 1948 | 56 | 2 | 2106 | 253 | 39.00 | 5 |
| | | | 1949 | 56 | 3 | 2426 | 210 | 45.77 | 7 |
| | | | 1950 | 59 | 5 | 2417 | 147 | 44.75 | 6 |
| Foster, R.E. | Worcestershire | | 1901 | 44 | 2 | 2128 | 136 | 50.66 | 6 |
| Fry, C.B. | Sussex | (6) | 1899 | 55 | 1 | 2366 | 181 | 43.81 | 5 |
| | | | 1900 | 41 | 3 | 2325 | 229 | 61.18 | 9 |
| | | | 1901 | 43 | 3 | 3147 | 244 | 78.67 | 13 |
| | | | 1903 | 40 | 7 | 2683 | 234 | 81.30 | 9 |
| | | | 1904 | 42 | 2 | 2824 | 229 | 70.60 | 10 |
| | | | 1905 | 44 | 4 | 2801 | 233 | 70.02 | 10 |
| Gale, R.A. | Middlesex | | 1962 | 58 | 1 | 2211 | 200 | 38.78 | 4 |
| Gatting, M.W. | Middlesex | | 1984 | 43 | 10 | 2257 | 258 | 68.39 | 8 |
| Gibbons, H.H.I. | Worcestershire | (3) | 1933 | 57 | 4 | 2008 | 155 | 37.88 | 4 |
| | | | 1934 | 57 | 6 | 2654 | 157 | 52.03 | 8 |
| | | | 1938 | 55 | 6 | 2120 | 178 | 43.26 | 6 |
| Gimblett, H. | Somerset | (2) | 1949 | 52 | 4 | 2093 | 156 | 43.60 | 5 |
| | | | 1952 | 55 | 1 | 2134 | 169 | 39.51 | 5 |
| Gooch, G.A. | Essex | (2) | 1984 | 45 | 7 | 2559 | 227 | 67.34 | 8 |
| | | | 1985 | 33 | 2 | 2208 | 202 | 71.22 | 7 |
| Grace, W.G. | Gloucestershire | (5) | 1871 | 39 | 4 | 2739 | 268 | 78.25 | 10 |
| | | | 1876 | 46 | 4 | 2622 | 344 | 62.42 | 7 |
| | | | 1887 | 46 | 8 | 2062 | 183* | 54.26 | 6 |
| | | | 1895 | 48 | 2 | 2346 | 288 | 51.00 | 5 |
| | | | 1896 | 54 | 4 | 2135 | 301 | 42.70 | 4 |
| Graveney, T.W. | Gloucestershire | (7) | 1951 | 50 | 3 | 2291 | 201 | 48.74 | 8 |
| | | | 1952 | 50 | 7 | 2066 | 171 | 48.04 | 6 |
| | | | 1955 | 51 | 2 | 2117 | 159 | 43.20 | 5 |
| | | | 1956 | 54 | 6 | 2397 | 200 | 49.93 | 9 |
| | | | 1957 | 53 | 5 | 2361 | 258 | 49.18 | 8 |
| | Worcestershire | | 1962 | 48 | 6 | 2269 | 164* | 54.02 | 9 |
| | | | 1964 | 51 | 7 | 2385 | 164 | 54.20 | 5 |

|  |  |  | Season | I | NO | Runs | HS | Avge | 100 |
|---|---|---|---|---|---|---|---|---|---|
| Gray, J.R. | Hampshire | (3) | 1959 | 57 | 5 | 2170 | 176* | 41.73 | 6 |
|  |  |  | 1961 | 66 | 3 | 2034 | 136 | 32.28 | 2 |
|  |  |  | 1962 | 61 | 6 | 2224 | 213* | 40.43 | 5 |
| Green, D.M. | Lancashire | (2) | 1965 | 63 | 1 | 2037 | 85 | 32.85 | – |
|  | Gloucestershire |  | 1968 | 54 | 1 | 2137 | 233 | 40.32 | 4 |
| Gregory, R.J. | Surrey | (2) | 1934 | 49 | 3 | 2379 | 180 | 51.71 | 8 |
|  |  |  | 1937 | 50 | 3 | 2166 | 154 | 46.08 | 7 |
| Grieves, K.J. | Lancashire |  | 1959 | 58 | 4 | 2253 | 202* | 41.72 | 4 |
| Gunn, W. | Nottinghamshire |  | 1893 | 51 | 3 | 2057 | 156 | 42.85 | 7 |
| Hallam, M.R. | Leicestershire | (3) | 1957 | 62 | 2 | 2068 | 176 | 34.46 | 6 |
|  |  |  | 1959 | 62 | 1 | 2070 | 210* | 33.93 | 4 |
|  |  |  | 1961 | 65 | 8 | 2262 | 203* | 39.68 | 5 |
| Hallows, C. | Lancashire | (3) | 1925 | 51 | 6 | 2354 | 163 | 52.31 | 8 |
|  |  |  | 1927 | 44 | 13 | 2343 | 233* | 75.58 | 7 |
|  |  |  | 1928 | 46 | 5 | 2645 | 232 | 64.51 | 11 |
| Hammond, W.R. | Gloucestershire | (12) | 1927 | 47 | 4 | 2969 | 197 | 69.04 | 12 |
|  |  |  | 1928 | 48 | 5 | 2825 | 244 | 65.69 | 9 |
|  |  |  | 1929 | 47 | 9 | 2456 | 238* | 64.63 | 10 |
|  |  |  | 1930 | 44 | 6 | 2032 | 211* | 53.47 | 5 |
|  |  |  | 1932 | 49 | 4 | 2528 | 264 | 56.17 | 8 |
|  |  |  | 1933 | 54 | 5 | 3323 | 264 | 67.81 | 13 |
|  |  |  | 1934 | 35 | 4 | 2366 | 302* | 76.32 | 8 |
|  |  |  | 1935 | 58 | 5 | 2616 | 252 | 49.35 | 7 |
|  |  |  | 1936 | 42 | 5 | 2107 | 317 | 56.94 | 5 |
|  |  |  | 1937 | 55 | 5 | 3252 | 217 | 65.04 | 13 |
|  |  |  | 1938 | 42 | 2 | 3011 | 271 | 75.27 | 15 |
|  |  |  | 1939 | 46 | 7 | 2479 | 302 | 63.56 | 7 |
| Hardinge, H.T.W. | Kent | (5) | 1913 | 56 | 7 | 2037 | 168 | 41.57 | 7 |
|  |  |  | 1921 | 52 | 7 | 2339 | 207 | 51.97 | 9 |
|  |  |  | 1922 | 48 | 8 | 2207 | 249* | 55.17 | 7 |
|  |  |  | 1926 | 52 | 5 | 2234 | 176 | 47.53 | 7 |
|  |  |  | 1928 | 46 | 5 | 2446 | 263* | 59.65 | 5 |
| Hardstaff, J., jr | Nottinghamshire | (4) | 1937 | 46 | 2 | 2540 | 266 | 57.72 | 8 |
|  |  |  | 1939 | 46 | 7 | 2129 | 159 | 54.58 | 5 |
|  |  |  | 1947 | 44 | 7 | 2396 | 221* | 64.75 | 7 |
|  |  |  | 1949 | 40 | 9 | 2251 | 162* | 72.61 | 8 |
| Harris, M.J. | Nottinghamshire |  | 1971 | 45 | 1 | 2238 | 177 | 50.86 | 9 |
| Harvey, R.N. | Australians |  | 1953 | 35 | 4 | 2040 | 202* | 65.80 | 10 |
| Hayes, E.G. | Surrey | (2) | 1906 | 56 | 5 | 2309 | 218 | 45.27 | 7 |
|  |  |  | 1909 | 65 | 5 | 2161 | 276 | 36.01 | 3 |
| Hayward, T.W. | Surrey | (10) | 1899 | 49 | 4 | 2647 | 273 | 58.82 | 7 |
|  |  |  | 1900 | 57 | 7 | 2693 | 193 | 53.86 | 10 |
|  |  |  | 1901 | 58 | 8 | 2535 | 181 | 50.70 | 2 |
|  |  |  | 1903 | 64 | 3 | 2177 | 156* | 35.68 | 3 |
|  |  |  | 1904 | 63 | 5 | 3170 | 203 | 54.65 | 11 |
|  |  |  | 1905 | 64 | 6 | 2592 | 129* | 44.68 | 5 |
|  |  |  | 1906 | 61 | 8 | 3518 | 219 | 66.37 | 13 |
|  |  |  | 1907 | 58 | 6 | 2353 | 161 | 45.25 | 7 |
|  |  |  | 1908 | 52 | 1 | 2337 | 175 | 45.82 | 5 |
|  |  |  | 1911 | 51 | 6 | 2149 | 202 | 47.75 | 5 |
| Headley, G.A. | West Indians |  | 1933 | 38 | 3 | 2320 | 224* | 66.28 | 7 |
| Headley, R.G.A. | Worcestershire |  | 1961 | 69 | 5 | 2040 | 150* | 31.87 | 4 |
| Hearne, J.W. | Middlesex | (4) | 1913 | 49 | 3 | 2036 | 189 | 44.26 | 6 |
|  |  |  | 1914 | 43 | 8 | 2116 | 204 | 60.45 | 8 |
|  |  |  | 1920 | 46 | 7 | 2148 | 215* | 55.07 | 6 |
|  |  |  | 1932 | 52 | 3 | 2151 | 176 | 43.89 | 6 |
| Hedges, B. | Glamorgan |  | 1961 | 65 | 2 | 2026 | 141 | 32.15 | 3 |
| Hendren, E.H. | Middlesex | (15) | 1920 | 47 | 6 | 2520 | 232 | 61.46 | 6 |
|  |  |  | 1921 | 53 | 5 | 2013 | 113 | 41.93 | 7 |
|  |  |  | 1922 | 38 | 7 | 2072 | 277* | 66.83 | 7 |
|  |  |  | 1923 | 51 | 12 | 3010 | 200* | 77.17 | 13 |
|  |  |  | 1924 | 48 | 11 | 2100 | 142 | 56.75 | 5 |
|  |  |  | 1925 | 50 | 6 | 2601 | 240 | 59.11 | 8 |
|  |  |  | 1926 | 53 | 11 | 2643 | 213 | 62.92 | 9 |
|  |  |  | 1927 | 43 | 5 | 2784 | 201* | 73.26 | 13 |
|  |  |  | 1928 | 54 | 7 | 3311 | 209* | 70.44 | 13 |

|  |  |  | Season | I | NO | Runs | HS | Avge | 100 |
|---|---|---|---|---|---|---|---|---|---|
| Hendren, E.H. *continued* |  |  | 1929 | 63 | 9 | 2213 | 156 | 40.98 | 5 |
|  |  |  | 1931 | 54 | 9 | 2548 | 232 | 56.62 | 7 |
|  |  |  | 1932 | 47 | 7 | 2041 | 194 | 51.02 | 5 |
|  |  |  | 1933 | 65 | 9 | 3186 | 301* | 56.89 | 11 |
|  |  |  | 1934 | 55 | 6 | 2213 | 135 | 45.16 | 7 |
|  |  |  | 1936 | 58 | 2 | 2654 | 202 | 47.39 | 9 |
| Hill, N.W. | Nottinghamshire | (2) | 1959 | 57 | 2 | 2129 | 167 | 38.70 | 6 |
|  |  |  | 1961 | 60 | 4 | 2239 | 201* | 39.98 | 6 |
| Hirst, G.H. | Yorkshire | (3) | 1904 | 50 | 4 | 2501 | 157 | 54.36 | 9 |
|  |  |  | 1905 | 52 | 10 | 2266 | 341 | 53.95 | 6 |
|  |  |  | 1906 | 58 | 6 | 2385 | 169 | 45.86 | 6 |
| Hobbs, J.B. | Surrey | (17) | 1907 | 63 | 6 | 2135 | 166* | 37.45 | 4 |
|  |  |  | 1909 | 54 | 2 | 2114 | 205 | 40.65 | 6 |
|  |  |  | 1911 | 60 | 3 | 2376 | 154* | 41.68 | 4 |
|  |  |  | 1912 | 60 | 6 | 2042 | 111 | 37.81 | 3 |
|  |  |  | 1913 | 57 | 5 | 2605 | 184 | 50.09 | 9 |
|  |  |  | 1914 | 48 | 2 | 2697 | 226 | 58.63 | 11 |
|  |  |  | 1919 | 49 | 6 | 2594 | 205* | 60.32 | 8 |
|  |  |  | 1920 | 50 | 2 | 2827 | 215 | 58.89 | 11 |
|  |  |  | 1922 | 46 | 5 | 2552 | 168 | 62.24 | 10 |
|  |  |  | 1923 | 59 | 4 | 2087 | 136 | 37.94 | 5 |
|  |  |  | 1924 | 43 | 7 | 2094 | 211 | 58.16 | 6 |
|  |  |  | 1925 | 48 | 5 | 3024 | 266* | 70.32 | 16 |
|  |  |  | 1926 | 41 | 3 | 2949 | 316* | 77.60 | 10 |
|  |  |  | 1928 | 38 | 7 | 2542 | 200* | 82.00 | 12 |
|  |  |  | 1929 | 39 | 5 | 2263 | 204 | 66.55 | 10 |
|  |  |  | 1930 | 43 | 2 | 2103 | 146* | 51.29 | 5 |
|  |  |  | 1931 | 49 | 6 | 2418 | 153 | 56.23 | 10 |
| Holmes, P. | Yorkshire | (7) | 1920 | 51 | 6 | 2254 | 302* | 50.08 | 7 |
|  |  |  | 1923 | 54 | 3 | 2001 | 199 | 39.23 | 3 |
|  |  |  | 1925 | 52 | 9 | 2453 | 315* | 57.04 | 6 |
|  |  |  | 1926 | 50 | 4 | 2006 | 143 | 43.60 | 4 |
|  |  |  | 1927 | 47 | 9 | 2174 | 180 | 57.21 | 6 |
|  |  |  | 1928 | 43 | 5 | 2220 | 275 | 58.42 | 6 |
|  |  |  | 1930 | 52 | 6 | 2003 | 132* | 43.54 | 4 |
| Horton, H. | Hampshire | (3) | 1959 | 59 | 8 | 2428 | 140* | 47.60 | 4 |
|  |  |  | 1960 | 59 | 9 | 2170 | 131 | 43.40 | 7 |
|  |  |  | 1961 | 65 | 4 | 2329 | 160* | 38.18 | 4 |
| Horton, M.J. | Worcestershire |  | 1959 | 58 | 3 | 2468 | 212 | 44.87 | 4 |
| Hutton, L. | Yorkshire | (9) | 1937 | 58 | 7 | 2888 | 271* | 56.62 | 10 |
|  |  |  | 1939 | 52 | 6 | 2883 | 280* | 62.67 | 12 |
|  |  |  | 1947 | 44 | 4 | 2585 | 270* | 64.62 | 11 |
|  |  |  | 1948 | 48 | 7 | 2654 | 176* | 64.73 | 10 |
|  |  |  | 1949 | 56 | 6 | 3429 | 269* | 68.58 | 12 |
|  |  |  | 1950 | 40 | 3 | 2128 | 202* | 57.51 | 6 |
|  |  |  | 1951 | 47 | 8 | 2145 | 194* | 55.00 | 7 |
|  |  |  | 1952 | 45 | 3 | 2567 | 189 | 61.11 | 11 |
|  |  |  | 1953 | 44 | 5 | 2458 | 241 | 63.02 | 8 |
| Ibadulla, K. | Warwickshire |  | 1962 | 64 | 2 | 2098 | 119 | 33.83 | 6 |
| Iddon, J. | Lancashire |  | 1934 | 51 | 6 | 2381 | 200* | 52.91 | 6 |
| Insole, D.J. | Essex | (3) | 1951 | 57 | 9 | 2032 | 186* | 42.33 | 3 |
|  |  |  | 1955 | 62 | 5 | 2427 | 142 | 42.57 | 9 |
|  |  |  | 1959 | 50 | 5 | 2045 | 180 | 45.44 | 5 |
| Javed Miandad | Glamorgan |  | 1981 | 37 | 7 | 2083 | 200* | 69.43 | 8 |
| Jessop, G.L. | Gloucestershire | (2) | 1900 | 58 | 3 | 2210 | 179 | 40.18 | 6 |
|  |  |  | 1901 | 58 | 1 | 2323 | 233 | 40.75 | 5 |
| Jones, A.O. | Nottinghamshire |  | 1901 | 51 | 2 | 2292 | 249 | 46.77 | 5 |
| Jupp, V.W.C. | Sussex |  | 1921 | 60 | 4 | 2169 | 179 | 38.73 | 7 |
| Kallicharran, A.I. | Warwickshire | (2) | 1982 | 37 | 5 | 2120 | 235 | 66.25 | 8 |
|  |  |  | 1984 | 50 | 6 | 2301 | 200* | 52.29 | 9 |
| Keeton, W.W. | Nottinghamshire | (6) | 1932 | 51 | 3 | 2062 | 242 | 42.95 | 7 |
|  |  |  | 1933 | 56 | 3 | 2258 | 168 | 42.60 | 6 |
|  |  |  | 1934 | 46 | 0 | 2006 | 261 | 43.60 | 3 |
|  |  |  | 1937 | 52 | 8 | 2004 | 136 | 45.54 | 4 |
|  |  |  | 1946 | 48 | 2 | 2021 | 160 | 43.93 | 5 |
|  |  |  | 1949 | 38 | 1 | 2049 | 210 | 55.37 | 6 |

| | | | Season | I | NO | Runs | HS | Avge | 100 |
|---|---|---|---|---|---|---|---|---|---|
| Kenyon, D. | Worcestershire | (7) | 1950 | 58 | 3 | 2351 | 163 | 42.74 | 6 |
| | | | 1951 | 59 | 6 | 2145 | 145 | 40.47 | 6 |
| | | | 1952 | 60 | 2 | 2489 | 171 | 42.91 | 7 |
| | | | 1953 | 58 | 3 | 2439 | 238* | 44.34 | 6 |
| | | | 1954 | 58 | 7 | 2636 | 253* | 51.68 | 6 |
| | | | 1955 | 64 | 3 | 2296 | 131 | 37.63 | 5 |
| | | | 1957 | 62 | 3 | 2231 | 200* | 37.81 | 6 |
| Kilner, N. | Warwickshire | | 1933 | 50 | 2 | 2159 | 197 | 44.97 | 6 |
| Lamb, A.J. | Northamptonshire | | 1981 | 43 | 9 | 2049 | 162 | 60.26 | 5 |
| Langridge, James | Sussex | | 1937 | 58 | 7 | 2082 | 150* | 40.82 | 1 |
| Langridge, J.G. | Sussex | (11) | 1933 | 51 | 6 | 2056 | 250* | 45.68 | 4 |
| | | | 1934 | 52 | 6 | 2256 | 232* | 49.04 | 4 |
| | | | 1935 | 56 | 4 | 2035 | 195 | 39.13 | 4 |
| | | | 1937 | 63 | 3 | 2514 | 175 | 41.90 | 10 |
| | | | 1938 | 54 | 4 | 2347 | 227 | 46.94 | 5 |
| | | | 1939 | 51 | 0 | 2106 | 202 | 41.29 | 6 |
| | | | 1947 | 57 | 5 | 2023 | 138* | 38.90 | 3 |
| | | | 1949 | 53 | 5 | 2914 | 234* | 60.70 | 12 |
| | | | 1950 | 65 | 5 | 2412 | 241 | 40.20 | 5 |
| | | | 1951 | 53 | 3 | 2041 | 200* | 40.82 | 5 |
| | | | 1952 | 60 | 4 | 2082 | 140 | 37.17 | 6 |
| Lawry, W.M. | Australians | | 1961 | 39 | 6 | 2019 | 165 | 61.18 | 9 |
| Lee, F.S. | Somerset | | 1938 | 51 | 6 | 2019 | 162 | 44.86 | 7 |
| Lenham, L.J. | Sussex | | 1961 | 68 | 6 | 2016 | 107 | 32.51 | 2 |
| Lewis, A.R. | Glamorgan | (2) | 1962 | 60 | 6 | 2188 | 151 | 40.51 | 5 |
| | | | 1966 | 61 | 8 | 2190 | 223 | 41.32 | 5 |
| Leyland, M. | Yorkshire | (3) | 1930 | 50 | 7 | 2175 | 211* | 50.58 | 6 |
| | | | 1933 | 50 | 4 | 2317 | 210* | 50.36 | 7 |
| | | | 1934 | 44 | 4 | 2142 | 182 | 53.55 | 7 |
| Livingston, L. | Northamptonshire | (3) | 1954 | 48 | 7 | 2269 | 207* | 55.34 | 6 |
| | | | 1955 | 58 | 5 | 2172 | 172* | 40.98 | 5 |
| | | | 1956 | 47 | 6 | 2006 | 188* | 48.92 | 2 |
| Lowson, F.A. | Yorkshire | | 1950 | 56 | 5 | 2152 | 141* | 42.19 | 5 |
| Macartney, C.G. | Australians | (2) | 1912 | 49 | 1 | 2187 | 208 | 45.56 | 6 |
| | | | 1921 | 41 | 2 | 2317 | 345 | 59.41 | 8 |
| McCabe, S.J. | Australians | | 1934 | 37 | 7 | 2078 | 240 | 69.26 | 8 |
| McEwan, K.S. | Essex | | 1983 | 39 | 5 | 2176 | 189* | 64.00 | 8 |
| Majid Khan | C.U. & Glamorgan | | 1972 | 38 | 4 | 2074 | 204 | 61.00 | 8 |
| Makepeace, J.W.H. | Lancashire | (2) | 1923 | 53 | 6 | 2310 | 203 | 49.14 | 6 |
| | | | 1926 | 54 | 5 | 2340 | 180 | 48.75 | 5 |
| Marshall, R.E. | Hampshire | (6) | 1955 | 60 | 4 | 2115 | 110* | 37.76 | 3 |
| | | | 1958 | 57 | 3 | 2118 | 193 | 39.22 | 5 |
| | | | 1959 | 63 | 1 | 2532 | 150 | 40.83 | 4 |
| | | | 1960 | 62 | 5 | 2380 | 168 | 41.75 | 5 |
| | | | 1961 | 62 | 2 | 2607 | 212 | 43.45 | 5 |
| | | | 1962 | 52 | 3 | 2124 | 228* | 43.34 | 6 |
| May, P.B.H. | Surrey | (5) | 1951 | 43 | 9 | 2339 | 178* | 68.79 | 9 |
| | | | 1952 | 47 | 7 | 2498 | 197 | 62.45 | 10 |
| | | | 1953 | 59 | 9 | 2554 | 159 | 51.08 | 8 |
| | | | 1957 | 41 | 3 | 2347 | 285* | 61.76 | 7 |
| | | | 1958 | 41 | 6 | 2231 | 174 | 63.74 | 8 |
| Mead, C.P. | Hampshire | (11) | 1911 | 52 | 5 | 2562 | 223 | 54.51 | 9 |
| | | | 1913 | 60 | 8 | 2627 | 171* | 50.51 | 9 |
| | | | 1914 | 53 | 5 | 2476 | 213 | 51.58 | 7 |
| | | | 1921 | 52 | 6 | 3179 | 280* | 69.10 | 10 |
| | | | 1922 | 50 | 10 | 2391 | 235 | 59.77 | 8 |
| | | | 1923 | 52 | 8 | 2604 | 222 | 59.18 | 7 |
| | | | 1926 | 45 | 8 | 2326 | 177* | 62.86 | 10 |
| | | | 1927 | 41 | 9 | 2385 | 200* | 74.53 | 8 |
| | | | 1928 | 50 | 10 | 3027 | 180 | 75.67 | 13 |
| | | | 1933 | 44 | 6 | 2576 | 227 | 67.78 | 10 |
| | | | 1934 | 46 | 8 | 2011 | 198 | 52.92 | 6 |
| Merchant, V.M. | Indians | | 1946 | 41 | 9 | 2385 | 242* | 74.53 | 7 |
| Milton, C.A. | Gloucestershire | | 1967 | 49 | 4 | 2089 | 145 | 46.42 | 7 |
| Mitchell, A. | Yorkshire | | 1933 | 51 | 12 | 2300 | 158 | 58.97 | 8 |
| Mitchell, B. | South Africans | | 1947 | 37 | 4 | 2014 | 189* | 61.03 | 8 |

| | | | Season | I | NO | Runs | HS | Avge | 100 |
|---|---|---|---|---|---|---|---|---|---|
| Nichol, M. | Worcestershire | | 1933 | 54 | 5 | 2154 | 165* | 43.95 | 8 |
| Nicholls, R.B. | Gloucestershire | | 1962 | 58 | 2 | 2059 | 217 | 36.76 | 4 |
| Noble, M.A. | Australians | | 1905 | 46 | 2 | 2053 | 267 | 46.65 | 6 |
| Oakman, A.S.M. | Sussex | (2) | 1961 | 67 | 4 | 2307 | 229* | 36.61 | 6 |
| | | | 1962 | 63 | 9 | 2008 | 177 | 37.18 | 3 |
| O'Connor, J. | Essex | (4) | 1928 | 53 | 4 | 2325 | 157 | 47.44 | 6 |
| | | | 1929 | 54 | 3 | 2288 | 168* | 44.86 | 9 |
| | | | 1933 | 52 | 5 | 2077 | 237 | 44.19 | 6 |
| | | | 1934 | 49 | 7 | 2350 | 248 | 55.95 | 9 |
| Oldfield, N. | Northamptonshire | | 1949 | 47 | 3 | 2192 | 168 | 49.81 | 4 |
| Padgett, D.E.V. | Yorkshire | | 1959 | 61 | 8 | 2181 | 161* | 41.15 | 4 |
| Palmer, C.H. | Leicestershire | | 1952 | 56 | 4 | 2071 | 127 | 39.82 | 4 |
| Parfitt, P.H. | Middlesex | (3) | 1961 | 59 | 8 | 2007 | 165* | 39.35 | 8 |
| | | | 1962 | 51 | 4 | 2121 | 138 | 45.12 | 8 |
| | | | 1966 | 57 | 8 | 2018 | 114* | 41.18 | 2 |
| Parkhouse, W.G.A. | Glamorgan | | 1959 | 49 | 3 | 2243 | 154 | 48.76 | 6 |
| Parks, H.W. | Sussex | | 1947 | 57 | 2 | 2122 | 170 | 38.58 | 5 |
| Parks, J.H. | Sussex | | 1937 | 63 | 4 | 3003 | 168 | 50.89 | 11 |
| Parks, J.M. | Sussex | (3) | 1955 | 63 | 8 | 2314 | 205* | 42.07 | 5 |
| | | | 1957 | 55 | 6 | 2171 | 132* | 44.30 | 4 |
| | | | 1959 | 56 | 11 | 2313 | 157* | 51.40 | 6 |
| Paynter, E. | Lancashire | (4) | 1932 | 55 | 1 | 2035 | 159 | 37.68 | 5 |
| | | | 1936 | 54 | 10 | 2016 | 177 | 45.81 | 4 |
| | | | 1937 | 58 | 4 | 2904 | 322 | 53.77 | 5 |
| | | | 1938 | 52 | 6 | 2691 | 291 | 58.50 | 8 |
| Place, W. | Lancashire | | 1947 | 47 | 7 | 2501 | 266* | 62.52 | 10 |
| Pullar, G. | Lancashire | (2) | 1959 | 55 | 7 | 2647 | 161 | 55.14 | 8 |
| | | | 1961 | 61 | 7 | 2344 | 165* | 43.40 | 5 |
| Quaife, W.G. | Warwickshire | | 1905 | 52 | 14 | 2060 | 255* | 54.21 | 6 |
| Randall, D.W. | Nottinghamshire | | 1985 | 47 | 7 | 2151 | 117 | 53.77 | 5 |
| Ranjitsinhji, K.S. | Sussex | (5) | 1896 | 55 | 7 | 2780 | 171* | 57.91 | 10 |
| | | | 1899 | 58 | 8 | 3159 | 197 | 63.18 | 8 |
| | | | 1900 | 40 | 5 | 3065 | 275 | 87.57 | 11 |
| | | | 1901 | 40 | 5 | 2468 | 285* | 70.51 | 8 |
| | | | 1904 | 34 | 6 | 2077 | 207* | 74.17 | 8 |
| Rhodes, W. | Yorkshire | (2) | 1909 | 59 | 7 | 2094 | 199 | 40.26 | 5 |
| | | | 1911 | 64 | 5 | 2261 | 128 | 38.32 | 5 |
| Richards, B.A. | Hampshire | | 1968 | 55 | 5 | 2395 | 206 | 47.90 | 5 |
| Richards, I.V.A. | Somerset | | 1977 | 35 | 2 | 2161 | 241* | 65.48 | 7 |
| Richardson, P.E. | Worcestershire | (4) | 1953 | 61 | 3 | 2294 | 171 | 39.55 | 3 |
| | Kent | | 1961 | 58 | 1 | 2152 | 171 | 37.75 | 4 |
| | | | 1962 | 54 | 0 | 2081 | 162 | 38.53 | 4 |
| | | | 1963 | 56 | 2 | 2110 | 172 | 39.07 | 5 |
| Robertson, J.D.B. | Middlesex | (9) | 1946 | 58 | 3 | 2114 | 128 | 38.43 | 5 |
| | | | 1947 | 57 | 4 | 2760 | 229 | 52.07 | 12 |
| | | | 1948 | 54 | 7 | 2366 | 154 | 50.34 | 7 |
| | | | 1949 | 57 | 1 | 2244 | 331* | 40.07 | 7 |
| | | | 1950 | 59 | 3 | 2093 | 138* | 37.37 | 4 |
| | | | 1951 | 56 | 4 | 2917 | 201* | 56.09 | 7 |
| | | | 1952 | 64 | 2 | 2337 | 162 | 37.69 | 2 |
| | | | 1955 | 64 | 0 | 2070 | 137 | 32.34 | 1 |
| | | | 1957 | 59 | 2 | 2155 | 201* | 37.80 | 4 |
| Robinson, R.T. | Nottinghamshire | | 1984 | 47 | 7 | 2032 | 171 | 50.80 | 5 |
| Rogers, N.H. | Hampshire | | 1952 | 58 | 3 | 2244 | 164 | 40.80 | 3 |
| Russell, C.A.G. | Essex | (5) | 1920 | 56 | 1 | 2432 | 197 | 44.21 | 3 |
| | | | 1921 | 44 | 3 | 2236 | 273 | 54.53 | 8 |
| | | | 1922 | 50 | 3 | 2575 | 172 | 54.78 | 9 |
| | | | 1925 | 47 | 4 | 2081 | 150 | 48.39 | 7 |
| | | | 1928 | 42 | 7 | 2243 | 182 | 64.08 | 8 |
| Russell, W.E. | Middlesex | (3) | 1960 | 63 | 9 | 2051 | 182 | 37.98 | 2 |
| | | | 1961 | 62 | 1 | 2014 | 156 | 33.01 | 4 |
| | | | 1964 | 56 | 5 | 2342 | 193 | 45.92 | 5 |
| Sandham, A. | Surrey | (8) | 1921 | 48 | 5 | 2117 | 292* | 49.23 | 7 |
| | | | 1924 | 37 | 2 | 2082 | 169 | 59.48 | 7 |
| | | | 1925 | 47 | 6 | 2255 | 181 | 55.00 | 7 |
| | | | 1927 | 46 | 6 | 2315 | 230 | 57.87 | 7 |

| | | | Season | I | NO | Runs | HS | Avge | 100 |
|---|---|---|---|---|---|---|---|---|---|
| Sandham, A. *continued* | | | 1928 | 47 | 4 | 2532 | 282* | 58.88 | 8 |
| | | | 1929 | 52 | 2 | 2565 | 187 | 51.30 | 6 |
| | | | 1930 | 50 | 4 | 2295 | 204 | 49.89 | 6 |
| | | | 1931 | 50 | 8 | 2209 | 175 | 52.59 | 9 |
| Seymour, James | Kent | | 1913 | 60 | 6 | 2088 | 124 | 38.66 | 5 |
| Sharp, J. | Lancashire | | 1911 | 55 | 3 | 2099 | 184* | 40.36 | 4 |
| Sharpe, P.J. | Yorkshire | | 1962 | 64 | 9 | 2252 | 138 | 40.94 | 7 |
| Shepherd, T.F. | Surrey | | 1927 | 45 | 6 | 2145 | 277* | 55.00 | 8 |
| Sheppard, D.S. | Sussex | (3) | 1951 | 43 | 3 | 2014 | 183 | 52.60 | 7 |
| | | | 1952 | 39 | 4 | 2262 | 239* | 64.62 | 10 |
| | | | 1953 | 57 | 7 | 2270 | 186* | 45.40 | 7 |
| Simpson, R.T. | Nottinghamshire | (5) | 1949 | 46 | 6 | 2525 | 238 | 63.12 | 6 |
| | | | 1950 | 47 | 6 | 2576 | 243* | 62.82 | 8 |
| | | | 1952 | 54 | 1 | 2222 | 216 | 41.92 | 5 |
| | | | 1953 | 60 | 5 | 2505 | 157 | 45.54 | 7 |
| | | | 1959 | 55 | 5 | 2033 | 132 | 40.66 | 5 |
| Smith, C.L. | Hampshire | | 1985 | 39 | 4 | 2000 | 143* | 57.14 | 7 |
| Smith, D. | Derbyshire | | 1935 | 61 | 6 | 2175 | 225 | 39.54 | 2 |
| Smith, D.V. | Sussex | | 1957 | 54 | 5 | 2088 | 166 | 42.61 | 5 |
| Smith, M.J.K. | Warwickshire | (6) | 1957 | 63 | 5 | 2125 | 127 | 36.63 | 3 |
| | | | 1958 | 51 | 3 | 2126 | 160 | 44.29 | 3 |
| | | | 1959 | 67 | 11 | 3245 | 200* | 57.94 | 8 |
| | | | 1960 | 63 | 7 | 2551 | 169* | 45.55 | 4 |
| | | | 1961 | 67 | 5 | 2587 | 145 | 41.72 | 5 |
| | | | 1962 | 64 | 12 | 2290 | 163 | 44.03 | 5 |
| Spooner, R.H. | Lancashire | | 1911 | 45 | 0 | 2312 | 224 | 51.37 | 7 |
| Stewart, M.J. | Surrey | | 1962 | 55 | 9 | 2045 | 200* | 44.45 | 5 |
| Stewart, W.J. | Warwickshire | | 1962 | 62 | 9 | 2318 | 182* | 43.73 | 7 |
| Stoddart, A.E. | Middlesex | | 1893 | 50 | 1 | 2072 | 195* | 42.28 | 4 |
| Stott, W.B. | Yorkshire | | 1959 | 56 | 2 | 2034 | 144* | 37.66 | 3 |
| Sutcliffe, B. | New Zealanders | | 1949 | 49 | 5 | 2627 | 243 | 59.70 | 7 |
| Sutcliffe, H. | Yorkshire | (15) | 1922 | 48 | 5 | 2020 | 232 | 46.97 | 4 |
| | | | 1923 | 60 | 6 | 2220 | 139 | 41.11 | 3 |
| | | | 1924 | 52 | 8 | 2142 | 255* | 48.68 | 6 |
| | | | 1925 | 51 | 8 | 2308 | 235 | 53.67 | 7 |
| | | | 1926 | 47 | 9 | 2528 | 200 | 66.52 | 8 |
| | | | 1927 | 49 | 6 | 2414 | 227 | 56.13 | 6 |
| | | | 1928 | 44 | 5 | 3002 | 228 | 76.97 | 13 |
| | | | 1929 | 46 | 4 | 2189 | 150 | 52.11 | 9 |
| | | | 1930 | 44 | 8 | 2312 | 173 | 64.22 | 6 |
| | | | 1931 | 42 | 11 | 3006 | 230 | 96.96 | 13 |
| | | | 1932 | 52 | 7 | 3336 | 313 | 74.13 | 14 |
| | | | 1933 | 52 | 5 | 2211 | 205 | 47.04 | 7 |
| | | | 1934 | 44 | 3 | 2023 | 203 | 49.34 | 4 |
| | | | 1935 | 54 | 3 | 2494 | 212 | 48.90 | 8 |
| | | | 1937 | 54 | 5 | 2162 | 189 | 44.12 | 4 |
| Suttle, K.G. | Sussex | | 1962 | 65 | 6 | 2326 | 204* | 39.42 | 3 |
| Tarrant, F.A. | Middlesex | | 1911 | 48 | 4 | 2030 | 207* | 46.13 | 5 |
| Todd, L.J. | Kent | | 1947 | 55 | 5 | 2312 | 173 | 46.24 | 7 |
| Tompkin, M. | Leicestershire | | 1955 | 62 | 3 | 2190 | 131 | 37.11 | 3 |
| Townsend, C.L. | Gloucestershire | | 1899 | 54 | 7 | 2440 | 224* | 51.91 | 9 |
| Townsend, L.F. | Derbyshire | | 1933 | 59 | 8 | 2268 | 233 | 44.47 | 6 |
| Tremlett, M.F. | Somerset | | 1951 | 59 | 0 | 2101 | 185 | 35.61 | 2 |
| Trumper, V.T. | Australians | | 1902 | 53 | 0 | 2570 | 128 | 48.49 | 11 |
| Turner, G.M. | Worcestershire | (3) | 1970 | 46 | 7 | 2379 | 154* | 61.00 | 10 |
| | | | 1973 | 44 | 8 | 2416 | 153* | 67.11 | 9 |
| | | | 1981 | 42 | 4 | 2101 | 168 | 55.28 | 9 |
| Tyldesley, G.E. | Lancashire | (6) | 1922 | 57 | 5 | 2168 | 178 | 41.69 | 4 |
| | | | 1923 | 60 | 6 | 2040 | 236 | 37.77 | 4 |
| | | | 1926 | 51 | 7 | 2826 | 226 | 64.22 | 10 |
| | | | 1928 | 48 | 10 | 3024 | 242 | 79.57 | 10 |
| | | | 1932 | 48 | 7 | 2420 | 225* | 59.02 | 8 |
| | | | 1934 | 51 | 8 | 2487 | 239 | 57.83 | 8 |
| Tyldesley, J.T. | Lancashire | (5) | 1901 | 60 | 5 | 3041 | 221 | 55.29 | 9 |
| | | | 1904 | 44 | 5 | 2439 | 225 | 62.53 | 8 |
| | | | 1906 | 52 | 3 | 2270 | 295* | 46.32 | 4 |

|  |  |  | Season | I | NO | Runs | HS | Avge | 100 |
|---|---|---|---|---|---|---|---|---|---|
| Tyldesley, J.T. continued |  |  | 1907 | 63 | 5 | 2132 | 209 | 36.75 | 5 |
|  |  |  | 1910 | 51 | 2 | 2265 | 158 | 46.22 | 7 |
| Virgin, R.T. | Somerset |  | 1970 | 47 | 0 | 2223 | 178 | 47.29 | 7 |
| Walters, C.F. | Worcestershire | (2) | 1933 | 52 | 3 | 2404 | 226 | 50.08 | 9 |
|  |  |  | 1934 | 48 | 4 | 2048 | 178 | 46.54 | 4 |
| Warner, P.F. | Middlesex |  | 1911 | 51 | 5 | 2123 | 244 | 46.15 | 5 |
| Washbrook, C. | Lancashire | (2) | 1946 | 43 | 8 | 2400 | 182 | 68.57 | 9 |
|  |  |  | 1947 | 47 | 8 | 2662 | 251* | 68.25 | 11 |
| Watson, F.B. | Lancashire | (3) | 1928 | 46 | 4 | 2583 | 300* | 61.05 | 9 |
|  |  |  | 1929 | 50 | 4 | 2137 | 207 | 46.45 | 6 |
|  |  |  | 1930 | 47 | 2 | 2031 | 135 | 45.13 | 3 |
| Watson, W. | Leicestershire |  | 1959 | 50 | 10 | 2212 | 173 | 55.30 | 7 |
| Weekes, E. de C. | West Indians |  | 1950 | 33 | 4 | 2310 | 304* | 79.65 | 7 |
| Wharton, A. | Lancashire |  | 1959 | 59 | 6 | 2157 | 199 | 40.69 | 4 |
| Whysall, W.W. | Nottinghamshire | (5) | 1926 | 56 | 5 | 2138 | 209 | 41.92 | 6 |
|  |  |  | 1927 | 50 | 5 | 2069 | 184 | 45.97 | 5 |
|  |  |  | 1928 | 51 | 2 | 2573 | 166 | 52.51 | 9 |
|  |  |  | 1929 | 56 | 3 | 2716 | 244 | 51.24 | 7 |
|  |  |  | 1930 | 47 | 3 | 2174 | 248 | 49.40 | 8 |
| Wight, P.B. | Somerset | (2) | 1960 | 62 | 5 | 2375 | 155* | 41.66 | 7 |
|  |  |  | 1962 | 55 | 9 | 2030 | 215 | 44.13 | 4 |
| Wilson, J.V. | Yorkshire |  | 1951 | 51 | 9 | 2027 | 223* | 48.26 | 6 |
| Wilson, R.C. | Kent |  | 1964 | 49 | 5 | 2038 | 156 | 46.31 | 4 |
| Wood, C.J.B. | Leicestershire |  | 1901 | 52 | 3 | 2033 | 156 | 41.48 | 3 |
| Woolley, F.E. | Kent | (13) | 1914 | 52 | 2 | 2272 | 160* | 45.44 | 6 |
|  |  |  | 1921 | 50 | 1 | 2101 | 174 | 42.87 | 6 |
|  |  |  | 1922 | 47 | 3 | 2022 | 188 | 45.95 | 5 |
|  |  |  | 1923 | 56 | 5 | 2091 | 270 | 41.00 | 5 |
|  |  |  | 1924 | 49 | 2 | 2344 | 202 | 49.87 | 8 |
|  |  |  | 1925 | 43 | 4 | 2190 | 215 | 56.15 | 5 |
|  |  |  | 1926 | 50 | 3 | 2183 | 217 | 46.44 | 6 |
|  |  |  | 1928 | 59 | 4 | 3352 | 198 | 60.94 | 12 |
|  |  |  | 1929 | 55 | 5 | 2804 | 176 | 56.08 | 11 |
|  |  |  | 1930 | 50 | 5 | 2023 | 120 | 44.95 | 5 |
|  |  |  | 1931 | 51 | 4 | 2301 | 224 | 48.95 | 5 |
|  |  |  | 1934 | 56 | 1 | 2643 | 176 | 48.05 | 10 |
|  |  |  | 1935 | 56 | 0 | 2339 | 229 | 41.76 | 6 |
| Wyatt, R.E.S. | Warwickshire | (5) | 1928 | 52 | 10 | 2408 | 177 | 57.33 | 6 |
|  |  |  | 1929 | 55 | 6 | 2630 | 161* | 53.67 | 10 |
|  |  |  | 1933 | 50 | 10 | 2379 | 187* | 59.47 | 8 |
|  |  |  | 1935 | 55 | 9 | 2019 | 149 | 43.89 | 4 |
|  |  |  | 1937 | 54 | 5 | 2625 | 232 | 53.57 | 9 |
| Young, D.M. | Gloucestershire | (2) | 1955 | 63 | 1 | 2106 | 170 | 33.96 | 4 |
|  |  |  | 1959 | 57 | 4 | 2179 | 148 | 41.11 | 6 |
| Zaheer Abbas | Gloucestershire | (2) | 1976 | 39 | 5 | 2554 | 230* | 75.11 | 11 |
|  |  |  | 1981 | 36 | 10 | 2306 | 215* | 88.69 | 10 |

*D.M. Green is the only player to score 2000 runs in a season without hitting a century. His highest innings in 1965 when he scored 2037 runs was only 85, but twenty of his innings were of 40 or more.*

*Three players have scored 2000 runs in a season while making only one century: James Langridge in 1937, T.C. Dodds in 1947, and J.D.B. Robertson in 1955.*

# 2000 RUNS IN AN OVERSEAS SEASON

The following batsmen achieved aggregates of 2000 runs in a season but played in more than one country:

|  | Venue | Season | I | NO | Runs | HS | Avge | 100 |
|---|---|---|---|---|---|---|---|---|
| M. Amarnath | P/I/WI | 1982–83 | 34 | 6 | 2234 | 207 | 79.78 | 9 |
| J.R. Reid | SA/A/NZ | 1961–62 | 40 | 2 | 2188 | 203 | 57.57 | 7 |
| S.M. Gavaskar | I/P | 1978–79 | 30 | 6 | 2121 | 205 | 88.37 | 10 |
| R.B. Simpson | I/P/A/WI | 1964–65 | 34 | 4 | 2063 | 201 | 68.76 | 8 |

# 1000 RUNS IN A SEASON IN AUSTRALIA

| | | | Season | I | NO | Runs | HS | Avge | 100 |
|---|---|---|---|---|---|---|---|---|---|
| Amarnath, L. | Indians | | 1947–48 | 23 | 3 | 1162 | 228* | 58.10 | 5 |
| Armstrong, W.W. | Victoria | (2) | 1907–08 | 16 | 2 | 1033 | 231 | 73.78 | 5 |
| | | | 1920–21 | 15 | 3 | 1069 | 245 | 89.08 | 5 |
| Barber, R.W. | MCC | | 1965–66 | 22 | 2 | 1001 | 185 | 50.05 | 3 |
| Bardsley, W. | NSW | | 1910–11 | 19 | 1 | 1233 | 191* | 68.50 | 3 |
| Barlow, E.J. | South Africans | | 1963–64 | 25 | 2 | 1523 | 209 | 66.21 | 6 |
| Barnes, S.G. | NSW | | 1940–41 | 14 | 0 | 1050 | 185 | 75.00 | 6 |
| Barnett, C.J. | MCC | | 1936–37 | 25 | 0 | 1375 | 259 | 55.00 | 5 |
| Barrington, K.F. | MCC | | 1962–63 | 22 | 5 | 1451 | 219* | 85.35 | 5 |
| Booth, B.C. | NSW | | 1963–64 | 17 | 4 | 1180 | 169* | 90.76 | 5 |
| Border, A.R. | NSW | (2) | 1978–79 | 25 | 3 | 1220 | 135 | 55.45 | 4 |
| | Queensland | | 1982–83 | 20 | 5 | 1081 | 165 | 72.06 | 2 |
| Boycott, G. | MCC | | 1970–71 | 22 | 6 | 1535 | 173 | 95.93 | 6 |
| Bradman, D.G. | NSW | (12) | 1928–29 | 24 | 6 | 1690 | 340* | 93.88 | 7 |
| | | | 1929–30 | 16 | 2 | 1586 | 452* | 113.28 | 5 |
| | | | 1930–31 | 18 | 0 | 1422 | 258 | 79.00 | 5 |
| | | | 1931–32 | 13 | 1 | 1403 | 299* | 116.91 | 7 |
| | | | 1932–33 | 21 | 2 | 1171 | 238 | 61.63 | 3 |
| | | | 1933–34 | 11 | 2 | 1192 | 253 | 132.44 | 5 |
| | South Australia | | 1935–36 | 9 | 0 | 1173 | 369 | 130.33 | 4 |
| | | | 1936–37 | 19 | 1 | 1552 | 270 | 86.22 | 6 |
| | | | 1937–38 | 18 | 2 | 1437 | 246 | 89.81 | 7 |
| | | | 1939–40 | 15 | 3 | 1475 | 267 | 122.91 | 5 |
| | | | 1946–47 | 14 | 1 | 1032 | 234 | 79.38 | 4 |
| | | | 1947–48 | 12 | 2 | 1296 | 201 | 129.60 | 8 |
| Brown, W.A. | Queensland | | 1938–39 | 11 | 1 | 1057 | 215 | 105.70 | 3 |
| Burge, P.J.P. | Queensland | (2) | 1960–61 | 22 | 1 | 1116 | 240 | 53.14 | 2 |
| | | | 1963–64 | 17 | 2 | 1144 | 283 | 76.26 | 3 |
| Butcher, B.F. | West Indians | | 1968–69 | 23 | 1 | 1191 | 172 | 54.13 | 5 |
| Chappell, G.S. | Queensland | (5) | 1973–74 | 18 | 3 | 1288 | 180 | 85.86 | 5 |
| | | | 1974–75 | 25 | 1 | 1484 | 159 | 61.83 | 5 |
| | | | 1975–76 | 26 | 8 | 1547 | 182* | 85.94 | 6 |
| | | | 1979–80 | 19 | 4 | 1066 | 185 | 71.06 | 4 |
| | | | 1980–81 | 22 | 2 | 1502 | 204 | 75.10 | 5 |
| Chappell, I.M. | South Australia | (6) | 1965–66 | 19 | 2 | 1019 | 134 | 59.94 | 4 |
| | | | 1968–69 | 21 | 3 | 1476 | 188* | 82.00 | 6 |
| | | | 1970–71 | 25 | 0 | 1210 | 129 | 48.40 | 3 |
| | | | 1971–72 | 21 | 2 | 1140 | 145 | 60.00 | 5 |
| | | | 1973–74 | 22 | 1 | 1074 | 141* | 51.14 | 3 |
| | | | 1975–76 | 26 | 4 | 1310 | 171 | 59.54 | 4 |
| Compton, D.C.S. | MCC | | 1946–47 | 25 | 3 | 1432 | 163 | 65.09 | 5 |
| Cowdrey, M.C. | MCC | | 1962–63 | 24 | 3 | 1028 | 307 | 48.95 | 2 |
| Cowper, R.M. | Victoria | | 1965–66 | 21 | 2 | 1418 | 307 | 74.63 | 4 |
| Darling, W.M. | South Australia | | 1981–82 | 17 | 3 | 1011 | 134 | 72.21 | 4 |
| Davison, B.F. | Tasmania | | 1983–84 | 20 | 4 | 1036 | 171 | 64.75 | 4 |
| Dexter, E.R. | MCC | | 1962–63 | 24 | 1 | 1023 | 102 | 44.47 | 1 |
| Dyson, J. | New South Wales | (2) | 1980–81 | 22 | 4 | 1028 | 152 | 57.11 | 3 |
| | | | 1983–84 | 19 | 3 | 1015 | 241 | 63.43 | 3 |
| Edrich, J.H. | MCC | | 1970–71 | 21 | 5 | 1097 | 130 | 68.56 | 3 |
| Endean, W.R. | South Africans | | 1952–53 | 27 | 3 | 1281 | 181* | 53.37 | 2 |
| Faulkner, G.A. | South Africans | | 1910–11 | 27 | 1 | 1534 | 204 | 59.00 | 3 |
| Goddard, T.L. | South Africans | | 1963–64 | 20 | 3 | 1054 | 194 | 62.00 | 1 |
| Hammond, W.R. | MCC | (2) | 1928–29 | 18 | 1 | 1553 | 251 | 91.35 | 7 |
| | | | 1936–37 | 20 | 2 | 1206 | 231* | 67.00 | 5 |
| Hardstaff, J., sr | MCC | | 1907–08 | 28 | 2 | 1360 | 135 | 52.30 | 3 |
| Harvey, R.N. | Victoria | (4) | 1950–51 | 25 | 1 | 1099 | 146 | 45.79 | 3 |
| | | | 1952–53 | 27 | 1 | 1659 | 205 | 63.80 | 5 |
| | | | 1954–55 | 24 | 2 | 1009 | 162 | 45.86 | 1 |
| | NSW | | 1962–63 | 22 | 2 | 1107 | 231* | 55.35 | 3 |
| Hassett, A.L. | Victoria | (2) | 1946–47 | 18 | 1 | 1213 | 200 | 71.35 | 5 |
| | | | 1950–51 | 25 | 3 | 1423 | 232 | 64.68 | 4 |
| Hazare, V.S. | Indians | | 1947–48 | 23 | 1 | 1056 | 145 | 48.00 | 4 |
| Headley, G.A. | West Indians | | 1930–31 | 25 | 1 | 1066 | 131 | 44.41 | 4 |
| Hendren, E.H. | MCC | (3) | 1920–21 | 20 | 1 | 1178 | 271 | 62.00 | 3 |

| | | | Season | I | NO | Runs | HS | Avge | 100 |
|---|---|---|---|---|---|---|---|---|---|
| Hendren, E.H. *contd.* | | | 1924–25 | 22 | 3 | 1233 | 168 | 64.89 | 4 |
| | | | 1928–29 | 17 | 1 | 1033 | 169 | 64.56 | 3 |
| Hilditch, A.M.J. | NSW | | 1978–79 | 25 | 0 | 1014 | 124 | 40.56 | 1 |
| Hill, C. | South Australia | (2) | 1897–98 | 19 | 1 | 1196 | 200 | 66.44 | 5 |
| | | | 1901–02 | 20 | 0 | 1035 | 107 | 51.75 | 1 |
| Hookes, D.W. | South Australia | | 1982–83 | 23 | 1 | 1424 | 193 | 64.72 | 4 |
| Hughes, K.J. | Western Australia | (2) | 1980–81 | 26 | 1 | 1036 | 213 | 41.44 | 2 |
| | | | 1982–83 | 21 | 1 | 1280 | 137 | 64.00 | 4 |
| Hutton, L. | MCC | (2) | 1946–47 | 21 | 3 | 1267 | 151* | 70.38 | 3 |
| | | | 1950–51 | 21 | 4 | 1199 | 156* | 70.52 | 5 |
| Jardine, D.R. | MCC | | 1928–29 | 19 | 1 | 1168 | 214 | 64.88 | 6 |
| Kanhai, R.B. | West Indians | | 1960–61 | 18 | 1 | 1093 | 252 | 64.29 | 4 |
| Kippax, A.F. | NSW | (2) | 1926–27 | 13 | 1 | 1039 | 217* | 86.58 | 5 |
| | | | 1928–29 | 19 | 2 | 1079 | 260* | 63.47 | 4 |
| Lawry, W.M. | Victoria | (4) | 1960–61 | 20 | 1 | 1042 | 266 | 54.84 | 2 |
| | | | 1963–64 | 24 | 4 | 1340 | 187* | 67.00 | 4 |
| | | | 1965–66 | 21 | 1 | 1445 | 166 | 72.25 | 6 |
| | | | 1968–69 | 20 | 2 | 1140 | 205 | 63.33 | 4 |
| McCosker, R.B. | NSW | (2) | 1974–75 | 24 | 1 | 1254 | 164 | 54.52 | 4 |
| | | | 1982–83 | 25 | 4 | 1153 | 124 | 54.90 | 3 |
| MacLaren, A.C. | A.E. Stoddart's XI | | 1897–98 | 20 | 1 | 1037 | 142 | 54.57 | 5 |
| May, P.B.H. | MCC | | 1958–59 | 22 | 1 | 1197 | 140 | 57.00 | 5 |
| Miller, K.R. | Victoria | (2) | 1946–47 | 19 | 3 | 1202 | 206* | 75.12 | 4 |
| | NSW | | 1950–51 | 20 | 3 | 1332 | 214 | 78.35 | 5 |
| Morris, A.R. | NSW | (3) | 1946–47 | 20 | 2 | 1234 | 155 | 68.55 | 5 |
| | | | 1948–49 | 17 | 1 | 1069 | 177 | 66.81 | 6 |
| | | | 1950–51 | 22 | 1 | 1221 | 206 | 58.14 | 6 |
| Mudassar Nazar | Pakistanis | | 1983–84 | 19 | 1 | 1071 | 139 | 59.50 | 5 |
| Noble, M.A. | NSW | | 1907–08 | 19 | 1 | 1071 | 176 | 59.50 | 3 |
| Nourse, A.W. | South Africans | | 1910–11 | 29 | 5 | 1454 | 201* | 60.58 | 5 |
| Ogilvie, A.D. | Queensland | | 1977–78 | 26 | 2 | 1215 | 194 | 50.62 | 6 |
| O'Neill, N.C. | NSW | (2) | 1957–58 | 14 | 2 | 1005 | 233 | 83.75 | 4 |
| | | | 1960–61 | 27 | 3 | 1288 | 181 | 53.66 | 5 |
| Pollock, R.G. | South Africans | | 1963–64 | 20 | 1 | 1018 | 175 | 53.57 | 5 |
| Ponsford, W.H. | Victoria | (2) | 1926–27 | 10 | 0 | 1229 | 352 | 122.90 | 6 |
| | | | 1927–28 | 8 | 0 | 1217 | 437 | 152.12 | 4 |
| Ranjitsinhji, K.S. | A.E. Stoddart's XI | | 1897–98 | 22 | 3 | 1157 | 189 | 60.89 | 3 |
| Rhodes, W. | MCC | | 1911–12 | 24 | 4 | 1098 | 179 | 54.90 | 4 |
| Redpath, I.R. | Victoria | | 1974–75 | 30 | 2 | 1150 | 163* | 41.07 | 3 |
| Richards, B.A. | South Australia | | 1970–71 | 16 | 2 | 1538 | 356 | 109.85 | 6 |
| Richards, I.V.A. | West Indians | | 1975–76 | 21 | 2 | 1107 | 175 | 58.26 | 4 |
| Ryder, J. | Victoria | | 1928–29 | 17 | 2 | 1045 | 175 | 69.66 | 3 |
| Sheahan, A.P. | Victoria | | 1972–73 | 15 | 3 | 1002 | 196* | 83.50 | 4 |
| Shepherd, B.K. | Western Australia | (2) | 1962–63 | 21 | 2 | 1001 | 219 | 52.68 | 2 |
| | | | 1963–64 | 23 | 1 | 1087 | 149 | 49.40 | 3 |
| Simpson, R.B. | Western Australia | (4) | 1960–61 | 26 | 2 | 1541 | 221* | 64.21 | 4 |
| | NSW | | 1962–63 | 24 | 2 | 1337 | 205 | 60.77 | 5 |
| | | | 1963–64 | 25 | 2 | 1524 | 359 | 66.26 | 4 |
| | | | 1967–68 | 20 | 1 | 1082 | 277 | 56.94 | 4 |
| Sobers, G.St A. | South Australia | (3) | 1962–63 | 18 | 2 | 1006 | 196 | 62.87 | 3 |
| | | | 1963–64 | 14 | 0 | 1128 | 195 | 80.57 | 6 |
| | West Indians | | 1968–69 | 17 | 2 | 1011 | 132 | 67.40 | 5 |
| Stackpole, K.R. | Victoria | | 1968–69 | 22 | 7 | 1009 | 140* | 67.26 | 5 |
| Sutcliffe, H. | MCC | (2) | 1924–25 | 18 | 0 | 1250 | 188 | 69.44 | 5 |
| | | | 1932–33 | 19 | 1 | 1318 | 194 | 73.22 | 5 |
| Taylor, M.D. | Victoria | | 1983–84 | 18 | 4 | 1010 | 172* | 72.14 | 4 |
| Thomas, G. | NSW | | 1965–66 | 20 | 0 | 1171 | 229 | 58.55 | 4 |
| Trimble, S.C. | Queensland | | 1963–64 | 14 | 2 | 1006 | 252* | 83.83 | 5 |
| Trumper, V.T. | NSW | | 1910–11 | 20 | 2 | 1246 | 214* | 69.22 | 5 |
| Walters, K.D. | NSW | (2) | 1965–66 | 21 | 2 | 1332 | 168 | 70.10 | 6 |
| | | | 1968–69 | 19 | 0 | 1078 | 242 | 56.73 | 5 |
| Wellham, D.M. | New South Wales | | 1982–83 | 23 | 5 | 1205 | 136* | 66.94 | 2 |
| Wessels, K.C. | Queensland | (3) | 1981–82 | 18 | 0 | 1094 | 220 | 60.77 | 5 |
| | | | 1982–83 | 23 | 0 | 1325 | 249 | 57.60 | 5 |
| | | | 1984–85 | 19 | 0 | 1020 | 173 | 53.68 | 3 |

| | | | Season | I | NO | Runs | HS | Avge | 100 |
|---|---|---|---|---|---|---|---|---|---|
| Yallop, G.N. | Victoria | (2) | 1982–83 | 22 | 1 | 1418 | 246 | 67.52 | 4 |
| | | | 1983–84 | 11 | 1 | 1132 | 268 | 113.20 | 5 |

*Only seven batsmen have scored 1000 runs in an Australian season when there were no matches against a visiting touring team: S.G. Barnes, D.G. Bradman, W.A. Brown, A.F. Kippax, A.R. Morris, N.C. O'Neill and W.H. Ponsford.*

### 1000 RUNS AGAINST A TOURING TEAM IN AUSTRALIA

| | Opponents | Season | I | NO | Runs | HS | Avge | 100 |
|---|---|---|---|---|---|---|---|---|
| Bradman, D.G. | South Africans | 1931–32 | 8 | 1 | 1190 | 299* | 170.00 | 6 |
| Chappell, I.M. | West Indians | 1968–69 | 12 | 1 | 1062 | 188* | 96.54 | 5 |

# 1000 RUNS IN A SEASON IN SOUTH AFRICA AND RHODESIA

| | | Season | I | NO | Runs | HS | Avge | 100 |
|---|---|---|---|---|---|---|---|---|
| J.R. Reid | New Zealanders | 1961–62 | 30 | 2 | 1915 | 203 | 68.39 | 7 |
| D.C.S. Compton | MCC | 1948–49 | 26 | 5 | 1781 | 300 | 84.80 | 8 |
| R.N. Harvey | Australians | 1949–50 | 25 | 5 | 1526 | 178 | 76.30 | 8 |
| J.B. Hobbs | MCC | 1913–14 | 22 | 2 | 1489 | 170 | 74.45 | 5 |
| L. Hutton | MCC | 1948–49 | 21 | 1 | 1477 | 174 | 73.85 | 5 |
| A.R. Morris | Australians | 1949–50 | 27 | 3 | 1411 | 157 | 58.79 | 8 |
| R.B. Simpson | Australians | 1966–67 | 26 | 4 | 1344 | 243 | 61.09 | 3 |
| J. Moroney | Australians | 1949–50 | 27 | 3 | 1331 | 160* | 55.45 | 6 |
| B.A. Richards | Natal | 1973–74 | 18 | 2 | 1285 | 186* | 80.31 | 4 |
| P.B.H. May | MCC | 1956–57 | 24 | 1 | 1270 | 206 | 55.21 | 6 |
| B.A. Richards | Natal | 1972–73 | 19 | 1 | 1247 | 197 | 69.27 | 5 |
| J.B. Hobbs | MCC | 1909–10 | 20 | 1 | 1194 | 187 | 62.84 | 3 |
| J.H.W. Fingleton | Australians | 1935–36 | 19 | 4 | 1192 | 167 | 79.46 | 6 |
| B.A. Richards | Natal | 1969–70 | 18 | 2 | 1172 | 169 | 73.25 | 6 |
| L. Hutton | MCC | 1938–39 | 19 | 1 | 1168 | 202 | 64.88 | 5 |
| B. Sutcliffe | New Zealanders | 1953–54 | 27 | 2 | 1155 | 196 | 46.20 | 1 |
| S.J. Cook | Transvaal | 1982–83 | 21 | 2 | 1142 | 201* | 60.10 | 4 |
| G. Boycott | MCC | 1964–65 | 25 | 5 | 1135 | 193* | 56.75 | 4 |
| G.E. Tyldesley | MCC | 1927–28 | 21 | 2 | 1130 | 161 | 59.47 | 4 |
| K.F. Barrington | MCC | 1964–65 | 18 | 5 | 1128 | 169* | 86.76 | 4 |
| R.G. Pollock | E. Province | 1974–75 | 21 | 5 | 1126 | 167* | 70.37 | 5 |
| C. Washbrook | MCC | 1948–49 | 23 | 2 | 1124 | 195 | 53.52 | 3 |
| R.M. Cowper | Australians | 1966–67 | 25 | 2 | 1116 | 201* | 48.52 | 2 |
| P. Holmes | MCC | 1927–28 | 22 | 3 | 1112 | 279* | 58.52 | 3 |
| B.A. Richards | Natal | 1971–72 | 15 | 1 | 1089 | 219 | 77.78 | 4 |
| P.N. Kirsten | W. Province | 1976–77 | 15 | 1 | 1074 | 173* | 76.71 | 6 |
| E. Paynter | MCC | 1938–39 | 14 | 0 | 1072 | 243 | 76.57 | 5 |
| W.A. Brown | Australians | 1935–36 | 19 | 2 | 1065 | 148 | 62.64 | 2 |
| B.A. Richards | Natal | 1975–76 | 21 | 4 | 1051 | 159 | 61.82 | 3 |
| K.C. Bland | Rhodesia | 1964–65 | 18 | 3 | 1048 | 151* | 69.86 | 3 |
| W.R. Hammond | MCC | 1930–31 | 19 | 2 | 1045 | 136* | 61.47 | 3 |
| I.R. Redpath | Australians | 1966–67 | 23 | 3 | 1045 | 154 | 52.25 | 2 |
| R.G. Pollock | E. Province | 1968–69 | 14 | 2 | 1043 | 196 | 86.91 | 3 |
| J.W. Burke | Australians | 1957–58 | 19 | 3 | 1041 | 189 | 65.06 | 4 |
| M.C. Cowdrey | MCC | 1956–57 | 27 | 1 | 1035 | 173 | 39.80 | 2 |
| H. Sutcliffe | MCC | 1927–28 | 23 | 3 | 1030 | 102 | 51.50 | 2 |
| W.R. Hammond | MCC | 1938–39 | 18 | 1 | 1025 | 181 | 60.29 | 4 |
| S.J. Cook | Transvaal | 1983–84 | 21 | 3 | 1016 | 166 | 56.44 | 2 |
| D.T. Lindsay | N.E. Transvaal | 1966–67 | 14 | 0 | 1014 | 216 | 72.42 | 4 |
| R.G. Pollock | E. Province | 1975–76 | 19 | 4 | 1013 | 194 | 67.53 | 3 |
| J.R. Reid | New Zealanders | 1953–54 | 27 | 0 | 1012 | 175 | 37.48 | 3 |
| R.G. Pollock | E. Province | 1969–70 | 16 | 0 | 1005 | 274 | 62.81 | 4 |

## 1000 RUNS IN A SEASON IN WEST INDIES

|  |  | Season | I | NO | Runs | HS | Avge | 100 |
|---|---|---|---|---|---|---|---|---|
| E.H. Hendren | MCC | 1929–30 | 18 | 5 | 1765 | 254* | 135.76 | 6 |
| A. Sandham | MCC | 1929–30 | 20 | 0 | 1281 | 325 | 64.05 | 6 |
| G.M. Turner | New Zealanders | 1971–72 | 16 | 2 | 1214 | 259 | 86.71 | 4 |
| S.M. Gavaskar | Indians | 1970–71 | 16 | 4 | 1169 | 220 | 97.41 | 5 |
| G. Boycott | MCC | 1967–68 | 16 | 2 | 1154 | 243 | 82.42 | 4 |
| D.L. Amiss | MCC | 1973–74 | 16 | 1 | 1120 | 262* | 74.66 | 5 |
| L.G. Rowe | Jamaica | 1973–74 | 15 | 1 | 1117 | 302 | 79.78 | 5 |
| G.S. Chappell | Australians | 1972–73 | 17 | 1 | 1109 | 154 | 69.31 | 4 |
| R.C. Fredericks | Guyana | 1971–72 | 19 | 2 | 1077 | 163 | 63.35 | 3 |
| R.C. Fredericks | Guyana | 1972–73 | 18 | 2 | 1076 | 158 | 67.25 | 3 |
| M.C. Cowdrey | MCC | 1959–60 | 18 | 2 | 1014 | 173 | 63.37 | 5 |
| G.St A. Sobers | Barbados | 1957–58 | 10 | 3 | 1007 | 365* | 143.85 | 4 |

## MOST RUNS IN A SEASON IN NEW ZEALAND

|  |  | Season | I | NO | Runs | HS | Avge | 100 |
|---|---|---|---|---|---|---|---|---|
| G.M. Turner | Otago | 1975–76 | 20 | 4 | 1244 | 177* | 77.75 | 5 |
| G.T. Dowling | Canterbury | 1967–68 | 18 | 1 | 968 | 239 | 56.94 | 4 |
| B.A. Edgar | Wellington | 1978–79 | 23 | 0 | 944 | 134 | 41.04 | 2 |
| E.de C. Weekes | West Indians | 1955–56 | 10 | 1 | 940 | 156 | 104.44 | 6 |
| B.A. Edgar | Wellington | 1981–82 | 19 | 1 | 934 | 161 | 51.88 | 3 |
| B.F. Hastings | Canterbury | 1968–69 | 15 | 4 | 872 | 117* | 79.27 | 4 |
| J.G. Wright | Northern Districts | 1981–82 | 18 | 0 | 872 | 141 | 48.44 | 4 |
| G.T. Dowling | Canterbury | 1966–67 | 18 | 2 | 871 | 102* | 54.43 | 1 |
| B. Sutcliffe | Otago | 1952–53 | 13 | 0 | 859 | 385 | 66.07 | 1 |
| R.W. Anderson | Northern Districts | 1977–78 | 22 | 0 | 849 | 123 | 38.59 | 2 |
| G.M. Turner | Otago | 1974–75 | 15 | 1 | 838 | 186* | 59.85 | 4 |
| S.M. Nurse | West Indians | 1968–69 | 9 | 0 | 826 | 258 | 91.77 | 3 |

## 1000 RUNS IN A SEASON IN INDIA, PAKISTAN AND SRI LANKA

|  |  | Season | I | NO | Runs | HS | Avge | 100 |
|---|---|---|---|---|---|---|---|---|
| Adhikari, S.G. |  | 1962–63 | 17 | 0 | 1028 | 173 | 60.47 | 5 |
| Aftab Baloch | (2) | 1973–74 | 32 | 4 | 1457 | 428 | 52.03 | 3 |
|  |  | 1974–75 | 20 | 3 | 1109 | 200* | 65.23 | 4 |
| Aftab Gul |  | 1973–74 | 27 | 2 | 1008 | 140 | 40.32 | 3 |
| Agha Zahid | (2) | 1981–82 | 24 | 3 | 1218 | 136 | 58.00 | 3 |
|  |  | 1982–83 | 23 | 2 | 1220 | 175 | 58.09 | 3 |
| Alimuddin |  | 1961–62 | 22 | 2 | 1020 | 131* | 51.00 | 4 |
| Ali Zia |  | 1983–84 | 25 | 1 | 1021 | 130 | 42.54 | 3 |
| Alley, W.E. | Commonwealth | 1949–50 | 28 | 9 | 1255 | 209* | 66.05 | 3 |
| Amarnath, L. |  | 1935–36 | 21 | 3 | 1071 | 149* | 59.50 | 2 |
| Amarnath, M. |  | 1978–79 | 26 | 7 | 1164 | 178* | 61.26 | 5 |
| Amarnath, S. |  | 1978–79 | 23 | 4 | 1044 | 144 | 54.94 | 3 |
| Anwar-ul-Haq |  | 1981–82 | 26 | 1 | 1037 | 147 | 41.48 | 4 |
| Arshad Pervez | (4) | 1977–78 | 17 | 1 | 1364 | 243* | 85.25 | 5 |
|  |  | 1981–82 | 24 | 4 | 1102 | 164 | 55.10 | 4 |
|  |  | 1983–84 | 20 | 2 | 1051 | 181 | 58.38 | 4 |
|  |  | 1984–85 | 27 | 5 | 1263 | 152* | 56.95 | 5 |
| Ashraf Ali |  | 1980–81 | 26 | 5 | 1033 | 136* | 49.19 | 1 |
| Azmat Rana |  | 1977–78 | 20 | 4 | 1495 | 206* | 93.43 | 6 |
| Bacchus, S.F.A.F. | West Indians | 1978–79 | 25 | 1 | 1030 | 250 | 42.91 | 2 |
| Barrington, K.F. | MCC | 1961–62 | 26 | 7 | 1329 | 172 | 69.94 | 5 |
| Borde, C.G. | (2) | 1964–65 | 28 | 3 | 1604 | 168 | 64.16 | 6 |
|  |  | 1966–67 | 24 | 3 | 1338 | 155* | 67.22 | 4 |
| Butcher, B.F. | West Indians | 1958–59 | 29 | 5 | 1133 | 142 | 47.20 | 2 |
| Chauhan, C.P.S. | (2) | 1972–73 | 18 | 3 | 1138 | 207 | 75.86 | 3 |
|  |  | 1978–79 | 30 | 1 | 1056 | 93 | 36.41 | – |
| Dexter, E.R. | MCC | 1961–62 | 27 | 5 | 1053 | 205 | 47.86 | 2 |
| Emmett, G.M. | Commonwealth | 1950–51 | 37 | 5 | 1296 | 104 | 40.50 | 2 |
| Engineer, F.M. |  | 1964–65 | 23 | 1 | 1050 | 142 | 47.72 | 2 |
| Fishlock, L.B. | Commonwealth | 1950–51 | 32 | 2 | 1123 | 138 | 37.43 | 3 |

| | | | Season | I | NO | Runs | HS | Avge | 100 |
|---|---|---|---|---|---|---|---|---|---|
| Fredericks, R.C. | West Indians | | 1974–75 | 21 | 1 | 1106 | 202 | 55.30 | 5 |
| Gaekwad, A.D. | | (2) | 1978–79 | 27 | 3 | 1047 | 151 | 43.62 | 5 |
| | | | 1983–84 | 27 | 2 | 1153 | 201 | 46.12 | 4 |
| Gatting, M.W. | England | | 1984–85 | 17 | 5 | 1029 | 207 | 85.75 | 3 |
| Gavaskar, S.M. | | (6) | 1972–73 | 34 | 4 | 1107 | 160 | 36.90 | 3 |
| | | | 1976–77 | 33 | 3 | 1444 | 228 | 48.13 | 4 |
| | | | 1978–79 | 30 | 5 | 2121 | 205 | 84.84 | 10 |
| | | | 1979–80 | 32 | 2 | 1518 | 166 | 50.60 | 4 |
| | | | 1981–82 | 21 | 4 | 1471 | 340 | 81.52 | 5 |
| | | | 1983–84 | 24 | 5 | 1310 | 206* | 68.94 | 5 |
| Ghulam Abbas | | | 1975–76 | 20 | 1 | 1069 | 276 | 56.26 | 3 |
| Gimblett, H. | Commonwealth | | 1950–51 | 38 | 6 | 1269 | 111 | 39.65 | 1 |
| Gomes, H.A. | West Indians | | 1978–79 | 23 | 2 | 1068 | 173* | 50.85 | 3 |
| Graveney, T.W. | MCC | | 1951–52 | 32 | 7 | 1393 | 175 | 55.72 | 6 |
| Grieves, K.J. | Commonwealth | | 1950–51 | 32 | 4 | 1193 | 155 | 42.60 | 2 |
| Hanif Mohammad | | (2) | 1952–53 | 20 | 5 | 1010 | 203* | 67.33 | 4 |
| | | | 1961–62 | 21 | 0 | 1250 | 189 | 59.52 | 5 |
| Hanumant Singh | | (3) | 1963–64 | 26 | 4 | 1234 | 179 | 56.09 | 5 |
| | | | 1964–65 | 30 | 5 | 1270 | 210 | 50.80 | 3 |
| | | | 1966–67 | 27 | 4 | 1586 | 213* | 68.95 | 6 |
| Haroon Rashid | | | 1975–76 | 24 | 4 | 1034 | 122* | 51.70 | 4 |
| Hazare, V.S. | | (4) | 1943–44 | 11 | 3 | 1423 | 309 | 177.87 | 5 |
| | | | 1948–49 | 21 | 3 | 1310 | 146 | 72.77 | 6 |
| | | | 1949–50 | 19 | 3 | 1364 | 195 | 85.24 | 5 |
| | | | 1950–51 | 20 | 3 | 1140 | 186 | 67.05 | 5 |
| Holt, J.K. | West Indians | | 1958–59 | 27 | 4 | 1001 | 123 | 43.52 | 3 |
| Hunte, C.C. | West Indians | | 1958–59 | 32 | 3 | 1127 | 137 | 38.86 | 1 |
| Ibrahim, K.C. | | | 1947–48 | 11 | 4 | 1171 | 234* | 167.28 | 4 |
| Ikin, J.T. | Commonwealth | | 1950–51 | 33 | 5 | 1292 | 111 | 46.14 | 2 |
| Imtiaz Ahmed | | | 1961–62 | 24 | 1 | 1142 | 251 | 49.65 | 4 |
| Jaisimha, M.L. | | (3) | 1959–60 | 23 | 2 | 1143 | 164 | 54.42 | 4 |
| | | | 1962–63 | 22 | 3 | 1003 | 124 | 52.78 | 3 |
| | | | 1964–65 | 31 | 0 | 1416 | 259 | 45.67 | 5 |
| Javed Miandad | | (4) | 1977–78 | 21 | 4 | 1315 | 172 | 77.35 | 5 |
| | | | 1979–80 | 24 | 7 | 1142 | 110* | 67.17 | 3 |
| | | | 1980–81 | 23 | 0 | 1039 | 130 | 45.17 | 3 |
| | | | 1982–83 | 16 | 2 | 1124 | 280* | 80.28 | 4 |
| Kallicharran, A.I. | West Indians | | 1974–75 | 25 | 3 | 1249 | 151 | 56.77 | 3 |
| Kanhai, R.B. | West Indians | | 1958–59 | 28 | 2 | 1518 | 256 | 58.38 | 4 |
| Khalid Irtiza | | | 1975–76 | 21 | 2 | 1016 | 290 | 53.47 | 2 |
| Kunderan, B.K. | | | 1963–64 | 29 | 1 | 1079 | 192 | 38.53 | 3 |
| Livingston, L. | Commonwealth | | 1949–50 | 25 | 5 | 1020 | 123 | 51.00 | 3 |
| Lloyd, C.H. | West Indians | | 1974–75 | 22 | 7 | 1363 | 242* | 90.86 | 3 |
| Lowson, F.A. | MCC | | 1951–52 | 28 | 5 | 1016 | 138 | 44.17 | 1 |
| Majid Khan | | | 1979–80 | 27 | 3 | 1068 | 156 | 44.50 | 3 |
| Manjrekar, V.L. | | | 1963–64 | 21 | 2 | 1077 | 283 | 56.68 | 5 |
| Mankad, A.V. | | (3) | 1969–70 | 28 | 5 | 1064 | 171 | 46.26 | 2 |
| | | | 1973–74 | 21 | 5 | 1034 | 124 | 64.62 | 4 |
| | | | 1976–77 | 22 | 8 | 1363 | 208* | 97.35 | 5 |
| Merchant, V.M. | | | 1944–45 | 15 | 3 | 1323 | 275 | 110.25 | 5 |
| Meuleman, K.D. | Commonwealth | | 1953–54 | 26 | 4 | 1158 | 131 | 52.63 | 3 |
| Modi, R.S. | | | 1944–45 | 15 | 3 | 1386 | 245* | 115.50 | 6 |
| Mohammad Shafiq | | | 1975–76 | 17 | 0 | 1014 | 271 | 59.64 | 3 |
| Mohsin Khan | | | 1981–82 | 20 | 1 | 1160 | 129 | 61.05 | 4 |
| Mudassar Nazar | | (3) | 1974–75 | 19 | 0 | 1106 | 165 | 58.21 | 6 |
| | | | 1977–78 | 22 | 2 | 1065 | 152* | 53.25 | 3 |
| | | | 1982–83 | 17 | 4 | 1110 | 231 | 85.38 | 4 |
| Mushtaq Mohammad | | | 1961–62 | 20 | 2 | 1112 | 229* | 61.77 | 4 |
| Nadkarni, R.G. | | | 1962–63 | 19 | 2 | 1190 | 219 | 70.00 | 2 |
| Parfitt, P.H. | MCC | | 1961–62 | 29 | 4 | 1043 | 166* | 41.72 | 3 |
| Parsons, J.H. | MCC | | 1926–27 | 28 | 2 | 1289 | 160 | 49.57 | 2 |
| Pataudi, Nawab of, jr | | (2) | 1963–64 | 31 | 1 | 1031 | 203* | 34.36 | 2 |
| | | | 1964–65 | 27 | 3 | 1415 | 154 | 58.96 | 7 |
| Patel, B.P. | | (3) | 1974–75 | 28 | 5 | 1042 | 106* | 45.30 | 2 |
| | | | 1976–77 | 26 | 1 | 1345 | 183 | 53.80 | 4 |
| | | | 1978–79 | 15 | 1 | 1029 | 216 | 73.50 | 6 |

|  |  |  | Season | I | NO | Runs | HS | Avge | 100 |
|---|---|---|---|---|---|---|---|---|---|
| Pullar, G. | MCC |  | 1961–62 | 25 | 1 | 1046 | 165 | 43.58 | 3 |
| Qasim Omar |  |  | 1982–83 | 18 | 4 | 1275 | 210* | 91.07 | 6 |
| Rae, A.F. | West Indians |  | 1948–49 | 25 | 0 | 1150 | 160 | 46.00 | 6 |
| Ramiz Raja |  |  | 1983–84 | 36 | 4 | 1294 | 149 | 40.43 | 4 |
| Reid, J.R. | New Zealanders |  | 1955–56 | 25 | 6 | 1024 | 150* | 53.89 | 3 |
| Richards, I.V.A. | West Indians |  | 1974–75 | 28 | 7 | 1267 | 192* | 60.33 | 4 |
| Richardson, P.E. | MCC |  | 1961–62 | 30 | 3 | 1003 | 147 | 37.14 | 1 |
| Rizwan-uz-Zaman |  | (2) | 1982–83 | 25 | 0 | 1358 | 152 | 54.32 | 4 |
|  |  |  | 1984–85 | 17 | 3 | 1101 | 166 | 78.64 | 5 |
| Robertson, J.D.B. | MCC |  | 1951–52 | 31 | 3 | 1173 | 183 | 41.89 | 3 |
| Saadat Ali |  | (2) | 1982–83 | 22 | 2 | 1013 | 206* | 50.65 | 3 |
|  |  |  | 1983–84 | 27 | 1 | 1649 | 208 | 63.42 | 4 |
| Sadiq Mohammad |  |  | 1982–83 | 21 | 2 | 1009 | 157 | 53.10 | 4 |
| Saeed Ahmed |  |  | 1970–71 | 20 | 2 | 1012 | 203* | 56.22 | 3 |
| Sajid Ali |  |  | 1983–84 | 24 | 0 | 1180 | 146 | 49.16 | 3 |
| Salim Malik |  |  | 1982–83 | 23 | 1 | 1013 | 124* | 46.04 | 6 |
| Salim Pervez |  |  | 1982–83 | 27 | 3 | 1136 | 102* | 47.33 | 2 |
| Sandham, A. | MCC |  | 1926–27 | 30 | 2 | 1756 | 150 | 62.71 | 7 |
| Sardesai, D.N. |  | (3) | 1963–64 | 29 | 2 | 1197 | 110 | 44.33 | 2 |
|  |  |  | 1964–65 | 27 | 4 | 1429 | 222 | 62.13 | 6 |
|  |  |  | 1966–67 | 20 | 1 | 1190 | 199 | 62.63 | 4 |
| Shafiq Ahmed |  | (7) | 1973–74 | 31 | 5 | 1152 | 117* | 44.31 | 1 |
|  |  |  | 1974–75 | 19 | 1 | 1335 | 200* | 74.16 | 5 |
|  |  |  | 1975–76 | 26 | 3 | 1198 | 122 | 52.08 | 3 |
|  |  |  | 1978–79 | 19 | 2 | 1409 | 217* | 82.88 | 6 |
|  |  |  | 1981–82 | 26 | 3 | 1058 | 161 | 46.00 | 4 |
|  |  |  | 1982–83 | 23 | 3 | 1104 | 118 | 55.20 | 3 |
|  |  |  | 1983–84 | 24 | 3 | 1052 | 125 | 50.09 | 2 |
| Shoaib Mohammad |  |  | 1983–84 | 26 | 3 | 1118 | 151* | 48.60 | 5 |
| Sobers, G.St A. | West Indians |  | 1958–59 | 26 | 5 | 1419 | 198 | 67.57 | 5 |
| Stollmeyer, J.B. | West Indians |  | 1948–49 | 22 | 5 | 1091 | 244* | 64.17 | 2 |
| Sutcliffe, B. | New Zealanders |  | 1955–56 | 28 | 4 | 1031 | 230* | 42.95 | 3 |
| Talat Ali |  |  | 1973–74 | 33 | 0 | 1124 | 112 | 34.06 | 1 |
| Tate, M.W. | MCC |  | 1926–27 | 33 | 0 | 1193 | 133 | 36.15 | 3 |
| Umrigar, P.R. |  | (2) | 1955–56 | 14 | 2 | 1028 | 223 | 85.66 | 3 |
|  |  |  | 1962–63 | 19 | 2 | 1065 | 124* | 62.64 | 4 |
| Vengsarkar, D.B. |  | (3) | 1978–79 | 29 | 5 | 1364 | 157* | 56.83 | 4 |
|  |  |  | 1979–80 | 28 | 2 | 1495 | 210 | 57.50 | 4 |
|  |  |  | 1983–84 | 20 | 2 | 1088 | 159 | 60.44 | 5 |
| Viswanath, G.R. |  | (3) | 1974–75 | 31 | 2 | 1538 | 200* | 53.03 | 4 |
|  |  |  | 1978–79 | 25 | 0 | 1356 | 179 | 54.24 | 5 |
|  |  |  | 1979–80 | 25 | 2 | 1051 | 161* | 45.69 | 3 |
| Wadekar, A.L. |  | (3) | 1965–66 | 22 | 4 | 1287 | 185 | 71.50 | 6 |
|  |  |  | 1966–67 | 23 | 1 | 1321 | 323 | 60.04 | 3 |
|  |  |  | 1972–73 | 25 | 2 | 1061 | 171 | 46.13 | 2 |
| Walcott, C.L. | West Indians |  | 1948–49 | 22 | 4 | 1366 | 152 | 75.88 | 5 |
| Wasim Raja |  |  | 1973–74 | 32 | 1 | 1010 | 165 | 32.58 | 1 |
| Wazir Ali, S. |  |  | 1935–36 | 18 | 3 | 1072 | 268* | 71.46 | 4 |
| Weekes, E. de C. | West Indians |  | 1948–49 | 19 | 4 | 1350 | 194 | 90.00 | 5 |
| Worrell, F.M.M. | Commonwealth | (2) | 1949–50 | 26 | 4 | 1640 | 223* | 74.54 | 5 |
|  |  |  | 1950–51 | 33 | 4 | 1900 | 285 | 63.33 | 5 |
| Wyatt, R.E.S. | MCC |  | 1926–27 | 37 | 4 | 1747 | 138 | 52.93 | 3 |
| Zaheer Abbas |  | (4) | 1973–74 | 24 | 5 | 1597 | 174 | 84.05 | 5 |
|  |  |  | 1975–76 | 23 | 1 | 1026 | 170 | 46.63 | 2 |
|  |  |  | 1980–81 | 22 | 10 | 1123 | 154* | 93.58 | 5 |
|  |  |  | 1982–83 | 15 | 1 | 1371 | 215 | 97.92 | 7 |

# MOST HUNDREDS IN A SEASON

W.G. Grace (1871) was the first batsman to score ten hundreds in an English season. Not until 1978–79 was this aggregate attained overseas (by S.M. Gavaskar in India and Pakistan), but the home record has progressed as follows: 12 – R. Abel (1900), 13 – C.B. Fry (1901), 16 – J.B. Hobbs (1925), and 18 – D.C.S. Compton (1947).

| 18 | D.C.S. Compton | Middlesex | 1947 | 15 | W.R. Hammond | Gloucestershire | 1938 |
|---|---|---|---|---|---|---|---|
| 16 | J.B. Hobbs | Surrey | 1925 | 14 | H. Sutcliffe | Yorkshire | 1932 |

| | | | | | | | | |
|---|---|---|---|---|---|---|---|---|
| 13 | D.G. Bradman | Australians | 1938 | 13 | G. Boycott | Yorkshire | 1971 |
| 13 | C.B. Fry | Sussex | 1901 | 12 | R. Abel | Surrey | 1900 |
| 13 | W.R. Hammond | Gloucestershire | 1933 | 12 | K.S. Duleepsinhji | Sussex | 1931 |
| 13 | W.R. Hammond | Gloucestershire | 1937 | 12 | W.J. Edrich | Middlesex | 1947 |
| 13 | T.W. Hayward | Surrey | 1906 | 12 | W.R. Hammond | Gloucestershire | 1927 |
| 13 | E.H. Hendren | Middlesex | 1923 | 12 | J.B. Hobbs | Surrey | 1928 |
| 13 | E.H. Hendren | Middlesex | 1927 | 12 | L. Hutton | Yorkshire | 1939 |
| 13 | E.H. Hendren | Middlesex | 1928 | 12 | L. Hutton | Yorkshire | 1949 |
| 13 | C.P. Mead | Hampshire | 1928 | 12 | J.G. Langridge | Sussex | 1949 |
| 13 | H. Sutcliffe | Yorkshire | 1928 | 12 | J.D.B. Robertson | Middlesex | 1947 |
| 13 | H. Sutcliffe | Yorkshire | 1931 | 12 | F.E. Woolley | Kent | 1928 |

# MOST HUNDREDS IN A SEASON OVERSEAS

| | | | | | |
|---|---|---|---|---|---|
| Australia | 8 | D.G. Bradman | South Australia | 1947–48 |
| South Africa | 8 | D.C.S. Compton | MCC | 1948–49 |
| | 8 | R.N. Harvey | Australians | 1949–50 |
| | 8 | A.R. Morris | Australians | 1949–50 |
| West Indies | 6 | E.H. Hendren | MCC | 1929–30 |
| | 6 | A. Sandham | MCC | 1929–30 |
| New Zealand | 6 | E.de C. Weekes | West Indians | 1955–56 |
| India | 7 | A. Sandham | MCC | 1926–27 |
| | 7 | Nawab of Pataudi, jr | Delhi | 1964–65 |
| | 7 | S.M. Gavaskar | Bombay | 1978–79 |
| Pakistan | 7 | Zaheer Abbas | PIA | 1982–83 |

# LEADING HOME BATSMEN OF THE ENGLISH SEASON 1894–1985

*Qualifications: 20 innings, highest average*

| | | | I | NO | Runs | HS | Avge | 100 |
|---|---|---|---|---|---|---|---|---|
| 1894 | W. Brockwell | Surrey | 45 | 6 | 1491 | 128 | 38.23 | 5 |
| 1895 | A.C. MacLaren | Lancashire | 24 | 0 | 1229 | 424 | 51.20 | 4 |
| 1896 | K.S. Ranjitsinhji | Sussex | 55 | 7 | 2780 | 171* | 57.91 | 10 |
| 1897 | N.F. Druce | C.U./Surrey | 20 | 2 | 928 | 227* | 51.55 | 3 |
| 1898 | W.G. Quaife | Warwickshire | 28 | 8 | 1219 | 157* | 60.95 | 3 |
| 1899 | R.M. Poore | Hampshire | 21 | 4 | 1551 | 304 | 91.23 | 7 |
| 1900 | K.S. Ranjitsinhji | Sussex | 40 | 5 | 3065 | 275 | 87.57 | 11 |
| 1901 | C.B. Fry | Sussex | 43 | 3 | 3147 | 244 | 78.67 | 13 |
| 1902 | A. Shrewsbury | Nottinghamshire | 32 | 7 | 1250 | 127* | 50.00 | 4 |
| 1903 | C.B. Fry | Sussex | 40 | 7 | 2683 | 234 | 81.30 | 9 |
| 1904 | K.S. Ranjitsinhji | Sussex | 34 | 6 | 2077 | 207* | 74.17 | 8 |
| 1905 | C.B. Fry | Sussex | 44 | 4 | 2801 | 233 | 70.02 | 10 |
| 1906 | C.J. Burnup | Kent | 21 | 3 | 1207 | 179 | 67.05 | 4 |
| 1907 | C.B. Fry | Sussex | 34 | 3 | 1449 | 187 | 46.74 | 4 |
| 1908 | B.J.T. Bosanquet | Middlesex | 22 | 2 | 1081 | 214 | 54.05 | 3 |
| 1909 | A.P. Day | Kent | 24 | 1 | 1014 | 177 | 44.08 | 3 |
| 1910 | J.T. Tyldesley | Lancashire | 51 | 2 | 2265 | 158 | 46.22 | 7 |
| 1911 | C.B. Fry | Hampshire | 26 | 2 | 1728 | 258* | 72.00 | 7 |
| 1912 | C.B. Fry | Hampshire | 31 | 3 | 1592 | 203* | 56.85 | 5 |
| 1913 | C.P. Mead | Hampshire | 60 | 8 | 2627 | 171* | 50.51 | 9 |
| 1914 | J.W. Hearne | Middlesex | 43 | 8 | 2116 | 204 | 60.45 | 8 |
| 1919 | G. Gunn | Nottinghamshire | 25 | 2 | 1451 | 185* | 63.08 | 5 |
| 1920 | E.H. Hendren | Middlesex | 47 | 6 | 2520 | 232 | 61.46 | 6 |
| 1921 | C.P. Mead | Hampshire | 52 | 6 | 3179 | 280* | 69.10 | 10 |
| 1922 | E.H. Hendren | Middlesex | 38 | 7 | 2072 | 277 | 66.83 | 7 |
| 1923 | E.H. Hendren | Middlesex | 51 | 12 | 3010 | 200* | 77.17 | 13 |
| 1924 | A. Sandham | Surrey | 37 | 2 | 2082 | 169 | 59.48 | 7 |
| 1925 | J.B. Hobbs | Surrey | 48 | 5 | 3024 | 266* | 70.32 | 16 |
| 1926 | J.B. Hobbs | Surrey | 41 | 3 | 2949 | 316* | 77.60 | 10 |
| 1927 | C. Hallows | Lancashire | 44 | 13 | 2343 | 233* | 75.58 | 7 |
| 1928 | J.B. Hobbs | Surrey | 38 | 7 | 2542 | 200* | 82.00 | 12 |
| 1929 | J.B. Hobbs | Surrey | 39 | 5 | 2263 | 204 | 66.55 | 10 |
| 1930 | H. Sutcliffe | Yorkshire | 44 | 8 | 2312 | 173 | 64.22 | 6 |
| 1931 | H. Sutcliffe | Yorkshire | 42 | 11 | 3006 | 230 | 96.96 | 13 |

| | | | *I* | *NO* | *Runs* | *HS* | *Avge* | *100* |
|---|---|---|---|---|---|---|---|---|
| 1932 | H. Sutcliffe | Yorkshire | 52 | 7 | 3336 | 313 | 74.13 | 14 |
| 1933 | W.R. Hammond | Gloucestershire | 54 | 5 | 3323 | 264 | 67.81 | 13 |
| 1934 | W.R. Hammond | Gloucestershire | 35 | 4 | 2366 | 302* | 76.32 | 8 |
| 1935 | W.R. Hammond | Gloucestershire | 58 | 5 | 2616 | 252 | 49.35 | 7 |
| 1936 | W.R. Hammond | Gloucestershire | 42 | 5 | 2107 | 317 | 56.94 | 5 |
| 1937 | W.R. Hammond | Gloucestershire | 55 | 5 | 3252 | 217 | 65.04 | 13 |
| 1938 | W.R. Hammond | Gloucestershire | 42 | 2 | 3011 | 271 | 75.27 | 15 |
| 1939 | W.R. Hammond | Gloucestershire | 46 | 7 | 2479 | 302 | 63.56 | 8 |
| 1946 | W.R. Hammond | Gloucestershire | 26 | 5 | 1783 | 214 | 84.90 | 7 |
| 1947 | D.C.S. Compton | Middlesex | 50 | 8 | 3816 | 246 | 90.85 | 18 |
| 1948 | C. Washbrook | Lancashire | 31 | 4 | 1900 | 200 | 70.37 | 7 |
| 1949 | J. Hardstaff, jr | Nottinghamshire | 40 | 9 | 2251 | 162* | 72.61 | 8 |
| 1950 | R.T. Simpson | Nottinghamshire | 47 | 6 | 2576 | 243* | 62.82 | 8 |
| 1951 | P.B.H. May | C.U./Surrey | 43 | 9 | 2339 | 178* | 68.79 | 9 |
| 1952 | D.S. Sheppard | C.U./Sussex | 39 | 4 | 2262 | 239* | 64.62 | 10 |
| 1953 | L. Hutton | Yorkshire | 44 | 5 | 2458 | 241 | 63.02 | 8 |
| 1954 | D.C.S. Compton | Middlesex | 28 | 2 | 1524 | 278 | 58.62 | 4 |
| 1955 | P.B.H. May | Surrey | 42 | 5 | 1902 | 125 | 51.40 | 5 |
| 1956 | T.W. Graveney | Gloucestershire | 54 | 6 | 2397 | 200 | 49.93 | 9 |
| 1957 | P.B.H. May | Surrey | 41 | 3 | 2347 | 285* | 61.76 | 7 |
| 1958 | P.B.H. May | Surrey | 41 | 6 | 2231 | 174 | 63.74 | 8 |
| 1959 | M.J.K. Smith | Warwickshire | 67 | 11 | 3245 | 200* | 57.94 | 8 |
| 1960 | R. Subba Row | Northamptonshire | 32 | 5 | 1503 | 147* | 55.66 | 4 |
| 1961 | K.F. Barrington | Surrey | 42 | 7 | 2070 | 163 | 59.14 | 4 |
| 1962 | R.T. Simpson | Nottinghamshire | 20 | 4 | 867 | 105 | 54.18 | 2 |
| 1963 | M.J.K. Smith | Warwickshire | 39 | 6 | 1566 | 144* | 47.45 | 3 |
| 1964 | K.F. Barrington | Surrey | 35 | 5 | 1872 | 256 | 62.40 | 4 |
| 1965 | M.C. Cowdrey | Kent | 43 | 10 | 2093 | 196* | 63.42 | 5 |
| 1966 | T.W. Graveney | Worcestershire | 40 | 6 | 1777 | 166 | 52.26 | 4 |
| 1967 | K.F. Barrington | Surrey | 40 | 10 | 2059 | 158* | 68.63 | 6 |
| 1968 | G. Boycott | Yorkshire | 30 | 7 | 1487 | 180* | 64.65 | 7 |
| 1969 | J.H. Edrich | Surrey | 39 | 7 | 2238 | 181 | 69.93 | 8 |
| 1970 | T.W. Graveney | Worcestershire | 34 | 13 | 1316 | 114 | 62.66 | 2 |
| 1971 | G. Boycott | Yorkshire | 30 | 5 | 2503 | 233 | 100.12 | 13 |
| 1972 | G. Boycott | Yorkshire | 22 | 5 | 1230 | 204* | 72.35 | 6 |
| 1973 | G. Boycott | Yorkshire | 30 | 6 | 1527 | 141* | 63.62 | 5 |
| 1974 | C.H. Lloyd | Lancashire | 31 | 8 | 1458 | 178* | 63.39 | 4 |
| 1975 | R.B. Kanhai | Warwickshire | 22 | 9 | 1073 | 178* | 82.53 | 3 |
| 1976 | Zaheer Abbas | Gloucestershire | 39 | 5 | 2554 | 230* | 75.11 | 11 |
| 1977 | G. Boycott | Yorkshire | 30 | 5 | 1701 | 191 | 68.04 | 7 |
| 1978 | C.E.B. Rice | Nottinghamshire | 37 | 9 | 1871 | 213* | 66.82 | 5 |
| 1979 | G. Boycott | Yorkshire | 20 | 5 | 1538 | 175* | 102.53 | 6 |
| 1980 | A.J. Lamb | Northamptonshire | 39 | 12 | 1797 | 152 | 66.55 | 5 |
| 1981 | Zaheer Abbas | Gloucestershire | 36 | 10 | 2306 | 215* | 88.69 | 10 |
| 1982 | Zaheer Abbas | Gloucestershire | 25 | 4 | 1475 | 162* | 70.23 | 5 |
| 1983 | I.V.A. Richards | Somerset | 20 | 4 | 1204 | 216 | 75.25 | 5 |
| 1984 | M.W. Gatting | Middlesex | 43 | 10 | 2257 | 258 | 68.39 | 8 |
| 1985 | I.V.A. Richards | Somerset | 24 | 0 | 1836 | 322 | 76.50 | 9 |

The following touring players achieved a higher average than that of the leading home batsman of the season:

| | | | *I* | *NO* | *Runs* | *HS* | *Avge* | *100* |
|---|---|---|---|---|---|---|---|---|
| 1909 | W. Bardsley | Australians | 49 | 4 | 2072 | 219 | 46.04 | 6 |
| 1930 | D.G. Bradman | Australians | 36 | 6 | 2960 | 334 | 98.66 | 10 |
| 1934 | D.G. Bradman | Australians | 27 | 3 | 2020 | 304 | 84.16 | 7 |
| 1934 | W.H. Ponsford | Australians | 27 | 4 | 1784 | 281* | 77.56 | 5 |
| 1938 | D.G. Bradman | Australians | 26 | 5 | 2429 | 278 | 115.66 | 13 |
| 1939 | G.A. Headley | West Indians | 30 | 6 | 1745 | 234* | 72.70 | 6 |
| 1948 | D.G. Bradman | Australians | 31 | 4 | 2428 | 187 | 89.92 | 11 |
| 1948 | A.L. Hassett | Australians | 27 | 6 | 1563 | 200* | 74.42 | 7 |
| 1948 | A.R. Morris | Australians | 29 | 2 | 1922 | 290 | 71.18 | 7 |
| 1950 | E.de C. Weekes | West Indians | 33 | 4 | 2310 | 304* | 79.65 | 7 |
| 1950 | F.M.M. Worrell | West Indians | 31 | 5 | 1775 | 261 | 68.26 | 6 |
| 1953 | R.N. Harvey | Australians | 35 | 4 | 2040 | 202* | 65.80 | 10 |
| 1955 | D.J. McGlew | South Africans | 34 | 2 | 1871 | 161 | 58.46 | 5 |
| 1956 | K.D. Mackay | Australians | 28 | 7 | 1103 | 163* | 52.52 | 3 |

| | | | I | NO | Runs | HS | Avge | 100 |
|---|---|---|---|---|---|---|---|---|
| 1961 | W.M. Lawry | Australians | 39 | 6 | 2019 | 165 | 61.18 | 9 |
| 1961 | N.C. O'Neill | Australians | 37 | 4 | 1981 | 162 | 60.03 | 7 |
| 1963 | G.St A. Sobers | West Indians | 34 | 6 | 1333 | 112 | 47.60 | 4 |
| 1966 | G.St A. Sobers | West Indians | 25 | 3 | 1349 | 174 | 61.31 | 4 |
| 1973 | M.L.C. Foster | West Indians | 20 | 7 | 828 | 127 | 63.69 | 1 |
| 1982 | Mohsin Khan | Pakistanis | 20 | 3 | 1248 | 203* | 73.41 | 4 |

# HIGHEST BATTING AVERAGES IN AN ENGLISH SEASON

*Qualifications: 12 innings, average 70.00*

G. Boycott, who achieved the feat twice, is the only English batsman to average over 100 in a home season. The first player to do so was D.G. Bradman, who holds the unique distinction of averaging over 80 on each of his four tours of Britain: 98.66, 84.16, 115.66 and 89.92 in 1930, 1934, 1938 and 1948 respectively. On each tour he exceeded the average of the leading home batsman of that season.

| | | Season | I | NO | Runs | HS | Avge | 100 |
|---|---|---|---|---|---|---|---|---|
| D.G. Bradman | Australians | 1938 | 26 | 5 | 2429 | 278 | 115.66 | 13 |
| G. Boycott | Yorkshire | 1979 | 20 | 5 | 1538 | 175* | 102.53 | 6 |
| W.A. Johnston | Australians | 1953 | 17 | 16 | 102 | 28* | 102.00 | – |
| G. Boycott | Yorkshire | 1971 | 30 | 5 | 2503 | 233 | 100.12 | 13 |
| D.G. Bradman | Australians | 1930 | 36 | 6 | 2960 | 334 | 98.66 | 10 |
| H. Sutcliffe | Yorkshire | 1931 | 42 | 11 | 3006 | 230 | 96.96 | 13 |
| R.M. Poore | Hampshire | 1899 | 21 | 4 | 1551 | 304 | 91.23 | 7 |
| D.R. Jardine | Surrey | 1927 | 14 | 3 | 1002 | 147 | 91.09 | 5 |
| D.C.S. Compton | Middlesex | 1947 | 50 | 8 | 3816 | 246 | 90.85 | 18 |
| G.M. Turner | Worcestershire | 1982 | 16 | 3 | 1171 | 311* | 90.07 | 5 |
| D.G. Bradman | Australians | 1948 | 31 | 4 | 2428 | 187 | 89.92 | 11 |
| Zaheer Abbas | Gloucestershire | 1981 | 36 | 10 | 2306 | 215* | 88.69 | 10 |
| K.S. Ranjitsinhji | Sussex | 1900 | 40 | 5 | 3065 | 275 | 87.57 | 11 |
| D.R. Jardine | Surrey | 1928 | 17 | 4 | 1133 | 193 | 87.15 | 3 |
| W.R. Hammond | Gloucestershire | 1946 | 26 | 5 | 1783 | 214 | 84.90 | 7 |
| D.G. Bradman | Australians | 1934 | 27 | 3 | 2020 | 304 | 84.16 | 7 |
| R.B. Kanhai | Warwickshire | 1975 | 22 | 9 | 1073 | 178* | 82.53 | 3 |
| Mudassar Nazar | Pakistanis | 1982 | 16 | 6 | 825 | 211* | 82.50 | 4 |
| C.G. Greenidge | West Indians | 1984 | 16 | 3 | 1069 | 223 | 82.23 | 4 |
| J.B. Hobbs | Surrey | 1928 | 38 | 7 | 2542 | 200* | 82.00 | 12 |
| C.B. Fry | Sussex | 1903 | 40 | 7 | 2683 | 234 | 81.30 | 9 |
| W.J. Edrich | Middlesex | 1947 | 52 | 8 | 3539 | 267* | 80.43 | 12 |
| E.de C. Weekes | West Indians | 1950 | 33 | 4 | 2310 | 304* | 79.65 | 7 |
| G.E. Tyldesley | Lancashire | 1928 | 48 | 10 | 3024 | 242 | 79.57 | 10 |
| Nawab of Pataudi, sr | Worcestershire | 1934 | 15 | 3 | 945 | 214* | 78.75 | 3 |
| A. Shrewsbury | Nottinghamshire | 1887 | 23 | 2 | 1653 | 267 | 78.71 | 8 |
| C.B. Fry | Sussex | 1901 | 43 | 3 | 3147 | 244 | 78.67 | 13 |
| W.G. Grace | Gloucestershire | 1871 | 39 | 4 | 2739 | 268 | 78.25 | 10 |
| J.B. Hobbs | Surrey | 1926 | 41 | 3 | 2949 | 316* | 77.60 | 10 |
| W.H. Ponsford | Australians | 1934 | 27 | 4 | 1784 | 281* | 77.56 | 5 |
| E.H. Hendren | Middlesex | 1923 | 51 | 12 | 3010 | 200* | 77.17 | 13 |
| H. Sutcliffe | Yorkshire | 1928 | 44 | 5 | 3002 | 228 | 76.97 | 13 |
| I.V.A. Richards | Somerset | 1985 | 24 | 0 | 1836 | 322 | 76.50 | 9 |
| W.R. Hammond | Gloucestershire | 1934 | 35 | 4 | 2366 | 302* | 76.32 | 8 |
| G.St A. Sobers | Notts/Rest of World | 1970 | 32 | 9 | 1742 | 183 | 75.73 | 7 |
| C.P. Mead | Hampshire | 1928 | 50 | 10 | 3027 | 180 | 75.67 | 13 |
| C. Hallows | Lancashire | 1927 | 44 | 13 | 2343 | 233* | 75.58 | 7 |
| G. Boycott | Yorkshire | 1985 | 34 | 12 | 1657 | 184 | 75.31 | 6 |
| W.R. Hammond | Gloucestershire | 1938 | 42 | 2 | 3011 | 271 | 75.27 | 15 |
| I.V.A. Richards | Somerset | 1983 | 20 | 4 | 1204 | 216 | 75.25 | 5 |
| Zaheer Abbas | Gloucestershire | 1976 | 39 | 5 | 2554 | 230* | 75.11 | 11 |
| C.P. Mead | Hampshire | 1927 | 41 | 9 | 2385 | 200* | 74.53 | 8 |
| V.M. Merchant | Indians | 1946 | 41 | 9 | 2385 | 242* | 74.53 | 7 |
| A.L. Hassett | Australians | 1948 | 27 | 6 | 1563 | 200* | 74.42 | 7 |
| K.S. Ranjitsinhji | Sussex | 1904 | 34 | 6 | 2077 | 207* | 74.17 | 8 |
| H. Sutcliffe | Yorkshire | 1932 | 52 | 7 | 3336 | 313 | 74.13 | 14 |
| G. Boycott | Yorkshire | 1975 | 34 | 8 | 1915 | 201* | 73.65 | 6 |
| Mohsin Khan | Pakistanis | 1982 | 20 | 3 | 1248 | 203* | 73.41 | 4 |

|  |  | Season | I | NO | Runs | HS | Avge | 100 |
|---|---|---|---|---|---|---|---|---|
| E.H. Hendren | Middlesex | 1927 | 43 | 5 | 2784 | 201* | 73.26 | 13 |
| G.A. Headley | West Indians | 1939 | 30 | 6 | 1745 | 234* | 72.70 | 6 |
| J. Hardstaff, jr | Nottinghamshire | 1949 | 40 | 9 | 2251 | 162* | 72.61 | 8 |
| K.R. Miller | Australian Services | 1945 | 13 | 3 | 725 | 185 | 72.50 | 3 |
| G. Boycott | Yorkshire | 1972 | 22 | 5 | 1230 | 204* | 72.35 | 6 |
| C.B. Fry | Hampshire | 1911 | 26 | 2 | 1728 | 258* | 72.00 | 7 |
| I.V.A. Richards | West Indians | 1976 | 25 | 1 | 1724 | 291 | 71.83 | 6 |
| R.P. Baker | Surrey | 1977 | 12 | 9 | 215 | 77* | 71.66 | – |
| A.R. Border | Australians | 1985 | 21 | 2 | 1355 | 196 | 71.31 | 8 |
| W.G. Grace | Gloucestershire | 1873 | 38 | 8 | 2139 | 192* | 71.30 | 7 |
| G.A. Gooch | Essex | 1985 | 33 | 2 | 2208 | 202 | 71.22 | 7 |
| A.R. Morris | Australians | 1948 | 29 | 2 | 1922 | 290 | 71.18 | 7 |
| C.B. Fry | Sussex | 1904 | 42 | 2 | 2824 | 229 | 70.60 | 10 |
| K.S. Ranjitsinhji | Sussex | 1901 | 40 | 5 | 2468 | 285* | 70.51 | 8 |
| E.H. Hendren | Middlesex | 1928 | 54 | 7 | 3311 | 209* | 70.44 | 13 |
| C. Washbrook | Lancashire | 1948 | 31 | 4 | 1900 | 200 | 70.37 | 7 |
| J.B. Hobbs | Surrey | 1925 | 48 | 5 | 3024 | 266* | 70.32 | 16 |
| Zaheer Abbas | Gloucs/Pakistanis | 1982 | 25 | 4 | 1475 | 162* | 70.23 | 5 |
| H.A. Gomes | West Indians | 1984 | 17 | 5 | 841 | 143 | 70.08 | 4 |
| C.B. Fry | Sussex | 1905 | 44 | 4 | 2801 | 233 | 70.02 | 10 |
| G.S. Chappell | Australians | 1972 | 28 | 10 | 1260 | 181 | 70.00 | 4 |

# 1000 RUNS IN SEASON OF FIRST-CLASS DEBUT

The following players scored 1000 runs in the season in which they made their first appearance in first-class cricket. The age listed is that at which they played their first match.

|  |  | Age | Season | I | NO | Runs | HS | Avge | 100 |
|---|---|---|---|---|---|---|---|---|---|
| W.L. Foster | Worcestershire | 24 | 1899 | 31 | 1 | 1041 | 172* | 34.70 | 3 |
| A.E. Relf | Sussex | 25 | 1900 | 48 | 3 | 1059 | 96 | 23.53 | — |
| A.P. Day | Kent | 20 | 1905 | 39 | 4 | 1149 | 107* | 32.82 | 2 |
| J.B. Hobbs | Surrey | 22 | 1905 | 54 | 3 | 1317 | 155 | 25.82 | 2 |
| R.A. Young | C.U./Sussex | 19 | 1905 | 33 | 0 | 1170 | 220 | 35.45 | 3 |
| H.L. Wilson | Sussex | 31 | 1913 | 47 | 1 | 1352 | 109 | 29.39 | 1 |
| H. Sutcliffe | Yorkshire | 24 | 1919 | 45 | 4 | 1839 | 174 | 44.85 | 5 |
| H.L.V. Day | Hampshire | 23 | 1922 | 27 | 0 | 1062 | 107 | 39.33 | 1 |
| D.N. Moore | Gloucestershire | 19 | 1930 | 34 | 2 | 1317 | 206 | 41.15 | 3 |
| F.C. de Saram | Oxford University | 21 | 1934 | 23 | 1 | 1119 | 208 | 50.86 | 3 |
| N. Oldfield | Lancashire | 24 | 1935 | 40 | 7 | 1066 | 111* | 32.30 | 2 |
| D.C.S. Compton | Middlesex | 18 | 1936 | 32 | 3 | 1004 | 100* | 34.62 | 1 |
| J.F. Crapp | Gloucestershire | 23 | 1936 | 48 | 8 | 1052 | 168 | 26.30 | 1, |
| K. Cranston | Lancashire | 29 | 1947 | 41 | 4 | 1228 | 155* | 33.18 | 1 |
| D.J. Insole | C.U./Essex | 21 | 1947 | 41 | 5 | 1237 | 161* | 34.36 | 2 |
| G.H.G. Doggart | C.U./Sussex | 23 | 1948 | 37 | 3 | 1169 | 215* | 34.38 | 3 |
| W.G.A. Parkhouse | Glamorgan | 22 | 1948 | 49 | 1 | 1204 | 117 | 25.08 | 2 |
| D.B. Close | Yorkshire | 18 | 1949 | 50 | 10 | 1098 | 88* | 27.45 | — |
| F.A. Lowson | Yorkshire | 23 | 1949 | 55 | 5 | 1799 | 104 | 35.98 | 1 |
| D.M. Green | O.U./Lancashire | 19 | 1959 | 45 | 3 | 1049 | 125 | 24.97 | 1 |
| D. Kirby | C.U./Leics | 20 | 1959 | 53 | 2 | 1102 | 109 | 21.60 | 1 |
| P.J. Watts | Northamptonshire | 18 | 1959 | 41 | 2 | 1118 | 113 | 28.66 | 2 |
| B.S. Crump | Northamptonshire | 22 | 1960 | 36 | 7 | 1000 | 90 | 34.48 | — |
| S.E.J. Russell | Middlesex | 22 | 1960 | 39 | 3 | 1119 | 129 | 31.08 | 1 |
| E.J. Craig | C.U./Lancashire | 19 | 1961 | 41 | 5 | 1528 | 208* | 42.44 | 5 |
| J.M. Brearley | C.U./Middlesex | 19 | 1961 | 40 | 6 | 1222 | 145* | 35.94 | 2 |
| J. Whitehouse | Warwickshire | 22 | 1971 | 36 | 2 | 1295 | 173 | 38.08 | 2 |
| P.A. Slocombe | Somerset | 20 | 1975 | 37 | 5 | 1125 | 132 | 35.15 | 2 |
| P.W.G. Parker | C.U./Sussex | 20 | 1976 | 42 | 3 | 1115 | 215 | 28.58 | 3 |

The following players appeared in only one or two matches in the season of their first-class debut but scored 1000 runs in their first full season:

| | | Season | Runs | Avge | Previous Matches | |
|---|---|---|---|---|---|---|
| C.P. Mead | Hampshire | 1906 | 1014 | 26.68 | 1 | 1905 |
| A.J. Holmes | Sussex | 1923 | 1020 | 20.00 | 2 | 1922 |
| L.E.G. Ames | Kent | 1927 | 1211 | 33.67 | 2 | 1926 |
| M. Nichol | Worcestershire | 1929 | 1494 | 29.29 | 1 | 1928 |
| J. Arnold | Hampshire | 1930 | 1186 | 32.05 | 1 | 1929 |
| E. Cooper | Worcestershire | 1937 | 1321 | 24.01 | 1 | 1936 |
| G.M. Emmett | Gloucestershire | 1938 | 1091 | 22.26 | 2 | 1936 & 1937 |
| W. Barron | Northamptonshire | 1946 | 1123 | 26.11 | 1 | 1945 |
| T.C. Dodds | Essex | 1946 | 1050 | 25.60 | 1 | 1943–44 |
| D.G.W. Fletcher | Surrey | 1947 | 1857 | 43.18 | 1 | 1946 |
| A. Hamer | Derbyshire | 1950 | 1133 | 29.81 | 2 | 1938 |
| R.G. Broadbent | Worcestershire | 1951 | 1385 | 38.47 | 1 | 1950 |
| L. Pickles | Somerset | 1956 | 1137 | 24.69 | 2 | 1955 |
| L.J. Lenham | Sussex | 1957 | 1401 | 27.47 | 1 | 1956 |
| R.C. White | Cambridge U./Gloucestershire | 1962 | 1696 | 29.24 | 1 | 1960–61 |
| K.W.R. Fletcher | Essex | 1963 | 1310 | 26.20 | 2 | 1962 |
| A.J.T. Miller | Oxford U./Middlesex | 1983 | 1002 | 43.56 | 1 | 1982 |

# 1000 RUNS IN A SEASON AVERAGING UNDER TWENTY

| | | Season | I | NO | Runs | HS | Avge |
|---|---|---|---|---|---|---|---|
| A.H.H. Gilligan | Sussex | 1923 | 70 | 3 | 1186 | 68 | 17.70 |
| J.J. Lyons | Australians | 1890 | 59 | 1 | 1029 | 99 | 17.74 |
| G.H.S. Trott | Australians | 1888 | 61 | 2 | 1081 | 73 | 18.32 |
| A.W. Wellard | Somerset | 1937 | 60 | 4 | 1049 | 91* | 18.73 |
| D. Kirby | Leicestershire | 1962 | 53 | 0 | 1007 | 118 | 19.00 |
| J.E. Timms | Northamptonshire | 1932 | 55 | 1 | 1032 | 97 | 19.11 |
| A.F.T. White | Worcestershire | 1947 | 54 | 2 | 1001 | 79 | 19.25 |
| W.E. Bates | Glamorgan | 1931 | 52 | 0 | 1001 | 74 | 19.25 |
| G. Ulyett | Yorkshire | 1886 | 52 | 0 | 1005 | 78 | 19.32 |
| M.W. Tate | Sussex | 1922 | 56 | 2 | 1050 | 88 | 19.44 |
| J.T. Murray | Middlesex | 1957 | 57 | 5 | 1025 | 120 | 19.71 |
| C.H. Bull | Worcestershire | 1936 | 54 | 0 | 1066 | 108 | 19.74 |
| J. Lawrence | Somerset | 1953 | 52 | 1 | 1015 | 89 | 19.90 |
| F.J. Titmus | Middlesex | 1957 | 56 | 3 | 1056 | 70 | 19.92 |
| J.B. Mortimore | Gloucestershire | 1964 | 58 | 2 | 1118 | 95 | 19.96 |

# 1000 RUNS IN A MONTH

| | | Month | Season | I | NO | Runs | HS | Avge |
|---|---|---|---|---|---|---|---|---|
| W.G. Grace | Gloucestershire | May | 1895 | 10 | 1 | 1016 | 288 | 112.88 |
| W.R. Hammond | Gloucestershire | | 1927 | 14 | 0 | 1042 | 192 | 74.42 |
| C. Hallows | Lancashire | | 1928 | 11 | 3 | 1000 | 232 | 125.00 |
| K.S. Ranjitsinhji | Sussex | June | 1899 | 15 | 2 | 1037 | 197 | 79.76 |
| C.B. Fry | Sussex | | 1901 | 11 | 2 | 1130 | 244 | 125.55 |
| J. Iremonger | Nottinghamshire | | 1904 | 11 | 1 | 1010 | 272 | 101.00 |
| C.P. Mead | Hampshire | | 1921 | 13 | 1 | 1159 | 280* | 96.58 |
| E.H. Hendren | Middlesex | | 1925 | 12 | 2 | 1122 | 240 | 112.20 |
| J.B. Hobbs | Surrey | | 1925 | 14 | 1 | 1112 | 215 | 85.53 |
| P. Holmes | Yorkshire | | 1925 | 12 | 2 | 1021 | 315* | 102.10 |
| H. Sutcliffe | Yorkshire | | 1932 | 14 | 3 | 1193 | 313 | 108.45 |
| L. Hutton | Yorkshire | | 1949 | 16 | 2 | 1294 | 201 | 92.42 |
| Zaheer Abbas | Gloucestershire | | 1981 | 14 | 5 | 1016 | 215* | 112.88 |
| K.S. Ranjitsinhji | Sussex | July | 1900 | 12 | 1 | 1059 | 275 | 96.27 |
| D. Denton | Yorkshire | | 1912 | 14 | 2 | 1023 | 221 | 85.25 |
| C.P. Mead | Hampshire | | 1923 | 13 | 6 | 1070 | 222 | 152.85 |
| G.E. Tyldesley | Lancashire | | 1926 | 9 | 1 | 1024 | 226 | 128.00 |
| A.E. Fagg | Kent | | 1938 | 15 | 1 | 1016 | 244 | 72.57 |
| C. Washbrook | Lancashire | | 1946 | 14 | 3 | 1079 | 162 | 98.09 |
| W.J. Edrich | Middlesex | | 1947 | 11 | 3 | 1047 | 267* | 130.87 |
| M.J.K. Smith | Warwickshire | | 1959 | 15 | 2 | 1209 | 200* | 93.00 |

|  |  | *Month* | *Season* | *I* | *NO* | *Runs* | *HS* | *Avge* |
|---|---|---|---|---|---|---|---|---|
| W.G. Grace | Gloucestershire | **August** | 1871 | 11 | 0 | 1024 | 268 | 93.09 |
| W.G. Grace | Gloucestershire |  | 1876 | 11 | 1 | 1278 | 344 | 127.80 |
| K.S. Ranjitsinhji | Sussex |  | 1899 | 14 | 1 | 1011 | 161 | 77.76 |
| C.B. Fry | Sussex |  | 1901 | 12 | 1 | 1116 | 209 | 101.45 |
| H. Sutcliffe | Yorkshire |  | 1932 | 13 | 1 | 1006 | 194 | 83.83 |
| M. Leyland | Yorkshire |  | 1932 | 13 | 1 | 1013 | 166 | 84.41 |
| E.H. Hendren | Middlesex |  | 1933 | 18 | 2 | 1110 | 222* | 69.37 |
| W.R. Hammond | Gloucestershire |  | 1933 | 13 | 3 | 1060 | 264 | 106.00 |
| W.W. Keeton | Nottinghamshire |  | 1933 | 15 | 2 | 1102 | 136* | 84.76 |
| W.R. Hammond | Gloucestershire |  | 1936 | 16 | 3 | 1281 | 317 | 98.53 |
| E.H. Hendren | Middlesex |  | 1936 | 14 | 0 | 1026 | 156 | 73.28 |
| J. Hardstaff, jr | Nottinghamshire |  | 1937 | 11 | 1 | 1150 | 266 | 115.00 |
| D.C.S. Compton | Middlesex |  | 1947 | 12 | 3 | 1039 | 178 | 115.44 |
| L. Hutton | Yorkshire |  | 1949 | 15 | 1 | 1050 | 269* | 75.00 |
| W.H. Ponsford | Victoria | **December** | 1927 | 5 | 0 | 1146 | 437 | 229.20 |

The following batsmen performed this feat twice in the same season:

| K.S. Ranjitsinhji | June and August | 1899 |
|---|---|---|
| C.B. Fry | June and August | 1901 |
| H. Sutcliffe | June and August | 1932 |
| L. Hutton | June and August | 1949 |

## 1000 RUNS IN MAY

Only three batsmen have scored 1000 runs within the month of May:

|  | *Days* | *I* | *Runs* | *Avge* |
|---|---|---|---|---|
| **W.G. Grace** (Gloucestershire), 9 to 30 May, 1895. | 22 | 10 | 1016 | 112.88 |

13, 103, 18, 25, 288, 52, 257, 73*, 18, 169.
*'W.G.' was aged 46 years 10 months.*

| **W.R. Hammond** (Gloucestershire), 7 to 31 May, 1927. | 25 | 14 | 1042 | 74.42 |
|---|---|---|---|---|

27, 135, 108, 128, 17, 11, 99, 187, 4, 30, 83, 7, 192, 14.
*He scored his 1000th run in his 13th innings and on 28 May, thus equalling Grace's record of 22 days.*

| **C. Hallows** (Lancashire), 5 to 31 May, 1928. | 27 | 11 | 1000 | 125.00 |
|---|---|---|---|---|

100, 101, 51*, 123, 101*, 22, 74, 104, 58, 34*, 232.

## 1000 RUNS BEFORE JUNE

Four other batsmen have scored 1000 runs before the end of May but only with the bonus of some innings in April:

|  | *Days* | *I* | *Runs* | *Avge* |
|---|---|---|---|---|
| **T.W. Hayward** (Surrey), 16 April to 31 May, 1900. | 46 | 13 | 1074 | 97.63 |

120*, 55, 108, 131*, 55, 193, 120, 5, 6, 3, 40, 146, 92.

| **D.G. Bradman** (Australians), 30 April to 31 May, 1930. | 32 | 11 | 1001 | 143.00 |
|---|---|---|---|---|

236, 185*, 78, 9, 48*, 66, 4, 44, 252*, 32, 47*.
*He scored 75* on 30 April.*

| **D.G. Bradman** (Australians), 30 April to 31 May, 1938. | 32 | 9 | 1056 | 150.85 |
|---|---|---|---|---|

258, 58, 137, 278, 2, 143, 145*, 5, 30*.
*He scored 258 on 30 April and his 1000th run on 27 May in 28 days but only 7 innings.*

| **W.J. Edrich** (Middlesex), 30 April to 31 May, 1938. | 32 | 15 | 1010 | 84.16 |
|---|---|---|---|---|

104, 37, 115, 63, 20*, 182, 71, 31, 53*, 45, 15, 245, 0, 9, 20*.
*He scored 21* on 30 April. All his runs were scored at Lord's. This is the only instance to include a duck.*

| **G.M. Turner** (New Zealanders), 24 April to 31 May, 1973. | 38 | 18 | 1018 | 78.30 |
|---|---|---|---|---|

41, 151*, 143, 85, 7, 8, 17*, 81, 13, 53, 44, 153*, 3, 2, 66*, 30, 10*, 111.
*He scored 683 runs in May.*

## EARLIEST DATES FOR SCORING 1000, 2000 AND 3000 RUNS

| **1000 runs** | **27 May 1938** | D.G. Bradman | Australians |
|---|---|---|---|
|  | 28 May 1927 | W.R. Hammond | Gloucestershire |

| | | | |
|---|---|---|---|
| **1000 runs** *contd.* | 30 May 1895 | W.G. Grace | Gloucestershire |
| | 31 May 1900 | T.W. Hayward | Surrey |
| | 31 May 1928 | C. Hallows | Lancashire |
| | 31 May 1930 | D.G. Bradman | Australians |
| | 31 May 1938 | W.J. Edrich | Middlesex |
| | 31 May 1973 | G.M. Turner | New Zealanders |
| **2000 runs** | **5 July 1906** | T.W. Hayward | Surrey |
| | 6 July 1927 | W.R. Hammond | Gloucestershire |
| | 11 July 1930 | D.G. Bradman | Australians |
| | 11 July 1949 | J.G. Langridge | Sussex |
| | 12 July 1921 | C.P. Mead | Hampshire |
| | 14 July 1937 | W.R. Hammond | Gloucestershire |
| **3000 runs** | **20 August 1906** | T.W. Hayward | Surrey |
| | **20 August 1937** | W.R. Hammond | Gloucestershire |
| | 21 August 1959 | M.J.K. Smith | Warwickshire |
| | 26 August 1921 | C.P. Mead | Hampshire |
| | 27 August 1947 | D.C.S. Compton | Middlesex |
| | 28 August 1947 | W.J. Edrich | Middlesex |

# PARTNERSHIP RECORDS

## WORLD RECORD FOR EACH WICKET

| | | | | | |
|---|---|---|---|---|---|
| 1st | 561 | Waheed Mirza, Mansoor Akhtar | Karachi Whites v Quetta | Karachi | 1976–77 |
| 2nd | 465* | J.A. Jameson, R.B. Kanhai | Warwicks v Gloucestershire | Birmingham | 1974 |
| 3rd | 456 | Khalid Irtiza, Aslam Ali | United Bank v Multan | Karachi | 1975–76 |
| 4th | 577 | V.S. Hazare, Gul Mahomed | Baroda v Holkar | Baroda | 1946–47 |
| 5th | 405 | S.G. Barnes, D.G. Bradman | Australia v England | Sydney | 1946–47 |
| 6th | 487* | G.A. Headley, C.C. Passailaigue | Jamaica v Ld Tennyson's XI | Kingston | 1931–32 |
| 7th | 347 | D.St E. Atkinson, C.C. Depeiza | West Indies v Australia | Bridgetown | 1954–55 |
| 8th | 433 | A. Sims, V.T. Trumper | Australian XI v Canterbury | Christchurch | 1913–14 |
| 9th | 283 | J. Chapman, A. Warren | Derbyshire v Warwickshire | Blackwell | 1910 |
| 10th | 307 | A.F. Kippax, J.E.H. Hooker | NSW v Victoria | Melbourne | 1928–29 |

*Australian batsmen hold three records, English, Pakistani and West Indian hold two each, and Indian batsmen hold one.*

## NATIONAL RECORDS FOR EACH WICKET

### HIGHEST BY ENGLISH TEAMS

| | | | | | |
|---|---|---|---|---|---|
| 1st | 555 | P. Holmes, H. Sutcliffe | Yorkshire v Essex | Leyton | 1932 |
| 2nd | 465* | J.A. Jameson, R.B. Kanhai | Warwicks v Gloucestershire | Birmingham | 1974 |
| 3rd | 424* | W.J. Edrich, D.C.S. Compton | Middlesex v Somerset | Lord's | 1948 |
| 4th | 470 | A.I. Kallicharran, G.W. Humpage | Warwickshire v Lancashire | Southport | 1982 |
| 5th | 393 | E.G. Arnold, W.B. Burns | Worcestershire v Warwicks | Birmingham | 1909 |
| 6th | 411 | R.M. Poore, E.G. Wynyard | Hampshire v Somerset | Taunton | 1899 |
| 7th | 344 | K.S. Ranjitsinhji, W. Newham | Sussex v Essex | Leyton | 1902 |
| 8th | 292 | R. Peel, Lord Hawke | Yorkshire v Warwickshire | Birmingham | 1896 |
| 9th | 283 | J. Chapman, A. Warren | Derbyshire v Warwickshire | Blackwell | 1910 |
| 10th | 235 | F.E. Woolley, A. Fielder | Kent v Worcestershire | Stourbridge | 1909 |

*All ten record partnerships occurred in County Championship matches.*

### HIGHEST BY AUSTRALIAN TEAMS

| | | | | | |
|---|---|---|---|---|---|
| 1st | 456 | W.H. Ponsford, E.R. Mayne | Victoria v Queensland | Melbourne | 1923–24 |
| 2nd | 451 | W.H. Ponsford, D.G. Bradman | Australia v England | Oval | 1934 |
| 3rd | 390* | J.M. Wiener, J.K. Moss | Victoria v W. Australia | Melbourne (St K) | 1981–82 |
| 4th | 424 | I.S. Lee, S.O. Quin | Victoria v Tasmania | Melbourne | 1933–34 |
| 5th | 405 | S.G. Barnes, D.G. Bradman | Australia v England | Sydney | 1946–47 |

| 6th | 428 | M.A. Noble, W.W. Armstrong | Australians v Sussex | Hove | 1902 |
|---|---|---|---|---|---|
| 7th | 335 | C.W. Andrews, E.C. Bensted | Queensland v NSW | Sydney | 1934–35 |
| 8th | 433 | A. Sims, V.T. Trumper | Australian XI v Canterbury | Christchurch | 1913–14 |
| 9th | 232 | C. Hill, E. Walkley | South Australia v NSW | Adelaide | 1900–01 |
| 10th | 307 | A.F. Kippax, J.E.H. Hooker | NSW v Victoria | Melbourne | 1928–29 |

## HIGHEST BY SOUTH AFRICAN TEAMS

| 1st | 424 | J.F.W. Nicolson, I.J. Siedle | Natal v OFS | Bloemfontein | 1926–27 |
|---|---|---|---|---|---|
| 2nd | 305 | S.K. Coen, J.M.M. Commaille | OFS v Natal | Bloemfontein | 1926–27 |
| 3rd | 341 | E.J. Barlow, R.G. Pollock | South Africa v Australia | Adelaide | 1963–64 |
| 4th | 342 | E.A.B. Rowan, P.J.M. Gibb | Transvaal v N.E. Transvaal | Johannesburg | 1952–53 |
| 5th | 338 | R.G. Pollock, A.L. Wilmot | E. Province v Natal | Port Elizabeth | 1975–76 |
| 6th | 244* | J.M.M. Commaille, A.W. Palm | W. Province v GW | Johannesburg | 1923–24 |
| 7th | 299 | B. Mitchell, A. Melville | Transvaal v GW | Kimberley | 1946–47 |
| 8th | 222 | D.P.B. Morkel, S.S.L. Steyn | W. Province v Border | Cape Town | 1929–30 |
| 9th | 221 | N.V. Lindsay, G.R. McCubbin | Transvaal v Rhodesia | Bulawayo | 1922–23 |
| 10th | 174 | H.R. Lance, D. Mackay-Coghill | Transvaal v Natal | Johannesburg | 1965–66 |

## HIGHEST BY WEST INDIAN TEAMS

| 1st | 390 | G.L. Wight, G.L.R. Gibbs | British Guiana v Barbados | Georgetown | 1951–52 |
|---|---|---|---|---|---|
| 2nd | 446 | C.C. Hunte, C.St A. Sobers | West Indies v Pakistan | Kingston | 1957–58 |
| 3rd | 434 | J.B. Stollmeyer, G.E. Gomez | Trinidad v British Guiana | Port-of-Spain | 1946–47 |
| 4th | 574* | C.L. Walcott, F.M.M. Worrell | Barbados v Trinidad | Port-of-Spain | 1945–46 |
| 5th | 335 | B.F. Butcher, C.H. Lloyd | West Indians v Glamorgan | Swansea | 1969 |
| 6th | 487* | G.A. Headley, C.C. Passailaigue | Jamaica v Ld Tennyson's XI | Kingston | 1931–32 |
| 7th | 347 | D.St E. Atkinson, C.C. Depeiza | West Indies v Australia | Bridgetown | 1954–55 |
| • 8th | 255 | E.A.V. Williams, E.A. Martindale | Barbados v Trinidad | Bridgetown | 1935–36 |
| 9th | 161 | C.H. Lloyd, A.M.E. Roberts | West Indies v India | Calcutta | 1983–84 |
| 10th | 138 | E.L.G. Hoad, H.C. Griffith | West Indians v Sussex | Hove | 1933 |

## HIGHEST BY NEW ZEALAND TEAMS

| 1st | 387 | G.M. Turner, T.W. Jarvis | New Zealand v West Indies | Georgetown | 1971–72 |
|---|---|---|---|---|---|
| 2nd | 317 | R.T. Hart, P.S. Briasco | Central Dists v Canterbury | New Plymouth | 1983–84 |
| 3rd | 445 | P.E. Whitelaw, W.N. Carson | Auckland v Otago | Dunedin | 1936–37 |
| 4th | 324 | J.R. Reid, W.M. Wallace | NZ v Cambridge U. | Cambridge | 1949 |
| 5th | 266 | B. Sutcliffe, W.S. Haig | Otago v Auckland | Dunedin | 1949–50 |
| 6th | 226 | E.J. Gray. R.W. Ormiston | Wellington v Central Dists | Wellington | 1981–82 |
| 7th | 265 | J.L. Powell, N. Dorreen | Canterbury v Otago | Christchurch | 1929–30 |
| 8th | 190* | J.E. Mills, C.F.W. Allcott | NZ v Civil Service | Chiswick | 1927 |
| 9th | 239 | H.B. Cave, I.B. Leggat | Central Districts v Otago | Dunedin | 1952–53 |
| 10th | 184 | R.C. Blunt, W. Hawksworth | Otago v Canterbury | Christchurch | 1931–32 |

## HIGHEST BY INDIAN TEAMS

| 1st | 451* | S. Desai, R.M.H. Binny | Karnataka v Kerala | Chickmagalur | 1977–78 |
|---|---|---|---|---|---|
| 2nd | 455 | K.V. Bhandarkar, B.B. Nimbalkar | Maharashtra v Kathiawar | Poona | 1948–49 |
| 3rd | 410 | L. Amarnath, R.S. Modi | India in England v Rest | Calcutta | 1946–47 |
| 4th | 577 | V.S. Hazare, Gul Mahomed | Baroda v Holkar | Baroda | 1946–47 |
| 5th | 360 | U.M. Merchant, M.N. Raiji | Bombay v Hyderabad | Bombay | 1947–48 |
| 6th | 371 | V.M. Merchant, R.S. Modi | Bombay v Maharashtra | Bombay | 1943–44 |
| 7th | 274 | K.C. Ibrahim, K.M. Rangnekar | Bijapur XI v Bengal XI | Bombay | 1942–43 |
| 8th | 236 | C.T. Sarwate, R.P. Singh | Holkar v Delhi | Delhi | 1949–50 |
| 9th | 245 | V.S. Hazare, N.D. Nagarwalla | Maharashtra v Baroda | Poona | 1939–40 |
| 10th | 249 | C.T. Sarwate, S.N. Banerjee | Indians v Surrey | Oval | 1946 |

## HIGHEST BY PAKISTANI TEAMS

| 1st | 561 | Waheed Mirza, Mansoor Akhtar | Karachi Whites v Quetta | Karachi | 1976–77 |
|---|---|---|---|---|---|
| 2nd | 426 | Arshad Pervez, Mohsin Khan | Habib Bank v Income Tax | Lahore | 1977–78 |
| 3rd | 456 | Khalid Irtiza, Aslam Ali | United Bank v Multan | Karachi | 1975–76 |
| 4th | 350 | Mushtaq Mohammad, Asif Iqbal | Pakistan v New Zealand | Dunedin | 1972–73 |
| 5th | 355 | Altaf Shah, Tariq Bashir | HBFC v Multan | Multan | 1976–77 |
| 6th | 353 | Salahuddin, Zaheer Abbas | Karachi v East Pakistan | Karachi | 1968–69 |
| 7th | 308 | Waqar Hassan, Imtiaz Ahmed | Pakistan v New Zealand | Lahore | 1955–56 |

| 8th | 240 | Gulfraz Khan, Raja Sarfraz | Railways v Universities | Lahore | 1976–77 |
| 9th | 190 | Asif Iqbal, Intikhab Alam | Pakistan v England | Oval | 1967 |
| 10th | 196* | Nadim Yousuf, Maqsood Kundi | MCB v National Bank | Lahore | 1981–82 |

# HIGHEST SCORE AT THE FALL OF EACH WICKET

| 1st | 561 | Karachi Whites (561-1d) v Quetta | Karachi | 1976–77 |
| 2nd | 594 | Victoria (1107) v New South Wales | Melbourne | 1926–27 |
| 3rd | 778 | Maharashtra (826-4) v Kathiawar | Poona | 1948–49 |
| 4th | 801 | Maharashtra (826-4) v Kathiawar | Poona | 1948–49 |
| 5th | 828 | Sind (951-7d) v Baluchistan | Karachi | 1973–74 |
| 6th | 834 | Victoria (1107) v New South Wales | Melbourne | 1926–27 |
| 7th | 956 | Victoria (1059) v Tasmania | Melbourne | 1922–23 |
| 8th | 1043 | Victoria (1107) v New South Wales | Melbourne | 1926–27 |
| 9th | 1046 | Victoria (1107) v New South Wales | Melbourne | 1926–27 |
| 10th | 1107 | Victoria (1107) v New South Wales | Melbourne | 1926–27 |

# PARTNERSHIPS OF 450 RUNS AND OVER

| Runs | Wkt | Partners | For | Venue | |
|------|-----|----------|-----|-------|--|
| 577 | 4th | V.S. Hazare, Gul Mahomed | Baroda | Baroda | 1946–47 |
| 574* | 4th | F.M.M. Worrell, C.L. Walcott | Barbados | Port-of-Spain | 1945–46 |
| 561 | 1st | Waheed Mirza, Mansoor Akhtar | Karachi Whites | Karachi | 1976–77 |
| 555 | 1st | P. Holmes, H. Sutcliffe | Yorkshire | Leyton | 1932 |
| 554 | 1st | J.T. Brown, J. Tunnicliffe | Yorkshire | Chesterfield | 1898 |
| 502* | 4th | F.M.M. Worrell, J.D.C. Goddard | Barbados | Bridgetown | 1943–44 |
| 490 | 1st | E.H. Bowley, J.G. Langridge | Sussex | Hove | 1933 |
| 487* | 6th | G.A. Headley, C.C. Passailaigue | Jamaica | Kingston | 1931–32 |
| 470 | 4th | A.I. Kallicharran, G.W. Humpage | Warwickshire | Southport | 1982 |
| 465* | 2nd | J.A. Jameson, R.B. Kanhai | Warwickshire | Birmingham | 1974 |
| 456 | 1st | W.H. Ponsford, E.R. Mayne | Victoria | Melbourne | 1923–24 |
| 456 | 3rd | Khalid Irtiza, Aslam Ali | United Bank | Karachi | 1975–76 |
| 455 | 2nd | K.V. Bhandarkar, B.B. Nimbalkar | Maharashtra | Poona | 1948–49 |
| 451* | 1st | S. Desai, R.M.H. Binny | Karnataka | Chickmagalur | 1977–78 |
| 451 | 2nd | D.G. Bradman, W.H. Ponsford | Australia | Oval | 1934 |
| 451 | 3rd | Mudassar Nazar, Javed Miandad | Pakistan | Hyderabad | 1982–83 |

# HIGHEST PARTNERSHIPS

The qualification for inclusion in these records is as follows:

| Wicket | Runs | | Wicket | Runs |
|--------|------|--|--------|------|
| 1st | 250 | | 6th | 225 |
| 2nd | 250 | | 7th | 200 |
| 3rd | 250 | | 8th | 175 |
| 4th | 250 | | 9th | 150 |
| 5th | 225 | | 10th | 100 |

So-called 'partnerships' which fulfil their respective qualification but involve more than two batsmen (because one of the original partners retires hurt), are not included. There being only two batsmen at the wicket at a time, their partnership ends in what is technically an unfinished state when one of them is forced to retire. The replacement batsman then begins a new partnership for the same wicket with the surviving partner. In the 1959–60 series between West Indies and England, the third wicket added 243 runs in the first West Indies innings. This total was composed of two century partnerships within that third wicket: Sobers and McMorris added 133 runs together before the latter retired hurt and was succeeded by Nurse, who helped Sobers to increase the score by a further 110. The records correctly show two partnerships for this wicket of 133 (unfinished) and 110. A school of thought accepting this as a three-man partnership worth 243 runs could produce an opening stand to which all members of the team had contributed with nine of them retiring hurt!

**FIRST WICKET**

| 561 | Waheed Mirza, Mansoor Akhtar | Karachi Whites v Quetta | Karachi | 1976–77 |
| 555 | P. Holmes, H. Sutcliffe | Yorkshire v Essex | Leyton | 1932 |
| 554 | J.T. Brown, J. Tunnicliffe | Yorkshire v Derbyshire | Chesterfield | 1898 |

| 490 | E.H. Bowley, J.G. Langridge | Sussex v Middlesex | Hove | 1933 |
|---|---|---|---|---|
| 456 | W.H. Ponsford, E.R. Mayne | Victoria v Queensland | Melbourne | 1923–24 |
| 451* | S. Desai, R.M.H. Binny | Karnataka v Kerala | Chickmagalur | 1977–78 |
| 428 | J.B. Hobbs, A. Sandham | Surrey v Oxford University | Oval | 1926 |
| 424 | J.F.W. Nicolson, I.J. Siedle | Natal v Orange Free State | Bloemfontein | 1926–27 |
| 421 | S.M. Gavaskar, G.A. Parkar | Bombay v Bengal | Bombay | 1981–82 |
| 418 | Kamal Najamuddin, Khalid Alvi | Karachi v Railways | Karachi | 1980–81 |
| 413 | M.H. Mankad, Pankaj Roy | India v New Zealand | Madras | 1955–56 |
| 405 | C.P.S. Chauhan, M.S. Gupte | Maharashtra v Vidarbha | Poona | 1972–73 |
| 395 | D.M. Young, R.B. Nicholls | Gloucestershire v Oxford U. | Oxford | 1962 |
| 391 | A.O. Jones, A. Shrewsbury | Nottinghamshire v Gloucs | Bristol | 1899 |
| 390 | G.L. Wight, G.L.R. Gibbs | British Guiana v Barbados | Georgetown | 1951–52 |
| 390 | B. Dudleston, J.F. Steele | Leicestershire v Derbyshire | Leicester | 1979 |
| 389 | Majid Khan, Shafiq Ahmed | Punjab v Sind | Karachi | 1974–75 |
| 389 | Mudassar Nazar, Mansoor Akhtar | United Bank v Rawalpindi | Lahore | 1981–82 |
| 388 | K.C. Wessels, R.B. Kerr | Queensland v Victoria | Melbourne | 1982–83 |
| 387 | G.M. Turner, T.W. Jarvis | New Zealand v West Indies | Georgetown | 1971–72 |
| 382 | W.M. Lawry, R.B. Simpson | Australia v West Indies | Bridgetown | 1964–65 |
| 380 | C.J.B. Wood, H. Whitehead | Leicestershire v Worcs | Worcester | 1906 |
| 379 | R. Abel, W. Brockwell | Surrey v Hampshire | Oval | 1897 |
| 378 | J.T. Brown, J. Tunnicliffe | Yorkshire v Sussex | Sheffield | 1897 |
| 377* | N.F. Horner, Khalid Ibadulla | Warwickshire v Surrey | Oval | 1960 |
| 375 | W.M. Woodfull, W.H. Ponsford | Victoria v New South Wales | Melbourne | 1926–27 |
| 373 | B. Sutcliffe, L. Watt | Otago v Auckland | Auckland | 1950–51 |
| 368 | A.C. MacLaren, R.H. Spooner | Lancashire v Gloucestershire | Liverpool | 1903 |
| 368 | E.H. Bowley, J.H. Parks | Sussex v Gloucestershire | Hove | 1929 |
| 367* | G.D. Barlow, W.N. Slack | Middlesex v Kent | Lord's | 1981 |
| 364 | R. Abel, D.L.A. Jephson | Surrey v Derbyshire | Oval | 1900 |
| 361 | N. Oldfield, V. Broderick | Northamptonshire v Scotland | Peterborough | 1953 |
| 359 | L. Hutton, C. Washbrook | England v South Africa | Johannesburg | 1948–49 |
| 355 | A.F. Rae, J.B. Stollmeyer | West Indians v Sussex | Hove | 1950 |
| 352 | T.W. Hayward, J.B. Hobbs | Surrey v Warwickshire | Oval | 1909 |
| 351 | G. Boycott, M.D. Moxon | Yorkshire v Worcestershire | Worcester | 1985 |
| 350* | C. Washbrook, W. Place | Lancashire v Sussex | Manchester | 1947 |
| 349 | J.G. Dewes, D.S. Sheppard | Cambridge U. v Sussex | Hove | 1950 |
| 347 | P. Holmes, H. Sutcliffe | Yorkshire v Hampshire | Portsmouth | 1920 |
| 346 | L.C.H. Palairet, H.T. Hewett | Somerset v Yorkshire | Taunton | 1892 |
| 343 | J.G. Dewes, D.S. Sheppard | Cambridge U. v West Indians | Cambridge | 1950 |
| 338 | T. Bowring, H. Teesdale | Oxford U. v Gents of England | Oxford | 1908 |
| 337 | C.C. McDonald, K.D. Meuleman | Victoria v South Australia | Adelaide | 1949–50 |
| 335 | B. Dudleston, J.F. Steele | Leicestershire v Glamorgan | Leicester | 1975 |
| 333 | J.F. Byrne, S. Kinneir | Warwickshire v Lancashire | Birmingham | 1905 |
| 331 | B.A. Courtice, R.B. Kerr | Queensland v Tasmania | Brisbane | 1984–85 |
| 330 | B. Mitchell, E.A.B. Rowan | South Africans v Surrey | Oval | 1935 |
| 330 | A. Jones, R.C. Fredericks | Glamorgan v Northants | Swansea | 1972 |
| 328 | C. Milburn, D. Chadwick | W. Australia v Queensland | Brisbane | 1968–69 |
| 325 | G. Bose, P. Nanda | Bengal v Bihar | Jamshedpur | 1973–74 |
| 323 | J.B. Hobbs, W. Rhodes | England v Australia | Melbourne | 1911–12 |
| 323 | P. Holmes, H. Sutcliffe | Yorkshire v Lancashire | Sheffield | 1931 |
| 322 | H. Storer, J. Bowden | Derbyshire v Essex | Derby | 1929 |
| 322 | G. Gunn, A. Sandham | MCC v Jamaica | Kingston | 1929–30 |
| 319 | R.B. McCosker, J. Dyson | NSW v Western Australia | Sydney | 1980–81 |
| 319 | Mudassar Nazar, Mohsin Khan | Pakistanis v Sussex | Hove | 1982 |
| 318 | W.W. Keeton, R.T. Simpson | Nottinghamshire v Lancs | Manchester | 1949 |
| 315 | H. Sutcliffe, L. Hutton | Yorkshire v Leicestershire | Hull | 1937 |
| 315 | H. Sutcliffe, L. Hutton | Yorkshire v Hampshire | Sheffield | 1939 |
| 315 | D.M. Green, C.A. Milton | Gloucestershire v Sussex | Hove | 1968 |
| 314 | A.C. MacLaren, T.W. Hayward | A.C. MacLaren's XI v NSW | Sydney | 1901–02 |
| 313 | T.W. Hayward, J.B. Hobbs | Surrey v Worcestershire | Worcester | 1913 |
| 313 | A.J. Richardson, L.T. Gun | S. Australia v W. Australia | Adelaide | 1925–26 |
| 312 | G.F. Dakin, C.G. Rushmere | E. Province v W. Province | Cape Town | 1962–63 |
| 312 | W.E. Russell, M.J. Harris | Middlesex v Pakistanis | Lord's | 1967 |
| 310 | J.D.B. Robertson, S.M. Brown | Middlesex v Nottinghamshire | Lord's | 1947 |
| 309 | H.K. Foster, F.L. Bowley | Worcestershire v Derbyshire | Derby | 1901 |
| 309 | P. Holmes, H. Sutcliffe | Yorkshire v Warwickshire | Birmingham | 1931 |
| 308 | R.B. Simpson, G. Thomas | NSW v Western Australia | Sydney | 1963–64 |
| 306 | L.A. Cuff, J.D. Lawrence | Canterbury v Auckland | Christchurch | 1893–94 |
| 306 | P.F. Warner, J. Douglas | Middlesex v Nottinghamshire | Nottingham | 1904 |

| | | | | |
|---|---|---|---|---|
| 306 | F.L. Bowley, F.A. Pearson | Worcestershire v Gloucs | Worcester | 1913 |
| 305 | J.G. Langridge, H.W. Greenwood | Sussex v Essex | Hove | 1935 |
| 303 | G.L. Wilson, F.J.W. Marlow | Sussex v Oxford University | Hove | 1895 |
| 303 | A.O. Jones, J. Iremonger | Nottinghamshire v Gloucs | Nottingham | 1904 |
| 301 | K.R. Stackpole, G.D. Watson | Australians v Hampshire | Southampton | 1972 |
| 301 | D.L. Amiss, J.M. Brearley | MCC v Leicestershire | Lord's | 1976 |
| 299 | D.V. Smith, M.J.K. Smith | MCC v Surrey | Lord's | 1958 |
| 299 | B. Wood, D. Lloyd | Lancashire v Leicestershire | Leicester | 1972 |
| 298 | V.T. Trumper, R.A. Duff | NSW v South Australia | Sydney | 1902–03 |
| 296 | C.G. Greenidge, D.L. Haynes | West Indies v India | St Johns | 1982–83 |
| 295 | C.J. Barnett, A.E. Fagg | MCC v Queensland | Brisbane | 1936–37 |
| 295 | J.G. Langridge, J.H. Parks | Sussex v Leicestershire | Hove | 1938 |
| 293 | V.M. Merchant, M.H. Mankad | Indians v Sussex | Hove | 1946 |
| 293 | R.M. Prideaux, C. Milburn | Northamptonshire v Essex | Clacton | 1966 |
| 293 | G.A. Gooch, L. Seeff | W. Province v E. Province | Cape Town | 1983–84 |
| 292 | G. Challenor, P.H. Tarilton | Barbados v Trinidad | Bridgetown | 1926–27 |
| 292 | Abdus Sami, Saadat Ali | Lahore C Whites v Faisalabad | Lahore | 1983–84 |
| 291 | G.M. Turner, J.A. Ormrod | Worcestershire v Warwicks | Worcester | 1982 |
| 290 | J.B. Hobbs, T.W. Hayward | Surrey v Yorkshire | Lord's | 1914 |
| 290 | P. Holmes, H. Sutcliffe | Yorkshire v Middlesex | Leeds | 1928 |
| 290 | D. Kenyon, P.E. Richardson | Worcestershire v Gloucs | Dudley | 1953 |
| 290 | G. Pullar, M.C. Cowdrey | England v South Africa | Oval | 1960 |
| 290 | R.B. Richardson, L.L. Lawrence | Leewards v Trinidad | St Johns | 1983–84 |
| 289 | R.B. Kerr, B.A. Courtice | Queensland v Victoria | Melbourne | 1983–84 |
| 288 | H.W. Bainbridge, W.G. Quaife | Warwickshire v Hampshire | Southampton | 1897 |
| 288 | G. Boycott, R.G. Lumb | Yorkshire v Somerset | Harrogate | 1979 |
| 287 | C.B. Fry, J. Vine | Sussex v Hampshire | Hove | 1904 |
| 286 | R.E.H. Hudson, C.P. Hamilton | Army v West Indians | Aldershot | 1933 |
| 286 | B. Sutcliffe, D.D. Taylor | Auckland v Canterbury | Auckland | 1948–49 |
| 286 | J.B. Stollmeyer, A.G. Ganteaume | Trinidad v Jamaica | Port-of-Spain | 1949–50 |
| 286 | L. Hutton, F.A. Lowson | Yorkshire v South Africans | Sheffield | 1951 |
| 285 | I.J. Siedle, H.F. Wade | Natal v E. Province | Pietermaritzburg | 1936–37 |
| 284 | J.W.H.T. Douglas, A.E. Knight | England XI v Australians | Blackpool | 1909 |
| 284 | R.T. Simpson, R.J. Giles | Nottinghamshire v Oxford U. | Oxford | 1951 |
| 283 | W.G. Grace, B.B. Cooper | Gents of South v Players of South | Oval | 1869 |
| 283 | J.B. Hobbs, H. Sutcliffe | England v Australia | Melbourne | 1924–25 |
| 283 | A.E. Fagg, P.R. Sunnucks | Kent v Essex | Colchester | 1938 |
| 283 | J.G. Wright, B. Wood | Derbyshire v Worcestershire | Chesterfield | 1981 |
| 282* | G. Wilson, W.W. Hill-Wood | MCC v Victoria | Melbourne | 1922–23 |
| 281* | W.B. Stott, K. Taylor | Yorkshire v Sussex | Hove | 1960 |
| 281 | G. Pullar, M.C. Cowdrey | MCC v British Guiana | Georgetown | 1959–60 |
| 281 | L.E. Favell, J.P. Causby | South Australia v NSW | Adelaide | 1967–68 |
| 279 | P. Holmes, H. Sutcliffe | Yorkshire v Northants | Northampton | 1919 |
| 279 | C.F. Walters, H.H.I. Gibbons | Worcestershire v Essex | Chelmsford | 1934 |
| 279 | S.M. Gavaskar, A.V. Mankad | Bombay v Rajasthan | Bombay | 1969–70 |
| 278* | C.F. Walters, H.H.I. Gibbons | Worcestershire v Leics | Worcester | 1934 |
| 278 | A.A. Jackson, W.H. Ponsford | J. Ryder's XI v W.M. Woodfull's XI | Sydney | 1929–30 |
| 278 | A.M. Taylor, R.E. Marshall | Barbados v Trinidad | Bridgetown | 1948–49 |
| 278 | G. Cook, W. Larkins | Northants v Yorkshire | Middlesbrough | 1982 |
| 278 | Qasim Omar, Anwar-ul-Haq | MCB v Railways | Lahore | 1982–83 |
| 277* | Hanif Mohammad, Alimuddin | Karachi v Sind | Karachi | 1957–58 |
| 277 | T.H. Fowler, H. Wrathall | Gloucs v London County | Crystal Palace | 1903 |
| 277 | G.T.S. Stevens, E.T. Killick | Middlesex v Warwickshire | Lord's | 1931 |
| 277 | W.W. Keeton, C.B. Harris | Nottinghamshire v Middlesex | Nottingham | 1933 |
| 277 | D. Kenyon, L. Outschoorn | Worcestershire v Kent | Gravesend | 1954 |
| 277 | M.R. Hallam, H.D. Bird | Leics v South Africans | Leicester | 1960 |
| 277 | G.S. Clinton, A.R. Butcher | Surrey v Yorkshire | Oval | 1984 |
| 276* | R.B. Simpson, N.C. O'Neill | NSW v South Australia | Sydney | 1964–65 |
| 276 | C.S. Dempster, J.E. Mills | New Zealand v England | Wellington | 1929–30 |
| 274 | H.K. Foster, F.L. Bowley | Worcestershire v Hampshire | Portsmouth | 1907 |
| 274 | P. Holmes, H. Sutcliffe | Yorkshire v Somerset | Hull | 1923 |
| 274 | P. Holmes, H. Sutcliffe | Yorkshire v Gloucestershire | Gloucester | 1927 |
| 274 | A.H. Dyson, D.E. Davies | Glamorgan v Leicestershire | Leicester | 1937 |
| 274 | E.A.B. Rowan, A.I. Taylor | Transvaal v Border | Johannesburg | 1952–53 |
| 273 | Nazar Mohammad, Jagadish Lal | Northern India v NWFP | Lahore | 1941–42 |
| 272 | P. Holmes, H. Sutcliffe | Yorkshire v Leicestershire | Hull | 1925 |

| | | | | |
|---|---|---|---|---|
| 272 | A.J.W. Croom, N. Kilner | Warwickshire v Worcs | Birmingham | 1934 |
| 272 | G. Pullar, B.J. Booth | Lancashire v Oxford U. | Oxford | 1962 |
| 270* | R. Abel, W. Brockwell | Surrey v Kent | Oval | 1900 |
| 270 | C. Hallows, J.W.H. Makepeace | Lancashire v Worcestershire | Worcester | 1922 |
| 270 | A.V. Avery, T.C. Dodds | Essex v Surrey | Oval | 1946 |
| 270 | N.J. Contractor, S.P. Gaekwad | West Zone v East Zone | Bombay | 1963–64 |
| 270 | K.R. Stackpole, A.P. Sheahan | Victoria v Pakistanis | Melbourne | 1972–73 |
| 269* | P. Holmes, H. Sutcliffe | North v South | Sheffield | 1927 |
| 269 | R.T. Simpson, W.W. Keeton | Nottinghamshire v Kent | Nottingham | 1951 |
| 269 | Imtiaz Ahmed, Shujauddin | Services v Karachi Blues | Karachi | 1961–62 |
| 269 | F.M. Engineer, S.G. Adhikari | Bombay v Bengal | Calcutta | 1962–63 |
| 268 | J.B. Hobbs, H. Sutcliffe | England v South Africa | Lord's | 1924 |
| 268 | P. Holmes, H. Sutcliffe | Yorkshire v Essex | Leyton | 1928 |
| 268 | E. Paynter, C. Washbrook | Lancashire v Sussex | Hove | 1937 |
| 268 | P.C. Davies, F.A. Seyfried | N.E. Transvaal v OFS | Bloemfontein | 1955–56 |
| 268 | R.A. Gripper, J.K. Clarke | Rhodesia v Orange Free State | Bloemfontein | 1967–68 |
| 268 | G.M. Turner, G.T. Dowling | NZ v President's XI | Montego Bay | 1971–72 |
| 268 | B.W. Luckhurst, D.L. Amiss | MCC v Victoria | Melbourne | 1974–75 |
| 267 | V.T. Trumper, R.A. Duff | New South Wales v Victoria | Sydney | 1902–03 |
| 267 | W. Barber, L. Hutton | Yorkshire v Kent | Leeds | 1934 |
| 267 | Zaki Ahmed, Saadat Ali | Income Tax v Bahawalpur | Bahawalpur | 1976–77 |
| 266 | A. Shrewsbury, A.E. Stoddart | England v MCC | Lord's | 1887 |
| 266 | A. Sandham, A. Jeacocke | Surrey v Northamptonshire | Oval | 1921 |
| 266 | N. Kilner, E.J. Smith | Warwickshire v Middlesex | Lord's | 1927 |
| 266 | A.R. Butcher, G.S. Clinton | Surrey v Cambridge U. | Cambridge | 1980 |
| 265* | P. Holmes, H. Sutcliffe | Yorkshire v Surrey | Oval | 1926 |
| 265 | R. Abel, W. Brockwell | Surrey v Warwickshire | Oval | 1898 |
| 265 | L.G. Brown, F.T. Prentice | Leics v New Zealanders | Leicester | 1937 |
| 265 | W.A. Brown, G.G. Cook | Queensland v NSW | Sydney | 1938–39 |
| 265 | D. Lloyd, B. Wood | Lancashire v Sussex | Blackpool | 1970 |
| 265 | B. Wood, D. Lloyd | Lancashire v Somerset | Taunton | 1974 |
| 265 | Shafiq Ahmed, Mudassar Nazar | Patron's XI v West Indians | Rawalpindi | 1974–75 |
| 265 | J. Dyson, W.J. Seabrook | NSW v Victoria | Melbourne | 1984–85 |
| 264 | J.B. Hobbs, A. Sandham | Surrey v Somerset | Taunton | 1932 |
| 264 | G. Boycott, R.G. Lumb | Yorkshire v Gloucestershire | Leeds | 1976 |
| 263 | J.B. Hobbs, H. Sutcliffe | Players v Gentlemen | Lord's | 1926 |
| 263 | L. Hutton, W.J. Edrich | MCC v Griqualand West | Kimberley | 1938–39 |
| 263 | G.A. Gooch, B.R. Hardie | Essex v Cambridge U. | Cambridge | 1983 |
| 262 | F.G. Mann, J.R. Thompson | Cambridge U. v Leics | Cambridge | 1939 |
| 262 | D.D. Dyer, S.J. Cook | Transvaal v N. Transvaal | Pretoria | 1980–81 |
| 261 | E.L.G. Hoad, P.H. Tarilton | Barbados v MCC | Bridgetown | 1929–30 |
| 261 | D.J. McGlew, T.L. Goddard | Natal v Rhodesia | Bulawayo | 1957–58 |
| 261 | Sadiq Mohammad, A.W. Stovold | Gloucestershire v Hampshire | Southampton | 1979 |
| 260 | F.B. Watson, C. Hallows | Lancashire v Hampshire | Liverpool | 1927 |
| 260 | B. Mitchell, I.J. Siedle | South Africa v England | Cape Town | 1930–31 |
| 260 | L.B. Fishlock, E.A. Bedser | Surrey v Somerset | Oval | 1949 |
| 259 | Hon H.G.H. Mulholland, D.C. Collins | Cambridge U. v Indians | Cambridge | 1911 |
| 259 | A.R. Morris, J. Moroney | Australians v Natal | Durban | 1949–50L |
| 259 | R.G.A. Headley, G.M. Turner | Worcestershire v Warwicks | Worcester | 1972 |
| 258 | A.E. Lewis, L.C.H. Palairet | Somerset v Sussex | Taunton | 1901 |
| 258 | J.G. Langridge, J.H. Parks | Sussex v Surrey | Horsham | 1934 |
| 258 | E.A.B. Rowan, R. Connell | E. Province v GW | Port Elizabeth | 1945–46 |
| 258 | A.F. Rae, E.D.A. St J. McMorris | Jamaica v Trinidad | Georgetown | 1959–60 |
| 258 | B.A. Richards, A.M. Short | Natal v Rhodesia | Durban | 1969–70 |
| 257 | J.A. Jameson, D.L. Amiss | Warwickshire v Lancashire | Birmingham | 1973 |
| 256 | A.J. Richardson, V.Y. Richardson | South Australia v MCC | Adelaide | 1922–23 |
| 256 | D.J. McGlew, T.L. Goddard | South Africans v Glamorgan | Cardiff | 1960 |
| 256 | S.C. Trimble, G.R. Reynolds | Queensland v S. Australia | Adelaide | 1963–64 |
| 256 | B.W. Luckhurst, G.W. Johnson | Kent v Derbyshire | Derby | 1973 |
| 255 | V.Y. Richardson, H.C. Nitschke | S. Australia v Queensland | Adelaide | 1934–35 |
| 255 | A.H. Dyson, D.E. Davies | Glamorgan v Gloucestershire | Newport | 1939 |
| 255 | R.C.E. Pratt, M.J. Stewart | Surrey v Cambridge U. | Guildford | 1956 |
| 255 | E.J. Barlow, A.J. Pithey | S. Africans v Combined XI | Perth | 1963–64 |
| 254 | G.M. Turner, J.A. Ormrod | Worcestershire v Surrey | Worcester | 1978 |
| 253* | J.B. Hobbs, A. Sandham | Surrey v West Indians | Oval | 1928 |
| 253 | P. Holmes, H. Sutcliffe | Yorkshire v Lancashire | Sheffield | 1919 |
| 253 | J.A. Hopkins, A. Jones | Glamorgan v Worcestershire | Worcester | 1977 |

| 252 | R.R. Relf, J. Vine | Sussex v Nottinghamshire | Hove | 1912 |
|---|---|---|---|---|
| 252 | G. Gunn, W.W. Whysall | Nottinghamshire v Kent | Nottingham | 1924 |
| 252 | B. Sutcliffe, V.J. Scott | New Zealand XI v Rest | Christchurch | 1948–49 |
| 252 | G. Boycott, D.L. Amiss | MCC v President's XI | Bridgetown | 1973–74 |
| 252 | C.P.S. Chauhan, V. Sunderam | Delhi v Haryana | Delhi | 1975–76 |
| 251 | L.J. Todd, A.E. Fagg | Kent v Leicestershire | Maidstone | 1949 |
| 251 | P. Roy, S. Bose | Bengal v Assam | Calcutta | 1951–52 |
| 251 | Agha Zahid, Sultan Rana | Habib Bank v Railways | Lahore | 1982–83 |
| 250* | B.A. Richards, A.J. Woodcock | South Australia v MCC | Adelaide | 1970–71 |
| 250* | C.G. Greenidge, D.L. Haynes | West Indies v Australia | Georgetown | 1983–84 |
| 250* | J.A. Hopkins, G.C. Holmes | Glamorgan v Worcestershire | Abergavenny | 1985 |
| 250 | R.A. Sinfield, C.J. Barnett | Gloucestershire v Glamorgan | Cardiff | 1935 |
| 250 | S.J. Cook, L. Seeff | S. African XI v Arosa Sri Lanka | Cape Town | 1982–83 |

## SECOND WICKET

| 465* | J.A. Jameson, R.B. Kanhai | Warwickshire v Gloucs | Birmingham | 1974 |
|---|---|---|---|---|
| 455 | K.V. Bhandarkar, B.B. Nimbalkar | Maharashtra v Kathiawar | Poona | 1948–49 |
| 451 | W.H. Ponsford, D.G. Bradman | Australia v England | Oval | 1934 |
| 446 | C.C. Hunte, G.St A. Sobers | West Indies v Pakistan | Kingston | 1957–58 |
| 429* | J.G. Dewes, G.H.G. Doggart | Cambridge U. v Essex | Cambridge | 1949 |
| 426 | Arshad Pervez, Mohsin Khan | Habib Bank v Income Tax | Lahore | 1977–78 |
| 398 | A. Shrewsbury, W. Gunn | Nottinghamshire v Sussex | Nottingham | 1890 |
| 385 | E.H. Bowley, M.W. Tate | Sussex v Northamptonshire | Hove | 1921 |
| 382 | L. Hutton, M. Leyland | England v Australia | Oval | 1938 |
| 380 | F.A. Tarrant, J.W. Hearne | Middlesex v Lancashire | Lord's | 1914 |
| 378 | L.A. Marks, K.D. Walters | NSW v South Australia | Adelaide | 1964–65 |
| 374 | R.B. Simpson, R.M. Cowper | Australians v N.E. Transvaal | Pretoria | 1966–67 |
| 371 | J.B. Hobbs, E.G. Hayes | Surrey v Hampshire | Oval | 1909 |
| 371 | F.B. Watson, G.E. Tyldesley | Lancashire v Surrey | Manchester | 1928 |
| 369 | J.H. Edrich, K.F. Barrington | England v New Zealand | Leeds | 1965 |
| 368 | A.C. MacLaren, A.G. Paul | Lancashire v Somerset | Taunton | 1895 |
| 368 | W. Rhodes, C.A.G. Russell | MCC v South Australia | Adelaide | 1920–21 |
| 358 | H.H.L. Kortlang, C. McKenzie | Victoria v Western Australia | Perth | 1909–10 |
| 356 | J.M. Brearley, D.L. Amiss | MCC v Pakistan XI | Dacca | 1966–67 |
| 352 | W.H. Ashdown, F.E. Woolley | Kent v Essex | Brentwood | 1934 |
| 351 | G.A. Gooch, D.I. Gower | England v Australia | Oval | 1985 |
| 349 | C.B. Fry, E.H. Killick | Sussex v Yorkshire | Hove | 1901 |
| 349 | C.S. Elliott, J.D. Eggar | Derbyshire v Notts | Nottingham | 1947 |
| 346 | W. Barber, M. Leyland | Yorkshire v Middlesex | Sheffield | 1932 |
| 344* | S.M. Gavaskar, D.B. Vengsarkar | India v West Indies | Calcutta | 1978–79 |
| 344 | J.H.G. Devey, S. Kinneir | Warwickshire v Derbyshire | Birmingham | 1900 |
| 344 | A. Sandham, R.J. Gregory | Surrey v Glamorgan | Oval | 1937 |
| 343 | F.A. Lowson, J.V. Wilson | Yorkshire v Oxford U. | Oxford | 1956 |
| 342 | W. Larkins, P. Willey | Northants v Lancashire | Northampton | 1983 |
| 336 | F.B. Watson, G.E. Tyldesley | Lancashire v Worcestershire | Worcester | 1929 |
| 334 | A. Jackson, D.G. Bradman | NSW v South Australia | Adelaide | 1930–31 |
| 333 | G.M. Lee, A.W. Carr | Nottinghamshire v Leics | Nottingham | 1913 |
| 333 | P. Holmes, E. Oldroyd | Yorkshire v Warwickshire | Birmingham | 1922 |
| 331* | W.K. Harbinson, E.T. Killick | Cambridge U. v Glamorgan | Cambridge | 1929 |
| 331 | R.T. Robinson, D.I. Gower | England v Australia | Birmingham | 1985 |
| 328 | L. Baichan, R.C. Fredericks | West Indians v Combined U's | Indore | 1974–75 |
| 327 | F.B. Watson, G.E. Tyldesley | Lancashire v Indians | Manchester | 1932 |
| 327 | S.M. Gavaskar, A.L. Wadekar | Indians v Worcestershire | Worcester | 1971 |
| 325 | G. Brann, K.S. Ranjitsinhji | Sussex v Surrey | Oval | 1899 |
| 325 | Salman Qazilbash, Ijaz Ahmed | Universities v Railways | Lahore | 1977–78 |
| 324* | M.C. Carew, R.C. Fredericks | West Indians v Leicestershire | Leicester | 1969 |
| 324 | I.D. Walker, Hon A. Lyttelton | Middlesex v Gloucestershire | Clifton | 1883 |
| 324 | S.M. Brown, W.J. Edrich | Middlesex v Warwickshire | Birmingham | 1954 |
| 323 | I.D. Craig, R.N. Harvey | NSW v Queensland | Sydney | 1960–61 |
| 322 | W. Larkins, R.G. Williams | Northamptonshire v Leics | Leicester | 1980 |
| 321* | J.G. Wright, P.N. Kirsten | Derbyshire v Lancashire | Manchester | 1980 |
| 321 | G. Brown, E.I.M. Barrett | Hampshire v Gloucestershire | Southampton | 1920 |
| 321 | G.A. Gooch, K.S. McEwan | Essex v Northamptonshire | Ilford | 1978 |
| 319 | H.W. Lee, G.O.B. Allen | Middlesex v Surrey | Oval | 1929 |
| 318 | R.E.H. Hudson, C.P. Hamilton | Army v Royal Air Force | Oval | 1932 |
| 318 | M.C. Cowdrey, A.S.M. Oakman | MCC v Orange Free State | Bloemfontein | 1956–57 |

| | | | | |
|---|---|---|---|---|
| 318 | C.W. Smith, S.M. Nurse | Barbados v Trinidad | Bridgetown | 1962–63 |
| 318 | D.L. Amiss, R.B. Kanhai | Warwickshire v Lancashire | Birmingham | 1972 |
| 317* | P. Nandy, Raja Mukherjee | Bengal v Assam | Calcutta | 1975–76 |
| 317 | H. Sutcliffe, C. Hallows | England v Rest | Bristol | 1927 |
| 317 | R.T. Hart, P.S. Briasco | Central Dists. v Canterbury | New Plymouth | 1983–84 |
| 316* | M.J. Stewart, K.F. Barrington | Surrey v Essex | Oval | 1962 |
| 316* | A.R. Butcher, D.M. Smith | Surrey v Warwickshire | Birmingham | 1982 |
| 316 | J.L. Hopwood, G.E. Tyldesley | Lancashire v Gloucestershire | Bristol | 1934 |
| 316 | G.R. Viswanath, Yashpal Sharma | India v England | Madras | 1981–82 |
| 316 | Ijaz Ahmed, Shaukat Mirza | PACO v Karachi | Karachi | 1984–85 |
| 315 | A.W. Thompson, W.J. Edrich | Middlesex v Worcestershire | Dudley | 1952 |
| 314 | H. Sutcliffe, E. Oldroyd | Yorkshire v Essex | Southend | 1924 |
| 314 | W.H. Ponsford, H.S.T.L. Hendry | Victoria v Queensland | Melbourne | 1927–28 |
| 314 | H.W. Lee, E.H. Hendren | Middlesex v Hampshire | Lord's | 1928 |
| 314 | M.S. Gupte, H.S. Kanitkar | Maharashtra v Rajasthan | Poona | 1970–71 |
| 312 | A. Shrewsbury, W. Gunn | Nottinghamshire v Sussex | Hove | 1891 |
| 308 | B.A. Richards, I.M. Chappell | S. Australia v W. Australia | Perth | 1970–71 |
| 308 | R.A. Austin, M.L.C. Foster | Jamaica v Trinidad | Montego Bay | 1976–77 |
| 308 | M. Bannerjee, Raju Mukherjee | Bengal v Orissa | Sambalpur | 1977–78 |
| 308 | T.A. Lloyd, A.I. Kallicharran | Warwickshire v Glamorgan | Birmingham | 1983 |
| 307 | H.T.W. Hardinge, James Seymour | Kent v Worcestershire | Kidderminster | 1922 |
| 307 | J.G. Langridge, H.W. Parks | Sussex v Kent | Tonbridge | 1939 |
| 306 | F.B. Watson, G.E. Tyldesley | Lancashire v Sussex | Hove | 1928 |
| 306 | C.L. Badcock, W. Horrocks | Combined XI v MCC | Perth | 1936–37 |
| 305 | J.W. Rothery, D. Denton | Yorkshire v Derbyshire | Chesterfield | 1910 |
| 305 | S.K. Coen, J.M.M. Commaille | Orange Free State v Natal | Bloemfontein | 1926–27 |
| 305 | F.B. Watson, J. Iddon | Lancashire v Somerset | Taunton | 1934 |
| 304 | W. Bardsley, M.A. Noble | New South Wales v Victoria | Sydney | 1908–09 |
| 304 | G.E.B. Abell, Agha Raza | Northern India v Army | Lahore | 1934–35 |
| 304 | C.L. Smith, R.M. Bentley | Natal B v N Transvaal B | Durban | 1982–83 |
| 303 | C.S. Dempster, C.F.W. Allcott | New Zealanders v Warwicks | Birmingham | 1927 |
| 302 | W. Watson, J.V. Wilson | Yorkshire v Derbyshire | Scarborough | 1948 |
| 302 | V.P. Terry, T.E. Jesty | Hampshire v Cambridge U | Cambridge | 1984 |
| 301 | A.R. Morris, D.G. Bradman | Australia v England | Leeds | 1948 |
| 301 | P.J. Sharpe, D.E.V. Padgett | Yorkshire v Glamorgan | Swansea | 1971 |
| 299* | L. Livingston, D.W. Barrick | Northamptonshire v Sussex | Northampton | 1953 |
| 299 | E.L. Bowley, J.T. Murray | South Australia v Queensland | Adelaide | 1923–24 |
| 299 | A. Sandham, A. Ducat | Surrey v Lancashire | Manchester | 1928 |
| 298 | W.M. Lawry, I.M. Chappell | Australia v West Indies | Melbourne | 1968–69 |
| 297 | R.C. Fredericks, A.I. Kallicharran | Guyana v Barbados | Bridgetown | 1974–75 |
| 297 | G.A. Parkar, A.V. Mankad | Bombay v Delhi | Bombay | 1980–81 |
| 297 | M.R. Srinivasaprasad, G.R. Viswanath | Karnataka v Kerala | Trivandrum | 1984–85 |
| 296 | E.J. Smith, L.T.A. Bates | Warwickshire v Kent | Coventry | 1927 |
| 296 | W.H. Ponsford, D.G. Bradman | Australian XI v Tasmania | Hobart | 1929–30 |
| 295 | A. Hartley, J.T. Tyldesley | Lancashire v Somerset | Manchester | 1910 |
| 295 | J.B. Stollmeyer, K.B. Trestrail | Trinidad v Jamaica | Port-of-Spain | 1949–50 |
| 295 | H. Praharaj, A. Jayaprakash | Orissa v Assam | Newgong | 1984–85 |
| 294 | W.A. Brown, D.G. Bradman | NSW v Queensland | Brisbane | 1933–34 |
| 294 | A.V. Avery, P.A. Gibb | Essex v Northamptonshire | Northampton | 1952 |
| 293 | L.E. Favell, R.B. Simpson | Australians v GW | Kimberley | 1957–58 |
| 293 | T.A. Lloyd, A.I. Kallicharran | Warwicks v Lancashire | Birmingham | 1983 |
| 292* | K.S. Ranjitsinhji, C.B. Fry | Sussex v Somerset | Taunton | 1901 |
| 292 | J.T. Ikin, G.A. Edrich | Lancashire v Oxford U. | Oxford | 1951 |
| 292 | J.M. Brearley, K.W.R. Fletcher | MCC v West Zone | Poona | 1976–77 |
| 291 | A. Sandham, H.S. Squires | Surrey v Yorkshire | Oval | 1933 |
| 291 | Zaheer Abbas, Mushtaq Mohd | Pakistan v England | Birmingham | 1971 |
| 291 | G.A. Parkar, G.M. Gupte | Bombay v Tamil Nadu | Madras | 1980–81 |
| 290 | J.C.W. MacBryan, M.D. Lyon | Somerset v Derbyshire | Burton upon Trent | 1924 |
| 290 | B. Wood, H. Pilling | Lancashire v Glamorgan | Liverpool | 1976 |
| 290 | D.R. Turner, M.C.J. Nicholas | Hampshire v Oxford U. | Oxford | 1983 |
| 289* | J.C. Balderstone, D.I. Gower | Leicestershire v Essex | Leicester | 1981 |
| 289 | A. Shrewsbury, W. Barnes | Nottinghamshire v Surrey | Oval | 1882 |
| 289 | Laxman Singh, P. Sharma | Rajasthan v Madhya Pradesh | Indore | 1974–75 |
| 289 | T.A. Lloyd, D.L. Amiss | Warwickshire v Gloucs | Birmingham | 1983 |
| 288* | G.J. Saville, K.W.R. Fletcher | Essex v Glamorgan | Swansea | 1972 |
| 288 | H. Sutcliffe, A. Mitchell | Yorkshire v Lancashire | Manchester | 1939 |
| 287* | C.G. Greenidge, H.A. Gomes | West Indies v England | Lord's | 1984 |

| 287 | W. Watson, A. Wharton | Leicestershire v Lancashire | Leicester | 1961 |
|---|---|---|---|---|
| 284 | P.J. Sharpe, F.R. Bailey | Minor Counties v Indians | Stoke | 1959 |
| 283 | A.J.Y. Hopkins, M.A. Noble | NSW v South Australia | Adelaide | 1908–09 |
| 283 | H.W. Taylor, R.H. Blake | Natal v Griqualand West | Durban | 1910–11 |
| 283 | I.J. Siedle, A. Melville | Natal v Border | Durban | 1928–29 |
| 283 | H. Sutcliffe, Nawab of Pataudi sr | MCC v Combined XI | Perth | 1932–33 |
| 283 | V.L. Mehra, B.K. Kunderan | Railways v Jammu & Kashmir | Delhi | 1959–60 |
| 282 | D. Brookes, L. Livingston | Northamptonshire v Kent | Maidstone | 1954 |
| 282 | J.W. Rutherford, R.N. Harvey | Australians v MCC | Lord's | 1956 |
| 281* | R.A Gripper, R.B. Ullyett | Rhodesia v Orange Free State | Bloemfontein | 1967–68 |
| 281 | W.G. Grace, J.M. Cotterill | South v North | Prince's | 1877 |
| 281 | A. Sandham, A. Ducat | Surrey v Nottinghamshire | Nottingham | 1930 |
| 281 | W.M. Woodfull, W.A. Brown | Australians v Lancashire | Manchester | 1934 |
| 281 | J.G. Langridge, H.W. Parks | Sussex v Glamorgan | Eastbourne | 1938 |
| 281 | C.L. Walcott, F.M.M. Worrell | West Indians v Tasmania | Hobart | 1951–52 |
| 280 | L. Hall, F. Lee | Yorkshire v Lancashire | Bradford | 1887 |
| 280 | G. Brown, E.I.M. Barrett | Hampshire v Warwickshire | Portsmouth | 1920 |
| 280 | P.A. Gibb, W.J. Edrich | England v South Africa | Durban | 1938–39 |
| 280 | J.W. Burke, R.N. Harvey | Australians v Warwickshire | Birmingham | 1956 |
| 280 | Kamal Najamuddin, Ishrat Zaidi | Karachi v National Bank | Karachi | 1980–81 |
| 280 | G. Cook, R.G. Williams | Northamptonshire v Sussex | Northampton | 1981 |
| 279 | G. Cook, D.S. Steele | Northants v Derbyshire | Northampton | 1978 |
| 277 | C.J.B. Wood, G.W. Beldam | London County v Surrey | Oval | 1901 |
| 277 | W.J. Edrich, D.C.S. Compton | Middlesex v Leicestershire | Leicester | 1947 |
| 277 | S.G. Adhikari, H.D. Amroliwalla | Bombay v Maharashtra | Poona | 1960–61 |
| 277 | R.B. McCosker, I.M. Chappell | Australia v England | Oval | 1975 |
| 277 | V. Sunderam, H. Gidwani | Delhi v Services | Delhi | 1977–78 |
| 277 | P.A. Hibbert, G.W. Richardson | Victoria v Queensland | Melbourne | 1983–84 |
| 276 | W. Bardsley, C.G. Macartney | Australians v Leicestershire | Leicester | 1921 |
| 276 | J.B. Hobbs, R.J. Gregory | Surrey v Hampshire | Southampton | 1926 |
| 275 | A.E. Fagg, F.G.H. Chalk | Kent v Worcestershire | Dudley | 1938 |
| 275 | C.C. McDonald, A.L. Hassett | Australia v South Africa | Adelaide | 1952–53 |
| 274 | A. Shrewsbury, W. Gunn | Nottinghamshire v Sussex | Hove | 1893 |
| 274 | W.M. Woodfull, D.G. Bradman | Australia v South Africa | Melbourne | 1931–32 |
| 274 | H.H.I. Gibbons, Pataudi sr | Worcestershire v Kent | Worcester | 1933 |
| 274 | H.H.I. Gibbons, Pataudi sr | Worcestershire v Glamorgan | Worcester | 1934 |
| 273 | J.L. Hopwood, G.E. Tyldesley | Lancashire v Glamorgan | Cardiff | 1934 |
| 273 | L.J. Todd, L.E.G. Ames | Kent v Essex | Maidstone | 1947 |
| 272 | R. Abel, E.G. Hayes | Surrey v Worcestershire | Oval | 1900 |
| 271 | M.R. Harvey, K.R. Miller | Victoria v New South Wales | Melbourne | 1946–47 |
| 271 | C. Washbrook, G.A. Edrich | Lancashire v Sussex | Manchester | 1951 |
| 271 | P.J. Muzzell, W.S. Farrer | Border v Orange Free State | Bloemfontein | 1968–69 |
| 271 | N. Juneja, A. Bhanot | Uttar Pradesh v Bengal | Kanpur | 1980–81 |
| 270 | H.L. Collins, T.J.E. Andrews | New South Wales v MCC | Sydney | 1924–25 |
| 270 | W.M. Woodfull, C.G. Macartney | Australians v Essex | Leyton | 1926 |
| 270 | D.N. Sardesai, A.L. Wadekar | Bombay v Mysore | Bombay | 1966–67 |
| 269 | Nazar Mohd, Murawat Hussain | Pakistan v Ceylon | Colombo | 1948–49 |
| 269 | G.St A. Sobers, C.L. Walcott | West Indies v Pakistan | Georgetown | 1957–58 |
| 269 | R.C. Fredericks, L.G. Rowe | West Indies v New Zealand | Kingston | 1971–72 |
| 269 | J.R.T. Barclay, K.C. Wessels | Sussex v Nottinghamshire | Eastbourne | 1980 |
| 268 | J.R.M. Mackay, M.A. Noble | New South Wales v Victoria | Melbourne | 1905–06 |
| 268 | Afzal Ahmed, Shafiq Ahmed | National Bank v PIA | Faisalabad | 1981–82 |
| 267 | M.H. Mankad, R.F. Surti | Rajasthan v Uttar Pradesh | Udaipur | 1959–60 |
| 266* | K. Taylor, D.E.V. Padgett | Yorkshire v Oxford U. | Oxford | 1962 |
| 266 | P.E. Richardson, T.W. Graveney | England v West Indies | Nottingham | 1957 |
| 266 | B.S. Groves, R.R. Collins | Natal B v Orange Free State | Bloemfontein | 1967–68 |
| 265* | M.S. Venter, H.R. Fotheringham | Transvaal v Arosa Sri Lanka | Johannesburg | 1982–83 |
| 265 | A. Ward, J.T. Tyldesley | Lancashire v Derbyshire | Derby | 1901 |
| 265 | G. Gunn, W. Walker | Notts v Hampshire | Bournemouth | 1928 |
| 265 | D. Brookes, W. Barron | Northants v Cambridge U. | Cambridge | 1948 |
| 265 | A.R. Morris, K.R. Miller | New South Wales v MCC | Sydney | 1950–51 |
| 265 | R.T. Robinson, D.W. Randall | Nottinghamshire v Yorkshire | Nottingham | 1984 |
| 264 | D.B Vengsarkar, S.M. Gavaskar | West Zone v Central Zone | Ahmedabad | 1977–78 |
| 263 | G.B.Y. Cox, H.B.G. Austin | Barbados v Trinidad | Bridgetown | 1897–98 |
| 263 | Sadiq Mohammad, Saeed Ahmed | Karachi Blues v PWD | Karachi | 1970–71 |
| 263 | D.L. Amiss, A.I. Kallicharran | Warwickshire v Middlesex | Birmingham | 1974 |
| 263 | N.R. Taylor, D.G. Aslett | Kent v Oxford University | Oxford | 1985 |
| 262 | J.M. Gregory, T.J.E. Andrews | NSW v New Zealanders | Sydney | 1927–28 |

| 262 | H.T.W. Hardinge, F.E. Woolley | Kent v Warwickshire | Tunbridge Wells | 1928 |
|---|---|---|---|---|
| 262 | W.P.J. Donaldson, K.R. Miller | NSW v Western Australia | Sydney | 1947–48 |
| 262 | R.T. Virgin, M.J. Kitchen | Somerset v Pakistanis | Taunton | 1967 |
| 261* | L. Hutton, J.V. Wilson | Yorkshire v Scotland | Hull | 1949 |
| 261 | E.W. Dillon, James Seymour | Kent v Somerset | Taunton | 1905 |
| 261 | A.R. Morris, S.G. Barnes | NSW v Queensland | Sydney | 1940–41 |
| 261 | N.W. Hill, J.D. Clay | Nottinghamshire v Yorkshire | Nottingham | 1959 |
| 261 | P.A. Hibbert, G.N. Yallop | Victoria v South Australia | Geelong | 1980–81 |
| 260 | A.E. Fagg, F.E. Woolley | Kent v Northamptonshire | Northampton | 1934 |
| 260 | F.M. Engineer, Zaheer Abbas | World XI v Combined XI | Hobart | 1971–72 |
| 260 | R.G. Lumb, K. Sharp | Yorkshire v Glamorgan | Cardiff | 1984 |
| 259* | R.T. Spooner, T.W. Graveney | MCC v Pakistan XI | Lahore | 1951–52 |
| 259 | T.W. Hayward, E.G. Hayes | Surrey v Yorkshire | Oval | 1911 |
| 259 | J.G. Langridge, A. Melville | Sussex v Indians | Hove | 1936 |
| 259 | D. Brookes, L. Livingston | Northamptonshire v Leics | Northampton | 1950 |
| 259 | Arshad Pervez, Tehsin Javed | Habib Bank v State Bank | Lahore | 1983–84 |
| 259 | W.B. Phillips, G.N. Yallop | Australia v Pakistan | Perth | 1983–84 |
| 258 | H. Sutcliffe, E. Oldroyd | Yorkshire v Kent | Folkestone | 1931 |
| 258 | Raja Mukherjee, P.C. Poddar | Bengal v Orissa | Rourkela | 1975–76 |
| 256* | G.P. Howarth, R.D.V. Knight | Surrey v Cambridge U. | Cambridge | 1978 |
| 256 | W.G. Grace, W. Chatterton | MCC v Cambridge University | Cambridge | 1894 |
| 256 | W.W. Whysall, W. Walker | Notts v Hampshire | Nottingham | 1930 |
| 256 | H.F. Wade, E.A.B. Rowan | South Africans v Glamorgan | Cardiff | 1935 |
| 256 | C.T.M. Pugh, T.W. Graveney | Gloucestershire v Derbyshire | Chesterfield | 1960 |
| 256 | Salim Asghar, Mohammad Arif | Rawalpindi v Peshawar | Rawalpindi | 1963–64 |
| 256 | R.W. Anderson, B.A. Edgar | New Zealanders v Scotland | Broughty Ferry | 1978 |
| 255 | A. Ward, A.E. Stoddart | Stoddart's XI v Queensland | Brisbane | 1894–95 |
| 255 | V.Y. Richardson, D.E. Pritchard | South Australia v MCC | Adelaide | 1928–29 |
| 255 | H.T.W. Hardinge, F.E. Woolley | Kent v Derbyshire | Chesterfield | 1929 |
| 255 | E.D.A.St J. McMorris, R.B. Kanhai | West Indies v India | Kingston | 1961–62 |
| 255 | D.L. Amiss, J.A. Jameson | Warwickshire v Oxford U. | Birmingham | 1964 |
| 255 | L. Baichan, T. Mohamed | Guyana v Combined I's | Rose Hall | 1978–79 |
| 255 | Arshad Pervez, Salim Malik | Habib Bank v HBFC | Lahore | 1983–84 |
| 255 | W. Larkins, R.J. Boyd-Moss | Northants v Worcestershire | Worcester | 1985 |
| 254* | G.L. Berry, N.F. Armstrong | Leics v L. Parkinson's XI | Blackpool | 1935 |
| 254* | W.M. Lawry, R.M. Cowper | Combined XI v MCC | Hobart | 1965–66 |
| 254 | C.P.S. Chauhan, D.B. Vengsarkar | Indians v Minor Counties | Wellington | 1979 |
| 253 | B.B. Wilson, D. Denton | Yorkshire v Warwickshire | Birmingham | 1912 |
| 253 | C.T. Sarwate, L. Amarnath | Indians v Tasmania | Launceston | 1947–48 |
| 253 | J.W. Burke, K.D. Mackay | Australians v E. Province | Port Elizabeth | 1957–58 |
| 253 | J.W. Burke, R.N. Harvey | NSW v Queensland | Brisbane | 1958–59 |
| 253 | J.G. Wright, P.N. Kirsten | Derbyshire v Northants | Derby | 1980 |
| 253 | J.C. Balderstone, D.I. Gower | Leicestershire v Australians | Leicester | 1985 |
| 252 | G. Brann, K.S. Ranjitsinhji | Sussex v Gloucestershire | Bristol | 1899 |
| 252 | W.K. Tyldesley, J.T. Tyldesley | Lancashire v Derbyshire | Derby | 1911 |
| 252 | W.A. Baker, E.M. Beechey | Wellington v Auckland | Wellington | 1918–19 |
| 252 | P.E. Palia, L. Amarnath | C.C. of India v Bombay | Bombay | 1934–35 |
| 252 | W.M. Lawry, J. Potter | Victoria v New South Wales | Sydney | 1960–61 |
| 251* | R.T. Simpson, C.J. Poole | Nottinghamshire v Leics | Nottingham | 1949 |
| 251 | J.C.W. MacBryan, A. Young | Somerset v Glamorgan | Taunton | 1923 |
| 251 | C.J. Barnett, W.R. Hammond | Gloucestershire v Sussex | Cheltenham | 1934 |
| 251 | Agha Zahid, Sultan Rana | Habib Bank v Railways | Lahore | 1982–83 |
| 250 | F.L. Bowley, H.K. Foster | Worcestershire v Somerset | Worcester | 1903 |
| 250 | A.C. Johnston, C.P. Mead | Hampshire v Warwickshire | Coventry | 1912 |
| 250 | H.T.W. Hardinge, James Seymour | Kent v Essex | Leyton | 1923 |
| 250 | D.J. McGlew, M.K. Elgie | Natal v Border | Durban | 1957–58 |
| 250 | A.V. Mankad, A.L. Wadekar | Bombay v Rest of India | Calcutta | 1970–71 |
| 250 | Mudassar Nazar, Qasim Omar | Pakistan v India | Faisalabad | 1984–85 |

## THIRD WICKET

| 456 | Khalid Irtiza, Aslam Ali | United Bank v Multan | Karachi | 1975–76 |
|---|---|---|---|---|
| 451 | Mudassar Nazar, Javed Miandad | Pakistan v India | Hyderabad | 1982–83 |
| 445 | P.E. Whitelaw, W.N. Carson | Auckland v Otago | Dunedin | 1936–37 |
| 434 | J.B. Stollmeyer, G.E. Gomez | Trinidad v British Guiana | Port-of-Spain | 1946–47 |
| 424* | W.J. Edrich, D.C.S. Compton | Middlesex v Somerset | Lord's | 1948 |

| | | | | |
|---|---|---|---|---|
| 410 | R.S. Modi, L. Amarnath | India in England v Rest | Calcutta | 1946–47 |
| 399 | R.T. Simpson, D.C.S. Compton | MCC v N.E. Transvaal | Benoni | 1948–49 |
| 390* | J.M. Wiener, J.K. Moss | Victoria v W. Australia | Melbourne (St K) | 1981–82 |
| 389 | W.H. Ponsford, S.J. McCabe | Australians v MCC | Lord's | 1934 |
| 388 | Salahuddin, W. Mathias | Karachi Blues v Hyderabad | Karachi | 1964–65 |
| 375 | J.W. Hearne, E.H. Hendren | Middlesex v Hampshire | Southampton | 1923 |
| 373 | V.M. Merchant, R.S. Modi | Bombay v W. India States | Bombay | 1944–45 |
| 370 | W.J. Edrich, D.C.S. Compton | England v South Africa | Lord's | 1947 |
| 369 | W. Gunn, J.R. Gunn | Nottinghamshire v Leics | Nottingham | 1903 |
| 365 | A.D. Gaekwad, N.Y. Satham | Baroda v Maharashtra | Baroda | 1980–81 |
| 363 | D.G. Bradman, A.F. Kippax | NSW v Queensland | Sydney | 1933–34 |
| 362 | W. Bardsley, C.G. Macartney | Australians v Essex | Leyton | 1912 |
| 356 | D.G. Bradman, R.A. Hamence | South Australia v Tasmania | Adelaide | 1935–36 |
| 355 | W. Bardsley, V.S. Ransford | Australians v Essex | Leyton | 1909 |
| 353 | A. Ducat, E.G. Hayes | Surrey v Hampshire | Southampton | 1919 |
| 350 | F.M.M. Worrell, E.de C. Weekes | West Indians v Cambridge U. | Cambridge | 1950 |
| 345 | W. Bardsley, J.M. Taylor | NSW v South Australia | Adelaide | 1920–21 |
| 345 | V.M. Merchant, H.R. Adhikari | Hindus v Rest | Bombay | 1943–44 |
| 344 | G. Brown, C.P. Mead | Hampshire v Yorkshire | Portsmouth | 1927 |
| 343 | P.A. Gibb, R. Horsfall | Essex v Kent | Blackheath | 1951 |
| 341 | E.J. Barlow, R.G. Pollock | South Africa v Australia | Adelaide | 1963–64 |
| 340* | F.M.M. Worrell, E.de C. Weekes | West Indians v Leicestershire | Leicester | 1950 |
| 338 | E.de C. Weekes, F.M.M. Worrell | West Indies v England | Port-of-Spain | 1953–54 |
| 338 | J.M. Brearley, M.W. Gatting | Middlesex v Derbyshire | Derby | 1981 |
| 336 | W.R. Hammond, B.H. Lyon | Gloucestershire v Leics | Leicester | 1933 |
| 335 | D.K. Gaekwad, C.G. Borde | Baroda v Maharashtra | Poona | 1959–60 |
| 333 | R.M. Taylor, J. O'Connor | Essex v Northamptonshire | Colchester | 1937 |
| 330 | A.E. Dipper, W.R. Hammond | Gloucestershire v Lancashire | Manchester | 1925 |
| 330 | G.M. Wood, G.R. Marsh | W. Australia v NSW | Sydney | 1983–84 |
| 328 | H. Carpenter, C.P. McGahey | Essex v Surrey | Oval | 1904 |
| 327 | S. Kinneir, W.G. Quaife | Warwickshire v Lancashire | Birmingham | 1901 |
| 323* | H. Sutcliffe, M. Leyland | Yorkshire v Glamorgan | Huddersfield | 1928 |
| 323 | C.P. McGahey, P.A. Perrin | Essex v Kent | Leyton | 1900 |
| 321* | A. Hearne, J.R. Mason | Kent v Nottinghamshire | Nottingham | 1899 |
| 321 | C.L. Smith, T.E. Jesty | Hampshire v Derbyshire | Derby | 1983 |
| 320 | W.W. Armstrong, M.A. Noble | Australians v Somerset | Bath | 1905 |
| 320 | L. Livingston, F. Jakeman | Northants v S. Africans | Northampton | 1951 |
| 320 | A.L. Wadekar, D.N. Sardesai | West Zone v Central Zone | Bombay | 1972–73 |
| 319 | A. Melville, A.D. Nourse | South Africa v England | Nottingham | 1947 |
| 319 | P.M. Roebuck, M.D. Crowe | Somerset v Leicestershire | Taunton | 1984 |
| 318 | G.A. Faulkner, A.W. Nourse | South Africans v NSW | Sydney | 1910–11 |
| 318 | T.W. Graveney, J.F. Crapp | Gloucestershire v Kent | Gillingham | 1953 |
| 318 | C.T. Radley, M.W. Gatting | Middlesex v New Zealanders | Lord's | 1983 |
| 317 | A. Ducat, T.F. Shepherd | Surrey v Essex | Leyton | 1928 |
| 316* | W. Watson, A. Wharton | Leicestershire v Somerset | Taunton | 1961 |
| 316 | G.R. Viswanath, Yashpal Sharma | India v England | Madras | 1981–82 |
| 315 | C.L. Badcock, A.L. Hassett | Australians v Leicestershire | Leicester | 1938 |
| 315 | K.M. Tiwari, V.L. Manjrekar | Uttar Pradesh v Madhya Pradesh | Indore | 1957–58 |
| 315 | L.G. Rowe, H.A. Gomes | West Indians v Derbyshire | Chesterfield | 1976 |
| 314 | M.J. Horton, T.W. Graveney | Worcestershire v Somerset | Worcester | 1962 |
| 313 | Umar Khan, Prithiviraj | W. India States v Bombay | Rajkot | 1943–44 |
| 313 | D.E. Davies, W.E. Jones | Glamorgan v Essex | Brentwood | 1948 |
| 312 | P.A. Perrin, C.P. McGahey | Essex v Derbyshire | Leyton | 1912 |
| 310 | A. Shrewsbury, W. Gunn | Non-Smokers v Smokers | East Melbourne | 1886–87 |
| 310 | Najam-ul-Haq, Parvez Mir | Lahore v Multan | Lahore | 1973–74 |
| 309* | C.B. Fry, A.C. MacLaren | Gentlemen v Players | Lord's | 1903 |
| 309 | Salahuddin, Aftab Baloch | PIA v Karachi | Karachi | 1977–78 |
| 308 | R.B. Richardson, I.V.A. Richards | West Indies v Australia | St John's | 1983–84 |
| 306 | R. Abel, F.C. Holland | Surrey v Cambridge U. | Oval | 1895 |
| 306 | L.G. Crawley, W.V. Fox | Worcestershire v Northants | Worcester | 1923 |
| 306 | E. Paynter, N. Oldfield | Lancashire v Hampshire | Southampton | 1938 |
| 306 | S.M. Nurse, G.St A. Sobers | Barbados v MCC | Bridgetown | 1959–60 |
| 305 | W.E. Roller, W.W. Read | Surrey v Lancashire | Manchester | 1887 |
| 305 | J.C. Balderstone, B.F. Davison | Leicestershire v Notts | Leicester | 1974 |
| 305 | C.W.J. Athey, P. Bainbridge | Gloucestershire v Derbyshire | Derby | 1985 |
| 304 | W.J. Edrich, D.C.S. Compton | Middlesex v Gloucestershire | Lord's | 1938 |
| 304 | A.H. Phebey, R.C. Wilson | Kent v Glamorgan | Blackheath | 1960 |

| 304 | K.C. Wessels, G.M. Ritchie | Queensland v Tasmania | Devonport | 1981–82 |
|---|---|---|---|---|
| 303 | H.K. Foster, R.E. Foster | Worcestershire v Kent | Worcester | 1907 |
| 303 | I.V.A. Richards, A.I. Kallicharran | West Indies v England | Nottingham | 1976 |
| 303 | H.A. Gomes, C.L. King | West Indians v Northants | Northampton | 1976 |
| 302 | Bashir Shana, Aftab Baloch | Sind v Baluchistan | Karachi | 1973–74 |
| 301* | Atma Singh, H.T. Dani | Services v Bengal | Delhi | 1957–58 |
| 301 | E.T. Killick, E.H. Hendren | Middlesex v Sussex | Hove | 1928 |
| 301 | H. Sutcliffe, M. Leyland | Yorkshire v Middlesex | Lord's | 1939 |
| 300 | G. Atkinson, P.B. Wight | Somerset v Glamorgan | Bath | 1960 |
| 300 | I.M. Chappell, G.S. Chappell | Australians v Barbados | Bridgetown | 1972–73 |
| 298 | K.S. Ranjitsinhji, E.H. Killick | Sussex v Lancashire | Hove | 1901 |
| 298 | J.B. Hobbs, E.H. Hendren | Players v Gentlemen | Scarborough | 1925 |
| 297 | P.B. Wight, W.E. Alley | Somerset v Surrey | Taunton | 1961 |
| 297 | J.H. Edrich, K.F. Barrington | Surrey v Middlesex | Oval | 1967 |
| 297 | G.A. Parkar, A.V. Mankad | Bombay v Delhi | Bombay | 1980–81 |
| 296 | R.H. Spooner, J. Hallows | Lancashire v Essex | Leyton | 1904 |
| 296 | W.J. Edrich, E.H. Hendren | MCC v Surrey | Lord's | 1936 |
| 296 | W.J. Edrich, D.C.S. Compton | Middlesex v Surrey | Lord's | 1946 |
| 295 | C.C. McDonald, R.N. Harvey | Australia v West Indies | Kingston | 1954–55 |
| 295 | K.D. Mackay, P.J.P. Burge | Queensland v South Australia | Adelaide | 1960–61 |
| 294 | J.M. Parks, James Langridge | Sussex v Kent | Tunbridge Wells | 1951 |
| 292 | A.C. Johnston, C.P. Mead | Hampshire v Warwickshire | Southampton | 1911 |
| 292 | D.N. Sardesai, V.H. Bhosle | Bombay v Baroda | Bombay | 1968–69 |
| 291 | A.E. Knight, J.H. King | Leicestershire v MCC | Lord's | 1904 |
| 291 | P.A. Perrin, F.H. Gillingham | Essex v Cambridge U. | Cambridge | 1910 |
| 291 | P.N. Kirsten, D.S. Steele | Derbyshire v Somerset | Taunton | 1981 |
| 290* | J.S. Solomon, B.F. Butcher | Berbice v MCC | Blairmont | 1959–60 |
| 290 | A.L. Wadekar, V.H. Bhosle | West Zone v East Zone | Calcutta | 1964–65 |
| 287* | W.J. Edrich, D.C.S. Compton | Middlesex v Surrey | Oval | 1947 |
| 287 | W.A. Hill, R.E.S. Wyatt | Warwickshire v Northants | Northampton | 1939 |
| 286* | W.J. van der Linden, N.T. Day | Transvaal B v Border | East London | 1976–77 |
| 286 | J.W. Hearne, E.H. Hendren | Middlesex v Somerset | Taunton | 1928 |
| 284 | E.T. Killick, G.C. Grant | Cambridge U. v Essex | Cambridge | 1929 |
| 283* | A. Malhotra, Premchand | Haryana v Jammu & Kashmir | Bhiwani | 1979–80 |
| 283 | H.T.W. Hardinge, F.E. Woolley | Kent v South Africans | Canterbury | 1924 |
| 283 | J.M. Parks, K.F. Barrington | MCC v Berbice | Blairmont | 1959–60 |
| 283 | R.C. Wilson, S.E. Leary | Kent v Northamptonshire | Kettering | 1963 |
| 282 | J. Whitehouse, A.I. Kallicharran | Warwickshire v Northants | Northampton | 1979 |
| 281 | W.G. Grace, L. Walker | London County v MCC | Crystal Palace | 1901 |
| 281 | K.E. Rigg, L.S. Darling | Victoria v South Australia | Adelaide | 1932–33 |
| 281 | L. Livingston, R. Subba Row | Northamptonshire v Notts | Nottingham | 1955 |
| 280 | James Seymour, F.E. Woolley | Kent v Lancashire | Dover | 1922 |
| 280 | O.W. Bill, A.F. Kippax | NSW v Queensland | Brisbane | 1930–31 |
| 280 | C. Richardson, D.J. Schonegevel | OFS v Transvaal B | Johannesburg | 1959–60 |
| 280 | T.L. Goddard, R.A. McLean | S. Africans v Northants | Northampton | 1960 |
| 279* | G.E. Tyldesley, J. Iddon | Lancashire v Worcestershire | Worcester | 1932 |
| 279 | J.W.H. Makepeace, G.E. Tyldesley | Lancashire v Notts | Manchester | 1926 |
| 279 | H.H.I. Gibbons, S.H. Martin | Worcestershire v Northants | Stourbridge | 1934 |
| 279 | D.S. Sheppard, G. Cox | Sussex v Yorkshire | Hastings | 1953 |
| 278 | A. Ward, F.H. Sugg | Lancashire v Somerset | Taunton | 1898 |
| 278 | C.J.B. Wood, A.E. Knight | Leicestershire v Hampshire | Southampton | 1905 |
| 278 | T.N. Pearce, M.P. Donnelly | MCC v Yorkshire | Scarborough | 1948 |
| 278 | J.A. Ormrod, Imran Khan | Worcestershire v Warwicks | Worcester | 1976 |
| 277* | G.R. Cass, T.J. Yardley | Worcestershire v Leics | Leicester | 1975 |
| 276 | W.L. Murdoch, G.H.S. Trott | Australians v Cambridge U. P. & P. | Leyton | 1890 |
| 276 | M.N. Harbottle, R.E.H. Hudson | Army v Oxford University | Camberley | 1938 |
| 276 | D.G. Bradman, A.L. Hassett | Australia v England | Brisbane | 1946–47 |
| 273 | F.L. Fane, G.J.V. Weigall | MCC v Cambridge University | Lord's | 1901 |
| 273 | H.T.W. Hardinge, F.E. Woolley | Kent v Hampshire | Southampton | 1922 |
| 273 | F.C. de Saram, N.S. Mitchell-Innes | Oxford U. v Gloucestershire | Oxford | 1934 |
| 273 | W.R. Hammond, B.O. Allen | Gloucestershire v Leics | Leicester | 1935 |
| 273 | W. Place, G.A. Edrich | Lancashire v Essex | Clacton | 1947 |
| 273 | V.L. Manjrekar, B.R. Irani | Bombay v Pakistanis | Bombay | 1952–53 |
| 273 | Hanif Mohd, V.L. Manjrekar | Hasan Mahmood's XI v AVM Cannon's XI | Karachi | 1953–54 |
| 273 | S.M. Nurse, R.B. Kanhai | West Indies v England | Port-of-Spain | 1967–68 |

| | | | | |
|---|---|---|---|---|
| 272 | C.P. Mead, E.H. Hendren | MCC Australian XI v Lord Hawke's XI | Scarborough | 1929 |
| 272 | D.G. Bradman, A.F. Kippax | NSW v Queensland | Sydney | 1929–30 |
| 272 | H. Horton, D.A. Livingstone | Hampshire v Middlesex | Bournemouth | 1966 |
| 272 | A.L. Jones, Javed Miandad | Glamorgan v Hampshire | Cardiff | 1984 |
| 271 | E. Paynter, N. Oldfield | Lancashire v Sussex | Hove | 1937 |
| 270 | D.W. Randall, C.E.B. Rice | Nottinghamshire v Yorks | Harrogate | 1980 |
| 270 | R.C. Ontong, Javed Miandad | Glamorgan v Gloucestershire | Bristol | 1981 |
| 269* | G. Brown, C.P. Mead | Hampshire v Yorkshire | Leeds | 1920 |
| 269 | B.O. Allen, W.R. Hammond | Gloucestershire v Worcs | Cheltenham | 1937 |
| 268 | H.O. Rock, A.F. Kippax | New South Wales v Victoria | Sydney | 1924–25 |
| 268 | N.F. Armstrong, C.S. Dempster | Leicester v Gloucestershire | Gloucester | 1937 |
| 268 | V.S. Hazare, R.S. Modi | West Zone v North Zone | Bombay | 1946–47 |
| 267* | R.E. Marshall, D.A. Livingstone | Hampshire v Pakistanis | Bournemouth | 1962 |
| 267 | R.J. Gregory, H.T. Barling | Surrey v Nottinghamshire | Oval | 1946 |
| 267 | W.J. Edrich, S.M. Brown | Middlesex v Oxford U. | Oxford | 1952 |
| 267 | P.R. Carlstein, J.H.B. Waite | Transvaal v Cavaliers | Johannesburg | 1962–63 |
| 266 | R. Aird, C.P. Mead | Hampshire v Sussex | Hastings | 1924 |
| 266 | C.B. Harris, J. Hardstaff jr | Nottinghamshire v Gloucs | Nottingham | 1936 |
| 266 | C.C. Hunte, G.St A. Sobers | West Indians v U's XI | Nagpur | 1958–59 |
| 266 | J.D. Inchmore, J.M. Parker | Worcestershire v Essex | Worcester | 1974 |
| 264* | C.B. Fry, E.I.M. Barrett | Hampshire v Oxford U. | Southampton | 1912 |
| 264 | F.E. Woolley, J.W. Hearne | MCC v Tasmania | Hobart | 1911–12 |
| 264 | J. Vine, R.R. Relf | Sussex v Oxford University | Hove | 1913 |
| 264 | L. Hutton, W.R. Hammond | England v West Indies | Oval | 1939 |
| 264 | I.M. Chappell, G.S. Chappell | Australia v New Zealand | Wellington | 1973–74 |
| 264 | Yashpal Sharma, M. Amarnath | N. Zone v West Indians | Jullundur | 1978–79 |
| 264 | J.A. Hopkins, Javed Miandad | Glamorgan v Warwickshire | Birmingham | 1980 |
| 263 | D.F. Pope, C.A.G. Russell | Essex v Sussex | Hove | 1930 |
| 263 | D.G.W. Fletcher, H.S. Squires | Surrey v Nottinghamshire | Nottingham | 1947 |
| 263 | D.W. Randall, C.E.B. Rice | Nottinghamshire v Yorkshire | Nottingham | 1981 |
| 262 | L.C.H. Palairet, C.A. Bernard | Somerset v Hampshire | Southampton | 1900 |
| 262 | W.R. Hammond, D.R. Jardine | England v Australia | Adelaide | 1928–29 |
| 261 | A. Ducat, T.F. Shepherd | Surrey v Leicestershire | Oval | 1926 |
| 261 | B. Constable, P.B.H. May | Surrey v Nottinghamshire | Nottingham | 1958 |
| 260 | W.W. Keeton, J. Hardstaff, jr | Nottinghamshire v Yorkshire | Sheffield | 1949 |
| 259* | J.C. Balderstone, T.J. Boon | Leicestershire v Derbyshire | Leicester | 1984 |
| 259 | C.L. Townsend, W. Troup | Gloucestershire v Essex | Clifton | 1899 |
| 259 | L.E.G. Ames, L.J. Todd | Kent v Gloucestershire | Folkestone | 1933 |
| 259 | J. Arnold, C.P. Mead | Hampshire v Derbyshire | Portsmouth | 1934 |
| 259 | D.S. Sheppard, G. Cox | Sussex v Glamorgan | Eastbourne | 1949 |
| 258* | J.T. Brown, F. Mitchell | Yorkshire v Warwickshire | Bradford | 1901 |
| 258* | E.de C. Weekes, C.L. Walcott | West Indians v Ceylon | Colombo | 1948–49 |
| 258 | E.S.B. Williams, G.J. Bryan | Army v Royal Navy | Lord's | 1928 |
| 256 | W.W. Whysall, A.W. Carr | Nottinghamshire v Leics | Leicester | 1928 |
| 255* | W.G. Grace, E.M. Knapp | Gloucestershire v Surrey | Clifton | 1873 |
| 255 | C.B. Fry, K.S. Ranjitsinhji | Sussex v Yorkshire | Sheffield | 1904 |
| 255 | J.S.F. Morrison, Hon H.G.H. Mulholland | Cambridge University v MCC | Cambridge | 1914 |
| 255 | J.W. Hearne, E.H. Hendren | Middlesex v Somerset | Taunton | 1934 |
| 255 | L. Amarnath, V.S. Hazare | Indians v Tasmania | Hobart | 1947–48 |
| 255 | O.C. Dawson, K.N. Kirton | Border v Rhodesia | East London | 1954–55 |
| 255 | C.H. Lloyd, C.A. Davis | West Indians v South Island | Dunedin | 1968–69 |
| 254 | B. Chowdhury, P. Roy | Bengal v Bihar | Calcutta | 1962–63 |
| 254 | Zaheer Abbas, A.J. Hignell | Gloucestershire v Somerset | Taunton | 1980 |
| 253 | C. Hill, D.R.A. Gehrs | South Australia v Victoria | Adelaide | 1909–10 |
| 253 | H.T.W. Hardinge, F.E. Woolley | Kent v Lancashire | Dover | 1926 |
| 252* | G.P. Howarth, A.D.G. Roberts | N. Districts v Pakistanis | Gisborne | 1978–79 |
| 252* | R.V. Mankad, A.V. Mankad | Bombay v Gujarat | Bombay | 1982–83 |
| 252 | C.L. Townsend, C.O.H. Sewell | Gloucestershire v Worcs | Cheltenham | 1906 |
| 252 | D.G. Bradman, K.R. Miller | Australian XI v Indians | Sydney | 1947–48 |
| 252 | D.E.V. Padgett, D.B. Close | Yorkshire v Nottinghamshire | Nottingham | 1959 |
| 252 | G. Barker, J. Milner | Essex v Leicestershire | Leicester | 1959 |
| 252 | Yajurvindra Singh, H.S. Kanitkar | Maharashtra v Karnataka | Bangalore | 1975–76 |
| 251* | C.G. Greenidge, T.E. Jesty | Hampshire v Glamorgan | Portsmouth | 1982 |
| 251 | R.C. Fredericks, B.F. Butcher | Guyana v Barbados | Georgetown | 1969–70 |
| 251 | Mohsin Khan, Javed Miandad | Sind v Punjab | Lahore | 1974–75 |
| 250* | H.T.W. Hardinge, James Seymour | Kent v Worcestershire | Tonbridge | 1921 |

| 250 | J. O'Connor, C.A.G. Russell | Essex v Leicestershire | Leyton | 1927 |
| 250 | E.H. Bowley, K.S. Duleepsinhji | Sussex v Surrey | Oval | 1931 |
| 250 | C.H. Bull, H.H.I. Gibbons | Worcestershire v Northants | Kidderminster | 1937 |
| 250 | R.J. Christiani, J.L. Thomas | British Guiana v Barbados | Georgetown | 1946–47 |
| 250 | M.K. Mantri, U.M. Merchant | Bombay v Maharashtra | Poona | 1948–49 |

## FOURTH WICKET

| 577 | V.S. Hazare, Gul Mahomed | Baroda v Holkar | Baroda | 1946–47 |
| 574* | C.L. Walcott, F.M.M. Worrell | Barbados v Trinidad | Port-of-Spain | 1945–46 |
| 502* | F.M.M. Worrell, J.D.C. Goddard | Barbados v Trinidad | Bridgetown | 1943–44 |
| 470 | A.I. Kallicharran, G.W. Humpage | Warwickshire v Lancashire | Southport | 1982 |
| 448 | R. Abel, T.W. Hayward | Surrey v Yorkshire | Oval | 1899 |
| 424 | I.S. Lee, S.O. Quin | Victoria v Tasmania | Melbourne | 1933–34 |
| 411 | P.B.H. May, M.C. Cowdrey | England v West Indies | Birmingham | 1957 |
| 410 | G. Abraham, B. Pandit | Kerala v Andhra | Palghat | 1959–60 |
| 402 | W. Watson, T.W. Graveney | MCC v British Guiana | Georgetown | 1953–54 |
| 402 | R.B. Kanhai, Khalid Ibadulla | Warwickshire v Notts | Nottingham | 1968 |
| 399 | G.St A. Sobers, F.M.M. Worrell | West Indies v England | Bridgetown | 1959–60 |
| 388 | W.H. Ponsford, D.G. Bradman | Australia v England | Leeds | 1934 |
| 382 | V.S. Hazare, V.M. Merchant | C.C. of India v Services XI | Bombay | 1944–45 |
| 381 | H.P. Bayley, C.S. Persaud | British Guiana v Barbados | Georgetown | 1937–38 |
| 377 | K.R. Miller, J.H. de Courcy | Australians v Combined Services | Kingston upon Thames | 1953 |
| 370 | R.T. Virgin, P. Willey | Northamptonshire v Somerset | Northampton | 1976 |
| 366* | P.R. Umrigar, V.S. Hazare | Indians v Oxford University | Oxford | 1952 |
| 361 | A.O. Jones, J.R. Gunn | Nottinghamshire v Essex | Leyton | 1905 |
| 350 | Mushtaq Mohammad, Asif Iqbal | Pakistan v New Zealand | Dunedin | 1972–73 |
| 346 | Zafar Altaf, Majid Khan | Lahore Greens v Bahawalpur | Lahore | 1965–66 |
| 342* | S.W. Sohoni, V.S. Hazare | Maharashtra v W. India States | Rajkot | 1940–41 |
| 342 | E.A.B. Rowan, P.J.M. Gibb | Transvaal v N.E. Transvaal | Johannesburg | 1952–53 |
| 336 | W.M. Lawry, K.D. Walters | Australia v West Indies | Sydney | 1968–69 |
| 334 | R. Abel, T.W. Hayward | Surrey v Somerset | Oval | 1899 |
| 333 | W.R. Hammond, E.H. Hendren | MCC v New South Wales | Sydney | 1928–29 |
| 330 | W. Barnes, W. Gunn | MCC v Yorkshire | Lord's | 1885 |
| 330 | Waqar Ahmed, Shafqat Rana | Lahore v Sargodha | Lahore | 1968–69 |
| 328 | P. Vaulkhard, D. Smith | Derbyshire v Notts | Nottingham | 1946 |
| 326* | James Langridge, G. Cox | Sussex v Yorkshire | Leeds | 1949 |
| 325 | J.W. Hearne, E.H. Hendren | Middlesex v Hampshire | Lord's | 1919 |
| 325 | N.C. O'Neill, B.C. Booth | New South Wales v Victoria | Sydney | 1957–58 |
| 324 | J.T. Tyldesley, A.C. MacLaren | Lancashire v Notts | Nottingham | 1904 |
| 324 | J.R. Reid, W.M. Wallace | NZ v Cambridge University | Cambridge | 1949 |
| 323 | A.W. Carr, W.R. Payton | Nottinghamshire v Kent | Nottingham | 1923 |
| 322 | V.S. Hazare, M.H. Mankad | Indians v Yorkshire | Sheffield | 1946 |
| 322 | D.K. Gaekwad, V.S. Hazare | Baroda v Bombay | Sholapur | 1957–58 |
| 321 | W.R. Hammond, W.L. Neale | Gloucestershire v Leics | Gloucester | 1937 |
| 319 | R.E.S. Wyatt, H.E. Dollery | Warwickshire v Lancashire | Birmingham | 1937 |
| 315 | M.A. Noble, S.E. Gregory | New South Wales v Victoria | Sydney | 1907–08 |
| 315 | W.G. Quaife, J.H. Parsons | Warwickshire v Glamorgan | Birmingham | 1927 |
| 312 | D. Denton, G.H. Hirst | Yorkshire v Hampshire | Southampton | 1914 |
| 310 | P.W. Denning, I.T. Botham | Somerset v Gloucestershire | Taunton | 1980 |
| 309 | S.M. Gavaskar, E.D. Solkar | Bombay v Bihar | Bombay | 1971–72 |
| 308 | G. Davidson, W. Storer | Derbyshire v Lancashire | Manchester | 1896 |
| 308 | A. Roy, S.S. Mitra | Bengal v Assam | Calcutta | 1969–70 |
| 306* | Javed Miandad, Younis Ahmed | Glamorgan v Australians | Neath | 1985 |
| 304 | D.C.S. Compton, F.G. Mann | Middlesex v Surrey | Lord's | 1947 |
| 303* | V.S. Hazare, H.R. Adhikari | Baroda v Maharashtra | Poona | 1944–45 |
| 302 | V.S. Hazare, Gul Mohamed | Bengal XI v Bijapur XI | Bombay | 1942–43 |
| 302 | U.M. Merchant, D.G. Phadkar | Bombay v Maharashtra | Poona | 1948–49 |
| 301 | L.P.J. O'Brien, L.S. Darling | Victoria v Queensland | Brisbane | 1932–33 |
| 301 | T.E. Bailey, P.B.H. May | MCC v Rhodesia | Salisbury | 1956–57 |
| 300 | G.E. Tyldesley, J. Iddon | Lancashire v Leicestershire | Leicester | 1928 |
| 300 | R.D. Brown, P.J. Allan | Rhodesia B v E. Province B | Salisbury | 1978–79 |
| 299 | P. Holmes, R. Kilner | Yorkshire v Northants | Harrogate | 1921 |
| 299 | W.M. Wallace, M.P. Donnelly | New Zealanders v Leics | Leicester | 1949 |
| 298 | A.V. Avery, R. Horsfall | Essex v Worcestershire | Clacton | 1948 |
| 297 | H.T.W. Hardinge, A.P.F. Chapman | Kent v Hampshire | Southampton | 1926 |

| | | | | |
|---|---|---|---|---|
| 297 | D.N. Sardesai, P.R. Umrigar | ACC XI v Indian Starlets | Hyderabad | 1964–65 |
| 296 | K.L. Hutchings, F.E. Woolley | Kent v Northamptonshire | Gravesend | 1908 |
| 295 | P.J.P. Burge, T.R. Veivers | Queensland v South Australia | Brisbane | 1962–63 |
| 294 | I.D. Walker, G.F. Grace | Gents of South v Gents of North | Beeston | 1870 |
| 294 | T.L. Goddard, H.M. Ackerman | N.E. Transvaal v W. Province | Cape Town | 1966–67 |
| 293 | R.A. Duff, M.A. Noble | NSW v South Australia | Sydney | 1903–04 |
| 293 | H.T. Barling, H.S. Squires | Surrey v Oxford University | Oval | 1932 |
| 293 | P.R. Umrigar, G. Kishenchand | Gujarat v Maharashtra | Kolhapur | 1951–52 |
| 291 | C.G. Macartney, C.E. Pellew | Australians v Notts | Nottingham | 1921 |
| 290* | P. Willey, T.J. Boon | Leicestershire v Warwicks | Leicester | 1984 |
| 290 | H.A. Gomes, A.L. Logie | West Indians v Leics | Leicester | 1984 |
| 289 | A. Ducat, T.F. Shepherd | Surrey v Gloucestershire | Oval | 1927 |
| 287 | L.G. Rowe, C.H. Lloyd | West Indians v Glamorgan | Swansea | 1976 |
| 287 | Javed Miandad, Zaheer Abbas | Pakistan v India | Faisalabad | 1982–83 |
| 285* | Fazal Abbas, Akhtar Hussain | Bahawalpur v Hyderabad | Hyderabad | 1971–72 |
| 285 | Arshad Pervez, Javed Miandad | Habib Bank v MCB | Lahore | 1977–78 |
| 283 | F.M.M. Worrell, E.de C. Weekes | West Indies v England | Nottingham | 1950 |
| 283 | R.G. Pollock, C.E.B. Rice | Transvaal v Natal | Durban | 1979–80 |
| 282 | A.C. Wilkinson, A.P.F. Chapman | MCC v Canterbury | Christchurch | 1922–23 |
| 282 | J. Hardstaff jr, D.C.S. Compton | MCC v Tasmania | Launceston | 1946–47 |
| 281 | T.E.R. Cook, James Langridge | Sussex v Surrey | Oval | 1930 |
| 281 | J.A. Ormrod, Younis Ahmed | Worcestershire v Notts | Nottingham | 1979 |
| 281 | Feroze Najamuddin, Zafar Ahmed | Karachi v MCB | Karachi | 1982–83 |
| 279 | R.E. Marshall, C.L. Walcott | West Indians v Surrey | Oval | 1950 |
| 278 | E.H. Hendren, L.E.G. Ames | MCC v British Guiana | Georgetown | 1929–30 |
| 278 | A.W. Roberts, M.L. Page | Canterbury v Wellington | Wellington | 1931–32 |
| 278 | G. Boycott, M.J.K. Smith | MCC v Eastern Province | Port Elizabeth | 1964–65 |
| 277 | H.H.I. Gibbons, B.W. Quaife | Worcestershire v Middlesex | Worcester | 1931 |
| 277 | D.G. Bradman, C.L. Badcock | Australians v Worcestershire | Worcester | 1938 |
| 277 | G.A. Hick, D.L. Houghton | Zimbabweans v Oxford U | Oxford | 1985 |
| 276 | P.G.T. Kingsley, N.M. Ford | Oxford University v Surrey | Oval | 1930 |
| 275 | R.de W.K. Winlaw, J.H. Human | Cambridge U. v Essex | Cambridge | 1934 |
| 275 | C.L. Badcock, A.L. Hassett | Australians v Cambridge U. | Cambridge | 1938 |
| 275 | F.C. Gardner, H.E. Dollery | Warwickshire v Somerset | Coventry | 1953 |
| 274* | R.G. Flockton, G. Thomas | NSW v South Australia | Sydney | 1959–60 |
| 274 | Azhar Khan, Sultan Rana | Habib Bank v Allied Bank | Lahore | 1983–84 |
| 273 | Mushtaq Mohd, W. Larkins | Northamptonshire v Essex | Chelmsford | 1975 |
| 273 | M. Amarnath, K. Azad | North Zone v East Zone | Bombay | 1982–83 |
| 271 | B.B. Wilson, W. Rhodes | Yorkshire v Sussex | Bradford | 1914 |
| 271 | J. O'Connor, T.N. Pearce | Essex v Lancashire | Clacton | 1931 |
| 271 | T.W. Graveney, B.L. D'Oliveira | Worcestershire v Essex | Worcester | 1966 |
| 270 | J.B. Hobbs, D.R. Jardine | Surrey v Middlesex | Lord's | 1926 |
| 270 | C.S. Dempster, G.S. Watson | Leicestershire v Yorkshire | Hull | 1937 |
| 268* | G.E. Tyldesley, J. Iddon | Lancashire v Glamorgan | Swansea | 1933 |
| 268 | H. Carpenter, T.M. Russell | Essex v Derbyshire | Derby | 1900 |
| 267 | C.L. Walcott, G.E. Gomez | West Indies v India | Delhi | 1948–49 |
| 266* | W.R. Payton, J.R. Gunn | Nottinghamshire v Gloucs | Nottingham | 1911 |
| 266* | J. Whitehouse, R.B. Kanhai | Warwickshire v Yorkshire | Birmingham | 1976 |
| 266 | W.R. Hammond, T.S. Worthington | England v India | Oval | 1936 |
| 266 | G. Cox, James Langridge | Sussex v Lancashire | Hove | 1939 |
| 266 | K.D. Walters, G.S. Chappell | Australians v Kent | Canterbury | 1972 |
| 266 | M.H. Denness, K.W.R. Fletcher | England v New Zealand | Auckland | 1974–75 |
| 265 | H.B. Cameron, Q. McMillan | Transvaal v OFS | Cape Town | 1928–29 |
| 265 | F.E. Woolley, M.J.L. Turnbull | MCC v New South Wales | Sydney | 1929–30 |
| 265 | P.A. Gibb, J.R. Thompson | C.U. v Free Foresters | Cambridge | 1938 |
| 265 | N. Rosendorff, S. Strydom | OFS v Transvaal B | Vereeniging | 1965–66 |
| 265 | K.P. Amarjit, D. Chopra | Punjab v Services | Delhi | 1984–85 |
| 264 | I.D. Craig, W. Watson | NSW v Western Australia | Perth | 1956–57 |
| 263 | G. Lavis, C.C. Smart | Glamorgan v Worcestershire | Cardiff | 1934 |
| 263 | J. Hardstaff jr, F.W. Stocks | Nottinghamshire v Northants | Nottingham | 1951 |
| 263 | R.E. Marshall, D.A. Livingstone | Hampshire v Middlesex | Lord's | 1970 |
| 262 | I.S. Lee, R.G. Gregory | Victoria v MCC | Melbourne | 1936–37 |
| 262 | M.L. Jaisimha, Pataudi jr | Hyderabad v Andhra | Hyderabad | 1967–68 |
| 262 | D.L. Amiss, A.I. Kallicharran | Warwickshire v Gloucs | Bristol | 1979 |
| 260* | I.M. Chappell, A.P. Sheahan | Combined XI v West Indians | Perth | 1968–69 |

| 260 | C.F. Walters, C.H. Bull | Worcestershire v Kent | Gravesend | 1933 |
|---|---|---|---|---|
| 260 | G.R. Marsh, C.S. Serjeant | Western Australia v NSW | Sydney | 1981–82 |
| 260 | C.E.B. Rice, P. Johnson | Nottinghamshire v Kent | Folkestone | 1984 |
| 259* | D.V. Smith, James Langridge | Sussex v Nottinghamshire | Nottingham | 1950 |
| 259 | A. Drake, G.H. Hirst | Yorkshire v Sussex | Hastings | 1911 |
| 259 | C.P. Mead, Hon L.H. Tennyson | Hampshire v Leicestershire | Portsmouth | 1921 |
| 259 | Hanif Mohammad, W. Mathias | Karachi v Bahawalpur | Karachi | 1958–59 |
| 259 | B.C. Francis, K.D. Walters | New South Wales v Victoria | Sydney | 1971–72 |
| 259 | A.E. Greenidge, C.L. King | Barbados v Trinidad | Bridgetown | 1978–79 |
| 259 | M.C.J. Nicholas, R.A. Smith | Hampshire v Leicestershire | Bournemouth | 1985 |
| 258 | J. Tunnicliffe, G.H. Hirst | Yorkshire v Hampshire | Portsmouth | 1904 |
| 258 | M.C. Datar, M.R. Rege | Maharashtra v Bombay | Poona | 1948–49 |
| 258 | K. Jayantilal, Wahid Yar Khan | Hyderabad v Andhra | Guntur | 1968–69 |
| 258 | K.S. McEwan, K.W.R. Fletcher | Essex v Sussex | Chelmsford | 1977 |
| 258 | S.M. Gavaskar, R.V. Mankad | Bombay v Bihar | Bombay | 1978–79 |
| 256* | P.J.P. Burge, G.M. Bizzell | Queensland v W. Australia | Brisbane | 1963–64 |
| 256 | R. Abel, F.C. Holland | Surrey v Essex | Oval | 1895 |
| 256 | A.E. Knight, H. Whitehead | Leicestershire v Sussex | Leicester | 1900 |
| 256 | E.H. Hendren, F.T. Mann | Middlesex v Essex | Leyton | 1923 |
| 256 | C.A.G. Russell, P.A. Perrin | Essex v Worcestershire | Worcester | 1923 |
| 256 | C.F. Walters, M. Nichol | Worcestershire v Hampshire | Bournemouth | 1933 |
| 256 | G. Cox, C. Oakes | Sussex v Northamptonshire | Northampton | 1950 |
| 256 | H.R. Adhikari, H.T. Dani | Services v Southern Punjab | Patiala | 1959–60 |
| 256 | Imran Khan, C.M. Wells | Sussex v Glamorgan | Swansea | 1980 |
| 255* | Hanif Mohd, Raees Mohd | Karachi v Sind | Karachi | 1954–55 |
| 255 | R.A. Pinnock, E.D.A.St J. McMorris | Jamaica v Guyana | Georgetown | 1966–67 |
| 255 | H. Pilling, D. Bailey | Lancashire v Kent | Manchester | 1969 |
| 255 | Zaheer Abbas, Javed Miandad | Pakistan v India | Faisalabad | 1978–79 |
| 254 | F. Chester, G.N. Foster | Worcestershire v Middlesex | Lord's | 1913 |
| 254 | K.G. Viljoen, J.C. Newton | OFS v Transvaal | Bloemfontein | 1933–34 |
| 254 | J.R. Reid, L.S.M. Miller | New Zealanders v Natal | Durban | 1953–54 |
| 254 | R.B. Simpson, G.R. Davies | NSW v Queensland | Sydney | 1967–68 |
| 253 | R.E.S. Wyatt, H.E. Dollery | Warwickshire v Derbyshire | Birmingham | 1937 |
| 253 | I.M. McLachlan, G.St A. Sobers | S. Australia v S. Africans | Adelaide | 1963–64 |
| 253 | D.M. Wellham, T.M. Chappell | NSW v Queensland | Sydney | 1982–83 |
| 252 | G. Boycott, B.L. D'Oliveira | England v India | Leeds | 1967 |
| 252 | Javed Miandad, Mushtaq Mohd | Pakistan v New Zealand | Karachi | 1976–77 |
| 251* | G.A. Edrich, K.J. Grieves | Lancashire v Notts | Manchester | 1951 |
| 251 | H.I. Moore, D.L. Murray | Nottinghamshire v Indians | Nottingham | 1967 |
| 251 | I.V.A. Richards, P.M. Roebuck | Somerset v Surrey | Weston-s-Mare | 1977 |
| 251 | G.M. Wood, C.S. Serjeant | Australia v West Indies | Georgetown | 1977–78 |
| 251 | C.J. Tavaré, A.G.E. Ealham | Kent v Worcestershire | Canterbury | 1979 |
| 251 | S.B. Smith, P.M. Toohey | NSW v Victoria | Melbourne | 1982–83 |
| 250 | H.H.I. Gibbons, M. Nichol | Worcestershire v Warwicks | Dudley | 1929 |
| 250 | H.P. Ward, R. Nailer | Europeans v Indians | Madras | 1931–32 |
| 250 | T.H. Clark, R.C.E. Pratt | Surrey v Kent | Oval | 1953 |
| 250 | H.L. Johnson, D.C. Morgan | Derbyshire v Somerset | Chesterfield | 1964 |
| 250 | R.B. Kanhai, G.St A. Sobers | West Indies v England | Georgetown | 1967–68 |

**FIFTH WICKET**

| 405 | S.G. Barnes, D.G. Bradman | Australia v England | Sydney | 1946–47 |
|---|---|---|---|---|
| 397 | W. Bardsley, C. Kelleway | NSW v South Australia | Sydney | 1920–21 |
| 393 | E.G. Arnold, W.B. Burns | Worcestershire v Warwicks | Birmingham | 1909 |
| 360 | U.M. Merchant, M.N. Raiji | Bombay v Hyderabad | Bombay | 1947–48 |
| 355 | Altaf Shah, Tariq Bashir | HBFC v Multan | Multan | 1976–77 |
| 347 | D. Brookes, D.W. Barrick | Northamptonshire v Essex | Northampton | 1952 |
| 344 | M.C. Cowdrey, T.W. Graveney | MCC v South Australia | Adelaide | 1962–63 |
| 343 | R.I. Maddocks, J. Hallebone | Victoria v Tasmania | Melbourne | 1951–52 |
| 340 | E. Wainwright, G.H. Hirst | Yorkshire v Surrey | Oval | 1899 |
| 338 | R.S. Lucas, T.C. O'Brien | Middlesex v Sussex | Hove | 1895 |
| 338 | R.G. Pollock, A.L. Wilmot | E. Province v Natal | Port Elizabeth | 1975–76 |
| 336 | W.H. Ponsford, H.S.B. Love | Victoria v Tasmania | Melbourne | 1922–23 |
| 335 | B.F. Butcher, C.H. Lloyd | West Indians v Glamorgan | Swansea | 1969 |
| 332 | E.H. Hendren, W.F.F. Price | Middlesex v Worcestershire | Dudley | 1933 |
| 332 | M.L. Jaisimha, B. Mahendra Kumar | Hyderabad v Bengal | Hyderabad | 1964–65 |

| 329 | F. Mitchell, E. Wainwright | Yorkshire v Leicestershire | Leicester | 1899 |
|---|---|---|---|---|
| 327 | P. Holmes, W.E. Astill | MCC v Jamaica | Kingston | 1925–26 |
| 327 | A.W. Briscoe, H.B. Cameron | Transvaal v Griqualand West | Johannesburg | 1934–35 |
| 325 | V.M. Merchant, K.M. Rangnekar | Bombay v Sind | Bombay | 1945–46 |
| 308 | J.N. Crawford, F.C. Holland | Surrey v Somerset | Oval | 1908 |
| 301* | C.E. Pellew, C.B. Willis | AIF v Worcestershire | Worcester | 1919 |
| 301* | R.B. Simpson, K.D. Meuleman | Western Australia v NSW | Perth | 1959–60 |
| 301 | F.M.M. Worrell, W.H.H. Sutcliffe | Commonwealth XI v Ceylon | Colombo | 1950–51 |
| 300 | D.W. Begbie, A.W. Briscoe | Transvaal v Orange Free State | Johannesburg | 1937–38 |
| 297 | J.H. Parks, H.W. Parks | Sussex v Hampshire | Portsmouth | 1937 |
| 297 | Khalid Irtiza, Nasir Valika | Sind v Universities | Lahore | 1975–76 |
| 291 | A.W. Nourse, J.M. Blanckenberg | Natal v Western Province | Johannesburg | 1923–24 |
| 290 | M.M. Sood, R. Saxena | Delhi v Southern Punjab | Delhi | 1960–61 |
| 289* | Pataudi sr, L.E.G. Ames | England v Rest | Lord's | 1934 |
| 289 | C.T. Radley, P.R. Downton | Middlesex v Northamptonshire | Uxbridge | 1985 |
| 288 | H.A. Peach, A. Ducat | Surrey v Northamptonshire | Northampton | 1920 |
| 287 | R. Abel, W. Lockwood | Surrey v Lancashire | Oval | 1899 |
| 287 | J. O'Connor, C.T. Ashton | Essex v Surrey | Brentwood | 1934 |
| 286 | M.A. Noble, S.E. Gregory | NSW v South Australia | Adelaide | 1899–00 |
| 285 | E.H. Hendren, J.H. Human | Middlesex v Surrey | Oval | 1935 |
| 283 | N.L. Bonitto, A.P. Binns | Jamaica v British Guiana | Georgetown | 1952–53 |
| 281 | C.L. Badcock, M.G. Waite | South Australia v Queensland | Adelaide | 1939–40 |
| 281 | Javed Miandad, Asif Iqbal | Pakistan v New Zealand | Lahore | 1976–77 |
| 279 | B. Versfeld, M.J. Procter | Natal v Transvaal | Durban | 1965–66 |
| 277 | F.E. Woolley, L.E.G. Ames | Kent v New Zealanders | Canterbury | 1931 |
| 276 | W. Rhodes, R. Kilner | Yorkshire v Northants | Northampton | 1921 |
| 276 | A.G. Kripal Singh, R.B. Alaganan | Madras v Travancore-Cochin | Ernakulam | 1954–55 |
| 275 | M.A. Noble, J. Darling | Australians v Sussex | Hove | 1905 |
| 273 | L. Hutton, N.W.D. Yardley | Yorkshire v Hampshire | Bournemouth | 1947 |
| 271 | A.J. Sieler, R.P. Rose | Victoria v Queensland | Brisbane | 1973–74 |
| 270 | L.C. Braund, J. Hardstaff sr | MCC v South Australia | Adelaide | 1907–08 |
| 270 | G.N. Yallop, D.M. Jones | Victoria v Queensland | Melbourne (St K) | 1982–83 |
| 268 | W.G. Quaife, W. Quaife | Warwickshire v Essex | Leyton | 1900 |
| 268 | R.G. Lloyd, I.M. McLachlan | South Australia v Queensland | Adelaide | 1960–61 |
| 268 | M.W. Gatting, J.E. Emburey | Middlesex v Essex | Chelmsford | 1983 |
| 267* | K.C. Bland, D.T. Lindsay | South Africa v Rest | Johannesburg | 1964–65 |
| 266 | A. Shrewsbury, W. Gunn | Nottinghamshire v Sussex | Hove | 1884 |
| 266 | C.E. Pellew, C.B. Willis | AIF v Leicestershire | Leicester | 1919 |
| 266 | R.E.S. Wyatt, A.J.W. Croom | Warwickshire v Somerset | Birmingham | 1928 |
| 266 | B. Sutcliffe, W.S. Haig | Otago v Auckland | Dunedin | 1949–50 |
| 265 | S.M. Nurse, G.St A. Sobers | West Indies v England | Leeds | 1966 |
| 264 | M. Robinson, S.W. Montgomery | Glamorgan v Hampshire | Bournemouth | 1949 |
| 264 | A.R. Morris, R. Benaud | NSW v Queensland | Brisbane | 1953–54 |
| 264 | D.W. Hookes, M.D. Haysman | South Australia v Victoria | Melbourne (St K) | 1982–83 |
| 263 | J.M. Taylor, A.F. Kippax | NSW v South Australia | Adelaide | 1922–23 |
| 263 | A.L. Wadekar, G.S. Ramchand | Bombay v Rajasthan | Bombay | 1961–62 |
| 263 | P.L.A. Bedford, G.D. Watson | Victoria v W. Australia | Melbourne | 1969–70 |
| 262 | A. Jeacocke, W.J. Abel | Surrey v Cambridge U. | Oval | 1923 |
| 262 | W.H. Ponsford, W.A. Brown | Australians v Cambridge U. | Cambridge | 1934 |
| 262 | K.G. Viljoen, H.B. Cameron | South Africans v Derbyshire | Ilkeston | 1935 |
| 262 | Javed Miandad, Wasim Raja | Pakistan XI v International XI | Lahore | 1981–82 |
| 261 | W.G. Grace, W.O. Moberley | Gloucestershire v Yorkshire | Cheltenham | 1876 |
| 261 | H.H.I. Gibbons, C.H. Palmer | Worcestershire v Northants | Dudley | 1939 |
| 258 | A.V. Mankad, E.D. Solkar | Bombay v Gujarat | Bombay | 1974–75 |
| 256* | R. Abel, D.L.A. Jephson | Surrey v Gloucestershire | Oval | 1898 |
| 256* | A.A. Baig, C.A. Fry | Oxford U. v Free Foresters | Oxford | 1959 |
| 256 | C.G. Macartney, N. Callaway | NSW v Queensland | Sydney | 1914–15 |
| 255* | J.A. Jameson, T.W. Cartwright | Warwicks v New Zealanders | Birmingham | 1965 |
| 255 | G.E.J. Healy, F. Vaughan | Victoria v Tasmania | Melbourne | 1909–10 |
| 255 | J.V. Coney, B.R. Taylor | Wellington v Otago | Dunedin | 1972–73 |
| 254 | E. Humphreys, A.P. Day | Kent v Lancashire | Tunbridge Wells | 1910 |
| 254 | K.W.R. Fletcher, A.W. Greig | England v India | Bombay | 1972–73 |
| 252 | A.J. Stewart, M.A. Lynch | Surrey v Kent | Canterbury | 1985 |
| 251* | G. Shipperd, R.W. Marsh | Western Australia v Victoria | Melbourne | 1983–84 |
| 251 | R.B. Kanhai, J.S. Solomon | British Guiana v Barbados | Georgetown | 1956–57 |
| 250 | T.W. Hayward, D.L.A. Jephson | Surrey v Derbyshire | Oval | 1901 |
| 249* | S. Amarnath, Madan Lal | Punjab v Madhya Pradesh | Jullundur | 1971–72 |

| | | | | |
|---|---|---|---|---|
| 249 | R.A. McLean, A.L. Upton | Natal v Orange Free State | Pietermaritzburg | 1954–55 |
| 249 | B. Wood, A. Kennedy | Lancashire v Warwickshire | Birmingham | 1975 |
| 249 | A.S. Bhansali, N.Y. Satham | Baroda v Rajasthan | Baroda | 1982–83 |
| 248* | R.W. Marsh, R.J. Inverarity | W. Australia v Pakistanis | Perth | 1972–73 |
| 248 | Majid Khan, Aamer Malik | Lahore v United Bank | Lahore | 1982–83 |
| 247* | J.F. Parker, E.R.T. Holmes | Surrey v Nottinghamshire | Nottingham | 1947 |
| 247 | J. Hardstaff jr, A. Staples | Nottinghamshire v Middlesex | Nottingham | 1937 |
| 247 | P.R. Umrigar, M.S. Hardikar | Bombay v Saurashtra | Poona | 1957–58 |
| 246* | M.J. Smedley, G.St A. Sobers | Notts v Glamorgan | Swansea | 1971 |
| 246 | K.S. Ranjitsinhji, A. Collins | Sussex v Kent | Hove | 1900 |
| 245* | H. Sutcliffe, W. Barber | Yorkshire v Northants | Northampton | 1939 |
| 245 | J.F. Crapp, A.E. Wilson | Gloucestershire v Worcs | Dudley | 1953 |
| 245 | K.C. Ibrahim, D.B. Satha | K.C. Ibrahim's XI v | | |
| | | M.K. Mantri's XI | Bombay | 1947–48 |
| 244 | F.H. Winrow, T.B. Reddick | Nottinghamshire v Kent | Nottingham | 1947 |
| 244 | J.R. Reid, M.E. Chapple | NZ v W. Province | Cape Town | 1961–62 |
| 243 | W.E. Alley, F.W. Freer | Commonwealth XI v | | |
| | | Cricket Club of India | Bombay | 1949–50 |
| 243 | I. Foulkes, G.L. Hayes | Border v Griqualand West | Kimberley | 1978–79 |
| 242 | W.R. Hammond, L.E.G. Ames | England v New Zealand | Christchurch | 1932–33 |
| 242 | W.R. Hammond, B.O. Allen | Gloucestershire v Somerset | Bristol | 1946 |
| 241* | F.E. Woolley, D.W. Jennings | Kent v Somerset | Tunbridge Wells | 1911 |
| 241 | M.H. Denness, M.C. Cowdrey | Kent v Somerset | Maidstone | 1973 |
| 241 | A.I. Kallicharran, C.H. Lloyd | Guyana v Jamaica | Kingston | 1973–74 |
| 240 | J.C. White, C.C.C. Case | Somerset v Gloucestershire | Taunton | 1927 |
| 240 | Pataudi jr, V. Subramanya | S. Zone v W. Zone | Bombay | 1967–68 |
| 239 | M.M. Naidu, C.S. Nayudu | Baroda v Rajputana | Baroda | 1942–43 |
| 238 | Hanumant Singh, A. Roy | State Bank v ACC XI | Hyderabad | 1971–72 |
| 237* | Mahmood Arshad, Ijaz Ahmed | National Bank v Rawalpindi | Lahore | 1981–82 |
| 237 | L.O.S. Poidevin, L.W. Pye | NSW v Queensland | Sydney | 1904–05 |
| 237 | D.C.S. Compton, N.W.D. Yardley | England v South Africa | Nottingham | 1947 |
| 237 | A. Malhotra, Aman Kumar | Haryana v Services | Delhi | 1982–83 |
| 237 | C.E.B. Rice, K.A. McKenzie | Transvaal v Natal | Durban | 1984–85 |
| 236 | G.J. Thompson, R. Haywood | Northamptonshire v Yorks | Dewsbury | 1911 |
| 236 | W.W. Keeton, A.W. Carr | Nottinghamshire v Essex | Nottingham | 1932 |
| 236 | D.C.H. Townsend, F.G.H. Chalk | Oxford U. v Free Foresters | Oxford | 1933 |
| 236 | Aftab Baloch, Nasir Valika | Sind v Baluchistan | Karachi | 1973–74 |
| 235* | W.M. Woodfull, V.S. Ransford | Victoria v New Zealand XI | Christchurch | 1924–25 |
| 235* | N. Oldfield, A.E. Nutter | Lancashire v Notts | Manchester | 1939 |
| 235 | B.J.T. Bosanquet, F.A. Tarrant | Rest v Yorkshire | Oval | 1908 |
| 235 | G. Hill, D.F. Walker | Hampshire v Sussex | Portsmouth | 1937 |
| 235 | M.L. Jaisimha, V. Subramanya | South Zone v West Zone | Bombay | 1966–67 |
| 234* | V.J. Scott, J.B. Morris | Auckland v Central Districts | Auckland | 1951–52 |
| 234 | P.F. Warner, C.B. Fry | Rest v Warwickshire | Oval | 1911 |
| 234 | D.G. Bradman, O.W. Bill | New South Wales v Victoria | Sydney | 1930–31 |
| 234 | J.M. Brearley, J.A. Ormrod | MCC U-25 XI v N. Zone | Peshawar | 1966–67 |
| 234 | Arun Lal, Madan Lal | Delhi v Rajasthan | Delhi | 1977–78 |
| 233* | S. Amarnath, M. Amarnath | Punjab v Delhi | Delhi | 1972–73 |
| 233* | D.A. Murray, S. Shivnarine | West Indians v East Zone | Jamshedpur | 1978–79 |
| 233 | D.A.R. Moloney, J.L. Kerr | N. Zealanders v England XI | Folkestone | 1937 |
| 233 | V. Sivaramakrishnan, | | | |
| | T.E. Srinivasan | Tamil Nadu v Karnataka | Madras | 1976–77 |
| 233 | N.E. Briers, R.W. Tolchard | Leicestershire v Somerset | Leicester | 1979 |
| 232 | H.W. Taylor, R.H. Catterall | S. Africans v Comb. Services | Portsmouth | 1924 |
| 232 | A.D. Nourse, D.F. Dowling | Natal v Griqualand West | Durban | 1947–48 |
| 232 | M.J.K. Smith, K.F. Barrington | MCC v Transvaal | Johannesburg | 1964–65 |
| 231 | C.B. Llewellyn, E.I.M. Barrett | Hampshire v Derbyshire | Southampton | 1903 |
| 231 | K.D. Mackay, R.G. Archer | Queensland v Victoria | Brisbane | 1953–54 |
| 230 | C. Baldwin, D.L.A. Jephson | Surrey v Kent | Oval | 1897 |
| 230 | James Seymour, J.R. Mason | Kent v Somerset | Taunton | 1907 |
| 230 | J. Iddon, T.M. Halliday | Lancashire v Surrey | Oval | 1928 |
| 230 | K.R. Miller, P.J.P. Burge | Australians v Leicestershire | Leicester | 1956 |
| 229* | C.E.B. Rice, M.J. Smedley | Nottinghamshire v Lancs | Nottingham | 1978 |
| 229 | Shafiq Ahmed, Maqsood Ahmed | National Bank v Karachi B | Karachi | 1978–79 |
| 228 | C.S. Baker, A.F.A. Lilley | Warwickshire v Worcs | Worcester | 1907 |
| 228 | G.A. Headley, C.A. Merry | West Indians v Warwickshire | Birmingham | 1933 |
| 228 | J. Hardstaff jr, F.W. Stocks | Nottinghamshire v Northants | Northampton | 1952 |

| 228 | B.C. Broad, A.J. Hignell | Gloucestershire v Northants | Bristol | 1979 |
|---|---|---|---|---|
| 228 | C.S. Cowdrey, E.A.E. Baptiste | Kent v Yorkshire | Sheffield | 1983 |
| 227 | W.G. Grace, P.E. Crutchley | MCC v Kent | Canterbury | 1876 |
| 227 | A.W. Nourse, S.S.L. Steyn | Western Province v Natal | Cape Town | 1932–33 |
| 227 | R.C. Wilson, M.C. Cowdrey | Kent v Northamptonshire | Tunbridge Wells | 1955 |
| 227 | I.V.A. Richards, D.B. Close | Somerset v Yorkshire | Harrogate | 1975 |
| 227 | P.J. Graves, R.J. East | Orange Free State v Border | East London | 1975–76 |
| 227 | T.S. Curtis, M.J. Weston | Worcestershire v Surrey | Worcester | 1985 |
| 226* | R. Macdonald, F. Geeson | Leicestershire v Derbyshire | Glossop | 1901 |
| 226* | T.E.R. Cook, A.J. Holmes | Sussex v Leicestershire | Leicester | 1937 |
| 226 | R.T. Dick, C.W. Travers | OFS v Griqualand West | Bloemfontein | 1934–35 |
| 226 | A. Malhotra, R. Chadda | Haryana v Services | Faridabad | 1981–82 |
| 225* | A.A. During, C.G. Stephens | Transvaal B v Border | Johannesburg | 1973–74 |
| 225 | V.M. Merchant, K.M. Rangnekar | Hindus v Parsees | Bombay | 1941–42 |

### SIXTH WICKET

| 487* | G.A. Headley, C.C. Passailaigue | Jamaica v Ld Tennyson's XI | Kingston | 1931–32 |
|---|---|---|---|---|
| 428 | W.W. Armstrong, M.A. Noble | Australians v Sussex | Hove | 1902 |
| 411 | R.M. Poore, E.G. Wynyard | Hampshire v Somerset | Taunton | 1899 |
| 376 | R. Subba Row, A. Lightfoot | Northamptonshire v Surrey | Oval | 1958 |
| 371 | V.M. Merchant, R.S. Modi | Bombay v Maharashtra | Bombay | 1943–44 |
| 353 | Salahuddin, Zaheer Abbas | Karachi v East Pakistan | Karachi | 1968–69 |
| 346 | J.H.W. Fingleton, D.G. Bradman | Australia v England | Melbourne | 1936–37 |
| 332 | N.G. Marks, G. Thomas | NSW v South Australia | Sydney | 1958–59 |
| 323 | E.H. Hendren, J.W.H.T. Douglas | MCC v Victoria | Melbourne | 1920–21 |
| 320 | J.H. Board, G.L. Jessop | Gloucestershire v Sussex | Hove | 1903 |
| 316* | H.R. Adhikari, A.K. Khanna | Services v Rajasthan | Ajmer | 1951–52 |
| 313 | J.A. Newman, Hon L.H. Tennyson | Hampshire v West Indians | Southampton | 1928 |
| 303* | F.H. Winrow, P.F. Harvey | Notts v Derbyshire | Nottingham | 1947 |
| 300 | Vijay S. Hazare, Vivek S. Hazare | Rest v Hindus | Bombay | 1943–44 |
| 298 | A. Sandham, H.S. Harrison | Surrey v Sussex | Oval | 1913 |
| 294 | D.R. Jardine, P.G.H. Fender | Surrey v Yorkshire | Bradford | 1928 |
| 289 | S.J.E. Loxton, D.T. Ring | Victoria v Queensland | Melbourne | 1946–47 |
| 285 | W.R. Hammond, B.H. Lyon | Gloucestershire v Surrey | Oval | 1928 |
| 284 | A.P.F. Chapman, G.B. Legge | Kent v Lancashire | Maidstone | 1927 |
| 280* | B.F. Butcher, J.S. Solomon | British Guiana v Jamaica | Georgetown | 1956–57 |
| 279 | A.L. Hassett, E.A. Williams | Australian Services v Prince's XI | Delhi | 1945–46 |
| 278 | J. Iddon, H.R.W. Butterworth | Lancashire v Sussex | Manchester | 1932 |
| 277 | O.G. Smith, A.P. Binns | Jamaica v Australians | Kingston | 1954–55 |
| 276 | M. Leyland, E. Robinson | Yorkshire v Glamorgan | Swansea | 1926 |
| 275 | A.G. Mathur, S. Anand | Uttar Pradesh v Railways | Allahabad | 1982–83 |
| 274* | G.St A. Sobers, D.A.J. Holford | West Indies v England | Lord's | 1966 |
| 270 | R.T. Simpson, A. Jepson | Nottinghamshire v Worcs | Nottingham | 1950 |
| 270 | D.R. Walsh, S.A. Westley | Oxford U. v Warwickshire | Oxford | 1969 |
| 269 | V.T. Trumper, C. Hill | Australians v NZ XI | Wellington | 1904–05 |
| 268 | J.N. Shepherd, D.A. Graveney | Gloucestershire v Warwicks | Birmingham | 1983 |
| 265 | W.E. Alley, K.E. Palmer | Somerset v Northants | Northampton | 1961 |
| 262 | A. Kenny, H.H.L. Kortlang | Victoria v Queensland | Brisbane | 1909–10 |
| 262 | A.T. Sharp, G.H.S. Fowke | Leicestershire v Derbyshire | Chesterfield | 1911 |
| 260 | J.N. Crawford, Lord Dalmeny | Surrey v Leicestershire | Oval | 1905 |
| 260 | A.C. MacLaren, R. Whitehead | Lancashire v Worcestershire | Worcester | 1910 |
| 260 | A. Wharton, K. Cranston | Lancashire v Warwickshire | Birmingham | 1948 |
| 259 | D. Brookes, E. Davis | Northamptonshire v Leics | Leicester | 1947 |
| 258 | V.T. Trumper, F.A. Iredale | New South Wales v Tasmania | Sydney | 1898–99 |
| 256* | C.J. Tavaré, A.P.E. Knott | Kent v Essex | Chelmsford | 1982 |
| 256 | S.C. Khanna, M. Amarnath | Delhi v Karnataka | Bangalore | 1978–79 |
| 255 | K.S. Duleepsinhji, M.W. Tate | Sussex v Northamptonshire | Hove | 1930 |
| 255 | G.St A. Sobers, B.N. Jarman | S. Australia v W. Australia | Perth | 1963–64 |
| 254 | E. Smith, C.E. de Trafford | North v South | Hastings | 1893 |
| 254 | C.A. Davis, G.St A. Sobers | West Indies v New Zealand | Bridgetown | 1971–72 |
| 254 | G.N. Yallop, R.D. Robinson | Victoria v W. Australia | Melbourne | 1976–77 |
| 253 | A.F. Kippax, J.G. Morgan | NSW v Queensland | Sydney | 1927–28 |
| 251 | C.P. Mead, J.A. Newman | Hampshire v Warwickshire | Bournemouth | 1928 |
| 250 | C.H. Lloyd, D.L. Murray | West Indies v India | Bombay | 1974–75 |
| 250 | S. Amarnath, K. Azad | Delhi v Bihar | Jamshedpur | 1981–82 |

| 248 | T.J.E. Andrews, W.W. Armstrong | Australians v South | Hastings | 1921 |
|---|---|---|---|---|
| 247* | W.R. Payton, W.A. Flint | Nottinghamshire v Northants | Nottingham | 1927 |
| 245 | J.L. Bryan, C.T. Ashton | Cambridge U. v Surrey | Oval | 1921 |
| 244* | J.M.M. Commaille, A.W. Palm | W. Province v GW | Johannesburg | 1923–24 |
| 244 | R. Benaud, A.K. Davidson | Australians v Natal | Pietermaritzburg | 1957–58 |
| 244 | J.T. Irvine, R. Edwards | W. Australia v NSW | Sydney | 1968–69 |
| 243 | W.R. Hammond, James Langridge | MCC v South Australia | Adelaide | 1946–47 |
| 241 | A.F.A. Lilley, W. Smith | London County v Cambridge University | Crystal Palace | 1901 |
| 241 | N.J. Contractor, R.H. Shodhan | Gujarat v Baroda | Baroda | 1952–53 |
| 240 | P.H. Parfitt, B.R. Knight | England v New Zealand | Auckland | 1962–63 |
| 238 | R. McDonald, O.W. Cowley | Queensland v Hawke's Bay | Napier | 1896–97 |
| 237* | R.W. Tolchard, B.J. Booth | Leicestershire v Surrey | Leicester | 1971 |
| 236 | E.R.T. Holmes, R.E.C. Butterworth | Oxford U. v Free Foresters | Oxford | 1927 |
| 234* | N. Gadkari, A.K. Seth | Services v Jammu & Kashmir | Delhi | 1984–85 |
| 234 | D.C.S. Compton, P.B.H. May | MCC v South Australia | Adelaide | 1954–55 |
| 233 | M.W. Booth, G.H. Hirst | Yorkshire v Worcestershire | Worcester | 1911 |
| 233 | J.N. Crawford, W.W. Armstrong | Australians v NZ XI | Auckland | 1913–14 |
| 233 | C.H. Knott, R.H.B. Bettington | Harlequins v West Indians | Eastbourne | 1928 |
| 233 | R. Mayes, W. Murray-Wood | Kent v Sussex | Tunbridge Wells | 1952 |
| 233 | A.J.S. Smith, P.H. Williams | Natal v N. Transvaal | Pretoria | 1979–80 |
| 232 | S.M. Gavaskar, S.V. Nayak | Bombay v Maharashtra | Bombay | 1979–80 |
| 232 | I.T. Botham, D.W. Randall | England v New Zealand | Wellington | 1983–84 |
| 231 | V.F.S. Crawford, T. Jayes | Leicestershire v Hampshire | Leicester | 1908 |
| 230 | W.E. Jones, B.L. Muncer | Glamorgan v Worcestershire | Worcester | 1953 |
| 230 | R.B. Kanhai, R.R. Ramnarace | Guyana v Jamaica | Georgetown | 1970–71 |
| 229 | W. Rhodes, N. Kilner | Yorkshire v Leicestershire | Leeds | 1921 |
| 228* | Qaisar Hussain, Yahya Toor | PACO v MCB | Sahiawal | 1983–84 |
| 228 | M.J.L. Turnbull, F.J. Seabrook | Cambridge U. v Sussex | Cambridge | 1928 |
| 227 | N.W.D. Yardley, H.T. Bartlett | MCC v Orange Free State | Bloemfontein | 1938–39 |
| 227 | C.T. Radley, F.J. Titmus | Middlesex v South Africans | Lord's | 1965 |
| 227 | E.J.O. Hemsley, D.N. Patel | Worcestershire v Oxford U. | Oxford | 1976 |
| 226* | V.S. Hazare, M.H. Mankad | Indians v Middlesex | Lord's | 1946 |
| 226* | W.R. Hammond, G.M. Emmett | Gloucestershire v Notts | Bristol | 1946 |
| 226 | K.C. Ibrahim, J.B. Khot | Bombay v W. India States | Bombay | 1941–42 |
| 226 | G. Cox, G. Potter | Sussex v Worcestershire | Worcester | 1954 |
| 226 | E.J. Gray, R.W. Ormiston | Wellington v Central Dists | Wellington | 1981–82 |
| 225 | E. Wainwright, Lord Hawke | Yorkshire v Hampshire | Southampton | 1899 |

**SEVENTH WICKET**

| 347 | D.St E. Atkinson, C.C. Depeiza | West Indies v Australia | Bridgetown | 1954–55 |
|---|---|---|---|---|
| 344 | K.S. Ranjitsinhji, W. Newham | Sussex v Essex | Leyton | 1902 |
| 340 | K.J. Key, H. Philipson | Oxford U. v Middlesex | Chiswick Park | 1887 |
| 336 | F.C.W. Newman, C.R.N. Maxwell | Sir J. Cahn's XI v Leics | Nottingham | 1935 |
| 335 | C.W. Andrews, E.C. Bensted | Queensland v NSW | Sydney | 1934–35 |
| 325 | G. Brown, C.H. Abercrombie | Hampshire v Essex | Leyton | 1913 |
| 323 | E.H. Hendren, L.F. Townsend | MCC v Barbados | Bridgetown | 1929–30 |
| 308 | Waqar Hassan, Imtiaz Ahmed | Pakistan v New Zealand | Lahore | 1955–56 |
| 299 | B. Mitchell, A. Melville | Transvaal v Griqualand West | Kimberley | 1946–47 |
| 289 | G. Goonesena, G.W. Cook | Cambridge U. v Oxford U. | Lord's | 1957 |
| 286 | A.I. Kallicharran, C.H. Lloyd | Guyana v Trinidad | Georgetown | 1980–81 |
| 274 | K.C. Ibrahim, K.M. Rangnekar | Bijapur XI v Bengal XI | Bombay | 1942–43 |
| 273* | W.W. Armstrong, J. Darling | Australians v Gents of England | Lord's | 1905 |
| 271* | E.H. Hendren, F.T. Mann | Middlesex v Notts | Nottingham | 1925 |
| 270 | C.P. Mead, J.P. Parker | Hampshire v Kent | Canterbury | 1926 |
| 268 | A.H. Kardar, Imtiaz Ahmed | N. Zone v Australian Services | Lahore | 1945–46 |
| 265 | J.L. Powell, N. Dorreen | Canterbury v Otago | Christchurch | 1929–30 |
| 262* | D.P.B. Morkel, A.W. Palm | Western Province v Natal | Cape Town | 1929–30 |
| 261 | J.W.H.T. Douglas, J.R. Freeman | Essex v Lancashire | Leyton | 1914 |
| 257 | J.T. Morgan, F.R. Brown | Cambridge U. v Surrey | Oval | 1930 |
| 255 | C.H. Knott, A.J. Evans | Harlequins v West Indians | Eastbourne | 1928 |
| 255 | G. Thomas, R. Benaud | New South Wales v Victoria | Melbourne | 1961–62 |
| 254 | D.C.F. Burton, W. Rhodes | Yorkshire v Hampshire | Dewsbury | 1919 |
| 252 | S.K. Girdhari, A.G. Roy | Assam v Orissa | Cuttack | 1957–58 |

| | | | | |
|---|---|---|---|---|
| 250 | H.E. Dollery, J.S. Ord | Warwickshire v Kent | Maidstone | 1953 |
| 249 | W.L. Murdoch, J.H.S. Hunt | Gentlemen v Players | Oval | 1904 |
| 248* | Pervez Akhtar, Mohd Sharif | Railways v Dera Ismail Khan | Lahore | 1964–65 |
| 248 | W.G. Grace, E.L. Thomas | Gloucestershire v Sussex | Hove | 1896 |
| 248 | A.P. Day, E. Humphreys | Kent v Somerset | Taunton | 1908 |
| 247 | P. Holmes, W. Rhodes | Yorkshire v Nottinghamshire | Nottingham | 1929 |
| 246 | J.F. Ireland, K.G. McLeod | Cambridge U. v Gentlemen | Eastbourne | 1908 |
| 246 | D.J. McGlew, A.R.A. Murray | South Africa v New Zealand | Wellington | 1952–53 |
| 246 | P. Bhandari, D.S. Saxena | Delhi v Punjab | Delhi | 1968–69 |
| 245 | J. Sharp, A.H. Hornby | Lancashire v Leicestershire | Manchester | 1912 |
| 244 | W.R. Patrick, C.F.W. Allcott | New Zealanders v NSW | Sydney | 1925–26 |
| 244 | T.W. Cartwright, A.C. Smith | Warwickshire v Middlesex | Nuneaton | 1962 |
| 244 | Javed Masood, Sukumar Guha | E. Pakistan v Hyderabad | Hyderabad | 1962–63 |
| 244 | A. Jabbar, L. Sivaramakrishnan | Tamil Nadu v Karnataka | Bangalore | 1983–84 |
| 241* | G.H. Pope, A.E.G. Rhodes | Derbyshire v Hampshire | Portsmouth | 1948 |
| 240 | S.M.J. Woods, V.T. Hill | Somerset v Kent | Taunton | 1898 |
| 240 | A.D. Nourse, L.W. Payn | Natal v Transvaal | Johannesburg | 1936–37 |
| 238 | Asif Ali, Nadim Yousuf | MCB v National Bank | Lahore | 1981–82 |
| 235* | Daljit Singh, A. Shukla | Bihar v Bengal | Jamshedpur | 1973–74 |
| 235 | R.J. Shastri, S.M.H. Kirmani | India v England | Bombay | 1984–85 |
| 232 | W. Bruce, H. Trumble | Australians v Oxford & | | |
| 232 | Mushtaq Mohammad, W. Mathias | Karachi Blues v Karachi U. | Karachi | 1967–68 |
| 229 | W.W. Timms, F.A. Walden | Northants v Warwicks | Northampton | 1926 |
| 229 | K.J. Schneider, W.A.S. Oldfield | Australians v Canterbury | Christchurch | 1927–28 |
| 229 | M.L. Jaisimha, | | | |
| | M.V. Narasimha Rao | Hyderabad v Maharashtra | Hyderabad | 1973–74 |
| 227 | Wasim Bari, Salim Altaf | PIA v Sind | Karachi | 1976–77 |
| 224 | C.F. Browne, K. Mason | Barbados v Trinidad | Bridgetown | 1919–20 |
| 224 | V.J. Scott, A.M. Matheson | Auckland v Canterbury | Auckland | 1937–38 |
| 222 | G.J. Thompson, R.A. Haywood | Northamptonshire v Gloucs | Northampton | 1911 |
| 221 | D.T. Lindsay, P.L. van der Merwe | South Africa v Australia | Johannesburg | 1966–67 |
| 220* | J.T. Murray, D. Bennett | Middlesex v Yorkshire | Leeds | 1964 |
| 220* | Aftab Baloch, Naeem Ahmed | National Bank v Baluchistan | Karachi | 1974–75 |
| 219 | B.W. Yuile, B.L. Hampton | C. Districts v Canterbury | Napier | 1967–68 |
| 219 | S. Amarnath, Madan Lal | Delhi v Rest of India | Delhi | 1980–81 |
| 218 | T.E.R. Cook, A.F. Wensley | Sussex v Worcestershire | Eastbourne | 1933 |
| 218 | J.H. Cameron, E.A.V. Williams | West Indians v Oxford U. | Oxford | 1939 |
| 217* | R.V. Mankad, S.V. Nayak | Bombay v Uttar Pradesh | Kanpur | 1980–81 |
| 217 | K.D. Walters, G.J. Gilmour | Australia v New Zealand | Christchurch | 1976–77 |
| 216 | D.B. Deodhar, M.N. Paranjpe | Maharashtra v Nawanagar | Poona | 1944–45 |
| 215 | E. Robinson, D.C.F. Burton | Yorkshire v Leicestershire | Leicester | 1921 |
| 214 | C.G. Borde, S.A. Durani | Chief Minister's XI v | | |
| | | Commonwealth XI | Calcutta | 1964–65 |
| 213* | K. Vasudevamurthy, D.D. Gupta | Mysore v Kerala | Mangalore | 1959–60 |
| 213 | S.J. Diwadkar, A.V. Mankad | Bombay v Rajasthan | Bombay | 1963–64 |
| 212 | W.A. Tester, J. Jones | Players of South v | | |
| | | Gents of South | Oval | 1885 |
| 208 | C.G. Macartney, A.J.Y. Hopkins | NSW v Queensland | Sydney | 1906–07 |
| 208 | R. Watson-Smith, D.F.L. Tricker | Border v Orange Free State | Bloemfontein | 1969–70 |
| 207 | G. Kishenchand, Fazal Mahmood | North Zone v South Zone | Bombay | 1946–47 |
| 207 | B. Mahendra Kumar, | | | |
| | Wahid Yar Khan | Hyderabad v Uttar Pradesh | Hyderabad | 1964–65 |
| 206 | A.H. Hornby, W.R. Cuttell | Lancashire v Somerset | Manchester | 1904 |
| 206 | B. Dudleston, J. Birkenshaw | Leicestershire v Kent | Canterbury | 1969 |
| 204 | M.J. Smedley, R.A. White | Nottinghamshire v Surrey | Oval | 1967 |
| 204 | G. Shipperd, T.J. Zoehrer | Western Australia v NSW | Perth | 1982–83 |
| 203* | B.F. Davison, P.I. Faulkner | Tasmania v W. Australia | Perth | 1983–84 |
| 203 | M.E.Z. Ghazali, Qamar Yusuf | Services v Karachi | Karachi | 1953–54 |
| 202 | A.E. Lawton, R.T. Crawford | Gentlemen v Oxford U. | Eastbourne | 1910 |
| 202 | S.J.E. Loxton, B.A. Barnett | Commonwealth XI v Bombay | Bombay | 1953–54 |
| 202 | B.A. Richards, M.N.S. Taylor | Hampshire v Notts | Nottingham | 1974 |
| 201 | R.H. Howitt, R. Bagguley | Nottinghamshire v Sussex | Nottingham | 1895 |
| 200 | T.F. Shepherd, J.W. Hitch | Surrey v Kent | Blackheath | 1921 |
| 200 | F.B. Watson, M.L. Taylor | Lancashire v Oxford U. | Oxford | 1930 |
| 200 | Maqsood Ahmed, | | | |
| | Mohammad Jamil | National Bank v Lahore | Lahore | 1981–82 |

## EIGHTH WICKET

| | | | | |
|---|---|---|---|---|
| 433 | A. Sims, V.T. Trumper | Australians v Canterbury | Christchurch | 1913–14 |
| 292 | R. Peel, Lord Hawke | Yorkshire v Warwicks | Birmingham | 1896 |
| 270 | V.T. Trumper, E.P. Barbour | New South Wales v Victoria | Sydney | 1912–13 |
| 263 | D.R. Wilcox, R.M. Taylor | Essex v Warwickshire | Southend | 1946 |
| 255 | E.A.V. Williams, E.A. Martindale | Barbados v Trinidad | Bridgetown | 1935–36 |
| 246 | L.E.G. Ames, G.O.B. Allen | England v New Zealand | Lord's | 1931 |
| 243 | R.J. Hartigan, C. Hill | Australia v England | Adelaide | 1907–08 |
| 240 | Gulfraz Khan, Raja Sarfraz | Railways v Universities | Lahore | 1976–77 |
| 239 | W.R. Hammond, A.E. Wilson | Gloucestershire v Lancs | Bristol | 1938 |
| 237 | W.V.D. Dickinson, R.St L. Fowler | Army v MCC | Lord's | 1920 |
| 236 | R.A. Duff, A.J.Y. Hopkins | NSW v Lord Hawke's XI | Sydney | 1902–03 |
| 236 | C.T. Sarwate, R.P. Singh | Holkar v Delhi | Delhi | 1949–50 |
| 234 | Ghulam Abbas, Naeem Ahmed | PIA v Punjab B | Karachi | 1975–76 |
| 229* | C.L.A. Smith, G. Brann | Sussex v Kent | Hove | 1902 |
| 228 | A.J.W. Croom, R.E.S. Wyatt | Warwickshire v Worcester | Dudley | 1925 |
| 227 | K.D. James, T.M. Tremlett | Hampshire v Somerset | Taunton | 1985 |
| 222 | S.S.L. Steyn, D.P.B. Morkel | W. Province v Border | Cape Town | 1929–30 |
| 222 | A.V. Mankad, K.D. Ghavri | Bombay v Uttar Pradesh | Bombay | 1978–79 |
| 220 | G.F.H. Heane, R. Winrow | Nottinghamshire v Somerset | Nottingham | 1935 |
| 220 | W.R. Kerr, J.C. Breakey | Transvaal B v N.E. Transvaal | Johannesburg | 1970–71 |
| 218 | C.G. Macartney, J.D. Scott | NSW v Queensland | Sydney | 1913–14 |
| 217 | C.K. Nayudu, N.D. Marshall | Indians v Warwickshire | Birmingham | 1932 |
| 217 | T.W. Graveney, J.T. Murray | England v West Indies | Oval | 1966 |
| 216 | C.A. Browne, E.L. Bartlett | Barbados v British Guiana | Bridgetown | 1926–27 |
| 215 | W.W. Armstrong, R.L. Park | Victoria v South Australia | Melbourne | 1919–20 |
| 214 | J.A. Cutmore, T.P.B. Smith | Essex v Indians | Brentwood | 1936 |
| 210 | V.M. Merchant, R.S. Cooper | Bombay v Maharashtra | Bombay | 1943–44 |
| 210 | M.M. Dalvi, V.R. Amladi | Bombay v Sind | Bombay | 1947–48 |
| 209 | G. Stannard, H.E. Roberts | Sussex v Worcestershire | Hove | 1920 |
| 209 | K.M. Rangnekar, J.N. Bhaya | Holkar v Hyderabad | Indore | 1950–51 |
| 206 | K.R. Pont, N. Smith | Essex v Somerset | Leyton | 1976 |
| 205 | Aftab Alam, Wasim Bari | Karachi v Khairpur | Karachi | 1968–69 |
| 204 | T.W. Hayward, L.C. Braund | Surrey v Lancashire | Oval | 1898 |
| 204 | W.A.S. Oldfield, C.O. Nicholls | New South Wales v Victoria | Sydney | 1927–28 |
| 204 | A. Shukla, Saghir Ahmed | Uttar Pradesh v Rajasthan | Udaipur | 1961–62 |
| 203 | G. Kishenchand, V. Desai | Gujarat v Services | Ahmedabad | 1950–51 |
| 203 | G.W. Humpage, W.A. Bourne | Warwickshire v Sussex | Birmingham | 1976 |
| 202 | D. Davies, J.J. Hills | Glamorgan v Sussex | Eastbourne | 1928 |
| 202 | R. Jadhav, Hyder Ali | Railways v Vidharba | Nagpur | 1984–85 |
| 198 | R.W. McLeod, F. Laver | Victoria v South Australia | Adelaide | 1892–93 |
| 198 | K.F. Barrington, J.C. Laker | Surrey v Gloucestershire | Oval | 1954 |
| 197 | H.T. Barling, A.V. Bedser | Surrey v Somerset | Taunton | 1947 |
| 197 | Moin Mumtaz, Ghaffar Kazmi | PACO v Allied Bank | Faisalabad | 1983–84 |
| 195 | W.R. Payton, T.W. Oates | Nottinghamshire v Kent | Nottingham | 1920 |
| 193 | W.W. Armstrong, A.E. Liddicut | Victoria v South Australia | Melbourne | 1920–21 |
| 192 | C. Hill, W.F. Giffen | South Australia v A.E. Stoddart's XI | Adelaide | 1894–95 |
| 192 | W.L. Neale, A.E. Wilson | Gloucestershire v Middlesex | Lord's | 1938 |
| 192 | S. Turner, R.N.S. Hobbs | Essex v Glamorgan | Ilford | 1968 |
| 191* | W. Rhodes, G.G. Macaulay | Yorkshire v Essex | Harrogate | 1922 |
| 190* | J. E. Mills, C.F.W. Allcott | NZ v Civil Service | Chiswick | 1927 |
| 190 | Javed Miandad, Azam Khan | Karachi Whites v National Bank | Karachi | 1974–75 |
| 189* | N.J. Falkner, K.T. Medlycott | Surrey v Cambridge U. | Banstead | 1984 |
| 189 | W.N. Carson, A.M. Matheson | Auckland v Wellington | Auckland | 1938–39 |
| 188 | H.S. Bush, V.F.S. Crawford | Surrey v Lancashire | Manchester | 1902 |
| 188 | R.L. Holdsworth, A.E.R. Gilligan | Sussex v Lancashire | Eastbourne | 1927 |
| 187 | J.D. Henderson, W.A. Edward | Scotland v Ireland | Paisley | 1954 |
| 186 | G.St A. Sobers, P.M. Pollock | World XI v Australia XI | Melbourne | 1971–72 |
| 186 | K.W.R. Fletcher, D.E. East | Essex v Gloucestershire | Southend | 1985 |
| 185* | J.D. Nel, J.H. Ferrandi | W. Province v E. Province | Port Elizabeth | 1952–53 |
| 184* | C.L. Bull, D.P. Isherwood | Canterbury v C. Districts | Nelson | 1971–72 |
| 184 | M.S. Nichols, T.P.B. Smith | Essex v Kent | Gravesend | 1938 |
| 183 | D.J. Insole, R. Smith | Essex v Worcestershire | Worcester | 1951 |
| 183 | T.E. Bailey, C. Griffiths | Essex v Kent | Tunbridge Wells | 1952 |

| | | | | |
|---|---|---|---|---|
| 182* | M.H.C. Doll, H.R. Murrell | Middlesex v Notts | Lord's | 1913 |
| 182 | R. Abel, W.E. Roller | Surrey v Kent | Oval | 1883 |
| 182 | G.N. Wyatt, H. Phillips | Sussex v Australians | Hove | 1884 |
| 182 | A.H.M. Jackson, W. Carter | Derbyshire v Leicestershire | Leicester | 1922 |
| 180 | W. Barber, T.F. Smailes | Yorkshire v Sussex | Leeds | 1935 |
| 179* | G. Leach, C.L.A. Smith | Sussex v Derbyshire | Hove | 1909 |
| 179 | L.D. Kemp, S.O. Quin | Victoria v Tasmania | Hobart | 1932–33 |
| 178 | C.P. Mead, C.P. Brutton | Hampshire v Worcestershire | Bournemouth | 1925 |
| 178 | Mohd Shafiq, Afzaal Ahmed | National Bank v Railways | Lahore | 1976–77 |
| 177 | W.G. Quaife, A.E.M Whittle | Warwickshire v Essex | Birmingham | 1904 |
| 176 | H.W. Parks, A.F. Wensley | Sussex v Cambridge U. | Cambridge | 1936 |
| 175 | E. Pooley, J. Southerton | Surrey v MCC | Oval | 1871 |
| 175 | A.J. Bowden, A.D. Fisher | NSW v Queensland | Sydney | 1907–08 |

## NINTH WICKET

| | | | | |
|---|---|---|---|---|
| 283 | J. Chapman, A. Warren | Derbyshire v Warwickshire | Blackwell | 1910 |
| 251 | J.W.H.T. Douglas, S.N. Hare | Essex v Derbyshire | Leyton | 1921 |
| 245 | V.S. Hazare, N.D. Nagarwalla | Maharashtra v Baroda | Poona | 1939–40 |
| 239 | H.B. Cave, I.B. Leggat | Central Districts v Otago | Dunedin | 1952–53 |
| 232 | C. Hill, E. Walkley | South Australia v NSW | Adelaide | 1900–01 |
| 231 | P. Sen, J. Mitter | Bengal v Bihar | Jamshedpur | 1950–51 |
| 230 | D.A. Livingstone, A.T. Castell | Hampshire v Surrey | Southampton | 1962 |
| 226 | C. Kelleway, W.A.S. Oldfield | New South Wales v Victoria | Melbourne | 1925–26 |
| 225 | W.W. Armstrong, E.A. Windsor | Australian XI v Rest | Sydney | 1907–08 |
| 221 | E.F. Waddy, W.P. Howell | NSW v South Australia | Adelaide | 1904–05 |
| 221 | N.V. Lindsay, G.R. McCubbin | Transvaal v Rhodesia | Bulawayo | 1922–23 |
| 217 | A.W. Nourse, B.C. Cooley | Natal v Western Province | Johannesburg | 1906–07 |
| 203* | J.J. Hills, J.C. Clay | Glamorgan v Worcestershire | Swansea | 1929 |
| 200 | E.B. Forssberg, H.S.B. Love | NSW v Queensland | Sydney | 1920–21 |
| 200 | G.W. Cook, C.S. Smith | Cambridge U. v Lancashire | Liverpool | 1957 |
| 197 | C.P. Mead, W.R. de la C. Shirley | Hampshire v Warwickshire | Birmingham | 1923 |
| 195 | Mohammad Shahid, Aslam Ali | Uttar Pradesh v Punjab | Mohan Nagar | 1977–78 |
| 193 | W.G. Grace, S.A.P. Kitcat | Gloucestershire v Sussex | Bristol | 1896 |
| 193 | G.O.B. Allen, N.E. Haig | Gentlemen v Players | Oval | 1925 |
| 192 | G.H. Hirst, S. Haigh | Yorkshire v Surrey | Bradford | 1898 |
| 190 | Asif Iqbal, Intikhab Alam | Pakistan v England | Oval | 1967 |
| 184 | C.A.G. Russell, L.C. Eastman | Essex v Middlesex | Lord's | 1920 |
| 183 | C.M.H. Greetham, H.W. Stephenson | Somerset v Leicestershire | Weston-s-Mare | 1963 |
| 181 | J.A. Cuffe, R.D. Burrows | Worcestershire v Gloucs | Worcester | 1907 |
| 181 | A. Bacher, J.T. Botten | South Africans v Leics | Leicester | 1965 |
| 181 | Rashid Israr, Abdur Raqeeb | Habib Bank v National Bank | Lahore | 1976–77 |
| 179* | N.F.M. Popplewell, D. Breakwell | Somerset v Kent | Taunton | 1980 |
| 179 | C.P. McGahey, C.P. Buckenham | Essex v Nottinghamshire | Leyton | 1904 |
| 179 | R.A. Hutton, G.A. Cope | Yorkshire v Pakistanis | Bradford | 1971 |
| 178 | H.W. Parks, A.F. Wensley | Sussex v Derbyshire | Horsham | 1930 |
| 177 | G. Brown, W.H. Livsey | Hampshire v Warwickshire | Birmingham | 1922 |
| 176* | R. Moorhouse, G.H. Hirst | Yorkshire v Gloucestershire | Bristol | 1894 |
| 173 | S. Haigh, W. Rhodes | Yorkshire v Sussex | Hove | 1902 |
| 173 | F.A. Tarrant, S. Aikut | Maharaja of Cooch Behar's XI v Lord Willingdon's XI | Poona | 1918–19 |
| 173 | Pankaj Roy, S.K. Girdhari | Governor's XI v West Indians | Calcutta | 1948–49 |
| 172 | R.G. Barlow, W. Flowers | Players v Australians | Nottingham | 1886 |
| 171 | D.P.B. Morkel, N.A. Quinn | S. Africans v W. Australia | Perth | 1931–32 |
| 170 | T.W. Garrett, T.R. McKibbin | NSW v South Australia | Sydney | 1896–97 |
| 169 | C.B. Willis, W.A.S. Oldfield | Australians v Notts | Nottingham | 1919 |
| 168 | L.G. Crawley, F.B. Watson | MCC v Jamaica | Kingston | 1925–26 |
| 168 | E.R.T. Holmes, E.W.J. Brooks | Surrey v Hampshire | Oval | 1936 |
| 167 | H. Verity, T.F. Smailes | Yorkshire v Somerset | Bath | 1936 |
| 166 | R.K. Muzzell, G.L.G. Watson | Transvaal v E. Province | Johannesburg | 1968–69 |
| 165 | W. McIntyre, G. Wootton | Nottinghamshire v Kent | Nottingham | 1869 |
| 165 | Mohd Nazir jr, Iqtidar Haider | Railways v Rawalpindi | Rawalpindi | 1969–70 |
| 164 | W.A.S. Oldfield, E.S. White | NSW v South Australia | Sydney | 1936–37 |
| 163* | M.C. Cowdrey, A.C. Smith | England v New Zealand | Wellington | 1962–63 |
| 162* | Aftab Baloch, Arshad Bashir | PWD v Hyderabad Blues | Karachi | 1969–70 |
| 162 | W. Rhodes, S. Haigh | Yorkshire v Lancashire | Manchester | 1904 |

| 161 | E. Smith, W. Rhodes | Yorkshire v Sussex | Sheffield | 1900 |
|---|---|---|---|---|
| 161 | B.R. Edrich, F. Ridgway | Kent v Sussex | Tunbridge Wells | 1949 |
| 161 | G.J. Whittaker, W.S. Surridge | Surrey v Glamorgan | Oval | 1951 |
| 161 | J.W. Ghorpade, C. Williams | Baroda v Bombay | Baroda | 1961–62 |
| 161 | C.H. Lloyd, A.M.E. Roberts | West Indies v India | Calcutta | 1983–84 |
| 161 | Zaheer Abbas, Sarfraz Nawaz | Pakistan v England | Lahore | 1983–84 |
| 160* | E.H. Hendren, F.J. Durston | Middlesex v Essex | Leyton | 1927 |
| 160 | R.T. Crawford, W.W. Odell | Leicestershire v Worcs | Leicester | 1902 |
| 160 | K.S. Ranjitsinhji, F.W. Tate | Sussex v Surrey | Hastings | 1902 |
| 160 | P.S. Arnott, C.V. Single | NSW v Western Australia | Sydney | 1912–13 |
| 160 | J.W.H.T. Douglas, H.W.F. Franklin | Essex v Middlesex | Leyton | 1923 |
| 160 | D.R. Wilcox, R. Smith | Essex v Yorkshire | Southend | 1947 |
| 159 | H.V. Page, W.O. Vizard | Gloucestershire v Notts | Cheltenham | 1883 |
| 159 | Saeed Ahmed, Rathod | Western India States v Sind | Karachi | 1939–40 |
| 158 | F. Marchant, E.B. Shine | Kent v Warwickshire | Tonbridge | 1897 |
| 158 | A.G.E. Ealham, A. Brown | Kent v Glamorgan | Folkestone | 1968 |
| 157 | C.P. Mead, W.H. Livsey | Hampshire v Notts | Southampton | 1921 |
| 157 | H.M. Garland-Wells, C.K.H. Hill-Wood | Oxford University v Kent | Oxford | 1928 |
| 157 | H.G. Gaekwad, K. Bhatnagar | Holkar v Bihar | Jamshedpur | 1948–49 |
| 156 | A. Street, F.E. Smith | Surrey v Leicestershire | Leicester | 1895 |
| 156 | T.W. Hayward, J.T. Hearne | Players v Gentlemen | Lord's | 1896 |
| 156 | H. Wrathall, W.S.A. Brown | Gloucestershire v Warwicks | Birmingham | 1898 |
| 156 | M.W. Payne, G.H.M.G. Cartwright | Free Foresters v Cambridge University | Cambridge | 1927 |
| 156 | R. Subba Row, S. Starkie | Northamptonshire v Lancs | Northampton | 1955 |
| 156 | S.K. Sahu, U.M. Kumre | Vidarbha v Uttar Pradesh | Nagpur | 1959–60 |
| 156 | P. Hansraj, S. Dhobi | Railways v Hyderabad | Hyderabad | 1975–76 |
| 155* | A. Persaud, K.C. Glasgow | Demerara v Berbice | Rose Hall | 1976–77 |
| 155 | F.R. Brown, M.J.C. Allom | Surrey v Middlesex | Oval | 1932 |
| 155 | S.J. Storey, R.D. Jackman | Surrey v Glamorgan | Cardiff | 1973 |
| 154 | S.E. Gregory, J.M. Blackham | Australia v England | Sydney | 1894–95 |
| 154 | G.W. Stephens, A.J.W. Croom | Warwickshire v Derbyshire | Birmingham | 1925 |
| 153 | J.S. Shepherd, R.M. Rutherford | Otago v Southland | Dunedin | 1913–14 |
| 152* | A.T.W. Grout, W.T. Walmsley | Queensland v NSW | Sydney | 1956–57 |
| 152 | E. Martin, H.R. Murrell | Middlesex v Essex | Leyton | 1919 |
| 152 | R. Chadda, Harminder Singh | Haryana v Jammu & Kashmir | Srinagar | 1972–73 |
| 151 | W.H. Scotton, W.W. Read | England v Australia | Oval | 1884 |
| 151 | D.J. Brickett, W.K. Watson | E. Province v N. Transvaal | Port Elizabeth | 1982–83 |
| 150 | H. Philipson, A.C.M. Croome | Oxford University v M.C.C. | Lord's | 1889 |
| 150 | A.E. Relf, S. Haigh | Lord Londesborough's XI v Australians | Scarborough | 1912 |
| 150 | E.A.E. Baptiste, M.A. Holding | West Indies v England | Birmingham | 1984 |

### TENTH WICKET

| 307 | A.F. Kippax, J.E.H. Hooker | New South Wales v Victoria | Melbourne | 1928–29 |
|---|---|---|---|---|
| 249 | C.T. Sarwate, S.N. Banerjee | Indians v Surrey | Oval | 1946 |
| 235 | F.E. Woolley, A. Fielder | Kent v Worcestershire | Stourbridge | 1909 |
| 230 | R.W. Nicholls, W. Roche | Middlesex v Kent | Lord's | 1899 |
| 228 | R. Illingworth, K. Higgs | Leicestershire v Northants | Leicester | 1977 |
| 218 | F.H. Vigar, T.P.B. Smith | Essex v Derbyshire | Chesterfield | 1947 |
| 211 | M. Ellis, T.J. Hastings | Victoria v South Australia | Melbourne | 1902–03 |
| 196* | Nadim Yousuf, Maqsood Kundi | MCB v National Bank | Lahore | 1981–82 |
| 192 | H.A.W. Bowell, W.H. Livsey | Hampshire v Worcestershire | Bournemouth | 1921 |
| 184 | R.C. Blunt, W. Hawksworth | Otago v Canterbury | Christchurch | 1931–32 |
| 177 | J.H. Naumann, A.E.R. Gilligan | Cambridge U. v Sussex | Hove | 1919 |
| 174 | H.R. Lance, D. Mackay-Coghill | Transvaal v Natal | Johannesburg | 1965–66 |
| 173 | J. Briggs, R. Pilling | Lancashire v Surrey | Liverpool | 1885 |
| 173 | A. Ducat, A. Sandham | Surrey v Essex | Leyton | 1921 |
| 172 | A. Needham, R.D. Jackman | Surrey v Lancashire | Manchester | 1982 |
| 169 | R.B. Minnett, C.G. McKew | New South Wales v Victoria | Sydney | 1911–12 |
| 167 | A.W.F. Somerset, W.C. Smith | MCC v Barbados | Bridgetown | 1912–13 |
| 157 | J. Parnham, J. White | North v South | Lord's | 1886 |
| 157 | C.A.G. Russell, A.B. Hipkin | Essex v Somerset | Taunton | 1926 |

| 157 | W.E. Astill, W.H. Marlow | Leicestershire v Gloucs | Cheltenham | 1933 |
|---|---|---|---|---|
| 156 | H.R. Butt, G.R. Cox | Sussex v Cambridge U. | Cambridge | 1908 |
| 154* | N.A. McDonald, K.C. Martin | Natal B v Griqualand West | Kimberley | 1965–66 |
| | *(This was Martin's only innings in first-class cricket)* | | | |
| 154 | F. Buttsworth, J.P. Lanigan | W. Australia v Victoria | Perth | 1921–22 |
| 152 | E.B. Alletson, W. Riley | Nottinghamshire v Essex | Hove | 1911 |
| 151 | B.F. Hastings, R.O. Collinge | New Zealand v Pakistan | Auckland | 1972–73 |
| 150* | Abdur Salaam, Ahsan-ul-Haq | Muslims v Sikhs | Lahore | 1923–24 |
| 149 | F.H. Hollins, B.A. Collins | Oxford University v MCC | Oxford | 1901 |
| 149 | K. Farnes, T.H. Wade | Essex v Somerset | Taunton | 1936 |
| 149 | G. Boycott, G.B. Stevenson | Yorkshire v Warwickshire | Birmingham | 1982 |
| 148 | Lord Hawke, D. Hunter | Yorkshire v Kent | Sheffield | 1898 |
| 148 | B.W. Bellamy, J.V. Murdin | Northants v Glamorgan | Northampton | 1925 |
| 147 | E.M. Sprot, A.E. Fielder | Hampshire v Gloucs | Bristol | 1911 |
| 147 | C.G. Macartney, S.C. Everett | Australian XI v Tasmania | Hobart | 1925–26 |
| 146 | Mahmood Ahmed, Tehsin Ilyas | United Bank v Railways | Lahore | 1976–77 |
| 145 | G.A. Rotherham, J.H. Naumann | Cambridge U. v AIF | Cambridge | 1919 |
| 145 | K.S. More, V. Patel | Baroda v Uttar Pradesh | Baroda | 1983–84 |
| 144 | S. Wazir Ali, J.G. Navle | Indians v Scotland | Dundee | 1932 |
| 144 | A. Sidebottom, A.L. Robinson | Yorkshire v Glamorgan | Cardiff | 1977 |
| 143 | H. Gibbs, J.J. Bridges | Somerset v Essex | Weston-s-Mare | 1919 |
| 143 | T. Davies, S.A.B. Daniels | Glamorgan v Gloucestershire | Swansea | 1982 |
| 141 | J.T. Tyldesley, W. Worsley | Lancashire v Notts | Nottingham | 1905 |
| 141 | J.R. Mason, C. Blythe | Kent v Surrey | Oval | 1909 |
| 140* | G.S. Boyes, A.E. Thomas | Players v Gentlemen | Folkestone | 1930 |
| 140* | R.C. Ontong, R.N.S. Hobbs | Glamorgan v Hampshire | Swansea | 1981 |
| 140 | S.J. Staples, T.L. Richmond | Notts v Derbyshire | Worksop | 1922 |
| 139 | P.R. Johnson, R.C. Robertson-Glasgow | Somerset v Surrey | Oval | 1926 |
| 138 | K.C. James, A.W.S. Brice | Wellington v Otago | Wellington | 1926–27 |
| 138 | E.L.G. Hoad, H.C. Griffith | West Indians v Sussex | Hove | 1933 |
| 138 | Yadvendrasinhji, S. Mubarak Ali | Nawanagar v Bengal | Bombay | 1936–37 |
| 138 | R.I. Jefferson, D.A.D. Sydenham | Surrey v Northamptonshire | Northampton | 1963 |
| 136 | J.P. O'Halloran, A.E. Johns | Victoria v South Australia | Melbourne | 1896–97 |
| 136 | K.S. Ranjitsinhji, P.R. May | London County v MCC | Crystal Palace | 1903 |
| 136 | G. Challenor, G.N. Francis | West Indians v Surrey | Oval | 1923 |
| 136 | H. Larwood, W. Voce | Nottinghamshire v Sussex | Nottingham | 1931 |
| 136 | J.S. Patel, H.A. Nakhuda | Gujarat v Holkar | Indore | 1950–51 |
| 136 | C. Shankar, D.G.C.A. Varma | Andhra v Kerala | Guntur | 1974–75 |
| 135 | T.W. Hayward, H.I. Young | Players v Gentlemen | Oval | 1899 |
| 135 | W.A.S. Oldfield, A.A. Mailey | NSW v South Australia | Adelaide | 1923–24 |
| 134 | A.E.R. Gilligan, M. Falcon | Gentlemen v Players | Oval | 1924 |
| 134 | H.G. Gaekwad, M. Salim Khan | Holkar v Delhi | Delhi | 1949–50 |
| 134 | W. Mathias, Afaq Hussain | Karachi v Karachi B | Karachi | 1962–63 |
| 134 | F.R.M. de S. Goonetilleke, G.R.A. de Silva | Sri Lanka v Tamil Nadu | Madras | 1976–77 |
| 133* | A. Sandham, W.J. Abel | Surrey v Middlesex | Oval | 1919 |
| 133* | G. Inder Dev, V.K. Tiwari | Delhi v Jammu & Kashmir | Delhi | 1961–62 |
| 133 | G.A. Bartlett, I.A. Colquhoun | Central Dists v Auckland | Auckland | 1959–60 |
| 133 | Wasim Raja, Wasim Bari | Pakistan v West Indies | Bridgetown | 1976–77 |
| 132 | R.W. McLeod, C.H. Ross | Victoria v South Australia | Adelaide | 1899–00 |
| 132 | V.A. Valentine, H.G. Griffith | West Indians v Middlesex | Lord's | 1933 |
| 131* | C.C. Smart, W.D. Hughes | Glamorgan v South Africans | Cardiff | 1935 |
| 131 | D.L.A. Jephson, F. Stedman | Surrey v Lancashire | Oval | 1900 |
| 131 | G.E. Tyldesley, R. Whitehead | Lancashire v Warwicks | Birmingham | 1914 |
| 131 | W.R. Gouldsworthy, J. Bessant | Gloucestershire v Somerset | Bristol | 1923 |
| 130 | G.W. Beldam, C. Headlam | Middlesex v Surrey | Lord's | 1902 |
| 130 | R.E. Foster, W. Rhodes | England v Australia | Sydney | 1903–04 |
| 130 | H. Strudwick, J.W. Hitch | Surrey v Warwickshire | Birmingham | 1911 |
| 130 | G.R. Cox, G. Stannard | Sussex v Essex | Hove | 1919 |
| 130 | N.J. Venkatesan, C.R. Rangachari | Madras v Madhya Pradesh | Madras | 1951–52 |
| 130 | Salahuddin, Arshad Bashir | Karachi v Railways | Karachi | 1967–68 |
| 130 | J. Abhiram, A.R. Bhat | Karnataka v Tamil Nadu | Bangalore | 1981–82 |
| 129 | E.G. Goatly, F. Stedman | Surrey v South Africans | Oval | 1904 |
| 129 | F. Caulfield, L.R. Tuckett | OFS v Western Province | Bloemfontein | 1925–26 |
| 128 | W. Mudie, T. Sewell | Surrey v Kent & Sussex | Oval | 1859 |
| 128 | H.D.G. Leveson Gower, G.K. Molineux | Gentlemen v Oxford U. | Eastbourne | 1908 |

| 128 | F.R. Santall, W. Sanders | Warwickshire v Yorkshire | Birmingham | 1930 |
|---|---|---|---|---|
| 128 | K. Higgs, J.A. Snow | England v West Indies | Oval | 1966 |
| 127 | C.P. Mead, G.S. Boyes | Hampshire v Worcestershire | Worcester | 1922 |
| 127 | J.M. Taylor, A.A. Mailey | Australia v England | Sydney | 1924–25 |
| 126 | J.W. Hearne, H. Strudwick | G.L. Jessop's XI v | | |
| | | P.F. Warner's XI | Sheffield | 1911 |
| 126 | R.E.S. Wyatt, J.H. Mayer | Warwickshire v Surrey | Oval | 1927 |
| 125 | A.L. Hosie, W.L. Budd | Hampshire v Glamorgan | Bournemouth | 1935 |
| 124 | W.A.S. Oldfield, A.A. Mailey | Australians v Warwicks | Birmingham | 1921 |
| 124 | Salahuddin, Niaz Ahmed | Pakistanis v Minor Counties | Swindon | 1967 |
| 123 | A.W.S. Brice, T. Beard | Wellington v Otago | Wellington | 1927–28 |
| 123 | R. Duckfield, J.C. Clay | Glamorgan v Leicestershire | Cardiff | 1933 |
| 123 | B. Dooland, A.K. Walker | Nottinghamshire v Somerset | Nottingham | 1956 |
| 122 | W.G. Ward, N. Dodds | Tasmania v Victoria | Hobart | 1898–99 |
| 122 | J.W. Hitch, H. Strudwick | Players v Gentlemen | Oval | 1914 |
| 122 | W. Reeves, G.M. Louden | Essex v Surrey | Leyton | 1919 |
| 122 | W.R. Hammond, C.I.J. Smith | MCC v Barbados | Bridgetown | 1934–35 |
| 122 | S. Turner, D.L. Acfield | Essex v Glamorgan | Swansea | 1974 |
| 122* | K.P. Tomlins, W.W. Daniel | Middlesex v Yorkshire | Lord's | 1981 |
| 121 | W. Bates, E. Peate | Under-30 v Over-30 | Lord's | 1882 |
| 121 | J.T. Brown, D. Hunter | Yorkshire v Liverpool & Dist | Liverpool | 1894 |
| 121 | W.L. Murdoch, J. Gilman | London County v | | |
| | | Cambridge University | Crystal Palace | 1900 |
| 120 | R.A. Duff, W.W. Armstrong | Australia v England | Melbourne | 1901–02 |
| 120 | A.J.Y. Hopkins, W. McIntyre | NSW v Queensland | Sydney | 1906–07 |
| 120 | G. Lavis, J. Mercer | Glamorgan v Surrey | Oval | 1934 |
| 120 | S.L. Saunders, P.M. Clough | Tasmania v W. Australia | Perth | 1981–82 |
| 119* | W.H. Ponsford, A.J. Richardson | Australians v MCC | Lord's | 1926 |
| 119* | E.A. Watts, J.V. Daley | Surrey v Hampshire | Bournemouth | 1936 |
| 119 | W.B. Burns, G.A. Wilson | Worcestershire v Somerset | Worcester | 1906 |
| 119 | C.D. McIver, C.U. Peat | H.D.G. Leveson Gower's XI | | |
| | | v Cambridge University | Eastbourne | 1921 |
| 119 | W.N. Carson, J. Cowie | Auckland v Otago | Auckland | 1937–38 |
| 118 | C. Calvert, T. Sewell | Surrey v Sussex | Hove | 1868 |
| 118 | Lord Hawke, D. Hunter | Yorkshire v Kent | Leeds | 1896 |
| 118 | C.H. Abercrombie, H.A.H. Smith | Hampshire v Worcs | Dudley | 1913 |
| 118 | A. Hurwood, P.M. Hornibrook | Australians v Sussex | Hove | 1930 |
| 118 | R.J.L. Hammond, | | | |
| | J.H.G. Deighton | Combined Services v Essex | Chelmsford | 1950 |
| 117* | R. Dare, R.O. Prouton | Hampshire v Worcestershire | Bournemouth | 1952 |
| 117* | P. Willey, R.G.D. Willis | England v West Indies | Oval | 1980 |
| 117 | V. Subramanya, | | | |
| | B.S. Chandrasekhar | Mysore v Madras | Madras | 1966–67 |
| 116 | C.I.J. Smith, I.A.R. Peebles | Middlesex v Kent | Canterbury | 1939 |
| 115 | W. Drysdale, M.C. Tandy | Europeans v Parsees | Poona | 1900–01 |
| 115 | L.G. Fuller, L.R. Tuckett | OFS v Western Province | Bloemfontein | 1925–26 |
| 115 | B.W. Malcolm, T. Bhattacharjee | Bengal v Madras | Calcutta | 1938–39 |
| 115 | S.W. Sohoni, S.G. Shinde | Hindus v Parsees | Bombay | 1945–46 |
| 115 | A.J. Watkins, D.J. Shepherd | Glamorgan v Northants | Northampton | 1958 |
| 115 | R.E. Hitchcock, R.B. Edmonds | Warwickshire v Northants | Northampton | 1964 |
| 115 | Hamid Khan, Khalid Begh | Peshawar v Income Tax | Lahore | 1977–78 |
| 115 | J. Stanworth, P.J.W. Allott | Lancashire v Gloucestershire | Bristol | 1985 |
| 114 | Wasim Bari, Iqbal Sikander | PIA v National Bank | Lahore | 1979–80 |
| 113* | E.W. Whitfield, J.F. Parker | Surrey v Indians | Oval | 1932 |
| 113* | Zakir Khan, Faridoon Khan | Peshawar v Hazara | Peshawar | 1983–84 |
| 113 | J.G. Greig, C. Robson | Hampshire v Lancashire | Liverpool | 1901 |
| 113 | G.R. Cox, H.R. Butt | Sussex v Hampshire | Chichester | 1906 |
| 113 | F.L.H. Mooney, E.C.V. Knapp | Wellington v Auckland | Wellington | 1943–44 |
| 113 | W. Mathias, Arshad Bashir | Karachi Blues v | | |
| | | Railway Greens | Karachi | 1965–66 |
| 113 | A.J.S. Smith, V.A.P. van der Bijl | South African Invitation XI v | | |
| | | D.H. Robins' XI | Durban | 1973–74 |
| 112* | E.E. Hemmings, R.D. Jackman | England XI v S. Australia | Adelaide | 1982–83 |
| 112 | J.J. Kelly, F. Laver | Australians v Gloucestershire | Bristol | 1905 |
| 112 | A.E. Dipper, E.G. Dennett | Gloucestershire v Sussex | Gloucester | 1908 |
| 112 | A.E. Relf, H.E. Roberts | Sussex v Lancashire | Eastbourne | 1914 |
| 112 | C. Kelleway, H. Carter | NSW v South Australia | Adelaide | 1920–21 |

| 112 | J.W. Lee, W.T. Luckes | Somerset v Kent | Taunton | 1934 |
|---|---|---|---|---|
| 112 | J.T. Botten, M.J. Macaulay | South African Colts v MCC | Benoni | 1964–65 |
| 112 | S. Keshwala, B.S. Sandhu | West Zone v South Zone | Bombay | 1982–83 |
| 111* | A.P.F. Chapman, F.T. Mann | South v North | Folkestone | 1927 |
| 111 | A. Ward, A.W. Mold | Lancashire v Leicestershire | Manchester | 1895 |
| 111 | M.A. Noble, W.P. Howell | New South Wales v Victoria | Sydney | 1896–97 |
| 111 | J.R. Gunn, W.A. Flint | Nottinghamshire v Middlesex | Nottingham | 1919 |
| 111 | J.F. Parker, A.R. Gover | Surrey v Indians | Oval | 1936 |
| 111 | Gulraiz Wali, Shanwar | Punjab U. v Railways | Lahore | 1964–65 |
| 111 | Maazullah Khan, Tariq Cheema | Peshawar v Lahore B | Lahore | 1973–74 |
| 110* | A.G. Marshall, G. Hunt | Somerset v Hampshire | Taunton | 1930 |
| 110* | F.W. Stocks, E.A. Meads | Nottinghamshire v Worcs | Nottingham | 1946 |
| 110 | J.S.E.C. Hood, C.E. Green | Cambridge U. v MCC | Lord's | 1867 |
| 110 | J.R. Sheffield, T.H. Wade | Essex v Warwickshire | Chelmsford | 1929 |
| 110 | N. Chanmugam, P.I. Pieris | Ceylon v West Indians | Colombo | 1966–67 |
| 109 | W. Gunn, R.G. Hardstaff | Nottinghamshire v Derbyshire | Derby | 1896 |
| 109 | A.L. Newell, W.P. Howell | NSW v A.E. Stoddart's XI | Sydney | 1897–98 |
| 109 | G. Dewhurst, C. Fraser | Trinidad v Barbados | Georgetown | 1922–23 |
| 109 | D.C.S. Compton, O.P. Rawal | Holkar v Bombay | Bombay | 1944–45 |
| 109 | H.R. Adhikari, Ghulam Ahmed | India v Pakistan | Delhi | 1952–53 |
| 108 | Lord Hawke, L. Whitehead | Yorkshire v Lancashire | Manchester | 1903 |
| 108 | R.G. Nadkarni, S.R. Patil | Maharashtra v Bombay | Bombay | 1953–54 |
| 108 | H. Ramoutar, Inshan Ali | Trinidad v Glamorgan | Port-of-Spain | 1969–70 |
| 108 | G. Boycott, M.K. Bore | Yorkshire v Nottinghamshire | Bradford | 1973 |
| 107 | A. Jaques, W.H. Livsey | Hampshire v Worcs | Southampton | 1914 |
| 107 | J.A. Small, G.N. Francis | West Indians v Harlequins | Eastbourne | 1928 |
| 107 | H.J. Enthoven, W.F.F. Price | Middlesex v Sussex | Lord's | 1930 |
| 107 | R.C. Motz, F.J. Cameron | New Zealanders v Worcs | Worcester | 1965 |
| 106 | G. Wootton, R.S. Forster | MCC v Sussex | Hove | 1863 |
| 106 | H. Wrathall, J.H. Board | Gloucestershire v Surrey | Oval | 1899 |
| 106 | E.R. Wilson, C.E. Hatfeild | MCC v Argentine | Hurlingham | 1911–12 |
| 106 | G. Brown, A.S. Kennedy | Hampshire v Yorkshire | Bournemouth | 1913 |
| 106 | R.C. Robertson-Glasgow, V.R. Price | Oxford U. v Somerset | Oxford | 1922 |
| 106 | F.W. Gilligan, M.S. Nichols | Essex v Kent | Canterbury | 1926 |
| 106 | E. Sim, H.J. O'Reilly | Rhodesia v Griqualand West | Kimberley | 1929–30 |
| 106 | E.H. Hendren, G.E. Hart | Middlesex v Somerset | Taunton | 1935 |
| 106 | A.B. Sellers, D.V. Brennan | Yorkshire v Worcestershire | Worcester | 1948 |
| 106 | D. Bennett, H.W. Tilly | MCC v Oxford University | Lord's | 1955 |
| 105* | W.T. Walmsley, J.E. Freeman | Queensland v NSW | Brisbane | 1957–58 |
| 105 | W. Brockwell, T. Richardson | Surrey v Gloucestershire | Oval | 1893 |
| 105 | L.W. Pye, A.J. Bowden | NSW v Queensland | Sydney | 1899–00 |
| 105 | R.W. Cherry, R.C. Torrance | Otago v Canterbury | Christchurch | 1925–26 |
| 105 | A. Wilson, R. Tattersall | Lancashire v Leicestershire | Manchester | 1958 |
| 105 | S. Abid Ali, P. Krishnamurthy | Hyderabad v Karnataka | Bangalore | 1973–74 |
| 104 | W.O. Reid, J.T. Hings | Transvaal v Natal | Pietermaritzburg | 1894–95 |
| 104 | W.S.A. Brown, F.G. Roberts | Gloucestershire v Sussex | Bristol | 1903 |
| 104 | C.K. Krishnaswami, C.R. Ganapathy | Indians v Europeans | Madras | 1920–21 |
| 104 | G. Brown, J. Mercer | MCC v Hindus-Muslims XI | Bombay | 1926–27 |
| 104 | K.C. James, H.B. Massey | Wellington v Australians | Wellington | 1927–28 |
| 104 | F.R. Brown, J.F. Parker | Surrey v Kent | Blackheath | 1932 |
| 104 | L. Michael, E. Pynor | South Australia v Victoria | Adelaide | 1949–50 |
| 104 | Zulfiqar Ahmed, Amir Elahi | Pakistan v India | Madras | 1952–53 |
| 103 | L.S. D'Ade, S. Rudder | Trinidad v A. Priestley's XI | Port-of-Spain | 1896–97 |
| 103 | P.A. McAlister, F.A. Tarrant | Victoria v New Zealanders | Melbourne | 1898–99 |
| 103 | James Seymour, A. Fielder | Kent v Worcestershire | Maidstone | 1904 |
| 103 | A. Dolphin, E. Smith | Yorkshire v Essex | Leyton | 1919 |
| 103 | H.G. Owen-Smith, A.J. Bell | South Africa v England | Leeds | 1929 |
| 103 | W. Voce, S.J. Staples | Nottinghamshire v Leics | Leicester | 1933 |
| 102 | D. Denton, D. Hunter | Yorkshire v Cambridge U. | Cambridge | 1895 |
| 102 | James Seymour, A. Fielder | Kent v Essex | Leyton | 1911 |
| 102 | P.T. Eckersley, W.E. Phillipson | Lancashire v Sussex | Manchester | 1933 |
| 102 | H.G. Gaekwad, O.P. Rawal | Holkar v Baroda | Indore | 1945–46 |
| 102 | Hanif Mohd, Pervez Sajjad | PIA v Railways | Lahore | 1973–74 |
| 101* | J.W.H.T. Douglas, B. Tremlin | Essex v Derbyshire | Leyton | 1914 |
| 101 | A.J.L. Hill, E.C. Streatfeild | Cambridge U. v Yorkshire | Cambridge | 1890 |

| | | | | |
|---|---|---|---|---|
| 101 | C.R. Hartley, A.W. Mold | Lancashire v Gloucs | Gloucester | 1901 |
| 101 | G. Giffen, J.F. Travers | South Australia v Victoria | Adelaide | 1902–03 |
| 101 | H.D.G. Leveson Gower, R.H. Fox | H.D.G. Leveson Gower's XI v Oxford University | Oxford | 1904 |
| 101 | W.W. Armstrong, F.G. Truman | Victoria v South Australia | Melbourne | 1918–19 |
| 101 | F.G. Travers, B. Howlett | Europeans v Muslims | Bombay | 1925–26 |
| 101 | W.W. Whysall, W. Voce | Nottinghamshire v Gloucs | Nottingham | 1929 |
| 101 | A.E. Wilson, T.W.J. Goddard | Gloucestershire v Somerset | Bristol | 1939 |
| 100* | D. Tallon, G. Noblet | D.G. Bradman's XI v A.L. Hassett's XI | Melbourne | 1948–49 |
| 100 | G.E. Palmer, W.H. Cooper | Victoria v NSW | Sydney | 1881–82 |
| 100 | P.H. Tarilton, H.W. Ince | Barbados v MCC | Bridgetown | 1912–13 |
| 100 | E.L. Dalton, A.L. Ochse | South Africans v Kent | Canterbury | 1929 |
| 100 | W.A. Sime, W. Voce | Notts v Cambridge U. | Cambridge | 1935 |
| 100 | S.N. Banerjee, C.S. Nayudu | Indians v Hampshire | Bournemouth | 1936 |
| 100 | D. Govindraj, Mumtaz Hussain | Hyderabad v Kerala | Cannanore | 1971–72 |

# FIRST-WICKET HUNDRED IN BOTH INNINGS

| | | | | | |
|---|---|---|---|---|---|
| 128 | 108 | L. Hall, G. Ulyett | Yorkshire v Sussex | Hove | 1885 |
| 139 | 147* | J.T. Brown, J. Tunnicliffe | Yorkshire v Middlesex | Lord's | 1896 |
| 135 | 148 | C.B. Fry, G. Brann | Sussex v Middlesex | Lord's | 1899 |
| 131 | 142 | W.G. Grace, C.J.B. Wood | London County v Surrey | Crystal Palace | 1901 |
| 108 | 100 | C.J. Burnup, E. Humphreys | Kent v South Africans | Beckenham | 1901 |
| 114 | 109 | R. Abel, D.L.A. Jephson | Surrey v Sussex | Hove | 1901 |
| 134 | 144* | A.O. Jones, J. Iremonger | Nottinghamshire v Surrey | Oval | 1901 |
| 170 | 179 | C.B. Fry, J. Vine | Sussex v Leicestershire | Hove | 1903 |
| 113 | 119* | V.T. Trumper, R.A. Duff | NSW v Victoria | Sydney | 1903–04 |
| 102 | 303 | A.O. Jones, J. Iremonger | Nottinghamshire v Gloucs | Nottingham | 1904 |
| 106 | 125 | T.W. Hayward, J.B. Hobbs | Surrey v Cambridge U. | Oval | 1907 |
| 147 | 105 | T.W. Hayward, J.B. Hobbs | Surrey v Middlesex | Lord's | 1907 |
| | | *These two instances occurred in the same week* | | | |
| 105 | 118 | T.W. Hayward, J.B. Hobbs | Surrey v Oxford University | Oval | 1908 |
| 103 | 100 | A. Hartley, W.K. Tyldesley | Lancashire v Hampshire | Southampton | 1910 |
| 122 | 121 | V.T. Trumper, W. Bardsley | NSW v South Africans | Sydney | 1910–11 |
| 141 | 193 | A.H. Hornby, J.W.H. Makepeace | Lancashire v Notts | Nottingham | 1912 |
| 127 | 136 | A.E. Dipper, C.S. Barnett | Gloucestershire v Somerset | Bristol | 1913 |
| 191 | 104 | C.A.G. Russell, F.A. Loveday | Essex v Lancashire | Leyton | 1921 |
| 122 | 140 | F.H. Gillingham, C.A.G. Russell | Essex v Surrey | Oval | 1922 |
| 154 | 155 | J.S. Shepherd, R.V.de R. Worker | Otago v Wellington | Dunedin | 1923–24 |
| 157 | 110 | J.B. Hobbs, H. Sutcliffe | England v Australia | Sydney | 1924–25 |
| 114 | 116 | J.W.H. Makepeace, C. Hallows | Lancashire v Australians | Liverpool | 1926 |
| 105 | 265* | P. Holmes, H. Sutcliffe | Yorkshire v Surrey | Oval | 1926 |
| 109 | 100 | J.A. Newman, H.L. Dales | F.S.G. Calthorpe's XI v L.H. Tennyson's XI | Folkestone | 1926 |
| 202 | 107* | F.B. Watson, C. Hallows | Lancashire v Glamorgan | Manchester | 1928 |
| 184 | 210* | P. Holmes, H. Sutcliffe | Yorkshire v Notts | Nottingham | 1928 |
| 106 | 368 | E.H. Bowley, J.H. Parks | Sussex v Gloucestershire | Hove | 1929 |
| 119 | 171 | R.H. Catterall, B. Mitchell | South Africa v England | Birmingham | 1929 |
| 129 | 109 | N.E. Haig, H.W. Lee | Middlesex v Leicestershire | Lord's | 1930 |
| 102 | 113 | D. Ayling, A.L.S. Jackson | South Americans v Sir J. Cahn's XI | Nottingham | 1932 |
| 125 | 128 | W.W. Keeton, C.B. Harris | Nottinghamshire v Kent | Nottingham | 1933 |
| 119 | 121 | A.W. Snowden, A.H. Bakewell | Northants v Warwicks | Birmingham | 1934 |
| | | *Both partnerships were recorded on the second day* | | | |
| 119 | 146 | J.W. Lee, F.S. Lee | Somerset v Sussex | Eastbourne | 1934 |
| 101 | 127 | W.H. Ashdown, A.E. Fagg | Kent v Glamorgan | Cardiff | 1935 |
| 111 | 109 | J.H. Parks, H.E. Hammond | Sussex v Hampshire | Portsmouth | 1936 |
| 109 | 102 | N. Kilner, A.J.W. Croom | Warwickshire v Worcs | Worcester | 1937 |
| 108 | 126* | E. Paynter, C. Washbrook | Lancashire v Notts | Nottingham | 1937 |
| 102 | 100 | N.T. McCorkell, J. Arnold | Hampshire v Kent | Southampton | 1938 |
| 116 | 105 | F.S. Lee, H. Gimblett | Somerset v Sussex | Taunton | 1939 |
| 152 | 169 | I.S. Lee, B.A. Barnett | Victoria v Queensland | Brisbane | 1939–40 |
| 129 | 170 | V.H. Stollmeyer, J.B. Stollmeyer | Trinidad v Barbados | Port-of-Spain | 1940–41 |

| | | | | | |
|---|---|---|---|---|---|
| 224 | 105* | V.H. Stollmeyer, J.B. Stollmeyer | Trinidad v Barbados | Port-of-Spain | 1941–42 |
| 123 | 136 | D. Brookes, P. Davis | Northamptonshire v Lancs | Northampton | 1946 |
| 137 | 100 | L. Hutton, C. Washbrook | England v Australia | Adelaide | 1946–47 |
| 110 | 117 | L. Hutton, W. Watson | Yorkshire v Lancashire | Manchester | 1947 |
| 121 | 116 | A.H. Dyson, D.E. Davies | Glamorgan v Sussex | Cardiff | 1947 |
| 121 | 176 | J.D.B. Robertson, S.M. Brown | Middlesex v Essex | Colchester | 1947 |
| 124 | 139 | G.L. Berry, G. Lester | Leicestershire v Middlesex | Leicester | 1948 |
| 168 | 129 | L. Hutton, C. Washbrook | England v Australia | Leeds | 1948 |
| 220 | 286 | B. Sutcliffe, D.D. Taylor | Auckland v Canterbury | Auckland | 1948–49 |
| 122 | 151* | W.W. Keeton, C.B. Harris | Notts v Northants | Northampton | 1950 |
| 199 | 109 | J.D.B. Robertson, S.M. Brown | Middlesex v Somerset | Lord's | 1951 |
| 166 | 108 | B.C. Khanna, R. Balasundaram | Uttar Pradesh v Madhya Pradesh | Nagpur | 1952–53 |
| 101 | 118 | C. Washbrook, J.T. Ikin | Lancashire v Hampshire | Manchester | 1953 |
| 107 | 132 | A.E. Fagg, A.H. Phebey | Kent v Gloucestershire | Gloucester | 1954 |
| 106 | 104 | D.V. Smith, A.S.M. Oakman | MCC v Oxford University | Lord's | 1956 |
| 122 | 230 | W.B. Stott, K. Taylor | Yorkshire v Notts | Nottingham | 1957 |
| 172 | 112 | G. Atkinson, R.T. Virgin | Somerset v Cambridge U. | Taunton | 1960 |
| 198 | 137 | R.M. Prideaux, A.R. Lewis | Cambridge U. v Somerset | Taunton | 1960 |
| 152 | 110 | M.J. Stewart, J.H. Edrich | Surrey v Somerset | Taunton | 1960 |
| 123 | 106 | N.F. Horner, Khalid Ibadulla | Warwickshire v Northants | Northampton | 1961 |
| 161 | 139* | I.D. Craig, R.B. Simpson | NSW v Victoria | Sydney | 1961–62 |
| 136 | 138 | J.B. Bolus, K. Taylor | Yorkshire v Cambridge U. | Cambridge | 1962 |
| 170 | 103 | B.J. Booth, K. Tebay | Lancashire v Worcs | Manchester | 1963 |
| 105 | 104 | G. Boycott, K. Taylor | Yorkshire v Leicestershire | Leicester | 1963 |
| 117 | 150 | M.J. Stewart, J.B. Bolus | MCC v President's XI | Bangalore | 1963–64 |
| 116 | 114* | J.H. Hampshire, K. Taylor | Yorkshire v Oxford U. | Oxford | 1964 |
| 157 | 142 | W.M. Lawry, I.R. Redpath | Victoria v S. Australia | Melbourne | 1964–65 |
| 143 | 204 | M.R. Hallam, B.J. Booth | Leicestershire v Worcs | Leicester | 1965 |
| 141 | 127* | C. Milburn, R.M. Prideaux | Northants v Sussex | Hove | 1966 |
| 111 | 127 | I.R. Redpath, R.J. Inverarity | Australians v Derbyshire | Chesterfield | 1968 |
| 131 | 140* | W.E. Russell, M.J. Smith | Middlesex v Oxford U. | Oxford | 1970 |
| 100 | 101 | D.M. Green, R.B. Nicholls | Gloucestershire v Sussex | Hove | 1970 |
| 172 | 154 | M.J. Harris, J.B. Bolus | Nottinghamshire v Lancs | Nottingham | 1970 |
| 143 | 115 | Nadeem Ahmed, Agha Zahid | Punjab U. v Rawalpindi Greens | Lahore | 1970–71 |
| 107 | 103 | G. Boycott, J.H. Edrich | England v Australia | Adelaide | 1970–71 |
| 123 | 140 | J.H. Edrich, M.J. Edwards | Surrey v Warwickshire | Oval | 1971 |
| 125 | 147 | R.G.A. Headley, P.J. Stimpson | Worcestershire v Northants | Worcester | 1971 |
| 102 | 128* | R.G.A. Headley, P.J. Stimpson | Worcestershire v Warwicks | Birmingham | 1971 |
| 161 | 163* | C.P.S. Chauhan, M.S. Gupte | Maharashtra v Bombay | Bombay | 1971–72 |
| 154 | 104 | R.C. Fredericks, L. Baichan | Guyana v Combined I's | Skeldon | 1971–72 |
| 105 | 108 | P.J. Graves, G.A. Greenidge | Sussex v Australians | Hove | 1972 |
| 102 | 155 | W.L. Blair, G.M. Turner | Otago v Auckland | Auckland | 1972–73 |
| 139 | 128* | R.C. Fredericks, G.S. Camacho | Guyana v Trinidad | Skeldon | 1972–73 |
| 138 | 181 | M.H. Denness, D. Lloyd | MCC v Warwickshire | Lord's | 1973 |
| 132 | 101 | G.M. Turner, J.M. Parker | Worcestershire v Sussex | Worcester | 1973 |
| 185 | 205 | L. Baichan, Romain Etwaroo | Berbice v Demerara | Georgetown | 1973–74 |
| 104 | 104 | G. Boycott, R.G. Lumb | Yorkshire v Sussex | Leeds | 1974 |
| 100 | 137* | Afzal Ahmed, Taslim Arif | National Bank v Railways | Lahore | 1974–75 |
| 126 | 103 | M.F. Rosen, R.B. McCosker | NSW v South Australia | Sydney | 1974–75 |
| 143 | 101* | L. Baichan, R.C. Fredericks | Guyana v Trinidad | Georgetown | 1974–75 |
| 115 | 158 | J.A. Ormrod, K.W. Wilkinson | Worcestershire v Gloucs | Worcester | 1975 |
| 103 | 185 | A. Turner, B.M. Laird | Australians v Essex | Chelmsford | 1975 |
| 115 | 115 | Shafiq Ahmed, Taslim Arif | National Bank v Punjab | Lahore | 1975–76 |
| 146 | 145 | J.A. Jameson, D.L. Amiss | Warwickshire v Worcs | Worcester | 1976 |
| 101 | 131 | M.J. Smith, J.M. Brearley | Middlesex v West Indians | Lord's | 1976 |
| 156 | 103* | B.C. Rose, P.W. Denning | Somerset v Kent | Taunton | 1976 |
| 121 | 112 | S.J. Bezuidenhout, C.P. Wilkins | E. Province v W. Province | Cape Town | 1976–77 |
| 165 | 146 | I.A. Payne, M.J. Mentis | W. Province B v N. Transvaal | Pretoria | 1976–77 |
| 123 | 142 | V. Chopra, K. Juneja | Uttar Pradesh v Madhya Pradesh | Lakshmipur | 1978–79 |
| 135 | 135 | K.C. Wessels, J.R.T. Barclay | Sussex v Somerset | Hove | 1979 |
| 150 | 112 | B.J. Whitfield, B. Plummer | Natal B v E. Province B | Port Elizabeth | 1979–80 |
| 114 | 131 | B. Wood, J.G. Wright | Derbyshire v Worcs | Worcester | 1980 |
| 104 | 106* | D.L. Amiss, K.D. Smith | Warwickshire v Somerset | Taunton | 1980 |

| 112 | 187 | I.R. McLean, W.B. Phillips | S. Australia v Victoria | Geelong | 1980–81 |
| 123 | 143 | J.M. Brearley, W.N. Slack | Middlesex v Warwickshire | Lord's | 1981 |
| 228 | 100 | W.M. Darling, W.B. Phillips | S. Australia v Pakistanis | Adelaide | 1981–82 |
| 127 | 171 | G.R. Marsh, S.C. Clements | W. Australia v Queensland | Perth | 1981–82 |
| 101 | 124 | L. Potter, N.R. Taylor | Kent v Indians | Canterbury | 1982 |
| 195 | 152* | P.M. Roebuck, J.W. Lloyds | Somerset v Northants | Northampton | 1982 |
| 196 | 163 | Rizwan-uz-Zaman, Shoaib Mohd | PIA v Railways | Lahore | 1982–83 |
| 119 | 207 | Qasim Omar, Anwar-ul-Haq | MCB v Karachi | Karachi | 1982–83 |
| 158 | 132 | C.L. Smith, V.P. Terry | Hampshire v Lancashire | Bournemouth | 1983 |
| 158 | 109 | I.S. Anderson, K.J. Barnett | Derbyshire v Kent | Chesterfield | 1983 |
| 180 | 118 | G.D. Barlow, A.J.T. Miller | Middlesex v Northants | Lord's | 1983 |
| 124 | 111 | S.C. Khanna, R. Lamba | Delhi v Bengal | Delhi | 1983–84 |
| 120 | 106 | S.I. Williams, L.L. Lawrence | Leeward Islands v Guyana | Berbice | 1983–84 |
| 101 | 113 | C.A. Best, T.A. Hunte | Barbados v Trinidad | Bridgetown | 1983–84 |
| 161 | 220* | R.T. Robinson, B.C. Broad | Nottinghamshire v Oxford U. | Oxford | 1984 |
| 163 | 120 | S.A.R. Silva, D.M. Vonhagt | Sri Lankans v Warwicks | Birmingham | 1984 |
| 104 | 139 | A.G. Elgar, I.M. Wingreen | W. Province B v Transvaal B | Johannesburg | 1984–85 |

## FIRST-WICKET HUNDRED IN BOTH INNINGS BUT WITH A CHANGE OF PARTNER

The following batsmen shared in two century opening partnerships in a match but changed their partner for the second innings:

| A. Sandham | 216 | J.B. Hobbs | Surrey v Essex | Leyton | 1925 |
| | 181 | A. Jeacocke | | | |
| F.W. Shipston | 113 | G. Gunn | Nottinghamshire v Gloucs | Bristol | 1932 |
| | 139 | C.B. Harris | | | |
| P.G.V. van der Bijl | 133 | A. Melville | South Africa v England | Durban | 1938–39 |
| | 191 | B. Mitchell | | | |
| W.H.H. Sutcliffe | 109 | F.A. Lowson | Yorkshire v Canadians | Scarborough | 1954 |
| | 143 | W. Watson | | | |
| A.S.M. Oakman | 109 | D.V. Smith | Sussex v Oxford University | Oxford | 1956 |
| | 100 | A.A.K. Lawrence | | | |
| D.J. Constant | 136 | B.J. Booth | Leicestershire v Oxford U. | Oxford | 1965 |
| | 101 | S. Greensword | | | |
| Daljit Singh | 192 | Robin Mukherjee | Bihar v Punjab | Jamshedpur | 1970–71 |
| | 100 | G. Tilak Raj | | | |
| B.W. Luckhurst | 124 | G. Boycott | England v Pakistan | Lord's | 1971 |
| | 117* | R.A. Hutton | | | |
| D.L. Amiss | 191 | G. Boycott | MCC v Guyana | Georgetown | 1973–74 |
| | 111 | M.H. Denness | | | |
| K.W. Wilkinson | 106 | G.M. Turner | Worcestershire v Oxford U. | Worcester | 1975 |
| | 141 | E.J.O. Hemsley | | | |
| G. Boycott | 109 | R.G. Lumb | Yorkshire v Northants | Bradford | 1977 |
| | 135 | J.H. Hampshire | | | |
| P.R.Downton | 160 | J.M. Brearley | Middlesex v Kent | Lord's | 1980 |
| | 109 | K.P. Tomlins | | | |

## TENTH-WICKET HUNDRED IN BOTH INNINGS

| L.R. Tuckett | 115 | L.G. Fuller | OFS v W. Province | Bloemfontein | 1925–26 |
| | 129 | F. Caulfield | | | |

*This was Caulfield's first first-class match.*

## CAREER RECORDS

All records are complete to the end of the 1985 English season. Dates in italics denote the first half of an overseas season, i.e. *1966* means 1966–67.

The column headed '1000' records the number of times that each batsman has scored 1000 runs in a season. The figures for J.B. Hobbs show that he scored 1000 runs in each of 24 English seasons and on two other occasions when playing overseas.

## 30,000 RUNS

| | Career | I | NO | Runs | HS | Avge | 100 | 1000 |
|---|---|---|---|---|---|---|---|---|
| J.B. Hobbs | 1905–1934 | 1315 | 106 | **61237** | 316* | 50.65 | 197 | 24+2 |
| F.E. Woolley | 1906–1938 | 1530 | 84 | **58959** | 305* | 40.77 | 145 | 28 |
| E.H. Hendren | 1907–1938 | 1300 | 166 | **57611** | 301* | 50.80 | 170 | 21+4 |
| C.P. Mead | 1905–1936 | 1340 | 185 | **55061** | 280* | 47.67 | 153 | 27 |
| W.G. Grace | 1865–1908 | 1493 | 105 | **54896** | 344 | 39.55 | 126 | 28 |
| W.R. Hammond | 1920–1951 | 1005 | 104 | **50551** | 336* | 56.10 | 167 | 17+5 |
| H. Sutcliffe | 1919–1945 | 1088 | 123 | **50138** | 313 | 51.95 | 149 | 21+3 |
| T.W. Graveney | 1948–*1971* | 1223 | 159 | **47793** | 258 | 44.91 | 122 | 20+2 |
| G. Boycott | 1962–1985 | 994 | 161 | **47434** | 261* | 56.94 | 149 | 23+3 |
| T.W. Hayward | 1893–1914 | 1138 | 96 | **43551** | 315* | 41.79 | 104 | 20 |
| M.C. Cowdrey | 1950–1976 | 1130 | 134 | **42719** | 307 | 42.89 | 107 | 21+6 |
| A. Sandham | 1911–*1937* | 1000 | 79 | **41284** | 325 | 44.82 | 107 | 18+2 |
| D.L. Amiss | 1960–1985 | 1048 | 117 | **40673** | 262* | 43.68 | 96 | 21+1 |
| L. Hutton | 1934–1960 | 814 | 91 | **40140** | 364 | 55.51 | 129 | 12+5 |
| M.J.K. Smith | 1951–1975 | 1091 | 139 | **39832** | 204 | 41.84 | 69 | 19+1 |
| W. Rhodes | 1898–1930 | 1526 | 236 | **39722** | 267* | 30.79 | 58 | 20+1 |
| J.H. Edrich | 1956–1978 | 979 | 104 | **39790** | 310* | 45.47 | 103 | 19+2 |
| R.E.S. Wyatt | 1923–1957 | 1141 | 157 | **39405** | 232 | 40.04 | 85 | 17+1 |
| D.C.S. Compton | 1936–1964 | 839 | 88 | **38942** | 300 | 51.85 | 123 | 14+3 |
| G.E. Tyldesley | 1909–1936 | 961 | 106 | **38874** | 256* | 45.46 | 102 | 18+1 |
| J.T. Tyldesley | 1895–1923 | 994 | 62 | **37897** | 295* | 40.66 | 86 | 19 |
| J.W. Hearne | 1909–1936 | 1025 | 116 | **37252** | 285* | 40.98 | 96 | 19 |
| L.E.G. Ames | 1926–1951 | 951 | 95 | **37248** | 295 | 43.51 | 102 | 17 |
| D. Kenyon | 1946–1967 | 1159 | 59 | **37002** | 259 | 33.63 | 74 | 19 |
| W.J. Edrich | 1934–1958 | 964 | 92 | **36965** | 267* | 42.39 | 86 | 15 |
| J.M. Parks | 1949–1976 | 1227 | 172 | **36673** | 205* | 34.76 | 51 | 20 |
| D. Denton | 1894–1920 | 1161 | 70 | **36440** | 221 | 33.40 | 69 | 21 |
| G.H. Hirst | 1891–1929 | 1214 | 151 | **36272** | 341 | 34.12 | 60 | 19 |
| A. Jones | 1957–1983 | 1168 | 72 | **36049** | 204* | 32.89 | 56 | 23 |
| W.G. Quaife | 1894–1928 | 1203 | 185 | **36012** | 255* | 35.37 | 72 | 24 |
| R.E. Marshall | *1945*–1972 | 1053 | 59 | **35725** | 228* | 35.94 | 68 | 18 |
| K.W.R. Fletcher | 1962–1985 | 1090 | 158 | **35701** | 228* | 38.30 | 62 | 20 |
| G. Gunn | 1902–1932 | 1061 | 82 | **35208** | 220 | 35.96 | 62 | 20 |
| D.B. Close | 1949–1985 | 1223 | 173 | **34968** | 198 | 33.30 | 52 | 20 |
| J.G. Langridge | 1928–1955 | 984 | 66 | **34380** | 250* | 37.45 | 76 | 17 |
| G.M. Turner | *1964–1982* | 792 | 101 | **34346** | 311* | 49.70 | 103 | 15+3 |
| Zaheer Abbas | *1965*–1985 | 746 | 89 | **34285** | 274 | 52.18 | 107 | 11+6 |
| C. Washbrook | 1933–1964 | 906 | 107 | **34101** | 251* | 42.67 | 76 | 17+3 |
| M. Leyland | 1920–1948 | 932 | 101 | **33659** | 263 | 40.50 | 80 | 17 |
| H.T.W. Hardinge | 1902–1933 | 1021 | 103 | **33519** | 263* | 36.51 | 75 | 18 |
| R. Abel | 1881–1904 | 1007 | 73 | **33124** | 357* | 35.46 | 74 | 14 |
| C.A. Milton | 1948–1974 | 1078 | 125 | **32150** | 170 | 33.73 | 56 | 16 |
| J.D.B. Robertson | 1937–1959 | 897 | 46 | **31914** | 331* | 37.50 | 67 | 14+1 |
| J. Hardstaff jr | 1930–1955 | 812 | 94 | **31847** | 266 | 44.35 | 83 | 13+1 |
| James Langridge | 1924–1953 | 1058 | 157 | **31716** | 167 | 35.20 | 42 | 20 |
| K.F. Barrington | 1953–1968 | 831 | 136 | **31714** | 256 | 45.63 | 76 | 12+3 |
| Mushtaq Mohammad | *1956*–1985 | 843 | 104 | **31091** | 303* | 42.07 | 72 | 12+3 |
| C.B. Fry | 1892–*1921* | 658 | 43 | **30886** | 258* | 50.22 | 94 | 12 |
| C.H. Lloyd | *1963*–1985 | 722 | 95 | **30885** | 242* | 49.25 | 78 | 10+4 |
| D. Brookes | 1934–1959 | 925 | 70 | **30874** | 257 | 36.10 | 71 | 17 |
| P. Holmes | 1913–1935 | 810 | 84 | **30574** | 315* | 42.11 | 67 | 14+1 |
| R.T. Simpson | *1944*–1963 | 852 | 55 | **30546** | 259 | 38.32 | 64 | 13+1 |
| G.L. Berry | 1924–1951 | 1056 | 57 | **30225** | 232 | 30.25 | 45 | 18 |
| K.G. Suttle | 1949–1971 | 1064 | 92 | **30225** | 204* | 31.09 | 49 | 17 |

## 10,000 RUNS

| | Career | I | NO | Runs | HS | Avge | 100 | 1000 |
|---|---|---|---|---|---|---|---|---|
| Abberley, R.N. | 1964–1979 | 439 | 27 | **10082** | 117* | 24.47 | 3 | 3 |
| Abel, R. | 1881–1904 | 1007 | 73 | **33124** | 357* | 35.46 | 74 | 14 |
| Ackerman, H.M. | *1963–1981* | 409 | 33 | **12219** | 208 | 32.49 | 20 | 3 |
| Agha Zahid | *1970–1984* | 262 | 17 | **10220** | 183* | 41.71 | 24 | 0+2 |
| Alderman, A.E. | 1928–1948 | 529 | 51 | **12376** | 175 | 25.89 | 12 | 6 |
| Allen, B.O. | 1932–1951 | 512 | 20 | **14195** | 220 | 28.85 | 14 | 6 |
| Alley, W.E. | *1945–1968* | 682 | 67 | **19612** | 221* | 31.88 | 31 | 10+1 |

| | Career | I | NO | Runs | HS | Avge | 100 | 1000 |
|---|---|---|---|---|---|---|---|---|
| Amarnath, L. | 1929–1963 | 281 | 33 | 10323 | 262 | 41.62 | 31 | 0+1 |
| Amarnath, M. | 1966–1984 | 316 | 53 | 11286 | 207 | 42.91 | 23 | 0+2 |
| Ames, L.E.G. | 1926–1951 | 951 | 95 | 37248 | 295 | 43.51 | 102 | 17 |
| Amiss, D.L. | 1960–1985 | 1048 | 117 | 40673 | 262* | 43.68 | 96 | 21+1 |
| Armstrong, N.F. | 1919–1939 | 637 | 61 | 19002 | 186 | 32.98 | 36 | 13 |
| Armstrong, W.W. | 1898–1921 | 406 | 61 | 16158 | 303* | 46.83 | 45 | 4+2 |
| Arnold, E.G. | 1899–1913 | 592 | 62 | 15853 | 215 | 29.91 | 24 | 10 |
| Arnold, J. | 1929–1950 | 710 | 45 | 21831 | 227 | 32.82 | 37 | 14 |
| Ashdown, W.H. | 1914–1947 | 812 | 77 | 22589 | 332 | 30.73 | 39 | 11 |
| Asif Iqbal | 1959–1982 | 703 | 76 | 23375 | 196 | 37.28 | 45 | 7+2 |
| Astill, W.E. | 1906–1939 | 1153 | 145 | 22731 | 164* | 22.55 | 15 | 11 |
| Athey, C.W.J. | 1976–1985 | 358 | 32 | 10057 | 170 | 30.84 | 20 | 4 |
| Atkinson, G. | 1954–1969 | 608 | 41 | 17654 | 190 | 31.13 | 27 | 9 |
| Avery, A.V. | 1935–1954 | 455 | 35 | 14137 | 224 | 33.65 | 25 | 7 |
| Baig, A.A. | 1954–1975 | 391 | 29 | 12367 | 224* | 34.16 | 21 | 3 |
| Bailey, T.E. | 1945–1967 | 1072 | 215 | 28642 | 205 | 33.42 | 28 | 17 |
| Bairstow, D.L. | 1970–1985 | 543 | 107 | 11466 | 145 | 26.29 | 7 | 3 |
| Bakewell, A.H. | 1928–1936 | 453 | 24 | 14570 | 257 | 33.96 | 31 | 8 |
| Balderstone, J.C. | 1961–1985 | 596 | 60 | 18624 | 181* | 34.74 | 31 | 11 |
| Barber, R.W. | 1954–1969 | 651 | 52 | 17631 | 185 | 29.43 | 17 | 7+1 |
| Barber, W. | 1926–1947 | 526 | 49 | 16402 | 255 | 34.38 | 29 | 8 |
| Bardsley, W. | 1903–1926 | 376 | 35 | 17025 | 264 | 49.92 | 53 | 4+1 |
| Barker, G. | 1954–1971 | 809 | 46 | 22288 | 181* | 29.21 | 30 | 15 |
| Barling, H.T. | 1927–1948 | 609 | 54 | 19209 | 269 | 34.61 | 34 | 9 |
| Barlow, E.J. | 1959–1982 | 493 | 28 | 18212 | 217 | 39.16 | 43 | 2+1 |
| Barlow, G.D. | 1969–1985 | 398 | 58 | 12193 | 177 | 35.86 | 25 | 7 |
| Barlow, R.G. | 1871–1891 | 608 | 64 | 11217 | 117 | 20.61 | 4 | 1 |
| Barnes, W. | 1875–1894 | 725 | 60 | 15425 | 160 | 23.19 | 21 | 5 |
| Barnett, C.J. | 1927–1953 | 821 | 45 | 25389 | 259 | 32.71 | 48 | 12+1 |
| Barrick, D.W. | 1949–1960 | 490 | 62 | 13970 | 211 | 32.64 | 20 | 7 |
| Barrington, K.F. | 1953–1968 | 831 | 136 | 31714 | 256 | 45.63 | 76 | 12+3 |
| Bartlett, H.T. | 1933–1951 | 350 | 34 | 10098 | 183 | 31.95 | 16 | 4 |
| Bates, L.T.A. | 1913–1935 | 749 | 53 | 19380 | 211 | 27.84 | 21 | 12 |
| Bates, W. | 1877–1887 | 495 | 20 | 10249 | 144* | 21.57 | 10 | 5 |
| Bates, W.E. | 1907–1931 | 688 | 31 | 16050 | 200* | 24.42 | 13 | 7 |
| Bear, M.J. | 1954–1968 | 562 | 44 | 12564 | 137 | 24.25 | 9 | 4 |
| Bedser, E.A. | 1939–1962 | 692 | 79 | 14716 | 163 | 24.00 | 10 | 6 |
| Benaud, R. | 1948–1967 | 365 | 44 | 11719 | 187 | 36.50 | 23 | — |
| Bennett, D. | 1950–1968 | 612 | 125 | 10656 | 117* | 21.88 | 4 | 2 |
| Berry, G.L. | 1924–1951 | 1056 | 57 | 30225 | 232 | 30.25 | 45 | 18 |
| Birkenshaw, J. | 1958–1981 | 665 | 123 | 12780 | 131 | 23.57 | 4 | — |
| Board, J.H. | 1891–1914 | 906 | 97 | 15674 | 214 | 19.37 | 9 | 6 |
| Bolus, J.B. | 1956–1975 | 833 | 81 | 25598 | 202* | 34.03 | 39 | 14 |
| Bond, J.D. | 1955–1974 | 548 | 80 | 12125 | 157 | 25.90 | 14 | 2 |
| Booth, B.C. | 1954–1968 | 283 | 35 | 11265 | 214* | 45.42 | 26 | 2+2 |
| Booth, B.J. | 1956–1973 | 600 | 52 | 15298 | 183* | 27.91 | 18 | 8 |
| Booth, R. | 1951–1970 | 671 | 134 | 10138 | 113* | 18.87 | 2 | 1 |
| Borde, C.G. | 1952–1973 | 370 | 57 | 12821 | 207* | 40.96 | 30 | 1+3 |
| Border, A.R. | 1976–1985 | 267 | 41 | 11821 | 200 | 52.30 | 33 | 1+4 |
| Bosanquet, B.J.T. | 1898–1919 | 382 | 32 | 11696 | 214 | 33.41 | 21 | 6 |
| Botham, I.T. | 1974–1985 | 414 | 31 | 13437 | 228 | 35.08 | 29 | 4 |
| Bowell, H.A.W. | 1902–1927 | 810 | 43 | 18509 | 204 | 24.13 | 25 | 8 |
| Bowley, E.H. | 1912–1934 | 859 | 47 | 28378 | 283 | 34.94 | 52 | 15 |
| Bowley, F.L. | 1899–1923 | 738 | 25 | 21121 | 276 | 29.62 | 39 | 14 |
| Boycott, G. | 1962–1985 | 994 | 161 | 47434 | 261* | 56.94 | 149 | 23+3 |
| Bradman, D.G. | 1927–1948 | 338 | 43 | 28067 | 452* | 95.14 | 117 | 4+12 |
| Brann, G. | 1885–1905 | 479 | 43 | 11205 | 161 | 25.69 | 25 | 2 |
| Braund, L.C. | 1896–1920 | 752 | 57 | 17801 | 257* | 25.61 | 25 | 7 |
| Brearley, J.M. | 1961–1983 | 768 | 102 | 25185 | 312* | 37.81 | 45 | 11 |
| Briggs, J. | 1879–1900 | 826 | 55 | 14092 | 186 | 18.27 | 10 | — |
| Broadbent, R.G. | 1950–1963 | 520 | 56 | 12800 | 155 | 27.58 | 13 | 7 |
| Brockwell, W. | 1886–1903 | 539 | 47 | 13285 | 225 | 27.00 | 21 | 6 |
| Brookes, D. | 1934–1959 | 925 | 70 | 30874 | 257 | 36.10 | 71 | 17 |
| Brown, A.S. | 1953–1976 | 808 | 99 | 12851 | 116 | 18.12 | 3 | 1 |
| Brown, F.R. | 1930–1961 | 536 | 49 | 13327 | 212 | 27.36 | 22 | 4 |
| Brown, G. | 1908–1933 | 1012 | 52 | 25649 | 232* | 26.71 | 37 | 11 |
| Brown, J.T. | 1889–1904 | 634 | 47 | 17920 | 311 | 30.52 | 29 | 10 |

| | Career | I | NO | Runs | HS | Avge | 100 | 1000 |
|---|---|---|---|---|---|---|---|---|
| Brown, S.M. | 1937–1955 | 580 | 40 | 15756 | 232* | 29.17 | 22 | 9 |
| Brown, W.A. | 1932–1949 | 284 | 15 | 13840 | 265* | 51.44 | 39 | 3+2 |
| Burge, P.J.P. | 1952–1967 | 354 | 46 | 14640 | 283 | 47.53 | 38 | 2+5 |
| Burgess, M.G. | 1963–1980 | 322 | 35 | 10281 | 146 | 35.82 | 20 | — |
| Burnup, C.J. | 1895–1907 | 395 | 25 | 13614 | 200 | 36.79 | 26 | 8 |
| Buse, H.T.F. | 1929–1953 | 523 | 54 | 10623 | 132 | 22.65 | 7 | 5 |
| Buss, M.A. | 1961–1978 | 547 | 47 | 11996 | 159 | 23.99 | 11 | 4 |
| Butcher, A.R. | 1972–1985 | 465 | 43 | 14100 | 216* | 33.41 | 28 | 7 |
| Butcher, B.F. | 1954–1971 | 262 | 29 | 11628 | 209* | 49.90 | 31 | 2+3 |
| Buxton, I.R. | 1959–1973 | 579 | 86 | 11803 | 118* | 23.94 | 5 | 5 |
| Cadman, S.W.A. | 1900–1926 | 690 | 34 | 14077 | 126 | 21.45 | 8 | 2 |
| Calthorpe, Hon F.S.G. | 1911–1935 | 576 | 52 | 12596 | 209 | 24.03 | 13 | 5 |
| Carpenter, H. | 1893–1920 | 551 | 26 | 14939 | 199 | 28.45 | 25 | 7 |
| Carr, A.W. | 1910–1935 | 709 | 42 | 21051 | 206 | 31.56 | 45 | 11 |
| Carr, D.B. | 1945–1968 | 745 | 72 | 19257 | 170 | 28.61 | 24 | 11 |
| Cartwright, T.W. | 1952–1977 | 737 | 94 | 13710 | 210 | 21.32 | 7 | 3 |
| Chapman, A.P.F. | 1920–1939 | 554 | 44 | 16309 | 260 | 31.97 | 27 | 3+1 |
| Chappell, G.S. | 1966–1983 | 542 | 72 | 24535 | 247* | 52.20 | 74 | 4+8 |
| Chappell, I.M. | 1961–1979 | 448 | 41 | 19680 | 209 | 48.35 | 59 | 3+8 |
| Charlesworth, C. | 1898–1921 | 632 | 27 | 14289 | 216 | 23.61 | 15 | 5 |
| Chatterton, W. | 1882–1902 | 510 | 39 | 10914 | 169 | 23.17 | 8 | 3 |
| Chauhan, C.P.S. | 1967–1984 | 299 | 22 | 11143 | 207 | 40.22 | 21 | 0+2 |
| Clark, T.H. | 1947–1959 | 426 | 35 | 11490 | 191 | 29.38 | 12 | 6 |
| Close, D.B. | 1949–1985 | 1223 | 173 | 34968 | 198 | 33.30 | 52 | 20 |
| Coe, S. | 1896–1923 | 775 | 69 | 17438 | 252* | 24.69 | 19 | 7 |
| Compton, D.C.S. | 1936–1964 | 839 | 88 | 38942 | 300 | 51.85 | 123 | 14+3 |
| Congdon, B.E. | 1960–1978 | 416 | 40 | 13101 | 202* | 34.84 | 23 | 1+1 |
| Constable, B. | 1939–1964 | 701 | 82 | 18849 | 205* | 30.45 | 27 | 12 |
| Cook, G. | 1971–1985 | 644 | 47 | 18913 | 172 | 31.68 | 27 | 10 |
| Cooke, T.E. | 1922–1937 | 730 | 65 | 20198 | 278 | 30.37 | 32 | 10 |
| Cooper, E. | 1936–1951 | 444 | 28 | 13304 | 216* | 31.98 | 18 | 9 |
| Cowdrey, M.C. | 1950–1976 | 1130 | 134 | 42719 | 307 | 42.89 | 107 | 21+6 |
| Cowper, R.M. | 1959–1969 | 228 | 31 | 10595 | 307 | 53.78 | 26 | 1+3 |
| Cox, G. | 1931–1961 | 754 | 57 | 22949 | 234* | 33.06 | 50 | 13 |
| Cox, G.R. | 1895–1928 | 978 | 197 | 14643 | 167* | 18.74 | 2 | 1 |
| Crapp, J.F. | 1936–1956 | 754 | 80 | 23615 | 175 | 35.03 | 38 | 14 |
| Crawford, V.F.S. | 1896–1910 | 479 | 32 | 11909 | 172* | 26.64 | 16 | 5 |
| Croom, A.J.W. | 1922–1939 | 628 | 65 | 17692 | 211 | 31.42 | 24 | 12 |
| Cutmore, J.A. | 1924–1936 | 593 | 36 | 15937 | 238* | 28.61 | 15 | 11 |
| Dacre, C.C.R. | 1914–1936 | 439 | 20 | 12230 | 223 | 29.18 | 24 | 7 |
| Daniell, J. | 1898–1927 | 530 | 53 | 10468 | 174* | 21.94 | 9 | — |
| Darling, J. | 1893–1907 | 333 | 25 | 10635 | 210 | 34.52 | 19 | 4 |
| Davies, D. | 1923–1939 | 698 | 62 | 15458 | 216 | 24.30 | 16 | 7 |
| Davies, D.E. | 1924–1954 | 1033 | 79 | 26566 | 287* | 27.84 | 32 | 16 |
| Davison, B.F. | 1967–1985 | 745 | 78 | 26923 | 189 | 40.36 | 53 | 13+1 |
| Dawkes, G.O. | 1937–1961 | 736 | 105 | 11411 | 143 | 18.08 | 1 | — |
| Dawson, E.W. | 1922–1934 | 482 | 17 | 12597 | 146 | 27.09 | 14 | 6 |
| Dempster, C.S. | 1921–1947 | 306 | 36 | 12145 | 212 | 44.98 | 35 | 5 |
| Denness, M.H. | 1959–1980 | 838 | 65 | 25886 | 195 | 33.48 | 33 | 14+1 |
| Denning, P.W. | 1969–1984 | 447 | 44 | 11559 | 184 | 28.68 | 8 | 6 |
| Denton, D. | 1894–1920 | 1161 | 70 | 36440 | 221 | 33.40 | 69 | 21 |
| Dews, G. | 1946–1961 | 642 | 53 | 16803 | 145 | 28.52 | 20 | 11 |
| Dexter, E.R. | 1956–1969 | 567 | 48 | 21150 | 205 | 40.75 | 51 | 8+2 |
| Dillon, E.W. | 1900–1923 | 414 | 25 | 11006 | 143 | 28.29 | 15 | 3 |
| Dipper, A.E. | 1908–1932 | 865 | 69 | 28075 | 252* | 35.27 | 53 | 15 |
| Dodds, T.C. | 1943–1961 | 693 | 18 | 19405 | 157 | 28.74 | 17 | 13 |
| Doggart, G.H.G. | 1948–1961 | 347 | 28 | 10054 | 219* | 31.51 | 20 | 4 |
| D'Oliveira, B.L. | 1964–1980 | 566 | 88 | 18919 | 227 | 39.57 | 43 | 9 |
| Dollery, H.E. | 1933–1955 | 717 | 66 | 24413 | 212 | 37.50 | 50 | 15 |
| Douglas, J.W.H.T. | 1901–1930 | 1035 | 156 | 24531 | 210* | 27.90 | 26 | 10 |
| Ducat, A. | 1906–1931 | 669 | 59 | 23373 | 306* | 38.31 | 52 | 14 |
| Dudleston, B. | 1966–1983 | 501 | 47 | 14747 | 202 | 32.48 | 32 | 8 |
| Duleepsinhji, K.S. | 1924–1932 | 333 | 23 | 15485 | 333 | 49.95 | 50 | 7 |
| Dyson, A.H. | 1926–1948 | 697 | 37 | 17922 | 208 | 27.15 | 24 | 10 |
| Eagar, E.D.R. | 1935–1958 | 599 | 42 | 12178 | 158* | 21.86 | 10 | 6 |
| Ealham, A.G.E. | 1966–1982 | 466 | 68 | 10996 | 153 | 27.62 | 7 | 3 |

| | Career | I | NO | Runs | HS | Avge | 100 | 1000 |
|---|---|---|---|---|---|---|---|---|
| Eastman, L.C. | 1920–1939 | 693 | 50 | 13385 | 161 | 20.81 | 7 | 5 |
| Edmeades, B.E.A. | 1961–1976 | 555 | 69 | 12593 | 163 | 25.91 | 14 | 5 |
| Edrich, G.A. | 1946–1958 | 508 | 60 | 15600 | 167* | 34.82 | 26 | 8 |
| Edrich, J.H. | 1956–1978 | 979 | 104 | 39790 | 310* | 45.47 | 103 | 19+2 |
| Edrich, W.J. | 1934–1958 | 964 | 92 | 36965 | 267* | 42.39 | 86 | 15 |
| Edwards, M.J. | 1961–1974 | 452 | 26 | 11378 | 137 | 26.70 | 12 | 5 |
| Elliott, C.S. | 1932–1953 | 468 | 29 | 11965 | 215 | 27.25 | 9 | 6 |
| Emmett, G.M. | 1936–1959 | 865 | 50 | 25602 | 188 | 31.41 | 37 | 13+1 |
| Engineer, F.M. | 1958–1976 | 510 | 55 | 13436 | 192 | 29.52 | 13 | — |
| Evans, T.G. | 1939–1969 | 753 | 52 | 14882 | 144 | 21.22 | 7 | 4 |
| Fagg, A.E. | 1932–1957 | 803 | 46 | 27291 | 269* | 36.05 | 58 | 13 |
| Fane, F.L. | 1895–1924 | 721 | 44 | 18548 | 217 | 27.39 | 25 | 5 |
| Favell, L.E. | 1951–1969 | 347 | 9 | 12380 | 190 | 36.62 | 26 | 0+2 |
| Featherstone, N.G. | 1967–1981 | 528 | 54 | 13922 | 147 | 29.37 | 10 | 4 |
| Fender, P.G.H. | 1910–1936 | 783 | 69 | 19034 | 185 | 26.65 | 21 | 9 |
| Fishlock, L.B. | 1931–1952 | 699 | 54 | 25376 | 253 | 39.34 | 56 | 12+1 |
| Fletcher, D.G.W. | 1946–1961 | 519 | 41 | 14461 | 194 | 30.25 | 22 | 4 |
| Fletcher, K.W.R. | 1962–1985 | 1090 | 158 | 35701 | 228* | 38.30 | 62 | 20 |
| Flowers, W. | 1877–1896 | 696 | 54 | 12891 | 173 | 20.07 | 9 | 2 |
| Foster, H.K. | 1894–1925 | 524 | 21 | 17154 | 216 | 34.10 | 29 | 8 |
| Fredericks, R.C. | 1963–1982 | 391 | 34 | 16384 | 250 | 45.89 | 40 | 3+2 |
| Freeman, J.R. | 1905–1928 | 579 | 56 | 14602 | 286 | 27.91 | 26 | 7 |
| Fry, C.B. | 1892–1921 | 658 | 43 | 30886 | 258* | 50.22 | 94 | 12 |
| Gale, R.A. | 1955–1968 | 439 | 13 | 12505 | 200 | 29.35 | 15 | 6 |
| Gardner, F.C. | 1947–1961 | 597 | 66 | 17905 | 215* | 33.71 | 29 | 10 |
| Gatting, M.W. | 1975–1985 | 398 | 66 | 15512 | 258 | 46.72 | 36 | 7+1 |
| Gavaskar, S.M. | 1966–1984 | 515 | 57 | 23539 | 340 | 51.39 | 74 | 2+10 |
| Geary, G. | 1912–1938 | 820 | 138 | 13504 | 122 | 19.80 | 8 | — |
| Gibb, P.A. | 1934–1956 | 479 | 33 | 12520 | 204 | 28.07 | 19 | 5 |
| Gibbons, H.H.I. | 1927–1946 | 671 | 57 | 21087 | 212* | 34.34 | 44 | 12 |
| Giffen, G. | 1877–1903 | 421 | 23 | 11758 | 271 | 29.54 | 18 | 4 |
| Gilliat, R.M.C. | 1964–1978 | 441 | 46 | 11589 | 223* | 29.33 | 18 | 4 |
| Gillingham, F.H. | 1903–1928 | 352 | 24 | 10050 | 201 | 30.64 | 19 | 1 |
| Gimblett, H. | 1935–1954 | 673 | 37 | 23007 | 310 | 36.17 | 50 | 12+1 |
| Goddard, T.L. | 1952–1969 | 297 | 19 | 11279 | 222 | 40.57 | 26 | 2+1 |
| Gooch, G.A. | 1973–1985 | 526 | 45 | 21171 | 227 | 44.01 | 54 | 9+1 |
| Gomes, H.A. | 1971–1984 | 331 | 47 | 11918 | 200* | 41.96 | 30 | 1+2 |
| Gower, D.I. | 1975–1985 | 422 | 38 | 15590 | 215 | 40.59 | 34 | 6 |
| Grace, E.M. | 1862–1896 | 558 | 18 | 10120 | 192* | 18.74 | 5 | — |
| Grace, W.G. | 1865–1908 | 1493 | 105 | 54986 | 344 | 39.45 | 126 | 28 |
| Graveney, T.W. | 1948–1971 | 1223 | 159 | 47793 | 258 | 44.91 | 122 | 20+2 |
| Graves, P.J. | 1965–1980 | 502 | 51 | 12076 | 145* | 26.77 | 14 | 5 |
| Gray, J.R. | 1948–1966 | 818 | 81 | 22650 | 213* | 30.73 | 30 | 13 |
| Green, D.M. | 1959–1972 | 479 | 15 | 13381 | 233 | 28.83 | 14 | 7 |
| Greenidge, C.G. | 1970–1985 | 695 | 59 | 28461 | 273* | 44.75 | 65 | 14+1 |
| Gregory, R.J. | 1925–1947 | 646 | 78 | 19495 | 243 | 34.32 | 39 | 9 |
| Gregory, S.E. | 1889–1912 | 587 | 55 | 15192 | 201 | 28.55 | 25 | 4 |
| Greig, A.W. | 1965–1978 | 579 | 45 | 16660 | 226 | 31.19 | 26 | 7+1 |
| Grieves, K.J. | 1945–1964 | 746 | 79 | 22454 | 224 | 33.66 | 29 | 13+1 |
| Gunn, G. | 1902–1932 | 1061 | 82 | 35208 | 220 | 35.96 | 62 | 20 |
| Gunn, G.V. | 1928–1950 | 395 | 43 | 10337 | 184 | 29.36 | 11 | 5 |
| Gunn, J.R. | 1896–1932 | 845 | 105 | 24557 | 294 | 33.18 | 40 | 11 |
| Gunn, W. | 1880–1904 | 850 | 72 | 25791 | 273 | 33.15 | 48 | 12 |
| Haig, N.E. | 1912–1936 | 779 | 51 | 15220 | 131 | 20.90 | 12 | 6 |
| Haigh, S. | 1895–1913 | 747 | 119 | 11715 | 159 | 18.65 | 4 | 1 |
| Hall, I.W. | 1959–1972 | 483 | 32 | 11666 | 136* | 25.86 | 9 | 5 |
| Hall, L. | 1873–1894 | 544 | 63 | 11095 | 160 | 23.06 | 12 | 4 |
| Hallam, M.R. | 1950–1970 | 905 | 56 | 24488 | 210* | 28.84 | 32 | 13 |
| Hallows, C. | 1914–1932 | 586 | 66 | 20926 | 233* | 40.24 | 55 | 11 |
| Hamer, A. | 1938–1960 | 515 | 19 | 15465 | 227 | 31.17 | 19 | 10 |
| Hammond, W.R. | 1920–1951 | 1005 | 104 | 50551 | 336* | 56.10 | 167 | 17+5 |
| Hampshire, J.H. | 1961–1984 | 924 | 112 | 28059 | 183* | 34.55 | 43 | 15 |
| Hanif Mohammad | 1951–1975 | 371 | 45 | 17059 | 499 | 52.32 | 55 | 2+3 |
| Hanumant Singh | 1956–1979 | 331 | 50 | 12338 | 213* | 43.90 | 29 | 0+3 |
| Hardie, B.R. | 1970–1985 | 466 | 58 | 13953 | 162 | 34.19 | 18 | 10 |
| Hardinge, H.T.W. | 1902–1933 | 1021 | 103 | 33519 | 263* | 36.51 | 75 | 18 |

| | Career | I | NO | Runs | HS | Avge | 100 | 1000 |
|---|---|---|---|---|---|---|---|---|
| Hardstaff, J. sr | 1902–1926 | 620 | 73 | **17146** | 213* | 31.34 | 26 | 7+1 |
| Hardstaff, J. jr | 1930–1955 | 812 | 94 | **31847** | 266 | 44.35 | 83 | 13+1 |
| Harris, C.B. | 1928–1951 | 601 | 64 | **18823** | 239* | 35.05 | 30 | 11 |
| Harris, Lord | 1870–1911 | 397 | 23 | **10058** | 176 | 26.89 | 11 | 1 |
| Harris, M.J. | 1964–1982 | 581 | 58 | **19196** | 201* | 36.70 | 41 | 11 |
| Harvey, R.N. | 1946–1962 | 461 | 35 | **21699** | 231* | 50.93 | 67 | 3+6 |
| Hassan, B. | 1963–1985 | 549 | 54 | **14394** | 182* | 29.07 | 15 | 5 |
| Hassett, A.L. | 1932–1953 | 322 | 32 | **16890** | 232 | 58.24 | 59 | 3+2 |
| Hawke, Lord | 1881–1911 | 936 | 105 | **16749** | 166 | 20.15 | 13 | 1 |
| Hayes, E.G. | 1896–1926 | 896 | 48 | **27318** | 276 | 32.21 | 48 | 16 |
| Hayes, F.C. | 1970–1984 | 421 | 58 | **13018** | 187 | 35.86 | 23 | 6 |
| Hayward, T.W. | 1893–1914 | 1138 | 96 | **43551** | 315* | 41.79 | 104 | 20 |
| Hazare, V.S. | 1934–1966 | 367 | 45 | **18635** | 316* | 57.87 | 60 | 2+5 |
| Headley, R.G.A. | 1958–1974 | 758 | 61 | **21695** | 187 | 31.12 | 32 | 13 |
| Hearne, A. | 1884–1910 | 833 | 78 | **16346** | 194 | 21.65 | 15 | 4 |
| Hearne, J.W. | 1909–1936 | 1025 | 116 | **37252** | 285* | 40.98 | 96 | 19 |
| Hedges, B. | 1950–1967 | 744 | 41 | **17733** | 182 | 25.22 | 21 | 9 |
| Hendren, E.H. | 1907–1938 | 1300 | 166 | **57611** | 301* | 50.80 | 170 | 21+4 |
| Hill, A. | 1972–1985 | 407 | 41 | **10918** | 160* | 29.83 | 15 | 4 |
| Hill, A.J.L. | 1890–1921 | 396 | 26 | **10353** | 199 | 27.98 | 19 | — |
| Hill, C. | 1892–1924 | 416 | 21 | **17213** | 365* | 43.57 | 45 | 3+2 |
| Hill, M. | 1953–1971 | 484 | 39 | **10722** | 137* | 24.09 | 7 | 6 |
| Hill, N.W. | 1953–1968 | 518 | 32 | **14303** | 201* | 29.43 | 23 | 8 |
| Hirst, G.H. | 1891–1929 | 1217 | 152 | **36356** | 341 | 34.13 | 60 | 19 |
| Hitchcock, R.E. | 1947–1964 | 517 | 71 | **12442** | 153* | 27.89 | 13 | 5 |
| Hobbs, J.B. | 1905–1934 | 1315 | 106 | **61237** | 316* | 50.65 | 197 | 24+2 |
| Holland, F.C. | 1894–1908 | 429 | 29 | **10384** | 171 | 25.96 | 12 | 4 |
| Holmes, E.R.T. | 1924–1955 | 465 | 51 | **13598** | 236 | 32.84 | 24 | 6 |
| Holmes, P. | 1913–1935 | 810 | 84 | **30574** | 315* | 42.11 | 67 | 14+1 |
| Hopkins, J.A. | 1970–1985 | 460 | 29 | **12099** | 230 | 28.07 | 17 | 7 |
| Hopwood, J.L. | 1923–1939 | 575 | 55 | **15548** | 220 | 29.90 | 27 | 8 |
| Hornby, A.N. | 1867–1899 | 712 | 41 | **16141** | 188 | 24.05 | 16 | 2 |
| Horner, N.F. | 1950–1965 | 656 | 34 | **18533** | 203* | 29.79 | 25 | 12 |
| Horton, H. | 1946–1967 | 744 | 84 | **21669** | 160* | 32.83 | 32 | 12 |
| Horton, M.J. | 1952–1970 | 724 | 49 | **19945** | 233 | 29.54 | 23 | 11 |
| Howarth, G.P. | 1968–1985 | 575 | 42 | **17126** | 183 | 32.13 | 32 | 4 |
| Howorth, R. | 1933–1951 | 611 | 56 | **11479** | 114 | 20.68 | 4 | 4 |
| Hubble, J.C. | 1904–1929 | 528 | 64 | **10939** | 189 | 23.57 | 5 | 1 |
| Hughes, K.J. | 1975–1984 | 298 | 15 | **10810** | 213 | 38.19 | 24 | 0+2 |
| Humpage, G.W. | 1974–1985 | 409 | 51 | **13239** | 254 | 36.98 | 25 | 8 |
| Humphreys, E. | 1899–1920 | 639 | 45 | **16603** | 208 | 27.95 | 21 | 8 |
| Hutchings, K.L. | 1902–1912 | 311 | 12 | **10054** | 176 | 33.62 | 22 | 6 |
| Hutton, L. | 1934–1960 | 814 | 91 | **40140** | 364 | 55.51 | 129 | 12+5 |
| Iddon, J. | 1924–1945 | 712 | 95 | **22681** | 222 | 36.76 | 46 | 13 |
| Ikin, J.T. | 1938–1964 | 554 | 66 | **17968** | 192 | 36.81 | 27 | 10+1 |
| Illingworth, R. | 1951–1983 | 1073 | 213 | **24134** | 162 | 28.06 | 22 | 8 |
| Imran Khan | 1969–1985 | 483 | 79 | **14464** | 170 | 35.80 | 23 | 4 |
| Imtiaz Ahmed | 1944–1973 | 311 | 32 | **10383** | 300* | 37.21 | 22 | 2+1 |
| Ingleby-Mackenzie, A.C.D. | 1951–1965 | 574 | 64 | **12421** | 132* | 24.35 | 11 | 5 |
| Inman, C.C. | 1956–1971 | 422 | 42 | **13112** | 178 | 34.50 | 21 | 8 |
| Insole, D.J. | 1947–1963 | 743 | 72 | **25237** | 219* | 37.61 | 54 | 13 |
| Intikhab Alam | 1957–1982 | 725 | 78 | **14331** | 182 | 22.14 | 9 | — |
| Inverarity, R.J. | 1962–1984 | 377 | 49 | **11777** | 187 | 35.90 | 26 | — |
| Iremonger, J. | 1899–1914 | 534 | 60 | **16622** | 272 | 35.06 | 31 | 9 |
| Jackson, Hon F.S. | 1890–1907 | 505 | 35 | **15901** | 160 | 33.83 | 31 | 10 |
| Jackson, G.R. | 1919–1936 | 468 | 22 | **10291** | 140 | 23.07 | 9 | 4 |
| Jackson, V.E. | 1936–1958 | 605 | 53 | **15698** | 170 | 28.43 | 21 | 11 |
| Jaisimha, M.L. | 1954–1976 | 387 | 27 | **13515** | 259 | 37.54 | 33 | 0+2 |
| Jameson, J.A. | 1960–1976 | 611 | 43 | **18941** | 240* | 33.34 | 33 | 11 |
| Jardine, D.R. | 1920–1948 | 378 | 61 | **14848** | 214 | 46.83 | 35 | 8+1 |
| Javed Miandad | 1973–1985 | 505 | 82 | **22534** | 311 | 53.27 | 63 | 5+8 |
| Jenkins, R.O. | 1938–1958 | 573 | 120 | **10073** | 109 | 22.23 | 1 | 4 |
| Jessop, G.L. | 1894–1914 | 855 | 37 | **26698** | 286 | 32.63 | 53 | 14 |
| Jesty, T.E. | 1966–1985 | 620 | 83 | **17186** | 248 | 32.00 | 31 | 8 |
| Johnson, G.W. | 1965–1985 | 605 | 78 | **12922** | 168 | 24.51 | 11 | 3 |
| Johnson, H.L. | 1949–1966 | 606 | 65 | **14286** | 154 | 26.40 | 16 | 6 |
| Johnson, P.R. | 1900–1927 | 488 | 24 | **11931** | 164 | 25.71 | 18 | 1 |

| | Career | I | NO | Runs | HS | Avge | 100 | 1000 |
|---|---|---|---|---|---|---|---|---|
| Jones, A. | 1957–1983 | 1168 | 72 | 36049 | 204* | 32.89 | 56 | 23 |
| Jones, A.O. | 1892–1914 | 774 | 47 | 22955 | 296 | 31.57 | 34 | 9 |
| Jones, W.E. | 1937–1958 | 563 | 64 | 13535 | 212* | 27.12 | 11 | 7 |
| Jupp, H. | 1862–1881 | 692 | 48 | 15319 | 165 | 23.78 | 12 | 6 |
| Jupp, V.W.C. | 1909–1938 | 876 | 84 | 23296 | 217 | 29.41 | 30 | 13 |
| Kallicharran, A.I. | 1966–1985 | 739 | 77 | 29770 | 243* | 44.96 | 78 | 11+1 |
| Kanhai, R.B. | 1954–1981 | 669 | 82 | 28774 | 256 | 49.01 | 83 | 10+2 |
| Keeton, W.W. | 1926–1952 | 657 | 43 | 24276 | 312* | 39.53 | 54 | 12 |
| Kennedy, A.S. | 1907–1936 | 1025 | 130 | 16586 | 163* | 18.53 | 10 | 5 |
| Kenyon, D. | 1946–1967 | 1159 | 59 | 37002 | 259 | 33.63 | 74 | 19 |
| Key, K.J. | 1882–1909 | 567 | 71 | 13008 | 281 | 26.22 | 13 | 3 |
| Khalid Ibadulla | 1952–1972 | 702 | 78 | 17039 | 171 | 27.30 | 22 | 6 |
| Killick, E.H. | 1893–1913 | 770 | 53 | 18768 | 200 | 26.17 | 22 | 11 |
| Kilner, N. | 1919–1937 | 619 | 42 | 17522 | 228 | 30.36 | 25 | 12 |
| Kilner, R. | 1911–1927 | 546 | 56 | 14707 | 206* | 30.01 | 17 | 10 |
| King, J.H. | 1895–1926 | 988 | 69 | 25122 | 227* | 27.33 | 34 | 14 |
| Kinneir, S. | 1898–1914 | 525 | 47 | 15641 | 268* | 32.72 | 26 | 8 |
| Kippax, A.F. | 1918–1935 | 256 | 33 | 12762 | 315* | 57.22 | 43 | 1+2 |
| Kirsten, P.N. | 1973–1984 | 375 | 43 | 15387 | 228 | 46.34 | 41 | 5+1 |
| Kitchen, M.J. | 1960–1979 | 612 | 32 | 15230 | 189 | 26.25 | 17 | 7 |
| Knight, A.E. | 1895–1912 | 702 | 40 | 19357 | 229* | 29.24 | 34 | 10 |
| Knight, B.R. | 1955–1969 | 602 | 83 | 13336 | 165 | 25.69 | 12 | 5 |
| Knight, R.D.V. | 1967–1984 | 668 | 59 | 19518 | 165* | 32.04 | 31 | 13 |
| Knott, A.P.E. | 1964–1985 | 745 | 134 | 18105 | 156 | 29.63 | 17 | 2 |
| Lamb, A.J. | 1972–1985 | 414 | 70 | 16402 | 178 | 47.68 | 41 | 6 |
| Langdon, T. | 1900–1914 | 519 | 14 | 10723 | 156 | 21.23 | 6 | 3 |
| Langridge, James | 1924–1953 | 1058 | 157 | 31716 | 167 | 35.20 | 42 | 20 |
| Langridge, J.G. | 1928–1955 | 984 | 66 | 34380 | 250* | 37.45 | 76 | 17 |
| Larkins, W. | 1972–1985 | 494 | 27 | 16214 | 252 | 34.71 | 37 | 8 |
| Lawry, W.M. | 1955–1971 | 417 | 49 | 18734 | 266 | 50.90 | 50 | 2+6 |
| Leary, S.E. | 1951–1971 | 627 | 96 | 16517 | 158 | 31.10 | 18 | 9 |
| Lee, C. | 1952–1964 | 472 | 16 | 12129 | 150 | 26.59 | 8 | 8 |
| Lee, F.S. | 1925–1947 | 586 | 38 | 15310 | 169 | 27.93 | 23 | 8 |
| Lee, G.M. | 1910–1933 | 624 | 47 | 14858 | 200* | 25.75 | 22 | 7 |
| Lee, H.W. | 1911–1934 | 720 | 49 | 20007 | 243* | 29.81 | 37 | 13 |
| Lenham, L.J. | 1956–1970 | 539 | 50 | 12796 | 191* | 26.16 | 7 | 6 |
| Lester, E.I. | 1945–1956 | 347 | 28 | 10912 | 186 | 34.20 | 25 | 6 |
| Lester, G. | 1937–1958 | 649 | 54 | 12857 | 143 | 21.60 | 9 | 5 |
| Lewis, A.R. | 1955–1974 | 708 | 76 | 20495 | 223 | 32.42 | 30 | 11 |
| Leyland, M. | 1920–1948 | 932 | 101 | 33659 | 263 | 40.50 | 80 | 17 |
| Lightfoot, A. | 1953–1970 | 495 | 61 | 12000 | 174* | 27.64 | 12 | 4 |
| Lilley, A.F.A. | 1891–1911 | 639 | 46 | 15591 | 171 | 26.29 | 16 | 3 |
| Lilley, B. | 1921–1937 | 513 | 79 | 10496 | 124 | 24.18 | 7 | 2 |
| Livingston, L. | 1941–1964 | 384 | 45 | 15260 | 210 | 45.01 | 34 | 7+1 |
| Livingstone, D.A. | 1959–1972 | 519 | 63 | 12722 | 200 | 27.89 | 16 | 6 |
| Llewellyn, C.B. | 1894–1912 | 461 | 34 | 11425 | 216 | 26.75 | 18 | 6 |
| Lloyd, C.H. | 1963–1985 | 722 | 95 | 30885 | 242* | 49.25 | 78 | 10+4 |
| Lloyd, D. | 1965–1983 | 652 | 74 | 19269 | 214* | 33.33 | 38 | 11 |
| Lock, G.A.R. | 1946–1970 | 812 | 161 | 10342 | 89 | 15.88 | — | — |
| Lockwood, E. | 1868–1884 | 569 | 39 | 12512 | 208 | 23.60 | 8 | 4 |
| Lockwood, W. | 1886–1904 | 531 | 45 | 10673 | 165 | 21.96 | 15 | 2 |
| Lowson, F.A. | 1949–1958 | 449 | 37 | 15321 | 259* | 37.18 | 31 | 8+1 |
| Lucas, A.P. | 1874–1907 | 435 | 46 | 10263 | 145 | 26.38 | 8 | — |
| Luckhurst, B.W. | 1958–1985 | 662 | 77 | 22303 | 215 | 38.12 | 48 | 14 |
| Lumb, R.G. | 1970–1984 | 406 | 30 | 11723 | 165* | 31.17 | 22 | 5 |
| Lyon, B.H. | 1921–1948 | 448 | 20 | 10694 | 189 | 24.98 | 16 | 4 |
| Macartney, C.G. | 1905–1935 | 360 | 32 | 15019 | 345 | 45.78 | 49 | 3 |
| MacBryan, J.C.W. | 1911–1936 | 362 | 12 | 10322 | 164 | 29.49 | 18 | 4 |
| McCabe, S.J. | 1928–1941 | 262 | 20 | 11951 | 240 | 49.38 | 29 | 3 |
| McCool, C.L. | 1939–1960 | 412 | 34 | 12421 | 172 | 32.85 | 18 | 5 |
| McCorkell, N. | 1932–1951 | 696 | 67 | 16107 | 203 | 25.60 | 17 | 9 |
| McDonald, C.C. | 1947–1962 | 307 | 26 | 11375 | 229 | 40.48 | 24 | 1 |
| McEwan, K.S. | 1972–1985 | 631 | 56 | 23135 | 218 | 40.23 | 61 | 12 |
| McGahey, C.P. | 1894–1921 | 751 | 65 | 20723 | 277 | 30.20 | 31 | 10 |
| McGlew, D.J. | 1947–1966 | 299 | 34 | 12170 | 255* | 45.92 | 27 | 3+1 |
| McIntyre, A.J.W. | 1938–1963 | 567 | 79 | 11145 | 143* | 22.83 | 7 | 3 |

| | Career | I | NO | Runs | HS | Avge | 100 | 1000 |
|---|---|---|---|---|---|---|---|---|
| Mackay, K.D. | 1946–1963 | 294 | 46 | 10823 | 223 | 43.64 | 23 | 1 |
| MacLaren, A.C. | 1890–1922 | 703 | 52 | 22237 | 424 | 34.15 | 47 | 8+1 |
| McLean, R.A. | 1949–1965 | 318 | 20 | 10969 | 207 | 36.80 | 22 | 2 |
| Majid Khan | 1961–1984 | 700 | 62 | 27444 | 241 | 43.01 | 73 | 8+1 |
| Makepeace, J.W.H. | 1906–1930 | 778 | 66 | 25799 | 203 | 36.23 | 43 | 13 |
| Manjrekar, V.L. | 1949–1972 | 295 | 38 | 12832 | 283 | 49.92 | 38 | 1+1 |
| Mankad, A.V. | 1963–1982 | 326 | 71 | 12980 | 265 | 50.90 | 31 | 0+3 |
| Mankad, M.H. | 1935–1961 | 358 | 27 | 11558 | 231 | 34.91 | 26 | 1 |
| Mann, F.T. | 1908–1933 | 612 | 47 | 13237 | 194 | 23.42 | 9 | 3 |
| Marner, P.T. | 1952–1970 | 680 | 62 | 17513 | 142* | 28.33 | 18 | 12 |
| Marsh, R.W. | 1968–1983 | 396 | 41 | 11067 | 236 | 31.17 | 12 | — |
| Marshall, R.E. | 1945–1972 | 1053 | 59 | 35725 | 228* | 35.94 | 68 | 18 |
| Martin, S.H. | 1925–1949 | 457 | 31 | 11491 | 191* | 26.97 | 13 | 7 |
| Mason, J.R. | 1893–1919 | 557 | 36 | 17337 | 183 | 33.27 | 34 | 8 |
| May, P.B.H. | 1948–1963 | 618 | 77 | 27592 | 285* | 51.00 | 85 | 11+3 |
| Mead, C.P. | 1905–1936 | 1340 | 185 | 55061 | 280* | 47.67 | 153 | 27 |
| Melville, A. | 1928–1948 | 295 | 15 | 10598 | 189 | 37.85 | 25 | 3 |
| Mendis, G.D. | 1974–1985 | 363 | 33 | 11621 | 209* | 35.21 | 23 | 6 |
| Merchant, V.M. | 1929–1951 | 229 | 43 | 13248 | 359* | 71.22 | 44 | 2+1 |
| Milburn, C. | 1960–1974 | 435 | 34 | 13262 | 243 | 33.07 | 23 | 6 |
| Miller, G. | 1973–1985 | 442 | 72 | 10188 | 130 | 27.53 | 2 | — |
| Miller, K.R. | 1937–1959 | 326 | 36 | 14183 | 281* | 48.90 | 41 | 2+2 |
| Milton, C.A. | 1948–1974 | 1078 | 125 | 32150 | 170 | 33.73 | 56 | 16 |
| Mitchell, A. | 1922–1947 | 593 | 72 | 19523 | 189 | 37.47 | 44 | 10 |
| Mitchell, B. | 1925–1949 | 281 | 30 | 11395 | 195 | 45.39 | 30 | 3+1 |
| Mohsin Khan | 1970–1984 | 302 | 29 | 10875 | 246 | 39.83 | 30 | 1+1 |
| Morgan, D.C. | 1950–1969 | 882 | 146 | 18356 | 147 | 24.94 | 9 | 8 |
| Morris, A.R. | 1940–1963 | 250 | 15 | 12614 | 290 | 53.67 | 46 | 2+4 |
| Mortimore, J.B. | 1950–1975 | 989 | 122 | 15891 | 149 | 18.32 | 4 | 5 |
| Morton, A. | 1903–1926 | 623 | 56 | 10957 | 131 | 19.32 | 6 | 1 |
| Mudassar Nazar | 1971–1984 | 276 | 26 | 11965 | 241 | 47.86 | 38 | 0+4 |
| Murdoch, W.L. | 1875–1904 | 679 | 48 | 16953 | 321 | 26.86 | 19 | 3 |
| Murray, D.L. | 1960–1980 | 554 | 85 | 13289 | 166* | 28.33 | 10 | 3 |
| Murray, J.T. | 1952–1975 | 939 | 136 | 18872 | 142 | 23.50 | 16 | 6 |
| Mushtaq Ali | 1930–1963 | 370 | 16 | 12815 | 233 | 36.20 | 30 | 1 |
| Mushtaq Mohammad | 1956–1985 | 843 | 104 | 31091 | 303* | 42.07 | 72 | 12+3 |
| Nayudu, C.K. | 1916–1963 | 333 | 15 | 11249 | 200 | 35.37 | 24 | 2 |
| Neale, P.A. | 1975–1985 | 383 | 51 | 11925 | 163* | 35.91 | 19 | 7 |
| Neale, W.L. | 1923–1948 | 700 | 79 | 14752 | 145* | 23.75 | 14 | 6 |
| Newham, W. | 1881–1905 | 643 | 43 | 14657 | 210* | 24.42 | 19 | 4 |
| Newman, J.A. | 1906–1930 | 837 | 129 | 15333 | 166* | 21.65 | 10 | 6 |
| Nicholls, R.B. | 1951–1975 | 954 | 52 | 23607 | 217 | 26.17 | 18 | 15 |
| Nichols, M.S. | 1924–1939 | 756 | 85 | 17827 | 205 | 26.56 | 20 | 9 |
| Noble, M.A. | 1893–1919 | 377 | 34 | 13975 | 284 | 40.94 | 37 | 4+1 |
| Norman, M.E.J.C. | 1952–1975 | 640 | 44 | 17441 | 221* | 29.26 | 24 | 8 |
| Nourse, A.W. | 1896–1935 | 371 | 39 | 14216 | 304* | 42.81 | 38 | 3+1 |
| Nourse, A.D. | 1931–1952 | 269 | 27 | 12472 | 260* | 51.53 | 41 | 2 |
| Oakes, C. | 1935–1954 | 474 | 40 | 10893 | 160 | 25.09 | 14 | 5 |
| Oakman, A.S.M. | 1947–1968 | 912 | 79 | 21800 | 229* | 26.17 | 22 | 9 |
| O'Brien, T.C. | 1881–1914 | 452 | 30 | 11397 | 202 | 27.00 | 15 | 2 |
| O'Connor, J. | 1921–1939 | 903 | 79 | 28764 | 248 | 34.90 | 72 | 16 |
| Oldfield, N. | 1935–1954 | 521 | 51 | 17811 | 168 | 37.89 | 38 | 11 |
| Oldroyd, E. | 1910–1931 | 511 | 58 | 15929 | 194 | 35.16 | 36 | 10 |
| O'Neill, N.C. | 1955–1967 | 306 | 34 | 13859 | 284 | 50.95 | 45 | 2+6 |
| Ontong, R.C. | 1972–1985 | 455 | 54 | 11896 | 204* | 29.66 | 18 | 5 |
| Ord, J.S. | 1933–1953 | 459 | 35 | 11788 | 187* | 27.80 | 16 | 6 |
| Ormrod, J.A. | 1962–1985 | 846 | 95 | 23205 | 204* | 30.89 | 32 | 13 |
| Outschoorn, L. | 1946–1959 | 595 | 53 | 15496 | 215* | 28.59 | 25 | 9 |
| Padgett, D.E.V. | 1951–1971 | 806 | 67 | 21124 | 161* | 28.58 | 32 | 12 |
| Page, M.H. | 1964–1975 | 451 | 47 | 11538 | 162 | 28.55 | 9 | 6 |
| Palairet, L.C.H. | 1890–1909 | 488 | 19 | 15777 | 292 | 33.63 | 27 | 7 |
| Palmer, C.H. | 1938–1959 | 588 | 38 | 17458 | 201 | 31.74 | 33 | 8 |
| Parfitt, P.H. | 1956–1973 | 845 | 104 | 26924 | 200* | 36.33 | 58 | 14+1 |
| Parker, J.F. | 1932–1952 | 523 | 71 | 14272 | 255 | 31.57 | 20 | 9 |
| Parker, J.M. | 1971–1983 | 362 | 39 | 11254 | 195 | 34.84 | 21 | 2 |
| Parker, P.W.G. | 1976–1985 | 371 | 52 | 11069 | 215 | 34.69 | 25 | 6 |

| | Career | I | NO | Runs | HS | Avge | 100 | 1000 |
|---|---|---|---|---|---|---|---|---|
| Parkhouse, W.G.A. | 1948–1964 | 791 | 49 | 23508 | 201 | 31.68 | 32 | 15 |
| Parks, H.W. | 1926–1949 | 745 | 98 | 21725 | 200* | 33.57 | 42 | 14 |
| Parks, J.H. | 1924–1952 | 758 | 63 | 21369 | 197 | 30.74 | 41 | 12 |
| Parks, J.M. | 1949–1976 | 1227 | 172 | 36673 | 205* | 34.76 | 51 | 20 |
| Parsons, J.H. | 1910–1936 | 555 | 52 | 17969 | 225 | 35.72 | 38 | 10+1 |
| Pataudi, Nawab of, jr | 1957–1975 | 499 | 41 | 15425 | 203* | 33.67 | 33 | 4+3 |
| Patel, B.P. | 1969–1984 | 283 | 42 | 10528 | 216 | 43.68 | 32 | 0+4 |
| Paynter, E. | 1926–1950 | 533 | 58 | 20075 | 322 | 42.26 | 45 | 9+1 |
| Payton, W.R. | 1905–1931 | 770 | 126 | 22132 | 169 | 34.36 | 39 | 9 |
| Pearce, T.N. | 1929–1952 | 406 | 54 | 12061 | 211* | 34.26 | 22 | 6 |
| Pearson, F.A. | 1900–1926 | 811 | 38 | 18735 | 167 | 24.23 | 22 | 8 |
| Peel, R. | 1882–1899 | 693 | 66 | 12191 | 210* | 19.44 | 7 | 1 |
| Perrin, P.A. | 1896–1928 | 918 | 91 | 29709 | 343* | 35.92 | 66 | 18 |
| Phebey, A.H. | 1946–1964 | 599 | 34 | 14643 | 157 | 25.91 | 13 | 9 |
| Pilling, H. | 1962–1980 | 542 | 68 | 15279 | 149* | 32.23 | 25 | 8 |
| Place, W. | 1937–1955 | 487 | 49 | 15609 | 266* | 35.63 | 36 | 8 |
| Pollock, R.G. | 1961–1984 | 414 | 51 | 19813 | 274 | 54.58 | 60 | 1+5 |
| Ponsford, W.H. | 1920–1934 | 235 | 23 | 13819 | 437 | 65.18 | 47 | 2+2 |
| Poole, C.J. | 1948–1962 | 637 | 42 | 19364 | 222* | 32.54 | 24 | 12 |
| Prentice, F.T. | 1934–1951 | 421 | 24 | 10997 | 191 | 27.70 | 17 | 5 |
| Pressdee, J.S. | 1949–1969 | 583 | 88 | 14267 | 150* | 28.82 | 13 | 6 |
| Prideaux, R.M. | 1958–1974 | 808 | 75 | 25136 | 202* | 34.29 | 41 | 13 |
| Procter, M.J. | 1965–1983 | 663 | 57 | 21904 | 254 | 36.14 | 48 | 9 |
| Pullar, G. | 1954–1970 | 672 | 63 | 21528 | 175 | 35.34 | 41 | 9+1 |
| Quaife, W.G. | 1894–1928 | 1203 | 185 | 36012 | 255* | 35.37 | 72 | 24 |
| Radley, C.T. | 1964–1985 | 834 | 125 | 25276 | 200 | 35.65 | 44 | 16 |
| Randall, D.W. | 1972–1985 | 596 | 55 | 20599 | 209 | 38.07 | 37 | 10 |
| Ranjitsinhji, K.S. | 1893–1920 | 500 | 62 | 24692 | 285* | 56.37 | 72 | 11+1 |
| Read, J.M. | 1880–1895 | 611 | 43 | 14010 | 186* | 24.66 | 11 | 2 |
| Read, W.W. | 1873–1897 | 749 | 52 | 22349 | 338 | 32.06 | 38 | 9 |
| Redpath, I.R. | 1961–1975 | 391 | 34 | 14993 | 261 | 41.99 | 32 | 2+5 |
| Reid, J.R. | 1947–1965 | 418 | 28 | 16128 | 296 | 41.35 | 39 | 2+3 |
| Relf, A.E. | 1900–1921 | 900 | 70 | 22238 | 189* | 26.79 | 26 | 11 |
| Relf, R.R. | 1905–1933 | 529 | 18 | 14522 | 272* | 28.41 | 24 | 6 |
| Revill, A.C. | 1946–1960 | 654 | 53 | 15917 | 156* | 26.48 | 16 | 9 |
| Reynolds, B.L. | 1950–1970 | 737 | 65 | 18824 | 169 | 28.01 | 21 | 10 |
| Rhodes, W. | 1898–1930 | 1526 | 236 | 39722 | 267* | 30.79 | 58 | 20+1 |
| Rice, C.E.B. | 1969–1985 | 607 | 94 | 21122 | 246 | 41.17 | 40 | 11 |
| Richards, B.A. | 1964–1982 | 576 | 58 | 28358 | 356 | 54.74 | 80 | 9+6 |
| Richards, I.V.A. | 1971–1985 | 572 | 38 | 26841 | 322 | 50.26 | 86 | 11+3 |
| Richardson, D.W. | 1952–1967 | 660 | 65 | 16303 | 169 | 27.40 | 16 | 9 |
| Richardson, P.E. | 1949–1965 | 794 | 41 | 26055 | 185 | 34.60 | 44 | 11+1 |
| Richardson, V.Y. | 1918–1937 | 297 | 12 | 10714 | 231 | 37.59 | 27 | — |
| Robertson, J.D.B. | 1937–1959 | 897 | 46 | 31914 | 331* | 37.50 | 67 | 14+1 |
| Robins, R.W.V. | 1925–1958 | 565 | 39 | 13884 | 140 | 26.39 | 11 | 4 |
| Robson, E. | 1895–1923 | 761 | 46 | 12620 | 163* | 17.65 | 5 | 1 |
| Roebuck, P.M. | 1974–1985 | 375 | 54 | 11245 | 159 | 35.03 | 15 | 5 |
| Rogers, N.H. | 1946–1955 | 529 | 28 | 16056 | 186 | 32.04 | 28 | 9 |
| Roope, G.R.J. | 1964–1985 | 645 | 129 | 19098 | 171 | 37.01 | 26 | 8 |
| Rose, B.C. | 1969–1985 | 421 | 45 | 12392 | 205 | 32.95 | 23 | 8 |
| Rowan, E.A.B. | 1929–1953 | 258 | 17 | 11710 | 306* | 48.58 | 30 | 2 |
| Roy, Pankaj | 1946–1967 | 298 | 18 | 11868 | 202* | 42.38 | 33 | 1 |
| Russell, C.A.G. | 1908–1930 | 717 | 59 | 27354 | 273 | 41.57 | 71 | 13 |
| Russell, W.E. | 1956–1972 | 796 | 64 | 25525 | 193 | 34.87 | 41 | 13 |
| Ryder, J. | 1912–1935 | 274 | 37 | 10499 | 295 | 44.29 | 24 | 0+1 |
| Sadiq Mohammad | 1959–1985 | 682 | 40 | 24046 | 203 | 37.45 | 50 | 7+3 |
| Saeed Ahmed | 1954–1977 | 346 | 25 | 12847 | 203* | 40.02 | 34 | 1+2 |
| Sainsbury, P.J. | 1954–1976 | 948 | 197 | 20176 | 163 | 26.86 | 7 | 6 |
| Sandham, A. | 1911–1937 | 1000 | 79 | 41284 | 325 | 44.82 | 107 | 18+2 |
| Santall, F.R. | 1919–1939 | 797 | 86 | 17730 | 201* | 24.93 | 21 | 7 |
| Sardesai, D.N. | 1960–1972 | 271 | 26 | 10231 | 222 | 41.75 | 25 | 0+4 |
| Seymour, James | 1900–1926 | 911 | 62 | 27238 | 218* | 32.08 | 53 | 16 |
| Shafiq Ahmed | 1967–1984 | 320 | 41 | 14379 | 217* | 51.53 | 43 | 0+5 |
| Sharp, J. | 1899–1925 | 805 | 75 | 22715 | 211 | 31.11 | 38 | 10 |
| Sharpe, P.J. | 1956–1976 | 811 | 78 | 22530 | 228 | 30.73 | 29 | 12 |
| Shepherd, D.R. | 1965–1979 | 476 | 40 | 10672 | 153 | 24.47 | 12 | 2 |

| | Career | I | NO | Runs | HS | Avge | 100 | 1000 |
|---|---|---|---|---|---|---|---|---|
| Shepherd, J.N. | 1964–1985 | 611 | 106 | **13353** | 170 | 26.44 | 10 | 2 |
| Shepherd, T.F. | 1919–1932 | 531 | 61 | **18715** | 277* | 39.81 | 42 | 12 |
| Sheppard, D.S. | 1947–1962 | 395 | 31 | **15838** | 239* | 43.51 | 45 | 6+1 |
| Shipman, A.W. | 1920–1936 | 661 | 72 | **13682** | 226 | 23.22 | 15 | 8 |
| Shrewsbury, A. | 1875–1902 | 813 | 90 | **26505** | 267 | 36.65 | 59 | 13 |
| Shuter, J. | 1874–1909 | 503 | 23 | **10206** | 135 | 21.26 | 8 | — |
| Simpson, R.B. | 1952–1977 | 436 | 62 | **21029** | 359 | 56.22 | 60 | 2+8 |
| Simpson, R.T. | 1944–1963 | 852 | 55 | **30546** | 259 | 38.32 | 64 | 13+1 |
| Sinfield, R.A. | 1921–1939 | 696 | 86 | **15674** | 209* | 25.69 | 16 | 10 |
| Smedley, M.J. | 1964–1979 | 604 | 76 | **16482** | 149 | 31.21 | 28 | 9 |
| Smith, A.C. | 1958–1974 | 612 | 85 | **11027** | 145 | 20.92 | 3 | 1 |
| Smith, D. | 1927–1952 | 753 | 63 | **21843** | 225 | 31.65 | 32 | 12 |
| Smith, D.V. | 1946–1962 | 625 | 66 | **16960** | 206* | 30.33 | 19 | 8 |
| Smith, E.J. | 1904–1930 | 814 | 55 | **16997** | 177 | 22.39 | 20 | 6 |
| Smith, H. | 1912–1935 | 656 | 56 | **13413** | 149 | 22.35 | 10 | 5 |
| Smith, M.J. | 1959–1980 | 704 | 78 | **19814** | 181 | 31.65 | 40 | 11 |
| Smith, M.J.K. | 1951–1975 | 1091 | 139 | **39832** | 204 | 41.84 | 69 | 19+1 |
| Smith, R. | 1934–1956 | 682 | 88 | **12042** | 147 | 20.27 | 8 | 4 |
| Smith, S.G. | 1899–1925 | 379 | 30 | **10920** | 256 | 31.28 | 14 | 4 |
| Smith, T.P.B. | 1929–1952 | 690 | 125 | **10161** | 163 | 17.98 | 8 | 1 |
| Sobers, G.St A. | 1952–1974 | 609 | 93 | **28315** | 365* | 54.87 | 86 | 9+6 |
| Spooner, R.H. | 1899–1923 | 393 | 16 | **13681** | 247 | 36.28 | 31 | 6 |
| Spooner, R.T. | 1948–1959 | 580 | 72 | **13851** | 168* | 27.26 | 12 | 6 |
| Sprot, E.M. | 1898–1914 | 458 | 28 | **12328** | 147 | 28.66 | 13 | 4 |
| Squires, H.S. | 1928–1949 | 658 | 44 | **19186** | 236 | 31.24 | 37 | 11 |
| Stackpole, K.R. | 1959–1973 | 279 | 22 | **10100** | 207 | 39.29 | 22 | 1+3 |
| Staples, A. | 1924–1938 | 512 | 59 | **12762** | 153* | 28.17 | 12 | 7 |
| Steele, D.S. | 1963–1984 | 812 | 124 | **22346** | 140* | 32.47 | 30 | 10 |
| Steele, J.F. | 1970–1985 | 588 | 80 | **14772** | 195 | 29.07 | 21 | 6 |
| Stephenson, H.W. | 1948–1964 | 747 | 91 | **13195** | 147* | 20.11 | 7 | 5 |
| Stevens, G.T.S. | 1919–1933 | 387 | 36 | **10376** | 182 | 29.56 | 12 | 2 |
| Stewart, M.J. | 1954–1972 | 898 | 93 | **26492** | 227* | 32.90 | 49 | 15 |
| Stewart, W.J. | 1955–1971 | 491 | 56 | **14826** | 182* | 34.08 | 25 | 6 |
| Stocks, F.W. | 1946–1957 | 430 | 45 | **11397** | 171 | 29.60 | 13 | 5 |
| Stoddart, A.E. | 1885–1900 | 537 | 16 | **16738** | 221 | 32.12 | 26 | 6 |
| Stone, J. | 1900–1923 | 524 | 63 | **10341** | 174 | 22.43 | 6 | 3 |
| Storer, H. | 1920–1936 | 517 | 29 | **13515** | 232 | 27.69 | 18 | 6 |
| Storer, W. | 1887–1905 | 490 | 41 | **12966** | 216* | 28.87 | 17 | 7 |
| Storey, S.J. | 1960–1978 | 492 | 62 | **10776** | 164 | 25.06 | 12 | 5 |
| Stovold, A.W. | 1973–1985 | 487 | 26 | **13986** | 212* | 30.33 | 17 | 6 |
| Subba Row, R. | 1951–1967 | 407 | 65 | **14182** | 300 | 41.46 | 30 | 6 |
| Sugg, F.H. | 1883–1899 | 515 | 30 | **11859** | 220 | 24.45 | 15 | 5 |
| Sutcliffe, B. | 1941–1965 | 405 | 39 | **17283** | 385 | 47.22 | 44 | 2+2 |
| Sutcliffe, H. | 1919–1945 | 1088 | 123 | **50138** | 313 | 51.95 | 149 | 21+3 |
| Suttle, K.G. | 1949–1971 | 1064 | 92 | **30225** | 204* | 31.09 | 49 | 17 |
| Tarrant, F.A. | 1898–1936 | 539 | 48 | **17857** | 250 | 36.36 | 33 | 9 |
| Tate, M.W. | 1912–1937 | 970 | 102 | **21717** | 203 | 25.01 | 23 | 11+1 |
| Tavaré, C.J. | 1974–1985 | 432 | 46 | **14685** | 168* | 38.04 | 28 | 9 |
| Taylor, B. | 1949–1973 | 949 | 73 | **19091** | 135 | 21.79 | 9 | 8 |
| Taylor, H.W. | 1909–1935 | 340 | 27 | **13105** | 250* | 41.86 | 30 | 3 |
| Taylor, K. | 1953–1968 | 524 | 36 | **13053** | 203* | 26.74 | 16 | 6 |
| Taylor, R.W. | 1960–1984 | 878 | 167 | **12040** | 100 | 16.93 | 1 | — |
| Tennyson, Lord | 1913–1937 | 759 | 38 | **16828** | 217 | 23.33 | 19 | 7 |
| Thompson, G.J. | 1897–1922 | 606 | 59 | **12018** | 131* | 21.97 | 9 | 3 |
| Timms, J.E. | 1925–1949 | 847 | 30 | **20457** | 213 | 25.03 | 31 | 11 |
| Titmus, F.J. | 1949–1982 | 1142 | 208 | **21588** | 137* | 23.11 | 6 | 8 |
| Todd, L.J. | 1927–1950 | 727 | 94 | **20087** | 174 | 31.73 | 38 | 10 |
| Tolchard, R.W. | 1965–1983 | 680 | 189 | **15288** | 126* | 31.13 | 12 | — |
| Tompkin, M. | 1938–1956 | 655 | 29 | **19927** | 186 | 31.83 | 31 | 10 |
| Townsend, A. | 1948–1960 | 553 | 70 | **12054** | 154 | 24.95 | 6 | 5 |
| Townsend, L.F. | 1922–1939 | 786 | 76 | **19555** | 233 | 27.54 | 22 | 9 |
| Tremlett, M.F. | 1947–1960 | 681 | 49 | **16038** | 185 | 25.37 | 16 | 10 |
| Tribe, G.E. | 1945–1959 | 454 | 82 | **10177** | 136* | 27.35 | 7 | 7 |
| Trimble, S.C. | 1959–1975 | 262 | 16 | **10282** | 252* | 41.79 | 26 | 0+3 |
| Trott, A.E. | 1892–1911 | 602 | 53 | **10696** | 164 | 19.48 | 8 | 2 |
| Trumper, V.T. | 1894–1913 | 401 | 21 | **16939** | 300* | 44.57 | 42 | 4+1 |

| | Career | I | NO | Runs | HS | Avge | 100 | 1000 |
|---|---|---|---|---|---|---|---|---|
| Tunnicliffe, J. | 1891–1907 | 811 | 59 | **20310** | 243 | 27.00 | 23 | 12 |
| Turnbull, M.J.L. | 1924–1939 | 626 | 37 | **17543** | 233 | 29.78 | 29 | 10 |
| Turner, D.R. | 1966–1985 | 590 | 55 | **15637** | 181* | 29.22 | 24 | 7 |
| Turner, G.M. | *1964–1982* | 792 | 101 | **34346** | 311* | 49.71 | 103 | 15+3 |
| Tyldesley, G.E. | 1909–1936 | 961 | 106 | **38874** | 256* | 45.46 | 102 | 18+1 |
| Tyldesley, J.T. | 1895–1923 | 994 | 62 | **37897** | 295* | 40.66 | 86 | 19 |
| Ulyett, G. | 1873–1893 | 928 | 40 | **20823** | 199* | 23.44 | 18 | 9 |
| Umrigar, P.R. | *1944–1967* | 350 | 41 | **16154** | 252* | 52.27 | 49 | 2+2 |
| Valentine, B.H. | 1927–1950 | 645 | 38 | **18306** | 242 | 30.15 | 35 | 9 |
| Vengsarkar, D.B. | *1975–1984* | 263 | 29 | **11192** | 210 | 47.82 | 31 | 0+4 |
| Vine, J. | 1896–1922 | 920 | 79 | **25171** | 202 | 29.92 | 34 | 14 |
| Virgin, R.T. | 1957–1977 | 773 | 39 | **21930** | 179* | 29.87 | 37 | 12 |
| Viswanath, G.R. | *1967–1984* | 464 | 43 | **17230** | 247 | 40.92 | 45 | 0+5 |
| Wadekar, A.L. | *1958–1974* | 360 | 33 | **15380** | 323 | 47.03 | 36 | 1+3 |
| Wainwright, E. | 1888–1902 | 607 | 31 | **12513** | 228 | 21.72 | 19 | 3 |
| Walcott, C.L. | *1941–1963* | 238 | 29 | **11820** | 314* | 56.55 | 40 | 2+2 |
| Walker, I.D. | 1862–1884 | 508 | 43 | **11400** | 179 | 24.51 | 7 | — |
| Walker, P.M. | 1956–1972 | 788 | 110 | **17650** | 152* | 26.03 | 13 | 11 |
| Walker, W. | 1913–1937 | 624 | 60 | **18259** | 165* | 32.37 | 31 | 10 |
| Walters, C.F. | 1923–1935 | 427 | 32 | **12145** | 226 | 30.74 | 21 | 5 |
| Walters, K.D. | *1962–1980* | 426 | 57 | **16180** | 253 | 43.84 | 45 | 0+3 |
| Ward, A. | 1886–1904 | 642 | 51 | **17809** | 219 | 30.13 | 29 | 9 |
| Warner, P.F. | 1894–1929 | 874 | 76 | **29024** | 244 | 36.37 | 60 | 14 |
| Washbrook, C. | 1933–1964 | 906 | 107 | **34101** | 251* | 42.67 | 76 | 17+3 |
| Wasim Raja | *1967–1984* | 372 | 53 | **11222** | 165 | 35.17 | 16 | 0+1 |
| Watkins, A.J. | 1939–1963 | 753 | 87 | **20362** | 170* | 30.57 | 32 | 13 |
| Watson, F.B. | 1920–1937 | 688 | 50 | **23596** | 300* | 36.98 | 50 | 12 |
| Watson, W. | 1939–1964 | 753 | 109 | **25670** | 257 | 39.86 | 55 | 14 |
| Watts, P.J. | 1959–1980 | 607 | 90 | **14449** | 145 | 27.94 | 10 | 7 |
| Webbe, A.J. | 1875–1900 | 641 | 58 | **14466** | 243* | 24.81 | 14 | 1 |
| Weekes, E.de C. | *1944–1964* | 241 | 24 | **12010** | 304* | 55.34 | 36 | 2+1 |
| Wellard, A.W. | 1927–1950 | 679 | 45 | **12515** | 112 | 19.73 | 2 | 4 |
| Wensley, A.F. | 1922–*1939* | 594 | 64 | **10849** | 154 | 20.46 | 9 | 3 |
| Wessels, K.C. | *1973–1984* | 289 | 23 | **13133** | 254 | 49.37 | 33 | 2+3 |
| Wharton, A. | 1946–1963 | 745 | 69 | **21796** | 199 | 32.24 | 31 | 11 |
| White, J.C. | 1909–1937 | 765 | 102 | **12202** | 192 | 18.40 | 6 | 2 |
| White, R.A. | 1958–1980 | 642 | 105 | **12452** | 116* | 23.18 | 5 | 1 |
| Whitehead, H. | 1898–1922 | 680 | 25 | **15112** | 174 | 23.07 | 14 | 4 |
| Whysall, W.W. | 1910–1930 | 601 | 44 | **21592** | 248 | 38.76 | 51 | 10 |
| Wight, P.B. | *1950*–1965 | 590 | 53 | **17773** | 222* | 33.09 | 28 | 10 |
| Wilkins, C.P. | *1962–1982* | 357 | 21 | **10966** | 156 | 32.63 | 18 | 3 |
| Willey, P. | 1966–1985 | 699 | 99 | **18371** | 227 | 30.61 | 34 | 6 |
| Wilson, A.E. | 1932–1955 | 502 | 77 | **10744** | 188 | 25.28 | 7 | 6 |
| Wilson, J.V. | 1946–1963 | 770 | 79 | **21650** | 230 | 31.33 | 30 | 14 |
| Wilson, R.C. | 1952–1967 | 647 | 39 | **19515** | 159* | 32.09 | 30 | 13 |
| Wolton, A.V. | 1947–1960 | 478 | 61 | **12930** | 165 | 31.00 | 12 | 7 |
| Wood, B. | 1964–1983 | 591 | 75 | **17453** | 198 | 33.82 | 30 | 8 |
| Wood, C.J.B. | 1896–1923 | 823 | 54 | **23879** | 225 | 31.05 | 37 | 13 |
| Woodfull, W.M. | *1921–1934* | 245 | 39 | **13388** | 284 | 64.99 | 49 | 3 |
| Woods, S.M.J. | 1886–1910 | 690 | 35 | **15345** | 215 | 23.42 | 19 | 4 |
| Wooller, W. | 1935–1962 | 679 | 77 | **13593** | 128 | 22.57 | 5 | 5 |
| Woolley, C.N. | 1909–1931 | 658 | 34 | **15395** | 204* | 24.67 | 13 | 7 |
| Woolley, F.E. | 1906–1938 | 1530 | 84 | **58959** | 305* | 40.77 | 145 | 28 |
| Woolmer, R.A. | 1968–1984 | 545 | 75 | **15771** | 203 | 33.55 | 34 | 5 |
| Worrell, F.M.M. | *1941–1964* | 326 | 49 | **15025** | 308* | 54.24 | 39 | 2+2 |
| Worthington, T.S. | 1924–1947 | 720 | 59 | **19221** | 238* | 29.07 | 31 | 10 |
| Wrathall, H. | 1894–1907 | 509 | 20 | **11023** | 176 | 22.54 | 9 | 4 |
| Wright, J.G. | *1975–1985* | 434 | 30 | **16641** | 190 | 41.91 | 40 | 6+1 |
| Wright, L.G. | 1883–1909 | 593 | 12 | **15166** | 195 | 26.10 | 20 | 6 |
| Wyatt, R.E.S. | 1923–1957 | 1141 | 157 | **39405** | 232 | 40.04 | 85 | 17+1 |
| Yallop, G.N. | *1972–1984* | 261 | 27 | **10791** | 268 | 46.11 | 29 | 0+2 |
| Yardley, N.W.D. | 1935–1955 | 658 | 75 | **18173** | 183* | 31.17 | 27 | 8 |
| Young, A. | 1911–1933 | 537 | 22 | **13159** | 198 | 25.55 | 11 | 5 |
| Young, D.M. | 1946–1964 | 842 | 42 | **24555** | 198 | 30.69 | 40 | 13 |
| Younis Ahmed | *1961*–1985 | 723 | 112 | **24543** | 221* | 40.16 | 43 | 13 |
| Zaheer Abbas | *1965*–1985 | 746 | 89 | **34285** | 274 | 52.18 | 107 | 11+6 |

*G.A.R. Lock and R.W. Taylor are the only players to score 10,000 runs in first-class cricket before making a hundred. Lock's average of 15.88 is the lowest by anyone scoring 10,000 runs.*

**1000 RUNS IN A SEASON MOST TIMES**
*Including seasons overseas*

| | |
|---|---|
| 28 | W.G. Grace, F.E. Woolley |
| 27 | M.C. Cowdrey, C.P. Mead |
| 26 | G. Boycott, J.B. Hobbs |
| 25 | E.H. Hendren |
| 24 | W.G. Quaife, H. Sutcliffe |
| 23 | A. Jones |
| 22 | D.L. Amiss, T.W. Graveney, W.R. Hammond |
| 21 | D. Denton, J.H. Edrich, W. Rhodes |
| 20 | D.B. Close, K.W.R. Fletcher, G. Gunn, T.W. Hayward, James Langridge, J.M. Parks, A. Sandham, M.J.K. Smith, C. Washbrook |

**MOST HUNDREDS**

| 100 | | Innings | 100 | | Innings |
|---|---|---|---|---|---|
| 197 | J.B. Hobbs | 1315 | 86 | J.T. Tyldesley | 994 |
| 170 | E.H. Hendren | 1300 | 85 | P.B.H. May | 618 |
| 167 | W.R. Hammond | 1005 | 85 | R.E.S. Wyatt | 1142 |
| 153 | C.P. Mead | 1340 | 83 | R.B. Kanhai | 669 |
| 149 | G. Boycott | 994 | 83 | J. Hardstaff, jr | 812 |
| 149 | H. Sutcliffe | 1088 | 80 | B.A. Richards | 576 |
| 145 | F.E. Woolley | 1532 | 80 | M. Leyland | 932 |
| 129 | L. Hutton | 814 | 78 | C.H. Lloyd | 722 |
| 126 | W.G. Grace | 1493 | 78 | A.I. Kallicharran | 739 |
| 123 | D.C.S. Compton | 839 | 76 | K.F. Barrington | 831 |
| 122 | T.W. Graveney | 1223 | 76 | C. Washbrook | 906 |
| 117 | D.G. Bradman | 338 | 76 | J.G. Langridge | 984 |
| 107 | Zaheer Abbas | 746 | 75 | H.T.W. Hardinge | 1021 |
| 107 | A. Sandham | 1000 | 74 | S.M. Gavaskar | 515 |
| 107 | M.C. Cowdrey | 1130 | 74 | G.S. Chappell | 542 |
| 104 | T.W. Hayward | 1138 | 74 | R. Abel | 1007 |
| 103 | G.M. Turner | 792 | 74 | D. Kenyon | 1159 |
| 103 | J.H. Edrich | 979 | 73 | Majid Khan | 700 |
| 102 | L.E.G. Ames | 951 | 72 | K.S. Ranjitsinhji | 500 |
| 102 | G.E. Tyldesley | 961 | 72 | Mushtaq Mohammad | 843 |
| 96 | J.W. Hearne | 1025 | 72 | J. O'Connor | 906 |
| 96 | D.L. Amiss | 1048 | 72 | W.G. Quaife | 1203 |
| 94 | C.B. Fry | 658 | 71 | C.A.G. Russell | 719 |
| 86 | I.V.A. Richards | 572 | 71 | D. Brookes | 925 |
| 86 | G.St A. Sobers | 609 | 69 | M.J.K. Smith | 1091 |
| 86 | W.J. Edrich | 964 | 69 | D. Denton | 1163 |
| 68 | R.E. Marshall | 1053 | 55 | Hanif Mohammad | 371 |
| 67 | R.N. Harvey | 461 | 55 | C. Hallows | 586 |
| 67 | P. Holmes | 810 | 55 | W. Watson | 753 |
| 67 | J.D.B. Robertson | 897 | 54 | G.A. Gooch | 526 |
| 66 | P.A. Perrin | 918 | 54 | W.W. Keeton | 657 |
| 65 | C.G. Greenidge | 695 | 54 | D.J. Insole | 743 |
| 64 | R.T. Simpson | 852 | 53 | W. Bardsley | 376 |
| 63 | Javed Miandad | 505 | 53 | B.F. Davison | 745 |
| 62 | G. Gunn | 1061 | 53 | G.L. Jessop | 855 |
| 62 | K.W.R. Fletcher | 1090 | 53 | A.E. Dipper | 865 |
| 61 | K.S. McEwan | 631 | 53 | James Seymour | 911 |
| 60 | V.S. Hazare | 367 | 52 | A. Ducat | 669 |
| 60 | R.G. Pollock | 414 | 52 | E.H. Bowley | 853 |
| 60 | R.B. Simpson | 436 | 52 | D.B. Close | 1223 |
| 60 | P.F. Warner | 874 | 51 | E.R. Dexter | 567 |
| 60 | G.H. Hirst | 1214 | 51 | W.W. Whysall | 601 |
| 59 | A.L. Hassett | 322 | 51 | J.M. Parks | 1227 |
| 59 | I.M. Chappell | 448 | 50 | K.S. Duleepsinhji | 333 |
| 59 | A. Shrewsbury | 811 | 50 | W.M. Lawry | 417 |
| 58 | A.E. Fagg | 803 | 50 | H. Gimblett | 673 |
| 58 | P.H. Parfitt | 845 | 50 | Sadiq Mohammad | 682 |

| *100* | | *Innings* | *100* | | *Innings* |
|---|---|---|---|---|---|
| **58** | W. Rhodes | 1526 | **50** | F.B. Watson | 688 |
| **56** | L.B. Fishlock | 699 | **50** | H.E. Dollery | 717 |
| **56** | C.A. Milton | 1078 | **50** | G. Cox | 752 |
| **56** | A. Jones | 1168 | | | |

# INDIVIDUAL RECORDS – BOWLING

## TEN WICKETS IN AN INNINGS

| O | M | R | | | | |
|---|---|---|---|---|---|---|
| | | | E. Hinkly | Kent v England | Lord's | 1848 |
| | | | J. Wisden | North v South | Lord's | 1850 |
| | | | *All bowled* | | | |
| 43 | 17 | 74 | V.E. Walker | England v Surrey | Oval | 1859 |
| 44.2 | 5 | 104 | V.E. Walker | Middlesex v Lancashire | Manchester | 1865 |
| 31.3 | 9 | 54 | G. Wootton | All England XI v Yorkshire | Sheffield | 1865 |
| 36.2 | 19 | 46 | W. Hickton | Lancashire v Hampshire | Manchester | 1870 |
| 24.1 | 11 | 38 | S.E. Butler | Oxford University v Cambridge U. | Lord's | 1871 |
| 60.2 | 22 | 129 | Jas. Lillywhite | South v North | Canterbury | 1872 |
| 36.2 | 8 | 73 | A. Shaw | MCC v North | Lord's | 1874 |
| 29 | 11 | 43 | E. Barratt | Players v Australians | Oval | 1878 |
| 26 | 10 | 66 | G. Giffen | Australian XI v Rest | Sydney | 1883–84 |
| 36.2 | 17 | 49 | W.G. Grace | MCC v Oxford University | Oxford | 1886 |
| 52.3 | 25 | 59 | G. Burton | Middlesex v Surrey | Oval | 1888 |
| 21.3 | 10 | 28 | A.E. Moss | Canterbury v Wellington | Christchurch | 1889–90 |
| | | | *On debut in first-class cricket* | | | |
| 31 | 6 | 69 | S.M.J. Woods | Cambridge U. v C.I. Thornton's XI | Cambridge | 1890 |
| 15.3 | 3 | 45 | T. Richardson | Surrey v Essex | Oval | 1894 |
| 27 | 11 | 32 | H. Pickett | Essex v Leicestershire | Leyton | 1895 |
| 34.3 | 15 | 49 | E.J. Tyler | Somerset v Surrey | Taunton | 1895 |
| 23.2 | 14 | 28 | W.P. Howell | Australians v Surrey | Oval | 1899 |
| 25.2 | 10 | 48 | C.H.G. Bland | Sussex v Kent | Tonbridge | 1899 |
| 28.5 | 7 | 55 | J. Briggs | Lancashire v Worcestershire | Manchester | 1900 |
| 14.2 | 5 | 42 | A.E. Trott | Middlesex v Somerset | Taunton | 1900 |
| 24.5 | 1 | 90 | A. Fielder | Players v Gentlemen | Lord's | 1906 |
| 19.4 | 7 | 40 | E.G. Dennett | Gloucestershire v Essex | Bristol | 1906 |
| 12 | 2 | 26 | A.E.E. Vogler | E. Province v Griqualand West | Johannesburg | 1906–07 |
| 16 | 7 | 30 | C. Blythe | Kent v Northamptonshire | Northampton | 1907 |
| 8.5 | 0 | 35 | A. Drake | Yorkshire v Somerset | Weston-s-Mare | 1914 |
| 35.4 | 4 | 90 | F.A. Tarrant | Maharaja of Cooch Behar's XI v Lord Willingdon's XI | Poona | 1918–19 |
| 42.2 | 11 | 76 | J.C. White | Somerset v Worcestershire | Worcester | 1921 |
| 19 | 2 | 40 | W. Bestwick | Derbyshire v Glamorgan | Cardiff | 1921 |
| 17.5 | 4 | 43 | T. Rushby | Surrey v Somerset | Taunton | 1921 |
| 40.3 | 13 | 79 | C.W.L. Parker | Gloucestershire v Somerset | Bristol | 1921 |
| 28.4 | 5 | 66 | A.A. Mailey | Australians v Gloucestershire | Cheltenham | 1921 |
| 19.3 | 4 | 65 | G.C. Collins | Kent v Nottinghamshire | Dover | 1922 |
| 25.1 | 5 | 51 | H. Howell | Warwickshire v Yorkshire | Birmingham | 1923 |
| 22.4 | 10 | 37 | A.S. Kennedy | Players v Gentlemen | Oval | 1927 |
| 25.3 | 10 | 40 | G.O.B. Allen | Middlesex v Lancashire | Lord's | 1929 |
| 42 | 9 | 131 | A.P. Freeman | Kent v Lancashire | Maidstone | 1929 |
| 16.2 | 8 | 18 | G. Geary | Leicestershire v Glamorgan | Pontypridd | 1929 |
| 22.3 | 8 | 37 | C.V. Grimmett | Australians v Yorkshire | Sheffield | 1930 |
| 30.4 | 8 | 53 | A.P. Freeman | Kent v Essex | Southend | 1930 |
| 18.4 | 6 | 36 | H. Verity | Yorkshire v Warwickshire | Leeds | 1931 |
| 36.1 | 9 | 79 | A.P. Freeman | Kent v Lancashire | Manchester | 1931 |
| 39 | 6 | 127 | V.W.C. Jupp | Northamptonshire v Kent | Tunbridge Wells | 1932 |
| 19.4 | 16 | 10 | H. Verity | Yorkshire v Nottinghamshire | Leeds | 1932 |
| 12.4 | 2 | 36 | T.W. Wall | South Australia v New South Wales | Sydney | 1932–33 |
| 19.1 | 4 | 64 | T.B. Mitchell | Derbyshire v Leicestershire | Leicester | 1935 |
| 26 | 10 | 51 | J. Mercer | Glamorgan v Worcestershire | Worcester | 1936 |
| 28.4 | 4 | 113 | T.W.J. Goddard | Gloucestershire v Worcestershire | Cheltenham | 1937 |
| 17.1 | 5 | 47 | T.F. Smailes | Yorkshire v Derbyshire | Sheffield | 1939 |
| 24.1 | 8 | 67 | E.A. Watts | Surrey v Warwickshire | Birmingham | 1939 |
| 20.4 | 4 | 49 | W.E. Hollies | Warwickshire v Nottinghamshire | Birmingham | 1946 |
| 18.4 | 2 | 90 | J.M. Sims | East v West | Kingston upon T. | 1948 |
| 18.4 | 2 | 66 | J.K.R. Graveney | Gloucestershire v Derbyshire | Chesterfield | 1949 |
| 39.4 | 9 | 90 | T.E. Bailey | Essex v Lancashire | Clacton | 1949 |
| 36.2 | 9 | 102 | R. Berry | Lancashire v Worcestershire | Blackpool | 1953 |

| O | M | R | | | | |
|---|---|---|---|---|---|---|
| 24.2 | 7 | 78 | S.P. Gupte | Bombay v Pakistan Services & Bahawalpur | Bombay | 1954–55 |
| 46 | 18 | 88 | J.C. Laker | Surrey v Australians | Oval | 1956 |
| 41.3 | 20 | 66 | K. Smales | Nottinghamshire v Gloucestershire | Stroud | 1956 |
| 29.1 | 18 | 54 | G.A.R. Lock | Surrey v Kent | Blackheath | 1956 |
| 51.2 | 23 | 53 | J.C. Laker | England v Australia | Manchester | 1956 |
| 19 | 11 | 20 | P. M. Chatterjee | Bengal v Assam | Jorhat | 1956–57 |
| 23.3 | 11 | 41 | J.D. Bannister | Warwickshire v Combined Services | Birmingham | 1959 |
| 30.3 | 8 | 78 | A.J.G. Pearson | Cambridge University v Leicestershire | Loughborough | 1961 |
| 34.2 | 19 | 49 | N.I. Thomson | Sussex v Warwickshire | Worthing | 1964 |
| 15.6 | 3 | 61 | P.J. Allan | Queensland v Victoria | Melbourne | 1965–66 |
| 17.6 | 4 | 44 | I.J. Brayshaw | Western Australia v Victoria | Perth | 1967–68 |
| 25 | 5 | 58 | Shahid Mahmood | Karachi Whites v Khairpur | Karachi | 1969–70 |
| 49.3 | 14 | 175 | E.E. Hemmings | International XI v West Indies XI | Kingston | 1982–83 |

# TEN WICKETS INCLUDING THE HAT-TRICK

| H. Verity (10-10) | | Yorkshire v Nottinghamshire | Leeds | 1932 |
|---|---|---|---|---|

# NINE OR TEN WICKETS IN AN INNINGS

| | | | | | |
|---|---|---|---|---|---|
| Abdul Qadir | (3) | 9–49 | Habib Bank v Rawalpindi | Rawalpindi | 1982–83 |
| | | 9–82 | Habib Bank v Karachi | Karachi | 1982–83 |
| | | 9–59 | Lahore C Blues v Sargodha | Lahore | 1984–85 |
| Afzaal Butt | | 9–41 | National Bank v PIA | Lahore | 1982–83 |
| Agnew, J.P. | | 9–70 | Leicestershire v Kent | Leicester | 1985 |
| Ahad Khan | | 9-7 | Railways v Dera Ismail Khan | Lahore | 1964–65 |
| Allan, P.J. | | 10-61 | Queensland v Victoria | Melbourne | 1965–66 |
| Allen, G.O.B. | | 10-40 | Middlesex v Lancashire | Lord's | 1929 |
| Allom, M.J.C. | | 9-55 | Cambridge University v Army | Cambridge | 1927 |
| Amarjit Singh | | 9-45 | Kerala v Andhra | Cannanore | 1971–72 |
| Appleby, A. | | 9-25 | Lancashire v Sussex | Hove | 1877 |
| Arnold, E.G. | | 9-64 | Worcestershire v Oxford University | Oxford | 1905 |
| Astill, W.E. | | 9-41 | Leicestershire v Warwickshire | Birmingham | 1923 |
| Attewell, W. | | 9-23 | Nottinghamshire v Sussex | Nottingham | 1886 |
| Bailey, T.E. | | 10-90 | Essex v Lancashire | Clacton | 1949 |
| Bannister, J.D. | (2) | 9-35 | Warwickshire v Yorkshire | Sheffield | 1955 |
| | | 10-41 | Warwickshire v Combined Services | Birmingham | 1959 |
| Baring, A.E.G. | | 9-26 | Hampshire v Essex | Colchester | 1931 |
| Barlow, R.G. | | 9-39 | Lancashire v Sussex | Manchester | 1886 |
| Barnes, S.F. | | 9-103 | England v South Africa | Johannesburg | 1913–14 |
| Barratt, E. | | 10-43 | Players v Australians | Oval | 1878 |
| Bennett, G. | | 9-113 | Kent v Sussex | Hove | 1871 |
| Berry, R. | | 10-102 | Lancashire v Worcestershire | Blackpool | 1953 |
| Bestwick, W. | (2) | 10-40 | Derbyshire v Glamorgan | Cardiff | 1921 |
| | | 9-65 | Derbyshire v Warwickshire | Birmingham | 1921 |
| Blair, R.W. | (2) | 9-75 | Wellington v Canterbury | Wellington | 1956–57 |
| | | 9-72 | Wellington v Auckland | Wellington | 1956–57 |
| Blanckenberg, J.M. | | 9-78 | Western Province v Transvaal | Johannesburg | 1920–21 |
| Bland, C.H.G. | | 10-48 | Sussex v Kent | Tonbridge | 1899 |
| Blythe, C. | (6) | 9-67 | Kent v Essex | Canterbury | 1903 |
| | | 9-30 | Kent v Hampshire | Tonbridge | 1904 |
| | | 10-30 | Kent v Northamptonshire | Northampton | 1907 |
| | | 9-42 | Kent v Leicestershire | Leicester | 1909 |
| | | 9-44 | Kent v Northamptonshire | Northampton | 1909 |
| | | 9-97 | Kent v Surrey | Lord's | 1914 |
| Bosanquet, B.J.T. | (2) | 9-31 | Oxford University v Sussex | Oxford | 1900 |
| | | 9-107 | MCC v South Africans | Lord's | 1904 |
| Botten, J.T. | (2) | 9-23 | N.E. Transvaal v Griqualand West | Pretoria | 1958–59 |
| | | 9-29 | N.E. Transvaal v Rhodesia | Pretoria | 1963–64 |
| Bowditch, M.H. | | 9-52 | Western Province v Natal | Cape Town | 1965–66 |
| | | | *His first bowl in first-class cricket* | | |
| Bowes, W.E. | | 9-121 | Yorkshire v Essex | Scarborough | 1932 |
| Bowley, E.H. | | 9-114 | Sussex v Derbyshire | Hove | 1929 |

| Boyce, K.D. | | 9-61 | Essex v Cambridge University | Brentwood | 1966 |
|---|---|---|---|---|---|
| Boyes, G.S. | | 9-57 | Hampshire v Somerset | Yeovil | 1938 |
| Bradley, W.M. | | 9-87 | Kent v Hampshire | Tonbridge | 1901 |
| Braund, L.C. | | 9-41 | Somerset v Yorkshire | Sheffield | 1902 |
| Brayshaw, I.J. | | 10-44 | Western Australia v Victoria | Perth | 1967–68 |
| Brearley, W. | (2) | 9-47 | Lancashire v Somerset | Manchester | 1905 |
| | | 9-80 | Lancashire v Yorkshire | Manchester | 1909 |
| Brice, A.W.S. | | 9-67 | Wellington v Auckland | Wellington | 1918–19 |
| Briggs, J. | (4) | 9-29 | Lancashire v Derbyshire | Derby | 1885 |
| | | 9-88 | Lancashire v Sussex | Manchester | 1888 |
| | | 9-31 | Londesborough's XI v Australians | Scarborough | 1890 |
| | | 10-55 | Lancashire v Worcestershire | Manchester | 1900 |
| Broderick, V. | | 9-35 | Northamptonshire v Sussex | Horsham | 1948 |
| Buchanan, D. | | 9-82 | Gentlemen v Players | Oval | 1868 |
| Bull, F.G. | | 9-93 | Essex v Surrey | Oval | 1897 |
| Burton, G. | | 10-59 | Middlesex v Surrey | Oval | 1888 |
| Butler, S.E. | | 10-38 | Oxford University v Cambridge U. | Lord's | 1871 |
| Caffyn, W. | | 9-29 | Surrey & Sussex v England | Oval | 1857 |
| Chandrasekhar, B.S. | | 9-72 | Mysore v Kerala | Bijapur | 1969–70 |
| Chatterjee, P.M. | | 10-20 | Bengal v Assam | Jorhat | 1956–57 |
| Chester, J. | | 9- | MCC v Cambridge University | Cambridge | 1850 |
| Childs, J.H. | | 9-56 | Gloucestershire v Somerset | Bristol | 1981 |
| Clarke, W. | (2) | 9- | Nottinghamshire v Kent | Town Malling | 1840 |
| | | 9-29 | Nottinghamshire v Kent | Nottingham | 1845 |
| Clay, J.C. | (3) | 9-54 | Glamorgan v Northamptonshire | Llanelly | 1935 |
| | | 9-59 | Glamorgan v Essex | Westcliff | 1937 |
| | | 9-66 | Glamorgan v Worcestershire | Swansea | 1937 |
| Collins, G.C. | | 10-65 | Kent v Nottinghamshire | Dover | 1922 |
| Connolly, A.N. | | 9-67 | Victoria v Queensland | Brisbane | 1964–65 |
| Conway, A.J. | | 9-38 | Worcestershire v Gloucestershire | Moreton-in-Marsh | 1914 |
| Cook, C. | | 9-42 | Gloucestershire v Yorkshire | Bristol | 1947 |
| Cooke, F.H. | | 9-73 | Otago v Canterbury | Christchurch | 1884–85 |
| Cordle, A.E. | | 9-49 | Glamorgan v Leicestershire | Colwyn Bay | 1969 |
| Cornford, J.H. | | 9-53 | Sussex v Northamptonshire | Rushden | 1949 |
| Cottam, R.M.H. | | 9-25 | Hampshire v Lancashire | Manchester | 1965 |
| Cotton, J. | | 9-29 | Leicestershire v Indians | Leicester | 1967 |
| Cowan, M.J. | | 9-43 | Yorkshire v Warwickshire | Birmingham | 1960 |
| Cox, G.R. | | 9-50 | Sussex v Warwickshire | Horsham | 1926 |
| Crisp, R.J. | | 9-64 | Western Province v Natal | Durban | 1933–34 |
| Cuffe, J.A. | | 9-38 | Worcestershire v Yorkshire | Bradford | 1907 |
| Daniel, W.W. | | 9-61 | Middlesex v Glamorgan | Swansea | 1982 |
| Davidson, G. | (2) | 9-42 | Derbyshire v Gloucestershire | Derby | 1886 |
| | | 9-39 | Derbyshire v Warwickshire | Derby | 1895 |
| Dean, H. | (6) | 9-46 | Lancashire v Derbyshire | Chesterfield | 1907 |
| | | 9-35 | Lancashire v Warwickshire | Liverpool | 1909 |
| | | 9-31 | Lancashire v Somerset | Manchester | 1909 |
| | | 9-77 | Lancashire v Somerset | Bath | 1910 |
| | | 9-109 | Lancashire v Leicestershire | Leicester | 1911 |
| | | 9-62 | Lancashire v Yorkshire | Liverpool | 1913 |
| Dean, J. | | 9-34 | MCC v Nottinghamshire | Nottingham | 1843 |
| Deas, L.M. | | 9-91 | Europeans v Hindus | Bombay | 1905–06 |
| Dennett, E.G. | (2) | 10-40 | Gloucestershire v Essex | Bristol | 1906 |
| | | 9-63 | Gloucestershire v Surrey | Bristol | 1913 |
| Dent, T.H. | | 9-47 | Hawke's Bay v Wellington | Napier | 1900–01 |
| Douglas, J.W.H.T. | (2) | 9-105 | Gentlemen v Players | Lord's | 1914 |
| | | 9-47 | Essex v Derbyshire | Leyton | 1921 |
| Drake, A. | | 10-35 | Yorkshire v Somerset | Weston-s-Mare | 1914 |
| Dwyer, J.E.B.B.P.Q.C. | (2) | 9-35 | Sussex v Derbyshire | Hove | 1906 |
| | | 9-44 | Sussex v Middlesex | Hove | 1906 |
| Eden, T. | | 9-43 | Nelson v Wellington | Wellington | 1875–76 |
| Ehteshamuddin | | 9-124 | United Bank v MCB | Lahore | 1984–85 |
| Elliott, G. | | 9-2 | Victoria v Tasmania | Launceston | 1857–58 |
| Emmett, T. | (2) | 9-34 | Yorkshire v Nottinghamshire | Dewsbury | 1868 |
| | | 9-23 | Yorkshire v Cambridgeshire | Hunslet, Leeds | 1869 |
| Evans, A.H. | | 9-59 | England XI v R. Daft's XI | Lord's | 1880 |
| Fazal Mahmood | | 9-43 | Punjab v Services | Lahore | 1956–57 |
| Fee, F. | | 9-26 | Ireland v Scotland | Dublin | 1957 |

| | | | | | |
|---|---|---|---|---|---|
| Fenner, F.P. | | 9- | Cambridge Town v Cambridge U. | Cambridge | 1844 |
| Field, E.F. | | 9-104 | Warwickshire v Leicestershire | Leicester | 1899 |
| Fielder, A. | (2) | 10-90 | Players v Gentlemen | Lord's | 1906 |
| | | 9-108 | Kent v Lancashire | Canterbury | 1907 |
| Fisher, A.H. | | 9-50 | Otago v Queensland | Dunedin | 1896–97 |
| Flanagan, M. | | 9-78 | MCC v Surrey | Lord's | 1876 |
| Flavell, J.A. | (3) | 9-122 | Worcestershire v Sussex | Hastings | 1954 |
| | | 9-30 | Worcestershire v Kent | Dover | 1955 |
| | | 9-56 | Worcestershire v Middlesex | Kidderminster | 1964 |
| Fleetwood-Smith, | (2) | 9-36 | Victoria v Tasmania | Melbourne | 1932–33 |
| L.O'B. | | 9-135 | Victoria v South Australia | Melbourne | 1937–38 |
| Foster, F.R. | | 9-118 | Warwickshire v Yorkshire | Birmingham | 1911 |
| Foster, T. | | 9-59 | Yorkshire v MCC | Lord's | 1894 |
| Freeman, A.P. | (8) | 9-87 | Kent v Sussex | Hastings | 1921 |
| | | 9-11 | Kent v Sussex | Hove | 1922 |
| | | 9-104 | Kent v West Indians | Canterbury | 1928 |
| | | 10-131 | Kent v Lancashire | Maidstone | 1929 |
| | | 9-50 | Kent v Derbyshire | Ilkeston | 1930 |
| | | 10-53 | Kent v Essex | Southend | 1930 |
| | | 10-79 | Kent v Lancashire | Manchester | 1931 |
| | | 9-61 | Kent v Warwickshire | Folkestone | 1932 |
| Geary, G. | (2) | 9-33 | Leicestershire v Lancashire | Ashby-de-la-Zouch | 1926 |
| | | 10-18 | Leicestershire v Glamorgan | Pontypridd | 1929 |
| Ghulam Ahmed | | 9-53 | Hyderabad v Madras | Secunderabad | 1947–48 |
| Giffen, G. | (5) | 10-66 | Australian XI v Rest | Sydney | 1883–84 |
| | | 9-91 | South Australia v Victoria | Adelaide | 1885–86 |
| | | 9-60 | Australians v Derbyshire | Derby | 1886 |
| | | 9-96 | South Australia v Victoria | Adelaide | 1891–92 |
| | | 9-147 | South Australia v Victoria | Adelaide | 1892–93 |
| Gill, G.C. | | 9-89 | Leicestershire v Warwickshire | Birmingham | 1905 |
| Gladwin, C. | (3) | 9-119 | Derbyshire v Lancashire | Buxton | 1947 |
| | | 9-64 | North v South | Kingston upon T. | 1951 |
| | | 9-41 | Derbyshire v Worcestershire | Stourbridge | 1952 |
| Goddard, T.W.J. | (9) | 9-21 | Gloucestershire v Cambridge U. | Cheltenham | 1929 |
| | | 9-37 | Gloucestershire v Leicestershire | Bristol | 1934 |
| | | 10-113 | Gloucestershire v Worcestershire | Cheltenham | 1937 |
| | | 9-55 | Gloucestershire v Worcestershire | Bristol | 1939 |
| | | 9-38 | Gloucestershire v Kent | Bristol | 1939 |
| | | 9-44 | Gloucestershire v Somerset | Bristol | 1939 |
| | | 9-82 | Gloucestershire v Surrey | Cheltenham | 1946 |
| | | 9-41 | Gloucestershire v Nottinghamshire | Bristol | 1947 |
| | | 9-61 | Gloucestershire v Derbyshire | Bristol | 1949 |
| Gomez, G.E. | | 9-24 | West Indians v South Zone | Madras | 1948–49 |
| Grace, W.G. | (4) | 9-48 | South v North | Loughborough | 1875 |
| | | 9-55 | Gloucestershire v Nottinghamshire | Cheltenham | 1877 |
| | | 9-20 | MCC v Nottinghamshire | Lord's | 1885 |
| | | 10-49 | MCC v Oxford University | Oxford | 1886 |
| Graveney, J.K.R. | | 10-66 | Gloucestershire v Derbyshire | Chesterfield | 1949 |
| Gregory, J.M. | | 9-32 | AIF v Natal | Durban | 1919–20 |
| Greswell, W.T. | | 9-62 | Somerset v Hampshire | Weston-s-Mare | 1928 |
| Griffith, G. | | 9-130 | Surrey v Lancashire | Oval | 1867 |
| Grimmett, C.V. | (3) | 10-37 | Australians v Yorkshire | Sheffield | 1930 |
| | | 9-74 | Australians v Cambridge University | Cambridge | 1934 |
| | | 9-180 | South Australia v Queensland | Adelaide | 1934–35 |
| Grove, C.W. | | 9-39 | Warwickshire v Sussex | Birmingham | 1952 |
| Grundy, J. | | 9-19 | Nottinghamshire v Kent | Nottingham | 1864 |
| Gupte, B.P. | | 9-55 | West Zone v South Zone | Calcutta | 1962–63 |
| Gupte, S.P. | (2) | 10-78 | Bombay v Pakistan Services & Bahawalpur | Bombay | 1954–55 |
| | | 9-102 | India v West Indies | Kanpur | 1958–59 |
| Gyaneshwar, T. | | 9-34 | Delhi v Jammu & Kashmir | Delhi | 1961–62 |
| Hagemann, A.F. | | 9-32 | Border v Griqualand West | Kimberley | 1960–61 |
| Haigh, S. | | 9-25 | Yorkshire v Gloucestershire | Leeds | 1912 |
| Halfyard, D.J. | (2) | 9-39 | Kent v Glamorgan | Neath | 1957 |
| | | 9-61 | Kent v Worcestershire | Maidstone | 1959 |
| Hall, G.G. | | 9-122 | South African U's v W. Province | Cape Town | 1960–61 |
| | | | *On debut in first-class cricket* | | |

| Hallows, J. | | 9-37 | Lancashire v Gloucestershire | Gloucester | 1904 |
|---|---|---|---|---|---|
| Hammond, W.R. | | 9-23 | Gloucestershire v Worcestershire | Cheltenham | 1928 |
| Hans, R.S. | | 9-152 | Uttar Pradesh v Karnataka | Mohan Nagar | 1977–78 |
| Hargreave, S. | | 9-35 | Warwickshire v Surrey | Oval | 1903 |
| Harry, F. | | 9-44 | Lancashire v Warwickshire | Manchester | 1906 |
| Hay, H. | | 9-67 | South Australia v Lord Hawke's XI | Adelaide (Unley) | 1902–03 |
| | | | *On debut in first-class cricket* | | |
| Heap, J.S. | | 9-43 | Lancashire v Northamptonshire | Northampton | 1910 |
| Hearne, J.T. | (8) | 9-32 | Middlesex v Nottinghamshire | Nottingham | 1891 |
| | | 9-41 | MCC v Nottinghamshire | Lord's | 1892 |
| | | 9-43 | MCC v Lancashire | Lord's | 1894 |
| | | 9-73 | MCC v Australians | Lord's | 1896 |
| | | 9-54 | MCC v Oxford University | Oxford | 1897 |
| | | 9-68 | Middlesex v Lancashire | Manchester | 1898 |
| | | 9-71 | MCC v Yorkshire | Lord's | 1900 |
| | | 9-78 | Middlesex v Yorkshire | Bradford | 1908 |
| Hearne, J.W. | (2) | 9-82 | Middlesex v Surrey | Lord's | 1911 |
| | | 9-61 | Middlesex v Derbyshire | Chesterfield | 1933 |
| Hemmings, E.E. | | 10-175 | International XI v West Indies XI | Kingston | 1982–83 |
| Hickton, W. | | 10-46 | Lancashire v Hampshire | Manchester | 1870 |
| Hinkly, E. | | 10- | Kent v England | Lord's | 1848 |
| Hirst, G.H. | (4) | 9-45 | Yorkshire v Middlesex | Sheffield | 1907 |
| | | 9-23 | Yorkshire v Lancashire | Leeds | 1910 |
| | | 9-41 | Yorkshire v Worcestershire | Worcester | 1911 |
| | | 9-69 | Yorkshire v MCC | Lord's | 1912 |
| Hobson, D.L. | | 9-64 | W. Province v E. Province | Cape Town | 1978–79 |
| Holland, R.G. | | 9-83 | New South Wales v S. Australia | Sydney | 1984–85 |
| Hollies, W.E. | (3) | 9-93 | Warwickshire v Glamorgan | Birmingham | 1939 |
| | | 10-49 | Warwickshire v Nottinghamshire | Birmingham | 1946 |
| | | 9-56 | Warwickshire v Northamptonshire | Birmingham | 1950 |
| Hopwood, J.L. | (2) | 9-33 | Lancashire v Leicestershire | Manchester | 1933 |
| | | 9-69 | Lancashire v Worcestershire | Blackpool | 1934 |
| Horton, M.J. | | 9-56 | Worcestershire v South Africans | Worcester | 1955 |
| Hourn, D.W. | | 9-77 | New South Wales v Victoria | Sydney | 1978–79 |
| Howell, H. | (3) | 10-51 | Warwickshire v Yorkshire | Birmingham | 1923 |
| | | 9-35 | Warwickshire v Somerset | Taunton | 1924 |
| | | 9-32 | Warwickshire v Hampshire | Birmingham | 1925 |
| Howell, W.P. | (3) | 10-28 | Australians v Surrey | Oval | 1899 |
| | | 9-23 | Australians v Western Province | Cape Town | 1902–03 |
| | | 9-52 | New South Wales v Victoria | Melbourne | 1902–03 |
| Huddleston, W. | | 9-36 | Lancashire v Nottinghamshire | Liverpool | 1906 |
| Huggins, J.H. | | 9-34 | Gloucestershire v Sussex | Bristol | 1904 |
| Hulme, J.J. | | 9-27 | Derbyshire v Yorkshire | Sheffield | 1894 |
| Hyder Ali | | 9-25 | Railways v Jammu & Kashmir | Delhi | 1969–70 |
| Iddon, J. | | 9-42 | Lancashire v Yorkshire | Sheffield | 1937 |
| Illingworth, R. | | 9-42 | Yorkshire v Worcestershire | Worcester | 1957 |
| Iqbal Qasim | | 9-80 | Pakistan XI v International XI | Lahore | 1981–82 |
| Iqbal Sikander | | 9-81 | PIA v Lahore | Lahore | 1981–82 |
| Israr Ali | | 9-58 | Bahawalpur v Punjab | Bahawalpur | 1957–58 |
| Jackson, J. | (3) | 9-27 | Kent v England | Lord's | 1858 |
| | | 9-35 | Kent v England | Canterbury | 1858 |
| | | 9-49 | Nottinghamshire v Surrey | Oval | 1860 |
| Jackson, H.L. | (2) | 9-60 | Derbyshire v Lancashire | Manchester | 1952 |
| | | 9-17 | Derbyshire v Cambridge University | Cambridge | 1959 |
| Jackson, P.F. | | 9-45 | Worcestershire v Somerset | Dudley | 1935 |
| James, A.E. | | 9-60 | Sussex v Yorkshire | Hove | 1955 |
| Jayes, T. | | 9-78 | Leicestershire v Derbyshire | Leicester | 1905 |
| Jones, A.A. | | 9-51 | Somerset v Sussex | Hove | 1972 |
| Julien, B.D. | | 9-97 | Trinidad v Jamaica | Port-of-Spain | 1981–82 |
| Jupp, V.W.C. | | 10-127 | Northamptonshire v Kent | Tunbridge Wells | 1932 |
| Kannan, K.S. | | 9-50 | Madras v Hyderabad | Secunderabad | 1947–48 |
| Kapil Dev | | 9-83 | India v West Indies | Ahmedabad | 1983–84 |
| Kennedy, A.S. | (3) | 9-33 | Hampshire v Lancashire | Liverpool | 1920 |
| | | 10-37 | Players v Gentlemen | Oval | 1927 |
| | | 9-46 | Hampshire v Derbyshire | Portsmouth | 1929 |
| Khalid Qureshi | | 9-28 | Lahore v Lahore Ed. Board | Lahore | 1960–61 |
| King, J.B. | (2) | 9-25 | Philadelphians v P.F. Warner's XI | Belmont | 1897–98 |

| | | | | | |
|---|---|---|---|---|---|
| King, J.B. *contd.* | | 9-62 | Philadelphians v Lancashire | Manchester | 1903 |
| Kirwan, J.H. | | 9- | Cambridge U. v Cambridge Town | Cambridge | 1836 |
| | | | *All bowled* | | |
| Knutton, H.J. | | 9-100 | England XI v Australians | Bradford | 1902 |
| Kumar, V.V. | | 9-76 | Madras v Kerala | Sankarnagar | 1969–70 |
| Laker, J.C. | (3) | 10-88 | Surrey v Australians | Oval | 1956 |
| | | 9-37 | England v Australians (*1st innings*) | Manchester | 1956 |
| | | 10-53 | England v Australians (*2nd innings*) | Manchester | 1956 |
| Lampard, A.W. | | 9-42 | AIF v Lancashire | Manchester | 1919 |
| Langford, B.A. | | 9-26 | Somerset v Lancashire | Weston-s-Mare | 1958 |
| Langridge, James | | 9-34 | Sussex v Yorkshire | Sheffield | 1934 |
| Larwood, H. | | 9-41 | Nottinghamshire v Kent | Nottingham | 1931 |
| Layne, O.H. | | 9-19 | Demerara v W.C. Shepherd's XI | Georgetown | 1909–10 |
| Lee, G.B. | | 9- | Oxford University v Cambridge U. | Lord's | 1839 |
| Lees, W.S. | | 9-81 | Surrey v Sussex | Eastbourne | 1905 |
| Lillywhite, James | (3) | 9-29 | Sussex v MCC | Lord's | 1862 |
| | | | *On debut in first-class cricket* | | |
| | | 9-73 | Sussex v Kent | Folkestone | 1863 |
| | | 10-129 | South v North | Canterbury | 1872 |
| Lillywhite, F.W. | (4) | 9- | Sussex v Hampshire & Surrey | Bramshill | 1826 |
| | | 9- | Players v Gentlemen | Lord's | 1837 |
| | | 9- | Slow Bowlers v Fast Bowlers | Lord's | 1841 |
| | | 9- | MCC v Cambridge University | Cambridge | 1846 |
| Lipscombe, R. | | 9-88 | Kent v MCC | Lord's | 1871 |
| Llewellyn, C.B. | | 9-55 | London County v Cambridge U. | Crystal Palace | 1902 |
| Loader, P.J. | (2) | 9-28 | Surrey v Kent | Blackheath | 1953 |
| | | 9-17 | Surrey v Warwickshire | Oval | 1958 |
| Lock, G.A.R. | (2) | 10-54 | Surrey v Kent | Blackheath | 1956 |
| | | 9-57 | Surrey v Oxford University | Guildford | 1960 |
| Lockwood, W. | (3) | 9-105 | Surrey v Gloucestershire | Cheltenham | 1899 |
| | | 9-94 | Surrey v Essex | Oval | 1900 |
| | | 9-59 | Surrey v Essex | Leyton | 1902 |
| Lohmann, G.A. | (2) | 9-67 | Surrey v Sussex | Hove | 1889 |
| | | 9-28 | England v South Africa | Johannesburg | 1895–96 |
| Luthra, S. | | 9-70 | Delhi v Services | Delhi | 1976–77 |
| McBeath, D.J. | | 9-56 | Canterbury v Auckland | Christchurch | 1918–19 |
| McCormick, E.L. | | 9-40 | Victoria v South Australia | Adelaide | 1936–37 |
| McIntyre, M. | | 9-33 | Nottinghamshire v Surrey | Oval | 1872 |
| McKibbin, T.R. | | 9-68 | New South Wales v Queensland | Brisbane | 1894–95 |
| McLaren, K. | | 9-54 | Griqualand West v Natal B | Umzinto | 1973–74 |
| McMillan, Q. | | 9-53 | South Africans v South Australia | Adelaide | 1931–32 |
| McNally, J.P. | | 9-91 | Griqualand West v Border | Kimberley | 1951–52 |
| | | | *His last first-class match* | | |
| McShane, P.G. | | 9-45 | Rest v Australian XI | Sydney | 1880–81 |
| Madan Lal | (2) | 9-31 | Delhi v Haryana | Delhi | 1979–80 |
| | | 9-50 | Delhi v Jammu & Kashmir | Delhi | 1984–85 |
| Mailey, A.A. | (3) | 9-121 | Australia v England | Melbourne | 1920–21 |
| | | 10-66 | Australians v Gloucestershire | Cheltenham | 1921 |
| | | 9-86 | Australians v Lancashire | Liverpool | 1926 |
| Marlar, R.G. | | 9-46 | Sussex v Lancashire | Hove | 1955 |
| Marsham, C.D.B. | | 9-64 | Gents of England v Gents of MCC | Lord's | 1855 |
| Matthews, F.C. | | 9-50 | Nottinghamshire v Northamptonshire | Nottingham | 1923 |
| Mead, W. | (3) | 9-52 | Essex v Hampshire | Southampton | 1895 |
| | | 9-75 | Essex v Leicestershire | Leyton | 1896 |
| | | 9-40 | Essex v Hampshire | Southampton | 1900 |
| Mee, R.J. | | 9-54 | Nottinghamshire v Sussex | Nottingham | 1893 |
| Melle, M.G. | | 9-22 | South Africans v Tasmania | Launceston | 1952–53 |
| Mercer, J. | (2) | 9-24 | Wales v Scotland | Perth | 1923 |
| | | 10-51 | Glamorgan v Worcestershire | Worcester | 1936 |
| Meyer, R.J.O. | | 9-160 | Europeans v Muslims | Bombay | 1927–28 |
| Mistri, K.B. | | 9-81 | Parsees v Europeans | Poona | 1906–07 |
| Mitchell, T.B. | | 10-64 | Derbyshire v Leicestershire | Leicester | 1935 |
| Mold, A.W. | (4) | 9-41 | Lancashire v Yorkshire | Huddersfield | 1890 |
| | | 9-43 | C.I. Thornton's XI v Australians | Barnes | 1890 |
| | | 9-29 | Lancashire v Kent | Tonbridge | 1892 |
| | | 9-62 | Lancashire v Kent | Manchester | 1895 |
| Morton, A. | | 9-71 | Derbyshire v Nottinghamshire | Blackwell | 1911 |

| | | | | | |
|---|---|---|---|---|---|
| Moss, A.E. | | 10-28 | Canterbury v Wellington | Christchurch | 1889–90 |
| | | | *On debut in first-class cricket* | | |
| Muncer, B.L. | (2) | 9-97 | Glamorgan v Surrey | Cardiff | 1947 |
| | | 9-62 | Glamorgan v Essex | Brentwood | 1948 |
| Mycroft, W. | (2) | 9-80 | Derbyshire v Lancashire | Derby | 1875 |
| | | 9-25 | Derbyshire v Hampshire | Southampton | 1876 |
| Mynn, A. | | 9- | Gents of Kent v Gents of England | Lord's | 1842 |
| Napier, G.G. | | 9-17 | Europeans v Parsees | Poona | 1909–10 |
| Nash, A.J. | | 9-93 | Glamorgan v Sussex | Swansea | 1922 |
| Nash, M.A. | | 9-56 | Glamorgan v Hampshire | Basingstoke | 1975 |
| Neill, R. | (2) | 9-75 | Auckland v Canterbury | Auckland | 1891–92 |
| | | 9-86 | Auckland v Canterbury | Auckland | 1897–98 |
| Newman, J.A. | | 9-131 | Hampshire v Essex | Bournemouth | 1921 |
| Nichols, M.S. | (4) | 9-59 | Essex v Hampshire | Chelmsford | 1927 |
| | | 9-116 | Essex v Middlesex | Leyton | 1930 |
| | | 9-32 | Essex v Nottinghamshire | Nottingham | 1936 |
| | | 9-37 | Essex v Gloucestershire | Gloucester | 1938 |
| Nicholson, A.G. | | 9-62 | Yorkshire v Sussex | Eastbourne | 1967 |
| Nixon, T. | | 9- | MCC v Middlesex | Lord's | 1851 |
| Noreiga, J.M. | | 9-95 | West Indies v India | Port-of-Spain | 1970–71 |
| Nupen, E.P. | | 9-48 | Transvaal v Griqualand West | Johannesburg | 1931–32 |
| O'Reilly, W.J. | (3) | 9-50 | New South Wales v Victoria | Melbourne | 1933–34 |
| | | 9-38 | Australians v Somerset | Taunton | 1934 |
| | | 9-41 | NSW v South Australia | Adelaide | 1937–38 |
| Oxenham, R.K. | | 9-18 | Australians v Ceylon | Colombo | 1935–36 |
| Pallett, H.J. | | 9-55 | Warwickshire v Essex | Leyton | 1894 |
| Palmer, K.E. | | 9-57 | Somerset v Nottinghamshire | Nottingham | 1963 |
| Parker, C.W.L. | (9) | 9-35 | Gloucestershire v Leicestershire | Cheltenham | 1920 |
| | | 10-79 | Gloucestershire v Somerset | Bristol | 1921 |
| | | 9-87 | Gloucestershire v Derbyshire | Gloucester | 1922 |
| | | 9-36 | Gloucestershire v Yorkshire | Bristol | 1922 |
| | | 9-44 | Gloucestershire v Essex | Gloucester | 1925 |
| | | 9-118 | Gloucestershire v Surrey | Gloucester | 1925 |
| | | 9-103 | Gloucestershire v Somerset | Bristol | 1927 |
| | | 9-46 | Gloucestershire v Northamptonshire | Northampton | 1927 |
| | | 9-44 | Gloucestershire v Warwickshire | Cheltenham | 1930 |
| Parkin, C.H. | (2) | 9-85 | Players v Gentlemen | Oval | 1920 |
| | | 9-32 | Lancashire v Leicestershire | Ashby-de-la-Z. | 1924 |
| Parry, D.R. | | 9-76 | Combined I's v Jamaica | Kingston | 1979–80 |
| Parsons, G.J. | | 9-72 | Boland v Transvaal B | Johannesburg | 1984–85 |
| Partridge, R.J. | | 9-66 | Northamptonshire v Warwickshire | Kettering | 1934 |
| Patel, J.M. | | 9-69 | India v Australia | Kanpur | 1959–60 |
| Pearson, A.J.G. | | 10-78 | Cambridge University v Leicestershire | Loughborough | 1961 |
| Pearson, F.A. | | 9-41 | H.K. Foster's XI v Oxford U. | Oxford | 1913 |
| Peel, R. | | 9-22 | Yorkshire v Somerset | Leeds | 1895 |
| Perks, R.T.D. | (2) | 9-40 | Worcestershire v Glamorgan | Stourbridge | 1939 |
| | | 9-42 | Worcestershire v Gloucestershire | Cheltenham | 1946 |
| Peth      P.J. | | 9-93 | Otago v Northern Districts | Dunedin | 1975–76 |
| Pick | | 10-32 | Essex v Leicestershire | Leyton | 1895 |
| Pocock, P. | | 9-57 | Surrey v Glamorgan | Cardiff | 1979 |
| Poug..., A... | | 9-34 | England XI v Surrey | Oval | 1895 |
| Powys, W.N. | | 9-42 | Cambridge University v MCC | Cambridge | 1871 |
| | | | *On debut in first-class cricket* | | |
| Pressdee, J.S. | | 9-43 | Glamorgan v Yorkshire | Swansea | 1965 |
| Preston, J.M. | | 9-28 | Yorkshire v MCC | Scarborough | 1888 |
| Procter, M.J. | | 9-71 | Rhodesia v Transvaal | Bulawayo | 1972–73 |
| Quilty, J. | | 9-55 | South Australia v Victoria | Adelaide | 1881–82 |
| | | | *On debut in first-class cricket* | | |
| Raikes, T.B. | | 9-38 | Oxford University v Army | Oxford | 1924 |
| Ranjane, V.B. | | 9-35 | Maharashtra v Saurashtra | Poona | 1956–57 |
| Rashid Khan | | 9-27 | PIA v Railways | Multan | 1980–81 |
| Relf, A.E. | | 9-95 | Sussex v Warwickshire | Hove | 1910 |
| Rhodes, W. | (3) | 9-28 | Yorkshire v Essex | Leyton | 1899 |
| | | 9-24 | C.I. Thornton's XI v Australians | Scarborough | 1899 |
| | | 9-39 | Yorkshire v Essex | Leyton | 1929 |
| Richardson, T. | (4) | 9-47 | Surrey v Yorkshire | Sheffield | 1893 |
| | | 10-45 | Surrey v Essex | Oval | 1894 |

| | | | | | |
|---|---|---|---|---|---|
| Richardson, T. *contd.* | | 9-49 | Surrey v Sussex | Oval | 1895 |
| | | 9-70 | Surrey v Hampshire | Oval | 1895 |
| Richmond, T.L. | (2) | 9-21 | Nottinghamshire v Hampshire | Nottingham | 1922 |
| | | 9-55 | Nottinghamshire v Northamptonshire | Nottingham | 1925 |
| Ringrose, W. | | 9-76 | Yorkshire v Australians | Bradford | 1905 |
| Robertson, W. | | 9-98 | Canterbury v Wellington | Christchurch | 1894–95 |
| Robertson-Glasgow, R.C. | | 9-38 | Somerset v Middlesex | Lord's | 1924 |
| Robinson, E. | | 9-36 | Yorkshire v Lancashire | Bradford | 1920 |
| Root, C.F. | (3) | 9-40 | Worcestershire v Essex | Worcester | 1924 |
| | | 9-81 | Worcestershire v Kent | Tunbridge Wells | 1930 |
| | | 9-23 | Worcestershire v Lancashire | Worcester | 1931 |
| Rowan, A.M.B. | | 9-19 | Transvaal v Australians | Johannesburg | 1949–50 |
| Rushby, T. | | 10-43 | Surrey v Somerset | Taunton | 1921 |
| Rylott, A. | | 9-30 | MCC v Cambridge University | Cambridge | 1873 |
| Saeed Anjum | | 9-38 | HBFC v Lahore | Lahore | 1980–81 |
| Safiullah Khan | | 9-62 | Peshawar v Railways B | Peshawar | 1971–72 |
| Sajjad Ahmed | | 9-80 | Peshawar v Services | Peshawar | 1958–59 |
| Sarfraz Nawaz | | 9-86 | Pakistan v Australia | Melbourne | 1978–79 |
| Sarwate, C.T. | | 9-61 | Holkar v Mysore | Indore | 1945–46 |
| Sekar, T.A.P. | | 9-54 | Tamil Nadu v Kerala | Palghat | 1982–83 |
| Shackleton, D. | (4) | 9-77 | Hampshire v Glamorgan | Newport | 1953 |
| | | 9-59 | Hampshire v Gloucestershire | Bristol | 1958 |
| | | 9-81 | Hampshire v Gloucestershire | Bristol | 1959 |
| | | 9-30 | Hampshire v Warwickshire | Portsmouth | 1960 |
| Shahid Mahmood | | 10-58 | Karachi Whites v Khairpur | Karachi | 1969–70 |
| Sharp, J. | | 9-77 | Lancashire v Worcestershire | Worcester | 1901 |
| Sharpe, J.W. | | 9-47 | Surrey v Middlesex | Oval | 1891 |
| Shastri, R.J. | | 9-101 | Bombay v Rest of India | Indore | 1981–82 |
| Shaw, A. | | 10-73 | MCC v North | Lord's | 1874 |
| Shaw, J.C. | | 9-86 | Nottinghamshire v Gloucestershire | Nottingham | 1871 |
| Shepherd, D.J. | (2) | 9-47 | Glamorgan v Northamptonshire | Cardiff | 1954 |
| | | 9-48 | Glamorgan v Yorkshire | Swansea | 1965 |
| Shipman, A.W. | | 9-83 | Leicestershire v Surrey | Oval | 1910 |
| Sims, J.M. | (2) | 9-92 | Middlesex v Lancashire | Manchester | 1934 |
| | | 10-90 | East v West | Kingston upon T. | 1948 |
| Sinfield, R.A. | | 9-111 | Gloucestershire v Middlesex | Lord's | 1936 |
| Smailes, T.F. | | 10-47 | Yorkshire v Derbyshire | Sheffield | 1939 |
| Smales, K. | | 10-66 | Nottinghamshire v Gloucestershire | Stroud | 1956 |
| Smith, E. | | 9-46 | Derbyshire v Scotland | Edinburgh | 1955 |
| Smith, S.G. | | 9-34 | West Indian XI v R.A. Bennett's XI | Port-of-Spain | 1901–02 |
| Smith, T.P.B. | (4) | 9-121 | MCC v New South Wales | Sydney | 1946–47 |
| | | 9-77 | Essex v Middlesex | Colchester | 1947 |
| | | 9-117 | Essex v Nottinghamshire | Southend | 1948 |
| | | 9-108 | Essex v Kent | Maidstone | 1948 |
| Smith, V.I. | | 9-88 | Natal v Border | Pietermaritzburg | 1946–47 |
| Smith, W.C. | | 9-31 | Surrey v Hampshire | Oval | 1904 |
| Sobers, G.St A. | | 9-49 | West Indians v Kent | Canterbury | 1966 |
| Southerton, J. | | 9-30 | South v North | Lord's | 1875 |
| Spencer, C.T. | | 9-63 | Leicestershire v Yorkshire | Huddersfield | 1954 |
| Spofforth, F.R. | (3) | 9-53 | Australians v Lancashire | Manchester | 1878 |
| | | 9-51 | Australians v Somerset | Taunton | 1882 |
| | | 9-18 | Australians v Oxford University | Oxford | 1886 |
| Staples, S.J. | | 9-141 | Nottinghamshire v Kent | Canterbury | 1927 |
| Steel, A.G. | | 9-63 | Lancashire v Yorkshire | Manchester | 1878 |
| Stephenson, J.W.A. | | 9-46 | Gentlemen v Players | Lord's | 1936 |
| Swarbrook, F.W. | | 9-20 | Derbyshire v Sussex | Hove | 1975 |
| Sydenham, D.A.D. | | 9-70 | Surrey v Gloucestershire | Oval | 1964 |
| Tahir Naqqash | | 9-45 | MCB v Karachi | Karachi | 1980–81 |
| Tarrant, F.A. | (7) | 9-57 | Middlesex v Yorkshire | Leeds | 1906 |
| | | 9-54 | Middlesex v Lancashire | Manchester | 1906 |
| | | 9-41 | Middlesex v Gloucestershire | Bristol | 1907 |
| | | 9-59 | Middlesex v Nottinghamshire | Lord's | 1907 |
| | | 9-105 | Middlesex v Lancashire | Manchester | 1914 |
| | | 9-99 | Europeans v Parsees | Bombay | 1916–17 |
| | | 10-90 | Maharaja of Cooch Behar's XI v Lord Willingdon's XI | Poona | 1918–19 |
| Tate, F.W. | | 9-73 | Sussex v Leicestershire | Leicester | 1902 |

| | | | | | |
|---|---|---|---|---|---|
| Tate, M.W. | | 9-71 | Sussex v Middlesex | Lord's | 1926 |
| Tattersall, R. | | 9-40 | Lancashire v Nottinghamshire | Manchester | 1953 |
| Tayfield, H.J. | | 9-113 | South Africa v England | Johannesburg | 1956–57 |
| Thomas, A.E. | | 9-30 | Northamptonshire v Yorkshire | Bradford | 1920 |
| Thompson, G.J. | (2) | 9-85 | Lord Hawke's XI v South Australia | Adelaide | 1902–03 |
| | | 9-64 | Northamptonshire v Derbyshire | Northampton | 1906 |
| Thompson, R.G. | | 9-65 | Warwickshire v Nottinghamshire | Birmingham | 1952 |
| Thomson, N.I. | | 10-49 | Sussex v Warwickshire | Worthing | 1964 |
| Titmus, F.J. | (2) | 9-52 | Middlesex v Cambridge University | Cambridge | 1962 |
| | | 9-57 | Middlesex v Lancashire | Lord's | 1964 |
| Townsend, C.L. | (2) | 9-48 | Gloucestershire v Middlesex | Lord's | 1898 |
| | | 9-128 | Gloucestershire v Warwickshire | Cheltenham | 1898 |
| Travers, J.F. | | 9-30 | South Australia v Victoria | Melbourne | 1900–01 |
| Tremlin, B. | | 9-126 | Essex v Derbyshire | Leyton | 1905 |
| Tribe, G.E. | (4) | 9-45 | Queensland v Victoria | Brisbane | 1945–46 |
| | | 9-50 | Commonwealth XI v Governor's XI | Calcutta | 1949–50 |
| | | 9-45 | Northamptonshire v Yorkshire | Bradford | 1955 |
| | | 9-43 | Northamptonshire v Worcestershire | Northampton | 1958 |
| Trott, A.E. | | 10-42 | Middlesex v Somerset | Taunton | 1900 |
| Trumble, H. | | 9-39 | Australians v South of England | Bournemouth | 1902 |
| Turner, C.T.B. | (2) | 9-15 | Australians v England XI | Stoke-on-Trent | 1888 |
| | | 9-37 | Australians v England XI | Hastings | 1888 |
| Tyler, E.J. | (3) | 9-33 | Somerset v Nottinghamshire | Taunton | 1892 |
| | | 10-49 | Somerset v Surrey | Taunton | 1895 |
| | | 9-83 | Somerset v Sussex | Hastings | 1907 |
| Underwood, D.L. | (3) | 9-28 | Kent v Sussex | Hastings | 1964 |
| | | 9-37 | Kent v Essex | Westcliff | 1966 |
| | | 9-32 | Kent v Surrey | Oval | 1978 |
| Venkataraghavan, S. | | 9-93 | Indians v Hampshire | Bournemouth | 1971 |
| Verity, H. | (9) | 9-60 | Yorkshire v Glamorgan | Swansea | 1930 |
| | | 10-36 | Yorkshire v Warwickshire | Leeds | 1931 |
| | | 10-10 | Yorkshire v Nottinghamshire | Leeds | 1932 |
| | | 9-44 | Yorkshire v Essex | Leyton | 1933 |
| | | 9-59 | Yorkshire v Kent | Dover | 1933 |
| | | 9-12 | Yorkshire v Kent | Sheffield | 1936 |
| | | 9-48 | Yorkshire v Essex | Westcliff | 1936 |
| | | 9-43 | Yorkshire v Warwickshire | Leeds | 1937 |
| | | 9-62 | Yorkshire v MCC | Lord's | 1939 |
| Vogler, A.E.E. | (2) | 9-44 | MCC v West Indians | Lord's | 1906 |
| | | 10-26 | E. Province v Griqualand West | Johannesburg | 1906–07 |
| Waddington, J.E. | | 9-105 | Griqualand West v E. Province | Port Elizabeth | 1954–55 |
| Wadkar, R.R. | | 9-38 | Bombay v Western India States | Jamnagar | 1937–38 |
| Wainwright, E. | | 9-66 | Yorkshire v Middlesex | Sheffield | 1894 |
| Walker, G.G. | | 9-68 | Derbyshire v Leicestershire | Leicester | 1895 |
| Walker, V.E. | (3) | 10-74 | England v Surrey | Oval | 1859 |
| | | 9-63 | Middlesex v Sussex | Islington | 1864 |
| | | 10-104 | Middlesex v Lancashire | Manchester | 1865 |
| Wall, T.W. | | 10-36 | South Australia v NSW | Sydney | 1932–33 |
| Walsh, J.E. | | 9-101 | Sir J. Cahn's XI v Glamorgan | Newport | 1938 |
| Wardle, J.H. | (2) | 9-48 | Yorkshire v Sussex | Hull | 1954 |
| | | 9-25 | Yorkshire v Lancashire | Manchester | 1954 |
| Warr, J.J. | | 9-65 | Middlesex v Kent | Lord's | 1956 |
| Wass, T.G. | (2) | 9-91 | Nottinghamshire v Surrey | Oval | 1902 |
| | | 9-67 | Nottinghamshire v Derbyshire | Blackwell | 1911 |
| Watson, A. | | 9-118 | Lancashire v Derbyshire | Manchester | 1874 |
| Watts, E.A. | | 10-67 | Surrey v Warwickshire | Birmingham | 1939 |
| Wells, G. | | 9-105 | Sussex v Surrey | Hove | 1860 |
| Wensley, A.F. | | 9-36 | Auckland v Otago | Auckland | 1929–30 |
| Wheatley, O.S. | | 9-60 | Glamorgan v Sussex | Ebbw Vale | 1968 |
| White, D.W. | | 9-44 | Hampshire v Leicestershire | Portsmouth | 1966 |
| White, J.C. | (5) | 9-46 | Somerset v Gloucestershire | Bristol | 1914 |
| | | 10-76 | Somerset v Worcestershire | Worcester | 1921 |
| | | 9-58 | Somerset v Warwickshire | Birmingham | 1922 |
| | | 9-71 | Somerset v Sussex | Eastbourne | 1931 |
| | | 9-51 | Somerset v Glamorgan | Bath | 1932 |
| Williams, A.C. | | 9-29 | Yorkshire v Hampshire | Dewsbury | 1919 |
| Wilson, G.A. | | 9-75 | Worcestershire v Oxford University | Oxford | 1904 |

| Wisden, J. | (2) | 10- | North v South | Lord's | 1850 |
|---|---|---|---|---|---|
| | | 9- | Young v Old | Lord's | 1850 |
| Woodcock, A. | | 9-28 | Leicestershire v MCC | Lord's | 1899 |
| Woods, S.M.J. | | 10-69 | Cambridge U. v C.I. Thornton's XI | Cambridge | 1890 |
| Wootton, G. | (3) | 9-37 | MCC v Oxford University | Lord's | 1865 |
| | | 10-54 | All England XI v Yorkshire | Sheffield | 1865 |
| | | 9-45 | MCC v England | Lord's | 1868 |
| Wright, D.V.P. | (2) | 9-47 | Kent v Gloucestershire | Bristol | 1939 |
| | | 9-51 | Kent v Leicestershire | Maidstone | 1949 |
| Wright, W. | | 9-72 | Kent v MCC | Lord's | 1889 |
| Young, J.A. | | 9-55 | England XI v Commonwealth XI | Hastings | 1951 |
| Yuile, B.W. | | 9-100 | Central Districts v Canterbury | New Plymouth | 1965–66 |

# MOST WICKETS IN A MATCH

### NINETEEN WICKETS IN A MATCH

| O | M | R | W | | | | |
|---|---|---|---|---|---|---|---|
| 68 | 27 | 90 | 19 | J.C. Laker | England v Australia | Manchester | 1956 |

### SEVENTEEN WICKETS IN A MATCH

| O | M | R | W | | | | |
|---|---|---|---|---|---|---|---|
| | | | 17 | F.P. Fenner | Cambridge Town v Cambridge U. | Cambridge | 1844 |
| 60 | 24 | 103 | 17 | W. Mycroft | Derbyshire v Hampshire | Southampton | 1876 |
| 76.1 | 36 | 89 | 17 | W.G. Grace | Gloucestershire v Nottinghamshire | Cheltenham | 1877 |
| 116.2 | 41 | 201 | 17 | G. Giffen | South Australia v Victoria | Adelaide | 1885–86 |
| 69 | 37 | 50 | 17 | C.T.B. Turner | Australians v England XI | Hastings | 1888 |
| 77.3 | 32 | 119 | 17 | W. Mead | Essex v Hampshire | Southampton | 1895 |
| 26.3 | 6 | 54 | 17 | W.P. Howell | Australians v Western Province | Cape Town | 1902–03 |
| 35.2 | 7 | 137 | 17 | W. Brearley | Lancashire v Somerset | Manchester | 1905 |
| 31.1 | 14 | 48 | 17 | C. Blythe | Kent v Northamptonshire | Northampton | 1907 |
| 47.4 | 10 | 91 | 17 | H. Dean | Lancashire v Yorkshire | Liverpool | 1913 |
| 65.3 | 16 | 159 | 17 | S.F. Barnes | England v South Africa | Johannesburg | 1913–14 |
| 33.5 | 10 | 67 | 17 | A.P. Freeman | Kent v Sussex | Hove | 1922 |
| 30 | 6 | 89 | 17 | F.C. Matthews | Nottinghamshire v Northamptonshire | Nottingham | 1923 |
| 48.3 | 23 | 56 | 17 | C.W.L. Parker | Gloucestershire v Essex | Gloucester | 1925 |
| 75.3 | 36 | 106 | 17 | G.R. Cox | Sussex v Warwickshire | Horsham | 1926 |
| 41.4 | 12 | 92 | 17 | A.P. Freeman | Kent v Warwickshire | Folkestone | 1932 |
| 41.1 | 13 | 91 | 17 | H. Verity | Yorkshire v Essex | Leyton | 1933 |
| 62.5 | 11 | 212 | 17 | J.C. Clay | Glamorgan v Worcestershire | Swansea | 1937 |
| 31.6 | 3 | 106 | 17 | T.W.J. Goddard | Gloucestershire v Kent | Bristol | 1939 |

*W. Mead took 17-205 for Essex v Australians at Leyton in 1893 – one year before the county was accorded first-class status.*

### FIFTEEN OR MORE WICKETS IN A MATCH

| Baldwin, H. | | 15-142 | Hampshire v Sussex | Hove | 1898 |
|---|---|---|---|---|---|
| Barnes, S.F. | | 17-159 | England v South Africa | Johannesburg | 1913–14 |
| Bennett, G. | | 15-115 | World XI v Surrey XI | Melbourne | 1861–62 |
| Blythe, C. | (5) | 15-76 | Kent v Hampshire | Tonbridge | 1904 |
| | | 15-99 | England v South Africa | Leeds | 1907 |
| | | 17-48 | Kent v Northamptonshire | Northampton | 1907 |
| | | 16-102 | Kent v Leicestershire | Leicester | 1909 |
| | | 15-45 | Kent v Leicestershire | Leicester | 1912 |
| Bosanquet, B.J.T. | | 15-65 | Oxford University v Sussex | Oxford | 1900 |
| Botten, J.T. | | 15-49 | N.E. Transvaal v Griqualand West | Pretoria | 1958–59 |
| Bowes, W.E. | | 16-35 | Yorkshire v Northamptonshire | Kettering | 1935 |
| Braund, L.C. | | 15-71 | Somerset v Yorkshire | Sheffield | 1902 |
| Brearley, W. | | 17-137 | Lancashire v Somerset | Manchester | 1905 |
| Briggs, J. | (2) | 15-28 | England v South Africa | Cape Town | 1888–89 |
| | | 15-57 | Londesborough's XI v Australians | Scarborough | 1890 |
| Brown, W. | | 15-73 | Tasmania v Victoria | Hobart | 1857–58 |
| Burton, G. | | 16-114 | Middlesex v Yorkshire | Sheffield | 1888 |

| Butler, S.E. | | 15-95 | Oxford University v Cambridge U. | Lord's | 1871 |
|---|---|---|---|---|---|
| Callaway, S.T. | (2) | 15-175 | NSW v New Zealand XI | Christchurch | 1895–96 |
| | | 15-60 | Canterbury v Hawke's Bay | Napier | 1903–04 |
| Cartwright, T.W. | | 15-89 | Warwickshire v Glamorgan | Swansea | 1967 |
| Chatterjee, P.M. | | 15-109 | Bengal v Madhya Pradesh | Calcutta | 1955–56 |
| Chester, J. | | 15- | MCC v Cambridge University | Cambridge | 1850 |
| Clarke, W. | (2) | 16- | Nottinghamshire v Kent | Nottingham | 1845 |
| | | 15-98 | North v South | Oval | 1851 |
| Clay, J.C. | (2) | 15-86 | Glamorgan v Northamptonshire | Llanelly | 1935 |
| | | 17-212 | Glamorgan v Worcestershire | Swansea | 1937 |
| Collins, G.C. | | 16-83 | Kent v Nottinghamshire | Dover | 1922 |
| Conway, A.J. | | 15-87 | Worcestershire v Gloucestershire | Moreton-in-Marsh | 1914 |
| Cooke, F.H. | | 15-94 | Otago v Canterbury | Christchurch | 1882–83 |
| Cox, G.R. | | 17-106 | Sussex v Warwickshire | Horsham | 1926 |
| Davidson, G. | | 15-116 | Derbyshire v Essex | Leyton | 1898 |
| Dean, H. | (3) | 16-103 | Lancashire v Somerset | Bath | 1910 |
| | | 15-108 | Lancashire v Kent | Manchester | 1912 |
| | | 17-91 | Lancashire v Yorkshire | Liverpool | 1913 |
| Deas, L.M. | | 15-166 | Europeans v Hindus | Bombay | · 1905–06 |
| Dennett, E.G. | (7) | 15-96 | Gloucestershire v Middlesex | Bristol | 1904 |
| | | 15-88 | Gloucestershire v Essex | Bristol | 1906 |
| | | 15-140 | Gloucestershire v Worcestershire | Cheltenham | 1906 |
| | | 15-21 | Gloucestershire v Northamptonshire | Gloucester | 1907 |
| | | | *All taken on June 11.* | | |
| | | 15-97 | Gloucestershire v Northamptonshire | Northampton | 1907 |
| | | 16-146 | Gloucestershire v Hampshire | Bristol | 1912 |
| | | 15-195 | Gloucestershire v Surrey | Bristol | 1913 |
| Dooland, B. | (2) | 16-83 | Nottinghamshire v Essex | Nottingham | 1954 |
| | | 15-193 | Nottinghamshire v Kent | Gravesend | 1956 |
| Dowson, E.M. | | 16-58 | R.A. Bennett's XI v Jamaica | Kingston | 1901–02 |
| Drake, A. | | 15-51 | Yorkshire v Somerset | Weston-s-Mare | 1914 |
| Dwyer, J.E.B.B.P.Q.C. | | 16-100 | Sussex v Middlesex | Hove | 1906 |
| East, R.E. | | 15-115 | Essex v Warwickshire | Leyton | 1968 |
| Ellis, C.H. | | 15-297 | Sussex v Surrey | Brighton | 1863 |
| Emmett, T. | | 16-38 | Yorkshire v Cambridgeshire | Hunslet, Leeds | 1869 |
| Farnes, K. | | 15-113 | Essex v Glamorgan | Clacton | 1938 |
| Fazal Mahmood | | 15-76 | Punjab v Services | Lahore | 1956–57 |
| Fenner, F.P. | | 17- | Cambridge Town v Cambridge U. | Cambridge | 1844 |
| Fleetwood-Smith, L.O'B. | (2) | 15-226 | Victoria v New South Wales | Sydney | 1934–35 |
| | | 15-96 | Victoria v Queensland | Melbourne | 1936–37 |
| Freeman, A.P. | (9) | 17-67 | Kent v Sussex | Hove | 1922 |
| | | 15-224 | Kent v Leicestershire | Tonbridge | 1928 |
| | | 16-94 | Kent v Essex | Southend | 1930 |
| | | 15-142 | Kent v Essex | Gravesend | 1931 |
| | | 15-144 | Kent v Leicestershire | Maidstone | 1931 |
| | | 15-94 | Kent v Somerset | Canterbury | 1931 |
| | | 17-92 | Kent v Warwickshire | Folkestone | 1932 |
| | | 16-82 | Kent v Northamptonshire | Tunbridge Wells | 1932 |
| | | 15-122 | Kent v Middlesex | Lord's | 1933 |
| Geary, G. | | 16-96 | Leicestershire v Glamorgan | Pontypridd | 1929 |
| Giffen, G. | (6) | 17-201 | South Australia v Victoria | Adelaide | 1885–86 |
| | | 16-101 | Australians v Derbyshire | Derby | 1886 |
| | | 16-65 | Australians v Lancashire | Manchester | 1886 |
| | | 16-166 | South Australia v Victoria | Adelaide | 1891–92 |
| | | 16-186 | South Australia v NSW | Adelaide | 1894–95 |
| | | 15-185 | South Australia v Victoria | Adelaide | 1902–03 |
| Gladwin, C. | | 16-84 | Derbyshire v Worcestershire | Stourbridge | 1952 |
| Glover, G.K. | | 15-68 | Griqualand West v E. Province | Cape Town | 1893–94 |
| Goddard, T.W.J. | (7) | 16-181 | Gloucestershire v Worcestershire | Cheltenham | 1937 |
| | | 16-99 | Gloucestershire v Worcestershire | Bristol | 1939 |
| | | 17-106 | Gloucestershire v Kent | Bristol | 1939 |
| | | 15-81 | Gloucestershire v Nottinghamshire | Bristol | 1947 |
| | | 15-134 | Gloucestershire v Leicestershire | Gloucester | 1947 |
| | | 15-156 | Gloucestershire v Middlesex | Cheltenham | 1947 |
| | | 15-107 | Gloucestershire v Derbyshire | Bristol | 1949 |
| Grace, W.G. | (5) | 15-79 | Gloucestershire v Yorkshire | Sheffield | 1872 |
| | | 15-147 | MCC v Kent | Canterbury | 1873 |

| | | | | | |
|---|---|---|---|---|---|
| Grace W.G. *contd.* | | 17-89 | Gloucestershire v Nottinghamshire | Cheltenham | 1877 |
| | | 15-116 | Gloucestershire v Surrey | Cirencester | 1879 |
| | | 16-60 | MCC v Nottinghamshire | Lord's | 1885 |
| Grimmett, C.V. | | 16-289 | South Australia v Queensland | Adelaide | 1934–35 |
| Gupte, S.P. | | 15-104 | Rajasthan v Vidarbha | Nagpur | 1962–63 |
| Halfyard, D.J. | | 15-117 | Kent v Worcestershire | Maidstone | 1959 |
| Hammond, W.R. | | 15-128 | Gloucestershire v Worcestershire | Cheltenham | 1928 |
| Hargreave, S. | | 15-76 | Warwickshire v Surrey | Oval | 1903 |
| Harry, F. | | 15-70 | Lancashire v Warwickshire | Manchester | 1906 |
| Hearne, J.T. | (4) | 15-154 | Middlesex v Nottinghamshire | Nottingham | 1893 |
| | | 15-110 | MCC v Oxford University | Oxford | 1897 |
| | | 16-114 | Middlesex v Lancashire | Manchester | 1898 |
| | | 15-93 | Middlesex v Somerset | Lord's | 1904 |
| Hearne, W. | | 15-114 | Kent v Lancashire | Manchester | 1893 |
| Henderson, R. | | 15-98 | Gentlemen of England v Oxford U. | Oxford | 1877 |
| Hillyer, W.R. | | 15- | England v Hampshire | Southampton | 1842 |
| Hinkly, E. | | 16- | Kent v England | Lord's | 1848 |
| Hirst, G.H. | | 15-63 | Yorkshire v Leicestershire | Hull | 1907 |
| Hopwood, J.L. | | 15-112 | Lancashire v Worcestershire | Blackpool | 1934 |
| Hordern, H.V. | | 16-96 | Philadelphians v Jamaica | Kingston | 1908–09 |
| Howell, W.P. | (2) | 15-57 | Australians v Surrey | Oval | 1899 |
| | | 17-54 | Australians v Western Province | Cape Town | 1902–03 |
| Humphreys, W.A. | | 15-193 | Sussex v Somerset | Taunton | 1893 |
| Illingworth, R. | | 15-123 | Yorkshire v Glamorgan | Swansea | 1960 |
| Jackson, J. | (2) | 15-91 | North v South | Lord's | 1857 |
| | | 15-73 | Nottinghamshire v Surrey | Oval | 1860 |
| Jenkins, R.O. | | 15-122 | Worcestershire v Sussex | Dudley | 1953 |
| Jupp, V.W.C. | | 15-52 | Northamptonshire v Glamorgan | Swansea | 1925 |
| Kennedy, A.S. | | 15-116 | Hampshire v Somerset | Bath | 1922 |
| Kirwan, J.H. | | 15- | Cambridge U. v Cambridge Town | Cambridge | 1836 |
| | | | *All bowled* | | |
| Laker, J.C. | (2) | 15-97 | Surrey v MCC | Lord's | 1954 |
| | | 19-90 | England v Australia | Manchester | 1956 |
| Langford, B.A. | | 15-54 | Somerset v Lancashire | Weston-s-Mare | 1958 |
| Lillywhite, F.W. | (2) | 16- | Sussex v Hampshire & Surrey | Bramshill | 1826 |
| | | 15- | England v Kent | Lord's | 1840 |
| Litteljohn, A.R. | | 15-189 | Middlesex v Lancashire | Lord's | 1911 |
| Lock, G.A.R. | (2) | 16-83 | Surrey v Kent | Blackheath | 1956 |
| | | 15-182 | Surrey v Kent | Blackheath | 1958 |
| Lockwood, W. | | 15-184 | Surrey v Gloucestershire | Cheltenham | 1899 |
| Lohmann, G.A. | (2) | 15-98 | Surrey v Sussex | Hove | 1889 |
| | | 15-45 | England v South Africa | Port Elizabeth | 1895–96 |
| McBeath, D.J. | | 15-168 | Canterbury v Auckland | Christchurch | 1918–19 |
| McDonald, E.A. | | 15-154 | Lancashire v Kent | Manchester | 1928 |
| McDonell, H.C. | | 15-138 | Cambridge University v Surrey | Cambridge | 1904 |
| McIntyre, W. | | 15-47 | Lancashire v Derbyshire | Derby | 1875 |
| McKibbin, T.R. | | 15-125 | NSW v South Australia | Adelaide | 1896–97 |
| Mailey, A.A. | | 15-193 | Australians v Nottinghamshire | Nottingham | 1926 |
| Marlar, R.G. | (2) | 15-133 | Sussex v Glamorgan | Swansea | 1952 |
| | | 15-119 | Sussex v Lancashire | Hove | 1955 |
| Marsham, C.D.B. | | 16-93 | Gents of England v Gents of MCC | Lord's | 1855 |
| Massie, R.A.L. | | 16-137 | Australia v England | Lord's | 1972 |
| Matthews, F.C. | | 17-89 | Nottinghamshire v Northamptonshire | Nottingham | 1923 |
| Mead, W. | (2) | 17-119 | Essex v Hampshire | Southampton | 1895 |
| | | 15-115 | Essex v Leicestershire | Leyton | 1903 |
| Meyer, R.J.O. | | 16-188 | Europeans v Muslims | Bombay | 1927–28 |
| Moir, A.M. | | 15-203 | Otago v Central Districts | New Plymouth | 1953–54 |
| Mold, A.W. | (4) | 15-131 | Lancashire v Somerset | Taunton | 1891 |
| | | 15-87 | Lancashire v Sussex | Hove | 1894 |
| | | 16-111 | Lancashire v Kent | Manchester | 1895 |
| | | 15-85 | Lancashire v Nottinghamshire | Nottingham | 1895 |
| Morley, F. | | 15-35 | Nottinghamshire v Kent | Town Malling | 1878 |
| Muncer, B.L. | (2) | 15-161 | Glamorgan v Essex | Brentwood | 1948 |
| | | 15-201 | Glamorgan v Sussex | Swansea | 1948 |
| Mycroft, W. | | 17-103 | Derbyshire v Hampshire | Southampton | 1876 |
| Mynn, A. | | 15-73 | Gents of Kent v Gents of England | Canterbury | 1843 |
| Nadeem Malik | | 15-102 | Lahore C v Sargodha | Lahore | 1973–74 |

| Name | | Figures | Match | Venue | Year |
|---|---|---|---|---|---|
| Nash, A.J. | | 15-116 | Glamorgan v Worcestershire | Swansea | 1921 |
| Newman, J.A. | | 16-88 | Hampshire v Somerset | Weston-s-Mare | 1927 |
| Nichols, M.S. | | 15-165 | Essex v Gloucestershire | Gloucester | 1938 |
| Nupen, E.P. | | 16-136 | Transvaal v Griqualand West | Johannesburg | 1931–32 |
| Parker, C.W.L. | (7) | 15-109 | Gloucestershire v Derbyshire | Derby | 1924 |
| | | 17-56 | Gloucestershire v Essex | Gloucester | 1925 |
| | | 16-154 | Gloucestershire v Somerset | Bristol | 1927 |
| | | 15-173 | Gloucestershire v Northamptonshire | Gloucester | 1927 |
| | | 16-109 | Gloucestershire v Middlesex | Cheltenham | 1930 |
| | | 15-91 | Gloucestershire v Surrey | Cheltenham | 1930 |
| | | 15-113 | Gloucestershire v Nottinghamshire | Bristol | 1931 |
| Parkin, C.H. | | 15-95 | Lancashire v Glamorgan | Blackpool | 1923 |
| Parris, F. | | 15-98 | Sussex v Gloucestershire | Bristol | 1894 |
| Parry, D.R. | | 15-101 | Combined I's v Jamaica | Kingston | 1979–80 |
| Peel, R. | | 15-50 | Yorkshire v Somerset | Leeds | 1895 |
| Perks, R.T.D. | | 15-106 | Worcestershire v Essex | Worcester | 1937 |
| Pervez Sajjad | | 15-112 | Karachi v Khairpur | Karachi | 1968–69 |
| Relf, A.E. | | 15-77 | Sussex v Leicestershire | Hove | 1912 |
| Rhodes, W. | (2) | 15-56 | Yorkshire v Essex | Leyton | 1899 |
| | | 15-124 | England v Australia | Melbourne | 1903–04 |
| Richardson, T. | (5) | 15-95 | Surrey v Essex | Oval | 1894 |
| | | 15-155 | Surrey v Hampshire | Oval | 1895 |
| | | 15-113 | Surrey v Leicestershire | Oval | 1896 |
| | | 15-154 | Surrey v Yorkshire | Leeds | 1897 |
| | | 15-83 | Surrey v Warwickshire | Oval | 1898 |
| Roberts, F.G. | | 15-123 | Gloucestershire v Kent | Maidstone | 1897 |
| Robinson, E.P. | | 15-78 | Somerset v Sussex | Weston-s-Mare | 1952 |
| Rowan, A.M.B. | | 15-68 | Transvaal v Australians | Johannesburg | 1949–50 |
| Shepherd, J.N. | | 15-147 | Kent v Sussex | Maidstone | 1975 |
| Smith, S.G. | | 16-85 | West Indian XI v R.A. Bennett's XI | Port-of-Spain | 1901–02 |
| Smith, T.P.B. | | 16-215 | Essex v Middlesex | Colchester | 1947 |
| Southerton, J. | | 16-52 | South v North | Lord's | 1875 |
| Spofforth, F.R. | | 15-36 | Australians v Oxford University | Oxford | 1886 |
| Statham, J.B. | (2) | 15-89 | Lancashire v Warwickshire | Coventry | 1957 |
| | | 15-108 | Lancashire v Leicestershire | Leicester | 1964 |
| Tarrant, F.A. | (2) | 15-47 | Middlesex v Hampshire | Lord's | 1913 |
| | | 16-176 | Middlesex v Lancashire | Manchester | 1914 |
| Tarrant, G. | | 15-56 | Cambridgeshire v Kent | Chatham | 1862 |
| Tate, F.W. | | 15-68 | Sussex v Middlesex | Lord's | 1902 |
| Tausif Ahmed | | 15-148 | United Bank v Railways | Lahore | 1984–85 |
| Thompson, G.J. | | 15-167 | Northamptonshire v Leicestershire | Northampton | 1906 |
| Thomson, N.I. | | 15-75 | Sussex v Warwickshire | Worthing | 1964 |
| Tinley, R.C. | | 15-78 | Nottinghamshire v Cambridgeshire | Nottingham | 1862 |
| Titmus, F.J. | | 15-95 | Middlesex v Somerset | Bath | 1955 |
| Townsend, C.L. | (5) | 16-122 | Gloucestershire v Nottinghamshire | Nottingham | 1895 |
| | | 15-184 | Gloucestershire v Yorkshire | Cheltenham | 1895 |
| | | 15-134 | Gloucestershire v Middlesex | Lord's | 1898 |
| | | 15-141 | Gloucestershire v Essex | Clifton | 1898 |
| | | 15-205 | Gloucestershire v Warwickshire | Cheltenham | 1898 |
| Tribe, G.E. | (2) | 15-75 | Northamptonshire v Yorkshire | Bradford | 1955 |
| | | 15-31 | Northamptonshire v Yorkshire | Northampton | 1958 |
| Trott, A.E. | | 15-187 | Middlesex v Sussex | Lord's | 1901 |
| Trumble, H. | (2) | 15-199 | Victoria v South Australia | Adelaide | 1888–89 |
| | | 15-68 | Australians v South of England | Bournemouth | 1902 |
| Turner, C.T.B. | (3) | 16-79 | NSW v A. Shrewsbury's XI | Sydney | 1887–88 |
| | | 17-50 | Australians v England XI | Hastings | 1888 |
| | | 15-174 | New South Wales v Victoria | Sydney | 1890–91 |
| Tyler, E.J. | (2) | 15-96 | Somerset v Nottinghamshire | Taunton | 1892 |
| | | 15-95 | Somerset v Sussex | Taunton | 1895 |
| Underwood, D.L. | | 15-43 | International XI v President's XI | Colombo | 1967-68 |
| Verity, H. | (5) | 17-91 | Yorkshire v Essex | Leyton | 1933 |
| | | 15-104 | England v Australia | Lord's | 1934 |
| | | 15-129 | Yorkshire v Oxford University | Oxford | 1936 |
| | | 15-38 | Yorkshire v Kent | Sheffield | 1936 |
| | | 15-100 | Yorkshire v Essex | Westcliff | 1936 |
| Vine, J. | | 15-161 | Sussex v Nottinghamshire | Nottingham | 1901 |
| Vogler, A.E.E. | | 16-38 | E. Province v Griqualand West | Johannesburg | 1906–07 |

| Walsh, J.E. | (3) | 15-100 | Leicestershire v Sussex | Hove | 1948 |
|---|---|---|---|---|---|
| | | 15-164 | Leicestershire v Nottinghamshire | Loughborough | 1949 |
| | | 16-225 | Leicestershire v Oxford University | Oxford | 1953 |
| Wardle, J.H. | | 16-112 | Yorkshire v Sussex | Hull | 1954 |
| Warren, A. | | 15-112 | Derbyshire v Nottinghamshire | Welbeck | 1904 |
| Wass, T.G. | (2) | 16-69 | Nottinghamshire v Lancashire | Liverpool | 1906 |
| | | 16-103 | Nottinghamshire v Essex | Nottingham | 1908 |
| Wellard, A.W. | | 15-101 | Somerset v Worcestershire | Bath | 1947 |
| White, J.C. | (3) | 16-83 | Somerset v Worcestershire | Bath | 1919 |
| | | 15-175 | Somerset v Worcestershire | Worcester | 1921 |
| | | 15-96 | Somerset v Glamorgan | Bath | 1932 |
| Wilson, G.A. | | 15-142 | Worcestershire v Somerset | Taunton | 1905 |
| Wisden, J. | | 15- | Sussex v Kent | Hove | 1848 |
| Woodcock, A. | | 15-136 | Leicestershire v Nottinghamshire | Leicester | 1894 |
| Woods, S.M.J. | (2) | 15-88 | Cambridge U. v C.I. Thornton's XI | Cambridge | 1890 |
| | | 15-86 | Lord Hawke's XI v Philadelphians | Philadelphia | 1891–92 |
| Wright, D.V.P. | (3) | 16-80 | Kent v Somerset | Bath | 1939 |
| | | 15-173 | Kent v Sussex | Hastings | 1947 |
| | | 15-163 | Kent v Leicestershire | Maidstone | 1949 |
| Young, H.I. | | 15-154 | Essex v Warwickshire | Birmingham | 1899 |

# SIXTEEN OR MORE WICKETS IN A DAY

| 17-48 | C. Blythe | Kent v Northamptonshire | Northampton | 1907 |
|---|---|---|---|---|
| 17-91 | H. Verity | Yorkshire v Essex | Leyton | 1933 |
| 17-106 | T.W.J. Goddard | Gloucestershire v Kent | Bristol | 1939 |
| 16-38 | T. Emmett | Yorkshire v Cambridgeshire | Hunslet, Leeds | 1869 |
| 16-38 | A.E.E. Vogler | Eastern Province v Griqualand West | Johannesburg | 1906–07 |
| 16-51 | J. Southerton | South v North | Lord's | 1875 |
| 16-69 | T.G. Wass | Nottinghamshire v Lancashire | Liverpool | 1906 |
| 16-83 | J.C. White | Somerset v Worcestershire | Bath | 1919 |
| 16-103 | T.G. Wass | Nottinghamshire v Essex | Nottingham | 1908 |

# OUTSTANDING INNINGS ANALYSES

### TEN WICKETS IN AN INNINGS

| O | M | R | W | | | | |
|---|---|---|---|---|---|---|---|
| 19.4 | 16 | 10 | 10 | H. Verity | Yorkshire v Nottinghamshire | Leeds | 1932 |
| 16.2 | 8 | 18 | 10 | G. Geary | Leicestershire v Glamorgan | Pontypridd | 1929 |
| 19 | 11 | 20 | 10 | P.M. Chatterjee | Bengal v Assam | Jorhat | 1956–57 |
| 12 | 2 | 26 | 10 | A.E.E. Vogler | Eastern Province v Griqualand West | Johannesburg | 1906–07 |
| 21.3 | 10 | 28 | 10 | A.E. Moss | Canterbury v Wellington | Christchurch | 1889–90 |
| 23.2 | 14 | 28 | 10 | W.P. Howell | Australians v Surrey | Oval | 1899 |
| 16 | 7 | 30 | 10 | C. Blythe | Kent v Northamptonshire | Northampton | 1907 |

### NINE WICKETS IN AN INNINGS

| O | M | R | W | | | | |
|---|---|---|---|---|---|---|---|
| 19 | 17 | 2 | 9 | G. Elliott | Victoria v Tasmania | Launceston | 1857–58 |
| 6.3 | 4 | 7 | 9 | Ahad Khan | Railways v Dera Ismail Khan | Lahore | 1964–65 |
| 10 | 4 | 11 | 9 | A.P. Freeman | Kent v Sussex | Hove | 1922 |
| 6.3 | 3 | 12 | 9 | H. Verity | Yorkshire v Kent | Sheffield | 1936 |
| 17.1 | 10 | 15 | 9 | C.T.B. Turner | Australians v England XI | Stoke-on-Trent | 1888 |
| 14.5 | 9 | 17 | 9 | G.G. Napier | Europeans v Parsees | Poona | 1909–10 |
| 15.5 | 6 | 17 | 9 | P.J. Loader | Surrey v Warwickshire | Oval | 1958 |
| 17.3 | 9 | 17 | 9 | H.L. Jackson | Derbyshire v Cambridge University | Cambridge | 1959 |
| 15.2 | 7 | 18 | 9 | F.R. Spofforth | Australians v Oxford University | Oxford | 1886 |
| 13 | 6 | 18 | 9 | R.K. Oxenham | Australians v Ceylon | Colombo | 1935–36 |
| 25 | 15 | 19 | 9 | J. Grundy | Nottinghamshire v Kent | Nottingham | 1864 |
| 15.4 | 3 | 19 | 9 | O.H. Layne | Demerara v W.C. Shepherd's XI | Georgetown | 1909–10 |
| 15.4 | 7 | 19 | 9 | A.M.B. Rowan | Transvaal v Australians | Johannesburg | 1949–50 |
| 35.1 | 25 | 20 | 9 | W.G. Grace | MCC v Nottinghamshire | Lord's | 1885 |
| 10 | 2 | 20 | 9 | F.W. Swarbrook | Derbyshire v Sussex | Hove | 1975 |

| O | M | R | W | | | | |
|---|---|---|---|---|---|---|---|
| 15.1 | 8 | 21 | 9 | T.L. Richmond | Nottinghamshire v Hampshire | Nottingham | 1922 |
| 13.5 | 8 | 21 | 9 | T.W.J. Goddard | Gloucestershire v Cambridge University | Cheltenham | 1929 |
| 21.3 | 10 | 22 | 9 | R. Peel | Yorkshire v Somerset | Leeds | 1895 |
| 10.3 | 2 | 22 | 9 | M.G. Melle | South Africans v Tasmania | Launceston | 1952–53 |

## EIGHT WICKETS IN AN INNINGS

| O | M | R | W | | | | |
|---|---|---|---|---|---|---|---|
| 14 | 12 | 2 | 8 | J.C. Laker | England v Rest | Bradford | 1950 |
| 11.1 | 7 | 4 | 8 | D. Shackleton | Hampshire v Somerset | Weston-s-Mare | 1955 |
| 16 | 11 | 5 | 8 | E. Peate | Yorkshire v Surrey | Holbeck | 1883 |
| 14 | | 7 | 8 | J. Bickley | England v Kent & Sussex | Lord's | 1856 |
| 9.4 | 5 | 7 | 8 | G.A. Lohmann | England v South Africa | Port Elizabeth | 1895–96 |
| 14 | 12 | 7 | 8 | C.H. Palmer | Leicestershire v Surrey | Leicester | 1955 |
| 6.7 | 2 | 8 | 8 | J.E.D. Sealy | Barbados v Trinidad | Bridgetown | 1941–42 |
| 12 | 7 | 8 | 8 | M.G. Melle | Transvaal v Griqualand West | Johannesburg | 1950–51 |
| 13.2 | 9 | 9 | 8 | G. Wootton | MCC v Sussex | Lord's | 1863 |
| 6 | 1 | 9 | 8 | E.G. Dennett | Gloucestershire v Northamptonshire | Gloucester | 1907 |
| 14.2 | 10 | 9 | 8 | G.E. Tribe | Northamptonshire v Yorkshire | Northampton | 1958 |
| 10.1 | 6 | 9 | 8 | D.L. Underwood | Kent v Sussex | Hastings | 1973 |
| 11.3 | 6 | 10 | 8 | D.L. Underwood | International XI v President's XI | Colombo | 1967–68 |
| 13 | 8 | 11 | 8 | G. Freeman | Yorkshire v Lancashire | Holbeck | 1868 |
| 14.2 | 5 | 11 | 8 | J. Briggs | England v South Africa | Cape Town | 1888–89 |
| 11.4 | 6 | 11 | 8 | B.M. Billimoria | Parsees v Europeans | Poona | 1895–96 |
| 13 | 7 | 11 | 8 | A.S. Kennedy | Hampshire v Glamorgan | Cardiff | 1921 |
| 8.2 | 2 | 11 | 8 | W.H. Copson | Derbyshire v Warwickshire | Derby | 1937 |
| 13 | 9 | 11 | 8 | I.J. Jones | Glamorgan v Leicestershire | Leicester | 1965 |
| 13.3 | | 12 | 8 | R.C. Tinley | Nottinghamshire v Cambridgeshire | Nottingham | 1862 |
| 20.2 | 13 | 12 | 8 | R. Peel | Yorkshire v Nottinghamshire | Sheffield | 1888 |
| 12 | 8 | 12 | 8 | R.W. Norden | Transvaal v Rhodesia | Johannesburg | 1904–05 |
| 17 | 10 | 12 | 8 | C.W.L. Parker | Gloucestershire v Essex | Gloucester | 1925 |
| 6.4 | 2 | 12 | 8 | W.H.R. Andrews | Somerset v Surrey | Oval | 1937 |
| 9.4 | 3 | 12 | 8 | G.S. Ramchand | Bombay v Saurashtra | Bombay | 1959–60 |
| 17.1 | 10 | 12 | 8 | R. Harman | Surrey v Nottinghamshire | Nottingham | 1964 |
| 13 | 6 | 13 | 8 | J.P. Firth | Wellington v Hawke's Bay | Wellington | 1883–84 |
| 21.3 | 12 | 13 | 8 | C.T.B. Turner | Australians v England XI | Hastings | 1888 |
| 9.1 | 3 | 13 | 8 | W.C. Smith | Surrey v Northamptonshire | Oval | 1910 |
| 13.2 | 5 | 13 | 8 | E. Robinson | Yorkshire v Cambridge University | Cambridge | 1928 |
| 8 | 2 | 13 | 8 | D.P.B. Morkel | South Africans v Western Australia | Perth | 1931–32 |
| 12 | 7 | 13 | 8 | Zafar Iqbal | Multan v Quetta | Multan | 1958–59 |
| 27.1 | 17 | 14 | 8 | A. Shaw | MCC v Derbyshire | Lord's | 1881 |
| 15.3 | 10 | 14 | 8 | G. Nash | Lancashire v Somerset | Manchester | 1882 |
| 19 | 12 | 14 | 8 | S.W. Austin | New South Wales v Hawke's Bay | Napier | 1893–94 |
| 7.5 | 1 | 14 | 8 | H.D. Kanga | Parsees v Europeans | Poona | 1913–14 |
| 9.3 | 3 | 14 | 8 | A.G. Ram Singh | Indians v Europeans | Madras | 1935–36 |
| 7.4 | 3 | 14 | 8 | V.D. Sondhi | Delhi v Jammu & Kashmir | Delhi | 1963–64 |
| 19.2 | 11 | 14 | 8 | R.M.H. Cottam | Northamptonshire v Oxford University | Oxford | 1972 |
| 33.3 | 23 | 15 | 8 | G. Wootton | MCC v Surrey | Lord's | 1867 |
| 29.3 | 21 | 15 | 8 | A. Rylott | MCC v Kent | Lord's | 1878 |
| 11 | 7 | 15 | 8 | A. Hearne | Kent v Gloucestershire | Tonbridge | 1903 |
| 17.2 | 11 | 15 | 8 | R.K. Tyldesley | Lancashire v Northamptonshire | Kettering | 1926 |
| 10.2 | 1 | 15 | 8 | Firasat Hussain | United Provinces v S. Punjab | Amritsar | 1936–37 |
| 14 | 8 | 15 | 8 | H.J. Butler | Nottinghamshire v Surrey | Nottingham | 1937 |
| 6.4 | 2 | 15 | 8 | S. Ramadhin | West Indians v Gloucestershire | Cheltenham | 1950 |

## SEVEN WICKETS IN AN INNINGS

| O | M | R | W | | | | |
|---|---|---|---|---|---|---|---|
| 8.3 | 6 | 3 | 7 | F.R. Spofforth | Australians v England XI | Birmingham | 1884 |
| 9.3 | 7 | 4 | 7 | W.A. Henderson | N.E. Transvaal v OFS | Bloemfontein | 1937–38 |
| 7 | 4 | 4 | 7 | R. Goel | Haryana v Jammu & Kashmir | Chandigarh | 1977–78 |
| 17.5 | 11 | 5 | 7 | B.S. Bedi | Delhi v Jammu & Kashmir | Delhi | 1974–75 |
| 21.2 | 18 | 6 | 7 | F. Morley | MCC v Oxford University | Oxford | 1877 |
| 7 | 4 | 6 | 7 | A. Waddington | Yorkshire v Sussex | Hull | 1922 |
| 14 | 12 | 6 | 7 | R.K. Tyldesley | Lancashire v Northamptonshire | Liverpool | 1924 |
| 12.4 | 6 | 6 | 7 | R.V. Webster | Warwickshire v Yorkshire | Birmingham | 1964 |

| O | M | R | W | | | | |
|---|---|---|---|---|---|---|---|
| 13 | 9 | 6 | 7 | R. Illingworth | Yorkshire v Gloucestershire | Harrogate | 1967 |
| 24 | 20 | 7 | 7 | W. Caffyn | Surrey v Kent | Canterbury | 1862 |
| 41.2 | 36 | 7 | 7 | A. Shaw | Nottinghamshire v MCC | Lord's | 1875 |
| 10.2 | 7 | 7 | 7 | F. Morley | Nottinghamshire v Derbyshire | Nottingham | 1879 |
| 6.4 | 3 | 7 | 7 | L.T. Driffield | Cambridge University v MCC | Cambridge | 1900 |
| 7 | 3 | 7 | 7 | J. Bailey | Hampshire v Nottinghamshire | Southampton | 1932 |
| 13.3 | 8 | 7 | 7 | G. Geary | Leicestershire v Warwickshire | Hinckley | 1936 |
| 9.1 | 6 | 7 | 7 | D.J. Shepherd | Glamorgan v Hampshire | Cardiff | 1966 |
| 8.1 | 4 | 7 | 7 | A. Bhattacharjee | Bengal v Assam | Jorhat | 1974–75 |
| 14 | 9 | 8 | 7 | L. Cook | Lancashire v Derbyshire | Chesterfield | 1920 |
| 16 | 9 | 8 | 7 | G.R. Cox | Sussex v Derbyshire | Hove | 1920 |
| 10 | 7 | 8 | 7 | A.S. Kennedy | Hampshire v Warwickshire | Portsmouth | 1927 |
| 11.5 | 7 | 8 | 7 | James Langridge | Sussex v Gloucestershire | Cheltenham | 1932 |
| 11.4 | 6 | 8 | 7 | G.D. McKenzie | Leicestershire v Glamorgan | Leicester | 1971 |
| 9.2 | 5 | 8 | 7 | P.G. Lee | Lancashire v Warwickshire | Birmingham | 1975 |
| 10 | | 9 | 7 | G. Bennett | Kent v Sussex | Hove | 1857 |
| 9.3 | 6 | 9 | 7 | T. Emmett | Yorkshire v Sussex | Hove | 1878 |
| 22 | 15 | 9 | 7 | F. Morley | Nottinghamshire v Kent | Town Malling | 1878 |
| 19.2 | 12 | 9 | 7 | F. Morley | Nottinghamshire v Surrey | Oval | 1880 |
| 6.3 | 3 | 9 | 7 | F.E. Woolley | Kent v Surrey | Oval | 1911 |
| 7.5 | 3 | 9 | 7 | C. Blythe | Kent v Leicestershire | Leicester | 1912 |
| 14 | 7 | 9 | 7 | G.G. Macaulay | Yorkshire v Northamptonshire | Kettering | 1933 |
| 6 | 1 | 9 | 7 | H. Verity | Yorkshire v Sussex | Hove | 1939 |
| 12.1 | 8 | 9 | 7 | J.T. Partridge | Rhodesia v Border | Bulawayo | 1959–60 |
| 10.1 | 6 | 9 | 7 | J.G. Bracewell | Otago v Canterbury | Dunedin | 1981–82 |
| 16 | | 10 | 7 | H. Stubberfield | Sussex v Kent | Hove | 1859 |
| 20.1 | 16 | 10 | 7 | A. Watson | England v MCC | Lord's | 1877 |
| 9 | 7 | 10 | 7 | A.W. Mold | Lancashire v Somerset | Manchester | 1894 |
| 8 | 2 | 10 | 7 | A.J.Y. Hopkins | Australians v Cambridge University | Cambridge | 1902 |
| 6.2 | 1 | 10 | 7 | A.C. King | Natal v Griqualand West | Johannesburg | 1906–07 |
| 8.2 | 4 | 10 | 7 | J.T. Newstead | Yorkshire v Worcestershire | Bradford | 1907 |
| 9 | 4 | 10 | 7 | J.C. White | Somerset v Gloucestershire | Bristol | 1920 |
| 5.3 | 2 | 10 | 7 | P.G.H. Fender | Surrey v Middlesex | Lord's | 1927 |
| 20.4 | 13 | 10 | 7 | F.M. Sibbles | Lancashire v Yorkshire | Bradford | 1932 |
| 17.2 | 14 | 10 | 7 | P.J. Robinson | Somerset v Nottinghamshire | Nottingham | 1966 |
| 6.2 | 3 | 10 | 7 | A. Bhattacharya | Bihar v Assam | Dhanbad | 1971–72 |

## SIX WICKETS IN AN INNINGS

| O | M | R | W | | | | |
|---|---|---|---|---|---|---|---|
| 21.1 | 20 | 1 | 6 | S. Cosstick | Victoria v Tasmania | Melbourne | 1868–69 |
| 4.5 | 3 | 1 | 6 | V.I. Smith | South Africans v Derbyshire | Derby | 1947 |
| 11 | 10 | 1 | 6 | Israr Ali | Bahawalpur v Dacca University | Bahawalpur | 1957–58 |
| 8.4 | 7 | 2 | 6 | E.F. Field | Warwickshire v Worcestershire | Dudley | 1914 |
| 8.1 | 6 | 3 | 6 | H.F. Boyle | Australians v MCC | Lord's | 1878 |
| 13.3 | 11 | 3 | 6 | A. Penn | Kent v Sussex | Tunbridge Wells | 1878 |
| 10.1 | 9 | 3 | 6 | R.G. Barlow | Lancashire v Derbyshire | Derby | 1881 |
| 4.4 | 3 | 3 | 6 | T.G. Wass | Nottinghamshire v MCC | Lord's | 1907 |
| 7 | 4 | 3 | 6 | G.G. Macaulay | Yorkshire v Derbyshire | Hull | 1921 |
| 8 | 5 | 3 | 6 | J. Cowie | New Zealanders v Ireland | Dublin | 1937 |
| 11 | 9 | 3 | 6 | T.L. Goddard | Natal v Border | East London | 1959–60 |
| 9 | 8 | 3 | 6 | Rajinder Pal | Delhi v Jammu & Kashmir | Srinagar | 1960–61 |
| 5.3 | 3 | 4 | 6 | F.R. Spofforth | Australians v MCC | Lord's | 1878 |
| 7.5 | 4 | 4 | 6 | W. Rhodes | Yorkshire v Nottinghamshire | Nottingham | 1901 |
| 8 | 5 | 4 | 6 | S.T. Callaway | Canterbury v Wellington | Wellington | 1903–04 |
| 7.3 | 4 | 4 | 6 | N. Phillip | Essex v Surrey | Chelmsford | 1983 |
| 7.2 | 3 | 4 | 6 | K.B. Ramamurthy | Andhra v Kerala | Vijayawada | 1984–85 |
| 6.2 | 4 | 5 | 6 | C.A. Reid | Victoria v Tasmania | Melbourne | 1870–71 |
| 9.2 | 3 | 5 | 6 | G. Bennett | Nelson v Wellington | Nelson | 1885–86 |
| 9.1 | 6 | 5 | 6 | G.S. Boyce | Hampshire v Derbyshire | Portsmouth | 1933 |
| 14 | 11 | 5 | 6 | J.C. Laker | Surrey v Nottinghamshire | Oval | 1955 |
| 16 | 14 | 5 | 6 | D.J. Shepherd | Glamorgan v Nottinghamshire | Newport | 1961 |
| 13 | 10 | 5 | 6 | F.J. Titmus | Middlesex v Oxford University | Oxford | 1968 |
| 8.4 | 5 | 6 | 6 | A.E. Bailey | Somerset v Warwickshire | Taunton | 1906 |
| 8 | 5 | 6 | 6 | C.H. Parkin | Lancashire v Glamorgan | Liverpool | 1924 |
| 9.4 | 7 | 6 | 6 | J.H. Wardle | Yorkshire v Gloucestershire | Bristol | 1955 |

| O | M | R | W | | | | |
|---|---|---|---|---|---|---|---|
| 4 | 0 | 6 | 6 | R. Goel | Southern Punjab v Northern Punjab | Patiala | 1962–63 |
| 16 | 11 | 6 | 6 | W.J.R. Haskell | Wellington v Otago | Wellington | 1967–68 |
| 7 | 4 | 6 | 6 | D.R. Doshi | Bengal v Assam | Jorhat | 1974–75 |
| 4.1 | 1 | 6 | 6 | Imran Khan | Sussex v Warwickshire | Birmingham | 1983 |

## FIVE WICKETS IN AN INNINGS

| O | M | R | W | | | | |
|---|---|---|---|---|---|---|---|
| 3 | 3 | 0 | 5 | A.D. Pougher | MCC v Australians | Lord's | 1896 |
| 6 | 6 | 0 | 5 | G.R. Cox | Sussex v Somerset | Weston-s-Mare | 1921 |
| 5 | 5 | 0 | 5 | R.K. Tyldesley | Lancashire v Leicestershire | Manchester | 1924 |
| 6.4 | 6 | 0 | 5 | P.T. Mills | Gloucestershire v Somerset | Bristol | 1928 |
| 4 | 3 | 1 | 5 | F.W. Tate | Sussex v Kent | Tonbridge | 1888 |
| 5.4 | 5 | 1 | 5 | J.S. Savage | Lancashire v Hampshire | Blackpool | 1967 |
| 15.2 | 13 | 2 | 5 | D. Ashby | Canterbury v Auckland | Auckland | 1877–78 |
| 6.1 | 4 | 2 | 5 | E.H. Killick | Sussex v Hampshire | Chichester | 1907 |
| 5.2 | 4 | 2 | 5 | J.C. Clay | Glamorgan v Somerset | Cardiff | 1922 |
| 2.3 | 1 | 2 | 5 | E.R.H. Toshack | Australia v India | Brisbane | 1947–48 |
| 5.3 | 4 | 2 | 5 | G.A.R. Lock | Surrey v Worcestershire | Oval | 1954 |
| 5.1 | 4 | 2 | 5 | W.B. Bridge | Warwickshire v Kent | Blackheath | 1961 |
| 4 | 2 | 2 | 5 | V.M. Muddiah | Services v Jammu & Kashmir | Delhi | 1961–62 |
| 10 | 8 | 2 | 5 | D.J. Shepherd | Glamorgan v Leicestershire | Ebbw Vale | 1965 |
| 10 | 9 | 2 | 5 | J.D. Gray | Warwickshire v Scotland | Birmingham | 1968 |
| 5.1 | 3 | 2 | 5 | N. Gifford | Warwickshire v Essex | Nuneaton | 1983 |
| 9.3 | 7 | 3 | 5 | R.G. Barlow | Lancashire v Kent | Manchester | 1878 |
| 11.3 | 8 | 3 | 5 | J. West | Yorkshire v Surrey | Sheffield | 1870 |
| 2.2 | 1 | 3 | 5 | B.D. Hylton-Stewart | Somerset v Worcestershire | Stourbridge | 1912 |
| 5 | 3 | 3 | 5 | C.F.W. Allcott | New Zealanders v Somerset | Taunton | 1927 |
| 3 | 1 | 3 | 5 | James Langridge | Sussex v Derbyshire | Derby | 1939 |
| 7.2 | 5 | 3 | 5 | T.E. Bailey | Essex v Cambridge University | Cambridge | 1965 |
| 7.6 | 6 | 3 | 5 | P. Willey | D.H. Robins' XI v Sri Lanka XI | Kandy | 1977–78 |
| 8.2 | 6 | 4 | 5 | R. Lang | Cambridge University v Oxford U. | Lord's | 1862 |
| 9 | 6 | 4 | 5 | W. Rhodes | Yorkshire v Worcestershire | Huddersfield | 1903 |
| 4.4 | 2 | 4 | 5 | G.A. Rotherham | Warwickshire v Northamptonshire | Northampton | 1921 |
| 7.1 | 4 | 4 | 5 | J.V. Murdin | Northamptonshire v Worcestershire | Northampton | 1921 |
| 4.4 | 1 | 4 | 5 | J.W.A. Stephenson | Essex v Somerset | Wells | 1939 |
| 3 | 1 | 4 | 5 | T.W.J. Goddard | Gloucestershire v Somerset | Bristol | 1947 |
| 8 | 4 | 4 | 5 | P.F. Jackson | Worcestershire v Warwickshire | Birmingham | 1950 |
| 10 | 8 | 4 | 5 | K. Bharathkumar | Tamil Nadu v Andhra | Coimbatore | 1978–79 |
| 7.3 | 4 | 4 | 5 | J.F. Steele | Leicestershire v Sussex | Hove | 1982 |
| 6 | 4 | 5 | 5 | Jas Lillywhite | Single v Married | Lord's | 1871 |
| 21.5 | 18 | 5 | 5 | J.W. Sharpe | Surrey v Oxford University | Oxford | 1889 |
| 14 | 10 | 5 | 5 | S. Rudder | Barbados v Trinidad | Bridgetown | 1897–98 |
| 4.4 | 2 | 5 | 5 | W. Rhodes | Yorkshire v Derbyshire | Bradford | 1910 |
| 7 | 3 | 5 | 5 | P.A. Wright | Cambridge University v Lancashire | Cambridge | 1922 |
| 8 | 5 | 5 | 5 | Firasat Hussain | United Provinces v Delhi | Agra | 1934–35 |
| 7 | 4 | 5 | 5 | C.J. Knott | Hampshire v Sussex | Eastbourne | 1950 |
| 15.4 | 12 | 5 | 5 | D. Shackleton | Hampshire v Somerset | Bournemouth | 1956 |
| 11 | 7 | 5 | 5 | S.P. Gupte | Bombay v Gujarat | Bombay | 1958–59 |
| 10.3 | 6 | 5 | 5 | R.J. Bright | Australians v Central Districts | Nelson | 1976–77 |

## FOUR WICKETS IN AN INNINGS

| O | M | R | W | | | | |
|---|---|---|---|---|---|---|---|
| 2 | 2 | 0 | 4 | Sir F.H.H. Bathurst | England v Kent | Lord's | 1843 |
| 3.2 | 3 | 0 | 4 | J.R. Napier | Lancashire v Yorkshire | Sheffield | 1888 |
| 5 | 5 | 0 | 4 | A. Hearne | Kent v Somerset | Taunton | 1893 |
| 0.5 | 0 | 0 | 4 | A.F. Borland | Natal v Griqualand West | Kimberley | 1926–27 |
| 2.1 | 2 | 0 | 4 | L.C. Eastman | Essex v Somerset | Weston-s-Mare | 1934 |
| 7 | 7 | 0 | 4 | L. Amarnath | Railways v Patiala | Patiala | 1958–59 |
| 6.1 | 5 | 1 | 4 | W. Barnes | A. Shrewsbury's XI v NSW | Sydney | 1884–85 |
| 6 | 5 | 1 | 4 | R.C.W. Burn | Lord Brackley's XI v Barbados | Bridgetown | 1904–05 |
| 3.3 | 2 | 1 | 4 | A.G. Slater | Derbyshire v Essex | Leyton | 1913 |
| 3 | 2 | 1 | 4 | C.A. Snedden | Auckland v Hawke's Bay | Auckland | 1920–21 |
| 4 | 3 | 1 | 4 | J.L. Hopwood | Lancashire v Gloucestershire | Manchester | 1931 |

| O | M | R | W | | | | |
|---|---|---|---|---|---|---|---|
| 10 | 9 | 1 | 4 | R.G. Garlick | Northamptonshire v Middlesex | Northampton | 1950 |
| 2.2 | 1 | 1 | 4 | E.J. Lewis | Glamorgan v Sussex | Cardiff | 1965 |
| 8.1 | 7 | 1 | 4 | K.J. Wheatley | Hampshire v Glamorgan | Southampton | 1968 |
| 8.1 | 7 | 2 | 4 | H.W. Fellows | M.C.C. v Hampshire | Lord's | 1861 |
| 8.3 | 6 | 2 | 4 | D.N. Writer | Parsees v Europeans | Bombay | 1894–95 |
| 3 | 2 | 2 | 4 | E.H. Killick | Sussex v Nottinghamshire | Nottingham | 1905 |
| 3 | 2 | 2 | 4 | H.L. Simms | Europeans v Muslims | Poona | 1915–16 |
| 5 | 3 | 2 | 4 | C.V. Grimmett | Australians v Worcestershire | Worcester | 1926 |
| 8 | 6 | 2 | 4 | H. Larwood | Nottinghamshire v Cambridge U. | Cambridge | 1926 |
| 7 | 5 | 2 | 4 | H.C. Chilvers | New South Wales v MCC | Sydney | 1936–37 |
| 7 | 5 | 2 | 4 | L. Amarnath | Southern Punjab v Sind | Patiala | 1938–39 |
| 5 | 3 | 2 | 4 | M.A. Sutton | Oxford U. v Combined Services | Oxford | 1947 |
| 6 | 5 | 2 | 4 | A.E.G. Rhodes | Derbyshire v Sussex | Horsham | 1947 |
| 6.4 | 5 | 2 | 4 | N. Puna | N. Districts v C. Districts | Hamilton | 1957–58 |
| 1.5 | 0 | 2 | 4 | S.E. Hankey | Transvaal B v Griqualand West | Johannesburg | 1965–66 |
| 4 | 2 | 2 | 4 | M. Bissex | Gloucestershire v Sussex | Cheltenham | 1968 |
| 7.5 | 5 | 2 | 4 | N. Gifford | Worcestershire v Kent | Worcester | 1974 |
| 8.2 | | 3 | 4 | S. Dakin | West of England v MCC | Bath | 1844 |
| 11 | 8 | 3 | 4 | W.J. Hammersley | Gents of England v Gents of Kent | Lord's | 1854 |
| 8 | 6 | 3 | 4 | W.H. Anstead | Surrey v Kent | Oval | 1870 |
| 6.3 | 4 | 3 | 4 | J. Young | Derbyshire v Nottinghamshire | Nottingham | 1900 |
| 10.2 | 7 | 3 | 4 | W.R. Cuttell | Lancashire v Kent | Manchester | 1904 |
| 2.2 | 0 | 3 | 4 | P. Compton | OFS v E. Province | Port Elizabeth | 1912–13 |
| 5 | 3 | 3 | 4 | J.A. Newman | Hampshire v Glamorgan | Swansea | 1922 |
| 6.2 | 4 | 3 | 4 | A. Young | Somerset v Glamorgan | Weston-s-Mare | 1930 |
| 7.3 | 5 | 3 | 4 | G.S. Boyes | Hampshire v Somerset | Southampton | 1936 |
| 5.4 | 4 | 3 | 4 | R.A. Sinfield | Gloucestershire v Lancashire | Preston | 1936 |
| 10.3 | 7 | 3 | 4 | L.F. Townsend | Derbyshire v Northants | Northampton | 1936 |
| 3.7 | 1 | 3 | 4 | F.A. Ward | South Australia v Queensland | Brisbane | 1936–37 |
| 8 | 5 | 3 | 4 | B.L. Muncer | Glamorgan v Kent | Swansea | 1949 |
| 7 | 5 | 3 | 4 | C.S. Matthews | Nottinghamshire v Somerset | Frome | 1957 |
| 5.5 | 4 | 3 | 4 | J.G. Lomax | Somerset v Cambridge University | Cambridge | 1959 |
| 4 | 2 | 3 | 4 | Tahir Ali | Khairpur v Hyderabad | Hyderabad | 1959–60 |
| 7 | 4 | 3 | 4 | T.W. Cartwright | Warwickshire v Surrey | Oval | 1962 |
| 5 | 4 | 3 | 4 | T.W. Cartwright | Warwickshire v Nottinghamshire | Nuneaton | 1964 |
| 4.2 | 2 | 3 | 4 | S.E. Leary | Kent v Oxford University | Canterbury | 1966 |
| 4.1 | 2 | 3 | 4 | L. Harris | Combined I's v Barbados | Basseterre | 1969–70 |
| 7 | 6 | 3 | 4 | S.M. Carrington | Northern Districts v Otago | Tauranga | 1982–83 |
| 7 | 5 | 3 | 4 | J.F. Steele | Leicestershire v Notts | Nottingham | 1983 |
| 10 | 6 | 4 | 4 | H.H. Stephenson | Surrey v Nottinghamshire | Nottingham | 1854 |
| 8.3 | 5 | 4 | 4 | W. Flowers | Nottinghamshire v Sussex | Hove | 1887 |
| 11 | 9 | 4 | 4 | J.T. Hearne | MCC v Australians | Lord's | 1896 |
| 3.1 | 1 | 4 | 4 | J.H. Vincett | Sussex v Gloucestershire | Bristol | 1909 |
| 4.3 | 1 | 4 | 4 | A. Drake | Yorkshire v Somerset | Bath | 1913 |
| 4 | 3 | 4 | 4 | F.S.G. Calthorpe | Warwickshire v Hampshire | Birmingham | 1922 |
| 8 | 5 | 4 | 4 | R.K. Tyldesley | Lancashire v Scotland | Manchester | 1925 |
| 7 | 4 | 4 | 4 | G. Wedel | Gloucestershire v Northamptonshire | Northampton | 1926 |
| 11 | 8 | 4 | 4 | S.J. Staples | Nottinghamshire v Hampshire | Southampton | 1932 |
| 2 | 0 | 4 | 4 | D.F. Dowling | Natal v Orange Free State | Pietermaritzburg | 1952–53 |
| 8.3 | 5 | 4 | 4 | E.A. Bedser | Surrey v Northamptonshire | Northampton | 1961 |
| 7.3 | 4 | 4 | 4 | K.S. Vaidyanathan | Madras v Kerala | Madras | 1965–66 |
| 7.5 | 4 | 4 | 4 | B.S. Chandrasekhar | Mysore v Andhra | Anantapur | 1965–66 |
| 4 | 2 | 4 | 4 | Ahad Khan | Railways v Peshawar | Lahore | 1969–70 |
| 5.3 | 2 | 4 | 4 | Izhar Ahmed | Lahore v PAF | Lahore | 1970–71 |
| 3.4 | 1 | 4 | 4 | S. Venkataraghavan | Indians v Nottinghamshire | Nottingham | 1979 |
| 6 | 3 | 4 | 4 | C.J.C. Rowe | Kent v Gloucestershire | Gloucester | 1979 |
| 10 | 6 | 4 | 4 | M. Hendrick | Nottinghamshire v Kent | Nottingham | 1982 |

*A. Drake returned analyses of 4.3-1-4-4 and 6.1-4-3-3 for Yorkshire v Somerset (Bath) 1913.*
*T.W. Hayward returned analyses of 0.3-0-0-1 and 0.3-0-0-2 for Surrey v Leicestershire (Leicester) 1895.*

## OUTSTANDING MATCH ANALYSES

### NINETEEN WICKETS IN A MATCH

| | | | | |
|---|---|---|---|---|
| 19-90 | (9-37, 10-53) J.C. Laker | England v Australia | Manchester | 1956 |

## SEVENTEEN WICKETS IN A MATCH

| | | | | | |
|---|---|---|---|---|---|
| 17-48 | (10-30, 7-18) | C. Blythe | Kent v Northamptonshire | Northampton | 1907 |
| 17-50 | (8-13, 9-37) | C.T.B. Turner | Australians v England XI | Hastings | 1888 |
| 17-54 | (8-31, 9-23) | W.P. Howell | Australians v Western Province | Cape Town | 1902–03 |
| 17-56 | (9-44, 8-12) | C.W.L. Parker | Gloucestershire v Essex | Gloucester | 1925 |
| 17-67 | (9-11, 8-56) | A.P. Freeman | Kent v Sussex | Hove | 1922 |
| 17-89 | (9-55, 8-34) | W.G. Grace | Gloucs v Nottinghamshire | Cheltenham | 1877 |
| 17-89 | (8-39, 9-50) | F.C. Matthews | Nottinghamshire v Northants | Nottingham | 1923 |
| 17-91 | (9-62, 8-29) | H. Dean | Lancashire v Yorkshire | Liverpool | 1913 |
| 17-91 | (8-47, 9-44) | H. Verity | Yorkshire v Essex | Leyton | 1933 |
| 17-92 | (8-31, 9-61) | A.P. Freeman | Kent v Warwickshire | Folkestone | 1932 |

## SIXTEEN WICKETS IN A MATCH

| | | | | | |
|---|---|---|---|---|---|
| 16-35 | (8-18, 8-17) | W.E. Bowes | Yorkshire v Northamptonshire | Kettering | 1935 |
| 16-38 | (7-15, 9-23) | T. Emmett | Yorkshire v Cambridgeshire | Hunslet, Leeds | 1869 |
| 16-38 | (6-12, 10-26) | A.E.E. Vogler | E. Province v Griqualand West | Johannesburg | 1906–07 |
| 16-52 | (9-30, 7-22) | J. Southerton | South v North | Lord's | 1875 |
| 16-58 | (8-21, 8-37) | E.M. Dowson | R.A. Bennett's XI v Jamaica | Kingston | 1901–02 |
| 16-60 | (7-40, 9-20) | W.G. Grace | MCC v Nottinghamshire | Lord's | 1885 |
| 16-65 | (8-23, 8-42) | G. Giffen | Australians v Lancashire | Manchester | 1886 |
| 16-69 | (8-25, 8-44) | T.G. Wass | Nottinghamshire v Lancashire | Liverpool | 1906 |
| 16-79 | (8-39, 8-40) | C.T.B. Turner | NSW v A. Shrewsbury's XI | Sydney | 1887–88 |
| 16-80 | (8-35, 8-45) | D.V.P. Wright | Kent v Somerset | Bath | 1939 |
| 16-82 | (8-38, 8-44) | A.P. Freeman | Kent v Northamptonshire | Tunbridge Wells | 1932 |
| 16-83 | (8-36, 8-47) | J.C. White | Somerset v Worcestershire | Bath | 1919 |
| 16-83 | (6-18, 10-65) | G.C. Collins | Kent v Nottinghamshire | Dover | 1922 |
| 16-83 | (8-39, 8-44) | B. Dooland | Nottinghamshire v Essex | Nottingham | 1954 |
| 16-83 | (6-29, 10-54) | G.A.R. Lock | Surrey v Kent | Blackheath | 1956 |
| 16-84 | (7-43, 9-41) | C. Gladwin | Derbyshire v Worcestershire | Stourbridge | 1952 |
| 16-85 | (9-34, 7-51) | S.G. Smith | West Indian XI v R.A. Bennett's XI | Port-of-Spain | 1901–02 |
| 16-88 | (8-65, 8-23) | J.A. Newman | Hampshire v Somerset | Weston-s-Mare | 1927 |

## FIFTEEN WICKETS IN A MATCH

| | | | | | |
|---|---|---|---|---|---|
| 15-21 | (8-9, 7-12) | E.G. Dennett | Gloucestershire v Northants | Gloucester | 1907 |
| 15-28 | (7-17, 8-11) | J. Briggs | England v South Africa | Cape Town | 1888–89 |
| 15-31 | (7-22, 8-9) | G.E. Tribe | Northamptonshire v Yorkshire | Northampton | 1958 |
| 15-35 | (7-9, 8-26) | F. Morley | Nottinghamshire v Kent | Town Malling | 1878 |
| 15-36 | (9-18, 6-18) | F.R. Spofforth | Australians v Oxford University | Oxford | 1886 |
| 15-38 | (6-26, 9-12) | H. Verity | Yorkshire v Kent | Sheffield | 1936 |
| 15-43 | (8-10, 7-33) | D.L. Underwood | International XI v President's XI | Colombo | 1967–68 |
| 15-45 | (7-38, 8-7) | G.A. Lohmann | England v South Africa | Port Elizabeth | 1895–96 |
| 15-45 | (7-9, 8-36) | C. Blythe | Kent v Leicestershire | Leicester | 1912 |
| 15-47 | (8-31, 7-16) | W. McIntyre | Lancashire v Derbyshire | Derby | 1877 |
| 15-47 | (7-27, 8-20) | F.A. Tarrant | Middlesex v Hampshire | Lord's | 1913 |
| 15-49 | (9-23, 6-26) | J.T. Botten | N.E. Transvaal v Griqualand West | Pretoria | 1958–59 |
| 15-50 | (9-22, 6-28) | R. Peel | Yorkshire v Somerset | Leeds | 1895 |
| 15-51 | (5-16, 10-35) | A. Drake | Yorkshire v Somerset | Weston-s-Mare | 1914 |
| 15-52 | (7-34, 8-18) | V.W.C. Jupp | Northamptonshire v Glamorgan | Swansea | 1925 |
| 15-54 | (9-26, 6-28) | B.A. Langford | Somerset v Lancashire | Weston-s-Mare | 1958 |
| 15-56 | (7-40, 8-16) | G. Tarrant | Cambridgeshire v Kent | Chatham | 1862 |
| 15-56 | (9-28, 6-28) | W. Rhodes | Yorkshire v Essex | Leyton | 1899 |
| 15-57 | (9-31, 6-26) | J. Briggs | Londesborough's XI v Australians | Scarborough | 1890 |
| 15-57 | (10-28, 5-29) | W.P. Howell | Australians v Surrey | Oval | 1899 |
| 15-60 | (8-33, 7-27) | S.T. Callaway | Canterbury v Hawke's Bay | Napier | 1903–04 |

## FOURTEEN WICKETS IN A MATCH

| | | | | | |
|---|---|---|---|---|---|
| 14-29 | (6-16, 8-13) | W.C. Smith | Surrey v Northamptonshire | Oval | 1910 |
| 14-29 | (8-4, 6-25) | D. Shackleton | Hampshire v Somerset | Weston-s-Mare | 1955 |
| 14-33 | (8-12, 6-21) | R. Peel | Yorkshire v Nottinghamshire | Sheffield | 1888 |
| 14-34 | (8-15, 6-19) | A. Rylott | MCC v Kent | Lord's | 1878 |
| 14-34 | (6-8, 8-26) | A. Rylott | MCC v Hampshire | Lord's | 1878 |
| 14-37 | (7-34, 7-3) | F.R. Spofforth | Australians v England XI | Birmingham | 1884 |

| 14-38 | (6-18, 8-20) | W. Mycroft | North v South | Loughborough | 1875 |
| 14-43 | (8-21, 6-22) | S. Haigh | Yorkshire v Hampshire | Southampton | 1898 |
| 14-43 | (7-23, 7-20) | W. Voce | Nottinghamshire v Northants | Nottingham | 1929 |
| 14-44 | (7-31, 7-13) | R.K. Oxenham | Australians v Central India & Rajputana | Ajmer | 1935–36 |
| 14-45 | (6-24, 8-21) | G.G. Hearne | Kent v MCC | Lord's | 1879 |
| 14-45 | (9-17, 5-28) | G.G. Napier | Europeans v Parsees | Poona | 1909–10 |
| 14-45 | (8-23, 6-22) | W.J. O'Reilly | NSW v Queensland | Sydney | 1939–40 |

## THIRTEEN WICKETS IN A MATCH

| 13-14 | (7-6, 6-8) | F. Morley | MCC v Oxford University | Oxford | 1877 |
| 13-29 | (7-  , 6- ) | C.R. Smith | Hawke's Bay v Taranaki | Hawera | 1891–92 |
| 13-29 | (6-25, 7-4) | R. Goel | Haryana v Jammu & Kashmir | Chandigarh | 1977–78 |
| 13-34 | (8-16, 5-18) | P.K. Shivalkar | Bombay v Tamil Nadu | Madras | 1972–73 |
| 13-34 | (6-29, 7-5) | B.S. Bedi | Delhi v Jammu & Kashmir | Delhi | 1974–75 |
| 13-35 | (7-13, 6-22) | W. Lankham | Auckland v Taranaki | Auckland | 1882–83 |
| 13-38 | (6-18, 7-20) | E. Wainwright | Yorkshire v Sussex | Dewsbury | 1894 |
| 13-38 | (6-27, 7-11) | T.R. McKibbin | Australians v Lancashire | Liverpool | 1896 |
| 13-39 | (6-22, 7-17) | H.R. Bromley-Davenport | R.S. Lucas's XI v Demerara | Georgetown | 1894–95 |
| 13-40 | (6-22, 7-18) | G. Howitt | United North v United South | Lord's | 1870 |
| 13-40 | (6-18, 7-22) | J. Briggs | Lord Londesborough's XI v Australians | Scarborough | 1888 |
| 13-40 | (8-17, 5-23) | T.G. Wass | Nottinghamshire v Derbyshire | Nottingham | 1901 |
| 13-40 | (6-27, 7-13) | S. Haigh | Yorkshire v Warwickshire | Sheffield | 1907 |
| 13-40 | (5-26, 8-14) | V.D. Sondhi | Delhi v Jammu & Kashmir | Delhi | 1963–64 |
| 13-41 | (4-5, 9-36) | W. Huddleston | Lancashire v Nottinghamshire | Liverpool | 1906 |
| 13-42 | (6-24, 7-18) | J. Jackson | North v South | Tunbridge Wells | 1857 |
| 13-43 | (6-36, 7-7) | G. Geary | Leicestershire v Warwickshire | Hinckley | 1936 |
| 13-44 | (5-16, 8-28) | H.H. Stephenson | England v Kent | Lord's | 1858 |
| 13-45 | (7-33, 6-12) | F. Morley | Nottinghamshire v Yorkshire | Sheffield | 1876 |
| 13-45 | (6-33, 7-12) | R. Henderson | I. Zingari v Yorkshire | Scarborough | 1877 |
| 13-45 | (7-24, 6-21) | W. Rhodes | Yorkshire v Somerset | Bath | 1898 |

## TWELVE WICKETS IN A MATCH

| 12-18 | (6-13, 6-5) | G. Bennett | Nelson v Wellington | Nelson | 1885–86 |
| 12-19 | (6-12, 6-7) | G.H. Hirst | Yorkshire v Northamptonshire | Northampton | 1908 |
| 12-20 | (5-6, 7-14) | T. Richardson | Surrey v Leicestershire | Leicester | 1897 |
| 12-23 | (8-11, 4-12) | G. Freeman | Yorkshire v Lancashire | Holbeck | 1868 |
| 12-28 | (6-19, 6-9) | E. Willsher | Kent v Yorkshire | Sheffield | 1865 |
| 12-29 | (7-13, 5-6) | G.A. Lohmann | Surrey v Hampshire | Oval | 1885 |
| 12-29 | (7-12, 5-17) | G.H. Hirst | Yorkshire v Essex | Leyton | 1901 |
| 12-30 | (6-11, 6-19) | T.B. Mitchell | Derbyshire v Sussex | Chesterfield | 1931 |
| 12-33 | (4-21, 8-12) | R.W. Norden | Transvaal v Rhodesia | Johannesburg | 1904–05 |
| 12-33 | (3-16, 9-17) | H.L. Jackson | Derbyshire v Cambridge U. | Cambridge | 1959 |
| 12-34 | (8-18, 4-16) | G.A. Lohmann | Surrey v Hampshire | Southampton | 1885 |
| 12-34 | (7-15, 5-19) | A. Cotter | Australians v Worcestershire | Worcester | 1905 |
| 12-34 | (6-20, 6-14) | G.A.R. Lock | Surrey v Glamorgan | Oval | 1957 |
| 12-34 | (7-27, 5-7) | M. Amarnath | Punjab v Jammu & Kashmir | Patiala | 1969–70 |
| 12-35 | (6-25, 6-10) | T.W.S. Wills | Victoria v Tasmania | Hobart | 1857–58 |
| 12-35 | (6-22, 6-13) | J.C. Shaw | Nottinghamshire v Kent | Crystal Palace | 1870 |
| 12-35 | (7-7, 5-28) | F. Morley | Nottinghamshire v Derbyshire | Nottingham | 1879 |
| 12-35 | (5-9, 7-26) | F.A. Tarrant | Maharaja of Cooch Bihar's XI v Bengal Governor's XI | Calcutta | 1917–18 |
| 12-35 | (8-18, 4-17) | A.V. Bedser | Surrey v Warwickshire | Oval | 1953 |
| 12-36 | (5-18, 7-18) | Y. Kumi | Punjab v Jammu & Kashmir | Jammu | 1972–73 |
| 12-38 | (5-15, 7-23) | W. McIntyre | Lancashire v Derbyshire | Derby | 1872 |
| 12-38 | (8-14, 4-24) | G. Nash | Lancashire v Somerset | Manchester | 1882 |
| 12-38 | (5-16, 7-22) | L.F. Townsend | MCC v Rajputana | Ajmer | 1933–34 |
| 12-38 | (7-19, 5-19) | M.A. Latif | E. Pakistan Greens v E. Railways | Dacca | 1967–68 |
| 12-39 | (5-12, 7-27) | Munir Malik | Rawalpindi v Peshawar | Rawalpindi | 1958–59 |
| 12-39 | (8-24, 4-15) | E.J. Chatfield | Wellington v N. Districts | Lower Hutt | 1979–80 |
| 12-40 | (7-16, 5-24) | E. O'Shaughnessy | Kent v Sussex | Hove | 1879 |
| 12-40 | (7-12, 5-28) | A.D. Downes | Otago v Canterbury | Dunedin | 1896–97 |
| 12-40 | (5-19, 7-21) | G.G. Macaulay | Yorkshire v Gloucestershire | Gloucester | 1924 |

## ELEVEN WICKETS IN A MATCH

| | | | | | |
|---|---|---|---|---|---|
| 11-17 | (8-17, 3-0) | G.A.R. Lock | MCC v East Pakistan | Chittagong | 1955–56 |
| 11-24 | (5-6, 6-18) | H. Ironmonger | Australia v South Africa | Melbourne | 1931–32 |
| 11-25 | (6-9, 5-16) | G. Fowler | Nelson v Wellington | Nelson | 1887–88 |
| 11-27 | (8-9, 3-18) | G. Wootton | MCC v Sussex | Lord's | 1863 |
| 11-29 | (7-12, 4-17) | F. Martin | MCC v Sussex | Lord's | 1894 |
| 11-30 | (8-5, 3-25) | E. Peate | Yorkshire v Surrey | Holbeck | 1883 |
| 11-30 | (4-19, 7-11) | P. Sitaram | Delhi v Jammu & Kashmir | Srinagar | 1960–61 |
| 11-31 | (5-12, 6-19) | W. McIntyre | Lancashire v Yorkshire | Sheffield | 1872 |
| 11-31 | (4-18, 7-13) | A.E. Trott | Middlesex v Somerset | Lord's | 1899 |
| 11-31 | (6-8, 5-23) | G.G. Macaulay | Yorkshire v Northamptonshire | Northampton | 1922 |
| 11-31 | (3-1, 8-30) | J.A. Newman | Hampshire v Northamptonshire | Northampton | 1926 |
| 11-31 | (9-18, 2-13) | R.K. Oxenham | Australians v Ceylon | Colombo | 1935–36 |
| 11-31 | (5-2, 6-29) | E.R.H. Toshack | Australia v India | Brisbane | 1947–48 |
| 11-31 | (5-16, 6-15) | Iqbal Awan | Bahawalpur v Khairpur | Bahawalpur | 1964–65 |
| 11-32 | (6-7, 5-25) | J.J. Ferris | MCC v Nottinghamshire | Lord's | 1891 |
| 11-33 | (5-8, 6-25) | I.R. Buxton | Derbyshire v Worcestershire | Derby | 1968 |
| 11-33 | (4-7, 7-29) | Nazir Khan | Railways v Peshawar | Lahore | 1969–70 |
| 11-33 | (7-24, 4-9) | V.A.P. van der Bijl | Natal v South African Universities | Durban | 1975–76 |
| 11-34 | (7-9, 4-25) | G.G. Macaulay | Yorkshire v Northamptonshire | Kettering | 1933 |
| 11-34 | (7-17, 4-17) | L.H. Gray | Middlesex v Hampshire | Lord's | 1946 |

## TEN WICKETS IN A MATCH

| | | | | | |
|---|---|---|---|---|---|
| 10-11 | (3-4, 7-7) | A. Bhattacharjee | Bengal v Assam | Jorhat | 1974–75 |
| 10-14 | (3-3, 7-11) | R.H.J. Lambert | Gentlemen of Ireland v Gentlemen of Scotland | Dublin | 1910 |
| 10-15 | (5-6, 5-9) | F.A. Tarrant | Europeans v Muslims | Poona | 1915–16 |
| 10-15 | (5-6, 5-9) | B.S. Bedi | Delhi v Services | Delhi | 1974–75 |
| 10-20 | (6-4, 4-16) | F.R. Spofforth | Australians v MCC | Lord's | 1878 |
| 10-21 | (3-12, 7-9) | T. Emmett | Yorkshire v Sussex | Hove | 1878 |
| 10-21 | (6-17, 4-4) | S.J. Staples | Nottinghamshire v Hampshire | Southampton | 1932 |
| 10-21 | (5-12, 5-9) | W.H. Copson | Derbyshire v Oxford University | Oxford | 1939 |
| 10-22 | (6-8, 4-14) | W.F. Downes | Otago v Canterbury | Christchurch | 1866–67 |
| 10-22 | (6-8, 4-14) | A. Shaw | Nottinghamshire v Surrey | Nottingham | 1875 |
| 10-23 | (5-10, 5-13) | G. Fowler | Nelson v Wellington | Nelson | 1883–84 |
| 10-24 | (4-11, 6-13) | G.F. Grace | United South v United North | Northampton | 1872 |
| 10-24 | (5-12, 5-12) | Naeem Ahmed | Rawalpindi v Dera Ismail Khan | Wah Cantt | 1984–85 |
| 10-25 | (6-12, 4-13) | G.H. Pope | Derbyshire v Yorkshire | Chesterfield | 1948 |
| 10-25 | (5-7, 5-18) | R. Goel | Haryana v Jammu & Kashmir | Rohtak | 1983–84 |
| 10-28 | (8-8, 2-20) | J.E.D. Sealy | Barbados v Trinidad | Bridgetown | 1942–43 |
| 10-29 | (3-11, 7-18) | J.T. Newstead | Yorkshire v Leicestershire | Leicester | 1908 |
| 10-30 | (5-13, 5-17) | H. Lawson | Wellington v Nelson | Nelson | 1883–84 |
| 10-30 | (5-8, 5-22) | F. Martin | MCC v Nottinghamshire | Lord's | 1894 |
| 10-30 | (2-22, 8-8) | M.G. Melle | Transvaal v Griqualand West | Johannesburg | 1950–51 |
| 10-30 | (5-13, 5-17) | Aftab Baloch | National Bank v Hyderabad | Hyderabad | 1974–75 |
| 10-30 | (3-12, 7-18) | A. Sidebottom | Yorkshire v Oxford University | Oxford | 1980 |

# MOST INEXPENSIVE ANALYSES

## FOUR-BALL OVERS

| O | M | R | W | | | | |
|---|---|---|---|---|---|---|---|
| 25.2 | 24 | 3 | 1 | W. Clarke | Middlesex v Nottinghamshire | Nottingham | 1882 |
| 26 | 23 | 3 | 0 | J. Beaumont | Surrey v Oxford University | Oxford | 1888 |
| 29 | 25 | 5 | 3 | A. Shaw | A. Shaw's XI v New South Wales | Sydney | 1881–82 |
| 40 | 35 | 7 | 0 | A. Shaw | Nottinghamshire v MCC | Lord's | 1882 |
| 41.2 | 36 | 7 | 7 | A. Shaw | Nottinghamshire v MCC | Lord's | 1875 |
| 48 | 40 | 12 | 3 | A. Shaw | Players v Gentlemen | Prince's | 1876 |
| 53 | 43 | 14 | 2 | E. Lockwood | Yorkshire v Nottinghamshire | Sheffield | 1876 |
| 60 | 47 | 14 | 4 | James Lillywhite | Sussex v Kent | Hove | 1879 |
| 83 | 66 | 25 | 5 | S. Cosstick | Victoria v New South Wales | Sydney | 1874–75 |
| 89 | 62 | 46 | 1 | W. Attewell | Nottinghamshire v Kent | Nottingham | 1888 |
| 98 | 69 | 58 | 3 | E. Peate | Yorkshire v Sussex | Hove | 1884 |

| 99 | 66 | **64** | 3 | A. Shaw | North v South | Nottingham | 1878 |
| 114 | 72 | **85** | 3 | A. Watson | Lancashire v MCC | Lord's | 1884 |
| 122.1 | 81 | **87** | 2 | J.T. Rawlin | G.F. Vernon's XI v S. Australia | Adelaide | 1887–88 |

**FIVE-BALL OVERS**

| O | M | R | W | | | | |
|---|---|---|---|---|---|---|---|
| 25 | 21 | **7** | 4 | W. Attewell | Nottinghamshire v Kent | Beckenham | 1889 |
| 30.4 | 22 | **17** | 5 | J. Briggs | Lancashire v Oxford University | Oxford | 1894 |
| 45 | 32 | **19** | 5 | W. Attewell | North v South | Oval | 1889 |
| 53 | 34 | **34** | 4 | W. Attewell | Nottinghamshire v Sussex | Nottingham | 1889 |
| 64 | 35 | **52** | 6 | W. Attewell | Nottinghamshire v Gloucestershire | Cheltenham | 1895 |
| 69 | 42 | **57** | 3 | W. Attewell | Nottinghamshire v Lancashire | Manchester | 1892 |
| 76 | 43 | **71** | 4 | W. Attewell | Nottinghamshire v Lancashire | Nottingham | 1889 |

**SIX-BALL OVERS**

| O | M | R | W | | | | |
|---|---|---|---|---|---|---|---|
| 11 | 11 | **0** | 1 | O. Corbie | Trinidad v Barbados | Port-of-Spain | 1960–61 |
| 11 | 10 | **2** | 2 | N.G. Cowley | Hampshire v Cambridge U | Cambridge | 1981 |
| 32 | 27 | **5** | 0 | R.G. Nadkarni | India v England | Madras | 1963–64 |
| 35 | 29 | **11** | 0 | W. Rhodes | Yorkshire v Nottinghamshire | Nottingham | 1929 |
| 36 | 27 | **17** | 3 | S.K. Girdhari | Bengal v Holkar | Calcutta | 1952–53 |
| 44 | 32 | **19** | 1 | W. Rhodes | Yorkshire v Lancashire | Leeds | 1930 |
| 47 | 29 | **30** | 6 | C. Cook | Gloucestershire v Leicestershire | Bristol | 1956 |
| 48 | 29 | **31** | 0 | R.G. Nadkarni | West Zone v South Zone | Delhi | 1963–64 |
| 53 | 37 | **34** | 4 | G.R. Beard | New South Wales v Victoria | Melbourne | 1980–81 |
| 53.3 | 37 | **38** | 8 | L.R. Gibbs | West Indies v India | Bridgetown | 1961–62 |
| 54 | 38 | **43** | 4 | B.W. Yuile | New Zealand v Pakistan | Auckland | 1964–65 |
| 62.3 | 39 | **50** | 4 | Dildar Awan | Services v Peshawar | Peshawar | 1961–62 |
| 63.2 | 38 | **57** | 4 | Saeed Ahmed | Western India States v Bombay | Rajkot | 1943–44 |
| 76 | 47 | **58** | 4 | M.H. Mankad | India v England | Delhi | 1951–52 |
| 79 | 39 | **90** | 2 | Mohammad Nazir | Railways v United Bank | Lahore | 1982–83 |
| 83 | 42 | **98** | 5 | R.W. McLeod | Victoria v New South Wales | Melbourne | 1892–93 |
| 89 | 25 | **132** | 1 | V.S. Pascall | Trinidad v Barbados | Bridgetown | 1926–27 |

**EIGHT-BALL OVERS**

| O | M | R | W | | | | |
|---|---|---|---|---|---|---|---|
| 18 | 13 | **5** | 2 | Iqbal Qasim | National Bank v PIA | Karachi | 1975–76 |
| 21 | 13 | **12** | 5 | R.L.A. McNamee | Australians v Auckland | Auckland | 1927–28 |
| 26 | 17 | **19** | 4 | L.W. Payn | Natal v Orange Free State | Bloemfontein | 1946–47 |
| 42 | 25 | **28** | 4 | N.B.F. Mann | Eastern Province v OFS | Port Elizabeth | 1950–51 |
| 43 | 23 | **36** | 4 | R.G. Nadkarni | Bombay v Rest of India | Bombay | 1962–63 |
| 57 | 26 | **55** | 3 | L.J. Heaney | Transvaal v Griqualand West | Johannesburg | 1947–48 |
| 67.6 | 38 | **69** | 6 | N.B.F. Mann | Eastern Province v Transvaal | Johannesburg | 1946–47 |

# MOST EXPENSIVE ANALYSES

**FIVE-BALL OVERS**

| O | M | R | W | | | | |
|---|---|---|---|---|---|---|---|
| 5 | 0 | **50** | 0 | W.G. Grace | South v North | Hastings | 1893 |
| 13 | 1 | **76** | 0 | W. Lockwood | C.I. Thornton's XI v Australians | Scarborough | 1893 |
| 14 | 0 | **94** | 0 | K.S. Ranjitsinhji | Sussex v Nottinghamshire | Nottingham | 1895 |
| 19 | 2 | **127** | 2 | J.B. Wood | Oxford University v MCC | Lord's | 1893 |
| 26 | 5 | **138** | 5 | E.J. Tyler | Somerset v Lancashire | Taunton | 1899 |
| 30 | 1 | **154** | 1 | A.C.S. Glover | Warwickshire v Yorkshire | Birmingham | 1896 |

**SIX-BALL OVERS**

| O | M | R | W | | | | |
|---|---|---|---|---|---|---|---|
| 1 | 0 | **32** | 0 | I.R. Snook | Central Districts v England XI | Palmerston North | 1983–84 |
| 2 | 0 | **50** | 0 | N.W. Hill | Nottinghamshire v Leicestershire | Nottingham | 1965 |
| | | | | | *Bowled slow full-tosses to give away runs quickly* | | |
| 3 | 0 | **52** | 0 | J.G. Leggat | Canterbury v Fijians | Christchurch | 1953–54 |
| 4 | 0 | **75** | 0 | I.J. Gould | Sussex v Yorkshire | Hove | 1985 |
| 8 | 1 | **87** | 0 | J.J. Whitaker | Leicestershire v Lancashire | Manchester | 1983 |
| 8.2 | 0 | **98** | 0 | T.W.J. Goddard | Gloucestershire v Kent | Dover | 1937 |

| O | M | R | W | | | | |
|---|---|---|---|---|---|---|---|
| 9 | 0 | **102** | 0 | D.I. Gower | Leicestershire v Lancashire | Manchester | 1983 |
| 13 | 0 | **112** | 1 | N.J.O. Carbutt | Army v Oxford University | Oxford | 1921 |
| 14 | 0 | **153** | 3 | J.R. Gunn | Nottinghamshire v Sussex | Hove | 1912 |
| 19.4 | 0 | **160** | 4 | D.B. Close | North v South | Blackpool | 1961 |
| 22 | 0 | **188** | 3 | A.E. Bailey | Somerset v Kent | Taunton | 1906 |
| 33 | 0 | **219** | 0 | Jehangir | Sind University v Punjab University | Karachi | 1958–59 |
| 38.4 | 3 | **220** | 7 | Kapil Dev | India v Pakistan | Faisalabad | 1982–83 |
| 40.2 | 2 | **227** | 5 | L.C. Braund | Somerset v Lancashire | Manchester | 1905 |
| 46 | 3 | **295** | 3 | Anwar | Dera Ismail Khan v Railways | Lahore | 1964–65 |

EIGHT-BALL OVERS

| O | M | R | W | | | | |
|---|---|---|---|---|---|---|---|
| 1 | 0 | **34** | 0 | M.C. Carew | West Indians v Governor-General's XI | Auckland | 1968–69 |
| 2.7 | 0 | **50** | 0 | J. Buchanan | E. Province v W. Province | Cape Town | 1937–38 |
| 4 | 1 | **62** | 0 | I.M. Chappell | S. Australia v New Zealanders | Adelaide | 1967–68 |
| 5.4 | 0 | **67** | 3 | A.T.E. Punch | New South Wales v M.C.C. | Sydney | 1924–25 |
| 6 | 0 | **71** | 2 | E.D.R. Eagar | Oxford University v MCC | Lord's | 1939 |
| 6.4 | 1 | **80** | 3 | V.V. Kumar | Chidambaram's XI v ACC XI | Hyderabad | 1962–63 |
| 7 | 0 | **85** | 3 | Sikander Bakht | Sind v Railways | Lahore | 1975–76 |
| 8 | 0 | **102** | 1 | Riaz Mahmood | Bahawalpur v Income Tax | Bahawalpur | 1976–77 |
| 10.4 | 1 | **125** | 1 | S.C. Everett | Australians v New South Wales | Sydney | 1925–26 |
| 12.7 | 0 | **149** | 5 | W.E. Merritt | Northamptonshire v Somerset | Taunton | 1939 |
| 16 | 0 | **155** | 4 | S.W.L. Putman | Tasmania v Australians | Hobart | 1937–38 |
| 18 | 1 | **182** | 4 | I.W. Johnson | A.L. Hassett's XI v A.R. Morris's XI | Melbourne | 1953–54 |
| 23.2 | 0 | **218** | 5 | W.E. Merritt | New Zealanders v NSW | Sydney | 1927–28 |
| 44 | 0 | **231** | 1 | Sabahat Hussain | Baluchistan v Sind | Karachi | 1973–74 |
| 64 | 0 | **362** | 4 | A.A. Mailey | New South Wales v Victoria | Melbourne | 1926–27 |

# MOST RUNS CONCEDED IN AN INNINGS

| O | M | R | W | | | | |
|---|---|---|---|---|---|---|---|
| 64 | 0 | **362** | 4 | A.A. Mailey | New South Wales v Victoria | Melbourne | 1926–27 |
| 87 | 12 | **309** | 5 | G. Giffen | South Australia v A.E. Stoddart's XI | Adelaide | 1894–95 |
| 69 | 7 | **301** | 4 | B.K. Garudachar | Mysore v Holkar | Indore | 1945–46 |
| 87 | 11 | **298** | 1 | L.O'B. Fleetwood-Smith | Australia v England | Oval | 1938 |
| 46 | 3 | **295** | 3 | Anwar | Dera Ismail Khan v Railways | Lahore | 1964–65 |
| 77.1 | 7 | **287** | 8 | G. Giffen | South Australia v NSW | Adelaide | 1899–00 |
| 59 | 2 | **279** | 1 | Inayat | Dera Ismail Khan v Railways | Lahore | 1964–65 |
| 88 | 15 | **275** | 5 | C.S. Nayudu | Holkar v Bombay | Bombay | 1944–45 |
| 49 | 2 | **268** | 3 | Sher Andaz | Sargodha v Lahore | Lahore | 1968–69 |
| 80.2 | 13 | **266** | 5 | O.C. Scott | West Indies v England | Kingston | 1929–30 |
| 64 | 4 | **261** | 4 | C.S. Nayudu | Baroda v Maharashtra | Poona | 1939–40 |
| 54 | 5 | **259** | 0 | Khan Mohammad | Pakistan v West Indies | Kingston | 1957–58 |
| 65 | 5 | **253** | 3 | A. Shukla | Uttar Pradesh v Hyderabad | Hyderabad | 1964–65 |
| 83 | 17 | **249** | 6 | J.A. O'Connor | South Australia v Victoria | Melbourne | 1907–08 |
| 85.2 | 20 | **247** | 2 | Fazal Mahmood | Pakistan v West Indies | Kingston | 1957–58 |
| 55 | 3 | **245** | 4 | A.P. Freeman | MCC v Victoria | Melbourne | 1928–29 |
| 92.3 | 21 | **245** | 4 | Ghulam Ahmed | Hyderabad v Holkar | Indore | 1950–51 |
| 57 | 1 | **242** | 5 | Rauf Ansari | E. Pakistan Greens v Karachi Blues | Karachi | 1967–68 |
| 52 | 8 | **236** | 3 | J.H. Wardle | North v South | Scarborough | 1947 |
| 56 | 7 | **232** | 3 | C.J. Eady | Tasmania v New South Wales | Sydney | 1898–99 |
| 63 | 10 | **231** | 6 | C.W.L. Parker | Gloucestershire v Somerset | Bristol | 1923 |
| 44 | 0 | **231** | 1 | Sabahat Hussain | Baluchistan v Sind | Karachi | 1973–74 |
| 65 | 4 | **230** | 1 | Asif Baloch | Baluchistan v PIA | Karachi | 1976–77 |
| 61.3 | 9 | **229** | 3 | Riaz Akhtar | Quetta v PWD | Quetta | 1969–70 |
| 38 | 1 | **228** | 2 | A.C. Facy | Tasmania v Victoria | Melbourne | 1922–23 |
| 48.7 | 4 | **228** | 5 | B.B.M. Gaskin | British Guiana v Trinidad | Port-of-Spain | 1946–47 |
| 82 | 17 | **228** | 5 | M.H. Mankad | India v West Indies | Kingston | 1952–53 |
| 40.2 | 2 | **227** | 5 | L.C. Braund | Somerset v Lancashire | Manchester | 1905 |
| 69 | 16 | **227** | 7 | Shahid Aziz | Punjab B v PIA | Karachi | 1975–76 |
| 59 | 11 | **226** | 6 | E.B. Shine | Kent v Surrey | Oval | 1897 |
| 64.2 | 8 | **226** | 6 | B.S. Bedi | India v England | Lord's | 1974 |
| 49 | 7 | **225** | 2 | F. Jarvis | South Australia v NSW | Sydney | 1900–01 |

# MOST RUNS CONCEDED IN A MATCH

| 428 | (6-153, 5-275) | C.S. Nayudu | Holkar v Bombay | Bombay | 1944–45 |
|---|---|---|---|---|---|
| 394 | (4-192, 6-202) | C.V. Grimmett | South Australia v New South Wales | Sydney | 1925–26 |
| 374 | (5-266, 4-108) | O.C. Scott | West Indies v England | Kingston | 1929–30 |
| 362 | (4-362) | A.A. Mailey | New South Wales v Victoria | Melbourne | 1926–27 |
| 359 | (3-149, 4-210) | D.G. Chowdhury | Maharashtra v Bombay | Poona | 1948–49 |
| 345 | (3-190, 0-155) | J.D. Scott | South Australia v New South Wales | Sydney | 1925–26 |
| 331 | (6-199, 2-132) | A.P. Freeman | Kent v MCC | Folkestone | 1934 |
| 326 | (6-134, 5-192) | N.L. Williams | South Australia v Victoria | Adelaide | 1928–29 |
| 322 | (5-309, 0-13) | G. Giffen | South Australia v A.E. Stoddart's XI | Adelaide | 1894–95 |
| 322 | (1-224, 1-98) | S.G. Shinde | Baroda v Bombay | Bombay | 1948–49 |
| 321 | (3-195, 1-126) | S.D. Dhanwade | Maharashtra v Bombay | Poona | 1948–49 |
| 320 | (3-142, 3-178) | D.G. Phadkar | Bombay v Maharashtra | Poona | 1948–49 |
| 308 | (4-129, 3-179) | A.A. Mailey | Australia v England | Sydney | 1924–25 |
| 306 | (2-174, 2-132) | J. Briggs | Lancashire v Sussex | Manchester | 1897 |
| 304 | (2-173, 0-131) | G.R. Dickinson | Otago v Wellington | Dunedin | 1923–24 |
| 303 | (2-118, 2-185) | Ijaz Ahmed | National Bank v Karachi Blues | Karachi | 1975–76 |
| 302 | (5-160, 5-142) | A.A. Mailey | Australia v England | Adelaide | 1920–21 |
| 301 | (4-301) | B.K. Garudachar | Mysore v Holkar | Indore | 1945–46 |
| 300 | (6-172, 4-128) | S.G. Smith | Auckland v Wellington | Wellington | 1923–24 |

# MOST BALLS BOWLED IN AN INNINGS

| Balls | O | M | R | W | | | | |
|---|---|---|---|---|---|---|---|---|
| 588 | 98 | 35 | 179 | 2 | S. Ramadhin | West Indies v England | Birmingham | 1957 |
| 571 | 95.1 | 36 | 155 | 3 | T.R. Veivers | Australia v England | Manchester | 1964 |
| | | | | | | *Including spell of 51 overs* | | |
| 564 | 94 | 26 | 180 | 1 | A.R. Bhat | Karnataka v Delhi | Delhi | 1981–82 |
| 555 | 92.3 | 21 | 245 | 4 | Ghulam Ahmed | Hyderabad v Holkar | Indore | 1950–51 |
| 552 | 92 | 49 | 140 | 3 | A.L. Valentine | West Indies v England | Nottingham | 1950 |
| 552 | 69 | 16 | 227 | 7 | Shahid Aziz | Punjab B v PIA | Karachi | 1975–76 |
| 545 | 90.5 | 32 | 165 | 2 | A.L. Valentine | Jamaica v British Guiana | Georgetown | 1956–57 |
| 542 | 67.6 | 38 | 69 | 6 | N.B.F. Mann | E. Province v Transvaal | Johannesburg | 1946–47 |
| 536 | 67 | 27 | 90 | 1 | A. Tayfield | Natal v Transvaal | Johannesburg | 1948–49 |
| 534 | 89 | 25 | 132 | 1 | V.R. Pascall | Trinidad v Barbados | Bridgetown | 1926–27 |
| 528 | 88 | 15 | 275 | 5 | C.S. Nayudu | Holkar v Bombay | Bombay | 1944–45 |
| 528 | 88 | 26 | 208 | 3 | Iqbal Ahwan | Bahawalpur v Karachi Blues | Karachi | 1964–65 |
| 527 | 87.5 | 18 | 204 | 3 | Maninder Singh | Delhi v Karnataka | Delhi | 1981–82 |
| 522 | 87 | 12 | 309 | 5 | G. Giffen | South Australia v A.E. Stoddart's XI | Adelaide | 1894–95 |
| 522 | 87 | 11 | 298 | 1 | L.O'B. Fleetwood-Smith | Australia v England | Oval | 1938 |
| 520 | 65 | 4 | 230 | 1 | Asif Baloch | Baluchistan v PIA | Karachi | 1976–77 |
| 518 | 64.6 | 18 | 96 | 4 | Zafar Medhi | Sind v Habib Bank | Karachi | 1977–78 |
| 512 | 64 | 0 | 362 | 4 | A.A. Mailey | NSW v Victoria | Melbourne | 1926–27 |
| 512 | 85.2 | 20 | 247 | 2 | Fazal Mahmood | Pakistan v West Indies | Kingston | 1957–58 |
| 512 | 64 | 17 | 109 | 2 | Nasir Ali | Hyderabad v PWD | Hyderabad | 1973–74 |
| 512 | 64 | 6 | 223 | 5 | Shahid Iqbal | Universities v Punjab | Lahore | 1973–74 |
| 510 | 85 | 26 | 178 | 3 | W.J. O'Reilly | Australia v England | Oval | 1938 |
| 510 | 85 | 11 | 209 | 3 | Ghulam Ahmed | Hyderabad v Bombay | Bombay | 1947–48 |
| 510 | 85 | 16 | 224 | 1 | S.G. Shinde | Baroda v Bombay | Bombay | 1948–49 |
| 504 | 84 | 18 | 168 | 4 | I.S. Madray | British Guiana v Jamaica | Georgetown | 1956–57 |
| 504 | 84 | 19 | 202 | 6 | Haseeb Ahsan | Pakistan v India | Madras | 1960–61 |
| 501 | 83.3 | 35 | 150 | 6 | G. Giffen | South Australia v NSW | Adelaide | 1890–91 |
| 501 | 100.1 | 31 | 168 | 4 | A. Shaw | Sussex v Nottinghamshire | Nottingham | 1895 |
| 498 | 83 | 42 | 98 | 5 | R.W. McLeod | Victoria v NSW | Melbourne | 1892–93 |
| 498 | 83 | 17 | 249 | 6 | J.A. O'Connor | South Australia v Victoria | Melbourne | 1907–08 |
| 498 | 83 | 31 | 143 | 4 | Maazullah Khan | NWFP v Railways | Peshawar | 1972–73 |
| 496 | 62 | 15 | 157 | 3 | L.W. Payn | Natal v Transvaal | Johannesburg | 1948–49 |
| 492 | 123 | 56 | 146 | 5 | D. Buchanan | Gents of England v Cambridge University | Cambridge | 1880 |
| 492 | 82 | 17 | 228 | 5 | M.H. Mankad | India v West Indies | Kingston | 1952–53 |
| 490 | 98 | 34 | 151 | 4 | F. Martin | Kent v Nottinghamshire | Nottingham | 1891 |
| 489 | 122.1 | 81 | 87 | 2 | J.T. Rawlin | G.F. Vernon's XI v South Australia | Adelaide | 1887–88 |

| Balls | O | M | R | W | | | | |
|---|---|---|---|---|---|---|---|---|
| **488** | 61 | 20 | 152 | 2 | W.H. Douglas | N.E. Transvaal v Transvaal | Benoni | 1947–48 |
| **488** | 81.2 | 25 | 135 | 5 | S. Ramadhin | West Indies v England | Nottingham | 1950 |
| **488** | 61 | 18 | 126 | 5 | L.F. Kline | Victoria v NSW | Sydney | 1956–57 |
| **488** | 61 | 12 | 178 | 2 | Naeem Ahmed | Universities v Punjab | Lahore | 1973–74 |
| **488** | 61 | 17 | 137 | 3 | Mohammad Nazir | Railways v Universities | Lahore | 1974–75 |
| **488** | 61 | 13 | 180 | 4 | Naeem Ahmed | National Bank v Karachi Whites | Karachi | 1974–75 |
| **486** | 81 | 36 | 105 | 5 | G. Geary | England v Australia | Melbourne | 1928–29 |
| **486** | 81 | 37 | 172 | 3 | J.H. Wardle | Yorkshire v Derbyshire | Bradford | 1949 |
| **482** | 80.2 | 13 | 266 | 5 | O.C. Scott | West Indies v England | Kingston | 1929–30 |
| **481** | 80.1 | 26 | 184 | 6 | Munawar Hussain | PWD v Karachi | Karachi | 1964–65 |
| **480** | 120 | 81 | 90 | 3 | W.G. Grace | Gloucestershire v Notts | Nottingham | 1885 |
| **480** | 80 | 22 | 187 | 3 | W. Huddleston | Lancashire v Warwickshire | Birmingham | 1901 |
| **480** | 80 | 28 | 138 | 3 | G.S. Boyes | Hampshire v Nottinghamshire | Southampton | 1934 |
| **480** | 80 | 12 | 178 | 4 | C.K. Nayudu | Holkar v Baroda | Baroda | 1946–47 |
| **480** | 60 | 9 | 167 | 5 | A.M.B. Rowan | South Africa v England | Port Elizabeth | 1948–49 |
| **480** | 80 | 21 | 174 | 2 | Maqsood Ahmed | Karachi Blues v Karachi Whites | Karachi | 1956–57 |
| **480** | 80 | 35 | 113 | 4 | L.R. Gibbs | British Guiana v Jamaica | Georgetown | 1956–57 |
| **478** | 59.6 | 15 | 148 | 5 | J.D. Higgs | Australia v England | Sydney | 1978–79 |
| **476** | 119 | 40 | 152 | 5 | J. Southerton | Surrey v Gloucestershire | Clifton | 1871 |
| **474** | 79 | 43 | 106 | 5 | J.C. White | Somerset v Hampshire | Taunton | 1930 |
| **474** | 79 | 19 | 184 | 3 | Nasim-ul-Ghani | Karachi Blues v Karachi Whites | Karachi | 1956–57 |
| **474** | 79 | 39 | 90 | 2 | Mohammad Nazir | Railways v United Bank | Lahore | 1982–83 |
| **472** | 59 | 24 | 94 | 3 | H.J. Tayfield | South Africa v Australia | Durban | 1957–58 |
| **472** | 59 | 16 | 129 | 3 | Shahid Aziz | United Bank v PIA | Karachi | 1977–78 |
| **470** | 78.2 | 21 | 156 | 6 | G. Giffen | Australia v England | Melbourne | 1894–95 |
| **468** | 78 | 30 | 143 | 0 | R. Goel | Haryana v Bombay | Bombay | 1976–77 |
| **465** | 93 | 33 | 134 | 3 | J.J. Ferris | Australians v Players | Lord's | 1890 |
| **464** | 58 | 14 | 138 | 6 | J.E. Waddington | Griqualand West v Transvaal | Kimberley | 1946–47 |
| **463** | 77.1 | 7 | 287 | 8 | G. Giffen | South Australia v NSW | Adelaide | 1899–00 |
| **462** | 77 | 44 | 99 | 3 | G.A.R. Lock | MCC v Pakistan XI | Lahore | 1955–56 |
| **462** | 77 | 26 | 139 | 3 | S.F. Rehman | Lahore v Railways & Quetta | Karachi | 1960–61 |
| **462** | 77 | 32 | 118 | 2 | T.W. Cartwright | England v Australia | Manchester | 1964 |
| **462** | 77 | 8 | 204 | 5 | Humayun Khan | Sargodha v Lahore | Lahore | 1968–69 |
| **462** | 57.6 | 11 | 166 | 6 | Khurshid Akhtar | United Bank v PIA | Karachi | 1975–76 |
| **462** | 77 | 13 | 132 | 8 | P.H. Edmonds | Middlesex v Gloucestershire | Lord's | 1977 |
| **460** | 76.4 | 35 | 128 | 7 | S.P. Gupte | India v New Zealand | Hyderabad | 1955–56 |
| **456** | 114 | 72 | 85 | 3 | A. Watson | Lancashire v MCC | Lord's | 1884 |
| **456** | 114 | 71 | 101 | 5 | W.A. Woof | Gloucestershire v Notts | Nottingham | 1885 |
| **456** | 57 | 6 | 139 | 3 | J.E. Waller | N.E. Transvaal v Transvaal | Benoni | 1947–48 |
| **456** | 57 | 26 | 55 | 3 | L.J. Heaney | Transvaal v Griqualand West | Johannesburg | 1947–48 |
| **456** | 76 | 47 | 58 | 4 | M.H. Mankad | India v England | Delhi | 1951–52 |
| **456** | 76 | 29 | 136 | 5 | J.H. Wardle | Yorkshire v Worcestershire | Worcester | 1953 |
| **456** | 57 | 25 | 93 | 1 | A.R.A. Murray | E. Province v Natal | Port Elizabeth | 1955–56 |
| **456** | 76 | 10 | 141 | 1 | Maqsood Husain | Hyderabad v Karachi Blues | Karachi | 1964–65 |
| **455** | 75.5 | 10 | 186 | 5 | S.G. Shinde | Maharashtra v Bombay | Bombay | 1943–44 |
| **455** | 75.5 | 40 | 94 | 6 | Nasim-ul-Ghani | Karachi v PIA | Karachi | 1962–63 |
| **454** | 113.2 | 71 | 118 | 4 | A. Watson | Lancashire v Yorkshire | Bradford | 1887 |
| **453** | 75.3 | 22 | 136 | 2 | J.C. White | England v Australia | Melbourne | 1928–29 |
| **453** | 113.1 | 63 | 126 | 6 | T.W. Garrett | NSW v Victoria | Melbourne | 1883–84 |
| **453** | 75.3 | 22 | 152 | 6 | Nasim-ul-Ghani | PWD v Punjab University | Karachi | 1971–72 |
| **452** | 113 | 66 | 108 | 6 | W. Flowers | Nottinghamshire v Lancashire | Manchester | 1886 |
| **451** | 75.1 | 16 | 190 | 7 | A.L. Newell | NSW v South Australia | Adelaide | 1893–94 |
| **450** | 75 | 25 | 164 | 4 | G. Giffen | Australia v England | Sydney | 1894–95 |
| **450** | 90 | 32 | 185 | 6 | J. Briggs | Lancashire v Derbyshire | Manchester | 1896 |
| **450** | 75 | 16 | 166 | 7 | C.S. Nayudu | Baroda v Bombay | Bombay | 1943–44 |
| **450** | 75 | 16 | 202 | 3 | M.H. Mankad | India v West Indies | Bombay | 1948–49 |
| **450** | 75 | 40 | 126 | 6 | D.N.F. Slade | Commonwealth XI v Pakistan | Lahore | 1963–64 |
| **450** | 75 | 16 | 119 | 3 | Ijaz Faqik | MCB v PACO | Sahiwal | 1983–84 |

# MOST BALLS BOWLED IN A MATCH

| | | | | | | | | |
|---|---|---|---|---|---|---|---|---|
| **917** | 152.5 | 25 | 428 | 11 | C.S. Nayudu | Holkar v Bombay | Bombay | 1944–45 |
| **848** | 106 | 14 | 394 | 10 | C.V. Grimmett | South Australia v NSW | Sydney | 1925–26 |

| Balls | *O* | *M* | *R* | *W* | | | | |
|---|---|---|---|---|---|---|---|---|
| 805 | 161 | 71 | 204 | 13 | J.H. Piton | Transvaal v Griqualand West | Johannesburg | 1890–91 |
| 774 | 129 | 51 | 228 | 9 | S. Ramadhin | West Indies v England | Birmingham | 1957 |
| 766 | 95.6 | 23 | 184 | 4 | H. Verity | England v South Africa | Durban | 1938–39 |
| 749 | 124.5 | 37 | 256 | 13 | J.C. White | England v Australia | Adelaide | 1928–29 |
| 748 | 92.7 | 22 | 255 | 10 | D.D. Blackie | Victoria v South Australia | Adelaide | 1926–27 |
| 738 | 92.2 | 17 | 256 | 1 | N. Gordon | South Africa v England | Durban | 1938–39 |
| 736 | 92 | 16 | 267 | 9 | C.V. Grimmett | South Australia v Victoria | Adelaide | 1924–25 |
| 730 | 91.2 | 33 | 190 | 10 | N.B.F. Mann | E. Province v W. Province | Cape Town | 1947–48 |
| 728 | 91 | 24 | 203 | 4 | A.B.C. Langton | South Africa v England | Durban | 1938–39 |
| 725 | 120.5 | 58 | 152 | 11 | R.W. McLeod | Victoria v New South Wales | Melbourne | 1892–93 |
| 720 | 120 | 30 | 299 | 9 | K.K. Tarapore | Bombay v Maharashtra | Poona | 1948–49 |
| 712 | 89 | 19 | 228 | 11 | M.W. Tate | England v Australia | Sydney | 1924–25 |
| 708 | 118 | 42 | 239 | 8 | G. Giffen | Australia v England | Sydney | 1894–95 |
| 696 | 116 | 75 | 127 | 7 | A.L. Valentine | West Indies v England | Lord's | 1950 |
| 695 | 115.5 | 50 | 191 | 11 | G. Giffen | South Australia v NSW | Adelaide | 1892–93 |
| 691 | 115.1 | 60 | 135 | 6 | M.H. Mankad | India v Pakistan | Peshawar | 1954–55 |
| 690 | 115 | 70 | 152 | 11 | S. Ramadhin | West Indies v England | Lord's | 1950 |
| 690 | 115 | 46 | 226 | 8 | G.A.R. Lock | England v Pakistan | Dacca | 1961–62 |
| 688 | 86 | 15 | 258 | 5 | A.P. Freeman | England v Australia | Sydney | 1924–25 |
| 686 | 85.6 | 44 | 123 | 9 | N.B.F. Mann | E. Province v Transvaal | Johannesburg | 1946–47 |
| 684 | 114 | 46 | 176 | 5 | Mohammad Nazir | Railways v United Bank | Lahore | 1982–83 |
| 683 | 113.5 | 50 | 171 | 6 | J.C. White | England v Australia | Melbourne | 1928–29 |
| 682 | 113.4 | 19 | 322 | 2 | S.G. Shinde | Baroda v Bombay | Bombay | 1948–49 |
| 680 | 85 | 22 | 174 | 12 | Iqbal Qasim | National Bank v MCB | Karachi | 1977–78 |
| 675 | 112.3 | 56 | 152 | 12 | S. Venkataraghavan | India v New Zealand | Delhi | 1964–65 |
| 672 | 84 | 15 | 266 | 7 | W.A. Johnston | Australia v South Africa | Melbourne | 1952–53 |
| 668 | 83.4 | 27 | 195 | 12 | H. Ironmonger | Victoria v South Australia | Adelaide | 1930–31 |
| 666 | 83.2 | 9 | 281 | 8 | A.A. Mailey | NSW v South Australia | Adelaide | 1926–27 |
| 664 | 83 | 19 | 191 | 9 | J.E. Waddington | GW v N.E. Transvaal | Pretoria | 1955–56 |
| 662 | 110.2 | 37 | 184 | 7 | S. Ramadhin | West Indies v England | Nottingham | 1950 |
| 662 | 110.2 | 44 | 167 | 7 | S.P. Gupte | India v Pakistan | Lahore | 1954–55 |
| 661 | 165.1 | 87 | 202 | 9 | T.W. Garrett | NSW v Victoria | Melbourne | 1883–84 |
| 660 | 110 | 55 | 183 | 5 | A.L. Valentine | West Indies v England | Nottingham | 1950 |
| 659 | 109.5 | 29 | 267 | 10 | M.H. Mankad | Gujarat v Holkar | Indore | 1950–51 |
| 656 | 109.2 | 30 | 225 | 5 | C.V. Grimmett | Australia v England | Oval | 1930 |
| 656 | 82 | 19 | 240 | 8 | F.A. Ward | Australia v England | Brisbane | 1936–37 |
| 655 | 109.1 | 43 | 192 | 14 | J.J. Ferris | NSW v South Australia | Adelaide | 1890–91 |
| 654 | 109 | 41 | 198 | 9 | H. Trumble | Australia v England | Adelaide | 1901–02 |
| 654 | 109 | 37 | 192 | 8 | C.V. Grimmett | Australia v South Africa | Melbourne | 1931–32 |
| 654 | 109 | 17 | 294 | 2 | C.T. Sarwate | Holkar v Bombay | Bombay | 1944–45 |
| 654 | 109 | 62 | 111 | 7 | M.H. Mankad | India v England | Delhi | 1951–52 |
| 651 | 108.3 | 36 | 253 | 8 | S.G. Shinde | India v England | Delhi | 1951–52 |
| 648 | 108 | 30 | 245 | 9 | G. Giffen | South Australia v Victoria | Adelaide | 1899–00 |
| 642 | 107 | 35 | 196 | 7 | K.D. Mackay | Australia v England | Oval | 1961 |
| 642 | 107 | 21 | 261 | 5 | Ijaz Faqih | MCB v PACO | Sahiwal | 1983–84 |
| 640 | 80 | 31 | 135 | 3 | H.J. Tayfield | South Africa v Australia | Durban | 1957–58 |
| 636 | 106 | 36 | 204 | 11 | A.L. Valentine | West Indies v England | Manchester | 1950 |
| 636 | 79.4 | 37 | 142 | 6 | L.R. Gibbs | West Indies v Australia | Melbourne | 1960–61 |
| 633 | 105.3 | 52 | 120 | 8 | C.V. Grimmett | Australia v England | Nottingham | 1934 |
| 632 | 79 | 12 | 207 | 9 | M.W. Tate | England v Australia | Sydney | 1924–25 |
| 632 | 105.2 | 13 | 374 | 9 | O.C. Scott | West Indies v England | Kingston | 1929–30 |
| 632 | 79 | 16 | 282 | 3 | Ilyas Khan | Sind v PIA | Karachi | 1976–77 |
| 630 | 105 | 45 | 165 | 8 | J.W. Sharpe | England v Australia | Melbourne | 1891–92 |
| 630 | 126 | 33 | 306 | 4 | J. Briggs | Lancashire v Sussex | Manchester | 1897 |
| 630 | 105 | 41 | 199 | 4 | J.C. Laker | England v West Indies | Nottingham | 1957 |
| 630 | 78.6 | 21 | 169 | 10 | Mohammad Nazir | Railways v United Bank | Lahore | 1976–77 |
| 629 | 104.5 | 44 | 178 | 9 | F.T. Badcock | Otago v Canterbury | Christchurch | 1933–34 |
| 629 | 78.5 | 26 | 166 | 8 | L.H. Drury | GW v N.E. Transvaal | Pretoria | 1955–56 |
| 627 | 78.3 | 18 | 241 | 9 | M.W. Tate | England v Australia | Melbourne | 1924–25 |
| 626 | 78.2 | 3 | 326 | 11 | N.L. Williams | South Australia v Victoria | Adelaide | 1928–29 |
| 625 | 78.1 | 14 | 178 | 6 | R. Kilner | England v Australia | Adelaide | 1924–25 |
| 625 | 104.1 | 27 | 219 | 6 | C.V. Grimmett | Australia v England | Adelaide | 1928–29 |
| 624 | 156 | 86 | 184 | 8 | W.G. Grace | Gentlemen v Players | Oval | 1876 |
| 624 | 104 | 28 | 163 | 3 | V.S. Pascall | Trinidad v Barbados | Bridgetown | 1926–27 |
| 624 | 78 | 11 | 222 | 5 | A.A. Mailey | NSW v South Australia | Adelaide | 1927–28 |
| 624 | 104 | 55 | 132 | 3 | C.S. Marriott | Kent v Northamptonshire | Dover | 1934 |

| Balls | O | M | R | W | | | | |
|---|---|---|---|---|---|---|---|---|
| 624 | 104 | 28 | 254 | 6 | M.H. Mankad | India v West Indies | Kingston | 1952–53 |
| 624 | 104 | 45 | 142 | 11 | C.W. Dickeson | N. Districts v Wellington | Hamilton | 1979–80 |
| 623 | 103.5 | 37 | 190 | 7 | A.H. McKinnon | E. Province v W. Province | Cape Town | 1962–63 |
| 622 | 77.6 | 19 | 190 | 8 | J.D. Higgs | Australia v England | Sydney | 1978–79 |
| 618 | 103 | 39 | 214 | 6 | E.J. Gray | Wellington v Otago | Wellington | 1984–85 |
| 617 | 77.1 | 12 | 209 | 10 | Mohammad Nazir | Railways v National Bank | Lahore | 1978–79 |
| 612 | 102 | 16 | 260 | 9 | E. Jones | South Australia v Victoria | Adelaide | 1898–99 |
| 612 | 102 | 28 | 182 | 8 | D.D. Parsana | West Zone v North Zone | Delhi | 1978–79 |
| 611 | 101.5 | 38 | 206 | 14 | A.P. Freeman | Kent v Northamptonshire | Dover | 1934 |
| 610 | 101.4 | 41 | 158 | 10 | E.G. Dennett | Gloucestershire v Notts | Nottingham | 1908 |
| 608 | 76 | 18 | 173 | 4 | R.L.A. McNamee | NSW v Queensland | Sydney | 1926–27 |
| 608 | 76 | 6 | 269 | 7 | Shahid Iqbal | Universities v Punjab | Lahore | 1973–74 |
| 608 | 76 | 14 | 170 | 7 | Mohammad Nazir | Railways v Punjab | Lahore | 1974–75 |
| 607 | 101.1 | 26 | 233 | 10 | A.L. Newell | NSW v South Australia | Adelaide | 1893–94 |
| 606 | 101 | 34 | 203 | 6 | J. Briggs | Lancashire v Kent | Manchester | 1900 |
| 606 | 101 | 41 | 136 | 6 | G. Geary | England v Australia | Melbourne | 1928–29 |
| 606 | 75.6 | 28 | 161 | 5 | W.J. O'Reilly | Australia v England | Brisbane | 1936–37 |
| 606 | 101 | 45 | 165 | 6 | Fazal Mahmood | Pakistan v West Indies | Port-of-Spain | 1957–58 |
| 604 | 75.4 | 15 | 244 | 7 | F.A. Ward | South Australia v NSW | Adelaide | 1935–36 |
| 603 | 100.3 | 40 | 161 | 6 | W.J. O'Reilly | Australia v England | Adelaide | 1932–33 |
| 602 | 100.2 | 38 | 191 | 6 | Mohammad Nazir | Railways v PIA | Lahore | 1982–83 |
| 601 | 100.1 | 44 | 171 | 13 | A.P. Freeman | Kent v Lancashire | Tonbridge | 1933 |
| 600 | 75 | 23 | 161 | 5 | C.F.W. Allcott | Auckland v Canterbury | Christchurch | 1924–25 |
| 600 | 100 | 39 | 180 | 0 | M.W. Tate | England v Australia | Melbourne | 1928–29 |
| 600 | 100 | 46 | 122 | 4 | L.C. Butler | Wellington v Auckland | Auckland | 1965–66 |
| 600 | 100 | 47 | 142 | 9 | D.A. Allen | Gloucestershire v Lancashire | Lydney | 1966 |

# FOUR WICKETS WITH CONSECUTIVE BALLS

| J. Wells | Kent v Sussex | Brighton | 1862 |
|---|---|---|---|
| G. Ulyett | Lord Harris' XI v New South Wales | Sydney | 1878–79 |
| G. Nash | Lancashire v Somerset | Manchester | 1882 |
| J.B. Hide | Sussex v MCC | Lord's | 1890 |
| F.J. Shacklock | Nottinghamshire v Somerset | Nottingham | 1893 |
| A.D. Downes | Otago v Auckland | Dunedin | 1893–94 |
| F. Martin | MCC v Derbyshire | Lord's | 1895 |
| A.W. Mold | Lancashire v Nottinghamshire | Nottingham | 1895 |
| W. Brearley | †Lancashire v Somerset | Manchester | 1905 |
| S. Haigh | MCC v Army | Pretoria | 1905–06 |
| A.E. Trott | ‡Middlesex v Somerset | Lord's | 1907 |
| F.A. Tarrant | Middlesex v Gloucestershire | Bristol | 1907 |
| A. Drake | Yorkshire v Derbyshire | Chesterfield | 1914 |
| S.G. Smith | Northamptonshire v Warwickshire | Birmingham | 1914 |
| H.A. Peach | Surrey v Sussex | Oval | 1924 |
| A.F. Borland | Natal v Griqualand West | Kimberley | 1926–27 |
| J.E.H. Hooker | †New South Wales v Victoria | Sydney | 1928–29 |
| R.K. Tyldesley | †Lancashire v Derbyshire | Derby | 1929 |
| R.J. Crisp | Western Province v Griqualand West | Johannesburg | 1931–32 |
| R.J. Crisp | Western Province v Natal | Durban | 1933–34 |
| A.R. Gover | Surrey v Worcestershire | Worcester | 1935 |
| W.H. Copson | Derbyshire v Warwickshire | Derby | 1937 |
| W.A. Henderson | N.E. Transvaal v Orange Free State | Bloemfontein | 1937–38 |
| F. Ridgway | Kent v Derbyshire | Folkestone | 1951 |
| A.K. Walker | †Nottinghamshire v Leicestershire | Leicester | 1956 |
| S.N. Mohol | President's XI v Combined XI | Poona | 1965–66 |
| P.I. Pocock | Surrey v Sussex | Eastbourne | 1972 |

† *Not all in the same innings.*
‡ *Trott achieved another hat-trick in the same innings of this, his benefit match.*

# HAT-TRICKS

## TWICE IN SAME INNINGS

| A.E. Trott | Middlesex v Somerset | Lord's | 1907 |
|---|---|---|---|
| J.S. Rao | Services v Northern Punjab | Amritsar | 1963–64 |

## IN BOTH INNINGS OF A MATCH

| | | | |
|---|---|---|---|
| A. Shaw | Nottinghamshire v Gloucestershire | Nottingham | 1884 |
| T.J. Matthews | Australia v South Africa | Manchester | 1912 |
| C.W.L. Parker | Gloucestershire v Middlesex | Bristol | 1924 |
| R.O. Jenkins | Worcestershire v Surrey | Worcester | 1949 |
| Amin Lakhani | Universities & Youth XI v Indians | Multan | 1978–79 |

## UNUSUAL SIMILARITIES OF DISMISSAL

### ALL LBW

| | | | |
|---|---|---|---|
| H. Fisher | Yorkshire v Somerset | Sheffield | 1932 |
| J.A. Flavell | Worcestershire v Lancashire | Manchester | 1963 |
| M.J. Procter | Gloucestershire v Essex | Westcliff | 1972 |
| B.J. Ikin | Griqualand West v Orange Free State | Kimberley | 1973–74 |
| M.J. Procter | Gloucestershire v Yorkshire | Cheltenham | 1979 |

### ALL CAUGHT

| | | | | |
|---|---|---|---|---|
| S.G. Smith | (c G.J. Thompson) | Northamptonshire v Warwickshire | Birmingham | 1914 |
| R. Beesly | (c C.White) | Border v Griqualand West | Queenstown | 1946–47 |
| H.L. Jackson | (c G.O. Dawkes) | Derbyshire v Worcestershire | Kidderminster | 1958 |

### ALL STUMPED

| | | | | |
|---|---|---|---|---|
| C.L. Townsend | (st W.H. Brain) | Gloucestershire v Somerset | Cheltenham | 1893 |

## MOST HAT-TRICKS

**7** D.V.P. Wright

**6** T.W.J. Goddard, C.W.L. Parker

**5** S. Haigh, V.W.C. Jupp, A.E.G. Rhodes, F.A. Tarrant

**4** R.G. Barlow, J.T. Hearne, J.C. Laker, G.A.R. Lock, G.G. Macaulay, T.J. Matthews, M.J. Procter, T. Richardson, F.R. Spofforth, F.S. Trueman

**3** W.M. Bradley, H.J. Butler, W.H. Copson, R.J. Crisp, J.W.H.T. Douglas, J.A. Flavell, A.P. Freeman, G. Giffen, K. Higgs, A. Hill, W.A. Humphreys, R.D. Jackman, R.O. Jenkins, A.S. Kennedy, W. Lockwood, E.A. McDonald, T.L. Pritchard, J.S. Rao, A. Shaw, J.B. Statham, M.W. Tate, H. Trumble, D. Wilson, G.A. Wilson.

## HAT-TRICKS

| | | | | |
|---|---|---|---|---|
| Abdul Qadir | | Habib Bank v Lahore | Faisalabad | 1981–82 |
| Abdul Wahab | | Karachi v Services | Karachi | 1954–55 |
| A'Court, D.G. | | Gloucestershire v Derbyshire | Gloucester | 1961 |
| Alabaster, G.D. | | Northern Districts v Canterbury | Hamilton | 1962–63 |
| Alleyne, H.L. | | Worcestershire v Middlesex | Lord's | 1981 |
| Allom, M.J.C. | | England v New Zealand | Christchurch | 1929–30 |
| | | *On Test match debut – 4 in 5* | | |
| Amin Lakhani | (2) | Combined XI v Indians *(1st inns)* | Multan | 1978–79 |
| | | Combined XI v Indians *(2nd inns)* | Multan | 1978–79 |
| Amjad Hussain | | Lahore B v Bahawalpur | Bahawalpur | 1962–63 |
| Anderson, I.D.E. | | Natal v Griqualand West | Durban | 1934–35 |
| Andrews, W.H.R. | | Somerset v Surrey | Oval | 1937 |
| Appleyard, R. | | Yorkshire v Gloucestershire | Sheffield | 1956 |
| Armstrong, W.W. | | Victoria v New South Wales | Melbourne | 1902–03 |
| Arnold, G.G. | | Surrey v Leicestershire | Leicester | 1974 |
| Arnott, T. | | Glamorgan v Somerset | Cardiff | 1926 |
| Arshad Khan | | Dacca U. v East Pakistan B | Dacca | 1957–58 |
| Asif Masood | | Pakistanis v Middlesex | Lord's | 1974 |
| Asim Butt | | Lahore City Blues v Lahore Division | Lahore | 1984–85 |
| Bailey, T.E. | | Essex v Glamorgan | Newport | 1950 |
| Baird, H.H.C. | | Army & Navy v Combined U's | Aldershot | 1910 |
| Balderstone, J.C. | | Leicestershire v Sussex | Eastbourne | 1976 |
| Banerjee, S.A. | | East Zone v West Zone | Bombay | 1948–49 |
| Banerjee, S.N. | | Bihar v Delhi | Jamshedpur | 1948–49 |
| Bannister, J.D. | | Warwickshire v Yorkshire | Sheffield | 1955 |
| Baqa Jilani, M. | | Northern India v Southern Punjab | Amritsar | 1934–35 |
| Barber, R.W. | | Warwickshire v Glamorgan | Birmingham | 1963 |
| Barclay, F. | | Auckland v Canterbury | Auckland | 1903–04 |
| Barlow, E.J. | | Rest of the World v England *(4 in 5)* | Leeds | 1970 |

| | | | | |
|---|---|---|---|---|
| Barlow, R.G. | (4) | Lancashire v Derbyshire | Manchester | 1879 |
| | | Lancashire v Derbyshire | Derby | 1881 |
| | | Players v Gentlemen | Oval | 1884 |
| | | Lancashire v Nottinghamshire | Manchester | 1886 |
| Barnes, S.F. | | England v Rest | Oval | 1912 |
| Bartlett, G.A. | | Central Districts v Northern Districts | Hamilton | 1959–60 |
| Bates, W. | | England v Australia | Melbourne | 1882–83 |
| Beaumont, J. | | South v North | Hastings | 1889 |
| Bedi, B.S. | | Delhi v Punjab | Delhi | 1968–69 |
| Bedser, A.V. | | Surrey v Essex | Oval | 1953 |
| Beesly, R. | | Border v Griqualand West | Queenstown | 1946–47 |
| Benskin, W.E. | (2) | Leicestershire v Essex | Southend | 1906 |
| | | Scotland v Oxford University | Oxford | 1913 |
| Bennett, J.H. | | Canterbury v Wellington | Wellington | 1911–12 |
| Bettington, R.H.B. | | Oxford University v Essex | Oxford | 1920 |
| Best, W.F. | | Kent v Somerset | Taunton | 1891 |
| Bhat, A.R. | | Karnataka v Bombay | Bangalore | 1981–82 |
| Birkenshaw, J. | (2) | Leicestershire v Worcestershire | Worcester | 1967 |
| | | Leicestershire v Cambridge University | Cambridge | 1968 |
| Blackman, W. | | Sussex v Surrey | Hove | 1881 |
| Blair, R.W. | | Wellington v Northern Districts | Wellington | 1962–63 |
| Blythe, C. | (2) | Kent v Surrey (4 in 5) | Blackheath | 1910 |
| | | Kent v Derbyshire | Gravesend | 1910 |
| Booth, M.W. | (2) | Yorkshire v Worcestershire | Bradford | 1911 |
| | | Yorkshire v Essex | Leyton | 1912 |
| Borland, A.F. | (2) | Natal v Griqualand West (4 in 4) | Kimberley | 1926–27 |
| | | Natal v Transvaal | Johannesburg | 1931–32 |
| Bosanquet, B.J.T. | | R.A. Bennett's XI v Barbados | Bridgetown | 1901–02 |
| Botham, I.T. | | MCC v Middlesex | Lord's | 1978 |
| Bowes, W.E. | | MCC v Cambridge University | Lord's | 1928 |
| Boyce, K.D. | | Essex v Warwickshire | Chelmsford | 1974 |
| Boyes, G.S. | (2) | Hampshire v Surrey | Portsmouth | 1925 |
| | | Hampshire v Warwickshire | Birmingham | 1926 |
| Boyle, C.W. | | Oxford University v Middlesex | Prince's | 1873 |
| Bradley, W.M. | (3) | Kent v Essex | Leyton | 1899 |
| | | Kent v Yorkshire | Tonbridge | 1899 |
| | | Kent v Somerset | Blackheath | 1900 |
| Braund, L.C. | | Somerset v Worcestershire | Worcester | 1906 |
| Brearley, W. | | Lancashire v Somerset (4 in 4) | Manchester | 1905 |
| Bridges, J. | | Somerset v Derbyshire | Burton upon Trent | 1924 |
| Briggs, J. | (2) | North v South | Scarborough | 1891 |
| | | England v Australia | Sydney | 1891–92 |
| Brockwell, W. | | Surrey v Yorkshire | Sheffield | 1900 |
| Bromley-Davenport, H.R. | | R.S. Lucas's XI v Demerara | Georgetown | 1894–95 |
| Brown, A.S. | | Gloucestershire v Glamorgan | Swansea | 1973 |
| Brown, J.T. | | Yorkshire v Derbyshire | Derby | 1896 |
| Browne, C.R. | | British Guiana v Barbados | Georgetown | 1937–38 |
| Browne, H.E. | | Europeans v Parsees | Poona | 1895–96 |
| Buchanan, D. | | Gentlemen v Cambridge University | Cambridge | 1874 |
| Budgen, E.A. | | Orange Free State v Griqualand West | Kimberley | 1921–22 |
| Bullough, J. | | Lancashire v Derbyshire | Derby | 1914 |
| Burns, W.B. | | Worcestershire v Gloucestershire | Worcester | 1913 |
| Buss, A. | (2) | Sussex v Cambridge University | Cambridge | 1965 |
| | | Sussex v Derbyshire | Hove | 1965 |
| Butler, H.J. | (3) | Nottinghamshire v Surrey | Nottingham | 1937 |
| | | Nottinghamshire v Leicestershire | Worksop | 1937 |
| | | Nottinghamshire v Hampshire | Nottingham | 1939 |
| Butler, S.E. | | Oxford University v MCC (4 in 5) | Oxford | 1871 |
| Buxton, I.R. | | Derbyshire v Oxford University | Derby | 1969 |
| Cameron, F.J. | | Otago v Northern Districts | Hamilton | 1962–63 |
| Carey, P.A.D. | | Sussex v Glamorgan | Hove | 1947 |
| Carter, R.G.M. | | Worcestershire v Lancashire | Worcester | 1965 |
| Cartwright, G.H.M.G. | | Free Foresters v Cambridge University | Cambridge | 1920 |
| Cartwright, T.W. | | Warwickshire v Somerset | Birmingham | 1969 |
| Chowdhury, N.R. | | General Stewart's XI v Bengal Governor's XI | Calcutta | 1944–45 |

| | | | | |
|---|---|---|---|---|
| Clark, E.W. | | Northamptonshire v West Indians | Northampton | 1923 |
| Clarke, S.T. | (2) | Barbados v Trinidad | Bridgetown | 1977–78 |
| | | Surrey v Nottinghamshire | Oval | 1980 |
| Clarke, W. | | England v Kent | Canterbury | 1844 |
| | | *Including the wicket of J.F. Fagge in both innings* | | |
| Clift, P.B. | (2) | Leicestershire v Yorkshire | Leicester | 1976 |
| | | Leicestershire v Derbyshire | Chesterfield | 1985 |
| Clough, P.M. | | Tasmania v New South Wales | Hobart | 1982–83 |
| Cobden, F.C. | | Cambridge U. v Oxford U. | Lord's | 1870 |
| Coldwell, L.J. | (2) | Worcestershire v Leicestershire | Stourbridge | 1957 |
| | | Worcestershire v Essex | Brentwood | 1965 |
| Constantine, L.N. | | West Indians v Northamptonshire | Northampton | 1928 |
| Cooke, R. | | Warwickshire v Kent *(4 in 5)* | Tunbridge Wells | 1925 |
| Cope, G.A. | | Yorkshire v Essex | Colchester | 1970 |
| Copson, W.H. | (3) | Derbyshire v Lancashire | Burton upon Trent | 1937 |
| | | Derbyshire v Warwickshire *(5 in 6)* | Derby | 1937 |
| | | Derbyshire v Oxford University *(4 in 5)* | Oxford | 1939 |
| Cotton, J. | | Leicestershire v Surrey | Oval | 1965 |
| Cousens, P. | | Essex v Combined Services | Chelmsford | 1950 |
| Cox, A.L. | | Northamptonshire v Lancashire *(4 in 5)* | Northampton | 1930 |
| Coxon, A. | | Yorkshire v Worcestershire | Leeds | 1946 |
| Crisp, R.J. | (3) | Western Province v GW *(4 in 4)* | Johannesburg | 1931–32 |
| | | Western Province v Transvaal *(4 in 5)* | Johannesburg | 1931–32 |
| | | Western Province v Natal *(4 in 4)* | Durban | 1933–34 |
| Cropper, W. | | Derbyshire v Hampshire | Southampton | 1885 |
| Crossland, J. | | Lancashire v Surrey | Oval | 1881 |
| Cuffe, J.A. | | Worcestershire v Hampshire | Bournemouth | 1910 |
| Cumbes, J. | | Worcestershire v Northamptonshire | Worcester | 1977 |
| Daniel, W.W. | | Middlesex v Lancashire | Southport | 1981 |
| Davey, J. | | Gloucestershire v Oxford University | Oxford | 1976 |
| Davidson, A.K. | | New South Wales v Western Australia | Perth | 1962–63 |
| Davidson, F. | | Derbyshire v Nottinghamshire | Derby | 1898 |
| Davidson, G. | (2) | Derbyshire v Lancashire | Derby | 1895 |
| | | Derbyshire v MCC | Lord's | 1898 |
| Davies, D.E. | | Glamorgan v Leicestershire | Leicester | 1937 |
| Davies, P.H. | | Oxford University v Middlesex | Oxford | 1914 |
| Davies, R.E. | | Natal v Western Province | Cape Town | 1934–35 |
| Dawson, O.C. | | South Africans v Northamptonshire | Northampton | 1947 |
| Dean, J. | | England v Nottinghamshire | Lord's | 1853 |
| Dean, T.A. | | Hampshire v Worcestershire *(4 in 5)* | Bournemouth | 1939 |
| Dench, C.E. | | Nottinghamshire v Gloucestershire | Bristol | 1899 |
| Dennett, E.G. | (2) | Gloucestershire v Northamptonshire | Gloucester | 1907 |
| | | Gloucestershire v Surrey | Bristol | 1913 |
| Dewdney, D.T. | | West Indians v Hampshire | Southampton | 1957 |
| Deyes, G. | | Yorkshire v Gentlemen of Ireland | Bray | 1907 |
| Dildar Awan | | Services v Sargodha | Lyallpur | 1961–62 |
| Dilley, G.R. | | Kent v Surrey | Oval | 1985 |
| Dilley, M.R. | (2) | Northamptonshire v Nottinghamshire | Nottingham | 1961 |
| | | Northamptonshire v Sussex | Hove | 1961 |
| Divecha, R.V. | | Indians v Surrey | Oval | 1952 |
| Dixon, J.A. | | Nottinghamshire v Lancashire | Nottingham | 1887 |
| Dollery, K.R. | (2) | Warwickshire v Gloucestershire | Bristol | 1953 |
| | | Warwickshire v Kent | Coventry | 1956 |
| Dooland, B. | | South Australia v Victoria | Melbourne | 1945–46 |
| Douglas, J.W.H.T. | (3) | Essex v Yorkshire | Leyton | 1905 |
| | | MCC v New South Wales | Sydney | 1920–21 |
| | | Essex v Sussex | Leyton | 1923 |
| Downes, A.D. | | Otago v Auckland *(4 in 4)* | Dunedin | 1893–94 |
| Drake, A. | (2) | Yorkshire v Essex | Huddersfield | 1912 |
| | | Yorkshire v Derbyshire *(4 in 4)* | Chesterfield | 1914 |
| Drybrough, C.D. | | Middlesex v Northamptonshire *(4 in 5)* | Northampton | 1964 |
| Durston, F.J. | (2) | Middlesex v Cambridge University | Cambridge | 1922 |
| | | Middlesex v Oxford University | Oxford | 1923 |
| East, R.E. | | Rest v MCC Touring XI | Hove | 1973 |
| Easter, J.N.C. | | Oxford University v Northamptonshire | Oxford | 1967 |
| Ebeling, H.I. | | Victoria v Queensland | Melbourne | 1928–29 |
| Edmonds, P.H. | | Middlesex v Leicestershire | Leicester | 1981 |

| | | | | |
|---|---|---|---|---|
| Enthoven, H.J. | (2) | Gentlemen v Players | Lord's | 1926 |
| | | Middlesex v Australians | Lord's | 1934 |
| Estwick, R.O. | | Barbados v Guyana | Bridgetown | 1981–82 |
| | | *On début in first-class cricket* | | |
| Evans, H. | | Derbyshire v Sussex | Hove | 1881 |
| Evans, W.H.B. | | Oxford University v Nottinghamshire | Oxford | 1905 |
| Fannin, H.A. | | Hawke's Bay v Taranaki | Napier | 1897–98 |
| Farnes, K. | | Essex v Nottinghamshire | Clacton | 1939 |
| Farrands, F.H. | | MCC v Cambridge University | Cambridge | 1872 |
| Faulkner, G.A. | (2) | Transvaal v Western Province | Cape Town | 1906–07 |
| | | Transvaal v Border | Cape Town | 1908–09 |
| Fender, P.G.H. | (2) | Surrey v Somerset | Oval | 1914 |
| | | Surrey v Gloucestershire | Oval | 1924 |
| Ferris, G.J.F. | | Leicestershire v Northamptonshire | Leicester | 1983 |
| Field, E.F. | | Warwickshire v Hampshire | Birmingham | 1911 |
| Fisher, H. | | Yorkshire v Somerset | Sheffield | 1932 |
| Flanagan, J.P.D. | | Transvaal B v Natal B | Ladysmith | 1971–72 |
| Flanagan, M. | | MCC v Surrey | Lord's | 1876 |
| Flavell, J.A. | (3) | Worcestershire v Kent | Kidderminster | 1951 |
| | | Worcestershire v Cambridge University | Cambridge | 1953 |
| | | Worcestershire v Lancashire | Manchester | 1963 |
| Fletcher, W. | | Yorkshire v MCC | Lord's | 1892 |
| Flowers, W. | (2) | Nottinghamshire v Kent | Maidstone | 1888 |
| | | MCC v Oxford University | Oxford | 1892 |
| Foster, D.G. | | Warwickshire v Hampshire | Birmingham | 1929 |
| Fowler, W.H. | | Somerset v MCC | Lord's | 1882 |
| Frederick, N. | | Ceylon v Madras | Colombo | 1963–64 |
| Freeman, A.P. | (3) | Kent v Middlesex | Canterbury | 1920 |
| | | MCC v South Australia | Adelaide | 1922–23 |
| | | Kent v Surrey | Blackheath | 1934 |
| Freeman, G. | (2) | Yorkshire v Lancashire | Holbeck, Leeds | 1868 |
| | | Yorkshire v Middlesex | Sheffield | 1868 |
| Frith, C. | | Otago v Canterbury | Dunedin | 1884–85 |
| Fry, C.B. | | Oxford University v MCC | Lord's | 1894 |
| Fulljames, R.E.G. | | RAF v Royal Navy | Oval | 1928 |
| Furlong, B.D.M. | | NZ U-23 XI v Canterbury | Christchurch | 1964–65 |
| Gaekwad, H.G. | | Madhya Pradesh v Rajasthan | Jabalpur | 1962–63 |
| Garner, J. | | Somerset v Worcestershire | Taunton | 1982 |
| Gattani, K.R. | | Rajasthan v Uttar Pradesh | Varanasi | 1969–70 |
| Geary, G. | | Leicestershire v Gloucestershire | Bristol | 1922 |
| Ghiasuddin Ahmed | | Bahawalpur v Khairpur | Bahawalpur | 1961–62 |
| Gibbs, K.L. | | Orange Free State v Eastern Province | Bloemfontein | 1952–53 |
| Gibbs, L.R. | | West Indies v Australia | Adelaide | 1960–61 |
| Gibson, D. | | Surrey v Northamptonshire | Northampton | 1961 |
| Giffen, G. | (3) | Australians v Lancashire | Manchester | 1884 |
| | | South Australia v G.F. Vernon's XI | Adelaide | 1887–88 |
| | | Australians v England XI | Wembley Park | 1896 |
| Gifford, N. | | Worcestershire v Derbyshire | Chesterfield | 1965 |
| Gilbert, D.R. | | New South Wales v Victoria | Sydney | 1984–85 |
| Gilbert, G.H.B. | | New South Wales v Victoria | Melbourne | 1857–58 |
| Gilligan, A.E.R. | | Sussex v Surrey | Oval | 1923 |
| Gladwin, C. | (2) | MCC v N.E. Transvaal *(4 in 5)* | Benoni | 1948–49 |
| | | Derbyshire v New Zealanders | Derby | 1958 |
| Goddard, T.L. | (2) | Natal v Border | East London | 1959–60 |
| | | Natal v Rhodesia | Salisbury | 1969–70 |
| Goddard, T.W.J. | (6) | Gloucestershire v Sussex | Eastbourne | 1924 |
| | | Gloucestershire v Glamorgan | Swansea | 1930 |
| | | England v South Africa | Johannesburg | 1938–39 |
| | | MCC v Rhodesia | Salisbury | 1938–39 |
| | | Gloucestershire v Glamorgan | Swansea | 1947 |
| | | Gloucestershire v Somerset | Bristol | 1947 |
| Gopalan, M.J. | | Madras v Ceylon *(4 in 5)* | Madras | 1932–33 |
| Gordon, N. | | Transvaal v Border | East London | 1937–38 |
| Gothard, E.J. | | Derbyshire v Middlesex | Derby | 1947 |
| Gover, A.R. | | Surrey v Worcestershire *(4 in 4)* | Worcester | 1935 |
| Graveney, D.A. | | Gloucestershire v Leicestershire | Leicester | 1983 |
| Gray, A.H. | | Surrey v Yorkshire *(4 in 5)* | Sheffield | 1985 |

| | | | | |
|---|---|---|---|---|
| Gregson, W.R. | | Lancashire v Leicestershire *(4 in 5)* | Blackpool | 1906 |
| Greig, A.W. | | Eastern Province v Natal | Port Elizabeth | 1971–72 |
| Griffin, G.M. | | South Africa v England | Lord's | 1960 |
| Grimmett, C.V. | | South Australia v Queensland | Brisbane | 1928–29 |
| Grove, C.W. | | Warwickshire v Somerset | Taunton | 1947 |
| Gunn, J.R. | (2) | Nottinghamshire v Middlesex | Lord's | 1899 |
| | | Nottinghamshire v Derbyshire | Chesterfield | 1904 |
| Hadlee, R.J. | | Canterbury v Central Districts | Nelson | 1971–72 |
| Haigh, S. | (5) | Yorkshire v Derbyshire | Bradford | 1897 |
| | | Lord Hawke's XI v Cape Colony | Cape Town | 1898–99 |
| | | Yorkshire v Somerset | Sheffield | 1902 |
| | | MCC v Army *(4 in 4)* | Pretoria | 1905–06 |
| | | Yorkshire v Lancashire | Manchester | 1909 |
| Halfyard, D.J. | (2) | Kent v Worcestershire | Folkestone | 1957 |
| | | Kent v Leicestershire | Gillingham | 1958 |
| Hall, W.W. | | West Indies v Pakistan | Lahore | 1958–59 |
| Hallam, A.W. | | Nottinghamshire v Leicestershire | Nottingham | 1907 |
| Hammersley, W.J. | | MCC v Surrey | Oval | 1848 |
| Hammond, H.E. | | Sussex v Warwickshire | Hove | 1946 |
| Hanley, R.W. | | Transvaal B v Border | East London | 1976–77 |
| Harman, R. | (2) | Surrey v Kent *(4 in 5)* | Blackheath | 1963 |
| | | Surrey v Derbyshire | Ilkeston | 1968 |
| Harvey, E. | | Cambridge University v MCC | Lord's | 1872 |
| Haslip, S.M. | | Middlesex v Nottinghamshire | Nottingham | 1919 |
| Hay, H. | | South Australia v Lord Hawke's XI | Unley, Adelaide | 1902–03 |
| | | *On début in first-class cricket* | | |
| Hayward, T. | | Players v Gentlemen | Lord's | 1870 |
| Hayward, T.W. | (2) | Surrey v Gloucestershire | Oval | 1899 |
| | | Surrey v Derbyshire | Chesterfield | 1899 |
| Hazare, V.S. | | Baroda v Maharashtra | Poona | 1941–42 |
| Hearne, A. | (2) | Kent v Gloucestershire | Clifton | 1900 |
| | | MCC v Yorkshire | Lord's | 1888 |
| Hearne, G.G. | | Kent v Lancashire | Manchester | 1875 |
| Hearne, J.T. | (4) | Middlesex v Kent | Tonbridge | 1896 |
| | | England v Australia | Leeds | 1899 |
| | | Middlesex v Essex *(4 in 5)* | Lord's | 1902 |
| | | Middlesex v Warwickshire | Lord's | 1912 |
| Hearne, J.W. | (2) | Middlesex v Essex | Lord's | 1911 |
| | | Middlesex v Essex | Leyton | 1922 |
| Hearne, T. | | Middlesex v Kent | Islington | 1868 |
| Hearne, W. | | Kent v Lancashire | Tonbridge | 1894 |
| Hemmings, E.E. | (2) | Warwickshire v Worcestershire | Birmingham | 1977 |
| | | Nottinghamshire v Northamptonshire | Nottingham | 1984 |
| Henderson, W.A. | | N.E. Transvaal v OFS *(5 in 6)* | Bloemfontein | 1937–38 |
| Hendrick, M. | | Derbyshire v West Indians | Chesterfield | 1980 |
| Herman, O.W. | | Hampshire v Glamorgan | Portsmouth | 1938 |
| Hesketh-Prichard, H. | | MCC v Philadelphians | Haverford | 1907–08 |
| Hide, J.B. | | Sussex v MCC *(4 in 4)* | Lord's | 1890 |
| Higgs, K. | (3) | Lancashire v Essex | Blackpool | 1960 |
| | | Lancashire v Yorkshire | Leeds | 1968 |
| | | Leicestershire v Hampshire | Leicester | 1977 |
| Hill, A. | (3) | Yorkshire v United South | Bradford | 1874 |
| | | Players v Gentlemen | Lord's | 1874 |
| | | Yorkshire v Surrey | Oval | 1880 |
| Hilton, J. | | Somerset v Hampshire | Weston-s-Mare | 1955 |
| Hipkin, A.B. | | Essex v Lancashire | Blackpool | 1924 |
| Hirst, G.H. | (2) | Yorkshire v Leicestershire | Leicester | 1895 |
| | | Yorkshire v Leicestershire | Hull | 1907 |
| Hitch, J.W. | (2) | Surrey v Cambridge University *(4 in 5)* | Oval | 1911 |
| | | Surrey v Warwickshire | Oval | 1914 |
| Holder, J.W. | | Hampshire v Kent | Southampton | 1972 |
| Hooker, J.E.H. | | New South Wales v Victoria *(4 in 4)* | Sydney | 1928–29 |
| Hopkins, A.J.Y. | (2) | Australians v Cambridge University | Cambridge | 1902 |
| | | New South Wales v South Australia | Sydney | 1903–04 |
| Horsley, J. | | Derbyshire v AIF | Derby | 1919 |
| Horton, M.J. | | Worcestershire v Somerset | Bath | 1956 |
| Howard, T.H. | | New South Wales v Queensland *(4 in 5)* | Sydney | 1902–03 |

| | | | | |
|---|---|---|---|---|
| Howell, W.P. | (2) | Australians v Western Province *(4 in 5)* | Cape Town | 1902–03 |
| | | Australians v New Zealand XI | Wellington | 1904–05 |
| Howorth, R. | | Worcestershire v Warwickshire | Birmingham | 1950 |
| Huggins, J.H. | | Gloucestershire v Nottinghamshire | Nottingham | 1903 |
| Humphreys, W.A. | (3) | Sussex v Australians | Hove | 1880 |
| | | Sussex v Australians | Hove | 1884 |
| | | Sussex v Hampshire | Southampton | 1885 |
| Hutton, R.A. | | MCC U-25 v North Zone | Peshawar | 1966–67 |
| Ikin, B.J. | | Griqualand West v Orange Free State | Kimberley | 1973–74 |
| Ikin, J.T. | | Lancashire v Somerset | Taunton | 1949 |
| Illingworth, R. | | Leicestershire v Surrey | Oval | 1975 |
| Imran Khan | | Sussex v Warwickshire | Birmingham | 1983 |
| Intikhab Alam | | Surrey v Yorkshire | Oval | 1972 |
| Iqbal Qasim | | National Bank v Allied Bank | Lahore | 1982–83 |
| Iqbal Sheikh | | Lahore Greens v Multan | Lahore | 1964–65 |
| Ireland, J.F. | | Cambridge U. v Oxford U. | Lord's | 1911 |
| Ironmonger, H. | | Victoria v MCC | Melbourne | 1924–25 |
| Ismail, A.A. | | Bombay v Saurashtra | Bombay | 1973–74 |
| Jackman, R.D. | (3) | Surrey v Kent | Canterbury | 1971 |
| | | Western Province v Natal | Pietermaritzburg | 1971–72 |
| | | Surrey v Yorkshire | Leeds | 1973 |
| Jackson, H.L. | (2) | Derbyshire v Worcestershire | Kidderminster | 1958 |
| | | Derbyshire v Worcestershire | Derby | 1960 |
| Jackson, P.F. | | Worcestershire v Glamorgan | Neath | 1936 |
| Jackson, V.E. | (2) | Leicestershire v Derbyshire | Derby | 1946 |
| | | Leicestershire v Surrey | Leicester | 1950 |
| Jalaluddin | | IDBP v Karachi | Karachi | 1981–82 |
| Jameson, J.A. | | Warwickshire v Gloucestershire | Birmingham | 1965 |
| Jarvis, P.W. | | Yorkshire v Derbyshire | Chesterfield | 1985 |
| Jayes, T. | (2) | Leicestershire v Northamptonshire | Leicester | 1906 |
| | | Leicestershire v Kent | Maidstone | 1907 |
| Jenkins, R.O. | (3) | Worcestershire v Surrey | Oval | 1948 |
| | | Worcestershire v Surrey *(1st inns)* | Worcester | 1949 |
| | | Worcestershire v Surrey *(2nd inns)* | Worcester | 1949 |
| Jephson, D.L.A. | | Surrey v Middlesex | Oval | 1904 |
| Jhanji, S.S. | | Uttar Pradesh v Vidharba | Nagpur | 1963–64 |
| Jones, I.J. | | Glamorgan v Yorkshire | Harrogate | 1962 |
| Jones, J.F. | | Wellington v Central Districts | Wellington | 1953–54 |
| Julien, B.D. | | North Trinidad v South Trinidad | Port-of-Spain | 1968–69 |
| Jupp, V.W.C. | (5) | Sussex v Surrey | Hove | 1911 |
| | | Sussex v Essex | Leyton | 1919 |
| | | Sussex v Essex | Colchester | 1921 |
| | | Northamptonshire v Glamorgan | Swansea | 1925 |
| | | Northamptonshire v Gloucestershire | Bristol | 1931 |
| Kalyanasundaram, B. | | Tamil Nadu v Bombay | Madras | 1972–73 |
| Kapil Dev | | North Zone v West Zone | Delhi | 1978–79 |
| Kennedy, A.S. | (3) | Hampshire v Gloucestershire | Southampton | 1920 |
| | | Hampshire v Somerset | Bournemouth | 1920 |
| | | Hampshire v Gloucestershire | Southampton | 1924 |
| Kermode, A. | | Lancashire v Leicestershire | Leicester | 1906 |
| Khalid Niazi | | Railways v MCB | Karachi | 1980–81 |
| Khanna, N. | | Southern Punjab v Jammu & Kashmir | Patiala | 1959–60 |
| Khot, J.B. | | Bombay v Baroda | Bombay | 1943–44 |
| King, J.H. | (2) | Leicestershire v Sussex | Hove | 1903 |
| | | Leicestershire v Somerset | Weston-s-Mare | 1920 |
| Kline, L.F. | | Australia v South Africa | Cape Town | 1957–58 |
| Knott, C.J. | | Gentlemen v Players | Lord's | 1950 |
| Kotze, J.J. | (2) | Transvaal v Griqualand West | Port Elizabeth | 1902–03 |
| | | Western Province v Eastern Province | Cape Town | 1904–05 |
| Kulkarni, U.N. | | Bombay v Gujarat | Vallabh Vidyanagar | 1963–64 |
| Laker, J.C. | (4) | P.F. Warner's XI v South of England | Hastings | 1947 |
| | | Surrey v Gloucestershire | Gloucester | 1951 |
| | | Surrey v Warwickshire | Oval | 1953 |
| | | Surrey v Cambridge University | Guildford | 1953 |
| Lambert, L.A. | | Berbice v Demerara | Berbice | 1982–83 |
| Langridge, James | | Sussex v Derbyshire | Derby | 1939 |
| Lankham, W. | | Auckland v Taranaki | Auckland | 1882–83 |

| | | | | |
|---|---|---|---|---|
| Larwood, H. | (2) | Nottinghamshire v Cambridge U. | Cambridge | 1926 |
| | | Nottinghamshire v Glamorgan | Nottingham | 1931 |
| Lawrence, J. | | Somerset v Yorkshire *(4 in 5)* | Taunton | 1948 |
| Lees, W.S. | | Surrey v Hampshire | Southampton | 1897 |
| Le Roux, G.S. | | Sussex v Warwickshire | Hove | 1981 |
| Lever P. | | Lancashire v Nottinghamshire | Manchester | 1969 |
| Lewis, C. | | Kent v Nottinghamshire | Nottingham | 1939 |
| Leyland, M. | | Yorkshire v Surrey | Sheffield | 1935 |
| Loader, P.J. | (2) | England v West Indies | Leeds | 1957 |
| | | Surrey v Leicestershire | Oval | 1963 |
| Lock, G.A.R. | (4) | Surrey v Somerset | Weston-s-Mare | 1955 |
| | | MCC v Bahawalpur XI | Bahawalpur | 1955–56 |
| | | MCC v Combined XI | Multan | 1955–56 |
| | | Leicestershire v Hampshire | Portsmouth | 1967 |
| | | *First hat-trick in England to be completed on a Sunday* | | |
| Lockwood, W. | (3) | Surrey v Cambridge University | Cambridge | 1893 |
| | | Surrey v Derbyshire | Oval | 1901 |
| | | Surrey v Yorkshire | Sheffield | 1903 |
| Lohmann, G.A. | | England v South Africa | Port Elizabeth | 1895–96 |
| Lomax, J.G. | | Somerset v Nottinghamshire | Weston-s-Mare | 1958 |
| Longfield, T.C. | | Bengal v Bihar | Calcutta | 1937–38 |
| Louden, G.M. | | Essex v Somerset | Southend | 1921 |
| Lowe, R.G.H. | | Cambridge U. v Oxford U. | Lord's | 1926 |
| Macaulay, G.G. | (4) | Yorkshire v Warwickshire | Birmingham | 1923 |
| | | Yorkshire v Leicestershire | Hull | 1930 |
| | | Yorkshire v Glamorgan | Cardiff | 1933 |
| | | Yorkshire v Lancashire *(4 in 5)* | Manchester | 1933 |
| Macaulay, M.J. | | South Africans v Kent | Canterbury | 1965 |
| McCarthy, C.N. | | South Africans v Sussex | Hove | 1951 |
| McConnon, J.E. | | Glamorgan v South Africans | Swansea | 1951 |
| McDonald, E.A. | (3) | Lancashire v Sussex | Hove | 1925 |
| | | Lancashire v Kent | Dover | 1926 |
| | | Lancashire v Warwickshire | Birmingham | 1930 |
| McGlew, D.J. | | Natal v Transvaal | Durban | 1963–64 |
| McKibbin, T.R. | | Australians v Lancashire | Liverpool | 1896 |
| Maguiness, S.J. | | Wellington v Central Districts | Wellington | 1983–84 |
| Maile, J.B.R. | | Western Province v Rhodesia | Salisbury | 1958–59 |
| Majid Khan | | Glamorgan v Oxford University | Oxford | 1969 |
| Marlar, R.G. | | Cambridge University v Essex | Cambridge | 1952 |
| Marlow, J. | | Derbyshire v Kent | Derby | 1884 |
| Marriott, C.S. | | MCC v Madras | Madras | 1933–34 |
| Marshall, M.D. | (2) | Barbados v Combined Islands | St John's | 1978–79 |
| | | Hampshire v Somerset *(4 in 5)* | Taunton | 1983 |
| Martin, F. | (2) | Kent v Surrey | Oval | 1890 |
| | | MCC v Derbyshire *(4 in 4)* | Lord's | 1895 |
| Matthews, T.J. | (4) | Victoria v Tasmania | Launceston | 1908–09 |
| | | Australia v South Africa *(1st inns)* | Manchester | 1912 |
| | | Australia v South Africa *(2nd inns)* | Manchester | 1912 |
| | | Australians v Philadelphians | Germantown | 1912–13 |
| Mehta, J.N. | | Hindus v Europeans | Lahore | 1923–24 |
| Melle, B.G. | | Oxford University v Scotland | Oxford | 1913 |
| Melville, A. | | Oxford U. v | | |
| | | H.D.G. Leveson Gower's XI | Eastbourne | 1932 |
| Mercer, J. | | Glamorgan v Surrey | Oval | 1932 |
| Merchant, V.M. | | Dr C.R. Pereira's XI v | | |
| | | Sir H. Mehta's XI | Bombay | 1946–47 |
| Middleton, F.S. | | Wellington v Hawke's Bay | Wellington | 1919–20 |
| Mills, P.T. | | Gloucestershire v Hampshire | Clifton | 1920 |
| Mohinder Kumar | | United Bank v Karachi B | Karachi | 1978–79 |
| Mohol, S.N. | | President's XI v Combined XI *(4 in 4)* | Poona | 1965–66 |
| Moir, A.M. | | Otago v Canterbury | Christchurch | 1950–51 |
| Mold, A.W. | (2) | Lancashire v Somerset | Manchester | 1894 |
| | | Lancashire v Nottinghamshire *(4 in 4)* | Nottingham | 1895 |
| Moore, F.W. | | Lancashire v Essex | Chelmsford | 1956 |
| More, R.E. | | B.J.T. Bosanquet's XI v Philadelphians | Philadelphia | 1901–02 |
| Morton, F.L. | | Victoria v Tasmania | Melbourne | 1931–32 |
| Morton, P.H. | | Cambridge U. v Oxford U. | Lord's | 1880 |

| | | | | |
|---|---|---|---|---|
| Moss, A.E. | | Middlesex v Gloucestershire | Lord's | 1956 |
| Mubarak Ali, S. | | Nawanagar v Western India States | Poona | 1936–37 |
| Muddiah, V.M. | | Services v East Punjab | Delhi | 1955–56 |
| Mulcock, E.T. | | Canterbury v Otago | Christchurch | 1937–38 |
| Munden, V.S. | | Leicestershire v Derbyshire | Ashby-de-la-Z. | 1953 |
| Murdin, J.V. | | Northamptonshire v Kent | Northampton | 1920 |
| Murray, R.M. | | Wellington v Otago | Wellington | 1949–50 |
| Mynn, A. | | Fast Bowlers v Slow Bowlers | Lord's | 1841 |
| Narottam, D. | | Kathiawar v Baroda | Dhrol | 1947–48 |
| Nash, G. | | Lancashire v Somerset *(4 in 4)* | Manchester | 1882 |
| Nayudu, C.S. | | Indians v Surrey | Oval | 1946 |
| Needham, P.G. | | Transvaal v Eastern Province | Johannesburg | 1951–52 |
| Neilson, D.R. | | Transvaal v Natal | Johannesburg | 1978–79 |
| Newman, J.A. | | Hampshire v Australians | Southampton | 1909 |
| Newstead, J.T. | | Yorkshire v Worcestershire | Bradford | 1907 |
| Nichols, M.S. | | Essex v Yorkshire | Leeds | 1931 |
| Noble, M.A. | | New South Wales v Tasmania | Sydney | 1898–99 |
| Nyalchand, S. | | Saurashtra v Baroda | Dhrangadhra | 1961–62 |
| Oakman, A.S.M. | | Sussex v Somerset | Hove | 1952 |
| O'Connor, J. | | Essex v Worcestershire | Worcester | 1925 |
| Odell, W.W. | (2) | London County v MCC | Lord's | 1904 |
| | | Leicestershire v Northamptonshire | Leicester | 1908 |
| Olliff, C. | | Auckland v Wellington | Auckland | 1912–13 |
| Orchard, S.A. | | Canterbury v Auckland | Auckland | 1909–10 |
| Orton, C.T. | | Europeans v Muslims | Bombay | 1938–39 |
| Overton, G.W.F. | | Otago v Canterbury | Christchurch | 1946–47 |
| Owen-Smith, H.G. | (2) | Oxford University v | | |
| | |    H.D.G. Leveson Gower's XI | Eastbourne | 1931 |
| | | Gentlemen v Players | Folkestone | 1935 |
| Oxenham, R.K. | | Australians v Ceylon | Colombo | 1935–36 |
| Paine, G.A.E. | (2) | Warwickshire v Middlesex | Lord's | 1932 |
| | | Warwickshire v Glamorgan | Cardiff | 1933 |
| Palmer, G.E. | (2) | Australians v Sussex | Hove | 1882 |
| | | Victoria v South Australia | Melbourne | 1882–83 |
| Parekh, M.D. | | Parsees v Hindus | Bombay | 1912–13 |
| Parker, C.W.L. | (6) | Gloucestershire v Yorkshire *(4 in 5)* | Bristol | 1922 |
| | | Gloucestershire v Middlesex (*1st inns*) | Bristol | 1924 |
| | | Gloucestershire v Middlesex (*2nd inns*) | Bristol | 1924 |
| | | Gloucestershire v Surrey | Oval | 1924 |
| | | Gloucestershire v Yorkshire | Hull | 1926 |
| | | Gloucestershire v Essex | Chelmsford | 1930 |
| Parthasarathi, G. | | Madras v Southern India | Pudokottah | 1936–37 |
| Partridge, R.J. | | Northamptonshire v Nottinghamshire | Nottingham | 1946 |
| Pascoe, L.S. | | New South Wales v South Australia | Adelaide | 1980–81 |
| Peach, H.A. | | Surrey v Sussex *(4 in 4)* | Oval | 1924 |
| Pearce, W. | | Kent v Derbyshire | Derby | 1878 |
| Pearson, F.A. | | Worcestershire v Surrey | Worcester | 1914 |
| Peate, E. | (2) | Yorkshire v Kent | Sheffield | 1882 |
| | | Yorkshire v Gloucestershire | Moreton-in-Marsh | 1884 |
| Peebles, I.A.R. | | Middlesex v Gloucestershire | Lord's | 1932 |
| Peel, R. | | Yorkshire v Kent | Halifax | 1897 |
| Pegler, S.J. | (2) | South Africans v MCC *(4 in 5)* | Lord's | 1912 |
| | | South Africans v Yorkshire | Huddersfield | 1912 |
| Pepper, C.G. | | Commonwealth XI v Holkar | Indore | 1949–50 |
| Perks, R.T.D. | (2) | Worcestershire v Kent | Stourbridge | 1931 |
| | | Worcestershire v Warwickshire | Birmingham | 1933 |
| Petherick, P.J. | | New Zealand v Pakistan | Lahore | 1976–77 |
| | | *On Test match debut* | | |
| Phillip, N. | | Essex v Northamptonshire | Wellingborough | 1983 |
| Phillips, R.R. | | Border v Eastern Province | Port Elizabeth | 1939–40 |
| | | *In his first over in first-class cricket* | | |
| Pieris, P.I. | | Cambridge U. v D.R. Jardine's XI | Eastbourne | 1958 |
| Pigott, A.C.S. | | Sussex v Surrey | Hove | 1978 |
| | | *His first wickets in first-class matches* | | |
| Platts, J.T.B.D. | | Derbyshire v Yorkshire | Derby | 1880 |
| Plowden, H.M. | | Cambridge University v MCC | Cambridge | 1862 |
| Pocock, P.I. | (2) | Surrey v Worcestershire | Guildford | 1971 |

| | | | | |
|---|---|---|---|---|
| Pocock, P.I. *continued* | | Surrey v Sussex *(5 in 6)* | Eastbourne | 1972 |
| Pollard, R. | (2) | Lancashire v Glamorgan | Preston | 1939 |
| | | Lancashire v Warwickshire | Blackpool | 1947 |
| Pope, G.H. | | Derbyshire v Nottinghamshire | Ilkeston | 1947 |
| Pougher, A.D. | | MCC v Cambridge University | Lord's | 1887 |
| Preece, C.R. | | Worcestershire v Warwickshire | Birmingham | 1924 |
| Prior, W. | | South Australia v New South Wales | Adelaide | 1975–76 |
| Pritchard, T.L. | (3) | Warwickshire v Leicestershire | Birmingham | 1948 |
| | | Warwickshire v Kent | Maidstone | 1949 |
| | | Warwickshire v Glamorgan | Birmingham | 1951 |
| Procter, M.J. | (4) | Gloucestershire v Essex | Westcliff | 1972 |
| | | Gloucestershire v Essex | Southend | 1977 |
| | | Gloucestershire v Leicestershire | Bristol | 1979 |
| | | Gloucestershire v Yorkshire | Cheltenham | 1979 |
| Ramadhin, S. | | West Indians v Hyderabad | Hyderabad | 1958–59 |
| Rangachari, C.R. | | Indians v Tasmania | Hobart | 1947–48 |
| Ranjane, V.B. | | Maharashtra v Saurashtra | Poona | 1956–57 |
| | | *On debut in first-class cricket* | | |
| Rao, J.S. | (3) | Services v Jammu & Kashmir | Delhi | 1963–64 |
| | | *On debut in first-class cricket* | | |
| | | Services v Northern Punjab | Amritsar | 1963–64 |
| | | Services v Northern Punjab | Amritsar | 1963–64 |
| | | *Two hat-tricks in the same innings and* | | |
| | | *three hat-tricks in two consecutive matches* | | |
| Rashid Khan | (2) | PIA v National Bank | Lahore | 1979–80 |
| | | Karachi Blues v Lahore City Blues | Karachi | 1983–84 |
| Ravinder Pal | | Southern Punjab v Delhi | Chandigarh | 1965–66 |
| Read, H.D. | | Essex v Gloucestershire | Bristol | 1935 |
| Read, W.W. | | Gentlemen v M. Sherwin's XI | Scarborough | 1891 |
| Reid, R.E. | | Wellington v Otago | Dunedin | 1958–59 |
| Relf, A.E. | | Sussex v Worcestershire | Hove | 1902 |
| Rhodes, A.E.G. | (5) | Derbyshire v Gentlemen of Ireland | Buxton | 1947 |
| | | MCC v Surrey | Lord's | 1948 |
| | | Derbyshire v Essex | Colchester | 1948 |
| | | Derbyshire v Oxford University | Oxford | 1950 |
| | | Derbyshire v Sussex | Derby | 1951 |
| Rhodes, H.J. | | Derbyshire v Oxford University | Buxton | 1961 |
| Rhodes, W. | (2) | Yorkshire v Kent | Canterbury | 1901 |
| | | Yorkshire v Derbyshire | Derby | 1920 |
| Richardson, T. | (4) | Surrey v Gloucestershire | Oval | 1893 |
| | | Surrey v Leicestershire | Oval | 1896 |
| | | Surrey v Warwickshire | Oval | 1898 |
| | | Surrey v Sussex | Hove | 1898 |
| Richmond, T.L. | | Nottinghamshire v Lancashire | Nottingham | 1926 |
| Ridgway, F. | (2) | Kent v Derbyshire *(4 in 4)* | Folkestone | 1951 |
| | | Kent v Oxford University | Oxford | 1958 |
| Ridley, A.W. | | Hampshire v Sussex | Hove | 1875 |
| Roberts, A.M.E. | (2) | Combined Islands v Jamaica | Basseterre | 1980–81 |
| | | Leeward Islands v Barbados | Bridgetown | 1982–83 |
| Robertson, J. | | Middlesex v Australians | Lord's | 1878 |
| Robins, D. | | South Australia v New South Wales | Adelaide | 1965–66 |
| Robins, R.W.V. | (2) | Middlesex v Leicestershire | Lord's | 1929 |
| | | Middlesex v Somerset | Lord's | 1937 |
| Robinson, A.L. | | Yorkshire v Nottinghamshire | Worksop | 1974 |
| Robinson, E. | (2) | Yorkshire v Sussex | Hull | 1928 |
| | | Yorkshire v Kent | Gravesend | 1930 |
| Robinson, E.P. | | Yorkshire v Kent | Leeds | 1939 |
| Robson, E. | (2) | Somerset v Hampshire | Bath | 1898 |
| | | Somerset v Yorkshire | Taunton | 1902 |
| Rodriguez, W.V. | | Trinidad v Windward Islands | Port-of-Spain | 1968–69 |
| Roller, W.E. | | Surrey v Sussex | Oval | 1885 |
| Rorke, G.F. | | New South Wales v Queensland | Sydney | 1958–59 |
| Rought-Rought, R.C. | | Cambridge University v Sussex | Hove | 1932 |
| Rylott, A. | | MCC v Derbyshire | Lord's | 1884 |
| Sadler, W.C.H. | | Surrey v Cambridge University | Oval | 1923 |
| Safiullah Khan | | Peshawar v PAF | Rawalpindi | 1969–70 |
| Salim Altaf | | Pakistanis v Leeward Islands | St John's | 1976–77 |

| Salmon, I.J. | | Wellington v Nelson | Wellington | 1873–74 |
|---|---|---|---|---|
| Sarwate, C.T. | | Holkar v Bihar | Jamshedpur | 1948–49 |
| Savage, J.S. | | Leicestershire v Somerset | Loughborough | 1961 |
| Sayer, D.M. | (2) | Oxford University v Kent | Oxford | 1958 |
| | | Kent v Glamorgan | Maidstone | 1964 |
| Sedgwick, H.A. | | Yorkshire v Worcestershire | Hull | 1906 |
| | | *On debut in first-class matches* | | |
| Sen, P. | | Bengal v Orissa | Cuttack | 1954–55 |
| | | *Began the match as a wicket-keeper* | | |
| Shacklock, F.J. | | Nottinghamshire v Somerset *(4 in 4)* | Nottingham | 1893 |
| Shaw, A. | (3) | Nottinghamshire v Derbyshire | Derby | 1875 |
| | | Nottinghamshire v Gloucs *(1st inns)* | Nottingham | 1884 |
| | | Nottinghamshire v Gloucs *(2nd inns)* | Nottingham | 1884 |
| Shepherd, D.J. | | Glamorgan v Northamptonshire | Swansea | 1964 |
| Shepherd, T.F. | | Surrey v Gloucestershire | Oval | 1926 |
| Shepstone, G.H. | | Transvaal v Border | Port Elizabeth | 1902–03 |
| Shipman, W. | | Leicestershire v Derbyshire | Leicester | 1909 |
| Shujauddin | | Services v Rawalpindi | Lahore | 1961–62 |
| Shuttleworth, K. | | Leicestershire v Surrey | Oval | 1977 |
| Simmons, J. | | Lancashire v Nottinghamshire | Liverpool | 1977 |
| Simms, H.L. | | Europeans v Muslims | Poona | 1915–16 |
| Sims, J.M. | | Middlesex v South Africans | Lord's | 1947 |
| Sincock, A.T. | | South Australia v Indians | Adelaide | 1977–78 |
| Smales, K. | | Nottinghamshire v Lancashire | Nottingham | 1955 |
| Smith, A.C. | | Warwickshire v Essex | Clacton | 1965 |
| | | *Began the match as a wicket-keeper* | | |
| Smith, C.I.J. | | Middlesex v Lancashire | Manchester | 1939 |
| Smith, D.V. | (2) | MCC v Oxford University | Lord's | 1956 |
| | | Sussex v Cambridge University | Cambridge | 1958 |
| Smith, S.G. | (2) | Northamptonshire v Leicestershire | Leicester | 1912 |
| | | Northants v Warwickshire *(4 in 4)* | Birmingham | 1914 |
| Smith, V.I. | (2) | Natal v Border | Pietermaritzburg | 1946–47 |
| | | South Africans v Derbyshire | Derby | 1947 |
| Smith, W.C. | (2) | Surrey v Hampshire | Oval | 1908 |
| | | Surrey v Northamptonshire | Oval | 1910 |
| Somers-Cocks, A. | | Barbados v A. Priestley's XI | Bridgetown | 1896–97 |
| Southerton, J. | | South v North | Sheffield | 1869 |
| Spofforth, F.R. | (4) | Australians v MCC | Lord's | 1878 |
| | | Australians v Players | Oval | 1878 |
| | | Australia v England | Melbourne | 1878–79 |
| | | Australians v South | Oval | 1884 |
| Statham, J.B. | (3) | Lancashire v Sussex | Manchester | 1956 |
| | | MCC v Transvaal | Johannesburg | 1956–57 |
| | | Lancashire v Leicestershire | Manchester | 1958 |
| Stead, B. | (2) | Nottinghamshire v Somerset | Nottingham | 1972 |
| | | Northern Transvaal v Transvaal B | Pretoria | 1975–76 |
| Steel, A.G. | | Cambridge U. v Oxford U. | Lord's | 1879 |
| Steele, D.S. | | Derbyshire v Glamorgan | Derby | 1980 |
| Stephenson, H.H. | | England v Kent | Lord's | 1858 |
| Storer, H. | | Derbyshire v Northamptonshire | Chesterfield | 1922 |
| Storey, S.J. | | Surrey v Glamorgan | Swansea | 1965 |
| Street, J. | | Surrey v Middlesex | Oval | 1868 |
| Strydom, W.T. | | Orange Free State v Transvaal B | Stilfontein | 1975–76 |
| Sully, H. | | Northamptonshire v Lancashire | Wellingborough | 1967 |
| Surti, R.F. | | Queensland v Western Australia | Perth | 1968–69 |
| Tariq Cheema | | Lahore Ed. Board v Railways | Lahore | 1964–65 |
| Tarrant, F.A. | (5) | Middlesex v Gloucestershire *(4 in 4)* | Bristol | 1907 |
| | | MCC v Cambridge University | Cambridge | 1908 |
| | | Middlesex v Surrey | Lord's | 1909 |
| | | Middlesex v Gloucestershire | Bristol | 1909 |
| | | Middlesex v Somerset | Bath | 1911 |
| Tate, F.W. | | Sussex v Surrey | Oval | 1901 |
| Tate, M.W. | (3) | Sussex v Middlesex | Lord's | 1926 |
| | | Rest of England v Lancashire | Oval | 1926 |
| | | Sussex v Northamptonshire | Peterborough | 1934 |
| Tattersall, R. | | Lancashire v Nottinghamshire | Manchester | 1953 |
| Tayfield, H.J. | (2) | Natal v Transvaal | Durban | 1946–47 |

| | | | | |
|---|---|---|---|---|
| Tayfield, H.J. *continued* | | South Africans v Victoria | Melbourne | 1952–53 |
| Taylor, L.B. | | Leicestershire v Middlesex | Leicester | 1979 |
| Taylor, M.N.S. | | Nottinghamshire v Kent | Dover | 1965 |
| Thomas, A.E. | | Northamptonshire v Leicestershire | Northampton | 1927 |
| Thompson, G.J. | | Northamptonshire v Lancashire | Manchester | 1907 |
| Thompson, R.G. | | Warwickshire v Sussex | Horsham | 1956 |
| Thomson, J.R. | | Queensland v Western Australia | Brisbane | 1984–85 |
| Thorbourn, D.O. | | Jamaica v Leeward Islands | Kingston | 1958–59 |
| Titmus, F.J. | | Middlesex v Somerset | Weston-s-Mare | 1966 |
| Toone, P.C.E. | | Essex v Kent | Leyton | 1920 |
| Townsend, C.L. | | Gloucestershire v Somerset | Cheltenham | 1893 |
| Townsend, L.F. | | Derbyshire v Northamptonshire | Northampton | 1931 |
| Toynbee, M.H. | | Central Districts v Northern Districts | Gisborne | 1979–80 |
| Treanor, J. | | New South Wales v Queensland | Brisbane | 1954–55 |
| Tremlin, B. | | Essex v Derbyshire | Derby | 1914 |
| Trott, A.E. | (2) | Middlesex v Somerset *(4 in 4)* | Lord's | 1907 |
| | | Middlesex v Somerset | Lord's | 1907 |
| | | *Twice in same innings* | | |
| Trueman, F.S. | (4) | Yorkshire v Nottinghamshire | Nottingham | 1951 |
| | | Yorkshire v Nottinghamshire | Scarborough | 1955 |
| | | Yorkshire v MCC | Lord's | 1958 |
| | | Yorkshire v Nottinghamshire | Bradford | 1963 |
| Trumble, H. | (3) | Australians v Gloucestershire | Cheltenham | 1896 |
| | | Australia v England | Melbourne | 1901–02 |
| | | Australia v England | Melbourne | 1903–04 |
| Turner, C.T.B. | | New South Wales v Victoria | Melbourne | 1886–87 |
| Turner, S. | | Essex v Surrey | Oval | 1971 |
| Tyldesley, J.D. | (2) | Lancashire v Derbyshire | Manchester | 1920 |
| | | Lancashire v Worcestershire | Manchester | 1922 |
| Tyldesley, R.K. | | Lancashire v Derbyshire *(4 in 4)* | Derby | 1929 |
| Tyler, E.J. | | Somerset v Yorkshire | Taunton | 1895 |
| Ulyett, G. | (2) | Lord Harris's XI v NSW *(4 in 4)* | Sydney | 1878–79 |
| | | Yorkshire v Lancashire | Sheffield | 1883 |
| Underwood, D.L. | | Kent v Sussex | Hove | 1977 |
| Van der Bijl, V.A.P. | | Natal v Eastern Province | Durban | 1978–79 |
| Van Heerden, C.J. | | Orange Free State v Griqualand West | Bloemfontein | 1981–82 |
| Van Wyk, M. | | Transvaal B v Northern Transvaal | Pretoria | 1972–73 |
| Verity, H. | (2) | Yorkshire v Nottinghamshire | Leeds | 1932 |
| | | MCC Australian XI v | | |
| | | H.D.G. Leveson Gower's XI | Scarborough | 1937 |
| Visser, P.J. | | Central Districts v Auckland | Nelson | 1983–84 |
| Waddington, A. | | Yorkshire v Northamptonshire *(4 in 5)* | Northampton | 1920 |
| Wainwright, E. | | Yorkshire v Sussex | Dewsbury | 1894 |
| Waite, M.G. | | South Australia v MCC | Adelaide | 1935–36 |
| Walker, A.K. | (2) | New South Wales v Queensland | Sydney | 1948–49 |
| | | Nottinghamshire v Leicestershire *(4 in 4)* | Leicester | 1956 |
| Walsh, J.E. | | Leicestershire v Nottinghamshire | Loughborough | 1949 |
| Ward, A.S. | | Griqualand West v Orange Free State | Kimberley | 1926–27 |
| Warr, J.J. | | Middlesex v Leicestershire | Loughborough | 1956 |
| Wass, T.G. | | Nottinghamshire v Essex | Nottingham | 1908 |
| Watson, A. | | Lancashire v Kent | Rochdale | 1876 |
| Weighell, W.B. | | Cambridge University v MCC | Lord's | 1866 |
| Wellard, A.W. | | Somerset v Leicestershire | Leicester | 1929 |
| Wells, J. | | Kent v Sussex *(4 in 4)* | Hove | 1862 |
| Wells, W. | | Northamptonshire v Nottinghamshire | Northampton | 1910 |
| Wensley, A.F. | | Sussex v Middlesex | Lord's | 1935 |
| Whateley, E.G. | | Oxford University v Philadelphians | Oxford | 1903 |
| Wheatley, O.S. | | Glamorgan v Somerset | Taunton | 1968 |
| White, D.W. | (2) | Hampshire v Sussex | Portsmouth | 1961 |
| | | Hampshire v Sussex | Hove | 1962 |
| White, G.C. | | South Africans v Kent | Canterbury | 1904 |
| White, J.C. | | Somerset v Middlesex | Lord's | 1923 |
| Whitehead, R. | | Lancashire v Surrey | Manchester | 1912 |
| Wilkinson, L.L. | | Lancashire v Sussex | Hove | 1938 |
| Williams, R.G. | | Northamptonshire v Gloucestershire | Northampton | 1980 |
| Willis, R.G.D. | (2) | Warwickshire v Derbyshire | Birmingham | 1972 |
| | | Warwickshire v West Indians | Birmingham | 1976 |

| Willsher, E. | | Players of South v Gentlemen of South | Oval | 1868 |
|---|---|---|---|---|
| Wilson, D. | (3) | Yorkshire v Nottinghamshire | Middlesbrough | 1959 |
| | | Yorkshire v Nottinghamshire | Worksop | 1966 |
| | | Yorkshire v Kent | Harrogate | 1966 |
| Wilson, E.R. | | Gentlemen v Players | Scarborough | 1919 |
| Wilson, G.A. | (3) | Worcestershire v London County | Worcester | 1900 |
| | | Worcestershire v Surrey | Worcester | 1901 |
| | | Worcestershire v Australians | Worcester | 1905 |
| Wiltshire, G.G.M. | | Gloucestershire v Yorkshire | Leeds | 1958 |
| Woods, S.M.J. | | Cambridge U. v C.I. Thornton's XI | Cambridge | 1888 |
| Woolley, C.N. | | Northamptonshire v Essex | Northampton | 1920 |
| Woolley, F.E. | | Kent v Surrey | Blackheath | 1919 |
| Woolmer, R.A. | | MCC v Australians | Lord's | 1975 |
| Wooster, R. | | Northamptonshire v Dublin University | Northampton | 1925 |
| Wootton, G. | | MCC v Sussex | Lord's | 1863 |
| Wright, A.C. | | Kent v Warwickshire | Tunbridge Wells | 1925 |
| Wright, D.V.P. | (7) | Kent v Worcestershire | Worcester | 1937 |
| | | Kent v Nottinghamshire | Nottingham | 1937 |
| | | Kent v Gloucestershire | Gillingham | 1938 |
| | | MCC v Border | East London | 1938–39 |
| | | Kent v Gloucestershire | Bristol | 1939 |
| | | Kent v Sussex | Hastings | 1947 |
| | | Kent v Hampshire | Canterbury | 1949 |
| Wyatt, R.E.S. | | MCC v Ceylon | Colombo | 1926–27 |
| Young, H.I. | | Essex v Leicestershire | Leyton | 1907 |
| Young, J.A. | (2) | Middlesex v Northamptonshire | Northampton | 1946 |
| | | Middlesex v Lancashire | Lord's | 1951 |

## FIVE WICKETS WITH SIX CONSECUTIVE BALLS

| W.H. Copson | Derbyshire v Warwickshire | Derby | 1937 |
|---|---|---|---|
| W.A. Henderson | N.E. Transvaal v Orange Free State | Bloemfontein | 1937–38 |
| P.I. Pocock | Surrey v Sussex | Eastbourne | 1972 |

## FOUR WICKETS WITH FIVE CONSECUTIVE BALLS

| J. Southerton | Surrey v Lancashire | Oval | 1869 |
|---|---|---|---|
| S.E. Butler | Oxford University v MCC | Oxford | 1871 |
| W.F. Neilson | Canterbury v Otago | Christchurch | 1876–77 |
| W. Flowers | A. Shaw's XI v T. Emmett's XI | Bradford | 1881 |
| G.A. Lohmann | Surrey v Lancashire | Manchester | 1888 |
| A.D. Downes | Otago v Canterbury | Dunedin | 1891–92 |
| J.T. Hearne | Middlesex v Essex | Lord's | 1902 |
| F.S. Jackson | Yorkshire v Australians | Leeds | 1902 |
| T.H. Howard | New South Wales v Queensland | Sydney | 1902–03 |
| W.P. Howell | Australians v Western Province | Cape Town | 1902–03 |
| G.A. Wilson | Worcestershire v Gloucestershire | Cheltenham | 1903 |
| G.J. Thompson | Northamptonshire v Leicestershire | Leicester | 1905 |
| W.R. Gregson | Lancashire v Leicestershire | Blackpool | 1906 |
| C. Blythe | Kent v Surrey | Blackheath | 1910 |
| J.W. Hitch | Surrey v Cambridge University | Oval | 1911 |
| S.J. Pegler | South Africans v MCC | Lord's | 1912 |
| H.B. Fawcus | Army v Royal Navy | Lord's | 1913 |
| M.F.S. Jewell | Worcestershire v Gloucestershire | Cheltenham | 1919 |
| C.W.L. Parker | Gloucestershire v Warwickshire | Bristol | 1920 |
| | *Hit the stumps with five successive balls – second one was a no-ball.* | | |
| A. Waddington | Yorkshire v Northamptonshire | Northampton | 1920 |
| W.E. Benskin | Leicestershire v Derbyshire | Leicester | 1921 |
| C.W.L. Parker | Gloucestershire v Yorkshire | Bristol | 1922 |
| M.W. Tate | England v Rest | Lord's | 1923 |
| L. Cook | J. Sharp's XI v Hon L.H. Tennyson's XI | Blackpool | 1923 |
| R. Cooke | Warwickshire v Kent | Tunbridge Wells | 1925 |
| P.G.H. Fender | Surrey v Middlesex | Lord's | 1927 |
| G.O.B. Allen | Middlesex v Lancashire | Lord's | 1929 |

| M.J.C. Allom | England v New Zealand | Christchurch | 1929–30 |
| A.L. Cox | Northamptonshire v Lancashire | Northampton | 1930 |
| R.J. Crisp | Western Province v Transvaal | Johannesburg | 1931–32 |
| M.P. Gopalan | Madras v Ceylon | Madras | 1932–33 |
| G.G. Macaulay | Yorkshire v Lancashire | Manchester | 1933 |
| T.A. Dean | Hampshire v Worcestershire | Bournemouth | 1939 |
| W.H. Copson | Derbyshire v Oxford University | Oxford | 1939 |
| James Langridge | Sussex v Somerset | Weston-s-Mare | 1948 |
| J. Lawrence | Somerset v Yorkshire | Taunton | 1948 |
| C. Gladwin | MCC v N.E. Transvaal | Benoni | 1948–49 |
| A.J. Watkins | Glamorgan v Derbyshire | Chesterfield | 1954 |
| A. Brown | Kent v Nottinghamshire | Folkestone | 1959 |
| D.W. White | Hampshire v Sussex | Portsmouth | 1961 |
| D.W. White | MCC v Services XI | Calcutta | 1961–62 |
| C.D. Drybrough | Middlesex v Somerset | Weston-s-Mare | 1962 |
| J.B. Mortimore | Gloucestershire v Lancashire | Cheltenham | 1962 |
| R. Harman | Surrey v Kent | Blackheath | 1963 |
| C.D. Drybrough | Middlesex v Northamptonshire | Northampton | 1964 |
| E.J. Barlow | Rest of the World v England | Leeds | 1970 |
| A.M.E. Roberts | Hampshire v Glamorgan | Cardiff | 1974 |
| C.M. Old | England v Pakistan | Birmingham | 1978 |
| Imran Khan | Sussex v Derbyshire | Eastbourne | 1981 |
| M.D. Marshall | Hampshire v Somerset | Taunton | 1983 |
| A.H. Gray | Surrey v Yorkshire | Sheffield | 1985 |

## OUTSTANDING SPELLS OF WICKET-TAKING

| Wkts | Balls | | | | |
|---|---|---|---|---|---|
| 10 | 42 | A. Drake | Yorkshire v Somerset | Weston-s-Mare | 1914 |
| 10 | 52 | H. Verity | Yorkshire v Nottinghamshire | Leeds | 1932 |
| 9 | 38 | A. Drake | Yorkshire v Somerset | Weston-s-Mare | 1914 |
| 9 | 39 | H. Verity | Yorkshire v Nottinghamshire | Leeds | 1932 |
| 9 | 39 | H. Verity | Yorkshire v Kent | Sheffield | 1936 |
| 9 | 39 | Ahad Khan | Railways v Dera Ismail Khan | Lahore | 1964–65 |
| 9 | 44 | T.W. Wall | South Australia v New South Wales | Sydney | 1932–33 |
| 9 | 47 | A.P. Freeman | Kent v Sussex | Hove | 1922 |
| 8 | 23 | A. Drake | Yorkshire v Somerset | Weston-s-Mare | 1914 |
| 8 | 24 | G.E. Tribe | Northamptonshire v Yorkshire | Northampton | 1958 |
| 8 | 32 | S. Ramadhin | West Indians v Gloucestershire | Cheltenham | 1950 |
| 8 | 34 | H. Verity | Yorkshire v Nottinghamshire | Leeds | 1932 |
| 8 | 34 | J.E.D. Sealy | Barbados v Trinidad | Bridgetown | 1941–42 |
| 8 | 36 | E.G. Dennett | Gloucestershire v Northamptonshire | Gloucester | 1907 |
| 8 | 36 | T.B. Mitchell | Derbyshire v Worcestershire | Stourbridge | 1934 |
| 8 | 36 | H. Verity | Yorkshire v Kent | Sheffield | 1936 |
| 8 | 39 | A.P. Freeman | Kent v Sussex | Hove | 1922 |
| 8 | 39 | W.H.R. Andrews | Somerset v Surrey | Oval | 1937 |
| 8 | 40 | W.G. Grace | Gloucestershire v Yorkshire | Clifton | 1877 |
| 7 | 11 | P.I. Pocock | Surrey v Sussex | Eastbourne | 1972 |
| 7 | 15 | H. Verity | Yorkshire v Nottinghamshire | Leeds | 1932 |
| 7 | 17 | W.G. Grace | Gloucestershire v Nottinghamshire | Cheltenham | 1877 |
| 7 | 19 | P.G.H. Fender | Surrey v Middlesex | Oval | 1927 |
| 7 | 19 | R. Tattersall | Lancashire v Nottinghamshire | Manchester | 1953 |
| 7 | 20 | A.W. Mold | Lancashire v Somerset | Manchester | 1894 |
| 7 | 20 | J.H. King | Leicestershire v Yorkshire | Leicester | 1911 |
| 7 | 20 | A. Drake | Yorkshire v Somerset | Weston-s-Mare | 1914 |
| 7 | 22 | R. Appleyard | Yorkshire v Somerset | Taunton | 1954 |
| 7 | 22 | J.C. Laker | England v Australia | Manchester | 1956 |
| 7 | 23 | W.H. Copson | Derbyshire v Warwickshire | Derby | 1937 |
| 7 | 24 | W. Rhodes | C.I. Thornton's XI v Australians | Scarborough | 1899 |
| 7 | 24 | F.E. Woolley | Kent v Surrey | Oval | 1911 |
| 7 | 24 | H. Verity | Yorkshire v Kent | Sheffield | 1936 |
| 7 | 25 | J.W. Hearne | Middlesex v Essex | Lord's | 1910 |
| 7 | 25 | V.W.C. Jupp | Northamptonshire v Glamorgan | Swansea | 1925 |
| 7 | 25 | T.W. Durnell | Warwickshire v Northamptonshire | Birmingham | 1927 |
| 7 | 25 | R.J. Crisp | Western Province v Griqualand West | Johannesburg | 1931–32 |
| 7 | 25 | A.P. Freeman | Kent v Somerset | Taunton | 1935 |

| Wkts | Balls | | | | |
|---|---|---|---|---|---|
| 7 | 26 | S. Ramadhin | West Indians v Gloucestershire | Cheltenham | 1950 |
| 7 | 26 | M.G. Melle | Transvaal v Griqualand West | Johannesburg | 1950–51 |
| 7 | 28 | A. Cotter | Australians v Worcestershire | Worcester | 1905 |
| 7 | 28 | W. Rhodes | Yorkshire v Essex | Leyton | 1929 |
| 7 | 29 | J.E.D. Sealy | Barbados v Trinidad | Bridgetown | 1941–42 |
| 7 | 29 | T.E. Bailey | Essex v Glamorgan | Brentwood | 1950 |
| 7 | 30 | T.G. Wass | Nottinghamshire v Sussex | Hove | 1902 |
| 6 | 9 | P.I. Pocock | Surrey v Sussex | Eastbourne | 1972 |
| 6 | 11 | G. Nash | Lancashire v Somerset | Manchester | 1882 |
| 6 | 12 | P.G.H. Fender | Surrey v Middlesex | Lord's | 1927 |
| 6 | 12 | R.J. Crisp | Western Province v Griqualand West | Johannesburg | 1931–32 |
| 6 | 13 | T.B. Mitchell | Derbyshire v Middlesex | Derby | 1934 |
| 6 | 13 | H. Verity | Yorkshire v Kent | Sheffield | 1936 |
| 6 | 13 | W.H. Copson | Derbyshire v Warwickshire | Derby | 1937 |
| 6 | 14 | S.E. Butler | Oxford U. v Cambridge U. | Lord's | 1871 |
| 6 | 14 | A.S. Kennedy | Hampshire v Warwickshire | Portsmouth | 1927 |
| 6 | 14 | H. Verity | Yorkshire v Nottinghamshire | Leeds | 1932 |
| 6 | 15 | P.G.H. Fender | Surrey v Middlesex | Lord's | 1927 |
| 5 | 6 | W.H. Copson | Derbyshire v Warwickshire | Derby | 1937 |
| 5 | 6 | W.A. Henderson | N.E. Transvaal v Orange Free State | Bloemfontein | 1937–38 |
| 5 | 6 | P.I. Pocock | Surrey v Sussex | Eastbourne | 1972 |
| 5 | 7 | G. Nash | Lancashire v Somerset | Manchester | 1882 |
| 5 | 7 | J. Briggs | Lancashire v Sussex | Manchester | 1890 |
| 5 | 7 | E. Wainwright | Yorkshire v Sussex | Dewsbury | 1894 |
| 5 | 7 | P.H. Clark | Philadelphians v B.J.T. Bosanquet's XI | Philadelphia | 1901–02 |
| 5 | 7 | P.G.H. Fender | Surrey v Middlesex | Lord's | 1927 |
| 5 | 7 | T.W.J. Goddard | Gloucestershire v Glamorgan | Swansea | 1930 |
| 5 | 7 | T.W.J. Goddard | Gloucestershire v Somerset | Bristol | 1947 |
| 5 | 8 | J.W.H.T. Douglas | Essex v Yorkshire | Leyton | 1905 |
| 5 | 8 | H. Verity | Yorkshire v Warwickshire | Leeds | 1931 |
| 5 | 8 | R.J. Crisp | Western Province v Griqualand West | Johannesburg | 1931–32 |
| 5 | 8 | G.A. Cope | Yorkshire v Essex | Colchester | 1970 |
| 5 | 9 | C.F. Root | Worcestershire v Gloucestershire | Cheltenham | 1924 |
| 5 | 9 | V.W.C. Jupp | Northamptonshire v Worcestershire | Dudley | 1928 |
| 5 | 9 | J.E. Walsh | Leicestershire v Nottinghamshire | Nottingham | 1946 |
| 5 | 9 | D. Shackleton | Hampshire v Leicestershire | Leicester | 1950 |
| 5 | 9 | T.E. Bailey | T.N. Pearce's XI v Indians | Scarborough | 1952 |
| 5 | 9 | D.K. Lillee | Australia v World XI | Perth | 1971–72 |
| 5 | 10 | S. Haigh | Yorkshire v Derbyshire | Bradford | 1897 |
| 5 | 10 | C. Blythe | Kent v Surrey | Blackheath | 1910 |
| 5 | 10 | J.N. Fraser | Oxford University v H.D.G. Leveson Gower's XI | Eastbourne | 1912 |
| 5 | 10 | C.W.L. Parker | Gloucestershire v Warwickshire | Bristol | 1920 |
| 5 | 10 | H. Verity | Yorkshire v Kent | Sheffield | 1936 |

# BOWLERS UNCHANGED THROUGHOUT BOTH COMPLETED INNINGS

These records illuminate the remarkable shift in the balance between bat and ball during the short history of first-class cricket. Poor batting surfaces produced many low innings totals in Victorian times and it was relatively commonplace for a pair of opening bowlers to operate throughout both innings of a match in which the opposition was dismissed twice. There were 224 recorded instances of this feat in Britain before the Great War. Such has been the improvement in pitches and batting techniques that there have been only 17 instances since 1918 and just three since 1945.

1836 SEASON
F.W. Lillywhite ( - ), G. Millyard ( - )    Sussex v Kent    Brighton

1840 SEASON
A. Mynn (7- ), W.R. Hillyer (12- )    Kent v England    Town Malling

1841 SEASON
A. Mynn (9- ), W.R. Hillyer (9- )    Kent v England    Lord's
A. Mynn (11- ), W.R. Hillyer (7- )    Kent v England    Bromley

1842 SEASON
| | | |
|---|---|---|
| A. Mynn (8- ), W.R. Hillyer (11- ) | Kent v Sussex | Canterbury |
| S. Redgate (9- ), T. Barker (10- ) | North v MCC | Lord's |
| W.R. Hillyer (10- ), J. Bayley (10- ) | MCC v North | Lord's |
| W.R. Hillyer (15- ), J. Dean (5- ) | England v Hampshire | Southampton |

1843 SEASON
| | | |
|---|---|---|
| W.R. Hillyer (8- ), T. Barker (9- ) | MCC v Sussex | Lord's |
| A. Mynn (7- ), F.W. Lillywhite (10- ) | England v MCC | Lord's |
| A. Mynn (15-73), J.F. Fagge (4-105) | Gentlemen of Kent v Gentlemen of England | Canterbury |

1845 SEASON
| | | |
|---|---|---|
| F.W. Lillywhite (11- ), W.R. Hillyer (8- ) | MCC v Oxford University | Oxford |
| W.R. Hillyer (11- ), T. Adams (7- ) | Kent v Nottinghamshire | Canterbury |

1846 SEASON
| | | |
|---|---|---|
| W.R. Hillyer (11-43), W. Martingell (9-48) | Kent v England | Canterbury |

1848 SEASON
| | | |
|---|---|---|
| W. Clarke (13- ), J. Jackson (7- ) | North v MCC | Lord's |

1849 SEASON
| | | |
|---|---|---|
| H.W. Fellows (10- ), T. Craven (7- ) | Gents of England v Gents of Kent | Lord's |

1850 SEASON
| | | |
|---|---|---|
| H.W. Fellows (11- ), J.G. Nash (7- ) | Gents of England v Gents of Kent | Lord's |
| W. Clarke (12- ), J. Wisden (8- ) | Players v Gentlemen | Lord's |

1851 SEASON
| | | |
|---|---|---|
| T. Sherman (10- ), G. Brockwell (9- ) | Surrey Club v MCC | Oval |
| J. Dean (8- ), J. Grundy (11- ) | MCC v Cambridge University | Lord's |

1852 SEASON
| | | |
|---|---|---|
| T. Nixon (12- ), J. Grundy (5- ) | MCC v Sussex | Lord's |
| J. Wisden (10-57), J. Dean (10-92) | Sussex v Kent | Hove |

1853 SEASON
| | | |
|---|---|---|
| Sir F.H.H. Bathurst (9- ), J.G. Nash (11- ) | Gents of England v Gents of Kent | Lord's |
| W.R. Hillyer (10-75), E. Hinkly (10-38) | South v North | Oval |
| W.R. Hillyer (12-57), W. Clarke (6-49) | MCC v England | Lord's |
| Sir F.H.H. Bathurst (11-50), M. Kempson (9-54) | Gentlemen v Players | Lord's |
| J. Dean (14- ), J. Grundy (5- ) | MCC v Surrey Club | Oval |
| W. Clarke (7-106), J. Wisden (8-36) | England v Kent | Canterbury |

1854 SEASON
| | | |
|---|---|---|
| J. Dean (8-89), J. Grundy (11-76) | MCC v Cambridge University | Cambridge |
| J. Grundy (6-39), T. Nixon (11-46) | MCC v Surrey Club | Lord's |

1855 SEASON
| | | |
|---|---|---|
| J. Grundy (10-73), J. Dean (9-76) | MCC v Surrey Club | Lord's |
| J. Wisden (12-92), J. Dean (6-77) | Sussex v MCC | Lord's |
| T. Sherman (8-71), John Lillywhite (11-70) | South v North | Tunbridge Wells |

1856 SEASON
| | | |
|---|---|---|
| E. Willsher (10-54), F. Hollands (9-54) | Kent v MCC | Lord's |
| W. Martingell (10-69), T. Sherman (7-82) | Surrey v Sussex | Oval |
| W. Martingell (10-67), G. Griffith (9-35) | Surrey v Kent | Tunbridge Wells |

1857 SEASON
| | | |
|---|---|---|
| W. Caffyn (9-28), G. Griffith (10-34) | Surrey v Sussex | Oval |
| J. Wisden (11-45), G. Griffith (8-35) | Surrey & Sussex v England | Hove |
| J. Jackson (13-42), W. Martingell (7-64) | North v South | Tunbridge Wells |
| W. Caffyn (8-71), G. Griffith (7-56) | Surrey v North | Sheffield |
| John Lillywhite (9-59), G. Hooker (10-65) | Sussex v MCC | St Leonard's |

**1857–58 SEASON**
T.W.S. Wills (12-35), G. Elliott (6-25)     Victoria v Tasmania          Hobart

**1858 SEASON**
C.D. Marsham (7-27), H.H. Stephenson (13-44)     England v Kent          Lord's

**1859 SEASON**
W. Caffyn (12-68), H.H. Stephenson (5-70)     Surrey Club v MCC          Oval
W. Caffyn (11-63), G. Atkinson (8-46)     United England XI v
                                              All England XI           Lord's
V.E. Walker (8-89), G. Wells (9-79)     Middlesex v Kent          Canterbury
J. Jackson (12-74), J. Grundy (8-96)     North v South          Canterbury

**1860 SEASON**
J. Grundy (9-51), A. Haygarth (11-56)     MCC v Sussex          Lord's
J. Jackson (7-57), R.C. Tinley (12-93)     North v Surrey          Oval
A.B. Rowley (10-48), J.B. Payne (8-75)     Gentlemen of North v
                                              Gentlemen of South       Manchester
C. Brampton (12-38), J. Grundy (8-52)     MCC v Sussex          Lewes

**1861 SEASON**
J. Jackson (11-99), E. Willsher (6-70)     Players v Gentlemen          Lord's
I. Hodgson (9-88), G.R. Atkinson (10-115)     Yorkshire v Surrey          Sheffield
C. Lawrence (10-86), V.E. Walker (9-104)     Middlesex v MCC          Lord's
I. Hodgson (8-52), R. Iddison (10-67)     Yorkshire & Durham v
                                              Cambridgeshire          Stockton-on-Tees

**1862 SEASON**
H. Stubberfield (6-40), James Lillywhite (14-57)     Sussex v MCC          Lord's

**1863 SEASON**
G. Wootton (11-55), J. Grundy (8-94)     MCC v Cambridge University  Cambridge
G. Wootton (11-27), J. Grundy (9-50)     MCC v Sussex          Lord's
J. Jackson (12-43), J. Grundy (8-48)     Nottinghamshire v Kent          Cranbrook

**1863–64 SEASON**
F. MacDonald (10-31), J. Mace (8-36)     Otago v Canterbury          Dunedin

**1864 SEASON**
V.E. Walker (14-111), T. Hearne (5-94)     Middlesex v Sussex          Islington
E. Willsher (9-55), G. Tarrant (11-49)     Players v Gentlemen          Lord's
T. Hearne (7-91), V.E. Walker (12-85)     Middlesex v MCC          Islington

**1864–65 SEASON**
F.B. Smith (10- ), A.E. Smith (8- )     Barbados v Demerara          Bridgetown

**1865 SEASON**
A.J.A. Wilkinson (8-69), T. Hearne (10-84)     Middlesex v Hampshire          Islington
W.G. Grace† (13-84), I.D. Walker (6-86)     Gentlemen of South v
                                              Players of South          Oval
G. Bennett (7-58), E. Willsher (12-28)     Kent v Yorkshire          Sheffield
† *On debut in first-class cricket when aged 16.*

**1866 SEASON**
G. Tarrant (13-77), F.R. Reynolds (6-75)     Cambridgeshire v Yorkshire  Bradford
J. Grundy (8-74), G. Wootton (10-68)     MCC v Hampshire          Lord's
G. Tarrant (12-84), T. Hayward (8-76)     Cambridgeshire v Middlesex  Islington
T. Hearne (12-76), R.D. Walker (8-73)     Middlesex v Nottinghamshire  Nottingham

**1867 SEASON**
G. Wootton (8-131), A. Shaw (10-47)     MCC v Oxford University          Oxford
James Lillywhite (6-41), J. Southerton (13-68)     Sussex v Kent          Gravesend
L. Greenwood (11-71), G. Freeman (8-73)     Yorkshire v Surrey          Oval
L. Greenwood (7-76), G. Freeman (12-51)     Yorkshire v Lancashire          Blackburn
G. Tarrant (9-108), G. Freeman (9-90)     North v Nottinghamshire          Nottingham

**1868 SEASON**

| | | |
|---|---|---|
| R.F. Miles (9-45), E.L. Fellowes (9-29) | Oxford University v MCC | Oxford |
| F. Silcock (7-75), E. Willsher (12-103) | England v MCC | Lord's |
| G. Freeman (12-23), T. Emmett (8-24) | Yorkshire v Lancashire | Holbeck |
| G. Freeman (12-61), T. Emmett (6-58) | Yorkshire v Middlesex | Sheffield |

**1868–69 SEASON**

| | | |
|---|---|---|
| E.G. Penalosa (9-86), W. Eccles (8-58) | Trinidad v Demerara | Port-of-Spain |

**1869 SEASON**

| | | |
|---|---|---|
| G. Freeman (13-60), T. Emmett (5-55) | Yorkshire v Surrey | Sheffield |
| G. Freeman (4-31), T. Emmett (16-38) | Yorkshire v Cambridgeshire | Hunslet, Leeds |

**1870 SEASON**

| | | |
|---|---|---|
| A. Shaw (13-58), G. Wootton (6-71) | MCC v Surrey | Oval |
| G. Freeman (10-43), T. Emmett (9-92) | Yorkshire v Surrey | Oval |

**1871 SEASON**

| | | |
|---|---|---|
| J. Southerton (14-67), James Lillywhite (6-64) | Sussex v Kent | Hove |
| G. Freeman (7-81), T. Emmett (11-85) | Yorkshire v Lancashire | Manchester |
| J. Southerton (11-67), James Lillywhite (8-44) | Sussex v Kent | Maidstone |
| J.C. Shaw (8-53), T. Emmett (10-70) | All England XI v United North | Bolton |
| T. Emmett (8-113), A. Hill (12-57) | Yorkshire v Surrey | Oval |
| J. Southerton (14-99), James Lillywhite (5-84) | Sussex v Surrey | Oval |

**1872 SEASON**

| | | |
|---|---|---|
| J. Southerton (13-71), James Lillywhite (6-34) | South v North | Liverpool |
| J.C. Shaw (4-49), E. Lockwood (13-82) | United North v United South | Bishop's Stortford |
| W. McIntyre (12-38), A. Watson (6-72) | Lancashire v Derbyshire | Derby |
| J. Southerton (12-100), James Lillywhite (6-71) | Sussex v Kent | Hove |
| J. Southerton (9-108), J. Street (11-61) | Surrey v Kent | Maidstone |

**1873 SEASON**

| | | |
|---|---|---|
| A. Shaw (7-49), A. Rylott (9-75) | MCC v Yorkshire | Lord's |
| T. Emmett (11-82), A. Hill (8-47) | Yorkshire v Lancashire | Manchester |
| James Lillywhite (7-101), R. Fillery (13-123) | Sussex v Surrey | Oval |
| James Lillywhite (11-88), R. Fillery (9-94) | Sussex v Kent | Lord's |
| James Lillywhite (12-99), R. Fillery (7-110) | Sussex v Gloucester | Hove |
| T. Emmett (12-84), A. Hill (8-55) | Yorkshire v Surrey | Sheffield |
| W. McIntyre (11-70), A. Watson (8-79) | Lancashire v Surrey | Manchester |
| W. McIntyre (11-54), A. Watson (8-47) | Lancashire v Surrey | Oval |
| James Lillywhite (8-84), R. Fillery (10-105) | Sussex v Kent | Eastbourne |

**1874 SEASON**

| | | |
|---|---|---|
| T. Emmett (9-87), A. Hill (10-96) | Yorkshire v Nottinghamshire | Nottingham |
| A. Hill (9-67), G. Ulyett (10-107) | Yorkshire v United South | Bradford |
| A. Hill (10-38), T. Emmett (8-74) | Yorkshire v Lancashire | Manchester |
| James Lillywhite (11-84), R. Fillery (7-71) | Sussex v Nottinghamshire | Hove |

**1875 SEASON**

| | | |
|---|---|---|
| James Lillywhite (10-91), R. Fillery (10-121) | Sussex v Hampshire | Hove |
| A. Hill (7-46), T. Armitage (12-61) | United North v Derbyshire XI | Chesterfield |

**1875–76 SEASON**

| | | |
|---|---|---|
| F.R. Spofforth (9-72), E. Evans (10-52) | New South Wales v Victoria | Sydney |

**1876 SEASON**

| | | |
|---|---|---|
| W. McIntyre (14-72), A. Watson (5-63) | Lancashire v Derbyshire | Manchester |
| W. McIntyre (9-96), A. Watson (10-83) | Lancashire v Derbyshire | Derby |

**1877 SEASON**

| | | |
|---|---|---|
| D. Buchanan (5-74), R. Henderson (15-98) | Gentlemen of England v Oxford University | Oxford |
| W. McIntyre (12-63), A. Watson (8-63) | Lancashire v Nottinghamshire | Manchester |

1877–78 SEASON
T. Eden (11- ), J. Wigzell (7- )  Nelson v Wellington  Wellington

1878 SEASON
A. Hill (10-80), E. Lockwood (8-41)  Players of North v England XI  Dewsbury
A. Shaw (11-55), F. Morley (8-72)  Nottinghamshire v Australians  Nottingham
A. Shaw (5-49), F. Morley (15-35)  Nottingham v Kent  Town Malling
A. Shaw (7-56), F. Morley (12-70)  Nottinghamshire v Surrey  Nottingham
A. Shaw (3-69), F. Morley (14-94)  Nottinghamshire v Yorkshire  Nottingham
W. Bates (9-34), T. Emmett (10-21)  Yorkshire v Sussex  Hove
W.G. Grace (12-109), W.R. Gilbert (8-106)  Gloucestershire v Lancashire  Clifton

1879 SEASON
A.G. Steel (9-43), A.H. Evans (10-74)  Gentlemen v Players  Oval
A. Shaw (8-25), F. Morley (12-35)  Nottinghamshire v Derbyshire  Nottingham
A. Shaw (5-36), F. Morley (14-53)  Nottinghamshire v Derbyshire  Derby

1880 SEASON
A. Shaw (12-53), F. Morley (8-62)  MCC v Oxford University  Oxford
A. Shaw (7-54), F. Morley (11-43)  MCC v Derbyshire  Lord's
H.F. Boyle (7-80), G.E. Palmer (11-89)  Australians v Players  Crystal Palace

1880–81 SEASON
F.R. Spofforth (12-105), G.E. Palmer (7-65)  Australian XI v Rest  Melbourne

1881 SEASON
A. Hill (6-85), E. Peate (14-77)  Yorkshire v Surrey  Huddersfield
E. Peate (8-57), W. Bates (11-47)  Yorkshire v Nottinghamshire  Nottingham
A. Penn (13-69), J. Wootton (7-41)  Kent v Sussex  Maidstone

1882 SEASON
G.E. Palmer (9-133), H.F. Boyle (11-107)  Australians v Liverpool Club  Liverpool
F.R. Spofforth (13-113), H.F. Boyle (7-106)  Australians v Somerset  Taunton

1882–83 SEASON
H.F. Boyle (8-46), G.E. Palmer (9-61)  Victoria v New South Wales  Sydney

1883 SEASON
E. Peate (8-59), G.P. Harrison (11-76)  Yorkshire v Kent  Dewsbury
R.G. Barlow (6-88), A. Watson (12-67)  Lancashire v Derbyshire  Derby

1884 SEASON
A. Shaw (14-65), W. Attewell (6-46)  Notts v Gloucestershire  Nottingham
G. Giffen (10-121), G.E. Palmer (10-72)  Australians v
  Lord Sheffield's XI  Sheffield Park
F.R. Spofforth (9-61), G.E. Palmer (11-54)  Australians v Yorkshire  Bradford
F.R. Spofforth (12-43), G.E. Palmer (7-72)  Australians v Middlesex  Lord's

1885 SEASON
W. Attewell (8-70), W. Gunn (11-85)  MCC v Hampshire  Lord's

1885–86 SEASON
F.H. Cooke (6-30), G. Bennett (12-18)  Nelson v Wellington  Nelson

1886 SEASON
F.R. Spofforth (15-36), T.W. Garrett (5-34)  Australians v Oxford U.  Oxford
E. Peate (12-50), A. Watson (7-34)  North v Australians  Manchester

1886–87 SEASON
D. Dunlop (10-36), R. Halley (9-52)  Canterbury v Wellington  Wellington

1887–88 SEASON
G.A. Lohmann (9-67), J. Briggs (11-58)  A. Shrewsbury's XI v
  Australian XI  Sydney

1888 SEASON
J. Briggs (12-45), R.G. Barlow (6-42)  Lancashire v Gloucestershire  Liverpool

C.T.B. Turner (11-59), J.J. Ferris (7-63)     Australians v Middlesex     Lord's
C.T.B. Turner (13-48), J.J. Ferris (6-48)     Australians v England XI     Stoke-on-T.

**1889 SEASON**
J. Beaumont (10-49), G.A. Lohmann (10-49)     Surrey v Kent     Oval
W. Wright (9-51), F. Martin (10-65)     Kent v Yorkshire     Maidstone

**1889–90 SEASON**
S.T. Callaway (12-58), W. McGlinchy (8-41)     New South Wales v Otago     Dunedin

**1890 SEASON**
G.A. Lohmann (13-54), J.W. Sharpe (7-50)     Surrey v Lancashire     Manchester
A. Watson (9-13), J. Briggs (10-41)     Lancashire v Sussex     Manchester
F. Martin (11-72), W. Wright (9-81)     Kent v Sussex     Town Malling
A. Watson (6-66), A.W. Mold (13-76)     Lancashire v Yorkshire     Huddersfield

**1891 SEASON**
G.A. Lohmann (11-40), J.W. Sharpe (9-31)     Surrey v Somerset     Oval
F. Martin (13-48), W. Wright (6-59)     Kent v Middlesex     Lord's
J. Briggs (8-54), A.W. Mold (11-65)     Lancashire v Sussex     Hove

**1891–92 SEASON**
C.R. Smith (13-29), J. Wolstenholme (5-35)     Hawke's Bay v Taranaki     Hawera

**1892 SEASON**
A.W. Mold (13-91), J. Briggs (5-54)     Lancashire v Kent     Tonbridge
A.W. Mold (14-159), A. Watson (4-67)     Lancashire v Sussex     Hove
J.T. Hearne (12-91), J.T. Rawlin (7-85)     Middlesex v Sussex     Hove
J.T. Hearne (7-61), F. Martin (13-51)     MCC v Sussex     Lord's

**1893 SEASON**
A. Coningham (9-100), R.W. McLeod (10-56)     Australians v Liverpool
                                              and District     Liverpool

**1894 SEASON**
T. Richardson (9-99), F.E. Smith (10-71)     Surrey v Gloucestershire     Oval
E. Wainwright (13-38), R. Peel (7-60)     Yorkshire v Sussex     Dewsbury
G. Davidson (9-54), J. Hulme (10-70)     Derbyshire v Yorkshire     Sheffield
W. Hearne (13-98), F. Martin (6-65)     Kent v Surrey     Catford
S.M.J. Woods (6-124), F.S. Jackson (12-77)     Gentlemen v Players     Lord's
J.T. Hearne (14-66), A.D. Pougher (5-60)     MCC v Kent     Lord's

**1894–95 SEASON**
F.W. Bush (7-70), H.R. Bromley-Davenport (13-39)     R.S. Lucas's XI v Demerara     Georgetown
F.W. Bush (14-71), H.R. Bromley-Davenport (7-35)     R.S. Lucas's XI v Jamaica     Kingston
F.W. Bush (11-91), H.R. Bromley-Davenport (9-68)     R.S. Lucas's XI v Jamaica     Kingston

**1895 SEASON**
J. Briggs (8-78), A.W. Mold (9-72)     Lancashire v Middlesex     Lord's
J. Briggs (12-51), A.W. Mold (8-97)     Lancashire v Leicestershire     Leicester
J. Briggs (4-62), A.W. Mold (15-85)     Lancashire v Nottinghamshire     Nottingham
T. Richardson (11-60), G.A. Lohmann (8-59)     Surrey v Derbyshire     Derby
T. Soar (11-113), H. Baldwin (8-93)     Hampshire v Derbyshire     Southampton

**1896 SEASON**
J.T. Hearne (12-90), J.T. Rawlin (7-69)     Middlesex v Surrey     Oval
H. Trumble (6-46), T.R. McKibbin (13-38)     Australians v Lancashire     Liverpool
J.T. Hearne (13-107), A.D. Pougher (7-103)     Earl de la Warr's XI v
                                               Australians     Bexhill

**1896–97 SEASON**
G.A. Lohmann (9-88), G.A. Rowe (10-48)     W. Province v GW     Johannesburg
A.H. Fisher (5-31), A.D. Downes (12-40)     Otago v Canterbury     Dunedin

**1897 SEASON**
T. Richardson (12-20), T.W. Hayward (7-43)     Surrey v Leicestershire     Leicester
C.H.G. Bland (14-72), F.W. Tate (6-113)     Sussex v Cambridge U.     Cambridge

| | | |
|---|---|---|
| **1899 SEASON** | | |
| J.T. Hearne (8-44), A.E. Trott (11-31) | Middlesex v Somerset | Lord's |
| E. Jones (10-84), C.E. McLeod (10-125) | Australians v Middlesex | Lord's |
| | | |
| **1899–1900 SEASON** | | |
| E.F. Upham (8-72), K.H. Tucker (10-89) | Wellington v Auckland | Auckland |
| | | |
| **1900 SEASON** | | |
| W. Rhodes (11-36), S. Haigh (7-49) | Yorkshire v Worcestershire | Bradford |
| W.R. Cuttell (8-46), S. Webb (11-41) | Lancashire v Hampshire | Manchester |
| | | |
| **1901 SEASON** | | |
| J. Sharp (11-105), S. Webb (8-68) | Lancashire v Kent | Manchester |
| G.A. Rowe (6-53), J.H. Sinclair (13-73) | South Africans v Gloucs | Clifton |
| C. Blythe (6-85), J.R. Mason (12-55) | Kent v Somerset | Taunton |
| G.H. Hirst (12-29), W. Rhodes (6-37) | Yorkshire v Essex | Leyton |
| | | |
| **1902 SEASON** | | |
| J. Hallows (13-71), W.R. Cuttell (7-50) | Lancashire v Kent | Tonbridge |
| F.W. Tate (8-109), E.G. Arnold (12-87) | South of England v Australians | Bournemouth |
| | | |
| **1902–03 SEASON** | | |
| J.J. Kotze (11-37), J.H. Sinclair (8-49) | Transvaal v GW | Port Elizabeth |
| | | |
| **1903 SEASON** | | |
| S. Haigh (12-52), W. Rhodes (7-55) | Yorkshire v Cambridge U. | Sheffield |
| S. Hargreave (15-76), S. Santall (5-66) | Warwickshire v Surrey | Oval |
| G.H. Hirst (10-67), W. Rhodes (10-81) | Yorkshire v Surrey | Oval |
| C. Blythe (12-67), A. Hearne (7-61) | Kent v Surrey | Oval |
| B. Cranfield (13-102), L.C. Braund (7-77) | Somerset v Gloucestershire | Gloucester |
| F.G. Roberts (11-93), E.G. Dennett (9-99) | Gloucestershire v Surrey | Bristol |
| | | |
| **1904 SEASON** | | |
| W. Rhodes (10-39), S. Haigh (10-49) | Yorkshire v Hampshire | Leeds |
| J.N. Crawford (10-78), H.C. McDonell (10-89) | Surrey v Gloucestershire | Cheltenham |
| | | |
| **1904–05 SEASON** | | |
| A.H. Mehta (9-36), M.D. Bulsara (8-43) | Parsees v Europeans | Bombay |
| | | |
| **1905 SEASON** | | |
| G.J. Thompson (13-105), H.B. Simpson (6-66) | Northamptonshire v Leics | Leicester |
| | | |
| **1906 SEASON** | | |
| W. Mead (10-73), A.E.E. Vogler (10-90) | MCC v Leicestershire | Lord's |
| E.G. Dennett (15-88), F.G. Roberts (5-111) | Gloucestershire v Essex | Bristol |
| E.G. Dennett (9-109), P.H. Ford (11-113) | Gloucestershire v Sussex | Cheltenham |
| G.G. Napier (7-88), P.R. May (12-66) | Cambridge U. v Yorkshire | Cambridge |
| | | |
| **1906–07 SEASON** | | |
| A.E.E. Vogler (14-58), A.T. Lyons (5-44) | E. Province v OFS | Johannesburg |
| | | |
| **1907 SEASON** | | |
| E.G. Arnold (7-66), J.A. Cuffe (13-76) | Worcestershire v Yorkshire | Bradford |
| J.N. Crawford (11-63), T. Rushby (6-67) | Surrey v Sussex | Oval |
| J.N. Crawford (6-52), W.C. Smith (11-65) | Surrey v Derbyshire | Derby |
| H. Dean (7-84), W. Huddleston (12-82) | Lancashire v Surrey | Manchester |
| W. Mead (12-73), W. Reeves (8-98) | Essex v Nottinghamshire | Leyton |
| S. Hargreave (8-82), S. Santall (11-91) | Warwickshire v Leicestershire | Coventry |
| G.J. Thompson (8-72), W. East (12-62) | Northamptonshire v Gloucs | Gloucester |
| T.G. Wass (9-69), A.W. Hallam (9-65) | Nottinghamshire v Northants | Northampton |
| T.G. Wass (10-67), A.W. Hallam (8-84) | Notts v Derbyshire | Chesterfield |
| G.H. Hirst (11-44), W. Rhodes (8-71) | Yorkshire v Derbyshire | Glossop |
| | | |
| **1908 SEASON** | | |
| W.S. Lees (8-104), T. Rushby (9-90) | Surrey v Lancashire | Manchester |
| T.G. Wass (16-103), A.W. Hallam (4-44) | Nottinghamshire v Essex | Nottingham |

G.H. Hirst (12-19), S. Haigh (6-19)            Yorkshire v Northamptonshire Northampton
F.A. Tarrant (10-46), A.E. Trott (9-59)        Middlesex v Philadelphians    Lord's

1909 SEASON
T.G. Wass (10-107), A.W. Hallam (10-63)        Nottinghamshire v Derbyshire Nottingham
W. Huddleston (8-101), H. Dean (11-102)        Lancashire v Essex           Liverpool

1910 SEASON
J.T. Hearne (12-70), F.A. Tarrant (8-59)       Middlesex v Gloucestershire   Lord's
H. Dean (11-67), W. Huddleston (9-38)          Lancashire v Worcestershire   Manchester
C. Blythe (11-95), F.E. Woolley (8-91)         Kent v Yorkshire              Maidstone

1912 SEASON
G.J. Thompson (9-55), S.G. Smith (10-72)       Northamptonshire v Essex      Northampton
C. Blythe (11-56), F.E. Woolley (9-58)         Kent v Nottinghamshire        Canterbury
C. Blythe (7-81), D.W. Carr (13-74)            Kent v Gloucestershire        Dover
H. Dean (10-66), W. Huddleston (10-83)         Lancashire v Leicestershire   Leicester

1913 SEASON
G.J. Thompson (10-104), S.G. Smith (10-95)     Northamptonshire v Sussex     Horsham
T.G. Wass (10-123), J. Iremonger (10-73)       Nottinghamshire v Derbyshire Chesterfield

1914 SEASON
J.W.H.T. Douglas (11-98), B. Tremlin (9-115)   Essex v Surrey                Oval
J.W.H.T. Douglas (9-62), B. Tremlin (10-52)    Essex v Derbyshire            Derby
A. Jaques (14-54), A.S. Kennedy (6-64)         Hampshire v Somerset          Bath
M.W. Booth (5-77), A. Drake (15-51)            Yorkshire v Somerset          Weston-s-Mare
M.W. Booth (12-89), A. Drake (8-81)            Yorkshire v Gloucestershire   Bristol

1917–18 SEASON
J.A. Newman (8-54), F.A. Tarrant (12-35)       Maharaja of Cooch Behar's
                                                 XI v Bengal Governor's XI   Calcutta

1918–19 SEASON
A.W. Alloo (10-50), V. Holderness (10-39)      Otago v Southland             Invercargill

1919 SEASON
E. Robson (8-107), J.C. White (11-114)         Somerset v Derbyshire         Derby
H.L. Collins (12-69), S.C. Winning (8-63)      AIF v Somerset                Taunton

1920 SEASON
A. Waddington (13-48), E. Robinson (6-34)      Yorkshire v Northamptonshire Northampton

1921 SEASON
A. Waddington (9-61), E. Robinson (10-70)      Yorkshire v Northamptonshire Harrogate
A.S. Kennedy (11-86), J.A. Newman (9-103)      Hampshire v Sussex            Portsmouth

1922 SEASON
P.T. Mills (9-43), C.W.L. Parker (11-50)       Gloucs v Worcestershire       Gloucester
W.E. Astill (10-65), G. Geary (10-68)          Leics v Gloucestershire       Bristol

1923 SEASON
A.S. Kennedy (12-72), J.A. Newman (7-62)       Hampshire v Somerset          Portsmouth

1924 SEASON
C.H. Parkin (10-78), R.K. Tyldesley (10-103)   Lancashire v Warwickshire     Manchester

1925 SEASON
W.E. Astill (8-35), G. Geary (11-61)           Leicestershire v Glamorgan    Leicester
M.W. Tate (14-58), A.F. Wensley (4-52)         Sussex v Glamorgan            Hove

1927 SEASON
G.G. Macaulay (12-50), E. Robinson (8-65)      Yorkshire v Worcestershire    Leeds

1932 SEASON
H. Larwood (10-88), W. Voce (10-35)            Nottinghamshire v Leics       Nottingham

**1935 SEASON**
H.A. Smith (11-91), G. Geary (9-62)          Leicestershire v Northants     Northampton

**1937–38 SEASON**
N. Gordon (9-50), F.J. Wickham (10-44)        Transvaal v E. Province        Port Elizabeth

**1952 SEASON**
D. Shackleton (12-67), V.H.D. Cannings (8-55)   Hampshire v Kent               Southampton

**1958 SEASON**
D. Shackleton (7-88), M. Heath (13-87)        Hampshire v Derbyshire         Burton upon Trent

**1960–61 SEASON**
Rajinder Pal (9-20), P. Sitaram (11-30)        Delhi v Jammu & Kashmir        Srinagar

**1967 SEASON**
B.S. Crump (12-74), R.R. Bailey (8-95)        Northants v Glamorgan          Cardiff

# MOST MAIDEN OVERS IN SUCCESSION

**FOUR-BALL OVERS**

| | | | | |
|---|---|---|---|---|
| 23 | A. Shaw | North v South | Nottingham | 1876 |
| 20 | A. Shaw | Nottinghamshire v MCC | Lord's | 1875 |
| 18 | W. Flowers | Nottinghamshire v Sussex | Hove | 1885 |
| 16 | J.C. Shaw | North v South | Canterbury | 1869 |
| 15 | W.G. Marten | Surrey v Sussex | Hove | 1871 |
| 15 | E. Willsher | South v North | Canterbury | 1871 |
| 15 | A. Shaw | MCC v Yorkshire | Scarborough | 1876 |
| 15 | C.F. Tufnell | Kent v Nottinghamshire | Nottingham | 1878 |
| 14 | A. Appleby | Gentlemen v Players | Lord's | 1870 |
| 14 | A. Shaw | Players v Gentlemen | Lord's | 1880 |

**FIVE-BALL OVERS**

| | | | | |
|---|---|---|---|---|
| 19 | J.W. Trumble | Victoria v New South Wales | Melbourne | 1885–86 |
| 10 | E. Robson | Somerset v Sussex | Hove | 1897 |

**SIX-BALL OVERS**

| | | | | |
|---|---|---|---|---|
| 21 | R.G. Nadkarni | India v England | Madras | 1963–64 |
| | | *131 balls without conceding a run* | | |
| 17 | H.L. Hazell | Somerset v Gloucestershire | Taunton | 1949 |
| | | *105 balls without conceding a run* | | |
| 17 | G.A.R. Lock | MCC v Governor-General's XI | Karachi | 1955–56 |
| | | *First 104 balls of innings bowled without conceding a run* | | |
| 16 | J.M. Cole | Natal v Eastern Province | Port Elizabeth | 1963–64 |
| 15 | W.S. Haig | Otago v Wellington | Dunedin | 1956–57 |
| 15 | M.C. Carew | West Indies v England | Port-of-Spain | 1967–68 |
| | | *90 balls without conceding a run* | | |
| 15 | D. Wilson | Yorkshire v Lancashire | Sheffield | 1969 |
| 14 | J.A. Young | Middlesex v Gloucestershire | Bristol | 1949 |
| 14 | W.E. Alley | Somerset v Essex | Yeovil | 1960 |
| 14 | B.A. Langford | Somerset v Glamorgan | Bath | 1960 |
| 14 | J.B. Mortimore | Gloucestershire v Glamorgan | Margam | 1962 |
| 14 | M.E. Scott | Northamptonshire v Cambridge U. | Cambridge | 1964 |
| 14 | P.M. Walker | Glamorgan v Somerset | Glastonbury | 1969 |

**EIGHT-BALL OVERS**

| | | | | |
|---|---|---|---|---|
| 16 | H.J. Tayfield | South Africa v England | Durban | 1956–57 |
| | | *137 balls without conceding a run* | | |
| 10 | R.W. Morgan | Auckland v Otago | Auckland | 1968–69 |
| 9 | H.J. Tayfield | South Africa v Australia | Melbourne | 1952–53 |
| 9 | P.J. Loader | MCC v Griqualand West | Kimberley | 1956–57 |

# MOST WICKETS IN CONSECUTIVE INNINGS

**THREE INNINGS**

| | | | | |
|---|---|---|---|---|
| 26 | C.W.L. Parker | (9-44, 8-12, 9-118) | Gloucestershire | 1925 |
| 25 | A.P. Freeman | (8-56, 8-31, 9-61) | Kent | 1932 |
| 25 | G. Giffen | (9-60, 8-56, 8-23) | Australians | · 1886 |
| 24 | H. Dean | (7-70, 9-62, 8-29) | Lancashire | 1913 |
| 24 | T.W.J. Goddard | (7-38, 9-38, 8-68) | Gloucestershire | 1939 |
| 24 | G.A. Lohmann | (7-38, 8-7, 9-28) | Lord Hawke's XI | 1895–96 |
| 24 | W. Mead | (8-67, 9-52, 7-73) | Essex | 1895 |
| 24 | C.W.L. Parker | (9-44, 8-38, 7-53) | Gloucestershire | 1930 |
| 24 | G.J. Thompson | (9-64, 7-72, 8-95) | Northamptonshire | 1906 |
| 24 | J.C. White | (7-52, 7-58, 10-76) | Somerset | 1921 |
| 24 | J. Wisden | (10-  , 9-  , 5-  ) | Sussex | 1850 |

**FOUR INNINGS**

| | | | | |
|---|---|---|---|---|
| 33 | G. Giffen | (9-60, 8-56, 8-23, 8-42) | Australians | 1886 |
| 32 | C.W.L. Parker | (6-61, 9-44, 8-12, 9-118) | Gloucestershire | 1925 |
| 30 | A.P. Freeman | (5-88, 8-56, 8-31, 9-61) | Kent | 1932 |
| 30 | A.P. Freeman | (8-56, 8-31, 9-61, 5-143) | Kent | 1932 |
| 30 | T.W.J. Goddard | (6-61, 7-38, 9-38, 8-68) | Gloucestershire | 1939 |
| 30 | C.L. Townsend | (8-67, 8-130, 7-54, 7-80) | Gloucestershire | 1895 |
| 30 | H. Verity | (7-35, 6-67, 8-47, 9-44) | Yorkshire | 1933 |

**FIVE INNINGS**

| | | | | |
|---|---|---|---|---|
| 40 | G. Giffen | (7-41, 9-60, 8-56, 8-23, 8-42) | Australians | 1886 |
| 38 | C.L. Townsend | (8-66, 9-128, 6-77, 8-64, 7-77) | Gloucestershire | 1898 |
| 38 | A.P. Freeman | (8-56, 8-31, 9-61, 5-143, 8-44) | Kent | 1932 |
| 37 | C.W.L. Parker | (5-19, 6-61, 9-44, 8-12, 9-118) | Gloucestershire | 1925 |
| 37 | H. Verity | (7-54, 7-35, 6-67, 8-47, 9-44) | Yorkshire | 1933 |

**SIX INNINGS**

| | | | | |
|---|---|---|---|---|
| 46 | G. Giffen | (6-71, 7-41, 9-60, 8-56, 8-23, 8-42) | Australians | 1886 |
| 46 | A.P. Freeman | (8-56, 8-31, 9-61, 5-143, 8-44, 8-38) | Kent | 1932 |
| 44 | H. Verity | (7-29, 7-54, 7-35, 6-67, 8-47, 9-44) | Yorkshire | 1933 |
| 42 | C.L. Townsend | (8-67, 8-130, 7-54, 7-80, 5-95, 7-122) | Gloucestershire | 1895 |
| 41 | A.P. Freeman | (6-97, 8-101, 8-70, 5-40, 8-71, 6-72) | Kent | 1930 |

**SEVEN INNINGS**

| | | | | |
|---|---|---|---|---|
| 51 | A.P. Freeman | (5-88, 8-56, 8-31, 9-61, 5-143, 8-44, 8-38) | Kent | 1932 |
| 50 | H. Verity | (7-29, 7-54, 7-35, 6-67, 8-47, 9-44, 6-103) | Yorkshire | 1933 |
| 50 | C.L. Townsend | (8-66, 9-128, 6-77, 8-64, 7-77, 5-51, 7-66) | Gloucestershire | 1898 |
| 47 | C.L. Townsend | (5-43, 8-67, 8-130, 7-54, 7-80, 5-95, 7-122) | Gloucestershire | 1895 |

# OUTSTANDING BOWLING ON DEBUT

**WICKET WITH FIRST BALL IN FIRST-CLASS CRICKET**

| | | | |
|---|---|---|---|
| H. Stubberfield | Sussex v Surrey | Hove | 1857 |
| G.P. Greenfield | Gentlemen of South v Players of South | Oval | 1866 |
| R.G. Barlow | Lancashire v Yorkshire | Sheffield | 1871 |
| G. McCanlis | Kent v Surrey | Oval | 1873 |
| J.J. Parfitt | Surrey v Yorkshire | Oval | 1881 |
| A.H. Grace | Gloucestershire v Sussex | Hove | 1886 |
| G. Waller | Yorkshire v Somerset | Sheffield | 1893 |
| M. Berkley | Essex v Yorkshire | Halifax | 1894 |
| T. Lancaster | Lancashire v Nottinghamshire | Manchester | 1894 |
| H.G. Curgenven | Derbyshire v Essex | Leyton | 1896 |
| C. Blythe | Kent v Yorkshire | Tonbridge | 1899 |
| H.J.J. Hodgkins | Gloucestershire v Somerset | Bristol | 1900 |
| R.B. Strange | Canterbury v Hawke's Bay | Christchurch | 1901–02 |
| J.H.S. Hunt | Middlesex v Somerset | Lord's | 1902 |
| C. Thorneycroft | Northamptonshire v Kent | Catford | 1907 |
| L. Cook | Lancashire v Essex | Manchester | 1907 |

| G.de L. Hough | Kent v Essex | Leyton | 1919 |
|---|---|---|---|
| C.F. Browne | Barbados v Trinidad | Bridgetown | 1919–20 |
| T.H. Collins | Nottinghamshire v Leicestershire | Nottingham | 1921 |
| J. John | Glamorgan v Somerset | Cardiff | 1922 |
| J.E. Phillips | Scotland v Ireland | Dublin | 1923 |
| A.E. Waters | Gloucestershire v Glamorgan | Cheltenham | 1923 |
| R.H. Sharp | Essex v Gloucestershire | Leyton | 1925 |
| S.C. Adams | Northamptonshire v Dublin University | Northampton | 1926 |
| J.G. O'Gorman | Surrey v Glamorgan | Oval | 1927 |
| B.N. Khanna | Northern India v Punjab Governor's XI | Lahore | 1927–28 |
| V.H.V. Goodwin | Queensland v New South Wales | Sydney | 1929–30 |
| W.H. Copson | Derbyshire v Surrey | Oval | 1932 |
| F.W. Stocks | Nottinghamshire v Lancashire | Manchester | 1946 |
| C. Cook | Gloucestershire v Oxford University | Oxford | 1946 |
| E.W. Tilley | Leicestershire v Derbyshire | Derby | 1946 |
| J. Lee | Leicestershire v Glamorgan | Cardiff | 1947 |
| R. Hiern | South Australia v Victoria | Melbourne | 1949–50 |
| G.A. Robertson | Cambridge University v Hampshire | Cambridge | 1950 |
| R. Flockton | New South Wales v Queensland | Brisbane | 1951–52 |
| D.H. Mitchell | Transvaal v Natal | Durban | 1954–55 |
| E.T.E. Hansen | Orange Free State v Western Province | Bloemfontein | 1952–53 |
| A.M. Patel | Gujarat v Bombay | Bombay | 1956–57 |
| W.G. Davies | Glamorgan v Surrey | Oval | 1957 |
| F.C. Brailsford | Derbyshire v Sussex | Derby | 1958 |
| N.T. Sawant | Baroda v Saurashtra | Baroda | 1960–61 |
| R.V. Webster | Scotland v MCC | Greenock | 1961 |
| K.M. Hill | New South Wales v South Australia | Adelaide | 1964–65 |
| U.C. Joshi | Saurashtra v Baroda | Rajkot | 1965–66 |
| B.A. Rothwell | New South Wales v MCC | Sydney | 1965–66 |
| A.R. Frost | South Australia v MCC | Adelaide | 1965–66 |
| K.R. Flint | Tasmania v MCC | Launceston | 1965–66 |
| R.L. Biffin | Tasmania v Indians | Hobart | 1967–68 |
| S.J. Gardiner | Orange Free State v Griqualand West | Bloemfontein | 1967–68 |
| Raju Mukerjee | Bengal v Maharashtra | Poona | 1972–73 |
| C. Jawahir | East Trinidad v Central Trinidad | Arima | 1975–76 |
| K.J. Hughes | Australians v Guyana | Georgetown | 1977–78 |
| Fuad Usman | Universities v United Bank | Peshawar | 1978–79 |
| T.A.P. Sekar | Tamil Nadu v Hyderabad | Hyderabad | 1980–81 |
| C. Lethbridge | Warwickshire v Yorkshire | Birmingham | 1981 |
| B.D.C. Logan | Natal B v Northern Transvaal B | Durban | 1982–83 |
| K.V.S.D. Kamaraju | Andhra v Tamil Nadu | Madras | 1982–83 |
| V. Vyas | Baroda v Bombay | Baroda | 1983–84 |
| M.A. Small | Barbados v Trinidad | Bridgetown | 1983–84 |
| S. Srivastava | Delhi v Haryana | Delhi | 1984–85 |

*S.C. Adams, playing for Northamptonshire v Dublin University (Northampton), 1926, took wickets with his first two balls, and three wickets for one run in his first over.*
*Both H.J. Roberts (Warwickshire v Middlesex, Birmingham, 1932) and R.B. Reid (Transvaal B v Border, East London, 1981–82) took two wickets during their first over in first-class cricket.*
*R.V. Webster (Scotland) also took a wicket with his first ball in the second innings (v MCC, Greenock, 1961).*
*R.J. Crisp, playing for Rhodesia v Transvaal (Bulawayo) 1929–30, took wickets with his second and third balls in first-class matches.*
*C.G. Fynn, playing for Hampshire v Lancashire (Bournemouth) 1930, took two wickets in his first over.*
*R.R. Phillips, playing for Border v Eastern Province (Port Elizabeth) 1939–40, performed the 'hat-trick' in his first over in first-class cricket. He had previously played in four matches without bowling.*
*J.M. Allan (Oxford University) bowled seven consecutive maidens for the wicket of J.V. Wilson v Yorkshire (Oxford) 1953, in his first match, and three more for the wickets of K.R. Miller and I.D. Craig in his second match v Australians (Oxford), before conceding his first first-class run in his 11th over.*
*R.J. Atkinson (Transvaal B), playing against Eastern Province B (Johannesburg) 1978–79, took a wicket with his first legitimate ball after bowling a wide and a no-ball.*
*P.R. Hart (Yorkshire) took the wicket of Intikhab Alam (Surrey) with his seventh ball and bowled 42 balls (7-7-0-1) before conceding his first run (Harrogate 1981).*

## TWELVE WICKETS IN FIRST MATCH

| | | | | |
|---|---|---|---|---|
| 15- | J.H. Kirwan | Cambridge U. v Cambridge Town | Cambridge | 1836 |
| 15-73 | W. Brown | Tasmania v Victoria | Hobart | 1857–58 |
| 15-102 | Nadim Malik | Lahore Reds v Sargodha | Lahore | 1973–74 |
| 14-57 | Jas Lillywhite | Sussex v MCC | Lord's | 1862 |
| 14-57 | C.E. Goodman | Barbados v Demerara | Bridgetown | 1891–92 |
| 14-59 | J. Bevan | South Australia v Tasmania | Adelaide | 1877–78 |
| 14-63 | A.W. Rees | Auckland v Otago | Dunedin | 1889–90 |
| 14-100 | F. Fee | Ireland v MCC | Dublin | 1956 |
| 14-107 | W. Robertson | Canterbury v Otago | Dunedin | 1893–94 |
| 14-112 | V.R. Price | Oxford University v Gents of England | Oxford | 1919 |
| 14-171 | F.G. Roberts | Gloucestershire v Yorkshire | Dewsbury | 1887 |
| 13-49 | B.M. Billimoria | Parsees v Europeans | Bombay | 1894–95 |
| 13-52 | T.W. Antill | Victoria v Tasmania | Launceston | 1850–51 |
| 13-57 | C.P. Cumberbatch | Trinidad v Barbados | Port-of-Spain | 1904–05 |
| 13-71 | V.B. Ranjane | Maharashtra v Saurashtra | Poona | 1956–57 |
| 13-72 | A.E. Moss | Canterbury v Wellington | Christchurch | 1889–90 |
| 13-80 | W.N. Powys | Cambridge University v MCC | Cambridge | 1871 |
| 13-80 | J.W. Toone | Jamaica v R.S. Lucas' XI | Kingston | 1894–95 |
| 13-84 | W.G. Grace | Gents of South v Players of South | Oval | 1865 |
| 13-107 | G.V. Kumar | Karnataka v Tamil Nadu | Bangalore | 1977–78 |
| 13-117 | J.H. Bruce-Lockhart | Cambridge U. v Yorkshire | Cambridge | 1909 |
| 13-146 | G.G. Hall | South African U's v W. Province | Cape Town | 1960–61 |
| 13-265 | G.M. Pierce | New South Wales v South Australia | Adelaide | 1892–93 |
| 12-18 | G. Bennett | Nelson v Wellington | Nelson | 1885–86 |
| 12-56 | Faqir Hussain | NWFP v Delhi | Peshawar | 1938–39 |
| 12-65 | S.G. Syeddin | PWD v Karachi Blues | Karachi | 1976–77 |
| 12-69 | E.A. Brice | Gloucestershire v Surrey | Oval | 1872 |
| 12-79 | Aftab Baloch | PWD v Hyderabad Blues | Karachi | 1969–70 |
| 12-87 | A.H.C. Fargus | Gloucestershire v Middlesex | Lord's | 1900 |
| 12-87 | M. Baqa Jilani | Northern India v Sind | Karachi | 1934–35 |
| 12-90 | W. Mills | Taranaki v Fijians | Hawera | 1894–95 |
| 12-97 | V.M. Muddiah | Services v Southern Punjab | Patiala | 1949–50 |
| 12-118 | W.A. Hay | Otago v Southland | Dunedin | 1917–18 |
| 12-121 | Ramesh Kapoor | Jammu & Kashmir v S. Punjab | Patiala | 1963–64 |
| 12-126 | J.T. Parnham | United England XI v Australians | Tunbridge Wells | 1882 |
| 12-132 | N. Dua | Madhya Pradesh v Uttar Pradesh | Indore | 1963–64 |
| 12-184 | Ghulam Hussain | Hyderabad v Sukkar | Hyderabad | 1984–85 |
| 12- | S.E. Butler | Oxford University v Gentlemen | Oxford | 1870 |

*The following took twelve or more wickets in their second match not having bowled in their first:*

| | | | | |
|---|---|---|---|---|
| 13-204 | J.H. Piton | Transvaal v Griqualand West | Johannesburg | 1890–91 |
| 12-120 | M.H. Bowditch | Western Province v Natal | Cape Town | 1965–66 |

## EIGHT WICKETS IN AN INNINGS OF FIRST MATCH

*Where both analyses qualify only the better one is listed*

| | | | | |
|---|---|---|---|---|
| 10-28 | A.E. Moss | Canterbury v Wellington | Christchurch | 1889–90 |
| 9- | J.H. Kirwan | Cambridge U. v Cambridge Town | Cambridge | 1836 |
| 9-29 | Jas Lillywhite | Sussex v MCC | Lord's | 1862 |
| 9-35 | V.B. Ranjane | Maharashtra v Saurashtra | Poona | 1956–57 |
| 9-42 | W.N. Powys | Cambridge University v MCC | Cambridge | 1871 |
| 9-45 | Amarjit Singh | Kerala v Andhra | Cannanore | 1971–72 |
| 9-55 | J. Quilty | South Australia v Victoria | Adelaide | 1881–82 |
| 9-67 | H. Hay | South Australia v Lord Hawke's XI | Unley, Adelaide | 1902–03 |
| 9-122 | G.G. Hall | South African U's v W. Province | Cape Town | 1960–61 |
| 8-17 | O. Weber | Demerara v Barbados | Bridgetown | 1891–92 |
| 8-30 | V.R. Price | Oxford University v Gents of England | Oxford | 1919 |
| 8-31 | W. Brown | Tasmania v Victoria | Hobart | 1857–58 |
| 8-33 | M. Jahangir Khan | Muslims v Europeans | Lahore | 1929–30 |
| 8-35 | R. Wilson | Queensland v Auckland | Auckland | 1896–97 |
| 8-36 | J. Bevan | South Australia v Tasmania | Adelaide | 1877–78 |
| 8-36 | A.W. Rees | Auckland v Otago | Dunedin | 1889–90 |
| 8-37 | H. Hole | Nelson v Wellington | Nelson | 1874–75 |
| 8-37 | V. Thambuswamy | Madras v Andhra | Guntur | 1967–68 |
| 8-39 | M.L. Horne | Barbados v R.A. Bennett's XI | Bridgetown | 1901–02 |
| 8-40 | W.G. Grace | Gents of South v Players of South | Oval | 1865 |

| | | | | |
|---|---|---|---|---|
| 8-42 | Bashir Ahmed | United Provinces v Bengal | Cawnpore | 1945–46 |
| 8-45 | J.H. Bruce-Lockhart | Cambridge U. v Yorkshire | Cambridge | 1909 |
| 8-47 | S.J. Whitehead | Warwickshire v Nottinghamshire | Nottingham | 1894 |
| 8-48 | W.J. O'Connell | Hawke's Bay v Wellington | Wellington | 1919–20 |
| 8-49 | Ramesh Kapoor | Jammu & Kashmir v S. Punjab | Patiala | 1963–64 |
| 8-50 | N.D. Bardhan | Orissa v Bihar | Jamshedpur | 1949–50 |
| 8-54 | V.M. Muddiah | Services v Southern Punjab | Patiala | 1949–50 |
| 8-58 | Nadim Malik | Lahore Reds v Sargodha | Lahore | 1973–74 |
| 8-59 | W. Robertson | Canterbury v Otago | Dunedin | 1893–94 |
| 8-60 | E. Barratt | South v North | Prince's | 1872 |
| 8-64 | W.B. Gadsden | Natal v Transvaal | Durban | 1928–29 |
| 8-70 | G.A. Wilson | Worcestershire v Yorkshire | Worcester | 1899 |
| 8-70 | W.A. Hay | Otago v Southland | Dunedin | 1917–18 |
| 8-77 | H.M. Hinde | Minor Counties v<br>  H.D.G. Leveson Gower's XI | Eastbourne | 1929 |
| 8-80 | W.R. Gregory | Ireland v Scotland | Dublin | 1912 |
| 8-81 | H.V. Hordern | New South Wales v Queensland | Sydney | 1905–06 |
| 8-89 | L.W. Payn | Natal v Orange Free State | Bloemfontein | 1936–37 |
| 8-91 | F. Barratt | Nottinghamshire v MCC | Lord's | 1914 |
| 8-111 | G.M. Pierce | New South Wales v South Australia | Adelaide | 1892–93 |
| 8-120 | C.L. Pouchet | R.S. Grant's XI v British Guiana | Georgetown | 1938–39 |

*The following took eight or more wickets in an innings in their second match not having bowled in their first:*

| | | | | |
|---|---|---|---|---|
| 9-52 | M.H. Bowditch | Western Province v Natal | Cape Town | 1965–66 |
| 8-88 | M.H.J. Allen | Northamptonshire v Nottinghamshire | Nottingham | 1956 |

*K.D. Boyce (Essex) had match figures of 13-108 (9-61 & 4-47) on his first appearance in English first-class cricket v Cambridge University (Brentwood) 1966. He had played in one previous first-class match for Barbados at Bridgetown in 1964–65.*
*J.W. Sharpe (Surrey) had an innings analysis of 5-5 on his debut v Oxford University (Oxford) 1889.*
*R. Roxby (NSW) took the first five wickets to fall in his debut match v South Australia (Adelaide) 1952–53, finishing with 5-84.*
*Nasim-ul-Ghani (Karachi Blues) had an innings analysis of 70-19-184-3 v Karachi Whites at Karachi on his debut in 1956–57.*B

# BOWLING EIGHT OR MORE BATSMEN IN AN INNINGS

**TEN**

| | | | | |
|---|---|---|---|---|
| J. Wisden | 10- | North v South | Lord's | 1850 |

**NINE**

| | | | | |
|---|---|---|---|---|
| J.H. Kirwan | 9- | Cambridge U. v Cambridge Town | Cambridge | 1836 |

**EIGHT**

| | | | | |
|---|---|---|---|---|
| J.H. Kirwan | 8- | Cambridge University v MCC | Cambridge | 1837 |
| C. Harenc | 8- | Gents of Kent v Gents of England | Lord's | 1849 |
| G. Griffiths | 8-36 | Surrey v North | Oval | 1857 |
| G.F. Tarrant | 8-26 | North v South | Lord's | 1862 |
| James Lillywhite | 8-55 | Sussex v MCC | Hove | 1867 |
| S.E. Butler | 10-38 | Oxford U. v Cambridge U. | Lord's | 1871 |
| M. Flanagan | 9-78 | MCC v Surrey | Lord's | 1876 |
| W. Mycroft | 9-25 | Derbyshire v Hampshire | Southampton | 1876 |
| W. Frith | 8-18 | Canterbury v Otago | Christchurch | 1880–81 |
| J. Briggs | 8-11 | England v South Africa | Cape Town | 1888–89 |
| J.T. Hearne | 8-22 | Middlesex v Lancashire | Lord's | 1891 |
| A.W. Mold | 8-49 | Lancashire v Sussex | Hove | 1893 |
| T.W. Foster | 9-59 | Yorkshire v MCC | Lord's | 1894 |
| T. Richardson | 10-45 | Surrey v Essex | Oval | 1894 |
| H.A. Fannin | 8-19 | Hawke's Bay v Auckland | Auckland | 1897–98 |
| S. Haigh | 8-34 | Lord Hawke's XI v Cape Province | Cape Town | 1898–99 |
| W.P. Howell | 10-28 | Australians v Surrey | Oval | 1899 |
| A. Woodcock | 9-28 | Leicestershire v MCC | Lord's | 1899 |
| J.T. Hearne | 8-42 | Middlesex v Lancashire | Manchester | 1900 |
| A.E. Trott | 8-47 | Middlesex v Gloucestershire | Clifton | 1900 |
| J.J. Kotze | 8-18 | Transvaal v Griqualand West | Port Elizabeth | 1902–03 |

| | | | | |
|---|---|---|---|---|
| J.B. King | 9-62 | Philadelphians v Lancashire | Manchester | 1903 |
| A.E.E. Vogler | 8-24 | Eastern Province v Orange Free State | Johannesburg | 1906–07 |
| G.H. Hirst | 9-23 | Yorkshire v Lancashire | Leeds | 1910 |
| A.J. McBeath | 9-56 | Canterbury v Auckland | Christchurch | 1918–19 |
| A.C. Williams | 9-29 | Yorkshire v Hampshire | Dewsbury | 1919 |
| H. Howell | 8-31 | Warwickshire v Northamptonshire | Northampton | 1922 |
| C.W.L. Parker | 9-87 | Gloucestershire v Derbyshire | Gloucester | 1922 |
| J.M. Blanckenberg | 8-97 | South Africans v Glamorgan | Cardiff | 1924 |
| G.O.B. Allen | 10-40 | Middlesex v Lancashire | Lord's | 1929 |
| A.J. Bell | 8-34 | W. Province v E. Province | Cape Town | 1929–30 |
| Riaz Akhtar | 8-70 | Quetta v Hyderabad | Hyderabad | 1962–63 |

# MOST WICKETS IN A SEASON

## 250 WICKETS IN A SEASON

| | Season | Balls in an over | Overs | Mdns | Runs | Wkts | Avge |
|---|---|---|---|---|---|---|---|
| A.P. Freeman | 1928 | 6 | 1976.1 | 423 | 5489 | 304 | 18.05 |
| A.P. Freeman | 1933 | 6 | 2039 | 651 | 4549 | 298 | 15.26 |
| T. Richardson | 1895 | 5 | 1690.1 | 463 | 4170 | 290 | 14.37 |
| C.T.B. Turner | 1888 | 4 | 2427.2 | 1127 | 3307 | 283 | 11.68 |
| A.P. Freeman | 1931 | 6 | 1618 | 360 | 4307 | 276 | 15.60 |
| A.P. Freeman | 1930 | 6 | 1914.3 | 472 | 4632 | 275 | 16.84 |
| T. Richardson | 1897 | 5 | 1603.4 | 495 | 3945 | 273 | 14.45 |
| A.P. Freeman | 1929 | 6 | 1670.5 | 381 | 4879 | 267 | 18.27 |
| W. Rhodes | 1900 | 6 | 1553 | 455 | 3606 | 261 | 13.81 |
| J.T. Hearne | 1896 | 5 | 2003.1 | 818 | 3670 | 257 | 14.28 |
| A.P. Freeman | 1932 | 6 | 1565.5 | 404 | 4149 | 253 | 16.39 |
| W. Rhodes | 1901 | 6 | 1565 | 505 | 3797 | 251 | 15.12 |

## 150 WICKETS IN A SEASON

| | | | Season | Overs | Mdns | Runs | Wkts | Avge |
|---|---|---|---|---|---|---|---|---|
| Appleyard, R. | Yorkshire | (2) | 1951 | 1313.2 | 391 | 2829 | 200 | 14.14 |
| | | | 1954 | 1026.3 | 315 | 2221 | 154 | 14.42 |
| Astill, W.E. | Leicestershire | | 1921 | 1226.3 | 316 | 3212 | 153 | 20.99 |
| Attewell, W. | Nottinghamshire | (2) | 1890 | 1581.2 | 820 | 1874 | 151 | 12.41 |
| | | | 1891 | 1514.3 | 706 | 2132 | 153 | 13.93 |
| Bedser, A.V. | Surrey | (2) | 1952 | 1184.4 | 296 | 2530 | 154 | 16.42 |
| | | | 1953 | 1253 | 340 | 2702 | 162 | 16.67 |
| Blythe, C. | Kent | (7) | 1907 | 1136.1 | 291 | 2822 | 183 | 15.42 |
| | | | 1908 | 1366.4 | 386 | 3326 | 197 | 16.88 |
| | | | 1909 | 1273.5 | 343 | 3128 | 215 | 14.54 |
| | | | 1910 | 1041.3 | 274 | 2497 | 175 | 14.26 |
| | | | 1912 | 919.3 | 241 | 2183 | 178 | 12.26 |
| | | | 1913 | 1120.2 | 289 | 2729 | 167 | 16.34 |
| | | | 1914 | 1008.4 | 280 | 2583 | 170 | 15.19 |
| Booth, M.W. | Yorkshire | (2) | 1913 | 1156.2 | 185 | 3342 | 181 | 18.46 |
| | | | 1914 | 983.5 | 178 | 2803 | 157 | 17.85 |
| Bowes, W.E. | Yorkshire | (3) | 1932 | 1194.2 | 271 | 2877 | 190 | 15.14 |
| | | | 1933 | 1010.4 | 226 | 2828 | 159 | 17.78 |
| | | | 1935 | 1286.5 | 342 | 2981 | 193 | 15.44 |
| Bradley, W.M. | Kent | | 1899 | 1257 | 414 | 2981 | 156 | 19.10 |
| Braund, L.C. | Somerset | | 1902 | 1100 | 250 | 3407 | 172 | 19.80 |
| Brearley, W. | Lancashire | (2) | 1905 | 1049.4 | 191 | 3486 | 181 | 19.25 |
| | | | 1908 | 856.2 | 165 | 2636 | 163 | 16.17 |
| Briggs, J. | Lancashire | (5) | 1888 | 1450.2 | 763 | 1679 | 160 | 10.49 |
| | | | 1890 | 1113.2 | 456 | 1950 | 158 | 12.34 |
| | | | 1893 | 1364 | 488 | 2639 | 166 | 15.89 |
| | | | 1896 | 1741.4 | 592 | 3253 | 165 | 19.71 |
| | | | 1897 | 1288 | 387 | 2560 | 155 | 16.51 |
| Clay, J.C. | Glamorgan | | 1937 | 1103.3 | 229 | 3052 | 176 | 17.34 |
| Coldwell, L.J. | Worcestershire | | 1962 | 1104 | 253 | 2722 | 152 | 17.90 |
| Cook, L. | Lancashire | (2) | 1920 | 1069.4 | 275 | 2322 | 156 | 14.88 |

| | | | Season | Overs | Mdns | Runs | Wkts | Avge |
|---|---|---|---|---|---|---|---|---|
| Cook, L. *continued* | | | 1921 | 1402 | 293 | 3472 | 151 | 22.99 |
| Copson, W.H. | Derbyshire | | 1936 | 946.4 | 239 | 2135 | 160 | 13.34 |
| Cox, G.R. | Sussex | (2) | 1905 | 1557.3 | 456 | 3719 | 170 | 21.87 |
| | | | 1907 | 1218.2 | 359 | 2900 | 164 | 17.68 |
| Dean, H. | Lancashire | (2) | 1911 | 1295.5 | 324 | 3191 | 183 | 17.43 |
| | | | 1912 | 1060 | 356 | 2216 | 162 | 13.67 |
| Dennett, E.G. | Gloucestershire | (6) | 1905 | 1161.3 | 280 | 3421 | 163 | 20.98 |
| | | | 1906 | 1145.5 | 256 | 3096 | 175 | 17.69 |
| | | | 1907 | 1216.2 | 305 | 3227 | 201 | 16.05 |
| | | | 1908 | 1317.1 | 409 | 3148 | 153 | 20.57 |
| | | | 1909 | 1039.5 | 242 | 2977 | 156 | 19.08 |
| | | | 1913 | 1175.1 | 289 | 3139 | 153 | 20.51 |
| Dooland, B. | Nottinghamshire | (3) | 1953 | 1332.3 | 461 | 2852 | 172 | 16.58 |
| | | | 1954 | 1287.1 | 408 | 3035 | 196 | 15.48 |
| | | | 1955 | 1245.3 | 327 | 3452 | 150 | 23.01 |
| Drake, A. | Yorkshire | | 1914 | 1017.2 | 283 | 2418 | 158 | 15.30 |
| Faulkner, G.A. | South Africans | | 1912 | 1015.1 | 207 | 2514 | 163 | 15.42 |
| Ferris, J.J. | Australians | (2) | 1888 | 2080.1 | 937 | 2934 | 199 | 14.74 |
| | | | 1890 | 1545.1 | 628 | 2657 | 186 | 14.28 |
| Fender, P.G.H. | Surrey | (2) | 1922 | 1116 | 208 | 3329 | 157 | 21.20 |
| | | | 1923 | 1324.2 | 307 | 3558 | 178 | 19.98 |
| Fielder, A. | Kent | (2) | 1906 | 1159.3 | 234 | 3756 | 186 | 20.19 |
| | | | 1907 | 977.3 | 197 | 2773 | 172 | 16.12 |
| Flavell, J.A. | Worcestershire | | 1961 | 1245.2 | 300 | 3043 | 171 | 17.79 |
| Freeman, A.P. | Kent | (14) | 1921 | 1017.2 | 217 | 3086 | 166 | 18.59 |
| | | | 1922 | 1101.1 | 270 | 2839 | 194 | 14.63 |
| | | | 1923 | 990 | 262 | 2642 | 157 | 16.82 |
| | | | 1924 | 1035.2 | 250 | 2518 | 167 | 15.07 |
| | | | 1926 | 1353.1 | 327 | 3740 | 180 | 20.77 |
| | | | 1927 | 1220.1 | 269 | 3330 | 181 | 18.39 |
| | | | 1928 | 1976.1 | 423 | 5489 | 304 | 18.05 |
| | | | 1929 | 1670.5 | 381 | 4879 | 267 | 18.27 |
| | | | 1930 | 1914.3 | 472 | 4632 | 275 | 16.84 |
| | | | 1931 | 1618 | 360 | 4307 | 276 | 15.60 |
| | | | 1932 | 1565.5 | 404 | 4149 | 253 | 16.39 |
| | | | 1933 | 2039 | 651 | 4549 | 298 | 15.26 |
| | | | 1934 | 1744.4 | 440 | 4753 | 205 | 23.18 |
| | | | 1935 | 1503.2 | 320 | 4562 | 212 | 21.51 |
| Geary, G. | Leicestershire | | 1929 | 1495.2 | 500 | 2980 | 152 | 19.60 |
| Giffen, G. | Australians | | 1886 | 1673.2 | 710 | 2674 | 154 | 17.36 |
| Gilligan, A.E.R. | Sussex | | 1923 | 1075.4 | 235 | 2853 | 163 | 17.50 |
| Gladwin, C. | Derbyshire | | 1952 | 1258.2 | 402 | 2917 | 152 | 19.19 |
| Goddard, T.W.J. | Gloucestershire | (10) | 1929 | 1285.1 | 357 | 3015 | 184 | 16.38 |
| | | | 1932 | 1316 | 343 | 3258 | 170 | 19.16 |
| | | | 1933 | 1371.5 | 414 | 3187 | 183 | 17.41 |
| | | | 1935 | 1553 | 384 | 4073 | 200 | 20.36 |
| | | | 1936 | 1425.2 | 323 | 3106 | 153 | 20.30 |
| | | | 1937 | 1478.1 | 359 | 4158 | 248 | 16.76 |
| | | | 1939 | 819 | 139 | 2973 | 200 | 14.86 |
| | | | 1946 | 1310.2 | 358 | 3095 | 177 | 17.48 |
| | | | 1947 | 1451.2 | 344 | 4119 | 238 | 17.30 |
| | | | 1949 | 1187.2 | 326 | 3069 | 160 | 19.18 |
| Gover, A.R. | Surrey | (2) | 1936 | 1159.2 | 185 | 3547 | 200 | 17.73 |
| | | | 1937 | 1219.4 | 191 | 3816 | 201 | 18.98 |
| Grace, W.G. | Gloucestershire | (3) | 1875 | 1689.1 | 698 | 2473 | 191 | 12.94 |
| | | | 1877 | 1801 | 772 | 2293 | 179 | 12.81 |
| | | | 1878 | 1660.2 | 733 | 2208 | 152 | 14.52 |
| Haigh, S. | Yorkshire | (3) | 1900 | 958.3 | 259 | 2416 | 163 | 14.82 |
| | | | 1902 | 799 | 219 | 1984 | 158 | 12.55 |
| | | | 1906 | 971.3 | 209 | 2540 | 174 | 14.59 |
| Hallam, A.W. | Nottinghamshire | | 1907 | 937.1 | 302 | 2133 | 168 | 12.69 |
| Hearne, J.T. | Middlesex | (6) | 1892 | 1360.3 | 527 | 2510 | 163 | 15.39 |
| | | | 1893 | 1741.4 | 667 | 3492 | 212 | 16.47 |
| | | | 1894 | 1486 | 600 | 2739 | 195 | 14.04 |
| | | | 1896 | 2003.1 | 818 | 3670 | 257 | 14.28 |
| | | | 1897 | 1619.3 | 647 | 3066 | 173 | 17.72 |
| | | | 1898 | 1802.2 | 781 | 3120 | 222 | 14.05 |

| | | | Season | Overs | Mdns | Runs | Wkts | Avge |
|---|---|---|---|---|---|---|---|---|
| Hillyer, W.R. | Kent | (2) | 1845 | | | | 174 | |
| | | | 1846 | | | | 151 | |
| | | | *(Full analyses not available)* | | | | | |
| Hilton, M.J. | Lancashire | | 1956 | 1199.5 | 558 | 2207 | 158 | 13.96 |
| Hirst, G.H. | Yorkshire | (6) | 1895 | 1262.1 | 429 | 2560 | 150 | 17.06 |
| | | | 1901 | 1135.3 | 261 | 2999 | 183 | 16.38 |
| | | | 1906 | 1306.1 | 271 | 3434 | 208 | 16.50 |
| | | | 1907 | 1167.4 | 269 | 2859 | 188 | 15.20 |
| | | | 1908 | 1121.5 | 290 | 2445 | 174 | 14.05 |
| | | | 1910 | 1021.2 | 252 | 2426 | 164 | 14.79 |
| Hitch, J.W. | Surrey | (3) | 1911 | 965.1 | 160 | 3477 | 151 | 23.02 |
| | | | 1913 | 958.4 | 169 | 3228 | 174 | 18.55 |
| | | | 1919 | 1009.3 | 198 | 3304 | 150 | 22.02 |
| Hollies, W.E. | Warwickshire | (2) | 1946 | 1528 | 433 | 2871 | 184 | 15.60 |
| | | | 1949 | 1627.4 | 484 | 3413 | 166 | 20.56 |
| Howell, H. | Warwickshire | (2) | 1920 | 1050.3 | 222 | 2885 | 161 | 17.91 |
| | | | 1923 | 1090.4 | 197 | 3126 | 152 | 20.56 |
| Howorth, R. | Worcestershire | | 1947 | 1254 | 375 | 2929 | 164 | 17.85 |
| Humphreys, W.A. | Sussex | | 1893 | 813.4 | 122 | 2598 | 150 | 17.32 |
| Jackson, H.L. | Derbyshire | | 1960 | 1082.2 | 310 | 2179 | 160 | 13.61 |
| Jenkins, R.O. | Worcestershire | | 1949 | 1146.1 | 187 | 3879 | 183 | 21.19 |
| Jupp, V.W.C. | Northamptonshire | | 1928 | 1023 | 192 | 3345 | 166 | 20.15 |
| Kennedy, A.S. | Hampshire | (6) | 1914 | 1289.4 | 331 | 3243 | 162 | 20.01 |
| | | | 1920 | 1179.4 | 279 | 3093 | 169 | 18.30 |
| | | | 1921 | 1427 | 316 | 4009 | 186 | 21.55 |
| | | | 1922 | 1346.4 | 366 | 3444 | 205 | 16.80 |
| | | | 1923 | 1376.5 | 370 | 3599 | 184 | 19.55 |
| | | | 1929 | 1178.5 | 344 | 2773 | 154 | 18.00 |
| Kilner, R. | Yorkshire | | 1923 | 1259.5 | 507 | 2040 | 158 | 12.91 |
| Laker, J.C. | Surrey | | 1950 | 1409.5 | 522 | 2544 | 166 | 15.32 |
| Langridge, James | Sussex | | 1933 | 1228.3 | 355 | 2617 | 158 | 16.56 |
| Larwood, H. | Nottinghamshire | | 1932 | 866.4 | 203 | 2084 | 162 | 12.86 |
| Lees, W.S. | Surrey | (2) | 1905 | 1388.2 | 387 | 3476 | 193 | 18.01 |
| | | | 1906 | 1258.5 | 321 | 3402 | 168 | 20.25 |
| Llewellyn, C.B. | Hampshire | (2) | 1902 | 1129.4 | 314 | 3164 | 170 | 18.61 |
| | | | 1910 | 951.3 | 161 | 2930 | 152 | 19.27 |
| Lock, G.A.R. | Surrey | (4) | 1955 | 1408.4 | 497 | 3109 | 216 | 14.39 |
| | | | 1956 | 1058.2 | 437 | 1932 | 155 | 12.46 |
| | | | 1957 | 1194.1 | 449 | 2550 | 212 | 12.02 |
| | | | 1958 | 1014.4 | 382 | 2055 | 170 | 12.08 |
| Lockwood, W. | Surrey | (3) | 1892 | 890.2 | 292 | 2054 | 151 | 13.60 |
| | | | 1893 | 931.2 | 267 | 2517 | 150 | 16.78 |
| | | | 1894 | 894.2 | 244 | 2233 | 150 | 14.88 |
| Lohmann, G.A. | Surrey | (7) | 1886 | 1715 | 809 | 2425 | 160 | 15.15 |
| | | | 1887 | 1634.2 | 737 | 2404 | 154 | 15.61 |
| | | | 1888 | 1649.1 | 783 | 2280 | 209 | 10.90 |
| | | | 1889 | 1614.1 | 646 | 2714 | 202 | 13.43 |
| | | | 1890 | 1759.1 | 737 | 2998 | 220 | 13.62 |
| | | | 1891 | 1189.3 | 445 | 2065 | 177 | 11.66 |
| | | | 1892 | 1213.4 | 431 | 2316 | 151 | 15.33 |
| Macaulay, G.G. | Yorkshire | (3) | 1923 | 1042.4 | 245 | 2297 | 166 | 13.83 |
| | | | 1924 | 1220.4 | 343 | 2514 | 190 | 13.23 |
| | | | 1925 | 1338.2 | 307 | 3268 | 211 | 15.48 |
| McDonald, E.A. | Lancashire | (4) | 1925 | 1249.4 | 282 | 3828 | 205 | 18.67 |
| | | | 1926 | 1177.4 | 222 | 3541 | 175 | 20.23 |
| | | | 1927 | 1137.3 | 223 | 3586 | 150 | 23.90 |
| | | | 1928 | 1254.1 | 266 | 3754 | 190 | 19.75 |
| Martin, F. | Kent | | 1890 | 1702.2 | 711 | 2480 | 190 | 13.05 |
| Mead, W. | Essex | | 1895 | 1206 | 390 | 2605 | 179 | 14.55 |
| Mitchell, T.B. | Derbyshire | (2) | 1934 | 986.1 | 202 | 3064 | 159 | 19.27 |
| | | | 1935 | 919.5 | 142 | 3448 | 171 | 20.16 |
| Mold, A.W. | Lancashire | (4) | 1893 | 1282.4 | 426 | 2817 | 166 | 16.97 |
| | | | 1894 | 1288.3 | 456 | 2548 | 207 | 12.30 |
| | | | 1895 | 1629 | 598 | 3400 | 213 | 15.96 |
| | | | 1896 | 1116.1 | 373 | 2719 | 150 | 18.12 |
| Morley, F. | Nottinghamshire | (2) | 1878 | 1997.3 | 1054 | 2386 | 197 | 12.11 |

| | | | Season | Overs | Mdns | Runs | Wkts | Avge |
|---|---|---|---|---|---|---|---|---|
| Morley, F. *continued* | | | 1880 | 1841 | 936 | 2257 | 184 | 12.59 |
| Muncer, B.L. | Glamorgan | | 1948 | 1289.2 | 381 | 2748 | 159 | 17.28 |
| Mycroft, W. | Derbyshire | | 1877 | 1374.1 | 659 | 1927 | 157 | 12.27 |
| Newman, J.A. | Hampshire | (3) | 1910 | 1012.1 | 192 | 2879 | 156 | 18.45 |
| | | | 1921 | 1234.1 | 260 | 3817 | 177 | 21.56 |
| | | | 1926 | 1277 | 267 | 3804 | 154 | 24.70 |
| Nichols, M.S. | Essex | (2) | 1935 | 972.3 | 196 | 2610 | 157 | 16.62 |
| | | | 1938 | 1228.1 | 264 | 3408 | 171 | 19.92 |
| Paine, G.A.E. | Warwickshire | | 1934 | 1285.5 | 463 | 2664 | 156 | 17.07 |
| Parker, C.W.L. | Gloucestershire | (10) | 1921 | 1178.5 | 381 | 2893 | 164 | 17.64 |
| | | | 1922 | 1294.5 | 445 | 2712 | 206 | 13.16 |
| | | | 1923 | 1420.2 | 520 | 3229 | 173 | 18.77 |
| | | | 1924 | 1303.5 | 411 | 2913 | 204 | 14.27 |
| | | | 1925 | 1512.3 | 478 | 3311 | 222 | 14.91 |
| | | | 1926 | 1739.5 | 556 | 3920 | 213 | 18.40 |
| | | | 1927 | 1727.4 | 540 | 3849 | 193 | 19.94 |
| | | | 1928 | 1474.2 | 470 | 3602 | 162 | 22.23 |
| | | | 1930 | 1016.3 | 301 | 2299 | 179 | 12.84 |
| | | | 1931 | 1320.4 | 386 | 3125 | 219 | 14.26 |
| Parkin, C.H. | Lancashire | (4) | 1922 | 1309.3 | 348 | 3300 | 189 | 17.46 |
| | | | 1923 | 1356.2 | 356 | 3543 | 209 | 16.94 |
| | | | 1924 | 1162.5 | 357 | 2735 | 200 | 13.67 |
| | | | 1925 | 1075.1 | 281 | 2935 | 152 | 19.30 |
| Peate, E. | Yorkshire | (2) | 1881 | 1712 | 760 | 2195 | 173 | 12.68 |
| | | | 1882 | 1853.1 | 868 | 2466 | 214 | 11.52 |
| Peel, R. | Yorkshire | (3) | 1888 | 1648.1 | 830 | 2091 | 171 | 12.22 |
| | | | 1890 | 1550.4 | 713 | 2233 | 171 | 13.05 |
| | | | 1895 | 1691.1 | 714 | 2695 | 180 | 14.97 |
| Pegler, S.J. | South Africans | | 1912 | 1286.5 | 352 | 2885 | 189 | 15.26 |
| Perks, R.T.D. | Worcestershire | | 1939 | 828 | 112 | 3057 | 159 | 19.22 |
| Pritchard, T.L. | Warwickshire | | 1948 | 1271.3 | 276 | 3225 | 172 | 18.75 |
| Relf, A.E. | Sussex | (2) | 1908 | 1301.3 | 428 | 2648 | 151 | 17.53 |
| | | | 1910 | 1360.3 | 448 | 3108 | 158 | 19.67 |
| Rhodes, W. | Yorkshire | (10) | 1898 | 1240 | 482 | 2249 | 154 | 14.60 |
| | | | 1899 | 1518.4 | 543 | 3062 | 179 | 17.10 |
| | | | 1900 | 1553 | 455 | 3606 | 261 | 13.81 |
| | | | 1901 | 1565 | 505 | 3797 | 251 | 15.12 |
| | | | 1902 | 1306.3 | 405 | 2801 | 213 | 13.15 |
| | | | 1903 | 1378 | 425 | 2813 | 193 | 14.57 |
| | | | 1905 | 1241.3 | 310 | 3085 | 182 | 16.95 |
| | | | 1907 | 1067.1 | 231 | 2757 | 177 | 15.57 |
| | | | 1919 | 1048.3 | 305 | 2365 | 164 | 14.42 |
| | | | 1920 | 1028.4 | 291 | 2123 | 161 | 13.18 |
| Richardson, T. | Surrey | (7) | 1893 | 993.4 | 288 | 2680 | 174 | 15.40 |
| | | | 1894 | 936.3 | 293 | 2024 | 196 | 10.32 |
| | | | 1895 | 1690.1 | 463 | 4170 | 290 | 14.37 |
| | | | 1896 | 1656.2 | 526 | 4015 | 246 | 16.32 |
| | | | 1897 | 1603.4 | 495 | 3945 | 273 | 14.45 |
| | | | 1898 | 1223.4 | 342 | 3147 | 161 | 19.54 |
| | | | 1901 | 1301.4 | 271 | 3697 | 159 | 23.25 |
| Richmond, T.L. | Nottinghamshire | (2) | 1920 | 949.4 | 162 | 2981 | 150 | 19.87 |
| | | | 1922 | 862.2 | 209 | 2279 | 169 | 13.48 |
| Robins, R.W.V. | Middlesex | | 1929 | 1154.4 | 159 | 3489 | 162 | 21.53 |
| Robinson, E.P. | Yorkshire | | 1946 | 1138.2 | 354 | 2498 | 167 | 14.95 |
| Root, C.F. | Worcestershire | (3) | 1923 | 1263.3 | 353 | 3498 | 170 | 20.52 |
| | | | 1924 | 1007.3 | 281 | 2508 | 153 | 16.39 |
| | | | 1925 | 1493.2 | 416 | 3770 | 219 | 17.21 |
| Shackleton, D. | Hampshire | (6) | 1953 | 1219.4 | 328 | 3070 | 150 | 20.46 |
| | | | 1955 | 1220.2 | 438 | 2183 | 159 | 13.72 |
| | | | 1957 | 1217.3 | 446 | 2429 | 155 | 15.67 |
| | | | 1958 | 1320.2 | 505 | 2549 | 165 | 15.44 |
| | | | 1961 | 1501.5 | 532 | 3017 | 158 | 19.09 |
| | | | 1962 | 1717.1 | 678 | 3467 | 172 | 20.15 |
| Shaw, A. | Nottinghamshire | (4) | 1875 | 1755.1 | 1023 | 1495 | 160 | 9.34 |
| | | | 1876 | 2631.2 | 1528 | 2601 | 191 | 13.61 |
| | | | 1878 | 2630 | 1586 | 2201 | 202 | 10.89 |

| | | | Season | Overs | Mdns | Runs | Wkts | Avge |
|---|---|---|---|---|---|---|---|---|
| Shaw, A. *continued* | | | 1880 | 2133 | 1257 | 1589 | 186 | 8.54 |
| Shepherd, D.J. | Glamorgan | | 1956 | 1226.5 | 433 | 2719 | 177 | 15.36 |
| Sims, J.M. | Middlesex | | 1939 | 775.4 | 72 | 3228 | 159 | 20.30 |
| Sinfield, R.A. | Gloucestershire | | 1936 | 1501 | 461 | 3082 | 161 | 19.14 |
| Smith, C.I.J. | Middlesex | | 1934 | 1398 | 346 | 3248 | 172 | 18.88 |
| Smith, H.A. | Leicestershire | | 1935 | 1103.2 | 230 | 2950 | 150 | 19.66 |
| Smith, T.P.B. | Essex | (2) | 1937 | 995.3 | 186 | 3039 | 155 | 19.60 |
| | | | 1947 | 1606 | 287 | 4667 | 172 | 27.13 |
| Smith, W.C. | Surrey | (2) | 1910 | 1423.3 | 420 | 3225 | 247 | 13.05 |
| | | | 1911 | 1283.4 | 368 | 3223 | 160 | 20.14 |
| Southerton, J. | Surrey | (4) | 1868 | 1096.2 | 334 | 2079 | 150 | 13.86 |
| | | | 1870 | 1876.5 | 709 | 3074 | 210 | 14.63 |
| | | | 1871 | 1633.1 | 643 | 2375 | 151 | 15.72 |
| | | | 1872 | 1570.1 | 629 | 2210 | 169 | 13.07 |
| Spofforth, F.R. | Australians | (2) | 1882 | 1470 | 646 | 2079 | 157 | 13.24 |
| | | | 1884 | 1577 | 653 | 2654 | 207 | 12.82 |
| Steel, A.G. | Lancashire | | 1878 | 1115.1 | 453 | 1547 | 164 | 9.43 |
| Tarrant, F.A. | Middlesex | (2) | 1907 | 1085.5 | 244 | 2874 | 183 | 15.70 |
| | | | 1908 | 1124.2 | 297 | 2819 | 169 | 16.68 |
| Tate, F.W. | Sussex | | 1902 | 1183.2 | 359 | 2828 | 180 | 15.71 |
| Tate, M.W. | Sussex | (6) | 1923 | 1608.5 | 331 | 3061 | 219 | 13.97 |
| | | | 1924 | 1469.5 | 465 | 2818 | 205 | 13.74 |
| | | | 1925 | 1694.3 | 472 | 3415 | 228 | 14.97 |
| | | | 1928 | 1584.2 | 491 | 3184 | 165 | 19.29 |
| | | | 1929 | 1420.1 | 393 | 2903 | 156 | 18.60 |
| | | | 1932 | 1380.1 | 440 | 2494 | 160 | 15.58 |
| Tattersall, R. | Lancashire | (2) | 1950 | 1404.4 | 502 | 2623 | 193 | 13.59 |
| | | | 1953 | 1186 | 345 | 2974 | 164 | 18.13 |
| Thompson, G.J. | Northamptonshire | | 1909 | 905.5 | 228 | 2392 | 163 | 14.67 |
| Titmus, F.J. | Middlesex | | 1955 | 1449.5 | 522 | 3117 | 191 | 16.31 |
| Tribe, G.E. | Northamptonshire | | 1955 | 1289 | 342 | 3366 | 176 | 19.12 |
| Trott, A.E. | Middlesex | (3) | 1899 | 1772.4 | 587 | 4086 | 239 | 17.09 |
| | | | 1900 | 1547.1 | 363 | 4923 | 211 | 23.33 |
| | | | 1901 | 1289.1 | 289 | 3835 | 176 | 21.78 |
| Trueman, F.S. | Yorkshire | (4) | 1955 | 996.5 | 214 | 2454 | 153 | 16.03 |
| | | | 1960 | 1068.4 | 275 | 2447 | 175 | 13.98 |
| | | | 1961 | 1180.1 | 302 | 3000 | 155 | 19.35 |
| | | | 1962 | 1141.5 | 273 | 2717 | 153 | 17.75 |
| Turner, C.T.B. | Australians | (2) | 1888 | 2427.2 | 1127 | 3307 | 283 | 11.68 |
| | | | 1890 | 1501.1 | 655 | 2544 | 179 | 14.21 |
| Tyldesley, R.K. | Lancashire | (2) | 1924 | 1075.3 | 346 | 2574 | 184 | 13.98 |
| | | | 1929 | 1114.3 | 350 | 2399 | 154 | 15.57 |
| Underwood, D.L. | Kent | | 1966 | 1104.5 | 475 | 2167 | 157 | 13.80 |
| Verity, H. | Yorkshire | (9) | 1931 | 1137.3 | 356 | 2542 | 188 | 13.52 |
| | | | 1932 | 1117.5 | 401 | 2250 | 162 | 13.88 |
| | | | 1933 | 1195.4 | 428 | 2553 | 190 | 13.43 |
| | | | 1934 | 1282.1 | 500 | 2645 | 150 | 17.63 |
| | | | 1935 | 1279.2 | 453 | 3032 | 211 | 14.36 |
| | | | 1936 | 1289.3 | 463 | 2847 | 216 | 13.18 |
| | | | 1937 | 1386.2 | 487 | 3168 | 202 | 15.68 |
| | | | 1938 | 1191.4 | 424 | 2476 | 158 | 15.67 |
| | | | 1939 | 936.3 | 270 | 2509 | 191 | 13.13 |
| Wainwright, E. | Yorkshire | | 1894 | 1087.3 | 413 | 2114 | 166 | 12.73 |
| Walsh, J.E. | Leicestershire | (2) | 1947 | 1032.1 | 135 | 3477 | 152 | 22.87 |
| | | | 1948 | 1175.3 | 193 | 3405 | 174 | 19.56 |
| Wardle, J.H. | Yorkshire | (6) | 1948 | 1283.4 | 483 | 2923 | 150 | 19.48 |
| | | | 1950 | 1627.1 | 741 | 2909 | 174 | 16.71 |
| | | | 1952 | 1857 | 810 | 3460 | 177 | 19.54 |
| | | | 1954 | 1262 | 520 | 2449 | 155 | 15.80 |
| | | | 1955 | 1486.4 | 572 | 3149 | 195 | 16.14 |
| | | | 1956 | 1230.2 | 464 | 2482 | 153 | 16.22 |
| Wass, T.G. | Nottinghamshire | | 1907 | 885 | 218 | 2328 | 163 | 14.28 |
| Wellard, A.W. | Somerset | (2) | 1937 | 1276.1 | 220 | 3675 | 156 | 23.55 |
| | | | 1938 | 1233.4 | 241 | 3491 | 172 | 20.29 |
| White, J.C. | Somerset | | 1929 | 1556.1 | 631 | 2648 | 168 | 15.76 |
| Wilkinson, L.L. | Lancashire | | 1938 | 1251.2 | 240 | 3531 | 151 | 23.38 |

| | | | Season | Overs | Mdns | Runs | Wkts | Avge |
|---|---|---|---|---|---|---|---|---|
| Woods, S.M.J. | Somerset | | 1892 | 1055.4 | 319 | 2576 | 153 | 16.83 |
| Woolley, F.E. | Kent | (3) | 1920 | 1135.4 | 315 | 2633 | 185 | 14.23 |
| | | | 1921 | 1163.1 | 367 | 2697 | 167 | 16.14 |
| | | | 1922 | 1233.1 | 370 | 2995 | 163 | 18.37 |
| Wright, D.V.P. | Kent | (2) | 1947 | 1175.5 | 252 | 3739 | 177 | 21.12 |
| | | | 1950 | 929.3 | 187 | 3140 | 151 | 20.79 |
| Young, J.A. | Middlesex | (4) | 1947 | 1291.1 | 416 | 2765 | 159 | 17.38 |
| | | | 1949 | 1453.3 | 526 | 2948 | 150 | 19.65 |
| | | | 1951 | 1680.2 | 741 | 2976 | 157 | 18.95 |
| | | | 1952 | 1448.1 | 511 | 3241 | 163 | 19.88 |

**MOST RECENT INSTANCES OF 250, 200 and 150 WICKETS**

| | | | |
|---|---|---|---|
| 250 wickets: | A.P. Freeman | Kent | 1933 |
| 200 wickets: | G.A.R. Lock | Surrey | 1957 |
| 150 wickets: | D.L. Underwood | Kent | 1966 |

The highest aggregate of first-class wickets in a season since 1966 is 134 by M.D. Marshall (Hampshire) in 1982.

**100 WICKETS IN A SEASON SINCE 1971**

The feat of taking a hundred first-class wickets in a season was achieved every year from 1864 to 1971 inclusive, war years excepted. A drastic pruning of the County Championship fixtures to 20 matches per county in 1972 reduced the number of instances to only six in the next five seasons. No bowler reached this aggregate in 1972 or 1976. The Championship programme was increased to 22 matches per county in 1977, and to 24 in 1983.

| | | | Season | Overs | Mdns | Runs | Wkts | Avge |
|---|---|---|---|---|---|---|---|---|
| Bedi, B.S. | Northamptonshire | (2) | 1973 | 864.2 | 309 | 1884 | 105 | 17.94 |
| | | | 1974 | 1085.3 | 307 | 2760 | 112 | 24.64 |
| Botham, I.T. | Somerset | | 1978 | 605.2 | 143 | 1640 | 100 | 16.40 |
| Doshi, D.R. | Warwickshire | | 1980 | 961.2 | 268 | 2700 | 101 | 26.73 |
| Emburey, J.E. | Middlesex | | 1983 | 935 | 328 | 1842 | 103 | 17.88 |
| Gifford, N. | Warwickshire | | 1983 | 1043.4 | 346 | 2393 | 104 | 23.00 |
| Hadlee, R.J. | Nottinghamshire | (2) | 1981 | 708.4 | 231 | 1564 | 105 | 14.89 |
| | | | 1984 | 772.2 | 245 | 1645 | 117 | 14.05 |
| Jackman, R.D. | Surrey | | 1980 | 746.2 | 220 | 1864 | 121 | 15.40 |
| Lee, P.G. | Lancashire | (2) | 1973 | 740.3 | 181 | 1901 | 101 | 18.82 |
| | | | 1975 | 799.5 | 199 | 2067 | 112 | 18.45 |
| Lever, J.K. | Essex | (4) | 1978 | 681.1 | 160 | 1610 | 106 | 15.18 |
| | | | 1979 | 700 | 166 | 1834 | 106 | 17.30 |
| | | | 1983 | 569 | 137 | 1726 | 106 | 16.28 |
| | | | 1984 | 874.5 | 195 | 2550 | 116 | 21.98 |
| Marshall, M.D. | Hampshire | | 1982 | 822 | 225 | 2108 | 134 | 15.73 |
| Procter, M.J. | Gloucestershire | | 1977 | 777.3 | 226 | 1967 | 109 | 18.04 |
| Radford, N.V. | Worcestershire | | 1985 | 779.4 | 130 | 2493 | 101 | 24.68 |
| Roberts, A.M.E. | Hampshire | | 1974 | 727.4 | 198 | 1621 | 119 | 13.62 |
| Sarfraz Nawaz | Northamptonshire | | 1975 | 728.4 | 175 | 2051 | 101 | 20.30 |
| Selvey, M.W.W. | Middlesex | | 1978 | 743.5 | 199 | 1929 | 101 | 19.09 |
| Underwood, D.L. | Kent | (3) | 1978 | 815.1 | 359 | 1594 | 110 | 14.49 |
| | | | 1979 | 799.2 | 335 | 1575 | 106 | 14.85 |
| | | | 1983 | 936.3 | 358 | 2044 | 106 | 19.28 |

# MOST WICKETS IN A SEASON OVERSEAS

**AUSTRALIA**

| | | Season | Overs | Mdns | Runs | Wkts | Avge |
|---|---|---|---|---|---|---|---|
| C.T.B. Turner | New South Wales | 1887–88 | 4267† | 473 | 1441 | 106 | 13.59 |
| G. Giffen | South Australia | 1894–95 | 808.5 | 195 | 2097 | 93 | 22.54 |
| C.V. Grimmett | South Australia | 1929–30 | 471.7 | 52 | 1943 | 82 | 23.69 |
| R. Benaud | New South Wales | 1958–59 | 559.5 | 146 | 1579 | 82 | 19.25 |

| | | Season | Overs | Mdns | Runs | Wkts | Avge |
|---|---|---|---|---|---|---|---|
| A.A. Mailey | New South Wales | 1920–21 | 2986† | 45 | 1825 | 81 | 22.53 |
| M.W. Tate | MCC | 1924–25 | 502.2 | 93 | 1464 | 77 | 19.01 |
| C.V. Grimmett | South Australia | 1931–32 | 588.4 | 166 | 1535 | 77 | 19.93 |
| E. Jones | South Australia | 1897–98 | 575.1 | 121 | 1653 | 76 | 21.75 |
| R.M. Hogg | South Australia | 1978–79 | 425 | 98 | 1249 | 76 | 16.43 |
| C.V. Grimmett | South Australia | 1930–31 | 449.6 | 99 | 1417 | 74 | 19.14 |
| C.V. Grimmett | South Australia | 1939–40 | 442.7 | 57 | 1654 | 73 | 22.65 |
| C.V. Grimmett | South Australia | 1928–29 | 5252† | 134 | 2432 | 71 | 34.25 |
| C.T.B. Turner | New South Wales | 1886–87 | 536.1 | 273 | 538 | 70 | 7.68 |
| W.J. Whitty | South Australia | 1910–11 | 493.3 | 99 | 1419 | 70 | 20.27 |
| H.J. Tayfield | South Africans | 1952–53 | 608.4 | 123 | 1954 | 70 | 27.91 |
| D.K. Lillee | Western Australia | 1976–77 | 350 | 58 | 1368 | 70 | 19.54 |
| T. Richardson | A.E. Stoddart's XI | 1894–95 | 592.2 | 148 | 1616 | 68 | 23.76 |
| D.K. Lillee | Western Australia | 1980–81 | 545 | 138 | 1462 | 69 | 21.18 |
| H. Ironmonger | Victoria | 1930–31 | 379.5 | 112 | 972 | 68 | 14.29 |
| J.N. Crawford | MCC | 1907–08 | 566 | 115 | 1663 | 66 | 25.19 |
| J.V. Saunders | Victoria | 1907–08 | 555.4 | 113 | 1587 | 66 | 24.04 |
| C.V. Grimmett | South Australia | 1933–34 | 420.5 | 68 | 1441 | 66 | 21.83 |
| W. Rhodes | MCC | 1903–04 | 423.3 | 112 | 1055 | 65 | 16.23 |
| J.C. White | MCC | 1928–29 | 5213† | 223 | 1471 | 65 | 22.63 |
| A.G. Hurst | Victoria | 1978–79 | 443.4 | 85 | 1353 | 65 | 20.81 |
| G.F. Lawson | New South Wales | 1982–83 | 495.4 | 110 | 1368 | 65 | 21.04 |
| L.O'B. Fleetwood-Smith | Victoria | 1937–38 | 395.1 | 29 | 1436 | 64 | 22.43 |
| W.J. O'Reilly | New South Wales | 1937–38 | 310.7 | 91 | 784 | 64 | 12.25 |
| G.A. Lohmann | A. Shrewsbury's XI | 1887–88 | 659.1 | 354 | 755 | 63 | 11.98 |
| H. Ironmonger | Victoria | 1931–32 | 491.5 | 178 | 1168 | 63 | 18.53 |
| L.O'B. Fleetwood-Smith | Victoria | 1934–35 | 291.4 | 26 | 1282 | 63 | 20.34 |
| L.S. Pascoe | New South Wales | 1980–81 | 451 | 105 | 1230 | 63 | 19.52 |
| L.C. Braund | A.C. MacLaren's XI | 1901–02 | 623.5 | 147 | 1779 | 62 | 28.69 |
| F.R. Foster | MCC | 1911–12 | 485.1 | 110 | 1252 | 62 | 20.19 |
| W.J. O'Reilly | New South Wales | 1932–33 | 642.5 | 237 | 1237 | 62 | 19.95 |
| A.A. Mallett | South Australia | 1972–73 | 410.2 | 105 | 1184 | 62 | 19.09 |
| D.K. Lillee | Western Australia | 1974–75 | 444.4 | 73 | 1559 | 62 | 25.14 |
| J.R. Thomson | Queensland | 1974–75 | 338.7 | 61 | 1201 | 62 | 19.37 |
| D.K. Lillee | Western Australia | 1975–76 | 312.3 | 29 | 1490 | 62 | 24.03 |
| J.R. Thomson | Queensland | 1975–76 | 330.4 | 39 | 1473 | 62 | 23.75 |
| B. Yardley | Western Australia | 1982–83 | 705 | 237 | 1782 | 61 | 29.21 |
| M.H. Mankad | Indians | 1947–48 | 494.3 | 76 | 1595 | 61 | 26.14 |
| A.N. Connolly | Victoria | 1967–68 | 398.7 | 96 | 1211 | 60 | 20.18 |
| G.D. McKenzie | Western Australia | 1968–69 | 458.6 | 68 | 1669 | 60 | 27.81 |

† *Balls bowled – six and eight-ball overs*

## SOUTH AFRICA AND RHODESIA

| | | | | | | | |
|---|---|---|---|---|---|---|---|
| R. Benaud | Australians | 1957–58 | 743.6 | 185 | 2056 | 106 | 19.39 |
| S.F. Barnes | MCC | 1913–14 | 460.2 | 129 | 1117 | 104 | 10.74 |
| W.J. O'Reilly | Australians | 1935–36 | 662.5 | 250 | 1289 | 95 | 13.56 |
| C.V. Grimmett | Australians | 1935–36 | 663.1 | 229 | 1362 | 92 | 14.80 |
| J.H. Wardle | MCC | 1956–57 | 380.3 | 94 | 1103 | 90 | 12.25 |
| J.C. Alabaster | New Zealanders | 1961–62 | 749 | 180 | 2219 | 86 | 25.80 |
| R.C. Motz | New Zealanders | 1961–62 | 579.4 | 155 | 1439 | 81 | 17.76 |
| I.W. Johnson | Australians | 1949–50 | 414.6 | 77 | 1280 | 77 | 16.62 |
| V.A.P. van der Bijl | Natal | 1981–82 | 507.3 | 153 | 1119 | 75 | 14.92 |
| A.K. Davidson | Australians | 1957–58 | 430.5 | 101 | 1090 | 72 | 15.13 |
| R.O. Jenkins | MCC | 1948–49 | 406.7 | 64 | 1508 | 71 | 21.23 |
| I.A.R. Peebles | MCC | 1930–31 | 444.4 | 80 | 1274 | 66 | 19.30 |
| A.S. Kennedy | Hon L.H. Tennyson's XI | 1924–25 | 480.2 | 121 | 1287 | 65 | 19.80 |
| V.A.P. van der Bijl | Natal | 1975–76 | 461.2 | 113 | 1084 | 65 | 16.67 |
| J.T. Partridge | Rhodesia | 1962–63 | 472.5 | 165 | 1064 | 64 | 16.62 |
| V.A.P. van der Bijl | Natal | 1973–74 | 486.2 | 132 | 1037 | 64 | 16.20 |
| J.T. Botten | N.E. Transvaal | 1958–59 | 261.3 | 68 | 664 | 63 | 10.53 |
| A.J. Kourie | Transvaal | 1982–83 | 573.1 | 157 | 1501 | 63 | 23.82 |
| F.J. Cameron | New Zealanders | 1961–62 | 633.2 | 203 | 1412 | 62 | 22.77 |
| A.S. Kennedy | MCC | 1922–23 | 478.5 | 168 | 1024 | 61 | 16.78 |
| M.J. Procter | Rhodesia | 1972–73 | 412.2 | 112 | 1049 | 60 | 17.48 |
| G. Geary | Hon L.H. Tennyson's XI | 1924–25 | 408 | 104 | 955 | 59 | 16.18 |

|  |  | Season | Overs | Mdns | Runs | Wkts | Avge |
|---|---|---|---|---|---|---|---|
| J.W. Gleeson | Australians | 1969–70 | 501 | 182 | 1150 | 59 | 19.49 |
| M.J. Procter | Natal | 1976–77 | 360.5 | 94 | 936 | 59 | 15.86 |
| P.G.H. Fender | MCC | 1922–23 | 380.1 | 81 | 1136 | 58 | 19.58 |
| S.T. Jefferies | Western Province | 1982–83 | 490.2 | 114 | 1386 | 58 | 23.89 |
| S.T. Clarke | Transvaal | 1984–85 | 329.4 | 88 | 738 | 58 | 12.72 |
| C. Blythe | MCC | 1905–06 | 481.2 | 167 | 1046 | 57 | 18.35 |
| P.H. Edmonds | E. Province/Int'l Wdrs. | 1975–76 | 615.3 | 193 | 1484 | 57 | 26.03 |
| W.A. Johnston | Australians | 1949–50 | 335.2 | 77 | 770 | 56 | 13.75 |
| G.A.R. Lock | MCC | 1956–57 | 352.7 | 120 | 833 | 56 | 14.87 |
| H.J. Tayfield | Natal/Transvaal | 1956–57 | 450.1 | 153 | 1036 | 56 | 18.50 |
| A.E.E. Vogler | Eastern Province | 1906–07 | 190.1 | 40 | 580 | 55 | 10.54 |
| J.J. Kotze | Western Province | 1906–07 | 196.1 | 38 | 585 | 54 | 10.83 |
| H.J. Tayfield | Natal | 1953–54 | 401.7 | 160 | 851 | 54 | 15.75 |
| L.F. Kline | Australians | 1957–58 | 423 | 122 | 1103 | 54 | 20.42 |
| V.A.P. van der Bijl | Natal | 1980–81 | 291 | 109 | 513 | 54 | 9.50 |
| J.E. Waddington | Griqualand West | 1952–53 | 303.6 | 59 | 893 | 53 | 16.84 |
| J.T. Partridge | Rhodesia | 1961–62 | 290.5 | 72 | 742 | 53 | 14.00 |
| G.S. Le Roux | Western Province | 1977–78 | 319.1 | 79 | 773 | 53 | 14.58 |
| A.E. Hall | Transvaal | 1926–27 | 277.4 | 60 | 650 | 52 | 12.50 |
| P.N.F. Mansell | Rhodesia | 1951–52 | 295.5 | 49 | 917 | 52 | 17.63 |
| M.J. Procter | Rhodesia | 1971–72 | 360.5 | 96 | 833 | 52 | 16.01 |
| A.J. Kourie | Transvaal | 1980–81 | 288.4 | 71 | 734 | 52 | 14.11 |
| S.T. Jefferies | Western Province | 1981–82 | 440.2 | 114 | 1166 | 52 | 22.42 |
| V.A.P. van der Bijl | Transvaal | 1982–83 | 460 | 133 | 976 | 52 | 18.76 |
| D.V.P. Wright | MCC | 1938–39 | 343.4 | 35 | 1453 | 51 | 28.49 |
| D.V.P. Wright | MCC | 1948–49 | 378.1 | 53 | 1544 | 51 | 30.27 |
| C.L. McCool | Australians | 1949–50 | 314.2 | 56 | 976 | 51 | 19.13 |
| J.R. Reid | New Zealanders | 1953–54 | 351.4 | 89 | 997 | 51 | 19.54 |
| G.B. Lawrence | Rhodesia | 1961–62 | 376.1 | 90 | 892 | 51 | 17.49 |
| F.J. Titmus | MCC | 1964–65 | 593.1 | 188 | 1240 | 51 | 24.31 |
| E.O. Simons | Northern Transvaal | 1984–85 | 309.4 | 68 | 859 | 51 | 16.84 |
| C. Blythe | MCC | 1909–10 | 373.1 | 120 | 783 | 50 | 15.66 |
| G.H.T. Simpson-Hayward | MCC | 1909–10 | 314.4 | 46 | 859 | 50 | 17.18 |
| A.E.E. Vogler | Transvaal | 1909–10 | 290.5 | 46 | 1016 | 50 | 20.32 |
| A.P. Freeman | MCC | 1927–28 | 325.3 | 73 | 965 | 50 | 19.30 |
| R.R. Lindwall | Australians | 1949–50 | 292.4 | 53 | 729 | 50 | 14.58 |
| H.J. Tayfield | Natal | 1951–52 | 387.2 | 121 | 889 | 50 | 17.78 |
| V.I. Smith | Natal | 1952–53 | 335.5 | 63 | 892 | 50 | 17.84 |
| A.R. MacGibbon | New Zealanders | 1953–54 | 342.6 | 70 | 971 | 50 | 19.42 |
| J.C. Laker | MCC | 1956–57 | 388.7 | 121 | 875 | 50 | 17.50 |
| P. Anker | Boland | 1981–82 | 295.3 | 86 | 731 | 50 | 14.62 |
| C.J.P.G. van Zyl | Orange Free State | 1984–85 | 232.4 | 40 | 676 | 50 | 13.52 |
| H.A. Page | Transvaal | 1984–85 | 292.1 | 74 | 775 | 50 | 15.50 |
| A.J. Kourie | Transvaal | 1984–85 | 365.3 | 89 | 1009 | 50 | 20.18 |

## WEST INDIES

|  |  |  |  |  |  |  |  |
|---|---|---|---|---|---|---|---|
| E.M. Dowson | R.A. Bennett's XI | 1901–02 | 404.5 | 121 | 997 | 80 | 12.46 |
| G.J. Thompson | Lord Brackley's XI | 1904–05 | 353.5 | 81 | 1048 | 75 | 13.97 |
| E.R. Wilson | R.A. Bennett's XI | 1901–02 | 414.1 | 144 | 767 | 67 | 11.44 |
| J.W. Hearne | MCC | 1910–11 | 398.4 | 62 | 1450 | 67 | 21.64 |
| C.E.H. Croft | Guyana | 1976–77 | 378 | 84 | 1283 | 59 | 21.74 |
| L.R. Gibbs | Guyana | 1972–73 | 577 | 186 | 1180 | 58 | 20.34 |
| J. Garner | Barbados | 1976–77 | 411.4 | 78 | 1294 | 58 | 22.31 |
| C.E. Goodman | Barbados | 1896–97 | 304.2 | 71 | 676 | 57 | 11.85 |
| H.R. Bromley-Davenport | R.S. Lucas's XI | 1894–95 | 317.2 | 95 | 561 | 56 | 10.01 |
| B.J.T. Bosanquet | R.A. Bennett's XI | 1901–02 | 338.3 | 92 | 906 | 55 | 16.47 |
| A.E. Stoddart | A. Priestley's XI | 1896–97 | 303.4 | 128 | 520 | 53 | 9.81 |
| E.T. Willett | Combined Islands | 1972–73 | 536.5 | 174 | 1162 | 53 | 21.92 |
| F.W. Bush | R.S. Lucas's XI | 1894–95 | 284.4 | 90 | 610 | 51 | 11.96 |
| S.P. Gupte | Indians | 1952–53 | 510 | 147 | 1182 | 50 | 23.64 |
| P.I. Philpott | Australians | 1964–65 | 447.1 | 99 | 1207 | 49 | 24.63 |
| R.R. Jumadeen | Trinidad | 1976–77 | 497.1 | 157 | 996 | 49 | 20.32 |
| S.G. Smith | Trinidad | 1901–02 | 220.5 | 36 | 568 | 48 | 11.83 |
| S.G. Smith | MCC | 1910–11 | 300.2 | 57 | 845 | 47 | 17.97 |
| B.R. Taylor | New Zealanders | 1971–72 | 352.3 | 68 | 974 | 46 | 21.17 |

|  |  | *Season* | *Overs* | *Mdns* | *Runs* | *Wkts* | *Avge* |
|---|---|---|---|---|---|---|---|
| A. Cumberbatch | Trinidad | 1896–97 | 231.1 | 84 | 529 | 45 | 11.75 |
| R.R. Jumadeen | Trinidad | 1977–78 | 514.2 | 140 | 1180 | 45 | 26.22 |
| C.G. Butts | Guyana | 1984–85 | 475.2 | 126 | 990 | 45 | 22.00 |
| W. Voce | MCC | 1929–30 | 387.2 | 68 | 1188 | 44 | 27.00 |
| D.R. Parry | Combined Islands | 1977–78 | 418.5 | 77 | 1153 | 44 | 26.20 |
| W. Williams | A. Priestley's XI | 1896–97 | 202.3 | 55 | 464 | 43 | 10.79 |
| Inshan Ali | Trinidad | 1973–74 | 307 | 80 | 749 | 42 | 17.83 |
| J.D. Higgs | Australians | 1977–78 | 354 | 90 | 934 | 42 | 22.23 |
| G. Mahabir | Trinidad | 1984–85 | 281.5 | 52 | 719 | 42 | 17.11 |
| C.R. Browne | Barbados | 1910–11 | 220.2 | 51 | 555 | 41 | 13.53 |
| S. Venkataraghavan | Indians | 1970–71 | 508.1 | 133 | 1278 | 41 | 31.17 |
| M.H.N. Walker | Australians | 1972–73 | 375 | 107 | 840 | 41 | 20.48 |
| B. Yardley | Australians | 1977–78 | 347.3 | 91 | 889 | 41 | 21.68 |
| E. Humphreys | MCC | 1912–13 | 249.1 | 57 | 660 | 40 | 16.50 |
| G.A.E. Paine | MCC | 1934–35 | 369 | 103 | 957 | 40 | 23.92 |
| L.R. Gibbs | British Guiana | 1961–62 | 438.1 | 132 | 937 | 40 | 23.42 |
| R.R. Jumadeen | Trinidad | 1976–77 | 415.2 | 134 | 853 | 40 | 21.32 |

## NEW ZEALAND

|  |  |  |  |  |  |  |  |
|---|---|---|---|---|---|---|---|
| S.L. Boock | Canterbury | 1977–78 | 479.4 | 167 | 1088 | 66 | 16.48 |
| R.J. Hadlee | Canterbury | 1981–82 | 424.2 | 131 | 867 | 59 | 14.69 |
| S.L. Boock | Otago | 1978–79 | 469.7 | 136 | 1238 | 58 | 21.34 |
| G.J. Thompson | Lord Hawke's XI | 1902–03 | 297 | 104 | 668 | 57 | 11.71 |
| S.T. Callaway | Canterbury | 1903–04 | 224.5 | 73 | 474 | 54 | 8.77 |
| R.W. Blair | Wellington | 1956–57 | 325.1 | 105 | 784 | 53 | 14.79 |
| W.W. Armstrong | Australians | 1913–14 | 307.4 | 81 | 789 | 52 | 15.17 |
| S. Austin | New South Wales | 1893–94 | 1751† | 86 | 612 | 52 | 11.76 |
| D.R. O'Sullivan | Central Districts | 1978–79 | 349.2 | 94 | 989 | 52 | 19.01 |
| E.J. Chatfield | Wellington | 1981–82 | 406.5 | 140 | 868 | 51 | 17.01 |
| J.W.H.T. Douglas | MCC | 1906–07 | 239.3 | 51 | 663 | 50 | 13.26 |
| R.J. Hadlee | Canterbury | 1978–79 | 299.1 | 56 | 909 | 50 | 18.18 |
| R.W. Blair | Wellington | 1957–58 | 302.2 | 103 | 606 | 49 | 12.36 |
| J.C. Alabaster | Otago | 1960–61 | 426.3 | 127 | 961 | 49 | 19.61 |
| R.W. Blair | Wellington | 1963–64 | 408.1 | 135 | 856 | 49 | 17.46 |
| H.J. Howarth | Auckland | 1972–73 | 373.1 | 84 | 1146 | 49 | 23.38 |
| B.L. Cairns | Otago | 1978–79 | 412.6 | 93 | 1253 | 49 | 25.57 |
| E.J. Chatfield | Wellington | 1979–80 | 298 | 130 | 530 | 49 | 10.81 |
| J.A. Hayes | Auckland | 1957–58 | 244.3 | 49 | 568 | 48 | 11.83 |
| B.W. Yuile | Central Districts | 1966–67 | 462.4 | 212 | 802 | 48 | 16.70 |
| E.J. Chatfield | Wellington | 1976–77 | 350.3 | 74 | 1073 | 48 | 22.35 |
| E.J. Gray | Wellington | 1984–85 | 437 | 149 | 1044 | 48 | 21.75 |
| W. Robertson | Canterbury | 1893–94 | 261.2 | 66 | 570 | 47 | 12.12 |
| P.M. Hornibrook | Australians | 1920–21 | 170 | 33 | 573 | 47 | 12.19 |
| C.V. Grimmett | Australians | 1927–28 | 319.4 | 65 | 795 | 47 | 16.91 |
| R.W. Blair | Central Districts | 1955–56 | 280.5 | 54 | 882 | 47 | 18.76 |
| J.C. Alabaster | Otago | 1959–60 | 313 | 78 | 824 | 47 | 17.53 |
| R.C. Motz | Canterbury | 1967–68 | 369.2 | 116 | 907 | 47 | 19.29 |
| K.W. Hough | Auckland | 1958–59 | 414.3 | 151 | 701 | 46 | 15.23 |
| B.W. Yuile | Central Districts | 1964–65 | 505.3 | 264 | 787 | 46 | 17.10 |
| F.J. Cameron | Otago | 1964–65 | 405 | 129 | 940 | 46 | 20.43 |
| P.R. May | MCC | 1906–07 | 248.4 | 47 | 719 | 45 | 15.97 |
| H. Ironmonger | Australians | 1920–21 | 198.3 | 40 | 593 | 45 | 13.17 |
| R.W. Barber | MCC | 1960–61 | 381.3 | 91 | 1070 | 45 | 23.77 |
| R.S. Cunis | Auckland | 1968–69 | 286.2 | 53 | 861 | 45 | 19.13 |
| P.J. Petherick | Otago | 1977–78 | 263.1 | 72 | 772 | 45 | 17.15 |
| S.R. Gillespie | Northern Districts | 1979–80 | 383.5 | 97 | 998 | 45 | 22.17 |

† *1751 balls bowled (85.3 five-ball overs, 220.3 six-ball overs)*

## INDIA, PAKISTAN AND SRI LANKA

|  |  |  |  |  |  |  |  |
|---|---|---|---|---|---|---|---|
| M.W. Tate | MCC | 1926–27 | 727.1 | 211 | 1599 | 116 | 13.78 |
| Abdul Qadir | Habib Bank | 1982–83 | 827.2 | 184 | 2367 | 103 | 22.98 |
| G.E. Tribe | Commonwealth | 1949–50 | 787.2 | 215 | 1805 | 99 | 18.23 |
| Wasim Raja | Punjab/Lahore | 1973–74 | 463.2 | 112 | 2219 | 99 | 22.41 |
| Abdur Raqib | Habib Bank | 1977–78 |  |  | 1191 | 90 | 13.23 |
| B.S. Bedi | Delhi | 1974–75 | 599.2 | 186 | 1305 | 88 | 14.82 |

| | | Season | Overs | Mdns | Runs | Wkts | Avge |
|---|---|---|---|---|---|---|---|
| B.S. Bedi | Delhi | 1976–77 | 897.3 | 319 | 1719 | 88 | 19.53 |
| W.W. Hall | West Indians | 1958–59 | 519.2 | 167 | 1312 | 87 | 15.08 |
| Tausif Ahmed | United Bank | 1981–82 | 715.1 | 195 | 1586 | 87 | 18.22 |
| Abdul Qadir | Habib Bank | 1981–82 | 596.4 | 132 | 1609 | 87 | 18.49 |
| R.K. Oxenham | Australians | 1935–36 | 323.3 | 149 | 586 | 86 | 6.81 |
| B.S. Chandrasekhar | Mysore | 1966–67 | 583.3 | 141 | 1624 | 85 | 19.10 |
| Khurshid Akhtar | United Bank | 1980–81 | 544.4 | 128 | 1254 | 84 | 14.92 |
| S. Venkataraghavan | Madras | 1967–68 | 750.1 | 223 | 1761 | 83 | 21.21 |
| K.D. Ghavri | Bombay | 1978–79 | 677.3 | 157 | 1910 | 83 | 23.01 |
| Tausif Ahmed | United Bank | 1984–85 | 546.2 | 125 | 1316 | 83 | 15.85 |
| S. Venkataraghavan | Tamil Nadu | 1971–72 | 450.3 | 103 | 1236 | 82 | 15.07 |
| P.K. Shivalkar | Bombay | 1972–73 | 570.5 | 183 | 1214 | 82 | 14.80 |
| Intikhab Alam | PIA | 1973–74 | 475.4 | 74 | 1668 | 82 | 20.34 |
| G. Geary | MCC | 1926–27 | 528.1 | 148 | 1162 | 81 | 14.34 |
| G.A.R. Lock | MCC | 1955–56 | 557 | 296 | 869 | 81 | 10.72 |
| S. Venkataraghavan | Tamil Nadu | 1972–73 | 605 | 147 | 1480 | 81 | 18.27 |
| S. Ramadhin | Commonwealth | 1950–51 | 754.3 | 261 | 1553 | 79 | 19.65 |
| Kapil Dev | Haryana | 1979–80 | 588.5 | 138 | 1580 | 79 | 20.00 |
| H. Verity | MCC | 1933–34 | 482.2 | 179 | 1180 | 78 | 15.12 |
| Khurshid Akhtar | United Bank | 1976–77 | 367.2 | 71 | 1140 | 78 | 14.61 |
| Intikhab Alam | Karachi/PWD | 1967–68 | 596.1 | 139 | 1686 | 77 | 21.89 |
| Pervez Sajjad | PIA | 1969–70 | 542.2 | 154 | 1254 | 77 | 16.28 |
| Ehteshamuddin | National Bank | 1981–82 | 436.5 | 88 | 1400 | 77 | 18.18 |
| G.E. Tribe | Commonwealth | 1950–51 | 592 | 127 | 1619 | 76 | 21.30 |
| B.P. Gupte | Bombay | 1962–63 | 442.3 | 76 | 1458 | 76 | 19.18 |
| Tanvir Ali | Karachi | 1984–85 | 663.3 | 141 | 1869 | 76 | 24.59 |
| Shahid Mahboob | PACO/Karachi | 1983–84 | 596.2 | 110 | 1939 | 74 | 26.20 |
| E.A.S. Prasanna | Karnataka | 1974–75 | 694 | 182 | 1757 | 73 | 24.06 |
| Iqbal Qasim | National Bank | 1977–78 | | | 1320 | 73 | 18.08 |
| S. Venkataraghavan | Madras | 1969–70 | 670.3 | 211 | 1423 | 72 | 19.76 |
| B.S. Chandrasekhar | Mysore | 1972–73 | 605.4 | 153 | 1511 | 72 | 20.98 |
| Abdul Qadir | Habib Bank | 1977–78 | | | 1259 | 72 | 17.48 |
| Abdul Qadir | Lahore/Habib Bank | 1984–85 | 471.5 | 106 | 1349 | 72 | 18.73 |
| W.E. Astill | MCC | 1926–27 | 567.4 | 151 | 1556 | 71 | 21.91 |
| L. Amar Singh | Nawanagar | 1937–38 | 473.2 | 120 | 1019 | 71 | 14.35 |
| G.E. Gomez | West Indians | 1948–49 | 729 | 238 | 1328 | 71 | 18.70 |
| R. Gilchrist | West Indians | 1958–59 | 386.5 | 117 | 964 | 71 | 13.57 |
| B.S. Bedi | Delhi | 1969–70 | 766.2 | 337 | 1263 | 70 | 18.04 |
| Mohammad Nazir | Railways | 1982–83 | 841.1 | 269 | 1451 | 70 | 20.72 |
| Rashid Khan | PIA | 1982–83 | 514.5 | 95 | 1772 | 70 | 25.31 |

# LEADING HOME BOWLERS OF THE ENGLISH SEASON 1894–1985

*Qualifications: 100 wickets, lowest average*

In 1972 the first-class programme was reduced to accommodate a third limited-overs competition. For 1972 and 1976 when no bowler took 100 wickets, the leading place is awarded to the player taking most wickets, the lower average deciding the 1972 entry.

| Season | | | Overs | Mdns | Runs | Wkts | Avge |
|---|---|---|---|---|---|---|---|
| 1894 | T. Richardson | Surrey | 936.3 | 293 | 2024 | 196 | 10.32 |
| 1895 | C.L. Townsend | Gloucestershire | 746.1 | 178 | 1827 | 131 | 13.94 |
| 1896 | J.T. Hearne | Middlesex | 2003.1 | 818 | 3670 | 257 | 14.28 |
| 1897 | T. Richardson | Surrey | 1603.4 | 495 | 3945 | 273 | 14.45 |
| 1898 | J.T. Hearne | Middlesex | 1802.2 | 781 | 3120 | 222 | 14.05 |
| 1899 | A.E. Trott | Middlesex | 1772.4 | 587 | 4086 | 239 | 17.09 |
| 1900 | W. Rhodes | Yorkshire | 1553 | 455 | 3606 | 261 | 13.81 |
| 1901 | W. Rhodes | Yorkshire | 1565 | 505 | 3797 | 251 | 15.12 |
| 1902 | S. Haigh | Yorkshire | 799 | 219 | 1984 | 158 | 12.55 |
| 1903 | W. Mead | Essex | 971.3 | 355 | 1791 | 131 | 13.67 |
| 1904 | J.T. Hearne | Middlesex | 1153.3 | 330 | 2732 | 145 | 18.84 |
| 1905 | S. Haigh | Yorkshire | 831.5 | 220 | 1983 | 120 | 15.37 |
| 1906 | S. Haigh | Yorkshire | 971.3 | 209 | 2540 | 174 | 14.59 |
| 1907 | A.W. Hallam | Nottinghamshire | 937.1 | 302 | 2133 | 168 | 12.69 |

| Season | | | Overs | Mdns | Runs | Wkts | Avge |
|---|---|---|---|---|---|---|---|
| 1908 | S. Haigh | Yorkshire | 623.2 | 176 | 1380 | 103 | 13.39 |
| 1909 | S. Haigh | Yorkshire | 844.2 | 205 | 1702 | 122 | 13.95 |
| 1910 | J.T. Hearne | Middlesex | 752 | 253 | 1523 | 119 | 12.79 |
| 1911 | G.J. Thompson | Northamptonshire | 735.5 | 199 | 1899 | 113 | 16.80 |
| 1912 | C. Blythe | Kent | 919.3 | 241 | 2183 | 178 | 12.26 |
| 1913 | C. Blythe | Kent | 1120.2 | 289 | 2729 | 167 | 16.34 |
| 1914 | C. Blythe | Kent | 1008.4 | 280 | 2583 | 170 | 15.19 |
| 1919 | W. Rhodes | Yorkshire | 1048.3 | 305 | 2365 | 164 | 14.42 |
| 1920 | W. Rhodes | Yorkshire | 1028.4 | 291 | 2123 | 161 | 13.18 |
| 1921 | W. Rhodes | Yorkshire | 963 | 316 | 1872 | 141 | 13.27 |
| 1922 | W. Rhodes | Yorkshire | 814.1 | 312 | 1451 | 119 | 12.19 |
| 1923 | W. Rhodes | Yorkshire | 929 | 345 | 1547 | 134 | 11.54 |
| 1924 | G.G. Macaulay | Yorkshire | 1220.4 | 343 | 2514 | 190 | 13.23 |
| 1925 | C.W.L. Parker | Gloucestershire | 1512.3 | 478 | 3311 | 222 | 14.91 |
| 1926 | W. Rhodes | Yorkshire | 892.4 | 315 | 1709 | 115 | 14.86 |
| 1927 | H. Larwood | Nottinghamshire | 629.2 | 147 | 1695 | 100 | 16.95 |
| 1928 | H. Larwood | Nottinghamshire | 834.5 | 204 | 2003 | 138 | 14.51 |
| 1929 | R.K. Tyldesley | Lancashire | 1114.3 | 350 | 2399 | 154 | 15.57 |
| 1930 | C.W.L. Parker | Gloucestershire | 1016.3 | 301 | 2299 | 179 | 12.84 |
| 1931 | H. Larwood | Nottinghamshire | 651.3 | 142 | 1553 | 129 | 12.03 |
| 1932 | H. Larwood | Nottinghamshire | 866.4 | 203 | 2084 | 162 | 12.86 |
| 1933 | H. Verity | Yorkshire | 1195.4 | 428 | 2553 | 190 | 13.43 |
| 1934 | G.A.E. Paine | Warwickshire | 1285.5 | 463 | 2664 | 156 | 17.07 |
| 1935 | H. Verity | Yorkshire | 1279.2 | 453 | 3032 | 211 | 14.36 |
| 1936 | H. Larwood | Nottinghamshire | 679.1 | 165 | 1544 | 119 | 12.97 |
| 1937 | H. Verity | Yorkshire | 1386.2 | 487 | 3168 | 202 | 15.68 |
| 1938 | W.E. Bowes | Yorkshire | 932.3 | 294 | 1844 | 121 | 15.23 |
| 1939 | H. Verity | Yorkshire | 936.3 | 270 | 2509 | 191 | 13.13 |
| 1946 | A. Booth | Yorkshire | 917.2 | 423 | 1289 | 111 | 11.61 |
| 1947 | T.W.J. Goddard | Gloucestershire | 1451.2 | 344 | 4119 | 238 | 17.30 |
| 1948 | C. Gladwin | Derbyshire | 954.5 | 266 | 2174 | 128 | 16.98 |
| 1949 | T.W.J. Goddard | Gloucestershire | 1187.2 | 326 | 3069 | 160 | 19.18 |
| 1950 | R. Tattersall | Lancashire | 1404.4 | 502 | 2623 | 193 | 13.59 |
| 1951 | R. Appleyard | Yorkshire | 1323.1 | 391 | 2829 | 200 | 14.14 |
| 1952 | A.V. Bedser | Surrey | 1184.4 | 296 | 2530 | 154 | 16.42 |
| 1953 | H.L. Jackson | Derbyshire | 741.4 | 229 | 1574 | 103 | 15.28 |
| 1954 | R. Appleyard | Yorkshire | 1026.3 | 315 | 2221 | 154 | 14.42 |
| 1955 | D. Shackleton | Hampshire | 1220.2 | 438 | 2183 | 159 | 13.72 |
| 1956 | G.A.R. Lock | Surrey | 1058.2 | 437 | 1932 | 155 | 12.46 |
| 1957 | G.A.R. Lock | Surrey | 1194.1 | 449 | 2550 | 212 | 12.02 |
| 1958 | H.L. Jackson | Derbyshire | 829 | 295 | 1572 | 143 | 10.99 |
| 1959 | J.B. Statham | Lancashire | 977.4 | 267 | 2087 | 139 | 15.01 |
| 1960 | J.B. Statham | Lancashire | 844.1 | 274 | 1662 | 135 | 12.31 |
| 1961 | J.A. Flavell | Worcestershire | 1245.2 | 300 | 3043 | 171 | 17.79 |
| 1962 | D.A.D. Sydenham | Surrey | 989.2 | 295 | 2030 | 115 | 17.65 |
| 1963 | F.S. Trueman | Yorkshire | 844.3 | 206 | 1955 | 129 | 15.15 |
| 1964 | T.W. Cartwright | Warwickshire | 1146.2 | 502 | 2141 | 134 | 15.97 |
| 1965 | H.J. Rhodes | Derbyshire | 646.5 | 187 | 1314 | 119 | 11.04 |
| 1966 | D.L. Underwood | Kent | 1104.5 | 475 | 2167 | 157 | 13.80 |
| 1967 | D.L. Underwood | Kent | 979.1 | 495 | 1686 | 136 | 12.39 |
| 1968 | D. Wilson | Yorkshire | 815.5 | 335 | 1521 | 109 | 13.95 |
| 1969 | M.J. Procter | Gloucestershire | 639.3 | 160 | 1623 | 108 | 15.02 |
| 1970 | D.J. Shepherd | Glamorgan | 1123.3 | 420 | 2031 | 106 | 19.16 |
| 1971 | P.J. Sainsbury | Hampshire | 850.5 | 332 | 1874 | 107 | 17.51 |
| 1972 | T.W. Cartwright | Somerset | 863 | 373 | 1827 | 98 | 18.64 |
| 1973 | B.S. Bedi | Northamptonshire | 864.2 | 309 | 1884 | 105 | 17.94 |
| 1974 | A.M.E. Roberts | Hampshire | 727.4 | 198 | 1621 | 119 | 13.62 |
| 1975 | P.G. Lee | Lancashire | 799.5 | 199 | 2067 | 112 | 18.45 |
| 1976 | G.A. Cope | Yorkshire | 916.4 | 288 | 2245 | 93 | 24.13 |
| 1977 | M.J. Procter | Gloucestershire | 777.3 | 226 | 1967 | 109 | 18.04 |
| 1978 | D.L. Underwood | Kent | 815.1 | 359 | 1594 | 110 | 14.49 |
| 1979 | D.L. Underwood | Kent | 799.2 | 335 | 1575 | 106 | 14.85 |
| 1980 | R.D. Jackman | Surrey | 746.2 | 220 | 1864 | 121 | 15.40 |
| 1981 | R.J. Hadlee | Nottinghamshire | 708.4 | 231 | 1564 | 105 | 14.89 |
| 1982 | M.D. Marshall | Hampshire | 822 | 225 | 2108 | 134 | 15.73 |
| 1983 | J.K. Lever | Essex | 569 | 137 | 1726 | 106 | 16.28 |

| Season | | | Overs | Mdns | Runs | Wkts | Avge |
|---|---|---|---|---|---|---|---|
| 1984 | R.J. Hadlee | Nottinghamshire | 772.2 | 245 | 1645 | 117 | 14.05 |
| 1985 | N.V. Radford | Worcestershire | 779.4 | 130 | 2493 | 101 | 24.68 |

The following touring players took one hundred wickets at an average lower than that of the leading home bowler of the season:

| Season | | | Overs | Mdns | Runs | Wkts | Avge |
|---|---|---|---|---|---|---|---|
| 1896 | T.R. McKibbin | Australians | 647.1 | 198 | 1441 | 101 | 14.26 |
| 1907 | R.O. Schwarz | South Africans | 711.3 | 153 | 1616 | 137 | 11.79 |
| 1934 | W.J. O'Reilly | Australians | 870 | 320 | 1858 | 109 | 17.04 |
| 1948 | W.A. Johnston | Australians | 850.1 | 279 | 1675 | 102 | 16.42 |
| 1963 | C.C. Griffith | West Indians | 701.2 | 192 | 1527 | 119 | 12.83 |

# OUTSTANDING BOWLING AVERAGES

| 1864–1899 | | Season | Overs | Mdns | Runs | Wkts | Avge |
|---|---|---|---|---|---|---|---|
| A. Shaw | Nottinghamshire | 1880 | 2133 | 1257 | 1589 | 186 | **8.54** |
| W. Caffyn | Surrey | 1857 | 832.1 | | 1134 | 125 | **9.07** |
| A. Shaw | Nottinghamshire | 1875 | 1755.1 | 1023 | 1495 | 160 | **9.34** |
| A.G. Steel | Lancashire | 1878 | 1223 | 447 | 1547 | 164 | **9.43** |
| A. Shaw | Nottinghamshire | 1879 | 1501 | 870 | 1232 | 128 | **9.62** |
| E. Willsher | Kent | 1868 | 979.2 | 529 | 1128 | 113 | **9.98** |
| J. Crossland | Lancashire | 1882 | 795 | 354 | 1127 | 112 | **10.06** |
| W. Mycroft | Derbyshire | 1878 | 1046.1 | 571 | 1196 | 116 | **10.31** |
| T. Richardson | Surrey | 1894 | 936.3 | 293 | 2024 | 196 | **10.32** |
| J. Briggs | Lancashire | 1888 | 1450.2 | 763 | 1679 | 160 | **10.49** |
| F. Morley | Nottinghamshire | 1879 | 1332 | 651 | 1516 | 143 | **10.60** |
| A. Shaw | Nottinghamshire | 1878 | 2465 | 1486 | 2044 | 189 | **10.81** |
| G.A. Lohmann | Surrey | 1888 | 1649.1 | 783 | 2280 | 209 | **10.90** |
| A. Shaw | Nottinghamshire | 1878 | 2573 | 1586 | 2201 | 201 | **10.95** |
| W. Attewell | Nottinghamshire | 1889 | 1346.2 | 673 | 1635 | 149 | **10.97** |

| 1900–1969 | | | | | | | |
|---|---|---|---|---|---|---|---|
| H.L. Jackson | Derbyshire | 1958 | 829 | 295 | 1572 | 143 | **10.99** |
| H.J. Rhodes | Derbyshire | 1965 | 646.5 | 187 | 1314 | 119 | **11.04** |
| W. Rhodes | Yorkshire | 1923 | 929 | 345 | 1547 | 134 | **11.54** |
| A. Booth | Yorkshire | 1946 | 917.2 | 423 | 1289 | 111 | **11.61** |
| R.O. Schwarz | South Africans | 1907 | 711.3 | 153 | 1616 | 137 | **11.79** |
| G.A.R. Lock | Surrey | 1957 | 1194.1 | 449 | 2550 | 212 | **12.02** |
| H. Larwood | Nottinghamshire | 1931 | 651.3 | 142 | 1553 | 129 | **12.03** |
| G.A.R. Lock | Surrey | 1958 | 1014.4 | 382 | 2055 | 170 | **12.08** |
| W. Rhodes | Yorkshire | 1922 | 814.1 | 312 | 1451 | 119 | **12.19** |
| C. Blythe | Kent | 1912 | 919.3 | 241 | 2183 | 178 | **12.26** |
| J.B. Statham | Lancashire | 1958 | 894.2 | 275 | 1648 | 134 | **12.29** |
| J.B. Statham | Lancashire | 1960 | 844.1 | 274 | 1662 | 135 | **12.31** |
| S. Haigh | Yorkshire | 1912 | 813.4 | 245 | 1541 | 125 | **12.32** |
| D.L. Underwood | Kent | 1967 | 979.1 | 459 | 1686 | 136 | **12.39** |
| A.B. Jackson | Derbyshire | 1965 | 807.5 | 262 | 1491 | 120 | **12.42** |
| G.A.R. Lock | Surrey | 1956 | 1058.2 | 437 | 1932 | 155 | **12.46** |
| J.B. Statham | Lancashire | 1965 | 771 | 205 | 1716 | 137 | **12.52** |
| S. Haigh | Yorkshire | 1902 | 799 | 219 | 1984 | 158 | **12.55** |
| S.G. Smith | Northamptonshire | 1912 | 559 | 165 | 1269 | 100 | **12.69** |
| J.T. Hearne | Middlesex | 1910 | 752 | 253 | 1523 | 119 | **12.79** |
| S. Haigh | Yorkshire | 1907 | 591.3 | 146 | 1308 | 102 | **12.82** |
| C.C. Griffith | West Indians | 1963 | 701.2 | 192 | 1527 | 119 | **12.83** |
| C.W.L. Parker | Gloucestershire | 1930 | 1016.3 | 301 | 2299 | 179 | **12.84** |
| H. Larwood | Nottinghamshire | 1932 | 866.4 | 203 | 2084 | 162 | **12.86** |
| R. Kilner | Yorkshire | 1923 | 1259.5 | 507 | 2040 | 158 | **12.91** |
| H. Larwood | Nottinghamshire | 1936 | 679.1 | 165 | 1544 | 119 | **12.97** |

| 1970–1985 | | | | | | | |
|---|---|---|---|---|---|---|---|
| A.M.E. Roberts | Hampshire | 1974 | 727.4 | 198 | 1621 | 119 | **13.62** |
| R.J. Hadlee | Nottinghamshire | 1984 | 772.2 | 245 | 1645 | 117 | **14.05** |
| D.L. Underwood | Kent | 1978 | 815.1 | 359 | 1594 | 110 | **14.49** |
| D.L. Underwood | Kent | 1979 | 799.2 | 335 | 1575 | 106 | **14.85** |
| R.J. Hadlee | Nottinghamshire | 1981 | 708.4 | 231 | 1564 | 105 | **14.89** |

# MOST EXPENSIVE HUNDRED WICKETS IN A SEASON

|  |  | Season | Overs | Mdns | Runs | Wkts | Avge |
|---|---|---|---|---|---|---|---|
| R. Smith | Essex | 1947 | 1557 | 324 | 4658 | 125 | **37.26** |
| R. Smith | Essex | 1950 | 1267 | 298 | 3547 | 102 | **34.77** |
| O.W. Herman | Hampshire | 1938 | 1098 | 198 | 3263 | 101 | **32.30** |
| C.W.L. Parker | Gloucestershire | 1934 | 1417.2 | 344 | 3724 | 117 | **31.82** |
| R. Smith | Essex | 1949 | 1185.5 | 252 | 3290 | 104 | **31.63** |
| L.C. Braund | Somerset | 1901 | 988.3 | 161 | 3675 | 120 | **30.62** |
| J.K. Nye | Sussex | 1939 | 769.1 | 56 | 3367 | 110 | **30.60** |
| R. Smith | Essex | 1948 | 1241 | 316 | 3157 | 104 | **30.35** |
| J.A. Newman | Hampshire | 1928 | 1118 | 199 | 3394 | 112 | **30.30** |
| D.W. White | Hampshire | 1964 | 1011 | 185 | 3149 | 104 | **30.27** |
| K. Higgs | Lancashire | 1961 | 1098.1 | 237 | 3080 | 102 | **30.19** |

# MOST RUNS CONCEDED IN A SEASON

|  |  | Season | Overs | Mdns | Runs | Wkts | Avge |
|---|---|---|---|---|---|---|---|
| A.P. Freeman | Kent | 1928 | 1976.1 | 423 | **5489** | 304 | 18.05 |
| A.E. Trott | Middlesex | 1900 | 1547.1 | 363 | **4923** | 211 | 23.33 |
| A.P. Freeman | Kent | 1929 | 1670.5 | 381 | **4879** | 267 | 18.27 |
| A.P. Freeman | Kent | 1934 | 1744.4 | 440 | **4753** | 205 | 23.18 |
| T.P.B. Smith | Essex | 1947 | 1606 | 287 | **4667** | 172 | 27.13 |
| R. Smith | Essex | 1947 | 1557 | 324 | **4658** | 125 | 37.26 |
| A.P. Freeman | Kent | 1930 | 1914.3 | 472 | **4632** | 275 | 16.84 |
| A.P. Freeman | Kent | 1935 | 1503.2 | 320 | **4562** | 212 | 21.51 |
| A.P. Freeman | Kent | 1933 | 2039 | 651 | **4549** | 298 | 15.26 |
| A.P. Freeman | Kent | 1931 | 1618 | 360 | **4307** | 276 | 15.60 |
| T. Richardson | Surrey | 1895 | 1690.1 | 463 | **4170** | 290 | 14.37 |
| T.W.J. Goddard | Gloucestershire | 1937 | 1478.1 | 359 | **4158** | 248 | 16.76 |
| A.P. Freeman | Kent | 1932 | 1565.5 | 404 | **4149** | 253 | 16.39 |
| T.W.J. Goddard | Gloucestershire | 1947 | 1451.2 | 344 | **4119** | 238 | 17.30 |
| A.E. Trott | Middlesex | 1899 | 1772.4 | 587 | **4086** | 239 | 17.09 |
| T.W.J. Goddard | Gloucestershire | 1935 | 1553 | 384 | **4073** | 200 | 20.36 |
| T. Richardson | Surrey | 1896 | 1656.2 | 526 | **4015** | 246 | 16.32 |
| A.S. Kennedy | Hampshire | 1921 | 1427 | 316 | **4009** | 186 | 21.55 |

# MOST BALLS BOWLED IN A SEASON

|  |  | Balls | Season | Overs | Mdns | Runs | Wkts | Avge |
|---|---|---|---|---|---|---|---|---|
| A.P. Freeman | Kent | **12234** | 1933 | 2039 | 651 | 4549 | 298 | 15.26 |
| A.P. Freeman | Kent | **11857** | 1928 | 1976.1 | 423 | 5489 | 304 | 18.05 |
| A.P. Freeman | Kent | **11487** | 1930 | 1914.3 | 472 | 4632 | 275 | 16.84 |
| J.H. Wardle | Yorkshire | **11142** | 1952 | 1857 | 810 | 3460 | 177 | 19.54 |
| A. Shaw | Nottinghamshire | **10526** | 1876 | 2631.2 | 1528 | 2601 | 190 | 13.68 |
| A.P. Freeman | Kent | **10468** | 1934 | 1744.4 | 440 | 4753 | 205 | 23.18 |
| C.W.L. Parker | Gloucestershire | **10439** | 1926 | 1739.5 | 556 | 3920 | 213 | 18.40 |
| C.W.L. Parker | Gloucestershire | **10366** | 1927 | 1727.4 | 540 | 3849 | 193 | 19.94 |
| D. Shackleton | Hampshire | **10303** | 1962 | 1717.1 | 678 | 3467 | 172 | 20.15 |
| M.W. Tate | Sussex | **10167** | 1925 | 1694.3 | 472 | 3415 | 228 | 14.97 |
| J.A. Young | Middlesex | **10082** | 1951 | 1680.2 | 741 | 2976 | 157 | 18.95 |
| A.P. Freeman | Kent | **10025** | 1929 | 1670.5 | 381 | 4879 | 267 | 18.27 |
| J.T. Hearne | Middlesex | **10016** | 1896 | 2003.1 | 818 | 3670 | 257 | 14.28 |

# HUNDRED WICKETS IN SEASON OF FIRST-CLASS DEBUT

The following bowlers have taken 100 wickets in the season in which they made their first appearance in first-class cricket (the age listed is that at the start of the season):

|  |  | Age | Season | Overs | Mdns | Runs | Wkts | Avge |
|---|---|---|---|---|---|---|---|---|
| G.P. Harrison | Yorkshire | 21 | 1883 | 786 | 328 | 1326 | 100 | 13.26 |
| A.W. Mold | Lancashire | 25 | 1889 | 678 | 262 | 1205 | 102 | 11.81 |
| C.H.G. Bland | Sussex | 24 | 1897 | 1140.2 | 337 | 2798 | 129 | 21.68 |
| W. Rhodes | Yorkshire | 20 | 1898 | 1240 | 482 | 2249 | 154 | 14.60 |

|  |  | Age | Season | Overs | Mdns | Runs | Wkts | Avge |
|---|---|---|---|---|---|---|---|---|
| F. Barratt | Nottinghamshire | 20 | 1914 | 920 | 192 | 2497 | 115 | 21.71 |
| A. Waddington | Yorkshire | 26 | 1919 | 718.1 | 186 | 1874 | 100 | 18.74 |
| J.M. Gregory | Australians | 23 | 1919 | 830 | 124 | 2383 | 131 | 18.19 |
| G.W. Brook | Worcestershire | 41 | 1930 | 974.4 | 165 | 2889 | 132 | 21.88 |
| C. Cook | Gloucestershire | 24 | 1946 | 1123.1 | 327 | 2477 | 133 | 18.62 |
| D.B. Close | Yorkshire | 18 | 1949 | 1245 | 324 | 3150 | 113 | 27.87 |
| D.L. Underwood | Kent | 17 | 1963 | 941.4 | 376 | 2134 | 101 | 21.12 |

*J.M. Gregory did not make his début in Australia until 1919–20.*

## HUNDRED WICKETS IN FIRST FULL SEASON

The following bowlers took 100 wickets in their first full season having previously played in less than five first-class matches:

|  |  | Season | Wkts | Avge | Previous Matches |
|---|---|---|---|---|---|
| A.G. Steel | Lancashire | 1878 | 164 | 9.40 | 1 |
| J. Beaumont | Surrey | 1885 | 112 | 17.83 | 4 |
| H. Baldwin | Hampshire | 1895 | 114 | 15.96 | 1 |
|  | *His first match was in 1877* |  |  |  |  |
| W.R. Cuttell | Lancashire | 1897 | 120 | 16.46 | 2 |
| A.J. Paish | Gloucestershire | 1899 | 137 | 18.54 | 1 |
| C. Blythe | Kent | 1900 | 114 | 18.47 | 4 |
| T. Jayes | Leicestershire | 1905 | 102 | 23.79 | 3 |
| N.A. Knox | Surrey | 1905 | 129 | 21.44 | 2 |
| P. Jeeves | Warwickshire | 1913 | 106 | 20.88 | 2 |
| F.J. Durston | Middlesex | 1920 | 113 | 21.88 | 4 |
| W.E. Merritt | New Zealanders | 1927 | 107 | 23.64 | 1 |
| A.W. Wellard | Somerset | 1929 | 131 | 21.38 | 2 |
| A.V. Bedser | Surrey | 1946 | 128 | 20.13 | 2 |
| C. Gladwin | Derbyshire | 1946 | 109 | 18.36 | 4 |
| S. Ramadhin | West Indians | 1950 | 135 | 14.28 | 2 |
| A.L. Valentine | West Indians | 1950 | 123 | 17.94 | 2 |
| R. Appleyard | Yorkshire | 1951 | 200 | 14.14 | 3 |

## EARLIEST DATES FOR TAKING 100, 200 AND 300 WICKETS

| 100 wickets | **12 June 1896** | J.T. Hearne | Middlesex |
|---|---|---|---|
|  | **12 June 1931** | C.W.L. Parker | Gloucestershire |
|  | 13 June 1931 | A.P. Freeman | Kent |
|  | 14 June 1930 | A.P. Freeman | Kent |
|  | 17 June 1925 | M.W. Tate | Sussex |
|  | 17 June 1932 | A.P. Freeman | Kent |
| 200 wickets | **27 July 1928** | A.P. Freeman | Kent |
|  | 1 August 1931 | A.P. Freeman | Kent |
|  | 6 August 1930 | A.P. Freeman | Kent |
|  | 7 August 1929 | A.P. Freeman | Kent |
|  | 14 August 1933 | A.P. Freeman | Kent |
| 300 wickets | **15 September 1928** | A.P. Freeman | Kent |

## NO-BALLED FOR THROWING

| J. Willes | Kent v MCC | Lord's | 1822 |
|---|---|---|---|
| *No-balled for bowling round-arm* |  |  |  |
| E. Willsher | England v Surrey | Oval | 1862 |
| *No-balled six times by John Lillywhite* |  |  |  |
| T.W.S. Wills | Victoria v New South Wales | Melbourne | 1871–72 |
| *No-balled three times by umpire Sellers* |  |  |  |
| — Burns | Nelson v Wellington | Nelson | 1881–82 |
| *No-balled once by J.H. Haughton* |  |  |  |
| R.W. Wardill | Victoria v Tasmania | Launceston | 1872–73 |
| *No-balled three times by W.L. Sidebottom* |  |  |  |

| | | | |
|---|---|---|---|
| D.W. Gregory | Rest of Australia v Victoria | Melbourne | 1872–73 |

*Once*

| | | | |
|---|---|---|---|
| G.E. Jowett | Lancashire v Surrey | Liverpool | 1885 |

*No-balled by umpire Platts*

| | | | |
|---|---|---|---|
| E.J. Coxon | Gentlemen of England v Oxford U. | Oxford | 1890 |
| E. Jones | Australia v England | Melbourne | 1897–98 |

*No-balled once by J. Phillips*

| | | | |
|---|---|---|---|
| E. Jones | South Australia v A.E. Stoddart's XI | Adelaide | 1897–98 |

*No-balled once by J. Phillips*

| | | | |
|---|---|---|---|
| C.B. Fry | Sussex v Nottinghamshire | Nottingham | 1898 |
| C.B. Fry | Sussex v Oxford University | Hove | 1898 |
| C.B. Fry | Sussex v Middlesex | Lord's | 1898 |
| F.J. Hopkins | Warwickshire v Kent | Tonbridge | 1898 |
| E.R.C. Bradford | Hampshire v Leicestershire | Leicester | 1899 |
| E.R.C. Bradford | Hampshire v Australians | Southampton | 1899 |

*No-balled by both umpires*

| | | | |
|---|---|---|---|
| R.G. Hardstaff | Nottinghamshire v Australians | Nottingham | 1899 |
| C.B. Fry | Sussex v Gloucestershire | Hove | 1900 |
| A.W. Mold | Lancashire v Nottinghamshire | Nottingham | 1900 |
| E.J. Tyler | Somerset v Surrey | Taunton | 1900 |

*No-balled twice in one over by J. Phillips*

| | | | |
|---|---|---|---|
| J.J. Marsh | New South Wales v Victoria | Melbourne | 1900–01 |

*No-balled three times by R.W. Crockett*

| | | | |
|---|---|---|---|
| J.J. Marsh | New South Wales v Victoria | Sydney | 1900–01 |

*No-balled 17 times by R.W. Crockett*

| | | | |
|---|---|---|---|
| T.H. Howard | New South Wales v Victoria | Sydney | 1900–01 |

*No-balled twice by R.W. Crockett*

| | | | |
|---|---|---|---|
| A.W. Mold | Lancashire v Somerset | Manchester | 1901 |

*No-balled 16 times in 10 overs by J. Phillips*

| | | | |
|---|---|---|---|
| A.D. Downes | New Zealand v Lord Hawke's XI | Christchurch | 1902–03 |
| A.J. Paish | Gloucestershire v Nottinghamshire | Bristol | 1903 |
| A.J. Paish | Gloucestershire v Yorkshire | Bristol | 1903 |

*No-balled by W.A.J. West in consecutive matches, on four occasions in second match*

| | | | |
|---|---|---|---|
| P.R. May | MCC v Otago | Dunedin | 1906–07 |

*No-balled once for taking a shy at the wicket*

| | | | |
|---|---|---|---|
| G.H.T. Simpson-<br>Hayward | Lord Brackley's XI v Barbados | Bridgetown | 1904–05 |

*No-balled once by J. Moss for taking a shy at the wicket*

| | | | |
|---|---|---|---|
| R. Whitehead | Lancashire v Nottinghamshire | Manchester | 1908 |

*His début match in first-class cricket, he also scored 131\**

| | | | |
|---|---|---|---|
| F.W. Pitcher | Victoria v South Africans | Melbourne | 1910–11 |

*No-balled four times in his first over by R.W. Crockett and once in his second, next day, by umpire Young*

| | | | |
|---|---|---|---|
| G. John | West Indian XI v MCC | Georgetown | 1910–11 |
| O.H. Gilkes | Barbados v Trinidad | Bridgetown | 1919–20 |

*No-balled once*

| | | | |
|---|---|---|---|
| R.A. Halcombe | Western Australia v Victoria | Melbourne | 1929–30 |

*No-balled by A.N. Barlow 8 times in succession in the only over he bowled*

| | | | |
|---|---|---|---|
| R.A. Halcombe | Western Australia v Tasmania | Hobart | 1929–30 |

*No-balled twice by F. Buttsworth and ten times in succession in one over by W. Lonergan*

| | | | |
|---|---|---|---|
| E. Gilbert | Queensland v Victoria | Melbourne | 1931–32 |

*No-balled by A.N. Barlow 8 times in 2 overs*

| | | | |
|---|---|---|---|
| S. Mubarak Ali | Trinidad v Barbados | Bridgetown | 1941–42 |

*No-balled 30 times in one innings*

| | | | |
|---|---|---|---|
| R.R. Frankish | Western Australia v Victoria | Melbourne | 1950–51 |
| M.R. Rege | Maharashtra v MCC | Poona | 1951–52 |

*No-balled twice in the only over he bowled by N.D. Nagarwalla from the bowler's end*

| | | | |
|---|---|---|---|
| C.N. McCarthy | Cambridge University v Worcestershire | Worcester | 1952 |

*No-balled by P. Corrall*

| | | | |
|---|---|---|---|
| D.J. Insole | Essex v Northamptonshire | Northampton | 1952 |
| G.A.R. Lock | Surrey v Indians | Oval | 1952 |

*No-balled 3 times by W.F.F. Price, twice in one over*

| | | | |
|---|---|---|---|
| G.A.R. Lock | England v West Indies | Kingston | 1953–54 |
| G.A.R. Lock | MCC v Barbados | Bridgetown | 1953–54 |

*No-balled by both umpires, once by one and twice in three balls by the other*

| | | | |
|---|---|---|---|
| D.B. Pearson | Worcestershire v Gloucestershire | Bristol | 1954 |
| K.N. Slater | Western Australia v Victoria | Melbourne | 1957–58 |
| G.M. Griffin | Natal v Transvaal | Durban | 1958–59 |

| G.M. Griffin | Natal v Border & Eastern Province | East London | 1958–59 |
| S.C. Stayers | British Guiana v Barbados | Bridgetown | 1958–59 |
| D.B. Pearson | Worcestershire v Indians | Worcester | 1959 |

*No-balled 5 times by J.S. Buller*

| D.B. Pearson | Worcestershire v Essex | Worcester | 1959 |
| G.A.R. Lock | Surrey v Glamorgan | Cardiff | 1959 |
| K.J. Aldridge | Worcestershire v Leicestershire | Kidderminster | 1959 |

*No-balled twice by J.S. Buller*

| J.J. McLaughlin | Queensland v New South Wales | Sydney | 1959–60 |

*No-balled once in his only over by J. Bowden*

| G.A.R. Lock | Surrey v Cambridge University | Cambridge | 1960 |
| K.J. Aldridge | Worcestershire v Glamorgan | Pontypridd | 1960 |
| H.J. Rhodes | Derbyshire v South Africans | Derby | 1960 |

*No-balled 6 times by P.A. Gibb*

| G.M. Griffin | South Africans v MCC | Lord's | 1960 |

*No-balled once by F.S. Lee and twice by J.G. Langridge. He was also called for dragging by F.S. Lee each time J.G. Langridge no-balled him for throwing*

| D.B. Pearson | Worcestershire v Northamptonshire | Dudley | 1960 |

*No-balled twice by T.J. Bartley*

| G.M. Griffin | South Africans v Nottinghamshire | Nottingham | 1960 |

*No-balled 11 times in the first innings, 5 times for throwing and 6 times for dragging. He was called 3 times for throwing by T.J. Bartley and twice by W.H. Copson. No-balled for throwing 3 times in the second innings*

| L.E. Bryant | Somerset v Gloucestershire | Bath | 1960 |

*No-balled 5 times by H. Yarnold, 4 times in one over*

| G.M. Griffin | South Africans v Hampshire | Southampton | 1960 |

*No-balled by both umpires, once each in first innings, and 4 times in the second innings, 3 times by J.H. Parks and once by H. Elliott*

| G.M. Griffin | South Africa v England | Lord's | 1960 |

*No-balled 11 times by F.S. Lee in England's only innings*

| D.W. White | Hampshire v Sussex | Hove | 1960 |

*No-balled 3 times by P.A. Gibb, twice in first innings and once in the second*

| R.T. Simpson | Nottinghamshire v Derbyshire | Nottingham | 1960 |

*No-balled once by H. Yarnold*

| B. Quigley | South Australia v Victoria | Adelaide | 1960–61 |

*No-balled twice by C.J. Egar from the bowler's end*

| R. Jairam | Hyderabad v Madras | Madras | 1960–61 |

*No-balled once*

| Haseeb Ahsan | Pakistan v India | Bombay | 1960–61 |
| B.K. Bose | East Zone v Pakistanis | Jamshedpur | 1960–61 |

*No-balled 3 times by S.K. Raghunatha Rao*

| H.J. Rhodes | Derbyshire v Northamptonshire | Derby | 1961 |

*No-balled 3 times in one over by P.A. Gibb*

| A. D'Souza | Karachi Blues v Lahore B | Lahore | 1961–62 |

*No-balled three times by Munawar Hussain*

| G.M. Griffin | Natal v Rhodesia | Salisbury | 1961–62 |
| P. Bhagwandas | Central Zone v MCC | Nagpur | 1961–62 |

*No-balled twice*

| G.V. Brooks | South Australia v New Zealanders | Adelaide | 1961–62 |

*No-balled by C.J. Egar*

| C.C. Griffith | Barbados v Indians | Bridgetown | 1961–62 |

*No-balled once by H.B. de C. Jordan*

| G.M. Griffin | Rhodesia v North-Eastern Transvaal | Salisbury | 1962–63 |

*No-balled 7 times by J. Fletcher*

| J. Khattar | Madhya Pradesh v Rajasthan | Jabalpur | 1962–63 |

*No-balled by N.D. Sane from the bowler's end*

| I. Meckiff | Victoria v South Australia | Adelaide | 1962–63 |

*No-balled once by J. Kierse*

| I. Meckiff | Victoria v Queensland | Brisbane | 1962–63 |

*No-balled once by W. Priem*

| K. Gillhouley | Nottinghamshire v Gloucestershire | Cheltenham | 1963 |

*No-balled 4 times in succession by J.S. Buller*

| I. Meckiff | Australia v South Africa | Brisbane | 1963–64 |

*No-balled 4 times in his only over by C.J. Egar and subsequently announced his retirement from all classes of cricket*

| P.J. Lawrence | Middlesex v Sussex | Lord's | 1964 |

*No-balled twice in one over by R. Aspinall*

| I.R. Redpath | Australians v Glamorgan | Cardiff | 1964 |

*No-balled once by J.G. Langridge*

| E.P. Illingworth | Victoria v South Australia | Adelaide | 1964–65 |

*No-balled twice by C.J. Egar and once by J.J. Ryan*

| K.N. Slater | Western Australia v New South Wales | Sydney | 1964–65 |

*No-balled once by E.F. Wykes*

| H.J. Rhodes | Derbyshire v South Africans | Chesterfield | 1965 |

*No-balled twice by J.S. Buller*

| D.W. White | Hampshire v Lancashire | Manchester | 1965 |

*No-balled once by J.S. Buller. White stumbled in the act of delivery and then flung the ball – apparently in fun – at D.M. Green, the batsman*

| R.C. Collymore | British Guiana v Jamaica | Kingston | 1965–66 |

*No-balled 5 times by D. Sang Hue*

| C.C. Griffith | West Indians v Lancashire | Manchester | 1966 |

*No-balled once by A.E. Fagg*

| P. Roberts | Trinidad v Jamaica | Kingston | 1966–67 |

*No-balled 3 times in one over by D. Sang Hue*

| D. Archer | Trinidad v Windward Islands | Port-of-Spain | 1966–67 |
| B. Fisher | Queensland v New South Wales | Sydney | 1967–68 |

*No-balled once by E.F. Wykes*

| S. Abid Ali | India v New Zealand | Christchurch | 1967–68 |

*No-balled once by F.R. Goodall; he deliberately threw one ball in protest against the action of G.A. Bartlett who had not been 'called'*

| J.D. Higgs | Australians v Leicestershire | Leicester | 1975 |
| S. Luthra | Delhi v Bihar | Delhi | 1975–76 |

*Four times*

| K.O. Cameron | Guyana v Jamaica | Montego Bay | 1975–76 |

*No-balled three times by W. Malcolm*

| G.V. Kumar | Karnataka v Uttar Pradesh | Mohan Nagar | 1977–78 |

*No-balled once from the bowler's end by Reporter*

| B. Yardley | Australians v Jamaica | Kingston | 1977–78 |

*No-balled twice by D. Sang Hue*

| Suresh Shanbal | Karnataka v Hyderabad | Hyderabad | 1979–80 |

*No-balled seven times*

| Kamal Das | East Zone v England XI | Jamshedpur | 1981–82 |

*No-balled once*

| G.A. Gooch | England XI v East Zone | Jamshedpur | 1981–82 |

*No-balled once whilst impersonating J.E. Emburey*

| M.F. Gill | Central Districts v Auckland | Auckland | 1981–82 |

*No-balled twice by B.V. Denison and once by J.D. Matheson*

| H.L. Alleyne | Barbados v Jamaica | Kingston | 1982–83 |

*No-balled twice by W. Malcolm*

| H.L. Alleyne | Barbados v Trinidad | Port-of-Spain | 1982–83 |

*No-balled twice by Mohammed Hosein*

| P.N. Webb | Auckland v Central Districts | Palmerston North | 1984–85 |

*No-balled twice*

| H. Joseph | Trinidad v Australians | Pointe-à-Pierre | 1984–85 |

# FURTHEST FLIGHTS FOR BAILS

The longest recorded distances for a bail to travel after a batsman has been bowled:

| Yd | In | Bowler | Batsman | | | |
|----|-----|--------------|----------------|-------------------------------|------------|---------|
| 67 | 6 | R.D. Burrows | W. Huddleston | Worcestershire v Lancashire | Manchester | 1911 |
| 66 | 0 | H. Larwood | G.W. Martin | MCC v Tasmania | Launceston | 1928–29 |
| 64 | 6 | R.D. Burrows | A.C. MacLaren | Worcestershire v Lancashire | Manchester | 1901 |
| 63 | 6 | A.W. Mold | G.A. Lohmann | Lancashire v Surrey | Oval | 1896 |

# CAREER RECORDS

## 2000 WICKETS

*1970* denotes the 1970–71 overseas season. '100w' shows the number of times the bowler has taken 100 wickets in a season.

| | Career | Runs | Wkts | Avge | 100w |
|---|---|---|---|---|---|
| W. Rhodes | 1898–1930 | 69993 | **4187** | 16.71 | 23 |
| A.P. Freeman | 1914–1936 | 69577 | **3776** | 18.42 | 17 |
| C.W.L. Parker | 1903–1935 | 63817 | **3278** | 19.46 | 16 |
| J.T. Hearne | 1888–1923 | 54361 | **3061** | 17.75 | 15 |
| T.W.J. Goddard | 1922–1952 | 59116 | **2979** | 19.84 | 16 |
| A.S. Kennedy | 1907–1936 | 61034 | **2874** | 21.43 | 15 |
| D. Shackleton | 1948–1969 | 53303 | **2857** | 18.65 | 20 |
| G.A.R. Lock | 1946–*1970* | 54710 | **2844** | 19.23 | 14 |
| F.J. Titmus | 1949–1982 | 63313 | **2830** | 22.37 | 16 |
| W.G. Grace | 1865–1908 | 51545 | **2876** | 17.92 | 9 |
| M.W. Tate | 1912–1937 | 50567 | **2784** | 18.16 | 13+1 |
| G.H. Hirst | 1891–1929 | 51372 | **2742** | 18.73 | 15 |
| C. Blythe | 1899–1914 | 42099 | **2503** | 16.81 | 14 |
| W.E. Astill | 1906–1939 | 57783 | **2431** | 23.76 | 9 |
| D.L. Underwood | 1963–1985 | 47327 | **2368** | 19.98 | 10 |
| J.C. White | 1909–1937 | 43759 | **2356** | 18.57 | 14 |
| W.E. Hollies | 1932–1957 | 48656 | **2323** | 20.94 | 14 |
| F.S. Trueman | 1949–1969 | 42154 | **2304** | 18.29 | 12 |
| J.B. Statham | 1950–1968 | 36995 | **2260** | 16.36 | 13 |
| R.T.D. Perks | 1930–1955 | 53770 | **2233** | 24.07 | 16 |
| J. Briggs | 1879–1900 | 35432 | **2221** | 15.95 | 12 |
| D.J. Shepherd | 1950–1972 | 47298 | **2218** | 21.32 | 12 |
| E.G. Dennett | 1903–1926 | 42640 | **2151** | 19.82 | 12 |
| T. Richardson | 1892–1905 | 38794 | **2105** | 18.42 | 10 |
| T.E. Bailey | 1945–1967 | 48170 | **2082** | 23.13 | 9 |
| R. Illingworth | 1951–1983 | 42023 | **2072** | 20.28 | 10 |
| F.E. Woolley | 1906–1938 | 41058 | **2066** | 19.87 | 8 |
| G. Geary | 1912–1938 | 41339 | **2063** | 20.03 | 11 |
| D.V.P. Wright | 1932–1957 | 49305 | **2056** | 23.98 | 10 |
| J.A. Newman | 1906–1930 | 51211 | **2032** | 25.20 | 9 |
| A. Shaw | 1864–1897 | 24579 | **2027** | 12.12 | 9 |
| S. Haigh | 1895–1913 | 32091 | **2012** | 15.94 | 11 |

## 1000 WICKETS

*1970* denotes the 1970–71 overseas season. '100w' shows the number of times the bowler has taken 100 wickets in a season.

| | Career | Runs | Wkts | Avge | 100w |
|---|---|---|---|---|---|
| Allen, D.A. | 1953–1972 | 28585 | **1209** | 23.64 | 1 |
| Arnold, E.G. | 1899–1913 | 24763 | **1069** | 23.16 | 4 |
| Arnold, G.G. | 1963–1982 | 24761 | **1130** | 21.91 | 1 |
| Astill, W.E. | 1906–1939 | 57783 | **2431** | 23.76 | 9 |
| Attewell, W. | 1881–1900 | 29896 | **1950** | 15.33 | 10 |
| Bailey, T.E. | 1945–1967 | 48170 | **2082** | 23.13 | 9 |
| Bannister, J.D. | 1950–1968 | 26258 | **1198** | 21.91 | 4 |
| Barratt, F. | 1914–1931 | 27803 | **1224** | 22.71 | 5 |
| Bedi, B.S. | 1961–*1980* | 33843 | **1560** | 21.69 | 2 |
| Bedser, A.V. | 1939–1960 | 39281 | **1924** | 20.41 | 11 |
| Bestwick, W. | 1898–1925 | 30998 | **1457** | 21.27 | 4 |
| Birkenshaw, J. | 1958–1981 | 29276 | **1073** | 27.28 | 2 |
| Blythe, C. | 1899–1914 | 42099 | **2503** | 16.81 | 14 |
| Bowes, W.E. | 1928–1947 | 27470 | **1639** | 16.76 | 9 |
| Boyes, G.S. | 1921–1939 | 34610 | **1472** | 23.51 | 3 |
| Braund, L.C. | 1896–1920 | 30388 | **1114** | 27.27 | 4 |
| Briggs, J. | 1879–1900 | 35432 | **2221** | 15.95 | 12 |
| Brown, A.S. | 1953–1976 | 31546 | **1230** | 25.64 | 2 |

| | Career | Runs | Wkts | Avge | 100w |
|---|---|---|---|---|---|
| Brown, D.J. | 1961–1982 | 28961 | **1165** | 24.85 | — |
| Brown, F.R. | 1930–1961 | 32007 | **1221** | 26.21 | 3 |
| Buckenham, C.P. | 1899–1914 | 29157 | **1152** | 25.30 | 6 |
| Cartwright, T.W. | 1952–1977 | 29357 | **1536** | 19.11 | 8 |
| Chandrasekhar, B.S. | *1963–1979* | 25547 | **1063** | 24.03 | — |
| Clark, E.W. | 1922–1947 | 25967 | **1208** | 21.49 | 2 |
| Clay, J.C. | 1921–1949 | 26028 | **1317** | 19.76 | 3 |
| Close, D.B. | 1949–1985 | 30876 | **1170** | 26.38 | 2 |
| Coldwell, L.J. | 1955–1969 | 22791 | **1076** | 21.18 | 2 |
| Cook, C. | 1946–1964 | 36578 | **1782** | 20.52 | 9 |
| Copson, W.H. | 1932–1950 | 20752 | **1094** | 18.96 | 3 |
| Cornford, J.H. | 1931–1952 | 26999 | **1019** | 26.49 | — |
| Cottam, R.M.H. | 1963–1976 | 21125 | **1010** | 20.91 | 3 |
| Cox, G.R. | 1895–1928 | 42138 | **1843** | 22.86 | 5 |
| Dean, H. | 1906–1921 | 23606 | **1301** | 18.14 | 8 |
| Dean, J. | 1835–1861 | — | **1140** | — | — |
| Dennett, E.G. | 1903–1926 | 42640 | **2151** | 19.82 | 12 |
| Dooland, B. | *1945*–1957 | 22332 | **1016** | 21.98 | 5 |
| Douglas, J.W.H.T. | 1901–1930 | 44159 | **1893** | 23.32 | 7 |
| Durston, F.J. | 1919–1933 | 29279 | **1329** | 22.03 | 6 |
| East, R.E. | 1965–1984 | 26210 | **1019** | 25.72 | — |
| Eastman, L.C. | 1920–1939 | 26941 | **1006** | 26.78 | — |
| Edmonds, P.H. | 1971–1985 | 28209 | **1129** | 24.98 | — |
| Emmett, T. | 1866–1888 | 21334 | **1572** | 13.57 | 4 |
| Fender, P.G.H. | 1910–1936 | 47440 | **1894** | 25.04 | 7 |
| Field, E.F. | 1897–1920 | 24091 | **1026** | 23.48 | 3 |
| Fielder, A. | 1900–1914 | 26852 | **1277** | 21.02 | 5 |
| Flavell, J.A. | 1949–1967 | 32847 | **1529** | 21.48 | 8 |
| Flowers, W. | 1877–1896 | 18887 | **1188** | 15.89 | 2 |
| Freeman, A.P. | 1914–1936 | 69577 | **3776** | 18.42 | 17 |
| Geary, G. | 1912–1938 | 41339 | **2063** | 20.03 | 11 |
| Gibbs, L.R. | *1953–1975* | 27878 | **1024** | 27.22 | 1 |
| Giffen, G. | *1877–1903* | 21782 | **1023** | 21.29 | 3 |
| Gifford, N. | 1960–1985 | 45097 | **1935** | 23.30 | 4 |
| Gladwin, C. | 1939–1958 | 30265 | **1653** | 18.30 | 12 |
| Goddard, T.W.J. | 1922–1952 | 59116 | **2979** | 19.84 | 16 |
| Gover, A.R. | 1928–1948 | 36753 | **1555** | 23.63 | 8 |
| Grace, W.G. | 1865–1908 | 50932 | **2809** | 18.13 | 9 |
| Grimmett, C.V. | *1911–1940* | 31740 | **1424** | 22.28 | 3 |
| Grundy, J. | 1850–1869 | — | **1126** | — | 1 |
| Gunn, J.R. | 1896–1932 | 30466 | **1242** | 24.52 | 4 |
| Hadlee, R.J. | *1971*–1985 | 20426 | **1092** | 18.70 | 2 |
| Haig, N.E. | 1912–1936 | 30698 | **1117** | 27.48 | 5 |
| Haigh, S. | 1895–1913 | 32091 | **2012** | 15.94 | 11 |
| Hallam, A.W. | 1895–1910 | 19255 | **1012** | 19.02 | 3 |
| Hearne, A. | 1884–1910 | 23120 | **1160** | 19.93 | — |
| Hearne, J.T. | 1888–1923 | 54361 | **3061** | 17.75 | 15 |
| Hearne, J.W. | 1909–1936 | 44944 | **1839** | 24.43 | 5 |
| Herman, O.W. | 1929–1948 | 28222 | **1045** | 27.00 | 5 |
| Higgs, K. | 1958–1982 | 36196 | **1531** | 23.64 | 5 |
| Hillyer, W.R. | 1835–1853 | — | **1475** | — | 7 |
| Hilton, M.J. | 1946–1961 | 19536 | **1006** | 19.41 | 4 |
| Hirst, G.H. | 1891–1929 | 51372 | **2742** | 18.73 | 15 |
| Hitch, J.W. | 1907–1925 | 29915 | **1387** | 21.56 | 7 |
| Hobbs, R.N.S. | 1961–1981 | 29776 | **1099** | 27.09 | 2 |
| Hollies, W.E. | 1932–1957 | 48656 | **2323** | 20.94 | 14 |
| Howorth, R. | 1933–1951 | 29427 | **1345** | 21.87 | 9 |
| Illingworth, R. | 1951–1983 | 42023 | **2072** | 20.28 | 10 |
| Imran Khan | *1969*–1985 | 23575 | **1074** | 21.95 | — |
| Intikhab Alam | *1957*–1982 | 43472 | **1571** | 27.67 | 1 |
| Jackman, R.D. | 1966–*1982* | 31978 | **1402** | 22.80 | 1 |
| Jackson, H.L. | 1947–1963 | 30101 | **1733** | 17.36 | 10 |
| Jackson, P.F. | 1929–1950 | 30521 | **1159** | 26.33 | 4 |
| Jenkins, R.O. | 1938–1958 | 30925 | **1309** | 23.62 | 5 |
| Jepson, A. | 1938–1959 | 30567 | **1051** | 29.08 | 1 |
| Jupp, V.W.C. | 1909–1938 | 38166 | **1658** | 23.01 | 10 |

|  | Career | Runs | Wkts | Avge | 100w |
|---|---|---|---|---|---|
| Kennedy, A.S. | 1907–1936 | 61034 | **2874** | 21.23 | 15 |
| King, J.H. | 1895–1925 | 30289 | **1204** | 25.15 | 2 |
| Knight, B.R. | 1955–1969 | 26203 | **1089** | 24.06 | 5 |
| Laker, J.C. | 1946–1964 | 35791 | **1944** | 18.41 | 11 |
| Langford, B.A. | 1953–1974 | 34964 | **1410** | 24.79 | 5 |
| Langridge, James | 1924–1953 | 34524 | **1530** | 22.56 | 6 |
| Larwood, H. | 1924–1938 | 24994 | **1427** | 17.51 | 8 |
| Lees, W.S. | 1896–1911 | 30008 | **1402** | 21.40 | 7 |
| Lever, J.K. | 1967–1985 | 36827 | **1549** | 23.77 | 4 |
| Lillywhite, James | 1862–1881 | 18436 | **1210** | 15.23 | 1 |
| Llewellyn, C.B. | 1894–1912 | 23715 | **1013** | 23.41 | 3 |
| Loader, P.J. | 1951–1963 | 25260 | **1326** | 19.04 | 7 |
| Lock, G.A.R. | 1946–1970 | 54710 | **2844** | 19.23 | 14 |
| Lockwood, W. | 1886–1904 | 25247 | **1376** | 18.34 | 7 |
| Lohmann, G.A. | 1884–1897 | 25298 | **1841** | 13.74 | 8 |
| Macaulay, G.G. | 1920–1935 | 32440 | **1837** | 17.65 | 10 |
| McDonald, E.A. | 1909–1935 | 28966 | **1395** | 20.76 | 7 |
| McKenzie, G.D. | 1959–1975 | 32868 | **1219** | 26.96 | — |
| Martin, F. | 1885–1900 | 22903 | **1317** | 17.39 | 6 |
| Mayer, J.H. | 1926–1939 | 25404 | **1144** | 22.20 | 2 |
| Mead, W. | 1892–1913 | 36388 | **1916** | 18.99 | 10 |
| Mercer, J. | 1919–1947 | 37210 | **1591** | 23.38 | 9 |
| Mitchell, T.B. | 1928–1939 | 30543 | **1483** | 20.59 | 10 |
| Mold, A.W. | 1889–1901 | 26012 | **1673** | 15.54 | 9 |
| Morgan, D.C. | 1950–1969 | 31302 | **1248** | 25.08 | — |
| Morley, F. | 1872–1883 | 17103 | **1274** | 13.42 | 7 |
| Mortimore, J.B. | 1950–1975 | 41904 | **1807** | 23.18 | 3 |
| Moss, A.E. | 1950–1968 | 27035 | **1301** | 20.78 | 5 |
| Mynn, A. | 1832–1859 | — | **1033** | — | — |
| Newman, J.A. | 1906–1930 | 51111 | **2032** | 25.15 | 9 |
| Nichols, M.S. | 1924–1939 | 39666 | **1833** | 21.63 | 11 |
| Old, C.M. | 1966–1985 | 25081 | **1071** | 23.41 | — |
| Paine, G.A.E. | 1926–1947 | 23334 | **1021** | 22.85 | 5 |
| Parker, C.W.L. | 1903–1935 | 63817 | **3278** | 19.46 | 16 |
| Parkin, C.H. | 1906–1926 | 18434 | **1048** | 17.58 | 4 |
| Peate, E. | 1879–1890 | 14511 | **1076** | 13.48 | 6 |
| Peel, R. | 1882–1899 | 28758 | **1776** | 16.19 | 8 |
| Perks, R.T.D. | 1930–1955 | 53770 | **2233** | 24.07 | 16 |
| Pocock, P.I. | 1964–1985 | 41553 | **1577** | 26.34 | 1 |
| Pollard, R. | 1933–1952 | 25314 | **1122** | 22.56 | 7 |
| Preston, K.C. | 1948–1964 | 30543 | **1160** | 26.33 | 1 |
| Procter, M.J. | 1965–1983 | 27249 | **1407** | 19.36 | 2 |
| Relf, A.E. | 1900–1921 | 39724 | **1897** | 20.94 | 11 |
| Rhodes, H.J. | 1953–1975 | 21145 | **1073** | 19.70 | 3 |
| Rhodes, W. | 1898–1930 | 69993 | **4187** | 16.71 | 23 |
| Richardson, T. | 1892–1905 | 38794 | **2105** | 18.42 | 10 |
| Richmond, T.L. | 1912–1932 | 24959 | **1176** | 21.22 | 7 |
| Ridgway, F. | 1946–1961 | 25381 | **1069** | 23.74 | 1 |
| Robinson, E.P. | 1934–1952 | 22784 | **1009** | 22.58 | 5 |
| Robson, E. | 1895–1923 | 30334 | **1147** | 26.44 | — |
| Root, C.F. | 1910–1933 | 31933 | **1512** | 21.11 | 9 |
| Ryan, F.P. | 1919–1931 | 21311 | **1013** | 21.03 | 5 |
| Sainsbury, P.J. | 1954–1976 | 31777 | **1316** | 24.14 | 2 |
| Santall, S. | 1894–1914 | 29250 | **1220** | 23.97 | 1 |
| Sarfraz Nawaz | 1967–1984 | 24744 | **1005** | 24.62 | 1 |
| Shackleton, D. | 1948–1969 | 53303 | **2857** | 18.65 | 20 |
| Shaw, A. | 1864–1897 | 24579 | **2028** | 12.12 | 9 |
| Shepherd, D.J. | 1950–1972 | 47298 | **2218** | 21.32 | 12 |
| Shepherd, J.N. | 1964–1985 | 31976 | **1155** | 27.68 | — |
| Sims, J.M. | 1929–1953 | 39401 | **1581** | 24.92 | 8 |
| Sinfield, R.A. | 1921–1939 | 28734 | **1173** | 24.49 | 4 |
| Smith, D.R. | 1956–1970 | 29655 | **1250** | 23.72 | 5 |
| Smith, E. | 1951–1971 | 31448 | **1217** | 25.84 | 1 |
| Smith, H.A. | 1925–1939 | 27968 | **1076** | 25.99 | 5 |
| Smith, R. | 1934–1956 | 41265 | **1350** | 30.56 | 7 |
| Smith, T.P.B. | 1929–1952 | 45059 | **1697** | 26.55 | 6 |

| | Career | Runs | Wkts | Avge | 100w |
|---|---|---|---|---|---|
| Smith, W.C. | 1900–1914 | 18910 | **1077** | 17.55 | 3 |
| Snow, J.A. | 1961–1977 | 26675 | **1174** | 22.72 | 2 |
| Sobers, G.St A. | *1952–1974* | 28941 | **1043** | 27.74 | — |
| Southerton, J. | 1854–1879 | 24310 | **1681** | 14.46 | 10 |
| Spencer, C.T. | 1952–1974 | 36486 | **1367** | 26.69 | 1 |
| Staples, S.J. | 1920–1934 | 30421 | **1331** | 22.85 | 5 |
| Statham, J.B. | 1950–1968 | 36995 | **2260** | 16.36 | 13 |
| Tarrant, F.A. | *1898–1936* | 26391 | **1511** | 17.46 | 8 |
| Tate, F.W. | 1887–1905 | 28690 | **1331**† | 21.55 | 5 |
| Tate, M.W. | 1912–1937 | 50567 | **2784** | 18.16 | 13+1 |
| Tattersall, R. | 1948–1964 | 24704 | **1369** | 18.04 | 8 |
| Thompson, G.J. | 1897–1922 | 30060 | **1591** | 18.89 | 8 |
| Thomson, N.I. | 1952–1972 | 32866 | **1597** | 20.57 | 12 |
| Titmus, F.J. | 1949–1982 | 63313 | **2830** | 22.37 | 16 |
| Townsend, L.F. | 1922–1939 | 22985 | **1088** | 21.12 | 4 |
| Tribe, G.E. | *1945–1959* | 28321 | **1378** | 20.55 | 8 |
| Trott, A.E. | *1892–1911* | 35316 | **1674** | 21.09 | 7 |
| Trueman, F.S. | 1949–1969 | 42154 | **2304** | 18.29 | 12 |
| Tyldesley, R.K. | 1919–1935 | 25980 | **1509** | 17.21 | 10 |
| Underwood, D.L. | 1963–1985 | 47327 | **2368** | 19.98 | 10 |
| Venkataraghavan, S. | *1963–1984* | 33588 | **1390** | 24.16 | — |
| Verity, H. | 1930–1939 | 29146 | **1956** | 14.90 | 9 |
| Voce, W. | 1927–1952 | 35961 | **1558** | 23.08 | 6 |
| Wainwright, E. | 1888–1902 | 19536 | **1071** | 18.24 | 5 |
| Walsh, J.E. | *1936–1956* | 29226 | **1190** | 24.55 | 7 |
| Wardle, J.H. | 1946–*1967* | 35027 | **1846** | 18.97 | 10 |
| Wass, T.G. | 1896–1920 | 34100 | **1666** | 20.46 | 10 |
| Watson, A. | 1872–1893 | 18425 | **1383** | 13.32 | 1 |
| Wellard, A.W. | 1927–1950 | 39302 | **1614** | 24.35 | 8 |
| Wensley, A.F. | 1922–*1939* | 30251 | **1142** | 26.48 | 5 |
| Wheatley, O.S. | 1956–*1969* | 22910 | **1099** | 20.84 | 5 |
| White, D.W. | 1957–1972 | 26913 | **1143** | 23.54 | 4 |
| White, J.C. | 1909–1937 | 43759 | **2356** | 18.57 | 14 |
| Willsher, E. | 1850–1875 | — | **1329** | — | 1 |
| Wilson, D. | 1957–1974 | 24977 | **1189** | 21.00 | 5 |
| Wisden, J. | 1845–1863 | — | **1109** | — | 3 |
| Woods, S.M.J. | 1886–1910 | 21653 | **1040** | 20.82 | 2 |
| Woolley, F.E. | 1906–1938 | 41058 | **2066** | 19.87 | 8 |
| Wright, D.V.P. | 1932–1957 | 49305 | **2056** | 23.98 | 10 |
| Young, J.A. | 1933–1956 | 26795 | **1361** | 19.68 | 8 |

† *Includes 5 wickets for which no analysis was published.*

## HUNDRED WICKETS IN A SEASON MOST TIMES

23   W. Rhodes
20   D. Shackleton
17   A.P. Freeman
16   T.W.J. Goddard, C.W.L. Parker, R.T.D. Perks, F.J. Titmus
15   J.T. Hearne, G.H. Hirst, A.S. Kennedy
14   C. Blythe, W.E. Hollies, G.A.R. Lock, M.W. Tate, J.C. White
13   J.B. Statham
12   J. Briggs, E.G. Dennett, C. Gladwin, D.J. Shepherd, N.I. Thomson, F.S. Trueman
11   A.V. Bedser, G. Geary, S. Haigh, J.C. Laker, M.S. Nichols, A.E. Relf
10   W. Attewell, R. Illingworth, H.L. Jackson, V.W.C. Jupp, G.G. Macaulay, W. Mead,
     T.B. Mitchell, T. Richardson, R.K. Tyldesley, D.L. Underwood, J.H. Wardle, T.G. Wass,
     D.V.P. Wright

## HUNDRED WICKETS IN MOST CONSECUTIVE SEASONS

20   D. Shackleton   1949 to 1968 inclusive

---

---

299

# INDIVIDUAL RECORDS – ALL-ROUND PERFORMANCES

## THE INNINGS DOUBLE

**100 RUNS AND 10 WICKETS**

| | | | | | |
|---|---|---|---|---|---|
| V.E. Walker | 108 | 10-74 | England v Surrey | Oval | 1859 |
| W.G. Grace | 104 & | 10-49 | MCC v Oxford University | Oxford | 1886 |
| F.A. Tarrant | 182* | 10-90 | Maharaja of Cooch Behar's XI v Lord Willingdon's XI | Poona | 1918–19 |

## THE MATCH DOUBLE

**HUNDRED IN EACH INNINGS AND FIVE WICKETS TWICE**

G.H. Hirst
111  117*  6-70  5-45  Yorkshire v Somerset  Bath  1906

**HUNDRED IN EACH INNINGS AND 10 WICKETS**

B.J.T. Bosanquet
103  100*  3-75  8-53  Middlesex v Sussex  Lord's  1905

**200 RUNS AND 16 WICKETS**

G. Giffen  271  9-96  7-70  South Australia v Victoria  Adelaide  1891–92

**100 RUNS AND 10 WICKETS**

Allen, G.O.B.
38  104*  7-120  3-36  MCC v New Zealanders  Lord's  1927
Amarnath, L.
83  63  7-60  3-56  Southern Punjab v United Provinces  Delhi  1935–36
Amar Singh, L.
103  55  6-48  4-35  Nawanagar v Sind  Ahmedabad  1936–37
Armstrong, W.W. (2)
126*  5-27  5-25  Australians v New Zealand XI  Christchurch  1904–05
55  50*  3-20  8-50  Australians v Middlesex  Lord's  1905
Arnold, E.G.
200*  3-70  7-44  Worcestershire v Warwickshire  Birmingham  1909
Ashton, C.T.
10  98  7-91  3-60  Cambridge University v Army  Cambridge  1923
Austin, R.A.
88  56  4-45  8-71  Jamaica v Trinidad  Port-of-Spain  1977–78
Bailey, J.
62  88  6-51  5-19  Hampshire v Leicestershire  Southampton  1948
Bailey, T.E. (2)
59  71*  6-32  8-49  Essex v Hampshire  Romford  1957
60*  46  7-40  5-61  Essex v Yorkshire  Leeds  1960
Balaskas, X.C. (2)
132  5-87  6-43  Griqualand West v E. Province  Kimberley  1929–30
101  6-142  6-93  Griqualand West v W. Province  Kimberley  1929–30
*In successive matches*
Barlow, R.G. (2)
71  39*  5-27  5-92  Lancashire v Surrey  Manchester  1883
10*  101  4-6  6-42  North v Australians  Nottingham  1884
Barnett, C.J.
168  5-63  6-40  Gloucestershire v Lancashire  Manchester  1938
Barrett, A.G.
102*  28  5-39  5-43  Jamaica v Combined Islands  Castries  1969–70

Bates, W.
| | | | | | | |
|---|---|---|---|---|---|---|
| 106 | 14 | 5-30 | 5-45 | Yorkshire v Derbyshire | Leeds | 1886 |

Bedser, E.A.
| | | | | | | |
|---|---|---|---|---|---|---|
| 71 | 30 | 7-142 | 3-89 | Surrey v Gloucestershire | Oval | 1951 |

Bettington, R.H.B.
| | | | | | | |
|---|---|---|---|---|---|---|
| 28 | 95 | 4-87 | 6-78 | Middlesex v Sussex | Lord's | 1928 |

Bosanquet, B.J.T.　(4)
| | | | | | | |
|---|---|---|---|---|---|---|
| 86 | 82* | 7-61 | 3-119 | H.D.G. Leveson Gower's XI v Oxford University | Oxford | 1902 |
| 71 | 41* | 6-109 | 4-61 | Middlesex v Kent | Tunbridge Wells | 1903 |
| 141 | | 5-112 | 5-136 | Middlesex v Yorkshire | Sheffield | 1904 |
| 103 | 100* | 3-75 | 8-53 | Middlesex v Sussex | Lord's | 1905 |

Botham, I.T.
| | | | | | | |
|---|---|---|---|---|---|---|
| 114 | | 6-58 | 7-48 | England v India | Bombay | 1979–80 |

Boyce, K.D.
| | | | | | | |
|---|---|---|---|---|---|---|
| 113 | | 6-25 | 6-48 | Essex v Leicestershire | Chelmsford | 1975 |

Briggs, J.　(3)
| | | | | | | |
|---|---|---|---|---|---|---|
| 129* | | 5-25 | 5-16 | Lancashire v Sussex | Manchester | 1890 |
| 115 | | 8-113 | 5-96 | Lancashire v Yorkshire | Manchester | 1892 |
| 112 | | 5-51 | 6-64 | Lancashire v Surrey | Oval | 1893 |

Brown, L.S.
| | | | | | | |
|---|---|---|---|---|---|---|
| 63 | 37 | 6-89 | 4-54 | N.E. Transvaal v Transvaal | Springs | 1937–38 |

Browne, C.R.　(2)
| | | | | | | |
|---|---|---|---|---|---|---|
| 102 | | 5-77 | 8-58 | British Guiana v Barbados | Port-of-Spain | 1925–26 |
| 83 | 24* | 5-56 | 6-134 | British Guiana v Trinidad | Georgetown | 1929–30 |

Buckland, F.M.
| | | | | | | |
|---|---|---|---|---|---|---|
| 104 | | 4-14 | 6-53 | Oxford University v Middlesex | Lord's | 1877 |

Bullock, P.W.
| | | | | | | |
|---|---|---|---|---|---|---|
| 31 | 148 | 7-70 | 3-29 | Assam v Orissa | Nowgong | 1951–52 |

Carlson, P.H.
| | | | | | | |
|---|---|---|---|---|---|---|
| 24 | 102* | 5-46 | 5-27 | Queensland v New South Wales | Brisbane | 1978–79 |

Christian, A.H.
| | | | | | | |
|---|---|---|---|---|---|---|
| 73 | 57 | 7-144 | 4-56 | Western Australia v South Australia | Fremantle | 1908–09 |

Clark, P.H.
| | | | | | | |
|---|---|---|---|---|---|---|
| 67 | 52 | 4-148 | 8-91 | Philadelphians v Worcestershire | Worcester | 1903 |

Compton, D.C.S.
| | | | | | | |
|---|---|---|---|---|---|---|
| 137* | | 6-94 | 6-80 | Middlesex v Surrey | Oval | 1947 |

Constantine, L.N.
| | | | | | | |
|---|---|---|---|---|---|---|
| 107 | | 7-45 | 6-67 | West Indians v Northamptonshire | Northampton | 1928 |

Crawford, J.N.　(3)
| | | | | | | |
|---|---|---|---|---|---|---|
| 148 | | 7-85 | 4-63 | Surrey v Gloucestershire | Bristol | 1906 |
| 91 | 40 | 5-89 | 5-71 | South Australia v New South Wales | Sydney | 1913–14 |
| 110 | 4* | 5-90 | 5-53 | Wellington v Auckland | Auckland | 1917–18 |

Crawford, R.T.
| | | | | | | |
|---|---|---|---|---|---|---|
| 20 | 90 | 5-61 | 5-46 | Gentlemen of England v Oxford U. | Eastbourne | 1910 |

Davidson, A.K.
| | | | | | | |
|---|---|---|---|---|---|---|
| 44 | 80 | 5-135 | 6-87 | Australia v West Indies | Brisbane | 1960–61 |

Dexter, E.R.　(2)
| | | | | | | |
|---|---|---|---|---|---|---|
| 113 | | 6-63 | 4-46 | Sussex v Kent | Tunbridge Wells | 1962 |
| 27 | 94 | 7-38 | 3-58 | Sussex v Surrey | Oval | 1962 |

Dooland, B.
| | | | | | | |
|---|---|---|---|---|---|---|
| 115* | 11 | 4-54 | 6-48 | Nottinghamshire v Sussex | Worthing | 1957 |

Douglas, J.W.H.T.　(2)
| | | | | | | |
|---|---|---|---|---|---|---|
| 8 | 123* | 7-91 | 7-65 | Essex v Worcestershire | Leyton | 1921 |
| 210* | | 9-47 | 2-0 | Essex v Derbyshire | Leyton | 1921 |

Dowson, E.M.
| | | | | | | |
|---|---|---|---|---|---|---|
| 71* | 50 | 3-47 | 8-68 | Cambridge University v Surrey | Oval | 1903 |

Eady, C.J.
| | | | | | | |
|---|---|---|---|---|---|---|
| 92 | 30 | 7-66 | 5-63 | Tasmania v Victoria | Hobart | 1898–99 |

Faulkner, G.A.　(2)
| | | | | | | |
|---|---|---|---|---|---|---|
| 42 | 68* | 6-72 | 4-94 | Transvaal v Western Province | Cape Town | 1908–09 |
| 54 | 73 | 5-32 | 5-106 | South Africans v Queensland | Brisbane | 1910–11 |

Fender, P.G.H.
| | | | | | | |
|---|---|---|---|---|---|---|
| 104 | | 3-48 | 7-76 | Surrey v Essex | Leyton | 1926 |

Flanagan, J.P.D.
| | | | | | | |
|---|---|---|---|---|---|---|
| 98 | 17 | 8-113 | 2-86 | Transvaal B v Natal B | Johannesburg | 1968–69 |

| Flowers, W. | (2) | | | | | |
|---|---|---|---|---|---|---|
| 131 | | 4-43 | 6-44 | MCC v Derbyshire | Lord's | 1883 |
| 107 | | 6-44 | 5-84 | Nottinghamshire v Lancashire | Manchester | 1893 |
| Foster, F.R. | | | | | | |
| 105 | 18 | 9-118 | 3-84 | Warwickshire v Yorkshire | Birmingham | 1911 |
| Foulkes, I. | | | | | | |
| 130 | | 3-62 | 7-54 | Border v Eastern Province B | East London | 1977–78 |
| Fry, C.B. | | | | | | |
| 89 | 65 | 5-81 | 5-66 | Sussex v Nottinghamshire | Nottingham | 1896 |
| Geeson, F. | | | | | | |
| 104* | | 6-128 | 6-111 | Leicestershire v Derbyshire | Glossop | 1901 |
| Giffen, G. | (9) | | | | | |
| 20 | 82 | 9-91 | 8-110 | South Australia v Victoria | Adelaide | 1885–86 |
| 166 | | 8-65 | 6-60 | South Australia v Victoria | Adelaide | 1887–88 |
| 135 | 19 | 6-82 | 7-77 | South Australia v Victoria | Melbourne | 1888–89 |
| 237 | | 5-89 | 7-103 | South Australia v Victoria | Melbourne | 1890–91 |
| 271 | | 9-96 | 7-70 | South Australia v Victoria | Adelaide | 1891–92 |
| 120 | | 7-122 | 5-28 | South Australia v New South Wales | Sydney | 1891–92 |
| 43 | 181 | 9-147 | 2-88 | South Australia v Victoria | Adelaide | 1892–93 |
| 64 | 58* | 5-175 | 6-49 | S. Australia v A.E. Stoddart's XI | Adelaide | 1894–95 |
| 81 | 97* | 7-75 | 8-110 | South Australia v Victoria | Adelaide | 1902–03 |
| Grace, W.G. | (15) | | | | | |
| 134* | | 6-50 | 4-31 | Gentlemen v Players | Lord's | 1868 |
| 81 | 42* | 6-68 | 4-83 | W.G. Grace's XI v Kent | Maidstone | 1871 |
| 114 | | 7-78 | 4-48 | South v North | Oval | 1872 |
| 150 | | 8-33 | 7-46 | Gloucestershire v Yorkshire | Sheffield | 1872 |
| 179 | | 5-76 | 7-82 | Gloucestershire v Sussex | Hove | 1874 |
| 23 | 110 | 3-61 | 7-58 | Gentlemen v Players | Prince's | 1874 |
| 167 | | 4-57 | 7-44 | Gloucestershire v Yorkshire | Sheffield | 1874 |
| 94 | 121 | 6-92 | 4-68 | Gloucestershire & Kent v England | Canterbury | 1874 |
| 127 | | 5-44 | 5-77 | Gloucestershire v Yorkshire | Clifton | 1874 |
| 7 | 152 | 7-64 | 5-61 | Gentlemen v Players | Lord's | 1875 |
| 261 | | 5-62 | 6-77 | South v North | Prince's | 1877 |
| 75 | 58 | 5-59 | 6-95 | Gloucestershire v Somerset | Taunton | 1883 |
| 89 | 35 | 5-64 | 7-92 | Gloucestershire v Middlesex | Lord's | 1883 |
| 221* | | 6-45 | 5-75 | Gloucestershire v Middlesex | Clifton | 1885 |
| 104 | | 2-60 | 10-49 | MCC v Oxford University | Oxford | 1886 |
| Gregory, R.J. | | | | | | |
| 171 | | 5-36 | 5-66 | Surrey v Middlesex | Lord's | 1930 |
| Greig, I.A. | | | | | | |
| 118* | | 6-75 | 4-57 | Sussex v Hampshire | Hove | 1981 |
| Gunn, J.R. | (2) | | | | | |
| 95 | 39* | 7-77 | 4-66 | Nottinghamshire v Gloucestershire | Gloucester | 1904 |
| 148 | 6* | 8-80 | 2-31 | Nottinghamshire v Lancashire | Nottingham | 1921 |
| Hartkopf, A.E.V. | | | | | | |
| 86 | 14* | 5-23 | 8-105 | Victoria v MCC | Melbourne | 1922–23 |
| Hearne, J.W. | (6) | | | | | |
| 54 | 88 | 7-83 | 4-104 | Middlesex v Worcestershire | Worcester | 1913 |
| 106* | | 7-54 | 7-92 | Middlesex v Essex | Leyton | 1914 |
| 88 | 37* | 5-78 | 5-91 | Middlesex v Essex | Lord's | 1914 |
| 79 | 28 | 6-74 | 4-73 | Middlesex v Nottinghamshire | Lord's | 1922 |
| 140 | 57* | 6-83 | 6-45 | Middlesex v Sussex | Lord's | 1923 |
| 14 | 93 | 5-38 | 6-36 | Middlesex v Gloucestershire | Lord's | 1924 |
| Hill, C.J. | | | | | | |
| 17 | 91 | 7-18 | 5-49 | New South Wales v Queensland | Sydney | 1932–33 |
| Hillyer, W.R. | | | | | | |
| 26 | 83 | 7- | 6- | MCC v Oxford University | Oxford | 1847 |
| Hirst, G.H. | (4) | | | | | |
| 86 | 18* | 7-55 | 4-28 | Yorkshire v MCC | Lord's | 1901 |
| 101 | 4 | 4-46 | 7-33 | Yorkshire v Kent | Catford | 1906 |
| 111 | 117* | 6-70 | 5-45 | Yorkshire v Somerset | Bath | 1906 |
| 100 | | 9-41 | 2-89 | Yorkshire v Worcestershire | Worcester | 1911 |
| Hopwood, J.L. | | | | | | |
| 110 | 45 | 1-20 | 9-33 | Lancashire v Leicestershire | Manchester | 1933 |
| Ijaz Faqih | | | | | | |
| 100* | 50* | 5-66 | 5-51 | MCB v Allied Bank | Lahore | 1983–84 |
| Ikin, J.T. | | | | | | |
| 67 | 85* | 5-98 | 6-21 | Lancashire v Nottinghamshire | Manchester | 1947 |

Illingworth, R.
| | | | | | |
|---|---|---|---|---|---|
| 135 | | 7-49 | 7-52 | Yorkshire v Kent | Dover | 1964 |

Imran Khan    (2)
| | | | | | |
|---|---|---|---|---|---|
| 111* | | 7-53 | 6-46 | Worcestershire v Lancashire | Worcester | 1976 |
| 117 | | 6-98 | 5-82 | Pakistan v India | Faisalabad | 1982–83 |

Intikhab Alam
| | | | | | |
|---|---|---|---|---|---|
| 12 | 90* | 5-61 | 6-113 | PIA v Sind B | Hyderabad | 1974–75 |

Jackson, J.
| | | | | | |
|---|---|---|---|---|---|
| 100 | | 6-23 | 6-20 | Nottinghamshire v Kent | Cranbrook | 1863 |

Jackson, V.E.
| | | | | | |
|---|---|---|---|---|---|
| 108 | 13 | 6-46 | 4-53 | Leicestershire v Kent | Gillingham | 1954 |

Javed Bhatti
| | | | | | |
|---|---|---|---|---|---|
| 109 | | 5-29 | 5-59 | Bahawalpur v Multan | Bahawalpur | 1962–63 |

Jenner, T.J.
| | | | | | |
|---|---|---|---|---|---|
| 59 | 47 | 4-43 | 7-127 | S. Australia v W. Australia | Adelaide | 1973–74 |

Jupp, V.W.C.    (3)
| | | | | | |
|---|---|---|---|---|---|
| 102 | 33* | 6-61 | 6-78 | Sussex v Essex | Colchester | 1921 |
| 56 | 70 | 5-34 | 7-71 | Northamptonshire v Essex | Colchester | 1925 |
| 113 | | 7-42 | 5-79 | Northamptonshire v Essex | Leyton | 1928 |

Lacey, F.E.
| | | | | | |
|---|---|---|---|---|---|
| 157 | 50* | 4-32 | 7-149 | Hampshire v Sussex | Hove | 1882 |

Langridge, James
| | | | | | |
|---|---|---|---|---|---|
| 13 | 103 | 7-58 | 4-66 | Sussex v Glamorgan | Swansea | 1929 |

Le Couteur, P.R.
| | | | | | |
|---|---|---|---|---|---|
| 160 | | 6-20 | 5-46 | Oxford University v Cambridge U. | Lord's | 1910 |

Lee, G.M.
| | | | | | |
|---|---|---|---|---|---|
| 100* | | 5-65 | 7-78 | Derbyshire v Northamptonshire | Northampton | 1927 |

Lee, H.W.
| | | | | | |
|---|---|---|---|---|---|
| 119 | | 5-21 | 6-47 | Middlesex v Sussex | Lord's | 1920 |

Lewis, A.E.
| | | | | | |
|---|---|---|---|---|---|
| 93 | 20 | 6-43 | 4-15 | Somerset v Hampshire | Bath | 1911 |

Liddle, J.R.
| | | | | | |
|---|---|---|---|---|---|
| 31 | 77 | 7-97 | 5-115 | Orange Free State v Rhodesia | Bulawayo | 1951–52 |

Llewellyn, C.B.
| | | | | | |
|---|---|---|---|---|---|
| 153 | | 5-115 | 5-68 | Hampshire v Somerset | Taunton | 1901 |

Lockwood, W.
| | | | | | |
|---|---|---|---|---|---|
| 63 | 37 | 6-48 | 6-48 | Surrey v Lancashire | Oval | 1902 |

McGahey, C.P.    (2)
| | | | | | |
|---|---|---|---|---|---|
| 66 | 91 | 6-86 | 6-71 | Essex v Gloucestershire | Clifton | 1901 |
| 89 | 14 | 7-27 | 3-37 | Essex v Nottinghamshire | Leyton | 1906 |

McIntyre, M.
| | | | | | |
|---|---|---|---|---|---|
| 88* | 27 | 9-33 | 3-66 | Nottinghamshire v Surrey | Oval | 1872 |

Mansell, P.N.F.
| | | | | | |
|---|---|---|---|---|---|
| 94* | 13* | 7-71 | 3-79 | Rhodesia v N.E. Transvaal | Pretoria | 1951–52 |

Mason, J.R.    (5)
| | | | | | |
|---|---|---|---|---|---|
| 72 | 46* | 4-23 | 6-34 | Kent v Middlesex | Tonbridge | 1900 |
| 145 | | 4-26 | 8-29 | Kent v Somerset | Taunton | 1901 |
| 126 | | 7-120 | 3-60 | Kent v Somerset | Beckenham | 1904 |
| 1 | 100 | 6-71 | 4-60 | Kent v Somerset | Taunton | 1904 |
| 133 | | 5-102 | 5-120 | Kent v Somerset | Taunton | 1905 |

Money, W.B.
| | | | | | |
|---|---|---|---|---|---|
| 89 | 13 | 6-66 | 6-104 | Cambridge University v Surrey | Oval | 1868 |

Monteith, J.D.
| | | | | | |
|---|---|---|---|---|---|
| 26 | 78 | 7-38 | 5-57 | Ireland v Scotland | Cork | 1973 |

Muncer, B.L.
| | | | | | |
|---|---|---|---|---|---|
| 107* | | 5-34 | 5-23 | Glamorgan v Derbyshire | Chesterfield | 1951 |

Murray, A.R.A.
| | | | | | |
|---|---|---|---|---|---|
| 78 | 44* | 5-77 | 5-54 | Eastern Province v Border | East London | 1953–54 |

Nasim-ul-Ghani
| | | | | | |
|---|---|---|---|---|---|
| 33 | 139 | 4-82 | 6-95 | PWD v Khairpur | Karachi | 1971–72 |

Nayudu, C.S.
| | | | | | |
|---|---|---|---|---|---|
| 127 | | 5-20 | 7-36 | Baroda v Rajputana | Baroda | 1942–43 |

Neill, R.
| | | | | | |
|---|---|---|---|---|---|
| 94 | 13 | 4-54 | 6-43 | Auckland v Wellington | Wellington | 1896–97 |

Newman, J.A.
| | | | | | |
|---|---|---|---|---|---|
| 66 | 42* | 8-61 | 6-87 | Hampshire v Gloucestershire | Bournemouth | 1926 |

Nichols, M.S.    (3)
| | | | | | |
|---|---|---|---|---|---|
| 73 | 33 | 5-67 | 5-37 | Essex v Sussex | Horsham | 1933 |

Nichols, M.S.  (3) *continued*

| | | | | | | |
|---|---|---|---|---|---|---|
| 146 | | 4-17 | 7-37 | Essex v Yorkshire | Huddersfield | 1935 |
| 159 | | 9-37 | 6-126 | Essex v Gloucestershire | Gloucester | 1938 |

Ontong, R.C.

| | | | | | | |
|---|---|---|---|---|---|---|
| 130 | | 5-39 | 8-67 | Glamorgan v Nottinghamshire | Nottingham | 1985 |

Phillip, N.

| | | | | | | |
|---|---|---|---|---|---|---|
| 70 | 90* | 5-59 | 5-71 | Combined Islands v Guyana | Georgetown | 1977–78 |

Pougher, A.D.

| | | | | | | |
|---|---|---|---|---|---|---|
| 5 | 109* | 6-29 | 8-60 | Leicestershire v Essex | Leyton | 1894 |

Procter, M.J.  (2)

| | | | | | | |
|---|---|---|---|---|---|---|
| 108 | | 7-35 | 6-38 | Gloucestershire v Worcestershire | Cheltenham | 1977 |
| 73 | 35 | 7-16 | 7-60 | Gloucestershire v Worcestershire | Cheltenham | 1980 |

Quaife, W.G.

| | | | | | | |
|---|---|---|---|---|---|---|
| 104* | | 5-51 | 7-76 | Warwickshire v Worcestershire | Birmingham | 1901 |

Ram Singh, A.G.  (2)

| | | | | | | |
|---|---|---|---|---|---|---|
| 74 | 70 | 5-88 | 6-71 | Madras v Hyderabad | Hyderabad | 1934–35 |
| 55 | 91 | 5-35 | 5-45 | Madras v Mysore | Madras | 1939–40 |

Ramchandra

| | | | | | | |
|---|---|---|---|---|---|---|
| 97* | 5 | 7-52 | 3-53 | Bengal v Mysore | Calcutta | 1941–42 |

Relf, A.E.  (2)

| | | | | | | |
|---|---|---|---|---|---|---|
| 42 | 83 | 6-22 | 6-25 | Auckland v Otago | Auckland | 1907–08 |
| 103* | | 8-41 | 7-36 | Sussex v Leicestershire | Hove | 1912 |

Rhodes, W.

| | | | | | | |
|---|---|---|---|---|---|---|
| 183 | | 5-26 | 7-33 | Europeans v Parsees | Bombay | 1921–22 |

Rice, C.E.B.

| | | | | | | |
|---|---|---|---|---|---|---|
| 90 | 11 | 7-62 | 4-50 | Transvaal v Western Province | Johannesburg | 1975–76 |

Ridley, A.W.

| | | | | | | |
|---|---|---|---|---|---|---|
| 104 | | 5-52 | 5-61 | Hampshire v Kent | Faversham | 1876 |

Robinson, E.

| | | | | | | |
|---|---|---|---|---|---|---|
| 108 | | 7-25 | 4-60 | Yorkshire v Hampshire | Bradford | 1930 |

Shastri, R.J.

| | | | | | | |
|---|---|---|---|---|---|---|
| 29 | 76 | 4-91 | 8-91 | Bombay v Delhi | Bombay | 1984–85 |

Shukla, A.  (2)

| | | | | | | |
|---|---|---|---|---|---|---|
| 168* | | 7-43 | 3-87 | Uttar Pradesh v Rajasthan | Udaipur | 1961–62 |
| 28 | 96 | 6-63 | 6-102 | Uttar Pradesh v Madhya Pradesh | Varanasi | 1964–65 |

Smith, S.G.  (2)

| | | | | | | |
|---|---|---|---|---|---|---|
| 5 | 136 | 2-3 | 8-39 | Northamptonshire v Somerset | Bath | 1912 |
| 82 | 20 | 6-82 | 4-25 | Northamptonshire v Derbyshire | Northampton | 1913 |

Smith, T.P.B.

| | | | | | | |
|---|---|---|---|---|---|---|
| 1 | 101 | 2-69 | 8-99 | Essex v Middlesex | Chelmsford | 1938 |

Sobers, G.St A.

| | | | | | | |
|---|---|---|---|---|---|---|
| 17 | 105* | 7-69 | 4-87 | Nottinghamshire v Kent | Dover | 1968 |

Steele, D.S.

| | | | | | | |
|---|---|---|---|---|---|---|
| 130 | | 6-36 | 5-39 | Northamptonshire v Derbyshire | Northampton | 1978 |

Stoddart, A.E.

| | | | | | | |
|---|---|---|---|---|---|---|
| 143 | | 7-67 | 3-10 | A. Priestleys' XI v Jamaica | Kingston | 1896–97 |

Studd, C.T.

| | | | | | | |
|---|---|---|---|---|---|---|
| 105* | | 6-79 | 4-45 | Middlesex v Kent | Canterbury | 1883 |

Tarrant, F.A.  (4)

| | | | | | | |
|---|---|---|---|---|---|---|
| 152 | 11 | 7-93 | 5-56 | Middlesex v Gloucestershire | Bristol | 1908 |
| 14 | 101* | 9-105 | 7-71 | Middlesex v Lancashire | Manchester | 1914 |
| 68* | 80 | 6-82 | 5-67 | Europeans v Hindus | Bombay | 1916–17 |
| 182* | 8* | 10-90 | 1-22 | Maharaja of Cooch Behar's XI v Lord Willingdon's XI | Poona | 1918–19 |

Tate, M.W.  (2)

| | | | | | | |
|---|---|---|---|---|---|---|
| 90 | 35 | 5-48 | 6-42 | Sussex v Oxford University | Hove | 1920 |
| 101 | | 6-52 | 4-43 | Sussex v Hampshire | Portsmouth | 1927 |

Thompson, G.J.

| | | | | | | |
|---|---|---|---|---|---|---|
| 5 | 131* | 6-72 | 4-71 | Northamptonshire v Somerset | Bath | 1913 |

Toogood, G.J.

| | | | | | | |
|---|---|---|---|---|---|---|
| 149 | | 8-42 | 2-41 | Oxford University v Cambridge U. | Lord's | 1985 |

Townsend, C.L.

| | | | | | | |
|---|---|---|---|---|---|---|
| 139 | | 5-121 | 5-83 | Gloucestershire v Warwickshire | Birmingham | 1898 |

Townsend, L.F.  (2)

| | | | | | | |
|---|---|---|---|---|---|---|
| 106* | | 6-66 | 5-64 | Derbyshire v Somerset | Weston-s-Mare | 1934 |
| 44 | 90* | 5-89 | 7-25 | Auckland v Wellington | Auckland | 1934–35 |

Trott, A.E.  (5)

| | | | | | | |
|---|---|---|---|---|---|---|
| 101* | | 7-74 | 4-66 | Lord Hawke's XI v Transvaal | Johannesburg | 1898–99 |

Trott, A.E. (5) *continued*

| | | | | | | |
|---|---|---|---|---|---|---|
| 64 | 69 | 6-57 | 5-56 | MCC v Sussex | Lord's | 1899 |
| 123 | 35* | 6-132 | 6-68 | Middlesex v Sussex | Lord's | 1899 |
| 112 | | 8-54 | 3-84 | Middlesex v Essex | Lord's | 1901 |
| 68 | 80* | 7-58 | 4-93 | Hawke's Bay v Canterbury | Christchurch | 1901–02 |

Vine, J.

| | | | | | | |
|---|---|---|---|---|---|---|
| 86 | 54 | 2-45 | 8-68 | Sussex v Oxford University | Eastbourne | 1906 |

Wainwright, E.

| | | | | | | |
|---|---|---|---|---|---|---|
| 10 | 104 | 7-66 | 4-57 | Yorkshire v Sussex | Sheffield | 1892 |

Walker, V.E.

| | | | | | | |
|---|---|---|---|---|---|---|
| 20* | 108 | 10-74 | 4-17 | England v Surrey | Oval | 1859 |

Wasim Raja (2)

| | | | | | | |
|---|---|---|---|---|---|---|
| 117 | | 5-77 | 5-23 | Universities v PWD | Lahore | 1972–73 |
| 85 | 50 | 6-118 | 8-65 | Pakistan U-25 XI v Sri Lanka U-25 XI | Colombo | 1973–74 |

Wellard, A.W. (2)

| | | | | | | |
|---|---|---|---|---|---|---|
| 75 | 55 | 6-82 | 5-93 | Somerset v Gloucestershire | Taunton | 1929 |
| 77 | 60 | 7-43 | 3-66 | Somerset v Hampshire | Portsmouth | 1933 |

Woolley, F.E. (6)

| | | | | | | |
|---|---|---|---|---|---|---|
| 77 | 111* | 7-66 | 5-56 | Kent v Gloucestershire | Gloucester | 1914 |
| 20 | 139* | 6-52 | 4-80 | Kent v Somerset | Horsham | 1920 |
| 174 | | 8-22 | 3-44 | Kent v Gloucestershire | Maidstone | 1921 |
| 15 | 109 | 7-40 | 3-76 | Kent v Nottinghamshire | Nottingham | 1921 |
| 156 | | 4-26 | 6-52 | Kent v Warwickshire | Tunbridge Wells | 1928 |
| 132 | | 6-50 | 4-38 | MCC v Otago | Dunedin | 1929–30 |

Young, A.

| | | | | | | |
|---|---|---|---|---|---|---|
| 63 | 70 | 3-47 | 8-30 | Somerset v Derbyshire | Taunton | 1930 |

# HUNDRED AND A HAT-TRICK

| | | | |
|---|---|---|---|
| G. Giffen (113) | Australians v Lancashire | Manchester | 1884 |
| W.E. Roller (204) | Surrey v Sussex | Oval | 1885 |
| W.B. Burns (102*) | Worcestershire v Gloucestershire | Worcester | 1913 |
| V.W.C. Jupp (102) | Sussex v Essex | Colchester | 1921 |
| R.E.S. Wyatt (124) | MCC v Ceylon | Colombo | 1926–27 |
| L.N. Constantine (107) | West Indians v Northamptonshire | Northampton | 1928 |
| D.E. Davies (139) | Glamorgan v Leicestershire | Leicester | 1937 |
| V.M. Merchant (142) | Dr C.R. Pereira's XI v Sir H. Mehta's XI | Bombay | 1946–47 |
| M.J. Procter (102) | Gloucestershire v Essex | Westcliff | 1972 |
| M.J. Procter (122) | Gloucestershire v Leicestershire | Bristol | 1979 |

# THE SEASON DOUBLE

The double of 1000 runs and 100 wickets in a first-class season was first achieved in 1874 by W.G. Grace. He repeated this performance in each of the next four seasons but it was not until 1882 that another player, C.T. Studd, emulated him. Apart from the war years, only two seasons (1951 and 1958) between 1895 and 1967 inclusive failed to produce at least one instance of a player doing the double. Mainly because of the reduced first-class fixtures list, only one player, R.J. Hadlee in 1984, has achieved this feat since 1967.

In 1949 D.B. Close of Yorkshire, aged 18, became the youngest player to do the double and the only one to achieve it in the season of his first appearance in first-class cricket.

V.W.C. Jupp (Sussex and Northamptonshire) and F.R. Brown (Surrey and Northamptonshire) are alone in achieving the double for two counties.

## OUTSTANDING DOUBLES

| | *Season* | *Runs* | *Wkts* |
|---|---|---|---|
| 2000 RUNS AND 200 WICKETS | | | |
| G.H. Hirst | 1906 | 2385 | 208 |
| | | | |
| 3000 RUNS AND 100 WICKETS | | | |
| J.H. Parks | 1937 | 3003 | 101 |
| | | | |
| 1000 RUNS AND 200 WICKETS | | | |
| A.E. Trott | 1899 | 1175 | 239 |
| A.E. Trott | 1900 | 1337 | 211 |
| A.S. Kennedy | 1922 | 1129 | 205 |

| | Season | Runs | Wkts |
|---|---|---|---|
| M.W. Tate | 1923 | 1168 | 219 |
| M.W. Tate | 1924 | 1419 | 205 |
| M.W. Tate | 1925 | 1290 | 228 |

### 2000 RUNS AND 100 WICKETS

| | Season | Runs | Wkts |
|---|---|---|---|
| W.G. Grace | 1876 | 2622 | 129 |
| C.L. Townsend | 1899 | 2440 | 101 |
| G.L. Jessop | 1900 | 2210 | 104 |
| G.H. Hirst | 1904 | 2501 | 132 |
| G.H. Hirst | 1905 | 2266 | 110 |
| W. Rhodes | 1909 | 2094 | 141 |
| W. Rhodes | 1911 | 2261 | 117 |
| F.A. Tarrant | 1911 | 2030 | 111 |
| J.W. Hearne | 1913 | 2036 | 124 |
| J.W. Hearne | 1914 | 2116 | 123 |
| F.E. Woolley | 1914 | 2272 | 125 |
| J.W. Hearne | 1920 | 2148 | 142 |
| V.W.C. Jupp | 1921 | 2169 | 121 |
| F.E. Woolley | 1921 | 2101 | 167 |
| F.E. Woolley | 1922 | 2022 | 163 |
| F.E. Woolley | 1923 | 2091 | 101 |
| L.F. Townsend | 1933 | 2268 | 100 |
| D.E. Davies | 1937 | 2012 | 103 |
| James Langridge | 1937 | 2082 | 101 |
| T.E. Bailey | 1959 | 2011 | 100 |

## FASTEST DOUBLES

G.H. Hirst completed the double in only 16 matches, on 28 June 1906.

| | | | |
|---|---|---|---|
| 28 June 1906 | G.H. Hirst | Yorkshire |
| 12 July 1901 | G.H. Hirst | Yorkshire |
| 15 July 1907 | F.A. Tarrant | Middlesex |
| 17 July 1928 | V.W.C. Jupp | Northamptonshire |
| 24 July 1908 | F.A. Tarrant | Middlesex |
| 24 July 1913 | A.E. Relf | Sussex |
| 25 July 1933 | Jas Langridge | Sussex |
| 25 July 1963 | B.R. Knight | Essex |
| 26 July 1875 | W.G. Grace | Gloucs |
| 26 July 1877 | W.G. Grace | Gloucs |
| 26 July 1920 | F.E. Woolley | Kent |
| 26 July 1923 | J.W. Hearne | Middlesex |
| 27 July 1905 | W. Rhodes | Yorkshire |
| 28 July 1922 | F.E. Woolley | Kent |
| 30 July 1928 | M.W. Tate | Sussex |
| 31 July 1914 | J.W.H.T. Douglas | Essex |
| 31 July 1926 | J.A. Newman | Hampshire |

## MOST DOUBLES

- 16  W. Rhodes
- 14  G.H. Hirst
- 10  V.W.C. Jupp
- 9  W.E. Astill
- 8  T.E. Bailey, M.S. Nichols, A.E. Relf, F.A. Tarrant, M.W. Tate, F.J. Titmus and F.E. Woolley

## MOST CONSECUTIVE DOUBLES

- 11  G.H. Hirst (1903–1913)
- 8  F.A. Tarrant (1907–1914) and M.W. Tate (1922–1929)
- 7  W. Rhodes, twice (1903–1909 & 1914–1924)
- 6  W.E. Astill (1921–1926), G. Tribe (1952–1957) and F.E. Woolley (1914–1923)

## 1000 RUNS AND 100 WICKETS IN A SEASON

| | | | Season | Runs | HS | Avge | 100 | Wkts | Avge |
|---|---|---|---|---|---|---|---|---|---|
| Allen, D.A. | Gloucestershire | | 1961 | 1001 | 121* | 25.02 | 1 | 124 | 19.43 |
| Alley, W.E. | Somerset | | 1962 | 1915 | 155 | 36.82 | 3 | 112 | 20.74 |
| Andrews, W.H.R. | Somerset | (2) | 1937 | 1141 | 80 | 20.74 | — | 143 | 20.53 |
| | | | 1938 | 1001 | 77* | 22.24 | — | 124 | 21.80 |
| Armstrong, W.W. | Australians | (3) | 1905 | 1902 | 303* | 50.05 | 4 | 122 | 18.20 |
| | | | 1909 | 1451 | 110* | 43.96 | 3 | 113 | 16.38 |
| | | | 1921 | 1213 | 182* | 41.82 | 3 | 100 | 14.44 |

| | | | Season | Runs | HS | Avge | 100 | Wkts | Avge |
|---|---|---|---|---|---|---|---|---|---|
| Arnold, E.G. | Worcestershire | (4) | 1902 | 1067 | 92 | 26.02 | — | 113 | 18.88 |
| | | | 1903 | 1157 | 128 | 30.44 | 2 | 143 | 17.44 |
| | | | 1904 | 1039 | 111 | 25.97 | 1 | 114 | 24.48 |
| | | | 1905 | 1148 | 134 | 37.03 | 3 | 115 | 22.32 |
| Astill, W.E. | Leicestershire | (9) | 1921 | 1380 | 115 | 27.05 | 2 | 153 | 20.99 |
| | | | 1922 | 1210 | 78 | 23.72 | — | 144 | 19.23 |
| | | | 1923 | 1307 | 106 | 27.80 | 2 | 114 | 23.50 |
| | | | 1924 | 1126 | 88 | 25.59 | — | 103 | 20.84 |
| | | | 1925 | 1601 | 109 | 32.02 | 1 | 105 | 20.99 |
| | | | 1926 | 1291 | 158* | 30.02 | 1 | 107 | 24.48 |
| | | | 1928 | 1127 | 89 | 24.50 | — | 130 | 22.33 |
| | | | 1929 | 1004 | 127 | 25.10 | 2 | 121 | 20.94 |
| | | | 1930 | 1022 | 84 | 24.92 | — | 111 | 22.25 |
| Bailey, J. | Hampshire | | 1948 | 1399 | 88 | 31.79 | — | 121 | 18.13 |
| Bailey, T.E. | Essex | (8) | 1949 | 1380 | 93 | 35.38 | — | 130 | 24.20 |
| | | | 1952 | 1513 | 155* | 36.90 | 1 | 103 | 29.09 |
| | | | 1954 | 1344 | 108* | 32.78 | 1 | 101 | 21.39 |
| | | | 1957 | 1322 | 132 | 38.88 | 2 | 104 | 17.02 |
| | | | 1959 | 2011 | 146 | 46.76 | 6 | 100 | 24.69 |
| | | | 1960 | 1639 | 118 | 39.02 | 1 | 117 | 20.25 |
| | | | 1961 | 1240 | 117* | 27.55 | 1 | 133 | 21.01 |
| | | | 1962 | 1460 | 124* | 35.60 | 1 | 125 | 20.59 |
| Barratt, F. | Nottinghamshire | | 1928 | 1167 | 139* | 29.17 | 2 | 114 | 25.18 |
| Booth, M.W. | Yorkshire | | 1913 | 1228 | 107* | 27.28 | 1 | 181 | 18.46 |
| Bosanquet, B.J.T. | Middlesex | | 1904 | 1405 | 145 | 36.02 | 4 | 132 | 21.62 |
| Braund, L.C. | Somerset | (3) | 1901 | 1587 | 115* | 36.06 | 4 | 120 | 30.62 |
| | | | 1902 | 1423 | 144 | 27.53 | 2 | 172 | 19.80 |
| | | | 1903 | 1425 | 132 | 32.38 | 3 | 134 | 21.01 |
| Brockwell, W. | Surrey | | 1899 | 1542 | 167 | 33.52 | 3 | 105 | 25.26 |
| Broderick, V. | Northamptonshire | | 1948 | 1066 | 135 | 26.65 | 2 | 100 | 22.77 |
| Brown, F.R. | Surrey | (2) | 1932 | 1135 | 212 | 32.42 | 3 | 120 | 20.46 |
| | Northamptonshire | | 1949 | 1077 | 94 | 24.47 | — | 111 | 27.00 |
| Calthorpe, Hon F.S.G. | Warwickshire | | 1920 | 1025 | 102 | 22.77 | 1 | 100 | 24.26 |
| Cartwright, T.W. | Warwickshire | | 1962 | 1176 | 210 | 33.60 | 1 | 106 | 20.05 |
| Close, D.B. | Yorkshire | (2) | 1949 | 1098 | 88* | 27.45 | — | 113 | 27.87 |
| | | | 1952 | 1192 | 87* | 33.11 | — | 114 | 24.08 |
| Collins, H.L. | Australians | | 1919 | 1615 | 127 | 38.45 | 5 | 106 | 16.55 |
| Constantine, L.N. | West Indians | | 1928 | 1381 | 130 | 34.52 | 3 | 107 | 22.95 |
| Crawford, J.N. | Surrey | (2) | 1906 | 1174 | 148 | 30.10 | 1 | 118 | 20.28 |
| | | | 1907 | 1158 | 103 | 30.47 | 1 | 124 | 16.95 |
| Cuffe, J.A. | Worcestershire | | 1911 | 1054 | 78 | 25.70 | — | 110 | 23.56 |
| Cuttell, W.R. | Lancashire | | 1898 | 1003 | 85* | 25.71 | — | 114 | 21.21 |
| Davidson, G. | Derbyshire | | 1895 | 1296 | 80 | 28.07 | — | 138 | 16.79 |
| Davies, D.E. | Glamorgan | (2) | 1935 | 1326 | 155* | 28.21 | 2 | 100 | 21.07 |
| | | | 1937 | 2012 | 140 | 40.24 | 3 | 103 | 23.03 |
| Dooland, B. | Nottinghamshire | (2) | 1954 | 1012 | 88 | 28.11 | — | 196 | 15.48 |
| | | | 1957 | 1604 | 115* | 28.64 | 1 | 141 | 23.21 |
| Douglas, J.W.H.T. | Essex | (5) | 1914 | 1288 | 146 | 35.77 | 2 | 138 | 19.10 |
| | | | 1919 | 1178 | 144 | 34.64 | 2 | 136 | 25.14 |
| | | | 1920 | 1328 | 147 | 32.39 | 2 | 147 | 21.38 |
| | | | 1921 | 1547 | 210* | 37.73 | 3 | 130 | 20.32 |
| | | | 1923 | 1110 | 147* | 29.21 | 2 | 146 | 22.35 |
| Drake, A. | Yorkshire | | 1913 | 1056 | 108 | 23.46 | 1 | 116 | 16.93 |
| Faulkner, G.A. | South Africans/MCC | | 1912 | 1206 | 145* | 26.21 | 3 | 163 | 15.42 |
| Fender, P.G.H. | Surrey | (6) | 1921 | 1152 | 101 | 21.33 | 1 | 134 | 26.58 |
| | | | 1922 | 1169 | 185 | 34.38 | 2 | 157 | 21.20 |
| | | | 1923 | 1427 | 124* | 29.12 | 2 | 178 | 19.98 |
| | | | 1925 | 1042 | 81* | 28.16 | — | 137 | 21.08 |
| | | | 1926 | 1043 | 104 | 30.67 | 1 | 112 | 24.54 |
| | | | 1928 | 1376 | 117 | 37.18 | 3 | 110 | 28.17 |
| Flowers, W. | Nottinghamshire | | 1883 | 1144 | 131 | 24.86 | 1 | 113 | 14.95 |
| Foster, F.R. | Warwickshire | (2) | 1911 | 1614 | 200 | 42.47 | 3 | 141 | 20.31 |
| | | | 1914 | 1460 | 305* | 34.76 | 1 | 122 | 18.62 |
| Giffen, G. | Australians | (3) | 1886 | 1424 | 119 | 26.86 | 1 | 154 | 17.36 |
| | | | 1893 | 1133 | 180 | 23.12 | 2 | 118 | 19.04 |
| | | | 1896 | 1208 | 130 | 25.17 | 2 | 117 | 19.29 |

| | | | Season | Runs | HS | Avge | 100 | Wkts | Avge |
|---|---|---|---|---|---|---|---|---|---|
| Gilligan, A.E.R. | Sussex | | 1923 | 1183 | 114* | 21.12 | 2 | 163 | 17.50 |
| Goonesena, G. | Nottinghamshire | (2) | 1955 | 1380 | 118 | 28.75 | 2 | 134 | 21.05 |
| | | | 1957 | 1156 | 211 | 26.88 | 1 | 110 | 23.26 |
| Grace, W.G. | Gloucestershire | (7) | 1874 | 1664 | 179 | 52.00 | 8 | 139 | 12.70 |
| | | | 1875 | 1498 | 152 | 32.56 | 3 | 191 | 12.92 |
| | | | 1876 | 2622 | 344 | 62.42 | 7 | 130 | 18.90 |
| | | | 1877 | 1474 | 261 | 39.83 | 2 | 179 | 12.81 |
| | | | 1878 | 1151 | 116 | 28.77 | 1 | 152 | 14.52 |
| | | | 1885 | 1688 | 221* | 43.28 | 4 | 117 | 18.79 |
| | | | 1886 | 1846 | 170 | 35.50 | 4 | 122 | 19.99 |
| Gregory, J.M. | Australians | | 1921 | 1135 | 107 | 36.61 | 3 | 116 | 16.58 |
| Gunn, J.R. | Nottinghamshire | (4) | 1903 | 1665 | 294 | 42.69 | 3 | 118 | 19.34 |
| | | | 1904 | 1225 | 100 | 30.62 | 1 | 123 | 25.27 |
| | | | 1905 | 1366 | 178 | 35.94 | 3 | 111 | 25.46 |
| | | | 1906 | 1395 | 112 | 35.76 | 2 | 112 | 21.66 |
| Hadlee, R.J. | Nottinghamshire | | 1984 | 1179 | 210* | 51.26 | 2 | 117 | 14.05 |
| Haig, N.E. | Middlesex | (3) | 1921 | 1009 | 108 | 22.95 | 1 | 111 | 23.10 |
| | | | 1927 | 1059 | 104* | 22.53 | 1 | 109 | 27.45 |
| | | | 1929 | 1552 | 130 | 25.02 | 2 | 129 | 24.17 |
| Haigh, S. | Yorkshire | | 1904 | 1055 | 138 | 26.37 | 2 | 121 | 19.85 |
| Hallows, J. | Lancashire | | 1904 | 1071 | 137* | 39.66 | 3 | 108 | 19.37 |
| Hayward, T.W. | Surrey | | 1897 | 1368 | 130 | 38.00 | 1 | 114 | 18.18 |
| Hearne, J.W. | Middlesex | (5) | 1911 | 1627 | 234* | 42.81 | 4 | 102 | 22.00 |
| | | | 1913 | 2036 | 189 | 44.26 | 6 | 124 | 22.26 |
| | | | 1914 | 2116 | 204 | 60.45 | 8 | 123 | 22.69 |
| | | | 1920 | 2148 | 215* | 55.07 | 6 | 142 | 17.83 |
| | | | 1923 | 1519 | 232 | 47.46 | 5 | 113 | 20.03 |
| Hirst, G.H. | Yorkshire | (14) | 1896 | 1122 | 107 | 28.05 | 1 | 104 | 21.61 |
| | | | 1897 | 1535 | 134 | 35.69 | 1 | 101 | 23.22 |
| | | | 1901 | 1950 | 214 | 42.39 | 3 | 183 | 16.38 |
| | | | 1903 | 1844 | 153 | 47.28 | 5 | 128 | 14.94 |
| | | | 1904 | 2501 | 157 | 54.36 | 9 | 132 | 21.09 |
| | | | 1905 | 2266 | 341 | 53.95 | 6 | 110 | 19.94 |
| | | | 1906 | 2385 | 169 | 45.86 | 6 | 208 | 16.50 |
| | | | 1907 | 1334 | 91* | 28.38 | — | 188 | 15.20 |
| | | | 1908 | 1598 | 128* | 38.97 | 1 | 174 | 14.05 |
| | | | 1909 | 1256 | 140 | 27.30 | 1 | 115 | 20.05 |
| | | | 1910 | 1840 | 158 | 32.85 | 3 | 164 | 14.79 |
| | | | 1911 | 1789 | 218 | 33.12 | 3 | 137 | 20.40 |
| | | | 1912 | 1133 | 109 | 25.75 | 1 | 118 | 17.37 |
| | | | 1913 | 1540 | 166* | 35.81 | 3 | 101 | 20.13 |
| Hopwood, J.L. | Lancashire | (2) | 1934 | 1672 | 220 | 38.00 | 3 | 111 | 20.69 |
| | | | 1935 | 1538 | 104 | 33.43 | 2 | 103 | 20.55 |
| Horton, M.J. | Worcestershire | (2) | 1955 | 1296 | 103 | 22.73 | 1 | 103 | 27.38 |
| | | | 1961 | 1808 | 124* | 28.25 | 4 | 101 | 21.64 |
| Howorth, R. | Worcestershire | (3) | 1939 | 1019 | 69 | 21.22 | — | 100 | 24.34 |
| | | | 1946 | 1201 | 114 | 24.51 | 2 | 114 | 19.35 |
| | | | 1947 | 1510 | 95 | 26.03 | — | 164 | 17.85 |
| Illingworth, R. | Yorkshire | (6) | 1957 | 1213 | 97 | 28.20 | — | 106 | 18.40 |
| | | | 1959 | 1726 | 162 | 46.64 | 5 | 110 | 21.46 |
| | | | 1960 | 1006 | 86 | 25.79 | — | 109 | 17.55 |
| | | | 1961 | 1153 | 75 | 24.53 | — | 128 | 17.90 |
| | | | 1962 | 1612 | 127 | 34.29 | 3 | 117 | 19.45 |
| | | | 1964 | 1301 | 135 | 37.17 | 2 | 122 | 17.46 |
| Jackson, F.S. | Yorkshire | | 1898 | 1566 | 160 | 41.21 | 5 | 104 | 15.67 |
| Jackson, V.E. | Leicestershire | | 1955 | 1582 | 121 | 29.29 | 4 | 112 | 21.71 |
| Jenkins, R.O. | Worcestershire | (2) | 1949 | 1183 | 91* | 28.16 | — | 183 | 21.19 |
| | | | 1952 | 1087 | 85 | 24.70 | — | 136 | 25.65 |
| Jessop, G.L. | Gloucestershire | (2) | 1897 | 1219 | 140 | 29.73 | 4 | 116 | 17.85 |
| | | | 1900 | 2210 | 179 | 40.18 | 6 | 104 | 21.00 |
| Jupp, V.W.C. | Sussex | (10) | 1920 | 1444 | 151 | 28.31 | 3 | 111 | 18.56 |
| | | | 1921 | 2169 | 179 | 38.73 | 7 | 121 | 22.78 |
| | Northamptonshire | | 1925 | 1306 | 144 | 27.78 | 1 | 116 | 20.68 |
| | | | 1926 | 1560 | 197 | 35.45 | 2 | 113 | 19.95 |
| | | | 1927 | 1519 | 116 | 38.94 | 3 | 121 | 20.42 |
| | | | 1928 | 1574 | 113 | 34.97 | 2 | 166 | 20.15 |

| | | | Season | Runs | HS | Avge | 100 | Wkts | Avge |
|---|---|---|---|---|---|---|---|---|---|
| Jupp, V.W.C. *continued* | | | 1930 | 1037 | 142* | 28.02 | 1 | 106 | 20.96 |
| | | | 1931 | 1540 | 128 | 28.00 | 2 | 131 | 24.91 |
| | | | 1932 | 1712 | 163 | 31.70 | 2 | 130 | 22.61 |
| | | | 1933 | 1155 | 121 | 28.17 | 1 | 108 | 29.46 |
| Kennedy, A.S. | Hampshire | (5) | 1921 | 1305 | 152* | 26.10 | 2 | 186 | 21.55 |
| | | | 1922 | 1129 | 110* | 22.13 | 1 | 205 | 16.80 |
| | | | 1923 | 1327 | 163* | 25.51 | 2 | 184 | 19.55 |
| | | | 1928 | 1437 | 128 | 26.61 | 2 | 105 | 28.38 |
| | | | 1930 | 1006 | 94* | 20.53 | — | 120 | 25.72 |
| Killick, E.H. | Sussex | | 1905 | 1392 | 104 | 26.26 | 1 | 108 | 21.93 |
| Kilner, R. | Yorkshire | (4) | 1922 | 1198 | 124 | 27.22 | 2 | 122 | 14.73 |
| | | | 1923 | 1404 | 79 | 34.24 | — | 158 | 12.91 |
| | | | 1925 | 1068 | 124 | 30.51 | 2 | 131 | 17.92 |
| | | | 1926 | 1187 | 150 | 37.09 | 1 | 107 | 22.52 |
| King, J.H. | Leicestershire | | 1912 | 1074 | 104* | 22.85 | 1 | 130 | 17.63 |
| Knight, B.R. | Essex | (4) | 1962 | 1689 | 165 | 34.46 | 2 | 100 | 24.05 |
| | | | 1963 | 1578 | 124 | 28.69 | 3 | 140 | 21.72 |
| | | | 1964 | 1209 | 97 | 23.25 | — | 100 | 27.02 |
| | | | 1965 | 1172 | 63 | 22.98 | — | 125 | 18.90 |
| Langridge, James | Sussex | (6) | 1930 | 1386 | 159* | 30.13 | 2 | 112 | 20.60 |
| | | | 1931 | 1007 | 92* | 28.77 | — | 102 | 18.60 |
| | | | 1932 | 1192 | 128 | 32.21 | 2 | 115 | 17.66 |
| | | | 1933 | 1578 | 159* | 37.57 | 5 | 158 | 16.56 |
| | | | 1935 | 1375 | 114* | 33.53 | 2 | 102 | 19.67 |
| | | | 1937 | 2082 | 150* | 40.82 | 1 | 101 | 22.92 |
| Llewellyn, C.B. | Hampshire | (3) | 1901 | 1025 | 216 | 31.06 | 2 | 134 | 22.53 |
| | | | 1908 | 1347 | 154 | 28.06 | 3 | 102 | 25.13 |
| | | | 1910 | 1232 | 107 | 29.33 | 2 | 152 | 19.27 |
| Lockwood, W. | Surrey | (2) | 1899 | 1272 | 131 | 37.14 | 3 | 117 | 19.52 |
| | | | 1900 | 1367 | 165 | 32.54 | 2 | 125 | 19.99 |
| Mankad, M.H. | Indians | | 1946 | 1120 | 132 | 28.00 | 3 | 129 | 20.76 |
| Martin, S.H. | Worcestershire | (2) | 1937 | 1130 | 92 | 21.73 | — | 114 | 20.25 |
| | | | 1939 | 1262 | 102* | 25.24 | 1 | 106 | 25.00 |
| Mason, J.R. | Kent | | 1901 | 1561 | 145 | 36.30 | 3 | 118 | 20.44 |
| Mortimore, J.B. | Gloucestershire | (3) | 1959 | 1060 | 76 | 20.78 | — | 113 | 18.28 |
| | | | 1963 | 1425 | 149 | 26.88 | 1 | 102 | 20.62 |
| | | | 1964 | 1118 | 95 | 19.96 | — | 104 | 21.44 |
| Muncer, B.L. | Glamorgan | | 1952 | 1097 | 135 | 24.37 | 1 | 105 | 17.29 |
| Newman, J.A. | Hampshire | (5) | 1921 | 1065 | 166* | 30.42 | 1 | 177 | 21.56 |
| | | | 1923 | 1006 | 130 | 22.86 | 1 | 148 | 25.35 |
| | | | 1926 | 1468 | 134 | 30.58 | 1 | 154 | 24.70 |
| | | | 1927 | 1448 | 102* | 32.17 | 2 | 115 | 23.19 |
| | | | 1928 | 1474 | 118 | 29.48 | 3 | 112 | 30.32 |
| Nichols, M.S. | Essex | (8) | 1929 | 1301 | 138 | 28.91 | 1 | 104 | 25.59 |
| | | | 1932 | 1430 | 105 | 31.77 | 1 | 115 | 24.92 |
| | | | 1933 | 1406 | 135 | 28.69 | 3 | 145 | 20.97 |
| | | | 1935 | 1249 | 146 | 23.56 | 1 | 157 | 16.62 |
| | | | 1936 | 1315 | 205 | 29.22 | 3 | 114 | 19.42 |
| | | | 1937 | 1247 | 120 | 25.44 | 2 | 148 | 18.52 |
| | | | 1938 | 1452 | 163 | 35.41 | 3 | 171 | 19.92 |
| | | | 1939 | 1387 | 146 | 35.56 | 2 | 121 | 18.87 |
| Palmer, K.E. | Somerset | | 1961 | 1036 | 125* | 25.90 | 1 | 114 | 20.32 |
| Parks, J.H. | Sussex | (2) | 1935 | 1633 | 156 | 33.32 | 4 | 103 | 19.57 |
| | | | 1937 | 3003 | 168 | 50.89 | 11 | 101 | 25.83 |
| Pearson, F.A. | Worcestershire | | 1923 | 1052 | 103* | 25.04 | 1 | 111 | 22.89 |
| Peel, R. | Yorkshire | | 1896 | 1206 | 210* | 30.15 | 3 | 128 | 17.50 |
| Pope, G.H. | Derbyshire | (2) | 1938 | 1040 | 85 | 29.71 | — | 103 | 24.13 |
| | | | 1948 | 1152 | 207* | 38.40 | 3 | 100 | 17.24 |
| Pressdee, J.S. | Glamorgan | (2) | 1963 | 1467 | 88* | 33.34 | — | 106 | 21.62 |
| | | | 1964 | 1606 | 133* | 37.34 | 1 | 105 | 19.39 |
| Relf, A.E. | Sussex | (8) | 1904 | 1214 | 154 | 28.23 | 2 | 102 | 26.04 |
| | | | 1905 | 1386 | 120 | 29.48 | 1 | 111 | 23.45 |
| | | | 1906 | 1256 | 189* | 25.63 | 2 | 106 | 23.24 |
| | | | 1908 | 1335 | 138 | 28.40 | 1 | 151 | 17.53 |
| | | | 1910 | 1296 | 87 | 23.56 | — | 158 | 19.67 |
| | | | 1911 | 1691 | 101* | 29.66 | 1 | 142 | 21.44 |

|  |  |  | Season | Runs | HS | Avge | 100 | Wkts | Avge |
|---|---|---|---|---|---|---|---|---|---|
| Relf, A.E. *continued* |  |  | 1912 | 1312 | 104 | 23.85 | 2 | 133 | 19.44 |
|  |  |  | 1913 | 1846 | 130 | 31.82 | 4 | 141 | 18.09 |
| Rhodes, W. | Yorkshire | (16) | 1903 | 1137 | 98* | 27.07 | — | 193 | 14.57 |
|  |  |  | 1904 | 1537 | 196 | 35.74 | 2 | 131 | 21.59 |
|  |  |  | 1905 | 1581 | 201 | 35.93 | 2 | 182 | 16.95 |
|  |  |  | 1906 | 1721 | 119 | 29.16 | 3 | 128 | 23.57 |
|  |  |  | 1907 | 1055 | 112 | 22.93 | 1 | 177 | 15.57 |
|  |  |  | 1908 | 1673 | 146 | 31.56 | 3 | 115 | 16.13 |
|  |  |  | 1909 | 2094 | 199 | 40.26 | 5 | 141 | 15.89 |
|  |  |  | 1911 | 2261 | 128 | 38.32 | 5 | 117 | 24.07 |
|  |  |  | 1914 | 1377 | 113 | 29.29 | 2 | 118 | 18.27 |
|  |  |  | 1919 | 1237 | 135 | 34.36 | 1 | 164 | 14.42 |
|  |  |  | 1920 | 1123 | 167* | 28.07 | 1 | 161 | 13.18 |
|  |  |  | 1921 | 1474 | 267* | 39.83 | 3 | 141 | 13.27 |
|  |  |  | 1922 | 1511 | 110 | 39.76 | 4 | 119 | 12.19 |
|  |  |  | 1923 | 1321 | 126 | 33.02 | 2 | 134 | 11.54 |
|  |  |  | 1924 | 1126 | 100 | 26.18 | 1 | 109 | 14.46 |
|  |  |  | 1926 | 1132 | 132 | 34.30 | 1 | 115 | 14.86 |
| Robins, R.W.V. | Middlesex |  | 1929 | 1134 | 106 | 26.37 | 1 | 162 | 21.53 |
| Root, C.F. | Worcestershire |  | 1928 | 1044 | 107 | 20.88 | 1 | 118 | 29.66 |
| Simms, H.L. | Sussex |  | 1912 | 1099 | 126 | 20.73 | 1 | 110 | 22.68 |
| Sinfield, R.A. | Gloucestershire | (2) | 1934 | 1228 | 83 | 31.48 | — | 122 | 23.40 |
|  |  |  | 1937 | 1001 | 74* | 24.41 | — | 129 | 22.92 |
| Smailes, T.F. | Yorkshire |  | 1938 | 1002 | 117 | 25.05 | 2 | 113 | 20.84 |
| Smith, R. | Essex | (3) | 1947 | 1386 | 86* | 28.87 | — | 125 | 37.26 |
|  |  |  | 1950 | 1149 | 80 | 23.93 | — | 102 | 34.77 |
|  |  |  | 1952 | 1044 | 107* | 24.27 | 1 | 136 | 28.87 |
| Smith, S.G. | Northamptonshire | (3) | 1909 | 1091 | 126 | 30.30 | 1 | 115 | 19.51 |
|  |  |  | 1913 | 1522 | 133 | 37.12 | 4 | 111 | 17.25 |
|  |  |  | 1914 | 1373 | 177 | 42.90 | 1 | 105 | 16.25 |
| Smith, T.P.B. | Essex |  | 1947 | 1065 | 163 | 23.66 | 1 | 172 | 27.13 |
| Storey, S.J. | Surrey |  | 1966 | 1013 | 109* | 24.70 | 1 | 104 | 18.39 |
| Studd, C.T. | Middlesex | (2) | 1882 | 1249 | 126* | 32.86 | 4 | 131 | 16.01 |
|  |  |  | 1883 | 1193 | 175* | 41.13 | 2 | 112 | 17.46 |
| Tarrant, F.A. | Middlesex | (8) | 1907 | 1552 | 147 | 32.33 | 2 | 183 | 15.70 |
|  |  |  | 1908 | 1724 | 157 | 41.04 | 5 | 169 | 16.68 |
|  |  |  | 1909 | 1643 | 138 | 32.86 | 2 | 125 | 19.26 |
|  |  |  | 1910 | 1425 | 142 | 36.53 | 3 | 137 | 16.18 |
|  |  |  | 1911 | 2030 | 207* | 46.13 | 5 | 111 | 19.23 |
|  |  |  | 1912 | 1492 | 140 | 30.44 | 2 | 140 | 14.78 |
|  |  |  | 1913 | 1630 | 142 | 40.75 | 3 | 136 | 17.08 |
|  |  |  | 1914 | 1879 | 250* | 45.82 | 5 | 138 | 18.84 |
| Tate, M.W. | Sussex | (8) | 1922 | 1050 | 88 | 19.44 | — | 119 | 17.42 |
|  |  |  | 1923 | 1168 | 97 | 22.03 | — | 219 | 13.97 |
|  |  |  | 1924 | 1419 | 164 | 29.56 | 2 | 205 | 13.74 |
|  |  |  | 1925 | 1290 | 121 | 23.45 | 2 | 228 | 14.97 |
|  |  |  | 1926 | 1347 | 93 | 32.07 | — | 147 | 17.51 |
|  |  |  | 1927 | 1713 | 146 | 36.44 | 3 | 147 | 20.53 |
|  |  |  | 1928 | 1469 | 126 | 30.60 | 3 | 165 | 19.29 |
|  |  |  | 1929 | 1161 | 100* | 25.80 | 1 | 156 | 18.60 |
| Thompson, G.J. | Northamptonshire | (2) | 1906 | 1014 | 103* | 25.35 | 1 | 136 | 22.20 |
|  |  |  | 1910 | 1021 | 101 | 23.74 | 2 | 129 | 17.86 |
| Titmus, F.J. | Middlesex | (8) | 1955 | 1235 | 104 | 24.70 | 1 | 191 | 16.31 |
|  |  |  | 1956 | 1227 | 96 | 28.53 | — | 105 | 20.84 |
|  |  |  | 1957 | 1056 | 70 | 19.92 | — | 106 | 19.74 |
|  |  |  | 1959 | 1273 | 90 | 25.75 | — | 104 | 24.83 |
|  |  |  | 1960 | 1205 | 105 | 27.38 | 1 | 117 | 19.83 |
|  |  |  | 1961 | 1703 | 120* | 37.02 | 1 | 127 | 23.11 |
|  |  |  | 1962 | 1238 | 74 | 30.95 | — | 136 | 20.76 |
|  |  |  | 1967 | 1093 | 81 | 36.43 | — | 106 | 20.35 |
| Todd, L.J. | Kent |  | 1936 | 1320 | 113 | 28.08 | 1 | 103 | 21.93 |
| Townsend, C.L. | Gloucestershire | (2) | 1898 | 1270 | 159 | 34.32 | 5 | 145 | 20.60 |
|  |  |  | 1899 | 2440 | 244* | 51.91 | 9 | 101 | 29.06 |
| Townsend, L.F. | Derbyshire | (3) | 1928 | 1001 | 98 | 29.44 | — | 104 | 23.56 |
|  |  |  | 1932 | 1497 | 153* | 31.18 | 1 | 117 | 18.45 |
|  |  |  | 1933 | 2268 | 233 | 44.47 | 6 | 100 | 18.71 |

| | | | Season | Runs | HS | Avge | 100 | Wkts | Avge |
|---|---|---|---|---|---|---|---|---|---|
| Tribe, G.E. | Northamptonshire | (7) | 1952 | 1039 | 78 | 29.68 | — | 126 | 25.61 |
| | | | 1953 | 1260 | 121 | 36.00 | 2 | 108 | 22.22 |
| | | | 1954 | 1117 | 136* | 27.92 | 1 | 149 | 19.79 |
| | | | 1955 | 1127 | 80* | 25.04 | — | 176 | 19.12 |
| | | | 1956 | 1204 | 116 | 32.54 | 1 | 126 | 19.02 |
| | | | 1957 | 1181 | 101 | 25.12 | 1 | 140 | 18.71 |
| | | | 1959 | 1082 | 105* | 26.39 | 1 | 122 | 23.95 |
| Trott, A.E. | Middlesex | (2) | 1899 | 1175 | 164 | 23.03 | 2 | 239 | 17.09 |
| | | | 1900 | 1357 | 112 | 23.87 | 2 | 211 | 23.33 |
| Trumble, H. | Australians | | 1899 | 1183 | 100 | 27.51 | 1 | 142 | 18.43 |
| Van Geloven, J. | Leicestershire | | 1962 | 1055 | 102* | 22.93 | 1 | 100 | 28.11 |
| Vine, J. | Sussex | | 1901 | 1190 | 94 | 28.33 | — | 113 | 29.72 |
| Wainwright, E. | Yorkshire | | 1897 | 1612 | 171 | 35.82 | 5 | 101 | 23.06 |
| Walker, P.M. | Glamorgan | | 1961 | 1347 | 112* | 24.94 | 1 | 101 | 24.04 |
| Walsh, J.E. | Leicestershire | | 1952 | 1106 | 102 | 24.04 | 1 | 122 | 25.87 |
| Watkins, A.J. | Glamorgan | (2) | 1954 | 1640 | 170* | 34.89 | 2 | 103 | 15.82 |
| | | | 1955 | 1160 | 111 | 24.16 | 2 | 114 | 20.49 |
| Wellard, A.W. | Somerset | (3) | 1933 | 1055 | 77 | 26.37 | — | 104 | 25.57 |
| | | | 1935 | 1347 | 112 | 31.32 | 1 | 114 | 20.68 |
| | | | 1937 | 1049 | 91* | 18.73 | — | 156 | 23.55 |
| Wensley, A.F. | Sussex | | 1929 | 1057 | 91 | 21.14 | — | 113 | 25.22 |
| White, J.C. | Somerset | (2) | 1929 | 1179 | 192 | 27.41 | 1 | 168 | 15.76 |
| | | | 1930 | 1050 | 97 | 26.25 | — | 123 | 19.51 |
| Wooller, W. | Glamorgan | | 1954 | 1059 | 71 | 24.06 | — | 107 | 18.42 |
| Woolley, F.E. | Kent | (8) | 1910 | 1101 | 120 | 24.46 | 3 | 136 | 14.50 |
| | | | 1912 | 1827 | 117 | 41.52 | 2 | 126 | 14.30 |
| | | | 1914 | 2272 | 160* | 45.44 | 6 | 125 | 19.45 |
| | | | 1919 | 1082 | 164 | 41.61 | 3 | 128 | 17.15 |
| | | | 1920 | 1924 | 158 | 40.93 | 5 | 185 | 14.23 |
| | | | 1921 | 2101 | 174 | 42.87 | 6 | 167 | 16.14 |
| | | | 1922 | 2022 | 188 | 45.95 | 5 | 163 | 18.37 |
| | | | 1923 | 2091 | 270 | 41.00 | 5 | 101 | 19.18 |

## 1000 RUNS AND 100 DISMISSALS

Only two players have achieved the wicket-keepers' double in a season.

| | | | Season | Runs | HS | Avge | 100 | Dis | Ct | St |
|---|---|---|---|---|---|---|---|---|---|---|
| L.E.G. Ames | Kent | (3) | 1928 | 1919 | 200 | 35.53 | 4 | 122 | 70 | 52 |
| | | | 1929 | 1795 | 145 | 35.90 | 5 | 128 | 79 | 49 |
| | | | 1932 | 2482 | 180 | 57.72 | 9 | 104 | 40 | 64 |
| J.T. Murray | Middlesex | | 1957 | 1025 | 120 | 19.71 | 1 | 104 | 82 | 22 |

# CAREER RECORDS

## 10,000 RUNS AND 1000 WICKETS

| | Career | Runs | Wkts | Double |
|---|---|---|---|---|
| Arnold, E.G. | 1899–1913 | 15853 | 1069 | 4 |
| Astill, W.E. | 1906–1939 | 22731 | 2431 | 9 |
| Bailey, T.E. | 1945–1967 | 28642 | 2082 | 8 |
| Birkenshaw, J. | 1958–1981 | 12780 | 1073 | — |
| Braund, L.C. | 1896–1920 | 17801 | 1114 | 3 |
| Briggs, J. | 1879–1900 | 14092 | 2221 | — |
| Brown, A.S. | 1953–1976 | 12851 | 1230 | — |
| Brown, F.R. | 1930–1961 | 13327 | 1221 | 2 |
| Cartwright, T.W. | 1952–1977 | 13710 | 1536 | 1 |
| Close, D.B. | 1949–1985 | 34968 | 1170 | 2 |
| Cox, G.R. | 1895–1928 | 14643 | 1843 | — |
| Douglas, J.W.H.T. | 1901–1930 | 24531 | 1893 | 5 |
| Eastman, L.C. | 1920–1939 | 13385 | 1006 | — |
| Fender, P.G.H. | 1910–1936 | 19034 | 1894 | 6 |
| Flowers, W. | 1877–1896 | 12891 | 1188 | 1 |
| Geary, G. | 1912–1938 | 13504 | 2063 | — |
| Giffen, G. | *1877–1903* | 11758 | 1023 | 3 |
| Grace, W.G. | 1865–1908 | 54896 | 2876 | 8 |
| Gunn, J.R. | 1896–1932 | 24557 | 1242 | 4 |

| | Career | Runs | Wkts | Doubles |
|---|---|---|---|---|
| Haig, N.E. | 1912–1936 | 15220 | 1117 | 3 |
| Haigh, S. | 1895–1913 | 11715 | 2012 | 1 |
| Hearne, A. | 1884–1910 | 16346 | 1160 | — |
| Hearne, J.W. | 1909–1936 | 37252 | 1839 | 5 |
| Hirst, G.H. | 1891–1929 | 36356 | 2742 | 14 |
| Howorth, R. | 1933–1951 | 11479 | 1345 | 3 |
| Illingworth, R. | 1951–1983 | 24134 | 2072 | 6 |
| Intikhab Alam | 1957–1982 | 14331 | 1571 | — |
| Imran Khan | 1969–1985 | 14464 | 1074 | — |
| Jenkins, R.O. | 1938–1958 | 10073 | 1309 | 2 |
| Jupp, V.W.C. | 1909–1938 | 23296 | 1658 | 10 |
| Kennedy, A.S. | 1907–1936 | 16586 | 2874 | 5 |
| King, J.H. | 1895–1925 | 25122 | 1204 | 1 |
| Knight, B.R. | 1955–1969 | 13336 | 1089 | 4 |
| Langridge, James | 1924–1953 | 31716 | 1530 | 6 |
| Llewellyn, C.B. | 1894–1912 | 11425 | 1013 | 3 |
| Lock, G.A.R. | 1946–1970 | 10342 | 2844 | — |
| Lockwood, W. | 1886–1904 | 10673 | 1376 | 2 |
| Morgan, D.C. | 1950–1969 | 18356 | 1248 | — |
| Mortimore, J.B. | 1950–1975 | 15891 | 1807 | 3 |
| Newman, J.A. | 1906–1930 | 15333 | 2032 | 5 |
| Nichols, M.S. | 1924–1939 | 17827 | 1833 | 8 |
| Peel, R. | 1882–1899 | 12191 | 1776 | 1 |
| Procter, M.J. | 1965–1983 | 21904 | 1407 | — |
| Relf, A.E. | 1900–1921 | 22238 | 1897 | 8 |
| Rhodes, W. | 1898–1930 | 39722 | 4187 | 16 |
| Robson, E. | 1895–1923 | 12620 | 1147 | — |
| Sainsbury, P.J. | 1954–1976 | 20176 | 1316 | — |
| Shepherd, J.N. | 1969–1985 | 13353 | 1155 | — |
| Sinfield, R.A. | 1921–1939 | 15674 | 1173 | 2 |
| Smith, R. | 1934–1956 | 12042 | 1350 | 3 |
| Smith, T.P.B. | 1929–1952 | 10161 | 1697 | 1 |
| Sobers, G.St A. | 1952–1974 | 28315 | 1043 | — |
| Tarrant, F.A. | 1898–1936 | 17857 | 1511 | 8 |
| Tate, M.W. | 1912–1937 | 21717 | 2784 | 8 |
| Thompson, G.J. | 1897–1922 | 12018 | 1591 | 2 |
| Titmus, F.J. | 1949–1982 | 21588 | 2830 | 8 |
| Townsend, L.F. | 1922–1939 | 19555 | 1088 | 3 |
| Tribe, G.E. | 1945–1959 | 10177 | 1378 | 7 |
| Trott, A.E. | 1892–1911 | 10696 | 1674 | 2 |
| Wainwright, E. | 1888–1902 | 12513 | 1071 | 1 |
| Wellard, A.W. | 1927–1950 | 12515 | 1614 | 3 |
| Wensley, A.F. | 1922–1939 | 10849 | 1141 | 1 |
| White, J.C. | 1909–1937 | 12202 | 2356 | 2 |
| Woods, S.M.J. | 1886–1910 | 15345 | 1040 | — |
| Woolley, F.E. | 1906–1938 | 58959 | 2066 | 8 |

## 10,000 RUNS AND 1000 DISMISSALS

| | Career | Runs | Dismissals | W-K Doubles |
|---|---|---|---|---|
| L.E.G. Ames | 1926–1951 | 37248 | 1121 | 3 |
| J.H. Board | 1891–1914 | 15674 | 1207 | — |
| R. Booth | 1951–1970 | 10138 | 1126 | — |
| G.O. Dawkes | 1937–1961 | 11411 | 1043 | — |
| T.G. Evans | 1939–1969 | 14882 | 1066 | — |
| A.P.E. Knott | 1964–1985 | 18105 | 1344 | — |
| J.T. Murray | 1952–1975 | 18872 | 1527 | 1 |
| J.M. Parks | 1949–1976 | 36673 | 1181 | — |
| H.W. Stephenson | 1948–1964 | 13195 | 1082 | — |
| B. Taylor | 1949–1973 | 19094 | 1294 | — |
| R.W. Taylor | 1960–1984 | 12040 | 1646 | — |
| R.W. Tolchard | 1965–1983 | 15288 | 1037 | — |

## 10,000 RUNS AND 1000 CATCHES

| | Career | Runs | Catches |
|---|---|---|---|
| F.E. Woolley | 1906–1938 | 58959 | 1018 |

# INDIVIDUAL RECORDS – WICKET-KEEPING

## MOST DISMISSALS IN AN INNINGS

### EIGHT DISMISSALS IN AN INNINGS

| | | Ct | St | | | |
|---|---|---|---|---|---|---|
| East, D.E. | | 8 | 0 | Essex v Somerset | Taunton | 1985 |
| | | | | *The first eight wickets to fall – on his 26th birthday* | | |
| Grout, A.T.W. | | 8 | 0 | Queensland v Western Australia | Brisbane | 1959–60 |

### SEVEN DISMISSALS IN AN INNINGS

| | | Ct | St | | | |
|---|---|---|---|---|---|---|
| Andrew, K.V. | | 7 | 0 | Northamptonshire v Lancashire | Manchester | 1962 |
| Arifuddin | | 3 | 4 | United Bank v PACO | Sahiwal | 1983–84 |
| Bairstow, D.L. | | 7 | 0 | Yorkshire v Derbyshire | Scarborough | 1982 |
| Benjamin, S. | | 6 | 1 | Central Zone v North Zone | Bombay | 1973–74 |
| Brown, J. | | 4 | 3 | Scotland v Ireland | Dublin | 1957 |
| East, R.J. | | 6 | 1 | OFS v Western Province B | Cape Town | 1984–85 |
| Farrimond, W. | | 6 | 1 | Lancashire v Kent | Manchester | 1930 |
| Jones, E.W. | | 6 | 1 | Glamorgan v Cambridge University | Cambridge | 1970 |
| Kirsten, N. | | 6 | 1 | Border v Rhodesia | East London | 1959–60 |
| Long, A. | | 7 | 0 | Surrey v Sussex | Hove | 1964 |
| Maclean, J.A. | | 7 | 0 | Queensland v Victoria | Melbourne | 1977–78 |
| Masood Iqbal | | 4 | 3 | Habib Bank v Lahore | Lahore | 1982–83 |
| Phillips, R.B. | | 6 | 1 | Queensland v New Zealanders | Bundaberg | 1982–83 |
| Price, W.F.F. | | 7 | 0 | Middlesex v Yorkshire | Lord's | 1937 |
| Saggers, R.A. | | 7 | 0 | New South Wales v Combined XI | Brisbane | 1940–41 |
| Schofield, R.M. | | 7 | 0 | Central Districts v Wellington | Wellington | 1964–65 |
| Shahid Israr | | 6 | 1 | Karachi Whites v Quetta | Karachi | 1976–77 |
| Smith, E.J. | | 4 | 3 | Warwickshire v Derbyshire | Birmingham | 1926 |
| Smith, M.S. | | 7 | 0 | Natal v Border | East London | 1959–60 |
| Taber, H.B. | | 6 | 1 | New South Wales v South Australia | Adelaide | 1968–69 |
| Tallon, D. | | 3 | 4 | Queensland v Victoria | Brisbane | 1938–39 |
| Taslim Arif | | 5 | 2 | National Bank v Punjab | Lahore | 1978–79 |
| Taylor, R.W. | (3) | 7 | 0 | Derbyshire v Glamorgan | Derby | 1966 |
| | | 7 | 0 | Derbyshire v Yorkshire | Chesterfield | 1975 |
| | | 7 | 0 | England v India | Bombay | 1979–80 |
| Wasim Bari | (2) | 4 | 3 | PIA v Sind | Lahore | 1977–78 |
| | | 7 | 0 | Pakistan v New Zealand | Auckland | 1978–79 |
| Yarnold, H. | | 1 | 6 | Worcestershire v Scotland | Broughty Ferry | 1951 |

### SIX DISMISSALS IN AN INNINGS

| | | Ct | St | | | |
|---|---|---|---|---|---|---|
| Allen, W.R. | | 2 | 4 | Yorkshire v Sussex | Hove | 1921 |
| Ames, L.E.G. | (2) | 4 | 2 | Kent v Sussex | Maidstone | 1929 |
| | | 5 | 1 | Kent v Sussex | Folkestone | 1930 |
| Anil Dalpat | | 4 | 2 | PIA v Karachi | Karachi | 1980–81 |
| Arifuddin | | 2 | 4 | United Bank v Karachi Whites | Karachi | 1975–76 |
| Bacher, A. | | 5 | 1 | Transvaal v Cavaliers | Johannesburg | 1960–61 |
| Bairstow, D.L. | (4) | 6 | 0 | Yorkshire v Lancashire | Manchester | 1971 |
| | | 6 | 0 | Yorkshire v Warwickshire | Bradford | 1978 |
| | | 5 | 1 | Yorkshire v Lancashire | Leeds | 1980 |
| | | 6 | 0 | Yorkshire v Derbyshire | Chesterfield | 1984 |
| Baker, E.A. | (2) | 6 | 0 | Victoria v New South Wales | Melbourne | 1946–47 |
| | | 1 | 5 | Victoria v New South Wales | Sydney | 1946–47 |
| Bale, E.W. | | 2 | 4 | Worcestershire v Australians | Worcester | 1909 |
| Barnard, J. | | 2 | 4 | MCC v Godalming | Lord's | 1822 |
| Becker, G.C. | | 6 | 0 | Western Australia v Victoria | Melbourne | 1965–66 |
| Bhandarkar, K.V. | | 5 | 1 | Holkar v Ceylon | Colombo | 1948–49 |
| Bhanot, A. | | 3 | 3 | Uttar Pradesh v Vidarbha | Agra | 1973–74 |
| Binks, J.G. | | 5 | 1 | Yorkshire v Lancashire | Leeds | 1962 |
| Binns, A.P. | | 3 | 3 | Jamaica v British Guiana | Georgetown | 1952–53 |

| | Ct | St | | | |
|---|---|---|---|---|---|
| Blundell, R.P. | 5 | 1 | South Australia v Queensland | Brisbane | 1969–70 |
| Bromham, C.G. | 6 | 0 | N.E. Transvaal v W. Province | Cape Town | 1939–40 |
| Brooks, E.W.J. | 6 | 0 | Surrey v Kent | Blackheath | 1935 |
| Buckingham, J. | 5 | 1 | Warwickshire v Sussex | Birmingham | 1939 |
| Butt, H.R. | (3) 6 | 0 | Sussex v Gloucestershire | Bristol | 1899 |
| | 6 | 0 | Sussex v Hampshire | Hove | 1901 |
| | 6 | 0 | Sussex v Leicestershire | Hove | 1909 |
| Cass, G.R. | 6 | 0 | Worcestershire v Essex | Worcester | 1973 |
| Clayton, G. | 6 | 0 | Somerset v Worcestershire | Kidderminster | 1965 |
| Compton, L.H. | 4 | 2 | Middlesex v Essex | Lord's | 1953 |
| Corrall, P. | (2) 4 | 2 | Leicestershire v Sussex | Hove | 1936 |
| | 3 | 3 | Leicestershire v Middlesex | Leicester | 1949 |
| Daljit Singh | 6 | 0 | Bihar v Bengal | Calcutta | 1978–79 |
| Davies, H.G. | 5 | 1 | Glamorgan v Leicestershire | Leicester | 1939 |
| Deshpande, D.D. | 3 | 3 | Services v Haryana | Delhi | 1972–73 |
| Dey, C.I. | 6 | 0 | Northern Transvaal v Natal B | Pretoria | 1974–75 |
| Downes, L.W. | 6 | 0 | Central Districts v Canterbury | Nelson | 1975–76 |
| Downton, P.R. | (2) 6 | 0 | England XI v Otago | Dunedin | 1977–78 |
| | 6 | 0 | Middlesex v Nottinghamshire | Nottingham | 1981 |
| Drummond, R.A. | 6 | 0 | W. Province v E. Province | Port Elizabeth | 1978–79 |
| Duckworth, G. | (2) 5 | 1 | Lancashire v Kent | Dover | 1926 |
| | 5 | 1 | Lancashire v Worcestershire | Worcester | 1936 |
| East, D.E. | 6 | 0 | Essex v Sussex | Hove | 1983 |
| East, R.J. | 6 | 0 | OFS v Griqualand West | Bloemfontein | 1978–79 |
| Elliott, H. | (3) 4 | 2 | Derbyshire v Worcestershire | Derby | 1931 |
| | 5 | 1 | Derbyshire v Middlesex | Derby | 1932 |
| | 4 | 2 | Derbyshire v Lancashire | Manchester | 1935 |
| Endean, W.R. | 6 | 0 | Transvaal v Rhodesia | Salisbury | 1950–51 |
| Engineer, F.M. | (2) 6 | 0 | Lancashire v Northamptonshire | Liverpool | 1970 |
| | 6 | 0 | Lancashire v Surrey | Oval | 1970 |
| Evans, D.G.L. | 6 | 0 | Glamorgan v Yorkshire | Swansea | 1967 |
| Findlay, T.M. | 3 | 3 | Windward I's v Leeward I's | Roseau | 1971–72 |
| Foster, T. | 6 | 0 | Derbyshire v Surrey | Oval | 1883 |
| French, B.N. | (3) 6 | 0 | Nottinghamshire v Essex | Nottingham | 1982 |
| | 6 | 0 | Nottinghamshire v Somerset | Taunton | 1984 |
| | 6 | 0 | Nottinghamshire v Derbyshire | Nottingham | 1985 |
| Gamsy, D. | 5 | 1 | Natal v Orange Free State | Pietermaritzburg | 1960–61 |
| Garnett, H.G. | 6 | 0 | Lancashire v Warwickshire | Birmingham | 1914 |
| Gaukrodger, G.W. | 4 | 2 | Worcestershire v Kent | Tunbridge Wells | 1907 |
| Ghosh, A. | 5 | 1 | Bihar v Assam | Bhagalpur | 1981–82 |
| Gibb, P.A. | 6 | 0 | Lord Tennyson's XI v Indian XI | Bombay | 1937–38 |
| Gibson, K.L. | 5 | 1 | Essex v Derbyshire | Leyton | 1911 |
| Gilligan, F.W. | 2 | 4 | Essex v Gloucestershire | Cheltenham | 1928 |
| Griffith, M.G. | 6 | 0 | Sussex v Essex | Clacton | 1964 |
| Griffith, S.C. | 6 | 0 | England v Australian Services | Manchester | 1945 |
| Grout, A.T.W. | (2) 6 | 0 | Queensland v New South Wales | Sydney | 1955–56 |
| | 6 | 0 | Australia v South Africa | Johannesburg | 1957–58 |
| Guillen, S.C. | 3 | 3 | West Indians v Tasmania | Launceston | 1951–52 |
| Hendricks, M. | 3 | 3 | New South Wales v South Australia | Adelaide | 1969–70 |
| Hubble, J.C. | 5 | 1 | Kent v Gloucestershire | Cheltenham | 1923 |
| Hudson, G.C. | 5 | 1 | Tasmania v West Indians | Launceston | 1960–61 |
| Huish, F.H. | 1 | 5 | Kent v Surrey | Oval | 1911 |
| Hunter, D. | (2) 5 | 1 | Yorkshire v Surrey | Sheffield | 1891 |
| | 6 | 0 | Yorkshire v Middlesex | Leeds | 1909 |
| Hunter, J. | 6 | 0 | Yorkshire v Gloucestershire | Gloucester | 1887 |
| Imtiaz Ahmed | 4 | 2 | Punjab University v W. Punjab Governor's XI | Lahore | 1948–49 |
| Indrajitsinhji, K.S. | 4 | 2 | Delhi v Bombay | Bombay | 1960–61 |
| Inkster, G.B. | 4 | 2 | South Australia v Victoria | Melbourne | 1926–27 |
| Irvine, B.L. | (2) 6 | 0 | Transvaal v Eastern Province | Johannesburg | 1969–70 |
| | 6 | 0 | Transvaal v Rhodesia | Johannesburg | 1974–75 |
| Jackson, P.B. | 6 | 0 | Ireland v Scotland | Glasgow | 1984 |
| James, K.C. | 6 | 0 | Northamptonshire v Glamorgan | Swansea | 1937 |
| Jarman, B.N. | (2) 5 | 1 | South Australia v Victoria | Melbourne | 1956–57 |
| | 5 | 1 | South Australia v New South Wales | Adelaide | 1961–62 |
| Jarvis, A.H. | 2 | 4 | Australian XI v Victoria | Melbourne | 1885–86 |

|  |  | Ct | St |  |  |  |
|---|---|---|---|---|---|---|
| Jennings, R.V. | (3) | 5 | 1 | Transvaal v Rhodesia | Bulawayo | 1979–80 |
|  |  | 6 | 0 | Transvaal v Eastern Province | Johannesburg | 1981–82 |
|  |  | 6 | 0 | Transvaal v Arosa Sri Lankans | Johannesburg | 1982–83 |
| Johnson, L.A. |  | 5 | 1 | Northamptonshire v Warwickshire | Birmingham | 1965 |
| Jones, E.W. |  | 6 | 0 | Glamorgan v Essex | Cardiff | 1982 |
| Jordon, R.C. |  | 6 | 0 | Victoria v Queensland | Melbourne | 1968–69 |
| Kirby, G.N.G. |  | 6 | 0 | Surrey v Cambridge University | Guildford | 1949 |
| Kirmani, S.M.H. |  | 5 | 1 | India v New Zealand | Christchurch | 1975–76 |
| Knott, A.P.E. | (7) | 4 | 2 | Kent v Middlesex | Gravesend | 1966 |
|  |  | 5 | 1 | Kent v Northamptonshire | Maidstone | 1966 |
|  |  | 6 | 0 | Kent v Lancashire | Folkestone | 1967 |
|  |  | 6 | 0 | MCC Tour XI v Rest | Hove | 1973 |
|  |  | 6 | 0 | Kent v Worcestershire | Dartford | 1973 |
|  |  | 6 | 0 | Kent v Hampshire | Southampton | 1975 |
|  |  | 6 | 0 | Kent v Hampshire | Maidstone | 1982 |
| Lambert, W. |  | 3 | 3 | MCC v Hampshire | Lord's | 1816 |
| Langley, G.R.A. |  | 5 | 1 | South Australia v Queensland | Brisbane | 1947–48 |
| Levett, W.H.V. | (2) | 4 | 2 | Kent v Northamptonshire | Northampton | 1934 |
|  |  | 5 | 1 | Kent v Glamorgan | Neath | 1939 |
| Lewis, E.B. |  | 6 | 0 | Warwickshire v Cambridge U. | Cambridge | 1956 |
| Lilley, A.F.A. |  | 4 | 2 | Warwickshire v Worcestershire | Birmingham | 1906 |
| Lilley, B. |  | 6 | 0 | Nottinghamshire v Somerset | Taunton | 1932 |
| Lindsay, D.T. |  | 6 | 0 | South Africa v Australia | Johannesburg | 1966–67 |
| Long, A. | (2) | 6 | 0 | Surrey v Lancashire | Manchester | 1967 |
|  |  | 5 | 1 | Surrey v Northamptonshire | Oval | 1968 |
| Love, H.S.B. |  | 5 | 1 | Australians v CP and Bihar | Nagpur | 1935–36 |
| Lovelock, O.I. |  | 3 | 3 | Western Australia v South Australia | Adelaide | 1937–38 |
| Maclean, J.A. |  | 6 | 0 | Queensland v Victoria | Melbourne | 1972–73 |
| Madsen, T.R. |  | 5 | 1 | Natal B v Orange Free State | Durban | 1981–82 |
| Marsh, R.W. | (6) | 6 | 0 | Western Australia v NSW | Perth | 1974–75 |
|  |  | 6 | 0 | Western Australia v Victoria | Perth | 1975–76 |
|  |  | 6 | 0 | Western Australia v S. Australia | Perth | 1976–77 |
|  |  | 6 | 0 | Western Australia v Queensland | Brisbane | 1979–80 |
|  |  | 6 | 0 | Western Australia v South Australia | Perth | 1980–81 |
|  |  | 6 | 0 | Australia v England | Brisbane | 1982–83 |
| Maqsood Kundi |  | 3 | 3 | Rawalpindi v National Bank | Rawalpindi | 1982–83 |
| Masood Iqbal |  | 6 | 0 | Habib Bank v Railways | Lahore | 1983–84 |
| Masroor Ali |  | 6 | 0 | Universities v Sind | Lahore | 1973–74 |
| Matthews, M.H. |  | 4 | 2 | Oxford University v Surrey | Oval | 1937 |
| Maynard, C. |  | 6 | 0 | Lancashire v Glamorgan | Swansea | 1983 |
| Meads, E.A. | (2) | 5 | 1 | Nottinghamshire v Derbyshire | Ilkeston | 1948 |
|  |  | 5 | 1 | Nottinghamshire v Kent | Nottingham | 1949 |
| Meyer, B.J. |  | 6 | 0 | Gloucestershire v Somerset | Taunton | 1962 |
| Millman, G. |  | 6 | 0 | Nottinghamshire v Northants | Nottingham | 1959 |
| Mooney, F.L.H. |  | 4 | 2 | New Zealanders v Worcestershire | Worcester | 1949 |
| Murray, D.A. |  | 6 | 0 | West Indian XI v South Africa | Port Elizabeth | 1983–84 |
| Murray, J.T. |  | 6 | 0 | England v India | Lord's | 1967 |
| Murrell, H.R. |  | 4 | 2 | Middlesex v Gloucestershire | Bristol | 1926 |
| Nicholls, D. |  | 6 | 0 | Kent v Nottinghamshire | Nottingham | 1974 |
| Nissar Ahmed |  | 6 | 0 | Gujranwala v Faisalabad | Faisalabad | 1983–84 |
| Oates, T.W. | (2) | 6 | 0 | Nottinghamshire v Middlesex | Nottingham | 1906 |
|  |  | 6 | 0 | Nottinghamshire v Leicestershire | Leicester | 1907 |
| Oldfield, W.A.S. |  | 3 | 3 | New South Wales v West Indians | Sydney | 1930–31 |
| Parkar, Z. |  | 5 | 1 | Bombay v Maharashtra | Bombay | 1981–82 |
| Parks, J.M. |  | 6 | 0 | Sussex v Worcestershire | Dudley | 1959 |
| Parks, R.J. | (2) | 6 | 0 | Hampshire v Derbyshire | Portsmouth | 1981 |
|  |  | 6 | 0 | Hampshire v Essex | Colchester | 1984 |
| Pfuhl, G.P. | (2) | 6 | 0 | Western Province v Rhodesia | Salisbury | 1970–71 |
|  |  | 6 | 0 | W. Province v E. Province | Cape Town | 1979–80 |
| Phillips, H. |  | 3 | 3 | Sussex v Surrey | Oval | 1872 |
| Phillips, L.M. |  | 6 | 0 | Griqualand West v OFS | Kimberley | 1984–85 |
| Pinnock, R.A. |  | 4 | 2 | Jamaica v Trinidad | Port-of-Spain | 1969–70 |
| Pooley, E. | (3) | 5 | 1 | Surrey v Sussex (1st inns) | Oval | 1868 |
|  |  | 3 | 3 | Surrey v Sussex (2nd inns) | Oval | 1868 |
|  |  | 1 | 5 | Surrey v Kent | Oval | 1878 |

|  |  | Ct | St |  |  |  |
|---|---|---|---|---|---|---|
| Price, W.F.F. | (2) | 3 | 3 | MCC v Kent | Folkestone | 1934 |
|  |  | 6 | 0 | Middlesex v Warwickshire | Lord's | 1938 |
| Reddy, B. |  | 6 | 0 | Tamil Nadu v Kerala | Palghat | 1982–83 |
| Robertson, T.J. |  | 4 | 2 | South Australia v NSW | Adelaide | 1978–79 |
| Robinson, R.D. | (2) | 5 | 1 | Victoria v Queensland | Brisbane | 1974–75 |
|  |  | 3 | 3 | Australians v Kent | Canterbury | 1975 |
| Russell, T.M. | (2) | 3 | 3 | Essex v Lancashire | Manchester | 1898 |
|  |  | 2 | 4 | Essex v Kent | Canterbury | 1901 |
| Rynners, N. |  | 5 | 1 | Transvaal B v Griqualand West | Kimberley | 1982–83 |
| Saggers, R.A. |  | 4 | 2 | New South Wales v Queensland | Sydney | 1946–47 |
| Sajid Abbasi |  | 3 | 3 | MCBank v IDBP | Karachi | 1980–81 |
| Salim Ahmed |  | 5 | 1 | Haryana v Services | Delhi | 1984–85 |
| Salim Yousuf |  | 3 | 3 | Allied Bank v HBFC | Multan | 1984–85 |
| Scattergood, J.H. |  | 5 | 1 | Philadelphians v P.F. Warner's XI | Philadelphia | 1897–98 |
| Sen, P. |  | 2 | 4 | Past v Present | Delhi | 1957–58 |
| Shahid Munir |  | 5 | 1 | Rawalpindi v PIA | Rawalpindi | 1975–76 |
| Shaw, A.A. |  | 3 | 3 | Sussex v Cambridge University | Hove | 1927 |
| Sismey, S.G. |  | 6 | 0 | New South Wales v Victoria | Sydney | 1949–50 |
| Smith, A.C. |  | 6 | 0 | Warwickshire v Derbyshire | Derby | 1970 |
| Smith, H. |  | 3 | 3 | Gloucestershire v Sussex | Bristol | 1923 |
| Spooner, R.T. |  | 6 | 0 | Warwickshire v Nottinghamshire | Birmingham | 1957 |
| Stephenson, G.R. |  | 5 | 1 | Hampshire v Middlesex | Lord's | 1976 |
| Stephenson, H.W. |  | 5 | 1 | Somerset v Glamorgan | Bath | 1962 |
| Strudwick, H. |  | 6 | 0 | Surrey v Sussex | Oval | 1914 |
| Swetman, R. | (3) | 6 | 0 | Surrey v Kent | Oval | 1960 |
|  |  | 6 | 0 | Surrey v Somerset | Taunton | 1960 |
|  |  | 4 | 2 | Cavaliers v Rhodesia | Salisbury | 1962–63 |
| Tallon, D. | (4) | 1 | 5 | Queensland v MCC | Brisbane | 1935–36 |
|  |  | 3 | 3 | Queensland v New South Wales | Brisbane | 1938–39 |
|  |  | 5 | 1 | Queensland v NSW (1st inns) | Sydney | 1938–39 |
|  |  | 4 | 2 | Queensland v NSW (2nd inns) | Sydney | 1938–39 |
| Tariq Khan |  | 6 | 0 | MC Bank v Karachi | Karachi | 1979–80 |
| Taylor, D.J.S. | (2) | 6 | 0 | Somerset v Essex | Taunton | 1981 |
|  |  | 6 | 0 | Somerset v Hampshire | Bath | 1982 |
| Taylor, R.W. | (2) | 6 | 0 | Derbyshire v Sussex | Chesterfield | 1963 |
|  |  | 6 | 0 | Derbyshire v Yorkshire | Sheffield | 1983 |
| Thomas, R. |  | 6 | 0 | Kerala v Tamil Nadu | Madras | 1981–82 |
| Timms, B.S.V. |  | 4 | 2 | Hampshire v Leicestershire | Portsmouth | 1964 |
| Tolchard, R.W. | (2) | 6 | 0 | Leicestershire v Yorkshire | Leeds | 1973 |
|  |  | 6 | 0 | Leicestershire v Hampshire | Southampton | 1980 |
| Trueman, G. |  | 5 | 1 | New South Wales v Queensland | Sydney | 1952–53 |
| Turner, M. | (2) | 3 | 3 | Gents of England v Oxford U. | Oxford | 1871 |
|  |  | 3 | 3 | Gents of England v Cambridge U. | Cambridge | 1876 |
| Ubsdell, G. |  | 1 | 5 | Hampshire v Surrey | Southampton | 1865 |
| Vance, R.H. |  | 6 | 0 | Wellington v Otago | Dunedin | 1977–78 |
| Viswanath, S. |  | 6 | 0 | South Zone v Central Zone | Kanpur | 1980–81 |
| Wade, T.H. |  | 4 | 2 | Essex v Lancashire | Clacton | 1947 |
| Wadsworth, K.J. |  | 5 | 1 | New Zealanders v Surrey | Oval | 1973 |
| Walker, C.W. |  | 2 | 4 | South Australia v New South Wales | Sydney | 1939–40 |
| Wasim Bari | (3) | 4 | 2 | Karachi v Lahore Ed Board | Lahore | 1964–65 |
|  |  | 3 | 3 | Pakistan U-25 v MCC U-25 | Karachi | 1966–67 |
|  |  | 6 | 0 | Pakistanis v Minor Counties | Jesmond | 1974 |
| Webb, R.T. | (2) | 3 | 3 | Sussex v Nottinghamshire | Hove | 1955 |
|  |  | 6 | 0 | Sussex v Somerset | Hove | 1960 |
| Wilcock, H.G. |  | 6 | 0 | Worcestershire v Hampshire | Portsmouth | 1974 |
| Wilson, A.E. |  | 6 | 0 | Gloucestershire v Hampshire | Portsmouth | 1953 |
| Worrall, N.C. |  | 6 | 0 | Barbados v Leeward Islands | Bridgetown | 1984–85 |
| Wright, K.J. |  | 6 | 0 | South Australia v Western Australia | Perth | 1982–83 |
| Yarnold, H. |  | 3 | 3 | Worcestershire v Hampshire | Worcester | 1949 |

*N.C. Tufnell (Cambridge University) stumped five batsmen in one innings off the bowling of J.H. Bruce Lockhart v Yorkshire at Cambridge in 1909.*
*B.A. Barnett stumped five batsmen in one innings off the bowling of J.S. Manning for A Commonwealth XI v An England XI at Hastings in 1960*

# MOST DISMISSALS IN A MATCH

## TWELVE DISMISSALS IN A MATCH

| | | Ct | St | | | |
|---|---|---|---|---|---|---|
| Pooley, E. | | 8 | 4 | Surrey v Sussex | Oval | 1868 |
| Taber, H.B. | | 9 | 3 | New South Wales v South Australia | Adelaide | 1968–69 |
| Tallon, D. | | 9 | 3 | Queensland v New South Wales | Sydney | 1938–39 |

## ELEVEN DISMISSALS IN A MATCH

| | | | | | | |
|---|---|---|---|---|---|---|
| Bairstow, D.L. | | 11 | 0 | Yorkshire v Derbyshire | Scarborough | 1982 |
| Long, A. | | 11 | 0 | Surrey v Sussex | Hove | 1964 |
| Marsh, R.W. | | 11 | 0 | Western Australia v Victoria | Perth | 1975–76 |

## TEN DISMISSALS IN A MATCH

| | | | | | | |
|---|---|---|---|---|---|---|
| Arifuddin | | 9 | 1 | United Bank v Karachi B | Karachi | 1978–79 |
| Azhar Abbas | | 7 | 3 | Bahawalpur v Lahore Greens | Bahawalpur | 1983–84 |
| Corrall, P. | | 7 | 3 | Leicestershire v Sussex | Hove | 1936 |
| Elliott, H. | | 8 | 2 | Derbyshire v Lancashire | Manchester | 1935 |
| French, B.N. | | 7 | 3 | Nottinghamshire v Oxford U. | Oxford | 1984 |
| Ghosh, A. | | 9 | 1 | Bihar v Assam | Bhagalpur | 1981–82 |
| Hubble, J.C. | | 9 | 1 | Kent v Gloucestershire | Cheltenham | 1923 |
| Huish, F.H. | | 1 | 9 | Kent v Surrey | Oval | 1911 |
| Jarman, B.N. | | 7 | 3 | South Australia v New South Wales | Adelaide | 1961–62 |
| Jennings, R.V. | | 10 | 0 | Transvaal v Arose Sri Lankans | Johannesburg | 1982–83 |
| Johnson, L.A. | (2) | 10 | 0 | Northamptonshire v Sussex | Worthing | 1963 |
| | | 8 | 2 | Northamptonshire v Warwickshire | Birmingham | 1965 |
| Jordon, R.C. | | 9 | 1 | Victoria v South Australia | Melbourne | 1970–71 |
| Kamal Najamuddin | | 9 | 1 | Karachi v Lahore | Lahore | 1982–83 |
| Marsh, R.W. | | 10 | 0 | Western Australia v S. Australia | Perth | 1976–77 |
| Murray, D.A. | | 10 | 0 | West Indian XI v South African XI | Port Elizabeth | 1983–84 |
| Oates, T.W. | | 9 | 1 | Nottinghamshire v Middlesex | Nottingham | 1906 |
| Parkar, Z. | | 8 | 2 | Bombay v Maharashtra | Bombay | 1981–82 |
| Parks, R.J. | | 10 | 0 | Hampshire v Derbyshire | Portsmouth | 1981 |
| Phillips, H. | | 5 | 5 | Sussex v Surrey | Oval | 1872 |
| Pooley, E. | | 2 | 8 | Surrey v Kent | Oval | 1878 |
| Ryall, R.J. | | 8 | 2 | Western Province v Transvaal | Cape Town | 1984–85 |
| Saggers, R.A. | | 9 | 1 | New South Wales v Combined XI | Brisbane | 1940–41 |
| Taslim Arif | | 6 | 4 | National Bank v Punjab | Lahore | 1978–79 |
| Taylor, R.W. | (2) | 10 | 0 | Derbyshire v Hampshire | Chesterfield | 1963 |
| | | 10 | 0 | England v India | Bombay | 1979–80 |
| Wilson, A.E. | | 10 | 0 | Gloucestershire v Hampshire | Portsmouth | 1953 |

## NINE DISMISSALS IN A MATCH

| | | | | | | |
|---|---|---|---|---|---|---|
| Ames, L.E.G. | (2) | 8 | 1 | Kent v Oxford University | Oxford | 1928 |
| | | 5 | 4 | Kent v Sussex | Maidstone | 1929 |
| Arifuddin | | 3 | 6 | United Bank v PACO | Sahiwal | 1983–84 |
| Bairstow, D.L. | | 9 | 0 | Yorkshire v Lancashire | Manchester | 1971 |
| Baker, E.A. | (2) | 2 | 7 | Victoria v New South Wales | Sydney | 1946–47 |
| | | 9 | 0 | Victoria v New South Wales | Melbourne | 1946–47 |
| Barnard, J. | | 2 | 7 | MCC v Godalming | Lord's | 1822 |
| Becker, G.C. | | 8 | 1 | Western Australia v Victoria | Melbourne | 1965–66 |
| Broadbridge, W. | | 2 | 7 | Sussex v Hampshire & Surrey | Bramshill | 1826 |
| Brown, J. | | 4 | 5 | Scotland v Ireland | Dublin | 1957 |
| Chatterton, E.V. | | 8 | 1 | Transvaal B v Natal B | Johannesburg | 1969–70 |
| Clayton, G. | | 8 | 1 | Lancashire v Gloucestershire | Gloucester | 1959 |
| Davidson, H. | | 6 | 3 | New South Wales v South Australia | Sydney | 1928–29 |
| Day, N.T. | (2) | 8 | 1 | Transvaal B v Eastern Province | Johannesburg | 1978–79 |
| | | 9 | 0 | Northern Transvaal v Natal | Pretoria | 1984–85 |
| Dolphin, A. | | 8 | 1 | Yorkshire v Derbyshire | Bradford | 1919 |
| East, D.E. | | 9 | 0 | Essex v Sussex | Hove | 1983 |
| East, R.J. | (2) | 9 | 0 | OFS v Griqualand West | Bloemfontein | 1976–77 |

|  |  | Ct | St |  |  |  |
|---|---|----|----|---|---|---|
| East, R.J. *continued* |  | 8 | 1 | OFS v Western Province B | Cape Town | 1984–85 |
| Evans, T.G. |  | 8 | 1 | Kent v New Zealanders | Canterbury | 1949 |
| Ferrandi, J.H. |  | 7 | 2 | Western Province v Transvaal | Johannesburg | 1958–59 |
| Findlay, T.M. |  | 7 | 2 | Combined Islands v Guyana | Rose Hall | 1973–74 |
| Ford, D.A. |  | 4 | 5 | New South Wales v Victoria | Sydney | 1963–64 |
| Gamsy, D. | (3) | 8 | 1 | Natal v Transvaal | Johannesburg | 1959–60 |
|  |  | 7 | 2 | Natal v Orange Free State | Pietermaritzburg | 1960–61 |
|  |  | 7 | 2 | Natal v N.E. Transvaal | Pretoria | 1967–68 |
| Gibson, K.L. |  | 7 | 2 | Essex v Derbyshire | Leyton | 1911 |
| Hunter, J. |  | 9 | 0 | Yorkshire v Gloucestershire | Gloucester | 1887 |
| Indrajitsinhji, K.S. |  | 5 | 4 | Saurashtra v Maharashtra | Nasik | 1965–66 |
| Inkster, G.B. |  | 4 | 5 | South Australia v Victoria | Melbourne | 1926–27 |
| Irvine, B.L. |  | 9 | 0 | Transvaal v Rhodesia | Johannesburg | 1974–75 |
| Jarman, B.N. |  | 9 | 0 | Australians v Nottinghamshire | Nottingham | 1964 |
| Jennings, R.V. | (2) | 9 | 0 | Transvaal v Eastern Province | Johannesburg | 1981–82 |
|  |  | 9 | 0 | Transvaal v SA Universities | Johannesburg | 1984–85 |
| Joshi, P.G. |  | 6 | 3 | Maharashtra v Gujarat | Ahmednagar | 1959–60 |
| Kirsten, N. |  | 7 | 2 | Border v Rhodesia | East London | 1959–60 |
| Knott, A.P.E. |  | 9 | 0 | Kent v Leicestershire | Maidstone | 1977 |
| Langley, G.R.A. |  | 8 | 1 | Australia v England | Lord's | 1956 |
| Levett, W.H.V. | (3) | 4 | 5 | Kent v Nottinghamshire | Maidstone | 1933 |
|  |  | 7 | 2 | Kent v Northamptonshire | Northampton | 1934 |
|  |  | 5 | 4 | Kent v Sussex | Tunbridge Wells | 1935 |
| Lewis, E.B. |  | 8 | 1 | Warwickshire v Oxford University | Birmingham | 1949 |
| Lilley, B. |  | 9 | 0 | Nottinghamshire v Somerset | Taunton | 1932 |
| Livsey, W.H. |  | 4 | 5 | Hampshire v Warwickshire | Southampton | 1914 |
| Maclean, J.A. |  | 9 | 0 | Queensland v Victoria | Melbourne | 1977–78 |
| McSweeney, E.B. |  | 8 | 1 | Wellington v Otago | Lower Hutt | 1983–84 |
| Mantri, M.K. |  | 4 | 5 | Bombay v Northern India | Lahore | 1941–42 |
| Marsh, R.W. | (2) | 9 | 0 | Western Australia v NSW | Perth | 1974–75 |
|  |  | 9 | 0 | Australia v England | Brisbane | 1982–83 |
| Maynard, C. |  | 8 | 1 | Lancashire v Somerset | Taunton | 1982 |
| Millman, G. |  | 8 | 1 | Nottinghamshire v Warwickshire | Nottingham | 1964 |
| Murray, D.A. |  | 9 | 0 | West Indies v Australia | Melbourne | 1981–82 |
| Murray, J.T. |  | 8 | 1 | Middlesex v Hampshire | Lord's | 1965 |
| Newton, A.E. |  | 6 | 3 | Somerset v Middlesex | Lord's | 1901 |
| Oldfield, W.A.S. |  | 4 | 5 | New South Wales v West Indians | Sydney | 1930–31 |
| Pandit, C.S. |  | 5 | 4 | President's XI v West Indians | Nagpur | 1983–84 |
| Pfuhl, G.P. |  | 8 | 1 | W. Province v E. Province | Cape Town | 1979–80 |
| Phillips, R.B. |  | 8 | 1 | Queensland v New Zealanders | Bundaberg | 1982–83 |
| Pope, C.W.S. |  | 9 | 0 | Border v Transvaal B | East London | 1971–72 |
| Robinson, R.D. | (2) | 8 | 1 | Victoria v New South Wales | Melbourne | 1973–74 |
|  |  | 8 | 1 | Victoria v South Australia | Adelaide | 1980–81 |
| Schofield, R.M. |  | 9 | 0 | Central Districts v Wellington | Wellington | 1964–65 |
| Stephenson, H.W. |  | 8 | 1 | Somerset v Yorkshire | Taunton | 1963 |
| Taber, H.B. |  | 8 | 1 | New South Wales v South Australia | Sydney | 1971–72 |
| Tallon, D. |  | 4 | 5 | Queensland v Victoria | Brisbane | 1938–39 |
| Taylor, R.W. |  | 9 | 0 | Derbyshire v Yorkshire | Chesterfield | 1975 |
| Turner, M. | (2) | 4 | 5 | Gentlemen of England v Oxford U. | Oxford | 1871 |
|  |  | 6 | 3 | Middlesex v Nottinghamshire | Prince's | 1875 |
| Vance, R.H. |  | 9 | 0 | Wellington v Otago | Wellington | 1977–78 |
| Walker, C.W. |  | 3 | 6 | South Australia v New South Wales | Sydney | 1939–40 |
| Wasim Bari | (3) | 7 | 2 | Karachi v Lahore Ed Board | Lahore | 1964–65 |
|  |  | 7 | 2 | Karachi Blues v Hyderabad | Karachi | 1965–66 |
|  |  | 8 | 1 | PIA v National Bank | Karachi | 1975–76 |
| Yagmich, D.B. |  | 9 | 0 | Western Australia v Queensland | Perth | 1973–74 |
| Yarnold, H. |  | 5 | 4 | Worcestershire v Hampshire | Worcester | 1949 |

## MOST DISMISSALS IN A SEASON

Only seven wicket-keepers have dismissed a hundred batsmen in a season. L.E.G. Ames – who achieved the feat three times – and F.H. Huish were each helped by great Kent slow bowlers; Huish by C. Blythe and Ames by A.P. Freeman.

|  |  | Season | **Total** | Ct | St |
|---|---|--------|-------|----|----|
| L.E.G. Ames | Kent | 1929 | **128** | 79 | 49 |
| L.E.G. Ames | Kent | 1928 | **122** | 70 | 52 |

|  |  | Season | Total | Ct | St |
|---|---|---|---|---|---|
| H. Yarnold | Worcestershire | 1949 | **110** | 63 | 47 |
| G. Duckworth | Lancashire | 1928 | **107** | 77 | 30 |
| J.G. Binks | Yorkshire | 1960 | **107** | 96 | 11 |
| L.E.G. Ames | Kent | 1932 | **104** | 40 | 64 |
| J.T. Murray | Middlesex | 1957 | **104** | 82 | 22 |
| F.H. Huish | Kent | 1913 | **102** | 69 | 33 |
| J.T. Murray | Middlesex | 1960 | **102** | 95 | 7 |
| F.H. Huish | Kent | 1911 | **101** | 62 | 39 |
| R. Booth | Worcestershire | 1960 | **101** | 85 | 16 |
| R. Booth | Worcestershire | 1964 | **100** | 91 | 9 |

**Most catches in a season**      96   J.G. Binks      Yorkshire      1960
**Most stumpings in a season**      64   L.E.G. Ames      Kent      1932

# HIGHEST TOTALS WITHOUT BYES

| | *Wicket-keeper* | | | |
|---|---|---|---|---|
| 672-7d | A.P. Wickham | Somerset v Hampshire | Taunton | 1899 |
| 659-8d | T.G. Evans | England v Australia | Sydney | 1946–47 |
| 652 | S.M.H. Kirmani | India v Pakistan | Faisalabad | 1982–83 |
| 647 | L.J. Alexander | Tasmania v Victoria | Melbourne | 1951–52 |
| 634-4d | Riaz Alam | Hyderabad v Karachi Blues | Karachi | 1964–65 |
| 619 | J.L. Hendriks | West Indies v Australia | Sydney | 1968–69 |
| 594-6d | J.H. Board | Gloucestershire v Hampshire | Southampton | 1911 |
| 589 | P. Marais | Natal v Australians | Durban | 1949–50 |
| 587 | W. Marais | Eastern Province v Natal | Pietermaritzburg | 1939–40 |
| 577-4 | A.E. Wilson | Gloucestershire v Glamorgan | Newport | 1939 |
| 575-9d | R.W. Marsh | Western Australia v S. Australia | Perth | 1970–71 |
| 574-7 | W.T. Luckes | Somerset v Glamorgan | Newport | 1939 |
| 570-8d | E.W.J. Brooks | Surrey v Essex | Brentwood | 1934 |
| 569 | S.O. Quin | Victoria v South Australia | Melbourne | 1935–36 |
| 559-9d | W.W. Wade | South Africa v England | Cape Town | 1938–39 |
| 558-7d | M.G. Dimattina | Victoria v West Indians | Melbourne | 1984–85 |
| 557-7d | H. Smith | Gloucestershire v Surrey | Oval | 1927 |
| 555-6d | S.C. Griffith | Sussex v South Africans | Hove | 1947 |
| 553 | C.I. Dey | N.E. Transvaal v Australians | Pretoria | 1966–67 |
| 552-7d | D.A. Murray | Barbados v Guyana | Bridgetown | 1974–75 |
| 551 | J.J. Kelly | Australia v England | Sydney | 1897–98 |
| 551-7 | D. Hunter | Yorkshire v Surrey | Oval | 1899 |
| 551-9d | A.P.E. Knott | England v New Zealand | Lord's | 1973 |
| 551-9d | S.J. Rixon | New South Wales v South Australia | Adelaide | 1981–82 |
| 546 | S.C. Griffith | Sussex v New Zealanders | Hove | 1937 |
| 544-5d | Imtiaz Ahmed | Pakistan v England | Birmingham | 1962 |
| 543-3d | T.M. Findlay | West Indies v New Zealand | Georgetown | 1971–72 |
| 540 | J.H.B. Waite | South Africans v Queensland | Brisbane | 1952–53 |
| 536-7d | R.B. Phillips | Queensland v Victoria | Geelong | 1981–82 |
| 536-4d | G.J. Miles | Victoria v Queensland | Melbourne (St K) | 1982–83 |
| 535-8d | N.T. McCorkell | Hampshire v Leicestershire | Leicester | 1938 |
| 534-6c | A.J. Brassington | Gloucestershire v Somerset | Taunton | 1980 |
| 533-5d | R. Swetman | MCC v Barbados | Bridgetown | 1959–60 |
| 533 | J.P. Harty | Eastern Province v Natal | Port Elizabeth | 1962–63 |
| 532-9d | A.P.E. Knott | England v Australia | Oval | 1975 |
| 531 | D.T. Lindsay | South Africa v England | Johannesburg | 1964–65 |
| 529-9 | J.H.B. Waite | South Africans v Combined XI | Perth | 1963–64 |
| 528 | H.B. Taber | New South Wales v South Australia | Adelaide | 1965–66 |
| 528 | S.M.H. Kirmani | India v Australia | Adelaide | 1980–81 |
| 527 | H.B. Taber | New South Wales v MCC | Sydney | 1965–66 |

*Taber performed this feat twice in consecutive matches and conceded no byes whilst 1580 runs were scored against New South Wales*

| 526-7d | A.P.E. Knott | England v West Indies | Port-of-Spain | 1967–68 |
|---|---|---|---|---|
| 521 | W.A.S. Oldfield | Australia v England | Brisbane | 1928–29 |
| 521-7d | B.W. Bellamy | Northamptonshire v Sussex | Hove | 1930 |
| 521-8d | J.L. Hendriks | Jamaica v Barbados | Bridgetown | 1966–67 |
| 520-8d | M. Patten | Free Foresters v Oxford University | Oxford | 1927 |
| 520 | J.H.B. Waite | South Africa v Australia | Melbourne | 1952–53 |
| 514-4d | R.G. de Alwis | Sri Lanka v Australia | Kandy | 1982–83 |

|        | *Wicket-keeper* |                                           |                 |         |
|--------|-----------------|-------------------------------------------|-----------------|---------|
| 512    | W.T. Luckes     | Somerset v Surrey                         | Oval            | 1936    |
| 512-8d | †J.D.P. Tanner  | Oxford University v Lancashire            | Oxford          | 1947    |
| 512    | J.M. Brearley   | Cambridge University v West Indians       | Cambridge       | 1963    |
| 512    | D.B. Yagmich    | South Australia v Victoria                | Melbourne       | 1976–77 |
| 511-4d | D.A. Murray     | President's XI v MCC                       | Bridgetown      | 1973–74 |
| 510    | J.L. Hendriks   | West Indies v Australia                    | Melbourne       | 1968–69 |
| 510    | R.B. Phillips   | Queensland v Victoria                     | Melbourne (St K) | 1982–83 |
| 509    | †P. Swanson     | Orange Free State v Border                | Bloemfontein    | 1969–70 |
| 509    | W.B. Phillips   | Australia v West Indies                   | Bridgetown      | 1983–84 |
| 507-6d | E.A. Meads      | Nottinghamshire v Kent                    | Nottingham      | 1953    |
| 507    | S.J. Katz       | Transvaal v Eastern Province              | Johannesburg    | 1966–67 |
| 507-6d | K.J. Wadsworth  | New Zealand v Pakistan                    | Dunedin         | 1972–73 |
| 507    | R.B. Phillips   | Queensland v Tasmania                     | Brisbane        | 1984–85 |
| 504-9d | A.W. Catt       | Western Province v Australians            | Cape Town       | 1966–67 |
| 504    | Daljit Singh    | Bihar v Bombay                            | Bombay          | 1971–72 |
| 503-8d | S.M.H. Kirmani  | India v Pakistan                          | Faisalabad      | 1978–79 |
| 501-6d | B.W. Bellamy    | Northamptonshire v Worcestershire         | Northampton     | 1930    |
| 501-8d | A.B. Wheat      | Nottinghamshire v Glamorgan               | Swansea         | 1939    |
| 500    | J.P. Whiteside  | Leicestershire v Surrey                   | Leicester       | 1900    |
| 500-4d | Daljit Singh    | East Zone v West Indians                  | Jamshedpur      | 1978–79 |

† *On début in first-class cricket.*
*K.V. Andrew did not concede a bye in the course of 2132 runs being scored against Northamptonshire in 1965.*

# CAREER RECORDS

**750 DISMISSALS**

|                | *Career*  | **Dismissals** | *Ct* | *St* |
|----------------|-----------|----------------|------|------|
| R.W. Taylor    | 1960–1984 | **1646**       | 1471 | 175  |
| J.T. Murray    | 1952–1975 | **1527**       | 1270 | 257  |
| H. Strudwick   | 1902–1927 | **1496**       | 1242 | 254  |
| A.P.E. Knott   | 1964–1985 | **1340**       | 1207 | 133  |
| F.H. Huish     | 1895–1914 | **1310**       | 933  | 377  |
| B. Taylor      | 1949–1973 | **1294**       | 1082 | 212  |
| D. Hunter      | 1889–1909 | **1265**       | 914  | 351  |
| H.R. Butt      | 1890–1912 | **1228**       | 953  | 275  |
| J.H. Board     | 1890–*1914* | **1207**     | 852  | 255  |
| H. Elliott     | 1920–1947 | **1206**       | 904  | 302  |
| J.M. Parks     | 1949–1976 | **1181**       | 1088 | 93   |
| R. Booth       | 1951–1970 | **1126**       | 949  | 177  |
| L.E.G. Ames    | 1926–1951 | **1121**       | 703  | 418  |
| G. Duckworth   | 1923–1947 | **1090**       | 751  | 339  |
| H.W. Stephenson | 1948–1964 | **1082**      | 748  | 334  |
| J.G. Binks     | 1955–1975 | **1071**       | 895  | 176  |
| T.G. Evans     | 1939–1969 | **1066**       | 816  | 250  |
| A. Long        | 1960–1979 | **1046**       | 922  | 124  |
| G.O. Dawkes    | 1937–1961 | **1043**       | 895  | 148  |
| R.W. Tolchard  | 1965–1983 | **1037**       | 912  | 125  |
| W.L. Cornford  | 1921–1947 | **1017**       | 673  | 344  |
| T.W. Oates     | 1897–1925 | **993**        | 758  | 235  |
| W.F.F. Price   | 1926–1947 | **987**        | 666  | 321  |
| D.L. Bairstow  | 1970–1985 | **944**        | 815  | 129  |
| E.W. Jones     | 1961–1983 | **933**        | 840  | 93   |
| A.F.A. Lilley  | 1891–1911 | **911**        | 717  | 194  |
| K.V. Andrew    | 1952–1966 | **905**        | 721  | 184  |
| A. Wood        | 1928–1947 | **888**        | 631  | 257  |
| E.J. Smith     | 1904–1930 | **878**        | 722  | 156  |
| A. Dolphin     | 1905–1927 | **881**        | 608  | 273  |
| R.W. Marsh     | *1968–1983* | **869**      | 803  | 66   |
| E. Pooley      | 1861–1883 | **854**        | 496  | 358  |
| D.L. Murray    | *1960–1980* | **849**      | 741  | 108  |
| M. Sherwin     | 1876–1896 | **836**        | 611  | 225  |
| H.R. Murrell   | 1899–1926 | **834**        | 565  | 269  |
| W.T. Luckes    | 1924–1949 | **827**        | 586  | 241  |

| | *Career* | **Dismissals** | *Ct* | *St* |
|---|---|---|---|---|
| B.J. Meyer | 1957–1971 | **827** | 709 | 118 |
| F.M. Engineer | *1958*–1976 | **824** | 703 | 121 |
| E.W.J. Brooks | 1925–1939 | **821** | 725 | 96 |
| Wasim Bari | *1964–1983* | **812** | 667 | 145 |
| A.J.W. McIntyre | 1938–1963 | **795** | 639 | 156 |
| B. Lilley | 1921–1937 | **789** | 657 | 132 |
| H.G. Davies | 1935–1958 | **788** | 584 | 204 |
| A.C. Smith | 1958–*1974* | **776** | 715 | 61 |
| R.T. Spooner | 1948–1959 | **767** | 589 | 178 |

*These figures include catches taken in the field.*

# INDIVIDUAL RECORDS – FIELDING

## MOST CATCHES IN AN INNINGS

### SEVEN CATCHES IN AN INNINGS

| | | | |
|---|---|---|---|
| Brown, A.S. | Gloucestershire v Nottinghamshire | Nottingham | 1966 |
| Stewart, M.J. | Surrey v Northamptonshire | Northampton | 1957 |

### SIX CATCHES IN AN INNINGS

| | | | |
|---|---|---|---|
| Bissex, M. | Gloucestershire v Sussex | Hove | 1968 |
| Broadbent, R.G. | Worcestershire v Glamorgan | Stourbridge | 1960 |
| Clay, J.D. | Nottinghamshire v Derbyshire | Nottingham | 1957 |
| Deas, L.M. | Europeans v Parsees | Poona | 1898–99 |
| Grieves, K.J. | Lancashire v Sussex | Manchester | 1951 |
| Griffith, G. | Surrey v Gentlemen of South | Oval | 1863 |
| Gulfraz Khan | Railways v MCB | Sialkot | 1981–82 |
| Hammond, W.R. (2) | Gloucestershire v Surrey | Cheltenham | 1928 |
| | Gloucestershire v Nottinghamshire | Bristol | 1933 |
| Leary, S.E. | Kent v Cambridge University | Cambridge | 1958 |
| Masood Anwar | Rawalpindi v Lahore Division | Rawalpindi | 1983–84 |
| Robinson, E.P. | Yorkshire v Leicestershire | Bradford | 1938 |
| Seymour, James | Kent v South Africans | Canterbury | 1904 |
| Sheppard, J.F. | Queensland v New South Wales | Brisbane | 1914–15 |
| Smith, M.J.K. | Warwickshire v Leicestershire | Hinckley | 1962 |
| Tarrant, F.A. | Middlesex v Essex | Leyton | 1906 |
| Tyldesley, R.K. | Lancashire v Hampshire | Liverpool | 1921 |
| Webbe, A.J. | Gentlemen v Players | Lord's | 1877 |

### FIVE CATCHES IN AN INNINGS

| | | | |
|---|---|---|---|
| Abel, R. | Surrey v Hampshire | Portsmouth | 1898 |
| Ali Zia (2) | National Bank v HBFC | Multan | 1980–81 |
| | National Bank v Rawalpindi | Rawalpindi | 1982–83 |
| Arshad Pervez | Habib Bank v Railways | Lahore | 1983–84 |
| Arun Lal | East Zone v South Zone | Cuttack | 1981–82 |
| Ashton, H. | Cambridge University v Surrey | Oval | 1922 |
| Astill, W.E. | Leicestershire v Somerset | Weston-s-Mare | 1920 |
| Atkinson, J.A. | Tasmania v Victoria | Melbourne | 1928–29 |
| Bakewell, A.H. | Northamptonshire v Essex | Leyton | 1928 |
| Barrow, A. | Transvaal B v Northern Transvaal B | Pietermaritzburg | 1982–83 |
| Barton, M.R. | Oxford University v Minor Counties | Oxford | 1937 |
| Bates, W.E. | Glamorgan v Warwickshire | Birmingham | 1928 |
| Boyle, H.F. | Australians v Yorkshire | Dewsbury | 1880 |
| Braund, L.C. | Somerset v Worcestershire | Taunton | 1909 |
| Brown, G. (2) | Hampshire v Somerset | Bath | 1914 |
| | Hampshire v Kent | Portsmouth | 1932 |
| Burbidge, F. | Gentlemen v Players | Oval | 1858 |
| Butcher, R.O. | Middlesex v Australians | Lord's | 1981 |
| Camacho, G.S. | Demerara v Berbice | Georgetown | 1971–72 |
| Carr, A.W. | Nottinghamshire v Leicestershire | Nottingham | 1933 |
| Clift, P.B. | Leicestershire v Worcestershire | Worcester | 1976 |
| Cowdrey, C.S. | Kent v Sussex | Hove | 1982 |
| Crapp, J.F. | Gloucestershire v Lancashire | Manchester | 1949 |
| Daniell, J. | Somerset v Kent | Taunton | 1901 |
| Davis, R.C. | Glamorgan v Northamptonshire | Cardiff | 1970 |
| Durity, O.M. (2) | Trinidad v Guyana | Georgetown | 1970–71 |
| | South Trinidad v East Trinidad | Pointe-à-Pierre | 1971–72 |
| Ealham, A.G.E. | Kent v Gloucestershire | Folkestone | 1966 |
| | *All off D.L. Underwood's bowling in the same position topographically – long-off to the right-handed batsman* | | |
| Evans, E. | New South Wales v Lord Harris' XI | Sydney | 1878–79 |
| Eyre, C.H. | Cambridge U. v G.J.V. Weigall's XI | Cambridge | 1904 |

| | | | |
|---|---|---|---|
| Fagg, A.E. | Kent v Hampshire | Southampton | 1952 |
| Faiz-ur-Rehman | Rajshahi v Dacca | Dacca | 1964–65 |
| Fishwick, T.S. | Warwickshire v South Africans | Birmingham | 1904 |
| Ford, F.G.J. | Cambridge University v MCC | Lord's | 1888 |
| Foster, R.E. | Oxford University v A.J. Webbe's XI | Oxford | 1898 |
| Gillingham, F.H. | Essex v Surrey | Oval | 1919 |
| Gooch, G.A. | Essex v Gloucestershire | Cheltenham | 1982 |
| Greenidge, G.A. | Sussex v Glamorgan | Hove | 1975 |
| Grieves, K.J.  (2) | Lancashire v Glamorgan | Blackpool | 1950 |
| | Lancashire v Gloucestershire | Bristol | 1954 |
| Gunn, G. | Nottinghamshire v Surrey | Nottingham | 1909 |
| Haig, N.E. | Middlesex v Nottinghamshire | Lord's | 1928 |
| Hallam, M.R. | Leicestershire v Northamptonshire | Leicester | 1964 |
| Hammond, W.R. | MCC West Indies XI v | | |
| | H.D.G. Leveson Gower's XI | Scarborough | 1935 |
| Hayes, E.G. | Surrey v London County | Oval | 1901 |
| Headley, R.G.A.  (2) | Worcestershire v Kent | Dartford | 1964 |
| | Worcestershire v Gloucestershire | Cheltenham | 1967 |
| Hignell, A.J. | Cambridge University v Derbyshire | Burton upon Trent | 1976 |
| Hopkins, J.A. | Glamorgan v Worcestershire | Cardiff | 1976 |
| Hughes, G. | Glamorgan v Essex | Swansea | 1964 |
| Hunt, G. | Somerset v Hampshire | Weston-super-Mare | 1928 |
| Hutton, L. | Players v Gentlemen | Lord's | 1952 |
| Ikin, J.T. | MCC v Auckland | Auckland | 1946–47 |
| Insole, D.J. | Essex v Lancashire | Blackpool | 1958 |
| Jameson, J.A. | Warwickshire v Indians | Birmingham | 1971 |
| Javed Miandad | Sussex v Oxford University | Pagham | 1976 |
| Jones, A.O. | Nottinghamshire v Sussex | Hove | 1907 |
| Jordaan, A.H. | Northern Transvaal v Border | East London | 1972–73 |
| Kanhai, R.B. | West Indians v Gloucestershire | Bristol | 1966 |
| Lamason, J.R.  (2) | Wellington v Otago | Dunedin | 1937–38 |
| | North Island Army v South Island Army | Wellington | 1942–43 |
| Langridge, J.G. | Sussex v Somerset | Taunton | 1950 |
| Lee, C. | Derbyshire v Lancashire | Chesterfield | 1960 |
| Lee, G.M. | Nottinghamshire v Hampshire | Southampton | 1913 |
| Lock, G.A.R. | Surrey v Lancashire | Manchester | 1953 |
| Lumb, R.G. | Yorkshire v Gloucestershire | Middlesbrough | 1972 |
| Lyon, B.H. | Gloucestershire v Leicestershire | Cheltenham | 1933 |
| McAlister, P.A. | Victoria v South Australia | Melbourne | 1901–02 |
| McCool, C.L. | New South Wales v Rest of Australia | Sydney | 1939–40 |
| MacDonald, G.K. | Canterbury v Pakistanis | Christchurch | 1984–85 |
| Mead, C.P. | Hampshire v Middlesex | Portsmouth | 1912 |
| Mehra, M. | Railways v Northern Punjab | Delhi | 1963–64 |
| Milton, C.A. | Gloucestershire v Pakistanis | Cheltenham | 1954 |
| Morgan, D.C. | Derbyshire v Glamorgan | Chesterfield | 1960 |
| Morrison, J.F.M. | Wellington v Central Districts | Wellington | 1980–81 |
| Mushtaq Mohammad | Northamptonshire v Leicestershire | Peterborough | 1968 |
| Nicholls, B.E. | Oxford University v Australians | Oxford | 1884 |
| Nichols, M.S. | Essex v Sussex | Hove | 1926 |
| Nicholson, J.H. | Northamptonshire v Worcestershire | Dudley | 1928 |
| Nourse, A.D. | Natal v Border | Durban | 1933–34 |
| Oakman, A.S.M.  (2) | Sussex v Glamorgan | Worthing | 1958 |
| | Sussex v Lancashire | Hastings | 1961 |
| Outschoorn, L. | Worcestershire v Derbyshire | Kidderminster | 1948 |
| Painter, J.R. | Gloucestershire v Sussex | Hove | 1891 |
| Parfitt, P.H. | MCC v South African Universities | Pietermaritzburg | 1964–65 |
| Paul, A. | Lancashire v Derbyshire | Derby | 1897 |
| Pierce, T.N. | Barbados v Trinidad | Bridgetown | 1941–42 |
| Pocock, N.E.J. | Hampshire v Oxford University | Oxford | 1979 |
| Pollock, J.S. | Ireland v MCC | Dublin | 1956 |
| Pratt, R.L. | Leicestershire v Derbyshire | Leicester | 1961 |
| Prodger, J.M.  (2) | Kent v Gloucestershire | Cheltenham | 1961 |
| | Kent v Lancashire | Blackpool | 1964 |
| Quinton, F.W.D. | Hampshire v Yorkshire | Harrogate | 1896 |
| Rabone, G.O. | New Zealanders v Oxford University | Oxford | 1949 |
| Reid, J.R. | New Zealanders v South Zone | Bangalore | 1955–56 |
| Richards, B.A. | Hampshire v Gloucestershire | Gloucester | 1972 |

| | | | | |
|---|---|---|---|---|
| Richards, I.V.A. | | Leeward Islands v Barbados | Basseterre | 1981–82 |
| Richardson, V.Y. | | Australia v South Africa | Durban | 1935–36 |
| Robinson, P.J. | | Somerset v Lancashire | Weston-s-Mare | 1968 |
| Roope, G.R.J. | | Surrey v Cambridge University | Cambridge | 1980 |
| Roy, Pranab | | Bengal v Orissa | Rourkela | 1983–84 |
| Russell, P.E. | | Derbyshire v Pakistanis | Chesterfield | 1978 |
| Ryder, J. | | Victoria v MCC | Melbourne | 1922–23 |
| Salahuddin | | Pakistan XI v Rest | Sahiwal | 1967–68 |
| Sellers, A.B. | | Yorkshire v Essex | Leyton | 1933 |
| Smith, M.J.K. | (2) | Warwickshire v Glamorgan | Swansea | 1961 |
| | | MCC v New South Wales | Sydney | 1965–66 |
| Solkar, E.D. | | Bombay v Rest of India | Bombay | 1968–69 |
| Steele, J.F. | | Leicestershire v Nottinghamshire | Nottingham | 1971 |
| Surridge, W.S. | | Surrey v Lancashire | Oval | 1955 |
| Tandon, R.P. | | Bombay v Gujarat | Bulsar | 1975–76 |
| Trumble, H. | (2) | Australians v Cambridge University | Cambridge | 1890 |
| | | Australians v Oxford University | Oxford | 1893 |
| Tunnicliffe, J. | (3) | Yorkshire v Leicestershire | Leeds | 1897 |
| | | Yorkshire v Leicestershire | Leicester | 1900 |
| | | Yorkshire v Leicestershire | Scarborough | 1901 |
| Vigar, F.H. | (3) | Essex v Middlesex | Westcliff | 1946 |
| | | Essex v Northamptonshire | Brentwood | 1946 |
| | | Essex v Surrey | Oval | 1951 |
| Walker, P.M. | (4) | Glamorgan v Leicestershire | Swansea | 1960 |
| | | Glamorgan v Derbyshire | Chesterfield | 1961 |
| | | Glamorgan v Nottinghamshire | Newport | 1961 |
| | | Glamorgan v Derbyshire | Swansea | 1970 |
| Walker, V.E. | | Middlesex v Surrey | Oval | 1865 |
| Watkins, A.J. | | MCC v South Zone | Bangalore | 1951–52 |
| Watson, A. | | Lancashire v Derbyshire | Manchester | 1881 |
| Wensley, A.F. | (2) | Sussex v Warwickshire | Birmingham | 1932 |
| | | Sussex v Surrey | Horsham | 1934 |
| White, C. | | Border v Griqualand West | Queenstown | 1946–47 |
| Whitehouse, J. | | Warwickshire v Oxford University | Oxford | 1975 |
| Williams, N.T. | | Auckland v Hawke's Bay | Napier | 1894–95 |
| Wilson, D. | | Yorkshire v Surrey | Oval | 1969 |
| Wood, A.M. | | Gents of Philadelphia v Australians | Haverford | 1896 |
| Wood, C.J.B. | | Leicestershire v Warwickshire | Hinckley | 1919 |
| Woolley, F.E. | (2) | Kent v Middlesex | Blackheath | 1926 |
| | | Kent v Hampshire | Canterbury | 1936 |
| Woolmer, R.A. | | Kent v Worcestershire | Worcester | 1976 |
| Wright, F.W. | | Oxford University v Surrey | Oval | 1865 |
| Yajurvindra Singh | | India v England | Bangalore | 1976–77 |
| Zaheer Abbas | | Dawood Industries v Lahore | Lahore | 1975–76 |

# MOST CATCHES IN A MATCH

## TEN CATCHES IN A MATCH

| | | | |
|---|---|---|---|
| Hammond, W.R. | Gloucestershire v Surrey | Cheltenham | 1928 |
| | *Eight held off the bowling of C.W.L. Parker* | | |

## EIGHT CATCHES IN A MATCH

| | | | |
|---|---|---|---|
| Bakewell, A.H. | Northamptonshire v Essex | Leyton | 1928 |
| Burns, W.B. | Worcestershire v Yorkshire | Bradford | 1907 |
| Grieves, K.J. | Lancashire v Sussex | Manchester | 1951 |
| Hammond, W.R. | Gloucestershire v Worcestershire | Cheltenham | 1932 |
| Javed Miandad | Habib Bank v Universities | Lahore | 1977–78 |
| Lock, G.A.R. | Surrey v Warwickshire | Oval | 1957 |
| Masood Anwar | Rawalpindi v Lahore Division | Rawalpindi | 1983–84 |
| Milton, C.A. | Gloucestershire v Sussex | Hove | 1952 |
| Prodger, J.M. | Kent v Gloucestershire | Cheltenham | 1961 |
| Walker, P.M. | Glamorgan v Derbyshire | Swansea | 1970 |

## SEVEN CATCHES IN A MATCH

| | | | | |
|---|---|---|---|---|
| Ashton, H. | | Cambridge University v Surrey | Oval | 1922 |
| Atkinson, J.A. | | Tasmania v Victoria | Melbourne | 1928–29 |
| Barrow, A. | | Transvaal B v N Transvaal B | Pietermaritzburg | 1982–83 |
| Broadbent, R.G. | | Worcestershire v Glamorgan | Stourbridge | 1960 |
| Brown, A.S. | | Gloucestershire v Nottinghamshire | Nottingham | 1966 |
| Chappell, G.S. | | Australia v England | Perth | 1974–75 |
| Cooper, G.C. | | Sussex v Nottinghamshire | Hove | 1961 |
| | | *Four were off his own bowling* | | |
| Crapp, J.F. | | Gloucestershire v Derbyshire | Bristol | 1950 |
| Dean, T.A. | | Hampshire v Essex | Colchester | 1947 |
| Deas, L.M. | | Europeans v Parsees | Poona | 1898–99 |
| De Vigne, S.P. | | N.E. Transvaal v Orange Free State | Benoni | 1950–51 |
| Dollery, H.E. | | Warwickshire v Hampshire | Portsmouth | 1953 |
| Dukanwala, S. | | Baroda v Saurashtra | Bhavnagar | 1981–82 |
| Ellis, C.H. | | Sussex v Surrey | Hove | 1863 |
| Fagg, A.E. | | Kent v Hampshire | Southampton | 1952 |
| Felix, N. | | Kent v England | Canterbury | 1847 |
| Ford, A.F.J. | | Middlesex v Gloucestershire | Lord's | 1882 |
| Freeman, E.W. | | South Australia v Western Australia | Adelaide | 1971–72 |
| Greig, J.G. | | Europeans v Parsees | Bombay | 1893–94 |
| Gulfraz Khan | | Railways v MCB | Sialkot | 1981–82 |
| Hughes, G. | | Glamorgan v Essex | Swansea | 1964 |
| Jones, A.O. | | Nottinghamshire v Gloucestershire | Nottingham | 1908 |
| Langridge, J.G. | | Sussex v Somerset | Taunton | 1950 |
| Leary, S.E. | | Kent v Cambridge University | Cambridge | 1958 |
| Lock, G.A.R. | | Surrey v Lancashire | Manchester | 1953 |
| Mason, J.R. | | Kent v Surrey | Oval | 1905 |
| Milton, C.A. | | Gloucestershire v Lancashire | Cheltenham | 1962 |
| More, H.K. | | Scotland v Pakistanis | Selkirk | 1971 |
| Morrison, J.F.M. | | Wellington v Northern Districts | Wellington | 1980–81 |
| Nicholls, B.E. | | Oxford University v Australians | Oxford | 1884 |
| Oakman, A.S.M. | | Sussex v Glamorgan | Worthing | 1958 |
| Parker, J.F. | | Surrey v Kent | Blackheath | 1952 |
| Pierce, T.N. | | Barbados v Trinidad | Bridgetown | 1941–42 |
| Poidevin, L.O.S. | | Lancashire v Yorkshire | Manchester | 1906 |
| Pratt, R.L. | | Leicestershire v Derbyshire | Leicester | 1961 |
| Robinson, E.P. | | Yorkshire v Leicestershire | Bradford | 1938 |
| Sellers, A.B. | | Yorkshire v Essex | Leyton | 1933 |
| Solkar, E.D. | | Bombay v Rest of India | Bombay | 1968–69 |
| Stanning, J. | | Cambridge University v MCC | Cambridge | 1900 |
| Stewart, M.J. | | Surrey v Northamptonshire | Northampton | 1957 |
| Surridge, W.S. | | South v North | Kingston upon T. | 1952 |
| Tarrant, F.A. | | Middlesex v Essex | Leyton | 1906 |
| Tennekoon, A.P.B. | | Sri Lankans v Railways | Sahiwal | 1973–74 |
| Tunnicliffe, J. | (2) | Yorkshire v Leicestershire | Leeds | 1897 |
| | | Yorkshire v Leicestershire | Leicester | 1900 |
| Voce, W. | | Nottinghamshire v Glamorgan | Pontypridd | 1929 |
| Walker, P.M. | (2) | Glamorgan v Northamptonshire | Northampton | 1960 |
| | | Glamorgan v Nottinghamshire | Newport | 1961 |
| Wensley, A.F. | | Sussex v Surrey | Horsham | 1934 |
| Whitehouse, J. | | Warwickshire v Oxford University | Oxford | 1975 |
| Yajurvindra Singh | | India v England | Bangalore | 1976–77 |

# MOST CATCHES IN A SEASON

| | | | | | | | | |
|---|---|---|---|---|---|---|---|---|
| 78 | W.R. Hammond | Gloucestershire | 1928 | | 65 | D.W. Richardson | Worcestershire | 1961 |
| 77 | M.J. Stewart | Surrey | 1957 | | 64 | K.F. Barrington | Surrey | 1957 |
| 73 | P.M. Walker | Glamorgan | 1961 | | 64 | G.A.R. Lock | Surrey | 1957 |
| 71 | P.J. Sharpe | Yorkshire | 1962 | | 63 | J. Tunnicliffe | Yorkshire | 1896 |
| 70 | J. Tunnicliffe | Yorkshire | 1901 | | 63 | J. Tunnicliffe | Yorkshire | 1904 |
| 69 | J.G. Langridge | Sussex | 1955 | | 63 | K.J. Grieves | Lancashire | 1950 |
| 69 | P.M. Walker | Glamorgan | 1960 | | 63 | C.A. Milton | Gloucestershire | 1956 |
| 66 | J. Tunnicliffe | Yorkshire | 1895 | | 61 | J.V. Wilson | Yorkshire | 1955 |
| 65 | W.R. Hammond | Gloucestershire | 1925 | | 61 | M.J. Stewart | Surrey | 1958 |
| 65 | P.M. Walker | Glamorgan | 1959 | | 59 | J.G. Langridge | Sussex | 1933 |

| | | | | | | | | |
|---|---|---|---|---|---|---|---|
| 59 | G.R.J. Roope | Surrey | 1971 | | 56 | C.A. Milton | Gloucestershire | 1959 |
| 58 | J.G. Langridge | Sussex | 1950 | | 55 | J.T. Ikin | Lancashire | 1946 |
| 58 | W.S. Surridge | Surrey | 1952 | | 55 | J.V. Wilson | Yorkshire | 1951 |
| 58 | M.R. Hallam | Leicestershire | 1961 | | 55 | C.A. Milton | Gloucestershire | 1952 |
| 57 | A.S.M. Oakman | Sussex | 1958 | | 55 | K.F. Barrington | Surrey | 1958 |
| 56 | W.S. Surridge | Surrey | 1955 | | 55 | M.J.K. Smith | Warwickshire | 1961 |
| 56 | P.J. Sainsbury | Hampshire | 1957 | | | | | |

# THROWING RECORDS

The following are the longest recorded distances for throwing a cricket ball:

| | | | |
|---|---|---|---|
| 140 yards 2 feet | Robert Percival | Durham Sands Racecourse, Co Durham | 1882 |
| 140 yards 9 inches | Ross Mackenzie | Toronto | 1872 |

Other notable throws:

| | | | |
|---|---|---|---|
| 132 yards | W.F. Forbes | Eton College | 1876 |
| 131 yards 1 foot | D.G. Foster | Denmark | 1930 |
| 118 yards | W.G. Grace | Oval | 1868 |

*He threw 116, 117 and 118 yards with successive throws*

# CAREER RECORDS

**500 CATCHES**

| | *Career* | **Catches** | | *Career* | **Catches** |
|---|---|---|---|---|---|
| F.E. Woolley | 1906–1938 | **1018** | G.R.J. Roope | 1964–1985 | **602** |
| W.G. Grace | 1865–1908 | **874** | P.G.H. Fender | 1910–1936 | **600** |
| G.A.R. Lock | 1946–*1970* | **831** | K.W.R. Fletcher | 1962–1985 | **597** |
| W.R. Hammond | 1920–1951 | **819** | A.S.M. Oakman | 1947–1968 | **594** |
| D.B. Close | 1949–1985 | **813** | M.J.K. Smith | 1951–1975 | **592** |
| J.G. Langridge | 1928–1955 | **786** | R. Abel | 1881–1904 | **586** |
| W. Rhodes | 1898–1930 | **764** | A.O. Jones | 1892–1914 | **577** |
| C.A. Milton | 1948–1974 | **758** | D.C. Morgan | 1950–1969 | **572** |
| E.H. Hendren | 1907–1938 | **754** | P.H. Parfitt | 1956–1974 | **564** |
| P.M. Walker | 1956–1972 | **697** | G.R. Cox | 1895–1928 | **551** |
| J. Tunnicliffe | 1891–1907 | **695** | T.W. Graveney | 1948–*1971* | **550** |
| James Seymour | 1900–1926 | **675** | J.V. Wilson | 1946–1963 | **548** |
| C.P. Mead | 1905–1936 | **671** | D.S. Steele | 1963–1984 | **546** |
| M.C. Cowdrey | 1950–1976 | **638** | L.C. Braund | 1896–1920 | **545** |
| M.J. Stewart | 1954–1972 | **634** | A.E. Relf | 1900–1921 | **537** |
| P.J. Sainsbury | 1954–1976 | **617** | W.J. Edrich | 1934–1958 | **529** |
| P.J. Sharpe | 1956–1976 | **616** | A.S. Kennedy | 1907–1936 | **528** |
| K.J. Grieves | *1945*–1964 | **610** | K.F. Barrington | 1953–1968 | **515** |
| E.G. Hayes | 1896–1926 | **609** | D.B. Carr | 1945–1968 | **501** |
| G.H. Hirst | 1891–1929 | **607** | | | |

# NATIONAL CRICKET

## ENGLAND
## THE COUNTY CHAMPIONSHIP

Few sporting topics can have provoked as much controversy and argument among historians as the pre-1890 County Championship. Space unfortunately allows only a brief summary of the subject but it is hoped that sufficient references have been included for you to draw your own conclusions – and possibly to compile your own list of early champions.

Until Peter Wynne-Thomas published the results of his own researches into 'The Early County Championship' in the December 1980 issue of *The Cricket Statistician* (the official journal of the Association of Cricket Statisticians, of which he is honorary secretary), most statisticians had accepted the list of champions compiled by Rowland Bowen and published within an article in the 1959 edition of *Wisden Cricketers' Almanack*. This extended and amended the previously accepted list of champions which began with the 1873 season for which rules governing playing qualifications were first agreed. In the centenary (1963) edition of *Wisden*, Bowen extended his list by one season to allow the start of the championship to coincide neatly with the first edition of the Almanack.

Wynne-Thomas has extended the list of champions to 1825 from his research into contemporary publications. The concept of a championship appears to have resulted from a sports journalist or a wealthy patron of cricket attempting to promote interest in certain inter-county matches in the same way that bare-knuckle prize-fights were publicised. In those pre-Victorian years only Northamptonshire (founded 1820) of the present county club organisations existed and they were not to warrant first-class status until 1905. In some of those seasons only two county matches were played, whereas 24 took place in 1864, the first of Bowen's championship years. Often such proclamations in the sporting press were not unanimous in their choice of champion and frequently the title was undecided as there was no generally accepted method of determining the holder. Although the 'least matches lost' method existed, it was not consistently applied. The playing quality of a team appears to have been as important as its results. Not until 1888 was an unofficial points system introduced.

Before 1864, references to county champions were very scattered and most usually found in the newspapers local to the county which claimed the title. From 1864 references became increasingly frequent but, as the following table shows, there was scant agreement among the contemporary cricket publications concerning the title-holders. In many of the years for which Bowen selected a champion it would have been more logical to have given joint winners or to have listed none.

On 10 December 1889 a private meeting of representatives of Gloucestershire, Kent, Lancashire, Middlesex, Nottinghamshire, Surrey, Sussex and Yorkshire took place at Lord's and agreed a method of deciding the championship. Only from 1890 was the competition officially constituted and the accolade awarded by the counties themselves. Only from that date can any authorised list of county champions commence.

**COUNTY CHAMPIONS 1825 to 1863 (as compiled by Peter Wynne-Thomas)**

| | | | |
|---|---|---|---|
| 1825 | — | 1845 | Sussex |
| 1826 | Sussex | 1846 | — |
| 1827 | Sussex | 1847 | Kent |
| 1828 | Kent | 1848 | Sussex |
| 1829 | — | 1849 | Kent |
| 1830 | Surrey | 1850 | Surrey |
| 1831 | Surrey | 1851 | Surrey |
| 1832 | — | 1852 | {Nottinghamshire |
| 1833 | Sussex | | {Sussex |
| 1834 | — | 1853 | Nottinghamshire |
| 1835 | — | 1854 | Surrey |
| 1836 | — | 1855 | Sussex |
| 1837 | Kent | 1856 | Surrey |
| 1838 | Kent | 1857 | Surrey |
| 1839 | Kent | 1858 | Surrey |
| 1840 | — | 1859 | — |
| 1841 | Kent | 1860 | — |
| 1842 | Kent | 1861 | — |
| 1843 | Kent | 1862 | Nottinghamshire |
| 1844 | — | 1863 | — |

## COUNTY CHAMPIONS 1864 to 1889 (As given by Rowland Bowen and by various contemporary sources)

| | Bowen | Wisden | Green Lillywhite | Red Lillywhite | Cricket | W.G. Grace | Holmes |
|---|---|---|---|---|---|---|---|
| 1864 | Surrey | — | — | — | — | Surrey | — |
| 1865 | Nottinghamshire | — | Nottinghamshire | — | — | Nottinghamshire | — |
| 1866 | Middlesex | — | Middlesex | — | — | Middlesex | — |
| 1867 | Yorkshire | — | Yorkshire | — | — | Yorkshire | — |
| 1868 | Nottinghamshire | — | | | Nottinghamshire | Yorkshire | — |
| 1869 | Notts/Yorkshire | — | Notts/Yorkshire | | Notts/Yorkshire | Nottinghamshire | — |
| 1870 | Yorkshire | Yorkshire | Yorkshire | | Notts/Yorkshire | Yorkshire | — |
| 1871 | Nottinghamshire | Nottinghamshire | Nottinghamshire | Nottinghamshire | Notts/Yorkshire | Nottinghamshire | — |
| 1872 | Nottinghamshire | Nottinghamshire | Nottinghamshire | Nottinghamshire | Notts/Yorkshire | Surrey | — |
| 1873 | Gloucs/Notts | Nottinghamshire | Gloucestershire | Gloucs/Notts | | Gloucs/Notts | Gloucs/Notts |
| 1874 | Gloucestershire | | Gloucestershire | Gloucestershire | | Gloucestershire | Derbyshire |
| 1875 | Nottinghamshire | Nottinghamshire | Nottinghamshire | Nottinghamshire | | Nottinghamshire | Nottinghamshire |
| 1876 | Gloucestershire | | Gloucestershire | Gloucestershire | | Gloucestershire | Gloucestershire |
| 1877 | Gloucestershire | | Gloucestershire | Gloucestershire | | Gloucestershire | Gloucestershire |
| 1878 | — | — | — | — | Middlesex | Nottinghamshire | Middlesex |
| 1879 | Nottinghamshire | Nottinghamshire | Lancashire/Notts | Lancashire/Notts | | Lancashire/Notts | Lancs/Notts |
| 1880 | Nottinghamshire | Nottinghamshire | Nottinghamshire | Nottinghamshire | — | Nottinghamshire | Nottinghamshire |
| 1881 | Lancashire | Lancashire | Lancashire | Lancashire | Lancashire | Lancashire | Lancashire |
| 1882 | Lancashire/Notts | Lancashire/Notts | Lancashire/Notts | Lancashire/Notts | | Lancashire/Notts | Lancs/Notts |
| 1883 | Nottinghamshire | Yorkshire | Nottinghamshire | Nottinghamshire | Notts/Yorkshire | Yorkshire | Nottinghamshire |
| 1884 | Nottinghamshire | Nottinghamshire | Nottinghamshire | Nottinghamshire | Nottinghamshire | Nottinghamshire | Nottinghamshire |
| 1885 | Nottinghamshire | Nottinghamshire | | Nottinghamshire | Nottinghamshire | Nottinghamshire | Nottinghamshire |
| 1886 | Nottinghamshire | Nottinghamshire | | Nottinghamshire | Nottinghamshire | Nottinghamshire | Nottinghamshire |
| 1887 | Surrey | Surrey | — | Surrey | Surrey | Surrey | Surrey |
| 1888 | Surrey | Surrey | — | Surrey | Surrey | Surrey | Surrey |
| 1889 | Lancs/Notts/Surrey | Lancs/Notts/Surrey | — | Lancs/Notts/Surrey | Lancs/Notts/Surrey | Lancs/Notts/Surrey | Lancs/Notts/Surrey |

The table includes the opinions of the four major cricketing publications of the 1880s and that of the greatest cricketer of the period.

Key:

**Wisden** — *Wisden Cricketers' Almanack.*

**Green Lillywhite** — John Lillywhite's *Cricketers' Companion* (incorporating Frederick Lillywhite's *Guide to Cricketers*).

**Red Lillywhite** — James Lillywhite's *Cricketers' Annual.*

**Cricket** — *Cricket* magazine. The details for 1868–72 are as listed in *Baily's Magazine.* The 1878 entry is from *Cricket & Football Times.*

**W.G. Grace** — List published in 1903 in *Cricket* edited by H.G. Hutchinson.

**Holmes** — Rev R.S. Holmes – his list was first published in *Cricket* 1894. From 1901 until Bowen's revision in 1959 this was accepted as the 'official' list of champions.

## COUNTY CHAMPIONS 1890 to 1985

| | | | | | |
|---|---|---|---|---|---|
| 1890 | Surrey | 1924 | Yorkshire | 1958 | Surrey |
| 1891 | Surrey | 1925 | Yorkshire | 1959 | Yorkshire |
| 1892 | Surrey | 1926 | Lancashire | 1960 | Yorkshire |
| 1893 | Yorkshire | 1927 | Lancashire | 1961 | Hampshire |
| 1894 | Surrey | 1928 | Lancashire | 1962 | Yorkshire |
| 1895 | Surrey | 1929 | Nottinghamshire | 1963 | Yorkshire |
| 1896 | Yorkshire | 1930 | Lancashire | 1964 | Worcestershire |
| 1897 | Lancashire | 1931 | Yorkshire | 1965 | Worcestershire |
| 1898 | Yorkshire | 1932 | Yorkshire | 1966 | Yorkshire |
| 1899 | Surrey | 1933 | Yorkshire | 1967 | Yorkshire |
| 1900 | Yorkshire | 1934 | Lancashire | 1968 | Yorkshire |
| 1901 | Yorkshire | 1935 | Yorkshire | 1969 | Glamorgan |
| 1902 | Yorkshire | 1936 | Derbyshire | 1970 | Kent |
| 1903 | Middlesex | 1937 | Yorkshire | 1971 | Surrey |
| 1904 | Lancashire | 1938 | Yorkshire | 1972 | Warwickshire |
| 1905 | Yorkshire | 1939 | Yorkshire | 1973 | Hampshire |
| 1906 | Kent | 1946 | Yorkshire | 1974 | Worcestershire |
| 1907 | Nottinghamshire | 1947 | Middlesex | 1975 | Leicestershire |
| 1908 | Yorkshire | 1948 | Glamorgan | 1976 | Middlesex |
| 1909 | Kent | 1949 | { Middlesex | 1977 | { Middlesex |
| 1910 | Kent | | Yorkshire | | Kent |
| 1911 | Warwickshire | 1950 | { Lancashire | 1978 | Kent |
| 1912 | Yorkshire | | Surrey | 1979 | Essex |
| 1913 | Kent | 1951 | Warwickshire | 1980 | Middlesex |
| 1914 | Surrey | 1952 | Surrey | 1981 | Nottinghamshire |
| 1919 | Yorkshire | 1953 | Surrey | 1982 | Middlesex |
| 1920 | Middlesex | 1954 | Surrey | 1983 | Essex |
| 1921 | Middlesex | 1955 | Surrey | 1984 | Essex |
| 1922 | Yorkshire | 1956 | Surrey | 1985 | Middlesex |
| 1923 | Yorkshire | 1957 | Surrey | | |

Most outright titles (1890 to date):   29 – Yorkshire
Earliest date for winning title:        12 August – Kent in 1910

From 1977 to 1983 the County Championship was sponsored by Schweppes, and since 1984 by Britannic Assurance.

## FINAL POSITIONS SINCE 1890

| | DERBYSHIRE | ESSEX | GLAMORGAN | GLOUCESTERSHIRE | HAMPSHIRE | KENT | LANCASHIRE | LEICESTERSHIRE | MIDDLESEX | NORTHAMPTONSHIRE | NOTTINGHAMSHIRE | SOMERSET | SURREY | SUSSEX | WARWICKSHIRE | WORCESTERSHIRE | YORKSHIRE |
|---|---|---|---|---|---|---|---|---|---|---|---|---|---|---|---|---|---|
| 1890 | — | — | — | 6 | — | 3 | 2 | — | 7 | — | 5 | — | 1 | 8 | — | — | 3 |
| 1891 | — | — | — | 9 | — | 5 | 2 | — | 3 | — | 4 | 5 | 1 | 7 | — | — | 8 |
| 1892 | — | — | — | 7 | — | 7 | 4 | — | 5 | — | 2 | 3 | 1 | 9 | — | — | 6 |
| 1893 | — | — | — | 9 | — | 4 | 2 | — | 3 | — | 6 | 8 | 5 | 7 | — | — | 1 |
| 1894 | — | — | — | 9 | — | 4 | 4 | — | 3 | — | 7 | 6 | 1 | 8 | — | — | 2 |
| 1895 | 5 | 9 | — | 4 | 10 | 14 | 2 | 12 | 6 | — | 12 | 8 | 1 | 11 | 6 | — | 3 |
| 1896 | 7 | 5 | — | 10 | 8 | 9 | 2 | 13 | 3 | — | 6 | 11 | 4 | 14 | 12 | — | 1 |
| 1897 | 14 | 3 | — | 5 | 9 | 12 | 1 | 13 | 8 | — | 10 | 11 | 2 | 6 | 7 | — | 4 |
| 1898 | 9 | 5 | — | 3 | 12 | 7 | 6 | 13 | 2 | — | 8 | 13 | 4 | 9 | 9 | — | 1 |
| 1899 | 15 | 6 | — | 9 | 10 | 8 | 4 | 13 | 2 | — | 10 | 13 | 1 | 5 | 7 | 12 | 3 |
| 1900 | 13 | 10 | — | 7 | 15 | 3 | 2 | 14 | 7 | — | 5 | 11 | 7 | 3 | 6 | 12 | 1 |
| 1901 | 15 | 10 | — | 14 | 7 | 7 | 3 | 12 | 2 | — | 9 | 12 | 6 | 4 | 5 | 11 | 1 |
| 1902 | 10 | 13 | — | 14 | 15 | 7 | 5 | 11 | 12 | — | 3 | 7 | 4 | 2 | 6 | 9 | 1 |
| 1903 | 12 | 8 | — | 13 | 14 | 8 | 4 | 14 | 1 | — | 5 | 10 | 11 | 2 | 7 | 6 | 3 |
| 1904 | 10 | 14 | — | 9 | 15 | 3 | 1 | 7 | 4 | — | 5 | 12 | 11 | 6 | 7 | 13 | 2 |
| 1905 | 14 | 12 | — | 8 | 16 | 6 | 2 | 5 | 11 | 13 | 10 | 15 | 4 | 3 | 7 | 8 | 1 |
| 1906 | 16 | 7 | — | 9 | 8 | 1 | 4 | 15 | 11 | 11 | 5 | 11 | 3 | 10 | 6 | 14 | 2 |
| 1907 | 16 | 7 | — | 10 | 12 | 8 | 6 | 11 | 5 | 15 | 1 | 14 | 4 | 13 | 9 | 2 | 2 |
| 1908 | 14 | 11 | — | 10 | 9 | 2 | 7 | 13 | 4 | 15 | 8 | 16 | 3 | 5 | 12 | 6 | 1 |
| 1909 | 15 | 14 | — | 16 | 8 | 1 | 2 | 13 | 6 | 7 | 10 | 11 | 5 | 4 | 12 | 8 | 3 |
| 1910 | 15 | 11 | — | 12 | 6 | 1 | 4 | 10 | 3 | 9 | 5 | 16 | 2 | 7 | 14 | 13 | 8 |

| | DERBYSHIRE | ESSEX | GLAMORGAN | GLOUCESTERSHIRE | HAMPSHIRE | KENT | LANCASHIRE | LEICESTERSHIRE | MIDDLESEX | NORTHAMPTONSHIRE | NOTTINGHAMSHIRE | SOMERSET | SURREY | SUSSEX | WARWICKSHIRE | WORCESTERSHIRE | YORKSHIRE |
|---|---|---|---|---|---|---|---|---|---|---|---|---|---|---|---|---|---|
| 1911 | 14 | 6 | — | 12 | 11 | 2 | 4 | 15 | 3 | 10 | 8 | 16 | 5 | 13 | 1 | 9 | 7 |
| 1912 | 12 | 15 | — | 11 | 6 | 3 | 4 | 13 | 5 | 2 | 8 | 14 | 7 | 10 | 9 | 16 | 1 |
| 1913 | 13 | 15 | — | 9 | 10 | 1 | 8 | 14 | 6 | 4 | 5 | 16 | 3 | 7 | 11 | 12 | 2 |
| 1914 | 12 | 8 | — | 16 | 5 | 3 | 11 | 13 | 2 | 9 | 10 | 15 | 1 | 6 | 7 | 14 | 4 |
| 1919 | 9 | 14 | — | 8 | 7 | 2 | 5 | 9 | 13 | 12 | 3 | 5 | 4 | 11 | 15 | — | 1 |
| 1920 | 16 | 9 | — | 8 | 11 | 5 | 2 | 13 | 1 | 14 | 7 | 10 | 3 | 6 | 12 | 15 | 4 |
| 1921 | 12 | 15 | 17 | 7 | 6 | 4 | 5 | 11 | 1 | 13 | 8 | 10 | 2 | 9 | 16 | 14 | 3 |
| 1922 | 11 | 8 | 16 | 13 | 6 | 4 | 5 | 14 | 7 | 15 | 2 | 10 | 3 | 9 | 12 | 17 | 1 |
| 1923 | 10 | 13 | 16 | 11 | 7 | 5 | 3 | 14 | 8 | 17 | 2 | 9 | 4 | 6 | 12 | 15 | 1 |
| 1924 | 17 | 15 | 13 | 6 | 12 | 5 | 4 | 11 | 2 | 16 | 6 | 8 | 3 | 10 | 9 | 14 | 1 |
| 1925 | 14 | 7 | 17 | 10 | 9 | 5 | 3 | 12 | 6 | 11 | 4 | 15 | 2 | 13 | 8 | 16 | 1 |
| 1926 | 11 | 9 | 8 | 15 | 7 | 3 | 1 | 13 | 6 | 16 | 4 | 14 | 5 | 10 | 12 | 17 | 2 |
| 1927 | 5 | 8 | 15 | 12 | 13 | 4 | 1 | 7 | 9 | 16 | 2 | 14 | 6 | 10 | 11 | 17 | 3 |
| 1928 | 10 | 16 | 15 | 5 | 12 | 2 | 1 | 9 | 8 | 13 | 3 | 14 | 6 | 7 | 11 | 17 | 4 |
| 1929 | 7 | 12 | 17 | 4 | 11 | 8 | 2 | 9 | 6 | 13 | 1 | 15 | 10 | 4 | 14 | 16 | 2 |
| 1930 | 9 | 6 | 11 | 2 | 13 | 5 | 1 | 12 | 16 | 17 | 4 | 13 | 8 | 7 | 15 | 10 | 3 |
| 1931 | 7 | 10 | 15 | 2 | 12 | 3 | 6 | 16 | 11 | 17 | 5 | 13 | 8 | 4 | 9 | 14 | 1 |
| 1932 | 10 | 14 | 15 | 13 | 8 | 3 | 6 | 12 | 10 | 16 | 4 | 7 | 5 | 2 | 9 | 17 | 1 |
| 1933 | 6 | 4 | 16 | 10 | 14 | 3 | 5 | 17 | 12 | 13 | 8 | 11 | 9 | 2 | 7 | 15 | 1 |
| 1934 | 3 | 8 | 13 | 7 | 14 | 5 | 1 | 12 | 10 | 17 | 9 | 15 | 11 | 2 | 4 | 16 | 5 |
| 1935 | 2 | 9 | 13 | 15 | 16 | 10 | 4 | 6 | 3 | 17 | 5 | 14 | 11 | 7 | 8 | 12 | 1 |
| 1936 | 1 | 9 | 16 | 4 | 10 | 8 | 11 | 15 | 2 | 17 | 5 | 7 | 6 | 14 | 13 | 12 | 3 |
| 1937 | 3 | 6 | 7 | 4 | 14 | 12 | 9 | 16 | 2 | 17 | 10 | 13 | 8 | 5 | 11 | 15 | 1 |
| 1938 | 5 | 6 | 16 | 10 | 14 | 9 | 4 | 15 | 2 | 17 | 12 | 7 | 3 | 8 | 13 | 11 | 1 |
| 1939 | 9 | 4 | 13 | 3 | 15 | 5 | 6 | 17 | 2 | 16 | 12 | 14 | 8 | 10 | 11 | 7 | 1 |
| 1946 | 15 | 8 | 6 | 5 | 10 | 6 | 3 | 11 | 2 | 16 | 13 | 4 | 11 | 17 | 14 | 8 | 1 |
| 1947 | 5 | 11 | 9 | 2 | 16 | 4 | 3 | 14 | 1 | 17 | 11 | 11 | 6 | 9 | 15 | 7 | 7 |
| 1948 | 6 | 13 | 1 | 8 | 9 | 15 | 5 | 11 | 3 | 17 | 14 | 12 | 2 | 16 | 7 | 10 | 4 |
| 1949 | 15 | 9 | 8 | 7 | 16 | 13 | 11 | 17 | 1 | 6 | 11 | 9 | 5 | 13 | 4 | 3 | 1 |
| 1950 | 5 | 17 | 11 | 7 | 12 | 9 | 1 | 16 | 14 | 10 | 15 | 7 | 1 | 13 | 4 | 6 | 3 |
| 1951 | 11 | 8 | 5 | 12 | 9 | 16 | 3 | 15 | 7 | 13 | 17 | 14 | 6 | 10 | 1 | 4 | 2 |
| 1952 | 4 | 10 | 7 | 9 | 12 | 15 | 3 | 6 | 5 | 8 | 16 | 17 | 1 | 13 | 10 | 14 | 2 |
| 1953 | 6 | 12 | 10 | 6 | 14 | 16 | 3 | 3 | 5 | 11 | 8 | 17 | 1 | 2 | 9 | 15 | 12 |
| 1954 | 3 | 15 | 4 | 13 | 14 | 11 | 10 | 16 | 7 | 7 | 5 | 17 | 1 | 9 | 6 | 11 | 2 |
| 1955 | 8 | 14 | 16 | 12 | 3 | 13 | 9 | 6 | 5 | 7 | 11 | 17 | 1 | 4 | 9 | 15 | 2 |
| 1956 | 12 | 11 | 13 | 3 | 6 | 16 | 2 | 17 | 5 | 4 | 8 | 15 | 1 | 9 | 14 | 9 | 7 |
| 1957 | 4 | 5 | 9 | 12 | 13 | 14 | 6 | 17 | 7 | 2 | 15 | 8 | 1 | 9 | 11 | 16 | 3 |
| 1958 | 5 | 6 | 15 | 14 | 2 | 8 | 7 | 12 | 10 | 4 | 17 | 3 | 1 | 13 | 16 | 9 | 11 |
| 1959 | 7 | 9 | 6 | 2 | 8 | 13 | 5 | 16 | 10 | 11 | 17 | 12 | 3 | 15 | 4 | 14 | 1 |
| 1960 | 5 | 6 | 11 | 8 | 12 | 10 | 2 | 17 | 3 | 9 | 16 | 14 | 7 | 4 | 15 | 13 | 1 |
| 1961 | 7 | 6 | 14 | 5 | 1 | 11 | 13 | 9 | 3 | 16 | 17 | 10 | 15 | 8 | 12 | 4 | 2 |
| 1962 | 7 | 9 | 14 | 4 | 10 | 16 | 11 | 17 | 13 | 8 | 15 | 6 | 5 | 12 | 3 | 2 | 1 |
| 1963 | 17 | 12 | 2 | 8 | 10 | 13 | 15 | 16 | 6 | 7 | 9 | 3 | 11 | 4 | 4 | 14 | 1 |
| 1964 | 12 | 10 | 11 | 17 | 12 | 7 | 14 | 16 | 6 | 3 | 15 | 8 | 4 | 9 | 2 | 1 | 5 |
| 1965 | 9 | 15 | 3 | 10 | 12 | 5 | 13 | 14 | 6 | 2 | 17 | 7 | 8 | 16 | 11 | 1 | 4 |
| 1966 | 9 | 16 | 14 | 15 | 11 | 4 | 12 | 8 | 12 | 5 | 17 | 3 | 7 | 10 | 6 | 2 | 1 |
| 1967 | 6 | 15 | 14 | 17 | 12 | 2 | 11 | 3 | 7 | 9 | 16 | 8 | 4 | 13 | 10 | 5 | 1 |
| 1968 | 8 | 14 | 3 | 16 | 5 | 2 | 6 | 9 | 10 | 13 | 4 | 12 | 15 | 17 | 11 | 7 | 1 |
| 1969 | 16 | 6 | 1 | 2 | 5 | 10 | 15 | 14 | 11 | 9 | 8 | 17 | 3 | 7 | 4 | 12 | 13 |
| 1970 | 7 | 12 | 2 | 17 | 10 | 1 | 3 | 15 | 16 | 14 | 11 | 13 | 5 | 9 | 7 | 6 | 4 |
| 1971 | 17 | 10 | 16 | 8 | 9 | 4 | 3 | 5 | 6 | 14 | 12 | 7 | 1 | 11 | 2 | 15 | 13 |
| 1972 | 17 | 5 | 13 | 3 | 9 | 2 | 15 | 6 | 8 | 4 | 14 | 11 | 12 | 16 | 1 | 7 | 10 |
| 1973 | 16 | 8 | 11 | 5 | 1 | 4 | 12 | 9 | 13 | 3 | 17 | 10 | 2 | 15 | 7 | 6 | 14 |
| 1974 | 17 | 12 | 16 | 14 | 2 | 10 | 8 | 4 | 6 | 3 | 15 | 5 | 7 | 13 | 9 | 1 | 11 |
| 1975 | 15 | 7 | 9 | 16 | 3 | 5 | 4 | 1 | 11 | 8 | 13 | 12 | 6 | 17 | 14 | 10 | 2 |
| 1976 | 15 | 6 | 17 | 3 | 12 | 14 | 16 | 4 | 1 | 2 | 13 | 7 | 9 | 10 | 5 | 11 | 8 |
| 1977 | 7 | 6 | 14 | 3 | 11 | 1 | 16 | 5 | 1 | 9 | 17 | 14 | 4 | 8 | 10 | 13 | 12 |
| 1978 | 14 | 2 | 13 | 10 | 8 | 1 | 12 | 6 | 3 | 17 | 7 | 5 | 16 | 9 | 11 | 15 | 4 |
| 1979 | 16 | 1 | 17 | 10 | 12 | 5 | 13 | 6 | 14 | 11 | 9 | 8 | 3 | 4 | 15 | 2 | 7 |
| 1980 | 9 | 8 | 13 | 7 | 17 | 16 | 15 | 9 | 1 | 12 | 3 | 5 | 2 | 4 | 14 | 11 | 6 |
| 1981 | 12 | 5 | 14 | 13 | 7 | 9 | 16 | 8 | 4 | 15 | 1 | 3 | 6 | 2 | 17 | 11 | 10 |
| 1982 | 11 | 7 | 16 | 15 | 3 | 13 | 12 | 2 | 1 | 9 | 4 | 6 | 5 | 8 | 17 | 14 | 10 |
| 1983 | 9 | 1 | 15 | 12 | 3 | 7 | 12 | 4 | 2 | 6 | 14 | 10 | 8 | 11 | 5 | 16 | 17 |
| 1984 | 12 | 1 | 13 | 17 | 15 | 5 | 16 | 4 | 3 | 11 | 2 | 7 | 8 | 6 | 9 | 10 | 14 |
| 1985 | 13 | 4 | 12 | 3 | 2 | 9 | 14 | 16 | 1 | 10 | 8 | 17 | 6 | 7 | 15 | 5 | 11 |

# FIRST-CLASS COUNTY CRICKET CLUBS

### DERBYSHIRE

**Present club formed:** 4 November 1870
**Colours:** Chocolate, amber and pale blue
**Badge:** Rose and crown
**Championships:** (1) 1936

### ESSEX

**Present club formed:** 14 January 1876
**Colours:** Blue, gold and red
**Badge:** Three seaxes above scroll bearing 'Essex'
**Championships:** (3) 1979, 1983, 1984

### GLAMORGAN

**Present club formed:** 6 July 1888
**Colours:** Blue and gold
**Badge:** Gold daffodil
**Championships:** (2) 1948, 1969

### GLOUCESTERSHIRE

**Present club formed:** 1871
**Colours:** Blue, gold, brown, silver, green and red
**Badge:** Coat of Arms of the city and county of Bristol
**Championships:** (0) Runners-up in 1930, 1931, 1947, 1959, 1969

### HAMPSHIRE

**Present club formed:** 12 August 1863
**Colours:** Blue, gold and white
**Badge:** Tudor rose and crown
**Championships:** (2) 1961, 1973

### KENT

**Present club formed:** 1 March 1859
**Substantially reorganised:** 6 December 1870
**Colours:** Maroon and white
**Badge:** White horse on a red ground
**Championships:** (6) 1906, 1909, 1910, 1913, 1970, 1978
**Joint championships:** (1) 1977

## LANCASHIRE

**Present club formed:** 12 January 1864
**Colours:** Red, green and blue
**Badge:** Red rose
**Championships:** (7) 1897, 1904, 1926, 1927, 1928, 1930, 1934
**Joint championships:** (1) 1950

## LEICESTERSHIRE

**Present club formed:** 25 March 1879
**Colours:** Dark green and scarlet
**Badge:** Gold running fox on green ground
**Championships:** (1) 1975

## MIDDLESEX

**Present club formed:** 2 February 1864
**Colours:** Blue
**Badge:** Three seaxes
**Championships:** (8) 1903, 1920, 1921, 1947, 1976, 1980, 1982, 1985
**Joint championships:** (2) 1949, 1977

## NORTHAMPTONSHIRE

**Present club formed:** 31 July 1878
**Colours:** Maroon
**Badge:** Tudor rose
**Championships:** (0) Runners-up in 1912, 1957, 1965, 1976

## NOTTINGHAMSHIRE

**Present club formed:** March/April 1841
**Substantially reorganised:** 11 December 1866
**Colours:** Green and gold
**Badge:** County badge of Nottinghamshire
**Championships:** (3) 1907, 1929, 1981

## SOMERSET

**Present club formed:** 18 August 1875
**Colours:** Black, white and maroon
**Badge:** Wessex Wyvern
**Championships:** (0) Third in 1892, 1958, 1963, 1966, 1981

### SURREY

**Present club formed:** 22 August 1845
**Colours:** Chocolate
**Badge:** Prince of Wales' feathers
**Championships:** (15) 1890, 1891, 1892, 1894, 1895, 1899, 1914, 1952, 1953, 1954, 1955, 1956, 1957, 1958, 1971
**Joint championships:** (1) 1950

### SUSSEX

**Present club formed:** 1 March 1839
**Substantially reorganised:** August 1857
**Colours:** Dark blue, light blue and gold
**Badge:** County Arms of six martlets
**Championships:** (0) Runners-up in 1902, 1903, 1932, 1933, 1934, 1953, 1981

### WARWICKSHIRE

**Present club formed:** 8 April 1882
**Substantially reorganised:** 19 January 1884
**Colours:** Dark blue, gold and silver
**Badge:** Bear and ragged staff
**Championships:** (3) 1911, 1951, 1972

### WORCESTERSHIRE

**Present club formed:** 11 March 1865
**Colours:** Dark green and black
**Badge:** Shield, *argent* bearing *fess* between three *pears sable*
**Championships:** (3) 1964, 1965, 1974

### YORKSHIRE

**Present club formed:** 8 January 1863
**Substantially reorganised:** 10 December 1891
**Colours:** Oxford blue, Cambridge blue and gold
**Badge:** White rose
**Championships:** (29) 1893, 1896, 1898, 1900, 1901, 1902, 1905, 1908, 1912, 1919, 1922, 1923, 1924, 1925, 1931, 1932, 1933, 1935, 1937, 1938, 1939, 1946, 1959, 1960, 1962, 1963, 1966, 1967, 1968
**Joint championships:** (1) 1949

# COUNTY CAPTAINS

Before the abolition of amateur status in first-class cricket after the 1962 season, it was unusual for a professional to be appointed officially as county captain. Professionals appointed before 1963 are listed in italics.

## DERBYSHIRE

| | | | |
|---|---|---|---|
| 1871–75 | S. Richardson | 1931–36 | A.W. Richardson |
| 1876–83 | R.P. Smith | 1937–39 | R.H.R. Buckston |
| 1884 | L.C. Docker | 1946 | G.F. Hodgkinson |
| 1885–86 | E.A.J. Maynard | 1947–48 | E.J. Gothard |
| 1887 | E.A.J. Maynard, W. Chatterton | 1949 | D.A. Skinner |
| 1888–89 | W. Chatterton | 1950 | P. Vaulkhard |
| 1890 | F.R. Spofforth | 1951–54 | G.L. Willatt |
| 1891–98 | S.H. Evershed | 1955–62 | D.B. Carr |
| 1899–01 | S.H. Hill-Wood | 1963–64 | C. Lee |
| 1902–03 | A.E. Lawton | 1965–69 | D.C. Morgan |
| 1904–05 | A.E. Lawton, E.M. Ashcroft | 1970–72 | I.R. Buxton |
| 1906 | A.E. Lawton, L.G. Wright | 1973–74 | J.B. Bolus |
| 1907 | L.G. Wright | 1975 | J.B. Bolus, R.W. Taylor |
| 1908 | A.E. Lawton, R.B. Rickman | 1976 | R.W. Taylor, E.J. Barlow |
| 1909 | A.E. Lawton | 1977–78 | E.J. Barlow |
| 1910–12 | J. Chapman | 1979 | D.S. Steele, G. Miller |
| 1913–14 | R.R.C. Baggallay | 1980 | G. Miller |
| 1919 | R.R.C. Baggallay, J. Chapman | 1981 | G. Miller, B. Wood |
| 1920 | J. Chapman, L. Oliver | 1982 | B. Wood |
| 1921 | G.M. Buckston | 1983 | B. Wood, K.J. Barnett |
| 1922–30 | G.R. Jackson | 1984– | K.J. Barnett |

## ESSEX

| | | | |
|---|---|---|---|
| 1894 | A.P. Lucas | 1933–38 | T.N. Pearce, D.R. Wilcox |
| 1895–00 | H.G.P. Owen | 1939 | D.R. Wilcox, F.St G. Unwin, |
| 1901 | H.G.P. Owen, A.P. Lucas | | J.W.A. Stephenson |
| 1902 | H.G.P. Owen | 1946–49 | T.N. Pearce |
| 1903 | C.J. Kortright | 1950 | T.N. Pearce, D.J. Insole |
| 1904–06 | F.L. Fane | 1951–60 | D.J. Insole |
| 1907–10 | C.P. McGahey | 1961–66 | T.E. Bailey |
| 1911–28 | J.W.H.T. Douglas | 1967–73 | B. Taylor |
| 1929–32 | H.M. Morris | 1974–85 | K.W.R. Fletcher |

## GLAMORGAN

| | | | |
|---|---|---|---|
| 1921 | N.V.H. Riches | 1967–72 | A.R. Lewis |
| 1922–23 | T.A.L. Whittington | 1973–75 | Majid Khan |
| 1924–27 | J.C. Clay | 1976 | Majid Khan, A. Jones |
| 1928 | T. Arnott | 1977–78 | A. Jones |
| 1929 | J.C. Clay, N.V.H. Riches | 1979 | R.N.S. Hobbs |
| 1930–39 | M.J.L. Turnbull | 1980–81 | M.A. Nash |
| 1946 | J.C. Clay | 1982 | Javed Miandad, B.J. Lloyd |
| 1947–60 | W. Wooller | 1983–84 | M.W.W. Selvey |
| 1961–66 | O.S. Wheatley | 1985– | R.C. Ontong |

## GLOUCESTERSHIRE

| | | | |
|---|---|---|---|
| 1871–98 | W.G. Grace | 1947–50 | B.O. Allen |
| 1899 | W.G. Grace, W. Troup | 1951–52 | Sir D.T.L. Bailey |
| 1900–12 | G.L. Jessop | 1953–54 | *J.F. Crapp* |
| 1913–14 | C.O.H. Sewell | 1955–58 | *G.M. Emmett* |
| 1919–21 | F.G. Robinson | 1959–60 | *T.W. Graveney* |
| 1922–23 | P.F.C. Williams | 1961–62 | C.T.M. Pugh |
| 1924–26 | D.C. Robinson | 1963–64 | J.K.R. Graveney |
| 1927–28 | W.H. Rowlands | 1965–67 | J.B. Mortimore |
| 1929–34 | B.H. Lyon | 1968 | C.A. Milton |
| 1935–36 | D.A.C. Page | 1969–76 | A.S. Brown |
| 1937–38 | B.O. Allen | 1977–81 | M.J. Procter |
| 1939–46 | W.R. Hammond | 1982– | D.A. Graveney |

## HAMPSHIRE

| | | | |
|---|---|---|---|
| 1864–69 | G.M. Ede | 1936–37 | R.H. Moore |
| 1870 | A.H. Wood | 1938 | C.G.A. Paris |
| 1875–78 | C. Booth | 1939 | G.R. Taylor |
| 1880–82 | H.W.R. Bencraft | 1946–57 | E.D.R. Eagar |
| 1883–85 | A.H. Wood | 1958–65 | A.C.D. Ingleby-Mackenzie |
| 1895 | H.W.R. Bencraft | 1966–70 | R.E. Marshall |
| 1896–99 | E.G. Wynyard | 1971–78 | R.M.C. Gilliat |
| 1900–02 | C. Robson | 1979 | G.R. Stephenson |
| 1903–14 | E.M. Sprot | 1980–84 | N.E.J. Pocock |
| 1919–33 | Lord (Hon L.H.) Tennyson | 1985– | M.C.J. Nicholas |
| 1934–35 | W.G.L.F. Lowndes | | |

## KENT

| | | | |
|---|---|---|---|
| 1859–70 | W.S. Norton | 1937 | R.T. Bryan, B.H. Valentine |
| 1871–74 | No official appointment | 1938–39 | F.G.H. Chalk |
| 1875–89 | Lord Harris | 1946–48 | B.H. Valentine |
| 1890–93 | F. Marchant, W.H. Patterson | 1949–51 | D.G. Clark |
| 1894–97 | F. Marchant | 1952–53 | W. Murray-Wood |
| 1898–02 | J.R. Mason | 1954–56 | *D.V.P. Wright* |
| 1903 | C.J. Burnup | 1957–71 | M.C. Cowdrey |
| 1904–08 | C.H.B. Marsham | 1972–76 | M.H. Denness |
| 1909–13 | E.W. Dillon | 1977 | Asif Iqbal |
| 1914–23 | L.H.W. Troughton | 1978–80 | A.G.E. Ealham |
| 1924–26 | W.S. Cornwallis | 1981–82 | Asif Iqbal |
| 1927 | A.J. Evans | 1983–84 | C.J. Tavaré |
| 1928–30 | G.B. Legge | 1985– | C.S. Cowdrey |
| 1931–36 | A.P.F. Chapman | | |

## LANCASHIRE

| | | | |
|---|---|---|---|
| 1866–79 | E.B. Rowley | 1947–48 | K. Cranston |
| 1880–91 | A.N. Hornby | 1949–53 | N.D. Howard |
| 1892–93 | A.N. Hornby, S.M. Crosfield | 1954–59 | *C. Washbrook* |
| 1894–96 | A.C. MacLaren | 1960–61 | R.W. Barber |
| 1897–98 | A.N. Hornby | 1962 | J.F. Blackledge |
| 1899 | A.C. MacLaren, G.R. Bardswell | 1963–64 | K.J. Grieves |
| 1900–07 | A.C. MacLaren | 1965–67 | J.B. Statham |
| 1908–14 | A.H. Hornby | 1968–72 | J.D. Bond |
| 1919–22 | M.N. Kenyon | 1973–77 | D. Lloyd |
| 1923–25 | J. Sharp | 1978–80 | F.C. Hayes |
| 1926–28 | L. Green | 1981–83 | C.H. Lloyd |
| 1929–35 | P.T. Eckersley | 1984–85 | J. Abrahams |
| 1936–39 | W.H.L. Lister | | |
| 1946 | J.A. Fallows | | |

## LEICESTERSHIRE

| | | | |
|---|---|---|---|
| 1879–85 | C. Marriott | 1936–38 | C.S. Dempster |
| 1886–89 | H.T. Arnall-Thompson | 1939 | M.St J. Packe |
| 1890–06 | C.E. de Trafford | 1946–48 | *G.L. Berry* |
| 1907–10 | Sir A.G. Hazlerigg | 1949 | S.J. Symington |
| 1911–13 | J. Shields | 1950–57 | C.H. Palmer |
| 1914–20 | C.J.B. Wood | 1958–61 | *W. Watson* |
| 1921 | A.T. Sharp | 1962 | D. Kirby |
| 1922–27 | G.H.S. Fowke | 1963–65 | M.R. Hallam |
| 1928–29 | E.W. Dawson | 1966–67 | G.A.R. Lock |
| 1930 | J.A.F.M.P. de Lisle | 1968 | M.R. Hallam |
| 1931 | E.W. Dawson | 1969–78 | R. Illingworth |
| 1932 | No official appointment | 1979 | K. Higgs |
| 1933 | E.W. Dawson | 1980 | B.F. Davison |
| 1934 | A.G. Hazlerigg | 1981–83 | R.W. Tolchard |
| 1935 | *W.E. Astill* | 1984– | D.I. Gower |

## MIDDLESEX

| | | | |
|---|---|---|---|
| 1864–72 | V.E. Walker | 1948–49 | F.G. Mann |
| 1873–84 | I.D. Walker | 1950 | R.W.V. Robins |
| 1885–97 | A.J. Webbe | 1951–52 | W.J. Edrich, *D.C.S. Compton* |
| 1898 | A.J. Webbe, A.E. Stoddart | 1953–57 | W.J. Edrich |
| 1899–07 | G. MacGregor | 1958–60 | J.J. Warr |
| 1908–20 | P.F. Warner | 1961–62 | P.I. Bedford |
| 1921–28 | F.T. Mann | 1963–64 | C.D. Drybrough |
| 1929–32 | N.E. Haig | 1965–67 | F.J. Titmus |
| 1933–34 | N.E. Haig, H.J. Enthoven | 1968 | F.J. Titmus, P.H. Parfitt |
| 1935–38 | R.W.V. Robins | 1969–70 | P.H. Parfitt |
| 1939 | I.A.R. Peebles | 1971–82 | J.M. Brearley |
| 1946–47 | R.W.V. Robins | 1983– | M.W. Gatting |

## NORTHAMPTONSHIRE

| | | | |
|---|---|---|---|
| 1905–06 | T. Horton | 1938–39 | R.P. Nelson |
| 1907 | E.M. Crosse | 1946 | P.E. Murray-Willis |
| 1908–10 | T.E. Manning | 1947–48 | A.W. Childs-Clarke |
| 1911–12 | G.A.T. Vials | 1949–53 | F.R. Brown |
| 1913 | G.A.T. Vials, S.G. Smith | 1954–57 | *D. Brookes* |
| 1914 | S.G. Smith | 1958–61 | R. Subba Row |
| 1919 | J.N. Beasley | 1962–66 | *K.V. Andrew* |
| 1920–21 | R.O. Raven | 1967–70 | R.M. Prideaux |
| 1922 | C.H. Tyler | 1971–74 | P.J. Watts |
| 1923–24 | A.H. Bull | 1975 | R.T. Virgin, P.J. Watts, |
| 1925–26 | J.M. Fitzroy | | Mushtaq Mohammad |
| 1927 | J.M. Fitzroy, V.W.C. Jupp | 1976–77 | Mushtaq Mohammad |
| 1928–31 | V.W.C. Jupp | 1978–80 | P.J. Watts |
| 1932–35 | W.C. Brown | 1981– | G. Cook |
| 1936–37 | G.B. Cuthbertson | | |

## NOTTINGHAMSHIRE

| | | | |
|---|---|---|---|
| 1835–55 | *W. Clarke* | 1947–50 | W.A. Sime |
| 1856–70 | *G. Parr* | 1951–60 | R.T. Simpson |
| 1871–80 | *R. Daft* | 1961 | *J.D. Clay* |
| 1881–82 | *W. Oscroft* | 1962 | A.J. Corran |
| 1883–86 | *A. Shaw* | 1963–65 | G. Millman |
| 1887–88 | *M. Sherwin* | 1966–67 | N.W. Hill |
| 1889–99 | J.A. Dixon | 1968–71 | G.St A. Sobers |
| 1900–12 | A.O. Jones | 1972 | J.B. Bolus |
| 1913 | A.O. Jones, G.O. Gauld | 1973 | G.St A. Sobers |
| 1914 | A.O. Jones | 1974 | J.D. Bond |
| 1919–34 | A.W. Carr | 1975–78 | M.J. Smedley |
| 1935 | G.F.H. Heane, S.D. Rhodes | 1979 | M.J. Smedley, C.E.B. Rice |
| 1936–46 | G.F.H. Heane | 1980– | C.E.B. Rice |

## SOMERSET

| | | | |
|---|---|---|---|
| 1891–93 | H.T. Hewett | 1949 | G.E.S. Woodhouse |
| 1894–06 | S.M.J. Woods | 1950–52 | S.S. Rogers |
| 1907 | L.C.H. Palairet | 1953–54 | B.G. Brocklehurst |
| 1908–12 | J. Daniell | 1955 | G.G. Tordoff |
| 1913–14 | E.S.M. Poyntz | 1956–59 | *M.F. Tremlett* |
| 1919–26 | J. Daniell | 1960–64 | *H.W. Stephenson* |
| 1927–31 | J.C. White | 1965–67 | C.R.M. Atkinson |
| 1932–37 | R.A. Ingle | 1968 | R.C. Kerslake |
| 1938–46 | E.F. Longrigg | 1969–71 | B.A. Langford |
| 1947 | R.J.O. Meyer | 1972–77 | D.B. Close |
| 1948 | N.S. Mitchell-Innes, | 1978–83 | B.C. Rose |
| | G.E.S. Woodhouse, J.W. Seamer | 1984–85 | I.T. Botham |

## SURREY

| | | | |
|---|---|---|---|
| 1846–50 | C.H. Hoare | 1910 | H.D.G. Leveson Gower, M.C. Bird |
| 1851–57 | F.P. Miller | 1911–13 | M.C. Bird |
| 1858–65 | F. Burbidge | 1914–19 | C.T.A. Wilkinson |
| 1866 | E. Dowson | 1920 | C.T.A. Wilkinson, P.G.H. Fender |
| 1867 | W.J. Collyer | 1921–31 | P.G.H. Fender |
| 1868 | C. Calvert | 1932–33 | D.R. Jardine |
| 1869–70 | S.H. Akroyd | 1934–38 | E.R.T. Holmes |
| 1871 | J.C. Gregory | 1939 | H.M. Garland-Wells |
| 1872–75 | G. Strachan | 1946 | N.H. Bennett |
| 1876 | A. Chandler | 1947–48 | E.R.T. Holmes |
| 1877–79 | G. Strachan | 1949–51 | M.R. Barton |
| 1880–93 | J. Shuter | 1952–56 | W.S. Surridge |
| 1894–99 | K.J.Key | 1957–62 | P.B.H. May† |
| 1900–02 | D.L.A. Jephson | 1963–72 | M.J. Stewart |
| 1903 | L. Walker | 1973–77 | J.H. Edrich |
| 1904 | No official appointment | 1978–83 | R.D.V. Knight |
| 1905–07 | Lord Dalmeny | 1984– | G.P. Howarth |
| 1908–09 | H.D.G. Leveson Gower | | |

† *P.B.H. May (ill) did not play in 1960, and A.V. Bedser (vice-captain) led the County.*

## SUSSEX

| | | | |
|---|---|---|---|
| 1839–46 | C.G. Taylor | 1909 | C.L.A. Smith |
| 1847–62 | E. Napper | 1910–14 | H.P. Chaplin |
| 1863 | J.H. Hale | 1919–21 | H.L. Wilson |
| 1864 | J.H. Hale, C.H. Smith | 1922–29 | A.E.R. Gilligan |
| 1865–73 | C.H. Smith | 1930 | A.H.H. Gilligan |
| 1874 | C.H. Smith, J.M. Cotterill | 1931–32 | K.S. Duleepsinhji |
| 1875 | J.M. Cotterill | 1933 | R.S.G. Scott |
| 1876–78 | F.F.J. Greenfield | 1934–35 | A. Melville |
| 1879 | C. Sharp | 1936–39 | A.J. Holmes |
| 1880 | R.T. Ellis | 1946 | S.C. Griffith |
| 1881–82 | F.F.J. Greenfield | 1947–49 | H.T. Bartlett |
| 1883–84 | H. Whitfeld | 1950–52 | *James Langridge* |
| 1885 | G.N. Wyatt | 1953 | D.S. Sheppard |
| 1886 | F.M. Lucas | 1954 | G.H.G. Doggart |
| 1887–88 | C.A. Smith | 1955–59 | R.G. Marlar |
| 1889 | W. Newham | 1960–65 | E.R. Dexter |
| 1890 | C.A. Smith | 1966 | Nawab of Pataudi, jr |
| 1891–92 | W. Newham | 1967 | J.M. Parks |
| 1893–98 | W.L. Murdoch | 1968 | J.M. Parks, M.G. Griffith |
| 1899 | W.L. Murdoch, K.S. Ranjitsinhji | 1969–72 | M.G. Griffith |
| 1900–03 | K.S. Ranjitsinhji | 1973–77 | A.W. Greig |
| 1904–05 | C.B. Fry | 1978–80 | A. Long |
| 1906 | C.B. Fry, C.L.A. Smith | 1981– | J.R.T. Barclay |
| 1907–08 | C.B. Fry | | |

## WARWICKSHIRE

| | | | |
|---|---|---|---|
| 1894–01 | H.W. Bainbridge | 1938–47 | P. Cranmer |
| 1902 | H.W. Bainbridge, T.S. Fishwick | 1948 | R.H. Maudsley, *H.E. Dollery* |
| 1903–06 | J.F. Byrne | 1949–55 | *H.E. Dollery* |
| 1907 | J.F. Byrne, T.S. Fishwick | 1956 | *W.E. Hollies* |
| 1908–09 | A.C.S. Glover | 1957–67 | M.J.K. Smith |
| 1910 | H.J. Goodwin | 1968–74 | A.C. Smith |
| 1911–14 | F.R. Foster | 1975–77 | D.J. Brown |
| 1919 | G.W. Stephens | 1978–79 | J. Whitehouse |
| 1920–29 | Hon F.S.G. Calthorpe | 1980–84 | R.G.D. Willis |
| 1930–37 | R.E.S. Wyatt | 1985– | N. Gifford |

## WORCESTERSHIRE

| | | | |
|---|---|---|---|
| 1899–00 | H.K. Foster | 1931–35 | C.F. Walters |
| 1901 | R.E. Foster | 1936–39 | Hon C.J. Lyttelton |
| 1902–10 | H.K. Foster | 1946 | A.P. Singleton |
| 1911–12 | G.H.T. Simpson-Hayward | 1947–48 | A.F.T. White |
| 1913 | H.K. Foster | 1949 | R.E.S. Wyatt, A.F.T. White |
| 1914 | W.H. Taylor | 1950–51 | R.E.S. Wyatt |
| 1920–21 | M.F.S. Jewell | 1952–54 | R.E. Bird |
| 1922 | W.H. Taylor | 1955 | *R.T.D. Perks* |
| 1923–25 | M.K. Foster | 1956–58 | P.E. Richardson |
| 1926 | M.F.S. Jewell | 1959–67 | *D. Kenyon* |
| 1927 | Hon C.B. Ponsonby | 1968–70 | T.W. Graveney |
| 1928 | M.F.S. Jewell | 1971–80 | N. Gifford |
| 1929 | M.F.S. Jewell, Hon J.B. Coventry | 1981 | G.M. Turner |
| 1930 | Hon J.B. Coventry | 1982– | P.A. Neale |

## YORKSHIRE

| | | | |
|---|---|---|---|
| 1863–70 | *R. Iddison* | 1933–47 | A.B. Sellers |
| 1871–75 | *J. Rowbotham* | 1948–55 | N.W.D. Yardley |
| 1876–77 | *E. Lockwood* | 1956–57 | W.H.H. Sutcliffe |
| 1878–82 | *T. Emmett* | 1958–59 | J.R. Burnet |
| 1883–10 | Lord Hawke | 1960–62 | *J.V. Wilson* |
| 1911 | E.J. Radcliffe | 1963–70 | D.B. Close |
| 1912–14 | Sir A.W. White | 1971–78 | G. Boycott |
| 1919–21 | D.C.F. Burton | 1979–80 | J.H. Hampshire |
| 1922–24 | G. Wilson | 1981 | C.M. Old |
| 1925–27 | A.W. Lupton | 1982 | C.M. Old, R. Illingworth |
| 1928–29 | W.A. Worsley | 1983 | R. Illingworth |
| 1930 | A.T. Barber | 1984– | D.L. Bairstow |
| 1931–32 | F.E. Greenwood | | |

# COUNTY CAPS

### CAPPED BY THREE COUNTIES

| | |
|---|---|
| **R. Berry** | Lancashire (1950), Worcestershire (1957), Derbyshire (1961) |
| **R. Swetman** | Surrey (1958), Nottinghamshire (1966), Gloucestershire (1972) |
| **J.B. Bolus** | Yorkshire (1960), Nottinghamshire (1963), Derbyshire (1973) |
| **R.D.V. Knight** | Gloucestershire (1971), Sussex (1976), Surrey (1978) |
| **Younis Ahmed** | Surrey (1969), Worcestershire (1979), Glamorgan (1985) |

### COUNTY CAPS AWARDED SINCE 1946

### DERBYSHIRE

| | | | |
|---|---|---|---|
| 1946 | J.D. Eggar, C. Gladwin, G.F. Hodgkinson, P. Vaulkhard | 1969 | A. Ward |
| 1947 | G.O. Dawkes, E.J. Gothard, E.A. Marsh, A.C. Revill | 1970 | C.P. Wilkins |
| | | 1972 | M. Hendrick |
| 1949 | H.L. Jackson, D.A. Skinner | 1973 | J.B. Bolus, F.E. Rumsey, S. Venkataraghavan |
| 1950 | A. Hamer, G.L. Willatt | | |
| 1951 | D.B. Carr, J.M. Kelly, D.C. Morgan, R. Sale | 1975 | P.E. Russell, F.W. Swarbrook |
| | | 1976 | E.J. Barlow, A. Hill, G. Miller |
| 1954 | E. Smith | 1977 | A.J. Borrington, C.J. Tunnicliffe, J.G. Wright |
| 1956 | C. Lee | | |
| 1958 | H.L. Johnson, H.J. Rhodes | 1978 | H. Cartwright, P.N. Kirsten |
| 1961 | R. Berry, I.W. Hall | 1979 | D.S. Steele |
| 1962 | I.R. Buxton, W.F. Oates, R.W. Taylor | 1980 | S. Oldham, B. Wood |
| 1963 | A.B. Jackson, G.W. Richardson | 1982 | K.J. Barnett, J.H. Hampshire |
| 1964 | M.H. Page | 1983 | M.A. Holding |
| 1967 | T.J.P. Eyre | 1985 | I.S. Anderson, R.J. Finney, D.G. Moir |
| 1968 | P.J.K. Gibbs, J.F. Harvey, D.H.K. Smith | | |

## ESSEX

| | |
|---|---|
| 1946 | H.P. Crabtree, T.C. Dodds, R.F.T. Paterson, F.H. Vigar |
| 1947 | T.E. Bailey, L.S. Clark, S.J. Cray |
| 1948 | R. Horsfall, F. Rist |
| 1949 | D.J. Insole, G.R. Pullinger |
| 1951 | P.A. Gibb, K.C. Preston |
| 1952 | W.T. Greensmith |
| 1954 | J.A. Bailey |
| 1955 | G. Barker |
| 1956 | B. Taylor |
| 1957 | L.H.R. Ralph |
| 1958 | M.J. Bear |
| 1959 | B.R. Knight, L.H. Savill |
| 1960 | G.J. Smith |
| 1961 | J. Milner |
| 1962 | J.C. Laker |
| 1963 | K.W.R. Fletcher |
| 1964 | R.N.S. Hobbs, P.J. Phelan |
| 1965 | B.E.A. Edmeades |
| 1967 | K.D. Boyce, R.E. East |
| 1968 | B.L. Irvine |
| 1970 | D.L. Acfield, J.K. Lever, G.J. Saville, S. Turner, B. Ward |
| 1971 | B.C. Francis |
| 1974 | B.R. Hardie, K.S. McEwan |
| 1975 | G.A. Gooch, N. Smith |
| 1976 | K.R. Pont |
| 1977 | M.H. Denness |
| 1978 | N. Phillip |
| 1982 | D.E. East, D.R. Pringle |
| 1983 | N.A. Foster |
| 1984 | C. Gladwin |

## GLAMORGAN

| | |
|---|---|
| 1946 | W.E. Jones, A. Porter, M. Robinson |
| 1947 | B.L. Muncer, A.J. Watkins |
| 1948 | P.B. Clift, J.T. Eaglestone, N.G. Hever, W.G.A. Parkhouse |
| 1951 | J.E. McConnon |
| 1952 | J.E. Pleass, D.J. Shepherd |
| 1954 | B. Hedges |
| 1955 | J.S. Pressdee |
| 1956 | L.N. Devereux |
| 1958 | P.M. Walker |
| 1959 | D.G.L. Evans |
| 1960 | J.B. Evans, A.R. Lewis |
| 1961 | D. Ward, O.S. Wheatley |
| 1962 | A. Jones |
| 1963 | A. Rees |
| 1965 | I.J. Jones, E.J. Lewis |
| 1967 | A.E. Cordle, E.W. Jones |
| 1968 | Majid Khan |
| 1969 | B.A. Davis, R.C. Davis, M.A. Nash |
| 1971 | R.C. Fredericks, D.L. Williams |
| 1973 | J.W. Solanky |
| 1974 | L.W. Hill |
| 1976 | G. Richards |
| 1977 | J.A. Hopkins, M.J. Llewellyn |
| 1979 | R.N.S. Hobbs, R.C. Ontong, P.D. Swart |
| 1980 | N.G. Featherstone, Javed Miandad |
| 1981 | E.A. Moseley |
| 1982 | D.A. Francis, B.J. Lloyd |
| 1983 | A.L. Jones, C.J.C. Rowe, M.W.W. Selvey |
| 1984 | J.F. Steele |
| 1985 | T. Davies, G.C. Holmes, Younis Ahmed |

## GLOUCESTERSHIRE

| | |
|---|---|
| 1946 | C. Cook |
| 1948 | T.W. Graveney |
| 1949 | Sir D.T.L. Bailey, J.K.R. Graveney, C.A. Milton |
| 1950 | D.M. Young |
| 1954 | F.P. McHugh, J.B. Mortimore, B.D. Wells |
| 1955 | P. Rochford |
| 1957 | A.S. Brown, D.G. Hawkins, R.B. Nicholls, D.R. Smith |
| 1958 | B.J. Meyer |
| 1959 | D.A. Allen |
| 1961 | D.G.A'Court, D. Carpenter, C.T.M. Pugh |
| 1965 | S.E.J. Russell, A.R. Windows |
| 1968 | D.M. Green, M.J. Procter |
| 1969 | D.R. Shepherd |
| 1970 | M. Bissex |
| 1971 | J. Davey, R.D.V. Knight |
| 1972 | R. Swetman |
| 1973 | Sadiq Mohammad |
| 1975 | Zaheer Abbas |
| 1976 | D.A. Graveney, A.W. Stovold |
| 1977 | B.M. Brain, J.H. Childs, A.J. Hignell |
| 1978 | A.J. Brassington |
| 1979 | J.C. Foat |
| 1981 | P. Bainbridge, B.C. Broad |
| 1983 | P.W. Romaines, J.N. Shepherd |
| 1985 | C.W.J. Athey, K.M. Curran, B.F. Davison, D.A. Lawrence, J.W. Lloyds, R.C. Russell, C.A. Walsh |

## HAMPSHIRE

| | |
|---|---|
| 1946 | E.D.R. Eagar, A.G. Holt |
| 1947 | N.H. Rogers |
| 1948 | G. Dawson |
| 1949 | V.J. Ransom, D. Shackleton, C. Walker |
| 1950 | V.H.D. Cannings |
| 1951 | J.R. Gray, L. Harrison |
| 1952 | A.W.H. Rayment |
| 1953 | D.E. Blake |
| 1954 | J.R. Bridger, R. Dare |
| 1955 | H.M. Barnard, M.D. Burden, H. Horton, R.E. Marshall, P.J. Sainsbury |
| 1957 | M. Heath, A.C.D. Ingleby-Mackenzie |
| 1959 | D.O. Baldry |
| 1960 | D.W. White |

## HAMPSHIRE *continued*

| | |
|---|---|
| 1961 | D.A. Livingstone |
| 1963 | B.S.V. Timms, A.R. Wassell |
| 1965 | R.M.H. Cottam |
| 1967 | B.L. Reed |
| 1968 | B.A. Richards |
| 1969 | R.M.C. Gilliat, G.R. Stephenson |
| 1970 | D.R. Turner |
| 1971 | T.E. Jesty |
| 1972 | C.G. Greenidge, R.S. Herman |
| 1973 | M.N.S. Taylor |

| | |
|---|---|
| 1974 | A.M.E. Roberts |
| 1975 | J.M. Rice |
| 1978 | N.G. Cowley, J.W. Southern |
| 1979 | K. Stevenson |
| 1980 | N.E.J. Pocock |
| 1981 | M.D. Marshall, C.L. Smith |
| 1982 | M.C.J. Nicholas, R.J. Parks |
| 1983 | V.P. Terry, T.M. Tremlett |
| 1985 | R.A. Smith |

## KENT

| | |
|---|---|
| 1946 | T.G. Evans, R.R. Dovey, J.W. Martin, H.A. Pawson |
| 1947 | N.W. Harding, P. Hearn, F. Ridgway |
| 1948 | E.E. Crush |
| 1949 | D.G. Clark, B.R. Edrich, A.W.H. Mallett |
| 1951 | M.C. Cowdrey, W. Murray-Wood |
| 1952 | R. Mayes, A.H. Phebey, A.C. Shirreff |
| 1953 | G. Smith |
| 1954 | J. Pettiford, R.C. Wilson |
| 1955 | J.M. Allan |
| 1956 | D.G. Ufton |
| 1957 | D.J. Halfyard, S.E. Leary, J.C.T. Page, J.F. Pretlove |
| 1960 | A.L. Dixon, P.E. Richardson |
| 1961 | A. Brown, P.H. Jones |
| 1962 | A.W. Catt, D.M. Sayer |
| 1963 | B.W. Luckhurst |
| 1964 | M.H. Denness, D.L. Underwood |

| | |
|---|---|
| 1965 | A.P.E. Knott, J.M. Prodger |
| 1966 | J.C.J. Dye |
| 1967 | J.N. Graham, J.N. Shepherd |
| 1968 | Asif Iqbal |
| 1969 | D. Nicholls |
| 1970 | A.G.E. Ealham, G.W. Johnson, R.A. Woolmer |
| 1972 | B.D. Julien |
| 1977 | R.W. Hills, K.B.S. Jarvis, C.J.C. Rowe |
| 1978 | C.J. Tavaré |
| 1979 | C.S. Cowdrey, P.R. Downton |
| 1980 | G.R. Dilley |
| 1981 | M.R. Benson |
| 1982 | N.R. Taylor |
| 1983 | D.G. Aslett, E.A.E. Baptiste, R.M. Ellison |
| 1984 | T.M. Alderman |
| 1985 | S.G. Hinks |

## LANCASHIRE

| | |
|---|---|
| 1946 | T.L. Brierley, G.A. Edrich, J.A. Fallows, J.T. Ikin, B.P. King, E. Price, A. Wharton |
| 1947 | K. Cranston, R.G. Garlick, B.J. Howard |
| 1948 | E.H. Edrich, N.D. Howard |
| 1949 | P. Greenwood, K.J. Grieves |
| 1950 | A.T. Barlow, R. Berry, M.J. Hilton, J.B. Statham, R. Tattersall |
| 1951 | A. Wilson |
| 1952 | J.G. Lomax |
| 1953 | F.D. Parr |
| 1956 | J. Dyson, T. Greenhough, J. Jordan, C.S. Smith |
| 1958 | R.W. Barber, P.T. Marner, G. Pullar |
| 1959 | K. Higgs |
| 1960 | G. Clayton |
| 1961 | J.D. Bond, B.J. Booth, R. Collins |
| 1962 | J.F. Blackledge, D.M. Green, C. Hilton |

| | |
|---|---|
| 1963 | R. Bennett |
| 1964 | S. Ramadhin |
| 1965 | K. Goodwin, P. Lever, H. Pilling |
| 1966 | D.R. Worsley |
| 1967 | G. Atkinson, G.K. Knox, J.S. Savage |
| 1968 | F.M. Engineer, D. Lloyd, K. Shuttleworth, B. Wood |
| 1969 | C.H. Lloyd, J. Sullivan |
| 1970 | D.P. Hughes |
| 1971 | J. Simmons, K.L. Snellgrove |
| 1972 | F.C. Hayes, P.G. Lee |
| 1975 | A. Kennedy, J. Lyon |
| 1976 | R.M. Ratcliffe |
| 1980 | B.W. Reidy |
| 1981 | P.J.W. Allott, G. Fowler |
| 1982 | J. Abrahams, C.E.H. Croft |
| 1984 | J.A. Ormrod |
| 1985 | N.H. Fairbrother, S.J. O'Shaughnessy |

## LEICESTERSHIRE

| | |
|---|---|
| 1946 | V.E. Jackson, G. Lester, M. Tompkin, J.E. Walsh |
| 1949 | G. Evans, S.J. Symington |
| 1950 | C.H. Palmer |
| 1951 | J. Firth, V.S. Munden, G.A. Smithson |
| 1952 | C.T. Spencer |
| 1953 | T.J. Goodwin |
| 1954 | M.R. Hallam |

| | |
|---|---|
| 1955 | M.J.K. Smith |
| 1958 | B.S. Boshier, A.C. Revill, J.S. Savage, W. Watson |
| 1959 | J. van Geloven |
| 1960 | H.D. Bird |
| 1961 | L.R. Gardner, R. Julian, A. Wharton |
| 1962 | D. Kirby |
| 1963 | C.C. Inman, S. Jayasinghe |

## LEICESTERSHIRE *continued*

| | |
|---|---|
| 1964 | B.J. Booth |
| 1965 | J. Birkenshaw, J. Cotton, G.A.R. Lock, P.T. Marner |
| 1966 | M.E.J.C. Norman, R.W. Tolchard |
| 1968 | B.R. Knight |
| 1969 | B. Dudleston, R. Illingworth, G.D. McKenzie |
| 1971 | B.F. Davison, J.F. Steele |
| 1972 | K. Higgs |

| | |
|---|---|
| 1973 | J.C. Balderstone |
| 1974 | N.M. McVicker |
| 1976 | P. Booth, P.B. Clift |
| 1977 | D.I. Gower, K. Shuttleworth, A. Ward |
| 1981 | N.E. Briers, L.B. Taylor |
| 1982 | N.G.B. Cook |
| 1984 | J.P. Agnew, I.P. Butcher, G.J. Parsons, |
| 1985 | P. Willey |

## MIDDLESEX

| | |
|---|---|
| 1946 | J.P. Mann, A. Thompson, J.A. Young |
| 1947 | L.H. Compton, A. Fairbairn |
| 1948 | P.I. Bedford, J.G. Dewes, E.A. Ingram, H.P.H. Sharp |
| 1949 | J.J. Warr |
| 1951 | R. Routledge |
| 1952 | D. Bennett, W. Knightley-Smith, A.E. Moss |
| 1953 | F.J. Titmus |
| 1955 | G.P.S. Delisle |
| 1956 | J.T. Murray |
| 1957 | R.A. Gale, R.J. Hurst, A.C. Walton |
| 1959 | R.W. Hooker, W.E. Russell |
| 1960 | P.H. Parfitt |
| 1961 | E.A. Clark |
| 1962 | C.D. Drybrough |
| 1963 | J.S.E. Price, R.A. White |

| | |
|---|---|
| 1964 | J.M. Brearley |
| 1965 | D. Bick |
| 1967 | M.J. Harris, C.T. Radley, M.J. Smith, M.O.C. Sturt |
| 1968 | A.H. Latchman |
| 1969 | A.N. Connolly, R.S. Herman |
| 1971 | N.G. Featherstone, K.V. Jones |
| 1973 | D.A. Marriott, M.W.W. Selvey |
| 1974 | P.H. Edmonds |
| 1976 | G.D. Barlow, A.A. Jones |
| 1977 | W.W. Daniel, J.E. Emburey, M.W. Gatting, I.J. Gould |
| 1979 | R.O. Butcher |
| 1980 | V.A.P. van der Bijl |
| 1981 | P.R. Downton, S.P. Hughes, W.N. Slack |
| 1983 | K.P. Tomlins |
| 1984 | N.G. Cowans, N.F. Williams |

## NORTHAMPTONSHIRE

| | |
|---|---|
| 1946 | W. Barron, P.E. Murray-Willis |
| 1947 | V. Broderick, A.W. Childs-Clarke, C.B. Clarke, K. Fiddling, J. Webster |
| 1948 | A.E. Nutter, N. Oldfield |
| 1949 | F.R. Brown, R.W. Clarke, R.G. Garlick |
| 1950 | L. Livingston |
| 1951 | F. Jakeman |
| 1952 | D.W. Barrick, G.E. Tribe |
| 1953 | E. Davis |
| 1954 | K.V. Andrew, S. Starkie, F.H. Tyson |
| 1955 | P. Arnold, R. Subba Row |
| 1956 | J.S. Manning, B.L. Reynolds |
| 1957 | M.J.H. Allen |
| 1960 | L.A. Johnson, M.E.J.C. Norman |
| 1961 | J.D.F. Larter, A. Lightfoot |
| 1962 | B.S. Crump, R.M. Prideaux, P.D. Watts, P.J. Watts |

| | |
|---|---|
| 1963 | C. Milburn |
| 1964 | M.E. Scott |
| 1965 | D.S. Steele |
| 1966 | H. Sully |
| 1967 | Mushtaq Mohammad |
| 1969 | H.M. Ackerman |
| 1971 | P. Willey |
| 1972 | B.S. Bedi, R.M.H. Cottam, J.C.J. Dye |
| 1973 | G. Sharp |
| 1974 | R.T. Virgin |
| 1975 | G. Cook, Sarfraz Nawaz |
| 1976 | A. Hodgson, W. Larkins |
| 1978 | B.J. Griffiths, A.J. Lamb, Hon T.M. Lamb, T.J. Yardley |
| 1979 | R.G. Williams |
| 1984 | R.J. Boyd-Moss, N.A. Mallender |
| 1985 | R.J. Bailey |

## NOTTINGHAMSHIRE

| | |
|---|---|
| 1946 | E.A. Meads, T.B. Reddick, R.T. Simpson, F.W. Stocks |
| 1947 | W.A. Sime, H. Winrow |
| 1949 | P.F. Harvey, C.J. Poole |
| 1951 | R.J. Giles |
| 1952 | J.D. Clay |
| 1953 | B. Dooland |
| 1954 | E.J. Martin, E.J. Rowe |
| 1955 | G. Goonesena, K. Smales |
| 1956 | A.K. Walker |
| 1957 | G. Millman |
| 1959 | N.W. Hill |
| 1960 | J. Cotton, J.D. Springall, B.D. Wells |

| | |
|---|---|
| 1961 | M. Hill |
| 1962 | A.J. Corran, I.J. Davison, H.M. Winfield |
| 1963 | J.B. Bolus |
| 1965 | C. Forbes, H.I. Moore |
| 1966 | M.J. Smedley, R. Swetman, R.A. White |
| 1967 | D.L. Murray, M.N.S. Taylor |
| 1968 | D.J. Halfyard, G.St A. Sobers |
| 1969 | B. Stead |
| 1970 | M.J. Harris, B. Hassan |
| 1971 | D.A. Pullan |
| 1973 | D.W. Randall |
| 1974 | J.D. Bond, P.A. Wilkinson |

## NOTTINGHAMSHIRE *continued*

| | | | |
|---|---|---|---|
| 1975 | P.D. Johnson, A.H. Latchman, C.E.B. Rice, W. Taylor | 1981 | J.D. Birch |
| 1977 | D.R. Doshi, P.A. Todd | 1982 | M. Hendrick |
| 1978 | R.J. Hadlee | 1983 | R.T. Robinson |
| 1980 | M.K. Bore, K.E. Cooper, B.N. French, P.J. Hacker, E.E. Hemmings | 1984 | B.C. Broad, K. Saxelby |

## SOMERSET

| | | | |
|---|---|---|---|
| 1946 | F. Castle, G.R. Langdale, J. Lawrence, M.M. Walford | 1964 | P.J. Eele |
| 1947 | M. Coope, M.F. Tremlett, H.E. Watts, G.E.S. Woodhouse | 1965 | G. Clayton |
| | | 1966 | M.J. Kitchen, P.J. Robinson |
| 1949 | E. Hill, S.S. Rogers, H.W. Stephenson | 1968 | T.I. Barwell, R.A. Brooks, G.I. Burgess, G.S. Chappell, A. Clarkson, R.C. Kerslake |
| 1950 | F.L. Angell, E.P. Robinson | | |
| 1951 | J. Redman | 1969 | R. Palmer |
| 1952 | G.G. Tordoff | 1970 | T.W. Cartwright |
| 1953 | B.G. Brocklehurst, T.A. Hall, C.G. Mitchell, Roy Smith | 1971 | D.B. Close, K.J. O'Keeffe, D.J.S. Taylor |
| 1954 | J.G. Lomax, J.W. McMahon, P.B. Wight, Yawar Saeed | 1972 | A.A. Jones, H.R. Moseley |
| | | 1973 | P.W. Denning, J.M. Parks |
| 1955 | B. Lobb | 1974 | I.V.A. Richards |
| 1956 | C.L. McCool, L. Pickles | 1975 | B.C. Rose |
| 1957 | W.E. Alley, B.A. Langford, D.R.W. Silk | 1976 | I.T. Botham, D. Breakwell |
| | | 1978 | C.H. Dredge, K.F. Jennings, P.M. Roebuck, P.A. Slocombe |
| 1958 | G. Atkinson, K.E. Palmer | | |
| 1959 | K.D. Biddulph | 1979 | J. Garner, V.J. Marks |
| 1960 | R.T. Virgin | 1980 | S.M. Gavaskar |
| 1961 | C.R.M. Atkinson, A.A. Baig | 1982 | J.W. Lloyds |
| 1962 | C.M.H. Greetham, B. Roe | 1983 | T. Gard, N.F.M. Popplewell |
| 1963 | F.E. Rumsey | 1984 | M.D. Crowe |

## SURREY

| | | | |
|---|---|---|---|
| 1946 | A.V. Bedser, N.H. Bennett, A.J.W. McIntyre | 1964 | R. Harman, R.I. Jefferson, S.J. Storey |
| | | 1966 | M.J. Edwards |
| 1947 | E.A. Bedser, D.G.W. Fletcher, J.C. Laker | 1967 | G.G. Arnold, P.I. Pocock |
| | | 1968 | W.A. Smith |
| 1948 | M.R. Barton, J.W. McMahon, W.S. Surridge | 1969 | Intikhab Alam, G.R.J. Roope, D.J.S. Taylor, Younis Ahmed |
| 1949 | G.J. Whittaker | 1970 | R.D. Jackman |
| 1950 | B. Constable, G.A.R. Lock, P.B.H. May | 1972 | C.E. Waller |
| 1952 | T.H. Clark | 1974 | G.P. Howarth |
| 1953 | P.J. Loader, R. Subba Row | 1975 | A.R. Butcher, L.E. Skinner |
| 1955 | K.F. Barrington, M.J. Stewart | 1978 | R.D.V. Knight, C.J. Richards |
| 1958 | R. Swetman | 1980 | S.T. Clarke, G.S. Clinton, D.M. Smith |
| 1959 | J.H. Edrich | 1982 | M.A. Lynch, D.J. Thomas |
| 1960 | D. Gibson | 1984 | G. Monkhouse |
| 1961 | A.B.D. Parsons | 1985 | A.H. Gray, T.E. Jesty, A. Needham, A.J. Stewart |
| 1962 | A. Long, D.A.D. Sydenham, R.A.E. Tindall, M.D. Willett | | |

## SUSSEX

| | | | |
|---|---|---|---|
| 1948 | P.D.S. Blake | 1964 | J.A. Snow |
| 1949 | G.H.G. Doggart, J. Oakes, D.S. Sheppard | 1965 | T. Gunn |
| | | 1966 | D.J. Foreman |
| 1950 | A.E. James, D.V. Smith, R.T. Webb | 1967 | M.A. Buss, A.W. Greig, M.G. Griffith, E.J. Lewis |
| 1951 | A.S.M. Oakman, J.M. Parks | | |
| 1952 | R.G. Marlar, K.G. Suttle | 1969 | P.J. Graves |
| 1953 | N.I. Thomson | 1970 | G.A. Greenidge |
| 1957 | D.L. Bates, L.J. Lenham | 1971 | U.C. Joshi, R.M. Prideaux |
| 1959 | E.R. Dexter | 1973 | J.D. Morley, J. Spencer |
| 1961 | R.V. Bell, G.C. Cooper, R.J. Langridge | 1976 | J.R.T. Barclay, R.D.V. Knight, A. Long, C.E. Waller |
| 1963 | A. Buss, Nawab of Pataudi, jr | | |

## SUSSEX *continued*

| | |
|---|---|
| 1977 | Javed Miandad, K.C. Wessels |
| 1978 | Imran Khan |
| 1979 | G.G. Arnold, P.W.G. Parker |
| 1980 | G.D. Mendis, C.P. Phillipson |

| | |
|---|---|
| 1981 | I.J. Gould, I.A. Greig, G.S. Le Roux |
| 1982 | A.C.S. Pigott, C.M. Wells |
| 1985 | A.M. Green |

## WARWICKSHIRE

| | |
|---|---|
| 1946 | W.E. Fantham, J.J. Hossell, J.M.A. Marshall, R.H. Maudsley, R. Sale, N.A. Shortland, K.A. Taylor |
| 1947 | V.H.D. Cannings, C.W. Grove, T.L. Pritchard, J.R. Thompson |
| 1948 | M.P. Donnelly, R.T. Spooner, A. Townsend |
| 1949 | F.C. Gardner, A.H. Kardar, A.V. Wolton |
| 1951 | R.E. Hitchcock, E.B. Lewis, R.T. Weeks |
| 1953 | N.F. Horner |
| 1954 | J.D. Bannister, K.R. Dollery |
| 1955 | R.G. Thompson |
| 1957 | K. Ibadulla, M.J.K. Smith, W.J. Stewart |
| 1958 | R.G. Carter, T.W. Cartwright |
| 1959 | O.S. Wheatley |
| 1961 | W.B. Bridge, A.C. Smith |
| 1962 | A. Wright |

| | |
|---|---|
| 1963 | R.W. Barber, E. Legard, R.V. Webster |
| 1964 | D.J. Brown, J.A. Jameson |
| 1965 | D.L. Amiss |
| 1966 | R.N. Abberley |
| 1968 | L.R. Gibbs, R.B. Kanhai |
| 1969 | W. Blenkiron |
| 1971 | N.M. McVicker, B.S.V. Timms |
| 1972 | A.I. Kallicharran, D.L. Murray, R.G.D. Willis |
| 1973 | J. Whitehouse |
| 1974 | E.E. Hemmings, S.J. Rouse |
| 1976 | G.W. Humpage |
| 1977 | S.P. Perryman |
| 1978 | K.D. Smith |
| 1980 | D.R. Doshi, T.A. Lloyd |
| 1982 | G.C. Small |
| 1983 | A.M. Ferreira, N. Gifford |
| 1984 | C.M. Old |

## WORCESTERSHIRE

| | |
|---|---|
| 1946 | R.E. Bird, A.F.T. White, R.E.S. Wyatt |
| 1947 | D. Kenyon, H. Yarnold |
| 1948 | L. Outschoorn |
| 1949 | M.L.Y. Ainsworth |
| 1950 | G.H. Chesterton, G. Dews |
| 1951 | R.G. Broadbent |
| 1952 | P.E. Richardson |
| 1955 | J.A. Flavell, M.J. Horton |
| 1956 | R. Booth, D.W. Richardson |
| 1957 | R. Berry |
| 1959 | K.J. Aldridge, L.J. Coldwell, D.B. Pearson |
| 1960 | D.N.F. Slade |
| 1961 | N. Gifford, R.G.A. Headley |
| 1962 | T.W. Graveney, J.A. Standen |

| | |
|---|---|
| 1965 | R.G.M. Carter, B.L. D'Oliveira |
| 1966 | B.M. Brain, J.A. Ormrod |
| 1968 | G.M. Turner |
| 1969 | E.J.O. Hemsley |
| 1970 | G.R. Cass, V.A. Holder |
| 1972 | T.J. Yardley |
| 1974 | J.M. Parker |
| 1976 | Imran Khan, J.D. Inchmore |
| 1978 | J. Cumbes, D.J. Humphries, P.A. Neale |
| 1979 | D.N. Patel, Younis Ahmed |
| 1980 | A.P. Pridgeon |
| 1981 | H.L. Alleyne |
| 1984 | T.S. Curtis, D.M. Smith |
| 1985 | D.B. D'Oliveira, N.V. Radford |

## YORKSHIRE

| | |
|---|---|
| 1946 | A. Booth |
| 1947 | D.V. Brennan, A. Coxon, G.A. Smithson, J.H. Wardle, W. Watson |
| 1948 | R. Aspinall, H. Halliday, E.I. Lester, J.V. Wilson |
| 1949 | D.B. Close, F.A. Lowson |
| 1951 | R. Appleyard, F.S. Trueman |
| 1952 | W.H.H. Sutcliffe |
| 1955 | R. Illingworth |
| 1957 | J.G. Binks, W.B. Stott, K. Taylor |
| 1958 | J.R. Burnet, D.E.V. Padgett |
| 1959 | R.K. Platt |
| 1960 | J.B. Bolus, M.J. Cowan, P.J. Sharpe, D. Wilson |

| | |
|---|---|
| 1962 | M. Ryan |
| 1963 | G. Boycott, J.H. Hampshire, A.G. Nicholson |
| 1964 | R.A. Hutton |
| 1969 | B. Leadbeater, C.M. Old |
| 1970 | G.A. Cope |
| 1973 | D.L. Bairstow |
| 1974 | R.G. Lumb |
| 1976 | P. Carrick, A.L. Robinson |
| 1978 | G.B. Stevenson |
| 1980 | C.W.J. Athey, J.D. Love, A. Sidebottom |
| 1982 | S.N. Hartley, K. Sharp |
| 1983 | S.J. Dennis |
| 1984 | M.D. Moxon |

# INDIVIDUAL COUNTY CAREER AGGREGATE RECORDS

The following records include performances in all first-class matches for the county and not in Championship matches alone.

## MOST RUNS IN A SEASON

| | | Season | I | NO | Runs | HS | Avge | 100 |
|---|---|---|---|---|---|---|---|---|
| Derbyshire | D.B. Carr | 1959 | 52 | 7 | **2165** | 156* | 48.11 | 5 |
| Essex | G.A. Gooch | 1984 | 45 | 7 | **2559** | 227 | 67.34 | 8 |
| Glamorgan | Javed Miandad | 1981 | 37 | 7 | **2083** | 200* | 69.43 | 8 |
| Gloucestershire | W.R. Hammond | 1933 | 46 | 5 | **2860** | 264 | 69.75 | 11 |
| Hampshire | C.P. Mead | 1928 | 45 | 9 | **2854** | 180 | 79.27 | 12 |
| Kent | F.E. Woolley | 1928 | 52 | 3 | **2894** | 198 | 59.06 | 10 |
| Lancashire | J.T. Tyldesley | 1901 | 51 | 4 | **2633** | 221 | 56.02 | 8 |
| Leicestershire | G.L. Berry | 1937 | 51 | 4 | **2446** | 184* | 52.04 | 7 |
| Middlesex | E.H. Hendren | 1923 | 42 | 10 | **2669** | 200* | 83.41 | 11 |
| Northamptonshire | D. Brookes | 1952 | 50 | 7 | **2198** | 204* | 51.11 | 6 |
| Nottinghamshire | W.W. Whysall | 1929 | 52 | 3 | **2620** | 244 | 53.46 | 7 |
| Somerset | W.E. Alley | 1961 | 58 | 11 | **2761** | 221* | 58.74 | 10 |
| Surrey | T.W. Hayward | 1906 | 53 | 8 | **3246** | 219 | 72.13 | 13 |
| Sussex | J.G. Langridge | 1949 | 49 | 5 | **2850** | 234* | 64.77 | 12 |
| Warwickshire | M.J.K. Smith | 1959 | 50 | 10 | **2417** | 200* | 60.42 | 6 |
| Worcestershire | H.H.I. Gibbons | 1934 | 57 | 6 | **2654** | 157 | 52.03 | 8 |
| Yorkshire | H. Sutcliffe | 1932 | 41 | 5 | **2883** | 313 | 80.08 | 12 |

## MOST HUNDREDS IN A SEASON

| | | | | |
|---|---|---|---|---|
| **Derbyshire** | 8 | P.N. Kirsten | 1982 |
| **Essex** | 9 | J. O'Connor | 1934 |
| | 9 | D.J. Insole | 1955 |
| **Glamorgan** | 8 | Javed Miandad | 1981 |
| **Gloucestershire** | 13 | W.R. Hammond | 1938 |
| **Hampshire** | 12 | C.P. Mead | 1928 |
| **Kent** | 10 | F.E. Woolley | 1928 |
| | 10 | F.E. Woolley | 1934 |
| **Lancashire** | 11 | C. Hallows | 1928 |
| **Leicestershire** | 7 | G.L. Berry | 1937 |
| | 7 | W. Watson | 1959 |
| | 7 | B.F. Davison | 1982 |
| **Middlesex** | 13 | D.C.S. Compton | 1947 |
| **Northamptonshire** | 8 | R.A. Haywood | 1921 |
| **Nottinghamshire** | 9 | W.W. Whysall | 1928 |
| | 9 | M.J. Harris | 1971 |
| **Somerset** | 10 | W.E. Alley | 1961 |
| **Surrey** | 13 | T.W. Hayward | 1906 |
| | 13 | J.B. Hobbs | 1925 |
| **Sussex** | 12 | J.G. Langridge | 1949 |
| **Warwickshire** | 9 | A.I. Kallicharran | 1984 |
| **Worcestershire** | 10 | G.M. Turner | 1970 |
| **Yorkshire** | 12 | H. Sutcliffe | 1932 |

## MOST WICKETS IN A SEASON

| | | Season | Overs | Mdns | Runs | Wkts | Avge |
|---|---|---|---|---|---|---|---|
| Derbyshire | T.B. Mitchell | 1935 | 866.5 | 134 | 3284 | **168** | 19.55 |
| Essex | T.P.B. Smith | 1947 | 1606 | 287 | 4667 | **172** | 27.13 |
| Glamorgan | J.C. Clay | 1937 | 1103.3 | 229 | 3052 | **176** | 17.34 |
| Gloucestershire | T.W.J. Goddard | 1937 | 1335 | 325 | 3730 | **222** | 16.80 |
| | | 1947 | 1327.1 | 323 | 3636 | **222** | 16.37 |
| Hampshire | A.S. Kennedy | 1922 | 1190.3 | 322 | 2967 | **190** | 15.61 |
| Kent | A.P. Freeman | 1933 | 1829.2 | 610 | 3862 | **262** | 14.74 |
| Lancashire | E.A. McDonald | 1925 | 1204.4 | 277 | 3674 | **198** | 18.55 |
| Leicestershire | J.E. Walsh | 1948 | 1124.3 | 185 | 3224 | **170** | 18.96 |
| Middlesex | F.J. Titmus | 1955 | 1179 | 443 | 2312 | **158** | 14.63 |
| Northamptonshire | G.E. Tribe | 1955 | 1272 | 341 | 3273 | **175** | 18.70 |

| | | Season | Overs | Mdns | Runs | Wkts | Avge |
|---|---|---|---|---|---|---|---|
| **Nottinghamshire** | B. Dooland | 1954 | 1197.4 | 393 | 2708 | **181** | 14.96 |
| **Somerset** | A.W. Wellard | 1938 | 1168.4 | 233 | 3152 | **169** | 19.24 |
| **Surrey** | T. Richardson | 1895 | 1444.4 | 394 | 3515 | **252** | 13.94 |
| **Sussex** | M.W. Tate | 1925 | 1440 | 416 | 2669 | **198** | 13.47 |
| **Warwickshire** | W.E. Hollies | 1946 | 1470 | 432 | 2725 | **180** | 15.13 |
| **Worcestershire** | C.F. Root | 1925 | 1440.5 | 404 | 3627 | **207** | 17.52 |
| **Yorkshire** | W. Rhodes | 1900 | 1366.4 | 411 | 3054 | **240** | 12.72 |

## MOST RUNS IN A CAREER

| | | Career | Runs | HS | Avge | 100 |
|---|---|---|---|---|---|---|
| **Derbyshire** | D. Smith | 1927–1952 | **20516** | 225 | 31.41 | **30** |
| **Essex** | P.A. Perrin | 1896–1928 | **29162** | 343* | 36.18 | **65** |
| **Glamorgan** | A. Jones | 1957–1983 | **34056** | 204* | 33.03 | **52** |
| **Gloucestershire** | W.R. Hammond | 1920–1951 | **33664** | 317 | 57.05 | **113** |
| **Hampshire** | C.P. Mead | 1905–1936 | **48892** | 280* | 48.84 | **138** |
| **Kent** | F.E. Woolley | 1906–1938 | **47868** | 270 | 41.77 | **122** |
| **Lancashire** | G.E. Tyldesley | 1909–1936 | **34222** | 256* | 45.20 | **90** |
| **Leicestershire** | G.L. Berry | 1924–1951 | **30143** | 232 | 30.32 | **45** |
| **Middlesex** | E.H. Hendren | 1907–1937 | **40302** | 301* | 48.82 | **119** |
| **Northamptonshire** | D. Brookes | 1934–1959 | **28980** | 257 | 36.13 | **67** |
| **Nottinghamshire** | G. Gunn | 1902–1932 | **31592** | 220 | 35.70 | **55** |
| **Somerset** | H. Gimblett | 1935–1954 | **21142** | 310 | 36.96 | **49** |
| **Surrey** | J.B. Hobbs | 1905–1934 | **43554** | 316* | 49.72 | **144** |
| **Sussex** | J.G. Langridge | 1928–1955 | **34152** | 250* | 37.69 | **76** |
| **Warwickshire** | W.G. Quaife | 1894–1928 | **33862** | 255* | 36.18 | **71** |
| **Worcestershire** | D. Kenyon | 1946–1967 | **34490** | 259 | 34.04 | **70** |
| **Yorkshire** | H. Sutcliffe | 1919–1945 | **38561** | 313 | 50.20 | **112** |

## MOST HUNDREDS IN A CAREER

With the following four exceptions the batsman scoring most runs for his county has also scored the most hundreds:

| | | | |
|---|---|---|---|
| **Essex** | **71** | J. O'Connor | 1921–1939 |
| **Nottinghamshire** | **65** | J. Hardstaff jr | 1930–1955 |
| **Warwickshire** | **72** | D.L. Amiss | 1960–85 |
| **Worcestershire** | **72** | G.M. Turner | 1967–82 |

## MOST WICKETS IN A CAREER

| | | Career | Wkts | Avge |
|---|---|---|---|---|
| **Derbyshire** | H.L. Jackson | 1947–1963 | **1670** | 17.11 |
| **Essex** | T.P.B. Smith | 1929–1951 | **1610** | 26.68 |
| **Glamorgan** | D.J. Shepherd | 1950–1972 | **2174** | 20.87 |
| **Gloucestershire** | C.W.L. Parker | 1903–1935 | **3170** | 19.43 |
| **Hampshire** | D. Shackleton | 1948–1969 | **2669** | 18.23 |
| **Kent** | A.P. Freeman | 1914–1936 | **3340** | 17.64 |
| **Lancashire** | J.B. Statham | 1950–1968 | **1816** | 15.12 |
| **Leicestershire** | W.E. Astill | 1906–1939 | **2130** | 23.19 |
| **Middlesex** | F.J. Titmus | 1949–1982 | **2361** | 21.27 |
| **Northamptonshire** | E.W. Clark | 1922–1947 | **1097** | 21.32 |
| **Nottinghamshire** | T.G. Wass | 1896–1920 | **1653** | 20.34 |
| **Somerset** | J.C. White | 1909–1937 | **2166** | 18.02 |
| **Surrey** | T. Richardson | 1892–1904 | **1775** | 17.88 |
| **Sussex** | M.W. Tate | 1912–1937 | **2223** | 16.34 |
| **Warwickshire** | W.E. Hollies | 1932–1957 | **2201** | 20.45 |
| **Worcestershire** | R.T.D. Perks | 1930–1955 | **2143** | 23.73 |
| **Yorkshire** | W. Rhodes | 1898–1930 | **3608** | 16.00 |

**RECORD NUMBER OF INDIVIDUAL AGGREGATES IN AN ENGLISH SEASON**

| BATTING PERFORMANCES | | | BOWLING PERFORMANCES | | |
|---|---|---|---|---|---|
| | *Most* | *Season* | | *Most* | *Season* |
| 3000 runs | 5 | 1928 | 300 wickets | 1 | 1928 |
| 2000 runs | 23 | 1959 | 200 wickets | 5 | 1925 |
| 1000 runs | 111 | 1961 | 100 wickets | 31 | 1961 |
| Triple-hundreds | 3 | 1899 | | | |
| | 3 | 1934 | | | |
| Double-hundreds | 34 | 1933 | ALL-ROUND PERFORMANCES | | |
| Hundreds | 414 | 1928 | Doubles | 12 | 1923 |

# UNIVERSITY CRICKET

### UNIVERSITY MATCH – OXFORD v CAMBRIDGE

This, the oldest surviving first-class fixture, dates from 1827 and, except for wartime interruptions, it has been played annually since 1838. Although the first match was played at Lord's, the fixture did not become established there until 1851 and five of the early matches were played in the Oxford area.

The most historic finish occurred in Cobden's Match in 1870. F.C. Cobden snatched a remarkable win for Cambridge by doing the hat-trick when Oxford needed only three runs for victory with three wickets in hand.

Blues are awarded for appearances in the 'Varsity Match' and, from the 1860s, these have been restricted to four per player. Not until 1976 did anyone gain blues for both universities, when D.W. Jarrett represented Cambridge after appearing for Oxford the previous year: after reading Classics at Worcester College, he moved to St Catharine's for a Certificate of Education course. He remains the only player to represent different universities in successive years, although S.M. Wookey appeared for Cambridge in 1975 and 1976 and for Oxford in 1978, and G. Pathmanathan, who gained four blues for Oxford (1975–76–77–78), appeared for Cambridge in 1983.

### UNIVERSITY MATCH RESULTS

Cambridge has won 53 and Oxford 46 of the 141 official matches played, the remaining 42 being drawn. With the exception of five matches played in the area of Oxford (1829, 1846 & 1848 at Magdalen; 1843 at Bullingdon Green; 1850 at Cowley Marsh), all the fixtures have taken place at Lord's.

| | | | | |
|---|---|---|---|---|
| 1827 | Drawn | | 1866 | Oxford: 12 runs |
| 1829 | Oxford: 115 runs | | 1867 | Cambridge: 5 wickets |
| 1836 | Oxford: 121 runs | | 1868 | Cambridge: 168 runs |
| 1838 | Oxford: 98 runs | | 1869 | Cambridge: 58 runs |
| 1839 | Cambridge: innings & 125 runs | | 1870 | Cambridge: 2 runs |
| 1840 | Cambridge: 63 runs | | 1871 | Oxford: 8 wickets |
| 1841 | Cambridge: 8 runs | | 1872 | Cambridge: innings & 166 runs |
| 1842 | Cambridge: 162 runs | | 1873 | Oxford: 3 wickets |
| 1843 | Cambridge: 54 runs | | 1874 | Oxford: innings & 92 runs |
| 1844 | Drawn | | 1875 | Oxford: 6 runs |
| 1845 | Cambridge: 6 wickets | | 1876 | Cambridge: 9 wickets |
| 1846 | Oxford: 3 wickets | | 1877 | Oxford: 10 wickets |
| 1847 | Cambridge: 138 runs | | 1878 | Cambridge: 238 runs |
| 1848 | Oxford: 23 runs | | 1879 | Cambridge: 9 wickets |
| 1849 | Cambridge: 3 wickets | | 1880 | Cambridge: 115 runs |
| 1850 | Oxford: 127 runs | | 1881 | Oxford: 135 runs |
| 1851 | Cambridge: innings & 4 runs | | 1882 | Cambridge: 7 wickets |
| 1852 | Oxford: innings & 77 runs | | 1883 | Cambridge: 7 wickets |
| 1853 | Oxford: innings & 19 runs | | 1884 | Oxford: 7 wickets |
| 1854 | Oxford: innings & 8 runs | | 1885 | Cambridge: 7 wickets |
| 1855 | Oxford: 3 wickets | | 1886 | Oxford: 133 runs |
| 1856 | Cambridge: 3 wickets | | 1887 | Oxford: 7 wickets |
| 1857 | Oxford: 81 runs | | 1888 | Drawn |
| 1858 | Oxford: innings & 38 runs | | 1889 | Cambridge: innings & 105 runs |
| 1859 | Cambridge: 28 runs | | 1890 | Cambridge: 7 wickets |
| 1860 | Cambridge: 3 wickets | | 1891 | Cambridge: 2 wickets |
| 1861 | Cambridge: 133 runs | | 1892 | Oxford: 5 wickets |
| 1862 | Cambridge: 8 wickets | | 1893 | Cambridge: 266 runs |
| 1863 | Oxford: 8 wickets | | 1894 | Oxford: 8 wickets |
| 1864 | Oxford: 4 wickets | | 1895 | Cambridge: 134 runs |
| 1865 | Oxford: 114 runs | | 1896 | Oxford: 4 wickets |

| | | | | |
|---|---|---|---|---|
| 1897 | Cambridge: 179 runs | | 1947 | Drawn |
| 1898 | Oxford: 9 wickets | | 1948 | Oxford: innings & 8 runs |
| 1899 | Drawn | | 1949 | Cambridge: 7 wickets |
| 1900 | Drawn | | 1950 | Drawn |
| 1901 | Drawn | | 1951 | Oxford: 21 runs |
| 1902 | Cambridge: 5 wickets | | 1952 | Drawn |
| 1903 | Oxford: 268 runs | | 1953 | Cambridge: 2 wickets |
| 1904 | Drawn | | 1954 | Drawn |
| 1905 | Cambridge: 40 runs | | 1955 | Drawn |
| 1906 | Cambridge: 94 runs | | 1956 | Drawn |
| 1907 | Cambridge: 5 wickets | | 1957 | Cambridge: innings & 186 runs |
| 1908 | Oxford: 2 wickets | | 1958 | Cambridge: 99 runs |
| 1909 | Drawn | | 1959 | Oxford: 85 runs |
| 1910 | Oxford: innings & 126 runs | | 1960 | Drawn |
| 1911 | Oxford: 74 runs | | 1961 | Drawn |
| 1912 | Cambridge: 3 wickets | | 1962 | Drawn |
| 1913 | Cambridge: 4 wickets | | 1963 | Drawn |
| 1914 | Oxford: 194 runs | | 1964 | Drawn |
| 1919 | Oxford: 45 runs | | 1965 | Drawn |
| 1920 | Drawn | | 1966 | Oxford: innings & 9 runs |
| 1921 | Cambridge: innings & 24 runs | | 1967 | Drawn |
| 1922 | Cambridge: innings & 100 runs | | 1968 | Drawn |
| 1923 | Oxford: innings & 227 runs | | 1969 | Drawn |
| 1924 | Cambridge: 9 wickets | | 1970 | Drawn |
| 1925 | Drawn | | 1971 | Drawn |
| 1926 | Cambridge: 34 runs | | 1972 | Cambridge: innings & 25 runs |
| 1927 | Cambridge: 116 runs | | 1973 | Drawn |
| 1928 | Drawn | | 1974 | Drawn |
| 1929 | Drawn | | 1975 | Drawn |
| 1930 | Cambridge: 205 runs | | 1976 | Oxford: 10 wickets |
| 1931 | Oxford: 8 wickets | | 1977 | Drawn |
| 1932 | Drawn | | 1978 | Drawn |
| 1933 | Drawn | | 1979 | Cambridge: innings & 52 runs |
| 1934 | Drawn | | 1980 | Drawn |
| 1935 | Cambridge: 195 runs | | 1981 | Drawn |
| 1936 | Cambridge: 8 wickets | | 1982 | Cambridge: 7 wickets |
| 1937 | Oxford: 7 wickets | | 1983 | Drawn |
| 1938 | Drawn | | 1984 | Oxford: 5 wickets |
| 1939 | Oxford: 45 runs | | 1985 | Drawn |
| 1946 | Oxford: 6 wickets | | | |

## RECORD TOTALS

| | Cambridge | | Oxford | |
|---|---|---|---|---|
| **Highest:** | 432-9d | 1936 | 503 | 1900 |
| **Lowest:** | 39 | 1858 | 32 | 1878 |

## UNIVERSITY MATCH RECORDS

| | | | |
|---|---|---|---|
| **Highest Scores:** | 238* | Nawab of Pataudi, sr (Oxford) 1931 | |
| | 211 | G. Goonesena (Cambridge) 1957 | |
| **Most Hundreds:** | 3 | M.J.K. Smith (Oxford) 1954–55–56 | |
| | 3 | R.J. Boyd-Moss (Cambridge) 1982–83 | |

## HUNDREDS

CAMBRIDGE (50)

| | | | | | | |
|---|---|---|---|---|---|---|
| 100 | W. Yardley | 1870 | | 118 | E.R. Wilson | 1901 |
| 130 | W. Yardley | 1872 | | 117* | S.H. Day | 1902 |
| 105* | W.S. Patterson | 1876 | | 172* | J.F. Marsh | 1904 |
| 120 | G.B. Studd | 1882 | | 107 | L.G. Colbeck | 1905 |
| 102 | C.W. Wright | 1883 | | 150 | R.A. Young | 1906 |
| 101 | H.W. Bainbridge | 1885 | | 118 | H. Ashton | 1921 |
| 103* | E. Crawley | 1887 | | 102* | A.P.F. Chapman | 1922 |
| 127 | H.J. Mordaunt | 1889 | | 104 | H.J. Enthoven | 1924 |
| 116 | E.C. Streatfeild | 1892 | | 129 | H.J. Enthoven | 1925 |
| 115 | C.E.M. Wilson | 1898 | | 124 | A.K. Judd | 1927 |

| 101* | R.W.V. Robins | 1928 | 211 | G. Goonesena | 1957 |
| 149 | J.T. Morgan | 1929 | 111* | G.W. Cook | 1957 |
| 136 | E.T. Killick | 1930 | 105 | E.J. Craig | 1961 |
| 201 | A. Ratcliffe | 1931 | 113* | J.M. Brearley | 1962 |
| 157 | D.R. Wilcox | 1932 | 103* | A.R. Lewis | 1962 |
| 124 | A. Ratcliffe | 1932 | 119 | J.M. Brearley | 1964 |
| 115 | A.W. Allen | 1934 | 100 | N.J. Cosh | 1967 |
| 101 | N.W.D. Yardley | 1937 | 200 | Majid Khan | 1970 |
| 122 | P.A. Gibb | 1938 | 146 | D.R. Owen-Thomas | 1971 |
| 100 | P.J. Dickinson | 1939 | 114* | D.R. Owen-Thomas | 1972 |
| 127 | D.S. Sheppard | 1952 | 158 | P.M. Roebuck | 1975 |
| 116* | D.R.W. Silk | 1953 | 103 | D.R. Pringle | 1979 |
| 118 | D.R.W. Silk | 1954 | 100 | R.J. Boyd-Moss | 1982 |
| 114 | J.F. Pretlove | 1955 | 139 | } R.J. Boyd-Moss | 1983 |
| 146 | R.P. O'Brien | 1956 | 124 | | |

OXFORD (40)

| 109 | W.H. Game | 1876 | 238* | Nawab of Pataudi, sr | 1931 |
| 117* | F.M. Buckland | 1877 | 167 | B.W. Hone | 1932 |
| 107* | W.H. Patterson | 1881 | 193 | D.C.H. Townsend | 1934 |
| 143 | K.J. Key | 1886 | 108 | F.G.H. Chalk | 1934 |
| 107 | W. Rashleigh | 1886 | 121 | J.N. Grover | 1937 |
| 100 | Lord G. Scott | 1887 | 142 | M.P. Donnelly | 1946 |
| 140 | M.R. Jardine | 1892 | 135 | H.A. Pawson | 1947 |
| 114 | V.T. Hill | 1892 | 145* | H.E. Webb | 1948 |
| 100* | C.B. Fry | 1894 | 116 | M.C. Cowdrey | 1953 |
| 121 | H.K. Foster | 1895 | 201* | M.J.K. Smith | 1954 |
| 132 | G.O. Smith | 1896 | 104 | M.J.K. Smith | 1955 |
| 109 | A. Eccles | 1898 | 117 | M.J.K. Smith | 1956 |
| 171 | R.E. Foster | 1900 | 131 | Nawab of Pataudi, jr | 1960 |
| 100* | C.H.B. Marsham | 1901 | 100* | M. Manasseh | 1964 |
| 130 | J.E. Raphael | 1903 | 145 | D.P.Toft | 1967 |
| 160 | P.R. le Couteur | 1910 | 155 | F.S. Goldstein | 1968 |
| 170 | M. Howell | 1919 | 112 | E.D. Fursdon | 1975 |
| 109 | C.H. Taylor | 1923 | 128 | A.J.T. Miller | 1984 |
| 113 | E.R.T. Holmes | 1927 | 109 | G.J. Toogood | 1984 |
| 106 | Nawab of Pataudi, sr | 1929 | 149 | G.J. Toogood | 1985 |

## HIGHEST PARTNERSHIPS

| 1st | 243 | K.J. Key | W. Rashleigh | Oxford | 1886 |
|---|---|---|---|---|---|
| 2nd | 226 | W.G. Keighley | H.A. Pawson | Oxford | 1947 |
| 3rd | 183 | A.T. Barber | E.R.T. Holmes | Oxford | 1927 |
| 4th | 230 | D.C.H. Townsend | F.G.H. Chalk | Oxford | 1934 |
| 5th | 191 | J.E. Raphael | E.L. Wright | Oxford | 1905 |
| 6th | 178 | M.R. Jardine | V.T. Hill | Oxford | 1892 |
| 7th | 289 | G. Goonesena | G.W. Cook | Cambridge | 1957 |
| 8th | 112 | H.E. Webb | A.W.H. Mallett | Oxford | 1948 |
| 9th | 97* | J.F. Marsh | F.J.V. Hopley | Cambridge | 1904 |
| 10th | 90 | W.J.H. Curwen | E.G. Martin | Oxford | 1906 |

## BEST BOWLING ANALYSIS

| Innings: | 10-38 | } S.E. Butler | Oxford | 1871 |
|---|---|---|---|---|
| Match: | 15-95 | | | |

## HAT-TRICKS

All for Cambridge: F.C. Cobden (1870), A.G. Steel (1879), P.H. Morton (1880), J.F. Ireland (1911), and R.G.H. Lowe (1926).

## MATCH DOUBLE

| P.R. le Couteur | 160 | 6-20 & 5-46 | Oxford | 1910 |
| G.J. Toogood | 149 | 8-42 & 2-41 | Oxford | 1985 |

## CAMBRIDGE UNIVERSITY BLUES

Abercrombie, J. (Tonbridge): 1838
Absolom, C.A. (Private): 1866–67–68–69
Acfield, D.L. (Brentwood): 1967–68
Aers, D.R. (Tonbridge): 1967
Aird, R. (Eton): 1923
Alexander, F.C.M. (Wolmer's College, Jamaica): 1952–53
Allbrook, M.E. (Tonbridge): 1975–76–77–78
Allen, A.W. (Eton): 1933–34
Allen, B.O. (Clifton): 1933
Allen, G.O.B. (Eton): 1922–23
Allom, M.J.C. (Wellington): 1927–28
Allsopp, H.T. (Cheltenham): 1876
Andrew, C.R. (Barnard Castle School): 1984–85 (Captain 1985)
Anson, T.A. (Eton): 1839–40–41–42 (Captain 1840–41–42)
Arkwright, H.A. (Harrow): 1858
Arnold, A.C.P. (Malvern): 1914
Ash, E.P. (Rugby): 1865
Ashton, C.T. (Winchester): 1921–22–23 (Captain 1923)
Ashton, G. (Winchester): 1919–20–21 (Captain 1921)
Ashton, H. (Winchester): 1920–21–22 (Captain 1922)
Atkins, G. (Dr Challoner's GS, Amersham): 1960
Austin, H.M. (Melbourne, Australia): 1924
Aworth, C.J. (Tiffin): 1973–74–75 (Captain 1975)

Baggallay, M.E.C. (Eton): 1911
Bagge, T.E. (Eton): 1859–60–61 (Captain 1861)
Bagnall, H.F. (Harrow): 1923
Bailey, T.E. (Dulwich): 1947–48
Baily, E.P. (Harrow): 1872–74
Baily, R.E.H. (Harrow): 1908
Bainbridge, H.W. (Eton): 1884–85–86 (Captain 1886)
Baker, E.C. (Brighton): 1912–14
Baker, R.K. (Brentwood): 1973–74
Balfour, R.D. (Bradfield & Westminster): 1863–64–65–66
Bannister, C.S. (Caterham): 1976
Barber, R.W. (Ruthin): 1956–57
Barchard, E. (Winchester): 1846–47–48
Barford, M.T. (Eastbourne): 1970–71
Barker, G. (Bury St Edmunds): 1840
Barnett, W.E. (Eton): 1849–50
Barrington, W.E.J. (Lancing): 1982
Bartlett, H.T. (Dulwich): 1934–35–36 (Captain 1936)
Bastard, J.H. (Winchester): 1838–40
Bateman, A. (Brighton): 1859–60–61
Bayford, R.A. (Kensington GS): 1857–58–59 (Captain 1859)
Beaumont, D.J. (West Bridgford GS & Bramshill College): 1978
Benke, A.F. (Cheltenham): 1962
Bennett, B.W.P. (Welbeck & RMA Sandhurst): 1979
Bennett, C.T. (Harrow): 1923–25 (Captain 1925)
Benthall, W.H. (Westminster & Marlborough): 1858–59–60
Bernard, J.R. (Clifton): 1958–59–60
Bhatia, A.N. (Doon School, Dehra Dun, India): 1969

Blacker, W. (Harrow): 1873–74–75–76
Blake, J.P. (Aldenham): 1939
Blaker, R.N. (Elizabeth College, Guernsey): 1842–43
Blaker, R.N.R. (Westminster): 1900–01–02
Blayds, E. (Harrow): 1846–47–48–49
Bligh, Hon I.F.W. (later Earl of Darnley) (Eton): 1878–79–80–81 (Captain 1881)
Block, S.A. (Marlborough): 1929
Blofeld, H.C. (Eton): 1959
Blore, E.W. (Eton): 1848–49–50–51 (Captain 1851)
Blundell, E.D. (Waitaki, N.Z.): 1928–29
Bodkin, P.E. (Bradfield): 1946 (Captain 1946)
Boldero, H.K. (Harrow): 1851–52–53
Booth, C. (Rugby): 1862–63–64–65 (Captain 1864)
Booth, H.W. (Eton): 1836 (Captain 1836)
Boudier, G.J. (Eton): 1841–43 (Joint-captain with T.L. French 1843)
Bourne, A.A. (Rugby): 1870
Boyd-Moss, R.J. (Bedford): 1980–81–82–83
Bray, E. (Westminster): 1871–72
Bray, E.H. (Charterhouse): 1896–97
Brearley, J.M. (City of London): 1961–62–63–64 (Captain 1963–64)
Breddy, M.N. (Cheltenham GS): 1984
Brereton, C.J. (Marlborough): 1858
Bridgeman, W.C. (Eton): 1887
Brocklebank, J.M. (Eton): 1936
Brodhurst, A.H. (Malvern): 1939
Brodie, J.B. (Union HS, South Africa): 1960
Brodrick, P.D. (Newcastle upon Tyne RGS): 1961
Bromley, R.C. (Christ's College, Christchurch & Canterbury U., N.Z.): 1970
Bromley-Davenport, H.R. (Eton): 1892–93
Brooker, M.E.W. (Lancaster RGS & Burnley GS): 1976
Brooke-Taylor, G.P. (Cheltenham): 1919–20
Broughton, R.J.P. (Harrow): 1836–38–39
Brown, F.R. (The Leys): 1930–31
Browne, F.B.R. (Aldro School & Eastbourne): 1922
Brune, C.J. (Godolphin, Hammersmith): 1867–68–69
Brunton, J. du V. (Lancaster GS): 1894
Bryan, J.L. (Rugby): 1921
Buchanan, D. (Rugby): 1850
Buchanan, J.N. (Charterhouse): 1906–07–08–09 (Captain 1909)
Buckston, G.M. (Eton): 1903
Bulwer, J.B.R. (King's, London): 1841
Burghley, Lord (later Marquess of Exeter) (Eton): 1847
Burnett, A.C. (Lancing): 1949
Burnley, I.D. (Queen Elizabeth College, Darlington): 1984
Burnup, C.J. (Malvern): 1896–97–98
Burr, G.F. (Maidstone): 1840
Burrough, J. (King's, Bruton & Shrewsbury): 1895
Bury, L. (Eton): 1877
Bury, T.W. (Winchester): 1855
Bury, W. (Private): 1861–62
Bushby, M.H. (Dulwich): 1952–53–54 (Captain 1954)
Butler, E.M. (Harrow): 1888–89

Butterworth, H.R.W. (Rydal Mount): 1929
Buxton, C.D. (Harrow): 1885–86–87–88 (Captain 1888)

Calthorpe, Hon F.S.G. (Repton): 1912–13–14–19
Calvert, C.T. (Shrewsbury): 1848
Cameron, J.H. (Taunton): 1935–36–37
Campbell, S.C. (Bury St Edmunds): 1845
Cangley, B.G.M. (Felsted): 1947
Carling, P.G. (Kingston upon Thames GS): 1968–70
Carris, B.D. (Harrow): 1938–39
Carris, H.E. (Mill Hill): 1930
Cawston, E. (Lancing): 1932
Chambers, R.E.J. (Forest): 1966
Chapman, A.P.F. (Oakham & Uppingham): 1920–21–22
Christopher, A.W.M. (Private): 1843
Christopherson, J.C. (Uppingham): 1931
Clement, R.A. (Rugby): 1854
Clissold, S.T. (Eton): 1844–46
Close, P.A. (Haileybury): 1965
Cobbold, P.W. (Eton): 1896
Cobbold, R.H. (Eton): 1927
Cobden, F.C. (Harrow): 1870–71–72
Cockburn-Hood, J.S.E. (Rugby): 1865–67
Cockett, J.A. (Aldenham): 1951
Coghlan, T.B.L. (Rugby): 1960
Colbeck, L.G. (Marlborough): 1905–06
Collins, D.C. (Wellington College, N.Z.): 1910–11
Collins, T. (Bury St Edmunds): 1863
Comber, J.T.H. (Marlborough): 1931–32–33
Conradi, E.R. (Oundle): 1946
Coode, A.T. (Fauconberge School, Beccles): 1898
Cook, G.W. (Dulwich): 1957–58
Cooke, C.R. (Eton & Ipswich): 1858
Cookesley, W.G. (Eton): 1827
Cooper, N.H.C. (St Brendan's, Bristol & East Anglia U.): 1979
Cosh, N.J. (Dulwich): 1966–67–68
Cotterell, T.A. (Downside): 1983–84–85
Cotterill, G.E. (Brighton): 1858–59–60
Cottrell, G.A. (Kingston upon Thames GS): 1966–67–68 (Captain 1968)
Cottrell, P.R. (Chislehurst and Sidcup, GS): 1979
Coverdale, S.P. (St Peter's, York): 1974–75–76–77
Cowie, A.G. (Charterhouse): 1910
Craig, E.J. (Charterhouse): 1961–62–63
Crawford, N.C. (Shrewsbury): 1979–80
Crawley, E. (Harrow): 1887–88–89
Crawley, L.G. (Harrow): 1923–24–25
Croft, P.D. (Gresham's): 1955
Crofts, C.D. (Winchester): 1843
Crookes, D.V. (Michaelhouse, S.A.): 1953
Cumberlege, B.S. (Durham): 1913
Currie, F.L. (Rugby): 1845
Curteis, T.S. (Felsted & Bury St Edmunds): 1864–65
Curtis, T.S. (Worcester RGS & Durham U.): 1983

Dale, J.W. (Tonbridge): 1868–69–70
Daniel, A.W.T. (Harrow): 1861–62–63–64
Daniell, J. (Clifton): 1899–1900–01
Daniels, D.M. (Rutlish): 1964–65
Datta, P.B. (Asutosh College, Calcutta): 1947
Davidson, J.E. (Penglais CS): 1985
Davies, A.G. (Birkenhead): 1984–85
Davies, G.B. (Rossall): 1913–14

Davies, J.G.W. (Tonbridge): 1933–34
Dawson, E.W. (Eton): 1924–25–26–27 (Captain 1927)
Day, S.H. (Malvern): 1899–1900–01–02 (Captain 1901)
De Gray, T. (later Lord Walsingham) (Eton): 1862–63
De Little, E.R. (Geelong GS, Australia): 1889
De Paravicini, P.J. (Eton): 1882–83–84–85
De St Croix, W. (Eton): 1839–40–41–42
De Zoete, H.W. (Eton): 1897–98
Deacon, W.S. (Eton): 1848–49–50 (Captain 1850)
Dewes, A.R. (Dulwich): 1978
Dewes, J.G. (Aldenham): 1948–49–50
Dewing, E.M. (Harrow): 1842–43–44–45 (Captain 1844–45)
Dexter, E.R. (Radley): 1956–57–58 (Captain 1958)
Dickinson, D.C. (Clifton): 1953
Dickinson, P.J. (KCS, Wimbledon): 1939
Doggart, A.G. (Bishop's Stortford): 1921–22
Doggart, G.H.G. (Winchester): 1948–49–50 (Captain 1950)
Doggart, S.J.G. (Winchester): 1980–81–82–83
Dolphin, J. (Eton): 1827
Dorman, A.W. (Dulwich): 1886
Douglas, J. (Dulwich): 1892–93–94
Douglas, R.N. (Dulwich): 1890–91–92
Douglas-Hamilton, H.A. (Wellington): 1873–75
Douglas-Pennant, S. (Eton): 1959
Downes, K.D. (Rydal): 1939
Dowson, E.M. (Harrow): 1900–01–02–03 (Captain 1903)
Drake, E.T. (Westminster): 1852–53–54
Driffield, L.T. (Leatherhead): 1902
Druce, N.F. (Marlborough): 1894–95–96–97 (Captain 1897)
Druce, W.G. (Marlborough): 1894–95 (Captain 1895)
Du Cane, A.R. (Harrow): 1854–55
Duleepsinhji, K.S. (Cheltenham): 1925–26–28
Dupuis, G.R. (Eton): 1857
Dyke, E.F. (Eton): 1865
Dykes, T. (Kingston College, Hull): 1844

Ebden, C.H.M. (Eton): 1902–03
Edmonds, P.H. (Gilbert Rennie HS, Lusaka, Zambia; Skinners' & Cranbrook): 1971–72–73 (Captain 1973)
Edwards, R.S. (Huntingdon GS & Christ's Hospital): 1850
Edwards, T.D.W. (Sherborne): 1981
Elgood, B.C. (Bradfield): 1948
Ellis, E.C. (Private): 1829
Ellison, C.C. (Tonbridge): 1982–83–85
Enthoven, H.J. (Harrow): 1923–24–25–26 (Captain 1926)
Estcourt, N.S.D. (Plumtree, Southern Rhodesia): 1954
Evans, R.G. (King Edward's, Bury St Edmunds): 1921
Eyre, C.H. (Harrow): 1904–05–06 (Captain 1906)

Fabian, A.H. (Highgate): 1929–30–31
Fairbairn, G.A. (Church of England GS, Geelong, Australia): 1913–14–19
Falcon, M. (Harrow): 1908–09–10–11 (Captain 1910)

Fargus, A.H.C. (Clifton & Haileybury): 1900–01
Farmer, A.A. (Winchester): 1836
Farnes, K. (Royal Liberty School, Romford): 1931–32–33
Fawcett, E.B. (Brighton): 1859–60
Fell, D.J. (The John Lyon School, Harrow): 1985
Fenn, S. (Blackheath Proprietary): 1851
Fenn, W.M. (Blackheath Proprietary): 1849–50–51
Fernie, A.E. (Wellingborough): 1897–1900
Fiddian-Green, C.A. (The Leys): 1921–22
Field, E. (Clifton): 1894
Field, M.N. (Bablake GS, Coventry): 1974
Fitzgerald, J.F. (St Brendan's, Bristol): 1968
FitzGerald, R.A. (Harrow): 1854–56
Foley, C.P. (Eton): 1889–90–91
Foley, C.W. (Eton): 1880
Ford, A.F.J. (Repton): 1878–79–80–81
Ford, F.G.J. (Repton): 1887–88–89–90 (Captain 1889)
Ford, W.J. (Repton): 1873
Fosh, M.K. (Harrow): 1977–78
Fowler, T.F. (Uppingham): 1864
Francis, T.E.S. (Tonbridge): 1925
Franklin, W.B. (Repton): 1912
Fraser, T.W. (Jeppe, S.A.): 1937
Freeman-Thomas, F. (later Lord Willingdon) (Eton): 1886–87–88–89
French, T.L. (Winchester): 1842–43–44 (Joint-captain with G.J. Boudier 1843)
Frere, J. (Eton): 1827
Fry, K.R.B. (Cheltenham): 1904
Fryer, C.W.H. (Rugby): 1854
Fryer, F.E.R. (Harrow): 1870–71–72–73 (Captain 1873)
Fuller, E.A. (Rugby): 1852
Fuller, J.M. (Marlborough): 1855–56–57–58 (Captain 1857–58)

Gaddum, F.D. (Uppingham & Rugby): 1882
Gardiner, S.J. (St Andrew's, Bloemfontein, S.A.): 1978
Garlick, P.L. (Sherborne): 1984
Gay, L.H. (Marlborough & Brighton): 1892–93
Gibb, P.A. (St Edward's, Oxford): 1935–36–37–38
Gibson, C.H. (Eton): 1920–21
Gibson, J.S. (Harrow): 1885
Gillespie, D.W. (Uppingham): 1939
Gilligan, A.E.R. (Dulwich): 1919–20
Gilman, J. (St Paul's): 1902
Godsell, R.T. (Clifton): 1903
Goldie, C.D. (Kensington GS): 1846
Goldie, C.F.E. (St Paul's): 1981–82
Goodfellow, A. (Marlborough): 1961–62
Goodwin, H.J. (Marlborough): 1907–08
Goonesena, G. (Royal College, Colombo, Ceylon): 1954–55–56–57 (Captain 1957)
Gordon, Hon F.A. (later Lord Francis Gordon) (Charterhouse): 1829
Gorman, S.R. (St Peter's, York): 1985
Gosling, R.C. (Eton): 1888–89–90
Grace, W.G. jr, (Clifton): 1895–96
Grant, G.C. (Trinidad): 1929–30
Grant, R.S. (Trinidad): 1933
Gray, H. (Perse): 1894–95
Grazebrook, H.G. (Winchester): 1829
Green, C.E. (Uppingham): 1865–66–67–68 (Captain 1868)

Green, D.J. (Burton GS): 1957–58–59 (Captain 1959)
Greenfield, F.F.J. (Hurstpierpoint): 1874–75–76 (Captain 1876)
Greig, I.A. (Queen's College, Queenstown, S.A.): 1977–78–79 (Captain 1979)
Grierson, H. (Bedford GS): 1911
Griffith, M.G. (Marlborough): 1963–64–65
Griffith, S.C. (Dulwich): 1935
Grifiths, W.H. (Charterhouse): 1946–47–48
Grimes, A.D.H. (Tonbridge): 1984
Grimshaw, J.W.T. (King William's, Isle of Man): 1934–35
Grimston, Hon F.S. (Harrow): 1843–44–45
Grout, J. (Private): 1838–39

Hadingham, A.W.G. (St Paul's): 1932
Hadley, R.J. (Sanfields CS): 1971–72–73
Hale, H. (Hutchin's School, Hobart, Tasmania): 1887–89–90
Hales, J. (Rugby): 1855–56
Hall, J.E. (Ardingly): 1969
Hall, P.J. (Geelong, Australia): 1949
Hammersley, W.J. (Private): 1847
Hammond, O. (Uppingham): 1855–56–57
Handley, E.H. (Harrow): 1827
Harbinson, W.K. (Marlborough): 1929
Hardy, J.R. (Charterhouse): 1829
Harenc, E.A.F. (Naval College, Portsmouth): 1841
Harper, L.V. (Rossall): 1901–02–03
Harris, J.E. (Sheffield Collegiate): 1859
Harrison, W.P. (Rugby): 1907
Harrison-Ward, E.E. (Bury St Edmunds): 1870–71
Hartopp, E.S.E. (Eton): 1841–42
Harvey, J.R.W. (Marlborough): 1965
Hawke, Hon M.B. (later Lord Hawke) (Eton): 1882–83–85 (Captain 1885)
Hawkins, H.H.B. (Whitgift): 1898–99
Hayes, P.J. (Brighton): 1974–75–77
Hays, D.L. (Highgate): 1966–68
Hayward, W.I.D. (St Peter's, Adelaide, Australia): 1950–51–53
Haywood, D.C. (Nottingham HS): 1968
Hazlerigg, A.G. (Eton): 1930–31–32 (Captain 1932)
Helm, G.F. (Marlborough): 1862–63
Hemingway, W.M. (Uppingham): 1895–96
Henderson, S.P. (Downside & Durham U.): 1982–83 (Captain 1983)
Henery, P.J.T. (Harrow): 1882–83
Hewan, G.E. (Marlborough): 1938
Hewitt, S.G.P. (Bradford GS): 1983
Hignell, A.J. (Denstone): 1975–76–77–78 (Captain 1977–78)
Hill, A.J.L. (Marlborough): 1890–91–92–93
Hill-Wood, W.W. (Eton): 1922
Hind, A.E. (Uppingham): 1898–99–1900–01
Hoare, A.M. (Private): 1844
*Hoare was appointed captain in 1846, but did not play because of illness.*
Hobson, B.S. (Taunton): 1946
Hodgson, E.F. (Eton): 1836
–Hodgson, K.I. (Oundle): 1981–82–83
Hodson, R.P. (Queen Elizabeth, GS, Wakefield): 1972–73
Holliday, D.C. (Oundle): 1979–80–81
Holloway, N.J. (The Leys): 1910–11–12
Hone, N.T. (Rugby): 1881

Hone-Goldney, G.H. (Eton): 1873
Hope-Grant, F.C. (Harrow): 1863
Hopley, F.J.V. (Harrow): 1904
Hopley, G.W.V. (Harrow): 1912
Horne, E.L. (Shrewsbury): 1855–57–58
Horsman, E. (Rugby): 1827–29
Hotchkin, N.S. (Eton): 1935
Howard-Smith, G. (Eton): 1903
Howat, M.G. (Abingdon): 1977–80
Howland, C.B. (Dulwich): 1958–59–60 (Captain 1960)
Hughes, G. (Cardiff HS): 1965
Hughes, O. (Malvern): 1910
Hughes, T.F. (Private): 1845
Human, J.H. (Repton): 1932–33–34 (Captain 1934)
Human, R.H.C. (Repton): 1930–31
Hume, A. (Eton): 1841–42
Hunt, R.G. (Aldenham): 1937
Hurd, A. (Chigwell): 1958–59–60
Hutton, R.A. (Repton): 1962–63–64
Huxter, R.J.A. (Magdalen College School, Oxford): 1981

Imlay, A.D. (Clifton): 1907
Ingram, C.P. (Westminster): 1854
Ingram, D.J. (Monoux, Walthamstow): 1947–48–49 (Captain 1949)
Ireland, J.F. (Marlborough): 1908–09–10–11 (Captain 1911)
Irvine, L.G. (Taunton): 1926–27

Jackson, E.J.W. (Winchester): 1974–75–76
Jackson, F.S. (later Hon Sir F.S. Jackson) (Harrow): 1890–91–92–93 (Captain 1892–93)
Jagger, S.T. (Malvern): 1925–26
Jahangir Khan, M. (Lahore, India): 1933–34–35–36
James, R.M. (St John's, Leatherhead): 1956–57–58
Jameson, T.E.N. (Taunton & Durham U.): 1970
Jarrett, D.W. (Wellington): 1976
*Gained blue for Oxford 1975*
Jarvis, L.K. (Harrow): 1877–78–79
Jefferson, R.I. (Winchester): 1961
Jeffery, G.E. (Rugby): 1873–74
Jenner, C.H. (Eton): 1829
Jenner, Herbert (Eton): 1827 (Captain 1827)
Jenner, H.L. (Harrow): 1841
Jenyns, G.F.G. (Private): 1849–50
Jephson, D.L.A. (Manor House, Clapham): 1890–91–92
Jessop, G.L. (Cheltenham GS): 1896–97–98–99 (Captain 1899)
Johnson, G.R. (Bury St Edmunds): 1855–56–57 (Captain 1855)
Johnson, P.D. (Nottingham HS): 1970–71–72
Johnson, P.R. (Eton): 1901
Johnstone, C.P. (Rugby): 1919–20
Jones, A.O. (Bedford Modern): 1893
Jones, R.S. (Chatham House, Ramsgate): 1879–80
Jones-Bateman, J.B. (Winchester): 1848
Jorden, A.M. (Monmouth): 1968–69–70 (Captain 1969–70)
Judd, A.K. (St Paul's): 1927

Kaye, M.A.C.P. (Harrow): 1938
Keigwin, R.P. (Clifton): 1903–04–05–06

Kelland, P.A. (Repton): 1950
Kemp, G.M. (later Lord Rochdale) (Mill Hill & Shrewsbury): 1885–86–88
Kempson, S.M.E. (Cheltenham): 1851–53
Kempson, W.J. (Rugby): 1855
Kemp-Welch, G.D. (Charterhouse): 1929–30–31 (Captain 1931)
Kendall, M.P. (Gillingham GS): 1972
Kenny, C.J.M. (Ampleforth): 1952
Kerslake, R.C. (Kingswood): 1963–64
Khanna, B.C. (Lahore, India): 1937
Kidd, E.L. (Wellington): 1910–11–12–13 (Captain 1912)
Killick, E.T. (St Paul's): 1928–29–30
King, F. (Dulwich): 1934
King, R.T. (Oakham): 1846–47–48–49 (Captain 1849)
Kingdon, S.N. (Eton): 1827
Kingston, F.W. (Abingdon House, Northampton): 1878
Kirby, D. (St Peter's, York): 1959–60–61 (Captain 1961)
Kirkman, M.C. (Dulwich): 1963
Kirwan, J.H. (Eton): 1839
Knatchbull-Hugessen, C.M. (later Lord Brabourne) (Eton): 1886
Knight, R.D.V. (Dulwich): 1967–68–69–70
Knightley-Smith, W. (Highgate): 1953
Koe, B.D. (Eton): 1838

Lacy, F.E. (Sherborne): 1882
Lacy-Scott, D.G. (Marlborough): 1946
Lagden, R.B. (Marlborough): 1912–13–14
Lancashire, O.P. (Lancing): 1880
Lang, A.H. (Harrow): 1913
Lang, R. (Harrow): 1860–61–62
Langley, J.D.A. (Stowe): 1938
Latham, P.M. (Malvern): 1892–93–94 (Captain 1894)
Latham, T. (Winchester): 1873–74
Lawrence, A.S. (Harrow): 1933
Lea, A.E. (High Arcal School): 1984–85
Leake, W.M. (Rugby): 1851–52–53–54
Lee, F. (Rugby): 1860
Lee, J.M. (Blackheath Proprietary & Oundle): 1846–47–48
Leith, J. (Private): 1848
Lewis, A.R. (Neath GS): 1960–61–62 (Captain 1962)
Lewis, L.K. (Taunton): 1953
Littlewood, D.J. (Enfield GS): 1978
Lockhart, J.H.B. (Sedbergh): 1909–10
Long, F.E. (Eton): 1836
Long, R.P. (Harrow): 1845–46
Longfield, T.C. (Aldenham): 1927–28
Longman, G.H. (Eton): 1872–73–74–75 (Captain 1874–75)
Longman, H.K. (Eton): 1901
Longrigg, E.F. (Rugby): 1927–28
Lowe, R.G.H. (Westminster): 1925–26–27
Lowe, W.W. (Malvern): 1895
Lowry, T.C. (Christ's College, Christchurch, N.Z.): 1923–24 (Captain 1924)
Lucas, A.P. (Uppingham): 1875–76–77–78
Luddington, H.T. (Uppingham): 1876–77
Lumsden, V.R. (Munro College, Jamaica): 1953–54–55
Lyon, M.D. (Rugby): 1921–22

Lyon, W.J. (Highstead, Torquay): 1861
Lyttelton, 4th Lord (Eton): 1838
Lyttelton, Hon Alfred (Eton): 1876–77–78–79 (Captain 1879)
Lyttelton, Hon C.F. (Eton): 1908–09
Lyttelton, Hon C.G. (later Lord Cobham) (Eton): 1861–62–63–64
Lyttelton, Hon Edward (Eton): 1875–76–77–78 (Captain 1878)
Lyttelton, Hon G.W.S. (Eton): 1866–67

McAdam, K.P.W.J. (Prince of Wales, Nairobi, Kenya & Millfield): 1965–66
Macan, G. (Harrow): 1874–75
MacBryan, J.C.W. (Exeter): 1920
McCarthy, C.N. (Maritzburg College, S.A.): 1952
McCormick, J. (Liverpool College & Bingley): 1854–56 (Captain 1856)
McDonell, H.C. (Winchester): 1903–04–05
McDowall, J.I. (Rugby): 1969
MacGregor, G. (Uppingham): 1888–89–90–91 (Captain 1891)
Machin, R.S. (Lancing): 1927
Mackinnon, F.A. (Harrow): 1870
McLachlan, A.A. (St Peter's, Adelaide, Australia): 1964–65
McLachlan, I.M. (St Peter's, Adelaide, Australia): 1957–58
Macleod, K.G. (Fettes): 1908–09
MacNiven, E. (Eton): 1846
Mainprice, H. (Blundell's): 1906
Majid Khan (Aitchison College, Lahore & Punjab U., Pakistan): 1970–71–72 (Captain 1971–72)
Makinson, J. (Huddersfield & Owen's College): 1856–57–58
Malalasekera, V.P. (Royal College, Colombo, Ceylon): 1966–67
Mann, E.W. (Harrow): 1903–04–05 (Captain 1905)
Mann, F.G. (Eton): 1938–39
Mann, F.T. (Malvern): 1909–10–11
Mann, J.E.F. (Geelong, Australia): 1924
Manners-Sutton, Hon J.H.T. (later Viscount Canterbury) (Eton): 1836
Mansfield, J.W. (Winchester): 1883–84
Maples, W. (Haileybury & Winchester): 1839
Marchant, F. (Rugby & Eton): 1884–85–86–87 (Captain 1887)
Marlar, R.G. (Harrow): 1951–52–53 (Captain 1953)
Marriott, C.S. (St Columba's): 1920–21
Marriott, H.H. (Malvern): 1895–96–97–98
Marsh, J.F. (Amersham Hall): 1904
Marshall, H.M. (Westminster): 1861–62–63–64
Marshall, J.H. (King Edward's, Birmingham): 1859
Marshall, J.W. (King Edward's, Birmingham): 1855–56–57
Martin, M.T. (Rugby): 1862–64
Martineau, L. (Uppingham): 1887
Massey, W. (Harrow): 1838–39
Mathews, K.P.A. (Felsted): 1951
Maule, W. (Tonbridge): 1853
May, P.B.H. (Charterhouse): 1950–51–52
May, P.R. (Private): 1905–06
Meetkerke, A. (Eton): 1840
Mellor, F.H. (Cheltenham): 1877
Melluish, M.E.L. (Rossall): 1954–55–56 (Captain 1956)

Meryweather, W.S.T.M. (Charterhouse): 1829
Meyer, R.J.O. (Haileybury): 1924–25–26
Meyrick-Jones, F. (Marlborough): 1888
Micklethwait, F.N. (Eton): 1836
Micklethwait, S.N. (Shrewsbury): 1843
Miller, M.E. (Prince Henry GS, Hohne, West Germany): 1963
Mills, J.M. (Oundle): 1946–47–48 (Captain 1948)
Mills, J.P.C. (Oundle): 1979–80–81–82 (Captain 1982)
Mills, W. (Harrow): 1840–41–42–43
Mischler, N.M. (St Paul's): 1946–47
Mitchell, F. (St Peter's, York): 1894–95–96–97 (Captain 1896)
Money, W.B. (Harrow): 1868–69–70–71 (Captain 1870)
Moon, L.J. (Westminster): 1899–1900
Morcom, A.F. (Repton): 1905–06–07
Mordaunt, H.J. (Eton): 1888–89
Morgan, J.T. (Charterhouse): 1928–29–30 (Captain 1930)
Morgan, M.N. (Marlborough): 1954
Morris, R.J. (Blundell's): 1949
Morrison, J.S.F. (Charterhouse): 1912–14–19 (Captain 1919)
Morse, C. (Dedham): 1842–43–44
Morton, P.H. (Rossall): 1878–79–80
Moses, G.H. (Ystalyfera GS): 1974
Moylan, A.C.D. (Clifton): 1977
Mubarak, A.M. (Royal College, Colombo & Sri Lanka, U.): 1978–79–80
Mugliston, F.H. (Rossall): 1907–08
Mulholland, Hon H.G.H. (Eton): 1911–12–13 (Captain 1913)
Murray, D.L. (Queen's Royal College, Trinidad): 1965–66 (Captain 1966)
Murrills, T.J. (The Leys): 1973–74–76 (Captain 1976)

Napier, G.G. (Marlborough): 1904–05–06–07
Nason, J.W.W. (University School, Hastings): 1909–10
Naumann, J.H. (Malvern): 1913–19
Nelson, R.P. (St George's, Harpenden): 1936
Nevin, M.R.S. (Winchester): 1969
Newton, S.C. (Victoria College, Jersey): 1876
Nicholson, J. (Rugby & Harrow): 1845
Norman, C.L. (Eton): 1852–53
Norman, F.H. (Eton): 1858–59–60 (Captain 1860)
Norris, D.W.W. (Harrow): 1967–68
Norris, W.A. (Eton): 1851
Northey, A.E. (Harrow): 1859–60
Nunn, F. (Bury St Edmunds): 1859

O'Brien, R.P. (Wellington): 1955–56
Oddie, H.H. (Eton): 1836
Odendaal, A. (Queen's College, Queenstown & Stellenbosch U., S.A.): 1980
Olivier, E. (Repton): 1908–09
Onslow, D.R. (Brighton): 1860–61
Orford, L.A. (Uppingham): 1886–87
Ottey, G.P. (Rugby): 1844–45–46–47
Owen-Thomas, D.R. (KCS, Wimbledon): 1969–70–71–72

Page, C.C. (Malvern): 1905–06
Palfreman, A.B. (Nottingham HS): 1966
Palmer, C. (Uppingham): 1907

Palmer, R.W.M. (Bedford): 1982
Parker, G.W. (Crypt, Gloucester): 1934–35 (Captain 1935)
Parker, H. (Maidstone): 1839
Parker, P.W.G. (Collyer's GS, Horsham): 1976–77–78
Parry, D.M. (Merchant Taylors'): 1931
Parsons, A.B.D. (Brighton): 1954–55
Partridge, N.E. (Malvern): 1920
Pathmanathan, G. (Royal College, Colombo & Sri Lanka U): 1983
*Gained blues for Oxford 1975–76–77–78*
Patterson, W.W. (Uppingham): 1875–76–77 (Captain 1877)
Paull, R.K. (Millfield): 1967
Pawle, J.H. (Harrow): 1936–37
Payne, A.U. (St Edmund's, Canterbury): 1925
Payne, M.W. (Wellington): 1904–05–06–07 (Captain 1907)
Payton, W.E.G. (Nottingham HS): 1937
Pearman, H. (King Alfred School, Hampstead & St Andrew's U.): 1969
Pearson, A.J.G. (Downside): 1961–62–63
Peck, I.G. (Bedford): 1980–81 (Captain 1980–81)
Pelham, A.G. (Eton): 1934
Pelham, Hon F.G. (later Earl of Chichester) (Eton): 1864–65–66–67 (Captain 1866–67)
Pell, O.C. (Rugby): 1844–45–46–47 (Captain 1847)
Penn, E.F. (Eton): 1899–1902
Pepper, J. (The Leys): 1946–47–48
Perkins, H. (Bury St Edmunds): 1854
Perkins, T.T.N. (Leatherhead): 1893–94
Phillips, E.S. (Marlborough): 1904
Pickering, E.H. (Eton): 1827–29 (Captain 1829)
Pickering, W.P. (Eton): 1840–42
Pieris, P.I. (St Thomas's, Colombo, Ceylon): 1957–58
Pigg, H. (Abingdon House, Northampton): 1877
Plowden, H.M. (Harrow): 1860–61–62–63 (Captain 1862–63)
Pollock, A.J. (Shrewsbury): 1982–83–84 (Captain 1984)
Ponniah, C.E.M. (St Thomas's, Colombo, Ceylon): 1967–68–69
Ponsonby, Hon F.G.B. (Harrow) (later Lord Bessborough): 1836
Pontifex, C. (KCS, London): 1851–53 (Captain 1853)
Pope, C.G. (Harrow): 1894
Popplewell, N.F.M. (Radley): 1977–78–79
Popplewell, O.B. (Charterhouse): 1949–50–51
Potter, A. (Private): 1849
Powell, A.G. (Charterhouse): 1934
Powys, W.N. (Private): 1871–72–74
Prest, E.B. (Eton): 1850
Prest, H.E.W. (Malvern): 1909–11
Preston, B. (Westminster): 1869
Pretlove, J.F. (Alleyn's): 1954–55–56
Price, D.G. (Haberdashers' Aske's): 1984–85
Prideaux, R.M. (Tonbridge): 1958–59–60
Pringle, D.R. (Felsted): 1979–80–81
*The elected captain for 1982, he represented England in the Second Test v India which coincided with the University Match.*
Pritchard, G.C. (King's, Canterbury): 1964
Pryer, B.J.K. (City of London): 1948
Pyemont, C.P. (Marlborough): 1967

Ramsay, R.C. (Harrow): 1882
Ranjitsinhji, K.S. (Rajkumar College, India): 1893
Ratcliffe, A. (Rydal): 1930–31–32
Raymond-Barker, H.B. (Winchester): 1844
Raynor, G.S. (Winchester): 1872
Reddy, N.S.K. (Doon School, Dehra Dun, India): 1959–60–61
Rees-Davies, W.R. (Eton): 1938
Reynolds, E.M. (Royal Institution, Liverpool): 1853–54
Richardson, H.A. (Tonbridge): 1867–68–69
Richardson, J.M. (Harrow): 1866–67–68
Riddell, V.H.H. (Clifton): 1926
Riley, W.N. (Worcester RGS): 1912
Rimell, A.G.J. (Charterhouse): 1949–50
Rippingall, S.F. (Rugby): 1845
Roberts, F.B. (Rossall): 1903
Robertson, W.P. (Harrow): 1901
Robbins, R.W.V. (Highgate): 1926–27–28
Robinson, J.J. (Appleby): 1894
Rock, C.W. (Launceston GS, Tasmania): 1884–85–86
Roe, W.N. (Clergy Orphan School, Canterbury): 1883
Roebuck, P.G.P. (Millfield): 1984–85
Roebuck, P.M. (Millfield): 1975–76–77
Romilly, E. (Bury St Edmunds): 1827
Roopnaraine, R. (Queen's College, British Guiana): 1965–66
Rose, M.H. (Pocklington): 1963–64
Ross, N.P.G. (Marlborough): 1969
Rotherham, G.A. (Rugby): 1919
Rought-Rought, D.C. (Private): 1937
Rought-Rought, R.C. (Private): 1930–32
Roundell, J. (Winchester): 1973
Rowe, F.C.C. (Harrow): 1881
Rowell, W.I. (Marlborough): 1891
Royston, Viscount (Harrow): 1857
Russell, D.P. (West Park GS, St Helens): 1974–75
Russell, S.G. (Tiffin): 1965–66–67 (Captain 1967)
Russom, N. (Huish's GS, Taunton): 1980–81

St John, E. (Private): 1829
Salter, H.W. (Private): 1861–62
Savile, Hon A. (Eton): 1840
Savile, G. (Eton & Rossall): 1868
Saville, S.H. (Marlborough): 1911–12–13–14 (Captain 1914)
Sayres, E. (Midhurst): 1838–39–40–41
Schultz, S.S. (later Storey) (Uppingham): 1877
Scott, A.M.G. (Seaford Head CS): 1985
Scott, A.T. (Brighton): 1870–71
Seabrook, F.J. (Haileybury): 1926–27–28 (Captain 1928)
Seager, C.P. (Peterhouse, Rhodesia): 1971
Seddon, R. (Bridgnorth GS): 1846–47
Selvey, M.W.W. (Battersea GS & Manchester U.): 1971
Sharpe, C.M. (Private): 1875
Shaw, V.K. (Haileybury): 1876
Shelmerdine, G.O. (Cheltenham): 1922
Sheppard, D.S. (later Right Reverend D.S. Sheppard) (Sherborne): 1950–51–52 (Captain 1952)
Sherwell, N.B. (Tonbridge): 1923–24–25
Shine, E.B. (King Edward VI, Saffron Walden): 1896–97
Shirley, W.R. de la C. (Eton): 1924
Shirreff, A.C. (Dulwich): 1939

Short, R.L. (Denstone): 1969
Shuttleworth, G.M. (Blackburn GS): 1946–47–48
Silk, D.R.W. (Christ's Hospital): 1953–54–55 (Captain 1955)
Simonds, H.J. (Eton): 1850
Sims, H.M. (St Peter's, York): 1873–74–75
Singh, S. (Khalsa College, Amritsar & Punjab U, Jullundur, India): 1955–56
Sinker, N.D. (Winchester): 1966
Sivewright, E. (Eton): 1829
Slack, J.K.E. (UCS, London): 1954
Smith, A.F. (Harrow & Wellington): 1875
Smith, C.A. (Charterhouse): 1882–83–84–85
Smith, C.S. (William Hulme's GS, Manchester): 1954–55–56–57
Smith, D.J. (Stockport GS): 1955–56
Smyth, R.I. (Sedbergh): 1973–74–75
Snowden, W. (Merchant Taylors', Crosby): 1972–73–74–75 (Captain 1974)
Southwell, H.G. (Harrow): 1852–53
Spencer, J. (Brighton, Hove and Sussex GS): 1970–71–72
Spencer, R. (Harrow): 1881
Spiro, D.G. (Harrow): 1884
Stacey, F.E. (Eton): 1853
Stanning, J. (Rugby): 1900
Stedman, H.C.P. (Private): 1871
Steel, A.G. (Marlborough): 1878–79–80–81 (Captain 1880)
Steel, D.Q. (Uppingham): 1876–77–78–79
Steele, H.K. (King's College, Auckland, N.Z.): 1971–72
Stevenson, M.H. (Rydal): 1949–50–51–52
Stogdon, J.H. (Harrow): 1897–98–99
Stow, M.H. (Harrow): 1867–68–69 (Captain 1869)
Streatfeild, E.C. (Charterhouse): 1890–91–92–93
Studd, C.T. (Eton): 1880–81–82–83 (Captain 1883)
Studd, G.B. (Eton): 1879–80–81–82 (Captain 1882)
Studd, J.E.K. (Eton): 1881–82–83–84 (Captain 1884)
Studd, P.M. (Harrow): 1937–38–39 (Captain 1939)
Studd, R.A. (Eton): 1895
Subba Row, R. (Whitgift): 1951–52–53
Surridge, D. (Richard Hale School, Hertford & Southampton U.): 1979
Sutthery, A.M. (Uppingham & Oundle): 1887
Swift, B.T. (St Peter's, Adelaide, Australia): 1957
Sykes, W. (Private): 1844

Tabor, A.S. (Eton): 1872–73–74
Taylor, C.G. (Eton): 1836–38–39 (Captain 1838–39)
Taylor, C.R.V. (Birkenhead): 1971–72–73
Taylor, T.L. (Uppingham): 1898–99–1900 (Captain 1900)
Templeton, C.H. (Winchester): 1827
Thackeray, F. (Eton): 1838–39–40
Thomas, A. (Winchester): 1838
Thompson, J.R. (Tonbridge): 1938–39
Thompson, W.T. (Ruthin): 1836
Thomson, R.H. (Bexhill): 1961–62
Thornewill, E.J. (Harrow): 1856
Thornton, C.I. (Eton): 1869–70–71–72 (Captain 1872)
Thwaites, I.G. (Eastbourne): 1964

Tillard, C. (Repton): 1873–74
Tindall, M. (Harrow): 1935–36–37 (Captain 1937)
Tobin, F. (Rugby): 1870–71–72
Tomblin, A.C. (Uppingham): 1857
Tomlinson, W.J.V. (Felsted): 1923
Topham, H.G. (Repton): 1883–84
Toppin, C. (Sedbergh): 1885–86–87
Tordoff, G.G. (Normanton GS): 1952
Townley, T.M. (Eton): 1847–48
Trapnell, B.M.W. (UCS, London): 1946
Tremlett, T.D. (Eton): 1854
Trevelyan, W.B. (Edinburgh Academy & Harrow): 1842–43
Tuck, G.H. (Eton): 1863–64–65–66 (Captain 1865)
Tufnell, N.C. (Eton): 1909–10
Turnbull, M.J.L. (Downside): 1926–28–29 (Captain 1929)
Turner, J.A. (Uppingham): 1883–84–85–86
Turner, J.B. (Blackheath Proprietary): 1841

Urquhart, J.R. (King Edward VI School, Chelmsford): 1948

Valentine, B.H. (Repton): 1929
Varey, D.W. (Birkenhead): 1982–83
*His twin, J.G. Varey, gained blues for Oxford, 1982–83.*
Vernon, H. (Harrow): 1850–51–52 (Captain 1852)
Vincent, H.G. (Haileybury): 1914

Wait, O.J. (Dulwich): 1949–51
Walker, Ashley (Westminster): 1864–65–66
Walker, F. (Private): 1849–50–51–52
Walker, John (Private): 1847–48–49 (Captain 1848)
Ward, A.R. (Private): 1853
*Ward was appointed captain in 1854 but did not play because of illness.*
Warner, W.S.O. (Torquay): 1867–68
Warr, J.J. (Ealing CGS): 1949–50–51–52 (Captain 1951)
Warren, C. (Oakham): 1866
Watts, H.E. (Downside): 1947
Webb, R.H. (Eton): 1827
Webster, J. (Bradford GS): 1939
Webster, W.H. (Highgate): 1932
Weedon, M.J.H. (Harrow): 1962
Weigall, G.J.V. (Wellington): 1891–92
Weighell, W.B. (Bedford GS): 1866–68–69
Wells, C.M. (Dulwich): 1891–92–93
Wells, T.U. (Kings, Auckland, N.Z.): 1950
Weston, J.S. (Rugby): 1851–52
Wheatley, O.S. (King Edward's, Birmingham): 1957–58
Wheelhouse, A. (Nottingham HS): 1959
White, A.F.T. (Uppingham): 1936
White, A.H. (Geelong, Australia): 1924
White, H.S. (Bury St Edmunds & Brighton): 1852
White, R.C. (Hilton College, S.A.): 1962–63–64–65 (Captain 1965)
Whitfeld, H. (Eton): 1878–79–80–81
Whymper, F.H. (Eton): 1849
Wilcox, D.R. (Dulwich): 1931–32–33 (Captain 1933)
Wild, J.V. (Taunton): 1938
Wilenkin, B.C.G. (Harrow): 1956

Wilkin, C.L.A. (St Kitts GS, Leeward Islands): 1970
Wilkins-Leir, E.J.P. (Marlborough): 1858
Willard, M.J.L. (Judd, Tonbridge): 1959–60–61
Willatt, G.L. (Repton): 1946–47 (Captain 1947)
Wills, T.W. (Rugby): 1856
*Wills had been entered at Cambridge and played as Cambridge were one short, but had never actually been in residence.*
Wilson, C.E.M. (Uppingham): 1895–96–97–98 (Captain 1898)
Wilson, C.P. (Uppingham & Marlborough): 1880–81
Wilson, E.R. (Rugby): 1899–1900–01–02 (Captain 1902)
Wilson, F.B. (Harrow): 1902–03–04 (Captain 1904)
Wilson, G. (Harrow): 1919
Wilson, T.W. (Repton): 1869
Windows, A.R. (Clifton): 1962–63–64
Wingfield, W. (Rossall): 1855–56–57
Winlaw, R. de W.K. (Winchester): 1932–33–34
Winter, A.H. (Westminster): 1865–66–67
Winter, C.E. (Uppingham): 1902

Winter, G.E. (Winchester): 1898–99
Winthorp, S. (Rugby): 1829
Wood, G.E.C. (Cheltenham): 1914–19–20 (Captain 1920)
Wood, H. (Sheffield Collegiate): 1879
Woodroffe, K.H.C. (Marlborough): 1913–14
Woods, S.M.J. (Brighton): 1888–89–90–91 (Captain 1890)
Wookey, S.M. (Malvern): 1975–76
*Gained blue for Oxford 1978*
Wooller, W. (Rydal): 1935–36
Wright, C.C.G. (Tonbridge): 1907–08
Wright, C.W. (Charterhouse): 1882–83–84–85
Wright, P.A. (Wellingborough): 1922–23–24
Wright, S. (Mill Hill): 1973
Wroth, H.T. (Uppingham): 1845
Wykes, N.G. (Oundle): 1928

Yardley, N.W.D. (St Peter's, York): 1935–36–37–38 (Captain 1938)
Yardley, W. (Rugby): 1869–70–71–72 (Captain 1871)
Young, R.A. (Repton): 1905–06–07–08 (Captain 1908)

## OXFORD UNIVERSITY BLUES

Aamer Hameed (Central Model HS, Lahore & Punjab U., Pakistan): 1979
Abell, G.E.B. (Marlborough): 1924–26–27
Ainslie, M.M. (Eton): 1843–44–45 (Captain 1844–45)
Aitken, H.M. (Eton): 1853
Aitken, J. (Eton): 1848–49–50 (Captain 1850)
Alington, H.G. (Rugby): 1859
Allan, J.M. (Edinburgh Academy): 1953–54–55–56
Allerton, J.W.O. (Stowe): 1969
Allison, D.F. (Greenmore College, Birmingham): 1970
Altham, H.S. (Repton): 1911–12
Arenhold, J.A. (Diocesan College, S.A.): 1954
Arkwright, H.A. (Eton): 1895
Armitstead, W.G. (Westminster): 1853–54–56–57
Arnall-Thompson, H.T. (Rugby): 1886
Asher, A.G.G. (Loretto): 1883
Awdry, R.W. (Winchester): 1904

Baig, A.A. (Aliya, Hyderabad & Osmania U., India): 1959–60–61–62
Baig, M.A. (Osmania U., India): 1962–63–64
Bailey, J.A. (Christ's Hospital): 1956–57–58 (Captain 1958)
Balfour, E. (Westminster): 1852–53–54
Ballance, T.G.L. (Uppingham): 1935–37
Bannon, B.D. (Tonbridge): 1898
Barber, A.T. (Shrewsbury): 1927–28–29 (Captain 1929)
Bardsley, R.V. (Shrewsbury): 1911–12–13
Bardswell, G.R. (Uppingham): 1894–96–97 (Captain 1897)
Barker, A.H. (Charterhouse): 1964–65–67
Barlow, E.A. (Shrewsbury): 1932–33–34
Barnard, F.H. (Charterhouse): 1922–24
Barnes, R.G. (Harrow): 1906–07
Bartholomew, A.C. (Marlborough): 1868
Bartlett, J.N. (Chichester): 1946–51

Barton, M.R. (Winchester): 1936–37
Bassett, H. (Bedford House, Oxford): 1889–90–91
Bastard, E.W. (Sherborne): 1883–84–85
Bateman, E.L. (Repton & Marlborough): 1854–55
Bathurst, F. (Winchester): 1848
Bathurst, L.C.V. (Radley): 1893–94
Bathurst, R.A. (Winchester): 1838–39
Bathurst, S.E. (Winchester): 1836
Bayly, C.H. (Winchester): 1827–29
Beauclerk, C.W. (Charterhouse): 1836
Belcher, T.H. (Magdalen College School, Oxford): 1870
Bell, G.F. (Repton): 1919
Belle, B.H. (Forest School): 1936
Benn, A. (Harrow): 1935
Bennett, G. (Winchester): 1856
Benson, E.T. (Blundell's): 1928–29
Bere, C.S. (Rugby): 1851
Berkeley, G.F.H. (Wellington): 1890–91–92–93
Bettington, R.H.B. (King's School, Parramatta, Australia): 1920–21–22–23 (Captain 1923)
Bickmore, A.F. (Clifton): 1920–21
Bird, J.W. (Winchester): 1827–29
Bird, W.S. (Malvern): 1904–05–06 (Captain 1906)
Birrell, H.B. (St Andrew's, S.A.): 1953–54
Blagg, P.H. (Shrewsbury): 1939
Blaikie, K.G. (Maritzburg College, S.A.): 1924
Blake, P.D.S. (Eton): 1950–51–52 (Captain 1952)
Bligh, E.V. (Eton): 1850
Bloy, N.C.F. (Dover): 1946–47
Boger, A.J. (Winchester): 1891
Bolitho, W.E.T. (Harrow): 1883–85
Bonham-Carter, M. (Winchester): 1902
Boobbyer, B. (Uppingham): 1949–50–51–52
Bosanquet, B.J.T. (Eton): 1898–99–1900
Boswell, W.G.K. (Eton): 1913–14
Botton, N.D. (King Edward's, Bath): 1974
Bowden-Smith, F.H. (Rugby): 1861
Bowman, R.C. (Fettes): 1957
Bowring, T. (Rugby): 1907–08

Boyle, C.E. (Charterhouse): 1865–66–67
Boyle, C.W. (Clifton): 1873
Bradby, H.C. (Rugby): 1890
Braddell, R.L. (Charterhouse): 1910–11
Bradshaw, W.H. (Malvern): 1930–31
Brain, J.H. (Clifton): 1884–85–86–87 (Captain 1887)
Brain, W.H. (Clifton): 1891–92–93
Brandt, D.R. (Harrow): 1907
Brandt, F. (Cheltenham): 1859–60–61 (Captain 1861)
Branston, G.T. (Charterhouse): 1904–05–06
Brett, P.J. (Winchester): 1929
Brettell, D.N. (Cheltenham): 1977
Briggs, R. (Winchester): 1875–76
Bristowe, O.C. (Eton): 1914
Bristowe, W.R. (Charterhouse): 1984–85
Bromley-Martin, G.E. (Eton): 1897–98
Brooke, R.H.J.(St Edward's, Oxford): 1932
Brooks, R.A. (Quintin, St John's Wood & Bristol U.): 1967
Brougham, H. (Wellington): 1911
Brownlee, L.D. (Clifton): 1904
Bruce, Hon C.N. (later Lord Aberdare) (Winchester): 1907–08
Buckland, E.H. (Marlborough): 1884–85–86–87
Buckland, F.M. (Eton): 1875–76–77
Bull, H.E. (Westminster): 1863
Bullock-Hall, W.H. (Rugby): 1857–58–60
Burchnall, R.L. (Winchester): 1970–71
Burn, R.C.W. (Winchester): 1902–03–04–05
Burton, M.St J.W. (Umtali HS, Rhodesia & Rhodes U.): 1969–70–71 (Captain 1970)
Bury, T.E.O. (Charterhouse): 1980
Bush, J.E. (Magdalen College School, Oxford): 1952
Butler, S.E. (Eton): 1870–71–72–73
Butterworth, R.E.C. (Harrow): 1927
Buxton, R.V. (Eton): 1906

Campbell, A.N. (Berkhamsted): 1970
Campbell, D. (Melbourne U., Australia): 1874–75–76
Campbell, I.P. (Canford): 1949–50
Campbell, I.P.F. (Repton): 1911–12–13 (Captain 1913)
Cantlay, C.P.T. (Radley): 1975
Carlisle, K.M. (Harrow): 1903–04–05 (Captain 1905)
Carpenter-Garnier, J. (Harrow): 1858
Carr, D.B. (Repton): 1949–50–51 (Captain 1950)
Carr, J.D. (Repton): 1983–84–85
Carroll, P.R. (Newington College, NSW & Sydney U., Australia): 1971
Carter, E.S. (Durham GS): 1866–67
Case, T. (Rugby): 1864–65–67
Case, T.B. (Winchester): 1891–92
*Case came into the game by permission of the Cambridge captain in 1891, after the Hon F.J.N. Thesiger had retired shortly after the start of the match.*
Cassan, E.J.P. (Bruton): 1859
Cator, W. (Bromsgrove GS): 1860
Cazalet, P.V.F. (Eton): 1927
Cazenove, A. (Private): 1851–52
Chalk, F.G.H. (Uppingham): 1931–32–33–34 (Captain 1934)

Champain, F.H.B. (Cheltenham): 1897–98–99–1900 (Captain 1899)
Cherry, G.C. (Harrow): 1841–42–43
Chesterton, G.H. (Malvern): 1949
Chitty, J.W. (Eton): 1848–49
Clarke, W.G. (Winchester): 1840
Claughton, J.A. (King Edward's, Birmingham): 1976–77–78–79 (Captain 1978)
Clement, R. (Rugby): 1853
Clements, S.M. (Ipswich): 1976–79 (Captain 1979)
Clube, S.V.M. (St John's, Leatherhead): 1956
Cobb, A.R. (Winchester): 1886
Cochrane, A.H.J. (Repton): 1885–86–88
Coker, J. (Winchester): 1840–42–43–44 (Captain 1842–43)
Colebrooke, E.L. (Charterhouse): 1880
Coleridge, C.E. (Eton): 1849–50
Coleridge, F.J. (Eton): 1847–50
Colley, R.H. (Bridgnorth GS): 1853–54–55
Collins, L.P. (Marlborough): 1899
Colman, G.R.R. (Eton): 1913–14
Commerell, W.A. (Harrow): 1843
Cooke, J. (Winchester): 1829
Coote, A. (Eton): 1838–39–40 (Captain 1838)
Corlett, S.C. (Worksop): 1971–72
Corran, A.J. (Gresham's): 1958–59–60
Coutts, I.D.F. (Dulwich): 1952
Cowan, R.S. (Lewes Priory CS): 1980–81–82
Cowburn, A. (Winchester): 1841
Cowdrey, M.C. (Tonbridge): 1952–53–54 (Captain 1954)
Coxon, A.J. (Harrow GCS): 1952
Crawford, J.W.F. (Merchant Taylors'): 1900–01
Crawley, A.M. (Harrow): 1927–28–29–30
Croome, A.C.M. (Wellington): 1888–89
Crutchley, G.E.V. (Harrow): 1912
Cullinan, M.R. (Hilton College & Cape Town U., S.A.): 1983–84
Cunliffe, F.H.E. (Eton): 1895–96–97–98 (Captain 1898)
Currer, C.S. (Harrow): 1847
Curteis, H.M. (Westminster): 1841–42
Curtis, I.J. (Whitgift GS): 1980–82
Curwen, W.J.H. (Charterhouse): 1906
Cushing, V.G.B. (KCS, Wimbledon): 1973
Cuthbertson, J.L. (Rugby): 1962–63

Darnell, N. (Winchester): 1838–39–40
Darwall-Smith, R.F.H. (Charterhouse): 1935–36–37–38
Daubeny, E.T. (Bromsgrove GS): 1861–62
Dauglish, M.J. (Harrow): 1889–90
Davenport, E. (Rugby): 1866
Davidson, W.W. (Brighton): 1947–48
Davies, P.H. (Brighton): 1913–14
Davies, W.H. (Charterhouse): 1846–47–48
Davis, F.J. (Blundell's): 1963
Delisle, G.P.S. (Stonyhurst): 1955–56
De Montmorency, R.H. (Cheltenham & St Paul's): 1899
Denison, H. (Eton): 1829
Denne, T. (Private): 1827
De Saram, F.C. (Royal College, Colombo, Ceylon): 1934–35
Des Vœux, H.D. (Harrow): 1844
Digby, K.E. (Harrow): 1857–58–59
Digby, R. (Harrow): 1867–68–69

Dillon, E.W. (Rugby): 1901–02
Divecha, R.V. (Podar HS & Bombay U., India): 1950–51
Dixon, E.J.H. (St Edward's, Oxford): 1937–38–39 (Captain 1939)
Dolphin, J.M. (Marlborough): 1860
Donnelly, M.P. (New Plymouth BHS & Canterbury U., N.Z.): 1946–47 (Captain 1947)
Dowding, A.L. (St Peter's, Adelaide, Australia): 1952–53 (Captain 1953)
Drybrough, C.D. (Highgate): 1960–61–62 (Captain 1961–62)
Dryden, A.E. (Winchester): 1841–42–43
Duff, A.R. (Radley): 1960–61
Durell, J.D. (Westminster): 1838
Dury, T.S. (Harrow): 1876
Dyer, A.W. (Mill Hill): 1965–66
Dyson, E.M. (Queen Elizabeth GS, Wakefield): 1958
Dyson, J.H. (Charterhouse): 1936

Eagar, E.D.R. (Cheltenham): 1939
Eagar, M.A. (Rugby): 1956–57–58–59
Easter, J.N.C. (St Edward's, Oxford): 1967–68
Eccles, A. (Repton): 1897–98–99
Edbrooke, R.M. (Queen Elizabeth's Hospital School, Bristol): 1984
Eden, F.M. (Rugby): 1850–51
Eggar, J.D. (Winchester): 1938
Ellis, R.G.P. (Haileybury): 1981–82–83 (Captain 1982)
Ellis, W.W. (Rugby): 1827
Elviss, R.W. (Leeds GS): 1966–67
Evans, A.H. (Rossall & Clifton): 1878–79–80–81 (Captain 1881)
Evans, A.J. (Winchester): 1909–10–11–12 (Captain 1911)
Evans, E.N. (Haileybury): 1932
Evans, F.R. (Cheltenham & Rugby): 1863–64–65
Evans, G. (St Asaph): 1939
Evans, W.H.B. (Malvern): 1902–03–04–05 (Captain 1904)
Evelyn, F.L. (Rugby): 1880
Evetts, W. (Harrow): 1868–69
Ezekowitz, R.A.B. (Westville BHS, Durban & Cape Town U., S.A.): 1980–81

Faber, M.J.J. (Eton): 1972
Fane, F.L. (Charterhouse): 1897–98
Fasken, D.K. (Wellington): 1953–54–55
Fellowes, E.L. (Marlborough): 1865–66–68 (Captain 1868)
Fellows, W. (Westminster): 1854–55–56–57
Fellows-Smith, J.P. (Durban HS, S.A.): 1953–54–55
Fiennes, W.S.T.W. (Winchester): 1856–57–58
Fillary, E.W.J. (St Lawrence): 1963–64–65
Findlay, W. (Eton): 1901–02–03 (Captain 1903)
Fisher, C.D. (Westminster): 1900
Fisher, P.B. (St Ignatius, Enfield): 1975–76–77–78
Foord-Kelcey, W. (Chatham House, Ramsgate): 1874–75
Forbes, D.H. (Eton): 1894
Ford, G.J. (King's College, London): 1839–40
Ford, N.M. (Harrow): 1928–29–30
Forster, H.W. (Eton): 1887–88–89
Fortescue, A.T. (Marlborough): 1868–69–70

Foster, G.N. (Malvern): 1905–06–07–08
Foster, H.K. (Malvern): 1894–95–96
Foster, R.E. (Malvern): 1897–98–99–1900 (Captain 1900)
Fowler, G. (Clifton): 1888
Fowler, H. (Clifton): 1877–79–80
Fox, R.W. (Wellington): 1897–98
Francis, C.K. (Rugby): 1870–71–72–73
Franklin, H.W.F. (Christ's Hospital): 1924
Franks, J.G. (Stamford): 1984–85
Fraser, J.N. (Church of England GS, Melbourne & Melbourne U., Australia): 1912–13
Frazer, J.E. (Winchester): 1924
Frederick, J.St J. (Eton): 1864–67
Fry, C.A. (Repton): 1959–60–61
Fry, C.B. (Repton): 1892–93–94–95 (Captain 1894)
Fuller, C.P. (Winchester): 1854–55
Fursdon, E.D. (Sherborne): 1974–75

Gamble, N.W. (Stockport GS): 1967
Game, W.H. (Sherborne): 1873–74–75–76 (Captain 1876)
Garland-Wells, H.M. (St Paul's): 1928–29–30
Garnett, C.A. (Cheltenham & Eton): 1860–62
Garnier, E.S. (Marlborough): 1873
Garnier, T.P. (Winchester): 1861–62–63
Garofall, A.R. (Latymer Upper): 1967–68
Garth, R. (Eton): 1839–40–41–42 (Captain 1840–41)
Garthwaite, P.F. (Wellington): 1929
Gibbon, J.H. (Harrow): 1869
Gibbs, P.J.K. (Hanley GS): 1964–65–66
Gibson, I. (Manchester GS): 1955–56–57–58
Gilbert, H.A. (Charterhouse): 1907–08–09
Gillett, H.H. (Winchester): 1857–58
Gilliat, I.A.W. (Charterhouse): 1925
Gilliat, R.M.C. (Charterhouse): 1964–65–66–67 (Captain 1966)
Gilligan, F.W. (Dulwich): 1919–20 (Captain 1920)
Glover, T.R. (Lancaster RGS): 1973–74–75 (Captain 1975)
Goldstein, F.S. (Falcon College, Bulawayo, Rhodesia): 1966–67–68–69 (Captain 1968–69)
Gordon, J.H. (Winchester): 1906–07
Goring, C. (Winchester): 1836
Green, D.M. (Manchester GS): 1959–60–61
Greene, A.D. (Clifton): 1877–78–79–80 (Captain 1880)
Greenstock, J.W. (Malvern): 1925–26–27
Gresson, F.H. (Winchester): 1887–88–89
Grimston, Hon E.H. (Harrow): 1836
Grimston, Hon R. (Harrow): 1838
Grover, J.N. (Winchester): 1936–37–38 (Captain 1938)
Groves, M.G.M. (Diocesan College, S.A.): 1964–65–66
Guest, M.R.J. (Rugby): 1964–65–66
Guise, J.L. (Winchester): 1924–25 (Captain 1925)
Gurr, D.R. (Aylesbury GS): 1976–77

Hadow, W.H. (Harrow): 1870–71–72
Hale, T.W. (Rugby): 1851–52
Halliday, J.G. (City of Oxford HS): 1935
Halliday, S.J. (Downside): 1980
Hamblin, C.B. (King's, Canterbury): 1971–72–73
Hamilton, A.C. (Charterhouse): 1975

Hamilton, W.D. (Haileybury): 1882
Hanbury, O.R. (Rugby): 1849
Hankey, R. (Harrow): 1853–55 (Captain 1855)
Hare, J.H.M. (Uppingham): 1879
Harris, C.R. (Buckingham RLS): 1964
Harris, Hon G.R.C. (later Lord Harris) (Eton): 1871–72–74
Harrison, G.C. (Malvern & Clifton): 1880–81
Hart, T.M. (Strathallan): 1931–32
Hartley, J.C. (Marlborough & Tonbridge): 1896–97
Haskett-Smith, A. (Eton): 1879
Hatfeild, C.E. (Eton): 1908
Hayes, K.A. (Queen Elizabeth's GS, Blackburn): 1981–82–83–84 (Captain 1984)
Haygarth, J.W (Winchester): 1862–63–64
Heal, M.G. (St Brendan's, Bristol): 1970–72
Heard, H. (Queen Elizabeth's Hospital School, Bristol): 1969–70
Heath, A.H. (Clifton): 1876–77–78–79
Hedges, L.P. (Tonbridge): 1920–21–22
Henderson, D. (St Edward's, Oxford): 1950
Henley, D.F. (later Henley-Welch) (Harrow): 1947
Henley, F.A.H. (Forest): 1905
Heseltine, P.J. (Barnsley & District Holgate GS): 1983
Hewetson, E.P. (Shrewsbury): 1923–24–25
Hewett, H.T. (Harrow): 1886
Hildyard, H.C.T. (Eton): 1845–46
Hildyard, L.D. (Private): 1884–85–86
Hill, F.H. (Bradfield): 1867–69–70
Hill, V.T. (Winchester): 1892
Hiller, R.B. (Bec): 1966
Hill-Wood, C.K.H. (Eton): 1928–29–30
Hill-Wood, D.J. (Eton): 1928
Hine-Haycock, T.R. (Wellington): 1883–84
Hirst, E.T. (Rugby): 1878–79–80
Hobbs, J.A.D. (Liverpool): 1957
Hodgkinson, G.L. (Harrow): 1857–58–59
Hofmeyr, M.B. (Pretoria, S.A.): 1949–50–51 (Captain 1951)
Holdsworth, R.L. (Repton): 1919–20–21–22
Hollins, A.M. (Eton): 1899
Hollins, F.H. (Eton): 1901
Holmes, E.R.T. (Malvern): 1925–26–27 (Captain 1927)
Hone, B.W. (Adelaide U, Australia): 1931–32–33 (Captain 1933)
Honywood, R. (Eton): 1845–46–47
Hooman, C.V.L. (Charterhouse): 1909–10
Hopkins, H.O. (St Peter's, Adelaide, Australia): 1923
Hore, A.H. (Tonbridge): 1851
Howell, M. (Repton): 1914–19 (Captain 1919)
Hughes, G.E. (Rugby): 1845
Hughes, T. (Rugby): 1842
Hume, E. (Marlborough): 1861–62
Hurst, C.S. (Uppingham): 1907–08–09 (Captain 1909)
Huxford, P.N. (Richard Hale School, Hertford): 1981

Imran Khan (Aitchison College, Lahore, Pakistan & Worcester RGS): 1973–74–75 (Captain 1974)
Inge, F.G. (Rossall & Charterhouse): 1861–62–63
Inge, W. (Shrewsbury): 1853
Isherwood, F.W. (Rugby): 1872

Jackson, K.L.T. (Rugby): 1934
Jacobson, T.R. (Charterhouse): 1961
Jardine, D.R. (Winchester): 1920–21–23
Jardine, M.R. (Fettes): 1889–90–91–92 (Captain 1891)
Jarrett, D.W. (Wellington): 1975
*Gained blue for Cambridge 1976*
Javed Burki (St Mary's, Rawalpindi & Punjab U., Pakistan): 1958–59–60
Jellicoe, F.G.G. (Haileybury): 1877–79
Jenkins, V.G.J. (Llandovery): 1933
Johns, R.L. (St Albans & Keele U.): 1970
Jones, A.K.C. (Solihull): 1971–72–73 (Captain 1973)
Jones, M. (Harrow): 1849–50
Jones, P.C.H. (Milton HS, Rhodesia & Rhodes U.): 1971–72 (Captain 1972)
Jones, R.T. (Eton): 1892
Jones, T.B. (Christ College, Brecon & Trinity College, Dublin): 1874
Jones-Bateman, R.L. (Winchester): 1846–48
Jose, A.D. (Adelaide U., Australia): 1950–51
Jowett, D.C.P.R. (Sherborne): 1952–53–54–55
Jowett, R.L. (Bradford GS): 1957–58–59

Kamm, A. (Charterhouse): 1954
Kardar, A.H. (formerly Abdul Hafeez) (Islamia College & Punjab U., India): 1947–48–49
Kayum, D.A. (Selhurst GS & Chatham House GS): 1977–78
Keighley, W.G. (Eton): 1947–48
Kelly, G.W.F. (Stonyhurst): 1901–02
Kemp, C.W.M. (Harrow): 1878
Kemp, M.C. (Harrow): 1881–82–83–84 (Captain 1883–84)
Kenney, E.M. (later Kenney-Herbert) (Rugby): 1866–67–68
Kentish, E.S.M. (Cornwall College, Jamaica): 1956 *(when aged 39)*
Ker, R.J.C.R. (Eton): 1842
Key, K.J. (Clifton): 1884–85–86–87
Khan, A.J. (Aitchison College, Lahore & Punjab U., Pakistan): 1968–69
Kimpton, R.C.M. (Melbourne U., Australia): 1935–37–38
Kingsley, P.G.T. (Winchester): 1928–29–30 (Captain 1930)
Kinkead-Weekes, R.C. (Eton): 1972
Knatchbull, H.E. (Winchester): 1827–29
Knight, D.J. (Malvern): 1914–19
Knight, J.M. (Oundle): 1979
Knight, N.S. (Uppingham): 1934
Knight, R.L. (Clifton): 1878
Knott, C.H. (Tonbridge): 1922–23–24 (Captain 1924)
Knott, F.H. (Tonbridge): 1912–13–14 (Captain 1914)
Knox, F.P. (Dulwich): 1899–1900–01 (Captain 1901)

Lagden, R.O. (Marlborough): 1909–10–11–12
Lamb, Hon T.M. (Shrewsbury): 1973–74
Lane, C.G. (Westminster): 1856–58–59–60 (Captain 1859–60)
Lang, T.W. (Edinburgh Academy & Clifton): 1874–75
Law, A.P. (Rugby): 1857

Law, W. (Harrow): 1871–72–73–74 (Captain 1874)
Lawrence, M.P. (Manchester GS): 1984–85
Lear, F. (Winchester): 1843–44
Le Couteur, P.R. (Warrnambool Academy & Melbourne U., Australia): 1909–10–11
Lee, E.C. (Winchester): 1898
Lee, G.B. (Winchester): 1838–39 (Captain 1839)
Lee, R.J. (Church of England GS, Sydney & Sydney U., Australia): 1972–73–74
Legard, A.R. (Winchester): 1932–35
Legge, G.B. (Malvern): 1925–26 (Captain 1926)
Leigh, E.C. (Harrow): 1852–53–54
Leslie, C.F.H. (Rugby): 1881–82–83
Leslie, J. (Harrow): 1843
L'Estrange, M.G. (St Aloysius College, Sydney & Sydney U., Australia): 1977–79
Leveson Gower, H.D.G. (Winchester): 1893–94–95–96 (Captain 1896)
Lewis, C.P. (Llandovery & King's, Gloucester): 1876
Lewis, D.J. (Cape Town U., S.A.): 1951
Lewis, R.P. (Winchester): 1894–95–96
Lewis, W.H. (Harrow): 1827
Lindsay, W.O. (Harrow): 1931
Linton, H. (Harrow): 1858–59
Linton, S. (Rugby): 1861–62
Lipscombe, W.H. (Marlborough): 1868
Llewelyn, W.D. (Eton): 1890–91
Lloyd, M.F.D. (Magdalen College School, Oxford): 1974
Loch, C.R.F. (Edinburgh Academy & Rugby): 1846–48
Loftus, Lord H.Y.A. (Harrow): 1841
Lomas, J.M. (Charterhouse): 1938–39
Longe, F.D. (Harrow): 1851–52
Lowe, J.C.M. (Uppingham): 1907–08–09
Lowndes, R. (Winchester): 1841
Lowndes, W.G.L.F. (Eton): 1921
Lowth, A.J. (Eton & Winchester): 1838–40–41
Luddington, R.S. (KCS, Wimbledon): 1982
Lyon, B.H. (Rugby): 1922–23
Lyon, G.W.F. (Brighton): 1925


McBride, W.N. (Westminster): 1926
McCanlis, M.A. (Cranleigh): 1926–27–28 (Captain 1928)
Macindoe, D.H. (Eton): 1937–38–39–46 (Captain 1946)
McIntosh, R.I.F. (Uppingham): 1927–28
McIver, C.D. (Forest): 1903–04
McKinna, G.H. (Manchester GS): 1953
M'Lachlan, N. (Loretto): 1879–80–81–82 (Captain 1882)
McLarnon, P.C. (Loughborough GS): 1985
Maitland, W.F. (Brighton & Harrow): 1864–65–66–67 (Captain 1867)
Majendie, N.L. (Winchester): 1962–63
Mallett, A.W.H. (Dulwich): 1947–48
Mallett, N.V.H. (St Andrew's, Grahamstown & Cape Town U., S.A.): 1981
Manasseh, M. (Epsom): 1964
Marcon, W. (Eton): 1844
Marie, G.V. (Western Australia U. & Reading U.): 1978
*Marie was the elected captain for 1979 but resigned in favour of S.M. Clements because of injury.*

Marks, V.J. (Blundell's): 1975–76–77–78 (Captain 1976–77)
Marriott, C. (Winchester): 1871
Marriott, G.S. (Winchester): 1878
Marsden, R. (Merchant Taylor's, Northwood): 1982
Marshall, J.C. (Rugby): 1953
Marsham, A.J.B. (Eton): 1939
Marsham, C.D.B. (Private): 1854–55–56–57–58 (Captain 1857–58)
Marsham, C.H.B. (Eton): 1900–01–02 (Captain 1902)
Marsham, C.J.B. (Private): 1851
Marsham, R.H.B. (Private): 1856
Marsland, G.P. (Rossall): 1954
Martin, E.G. (Eton): 1903–04–05–06
Martin, J.D. (Magdalen College School, Oxford): 1962–63–65 (Captain 1965)
Martyn, H. (Exeter GS): 1899–1900
Mathews, E. (Harrow): 1868–69
Matthews, M.H. (Westminster): 1936–37
Maude, J. (Eton): 1873
Maudsley, R.H. (Malvern): 1946–47
May, B. (Prince Edward School, Salisbury, Rhodesia & Cape Town U., S.A.): 1970–71–72 (Captain 1971)
Mayhew, J.F.N. (Eton): 1930
Medlicott, W.S. (Harrow): 1902
Melle, B.G. von B. (S.A. College School & S.A. College, Cape Town): 1913–14
Melville, A. (Michaelhouse, S.A.): 1930–31–32–33 (Captain 1931–32)
Melville, C.D.M. (Michaelhouse, S.A.): 1957
Metcalfe, S.G. (Leeds GS): 1956
Miles, R.F. (Marlborough): 1867–68–69
Millener, D.J. (Auckland GS & Auckland U., N.Z.): 1969–70
Miller, A.J.T. (Haileybury): 1983–84–85 (Captain 1985)
Mills, B.S.T. (Harrow): 1841–42–43
Minns, R.E.F. (King's, Canterbury): 1962–63
Mitchell, R.A.H. (Eton): 1862–63–64–65 (Captain 1863–64–65)
Mitchell, W.M. (Dulwich): 1951–52
Mitchell-Innes, N.S. (Sedbergh): 1934–35–36–37 (Captain 1936)
Moberley, H.E. (Winchester): 1842–43–44–45
Monro, R.W. (Harrow): 1860
Moore, D.N. (Shrewsbury): 1930
*Moore was the appointed captain in 1931, but was unable to play because of illness.*
Mordaunt, G.J. (Wellington): 1893–94–95–96 (Captain 1895)
More, R.E. (Westminster): 1900–01
Morgan, A.H. (Hastings GS): 1969
Morley, J.W. (Marlborough): 1859–60
Morres, E.J. (Winchester): 1850
Morrill, N.D. (Sandown GS & Millfield): 1979
Moss, R.H. (Radley): 1889
Moulding, R.P. (Haberdashers' Aske's): 1978–79–80–81–82–83 (Captain 1981)
Mountford, P.N.G. (Bromsgrove): 1963
Munn, J.S. (Forest): 1901
Murray-Wood, W. (Mill Hill): 1936
Musters, W.M. (Eton): 1829

Napier, C.W.A. (Harrow): 1838–39

Naumann, F.C.G. (Malvern): 1914–19
Neate, F.W. (St Paul's): 1961–62
Nepean, C.E.B. (Charterhouse): 1873
Nepean, E.A. (Sherborne): 1887–88
Neser, V.H. (S.A. College, Cape Town): 1921
Nethercote, H.O. (Charterhouse & Harrow): 1840–41
Newman, G.C. (Eton): 1926–27
Newton, A.E. (Eton): 1885
Newton-Thompson, J.O. (Diocesan College, S.A.): 1946
Nicholls, B.E. (Winchester): 1884
Niven, R.A. (Berkhamsted): 1968–69–73
Nunn, J.A. (Sherborne): 1926–27

O'Brien, T.C. (St Charles' College, Notting Hill): 1884–85
Oldfield, P.C. (Repton): 1932–33
Oliver, F.W. (Westminster): 1856–57
Orders, J.O.D. (Winchester): 1978–79–80–81
Ottaway, C.J. (Eton): 1870–71–72–73 (Captain 1873)
Owen-Smith, H.G. (Diocesan College, S.A.): 1931–32–33

Page, H.V. (Cheltenham): 1883–84–85–86 (Captain 1885–86)
Palairet, L.C.H. (Repton): 1890–91–92–93 (Captain 1892–93)
Palairet, R.C.N. (Repton): 1893–94
Papillon, J. (Winchester): 1827
Parker, W.W. (Rugby): 1852–53–55
Pataudi, Nawab of, sr (Chief's College, Lahore, India): 1929–30–31
Pataudi, Nawab of, jr (Winchester): 1960–63 (Captain 1963)
*Pataudi was also the appointed captain in 1961, but was unable to play because of injuries received in a car accident.*
Pathmanathan, G. (Royal College, Colombo & Sri Lanka U.): 1975–76–77–78
Patten, M. (Winchester): 1922–23
Patterson, J.I. (Chatham House, Ramsgate): 1882
Patterson, W.H. (Chatham House, Ramsgate & Harrow): 1880–81
Patteson, J.C. (Eton): 1849
Pauncefote, B. (Rugby): 1868–69–70–71 (Captain 1869–70)
Paver, R.G.L. (Fort Victoria HS, Rhodesia & Rhodes U.): 1973–74
Pawson, A.C. (Winchester): 1903
Pawson, A.G. (Winchester): 1908–09–10–11 (Captain 1910)
Pawson, H.A. (Winchester): 1947–48 (Captain 1948)
Payne, A. (Private): 1852–54–55–56 (Captain 1856)
Payne, A.F. (Private): 1855
Payne, C.A.L. (Charterhouse): 1906–07
Peake, E. (Marlborough): 1881–82–83
Pearce, J.P. (Ampleforth): 1979
Pearse, G.V. (Maritzburg College, S.A.): 1919
Pearson, A. (Loretto & Rugby): 1876–77
Peat, C.U. (Sedbergh): 1913
Peebles, I.A.R. (Glasgow Academy): 1930
Peel, H.R. (Eton): 1851–52
Pelham, S. (Harrow): 1871

Pepys, J.A. (Eton): 1861
Pershke, W.J. (Uppingham): 1938
Petchey, M.D. (Latymer Upper & Sussex U.): 1983
Pether, S. (Magdalen College School, Oxford): 1939
Philipson, H. (Eton): 1887–88–89 (Captain 1889)
Phillips, F.A. (Rossall): 1892–94–95
Phillips, J.B.M. (King's, Canterbury): 1955
Piachaud, J.D. (St Thomas's, Colombo, Ceylon): 1958–59–60–61
Pilkington, C.C. (Eton): 1896
Pilkington, H.C. (Eton): 1899–1900
Pilkington, W. (Midhurst): 1827
Pithey, D.B. (Plumtree HS & Cape Town U., S.A.): 1961–62
Pole, E. (Winchester): 1827
Popham, F.L. (Harrow): 1829
Porter, S.R. (Peers School, Littlemore, Oxon): 1973
Potter, I.C. (King's, Canterbury): 1961–62
Potts, H.J. (Stand GS): 1950
Price, R. (Winchester): 1827–29
Price, V.R. (Bishop's Stortford): 1919–20–21–22 (Captain 1921)
Proud, R.B. (Winchester): 1939
Pulman, W.W. (Marlborough): 1874–75
Pycroft, J. (Bath): 1836

Quinlan, J.D. (Sherborne): 1985

Raikes, D.C.G. (Shrewsbury): 1931
Raikes, G.B. (Shrewsbury): 1894–95
Raikes, T.B. (Winchester): 1922–23–24
Randolph, B.M. (Charterhouse): 1855–56
Randolph, C. (Eton): 1844–45
Randolph, J. (Westminster): 1843
Randolph, L.C. (Westminster): 1845
Ranken, R.B. (Edinburgh Academy): 1860
Raphael, J.E. (Merchant Taylors'): 1903–04–05
Rashleigh, J. (Harrow): 1842
*Rashleigh fielded substitute for R. Garth in the 1842 match and was allowed to bowl. R. Garth batted.*
Rashleigh, W. (Tonbridge): 1886–87–88–89 (Captain 1888)
Rawlinson, G. (Ealing): 1836
Rawlinson, H.T. (Eton): 1983–84
Raybould, J.G. (Leeds GS): 1959
Reade, H.St J. (Tonbridge): 1861–62 (Captain 1862)
Reid, R.T. (Cheltenham): 1866–67–68
Rice, R.W. (Cardiff): 1893
Richardson, J.V. (Uppingham): 1925
Ricketts, G.W. (Winchester): 1887
Ridding, A. (Winchester): 1846–47–48–49–50 (Captain 1849)
Ridding, C.H. (Winchester): 1845–46–47–48–49
Ridding, W. (Winchester): 1849–50–52–53 (Captain 1852)
*Ridding was also appointed captain in 1851, but was unable to play because of illness.*
Ridge, S.P. (Dr Challoner's GS, Amersham): 1982
Ridley, A.W. (Eton): 1872–73–74–75 (Captain 1875)
Ridley, G.N.S. (Milton HS, Rhodesia): 1965–66–67–68 (Captain 1967)
Ridley, R.M. (Clifton): 1968–69–70
Ridsdale, S.O.B. (Tonbridge): 1862

Robertson, G.P. (Rugby): 1866
Robertson, J.C. (Winchester): 1829
Robertson-Glasgow, R.C. (Charterhouse): 1920–21–22–23
Robinson, G.A. (Preston Catholic College): 1971
Robinson, G.E. (Burton): 1881–82–83
Robinson, H.B.O. (North Shore, Vancouver, Canada): 1947–48
Robinson, R.L. (St Peter's, Adelaide & Adelaide U., Australia): 1908–09
Rogers, J.J. (Sedbergh): 1979–80–81
Ross, C.J. (Wanganui Collegiate School & Wellington U., N.Z.): 1978–79–80 (Captain 1980)
Royle, V.P.F.A. (Rossall): 1875–76
Rucker, C.E.S. (Charterhouse): 1914
Rucker, P.W. (Charterhouse): 1919
Rudd, C.R.D. (Eton): 1949
Ruggles-Brise, H.G. (Winchester): 1883
Rumbold, J.S. (St Andrew's, Christchurch, N.Z.): 1946
Russell, H.S. (Harrow): 1839
Rutnagur, R.S. (Westminster): 1985
Ryle, J.C. (Eton): 1836–38

Sabine, P.N.B. (Marlborough): 1963
Sale, R., sr (Repton): 1910
Sale, R., jr (Repton): 1939–46
Salter, M.G. (Cheltenham): 1909–10
Samson, O.M. (Cheltenham): 1903
Sanderson, J.F.W. (Westminster): 1980
Sandford, E.G. (Rugby): 1859–61
Sankey, P.M. (King's, Canterbury): 1852
Saunders, C.J. (Lancing): 1964
Savage, R. le Q. (Marlborough): 1976–77–78
Savory, J.H. (Winchester): 1877–78
Sayer, D.M. (Maidstone GS): 1958–59–60
Schwann, H.S. (Clifton): 1890
Scott, Lord G. (Eton): 1887–88–89
Scott, J. (Bruce Castle): 1863
Scott, K.B. (Winchester): 1937
Scott, M.D. (Winchester): 1957
Scott, R.S.G. (Winchester): 1931
Seamer, J.W. (Marlborough): 1934–35–36
Seitz, J.A. (Geelong & Melbourne U., Australia): 1909
Shaw, E.A. (Marlborough): 1912–14
Shaw, E.D. (Forest): 1882
Sibthorpe, G.T.W. (Harrow): 1836
Simpson, E.T.B. (Harrow): 1888
Sinclair, E.H. (Winchester): 1924
Singleton, A.P. (Shrewsbury): 1934–35–36–37 (Captain 1937)
Siviter, K. (Liverpool): 1976
Skeet, C.H.L. (St Paul's): 1920
Skene, R.W. (Sedbergh): 1928
Smith, A.C. (King Edward's, Birmingham): 1958–59–60 (Captain 1959–60)
Smith, E. (Clifton): 1890–91
Smith, G.O. (Charterhouse): 1895–96
Smith, M.J.K. (Stamford): 1954–55–56 (Captain 1956)
Smith, V.S.C. (Winchester): 1844–45–46–47 (Captain 1846–47)
Soames, S. (Rugby): 1846–47
Spencer-Smith, O. (Eton): 1866
Spinks, T. (Merchant Taylors'): 1840
Stainton, R.G. (Malvern): 1933

Stallibrass, M.J.D. (Lancing): 1974
Stanning, J. (Winchester): 1939
Stephenson, J.S. (Shrewsbury): 1925–26
Stevens, G.T.S. (UCS, London): 1920–21–22–23 (Captain 1922)
Stewart, W.A. (Winchester): 1869–70
Stewart-Brown, P.H. (Harrow): 1925–26
Stocks, F.W. (Lancing & Denstone): 1898–99
Sutcliffe, S.P. (King George V GS, Southport): 1980–81
Sutton, M.A. (Ampleforth): 1946

Taswell, H.J. (Rugby): 1851
Tavaré, C.J. (Sevenoaks): 1975–76–77
Taylor, C.H. (Westminster): 1923–24–25–26
Taylor, T.J. (Stockport GS): 1981–82
Teape, A.S. (Eton): 1863–64–65
Teesdale, H. (Winchester): 1908
Thackeray, P.R. (St Edward's, Oxford & Exeter U.): 1974
Thesiger, Hon F.J.N. (Winchester): 1888–90 (Captain 1890)
*Thesiger (1st Viscount Chelmsford) retired hurt in the 1891 match, his place being taken by T.B. Case.*
Thomas, R.J.A. (Radley): 1965
Thorne, D.A. (Coventry School, Bablake): 1984–85
Thornton, W.A. (Winchester): 1879–80–81–82
Tindall, R.G. (Winchester): 1933–34
Toft, D.P. (Tonbridge): 1966–67
Toogood, G.J. (North Bromsgrove HS): 1982–83–84–85 (Captain 1983)
Tooley, C.D.M. (St Dunstan's): 1985
Topham, R.D.N. (Shrewsbury & Australian National U., Canberra): 1976
Torre, H.J. (Harrow): 1839–40
Townsend, D.C.H. (Winchester): 1933–34
Townsend, W.H. (Rugby): 1842–43
Townshend, W. (Rossall): 1870–71–72
Traill, W.F. (Merchant Taylors'): 1858–59–60
Travers, B.H. (Sydney U., Australia): 1946–48
Trevor, A.H. (Winchester): 1880–81
Tritton, E.W. (Eton): 1864–65–66–67 (Captain 1866)
Trower, C.F. (Winchester): 1838
Tuff, F.N. (Malvern): 1910
Twining, R.H. (Eton): 1910–11–12–13 (Captain 1912)
Tylecote, E.F.S. (Clifton): 1869–70–71–72 (Captain 1871–72)
Tylecote, H.G. (Clifton): 1874–75–76–77

Udal, N.R. (Winchester): 1905–06

Vance, G. (Eton): 1836–38
Van der Bijl, P.G. (Diocesan College, S.A.): 1932
Van Ryneveld, C.B. (Diocesan College, S.A.): 1948–49–50 (Captain 1949)
Varey, J.G. (Birkenhead): 1982–83
*His twin, D.W. Varey, gained blues for Cambridge 1982–83*
Veitch, H.G.J. (Twyford): 1854–55–56
Vidler, J.L.S. (Repton): 1910–11–12
Von Ernsthausen, A.C. (Uppingham): 1902–03–04
Voules, S.C. (Marlborough): 1863–64–65–66

Waddy, P.S. (King's School, Parramatta, Australia): 1896–97
Wagstaffe, M.C. (Rossall & Exeter U.): 1972
Waldock, F.A. (Uppingham): 1919–20
Walford, M.M. (Rugby): 1936–38
Walker, D.F. (Uppingham): 1933–34–35 (Captain 1935)
Walker, J.G. (Loretto): 1882–83
Walker, R.D. (Harrow): 1861–62–63–64–65
Wallace, A. (Winchester): 1851
Waller, G. de W. (Hurstpierpoint): 1974
Wallington, E.W. (Sherborne): 1877
Wallroth, C.A. (Harrow): 1872–73–74
Walsh, D.R. (Marlborough): 1967–68–69
Walshe, A.P. (Milton HS, Rhodesia): 1953–55–56
Walter, A.F. (Eton): 1869
Walton, A.C. (Radley): 1955–56–57 (Captain 1957)
Ward, H.P. (Shrewsbury): 1919–21
Ward, J.M. (Newcastle-under-Lyme HS): 1971–72–73
Ward, Lord (later Earl of Dudley) (Eton): 1841–42
Warner, P.F. (Rugby): 1895–96
Waters, R.H.C. (Shrewsbury) *was awarded a blue in 1961 but was unable to play in the University Match because of injuries sustained in a car accident.*
Watson, A.G.M. (St Lawrence): 1965–66–68
Watson, A.K. (Harrow): 1889
Watson, H.D. (Harrow): 1891
Waud, B.W. (Eton): 1857–58–59–60
Webb, H.E. (Winchester): 1948
Webbe, A.J. (Harrow): 1875–76–77–78 (Captain 1877–78)
Webbe, H.R. (Winchester): 1877–78–79 (Captain 1879)
Wellings, E.M. (Cheltenham): 1929–31
Westley, S.A. (Lancaster RGS): 1968–69
Wheatley, G.A. (Uppingham): 1946
Whitby, H.O. (Leamington): 1884–85–86–87
Whitcombe, P.A. (Winchester): 1947–48–49
Whitcombe, P.J. (Worcester RGS): 1951–52
White, H. (Denstone): 1900
Whitehouse, P.M. (Marlborough): 1938
Whiting, A.O. (Charterhouse & Sherborne): 1881–82

Wickham, A.P. (Marlborough): 1878
Wiley, W.G.A. (Diocesan College, S.A.): 1952
Wilkinson, W.A.C. (Eton): 1913
Willes, E.H.L. (Winchester): 1852–53–54 (Captain 1853–54)
Williams, C.C.P. (Westminster): 1953–54–55 (Captain 1955)
Williams, P. (Winchester): 1844–45–46–47
Williams, R.A. (Winchester): 1901–02
Willis, C.F. (Tonbridge): 1847–48–49
Wilson, A. (Rugby): 1848–49–50
Wilson, G.L. (Repton & Brighton): 1890–91
Wilson, P.R.B. (Milton HS, Rhodesia & Cape Town U, South Africa): 1968–70
Wilson, R.W. (Warwick): 1957
Wilson, T.S.B. (Bath): 1892–93
Wingfield Digby, A.R. (Sherborne): 1971–75–76–77
Winn, C.E. (KCS, Wimbledon): 1948–49–50–51
Wood, J.B. (Marlborough): 1892–93
Woodcock, R.G. (Worcester RGS): 1957–58
Wookey, S.M. (Malvern): 1978
*Gained blues for Cambridge 1975–76*
Wordsworth, Charles (Harrow): 1827–29 (Captain 1827–29)
Worsley, D.R. (Bolton): 1961–62–63–64 (Captain 1964)
Worthington, G. (Tonbridge): 1844
Wright, E.C. (Clergy Orphan School, Canterbury): 1897
Wright, E.L. (Winchester): 1905–06–07–08 (Captain 1907–08)
Wright, F.B. (Winchester): 1829
Wright, F.W. (Rossall): 1863–64–65
Wrigley, M.H. (Harrow): 1949
Wyatt, M.T.H. (Private): 1850–51 (Acting Captain 1851)
Wyld, H.J. (Harrow): 1901–02–03
Wynne, J.H.G. (Eton): 1839–40
Wynne-Finch, C.G. (Eton): 1836

Yonge, C.D. (Eton): 1836
Yonge, G.E. (Eton): 1844–45–46–47–48 (Captain 1848)
Young, D.E. (KCS, Wimbledon): 1938

# UNIVERSITY CRICKET RECORDS

These records do not include performances for combined Oxford and Cambridge University teams.

### 1000 RUNS IN A UNIVERSITY SEASON

|  |  | Season | I | NO | Runs | HS | Avge | 100 |
|---|---|---|---|---|---|---|---|---|
| D.S. Sheppard | Cambridge | 1952 | 23 | 3 | 1581 | 239* | 79.05 | 7 |
| A.R. Lewis | Cambridge | 1962 | 31 | 3 | 1365 | 148 | 48.75 | 3 |
| E.J. Craig | Cambridge | 1961 | 32 | 4 | 1342 | 208* | 47.92 | 5 |
| J.M. Brearley | Cambridge | 1964 | 26 | 3 | 1313 | 169 | 57.08 | 4 |
| R.M. Prideaux | Cambridge | 1960 | 34 | 0 | 1311 | 140 | 38.55 | 4 |
| Nawab of Pataudi sr | Oxford | 1931 | 16 | 2 | 1307 | 238* | 93.35 | 6 |
| A.R. Lewis | Cambridge | 1960 | 32 | 2 | 1307 | 125 | 43.56 | 2 |
| P.B.H. May | Cambridge | 1951 | 24 | 6 | 1286 | 178* | 71.44 | 4 |
| G.H.G. Doggart | Cambridge | 1949 | 24 | 5 | 1280 | 219* | 67.36 | 3 |
| J.G. Dewes | Cambridge | 1950 | 20 | 4 | 1262 | 212 | 78.87 | 5 |
| M.P. Donnelly | Oxford | 1946 | 22 | 2 | 1256 | 142 | 62.80 | 6 |
| E.R. Dexter | Cambridge | 1958 | 32 | 2 | 1256 | 114 | 41.86 | 3 |

| | | Seasons | I | NO | Runs | HS | Avge | 100 |
|---|---|---|---|---|---|---|---|---|
| Nawab of Pataudi jr | Oxford | 1961 | 24 | 2 | 1216 | 144 | 55.27 | 4 |
| Majid Khan | Cambridge | 1970 | 23 | 1 | 1216 | 200 | 55.27 | 5 |
| E.R. Dexter | Cambridge | 1957 | 32 | 1 | 1209 | 185 | 39.00 | 2 |
| J.G. Dewes | Cambridge | 1949 | 22 | 2 | 1175 | 204* | 58.75 | 1 |
| J.H. Human | Cambridge | 1934 | 21 | 3 | 1160 | 146* | 64.44 | 5 |
| J.M. Brearley | Cambridge | 1961 | 32 | 6 | 1158 | 145* | 44.53 | 2 |
| A.A. Baig | Oxford | 1959 | 29 | 4 | 1148 | 221* | 45.92 | 3 |
| M.P. Donnelly | Oxford | 1947 | 21 | 4 | 1144 | 154* | 67.29 | 3 |
| A.M. Crawley | Oxford | 1928 | 21 | 0 | 1137 | 167 | 54.14 | 5 |
| A.C. Walton | Oxford | 1956 | 29 | 2 | 1128 | 152 | 41.77 | 3 |
| M.C. Cowdrey | Oxford | 1953 | 24 | 2 | 1124 | 154 | 51.09 | 3 |
| F.C. de Saram | Oxford | 1934 | 23 | 1 | 1119 | 208 | 50.86 | 3 |
| E.J. Craig | Cambridge | 1962 | 31 | 1 | 1113 | 157* | 37.10 | 2 |
| G.D. Kemp-Welch | Cambridge | 1931 | 24 | 1 | 1111 | 126 | 48.30 | 3 |
| R.C. White | Cambridge | 1962 | 34 | 1 | 1103 | 125 | 33.42 | 2 |
| P.A. Gibb | Cambridge | 1938 | 17 | 1 | 1075 | 204 | 67.18 | 4 |
| T.C. Lowry | Cambridge | 1923 | 24 | 2 | 1077 | 161 | 48.95 | 4 |
| D.S. Sheppard | Cambridge | 1950 | 20 | 1 | 1072 | 227 | 56.42 | 4 |
| M.J.K. Smith | Oxford | 1954 | 26 | 4 | 1065 | 201* | 48.40 | 2 |
| M.B. Hofmeyr | Oxford | 1950 | 21 | 2 | 1063 | 162 | 55.94 | 4 |
| M.J.L. Turnbull | Cambridge | 1929 | 24 | 4 | 1001 | 167* | 50.05 | 3 |
| M.J.K. Smith | Oxford | 1956 | 27 | 2 | 1001 | 126 | 40.04 | 3 |

## 2000 RUNS IN A UNIVERSITY CAREER

| | | Seasons | I | NO | Runs | HS | Avge | 100 |
|---|---|---|---|---|---|---|---|---|
| J.M. Brearley | Cambridge | 1961–1968 | 125 | 13 | 4310 | 169 | 38.48 | 10 |
| D.S. Sheppard | Cambridge | 1950–1952 | 62 | 5 | 3545 | 239* | 62.19 | 14 |
| N.S. Mitchell-Innes | Oxford | 1934–1937 | 78 | 8 | 3319 | 207 | 47.41 | 9 |
| E.R. Dexter | Cambridge | 1956–1958 | 92 | 5 | 3298 | 185 | 37.90 | 7 |
| J.G. Dewes | Cambridge | 1948–1950 | 62 | 8 | 3247 | 212 | 60.12 | 7 |
| A.A. Baig | Oxford | 1959–1962 | 96 | 6 | 3182 | 221* | 35.35 | 6 |
| A.R. Lewis | Cambridge | 1960–1962 | 81 | 6 | 3167 | 148 | 42.22 | 6 |
| M.J.K. Smith | Oxford | 1954–1956 | 80 | 7 | 3049 | 201* | 41.76 | 8 |
| F.S. Goldstein | Oxford | 1966–1969 | 88 | 1 | 2964 | 155 | 34.06 | 1 |
| Nawab of Pataudi jr | Oxford | 1960–1963 | 75 | 6 | 2932 | 153 | 42.49 | 8 |
| A.M. Crawley | Oxford | 1927–1930 | 63 | 3 | 2914 | 204 | 48.56 | 9 |
| E.J. Craig | Cambridge | 1961–1963 | 78 | 6 | 2879 | 208* | 39.98 | 7 |
| P.B.H. May | Cambridge | 1950–1952 | 58 | 12 | 2861 | 227* | 62.19 | 9 |
| M.C. Cowdrey | Oxford | 1952–1954 | 70 | 5 | 2848 | 154 | 43.81 | 5 |
| Nawab of Pataudi sr | Oxford | 1928–1931 | 59 | 5 | 2744 | 238* | 50.81 | 9 |
| R.C. White | Cambridge | 1962–1965 | 96 | 2 | 2715 | 151 | 28.88 | 3 |
| R.M. Prideaux | Cambridge | 1958–1960 | 92 | 5 | 2684 | 143 | 30.85 | 6 |
| G.H.G. Doggart | Cambridge | 1948–1950 | 56 | 9 | 2599 | 219* | 55.29 | 7 |
| E.W. Dawson | Cambridge | 1924–1927 | 87 | 4 | 2581 | 140 | 31.09 | 4 |
| D.R. Worsley | Oxford | 1961–1964 | 97 | 2 | 2554 | 139 | 26.88 | 2 |
| Majid Khan | Cambridge | 1970–1972 | 52 | 4 | 2545 | 200 | 53.02 | 9 |
| E.T. Killick | Cambridge | 1927–1930 | 59 | 3 | 2534 | 201 | 45.25 | 8 |
| M.B. Hofmeyr | Oxford | 1949–1951 | 65 | 8 | 2495 | 161 | 43.77 | 5 |
| G.T.S. Stevens | Oxford | 1920–1923 | 72 | 8 | 2484 | 182 | 38.81 | 2 |
| R.D.V. Knight | Cambridge | 1967–1970 | 90 | 5 | 2428 | 164* | 28.56 | 2 |
| R.C.M. Kimpton | Oxford | 1935–1938 | 68 | 7 | 2412 | 160 | 39.54 | 5 |
| M.P. Donnelly | Oxford | 1946–1947 | 43 | 6 | 2400 | 154* | 64.86 | 9 |
| K.S. Duleepsinhji | Cambridge | 1925–1928 | 57 | 4 | 2333 | 254* | 44.02 | 5 |
| G. Goonesena | Cambridge | 1954–1957 | 87 | 8 | 2309 | 211 | 29.22 | 2 |
| C.C.P. Williams | Oxford | 1952–1955 | 75 | 4 | 2301 | 139* | 32.40 | 4 |
| M.A. Eagar | Oxford | 1956–1959 | 93 | 8 | 2298 | 125 | 27.03 | 1 |
| Javed Burki | Oxford | 1958–1960 | 78 | 9 | 2272 | 144* | 32.92 | 5 |
| H. Ashton | Cambridge | 1920–1922 | 43 | 8 | 2258 | 236 | 64.51 | 7 |
| A.C. Walton | Oxford | 1955–1957 | 80 | 2 | 2254 | 152 | 28.89 | 3 |
| D.R. Owen-Thomas | Cambridge | 1969–1972 | 66 | 6 | 2214 | 182* | 37.86 | 5 |
| J.H. Human | Cambridge | 1932–1934 | 48 | 8 | 2205 | 158* | 55.12 | 10 |
| D.B. Carr | Oxford | 1948–1951 | 67 | 4 | 2200 | 170 | 34.92 | 5 |
| P.A. Gibb | Cambridge | 1935–1938 | 73 | 8 | 2199 | 204 | 33.83 | 5 |
| F.G.H. Chalk | Oxford | 1931–1934 | 77 | 7 | 2141 | 149 | 30.58 | 6 |

| | | Seasons | I | NO | Runs | HS | Avge | 100 |
|---|---|---|---|---|---|---|---|---|
| N.F. Druce | Cambridge | 1894–1897 | 51 | 4 | 2121 | 227* | 45.12 | 7 |
| N.W.D. Yardley | Cambridge | 1935–1938 | 77 | 5 | 2099 | 116* | 29.15 | 4 |
| R.J. Boyd-Moss | Cambridge | 1980–1983 | 65 | 2 | 2090 | 139 | 33.17 | 5 |
| R.A. Hutton | Cambridge | 1962–1964 | 82 | 7 | 2026 | 163* | 27.01 | 1 |
| H.J. Enthoven | Cambridge | 1923–1926 | 68 | 8 | 2024 | 129 | 33.73 | 2 |
| N.M. Ford | Oxford | 1928–1930 | 62 | 8 | 2016 | 183 | 37.33 | 5 |

## HIGHEST INDIVIDUAL SCORES

| | | | | | | |
|---|---|---|---|---|---|---|
| Oxford | 281 | K.J. Key | Middlesex | Chiswick Park | | 1887 |
| Cambridge | 254* | K.S. Duleepsinhji | Middlesex | Cambridge | | 1927 |

## MOST WICKETS IN A UNIVERSITY SEASON

| | | Season | Overs | Mdns | Runs | Wkts | Avge |
|---|---|---|---|---|---|---|---|
| O.S. Wheatley | Cambridge | 1958 | 578.1 | 149 | 1411 | 80 | 17.63 |
| A.G. Steel | Cambridge | 1878 | 456 | 212 | 557 | 75 | 7.42 |
| I.A.R. Peebles | Oxford | 1930 | 442.2 | 77 | 1271 | 70 | 18.15 |
| C.M. Sharpe | Cambridge | 1875 | 546.3 | 168 | 848 | 66 | 12.84 |
| F.R. Brown | Cambridge | 1931 | 499.2 | 104 | 1461 | 66 | 22.13 |
| C.W. Rock | Cambridge | 1886 | 696.2 | 326 | 868 | 65 | 13.35 |
| E.M. Dowson | Cambridge | 1902 | 420.3 | 95 | 1174 | 65 | 18.06 |
| D.M. Sayer | Oxford | 1959 | 509.2 | 103 | 1470 | 64 | 22.96 |
| D.M. Sayer | Oxford | 1958 | 408.4 | 129 | 831 | 62 | 13.40 |
| R.H.B. Bettington | Oxford | 1923 | 303.4 | 60 | 1010 | 61 | 16.55 |
| R.G. Marlar | Cambridge | 1953 | 610.1 | 172 | 1619 | 61 | 26.54 |
| S.M.J. Woods | Cambridge | 1888 | 500 | 176 | 990 | 60 | 16.50 |
| F.H.E. Cunliffe | Oxford | 1896 | 471.4 | 168 | 984 | 60 | 16.40 |
| M.J.C. Allom | Cambridge | 1927 | 465.5 | 95 | 1345 | 60 | 22.41 |
| G. Goonesena | Cambridge | 1955 | 520.2 | 140 | 1290 | 60 | 21.50 |
| C.D. Drybrough | Oxford | 1961 | 710.5 | 247 | 1667 | 60 | 27.78 |
| P.R. le Couteur | Oxford | 1910 | 243.4 | 39 | 845 | 59 | 14.32 |
| A. Hurd | Cambridge | 1960 | 723.2 | 214 | 1883 | 59 | 31.91 |
| R.C. Ramsay | Cambridge | 1882 | 534 | 215 | 856 | 58 | 14.75 |
| A. Hurd | Cambridge | 1959 | 714.2 | 217 | 1888 | 58 | 32.58 |
| F.S. Jackson | Cambridge | 1892 | 327.2 | 98 | 829 | 57 | 14.54 |
| H.A. Gilbert | Oxford | 1909 | 350.5 | 112 | 756 | 57 | 13.26 |
| C.S. Marriott | Cambridge | 1921 | 443.3 | 128 | 1064 | 57 | 18.66 |
| G. Goonesena | Cambridge | 1954 | 587.3 | 170 | 1336 | 57 | 23.43 |
| G.G. Napier | Cambridge | 1905 | 338.1 | 75 | 973 | 56 | 17.37 |
| R.H.B. Bettington | Oxford | 1920 | 292.3 | 65 | 847 | 56 | 15.12 |
| P.A. Wright | Cambridge | 1924 | 394.2 | 127 | 888 | 56 | 15.85 |
| R.F.H. Darwall-Smith | Oxford | 1937 | 394.3 | 77 | 1102 | 56 | 19.67 |

## HUNDRED WICKETS IN A UNIVERSITY CAREER

| | | Career | Runs | Wkts | Avge |
|---|---|---|---|---|---|
| G. Goonesena | Cambridge | 1954–1957 | 4540 | 208 | 21.82 |
| G.G. Napier | Cambridge | 1904–1907 | 3904 | 205 | 19.04 |
| A.G. Steel | Cambridge | 1878–1881 | 2202 | 198 | 11.12 |
| S.M.J. Woods | Cambridge | 1888–1891 | 2838 | 190 | 14.93 |
| E.M. Dowson | Cambridge | 1900–1903 | 4656 | 186 | 25.03 |
| R.H.B. Bettington | Oxford | 1920–1923 | 3528 | 182 | 19.38 |
| J.J. Warr | Cambridge | 1949–1952 | 3562 | 169 | 21.07 |
| C.S. Smith | Cambridge | 1954–1957 | 4277 | 160 | 26.73 |
| P.A. Wright | Cambridge | 1922–1924 | 2910 | 157 | 18.53 |
| A. Hurd | Cambridge | 1958–1960 | 5012 | 156 | 32.12 |
| F.S. Jackson | Cambridge | 1890–1893 | 2713 | 153 | 17.73 |
| J.M. Allan | Oxford | 1953–1956 | 3935 | 151 | 26.05 |
| J.D. Piachaud | Oxford | 1958–1961 | 3763 | 149 | 25.25 |
| R.G. Marlar | Cambridge | 1951–1953 | 4100 | 147 | 27.89 |
| G.T.S. Stevens | Oxford | 1920–1923 | 2907 | 146 | 19.91 |
| R.C. Robertson-Glasgow | Oxford | 1920–1923 | 3077 | 146 | 21.07 |
| D.M. Sayer | Oxford | 1958–1960 | 3093 | 146 | 21.18 |

| | | Career | Runs | Wkts | Avge |
|---|---|---|---|---|---|
| F.H.E. Cunliffe | Oxford | 1895–1897 | 2752 | 143 | 19.24 |
| E.R. Wilson | Cambridge | 1899–1902 | 3177 | 142 | 22.37 |
| H.A. Gilbert | Oxford | 1907–1909 | 2341 | 142 | 16.48 |
| R.F.H. Darwall-Smith | Oxford | 1935–1938 | 3767 | 140 | 26.90 |
| Jahangir Khan | Cambridge | 1933–1936 | 3414 | 134 | 25.47 |
| R.J.O. Meyer | Cambridge | 1924–1926 | 3148 | 133 | 23.66 |
| T.B. Raikes | Oxford | 1922–1925 | 3305 | 132 | 25.03 |
| C.K.H. Hill-Wood | Oxford | 1928–1930 | 3991 | 132 | 30.23 |
| A.P. Singleton | Oxford | 1934–1937 | 4029 | 132 | 30.52 |
| C.T. Studd | Cambridge | 1880–1883 | 2119 | 130 | 16.30 |
| G.L. Jessop | Cambridge | 1896–1899 | 2729 | 127 | 21.48 |
| A.H. Kardar | Oxford | 1947–1949 | 2174 | 124 | 17.53 |
| R.V. Divecha | Oxford | 1948–1951 | 2818 | 121 | 23.28 |
| O.S. Wheatley | Cambridge | 1957–1958 | 2651 | 121 | 21.90 |
| G.N.S. Ridley | Oxford | 1965–1968 | 2889 | 121 | 23.87 |
| W.H.B. Evans | Oxford | 1902–1905 | 2382 | 120 | 19.85 |
| H.J. Enthoven | Cambridge | 1923–1926 | 2726 | 118 | 23.10 |
| D.C.P.R. Jowett | Oxford | 1952–1955 | 3800 | 118 | 32.20 |
| J.A. Bailey | Oxford | 1956–1958 | 2409 | 118 | 20.41 |
| R.A. Hutton | Cambridge | 1962–1964 | 3260 | 118 | 27.62 |
| H.C. McDonell | Cambridge | 1902–1905 | 2358 | 117 | 20.15 |
| Hon F.S.G. Calthorpe | Cambridge | 1912–1919 | 2694 | 117 | 23.02 |
| C.W. Rock | Cambridge | 1884–1886 | 1781 | 116 | 15.35 |
| P.R. May | Cambridge | 1903–1906 | 2792 | 115 | 24.27 |
| J.W. Greenstock | Oxford | 1925–1927 | 2675 | 113 | 23.67 |
| K. Farnes | Cambridge | 1931–1933 | 2292 | 113 | 20.28 |
| A.J.G. Pearson | Cambridge | 1961–1963 | 3411 | 113 | 30.18 |
| H.G. Owen-Smith | Oxford | 1931–1933 | 2518 | 112 | 22.48 |
| B.J.T. Bosanquet | Oxford | 1898–1900 | 2183 | 112 | 19.49 |
| M.J.C. Allom | Cambridge | 1926–1928 | 2506 | 111 | 22.57 |
| V.R. Price | Oxford | 1919–1922 | 2806 | 109 | 25.74 |
| P.R. le Couteur | Oxford | 1909–1911 | 1747 | 108 | 16.17 |
| A.J. Corran | Oxford | 1958–1960 | 2213 | 108 | 20.49 |
| C.S. Marriott | Cambridge | 1920–1921 | 1743 | 107 | 16.28 |
| C.A. Absolom | Cambridge | 1866–1869 | 1554 | 107 | 14.52 |
| E.G. Martin | Oxford | 1903–1906 | 2369 | 105 | 22.56 |
| J.C.M. Lowe | Oxford | 1907–1910 | 2725 | 105 | 25.95 |
| R.C. Rought-Rought | Cambridge | 1930–1932 | 2294 | 105 | 21.84 |
| W.S. Patterson | Cambridge | 1874–1877 | 1681 | 104 | 16.16 |
| C.E.M. Wilson | Cambridge | 1895–1898 | 1918 | 104 | 18.44 |
| R.C.W. Burn | Oxford | 1902–1905 | 2774 | 104 | 26.67 |
| J.H.B. Lockhart | Cambridge | 1909–1911 | 2101 | 103 | 20.39 |
| C.D. Drybrough | Oxford | 1960–1962 | 3302 | 103 | 32.05 |
| E.D. Blundell | Cambridge | 1928–1929 | 2336 | 102 | 22.90 |
| H.M. Plowden | Cambridge | 1860–1863 | 1144 | 101 | 11.32 |
| A.R. Windows | Cambridge | 1962–1964 | 3295 | 101 | 32.62 |
| F.G.J. Ford | Cambridge | 1887–1890 | 2020 | 100 | 20.20 |
| F.R. Brown | Cambridge | 1930–1932 | 2343 | 100 | 23.43 |

**BEST INDIVIDUAL ANALYSES**

| INNINGS | | | Opponents | | |
|---|---|---|---|---|---|
| Oxford | 10-38 | S.E. Butler | Cambridge University | Lord's | 1871 |
| Cambridge | 10-69 | S.M.J. Woods | C.I. Thornton's XI | Cambridge | 1890 |

| MATCH | | | | | |
|---|---|---|---|---|---|
| Oxford | 15-65 | B.J.T. Bosanquet | Sussex | Oxford | 1900 |
| Cambridge | 15-88 | S.M.J. Woods | C.I. Thornton's XI | Cambridge | 1890 |

# GENTLEMEN v PLAYERS MATCHES

This series of matches between amateurs and professionals began in 1806 and ended with the abolition of amateur status in first-class cricket after the 1962 season.

Before Test matches became annual events the highlight of the English season was the Lord's match between the Gentlemen and the Players. The MCC selected the teams for the fixture at Lord's, and an invitation to play was regarded as an honour equal almost to the award of an England cap. Until 1952, when the first professional England captain of modern times (L. Hutton) was appointed, captaincy of the Players was the greatest honour available to a professional cricketer. Eventually the match at Lord's became almost a Test trial.

For many years additional matches in this series were played at Kennington Oval and during the Scarborough Festival. In 1919, J.B. Hobbs scored a hundred in each of the three fixtures. Other matches were occasionally staged under this title at Blackpool, Bournemouth, Folkestone, Hastings, Hove and Prince's.

## HIGHEST INDIVIDUAL INNINGS

| 266* | J.B. Hobbs | Players | Scarborough | 1925 |
|------|------------|---------|-------------|------|
| 247 | R. Abel | Players | Oval | 1901 |
| 241 | L. Hutton | Players | Scarborough | 1951 |
| 232* | C.B. Fry | Gentlemen | Lord's | 1903 |
| 223 | C.P. Mead | Players | Scarborough | 1913 |
| 217 | W.G. Grace | Gentlemen | Hove | 1873 |
| 215 | W.G. Grace | Gentlemen | Oval | 1870 |
| 203 | T.W. Hayward | Players | Oval | 1904 |
| 201 | L.E.G. Ames | Players | Folkestone | 1933 |

## HIGHEST INNINGS TOTALS

| 651-7d | Players | Oval | 1934 |
|--------|---------|------|------|
| 647 | Players | Oval | 1899 |
| 608-8d | Players | Oval | 1921 |
| 579 | Players | Lord's | 1926 |
| 578 | Gentlemen | Oval | 1904 |
| 561-6d | Players | Folkestone | 1927 |
| 552-8d | Players | Folkestone | 1933 |

## LOWEST INNINGS TOTALS

| 24 | Players | Lord's | 1829 |
|----|---------|--------|------|
| 31 | Gentlemen | Lord's | 1848 |
| 35 | Gentlemen | Lord's | 1837 |
| 36 | Gentlemen | Lord's | 1831 |
| 37 | Players | Lord's | 1829 |
| 37 | Gentlemen | Lord's | 1853 |
| 39 | Gentlemen | Lord's | 1840 |

## RESULTS OF MATCHES AT LORD'S

137 matches were played at Lord's between 1806 and 1962. The Players won 68, the Gentlemen won 41 and 28 were drawn.

RESULTS 1919 to 1962:

| | | | Captain | |
|--------|--------|--------|-----------|---------|
| Season | Result | | Gentlemen | Players |
| 1919 | Drawn | | P.F. Warner | G.H. Hirst |
| 1920 | Players: | 7 wickets | J.W.H.T. Douglas | W. Rhodes |
| 1921 | Players: | 9 wickets | Hon L.H. Tennyson | W. Rhodes |
| 1922 | Drawn | | F.T. Mann | J.B. Hobbs |
| 1923 | Drawn | | F.T. Mann | J.B. Hobbs |
| 1924 | Players: | innings & 231 runs | A.E.R. Gilligan | J.B. Hobbs |
| 1925 | Drawn | | A.W. Carr | J.B. Hobbs |
| 1926 | Drawn | | A.W. Carr | J.B. Hobbs |
| 1927 | Drawn | | A.P.F. Chapman | F.E. Woolley |
| 1928 | Players: | 9 wickets | A.P.F. Chapman | F.E. Woolley |
| 1929 | Players: | 7 wickets | J.C. White | F.E. Woolley |
| 1930 | Drawn | | A.P.F. Chapman | J.B. Hobbs |
| 1931 | Drawn | | D.R. Jardine | H. Sutcliffe |
| 1932 | Drawn | | D.R. Jardine | J.B. Hobbs |
| 1933 | Players: | 10 wickets | D.R. Jardine | H. Sutcliffe |
| 1934 | Gentlemen: | 7 wickets | R.E.S. Wyatt | E.H. Hendren |
| 1935 | Players: | 9 wickets | R.E.S. Wyatt | W.R. Hammond |
| 1936 | Drawn | | G.O.B. Allen | W.R. Hammond |
| 1937 | Players: | 8 wickets | A.B. Sellers | W.R. Hammond |

|          |          |                  | Captain          |                  |
| Season   | Result   |                  | Gentlemen        | Players          |
|----------|----------|------------------|------------------|------------------|
| 1938     | Gentlemen: | 133 runs       | W.R. Hammond     | F.E. Woolley     |
| 1939     | Players: | 160 runs         | W.R. Hammond     | E. Paynter       |
| 1946     | Players: | innings & 140 runs | W.R. Hammond   | J. Hardstaff, jr |
| 1947     | Drawn    |                  | N.W.D. Yardley   | L.E.G. Ames      |
| 1948     | Players: | 7 wickets        | N.W.D. Yardley   | L. Hutton        |
| 1949     | Players: | 4 wickets        | F.G. Mann        | D.C.S. Compton   |
| 1950     | Drawn    |                  | F.R. Brown       | H.E. Dollery     |
| 1951     | Players: | 21 runs          | N.D. Howard      | D.C.S. Compton   |
| 1952     | Players: | 2 runs           | F.R. Brown       | L. Hutton        |
| 1953     | Gentlemen: | 95 runs        | F.R. Brown       | C. Washbrook     |
| 1954     | Players: | 49 runs          | D.S. Sheppard    | D.C.S. Compton   |
| 1955     | Players: | 20 runs          | D.J. Insole      | A.V. Bedser      |
| 1956     | Drawn    |                  | C.H. Palmer      | C. Washbrook     |
| 1957     | Drawn    |                  | P.B.H. May       | D.C.S. Compton   |
| 1958     | Drawn    |                  | D.J. Insole      | T.G. Evans       |
| 1959     | Drawn    |                  | P.B.H. May       | D. Brookes       |
| 1960     | Drawn    |                  | M.C. Cowdrey     | J.B. Statham     |
| 1961     | Players: | 172 runs         | P.B.H. May       | W. Watson        |
| 1962     | Drawn    |                  | E.R. Dexter      | F.S. Trueman     |

# AUSTRALIA

## THE SHEFFIELD SHIELD

Although the first inter-colonial match to be accorded first-class status by modern statisticians took place in 1850–51, no regular competition existed when the Earl of Sheffield toured Australia in 1891–92 with a team captained by W.G. Grace. This visit was so enthusiastically received that the Earl donated 150 guineas for the promotion of cricket in Australia. The newly-formed Australian Cricket Council instituted a Shield to be competed for by the three leading cricket colonies in an annual championship which began the following season.

New South Wales, Victoria and South Australia contested the Shield until 1926–27 when Queensland were admitted, and from which time all matches were played on a time basis instead of to a finish as previously. Western Australia were admitted on an experimental basis in 1947–48, playing the other states once only. Although they won the Shield in their first season, they were not admitted to full membership until 1956–57. Tasmania were admitted on a similar experimental basis in 1977–78, playing the other states once only each season until becoming fully integrated in 1982–83. Since that season the competition has been decided by a final between the first two teams in the Shield table.

HOLDERS

| 1892–93 | Victoria        | 1919–20 | New South Wales   |
|---------|-----------------|---------|-------------------|
| 1893–94 | South Australia | 1920–21 | New South Wales   |
| 1894–95 | Victoria        | 1921–22 | Victoria          |
| 1895–96 | New South Wales | 1922–23 | New South Wales   |
| 1896–97 | New South Wales | 1923–24 | Victoria          |
| 1897–98 | Victoria        | 1924–25 | Victoria          |
| 1898–99 | Victoria        | 1925–26 | New South Wales   |
| 1899–00 | New South Wales | 1926–27 | South Australia   |
| 1900–01 | Victoria        | 1927–28 | Victoria          |
| 1901–02 | New South Wales | 1928–29 | New South Wales   |
| 1902–03 | New South Wales | 1929–30 | Victoria          |
| 1903–04 | New South Wales | 1930–31 | Victoria          |
| 1904–05 | New South Wales | 1931–32 | New South Wales   |
| 1905–06 | New South Wales | 1932–33 | New South Wales   |
| 1906–07 | New South Wales | 1933–34 | Victoria          |
| 1907–08 | Victoria        | 1934–35 | Victoria          |
| 1908–09 | New South Wales | 1935–36 | South Australia   |
| 1909–10 | South Australia | 1936–37 | Victoria          |
| 1910–11 | New South Wales | 1937–38 | New South Wales   |
| 1911–12 | New South Wales | 1938–39 | South Australia   |
| 1912–13 | South Australia | 1939–40 | New South Wales   |
| 1913–14 | New South Wales | 1940–46 | No competition    |
| 1914–15 | Victoria        | 1946–47 | Victoria          |
| 1915–19 | No competition  | 1947–48 | Western Australia |

| | | | | |
|---|---|---|---|---|
| 1948–49 | New South Wales | | 1967–68 | Western Australia |
| 1949–50 | New South Wales | | 1968–69 | South Australia |
| 1950–51 | Victoria | | 1969–70 | Victoria |
| 1951–52 | New South Wales | | 1970–71 | South Australia |
| 1952–53 | South Australia | | 1971–72 | Western Australia |
| 1953–54 | New South Wales | | 1972–73 | Western Australia |
| 1954–55 | New South Wales | | 1973–74 | Victoria |
| 1955–56 | New South Wales | | 1974–75 | Western Australia |
| 1956–57 | New South Wales | | 1975–76 | South Australia |
| 1957–58 | New South Wales | | 1976–77 | Western Australia |
| 1958–59 | New South Wales | | 1977–78 | Western Australia |
| 1959–60 | New South Wales | | 1978–79 | Victoria |
| 1960–61 | New South Wales | | 1979–80 | Victoria |
| 1961–62 | New South Wales | | 1980–81 | Western Australia |
| 1962–63 | Victoria | | 1981–82 | South Australia |
| 1963–64 | South Australia | | 1982–83 | New South Wales |
| 1964–65 | New South Wales | | 1983–84 | Western Australia |
| 1965–66 | New South Wales | | 1984–85 | New South Wales |
| 1966–67 | Victoria | | | |

Wins:     New South Wales 38,     Victoria 24,     South Australia 12,     Western Australia 9.

**RESULTS SUMMARY 1892–93 to 1984–85**

| | *First Match* | P | W | L | D | T |
|---|---|---|---|---|---|---|
| New South Wales | 1892–93 | 513 | 240 | 130 | 142 | 1 |
| Victoria | 1892–93 | 507 | 204 | 152 | 150 | 1 |
| South Australia | 1892–93 | 507 | 149 | 236 | 121 | 1 |
| Queensland | 1926–27 | 391 | 91 | 156 | 143 | 1 |
| Western Australia | 1947–48 | 279 | 91 | 85 | 103 | — |
| Tasmania | 1977–78 | 55 | 5 | 21 | 29 | — |
| | | 2252 | 780 | 780 | 688 | 4 |

*Matches abandoned without a ball being bowled are excluded.*

# SOUTH AFRICA

### THE CURRIE CUP

This trophy was donated by Sir Donald Currie, head of the Castle Mail Packets Company whose ship brought the first English team to South Africa in 1888, as a Challenge Cup to be awarded first to the team which excelled most against the pioneer tourists and thereafter to be competed for by the provinces. It was duly presented to Kimberley (later to be renamed Griqualand West) but they lost the inaugural Currie Cup match the following season against their sole challengers, the Transvaal, who thus became the first winners of the competition.

Until 1966–67 the Currie Cup competition was not normally held when a touring team visited South Africa, occasional friendly inter-provincial matches being played instead.

In 1951–52 the teams were divided into two sections (A: Eastern Province, Natal, Transvaal and Western Province; B: Border, Griqualand West, North-Eastern Transvaal, Orange Free State and Rhodesia) and a system of promotion and relegation instituted. The two-section tournament was abandoned in 1960–61 but was resumed when the competition was next held, in 1962–63. The number of teams in each section has varied as B (2nd) teams were ineligible for promotion and A (1st) teams could not be relegated.

As a result of sponsorship the competition amended its name to the South African Breweries Currie Cup from 1972–73 to 1975–76 and again in 1979–80, and to the Castle Currie Cup from 1976–77 to 1978–79 and from 1983–84 to date.

The B Section competition was renamed the Castle Bowl in 1977–78, after the trophy presented by South African Breweries, and its number of teams increased to nine by the admission of B sides from Eastern Province and Rhodesia. Since 1980–81 it has been the SAB Bowl. In 1978–79 the five B teams played in a separate league known as the President's Competition, but this arrangement was shelved after one season.

Rhodesia, who played as 'Zimbabwe-Rhodesia' in 1979–80, withdrew from both competitions when that country became independent Zimbabwe in 1980.

## HOLDERS

| | | | |
|---|---|---|---|
| 1889–90 | Transvaal | 1951–52 | Natal |
| 1890–91 | Kimberley | 1952–53 | Western Province |
| 1892–93 | Western Province | 1954–55 | Natal |
| 1893–94 | Western Province | 1955–56 | Western Province |
| 1894–95 | Transvaal | 1958–59 | Transvaal |
| 1896–97 | Western Province | 1959–60 | Natal |
| 1897–98 | Western Province | 1960–61 | Natal |
| 1902–03 | Transvaal | 1962–63 | Natal |
| 1903–04 | Transvaal | 1963–64 | Natal |
| 1904–05 | Transvaal | 1965–66 { | Natal |
| 1906–07 | Transvaal | | Transvaal |
| 1908–09 | Western Province | 1966–67 | Natal |
| 1910–11 | Natal | 1967–68 | Natal |
| 1912–13 | Natal | 1968–69 | Transvaal |
| 1920–21 | Western Province | 1969–70 { | Transvaal |
| 1921–22 { | Natal | | Western Province |
| | Transvaal | 1970–71 | Transvaal |
| | Western Province | 1971–72 | Transvaal |
| 1923–24 | Transvaal | 1972–73 | Transvaal |
| 1925–26 | Transvaal | 1973–74 | Natal |
| 1926–27 | Transvaal | 1974–75 | Western Province |
| 1929–30 | Transvaal | 1975–76 | Natal |
| 1931–32 | Western Province | 1976–77 | Natal |
| 1933–34 | Natal | 1977–78 | Western Province |
| 1934–35 | Transvaal | 1978–79 | Transvaal |
| 1936–37 | Natal | 1979–80 | Transvaal |
| 1937–38 { | Natal | 1980–81 | Natal |
| | Transvaal | 1981–82 | Western Province |
| 1946–47 | Natal | 1982–83 | Transvaal |
| 1947–48 | Natal | 1983–84 | Transvaal |
| 1950–51 | Transvaal | 1984–85 | Transvaal |

Outright wins: Transvaal 22, Natal 18, Western Province 12, Kimberley (now Griqualand West) 1.
Shared wins: Transvaal 4, Natal 3, Western Province 2.

## SECTION B WINNERS (CASTLE BOWL from 1977–78)

| | | | |
|---|---|---|---|
| 1951–52 | Orange Free State | 1971–72 | Northern Transvaal |
| 1952–53 | Transvaal | 1972–73 | Transvaal B |
| 1954–55 | Eastern Province | 1973–74 | Natal B |
| 1955–56 | Rhodesia | 1974–75 | Transvaal B |
| 1958–59 | Border | 1975–76 | Orange Free State |
| 1959–60 { | Eastern Province | 1976–77 | Transvaal B |
| | Transvaal B | 1977–78 | Northern Transvaal |
| 1962–63 | Transvaal B | 1978–79 | Northern Transvaal |
| 1963–64 | Rhodesia | 1979–80 | Natal B |
| 1965–66 | North-Eastern Transvaal | 1980–81 | Western Province B |
| 1966–67 | North-Eastern Transvaal | 1981–82 | Boland |
| 1967–68 | Rhodesia | 1982–83 | Western Province B |
| 1968–69 | Western Province | 1983–84 | Western Province B |
| 1969–70 | Transvaal B | 1984–85 | Transvaal B |
| 1970–71 | Rhodesia | | |

## PRESIDENT'S COMPETITION WINNER

1978–79   Transvaal B

## RESULTS SUMMARY 1889–90 to 1984–85

| | First Match | P | W | L | D | T |
|---|---|---|---|---|---|---|
| Boland | 1980–81 | 31 | 12 | 10 | 9 | — |
| Border | 1897–98 | 250 | 77 | 115 | 58 | — |
| Eastern Province | 1893–94 | 286 | 64 | 133 | 88 | 1 |
| Eastern Province B | 1977–78 | 44 | 7 | 19 | 18 | — |
| Griqualand West (Kimberley) | 1889–90 | 264 | 39 | 150 | 75 | — |
| Natal | 1893–94 | 302 | 145 | 59 | 98 | — |
| Natal B | 1965–66 | 107 | 34 | 29 | 44 | — |
| Northern (N-E) Transvaal | 1937–38 | 196 | 55 | 79 | 62 | — |

|                        | First-Match | P    | W   | L   | D   | T |
|------------------------|-------------|------|-----|-----|-----|---|
| Northern Transvaal B   | 1981–82     | 24   | 9   | 8   | 7   | — |
| Orange Free State      | 1903–04     | 256  | 63  | 126 | 66  | 1 |
| Rhodesia (Zimbabwe)    | 1904–05     | 183  | 58  | 64  | 61  | — |
| Rhodesia (Zimbabwe) B  | 1977–78     | 14   | 2   | 8   | 4   | — |
| South-Western Districts| 1904–05     | 1    | —   | 1   | —   | — |
| Transvaal              | 1889–90     | 321  | 175 | 45  | 101 | — |
| Transvaal B            | 1959–60     | 132  | 67  | 34  | 31  | — |
| Western Province       | 1892–93     | 309  | 137 | 86  | 86  | — |
| Western Province B     | 1975–76     | 58   | 32  | 10  | 16  | — |
|                        |             | 2778 | 976 | 976 | 824 | 2 |

*Matches abandoned without a ball being bowled are excluded.*

# WEST INDIES

Administrators of West Indian domestic cricket have always been hampered by the immense distances separating the various countries. Although most tournaments in the Caribbean have been failures financially, there is always the need to maintain playing interest throughout the region and to develop prospective candidates for Test selection.

Until 1963–64, the countries had either met at one centre and played a knock-out tournament, or two countries had held private two-match series, or two matches had been played at two different venues simultaneously.

### INTER-COLONIAL TOURNAMENT

Coming under the first of the categories mentioned above, this was a triangular knock-out tournament between Barbados, Demerara (later to compete as British Guiana), and Trinidad (distant Jamaica not competing) played on each home ground in turn. Although Barbados beat Trinidad in 1891–92, Demerara did not compete and the tournament is not considered to have been inaugurated until the following season. It continued until the last war but was not resumed afterwards.

WINNERS

| | | | | | |
|---|---|---|---|---|---|
| 1892–93 | Barbados | Port-of-Spain | 1923–24 | Barbados | Bridgetown |
| 1895–96 | Demerara | Georgetown | 1924–25 | Trinidad | Port-of-Spain |
| 1897–98 | Barbados | Bridgetown | 1925–26 | Trinidad | Georgetown |
| 1899–00 | Barbados | Port-of-Spain | 1926–27 | Barbados | Bridgetown |
| 1901–02 | Trinidad | Georgetown | 1928–29 | Trinidad | Port-of-Spain |
| 1903–04 | Trinidad | Bridgetown | 1929–30 | British Guiana | Georgetown |
| 1905–06 | Barbados | Port-of-Spain | 1931–32 | Trinidad | Bridgetown |
| 1907–08 | Trinidad | Georgetown | 1933–34 | Trinidad | Port-of-Spain |
| 1908–09 | Barbados | Bridgetown | 1934–35 | British Guiana | Georgetown |
| 1909–10 | Trinidad | Port-of-Spain | 1935–36 | British Guiana | Bridgetown |
| 1910–11 | Barbados | Georgetown | 1936–37 | Trinidad | Port-of-Spain |
| 1911–12 | Barbados | Bridgetown | 1937–38 | British Guiana | Georgetown |
| 1921–22 | No result | Port-of-Spain | 1938–39 | Trinidad | Bridgetown |
| 1922–23 | Barbados | Georgetown | | | |

### 1956–57 QUADRANGULAR TOURNAMENT

For the first time all four major countries met in a knock-out tournament held at one venue – Georgetown.
Final: British Guiana beat Barbados on first innings.

### 1961–62 PENTANGULAR TOURNAMENT

A fifth team, Leeward and Windward Islands, competed in this knock-out tournament held at Georgetown.
Final: British Guiana beat Barbados by 4 wickets.

### 1963–64 REGIONAL TOURNAMENT

For the first time a tournament was staged in more than two centres, the four major countries meeting each other once in a league championship with the six matches being divided equally between Bridgetown, Port-of-Spain and Georgetown.
Champions: British Guiana.

## THE SHELL SHIELD

Sponsored by Shell Oil, 'The Shell Shield for Caribbean Regional Cricket Tournament' was instituted in 1965–66. In its first season five teams participated but the combined Leeward and Windward Islands side did not compete for points. In 1966–67 and 1968–69 the Leeward Islands and Windwards Islands took part as separate teams, playing two matches each without competing for points. The Combined Islands were admitted to full membership in 1969–70, the five teams playing each other once on a league basis. After winning the Shield in 1981, the Combined Islands separated, extending the competition to a six-team championship, with both Leeward Islands and Windward Islands enjoying full membership.

Because of the MCC tour, the competition was not held in 1967–68.

In 1975–76 the match between Guyana and Barbados was abandoned when Barbados withdrew its team following a political ban on one of its players by the Guyana government. G.A. Greenidge was prevented from entering Guyana for the match because he had played cricket in Rhodesia and South Africa.

### HOLDERS

| | | | |
|---|---|---|---|
| 1965–66 | Barbados | 1976–77 | Barbados |
| 1966–67 | Barbados | 1977–78 | Barbados |
| 1968–69 | Jamaica | 1978–79 | Barbados |
| 1969–70 | Trinidad | 1979–80 | Barbados |
| 1970–71 | Trinidad | 1980–81 | Combined Islands |
| 1971–72 | Barbados | 1981–82 | Barbados |
| 1972–73 | Guyana | 1982–83 | Guyana |
| 1973–74 | Barbados | 1983–84 | Barbados |
| 1974–75 | Guyana | 1984–85 | Trinidad |
| 1975–76 { | Barbados<br>Trinidad | | |

### RESULTS SUMMARY 1965–66 to 1984–85

| | P | W | L | D |
|---|---|---|---|---|
| Barbados | 79 | 39 | 12 | 28 |
| Guyana (British Guiana) | 77 | 16 | 19 | 42 |
| Jamaica | 80 | 15 | 26 | 39 |
| Trinidad | 80 | 21 | 22 | 37 |
| Combined Islands | 52 | 11 | 22 | 19 |
| Leeward Islands | 23 | 6 | 9 | 8 |
| Windward Islands | 23 | 8 | 6 | 9 |
| | 414 | 116 | 116 | 182 |

*Matches abandoned without a ball being bowled are excluded.*

# NEW ZEALAND

## THE PLUNKET SHIELD

The Shield was presented by the Governor-General of New Zealand, Lord Plunket, in 1906–07 and was awarded by the New Zealand Cricket Council to Canterbury as the association with the best record in that season. Initially the Shield was contested on a challenge match basis but in 1921 it was reorganised as a league championship in which Auckland, Canterbury, Otago and Wellington competed. Apart from two isolated appearances by Hawke's Bay in 1914–15, the competition's structure remained unchanged until Central Districts and Northern Districts were admitted in 1950–51 and 1956–57 respectively.

After the 1974–75 season the Plunket Shield was replaced as New Zealand's major championship by an expanded league/knock-out competition. The trophy itself was reallocated to the North v South Island fixture.

| HOLDERS (Challenge System) | | *Challenges defeated* |
|---|---|---|
| Canterbury | 1906–07 to December 1907 | 0 |
| Auckland | December 1907 to February 1911 | 7 |
| Canterbury | February 1911 to February 1912 | 2 |
| Auckland | February 1912 to January 1913 | 1 |
| Canterbury | January 1913 to December 1918 | 9 |
| Wellington | December 1918 to January 1919 | 0 |
| Canterbury | January 1919 to January 1920 | 2 |
| Auckland | January 1920 to January 1921 | 3 |
| Wellington | January 1921 – challenge system ended | 0 |

HOLDERS (League System)

| | | | |
|---|---|---|---|
| 1921–22 | Auckland | 1951–52 | Canterbury |
| 1922–23 | Canterbury | 1952–53 | Otago |
| 1923–24 | Wellington | 1953–54 | Central Districts |
| 1924–25 | Otago | 1954–55 | Wellington |
| 1925–26 | Wellington | 1955–56 | Canterbury |
| 1926–27 | Auckland | 1956–57 | Wellington |
| 1927–28 | Wellington | 1957–58 | Otago |
| 1928–29 | Auckland | 1958–59 | Auckland |
| 1929–30 | Wellington | 1959–60 | Canterbury |
| 1930–31 | Canterbury | 1960–61 | Wellington |
| 1931–32 | Wellington | 1961–62 | Wellington |
| 1932–33 | Otago | 1962–63 | Northern Districts |
| 1933–34 | Auckland | 1963–64 | Auckland |
| 1934–35 | Canterbury | 1964–65 | Canterbury |
| 1935–36 | Wellington | 1965–66 | Wellington |
| 1936–37 | Auckland | 1966–67 | Central Districts |
| 1937–38 | Auckland | 1967–68 | Central Districts |
| 1938–39 | Auckland | 1968–69 | Auckland |
| 1939–40 | Auckland | 1969–70 | Otago |
| 1945–46 | Canterbury | 1970–71 | Central Districts |
| 1946–47 | Auckland | 1971–72 | Otago |
| 1947–48 | Otago | 1972–73 | Wellington |
| 1948–49 | Canterbury | 1973–74 | Wellington |
| 1949–50 | Wellington | 1974–75 | Otago |
| 1950–51 | Otago | | |

**RESULTS SUMMARY 1907–08 to 1974–75**

| | *First Match* | *P* | *W* | *L* | *D* |
|---|---|---|---|---|---|
| Auckland | 1907–08 | 211 | 95 | 52 | 64 |
| Canterbury | 1907–08 | 214 | 86 | 68 | 60 |
| Otago | 1907–08 | 199 | 56 | 95 | 48 |
| Wellington | 1907–08 | 202 | 85 | 68 | 49 |
| Hawke's Bay | 1914–15 | 2 | — | 2 | — |
| Central Districts | 1950–51 | 118 | 35 | 34 | 49 |
| Northern Districts | 1956–57 | 94 | 10 | 48 | 36 |
| | | 1040 | 367 | 367 | 306 |

*Matches abandoned without a ball being bowled are excluded.*

**THE SHELL SERIES**

A new league-cup competition, sponsored by Shell Oil and with two separate trophies, replaced the Plunket Shield in 1975–76. It increased the amount of first-class cricket played in New Zealand and had the added attraction of culminating in a final.

**SHELL CUP**

Organised on a league basis like the Plunket Shield, this competition formed the first round of the series with each team playing the others once and the one with most points winning the Cup. It was not competed for in 1979–80 and has been awarded to the winners of a national limited-overs knock-out tournament since 1980–81.

HOLDERS

| | |
|---|---|
| 1975–76 | Canterbury |
| 1976–77 | Northern Districts |
| 1977–78 | Canterbury |
| 1978–79 | Otago |

**SHELL TROPHY**

This competition has been reorganised three times in five years. Originally the six teams divided into two sections according to their positions in the Shell Cup. Points gained in that first round were carried through and the section winners then contested a four-day final for the Trophy.

In 1976–77 this competition was played entirely on a knock-out basis with the Shell Cup winner and runner-up receiving a bye in the quarter-finals. Drawn matches were awarded to the teams leading on first innings.

The original two-section system was reinstituted for the next two seasons but the composition of those sections was decided before the Shell Cup was played. Points gained in the first competition were not carried through.

After four seasons of two-trophy first-class cricket, New Zealand returned to a single league competition on expanded Plunket Shield lines in 1979–80.

HOLDERS

| | | |
|---|---|---|
| 1975–76 | Canterbury | (beat Otago by 9 wickets) |
| 1976–77 | Otago | (beat Central Districts by 65 runs) |
| 1977–78 | Auckland | (beat Canterbury on first innings) |
| 1978–79 | Otago | (beat Central Districts on first innings) |
| 1979–80 | Northern Districts | |
| 1980–81 | Auckland | |
| 1981–82 | Wellington | |
| 1982–83 | Wellington | |
| 1983–84 | Canterbury | |
| 1984–85 | Wellington | |

RESULTS SUMMARY 1975–76 to 1984–85

| | P | W | L | D |
|---|---|---|---|---|
| Auckland | 73 | 21 | 13 | 39 |
| Canterbury | 74 | 25 | 25 | 24 |
| Central Districts | 75 | 13 | 25 | 37 |
| Northern Districts | 72 | 19 | 15 | 38 |
| Otago | 76 | 17 | 29 | 30 |
| Wellington | 72 | 27 | 15 | 30 |
| | 442 | 122 | 122 | 198 |

# INDIA

### BOMBAY PENTANGULAR TOURNAMENT

Originated in 1892 as the Presidency Match between the Parsees, who provided India's earliest cricketers, and the Europeans, this tournament was India's premier championship until 1946. The tournament became triangular when the Hindus entered in 1907, quadrangular when the Muslims joined in 1912, and pentangular in 1937 when a fifth team, the Rest, was formed. The tournament was abandoned as a major event after the 1945–46 season because of political agitation.

PRESIDENCY MATCH RESULTS (Parsees v Europeans)

| | Winners | Venue | | Winners | Venue |
|---|---|---|---|---|---|
| 1892–93 | Drawn | Bombay | 1900–01 | Parsees | Bombay |
| 1893–94 | Drawn | Bombay | | Drawn | Poona |
| 1894–95 | Parsees | Bombay | 1901–02 | Parsees | Bombay |
| 1895–96 | Europeans | Bombay | | Europeans | Poona |
| | Parsees | Poona | 1902–03 | Parsees | Bombay |
| 1896–97 | Europeans | Bombay | | Europeans | Poona |
| | Europeans | Poona | 1903–04 | Parsees | Bombay |
| 1897–98 | Drawn | Bombay | | Parsees | Poona |
| | Parsees | Poona | 1904–05 | Parsees | Bombay |
| 1898–99 | Europeans | Bombay | | Abandoned | Poona |
| | Europeans | Poona | 1905–06 | Parsees | Poona |
| 1899–00 | Drawn | Bombay | 1906–07 | Europeans | Poona |

### THE TOURNAMENTS – Results of Finals

TRIANGULAR

| | | |
|---|---|---|
| 1907–08 | Parsees beat Europeans by 143 runs | Bombay |
| 1908–09† | Europeans beat Parsees by 176 runs | Bombay |
| 1909–10 | Drawn (Europeans v Parsees) | Bombay |
| 1910–11 | Drawn (Europeans v Hindus) | Bombay |
| 1911–12 | Parsees beat Europeans by 2 wickets | Bombay |

QUADRANGULAR

| | | |
|---|---|---|
| 1912–13 | Parsees beat Muslims by an innings and 177 runs | Bombay |
| 1913–14 | Drawn (Hindus v Muslims) | Bombay |

| | | |
|---|---|---|
| 1914–15 | Abandoned (Hindus v Parsees) | Bombay |
| 1915–16 | Europeans beat Hindus by 10 wickets | Poona |
| 1916–17 | Drawn (Europeans v Parsees) | Bombay |
| 1917–18 | Drawn (Hindus v Parsees) | Bombay |
| 1918–19 | Europeans beat Parsees by 91 runs | Poona |
| 1919–20 | Hindus beat Muslims by an innings and 13 runs | Bombay |
| 1920–21 | Drawn (Hindus v Parsees) | Bombay |
| 1921–22 | Europeans beat Parsees by an innings and 297 runs | Bombay |
| 1922–23 | Parsees beat Hindus by 121 runs | Poona |
| 1923–24 | Hindus beat Europeans by 9 wickets | Bombay |
| 1924–25 | Muslims beat Hindus by 5 wickets | Bombay |
| 1925–26 | Hindus beat Europeans by 4 wickets | Bombay |
| 1926–27 | Hindus beat Europeans by 11 runs | Poona |
| 1927–28 | Europeans beat Muslims by 4 wickets | Bombay |
| 1928–29 | Parsees beat Europeans by 134 runs | Bombay |
| 1929–30 | Hindus beat Parsees by 5 wickets | Bombay |
| 1930–34 | *Not played* | |
| 1934–35 | Muslims beat Hindus by 91 runs | Bombay |
| 1935–36 | Muslims beat Hindus by 221 runs | Bombay |
| 1936–37 | Hindus beat Europeans by 257 runs | Bombay |

## PENTANGULAR

| | | |
|---|---|---|
| 1937–38† | Muslims beat Europeans by an innings and 91 runs | Bombay |
| 1938–39 | Muslims beat Hindus by 6 wickets | Bombay |
| 1939–40 | Hindus beat Muslims by 5 wickets | Bombay |
| 1940–41† | Muslims beat Rest by 7 wickets | Bombay |
| 1941–42 | Hindus beat Parsees by 10 wickets | Bombay |
| 1942–43 | *Not played* | |
| 1943–44 | Hindus beat Rest by an innings and 61 runs | Bombay |
| 1944–45 | Muslims beat Hindus by 1 wicket | Bombay |
| 1945–46 | Hindus beat Parsees by 310 runs | Bombay |

† *Hindus did not compete.*

## THE RANJI TROPHY

This championship was instituted in 1934 to commemorate the great 'Ranji' – Prince Kumar Shri Ranjitsinhji, the Jam Sahib of Nawanagar – who had died during the previous year.

To avoid teams having to travel vast distances, India was divided into zones, originally four in number (North, East, South and West) but with a fifth (Central) introduced in 1953–54. Each zone held a knock-out competition of four-day matches to produce champions to contest the final rounds which were played to a finish. An open draw was experimented with, unsuccessfully, as an alternative to the zonal system in 1948–49.

A league system replaced the knock-out competition in the zonal stage of the championship in 1957–1958. Originally this produced five champions to contest the final knock-out stages but in 1970–71 this was extended to 10 teams by including the runners-up.

## FINALISTS

| | | |
|---|---|---|
| 1934–35 | Bombay beat Northern India by 208 runs | Bombay |
| 1935–36 | Bombay beat Madras by 190 runs | Delhi |
| 1936–37 | Nawanagar beat Bengal by 256 runs | Bombay |
| 1937–38 | Hyderabad beat Nawanagar by 1 wicket | Bombay |
| 1938–39 | Bengal beat Southern Punjab by 178 runs | Calcutta |
| 1939–40 | Maharashtra beat United Provinces by 10 wickets | Poona |
| 1940–41 | Maharashtra beat Madras by 6 wickets | Madras |
| 1941–42 | Bombay beat Mysore by an innings and 281 runs | Bombay |
| 1942–43 | Baroda beat Hyderabad by 307 runs | Secunderabad |
| 1943–44 | Western India States beat Bengal by an innings and 23 runs | Bombay |
| 1944–45 | Bombay beat Holkar by 374 runs | Bombay |
| 1945–46 | Holkar beat Baroda by 56 runs | Indore |
| 1946–47 | Baroda beat Holkar by an innings and 409 runs | Baroda |
| 1947–48 | Holkar beat Bombay by 9 wickets | Indore |
| 1948–49 | Bombay beat Baroda by 468 runs | Bombay |
| 1949–50 | Baroda beat Holkar by 4 wickets | Baroda |
| 1950–51 | Holkar beat Gujarat by 189 runs | Indore |
| 1951–52 | Bombay beat Holkar by 531 runs | Bombay |
| 1952–53 | Holkar beat Bengal on first innings | Calcutta |
| 1953–54 | Bombay beat Holkar by 8 wickets | Indore |

| | | |
|---|---|---|
| 1954–55 | Madras beat Holkar by 46 runs | Indore |
| 1955–56 | Bombay beat Bengal by 8 wickets | Calcutta |
| 1956–57 | Bombay beat Services by an innings and 38 runs | Delhi |
| 1957–58 | Baroda beat Services by an innings and 51 runs | Baroda |
| 1958–59 | Bombay beat Bengal by 420 runs | Bombay |
| 1959–60 | Bombay beat Mysore by an innings and 22 runs | Bombay |
| 1960–61 | Bombay beat Rajasthan by 7 wickets | Udaipur |
| 1961–62 | Bombay beat Rajasthan by an innings and 287 runs | Bombay |
| 1962–63 | Bombay beat Rajasthan by an innings and 19 runs | Jaipur |
| 1963–64 | Bombay beat Rajasthan by 9 wickets | Bombay |
| 1964–65 | Bombay beat Hyderabad by an innings and 126 runs | Hyderabad |
| 1965–66 | Bombay beat Rajasthan by 8 wickets | Jaipur |
| 1966–67 | Bombay beat Rajasthan on first innings | Bombay |
| 1967–68 | Bombay beat Madras on first innings | Bombay |
| 1968–69 | Bombay beat Bengal on first innings | Bombay |
| 1969–70 | Bombay beat Rajasthan by an innings and 59 runs | Bombay |
| 1970–71 | Bombay beat Maharashtra by 48 runs | Bombay |
| 1971–72 | Bombay beat Bengal by 246 runs | Bombay |
| 1972–73 | Bombay beat Tamil Nadu by 123 runs | Madras |

*World record for any national championship of 15 consecutive wins.*
*Bombay lost to Karnataka on first innings in the 1973–74 semi-finals.*

| | | |
|---|---|---|
| 1973–74 | Karnataka beat Rajasthan by 185 runs | Jaipur |
| 1974–75 | Bombay beat Karnataka by 7 wickets | Bombay |
| 1975–76 | Bombay beat Bihar by 10 wickets | Jamshedpur |
| 1976–77 | Bombay beat Delhi by 129 runs | Delhi |
| 1977–78 | Karnataka beat Uttar Pradesh by an innings and 193 runs | Mohan Nagar |
| 1978–79 | Delhi beat Karnataka by 399 runs | Bangalore |
| 1979–80 | Delhi beat Bombay by 240 runs | Delhi |
| 1980–81 | Bombay beat Delhi by an innings and 46 runs | Bombay |
| 1981–82 | Delhi beat Karnataka on first innings | Delhi |
| 1982–83 | Karnataka beat Bombay on first innings | Bombay |
| 1983–84 | Bombay beat Delhi on first innings | Bombay |
| 1984–85 | Bombay beat Delhi by 90 runs | Bombay |

Wins: 30 – Bombay. 4 – Baroda, Holkar. 3 – Delhi, Karnataka (Mysore). 2 – Maharashtra. 1 – Bengal, Hyderabad, Madras (Tamil Nadu), Nawanagar, Western India States.

## THE DULEEP TROPHY

Named after K.S. Duleepsinhji, Ranji's nephew, this inter-zonal tournament was introduced in 1961–1962. It is organised on a knock-out system, and has usually formed the basis for selection for Test matches and tours abroad.

FINALISTS

| | | |
|---|---|---|
| 1961–62 | West beat South by 10 wickets | Bombay |
| 1962–63 | West beat South by an innings and 20 runs | Calcutta |
| 1963–64 | South and West drew – trophy shared | Delhi |
| 1964–65 | West beat Central by an innings and 89 runs | Bombay |
| 1965–66 | South beat Central by an innings and 20 runs | Madras |
| 1966–67 | South beat West on first innings | Bombay |
| 1967–68 | South beat West on first innings | Bombay |
| 1968–69 | South beat South on first innings | Hyderabad |
| 1969–70 | West beat North by an innings and 81 runs | Ahmedabad |
| 1970–71 | South beat East by 10 wickets | Bombay |
| 1971–72 | Central beat West by 2 wickets | Bangalore |
| 1972–73 | West beat Central by an innings and 172 runs | Bombay |
| 1973–74 | North beat Central by 76 runs | Bombay |
| 1974–75 | South beat West by 9 wickets | Hyderabad |
| 1975–76 | South beat North by 37 runs | Madras |
| 1976–77 | West beat North by 9 wickets | Baroda |
| 1977–78 | West beat North on first innings | Bombay |
| 1978–79 | North beat West on first innings | Delhi |
| 1979–80 | North beat West by 104 runs | Bombay |
| 1980–81 | West beat East on first innings | Calcutta |
| 1981–82 | West beat East on first innings | Bombay |
| 1982–83 | North beat West by 8 wickets | Bombay |
| 1983–84 | North beat West on first innings | Cuttack |
| 1984–85 | South beat North by 73 runs | Delhi |

# PAKISTAN

## THE QAID-E-AZAM TROPHY

Qaid-e-Azam ('The Great Leader') was the title given to Mohammad Ali Jinnah (1876–1948), head of the All-India Muslim League and the main creator of Pakistan.

This competition was inaugurated as Pakistan's national championship in 1953 and, although its structure and number of teams have varied, it was originally organised on similar lines to the Ranji Trophy with zonal knock-out or league champions contesting the final knock-out stages. In 1979–80 it was reorganised on a league basis with three groups, the winners of which met in a final three-match round decided on points. From 1980–81 to 1983–84 it was contested on a single league basis by the top ten national teams. In 1984–85 a 12-team two-league competition culminated in a knock-out tournament involving both sets of winners and runners-up.

FINALISTS

| | | |
|---|---|---|
| 1953–54 | Bahawalpur beat Punjab by 8 wickets | Karachi |
| 1954–55 | Karachi beat Services by 9 wickets | Karachi |
| 1956–57 | Punjab beat Karachi Whites by 43 runs | Lahore |
| 1957–58 | Bahawalpur beat Karachi C by 211 runs | Bahawalpur |
| 1958–59 | Karachi beat Services by 279 runs | Karachi |
| 1959–60 | Karachi beat Lahore by 99 runs | Karachi |
| 1961–62 | Karachi Blues beat Services by 4 wickets | Karachi |
| 1962–63 | Karachi beat Karachi B by an innings and 163 runs | Karachi |
| 1963–64 | Karachi Blues beat Karachi Whites by 18 runs | Karachi |
| 1964–65 | Karachi Blues beat Lahore Greens by 105 runs | Karachi |
| 1966–67 | Karachi beat Railways by 10 wickets | Karachi |
| 1968–69 | Lahore beat Karachi on first innings | Lahore |
| 1969–70 | PIA beat PWD by 195 runs | Karachi |
| 1970–71 | Karachi Blues beat Punjab University on first innings | Lahore |
| 1972–73 | Railways beat Sind by an innings and 69 runs | Karachi |
| 1973–74 | Railways beat Sind by 274 runs | Lahore |
| 1974–75 | Punjab beat Sind by an innings and 248 runs | Karachi |
| 1975–76 | National Bank beat Punjab by 9 wickets | Lahore |
| 1976–77 | United Bank beat National Bank on first innings | Lahore |
| 1977–78 | Habib Bank beat National Bank by 127 runs | Lahore |
| 1978–79 | National Bank beat Habib Bank by 384 runs | Karachi |
| 1979–80 | PIA beat National Bank and Habib Bank | Lahore |
| 1980–81 | United Bank | |
| 1981–82 | National Bank | |
| 1982–83 | United Bank | |
| 1983–84 | National Bank | |
| 1984–85 | United Bank beat Railways on first innings | Lahore |

## THE AYUB TROPHY

Introduced in 1960–61 when Pakistan's leading players were touring India, this competition was run on a knock-out basis with the winners and runners-up of the zonal stage contesting the final rounds. The trophy was named after its donor, Field-Marshal Mohammad Ayub Khan, President of Pakistan.

The competition was suspended in favour of the BCCP Trophy after 1970.

FINALISTS

| | | |
|---|---|---|
| 1960–61 | Railways & Quetta beat Lahore on first innings | Karachi |
| 1961–62 | Karachi beat North Zone by 316 runs | Karachi |
| 1962–63 | Karachi beat PIA on first innings | Karachi |
| 1964–65 | Karachi beat Lahore Education Board by an innings and 91 runs | Lahore |
| 1965–66 | Karachi Blues beat Lahore Greens by 10 wickets | Lahore |
| 1967–68 | Karachi Blues beat Rawalpindi by 10 wickets | Rawalpindi |
| 1969–70 | PIA beat Karachi Blues on first innings | Karachi |

## THE BCCP TROPHY

Introduced by the Board of Control for Cricket in Pakistan, this competition replaced the suspended Ayub Trophy but was organised on the same lines.

| | | |
|---|---|---|
| 1970–71 | PIA beat Karachi Blues by 8 wickets | Karachi |
| 1971–72 | PIA beat Karachi Blues on first innings | Karachi |

## THE BCCP PATRON'S TROPHY

In 1972, after two seasons, the BCCP Trophy was renamed the Patron's Trophy. It lost its first-class status for the seasons 1979–80 to 1982–83 inclusive, being used merely as a qualifying competition for the Qaid-e-Azam Trophy. In 1983–84 its status and former make-up were restored.

| | | |
|---|---|---|
| 1972–73 | Karachi Blues beat Railways on first innings | Lahore |
| 1973–74 | Railways beat PIA by 127 runs | Lahore |
| 1974–75 | National Bank beat Railways by 10 wickets | Lahore |
| 1975–76 | National Bank beat PIA on first innings | Karachi |
| 1976–77 | Habib Bank beat National Bank on first innings | Lahore |
| 1977–78 | Habib Bank beat MC Bank by an innings and 132 runs | Lahore |
| 1978–79 | National Bank beat MC Bank on first innings | Karachi |
| 1983–84 | Karachi Blues beat Lahore City Whites by 3 wickets | Lahore |
| 1984–85 | Karachi Whites beat Rawalpindi by 10 wickets | Karachi |

## BCCP PENTANGULAR TOURNAMENT/BCCP INVITATION TROPHY/PACO CUP

Originated as a league competition for five teams, this competition was converted into a knock-out tournament after three seasons and replaced by the BCCP Invitation Trophy in 1977–78. Since 1980–81 it has been restored to a league competition involving the leading five Qaid-e-Azam teams, sponsored by the Pakistan Automobile Company and renamed the PACO Cup. It was not held in 1983–84.

HOLDERS/FINALISTS

| | | |
|---|---|---|
| 1973–74 | PIA | |
| 1974–75 | National Bank | |
| 1975–76 | PIA | |
| 1976–77 | PIA beat National Bank on first innings | Lahore |
| 1977–78 | Habib Bank beat PIA by 218 runs | Lahore |
| 1978–79 | Habib Bank drew with PIA (rain) | Lahore |
| 1979–80 | PIA beat Habib Bank by 5 wickets | Lahore |
| 1980–81 | PIA | |
| 1981–82 | Habib Bank | |
| 1982–83 | Habib Bank | |
| 1984–85 | United Bank | |

## OTHER TOURNAMENT WINNERS

S.A. BHUTTO MEMORIAL TOURNAMENT

| | | | | | | | |
|---|---|---|---|---|---|---|---|
| 1972–73 | PIA | 1973–74 | PIA | 1975–76 | PIA | 1976–77 | United Bank |

A.S. PIRZADA MEMORIAL TOURNAMENT

| | | | |
|---|---|---|---|
| 1974–75 | National Bank | 1975–76 | National Bank |

PUNJAB TOURNAMENT

| | | | | | |
|---|---|---|---|---|---|
| 1973–74 | Lahore | 1974–75 | Lahore | 1975–76 | Lahore |

# TOURING TEAM RECORDS

Minor tours since 1900 in which no first-class matches were played are excluded from these results. Also omitted are short tours within the Indian sub-continent in which a specific annual tournament is involved, such as the Gopalan Trophy matches between Tamil Nadu and Sri Lanka.

All matches abandoned without a ball being bowled are excluded from these records. The fact that the toss may have been made is totally irrelevant.

*Denotes an official MCC/England tour throughout section.

## ENGLISH TEAMS IN AUSTRALIA

| Season | Captain | First-class Matches P | W | L | D | T | All Matches P | W | L | D | T |
|---|---|---|---|---|---|---|---|---|---|---|---|
| 1861–62 | H.H. Stephenson | — | — | — | — | — | 12 | 6 | 2 | 4 | — |
| 1863–64† | G. Parr | — | — | — | — | — | 12 | 7 | — | 5 | — |
| 1873–74 | W.G. Grace | — | — | — | — | — | 15 | 10 | 3 | 2 | — |
| 1876–77† | James Lillywhite | 3 | 1 | 1 | 1 | — | 15 | 5 | 4 | 6 | — |
| 1878–79 | Lord Harris | 5 | 2 | 3 | — | — | 13 | 5 | 3 | 5 | — |
| 1881–82† | A. Shaw | 7 | 3 | 2 | 2 | — | 18 | 8 | 3 | 7 | — |
| 1882–83 | Hon I.F.W. Bligh | 7 | 4 | 3 | — | — | 17 | 9 | 3 | 5 | — |
| 1884–85 | A. Shrewsbury | 8 | 6 | 2 | — | — | 33 | 16 | 2 | 15 | — |
| 1886–87 | A. Shrewsbury | 10 | 6 | 2 | 2 | — | 29 | 12 | 2 | 15 | — |
| 1887–88a | G.F. Vernon | 8 | 6 | 1 | 1 | — | 26 | 11 | 1 | 14 | — |
| 1887–88†b | A. Shrewsbury | 7 | 5 | 2 | — | — | 22 | 14 | 2 | 6 | — |
| 1887–88c | Combined team | 1 | 1 | — | — | — | 1 | 1 | — | — | — |
| 1891–92 | W.G. Grace | 8 | 6 | 2 | — | — | 27 | 12 | 2 | 13 | — |
| 1894–95 | A.E. Stoddart | 12 | 8 | 4 | — | — | 23 | 9 | 4 | 10 | — |
| 1897–98 | A.E. Stoddart | 12 | 4 | 5 | 3 | — | 22 | 6 | 5 | 11 | — |
| 1901–02 | A.C. MacLaren | 11 | 5 | 6 | — | — | 22 | 8 | 6 | 8 | — |
| 1902–03† | P.F. Warner | 3 | — | 2 | 1 | — | 3 | — | 2 | 1 | — |
| 1903–04 | P.F. Warner* | 14 | 9 | 2 | 3 | — | 20 | 10 | 2 | 8 | — |
| 1907–08 | A.O. Jones* | 18 | 7 | 4 | 7 | — | 19 | 7 | 4 | 8 | — |
| 1911–12 | J.W.H.T. Douglas* | 14 | 11 | 1 | 2 | — | 18 | 12 | 1 | 5 | — |
| 1920–21 | J.W.H.T. Douglas* | 13 | 5 | 6 | 2 | — | 22 | 9 | 6 | 7 | — |
| 1922–23† | A.C. MacLaren* | 7 | — | 3 | 4 | — | 8 | — | 3 | 5 | — |
| 1924–25 | A.E.R. Gilligan* | 17 | 7 | 6 | 4 | — | 23 | 8 | 6 | 9 | — |
| 1928–29 | A.P.F. Chapman* | 17 | 8 | 1 | 8 | — | 24 | 10 | 1 | 13 | — |
| 1929–30† | A.H.H. Gilligan | 5 | 2 | 2 | 1 | — | 5 | 2 | 2 | 1 | — |
| 1932–33† | D.R. Jardine* | 17 | 10 | 1 | 5 | 1 | 22 | 10 | 1 | 10 | 1 |
| 1935–36† | E.R.T. Holmes* | 6 | 3 | 1 | 2 | — | 6 | 3 | 1 | 2 | — |
| 1936–37† | G.O.B. Allen* | 17 | 5 | 5 | 7 | — | 24 | 7 | 5 | 12 | — |
| 1946–47† | W.R. Hammond* | 17 | 1 | 3 | 13 | — | 25 | 4 | 3 | 18 | — |
| 1950–51† | F.R. Brown* | 16 | 5 | 4 | 7 | — | 25 | 7 | 4 | 14 | — |
| 1954–55† | L. Hutton* | 17 | 8 | 2 | 7 | — | 23 | 13 | 2 | 8 | — |
| 1958–59† | P.B.H. May* | 17 | 4 | 4 | 9 | — | 20 | 7 | 4 | 9 | — |
| 1962–63† | E.R. Dexter* | 15 | 4 | 3 | 8 | — | 32 | 12 | 3 | 17 | — |
| 1965–66† | M.J.K. Smith* | 15 | 5 | 2 | 8 | — | 24 | 13 | 2 | 9 | — |
| 1970–71† | R. Illingworth* | 14 | 3 | 1 | 10 | — | 24 | 10 | 2 | 12 | — |
| 1974–75† | M.H. Denness* | 15 | 5 | 5 | 5 | — | 23 | 8 | 9 | 6 | — |
| 1976–77 | A.W. Greig* | 2 | — | 1 | 1 | — | 2 | — | 1 | 1 | — |
| 1978–79 | J.M. Brearley* | 13 | 8 | 2 | 3 | — | 26 | 17 | 4 | 5 | — |
| 1979–80 | J.M. Brearley* | 8 | 3 | 3 | 2 | — | 20 | 10 | 7 | 3 | — |
| 1982–83 | R.G.D. Willis* | 11 | 4 | 3 | 4 | — | 23 | 10 | 9 | 4 | — |
| | | 407 | 174 | 100 | 132 | 1 | 768 | 328 | 126 | 313 | 1 |

*Two teams toured Australia in 1887–88; one captained by G.F. Vernon (a) and the other by A. Shrewsbury (b). They combined to play one Test match (c).*

† *Tour combined with New Zealand.*

# ENGLISH TEAMS IN SOUTH AFRICA AND RHODESIA

| Season | Captain | First-class Matches | | | | All Matches | | | |
|--------|---------|---|---|---|---|---|---|---|---|
| | | P | W | L | D | P | W | L | D |
| 1888–89 | C.A. Smith | 2 | 2 | — | — | 19 | 13 | 4 | 2 |
| 1891–92 | W.W. Read | 1 | 1 | — | — | 21 | 14 | — | 7 |
| 1895–96 | Lord Hawke | 4 | 3 | — | 1 | 18 | 7 | 3 | 8 |
| 1898–99 | Lord Hawke | 5 | 5 | — | — | 17 | 15 | — | 2 |
| 1905–06 | P.F. Warner* | 12 | 7 | 5 | — | 26 | 17 | 5 | 4 |
| 1909–10R | H.D.G. Leveson Gower* | 14 | 7 | 4 | 3 | 18 | 10 | 4 | 4 |
| 1913–14 | J.W.H.T. Douglas* | 18 | 9 | 1 | 8 | 22 | 12 | 1 | 9 |
| 1922–23 | F.T. Mann* | 14 | 10 | 1 | 3 | 22 | 14 | 1 | 7 |
| 1924–25 | Hon L.H. Tennyson | 14 | 5 | 2 | 7 | 21 | 8 | 2 | 11 |
| 1927–28 | R.T. Stanyforth* | 16 | 7 | 2 | 7 | 18 | 7 | 2 | 9 |
| 1930–31 | A.P.F. Chapman* | 16 | 5 | 1 | 10 | 20 | 7 | 1 | 12 |
| 1938–39 | W.R. Hammond* | 17 | 8 | — | 9 | 18 | 9 | — | 9 |
| 1948–49 | F.G. Mann* | 20 | 9 | — | 11 | 23 | 11 | — | 12 |
| 1956–57 | P.B.H. May* | 20 | 11 | 3 | 6 | 22 | 13 | 3 | 6 |
| 1959–60R | W.S. Surridge (Surrey) | 2 | — | 1 | 1 | 2 | — | 1 | 1 |
| 1964–65 | M.J.K. Smith* | 17 | 10 | — | 7 | 19 | 11 | — | 8 |
| 1964–65R | D. Kenyon (Worcestershire) | 2 | 1 | 1 | — | 3 | 2 | 1 | — |
| | | 194 | 100 | 21 | 73 | 309 | 170 | 28 | 111 |

R  *Toured Rhodesia only*

# ENGLISH TEAMS IN WEST INDIES AND BERMUDA

| Season | Captain | First-class Matches | | | | | All Matches | | | | |
|--------|---------|---|---|---|---|---|---|---|---|---|---|
| | | P | W | L | D | T | P | W | L | D | T |
| 1894–95 | R.S. Lucas | 8 | 3 | 3 | 2 | — | 17 | 10 | 4 | 3 | — |
| 1896–97 | Lord Hawke | 7 | 3 | 2 | 2 | — | 14 | 9 | 2 | 3 | — |
| 1896–97 | A. Priestley | 9 | 4 | 5 | — | — | 16 | 10 | 5 | 1 | — |
| 1901–02 | R.A. Bennett | 13 | 8 | 5 | — | — | 19 | 13 | 5 | 1 | — |
| 1904–05 | Lord Brackley | 10 | 6 | 3 | 1 | — | 20 | 11 | 3 | 6 | — |
| 1910–11 | A.F. Somerset* | 11 | 3 | 4 | 3 | 1 | 13 | 5 | 4 | 3 | 1 |
| 1912–13 | A.F. Somerset* | 9 | 5 | 3 | 1 | — | 9 | 5 | 3 | 1 | — |
| 1925–26 | Hon F.S.G. Calthorpe* | 12 | 2 | 1 | 9 | — | 13 | 2 | 1 | 10 | — |
| 1926–27J | Hon L.H. Tennyson | 3 | — | — | 3 | — | 7 | 1 | — | 6 | — |
| 1927–28J | Hon L.H. Tennyson | 3 | — | 2 | 1 | — | 5 | 1 | 2 | 2 | — |
| 1928–29J | Sir J. Cahn | 3 | — | 2 | 1 | — | 5 | — | 2 | 3 | — |
| 1929–30 | Hon F.S.G. Calthorpe* | 12 | 4 | 2 | 6 | — | 13 | 4 | 2 | 7 | — |
| 1931–32J | Lord Tennyson | 3 | — | 3 | — | — | 6 | 1 | 3 | 2 | — |
| 1934–35 | R.E.S. Wyatt* | 12 | 2 | 2 | 8 | — | 12 | 2 | 2 | 8 | — |
| 1935–36J | P.A. Gibb (Yorkshire) | 3 | 1 | — | 2 | — | 6 | 1 | — | 5 | — |
| 1938–39J | E.J.H. Dixon (Combined U's) | 2 | — | 1 | 1 | — | 7 | 2 | 1 | 4 | — |
| 1947–48 | G.O.B. Allen* | 11 | — | 2 | 9 | — | 11 | — | 2 | 9 | — |
| 1953–54 | L. Hutton* | 10 | 6 | 2 | 2 | — | 17 | 8 | 2 | 7 | — |
| 1955–56 | M.C. Cowdrey (EWS) | 4 | 1 | 2 | 1 | — | 6 | 2 | 2 | 2 | — |
| 1956–57J | E.D.R. Eagar (D of N) | 3 | 2 | — | 1 | — | 10 | 4 | — | 6 | — |
| 1959–60 | P.B.H. May* | 13 | 4 | 1 | 8 | — | 15 | 4 | 1 | 10 | — |
| 1960–61 | A.C.D. Ingleby-Mackenzie (EWS) | 4 | 2 | 1 | 1 | — | 9 | 5 | 1 | 3 | — |
| 1963–64J | D.C.S. Compton (Cavaliers) | 3 | 2 | — | 1 | — | 5 | 3 | — | 2 | — |
| 1964–65 | T.E. Bailey (Cavaliers) | 4 | — | 1 | 3 | — | 7 | 1 | 1 | 5 | — |
| 1965–66J | D. Kenyon (Worcestershire) | 1 | — | — | 1 | — | 5 | — | — | 5 | — |
| 1967–68 | M.C. Cowdrey* | 12 | 3 | — | 9 | — | 16 | 4 | — | 12 | — |
| 1969–70J | M.C. Cowdrey (Cavaliers) | 1 | — | — | 1 | — | 4 | 1 | — | 3 | — |
| 1969–70 | M.C. Cowdrey (D of N) | 3 | 1 | 1 | 1 | — | 9 | 5 | 2 | 2 | — |
| 1969–70 | A.R. Lewis (Glamorgan) | 2 | — | 1 | 1 | — | 6 | 1 | 2 | 3 | — |
| 1973–74 | M.H. Denness* | 11 | 1 | 2 | 8 | — | 16 | 3 | 3 | 10 | — |
| 1980–81 | I.T. Botham* | 9 | 2 | 2 | 5 | — | 14 | 5 | 4 | 5 | — |
| | | 211 | 65 | 53 | 92 | 1 | 332 | 123 | 59 | 149 | 1 |

J  *Toured Jamaica only*
D of N  *Duke of Norfolk's XI;*   EWS  *E.W. Swanton's XI*

# ENGLISH TEAMS IN NEW ZEALAND

| Season | Captain | First-class Matches | | | | | All Matches | | | | |
|---|---|---|---|---|---|---|---|---|---|---|---|
| | | P | W | L | D | T | P | W | L | D | T |
| 1863–64† | G. Parr | — | — | — | — | — | 4 | 3 | — | 1 | — |
| 1876–77† | James Lillywhite | — | — | — | — | — | 8 | 6 | — | 2 | — |
| 1881–82† | A. Shaw | — | — | — | — | — | 7 | 5 | — | 2 | — |
| 1887–88† | C.A. Smith (A. Shrewsbury's XI) | — | — | — | — | — | 3 | — | — | 3 | — |
| 1902–03† | P.F. Warner | 7 | 7 | — | — | — | 18 | 18 | — | — | — |
| 1906–07 | E.G. Wynyard* | 11 | 6 | 2 | 3 | — | 16 | 10 | 2 | 4 | — |
| 1922–23† | A.C. MacLaren* | 8 | 6 | — | 2 | — | 14 | 11 | — | 3 | — |
| 1929–30† | A.H.H. Gilligan* | 8 | 2 | — | 6 | — | 17 | 9 | — | 8 | — |
| 1932–33† | D.R. Jardine* | 3 | — | — | 3 | — | 3 | — | — | 3 | — |
| 1935–36† | E.R.T. Holmes* | 8 | 2 | 1 | 5 | — | 18 | 5 | 1 | 12 | — |
| 1936–37† | G.O.B. Allen* | 3 | 1 | — | 2 | — | 3 | 1 | — | 2 | — |
| 1938–39 | Sir J. Cahn | 1 | — | — | 1 | — | 10 | 2 | — | 8 | — |
| 1946–47† | W.R. Hammond* | 4 | 2 | — | 2 | — | 4 | 2 | — | 2 | — |
| 1950–51† | F.R. Brown* | 4 | 3 | — | 1 | — | 4 | 3 | — | 1 | — |
| 1954–55† | L. Hutton* | 4 | 4 | — | — | — | 4 | 4 | — | — | — |
| 1958–59† | P.B.H. May* | 5 | 3 | — | 2 | — | 5 | 3 | — | 2 | — |
| 1960–61 | D.R.W. Silk* | 10 | 4 | 1 | 5 | — | 21 | 10 | 1 | 10 | — |
| 1962–63† | E.R. Dexter* | 4 | 4 | — | — | — | 4 | 4 | — | — | — |
| 1965–66† | M.J.K. Smith* | 4 | — | — | 4 | — | 4 | — | — | 4 | — |
| 1970–71† | R. Illingworth* | 2 | 1 | — | 1 | — | 5 | 3 | 1 | 1 | — |
| 1974–75† | M.H. Denness* | 3 | 1 | — | 2 | — | 5 | 1 | — | 4 | — |
| 1977–78 | G. Boycott* | 8 | 3 | 1 | 3 | 1 | 9 | 4 | 1 | 3 | 1 |
| 1979–80† | C.S. Cowdrey (D.H. Robins' XI) | 2 | — | — | 2 | — | 8 | 5 | 1 | 2 | — |
| 1983–84 | R.G.D. Willis* | 7 | 1 | 1 | 5 | — | 11 | 4 | 2 | 5 | — |
| | | 106 | 50 | 6 | 49 | 1 | 205 | 113 | 9 | 82 | 1 |

† Tour combined with Australia.

# ENGLISH TEAMS IN INDIA, PAKISTAN AND SRI LANKA

| Season | Captain | First-class Matches | | | | All Matches | | | |
|---|---|---|---|---|---|---|---|---|---|
| | | P | W | L | D | P | W | L | D |
| 1892–93[I] | Lord Hawke | 4 | 3 | 1 | — | 23 | 15 | 2 | 6 |
| 1902–03[I] | K.J. Key (OU Auths) | 3 | 1 | 2 | — | 19 | 12 | 2 | 5 |
| 1926–27 | A.E.R. Gilligan* | 30 | 10 | — | 20 | 34 | 11 | — | 23 |
| 1933–34 | D.R. Jardine* | 18 | 10 | 1 | 7 | 34 | 17 | 1 | 16 |
| 1936–37 | Sir J. Cahn | 1 | 1 | — | — | 9 | 3 | — | 6 |
| 1937–38 | Lord Tennyson | 15 | 4 | 5 | 6 | 24 | 8 | 5 | 11 |
| 1951–52 | N.D. Howard* | 23 | 7 | 3 | 13 | 27 | 10 | 3 | 14 |
| 1955–56[P] | D.B. Carr* | 14 | 7 | 2 | 5 | 16 | 7 | 2 | 7 |
| 1956–57[I] | W.J. Edrich (C.G. Howard's XI) | 2 | 1 | 1 | — | 2 | 1 | 1 | — |
| 1961–62 | E.R. Dexter* | 22 | 7 | 2 | 13 | 24 | 8 | 2 | 14 |
| 1963–64[I] | M.J.K. Smith* | 10 | 1 | — | 9 | 10 | 1 | — | 9 |
| 1966–67[P] | J.M. Brearley* | 7 | 4 | — | 3 | 8 | 4 | — | 4 |
| 1968–69[PS] | M.C. Cowdrey* | 7 | — | 7 | — | 10 | 2 | 7 | 1 |
| 1969–70[S] | A.R. Lewis* | 1 | 1 | — | — | 1 | 1 | — | — |
| 1972–73 | A.R. Lewis* | 16 | 3 | 2 | 11 | 17 | 4 | 2 | 11 |
| 1976–77[IS] | A.W. Greig* | 13 | 4 | 1 | 8 | 16 | 5 | 2 | 9 |
| 1977–78[P] | J.M. Brearley* | 7 | 1 | — | 6 | 12 | 4 | 2 | 6 |
| 1979–80[I] | J.M. Brearley* | 1 | 1 | — | — | 1 | 1 | — | — |
| 1981–82[IS] | K.W.R. Fletcher* | 15 | 3 | 1 | 11 | 21 | 6 | 4 | 11 |
| 1983–84[P] | R.G.D. Willis* | 3 | — | 1 | 2 | 5 | 1 | 2 | 2 |
| 1984–85[IS] | D.I. Gower* | 12 | 3 | 2 | 7 | 18 | 7 | 2 | 9 |
| | | 224 | 72 | 31 | 121 | 331 | 128 | 39 | 164 |

[I]    Toured India only                          [PS]    Toured Pakistan and Sri Lanka only
[IS]   Toured India and Sri Lanka only     [S]    Toured Sri Lanka only
[P]    Toured Pakistan only

# ENGLISH TEAMS IN NORTH AMERICA

| Season | Captain | First-class Matches | | | | All Matches | | | |
|--------|---------|---|---|---|---|---|---|---|---|
| | | P | W | L | D | P | W | L | D |
| 1859 | G. Parr | — | — | — | — | 5 | 5 | — | — |
| 1868 | E. Willsher | — | — | — | — | 6 | 5 | — | 1 |
| 1872 | R.A. Fitzgerald | — | — | — | — | 8 | 7 | — | 1 |
| 1879 | Lord Harris | — | — | — | — | 1 | 1 | — | — |
| 1879 | R. Daft | — | — | — | — | 12 | 9 | — | 3 |
| 1881 | A. Shaw | — | — | — | — | 5 | 2 | — | 3 |
| 1885 | E.J. Sandars | 2 | 1 | 1 | — | 10 | 8 | 1 | 1 |
| 1886 | E.J. Sandars | 2 | 2 | — | — | 9 | 8 | — | 1 |
| 1891 | Lord Hawke | 2 | 1 | 1 | — | 8 | 6 | 1 | 1 |
| 1894 | Lord Hawke | 2 | 2 | — | — | 5 | 3 | — | 2 |
| 1895 | F. Mitchell | 2 | 1 | 1 | — | 5 | 2 | 2 | 1 |
| 1897 | P.F. Warner | 2 | 1 | 1 | — | 6 | 2 | 1 | 3 |
| 1898 | P.F. Warner | 2 | 2 | — | — | 8 | 6 | — | 2 |
| 1899 | K.S. Ranjitsinhji | 2 | 2 | — | — | 5 | 3 | — | 2 |
| 1901 | B.J.T. Bosanquet | 2 | 1 | 1 | — | 5 | 3 | 2 | — |
| 1903 | C.J. Burnup (Kent) | 2 | 2 | — | — | 4 | 4 | — | — |
| 1905 | E.W. Mann* | 2 | 1 | 1 | — | 8 | 5 | 1 | 2 |
| 1907 | H. Hesketh-Prichard* | 2 | — | — | 2 | 5 | 1 | — | 4 |
| 1937 | G.C. Newman* | — | — | — | — | 19 | 12 | 1 | 6 |
| 1951 | R.W.V. Robins* | 1 | 1 | — | — | 22 | 18 | 2 | 2 |
| 1959 | D.R.W. Silk* | — | — | — | — | 24 | 20 | — | 4 |
| 1967 | D.R.W. Silk* | — | — | — | — | 25 | 21 | — | 4 |
| | | 25 | 17 | 6 | 2 | 205 | 151 | 11 | 43 |

# ENGLISH TEAMS IN SOUTH AMERICA

| Season | Captain | First-class Matches | | | | All Matches | | | |
|--------|---------|---|---|---|---|---|---|---|---|
| | | P | W | L | D | P | W | L | D |
| 1911–12 | Lord Hawke* | 3 | 2 | 1 | — | 9 | 6 | 1 | 2 |
| 1926–27 | P.F. Warner* | 4 | 2 | 1 | 1 | 10 | 6 | 1 | 3 |
| 1929–30 | Sir J. Cahn | 3 | 1 | — | 2 | 6 | 2 | 1 | 3 |
| 1937–38 | Sir T.E.W. Brinckman | 3 | 1 | 1 | 1 | 11 | 4 | 1 | 6 |
| 1958–59 | G.H.G. Doggart* | — | — | — | — | 10 | 9 | — | 1 |
| 1964–65 | A.C. Smith* | — | — | — | — | 15 | 14 | — | 1 |
| | | 13 | 6 | 3 | 4 | 61 | 41 | 4 | 16 |

# ENGLISH TEAMS IN EAST AFRICA

| Season | Captain | First-class Matches | | | | All Matches | | | |
|--------|---------|---|---|---|---|---|---|---|---|
| | | P | W | L | D | P | W | L | D |
| 1963–64 | M.J.K. Smith* | 1 | 1 | — | — | 11 | 7 | — | 4 |
| 1973–74 | J.M. Brearley* | 1 | 1 | — | — | 8 | 5 | — | 3 |
| | | 2 | 2 | — | — | 19 | 12 | — | 7 |

# ENGLISH TEAMS IN ZIMBABWE

| Season | Captain | First-class Matches | | | | | All Matches | | | | |
|--------|---------|---|---|---|---|---|---|---|---|---|---|
| | | P | W | L | D | T | P | W | L | D | T |
| 1980–81 | J.M. Brearley (Middx) | 3 | 1 | 1 | 1 | — | 6 | 3 | 1 | 1 | 1 |
| 1980–81 | R.W. Tolchard (Leics) | 3 | — | — | 3 | — | 5 | 1 | 1 | 3 | — |
| 1984–85 | M.C.J. Nicholas (Eng. Cos.) | 2 | 1 | 1 | — | — | 12 | 6 | 6 | — | — |
| | | 8 | 2 | 2 | 4 | — | 23 | 10 | 8 | 4 | 1 |

# AUSTRALIAN TEAMS IN BRITAIN

| Season | Captain | First-class Matches | | | | | All Matches | | | | |
|--------|---------|---|---|---|---|---|---|---|---|---|---|
| | | P | W | L | D | T | P | W | L | D | T |
| 1868 | C. Lawrence (Aborigines) | — | — | — | — | — | 47 | 14 | 14 | 19 | — |
| 1878 | D.W. Gregory | 15 | 7 | 4 | 4 | — | 37 | 18 | 7 | 12 | — |
| 1880 | W.L. Murdoch | 10 | 5 | 2 | 3 | — | 37 | 21 | 4 | 12 | — |
| 1882 | W.L. Murdoch | 32 | 17 | 4 | 11 | — | 38 | 23 | 4 | 11 | — |
| 1884 | W.L. Murdoch | 31 | 17 | 7 | 7 | — | 32 | 18 | 7 | 7 | — |
| 1886 | H.J.H. Scott | 37 | 9 | 7 | 21 | — | 39 | 9 | 8 | 22 | — |
| 1888 | P.S. McDonnell | 37 | 17 | 13 | 7 | — | 40 | 19 | 14 | 7 | — |
| 1890 | W.L. Murdoch | 34 | 10 | 16 | 8 | — | 38 | 13 | 16 | 9 | — |
| 1893 | J.M. Blackham | 31 | 14 | 10 | 7 | — | 36 | 18 | 10 | 8 | — |
| 1896 | G.H.S. Trott | 34 | 19 | 6 | 9 | — | 34 | 19 | 6 | 9 | — |
| 1899 | J. Darling | 35 | 16 | 3 | 16 | — | 35 | 16 | 3 | 16 | — |
| 1902 | J. Darling | 38 | 22 | 2 | 14 | — | 39 | 23 | 2 | 14 | — |
| 1905 | J. Darling | 35 | 15 | 3 | 17 | — | 38 | 16 | 3 | 19 | — |
| 1909 | M.A. Noble | 37 | 11 | 4 | 22 | — | 39 | 13 | 4 | 22 | — |
| 1912 | S.E. Gregory | 36 | 9 | 8 | 19 | — | 37 | 9 | 8 | 20 | — |
| 1919 | H.L. Collins (AIF) | 28 | 12 | 4 | 12 | — | 32 | 13 | 4 | 15 | — |
| 1921 | W.W. Armstrong | 34 | 21 | 2 | 11 | — | 39 | 23 | 2 | 14 | — |
| 1926 | H.L. Collins | 33 | 9 | 1 | 23 | — | 40 | 12 | 1 | 27 | — |
| 1930 | W.M. Woodfull | 31 | 11 | 1 | 18 | 1 | 33 | 12 | 1 | 19 | 1 |
| 1934 | W.M. Woodfull | 30 | 13 | 1 | 16 | — | 34 | 15 | 1 | 18 | — |
| 1938 | D.G. Bradman | 29 | 15 | 2 | 12 | — | 35 | 20 | 2 | 13 | — |
| 1948 | D.G. Bradman | 31 | 23 | — | 8 | — | 34 | 25 | — | 9 | — |
| 1953 | A.L. Hassett | 33 | 16 | 1 | 16 | — | 35 | 16 | 1 | 18 | — |
| 1956 | I.W. Johnson | 31 | 9 | 3 | 19 | — | 34 | 11 | 3 | 20 | — |
| 1961 | R. Benaud | 32 | 13 | 1 | 18 | — | 37 | 14 | 2 | 21 | — |
| 1964 | R.B. Simpson | 30 | 11 | 3 | 16 | — | 35 | 14 | 3 | 18 | — |
| 1968 | W.M. Lawry | 25 | 8 | 3 | 14 | — | 29 | 10 | 3 | 16 | — |
| 1972 | I.M. Chappell | 26 | 11 | 5 | 10 | — | 37 | 14 | 10 | 13 | — |
| 1975 | I.M. Chappell | 15 | 8 | 2 | 5 | — | 21 | 12 | 4 | 5 | — |
| 1977 | G.S. Chappell | 22 | 5 | 4 | 13 | — | 31 | 8 | 8 | 15 | — |
| 1980 | G.S. Chappell | 5 | 1 | 2 | 2 | — | 8 | 1 | 4 | 3 | — |
| 1981 | K.J. Hughes | 17 | 3 | 3 | 11 | — | 25 | 7 | 6 | 12 | — |
| 1985 | A.R. Border | 20 | 4 | 3 | 13 | — | 24 | 6 | 4 | 14 | — |
| | | 914 | 381 | 130 | 402 | 1 | 1129 | 482 | 169 | 477 | 1 |

# AUSTRALIAN TEAMS IN SOUTH AFRICA AND RHODESIA

| Season | Captain | First-class Matches | | | | All Matches | | | |
|--------|---------|---|---|---|---|---|---|---|---|
| | | P | W | L | D | P | W | L | D |
| 1902–03 | J. Darling | 4 | 3 | — | 1 | 6 | 3 | — | 3 |
| 1919–20 | H.L. Collins (AIF) | 8 | 6 | — | 2 | 9 | 7 | — | 2 |
| 1921–22 | H.L. Collins | 6 | 4 | — | 2 | 6 | 4 | — | 2 |
| 1935–36 | V.Y. Richardson | 16 | 13 | — | 3 | 16 | 13 | — | 3 |
| 1949–50 | A.L. Hassett | 21 | 14 | — | 7 | 25 | 18 | — | 7 |
| 1957–58 | I.D. Craig | 20 | 11 | — | 9 | 22 | 11 | — | 11 |
| 1966–67 | R.B. Simpson | 17 | 7 | 5 | 5 | 23 | 11 | 5 | 7 |
| 1969–70 | W.M. Lawry | 12 | 4 | 4 | 4 | 12 | 4 | 4 | 4 |
| | | 104 | 62 | 9 | 33 | 119 | 71 | 9 | 39 |

# AUSTRALIAN TEAMS IN WEST INDIES

| Season | Captain | First-class Matches | | | | All Matches | | | |
|--------|---------|---|---|---|---|---|---|---|---|
| | | P | W | L | D | P | W | L | D |
| 1954–55 | I.W. Johnson | 9 | 5 | — | 4 | 12 | 6 | — | 6 |
| 1964–65 | R.B. Simpson | 11 | 3 | 2 | 6 | 16 | 4 | 3 | 9 |
| 1972–73 | I.M. Chappell | 12 | 7 | — | 5 | 15 | 10 | — | 5 |
| 1977–78 | R.B. Simpson | 11 | 5 | 3 | 3 | 13 | 6 | 4 | 3 |
| 1983–84 | K.J. Hughes | 10 | 1 | 3 | 6 | 15 | 2 | 6 | 7 |
| | | 53 | 21 | 8 | 24 | 71 | 28 | 13 | 30 |

# AUSTRALIAN TEAMS IN NEW ZEALAND

| Season | Captain | First-class Matches P | W | L | D | All Matches P | W | L | D |
|---|---|---|---|---|---|---|---|---|---|
| 1877–78 | D.W. Gregory | — | — | — | — | 7 | 5 | 1 | 1 |
| 1880–81 | W.L. Murdoch | — | — | — | — | 10 | 6 | 1 | 3 |
| 1883–84 | J.G. Davis (Tasmania) | 4 | — | 3 | 1 | 7 | 2 | 3 | 2 |
| 1886–87 | H.J.H. Scott | — | — | — | — | 5 | 2 | — | 3 |
| 1889–90 | J. Davis (New South Wales) | 5 | 4 | — | 1 | 7 | 6 | — | 1 |
| 1893–94 | J. Davis (New South Wales) | 7 | 4 | 1 | 2 | 8 | 4 | 1 | 3 |
| 1895–96 | L.T. Cobcroft (NSW) | 5 | 3 | 1 | 1 | 5 | 3 | 1 | 1 |
| 1896–97 | G.H.S. Trott | — | — | — | — | 5 | 3 | — | 2 |
| 1896–97 | O.C. Hitchcock (Queensland) | 5 | 3 | 1 | 1 | 8 | 4 | 1 | 3 |
| 1904–05 | M.A. Noble | 4 | 3 | — | 1 | 6 | 4 | — | 2 |
| 1909–10 | W.W. Armstrong | 6 | 5 | — | 1 | 9 | 7 | — | 2 |
| 1913–14 | A. Sims | 8 | 6 | — | 2 | 16 | 8 | — | 8 |
| 1920–21 | V.S. Ransford | 9 | 6 | — | 3 | 15 | 12 | — | 3 |
| 1923–24 | C.G. Macartney (NSW) | 6 | 5 | — | 1 | 12 | 8 | — | 4 |
| 1924–25 | E.R. Mayne (Victoria) | 6 | 1 | 1 | 4 | 12 | 4 | 1 | 7 |
| 1927–28 | V.Y. Richardson | 6 | 4 | — | 2 | 13 | 6 | — | 7 |
| 1945–46 | W.A. Brown | 5 | 5 | — | — | 5 | 5 | — | — |
| 1949–50 | W.A. Brown | 5 | 3 | — | 2 | 14 | 9 | — | 5 |
| 1956–57 | I.D. Craig | 7 | 5 | — | 2 | 12 | 7 | — | 5 |
| 1959–60 | I.D. Craig | 6 | 2 | — | 4 | 9 | 4 | — | 5 |
| 1966–67 | L.E. Favell | 9 | 1 | 2 | 6 | 10 | 2 | 2 | 6 |
| 1969–70 | S.C. Trimble | 8 | 2 | — | 6 | 8 | 2 | — | 6 |
| 1973–74 | I.M. Chappell | 7 | 2 | 1 | 4 | 11 | 6 | 1 | 4 |
| 1976–77 | G.S. Chappell | 6 | 5 | — | 1 | 8 | 5 | 2 | 1 |
| 1981–82 | G.S. Chappell | 5 | 1 | 1 | 3 | 11 | 4 | 4 | 3 |
| | | 129 | 70 | 11 | 48 | 233 | 128 | 18 | 87 |

# AUSTRALIAN TEAMS IN INDIA, PAKISTAN AND SRI LANKA

| Season | Captain | First-class Matches P | W | L | D | All Matches P | W | L | D |
|---|---|---|---|---|---|---|---|---|---|
| 1935–36† | J. Ryder | 17 | 11 | 3 | 3 | 23 | 11 | 3 | 9 |
| 1945–46 | A.L. Hassett (Services) | 9 | 2 | 2 | 5 | 10 | 2 | 2 | 6 |
| 1956–57IP | I.W. Johnson | 4 | 2 | 1 | 1 | 4 | 2 | 1 | 1 |
| 1959–60IP | R. Benaud | 11 | 5 | 1 | 5 | 11 | 5 | 1 | 5 |
| 1964–65IP | R.B. Simpson | 4 | 1 | 1 | 2 | 4 | 1 | 1 | 2 |
| 1969–70IS | W.M. Lawry | 11 | 5 | 1 | 5 | 14 | 6 | 1 | 7 |
| 1979–80I | K.J. Hughes | 11 | — | 3 | 8 | 11 | — | 3 | 8 |
| 1979–80P | G.S. Chappell | 5 | — | 1 | 4 | 5 | — | 1 | 4 |
| 1980–81S | K.J. Hughes | 1 | — | — | 1 | 4 | 2 | 1 | 1 |
| 1982–83P | K.J. Hughes | 6 | — | 3 | 3 | 9 | — | 5 | 4 |
| 1982–83S | G.S. Chappell | 2 | 1 | — | 1 | 6 | 1 | 2 | 3 |
| | | 81 | 27 | 16 | 38 | 101 | 30 | 21 | 50 |

I   Toured India only      IP   Toured India and Pakistan only   S   Toured Sri Lanka only
IS   Toured India and Sri Lanka only    P   Toured Pakistan only
†   Unofficial Australian team managed by F.A. Tarrant

# AUSTRALIAN TEAMS IN NORTH AMERICA

| Season | Captain | First-class Matches P | W | L | D | All Matches P | W | L | D |
|---|---|---|---|---|---|---|---|---|---|
| 1878–79 | D.W. Gregory | 1 | — | — | 1 | 6 | 4 | — | 2 |
| 1882–83 | W.L. Murdoch | — | — | — | — | 2 | 2 | — | — |
| 1893–94 | J.M. Blackham | 2 | 1 | 1 | — | 6 | 4 | 1 | 1 |
| 1896–97 | G.H.S. Trott | 3 | 2 | 1 | — | 6 | 4 | 1 | 1 |
| 1912–13 | S.E. Gregory | 2 | 1 | 1 | — | 6 | 4 | 1 | 1 |
| 1913–14 | A. Diamond | 5 | 4 | — | 1 | 48 | 45 | 1 | 2 |
| 1932–33 | V.Y. Richardson | — | — | — | — | 52 | 45 | 1 | 6 |
| | | 13 | 8 | 3 | 2 | 126 | 108 | 5 | 13 |

# AUSTRALIAN TEAMS IN ZIMBABWE

| Season | Captain | First-class Matches | | | | | All Matches | | | | |
|--------|---------|---|---|---|---|---|---|---|---|---|---|
| | | P | W | L | D | | P | W | L | D | |
| 1982–83 | D.M. Wellham | 2 | 1 | 1 | — | | 7 | 5 | 2 | — | |

# SOUTH AFRICAN TEAMS IN BRITAIN

| Season | Captain | First-class Matches | | | | | All Matches | | | | |
|--------|---------|---|---|---|---|---|---|---|---|---|---|
| | | P | W | L | D | T | P | W | L | D | T |
| 1894 | H.H. Castens | — | — | — | — | — | 24 | 12 | 5 | 7 | — |
| 1901 | M. Bisset | 15 | 5 | 9 | — | 1 | 25 | 13 | 9 | 2 | 1 |
| 1904 | F. Mitchell | 22 | 10 | 2 | 9 | 1 | 26 | 13 | 3 | 9 | 1 |
| 1907 | P.W. Sherwell | 27 | 17 | 4 | 6 | — | 31 | 21 | 4 | 6 | — |
| 1912 | F. Mitchell | 37 | 13 | 8 | 16 | — | 37 | 13 | 8 | 16 | — |
| 1924 | H.W. Taylor | 35 | 8 | 9 | 18 | — | 38 | 8 | 9 | 21 | — |
| 1929 | H.G. Deane | 34 | 9 | 7 | 18 | — | 37 | 11 | 7 | 19 | — |
| 1935 | H.F. Wade | 31 | 17 | 2 | 12 | — | 39 | 22 | 2 | 15 | — |
| 1947 | A. Melville | 28 | 14 | 5 | 9 | — | 33 | 16 | 5 | 12 | — |
| 1951 | A.D. Nourse | 30 | 5 | 5 | 20 | — | 34 | 8 | 5 | 21 | — |
| 1955 | J.E. Cheetham | 28 | 15 | 4 | 9 | — | 31 | 16 | 4 | 11 | — |
| 1960 | D.J. McGlew | 30 | 14 | 5 | 11 | — | 31 | 15 | 5 | 11 | — |
| 1961 | R.A. McLean (Fezelas) | 3 | 3 | — | — | — | 21 | 14 | — | 7 | — |
| 1965 | P.L. van der Merwe | 18 | 5 | 2 | 11 | — | 19 | 5 | 3 | 11 | — |
| 1967 | W. McAdam (South African U's) | 2 | 1 | — | 1 | — | 21 | 10 | 1 | 10 | — |
| | | 340 | 136 | 62 | 140 | 2 | 447 | 197 | 70 | 178 | 2 |

# SOUTH AFRICAN TEAMS IN AUSTRALIA

| Season | Captain | First-class Matches | | | | All Matches | | | |
|--------|---------|---|---|---|---|---|---|---|---|
| | | P | W | L | D | P | W | L | D |
| 1910–11 | P.W. Sherwell | 15 | 6 | 7 | 2 | 22 | 12 | 7 | 3 |
| 1931–32† | H.B. Cameron | 16 | 4 | 6 | 6 | 18 | 6 | 6 | 6 |
| 1952–53† | J.E. Cheetham | 16 | 4 | 3 | 9 | 21 | 7 | 3 | 11 |
| 1963–64† | T.L. Goddard | 14 | 5 | 3 | 6 | 28 | 16 | 4 | 8 |
| | | 61 | 19 | 19 | 23 | 89 | 41 | 20 | 28 |

† Tour combined with New Zealand

# SOUTH AFRICAN TEAMS IN NEW ZEALAND

| Season | Captain | First-class Matches | | | | All Matches | | | |
|--------|---------|---|---|---|---|---|---|---|---|
| | | P | W | L | D | P | W | L | D |
| 1931–32† | H.B. Cameron | 3 | 3 | — | — | 3 | 3 | — | — |
| 1952–53† | J.E. Cheetham | 4 | 1 | — | 3 | 5 | 1 | — | 4 |
| 1963–64† | T.L. Goddard | 4 | 1 | — | 3 | 7 | 1 | — | 6 |
| | | 11 | 5 | — | 6 | 15 | 5 | — | 10 |

† Tour combined with Australia

# WEST INDIAN TEAMS IN BRITAIN

| Season | Captain | First-class Matches | | | | All Matches | | | |
|--------|---------|---|---|---|---|---|---|---|---|
| | | P | W | L | D | P | W | L | D |
| 1900 | R.S.A. Warner | — | — | — | — | 17 | 5 | 8 | 4 |
| 1906 | H.B.G. Austin | 13 | 3 | 8 | 2 | 19 | 7 | 10 | 2 |
| 1923 | H.B.G. Austin | 20 | 6 | 7 | 7 | 26 | 12 | 7 | 7 |
| 1928 | R.K. Nunes | 30 | 5 | 12 | 13 | 38 | 8 | 12 | 18 |
| 1933 | G.C. Grant | 30 | 5 | 9 | 16 | 43 | 9 | 9 | 25 |
| 1939 | R.S. Grant | 25 | 8 | 6 | 11 | 33 | 10 | 6 | 17 |
| 1950 | J.D.C. Goddard | 31 | 17 | 3 | 11 | 38 | 19 | 3 | 16 |
| 1957 | J.D.C. Goddard | 30 | 14 | 3 | 13 | 34 | 16 | 3 | 15 |
| 1963 | F.M.M. Worrell | 30 | 15 | 2 | 13 | 38 | 19 | 3 | 16 |
| 1964 | Sir F.M.M. Worrell | 3 | 1 | — | 2 | 3 | 1 | — | 2 |
| 1966 | G.St A. Sobers | 27 | 8 | 4 | 15 | 34 | 13 | 5 | 16 |
| 1969 | G.St A. Sobers | 19 | 2 | 3 | 14 | 23 | 3 | 4 | 16 |
| 1969 | S.M. Nurse (Barbados) | 2 | — | 1 | 1 | 7 | 3 | 3 | 1 |
| 1970 | E.D.A.S. McMorris (Jamaica) | 4 | 1 | — | 3 | 12 | 2 | 2 | 8 |
| 1973 | R.B. Kanhai | 17 | 6 | 1 | 10 | 25 | 11 | 3 | 11 |
| 1976 | C.H. Lloyd | 26 | 18 | 2 | 6 | 34 | 25 | 2 | 7 |
| 1980 | C.H. Lloyd | 16 | 8 | — | 8 | 29 | 16 | 2 | 11 |
| 1984 | C.H. Lloyd | 14 | 8 | — | 6 | 23 | 12 | 1 | 10 |
| | | 337 | 125 | 61 | 151 | 476 | 191 | 83 | 202 |

# WEST INDIAN TEAMS IN AUSTRALIA

| Season | Captain | First-class Matches | | | | | All Matches | | | | |
|--------|---------|---|---|---|---|---|---|---|---|---|---|
| | | P | W | L | D | T | P | W | L | D | T |
| 1930–31 | G.C. Grant | 14 | 4 | 8 | 2 | — | 16 | 5 | 8 | 3 | — |
| 1951–52† | J.D.C. Goddard | 13 | 4 | 8 | 1 | — | 15 | 5 | 8 | 2 | — |
| 1960–61 | F.M.M. Worrell | 14 | 4 | 5 | 4 | 1 | 22 | 10 | 5 | 5 | 2 |
| 1968–69† | G.St A. Sobers | 15 | 4 | 5 | 6 | — | 23 | 9 | 5 | 9 | — |
| 1975–76 | C.H. Lloyd | 13 | 3 | 6 | 4 | — | 21 | 8 | 7 | 6 | — |
| 1979–80† | C.H. Lloyd | 7 | 5 | 1 | 1 | — | 21 | 13 | 5 | 3 | — |
| 1981–82 | C.H. Lloyd | 7 | 4 | 1 | 2 | — | 24 | 16 | 5 | 3 | — |
| 1984–85 | C.H. Lloyd | 11 | 4 | 2 | 5 | — | 33 | 24 | 4 | 5 | — |
| | | 94 | 32 | 36 | 25 | 1 | 175 | 90 | 47 | 36 | 2 |

† Tour combined with New Zealand

# WEST INDIAN TEAMS IN NEW ZEALAND

| Season | Captain | First-class Matches | | | | All Matches | | | |
|--------|---------|---|---|---|---|---|---|---|---|
| | | P | W | L | D | P | W | L | D |
| 1951–52† | J.D.C. Goddard | 4 | 2 | — | 2 | 5 | 3 | — | 2 |
| 1955–56 | D.St E. Atkinson | 8 | 6 | 1 | 1 | 15 | 11 | 1 | 3 |
| 1968–69† | G.St A. Sobers | 6 | 1 | 2 | 3 | 7 | 1 | 2 | 4 |
| 1979–80† | C.H. Lloyd | 5 | — | 2 | 3 | 8 | 2 | 3 | 3 |
| | | 23 | 9 | 5 | 9 | 35 | 17 | 6 | 12 |

† Tour combined with Australia

## WEST INDIAN TEAMS IN INDIA, PAKISTAN AND SRI LANKA

| | | First-class Matches | | | | All Matches | | | |
|---|---|---|---|---|---|---|---|---|---|
| Season | Captain | P | W | L | D | P | W | L | D |
| 1948–49 | J.D.C. Goddard | 19 | 6 | 1 | 12 | 23 | 7 | 1 | 15 |
| 1958–59IP | F.C.M. Alexander | 23 | 13 | 2 | 8 | 23 | 13 | 2 | 8 |
| 1966–67IS | G.St A. Sobers | 9 | 4 | 1 | 4 | 9 | 4 | 1 | 4 |
| 1974–75 | C.H. Lloyd | 18 | 6 | 2 | 10 | 20 | 6 | 4 | 10 |
| 1978–79IS | A.I. Kallicharran | 16 | 2 | 2 | 12 | 19 | 4 | 3 | 12 |
| 1980–81P | C.H. Lloyd | 9 | 3 | 1 | 5 | 12 | 6 | 1 | 5 |
| 1983–84I | C.H. Lloyd | 12 | 4 | — | 8 | 19 | 10 | — | 9 |
| | | 106 | 38 | 9 | 59 | 125 | 50 | 12 | 63 |

IS    *Toured India and Sri Lanka only*             IP    *Toured India and Pakistan only*
I    *Toured India only*                              P    *Toured Pakistan only*

## WEST INDIAN TEAMS IN ZIMBABWE

| | | First-class Matches | | | | All Matches | | | |
|---|---|---|---|---|---|---|---|---|---|
| Season | Captain | P | W | L | D | P | W | L | D |
| 1981–82 | S.F.A.F. Bacchus | 3 | 1 | — | 2 | 9 | 6 | 1 | 2 |
| 1983–84 | T. Mohamed | 2 | — | 2 | — | 9 | 3 | 6 | — |
| | | 5 | 1 | 2 | 2 | 18 | 9 | 7 | 2 |

## NEW ZEALAND TEAMS IN BRITAIN

| | | First-class Matches | | | | | All Matches | | | | |
|---|---|---|---|---|---|---|---|---|---|---|---|
| Season | Captain | P | W | L | D | T | P | W | L | D | T |
| 1927 | T.C. Lowry | 26 | 7 | 5 | 14 | — | 38 | 13 | 5 | 20 | — |
| 1931 | T.C. Lowry | 32 | 6 | 3 | 23 | — | 36 | 7 | 3 | 26 | — |
| 1937 | M.L. Page | 32 | 9 | 9 | 14 | — | 37 | 13 | 9 | 15 | — |
| 1949 | W.A. Hadlee | 32 | 13 | 1 | 18 | — | 35 | 14 | 1 | 20 | — |
| 1958 | J.R. Reid | 31 | 7 | 6 | 17 | 1 | 35 | 7 | 6 | 21 | 1 |
| 1965 | J.R. Reid | 19 | 3 | 6 | 10 | — | 21 | 4 | 6 | 11 | — |
| 1969 | G.T. Dowling | 18 | 4 | 3 | 11 | — | 22 | 5 | 4 | 13 | — |
| 1973 | B.E. Congdon | 19 | 3 | 2 | 14 | — | 23 | 4 | 3 | 16 | — |
| 1978 | M.G. Burgess | 16 | 5 | 4 | 7 | — | 20 | 5 | 8 | 7 | — |
| 1983 | G.P. Howarth | 13 | 7 | 3 | 3 | — | 15 | 8 | 3 | 4 | — |
| | | 238 | 64 | 42 | 131 | 1 | 282 | 80 | 48 | 153 | 1 |

## NEW ZEALAND TEAMS IN AUSTRALIA

| | | First-class Matches | | | | | All Matches | | | | |
|---|---|---|---|---|---|---|---|---|---|---|---|
| Season | Captain | P | W | L | D | T | P | W | L | D | T |
| 1898–99 | L.T. Cobcroft | 2 | — | 2 | — | — | 4 | 1 | 2 | 1 | — |
| 1913–14 | D. Reese | 4 | 1 | 2 | 1 | — | 9 | 5 | 2 | 2 | — |
| 1925–26 | W.R. Patrick | 4 | — | 1 | 3 | — | 9 | 3 | 1 | 5 | — |
| 1927–28 | T.C. Lowry | 1 | — | 1 | — | — | 1 | — | 1 | — | — |
| 1937–38 | M.L. Page | 3 | — | 3 | — | — | 3 | — | 3 | — | — |
| 1953–54 | B. Sutcliffe | 3 | 2 | — | 1 | — | 3 | 2 | — | 1 | — |
| 1961–62 | J.R. Reid | 3 | — | 2 | 1 | — | 3 | — | 2 | 1 | — |
| 1967–68 | B.W. Sinclair | 4 | — | 2 | 2 | — | 7 | 2 | 2 | 3 | — |
| 1969–70 | G.T. Dowling | 3 | — | — | 3 | — | 8 | 3 | — | 5 | — |
| 1970–71 | G.T. Dowling | 1 | — | — | 1 | — | 2 | — | 1 | 1 | — |
| 1972–73 | B.E. Congdon | 1 | — | — | 1 | — | 3 | 2 | — | 1 | — |
| 1973–74 | B.E. Congdon | 9 | 2 | 5 | 2 | — | 13 | 5 | 6 | 2 | — |
| 1980–81 | G.P. Howarth | 7 | 1 | 2 | 4 | — | 29 | 14 | 9 | 6 | — |
| 1982–83 | G.P. Howarth | 2 | — | — | 1 | 1 | 9 | 6 | 1 | 1 | 1 |
| | | 47 | 6 | 20 | 20 | 1 | 103 | 43 | 30 | 29 | 1 |

# NEW ZEALAND TEAMS IN SOUTH AFRICA

| Season | Captain | First-class Matches | | | | All Matches | | | |
|---|---|---|---|---|---|---|---|---|---|
| | | P | W | L | D | P | W | L | D |
| 1953–54 | G.O. Rabone | 16 | 3 | 4 | 9 | 17 | 3 | 4 | 10 |
| 1961–62 | J.R. Reid | 18 | 5 | 2 | 11 | 24 | 7 | 2 | 15 |
| | | 34 | 8 | 6 | 20 | 41 | 10 | 6 | 25 |

# NEW ZEALAND TEAMS IN WEST INDIES AND BERMUDA

| Season | Captain | First-class Matches | | | | All Matches | | | |
|---|---|---|---|---|---|---|---|---|---|
| | | P | W | L | D | P | W | L | D |
| 1971–72 | G.T. Dowling | 13 | 1 | — | 12 | 16 | 4 | — | 12 |
| 1984–85 | G.P. Howarth | 7 | — | 2 | 5 | 12 | — | 7 | 5 |
| | | 20 | 1 | 2 | 17 | 28 | 4 | 7 | 17 |

# NEW ZEALAND TEAMS IN INDIA AND PAKISTAN

| Season | Captain | First-class Matches | | | | All Matches | | | |
|---|---|---|---|---|---|---|---|---|---|
| | | P | W | L | D | P | W | L | D |
| 1955–56 | H.B. Cave | 16 | 3 | 6 | 7 | 16 | 3 | 6 | 7 |
| 1964–65 | J.R. Reid | 7 | — | 3 | 4 | 7 | — | 3 | 4 |
| 1969–70 | G.T. Dowling | 9 | 2 | 1 | 6 | 9 | 2 | 1 | 6 |
| 1976–77 | G.M. Turner | 9 | 1 | 5 | 3 | 10 | 2 | 5 | 3 |
| 1983–84s | G.P. Howarth | 5 | 3 | — | 2 | 8 | 5 | 1 | 2 |
| 1984–85p | J.V. Coney | 5 | — | 2 | 3 | 9 | 1 | 5 | 3 |
| | | 51 | 9 | 17 | 25 | 59 | 13 | 21 | 25 |

p   *Toured Pakistan only*                                   s   *Toured Sri Lanka only*

# NEW ZEALAND TEAMS IN ZIMBABWE

| Season | Captain | First-class Matches | | | | All Matches | | | |
|---|---|---|---|---|---|---|---|---|---|
| | | P | W | L | D | P | W | L | D |
| 1984–85 | J.J. Crowe | 4 | 1 | — | 3 | 11 | 5 | 3 | 3 |

# INDIAN TEAMS IN BRITAIN

| Season | Captain | First-class Matches | | | | All Matches | | | |
|---|---|---|---|---|---|---|---|---|---|
| | | P | W | L | D | P | W | L | D |
| 1911 | Maharajah of Patiala | 14 | 2 | 10 | 2 | 23 | 6 | 15 | 2 |
| 1932 | Maharajah of Porbandar | 26 | 9 | 8 | 9 | 36 | 13 | 9 | 14 |
| 1936 | Maharajah of Vizianagram | 28 | 4 | 12 | 12 | 31 | 5 | 13 | 13 |
| 1946 | Nawab of Pataudi, sr | 29 | 11 | 4 | 14 | 33 | 13 | 4 | 16 |
| 1952 | V.S. Hazare | 29 | 4 | 5 | 20 | 34 | 6 | 5 | 23 |
| 1959 | D.K. Gaekwad | 33 | 6 | 11 | 16 | 35 | 7 | 11 | 17 |
| 1967 | Nawab of Pataudi, jr | 18 | 2 | 7 | 9 | 21 | 4 | 7 | 10 |
| 1971 | A.L. Wadekar | 19 | 7 | 1 | 11 | 19 | 7 | 1 | 11 |
| 1974 | A.L. Wadekar | 18 | 4 | 3 | 11 | 21 | 5 | 5 | 11 |
| 1979 | S. Venkataraghavan | 16 | 1 | 3 | 12 | 19 | 1 | 6 | 12 |
| 1982 | S.M. Gavaskar | 12 | 1 | 1 | 10 | 18 | 2 | 4 | 12 |
| | | 242 | 51 | 65 | 126 | 290 | 69 | 80 | 141 |

# INDIAN TEAMS IN AUSTRALIA

| Season | Captain | First-class Matches | | | | All Matches | | | |
|---|---|---|---|---|---|---|---|---|---|
| | | P | W | L | D | P | W | L | D |
| 1947–48 | L. Amarnath | 14 | 2 | 7 | 5 | 20 | 5 | 7 | 8 |
| 1967–68† | Nawab of Pataudi, jr | 9 | — | 6 | 3 | 15 | 4 | 6 | 5 |
| 1977–78 | B.S. Bedi | 11 | 6 | 5 | — | 20 | 12 | 6 | 2 |
| 1980–81 | S.M. Gavaskar | 8 | 2 | 2 | 4 | 25 | 8 | 11 | 6 |
| | | 42 | 10 | 20 | 12 | 80 | 29 | 30 | 21 |

† Tour combined with New Zealand

# INDIAN TEAMS IN WEST INDIES

| Season | Captain | First-class Matches | | | | All Matches | | | |
|---|---|---|---|---|---|---|---|---|---|
| | | P | W | L | D | P | W | L | D |
| 1952–53 | V.S. Hazare | 9 | 1 | 1 | 7 | 10 | 1 | 1 | 8 |
| 1961–62 | N.J. Contractor | 9 | 1 | 6 | 2 | 12 | 2 | 6 | 4 |
| 1970–71 | A.L. Wadekar | 12 | 2 | 1 | 9 | 13 | 3 | 1 | 9 |
| 1975–76 | B.S. Bedi | 9 | 1 | 3 | 5 | 9 | 1 | 3 | 5 |
| 1982–83 | Kapil Dev | 10 | 3 | 2 | 5 | 14 | 4 | 4 | 6 |
| | | 49 | 8 | 13 | 28 | 58 | 11 | 15 | 32 |

# INDIAN TEAMS IN NEW ZEALAND

| Season | Captain | First-class Matches | | | | All Matches | | | |
|---|---|---|---|---|---|---|---|---|---|
| | | P | W | L | D | P | W | L | D |
| 1967–68† | Nawab of Pataudi, jr | 6 | 4 | 1 | 1 | 6 | 4 | 1 | 1 |
| 1975–76 | B.S. Bedi | 6 | 3 | 1 | 2 | 9 | 3 | 4 | 2 |
| 1980–81 | S.M. Gavaskar | 5 | 1 | 1 | 3 | 7 | 1 | 3 | 3 |
| | | 17 | 8 | 3 | 6 | 22 | 8 | 8 | 6 |

† Tour combined with Australia.

# INDIAN TEAMS IN PAKISTAN

| Season | Captain | First-class Matches | | | | All Matches | | | |
|---|---|---|---|---|---|---|---|---|---|
| | | P | W | L | D | P | W | L | D |
| 1954–55 | M.H. Mankad | 14 | 5 | — | 9 | 14 | 5 | — | 9 |
| 1978–79 | B.S. Bedi | 9 | 2 | 2 | 5 | 12 | 3 | 4 | 5 |
| 1982–83 | S.M. Gavaskar | 10 | 1 | 3 | 6 | 15 | 3 | 6 | 6 |
| 1984–85 | S.M. Gavaskar | 2 | — | — | 2 | 5 | 1 | 1 | 3 |
| | | 35 | 8 | 5 | 22 | 46 | 12 | 11 | 23 |

# INDIAN TEAMS IN SRI LANKA

*Major tours only*

| Season | Captain | First-class Matches | | | | All Matches | | | |
|---|---|---|---|---|---|---|---|---|---|
| | | P | W | L | D | P | W | L | D |
| 1944–45 | V.M. Merchant | 1 | — | — | 1 | 5 | 2 | — | 3 |
| 1956–57 | P.R. Umrigar | 2 | — | — | 2 | 3 | 1 | — | 2 |
| 1973–74 | A.L. Wadekar | 4 | 1 | — | 3 | 7 | 3 | — | 4 |
| | | 7 | 1 | — | 7 | 15 | 6 | — | 9 |

## INDIAN TEAM IN EAST AFRICA

| Season | Captain | First-class Matches | | | | All Matches | | | |
|---|---|---|---|---|---|---|---|---|---|
| | | P | W | L | D | P | W | L | D |
| 1967 | Nawab of Pataudi, jr | 1 | 1 | — | — | 7 | 5 | — | 2 |

## INDIAN TEAMS IN ZIMBABWE

| Season | Captain | First-class Matches | | | | All Matches | | | |
|---|---|---|---|---|---|---|---|---|---|
| | | P | W | L | D | P | W | L | D |
| 1983–84 | R.J. Shastri | 2 | 1 | 1 | — | 10 | 6 | 4 | — |

## PAKISTANI TEAMS IN BRITAIN

| Season | Captain | First-class Matches | | | | All Matches | | | |
|---|---|---|---|---|---|---|---|---|---|
| | | P | W | L | D | P | W | L | D |
| 1954 | A.H. Kardar | 30 | 9 | 3 | 18 | 32 | 10 | 3 | 19 |
| 1962 | Javed Burki | 29 | 4 | 8 | 17 | 35 | 6 | 8 | 21 |
| 1963 | Wazir Mohammad (Eaglets) | 8 | 2 | 2 | 4 | 20 | 11 | 2 | 7 |
| 1967 | Hanif Mohammad | 17 | 3 | 3 | 11 | 22 | 3 | 6 | 13 |
| 1971 | Intikhab Alam | 19 | 5 | 4 | 10 | 19 | 5 | 4 | 10 |
| 1974 | Intikhab Alam | 16 | 9 | — | 7 | 23 | 16 | — | 7 |
| 1978 | Wasim Bari | 13 | 1 | 2 | 10 | 16 | 1 | 4 | 11 |
| 1982 | Imran Khan | 15 | 5 | 4 | 6 | 19 | 6 | 6 | 7 |
| | | 147 | 38 | 26 | 83 | 186 | 58 | 33 | 95 |

## PAKISTANI TEAMS IN AUSTRALIA

| Season | Captain | First-class Matches | | | | All Matches | | | |
|---|---|---|---|---|---|---|---|---|---|
| | | P | W | L | D | P | W | L | D |
| 1964–65† | Hanif Mohammad | 4 | — | — | 4 | 4 | — | — | 4 |
| 1972–73† | Intikhab Alam | 8 | 2 | 5 | 1 | 13 | 5 | 6 | 2 |
| 1976–77 | Mushtaq Mohammad | 5 | 1 | 2 | 2 | 5 | 1 | 2 | 2 |
| 1978–79† | Mushtaq Mohammad | 4 | 1 | 1 | 2 | 5 | 2 | 1 | 2 |
| 1981–82 | Javed Miandad | 8 | 2 | 2 | 4 | 21 | 8 | 8 | 5 |
| 1983–84 | Imran Khan | 11 | 3 | 3 | 5 | 24 | 7 | 11 | 6 |
| | | 40 | 9 | 13 | 18 | 72 | 23 | 28 | 21 |

† Tour combined with New Zealand.

## PAKISTANI TEAMS IN WEST INDIES

| Season | Captain | First-class Matches | | | | All Matches | | | |
|---|---|---|---|---|---|---|---|---|---|
| | | P | W | L | D | P | W | L | D |
| 1957–58 | A.H. Kardar | 9 | 1 | 3 | 5 | 16 | 3 | 3 | 10 |
| 1976–77 | Mushtaq Mohammad | 12 | 4 | 3 | 5 | 13 | 4 | 4 | 5 |
| | | 21 | 5 | 6 | 10 | 29 | 7 | 7 | 15 |

## PAKISTANI TEAMS IN NEW ZEALAND

| Season | Captain | First-class Matches | | | | All Matches | | | |
|---|---|---|---|---|---|---|---|---|---|
| | | P | W | L | D | P | W | L | D |
| 1964–65† | Hanif Mohammad | 10 | 2 | — | 8 | 12 | 4 | — | 8 |
| 1972–73† | Intikhab Alam | 8 | 5 | 1 | 2 | 11 | 6 | 3 | 2 |
| 1978–79† | Mushtaq Mohammad | 8 | 5 | — | 3 | 10 | 6 | 1 | 3 |
| 1984–85 | Javed Miandad | 5 | 1 | 2 | 2 | 9 | 1 | 5 | 3 |
| | | 31 | 13 | 3 | 15 | 42 | 17 | 9 | 16 |

† Tour combined with Australia.

# PAKISTANI TEAMS IN INDIA

*Major tours only*

| Season | Captain | First-class Matches | | | | All Matches | | | |
|---|---|---|---|---|---|---|---|---|---|
| | | P | W | L | D | P | W | L | D |
| 1952–53 | A.H. Kardar | 12 | 1 | 2 | 9 | 12 | 1 | 2 | 9 |
| 1960–61 | Fazal Mahmood | 15 | — | — | 15 | 15 | — | — | 15 |
| 1979–80 | Asif Iqbal | 12 | 1 | 2 | 9 | 13 | 1 | 2 | 10 |
| 1983–84 | Zaheer Abbas | 3 | — | — | 3 | 6 | — | 3 | 3 |
| | | 42 | 2 | 4 | 36 | 46 | 2 | 7 | 37 |

# PAKISTANI TEAMS IN SRI LANKA

*Major tours only*

| Season | Captain | First-class Matches | | | | All Matches | | | |
|---|---|---|---|---|---|---|---|---|---|
| | | P | W | L | D | P | W | L | D |
| 1948–49 | Mohammad Saeed | 2 | 2 | — | — | 4 | 2 | — | 2 |
| 1953–54 | A.H. Kardar (Services) | 1 | 1 | — | — | 6 | 2 | — | 4 |
| 1960–61 | Shujauddin (Eaglets) | 1 | — | — | 1 | 4 | — | 1 | 3 |
| 1964 | Imtiaz Ahmed (Pakistan A) | 2 | — | 2 | — | 4 | 1 | 3 | — |
| 1972–73 | Intikhab Alam | 1 | — | — | 1 | 1 | — | — | 1 |
| 1973–74 | Wasim Raja (Under-25 XI) | 4 | 3 | — | 1 | 7 | 3 | — | 4 |
| 1975–76 | Intikhab Alam | 3 | 2 | 1 | — | 6 | 2 | 3 | 1 |
| | | 14 | 8 | 3 | 3 | 32 | 10 | 7 | 15 |

# PAKISTANI TEAM IN EAST AFRICA

| Season | Captain | First-class Matches | | | | All Matches | | | |
|---|---|---|---|---|---|---|---|---|---|
| | | P | W | L | D | P | W | L | D |
| 1964 | Hanif Mohammad (PIA) | 1 | 1 | — | — | 9 | 5 | 1 | 3 |

# PAKISTANI TEAMS IN ZIMBABWE

| Season | Captain | First-class Matches | | | | | All Matches | | | | |
|---|---|---|---|---|---|---|---|---|---|---|---|
| | | P | W | L | D | T | P | W | L | D | T |
| 1981–82 | Aftab Baloch (PIA) | 2 | — | 1 | 1 | — | 9 | 2 | 3 | 3 | 1 |

# SRI LANKAN TEAMS IN BRITAIN

| Season | Captain | First-class Matches | | | | All Matches | | | |
|---|---|---|---|---|---|---|---|---|---|
| | | P | W | L | D | P | W | L | D |
| 1975 | A.P.B. Tennekoon | 1 | 1 | — | — | 4 | 1 | 3 | — |
| 1979 | A.P.B. Tennekoon | 9 | 1 | 1 | 7 | 16 | 6 | 3 | 7 |
| 1981 | B. Warnapura | 13 | 1 | 1 | 11 | 15 | 3 | 1 | 11 |
| 1984 | L.R.D. Mendis | 9 | — | 1 | 8 | 10 | 1 | 1 | 8 |
| | | 32 | 3 | 3 | 26 | 45 | 11 | 8 | 26 |

# SRI LANKAN TEAMS IN AUSTRALIA

| Season | Captain | First-class Matches | | | | All Matches | | | |
|---|---|---|---|---|---|---|---|---|---|
| | | P | W | L | D | P | W | L | D |
| 1982–83 | L.R.D. Mendis | 2 | — | — | 2 | 5 | 1 | 1 | 3 |
| 1984–85 | L.R.D. Mendis | 1 | 1 | — | — | 13 | 2 | 11 | — |
| | | 3 | 1 | — | 2 | 18 | 3 | 12 | 3 |

## SRI LANKAN TEAM IN NEW ZEALAND

| Season | Captain | First-class Matches | | | | All Matches | | | |
|---|---|---|---|---|---|---|---|---|---|
| | | P | W | L | D | P | W | L | D |
| 1982–83 | L.R.D. Mendis | 4 | — | 3 | 1 | 9 | 1 | 7 | 1 |

## SRI LANKAN TEAMS IN INDIA

*Major tours only*

| Season | Captain | First-class Matches | | | | All Matches | | | |
|---|---|---|---|---|---|---|---|---|---|
| | | P | W | L | D | P | W | L | D |
| 1932–33 | C.H. Gunasekara | 6 | 2 | 1 | 3 | 10 | 2 | 1 | 7 |
| 1940–41 | S.S. Jayawickreme | 3 | 1 | 1 | 1 | 5 | 1 | 1 | 3 |
| 1964–65 | M.H. Tissera | 8 | 1 | 3 | 4 | 8 | 1 | 3 | 4 |
| 1975–76 | A.P.B. Tennekoon | 9 | — | 3 | 6 | 9 | — | 3 | 6 |
| 1982–83 | B. Warnapura | 1 | — | — | 1 | 5 | 1 | 3 | 1 |
| | | 27 | 4 | 8 | 15 | 37 | 5 | 11 | 21 |

## SRI LANKAN TEAMS IN PAKISTAN

*Major tours only*

| Season | Captain | First-class Matches | | | | All Matches | | | |
|---|---|---|---|---|---|---|---|---|---|
| | | P | W | L | D | P | W | L | D |
| 1949–50 | S.S. Jayawickreme | 5 | — | 3 | 2 | 6 | — | 3 | 3 |
| 1966–67 | M.H. Tissera | 5 | — | 3 | 2 | 6 | — | 3 | 3 |
| 1973–74 | A.P.B. Tennekoon | 8 | 2 | 1 | 5 | 10 | 2 | 3 | 5 |
| 1981–82 | B. Warnapura | 3 | — | 2 | 1 | 6 | 1 | 4 | 1 |
| | | 21 | 2 | 9 | 10 | 28 | 3 | 13 | 12 |

## SRI LANKAN TEAMS IN ZIMBABWE

| Season | Captain | First-class Matches | | | | All Matches | | | |
|---|---|---|---|---|---|---|---|---|---|
| | | P | W | L | D | P | W | L | D |
| 1982–83 | L.R.D. Mendis | 2 | — | 1 | 1 | 7 | 2 | 4 | 1 |

## PHILADELPHIAN TEAMS IN BRITAIN

| Season | Captain | First-class Matches | | | | All Matches | | | |
|---|---|---|---|---|---|---|---|---|---|
| | | P | W | L | D | P | W | L | D |
| 1884 | R.S. Newhall | — | — | — | — | 18 | 8 | 5 | 5 |
| 1889 | D.S. Newhall | — | — | — | — | 12 | 4 | 3 | 5 |
| 1897 | G.S. Patterson | 15 | 2 | 9 | 4 | 15 | 2 | 9 | 4 |
| 1903 | J.A. Lester | 15 | 6 | 6 | 3 | 20 | 10 | 6 | 4 |
| 1908 | J.B. King | 9 | 3 | 6 | — | 16 | 7 | 6 | 3 |
| | | 39 | 11 | 21 | 7 | 81 | 31 | 29 | 21 |

## SOUTH AMERICAN TEAM IN BRITAIN

| Season | Captain | First-class Matches | | | | All Matches | | | |
|---|---|---|---|---|---|---|---|---|---|
| | | P | W | L | D | P | W | L | D |
| 1932 | C.H. Gibson | 6 | 2 | 3 | 1 | 18 | 2 | 5 | 11 |

# FIJIAN TEAMS IN NEW ZEALAND

| Season | Captain | First-class Matches P | W | L | D | All Matches P | W | L | D |
|--------|---------|---|---|---|---|---|---|---|---|
| 1894–95 | J.S. Udal | 6 | 1 | 3 | 2 | 8 | 4 | 2 | 2 |
| 1947–48 | P.A. Snow | — | — | — | — | 17 | 6 | 3 | 8 |
| 1953–54 | P.T. Raddock | 4 | 1 | 3 | — | 17 | 8 | 6 | 3 |
| 1961–62 | S.E.B. Snowsill | — | — | — | — | 22 | 9 | 9 | 4 |
| 1967–68 | N. Uluiviti | — | — | — | — | 25 | 12 | 7 | 6 |
| 1977–78 | F.L.C. Valentine | — | — | — | — | 15 | 5 | 4 | 6 |
| | | 10 | 2 | 6 | 2 | 104 | 44 | 31 | 29 |

# CANADIAN TEAMS IN BRITAIN

| Season | Captain | First-class Matches P | W | L | D | All Matches P | W | L | D |
|--------|---------|---|---|---|---|---|---|---|---|
| 1954 | H.B. Robinson | 4 | — | 2 | 2 | 15 | 4 | 3 | 8 |
| 1974 | R.J. Stevens | — | — | — | — | 16 | 5 | 6 | 5 |
| | | 4 | — | 2 | 2 | 31 | 9 | 9 | 13 |

# ZIMBABWEAN TEAMS IN BRITAIN

| Season | Captain | First-class Matches P | W | L | D | All Matches P | W | L | D |
|--------|---------|---|---|---|---|---|---|---|---|
| 1982 | D.A.G. Fletcher | 2 | — | — | 2 | 13 | 7 | 2 | 4 |
| 1985 | A.J. Pycroft | 6 | — | 1 | 5 | 13 | 5 | 3 | 5 |
| | | 8 | — | 1 | 7 | 26 | 12 | 5 | 9 |

# ZIMBABWEAN TEAMS IN SRI LANKA

| Season | Captain | First-class Matches P | W | L | D | All Matches P | W | L | D |
|--------|---------|---|---|---|---|---|---|---|---|
| 1983–84 | A.J. Traicos | 2 | — | — | 2 | 6 | — | 1 | 5 |

# REST OF THE WORLD TEAMS IN BRITAIN

| Season | Captain | First-class Matches P | W | L | D | All Matches P | W | L | D |
|--------|---------|---|---|---|---|---|---|---|---|
| 1965 | J.R. Reid | 1 | — | — | 1 | 2 | 1 | — | 1 |
| 1966 | R.B. Simpson | 1 | — | 1 | — | 3 | — | 3 | — |
| 1967 | G.St A. Sobers | 2 | — | — | 2 | 4 | 2 | — | 2 |
| 1968 | Nawab of Pataudi, jr | 4 | 1 | 3 | — | 5 | 2 | 3 | — |
| 1970 | G.St A. Sobers | 5 | 4 | 1 | — | 5 | 4 | 1 | — |
| | | 13 | 5 | 5 | 3 | 19 | 9 | 7 | 3 |

# REST OF THE WORLD TEAM IN AUSTRALIA

| Season | Captain | First-class Matches P | W | L | D | All Matches P | W | L | D |
|--------|---------|---|---|---|---|---|---|---|---|
| 1971–72 | G.St A. Sobers | 12 | 5 | 2 | 5 | 15 | 5 | 3 | 7 |

# INTERNATIONAL TEAMS IN SOUTH AFRICA AND RHODESIA

| Season | Captain | Team | First-class Matches | | | | All Matches | | | |
|--------|---------|------|---|---|---|---|---|---|---|---|
| | | | P | W | L | D | P | W | L | D |
| 1959–60 | D.C.S. Compton | CW | 3 | 1 | — | 2 | 5 | 2 | — | 3 |
| 1960–61 | R. Benaud | CW | 4 | 4 | — | — | 5 | 4 | — | 1 |
| 1961–62R | E. de C. Weekes | CW | 3 | 1 | 1 | 1 | 3 | 1 | 1 | 1 |
| 1962–63R | W. Watson | CW | 2 | — | 1 | 1 | 3 | — | 1 | 2 |
| 1962–63 | R. Benaud | CW | 5 | 1 | 2 | 2 | 7 | 2 | 3 | 2 |
| 1972–73R | D.B. Close | IW | 2 | — | 1 | 1 | 3 | 1 | 1 | 1 |
| 1972–73 | D.J. Brown | DHR | 6 | 1 | 3 | 2 | 10 | 4 | 4 | 2 |
| 1973–74 | D.B. Close | DHR | 7 | 2 | 1 | 4 | 13 | 8 | 1 | 4 |
| 1974–75 | D.B. Close | IW | 2 | 2 | — | — | 6 | 6 | — | — |
| 1974–75 | D.B. Close | DHR | 5 | — | 2 | 3 | 8 | 3 | 2 | 3 |
| 1975–76R | G.M. Turner | IW | 2 | 1 | 1 | — | 5 | 2 | 3 | — |
| 1975–76 | D. Lloyd | DHR | 4 | 2 | 2 | — | 10 | 4 | 3 | 3 |
| 1975–76 | G.S. Chappell | IW | 4 | 2 | — | 2 | 7 | 4 | — | 3 |
| | | | 49 | 17 | 14 | 18 | 85 | 41 | 19 | 25 |

R   *Toured Rhodesia only*
*Teams:* CW – *Commonwealth XI;* IW – *International Wanderers;* DHR – *D.H. Robins' XI*

# INTERNATIONAL TEAMS IN WEST INDIES

| Season | Captain | Team | First-class Matches | | | | All Matches | | | |
|--------|---------|------|---|---|---|---|---|---|---|---|
| | | | P | W | L | D | P | W | L | D |
| 1966–67 B | W.M. Lawry | RW | 1 | 1 | — | — | 2 | 2 | — | — |
| 1982–83 J | J.G. Wright | INT | 1 | — | — | 1 | 1 | — | — | 1 |
| | | | 2 | 1 | — | 1 | 3 | 2 | — | 1 |

B   *Played in Barbados only*
J   *Played in Jamaica only*
RW– *Rest of the World XI*
INT – *International XI*

# INTERNATIONAL TEAM IN NEW ZEALAND

| Season | Captain | Team | First-class Matches | | | | All Matches | | | |
|--------|---------|------|---|---|---|---|---|---|---|---|
| | | | P | W | L | D | P | W | L | D |
| 1961–62 | R. Benaud | CW | 2 | 2 | — | — | 3 | 2 | — | 1 |

CW – *Commonwealth XI*

# INTERNATIONAL TEAMS IN INDIA, PAKISTAN AND SRI LANKA

| Season | Captain | Team | First-class Matches | | | | All Matches | | | |
|--------|---------|------|---|---|---|---|---|---|---|---|
| | | | P | W | L | D | P | W | L | D |
| 1949–50 | L. Livingston | CW | 21 | 10 | 2 | 9 | 28 | 12 | 2 | 14 |
| 1950–51ɪs | L.E.G. Ames | CW | 27 | 13 | — | 14 | 29 | 14 | — | 15 |
| 1953–54ɪ | B.A. Barnett | CW | 21 | 3 | 5 | 13 | 21 | 3 | 5 | 13 |
| 1961–62ɪᴘ | R. Benaud | IC | 3 | 1 | — | 2 | 3 | 1 | — | 2 |
| 1962–63ɪ | R. Benaud | IC | 1 | 1 | — | — | 1 | 1 | — | — |
| 1963–64ᴘ | P.E. Richardson | CW | 6 | 1 | — | 5 | 6 | 1 | — | 5 |
| 1963–64ɪ | A.C.D. Ingleby -Mackenzie | EWS | 1 | 1 | — | — | 1 | 1 | — | — |
| 1964–65ɪ | P.E. Richardson | CW | 1 | 1 | — | — | 2 | 1 | — | 1 |
| 1967–68 | M.J. Stewart | INT | 4 | 4 | — | — | 5 | 4 | — | 1 |
| 1967–68ᴘ | R. Benaud | CW | 8 | 3 | 2 | 3 | 8 | 3 | 2 | 3 |
| 1970–71ᴘ | M.J. Stewart | CW | 3 | — | 1 | 2 | 3 | — | 1 | 2 |
| 1970–71ᴘ | G.St A. Sobers | RW | 1 | — | 1 | — | 1 | — | 1 | — |
| 1980–81ɪ | J.M. Brearley | INT | 1 | — | 1 | — | 1 | — | 1 | — |
| 1981–82ᴘ | R.B. Kanhai | INT | 3 | 1 | 2 | — | 6 | 2 | 4 | — |
| | | | 101 | 39 | 14 | 48 | 115 | 43 | 16 | 56 |

ɪ    *Toured India only*
ɪᴘ   *Toured India and Pakistan only*
ᴘ    *Toured Pakistan only*
ɪs   *Toured India and Sri Lanka only*
*Teams:*    CW—*Commonwealth XI;* IC—*International Cavaliers;* EWS—*E.W. Swanton's XI;*
            INT—*International XI;* RW—*Rest of the World XI*

# 'UNOFFICIAL' TOURING TEAMS IN SOUTH AFRICA

| Season | Captain | Team | First-class Matches | | | | All Matches | | | |
|--------|---------|------|---|---|---|---|---|---|---|---|
| | | | P | W | L | D | P | W | L | D |
| 1981–82 | G.A. Gooch | ENG | 4 | — | 1 | 3 | 8 | — | 4 | 4 |
| 1982–83 | B. Warnapura | SL | 6 | — | 4 | 2 | 12 | — | 10 | 2 |
| 1982–83 | L.G. Rowe | WI | 2 | 1 | 1 | — | 12 | 6 | 6 | — |
| 1983–84 | L.G. Rowe | WI | 9 | 2 | 2 | 5 | 19 | 10 | 4 | 5 |
| | | | 21 | 3 | 8 | 10 | 51 | 16 | 24 | 11 |

# TEST MATCH RECORDS 1876-77 TO 1985

The term 'Test match' was coined during the first English tour to Australia in 1861–62 to describe games between H. H. Stephenson's team and each of the colonies. Those matches were against odds, i.e. with the opposition batting and fielding more than 11 men. It was not until the fourth expedition to Australia, by James Lillywhite's professionals in 1876–77, that an English team played on level terms overseas. The first such contest, against a combined XI from Melbourne and Sydney, has become accepted as the first official Test match.

*The Wisden Book of Test Cricket 1876–77 to 1977–78,* published in 1979 as the first volume of the Wisden Cricket Library, contained the full scores of the 824 official Test matches played up to the start of the 1978 English season. Such has been the proliferation of Test cricket that 61 more matches were played in the subsequent 27 months. During that period Kapil Dev played 26 Tests for India and achieved the career double of 1000 runs and 100 wickets in record time. Half of those matches were staged in India during the 1979–80 season – an alarming example of 'overkill' that makes a mockery of aggregate records. The second edition of *Test Cricket,* which contained scores of all Tests to the end of the 1984 English season, had to encompass an additional 170 matches.

The frequency of Test matches has increased dramatically since 1945:

| Inclusive Period | Years | Tests | Average per Year |
|---|---|---|---|
| 1877–1899 | 23 | 64 | 2.78 |
| 1900–1914 | 15 | 70 | 4.66 |
| 1920–1939 | 20 | 140 | 7.00 |
| 1945–1960 | 16 | 225 | 14.06 |
| 1961–1970 | 10 | 176 | 17.60 |
| 1971–1980 | 10 | 217 | 21.70 |
| 1981–1985 | 5 | 141 | 28.00 |

Pressure of space in *Test Cricket* compelled a severe pruning of the records section. Here it has been updated to the end of the 1985 English season and expanded to include many of the items which had to be omitted. The section begins with a summary of scores and results of all Test matches series by series. The chronological reference numbers allotted to each match in *Test Cricket* are included to facilitate access to the full scorecard in that volume. Numbers after 994 have been allotted to matches since 1984 for future editions of *Test Cricket.*

**BILL FRINDALL**

## KEY TO SYMBOLS
* denotes a 'not out' innings or an unbroken partnership.
• denotes the side batting first and is used only in the summarised scores section.
All other symbols are explained within the section in which they appear.

## KEY TO TEST MATCH GROUNDS
(Where more than one ground has been used in a city)

| | |
|---|---|
| Bombay[1] | Gymkhana Ground |
| Bombay[2] | Brabourne Stadium |
| Bombay[3] | Wankhede Stadium |
| Brisbane[1] | Exhibition Ground |
| Brisbane[2] | Woolloongabba |
| Colombo (SO) | Saravanamuttu (Colombo) Oval |
| Colombo (SSC) | Sinhalese Sports Club Ground |
| Colombo (CCC) | Colombo Cricket Club Ground |
| Durban[1] | Lord's |
| Durban[2] | Kingsmead |
| Johannesburg[1] | Old Wanderers |
| Johannesburg[2] | Ellis Park |
| Johannesburg[3] | Wanderers Stadium |
| Lahore[1] | Bagh-i-Jinnah |
| Lahore[2] | Gaddafi Stadium |
| Madras[1] | Chepauk Stadium |
| Madras[2] | Corporation (Nehru) Stadium |

This system has not been applied to London where Test cricket has been staged on two grounds concurrently since 1884.

## NUMBER OF BALLS TO AN OVER IN TEST MATCHES

| In England | Balls |
|---|---|
| 1880–1888 | 4 |
| 1890–1899 | 5 |
| 1902–1938 | 6 |
| 1939 | 8 |
| 1946 to date | 6 |

| In Australia | |
|---|---|
| 1876–77 to 1887–88 | 4 |
| 1891–92 to 1920–21 | 6 |
| 1924–25 | 8 |
| 1928–29 to 1932–33 | 6 |
| 1936–37 to 1978–79 | 8 |
| 1979–80 to date | 6 |

| In South Africa | |
|---|---|
| 1888–89 | 4 |
| 1891–92 to 1898–99 | 5 |
| 1902–03 to 1935–36 | 6 |
| 1938–39 to 1957–58 | 8 |
| 1961–62 to 1969–70 | 6 |

| In West Indies | Balls |
|---|---|
| 1929–30 to date | 6 |

| In New Zealand | |
|---|---|
| 1929–30 to 1967–68 | 6 |
| 1968–69 to 1978–79 | 8 |
| 1979–80 to date | 6 |

| In India | |
|---|---|
| 1933–34 to date | 6 |

| In Pakistan | |
|---|---|
| 1954–55 to 1972–73 | 6 |
| 1974–75 to 1977–78 | 8 |
| 1978–79 to date | 6 |

| In Sri Lanka | |
|---|---|
| 1981–82 to date | 6 |

# RESULTS SUMMARY

## RESULTS SUMMARY OF ALL TEST MATCHES 1876–77 to 1985
(1,022 MATCHES)

| | | Tests | E | A | SA | WI | NZ | I | P | SL | Tied | Drawn |
|---|---|---|---|---|---|---|---|---|---|---|---|---|
| | | | | | | Won by | | | | | | |
| England | v Australia | 257 | 86 | 96 | – | – | – | – | – | – | – | 75 |
| | v South Africa | 102 | 46 | – | 18 | – | – | – | – | – | – | 38 |
| | v West Indies | 85 | 21 | – | – | 30 | – | – | – | – | – | 34 |
| | v New Zealand | 60 | 30 | – | – | – | 3 | – | – | – | – | 27 |
| | v India | 72 | 30 | – | – | – | – | 9 | – | – | – | 33 |
| | v Pakistan | 39 | 13 | – | – | – | – | – | 3 | – | – | 23 |
| | v Sri Lanka | 2 | 1 | – | – | – | – | – | – | – | – | 1 |
| Australia | v South Africa | 53 | – | 29 | 11 | – | – | – | – | – | – | 13 |
| | v West Indies | 62 | – | 27 | – | 19 | – | – | – | – | 1 | 15 |
| | v New Zealand | 15 | – | 8 | – | – | 2 | – | – | – | – | 5 |
| | v India | 39 | – | 20 | – | – | – | 8 | – | – | – | 11 |
| | v Pakistan | 28 | – | 11 | – | – | – | – | 8 | – | – | 9 |
| | v Sri Lanka | 1 | – | 1 | – | – | – | – | – | – | – | – |
| South Africa | v New Zealand | 17 | – | – | 9 | – | 2 | – | – | – | – | 6 |
| West Indies | v New Zealand | 21 | – | – | – | 7 | 3 | – | – | – | – | 11 |
| | v India | 54 | – | – | – | 22 | – | 5 | – | – | – | 27 |
| | v Pakistan | 19 | – | – | – | 7 | – | – | 4 | – | – | 8 |
| New Zealand | v India | 25 | – | – | – | – | 4 | 10 | – | – | – | 11 |
| | v Pakistan | 27 | – | – | – | – | 3 | – | 10 | – | – | 14 |
| | v Sri Lanka | 5 | – | – | – | – | 4 | – | – | – | – | 1 |
| India | v Pakistan | 35 | – | – | – | – | – | 4 | 6 | – | – | 25 |
| | v Sri Lanka | 1 | – | – | – | – | – | – | – | – | – | 1 |
| Pakistan | v Sri Lanka | 3 | – | – | – | – | – | – | 2 | – | – | 1 |
| | | 1,022 | 227 | 192 | 38 | 85 | 21 | 36 | 33 | – | 1 | 389 |

| | Tests | Won | Lost | Drawn | Tied | Toss Won |
|---|---|---|---|---|---|---|
| England | 617 | 227 | 159 | 231 | – | 303 |
| Australia | 455 | 192 | 134 | 128 | 1 | 228 |
| South Africa | 172 | 38 | 77 | 57 | – | 80 |
| West Indies | 241 | 85 | 60 | 95 | 1 | 130 |
| New Zealand | 170 | 21 | 74 | 75 | – | 83 |
| India | 226 | 36 | 82 | 108 | – | 113 |
| Pakistan | 151 | 33 | 38 | 80 | – | 80 |
| Sri Lanka | 12 | – | 8 | 4 | – | 5 |

# ENGLAND v AUSTRALIA

† Reference number in The Wisden Book of Test Cricket
• Batted first

‡ Where a captain's name appears only once, he was captain throughout that series

| Test No.† | Venue and Result | England | | Australia | | Captains‡ | |
|---|---|---|---|---|---|---|---|
| | | 1st | 2nd | 1st | 2nd | England | Australia |
| | **1876–77 in Australia** | | | | | | |
| 1 | Melbourne – Australia 45 runs | 196 | 108 | •245 | 104 | J. Lillywhite | D.W. Gregory |
| 2 | Melbourne – England 4 wkts | 261 | 122-6 | •122 | 259 | | |
| | **1878–79 in Australia** | | | | | | |
| 3 | Melbourne – Australia 10 wkts | •113 | 160 | 256 | 19-0 | Lord Harris | D.W. Gregory |
| | **1880 in England** | | | | | | |
| 4 | Oval – England 5 wkts | •420 | 57-5 | 149 | 327 | Lord Harris | W.L. Murdoch |
| | **1881–82 in Australia** | | | | | | |
| 5 | Melbourne – Drawn | •294 | 308 | 320 | 127-3 | | |
| 6 | Sydney – Australia 5 wkts | •133 | 232 | 197 | 169-5 | A. Shaw | W.L. Murdoch |
| 7 | Sydney – Australia 6 wkts | •188 | 134 | 260 | 66-4 | | |
| 8 | Melbourne – Drawn | •309 | 234-2 | 300 | — | | |
| | **1882 in England** | | | | | | |
| 9 | Oval – Australia 7 runs | 101 | 77 | •63 | 122 | A.N. Hornby | W.L. Murdoch |
| | **1882–83 in Australia** | | | | | | |
| 10 | Melbourne – Australia 9 wkts | 177 | 169 | •291 | 58-1 | | |
| 11 | Melbourne – England inns & 27 runs | •294 | — | 114 | 153 | Hon I.F.W. Bligh | W.L. Murdoch |
| 12 | Sydney – England 69 runs | •247 | 123 | 218 | 83 | | |
| 13 | Sydney – Australia 4 wkts | •263 | 197 | 262 | 199-6 | | |
| | **1884 in England** | | | | | | |
| 14 | Manchester – Drawn | •95 | 180-9 | 182 | — | A.N. Hornby | |
| 15 | Lord's – England inns & 5 runs | 379 | — | •229 | 145 | Lord Harris | W.L. Murdoch |
| 16 | Oval – Drawn | 346 | 85-2 | •551 | — | Lord Harris | |

| Test No. | Venue and Result | England 1st | England 2nd | Australia 1st | Australia 2nd | Captains England | Captains Australia |
|---|---|---|---|---|---|---|---|
| | **1884–85 in Australia** | | | | | | |
| 17 | Adelaide – England 8 wkts | •369 | 67-2 | •243 | 191 | A. Shrewsbury | W.L. Murdoch |
| 18 | Melbourne – England 10 wkts | •401 | 7-0 | •279 | 126 | | T.P. Horan |
| 19 | Sydney – Australia 6 runs | 133 | 207 | •181 | 165 | | H.H. Massie |
| 20 | Sydney – Australia 8 wkts | •269 | 77 | 309 | 40-2 | | J.M. Blackham |
| 21 | Melbourne – England inns & 98 runs | 386 | — | •163 | 125 | | T.P. Horan |
| | **1886 in England** | | | | | | |
| 22 | Manchester – England 4 wkts | 223 | 107-6 | •205 | 123 | A.G. Steel | H.J.H. Scott |
| 23 | Lord's – England inns & 106 runs | •353 | — | 121 | 126 | | |
| 24 | Oval – England inns & 217 runs | •434 | — | 68 | 149 | | |
| | **1886–87 in Australia** | | | | | | |
| 25 | Sydney – England 13 runs | •45 | 184 | 119 | 97 | A. Shrewsbury | P.S. McDonnell |
| 26 | Sydney – England 71 runs | •151 | 154 | 84 | 150 | | |
| | **1887–88 in Australia** | | | | | | |
| 27 | Sydney – England 126 runs | •113 | 137 | 42 | 82 | W.W. Read | P.S. McDonnell |
| | **1888 in England** | | | | | | |
| 28 | Lord's – Australia 61 runs | 53 | 62 | •116 | 60 | A.G. Steel | P.S. McDonnell |
| 29 | Oval – England inns & 137 runs | 317 | — | •80 | 100 | W.G. Grace | |
| 30 | Manchester – England inns & 21 runs | •172 | — | 81 | 70 | W.G. Grace | |
| | **1890 in England** | | | | | | |
| 33 | Lord's – England 7 wkts | 173 | 137-3 | •132 | 176 | W.G. Grace | W.L. Murdoch |
| 34 | Oval – England 2 wkts | 100 | 95-8 | •92 | 102 | | |
| — | Manchester – Abandoned | — | — | — | — | | |
| | **1891–92 in Australia** | | | | | | |
| 35 | Melbourne – Australia 54 runs | 264 | 158 | •240 | 236 | W.G. Grace | J.M. Blackham |
| 36 | Sydney – Australia 72 runs | 307 | 157 | •145 | 391 | | |
| 37 | Adelaide – England inns & 230 runs | •499 | — | 100 | 169 | | |
| | **1893 in England** | | | | | | |
| 39 | Lord's – Drawn | •334 | 234-8d | 269 | — | A.E. Stoddart | J.M. Blackham |
| 40 | Oval – England inns & 43 runs | •483 | — | 91 | 349 | W.G. Grace | |
| 41 | Manchester – Drawn | 243 | 118-4 | •204 | 236 | W.G. Grace | |

| Test No. | Venue and Result | England 1st | England 2nd | Australia 1st | Australia 2nd | Captains England | Captains Australia |
|---|---|---|---|---|---|---|---|
| | **1894–95 in Australia** | | | | | | |
| 42 | Sydney – England 10 runs | 325 | 437 | •586 | 166 | A.E. Stoddart | J.M. Blackham |
| 43 | Melbourne – England 94 runs | •75 | 475 | 123 | 333 | | G. Giffen |
| 44 | Adelaide – Australia 382 runs | 124 | 143 | 238 | 411 | | G. Giffen |
| 45 | Sydney – Australia inns & 147 runs | 65 | 72 | •284 | — | | G. Giffen |
| 46 | Melbourne – England 6 wkts | 385 | 298-4 | •414 | 267 | | G. Giffen |
| | **1896 in England** | | | | | | |
| 50 | Lord's – England 6 wkts | 292 | 111-4 | •53 | 347 | W.G. Grace | G.H.S. Trott |
| 51 | Manchester – Australia 3 wkts | 231 | 305 | •412 | 125-7 | | |
| 52 | Oval – England 66 runs | •145 | 84 | 119 | 44 | | |
| | **1897–98 in Australia** | | | | | | |
| 53 | Sydney – England 9 wkts | •551 | 96-1 | 237 | 408 | A.C. MacLaren | G.H.S. Trott |
| 54 | Melbourne – Australia inns & 55 runs | 315 | 150 | •520 | — | A.C. MacLaren | |
| 55 | Adelaide – Australia inns & 13 runs | 278 | 282 | 573 | — | A.E. Stoddart | |
| 56 | Melbourne – Australia 8 wkts | 174 | 263 | 323 | 115-2 | A.E. Stoddart | |
| 57 | Sydney – Australia 6 wkts | •335 | 178 | 239 | 276-4 | A.C. MacLaren | |
| | **1899 in England** | | | | | | |
| 60 | Nottingham – Drawn | 193 | 155-7 | •252 | 230-8d | W.G. Grace | J. Darling |
| 61 | Lord's – Australia 10 wkts | •206 | 240 | 421 | 28-0 | A.C. MacLaren | |
| 62 | Leeds – Drawn | •220 | 19-0 | 172 | 224 | A.C. MacLaren | |
| 63 | Manchester – Drawn | •372 | 94-3 | 196 | 346-7d | A.C. MacLaren | |
| 64 | Oval – Drawn | 576 | — | 352 | 254-5 | A.C. MacLaren | |
| | **1901–02 in Australia** | | | | | | |
| 65 | Sydney – England inns & 124 runs | •464 | — | 168 | 172 | A.C. MacLaren | J. Darling |
| 66 | Melbourne – Australia 229 runs | 61 | 175 | •112 | 353 | | J. Darling |
| 67 | Adelaide – Australia 4 wkts | •388 | 247 | 321 | 315-6 | | J. Darling |
| 68 | Sydney – Australia 7 wkts | 317 | 99 | 299 | 121-3 | | H. Trumble |
| 69 | Melbourne – Australia 32 runs | 189 | 178 | •144 | 255 | | H. Trumble |
| | **1902 in England** | | | | | | |
| 70 | Birmingham – Drawn | •376-9d | — | 36 | 46-2 | A.C. MacLaren | J. Darling |
| 71 | Lord's – Drawn | 102-2 | — | — | — | | |
| 72 | Sheffield – Australia 143 runs | 145 | 195 | •194 | 289 | | |
| 73 | Manchester – Australia 3 runs | 262 | 120 | •299 | 86 | | |
| 74 | Oval – England 1 wkt | 183 | 263-9 | •324 | 121 | | |

| Test No. | Venue and Result | England 1st | England 2nd | Australia 1st | Australia 2nd | Captains England | Captains Australia |
|---|---|---|---|---|---|---|---|
| | **1903–04** in Australia | | | | | | |
| 78 | Sydney – England 5 wkts | 577 | 194-5 | •285 | 485 | P.F. Warner | M.A. Noble |
| 79 | Melbourne – England 185 runs | •315 | 103 | 122 | 111 | | |
| 80 | Adelaide – Australia 216 runs | 245 | 278 | •388 | 351 | | |
| 81 | Sydney – England 157 runs | •249 | 210 | 131 | 171 | | |
| 82 | Melbourne – Australia 218 runs | 61 | 101 | •247 | 133 | | |
| | **1905** in England | | | | | | |
| 83 | Nottingham – England 213 runs | •196 | 426-5d | 221 | 188 | Hon F.S. Jackson | J. Darling |
| 84 | Lord's – Drawn | 282 | 151-5 | 181 | — | | |
| 85 | Leeds – Drawn | •301 | 295-5d | 195 | 224-7 | | |
| 86 | Manchester – England inns & 80 runs | •446 | — | 197 | 169 | | |
| 87 | Oval – Drawn | •430 | 261-6d | 363 | 124-4 | | |
| | **1907–08** in Australia | | | | | | |
| 96 | Sydney – Australia 2 wkts | •273 | 300 | 300 | 275-8 | F.L. Fane | M.A. Noble |
| 97 | Melbourne – England 1 wkt | 382 | 282-9 | 266 | 397 | F.L. Fane | |
| 98 | Adelaide – Australia 245 runs | 363 | 183 | •285 | 506 | F.L. Fane | |
| 99 | Melbourne – Australia 308 runs | 105 | 186 | 214 | 385 | A.O. Jones | |
| 100 | Sydney – Australia 49 runs | 281 | 229 | •137 | 422 | A.O. Jones | |
| | **1909** in England | | | | | | |
| 101 | Birmingham – England 10 wkts | 121 | 105-0 | •74 | 151 | A.C. MacLaren | M.A. Noble |
| 102 | Lord's – Australia 9 wkts | •269 | 121 | 350 | 41-1 | | |
| 103 | Leeds – Australia 126 runs | 182 | 87 | •188 | 207 | | |
| 104 | Manchester – Drawn | 119 | 108-3 | 147 | 279-9d | | |
| 105 | Oval – Drawn | 352 | 104-3 | •325 | 339-5d | | |
| | **1911–12** in Australia | | | | | | |
| 116 | Sydney – Australia 146 runs | 318 | 291 | •447 | 308 | J.W.H.T. Douglas | C. Hill |
| 117 | Melbourne – England 8 wkts | 265 | 219-2 | •184 | 299 | | |
| 118 | Adelaide – England 7 wkts | 501 | 112-3 | •133 | 476 | | |
| 119 | Melbourne – England inns & 225 runs | 589 | — | 191 | 173 | | |
| 120 | Sydney – England 70 runs | •324 | 214 | 176 | 292 | | |

| Test No. | Venue and Result | England 1st | England 2nd | Australia 1st | Australia 2nd | Captains England | Captains Australia |
|---|---|---|---|---|---|---|---|
| | **1912 in England** | | | | | | |
| 123 | Lord's – Drawn | •310-7d | — | 282-7 | — | C.B. Fry | S.E. Gregory |
| 126 | Manchester – Drawn | •203 | — | 14-0 | — | | |
| 129 | Oval – England 244 runs | •245 | 175 | 111 | 65 | | |
| | **1920–21 in Australia** | | | | | | |
| 135 | Sydney – Australia 377 runs | 190 | 281 | •267 | 581 | J.W.H.T. Douglas | W.W. Armstrong |
| 136 | Melbourne – Australia inns & 91 runs | 251 | 157 | •499 | — | | |
| 137 | Adelaide – Australia 119 runs | 447 | 370 | 354 | 582 | | |
| 138 | Melbourne – Australia 8 wkts | •284 | 315 | 389 | 211-2 | | |
| 139 | Sydney – Australia 9 wkts | •204 | 280 | 392 | 93-1 | | |
| | **1921 in England** | | | | | | |
| 140 | Nottingham – Australia 10 wkts | •112 | 147 | 232 | 30-0 | J.W.H.T. Douglas | W.W. Armstrong |
| 141 | Lord's – Australia 8 wkts | •187 | 283 | 342 | 131-2 | J.W.H.T. Douglas | |
| 142 | Leeds – Australia 219 runs | 259 | 202 | 407 | 273-7d | Hon L.H. Tennyson | |
| 143 | Manchester – Drawn | •362-4d | 44-1 | 175 | — | Hon L.H. Tennyson | |
| 144 | Oval – Drawn | 403-8d | 244-2 | 389 | — | Hon L.H. Tennyson | |
| | **1924–25 in Australia** | | | | | | |
| 158 | Sydney – Australia 193 runs | 298 | 411 | •450 | 452 | A.E.R. Gilligan | H.L. Collins |
| 159 | Melbourne – Australia 81 runs | 479 | 290 | •600 | 250 | | |
| 160 | Adelaide – Australia 11 runs | 365 | 363 | 489 | 250 | | |
| 161 | Melbourne – England inns & 29 runs | •548 | — | 269 | 250 | | |
| 162 | Sydney – Australia 307 runs | 167 | 146 | •295 | 325 | | |
| | **1926 in England** | | | | | | |
| 163 | Nottingham – Drawn | •32-0 | — | — | — | A.W. Carr | H.L. Collins |
| 164 | Lord's – Drawn | 475-3d | — | •383 | 194-5 | A.W. Carr | H.L. Collins |
| 165 | Leeds – Drawn | 294 | 254-3 | •494 | — | A.W. Carr | W. Bardsley |
| 166 | Manchester – Drawn | 305-5 | — | 335 | — | A.W. Carr | W. Bardsley |
| 167 | Oval – England 289 runs | •280 | 436 | 302 | 125 | A.P.F. Chapman | H.L. Collins |
| | **1928–29 in Australia** | | | | | | |
| 176 | Brisbane[1] – England 675 runs | •521 | 342-8d | 122 | 66 | A.P.F. Chapman | J. Ryder |
| 177 | Sydney – England 8 wkts | 636 | 16-2 | •253 | 397 | A.P.F. Chapman | |
| 178 | Melbourne – England 3 wkts | 417 | 332-7 | 397 | 351 | A.P.F. Chapman | |
| 179 | Adelaide – England 12 runs | •334 | 383 | 369 | 336 | A.P.F. Chapman | |
| 180 | Melbourne – Australia 5 wkts | •519 | 257 | 491 | 287-5 | J.C. White | |

| Test No. | Venue and Result | England 1st | England 2nd | Australia 1st | Australia 2nd | Captains England | Captains Australia |
|---|---|---|---|---|---|---|---|
| | **1930 in England** | | | | | | |
| 194 | Nottingham – England 93 runs | •270 | 302 | 144 | 335 | A.P.F. Chapman | W.M. Woodfull |
| 195 | Lord's – Australia 7 wkts | 425 | 375 | 729-6d | 72-3 | A.P.F. Chapman | |
| 196 | Leeds – Drawn | 391 | 95-3 | 566 | — | A.P.F. Chapman | |
| 197 | Manchester – Drawn | 251-8 | — | 345 | — | A.P.F. Chapman | |
| 198 | Oval – Australia inns & 39 runs | •405 | 251 | 695 | — | R.E.S. Wyatt | |
| | **1932–33 in Australia** | | | | | | |
| 220 | Sydney – England 10 wkts | 524 | 1-0 | •360 | 164 | D.R. Jardine | W.M. Woodfull |
| 221 | Melbourne – Australia 111 runs | 169 | 139 | •228 | 191 | | |
| 222 | Adelaide – England 338 runs | •341 | 412 | 222 | 193 | | |
| 223 | Brisbane² – England 6 wkts | 356 | 162-4 | •340 | 175 | | |
| 224 | Sydney – England 8 wkts | 454 | 168-2 | 435 | 182 | | |
| | **1934 in England** | | | | | | |
| 233 | Nottingham – Australia 238 runs | 268 | 141 | •374 | 273-8d | C.F. Walters | W.M. Woodfull |
| 234 | Lord's – England inns & 38 runs | •440 | — | 284 | 118 | R.E.S. Wyatt | |
| 235 | Manchester – Drawn | •627-9d | 123-0d | 491 | 66-1 | R.E.S. Wyatt | |
| 236 | Leeds – Drawn | •200 | 229-6 | 584 | — | R.E.S. Wyatt | |
| 237 | Oval – Australia 562 runs | 321 | 145 | •701 | 327 | R.E.S. Wyatt | |
| | **1936–37 in Australia** | | | | | | |
| 255 | Brisbane² – England 322 runs | •358 | 256 | 234 | 58 | G.O.B. Allen | D.G. Bradman |
| 256 | Sydney – England inns & 22 runs | 426-6d | — | 80 | 324 | | |
| 257 | Melbourne – Australia 365 runs | 76-9d | 323 | •200-9d | 564 | | |
| 258 | Adelaide – Australia 148 runs | 330 | 243 | •288 | 433 | | |
| 259 | Melbourne – Australia inns & 200 runs | 239 | 165 | •604 | — | | |
| | **1938 in England** | | | | | | |
| 263 | Nottingham – Drawn | •658-8d | — | 411 | 427-6 | W.R. Hammond | D.G. Bradman |
| 264 | Lord's – Drawn | 494 | 242-8d | 422 | 204-6 | | |
| — | Manchester – Abandoned | | | — | — | | |
| 265 | Leeds – Australia 5 wkts | •223 | 123 | 242 | 107-5 | | |
| 266 | Oval – England inns & 579 runs | •903-7d | — | 201 | 123 | | |

| Test No. | Venue and Result | England 1st | England 2nd | Australia 1st | Australia 2nd | Captains England | Captains Australia |
|---|---|---|---|---|---|---|---|
| | **1946–47 in Australia** | | | | | | |
| 279 | Brisbane[2] – Australia inns & 332 runs | 141 | 172 | •645 | — | W.R. Hammond | D.G. Bradman |
| 280 | Sydney – Australia inns & 33 runs | •255 | 371 | 659-8d | — | W.R. Hammond | |
| 281 | Melbourne – Drawn | 351 | 310-7 | •365 | 536 | W.R. Hammond | |
| 282 | Adelaide – Drawn | •460 | 340-8d | 487 | 215-1 | W.R. Hammond | |
| 283 | Sydney – Australia 5 wkts | •280 | 186 | 253 | 214-5 | N.W.D. Yardley | |
| | **1948 in England** | | | | | | |
| 299 | Nottingham – Australia 8 wkts | •165 | 441 | 509 | 98-2 | N.W.D. Yardley | D.G. Bradman |
| 300 | Lord's – Australia 409 runs | 215 | 186 | •350 | 460-7d | | |
| 301 | Manchester – Drawn | •363 | 174-3d | 221 | 92-1 | | |
| 302 | Leeds – Australia 7 wkts | •496 | 365-8d | 458 | 404-3 | | |
| 303 | Oval – Australia inns & 149 runs | •52 | 188 | 389 | — | | |
| | **1950–51 in Australia** | | | | | | |
| 327 | Brisbane[2] – Australia 70 runs | 68-7d | 122 | •228 | 32-7d | F.R. Brown | A.L. Hassett |
| 328 | Melbourne – Australia 28 runs | 197 | 150 | •194 | 181 | | |
| 329 | Sydney – Australia inns & 13 runs | •290 | 123 | 426 | — | | |
| 330 | Adelaide – Australia 274 runs | 272 | 228 | •371 | 403-8d | | |
| 331 | Melbourne – England 8 wkts | 320 | 95-2 | •217 | 197 | | |
| | **1953 in England** | | | | | | |
| 372 | Nottingham – Drawn | 144 | 120-1 | •249 | 123 | L. Hutton | A.L. Hassett |
| 373 | Lord's – Drawn | 372 | 282-7 | 346 | 368 | | |
| 374 | Manchester – Drawn | 276 | — | •318 | 35-8 | | |
| 375 | Leeds – Drawn | •167 | 275 | 266 | 147-4 | | |
| 376 | Oval – England 8 wkts | 306 | 132-2 | •275 | 162 | | |
| | **1954–55 in Australia** | | | | | | |
| 391 | Brisbane[2] – Australia inns & 154 runs | 190 | 257 | •601-8d | — | L. Hutton | I.W. Johnson |
| 392 | Sydney – England 38 runs | •154 | 296 | 228 | 184 | | A.R. Morris |
| 393 | Melbourne – England 128 runs | •191 | 279 | 231 | 111 | | I.W. Johnson |
| 394 | Adelaide – England 5 wkts | 341 | 97-5 | •323 | 111 | | I.W. Johnson |
| 395 | Sydney – Drawn | 371-7d | — | 221 | 118-6 | | I.W. Johnson |

| Test No. | Venue and Result | England 1st | England 2nd | Australia 1st | Australia 2nd | Captains England | Captains Australia |
|---|---|---|---|---|---|---|---|
| | **1956 in England** | | | | | | |
| 425 | Nottingham – Drawn | •217-8d | 188-3d | 148 | 120-3 | P.B.H. May | I.W. Johnson |
| 426 | Lord's – Australia 185 runs | 171 | 186 | 285 | 257 | | |
| 427 | Leeds – England inns & 42 runs | 325 | — | 143 | 140 | | |
| 428 | Manchester – England inns & 170 runs | 459 | — | 84 | 205 | | |
| 429 | Oval – Drawn | •247 | 182-3d | 202 | 27-5 | | |
| | **1958–59 in Australia** | | | | | | |
| 464 | Brisbane[2] – Australia 8 wkts | •134 | 198 | 186 | 147-2 | P.B.H. May | R. Benaud |
| 465 | Melbourne – Australia 8 wkts | •259 | 87 | 308 | 42-2 | | |
| 466 | Sydney – Drawn | •219 | 287-7d | 357 | 54-2 | | |
| 467 | Adelaide – Australia 10 wkts | 240 | 270 | •476 | 36-0 | | |
| 468 | Melbourne – Australia 9 wkts | •205 | 214 | 351 | 69-1 | | |
| | **1961 in England** | | | | | | |
| 507 | Birmingham – Drawn | •195 | 401-4 | 516-9d | — | M.C. Cowdrey | R. Benaud |
| 508 | Lord's – Australia 5 wkts | 206 | 202 | 340 | 71-5 | M.C. Cowdrey | R.N. Harvey |
| 509 | Leeds – England 8 wkts | 299 | 62-2 | •237 | 120 | P.B.H. May | R. Benaud |
| 510 | Manchester – Australia 54 runs | 367 | 201 | •190 | 432 | P.B.H. May | R. Benaud |
| 511 | Oval – Drawn | •256 | 370-8 | 494 | — | P.B.H. May | R. Benaud |
| | **1962–63 in Australia** | | | | | | |
| 535 | Brisbane[2] – Drawn | 389 | 278-6 | •404 | 362-4d | E.R. Dexter | R. Benaud |
| 536 | Melbourne – England 7 wkts | 331 | 237-3 | 316 | 248 | | |
| 537 | Sydney – Australia 8 wkts | •279 | 104 | 319 | 67-2 | | |
| 538 | Adelaide – Drawn | 331 | 223-4 | 393 | 293 | | |
| 539 | Sydney – Drawn | •321 | 268-8d | 349 | 152-4 | | |
| | **1964 in England** | | | | | | |
| 561 | Nottingham – Drawn | •216-8d | 193-9d | 168 | 40-2 | E.R. Dexter | R.B. Simpson |
| 562 | Lord's – Drawn | 246 | — | •176 | 168-4 | | |
| 563 | Leeds – Australia 7 wkts | 268 | 229 | 389 | 111-3 | | |
| 564 | Manchester – Drawn | 611 | — | •656-8d | 4-0 | | |
| 565 | Oval – Drawn | •182 | 381-4 | 379 | — | | |

| Test No. | Venue and Result | England 1st | England 2nd | Australia 1st | Australia 2nd | Captains England | Captains Australia |
|---|---|---|---|---|---|---|---|
| | **1965–66** in Australia | | | | | | |
| 597 | Brisbane² – Drawn | 280 | 186-3 | •443-6d | — | | B.C. Booth |
| 598 | Melbourne – Drawn | 558 | 5-0 | •358 | 426 | | R.B. Simpson |
| 599 | Sydney – England inns & 93 runs | •488 | — | 221 | 174 | M.J.K. Smith | B.C. Booth |
| 600 | Adelaide – Australia inns & 9 runs | 241 | 266 | 516 | — | | R.B. Simpson |
| 601 | Melbourne – Drawn | •485-9d | 69-3 | 543-8d | — | | R.B. Simpson |
| | **1968** in England | | | | | | |
| 637 | Manchester – Australia 159 runs | 165 | 253 | •357 | 220 | M.C. Cowdrey | W.M. Lawry |
| 638 | Lord's – Drawn | •351-7d | — | 78 | 127-4 | M.C. Cowdrey | W.M. Lawry |
| 639 | Birmingham – Drawn | •409 | 142-3d | 222 | 68-1 | M.C. Cowdrey | W.M. Lawry |
| 640 | Leeds – Drawn | 302 | 230-4 | 315 | 312 | T.W. Graveney | B.N. Jarman |
| 641 | Oval – England 226 runs | •494 | 181 | 324 | 125 | M.C. Cowdrey | W.M. Lawry |
| | **1970–71** in Australia | | | | | | |
| 674 | Brisbane² – Drawn | 464 | 39-1 | •433 | 214 | | W.M. Lawry |
| 675 | Perth – Drawn | •397 | 287-6d | 440 | 100-3 | | W.M. Lawry |
| — | Melbourne – Abandoned | | | | | | W.M. Lawry |
| 676 | Sydney – England 299 runs | •332 | 319-5d | 236 | 116 | R. Illingworth | W.M. Lawry |
| 677 | Melbourne – Drawn | 392 | 161-0 | •493-9d | 169-4d | | W.M. Lawry |
| 678 | Adelaide – Drawn | •470 | 233-4d | 235 | 328-3 | | W.M. Lawry |
| 679 | Sydney – England 62 runs | •184 | 302 | 264 | 160 | | I.M. Chappell |
| | **1972** in England | | | | | | |
| 698 | Manchester – England 89 runs | •249 | 234 | 142 | 252 | | |
| 699 | Lord's – Australia 8 wkts | •272 | 116 | 308 | 81-2 | | |
| 700 | Nottingham – Drawn | 189 | 290-4 | •315 | 324-4d | R. Illingworth | I.M. Chappell |
| 701 | Leeds – England 9 wkts | 263 | 21-1 | 146 | 136 | | |
| 702 | Oval – Australia 5 wkts | •284 | 356 | 399 | 242-5 | | |
| | **1974–75** in Australia | | | | | | |
| 750 | Brisbane² – Australia 166 runs | 265 | 166 | •309 | 288-5d | M.H. Denness | |
| 751 | Perth – Australia 9 wkts | •208 | 293 | 481 | 23-1 | M.H. Denness | |
| 752 | Melbourne – Drawn | 242 | 244 | •241 | 238-8 | M.H. Denness | I.M. Chappell |
| 753 | Sydney – Australia 171 runs | 295 | 228 | •405 | 289-4d | J.H. Edrich | |
| 754 | Adelaide – Australia 163 runs | 172 | 241 | •304 | 272-5d | M.H. Denness | |
| 755 | Melbourne – England inns & 4 runs | 529 | — | •152 | 373 | M.H. Denness | |

| Test No. | Venue and Result | England 1st | England 2nd | Australia 1st | Australia 2nd | Captains England | Captains Australia |
|---|---|---|---|---|---|---|---|
| | **1975 in England** | | | | | | |
| 760 | Birmingham – Australia inns & 85 runs | 101 | 173 | •359 | — | M.H. Denness | I.M. Chappell |
| 761 | Lord's – Drawn | •315 | 436-7d | 268 | 329-3 | A.W. Greig | |
| 762 | Leeds – Drawn | •288 | 291 | 135 | 220-3 | A.W. Greig | |
| 763 | Oval – Drawn | 191 | 538 | •532-9d | 40-2 | A.W. Greig | |
| | **1976–77 in Australia (Centenary Test)** | | | | | | |
| 803 | Melbourne – Australia 45 runs | 95 | 417 | •138 | 419-9d | A.W. Greig | G.S. Chappell |
| | **1977 in England** | | | | | | |
| 804 | Lord's – Drawn | •216 | 305 | 296 | 114-6 | J.M. Brearley | G.S. Chappell |
| 805 | Manchester – England 9 wkts | 437 | 82-1 | 297 | 218 | | |
| 806 | Nottingham – England 7 wkts | 364 | 189-3 | •243 | 309 | | |
| 807 | Leeds – England inns & 85 runs | •436 | — | 103 | 248 | | |
| 808 | Oval – Drawn | •214 | 57-2 | 385 | — | | |
| | **1978–79 in Australia** | | | | | | |
| 834 | Brisbane[2] – England 7 wkts | 286 | 170-3 | •116 | 339 | J.M. Brearley | G.N. Yallop |
| 835 | Perth – England 166 runs | •309 | 208 | 190 | 161 | | |
| 836 | Melbourne – Australia 103 runs | 143 | 179 | •258 | 167 | | |
| 837 | Sydney – England 93 runs | •152 | 346 | 294 | 111 | | |
| 838 | Adelaide – England 205 runs | •169 | 360 | 164 | 160 | | |
| 839 | Sydney – England 9 wkts | 308 | 35-1 | •198 | 143 | | |
| | **1979–80 in Australia** | | | | | | |
| 868 | Perth – Australia 138 runs | 228 | 215 | •244 | 337 | J.M. Brearley | G.S. Chappell |
| 870 | Sydney – Australia 6 wkts | •123 | 237 | 145 | 219-4 | | |
| 872 | Melbourne – Australia 8 wkts | •306 | 273 | 477 | 103-2 | | |
| | **1980 in England (Centenary Test)** | | | | | | |
| 885 | Lord's – Drawn | 205 | 244-3 | •385-5d | 189-4d | I.T. Botham | G.S. Chappell |
| | **1981 in England** | | | | | | |
| 903 | Nottingham – Australia 4 wkts | •185 | 125 | 179 | 132-6 | I.T. Botham | K.J. Hughes |
| 904 | Lord's – Drawn | •311 | 265-8d | 345 | 90-4 | I.T. Botham | |
| 905 | Leeds – England 18 runs | 174 | 356 | •401-9d | 111 | J.M. Brearley | |
| 906 | Birmingham – England 29 runs | •189 | 219 | 258 | 121 | J.M. Brearley | |
| 907 | Manchester – England 103 runs | •231 | 404 | 130 | 402 | J.M. Brearley | |
| 908 | Oval – Drawn | 314 | 261-7 | •352 | 344-9d | J.M. Brearley | |

| Test No. | Venue and Result | England 1st | England 2nd | Australia 1st | Australia 2nd | Captains England | Captains Australia |
|---|---|---|---|---|---|---|---|
| | **1982–83** in Australia | | | | | | |
| 938 | Perth – Drawn | •411 | 358 | 424-9d | 73-2 | | |
| 939 | Brisbane – Australia 7 wkts | •219 | 309 | 341 | 190-3 | | |
| 940 | Adelaide – Australia 8 wkts | 216 | 304 | •438 | 83-2 | R.G.D. Willis | G.S. Chappell |
| 941 | Melbourne – England 3 runs | •284 | 294 | 287 | 288 | | |
| 942 | Sydney – Drawn | 237 | 314-7 | •314 | 382 | | |
| | **1985** in England | | | | | | |
| 1017 | Leeds – England 5 wkts | 533 | 123-5 | •331 | 324 | | |
| 1018 | Lord's – Australia 4 wkts | •290 | 261 | 425 | 127-6 | | |
| 1019 | Nottingham – Drawn | •456 | 196-2 | 539 | — | D.I. Gower | A.R. Border |
| 1020 | Manchester – Drawn | 482-9d | — | •257 | 340-5 | | |
| 1021 | Birmingham – England inns & 118 runs | 595-5d | — | •335 | 142 | | |
| 1022 | Oval – England inns & 94 runs | •464 | — | 241 | 129 | | |

# RESULTS SUMMARY

## ENGLAND v AUSTRALIA – IN ENGLAND

| | | Result | | | Oval | | | Manchester | | | Lord's | | | Nottingham | | | Leeds | | | Birmingham | | | Sheffield | | |
|---|---|---|---|---|---|---|---|---|---|---|---|---|---|---|---|---|---|---|---|---|---|---|---|---|---|---|
| *Year* | *Tests* | E | A | *Drawn* | E | A | *Drawn* | E | A | *Drawn* | E | A | *Drawn* | E | A | *Drawn* | E | A | *Drawn* | E | A | *Drawn* | E | A | *Drawn* |
| 1880 | 1 | 1 | – | – | 1 | – | – | – | – | – | – | – | – | – | – | – | – | – | – | – | – | – | – | – | – |
| 1882 | 1 | – | 1 | – | – | 1 | – | – | – | – | – | – | – | – | – | – | – | – | – | – | – | – | – | – | – |
| 1884 | 3 | 1 | – | 2 | – | – | 1 | – | – | 1 | 1 | – | – | – | – | – | – | – | – | – | – | – | – | – | – |
| 1886 | 3 | 3 | – | – | 1 | – | – | 1 | – | – | 1 | – | – | – | – | – | – | – | – | – | – | – | – | – | – |
| 1888 | 3 | 2 | 1 | – | 1 | – | – | 1 | – | – | – | 1 | – | – | – | – | – | – | – | – | – | – | – | – | – |
| 1890 | 2 | 2 | – | – | 1 | – | – | – | – | – | 1 | – | – | – | – | – | – | – | – | – | – | – | – | – | – |
| 1893 | 3 | 1 | – | 2 | 1 | – | – | – | – | 1 | – | – | 1 | – | – | – | – | – | – | – | – | – | – | – | – |
| 1896 | 3 | 2 | 1 | – | 1 | – | – | – | 1 | – | 1 | – | – | – | – | – | – | – | – | – | – | – | – | – | – |
| 1899 | 5 | – | 1 | 4 | – | – | 1 | – | – | 1 | – | 1 | – | – | – | 1 | – | – | 1 | – | – | – | – | – | – |
| 1902 | 5 | 1 | 2 | 2 | 1 | – | – | – | 1 | – | – | – | 1 | – | – | – | – | – | – | – | – | 1 | – | 1 | – |
| 1905 | 5 | 2 | – | 3 | – | – | 1 | 1 | – | – | – | – | 1 | 1 | – | – | – | – | 1 | – | – | – | – | – | – |
| 1909 | 5 | 1 | 2 | 2 | – | – | 1 | – | – | 1 | – | 1 | – | – | – | – | – | 1 | – | 1 | – | – | – | – | – |
| 1912 | 3 | 1 | – | 2 | 1 | – | – | – | – | 1 | – | – | 1 | – | – | – | – | – | – | – | – | – | – | – | – |
| 1921 | 5 | – | 3 | 2 | – | – | 1 | – | – | 1 | – | 1 | – | – | 1 | – | – | 1 | – | – | – | – | – | – | – |
| 1926 | 5 | 1 | – | 4 | 1 | – | – | – | – | 1 | – | – | 1 | – | – | 1 | – | – | 1 | – | – | – | – | – | – |
| 1930 | 5 | 1 | 2 | 2 | – | 1 | – | – | – | 1 | – | 1 | – | 1 | – | – | – | – | 1 | – | – | – | – | – | – |
| 1934 | 5 | 1 | 2 | 2 | – | 1 | – | – | – | 1 | 1 | – | – | – | 1 | – | – | – | 1 | – | – | – | – | – | – |
| 1938 | 4 | 1 | 1 | 2 | 1 | – | – | – | – | – | – | – | 1 | – | – | 1 | – | 1 | – | – | – | – | – | – | – |
| 1948 | 5 | – | 4 | 1 | – | 1 | – | – | – | 1 | – | 1 | – | – | 1 | – | – | 1 | – | – | – | – | – | – | – |
| 1953 | 5 | 1 | – | 4 | 1 | – | – | – | – | 1 | – | – | 1 | – | – | 1 | – | – | 1 | – | – | – | – | – | – |
| 1956 | 5 | 2 | 1 | 2 | – | – | 1 | 1 | – | – | – | 1 | – | – | – | 1 | 1 | – | – | – | – | – | – | – | – |
| 1961 | 5 | 1 | 2 | 2 | – | – | 1 | – | 1 | – | – | 1 | – | – | – | – | 1 | – | – | – | – | 1 | – | – | – |
| 1964 | 5 | – | 1 | 4 | – | – | 1 | – | – | 1 | – | – | 1 | – | – | 1 | – | 1 | – | – | – | – | – | – | – |
| 1968 | 5 | 1 | 1 | 3 | 1 | – | – | – | 1 | – | – | – | 1 | – | – | – | – | – | 1 | – | – | 1 | – | – | – |
| 1972 | 5 | 2 | 2 | 1 | – | 1 | – | 1 | – | – | – | 1 | – | – | – | 1 | 1 | – | – | – | – | – | – | – | – |
| 1975 | 4 | – | 1 | 3 | – | – | 1 | – | – | – | – | – | 1 | – | – | – | – | – | 1 | – | 1 | – | – | – | – |
| 1977 | 5 | 3 | – | 2 | – | – | 1 | 1 | – | – | – | – | 1 | 1 | – | – | 1 | – | – | – | – | – | – | – | – |
| 1980 | 1 | – | – | 1 | – | – | – | – | – | – | – | – | 1 | – | – | – | – | – | – | – | – | – | – | – | – |
| 1981 | 6 | 3 | 1 | 2 | – | – | 1 | 1 | – | – | – | – | 1 | – | 1 | – | 1 | – | – | 1 | – | – | – | – | – |
| 1985 | 6 | 3 | 1 | 2 | 1 | – | – | – | – | 1 | – | 1 | – | – | – | 1 | 1 | – | – | 1 | – | – | – | – | – |
| **123** | | **37** | **30** | **56** | **13** | **5** | **11** | **7** | **4** | **13** | **5** | **10** | **13** | **3** | **4** | **8** | **6** | **5** | **8** | **3** | **1** | **3** | **–** | **1** | **–** |

## ENGLAND v AUSTRALIA – IN AUSTRALIA

| Season | Result E | A | Drawn | Tests | Melbourne E | A | Drawn | Sydney E | A | Drawn | Adelaide E | A | Drawn | Brisbane E | A | Drawn | Perth E | A | Drawn |
|---|---|---|---|---|---|---|---|---|---|---|---|---|---|---|---|---|---|---|---|
| 1876–77 | 1 | 1 | – | 2 | 1 | 1 | – | – | – | – | – | – | – | – | – | – | – | – | – |
| 1878–79 | – | 1 | – | 1 | – | 1 | – | – | – | – | – | – | – | – | – | – | – | – | – |
| 1881–82 | – | 2 | 2 | 4 | – | – | 2 | – | 2 | – | – | – | – | – | – | – | – | – | – |
| 1882–83 | 2 | 2 | – | 4 | – | 1 | – | 2 | 1 | – | – | – | – | – | – | – | – | – | – |
| 1884–85 | 3 | 2 | – | 5 | 2 | – | – | – | 2 | – | 1 | – | – | – | – | – | – | – | – |
| 1886–87 | 2 | – | – | 2 | – | – | – | 2 | – | – | – | – | – | – | – | – | – | – | – |
| 1887–88 | 1 | – | – | 1 | – | – | – | 1 | – | – | – | – | – | – | – | – | – | – | – |
| 1891–92 | 1 | 2 | – | 3 | – | 1 | – | – | 1 | – | 1 | – | – | – | – | – | – | – | – |
| 1894–95 | 3 | 2 | – | 5 | 1 | 1 | – | 1 | 1 | – | 1 | – | – | – | – | – | – | – | – |
| 1897–98 | 1 | 4 | – | 5 | – | 2 | – | 1 | 1 | – | – | 1 | – | – | – | – | – | – | – |
| 1901–02 | 1 | 4 | – | 5 | – | 2 | – | 1 | 1 | – | – | 1 | – | – | – | – | – | – | – |
| 1903–04 | 3 | 2 | – | 5 | 1 | 1 | – | 2 | – | – | – | 1 | – | – | – | – | – | – | – |
| 1907–08 | 1 | 4 | – | 5 | 1 | 1 | – | – | 2 | – | – | 1 | – | – | – | – | – | – | – |
| 1911–12 | 4 | 1 | – | 5 | 2 | – | – | 1 | 1 | – | 1 | – | – | – | – | – | – | – | – |
| 1920–21 | – | 5 | – | 5 | – | 2 | – | – | 2 | – | – | 1 | – | – | – | – | – | – | – |
| 1924–25 | 1 | 4 | – | 5 | 1 | 1 | – | – | 2 | – | – | 1 | – | – | – | – | – | – | – |
| 1928–29 | 4 | 1 | – | 5 | 1 | 1 | – | 1 | – | – | 1 | – | – | 1 | – | – | – | – | – |
| 1932–33 | 4 | 1 | – | 5 | – | 1 | – | 2 | – | – | 1 | – | – | 1 | – | – | – | – | – |
| 1936–37 | 2 | 3 | – | 5 | – | 2 | – | 1 | – | – | – | 1 | – | 1 | – | – | – | – | – |
| 1946–47 | – | 3 | 2 | 5 | – | – | 1 | – | 2 | – | – | – | 1 | – | 1 | – | – | – | – |
| 1950–51 | 1 | 4 | – | 5 | 1 | 1 | – | – | 1 | – | – | 1 | – | – | 1 | – | – | – | – |
| 1954–55 | 3 | 1 | 1 | 5 | 1 | – | – | 1 | – | 1 | 1 | – | – | – | 1 | – | – | – | – |
| 1958–59 | – | 4 | 1 | 5 | – | 2 | – | – | – | 1 | – | 1 | – | – | 1 | – | – | – | – |
| 1962–63 | 1 | 1 | 3 | 5 | 1 | – | – | – | 1 | 1 | – | – | 1 | – | – | 1 | – | – | – |
| 1965–66 | 1 | 1 | 3 | 5 | – | – | 2 | 1 | – | – | – | 1 | – | – | – | 1 | – | – | – |
| 1970–71 | 2 | – | 4 | 6 | – | – | 1 | 2 | – | – | – | – | 1 | – | – | 1 | – | – | 1 |
| 1974–75 | 1 | 4 | 1 | 6 | 1 | – | 1 | – | 1 | – | – | 1 | – | – | 1 | – | – | 1 | – |
| 1976–77 | – | 1 | – | 1 | – | 1 | – | – | – | – | – | – | – | – | – | – | – | – | – |
| 1978–79 | 5 | 1 | – | 6 | – | 1 | – | 2 | – | – | 1 | – | – | 1 | – | – | 1 | – | – |
| 1979–80 | – | 3 | – | 3 | – | 1 | – | – | 1 | – | – | – | – | – | – | – | – | 1 | – |
| 1982–83 | 1 | 2 | 2 | 5 | 1 | – | – | – | – | 1 | – | 1 | – | – | 1 | – | – | – | 1 |
| **Totals** | **49** | **66** | **19** | **134** | **17** | **23** | **7** | **20** | **22** | **4** | **7** | **13** | **3** | **4** | **6** | **3** | **1** | **2** | **2** |

## HIGHEST INNINGS TOTALS

| | | | | | |
|---|---|---|---|---|---|
| England | in England | 903-7d | | Oval | 1938 |
| | in Australia | 636 | | Sydney | 1928–29 |
| Australia | in England | 729-6d | | Lord's | 1930 |
| | in Australia | 659-8d | | Sydney | 1946–47 |

## LOWEST INNINGS TOTALS

| | | | | | |
|---|---|---|---|---|---|
| England | in England | 52 | | Oval | 1948 |
| | in Australia | 45 | | Sydney | 1886–87 |
| Australia | in England | 36 | | Birmingham | 1902 |
| | in Australia | 42 | | Sydney | 1887–88 |

| | | | |
|---|---|---|---|
| **HIGHEST MATCH AGGREGATE** | 1753 for 40 wickets | Adelaide | 1920–21 |
| **LOWEST MATCH AGGREGATE** | 291 for 40 wickets | Lord's | 1888 |

## HIGHEST INDIVIDUAL INNINGS

| | | | | | |
|---|---|---|---|---|---|
| England | in England | 364 | L. Hutton | Oval | 1938 |
| | in Australia | 287 | R.E. Foster | Sydney | 1903–04 |
| Australia | in England | 334 | D.G. Bradman | Leeds | 1930 |
| | in Australia | 307 | R.M. Cowper | Melbourne | 1965–66 |

## HIGHEST AGGREGATE OF RUNS IN A SERIES

| | | | | | |
|---|---|---|---|---|---|
| England | in England | 732 (av 81.33) | D.I. Gower | | 1985 |
| | in Australia | 905 (av 113.12) | W.R. Hammond | | 1928–29 |
| Australia | in England | 974 (av 139.14) | D.G. Bradman | | 1930 |
| | in Australia | 810 (av 90.00) | D.G. Bradman | | 1936–37 |

## RECORD WICKET PARTNERSHIPS — ENGLAND

| | | | | |
|---|---|---|---|---|
| 1st | 323 | J.B. Hobbs (178), W. Rhodes (179) | Melbourne | 1911–12 |
| 2nd | 382 | L. Hutton (364), M. Leyland (187) | Oval | 1938 |
| 3rd | 262 | W.R. Hammond (177), D.R. Jardine (98) | Adelaide | 1928–29 |
| 4th | 222 | W.R. Hammond (240), E. Paynter (99) | Lord's | 1938 |
| 5th | 206 | E. Paynter (216*), D.C.S. Compton (102) | Nottingham | 1938 |
| 6th | 215 | L. Hutton (364), J. Hardstaff, jr (169*) | Oval | 1938 |
| | 215 | G. Boycott (107), A.P.E. Knott (135) | Nottingham | 1977 |
| 7th | 143 | F.E. Woolley (133*), J.Vine (36) | Sydney | 1911–12 |
| 8th | 124 | E.H. Hendren (169), H. Larwood (70) | Brisbane[1] | 1928–29 |
| 9th | 151 | W.H. Scotton (90), W.W. Read (117) | Oval | 1884 |
| 10th | 130 | R.E. Foster (287), W. Rhodes (40*) | Sydney | 1903–04 |

## RECORD WICKET PARTNERSHIPS — AUSTRALIA

| | | | | |
|---|---|---|---|---|
| 1st | 244 | R.B. Simpson (225), W.M. Lawry (119) | Adelaide | 1965–66 |
| 2nd | 451 | W.H. Ponsford (266), D.G. Bradman (244) | Oval | 1934 |
| 3rd | 276 | D.G. Bradman (187), A.L. Hassett (128) | Brisbane[2] | 1946–47 |
| 4th | 388 | W.H. Ponsford (181), D.G. Bradman (304) | Leeds | 1934 |
| 5th | 405 | S.G. Barnes (234), D.G. Bradman (234) | Sydney | 1946–47 |
| 6th | 346 | J.H.W. Fingleton (136), D.G. Bradman (270) | Melbourne | 1936–37 |
| 7th | 165 | C. Hill (188), H. Trumble (46) | Melbourne | 1897–98 |
| 8th | 243 | R.J. Hartigan (113), C. Hill (160) | Adelaide | 1907–08 |
| 9th | 154 | S.E. Gregory (201), J.M. Blackham (74) | Sydney | 1894–95 |
| 10th | 127 | J.M. Taylor (108), A.A. Mailey (46*) | Sydney | 1924–25 |

## BEST INNINGS BOWLING ANALYSIS

| | | | | | |
|---|---|---|---|---|---|
| England | in England | 10-53 | J.C. Laker | Manchester | 1956 |
| | in Australia | 8-35 | G.A. Lohmann | Sydney | 1886–87 |
| Australia | in England | 8-31 | F. Laver | Manchester | 1909 |
| | in Australia | 9-121 | A.A. Mailey | Melbourne | 1920–21 |

## BEST MATCH BOWLING ANALYSIS

| | | | | | |
|---|---|---|---|---|---|
| England | in England | 19-90 | J.C. Laker | Manchester | 1956 |
| | in Australia | 15-124 | W. Rhodes | Melbourne | 1903–04 |
| Australia | in England | 16-137 | R.A.L. Massie | Lord's | 1972 |
| | in Australia | 13-77 | M.A. Noble | Melbourne | 1901–02 |

## HIGHEST AGGREGATE OF WICKETS IN A SERIES

| | | | | | |
|---|---|---|---|---|---|
| England | in England | 46 (av 9.60) | J.C. Laker | | 1956 |
| | in Australia | 38 (av 23.18) | M.W. Tate | | 1924–25 |
| Australia | in England | 42 (av 21.26) | T.M. Alderman | | 1981 |
| | in Australia | 41 (av 12.85) | R.M. Hogg | | 1978–79 |

## MOST RUNS

| | Tests | I | NO | Runs | HS | Avge |
|---|---|---|---|---|---|---|
| D.G. Bradman (A) | 37 | 63 | 7 | **5028** | 334 | 89.78 |
| J.B. Hobbs (E) | 41 | 71 | 4 | **3636** | 187 | 54.26 |
| G. Boycott (E) | 38 | 71 | 9 | **2945** | 191 | 47.50 |
| W.R. Hammond (E) | 33 | 58 | 3 | **2852** | 251 | 51.85 |
| H. Sutcliffe (E) | 27 | 46 | 5 | **2741** | 194 | 66.85 |
| C. Hill (A) | 41 | 76 | 1 | **2660** | 188 | 35.46 |
| J.H. Edrich (E) | 32 | 57 | 3 | **2644** | 175 | 48.96 |
| G.S. Chappell (A) | 35 | 65 | 8 | **2619** | 144 | 45.94 |
| M.C. Cowdrey (E) | 43 | 75 | 4 | **2433** | 113 | 34.26 |
| L. Hutton (E) | 27 | 49 | 6 | **2428** | 364 | 56.46 |
| R.N. Harvey (A) | 37 | 68 | 5 | **2416** | 167 | 38.34 |
| V.T. Trumper (A) | 40 | 74 | 5 | **2263** | 185* | 32.79 |
| W.M. Lawry (A) | 29 | 51 | 5 | **2233** | 166 | 48.54 |
| S.E. Gregory (A) | 52 | 92 | 7 | **2193** | 201 | 25.80 |
| W.W. Armstrong (A) | 42 | 71 | 9 | **2172** | 158 | 35.03 |
| I.M. Chappell (A) | 30 | 56 | 4 | **2138** | 192 | 41.11 |
| K.F. Barrington (E) | 23 | 39 | 6 | **2111** | 256 | 63.96 |
| A.R. Morris (A) | 24 | 43 | 2 | **2080** | 206 | 50.73 |
| D.I. Gower (E) | 26 | 48 | 2 | **2075** | 215 | 45.10 |

*D.G. Bradman holds the unique record of scoring 2000 runs in both countries in this series (2674 runs in England and 2354 in Australia). J.B. Hobbs is the only other batsman to score 2000 runs in either country (2493 runs in Australia).*

## MOST WICKETS

| | Tests | Balls | Runs | Wkts | BB | 5wI | Avge |
|---|---|---|---|---|---|---|---|
| D.K. Lillee (A) | 29 | 8516 | 3507 | **167** | 7-89 | 11 | 21.00 |
| H. Trumble (A) | 31 | 7895 | 2945 | **141** | 8-65 | 9 | 20.88 |
| I.T. Botham (E) | 29 | 7361 | 3556 | **136** | 6-78 | 8 | 26.14 |
| R.G.D. Willis (E) | 35 | 7294 | 3346 | **128** | 8-43 | 7 | 26.14 |
| M.A. Noble (A) | 39 | 6845 | 2860 | **115** | 7-17 | 9 | 24.86 |
| R.R. Lindwall (A) | 29 | 6728 | 2559 | **114** | 7-63 | 6 | 22.44 |
| W. Rhodes (E) | 41 | 5791 | 2616 | **109** | 8-68 | 6 | 24.00 |
| S.F. Barnes (E) | 20 | 5749 | 2288 | **106** | 7-60 | 12 | 21.58 |
| C.V. Grimmett (A) | 22 | 9224 | 3439 | **106** | 6-37 | 11 | 32.44 |
| D.L. Underwood (E) | 29 | 8000 | 2770 | **105** | 7-50 | 4 | 26.38 |
| A.V. Bedser (E) | 21 | 7065 | 2859 | **104** | 7-44 | 7 | 27.49 |
| G. Giffen (A) | 31 | 6325 | 2791 | **103** | 7-117 | 7 | 27.09 |
| W.J.O'Reilly (A) | 19 | 7864 | 2587 | **102** | 7-54 | 8 | 25.36 |
| R. Peel (E) | 20 | 5216 | 1715 | **102** | 7-31 | 6 | 16.81 |
| C.T.B. Turner (A) | 17 | 5195 | 1670 | **101** | 7-43 | 11 | 16.53 |
| J.R. Thomson (A) | 21 | 4951 | 2418 | **100** | 6-46 | 5 | 24.18 |

## MOST WICKET-KEEPING DISMISSALS

| | Tests | Ct | St | Total |
|---|---|---|---|---|
| R.W. Marsh (A) | 42 | 141 | 7 | **148** |
| A.P.E. Knott (E) | 34 | 97 | 8 | **105** |
| W.A.S. Oldfield (A) | 38 | 59 | 31 | **90** |
| A.F.A. Lilley (E) | 32 | 65 | 19 | **84** |
| A.T.W. Grout (A) | 22 | 69 | 7 | **76** |
| T.G. Evans (E) | 31 | 63 | 12 | **75** |

# ENGLAND v SOUTH AFRICA

| Test No. | Venue and Result | England 1st | England 2nd | South Africa 1st | South Africa 2nd | Captains England | Captains South Africa |
|---|---|---|---|---|---|---|---|
| | **1888–89 in South Africa** | | | | | | |
| 31 | Port Elizabeth – England 8 wkts | 148 | 67-2 | •84 | 129 | C.A. Smith | O.R. Dunell |
| 32 | Cape Town – England inns & 202 runs | •292 | — | 47 | 43 | M.P. Bowden | W.H. Milton |
| | **1891–92 in South Africa** | | | | | | |
| 38 | Cape Town – England inns & 189 runs | 369 | — | •97 | 83 | W.W. Read | W.H. Milton |
| | **1895–96 in South Africa** | | | | | | |
| 47 | Port Elizabeth – England 288 runs | •185 | 226 | 93 | 30 | Sir T.C. O'Brien | E.A. Halliwell |
| 48 | Johannesburg1 – England inns & 197 runs | •482 | — | 151 | 134 | Lord Hawke | E.A. Halliwell |
| 49 | Cape Town – England inns & 33 runs | 265 | — | •115 | 117 | Lord Hawke | A.R. Richards |
| | **1898–99 in South Africa** | | | | | | |
| 58 | Johannesburg1 – England 32 runs | •145 | 237 | 251 | 99 | Lord Hawke | M. Bisset |
| 59 | Cape Town – England 210 runs | •92 | 330 | 177 | 35 | | |
| | **1905–06 in South Africa** | | | | | | |
| 88 | Johannesburg1 – South Africa 1 wkt | •184 | 190 | 91 | 287-9 | | |
| 89 | Johannesburg1 – South Africa 9 wkts | •148 | 160 | 277 | 33-1 | | |
| 90 | Johannesburg1 – South Africa 243 runs | 295 | 196 | •385 | 349-5d | P.F. Warner | P.W. Sherwell |
| 91 | Cape Town – England 4 wkts | 198 | 160-6 | 218 | 138 | | |
| 92 | Cape Town – South Africa inns & 16 runs | •187 | 130 | 333 | — | | |
| | **1907 in England** | | | | | | |
| 93 | Lord's – Drawn | •428 | — | 140 | 185-3 | | |
| 94 | Leeds – England 53 runs | •76 | 162 | 110 | 75 | R.E. Foster | P.W. Sherwell |
| 95 | Oval – Drawn | •295 | 138 | 178 | 159-5 | | |
| | **1909–10 in South Africa** | | | | | | |
| 106 | Johannesburg1 – South Africa 19 runs | 310 | 224 | •208 | 345 | H.D.G. Leveson Gower | |
| 107 | Durban1 – South Africa 95 runs | 199 | 252 | •199 | 347 | H.D.G. Leveson Gower | |
| 108 | Johannesburg1 – England 3 wkts | 322 | 221-7 | 305 | 237 | H.D.G. Leveson Gower | S.J. Snooke |
| 109 | Cape Town – South Africa 4 wkts | •203 | 178 | 207 | 175-6 | F.L. Fane | |
| 110 | Cape Town – England 9 wkts | •417 | 16-1 | 103 | 327 | F.L. Fane | |

| Test No. | Venue and Result | England 1st | England 2nd | South Africa 1st | South Africa 2nd | Captains England | Captains South Africa |
|---|---|---|---|---|---|---|---|
| | **1912 in England** | | | | | | |
| 122 | Lord's – England inns & 62 runs | 337 | — | •58 | 217 | C.B. Fry | F. Mitchell |
| 124 | Leeds – England 174 runs | •242 | 238 | 147 | 159 | C.B. Fry | L.J. Tancred |
| 128 | Oval – England 10 wkts | 176 | 14-0 | •95 | 93 | C.B. Fry | L.J. Tancred |
| | **1913–14 in South Africa** | | | | | | |
| 130 | Durban¹ – England inns & 157 runs | 450 | — | •182 | 111 | J.W.H.T. Douglas | H.W. Taylor |
| 131 | Johannesburg¹ – England inns & 12 runs | 403 | — | •160 | 231 | J.W.H.T. Douglas | H.W. Taylor |
| 132 | Johannesburg¹ – England 91 runs | •238 | 308 | 151 | 304 | J.W.H.T. Douglas | H.W. Taylor |
| 133 | Durban¹ – Drawn | 163 | 154-5 | 170 | 305-9d | J.W.H.T. Douglas | H.W. Taylor |
| 134 | Port Elizabeth – England 10 wkts | 411 | 11-0 | •193 | 228 | J.W.H.T. Douglas | H.W. Taylor |
| | **1922–23 in South Africa** | | | | | | |
| 148 | Johannesburg¹ – South Africa 168 runs | 182 | 218 | •148 | 420 | F.T. Mann | H.W. Taylor |
| 149 | Cape Town – England 1 wkt | 183 | 173-9 | •113 | 242 | F.T. Mann | H.W. Taylor |
| 150 | Durban² – Drawn | •428 | 11-1 | 368 | — | F.T. Mann | H.W. Taylor |
| 151 | Johannesburg¹ – Drawn | •244 | 376-6d | 295 | 247-4 | F.T. Mann | H.W. Taylor |
| 152 | Durban² – England 109 runs | •281 | 241 | 179 | 234 | F.T. Mann | H.W. Taylor |
| | **1924 in England** | | | | | | |
| 153 | Birmingham – England inns & 18 runs | •438 | — | 30 | 390 | A.E.R. Gilligan | H.W. Taylor |
| 154 | Lord's – England inns & 18 runs | 531-2d | — | •273 | 240 | A.E.R. Gilligan | H.W. Taylor |
| 155 | Leeds – England 9 wkts | 396 | 60-1 | 132 | 323 | A.E.R. Gilligan | H.W. Taylor |
| 156 | Manchester – Drawn | — | — | •116-4 | — | J.W.H.T. Douglas | H.W. Taylor |
| 157 | Oval – Drawn | 421-8 | — | •342 | — | A.E.R. Gilligan | H.W. Taylor |
| | **1927–28 in South Africa** | | | | | | |
| 168 | Johannesburg¹ – England 10 wkts | 313 | 57-0 | •196 | 170 | R.T. Stanyforth | H.G. Deane |
| 169 | Cape Town – England 87 runs | •133 | 428 | 250 | 224 | R.T. Stanyforth | H.G. Deane |
| 170 | Durban² – Drawn | 430 | 132-2 | •246 | 464-8d | R.T. Stanyforth | H.G. Deane |
| 171 | Johannesburg¹ – South Africa 4 wkts | •265 | 215 | 328 | 156-6 | R.T. Stanyforth | H.G. Deane |
| 172 | Durban² – South Africa 8 wkts | •282 | 118 | 332-7d | 69-2 | G.T.S. Stevens | H.G. Deane |
| | **1929 in England** | | | | | | |
| 181 | Birmingham – Drawn | •245 | 308-4d | 250 | 171-1 | J.C. White | H.G. Deane |
| 182 | Lord's – Drawn | 302 | 312-8d | 322 | 90-5 | J.C. White | H.G. Deane |
| 183 | Leeds – England 5 wkts | 328 | 186-5 | 236 | 275 | J.C. White | H.G. Deane |
| 184 | Manchester – England inns & 32 runs | •427-7d | — | 130 | 265 | A.W. Carr | H.G. Deane |
| 185 | Oval – Drawn | •258 | 264-1 | 492-8d | — | A.W. Carr | H.G. Deane |

| Test No. | Venue and Result | England 1st | England 2nd | South Africa 1st | South Africa 2nd | Captains England | Captains South Africa |
|---|---|---|---|---|---|---|---|
| | **1930–31 in South Africa** | | | | | | |
| 204 | Johannesburg¹ – South Africa 28 runs | 193 | 211 | •126 | 306 | A.P.F. Chapman | E.P. Nupen |
| 205 | Cape Town – Drawn | 350 | 252 | •513-8d | — | | H.G. Deane |
| 206 | Durban² – Drawn | 223-1d | — | 177 | 145-8 | | H.G. Deane |
| 207 | Johannesburg¹ – Drawn | •442 | 169-9d | 295 | 280-7 | | H.B. Cameron |
| 208 | Durban² – Drawn | 230 | 72-4 | •252 | 219-7d | | H.B. Cameron |
| | **1935 in England** | | | | | | |
| 242 | Nottingham – Drawn | •384-7d | — | 220 | 17-1 | R.E.S. Wyatt | H.F. Wade |
| 243 | Lord's – South Africa 157 runs | 198 | 151 | 228 | 278-7d | | |
| 244 | Leeds – Drawn | 216 | 294-7d | 171 | 194-5 | | |
| 245 | Manchester – Drawn | 357 | 231-6d | 318 | 169-2 | | |
| 246 | Oval – Drawn | 534-6d | — | •476 | 287-6 | | |
| | **1938–39 in South Africa** | | | | | | |
| 267 | Johannesburg¹ – Drawn | •422 | 291-4d | 390 | 108-1 | W.R. Hammond | A. Melville |
| 268 | Cape Town – Drawn | 559-9d | — | 286 | 201-2 | | |
| 269 | Durban² – England inns & 13 runs | •469-4d | — | 103 | 353 | | |
| 270 | Johannesburg¹ – Drawn | •215 | 203-4 | 349-8d | — | | |
| 271 | Durban² – Drawn | 316 | 654-5 | 530 | 481 | | |
| | **1947 in England** | | | | | | |
| 285 | Nottingham – Drawn | 208 | 551 | •533 | 166-1 | N.W.D. Yardley | A. Melville |
| 286 | Lord's – England 10 wkts | 554-8d | 26-0 | 327 | 252 | | |
| 287 | Manchester – England 7 wkts | 478 | 130-3 | •339 | 267 | | |
| 288 | Leeds – England 10 wkts | 317-7d | 47-0 | •175 | 184 | | |
| 289 | Oval – Drawn | •427 | 325-6d | 302 | 423-7 | | |
| | **1948–49 in South Africa** | | | | | | |
| 309 | Durban² – England 2 wkts | 253 | 128-8 | •161 | 219 | F.G. Mann | A.D. Nourse |
| 310 | Johannesburg² – Drawn | •608 | — | 315 | 270-2 | | |
| 311 | Cape Town – Drawn | •308 | 276-3d | 356 | 142-4 | | |
| 312 | Johannesburg² – Drawn | 379 | 253-7d | 257-9d | 194-4 | | |
| 313 | Port Elizabeth – England 3 wkts | 395 | 174-7 | •379 | 187-3d | | |

| Test No. | Venue and Result | England 1st | England 2nd | South Africa 1st | South Africa 2nd | Captains England | Captains South Africa |
|---|---|---|---|---|---|---|---|
| | **1951 in England** | | | | | | |
| 334 | Nottingham – South Africa 71 runs | •419-9d | 114 | •483-9d | 121 | | |
| 335 | Lord's – England 10 wkts | •311 | 16-0 | 115 | 211 | | |
| 336 | Manchester – England 9 wkts | 211 | 142-1 | •158 | 191 | F.R. Brown | A.D. Nourse |
| 337 | Leeds – Drawn | 505 | — | •538 | 87-0 | | |
| 338 | Oval – England 4 wkts | 194 | 164-6 | •202 | 154 | | |
| | **1955 in England** | | | | | | |
| 408 | Nottingham – England inns & 5 runs | •334 | — | 181 | 148 | | J.E. Cheetham |
| 409 | Lord's – England 71 runs | •133 | 353 | 304 | 111 | | J.E. Cheetham |
| 410 | Manchester – South Africa 3 wkts | •284 | 381 | 521-8d | 145-7 | P.B.H. May | D.J. McGlew |
| 411 | Leeds – South Africa 224 runs | 191 | 256 | 171 | 500 | | D.J. McGlew |
| 412 | Oval – England 92 runs | •151 | 204 | 112 | 151 | | J.E. Cheetham |
| | **1956–57 in South Africa** | | | | | | |
| 434 | Johannesburg[3] – England 131 runs | •268 | 150 | 215 | 72 | | C.B. van Ryneveld |
| 435 | Cape Town – England 312 runs | 369 | 220-6d | 205 | 72 | | D.J. McGlew |
| 436 | Durban[2] – Drawn | •218 | 254 | 283 | 142-6 | P.B.H. May | C.B. van Ryneveld |
| 437 | Johannesburg[3] – South Africa 17 runs | 251 | 214 | •340 | 142 | | C.B. van Ryneveld |
| 438 | Port Elizabeth – South Africa 58 runs | 110 | 130 | •164 | 134 | | C.B. van Ryneveld |
| | **1960 in England** | | | | | | |
| 492 | Birmingham – England 100 runs | •292 | 203 | 186 | 209 | | |
| 493 | Lord's – England inns & 73 runs | •362-8d | — | 152 | 137 | | |
| 494 | Nottingham – England 8 wkts | •287 | 49-2 | 88 | 247 | M.C. Cowdrey | D.J. McGlew |
| 495 | Manchester – Drawn | •260 | 153-7d | 229 | 46-0 | | |
| 496 | Oval – Drawn | •155 | 479-9d | 419 | 97-4 | | |
| | **1964-65 in South Africa** | | | | | | |
| 571 | Durban[2] – England inns & 104 runs | •485-5d | — | 155 | 226 | | |
| 572 | Johannesburg[3] – Drawn | 531 | — | 317 | 336-6 | | |
| 573 | Cape Town – Drawn | 442 | 15-0 | 501-7d | 346 | M.J.K. Smith | T.L. Goddard |
| 574 | Johannesburg[3] – Drawn | 384 | 153-6 | •390-6d | 307-3d | | |
| 575 | Port Elizabeth – Drawn | 435 | 29-1 | 502 | 178-4d | | |
| | **1965 in England** | | | | | | |
| 594 | Lord's – Drawn | 338 | 145-7 | •280 | 248 | | |
| 595 | Nottingham – South Africa 94 runs | 240 | 224 | •269 | 289 | M.J.K. Smith | P.L. van der Merwe |
| 596 | Oval – Drawn | 202 | 308-4 | •208 | 392 | | |

| Year | Tests | Result E | Result SA | Result Drawn | Lord's E | Lord's SA | Lord's Drawn | Leeds E | Leeds SA | Leeds Drawn | Oval E | Oval SA | Oval Drawn | Birmingham E | Birmingham SA | Birmingham Drawn | Manchester E | Manchester SA | Manchester Drawn | Nottingham E | Nottingham SA | Nottingham Drawn |
|---|---|---|---|---|---|---|---|---|---|---|---|---|---|---|---|---|---|---|---|---|---|---|
| 1907 | 3 | 1 | – | 2 | – | – | 1 | 1 | – | – | – | – | 1 | – | – | – | – | – | – | – | – | – |
| 1912 | 3 | 3 | – | – | 1 | – | – | 1 | – | – | 1 | – | – | – | – | – | – | – | – | – | – | – |
| 1924 | 5 | 3 | – | 2 | 1 | – | – | 1 | – | – | – | – | 1 | 1 | – | – | – | – | 1 | – | – | – |
| 1929 | 5 | 2 | – | 3 | – | – | 1 | 1 | – | – | – | – | 1 | – | – | 1 | 1 | – | – | – | – | – |
| 1935 | 5 | – | 1 | 4 | – | 1 | – | – | – | 1 | – | – | 1 | – | – | – | – | – | 1 | – | – | 1 |
| 1947 | 5 | 3 | – | 2 | 1 | – | – | 1 | – | – | – | – | 1 | – | – | – | 1 | – | – | – | – | 1 |
| 1951 | 5 | 3 | 1 | 1 | 1 | – | – | – | – | 1 | 1 | – | – | – | – | – | 1 | – | – | – | 1 | – |
| 1955 | 5 | 3 | 2 | – | 1 | – | – | – | 1 | – | 1 | – | – | – | – | – | – | 1 | – | 1 | – | – |
| 1960 | 5 | 3 | – | 2 | 1 | – | – | – | – | – | – | – | 1 | 1 | – | – | – | – | 1 | 1 | – | – |
| 1965 | 3 | – | 1 | 2 | – | – | 1 | – | – | – | – | – | 1 | – | – | – | – | – | – | – | 1 | – |
| **44** | | **21** | **5** | **18** | **6** | **1** | **3** | **5** | **1** | **2** | **3** | **–** | **7** | **2** | **–** | **1** | **3** | **1** | **3** | **2** | **2** | **2** |

## ENGLAND v SOUTH AFRICA – IN SOUTH AFRICA

| Year | Tests | Result E | Result SA | Result Drawn | Port Elizabeth E | Port Elizabeth SA | Port Elizabeth Drawn | Cape Town E | Cape Town SA | Cape Town Drawn | Johannesburg E | Johannesburg SA | Johannesburg Drawn | Durban E | Durban SA | Durban Drawn |
|---|---|---|---|---|---|---|---|---|---|---|---|---|---|---|---|---|
| 1888–89 | 2 | 2 | – | – | 1 | – | – | 1 | – | – | – | – | – | – | – | – |
| 1891–92 | 1 | 1 | – | – | – | – | – | 1 | – | – | – | – | – | – | – | – |
| 1895–96 | 3 | 3 | – | – | 1 | – | – | 1 | – | – | 1 | – | – | – | – | – |
| 1898–99 | 2 | 2 | – | – | – | – | – | 1 | – | – | 1 | – | – | – | – | – |
| 1905–06 | 5 | 1 | 4 | – | – | – | – | 1 | 1 | – | – | 3 | – | – | – | – |
| 1909–10 | 5 | 2 | 3 | – | – | – | – | 1 | 1 | – | 1 | 1 | – | – | 1 | – |
| 1913–14 | 5 | 4 | – | 1 | 1 | – | – | – | – | – | 2 | – | – | 1 | – | 1 |
| 1922–23 | 5 | 2 | 1 | 2 | – | – | – | 1 | – | – | – | 1 | 1 | 1 | – | 1 |
| 1927–28 | 5 | 2 | 2 | 1 | – | – | – | 1 | – | – | 1 | 1 | – | – | 1 | 1 |
| 1930–31 | 5 | – | 1 | 4 | – | – | – | – | – | 1 | – | 1 | 1 | – | – | 2 |
| 1938–39 | 5 | 1 | – | 4 | – | – | – | – | – | 1 | – | – | 2 | 1 | – | 1 |
| 1948–49 | 5 | 2 | – | 3 | 1 | – | – | – | – | 1 | – | – | 2 | 1 | – | – |
| 1956–57 | 5 | 2 | 2 | 1 | – | 1 | – | 1 | – | – | 1 | 1 | – | – | – | 1 |
| 1964–65 | 5 | 1 | – | 4 | – | – | 1 | – | – | 1 | – | – | 2 | 1 | – | – |
| **58** | | **25** | **13** | **20** | **4** | **1** | **1** | **9** | **2** | **4** | **7** | **8** | **8** | **5** | **2** | **7** |
| **Totals 102** | | **46** | **18** | **38** | | | | | | | | | | | | |

## HIGHEST INNINGS TOTALS

| | | | | |
|---|---|---|---|---|
| England | in England | 554-8d | Lord's | 1947 |
| | in South Africa | 654-5 | Durban[2] | 1938–39 |
| South Africa | in England | 538 | Leeds | 1951 |
| | in South Africa | 530 | Durban[2] | 1938–39 |

## LOWEST INNINGS TOTALS

| | | | | |
|---|---|---|---|---|
| England | in England | 76 | Leeds | 1907 |
| | in South Africa | 92 | Cape Town | 1898–99 |
| South Africa | in England | 30 | Birmingham | 1924 |
| | in South Africa | 30 | Port Elizabeth | 1895–96 |

| | | | |
|---|---|---|---|
| **HIGHEST MATCH AGGREGATE** | 1981 for 35 wickets | Durban[2] | 1938–39 |
| **LOWEST MATCH AGGREGATE** | 378 for 30 wickets | Oval | 1912 |

## HIGHEST INDIVIDUAL INNINGS

| | | | | | |
|---|---|---|---|---|---|
| England | in England | 211 | J.B. Hobbs | Lord's | 1924 |
| | in South Africa | 243 | E. Paynter | Durban[2] | 1938–39 |
| South Africa | in England | 236 | E.A.B. Rowan | Leeds | 1951 |
| | in South Africa | 176 | H.W. Taylor | Johannesburg[1] | 1922–23 |

## HIGHEST AGGREGATE OF RUNS IN A SERIES

| | | | | |
|---|---|---|---|---|
| England | in England | 753 (av 94.12) | D.C.S. Compton | 1947 |
| | in South Africa | 653 (av 81.62) | E. Paynter | 1938–39 |
| South Africa | in England | 621 (av 69.00) | A.D. Nourse | 1947 |
| | in South Africa | 582 (av 64.66) | H.W. Taylor | 1922–23 |

## RECORD WICKET PARTNERSHIPS — ENGLAND

| | | | | |
|---|---|---|---|---|
| 1st | 359 | L. Hutton (158), C. Washbrook (195) | Johannesburg[2] | 1948–49 |
| 2nd | 280 | P.A. Gibb (120), W.J. Edrich (219) | Durban[2] | 1938–39 |
| 3rd | 370 | W.J. Edrich (189), D.C.S. Compton (208) | Lord's | 1947 |
| 4th | 197 | W.R. Hammond (181), L.E.G. Ames (115) | Cape Town | 1938–39 |
| 5th | 237 | D.C.S. Compton (163), N.W.D. Yardley (99) | Nottingham | 1947 |
| 6th | 206* | K.F. Barrington (148*), J.M. Parks (108*) | Durban[2] | 1964–65 |
| 7th | 115 | J.W.H.T. Douglas (119), M.C. Bird (61) | Durban[1] | 1913–14 |
| 8th | 154 | C.W. Wright (71), H.R. Bromley-Davenport (84) | Johannesburg[1] | 1895–96 |
| 9th | 71 | H. Wood (134*), J.T. Hearne (40) | Cape Town | 1891–92 |
| 10th | 92 | C.A.G. Russell (111), A.E.R. Gilligan (39*) | Durban[2] | 1922–23 |

## RECORD WICKET PARTNERSHIPS — SOUTH AFRICA

| | | | | |
|---|---|---|---|---|
| 1st | 260 | B. Mitchell (123), I.J. Siedle (141) | Cape Town | 1930–31 |
| 2nd | 198 | E.A.B. Rowan (236), C.B. van Ryneveld (83) | Leeds | 1951 |
| 3rd | 319 | A. Melville (189), A.D. Nourse (149) | Nottingham | 1947 |
| 4th | 214 | H.W. Taylor (121), H.G. Deane (93) | Oval | 1929 |
| 5th | 157 | A.J. Pithey (95), J.H.B. Waite (64) | Johannesburg[3] | 1964–65 |
| 6th | 171 | J.H.B. Waite (113), P.L. Winslow (108) | Manchester | 1955 |
| 7th | 123 | H.G. Deane (73), E.P. Nupen (69) | Durban[2] | 1927–28 |
| 8th | 109* | B. Mitchell (189*), L. Tuckett (40*) | Oval | 1947 |
| 9th | 137 | E.L. Dalton (117), A.B.C. Langton (73*) | Oval | 1935 |
| 10th | 103 | H.G. Owen-Smith (129), A.J. Bell (26*) | Leeds | 1929 |

## BEST INNINGS BOWLING ANALYSIS

| | | | | | |
|---|---|---|---|---|---|
| England | in England | 8-29 | S.F. Barnes | Oval | 1912 |
| | in South Africa | 9-28 | G.A. Lohmann | Johannesburg[1] | 1895–96 |
| South Africa | in England | 7-65 | S.J. Pegler | Lord's | 1912 |
| | in South Africa | 9-113 | H.J. Tayfield | Johannesburg[3] | 1956–57 |

## BEST MATCH BOWLING ANALYSIS

| | | | | | |
|---|---|---|---|---|---|
| England | in England | 15-99 | C. Blythe | Leeds | 1907 |
| | in South Africa | 17-159 | S.F. Barnes | Johannesburg[1] | 1913–14 |
| South Africa | in England | 10-87 | P.M. Pollock | Nottingham | 1965 |
| | in South Africa | 13-192 | H.J. Tayfield | Johannesburg[3] | 1956–57 |

## HIGHEST AGGREGATE OF WICKETS IN A SERIES

| | | | | |
|---|---|---|---|---|
| England | in England | 34 (av 8.29) | S.F. Barnes | 1912 |
| | in South Africa | 49 (av 10.93) | S.F. Barnes | 1913–14 |
| South Africa | in England | 26 (av 21.84) | H.J. Tayfield | 1955 |
| | | 26 (av 22.57) | N.A.T. Adcock | 1960 |
| | in South Africa | 37 (av 17.18) | H.J. Tayfield | 1956–57 |

# ENGLAND v WEST INDIES

| Test No. | Venue and Result | England 1st | England 2nd | West Indies 1st | West Indies 2nd | Captains England | Captains West Indies |
|---|---|---|---|---|---|---|---|
| | **1928** in England | | | | | A.P.F. Chapman | R.K. Nunes |
| 173 | Lord's – England inns & 58 runs | •401 | — | 177 | 166 | | |
| 174 | Manchester – England inns & 30 runs | 351 | — | •206 | 115 | | |
| 175 | Oval – England inns & 71 runs | 438 | — | •238 | 129 | | |
| | **1929–30** in West Indies | | | | | Hon F.S.G. Calthorpe | |
| 190 | Bridgetown – Drawn | 467 | 167-3 | •369 | 384 | | E.L.G. Hoad |
| 191 | Port-of-Spain – England 167 runs | •208 | 425-8d | 254 | 212 | | N. Betancourt |
| 192 | Georgetown – West Indies 289 runs | 145 | 327 | •471 | 290 | | M.P. Fernandes |
| 193 | Kingston – Drawn | •849 | 272-9d | 286 | 408-5 | | R.K. Nunes |
| | **1933** in England | | | | | | G.C. Grant |
| 227 | Lord's – England inns & 27 runs | •296 | — | 97 | 172 | D.R. Jardine | |
| 228 | Manchester – Drawn | 374 | — | •375 | 225 | D.R. Jardine | |
| 229 | Oval – England inns & 17 runs | •312 | — | 100 | 195 | R.E.S. Wyatt | |
| | **1934–35** in West Indies | | | | | R.E.S. Wyatt | G.C. Grant |
| 238 | Bridgetown – England 4 wkts | 81-7d | 75-6 | •102 | 51-6d | | |
| 239 | Port-of-Spain – West Indies 217 runs | 258 | 107 | 302 | 280-6d | | |
| 240 | Georgetown – Drawn | •226 | 160-6d | 184 | 104-5 | | |
| 241 | Kingston – West Indies inns & 161 runs | 271 | 103 | •535-7d | — | | |
| | **1939** in England | | | | | W.R. Hammond | R.S. Grant |
| 272 | Lord's – England 8 wkts | 404-5d | 100-2 | •277 | 225 | | |
| 273 | Manchester – Drawn | •164-7d | 128-6d | 133 | 43-4 | | |
| 274 | Oval – Drawn | •352 | 366-3 | 498 | — | | |
| | **1947–48** in West Indies | | | | | | |
| 295 | Bridgetown – Drawn | 253 | 86-4 | •296 | 351-9d | K. Cranston | G.A. Headley |
| 296 | Port-of-Spain – Drawn | •362 | 275 | 497 | 72-3 | G.O.B. Allen | G.E. Gomez |
| 297 | Georgetown – West Indies 7 wkts | 111 | 263 | •297-8d | 78-3 | G.O.B. Allen | J.D.C. Goddard |
| 298 | Kingston – West Indies 10 wkts | •227 | 336 | 490 | 76-0 | G.O.B. Allen | J.D.C. Goddard |

| Test No. | Venue and Result | England 1st | England 2nd | West Indies 1st | West Indies 2nd | Captains England | Captains West Indies |
|---|---|---|---|---|---|---|---|
| | **1950 in England** | | | | | | |
| 323 | Manchester – England 202 runs | •312 | 288 | 215 | 183 | N.W.D. Yardley | J.D.C. Goddard |
| 324 | Lord's – West Indies 326 runs | 151 | 274 | •326 | 425-6d | N.W.D. Yardley | |
| 325 | Nottingham – West Indies 10 wkts | •223 | 436 | 558 | 103-0 | N.W.D. Yardley | |
| 326 | Oval – West Indies inns & 56 runs | 344 | 103 | •503 | — | F.R. Brown | |
| | **1953–54 in West Indies** | | | | | | |
| 382 | Kingston – West Indies 140 runs | 170 | 316 | •417 | 209-6d | L. Hutton | J.B. Stollmeyer |
| 383 | Bridgetown – West Indies 181 runs | 181 | 313 | 383 | 292-2d | | |
| 384 | Georgetown – England 9 wkts | •435 | 75-1 | 251 | 256 | | |
| 385 | Port-of-Spain – Drawn | 537 | 98-3 | •681-8d | 212-4d | | |
| 386 | Kingston – England 9 wkts | 414 | 72-1 | •139 | 346 | | |
| | **1957 in England** | | | | | | |
| 439 | Birmingham – Drawn | •186 | 583-4d | 474 | 72-7 | P.B.H. May | J.D.C. Goddard |
| 440 | Lord's – England inns & 36 runs | 424 | — | •127 | 261 | | |
| 441 | Nottingham – Drawn | •619-6d | 64-1 | 372 | 367 | | |
| 442 | Leeds – England inns & 5 runs | 279 | — | •142 | 132 | | |
| 443 | Oval – England inns & 237 runs | •412 | — | 89 | 86 | | |
| | **1959–60 in West Indies** | | | | | | |
| 487 | Bridgetown – Drawn | •482 | 71-0 | 563-8d | — | P.B.H. May | F.C.M. Alexander |
| 488 | Port-of-Spain – England 256 runs | •382 | 230-9d | 112 | 244 | P.B.H. May | |
| 489 | Kingston – Drawn | •277 | 305 | 353 | 175-6 | P.B.H. May | |
| 490 | Georgetown – Drawn | •295 | 334-8 | 402-8d | — | M.C. Cowdrey | |
| 491 | Port-of-Spain – Drawn | •393 | 350-7d | 338-8d | 209-5 | M.C. Cowdrey | |
| | **1963 in England** | | | | | | |
| 543 | Manchester – West Indies 10 wkts | 205 | 296 | •501-6d | 1-0 | E.R. Dexter | F.M.M. Worrell |
| 544 | Lord's – Drawn | 297 | 228-9 | 301 | 229 | | |
| 545 | Birmingham – England 217 runs | •216 | 278-9d | 186 | 91 | | |
| 546 | Leeds – West Indies 221 runs | 174 | 231 | 397 | 229 | | |
| 547 | Oval – West Indies 8 wkts | •275 | 223 | 246 | 255-2 | | |
| | **1966 in England** | | | | | | |
| 605 | Manchester – West Indies inns & 40 runs | 167 | 277 | •484 | — | M.J.K. Smith | G.St A. Sobers |
| 606 | Lord's – Drawn | 355 | 197-4 | •269 | 369-5d | M.C. Cowdrey | |
| 607 | Nottingham – West Indies 139 runs | 325 | 253 | •235 | 482-8d | M.C. Cowdrey | |
| 608 | Leeds – West Indies inns & 55 runs | 240 | 205 | •500-9d | — | M.C. Cowdrey | |
| 609 | Oval – England inns & 34 runs | 527 | | •268 | 225 | D.B. Close | |

| Test No. | Venue and Result | England 1st | England 2nd | West Indies 1st | West Indies 2nd | Captains England | Captains West Indies |
|---|---|---|---|---|---|---|---|
| | **1967–68** in West Indies | | | | | | |
| 628 | Port-of-Spain – Drawn | •568 | — | 363 | 243-8 | | |
| 629 | Kingston – Drawn | 376 | 68-8 | 143 | 391-9d | | |
| 630 | Bridgetown – Drawn | 449 | — | 349 | 284-6 | M.C. Cowdrey | G.St A. Sobers |
| 631 | Port-of-Spain – England 7 wkts | 404 | 215-3 | •526-7d | 92-2d | | |
| 632 | Georgetown – Drawn | 371 | 206-9 | •414 | 264 | | |
| | **1969** in England | | | | | | |
| 653 | Manchester – England 10 wkts | •413 | 12-0 | 147 | 275 | | |
| 654 | Lord's – Drawn | 344 | 295-7 | •380 | 295-9d | R. Illingworth | G.St A. Sobers |
| 655 | Leeds – England 30 runs | •223 | 240 | 161 | 272 | | |
| | **1973** in England | | | | | | |
| 725 | Oval – West Indies 158 runs | 257 | 255 | •415 | 255 | | |
| 726 | Birmingham – Drawn | 305 | 182-2 | •327 | 302 | R. Illingworth | R.B. Kanhai |
| 727 | Lord's – West Indies inns & 226 runs | 233 | 193 | •652-8d | — | | |
| | **1973–74** in West Indies | | | | | | |
| 731 | Port-of-Spain – West Indies 7 wkts | •131 | 392 | 392 | 132-3 | | |
| 732 | Kingston – Drawn | •353 | 432-9 | 583-9d | — | | |
| 733 | Bridgetown – Drawn | •395 | 277-7 | 596-8d | — | M.H. Denness | R.B. Kanhai |
| 734 | Georgetown – Drawn | •448 | — | 198-4 | — | | |
| 735 | Port-of-Spain – England 26 runs | •267 | 263 | 305 | 199 | | |
| | **1976** in England | | | | | | |
| 777 | Nottingham – Drawn | 332 | 156-2 | •494 | 176-5d | | |
| 778 | Lord's – Drawn | •250 | 254 | 182 | 241-6 | | |
| 779 | Manchester – West Indies 425 runs | 71 | 126 | •211 | 411-5d | A.W. Greig | C.H. Lloyd |
| 780 | Leeds – West Indies 55 runs | 387 | 204 | •450 | 196 | | |
| 781 | Oval – West Indies 231 runs | 435 | 203 | •687-8d | 182-0d | | |
| | **1980** in England | | | | | | |
| 880 | Nottingham – West Indies 2 wkts | •263 | 252 | 308 | 209-8 | | C.H. Lloyd |
| 881 | Lord's – Drawn | •269 | 133-2 | 518 | — | | C.H. Lloyd |
| 882 | Manchester – Drawn | •150 | 391-7 | 260 | — | I.T. Botham | C.H. Lloyd |
| 883 | Oval – Drawn | •370 | 209-9d | 265 | — | | C.H. Lloyd |
| 884 | Leeds – Drawn | •143 | 227-6d | 245 | — | | I.V.A. Richards |

| Test No. | Venue and Result | England | | West Indies | | Captains | |
|---|---|---|---|---|---|---|---|
| | | 1st | 2nd | 1st | 2nd | England | West Indies |
| | **1980–81** in West Indies | | | | | | |
| 896 | Port-of-Spain – West Indies inns & 79 runs | 178 | 169 | •426-9d | — | I.T. Botham | C.H. Lloyd |
| — | Georgetown – Cancelled | — | — | — | — | | |
| 897 | Bridgetown – West Indies 298 runs | 122 | 224 | •265 | 379-7d | | |
| 898 | St John's – Drawn | •271 | 234-3 | 468-9d | — | | |
| 899 | Kingston – Drawn | •285 | 302-6d | 442 | — | | |
| | **1984** in England | | | | | | |
| 989 | Birmingham – West Indies inns & 180 runs | •191 | 235 | 606 | — | D.I. Gower | C.H. Lloyd |
| 990 | Lord's – West Indies 9 wkts | •286 | 300-9d | 245 | 344-1 | | |
| 991 | Leeds – West Indies 8 wkts | •270 | 159 | 302 | 131-2 | | |
| 992 | Manchester – West Indies inns & 64 runs | 280 | 156 | •500 | — | | |
| 993 | Oval – West Indies 172 runs | 162 | 202 | •190 | 346 | | |

# RESULTS SUMMARY

## ENGLAND v WEST INDIES – IN ENGLAND

| | Tests | Result E | WI | Drawn | Lord's E | WI | Drawn | Manchester E | WI | Drawn | Oval E | WI | Drawn | Nottingham E | WI | Drawn | Birmingham E | WI | Drawn | Leeds E | WI | Drawn |
|---|---|---|---|---|---|---|---|---|---|---|---|---|---|---|---|---|---|---|---|---|---|---|
| 1928 | 3 | 3 | – | – | 1 | – | – | 1 | – | – | 1 | – | – | – | – | – | – | – | – | – | – | – |
| 1933 | 3 | 2 | – | 1 | 1 | – | – | – | – | 1 | 1 | – | – | – | – | – | – | – | – | – | – | – |
| 1939 | 3 | 1 | – | 2 | 1 | – | – | – | – | 1 | – | – | 1 | – | – | – | – | – | – | – | – | – |
| 1950 | 4 | 1 | 3 | – | – | 1 | – | 1 | – | – | – | 1 | – | – | 1 | – | – | – | – | – | – | – |
| 1957 | 5 | 3 | – | 2 | 1 | – | – | – | – | – | 1 | – | – | – | – | 1 | – | – | 1 | 1 | – | – |
| 1963 | 5 | 1 | 3 | 1 | – | – | 1 | – | 1 | – | – | 1 | – | – | – | – | 1 | – | – | – | 1 | – |
| 1966 | 5 | 1 | 3 | 1 | – | – | 1 | – | 1 | – | 1 | – | – | – | 1 | – | – | – | – | – | 1 | – |
| 1969 | 3 | 2 | – | 1 | – | – | 1 | 1 | – | – | – | – | – | – | – | – | – | – | – | 1 | – | – |
| 1973 | 3 | – | 2 | 1 | – | 1 | – | – | – | – | – | 1 | – | – | – | – | – | – | 1 | – | – | – |
| 1976 | 5 | – | 3 | 2 | – | – | 1 | – | 1 | – | – | 1 | – | – | – | 1 | – | – | – | – | 1 | – |
| 1980 | 5 | – | 1 | 4 | – | – | 1 | – | – | 1 | – | – | 1 | – | 1 | – | – | – | – | – | – | 1 |
| 1984 | 5 | – | 5 | – | – | 1 | – | – | 1 | – | – | 1 | – | – | – | – | – | 1 | – | – | 1 | – |
| **49** | **49** | **14** | **20** | **15** | **4** | **3** | **5** | **3** | **4** | **3** | **4** | **5** | **2** | **–** | **3** | **2** | **1** | **1** | **2** | **2** | **4** | **1** |

## ENGLAND v WEST INDIES – IN WEST INDIES

| | Tests | Result E | WI | Drawn | Bridgetown E | WI | Drawn | Port-of-Spain E | WI | Drawn | Georgetown E | WI | Drawn | Kingston E | WI | Drawn | St John's E | WI | Drawn |
|---|---|---|---|---|---|---|---|---|---|---|---|---|---|---|---|---|---|---|---|
| 1929–30 | 4 | 1 | 1 | 2 | – | – | 1 | 1 | – | – | – | 1 | – | – | – | 1 | – | – | – |
| 1934–35 | 4 | 1 | 2 | 1 | 1 | – | – | – | 1 | – | – | – | 1 | – | 1 | – | – | – | – |
| 1947–48 | 4 | – | 2 | 2 | – | – | 1 | – | – | 1 | – | 1 | – | – | 1 | – | – | – | – |
| 1953–54 | 5 | 2 | 2 | 1 | – | 1 | – | – | – | 1 | 1 | – | – | 1 | 1 | – | – | – | – |
| 1959–60 | 5 | 1 | – | 4 | – | – | 1 | 1 | – | 1 | – | – | 1 | – | – | 1 | – | – | – |
| 1967–68 | 5 | 1 | – | 4 | – | – | 1 | 1 | – | 1 | – | – | 1 | – | – | 1 | – | – | – |
| 1973–74 | 5 | 1 | 1 | 3 | – | – | 1 | 1 | 1 | – | – | – | 1 | – | – | 1 | – | – | – |
| 1980–81 | 4 | – | 2 | 2 | – | 1 | – | – | 1 | – | – | – | – | – | – | 1 | – | – | 1 |
| **36** | **36** | **7** | **10** | **19** | **1** | **2** | **5** | **4** | **3** | **4** | **1** | **2** | **4** | **1** | **3** | **5** | **–** | **–** | **1** |

**Totals   85   21   30   34**

## HIGHEST INNINGS TOTALS

| | | | | |
|---|---|---|---|---|
| England | in England | 619-6d | Nottingham | 1957 |
| | in West Indies | 849 | Kingston | 1929–30 |
| West Indies | in England | 687-8d | Oval | 1976 |
| | in West Indies | 681-8d | Port-of-Spain | 1953–54 |

## LOWEST INNINGS TOTALS

| | | | | |
|---|---|---|---|---|
| England | in England | 71 | Manchester | 1976 |
| | in West Indies | 103 | Kingston | 1934–35 |
| West Indies | in England | 86 | Oval | 1957 |
| | in West Indies | 102 | Bridgetown | 1934–35 |

| | | | |
|---|---|---|---|
| **HIGHEST MATCH AGGREGATE** | 1815 for 34 wickets | Kingston | 1929–30 |
| **LOWEST MATCH AGGREGATE** | 309 for 29 wickets | Bridgetown | 1934–35 |

## HIGHEST INDIVIDUAL INNINGS

| | | | | | |
|---|---|---|---|---|---|
| England | in England | 285* | P.B.H. May | Birmingham | 1957 |
| | in West Indies | 325 | A. Sandham | Kingston | 1929–30 |
| West Indies | in England | 291 | I.V.A. Richards | Oval | 1976 |
| | in West Indies | 302 | L.G. Rowe | Bridgetown | 1973–74 |

## HIGHEST AGGREGATE OF RUNS IN A SERIES

| | | | | | |
|---|---|---|---|---|---|
| England | in England | 489 (av 97.80) | P.B.H. May | | 1957 |
| | in West Indies | 693 (av 115.50) | E.H. Hendren | | 1929–30 |
| West Indies | in England | 829 (av 118.42) | I.V.A. Richards | | 1976 |
| | in West Indies | 709 (av 101.28) | G.St A. Sobers | | 1959–60 |

## RECORD WICKET PARTNERSHIPS — ENGLAND

| | | | | |
|---|---|---|---|---|
| 1st | 212 | C. Washbrook (102), R.T. Simpson (94) | Nottingham | 1950 |
| 2nd | 266 | P.E. Richardson (126), T.W. Graveney (258) | Nottingham | 1957 |
| 3rd | 264 | L. Hutton (165*), W.R. Hammond (138) | Oval | 1939 |
| 4th | 411 | P.B.H. May (285*), M.C. Cowdrey (154) | Birmingham | 1957 |
| 5th | 130* | C. Milburn (126*), T.W. Graveney (30*) | Lord's | 1966 |
| 6th | 163 | A.W. Greig (148), A.P.E. Knott (87) | Bridgetown | 1973–74 |
| 7th | 197 | M.J.K. Smith (96), J.M. Parks (101*) | Port-of-Spain | 1959–60 |
| 8th | 217 | T.W. Graveney (165), J.T. Murray (112) | Oval | 1966 |
| 9th | 109 | G.A.R. Lock (89), P.I. Pocock (13) | Georgetown | 1967–68 |
| 10th | 128 | K. Higgs (63), J.A. Snow (59*) | Oval | 1966 |

## RECORD WICKET PARTNERSHIPS — WEST INDIES

| | | | | |
|---|---|---|---|---|
| 1st | 206 | R.C. Fredericks (94), L.G. Rowe (120) | Kingston | 1973–74 |
| 2nd | 287* | C.G. Greenidge (214*), H.A. Gomes (92*) | Lord's | 1984 |
| 3rd | 338 | E.de C. Weekes (206), F.M.M. Worrell (167) | Port-of-Spain | 1953–54 |
| 4th | 399 | G.St A. Sobers (226), F.M.M. Worrell (197*) | Bridgetown | 1959–60 |
| 5th | 265 | S.M. Nurse (137), G.St A. Sobers (174) | Leeds | 1966 |
| 6th | 274* | G.St A. Sobers (163*), D.A.J. Holford (105*) | Lord's | 1966 |
| 7th | 155*† | G.St A. Sobers (150*), B.D. Julien (121) | Lord's | 1973 |
| 8th | 99 | C.A. McWatt (54), J.K. Holt (48*) | Georgetown | 1953–54 |
| 9th | 150 | E.A.E. Baptiste (87*), M.A. Holding (69) | Birmingham | 1984 |
| 10th | 67* | M.A. Holding (58*), C.E.H. Croft (17*) | St John's | 1980–81 |

## BEST INNINGS BOWLING ANALYSIS

| | | | | | |
|---|---|---|---|---|---|
| England | in England | 8-103 | I.T. Botham | Lord's | 1984 |
| | in West Indies | 8-86 | A.W. Greig | Port-of-Spain | 1973–74 |
| West Indies | in England | 8-92 | M.A. Holding | Oval | 1976 |
| | in West Indies | 7-69 | W.W. Hall | Kingston | 1959–60 |

## BEST MATCH BOWLING ANALYSIS

| | | | | | |
|---|---|---|---|---|---|
| England | in England | 12-119 | F.S. Trueman | Birmingham | 1963 |
| | in West Indies | 13-156 | A.W. Greig | Port-of-Spain | 1973–74 |
| West Indies | in England | 14-149 | M.A. Holding | Oval | 1976 |
| | in West Indies | 11-229 | W. Ferguson | Port-of-Spain | 1947–48 |

## HIGHEST AGGREGATE OF WICKETS IN A SERIES

| | | | | | |
|---|---|---|---|---|---|
| England | in England | 34 (av 17.47) | F.S. Trueman | | 1963 |
| | in West Indies | 27 (av 18.66) | J.A. Snow | | 1967–68 |
| West Indies | in England | 33 (av 20.42) | A.L. Valentine | | 1950 |
| | in West Indies | 24 (av 18.95) | C.E.H. Croft | | 1980–81 |

† *231 runs were added for this wicket, G.St A. Sobers retired ill and was succeeded by K.D. Boyce after 155 had been scored.*

# ENGLAND v NEW ZEALAND

| Test No. | Venue and Result | England 1st | England 2nd | New Zealand 1st | New Zealand 2nd | Captains England | Captains New Zealand |
|---|---|---|---|---|---|---|---|
| | **1929–30 in New Zealand** | | | | | | |
| 186 | Christchurch – England 8 wkts | 181 | 66-2 | •112 | 131 | A.H.H. Gilligan | T.C. Lowry |
| 187 | Wellington – Drawn | 320 | 107-4 | •440 | 164-4d | | |
| 188 | Auckland – Drawn | •330-4d | — | 96-1 | — | | |
| 189 | Auckland – Drawn | •540 | 22-3 | 387 | — | | |
| | **1931 in England** | | | | | | |
| 209 | Lord's – Drawn | 454 | 146-5 | •224 | 469-9d | D.R. Jardine | T.C. Lowry |
| 210 | Oval – England inns & 26 runs | •416-4d | — | 193 | 197 | | |
| 211 | Manchester – Drawn | •224-3 | — | — | — | | |
| | **1932–33 in New Zealand** | | | | | | |
| 225 | Christchurch – Drawn | •560-8d | — | 223 | 35-0 | D.R. Jardine | M.L. Page |
| 226 | Auckland – Drawn | 548-7d | — | •158 | 16-0 | R.E.S. Wyatt | |
| | **1937 in England** | | | | | | |
| 260 | Lord's – Drawn | •424 | 226-4d | 295 | 175-8 | R.W.V. Robins | M.L. Page |
| 261 | Manchester – England 130 runs | •358-9d | 187 | 281 | 134 | | |
| 262 | Oval – Drawn | 254-7d | 31-1 | •249 | 187 | | |
| | **1946–47 in New Zealand** | | | | | | |
| 284 | Christchurch – Drawn | 265-7d | — | •345-9d | — | W.R. Hammond | W.A. Hadlee |
| | **1949 in England** | | | | | | |
| 314 | Leeds – Drawn | •372 | 267-4d | 341 | 195-2 | F.G. Mann | W.A. Hadlee |
| 315 | Lord's – Drawn | •313-9d | 306-5 | 484 | — | F.G. Mann | |
| 316 | Manchester – Drawn | 440-9d | — | •293 | 348-7 | F.R. Brown | |
| 317 | Oval – Drawn | 482 | — | •345 | 308-9d | F.R. Brown | |
| | **1950–51 in New Zealand** | | | | | | |
| 332 | Christchurch – Drawn | 550 | — | •417-8d | 46-3 | F.R. Brown | W.A. Hadlee |
| 333 | Wellington – England 6 wkts | 227 | 91-4 | •125 | 189 | | |

| Test No. | Venue and Result | England 1st | England 2nd | New Zealand 1st | New Zealand 2nd | Captains England | Captains New Zealand |
|---|---|---|---|---|---|---|---|
| | **1954–55 in New Zealand** | | | | | | |
| 401 | Dunedin – England 8 wkts | 209-8d | 49-2 | •125 | 132 | L. Hutton | G.O. Rabone |
| 402 | Auckland – England inns & 20 runs | 246 | — | •200 | 26 | | |
| | **1958 in England** | | | | | | |
| 454 | Birmingham – England 205 runs | •221 | 215-6d | 94 | 137 | P.B.H. May | J.R. Reid |
| 455 | Lord's – England inns & 148 runs | 269 | — | 47 | 74 | | |
| 456 | Leeds – England inns & 71 runs | 267-2d | — | • 67 | 129 | | |
| 457 | Manchester – England inns & 13 runs | 365-9d | — | •267 | 85 | | |
| 458 | Oval – Drawn | 219-9d | — | •161 | 91-3 | | |
| | **1958–59 in New Zealand** | | | | | | |
| 472 | Christchurch – England inns & 99 runs | •374 | — | 142 | 133 | P.B.H. May | J.R. Reid |
| 473 | Auckland – Drawn | 311-7 | — | •181 | — | | |
| | **1962–63 in New Zealand** | | | | | | |
| 540 | Auckland – England inns & 215 runs | •562-7d | — | 258 | 89 | E.R. Dexter | J.R. Reid |
| 541 | Wellington – England inns & 47 runs | 428-8d | — | •194 | 187 | | |
| 542 | Christchurch – England 7 wkts | 253 | 173-3 | •266 | 159 | | |
| | **1965 in England** | | | | | | |
| 591 | Birmingham – England 9 wkts | •435 | 96-1 | 116 | 413 | M.J.K. Smith | J.R. Reid |
| 592 | Lord's – England 7 wkts | 307 | 218-3 | 175 | 347 | | |
| 593 | Leeds – England inns & 187 runs | •546-4d | — | 193 | 166 | | |
| | **1965–66 in New Zealand** | | | | | | |
| 602 | Christchurch – Drawn | •342 | 201-5d | 347 | 48-8 | M.J.K. Smith | M.E. Chapple |
| 603 | Dunedin – Drawn | 254-8d | — | 192 | 147-9 | | B.W. Sinclair |
| 604 | Auckland – Drawn | 222 | 159-4 | •296 | 129 | | B.W. Sinclair |
| | **1969 in England** | | | | | | |
| 656 | Lord's – England 230 runs | •190 | 340 | 169 | 131 | R. Illingworth | G.T. Dowling |
| 657 | Nottingham – Drawn | 451-8d | — | •294 | 66-1 | | |
| 658 | Oval – England 8 wkts | 242 | 138-2 | •150 | 229 | | |
| | **1970–71 in New Zealand** | | | | | | |
| 685 | Christchurch – England 8 wkts | 231 | 89-2 | • 65 | 254 | R. Illingworth | G.T. Dowling |
| 686 | Auckland – Drawn | •321 | 237 | 313-7d | 40-0 | | |

| Test No. | Venue and Result | England 1st | England 2nd | New Zealand 1st | New Zealand 2nd | Captains England | Captains New Zealand |
|---|---|---|---|---|---|---|---|
| | **1973 in England** | | | | | | |
| 722 | Nottingham – England 38 runs | •250 | 325-8d | 97 | 440 | R. Illingworth | B.E. Congdon |
| 723 | Lord's – Drawn | •253 | 463-9 | 551-9d | — | | |
| 724 | Leeds – England inns & 1 run | 419 | — | •276 | 142 | | |
| | **1974–75 in New Zealand** | | | | | | |
| 758 | Auckland – England inns & 83 runs | •593-6d | — | 326 | 184 | M.H. Denness | B.E. Congdon |
| 759 | Christchurch – Drawn | 272-2 | — | •342 | — | | |
| | **1977–78 in New Zealand** | | | | | | |
| 817 | Wellington – New Zealand 72 runs | 215 | 64 | •228 | 123 | G. Boycott | M.G. Burgess |
| 818 | Christchurch – England 174 runs | •418 | 96-4d | 235 | 105 | | |
| 819 | Auckland – Drawn | 429 | — | •315 | 382-8 | | |
| | **1978 in England** | | | | | | |
| 828 | Oval – England 7 wkts | 279 | 138-3 | •234 | 182 | J.M. Brearley | M.G. Burgess |
| 829 | Nottingham – England inns & 119 runs | •429 | — | 120 | 190 | | |
| 830 | Lord's – England 7 wkts | 289 | 118-3 | •339 | 67 | | |
| | **1983 in England** | | | | | | |
| 957 | Oval – England 189 runs | •209 | 446-6d | 196 | 270 | R.G.D. Willis | G.P. Howarth |
| 958 | Leeds – New Zealand 5 wkts | •225 | 252 | 377 | 103-5 | | |
| 959 | Lord's – England 127 runs | •326 | 211 | 191 | 219 | | |
| 960 | Nottingham – England 165 runs | •420 | 297 | 207 | 345 | | |
| | **1983–84 in New Zealand** | | | | | | |
| 975 | Wellington – Drawn | 463 | 69-0 | •219 | 537 | R.G.D. Willis | G.P. Howarth |
| 976 | Christchurch – New Zealand inns & 132 runs | 82 | 93 | •307 | — | | |
| 977 | Auckland – Drawn | 439 | — | •496-9d | 16-0 | | |

# RESULTS SUMMARY

## ENGLAND v NEW ZEALAND – IN ENGLAND

| | | Result | | | Lord's | | | Oval | | | Manchester | | | Leeds | | | Birmingham | | | Nottingham | | |
|---|---|---|---|---|---|---|---|---|---|---|---|---|---|---|---|---|---|---|---|---|---|---|
| | Tests | E | NZ | Drawn | E | NZ | Drawn | E | NZ | Drawn | E | NZ | Drawn | E | NZ | Drawn | E | NZ | Drawn | E | NZ | Drawn |
| 1931 | 3 | 1 | – | 2 | – | – | 1 | 1 | – | – | – | – | 1 | – | – | – | – | – | – | – | – | – |
| 1937 | 3 | 1 | – | 2 | – | – | 1 | – | – | 1 | 1 | – | – | – | – | – | – | – | – | – | – | – |
| 1949 | 4 | – | – | 4 | – | – | 1 | – | – | 1 | – | – | 1 | – | – | 1 | – | – | – | – | – | – |
| 1958 | 5 | 4 | – | 1 | 1 | – | – | – | – | 1 | 1 | – | – | 1 | – | – | 1 | – | – | – | – | – |
| 1965 | 3 | 3 | – | – | 1 | – | – | – | – | – | – | – | – | 1 | – | – | 1 | – | – | – | – | – |
| 1969 | 3 | 2 | – | 1 | 1 | – | – | 1 | – | – | – | – | – | – | – | – | – | – | – | – | – | 1 |
| 1973 | 3 | 2 | – | 1 | – | – | 1 | – | – | – | – | – | – | 1 | – | – | – | – | – | 1 | – | – |
| 1978 | 3 | 3 | – | – | 1 | – | – | 1 | – | – | – | – | – | – | – | – | – | – | – | 1 | – | – |
| 1983 | 4 | 3 | 1 | – | 1 | – | – | 1 | – | – | – | – | – | – | 1 | – | – | – | – | 1 | – | – |
| **31** | | **19** | **1** | **11** | **5** | **–** | **4** | **4** | **–** | **3** | **2** | **–** | **2** | **3** | **1** | **1** | **2** | **–** | **–** | **3** | **–** | **1** |

## ENGLAND v NEW ZEALAND – IN NEW ZEALAND

| | | Result | | | Christchurch | | | Wellington | | | Auckland | | | Dunedin | | |
|---|---|---|---|---|---|---|---|---|---|---|---|---|---|---|---|---|---|
| | Tests | E | NZ | Drawn | E | NZ | Drawn | E | NZ | Drawn | E | NZ | Drawn | E | NZ | Drawn |
| 1929–30 | 4 | 1 | – | 3 | 1 | – | – | – | – | 1 | – | – | 2 | – | – | – |
| 1932–33 | 2 | – | – | 2 | – | – | 1 | – | – | – | – | – | 1 | – | – | – |
| 1946–47 | 1 | – | – | 1 | – | – | 1 | – | – | – | – | – | – | – | – | – |
| 1950–51 | 2 | 1 | – | 1 | – | – | 1 | 1 | – | – | – | – | – | – | – | – |
| 1954–55 | 2 | 2 | – | – | – | – | – | – | – | – | 1 | – | – | 1 | – | – |
| 1958–59 | 2 | 1 | – | 1 | 1 | – | – | – | – | – | – | – | 1 | – | – | – |
| 1962–63 | 3 | 3 | – | – | 1 | – | – | 1 | – | – | 1 | – | – | – | – | – |
| 1965–66 | 3 | – | – | 3 | – | – | 1 | – | – | – | – | – | 1 | – | – | 1 |
| 1970–71 | 2 | 1 | – | 1 | 1 | – | – | – | – | – | – | – | 1 | – | – | – |
| 1974–75 | 2 | 1 | – | 1 | – | – | 1 | – | – | – | 1 | – | – | – | – | – |
| 1977–78 | 3 | 1 | 1 | 1 | 1 | – | – | – | 1 | – | – | – | 1 | – | – | – |
| 1983–84 | 3 | – | 1 | 2 | – | 1 | – | – | – | 1 | – | – | 1 | – | – | – |
| **29** | | **11** | **2** | **16** | **5** | **1** | **5** | **2** | **1** | **2** | **3** | **–** | **8** | **1** | **–** | **1** |

| Totals | | | | |
|---|---|---|---|---|
| **60** | | **30** | **3** | **27** |

## HIGHEST INNINGS TOTALS

| | | | | | |
|---|---|---|---|---|---|
| England | in England | 546-4d | | Leeds | 1965 |
| | in New Zealand | 593-6d | | Auckland | 1974–75 |
| New Zealand | in England | 551-9d | | Lord's | 1973 |
| | in New Zealand | 537 | | Wellington | 1983–84 |

## LOWEST INNINGS TOTALS

| | | | | | |
|---|---|---|---|---|---|
| England | in England | 187 | | Manchester | 1937 |
| | in New Zealand | 64 | | Wellington | 1977–78 |
| New Zealand | in England | 47 | | Lord's | 1958 |
| | in New Zealand | 26 | | Auckland | 1954–55 |

| | | | |
|---|---|---|---|
| **HIGHEST MATCH AGGREGATE** | 1293 for 34 wickets | Lord's | 1931 |
| **LOWEST MATCH AGGREGATE** | 390 for 30 wickets | Lord's | 1958 |

## HIGHEST INDIVIDUAL INNINGS

| | | | | | |
|---|---|---|---|---|---|
| England | in England | 310* | J.H. Edrich | Leeds | 1965 |
| | in New Zealand | 336* | W.R. Hammond | Auckland | 1932–33 |
| New Zealand | in England | 206 | M.P. Donnelly | Lord's | 1949 |
| | in New Zealand | 174* | J.V. Coney | Wellington | 1983–84 |

## HIGHEST AGGREGATE OF RUNS IN A SERIES

| | | | | |
|---|---|---|---|---|
| England | in England | 469 (av 78.16) | L. Hutton | 1949 |
| | in New Zealand | 563 (av 563.00) | W.R. Hammond | 1932–33 |
| New Zealand | in England | 462 (av 77.00) | M.P. Donnelly | 1949 |
| | in New Zealand | 341 (av 85.25) | C.S. Dempster | 1929–30 |

## RECORD WICKET PARTNERSHIPS — ENGLAND

| | | | | |
|---|---|---|---|---|
| 1st | 223 | G. Fowler (105), C.J. Tavaré (109) | Oval | 1983 |
| 2nd | 369 | J.H. Edrich (310*), K.F. Barrington (163) | Leeds | 1965 |
| 3rd | 245 | J. Hardstaff, jr (114), W.R. Hammond (140) | Lord's | 1937 |
| 4th | 266 | M.H. Denness (188), K.W.R. Fletcher (216) | Auckland | 1974–75 |
| 5th | 242 | W.R. Hammond (227), L.E.G. Ames (103) | Christchurch | 1932–33 |
| 6th | 240 | P.H. Parfitt (131*), B.R. Knight (125) | Auckland | 1962–63 |
| 7th | 149 | A.P.E. Knott (104), P. Lever (64) | Auckland | 1970–71 |
| 8th | 246 | L.E.G. Ames (137), G.O.B. Allen (122) | Lord's | 1931 |
| 9th | 163* | M.C. Cowdrey (128*), A.C. Smith (69*) | Wellington | 1962–63 |
| 10th | 59 | A.P.E. Knott (49), N. Gifford (25*) | Nottingham | 1973 |

## RECORD WICKET PARTNERSHIPS — NEW ZEALAND

| | | | | |
|---|---|---|---|---|
| 1st | 276 | C.S. Dempster (136), J.E. Mills (117) | Wellington | 1929–30 |
| 2nd | 131 | B. Sutcliffe (116), J.R. Reid (50) | Christchurch | 1950–51 |
| 3rd | 190 | B.E. Congdon (175), B.F. Hastings (86) | Lord's | 1973 |
| 4th | 154 | J.G. Wright (130), J.J. Crowe (128) | Auckland | 1983–84 |
| 5th | 177 | B.E. Congdon (176), V. Pollard (116) | Nottingham | 1973 |
| 6th | 117 | M.G. Burgess (105), V. Pollard (105*) | Lord's | 1973 |
| 7th | 104 | B. Sutcliffe (53), V. Pollard (81*) | Birmingham | 1965 |
| 8th | 104 | D.A.R. Moloney (64), A.W. Roberts (66*) | Lord's | 1937 |
| 9th | 118 | J.V. Coney (174*), B.L. Cairns (64) | Wellington | 1983–84 |
| 10th | 57 | F.L.H. Mooney (46), J. Cowie (26*) | Leeds | 1949 |

## BEST INNINGS BOWLING ANALYSIS

| | | | | | |
|---|---|---|---|---|---|
| England | in England | 7-32 | D.L. Underwood | Lord's | 1969 |
| | in New Zealand | 7-75 | F.S. Trueman | Christchurch | 1962–63 |
| New Zealand | in England | 7-74 | B.L. Cairns | Leeds | 1983 |
| | in New Zealand | 7-143 | B.L. Cairns | Wellington | 1983–84 |

## BEST MATCH BOWLING ANALYSIS

| | | | | | |
|---|---|---|---|---|---|
| England | in England | 12-101 | D.L. Underwood | Oval | 1969 |
| | in New Zealand | 12-97 | D.L. Underwood | Christchurch | 1970–71 |
| New Zealand | in England | 10-140 | J. Cowie | Manchester | 1937 |
| | in New Zealand | 10-100 | R.J. Hadlee | Wellington | 1977–78 |

## HIGHEST AGGREGATE OF WICKETS IN A SERIES

| | | | | |
|---|---|---|---|---|
| England | in England | 34 (av 7.47) | G.A.R. Lock | 1958 |
| | in New Zealand | 17 (av 9.34) | K. Higgs | 1965–66 |
| | | 17 (av 12.05) | D.L. Underwood | 1970–71 |
| | | 17 (av 18.29) | I.T. Botham | 1977–78 |
| New Zealand | in England | 21 (av 26.61) | R.J. Hadlee | 1983 |
| | in New Zealand | 15 (av 19.53) | R.O. Collinge | 1977–78 |
| | | 15 (av 24.73) | R.J. Hadlee | 1977–78 |

# ENGLAND v INDIA

| Test No. | Venue and Result | England 1st | England 2nd | India 1st | India 2nd | Captains England | Captains India |
|---|---|---|---|---|---|---|---|
| | **1932 in England** | | | | | | |
| 219 | Lord's – England 158 runs | *259 | 275-8d | 189 | 187 | D.R. Jardine | C.K. Nayudu |
| | **1933–34 in India** | | | | | | |
| 230 | Bombay[1] – England 9 wkts | 438 | 40-1 | *219 | 258 | D.R. Jardine | C.K. Nayudu |
| 231 | Calcutta – Drawn | *403 | 7-2 | 247 | 237 | | |
| 232 | Madras[1] – England 202 runs | *335 | 261-7d | 145 | 249 | | |
| | **1936 in England** | | | | | | |
| 252 | Lord's – England 9 wkts | 134 | 108-1 | *147 | 93 | G.O.B. Allen | Maharajkumar of Vizianagram |
| 253 | Manchester – Drawn | 571-8d | — | *203 | 390-5 | | |
| 254 | Oval – England 9 wkts | *471-8d | 64-1 | 222 | 312 | | |
| | **1946 in England** | | | | | | |
| 276 | Lord's – England 10 wkts | 428 | 48-0 | *200 | 275 | W.R. Hammond | Nawab of Pataudi, sr |
| 277 | Manchester – Drawn | *294 | 153-5d | 170 | 152-9 | | |
| 278 | Oval – Drawn | 95-3 | — | *331 | — | | |
| | **1951–52 in India** | | | | | | |
| 339 | Delhi – Drawn | *203 | 368-6 | 418-6d | — | N.D. Howard | V.S. Hazare |
| 340 | Bombay[2] – Drawn | 456 | 55-2 | *485-9d | 208 | N.D. Howard | |
| 341 | Calcutta – Drawn | *342 | 252-5d | 344 | 103-0 | N.D. Howard | |
| 342 | Kanpur – England 8 wkts | 203 | 76-2 | *121 | 157 | N.D. Howard | |
| 343 | Madras[1] – India inns & 8 runs | *266 | 183 | 457-9d | — | D.B. Carr | |
| | **1952 in England** | | | | | | |
| 351 | Leeds – England 7 wkts | 334 | 128-3 | *293 | 165 | L. Hutton | V.S. Hazare |
| 352 | Lord's – England 8 wkts | 537 | 79-2 | *235 | 378 | | |
| 353 | Manchester – England inns & 207 runs | *347-9d | — | 58 | 82 | | |
| 354 | Oval – Drawn | *326-6d | — | 98 | — | | |

| Test No. | Venue and Result | England 1st | England 2nd | India 1st | India 2nd | Captains England | Captains India |
|---|---|---|---|---|---|---|---|
| | **1959** in England | | | | | | |
| 474 | Nottingham – England inns & 59 runs | •422 | — | 206 | 157 | P.B.H. May | D.K. Gaekwad |
| 475 | Lord's – England 8 wkts | 226 | 108-2 | •168 | 165 | P.B.H. May | P. Roy |
| 476 | Leeds – England inns & 173 runs | 483-8d | — | 161 | 149 | P.B.H. May | D.K. Gaekwad |
| 477 | Manchester – England 171 runs | 490 | 265-8d | 208 | 376 | M.C. Cowdrey | D.K. Gaekwad |
| 478 | Oval – England inns & 27 runs | 361 | — | •140 | 194 | M.C. Cowdrey | D.K. Gaekwad |
| | **1961–62** in India | | | | | | |
| 513 | Bombay² – Drawn | •500-8d | 184-5d | 390 | 180-5 | E.R. Dexter | N.J. Contractor |
| 514 | Kanpur – Drawn | 244 | 497-5 | •467-8d | — | | |
| 515 | Delhi – Drawn | 256-3 | — | •466 | — | | |
| 516 | Calcutta – India 187 runs | 212 | 233 | •380 | 252 | | |
| 517 | Madras² – India 128 runs | 281 | 209 | •428 | 190 | | |
| | **1963–64** in India | | | | | | |
| 553 | Madras² – Drawn | 317 | 241-5 | •457-7d | 152-9d | M.J.K. Smith | Nawab of Pataudi, jr |
| 554 | Bombay² – Drawn | 233 | 206-3 | •300 | 249-8d | | |
| 555 | Calcutta – Drawn | 267 | 145-2 | •241 | 300-7d | | |
| 556 | Delhi – Drawn | 451 | — | 344 | 463-4 | | |
| 557 | Kanpur – Drawn | •559-8d | — | 266 | 347-3 | | |
| | **1967** in England | | | | | | |
| 618 | Leeds – England 6 wkts | •550-4d | 126-4 | 164 | 510 | D.B. Close | Nawab of Pataudi, jr |
| 619 | Lord's – England inns & 124 runs | 386 | — | •152 | 110 | | |
| 620 | Birmingham – England 132 runs | •298 | 203 | 92 | 277 | | |
| | **1971** in England | | | | | | |
| 690 | Lord's – Drawn | •304 | 191 | 313 | 145-8 | R. Illingworth | A.L. Wadekar |
| 691 | Manchester – Drawn | •386 | 245-3d | 212 | 65-3 | | |
| 692 | Oval – India 4 wkts | •355 | 101 | 284 | 174-6 | | |
| | **1972–73** in India | | | | | | |
| 703 | Delhi – England 6 wkts | 200 | 208-4 | •173 | 233 | A.R. Lewis | A.L. Wadekar |
| 704 | Calcutta – India 28 runs | 174 | 163 | •210 | 155 | | |
| 705 | Madras¹ – India 4 wkts | 242 | 159 | 316 | 86-6 | | |
| 706 | Kanpur – Drawn | 397 | 67-2 | •357 | 186-6 | | |
| 707 | Bombay² – Drawn | 480 | — | •448 | 244-5d | | |

| Test No. | Venue and Result | England 1st | England 2nd | India 1st | India 2nd | Captains England | Captains India |
|---|---|---|---|---|---|---|---|
| | **1974 in England** | | | | | | |
| 739 | Manchester – England 113 runs | 328-9d | 213-3d | 246 | 182 | M.H. Denness | A.L. Wadekar |
| 740 | Lord's – England inns & 285 runs | 629 | — | 302 | 42 | | |
| 741 | Birmingham – England inns & 78 runs | 459-2d | — | 165 | 216 | | |
| | **1976–77 in India** | | | | | | |
| 788 | Delhi – England inns & 25 runs | 381 | — | 122 | 234 | A.W. Greig | B.S. Bedi |
| 789 | Calcutta – England 10 wkts | 321 | 16-0 | 155 | 181 | | |
| 790 | Madras[1] – England 200 runs | 262 | 185-9d | 164 | 83 | | |
| 791 | Bangalore – India 140 runs | 195 | 177 | 253 | 259-9d | | |
| 792 | Bombay[3] – Drawn | 317 | 152-7 | 338 | 192 | | |
| | **1979 in England** | | | | | | |
| 851 | Birmingham – England inns & 83 runs | 633-5d | — | 297 | 253 | J.M. Brearley | S. Venkataraghavan |
| 852 | Lord's – Drawn | 419-9d | — | 96 | 318-4 | | |
| 853 | Leeds – Drawn | 270 | — | 223-6 | — | | |
| 854 | Oval – Drawn | 305 | 334-8d | 202 | 429-8 | | |
| | **1979–80 in India** | | | | | | |
| 876 | Bombay[3] – England 10 wkts | 296 | 98-0 | 242 | 149 | J.M. Brearley | G.R. Viswanath |
| | **1981–82 in India** | | | | | | |
| 912 | Bombay[3] – India 138 runs | 166 | 102 | 179 | 227 | K.W.R. Fletcher | S.M. Gavaskar |
| 913 | Bangalore – Drawn | 400 | 174-3d | 428 | — | | |
| 914 | Delhi – Drawn | 476-9d | 68-0d | 487 | — | | |
| 915 | Calcutta – Drawn | 248 | 265-5d | 208 | 170-3 | | |
| 916 | Madras[1] – Drawn | 328 | — | 481-4d | 160-3d | | |
| 917 | Kanpur – Drawn | 378-9d | — | 377-7d | — | | |
| | **1982 in England** | | | | | | |
| 928 | Lord's – England 7 wkts | 433 | 67-3 | 128 | 369 | R.G.D. Willis | S.M. Gavaskar |
| 929 | Manchester – Drawn | 425 | — | 379-8 | — | | |
| 930 | Oval – Drawn | 594 | 191-3d | 410 | 111-3 | | |
| | **1984–85 in India** | | | | | | |
| 1005 | Bombay[3] – India 8 wkts | 195 | 317 | 465-8d | 51-2 | D.I. Gower | S.M. Gavaskar |
| 1006 | Delhi – England 8 wkts | 418 | 127-2 | 307 | 235 | | |
| 1007 | Calcutta – Drawn | 276 | — | 437-7d | 29-1 | | |
| 1008 | Madras[1] – England 9 wkts | 652-7d | 35-1 | 272 | 412 | | |
| 1009 | Kanpur – Drawn | 417 | 91-0 | 553-8d | 97-1d | | |

# RESULTS SUMMARY

## ENGLAND v INDIA – IN ENGLAND

| | Result | | | | Lord's | | | Manchester | | | Oval | | | Leeds | | | Nottingham | | | Birmingham | | |
|---|---|---|---|---|---|---|---|---|---|---|---|---|---|---|---|---|---|---|---|---|---|---|
| | *Tests* | *E* | *I* | *Drawn* | *E* | *I* | *Drawn* | *E* | *I* | *Drawn* | *E* | *I* | *Drawn* | *E* | *I* | *Drawn* | *E* | *I* | *Drawn* | *E* | *I* | *Drawn* |
| 1932 | 1 | 1 | – | – | 1 | – | – | – | – | – | – | – | – | – | – | – | – | – | – | – | – | – |
| 1936 | 3 | 2 | – | 1 | 1 | – | – | – | – | 1 | 1 | – | – | – | – | – | – | – | – | – | – | – |
| 1946 | 3 | 1 | – | 2 | 1 | – | – | – | – | 1 | – | – | 1 | – | – | – | – | – | – | – | – | – |
| 1952 | 4 | 3 | – | 1 | 1 | – | – | 1 | – | – | – | – | 1 | 1 | – | – | – | – | – | – | – | – |
| 1959 | 5 | 5 | – | – | 1 | – | – | 1 | – | – | 1 | – | – | 1 | – | – | 1 | – | – | – | – | – |
| 1967 | 3 | 3 | – | – | 1 | – | – | – | – | – | – | – | – | 1 | – | – | – | – | – | 1 | – | – |
| 1971 | 3 | – | 1 | 2 | – | – | 1 | – | – | 1 | – | 1 | – | – | – | – | – | – | – | – | – | – |
| 1974 | 3 | 3 | – | – | 1 | – | – | 1 | – | – | – | – | – | – | – | – | – | – | – | 1 | – | – |
| 1979 | 4 | 1 | – | 3 | – | – | 1 | – | – | – | – | – | 1 | – | – | 1 | – | – | – | 1 | – | – |
| 1982 | 3 | 1 | – | 2 | 1 | – | – | – | – | 1 | – | – | 1 | – | – | – | – | – | – | – | – | – |
| **Totals** | **32** | 20 | 1 | 11 | 8 | – | 2 | 3 | – | 4 | 2 | 1 | 4 | 3 | – | 1 | 1 | – | – | 3 | – | – |

## ENGLAND v INDIA – IN INDIA

| | Result | | | | Bombay | | | Calcutta | | | Madras | | | Delhi | | | Kanpur | | | Bangalore | | |
|---|---|---|---|---|---|---|---|---|---|---|---|---|---|---|---|---|---|---|---|---|---|---|
| | *Tests* | *E* | *I* | *Drawn* | *E* | *I* | *Drawn* | *E* | *I* | *Drawn* | *E* | *I* | *Drawn* | *E* | *I* | *Drawn* | *E* | *I* | *Drawn* | *E* | *I* | *Drawn* |
| 1933–34 | 3 | 2 | – | 1 | 1 | – | – | – | – | 1 | 1 | – | – | – | – | – | – | – | – | – | – | – |
| 1951–52 | 5 | 1 | 1 | 3 | – | – | 1 | – | – | 1 | – | 1 | – | – | – | 1 | 1 | – | – | – | – | – |
| 1961–62 | 5 | – | 2 | 3 | – | – | 1 | – | 1 | – | – | 1 | – | – | – | 1 | – | – | 1 | – | – | – |
| 1963–64 | 5 | – | – | 5 | – | – | 1 | – | – | 1 | – | – | 1 | – | – | 1 | – | – | 1 | – | – | – |
| 1972–73 | 5 | 1 | 2 | 2 | – | – | 1 | – | 1 | – | – | 1 | – | 1 | – | – | – | – | 1 | – | – | – |
| 1976–77 | 5 | 3 | 1 | 1 | – | – | 1 | 1 | – | – | 1 | – | – | 1 | – | – | – | – | – | – | 1 | – |
| 1979–80 | 1 | 1 | – | – | 1 | – | – | – | – | – | – | – | – | – | – | – | – | – | – | – | – | – |
| 1981–82 | 6 | – | 1 | 5 | – | 1 | – | – | – | 1 | – | – | 1 | – | – | 1 | – | – | 1 | – | – | 1 |
| 1984–85 | 5 | 2 | 1 | 2 | – | 1 | – | – | – | 1 | 1 | – | – | 1 | – | – | – | – | 1 | – | – | – |
| **Totals** | **40** | 10 | 8 | 22 | 2 | 2 | 5 | 1 | 2 | 5 | 3 | 3 | 2 | 3 | – | 4 | 1 | – | 5 | – | 1 | 1 |
| **72** | 30 | 9 | 33 | | | | | | | | | | | | | | | | | | | |

## HIGHEST INNINGS TOTALS

| England | in England | 633-5d | | | Birmingham | 1979 |
|---|---|---|---|---|---|---|
| | in India | 652-7d | | | Madras[1] | 1984–85 |
| India | in England | 510 | | | Leeds | 1967 |
| | in India | 553-8d | | | Kanpur | 1984–85 |

## LOWEST INNINGS TOTALS

| England | in England | 101 | | | Oval | 1971 |
|---|---|---|---|---|---|---|
| | in India | 102 | | | Bombay[3] | 1981–82 |
| India | in England | 42 | | | Lord's | 1974 |
| | in India | 83 | | | Madras[1] | 1976–77 |

| **HIGHEST MATCH AGGREGATE** | 1371 for 28 wickets | Madras[1] | 1984–85 |
|---|---|---|---|
| **LOWEST MATCH AGGREGATE** | 482 for 31 wickets | Lord's | 1936 |

## HIGHEST INDIVIDUAL INNINGS

| England | in England | 246* | G. Boycott | Leeds | 1967 |
|---|---|---|---|---|---|
| | in India | 207 | M.W. Gatting | Madras[1] | 1984–85 |
| India | in England | 221 | S.M. Gavaskar | Oval | 1979 |
| | in India | 222 | G.R. Viswanath | Madras[1] | 1981–82 |

## HIGHEST AGGREGATE OF RUNS IN A SERIES

| England | in England | 403 (av 134.33) | I.T. Botham | | 1982 |
|---|---|---|---|---|---|
| | in India | 594 (av 99.00) | K.F. Barrington | | 1961–62 |
| India | in England | 542 (av 77.42) | S.M. Gavaskar | | 1979 |
| | in India | 586 (av 83.71) | V.L. Manjrekar | | 1961–62 |

## RECORD WICKET PARTNERSHIPS — ENGLAND

| 1st | 178 | G. Fowler (201), R.T. Robinson (74) | Madras[1] | 1984–85 |
|---|---|---|---|---|
| 2nd | 241 | G. Fowler (201), M.W. Gatting (207) | Madras[1] | 1984–85 |
| 3rd | 169 | R. Subba Row (94), M.J.K. Smith (98) | Oval | 1959 |
| 4th | 266 | W.R. Hammond (217), T.S. Worthington (128) | Oval | 1936 |
| 5th | 254 | K.W.R. Fletcher (113), A.W. Greig (148) | Bombay[2] | 1972–73 |
| 6th | 171 | I.T. Botham (114), R.W. Taylor (43) | Bombay[3] | 1979–80 |
| 7th | 125 | D.W. Randall (126), P.H. Edmonds (64) | Lord's | 1982 |
| 8th | 168 | R. Illingworth (107), P. Lever (88*) | Manchester | 1971 |
| 9th | 83 | K.W.R. Fletcher (97*), N. Gifford (19) | Madras[1] | 1972–73 |
| 10th | 70 | P.J.W. Allott (41*), R.G.D. Willis (28) | Lord's | 1982 |

## RECORD WICKET PARTNERSHIPS — INDIA

| 1st | 213 | S.M. Gavaskar (221), C.P.S. Chauhan (80) | Oval | 1979 |
|---|---|---|---|---|
| 2nd | 192 | F.M. Engineer (121), A.L. Wadekar (87) | Bombay[2] | 1972–73 |
| 3rd | 316† | G.R. Viswanath (222), Yashpal Sharma (140) | Madras[1] | 1981–82 |
| 4th | 222 | V.S. Hazare (89), V.L. Manjrekar (133) | Leeds | 1952 |
| 5th | 214 | M. Azharuddin (110), R.J. Shastri (111) | Calcutta | 1984–85 |
| 6th | 130 | S.M.H. Kirmani (43), Kapil Dev (97) | Oval | 1982 |
| 7th | 235 | R.J. Shastri (142), S.M.H. Kirmani (102) | Bombay[3] | 1984–85 |
| 8th | 128 | R.J. Shastri (93), S.M.H. Kirmani (67) | Delhi | 1981–82 |
| 9th | 104 | R.J. Shastri (93), Madan Lal (44) | Delhi | 1981–82 |
| 10th | { 51 | R.G. Nadkarni (43*), B.S. Chandrasekhar (16) | Calcutta | 1963–64 |
| | { 51 | S.M.H. Kirmani (75), C. Sharma (17*) | Madras[1] | 1984–85 |

## BEST INNINGS BOWLING ANALYSIS

| England | in England | 8-31 | F.S. Trueman | Manchester | 1952 |
|---|---|---|---|---|---|
| | in India | 7-46 | J.K. Lever | Delhi | 1976–77 |
| India | in England | 6-35 | L. Amar Singh | Lord's | 1936 |
| | in India | 8-55 | M.H. Mankad | Madras[1] | 1951–52 |

## BEST MATCH BOWLING ANALYSIS

| England | in England | 11-93 | A.V. Bedser | Manchester | 1946 |
|---|---|---|---|---|---|
| | in India | 13-106 | I.T. Botham | Bombay[3] | 1979–80 |
| India | in England | 8-114 | B.S. Chandrasekhar | Oval | 1971 |
| | in India | 12-108 | M.H. Mankad | Madras[1] | 1951–52 |

## HIGHEST AGGREGATE OF WICKETS IN A SERIES

| England | in England | 29 (av 13.31) | F.S. Trueman | | 1952 |
|---|---|---|---|---|---|
| | in India | 29 (av 17.55) | D.L. Underwood | | 1976–77 |
| India | in England | 17 (av 34.64) | S.P. Gupte | | 1959 |
| | in India | 35 (av 18.91) | B.S. Chandrasekhar | | 1972–73 |

*†415 runs were added for this wicket. D.B. Vengsarkar retired hurt and was replaced by Yashpal Sharma after 99 had been scored.*

# ENGLAND v PAKISTAN

| Test No. | Venue and Result | England 1st | England 2nd | Pakistan 1st | Pakistan 2nd | Captains England | Captains Pakistan |
|---|---|---|---|---|---|---|---|
| | **1954** in England | | | | | | |
| 387 | Lord's – Drawn | 117-9d | — | •87 | 121-3 | L. Hutton | A.H. Kardar |
| 388 | Nottingham – England inns & 129 runs | 558-6d | — | •157 | 272 | D.S. Sheppard | |
| 389 | Manchester – Drawn | •359-8d | — | 90 | 25-4 | D.S. Sheppard | |
| 390 | Oval – Pakistan 24 runs | 130 | 143 | •133 | 164 | L. Hutton | |
| | **1961–62** in Pakistan | | | | | | |
| 512 | Lahore[2] – England 5 wkts | 380 | 209-5 | •387-9d | 200 | E.R. Dexter | Imtiaz Ahmed |
| 518 | Dacca – Drawn | 439 | 38-0 | •393-7d | 216 | | |
| 519 | Karachi – Drawn | 507 | — | •253 | 404-8 | | |
| | **1962** in England | | | | | | |
| 530 | Birmingham – England inns & 24 runs | •544-5d | — | 246 | 274 | E.R. Dexter | Javed Burki |
| 531 | Lord's – England 9 wkts | 370 | 86-1 | 100 | 355 | E.R. Dexter | |
| 532 | Leeds – England inns & 117 runs | 428 | — | 131 | 180 | M.C. Cowdrey | |
| 533 | Nottingham – Drawn | •428-5d | — | 219 | 216-6 | E.R. Dexter | |
| 534 | Oval – England 10 wkts | •480-5d | 27-0 | 183 | 323 | E.R. Dexter | |
| | **1967** in England | | | | | | |
| 621 | Lord's – Drawn | •369 | 241-9d | 354 | 88-3 | D.B. Close | Hanif Mohammad |
| 622 | Nottingham – England 10 wkts | 252-8d | 3-0 | •140 | 114 | | |
| 623 | Oval – England 8 wkts | 440 | 34-2 | •216 | 255 | | |
| | **1968–69** in Pakistan | | | | | | |
| 647 | Lahore[2] – Drawn | •306 | 225-9d | 209 | 203-5 | M.C. Cowdrey | Saeed Ahmed |
| 648 | Dacca – Drawn | 274 | 33-0 | •246 | 195-6d | | |
| 649 | Karachi – Drawn | •502-7 | — | — | — | | |
| | **1971** in England | | | | | | |
| 687 | Birmingham – Drawn | 353 | 229-5 | •608-7d | — | R. Illingworth | Intikhab Alam |
| 688 | Lord's – Drawn | •241-2d | 117-0 | 148 | — | | |
| 689 | Leeds – England 25 runs | •316 | 264 | 350 | 205 | | |

| Test No. | Venue and Result | England | | Pakistan | | Captains | |
|---|---|---|---|---|---|---|---|
| | | *1st* | *2nd* | *1st* | *2nd* | *England* | *Pakistan* |
| | **1972–73 in Pakistan** | | | | | | |
| 719 | Lahore² – Drawn | •355 | 306-7d | 422 | 124-3 | A.R. Lewis | Majid Khan |
| 720 | Hyderabad – Drawn | •487 | 218-6 | 569-9d | — | | |
| 721 | Karachi – Drawn | 386 | 30-1 | •445-6d | 199 | | |
| | **1974 in England** | | | | | | |
| 742 | Leeds – Drawn | 183 | 238-6 | •285 | 179 | M.H. Denness | Intikhab Alam |
| 743 | Lord's – Drawn | 270 | 27-0 | •130-9d | 226 | | |
| 744 | Oval – Drawn | 545 | — | 600-7d | 94-4 | | |
| | **1977–78 in Pakistan** | | | | | | |
| 814 | Lahore² – Drawn | 288 | — | •407-9d | 106-3 | J.M. Brearley | Wasim Bari |
| 815 | Hyderabad – Drawn | 191 | 186-1 | •275 | 259-4d | J.M. Brearley | |
| 816 | Karachi – Drawn | •266 | 222-5 | 281 | — | G. Boycott | |
| | **1978 in England** | | | | | | |
| 825 | Birmingham – England inns & 57 runs | 452-8d | — | •164 | 231 | J.M. Brearley | Wasim Bari |
| 826 | Lord's – England inns & 120 runs | •364 | — | 105 | 139 | | |
| 827 | Leeds – Drawn | 119-7 | — | •201 | — | | |
| | **1982 in England** | | | | | | |
| 931 | Birmingham – England 113 runs | •272 | 291 | 251 | 199 | R.G.D. Willis | Imran Khan |
| 932 | Lord's – Pakistan 10 wkts | 227 | 276 | •428-8d | 77-0 | D.I. Gower | |
| 933 | Leeds – England 3 wkts | 256 | 219-7 | •275 | 199 | R.G.D. Willis | |
| | **1983–84 in Pakistan** | | | | | | |
| 978 | Karachi – Pakistan 3 wkts | •182 | 159 | 277 | 66-7 | R.G.D. Willis | Zaheer Abbas |
| 979 | Faisalabad – Drawn | 546-8d | — | •449-8d | 137-4 | D.I. Gower | |
| 980 | Lahore² – Drawn | •241 | 344-9d | 343 | 217-6 | D.I. Gower | |

# RESULTS SUMMARY

## ENGLAND v PAKISTAN – IN ENGLAND

| | Result | | | | Lord's | | | Nottingham | | | Manchester | | | Oval | | | Birmingham | | | Leeds | | |
|---|---|---|---|---|---|---|---|---|---|---|---|---|---|---|---|---|---|---|---|---|---|---|
| | Tests | E | P | Drawn | E | P | Drawn | E | P | Drawn | E | P | Drawn | E | P | Drawn | E | P | Drawn | E | P | Drawn |
| 1954 | 4 | 1 | 1 | 2 | – | – | 1 | 1 | – | – | – | – | 1 | – | 1 | – | – | – | – | – | – | – |
| 1962 | 5 | 4 | – | 1 | 1 | – | – | – | – | 1 | – | – | – | 1 | – | – | 1 | – | – | 1 | – | – |
| 1967 | 3 | 2 | – | 1 | – | – | 1 | 1 | – | – | – | – | – | 1 | – | – | – | – | – | – | – | – |
| 1971 | 3 | 1 | – | 2 | – | – | 1 | – | – | – | – | – | – | – | – | – | – | – | 1 | 1 | – | – |
| 1974 | 3 | – | – | 3 | – | – | 1 | – | – | – | – | – | – | – | – | 1 | – | – | – | – | – | 1 |
| 1978 | 3 | 2 | – | 1 | 1 | – | – | – | – | – | – | – | – | – | – | – | 1 | – | – | – | – | 1 |
| 1982 | 3 | 2 | 1 | – | – | 1 | – | – | – | – | – | – | – | – | – | – | 1 | – | – | 1 | – | – |
| | **24** | **12** | **2** | **10** | **2** | **1** | **4** | **2** | **–** | **1** | **–** | **–** | **1** | **2** | **1** | **1** | **3** | **–** | **1** | **3** | **–** | **2** |

## ENGLAND v PAKISTAN – IN PAKISTAN

| | Result | | | | Lahore | | | Dacca | | | Karachi | | | Hyderabad | | | Faisalabad | | |
|---|---|---|---|---|---|---|---|---|---|---|---|---|---|---|---|---|---|---|---|---|
| | Tests | E | P | Drawn | E | P | Drawn | E | P | Drawn | E | P | Drawn | E | P | Drawn | E | P | Drawn |
| 1961–62 | 3 | 1 | – | 2 | 1 | – | – | – | – | 1 | – | – | 1 | – | – | – | – | – | – |
| 1968–69 | 3 | – | – | 3 | – | – | 1 | – | – | 1 | – | – | 1 | – | – | – | – | – | – |
| 1972–73 | 3 | – | – | 3 | – | – | 1 | – | – | – | – | – | 1 | – | – | 1 | – | – | – |
| 1977–78 | 3 | – | – | 3 | – | – | 1 | – | – | – | – | – | 1 | – | – | 1 | – | – | – |
| 1983–84 | 3 | – | 1 | 2 | – | – | 1 | – | – | – | – | 1 | – | – | – | – | – | – | 1 |
| **Totals** | **15** | **1** | **1** | **13** | **1** | **–** | **4** | **–** | **–** | **2** | **–** | **1** | **4** | **–** | **–** | **2** | **–** | **–** | **1** |

Totals   **39**   **13**   **3**   **23**

## HIGHEST INNINGS TOTALS

| | | | | | |
|---|---|---|---|---|---|
| England | in England | 558-6d | | Nottingham | 1954 |
| | in Pakistan | 546-8d | | Faisalabad | 1983–84 |
| Pakistan | in England | 608-7d | | Birmingham | 1971 |
| | in Pakistan | 569-9d | | Hyderabad | 1972–73 |

## LOWEST INNINGS TOTALS

| | | | | | |
|---|---|---|---|---|---|
| England | in England | 130 | | Oval | 1954 |
| | in Pakistan | 159 | | Karachi | 1983–84 |
| Pakistan | in England | 87 | | Lord's | 1954 |
| | in Pakistan | 199 | | Karachi | 1972–73 |

| | | | | |
|---|---|---|---|---|
| **HIGHEST MATCH AGGREGATE** | 1274 for 25 wickets | | Hyderabad | 1972–73 |
| **LOWEST MATCH AGGREGATE** | 509 for 28 wickets | | Nottingham | 1967 |

## HIGHEST INDIVIDUAL INNINGS

| | | | | | |
|---|---|---|---|---|---|
| England | in England | 278 | D.C.S. Compton | Nottingham | 1954 |
| | in Pakistan | 205 | E.R. Dexter | Karachi | 1961–62 |
| Pakistan | in England | 274 | Zaheer Abbas | Birmingham | 1971 |
| | in Pakistan | 157 | Mushtaq Mohammad | Hyderabad | 1972–73 |

## HIGHEST AGGREGATE OF RUNS IN A SERIES

| | | | | | |
|---|---|---|---|---|---|
| England | in England | 453 (av 90.60) | D.C.S. Compton | | 1954 |
| | in Pakistan | 449 (av 112.25) | D.I. Gower | | 1983–84 |
| Pakistan | in England | 401 (av 44.55) | Mushtaq Mohammad | | 1962 |
| | in Pakistan | 407 (av 67.83) | Hanif Mohammad | | 1961–62 |

## RECORD WICKET PARTNERSHIPS — ENGLAND

| | | | | |
|---|---|---|---|---|
| 1st | 198 | G. Pullar (165), R.W. Barber (86) | Dacca | 1961–62 |
| 2nd | 248 | M.C. Cowdrey (182), E.R. Dexter (172) | Oval | 1962 |
| 3rd | 201 | K.F. Barrington (148), T.W. Graveney (81) | Lord's | 1967 |
| 4th | 188 | E.R. Dexter (205), P.H. Parfitt (111) | Karachi | 1961–62 |
| 5th | 192 | D.C.S. Compton (278), T.E. Bailey (36*) | Nottingham | 1954 |
| 6th | 153* | P.H. Parfitt (101*), D.A. Allen (79*) | Birmingham | 1962 |
| 7th | 167 | D.I. Gower (152), V.J. Marks (83) | Faisalabad | 1983–84 |
| 8th | 99 | P.H. Parfitt (119), D.A. Allen (62) | Leeds | 1962 |
| 9th | 76 | T.W. Graveney (153), F.S. Trueman (29) | Lord's | 1962 |
| 10th | 79 | R.W. Taylor (54), R.G.D. Willis (28*) | Birmingham | 1982 |

## RECORD WICKET PARTNERSHIPS — PAKISTAN

| | | | | |
|---|---|---|---|---|
| 1st | 173 | Mohsin Khan (104), Shoaib Mohammad (80) | Lahore[2] | 1983–84 |
| 2nd | 291 | Zaheer Abbas (274), Mushtaq Mohammad (100) | Birmingham | 1971 |
| 3rd | 180 | Mudassar Nazar (114), Haroon Rashid (122) | Lahore[2] | 1977–78 |
| 4th | 153 | Javed Burki (138), Mushtaq Mohammad (76) | Lahore[2] | 1961–62 |
| | 153 | Mohsin Khan (200), Zaheer Abbas (75) | Lord's | 1982 |
| 5th | 197 | Javed Burki (101), Nasim-ul-Ghani (101) | Lord's | 1962 |
| 6th | 145 | Mushtaq Mohammad (157), Intikhab Alam (138) | Hyderabad | 1972–73 |
| 7th | 75 | Salim Malik (74), Abdul Qadir (40) | Karachi | 1983–84 |
| 8th | 130 | Hanif Mohammad (187*), Asif Iqbal (76) | Lord's | 1967 |
| 9th | 190 | Asif Iqbal (146), Intikhab Alam (51) | Oval | 1967 |
| 10th | 62 | Sarfraz Nawaz (53), Asif Masood (4*) | Leeds | 1974 |

## BEST INNINGS BOWLING ANALYSIS

| | | | | | |
|---|---|---|---|---|---|
| England | in England | 8-34 | I.T. Botham | Lord's | 1978 |
| | in Pakistan | 7-66 | P.H. Edmonds | Karachi | 1977–78 |
| Pakistan | in England | 7-52 | Imran Khan | Birmingham | 1982 |
| | in Pakistan | 6-44 | Abdul Qadir | Hyderabad | 1977–78 |

## BEST MATCH BOWLING ANALYSIS

| | | | | | |
|---|---|---|---|---|---|
| England | in England | 13-71 | D.L. Underwood | Lord's | 1974 |
| | in Pakistan | 11-83 | N.G.B. Cook | Karachi | 1983–84 |
| Pakistan | in England | 12-99 | Fazal Mahmood | Oval | 1954 |
| | in Pakistan | 10-194 | Abdul Qadir | Lahore[2] | 1983–84 |

## HIGHEST AGGREGATE OF WICKETS IN A SERIES

| | | | | | |
|---|---|---|---|---|---|
| England | in England | 22 (av 19.95) | F.S. Trueman | | 1962 |
| | in Pakistan | 14 (av 31.71) | N.G.B. Cook | | 1983–84 |
| Pakistan | in England | 21 (av 18.57) | Imran Khan | | 1982 |
| | in Pakistan | 19 (av 23.73) | Abdul Qadir | | 1983–84 |

# ENGLAND v SRI LANKA

| Test No. | Venue and Result | England 1st | 2nd | Sri Lanka 1st | 2nd | Captains England | Sri Lanka |
|---|---|---|---|---|---|---|---|
| 921 | **1981–82** in Sri Lanka<br>Colombo (SO) – England 7 wkts | 223 | 171-3 | *218 | 175 | K.W.R. Fletcher | B. Warnapura |
| 994 | **1984** in England<br>Lord's – Drawn | 370 | — | *491-7d | 294-7d | D.I. Gower | L.R.D. Mendis |

## RESULTS SUMMARY

ENGLAND v SRI LANKA – IN ENGLAND

| | Tests | Result E | SL | Drawn | | Lord's E | SL | Drawn |
|---|---|---|---|---|---|---|---|---|
| 1984 | 1 | – | – | 1 | | – | – | 1 |

ENGLAND v SRI LANKA – IN SRI LANKA

| | Tests | Result E | SL | Drawn | | Colombo (SO) E | SL | Drawn |
|---|---|---|---|---|---|---|---|---|
| 1981–82 | 1 | 1 | – | – | | 1 | – | – |
| Totals | 2 | 1 | – | 1 | | | | |

## HIGHEST INNINGS TOTALS

| England | in England | 370 | | Lord's | 1984 |
|---|---|---|---|---|---|
| | in Sri Lanka | 223 | | Colombo (SO) | 1981–82 |
| Sri Lanka | in England | 491-7d | | Lord's | 1984 |
| | in Sri Lanka | 218 | | Colombo (SO) | 1981–82 |

## LOWEST INNINGS TOTALS

| England | in England | 370 | | Lord's | 1984 |
|---|---|---|---|---|---|
| | in Sri Lanka | 223 | | Colombo (SO) | 1981–82 |
| Sri Lanka | in England | 294-7d | | Lord's | 1984 |
| | in Sri Lanka | 175 | | Colombo (SO) | 1981–82 |

| HIGHEST MATCH AGGREGATE | 1155 for 24 wickets | Lord's | 1984 |
|---|---|---|---|
| LOWEST MATCH AGGREGATE | 787 for 33 wickets | Colombo (SO) | 1981–82 |

## HIGHEST INDIVIDUAL INNINGS

| England | in England | 107 | A.J. Lamb | Lord's | 1984 |
|---|---|---|---|---|---|
| | in Sri Lanka | 89 | D.I. Gower | Colombo (SO) | 1981–82 |
| Sri Lanka | in England | 190 | S. Wettimuny | Lord's | 1984 |
| | in Sri Lanka | 77 | R.L. Dias | Colombo (SO) | 1981–82 |

## HIGHEST AGGREGATE OF RUNS IN A SERIES

| England | in England | 107 | A.J. Lamb | 1984 |
|---|---|---|---|---|
| | in Sri Lanka | 131 | D.I. Gower | 1981–82 |
| Sri Lanka | in England | 205 | L.R.D. Mendis | 1984 |
| | in Sri Lanka | 77 | R.L. Dias | 1981–82 |

## RECORD WICKET PARTNERSHIPS — ENGLAND

| 1st | 49 | G. Fowler (25), B.C. Broad (86) | Lord's | 1984 |
|---|---|---|---|---|
| 2nd | 81 | G.A. Gooch (31), C.J. Tavaré (85) | Colombo (SO) | 1981–82 |
| 3rd | 85 | B.C. Broad (86), D.I. Gower (55) | Lord's | 1984 |
| 4th | 80 | D.I. Gower (89), K.W.R. Fletcher (45) | Colombo (SO) | 1981–82 |
| 5th | 31 | D.I. Gower (89), I.T. Botham (13) | Colombo (SO) | 1981–82 |
| 6th | 87 | A.J. Lamb (107), R.M. Ellison (41) | Lord's | 1984 |
| 7th | 49 | A.J. Lamb (107), P.R. Downton (10) | Lord's | 1984 |
| 8th | 9 | R.W. Taylor (31*), P.J.W. Allott (3) | Colombo (SO) | 1981–82 |
| 9th | 15 | A.J. Lamb (107), P.I. Pocock (2) | Lord's | 1984 |
| 10th | 7 | R.W. Taylor (31*), R.G.D. Willis (0) | Colombo (SO) | 1981–82 |

## RECORD WICKET PARTNERSHIPS — SRI LANKA

| 1st | 30 | B. Warnapura (38), S. Wettimuny (19) | Colombo (SO) | 1981–82 |
|---|---|---|---|---|
| 2nd | 83 | B. Warnapura (38), R.L. Dias (77) | Colombo (SO) | 1981–82 |
| 3rd | 101 | S. Wettimuny (190), R.L. Dias (32) | Lord's | 1984 |
| 4th | 148 | S. Wettimuny (190), A. Ranatunga (84) | Lord's | 1984 |
| 5th | 150 | S. Wettimuny (190), L.R.D. Mendis (111) | Lord's | 1984 |
| 6th | 138 | S.A.R. Silva (102*), L.R.D. Mendis (94) | Lord's | 1984 |
| 7th | 32 | R.S. Madugalle (65), A.L.F. De Mel (19) | Colombo (SO) | 1981–82 |
| 8th | 27* | A.L.F. De Mel (20*), J.R. Ratnayeke (5*) | Lord's | 1984 |
| 9th | 7 | R.S. Madugalle (65), H.M. Goonatillake (22*) | Colombo (SO) | 1981–82 |
| 10th | 28 | H.M. Goonatillake (22*), G.R.A. De Silva (12) | Colombo (SO) | 1981–82 |

## BEST INNINGS BOWLING ANALYSIS

| England | in England | 6-90 | I.T. Botham | Lord's | 1984 |
|---|---|---|---|---|---|
| | in Sri Lanka | 6-33 | J.E. Emburey | Colombo (SO) | 1981–82 |
| Sri Lanka | in England | 4-98 | V.B. John | Lord's | 1984 |
| | in Sri Lanka | 4-70 | A.L.F. De Mel | Colombo (SO) | 1981–82 |

## BEST MATCH BOWLING ANALYSIS

| England | in England | 7-204 | I.T. Botham | Lord's | 1984 |
|---|---|---|---|---|---|
| | in Sri Lanka | 8-95 | D.L. Underwood | Colombo (SO) | 1981–82 |
| Sri Lanka | in England | 4-98 | V.B. John | Lord's | 1984 |
| | in Sri Lanka | 5-103 | A.L.F. De Mel | Colombo (SO) | 1981–82 |

## HIGHEST AGGREGATE OF WICKETS IN A SERIES

| England | in England | 7 (av 29.14) | I.T. Botham | 1984 |
|---|---|---|---|---|
| | in Sri Lanka | 8 (av 11.87) | D.L. Underwood | 1981–82 |
| Sri Lanka | in England | { 4 (av 24.50) | V.B. John | 1984 |
| | | { 4 (av 27.50) | A.L.F. De Mel | 1984 |
| | in Sri Lanka | 5 (av 20.60) | A.L.F. De Mel | 1981–82 |

# AUSTRALIA v SOUTH AFRICA

| Test No. | Venue and Result | Australia 1st | Australia 2nd | South Africa 1st | South Africa 2nd | Captains Australia | Captains South Africa |
|---|---|---|---|---|---|---|---|
| | **1902–03** in South Africa | | | | | | |
| 75 | Johannesburg[1] – Drawn | 296 | 372-7d | •454 | 101-4 | J. Darling | H.M. Taberer |
| 76 | Johannesburg[1] – Australia 159 runs | •175 | 309 | 240 | 85 | | J.H. Anderson |
| 77 | Cape Town – Australia 10 wkts | •252 | 59-0 | 85 | 225 | | E.A. Halliwell |
| | **1910–11** in Australia | | | | | | |
| 111 | Sydney – Australia inns & 114 runs | •528 | — | 174 | 240 | | |
| 112 | Melbourne – Australia 89 runs | 348 | 327 | 506 | 80 | C. Hill | P.W. Sherwell |
| 113 | Adelaide – South Africa 38 runs | 465 | 339 | •482 | 360 | | |
| 114 | Melbourne – Australia 530 runs | •328 | 578 | 205 | 171 | | |
| 115 | Sydney – Australia 7 wkts | 364 | 198-3 | 160 | 401 | | |
| | **1912** in England | | | | | | |
| 121 | Manchester – Australia inns & 88 runs | •448 | — | 265 | 95 | | F. Mitchell |
| 125 | Lord's – Australia 10 wkts | 390 | 48-0 | •263 | 173 | S.E. Gregory | F. Mitchell |
| 127 | Nottingham – Drawn | 219 | — | 329 | — | | L.J. Tancred |
| | **1921–22** in South Africa | | | | | | |
| 145 | Durban[1] – Drawn | •299 | 324-7d | 232 | 184-7 | | |
| 146 | Johannesburg[1] – Drawn | •450 | 7-0 | 243 | 472-8d | H.L. Collins | H.W. Taylor |
| 147 | Cape Town – Australia 10 wkts | 396 | 1-0 | •180 | 216 | | |
| | **1931–32** in Australia | | | | | | |
| 212 | Brisbane[2] – Australia inns & 163 runs | •450 | — | 170 | 117 | | |
| 213 | Sydney – Australia inns & 155 runs | 469 | — | •153 | 161 | | |
| 214 | Melbourne – Australia 169 runs | •198 | 554 | 358 | 225 | W.M. Woodfull | H.B. Cameron |
| 215 | Adelaide – Australia 10 wkts | 513 | 73-0 | •308 | 274 | | |
| 216 | Melbourne – Australia inns & 72 runs | 153 | — | •36 | 45 | | |
| | **1935–36** in South Africa | | | | | | |
| 247 | Durban[2] – Australia 9 wkts | 429 | 102-1 | •248 | 282 | | |
| 248 | Johannesburg[1] – Drawn | 250 | 274-2 | •157 | 491 | | |
| 249 | Cape Town – Australia inns & 78 runs | •362-8d | — | 102 | 182 | V.Y. Richardson | H.F. Wade |
| 250 | Johannesburg[1] – Australia inns & 184 runs | 439 | — | •157 | 98 | | |
| 251 | Durban[2] – Australia inns & 6 runs | 455 | — | •222 | 227 | | |

| Test No. | Venue and Result | Australia 1st | Australia 2nd | South Africa 1st | South Africa 2nd | Captains Australia | Captains South Africa |
|---|---|---|---|---|---|---|---|
| | **1949–50 in South Africa** | | | | | | |
| 318 | Johannesburg² – Australia inns & 85 runs | •413 | — | 137 | 191 | | |
| 319 | Cape Town – Australia 8 wkts | •526-7d | 87-2 | 278 | 333 | A.L. Hassett | A.D. Nourse |
| 320 | Durban² – Australia 5 wkts | 75 | 336-5 | •311 | 99 | | |
| 321 | Johannesburg² – Drawn | •465-8d | 259-2 | 352 | — | | |
| 322 | Port Elizabeth – Australia inns & 259 runs | •549-7d | — | 158 | 132 | | |
| | **1952–53 in Australia** | | | | | | |
| 360 | Brisbane² – Australia 96 runs | •280 | 277 | 221 | 240 | | |
| 361 | Melbourne – South Africa 82 runs | 243 | 290 | •227 | 388 | | |
| 362 | Sydney – Australia inns & 38 runs | 443 | — | •173 | 232 | A.L. Hassett | J.E. Cheetham |
| 363 | Adelaide – Drawn | •530 | 233-3d | 387 | 177-6 | | |
| 364 | Melbourne – South Africa 6 wkts | •520 | 209 | 435 | 297-4 | | |
| | **1957–58 in South Africa** | | | | | | |
| 444 | Johannesburg³ – Drawn | 368 | 162-3 | •470-9d | 201 | | D.J. McGlew |
| 445 | Cape Town – Australia inns & 141 runs | •449 | — | 209 | 99 | | C.B. van Ryneveld |
| 446 | Durban² – Drawn | •163 | 292-7 | 384 | — | I.D. Craig | C.B. van Ryneveld |
| 447 | Johannesburg³ – Australia 10 wkts | 401 | 1-0 | 203 | 198 | | C.B. van Ryneveld |
| 448 | Port Elizabeth – Australia 8 wkts | 291 | 68-2 | •214 | 144 | | C.B. van Ryneveld |
| | **1963–64 in Australia** | | | | | | |
| 548 | Brisbane² – Drawn | •435 | 144-1d | 346 | 13-1 | R. Benaud | |
| 549 | Melbourne – Australia 8 wkts | 447 | 136-2 | •274 | 306 | R.B. Simpson | |
| 550 | Sydney – Drawn | •260 | 450-9d | 302 | 326-5 | R.B. Simpson | T.L. Goddard |
| 551 | Adelaide – South Africa 10 wkts | •345 | 331 | 595 | 82-0 | R.B. Simpson | |
| 552 | Sydney – Drawn | •311 | 270 | 411 | 76-0 | R.B. Simpson | |
| | **1966–67 in South Africa** | | | | | | |
| 613 | Johannesburg³ – South Africa 233 runs | 325 | 261 | •199 | 620 | | |
| 614 | Cape Town – Australia 6 wkts | •542 | 180-4 | 353 | 367 | | |
| 615 | Durban² – South Africa 8 wkts | 147 | 334 | •300 | 185-2 | R.B. Simpson | P.L. van der Merwe |
| 616 | Johannesburg³ – Drawn | •143 | 148-8 | 332-9d | — | | |
| 617 | Port Elizabeth – South Africa 7 wkts | •173 | 278 | 276 | 179-3 | | |
| | **1969–70 in South Africa** | | | | | | |
| 670 | Cape Town – South Africa 170 runs | 164 | 280 | •382 | 232 | | |
| 671 | Durban² – South Africa inns & 129 runs | 157 | 336 | •622-9d | — | W.M. Lawry | A. Bacher |
| 672 | Johannesburg³ – South Africa 307 runs | 202 | 178 | •279 | 408 | | |
| 673 | Port Elizabeth – South Africa 323 runs | 212 | 246 | •311 | 470-8d | | |

# RESULTS SUMMARY

## AUSTRALIA v SOUTH AFRICA – IN AUSTRALIA

| | | Result | | | Sydney | | | Melbourne | | | Adelaide | | | Brisbane | | |
|---|---|---|---|---|---|---|---|---|---|---|---|---|---|---|---|---|
| | *Tests* | *A* | *SA* | *Drawn* | *A* | *SA* | *Drawn* | *A* | *SA* | *Drawn* | *A* | *SA* | *Drawn* | *A* | *SA* | *Drawn* |
| 1910–11 | **5** | 4 | 1 | – | 2 | – | – | 2 | – | – | – | 1 | – | – | – | – |
| 1931–32 | **5** | 5 | – | – | 1 | – | – | 2 | – | – | 1 | – | – | 1 | – | – |
| 1952–53 | **5** | 2 | 2 | 1 | 1 | – | – | – | 2 | – | – | – | 1 | 1 | – | – |
| 1963–64 | **5** | 1 | 1 | 3 | – | – | 2 | 1 | – | – | – | 1 | – | – | – | 1 |
| | **20** | 12 | 4 | 4 | 4 | – | 2 | 5 | 2 | – | 1 | 2 | 1 | 2 | – | 1 |

## AUSTRALIA v SOUTH AFRICA – IN SOUTH AFRICA

| | | Result | | | Johannesburg | | | Cape Town | | | Durban | | | Port Elizabeth | | |
|---|---|---|---|---|---|---|---|---|---|---|---|---|---|---|---|---|
| | *Tests* | *A* | *SA* | *Drawn* | *A* | *SA* | *Drawn* | *A* | *SA* | *Drawn* | *A* | *SA* | *Drawn* | *A* | *SA* | *Drawn* |
| 1902–03 | **3** | 2 | – | 1 | 1 | – | 1 | 1 | – | – | – | – | – | – | – | – |
| 1921–22 | **3** | 1 | – | 2 | – | – | 1 | 1 | – | – | – | – | 1 | – | – | – |
| 1935–36 | **5** | 4 | – | 1 | 1 | – | 1 | 1 | – | – | 2 | – | – | – | – | – |
| 1949–50 | **5** | 4 | – | 1 | 1 | – | 1 | 1 | – | – | 1 | – | – | 1 | – | – |
| 1957–58 | **5** | 3 | – | 2 | 1 | – | 1 | 1 | – | – | – | – | 1 | 1 | – | – |
| 1966–67 | **5** | 1 | 3 | 1 | – | 1 | 1 | 1 | – | – | – | 1 | – | – | 1 | – |
| 1969–70 | **4** | – | 4 | – | – | 1 | – | – | 1 | – | – | 1 | – | – | 1 | – |
| | **30** | 15 | 7 | 8 | 4 | 2 | 6 | 6 | 1 | – | 3 | 2 | 2 | 2 | 2 | – |

## AUSTRALIA v SOUTH AFRICA – IN ENGLAND

| | | Result | | | Manchester | | | Lord's | | | Nottingham | | |
|---|---|---|---|---|---|---|---|---|---|---|---|---|---|
| | *Tests* | *A* | *SA* | *Drawn* | *A* | *SA* | *Drawn* | *A* | *SA* | *Drawn* | *A* | *SA* | *Drawn* |
| 1912 | **3** | 2 | – | 1 | 1 | – | – | 1 | – | – | – | – | 1 |
| Totals | **53** | 29 | 11 | 13 | | | | | | | | | |

## HIGHEST INNINGS TOTALS

| | | | | | |
|---|---|---|---|---|---|
| Australia | in Australia | 578 | | Melbourne | 1910–11 |
| | in South Africa | 549-7d | | Port Elizabeth | 1949–50 |
| South Africa | in Australia | 595 | | Adelaide | 1963–64 |
| | in South Africa | 622-9d | | Durban[2] | 1969–70 |

## LOWEST INNINGS TOTALS

| | | | | | |
|---|---|---|---|---|---|
| Australia | in Australia | 153 | | Melbourne | 1931–32 |
| | in South Africa | 75 | | Durban[2] | 1949–50 |
| South Africa | in Australia | 36 | | Melbourne | 1931–32 |
| | in South Africa | {85 | | Johannesburg[1] | 1902–03 |
| | | {85 | | Cape Town | 1902–03 |

| | | | | |
|---|---|---|---|---|
| **HIGHEST MATCH AGGREGATE** | 1646 for 40 wickets | | Adelaide | 1910–11 |
| **LOWEST MATCH AGGREGATE** | 234 for 29 wickets | | Melbourne | 1931–32 |

## HIGHEST INDIVIDUAL INNINGS

| | | | | | |
|---|---|---|---|---|---|
| Australia | in Australia | 299* | D.G. Bradman | Adelaide | 1931–32 |
| | in South Africa | 203 | H.L. Collins | Johannesburg[1] | 1921–22 |
| South Africa | in Australia | 204 | G.A. Faulkner | Melbourne | 1910–11 |
| | in South Africa | 274 | R.G. Pollock | Durban[2] | 1969–70 |

## HIGHEST AGGREGATE OF RUNS IN A SERIES

| | | | | |
|---|---|---|---|---|
| Australia | in Australia | 834 (av 92.66) | R.N. Harvey | 1952–53 |
| | in South Africa | 660 (av 132.00) | R.N. Harvey | 1949–50 |
| South Africa | in Australia | 732 (av 73.20) | G.A. Faulkner | 1910–11 |
| | in South Africa | 606 (av 86.57) | D.T. Lindsay | 1966–67 |

## RECORD WICKET PARTNERSHIPS — AUSTRALIA

| | | | | |
|---|---|---|---|---|
| 1st | 233 | J.H.W. Fingleton (112), W.A. Brown (121) | Cape Town | 1935–36 |
| 2nd | 275 | C.C. McDonald (154), A.L. Hassett (163) | Adelaide | 1952–53 |
| 3rd | 242 | C. Kelleway (102), W. Bardsley (164) | Lord's | 1912 |
| 4th | 168 | R.N. Harvey (190), K.R. Miller (55) | Sydney | 1952–53 |
| 5th | 143 | W.W. Armstrong (132), V.T. Trumper (87) | Melbourne | 1910–11 |
| 6th | 107 | C. Kelleway (59), V.S. Ransford (75) | Melbourne | 1910–11 |
| 7th | 160 | R. Benaud (90), G.D. McKenzie (76) | Sydney | 1963–64 |
| 8th | 83 | A.G. Chipperfield (109), C.V. Grimmett (15) | Durban[2] | 1935–36 |
| 9th | {78 | D.G. Bradman (299*), W.J. O'Reilly (23) | Adelaide | 1931–32 |
| | {78 | K.D. Mackay (83*), I. Meckiff (26) | Johannesburg[3] | 1957–58 |
| 10th | 82 | V.S. Ransford (95), W.J. Whitty (39*) | Melbourne | 1910–11 |

## RECORD WICKET PARTNERSHIPS — SOUTH AFRICA

| | | | | |
|---|---|---|---|---|
| 1st | 176 | D.J. McGlew (108), T.L. Goddard (90) | Johannesburg[3] | 1957–58 |
| 2nd | 173 | L.J. Tancred (97), C.B. Llewellyn (90) | Johannesburg[1] | 1902–03 |
| 3rd | 341 | E.J. Barlow (201), R.G. Pollock (175) | Adelaide | 1963–64 |
| 4th | 206 | C.N. Frank (152), A.W. Nourse (111) | Johannesburg[1] | 1921–22 |
| 5th | 129 | J.H.B. Waite (59), W.R. Endean (77) | Johannesburg[3] | 1957–58 |
| 6th | 200 | R.G. Pollock (274), H.R. Lance (61) | Durban[2] | 1969–70 |
| 7th | 221 | D.T. Lindsay (182), P.L. van der Merwe (76) | Johannesburg[3] | 1966–67 |
| 8th | 124 | A.W. Nourse (72), E.A. Halliwell (57) | Johannesburg[1] | 1902–03 |
| 9th | 85 | R.G. Pollock (209), P.M. Pollock (41) | Cape Town | 1966–67 |
| 10th | 53 | L.A. Stricker (48), S.J. Pegler (24*) | Adelaide | 1910–11 |

## BEST INNINGS BOWLING ANALYSIS

| | | | | | |
|---|---|---|---|---|---|
| Australia | in Australia | 7–83 | C.V. Grimmett | Adelaide | 1931–32 |
| | in South Africa | 7–34 | J.V. Saunders | Johannesburg[1] | 1902–03 |
| South Africa | in Australia | 7–81 | H.J. Tayfield | Melbourne | 1952–53 |
| | in South Africa | 7–23 | H.J. Tayfield | Durban[2] | 1949–50 |

## BEST MATCH BOWLING ANALYSIS

| | | | | | |
|---|---|---|---|---|---|
| Australia | in Australia | 14–199 | C.V. Grimmett | Adelaide | 1931–32 |
| | in South Africa | 13–173 | C.V. Grimmett | Durban[2] | 1935–36 |
| South Africa | in Australia | 13–165 | H.J. Tayfield | Melbourne | 1952–53 |
| | in South Africa | 10–116 | C.B. Llewellyn | Johannesburg[1] | 1902–03 |

## HIGHEST AGGREGATE OF WICKETS IN A SERIES

| | | | | |
|---|---|---|---|---|
| Australia | in Australia | 37 (av 17.08) | W.J. Whitty | 1910–11 |
| | in South Africa | 44 (av 14.59) | C.V. Grimmett | 1935–36 |
| South Africa | in Australia | 30 (av 28.10) | H.J. Tayfield | 1952–53 |
| | in South Africa | {26 (av 16.23) | T.L. Goddard | 1966–67 |
| | | {26 (av 13.57) | M.J. Procter | 1969–70 |

# AUSTRALIA v WEST INDIES

| Test No. | Venue and Result | Australia 1st | Australia 2nd | West Indies 1st | West Indies 2nd | Captains Australia | Captains West Indies |
|---|---|---|---|---|---|---|---|
| | **1930–31 in Australia** | | | | | | |
| 199 | Adelaide – Australia 10 wkts | 376 | 172-0 | •296 | 249 | W.M. Woodfull | G.C. Grant |
| 200 | Sydney – Australia inns & 172 runs | 369 | — | 107 | 90 | | |
| 201 | Brisbane[1] – Australia inns & 217 runs | •558 | — | 193 | 148 | | |
| 202 | Melbourne – Australia inns & 122 runs | 328-8d | — | •99 | 107 | | |
| 203 | Sydney – West Indies 30 runs | 224 | 220 | •350-6d | 124-5d | | |
| | **1951–52 in Australia** | | | | | | |
| 344 | Brisbane[2] – Australia 3 wkts | 226 | 236-7 | •216 | 245 | A.L. Hassett | J.D.C. Goddard |
| 345 | Sydney – Australia 7 wkts | 517 | 137-3 | 362 | 290 | A.L. Hassett | J.D.C. Goddard |
| 346 | Adelaide – West Indies 6 wkts | •82 | 255 | 105 | 233-4 | A.R. Morris | J.D.C. Goddard |
| 347 | Melbourne – Australia 1 wkt | 216 | 260-9 | 272 | 203 | A.L. Hassett | J.D.C. Goddard |
| 348 | Sydney – Australia 202 runs | •116 | 377 | 78 | 213 | A.L. Hassett | J.B. Stollmeyer |
| | **1954–55 in West Indies** | | | | | | |
| 403 | Kingston – Australia 9 wkts | •515-9d | 20-1 | 259 | 275 | I.W. Johnson | D.St E. Atkinson |
| 404 | Port-of-Spain – Drawn | 600-9d | — | •382 | 273-4 | | J.B. Stollmeyer |
| 405 | Georgetown – Australia 8 wkts | 257 | 133-2 | •182 | 207 | | J.B. Stollmeyer |
| 406 | Bridgetown – Drawn | •668 | 249 | 510 | 234-6 | | D.St E. Atkinson |
| 407 | Kingston – Australia inns & 82 runs | 758-8d | — | •357 | 319 | | D.St E. Atkinson |
| | **1960–61 in Australia** | | | | | | |
| 502 | Brisbane[2] – Tied | 505 | 232 | •453 | 284 | R. Benaud | F.M.M. Worrell |
| 503 | Melbourne – Australia 7 wkts | 348 | 70-3 | 181 | 233 | | |
| 504 | Sydney – West Indies 222 runs | 202 | 241 | •339 | 326 | | |
| 505 | Adelaide – Drawn | 366 | 273-9 | •393 | 432-6d | | |
| 506 | Melbourne – Australia 2 wkts | 356 | 258-8 | 292 | 321 | | |
| | **1964–65 in West Indies** | | | | | | |
| 583 | Kingston – West Indies 179 runs | 217 | 216 | •239 | 373 | R.B. Simpson | G.St A. Sobers |
| 584 | Port-of-Spain – Drawn | 516 | — | •429 | 386 | | |
| 585 | Georgetown – West Indies 212 runs | 179 | 144 | •355 | 180 | | |
| 586 | Bridgetown – Drawn | •650-6d | 175-4d | 573 | 242-5 | | |
| 587 | Port-of-Spain – Australia 10 wkts | 294 | 63-0 | •224 | 131 | | |

| Test No. | Venue and Result | Australia 1st | Australia 2nd | West Indies 1st | West Indies 2nd | Captains Australia | Captains West Indies |
|---|---|---|---|---|---|---|---|
| | **1968–69 in Australia** | | | | | | |
| 642 | Brisbane[2] – West Indies 125 runs | 284 | 240 | •296 | 353 | W.M. Lawry | G.St A. Sobers |
| 643 | Melbourne – Australia inns & 30 runs | 510 | — | •200 | 280 | | |
| 644 | Sydney – Australia 10 wkts | 547 | 42-0 | •264 | 324 | | |
| 645 | Adelaide – Drawn | 533 | 339-9 | •276 | 616 | | |
| 646 | Sydney – Australia 382 runs | •619 | 394-8d | 279 | 352 | | |
| | **1972–73 in West Indies** | | | | | | |
| 714 | Kingston – Drawn | •428-7d | 260-2d | 428 | 67-3 | I.M. Chappell | R.B. Kanhai |
| 715 | Bridgetown – Drawn | •324 | 300-2d | 391 | 36-0 | | |
| 716 | Port-of-Spain – Australia 44 runs | 332 | 281 | •280 | 289 | | |
| 717 | Georgetown – Australia 10 wkts | 341 | 135-0 | •366 | 109 | | |
| 718 | Port-of-Spain – Drawn | •419-8d | 218-7d | 319 | 135-5 | | |
| | **1975–76 in Australia** | | | | | | |
| 764 | Brisbane[2] – Australia 8 wkts | 366 | 219-2 | •214 | 370 | G.S. Chappell | C.H. Lloyd |
| 765 | Perth – West Indies inns & 87 runs | •329 | 169 | 585 | — | | |
| 766 | Melbourne – Australia 8 wkts | 485 | 55-2 | •224 | 312 | | |
| 767 | Sydney – Australia 7 wkts | 405 | 82-3 | 355 | 128 | | |
| 768 | Adelaide – Australia 190 runs | •418 | 345-7d | 274 | 299 | | |
| 769 | Melbourne – Australia 165 runs | •351 | 300-3d | 160 | 326 | | |
| | **1977–78 in West Indies** | | | | | | |
| 820 | Port-of-Spain – West Indies inns & 106 runs | •90 | 209 | 405 | — | R.B. Simpson | C.H. Lloyd |
| 821 | Bridgetown – West Indies 9 wkts | •250 | 178 | 288 | 141-1 | | C.H. Lloyd |
| 822 | Georgetown – Australia 3 wkts | 286 | 362-7 | •205 | 439 | | A.I. Kallicharran |
| 823 | Port-of-Spain – West Indies 198 runs | 290 | 94 | •292 | 290 | | A.I. Kallicharran |
| 824 | Kingston – Drawn | •343 | 305-3d | 280 | 258-9 | | A.I. Kallicharran |
| | **1979–80 in Australia** | | | | | | |
| 867 | Brisbane[2] – Drawn | •268 | 448-6d | 441 | 40-3 | G.S. Chappell | D.L. Murray |
| 869 | Melbourne – West Indies 10 wkts | •156 | 259 | 397 | 22-0 | | C.H. Lloyd |
| 871 | Adelaide – West Indies 408 runs | 203 | 165 | •328 | 448 | | C.H. Lloyd |
| | **1981–82 in Australia** | | | | | | |
| 918 | Melbourne – Australia 58 runs | •198 | 222 | 201 | 161 | G.S. Chappell | C.H. Lloyd |
| 919 | Sydney – Drawn | 267 | 200-4 | •384 | 255 | | |
| 920 | Adelaide – West Indies 5 wkts | •238 | 386 | 389 | 239-5 | | |

| Test No. | Venue and Result | Australia | | West Indies | | Captains | |
|---|---|---|---|---|---|---|---|
| | | 1st | 2nd | 1st | 2nd | Australia | West Indies |
| | **1983–84** in West Indies | | | | | | |
| 981 | Georgetown – Drawn | •279 | 273-9d | 230 | 250-0 | | C.H. Lloyd |
| 982 | Port-of-Spain – Drawn | •255 | 299-9 | 468-8d | — | | I.V.A. Richards |
| 983 | Bridgetown – West Indies 10 wkts | •429 | 97 | 509 | 21-0 | K. J. Hughes | C.H. Lloyd |
| 984 | St John's – West Indies inns & 36 runs | •262 | 200 | 498 | — | | C.H. Lloyd |
| 985 | Kingston – West Indies 10 wkts | •199 | 160 | 305 | 55-0 | | C.H. Lloyd |
| | **1984–85** in Australia | | | | | | |
| 997 | Perth – West Indies inns & 112 runs | 76 | 228 | •416 | — | K.J. Hughes | |
| 998 | Brisbane[2] – West Indies 8 wkts | •175 | 271 | 424 | 26-2 | K.J. Hughes | |
| 999 | Adelaide – West Indies 191 runs | 284 | 173 | •356 | 292-7d | A.R. Border | C.H. Lloyd |
| 1000 | Melbourne – Drawn | 296 | 198-8 | •479 | 186-5d | A.R. Border | |
| 1001 | Sydney – Australia inns & 55 runs | •471-9d | — | 163 | 253 | A.R. Border | |

# RESULTS SUMMARY

## AUSTRALIA v WEST INDIES – IN AUSTRALIA

| | | Result | | | | Adelaide | | | Sydney | | | Brisbane | | | | Melbourne | | | Perth | | |
|---|---|---|---|---|---|---|---|---|---|---|---|---|---|---|---|---|---|---|---|---|---|
| | Tests | A | WI | Drawn | Tied | A | WI | Drawn | A | WI | Drawn | A | WI | Drawn | Tied | A | WI | Drawn | A | WI | Drawn |
| 1930–31 | 5 | 4 | 1 | – | – | 1 | – | – | 1 | 1 | – | 1 | – | – | – | 1 | – | – | – | – | – |
| 1951–52 | 5 | 4 | 1 | – | – | – | 1 | – | 2 | – | – | 1 | – | – | – | 1 | – | – | – | – | – |
| 1960–61 | 5 | 2 | 1 | 1 | 1 | – | – | 1 | – | 1 | – | – | – | – | 1 | 2 | – | – | – | – | – |
| 1968–69 | 5 | 3 | 1 | 1 | – | – | – | 1 | 2 | – | – | – | 1 | – | – | 1 | – | – | – | – | – |
| 1975–76 | 6 | 5 | 1 | – | – | 1 | – | – | 1 | – | – | 1 | – | – | – | 2 | – | – | – | 1 | – |
| 1979–80 | 3 | – | 2 | 1 | – | – | 1 | – | – | – | – | – | – | 1 | – | – | 1 | – | – | – | – |
| 1981–82 | 3 | 1 | 1 | 1 | – | – | 1 | – | – | – | 1 | – | – | – | – | 1 | – | – | – | – | – |
| 1984–85 | 5 | 1 | 3 | 1 | – | – | 1 | – | 1 | – | – | – | 1 | – | – | – | – | 1 | – | 1 | – |
| | **37** | **20** | **11** | **5** | **1** | **2** | **4** | **2** | **7** | **2** | **1** | **3** | **2** | **1** | **1** | **8** | **1** | **1** | **–** | **2** | **–** |

## AUSTRALIA v WEST INDIES – IN WEST INDIES

| | | Result | | | | Kingston | | | Port-of-Spain | | | Georgetown | | | Bridgetown | | | St John's | | |
|---|---|---|---|---|---|---|---|---|---|---|---|---|---|---|---|---|---|---|---|---|---|
| | Tests | A | WI | Drawn | Tied | A | WI | Drawn | A | WI | Drawn | A | WI | Drawn | A | WI | Drawn | A | WI | Drawn |
| 1954–55 | 5 | 3 | – | 2 | – | 2 | – | – | – | – | 1 | 1 | – | – | – | – | 1 | – | – | – |
| 1964–65 | 5 | 1 | 2 | 2 | – | – | 1 | – | 1 | – | 1 | – | 1 | – | – | – | 1 | – | – | – |
| 1972–73 | 5 | 2 | – | 3 | – | – | – | 1 | 1 | – | 1 | 1 | – | – | – | – | 1 | – | – | – |
| 1977–78 | 5 | 1 | 3 | 1 | – | – | – | 1 | – | 2 | – | 1 | – | – | – | 1 | – | – | – | – |
| 1983–84 | 5 | – | 3 | 2 | – | – | 1 | – | – | – | 1 | – | – | 1 | – | 1 | – | – | 1 | – |
| Totals | **25** | **7** | **8** | **10** | **–** | **2** | **2** | **2** | **2** | **2** | **4** | **3** | **1** | **1** | **–** | **2** | **3** | **–** | **1** | **–** |
| | **62** | **27** | **19** | **15** | **1** | | | | | | | | | | | | | | | | |

## HIGHEST INNINGS TOTALS

| Australia | in Australia | 619 | | Sydney | 1968–69 |
| | in West Indies | 758-8d | | Kingston | 1954–55 |
| West Indies | in Australia | 616 | | Adelaide | 1968–69 |
| | in West Indies | 573 | | Bridgetown | 1964–65 |

## LOWEST INNINGS TOTALS

| Australia | in Australia | 76 | | Perth | 1984–85 |
| | in West Indies | 90 | | Port-of-Spain | 1977–78 |
| West Indies | in Australia | 78 | | Sydney | 1951–52 |
| | in West Indies | 109 | | Georgetown | 1972–73 |

| **HIGHEST MATCH AGGREGATE** | 1764 for 39 wickets | Adelaide | 1968–69 |
| **LOWEST MATCH AGGREGATE** | 534 for 28 wickets | Melbourne | 1930–31 |

## HIGHEST INDIVIDUAL INNINGS

| Australia | in Australia | 242 | K.D. Walters | Sydney | 1968–69 |
| | in West Indies | 210 | W.M. Lawry | Bridgetown | 1964–65 |
| West Indies | in Australia | 208 | I.V.A. Richards | Melbourne | 1984–85 |
| | in West Indies | 219 | D.St E. Atkinson | Bridgetown | 1954–55 |

## HIGHEST AGGREGATE OF RUNS IN A SERIES

| Australia | in Australia | 702 (av 117.00) | G.S. Chappell | 1975–76 |
| | in West Indies | 650 (av 108.33) | R.N. Harvey | 1954–55 |
| West Indies | in Australia | 503 (av 50.30) | R.B. Kanhai | 1960–61 |
| | in West Indies | 827 (av 82.70) | C.L. Walcott | 1954–55 |

## RECORD WICKET PARTNERSHIPS — AUSTRALIA

| 1st | 382 | W.M. Lawry (210), R.B. Simpson (201) | Bridgetown | 1964–65 |
| 2nd | 298 | W.M. Lawry (205), I.M. Chappell (165) | Melbourne | 1968–69 |
| 3rd | 295 | C.C. McDonald (127), R.N. Harvey (204) | Kingston | 1954–55 |
| 4th | 336 | W.M. Lawry (151), K.D. Walters (242) | Sydney | 1968–69 |
| 5th | 220 | K.R. Miller (109), R.G. Archer (128) | Kingston | 1954–55 |
| 6th | 206 | K.R. Miller (137), R.G. Archer (98) | Bridgetown | 1954–55 |
| 7th | 134 | A.K. Davidson (80), R. Benaud (52) | Brisbane[2] | 1960–61 |
| 8th | 137 | R. Benaud (128), I.W. Johnson (27*) | Kingston | 1954–55 |
| 9th | 97 | K.D. Mackay (74), J.W. Martin (55) | Melbourne | 1960–61 |
| 10th | 97 | T.G. Hogan (42*), R.M. Hogg (52) | Georgetown | 1983–84 |

## RECORD WICKET PARTNERSHIPS — WEST INDIES

| 1st | 250* | C.G. Greenidge (120*), D.L. Haynes (103*) | Georgetown | 1983–84 |
| 2nd | 165 | M.C. Carew (83), R.B. Kanhai (94) | Brisbane[2] | 1968–69 |
| 3rd | 308 | R.B. Richardson (154), I.V.A. Richards (178) | St John's | 1983–84 |
| 4th | 198 | L.G. Rowe (107), A.I. Kallicharran (101) | Brisbane[2] | 1975–76 |
| 5th | 210 | R.B. Kanhai (84), M.L.C. Foster (125) | Kingston | 1972–73 |
| 6th | 165 | R.B. Kanhai (105), D.L. Murray (90) | Bridgetown | 1972–73 |
| 7th | 347 | D.St E. Atkinson (219), C.C. Depeiza (122) | Bridgetown | 1954–55 |
| 8th | 82 | H.A. Gomes (124*), A.M.E. Roberts (42) | Adelaide | 1981–82 |
| 9th | 122 | D.A.J. Holford (80), J.L. Hendriks (37*) | Adelaide | 1968–69 |
| 10th | 56 | J. Garner (60), C.E.H. Croft (2*) | Brisbane[2] | 1979–80 |

## BEST INNINGS BOWLING ANALYSIS

| Australia | in Australia | 8-71 | G.D. McKenzie | Melbourne | 1968–69 |
| | in West Indies | 7-44 | I.W. Johnson | Georgetown | 1954–55 |
| West Indies | in Australia | 7-54 | A.M.E. Roberts | Perth | 1975–76 |
| | in West Indies | 6-29 | L.R. Gibbs | Georgetown | 1964–65 |

## BEST MATCH BOWLING ANALYSIS

| Australia | in Australia | 11-79 | H. Ironmonger | Melbourne | 1930–31 |
| | in West Indies | 10-115 | N.J.N. Hawke | Georgetown | 1964–65 |
| West Indies | in Australia | 11-107 | M.A. Holding | Melbourne | 1981–82 |
| | in West Indies | 9-80 | L.R. Gibbs | Georgetown | 1964–65 |

## HIGHEST AGGREGATE OF WICKETS IN A SERIES

| Australia | in Australia | { 33 (av 17.96) | C.V. Grimmett | 1930–31 |
| | | { 33 (av 18.54) | A.K. Davidson | 1960–61 |
| | in West Indies | 26 (av 20.73) | M.H.N. Walker | 1972–73 |
| West Indies | in Australia | 28 (av 19.78) | M.D. Marshall | 1984–85 |
| | in West Indies | 31 (av 16.87) | J. Garner | 1983–84 |

# AUSTRALIA v NEW ZEALAND

| Test No. | Venue and Result | Australia 1st | 2nd | New Zealand 1st | 2nd | Captains Australia | New Zealand |
|---|---|---|---|---|---|---|---|
| | **1945–46 in New Zealand** | | | | | | |
| 275 | Wellington – Australia inns & 103 runs | 199-8d | — | •42 | 54 | W.A. Brown | W.A. Hadlee |
| | **1973–74 in Australia** | | | | | | |
| 728 | Melbourne – Australia inns & 25 runs | •462-8d | — | 237 | 200 | I.M. Chappell | B.E. Congdon |
| 729 | Sydney – Drawn | 162 | 30-2 | •312 | 305-9d | | |
| 730 | Adelaide – Australia inns & 57 runs | •477 | — | 218 | 202 | | |
| | **1973–74 in New Zealand** | | | | | | |
| 736 | Wellington – Drawn | •511-6d | 460-8 | •484 | — | I.M. Chappell | B.E. Congdon |
| 737 | Christchurch – New Zealand 5 wkts | •223 | 259 | 255 | 230-5 | | |
| 738 | Auckland – Australia 297 runs | •221 | 346 | 112 | 158 | | |
| | **1976–77 in New Zealand** | | | | | | |
| 796 | Christchurch – Drawn | •552 | 154-4d | 357 | 293-8 | G.S. Chappell | G.M. Turner |
| 797 | Auckland – Australia 10 wkts | 377 | 28-0 | •229 | 175 | | |
| | **1980–81 in Australia** | | | | | | |
| 890 | Brisbane[2] – Australia 10 wkts | 305 | 63-0 | •225 | 142 | G.S. Chappell | G.P. Howarth |
| 891 | Perth – Australia 8 wkts | 265 | 55-2 | •196 | 121 | | M.G. Burgess |
| 892 | Melbourne – Drawn | •321 | 188 | 317 | 128-6 | | G.P. Howarth |
| | **1981–82 in New Zealand** | | | | | | |
| 922 | Wellington – Drawn | 85-1 | — | •266-7d | — | G.S. Chappell | G.P. Howarth |
| 923 | Auckland – New Zealand 5 wkts | •210 | 280 | 387 | 109-5 | | |
| 924 | Christchurch – Australia 8 wkts | •353 | 69-2 | 149 | 272 | | |

# RESULTS SUMMARY

## AUSTRALIA v NEW ZEALAND – IN AUSTRALIA

| | Tests | Result | | | Melbourne | | | Sydney | | | Adelaide | | | Brisbane | | | Perth | | |
|---|---|---|---|---|---|---|---|---|---|---|---|---|---|---|---|---|---|---|---|
| | | A | NZ | Drawn | A | NZ | Drawn | A | NZ | Drawn | A | NZ | Drawn | A | NZ | Drawn | A | NZ | Drawn |
| 1973–74 | 3 | 2 | – | 1 | 1 | – | – | – | – | 1 | 1 | – | – | – | – | – | – | – | – |
| 1980–81 | 3 | 2 | – | 1 | – | – | 1 | – | – | – | – | – | – | 1 | – | – | 1 | – | – |
| | 6 | 4 | – | 2 | 1 | – | 1 | – | – | 1 | 1 | – | – | 1 | – | – | 1 | – | – |

## AUSTRALIA v NEW ZEALAND – IN NEW ZEALAND

| | Tests | Result | | | Wellington | | | Christchurch | | | Auckland | | |
|---|---|---|---|---|---|---|---|---|---|---|---|---|---|
| | | A | NZ | Drawn | A | NZ | Drawn | A | NZ | Drawn | A | NZ | Drawn |
| 1945–46 | 1 | 1 | – | – | 1 | – | – | – | – | – | – | – | – |
| 1973–74 | 3 | 1 | 1 | 1 | – | – | 1 | – | 1 | – | 1 | – | – |
| 1976–77 | 2 | 1 | – | 1 | – | – | – | – | – | 1 | 1 | – | – |
| 1981–82 | 3 | 1 | 1 | 1 | – | – | 1 | 1 | – | – | – | 1 | – |
| | 9 | 4 | 2 | 3 | 1 | – | 2 | 1 | 1 | 1 | 2 | 1 | – |
| **Totals** | **15** | **8** | **2** | **5** | | | | | | | | | |

## HIGHEST INNINGS TOTALS

| Australia | in Australia | 477 | | Adelaide | 1973–74 |
|---|---|---|---|---|---|
| | in New Zealand | 552 | | Christchurch | 1976–77 |
| New Zealand | in Australia | 317 | | Melbourne | 1980–81 |
| | in New Zealand | 484 | | Wellington | 1973–74 |

## LOWEST INNINGS TOTALS

| Australia | in Australia | 162 | | Sydney | 1973–74 |
|---|---|---|---|---|---|
| | in New Zealand | 210 | | Auckland | 1981–82 |
| New Zealand | in Australia | 121 | | Perth | 1980–81 |
| | in New Zealand | 42 | | Wellington | 1945–46 |

| HIGHEST MATCH AGGREGATE | 1455 for 24 wickets | | Wellington | 1973–74 |
|---|---|---|---|---|
| LOWEST MATCH AGGREGATE | 295 for 28 wickets | | Wellington | 1945–46 |

## HIGHEST INDIVIDUAL INNINGS

| Australia | in Australia | 132 | R.W. Marsh | Adelaide | 1973–74 |
|---|---|---|---|---|---|
| | in New Zealand | 250 | K.D. Walters | Christchurch | 1976–77 |
| New Zealand | in Australia | 117 | J.F.M. Morrison | Sydney | 1973–74 |
| | in New Zealand | 161 | B.A. Edgar | Auckland | 1981–82 |

## HIGHEST AGGREGATE OF RUNS IN A SERIES

| Australia | in Australia | 214 (av 71.33) | K.D. Walters | | 1973–74 |
|---|---|---|---|---|---|
| | in New Zealand | 449 (av 89.80) | G.S. Chappell | | 1973–74 |
| New Zealand | in Australia | 249 (av 41.50) | J.F.M. Morrison | | 1973–74 |
| | in New Zealand | 403 (av 100.75) | G.M. Turner | | 1973–74 |

## RECORD WICKET PARTNERSHIPS — AUSTRALIA

| 1st | 106 | B.M. Laird (39), G.M. Wood (100) | Auckland | 1981–82 |
|---|---|---|---|---|
| 2nd | 141 | I.R. Redpath (93), I.M. Chappell (121) | Wellington | 1973–74 |
| 3rd | 264 | I.M. Chappell (145), G.S. Chappell (247*) | Wellington | 1973–74 |
| 4th | 106 | I.R. Redpath (58), I.C. Davis (50) | Christchurch | 1973–74 |
| 5th | 93 | G.S. Chappell (44), K.D. Walters (250) | Christchurch | 1976–77 |
| 6th | 92 | G.S. Chappell (176), R.W. Marsh (23) | Christchurch | 1981–82 |
| 7th | 217 | K.D. Walters (250), G.J. Gilmour (101) | Christchurch | 1976–77 |
| 8th | 93 | G.J. Gilmour (64), K.J. O'Keeffe (32) | Auckland | 1976–77 |
| 9th | 57 | R.W. Marsh (91), L.S. Pascoe (30*) | Perth | 1980–81 |
| 10th | 60 | K.D. Walters (107), J.D. Higgs (6*) | Melbourne | 1980–81 |

## RECORD WICKET PARTNERSHIPS — NEW ZEALAND

| 1st | 107 | G.M. Turner (72), J.M. Parker (34) | Auckland | 1973–74 |
|---|---|---|---|---|
| 2nd | 108 | G.M. Turner (79), J.F.M. Morrison (66) | Wellington | 1973–74 |
| 3rd | 125 | G.P. Howarth (65), J.M. Parker (56) | Melbourne | 1980–81 |
| 4th | 229 | B.E. Congdon (132), B.F. Hastings (101) | Wellington | 1973–74 |
| 5th | 88 | J.V. Coney (71), M.G. Burgess (43) | Perth | 1980–81 |
| 6th | 105 | M.G. Burgess (38), R.J. Hadlee (81) | Auckland | 1976–77 |
| 7th | 66 | K.J. Wadsworth (48), D.R. Hadlee (29) | Adelaide | 1973–74 |
| 8th | 53 | B.A. Edgar (51), R.J. Hadlee (51*) | Brisbane[2] | 1980–81 |
| 9th | 73 | H.J. Howarth (61), D.R. Hadlee (37) | Christchurch | 1976–77 |
| 10th | 47 | H.J. Howarth (29*), M.G. Webb (12) | Wellington | 1973–74 |

## BEST INNINGS BOWLING ANALYSIS

| Australia | in Australia | 6-53 | D.K. Lillee | Brisbane[2] | 1980–81 |
|---|---|---|---|---|---|
| | in New Zealand | 6-72 | D.K. Lillee | Auckland | 1976–77 |
| New Zealand | in Australia | 6-57 | R.J. Hadlee | Melbourne | 1980–81 |
| | in New Zealand | 6-40 | J. Cowie | Wellington | 1945–46 |

## BEST MATCH BOWLING ANALYSIS

| Australia | in Australia | 8-89 | D.K. Lillee | Brisbane[2] | 1980–81 |
|---|---|---|---|---|---|
| | in New Zealand | 11-123 | D.K. Lillee | Auckland | 1976–77 |
| New Zealand | in Australia | 9-146 | R.J. Hadlee | Melbourne | 1980–81 |
| | in New Zealand | 9-166 | R.O. Collinge | Auckland | 1973–74 |

## HIGHEST AGGREGATE OF WICKETS IN A SERIES

| Australia | in Australia | 16 (av 15.31) | D.K. Lillee | | 1980–81 |
|---|---|---|---|---|---|
| | in New Zealand | 15 (av 20.80) | D.K. Lillee | | 1976–77 |
| New Zealand | in Australia | 19 (av 19.15) | R.J. Hadlee | | 1980–81 |
| | in New Zealand | 17 (av 25.64) | R.O. Collinge | | 1973–74 |

# AUSTRALIA v INDIA

| Test No. | Venue and Result | Australia 1st | Australia 2nd | India 1st | India 2nd | Captains Australia | Captains India |
|---|---|---|---|---|---|---|---|
| | **1947–48 in Australia** | | | | | | |
| 290 | Brisbane² – Australia inns & 226 runs | •382-8d | — | •58 | 98 | D.G. Bradman | L. Amarnath |
| 291 | Sydney – Drawn | 107 | — | 188 | 61-7 | | |
| 292 | Melbourne – Australia 233 runs | •394 | 255-4d | 291-9d | 125 | | |
| 293 | Adelaide – Australia inns & 16 runs | •674 | — | 381 | 277 | | |
| 294 | Melbourne – Australia inns & 177 runs | •575-8d | — | 331 | 67 | | |
| | **1956–57 in India** | | | | | | |
| 431 | Madras² – Australia inns & 5 runs | 319 | — | •161 | 153 | I.W. Johnson | P.R. Umrigar |
| 432 | Bombay² – Drawn | 523-7d | — | •251 | 250-5 | R.R. Lindwall | |
| 433 | Calcutta – Australia 94 runs | •177 | 189-9d | 136 | 136 | I.W. Johnson | |
| | **1959–60 in India** | | | | | | |
| 482 | Delhi – Australia inns & 127 runs | 468 | — | •135 | 206 | R. Benaud | G.S. Ramchand |
| 483 | Kanpur – India 119 runs | 219 | 105 | •152 | 291 | | |
| 484 | Bombay² – Drawn | 387-8d | 34-1 | •289 | 226-5d | | |
| 485 | Madras² – Australia inns & 55 runs | •342 | — | 149 | 138 | | |
| 486 | Calcutta – Drawn | 331 | 121-2 | •194 | 339 | | |
| | **1964–65 in India** | | | | | | |
| 566 | Madras² – Australia 139 runs | •211 | 397 | 276 | 193 | R.B. Simpson | Nawab of Pataudi, jr |
| 567 | Bombay² – India 2 wkts | 320 | 274 | 341 | 256-8 | | |
| 568 | Calcutta – Drawn | •174 | 143-1 | 235 | — | | |
| | **1967–68 in Australia** | | | | | | |
| 624 | Adelaide – Australia 146 runs | •335 | 369 | 307 | 251 | R.B. Simpson | C.G. Borde |
| 625 | Melbourne – Australia inns & 4 runs | 529 | — | •173 | 352 | R.B. Simpson | Nawab of Pataudi, jr |
| 626 | Brisbane² – Australia 39 runs | •379 | 294 | 279 | 355 | W.M. Lawry | Nawab of Pataudi, jr |
| 627 | Sydney – Australia 144 runs | 317 | 292 | 268 | 197 | W.M. Lawry | Nawab of Pataudi, jr |
| | **1969–70 in India** | | | | | | |
| 665 | Bombay² – Australia 8 wkts | 345 | 67-2 | •271 | 137 | W.M. Lawry | Nawab of Pataudi, jr |
| 666 | Kanpur – Drawn | 348 | 95-0 | •320 | 312-7d | | |
| 667 | Delhi – India 7 wkts | •296 | 107 | 223 | 181-3 | | |
| 668 | Calcutta – Australia 10 wkts | 335 | 42-0 | •212 | 161 | | |
| 669 | Madras¹ – Australia 77 runs | •258 | 153 | 163 | 171 | | |

| Test No. | Venue and Result | Australia 1st | Australia 2nd | India 1st | India 2nd | Captains Australia | India |
|---|---|---|---|---|---|---|---|
| | **1977–78** in Australia | | | | | | |
| 809 | Brisbane[2] – Australia 16 runs | •166 | 327 | 153 | 324 | | |
| 810 | Perth – Australia 2 wkts | 394 | 342-8 | •402 | 330-9d | R.B. Simpson | B.S. Bedi |
| 811 | Melbourne – India 222 runs | 213 | 164 | •256 | 343 | | |
| 812 | Sydney – India inns & 2 runs | •131 | 263 | 396-8d | — | | |
| 813 | Adelaide – Australia 47 runs | •505 | 256 | 269 | 445 | | |
| | **1979–80** in India | | | | | | |
| 855 | Madras[1] – Drawn | •390 | 212-7 | 425 | — | | |
| 856 | Bangalore – Drawn | •333 | 77-3 | 457-5d | — | | |
| 857 | Kanpur – India 153 runs | 304 | 125 | •271 | 311 | | |
| 858 | Delhi – Drawn | 298 | 413 | •510-7d | — | K.J. Hughes | S.M. Gavaskar |
| 859 | Calcutta – Drawn | •442 | 151-6d | 347 | 200-4 | | |
| 860 | Bombay[3] – India inns & 100 runs | 160 | 198 | •458-8d | — | | |
| | **1980–81** in Australia | | | | | | |
| 893 | Sydney – Australia inns & 4 runs | 406 | — | •201 | 201 | | |
| 894 | Adelaide – Drawn | •528 | 221-7d | 419 | 135-8 | G.S. Chappell | S.M. Gavaskar |
| 895 | Melbourne – India 59 runs | 419 | 83 | •237 | 324 | | |

# RESULTS SUMMARY

## AUSTRALIA v INDIA – IN AUSTRALIA

| | Result | | | Brisbane | | | Sydney | | | Melbourne | | | Adelaide | | | Perth | | |
| --- | --- | --- | --- | --- | --- | --- | --- | --- | --- | --- | --- | --- | --- | --- | --- | --- | --- | --- |
| Tests | A | I | Drawn | A | I | Drawn | A | I | Drawn | A | I | Drawn | A | I | Drawn | A | I | Drawn |
| 1947–48 | 5 | 4 | – | 1 | 1 | – | – | – | – | 1 | 2 | – | – | 1 | – | – | – | – | – |
| 1967–68 | 4 | 4 | – | – | 1 | – | – | 1 | – | – | 1 | – | – | 1 | – | – | – | – | – |
| 1977–78 | 5 | 3 | 2 | – | 1 | – | – | – | 1 | – | – | 1 | – | 1 | – | – | 1 | 1 | – |
| 1980–81 | 3 | 1 | 1 | 1 | – | – | – | 1 | – | 1 | – | 1 | 1 | – | – | 1 | – | – | – |
| | **17** | 12 | 3 | 2 | 3 | – | – | 2 | 1 | 1 | 3 | 2 | – | 3 | – | 1 | 1 | – | – |

## AUSTRALIA v INDIA – IN INDIA

| | Result | | | Madras | | | Bombay | | | Calcutta | | | Delhi | | | Kanpur | | | Bangalore | | |
| --- | --- | --- | --- | --- | --- | --- | --- | --- | --- | --- | --- | --- | --- | --- | --- | --- | --- | --- | --- | --- | --- |
| Tests | A | I | Drawn | A | I | Drawn | A | I | Drawn | A | I | Drawn | A | I | Drawn | A | I | Drawn | A | I | Drawn |
| 1956–57 | 3 | 2 | – | 1 | 1 | – | – | – | – | 1 | 1 | – | – | – | – | – | – | – | – | – | – | – |
| 1959–60 | 5 | 2 | 1 | 2 | 1 | – | – | – | – | 1 | – | – | 1 | 1 | – | – | – | 1 | – | – | – | – |
| 1964–65 | 3 | 1 | 1 | 1 | 1 | – | – | – | 1 | – | – | – | 1 | – | – | – | – | – | – | – | – | – |
| 1969–70 | 5 | 3 | 1 | 1 | 1 | – | – | 1 | – | – | 1 | – | – | – | 1 | – | – | – | 1 | – | – | – |
| 1979–80 | 6 | – | 2 | 4 | – | – | 1 | – | 1 | – | – | – | 1 | – | – | 1 | – | 1 | – | – | – | 1 |
| | **22** | 8 | 5 | 9 | 4 | – | 1 | 1 | 2 | 2 | 2 | – | 3 | 1 | 1 | 1 | – | 2 | 1 | – | – | 1 |
| Totals | **39** | 20 | 8 | 11 | | | | | | | | | | | | | | | | | | |

## HIGHEST INNINGS TOTALS

| | | | | |
|---|---|---|---|---|
| Australia | in Australia | 674 | Adelaide | 1947–48 |
| | in India | 523-7d | Bombay[2] | 1956–57 |
| India | in Australia | 445 | Adelaide | 1977–78 |
| | in India | 510-7d | Delhi | 1979–80 |

## LOWEST INNINGS TOTALS

| | | | | |
|---|---|---|---|---|
| Australia | in Australia | 83 | Melbourne | 1980–81 |
| | in India | 105 | Kanpur | 1959–60 |
| India | in Australia | 58 | Brisbane[2] | 1947–48 |
| | in India | 135 | Delhi | 1959–60 |

| | | | |
|---|---|---|---|
| **HIGHEST MATCH AGGREGATE** | 1475 for 40 wickets | Adelaide | 1977–78 |
| **LOWEST MATCH AGGREGATE** | 538 for 28 wickets | Brisbane[2] | 1947–48 |

## HIGHEST INDIVIDUAL INNINGS

| | | | | | |
|---|---|---|---|---|---|
| Australia | in Australia | 213 | K.J. Hughes | Adelaide | 1980–81 |
| | in India | 167 | G.N. Yallop | Calcutta | 1979–80 |
| India | in Australia | 174 | S.M. Patil | Adelaide | 1980–81 |
| | in India | 161* | G.R. Viswanath | Bangalore | 1979–80 |

## HIGHEST AGGREGATE OF RUNS IN A SERIES

| | | | | |
|---|---|---|---|---|
| Australia | in Australia | 715 (av 178.75) | D.G. Bradman | 1947–48 |
| | in India | 594 (av 59.40) | K.J. Hughes | 1979–80 |
| India | in Australia | 473 (av 52.55) | G.R. Viswanath | 1977–78 |
| | in India | 518 (av 74.00) | G.R. Viswanath | 1979–80 |

## RECORD WICKET PARTNERSHIPS — AUSTRALIA

| | | | | |
|---|---|---|---|---|
| 1st | 191 | R.B. Simpson (109), W.M. Lawry (100) | Melbourne | 1967–68 |
| 2nd | 236 | S.G. Barnes (112), D.G. Bradman (201) | Adelaide | 1947–48 |
| 3rd | 222 | A.R. Border (162), K.J. Hughes (100) | Madras[1] | 1979–80 |
| 4th | 159 | R.N. Harvey (153), S.J.E. Loxton (80) | Melbourne | 1947–48 |
| 5th | 223* | A.R. Morris (100*), D.G. Bradman (127*) | Melbourne | 1947–48 |
| 6th | 151 | T.R. Veivers (67), B.N. Jarman (78) | Bombay[2] | 1964–65 |
| 7th | 64 | T.R. Veivers (74), J.W. Martin (39) | Madras[2] | 1964–65 |
| 8th | 73 | T.R. Veivers (74), G.D. McKenzie (27) | Madras[2] | 1964–65 |
| 9th | 87 | I.W. Johnson (73), W.P.A. Crawford (34) | Madras[2] | 1956–57 |
| 10th | 52 | K.J. Wright (55*), J.D. Higgs (11) | Delhi | 1979–80 |

## RECORD WICKET PARTNERSHIPS — INDIA

| | | | | |
|---|---|---|---|---|
| 1st | 192 | S.M. Gavaskar (123), C.P.S. Chauhan (73) | Bombay[3] | 1979–80 |
| 2nd | 193 | S.M. Gavaskar (127), M. Amarnath (100) | Perth | 1977–78 |
| 3rd | 159 | S.M. Gavaskar (115), G.R. Viswanath (131) | Delhi | 1979–80 |
| 4th | 159 | D.B. Vengsarkar (112), G.R. Viswanath (161*) | Bangalore | 1979–80 |
| 5th | 109 | A.A. Baig (58), R.B. Kenny (55*) | Bombay[2] | 1959–60 |
| 6th | 188 | V.S. Hazare (116), D.G. Phadkar (123) | Adelaide | 1947–48 |
| 7th | 132 | V.S. Hazare (145), H.R. Adhikari (51) | Adelaide | 1947–48 |
| 8th | 127 | S.M.H. Kirmani (101*), K.D. Ghavri (86) | Bombay[3] | 1979–80 |
| 9th | 57 | S.M.H. Kirmani (43*), K.D. Ghavri (21) | Sydney | 1980–81 |
| 10th | 39 | C.G. Borde (68*), B.S. Chandrasekhar (1) | Calcutta | 1964–65 |

## BEST INNINGS BOWLING ANALYSIS

| | | | | | |
|---|---|---|---|---|---|
| Australia | in Australia | 7-38 | R.R. Lindwall | Adelaide | 1947–48 |
| | in India | 7-43 | R.R. Lindwall | Madras[2] | 1956–57 |
| India | in Australia | 6-52 | B.S. Chandrasekhar | Melbourne | 1977–78 |
| | in India | 9-69 | J.M. Patel | Kanpur | 1959–60 |

## BEST MATCH BOWLING ANALYSIS

| | | | | | |
|---|---|---|---|---|---|
| Australia | in Australia | 11-31 | E.R.H. Toshack | Brisbane[2] | 1947–48 |
| | in India | 12-124 | A.K. Davidson | Kanpur | 1959–60 |
| India | in Australia | 12-104 | B.S. Chandrasekhar | Melbourne | 1977–78 |
| | in India | 14-124 | J.M. Patel | Kanpur | 1959–60 |

## HIGHEST AGGREGATE OF WICKETS IN A SERIES

| | | | | |
|---|---|---|---|---|
| Australia | in Australia | 28 (av 25.03) | W.M. Clark | 1977–78 |
| | in India | 29 (av 14.86) | A.K. Davidson | 1959–60 |
| | | 29 (av 19.58) | R. Benaud | 1959–60 |
| India | in Australia | 31 (av 23.87) | B.S. Bedi | 1977–78 |
| | in India | 28 (av 22.32) | Kapil Dev | 1979–80 |

# AUSTRALIA v PAKISTAN

| Test No. | Venue and Result | Australia 1st | Australia 2nd | Pakistan 1st | Pakistan 2nd | Captains Australia | Captains Pakistan |
|---|---|---|---|---|---|---|---|
| 430 | **1956–57** in Pakistan<br>Karachi – Pakistan 9 wkts | •80 | 187 | 199 | 69-1 | I.W. Johnson | A.H. Kardar |
| 479<br>480<br>481 | **1959–60** in Pakistan<br>Dacca – Australia 8 wkts<br>Lahore² – Australia 7 wkts<br>Karachi – Drawn | 225<br>391-9d<br>257 | 112-2<br>123-3<br>83-2 | •200<br>•146<br>•287 | 134<br>366<br>194-8d | R. Benaud | Fazal Mahmood<br>Imtiaz Ahmed<br>Fazal Mahmood |
| 569 | **1964–65** in Pakistan<br>Karachi – Drawn | 352 | 227-2 | •414 | 279-8d | R.B. Simpson | Hanif Mohammad |
| 570 | **1964–65** in Australia<br>Melbourne – Drawn | 448 | 88-2 | •287 | 326 | R.B. Simpson | Hanif Mohammad |
| 708<br>709<br>710 | **1972–73** in Australia<br>Adelaide – Australia inns & 114 runs<br>Melbourne – Australia 92 runs<br>Sydney – Australia 52 runs | 585<br>•441-5d<br>•334 | —<br>425<br>184 | •257<br>574-8d<br>360 | 214<br>200<br>106 | I.M. Chappell | Intikhab Alam |
| 793<br>794<br>795 | **1976–77** in Australia<br>Adelaide – Drawn<br>Melbourne – Australia 348 runs<br>Sydney – Pakistan 8 wkts | 454<br>•517-8d<br>•211 | 261-6<br>315-8d<br>180 | •272<br>333<br>360 | 466<br>151<br>32-2 | G.S. Chappell | Mushtaq<br>Mohammad |
| 849<br>850 | **1978–79** in Australia<br>Melbourne – Pakistan 71 runs<br>Perth – Australia 7 wkts | 168<br>327 | 310<br>236-3 | •196<br>•277 | 353-9d<br>285 | G.N. Yallop<br>K.J. Hughes | Mushtaq<br>Mohammad |
| 877<br>878<br>879 | **1979–80** in Pakistan<br>Karachi – Pakistan 7 wkts<br>Faisalabad – Drawn<br>Lahore² – Drawn | •225<br>617<br>•407-7d | 140<br>—<br>391-8 | 292<br>382-2<br>420-9d | 76-3<br>—<br>— | G.S. Chappell | Javed Miandad |

| Test No. | Venue and Result | Australia | | Pakistan | | Captains | |
|---|---|---|---|---|---|---|---|
| | | 1st | 2nd | 1st | 2nd | Australia | Pakistan |
| | **1981–82 in Australia** | | | | | | |
| 909 | Perth – Australia 286 runs | •180 | 424-8d | 62 | 256 | G.S. Chappell | Javed Miandad |
| 910 | Brisbane² – Australia 10 wkts | 512-9d | 3-0 | •291 | 223 | | |
| 911 | Melbourne – Pakistan inns & 82 runs | 293 | 125 | •500-8d | — | | |
| | **1982–83 in Pakistan** | | | | | | |
| 935 | Karachi – Pakistan 9 wkts | •284 | 179 | 419-9d | 47-1 | K.J. Hughes | Imran Khan |
| 936 | Faisalabad – Pakistan inns & 3 runs | 168 | 330 | •501-6d | — | | |
| 937 | Lahore² – Pakistan 9 wkts | •316 | 214 | 467-7d | 64-1 | | |
| | **1983–84 in Australia** | | | | | | |
| 970 | Perth – Australia inns & 9 runs | •436-9d | — | 129 | 298 | K.J. Hughes | Zaheer Abbas |
| 971 | Brisbane² – Drawn | 509-7d | — | •156 | 82-3 | | Zaheer Abbas |
| 972 | Adelaide – Drawn | •465 | 310-7 | 624 | — | | Zaheer Abbas |
| 973 | Melbourne – Drawn | 555 | — | •470 | 238-7 | | Imran Khan |
| 974 | Sydney – Australia 10 wkts | 454-6d | 35-0 | •278 | 210 | | Imran Khan |

# RESULTS SUMMARY

## AUSTRALIA v PAKISTAN – IN AUSTRALIA

| | Tests | Result | | | Melbourne | | | Adelaide | | | Sydney | | | Perth | | | Brisbane | | |
|---|---|---|---|---|---|---|---|---|---|---|---|---|---|---|---|---|---|---|---|
| | | A | P | Drawn | A | P | Drawn | A | P | Drawn | A | P | Drawn | A | P | Drawn | A | P | Drawn |
| 1964–65 | 1 | – | – | 1 | – | – | 1 | – | – | – | – | – | – | – | – | – | – | – | – |
| 1972–73 | 3 | 3 | – | – | 1 | – | – | 1 | – | – | 1 | – | – | – | – | – | – | – | – |
| 1976–77 | 3 | 1 | 1 | 1 | 1 | – | – | – | – | 1 | – | 1 | – | – | – | – | – | – | – |
| 1978–79 | 2 | 1 | 1 | – | – | 1 | – | – | – | – | – | – | – | 1 | – | – | – | – | – |
| 1981–82 | 3 | 2 | 1 | – | – | 1 | – | – | – | – | – | – | – | 1 | – | – | 1 | – | – |
| 1983–84 | 5 | 2 | – | 3 | – | – | 1 | – | – | 1 | 1 | – | – | 1 | – | – | – | – | 1 |
| | **17** | 9 | 3 | 5 | 2 | 2 | 2 | 1 | – | 2 | 2 | 1 | – | 3 | – | – | 1 | – | 1 |

## AUSTRALIA v PAKISTAN – IN PAKISTAN

| | Tests | Result | | | Karachi | | | Dacca | | | Lahore | | | Faisalabad | | |
|---|---|---|---|---|---|---|---|---|---|---|---|---|---|---|---|---|---|
| | | A | P | Drawn | A | P | Drawn | A | P | Drawn | A | P | Drawn | A | P | Drawn |
| 1956–57 | 1 | – | 1 | – | – | 1 | – | – | – | – | – | – | – | – | – | – |
| 1959–60 | 3 | 2 | – | 1 | – | – | 1 | 1 | – | – | 1 | – | – | – | – | – |
| 1964–65 | 1 | – | – | 1 | – | – | 1 | – | – | – | – | – | – | – | – | – |
| 1979–80 | 3 | – | 1 | 2 | – | 1 | – | – | – | – | – | – | 1 | – | – | 1 |
| 1982–83 | 3 | – | 3 | – | – | 1 | – | – | – | – | – | 1 | – | – | 1 | – |
| | **11** | 2 | 5 | 4 | – | 3 | 2 | 1 | – | – | 1 | 1 | 1 | – | 1 | 1 |
| Totals | **28** | 11 | 8 | 9 | | | | | | | | | | | | |

## HIGHEST INNINGS TOTALS

| | | | | | |
|---|---|---|---|---|---|
| Australia | in Australia | 585 | | Adelaide | 1972–73 |
| | in Pakistan | 617 | | Faisalabad | 1979–80 |
| Pakistan | in Australia | 624 | | Adelaide | 1983–84 |
| | in Pakistan | 501-6d | | Faisalabad | 1982–83 |

## LOWEST INNINGS TOTALS

| | | | | | |
|---|---|---|---|---|---|
| Australia | in Australia | 125 | | Melbourne | 1981–82 |
| | in Pakistan | 80 | | Karachi | 1956–57 |
| Pakistan | in Australia | 62 | | Perth | 1981–82 |
| | in Pakistan | 134 | | Dacca | 1959–60 |

| | | | | |
|---|---|---|---|---|
| **HIGHEST MATCH AGGREGATE** | 1640 for 33 wickets | | Melbourne | 1972–73 |
| **LOWEST MATCH AGGREGATE** | 535 for 31 wickets | | Karachi | 1956–57 |

## HIGHEST INDIVIDUAL INNINGS

| | | | | | |
|---|---|---|---|---|---|
| Australia | in Australia | 268 | G.N. Yallop | Melbourne | 1983–84 |
| | in Pakistan | 235 | G.S. Chappell | Faisalabad | 1979–80 |
| Pakistan | in Australia | 158 | Majid Khan | Melbourne | 1972–73 |
| | in Pakistan | 210* | Taslim Arif | Faisalabad | 1979–80 |

## HIGHEST AGGREGATE OF RUNS IN A SERIES

| | | | | | |
|---|---|---|---|---|---|
| Australia | in Australia | 554 (av 92.33) | G.N. Yallop | | 1983–84 |
| | in Pakistan | 395 (av 131.66) | A.R. Border | | 1979–80 |
| Pakistan | in Australia | 390 (av 43.33) | Mohsin Khan | | 1983–84 |
| | in Pakistan | 334 (av 55.66) | Saeed Ahmed | | 1959–60 |

## RECORD WICKET PARTNERSHIPS — AUSTRALIA

| | | | | |
|---|---|---|---|---|
| 1st | 134 | I.C. Davis (56), A. Turner (82) | Melbourne | 1976–77 |
| 2nd | 259 | W.B. Phillips (159), G.N. Yallop (141) | Perth | 1983–84 |
| 3rd | 203 | G.N. Yallop (268), K.J. Hughes (94) | Melbourne | 1983–84 |
| 4th | 217 | G.S. Chappell (235), G.N. Yallop (172) | Faisalabad | 1979–80 |
| 5th | 171 | G.S. Chappell (121), G.J. Cosier (168) | Melbourne | 1976–77 |
| | 171 | A.R. Border (118), G.S. Chappell (150*) | Brisbane[2] | 1983–84 |
| 6th | 139 | R.M. Cowper (83), T.R. Veivers (88) | Melbourne | 1964–65 |
| 7th | 185 | G.N. Yallop (268), G.R.J. Matthews (75) | Melbourne | 1983–84 |
| 8th | 117 | G.J. Cosier (168), K.J. O'Keeffe (28*) | Melbourne | 1976–77 |
| 9th | 83 | J.R. Watkins (36), R.A.L. Massie (42) | Sydney | 1972–73 |
| 10th | 52 | D.K. Lillee (14), M.H.N. Walker (34*) | Sydney | 1976–77 |
| | 52 | G.F. Lawson (57*), T.M. Alderman (7) | Lahore[2] | 1982–83 |

## RECORD WICKET PARTNERSHIPS — PAKISTAN

| | | | | |
|---|---|---|---|---|
| 1st | 249 | Khalid Ibadulla (166), Abdul Kadir (95) | Karachi | 1964–65 |
| 2nd | 233 | Mohsin Khan (149), Qasim Omar (113) | Adelaide | 1983–84 |
| 3rd | 223* | Taslim Arif (210*), Javed Miandad (106*) | Faisalabad | 1979–80 |
| 4th | 155 | Mansoor Akhtar (111), Zaheer Abbas (126) | Faisalabad | 1982–83 |
| 5th | 186 | Javed Miandad (131), Salim Malik (77) | Adelaide | 1983–84 |
| 6th | 115 | Asif Iqbal (120), Javed Miandad (64) | Sydney | 1976–77 |
| 7th | 104 | Intikhab Alam (64), Wasim Bari (72) | Melbourne | 1976–77 |
| 8th | 111 | Majid Khan (110*), Imran Khan (56) | Lahore[2] | 1979–80 |
| 9th | 56 | Intikhab Alam (61), Afaq Hussain (13*) | Melbourne | 1964–65 |
| 10th | 87 | Asif Iqbal (152*), Iqbal Qasim (4) | Adelaide | 1976–77 |

## BEST INNINGS BOWLING ANALYSIS

| | | | | | |
|---|---|---|---|---|---|
| Australia | in Australia | 8-59 | A.A. Mallett | Adelaide | 1972–73 |
| | in Pakistan | 7-75 | L.F. Kline | Lahore[2] | 1959–60 |
| Pakistan | in Australia | 9-86 | Sarfraz Nawaz | Melbourne | 1978–79 |
| | in Pakistan | 7-49 | Iqbal Qasim | Karachi | 1979–80 |

## BEST MATCH BOWLING ANALYSIS

| | | | | | |
|---|---|---|---|---|---|
| Australia | in Australia | 11-118 | C.G. Rackemann | Perth | 1983–84 |
| | in Pakistan | 10-111 | R.J. Bright | Karachi | 1979–80 |
| Pakistan | in Australia | 12-165 | Imran Khan | Sydney | 1976–77 |
| | in Pakistan | 13-114 | Fazal Mahmood | Karachi | 1956–57 |

## HIGHEST AGGREGATE OF WICKETS IN A SERIES

| | | | | | |
|---|---|---|---|---|---|
| Australia | in Australia | 24 (av 24.16) | G.F. Lawson | | 1983–84 |
| | in Pakistan | 18 (av 21.05) | R. Benaud | | 1959–60 |
| Pakistan | in Australia | 19 (av 38.52) | Azeem Hafeez | | 1983–84 |
| | in Pakistan | 22 (av 25.54) | Abdul Qadir | | 1982–83 |

# AUSTRALIA v SRI LANKA

| Test No. | Venue and Result | Australia 1st | Australia 2nd | Sri Lanka 1st | Sri Lanka 2nd | Captains Australia | Captains Sri Lanka |
|---|---|---|---|---|---|---|---|
| 956 | **1982–83** in Sri Lanka Kandy – Australia inns & 38 runs | °514-4d | — | 271 | 205 | G.S. Chappell | L.R.D. Mendis |

## RESULTS SUMMARY

AUSTRALIA v SRI LANKA – IN SRI LANKA

|  |  | Result | | |
|---|---|---|---|---|
|  | Tests | A | SL | Drawn |
| 1982–83 | 1 | 1 | – | – |

| Kandy | | |
|---|---|---|
| A | SL | Drawn |
| 1 | – | – |

**HIGHEST INDIVIDUAL INNINGS**
Australia       143*     D.W. Hookes
Sri Lanka        96      S. Wettimuny

**RECORD WICKET PARTNERSHIPS — AUSTRALIA**
2nd    170    K.C. Wessels (141), G.N. Yallop (98)
4th    155*   D.W. Hookes (143*), A.R. Border (47*)

**RECORD WICKET PARTNERSHIP — SRI LANKA**
5th     96    L.R.D. Mendis (74), A. Ranatunga (90)

**BEST INNINGS BOWLING ANALYSIS**
Australia                    5-66              T.G. Hogan
Sri Lanka                    2-113             A.L.F. De Mel

**BEST MATCH BOWLING ANALYSIS**
Australia                    7-166             B. Yardley
Sri Lanka                    2-113             A.L.F. De Mel

# SOUTH AFRICA v NEW ZEALAND

| Test No. | Venue and Result | South Africa | | New Zealand | | Captains | |
|---|---|---|---|---|---|---|---|
| | | 1st | 2nd | 1st | 2nd | South Africa | New Zealand |
| | **1931–32 in New Zealand** | | | | | | |
| 217 | Christchurch – South Africa inns & 12 runs | 451 | — | •293 | 146 | H.B. Cameron | M.L. Page |
| 218 | Wellington – South Africa 8 wkts | 410 | 150-2 | •364 | 193 | | |
| | **1952–53 in New Zealand** | | | | | | |
| 370 | Wellington – South Africa inns & 180 runs | •524-8d | — | 172 | 172 | J.E. Cheetham | W.M. Wallace |
| 371 | Auckland – Drawn | 377 | 200-5d | 245 | 31-2 | | |
| | **1953–54 in South Africa** | | | | | | |
| 377 | Durban[2] – South Africa inns & 58 runs | •437-9d | — | 230 | 149 | J.E. Cheetham | G.O. Rabone |
| 378 | Johannesburg[2] – South Africa 132 runs | 271 | 148 | 187 | 100 | | G.O. Rabone |
| 379 | Cape Town – Drawn | 326 | 159-3 | •505 | — | | G.O. Rabone |
| 380 | Johannesburg[2] – South Africa 9 wkts | •243 | 25-1 | 79 | 188 | | B. Sutcliffe |
| 381 | Port Elizabeth – South Africa 5 wkts | 237 | 215-5 | •226 | 222 | | B. Sutcliffe |
| | **1961–62 in South Africa** | | | | | | |
| 520 | Durban[2] – South Africa 30 runs | •292 | 149 | 245 | 166 | D.J. McGlew | J.R. Reid |
| 521 | Johannesburg[3] – Drawn | 322 | 178-6d | 223 | 165-4 | | |
| 522 | Cape Town – New Zealand 72 runs | 190 | 335 | •385 | 212-9d | | |
| 523 | Johannesburg[3] – South Africa inns & 51 runs | 464 | — | 164 | 249 | | |
| 524 | Port Elizabeth – New Zealand 40 runs | 190 | 273 | •275 | 228 | | |
| | **1963–64 in New Zealand** | | | | | | |
| 558 | Wellington – Drawn | •302 | 218-2d | 253 | 138-6 | T.L. Goddard | J.R. Reid |
| 559 | Dunedin – Drawn | 223 | 42-3 | •149 | 138 | | |
| 560 | Auckland – Drawn | 371 | 200-5d | 263 | 191-8 | | |

# RESULTS SUMMARY

## SOUTH AFRICA v NEW ZEALAND – IN SOUTH AFRICA

|         |       | Result | | | Durban | | | Johannesburg | | | Cape Town | | | Port Elizabeth | | |
|---------|-------|----|----|-------|----|----|-------|----|----|-------|----|----|-------|----|----|-------|
|         | Tests | SA | NZ | Drawn | SA | NZ | Drawn | SA | NZ | Drawn | SA | NZ | Drawn | SA | NZ | Drawn |
| 1953–54 | 5     | 4  | –  | 1     | 1  | –  | –     | 2  | –  | –     | –  | –  | 1     | 1  | –  | –     |
| 1961–62 | 5     | 2  | 2  | 1     | 1  | –  | –     | 1  | –  | 1     | –  | 1  | –     | –  | 1  | –     |
|         | 10    | 6  | 2  | 2     | 2  | –  | –     | 3  | –  | 1     | –  | 1  | 1     | 1  | 1  | –     |

## SOUTH AFRICA v NEW ZEALAND – IN NEW ZEALAND

|         |       | Result | | | Christchurch | | | Wellington | | | Auckland | | | Dunedin | | |
|---------|-------|----|----|-------|----|----|-------|----|----|-------|----|----|-------|----|----|-------|
|         | Tests | SA | NZ | Drawn | SA | NZ | Drawn | SA | NZ | Drawn | SA | NZ | Drawn | SA | NZ | Drawn |
| 1931–32 | 2     | 2  | –  | –     | 1  | –  | –     | 1  | –  | –     | –  | –  | –     | –  | –  | –     |
| 1952–53 | 2     | 1  | –  | 1     | –  | –  | –     | 1  | –  | –     | –  | –  | 1     | –  | –  | –     |
| 1963–64 | 3     | –  | –  | 3     | –  | –  | –     | –  | –  | 1     | –  | –  | 1     | –  | –  | 1     |
|         | 7     | 3  | –  | 4     | 1  | –  | –     | 2  | –  | 1     | –  | –  | 2     | –  | –  | 1     |
| Totals  | 17    | 9  | 2  | 6     |    |    |       |    |    |       |    |    |       |    |    |       |

## HIGHEST INNINGS TOTALS

| | | | | |
|---|---|---|---|---|
| South Africa | in South Africa | 464 | | Johannesburg[3] | 1961–62 |
| | in New Zealand | 524-8d | | Wellington | 1952–53 |
| New Zealand | in South Africa | 505 | | Cape Town | 1953–54 |
| | in New Zealand | 364 | | Wellington | 1931–32 |

## LOWEST INNINGS TOTALS

| | | | | | |
|---|---|---|---|---|---|
| South Africa | in South Africa | 148 | | Johannesburg[2] | 1953–54 |
| | in New Zealand | 223 | | Dunedin | 1963–64 |
| New Zealand | in South Africa | 79 | | Johannesburg[2] | 1953–54 |
| | in New Zealand | 138 | | Dunedin | 1963–64 |

**HIGHEST MATCH AGGREGATE**   1122 for 39 wickets        Cape Town   1961–62
**LOWEST MATCH AGGREGATE**     535 for 31 wickets         Johannesburg[2]   1953–54

## HIGHEST INDIVIDUAL INNINGS

| | | | | | |
|---|---|---|---|---|---|
| South Africa | in South Africa | 127* | D.J. McGlew | Durban[2] | 1961–62 |
| | in New Zealand | 255* | D.J. McGlew | Wellington | 1952–53 |
| New Zealand | in South Africa | 142 | J.R. Reid | Johannesburg[3] | 1961–62 |
| | in New Zealand | 138 | B.W. Sinclair | Auckland | 1963–64 |

## HIGHEST AGGREGATE OF RUNS IN A SERIES

| | | | | | |
|---|---|---|---|---|---|
| South Africa | in South Africa | 426 (av 60.85) | D.J. McGlew | | 1961–62 |
| | in New Zealand | 323 (av 161.50) | D.J. McGlew | | 1952–53 |
| New Zealand | in South Africa | 546 (av 60.66) | J.R. Reid | | 1961–62 |
| | in New Zealand | 264 (av 44.00) | B.W. Sinclair | | 1963–64 |

## RECORD WICKET PARTNERSHIPS — SOUTH AFRICA

| | | | | |
|---|---|---|---|---|
| 1st | 196 | J.A.J. Christy (103), B. Mitchell (113) | Christchurch | 1931–32 |
| 2nd | 76 | J.A.J. Christy (62), H.B. Cameron (44) | Wellington | 1931–32 |
| 3rd | 112 | D.J. McGlew (120), R.A. McLean (78) | Johannesburg[3] | 1961–62 |
| 4th | 135 | K.J. Funston (39), R.A. McLean (101) | Durban[2] | 1953–54 |
| 5th | 130 | W.R. Endean (116), J.E. Cheetham (54) | Auckland | 1952–53 |
| 6th | 83 | K.C. Bland (83), D.T. Lindsay (37) | Auckland | 1963–64 |
| 7th | 246 | D.J. McGlew (255*), A.R.A. Murray (109) | Wellington | 1952–53 |
| 8th | 95 | J.E. Cheetham (89), H.J. Tayfield (34) | Cape Town | 1953–54 |
| 9th | 60 | P.M. Pollock (54*), N.A.T. Adcock (24) | Port Elizabeth | 1961–62 |
| 10th | 47 | D.J. McGlew (28*), H.D. Bromfield (21) | Port Elizabeth | 1961–62 |

## RECORD WICKET PARTNERSHIPS — NEW ZEALAND

| | | | | |
|---|---|---|---|---|
| 1st | 126 | G.O. Rabone (56), M.E. Chapple (76) | Cape Town | 1953–54 |
| 2nd | 51 | W.P. Bradburn (32), B.W. Sinclair (52) | Dunedin | 1963–64 |
| 3rd | 94 | M.B. Poore (44), B. Sutcliffe (66) | Cape Town | 1953–54 |
| 4th | 171 | B.W. Sinclair (138), S.N. McGregor (62) | Auckland | 1963–64 |
| 5th | 174 | J.R. Reid (135), J.E.F. Beck (99) | Cape Town | 1953–54 |
| 6th | 100 | H.G. Vivian (100), F.T. Badcock (53) | Wellington | 1931–32 |
| 7th | 84 | J.R. Reid (142), G.A. Bartlett (33) | Johannesburg[2] | 1961–62 |
| 8th | 73 | P.G.Z. Harris (74), G.A. Bartlett (40) | Durban[2] | 1961–62 |
| 9th | 69 | C.F.W. Allcott (26), I.B. Cromb (51*) | Wellington | 1931–32 |
| 10th | 49* | A.E. Dick (50*), F.J. Cameron (10*) | Cape Town | 1961–62 |

## BEST INNINGS BOWLING ANALYSIS

| | | | | | |
|---|---|---|---|---|---|
| South Africa | in South Africa | 8-53 | G.B. Lawrence | Johannesburg[3] | 1961–62 |
| | in New Zealand | 6-47 | P.M. Pollock | Wellington | 1963–64 |
| New Zealand | in South Africa | 6-68 | G.O. Rabone | Cape Town | 1953–54 |
| | in New Zealand | 6-60 | J.R. Reid | Dunedin | 1963–64 |

## BEST MATCH BOWLING ANALYSIS

| | | | | | |
|---|---|---|---|---|---|
| South Africa | in South Africa | 11-196 | S.F. Burke | Cape Town | 1961–62 |
| | in New Zealand | 9-127 | Q. McMillan | Christchurch | 1931–32 |
| New Zealand | in South Africa | 8-180 | J.C. Alabaster | Cape Town | 1961–62 |
| | in New Zealand | 7-142 | R.W. Blair | Auckland | 1963–64 |

## HIGHEST AGGREGATE OF WICKETS IN A SERIES

| | | | | | |
|---|---|---|---|---|---|
| South Africa | in South Africa | 28 (av 18.28) | G.B. Lawrence | | 1961–62 |
| | in New Zealand | 16 (av 20.18) | Q. McMillan | | 1931–32 |
| New Zealand | in South Africa | 22 (av 20.63) | A.R. MacGibbon | | 1953–54 |
| | | 22 (av 28.04) | J.C. Alabaster | | 1961–62 |
| | in New Zealand | 12 (av 23.16) | J.R. Reid | | 1963–64 |
| | | 12 (av 27.16) | R.W. Blair | | 1963–64 |

# WEST INDIES v NEW ZEALAND

| Test No. | Venue and Result | West Indies 1st | West Indies 2nd | New Zealand 1st | New Zealand 2nd | Captains West Indies | Captains New Zealand |
|---|---|---|---|---|---|---|---|
| | **1951–52 in New Zealand** | | | | | | |
| 349 | Christchurch – West Indies 5 wkts | 287 | 142-5 | •236 | 189 | J.D.C. Goddard | B. Sutcliffe |
| 350 | Auckland – Drawn | •546-6d | — | 160 | 17-1 | | |
| | **1955–56 in New Zealand** | | | | | | |
| 421 | Dunedin – West Indies inns & 71 runs | 353 | — | •74 | 208 | | H.B Cave |
| 422 | Christchurch – West Indies inns & 64 runs | •386 | — | 158 | 164 | D.St E. Atkinson | J.R. Reid |
| 423 | Wellington – West Indies 9 wkts | •404 | 13-1 | 208 | 208 | | J.R. Reid |
| 424 | Auckland – New Zealand 190 runs | 145 | 77 | •255 | 157-9d | | J.R. Reid |
| | **1968–69 in New Zealand** | | | | | | |
| 650 | Auckland – West Indies 5 wkts | 276 | 348-5 | •323 | 297-8d | | G.T. Dowling |
| 651 | Wellington – New Zealand 6 wkts | •297 | 148 | 282 | 166-4 | G.St A. Sobers | |
| 652 | Christchurch – Drawn | •417 | — | 217 | 367-6 | | |
| | **1971–72 in West Indies** | | | | | | |
| 693 | Kingston – Drawn | •508-4d | 218-3d | •386 | 236-6 | | G.T. Dowling |
| 694 | Port-of-Spain – Drawn | 341 | 121-5 | •348 | 288-3d | | G.T. Dowling |
| 695 | Bridgetown – Drawn | 133 | 564-8 | 422 | — | G.St A. Sobers | B.E. Congdon |
| 696 | Georgetown – Drawn | •365-7d | 86-0 | 543-3d | — | | B.E. Congdon |
| 697 | Port-of-Spain – Drawn | •368 | 194 | 162 | 253-7 | | B.E. Congdon |
| | **1979–80 in New Zealand** | | | | | | |
| 873 | Dunedin – New Zealand 1 wkt | •140 | 212 | 249 | 104-9 | | G.P. Howarth |
| 874 | Christchurch – Drawn | •228 | 447-5d | 460 | — | C.H. Lloyd | |
| 875 | Auckland – Drawn | •220 | 264-9d | 305 | 73-4 | | |
| | **1984–85 in West Indies** | | | | | | |
| 1013 | Port-of-Spain – Drawn | •307 | 261-8d | 262 | 187-6 | | G.P. Howarth |
| 1014 | Georgetown – Drawn | •511-6d | 268-6d | 440 | — | I.V.A. Richards | |
| 1015 | Bridgetown – West Indies 10 wkts | 336 | 10-0 | •94 | 248 | | |
| 1016 | Kingston – West Indies 10 wkts | •363 | 59-0 | 138 | 283 | | |

# RESULTS SUMMARY

## WEST INDIES v NEW ZEALAND – IN WEST INDIES

| | Result | | | | Kingston | | | Port-of-Spain | | | Bridgetown | | | Georgetown | | |
|---|---|---|---|---|---|---|---|---|---|---|---|---|---|---|---|---|
| | *Tests* | *WI* | *NZ* | *Drawn* | *WI* | *NZ* | *Drawn* | *WI* | *NZ* | *Drawn* | *WI* | *NZ* | *Drawn* | *WI* | *NZ* | *Drawn* |
| 1971–72 | **5** | – | – | 5 | – | – | 1 | – | – | 2 | – | – | 1 | – | – | 1 |
| 1984–85 | **4** | 2 | – | 2 | 1 | – | – | – | – | 1 | 1 | – | – | – | – | 1 |
| | **9** | 2 | – | 7 | 1 | – | 1 | – | – | 3 | 1 | – | 1 | – | – | 2 |

## WEST INDIES v NEW ZEALAND – IN NEW ZEALAND

| | Result | | | | Christchurch | | | Auckland | | | Dunedin | | | Wellington | | |
|---|---|---|---|---|---|---|---|---|---|---|---|---|---|---|---|---|
| | *Tests* | *WI* | *NZ* | *Drawn* | *WI* | *NZ* | *Drawn* | *WI* | *NZ* | *Drawn* | *WI* | *NZ* | *Drawn* | *WI* | *NZ* | *Drawn* |
| 1951–52 | **2** | 1 | – | 1 | 1 | – | – | – | – | 1 | – | – | – | – | – | – |
| 1955–56 | **4** | 3 | 1 | – | 1 | – | – | – | 1 | – | 1 | – | – | 1 | – | – |
| 1968–69 | **3** | 1 | 1 | 1 | – | – | 1 | 1 | – | – | – | – | – | – | 1 | – |
| 1979–80 | **3** | – | 1 | 2 | – | – | 1 | – | – | 1 | – | 1 | – | – | – | – |
| | **12** | 5 | 3 | 4 | 2 | – | 2 | 1 | 1 | 2 | 1 | 1 | – | 1 | 1 | – |
| Totals | **21** | 7 | 3 | 11 | 2 | – | 2 | 1 | 1 | 2 | 1 | 1 | – | 1 | 1 | – |

## HIGHEST INNINGS TOTALS

| West Indies | in West Indies | 564-8 | | Bridgetown | 1971–72 |
|---|---|---|---|---|---|
| | in New Zealand | 546-6d | | Auckland | 1951–52 |
| New Zealand | in West Indies | 543-3d | | Georgetown | 1971–72 |
| | in New Zealand | 460 | | Christchurch | 1979–80 |

## LOWEST INNINGS TOTALS

| West Indies | in West Indies | 133 | | Bridgetown | 1971–72 |
|---|---|---|---|---|---|
| | in New Zealand | 77 | | Auckland | 1955–56 |
| New Zealand | in West Indies | 94 | | Bridgetown | 1984–85 |
| | in New Zealand | 74 | | Dunedin | 1955–56 |

| **HIGHEST MATCH AGGREGATE** | 1348 for 23 wickets | Kingston | 1971–72 |
|---|---|---|---|
| **LOWEST MATCH AGGREGATE** | 634 for 39 wickets | Auckland | 1955–56 |

## HIGHEST INDIVIDUAL INNINGS

| West Indies | in West Indies | 214 | L.G. Rowe | Kingston | 1971–72 |
|---|---|---|---|---|---|
| | in New Zealand | 258 | S.M. Nurse | Christchurch | 1968–69 |
| New Zealand | in West Indies | 259 | G.M. Turner | Georgetown | 1971–72 |
| | in New Zealand | 147 | G.P. Howarth | Christchurch | 1979–80 |

## HIGHEST AGGREGATE OF RUNS IN A SERIES

| West Indies | in West Indies | 487 (av 54.11) | R.C. Fredericks | | 1971–72 |
|---|---|---|---|---|---|
| | in New Zealand | 558 (av 111.60) | S.M. Nurse | | 1968–69 |
| New Zealand | in West Indies | 672 (av 96.00) | G.M. Turner | | 1971–72 |
| | in New Zealand | 241 (av 60.25) | B.A. Edgar | | 1979–80 |

## RECORD WICKET PARTNERSHIPS — WEST INDIES

| 1st | 225 | C.G. Greenidge (97), D.L. Haynes (122) | Christchurch | 1979–80 |
|---|---|---|---|---|
| 2nd | 269 | R.C. Fredericks (163), L.G. Rowe (214) | Kingston | 1971–72 |
| 3rd | 185 | C.G. Greenidge (100), R.B. Richardson (78) | Port-of-Spain | 1984–85 |
| 4th | 162 | E. de C. Weekes (123), O.G. Smith (64) | Dunedin | 1955–56 |
| | 162 | C.G. Greenidge (91), A.I. Kallicharran (75) | Christchurch | 1979–80 |
| 5th | 189 | F.M.M. Worrell (100), C.L. Walcott (115) | Auckland | 1951–52 |
| 6th | 254 | C.A. Davis (183), G.St A. Sobers (142) | Bridgetown | 1971–72 |
| 7th | 143 | D. St E. Atkinson (85), J.D.C. Goddard (83*) | Christchurch | 1955–56 |
| 8th | 83 | I.V.A. Richards (105), M.D. Marshall (63) | Bridgetown | 1984–85 |
| 9th | 70 | M.D. Marshall (63), J. Garner (37*) | Bridgetown | 1984–85 |
| 10th | 31 | T.M. Findlay (44*), G.C. Shillingford (15) | Bridgetown | 1971–72 |

## RECORD WICKET PARTNERSHIPS — NEW ZEALAND

| 1st | 387 | G.M. Turner (259), T.W. Jarvis (182) | Georgetown | 1971–72 |
|---|---|---|---|---|
| 2nd | 210 | G.P. Howarth (84), J.J. Crowe (112) | Kingston | 1984–85 |
| 3rd | 75 | B.E. Congdon (43), B.F. Hastings (117*) | Christchurch | 1968–69 |
| 4th | 175 | B.E. Congdon (126), B.F. Hastings (105) | Bridgetown | 1971–72 |
| 5th | 142 | M.D. Crowe (188), J.V. Coney (73) | Georgetown | 1984–85 |
| 6th | 220 | G.M. Turner (223*), K.J. Wadsworth (78) | Kingston | 1971–72 |
| 7th | 143 | M.D. Crowe (188), I.D.S. Smith (53) | Georgetown | 1984–85 |
| 8th | 136 | B.E. Congdon (166*), R.S. Cunis (51) | Port-of-Spain | 1971–72 |
| 9th | 62* | V. Pollard (51*), R.S. Cunis (20*) | Auckland | 1968–69 |
| 10th | 41 | B.E. Congdon (166*), J.C. Alabaster (18) | Port-of-Spain | 1971–72 |

## BEST INNINGS BOWLING ANALYSIS

| West Indies | in West Indies | 7-80 | M.D. Marshall | Bridgetown | 1984–85 |
|---|---|---|---|---|---|
| | in New Zealand | 7-53 | D.St E. Atkinson | Auckland | 1955–56 |
| New Zealand | in West Indies | 7-74 | B.R. Taylor | Bridgetown | 1971–72 |
| | in New Zealand | 6-68 | R.J. Hadlee | Dunedin | 1979–80 |

## BEST MATCH BOWLING ANALYSIS

| West Indies | in West Indies | 11-120 | M.D. Marshall | Bridgetown | 1984–85 |
|---|---|---|---|---|---|
| | in New Zealand | 9-81 | S. Ramadhin | Dunedin | 1955–56 |
| New Zealand | in West Indies | 10-124 | E.J. Chatfield | Port-of-Spain | 1984–85 |
| | in New Zealand | 11-102 | R.J. Hadlee | Dunedin | 1979–80 |

## HIGHEST AGGREGATE OF WICKETS IN A SERIES

| West Indies | in West Indies | 27 (av 18.00) | M.D. Marshall | | 1984–85 |
|---|---|---|---|---|---|
| | in New Zealand | 20 (av 15.80) | S. Ramadhin | | 1955–56 |
| New Zealand | in West Indies | 27 (av 17.70) | B.R. Taylor | | 1971–72 |
| | in New Zealand | 19 (av 19.00) | R.J. Hadlee | | 1979–80 |

# WEST INDIES v INDIA

| Test No. | Venue and Result | West Indies 1st | West Indies 2nd | India 1st | India 2nd | Captains West Indies | Captains India |
|---|---|---|---|---|---|---|---|
| | **1948–49 in India** | | | | | | |
| 304 | Delhi – Drawn | •631 | — | 454 | 220-6 | | |
| 305 | Bombay² – Drawn | •629-6d | — | 273 | 333-3 | J.D.C. Goddard | L. Amarnath |
| 306 | Calcutta – Drawn | 366 | 336-9d | 272 | 325-3 | | |
| 307 | Madras¹ – West Indies inns & 193 runs | 582 | — | 245 | 144 | | |
| 308 | Bombay² – Drawn | •286 | 267 | 193 | 355-8 | | |
| | **1952–53 in West Indies** | | | | | | |
| 365 | Port-of-Spain – Drawn | 438 | 142-0 | •417 | 294 | | |
| 366 | Bridgetown – West Indies 142 runs | •296 | 228 | 253 | 129 | | |
| 367 | Port-of-Spain – Drawn | 315 | 192-2 | •279 | 362-7d | J.B. Stollmeyer | V.S. Hazare |
| 368 | Georgetown – Drawn | 364 | — | •262 | 190-5 | | |
| 369 | Kingston – Drawn | 576 | 92-4 | •312 | 444 | | |
| | **1958–59 in India** | | | | | | |
| 459 | Bombay² – Drawn | •227 | 323-4d | 152 | 289-5 | | P.R. Umrigar |
| 460 | Kanpur – West Indies 203 runs | •222 | 443-7d | 222 | 240 | | Ghulam Ahmed |
| 461 | Calcutta – West Indies inns & 336 runs | •614-5d | — | 124 | 154 | F.C.M. Alexander | Ghulam Ahmed |
| 462 | Madras² – West Indies 295 runs | •500 | 168-5d | 222 | 151 | | M.H. Mankad |
| 463 | Delhi – Drawn | 644-8d | — | •415 | 275 | | H.R. Adhikari |
| | **1961–62 in West Indies** | | | | | | |
| 525 | Port-of-Spain – West Indies 10 wkts | 289 | 15-0 | •203 | 98 | | N.J. Contractor |
| 526 | Kingston – West Indies inns & 18 runs | 631-8d | — | •395 | 218 | | N.J. Contractor |
| 527 | Bridgetown – West Indies inns & 30 runs | 475 | — | •258 | 187 | F.M.M. Worrell | Nawab of Pataudi, jr |
| 528 | Port-of-Spain – West Indies 7 wkts | •444-9d | 176-3 | 197 | 422 | | Nawab of Pataudi, jr |
| 529 | Kingston – West Indies 123 runs | •253 | 283 | 178 | 235 | | Nawab of Pataudi, jr |
| | **1966–67 in India** | | | | | | |
| 610 | Bombay² – West Indies 6 wkts | 421 | 192-4 | •296 | 316 | | |
| 611 | Calcutta – West Indies inns & 45 runs | •390 | — | 167 | 178 | G.St A. Sobers | Nawab of Pataudi, jr |
| 612 | Madras¹ – Drawn | 406 | 270-7 | •404 | 323 | | |

| Test No. | Venue and Result | West Indies 1st | West Indies 2nd | India 1st | India 2nd | Captains West Indies | Captains India |
|---|---|---|---|---|---|---|---|
| | **1970–71** in West Indies | | | | | | |
| 680 | Kingston – Drawn | 217 | 385-5 | •387 | — | G.St A. Sobers | A.L. Wadekar |
| 681 | Port-of-Spain – India 7 wkts | •214 | 261 | 352 | 125-3 | | |
| 682 | Georgetown – Drawn | 363 | 307-3d | 376 | 123-0 | | |
| 683 | Bridgetown – Drawn | •501-5d | 180-6d | 347 | 221-5 | | |
| 684 | Port-of-Spain – Drawn | 526 | 165-8 | •360 | 427 | | |
| | **1974–75** in India | | | | | | |
| 745 | Bangalore – West Indies 267 runs | •289 | 356-6d | 260 | 118 | C.H. Lloyd | Nawab of Pataudi, jr |
| 746 | Delhi – West Indies inns & 17 runs | 493 | — | •220 | 256 | | S. Venkataraghavan |
| 747 | Calcutta – India 85 runs | 240 | 224 | •233 | 316 | | Nawab of Pataudi, jr |
| 748 | Madras[1] – India 100 runs | 192 | 154 | •190 | 256 | | Nawab of Pataudi, jr |
| 749 | Bombay[3] – West Indies 201 runs | •604-6d | 205-3d | 406 | 202 | | Nawab of Pataudi, jr |
| | **1975–76** in West Indies | | | | | | |
| 773 | Bridgetown – West Indies inns & 97 runs | 488-9d | — | •177 | 214 | C.H. Lloyd | B.S. Bedi |
| 774 | Port-of-Spain – Drawn | •241 | 215-8 | 402-5d | — | | |
| 775 | Port-of-Spain – India 6 wkts | •359 | 271-6d | 228 | 406-4 | | |
| 776 | Kingston – West Indies 10 wkts | 391 | 13-0 | •306-6d | 97 | | |
| | **1978–79** in India | | | | | | |
| 840 | Bombay[3] – Drawn | 493 | — | •424 | 224-2 | A.I. Kallicharran | S.M. Gavaskar |
| 841 | Bangalore – Drawn | •437 | 200-8 | 371 | — | | |
| 842 | Calcutta – Drawn | 327 | 197-9 | 300 | 361-1d | | |
| 843 | Madras[1] – India 3 wkts | •228 | 151 | 255 | 125-7 | | |
| 844 | Delhi – Drawn | 172 | 179-3 | •566-8d | — | | |
| 845 | Kanpur – Drawn | 452-8 | — | •644-7d | — | | |
| | **1982-83** in West Indies | | | | | | |
| 949 | Kingston – West Indies 4 wkts | 254 | 173-6d | •251 | 174 | C.H. Lloyd | Kapil Dev |
| 950 | Port-of-Spain – Drawn | 394 | — | •175 | 469-7 | | |
| 951 | Georgetown – Drawn | 470 | — | 284-3 | — | | |
| 952 | Bridgetown – West Indies 10 wkts | 486 | 1-0 | •209 | 277 | | |
| 953 | St John's – Drawn | 550 | — | •457 | 247-5d | | |

| Test No. | Venue and Result | West Indies | | India | | Captains | |
|---|---|---|---|---|---|---|---|
| | | *1st* | *2nd* | *1st* | *2nd* | *West Indies* | *India* |
| | **1983–84** in India | | | | | | |
| 964 | Kanpur – West Indies inns & 83 runs | •454 | — | 207 | 164 | | |
| 965 | Delhi – Drawn | 384 | 120-2 | •464 | 233 | | |
| 966 | Ahmedabad – West Indies 138 runs | •281 | 201 | 241 | 103 | C.H. Lloyd | Kapil Dev |
| 967 | Bombay[3] – Drawn | 393 | 104-4 | •463 | 173-5d | | |
| 968 | Calcutta – West Indies inns & 46 runs | 377 | — | •241 | 90 | | |
| 969 | Madras[1] – Drawn | •313 | 64-1 | 451-8d | — | | |

# RESULTS SUMMARY

## WEST INDIES v INDIA – IN WEST INDIES

| | Tests | Result | | | Port-of-Spain | | | Bridgetown | | | Georgetown | | | Kingston | | | St John's | | |
|---|---|---|---|---|---|---|---|---|---|---|---|---|---|---|---|---|---|---|---|
| | | WI | I | Drawn | WI | I | Drawn | WI | I | Drawn | WI | I | Drawn | WI | I | Drawn | WI | I | Drawn |
| 1952–53 | 5 | 1 | — | 4 | — | — | 2 | 1 | — | — | — | — | 1 | — | — | 1 | — | — | — |
| 1961–62 | 5 | 5 | — | — | 1 | — | — | 2 | — | — | 1 | — | — | 1 | — | — | — | — | — |
| 1970–71 | 5 | — | 1 | 4 | — | 1 | 1 | — | — | 1 | — | — | 1 | — | — | 1 | — | — | — |
| 1975–76 | 4 | 2 | 1 | 1 | 1 | 1 | 1 | — | — | — | — | — | — | 1 | — | — | — | — | — |
| 1982–83 | 5 | 2 | — | 3 | — | — | 1 | 1 | — | — | — | — | 1 | 1 | — | — | — | — | 1 |
| | 24 | 10 | 2 | 12 | 2 | 2 | 5 | 4 | — | 1 | 1 | — | 3 | 3 | — | 2 | — | — | 1 |

## WEST INDIES v INDIA – IN INDIA

| | Tests | Result | | | Bombay | | | Delhi | | | Calcutta | | | Kanpur | | | Madras | | | Bangalore | | | Ahmedabad | | |
|---|---|---|---|---|---|---|---|---|---|---|---|---|---|---|---|---|---|---|---|---|---|---|---|---|---|
| | | WI | I | Drawn | WI | I | Drawn | WI | I | Drawn | WI | I | Drawn | WI | I | Drawn | WI | I | Drawn | WI | I | Drawn | WI | I | Drawn |
| 1948–49 | 5 | 1 | — | 4 | — | — | 2 | — | — | 1 | — | — | 1 | — | — | — | 1 | — | — | — | — | — | — | — | — |
| 1958–59 | 5 | 3 | — | 2 | — | — | 1 | — | — | 1 | 1 | — | — | 1 | — | — | 1 | — | — | — | — | — | — | — | — |
| 1966–67 | 3 | 2 | — | 1 | — | — | — | — | — | — | 1 | — | — | 1 | — | — | — | — | 1 | — | — | — | — | — | — |
| 1974–75 | 5 | 3 | 2 | — | 1 | — | — | 1 | — | — | — | 1 | — | — | — | — | — | 1 | — | 1 | — | — | — | — | — |
| 1978–79 | 6 | — | 1 | 5 | — | — | 1 | — | — | 1 | — | — | 1 | — | — | 1 | — | 1 | — | — | — | 1 | — | — | — |
| 1983–84 | 6 | 3 | — | 3 | 1 | — | 1 | — | — | 1 | 1 | — | — | — | — | — | — | — | 1 | — | — | — | 1 | — | — |
| | 30 | 12 | 3 | 15 | 2 | — | 5 | 1 | — | 4 | 3 | 1 | 2 | 2 | — | 1 | 2 | 2 | 2 | 1 | — | 1 | 1 | — | — |
| Totals | 54 | 22 | 5 | 27 | | | | | | | | | | | | | | | | | | | | | |

## HIGHEST INNINGS TOTALS

| | | | | | |
|---|---|---|---|---|---|
| West Indies | in West Indies | 631-8d | | Kingston | 1961–62 |
| | in India | 644-8d | | Delhi | 1958–59 |
| India | in West Indies | 469-7 | | Port-of-Spain | 1982–83 |
| | in India | 644-7d | | Kanpur | 1978–79 |

## LOWEST INNINGS TOTALS

| | | | | | |
|---|---|---|---|---|---|
| West Indies | in West Indies | 214 | | Port-of-Spain | 1970–71 |
| | in India | 151 | | Madras[1] | 1978–79 |
| India | in West Indies | 97 | | Kingston | 1975–76 |
| | in India | 90 | | Calcutta | 1983–84 |

| | | | |
|---|---|---|---|
| **HIGHEST MATCH AGGREGATE** | 1478 for 38 wickets | Port-of-Spain | 1970–71 |
| **LOWEST MATCH AGGREGATE** | 605 for 30 wickets | Port-of-Spain | 1961–62 |

## HIGHEST INDIVIDUAL INNINGS

| | | | | | |
|---|---|---|---|---|---|
| West Indies | in West Indies | 237 | F.M.M. Worrell | Kingston | 1952–53 |
| | in India | 256 | R.B. Kanhai | Calcutta | 1958–59 |
| India | in West Indies | 220 | S.M. Gavaskar | Port-of-Spain | 1970–71 |
| | in India | 236* | S.M. Gavaskar | Madras[1] | 1983–84 |

## HIGHEST AGGREGATE OF RUNS IN A SERIES

| | | | | | |
|---|---|---|---|---|---|
| West Indies | in West Indies | 716 (av 102.28) | E. de C. Weekes | | 1952–53 |
| | in India | 779 (av 111.28) | E. de C. Weekes | | 1948–49 |
| India | in West Indies | 774 (av 154.80) | S.M. Gavaskar | | 1970–71 |
| | in India | 732 (av 91.50) | S.M. Gavaskar | | 1978–79 |

## RECORD WICKET PARTNERSHIPS — WEST INDIES

| | | | | |
|---|---|---|---|---|
| 1st | 296 | C.G. Greenidge (154*), D.L. Haynes (136) | St John's | 1982–83 |
| 2nd | 255 | E.D.A.St J. McMorris (125), R.B. Kanhai (158) | Kingston | 1961–62 |
| 3rd | 220 | I.V.A. Richards (142), A.I. Kallicharran (93) | Bridgetown | 1975–76 |
| 4th | 267 | C.L. Walcott (152), G.E. Gomez (101) | Delhi | 1948–49 |
| 5th | 219 | E. de C. Weekes (207), B.H. Pairaudeau (115) | Port-of-Spain | 1952–53 |
| 6th | 250 | C.H. Lloyd (242*), D.L. Murray (91) | Bombay[3] | 1974–75 |
| 7th | 130 | C.G. Greenidge (194), M.D. Marshall (92) | Kanpur | 1983–84 |
| 8th | 124 | I.V.A. Richards (192*), K.D. Boyce (68) | Delhi | 1974–75 |
| 9th | 161 | C.H. Lloyd (161*), A.M.E. Roberts (68) | Calcutta | 1983–84 |
| 10th | 98* | F.M.M. Worrell (73*), W.W. Hall (50*) | Port-of-Spain | 1961–62 |

## RECORD WICKET PARTNERSHIPS — INDIA

| | | | | |
|---|---|---|---|---|
| 1st | 153 | S.M. Gavaskar (73), C.P.S. Chauhan (84) | Bombay[3] | 1978–79 |
| 2nd | 344* | S.M. Gavaskar (182*), D.B. Vengsarkar (157*) | Calcutta | 1978–79 |
| 3rd | 159 | M. Amarnath (85), G.R. Viswanath (112) | Port-of-Spain | 1975–76 |
| 4th | 172 | G.R. Viswanath (179), A.D. Gaekwad (102) | Kanpur | 1978–79 |
| 5th | 204 | S.M. Gavaskar (156), B.P. Patel (115*) | Port-of-Spain | 1975–76 |
| 6th | 170 | S.M. Gavaskar (236*), R.J. Shastri (72) | Madras[1] | 1983–84 |
| 7th | 186 | D.N. Sardesai (150), E.D. Solkar (65) | Bridgetown | 1970–71 |
| 8th | 107 | Yashpal Sharma (63), B.S. Sandhu (68) | Kingston | 1982–83 |
| 9th | 143* | S.M. Gavaskar (236*), S.M.H. Kirmani (63*) | Madras[1] | 1983–84 |
| 10th | 62 | D.N. Sardesai (150), B.S. Bedi (20*) | Bridgetown | 1970–71 |

## BEST INNINGS BOWLING ANALYSIS

| | | | | | |
|---|---|---|---|---|---|
| West Indies | in West Indies | 9-95 | J.M. Noreiga | Port-of-Spain | 1970–71 |
| | in India | 7-64 | A.M.E. Roberts | Madras[1] | 1974–75 |
| India | in West Indies | 7-162 | S.P. Gupte | Port-of-Spain | 1952–53 |
| | in India | 9-83 | Kapil Dev | Ahmedabad | 1983–84 |

## BEST MATCH BOWLING ANALYSIS

| | | | | | |
|---|---|---|---|---|---|
| West Indies | in West Indies | 9-63 | L.R. Gibbs | Bridgetown | 1961–62 |
| | in India | 12-121 | A.M.E. Roberts | Madras[1] | 1974–75 |
| India | in West Indies | 8-118 | Kapil Dev | Kingston | 1982–83 |
| | in India | 11-235 | B.S. Chandrasekhar | Bombay[2] | 1966–67 |

## HIGHEST AGGREGATE OF WICKETS IN A SERIES

| | | | | | |
|---|---|---|---|---|---|
| West Indies | in West Indies | 28 (av 29.57) | A.L. Valentine | | 1952–53 |
| | in India | 33 (av 18.81) | M.D. Marshall | | 1983–84 |
| India | in West Indies | 27 (av 29.22) | S.P. Gupte | | 1952–53 |
| | in India | 29 (av 18.51) | Kapil Dev | | 1983–84 |

# WEST INDIES v PAKISTAN

| Test No. | Venue and Result | West Indies 1st | West Indies 2nd | Pakistan 1st | Pakistan 2nd | Captains West Indies | Captains Pakistan |
|---|---|---|---|---|---|---|---|
| | **1957–58 in West Indies** | | | | | | |
| 449 | Bridgetown – Drawn | •579-9d | 28-0 | 106 | 657-8d | F.C.M. Alexander | A.H. Kardar |
| 450 | Port-of-Spain – West Indies 120 runs | 325 | 312 | 282 | 235 | | |
| 451 | Kingston – West Indies inns & 174 runs | 790-3d | — | •328 | 288 | | |
| 452 | Georgetown – West Indies 8 wkts | 410 | 317-2 | •408 | 318 | | |
| 453 | Port-of-Spain – Pakistan inns & 1 run | •268 | 227 | 496 | — | | |
| | **1958–59 in Pakistan** | | | | | | |
| 469 | Karachi – Pakistan 10 wkts | •146 | 245 | 304 | 88-0 | F.C.M. Alexander | Fazal Mahmood |
| 470 | Dacca – Pakistan 41 runs | 76 | 172 | •145 | 144 | | |
| 471 | Lahore[1] – West Indies inns & 156 runs | •469 | — | 209 | 104 | | |
| | **1974–75 in Pakistan** | | | | | | |
| 756 | Lahore[2] – Drawn | 214 | 258-4 | •199 | 373-7d | C.H. Lloyd | Intikhab Alam |
| 757 | Karachi – Drawn | 493 | 1-0 | •406-8d | 256 | | |
| | **1976–77 in West Indies** | | | | | | |
| 798 | Bridgetown – Drawn | 421 | 251-9 | •435 | 291 | C.H. Lloyd | Mushtaq Mohammad |
| 799 | Port-of-Spain – West Indies 6 wkts | 316 | 206-4 | •180 | 340 | | |
| 800 | Georgetown – Drawn | 448 | 154-1 | •194 | 540 | | |
| 801 | Port-of-Spain – Pakistan 266 runs | 154 | 222 | •341 | 301-9d | | |
| 802 | Kingston – West Indies 140 runs | •280 | 359 | 198 | 301 | | |
| | **1980–81 in Pakistan** | | | | | | |
| 886 | Lahore[2] – Drawn | 297 | — | •369 | 156-7 | C.H. Lloyd | Javed Miandad |
| 887 | Faisalabad – West Indies 156 runs | •235 | 242 | 176 | 145 | | |
| 888 | Karachi – Drawn | 169 | — | •128 | 204-9 | | |
| 889 | Multan – Drawn | •249 | 116-5 | 166 | — | | |

# RESULTS SUMMARY

## WEST INDIES v PAKISTAN – IN WEST INDIES

| | Result | | | | Bridgetown | | | Port-of-Spain | | | Kingston | | | Georgetown | | |
|---|---|---|---|---|---|---|---|---|---|---|---|---|---|---|---|---|
| | Tests | WI | P | Drawn | WI | P | Drawn | WI | P | Drawn | WI | P | Drawn | WI | P | Drawn |
| 1957–58 | 5 | 3 | 1 | 1 | – | – | 1 | 1 | 1 | – | 1 | – | – | 1 | – | – |
| 1976–77 | 5 | 2 | 1 | 2 | – | – | 1 | 1 | 1 | – | 1 | – | – | – | – | 1 |
| | 10 | 5 | 2 | 3 | – | – | 2 | 2 | 2 | – | 2 | – | – | 1 | – | 1 |

## WEST INDIES v PAKISTAN – IN PAKISTAN

| | Result | | | | Karachi | | | Dacca | | | Lahore | | | Faisalabad | | | Multan | | |
|---|---|---|---|---|---|---|---|---|---|---|---|---|---|---|---|---|---|---|---|
| | Tests | WI | P | Drawn | WI | P | Drawn | WI | P | Drawn | WI | P | Drawn | WI | P | Drawn | WI | P | Drawn |
| 1958–59 | 3 | 1 | 2 | – | 1 | 1 | – | – | 1 | – | 1 | – | – | – | – | – | – | – | – |
| 1974–75 | 2 | – | – | 2 | – | – | 1 | – | – | – | – | – | 1 | – | – | – | – | – | – |
| 1980–81 | 4 | 1 | – | 3 | – | – | 1 | – | – | – | – | – | 1 | 1 | – | – | – | – | 1 |
| | 9 | 2 | 2 | 5 | 1 | 1 | 2 | – | 1 | – | 1 | – | 2 | 1 | – | – | – | – | 1 |
| Totals | 19 | 7 | 4 | 8 | | | | | | | | | | | | | | | |

## HIGHEST INNINGS TOTALS

| | | | | | |
|---|---|---|---|---|---|
| West Indies | in West Indies | 790-3d | | Kingston | 1957–58 |
| | in Pakistan | 493 | | Karachi | 1974–75 |
| Pakistan | in West Indies | 657-8d | | Bridgetown | 1957–58 |
| | in Pakistan | 406-8d | | Karachi | 1974–75 |

## LOWEST INNINGS TOTALS

| | | | | | |
|---|---|---|---|---|---|
| West Indies | in West Indies | 154 | | Port-of-Spain | 1976–77 |
| | in Pakistan | 76 | | Dacca | 1958–59 |
| Pakistan | in West Indies | 106 | | Bridgetown | 1957–58 |
| | in Pakistan | 104 | | Lahore[1] | 1958–59 |

| | | | |
|---|---|---|---|
| **HIGHEST MATCH AGGREGATE** | 1453 for 32 wickets | Georgetown | 1957–58 |
| **LOWEST MATCH AGGREGATE** | 537 for 40 wickets | Dacca | 1958–59 |

## HIGHEST INDIVIDUAL INNINGS

| | | | | | |
|---|---|---|---|---|---|
| West Indies | in West Indies | 365* | G. St A. Sobers | Kingston | 1957–58 |
| | in Pakistan | 217 | R.B. Kanhai | Lahore[1] | 1958–59 |
| Pakistan | in West Indies | 337 | Hanif Mohammad | Bridgetown | 1957–58 |
| | {in Pakistan | 123 | Mushtaq Mohammad | Lahore[2] | 1974–75 |
| | | 123 | Imran Khan | Lahore[2] | 1980–81 |

## HIGHEST AGGREGATE OF RUNS IN A SERIES

| | | | | |
|---|---|---|---|---|
| West Indies | in West Indies | 824 (av 137.33) | G. St A. Sobers | 1957–58 |
| | in Pakistan | 364 (av 72.80) | I.V.A. Richards | 1980–81 |
| Pakistan | in West Indies | 628 (av 69.77) | Hanif Mohammad | 1957–58 |
| | in Pakistan | 246 (av 61.50) | Wasim Raja | 1980–81 |

## RECORD WICKET PARTNERSHIPS — WEST INDIES

| | | | | |
|---|---|---|---|---|
| 1st | 182 | R.C. Fredericks (83), C.G. Greenidge (82) | Kingston | 1976–77 |
| 2nd | 446 | C.C. Hunte (260), G. St A. Sobers (365*) | Kingston | 1957–58 |
| 3rd | 162 | R.B. Kanhai (217), G. St A. Sobers (72) | Lahore[1] | 1958–59 |
| 4th | 188* | G. St A. Sobers (365*), C.L. Walcott (88*) | Kingston | 1957–58 |
| 5th | 185 | E. de C. Weekes (197), O.G. Smith (78) | Bridgetown | 1957–58 |
| 6th | 151 | C.H. Lloyd (157), D.L. Murray (52) | Bridgetown | 1976–77 |
| 7th | 70 | C.H. Lloyd (157), J. Garner (43) | Bridgetown | 1976–77 |
| 8th | 50 | B.D. Julien (101), V.A. Holder (29) | Karachi | 1974–75 |
| 9th | 46 | J. Garner (36), C.E.H. Croft (23*) | Port-of-Spain | 1976–77 |
| 10th | 44 | R. Nanan (8), S.T. Clarke (35*) | Faisalabad | 1980–81 |

## RECORD WICKET PARTNERSHIPS — PAKISTAN

| | | | | |
|---|---|---|---|---|
| 1st | 159† | Majid Khan (167), Zaheer Abbas (80) | Georgetown | 1976–77 |
| 2nd | 178 | Hanif Mohammad (103), Saeed Ahmed (78) | Karachi | 1958–59 |
| 3rd | 169 | Saeed Ahmed (97), Wazir Mohammad (189) | Port-of-Spain | 1957–58 |
| 4th | 154 | Wazir Mohammad (189), Hanif Mohammad (54) | Port-of-Spain | 1957–58 |
| 5th | 87 | Mushtaq Mohammad (17), Asif Iqbal (135) | Kingston | 1976–77 |
| 6th | 166 | Wazir Mohammad (106), A.H. Kardar (57) | Kingston | 1957–58 |
| 7th | 128 | Wasim Raja (107*), Wasim Bari (58) | Karachi | 1974–75 |
| 8th | 73 | Imran Khan (30), Sarfraz Nawaz (51) | Port-of-Spain | 1976–77 |
| 9th | 73 | Wasim Raja (117*), Sarfraz Nawaz (38) | Bridgetown | 1976–77 |
| 10th | 133 | Wasim Raja (71), Wasim Bari (60*) | Bridgetown | 1976–77 |

## BEST INNINGS BOWLING ANALYSIS

| | | | | | |
|---|---|---|---|---|---|
| West Indies | in West Indies | 8-29 | C.E.H. Croft | Port-of-Spain | 1976–77 |
| | in Pakistan | 5-66 | A.M.E. Roberts | Lahore[2] | 1974–75 |
| Pakistan | in West Indies | 6-67 | Nasim-ul-Ghani | Port-of-Spain | 1957–58 |
| | in Pakistan | 6-34 | Fazal Mahmood | Dacca | 1958–59 |

## BEST MATCH BOWLING ANALYSIS

| | | | | | |
|---|---|---|---|---|---|
| West Indies | in West Indies | 9-95 | C.E.H. Croft | Port-of-Spain | 1976–77 |
| | in Pakistan | 9-187 | A.M.E. Roberts | Lahore[2] | 1974–75 |
| Pakistan | in West Indies | 8-97 | Mushtaq Mohammad | Port-of-Spain | 1976–77 |
| | in Pakistan | 12-100 | Fazal Mahmood | Dacca | 1959–60 |

## HIGHEST AGGREGATE OF WICKETS IN A SERIES

| | | | | |
|---|---|---|---|---|
| West Indies | in West Indies | 33 (av 20.48) | C.E.H. Croft | 1976–77 |
| | in Pakistan | 17 (av 17.76) | C.E.H. Croft | 1980–81 |
| Pakistan | in West Indies | 25 (av 31.60) | Imran Khan | 1976–77 |
| | in Pakistan | 21 (av 15.85) | Fazal Mahmood | 1958–59 |

† *219 runs were added for this wicket in two separate partnerships, Sadiq Mohammad retired hurt and was succeeded by Zaheer Abbas when 60 had been scored.*

| Test No. | Venue and Result | New Zealand 1st | New Zealand 2nd | India 1st | India 2nd | Captains New Zealand | Captains India |
|---|---|---|---|---|---|---|---|
| | **1955–56 in India** | | | | | | |
| 416 | Hyderabad – Drawn | 326 | 212-2 | •498-4d | — | | Ghulam Ahmed |
| 417 | Bombay² – India inns & 27 runs | 258 | 136 | 421-8d | — | H.B. Cave | P.R. Umrigar |
| 418 | Delhi – Drawn | •450-2d | 112-1 | 531-7d | — | | P.R. Umrigar |
| 419 | Calcutta – Drawn | 336 | 75-6 | •132 | 438-7d | | P.R. Umrigar |
| 420 | Madras² – India inns & 109 runs | 209 | 219 | •537-3d | — | | P.R. Umrigar |
| | **1964–65 in India** | | | | | | |
| 579 | Madras² – Drawn | 315 | 62-0 | •397 | 199-2d | | Nawab of Pataudi, jr |
| 580 | Calcutta – Drawn | •462-9d | 191-9d | 380 | 92-3 | J.R. Reid | |
| 581 | Bombay² – Drawn | •297 | 80-8 | 88 | 463-5d | | |
| 582 | Delhi – India 7 wkts | •262 | 272 | 465-8d | 73-3 | | |
| | **1967–68 in New Zealand** | | | | | | |
| 633 | Dunedin – India 5 wkts | •350 | 208 | 359 | 200-5 | B.W. Sinclair | Nawab of Pataudi, jr |
| 634 | Christchurch – New Zealand 6 wkts | •502 | 88-4 | 288 | 301 | G.T. Dowling | |
| 635 | Wellington – India 8 wkts | •186 | 199 | 327 | 59-2 | G.T. Dowling | |
| 636 | Auckland – India 272 runs | 140 | 101 | •252 | 261-5d | G.T. Dowling | |
| | **1969–70 in India** | | | | | | |
| 659 | Bombay² – India 60 runs | 229 | 127 | •156 | 260 | G.T. Dowling | Nawab of Pataudi, jr |
| 660 | Nagpur – New Zealand 167 runs | •319 | 214 | 257 | 109 | | |
| 661 | Hyderabad – Drawn | •181 | 175-8d | 89 | 76-7 | | |
| | **1975–76 in New Zealand** | | | | | | |
| 770 | Auckland – India 8 wkts | •266 | 215 | 414 | 71-2 | G.M. Turner | S.M. Gavaskar |
| 771 | Christchurch – Drawn | 403 | — | •270 | 255-6 | | B.S. Bedi |
| 772 | Wellington – New Zealand inns & 33 runs | 334 | — | •220 | 81 | | B.S. Bedi |
| | **1976–77 in India** | | | | | | |
| 785 | Bombay³ – India 162 runs | 298 | 141 | •399 | 202-4d | G.M. Turner | B.S. Bedi |
| 786 | Kanpur – Drawn | 350 | 193-7 | •524-9d | 208-2d | | |
| 787 | Madras¹ – India 216 runs | 140 | 143 | •298 | 201-5d | | |
| | **1980–81 in New Zealand** | | | | | | |
| 900 | Wellington – New Zealand 62 runs | •375 | 100 | 223 | 190 | G.P. Howarth | S.M. Gavaskar |
| 901 | Christchurch – Drawn | 286-5 | — | •255 | — | | |
| 902 | Auckland – Drawn | 366 | 95-5 | •238 | 284 | | |

# RESULTS SUMMARY

## NEW ZEALAND v INDIA – IN NEW ZEALAND

|  | Tests | Result | | | Dunedin | | | Christchurch | | | Wellington | | | Auckland | | |
|---|---|---|---|---|---|---|---|---|---|---|---|---|---|---|---|---|
|  |  | NZ | I | Drawn | NZ | I | Drawn | NZ | I | Drawn | NZ | I | Drawn | NZ | I | Drawn |
| 1967–68 | 4 | 1 | 3 | – | – | 1 | – | 1 | – | – | – | 1 | – | – | 1 | – |
| 1975–76 | 3 | 1 | 1 | 1 | – | – | – | – | – | 1 | 1 | – | – | – | 1 | – |
| 1980–81 | 3 | 1 | – | 2 | – | – | – | – | – | 1 | 1 | – | – | – | – | 1 |
|  | **10** | 3 | 4 | 3 | – | 1 | – | 1 | – | 2 | 2 | 1 | – | – | 2 | 1 |

## NEW ZEALAND v INDIA – IN INDIA

|  | Tests | Result | | | Hyderabad | | | Bombay | | | Delhi | | | Calcutta | | | Madras | | | Nagpur | | | Kanpur | | |
|---|---|---|---|---|---|---|---|---|---|---|---|---|---|---|---|---|---|---|---|---|---|---|---|---|---|
|  |  | NZ | I | Drawn | NZ | I | Drawn | NZ | I | Drawn | NZ | I | Drawn | NZ | I | Drawn | NZ | I | Drawn | NZ | I | Drawn | NZ | I | Drawn |
| 1955–56 | 5 | – | 2 | 3 | – | – | 1 | – | 1 | – | – | – | 1 | – | – | 1 | – | 1 | – | – | – | – | – | – | – |
| 1964–65 | 4 | – | 1 | 3 | – | – | – | – | – | 1 | – | 1 | – | – | – | 1 | – | – | 1 | – | – | – | – | – | – |
| 1969–70 | 3 | 1 | 1 | 1 | – | – | 1 | – | 1 | – | – | – | – | – | – | – | – | – | – | 1 | – | – | – | – | – |
| 1976–77 | 3 | – | 2 | 1 | – | – | – | – | 1 | – | – | – | – | – | – | – | – | 1 | – | – | – | – | – | – | 1 |
|  | **15** | 1 | 6 | 8 | – | – | 2 | – | 3 | 1 | – | 1 | 1 | – | – | 2 | – | 2 | 1 | 1 | – | – | – | – | 1 |
| Totals | **25** | 4 | 10 | 11 | | | | | | | | | | | | | | | | | | | | | |

## HIGHEST INNINGS TOTALS

| | | | | |
|---|---|---|---|---|
| New Zealand | in New Zealand | 502 | Christchurch | 1967–68 |
| | in India | 462-9d | Calcutta | 1964–65 |
| India | in New Zealand | 414 | Auckland | 1975–76 |
| | in India | 537-3d | Madras² | 1955–56 |

## LOWEST INNINGS TOTALS

| | | | | |
|---|---|---|---|---|
| New Zealand | in New Zealand | 100 | Wellington | 1980–81 |
| | in India | 127 | Bombay² | 1969–70 |
| India | in New Zealand | 81 | Wellington | 1975–76 |
| | in India | 88 | Bombay² | 1964–65 |

| | | | |
|---|---|---|---|
| **HIGHEST MATCH AGGREGATE** | 1275 for 28 wickets | Kanpur | 1976–77 |
| **LOWEST MATCH AGGREGATE** | 635 for 29 wickets | Wellington | 1975–76 |

## HIGHEST INDIVIDUAL INNINGS

| | | | | | |
|---|---|---|---|---|---|
| New Zealand | in New Zealand | 239 | G.T. Dowling | Christchurch | 1967–68 |
| | in India | 230* | B. Sutcliffe | Delhi | 1955–56 |
| India | in New Zealand | 143 | A.L. Wadekar | Wellington | 1967–68 |
| | in India | 231 | M.H. Mankad | Madras² | 1955–56 |

## HIGHEST AGGREGATE OF RUNS IN A SERIES

| | | | | | |
|---|---|---|---|---|---|
| New Zealand | in New Zealand | 471 (av 58.87) | G.T. Dowling | | 1967–68 |
| | in India | 611 (av 87.28) | B. Sutcliffe | | 1955–56 |
| India | in New Zealand | 330 (av 47.14) | A.L. Wadekar | | 1967–68 |
| | in India | 526 (av 105.20) | M.H. Mankad | | 1955–56 |

## RECORD WICKET PARTNERSHIPS — NEW ZEALAND

| | | | | |
|---|---|---|---|---|
| 1st | 126 | B.A.G. Murray (74), G.T. Dowling (239) | Christchurch | 1967–68 |
| 2nd | 155 | G.T. Dowling (143), B.E. Congdon (58) | Dunedin | 1967–68 |
| 3rd | 222* | B. Sutcliffe (230*), J.R. Reid (119*) | Delhi | 1955–56 |
| 4th | 103 | G.T. Dowling (239), M.G. Burgess (26) | Christchurch | 1967–68 |
| 5th | 119 | G.T. Dowling (239), K. Thomson (69) | Christchurch | 1967–68 |
| 6th | 87 | J.W. Guy (102), A.R. MacGibbon (59) | Hyderabad | 1955–56 |
| 7th | 163 | B. Sutcliffe (151*), B.R. Taylor (105) | Calcutta | 1964–65 |
| 8th | 81 | V. Pollard (43), G.E. Vivian (43) | Calcutta | 1964–65 |
| 9th | 69 | M.G. Burgess (50), J.C. Alabaster (34) | Dunedin | 1967–68 |
| 10th | 61 | J.T. Ward (35*), R.O. Collinge (34) | Madras² | 1964–65 |

## RECORD WICKET PARTNERSHIPS — INDIA

| | | | | |
|---|---|---|---|---|
| 1st | 413 | M.H. Mankad (231), P. Roy (173) | Madras² | 1955–56 |
| 2nd | 204 | S.M. Gavaskar (116), S. Amarnath (124) | Auckland | 1975–76 |
| 3rd | 238 | P.R. Umrigar (223), V.L. Manjrekar (118) | Hyderabad | 1955–56 |
| 4th | 171 | P.R. Umrigar (223), A.G. Kripal Singh (100*) | Hyderabad | 1955–56 |
| 5th | 127 | V.L. Manjrekar (177), G.S. Ramchand (72) | Delhi | 1955–56 |
| 6th | 193* | D.N. Sardesai (200*), Hanumant Singh (75*) | Bombay² | 1964–65 |
| 7th | 116 | B.P. Patel (81), S.M.H. Kirmani (49) | Wellington | 1975–76 |
| 8th | 143 | R.G. Nadkarni (75), F.M. Engineer (90) | Madras² | 1964–65 |
| 9th | {105 | S.M.H. Kirmani (88), B.S. Bedi (36) | Bombay³ | 1976–77 |
| | {105 | S.M.H. Kirmani (78), N.S. Yadav (43) | Auckland | 1980–81 |
| 10th | 57 | R.B. Desai (32*), B.S. Bedi (22) | Dunedin | 1967–68 |

## BEST INNINGS BOWLING ANALYSIS

| | | | | | |
|---|---|---|---|---|---|
| New Zealand | in New Zealand | 7-23 | R.J. Hadlee | Wellington | 1975–76 |
| | in India | 5-26 | B.R. Taylor | Bombay² | 1964–65 |
| India | in New Zealand | 8-76 | E.A.S. Prasanna | Auckland | 1975–76 |
| | in India | 8-72 | S. Venkataraghavan | Delhi | 1964–65 |

## BEST MATCH BOWLING ANALYSIS

| | | | | | |
|---|---|---|---|---|---|
| New Zealand | in New Zealand | 11-58 | R.J. Hadlee | Wellington | 1975–76 |
| | in India | 9-100 | H.J. Howarth | Nagpur | 1969–70 |
| India | in New Zealand | 11-140 | E.A.S. Prasanna | Auckland | 1975–76 |
| | in India | 12-152 | S. Venkataraghavan | Delhi | 1964–65 |

## HIGHEST AGGREGATE OF WICKETS IN A SERIES

| | | | | | |
|---|---|---|---|---|---|
| New Zealand | in New Zealand | 15 (av 26.86) | R.C. Motz | | 1967–68 |
| | in India | 15 (av 18.40) | B.R. Taylor | | 1964–65 |
| India | in New Zealand | 24 (av 18.79) | E.A.S. Prasanna | | 1967–68 |
| | in India | 34 (av 19.67) | S.P. Gupte | | 1955–56 |

# NEW ZEALAND v PAKISTAN

| Test No. | Venue and Result | New Zealand 1st | New Zealand 2nd | Pakistan 1st | Pakistan 2nd | Captains New Zealand | Captains Pakistan |
|---|---|---|---|---|---|---|---|
| | **1955–56 in Pakistan** | | | | | | |
| 413 | Karachi – Pakistan inns & 1 run | *164 | 124 | 289 | — | H.B. Cave | A.H. Kardar |
| 414 | Lahore[1] – Pakistan 4 wkts | *348 | 328 | 561 | 117-6 | | |
| 415 | Dacca – Drawn | *70 | 69-6 | 195-6d | — | | |
| | **1964–65 in New Zealand** | | | | | | |
| 576 | Wellington – Drawn | *266 | 179-7d | 187 | 140-7 | J.R. Reid | Hanif Mohammad |
| 577 | Auckland – Drawn | 214 | 166-7 | *226 | 207 | | |
| 578 | Christchurch – Drawn | 202 | 223-5 | *206 | 309-8d | | |
| | **1964–65 in Pakistan** | | | | | | |
| 588 | Rawalpindi – Pakistan inns & 64 runs | *175 | 79 | 318 | — | J.R. Reid | Hanif Mohammad |
| 589 | Lahore[2] – Drawn | 482-6d | — | *385-7d | 194-8d | | |
| 590 | Karachi – Pakistan 8 wkts | *285 | 223 | 307-8d | 202-2 | | |
| | **1969–70 in Pakistan** | | | | | | |
| 662 | Karachi – Drawn | 274 | 112-5 | *220 | 283-8d | G.T. Dowling | Intikhab Alam |
| 663 | Lahore[2] – New Zealand 5 wkts | 241 | 82-5 | *114 | 208 | | |
| 664 | Dacca – Drawn | *273 | 200 | 290-7d | 51-4 | | |
| | **1972–73 in New Zealand** | | | | | | |
| 711 | Wellington – Drawn | 325 | 78-3 | *357 | 290-6d | B.E. Congdon | Intikhab Alam |
| 712 | Dunedin – Pakistan inns & 166 runs | 156 | 185 | *507-6d | — | | |
| 713 | Auckland – Drawn | 402 | 92-3 | *402 | 271 | | |
| | **1976–77 in Pakistan** | | | | | | |
| 782 | Lahore[2] – Pakistan 6 wkts | 157 | 360 | *417 | 105-4 | G.M. Turner | Mushtaq Mohammad |
| 783 | Hyderabad – Pakistan 10 wkts | 219 | 254 | *473-8d | 4-0 | G.M. Turner | |
| 784 | Karachi – Drawn | 468 | 262-7 | *565-9d | 290-5d | J.M. Parker | |
| | **1978–79 in New Zealand** | | | | | | |
| 846 | Christchurch – Pakistan 128 runs | 290 | 176 | *271 | 323-6d | M.G. Burgess | Mushtaq Mohammad |
| 847 | Napier – Drawn | 402 | — | *360 | 234-3d | | |
| 848 | Auckland – Drawn | *254 | 281-8d | 359 | 8-0 | | |

| Test No. | Venue and Result | New Zealand | | Pakistan | | Captains | |
|---|---|---|---|---|---|---|---|
| | | 1st | 2nd | 1st | 2nd | New Zealand | Pakistan |
| | **1984–85** in Pakistan | | | | | | |
| 1002 | Lahore[2] – Pakistan 6 wkts | •157 | 241 | 221 | 181-4 | J.V. Coney | Zaheer Abbas |
| 1003 | Hyderabad – Pakistan 7 wkts | •267 | 189 | 230 | 230-3 | | |
| 1004 | Karachi – Drawn | 426 | — | •328 | 308-5 | | |
| | **1984–85** in New Zealand | | | | | | |
| 1010 | Wellington – Drawn | •492 | 103-4 | 322 | — | G.P. Howarth | Javed Miandad |
| 1011 | Auckland – New Zealand inns & 99 runs | 451-9d | — | •169 | 183 | | |
| 1012 | Dunedin – New Zealand 2 wkts | 220 | 278-8 | •274 | 223 | | |

# RESULTS SUMMARY

## NEW ZEALAND v PAKISTAN – IN NEW ZEALAND

| | Tests | Result | | | Wellington | | | Auckland | | | Christchurch | | | Dunedin | | | Napier | | |
|---|---|---|---|---|---|---|---|---|---|---|---|---|---|---|---|---|---|---|---|
| | | NZ | P | Drawn | NZ | P | Drawn | NZ | P | Drawn | NZ | P | Drawn | NZ | P | Drawn | NZ | P | Drawn |
| 1964–65 | 3 | – | – | 3 | – | – | 1 | – | – | 1 | – | – | 1 | – | – | – | – | – | – |
| 1972–73 | 3 | – | 1 | 2 | – | – | 1 | – | – | 1 | – | – | – | – | 1 | – | – | – | – |
| 1978–79 | 3 | – | 1 | 2 | – | – | – | – | – | 1 | – | 1 | – | – | – | – | – | – | 1 |
| 1984–85 | 3 | 2 | – | 1 | – | – | 1 | 1 | – | – | – | – | – | 1 | – | – | – | – | – |
| | **12** | 2 | 2 | 8 | – | – | 3 | 1 | – | 3 | – | 1 | 1 | 1 | 1 | – | – | – | 1 |

## NEW ZEALAND v PAKISTAN – IN PAKISTAN

| | Tests | Result | | | Karachi | | | Lahore | | | Dacca | | | Rawalpindi | | | Hyderabad | | |
|---|---|---|---|---|---|---|---|---|---|---|---|---|---|---|---|---|---|---|---|
| | | NZ | P | Drawn | NZ | P | Drawn | NZ | P | Drawn | NZ | P | Drawn | NZ | P | Drawn | NZ | P | Drawn |
| 1955–56 | 3 | – | 2 | 1 | – | 1 | – | – | 1 | – | – | – | 1 | – | – | – | – | – | – |
| 1964–65 | 3 | – | 2 | 1 | – | – | 1 | – | 1 | – | – | – | – | – | 1 | – | – | – | – |
| 1969–70 | 3 | 1 | – | 2 | – | – | 1 | 1 | – | – | – | – | 1 | – | – | – | – | – | – |
| 1976–77 | 3 | – | 2 | 1 | – | – | 1 | – | 1 | – | – | – | – | – | – | – | – | 1 | – |
| 1984–85 | 3 | – | 2 | 1 | – | 1 | – | – | – | 1 | – | – | – | – | – | – | – | 1 | – |
| | **15** | 1 | 8 | 6 | – | 2 | 3 | 1 | 3 | 1 | – | – | 2 | – | 1 | – | – | 2 | – |
| Totals | **27** | 3 | 10 | 14 | | | | | | | | | | | | | | | |

## HIGHEST INNINGS TOTALS

| | | | | |
|---|---|---|---|---|
| New Zealand | in New Zealand | 492 | Wellington | 1984–85 |
| | in Pakistan | 482-6d | Lahore² | 1964–65 |
| Pakistan | in New Zealand | 507-6d | Dunedin | 1972–73 |
| | in Pakistan | 565-9d | Karachi | 1976–77 |

## LOWEST INNINGS TOTALS

| | | | | |
|---|---|---|---|---|
| New Zealand | in New Zealand | 156 | Dunedin | 1972–73 |
| | in Pakistan | 70 | Dacca | 1955–56 |
| Pakistan | in New Zealand | 169 | Auckland | 1984–85 |
| | in Pakistan | 114 | Lahore² | 1969–70 |

| | | | |
|---|---|---|---|
| **HIGHEST MATCH AGGREGATE** | 1585 for 31 wickets | Karachi | 1976–77 |
| **LOWEST MATCH AGGREGATE** | 572 for 30 wickets | Rawalpindi | 1964–65 |

## HIGHEST INDIVIDUAL INNINGS

| | | | | | |
|---|---|---|---|---|---|
| New Zealand | in New Zealand | 158* | J.F. Reid | Auckland | 1984–85 |
| | in Pakistan | 152 | W.K. Lees | Karachi | 1976–77 |
| Pakistan | in New Zealand | 201 | Mushtaq Mohammad | Dunedin | 1972–73 |
| | in Pakistan | 209 | Imtiaz Ahmed | Lahore¹ | 1955–56 |

## HIGHEST AGGREGATE OF RUNS IN A SERIES

| | | | | | |
|---|---|---|---|---|---|
| New Zealand | in New Zealand | 333 (av 83.25) | J.F. Reid | | 1984–85 |
| | in Pakistan | 296 (av 59.20) | J.R. Reid | | 1964–65 |
| Pakistan | in New Zealand | 366 (av 73.20) | Sadiq Mohammad | | 1972–73 |
| | in Pakistan | 504 (av 126.00) | Javed Miandad | | 1976–77 |

## RECORD WICKET PARTNERSHIPS — NEW ZEALAND

| | | | | |
|---|---|---|---|---|
| 1st | 159 | R.E. Redmond (107), G.M. Turner (58) | Auckland | 1972–73 |
| 2nd | 195 | J.G. Wright (88), G.P. Howarth (114) | Napier | 1978–79 |
| 3rd | 178 | B.W. Sinclair (130), J.R. Reid (88) | Lahore² | 1964–65 |
| 4th | 128 | B.F. Hastings (72), M.G. Burgess (79) | Wellington | 1972–73 |
| 5th | 183 | M.G. Burgess (111), R.W. Anderson (92) | Lahore² | 1976–77 |
| 6th | 145 | J.F. Reid (148), R.J. Hadlee (89) | Wellington | 1984–85 |
| 7th | 186 | W.K. Lees (152), R.J. Hadlee (87) | Karachi | 1976–77 |
| 8th | 100 | B.W. Yuile (47*), D.R. Hadlee (56) | Karachi | 1969–70 |
| 9th | 96 | M.G. Burgess (119*), R.S. Cunis (23) | Dacca | 1969–70 |
| 10th | 151 | B.F. Hastings (110), R.O. Collinge (68*) | Auckland | 1972–73 |

## RECORD WICKET PARTNERSHIPS — PAKISTAN

| | | | | |
|---|---|---|---|---|
| 1st | 147 | Sadiq Mohammad (34), Majid Khan (112) | Karachi | 1976–77 |
| 2nd | 114 | Mohammad Ilyas (56), Saeed Ahmed (68) | Rawalpindi | 1964–65 |
| 3rd | 212 | Mudassar Nazar (106), Javed Miandad (103*) | Hyderabad | 1984–85 |
| 4th | 350 | Mushtaq Mohammad (201), Asif Iqbal (175) | Dunedin | 1972–73 |
| 5th | 281 | Javed Miandad (163), Asif Iqbal (166) | Lahore² | 1976–77 |
| 6th | 217 | Hanif Mohammad (203*), Majid Khan (80) | Lahore² | 1964–65 |
| 7th | 308 | Waqar Hassan (189), Imtiaz Ahmed (209) | Lahore¹ | 1955–56 |
| 8th | 89 | Anil Dalpat (52), Iqbal Qasim (45*) | Karachi | 1984–85 |
| 9th | 52 | Intikhab Alam (45), Arif Butt (20) | Auckland | 1964–65 |
| 10th | 65 | Salahuddin (34*), Mohammad Farooq (47) | Rawalpindi | 1964–65 |

## BEST INNINGS BOWLING ANALYSIS

| | | | | | |
|---|---|---|---|---|---|
| New Zealand | in New Zealand | 6-51 | R.J. Hadlee | Dunedin | 1984–85 |
| | in Pakistan | 7-87 | S.L. Boock | Hyderabad | 1984–85 |
| Pakistan | in New Zealand | 7-52 | Intikhab Alam | Dunedin | 1972–73 |
| | in Pakistan | 7-74 | Pervez Sajjad | Lahore² | 1969–70 |

## BEST MATCH BOWLING ANALYSIS

| | | | | | |
|---|---|---|---|---|---|
| New Zealand | in New Zealand | 9-70 | F.J. Cameron | Auckland | 1964–65 |
| | in Pakistan | 8-156 | S.L. Boock | Hyderabad | 1984–85 |
| Pakistan | in New Zealand | 11-130 | Intikhab Alam | Dunedin | 1972–73 |
| | in Pakistan | 11-79 | Zulfiqar Ahmed | Karachi | 1955–56 |

## HIGHEST AGGREGATE OF WICKETS IN A SERIES

| | | | | | |
|---|---|---|---|---|---|
| New Zealand | in New Zealand | 18 (av 23.00) | R.J. Hadlee | | 1978–79 |
| | in Pakistan | 17 (av 25.35) | S.L. Boock | | 1984–85 |
| Pakistan | in New Zealand | {18 (av 13.77) | Asif Iqbal | | 1964–65 |
| | | {18 (av 17.94) | Intikhab Alam | | 1972–73 |
| | in Pakistan | 22 (av 15.63) | Pervez Sajjad | | 1969–70 |

# NEW ZEALAND v SRI LANKA

| Test No. | Venue and Result | New Zealand 1st | New Zealand 2nd | Sri Lanka 1st | Sri Lanka 2nd | Captains New Zealand | Sri Lanka |
|---|---|---|---|---|---|---|---|
| | **1982–83 in New Zealand** | | | | | | |
| 954 | Christchurch – New Zealand inns & 25 runs | *344 | — | 144 | 175 | G.P. Howarth | D.S. De Silva |
| 955 | Wellington – New Zealand 6 wkts | 201 | 134-4 | *240 | 93 | | |
| | **1983–84 in Sri Lanka** | | | | | | |
| 986 | Kandy – New Zealand 165 runs | *276 | 201-8d | 215 | 97 | G.P. Howarth | L.R.D. Mendis |
| 987 | Colombo (SSC) – Drawn | 198 | 123-4 | *174 | 289-9d | | |
| 988 | Colombo (CCC) – New Zealand inns & 61 runs | 459 | — | *256 | 142 | | |

# RESULTS SUMMARY

## NEW ZEALAND v SRI LANKA – IN NEW ZEALAND

| | Tests | Result NZ | SL | Drawn |
|---|---|---|---|---|
| 1982–83 | 2 | 2 | – | – |

## NEW ZEALAND v SRI LANKA – IN SRI LANKA

| | Tests | Result NZ | SL | Drawn |
|---|---|---|---|---|
| 1983–84 | 3 | 2 | – | 1 |
| Totals | 5 | 4 | – | 1 |

| Christchurch NZ | SL | Drawn | Wellington NZ | SL | Drawn |
|---|---|---|---|---|---|
| 1 | – | – | 1 | – | – |

| Kandy NZ | SL | Drawn | Colombo (SSC) NZ | SL | Drawn | Colombo (CCC) NZ | SL | Drawn |
|---|---|---|---|---|---|---|---|---|
| 1 | – | – | – | – | 1 | 1 | – | – |

## HIGHEST INNINGS TOTALS

| | | | | |
|---|---|---|---|---|
| New Zealand | in New Zealand | 344 | Christchurch | 1982–83 |
| | in Sri Lanka | 459 | Colombo (CCC) | 1983–84 |
| Sri Lanka | in New Zealand | 240 | Wellington | 1982–83 |
| | in Sri Lanka | 289–9d | Colombo (SSC) | 1983–84 |

## LOWEST INNINGS TOTALS

| | | | | |
|---|---|---|---|---|
| New Zealand | in New Zealand | 201 | Wellington | 1982–83 |
| | in Sri Lanka | 198 | Colombo (SSC) | 1983–84 |
| Sri Lanka | in New Zealand | 93 | Wellington | 1982–83 |
| | in Sri Lanka | 97 | Kandy | 1983–84 |

| | | | | |
|---|---|---|---|---|
| **HIGHEST MATCH AGGREGATE** | 857 for 29 wickets | | Colombo (CCC) | 1983–84 |
| **LOWEST MATCH AGGREGATE** | 663 for 30 wickets | | Christchurch | 1982–83 |

## HIGHEST INDIVIDUAL INNINGS

| | | | | | |
|---|---|---|---|---|---|
| New Zealand | in New Zealand | 89 | W.K. Lees | Christchurch | 1982–83 |
| | in Sri Lanka | 180 | J.F. Reid | Colombo (CCC) | 1983–84 |
| Sri Lanka | in New Zealand | 79 | R.S. Madugalle | Wellington | 1982–83 |
| | in Sri Lanka | 108 | R.L. Dias | Colombo (SSC) | 1983–84 |

## HIGHEST AGGREGATE OF RUNS IN A SERIES

| | | | | |
|---|---|---|---|---|
| New Zealand | in New Zealand | 103 (av 34.33) | J.V. Coney | 1982–83 |
| | in Sri Lanka | 243 (av 48.60) | J.F. Reid | 1983–84 |
| Sri Lanka | in New Zealand | 149 (av 37.25) | R.S. Madugalle | 1982–83 |
| | in Sri Lanka | 242 (av 60.50) | R.S. Madugalle | 1983–84 |

## RECORD WICKET PARTNERSHIPS — NEW ZEALAND

| | | | | |
|---|---|---|---|---|
| 1st | 97 | G.P. Howarth (62), J.G. Wright (45) | Kandy | 1983–84 |
| 2nd | 61 | G.P. Howarth (60), J.F. Reid (30) | Kandy | 1983–84 |
| 3rd | 100 | J.F. Reid (180), M.D. Crowe (45) | Colombo (CCC) | 1983–84 |
| 4th | 82 | J.F. Reid (180), S.L. Boock (35) | Colombo (CCC) | 1983–84 |
| 5th | 44 | J.J. Crowe (12), J.V. Coney (84) | Christchurch | 1982–83 |
| 6th | 133 | J.F. Reid (180), J.V. Coney (92) | Colombo (CCC) | 1983–84 |
| 7th | { 30 | R.J. Hadlee (29), I.D.S. Smith (30) | Kandy | 1983–84 |
| | { 30 | R.J. Hadlee (27), J.J. Crowe (9) | Kandy | 1983–84 |
| 8th | 79 | J.V. Coney (84), W.K. Lees (89) | Christchurch | 1982–83 |
| 9th | 42 | W.K. Lees (89), M.C. Snedden (22) | Christchurch | 1982–83 |
| 10th | 52 | W.K. Lees (89), E.J. Chatfield (10*) | Christchurch | 1982–83 |

## RECORD WICKET PARTNERSHIPS — SRI LANKA

| | | | | |
|---|---|---|---|---|
| 1st | 49 | M. de S. Wettimuny (17), S. Wettimuny (63*) | Christchurch | 1982–83 |
| 2nd | 57 | S.M.S. Kaluperuma (18), R.S. Madugalle (38) | Colombo (CCC) | 1983–84 |
| 3rd | 159*† | S. Wettimuny (65), R.L. Dias (108) | Colombo (SSC) | 1983–84 |
| 4th | 49 | E.R.N.S. Fernando (46), R.S. Madugalle (23) | Christchurch | 1982–83 |
| 5th | 130 | R.S. Madugalle (79), D.S. De Silva (61) | Wellington | 1982–83 |
| 6th | 109*‡ | R.S. Madugalle (89*), A. Ranatunga (37) | Colombo (CCC) | 1983–84 |
| 7th | 41 | R.S. Madugalle (44*), J.R. Ratnayeke (22) | Colombo (SSC) | 1983–84 |
| 8th | 42 | A. Ranatunga (51), R.J. Ratnayake (12) | Kandy | 1983–84 |
| 9th | 23 | R.G. de Alwis (26), V.B. John (27*) | Kandy | 1983–84 |
| 10th | 60 | V.B. John (27*), M.J.G. Amerasinghe (34) | Kandy | 1983–84 |

## BEST INNINGS BOWLING ANALYSIS

| | | | | | |
|---|---|---|---|---|---|
| New Zealand | in New Zealand | 4-33 | R.J. Hadlee | Christchurch | 1982–83 |
| | in Sri Lanka | 5-28 | S.L. Boock | Kandy | 1983–84 |
| Sri Lanka | in New Zealand | 5-60 | V.B. John | Wellington | 1982–83 |
| | in Sri Lanka | 5-42 | J.R. Ratnayeke | Colombo (SSC) | 1983–84 |

## BEST MATCH BOWLING ANALYSIS

| | | | | | |
|---|---|---|---|---|---|
| New Zealand | in New Zealand | 8-96 | B.L. Cairns | Christchurch | 1982–83 |
| | in Sri Lanka | 10-102 | R.J. Hadlee | Colombo (CCC) | 1983–84 |
| Sri Lanka | in New Zealand | 6-98 | V.B. John | Wellington | 1982–83 |
| | in Sri Lanka | 8-159 | V.B. John | Kandy | 1983–84 |

## HIGHEST AGGREGATE OF WICKETS IN A SERIES

| | | | | |
|---|---|---|---|---|
| New Zealand | in New Zealand | { 10 (av 14.10) | E.J. Chatfield | 1982–83 |
| | | { 10 (av 14.10) | R.J. Hadlee | 1982–83 |
| | in Sri Lanka | 23 (av 10.00) | R.J. Hadlee | 1983–84 |
| Sri Lanka | in New Zealand | 8 (av 17.87) | V.B. John | 1982–83 |
| | in Sri Lanka | 16 (av 23.31) | V.B. John | 1983–84 |

†*163 runs were added for this wicket, S. Wettimuny retiring hurt and being succeeded by L.R.D. Mendis after 159 had been scored.*
‡*119 runs were added for this wicket, R.S. Madugalle retiring hurt and being succeeded by D.S. De Silva after 109 had been scored.*

# INDIA v PAKISTAN

| Test No. | Venue and Result | India 1st | India 2nd | Pakistan 1st | Pakistan 2nd | Captains India | Captains Pakistan |
|---|---|---|---|---|---|---|---|
| | **1952–53 in India** | | | | | | |
| 355 | Delhi – India inns & 70 runs | •372 | — | 150 | 152 | L. Amarnath | A.H. Kardar |
| 356 | Lucknow – Pakistan inns & 43 runs | •106 | 182 | 331 | — | | |
| 357 | Bombay[2] – India 10 wkts | 387-4d | 45-0 | •186 | 242 | | |
| 358 | Madras[1] – Drawn | 175-6 | — | •344 | — | | |
| 359 | Calcutta – Drawn | 397 | 28-0 | •257 | 236-7d | | |
| | **1954–55 in Pakistan** | | | | | | |
| 396 | Dacca – Drawn | 148 | 147-2 | •257 | 158 | M.H. Mankad | A.H. Kardar |
| 397 | Bahawalpur – Drawn | •235 | 209-5 | 312-9d | — | | |
| 398 | Lahore[1] – Drawn | 251 | 74-2 | •328 | 136-5d | | |
| 399 | Peshawar – Drawn | 245 | 23-1 | •188 | 182 | | |
| 400 | Karachi – Drawn | 145 | 69-2 | •162 | 241-5d | | |
| | **1960–61 in India** | | | | | | |
| 497 | Bombay[2] – Drawn | 449-9d | — | •350 | 166-4 | N.J. Contractor | Fazal Mahmood |
| 498 | Kanpur – Drawn | 404 | — | •335 | 140-3 | | |
| 499 | Calcutta – Drawn | 180 | 127-4 | 301 | 146-3d | | |
| 500 | Madras[2] – Drawn | 539-9d | — | 448-8d | 59-0 | | |
| 501 | Delhi – Drawn | •463 | 16-0 | 286 | 250 | | |
| | **1978–79 in Pakistan** | | | | | | |
| 831 | Faisalabad – Drawn | 462-9d | 43-0 | •503-8d | 264-4d | B.S. Bedi | Mushtaq Mohammad |
| 832 | Lahore[2] – Pakistan 8 wkts | •199 | 465 | 539-6d | 128-2 | | |
| 833 | Karachi – Pakistan 8 wkts | •344 | 300 | 481-9d | 164-2 | | |
| | **1979–80 in India** | | | | | | |
| 861 | Bangalore – Drawn | 416 | — | •431-9d | 108-2 | S.M. Gavaskar | Asif Iqbal |
| 862 | Delhi – Drawn | 126 | 364-6 | 273 | 242 | S.M. Gavaskar | |
| 863 | Bombay[3] – India 131 runs | •334 | 160 | 173 | 190 | S.M. Gavaskar | |
| 864 | Kanpur – Drawn | •162 | 193-2 | 249 | — | S.M. Gavaskar | |
| 865 | Madras[1] – India 10 wkts | 430 | 78-0 | •272 | 233 | S.M. Gavaskar | |
| 866 | Calcutta – Drawn | •331 | 205 | 272-4d | 179-6 | G.R. Viswanath | |

| Test No. | Venue and Result | India 1st | India 2nd | Pakistan 1st | Pakistan 2nd | Captains India | Captains Pakistan |
|---|---|---|---|---|---|---|---|
| | **1982–83 in Pakistan** | | | | | | |
| 943 | Lahore² – Drawn | 379 | — | *485 | 135-1 | S.M. Gavaskar | Imran Khan |
| 944 | Karachi – Pakistan inns & 86 runs | *169 | 197 | 452 | — | | |
| 945 | Faisalabad – Pakistan 10 wkts | *372 | 286 | 652 | 10-0 | | |
| 946 | Hyderabad – Pakistan inns & 119 runs | 189 | 273 | *581-3d | — | | |
| 947 | Lahore² – Drawn | 235-3 | — | *323 | — | | |
| 948 | Karachi – Drawn | *393-8d | 224-2 | 420-6d | — | | |
| | **1983–84 in India** | | | | | | |
| 961 | Bangalore – Drawn | *275 | 176-0 | 288 | — | Kapil Dev | Zaheer Abbas |
| 962 | Jullundur – Drawn | 374 | — | *337 | 16-0 | | |
| 963 | Nagpur – Drawn | *245 | 262-8d | 322 | 42-1 | | |
| | **1984–85 in Pakistan** | | | | | | |
| 995 | Lahore² – Drawn | 156 | 371-6 | *428-9d | — | S.M. Gavaskar | Zaheer Abbas |
| 996 | Faisalabad – Drawn | *500 | — | 674-6 | — | | |

# RESULTS SUMMARY

## INDIA v PAKISTAN – IN INDIA

| | Tests | Result | | | Delhi | | | Lucknow | | | Bombay | | | Madras | | | Calcutta | | | Kanpur | | | Bangalore | | | Jullundur | | | Nagpur | | |
|---|---|---|---|---|---|---|---|---|---|---|---|---|---|---|---|---|---|---|---|---|---|---|---|---|---|---|---|---|---|---|---|---|
| | | I | P | Drawn | I | P | D | I | P | D | I | P | D | I | P | D | I | P | D | I | P | D | I | P | D | I | P | D | I | P | D |
| 1952–53 | 5 | 2 | 1 | 2 | 1 | – | – | – | 1 | – | 1 | – | – | – | – | 1 | – | – | 1 | | | | | | | | | | | | |
| 1960–61 | 5 | – | – | 5 | – | – | 1 | | | | – | – | 1 | – | – | 1 | – | – | 1 | – | – | 1 | | | | | | | | | |
| 1979–80 | 6 | 2 | – | 4 | – | – | 1 | | | | 1 | – | – | 1 | – | – | – | – | 1 | – | – | 1 | – | – | 1 | | | | | | |
| 1983–84 | 3 | – | – | 3 | | | | | | | | | | | | | | | | | | | – | – | 1 | – | – | 1 | – | – | 1 |
| | **19** | 4 | 1 | 14 | 1 | – | 2 | – | 1 | – | 2 | – | 1 | 1 | – | 2 | – | – | 3 | – | – | 2 | – | – | 2 | – | – | 1 | – | – | 1 |

## INDIA v PAKISTAN – IN PAKISTAN

| | Tests | Result | | | Dacca | | | Bahawalpur | | | Lahore | | | Peshawar | | | Karachi | | | Faisalabad | | | Hyderabad | | |
|---|---|---|---|---|---|---|---|---|---|---|---|---|---|---|---|---|---|---|---|---|---|---|---|---|---|---|---|
| | | I | P | Drawn | I | P | D | I | P | D | I | P | D | I | P | D | I | P | D | I | P | D | I | P | D |
| 1954–55 | 5 | – | – | 5 | – | – | 1 | – | – | 1 | – | – | 1 | – | – | 1 | – | – | 1 | | | | | | |
| 1978–79 | 3 | – | 2 | 1 | | | | | | | – | – | 1 | | | | – | 1 | – | – | 1 | – | | | |
| 1982–83 | 6 | – | 3 | 3 | | | | | | | – | 1 | 1 | | | | – | 1 | 1 | – | – | 1 | – | 1 | – |
| 1984–85 | 2 | – | – | 2 | | | | | | | – | – | 1 | | | | | | | – | – | 1 | | | |
| | **16** | – | 5 | 11 | – | – | 1 | – | – | 1 | – | 1 | 4 | – | – | 1 | – | 2 | 2 | – | 1 | 2 | – | 1 | – |
| Totals | **35** | 4 | 6 | 25 | | | | | | | | | | | | | | | | | | | | | |

## HIGHEST INNINGS TOTALS

| | | | | |
|---|---|---|---|---|
| India | in India | 539-9d | Madras[2] | 1960–61 |
| | in Pakistan | 500 | Faisalabad | 1984–85 |
| Pakistan | in India | 448-8d | Madras[2] | 1960–61 |
| | in Pakistan | 674-6 | Faisalabad | 1984–85 |

## LOWEST INNINGS TOTALS

| | | | | |
|---|---|---|---|---|
| India | in India | 106 | Lucknow | 1952–53 |
| | in Pakistan | 145 | Karachi | 1954–55 |
| Pakistan | in India | 150 | Delhi | 1952–53 |
| | in Pakistan | 158 | Dacca | 1954–55 |

| | | | |
|---|---|---|---|
| **HIGHEST MATCH AGGREGATE** | 1331 for 28 wickets | Lahore[2] | 1978–79 |
| **LOWEST MATCH AGGREGATE** | 619 for 30 wickets | Lucknow | 1952–53 |

## HIGHEST INDIVIDUAL INNINGS

| | | | | | |
|---|---|---|---|---|---|
| India | in India | 201 | A.D. Gaekwad | Jullundur | 1983–84 |
| | in Pakistan | 145 | G.R. Viswanath | Faisalabad | 1978–79 |
| Pakistan | in India | 160 | Hanif Mohammad | Bombay[2] | 1960–61 |
| | in Pakistan | 280* | Javed Miandad | Hyderabad | 1982–83 |

## HIGHEST AGGREGATE OF RUNS IN A SERIES

| | | | | |
|---|---|---|---|---|
| India | in India | 529 (av  52.90) | S.M. Gavaskar | 1979–80 |
| | in Pakistan | 584 (av  73.00) | M. Amarnath | 1982–83 |
| Pakistan | in India | 460 (av  51.11) | Saeed Ahmed | 1960–61 |
| | in Pakistan | 761 (av 126.83) | Mudassar Nazar | 1982–83 |

## RECORD WICKET PARTNERSHIPS — INDIA

| | | | | |
|---|---|---|---|---|
| 1st | 192 | S.M. Gavaskar (97), C.P.S. Chauhan (93) | Lahore[2] | 1978–79 |
| 2nd | 125 | S.M. Gavaskar (60), M. Amarnath (64) | Hyderabad | 1982–83 |
| 3rd | 190 | M. Amarnath (120), Yashpal Sharma (63*) | Lahore[2] | 1982–83 |
| 4th | 183 | V.S. Hazare (146*), P.R. Umrigar (102) | Bombay[2] | 1952–53 |
| 5th | 200 | S.M. Patil (127), R.J. Shastri (139) | Faisalabad | 1984–85 |
| 6th | 121 | A.D. Gaekwad (201), R.M.H. Binny (54) | Jullundur | 1983–84 |
| 7th | 155 | R.M.H. Binny (83*), Madan Lal (74) | Bangalore | 1983–84 |
| 8th | 122 | S.M.H. Kirmani (66), Madan Lal (54) | Faisalabad | 1982–83 |
| 9th | 149 | P.G. Joshi (52*), R.B. Desai (85) | Bombay[2] | 1960–61 |
| 10th | 109 | H.R. Adhikari (81*), Ghulam Ahmed (50) | Delhi | 1952–53 |

## RECORD WICKET PARTNERSHIPS — PAKISTAN

| | | | | |
|---|---|---|---|---|
| 1st | 162 | Hanif Mohammad (62), Imtiaz Ahmed (135) | Madras[2] | 1960–61 |
| 2nd | 250 | Mudassar Nazar (199), Qasim Omar (210) | Faisalabad | 1984–85 |
| 3rd | 451 | Mudassar Nazar (230), Javed Miandad (280*) | Hyderabad | 1982–83 |
| 4th | 287 | Javed Miandad (126), Zaheer Abbas (168) | Faisalabad | 1982–83 |
| 5th | 213 | Zaheer Abbas (186), Mudassar Nazar (119) | Karachi | 1982–83 |
| 6th | 207 | Salim Malik (107), Imran Khan (117) | Faisalabad | 1982–83 |
| 7th | 142 | Zaheer Abbas (168*), Ashraf Ali (65) | Lahore[2] | 1984–85 |
| 8th | 95 | Wasim Raja (125), Tahir Naqqash (37) | Jullundur | 1983–84 |
| 9th | 60 | Wasim Bari (49*), Iqbal Qasim (20) | Bangalore | 1979–80 |
| 10th | 104 | Zulfiqar Ahmed (63*), Amir Elahi (47) | Madras[1] | 1952–53 |

## BEST INNINGS BOWLING ANALYSIS

| | | | | | |
|---|---|---|---|---|---|
| India | in India | 8-52 | M.H. Mankad | Delhi | 1952–53 |
| | in Pakistan | 8-85 | Kapil Dev | Lahore[2] | 1982–83 |
| Pakistan | in India | 8-69 | Sikander Bakht | Delhi | 1979–80 |
| | in Pakistan | 8-60 | Imran Khan | Karachi | 1982–83 |

## BEST MATCH BOWLING ANALYSIS

| | | | | | |
|---|---|---|---|---|---|
| India | in India | 13-131 | M.H. Mankad | Delhi | 1952–53 |
| | in Pakistan | 8-85 | Kapil Dev | Lahore[2] | 1982–83 |
| Pakistan | in India | 12-94 | Fazal Mahmood | Lucknow | 1952–53 |
| | in Pakistan | 11-79 | Imran Khan | Karachi | 1982–83 |

## HIGHEST AGGREGATE OF WICKETS IN A SERIES

| | | | | |
|---|---|---|---|---|
| India | in India | 32 (av 17.68) | Kapil Dev | 1979–80 |
| | in Pakistan | 24 (av 34.62) | Kapil Dev | 1982–83 |
| Pakistan | in India | 24 (av 26.70) | Sikander Bakht | 1979–80 |
| | in Pakistan | 40 (av 13.95) | Imran Khan | 1982–83 |

# INDIA v SRI LANKA

| Test No. | Venue and Result | India | | Sri Lanka | | Captains | |
|---|---|---|---|---|---|---|---|
| | | *1st* | *2nd* | *1st* | *2nd* | *India* | *Sri Lanka* |
| 934 | **1982–83** in India<br>Madras[1] – Drawn | 566-6d | 135-7 | °346 | 394 | S.M. Gavaskar | B. Warnapura |

## RESULTS SUMMARY

### INDIA v SRI LANKA – IN INDIA

| | | Result | | Madras | | |
|---|---|---|---|---|---|---|
| | *Tests* | *I* | *SL* | *Drawn* | *I* | *SL* | *Drawn* |
| 1982–83 | 1 | – | – | 1 | – | – | 1 |

## HIGHEST INDIVIDUAL INNINGS
India        155      S.M. Gavaskar
Sri Lanka 105        L.R.D. Mendis (twice)

## RECORD WICKET PARTNERSHIPS — INDIA
1st    156    S.M. Gavaskar (155), Arun Lal (63)
2nd   173    S.M. Gavaskar (155), D.B. Vengsarkar (90)

## RECORD WICKET PARTNERSHIPS — SRI LANKA
3rd    153    R.L. Dias (60), L.R.D. Mendis (105)
3rd    110    R.L. Dias (97), L.R.D. Mendis (105)

## BEST INNINGS BOWLING ANALYSIS
India                        5-85              D.R. Doshi
Sri Lanka                  5-68              A.L.F. De Mel

## BEST MATCH BOWLING ANALYSIS
India                        8-207            Kapil Dev
Sri Lanka                  7-201            A.L.F. De Mel

# PAKISTAN v SRI LANKA

| Test No. | Venue and Result | Pakistan 1st | 2nd | Sri Lanka 1st | 2nd | Captains Pakistan | Sri Lanka |
|---|---|---|---|---|---|---|---|
| | **1981–82** in Pakistan | | | | | | |
| 925 | Karachi – Pakistan 204 runs | •396 | 301-4d | 344 | 149 | Javed Miandad | B. Warnapura |
| 926 | Faisalabad – Drawn | 270 | 186-7 | •454 | 154-8d | | L.R.D. Mendis |
| 927 | Lahore[2] – Pakistan inns & 102 runs | 500-7d | — | •240 | 158 | | B. Warnapura |

## RESULTS SUMMARY

PAKISTAN v SRI LANKA – IN PAKISTAN

| | Tests | Result P | SL | Drawn |
|---|---|---|---|---|
| 1981–82 | 3 | 2 | – | 1 |

| Karachi P | SL | Drawn | Faisalabad P | SL | Drawn | Lahore P | SL | Drawn |
|---|---|---|---|---|---|---|---|---|
| 1 | – | – | – | – | 1 | 1 | – | – |

**HIGHEST INDIVIDUAL INNINGS**

| | | | |
|---|---|---|---|
| Pakistan | 153 | Haroon Rashid | Karachi |
| Sri Lanka | 157 | S. Wettimuny | Faisalabad |

**RECORD WICKET PARTNERSHIPS — PAKISTAN**

| | | | |
|---|---|---|---|
| 2nd | 151 | Mohsin Khan (129), Majid Khan (63) | Lahore[2] |
| 4th | 162 | Salim Malik (100)*, Javed Miandad (92) | Karachi |
| 6th | 100 | Zaheer Abbas (134), Imran Khan (39) | Lahore[2] |
| 7th | 104 | Haroon Rashid (153), Tahir Naqqash (57) | Karachi |
| 9th | 127 | Haroon Rashid (153), Rashid Khan (59) | Karachi |

**RECORD WICKET PARTNERSHIPS — SRI LANKA**

| | | | |
|---|---|---|---|
| 2nd | 217 | S. Wettimuny (157), R.L. Dias (97) | Faisalabad |

**BEST INNINGS BOWLING ANALYSIS**

| | | | |
|---|---|---|---|
| Pakistan | 8-58 | Imran Khan | Lahore[2] |
| Sri Lanka | 5-59 | D.S. De Silva | Faisalabad |

**BEST MATCH BOWLING ANALYSIS**

| | | | |
|---|---|---|---|
| Pakistan | 14-116 | Imran Khan | Lahore[2] |
| Sri Lanka | 9-162 | D.S. De Silva | Faisalabad |

494

# TEST MATCH GROUNDS

## TEST MATCH GROUNDS

Official Test matches have been played on 58 grounds and at 48 centres – if the two London grounds, Lord's and The Oval, are treated as separate Test centres. Seven centres, excluding London, have staged Test matches on more than one ground; Johannesburg, Bombay and Colombo have used three, while Brisbane, Durban, Madras and Lahore have each played Test cricket on two different grounds.

Where any of these seven centres appears in this Records section, the exact ground is denoted by an indicator number (e.g. Bombay[3]) except for Colombo, where the ground appears in brackets. This number refers to the key included in the following tables and which is summarised in the key to Test match grounds in the introduction to this section.

The following tables show the full title, date of the first day's play and number of Tests staged for each ground. The records are those for each centre.

| Test Match Centres | Grounds | First Test Match Day | No. of Tests | |
|---|---|---|---|---|
| **ENGLAND** | | | (307) | |
| Birmingham | Edgbaston | 29.5.1902 | 23 | |
| Leeds | Headingley | 29.6.1899 | 48 | |
| Lord's, London | Lord's Cricket Ground | 21.7.1884 | 78 | |
| Manchester | Old Trafford | 10.7.1884 † | 54 | |
| Nottingham | Trent Bridge | 1.6.1899 | 35 | |
| Oval, London | Kennington Oval | 6.9.1880 | 68 | |
| Sheffield | Bramall Lane | 3.7.1902 | 1 | |
| **AUSTRALIA** | | | (231) | |
| Adelaide | Adelaide Oval | 12.12.1884 | 43 | |
| Brisbane | [1]Exhibition Ground (1928–29 to 1930–31) | 30.11.1928 | 29 | (2) |
| | [2]Woolloongabba | 27.11.1931 | | (27) |
| Melbourne | Melbourne Cricket Ground | 15.3.1877 | 77 | |
| Perth | Western Australia Cricket Association (WACA) Ground | 11.12.1970 | 12 | |
| Sydney | Sydney Cricket Ground (No. 1) | 17.2.1882 | 70 | |
| **SOUTH AFRICA** | | | (98) | |
| Cape Town | Newlands | 25.3.1889 | 24 | |
| Durban | [1]Lord's (1909–10 to 1921–22) | 21.1.1910 | 23 | (4) |
| | [2]Kingsmead | 18.1.1923 | | (19) |
| Johannesburg | [1]Old Wanderers (1895–96 to 1938–39) | 2.3.1896 | 39 | (22) |
| | [2]Ellis Park (1948–49 to 1953–54) | 27.12.1948 | | (6) |
| | [3]Wanderers Stadium | 24.12.1956 | | (11) |
| Port Elizabeth | St George's Park | 12.3.1889 | 12 | |
| **WEST INDIES** | | | (104) | |
| Bridgetown, Barbados | Kensington Oval | 11.1.1930 | 22 | |
| Georgetown, Guyana | Bourda | 21.2.1930 | 19 | |
| Kingston, Jamaica | Sabina Park | 3.4.1930 | 25 | |
| Port-of-Spain, Trinidad | Queen's Park Oval | 1.2.1930 | 35 | |
| St John's, Antigua | Recreation Ground | 27.3.1981 | 3 | |
| **NEW ZEALAND** | | | (81) | |
| Auckland | Eden Park | 14.2.1930 ‡ | 27 | |
| Christchurch | Lancaster Park | 10.1.1930 | 25 | |
| Dunedin | Carisbrook | 11.3.1955 | 8 | |
| Napier | McLean Park | 16.2.1979 | 1 | |
| Wellington | Basin Reserve | 24.1.1930 | 20 | |

| *Test Match Centres* | *Grounds* | *First Test Match Day* | *No. of Tests* | |
|---|---|---|---|---|
| **INDIA** | | | (127) | |
| Ahmedabad | Gujarat Stadium | 12.11.1983 | 1 | |
| Bangalore | Karnataka State Cricket Association Stadium | 22.11.1974 | 7 | |
| Bombay | [1]Gymkhana (1933–34 only) | 15.12.1933 | 28 | (1) |
| | [2]Brabourne Stadium (1948–49 to 1972–73) | 9.12.1948 | | (17) |
| | [3]Wankhede Stadium | 23.1.1975 | | (10) |
| Calcutta | Eden Gardens | 5.1.1934 | 24 | |
| Delhi | Feroz Shah Kotla | 10.11.1948 | 20 | |
| Hyderabad (Deccan) | Fateh Maidan (Lal Bahadur Stadium) | 19.11.1955 | 2 | |
| Jullundur | Burlton Park | 24.9.1983 | 1 | |
| Kanpur | Green Park (Modi Stadium) | 12.1.1952 | 15 | |
| Lucknow | University Ground | 23.10.1952 | 1 | |
| Madras | [1]Chepauk (Chidambaram Stadium) | 10.2.1934 | 26 | (17) |
| | [2]Corporation (Nehru) Stadium (1955–56 to 1964–65) | 6.1.1956 | | (9) |
| Nagpur | Vidarbha Cricket Association Ground | 3.10.1969 | 2 | |
| **PAKISTAN** | | | (69) | |
| Bahawalpur | Dring Stadium | 15.1.1955 | 1 | |
| Dacca | Dacca Stadium | 1.1.1955 | 7 | |
| Faisalabad | Iqbal Stadium | 16.10.1978 | 8 | |
| Hyderabad (Sind) | Niaz Stadium | 16.3.1973 | 5 | |
| Karachi | National Stadium | 26.2.1955 | 23 | |
| Lahore | [1]Lawrence Gardens (Bagh-i-Jinnah) (1954–55 to 1958–59) | 29.1.1955 | 22 | (3) |
| | [2]Lahore (Gaddafi) Stadium | 21.11.1959 | | (19) |
| Multan | Ibn-e-Qasim Bagh Stadium | 30.12.1980 | 1 | |
| Peshawar | Peshawar Club Ground | 13.2.1955 | 1 | |
| Rawalpindi | Pindi Club Ground | 27.3.1965 | 1 | |
| **SRI LANKA** | | | (5) | |
| Colombo | P. Saravanamuttu (Colombo) Oval (SO) | 17.2.1982 | 3 | (1) |
| | Sinhalese Sports Club Ground (SSC) | | | |
| | Colombo Cricket Club Ground (CCC) | 16.3.1984 | | (1) |
| | Asgiriya Stadium | 24.3.1984 | | (1) |
| Kandy | | 22.4.1983 | 2 | |

† Rain prevented play until 11.7.1884.
‡ Rain prevented play until 17.2.1930.
The 1890 and 1938 Tests at Manchester and the 1970–71 Third Test at Melbourne, all abandoned without a ball being bowled, plus the cancelled 1980–81 Second Test at Georgetown, are excluded from these figures.

# RECORD TOTALS FOR EACH TEST MATCH CENTRE

| Centre | Highest Total | | | Lowest Total‡ | | |
|---|---|---|---|---|---|---|
| Birmingham | 633-5d | England v India | 1979 | 30 | S. Africa v England | 1924 |
| Leeds | 584 | Australia v England | 1934 | 67 | N. Zealand v England | 1958 |
| Lord's | 729-6d | Australia v England | 1930 | 42 | India v England | 1974 |
| Manchester | 656-8d | Australia v England | 1964 | 58 | India v England | 1952 |
| Nottingham | 658-8d | England v Australia | 1938 | 88 | S. Africa v England | 1960 |
| Oval | 903-7d | England v Australia | 1938 | 44 | Australia v England | 1896 |
| Sheffield | 289 | Australia v England | 1902 | 145 | England v Australia | 1902 |
| Adelaide | 674 | Australia v India | 1947–48 | 82 | Australia v W. Indies | 1951–52 |
| Brisbane | 645 | Australia v England | 1946–47 | 58 | { Australia v England | 1936–37 |
| | | | | | { India v Australia | 1947–48 |
| Melbourne | 604 | Australia v England | 1936–37 | 36 | S. Africa v Australia | 1931–32 |
| Perth | 585 | W. Indies v Australia | 1975–76 | 62 | Pakistan v Australia | 1981–82 |
| Sydney | 659-8d | Australia v England | 1946–47 | 42 | Australia v England | 1887–88 |
| Cape Town | 559-9d | England v S. Africa | 1938–39 | 35 | S. Africa v England | 1898–99 |
| Durban | 654-5 | England v S. Africa | 1938–39 | 75 | Australia v S. Africa | 1949–50 |
| Johannesburg | 620 | S. Africa v Australia | 1966–67 | 72 | S. Africa v England | 1956–57 |
| Port Elizabeth | 549-7d | Australia v S. Africa | 1949–50 | 30 | S. Africa v England | 1895–96 |
| Bridgetown | 668 | Australia v W. Indies | 1954–55 | 94 | N. Zealand v W. Indies | 1984–85 |
| Georgetown | 543-3d | N. Zealand v W. Indies | 1971–72 | 109 | W. Indies v Australia | 1972–73 |
| Kingston | 849 | England v W. Indies | 1929–30 | 97† | India v W. Indies | 1975–76 |
| Port-of-Spain | 681-8d | W. Indies v England | 1953–54 | 90 | Australia v W. Indies | 1977–78 |
| St John's | 550 | W. Indies v India | 1982–83 | 200 | Australia v. W. Indies | 1983–84 |
| Auckland | 593-6d | England v N. Zealand | 1974–75 | 26 | N. Zealand v England | 1954–55 |
| Christchurch | 560-8d | England v N. Zealand | 1932–33 | 65 | N. Zealand v England | 1970–71 |
| Dunedin | 507-6d | Pakistan v N. Zealand | 1972–73 | 74 | N. Zealand v W. Indies | 1955–56 |
| Napier | 402 | N. Zealand v Pakistan | 1978–79 | 360 | Pakistan v N. Zealand | 1978–79 |
| Wellington | 537 | N. Zealand v England | 1983–84 | 42 | N. Zealand v Australia | 1945–46 |
| Ahmedabad | 281 | W. Indies v India | 1983–84 | 103 | India v W. Indies | 1983–84 |
| Bangalore | 457-5d | India v Australia | 1979–80 | 118 | India v W. Indies | 1974–75 |
| Bombay | 629-6d | W. Indies v India | 1948–49 | 88 | India v N. Zealand | 1964–65 |
| Calcutta | 614-5d | W. Indies v India | 1958–59 | 90 | India v W. Indies | 1983–84 |
| Delhi | 644-8d | W. Indies v India | 1958–59 | 107 | Australia v India | 1969–70 |
| Hyderabad | 498-4d | India v N. Zealand | 1955–56 | 89 | India v N. Zealand | 1969–70 |
| Jullundur | 374 | India v Pakistan | 1983–84 | 337 | Pakistan v India | 1983–84 |
| Kanpur | 644-7d | India v W. Indies | 1978–79 | 105 | Australia v India | 1959–60 |
| Lucknow | 331 | Pakistan v India | 1952–53 | 106 | India v Pakistan | 1952–53 |
| Madras | 652-7d | England v India | 1984–85 | 83 | India v England | 1976–77 |
| Nagpur | 322 | Pakistan v India | 1983–84 | 109 | India v N. Zealand | 1969–70 |
| Bahawalpur | 312-9d | Pakistan v India | 1954–55 | 235 | India v Pakistan | 1954–55 |
| Dacca | 439 | England v Pakistan | 1961–62 | 70 | N. Zealand v Pakistan | 1955–56 |
| Faisalabad | 674-6 | Pakistan v India | 1984–85 | 145 | Pakistan v W. Indies | 1980–81 |
| Hyderabad | 581-3d | Pakistan v India | 1982–83 | 189 | { India v Pakistan | 1982–83 |
| | | | | | { N. Zealand v Pakistan | 1984–85. |
| Karachi | 565-9d | Pakistan v N. Zealand | 1976–77 | 80 | Australia v Pakistan | 1956–57 |
| Lahore | 561 | Pakistan v N. Zealand | 1955–56 | 104 | Pakistan v W. Indies | 1958–59 |
| Multan | 249 | W. Indies v Pakistan | 1980–81 | 166 | Pakistan v W. Indies | 1980–81 |
| Peshawar | 245 | India v Pakistan | 1954–55 | 182 | Pakistan v India | 1954–55 |
| Rawalpindi | 318 | Pakistan v N. Zealand | 1964–65 | 79 | N. Zealand v Pakistan | 1964–65 |
| Colombo (SO) | 223 | England v Sri Lanka | 1981–82 | 175 | Sri Lanka v England | 1981–82 |
| Colombo (SSC) | 289-9d | Sri Lanka v N. Zealand | 1983–84 | 174 | Sri Lanka v N. Zealand | 1983–84 |
| Colombo (CCC) | 459 | N. Zealand v Sri Lanka | 1983–84 | 142 | Sri Lanka v N. Zealand | 1983–84 |
| Kandy | 514-4d | Australia v Sri Lanka | 1982–83 | 97 | Sri Lanka v N. Zealand | 1983–84 |

†Five men were absent hurt. The second lowest total at Kingston is 103 by England in 1934–35.
‡Completed innings.

# HIGHEST INDIVIDUAL SCORE FOR EACH CENTRE

| | | | | |
|---|---|---|---|---|
| Birmingham | 285* | P.B.H. May | England v West Indies | 1957 |
| Leeds | 334 | D.G. Bradman | Australia v England | 1930 |
| Lord's | 254 | D.G. Bradman | Australia v England | 1930 |
| Manchester | 311 | R.B. Simpson | Australia v England | 1964 |
| Nottingham | 278 | D.C.S. Compton | England v Pakistan | 1954 |
| Oval | 364 | L. Hutton | England v Australia | 1938 |
| Sheffield | 119 | C. Hill | Australia v England | 1902 |
| | | | | |
| Adelaide | 299* | D.G. Bradman | Australia v South Africa | 1931–32 |
| Brisbane | 226 | D.G. Bradman | Australia v South Africa | 1931–32 |
| Melbourne | 307 | R.M. Cowper | Australia v England | 1965–66 |
| Perth | 176 | R.B. Simpson | Australia v India | 1977–78 |
| Sydney | 287 | R.E. Foster | England v Australia | 1903–04 |
| | | | | |
| Cape Town | 209 | R.G. Pollock | South Africa v Australia | 1966–67 |
| Durban | 274 | R.G. Pollock | South Africa v Australia | 1969–70 |
| Johannesburg | 231 | A.D. Nourse | South Africa v Australia | 1935–36 |
| Port Elizabeth | 167 | A.L. Hassett | Australia v South Africa | 1949–50 |
| | | | | |
| Bridgetown | 337 | Hanif Mohammad | Pakistan v West Indies | 1957–58 |
| Georgetown | 259 | G.M. Turner | New Zealand v West Indies | 1971–72 |
| Kingston | 365* | G.St A. Sobers | West Indies v Pakistan | 1957–58 |
| Port-of-Spain | 220 | S.M. Gavaskar | India v West Indies | 1970–71 |
| St John's | 178 | I.V.A. Richards | West Indies v Australia | 1983–84 |
| | | | | |
| Auckland | 336* | W.R. Hammond | England v New Zealand | 1932–33 |
| Christchurch | 258 | S.M. Nurse | West Indies v New Zealand | 1968–69 |
| Dunedin | 201 | Mushtaq Mohammad | Pakistan v New Zealand | 1972–73 |
| Napier | 119* | Majid Khan | Pakistan v New Zealand | 1978–79 |
| Wellington | 255* | D.J. McGlew | South Africa v New Zealand | 1952–53 |
| | | | | |
| Ahmedabad | 98 | P.J.L. Dujon | West Indies v India | 1983–84 |
| Bangalore | 172 | S.M. Gavaskar | India v England | 1981–82 |
| Bombay | 242* | C.H. Lloyd | West Indies v India | 1974–75 |
| Calcutta | 256 | R.B. Kanhai | West Indies v India | 1958–59 |
| Delhi | 230* | B. Sutcliffe | New Zealand v India | 1955–56 |
| Hyderabad | 223 | P.R. Umrigar | India v New Zealand | 1955–56 |
| Jullundur | 201 | A.D. Gaekwad | India v Pakistan | 1983–84 |
| Kanpur | 250 | S.F.A.F. Bacchus | West Indies v India | 1978–79 |
| Lucknow | 124* | Nazar Mohammad | Pakistan v India | 1952–53 |
| Madras | 236* | S.M. Gavaskar | India v West Indies | 1983–84 |
| Nagpur | 89 | M.G. Burgess | New Zealand v India | 1969–70 |
| | | | | |
| Bahawalpur | 142 | Hanif Mohammad | Pakistan v India | 1954–55 |
| Dacca | 165 | G. Pullar | England v Pakistan | 1961–62 |
| Faisalabad | 235 | G.S. Chappell | Australia v Pakistan | 1979–80 |
| Hyderabad | 280* | Javed Miandad | Pakistan v India | 1982–83 |
| Karachi | 206 | Javed Miandad | Pakistan v New Zealand | 1976–77 |
| Lahore | 235* | Zaheer Abbas | Pakistan v India | 1978–79 |
| Multan | 120* | I.V.A. Richards | West Indies v Pakistan | 1980–81 |
| Peshawar | 108 | P.R. Umrigar | India v Pakistan | 1954–55 |
| Rawalpindi | 76 | B.R. Taylor | New Zealand v Pakistan | 1964–65 |
| | | | | |
| Colombo (SO) | 89 | D.I. Gower | England v Sri Lanka | 1981–82 |
| Colombo (SSC) | 108 | R.L. Dias | Sri Lanka v New Zealand | 1983–84 |
| Colombo (CCC) | 180 | J.F. Reid | New Zealand v Sri Lanka | 1983–84 |
| Kandy | 143* | D.W. Hookes | Australia v Sri Lanka | 1982–83 |

# HIGHEST WICKET PARTNERSHIPS FOR EACH TEST MATCH CENTRE

|  | Runs | Wkt |  |  |  |  |
|---|---|---|---|---|---|---|
| Birmingham | 411 | 4th | P.B.H. May, M.C. Cowdrey | E | v WI | 1957 |
| Leeds | 388 | 4th | W.H. Ponsford, D.G. Bradman | A | v E | 1934 |
| Lord's | 370 | 3rd | W.J. Edrich, D.C.S. Compton | E | v SA | 1947 |
| Manchester | 246 | 3rd | E.R. Dexter, K.F. Barrington | E | v A | 1964 |
| Nottingham | 319 | 3rd | A. Melville, A.D. Nourse | SA | v E | 1947 |
| Oval | 451 | 2nd | W.H. Ponsford, D.G. Bradman | A | v E | 1934 |
| Sheffield | 107 | 4th | C. Hill, S.E. Gregory | A | v E | 1902 |
| | | | | | | |
| Adelaide | 341 | 3rd | E.J. Barlow, R.G. Pollock | SA | v A | 1963–64 |
| Brisbane | 276 | 3rd | D.G. Bradman, A.L. Hassett | A | v E | 1946–47 |
| Melbourne | 346 | 6th | J.H.W. Fingleton, D.G. Bradman | A | v E | 1936–37 |
| Perth | 259 | 2nd | W.B. Phillips, G.N. Yallop | A | v P | 1983–84 |
| Sydney | 405 | 5th | S.G. Barnes, D.G. Bradman | A | v E | 1946–47 |
| | | | | | | |
| Cape Town | 260 | 1st | B. Mitchell, I.J. Siedle | SA | v E | 1930–31 |
| Durban | 280 | 2nd | P.A. Gibb, W.J. Edrich | E | v SA | 1938–39 |
| Johannesburg | 359 | 1st | L. Hutton, C. Washbrook | E | v SA | 1948–49 |
| Port Elizabeth | 187 | 3rd | A.R. Morris, R.N. Harvey | A | v SA | 1949–50 |
| | | | | | | |
| Bridgetown | 399 | 4th | G.St A. Sobers, F.M.M. Worrell | WI | v E | 1959–60 |
| Georgetown | 387 | 1st | G.M. Turner, T.W. Jarvis | NZ | v WI | 1971–72 |
| Kingston | 446 | 2nd | C.C. Hunte, G.St A. Sobers | WI | v P | 1957–58 |
| Port-of-Spain | 338 | 3rd | E.de C. Weekes, F.M.M. Worrell | WI | v E | 1953–54 |
| St John's | 308 | 3rd | R.B. Richardson, I.V.A. Richards | WI | v A | 1983–84 |
| | | | | | | |
| Auckland | 266 | 4th | M.H. Denness, K.W.R. Fletcher | E | v NZ | 1974–75 |
| Christchurch | 242 | 5th | W.R. Hammond, L.E.G. Ames | E | v NZ | 1932–33 |
| Dunedin | 350 | 4th | Mushtaq Mohammad, Asif Iqbal | P | v NZ | 1972–73 |
| Napier | 195 | 2nd | J.G. Wright, G.P. Howarth | NZ | v P | 1978–79 |
| Wellington | 276 | 1st | C.S. Dempster, J.E. Mills | NZ | v E | 1929–30 |
| | | | | | | |
| Ahmedabad | 127 | 1st | S.M. Gavaskar, A.D. Gaekwad | I | v WI | 1983–84 |
| Bangalore | 207 | 4th | C.G. Greenidge, C.H. Lloyd | WI | v I | 1974–75 |
| Bombay | 254 | 5th | K.W.R. Fletcher, A.W. Greig | E | v I | 1972–73 |
| Calcutta | 344* | 2nd | S.M. Gavaskar, D.B. Vengsarkar | I | v WI | 1978–79 |
| Delhi | 267 | 4th | C.L. Walcott, G.E. Gomez | WI | v I | 1948–49 |
| Hyderabad | 238 | 3rd | P.R. Umrigar, V.L. Manjrekar | I | v NZ | 1955–56 |
| Jullundur | 121 | 6th | A.D. Gaekwad, R.M.H. Binny | I | v P | 1983–84 |
| Kanpur | 206 | 4th | K.F. Barrington, E.R. Dexter | E | v I | 1961–62 |
| Lucknow | 63 | 8th | Nazar Mohammad, Zulfiqar Ahmed | P | v I | 1952–53 |
| Madras | 413 | 1st | M.H. Mankad, P. Roy | I | v NZ | 1955–56 |
| Nagpur | 101 | 5th | Zaheer Abbas, Mudassar Nazar | P | v I | 1983–84 |
| | | | | | | |
| Bahawalpur | 127 | 1st | Hanif Mohammad, Alimuddin | P | v I | 1954–55 |
| Dacca | 198 | 1st | G. Pullar, R.W. Barber | E | v P | 1961–62 |
| Faisalabad | 287 | 4th | Javed Miandad, Zaheer Abbas | P | v I | 1982–83 |
| Hyderabad | 451 | 3rd | Mudassar Nazar, Javed Miandad | P | v I | 1982–83 |
| Karachi | 252 | 4th | Javed Miandad, Mushtaq Mohammad | P | v NZ | 1976–77 |
| Lahore | 308 | 7th | Waqar Hassan, Imtiaz Ahmed | P | v NZ | 1955–56 |
| Multan | 100 | 3rd | Majid Khan, Javed Miandad | P | v WI | 1980–81 |
| Peshawar | 91 | 3rd | P.R. Umrigar, V.L. Manjrekar | I | v P | 1954–55 |
| Rawalpindi | 114 | 2nd | Mohammad Ilyas, Saeed Ahmed | P | v NZ | 1964–65 |
| | | | | | | |
| Colombo (SO) | 99 | 5th | R.S. Madugalle, A. Ranatunga | SL | v E | 1981–82 |
| Colombo (SSC) | 159* | 3rd | S. Wettimuny, R.L. Dias | SL | v NZ | 1983–84 |
| Colombo (CCC) | 133 | 6th | J.F. Reid, J.V. Coney | NZ | v SL | 1983–84 |
| Kandy | 170 | 2nd | K.C. Wessels, G.N. Yallop | A | v SL | 1982–83 |

# BEST INNINGS BOWLING ANALYSIS FOR EACH CENTRE

| | | | | |
|---|---|---|---|---|
| Birmingham | 7-17 | W. Rhodes | England v Australia | 1902 |
| Leeds | 8-43 | R.G.D. Willis | England v Australia | 1981 |
| Lord's | 8-34 | I.T. Botham | England v Pakistan | 1978 |
| Manchester | 10-53 | J.C. Laker | England v Australia | 1956 |
| Nottingham | 8-107 | B.J.T. Bosanquet | England v Australia | 1905 |
| Oval | 8-29 | S.F. Barnes | England v South Africa | 1912 |
| Sheffield | 6-49 | S.F. Barnes | England v Australia | 1902 |
| | | | | |
| Adelaide | 8-43 | A.E. Trott | Australia v England | 1894–95 |
| Brisbane | 7-60 | K.R. Miller | Australia v England | 1946–47 |
| Melbourne | 9-86 | Sarfraz Nawaz | Pakistan v Australia | 1978–79 |
| Perth | 7-54 | A.M.E. Roberts | West Indies v Australia | 1975–76 |
| Sydney | 8-35 | G.A. Lohmann | England v Australia | 1886–87 |
| | | | | |
| Cape Town | 8-11 | J. Briggs | England v South Africa | 1888–89 |
| Durban | 8-69 | H.J. Tayfield | South Africa v England | 1956–57 |
| Johannesburg | 9-28 | G.A. Lohmann | England v South Africa | 1895–96 |
| Port Elizabeth | 8-7 | G.A. Lohmann | England v South Africa | 1895–96 |
| | | | | |
| Bridgetown | 8-38 | L.R. Gibbs | West Indies v India | 1961–62 |
| Georgetown | 7-44 | I.W. Johnson | Australia v West Indies | 1954–55 |
| Kingston | 7-34 | T.E. Bailey | England v West Indies | 1953–54 |
| Port-of-Spain | 9-95 | J.M. Noreiga | West Indies v India | 1970–71 |
| St John's | 6-74 | C.E.H. Croft | West Indies v England | 1980–81 |
| | | | | |
| Auckland | 8-76 | E.A.S. Prasanna | India v New Zealand | 1975–76 |
| Christchurch | 7-75 | F.S. Trueman | England v New Zealand | 1962–63 |
| Dunedin | 7-52 | Intikhab Alam | Pakistan v New Zealand | 1972–73 |
| Napier | 5-106 | Imran Khan | Pakistan v New Zealand | 1978–79 |
| Wellington | 7-23 | R.J. Hadlee | New Zealand v India | 1975–76 |
| | | | | |
| Ahmedabad | 9-83 | Kapil Dev | India v West Indies | 1983–84 |
| Bangalore | 6-53 | R.G.D. Willis | England v India | 1976–77 |
| Bombay | 7-48 | I.T. Botham | England v India | 1979–80 |
| Calcutta | 7-49 | Ghulam Ahmed | India v Australia | 1956–57 |
| Delhi | 8-52 | M.H. Mankad | India v Pakistan | 1952–53 |
| Hyderabad | 7-128 | S.P. Gupte | India v New Zealand | 1955–56 |
| Jullundur | 4-50 | Wasim Raja | Pakistan v India | 1983–84 |
| Kanpur | 9-69 | J.M. Patel | India v Australia | 1959–60 |
| Lucknow | 7-42 | Fazal Mahmood | Pakistan v India | 1952–53 |
| Madras | 8-55 | M.H. Mankad | India v England | 1951–52 |
| Nagpur | 6-74 | S. Venkataraghavan | India v New Zealand | 1969–70 |
| | | | | |
| Bahawalpur | 6-74 | P.R. Umrigar | India v Pakistan | 1954–55 |
| Dacca | 6-21 | Khan Mohammad | Pakistan v New Zealand | 1955–56 |
| Faisalabad | 7-142 | Abdul Qadir | Pakistan v Australia | 1982–83 |
| Hyderabad | 7-87 | S.L. Boock | New Zealand v Pakistan | 1984–85 |
| Karachi | 8-60 | Imran Khan | Pakistan v India | 1982–83 |
| Lahore | 8-58 | Imran Khan | Pakistan v Sri Lanka | 1981–82 |
| Multan | 5-62 | Imran Khan | Pakistan v West Indies | 1980–81 |
| Peshawar | 5-63 | S.P. Gupte | India v Pakistan | 1954–55 |
| Rawalpindi | 4-5 | Pervez Sajjad | Pakistan v New Zealand | 1964–65 |
| | | | | |
| Colombo (SO) | 6-33 | J.E. Emburey | England v Sri Lanka | 1981–82 |
| Colombo (SSC) | 5-42 | J.R. Ratnayeke | Sri Lanka v New Zealand | 1983–84 |
| Colombo (CCC) | 5-29 | R.J. Hadlee | New Zealand v Sri Lanka | 1983–84 |
| Kandy | 5-28 | S.L. Boock | New Zealand v Sri Lanka | 1983–84 |

# BEST MATCH BOWLING ANALYSIS FOR EACH CENTRE

| | | | | |
|---|---|---|---|---|
| Birmingham | 12-119 | F.S. Trueman | England v West Indies | 1963 |
| Leeds | 15-99 | C. Blythe | England v South Africa | 1907 |
| Lord's | 16-137 | R.A.L. Massie | Australia v England | 1972 |
| Manchester | 19-90 | J.C. Laker | England v Australia | 1956 |
| Nottingham | 14-99 | A.V. Bedser | England v Australia | 1953 |
| Oval | 14-90 | F.R. Spofforth | Australia v England | 1882 |
| Sheffield | 11-103 | M.A. Noble | Australia v England | 1902 |
| | | | | |
| Adelaide | 14-199 | C.V. Grimmett | Australia v South Africa | 1931–32 |
| Brisbane | 11-31 | E.R.H. Toshack | Australia v India | 1947–48 |
| Melbourne | 15-124 | W. Rhodes | England v Australia | 1903–04 |
| Perth | 11-118 | C.G. Rackemann | Australia v Pakistan | 1983–84 |
| Sydney | 12-87 | C.T.B. Turner | Australia v England | 1887–88 |
| | | | | |
| Cape Town | 15-28 | J. Briggs | England v South Africa | 1888–89 |
| Durban | 14-144 | S.F. Barnes | England v South Africa | 1913–14 |
| Johannesburg | 17-159 | S.F. Barnes | England v South Africa | 1913–14 |
| Port Elizabeth | 15-45 | G.A. Lohmann | England v South Africa | 1895–96 |
| | | | | |
| Bridgetown | 11-120 | M.D. Marshall | West Indies v New Zealand | 1984–85 |
| Georgetown | 10-115 | N.J.N. Hawke | Australia v West Indies | 1964–65 |
| Kingston | 10-96 | H.H.H. Johnson | West Indies v England | 1947–48 |
| Port-of-Spain | 13-156 | A.W. Greig | England v West Indies | 1973–74 |
| St John's | 8-113 | C.E.H. Croft | West Indies v England | 1980–81 |
| | | | | |
| Auckland | 11-123 | D.K. Lillee | Australia v New Zealand | 1976–77 |
| Christchurch | 12-97 | D.L. Underwood | England v New Zealand | 1970–71 |
| Dunedin | 11-102 | R.J. Hadlee | New Zealand v West Indies | 1979–80 |
| Napier | 5-106 | Imran Khan | Pakistan v New Zealand | 1978–79 |
| Wellington | 11-58 | R.J. Hadlee | New Zealand v India | 1975–76 |
| | | | | |
| Ahmedabad | 10-135 | Kapil Dev | India v West Indies | 1983–84 |
| Bangalore | 9-131 | B.S. Chandrasekhar | India v England | 1976–77 |
| Bombay | 13-106 | I.T. Botham | England v India | 1979–80 |
| Calcutta | 11-105 | R. Benaud | Australia v India | 1956–57 |
| Delhi | 13-131 | M.H. Mankad | India v Pakistan | 1952–53 |
| Hyderabad | 8-109 | E.A.S. Prasanna | India v New Zealand | 1969–70 |
| Jullundur | 4-50 | Wasim Raja | Pakistan v India | 1983–84 |
| Kanpur | 14-124 | J.M. Patel | India v Australia | 1959–60 |
| Lucknow | 12-94 | Fazal Mahmood | Pakistan v India | 1952–53 |
| Madras | 12-108 | M.H. Mankad | India v England | 1951–52 |
| Nagpur | 9-100 | H.J. Howarth | New Zealand v India | 1969–70 |
| | | | | |
| Bahawalpur | 7-124 | Khan Mohammad | Pakistan v India | 1954–55 |
| Dacca | 12-100 | Fazal Mahmood | Pakistan v West Indies | 1958–59 |
| Faisalabad | 11-180 | Imran Khan | Pakistan v India | 1982–83 |
| Hyderabad | 8-80 | Imran Khan | Pakistan v India | 1982–83 |
| Karachi | 13-114 | Fazal Mahmood | Pakistan v Australia | 1956–57 |
| Lahore | 14-116 | Imran Khan | Pakistan v Sri Lanka | 1981–82 |
| Multan | 5-89 | Imran Khan | Pakistan v West Indies | 1980–81 |
| Peshawar | 6-115 | S.P. Gupte | India v Pakistan | 1954–55 |
| Rawalpindi | 8-47 | Pervez Sajjad | Pakistan v New Zealand | 1964–65 |
| | | | | |
| Colombo (SO) | 8-95 | D.L. Underwood | England v Sri Lanka | 1981–82 |
| Colombo (SSC) | 5-59 | J.R. Ratnayeke | Sri Lanka v New Zealand | 1983–84 |
| Colombo (CCC) | 10-102 | R.J. Hadlee | New Zealand v Sri Lanka | 1983–84 |
| Kandy | 8-43 | R.J. Hadlee | New Zealand v Sri Lanka | 1983–84 |

# TEAM RECORDS

## HIGHEST INNINGS TOTALS

| | | | |
|---|---|---|---:|
| 903-7d | England v Australia | Oval | 1938 |
| 849 | England v West Indies | Kingston | 1929–30 |
| 790-3d | West Indies v Pakistan | Kingston | 1957–58 |
| 758-8d | Australia v West Indies | Kingston | 1954–55 |
| 729-6d | Australia v England | Lord's | 1930 |
| 701 | Australia v England | Oval | 1934 |
| 695 | Australia v England | Oval | 1930 |
| 687-8d | West Indies v England | Oval | 1976 |
| 681-8d | West Indies v England | Port-of-Spain | 1953–54 |
| 674-6 | Pakistan v India | Faisalabad | 1984–85 |
| 674 | Australia v India | Adelaide | 1947–48 |
| 668 | Australia v West Indies | Bridgetown | 1954–55 |
| 659-8d | Australia v England | Sydney | 1946–47 |
| 658-8d | England v Australia | Nottingham | 1938 |
| 657-8d | Pakistan v West Indies | Bridgetown | 1957–58 |
| 656-8d | Australia v England | Manchester | 1964 |
| 654-5 | England v South Africa | Durban[2] | 1938–39 |
| 652-8d | West Indies v England | Lord's | 1973 |
| 652-7d | England v India | Madras | 1984–85 |
| 652 | Pakistan v India | Faisalabad | 1982–83 |
| 650-6d | Australia v West Indies | Bridgetown | 1964–65 |
| 645 | Australia v England | Brisbane[2] | 1946–47 |
| 644-7d | India v West Indies | Kanpur | 1978–79 |
| 644-8d | West Indies v India | Delhi | 1958–59 |
| 636 | England v Australia | Sydney | 1928–29 |
| 633-5d | England v India | Birmingham | 1979 |
| 631-8d | West Indies v India | Kingston | 1961–62 |
| 631 | West Indies v India | Delhi | 1948–49 |
| 629-6d | West Indies v India | Bombay[2] | 1948–49 |
| 629 | England v India | Lord's | 1974 |
| 627-9d | England v Australia | Manchester | 1934 |
| 624 | Pakistan v Australia | Adelaide | 1983–84 |
| 622-9d | South Africa v Australia | Durban[2] | 1969–70 |
| 620 | South Africa v Australia | Johannesburg[3] | 1966–67 |
| 619-6d | England v West Indies | Nottingham | 1957 |
| 619 | Australia v West Indies | Sydney | 1968–69 |
| 617 | Australia v Pakistan | Faisalabad | 1979–80 |
| 616 | West Indies v Australia | Adelaide | 1968–69 |
| 614-5d | West Indies v India | Calcutta | 1958–59 |
| 611 | England v Australia | Manchester | 1964 |
| 608-7d | Pakistan v England | Birmingham | 1971 |
| 608 | England v South Africa | Johannesburg[2] | 1948–49 |
| 606 | West Indies v England | Birmingham | 1984 |
| 604-6d | West Indies v India | Bombay[3] | 1974–75 |
| 604 | Australia v England | Melbourne | 1936–37 |
| 601-8d | Australia v England | Brisbane[2] | 1954–55 |
| 600-7d | Pakistan v England | Oval | 1974 |
| 600-9d | Australia v West Indies | Port-of-Spain | 1954–55 |
| 600 | Australia v England | Melbourne | 1924–25 |

*The highest totals by New Zealand and Sri Lanka are:*

| | | | |
|---|---|---|---:|
| 551-9d | New Zealand v England | Lord's | 1973 |
| 491-7d | Sri Lanka v England | Lord's | 1984 |

**BOTH TEAMS SCORING 600**

| | | |
|---|---|---:|
| Australia (656-8d) v England (611) | Manchester | 1964 |

# HIGHEST SECOND INNINGS TOTALS
*First innings in brackets*

| | | | | |
|---|---|---|---|---|
| 657-8d† | (106) | Pakistan v West Indies | Bridgetown | 1957–58 |
| 654-5 | (316) | England v South Africa | Durban[2] | 1938–39 |
| 620 | (199) | South Africa v Australia | Johannesburg[3] | 1966–67 |
| 616 | (276) | West Indies v Australia | Adelaide | 1968–69 |
| 583-4d | (186) | England v West Indies | Birmingham | 1957 |
| 582 | (354) | Australia v England | Adelaide | 1920–21 |
| 581 | (267) | Australia v England | Sydney | 1920–21 |
| 578 | (328) | Australia v South Africa | Melbourne | 1910–11 |
| 564-8 | (133) | West Indies v New Zealand | Bridgetown | 1971–72 |
| 564 | (200-9d) | Australia v England | Melbourne | 1936–37 |
| 554 | (198) | Australia v South Africa | Melbourne | 1931–32 |
| 551† | (208) | England v South Africa | Nottingham | 1947 |

†*After following on.*

# HIGHEST FOURTH INNINGS TOTALS

**TO WIN**

| | | | |
|---|---|---|---|
| 406-4 | India v West Indies | Port-of-Spain | 1975–76 |
| 404-3 | Australia v England | Leeds | 1948 |
| 362-7 | Australia v West Indies | Georgetown | 1977–78 |
| 348-5 | West Indies v New Zealand | Auckland | 1968–69 |
| 344-1 | West Indies v England | Lord's | 1984 |
| 342-8 | Australia v India | Perth | 1977–78 |
| 336-5 | Australia v South Africa | Durban[2] | 1949–50 |
| 332-7 | England v Australia | Melbourne | 1928–29 |
| 317-2 | West Indies v Pakistan | Georgetown | 1957–58 |
| 315-6 | Australia v England | Adelaide | 1901–02 |

| | | | | Runs set in 4th innings |
|---|---|---|---|---|
| **TO DRAW** | | | | |
| 654-5 | England v South Africa | Durban[2] | 1938–39 | 696 |
| 429-8 | India v England | Oval | 1979 | 438 |
| 423-7 | South Africa v England | Oval | 1947 | 451 |
| 408-5 | West Indies v England | Kingston | 1929–30 | 836 |
| 364-6 | India v Pakistan | Delhi | 1979–80 | 390 |
| 355-8 | India v West Indies | Bombay[2] | 1948–49 | 361 |
| 339-9 | Australia v West Indies | Adelaide | 1968–69 | 360 |
| 329-3 | Australia v England | Lord's | 1975 | 484 |
| 328-3 | Australia v England | Adelaide | 1970–71 | 469 |
| 326-5 | South Africa v Australia | Sydney | 1963–64 | 409 |
| 325-3 | India v West Indies | Calcutta | 1948–49 | 431 |
| 314-7 | England v Australia | Sydney | 1982–83 | 460 |
| 310-7 | England v Australia | Melbourne | 1946–47 | 551 |
| 308-4 | England v South Africa | Oval | 1965 | 399 |

| | | | | Losing Margin |
|---|---|---|---|---|
| **TO LOSE** | | | | |
| 445 | India v Australia | Adelaide | 1977–78 | 47 |
| 440 | New Zealand v England | Nottingham | 1973 | 38 |
| 417 | England v Australia | Melbourne | 1976–77 | 45 |
| 411 | England v Australia | Sydney | 1924–25 | 193 |
| 402 | Australia v England | Manchester | 1981 | 103 |
| 376 | India v England | Manchester | 1959 | 171 |
| 370 | England v Australia | Adelaide | 1920–21 | 119 |
| 363 | England v Australia | Adelaide | 1924–25 | 11 |
| 355 | India v Australia | Brisbane[2] | 1967–68 | 39 |
| 352 | West Indies v Australia | Sydney | 1968–69 | 382 |
| 345 | New Zealand v England | Nottingham | 1983 | 511 |
| 339 | Australia v South Africa | Adelaide | 1910–11 | 38 |
| 336 | Australia v England | Adelaide | 1928–29 | 12 |
| 335 | Australia v England | Nottingham | 1930 | 93 |
| 335 | South Africa v New Zealand | Cape Town | 1961–62 | 72 |

| | | | | Losing Margin |
|---|---|---|---|---|
| TO LOSE *continued* | | | | |
| 333 | Australia v England | Melbourne | 1894–95 | 94 |
| 327 | England v West Indies | Georgetown | 1929–30 | 289 |
| 326 | West Indies v Australia | Melbourne | 1975–76 | 165 |
| 324 | India v Australia | Brisbane[2] | 1977–78 | 16 |
| 323 | England v Australia | Melbourne | 1936–37 | 365 |
| 316 | England v West Indies | Kingston | 1953–54 | 140 |
| 313 | England v West Indies | Bridgetown | 1953–54 | 181 |
| 310 | Australia v Pakistan | Melbourne | 1978–79 | 71 |
| 304 | South Africa v England | Johannesburg[1] | 1913-14 | 91 |
| 301 | Pakistan v West Indies | Kingston | 1976-77 | 140 |

# HIGHEST MATCH AGGREGATES

## BOTH SIDES

| Runs | Wkts | | | | Days Played |
|---|---|---|---|---|---|
| 1981 | 35 | South Africa v England | Durban[2] | 1938–39 | 10† |
| 1815 | 34 | West Indies v England | Kingston | 1929–30 | 9‡ |
| 1764 | 39 | Australia v West Indies | Adelaide | 1968–69 | 5 |
| 1753 | 40 | Australia v England | Adelaide | 1920–21 | 6 |
| 1723 | 31 | England v Australia | Leeds | 1948 | 5 |
| 1661 | 36 | West Indies v Australia | Bridgetown | 1954–55 | 6 |
| 1646 | 40 | Australia v South Africa | Adelaide | 1910–11 | 6 |
| 1644 | 38 | Australia v West Indies | Sydney | 1968–69 | 6 |
| 1640 | 24 | West Indies v Australia | Bridgetown | 1964–65 | 6 |
| 1640 | 33 | Australia v Pakistan | Melbourne | 1972–73 | 5 |
| 1619 | 40 | Australia v England | Melbourne | 1924–25 | 7 |
| 1611 | 40 | Australia v England | Sydney | 1924–25 | 7 |
| 1601 | 29 | England v Australia | Lord's | 1930 | 4 |
| 1585 | 31 | Pakistan v New Zealand | Karachi | 1976–77 | 5 |
| 1562 | 37 | Australia v England | Melbourne | 1946–47 | 6 |
| 1554 | 35 | Australia v England | Melbourne | 1928–29 | 8 |
| 1541 | 35 | Australia v England | Sydney | 1903–04 | 6 |
| 1528 | 24 | West Indies v England | Port-of-Spain | 1953–54 | 6 |
| 1514 | 40 | Australia v England | Sydney | 1894–95 | 6 |
| 1507 | 28 | England v West Indies | Oval | 1976 | 5 |
| 1502 | 29 | Australia v England | Adelaide | 1946–47 | 6 |

†*No play on one day*   ‡*No play on two days*

## ONE SIDE

| Runs | Wkts | | | |
|---|---|---|---|---|
| 1121 | 19 | England v West Indies | Kingston | 1929–30 |
| 1028 | 20 | Australia v England | Oval | 1934 |
| 1013 | 18 | Australia v West Indies | Sydney | 1968–69 |
| 1011 | 20 | South Africa v England | Durban[2] | 1938–39 |

# LOWEST INNINGS TOTALS

| | | | |
|---|---|---|---|
| 26 | New Zealand v England | Auckland | 1954–55 |
| 30 | South Africa v England | Port Elizabeth | 1895–96 |
| 30 | South Africa v England | Birmingham | 1924 |
| 35 | South Africa v England | Cape Town | 1898–99 |
| 36 | Australia v England | Birmingham | 1902 |
| 36 | South Africa v Australia | Melbourne | 1931–32 |
| 42 | Australia v England | Sydney | 1887–88 |
| 42 | New Zealand v Australia | Wellington | 1945–46 |
| 42† | India v England | Lord's | 1974 |
| 43 | South Africa v England | Cape Town | 1888–89 |
| 44 | Australia v England | Oval | 1896 |
| 45 | England v Australia | Sydney | 1886–87 |

| 45 | South Africa v Australia | Melbourne | 1931–32 |
|----|----|----|----|
| 47 | South Africa v England | Cape Town | 1888–89 |
| 47 | New Zealand v England | Lord's | 1958 |
| 52 | England v Australia | Oval | 1948 |
| 53 | England v Australia | Lord's | 1888 |
| 53 | Australia v England | Lord's | 1896 |
| 54 | New Zealand v Australia | Wellington | 1945–46 |
| 58 | South Africa v England | Lord's | 1912 |
| 58† | Australia v England | Brisbane² | 1936–37 |
| 58 | India v Australia | Brisbane² | 1947–48 |
| 58 | India v England | Manchester | 1952 |
| 60 | Australia v England | Lord's | 1888 |

†*One batsman absent hurt/ill.*

*The lowest innings totals by Pakistan, West Indies and Sri Lanka are:*

| 62 | Pakistan v Australia | Perth | 1981–82 |
|----|----|----|----|
| 76 | West Indies v Pakistan | Dacca | 1958–59 |
| 93 | Sri Lanka v New Zealand | Wellington | 1982–83 |

*The following innings closed at a low total:*

| 32-7d | Australia v England | Brisbane² | 1950–51 |
|----|----|----|----|
| 35-8 | Australia v England | Manchester | 1953 |
| 48-8 | New Zealand v England | Christchurch | 1965–66 |
| 51-6d | West Indies v England | Bridgetown | 1934–35 |

DISMISSED FOR UNDER 100 IN BOTH INNINGS

| 42 & 82 | Australia v England | Sydney | 1887–88 |
|----|----|----|----|
| 53 & 62 | England v Australia | Lord's | 1888 |
| 81 & 70 | Australia v England | Manchester | 1888 |
| 47 & 43 | South Africa v England | Cape Town | 1888–89 |
| 97 & 83 | South Africa v England | Cape Town | 1891–92 |
| 65 & 72 | England v Australia | Sydney | 1894–95 |
| 93 & 30 | South Africa v England | Port Elizabeth | 1895–96 |
| 95 & 93 | South Africa v England | Oval | 1912 |
| 36 & 45 | South Africa v Australia | Melbourne | 1931–32 |
| 42 & 54 | New Zealand v Australia | Wellington | 1945–46 |
| 58 & 98 | India v Australia | Brisbane² | 1947–48 |
| 58 & 82 | India v England | Manchester | 1952 |
| 89 & 86 | West Indies v England | Oval | 1957 |
| 47 & 74 | New Zealand v England | Lord's | 1958 |
| 82 & 93 | England v New Zealand | Christchurch | 1983–84 |

# LOWEST MATCH AGGREGATES
*Completed match*

| Runs | Wkts | | | | Days Played |
|----|----|----|----|----|----|
| 234 | 29 | Australia v South Africa | Melbourne | 1931–32 | 3† |
| 291 | 40 | England v Australia | Lord's | 1888 | 2 |
| 295 | 28 | New Zealand v Australia | Wellington | 1945–46 | 2 |
| 309 | 29 | West Indies v England | Bridgetown | 1934–35 | 3 |
| 323 | 30 | England v Australia | Manchester | 1888 | 2 |
| 363 | 40 | England v Australia | Oval | 1882 | 2 |
| 374 | 40 | Australia v England | Sydney | 1887–88 | 5‡ |
| 378 | 30 | England v South Africa | Oval | 1912 | 2 |
| 382 | 30 | South Africa v England | Cape Town | 1888–89 | 2 |
| 389 | 38 | England v Australia | Oval | 1890 | 2 |
| 390 | 30 | England v New Zealand | Lord's | 1958 | 3 |
| 392 | 40 | England v Australia | Oval | 1896 | 3 |

†*No play on one day*    ‡*No play on two days*

# LARGEST MARGINS OF VICTORY

| Inns and 579 runs | England v Australia | Oval | 1938 |
|----|----|----|----|
| Inns and 336 runs | West Indies v India | Calcutta | 1958–59 |

| | | | |
|---|---|---|---|
| Inns and 332 runs | Australia v England | Brisbane[2] | 1946–47 |
| Inns and 285 runs | England v India | Lord's | 1974 |
| Inns and 259 runs | Australia v South Africa | Port Elizabeth | 1949–50 |
| Inns and 237 runs | England v West Indies | Oval | 1957 |
| Inns and 230 runs | England v Australia | Adelaide | 1891–92 |
| Inns and 226 runs | Australia v India | Brisbane[2] | 1947–48 |
| Inns and 226 runs | West Indies v England | Lord's | 1973 |
| Inns and 225 runs | England v Australia | Melbourne | 1911–12 |
| Inns and 217 runs | England v Australia | Oval | 1886 |
| Inns and 217 runs | Australia v West Indies | Brisbane[1] | 1930–31 |
| Inns and 215 runs | England v New Zealand | Auckland | 1962–63 |
| Inns and 207 runs | England v India | Manchester | 1952 |
| Inns and 202 runs | England v South Africa | Cape Town | 1888–89 |
| Inns and 200 runs | Australia v England | Melbourne | 1936–37 |
| 675 runs | England v Australia | Brisbane[1] | 1928–29 |
| 562 runs | Australia v England | Oval | 1934 |
| 530 runs | Australia v South Africa | Melbourne | 1910–11 |
| 425 runs | West Indies v England | Manchester | 1976 |
| 409 runs | Australia v England | Lord's | 1948 |
| 408 runs | West Indies v Australia | Adelaide | 1979–80 |
| 382 runs | Australia v England | Adelaide | 1894–95 |
| 382 runs | Australia v West Indies | Sydney | 1968–69 |
| 377 runs | Australia v England | Sydney | 1920–21 |
| 365 runs | Australia v England | Melbourne | 1936–37 |
| 348 runs | Australia v Pakistan | Melbourne | 1976–77 |
| 338 runs | England v Australia | Adelaide | 1932–33 |
| 326 runs | West Indies v England | Lord's | 1950 |
| 323 runs | South Africa v Australia | Port Elizabeth | 1969–70 |
| 322 runs | England v Australia | Brisbane[2] | 1936–37 |
| 312 runs | England v South Africa | Cape Town | 1956–57 |
| 308 runs | Australia v England | Melbourne | 1907–08 |
| 307 runs | Australia v England | Sydney | 1924–25 |
| 307 runs | South Africa v Australia | Johannesburg[3] | 1969–70 |

# VICTORY LOSING FEWEST WICKETS

TWO WICKETS

| | | |
|---|---|---|
| England (531-2d) v South Africa (273 & 240) | Lord's | 1924 |
| England (267-2d) v New Zealand (67 & 129) | Leeds | 1958 |
| England (459-2d) v India (165 & 216) | Birmingham | 1974 |

# RESULTS BY NARROW MARGINS

TIE

| | | |
|---|---|---|
| Australia v West Indies | Brisbane[2] | 1960–61 |

WON BY ONE WICKET

| | | 10th Wicket Partnership | |
|---|---|---|---|
| England v Australia | Oval | 15* | 1902 |
| South Africa v England | Johannesburg[1] | 48* | 1905–06 |
| England v Australia | Melbourne | 39* | 1907–08 |
| England v South Africa | Cape Town | 5* | 1922–23 |
| Australia v West Indies | Melbourne | 38* | 1951–52 |
| New Zealand v West Indies | Dunedin | 4* | 1979–80 |
| | | (*unbroken) | |

WON BY TWO WICKETS

| | | |
|---|---|---|
| England v Australia | Oval | 1890 |
| Australia v England | Sydney | 1907–08 |
| †England v South Africa | Durban[2] | 1948–49 |
| Australia v West Indies | Melbourne | 1960–61 |
| India v Australia | Bombay[2] | 1964–65 |
| Australia v India | Perth | 1977–78 |
| West Indies v England | Nottingham | 1980 |
| New Zealand v Pakistan | Dunedin | 1984–85 |

†England won by a leg bye off the last possible ball

LESS THAN TWENTY RUNS

| | | | |
|---|---|---|---|
| 3 | Australia v England | Manchester | 1902 |
| 3 | England v Australia | Melbourne | 1982–83 |
| 6 | Australia v England | Sydney | 1884–85 |
| 7 | Australia v England | Oval | 1882 |
| 10 | England v Australia | Sydney | 1894–95 |
| 11 | Australia v England | Adelaide | 1924–25 |
| 12 | England v Australia | Adelaide | 1928–29 |
| 13 | England v Australia | Sydney | 1886–87 |
| 16 | Australia v India | Brisbane[2] | 1977–78 |
| 17 | South Africa v England | Johannesburg[3] | 1956–57 |
| 18 | England v Australia | Leeds | 1981 |
| 19 | South Africa v England | Johannesburg[1] | 1909–10 |

*At Port-of-Spain in 1934–35, West Indies took England's last second innings wicket with the fifth ball of the last possible over to win by 217 runs.*

DRAWS

| | Total | Target | Opponents | | |
|---|---|---|---|---|---|
| India | 355-8 | 361 | West Indies | Bombay[2] | 1948–49 |
| England | 228-9 | 234 | West Indies | Lord's | 1963 |
| Australia | 339-9 | 360 | West Indies | Adelaide | 1968–69 |
| Australia | 238-8 | 246 | England | Melbourne | 1974–75 |

# VICTORY AFTER FOLLOWING-ON

| | | |
|---|---|---|
| England (325 & 437) beat Australia (586 & 166) by 10 runs | Sydney | 1894–95 |
| England (174 & 356) beat Australia (401-9d & 111) by 18 runs | Leeds | 1981 |

# LONGEST MATCHES

| | | | |
|---|---|---|---|
| 10 days | South Africa v England | Durban[2] | 1938–39 |
| 9 days | West Indies v England | Kingston | 1929–30 |
| 8 days | Australia v England | Melbourne | 1928–29 |

# MATCHES COMPLETED IN TWO DAYS

| | | |
|---|---|---|
| England (101 & 77) v Australia (63 & 122) | Oval | 1882 |
| England (53 & 62) v Australia (116 & 60) | Lord's | 1888 |
| England (317) v Australia (80 & 100) | Oval | 1888 |
| England (172) v Australia (81 & 70) | Manchester | 1888 |
| South Africa (84 & 129) v England (148 & 67-2) | Port Elizabeth | 1888–89 |
| South Africa (47 & 43) v England (292) | Cape Town | 1888–89 |
| England (100 & 95-8) v Australia (92 & 102) | Oval | 1890 |
| South Africa (93 & 30) v England (185 & 226) | Port Elizabeth | 1895–96 |
| South Africa (115 & 117) v England (265) | Cape Town | 1895–96 |
| England (176 & 14-0) v South Africa (95 & 93) | Oval | 1912 |
| Australia (448) v South Africa (265 & 95) | Manchester | 1912 |
| England (112 & 147) v Australia (232 & 30-0) | Nottingham | 1921 |
| Australia (328-8d) v West Indies (99 & 107) | Melbourne | 1930–31 |
| South Africa (157 & 98) v Australia (439) | Johannesburg[1] | 1935–36 |
| New Zealand (42 & 54) v Australia (199-8d) | Wellington | 1945–46 |

# COMPLETE SIDE DISMISSED TWICE IN A DAY

| | | Day | |
|---|---|---|---|
| India (58 & 82) v England | Manchester | 3rd | 1952 |

# MOST RUNS IN ONE DAY

BY ONE TEAM

|  |  |  | Day |  |
|---|---|---|---|---|
| 503-2 | England v South Africa | Lord's | 2nd | 1924 |
| 494-6 | Australia v South Africa | Sydney | 1st | 1910–11 |
| 475-2 | Australia v England | Oval | 1st | 1934 |
| 471-8 | England v India | Oval | 1st | 1936 |
| 458-3 | Australia v England | Leeds | 1st | 1930 |
| 455-1 | Australia v England | Leeds | 2nd | 1934 |
| 450-10 | Australia v South Africa | Johannesburg[1] | 1st | 1921–22 |

BY BOTH TEAMS

| 588-6 | England (398-6) v India (190-0) | Manchester | 2nd | 1936 |
|---|---|---|---|---|
| 522-2 | England (503-2) v South Africa (19-0) | Lord's | 2nd | 1924 |
| 508-8 | England (221-2) v South Africa (287-6) | Oval | 3rd | 1935 |
| 496-4 | England (437-4) v Pakistan (59-0) | Nottingham | 2nd | 1954 |
| 491-7 | New Zealand (29-1 & 195-2) v England (267-4d) | Leeds | 3rd | 1949 |
| 473-4 | England (264-1) v South Africa (209-3) | Oval | 3rd | 1929 |
| 471-9 | England (244-2) v Australia (227-7) | Oval | 3rd | 1921 |
| 469-7 | England (366-3) v West Indies (103-4) | Oval | 3rd | 1939 |
| 464-11 | Australia (448) v South Africa (16-1) | Manchester | 1st | 1912 |
| 458-12 | Australia (155-5) v West Indies (303-7) | Sydney | 5th | 1968–69 |

# FEWEST RUNS IN A FULL DAY'S PLAY

|  |  |  | Day |  |
|---|---|---|---|---|
| 95 | Australia (80) v Pakistan (15-2) | Karachi | 1st | 1956–57 |
| 104 | Pakistan (104-5) v Australia | Karachi | 4th | 1959–60 |
| 106 | England (92-2 to 198 out) v Australia | Brisbane[2] | 4th | 1958–59 |
| 112 | Australia (138-6 to 187 out) v Pakistan (63-1) | Karachi | 4th | 1956–57 |
| 117 | India (117-5) v Australia | Madras[2] | 1st | 1956–57 |
| 117 | New Zealand (6-0 to 123-4) v Sri Lanka | Colombo (SSC) | 5th | 1983–84 |

*In England:*
| 151 | England (175-2 to 289 out) v New Zealand (37-7) | Lord's | 3rd | 1978 |
|---|---|---|---|---|

# MOST WICKETS IN ONE DAY

| 27 | England (18-3 to 53 out & 62) v Australia (60) | 2nd day | Lord's | 1888 |
|---|---|---|---|---|
| 25 | Australia (112 & 48-5) v England (61) | 1st day | Melbourne | 1901–02 |

# MOST WICKETS BEFORE LUNCH

| 18 | Australia (32-2 to 81 out & 70) v England | 2nd day | Manchester | 1888 |
|---|---|---|---|---|

# NO WICKETS IN A FULL DAY'S PLAY

| England (283-0) v Australia | 3rd day | Melbourne | 1924–25 |
|---|---|---|---|
| West Indies (187-6 to 494-6) v Australia | 4th day | Bridgetown | 1954–55 |
| India (234-0) v New Zealand | 1st day | Madras[2] | 1955–56 |
| West Indies (147-1 to 504-1) v Pakistan | 3rd day | Kingston | 1957–58 |
| West Indies (279-3 to 486-3) v England | 5th day | Bridgetown | 1959–60† |
| Australia (263-0) v West Indies | 1st day | Bridgetown | 1964–65 |
| West Indies (310-7 to 365-7d) v New Zealand (163-0) | 3rd day | Georgetown | 1971–72 |
| India (70-1 to 361-1d) v West Indies (15-0) | 4th day | Calcutta | 1978–79 |
| India (178-2 to 395-2) v England | 2nd day | Madras[1] | 1981–82 |

†*G.St A. Sobers (226) and F.M.M. Worrell (197\*) added 399 for the fourth wicket in the longest partnership in Test cricket (579 minutes) and remain the only pair of batsmen to bat throughout two consecutive days of Test cricket, although the final hour of the fourth day was lost to rain and a rest day intervened.*

*The following pairs of batsmen have batted throughout one full day's play in the above matches: J.B. Hobbs and H. Sutcliffe (1924–25), D.St E. Atkinson and C.C. Depeiza (1954–55), M.H. Mankad and Pankaj Roy (1955–56), C.C. Hunte and G.St A. Sobers (1957–58), W.M. Lawry and R.B. Simpson (1964–65), and G.R. Viswanath and Yashpal Sharma-(1981–82).*

## BATSMEN'S MATCHES
*Over 60 runs per wicket*

| Runs/Wkt | Runs-Wkts | | | |
|---|---|---|---|---|
| 109.30 | (1093-10) | India v New Zealand | Delhi | 1955–56 |
| 99.40 | (994-10) | West Indies v New Zealand | Georgetown | 1971–72 |
| 83.25 | (999-12) | Pakistan v Australia | Faisalabad | 1979–80 |
| 73.37 | (1174-16) | Pakistan v India | Faisalabad | 1984–85 |
| 73.06 | (1096-15) | India v West Indies | Kanpur | 1978–79 |
| 70.61 | (1271-18) | England v Australia | Manchester | 1964 |
| 68.33 | (1640-24) | West Indies v Australia | Bridgetown | 1964–65 |
| 66.95 | (1406-21) | West Indies v Pakistan | Kingston | 1957–58 |
| 65.35 | (1307-20) | England v Australia | Manchester | 1934 |
| 65.00 | (1235-19) | India v West Indies | Bombay[2] | 1948–49 |
| 64.75 | (1036-16) | India v New Zealand | Hyderabad | 1955–56 |
| 63.66 | (1528-24) | West Indies v England | Port-of-Spain | 1953–54 |
| 62.33 | (1496-24) | England v Australia | Nottingham | 1938 |
| 62.00 | (1116-18) | West Indies v England | Bridgetown | 1959–60 |
| 61.52 | (1046-17) | India v Pakistan | Madras[2] | 1960–61 |
| 60.94 | (1158-19) | India v England | Kanpur | 1984–85 |
| 60.62 | (1455-24) | New Zealand v Australia | Wellington | 1973–74 |
| 60.57 | (1272-21) | Pakistan v India | Faisalabad | 1978–79 |

## HIGHEST SCORES FOR EACH BATTING POSITION

| No. | | | | | |
|---|---|---|---|---|---|
| 1 | 364 | L. Hutton | England v Australia | Oval | 1938 |
| 2 | 325 | A. Sandham | England v West Indies | Kingston | 1929–30 |
| 3 | 365* | G.St A. Sobers | West Indies v Pakistan | Kingston | 1957–58 |
| 4 | 307 | R.M. Cowper | Australia v England | Melbourne | 1965–66 |
| 5 | 304 | D.G. Bradman | Australia v England | Leeds | 1934 |
| 6 | 250 | K.D. Walters | Australia v New Zealand | Christchurch | 1976–77 |
| 7 | 270 | D.G. Bradman | Australia v England | Melbourne | 1936–37 |
| 8 | 209 | Imtiaz Ahmed | Pakistan v New Zealand | Lahore[1] | 1955–56 |
| 9 | 160 | C. Hill | Australia v England | Adelaide | 1907–08 |
| 10 | 117 | W.W. Read | England v Australia | Oval | 1884 |
| 11 | 68* | R.O. Collinge | New Zealand v Pakistan | Auckland | 1972–73 |

## HIGHEST SCORE AT THE FALL OF EACH WICKET

| 1st | 413 | India (537-3d) v New Zealand | Madras[2] | 1955–56 |
|---|---|---|---|---|
| 2nd | 533 | West Indies (790-3d) v Pakistan | Kingston | 1957–58 |
| 3rd | 602 | West Indies (790-3d) v Pakistan | Kingston | 1957–58 |
| 4th | 667 | England (849) v West Indies | Kingston | 1929–30 |
| 5th | 720 | England (849) v West Indies | Kingston | 1929–30 |
| 6th | 770 | England (903-7d) v Australia | Oval | 1938 |
| 7th | 876 | England (903-7d) v Australia | Oval | 1938 |
| 8th | 813 | England (849) v West Indies | Kingston | 1929–30 |
| 9th | 821 | England (849) v West Indies | Kingston | 1929–30 |
| 10th | 849 | England (849) v West Indies | Kingston | 1929–30 |

## LOWEST SCORE AT THE FALL OF EACH WICKET

| 1st | 0 | | | |
|---|---|---|---|---|
| 2nd | 0 | | | |
| 3rd | 0 | ⎰ Australia (32-7d) v England | Brisbane[2] | 1950–51 |
| | | ⎱ India (165) v England | Leeds | 1952 |
| 4th | 0 | India (165) v England | Leeds | 1952 |

| 5th | 6 | India (98) v England | Oval | 1952 |
| 6th | 7 | Australia (70) v England | Manchester | 1888 |
| 7th | 14 | Australia (44) v England | Oval | 1896 |
| 8th | 19 | Australia (44) v England | Oval | 1896 |
| 9th | 25 | Australia (44) v England | Oval | 1896 |
| 10th | 26 | New Zealand (26) v England | Auckland | 1954–55 |

# MOST HUNDREDS IN AN INNINGS

| 5 | Australia (758-8d) v West Indies | Kingston | 1954–55 |
| 4 | England (658-8d) v Australia | Nottingham | 1938 |
| 4 | West Indies (631) v India | Delhi | 1948–49 |
| 4 | Pakistan (652) v India | Faisalabad | 1982–83 |
| 4 | West Indies (550) v India | St John's | 1982–83 |

*The record number of fifties in a Test innings is seven by England (627-9d) v Australia at Manchester in 1934.*

# MOST HUNDREDS IN A MATCH (BOTH TEAMS)

| 7 | England (4) v Australia (3) | Nottingham | 1938 |
| 7 | West Indies (2) v Australia (5) | Kingston | 1954–55 |

*The record number of fifties in a Test match is 17 by Australia (10) and West Indies (7) at Adelaide in 1968–69.*

# MOST HUNDREDS IN A SERIES (ONE TEAM)

|  |  | Venue | Tests |  |
| --- | --- | --- | --- | --- |
| 12 | Australia v West Indies | West Indies | 5 | 1954–55 |
| 12 | Pakistan v India | Pakistan | 6 | 1982–83 |
| 11 | England v South Africa | South Africa | 5 | 1938–39 |
| 11 | West Indies v India | India | 5 | 1948–49 |
| 11 | Australia v South Africa | South Africa | 5 | 1949–50 |
| 11 | India v West Indies | India | 6 | 1978–79 |

# MOST HUNDREDS IN A SERIES (BOTH TEAMS)

|  |  | Venue | Tests |  |
| --- | --- | --- | --- | --- |
| 21 | West Indies (9) v Australia (12) | West Indies | 5 | 1954–55 |
| 17 | Australia (9) v England (8) | Australia | 5 | 1928–29 |
| 17 | South Africa (6) v England (11) | South Africa | 5 | 1938–39 |
| 17 | Pakistan (12) v India (5) | Pakistan | 6 | 1982–83 |
| 16 | India (5) v West Indies (11) | India | 5 | 1948–49 |
| 16 | Australia (10) v West Indies (6) | Australia | 5 | 1968–69 |
| 16 | Australia (10) v West Indies (6) | Australia | 6 | 1975–76 |
| 15 | Australia (10) v England (5) | Australia | 5 | 1946–47 |

# TEAM UNCHANGED THROUGHOUT A SERIES

| Tests |  | Venue |  |
| --- | --- | --- | --- |
| 5 | England v Australia | Australia | 1884–85 |
| 5 | South Africa v England | South Africa | 1905–06 |
| 4 | England v Australia | Australia | 1881–82 |
| 3 | Australia v England | England | 1884 |
| 3 | Australia v England | England | 1893 |
| 3 | Pakistan v New Zealand | Pakistan | 1964–65 |
| 3 | India v England | England | 1971 |
| 3 | Australia v New Zealand | New Zealand | 1981–82 |

# MOST PLAYERS ENGAGED BY ONE SIDE IN A SERIES

|  |  | Venue |  |
|---|---|---|---|
| 30 in 5 Tests | England v Australia | England | 1921 |
| 28 in 5 Tests | Australia v England | Australia | 1884–85 |
| 27 in 4 Tests | West Indies v England | West Indies | 1929–30 |
| 26 in 5 Tests | India v Pakistan | India | 1952–53 |
| 25 in 4 Tests | England v West Indies | England | 1950 |
| 25 in 5 Tests | England v Australia | England | 1909 |
| 25 in 5 Tests | England v South Africa | England | 1935 |
| 25 in 5 Tests | England v South Africa | England | 1955 |

*South Africa used 20 players in the 3-match rubber of 1895–96 against England in South Africa.*

# WINNING EVERY TEST IN A SERIES
*Minimum: 4 matches*

|  |  | Venue | Tests |
|---|---|---|---|
| 1920–21 | Australia v England | Australia | 5 |
| 1931–32 | Australia v South Africa | Australia | 5 |
| 1959 | England v India | England | 5 |
| 1961–62 | West Indies v India | West Indies | 5 |
| 1967–68 | Australia v India | Australia | 4 |
| 1969–70 | South Africa v Australia | South Africa | 4 |
| 1984 | West Indies v England | England | 5 |

*The following countries won 6-match series in Australia by 5 Tests to one: Australia (v West Indies 1975–76); England (v Australia 1978–79).*

# MOST CONSECUTIVE WINS

| 11 | West Indies | Bridgetown 1983–84 to Adelaide 1984–85 |
|---|---|---|
| 8 | Australia | Sydney 1920–21 to Leeds 1921 |
| 7 | England | Melbourne 1884–85 to Sydney 1887–88 |
| 7 | England | Lord's 1928 to Adelaide 1928–29 |
| 6 | England | Oval 1888 to Oval 1890 |
| 6 | England | Leeds 1957 to Manchester 1958 |
| 6 | West Indies | Port-of-Spain 1961–62 to Manchester 1963 |

# MOST CONSECUTIVE MATCHES WITHOUT DEFEAT

| 27 | West Indies | Sydney 1981–82 to Melbourne 1984–85 |
|---|---|---|
| 26 | England | Lord's 1968 to Manchester 1971 |
| 25 | Australia | Wellington 1945–46 to Adelaide 1950–51 |
| 18 | England | Christchurch 1958–59 to Birmingham 1961 |
| 17 | Australia | Madras[2] 1956–57 to Delhi 1959–60 |
| 16 | Australia | Sydney 1920–21 to Adelaide 1924–25 |
| 15 | England | Melbourne 1911–12 to Port Elizabeth 1913–14 |
| 15 | Pakistan | Wellington 1972–73 to Adelaide 1976–77 |
| 15 | India | Lord's 1979 to Calcutta 1979–80 |
| 13 | India | Port-of-Spain 1952–53 to Madras[2] 1955–56 |
| 13 | Australia | Oval 1972 to Wellington 1973–74 |
| 12 | England | Oval 1938 to Oval 1946 |
| 12 | Pakistan | Manchester 1954 to Bridgetown 1957–58 |
| 12 | England | Oval 1966 to Georgetown 1967–68 |
| 12 | Pakistan | Karachi 1982–83 to Nagpur 1983–84 |

# MOST CONSECUTIVE DEFEATS

| 8 | South Africa | Port Elizabeth 1888–89 to Cape Town 1898–99 (*their first 8 Tests*) |
|---|---|---|
| 8 | England | Sydney 1920–21 to Leeds 1921 |
| 7 | Australia | Melbourne 1884–85 to Sydney 1887–88 |
| 7 | England | Lord's 1950 to Adelaide 1950–51 |
| 7 | India | Leeds 1967 to Sydney 1967–68 |

| 6 | South Africa | Melbourne 1910–11 to Lord's 1912 |
| 6 | New Zealand | Johannesburg[2] 1953–54 to Lahore[1] 1955–56 |
| 6 | India | Nottingham 1959 to Delhi 1959–60 |
| 6 | Australia | Bridgetown 1983–84 to Adelaide 1984–85 |

# MOST CONSECUTIVE MATCHES WITHOUT VICTORY

| 44 | New Zealand | Christchurch 1929–30 to Wellington 1955–56 |
| 31 | India | Bangalore 1981–82 to Faisalabad 1984–85 |
| 28 | South Africa | Leeds 1935 to Port Elizabeth 1949–50 |
| 24 | India | Lord's 1932 to Kanpur 1951–52 |
| 23 | New Zealand | Auckland 1962–63 to Dunedin 1967–68 |
| 22 | Pakistan | Lahore[1] 1958–59 to Christchurch 1964–65 |
| 20 | West Indies | Wellington 1968–69 to Port-of-Spain 1972–73 |
| 18 | New Zealand | Dacca 1969–70 to Wellington 1973–74 |
| 16 | South Africa | Melbourne 1910–11 to Cape Town 1921–22 |
| 16 | Pakistan | Lord's 1967 to Wellington 1972–73 |
| 14 | India | Madras[2] 1956–57 to Delhi 1959–60 |
| 13 | India | Madras[1] 1952–53 to Hyderabad 1955–56 |
| 13 | England | Wellington 1983–84 to Bombay[3] 1984–85 |
| 12 | South Africa | Cape Town 1922–23 to Durban[2] 1927–28 |
| 12 | England | Leeds 1963 to Oval 1964 |
| 12 | England | Nottingham 1980 to Lord's 1981 |
| 12 | Sri Lanka | Colombo (SO) 1981–82 to Lord's 1984 |

# MOST CONSECUTIVE DRAWS

| 10 | West Indies | Georgetown 1970–71 to Bridgetown 1972–73 |
| 9 | India | Port-of-Spain 1952–53 to Hyderabad 1955–56 |
| 9 | India | Calcutta 1959–60 to Delhi 1961–62 |

# DRAWING EVERY TEST IN A FIVE-MATCH SERIES

| 1954–55 | Pakistan v India |
| 1960–61 | India v Pakistan |
| 1963–64 | India v England |
| 1971–72 | West Indies v New Zealand |

# ELEVEN BATSMEN REACHING DOUBLE FIGURES IN AN INNINGS

| | | *Venue* | *Lowest Score* |
|---|---|---|---|
| 1894–95 | England (475) v Australia | Melbourne | 11 |
| 1905–06 | South Africa (385) v England | Johannesburg[1] | 10 |
| 1928–29 | England (636) v Australia | Sydney | 11 |
| 1931–32 | South Africa (358) v Australia | Melbourne | 10* |
| 1947–48 | Australia (575-9d) v India | Melbourne | 11 |
| 1952–53 | India (397) v Pakistan | Calcutta | 11 |
| 1967–68 | India (359) v New Zealand | Dunedin | 12 |
| 1976–77 | India (524-9d) v New Zealand | Kanpur | 10* |

# NO BATSMAN REACHING DOUBLE FIGURES IN A COMPLETED INNINGS

| South Africa (30 – highest score 7) v England | Birmingham | 1924 |

# ONLY FOUR BOWLERS IN AN INNINGS OF OVER 400 RUNS

| | *Opponents* | | |
|---|---|---|---|
| Australia | England (403-8d) | Oval | 1921 |

| | | | |
|---|---|---|---|
| South Africa | England (421-8) | Oval | 1924 |
| New Zealand | England (482) | Oval | 1949 |
| England | Australia (426) | Sydney | 1950–51 |
| India | England (419-9d) | Lord's | 1979 |
| India | Australia (528) | Adelaide | 1980–81 |
| Australia | England (404) | Manchester | 1981 |
| England | India (428) | Bangalore | 1981–82 |
| Sri Lanka | Pakistan (500-7d) | Lahore[2] | 1981–82 |
| Pakistan | Australia (454-6d) | Sydney | 1983–84 |
| Australia | West Indies (468-8d) | Port-of-Spain | 1983–84 |
| Australia | West Indies (498) | St John's | 1983–84 |
| Australia | West Indies (416) | Perth | 1984–85 |
| Australia | England (456) | Nottingham | 1985 |

# ELEVEN BOWLERS IN AN INNINGS

| | | | |
|---|---|---|---|
| England | Australia (551) | Oval | 1884 |
| Australia | Pakistan (382-2) | Faisalabad | 1979–80 |

# TWENTY BOWLERS IN A MATCH

| | | |
|---|---|---|
| South Africa (501-7d, 346) v England (442, 15-0) | Cape Town | 1964–65 |

# EXTRAS BEING HIGHEST SCORER IN A COMPLETED INNINGS

| | Total | Highest Score | Extras | Opponents | | |
|---|---|---|---|---|---|---|
| South Africa | 58 | 13 | 17 | England | Lord's | 1912 |
| South Africa | 30 | 7 | 11 | England | Birmingham | 1924 |
| New Zealand | 97 | 19 | 20 | England | Nottingham | 1973 |
| England | 126 | 24 | 25 | West Indies | Manchester | 1976 |
| England | 227 | 33 | 46 | Pakistan | Lord's | 1982 |
| Australia | 200 | 29 | 36 | West Indies | St John's | 1983–84 |

# MOST EXTRAS IN AN INNINGS

| | | | |
|---|---|---|---|
| 68 | (B 29, LB 11, NB 28) Pakistan (291) v West Indies | Bridgetown | 1976–77 |

**MOST BYES**

| | | | |
|---|---|---|---|
| 37 | Australia (327) v England | Oval | 1934 |

**MOST LEG BYES**

| | | | |
|---|---|---|---|
| 30 | West Indies (411-5d) v England | Manchester | 1976 |

**MOST WIDES**

| | | | |
|---|---|---|---|
| 13 | England (227) v Pakistan | Lord's | 1982 |

**MOST NO BALLS** (Off which no runs were scored by batsmen)

| | | | |
|---|---|---|---|
| 35 | West Indies (596-8d) v England | Bridgetown | 1973–74 |
| 35 | England (309) v Australia | Brisbane[2] | 1982–83 |

# MOST EXTRAS IN A MATCH

| | | | |
|---|---|---|---|
| 173 | (B 37, LB 31, W 2, NB 103) West Indies v Pakistan | Bridgetown | 1976–77 |

*The highest total without an extra is Pakistan's 328 v India at Lahore in 1954–55.*

# UNUSUAL DISMISSALS

### HANDLED THE BALL

| | | | |
|---|---|---|---|
| W.R. Endean (3) | SA v E | Cape Town | 1956–57 |
| A.M.J. Hilditch (29) | A v P | Perth | 1978–79 |
| Mohsin Khan (58) | P v A | Karachi | 1982–83 |
| D.L. Haynes (55) | WI v I | Bombay[3] | 1983–84 |

### HIT THE BALL TWICE

No instance

### OBSTRUCTING THE FIELD

| | | | |
|---|---|---|---|
| L. Hutton (27) | E v SA | Oval | 1951 |

### RUN OUT BY THE BOWLER (while backing up before the ball had been bowled)

| | | | |
|---|---|---|---|
| W.A. Brown (18) by M.H. Mankad | A v I | Sydney | 1947–48 |
| I.R. Redpath (9) by C.C. Griffith | A v WI | Adelaide | 1968–69 |
| D.W. Randall (13) by E.J. Chatfield | E v NZ | Christchurch | 1977–78 |
| Sikander Bakht (0) by A.G. Hurst | P v A | Perth | 1978–79 |

### STUMPED BY A SUBSTITUTE

| | | | |
|---|---|---|---|
| S.J. Snooke by N.C. Tufnell (sub for H. Strudwick) | SA v E | Durban[1] | 1909–10 |
| Pervez Sajjad by B.E. Congdon (sub for A.E. Dick) | P v NZ | Lahore[2] | 1964–65 |

# SIMILARITY OF DISMISSAL

### TEN BATSMEN CAUGHT IN AN INNINGS

| | | |
|---|---|---|
| Australia v England | Melbourne | 1903–04 |
| South Africa v Australia | Melbourne | 1931–32 |
| England v South Africa | Durban[2] | 1948–49 |
| New Zealand v England | Leeds | 1949 |
| England v Pakistan | Oval | 1954 |
| England v Australia | Melbourne | 1958–59 |
| West Indies v Australia | Sydney | 1960–61 |
| New Zealand v India | Wellington | 1967–68 |
| New Zealand v West Indies | Auckland | 1968–69 |
| New Zealand v India | Bombay[2] | 1969–70 |
| India v West Indies | Port-of-Spain | 1970–71 |
| India v England | Lord's | 1971 |
| Australia v England | Nottingham | 1972 |
| England v India | Madras[1] | 1972–73 |
| England v West Indies | Lord's | 1973 |
| Australia v New Zealand | Auckland | 1973–74 |
| New Zealand v Pakistan | Auckland | 1978–79 |
| †England v Australia | Brisbane[2] | 1982–83 |
| England v Australia | Melbourne | 1982–83 |
| India v West Indies | Bridgetown | 1982–83 |
| West Indies v India | Bridgetown | 1982–83 |
| Sri Lanka v Australia | Kandy | 1982–83 |

† *Australia held nine catches in England's second innings to become the only side to hold 19 catches in a Test.*

### MOST BATSMEN CAUGHT IN A MATCH

| | | | |
|---|---|---|---|
| 32 | England v Pakistan | Leeds | 1971 |

### MOST BATSMEN BOWLED IN AN INNINGS

| | | | |
|---|---|---|---|
| 9 | South Africa v England | Cape Town | 1888–89 |

**MOST BATSMEN BOWLED IN A MATCH**

| | | | |
|---|---|---|---|
| 23 | South Africa v England | Port Elizabeth | 1895–96 |

**MOST BATSMEN LBW IN AN INNINGS**

| | | | |
|---|---|---|---|
| 6 | England v South Africa | Leeds | 1955 |
| 6 | England v West Indies | Kingston | 1959–60 |
| 6 | England v Pakistan | Karachi | 1977–78 |

**MOST BATSMEN LBW IN A MATCH**

| | | | |
|---|---|---|---|
| 12 | New Zealand v West Indies | Dunedin | 1979–80 |
| 12 | England v West Indies | Lord's | 1984 |

**MOST BATSMEN RUN OUT IN AN INNINGS**

| | | | |
|---|---|---|---|
| 4 | India v Pakistan | Peshawar | 1954–55 |
| 4 | Australia v West Indies | Adelaide | 1968–69 |

**MOST BATSMEN RUN OUT IN A MATCH**

| | | | |
|---|---|---|---|
| 7 | Australia v Pakistan | Melbourne | 1972–73 |

**MOST BATSMEN STUMPED IN AN INNINGS**

| | | | |
|---|---|---|---|
| 4 | England v Australia (W.A.S. Oldfield) | Melbourne | 1924–25 |
| 4 | England v India (P. Sen) | Madras[1] | 1951–52 |

**MOST BATSMEN STUMPED IN A MATCH**

| | | | |
|---|---|---|---|
| 6 | Australia v England | Sydney | 1894–95 |
| 6 | India v England | Madras[1] | 1951–52 |

# INDIVIDUAL RECORDS – BATTING

## 2000 RUNS IN TESTS

| ENGLAND | M | I | Runs | Opponents A | SA | WI | NZ | I | P | SL |
|---|---|---|---|---|---|---|---|---|---|---|
| G. Boycott | 108 | 193 | **8114** | 2945 | 373 | 2205 | 916 | 1084 | 591 | — |
| M.C. Cowdrey | 114 | 188 | **7624** | 2433 | 1021 | 1751 | 1133 | 653 | 633 | — |
| W.R. Hammond | 85 | 140 | **7249** | 2852 | 2188 | 639 | 1015 | 555 | — | — |
| L. Hutton | 79 | 138 | **6971** | 2428 | 1564 | 1661 | 777 | 522 | 19 | — |
| K.F. Barrington | 82 | 131 | **6806** | 2111 | 989 | 1042 | 594 | 1355 | 715 | — |
| D.C.S. Compton | 78 | 131 | **5807** | 1842 | 2205 | 592 | 510 | 205 | 453 | — |
| J.B. Hobbs | 61 | 102 | **5410** | 3636 | 1562 | 212 | — | — | — | — |
| D.I. Gower | 76 | 129 | **5385** | 2075 | — | 568 | 758 | 999 | 799 | 186 |
| J.H. Edrich | 77 | 127 | **5138** | 2644 | 7 | 792 | 840 | 494 | 361 | — |
| T.W. Graveney | 79 | 123 | **4882** | 1075 | 234 | 1532 | 293 | 805 | 943 | — |
| H. Sutcliffe | 54 | 84 | **4555** | 2741 | 1336 | 206 | 250 | 22 | — | — |
| P.B.H. May | 66 | 106 | **4537** | 1566 | 906 | 986 | 603 | 356 | 120 | — |
| E.R. Dexter | 62 | 102 | **4502** | 1358 | 585 | 866 | 477 | 467 | 749 | — |
| I.T. Botham | 79 | 125 | **4409** | 1422 | — | 589 | 771 | 1201 | 407 | 19 |
| A.P.E. Knott | 95 | 149 | **4389** | 1682 | — | 994 | 352 | 685 | 676 | — |
| D.L. Amiss | 50 | 88 | **3612** | 305 | — | 1130 | 433 | 965 | 779 | — |
| A.W. Greig | 58 | 93 | **3599** | 1303 | — | 795 | 267 | 883 | 351 | — |
| E.H. Hendren | 51 | 83 | **3525** | 1740 | 876 | 909 | — | — | — | — |
| F.E. Woolley | 64 | 98 | **3283** | 1664 | 1354 | — | 235 | 30 | — | — |
| G.A. Gooch | 48 | 84 | **3027** | 1105 | — | 854 | 190 | 751 | 74 | 53 |
| K.W.R. Fletcher | 59 | 96 | **3272** | 661 | — | 528 | 578 | 874 | 586 | 45 |
| M. Leyland | 41 | 65 | **2764** | 1705 | 936 | 37 | — | 86 | — | — |
| C. Washbrook | 37 | 66 | **2569** | 996 | 938 | 255 | 234 | 146 | — | — |
| B.L. D'Oliveira | 44 | 70 | **2484** | 865 | — | 555 | 258 | 254 | 552 | — |
| D.W. Randall | 47 | 79 | **2470** | 1161 | — | 1 | 543 | 390 | 375 | — |
| W.J. Edrich | 39 | 63 | **2440** | 1184 | 792 | 94 | 366 | — | 4 | — |
| T.G. Evans | 91 | 133 | **2439** | 783 | 511 | 625 | 142 | 315 | 63 | — |
| L.E.G. Ames | 47 | 72 | **2434** | 675 | 530 | 748 | 410 | 71 | — | — |
| W. Rhodes | 58 | 98 | **2325** | 1706 | 568 | 51 | — | — | — | — |
| T.E. Bailey | 61 | 91 | **2290** | 875 | 552 | 343 | 439 | — | 81 | — |
| M.J.K. Smith | 50 | 78 | **2278** | 248 | 561 | 319 | 312 | 639 | 199 | — |
| M.W. Gatting | 41 | 70 | **2246** | 960 | — | 204 | 159 | 643 | 280 | — |
| A.J. Lamb | 38 | 64 | **2211** | 670 | — | 386 | 474 | 448 | 126 | 107 |
| P.E. Richardson | 34 | 56 | **2061** | 526 | 369 | 427 | 317 | 304 | 118 | — |

| AUSTRALIA | M | I | Runs | Opponents E | SA | WI | NZ | I | P | SL |
|---|---|---|---|---|---|---|---|---|---|---|
| G.S. Chappell | 87 | 151 | **7110** | 2619 | — | 1400 | 1076 | 368 | 1581 | 66 |
| D.G. Bradman | 52 | 80 | **6996** | 5028 | 806 | 447 | — | 715 | — | — |
| R.N. Harvey | 79 | 137 | **6149** | 2416 | 1625 | 1054 | — | 775 | 279 | — |
| K.D. Walters | 74 | 125 | **5357** | 1981 | 258 | 1196 | 901 | 756 | 265 | — |
| I.M. Chappell | 75 | 136 | **5345** | 2138 | 288 | 1545 | 486 | 536 | 352 | — |
| A.R. Border | 72 | 127 | **5332** | 1869 | — | 1221 | 144 | 749 | 1302 | 47 |
| W.M. Lawry | 67 | 123 | **5234** | 2233 | 985 | 1035 | — | 892 | 89 | — |
| R.B. Simpson | 62 | 111 | **4869** | 1405 | 980 | 1043 | — | 1125 | 316 | — |
| I.R. Redpath | 66 | 120 | **4737** | 1512 | 791 | 1247 | 413 | 475 | 299 | — |
| K.J. Hughes | 70 | 124 | **4415** | 1499 | — | 774 | 138 | 988 | 1016 | — |
| R.W. Marsh | 96 | 150 | **3633** | 1633 | — | 707 | 486 | 83 | 724 | — |
| A.R. Morris | 46 | 79 | **3533** | 2080 | 792 | 452 | — | 209 | — | — |
| C. Hill | 49 | 89 | **3412** | 2660 | 752 | — | — | — | — | — |
| V.T. Trumper | 48 | 89 | **3163** | 2263 | 900 | — | — | — | — | — |
| G.M. Wood | 53 | 101 | **3109** | 1063 | — | 899 | 393 | 287 | 463 | 4 |
| C.C. McDonald | 47 | 83 | **3107** | 1043 | 786 | 880 | — | 224 | 174 | — |
| A.L. Hassett | 43 | 69 | **3073** | 1572 | 748 | 402 | 19 | 332 | — | — |
| K.R. Miller | 55 | 87 | **2958** | 1511 | 399 | 801 | 30 | 185 | 32 | — |
| W.W. Armstrong | 50 | 84 | **2863** | 2172 | 691 | — | — | — | — | — |
| K.R. Stackpole | 43 | 80 | **2807** | 1164 | 441 | 600 | 197 | 368 | 37 | — |
| N.C. O'Neill | 42 | 69 | **2779** | 1072 | 285 | 788 | — | 416 | 218 | — |

**AUSTRALIA** *continued*

| | M | I | Runs | *Opponents* | | | | | | |
| | | | | E | SA | WI | NZ | I | P | SL |
|---|---|---|---|---|---|---|---|---|---|---|
| G.N. Yallop | 39 | 70 | **2756** | 709 | — | 499 | — | 568 | 882 | 98 |
| S.J. McCabe | 39 | 62 | **2748** | 1922 | 621 | 205 | — | — | — | — |
| W. Bardsley | 41 | 66 | **2469** | 1487 | 982 | — | — | — | — | — |
| W.M. Woodfull | 35 | 54 | **2300** | 1684 | 421 | 195 | — | — | — | — |
| P.J.P. Burge | 42 | 68 | **2290** | 1179 | 331 | 229 | — | 457 | 94 | — |
| S.E. Gregory | 58 | 100 | **2282** | 2193 | 89 | — | — | — | — | — |
| R. Benaud | 63 | 97 | **2201** | 767 | 684 | 462 | — | 144 | 144 | — |
| C.G. Macartney | 35 | 55 | **2131** | 1640 | 491 | — | — | — | — | — |
| W.H. Ponsford | 29 | 48 | **2122** | 1558 | 97 | 467 | — | — | — | — |
| R.M. Cowper | 27 | 46 | **2061** | 686 | 255 | 417 | — | 604 | 99 | — |

**SOUTH AFRICA**

| | M | I | Runs | *Opponents* | | |
| | | | | E | A | NZ |
|---|---|---|---|---|---|---|
| B. Mitchell | 42 | 80 | **3471** | 2732 | 573 | 166 |
| A.D. Nourse | 34 | 62 | **2960** | 2037 | 923 | — |
| H.W. Taylor | 42 | 76 | **2936** | 2287 | 640 | 9 |
| E.J. Barlow | 30 | 57 | **2516** | 742 | 1149 | 625 |
| T.L. Goddard | 41 | 78 | **2516** | 1193 | 1090 | 233 |
| D.J. McGlew | 34 | 64 | **2440** | 736 | 604 | 1100 |
| J.H.B. Waite | 50 | 86 | **2405** | 923 | 839 | 643 |
| R.G. Pollock | 23 | 41 | **2256** | 750 | 1453 | 53 |
| A.W. Nourse | 45 | 83 | **2234** | 1415 | 819 | — |
| R.A. McLean | 40 | 73 | **2120** | 1068 | 480 | 572 |

**WEST INDIES**

| | M | I | Runs | *Opponents* | | | | |
| | | | | E | A | NZ | I | P |
|---|---|---|---|---|---|---|---|---|
| G.St A. Sobers | 93 | 160 | **8032** | 3214 | 1510 | 404 | 1920 | 984 |
| C.H. Lloyd | 110 | 175 | **7515** | 2120 | 2211 | 234 | 2344 | 606 |
| R.B. Kanhai | 79 | 137 | **6227** | 2267 | 1694 | — | 1693 | 573 |
| I.V.A. Richards | 77 | 116 | **5889** | 1798 | 1646 | 310 | 1497 | 638 |
| C.G. Greenidge | 66 | 111 | **4816** | 1511 | 1056 | 538 | 1175 | 536 |
| E. de C. Weekes | 48 | 81 | **4455** | 1313 | 714 | 478 | 1495 | 455 |
| A.I. Kallicharran | 66 | 109 | **4399** | 891 | 1325 | 365 | 1229 | 589 |
| R.C. Fredericks | 59 | 109 | **4334** | 1369 | 1069 | 537 | 767 | 592 |
| F.M.M. Worrell | 51 | 87 | **3860** | 1979 | 918 | 233 | 730 | — |
| C.L. Walcott | 44 | 74 | **3798** | 1391 | 914 | 199 | 909 | 385 |
| C.C. Hunte | 44 | 78 | **3245** | 1005 | 927 | — | 670 | 643 |
| D.L. Haynes | 54 | 88 | **3234** | 777 | 1161 | 683 | 509 | 104 |
| B.F. Butcher | 44 | 78 | **3104** | 1373 | 810 | 216 | 572 | 133 |
| H.A. Gomes | 49 | 75 | **2841** | 610 | 1122 | 158 | 806 | 145 |
| S.M. Nurse | 29 | 54 | **2523** | 1016 | 820 | 558 | 129 | — |
| G.A. Headley | 22 | 40 | **2190** | 1852 | 336 | — | 2 | — |
| J.B. Stollmeyer | 32 | 56 | **2159** | 858 | 417 | 188 | 696 | — |
| L.G. Rowe | 30 | 49 | **2047** | 742 | 528 | 598 | 179 | — |

**NEW ZEALAND**

| | M | I | Runs | *Opponents* | | | | | | |
| | | | | E | A | SA | WI | I | P | SL |
|---|---|---|---|---|---|---|---|---|---|---|
| B.E. Congdon | 61 | 114 | **3448** | 1143 | 456 | — | 764 | 713 | 372 | — |
| J.R. Reid | 58 | 108 | **3428** | 953 | — | 914 | 212 | 691 | 658 | — |
| G.M. Turner | 41 | 73 | **2991** | 510 | 541 | — | 855 | 583 | 431 | 71 |
| B. Sutcliffe | 42 | 76 | **2727** | 1049 | — | 455 | 196 | 885 | 142 | — |
| M.G. Burgess | 50 | 92 | **2684** | 610 | 279 | — | 317 | 725 | 753 | — |
| G.P. Howarth | 47 | 83 | **2531** | 910 | 468 | — | 397 | 216 | 340 | 200 |
| G.T. Dowling | 39 | 77 | **2306** | 517 | — | 271 | 277 | 964 | 277 | — |
| J.G. Wright | 41 | 71 | **2133** | 671 | 291 | — | 296 | 201 | 512 | 162 |
| J.V. Coney | 40 | 67 | **2094** | 489 | 331 | — | 381 | 92 | 528 | 273 |
| R.J. Hadlee | 57 | 96 | **2088** | 561 | 438 | — | 315 | 134 | 506 | 134 |

| **INDIA** | | | *Opponents* | | | | | |
|---|---|---|---|---|---|---|---|---|
| | *M* | *I* | **Runs** | *E* | *A* | *WI* | *NZ* | *P* | *SL* |
| S.M. Gavaskar | 106 | 185 | **8654** | 2308 | 993 | 2749 | 651 | 1794 | 159 |
| G.R. Viswanath | 91 | 155 | **6080** | 1880 | 1538 | 1455 | 585 | 611 | 11 |
| D.B. Vengsarkar | 76 | 124 | **4328** | 1071 | 840 | 1181 | 261 | 880 | 95 |
| P.R. Umrigar | 59 | 94 | **3631** | 770 | 227 | 1372 | 351 | 911 | — |
| M. Amarnath | 49 | 83 | **3241** | 484 | 463 | 1020 | 407 | 867 | — |
| V.L. Manjrekar | 55 | 92 | **3208** | 1181 | 377 | 569 | 507 | 574 | — |
| C.G. Borde | 55 | 97 | **3061** | 746 | 502 | 870 | 613 | 330 | — |
| Nawab of Pataudi, jr | 46 | 83 | **2793** | 946 | 829 | 352 | 666 | — | — |
| Kapil Dev | 68 | 101 | **2788** | 953 | 267 | 767 | 27 | 713 | 61 |
| S.M.H. Kirmani | 85 | 122 | **2717** | 707 | 714 | 469 | 400 | 422 | 5 |
| F.M. Engineer | 46 | 87 | **2611** | 1113 | 449 | 465 | 584 | — | — |
| Pankaj Roy | 43 | 79 | **2442** | 620 | 432 | 717 | 301 | 372 | — |
| V.S. Hazare | 30 | 52 | **2192** | 803 | 429 | 737 | — | 223 | — |
| A.L. Wadekar | 37 | 71 | **2113** | 840 | 548 | 230 | 495 | — | — |
| M.H. Mankad | 44 | 72 | **2109** | 618 | 388 | 397 | 526 | 180 | — |
| C.P.S. Chauhan | 40 | 68 | **2084** | 213 | 878 | 331 | 224 | 438 | — |
| M.L. Jaisimha | 39 | 71 | **2056** | 852 | 434 | 276 | 268 | 226 | — |
| D.N. Sardesai | 30 | 55 | **2001** | 674 | 156 | 811 | 360 | — | — |

| **PAKISTAN** | | | *Opponents* | | | | | |
|---|---|---|---|---|---|---|---|---|
| | *M* | *I* | **Runs** | *E* | *A* | *WI* | *NZ* | *I* | *SL* |
| Zaheer Abbas | 76 | 123 | **5058** | 1086 | 1411 | 259 | 428 | 1740 | 134 |
| Javed Miandad | 68 | 108 | **5044** | 517 | 1195 | 233 | 1276 | 1647 | 176 |
| Majid Khan | 63 | 106 | **3931** | 751 | 915 | 821 | 936 | 445 | 63 |
| Hanif Mohammad | 55 | 97 | **3915** | 1039 | 548 | 736 | 622 | 970 | — |
| Mushtaq Mohammad | 57 | 100 | **3643** | 1554 | 409 | 488 | 779 | 413 | — |
| Asif Iqbal | 58 | 99 | **3575** | 822 | 758 | 416 | 1113 | 466 | — |
| Mudassar Nazar | 52 | 81 | **3099** | 496 | 781 | — | 354 | 1431 | 37 |
| Saeed Ahmed | 41 | 78 | **2991** | 791 | 611 | 707 | 422 | 460 | — |
| Wasim Raja | 57 | 92 | **2821** | 488 | 334 | 919 | 371 | 643 | 66 |
| Sadiq Mohammad | 41 | 74 | **2579** | 820 | 400 | 456 | 740 | 163 | — |
| Mohsin Khan | 40 | 65 | **2468** | 736 | 786 | — | 259 | 472 | 215 |
| Imtiaz Ahmed | 41 | 72 | **2079** | 488 | 131 | 423 | 284 | 753 | — |
| Imran Khan | 51 | 77 | **2023** | 309 | 583 | 419 | 168 | 505 | 39 |

# HIGHEST BATTING AVERAGES

*Qualification: 15 innings*

| | Country | Tests | I | NO | HS | Runs | Av | 100 | 50 |
|---|---|---|---|---|---|---|---|---|---|
| D.G. Bradman | Australia | 52 | 80 | 10 | 334 | 6996 | **99.94** | 29 | 13 |
| C.S. Dempster | New Zealand | 10 | 15 | 4 | 136 | 723 | **65.72** | 2 | 5 |
| S.G. Barnes | Australia | 13 | 19 | 2 | 234 | 1072 | **63.05** | 3 | 5 |
| R.T. Robinson | England | 11 | 18 | 3 | 175 | 934 | **62.26** | 3 | 3 |
| R.G. Pollock | South Africa | 23 | 41 | 4 | 274 | 2256 | **60.97** | 7 | 11 |
| G.A. Headley | West Indies | 22 | 40 | 4 | 270* | 2190 | **60.83** | 10 | 5 |
| H. Sutcliffe | England | 54 | 84 | 9 | 194 | 4555 | **60.73** | 16 | 23 |
| E. Paynter | England | 20 | 31 | 5 | 243 | 1540 | **59.23** | 4 | 7 |
| K.F. Barrington | England | 82 | 131 | 15 | 256 | 6806 | **58.67** | 20 | 35 |
| E. de C. Weekes | West Indies | 48 | 81 | 5 | 207 | 4455 | **58.61** | 15 | 19 |
| K.S. Duleepsinhji | England | 12 | 19 | 2 | 173 | 995 | **58.52** | 3 | 5 |
| W.R. Hammond | England | 85 | 140 | 16 | 336* | 7249 | **58.45** | 22 | 24 |
| G.St A. Sobers | West Indies | 93 | 160 | 21 | 365* | 8032 | **57.78** | 26 | 30 |
| J.B. Hobbs | England | 61 | 102 | 7 | 211 | 5410 | **56.94** | 15 | 28 |
| C.A.G. Russell | England | 10 | 18 | 2 | 140 | 910 | **56.87** | 5 | 2 |
| C.L. Walcott | West Indies | 44 | 74 | 7 | 220 | 3798 | **56.68** | 15 | 14 |
| L. Hutton | England | 79 | 138 | 15 | 364 | 6971 | **56.67** | 19 | 33 |
| G.E. Tyldesley | England | 14 | 20 | 2 | 122 | 990 | **55.00** | 3 | 6 |
| Javed Miandad | Pakistan | 68 | 108 | 16 | 280* | 5044 | **54.92** | 13 | 27 |
| C.A. Davis | West Indies | 15 | 29 | 5 | 183 | 1301 | **54.20** | 4 | 4 |
| I.V.A. Richards | West Indies | 77 | 116 | 7 | 291 | 5889 | **54.02** | 19 | 25 |
| G.S. Chappell | Australia | 87 | 151 | 19 | 247* | 7110 | **53.86** | 24 | 31 |
| J.F. Reid | New Zealand | 13 | 22 | 2 | 180 | 1077 | **53.85** | 5 | 2 |
| A.D. Nourse | South Africa | 34 | 62 | 7 | 231 | 2960 | **53.81** | 9 | 14 |
| A. Melville | South Africa | 11 | 19 | 2 | 189 | 894 | **52.58** | 4 | 3 |
| C.F. Walters | England | 11 | 18 | 3 | 102 | 784 | **52.26** | 1 | 7 |
| J. Ryder | Australia | 20 | 32 | 5 | 201* | 1394 | **51.62** | 3 | 9 |
| A.R. Border | Australia | 72 | 127 | 22 | 196 | 5332 | **50.78** | 14 | 29 |
| S.M. Gavaskar | India | 106 | 185 | 14 | 236* | 8654 | **50.60** | 30 | 37 |
| D.C.S. Compton | England | 78 | 131 | 15 | 278 | 5807 | **50.06** | 17 | 28 |

# HIGHEST AGGREGATES IN A SERIES

| | | | M | I | NO | HS | Runs | Av | 100 | 50 |
|---|---|---|---|---|---|---|---|---|---|---|
| D.G. Bradman | A v E | 1930 | 5 | 7 | 0 | 334 | **974** | 139.14 | 4 | – |
| W.R. Hammond | E v A | 1928–29 | 5 | 9 | 1 | 251 | **905** | 113.12 | 4 | – |
| R.N. Harvey | A v SA | 1952–53 | 5 | 9 | 0 | 205 | **834** | 92.66 | 4 | 3 |
| I.V.A. Richards | WI v E | 1976 | 4 | 7 | 0 | 291 | **829** | 118.42 | 3 | 2 |
| C.L. Walcott | WI v A | 1954–55 | 5 | 10 | 0 | 155 | **827** | 82.70 | 5 | 2 |
| G.St A. Sobers | WI v P | 1957–58 | 5 | 8 | 2 | 365* | **824** | 137.33 | 3 | 3 |
| D.G. Bradman | A v E | 1936–37 | 5 | 9 | 0 | 270 | **810** | 90.00 | 3 | 1 |
| D.G. Bradman | A v SA | 1931–32 | 5 | 5 | 1 | 299* | **806** | 201.50 | 4 | – |
| E. de C. Weekes | WI v I | 1948–49 | 5 | 7 | 0 | 194 | **779** | 111.28 | 4 | 3 |
| S.M. Gavaskar | I v WI | 1970–71 | 4 | 8 | 3 | 220 | **774** | 154.80 | 4 | 3 |
| Mudassar Nazar | P v I | 1982–83 | 6 | 8 | 2 | 231 | **761** | 126.83 | 4 | 1 |
| D.G. Bradman | A v E | 1934 | 5 | 8 | 0 | 304 | **758** | 94.75 | 2 | 1 |
| D.C.S. Compton | E v SA | 1947 | 5 | 8 | 0 | 208 | **753** | 94.12 | 4 | 2 |
| H. Sutcliffe | E v A | 1924–25 | 5 | 9 | 0 | 176 | **734** | 81.55 | 4 | 2 |
| G.A. Faulkner | SA v A | 1910–11 | 5 | 10 | 0 | 204 | **732** | 73.20 | 2 | 5 |
| S.M. Gavaskar | I v WI | 1978–79 | 6 | 9 | 1 | 205 | **732** | 91.50 | 4 | 1 |
| D.I. Gower | E v A | 1985 | 6 | 9 | 0 | 215 | **732** | 81.33 | 3 | 1 |
| G.St A. Sobers | WI v E | 1966 | 5 | 8 | 1 | 174 | **722** | 103.14 | 3 | 2 |
| E. de C. Weekes | WI v I | 1952–53 | 5 | 8 | 1 | 207 | **716** | 102.28 | 3 | 2 |
| D.G. Bradman | A v I | 1947–48 | 5 | 6 | 2 | 201 | **715** | 178.75 | 4 | 1 |
| G.St A. Sobers | WI v E | 1959–60 | 5 | 8 | 1 | 226 | **709** | 101.28 | 3 | 1 |
| G.A. Headley | WI v E | 1929–30 | 4 | 8 | 0 | 223 | **703** | 87.87 | 4 | – |
| G.S. Chappell | A v WI | 1975–76 | 6 | 11 | 5 | 182* | **702** | 117.00 | 3 | 3 |
| K.D. Walters | A v WI | 1968–69 | 4 | 6 | 0 | 242 | **699** | 116.50 | 4 | 2 |

| | Country | | M | I | NO | HS | Runs | Av | 100 | 50 |
|---|---|---|---|---|---|---|---|---|---|---|
| C.L. Walcott | WI v E | 1953–54 | 5 | 10 | 2 | 220 | 698 | 87.25 | 3 | 3 |
| A.R. Morris | A v E | 1948 | 5 | 9 | 1 | 196 | 696 | 87.00 | 3 | 3 |
| E.H. Hendren | E v WI | 1929–30 | 4 | 8 | 2 | 205* | 693 | 115.50 | 2 | 5 |
| D.G. Bradman | A v E | 1946–47 | 5 | 8 | 1 | 234 | 680 | 97.14 | 2 | 3 |
| L. Hutton | E v WI | 1953–54 | 5 | 8 | 1 | 205 | 677 | 96.71 | 2 | 3 |
| G.M. Turner | NZ v WI | 1971–72 | 5 | 8 | 1 | 259 | 672 | 96.00 | 2 | 2 |
| W.M. Lawry | A v WI | 1968–69 | 5 | 8 | 0 | 205 | 667 | 83.37 | 3 | 2 |
| D.L. Amiss | E v WI | 1973–74 | 5 | 9 | 1 | 262* | 663 | 82.87 | 3 | – |
| J.B. Hobbs | E v A | 1911–12 | 5 | 9 | 1 | 187 | 662 | 82.75 | 3 | 1 |
| V.T. Trumper | A v SA | 1910–11 | 5 | 9 | 2 | 214* | 661 | 94.42 | 2 | 2 |
| R.N. Harvey | A v SA | 1949–50 | 5 | 8 | 3 | 178 | 660 | 132.00 | 4 | 1 |
| G. Boycott | E v A | 1970–71 | 5 | 10 | 3 | 142* | 657 | 93.85 | 2 | 5 |
| E. Paynter | E v SA | 1938–39 | 5 | 8 | 0 | 243 | 653 | 81.62 | 3 | 2 |
| R.N. Harvey | A v WI | 1954–55 | 5 | 7 | 1 | 204 | 650 | 108.33 | 3 | 1 |
| Zaheer Abbas | P v I | 1982–83 | 6 | 6 | 1 | 215 | 650 | 130.00 | 3 | – |
| J.H. Edrich | E v A | 1970–71 | 6 | 11 | 2 | 130 | 648 | 72.00 | 2 | 4 |
| D.N. Sardesai | I v WI | 1970–71 | 5 | 8 | 0 | 212 | 642 | 80.25 | 1 | 1 |
| C.H. Lloyd | WI v I | 1974–75 | 5 | 9 | 1 | 242* | 636 | 79.20 | 2 | 1 |
| Hanif Mohammad | P v WI | 1957–58 | 5 | 9 | 0 | 337 | 628 | 69.77 | 1 | 3 |
| K.R. Stackpole | A v E | 1970–71 | 6 | 12 | 0 | 207 | 627 | 52.25 | 2 | 2 |
| C.C. Hunte | WI v P | 1957–58 | 5 | 9 | 1 | 260 | 622 | 77.75 | 3 | – |
| A.D. Nourse | SA v E | 1947 | 5 | 9 | 0 | 149 | 621 | 69.00 | 2 | 5 |
| L.G. Rowe | WI v E | 1973–74 | 5 | 7 | 0 | 302 | 616 | 88.00 | 3 | – |
| B. Sutcliffe | NZ v I | 1955–56 | 5 | 9 | 2 | 230* | 611 | 87.28 | 2 | 1 |
| W.R. Hammond | E v SA | 1938–39 | 5 | 8 | 1 | 181 | 609 | 87.00 | 3 | 2 |
| G.S. Chappell | A v E | 1974–75 | 6 | 11 | 0 | 144 | 608 | 55.27 | 2 | 5 |
| D.T. Lindsay | SA v A | 1966–67 | 5 | 7 | 0 | 182 | 606 | 86.57 | 3 | 2 |
| E.J. Barlow | SA v A | 1963–64 | 5 | 10 | 2 | 201 | 603 | 75.37 | 3 | 1 |

*Zaheer Abbas scored 583 runs, average 194.33, in 5 innings in the 3-match series against India in Pakistan in 1978–79.*

## MOST RUNS IN A MATCH

| | | | | |
|---|---|---|---|---|
| 380 | G.S. Chappell (247*, 133) | Australia v New Zealand | Wellington | 1973–74 |
| 375 | A. Sandham (325, 50) | England v West Indies | Kingston | 1929–30 |
| 365 | G.St A. Sobers (365*) | West Indies v Pakistan | Kingston | 1957–58 |
| 364 | L. Hutton (364) | England v Australia | Oval | 1938 |
| 354 | Hanif Mohammad (17, 337) | Pakistan v West Indies | Bridgetown | 1957–58 |

## CARRYING BAT THROUGH A COMPLETED INNINGS

| ENGLAND | Score | Total | Opponents | | |
|---|---|---|---|---|---|
| R. Abel | 132* | 307 | Australia | Sydney | 1891–92 |
| P.F. Warner† | 132* | 237 | South Africa | Johannesburg[1] | 1898–99 |
| L. Hutton | 202* | 344 | West Indies | Oval | 1950 |
| L. Hutton | 156* | 272 | Australia | Adelaide | 1950–51 |
| G. Boycott | 99* | 215 | Australia | Perth | 1979–80 |

| AUSTRALIA | | | | | |
|---|---|---|---|---|---|
| J.E. Barrett† | 67* | 176 | England | Lord's | 1890 |
| W.W. Armstrong | 159* | 309 | South Africa | Johannesburg[1] | 1902–03 |
| W. Bardsley | 193* | 383 | England | Lord's | 1926 |
| W.M. Woodfull | 30* | 66‡ | England | Brisbane[1] | 1928–29 |
| W.M. Woodfull | 73* | 193‡ | England | Adelaide | 1932–33 |
| W.A. Brown | 206* | 422 | England | Lord's | 1938 |
| W.M. Lawry | 49* | 107 | India | Delhi | 1969–70 |
| W.M. Lawry | 60* | 116‡ | England | Sydney | 1970–71 |
| I.R. Redpath | 159* | 346 | New Zealand | Auckland | 1973–74 |

| SOUTH AFRICA | Score | Total | Opponents | | |
|---|---|---|---|---|---|
| A.B. Tancred | 26* | 47 | England | Cape Town | 1888–89 |
| J.W. Zulch | 43* | 103 | England | Cape Town | 1909–10 |
| T.L. Goddard | 56* | 99 | Australia | Cape Town | 1957–58 |
| D.J. McGlew | 127* | 292 | New Zealand | Durban² | 1961–62 |

| WEST INDIES | | | | | |
|---|---|---|---|---|---|
| F.M.M. Worrell | 191* | 372 | England | Nottingham | 1957 |
| C.C. Hunte | 60* | 131 | Australia | Port-of-Spain | 1964–65 |

| NEW ZEALAND | | | | | |
|---|---|---|---|---|---|
| G.M. Turner | 43* | 131 | England | Lord's | 1969 |
| G.M. Turner | 223* | 386 | West Indies | Kingston | 1971–72 |

| INDIA | | | | | |
|---|---|---|---|---|---|
| S.M. Gavaskar | 127* | 286 | Pakistan | Faisalabad | 1982–83 |

| PAKISTAN | | | | | |
|---|---|---|---|---|---|
| Nazar Mohammad | 124* | 331 | India | Lucknow | 1952–53 |
| Mudassar Nazar | 152* | 323 | India | Lahore² | 1982–83 |

| SRI LANKA | | | | | |
|---|---|---|---|---|---|
| S. Wettimuny | 63* | 144 | New Zealand | Christchurch | 1982–83 |

† On debut in Test cricket.
‡ Completed innings in which one or more batsmen were retired or absent.
*G.M. Turner is the youngest player to carry his bat through a Test match innings; he was 22 years and 63 days old when he first achieved this feat.*
*Nazar Mohammad and his son Mudassar Nazar are the only related players to achieve this feat at Test level.*
*D.L. Amiss (262\*) batted throughout England's innings of 432-9 against West Indies at Kingston in 1973-74. His unbroken tenth-wicket partnership with R.G.D. Willis (3\*) added 40 runs in 53 minutes.*
*D.L. Haynes (55 and 105) batted throughout both innings for West Indies v New Zealand at Dunedin in 1979-80.*

# HIGHEST INDIVIDUAL INNINGS

| | | | | |
|---|---|---|---|---|
| 365* | G.St A. Sobers | West Indies v Pakistan | Kingston | 1957–58 |
| 364 | L. Hutton | England v Australia | Oval | 1938 |
| 337 | Hanif Mohammad | Pakistan v West Indies | Bridgetown | 1957–58 |
| 336* | W.R. Hammond | England v New Zealand | Auckland | 1932–33 |
| 334 | D.G. Bradman | Australia v England | Leeds | 1930 |
| 325 | A. Sandham | England v West Indies | Kingston | 1929–30 |
| 311 | R.B. Simpson | Australia v England | Manchester | 1964 |
| 310* | J.H. Edrich | England v New Zealand | Leeds | 1965 |
| 307 | R.M. Cowper | Australia v England | Melbourne | 1965–66 |
| 304 | D.G. Bradman | Australia v England | Leeds | 1934 |
| 302 | L.G. Rowe | West Indies v England | Bridgetown | 1973–74 |
| 299* | D.G. Bradman | Australia v South Africa | Adelaide | 1931–32 |
| 291 | I.V.A. Richards | West Indies v England | Oval | 1976 |
| 287 | R.E. Foster | England v Australia | Sydney | 1903–04 |
| 285* | P.B.H. May | England v West Indies | Birmingham | 1957 |
| 280* | Javed Miandad | Pakistan v India | Hyderabad | 1982–83 |
| 278 | D.C.S. Compton | England v Pakistan | Nottingham | 1954 |
| 274 | R.G. Pollock | South Africa v Australia | Durban² | 1969–70 |
| 274 | Zaheer Abbas | Pakistan v England | Birmingham | 1971 |
| 270* | G.A. Headley | West Indies v England | Kingston | 1934–35 |
| 270 | D.G. Bradman | Australia v England | Melbourne | 1936–37 |
| 268 | G.N. Yallop | Australia v Pakistan | Melbourne | 1983–84 |
| 266 | W.H. Ponsford | Australia v England | Oval | 1934 |
| 262* | D.L. Amiss | England v West Indies | Kingston | 1973–74 |
| 261 | F.M.M. Worrell | West Indies v England | Nottingham | 1950 |
| 260 | C.C. Hunte | West Indies v Pakistan | Kingston | 1957–58 |

| 259 | G.M. Turner | New Zealand v West Indies | Georgetown | 1971–72 |
|---|---|---|---|---|
| 258 | T.W. Graveney | England v West Indies | Nottingham | 1957 |
| 258 | S.M. Nurse | West Indies v New Zealand | Christchurch | 1968–69 |
| 256 | R.B. Kanhai | West Indies v India | Calcutta | 1958–59 |
| 256 | K.F. Barrington | England v Australia | Manchester | 1964 |
| 255* | D.J. McGlew | South Africa v New Zealand | Wellington | 1952–53 |
| 254 | D.G. Bradman | Australia v England | Lord's | 1930 |
| 251 | W.R. Hammond | England v Australia | Sydney | 1928–29 |
| 250 | K.D. Walters | Australia v New Zealand | Christchurch | 1976–77 |
| 250 | S.F.A.F. Bacchus | West Indies v India | Kanpur | 1978–79 |
| 247* | G.S. Chappell | Australia v New Zealand | Wellington | 1973–74 |
| 246* | G. Boycott | England v India | Leeds | 1967 |
| 244 | D.G. Bradman | Australia v England | Oval | 1934 |
| 243 | E. Paynter | England v South Africa | Durban[2] | 1938–39 |
| 242* | C.H. Lloyd | West Indies v India | Bombay[3] | 1974–75 |
| 242 | K.D. Walters | Australia v West Indies | Sydney | 1968–69 |
| 240 | W.R. Hammond | England v Australia | Lord's | 1938 |
| 240 | Zaheer Abbas | Pakistan v England | Oval | 1974 |
| 239 | G.T. Dowling | New Zealand v India | Christchurch | 1967–68 |
| 237 | F.M.M. Worrell | West Indies v India | Kingston | 1952–53 |
| 236* | S.M. Gavaskar | India v West Indies | Madras[1] | 1983–84 |
| 236 | E.A.B. Rowan | South Africa v England | Leeds | 1951 |
| 235* | Zaheer Abbas | Pakistan v India | Lahore[2] | 1978–79 |
| 235 | G.S. Chappell | Australia v Pakistan | Faisalabad | 1979–80 |
| 234 | D.G. Bradman | Australia v England | Sydney | 1946–47 |
| 234 | S.G. Barnes | Australia v England | Sydney | 1946–47 |
| 232 | D.G. Bradman | Australia v England | Oval | 1930 |
| 232 | S.J. McCabe | Australia v England | Nottingham | 1938 |
| 232 | I.V.A. Richards | West Indies v England | Nottingham | 1976 |
| 231* | W.R. Hammond | England v Australia | Sydney | 1936–37 |
| 231 | A.D. Nourse | South Africa v Australia | Johannesburg[1] | 1935–36 |
| 231 | M.H. Mankad | India v New Zealand | Madras[2] | 1955–56 |
| 231 | Mudassar Nazar | Pakistan v India | Hyderabad | 1982–83 |
| 230* | B. Sutcliffe | New Zealand v India | Delhi | 1955–56 |
| 227 | W.R. Hammond | England v New Zealand | Christchurch | 1932–33 |
| 226 | D.G. Bradman | Australia v South Africa | Brisbane[2] | 1931–32 |
| 226 | G.St A. Sobers | West Indies v England | Bridgetown | 1959–60 |
| 225 | R.B. Simpson | Australia v England | Adelaide | 1965–66 |
| 223* | G.M. Turner | New Zealand v West Indies | Kingston | 1971–72 |
| 223 | G.A. Headley | West Indies v England | Kingston | 1929–30 |
| 223 | D.G. Bradman | Australia v West Indies | Brisbane[1] | 1930–31 |
| 223 | P.R. Umrigar | India v New Zealand | Hyderabad | 1955–56 |
| 223 | M.H. Mankad | India v New Zealand | Bombay[2] | 1955–56 |
| 223 | C.G. Greenidge | West Indies v England | Manchester | 1984 |
| 222 | G.R. Viswanath | India v England | Madras[1] | 1981–82 |
| 221 | S.M. Gavaskar | India v England | Oval | 1979 |
| 220 | C.L. Walcott | West Indies v England | Bridgetown | 1953–54 |
| 220 | S.M. Gavaskar | India v West Indies | Port-of-Spain | 1970–71 |
| 219 | W.J. Edrich | England v South Africa | Durban[2] | 1938–39 |
| 219 | D.St E. Atkinson | West Indies v Australia | Bridgetown | 1954–55 |
| 217 | W.R. Hammond | England v India | Oval | 1936 |
| 217 | R.B. Kanhai | West Indies v Pakistan | Lahore[1] | 1958–59 |
| 216* | E. Paynter | England v Australia | Nottingham | 1938 |
| 216 | K.W.R. Fletcher | England v New Zealand | Auckland | 1974–75 |
| 215 | Zaheer Abbas | Pakistan v India | Lahore[2] | 1982–83 |
| 215 | D.I. Gower | England v Australia | Birmingham | 1985 |
| 214* | V.T. Trumper | Australia v South Africa | Adelaide | 1910–11 |
| 214* | D. Lloyd | England v India | Birmingham | 1974 |
| 214 | L.G. Rowe | West Indies v New Zealand | Kingston | 1971–72 |
| 214* | C.G. Greenidge | West Indies v England | Lord's | 1984 |
| 213 | K.J. Hughes | Australia v India | Adelaide | 1980–81 |
| 212 | D.G. Bradman | Australia v England | Adelaide | 1936–37 |
| 212 | D.N. Sardesai | India v West Indies | Kingston | 1970–71 |
| 211 | W.L. Murdoch | Australia v England | Oval | 1884 |
| 211 | J.B. Hobbs | England v South Africa | Lord's | 1924 |
| 210* | Taslim Arif | Pakistan v Australia | Faisalabad | 1979–80 |
| 210 | W.M. Lawry | Australia v West Indies | Bridgetown | 1964–65 |

| | | | | |
|---|---|---|---|---|
| 210 | Qasim Omar | Pakistan v India | Faisalabad | 1984–85 |
| 209* | B.F. Butcher | West Indies v England | Nottingham | 1966 |
| 209 | C.A. Roach | West Indies v England | Georgetown | 1929–30 |
| 209 | Imtiaz Ahmed | Pakistan v New Zealand | Lahore[1] | 1955–56 |
| 209 | R.G. Pollock | South Africa v Australia | Cape Town | 1966–67 |
| 208 | D.C.S. Compton | England v South Africa | Lord's | 1947 |
| 208 | A.D. Nourse | South Africa v England | Nottingham | 1951 |
| 208 | I.T. Botham | England v India | Oval | 1982 |
| 208 | I.V.A. Richards | West Indies v Australia | Melbourne | 1984–85 |
| 207 | E. de C. Weekes | West Indies v India | Port-of-Spain | 1952–53 |
| 207 | K.R. Stackpole | Australia v England | Brisbane[2] | 1970–71 |
| 207 | M.W. Gatting | England v India | Madras[1] | 1984–85 |
| 206* | W.A. Brown | Australia v England | Lord's | 1938 |
| 206 | M.P. Donnelly | New Zealand v England | Lord's | 1949 |
| 206 | L. Hutton | England v New Zealand | Oval | 1949 |
| 206 | A.R. Morris | Australia v England | Adelaide | 1950–51 |
| 206 | E. de C. Weekes | West Indies v England | Port-of-Spain | 1953–54 |
| 206 | Javed Miandad | Pakistan v New Zealand | Karachi | 1976–77 |
| 205* | E.H. Hendren | England v West Indies | Port-of-Spain | 1929–30 |
| 205* | J. Hardstaff, jr | England v India | Lord's | 1946 |
| 205 | R.N. Harvey | Australia v South Africa | Melbourne | 1952–53 |
| 205 | L. Hutton | England v West Indies | Kingston | 1953–54 |
| 205 | E.R. Dexter | England v Pakistan | Karachi | 1961–62 |
| 205 | W.M. Lawry | Australia v West Indies | Melbourne | 1968–69 |
| 205 | S.M. Gavaskar | India v West Indies | Bombay[3] | 1978–79 |
| 204 | G.A. Faulkner | South Africa v Australia | Melbourne | 1910–11 |
| 204 | R.N. Harvey | Australia v West Indies | Kingston | 1954–55 |
| 204 | G.S. Chappell | Australia v India | Sydney | 1980–81 |
| 203* | Nawab of Pataudi, jr | India v England | Delhi | 1963–64 |
| 203* | Hanif Mohammad | Pakistan v New Zealand | Lahore[2] | 1964–65 |
| 203 | H.L. Collins | Australia v South Africa | Johannesburg[1] | 1921–22 |
| 203 | D.L. Amiss | England v West Indies | Oval | 1976 |
| 202* | L. Hutton | England v West Indies | Oval | 1950 |
| 201* | J. Ryder | Australia v England | Adelaide | 1924–25 |
| 201 | S.E. Gregory | Australia v England | Sydney | 1894–95 |
| 201 | D.G. Bradman | Australia v India | Adelaide | 1947–48 |
| 201 | E.J. Barlow | South Africa v Australia | Adelaide | 1963–64 |
| 201 | R.B. Simpson | Australia v West Indies | Bridgetown | 1964–65 |
| 201 | S.M. Nurse | West Indies v Australia | Bridgetown | 1964–65 |
| 201 | Mushtaq Mohammad | Pakistan v New Zealand | Dunedin | 1972–73 |
| 201 | G.S. Chappell | Australia v Pakistan | Brisbane[2] | 1981–82 |
| 201 | A.D. Gaekwad | India v Pakistan | Jullundur | 1983–84 |
| 201 | G. Fowler | England v India | Madras[1] | 1984–85 |
| 200* | D.N. Sardesai | India v New Zealand | Bombay[2] | 1964–65 |
| 200* | D.I. Gower | England v India | Birmingham | 1979 |
| 200 | W.R. Hammond | England v Australia | Melbourne | 1928–29 |
| 200 | Mohsin Khan | Pakistan v England | Lord's | 1982 |

## MOST HUNDREDS

| | | | | Opponents | | | | | | |
|---|---|---|---|---|---|---|---|---|---|---|
| | | 100 | I | E | A | SA | WI | NZ | I | P | SL |
| S.M. Gavaskar | India | 30 | 185 | 4 | 5 | – | 13 | 2 | – | 5 | 1 |
| D.G. Bradman | Australia | 29 | 80 | 19 | – | 4 | 2 | – | 4 | – | – |
| G.St A. Sobers | West Indies | 26 | 160 | 10 | 4 | – | – | 1 | 8 | 3 | – |
| G.S. Chappell | Australia | 24 | 151 | 9 | – | – | 5 | 3 | 1 | 6 | – |
| G. Boycott | England | 22 | 193 | – | 7 | 1 | 5 | 2 | 4 | 3 | – |
| M.C. Cowdrey | England | 22 | 188 | – | 5 | 3 | 6 | 2 | 3 | 3 | – |
| W.R. Hammond | England | 22 | 140 | – | 9 | 6 | 1 | 4 | 2 | – | – |
| R.N. Harvey | Australia | 21 | 137 | 6 | – | 8 | 3 | – | 4 | – | – |
| K.F. Barrington | England | 20 | 131 | – | 5 | 2 | 3 | 3 | 3 | 4 | – |
| L. Hutton | England | 19 | 138 | – | 5 | 4 | 5 | 3 | 2 | – | – |
| C.H. Lloyd | West Indies | 19 | 175 | 5 | 6 | – | – | – | 7 | 1 | – |
| I.V.A. Richards | West Indies | 19 | 116 | 7 | 4 | – | – | 1 | 6 | 1 | – |
| D.C.S. Compton | England | 17 | 131 | – | 5 | 7 | 2 | 2 | – | 1 | – |
| H. Sutcliffe | England | 16 | 84 | – | 8 | 6 | – | 2 | – | – | – |

| | | 100 | I | Opponents E | A | SA | WI | NZ | I | P | SL |
|---|---|---|---|---|---|---|---|---|---|---|---|
| J.B. Hobbs | England | 15 | 102 | – | 12 | 2 | 1 | – | – | – | – |
| R.B. Kanhai | West Indies | 15 | 137 | 5 | 5 | – | – | – | 4 | 1 | – |
| C.L. Walcott | West Indies | 15 | 74 | 4 | 5 | – | – | 1 | 4 | 1 | – |
| K.D. Walters | Australia | 15 | 125 | 4 | – | – | 6 | 3 | 1 | 1 | – |
| E. de C. Weekes | West Indies | 15 | 81 | 3 | 1 | – | – | 3 | 7 | 1 | – |
| A.R. Border | Australia | 14 | 127 | 5 | – | – | 2 | – | 2 | 5 | – |
| I.M. Chappell | Australia | 14 | 136 | 4 | – | – | 5 | 2 | 2 | 1 | – |
| G.R. Viswanath | India | 14 | 155 | 4 | 4 | – | 4 | 1 | – | 1 | – |
| I.T. Botham | England | 13 | 125 | – | 3 | – | – | 3 | 5 | 2 | – |
| Javed Miandad | Pakistan | 13 | 108 | – | 4 | – | – | 5 | 4 | – | – |
| W.M. Lawry | Australia | 13 | 123 | 7 | – | 1 | 4 | – | 1 | – | – |
| P.B.H. May | England | 13 | 106 | – | 3 | 3 | 3 | 3 | 1 | – | – |
| J.H. Edrich | England | 12 | 127 | – | 7 | – | 1 | 3 | 1 | – | – |
| D.I. Gower | England | 12 | 129 | – | 5 | – | 1 | 3 | 1 | 2 | – |
| C.G. Greenidge | West Indies | 12 | 111 | 5 | 2 | – | – | 1 | 3 | 1 | – |
| Hanif Mohammad | Pakistan | 12 | 97 | 3 | 2 | – | 2 | 3 | 2 | – | – |
| A.I. Kallicharran | West Indies | 12 | 109 | 2 | 4 | – | – | 2 | 3 | 1 | – |
| A.R. Morris | Australia | 12 | 79 | 8 | – | 2 | 1 | – | 1 | – | – |
| P.R. Umrigar | India | 12 | 94 | 3 | – | – | 3 | 1 | – | 5 | – |
| Zaheer Abbas | Pakistan | 12 | 123 | 2 | 2 | – | – | 1 | 6 | – | 1 |
| D.L. Amiss | England | 11 | 88 | – | – | – | 4 | 2 | 2 | 3 | – |
| Asif Iqbal | Pakistan | 11 | 99 | 3 | 3 | – | 1 | 3 | 1 | – | – |
| T.W. Graveney | England | 11 | 123 | – | 1 | – | 5 | – | 2 | 3 | – |
| A.L. Hassett | Australia | 10 | 69 | 4 | – | 3 | 2 | – | 1 | – | – |
| G.A. Headley | West Indies | 10 | 40 | 8 | 2 | – | – | – | – | – | – |
| Mushtaq Mohammad | Pakistan | 10 | 100 | 3 | 1 | – | 2 | 3 | 1 | – | – |
| R.B. Simpson | Australia | 10 | 111 | 2 | – | 1 | 1 | – | 4 | 2 | – |

*The leading century-maker for South Africa is A.D. Nourse (9 in 62 innings), for New Zealand B.E. Congdon (7 in 114 innings) and G.M. Turner (7 in 70 innings), and for Sri Lanka L.R.D. Mendis (3 in 20 innings).*

# MOST HUNDREDS IN A SERIES

**FIVE**

| C.L. Walcott | | West Indies v Australia | 1954–55 |
|---|---|---|---|

**FOUR**

| D.G. Bradman | (3) | Australia v England | 1930 |
|---|---|---|---|
| | | Australia v South Africa | 1931–32 |
| | | Australia v India | 1947–48 |
| D.C.S. Compton | | England v South Africa | 1947 |
| S.M. Gavaskar | (2) | India v West Indies | 1970–71 |
| | | India v West Indies | 1978–79 |
| W.R. Hammond | | England v Australia | 1928–29 |
| R.N. Harvey | (2) | Australia v South Africa | 1949–50 |
| | | Australia v South Africa | 1952–53 |
| G.A. Headley | | West Indies v England | 1929–30 |
| Mudassar Nazar | | Pakistan v India | 1982–83 |
| H. Sutcliffe | (2) | England v Australia | 1924–25 |
| | | England v South Africa | 1929 |
| K.D. Walters | | Australia v West Indies | 1968–69 |
| E. de C. Weekes | | West Indies v India | 1948–49 |

# MOST DOUBLE HUNDREDS IN A SERIES

**THREE**

| D.G. Bradman | Australia v England | 1930 |
|---|---|---|

**TWO**

| D.G. Bradman | (3) | Australia v South Africa | 1931–32 |
|---|---|---|---|
| | | Australia v England | 1934 |
| | | Australia v England | 1936–37 |
| C.G. Greenidge | | West Indies v England | 1984 |
| W.R. Hammond | (2) | England v Australia | 1928–29 |
| | | England v New Zealand | 1932–33 |
| M.H. Mankad | | India v New Zealand | 1955–56 |
| I.V.A. Richards | | West Indies v England | 1976 |
| G.M. Turner | | New Zealand v West Indies | 1971–72 |

# HUNDREDS IN MOST CONSECUTIVE INNINGS

**FIVE**

| | | | Opponents | | |
|---|---|---|---|---|---|
| E. de C. Weekes | West Indies | 141 | England | Kingston | 1947–48 |
| | | 128 | India | Delhi | 1948–49 |
| | | 194 | India | Bombay[2] | 1948–49 |
| | | 162 }<br>101 } | India | Calcutta | 1948–49 |

*Weekes was run out for 90 in his next innings (Madras[1] 1948–49).*

**FOUR**

| | | | | | |
|---|---|---|---|---|---|
| J.H.W. Fingleton | Australia | 112 | South Africa | Cape Town | 1935–36 |
| | | 108 | South Africa | Johannesburg[1] | 1935–36 |
| | | 118 | South Africa | Durban[2] | 1935–36 |
| | | 100 | England | Brisbane[2] | 1936–37 |
| A. Melville | South Africa | 103 | England | Durban[2] | 1938–39 |
| | | 189 }<br>104* } | England | Nottingham | 1947 |
| | | 117 | England | Lord's | 1947 |

**THREE**

| | | | | | |
|---|---|---|---|---|---|
| W. Bardsley | Australia | 136 }<br>130 } | England | Oval | 1909 |
| | | 132 | South Africa | Sydney | 1910–11 |
| G. Boycott | England | 119* | Australia | Adelaide | 1970–71 |
| | | 121* | Pakistan | Lord's | 1971 |
| | | 112 | Pakistan | Leeds | 1971 |
| D.G. Bradman | Australia | 132 }<br>127* } | India | Melbourne | 1947–48 |
| | | 201 | India | Adelaide | 1947–48 |
| D.C.S. Compton | England | 163 | South Africa | Nottingham | 1947 |
| | | 208 | South Africa | Lord's | 1947 |
| | | 115 | South Africa | Manchester | 1947 |
| S.M. Gavaskar (2) | India | 117* | West Indies | Bridgetown | 1970–71 |
| | | 124 }<br>220 } | West Indies | Port-of-Spain | 1970–71 |
| | | 111 }<br>137 } | Pakistan | Karachi | 1978–79 |
| | | 205 | West Indies | Bombay[3] | 1978–79 |
| C.G. Greenidge | West Indies | 134 }<br>101 } | England | Manchester | 1976 |
| | | 115 | England | Leeds | 1976 |
| V.S. Hazare | India | 122 | West Indies | Bombay[2] | 1948–49 |
| | | 164* | England | Delhi | 1951–52 |
| | | 155 | England | Bombay[2] | 1951–52 |
| G.A. Headley | West Indies | 270* | England | Kingston | 1934–35 |
| | | 106 }<br>107 } | England | Lord's | 1939 |
| C.G. Macartney | Australia | 133* | England | Lord's | 1926 |
| | | 151 | England | Leeds | 1926 |
| | | 109 | England | Manchester | 1926 |

| A.R. Morris | Australia | 155 | England | Melbourne | 1946–47 |
|---|---|---|---|---|---|
| | | 122 ⎫<br>124* ⎭ | England | Adelaide | 1946–47 |
| Mudassar Nazar | Pakistan | 231 | India | Hyderabad | 1982–83 |
| | | 152*' | India | Lahore | 1982–83 |
| | | 152 | India | Karachi | 1982–83 |
| G.St A. Sobers | West Indies | 365* | Pakistan | Kingston | 1957–58 |
| | | 125 ⎫<br>109* ⎭ | Pakistan | Georgetown | 1957–58 |
| H. Sutcliffe | England | 115 | Australia | Sydney | 1924–25 |
| | | 176⎫<br>127⎭ | Australia | Melbourne | 1924–25 |
| P.R. Umrigar | India | 117 | Pakistan | Madras[2] | 1960–61 |
| | | 112 | Pakistan | Delhi | 1960–61 |
| | | 147* | England | Kanpur | 1961–62 |
| E. de C. Weekes | West Indies | 123 | New Zealand | Dunedin | 1955–56 |
| | | 103 | New Zealand | Christchurch | 1955–56 |
| | | 156 | New Zealand | Wellington | 1955–56 |
| Zaheer Abbas | Pakistan | 215 | India | Lahore | 1982–83 |
| | | 186 | India | Karachi | 1982–83 |
| | | 168 | India | Faisalabad | 1982–83 |

# HUNDRED IN EACH INNINGS OF A MATCH

**ENGLAND**

| | | | *Opponents* | | |
|---|---|---|---|---|---|
| C.A.G. Russell | 140 | 111 | South Africa | Durban[2] | 1922–23 |
| H. Sutcliffe | 176 | 127 | Australia | Melbourne | 1924–25 |
| W.R. Hammond | 119* | 177 | Australia | Adelaide | 1928–29 |
| H. Sutcliffe | 104 | 109* | South Africa | Oval | 1929 |
| E. Paynter | 117 | 100 | South Africa | Johannesburg[1] | 1938–39 |
| D.C.S. Compton | 147 | 103* | Australia | Adelaide | 1946–47 |

**AUSTRALIA**

| | | | | | |
|---|---|---|---|---|---|
| W. Bardsley | 136 | 130 | England | Oval | 1909 |
| A.R. Morris | 122 | 124* | England | Adelaide | 1946–47 |
| D.G. Bradman | 132 | 127* | India | Melbourne | 1947–48 |
| J. Moroney | 118 | 101* | South Africa | Johannesburg[2] | 1949–50 |
| R.B. Simpson | 153 | 115 | Pakistan | Karachi | 1964–65 |
| K.D. Walters | 242 | 103 | West Indies | Sydney | 1968–69 |
| I.M. Chappell | 145 | 121 | New Zealand | Wellington | 1973–74 |
| G.S. Chappell | 247* | 133 | New Zealand | Wellington | 1973–74 |
| G.S. Chappell | 123 | 109* | West Indies | Brisbane[2] | 1975–76 |
| A.R. Border | 150* | 153 | Pakistan | Lahore[2] | 1979–80 |

**SOUTH AFRICA**

| | | | | | |
|---|---|---|---|---|---|
| A. Melville | 189 | 104* | England | Nottingham | 1947 |
| B. Mitchell | 120 | 189* | England | Oval | 1947 |

**WEST INDIES**

| | | | | | |
|---|---|---|---|---|---|
| G.A. Headley | 114 | 112 | England | Georgetown | 1929–30 |
| G.A. Headley | 106 | 107 | England | Lord's | 1939 |
| E. de C. Weekes | 162 | 101 | India | Calcutta | 1948–49 |
| C.L. Walcott | 126 | 110 | Australia | Port-of-Spain | 1954–55 |
| C.L. Walcott | 155 | 110 | Australia | Kingston | 1954–55 |
| G.St A. Sobers | 125 | 109* | Pakistan | Georgetown | 1957–58 |
| R.B. Kanhai | 117 | 115 | Australia | Adelaide | 1960–61 |
| L.G. Rowe | 214 | 100* | New Zealand | Kingston | 1971–72 |
| C.G. Greenidge | 134 | 101 | England | Manchester | 1976 |

**NEW ZEALAND**

| | | | | | |
|---|---|---|---|---|---|
| G.M. Turner | 101 | 110* | Australia | Christchurch | 1973–74 |
| G.P. Howarth | 122 | 102 | England | Auckland | 1977–78 |

| INDIA | | | Opponents | | |
|---|---|---|---|---|---|
| V.S. Hazare | 116 | 145 | Australia | Adelaide | 1947–48 |
| S.M. Gavaskar | 124 | 220 | West Indies | Port-of-Spain | 1970–71 |
| S.M. Gavaskar | 111 | 137 | Pakistan | Karachi | 1978–79 |
| S.M. Gavaskar | 107 | 182* | West Indies | Calcutta | 1978–79 |
| | | | | | |
| PAKISTAN | | | | | |
| Hanif Mohammad | 111 | 104 | England | Dacca | 1961–62 |
| Javed Miandad | 104 | 103* | New Zealand | Hyderabad | 1984–85 |
| | | | | | |
| SRI LANKA | | | | | |
| L.R.D. Mendis | 105 | 105 | India | Madras[1] | 1982–83 |

L.G. Rowe achieved this feat in his first Test match.
V.S. Hazare scored two separate hundreds on successive days – 108* (3rd day) and 102* (4th day).
L.R.D. Mendis is alone in making the same three-figure score twice in a Test match.
G. Boycott scored 99 and 112 for England v West Indies at Port-of-Spain in 1973–74.

# HUNDREDS IN MOST CONSECUTIVE MATCHES
SIX
D.G. Bradman    Australia    270, 212, 169, 144*, 102*, 103                1936–37 to 1938

Because of injury Bradman was unable to bat in his next Test but scored 187 and 234 in his following two matches in 1946–47.

# HUNDRED ON DEBUT

IN BOTH INNINGS

L.G. Rowe              214 ⎱
                       100* ⎰   West Indies v New Zealand          Kingston          1971–72

IN FIRST INNINGS

| C. Bannerman | 165* | Australia v England | Melbourne | 1876–77 |
|---|---|---|---|---|
| W.G. Grace | 152 | England v Australia | Oval | 1880 |
| H. Graham | 107 | Australia v England | Lord's | 1893 |
| R.E. Foster | 287 | England v Australia | Sydney | 1903–04 |
| G. Gunn | 119 | England v Australia | Sydney | 1907–08 |
| W.H. Ponsford | 110 | Australia v England | Sydney | 1924–25 |
| A.A. Jackson | 164 | Australia v England | Adelaide | 1928–29 |
| J.E. Mills | 117 | New Zealand v England | Wellington | 1929–30 |
| Nawab of Pataudi, sr | 102 | England v Australia | Sydney | 1932–33 |
| B.H. Valentine | 136 | England v India | Bombay[1] | 1933–34 |
| S.C. Griffith | 140 | England v West Indies | Port-of-Spain | 1947–48 |
| A.G. Ganteaume | 112 | West Indies v England | Port-of-Spain | 1947–48 |
| P.B.H. May | 138 | England v South Africa | Leeds | 1951 |
| R.H. Shodhan | 110 | India v Pakistan | Calcutta | 1952–53 |
| B.H. Pairaudeau | 115 | West Indies v India | Port-of-Spain | 1952–53 |
| A.G. Kripal Singh | 100* | India v New Zealand | Hyderabad | 1955–56 |
| C.C. Hunte | 142 | West Indies v Pakistan | Bridgetown | 1957–58 |
| C.A. Milton | 104* | England v New Zealand | Leeds | 1958 |
| Hanumant Singh | 105 | India v England | Delhi | 1963–64 |
| Khalid Ibadulla | 166 | Pakistan v Australia | Karachi | 1964–65 |
| B.R. Taylor | 105 | New Zealand v India | Calcutta | 1964–65 |
| K.D. Walters | 155 | Australia v England | Brisbane[2] | 1965–66 |
| J.H. Hampshire | 107 | England v West Indies | Lord's | 1969 |
| G.S. Chappell | 108 | Australia v England | Perth | 1970–71 |
| A.I. Kallicharran | 100* | West Indies v New Zealand | Georgetown | 1971–72 |
| R.E. Redmond | 107 | New Zealand v Pakistan | Auckland | 1972–73 |
| G.J. Cosier | 109 | Australia v West Indies | Melbourne | 1975–76 |
| S. Amarnath | 124 | India v New Zealand | Auckland | 1975–76 |
| Javed Miandad | 163 | Pakistan v New Zealand | Lahore[2] | 1976–77 |
| K.C. Wessels | 162 | Australia v England | Brisbane[2] | 1982–83 |
| W.B. Phillips | 159 | Australia v Pakistan | Perth | 1983–84 |
| M. Azharuddin | 110 | India v England | Calcutta | 1984–85 |

IN SECOND INNINGS

| K.S. Ranjitsinhji | 154* | England v Australia | Manchester | 1896 |
| P.F. Warner | 132* | England v South Africa | Johannesburg[1] | 1898–99 |
| R.A. Duff | 104 | Australia v England | Melbourne | 1901–02 |
| R.J. Hartigan | 116 | Australia v England | Adelaide | 1907–08 |
| H.L. Collins | 104 | Australia v England | Sydney | 1920–21 |
| G.A. Headley | 176 | West Indies v England | Bridgetown | 1929–30 |
| L. Amarnath | 118 | India v England | Bombay[1] | 1933–34 |
| P.A. Gibb | 106 | England v South Africa | Johannesburg[1] | 1938–39 |
| J.W. Burke | 101* | Australia v England | Adelaide | 1950–51 |
| O.G. Smith | 104 | West Indies v Australia | Kingston | 1954–55 |
| A.A. Baig | 112 | India v England | Manchester | 1959 |
| G.R. Viswanath | 137 | India v Australia | Kanpur | 1969–70 |
| F.C. Hayes | 106* | England v West Indies | Oval | 1973 |
| C.G. Greenidge | 107 | West Indies v India | Bangalore | 1974–75 |
| L. Baichan | 105* | West Indies v Pakistan | Lahore[2] | 1974–75 |
| A.B. Williams | 100 | West Indies v Australia | Georgetown | 1977–78 |
| D.M. Wellham | 103 | Australia v England | Oval | 1981 |
| Salim Malik | 100* | Pakistan v Sri Lanka | Karachi | 1981–82 |

*A.I. Kallicharran also scored a hundred in his second Test innings – 101 v New Zealand at Port-of-Spain, 1971–72.*
*M. Azharuddin scored hundreds in each of his first three Test matches, v England in 1984–85, his full scoring sequence being 110 at Calcutta, 48 and 105 at Madras[1], and 122 and 54\* at Kanpur.*
*The following scored 99 in their debut match:*
| A.G. Chipperfield | (1st innings) | Australia v England | Nottingham | 1934 |
| R.J. Christiani | (2nd innings) | West Indies v England | Bridgetown | 1947–48 |
*The highest score by a South African on debut is 97 by L.J. Tancred v Australia at Johannesburg[1] in 1902–03, while the highest by a Sri Lankan on first appearance is 77 by R.L. Dias v England at Colombo (SO) in 1981–82.*

## MOST RUNS IN FIRST TEST MATCH

| 314 | L.G. Rowe | (214, 100*) | West Indies v New Zealand | Kingston | 1971–72 |
| 306 | R.E. Foster | (287, 19) | England v Australia | Sydney | 1903–04 |

*B.M. Laird (92 and 75) scored 167 runs for Australia v West Indies at Brisbane[2] in 1979–80 – the highest aggregate without a hundred by any player in his first Test.*

## MAIDEN FIRST-CLASS HUNDRED IN A TEST MATCH

| C. Bannerman†‡ | 165* | Australia v England | Melbourne | 1876–77 |
| W.L. Murdoch | 153* | Australia v England | Oval | 1880 |
| P.S. McDonnell | 147 | Australia v England | Sydney | 1881–82 |
| H. Wood‡ | 134* | England v South Africa | Cape Town | 1891–92 |
| H. Graham† | 107 | Australia v England | Lord's | 1893 |
| A.J.L. Hill | 124 | England v South Africa | Cape Town | 1895–96 |
| J.H. Sinclair | 106 | South Africa v England | Cape Town | 1898–99 |
| P.W. Sherwell | 115 | South Africa v England | Lord's | 1907 |
| H.G. Owen-Smith | 129 | South Africa v England | Leeds | 1929 |
| C.A. Roach | 122 | West Indies v England | Bridgetown | 1929–30 |
| S.C. Griffith† | 140 | England v West Indies | Port-of-Spain | 1947–48 |
| V.L. Manjrekar | 133 | India v England | Leeds | 1952 |
| C.C. Depeiza‡ | 122 | West Indies v Australia | Bridgetown | 1954–55 |
| P.L. Winslow | 108 | South Africa v England | Manchester | 1955 |
| S.N. McGregor | 111 | New Zealand v Pakistan | Lahore[1] | 1955–56 |
| F.C.M. Alexander‡ | 108 | West Indies v Australia | Sydney | 1960–61 |
| Nasim-ul-Ghani | 101 | Pakistan v England | Lord's | 1962 |
| B.R. Taylor† | 105 | New Zealand v India | Calcutta | 1964–65 |
| B.D. Julien | 121 | West Indies v England | Lord's | 1973 |
| W.K. Lees | 152 | New Zealand v Pakistan | Karachi | 1976–77 |
| Kapil Dev | 126* | India v West Indies | Delhi | 1978–79 |
| S. Wettimuny | 157 | Sri Lanka v Pakistan | Faisalabad | 1981–82 |
| S.A.R. Silva | 102* | Sri Lanka v England | Lord's | 1984 |

*† On Test debut   ‡ Only hundred in first-class cricket*
*H. Graham (105 v England at Sydney in 1894–95), C.A. Roach (209 v England at Georgetown in 1929–1930) and B.R. Taylor (124 v West Indies at Auckland in 1968–69) also scored their second first-class hundred in a Test match.*

# YOUNGEST PLAYERS TO SCORE A HUNDRED

| Years | Days | | | | | |
|---|---|---|---|---|---|---|
| 17 | 82 | Mushtaq Mohammad | 101 | Pakistan v India | Delhi | 1960–6 |
| 18 | 328 | Salim Malik | 100* | Pakistan v Sri Lanka | Karachi | 1981–8 |
| 19 | 26 | Mohammad Ilyas | 126 | Pakistan v New Zealand | Karachi | 1964–6 |
| 19 | 119 | Javed Miandad | 163 | Pakistan v New Zealand | Lahore² | 1976–7 |
| 19 | 121 | H.G. Vivian | 100 | New Zealand v South Africa | Wellington | 1931–3 |
| 19 | 121 | R.N. Harvey | 153 | Australia v India | Melbourne | 1947–4 |
| 19 | 152 | A.A. Jackson | 164 | Australia v England | Adelaide | 1928–2 |
| 19 | 318 | R.G. Pollock | 122 | South Africa v Australia | Sydney | 1963–6 |
| 19 | 357 | K.D. Walters | 155 | Australia v England | Brisbane² | 1965–6 |
| 20 | 19 | D.C.S. Compton | 102 | England v Australia | Nottingham | 193 |
| 20 | 21 | Kapil Dev | 126* | India v West Indies | Delhi | 1978–7 |
| 20 | 58 | Hanif Mohammad | 142 | Pakistan v India | Bahawalpur | 1954–5 |
| 20 | 129 | D.G. Bradman | 112 | Australia v England | Melbourne | 1928–2 |
| 20 | 131 | A.A. Baig | 112 | India v England | Manchester | 195 |
| 20 | 148 | H.G. Owen-Smith | 129 | South Africa v England | Leeds | 192 |
| 20 | 154 | Saeed Ahmed | 150 | Pakistan v West Indies | Georgetown | 1957–5 |
| 20 | 230 | G.A. Headley | 176 | West Indies v England | Bridgetown | 1929–3 |
| 20 | 240 | J.W. Burke | 101* | Australia v England | Adelaide | 1950–5 |
| 20 | 249 | R.J. Shastri | 128 | India v Pakistan | Karachi | 1982–8 |
| 20 | 253 | V.L. Manjrekar | 133 | India v England | Leeds | 195 |
| 20 | 281 | G.R. Viswanath | 137 | India v Australia | Kanpur | 1969–7 |
| 20 | 317 | C. Hill | 188 | Australia v England | Melbourne | 1897–9 |
| 20 | 324 | J.W. Hearne | 114 | England v Australia | Melbourne | 1911–1 |
| 20 | 330 | O.G. Smith | 104 | West Indies v Australia | Kingston | 1954–5 |

*Only the first hundred is listed for each player. Mushtaq Mohammad scored two hundreds before his 19th birthday, R.N. Harvey, R.G. Pollock, Javed Miandad and Salim Malik each scored two before their 20th and G.A. Headley scored four before his 21st.*

## YOUNGEST PLAYERS TO SCORE A DOUBLE HUNDRED

| Years | Days | | | | | |
|---|---|---|---|---|---|---|
| 19 | 141 | Javed Miandad | 206 | Pakistan v New Zealand | Karachi | 1976–77 |
| 20 | 315 | G.A. Headley | 223 | West Indies v England | Kingston | 1929–30 |

## YOUNGEST PLAYERS TO SCORE A TRIPLE HUNDRED

| Years | Days | | | | | |
|---|---|---|---|---|---|---|
| 21 | 216 | G.St A. Sobers | 365* | West Indies v Pakistan | Kingston | 1957–58 |
| 21 | 318 | D.G. Bradman | 334 | Australia v England | Leeds | 1930 |

## OLDEST PLAYERS TO SCORE A HUNDRED

| Years | Days | | | | | |
|---|---|---|---|---|---|---|
| 46 | 82 | J.B. Hobbs | 142 | England v Australia | Melbourne | 1928–29 |
| 45 | 240 | J.B. Hobbs | 159 | England v West Indies | Oval | 1928 |
| 45 | 151 | E.H. Hendren | 132 | England v Australia | Manchester | 1934 |

*The ages of Indian and Pakistani players have not been confirmed.*

# DISTRIBUTION OF TEST MATCH HUNDREDS

| Conceded By | E | A | SA | Scored For WI | NZ | I | P | SL | Total Conceded |
|---|---|---|---|---|---|---|---|---|---|
| England | – | 198 | 58 | 87 | 26 | 48 | 25 | 3 | 445 |
| Australia | 179 | – | 36 | 63 | 9 | 23 | 25 | 0 | 335 |
| South Africa | 87 | 55 | – | – | 7 | – | – | – | 149 |
| West Indies | 81 | 64 | – | – | 14 | 49 | 14 | – | 222 |
| New Zealand | 65 | 14 | 11 | 23 | – | 20 | 26 | 1 | 160 |
| India | 59 | 36 | – | 67 | 16 | – | 31 | 2 | 211 |
| Pakistan | 36 | 32 | – | 17 | 16 | 23 | – | 2 | 126 |
| Sri Lanka | 1 | 2 | – | – | 1 | 2 | 4 | – | 10 |
| Total Scored | 508 | 401 | 105 | 257 | 89 | 165 | 125 | 8 | 1658 |

# HUNDREDS IN TEST CRICKET

† *Denotes hundred on first appearance against that country.*

## ENGLAND (508)

| | | | Opponents | | |
|---|---|---|---|---|---|
| Abel, R. | (2) | 120 | South Africa | Cape Town | 1888–89 |
| | | 132* | Australia | Sydney | 1891–92 |
| Allen, G.O.B. | | 122† | New Zealand | Lord's | 1931 |
| Ames, L.E.G. | (8) | 105 | West Indies | Port-of-Spain | 1929–30 |
| | | 149 | West Indies | Kingston | 1929–30 |
| | | 137† | New Zealand | Lord's | 1931 |
| | | 103 | New Zealand | Christchurch | 1932–33 |
| | | 120 | Australia | Lord's | 1934 |
| | | 126 | West Indies | Kingston | 1934–35 |
| | | 148* | South Africa | Oval | 1935 |
| | | 115 | South Africa | Cape Town | 1938–39 |
| Amiss, D.L. | (11) | 112 | Pakistan | Lahore[2] | 1972–73 |
| | | 158 | Pakistan | Hyderabad | 1972–73 |
| | | 138*† | New Zealand | Nottingham | 1973 |
| | | 174 | West Indies | Port-of-Spain | 1973–74 |
| | | 262* | West Indies | Kingston | 1973–74 |
| | | 118 | West Indies | Georgetown | 1973–74 |
| | | 188 | India | Lord's | 1974 |
| | | 183 | Pakistan | Oval | 1974 |
| | | 164* | New Zealand | Christchurch | 1974–75 |
| | | 203 | West Indies | Oval | 1976 |
| | | 179 | India | Delhi | 1976–77 |
| Bailey, T.E. | | 134* | New Zealand | Christchurch | 1950–51 |
| Bakewell, A.H. | | 107† | West Indies | Oval | 1933 |
| Barber, R.W. | | 185 | Australia | Sydney | 1965–66 |
| Barnes, W. | | 134 | Australia | Adelaide | 1884–85 |
| Barnett, C.J. | (2) | 129 | Australia | Adelaide | 1936–37 |
| | | 126 | Australia | Nottingham | 1938 |
| Barrington, K.F. | (20) | 128† | West Indies | Bridgetown | 1959–60 |
| | | 121 | West Indies | Port-of-Spain | 1959–60 |
| | | 139† | Pakistan | Lahore[2] | 1961–62 |
| | | 151* | India | Bombay[2] | 1961–62 |
| | | 172 | India | Kanpur | 1961–62 |
| | | 113* | India | Delhi | 1961–62 |
| | | 132* | Australia | Adelaide | 1962–63 |
| | | 101 | Australia | Sydney | 1962–63 |
| | | 126† | New Zealand | Auckland | 1962–63 |
| | | 256 | Australia | Manchester | 1964 |
| | | 148* | South Africa | Durban[2] | 1964–65 |
| | | 121 | South Africa | Johannesburg[3] | 1964–65 |
| | | 137 | New Zealand | Birmingham | 1965 |
| | | 163 | New Zealand | Leeds | 1965 |

| | | | Opponents | | |
|---|---|---|---|---|---|
| Barrington, K. F. *continued* | | 102 | Australia | Adelaide | 1965–6 |
| | | 115 | Australia | Melbourne | 1965–6 |
| | | 148 | Pakistan | Lord's | 196 |
| | | 109* | Pakistan | Nottingham | 196 |
| | | 142 | Pakistan | Oval | 196 |
| | | 143 | West Indies | Port-of-Spain | 1967–6 |
| Botham, I.T. | (13) | 103 | New Zealand | Christchurch | 1977–7 |
| | | 100† | Pakistan | Birmingham | 197 |
| | | 108 | Pakistan | Lord's | 197 |
| | | 137 | India | Leeds | 197 |
| | | 119* | Australia | Melbourne | 1979–8 |
| | | 114 | India | Bombay[3] | 1979–8 |
| | | 149* | Australia | Leeds | 198 |
| | | 118 | Australia | Manchester | 198 |
| | | 142 | India | Kanpur | 1981–8 |
| | | 128 | India | Manchester | 198 |
| | | 208 | India | Oval | 198 |
| | | 103 | New Zealand | Nottingham | 198 |
| | | 138 | New Zealand | Wellington | 1983–8 |
| Bowley, E.H. | | 109 | New Zealand | Auckland | 1929–3 |
| Boycott, G. | (22) | 113 | Australia | Oval | 196 |
| | | 117 | South Africa | Port Elizabeth | 1964–6 |
| | | 246*† | India | Leeds | 196 |
| | | 116 | West Indies | Georgetown | 1967–6 |
| | | 128 | West Indies | Manchester | 196 |
| | | 106 | West Indies | Lord's | 196 |
| | | 142* | Australia | Sydney | 1970–7 |
| | | 119* | Australia | Adelaide | 1970–7 |
| | | 121* | Pakistan | Lord's | 197 |
| | | 112 | Pakistan | Leeds | 197 |
| | | 115 | New Zealand | Leeds | 197 |
| | | 112 | West Indies | Port-of-Spain | 1973–7 |
| | | 107 | Australia | Nottingham | 197 |
| | | 191 | Australia | Leeds | 197 |
| | | | *(His 100th first-class hundred)* | | |
| | | 100* | Pakistan | Hyderabad | 1977–7 |
| | | 131 | New Zealand | Nottingham | 197 |
| | | 155 | India | Birmingham | 197 |
| | | 125 | India | Oval | 197 |
| | | 128* | Australia | Lord's | 198 |
| | | 104* | West Indies | St John's | 1980–8 |
| | | 137 | Australia | Oval | 198 |
| | | 105 | India | Delhi | 1981–8 |
| Braund, L.C. | (3) | 103* | Australia | Adelaide | 1901–0 |
| | | 102 | Australia | Sydney | 1903–0 |
| | | 104† | South Africa | Lord's | 190 |
| Briggs, J. | | 121 | Australia | Melbourne | 1884–8 |
| Brown, J.T. | | 140 | Australia | Melbourne | 1894–9 |
| Chapman, A.P.F. | | 121 | Australia | Lord's | 193 |
| Compton, D.C.S. | (17) | 102† | Australia | Nottingham | 193 |
| | | 120† | West Indies | Lord's | 193 |
| | | 147 ⎫ 103* ⎭ | Australia | Adelaide | 1946–4 |
| | | 163† | South Africa | Nottingham | 194 |
| | | 208 | South Africa | Lord's | 194 |
| | | 115 | South Africa | Manchester | 194 |
| | | 113 | South Africa | Oval | 194 |
| | | 184 | Australia | Nottingham | 194 |
| | | 145* | Australia | Manchester | 194 |
| | | 114 | South Africa | Johannesburg[2] | 1948–4 |
| | | 114 | New Zealand | Leeds | 194 |
| | | 116 | New Zealand | Lord's | 194 |
| | | 112 | South Africa | Nottingham | 195 |
| | | 133 | West Indies | Port-of-Spain | 1953–5 |
| | | 278 | Pakistan | Nottingham | 195 |
| | | 158 | South Africa | Manchester | 195 |

|  |  |  | *Opponents* |  |  |
|---|---|---|---|---|---|
| Cowdrey, M.C. | (22) | 102 | Australia | Melbourne | 1954–55 |
|  |  | 101 | South Africa | Cape Town | 1956–57 |
|  |  | 154† | West Indies | Birmingham | 1957 |
|  |  | 152 | West Indies | Lord's | 1957 |
|  |  | 100* | Australia | Sydney | 1958–59 |
|  |  | 160 | India | Leeds | 1959 |
|  |  | 114 | West Indies | Kingston | 1959–60 |
|  |  | 119 | West Indies | Port-of-Spain | 1959–60 |
|  |  | 155 | South Africa | Oval | 1960 |
|  |  | 159† | Pakistan | Birmingham | 1962 |
|  |  | 182 | Pakistan | Oval | 1962 |
|  |  | 113 | Australia | Melbourne | 1962–63 |
|  |  | 128* | New Zealand | Wellington | 1962–63 |
|  |  | 107 | India | Calcutta | 1963–64 |
|  |  | 151 | India | Delhi | 1963–64 |
|  |  | 119 | New Zealand | Lord's | 1965 |
|  |  | 105 | South Africa | Nottingham | 1965 |
|  |  | 104 | Australia | Melbourne | 1965–66 |
|  |  | 101 | West Indies | Kingston | 1967–68 |
|  |  | 148 | West Indies | Port-of-Spain | 1967–68 |
|  |  | 104 | Australia | Birmingham | 1968 |
|  |  |  | *(In his 100th Test match)* |  |  |
|  |  | 100 | Pakistan | Lahore[2] | 1968–69 |
| Denness, M.H. | (4) | 118 | India | Lord's | 1974 |
|  |  | 100 | India | Birmingham | 1974 |
|  |  | 188 | Australia | Melbourne | 1974–75 |
|  |  | 181 | New Zealand | Auckland | 1974–75 |
| Denton, D. |  | 104 | South Africa | Johannesburg[1] | 1909–10 |
| Dexter, E.R. | (9) | 141 | New Zealand | Christchurch | 1958–59 |
|  |  | 136*† | West Indies | Bridgetown | 1959–60 |
|  |  | 110 | West Indies | Georgetown | 1959–60 |
|  |  | 180 | Australia | Birmingham | 1961 |
|  |  | 126* | India | Kanpur | 1961–62 |
|  |  | 205 | Pakistan | Karachi | 1961–62 |
|  |  | 172 | Pakistan | Oval | 1962 |
|  |  | 174 | Australia | Manchester | 1964 |
|  |  | 172 | South Africa | Johannesburg[3] | 1964–65 |
| D'Oliveira, B.L. | (5) | 109† | India | Leeds | 1967 |
|  |  | 158 | Australia | Oval | 1968 |
|  |  | 114* | Pakistan | Dacca | 1968–69 |
|  |  | 117 | Australia | Melbourne | 1970–71 |
|  |  | 100 | New Zealand | Christchurch | 1970–71 |
| Douglas, J.W.H.T. |  | 119† | South Africa | Durban[1] | 1913–14 |
| Duleepsinhji, K.S. | (3) | 117 | New Zealand | Auckland | 1929–30 |
|  |  | 173† | Australia | Lord's | 1930 |
|  |  | 109 | New Zealand | Oval | 1931 |
| Edrich, J.H. | (12) | 120† | Australia | Lord's | 1964 |
|  |  | 310*† | New Zealand | Leeds | 1965 |
|  |  | 109 | Australia | Melbourne | 1965–66 |
|  |  | 103 | Australia | Sydney | 1965–66 |
|  |  | 146 | West Indies | Bridgetown | 1967–68 |
|  |  | 164 | Australia | Oval | 1968 |
|  |  | 115 | New Zealand | Lord's | 1969 |
|  |  | 115 | New Zealand | Nottingham | 1969 |
|  |  | 115* | Australia | Perth | 1970–71 |
|  |  | 130 | Australia | Adelaide | 1970–71 |
|  |  | 100* | India | Manchester | 1974 |
|  |  | 175 | Australia | Lord's | 1975 |
| Edrich, W.J. | (6) | 219 | South Africa | Durban[2] | 1938–39 |
|  |  | 119 | Australia | Sydney | 1946–47 |
|  |  | 189 | South Africa | Lord's | 1947 |
|  |  | 191 | South Africa | Manchester | 1947 |
|  |  | 111 | Australia | Leeds | 1948 |
|  |  | 100 | New Zealand | Oval | 1949 |
| Evans, T.G. | (2) | 104 | West Indies | Manchester | 1950 |
|  |  | 104 | India | Lord's | 1952 |

|  |  |  | *Opponents* |  |  |
|---|---|---|---|---|---|
| Fane, F.L. |  | 143 | South Africa | Johannesburg[1] | 1905–06 |
| Fletcher, K.W.R. | (7) | 113 | India | Bombay[2] | 1972–73 |
|  |  | 178 | New Zealand | Lord's | 1973 |
|  |  | 129* | West Indies | Bridgetown | 1973–74 |
|  |  | 123* | India | Manchester | 1974 |
|  |  | 122 | Pakistan | Oval | 1974 |
|  |  | 146 | Australia | Melbourne | 1974–75 |
|  |  | 216 | New Zealand | Auckland | 1974–75 |
| Foster, R.E. |  | 287† | Australia | Sydney | 1903–04 |
| Fowler, G. | (3) | 105† | New Zealand | Oval | 1983 |
|  |  | 106 | West Indies | Lord's | 1984 |
|  |  | 201 | India | Madras[1] | 1984–85 |
| Fry, C.B. | (2) | 144 | Australia | Oval | 1905 |
|  |  | 129 | South Africa | Oval | 1907 |
| Gatting, M.W. | (4) | 136 | India | Bombay[3] | 1984–85 |
|  |  | 207 | India | Madras[1] | 1984–85 |
|  |  | 100* | Australia | Birmingham | 1985 |
|  |  | 160 | Australia | Manchester | 1985 |
| Gibb, P.A. | (2) | 106† | South Africa | Johannesburg[1] | 1938–39 |
|  |  | 120 | South Africa | Durban[2] | 1938–39 |
| Gooch, G.A. | (5) | 123 | West Indies | Lord's | 1980 |
|  |  | 116 | West Indies | Bridgetown | 1980–81 |
|  |  | 153 | West Indies | Kingston | 1980–81 |
|  |  | 127 | India | Madras[1] | 1981–82 |
|  |  | 196 | Australia | Oval | 1985 |
| Gower, D.I. | (12) | 111† | New Zealand | Oval | 1978 |
|  |  | 102 | Australia | Perth | 1978–79 |
|  |  | 200*† | India | Birmingham | 1979 |
|  |  | 154* | West Indies | Kingston | 1980–81 |
|  |  | 114 | Australia | Adelaide | 1982–83 |
|  |  | 112* | New Zealand | Leeds | 1983 |
|  |  | 108 | New Zealand | Lord's | 1983 |
|  |  | 152 | Pakistan | Faisalabad | 1983–84 |
|  |  | 173* | Pakistan | Lahore[2] | 1983–84 |
|  |  | 166 | Australia | Nottingham | 1985 |
|  |  | 215 | Australia | Birmingham | 1985 |
|  |  | 157 | Australia | Oval | 1985 |
| Grace, W.G. | (2) | 152† | Australia | Oval | 1880 |
|  |  | 170 | Australia | Oval | 1886 |
| Graveney, T.W. | (11) | 175† | India | Bombay[2] | 1951–52 |
|  |  | 111 | Australia | Sydney | 1954–55 |
|  |  | 258 | West Indies | Nottingham | 1957 |
|  |  | 164 | West Indies | Oval | 1957 |
|  |  | 153 | Pakistan | Lord's | 1962 |
|  |  | 114 | Pakistan | Nottingham | 1962 |
|  |  | 109 | West Indies | Nottingham | 1966 |
|  |  | 165 | West Indies | Oval | 1966 |
|  |  | 151 | India | Lord's | 1967 |
|  |  | 118 | West Indies | Port-of-Spain | 1967–68 |
|  |  | 105 | Pakistan | Karachi | 1968–69 |
| Greig, A.W. | (8) | 148 | India | Bombay[2] | 1972–73 |
|  |  | 139† | New Zealand | Nottingham | 1973 |
|  |  | 148 | West Indies | Bridgetown | 1973–74 |
|  |  | 121 | West Indies | Georgetown | 1973–74 |
|  |  | 106 | India | Lord's | 1974 |
|  |  | 110 | Australia | Brisbane[2] | 1974–75 |
|  |  | 116 | West Indies | Leeds | 1976 |
|  |  | 103 | India | Calcutta | 1976–77 |
| Griffith, S.C. |  | 140† | West Indies | Port-of-Spain | 1947–48 |
| Gunn, G. | (2) | 119† | Australia | Sydney | 1907–08 |
|  |  | 122* | Australia | Sydney | 1907–08 |
| Gunn, W. |  | 102* | Australia | Manchester | 1893 |
| Hammond, W.R. | (22) | 251 | Australia | Sydney | 1928–29 |
|  |  | 200 | Australia | Melbourne | 1928–29 |
|  |  | 119* / 177 | Australia | Adelaide | 1928–29 |

|  |  |  | *Opponents* |  |  |
|---|---|---|---|---|---|
| Hammond W.R. *continued* |  | 138* | South Africa | Birmingham | 1929 |
|  |  | 101* | South Africa | Oval | 1929 |
|  |  | 113 | Australia | Leeds | 1930 |
|  |  | 136* | South Africa | Durban[2] | 1930–31 |
|  |  | 100* | New Zealand | Oval | 1931 |
|  |  | 112 | Australia | Sydney | 1932–33 |
|  |  | 101 | Australia | Sydney | 1932–33 |
|  |  | 227 | New Zealand | Christchurch | 1932–33 |
|  |  | 336* | New Zealand | Auckland | 1932–33 |
|  |  | 167 | India | Manchester | 1936 |
|  |  | 217 | India | Oval | 1936 |
|  |  | 231* | Australia | Sydney | 1936–37 |
|  |  | 140 | New Zealand | Lord's | 1937 |
|  |  | 240 | Australia | Lord's | 1938 |
|  |  | 181 | South Africa | Cape Town | 1938–39 |
|  |  | 120 | South Africa | Durban[2] | 1938–39 |
|  |  | 140 | South Africa | Durban[2] | 1938–39 |
|  |  | 138 | West Indies | Oval | 1939 |
| Hampshire, J.H. |  | 107† | West Indies | Lord's | 1969 |
| Hardstaff, J., jr | (4) | 114† | New Zealand | Lord's | 1937 |
|  |  | 103 | New Zealand | Oval | 1937 |
|  |  | 169* | Australia | Oval | 1938 |
|  |  | 205* | India | Lord's | 1946 |
| Hayes, F.C. |  | 106*† | West Indies | Oval | 1973 |
| Hayward, T.W. | (3) | 122 | South Africa | Johannesburg[1] | 1895–96 |
|  |  | 130 | Australia | Manchester | 1899 |
|  |  | 137 | Australia | Oval | 1899 |
| Hearne, J.W. |  | 114 | Australia | Melbourne | 1911–12 |
| Hendren, E.H. | (7) | 132 | South Africa | Leeds | 1924 |
|  |  | 142 | South Africa | Oval | 1924 |
|  |  | 127* | Australia | Lord's | 1926 |
|  |  | 169 | Australia | Brisbane[1] | 1928–29 |
|  |  | 205* | West Indies | Port-of-Spain | 1929–30 |
|  |  | 123 | West Indies | Georgetown | 1929–30 |
|  |  | 132 | Australia | Manchester | 1934 |
| Hill, A.J.L. |  | 124 | South Africa | Cape Town | 1895–96 |
| Hobbs, J.B. | (15) | 187 | South Africa | Cape Town | 1909–10 |
|  |  | 126* | Australia | Melbourne | 1911–12 |
|  |  | 187 | Australia | Adelaide | 1911–12 |
|  |  | 178 | Australia | Melbourne | 1911–12 |
|  |  | 107 | Australia | Lord's | 1912 |
|  |  | 122 | Australia | Melbourne | 1920–21 |
|  |  | 123 | Australia | Adelaide | 1920–21 |
|  |  | 211 | South Africa | Lord's | 1924 |
|  |  | 115 | Australia | Sydney | 1924–25 |
|  |  | 154 | Australia | Melbourne | 1924–25 |
|  |  | 119 | Australia | Adelaide | 1924–25 |
|  |  | 119 | Australia | Lord's | 1926 |
|  |  | 100 | Australia | Oval | 1926 |
|  |  | 159 | West Indies | Oval | 1928 |
|  |  | 142 | Australia | Melbourne | 1928–29 |
| Hutchings, K.L. |  | 126 | Australia | Melbourne | 1907–08 |
| Hutton, L. | (19) | 100 | New Zealand | Manchester | 1937 |
|  |  | 100† | Australia | Nottingham | 1938 |
|  |  | 364 | Australia | Oval | 1938 |
|  |  | 196† | West Indies | Lord's | 1939 |
|  |  | 165* | West Indies | Oval | 1939 |
|  |  | 122* | Australia | Sydney | 1946–47 |
|  |  | 100 | South Africa | Leeds | 1947 |
|  |  | 158 | South Africa | Johannesburg[2] | 1948–49 |
|  |  | 123 | South Africa | Johannesburg[2] | 1948–49 |
|  |  | 101 | New Zealand | Leeds | 1949 |
|  |  | 206 | New Zealand | Oval | 1949 |
|  |  | 202* | West Indies | Oval | 1950 |
|  |  | 156* | Australia | Adelaide | 1950–51 |
|  |  | 100 | South Africa | Leeds | 1951 |

| | | | *Opponents* | | |
|---|---|---|---|---|---|
| Hutton, L. *continued* | | 150 | India | Lord's | 1952 |
| | | 104 | India | Manchester | 1952 |
| | | 145 | Australia | Lord's | 1953 |
| | | 169 | West Indies | Georgetown | 1953–54 |
| | | 205 | West Indies | Kingston | 1953–54 |
| Illingworth, R. | (2) | 113 | West Indies | Lord's | 1969 |
| | | 107 | India | Manchester | 1971 |
| Insole, D.J. | | 110* | South Africa | Durban[2] | 1956–57 |
| Jackson, Hon F.S. | (5) | 103 | Australia | Oval | 1893 |
| | | 118 | Australia | Oval | 1899 |
| | | 128 | Australia | Manchester | 1902 |
| | | 144* | Australia | Leeds | 1905 |
| | | 113 | Australia | Manchester | 1905 |
| Jardine, D.R. | | 127 | West Indies | Manchester | 1933 |
| Jessop, G.L. | | 104 | Australia | Oval | 1902 |
| Knight, B.R. | (2) | 125† | New Zealand | Auckland | 1962–63 |
| | | 127 | India | Kanpur | 1963–64 |
| Knott, A.P.E. | (5) | 101 | New Zealand | Auckland | 1970–71 |
| | | 116 | Pakistan | Birmingham | 1971 |
| | | 106* | Australia | Adelaide | 1974–75 |
| | | 116 | West Indies | Leeds | 1976 |
| | | 135 | Australia | Nottingham | 1977 |
| Lamb, A.J. | (7) | 107 | India | Oval | 1982 |
| | | 102*† | New Zealand | Oval | 1983 |
| | | 137* | New Zealand | Nottingham | 1983 |
| | | 110 | West Indies | Lord's | 1984 |
| | | 100 | West Indies | Leeds | 1984 |
| | | 100* | West Indies | Manchester | 1984 |
| | | 107† | Sri Lanka | Lord's | 1984 |
| Legge, G.B. | | 196 | New Zealand | Auckland | 1929–30 |
| Lewis, A.R. | | 125 | India | Kanpur | 1972–7. |
| Leyland, M. | (9) | 137† | Australia | Melbourne | 1928–2 |
| | | 102 | South Africa | Lord's | 1929 |
| | | 109 | Australia | Lord's | 1934 |
| | | 153 | Australia | Manchester | 1934 |
| | | 110 | Australia | Oval | 1934 |
| | | 161 | South Africa | Oval | 1935 |
| | | 126 | Australia | Brisbane[2] | 1936–3. |
| | | 111* | Australia | Melbourne | 1936–3 |
| | | 187 | Australia | Oval | 1938 |
| Lloyd, D. | | 214* | India | Birmingham | 1974 |
| Luckhurst, B.W. | (4) | 131 | Australia | Perth | 1970–71 |
| | | 109 | Australia | Melbourne | 1970–71 |
| | | 108*† | Pakistan | Birmingham | 1971 |
| | | 101 | India | Manchester | 1971 |
| MacLaren, A.C. | (5) | 120 | Australia | Melbourne | 1894–9. |
| | | 109 | Australia | Sydney | 1897–98 |
| | | 124 | Australia | Adelaide | 1897–98 |
| | | 116 | Australia | Sydney | 1901–0. |
| | | 140 | Australia | Nottingham | 1905 |
| Makepeace, J.W.H. | | 117 | Australia | Melbourne | 1920–21 |
| Mann, F.G. | | 136* | South Africa | Port Elizabeth | 1948–4 |
| May, P.B.H. | (13) | 138† | South Africa | Leeds | 1951 |
| | | 135 | West Indies | Port-of-Spain | 1953–54 |
| | | 104 | Australia | Sydney | 1954–55 |
| | | 112 | South Africa | Lord's | 1955 |
| | | 117 | South Africa | Manchester | 1955 |
| | | 101 | Australia | Leeds | 1956 |
| | | 285* | West Indies | Birmingham | 1957 |
| | | 104 | West Indies | Nottingham | 1957 |
| | | 113* | New Zealand | Leeds | 1958 |
| | | 101 | New Zealand | Manchester | 1958 |
| | | 113 | Australia | Melbourne | 1958–59 |
| | | 124* | New Zealand | Auckland | 1958–59 |
| | | 106 | India | Nottingham | 1959 |
| Mead, C.P. | (4) | 102 | South Africa | Johannesburg[1] | 1913–1 |

|  |  | | *Opponents* | | |
|---|---|---|---|---|---|
| Mead, C.P. *continued* |  | 117 | South Africa | Port Elizabeth | 1913–14 |
|  |  | 182* | Australia | Oval | 1921 |
|  |  | 181 | South Africa | Durban[2] | 1922–23 |
| Milburn, C. | (2) | 126* | West Indies | Lord's | 1966 |
|  |  | 139 | Pakistan | Karachi | 1968–69 |
| Milton, C.A. |  | 104*† | New Zealand | Leeds | 1958 |
| Murray, J.T. |  | 112† | West Indies | Oval | 1966 |
| Parfitt, P.H. | (7) | 111 | Pakistan | Karachi | 1961–62 |
|  |  | 101* | Pakistan | Birmingham | 1962 |
|  |  | 119 | Pakistan | Leeds | 1962 |
|  |  | 101* | Pakistan | Nottingham | 1962 |
|  |  | 131*† | New Zealand | Auckland | 1962–63 |
|  |  | 121 | India | Kanpur | 1963–64 |
|  |  | 122* | South Africa | Johannesburg[3] | 1964–65 |
| Parks, J.M. | (2) | 101*† | West Indies | Port-of-Spain | 1959–60 |
|  |  | 108* | South Africa | Durban[2] | 1964–65 |
| Pataudi, Nawab of, sr |  | 102† | Australia | Sydney | 1932–33 |
| Paynter, E. | (4) | 216* | Australia | Nottingham | 1938 |
|  |  | 117†⎫<br>100†⎭ | South Africa | Johannesburg[1] | 1938–39 |
|  |  | 243 | South Africa | Durban[2] | 1938–39 |
| Place, W. |  | 107 | West Indies | Kingston | 1947–48 |
| Pullar, G. | (4) | 131 | India | Manchester | 1959 |
|  |  | 175 | South Africa | Oval | 1960 |
|  |  | 119 | India | Kanpur | 1961–62 |
|  |  | 165 | Pakistan | Dacca | 1961–62 |
| Radley, C.T. | (2) | 158 | New Zealand | Auckland | 1977–78 |
|  |  | 106† | Pakistan | Birmingham | 1978 |
| Randall, D.W. | (7) | 174† | Australia | Melbourne | 1976–77 |
|  |  | 150 | Australia | Sydney | 1978–79 |
|  |  | 126 | India | Lord's | 1982 |
|  |  | 105 | Pakistan | Birmingham | 1982 |
|  |  | 115 | Australia | Perth | 1982–83 |
|  |  | 164 | New Zealand | Wellington | 1983–84 |
|  |  | 104 | New Zealand | Auckland | 1983–84 |
| Ranjitsinhji, K.S. | (2) | 154*† | Australia | Manchester | 1896 |
|  |  | 175 | Australia | Sydney | 1897–98 |
| Read, W.W. |  | 117 | Australia | Oval | 1884 |
| Rhodes, W. | (2) | 179 | Australia | Melbourne | 1911–12 |
|  |  | 152 | South Africa | Johannesburg[1] | 1913–14 |
| Richardson, P.E. | (5) | 104 | Australia | Manchester | 1956 |
|  |  | 117† | South Africa | Johannesburg[3] | 1956–57 |
|  |  | 126 | West Indies | Nottingham | 1957 |
|  |  | 107 | West Indies | Oval | 1957 |
|  |  | 100† | New Zealand | Birmingham | 1958 |
| Robertson, J.D.B. | (2) | 133 | West Indies | Port-of-Spain | 1947–48 |
|  |  | 121† | New Zealand | Lord's | 1949 |
| Robins, R.W.V. |  | 108 | South Africa | Manchester | 1935 |
| Robinson, R.T. | (3) | 160 | India | Delhi | 1984–85 |
|  |  | 175† | Australia | Leeds | 1985 |
|  |  | 148 | Australia | Birmingham | 1985 |
| Russell, C.A.G. | (5) | 135* | Australia | Adelaide | 1920–21 |
|  |  | 101 | Australia | Manchester | 1921 |
|  |  | 102* | Australia | Oval | 1921 |
|  |  | 140⎫<br>111⎭ | South Africa | Durban[2] | 1922–23 |
| Sandham, A. | (2) | 152† | West Indies | Bridgetown | 1929–30 |
|  |  | 325 | West Indies | Kingston | 1929–30 |
| Sharp, J. |  | 105 | Australia | Oval | 1909 |
| Sharpe, P.J. |  | 111 | New Zealand | Nottingham | 1969 |
| Sheppard, Rev D.S. | (3) | 119 | India | Oval | 1952 |
|  |  | 113 | Australia | Manchester | 1956 |
|  |  | 113 | Australia | Melbourne | 1962–63 |
| Shrewsbury, A. | (3) | 105* | Australia | Melbourne | 1884–85 |
|  |  | 164 | Australia | Lord's | 1886 |
|  |  | 106 | Australia | Lord's | 1893 |

|  |  |  | *Opponents* |  |  |
|---|---|---|---|---|---|
| Simpson, R.T. | (4) | 103† | New Zealand | Manchester | 1949 |
|  |  | 156* | Australia | Melbourne | 1950–51 |
|  |  | 137 | South Africa | Nottingham | 1951 |
|  |  | 101 | Pakistan | Nottingham | 1954 |
| Smith, M.J.K. | (3) | 100† | India | Manchester | 1959 |
|  |  | 108 | West Indies | Port-of-Spain | 1959–60 |
|  |  | 121 | South Africa | Cape Town | 1964–65 |
| Spooner, R.H. |  | 119† | South Africa | Lord's | 1912 |
| Steel, A.G. | (2) | 135* | Australia | Sydney | 1882–83 |
|  |  | 148 | Australia | Lord's | 1884 |
| Steele, D.S. |  | 106† | West Indies | Nottingham | 1976 |
| Stoddart, A.E. | (2) | 134 | Australia | Adelaide | 1891–92 |
|  |  | 173 | Australia | Melbourne | 1894–95 |
| Subba Row, R. | (3) | 100† | West Indies | Georgetown | 1959–60 |
|  |  | 112† | Australia | Birmingham | 1961 |
|  |  | 137 | Australia | Oval | 1961 |
| Sutcliffe, H. | (16) | 122 | South Africa | Lord's | 1924 |
|  |  | 115† | Australia | Sydney | 1924–25 |
|  |  | 176⎱<br>127⎰ | Australia | Melbourne | 1924–25 |
|  |  | 143 | Australia | Melbourne | 1924–25 |
|  |  | 161 | Australia | Oval | 1926 |
|  |  | 102 | South Africa | Johannesburg[1] | 1927–28 |
|  |  | 135 | Australia | Melbourne | 1928–29 |
|  |  | 114 | South Africa | Birmingham | 1929 |
|  |  | 100 | South Africa | Lord's | 1929 |
|  |  | 104 ⎱<br>109*⎰ | South Africa | Oval | 1929 |
|  |  | 161 | Australia | Oval | 1930 |
|  |  | 117† | New Zealand | Oval | 1931 |
|  |  | 109* | New Zealand | Manchester | 1931 |
|  |  | 194 | Australia | Sydney | 1932–33 |
| Tate, M.W. |  | 100* | South Africa | Lord's | 1929 |
| Tavaré, C.J. | (2) | 149 | India | Delhi | 1981–82 |
|  |  | 109† | New Zealand | Oval | 1983 |
| Tyldesley, G.E. | (3) | 122† | South Africa | Johannesburg[1] | 1927–28 |
|  |  | 100 | South Africa | Durban[2] | 1927–28 |
|  |  | 122 | West Indies | Lord's | 1928 |
| Tyldesley, J.T. | (4) | 112 | South Africa | Cape Town | 1898–99 |
|  |  | 138 | Australia | Birmingham | 1902 |
|  |  | 100 | Australia | Leeds | 1905 |
|  |  | 112* | Australia | Oval | 1905 |
| Ulyett, G. |  | 149 | Australia | Melbourne | 1881–82 |
| Valentine, B.H. | (2) | 136† | India | Bombay[1] | 1933–34 |
|  |  | 112 | South Africa | Cape Town | 1938–39 |
| Walters, C.F. |  | 102 | India | Madras[1] | 1933–34 |
| Ward, Albert |  | 117 | Australia | Sydney | 1894–95 |
| Warner, P.F. |  | 132*† | South Africa | Johannesburg[1] | 1898–99 |
| Washbrook, C. | (6) | 112 | Australia | Melbourne | 1946–47 |
|  |  | 143 | ˏAustralia | Leeds | 1948 |
|  |  | 195 | South Africa | Johannesburg[2] | 1948–49 |
|  |  | 103* | New Zealand | Leeds | 1949 |
|  |  | 114† | West Indies | Lord's | 1950 |
|  |  | 102 | West Indies | Nottingham | 1950 |
| Watkins, A.J. | (2) | 111 | South Africa | Johannesburg[2] | 1948–49 |
|  |  | 137*† | India | Delhi | 1951–52 |
| Watson, W. | (2) | 109† | Australia | Lord's | 1953 |
|  |  | 116† | West Indies | Kingston | 1953–54 |
| Willey, P. | (2) | 100* | West Indies | Oval | 1980 |
|  |  | 102* | West Indies | St John's | 1980–81 |
| Wood, H. |  | 134* | South Africa | Cape Town | 1891–92 |
| Woolley, F.E. | (5) | 133* | Australia | Sydney | 1911–12 |
|  |  | 115* | South Africa | Johannesburg[1] | 1922–23 |
|  |  | 134* | South Africa | Lord's | 1924 |
|  |  | 123 | Australia | Sydney | 1924–25 |
|  |  | 154 | South Africa | Manchester | 1929 |

|  |  |  | *Opponents* |  |  |
|---|---|---|---|---|---|
| Woolmer, R.A. | (3) | 149 | Australia | Oval | 1975 |
|  |  | 120 | Australia | Lord's | 1977 |
|  |  | 137 | Australia | Manchester | 1977 |
| Worthington, T.S. |  | 128 | India | Oval | 1936 |
| Wyatt, R.E.S. | (2) | 113 | South Africa | Manchester | 1929 |
|  |  | 149 | South Africa | Nottingham | 1935 |

### AUSTRALIA (401)

|  |  |  |  |  |  |
|---|---|---|---|---|---|
| Archer, R.G. |  | 128 | West Indies | Kingston | 1954–55 |
| Armstrong, W.W. | (6) | 159* | South Africa | Johannesburg[1] | 1902–03 |
|  |  | 133* | England | Melbourne | 1907–08 |
|  |  | 132 | South Africa | Melbourne | 1910–11 |
|  |  | 158 | England | Sydney | 1920–21 |
|  |  | 121 | England | Adelaide | 1920–21 |
|  |  | 123* | England | Melbourne | 1920–21 |
| Badcock, C.L. |  | 118 | England | Melbourne | 1936–37 |
| Bannerman, C. |  | 165*† | England | Melbourne | 1876–77 |
|  |  |  | *The first hundred in Test cricket* |  |  |
| Bardsley, W. | (6) | 136 ⎱ 130 ⎰ | England | Oval | 1909 |
|  |  | 132† | South Africa | Sydney | 1910–11 |
|  |  | 121 | South Africa | Manchester | 1912 |
|  |  | 164 | South Africa | Lord's | 1912 |
|  |  | 193* | England | Lord's | 1926 |
| Barnes, S.G. | (3) | 234 | England | Sydney | 1946–47 |
|  |  | 112 | India | Adelaide | 1947–48 |
|  |  | 141 | England | Lord's | 1948 |
| Benaud, J. |  | 142 | Pakistan | Melbourne | 1972–73 |
| Benaud, R. | (3) | 121 | West Indies | Kingston | 1954–55 |
|  |  | 122 | South Africa | Johannesburg[3] | 1957–58 |
|  |  | 100 | South Africa | Johannesburg[3] | 1957–58 |
| Bonnor, G.J. |  | 128 | England | Sydney | 1884–85 |
| Booth, B.C. | (5) | 112 | England | Brisbane[2] | 1962–63 |
|  |  | 103 | England | Melbourne | 1962–63 |
|  |  | 169† | South Africa | Brisbane[2] | 1963–64 |
|  |  | 102* | South Africa | Sydney | 1963–64 |
|  |  | 117 | West Indies | Port-of-Spain | 1964–65 |
| Border, A.R. | (14) | 105† | Pakistan | Melbourne | 1978–79 |
|  |  | 162† | India | Madras[1] | 1979–80 |
|  |  | 115 | England | Perth | 1979–80 |
|  |  | 150* ⎱ 153 ⎰ | Pakistan | Lahore[2] | 1979–80 |
|  |  | 124 | India | Melbourne | 1980–81 |
|  |  | 123* | England | Manchester | 1981 |
|  |  | 106* | England | Oval | 1981 |
|  |  | 126 | West Indies | Adelaide | 1981–82 |
|  |  | 118 | Pakistan | Brisbane[2] | 1983–84 |
|  |  | 117* | Pakistan | Adelaide | 1983–84 |
|  |  | 100* | West Indies | Port-of-Spain | 1983–84 |
|  |  | 196 | England | Lord's | 1985 |
|  |  | 146* | England | Manchester | 1985 |
| Bradman, D.G. | (29) | 112 | England | Melbourne | 1928–29 |
|  |  | 123 | England | Melbourne | 1928–29 |
|  |  | 131 | England | Nottingham | 1930 |
|  |  | 254 | England | Lord's | 1930 |
|  |  | 334 | England | Leeds | 1930 |
|  |  | 232 | England | Oval | 1930 |
|  |  | 223 | West Indies | Brisbane[1] | 1930–31 |
|  |  | 152 | West Indies | Melbourne | 1930–31 |
|  |  | 226† | South Africa | Brisbane[2] | 1931–32 |
|  |  | 112 | South Africa | Sydney | 1931–32 |
|  |  | 167 | South Africa | Melbourne | 1931–32 |
|  |  | 299* | South Africa | Adelaide | 1931–32 |

|  |  |  | *Opponents* |  |  |
|---|---|---|---|---|---|
| Bradman, D.G. *continued* |  | 103* | England | Melbourne | 1932–33 |
|  |  | 304 | England | Leeds | 1934 |
|  |  | 244 | England | Oval | 1934 |
|  |  | 270 | England | Melbourne | 1936–37 |
|  |  | 212 | England | Adelaide | 1936–37 |
|  |  | 169 | England | Melbourne | 1936–37 |
|  |  | 144* | England | Nottingham | 1938 |
|  |  | 102* | England | Lord's | 1938 |
|  |  | 103 | England | Leeds | 1938 |
|  |  | 187 | England | Brisbane² | 1946–47 |
|  |  | 234 | England | Sydney | 1946–47 |
|  |  | 185† | India | Brisbane² | 1947–48 |
|  |  | 132 } 127* | India | Melbourne | 1947–48 |
|  |  | 201 | India | Adelaide | 1947–48 |
|  |  | 138 | England | Nottingham | 1948 |
|  |  | 173* | England | Leeds | 1948 |
| Brown, W.A. | (4) | 105 | England | Lord's | 1934 |
|  |  | 121 | South Africa | Cape Town | 1935–36 |
|  |  | 133 | England | Nottingham | 1938 |
|  |  | 206* | England | Lord's | 1938 |
| Burge, P.J.P. | (4) | 181 | England | Oval | 1961 |
|  |  | 103 | England | Sydney | 1962–63 |
|  |  | 160 | England | Leeds | 1964 |
|  |  | 120 | England | Melbourne | 1965–66 |
| Burke, J.W. | (3) | 101*† | England | Adelaide | 1950–51 |
|  |  | 161 | India | Bombay² | 1956–57 |
|  |  | 189 | South Africa | Cape Town | 1957–58 |
| Chappell, G.S. | (24) | 108† | England | Perth | 1970–71 |
|  |  | 131 | England | Lord's | 1972 |
|  |  | 113 | England | Oval | 1972 |
|  |  | 116* | Pakistan | Melbourne | 1972–73 |
|  |  | 106 | West Indies | Bridgetown | 1972–73 |
|  |  | 247* } 133 | New Zealand | Wellington | 1973–74 |
|  |  | 144 | England | Sydney | 1974–75 |
|  |  | 102 | England | Melbourne | 1974–75 |
|  |  | 123 } 109* | West Indies | Brisbane² | 1975–76 |
|  |  | 182* | West Indies | Sydney | 1975–76 |
|  |  | 121 | Pakistan | Melbourne | 1976–77 |
|  |  | 112 | England | Manchester | 1977 |
|  |  | 124 | West Indies | Brisbane² | 1979–80 |
|  |  | 114 | England | Melbourne | 1979–80 |
|  |  | 235 | Pakistan | Faisalabad | 1979–80 |
|  |  | 204† | India | Sydney | 1980–81 |
|  |  | 201 | Pakistan | Brisbane² | 1981–82 |
|  |  | 176 | New Zealand | Christchurch | 1981–82 |
|  |  | 117 | England | Perth | 1982–83 |
|  |  | 115 | England | Adelaide | 1982–83 |
|  |  | 150* | Pakistan | Brisbane² | 1983–84 |
|  |  | 182 | Pakistan | Sydney | 1983–84 |
| Chappell, I.M. | (14) | 151 | India | Melbourne | 1967–68 |
|  |  | 117† | West Indies | Brisbane² | 1968–69 |
|  |  | 165 | West Indies | Melbourne | 1968–69 |
|  |  | 138 | India | Delhi | 1969–70 |
|  |  | 111 | England | Melbourne | 1970–71 |
|  |  | 104 | England | Adelaide | 1970–71 |
|  |  | 118 | England | Oval | 1972 |
|  |  | 196 | Pakistan | Adelaide | 1972–73 |
|  |  | 106* | West Indies | Bridgetown | 1972–73 |
|  |  | 109 | West Indies | Georgetown | 1972–73 |
|  |  | 145 } 121 | New Zealand | Wellington | 1973–74 |
|  |  | 192 | England | Oval | 1975 |
|  |  | 156 | West Indies | Perth | 1975–76 |

|  |  |  | *Opponents* |  |  |
|---|---|---|---|---|---|
| Chipperfield, A.G. |  | 109† | South Africa | Durban² | 1935–36 |
| Collins, H.L. | (4) | 104† | England | Sydney | 1920–21 |
|  |  | 162 | England | Adelaide | 1920–21 |
|  |  | 203 | South Africa | Johannesburg¹ | 1921–22 |
|  |  | 114 | England | Sydney | 1924–25 |
| Cosier, G.J. | (2) | 109† | West Indies | Melbourne | 1975–76 |
|  |  | 168 | Pakistan | Melbourne | 1976–77 |
| Cowper, R.M. | (5) | 143 | West Indies | Port-of-Spain | 1964–65 |
|  |  | 102 | West Indies | Bridgetown | 1964–65 |
|  |  | 307 | England | Melbourne | 1965–66 |
|  |  | 108 | India | Adelaide | 1967–68 |
|  |  | 165 | India | Sydney | 1967–68 |
| Darling, J. | (3) | 101 | England | Sydney | 1897–98 |
|  |  | 178 | England | Adelaide | 1897–98 |
|  |  | 160 | England | Sydney | 1897–98 |
| Davis, I.C. |  | 105† | Pakistan | Adelaide | 1976–77 |
| Duff, R.A. | (2) | 104† | England | Melbourne | 1901–02 |
|  |  | 146 | England | Oval | 1905 |
| Dyson, J. | (2) | 102 | England | Leeds | 1981 |
|  |  | 127*† | West Indies | Sydney | 1981–82 |
| Edwards, R. | (2) | 170* | England | Nottingham | 1972 |
|  |  | 115 | England | Perth | 1974–75 |
| Favell, L.E. |  | 101 | India | Madras² | 1959–60 |
| Fingleton, J.H.W. | (5) | 112 | South Africa | Cape Town | 1935–36 |
|  |  | 108 | South Africa | Johannesburg¹ | 1935–36 |
|  |  | 118 | South Africa | Durban² | 1935–36 |
|  |  | 100 | England | Brisbane² | 1936–37 |
|  |  | 136 | England | Melbourne | 1936–37 |
| Giffen, G. |  | 161 | England | Sydney | 1894–95 |
| Gilmour, G.J. |  | 101 | New Zealand | Christchurch | 1976–77 |
| Graham, H. | (2) | 107† | England | Lord's | 1893 |
|  |  | 105 | England | Sydney | 1894–95 |
| Gregory, J.M. | (2) | 100 | England | Melbourne | 1920–21 |
|  |  | 119 | South Africa | Johannesburg¹ | 1921–22 |
|  |  | | *Including the fastest Test hundred in 70 minutes* | | |
| Gregory, S.E. | (4) | 201 | England | Sydney | 1894–95 |
|  |  | 103 | England | Lord's | 1896 |
|  |  | 117 | England | Oval | 1899 |
|  |  | 112 | England | Adelaide | 1903–04 |
| Hartigan, R.J. |  | 116† | England | Adelaide | 1907–08 |
| Harvey, R.N. | (21) | 153 | India | Melbourne | 1947–48 |
|  |  | 112† | England | Leeds | 1948 |
|  |  | 178 | South Africa | Cape Town | 1949–50 |
|  |  | 151* | South Africa | Durban² | 1949–50 |
|  |  | 100 | South Africa | Johannesburg² | 1949–50 |
|  |  | 116 | South Africa | Port Elizabeth | 1949–50 |
|  |  | 109 | South Africa | Brisbane² | 1952–53 |
|  |  | 190 | South Africa | Sydney | 1952–53 |
|  |  | 116 | South Africa | Adelaide | 1952–53 |
|  |  | 205 | South Africa | Melbourne | 1952–53 |
|  |  | 122 | England | Manchester | 1953 |
|  |  | 162 | England | Brisbane² | 1954–55 |
|  |  | 133 | West Indies | Kingston | 1954–55 |
|  |  | 133 | West Indies | Port-of-Spain | 1954–55 |
|  |  | 204 | West Indies | Kingston | 1954–55 |
|  |  | 140 | India | Bombay² | 1956–57 |
|  |  | 167 | England | Melbourne | 1958–59 |
|  |  | 114 | India | Delhi | 1959–60 |
|  |  | 102 | India | Bombay² | 1959–60 |
|  |  | 114 | England | Birmingham | 1961 |
|  |  | 154 | England | Adelaide | 1962–63 |
| Hassett, A.L. | (10) | 128 | England | Brisbane² | 1946–47 |
|  |  | 198* | India | Adelaide | 1947–48 |
|  |  | 137 | England | Nottingham | 1948 |
|  |  | 112† | South Africa | Johannesburg² | 1949–50 |
|  |  | 167 | South Africa | Port Elizabeth | 1949–50 |

|  |  |  | *Opponents* |  |  |
|---|---|---|---|---|---|
| Hassett, A.L. *continued* |  | 132 | West Indies | Sydney | 1951–52 |
|  |  | 102 | West Indies | Melbourne | 1951–52 |
|  |  | 163 | South Africa | Adelaide | 1952–53 |
|  |  | 115 | England | Nottingham | 1953 |
|  |  | 104 | England | Lord's | 1953 |
| Hendry, H.S.T.L. |  | 112 | England | Sydney | 1928–29 |
| Hilditch, A.M.J. | (2) | 113† | West Indies | Melbourne | 1984–85 |
|  |  | 119 | England | Leeds | 1985 |
| Hill, C. | (7) | 188 | England | Melbourne | 1897–98 |
|  |  | 135 | England | Lord's | 1899 |
|  |  | 119 | England | Sheffield | 1902 |
|  |  | 142† | South Africa | Johannesburg[1] | 1902–03 |
|  |  | 160 | England | Adelaide | 1907–08 |
|  |  | 191 | South Africa | Sydney | 1910–11 |
|  |  | 100 | South Africa | Melbourne | 1910–11 |
| Hookes, D.W. |  | 143*† | Sri Lanka | Kandy | 1982–83 |
| Horan, T.P. |  | 124 | England | Melbourne | 1881–82 |
| Hughes, K.J. | (9) | 129 | England | Brisbane[2] | 1978–79 |
|  |  | 100 | India | Madras[1] | 1979–80 |
|  |  | 130*† | West Indies | Brisbane[2] | 1979–80 |
|  |  | 117 | England | Lord's | 1980 |
|  |  | 213 | India | Adelaide | 1980–81 |
|  |  | 106 | Pakistan | Perth | 1981–82 |
|  |  | 100* | West Indies | Melbourne | 1981–82 |
|  |  | 137 | England | Sydney | 1982–83 |
|  |  | 106 | Pakistan | Adelaide | 1983–84 |
| Iredale, F.A. | (2) | 140 | England | Adelaide | 1894–95 |
|  |  | 108 | England | Manchester | 1896 |
| Jackson, A.A. |  | 164† | England | Adelaide | 1928–29 |
| Kelleway, C. | (3) | 114 | South Africa | Manchester | 1912 |
|  |  | 102 | South Africa | Lord's | 1912 |
|  |  | 147 | England | Adelaide | 1920–21 |
| Kippax, A.F. | (2) | 100 | England | Melbourne | 1928–29 |
|  |  | 146† | West Indies | Adelaide | 1930–31 |
| Lawry, W.M. | (13) | 130 | England | Lord's | 1961 |
|  |  | 102 | England | Manchester | 1961 |
|  |  | 157 | South Africa | Melbourne | 1963–64 |
|  |  | 106 | England | Manchester | 1964 |
|  |  | 210 | West Indies | Bridgetown | 1964–65 |
|  |  | 166 | England | Brisbane[2] | 1965–66 |
|  |  | 119 | England | Adelaide | 1965–66 |
|  |  | 108 | England | Melbourne | 1965–66 |
|  |  | 100 | India | Melbourne | 1967–68 |
|  |  | 135 | England | Oval | 1968 |
|  |  | 105 | West Indies | Brisbane[2] | 1968–69 |
|  |  | 205 | West Indies | Melbourne | 1968–69 |
|  |  | 151 | West Indies | Sydney | 1968–69 |
| Lindwall, R.R. | (2) | 100 | England | Melbourne | 1946–47 |
|  |  | 118 | West Indies | Bridgetown | 1954–55 |
| Loxton, S.J.E. |  | 101† | South Africa | Johannesburg[2] | 1949–50 |
| Lyons, J.J. |  | 134 | England | Sydney | 1891–92 |
| Macartney, C.G. | (7) | 137 | South Africa | Sydney | 1910–11 |
|  |  | 170 | England | Sydney | 1920–21 |
|  |  | 115 | England | Leeds | 1921 |
|  |  | 116 | South Africa | Durban[1] | 1921–22 |
|  |  | 133* | England | Lord's | 1926 |
|  |  | 151 | England | Leeds | 1926 |
|  |  | 109 | England | Manchester | 1926 |
| McCabe, S.J. | (6) | 187* | England | Sydney | 1932–33 |
|  |  | 137 | England | Manchester | 1934 |
|  |  | 149 | South Africa | Durban[2] | 1935–36 |
|  |  | 189* | South Africa | Johannesburg[1] | 1935–36 |
|  |  | 112 | England | Melbourne | 1936–37 |
|  |  | 232 | England | Nottingham | 1938 |
| McCool, C.L. |  | 104* | England | Melbourne | 1946–47 |

| | | | | *Opponents* | | |
|---|---|---|---|---|---|---|
| McCosker, R.B. | (4) | 127 | England | Oval | 1975 |
| | | 109* | West Indies | Melbourne | 1975–76 |
| | | 105 | Pakistan | Melbourne | 1976–77 |
| | | 107 | England | Nottingham | 1977 |
| McDonald, C.C. | (5) | 154 | South Africa | Adelaide | 1952–53 |
| | | 110 | West Indies | Port-of-Spain | 1954–55 |
| | | 127 | West Indies | Kingston | 1954–55 |
| | | 170 | England | Adelaide | 1958–59 |
| | | 133 | England | Melbourne | 1958–59 |
| McDonnell, P.S. | (3) | 147 | England | Sydney | 1881–82 |
| | | 103 | England | Oval | 1884 |
| | | 124 | England | Adelaide | 1884–85 |
| McLeod, C.E. | | 112 | England | Melbourne | 1897–98 |
| Mann, A.L. | | 105 | India | Perth | 1977–78 |
| Marsh, R.W. | (3) | 118† | Pakistan | Adelaide | 1972–73 |
| | | 132 | New Zealand | Adelaide | 1973–74 |
| | | 110* | England | Melbourne | 1976–77 |
| Miller, K.R. | (7) | 141* | England | Adelaide | 1946–47 |
| | | 145* | England | Sydney | 1950–51 |
| | | 129 | West Indies | Sydney | 1951–52 |
| | | 109 | England | Lord's | 1953 |
| | | 147 | West Indies | Kingston | 1954–55 |
| | | 137 | West Indies | Bridgetown | 1954–55 |
| | | 109 | West Indies | Kingston | 1954–55 |
| Moroney, J. | (2) | 118 ⎱ 101* ⎰ | South Africa | Johannesburg[2] | 1949–50 |
| Morris, A.R. | (12) | 155 | England | Melbourne | 1946–47 |
| | | 122 ⎱ 124* ⎰ | England | Adelaide | 1946–47 |
| | | 100* | India | Melbourne | 1947–48 |
| | | 105 | England | Lord's | 1948 |
| | | 182 | England | Leeds | 1948 |
| | | 196 | England | Oval | 1948 |
| | | 111 | South Africa | Johannesburg[2] | 1949–50 |
| | | 157 | South Africa | Port Elizabeth | 1949–50 |
| | | 206 | England | Adelaide | 1950–51 |
| | | 153 | England | Brisbane[2] | 1954–55 |
| | | 111 | West Indies | Port-of-Spain | 1954–55 |
| Murdoch, W.L. | (2) | 153* | England | Oval | 1880 |
| | | 211 | England | Oval | 1884 |
| Noble, M.A. | | 133 | England | Sydney | 1903–04 |
| O'Neill, N.C. | (6) | 134 | Pakistan | Lahore[2] | 1959–60 |
| | | 163 | India | Bombay[2] | 1959–60 |
| | | 113 | India | Calcutta | 1959–60 |
| | | 181† | West Indies | Brisbane[2] | 1960–61 |
| | | 117 | England | Oval | 1961 |
| | | 100 | England | Adelaide | 1962–63 |
| Pellew, C.E. | (2) | 116 | England | Melbourne | 1920–21 |
| | | 104 | England | Adelaide | 1920–21 |
| Phillips, W.B. | (2) | 159† | Pakistan | Perth | 1983–84 |
| | | 120 | West Indies | Bridgetown | 1983–84 |
| Ponsford, W.H. | (7) | 110† | England | Sydney | 1924–25 |
| | | 128 | England | Melbourne | 1924–25 |
| | | 110 | England | Oval | 1930 |
| | | 183 | West Indies | Sydney | 1930–31 |
| | | 109 | West Indies | Brisbane[1] | 1930–31 |
| | | 181 | England | Leeds | 1934 |
| | | 266 | England | Oval | 1934 |
| Ransford, V.S. | | 143* | England | Lord's | 1909 |
| Redpath, I.R. | (8) | 132 | West Indies | Sydney | 1968–69 |
| | | 171 | England | Perth | 1970–71 |
| | | 135 | Pakistan | Melbourne | 1972–73 |
| | | 159* | New Zealand | Auckland | 1973–74 |
| | | 105 | England | Sydney | 1974–75 |
| | | 102 | West Indies | Melbourne | 1975–76 |
| | | 103 | West Indies | Adelaide | 1975–76 |

|  |  |  | *Opponents* |  |  |
|---|---|---|---|---|---|
| Redpath, I.R. *continued* |  | 101 | West Indies | Melbourne | 1975–76 |
| Richardson, A.J. |  | 100 | England | Leeds | 1926 |
| Richardson, V.Y. |  | 138 | England | Melbourne | 1924–25 |
| Rigg, K.E. |  | 127† | South Africa | Sydney | 1931–32 |
| Ritchie, G.M. | (2) | 106* | Pakistan | Faisalabad | 1982–83 |
|  |  | 146 | England | Nottingham | 1985 |
| Ryder, J. | (3) | 142 | South Africa | Cape Town | 1921–22 |
|  |  | 201* | England | Adelaide | 1924–25 |
|  |  | 112 | England | Melbourne | 1928–29 |
| Scott, H.J.H. |  | 102 | England | Oval | 1884 |
| Serjeant, C.S. |  | 124 | West Indies | Georgetown | 1977–78 |
| Sheahan, A.P. | (2) | 114 | India | Kanpur | 1969–70 |
|  |  | 127 | Pakistan | Melbourne | 1972–73 |
| Simpson, R.B. | (10) | 311 | England | Manchester | 1964 |
|  |  | 153†⎫ 115†⎭ | Pakistan | Karachi | 1964–65 |
|  |  | 201 | West Indies | Bridgetown | 1964–65 |
|  |  | 225 | England | Adelaide | 1965–66 |
|  |  | 153 | South Africa | Cape Town | 1966–67 |
|  |  | 103 | India | Adelaide | 1967–68 |
|  |  | 109 | India | Melbourne | 1967–68 |
|  |  | 176 | India | Perth | 1977–78 |
|  |  | 100 | India | Adelaide | 1977–78 |
| Stackpole, K.R. | (7) | 134 | South Africa | Cape Town | 1966–67 |
|  |  | 103† | India | Bombay[2] | 1969–70 |
|  |  | 207 | England | Brisbane[2] | 1970–71 |
|  |  | 136 | England | Adelaide | 1970–71 |
|  |  | 114 | England | Nottingham | 1972 |
|  |  | 142 | West Indies | Kingston | 1972–73 |
|  |  | 122† | New Zealand | Melbourne | 1973–74 |
| Taylor, J.M. |  | 108 | England | Sydney | 1924–25 |
| Toohey, P.M. |  | 122 | West Indies | Kingston | 1977–78 |
| Trott, G.H.S. |  | 143 | England | Lord's | 1896 |
| Trumper, V.T. | (8) | 135* | England | Lord's | 1899 |
|  |  | 104 | England | Manchester | 1902 |
|  |  | 185* | England | Sydney | 1903–04 |
|  |  | 113 | England | Adelaide | 1903–04 |
|  |  | 166 | England | Sydney | 1907–08 |
|  |  | 159 | South Africa | Melbourne | 1910–11 |
|  |  | 214* | South Africa | Adelaide | 1910–11 |
|  |  | 113 | England | Sydney | 1911–12 |
| Turner, A. |  | 136 | West Indies | Adelaide | 1975–76 |
| Walters, K.D. | (15) | 155† | England | Brisbane[2] | 1965–66 |
|  |  | 115 | England | Melbourne | 1965–66 |
|  |  | 118 | West Indies | Sydney | 1968–69 |
|  |  | 110 | West Indies | Adelaide | 1968–69 |
|  |  | 242⎫ 103⎭ | West Indies | Sydney | 1968–69 |
|  |  | 102 | India | Madras[1] | 1969–70 |
|  |  | 112 | England | Brisbane[2] | 1970–71 |
|  |  | 102* | West Indies | Bridgetown | 1972–73 |
|  |  | 112 | West Indies | Port-of-Spain | 1972–73 |
|  |  | 104* | New Zealand | Auckland | 1973–74 |
|  |  | 103 | England | Perth | 1974–75 |
|  |  | 107 | Pakistan | Adelaide | 1976–77 |
|  |  | 250 | New Zealand | Christchurch | 1976–77 |
|  |  | 107 | New Zealand | Melbourne | 1980–81 |
| Wellham, D.M. |  | 103† | England | Oval | 1981 |
| Wessels, K.C. | (4) | 162† | England | Brisbane[2] | 1982–83 |
|  |  | 141† | Sri Lanka | Kandy | 1982–83 |
|  |  | 179 | Pakistan | Adelaide | 1983–84 |
|  |  | 173 | West Indies | Sydney | 1984–85 |
| Wood, G.M. | (8) | 126 | West Indies | Georgetown | 1977–78 |
|  |  | 100 | England | Melbourne | 1978–79 |
|  |  | 112 | England | Lord's | 1980 |
|  |  | 111† | New Zealand | Brisbane[2] | 1980–81 |

|  |  |  | *Opponents* |  |  |
|---|---|---|---|---|---|
| Wood, G.M. *continued* |  | 125 | India | Adelaide | 1980–81 |
|  |  | 100 | Pakistan | Melbourne | 1981–82 |
|  |  | 100 | New Zealand | Auckland | 1981–82 |
|  |  | 172 | England | Nottingham | 1985 |
| Woodfull, W.M. | (7) | 141 | England | Leeds | 1926 |
|  |  | 117 | England | Manchester | 1926 |
|  |  | 111 | England | Sydney | 1928–29 |
|  |  | 107 | England | Melbourne | 1928–29 |
|  |  | 102 | England | Melbourne | 1928–29 |
|  |  | 155 | England | Lord's | 1930 |
|  |  | 161 | South Africa | Melbourne | 1931–32 |
| Yallop, G.N. | (8) | 121† | India | Adelaide | 1977–78 |
|  |  | 102† | England | Brisbane[2] | 1978–79 |
|  |  | 121 | England | Sydney | 1978–79 |
|  |  | 167 | India | Calcutta | 1979–80 |
|  |  | 172 | Pakistan | Faisalabad | 1979–80 |
|  |  | 114 | England | Manchester | 1981 |
|  |  | 141 | Pakistan | Perth | 1983–84 |
|  |  | 268 | Pakistan | Melbourne | 1983–84 |

## SOUTH AFRICA (105)

|  |  |  |  |  |  |
|---|---|---|---|---|---|
| Balaskas, X.C. |  | 122* | New Zealand | Wellington | 1931–32 |
| Barlow, E.J. | (6) | 114† | Australia | Brisbane[2] | 1963–64 |
|  |  | 109 | Australia | Melbourne | 1963–64 |
|  |  | 201 | Australia | Adelaide | 1963–64 |
|  |  | 138 | England | Cape Town | 1964–65 |
|  |  | 127 | Australia | Cape Town | 1969–70 |
|  |  | 110 | Australia | Johannesburg[3] | 1969–70 |
| Bland, K.C. | (3) | 126 | Australia | Sydney | 1963–64 |
|  |  | 144* | England | Johannesburg[3] | 1964–65 |
|  |  | 127 | England | Oval | 1965 |
| Catterall, R.H. | (3) | 120 | England | Birmingham | 1924 |
|  |  | 120 | England | Lord's | 1924 |
|  |  | 119 | England | Durban[2] | 1927–28 |
| Christy, J.A.J. |  | 103† | New Zealand | Christchurch | 1931–32 |
| Dalton, E.L. | (2) | 117 | England | Oval | 1935 |
|  |  | 102 | England | Johannesburg[1] | 1938–39 |
| Endean, W.R. | (3) | 162* | Australia | Melbourne | 1952–53 |
|  |  | 116 | New Zealand | Auckland | 1952–53 |
|  |  | 116* | England | Leeds | 1955 |
| Faulkner, G.A. | (4) | 123 | England | Johannesburg[1] | 1909–10 |
|  |  | 204 | Australia | Melbourne | 1910–11 |
|  |  | 115 | Australia | Adelaide | 1910–11 |
|  |  | 122* | Australia | Manchester | 1912 |
| Frank, C.N. |  | 152 | Australia | Johannesburg[1] | 1921–22 |
| Goddard, T.L. |  | 112 | England | Johannesburg[3] | 1964–65 |
| Hathorn, C.M.H. |  | 102 | England | Johannesburg[1] | 1905–06 |
| Irvine, B.L. |  | 102 | Australia | Port Elizabeth | 1969–70 |
| Lindsay, D.T. | (3) | 182 | Australia | Johannesburg[3] | 1966–67 |
|  |  | 137 | Australia | Durban[2] | 1966–67 |
|  |  | 131 | Australia | Johannesburg[3] | 1966–67 |
| McGlew, D.J. | (7) | 255*† | New Zealand | Wellington | 1952–53 |
|  |  | 104* | England | Manchester | 1955 |
|  |  | 133 | England | Leeds | 1955 |
|  |  | 108 | Australia | Johannesburg[3] | 1957–58 |
|  |  | 105 | Australia | Durban[2] | 1957–58 |
|  |  | 127* | New Zealand | Durban[2] | 1961–62 |
|  |  | 120 | New Zealand | Johannesburg[3] | 1961–62 |
| McLean, R.A. | (5) | 101 | New Zealand | Durban[2] | 1953–54 |
|  |  | 142 | England | Lord's | 1955 |
|  |  | 100 | England | Durban[2] | 1956–57 |
|  |  | 109 | England | Manchester | 1960 |
|  |  | 113 | New Zealand | Cape Town | 1961–62 |

|  |  |  | *Opponents* |  |  |
|---|---|---|---|---|---|
| Melville, A. | (4) | 103 | England | Durban[2] | 1938–39 |
|  |  | 189 189 104* | England | Nottingham | 1947 |
|  |  | 117 | England | Lord's | 1947 |
| Mitchell, B. | (8) | 123 | England | Cape Town | 1930–31 |
|  |  | 113† | New Zealand | Christchurch | 1931–32 |
|  |  | 164* | England | Lord's | 1935 |
|  |  | 128 | England | Oval | 1935 |
|  |  | 109 | England | Durban[2] | 1938–39 |
|  |  | 120 189* | England | Oval | 1947 |
|  |  | 120 | England | Cape Town | 1948–49 |
| Murray, A.R.A. |  | 109† | New Zealand | Wellington | 1952–53 |
| Nourse, A.D. | (9) | 231 | Australia | Johannesburg[1] | 1935–36 |
|  |  | 120 | England | Cape Town | 1938–39 |
|  |  | 103 | England | Durban[2] | 1938–39 |
|  |  | 149 | England | Nottingham | 1947 |
|  |  | 115 | England | Manchester | 1947 |
|  |  | 112 | England | Cape Town | 1948–49 |
|  |  | 129* | England | Johannesburg[2] | 1948–49 |
|  |  | 114 | Australia | Cape Town | 1949–50 |
|  |  | 208 | England | Nottingham | 1951 |
| Nourse, A.W. |  | 111 | Australia | Johannesburg[1] | 1921–22 |
| Owen-Smith, H.G. |  | 129 | England | Leeds | 1929 |
| Pithey, A.J. |  | 154 | England | Cape Town | 1964–65 |
| Pollock, R.G. | (7) | 122 | Australia | Sydney | 1963–64 |
|  |  | 175 | Australia | Adelaide | 1963–64 |
|  |  | 137 | England | Port Elizabeth | 1964–65 |
|  |  | 125 | England | Nottingham | 1965 |
|  |  | 209 | Australia | Cape Town | 1966–67 |
|  |  | 105 | Australia | Port Elizabeth | 1966–67 |
|  |  | 274 | Australia | Durban[2] | 1969–70 |
| Richards, B.A. | (2) | 140 | Australia | Durban[2] | 1969–70 |
|  |  | 126 | Australia | Port Elizabeth | 1969–70 |
| Rowan, E.A.B. | (3) | 156* | England | Johannesburg[2] | 1948–49 |
|  |  | 143 | Australia | Durban[2] | 1949–50 |
|  |  | 236 | England | Leeds | 1951 |
| Sherwell, P.W. |  | 115 | England | Lord's | 1907 |
| Siedle, I.J. |  | 141 | England | Cape Town | 1930–31 |
| Sinclair, J.H. | (3) | 106 | England | Cape Town | 1898–99 |
|  |  | 101 | Australia | Johannesburg[1] | 1902–03 |
|  |  | 104 | Australia | Cape Town | 1902–03 |
| Snooke, S.J. |  | 103 | Australia | Adelaide | 1910–11 |
| Taylor, H.W. | (7) | 109 | England | Durban[1] | 1913–14 |
|  |  | 176 | England | Johannesburg[1] | 1922–23 |
|  |  | 101 | England | Johannesburg[1] | 1922–23 |
|  |  | 102 | England | Durban[2] | 1922–23 |
|  |  | 101 | England | Johannesburg[1] | 1927–28 |
|  |  | 121 | England | Oval | 1929 |
|  |  | 117 | England | Cape Town | 1930–31 |
| Van der Bijl, P.G.V. |  | 125 | England | Durban[2] | 1938–39 |
| Viljoen, K.G. | (2) | 111 | Australia | Melbourne | 1931–32 |
|  |  | 124 | England | Manchester | 1935 |
| Wade, W.W. |  | 125 | England | Port Elizabeth | 1948–49 |
| Waite, J.H.B. | (4) | 113 | England | Manchester | 1955 |
|  |  | 115 | Australia | Johannesburg[3] | 1957–58 |
|  |  | 134 | Australia | Durban[2] | 1957–58 |
|  |  | 101 | New Zealand | Johannesburg[3] | 1961–62 |
| White, G.C. | (2) | 147 | England | Johannesburg[1] | 1905–06 |
|  |  | 118 | England | Durban[1] | 1909–10 |
| Winslow, P.L. |  | 108 | England | Manchester | 1955 |
| Zulch, J.W. | (2) | 105 | Australia | Adelaide | 1910–11 |
|  |  | 150 | Australia | Sydney | 1910–11 |

**WEST INDIES (257)**

|  |  |  | *Opponents* |  |  |
|---|---|---|---|---|---|
| Alexander, F.C.M. |  | 108 | Australia | Sydney | 1960–61 |
| Atkinson, D.St E. |  | 219 | Australia | Bridgetown | 1954–55 |
| Bacchus, S.F.A.F. |  | 250 | India | Kanpur | 1978–79 |
| Baichan, L. |  | 105*† | Pakistan | Lahore² | 1974–75 |
| Barrow, I. |  | 105 | England | Manchester | 1933 |
| Butcher, B.F. | (7) | 103 | India | Calcutta | 1958–59 |
|  |  | 142 | India | Madras² | 1958–59 |
|  |  | 133 | England | Lord's | 1963 |
|  |  | 117 | Australia | Port-of-Spain | 1964–65 |
|  |  | 209* | England | Nottingham | 1966 |
|  |  | 101 | Australia | Sydney | 1968–69 |
|  |  | 118 | Australia | Adelaide | 1968–69 |
| Carew, G.M. |  | 107 | England | Port-of-Spain | 1947–48 |
| Carew, M.C. |  | 109† | New Zealand | Auckland | 1968–69 |
| Christiani, R.J. |  | 107† | India | Delhi | 1948–49 |
| Davis, C.A. | (4) | 103 | England | Lord's | 1969 |
|  |  | 125* | India | Georgetown | 1970–71 |
|  |  | 105 | India | Port-of-Spain | 1970–71 |
|  |  | 183 | New Zealand | Bridgetown | 1971–72 |
| Depeiza, C.C. |  | 122 | Australia | Bridgetown | 1954–55 |
| Dujon, P.J.L. | (4) | 110 | India | St John's | 1982–83 |
|  |  | 130 | Australia | Port-of-Spain | 1983–84 |
|  |  | 101 | England | Manchester | 1984 |
|  |  | 139 | Australia | Perth | 1984–85 |
| Foster, M.L.C. |  | 125† | Australia | Kingston | 1972–73 |
| Fredericks, R.C. | (8) | 163 | New Zealand | Kingston | 1971–72 |
|  |  | 150 | England | Birmingham | 1973 |
|  |  | 100 | India | Calcutta | 1974–75 |
|  |  | 104 | India | Bombay³ | 1974–75 |
|  |  | 169 | Australia | Perth | 1975–76 |
|  |  | 138 | England | Lord's | 1976 |
|  |  | 109 | England | Leeds | 1976 |
|  |  | 120 | Pakistan | Port-of-Spain | 1976–77 |
| Ganteaume, A.G. |  | 112† | England | Port-of-Spain | 1947–48 |
| Gomes, H.A. | (9) | 101† | Australia | Georgetown | 1977–78 |
|  |  | 115 | Australia | Kingston | 1977–78 |
|  |  | 126 | Australia | Sydney | 1981–82 |
|  |  | 124* | Australia | Adelaide | 1981–82 |
|  |  | 123 | India | Port-of-Spain | 1982–83 |
|  |  | 143 | England | Birmingham | 1984 |
|  |  | 104* | England | Leeds | 1984 |
|  |  | 127 | Australia | Perth | 1984–85 |
|  |  | 120* | Australia | Adelaide | 1984–85 |
| Gomez, G.E. |  | 101† | India | Delhi | 1948–49 |
| Greenidge, C.G. | (12) | 107† | India | Bangalore | 1974–75 |
|  |  | 134⎱ 101⎰ | England | Manchester | 1976 |
|  |  | 115 | England | Leeds | 1976 |
|  |  | 100 | Pakistan | Kingston | 1976–77 |
|  |  | 154* | India | St John's | 1982–83 |
|  |  | 194 | India | Kanpur | 1983–84 |
|  |  | 120* | Australia | Georgetown | 1983–84 |
|  |  | 127 | Australia | Kingston | 1983–84 |
|  |  | 214* | England | Lord's | 1984 |
|  |  | 223 | England | Manchester | 1984 |
|  |  | 100 | New Zealand | Port-of-Spain | 1984–85 |
| Haynes, D.L. | (7) | 105† | New Zealand | Dunedin | 1979–80 |
|  |  | 122 | New Zealand | Christchurch | 1979–80 |
|  |  | 184 | England | Lord's | 1980 |
|  |  | 136 | India | St John's | 1982–83 |
|  |  | 103* | Australia | Georgetown | 1983–84 |
|  |  | 145 | Australia | Bridgetown | 1983–84 |
|  |  | 125 | England | Oval | 1984 |

|  |  |  | *Opponents* |  |  |
|---|---|---|---|---|---|
| Headley, G.A. | (10) | 176† | England | Bridgetown | 1929–30 |
|  |  | 114⎫<br>112⎭ | England | Georgetown | 1929–30 |
|  |  | 223 | England | Kingston | 1929–30 |
|  |  | 102* | Australia | Brisbane[1] | 1930–31 |
|  |  | 105 | Australia | Sydney | 1930–31 |
|  |  | 169* | England | Manchester | 1933 |
|  |  | 270* | England | Kingston | 1934–35 |
|  |  | 106⎫<br>107⎭ | England | Lord's | 1939 |
| Holford, D.A.J. |  | 105* | England | Lord's | 1966 |
| Holt, J.K. | (2) | 166 | England | Bridgetown | 1953–54 |
|  |  | 123 | India | Delhi | 1958–59 |
| Hunte, C.C. | (8) | 142† | Pakistan | Bridgetown | 1957–58 |
|  |  | 260 | Pakistan | Kingston | 1957–58 |
|  |  | 114 | Pakistan | Georgetown | 1957–58 |
|  |  | 110 | Australia | Melbourne | 1960–61 |
|  |  | 182 | England | Manchester | 1963 |
|  |  | 108* | England | Oval | 1963 |
|  |  | 135 | England | Manchester | 1966 |
|  |  | 101 | India | Bombay[2] | 1966–67 |
| Julien, B.D. | (2) | 121 | England | Lord's | 1973 |
|  |  | 101 | Pakistan | Karachi | 1974–75 |
| Kallicharran, A.I. | (12) | 100*† | New Zealand | Georgetown | 1971–72 |
|  |  | 101 | New Zealand | Port-of-Spain | 1971–72 |
|  |  | 158 | England | Port-of-Spain | 1973–74 |
|  |  | 119 | England | Bridgetown | 1973–74 |
|  |  | 124† | India | Bangalore | 1974–75 |
|  |  | 115 | Pakistan | Karachi | 1974–75 |
|  |  | 101 | Australia | Brisbane[2] | 1975–76 |
|  |  | 103* | India | Port-of-Spain | 1975–76 |
|  |  | 127 | Australia | Port-of-Spain | 1977–78 |
|  |  | 126 | Australia | Kingston | 1977–78 |
|  |  | 187 | India | Bombay[3] | 1978–79 |
|  |  | 106 | Australia | Adelaide | 1979–80 |
| Kanhai, R.B. | (15) | 256 | India | Calcutta | 1958–59 |
|  |  | 217 | Pakistan | Lahore[1] | 1958–59 |
|  |  | 110 | England | Port-of-Spain | 1959–60 |
|  |  | 117⎫<br>115⎭ | Australia | Adelaide | 1960–61 |
|  |  | 138 | India | Kingston | 1961–62 |
|  |  | 139 | India | Port-of-Spain | 1961–62 |
|  |  | 129 | Australia | Bridgetown | 1964–65 |
|  |  | 121 | Australia | Port-of-Spain | 1964–65 |
|  |  | 104 | England | Oval | 1966 |
|  |  | 153 | England | Port-of-Spain | 1967–68 |
|  |  | 150 | England | Georgetown | 1967–68 |
|  |  | 158* | India | Kingston | 1970–71 |
|  |  | 105 | Australia | Bridgetown | 1972–73 |
|  |  | 157 | England | Lord's | 1973 |
| King, C.L. |  | 100* | New Zealand | Christchurch | 1979–80 |
| Lloyd, C.H. | (19) | 118† | England | Port-of-Spain | 1967–68 |
|  |  | 113* | England | Bridgetown | 1967–68 |
|  |  | 129† | Australia | Brisbane[2] | 1968–69 |
|  |  | 178 | Australia | Georgetown | 1972–73 |
|  |  | 132 | England | Oval | 1973 |
|  |  | 163 | India | Bangalore | 1974–75 |
|  |  | 242* | India | Bombay[3] | 1974–75 |
|  |  | 149 | Australia | Perth | 1975–76 |
|  |  | 102 | Australia | Melbourne | 1975–76 |
|  |  | 102 | India | Bridgetown | 1975–76 |
|  |  | 157 | Pakistan | Bridgetown | 1976–77 |
|  |  | 121 | Australia | Adelaide | 1979–80 |
|  |  | 101 | England | Manchester | 1980 |
|  |  | 100 | England | Bridgetown | 1980–81 |
|  |  | 143 | India | Port-of-Spain | 1982–83 |

| | | | *Opponents* | | |
|---|---|---|---|---|---|
| Lloyd, C.H. *continued* | | 106 | India | St John's | 1982–83 |
| | | 103 | India | Delhi | 1983–84 |
| | | 161* | India | Calcutta | 1983–84 |
| | | 114 | Australia | Brisbane[2] | 1984–85 |
| Logie, A.L. | | 130 | India | Bridgetown | 1982–83 |
| McMorris, E.D.A.St J. | | 125† | India | Kingston | 1961–62 |
| Martin, F.R. | | 123* | Australia | Sydney | 1930–31 |
| Nurse, S.M. | (6) | 201 | Australia | Bridgetown | 1964–65 |
| | | 137 | England | Leeds | 1966 |
| | | 136 | England | Port-of-Spain | 1967–68 |
| | | 137 | Australia | Sydney | 1968–69 |
| | | 168† | New Zealand | Auckland | 1968–69 |
| | | 258 | New Zealand | Christchurch | 1968–69 |
| Pairaudeau, B.H. | | 115† | India | Port-of-Spain | 1952–53 |
| Rae, A.F. | (4) | 104 | India | Bombay[2] | 1948–49 |
| | | 109 | India | Madras[1] | 1948–49 |
| | | 106 | England | Lord's | 1950 |
| | | 109 | England | Oval | 1950 |
| Richards, I.V.A. | (19) | 192* | India | Delhi | 1974–75 |
| | | 101 | Australia | Adelaide | 1975–76 |
| | | 142 | India | Bridgetown | 1975–76 |
| | | 130 | India | Port-of-Spain | 1975–76 |
| | | 177 | India | Port-of-Spain | 1975–76 |
| | | 232† | England | Nottingham | 1976 |
| | | 135 | England | Manchester | 1976 |
| | | 291 | England | Oval | 1976 |
| | | 140 | Australia | Brisbane[2] | 1979–80 |
| | | 145 | England | Lord's | 1980 |
| | | 120 | Pakistan | Multan | 1980–81 |
| | | 182* | England | Bridgetown | 1980–81 |
| | | 114 | England | St John's | 1980–81 |
| | | 109 | India | Georgetown | 1982–83 |
| | | 120 | India | Bombay[3] | 1983–84 |
| | | 178 | Australia | St John's | 1983–84 |
| | | 117 | England | Birmingham | 1984 |
| | | 208 | Australia | Melbourne | 1984–85 |
| | | 105 | New Zealand | Bridgetown | 1984–85 |
| Richardson, R.B. | (4) | 131* | Australia | Bridgetown | 1983–84 |
| | | 154 | Australia | St John's | 1983–84 |
| | | 138 | Australia | Brisbane[2] | 1984–85 |
| | | 185 | New Zealand | Georgetown | 1984–85 |
| Roach, C.A. | (2) | 122 | England | Bridgetown | 1929–30 |
| | | 209 | England | Georgetown | 1929–30 |
| Rowe, L.G. | (7) | 214† ⎫ 100*† ⎭ | New Zealand | Kingston | 1971–72 |
| | | 120 | England | Kingston | 1973–74 |
| | | 302 | England | Bridgetown | 1973–74 |
| | | 123 | England | Port-of-Spain | 1973–74 |
| | | 107 | Australia | Brisbane[2] | 1975–76 |
| | | 100 | New Zealand | Christchurch | 1979–80 |
| Shillingford, I.T. | | 120 | Pakistan | Georgetown | 1976–77 |
| Smith, O.G. | (4) | 104† | Australia | Kingston | 1954–55 |
| | | 161† | England | Birmingham | 1957 |
| | | 168 | England | Nottingham | 1957 |
| | | 100 | India | Delhi | 1958–59 |
| Sobers, G.St A. | (26) | 365* | Pakistan | Kingston | 1957–58 |
| | | 125 ⎫ 109* ⎭ | Pakistan | Georgetown | 1957–58 |
| | | 142*† | India | Bombay[2] | 1958–59 |
| | | 198 | India | Kanpur | 1958–59 |
| | | 106* | India | Calcutta | 1958–59 |
| | | 226 | England | Bridgetown | 1959–60 |
| | | 147 | England | Kingston | 1959–60 |
| | | 145 | England | Georgetown | 1959–60 |
| | | 132 | Australia | Brisbane[2] | 1960–61 |
| | | 168 | Australia | Sydney | 1960–61 |

| | | | *Opponents* | | |
|---|---|---|---|---|---|
| Sobers, G. St A. *continued* | | 153 | India | Kingston | 1961–62 |
| | | 104 | India | Kingston | 1961–62 |
| | | 102 | England | Leeds | 1963 |
| | | 161 | England | Manchester | 1966 |
| | | 163* | England | Lord's | 1966 |
| | | 174 | England | Leeds | 1966 |
| | | 113* | England | Kingston | 1967–68 |
| | | 152 | England | Georgetown | 1967–68 |
| | | 110 | Australia | Adelaide | 1968–69 |
| | | 113 | Australia | Sydney | 1968–69 |
| | | 108* | India | Georgetown | 1970–71 |
| | | 178 | India | Bridgetown | 1970–71 |
| | | 132 | India | Port-of-Spain | 1970–71 |
| | | 142 | New Zealand | Bridgetown | 1971–72 |
| | | 150* | England | Lord's | 1973 |
| Solomon, J.S. | | 100* | India | Delhi | 1958–59 |
| Stollmeyer, J.B. | (4) | 160 | India | Madras$^2$ | 1948–49 |
| | | 104 | Australia | Sydney | 1951–52 |
| | | 152 | New Zealand | Auckland | 1951–52 |
| | | 104* | India | Port-of-Spain | 1952–53 |
| Walcott, C.L. | (15) | 152† | India | Delhi | 1948–49 |
| | | 108 | India | Calcutta | 1948–49 |
| | | 168* | England | Lord's | 1950 |
| | | 115 | New Zealand | Auckland | 1951–52 |
| | | 125 | India | Georgetown | 1952–53 |
| | | 118 | India | Kingston | 1952–53 |
| | | 220 | England | Bridgetown | 1953–54 |
| | | 124 | England | Port-of-Spain | 1953–54 |
| | | 116 | England | Kingston | 1953–54 |
| | | 108 | Australia | Kingston | 1954–55 |
| | | 126⎱ 110⎰ | Australia | Port-of-Spain | 1954–55 |
| | | 155⎱ 110⎰ | Australia | Kingston | 1954–55 |
| | | 145 | Pakistan | Georgetown | 1957–58 |
| Weekes, E. de C. | (15) | 141 | England | Kingston | 1947–48 |
| | | 128† | India | Delhi | 1948–49 |
| | | 194 | India | Bombay$^2$ | 1948–49 |
| | | 162⎱ 101⎰ | India | Calcutta | 1948–49 |
| | | 129 | England | Nottingham | 1950 |
| | | 207 | India | Port-of-Spain | 1952–53 |
| | | 161 | India | Port-of-Spain | 1952–53 |
| | | 109 | India | Kingston | 1952–53 |
| | | 206 | England | Port-of-Spain | 1953–54 |
| | | 139 | Australia | Port-of-Spain | 1954–55 |
| | | 123 | New Zealand | Dunedin | 1955–56 |
| | | 103 | New Zealand | Christchurch | 1955–56 |
| | | 156 | New Zealand | Wellington | 1955–56 |
| | | 197† | Pakistan | Bridgetown | 1957–58 |
| Weekes, K.H. | | 137 | England | Oval | 1939 |
| Williams, A.B. | (2) | 100† | Australia | Georgetown | 1977–78 |
| | | 111 | India | Calcutta | 1978–79 |
| Worrell, F.M.M. | (9) | 131* | England | Georgetown | 1947–48 |
| | | 261 | England | Nottingham | 1950 |
| | | 138 | England | Oval | 1950 |
| | | 108 | Australia | Melbourne | 1951–52 |
| | | 100 | New Zealand | Auckland | 1951–52 |
| | | 237 | India | Kingston | 1952–53 |
| | | 167 | England | Port-of-Spain | 1953–54 |
| | | 191* | England | Nottingham | 1957 |
| | | 197* | England | Bridgetown | 1959–60 |

## NEW ZEALAND (89)

| | | | Opponents | | |
|---|---|---|---|---|---|
| Barton, P.T. | | 109 | South Africa | Port Elizabeth | 1961–62 |
| Burgess, M.G. | (5) | 119* | Pakistan | Dacca | 1969–70 |
| | | 104 | England | Auckland | 1970–71 |
| | | 101 | West Indies | Kingston | 1971–72 |
| | | 105 | England | Lord's | 1973 |
| | | 111 | Pakistan | Lahore[2] | 1976–77 |
| Coney, J.V. | (2) | 174* | England | Wellington | 1983–84 |
| | | 111* | Pakistan | Dunedin | 1984–85 |
| Congdon, B.E. | (7) | 104 | England | Christchurch | 1965–66 |
| | | 166* | West Indies | Port-of-Spain | 1971–72 |
| | | 126 | West Indies | Bridgetown | 1971–72 |
| | | 176 | England | Nottingham | 1973 |
| | | 175 | England | Lord's | 1973 |
| | | 132 | Australia | Wellington | 1973–74 |
| | | 107* | Australia | Christchurch | 1976–77 |
| Crowe, J.J. | (2) | 128 | England | Auckland | 1983–84 |
| | | 112 | West Indies | Kingston | 1984–85 |
| Crowe, M.D. | (2) | 100 | England | Wellington | 1983–84 |
| | | 188 | West Indies | Georgetown | 1984–85 |
| Dempster, C.S. | (2) | 136 | England | Wellington | 1929–30 |
| | | 120 | England | Lord's | 1931 |
| Donnelly, M.P. | | 206 | England | Lord's | 1949 |
| Dowling, G.T. | (3) | 129 | India | Bombay[2] | 1964–65 |
| | | 143 | India | Dunedin | 1967–68 |
| | | 239 | India | Christchurch | 1967–68 |
| Edgar, B.A. | (3) | 129† | Pakistan | Christchurch | 1978–79 |
| | | 127 | West Indies | Auckland | 1979–80 |
| | | 161 | Australia | Auckland | 1981–82 |
| Guy, J.W. | | 102† | India | Hyderabad | 1955–56 |
| Hadlee, R.J. | | 103 | West Indies | Christchurch | 1979–80 |
| Hadlee, W.A. | | 116 | England | Christchurch | 1946–47 |
| Harris, P.G.Z. | | 101 | South Africa | Cape Town | 1961–62 |
| Hastings, B.F. | (4) | 117* | West Indies | Christchurch | 1968–69 |
| | | 105 | West Indies | Bridgetown | 1971–72 |
| | | 110 | Pakistan | Auckland | 1972–73 |
| | | 101 | Australia | Wellington | 1973–74 |
| Howarth, G.P. | (6) | 122⎱ 102⎰ | England | Auckland | 1977–78 |
| | | 123 | England | Lord's | 1978 |
| | | 114 | Pakistan | Napier | 1978–79 |
| | | 147 | West Indies | Christchurch | 1979–80 |
| | | 137* | India | Wellington | 1980–81 |
| Jarvis, T.W. | | 182 | West Indies | Georgetown | 1971–72 |
| Lees, W.K. | | 152 | Pakistan | Karachi | 1976–77 |
| McGregor, S.N. | | 111 | Pakistan | Lahore[1] | 1955–56 |
| Mills, J.E. | | 117† | England | Wellington | 1929–30 |
| Morrison, J.F.M. | | 117 | Australia | Sydney | 1973–74 |
| Page, M.L. | | 104 | England | Lord's | 1931 |
| Parker, J.M. | (3) | 108 | Australia | Sydney | 1973–74 |
| | | 121 | England | Auckland | 1974–75 |
| | | 104 | India | Bombay[3] | 1976–77 |
| Pollard, V. | (2) | 116 | England | Nottingham | 1973 |
| | | 105* | England | Lord's | 1973 |
| Rabone, G.O. | | 107 | South Africa | Durban[2] | 1953–54 |
| Redmond, R.E. | | 107† | Pakistan | Auckland | 1972–73 |
| Reid, J.F. | (5) | 123* | India | Christchurch | 1980–81 |
| | | 180 | Sri Lanka | Colombo (CCC) | 1983–84 |
| | | 106 | Pakistan | Hyderabad | 1984–85 |
| | | 148 | Pakistan | Wellington | 1984–85 |
| | | 158* | Pakistan | Auckland | 1984–85 |
| Reid, J.R. | (6) | 135 | South Africa | Cape Town | 1953–54 |
| | | 119* | India | Delhi | 1955–56 |
| | | 120 | India | Calcutta | 1955–56 |
| | | 142 | South Africa | Johannesburg[3] | 1961–62 |

| | | | Opponents | | |
|---|---|---|---|---|---|
| Reid, J.R. *continued* | | 100 | England | Christchurch | 1962–63 |
| | | 128 | Pakistan | Karachi | 1964–65 |
| Sinclair, B.W. | (3) | 138 | South Africa | Auckland | 1963–64 |
| | | 130 | Pakistan | Lahore² | 1964–65 |
| | | 114 | England | Auckland | 1965–66 |
| Smith, I.D.S. | | 113* | England | Auckland | 1983–84 |
| Sutcliffe, B. | (5) | 101 | England | Manchester | 1949 |
| | | 116 | England | Christchurch | 1950–51 |
| | | 137*† | India | Hyderabad | 1955–56 |
| | | 230* | India | Delhi | 1955–56 |
| | | 151* | India | Calcutta | 1964–65 |
| Taylor, B.R. | (2) | 105† | India | Calcutta | 1964–65 |
| | | 124† | West Indies | Auckland | 1968–69 |
| Turner, G.M. | (7) | 110† | Pakistan | Dacca | 1969–70 |
| | | 223* | West Indies | Kingston | 1971–72 |
| | | 259 | West Indies | Georgetown | 1971–72 |
| | | 101 } 110* } | Australia | Christchurch | 1973–74 |
| | | 117 | India | Christchurch | 1975–76 |
| | | 113 | India | Kanpur | 1976–77 |
| Vivian, H.G. | | 100† | South Africa | Wellington | 1931–32 |
| Wright, J.G. | (4) | 110 | India | Auckland | 1980–81 |
| | | 141 | Australia | Christchurch | 1981–82 |
| | | 130 | England | Auckland | 1983–84 |
| | | 107 | Pakistan | Karachi | 1984–85 |

## INDIA (165)

| | | | | | |
|---|---|---|---|---|---|
| Adhikari, H.R. | | 114*† | West Indies | Delhi | 1948–49 |
| Amarnath, L. | | 118† | England | Bombay¹ | 1933–34 |
| Amarnath, M. | (8) | 100 | Australia | Perth | 1977–78 |
| | | 101* | West Indies | Kanpur | 1978–79 |
| | | 109* | Pakistan | Lahore² | 1982–83 |
| | | 120 | Pakistan | Lahore² | 1982–83 |
| | | 103* | Pakistan | Karachi | 1982–83 |
| | | 117 | West Indies | Port-of-Spain | 1982–83 |
| | | 116 | West Indies | St John's | 1982–83 |
| | | 101* | Pakistan | Lahore² | 1984–85 |
| Amarnath, S. | | 124† | New Zealand | Auckland | 1975–76 |
| Apte, M.L. | | 163* | West Indies | Port-of-Spain | 1952–53 |
| Azharuddin, M. | (3) | 110† | England | Calcutta | 1984–85 |
| | | 105 | England | Madras¹ | 1984–85 |
| | | 122 | England | Kanpur | 1984–85 |
| Baig, A.A. | | 112† | England | Manchester | 1959 |
| Borde, C.G. | (5) | 109 | West Indies | Delhi | 1958–59 |
| | | 177* | Pakistan | Madras² | 1960–61 |
| | | 109 | New Zealand | Bombay² | 1964–65 |
| | | 121 | West Indies | Bombay² | 1966–67 |
| | | 125 | West Indies | Madras¹ | 1966–67 |
| Contractor, N.J. | | 108 | Australia | Bombay² | 1959–60 |
| Durani, S.A. | | 104 | West Indies | Port-of-Spain | 1961–62 |
| Engineer, F.M. | (2) | 109 | West Indies | Madras¹ | 1966–67 |
| | | 121 | England | Bombay² | 1972–73 |
| Gaekwad, A.D. | (2) | 102 | West Indies | Kanpur | 1978–79 |
| | | 201 | Pakistan | Jullundur | 1983–84 |
| Gavaskar, S.M. | (30) | 116 | West Indies | Georgetown | 1970–71 |
| | | 117* | West Indies | Bridgetown | 1970–71 |
| | | 124 } 220 } | West Indies | Port-of-Spain | 1970–71 |
| | | 101 | England | Manchester | 1974 |
| | | 116† | New Zealand | Auckland | 1975–76 |
| | | 156 | West Indies | Port-of-Spain | 1975–76 |
| | | 102 | West Indies | Port-of-Spain | 1975–76 |
| | | 119 | New Zealand | Bombay³ | 1976–77 |
| | | 108 | England | Bombay³ | 1976–77 |
| | | 113† | Australia | Brisbane² | 1977–78 |
| | | 127 | Australia | Perth | 1977–78 |

|  |  |  | *Opponents* |  |  |
|---|---|---|---|---|---|
| Gavaskar, S.M. *continued* |  | 118 | Australia | Melbourne | 1977–78 |
|  |  | 111⎱<br>137⎰ | Pakistan | Karachi | 1978–79 |
|  |  | 205 | West Indies | Bombay³ | 1978–79 |
|  |  | 107 ⎱<br>182*⎰ | West Indies | Calcutta | 1978–79 |
|  |  | 120 | West Indies | Delhi | 1978–79 |
|  |  | 221 | England | Oval | 1979 |
|  |  | 115 | Australia | Delhi | 1979–80 |
|  |  | 123 | Australia | Bombay³ | 1979–80 |
|  |  | 166 | Pakistan | Madras¹ | 1979–80 |
|  |  | 172 | England | Bangalore | 1981–82 |
|  |  | 155† | Sri Lanka | Madras¹ | 1982–83 |
|  |  | 127* | Pakistan | Faisalabad | 1982–83 |
|  |  | 147* | West Indies | Georgetown | 1982–83 |
|  |  | 103* | Pakistan | Bangalore | 1983–84 |
|  |  | 121 | West Indies | Delhi | 1983–84 |
|  |  | 236* | West Indies | Madras¹ | 1983–84 |
| Hanumant Singh |  | 105† | England | Delhi | 1963–64 |
| Hazare, V.S. | (7) | 116⎱<br>145⎰ | Australia | Adelaide | 1947–48 |
|  |  | 134* | West Indies | Bombay² | 1948–49 |
|  |  | 122 | West Indies | Bombay² | 1948–49 |
|  |  | 164* | England | Delhi | 1951–52 |
|  |  | 155 | England | Bombay² | 1951–52 |
|  |  | 146* | Pakistan | Bombay² | 1952–53 |
| Jaisimha, M.L. | (3) | 127 | England | Delhi | 1961–62 |
|  |  | 129 | England | Calcutta | 1963–64 |
|  |  | 101 | Australia | Brisbane² | 1967–68 |
| Kapil Dev | (3) | 126* | West Indies | Delhi | 1978–79 |
|  |  | 116 | England | Kanpur | 1981–82 |
|  |  | 100* | West Indies | Port-of-Spain | 1982–83 |
| Kirmani, S.M.H. | (2) | 101* | Australia | Bombay³ | 1979–80 |
|  |  | 102 | England | Bombay³ | 1984–85 |
| Kripal Singh, A.G. |  | 100*† | New Zealand | Hyderabad | 1955–56 |
| Kunderan, B.K. | (2) | 192 | England | Madras² | 1963–64 |
|  |  | 100 | England | Delhi | 1963–64 |
| Manjrekar, V.L. | (7) | 133 | England | Leeds | 1952 |
|  |  | 118 | West Indies | Kingston | 1952–53 |
|  |  | 118† | New Zealand | Hyderabad | 1955–56 |
|  |  | 177 | New Zealand | Delhi | 1955–56 |
|  |  | 189* | England | Delhi | 1961–62 |
|  |  | 108 | England | Madras² | 1963–64 |
|  |  | 102* | New Zealand | Madras² | 1964–65 |
| Mankad, M.H. | (5) | 116 | Australia | Melbourne | 1947–48 |
|  |  | 111 | Australia | Melbourne | 1947–48 |
|  |  | 184 | England | Lord's | 1952 |
|  |  | 223 | New Zealand | Bombay² | 1955–56 |
|  |  | 231 | New Zealand | Madras² | 1955–56 |
| Merchant, V.M. | (3) | 114 | England | Manchester | 1936 |
|  |  | 128 | England | Oval | 1946 |
|  |  | 154 | England | Delhi | 1951–52 |
| Modi, R.S. |  | 112 | West Indies | Bombay² | 1948–49 |
| Mushtaq Ali | (2) | 112 | England | Manchester | 1936 |
|  |  | 106† | West Indies | Calcutta | 1948–49 |
| Nadkarni, R.G. |  | 122* | England | Kanpur | 1963–64 |
| Pataudi, Nawab of, jr | (6) | 103 | England | Madras² | 1961–62 |
|  |  | 203* | England | Delhi | 1963–64 |
|  |  | 128*† | Australia | Madras² | 1964–65 |
|  |  | 153 | New Zealand | Calcutta | 1964–65 |
|  |  | 113 | New Zealand | Delhi | 1964–65 |
|  |  | 148 | England | Leeds | 1967 |
| Patel, B.P. |  | 115* | West Indies | Port-of-Spain | 1975–76 |
| Patil, S.M. | (4) | 174 | Australia | Adelaide | 1980–81 |
|  |  | 129* | England | Manchester | 1982 |
|  |  | 114*† | Sri Lanka | Madras¹ | 1982–83 |

|  |  |  | *Opponents* |  |  |
|---|---|---|---|---|---|
|  |  | 127 | Pakistan | Faisalabad | 1984–85 |
| Phadkar, D.G. | (2) | 123 | Australia | Adelaide | 1947–48 |
|  |  | 115 | England | Calcutta | 1951–52 |
| Ramchand, G.S. | (2) | 106* | New Zealand | Calcutta | 1955–56 |
|  |  | 109 | Australia | Bombay² | 1956–57 |
| Roy, Pankaj | (5) | 140 | England | Bombay² | 1951–52 |
|  |  | 111 | England | Madras¹ | 1951–52 |
|  |  | 150 | West Indies | Kingston | 1952–53 |
|  |  | 100 | New Zealand | Calcutta | 1955–56 |
|  |  | 173 | New Zealand | Madras² | 1955–56 |
| Sardesai, D.N. | (5) | 200* | New Zealand | Bombay² | 1964–65 |
|  |  | 106 | New Zealand | Delhi | 1964–65 |
|  |  | 212 | West Indies | Kingston | 1970–71 |
|  |  | 112 | West Indies | Port-of-Spain | 1970–71 |
|  |  | 150 | West Indies | Bridgetown | 1970–71 |
| Shastri, R.J. | (5) | 128 | Pakistan | Karachi | 1982–83 |
|  |  | 102 | West Indies | St John's | 1982–83 |
|  |  | 139 | Pakistan | Faisalabad | 1984–85 |
|  |  | 142 | England | Bombay³ | 1984–85 |
|  |  | 111 | England | Calcutta | 1984–85 |
| Shodhan, R.H. | | 110† | Pakistan | Calcutta | 1952–53 |
| Solkar, E.D. | | 102 | West Indies | Bombay³ | 1974–75 |
| Umrigar, P.R. | (12) | 130* | England | Madras¹ | 1951–52 |
|  |  | 102 | Pakistan | Bombay² | 1952–53 |
|  |  | 130 | West Indies | Port-of-Spain | 1952–53 |
|  |  | 117 | West Indies | Kingston | 1952–53 |
|  |  | 108 | Pakistan | Peshawar | 1954–55 |
|  |  | 223† | New Zealand | Hyderabad | 1955–56 |
|  |  | 118 | England | Manchester | 1959 |
|  |  | 115 | Pakistan | Kanpur | 1960–61 |
|  |  | 117 | Pakistan | Madras² | 1960–61 |
|  |  | 112 | Pakistan | Delhi | 1960–61 |
|  |  | 147* | England | Kanpur | 1961–62 |
|  |  | 172* | West Indies | Port-of-Spain | 1961–62 |
| Vengsarkar, D.B. | (9) | 157* | West Indies | Calcutta | 1978–79 |
|  |  | 109 | West Indies | Delhi | 1978–79 |
|  |  | 103 | England | Lord's | 1979 |
|  |  | 112 | Australia | Bangalore | 1979–80 |
|  |  | 146* | Pakistan | Delhi | 1979–80 |
|  |  | 157 | England | Lord's | 1982 |
|  |  | 159 | West Indies | Delhi | 1983–84 |
|  |  | 100 | West Indies | Bombay³ | 1983–84 |
|  |  | 137 | England | Kanpur | 1984–85 |
| Viswanath, G.R. | (14) | 137† | Australia | Kanpur | 1969–70 |
|  |  | 113 | England | Bombay² | 1972–73 |
|  |  | 139 | West Indies | Calcutta | 1974–75 |
|  |  | 112 | West Indies | Port-of-Spain | 1975–76 |
|  |  | 103* | New Zealand | Kanpur | 1976–77 |
|  |  | 145† | Pakistan | Faisalabad | 1978–79 |
|  |  | 124 | West Indies | Madras¹ | 1978–79 |
|  |  | 179 | West Indies | Kanpur | 1978–79 |
|  |  | 113 | England | Lord's | 1979 |
|  |  | 161* | Australia | Bangalore | 1979–80 |
|  |  | 131 | Australia | Delhi | 1979–80 |
|  |  | 114 | Australia | Melbourne | 1980–81 |
|  |  | 107 | England | Delhi | 1981–82 |
|  |  | 222 | England | Madras¹ | 1981–82 |
| Wadekar, A.L. | | 143 | New Zealand | Wellington | 1967–68 |
| Yashpal Sharma | (2) | 100* | Australia | Delhi | 1979–80 |
|  |  | 140 | England | Madras¹ | 1981–82 |

**PAKISTAN (125)**

| | | | | | |
|---|---|---|---|---|---|
| Alimuddin | (2) | 103* | India | Karachi | 1954–55 |
|  |  | 109 | England | Karachi | 1961–62 |

*Opponents*

| | | | | | |
|---|---|---|---|---|---|
| Asif Iqbal | (11) | 146 | England | Oval | 1967 |
| | | 104* | England | Birmingham | 1971 |
| | | 175 | New Zealand | Dunedin | 1972–73 |
| | | 102 | England | Lahore$^2$ | 1972–73 |
| | | 166 | New Zealand | Lahore$^2$ | 1976–77 |
| | | 152* | Australia | Adelaide | 1976–77 |
| | | 120 | Australia | Sydney | 1976–77 |
| | | 135 | West Indies | Kingston | 1976–77 |
| | | 104† | India | Faisalabad | 1978–79 |
| | | 104 | New Zealand | Napier | 1978–79 |
| | | 134* | Australia | Perth | 1978–79 |
| Hanif Mohammad | (12) | 142 | India | Bahawalpur | 1954–55 |
| | | 103 | New Zealand | Dacca | 1955–56 |
| | | 337† | West Indies | Bridgetown | 1957–58 |
| | | 103 | West Indies | Karachi | 1958–59 |
| | | 101* | Australia | Karachi | 1959–60 |
| | | 160 | India | Bombay$^2$ | 1960–61 |
| | | 111 ⎫<br>104 ⎭ | England | Dacca | 1961–62 |
| | | 104 | Australia | Melbourne | 1964–65 |
| | | 100* | New Zealand | Christchurch | 1964–65 |
| | | 203* | New Zealand | Lahore$^2$ | 1964–65 |
| | | 187* | England | Lord's | 1967 |
| Haroon Rashid | (3) | 122† | England | Lahore$^2$ | 1977–78 |
| | | 108 | England | Hyderabad | 1977–78 |
| | | 153† | Sri Lanka | Karachi | 1981–82 |
| Imran Khan | (2) | 123 | West Indies | Lahore$^2$ | 1980–81 |
| | | 117 | India | Faisalabad | 1982–83 |
| Imtiaz Ahmed | (3) | 209 | New Zealand | Lahore$^1$ | 1955–56 |
| | | 122 | West Indies | Kingston | 1957–58 |
| | | 135 | India | Madras$^2$ | 1960–61 |
| Intikhab Alam | | 138 | England | Hyderabad | 1972–73 |
| Javed Burki | (3) | 138† | England | Lahore$^2$ | 1961–62 |
| | | 140 | England | Dacca | 1961–62 |
| | | 101 | England | Lord's | 1962 |
| Javed Miandad | (13) | 163† | New Zealand | Lahore$^2$ | 1976–77 |
| | | 206 | New Zealand | Karachi | 1976–77 |
| | | 154*† | India | Faisalabad | 1978–79 |
| | | 100 | India | Karachi | 1978–79 |
| | | 160* | New Zealand | Christchurch | 1978–79 |
| | | 129* | Australia | Perth | 1978–79 |
| | | 106* | Australia | Faisalabad | 1979–80 |
| | | 138 | Australia | Lahore$^2$ | 1982–83 |
| | | 126 | India | Faisalabad | 1982–83 |
| | | 280* | India | Hyderabad | 1982–83 |
| | | 131 | Australia | Adelaide | 1983–84 |
| | | 104 ⎫<br>103* ⎭ | New Zealand | Hyderabad | 1984–85 |
| Khalid Ibadulla | | 166† | Australia | Karachi | 1964–65 |
| Majid Khan | (8) | 158 | Australia | Melbourne | 1972–73 |
| | | 110 | New Zealand | Auckland | 1972–73 |
| | | 100 | West Indies | Karachi | 1974–75 |
| | | 112 | New Zealand | Karachi | 1976–77 |
| | | 167 | West Indies | Georgetown | 1976–77 |
| | | 119* | New Zealand | Napier | 1978–79 |
| | | 108 | Australia | Melbourne | 1978–79 |
| | | 110* | Australia | Lahore$^2$ | 1979–80 |
| Mansoor Akhtar | (1) | 111 | Australia | Faisalabad | 1982–83 |
| Mohammad Ilyas | | 126 | New Zealand | Karachi | 1964–65 |
| Mohsin Khan | (7) | 129 | Sri Lanka | Lahore$^2$ | 1981–82 |
| | | 200 | England | Lord's | 1982 |
| | | 135 | Australia | Lahore$^2$ | 1982–83 |
| | | 101* | India | Lahore$^2$ | 1982–83 |
| | | 149 | Australia | Adelaide | 1983–84 |
| | | 152 | Australia | Melbourne | 1983–84 |
| | | 104 | England | Lahore$^2$ | 1983–84 |

| | | | Opponents | | |
|---|---|---|---|---|---|
| Mudassar Nazar | (8) | 114† | England | Lahore[2] | 1977–78 |
| | | 126 | India | Bangalore | 1979–80 |
| | | 119 | India | Karachi | 1982–83 |
| | | 231 | India | Hyderabad | 1982–83 |
| | | 152* | India | Lahore[2] | 1982–83 |
| | | 152 | India | Karachi | 1982–83 |
| | | 199 | India | Faisalabad | 1984–85 |
| | | 106 | New Zealand | Hyderabad | 1984–85 |
| Mushtaq Mohammad | (10) | 101 | India | Delhi | 1960–61 |
| | | 100* | England | Nottingham | 1962 |
| | | 100 | England | Birmingham | 1971 |
| | | 121 | Australia | Sydney | 1972–73 |
| | | 201 | New Zealand | Dunedin | 1972–73 |
| | | 157 | England | Hyderabad | 1972–73 |
| | | 123 | West Indies | Lahore[2] | 1974–75 |
| | | 101 | New Zealand | Hyderabad | 1976–77 |
| | | 107 | New Zealand | Karachi | 1976–77 |
| | | 121 | West Indies | Port-of-Spain | 1976–77 |
| Nasim-ul-Ghani | | 101 | England | Lord's | 1962 |
| Nazar Mohammad | | 124* | India | Lucknow | 1952–53 |
| Qasim Omar | (2) | 113 | Australia | Adelaide | 1983–84 |
| | | 210 | India | Faisalabad | 1984–85 |
| Sadiq Mohammad | (5) | 137 | Australia | Melbourne | 1972–73 |
| | | 166 | New Zealand | Wellington | 1972–73 |
| | | 119 | England | Lahore[2] | 1972–73 |
| | | 103* | New Zealand | Hyderabad | 1976–77 |
| | | 105 | Australia | Melbourne | 1976–77 |
| Saeed Ahmed | (5) | 150 | West Indies | Georgetown | 1957–58 |
| | | 166 | Australia | Lahore[2] | 1959–60 |
| | | 121† | India | Bombay[2] | 1960–61 |
| | | 103 | India | Madras[2] | 1960–61 |
| | | 172 | New Zealand | Karachi | 1964–65 |
| Salim Malik | (5) | 100*† | Sri Lanka | Karachi | 1981–82 |
| | | 107 | India | Faisalabad | 1982–83 |
| | | 116 | England | Faisalabad | 1983–84 |
| | | 102* | India | Faisalabad | 1984–85 |
| | | 119* | New Zealand | Karachi | 1984–85 |
| Taslim Arif | | 210* | Australia | Faisalabad | 1979–80 |
| Waqar Hassan | | 189 | New Zealand | Lahore[1] | 1955–56 |
| Wasim Raja | (4) | 107* | West Indies | Karachi | 1974–75 |
| | | 117* | West Indies | Bridgetown | 1976–77 |
| | | 125 | India | Jullundur | 1983–84 |
| | | 112 | England | Faisalabad | 1983–84 |
| Wazir Mohammad | (2) | 106 | West Indies | Kingston | 1957–58 |
| | | 189 | West Indies | Port-of-Spain | 1957–58 |
| Zaheer Abbas | (12) | 274† | England | Birmingham | 1971 |
| | | 240 | England | Oval | 1974 |
| | | 101 | Australia | Adelaide | 1976–77 |
| | | 176† | India | Faisalabad | 1978–79 |
| | | 235* | India | Lahore[2] | 1978–79 |
| | | 135 | New Zealand | Auckland | 1978–79 |
| | | 134† | Sri Lanka | Lahore[2] | 1981–82 |
| | | 126 | Australia | Faisalabad | 1982–83 |
| | | 215 | India | Lahore[2] | 1982–83 |
| | | 186 | India | Karachi | 1982–83 |
| | | 168 | India | Faisalabad | 1982–83 |
| | | 168* | India | Lahore[2] | 1984–85 |

**SRI LANKA (8)**

| | | | | | |
|---|---|---|---|---|---|
| Dias, R.L. | (2) | 109 | Pakistan | Lahore[2] | 1981–82 |
| | | 108 | New Zealand | Colombo (SSC) | 1983–84 |
| Mendis, L.R.D. | (3) | 105† ⎫<br>105† ⎭ | India | Madras[1] | 1982–83 |
| | | 111 | England | Lord's | 1984 |
| Silva, S.A.R. | (1) | 102* | England | Lord's | 1984 |
| Wettimuny, S. | (2) | 157 | Pakistan | Faisalabad | 1981–82 |
| | | 190 | England | Lord's | 1984 |

# NOUGHT AND A HUNDRED IN THE SAME MATCH

| ENGLAND | Scores | | Opponents | | |
|---|---|---|---|---|---|
| L.C. Braund | 102 | 0 | Australia | Sydney | 1903–04 |
| J.T. Tyldesley | 0 | 100 | Australia | Leeds | 1905 |
| G. Gunn | 122* | 0 | Australia | Sydney | 1907–08 |
| F.E. Woolley | 0 | 123 | Australia | Sydney | 1924–25 |
| G.B. Legge | 196 | 0 | New Zealand | Auckland | 1929–30 |
| D.C.S. Compton | 145* | 0 | Australia | Manchester | 1948 |
| L. Hutton | 101 | 0 | New Zealand | Leeds | 1949 |
| P.B.H. May | 0 | 112 | South Africa | Lord's | 1955 |
| M.C. Cowdrey | 119 | 0 | West Indies | Port-of-Spain | 1959–60 |
| Rev D.S. Sheppard | 0 | 113 | Australia | Melbourne | 1962–63 |
| M.C. Cowdrey | 101 | 0 | West Indies | Kingston | 1967–68 |
| D.L. Amiss | 158 | 0 | Pakistan | Hyderabad | 1972–73 |
| D.W. Randall | 0 | 150 | Australia | Sydney | 1978–79 |
| I.T. Botham | 0 | 118 | Australia | Manchester | 1981 |
| G. Boycott | 137 | 0 | Australia | Oval | 1981 |

| AUSTRALIA | | | | | |
|---|---|---|---|---|---|
| W.L. Murdoch | 0 | 153* | England | Oval | 1880 |
| G.H.S. Trott | 0 | 143 | England | Lord's | 1896 |
| C. Hill | 188 | 0 | England | Melbourne | 1897–98 |
| D.G. Bradman | 0 | 103* | England | Melbourne | 1932–33 |
| J.H.W. Fingleton | 100 | 0 | England | Brisbane[2] | 1936–37 |
| D.G. Bradman | 138 | 0 | England | Nottingham | 1948 |
| S.G. Barnes | 0 | 141 | England | Lord's | 1948 |
| R.N. Harvey | 122 | 0 | England | Manchester | 1953 |
| I.R. Redpath | 0 | 132 | West Indies | Sydney | 1968–69 |
| I.M. Chappell | 138 | 0 | India | Delhi | 1969–70 |
| I.C. Davis | 105 | 0 | Pakistan | Adelaide | 1976–77 |
| R.B. McCosker | 0 | 105 | Pakistan | Melbourne | 1976–77 |
| C.S. Serjeant | 0 | 124 | West Indies | Georgetown | 1977–78 |
| G.N. Yallop | 0 | 114 | England | Manchester | 1981 |

| SOUTH AFRICA | | | | | |
|---|---|---|---|---|---|
| J.H. Sinclair | 0 | 104 | Australia | Cape Town | 1902–03 |
| G.A. Faulkner | 122* | 0 | Australia | Manchester | 1912 |
| R.H. Catterall | 0 | 120 | England | Birmingham | 1924 |
| A.D. Nourse | 0 | 231 | Australia | Johannesburg[1] | 1935–36 |
| E.J. Barlow | 114 | 0 | Australia | Brisbane[2] | 1963–64 |

| WEST INDIES | | | | | |
|---|---|---|---|---|---|
| I. Barrow | 105 | 0 | England | Manchester | 1933 |
| F.C.M. Alexander | 0 | 108 | Australia | Sydney | 1960–61 |
| S.M. Nurse | 201 | 0 | Australia | Bridgetown | 1964–65 |
| G.St A. Sobers | 0 | 113* | England | Kingston | 1967–68 |
| C.A. Davis | 103 | 0 | England | Lord's | 1969 |
| G.St A. Sobers | 132 | 0 | India | Port-of-Spain | 1970–71 |
| A.I. Kallicharran | 0 | 103* | India | Port-of-Spain | 1975–76 |
| R.C. Fredericks | 0 | 138 | England | Lord's | 1976 |
| D.L. Haynes | 0 | 122 | New Zealand | Christchurch | 1979–80 |
| C.L. King | 0 | 100* | New Zealand | Christchurch | 1979–80 |
| I.V.A. Richards | 0 | 182* | England | Bridgetown | 1980–81 |
| I.V.A. Richards | 208 | 0 | Australia | Melbourne | 1984–85 |

| NEW ZEALAND | | | | | |
|---|---|---|---|---|---|
| G.T. Dowling | 129 | 0 | India | Bombay[2] | 1964–65 |
| B.F. Hastings | 0 | 117* | West Indies | Christchurch | 1968–69 |

| INDIA | Scores | | Opponents | | |
|---|---|---|---|---|---|
| M.H. Mankad | 111 | 0 | Australia | Melbourne | 1947–48 |
| Pankaj Roy | 140 | 0 | England | Bombay[2] | 1951–52 |
| V.L. Manjrekar | 133 | 0 | England | Leeds | 1952 |
| M.L. Apte | 0 | 163* | West Indies | Port-of-Spain | 1952–53 |
| V.L. Manjrekar | 108 | 0 | England | Madras[2] | 1963–64 |
| G.R. Viswanath | 0 | 137 | Australia | Kanpur | 1969–70 |
| S.M. Gavaskar | 0 | 118 | Australia | Melbourne | 1977–78 |
| D.B. Vengsarkar | 0 | 103 | England | Lord's | 1979 |
| **PAKISTAN** | | | | | |
| Imtiaz Ahmed | 209 | 0 | New Zealand | Lahore[1] | 1955–56 |
| Imtiaz Ahmed | 122 | 0 | West Indies | Kingston | 1957–58 |
| Hanif Mohammad | 160 | 0 | India | Bombay[2] | 1960–61 |
| Javed Burki | 140 | 0 | England | Dacca | 1961–62 |
| Asif Iqbal | 0 | 152* | Australia | Adelaide | 1976–77 |
| Sadiq Mohammad | 105 | 0 | Australia | Melbourne | 1976–77 |
| Asif Iqbal | 0 | 104 | India | Faisalabad | 1978–79 |

# NINETY-NINES IN TEST MATCHES

| ENGLAND | Batting Position | How Out | Opponents | | |
|---|---|---|---|---|---|
| H. Sutcliffe | 2 | Bowled | South Africa | Cape Town | 1927–28 |
| E. Paynter | 5 | Lbw | Australia | Lord's | 1938 |
| N.W.D. Yardley | 6 | Ct | South Africa | Nottingham | 1947 |
| M.J.K. Smith | 5 | Ct (wk) | South Africa | Lord's | 1960 |
| M.J.K. Smith | 4 | Run out | Pakistan | Lahore[2] | 1961–62 |
| E.R. Dexter | 3 | Bowled | Australia | Brisbane[2] | 1962–63 |
| D.L. Amiss | 2 | Ct | Pakistan | Karachi | 1972–73 |
| G. Boycott | 1 | Ct (wk) | West Indies | Port-of-Spain | 1973–74 |
| G. Boycott | 2 | Not out | Australia | Perth | 1979–80 |
| G.A. Gooch | 1 | Run out | Australia | Melbourne | 1979–80 |
| **AUSTRALIA** | | | | | |
| C. Hill | 7 | Ct | England | Melbourne | 1901–02 |
| C.G. Macartney | 3 | Ct (wk) | England | Lord's | 1912 |
| A.G. Chipperfield† | 7 | Ct (wk) | England | Nottingham | 1934 |
| W.A. Brown | 2 | Run out | India | Melbourne | 1947–48 |
| K.R. Miller | 5 | Bowled | England | Adelaide | 1950–51 |
| A.R. Morris | 2 | Run out | South Africa | Melbourne | 1952–53 |
| C.C. McDonald | 1 | Ct (wk) | South Africa | Cape Town | 1957–58 |
| R.M. Cowper | 4 | Ct | England | Melbourne | 1965–66 |
| I.M. Chappell | 3 | Ct | India | Calcutta | 1969–70 |
| R. Edwards | 5 | Lbw | England | Lord's | 1975 |
| K.J. Hughes | 5 | Ct | England | Perth | 1979–80 |
| **SOUTH AFRICA** | | | | | |
| G.A. Faulkner | 5 | Ct | England | Cape Town | 1909–10 |
| B. Mitchell | 1 | Ct (wk) | England | Port Elizabeth | 1948–49 |
| T.L. Goddard | 2 | Ct | England | Oval | 1960 |
| **WEST INDIES** | | | | | |
| R.J. Christiani† | 6 | Lbw | England | Bridgetown | 1947–48 |
| A.F. Rae | 2 | Bowled | New Zealand | Auckland | 1951–52 |
| R.B. Kanhai | 3 | Run out | India | Madras[2] | 1958–59 |
| M.L.C. Foster | 7 | Bowled | India | Port-of-Spain | 1970–71 |
| **NEW ZEALAND** | | | | | |
| J.E.F. Beck | 6 | Run out | South Africa | Cape Town | 1953–54 |
| R.J. Hadlee | 7 | Ct (wk) | England | Christchurch | 1983–84 |

| INDIA | Batting Position | How Out | Opponents | | |
|---|---|---|---|---|---|
| Pankaj Roy | 1 | Ct | Australia | Delhi | 1959–60 |
| M.L. Jaisimha | 2 | Run out | Pakistan | Kanpur | 1960–61 |
| A.L. Wadekar | 3 | Ct | Australia | Melbourne | 1967–68 |
| R.F. Surti | 4 | Ct | New Zealand | Auckland | 1967–68 |
| **PAKISTAN** | | | | | |
| Maqsood Ahmed | 4 | Stumped | India | Lahore[1] | 1954–55 |
| Majid Khan | 3 | Ct | England | Karachi | 1972–73 |
| Mushtaq Mohammad | 4 | Run out | England | Karachi | 1972–73 |
| Javed Miandad | 4 | Ct | India | Bangalore | 1983–84 |

† on debut

C. Hill, the first player to be dismissed for 99 in Test cricket, scored 98 and 97 in his next two innings.
M.J.K. Smith and G. Boycott are the only batsmen to score 99 on two occasions. Boycott holds two unique records: no other player has scored 99 not out in Test matches, nor has his performance of scoring 99 and a hundred (112) at Port-of-Spain in 1973–74 been equalled.
Majid Khan, Mushtaq Mohammad and D.L. Amiss were dismissed for 99 in the same Test.

# MOST FIFTIES

*All scores of 50 and over*

| | | | | Opponents | | | | | | | |
|---|---|---|---|---|---|---|---|---|---|---|---|
| | | **50s** | E | A | SA | WI | NZ | I | P | SL | |
| S.M. Gavaskar | India | **67** | 19 | 8 | – | 20 | 5 | – | 14 | 1 | |
| G. Boycott | England | **64** | – | 21 | 3 | 20 | 8 | 6 | 6 | – | |
| M.C. Cowdrey | England | **60** | – | 16 | 10 | 16 | 10 | 5 | 3 | – | |
| C.H. Lloyd | West Indies | **58** | 18 | 18 | – | – | – | 19 | 3 | – | |
| G.St A. Sobers | West Indies | **56** | 23 | 10 | – | – | 1 | 15 | 7 | – | |
| K.F. Barrington | England | **55** | – | 18 | 8 | 7 | 4 | 12 | 6 | – | |
| G.S. Chappell | Australia | **55** | 21 | – | – | 12 | 6 | 3 | 12 | 1 | |
| L. Hutton | England | **52** | – | 19 | 11 | 11 | 7 | 4 | – | – | |

# MOST CONSECUTIVE FIFTIES

**SEVEN**

| E. de C. Weekes | West Indies | 141 | 128 | 194 | 162 | 101 | 90 | 56 | 1947–48 to 1948–49 |
|---|---|---|---|---|---|---|---|---|---|

**SIX**

| J. Ryder | Australia | 78* | 58 | 56 | 142 | 201* | 88 | | 1921–22 to 1924–25 |
|---|---|---|---|---|---|---|---|---|---|
| E.H. Hendren | England | 77 | 205* | 56 | 123 | 61 | 55 | | 1929–30 |
| G.A. Headley | West Indies | 93 | 53 | 270* | 106 | 107 | 51 | | 1934–35 to 1939 |
| A. Melville | South Africa | 67 | 78 | 103 | 189 | 104* | 117 | | 1938–39 to 1947 |
| G.St A. Sobers | West Indies | 52 | 52 | 80 | 365* | 125 | 109* | | 1957–58 |
| E.R. Dexter | England | 85 | 172 | 70 | 99 | 93 | 52 | | 1962 to 1962–63 |
| K.F. Barrington | England | 63 | 132* | 101 | 94 | 126 | 76 | | 1962–63 |
| K.D. Walters | Australia | 76 | 118 | 110 | 50 | 242 | 103 | | 1968–69 |
| G.S. Chappell | Australia | 68 | 54* | 52 | 70 | 121 | 67 | | 1975–76 to 1976–77 |
| G.R. Viswanath | India | 59 | 54 | 79 | 89 | 73 | 145 | | 1977–78 to 1978–79 |

G. Boycott (England) scored nine fifties in ten innings in 1970–71 and 1971: 70, 50, 77, 142*, 12, 76*, 58, 119*, 121*, 112.
M.A. Noble (Australia) is the only player to score two separate fifties on the same day: 60* and 59* v England at Manchester in 1899 on the second day.

# OVER 60% OF A COMPLETED INNINGS TOTAL

| % | | | | | |
|---|---|---|---|---|---|
| **67.34** | C. Bannerman | 165*/245 | Australia v England | Melbourne | 1876–77 |
| **63.50** | C.G. Greenidge | 134/211 | West Indies v England | Manchester | 1976 |
| **62.89** | J.R. Reid | 100/159 | New Zealand v England | Christchurch | 1962–63 |
| **61.87** | S.M. Nurse | 258/417 | West Indies v New Zealand | Christchurch | 1968–69 |

| 61.85 | M. Amarnath | 60/97† | India v West Indies | Kingston | 1975–76 |
|---|---|---|---|---|---|
| 61.11 | G.N. Yallop | 121/198 | Australia v England | Sydney | 1978–79 |
| 60.65 | V.T. Trumper | 74/122 | Australia v England | Melbourne | 1903–04 |
| 60.26 | H.A. Gomes | 91/151 | West Indies v India | Madras[1] | 1978–79 |
| 60.19 | J.T. Tyldesley | 62/103 | England v Australia | Melbourne | 1903–04 |

† *Five men were absent hurt.*

*D.L. Amiss (262\*) scored 60.64% of England's total of 432 for 9 against West Indies at Kingston in 1973–1974.*

# OVER 50% OF COMPLETED INNINGS TOTALS IN A MATCH

| % | | | | | |
|---|---|---|---|---|---|
| 51.88 | J.H. Sinclair | 106/177<br>4/35 | South Africa v England | Cape Town | 1898–99 |

# OVER 600 RUNS ADDED DURING ONE BATSMAN'S INNINGS

| 770 | L. Hutton | 364 | England v Australia | Oval | 1938 |
|---|---|---|---|---|---|
| 720 | A. Sandham | 325 | England v West Indies | Kingston | 1929–30 |
| 703 | G.St A. Sobers | 365* | West Indies v Pakistan | Kingston | 1957–58 |
| 646 | R.B. Simpson | 311 | Australia v England | Manchester | 1964 |
| 628 | Hanif Mohammad | 337 | Pakistan v West Indies | Bridgetown | 1957–58 |

# LONGEST INNINGS FOR EACH COUNTRY

| For | Min | | Opponents | | |
|---|---|---|---|---|---|
| England | 797 | L. Hutton (364) | Australia | Oval | 1938 |
| Australia | 762 | R.B. Simpson (311) | England | Manchester | 1964 |
| South Africa | 575 | D.J. McGlew (105) | Australia | Durban[2] | 1957–58 |
| West Indies | 682 | F.M.M. Worrell (197*) | England | Bridgetown | 1959–60 |
| New Zealand | 704 | G.M. Turner (259) | West Indies | Georgetown | 1971–72 |
| India | 708 | S.M. Gavaskar (172) | England | Bangalore | 1981–82 |
| Pakistan | 970 | Hanif Mohammad (337) | West Indies | Bridgetown | 1957–58 |

# BATTED ON EACH DAY OF A FIVE-DAY MATCH

| | Scores | | | | |
|---|---|---|---|---|---|
| M.L. Jaisimha | 20* | 74 | I v A | Calcutta | 1959–60 |
| G. Boycott | 107 | 80* | E v A | Nottingham | 1977 |
| K.J. Hughes | 117 | 84 | A v E | Lord's | 1980 |
| A.J. Lamb | 23 | 110 | E v WI | Lord's | 1984 |
| R.J. Shastri | 111 | 7* | I v E | Calcutta | 1984–85 |

# MOST RUNS FROM STROKES WORTH FOUR OR MORE IN AN INNINGS

| | 6s | 5s | 4s | | | | | |
|---|---|---|---|---|---|---|---|---|
| 238 | 5 | – | 52 | J.H. Edrich | 310* | E v NZ | Leeds | 1965 |
| 196 | 10 | – | 34 | W.R. Hammond | 336* | E v NZ | Auckland | 1932–33 |
| 184 | – | – | 46 | D.G. Bradman | 334 | A v E | Leeds | 1930 |
| 184 | 2 | – | 43 | D.G. Bradman | 304 | A v E | Leeds | 1934 |
| 177 | – | 1 | 43 | R.G. Pollock | 274 | SA v A | Durban[2] | 1969–70 |
| 168 | – | – | 42 | R.B. Kanhai | 256 | WI v I | Calcutta | 1958–59 |
| 166 | 1 | – | 40 | D.L. Amiss | 262* | E v WI | Kingston | 1973–74 |
| 157 | – | 1 | 38 | G.St A. Sobers | 365* | WI v P | Kingston | 1957–58 |
| 152 | 2 | – | 35 | F.M.M. Worrell | 261 | WI v E | Nottingham | 1950 |
| 152 | – | – | 38 | Zaheer Abbas | 274 | P v E | Birmingham | 1971 |
| 152 | – | – | 38 | I.V.A. Richards | 291 | WI v E | Oval | 1976 |
| 150 | 1 | – | 36 | L.G. Rowe | 302 | WI v E | Bridgetown | 1973–74 |

# MOST SIXES IN AN INNINGS

| | | | | |
|---|---|---|---|---|
| TEN | W.R. Hammond (336*) | E v NZ | Auckland | 1932–33 |
| SEVEN | B. Sutcliffe (80*) | NZ v SA | Johannesburg[2] | 1953–54 |
| SIX | J.H. Sinclair (104) | SA v A | Cape Town | 1902–03 |
| | I.V.A. Richards (192*) | WI v I | Delhi | 1974–75 |
| | Haroon Rashid (108) | P v E | Hyderabad | 1977–78 |
| | I.T. Botham (118) | E v A | Manchester | 1981 |

# MOST SIXES OFF CONSECUTIVE BALLS

| | | | | |
|---|---|---|---|---|
| THREE | W.R. Hammond (336*) off J. Newman | E v NZ | Auckland | 1932–33 |
| | S.T. Clarke (35*) off Mohammad Nazir | WI v P | Faisalabad | 1980–81 |

# MOST FOURS OFF CONSECUTIVE BALLS

| | | | | |
|---|---|---|---|---|
| FIVE | D.T. Lindsay (60) off J.W. Gleeson | SA v A | Port Elizabeth | 1969–70 |
| | R.E. Redmond (107) off Majid Khan | NZ v P | Auckland | 1972–73 |
| | D.W. Hookes (56) off A.W. Greig | A v E | Melbourne | 1976–77 |

# MOST RUNS OFF ONE OVER

EIGHT-BALL

| | | | | |
|---|---|---|---|---|
| 25 (66061600) | B. Sutcliffe and R.W. Blair (off H.J. Tayfield) | NZ v SA | Johannesburg[2] | 1953–54 |

SIX-BALL

| | | | | |
|---|---|---|---|---|
| 24 (462660†) (†1 leg-bye) | A.M.E. Roberts (off I.T. Botham) | WI v E | Port-of-Spain | 1980–81 |
| 24 (444†0444) (†no-ball) | S.M. Patil (off R.G.D. Willis) | I v E | Manchester | 1982 |

# FASTEST FIFTIES

| Min | Balls | | | | |
|---|---|---|---|---|---|
| 28 | | J.T. Brown (140) | England v Australia | Melbourne | 1894–95 |
| 29 | | S.A. Durani (61*) | India v England | Kanpur | 1963–64 |
| 30 | | E.A.V. Williams (72) | West Indies v England | Bridgetown | 1947–48 |
| 30 | 36 | B.R. Taylor (124) | New Zealand v West Indies | Auckland | 1968–69 |
| 33 | | C.A. Roach (56) | West Indies v England | Oval | 1933 |
| 34 | | C.R. Browne (70*) | West Indies v England | Georgetown | 1929–30 |
| 35 | | J.H. Sinclair (104) | South Africa v Australia | Cape Town | 1902–03 |
| 35 | | C.G. Macartney (56) | Australia v South Africa | Sydney | 1910–11 |
| 35 | | J.W. Hitch (51*) | England v Australia | Oval | 1921 |
| 35 | | J.M. Gregory (119) | Australia v South Africa | Johannesburg[1] | 1921–22 |

*R.C. Fredericks (169) scored his first fifty off 33 balls (45 minutes) for West Indies v Australia at Perth in 1975–76.*
*F.G. Mann scored 49\* in 24 minutes for England v New Zealand at Leeds in 1949.*
*Kapil Dev (65) scored 50 off 33 balls in 44 minutes for India v England at Manchester in 1982.*

# FASTEST HUNDREDS

| Min | Balls | | | | |
|---|---|---|---|---|---|
| 70 | 67 | J.M. Gregory (119) | Australia v South Africa | Johannesburg[1] | 1921–22 |
| 75 | 75 | G.L. Jessop (104) | England v Australia | Oval | 1902 |
| 78 | | R. Benaud (121) | Australia v West Indies | Kingston | 1954–55 |
| 80 | | J.H. Sinclair (104) | South Africa v Australia | Cape Town | 1902–03 |
| 86 | 83 | B.R. Taylor (124) | New Zealand v West Indies | Auckland | 1968–69 |
| 91 | | J. Darling (160) | Australia v England | Sydney | 1897–98 |
| 91 | | S.J. McCabe (189*) | Australia v South Africa | Johannesburg[1] | 1935–36 |
| 94 | | V.T. Trumper (185*) | Australia v England | Sydney | 1903–04 |

*Minutes*

| | | | | |
|---|---|---|---|---|
| 95 | J.T. Brown (140) | England v Australia | Melbourne | 1894–95 |
| 95 | P.W. Sherwell (115) | South Africa v England | Lord's | 1907 |

*R.C. Fredericks (169) scored his hundred off 71 balls (116 minutes) for West Indies v Australia at Perth in 1975–76.*

*Majid Khan (112) scored his hundred off 74 balls (113 minutes) before lunch for Pakistan v New Zealand at Karachi in 1976–77.*

## HUNDRED BEFORE LUNCH

FIRST DAY

| | Lunch score | | | |
|---|---|---|---|---|
| V.T. Trumper (104) | 103* | Australia v England | Manchester | 1902 |
| C.G. Macartney (151) | 112* | Australia v England | Leeds | 1926 |
| D.G. Bradman (334) | 105* | Australia v England | Leeds | 1930 |
| Majid Khan (112) | 108* | Pakistan v New Zealand | Karachi | 1976–77 |

| | Overnight | Lunch | | | |
|---|---|---|---|---|---|
| OTHER DAYS | score | score | | | Day |
| K.S. Ranjitsinhji (154*) | 41* | 154* | E v A | Manchester | 3 | 1896 |
| C. Hill (142) | 22* | 138* | A v SA | Johannesburg[1] | 3 | 1902–03 |
| W. Bardsley (164) | 32* | 150* | A v SA | Lord's | 2 | 1912 |
| C.P. Mead (182*) | 19* | 128* | E v A | Oval | 2 | 1921 |
| J.B. Hobbs (211) | 12* | 114* | E v SA | Lord's | 2 | 1924 |
| H.G. Owen-Smith (129) | 27* | 129 | SA v E | Leeds | 3 | 1929 |
| W.R. Hammond (336*) | 41* | 152* | E v NZ | Auckland | 2 | 1932–33 |
| L.E.G. Ames (148*) | 25* | 148* | E v SA | Oval | 3 | 1935 |
| S.J. McCabe (189*) | 59* | 159* | A v SA | Johannesburg[1] | 4 | 1935–36 |
| G.S. Chappell (176) | 76* | 176 | A v NZ | Christchurch | 2 | 1981–82 |

*I.T. Botham (9* to 108*) scored 99 before lunch on the 4th day for England v India at Leeds in 1979.*

## FASTEST DOUBLE HUNDREDS

*Minutes*

| | | | | |
|---|---|---|---|---|
| 214 | D.G. Bradman (334) | Australia v England | Leeds | 1930 |
| 223 | S.J. McCabe (232) | Australia v England | Nottingham | 1938 |
| 226 | V.T. Trumper (214*) | Australia v South Africa | Adelaide | 1910–11 |
| 234 | D.G. Bradman (254) | Australia v England | Lord's | 1930 |
| 240 | W.R. Hammond (336*) | England v New Zealand | Auckland | 1932–33 |
| 241 | S.E. Gregory (201) | Australia v England | Sydney | 1894–95 |
| 245 | D.C.S. Compton (278) | England v Pakistan | Nottingham | 1954 |
| 251 | D.G. Bradman (223) | Australia v West Indies | Brisbane[1] | 1930–31 |
| 253 | D.G. Bradman (226) | Australia v South Africa | Brisbane[2] | 1931–32 |

*I.T. Botham (208) reached his double century off 220 balls (268 minutes) for England v India at The Oval in 1982.*

## FASTEST TRIPLE HUNDREDS

*Minutes*

| | | | | |
|---|---|---|---|---|
| 288 | W.R. Hammond (336*) | England v New Zealand | Auckland | 1932–33 |
| 336 | D.G. Bradman (334) | Australia v England | Leeds | 1930 |

*W.R. Hammond's third hundred was scored in 47 minutes.*

*D.G. Bradman scored his three hundreds in 99, 115 and 122 minutes respectively and reached 309* at the end of the first day.*

## MOST RUNS IN A DAY

| | | | | | |
|---|---|---|---|---|---|
| 309 | (0-309*) | D.G. Bradman (334) | A v E | Leeds | 1930 |
| 295 | (41*-336*) | W.R. Hammond (336*) | E v NZ | Auckland | 1932–33 |
| 273 | (5*-278) | D.C.S. Compton (278) | E v P | Nottingham | 1954 |

| 271 | (0-271*) | D.G. Bradman (304) | A v E | Leeds | 1934 |
|---|---|---|---|---|---|
| 244 | (0-244) | D.G. Bradman (244) | A v E | Oval | 1934 |
| 239 | (0-239*) | F.M.M. Worrell (261) | WI v E | Nottingham | 1950 |
| 223 | (0-223*) | W.R. Hammond (227) | E v NZ | Christchurch | 1932–33 |
| 223 | (0-223*) | D.G. Bradman (223) | A v WI | Brisbane[1] | 1930–31 |
| 217 | (0-217) | W.R. Hammond (217) | E v I | Oval | 1936 |
| 214 | (73*-287) | R.E. Foster (287) | E v A | Sydney | 1903–04 |
| 213 | (19*-232) | S.J. McCabe (232) | A v E | Nottingham | 1938 |
| 210 | (0-210*) | W.R. Hammond (240) | E v A | Lord's | 1938 |
| 209 | (0-209) | C.A. Roach (209) | WI v E | Georgetown | 1929–30 |
| 208 | (20*-228*) | G.St A. Sobers (365*) | WI v P | Kingston | 1957–58 |
| 208 | (0-208*) | V.T. Trumper (214*) | A v SA | Adelaide | 1910–11 |
| 206 | (0-206) | L. Hutton (206) | E v NZ | Oval | 1949 |
| 205 | (0-205*) | W.H. Ponsford (266) | A v E | Oval | 1934 |
| 203 | (0-203) | H.L. Collins (203) | A v SA | Johannesburg[1] | 1921–22 |
| 203 | (0-203*) | R.B. Kanhai (256) | WI v I | Calcutta | 1958–59 |
| 201 | (0-201) | D.G. Bradman (201) | A v I | Adelaide | 1947–48 |
| 200 | (0-200*) | D.G. Bradman (226) | A v SA | Brisbane[2] | 1931–32 |
| 200 | (0-200*) | I.V.A. Richards (291) | WI v E | Oval | 1976 |

## FAST INNINGS

| Runs | Min | | | | |
|---|---|---|---|---|---|
| 35 | 14 | W.P. Howell | A v E | Sydney | 1901–02 |
| 49* | 24 | F.G. Mann | E v NZ | Leeds | 1949 |
| 61* | 34 | S.A. Durani | I v E | Kanpur | 1963–64 |
| 63 | 50 | V.T. Trumper | A v SA | Johannesburg[1] | 1902–03 |
| 72 | 63 | E.A.V. Williams | WI v E | Bridgetown | 1947–48 |
| 104 | 77 | G.L. Jessop | E v A | Oval | 1902 |
| 119 | 97 | J.M. Gregory | A v SA | Johannesburg[1] | 1921–22 |
| 124 | 110 | B.R. Taylor | NZ v WI | Auckland | 1968–69 |
| 128 | 115 | G.J. Bonnor | A v E | Sydney | 1884–85 |
| 137 | 135 | K.H. Weekes | WI v E | Oval | 1939 |
| 189* | 165 | S.J. McCabe | A v SA | Johannesburg[1] | 1935–36 |
| 191 | 202 | C. Hill | A v SA | Sydney | 1910–11 |
| 232 | 235 | S.J. McCabe | A v E | Nottingham | 1938 |
| 278 | 290 | D.C.S. Compton | E v P | Nottingham | 1954 |
| 336* | 318 | W.R. Hammond | E v NZ | Auckland | 1932–33 |

## FAST PARTNERSHIPS

| Runs | Min | Wkt | | | | |
|---|---|---|---|---|---|---|
| 42* | 16 | 9th | F.W. Freer (28*), G.E. Tribe (25*) | A v E | Sydney | 1946–47 |
| 66* | 24 | 5th | C. Washbrook (103*), F.G. Mann (49*) | E v NZ | Leeds | 1949 |
| 77 | 28 | 10th | S.J. McCabe (232), L.O. Fleetwood-Smith (5*) | A v E | Nottingham | 1938 |
| 80 | 41 | 7th | B.W. Yuile (20), B.R. Taylor (124) | NZ v WI | Auckland | 1968–69 |
| 86 | 44 | 3rd | I.M. Chappell (121), G.S. Chappell (133) | A v NZ | Wellington | 1973–74 |
| 108 | 45 | 7th | F.R. Brown (74), W. Voce (66) | E v NZ | Christchurch | 1932–33 |
| 121* | 55 | 3rd | F.E. Woolley (134*), E.H. Hendren (50*) | E v SA | Lord's | 1924 |
| 144 | 64 | 3rd | C. Hill (191), D.R.A. Gehrs (67) | A v SA | Sydney | 1910–11 |
| 154 | 73 | 9th | S.E. Gregory (201), J.M. Blackham (74) | A v E | Sydney | 1894–95 |
| 158 | 90 | 6th | J.T. Tyldesley (112*), R.H. Spooner (79) | E v A | Oval | 1905 |
| 209 | 97 | 3rd | H.L. Collins (203), J.M. Gregory (119) | A v SA | Johannesburg[1] | 1921–22 |
| 224 | 115 | 2nd | W. Bardsley (132), C. Hill (191) | A v SA | Sydney | 1910–11 |
| 248 | 140 | 4th | L. Hutton (196), D.C.S. Compton (120) | E v WI | Lord's | 1939 |
| 249 | 163 | 3rd | D.G. Bradman (169), S.J. McCabe (112) | A v E | Melbourne | 1936–37 |
| 264 | 180 | 3rd | L. Hutton (165*), W.R. Hammond (138) | E v WI | Oval | 1939 |
| 301 | 217 | 2nd | A.R. Morris (182), D.G. Bradman (173*) | A v E | Leeds | 1948 |
| 350 | 274 | 4th | Mushtaq Mohammad (201), Asif Iqbal (175) | P v NZ | Dunedin | 1972–73 |
| 451 | 316 | 2nd | W.H. Ponsford (266), D.G. Bradman (244) | A v E | Oval | 1934 |

# SLOWEST FIFTIES

| Min | Balls | | | | |
|-----|-------|---|---|---|---|
| 357 | | T.E. Bailey (68) | E v A | Brisbane[2] | 1958-5 |
| 350 | 236 | C.J. Tavaré (82) | E v P | Lord's | 198 |
| 316 | | C.P.S. Chauhan (61) | I v P | Kanpur | 1979-8 |
| 313 | | D.J. McGlew (70) | SA v A | Johannesburg[3] | 1957-5 |
| 310 | | B.A. Edgar (55) | NZ v A | Wellington | 1981-8 |
| 306 | 219 | C.J. Tavaré (78) | E v A | Manchester | 198 |
| 302 | | D.N. Sardesai (60) | I v WI | Bridgetown | 1961-6 |
| 300 | | G.S. Camacho (57) | WI v E | Bridgetown | 1967-6 |
| 290 | 207 | G. Boycott (63) | E v P | Lahore[2] | 1977-7 |
| 289 | 219 | C.J. Tavaré (56) | E v I | Bombay[3] | 1981-8 |
| 282 | | E.D.A.St J. McMorris (73) | WI v E | Kingston | 1959-6 |
| 280 | | P.E. Richardson (117) | E v SA | Johannesburg[3] | 1956-5 |
| 280 | 218 | G. Boycott (77) | E v A | Perth | 1978-7 |

# SLOWEST HUNDREDS

| Min | Balls | | | | |
|-----|-------|---|---|---|---|
| 557 | 420 | Mudassar Nazar (114) | P v E | Lahore[2] | 1977-7 |
| 545 | | D.J. McGlew (105) | SA v A | Durban[2] | 1957-5 |
| 488 | | P.E. Richardson (117) | E v SA | Johannesburg[3] | 1956-5 |
| 487 | 397 | C.T. Radley (158) | E v NZ | Auckland | 1977-7 |
| 468 | | Hanif Mohammad (142) | P v I | Bahawalpur | 1954-5 |
| 460 | | Hanif Mohammad (111) | P v E | Dacca | 1961-6 |
| 458 | 329 | K.W.R. Fletcher (122) | E v P | Oval | 197 |
| 455 | 307 | G.P. Howarth (122) | NZ v E | Auckland | 1977-7 |
| 437 | | D.B. Vengsarkar (146*) | I v P | Delhi | 1979-8 |
| 435 | | J.W. Guy (102) | NZ v I | Hyderabad | 1955-5 |
| 434 | | M.C. Cowdrey (154) | E v WI | Birmingham | 195 |
| 428 | 280 | S.M. Gavaskar (172) | I v E | Bangalore | 1981-8 |
| 414 | | J.H.B. Waite (134) | SA v A | Durban[2] | 1957-5 |
| 414 | 321 | A.W. Greig (103) | E v I | Calcutta | 1976-7 |

*The slowest hundreds in matches between England and Australia are:*

| Min | Balls | | | | |
|-----|-------|---|---|---|---|
| 406 | 353 | D.W. Randall (150) | E v A | Sydney | 1978-7 |
| 377 | 314 | A.R. Border (123*) | A v E | Manchester | 198 |
| 374 | 297 | K.J. Hughes (129) | A v E | Brisbane[2] | 1978-7 |

# SLOWEST DOUBLE HUNDREDS

| Min | Balls | | | | |
|-----|-------|---|---|---|---|
| 652 | 426 | A.D. Gaekwad (201) | I v P | Jullundur | 1983-8 |
| 608 | | R.B. Simpson (311) | A v E | Manchester | 196 |
| 595 | | G.St A. Sobers (226) | WI v E | Bridgetown | 1959-6 |
| 584 | | Hanif Mohammad (337) | P v WI | Bridgetown | 1957-58 |
| 570 | | S.G. Barnes (234) | A v E | Sydney | 1946-4 |
| 568 | 348 | G.R. Viswanath (222) | I v E | Madras[1] | 1981-8 |

# SLOWEST TRIPLE HUNDREDS

| Minutes | | | | |
|---------|---|---|---|---|
| 858 | Hanif Mohammad (337) | P v WI | Bridgetown | 1957-58 |
| 753 | R.B. Simpson (311) | A v E | Manchester | 196 |

# SLOWEST INNINGS

| Runs | Minutes | | | | |
|------|---------|---|---|---|---|
| 2* | 80 | C.E.H. Croft | WI v A | Brisbane[2] | 1979-80 |
| 3* | 100 | J.T. Murray *(injured)* | E v A | Sydney | 1962-63 |

| Runs | Minutes | | | | |
|------|---------|--|--|--|--|
| 5 | 102 | Nawab of Pataudi, jr | I v E | Bombay[2] | 1972–73 |
| 7 | 123 | G. Miller | E v A | Melbourne | 1978–79 |
| 9 | 125 | T.W. Jarvis | NZ v I | Madras[1] | 1964–65 |
| 10* | 133 | T.G. Evans | E v A | Adelaide | 1946–47 |
| 16* | 147 | D.B. Vengsarkar | I v P | Kanpur | 1979–80 |
| 18 | 194 | W.R. Playle | NZ v E | Leeds | 1958 |
| 19 | 217 | M.D. Crowe | NZ v SL | Colombo (SSC) | 1983–84 |
| 28* | 250 | J.W. Burke | A v E | Brisbane[2] | 1958–59 |
| 31 | 264 | K.D. Mackay | A v E | Lord's | 1956 |
| 40 | 289 | H.L. Collins | A v E | Manchester | 1921 |
| 42 | 294 | C.J. Tavaré | E v WI | Lord's | 1980 |
| 45 | 318 | Shujauddin | P v A | Lahore[2] | 1959–60 |
| 55 | 336 | B.A. Edgar | NZ v A | Wellington | 1981–82 |
| 57 | 346 | G.S. Camacho | WI v E | Bridgetown | 1967–68 |
| 58 | 367 | Ijaz Butt | P v A | Karachi | 1959–60 |
| 60 | 390 | D.N. Sardesai | I v WI | Bridgetown | 1961–62 |
| 68 | 458 | T.E. Bailey | E v A | Brisbane[2] | 1958–59 |
| 99 | 505 | M.L. Jaisimha | I v P | Kanpur | 1960–61 |
| 105 | 575 | D.J. McGlew | SA v A | Durban[2] | 1957–58 |
| 114 | 591 | Mudassar Nazar | P v E | Lahore[2] | 1977–78 |
| 158 | 648 | C.T. Radley | E v NZ | Auckland | 1977–78 |
| 172 | •708 | S.M. Gavaskar | I v E | Bangalore | 1981–82 |
| 337 | 970 | Hanif Mohammad | P v WI | Bridgetown | 1957–58 |

*C.E.H. Croft faced 73 balls and added 56 for the tenth wicket with J. Garner (60).*

# FEWEST BOUNDARIES IN AN INNINGS

| Runs | Fours | | | | |
|------|-------|--|--|--|--|
| 84 | 0 | W.M. Lawry | A v E | Brisbane[2] | 1970–71 |
| 77 | 0 | G. Boycott | E v A | Perth | 1978–79 |
| 67 | 0 | E.A.B. Rowan | SA v E | Durban[2] | 1938–39 |
| 120 | 2 | P.A. Gibb | E v SA | Durban[2] | 1938–39 |
| 94 | 2 | K.F. Barrington | E v A | Sydney | 1962–63 |
| 102 | 3 | W.M. Woodfull | A v E | Melbourne | 1928–29 |
| 161 | 5 | W.M. Woodfull | A v SA | Melbourne | 1931–32 |

*G. Boycott's innings included one four but it was all-run and included two runs from an overthrow.*

# AN HOUR BEFORE SCORING FIRST RUN

| Minutes | | | | |
|---------|--|--|--|--|
| 97 | T.G. Evans (10*) | E v A | Adelaide | 1946–47 |
| 82 | P.I. Pocock (13) | E v WI | Georgetown | 1967–68 |
| 74 | J.T. Murray (3*) | E v A | Sydney | 1962–63 |
| 70 | W.L. Murdoch (17) | A v E | Sydney | 1882–83 |
| 69 | R.M. Hogg (7*) | A v WI | Adelaide | 1984–85 |
| 67 | C.J. Tavaré (82) | E v P | Lord's | 1982 |
| 66 | J.G. Wright (38) | NZ v A | Wellington | 1981–82 |
| 65 | Shujauddin (45) | P v A | Lahore[2] | 1959–60 |
| 63 | C.J. Tavaré (9) | E v A | Perth | 1982–83 |

# AN HOUR WITHOUT ADDING TO A SCORE

| Minutes | | | | |
|---------|--|--|--|--|
| 90 | B. Mitchell (58) | SA v A | Brisbane[2] | 1931–32 |
| 90 | C.J. Tavaré (89) | E v A | Perth | 1982–83 |
| 79 | T.E. Bailey (8) | E v SA | Leeds | 1955 |
| 77 | D.B. Close (20) | E v WI | Manchester | 1976 |
| 75 | A. Ranatunga (37) | SL v NZ | Colombo (CCC) | 1983–84 |
| 70 | D.L. Haynes (9) | WI v NZ | Auckland | 1979–80 |

*Minutes*

| | | | | |
|---|---|---|---|---|
| 67 | W.H. Scotton (34) | E v A | Oval | 1886 |
| 65 | Nawab of Pataudi, jr (5) | I v E | Bombay[2] | 1972–73 |
| 64 | Anil Dalpat (15) | P v NZ | Wellington | 1984–85 |
| 63 | D.R. Jardine (24) | E v A | Brisbane[2] | 1932–33 |
| 63 | W.R. Endean (18) | SA v E | Johannesburg[3] | 1956–57 |
| 63 | W.R. Playle (18) | NZ v E | Leeds | 1958 |
| 63 | J.M. Brearley (48) | E v A | Birmingham | 1981 |
| 62 | K.F. Barrington (137) | E v NZ | Birmingham | 1965 |
| 61 | J.F. Reid (148) | NZ v P | Wellington | 1984–85 |
| 60 | B. Mitchell (73) | SA v E | Johannesburg[1] | 1938–39 |
| 60 | T.E. Bailey (80) | E v SA | Durban[2] | 1956–57 |
| 60 | C.J. Tavaré (82) | E v P | Lord's | 1982 |
| 60 | A.R. Border (9) | A v P | Faisalabad | 1982–83 |

# FEWEST RUNS IN A DAY

| | | | | |
|---|---|---|---|---|
| **49** | (5*–54*) | M.L. Jaisimha (99) | I v P | Kanpur | 1960–61 |
| **52** | (52*) | Mudassar Nazar (114) | P v E | Lahore[2] | 1977–78 |
| **56** | (1*–57*) | D.J. McGlew (70) | SA v A | Johannesburg[3] | 1957–58 |
| **59** | (0*–59*) | M.L. Jaisimha (74) | I v A | Calcutta | 1959–60 |

# DISMISSED BY THE FIRST BALL OF A MATCH

| *Batsman* | *Bowler* | | | |
|---|---|---|---|---|
| A.C. MacLaren | A. Coningham | E v A | Melbourne | 1894–95 |
| T.W. Hayward | A.E.E. Vogler | E v SA | Oval | 1907 |
| W. Bardsley | M.W. Tate | A v E | Leeds | 1926 |
| H. Sutcliffe | F.T. Badcock | E v NZ | Christchurch | 1932–33 |
| T.S. Worthington | E.L. McCormick | E v A | Brisbane[2] | 1936–37 |
| C.C. Hunte | Fazal Mahmood | WI v P | Port-of-Spain | 1957–58 |
| E.J. Barlow | G.D. McKenzie | SA v A | Durban[2] | 1966–67 |
| R.C. Fredericks | S. Abid Ali | WI v I | Port-of-Spain | 1970–71 |
| K.R. Stackpole | R.J. Hadlee | A v NZ | Auckland | 1973–74 |
| S.M. Gavaskar | G.G. Arnold | I v E | Birmingham | 1974 |
| S.S. Naik | A.M.E. Roberts | I v WI | Calcutta | 1974–75 |
| J.F.M. Morrison | G.G. Arnold | NZ v E | Christchurch | 1974–75 |
| S.M. Gavaskar | M.D. Marshall | I v WI | Calcutta | 1983–84 |

# BATSMEN DISMISSED FOR A PAIR

**FOUR TIMES**

B.S. Chandrasekhar (India): v E 1976–77; v A 1977–78 (twice); v NZ 1975–76.

**THREE TIMES**

R. Peel (England): v A 1894–95 (twice), 1896.
R.W. Blair (New Zealand): v E 1962–63; v SA 1963–64; v WI 1955–56.
D.L. Underwood (England): v A 1974–75; v WI 1966, 1976.
B.S. Bedi (India): v E 1974, 1976–77; v WI 1974–75.
A.G. Hurst (Australia): v E 1978–79 (twice); v P 1978–79.

**TWICE**

ENGLAND: A.V. Bedser v A 1948; v WI 1950. D.L. Amiss v A 1968, 1974–75. P.I. Pocock v WI 1984 (twice).

AUSTRALIA: K.D. Mackay v E 1956; v I 1959–60. G.D. McKenzie v E 1968; v SA 1963–64. J.W. Gleeson v E 1970–71; v SA 1969–70. W.M. Clark v WI 1977–78 (twice). R.M. Hogg v I 1979–80; v WI 1984–85.

SOUTH AFRICA: L.J. Tancred v E 1907, 1912. Q. McMillan v A 1931–32 (twice). R.J. Crisp v A 1935–36 (twice).

WEST INDIES: C.A. Roach v E 1929–30, 1933. A.L. Valentine v E 1950, 1953–54. A.I. Kallicharran v E 1973–74, v NZ 1979–80.
INDIA: D.R. Doshi v A 1980–81; v P 1982–83. M. Amarnath v WI 1983–84 (twice).

---

## ONCE

ENGLAND: G.F. Grace v A 1880. W. Attewell v A 1891–92. G.A. Lohmann v SA 1895–96. E.G. Arnold v A 1903–04. A.E. Knight v A 1903–04. E.G. Hayes v SA 1905–06. M.C. Bird v SA 1909–10. H. Strudwick v A 1921. P. Holmes v SA 1927–28. C.I.J. Smith v WI 1934–35. J.T. Ikin v A 1946–47. J.J. Warr v A 1950–51. F. Ridgway v I 1951–52. R.T. Spooner v SA 1955. J.H. Wardle v A 1956. F.S. Trueman v A 1958–59. T.E. Bailey v A 1958–59. G. Pullar v P 1961–62. M.J.K. Smith v I 1961–62. J.T. Murray v P 1967. B.W. Luckhurst v P 1971. A.P.E. Knott v NZ 1973. G.G. Arnold v A 1974–75. G.A. Gooch v A 1975. A. Ward v WI 1976. J.C. Balderstone v WI 1976. M. Hendrick v NZ 1977–78. R.A. Woolmer v A 1981. I.T. Botham v A 1981. E.E. Hemmings v A 1982–83. N.G. Cowans v I 1984–85.

AUSTRALIA: P.S. McDonnell v E 1882–83. T.W. Garrett v E 1882–83. E. Evans v E 1886. P.G. McShane v E 1887–88. A.C. Bannerman v E 1888. M.A. Noble v E 1899. S.E. Gregory v E 1899. C.E. McLeod v E 1901–02. J. Darling v E 1902. J.J. Kelly v E 1902. H. Trumble v E 1903–04. V.T. Trumper v E 1907–08. J.V. Saunders v E 1907–08. C.V. Grimmett v E 1930. W.A.S. Oldfield v SA 1931–32. J.H.W. Fingleton v E 1932–33. V.Y. Richardson v E 1932–33. C.L. Badcock v E 1938. I.W. Johnson v E 1946–47. J. Moroney v E 1950–51. J.B. Iverson v E 1950–51. L.V. Maddocks v E 1956. R.N. Harvey v E 1956. A.T.W. Grout v WI 1960–61. R. Benaud v E 1961. A.N. Connolly v WI 1968–69. R. Edwards v E 1972. K.R. Stackpole v NZ 1973–74. G. Dymock v E 1974–75. R.W. Marsh v E 1977. J.R. Thomson v E 1977. C.S. Serjeant v I 1977–78. A.L. Mann v I 1977–78. D.W. Hookes v P 1979–80. G.M. Wood v NZ 1980–81. M.R. Whitney v E 1981. B. Yardley v P 1982–83. R.J. Bright v P 1982–83. C.G. Rackemann v WI 1984–85. K.J. Hughes v WI 1984–85. R.G. Holland v E 1985.

SOUTH AFRICA: C.S. Wimble v E 1891–92. J.T. Willoughby v E 1895–96. J.J. Kotze v A 1902–03. P.S.T. Jones v A 1902–03. A.E.E. Vogler v A 1910–11. T.A. Ward v A 1912. C.B. Llewellyn v E 1912. P.T. Lewis v E 1913–14. J.L. Cox v E 1913–14. C.D. Dixon v E 1913–14. G.A.L. Hearne v E 1922–23. A.E. Hall v E 1922–23. F. Nicholson v A 1935–36. X.C. Balaskas v A 1935–36. C.N. McCarthy v E 1948–49. D.J. McGlew v E 1955. W.R. Endean v E 1955. P.S. Heine v E 1956–57. C. Wesley v E 1960. M.A. Seymour v A 1969–70.

WEST INDIES: C.R. Browne v E 1929–30. H.C. Griffith v E 1933. E.E. Achong v E 1934–35. J. Trim v A 1951–52. A.P. Binns v A 1954–55. O.G. Smith v A 1954–55. S. Ramadhin v E 1957. E. de C. Weekes v E 1957. F.C.M. Alexander v E 1957. L.R. Gibbs v P 1958–59. F.M.M. Worrell v A 1960–61. J.S. Solomon v I 1961–62. J.L. Hendriks v E 1966. W.W. Hall v E 1967–68. D.L. Murray v I 1974–75. C.G. Greenidge v A 1975–76. J. Garner v P 1976–77. D.A. Murray v P 1980–81. A.L. Logie v I 1983–84. M.A. Holding v A 1984–85.

NEW ZEALAND: K.C. James v E 1929–30. F.T. Badcock v E 1929–30. J. Cowie v E 1937. C.G. Rowe v A 1945–46. L.A. Butterfield v A 1945–46. L.S.M. Miller v SA 1953–54. M.B. Poore v E 1954–55. I.A. Colquhoun v E 1954–55. J.A. Hayes v E 1954–55. A.R. MacGibbon v I 1955–56. H.B. Cave v WI 1955–56. N.S. Harford v E 1958. R.C. Motz v SA 1961–62. M.J.F. Shrimpton v SA 1963–64. A.E. Dick v P 1964–65. G.A. Bartlett v E 1965–66. T.W. Jarvis v P 1972–73. W.K. Lees v E 1977–78. B.P. Bracewell v E 1978. B.L. Cairns v A 1980–81. B.A. Edgar v A 1980–81. G.B. Troup v I 1980–81. J.V. Coney v A 1981–82. I.D.S. Smith v A 1981–82. J.G. Bracewell v P 1984–85. K.R. Rutherford v WI 1984–85.

INDIA: V.S. Hazare v E 1951–52. G.S. Ramchand v E 1952. Pankaj Roy v E 1952. P.G. Joshi v WI 1952–53. C.V. Gadkari v WI 1952–53. N.S. Tamhane v WI 1958–59. Surendranath v E 1959. R.B. Desai v A 1959–60. D.N. Sardesai v WI 1961–62. M.L. Jaisimha v NZ 1969–70. E.A.S. Prasanna v WI 1974–75. F.M. Engineer v WI 1974–75. D.B. Vengsarkar v WI 1978–79. Yashpal Sharma v A 1979–80. R.M.H. Binny v P 1979–80. Maninder Singh v P 1982–83. S. Venkataraghavan v WI 1982–83.

PAKISTAN: M.E.Z. Ghazali v E 1954. Nasim-ul-Ghani v WI 1957–58. Wazir Mohammad v WI 1957–58. Imtiaz Ahmed v E 1961–62. Javed Burki v NZ 1964–65. Salim Altaf v A 1976–77. Iqbal Qasim v E 1978. Majid Khan v A 1978–79. Wasim Bari v A 1978–79. Sikander Bakht v A 1978–79. Mudassar Nazar v E 1982.

SRI LANKA: no instance.

---

# FASTEST PAIRS

*Timed from the start of their first innings to their dismissal in the second innings.*

| Minutes | | | | |
|---|---|---|---|---|
| 120 | M.E.Z. Ghazali | Pakistan v England | Manchester | 1954 |
| 124 | R.N. Harvey | Australia v England | Manchester | 1956 |
| 164 | Pankaj Roy | India v England | Manchester | 1952 |

# DISMISSED FOR A PAIR BY THE SAME FIELDING COMBINATION

| R. Peel | st Jarvis b Turner | E v A | Sydney | 1894–95 |
|---|---|---|---|---|
| J. Darling | c Braund b Barnes | A v E | Sheffield | 1902 |
| P.T. Lewis | c Woolley b Barnes | SA v E | Durban[1] | 1913–14 |
| P.G. Joshi | c Worrell b Valentine | I v WI | Bridgetown | 1952–53 |
| K.D. Mackay | c Oakman b Laker | A v E | Manchester | 1956 |

# THREE PAIRS IN A MATCH BY THE SAME TEAM

| M.B. Poore, I.A. Colquhoun, J.A. Hayes | NZ v E | Auckland | 1954–55 |
|---|---|---|---|
| D.L. Amiss, D.L. Underwood, G.G. Arnold | E v A | Adelaide | 1974–75 |
| Majid Khan, Wasim Bari, Sikander Bakht | P v A | Perth | 1978–79 |

# MOST CONSECUTIVE DUCKS

| FOUR | | | |
|---|---|---|---|
| R. Peel | (2 pairs in consecutive Tests) | E v A | 1894–95 |
| R.J. Crisp | (2 pairs in consecutive Tests) | SA v A | 1935–36 |
| Pankaj Roy | (including one pair) | I v E | 1952 |
| L.S.M. Miller | (including one pair) | NZ v SA | 1953–54 |
| W.M. Clark | (2 pairs in consecutive Tests) | A v WI | 1977–78 |
| P.I. Pocock | (2 pairs in consecutive Tests) | E v WI | 1984 |

*R.J. Crisp was dismissed four times in five balls.*

# MOST DUCKS IN A SERIES

| | | | Innings | |
|---|---|---|---|---|
| SIX | A.G. Hurst | Australia v England | 12 | 1978–79 |
| FIVE | Pankaj Roy | India v England | 7 | 1952 |
| | R.C. Motz | New Zealand v South Africa | 9 | 1961–62 |
| | W.M. Clark | Australia v West Indies | 7 | 1977–78 |
| | M. Amarnath | India v West Indies | 6 | 1983–84 |

# FEWEST DUCKS IN A CAREER

| Ducks | Innings | | | |
|---|---|---|---|---|
| 1 | 74 | C.L. Walcott | West Indies | 1947–48 to 1959–60 |
| 1 | 73 | G.M. Turner | New Zealand | 1968–69 to 1982–83 |
| 2 | 84 | H. Sutcliffe | England | 1924 to 1935 |
| 2 | 83 | C.C. McDonald | Australia | 1951–52 to 1961 |
| 4 | 175 | C.H. Lloyd | West Indies | 1966–67 to 1984–85 |
| 4 | 140 | W.R. Hammond | England | 1927–28 to 1946–47 |
| 5 | 131 | K.F. Barrington | England | 1955 to 1968 |

# MOST INNINGS BEFORE FIRST DUCK

| 58 | C.H. Lloyd | West Indies | 1966–67 to 1973–74 |
|---|---|---|---|
| 46 | B.F. Butcher | West Indies | 1958–59 to 1966–67 |
| 41 | R.N. Harvey | Australia | 1947–48 to 1953 |
| 40 | W.H. Ponsford | Australia | 1924–25 to 1932–33 |

# MOST CONSECUTIVE INNINGS WITHOUT A DUCK

| | | | |
|---|---|---|---|
| 78 | K.F. Barrington | England | 1962 to 1967–68 |
| 74 | C.H. Lloyd | West Indies | 1976 to 1984 |
| 72 | H.W. Taylor | South Africa | 1912 to 1931–32 |
| 72 | G.M. Turner | New Zealand | 1968–69 to 1982–83 |
| 68 | K.D. Walters | Australia | 1969–70 to 1976–77 |
| 67 | W.R. Hammond | England | 1929 to 1936 |
| 67 | G. Boycott | England | 1969 to 1978–79 |

# PARTNERSHIP RECORDS

*Throughout these records partnerships involving more than two batsmen are excluded unless two of the partners added at least 100 runs together.*

## HIGHEST PARTNERSHIPS FOR EACH WICKET

| | | | | | |
|---|---|---|---|---|---|
| 1st | 413 | M.H. Mankad (231), Pankaj Roy (173) | I v NZ | Madras[2] | 1955–56 |
| 2nd | 451 | W.H. Ponsford (266), D.G. Bradman (244) | A v E | Oval | 1934 |
| 3rd | 451 | Mudassar Nazar (231), Javed Miandad (280*) | P v I | Hyderabad | 1982–83 |
| 4th | 411 | P.B.H. May (285*), M.C. Cowdrey ('54) | E v WI | Birmingham | 1957 |
| 5th | 405 | S.G. Barnes (234), D.G. Bradman (234) | A v E | Sydney | 1946–47 |
| 6th | 346 | J.H.W. Fingleton (136), D.G. Bradman (270) | A v E | Melbourne | 1936–37 |
| 7th | 347 | D.St E. Atkinson (219), C.C. Depeiza (122) | WI v A | Bridgetown | 1954–55 |
| 8th | 246 | L.E.G. Ames (137), G.O.B. Allen (122) | E v NZ | Lord's | 1931 |
| 9th | 190 | Asif Iqbal (146), Intikhab Alam (51) | P v E | Oval | 1967 |
| 10th | 151 | B.F. Hastings (110), R.O. Collinge (68*) | NZ v P | Auckland | 1972–73 |

## PARTNERSHIPS OF 300 AND OVER

| Runs | Wkt | | | | |
|---|---|---|---|---|---|
| 451 | 2nd | W.H. Ponsford (266), D.G. Bradman (244) | A v E | Oval | 1934 |
| 451 | 3rd | Mudassar Nazar (231), Javed Miandad (280*) | P v I | Hyderabad | 1982–83 |
| 446 | 2nd | C.C. Hunte (260), G.St A. Sobers (365*) | WI v P | Kingston | 1957–58 |
| 413 | 1st | M.H. Mankad (231), Pankaj Roy (173) | I v NZ | Madras[2] | 1955–56 |
| 411 | 4th | P.B.H. May (285*), M.C. Cowdrey (154) | E v WI | Birmingham | 1957 |
| 405 | 5th | S.G. Barnes (234), D.G. Bradman (234) | A v E | Sydney | 1946–47 |
| 399 | 4th | G.St A. Sobers (226), F.M.M. Worrell (197*) | WI v E | Bridgetown | 1959–60 |
| 388 | 4th | W.H. Ponsford (181), D.G. Bradman (304) | A v E | Leeds | 1934 |
| 387 | 1st | G.M. Turner (259), T.W. Jarvis (182) | NZ v WI | Georgetown | 1971–72 |
| 382 | 2nd | L. Hutton (364), M. Leyland (187) | E v A | Oval | 1938 |
| 382 | 1st | W.M. Lawry (210), R.B. Simpson (201) | A v WI | Bridgetown | 1964–65 |
| 370 | 3rd | W.J. Edrich (189), D.C.S. Compton (208) | E v SA | Lord's | 1947 |
| 369 | 2nd | J.H. Edrich (310*), K.F. Barrington (163) | E v NZ | Leeds | 1965 |
| 359 | 1st | L. Hutton (158), C. Washbrook (195) | E v SA | Johannesburg[2] | 1948–49 |
| 351 | 2nd | G.A. Gooch (196), D.I. Gower (157) | E v A | Oval | 1985 |
| 350 | 4th | Mushtaq Mohammad (201), Asif Iqbal (175) | P v NZ | Dunedin | 1972–73 |
| 347 | 7th | D.St E. Atkinson (219), C.C. Depeiza (122) | WI v A | Bridgetown | 1954–55 |
| 346 | 6th | J.H.W. Fingleton (136), D.G. Bradman (270) | A v E | Melbourne | 1936–37 |
| 344* | 2nd | S.M. Gavaskar (182*), D.B. Vengsarkar (157*) | I v WI | Calcutta | 1978–79 |
| 341 | 3rd | E.J. Barlow (201), R.G. Pollock (175) | SA v A | Adelaide | 1963–64 |
| 338 | 3rd | E. de C. Weekes (206), F.M.M. Worrell (167) | WI v E | Port-of-Spain | 1953–54 |
| 336 | 4th | W.M. Lawry (151), K.D. Walters (242) | A v WI | Sydney | 1968–69 |
| 331 | 2nd | R.T. Robinson (148), D.I. Gower (215) | E v A | Birmingham | 1985 |
| 323 | 1st | J.B. Hobbs (178), W. Rhodes (179) | E v A | Melbourne | 1911–12 |
| 319 | 3rd | A. Melville (189), A.D. Nourse (149) | SA v E | Nottingham | 1947 |
| 316† | 3rd | G.R. Viswanath (222), Yashpal Sharma (140) | I v E | Madras[1] | 1981–82 |
| 308 | 7th | Waqar Hassan (189), Imtiaz Ahmed (209) | P v NZ | Lahore[1] | 1955–56 |
| 308 | 3rd | R.B. Richardson (154), I.V.A. Richards (178) | WI v A | St John's | 1983–84 |
| 303 | 3rd | I.V.A. Richards (232), A.I. Kallicharran (97) | WI v E | Nottingham | 1976 |
| 301 | 2nd | A.R. Morris (182), D.G. Bradman (173*) | A v E | Leeds | 1948 |

*†415 runs were added for this wicket in two separate partnerships, D.B. Vengsarkar retiring hurt and being succeeded by Yashpal Sharma when 99 runs had been added.*

# MOST HUNDRED PARTNERSHIPS IN ONE INNINGS

FOUR                                       *Opponents*

| | | | | |
|---|---|---|---|---|
| England | 382 (2nd), 135 (3rd), 215 (6th), 106 (7th) | Australia | Oval | 1938 |
| West Indies | 267 (4th), 101 (6th), 118 (7th), 106 (9th) | India | Delhi | 1948–49 |
| Pakistan | 152 (1st), 112 (2nd), 154 (3rd), 121 (4th) | West Indies | Bridgetown | 1957–58 |
| India | 144 (3rd), 172 (4th), 109 (5th), 102 (6th) | West Indies | Kanpur | 1978–79 |

## SUMMARY OF HUNDRED PARTNERSHIPS

| | *1st* | *2nd* | *3rd* | *4th* | *5th* | *6th* | *7th* | *8th* | *9th* | *10th* | *Total* |
|---|---|---|---|---|---|---|---|---|---|---|---|
| England | 115 | 113 | 99 | 92 | 59 | 65 | 28 | 11 | 7 | 3 | 592 |
| Australia | 53 | 93 | 82 | 79 | 57 | 25 | 18 | 12 | 5 | 2 | 426 |
| South Africa | 28 | 19 | 26 | 22 | 11 | 10 | 11 | 5 | 1 | 1 | 134 |
| West Indies | 35 | 45 | 54 | 46 | 37 | 40 | 15 | 1 | 4 | – | 277 |
| New Zealand | 14 | 15 | 16 | 16 | 16 | 7 | 5 | 3 | 1 | 1 | 94 |
| India | 30 | 37 | 35 | 33 | 24 | 18 | 9 | 6 | 7 | 1 | 200 |
| Pakistan | 16 | 22 | 25 | 24 | 16 | 13 | 6 | 3 | 3 | 2 | 130 |
| Sri Lanka | – | 1 | 4 | 1 | 2 | 2 | – | – | – | – | 10 |
| | | | | | | | | | | | |
| Totals | 291 | 345 | 341 | 313 | 222 | 180 | 92 | 41 | 28 | 10 | 1863 |

## BATSMEN SHARING IN MOST HUNDRED PARTNERSHIPS

| | | *Total* | *1st* | *2nd* | *3rd* | *4th* | *5th* | *6th* | *7th* | *8th* | *9th* | *10th* |
|---|---|---|---|---|---|---|---|---|---|---|---|---|
| S.M. Gavaskar | I | **50** | 20 | 16 | 6 | 4 | 2 | 1 | – | – | 1 | – |
| G. Boycott | E | **47** | 20 | 8 | 9 | 8 | – | 2 | – | – | – | – |
| G.S. Chappell | A | **44** | – | 2 | 15 | 13 | 11 | 2 | 1 | – | – | – |
| G.St A. Sobers | WI | **43** | – | 3 | 4 | 12 | 12 | 10 | 2 | – | – | – |
| M.C. Cowdrey | E | **42** | 5 | 9 | 6 | 13 | 4 | 3 | 1 | – | 1 | – |
| L. Hutton | E | **41** | 17 | 13 | 7 | 1 | – | 2 | 1 | – | – | – |
| C.H. Lloyd | WI | **41** | – | – | 6 | 14 | 9 | 10 | 1 | – | 1 | – |
| K.F. Barrington | E | **35** | – | 6 | 10 | 14 | 4 | 1 | – | – | – | – |
| D.G. Bradman | A | **35** | – | 14 | 11 | 3 | 6 | 1 | – | – | – | – |
| R.B. Kanhai | WI | **34** | 2 | 9 | 11 | 7 | 3 | 2 | – | – | – | – |
| W.R. Hammond | E | **33** | 1 | 6 | 12 | 11 | 2 | 1 | – | – | – | – |
| I.V.A. Richards | WI | **33** | – | 11 | 11 | 4 | 3 | 2 | 1 | 1 | – | – |
| H. Sutcliffe | E | **33** | 21 | 10 | 1 | – | – | 1 | – | – | – | – |
| J.H. Edrich | E | **32** | 9 | 11 | 6 | 5 | 1 | – | – | – | – | – |
| R.N. Harvey | A | **32** | – | 6 | 13 | 9 | 3 | 1 | – | – | – | – |
| J.B. Hobbs | E | **32** | 24 | 6 | 1 | – | – | – | 1 | – | – | – |
| C.G. Greenidge | WI | **31** | 15 | 6 | 3 | 2 | 2 | 2 | 1 | – | ... | – |
| I.M. Chappell | A | **30** | – | 18 | 8 | 1 | 1 | 2 | – | – | – | – |
| D.C.S. Compton | E | **30** | – | – | 14 | 7 | 7 | 1 | – | 1 | – | – |

*The most for South Africa, New Zealand, Pakistan and Sri Lanka is:*

| | | *Total* | *1st* | *2nd* | *3rd* | *4th* | *5th* | *6th* | *7th* | *8th* | *9th* | *10th* |
|---|---|---|---|---|---|---|---|---|---|---|---|---|
| B. Mitchell | SA | **24** | 9 | 3 | 8 | 2 | – | 1 | 1 | 1 | – | – |
| G.M. Turner | NZ | **13** | 5 | 4 | 1 | 2 | – | 1 | – | – | – | – |
| Javed Miandad | P | **28** | – | 2 | 10 | 9 | 5 | 2 | – | – | – | – |
| Zaheer Abbas | P | **28** | 1 | 4 | 3 | 10 | 5 | 2 | 2 | – | 1 | – |
| R.L. Dias | SL | **5** | – | – | 1 | 4 | – | – | – | – | – | – |
| S. Wettimuny | SL | **5** | 1 | 2 | 1 | 1 | – | – | – | – | – | – |

# HUNDRED PARTNERSHIPS

**ENGLAND – (592) – 1st Wicket**

| | | | *A* | *SA* | *WI* | *NZ* | *I* | *P* | *SL* |
|---|---|---|---|---|---|---|---|---|---|
| L. Hutton (158), C. Washbrook (195) | Johannesburg[2] | 1948–49 | – | 359 | – | – | – | – | – |
| J.B. Hobbs (178), W. Rhodes (179) | Melbourne | 1911–12 | 323 | – | – | – | – | – | – |
| G. Pullar (175), M.C. Cowdrey (155) | Oval | 1960 | – | 290 | – | – | – | – | – |
| J.B. Hobbs (154), H. Sutcliffe (176) | Melbourne | 1924–25 | 283 | – | – | – | – | – | – |
| J.B. Hobbs (211), H. Sutcliffe (122) | Lord's | 1924 | – | 268 | – | – | – | – | – |
| G. Boycott (84), R.W. Barber (185) | Sydney | 1965–66 | 234 | – | – | – | – | – | – |

**1st Wicket** *continued*

| | | | A | SA | WI | NZ | I | P | SL |
|---|---|---|---|---|---|---|---|---|---|
| G. Fowler (105), C.J. Tavaré (109) | Oval | 1983 | – | – | – | 223 | – | – | – |
| J.B. Hobbs (187), W. Rhodes (77) | Cape Town | 1909–10 | – | 221 | – | – | – | – | – |
| C.J. Barnett (126), L. Hutton (100) | Nottingham | 1938 | 219 | – | – | – | – | – | – |
| C. Washbrook (102), R.T. Simpson (94) | Nottingham | 1950 | – | – | 212 | – | – | – | – |
| G. Boycott (93), D.L. Amiss (174) | Port-of-Spain | 1973–74 | – | – | 209 | – | – | – | – |
| G. Pullar (165), R.W. Barber (86) | Dacca | 1961–62 | – | – | – | – | – | 198 | – |
| T.W. Hayward (137), F.S. Jackson (118) | Oval | 1899 | 185 | – | – | – | – | – | – |
| G. Boycott (100*), J.M. Brearley (74) | Hyderabad | 1977–78 | – | – | – | – | – | 185 | – |
| J.B. Hobbs (119), H. Sutcliffe (82) | Lord's | 1926 | 182 | – | – | – | – | – | – |
| G. Fowler (201), R.T. Robinson (74) | Madras[1] | 1984–85 | – | – | – | – | 178 | – | – |
| M.C. Cowdrey (97), G. Pullar (66) | Kingston | 1959–60 | – | – | 177 | – | – | – | – |
| P.E. Richardson (104), M.C. Cowdrey (80) | Manchester | 1956 | 174 | – | – | – | – | – | – |
| G. Gunn (85), A. Sandham (325) | Kingston | 1929–30 | – | – | 173 | – | – | – | – |
| J.B. Hobbs (100), H. Sutcliffe (161) | Oval | 1926 | 172 | – | – | – | – | – | – |
| J.H. Edrich (146), G. Boycott (90) | Bridgetown | 1967–68 | – | – | 172 | – | – | – | – |
| G. Boycott (70), B.W. Luckhurst (131) | Perth | 1970–71 | 171 | – | – | – | – | – | – |
| W.G. Grace (170), W.H. Scotton (34) | Oval | 1886 | 170 | – | – | – | – | – | – |
| L. Hutton (81), C. Washbrook (143) | Leeds | 1948 | 168 | – | – | – | – | – | – |
| G. Boycott (76*), J.H. Edrich (74*) | Melbourne | 1970–71 | 161* | – | – | – | – | – | – |
| R.E.S. Wyatt (54), W.R. Hammond (136*) | Durban[2] | 1930–31 | – | 160 | – | – | – | – | – |
| J.B. Hobbs (89), W. Rhodes (66) | Johannesburg[1] | 1909–10 | – | 159 | – | – | – | – | – |
| P.E. Richardson (71), G. Pullar (83) | Bombay[2] | 1961–62 | – | – | – | – | 159 | – | – |
| C.A.G. Russell (102*), G. Brown (84) | Oval | 1921 | 158 | – | – | – | – | – | – |
| J.B. Hobbs (115), H. Sutcliffe (59) | Sydney | 1924–25 | 157 | – | – | – | – | – | – |
| D.L. Amiss (79), D. Lloyd (214*) | Birmingham | 1974 | – | – | – | – | 157 | – | – |
| J.B. Hobbs (88), H. Sutcliffe (94) | Leeds | 1926 | 156 | – | – | – | – | – | – |
| G. Fowler (69), R.T. Robinson (96) | Kanpur | 1984–85 | – | – | – | – | 156 | – | – |
| J.B. Hobbs (159), H. Sutcliffe (63) | Oval | 1928 | – | – | 155 | – | – | – | – |
| G.A. Gooch (127), C.J. Tavaré (35) | Madras[1] | 1981–82 | – | – | – | – | 155 | – | – |
| A.C. MacLaren (116), T.W. Hayward (69) | Sydney | 1901–02 | 154 | – | – | – | – | – | – |
| J.M. Brearley (81), G. Boycott (80*) | Nottingham | 1977 | 154 | – | – | – | – | – | – |
| A. Sandham (58), C.A.G. Russell (96) | Johannesburg[1] | 1922–23 | – | 153 | – | – | – | – | – |
| W.G. Grace (68), A.E. Stoddart (83) | Oval | 1893 | 151 | – | – | – | – | – | – |
| P.E. Richardson (73), M.C. Cowdrey (81) | Nottingham | 1956 | 151 | – | – | – | – | – | – |
| T.W. Hayward (90), A.C. MacLaren (67) | Adelaide | 1901–02 | 149 | – | – | – | – | – | – |
| T.W. Hayward (67), P.F. Warner (79) | Adelaide | 1903–04 | 148 | – | – | – | – | – | – |
| J.B. Hobbs (187), W. Rhodes (59) | Adelaide | 1911–12 | 147 | – | – | – | – | – | – |
| L. Hutton (206), R.T. Simpson (68) | Oval | 1949 | – | – | – | – | 147 | – | – |
| W.G.A. Parkhouse (78), G. Pullar (75) | Leeds | 1959 | – | – | – | – | 146 | – | – |
| D.L. Amiss (50), J.M. Brearley (91) | Bombay[3] | 1976–77 | – | – | – | – | 146 | – | – |
| G.A. Gooch (83), B.C. Rose (50) | Oval | 1980 | – | – | 146† | – | – | – | – |
| T.W. Hayward (47), A.C. MacLaren (140) | Nottingham | 1905 | 145 | – | – | – | – | – | – |
| G.A. Gooch (83), G. Boycott (104*) | St John's | 1980–81 | – | – | 144 | – | – | – | – |
| J.B. Hobbs (74), H. Sutcliffe (64) | Adelaide | 1928–29 | 143 | – | – | – | – | – | – |
| L. Hutton (66), J.D.B. Robertson (121) | Lord's | 1949 | – | – | – | – | 143 | – | – |
| L. Hutton (86), D.S. Sheppard (119) | Oval | 1952 | – | – | – | – | 143 | – | – |
| W. Rhodes (152), A.E. Relf (63) | Johannesburg[1] | 1913–14 | – | 141 | – | – | – | – | – |
| L. Hutton (100), C. Washbrook (75) | Leeds | 1947 | – | 141 | – | – | – | – | – |
| P. Holmes (88), H. Sutcliffe (99) | Cape Town | 1927–28 | – | 140 | – | – | – | – | – |
| L. Hutton (40), C. Washbrook (112) | Melbourne | 1946–47 | 138 | – | – | – | – | – | – |
| L. Hutton (94), C. Washbrook (65) | Adelaide | 1946–47 | 137 | – | – | – | – | – | – |
| J.B. Hobbs (76), H. Sutcliffe (64) | Birmingham | 1924 | – | 136 | – | – | – | – | – |
| J.B. Hobbs (97), W. Rhodes (35) | Durban[1] | 1913–14 | – | 133 | – | – | – | – | – |
| G.A. Gooch (71), G. Boycott (105) | Delhi | 1981–82 | – | – | – | – | 132 | – | – |
| L. Hutton (56), W. Watson (116) | Kingston | 1953–54 | – | – | 130 | – | – | – | – |
| L. Hutton (56), J.D.B. Robertson (64) | Kingston | 1947–48 | – | – | 129 | – | – | – | – |
| L. Hutton (57), C. Washbrook (65) | Leeds | 1948 | 129 | – | – | – | – | – | – |
| D. Smith (57), A. Mitchell (72) | Leeds | 1935 | – | 128 | – | – | – | – | – |
| C.L. Smith (66), M.W. Gatting (75) | Faisalabad | 1983–84 | – | – | – | – | – | 127 | – |
| J.B. Hobbs (66), H. Sutcliffe (143) | Melbourne | 1924–25 | 126 | – | – | – | – | – | – |
| P.E. Richardson (74), W. Watson (66) | Manchester | 1958 | – | – | – | – | 126 | – | – |
| J.B. Hobbs (74), H. Sutcliffe (58*) | Nottingham | 1930 | 125 | – | – | – | – | – | – |
| J.B. Bolus (57), G.J. Binks (55) | Bombay[2] | 1963–64 | – | – | – | – | 125 | – | – |
| G. Boycott (47), J.H. Edrich (115) | Lord's | 1969 | – | – | – | – | 125 | – | – |
| G. Boycott (121*), B.W. Luckhurst (46) | Lord's | 1971 | – | – | – | – | – | 124 | – |
| C.F. Walters (50*), H. Sutcliffe (69*) | Manchester | 1934 | 123* | – | – | – | – | – | – |

### 1st Wicket continued

| | | | A | SA | WI | NZ | I | P | SL |
|---|---|---|---|---|---|---|---|---|---|
| J.H. Edrich (62), R.M. Prideaux (64) | Leeds | 1968 | 123 | – | – | – | – | – | – |
| G. Ulyett (67), R.G. Barlow (62) | Sydney | 1881–82 | 122 | – | – | – | – | – | – |
| P.F. Warner (68), T.W. Hayward (58) | Melbourne | 1903–04 | 122 | – | – | – | – | – | – |
| L. Hutton (98*), J.T. Ikin (38) | Manchester | 1951 | – | 121 | – | – | – | – | – |
| G. Boycott (73), R.W. Barber (74) | Durban[2] | 1964–65 | – | 120 | – | – | – | – | – |
| J.B. Hobbs (53), H. Sutcliffe (54) | Manchester | 1928 | – | – | 119 | – | – | – | – |
| H. Sutcliffe (61), R.E.S. Wyatt (149) | Nottingham | 1935 | – | 118 | – | – | – | – | – |
| B.W. Luckhurst (53*), R.A. Hutton (58*) | Lord's | 1971 | – | – | – | – | – | 117* | – |
| Rev D.S. Sheppard (57), M.C. Cowdrey (182) | Oval | 1962 | – | – | – | – | – | 117 | – |
| G. Boycott (77), B.W. Luckhurst (38) | Sydney | 1970–71 | 116 | – | – | – | – | – | – |
| D.L. Amiss (188), D. Lloyd (46) | Lord's | 1974 | – | – | – | – | 116 | – | – |
| G.A. Gooch (99), G. Boycott (44) | Melbourne | 1979–80 | 116 | – | – | – | – | – | – |
| P.E. Richardson (68), T.E. Bailey (80) | Durban[2] | 1956–57 | – | 115 | – | – | – | – | – |
| D.L. Amiss (90), D. Lloyd (44) | Melbourne | 1974–75 | 115 | – | – | – | – | – | – |
| H. Sutcliffe (86), D.R. Jardine (46) | Brisbane[2] | 1932–33 | 114 | – | – | – | – | – | – |
| Rev D.S. Sheppard (53), G. Pullar (56) | Brisbane[2] | 1962–63 | 114 | – | – | – | – | – | – |
| J.B. Hobbs (107), W. Rhodes (59) | Lord's | 1912 | 112 | – | – | – | – | – | – |
| H. Sutcliffe (194), R.E.S. Wyatt (38) | Sydney | 1932–33 | 112 | – | – | – | – | – | – |
| J.H. Edrich (58), G. Boycott (128) | Manchester | 1969 | – | – | 112 | – | – | – | – |
| G. Boycott (92), D. Amiss (53) | Lord's | 1973 | – | – | – | 112 | – | – | – |
| A.C. MacLaren (65), E. Wainwright (49) | Sydney | 1897–98 | 111 | – | – | – | – | – | – |
| A.H. Bakewell (85), C.F. Walters (59) | Madras[1] | 1933–34 | – | – | – | – | 111 | – | – |
| B. Wood (52), J.H. Edrich (175) | Lord's | 1975 | 111 | – | – | – | – | – | – |
| G.A. Gooch (55), G. Boycott (131) | Nottingham | 1978 | – | – | – | 111 | – | – | – |
| J.B. Hobbs (57), H. Sutcliffe (115) | Sydney | 1924–25 | 110 | – | – | – | – | – | – |
| J.B. Hobbs (31), H. Sutcliffe (74) | Manchester | 1930 | 108 | – | – | – | – | – | – |
| J.B. Hobbs (66), W. Rhodes (49) | Oval | 1912 | 107 | – | – | – | – | – | – |
| G. Boycott (58), J.H. Edrich (130) | Adelaide | 1970–71 | 107 | – | – | – | – | – | – |
| L. Hutton (150), R.T. Simpson (53) | Lord's | 1952 | – | – | – | 106 | – | – | – |
| G. Cook (66), C.J. Tavaré (57) | Manchester | 1982 | – | – | – | 106 | – | – | – |
| J.B. Hobbs (62*), C.B. Fry (35*) | Birmingham | 1909 | 105* | – | – | – | – | – | – |
| G. Boycott (56*), D.L. Amiss (56) | Birmingham | 1973 | – | – | 105*‡ | – | – | – | – |
| J.B. Hobbs (49), H. Sutcliffe (135) | Melbourne | 1928–29 | 105 | – | – | – | – | – | – |
| M.H. Denness (50), D.L. Amiss (112) | Lahore[2] | 1972–73 | – | – | – | – | – | 105 | – |
| C.F. Walters (64), H. Sutcliffe (38) | Oval | 1934 | 104 | – | – | – | – | – | – |
| L. Hutton (73), C. Washbrook (44) | Manchester | 1949 | – | – | – | 103 | – | – | – |
| G. Boycott (119*), J.H. Edrich (40) | Adelaide | 1970–71 | 103 | – | – | – | – | – | – |
| C.J. Tavaré (33), G. Fowler (86) | Leeds | 1982 | – | – | – | – | – | 103 | – |
| J.B. Bolus (58), J.H. Edrich (41) | Delhi | 1963–64 | – | – | – | – | 101 | – | – |
| G. Fowler (106), B.C. Broad (55) | Lord's | 1984 | – | – | 101 | – | – | – | – |
| J.B. Hobbs (92), W. Rhodes (35) | Johannesburg[1] | 1913–14 | – | 100 | – | – | – | – | – |
| L. Hutton (100), C.J. Barnett (62) | Manchester | 1937 | – | – | – | 100 | – | – | – |
| L. Hutton (76), C. Washbrook (39) | Adelaide | 1946–47 | 100 | – | – | – | – | – | – |
| Totals: (115) | | | 51 | 18 | 14 | 9 | 15 | 8 | – |

† 155 runs were added for this wicket in two separate partnerships, G. Boycott retiring hurt and being succeeded by B.C. Rose when the score was 9.
‡ 119 runs were added for this wicket in two partnerships, G. Boycott retiring hurt and being succeeded by B.W. Luckhurst when 105 runs had been scored.

### ENGLAND – 2nd Wicket

| | | | A | SA | WI | NZ | I | P | SL |
|---|---|---|---|---|---|---|---|---|---|
| L. Hutton (364), M. Leyland (187) | Oval | 1938 | 382 | – | – | – | – | – | – |
| J.H. Edrich (310*), K.F. Barrington (163) | Leeds | 1965 | – | – | – | 369 | – | – | – |
| G.A. Gooch (196), D.I. Gower (157) | Oval | 1985 | 351 | – | – | – | – | – | – |
| R.T. Robinson (148), D.I. Gower (215) | Birmingham | 1985 | 331 | – | – | – | – | – | – |
| P.A. Gibb (120), W.J. Edrich (219) | Durban[2] | 1938–39 | – | 280 | – | – | – | – | – |
| P.E. Richardson (126), T.W. Graveney (258) | Nottingham | 1957 | – | – | 266 | – | – | – | – |
| J.H. Edrich (155), P.J. Sharpe (111) | Nottingham | 1969 | – | – | – | 249 | – | – | – |
| M.C. Cowdrey (182), E.R. Dexter (172) | Oval | 1962 | – | – | – | – | – | 248 | – |
| G. Fowler (201), M.W. Gatting (207) | Madras[1] | 1984–85 | – | – | – | – | 241 | – | – |
| H. Sutcliffe (102), G.E. Tyldesley (122) | Johannesburg[1] | 1927–28 | – | 230 | – | – | – | – | – |
| H. Sutcliffe (114), W.R. Hammond (138*) | Birmingham | 1929 | – | 221 | – | – | – | – | – |
| D.L. Amiss (188), J.H. Edrich (96) | Lord's | 1974 | – | – | – | – | 221 | – | – |
| L. Hutton (206), W.J. Edrich (100) | Oval | 1949 | – | – | – | 218 | – | – | – |
| D. Lloyd (214*), M.H. Denness (100) | Birmingham | 1974 | – | – | – | – | 211 | – | – |

**2nd Wicket** *continued*

| | | | A | SA | WI | NZ | I | P | SL |
|---|---|---|---|---|---|---|---|---|---|
| M.C. Cowdrey (119), E.R. Dexter (76) | Port-of-Spain | 1959–60 | – | – | 191 | – | – | – | – |
| H. Sutcliffe (194), W.R. Hammond (112) | Sydney | 1932–33 | 188 | – | – | – | – | – | – |
| H. Sutcliffe (109*), W.R. Hammond (101*) | Oval | 1929 | – | 187* | – | – | – | – | – |
| P.A. Gibb (93), E. Paynter (117) | Johannesburg[1] | 1938–39 | – | 184 | – | – | – | – | – |
| T.W. Graveney (111), P.B.H. May (79) | Sydney | 1954–55 | 182 | – | – | – | – | – | – |
| H. Sutcliffe (117), K.S. Duleepsinhji (109) | Oval | 1931 | – | – | – | 178 | – | – | – |
| G. Boycott (116), M.C. Cowdrey (59) | Georgetown | 1967–68 | – | – | 172 | – | – | – | – |
| J.H. Edrich (130), K.W.R. Fletcher (80) | Adelaide | 1970–71 | 169 | – | – | – | – | – | – |
| P.A. Gibb (106), E. Paynter (100) | Johannesburg[1] | 1938–39 | – | 168 | – | – | – | – | – |
| L. Hutton (145), T.W. Graveney (78) | Lord's | 1953 | 168 | – | – | – | – | – | – |
| D.L. Amiss (158), K.W.R. Fletcher (78) | Hyderabad | 1972–73 | – | – | – | – | 168 | – | – |
| M.C. Cowdrey (159), E.R. Dexter (72) | Birmingham | 1962 | – | – | – | – | 166 | – | – |
| G. Pullar (89), K.F. Barrington (113*) | Delhi | 1961–62 | – | – | – | – | 164 | – | – |
| Rev D.S. Sheppard (83), E.R. Dexter (85) | Nottingham | 1962 | – | – | – | – | 161 | – | – |
| L. Hutton (150), P.B.H. May (74) | Lord's | 1952 | – | – | – | – | 158 | – | – |
| C. Milburn (139), T.W. Graveney (105) | Karachi | 1968–69 | – | – | – | – | – | 156 | – |
| A. Shrewsbury (81), W. Gunn (77) | Lord's | 1893 | 152 | – | – | – | – | – | – |
| L. Hutton (122*), W.J. Edrich (60) | Sydney | 1946–47 | 150 | – | – | – | – | – | – |
| C.J. Tavaré (51), D.I. Gower (108) | Lord's | 1983 | – | – | – | 149 | – | – | – |
| A. Sandham (325), R.E.S. Wyatt (58) | Kingston | 1929–30 | – | – | 148 | – | – | – | – |
| C. Washbrook (62), W.J. Edrich (89) | Melbourne | 1946–47 | 147 | – | – | – | – | – | – |
| G. Pullar (165), K.F. Barrington (84) | Dacca | 1961–62 | – | – | – | – | – | 147 | – |
| P.E. Richardson (107), T.W. Graveney (164) | Oval | 1957 | – | – | 146 | – | – | – | – |
| G.A. Gooch (123), C.J. Tavaré (42) | Lord's | 1980 | – | – | 145 | – | – | – | – |
| L. Hutton (63), R.T. Simpson (137) | Nottingham | 1951 | – | 144 | – | – | – | – | – |
| A.C. MacLaren (124), K.S. Ranjitsinhji (77) | Adelaide | 1897–98 | 142 | – | – | – | – | – | – |
| J.B. Hobbs (211), F.E. Woolley (134*) | Lord's | 1924 | – | 142 | – | – | – | – | – |
| G. Pullar (119), K.F. Barrington (172) | Kanpur | 1961–62 | – | – | – | – | 139 | – | – |
| G. Boycott (246*), K.F. Barrington (93) | Leeds | 1967 | – | – | – | – | 139 | – | – |
| G. Ulyett (87), J. Selby (55) | Melbourne | 1881–82 | 137 | – | – | – | – | – | – |
| A.C. MacLaren (109), T.W. Hayward (72) | Sydney | 1897–98 | 136 | – | – | – | – | – | – |
| R.W. Barber (97), E.R. Dexter (172) | Johannesburg[3] | 1964–65 | – | 136 | – | – | – | – | – |
| G. Fowler (55), M.W. Gatting (136) | Bombay[3] | 1984–85 | – | – | – | – | 135 | – | – |
| J.B. Hobbs (72), G. Gunn (122*) | Sydney | 1907–08 | 134 | – | – | – | – | – | – |
| A.E. Fagg (39), W.R. Hammond (167) | Manchester | 1936 | – | – | – | – | 134 | – | – |
| L. Hutton (87), J.F. Crapp (54) | Cape Town | 1948–49 | – | 134 | – | – | – | – | – |
| H. Sutcliffe (58), W.R. Hammond (200) | Melbourne | 1928–29 | 133 | – | – | – | – | – | – |
| T.W. Graveney (60), P.B.H. May (112) | Lord's | 1955 | – | 132 | – | – | – | – | – |
| G. Boycott (49), C. Milburn (83) | Lord's | 1968 | 132 | – | – | – | – | – | – |
| J.M. Brearley (49), R.A. Woolmer (120) | Lord's | 1977 | 132 | – | – | – | – | – | – |
| T.W. Hayward (137), K.S. Ranjitsinhji (54) | Oval | 1899 | 131 | – | – | – | – | – | – |
| L. Hutton (73), N. Oldfield (80) | Oval | 1939 | – | – | 131 | – | – | – | – |
| L. Hutton (79), R.T. Simpson (156*) | Melbourne | 1950–51 | 131 | – | – | – | – | – | – |
| G. Pullar (131), M.C. Cowdrey (67) | Manchester | 1959 | – | – | – | – | 131 | – | – |
| H. Sutcliffe (51), G.E. Tyldesley (100) | Durban[2] | 1927–28 | – | 130 | – | – | – | – | – |
| D.L. Amiss (99), K.W.R. Fletcher (54) | Karachi | 1972–73 | – | – | – | – | – | 130 | – |
| J.B. Hobbs (100), G.E. Tyldesley (73) | Oval | 1928 | – | 129 | – | – | – | – | – |
| L. Hutton (100), P.B.H. May (138) | Leeds | 1951 | – | 129 | – | – | – | – | – |
| J.H. Edrich (96), M.C. Cowdrey (101) | Kingston | 1967–68 | – | – | 129 | – | – | – | – |
| D.L. Amiss (183), D.L. Underwood (43) | Oval | 1974 | – | – | – | – | – | 129 | – |
| G. Boycott (131), C.T. Radley (59) | Nottingham | 1978 | – | – | – | 129 | – | – | – |
| L. Hutton (100), J. Hardstaff, jr (58) | Manchester | 1937 | – | – | – | 128 | – | – | – |
| W. Rhodes (61), J.W. Hearne (114) | Melbourne | 1911–12 | 127 | – | – | – | – | – | – |
| H. Sutcliffe (109*), K.S. Duleepsinhji (63) | Manchester | 1931 | – | – | – | 126 | – | – | – |
| J.H. Edrich (96), D.S. Steele (66) | Oval | 1975 | 125 | – | – | – | – | – | – |
| W. Rhodes (36), R.H. Spooner (119) | Lord's | 1912 | – | 124 | – | – | – | – | – |
| C. Washbrook (85*), W.J. Edrich (53) | Manchester | 1948 | 124 | – | – | – | – | – | – |
| Rev D.S. Sheppard (113), E.R. Dexter (52) | Melbourne | 1962–63 | 124 | – | – | – | – | – | – |
| B.W. Luckhurst (101), J.H. Edrich (59) | Manchester | 1971 | – | – | – | – | 123 | – | – |
| H. Sutcliffe (56), W.R. Hammond (101) | Sydney | 1932–33 | 122 | – | – | – | – | – | – |
| G.A. Gooch (74), D.I. Gower (47) | Manchester | 1985 | 121 | – | – | – | – | – | – |
| W.G. Grace (152), A.P. Lucas (55) | Oval | 1880 | 120 | – | – | – | – | – | – |
| C. Washbrook (97), J.F. Crapp (51) | Johannesburg[2] | 1948–49 | – | 120 | – | – | – | – | – |
| D.L. Amiss (174), M.H. Denness (44) | Port-of-Spain | 1973–74 | – | – | 119 | – | – | – | – |
| C. Washbrook (103*), W.J. Edrich (70) | Leeds | 1949 | – | – | – | 118 | – | – | – |
| Rev D.S. Sheppard (119), J.T. Ikin (53) | Oval | 1952 | – | – | – | – | 118 | – | – |

**2nd Wicket** *continued*

| | | | A | SA | WI | NZ | I | P | SL |
|---|---|---|---|---|---|---|---|---|---|
| W.E. Russell (56), M.C. Cowdrey (59) | Auckland | 1965–66 | – | – | – | 118 | – | – | – |
| G. Boycott (80*), M.C. Cowdrey (71) | Port-of-Spain | 1967–68 | – | – | 118 | – | – | – | – |
| B.W. Luckhurst (96), P.H. Parfitt (46) | Nottingham | 1972 | 117 | – | – | – | – | – | – |
| A. Shrewsbury (72), W. Barnes (58) | Melbourne | 1884–85 | 116 | – | – | – | – | – | – |
| G. Boycott (105), C.J. Tavaré (149) | Delhi | 1981–82 | – | – | – | – | 116 | – | – |
| G.A. Gooch (70), D.I. Gower (166) | Nottingham | 1985 | 116 | – | – | – | – | – | – |
| P.A. Gibb (38), E. Paynter (243) | Durban[2] | 1938–39 | – | 115 | – | – | – | – | – |
| G. Boycott (60), T.W. Graveney (96) | Lord's | 1966 | – | – | 115 | – | – | – | – |
| W. Rhodes (73), J.W.H. Makepeace (54) | Melbourne | 1920–21 | 113 | – | – | – | – | – | – |
| J.B. Hobbs (126*), G. Gunn (43) | Melbourne | 1911–12 | 112 | – | – | – | – | – | – |
| J.H. Edrich (62), D.S. Steele (73) | Leeds | 1975 | 112 | – | – | – | – | – | – |
| E.H. Bowley (109), K.S. Duleepsinhji (117) | Auckland | 1929–30 | – | – | – | 111 | – | – | – |
| G. Boycott (58), E.R. Dexter (174) | Manchester | 1964 | 111 | – | – | – | – | – | – |
| J.M. Brearley (53), D.W. Randall (150) | Sydney | 1978–79 | 111 | – | – | – | – | – | – |
| R. Subba Row (49), E.R. Dexter (76) | Manchester | 1961 | 110 | – | – | – | – | – | – |
| R. Subba Row (112), E.R. Dexter (180) | Birmingham | 1961 | 109 | – | – | – | – | – | – |
| H. Gimblett (67*), M.J.L. Turnbull (37*) | Lord's | 1936 | – | – | – | – | 108* | – | – |
| J.H. Edrich (88), M.C. Cowdrey (104) | Birmingham | 1968 | 108 | – | – | – | – | – | – |
| L. Hutton (77), P.B.H. May (62) | Bridgetown | 1953–54 | – | – | 107 | – | – | – | – |
| A.C. MacLaren (92), J.T. Tyldesley (79) | Sydney | 1901–02 | 106 | – | – | – | – | – | – |
| H. Sutcliffe (143), J.W. Hearne (44) | Melbourne | 1924–25 | 106 | – | – | – | – | – | – |
| J.A. Jameson (82), J.H. Edrich (41) | Oval | 1971 | – | – | – | – | 106 | – | – |
| W.G. Grace (66), R. Abel (94) | Lord's | 1896 | 105 | – | – | – | – | – | – |
| J.B. Hobbs (123), J.W.H. Makepeace (30) | Adelaide | 1920–21 | 105 | – | – | – | – | – | – |
| Albert Ward (32), A.E. Stoddart (68) | Melbourne | 1894–95 | 104 | – | – | – | – | – | – |
| J.H. Edrich (175), D.S. Steele (45) | Lord's | 1975 | 104 | – | – | – | – | – | – |
| G. Pullar (65), K.F. Barrington (128) | Bridgetown | 1959–60 | – | – | 103 | – | – | – | – |
| W. Rhodes (179), G. Gunn (75) | Melbourne | 1911–12 | 102 | – | – | – | – | – | – |
| P. Holmes (56), G.E. Tyldesley (62*) | Durban[2] | 1927–28 | – | 102 | – | – | – | – | – |
| J.B. Hobbs (59), J.W. Hearne (57) | Sydney | 1920–21 | 100 | – | – | – | – | – | – |
| C. Washbrook (143), W.J. Edrich (111) | Leeds | 1948 | 100 | – | – | – | – | – | – |
| L. Hutton (82), P.B.H. May (39) | Oval | 1953 | 100 | – | – | – | – | – | – |
| D.L. Amiss (203), D.S. Steele (44) | Oval | 1976 | – | – | 100 | – | – | – | – |
| *Totals: (113)* | | | 47 | 17 | 15 | 11 | 15 | 8 | – |

**ENGLAND – 3rd Wicket**

| | | | A | SA | WI | NZ | I | P | SL |
|---|---|---|---|---|---|---|---|---|---|
| W.J. Edrich (189), D.C.S. Compton (208) | Lord's | 1947 | – | 370 | – | – | – | – | – |
| L. Hutton (165*), W.R. Hammond (138) | Oval | 1939 | – | – | 264 | – | – | – | – |
| W.R. Hammond (177), D.R. Jardine (98) | Adelaide | 1928–29 | 262 | – | – | – | – | – | – |
| E.R. Dexter (174), K.F. Barrington (256) | Manchester | 1964 | 246 | – | – | – | – | – | – |
| R.E.S. Wyatt (113), F.E. Woolley (154) | Manchester | 1929 | – | 245 | – | – | – | – | – |
| J. Hardstaff, jr (114), W.R. Hammond (140) | Lord's | 1937 | – | – | – | 245 | – | – | – |
| E. Paynter (243), W.R. Hammond (120) | Durban[2] | 1938–39 | – | 242 | – | – | – | – | – |
| W.J. Edrich (191), D.C.S. Compton (115) | Manchester | 1947 | – | 228 | – | – | – | – | – |
| Albert Ward (93), J.T. Brown (140) | Melbourne | 1894–95 | 210 | – | – | – | – | – | – |
| T.W. Graveney (258), P.B.H. May (104) | Nottingham | 1957 | – | 207 | – | – | – | – | – |
| K.F. Barrington (148), T.W. Graveney (81) | Lord's | 1967 | – | – | – | – | – | 201 | – |
| C.A. Milton (104*), P.B.H. May (113*) | Leeds | 1958 | – | – | 194* | – | – | – | – |
| K.F. Barrington (139), M.J.K. Smith (99) | Lahore[2] | 1961–62 | – | – | – | – | – | 192 | – |
| E.R. Dexter (172), K.F. Barrington (121) | Johannesburg[3] | 1964–65 | – | 191 | – | – | – | – | – |
| D.I. Gower (166), M.W. Gatting (74) | Nottingham | 1985 | 187 | – | – | – | – | – | – |
| J.H. Edrich (85), K.F. Barrington (115) | Melbourne | 1965–66 | 178 | – | – | – | – | – | – |
| W.H. Scotton (82), W. Barnes (134) | Adelaide | 1884–85 | 175 | – | – | – | – | – | – |
| E.R. Dexter (93), M.C. Cowdrey (113) | Melbourne | 1962–63 | 175 | – | – | – | – | – | – |
| R. Subba Row (94), M.J.K. Smith (98) | Oval | 1959 | – | – | – | – | 169 | – | – |
| A. Sandham (152), E.H. Hendren (80) | Bridgetown | 1929–30 | – | – | 168 | – | – | – | – |
| P.B.H. May (135), D.C.S. Compton (133) | Port-of-Spain | 1953–54 | – | – | 166 | – | – | – | – |
| D.W. Randall (174), D.L. Amiss (64) | Melbourne | 1976–77 | 166 | – | – | – | – | – | – |
| W.J. Edrich (111), A.V. Bedser (79) | Leeds | 1948 | 155 | – | – | – | – | – | – |
| W. Rhodes (152), C.P. Mead (102) | Johannesburg[1] | 1913–14 | – | 152 | – | – | – | – | – |
| D.L. Amiss (164*), M.H. Denness (59*) | Christchurch | 1974–75 | – | – | – | 151* | – | – | – |
| J.F. Crapp (56), D.C.S. Compton (114) | Johannesburg[2] | 1948–49 | – | 150 | – | – | – | – | – |
| L. Hutton (169), D.C.S. Compton (64) | Georgetown | 1953–54 | – | – | 150 | – | – | – | – |
| W.R. Hammond (336*), E. Paynter (36) | Auckland | 1932–33 | – | – | – | 149 | – | – | – |

**3rd Wicket** *continued*

| | | | A | SA | WI | NZ | I | P | SL |
|---|---|---|---|---|---|---|---|---|---|
| J.H. Edrich (70), M.H. Denness (188) | Melbourne | 1974–75 | 149 | – | – | – | – | – | – |
| E.R. Dexter (110), R. Subba Row (100) | Georgetown | 1959–60 | – | – | 148 | – | – | – | – |
| G. Boycott (155), G.A. Gooch (83) | Birmingham | 1979 | – | – | – | – | 145 | – | – |
| M.W. Gatting (207), A.J. Lamb (62) | Madras[1] | 1984–85 | – | – | – | – | 144 | – | – |
| E.R. Dexter (205), M.J.K. Smith (56) | Karachi | 1961–62 | – | – | – | – | – | 143 | – |
| J.B. Hobbs (122), E.H. Hendren (67) | Melbourne | 1920–21 | 142 | – | – | – | – | – | – |
| R.A. Woolmer (137), D.W. Randall (79) | Manchester | 1977 | 142 | – | – | – | – | – | – |
| K.F. Barrington (142), T.W. Graveney (77) | Oval | 1967 | – | – | – | – | – | 141 | – |
| F.E. Woolley (87), E.H. Hendren (127*) | Lord's | 1926 | 140 | – | – | – | – | – | – |
| C.A.G. Russell (140), C.P. Mead (66) | Durban[2] | 1922–23 | – | 139 | – | – | – | – | – |
| C.T. Radley (158), G.R.J. Roope (68) | Auckland | 1977–78 | – | – | – | 139 | – | – | – |
| A. Shrewsbury (106), Hon F.S. Jackson (91) | Lord's | 1893 | 137 | – | – | – | – | – | – |
| M.W. Gatting (53), D.I. Gower (173*) | Lahore[2] | 1983–84 | – | – | – | – | – | 137 | – |
| R.T. Robinson (175), M.W. Gatting (53) | Leeds | 1985 | 136 | – | – | – | – | – | – |
| L. Hutton (364), W.R. Hammond (59) | Oval | 1938 | 135 | – | – | – | – | – | – |
| M.C. Cowdrey (72), K.F. Barrington (143) | Port-of-Spain | 1967–68 | – | – | 134 | – | – | – | – |
| M.C. Cowdrey (148), K.F. Barrington (48) | Port-of-Spain | 1967–68 | – | – | 133 | – | – | – | – |
| W.R. Hammond (231*), M. Leyland (42) | Sydney | 1936–37 | 129 | – | – | – | – | – | – |
| R.T. Simpson (81), D.C.S. Compton (79) | Christchurch | 1950–51 | – | – | – | 129 | – | – | – |
| G. Boycott (128), T.W. Graveney (73) | Manchester | 1969 | – | – | 128 | – | – | – | – |
| G.E. Tyldesley (78), W.R. Hammond (90) | Durban[2] | 1927–28 | – | 127 | – | – | – | – | – |
| W.R. Hammond (167), T.S. Worthington (87) | Manchester | 1936 | – | – | – | – | 127 | – | – |
| C.J. Tavaré (54), D.I. Gower (74) | Birmingham | 1982 | – | – | – | – | – | 127 | – |
| G. Boycott (76), E.R. Dexter (80*) | Lord's | 1965 | – | – | – | 126 | – | – | – |
| R.E.S. Wyatt (61*), W.R. Hammond (75*) | Sydney | 1932–33 | 125* | – | – | – | – | – | – |
| W.J. Edrich (88), P.B.H. May (44) | Brisbane[2] | 1954–55 | 124 | – | – | – | – | – | – |
| P.B.H. May (117), D.C.S. Compton (71) | Manchester | 1955 | – | 124 | – | – | – | – | – |
| H. Sutcliffe (194), Nawab of Pataudi, sr (102) | Sydney | 1932–33 | 123 | – | – | – | – | – | – |
| G. Boycott (60), D.I. Gower (89) | Lord's | 1981 | 123 | – | – | – | – | – | – |
| F.E. Woolley (134*), E.H. Hendren (50*) | Lord's | 1924 | – | 121* | – | – | – | – | – |
| G.A. Gooch (116), D.I. Gower (54) | Bridgetown | 1980–81 | – | – | 120 | – | – | – | – |
| T.W. Hayward (122), C.B. Fry (64) | Johannesburg[1] | 1895–96 | – | 119 | – | – | – | – | – |
| W.R. Hammond (75), E.H. Hendren (64) | Johannesburg[1] | 1930–31 | – | 119 | – | – | – | – | – |
| G. Boycott (115), K.W.R. Fletcher (81) | Leeds | 1973 | – | – | – | 119 | – | – | – |
| D.I. Gower (60), A.J. Lamb (82) | Adelaide | 1982–83 | 119 | – | – | – | – | – | – |
| J.H. Edrich (109), K.F. Barrington (63) | Melbourne | 1965–66 | 118 | – | – | – | – | – | – |
| J.H. Edrich (64), M.H. Denness (181) | Auckland | 1974–75 | – | – | – | 117 | – | – | – |
| C.T. Radley (49), D.I. Gower (111) | Oval | 1978 | – | – | – | 116 | – | – | – |
| G. Boycott (137), M.W. Gatting (53) | Oval | 1981 | 115 | – | – | – | – | – | – |
| C.T. Radley (77), D.I. Gower (71) | Lord's | 1978 | – | – | – | 114 | – | – | – |
| W. Place (107), J. Hardstaff, jr (64) | Kingston | 1947–48 | – | – | 113 | – | – | – | – |
| L. Hutton (74), D.C.S. Compton (184) | Nottingham | 1948 | 111 | – | – | – | – | – | – |
| G. Pullar (63), P.B.H. May (95) | Manchester | 1961 | 111 | – | – | – | – | – | – |
| R.T. Robinson (160), A.J. Lamb (52) | Delhi | 1984–85 | – | – | – | – | 110 | – | – |
| P.A. Gibb (58), W.R. Hammond (181) | Cape Town | 1938–39 | – | 109 | – | – | – | – | – |
| L. Hutton (202*), D.C.S. Compton (44) | Oval | 1950 | – | – | 109 | – | – | – | – |
| A.P.E. Knott (73), J.H. Edrich (79) | Brisbane[2] | 1970–71 | 109 | – | – | – | – | – | – |
| P.E. Richardson (81), P.B.H. May (73) | Nottingham | 1956 | 108 | – | – | – | – | – | – |
| M.C. Cowdrey (159), T.W. Graveney (97) | Birmingham | 1962 | – | – | – | – | – | 107 | – |
| G. Boycott (246*), T.W. Graveney (59) | Leeds | 1967 | – | – | – | – | 107 | – | – |
| J.T. Tyldesley (55), J. Sharp (61) | Leeds | 1909 | 106 | – | – | – | – | – | – |
| W.J. Edrich (57), D.C.S. Compton (65) | Nottingham | 1947 | – | 106 | – | – | – | – | – |
| W.G.A. Parkhouse (69), J.G. Dewes (67) | Nottingham | 1950 | – | – | *106 | – | – | – | – |
| G. Boycott (75), R.A. Woolmer (29) | Nottingham | 1980 | – | – | 106 | – | – | – | – |
| W. Rhodes (66), C.B. Fry (62) | Oval | 1909 | 104 | – | – | – | – | – | – |
| J. Hardstaff, jr (64), C.J. Barnett (83*) | Lord's | 1937 | – | – | – | 104 | – | – | – |
| Rev D.S. Sheppard (113), M.C. Cowdrey (58*) | Melbourne | 1962–63 | 104 | – | – | – | – | – | – |
| W.J. Edrich (54), D.C.S. Compton (66) | Leeds | 1948 | 103 | – | – | – | – | – | – |
| A.C. MacLaren (47*), Hon F.S. Jackson (55*) | Lord's | 1902 | 102* | – | – | – | – | – | – |
| Albert Ward (117), J.T. Brown (53) | Sydney | 1894–95 | 102 | – | – | – | – | – | – |
| W.J. Edrich (119), D.C.S. Compton (54) | Sydney | 1946–47 | 102 | – | – | – | – | – | – |
| L. Hutton (101), D.C.S. Compton (114) | Leeds | 1949 | – | – | – | 102 | – | – | – |
| L. Hutton (145), D.C.S. Compton (57) | Lord's | 1953 | 102 | – | – | – | – | – | – |
| J.H. Edrich (76*), D.B. Close (36*) | Nottingham | 1976 | – | – | 101* | – | – | – | – |
| P.B.H. May (97), D.J. Insole (47) | Leeds | 1955 | – | 101 | – | – | – | – | – |
| M.C. Cowdrey (101), K.F. Barrington (63) | Kingston | 1967–68 | – | – | 101 | – | – | – | – |

**3rd Wicket** *continued*

| | | | A | SA | WI | NZ | I | P | SL |
|---|---|---|---|---|---|---|---|---|---|
| G. Boycott (112), K.W.R. Fletcher (45) | Port-of-Spain | 1973–74 | – | – | 101 | – | – | – | – |
| G.A. Gooch (54), D.I. Gower (56) | Lord's | 1978 | – | – | – | – | – | 101 | – |
| T.W. Hayward (59), C.B. Fry (144) | Oval | 1905 | 100 | – | – | – | – | – | – |
| D.L. Amiss (118), K.W.R. Fletcher (41) | Georgetown | 1973–74 | – | – | 100 | – | – | – | – |
| C.J. Tavaré (69), A.J. Lamb (58) | Leeds | 1983 | – | – | – | 100 | – | – | – |
| | *Totals: (99)* | | *37* | *16* | *18* | *14* | *6* | *8* | *–* |

*Although the 3rd wicket added 145 against Australia (2nd Test – Melbourne) in 1903–04, this consisted of two partnerships: J.T. Tyldesley added 89\* with R.E. Foster (retired ill) and a further 56 with L.C. Braund.*

**ENGLAND – 4th Wicket**

| | | | A | SA | WI | NZ | I | P | SL |
|---|---|---|---|---|---|---|---|---|---|
| P.B.H. May (285*), M.C. Cowdrey (154) | Birmingham | 1957 | – | – | 411 | – | – | – | – |
| W.R. Hammond (217), T.S. Worthington (128) | Oval | 1936 | – | – | – | – | 266 | – | – |
| M.H. Denness (181), K.W.R. Fletcher (216) | Auckland | 1974–75 | – | – | – | 266 | – | – | – |
| G. Boycott (246*), B.L. D'Oliveira (109) | Leeds | 1967 | – | – | – | – | 252 | – | – |
| A. Sandham (325), L.E.G. Ames (149) | Kingston | 1929–30 | – | – | 249 | – | – | – | – |
| L. Hutton (196), D.C.S. Compton (120) | Lord's | 1939 | – | – | 248 | – | – | – | – |
| E.H. Hendren (205*), L.E.G. Ames (105) | Port-of-Spain | 1929–30 | – | – | 237 | – | – | – | – |
| W.R. Hammond (240), E. Paynter (99) | Lord's | 1938 | 222 | – | – | – | – | – | – |
| K.F. Barrington (172), E.R. Dexter (126*) | Kanpur | 1961–62 | – | – | – | – | 206 | – | – |
| W.R. Hammond (181), L.E.G. Ames (115) | Cape Town | 1938–39 | – | 197 | – | – | – | – | – |
| M.C. Cowdrey (160), K.F. Barrington (80) | Leeds | 1959 | – | – | – | – | 193 | – | – |
| M.H. Denness (188), K.W.R. Fletcher (146) | Melbourne | 1974–75 | 192 | – | – | – | – | – | – |
| B.R. Knight (127), P.H. Parfitt (121) | Kanpur | 1963–64 | – | – | – | – | 191 | – | – |
| G. Boycott (155), D.I. Gower (200*) | Birmingham | 1979 | – | – | – | – | 191 | – | – |
| E.R. Dexter (205), P.H. Parfitt (111) | Karachi | 1961–62 | – | – | – | – | – | 188 | – |
| K.F. Barrington (143), T.W. Graveney (118) | Port-of-Spain | 1967–68 | – | – | 188 | – | – | – | – |
| P.B.H. May (101), C. Washbrook (98) | Leeds | 1956 | 187 | – | – | – | – | – | – |
| T.W. Graveney (114), P.H. Parfitt (101*) | Nottingham | 1962 | – | – | – | – | – | 184 | – |
| P.B.H. May (92), M.C. Cowdrey (100*) | Sydney | 1958–59 | 182 | – | – | – | – | – | – |
| A.J. Lamb (107), I.T. Botham (208) | Oval | 1982 | – | – | – | – | 176 | – | – |
| T.W. Graveney (109), M.C. Cowdrey (96) | Nottingham | 1966 | – | – | 169 | – | – | – | – |
| T.W. Graveney (114), P.H. Parfitt (101*) | Oval | 1982 | – | – | – | – | 176 | – | – |
| K.F. Barrington (126), M.C. Cowdrey (86) | Auckland | 1962–63 | – | – | – | 166 | – | – | – |
| W.R. Hammond (140), E. Paynter (75) | Durban² | 1938–39 | – | 164 | – | – | – | – | – |
| E.R. Dexter (180), K.F. Barrington (48*) | Birmingham | 1961 | 161 | – | – | – | – | – | – |
| K.F. Barrington (151*), E.R. Dexter (85) | Bombay² | 1961–62 | – | – | – | – | 161 | – | – |
| C.J. Tavaré (89), A.J. Lamb (83) | Melbourne | 1982–83 | 161 | – | – | – | – | – | – |
| R.A. Woolmer (137), A.W. Greig (76) | Manchester | 1977 | 160 | – | – | – | – | – | – |
| A.J. Watkins (137*), D.B. Carr (76) | Delhi | 1951–52 | – | – | – | – | 158 | – | – |
| G. Boycott (77), D.I. Gower (102) | Perth | 1978–79 | 158 | – | – | – | – | – | – |
| G. Boycott (117), K.F. Barrington (72) | Port Elizabeth | 1964–65 | – | 157 | – | – | – | – | – |
| P.B.H. May (83*), D.C.S. Compton (94) | Oval | 1956 | 156 | – | – | – | – | – | – |
| M.W. Gatting (160), A.J. Lamb (67) | Manchester | 1985 | 156 | – | – | – | – | – | – |
| D.C.S. Compton (278), T.W. Graveney (84) | Nottingham | 1954 | – | – | – | – | – | 154 | – |
| C.B. Fry (144), Hon F.S. Jackson (76) | Oval | 1905 | 151 | – | – | – | – | – | – |
| W.R. Hammond (65), M. Leyland (161) | Oval | 1935 | – | 151 | – | – | – | – | – |
| W.R. Hammond (251), E.H. Hendren (74) | Sydney | 1928–29 | 145 | – | – | – | – | – | – |
| A.R. Lewis (125), K.W.R. Fletcher (58) | Kanpur | 1972–73 | – | – | – | – | 144 | – | – |
| K.F. Barrington (121), E.R. Dexter (77) | Port-of-Spain | 1959–60 | – | – | 142 | – | – | – | – |
| D.C.S. Compton (112), W. Watson (57) | Nottingham | 1951 | – | 141 | – | – | – | – | – |
| B.W. Luckhurst (109), B.L. D'Oliveira (117) | Melbourne | 1970–71 | 140 | – | – | – | – | – | – |
| R.E.S. Wyatt (149), M. Leyland (69) | Nottingham | 1935 | – | 139 | – | – | – | – | – |
| K.F. Barrington (137), M.C. Cowdrey (85) | Birmingham | 1965 | – | – | – | 136 | – | – | – |
| D.I. Gower (154*), P. Willey (67) | Kingston | 1980–81 | – | – | 136 | – | – | – | – |
| K.F. Barrington (73), M.C. Cowdrey (78*) | Oval | 1965 | – | 135 | – | – | – | – | – |
| G. Boycott (112), B.L. D'Oliveira (74) | Leeds | 1971 | – | – | – | – | – | 135 | – |
| G. Boycott (142*), B.L. D'Oliveira (56) | Sydney | 1970–71 | 133 | – | – | – | – | – | – |
| W.R. Hammond (100*), L.E.G. Ames (41) | Oval | 1931 | – | – | – | 130 | – | – | – |
| W.R. Hammond (87*), R.E.S. Wyatt (44) | Leeds | 1935 | – | 129 | – | – | – | – | – |
| D.L. Amiss (203), P. Willey (33) | Oval | 1976 | – | – | 128 | – | – | – | – |
| D.I. Gower (85), I.T. Botham (142) | Kanpur | 1981–82 | – | – | – | – | 127 | – | – |
| G. Boycott (106), P.J. Sharpe (86) | Lord's | 1969 | – | – | 126 | – | – | – | – |
| D.C.S. Compton (65), J. Hardstaff, jr (103) | Oval | 1937 | – | – | – | 125 | – | – | – |
| P.B.H. May (106), K.F. Barrington (56) | Nottingham | 1959 | – | – | – | – | 125 | – | – |

**4th Wicket** *continued*

| | | | A | SA | WI | NZ | I | P | SL |
|---|---|---|---|---|---|---|---|---|---|
| J.H. Edrich (164), T.W. Graveney (63) | Oval | 1968 | 125 | – | – | – | – | – | – |
| T.W. Hayward (122), A.J.L. Hill (65) | Johannesburg[1] | 1895–96 | – | 122 | – | – | – | – | – |
| D.C.S. Compton (79), W. Watson (79) | Lord's | 1951 | – | 122 | – | – | – | – | – |
| T.W. Graveney (151), B.L. D'Oliveira (33) | Lord's | 1967 | – | – | – | – | 122 | – | – |
| G.R.J. Roope (77), R.A. Woolmer (149) | Oval | 1975 | 122 | – | – | – | – | – | – |
| D.I. Gower (70), D.W. Randall (70) | Sydney | 1982–83 | 122 | – | – | – | – | – | – |
| P.E. Richardson (117), M.C. Cowdrey (59) | Johannesburg[3] | 1956–57 | – | 121 | – | – | – | – | – |
| P.B.H. May (84), M.C. Cowdrey (81) | Birmingham | 1958 | – | – | – | 121 | – | – | – |
| D.S. Steele (106), R.A. Woolmer (82) | Nottingham | 1976 | – | – | 121 | – | – | – | – |
| G. Boycott (128*), M.W. Gatting (51*) | Lord's | 1980 | 120* | – | – | – | – | – | – |
| W.R. Hammond (63), D.R. Jardine (83) | Manchester | 1928 | – | – | 120 | – | – | – | – |
| C.J. Tavaré (149), K.W.R. Fletcher (51) | Delhi | 1981–82 | – | – | – | – | 120 | – | – |
| J.B. Bolus (88), K.F. Barrington (80) | Madras[2] | 1963–64 | – | – | – | – | 119 | – | – |
| D.I. Gower (114), I.T. Botham (58) | Adelaide | 1982–83 | 118 | – | – | – | – | – | – |
| G. Gunn (119), L.C. Braund (30) | Sydney | 1907–08 | 117 | – | – | – | – | – | – |
| E.H. Hendren (127*), A.P.F. Chapman (50*) | Lord's | 1926 | 116* | – | – | – | – | – | – |
| P.B.H. May (104), M.C. Cowdrey (54) | Sydney | 1954–55 | 116 | – | – | – | – | – | – |
| D.I. Gower (82), D.W. Randall (57) | Lord's | 1979 | – | – | – | – | 114 | – | – |
| G. Gunn (74), J. Hardstaff, sr (63) | Sydney | 1907–08 | 113 | – | – | – | – | – | – |
| L.C. Braund (47), J. Hardstaff, sr (72) | Adelaide | 1907–08 | 113 | – | – | – | – | – | – |
| C.J. Tavaré (82), I.T. Botham (69) | Lord's | 1982 | – | – | – | – | – | 112 | – |
| D.C.S. Compton (51*), A.J. Watkins (64*) | Cape Town | 1948–49 | – | 111* | – | – | – | – | – |
| C.B. Fry (60), A.C. MacLaren (49) | Oval | 1899 | 110 | – | – | – | – | – | – |
| J.H. Edrich (100*), M.H. Denness (45*) | Manchester | 1974 | – | – | – | – | 109* | – | – |
| M.J.K. Smith (100), K.F. Barrington (87) | Manchester | 1959 | – | – | – | – | 109 | – | – |
| J.H. Edrich (310*), P.H. Parfitt (32) | Leeds | 1965 | – | – | – | 109 | – | – | – |
| J.H. Edrich (146), T.W. Graveney (55) | Bridgetown | 1967–68 | – | – | 109 | – | – | – | – |
| J.M. Brearley (59), A.W. Greig (54) | Madras[1] | 1976–77 | – | – | – | – | 109† | – | – |
| M.W. Gatting (100*), A.J. Lamb (46) | Birmingham | 1985 | 109 | – | – | – | – | – | – |
| K.L. Hutchings (126), L.C. Braund (49) | Melbourne | 1907–08 | 108 | – | – | – | – | – | – |
| P.B.H. May (117), M.C. Cowdrey (50) | Manchester | 1955 | – | 108 | – | – | – | – | – |
| J.H. Edrich (109), M.C. Cowdrey (104) | Melbourne | 1965–66 | 105 | – | – | – | – | – | – |
| K.S. Duleepsinhji (173), E.H. Hendren (48) | Lord's | 1930 | 104 | – | – | – | – | – | – |
| W.R. Hammond (231*), L.E.G. Ames (29) | Sydney | 1936–37 | 104 | – | – | – | – | – | – |
| P.E. Richardson (100), M.C. Cowdrey (70) | Birmingham | 1958 | – | – | – | 104 | – | – | – |
| A. Shrewsbury (66), Albert Ward (55) | Oval | 1893 | 103 | – | – | – | – | – | – |
| W.R. Hammond (63), M.J.L. Turnbull (61) | Johannesburg[1] | 1930–31 | – | 101 | – | – | – | – | – |
| F.L. Fane (37), F.E. Woolley (64) | Cape Town | 1909–10 | – | 100 | – | – | – | – | – |
| K.F. Barrington (93), P.H. Parfitt (122*) | Johannesburg[3] | 1964–65 | – | 100 | – | – | – | – | – |
| | Totals: | (92) | 31 | 16 | 13 | 8 | 19 | 5 | – |

†*111 runs were added for this wicket in two partnerships, R.W. Tolchard retiring hurt and being succeeded by A.W.
Greig after 2 runs had been scored.
Although the 4th wicket added 101 against New Zealand (Christchurch) in 1977–78, this consisted of two partnerships:
G.R.J. Roope added 77\* with G. Miller (retired hurt) and a further 24 with C.T. Radley.*

**ENGLAND – 5th Wicket**

| | | | A | SA | WI | NZ | I | P | SL |
|---|---|---|---|---|---|---|---|---|---|
| K.W.R. Fletcher (113), A.W. Greig (148) | Bombay[2] | 1972–73 | – | – | – | – | 254 | – | – |
| W.R. Hammond (227), L.E.G. Ames (103) | Christchurch | 1932–33 | – | – | – | 242 | – | – | – |
| D.C.S. Compton (163), N.W.D. Yardley (99) | Nottingham | 1947 | – | 237 | – | – | – | – | – |
| D.L. Amiss (138*), A.W. Greig (139) | Nottingham | 1973 | – | – | – | 210 | – | – | – |
| E. Paynter (216*), D.C.S. Compton (102) | Nottingham | 1938 | 206 | – | – | – | – | – | – |
| M.H. Denness (118), A.W. Greig (106) | Lord's | 1974 | – | – | – | – | 202 | – | – |
| R.E. Foster (287), L.C. Braund (102) | Sydney | 1903–04 | 192 | – | – | – | – | – | – |
| D.C.S. Compton (278), T.E. Bailey (36*) | Nottingham | 1954 | – | – | – | – | – | 192 | – |
| E.H. Hendren (132), M. Leyland (153) | Manchester | 1934 | 191 | – | – | – | – | – | – |
| G.B. Legge (196), M.S. Nichols (75) | Auckland | 1929–30 | – | – | – | 184 | – | – | – |
| J. Hardstaff, jr (205*), P.A. Gibb (60) | Lord's | 1946 | – | – | – | – | 182 | – | – |
| M. Leyland (161), L.E.G. Ames (148*) | Oval | 1935 | – | 179 | – | – | – | – | – |
| R. Subba Row (137), K.F. Barrington (83) | Oval | 1961 | 172 | – | – | – | – | – | – |
| W. Watson (109), T.E. Bailey (71) | Lord's | 1953 | 163 | – | – | – | – | – | – |
| A.C. MacLaren (164), R. Peel (73) | Melbourne | 1894–95 | 162 | – | – | – | – | – | – |
| A. Shrewsbury (164), W. Barnes (58) | Lord's | 1886 | 161 | – | – | – | – | – | – |
| M. Leyland (83), R.E.S. Wyatt (78) | Adelaide | 1932–33 | 156 | – | – | – | – | – | – |
| C.P. Mead (181), P.G.H. Fender (60) | Durban[2] | 1922–23 | – | 154 | – | – | – | – | – |
| I.T. Botham (208), D.W. Randall (95) | Oval | 1982 | – | – | – | – | 151 | – | – |

**5th Wicket** *continued*

| | | | A | SA | WI | NZ | I | P | SL |
|---|---|---|---|---|---|---|---|---|---|
| T.W. Graveney (175), A.J. Watkins (80) | Bombay² | 1951–52 | – | – | – | – | 148 | – | – |
| K.W.R. Fletcher (146), A.W. Greig (89) | Melbourne | 1974–75 | 148 | – | – | – | – | – | – |
| D.R. Jardine (61), B.H. Valentine (136) | Bombay¹ | 1933–34 | – | – | – | – | 145 | – | – |
| D.C.S. Compton (158), T.E. Bailey (44) | Manchester | 1955 | – | 144 | – | – | – | – | – |
| K.F. Barrington (256), J.M. Parks (60) | Manchester | 1964 | 143 | – | – | – | – | – | – |
| R.W. Tolchard (67), A.W. Greig (103) | Calcutta | 1976–77 | – | – | – | – | 142 | – | – |
| D.C.S. Compton (84), T.E. Bailey (72) | Sydney | 1954–55 | 134 | – | – | – | – | – | – |
| C. Milburn (126*), T.W. Graveney (30*) | Lord's | 1966 | – | – | 130* | – | – | – | – |
| A.J. Lamb (110), I.T. Botham (81) | Lord's | 1984 | – | – | 128 | – | – | – | – |
| M.C. Cowdrey (93*), K.F. Barrington (54*) | Oval | 1964 | 126* | – | – | – | – | – | – |
| W.R. Hammond (200), D.R. Jardine (62) | Melbourne | 1928–29 | 126 | – | – | – | – | – | – |
| Hon F.S. Jackson (113), R.H. Spooner (52) | Manchester | 1905 | 125 | – | – | – | – | – | – |
| M.J.K. Smith (87), P.H. Parfitt (46*) | Christchurch | 1965–66 | – | – | – | 125 | – | – | – |
| J.H. Edrich (164), B.L. D'Oliveira (158) | Oval | 1968 | 121 | – | – | – | – | – | – |
| D.C.S. Compton (147), J. Hardstaff, jr (67) | Adelaide | 1946–47 | 118 | – | – | – | – | – | – |
| P.B.H. May (113), M.C. Cowdrey (44) | Melbourne | 1958–59 | 118 | – | – | – | – | – | – |
| D.I. Gower (152), G. Fowler (57) | Faisalabad | 1983–84 | – | – | – | – | – | 116 | – |
| P.H. Parfitt (67), M.C. Cowdrey (151) | Delhi | 1963–64 | – | – | – | – | 115 | – | – |
| P.F. Warner (39), F.E. Woolley (73) | Lord's | 1912 | – | 113 | – | – | – | – | – |
| M.J.K. Smith (54), P.H. Parfitt (54) | Christchurch | 1965–66 | – | – | – | 113 | – | – | – |
| R. Abel (70), W. Barnes (62) | Oval | 1888 | 112 | – | – | – | – | – | – |
| J.W. Hearne (45), F.E. Woolley (57) | Leeds | 1912 | – | 111 | – | – | – | – | – |
| D.C.S. Compton (133), T.W. Graveney (92) | Port-of-Spain | 1953–54 | – | – | 110 | – | – | – | – |
| A.J. Watkins (68), C.J. Poole (55) | Calcutta | 1951–52 | – | – | – | – | 107 | – | – |
| J.W.H. Makepeace (117), J.W.H.T. Douglas (50) | Melbourne | 1920–21 | 106 | – | – | – | – | – | – |
| R. Abel (120), H. Wood (59) | Cape Town | 1888–89 | – | 105 | – | – | – | – | – |
| R.T. Simpson (103), T.E. Bailey (72*) | Manchester | 1949 | – | – | – | 105 | – | – | – |
| M.C. Cowdrey (119), M.J.K. Smith (44) | Lord's | 1965 | – | – | – | 105 | – | – | – |
| D.I. Gower (74), K.W.R. Fletcher (60*) | Calcutta | 1981–82 | – | – | – | – | 105 | – | – |
| C.P. Mead (117), F.E. Woolley (54) | Port Elizabeth | 1913–14 | – | 104 | – | – | – | – | – |
| B.L. D'Oliveira (81*), D.B. Close (36) | Lord's | 1967 | – | – | – | – | – | 104 | – |
| G.E. Tyldesley (78*), P.G.H. Fender (44*) | Manchester | 1921 | 102* | – | – | – | – | – | – |
| K.F. Barrington (132*), T.W. Graveney (36*) | Adelaide | 1962–63 | 101* | – | – | – | – | – | – |
| A.R. Lewis (70*), A.W. Greig (40*) | Delhi | 1972–73 | – | – | – | – | 101* | – | – |
| A. Sandham (46), E.H. Hendren (142) | Oval | 1924 | – | 101 | – | – | – | – | – |
| E.R. Dexter (57), P.J. Sharpe (85*) | Birmingham | 1963 | – | – | 101 | – | – | – | – |
| D.B. Close (46), P.J. Sharpe (63) | Oval | 1963 | – | – | 101 | – | – | – | – |
| I.T. Botham (142), M.W. Gatting (32) | Kanpur | 1981–82 | – | – | – | – | 101 | – | – |
| A.R. Lewis (88), A.W. Greig (48) | Karachi | 1972–73 | – | – | – | – | – | 100† | – |
| C.J. Tavaré (89), D.W. Randall (78) | Perth | 1982–83 | 100 | – | – | – | – | – | – |
| *Totals: (59)* | | | 22 | 9 | 5 | 7 | 12 | 4 | – |

†*103 runs were added for this wicket in two partnerships, P.I. Pocock retiring hurt after 3 runs had been scored. Although the 5th wicket added 115 v Australia in 1884–85 (5th Test – Melbourne), this consisted of two partnerships: A. Shrewsbury added 73* with W. Bates (retired ill) and a further 42 with W. Flowers. Similarly, in the Oval Test v Pakistan in 1974, 139 runs were added in two partnerships for the 5th wicket, K.W.R. Fletcher adding 61* with D.L. Amiss (retired hurt) and a further 78 with A.W. Greig.*

**ENGLAND – 6th Wicket**

| | | | A | SA | WI | NZ | I | P | SL |
|---|---|---|---|---|---|---|---|---|---|
| P.H. Parfitt (131*), B.R. Knight (125) | Auckland | 1962–63 | – | – | – | 240 | – | – | – |
| I.T. Botham (138), D.W. Randall (164) | Wellington | 1983–84 | – | – | – | 232 | – | – | – |
| L. Hutton (364), J. Hardstaff, jr (169*) | Oval | 1938 | 215 | – | – | – | – | – | – |
| G. Boycott (107), A.P.E. Knott (135) | Nottingham | 1977 | 215 | – | – | – | – | – | – |
| K.F. Barrington (148*), J.M. Parks (108*) | Durban² | 1964–65 | – | 206* | – | – | – | – | – |
| D.C.S. Compton (116), T.E. Bailey (93) | Lord's | 1949 | – | – | – | 189 | – | – | – |
| W.R. Hammond (240), L.E.G. Ames (83) | Lord's | 1938 | 186 | – | – | – | – | – | – |
| I.T. Botham (103), D.W. Randall (83) | Nottingham | 1983 | – | – | – | 186 | – | – | – |
| I.T. Botham (114), R.W. Taylor (43) | Bombay³ | 1979–80 | – | – | – | – | 171 | – | – |
| H. Sutcliffe (161), R.E.S. Wyatt (64) | Oval | 1930 | 170 | – | – | – | – | – | – |
| I.T. Botham (128), G. Miller (98) | Manchester | 1982 | – | – | – | – | 169 | – | – |
| D.I. Gower (200*), G. Miller (63*) | Birmingham | 1979 | – | – | – | – | 165* | – | – |
| A.W. Greig (148), A.P.E. Knott (87) | Bridgetown | 1973–74 | – | – | 163 | – | – | – | – |
| T.E. Bailey (82*), T.G. Evans (104) | Manchester | 1950 | – | – | 161 | – | – | – | – |
| I.T. Botham (103), R.W. Taylor (45) | Christchurch | 1977–78 | – | – | – | 160 | – | – | – |

**6th Wicket** *continued*

| | | | A | SA | WI | NZ | I | P | SL |
|---|---|---|---|---|---|---|---|---|---|
| T.W. Graveney (73), T.G. Evans (104) | Lord's | 1952 | – | – | – | – | 159 | – | – |
| J.T. Tyldesley (112*), R.H. Spooner (79) | Oval | 1905 | 158 | – | – | – | – | – | – |
| L.E.G. Ames (126), J. Iddon (54) | Kingston | 1934–35 | – | – | 157 | – | – | – | – |
| C.P. Mead (181), F.T. Mann (84) | Durban² | 1922–23 | – | 156 | – | – | – | – | – |
| P.H. Parfitt (101*), D.A. Allen (79*) | Birmingham | 1962 | – | – | – | – | – | 153* | – |
| A.W. Greig (116), A.P.E. Knott (116) | Leeds | 1976 | – | – | 152 | – | – | – | – |
| R.A. Woolmer (149), A.P.E. Knott (64) | Oval | 1975 | 151 | – | – | – | – | – | – |
| C.J. Tavaré (78), I.T. Botham (118) | Manchester | 1981 | 149 | – | – | – | – | – | – |
| L.C. Braund (104), G.L. Jessop (93) | Lord's | 1907 | – | 145 | – | – | – | – | – |
| M. Leyland (153), L.E.G. Ames (72) | Manchester | 1934 | 142 | – | – | – | – | – | – |
| K.W.R. Fletcher (129*), A.P.E. Knott (67) | Bridgetown | 1973–74 | – | – | 142 | – | – | – | – |
| Hon F.S. Jackson (128), L.C. Braund (65) | Manchester | 1902 | 141 | – | – | – | – | – | – |
| E.H. Hendren (95), M. Leyland (137) | Melbourne | 1928–29 | 140 | – | – | – | – | – | – |
| M.C. Cowdrey (79), J.M. Parks (89) | Melbourne | 1965–66 | 138 | – | – | – | – | – | – |
| W.W. Read (52), Hon F.S. Jackson (103) | Oval | 1893 | 131 | – | – | – | – | – | – |
| M. Leyland (102), M.W. Tate (100*) | Lord's | 1929 | – | 129 | – | – | – | – | – |
| M. Leyland (109), L.E.G. Ames (120) | Lord's | 1934 | 129 | – | – | – | – | – | – |
| J.H. Hampshire (107), A.P.E. Knott (53) | Lord's | 1969 | – | – | 128 | – | – | – | – |
| M.C. Cowdrey (82), A.P.E. Knott (73*) | Georgetown | 1967–68 | – | – | 127 | – | – | – | – |
| A.P.F. Chapman (121), G.O.B. Allen (57) | Lord's | 1930 | 125 | – | – | – | – | – | – |
| G.H. Hirst (62), K.S. Ranjitsinhji (175) | Sydney | 1897–98 | 124 | – | – | – | – | – | – |
| C.A.G. Russell (135*), J.W.H.T. Douglas (60) | Adelaide | 1920–21 | 124 | – | – | – | – | – | – |
| F.E. Woolley (115*), F.T. Mann (59) | Johannesburg¹ | 1922–23 | – | 124 | – | – | – | – | – |
| G. Boycott (191), A.P.E. Knott (57) | Leeds | 1977 | 123 | – | – | – | – | – | – |
| G. Miller (48), I.T. Botham (100) | Birmingham | 1978 | – | – | – | – | – | 123 | – |
| C.P. Mead (182), Hon L.H. Tennyson (51) | Oval | 1921 | 121 | – | – | – | – | – | – |
| M.J.K. Smith (99), P.M. Walker (52) | Lord's | 1960 | – | 120 | – | – | – | – | – |
| G. Fowler (58), V.J. Marks (74) | Lahore² | 1983–84 | – | – | – | – | – | 120 | – |
| A.W. Greig (121), A.P.E. Knott (61) | Georgetown | 1973–74 | – | – | 119 | – | – | – | – |
| D.I. Gower (173*), V.J. Marks (55) | Lahore² | 1983–84 | – | – | – | – | – | 119 | – |
| G.R.J. Roope (69), I.T. Botham (108) | Lord's | 1978 | – | – | – | – | – | 118 | – |
| M.J.K. Smith (121), J.M. Parks (59) | Cape Town | 1964–65 | – | 117 | – | – | – | – | – |
| W.W. Read (66), E.F.S. Tylecote (66) | Sydney | 1882–83 | 116 | – | – | – | – | – | – |
| Hon F.S. Jackson (82*), W. Rhodes (39*) | Nottingham | 1905 | 113* | – | – | – | – | – | – |
| J.T. Ikin (48), N.W.D. Yardley (61) | Melbourne | 1946–47 | 113 | – | – | – | – | – | – |
| M.C. Cowdrey (148), A.P.E. Knott (69*) | Port-of-Spain | 1967–68 | – | – | 113 | – | – | – | – |
| A.W. Greig (64), A.P.E. Knott (63*) | Hyderabad | 1972–73 | – | – | – | – | – | 112 | – |
| Hon F.S. Jackson (49), G.L. Jessop (104) | Oval | 1902 | 109 | – | – | – | – | – | – |
| W.G. Quaife (68), L.C. Braund (103*) | Adelaide | 1901–02 | 108 | – | – | – | – | – | – |
| L. Hutton (205), T.G. Evans (28) | Kingston | 1953–54 | – | – | 108 | – | – | – | – |
| F.E. Woolley (83), M. Leyland (45) | Leeds | 1929 | – | 106 | – | – | – | – | – |
| M.J. Horton (58), T.G. Evans (73) | Nottingham | 1959 | – | – | – | – | 106 | – | – |
| B.L. D'Oliveira (72), R. Illingworth (45) | Leeds | 1971 | – | – | – | – | – | 106 | – |
| R.T. Robinson (160), P.R. Downton (74) | Delhi | 1984–85 | – | – | – | – | 106 | – | – |
| M. Leyland (53), R.W.V. Robins (108) | Manchester | 1935 | – | 105 | – | – | – | – | – |
| J.W.H.T. Douglas (60), P.G.H. Fender (59) | Melbourne | 1920–21 | 104 | – | – | – | – | – | – |
| K.W.R. Fletcher (123*), A.W. Greig (53) | Manchester | 1974 | – | – | – | – | 104 | – | – |
| E.R. Dexter (66*), R.W. Barber (39*) | Lahore² | 1961–62 | – | – | – | – | – | 101* | – |
| D.L. Amiss (179), A.P.E. Knott (75) | Delhi | 1976–77 | – | – | – | – | 101 | – | – |
| F.G. Mann (136*), R.O. Jenkins (29) | Port Elizabeth | 1948–49 | – | 100 | – | – | – | – | – |
| *Totals:* (65) | | | 24 | 10 | 10 | 5 | 8 | 8 | – |

*Although the 6th wicket added 121 v Australia (Oval) 1934, this consisted of two partnerships: M. Leyland added 85\* with L.E.G. Ames (retired hurt) and a further 36 with G.O.B. Allen.*

**ENGLAND – 7th Wicket**

| | | | A | SA | WI | NZ | I | P | SL |
|---|---|---|---|---|---|---|---|---|---|
| M.J.K. Smith (96), J.M. Parks (101*) | Port-of-Spain | 1959–60 | – | – | 197 | – | – | – | – |
| M.C. Cowdrey (152), T.G. Evans (82) | Lord's | 1957 | – | – | 174 | – | – | – | – |
| D.I. Gower (152), V.J. Marks (83) | Faisalabad | 1983–84 | – | – | – | – | – | 167 | – |
| A.P.E. Knott (116), P. Lever (47) | Birmingham | 1971 | – | – | – | – | – | 159 | – |
| A.P.E. Knott (104), P. Lever (64) | Auckland | 1970–71 | – | – | – | 149 | – | – | – |
| F.E. Woolley (133*), J. Vine (36) | Sydney | 1911–12 | 143 | – | – | – | – | – | – |
| J. Sharp (105), K.L. Hutchings (59) | Oval | 1909 | 142 | – | – | – | – | – | – |
| D.R. Jardine (128), R.W.V. Robins (55) | Manchester | 1933 | – | – | 140 | – | – | – | – |
| G. Miller (64), R.W. Taylor (97) | Adelaide | 1978–79 | 135 | – | – | – | – | – | – |
| W.W. Whysall (76), R. Kilner (74) | Melbourne | 1924–25 | 133 | – | – | – | – | – | – |

**7th Wicket** *continued*

| | | | A | SA | WI | NZ | I | P | SL |
|---|---|---|---|---|---|---|---|---|---|
| M.W. Gatting (75*), I.T. Botham (85) | Lord's | 1985 | 131 | – | – | – | – | – | – |
| K.W.R. Fletcher (122), C.M. Old (65) | Oval | 1974 | – | – | – | – | – | 130 | – |
| D.W. Randall (126), P.H. Edmonds (64) | Lord's | 1982 | – | – | – | – | 125 | – | – |
| A.F.A. Lilley (84), L.C. Braund (58) | Sydney | 1901–02 | 124 | – | – | – | – | – | – |
| E.R. Dexter (136*), R. Swetman (45) | Bridgetown | 1959–60 | – | – | 123 | – | – | – | – |
| J.B. Hobbs (119), E.H. Hendren (92) | Adelaide | 1924–25 | 117 | – | – | – | – | – | – |
| J.W.H.T. Douglas (119), M.C. Bird (61) | Durban[1] | 1913–14 | – | 115 | – | – | – | – | – |
| T.W. Hayward (130), A.F.A. Lilley (58) | Manchester | 1899 | 113 | – | – | – | – | – | – |
| M. Leyland (111*), R.W.V. Robins (61) | Melbourne | 1936–37 | 111 | – | – | – | – | – | – |
| A.J. Lamb (102*), P.H. Edmonds (43*) | Oval | 1983 | – | – | – | 110* | – | – | – |
| F.R. Brown (74), W. Voce (66) | Christchurch | 1932–33 | – | – | – | 108 | – | – | – |
| J. Hardstaff, jr (169*), A. Wood (53) | Oval | 1938 | 106 | – | – | – | – | – | – |
| L. Hutton (205), J.H. Wardle (66) | Kingston | 1953–54 | – | – | 105 | – | – | – | – |
| A.P.E. Knott (90), R.A. Hutton (81) | Oval | 1971 | – | – | – | – | 103 | – | – |
| W. Flowers (56), J.M. Read (56) | Sydney | 1884–85 | 102 | – | – | – | – | – | – |
| R. Illingworth (50), R. Swetman (65) | Oval | 1959 | – | – | – | – | 102 | – | – |
| E.H. Hendren (79), G. Geary (53) | Nottingham | 1934 | 101 | – | – | – | – | – | – |
| D.I. Gower (78), P.H. Edmonds (49) | Kanpur | 1984–85 | – | – | – | – | 100 | – | – |
| *Totals: (28)* | | | *12* | *1* | *5* | *3* | *4* | *3* | *–* |

**ENGLAND – 8th Wicket**

| | | | A | SA | WI | NZ | I | P | SL |
|---|---|---|---|---|---|---|---|---|---|
| L.E.G. Ames (137), G.O.B. Allen (122) | Lord's | 1931 | – | – | – | 246 | – | – | – |
| T.W. Graveney (165), J.T. Murray (112) | Oval | 1966 | – | – | 217 | – | – | – | – |
| R. Illingworth (107), P. Lever (88*) | Manchester | 1971 | – | – | – | – | 168 | – | – |
| C.W. Wright (71), H.R. Bromley-Davenport (84) | Johannesburg[1] | 1895–96 | – | 154 | – | – | – | – | – |
| R.W.V. Robins (76), H. Verity (66*) | Manchester | 1936 | – | – | – | – | 138 | – | – |
| E.H. Hendren (169), H. Larwood (70) | Brisbane[1] | 1928–29 | 124 | – | – | – | – | – | – |
| D.C.S. Compton (145*), A.V. Bedser (37) | Manchester | 1948 | 121 | – | – | – | – | – | – |
| I.T. Botham (149*), G.R. Dilley (56) | Leeds | 1981 | 117 | – | – | – | – | – | – |
| D.A. Allen (88), D.J. Brown (44) | Christchurch | 1965–66 | – | – | – | 107 | – | – | – |
| R. Illingworth (57), J.A. Snow (48) | Leeds | 1972 | 104 | – | – | – | – | – | – |
| G. Miller (62), R.W. Taylor (64) | Lord's | 1979 | – | – | – | – | 103 | – | – |
| *Totals: (11)* | | | *4* | *1* | *1* | *2* | *3* | *–* | *–* |

**ENGLAND – 9th Wicket**

| | | | A | SA | WI | NZ | I | P | SL |
|---|---|---|---|---|---|---|---|---|---|
| M.C. Cowdrey (128*), A.C. Smith (69*) | Wellington | 1962–63 | – | – | – | 163* | – | – | – |
| W.H. Scotton (90), W.W. Read (117) | Oval | 1884 | 151 | – | – | – | – | – | – |
| F.E. Woolley (123), A.P. Freeman (50*) | Sydney | 1924–25 | 128 | – | – | – | – | – | – |
| T.E. Bailey (134*), D.V.P. Wright (45) | Christchurch | 1950–51 | – | – | – | 117 | – | – | – |
| R.E. Foster (287), A.E. Relf (31) | Sydney | 1903–04 | 115 | – | – | – | – | – | – |
| G.A.R. Lock (89), P.I. Pocock (13) | Georgetown | 1967–68 | – | – | 109 | – | – | – | – |
| G. Geary (35*), G.G. Macaulay (76) | Leeds | 1926 | 108 | – | – | – | – | – | – |
| *Totals: (7)* | | | *4* | *–* | *1* | *2* | *–* | *–* | *–* |

**ENGLAND – 10th Wicket**

| | | | A | SA | WI | NZ | I | P | SL |
|---|---|---|---|---|---|---|---|---|---|
| R.E. Foster (287), W. Rhodes (40*) | Sydney | 1903–04 | 130 | – | – | – | – | – | – |
| K. Higgs (63), J.A. Snow (59*) | Oval | 1966 | – | – | 128 | – | – | – | – |
| P. Willey (100*), R.G.D. Willis (24*) | Oval | 1980 | – | – | 117* | – | – | – | – |
| *Totals: (3)* | | | *1* | *–* | *2* | *–* | *–* | *–* | *–* |

**AUSTRALIA – (426) – 1st Wicket**

| | | | E | SA | WI | NZ | I | P | SL |
|---|---|---|---|---|---|---|---|---|---|
| W.M. Lawry (210), R.B. Simpson (201) | Bridgetown | 1964–65 | – | – | 382 | – | – | – | – |
| R.B. Simpson (225), W.M. Lawry (119) | Adelaide | 1965–66 | 244 | – | – | – | – | – | – |
| J.H.W. Fingleton (112), W.A. Brown (121) | Cape Town | 1935–36 | – | 233 | – | – | – | – | – |
| W.M. Lawry (157), I.R. Redpath (97) | Melbourne | 1963–64 | – | 219 | – | – | – | – | – |
| A.R. Morris (111), J. Moroney (118) | Johannesburg[2] | 1949–50 | – | 214 | – | – | – | – | – |
| W.M. Lawry (106), R.B. Simpson (311) | Manchester | 1964 | 201 | – | – | – | – | – | – |
| C.C. McDonald (110), A.R. Morris (111) | Port-of-Spain | 1954–55 | – | – | 191 | – | – | – | – |
| R.B. Simpson (109), W.M. Lawry (100) | Melbourne | 1967–68 | – | – | – | – | 191 | – | – |
| C.C. McDonald (99), J.W. Burke (189) | Cape Town | 1957–58 | – | 190 | – | – | – | – | – |
| W. Bardsley (130), S.E. Gregory (74) | Oval | 1909 | 180 | – | – | – | – | – | – |
| W.H. Ponsford (92*), A. Jackson (70*) | Adelaide | 1930–31 | – | – | 172* | – | – | – | – |

**1st Wicket** *continued*

| | | | E | SA | WI | NZ | I | P | SL |
|---|---|---|---|---|---|---|---|---|---|
| C.C. McDonald (170), J.W. Burke (66) | Adelaide | 1958–59 | 171 | – | – | – | – | – | – |
| W.M. Woodfull (155), W.H. Ponsford (81) | Lord's | 1930 | 162 | – | – | – | – | – | – |
| J.H.W. Fingleton (118), W.A. Brown (84) | Durban[2] | 1935–36 | – | 162 | – | – | – | – | – |
| K.R. Stackpole (142), I.R. Redpath (60) | Kingston | 1972–73 | – | – | 161 | – | – | – | – |
| W.M. Woodfull (54), W.H. Ponsford (110) | Oval | 1930 | 159 | – | – | – | – | – | – |
| I.R. Redpath (65), A. Turner (136) | Adelaide | 1975–76 | – | – | 148 | – | – | – | – |
| C.C. McDonald (91), R.B. Simpson (75) | Melbourne | 1960–61 | – | – | 146 | – | – | – | – |
| C.C. McDonald (78), J.W. Burke (65) | Lord's | 1956 | 137 | – | – | – | – | – | – |
| W.M. Lawry (98), R.B. Simpson (71) | Brisbane[2] | 1962–63 | 136 | – | – | – | – | – | – |
| K.P. Stackpole (76*), I.R. Redpath (57*) | Georgetown | 1972–73 | – | – | 135* | – | – | – | – |
| V.T. Trumper (104), R.A. Duff (54) | Manchester | 1902 | 135 | – | – | – | – | – | – |
| I.C. Davis (56), A. Turner (82) | Melbourne | 1976–77 | – | – | – | – | – | 134 | – |
| W.M. Woodfull (67), V.Y. Richardson (83) | Brisbane[2] | 1932–33 | 133 | – | – | – | – | – | – |
| V.T. Trumper (113), R.A. Duff (79) | Adelaide | 1903–04 | 129 | – | – | – | – | – | – |
| V.T. Trumper (63), M.A. Noble (64) | Melbourne | 1907–08 | 126 | – | – | – | – | – | – |
| S.G. Barnes (71), A.R. Morris (57) | Sydney | 1946–47 | 126 | – | – | – | – | – | – |
| H.L. Collins (104), W. Bardsley (57) | Sydney | 1920–21 | 123 | – | – | – | – | – | – |
| S.G. Barnes (141), A.R. Morris (57) | Lord's | 1948 | 122 | – | – | – | – | – | – |
| C.C. McDonald (41), A.R. Morris (99) | Melbourne | 1952–53 | – | 122 | – | – | – | – | – |
| R.B. Simpson (67), W.M. Lawry (78) | Melbourne | 1965–66 | 120 | – | – | – | – | – | – |
| G.M. Wood (66), M.F. Kent (54) | Oval | 1981 | 120 | – | – | – | – | – | – |
| R.B. Simpson (65), W.M. Lawry (98) | Johannesburg[3] | 1966–67 | – | 118 | – | – | – | – | – |
| H.L. Collins (59), W. Bardsley (56) | Melbourne | 1920–21 | 117 | – | – | – | – | – | – |
| S.G. Barnes (61), A.R. Morris (196) | Oval | 1948 | 117 | – | – | – | – | – | – |
| C.E. McLeod (77), J. Worrall (75) | Oval | 1899 | 116 | – | – | – | – | – | – |
| H.L. Collins (64), W. Bardsley (51) | Melbourne | 1920–21 | 116 | – | – | – | – | – | – |
| A.R. Morris (124*), M.R. Harvey (31) | Adelaide | 1946–47 | 116 | – | – | – | – | – | – |
| W.M. Lawry (45), I.R. Redpath (79) | Brisbane[2] | 1967–68 | – | – | – | – | 116 | – | – |
| W.M. Lawry (47*), R.B. Simpson (71) | Calcutta | 1964–65 | – | – | – | – | 115 | – | – |
| W.M. Lawry (102), R.B. Simpson (51) | Manchester | 1961 | 113 | – | – | – | – | – | – |
| W.M. Lawry (52), R.M. Cowper (165) | Sydney | 1967–68 | – | – | – | – | 111 | – | – |
| I.R. Redpath (83), R.B. McCosker (76) | Melbourne | 1974–75 | 111 | – | – | – | – | – | – |
| A.C. Bannerman (37), W.L. Murdoch (85) | Melbourne | 1881–82 | 110 | – | – | – | – | – | – |
| B.M. Laird (44), G.M. Wood (72) | Brisbane[2] | 1981–82 | – | – | – | – | – | 109 | – |
| C.C. McDonald (46), L.E. Favell (72) | Bridgetown | 1954–55 | – | – | 108 | – | – | – | – |
| W.M. Woodfull (54), W.H. Ponsford (83) | Manchester | 1930 | 106 | – | – | – | – | – | – |
| B.M. Laird (39), G.M. Wood (100) | Auckland | 1981–82 | – | – | – | 106 | – | – | – |
| J.H.W. Fingleton (62), W.A. Brown (51) | Johannesburg[1] | 1935–36 | – | 105 | – | – | – | – | – |
| B.M. Laird (38), J. Dyson (127*) | Sydney | 1981–82 | – | – | – | 104 | – | – | – |
| W. Bardsley (63*), T.J.E. Andrews (49) | Lord's | 1921 | 103 | – | – | – | – | – | – |
| C.C. McDonald (50), A.R. Morris (65) | Kingston | 1954–55 | – | – | 102 | – | – | – | – |
| V.T. Trumper (70), R.A. Duff (34) | Cape Town | 1902–03 | – | 100 | – | – | – | – | – |
| | *Totals: (53)* | | 27 | 9 | 10 | 1 | 4 | 2 | – |

**AUSTRALIA – 2nd Wicket**

| | | | E | SA | WI | NZ | I | P | SL |
|---|---|---|---|---|---|---|---|---|---|
| W.H. Ponsford (266), D.G. Bradman (244) | Oval | 1934 | 451 | – | – | – | – | – | – |
| A.R. Morris (182), D.G. Bradman (173*) | Leeds | 1948 | 301 | – | – | – | – | – | – |
| W.M. Lawry (205), I.M. Chappell (165) | Melbourne | 1968–69 | – | – | 298 | – | – | – | – |
| R.B. McCosker (127), I.M. Chappell (192) | Oval | 1975 | 277 | – | – | – | – | – | – |
| C.C. McDonald (154), A.L. Hassett (163) | Adelaide | 1952–53 | – | 275 | – | – | – | – | – |
| W.M. Woodfull (161), D.G. Bradman (167) | Melbourne | 1931–32 | – | 274 | – | – | – | – | – |
| W.B. Phillips (159), G.N. Yallop (141) | Perth | 1983–84 | – | – | – | – | – | 259 | – |
| S.G. Barnes (112), D.G. Bradman (201) | Adelaide | 1947–48 | – | – | – | – | 236 | – | – |
| W.M. Woodfull (141), C.G. Macartney (151) | Leeds | 1926 | 235 | – | – | – | – | – | – |
| A.P. Sheahan (127), J. Benaud (142) | Melbourne | 1972–73 | – | – | – | – | – | 233 | – |
| W.M. Woodfull (155), D.G. Bradman (254) | Lord's | 1930 | 231 | – | – | – | – | – | – |
| W.H. Ponsford (109), D.G. Bradman (223) | Brisbane[1] | 1930–31 | – | – | 229 | – | – | – | – |
| W. Bardsley (132), C. Hill (191) | Sydney | 1910–11 | – | 224 | – | – | – | – | – |
| I.R. Redpath (105), G.S. Chappell (144) | Sydney | 1974–75 | 220 | – | – | – | – | – | – |
| W.M. Lawry (105), I.M. Chappell (117) | Brisbane[2] | 1968–69 | – | – | 217 | – | – | – | – |
| W.M. Woodfull (111), H.S.T.L. Hendry (112) | Sydney | 1928–29 | 215 | – | – | – | – | – | – |
| J.W. Burke (161), R.N. Harvey (140) | Bombay[2] | 1956–57 | – | – | – | – | 204 | – | – |
| K.R. Stackpole (136), I.M. Chappell (104) | Adelaide | 1970–71 | 202 | – | – | – | – | – | – |
| W.A. Brown (72), S.J. McCabe (137) | Manchester | 1934 | 196 | – | – | – | – | – | – |
| W.M. Woodfull (117), C.G. Macartney (109) | Manchester | 1926 | 192 | – | – | – | – | – | – |
| W.M. Woodfull (50), D.G. Bradman (334) | Leeds | 1930 | 192 | – | – | – | – | – | – |

**2nd Wicket** *continued*

| | | | E | SA | WI | NZ | I | P | SL |
|---|---|---|---|---|---|---|---|---|---|
| H.L. Collins (114), W.H. Ponsford (110) | Sydney | 1924–25 | 190 | – | – | – | – | – | – |
| I.R. Redpath (72), I.M. Chappell (111) | Melbourne | 1970–71 | 180† | – | – | – | – | – | – |
| G.M. Wood (90), P.M. Toohey (97) | Kingston | 1977–78 | – | – | 180 | – | – | – | – |
| J.H.W. Fingleton (40), S.J. McCabe (189*) | Johannesburg[1] | 1935–36 | – | 177 | – | – | – | – | – |
| W.M. Woodfull (82), D.G. Bradman (299*) | Adelaide | 1931–32 | – | 176 | – | – | – | – | – |
| I.C. Davis (88), R.B. McCosker (105) | Melbourne | 1976–77 | – | – | – | – | – | 176 | – |
| A.C. Bannerman (91), J.J. Lyons (134) | Sydney | 1891–92 | 174 | – | – | – | – | – | – |
| S.G. Barnes (141), D.G. Bradman (89) | Lord's | 1948 | 174 | – | – | – | – | – | – |
| W.A. Brown (133), D.G. Bradman (144*) | Nottingham | 1938 | 170 | – | – | – | – | – | – |
| J. Moroney (101*), R.N. Harvey (100) | Johannesburg[2] | 1949–50 | – | 170 | – | – | – | – | – |
| K.C. Wessels (141), G.N. Yallop (98) | Kandy | 1982–83 | – | – | – | – | – | – | 170 |
| A.R. Morris (89), K.R. Miller (109) | Lord's | 1953 | 165 | – | – | – | – | – | – |
| W.M. Woodfull (76), D.G. Bradman (226) | Brisbane[2] | 1931–32 | – | 163 | – | – | – | – | – |
| W.A. Brown (66), S.J. McCabe (149) | Durban[2] | 1935–36 | – | 161 | – | – | – | – | – |
| R.B. Simpson (91), R.N. Harvey (64) | Sydney | 1962–63 | 160 | – | – | – | – | – | – |
| A.R. Morris (77), R.N. Harvey (116) | Adelaide | 1952–53 | – | 157 | – | – | – | – | – |
| W.M. Woodfull (83), D.G. Bradman (152) | Melbourne | 1930–31 | – | – | 156 | – | – | – | – |
| K.R. Stackpole (207), I.M. Chappell (59) | Brisbane[2] | 1970–71 | 151 | – | – | – | – | – | – |
| J. Darling (178), C. Hill (81) | Adelaide | 1897–98 | 148 | – | – | – | – | – | – |
| C. Kelleway (61), C.G. Macartney (99) | Lord's | 1912 | 146 | – | – | – | – | – | – |
| P.S. McDonnell (103), W.L. Murdoch (211) | Oval | 1884 | 143 | – | – | – | – | – | – |
| V.T. Trumper (113), C. Hill (88) | Adelaide | 1903–04 | 143 | – | – | – | – | – | – |
| K.C. Wessels (179), G.N. Yallop (68) | Adelaide | 1983–84 | – | – | – | – | – | 142 | – |
| I.R. Redpath (93), I.M. Chappell (121) | Wellington | 1973–74 | – | – | – | 141 | – | – | – |
| W.M. Lawry (89), N.C. O'Neill (88) | Sydney | 1963–64 | – | 140 | – | – | – | – | – |
| W.M. Lawry (210), R.M. Cowper (102) | Bridgetown | 1964–65 | – | – | 140 | – | – | – | – |
| A.M.J. Hilditch (80), K.C. Wessels (64) | Leeds | 1985 | 139 | – | – | – | – | – | – |
| R.B. Simpson (72), R.M. Cowper (69) | Port-of-Spain | 1964–65 | – | – | 138 | – | – | – | – |
| W.M. Woodfull (58), K.E. Rigg (127) | Sydney | 1931–32 | – | 137 | – | – | – | – | – |
| V.T. Trumper (65), C. Hill (98) | Adelaide | 1901–02 | 136 | – | – | – | – | – | – |
| A.M.J. Hilditch (119), K.C. Wessels (36) | Leeds | 1985 | 132 | – | – | – | – | – | – |
| F.A. Iredale (108), G. Giffen (80) | Manchester | 1896 | 131 | – | – | – | – | – | – |
| W.M. Lawry (135), I.R. Redpath (67) | Oval | 1968 | 129 | – | – | – | – | – | – |
| K.R. Stackpole (122), I.M. Chappell (54) | Melbourne | 1973–74 | – | – | – | 128 | – | – | – |
| I.R. Redpath (103), G.N. Yallop (47) | Adelaide | 1975–76 | – | – | 128 | – | – | – | – |
| A.M.J. Hilditch (85), A.R. Border (46) | Delhi | 1979–80 | – | – | – | – | 127 | – | – |
| B.M. Laird (74), I.M. Chappell (75) | Melbourne | 1979–80 | 127 | – | – | – | – | – | – |
| C.C. McDonald (47), R.N. Harvey (167) | Melbourne | 1958–59 | 126 | – | – | – | – | – | – |
| A.L. Hassett (104), R.N. Harvey (59) | Lord's | 1953 | 125 | – | – | – | – | – | – |
| I.C. Davis (105), R.B. McCosker (65) | Adelaide | 1976–77 | – | – | – | – | – | 125 | – |
| W.M. Darling (91), K.J. Hughes (48) | Sydney | 1978–79 | 125 | – | – | – | – | – | – |
| C.E. McLeod (112), C. Hill (58) | Melbourne | 1897–98 | 124 | – | – | – | – | – | – |
| C.G. Macartney (137), H.V. Hordern (50) | Sydney | 1910–11 | – | 124 | – | – | – | – | – |
| J.H.W. Fingleton (73), D.G. Bradman (82) | Sydney | 1936–37 | 124 | – | – | – | – | – | – |
| R. Edwards (170*), I.M. Chappell (50) | Nottingham | 1972 | 124 | – | – | – | – | – | – |
| H.L. Collins (24), C.G. Macartney (133*) | Lord's | 1926 | 123 | – | – | – | – | – | – |
| I.R. Redpath (135), I.M. Chappell (66) | Melbourne | 1972–73 | – | – | – | – | – | 123 | – |
| A.M.J. Hilditch (70), K.C. Wessels (90) | Melbourne | 1984–85 | – | – | 123 | – | – | – | – |
| A.R. Morris (67), A.L. Hassett (115) | Nottingham | 1953 | 122 | – | – | – | – | – | – |
| C. Kelleway (70), C. Hill (65) | Sydney | 1911–12 | 121 | – | – | – | – | – | – |
| K.A. Archer (48), A.L. Hassett (70) | Sydney | 1950–51 | 121 | – | – | – | – | – | – |
| R.B. Simpson (91), I.R. Redpath (40*) | Karachi | 1964–65 | – | – | – | – | – | 119 | – |
| R.B. McCosker (79), I.M. Chappell (86) | Lord's | 1975 | 119† | – | – | – | – | – | – |
| R.B. Simpson (153), I.R. Redpath (54) | Cape Town | 1966–67 | – | 117 | – | – | – | – | – |
| K.R. Stackpole (79), I.M. Chappell (37) | Oval | 1972 | 116 | – | – | – | – | – | – |
| W.M. Woodfull (67), D.G. Bradman (71) | Sydney | 1932–33 | 115 | – | – | – | – | – | – |
| G.M. Wood (45), K.C. Wessels (173) | Sydney | 1984–85 | – | – | 114 | – | – | – | – |
| H.L. Collins (203), J. Ryder (56) | Johannesburg[1] | 1921–22 | – | 113 | – | – | – | – | – |
| H.L. Collins (104), C.G. Macartney (69) | Sydney | 1920–21 | 111 | – | – | – | – | – | – |
| R.M. Cowper (57), I.M. Chappell (71) | Birmingham | 1968 | 111 | – | – | – | – | – | – |
| W.A. Brown (67), S.G. Barnes (54) | Wellington | 1945–46 | – | – | – | 109 | – | – | – |
| R. Edwards (74), I.M. Chappell (56) | Port-of-Spain | 1972–73 | – | – | 109 | – | – | – | – |
| I.R. Redpath (66), G.S. Chappell (56) | Port-of-Spain | 1972–73 | – | – | 107 | – | – | – | – |
| M.A. Noble (50), C. Hill (54) | Nottingham | 1905 | 106‡ | – | – | – | – | – | – |
| R.B. McCosker (95*), I.M. Chappell (62) | Leeds | 1975 | 106 | – | – | – | – | – | – |
| A. Turner (136), G.N. Yallop (43) | Adelaide | 1975–76 | – | – | 105 | – | – | – | – |

| 2nd Wicket continued | | | E | SA | WI | NZ | I | P | SL |
|---|---|---|---|---|---|---|---|---|---|
| J. Moroney (87), K.R. Miller (58) | Cape Town | 1949–50 | – | 104 | – | – | – | – | – |
| I.R. Redpath (83), I.M. Chappell (50) | Melbourne | 1974–75 | 104 | – | – | – | – | – | – |
| G.M. Wood (68), G.M. Ritchie (57) | Bridgetown | 1983–84 | – | – | 103 | – | – | – | – |
| W. Bardsley (85), C. Hill (39) | Melbourne | 1910–11 | – | 101 | – | – | – | – | – |
| A.M.J. Hilditch (55), A.R. Border (50) | Madras[1] | 1979–80 | – | – | – | – | 101 | – | – |
| A.P. Sheahan (44), I.M. Chappell (196) | Adelaide | 1972–73 | – | – | – | – | – | 100 | – |
| Totals: (93) | | | 47 | 16 | 14 | 3 | 4 | 8 | 1 |

†202 runs were added for this wicket; W.M. Lawry retired hurt and was succeeded by I.R. Redpath after 22 runs had been scored.
‡128 runs were added for this wicket; V.T. Trumper retired hurt and was succeeded by M.A. Noble after 22 runs had been scored.
Although the 2nd wicket added 134 v India at Melbourne in 1947–48, this consisted of two partnerships: W.A. Brown added 92* with D.G. Bradman (retired hurt) and a further 42 with K.R. Miller. Similarly, 105 were added v England at Adelaide in 1958–59, R.N. Harvey scoring 97* with C.C. McDonald (retired hurt) and a further 8 with N.C. O'Neill.

### AUSTRALIA – 3rd Wicket

| | | | E | SA | WI | NZ | I | P | SL |
|---|---|---|---|---|---|---|---|---|---|
| C.C. McDonald (127), R.N. Harvey (204) | Kingston | 1954–55 | – | – | 295 | – | – | – | – |
| D.G. Bradman (187), A.L. Hassett (128) | Brisbane[2] | 1946–47 | 276 | – | – | – | – | – | – |
| I.M. Chappell (145), G.S. Chappell (247*) | Wellington | 1973–74 | – | – | – | 264 | – | – | – |
| D.G. Bradman (169), S.J. McCabe (112) | Melbourne | 1936–37 | 249 | – | – | – | – | – | – |
| C. Kelleway (102), W. Bardsley (164) | Lord's | 1912 | – | 242 | – | – | – | – | – |
| D.G. Bradman (334), A.F. Kippax (77) | Leeds | 1930 | 229 | – | – | – | – | – | – |
| R.M. Cowper (143), B.C. Booth (117) | Port-of-Spain | 1964–65 | – | – | 225† | – | – | – | – |
| R.N. Harvey (133), K.R. Miller (147) | Kingston | 1954–55 | – | – | 224 | – | – | – | – |
| A.R. Border (162), K.J. Hughes (100) | Madras[1] | 1979–80 | – | – | – | – | 222 | – | – |
| W.M. Lawry (108), R.M. Cowper (307) | Melbourne | 1965–66 | 212 | – | – | – | – | – | – |
| H.L. Collins (203), J.M. Gregory (119) | Johannesburg[1] | 1921–22 | – | 209 | – | – | – | – | – |
| K.R. Stackpole (207), K.D. Walters (112) | Brisbane[2] | 1970–71 | 209 | – | – | – | – | – | – |
| W.L. Murdoch (211), H.J.H. Scott (102) | Oval | 1884 | 207 | – | – | – | – | – | – |
| R.N. Harvey (102), N.C. O'Neill (163) | Bombay[2] | 1959–60 | – | – | – | – | 207 | – | – |
| G.N. Yallop (167), K.J. Hughes (92) | Calcutta | 1979–80 | – | – | – | – | 206 | – | – |
| G.N. Yallop (268), K.J. Hughes (94) | Melbourne | 1983–84 | – | – | – | – | 203 | – |
| C. Kelleway (114), W. Bardsley (121) | Manchester | 1912 | – | 202 | – | – | – | – | – |
| A.R. Morris (153), R.N. Harvey (162) | Brisbane[2] | 1954–55 | 202 | – | – | – | – | – | – |
| I.M. Chappell (118), G.S. Chappell (113) | Oval | 1972 | 201 | – | – | – | – | – | – |
| J. Darling (160), J. Worrall (62) | Sydney | 1897–98 | 193 | – | – | – | – | – | – |
| D.G. Bradman (223), A.F. Kippax (84) | Brisbane[1] | 1930–31 | – | – | 193 | – | – | – | – |
| I.M. Chappell (106*), K.D. Walters (102*) | Bridgetown | 1972–73 | – | – | 192* | – | – | – | – |
| D.G. Bradman (254), A.F. Kippax (83) | Lord's | 1930 | 192 | – | – | – | – | – | – |
| A.R. Morris (122), A.L. Hassett (78) | Adelaide | 1946–47 | 189 | – | – | – | – | – | – |
| A.R. Morris (157), R.N. Harvey (116) | Port Elizabeth | 1949–50 | – | 187 | – | – | – | – | – |
| K.J. Hughes (88), G.S. Chappell (235) | Faisalabad | 1979–80 | – | – | – | – | – | 179 | – |
| R.B. Simpson (103), R.M. Cowper (108) | Adelaide | 1967–68 | – | – | – | – | 172 | – | – |
| D.G. Bradman (132), A.L. Hassett (80) | Melbourne | 1947–48 | – | – | – | – | 169 | – | – |
| B.M. Laird (78), A.R. Border (126) | Adelaide | 1981–82 | – | – | 166 | – | – | – | – |
| W.W. Armstrong (59), C. Hill (142) | Johannesburg[1] | 1902–03 | – | 164 | – | – | – | – | – |
| I.M. Chappell (74*), G.S. Chappell (109*) | Brisbane[2] | 1975–76 | – | – | 159* | – | – | – | – |
| J.W. Burke (81), R. Benaud (100) | Johannesburg[3] | 1957–58 | – | 158 | – | – | – | – | – |
| H. Carter (72), C. Hill (98) | Adelaide | 1911–12 | 157 | – | – | – | – | – | – |
| R.N. Harvey (109), A.L. Hassett (55) | Brisbane[2] | 1952–53 | – | 155 | – | – | – | – | – |
| D.G. Bradman (77), S.J. McCabe (70) | Oval | 1934 | 150 | – | – | – | – | – | – |
| R.N. Harvey (114), N.C. O'Neill (82) | Birmingham | 1961 | 146 | – | – | – | – | – | – |
| R. Edwards (170*), G.S. Chappell (72) | Nottingham | 1972 | 146 | – | – | – | – | – | – |
| C.G. Macartney (137), W. Bardsley (94) | Sydney | 1910–11 | – | 145 | – | – | – | – | – |
| C. Hill (191), D.R.A. Gehrs (67) | Sydney | 1910–11 | – | 144 | – | – | – | – | – |
| W.M. Lawry (81), K.D. Walters (81) | Manchester | 1968 | 144 | – | – | – | – | – | – |
| K.C. Wessels (173), A.R. Border (69) | Sydney | 1984–85 | – | – | 144‡ | – | – | – | – |
| A.L. Mann (105), A.D. Ogilvie (47) | Perth | 1977–78 | – | – | – | – | 139 | – | – |
| J.W. Burke (161), P.J.P. Burge (83) | Bombay[2] | 1956–57 | – | – | – | – | 137 | – | – |
| R.B. Simpson (71), B.C. Booth (77) | Adelaide | 1962–63 | 133 | – | – | – | – | – | – |
| P.M. Toohey (122), G.N. Yallop (57) | Kingston | 1977–78 | – | – | 133 | – | – | – | – |
| A.R. Border (67), K.J. Hughes (80) | Bombay[3] | 1979–80 | – | – | – | – | 132 | – | – |
| J. Ryder (52*), J.M. Gregory (76*) | Melbourne | 1920–21 | 130* | – | – | – | – | – | – |
| B.M. Laird (92), G.S. Chappell (74) | Brisbane[2] | 1979–80 | – | – | 130 | – | – | – | – |

**3rd Wicket** *continued*

| | | | E | SA | WI | NZ | I | P | SL |
|---|---|---|---|---|---|---|---|---|---|
| I.M. Chappell (72), G.S. Chappell (106) | Bridgetown | 1972–73 | – | – | 129 | – | – | – | – |
| W.M. Lawry (58*), N.C. O'Neill (74*) | Bridgetown | 1964–65 | – | – | 126*§ | – | – | – | – |
| G.S. Chappell (115), K.J. Hughes (88) | Adelaide | 1982–83 | 126 | – | – | – | – | – | – |
| B.M. Laird (75), G.S. Chappell (124) | Brisbane² | 1979–80 | – | – | 124 | – | – | – | – |
| W.M. Lawry (205), K.D. Walters (76) | Melbourne | 1968–69 | – | – | 123 | – | – | – | – |
| I.M. Chappell (109), G.S. Chappell (51) | Georgetown | 1972–73 | – | – | 121 | – | – | – | – |
| G.N. Yallop (121), P.M. Toohey (60) | Adelaide | 1977–78 | – | – | – | – | 120 | – | – |
| R.N. Harvey (167), N.C. O'Neill (37) | Melbourne | 1958–59 | 118 | – | – | – | – | – | – |
| A.P. Sheahan (81), R.M. Cowper (92) | Adelaide | 1967–68 | – | – | – | – | 118 | – | – |
| R.B. Simpson (153), P.J.P. Burge (54) | Karachi | 1964–65 | – | – | – | – | – | 116 | – |
| R.A. Duff (146), M.A. Noble (25) | Oval | 1905 | 115 | – | – | – | – | – | – |
| R.B. McCosker (84), G.S. Chappell (58) | Auckland | 1976–77 | – | – | – | 115 | – | – | – |
| V.T. Trumper (166), S.E. Gregory (56) | Sydney | 1907–08 | 114 | – | – | – | – | – | – |
| C.C. McDonald (67), R.N. Harvey (190) | Sydney | 1952–53 | – | 113 | – | – | – | – | – |
| K.E. Rigg (127), D.G. Bradman (112) | Sydney | 1931–32 | – | 111 | – | – | – | – | – |
| G.S. Chappell (59), K.J. Hughes (84) | Lord's | 1980 | 111 | – | – | – | – | – | – |
| A.R. Morris (206), R.N. Harvey (43) | Adelaide | 1950–51 | 110 | – | – | – | – | – | – |
| G.M. Wood (112), K.J. Hughes (117) | Lord's | 1980 | 110 | – | – | – | – | – | – |
| D.G. Bradman (212), S.J. McCabe (55) | Adelaide | 1936–37 | 109 | – | – | – | – | – | – |
| A.R. Morris (196), A.L. Hassett (37) | Oval | 1948 | 109 | – | – | – | – | – | – |
| C.G. Macartney (61), T.J.E. Andrews (94) | Oval | 1921 | 108 | – | – | – | – | – | – |
| R.N. Harvey (85), N.C. O'Neill (70) | Sydney | 1960–61 | – | – | 108 | – | – | – | – |
| B.M. Laird (63), G.S. Chappell (57) | Lahore² | 1979–80 | – | – | – | – | – | 108 | – |
| D.G. Bradman (201), A.L. Hassett (198*) | Adelaide | 1947–48 | – | – | – | – | 105 | – | – |
| R.B. Simpson (78), P.J.P. Burge (81) | Adelaide | 1963–64 | – | 104 | – | – | – | – | – |
| G.J. Cosier (67), C.S. Serjeant (85) | Melbourne | 1977–78 | – | – | – | – | 104 | – | – |
| R.N. Harvey (205), A.L. Hassett (40) | Melbourne | 1952–53 | – | 103 | – | – | – | – | – |
| W. Bardsley (82), W.W. Armstrong (48) | Melbourne | 1910–11 | – | 102 | – | – | – | – | – |
| C.G. Macartney (115), C.E. Pellew (52) | Leeds | 1921 | 101 | – | – | – | – | – | – |
| D.G. Bradman (185), A.L. Hassett (48) | Brisbane² | 1947–48 | – | – | – | – | 101 | – | – |
| I.M. Chappell (99), K.D. Walters (56) | Calcutta | 1969–70 | – | – | – | – | 101 | – | – |
| I.R. Redpath (39), G.S. Chappell (61) | Melbourne | 1974–75 | 101 | – | – | – | – | – | – |
| R.N. Harvey (74), W.J. Watson (30) | Bridgetown | 1954–55 | – | – | 100 | – | – | – | – |
| I.M. Chappell (90), G.S. Chappell (58) | Brisbane² | 1974–75 | 100 | – | – | – | – | – | – |
| *Totals: (82)* | | | *31* | *14* | *17* | *2* | *14* | *4* | *–* |

†*228 runs were added for this wicket, N.C. O'Neill retiring hurt and being succeeded by B.C. Booth after 3 runs had been scored.*
‡*212 runs were added for the third wicket, G.M. Ritchie retiring hurt and being succeeded by A.R. Border after 68 had been scored.*
§*147 runs were added for this wicket, W.M. Lawry retiring hurt and being succeeded by B.C. Booth after 126 runs had been scored.*

**AUSTRALIA – 4th Wicket**

| | | | E | SA | WI | NZ | I | P | SL |
|---|---|---|---|---|---|---|---|---|---|
| W.H. Ponsford (181), D.G. Bradman (304) | Leeds | 1934 | 388 | – | – | – | – | – | – |
| W.M. Lawry (151), K.D. Walters (242) | Sydney | 1968–69 | – | – | 336 | – | – | – | – |
| G.M. Wood (126), C.S. Serjeant (124) | Georgetown | 1977–78 | – | – | 251 | – | – | – | – |
| D.G. Bradman (232), A.A. Jackson (73) | Oval | 1930 | 243 | – | – | – | – | – | – |
| A.L. Hassett (132), K.R. Miller (129) | Sydney | 1951–52 | – | – | 235 | – | – | – | – |
| G.H.S. Trott (143), S.E. Gregory (103) | Lord's | 1896 | 221 | – | – | – | – | – | – |
| G.S. Chappell (235), G.N. Yallop (172) | Faisalabad | 1979–80 | – | – | – | – | – | 217 | – |
| I.R. Redpath (132), K.D. Walters (103) | Sydney | 1968–69 | – | – | 210 | – | – | – | – |
| A.C. Bannerman (70), P.S. McDonnell (147) | Sydney | 1881–82 | 199 | – | – | – | – | – | – |
| C.G. Macartney (170), J.M. Gregory (93) | Sydney | 1920–21 | 198 | – | – | – | – | – | – |
| C. Kelleway (147), W.W. Armstrong (121) | Adelaide | 1920–21 | 194 | – | – | – | – | – | – |
| R.N. Harvey (154), N.C. O'Neill (100) | Adelaide | 1962–63 | 194 | – | – | – | – | – | – |
| A.F. Kippax (146), S.J. McCabe (90) | Adelaide | 1930–31 | – | – | 182 | – | – | – | – |
| A.R. Border (105), K.J. Hughes (84) | Melbourne | 1978–79 | – | – | – | – | – | 177 | – |
| R.N. Harvey (122), G.B. Hole (66) | Manchester | 1953 | 173 | – | – | – | – | – | – |
| R.M. Cowper (307), K.D. Walters (60) | Melbourne | 1965–66 | 172 | – | – | – | – | – | – |
| I.M. Chappell (196), R. Edwards (89) | Adelaide | 1972–73 | – | – | – | – | 172 | – | – |
| G. Giffen (161), F.A. Iredale (81) | Sydney | 1894–95 | 171 | – | – | – | – | – | – |
| G.S. Chappell (182), K.J. Hughes (76) | Sydney | 1983–84 | – | – | – | – | – | 171 | – |
| G.N. Yallop (102), K.J. Hughes (129) | Brisbane² | 1978–79 | 170 | – | – | – | – | – | – |

**4th Wicket** *continued*

| | | | E | SA | WI | NZ | I | P | SL |
|---|---|---|---|---|---|---|---|---|---|
| R.N. Harvey (190), K.R. Miller (55) | Sydney | 1952–53 | – | 168 | – | – | – | – | – |
| M.A. Noble (65), S.E. Gregory (112) | Adelaide | 1903–04 | 162 | – | – | – | – | – | – |
| W.H. Ponsford (128), J.M. Taylor (72) | Melbourne | 1924–25 | 161 | – | – | – | – | – | – |
| A.F. Kippax (100), J. Ryder (112) | Melbourne | 1928–29 | 161 | – | – | – | – | – | – |
| R.N. Harvey (153), S.J.E. Loxton (80) | Melbourne | 1947–48 | – | – | – | – | 159 | – | – |
| W.W. Armstrong (132), C. Hill (100) | Melbourne | 1910–11 | – | 154 | – | – | – | – | – |
| N.C. O'Neill (113), P.J.P. Burge (60) | Calcutta | 1959–60 | – | – | – | – | 150 | – | – |
| R.N. Harvey (205), I.D. Craig (53) | Melbourne | 1952–53 | – | 148 | – | – | – | – | – |
| A.L. Hassett (198*), K.R. Miller (67) | Adelaide | 1947–48 | – | – | – | – | 142 | – | – |
| G.S. Chappell (117), K.J. Hughes (62) | Perth | 1982–83 | 141 | – | – | – | – | – | – |
| A.F. Kippax (51), J. Ryder (87) | Adelaide | 1928–29 | 137 | – | – | – | – | – | – |
| K.C. Wessels (179), A.R. Border (117*) | Adelaide | 1983–84 | – | – | – | – | – | 134 | – |
| R.N. Harvey (114), K.D. Mackay (78) | Delhi | 1959–60 | – | – | – | – | 132 | – | – |
| R.N. Harvey (162), G.B. Hole (57) | Brisbane² | 1954–55 | 131 | – | – | – | – | – | – |
| C. Hill (135), M.A. Noble (54) | Lord's | 1899 | 130 | – | – | – | – | – | – |
| J.W. Burke (189), K.D. Mackay (63) | Cape Town | 1957–58 | – | 130 | – | – | – | – | – |
| W.M. Woodfull (141), A.J. Richardson (100) | Leeds | 1926 | 129 | – | – | – | – | – | – |
| K.J. Hughes (213), A.R. Border (57) | Adelaide | 1980–81 | – | – | – | – | 129 | – | – |
| A.A. Jackson (164), J. Ryder (63) | Adelaide | 1928–29 | 126 | – | – | – | – | – | – |
| R.M. Cowper (81), B.C. Booth (74) | Bombay² | 1964–65 | – | – | – | – | 125 | – | – |
| W.A. Brown (206*), A.L.Hassett (56) | Lord's | 1938 | 124 | – | – | – | – | – | – |
| R.N. Harvey (83), K.R. Miller (47) | Melbourne | 1951–52 | – | – | 124 | – | – | – | – |
| I.R. Redpath (101), G.S. Chappell (68) | Melbourne | 1975–76 | – | – | 124 | – | – | – | – |
| N.C. O'Neill (117), P.J.P. Burge (181) | Oval | 1961 | 123 | – | – | – | – | – | – |
| K.R. Miller (58), R.N. Harvey (112) | Leeds | 1948 | 121 | – | – | – | – | – | – |
| D.G. Bradman (185), K.R. Miller (58) | Brisbane² | 1947–48 | – | – | – | – | 120 | – | – |
| N.C. O'Neill (82), B.C. Booth (169) | Brisbane² | 1963–64 | – | 120 | – | – | – | – | – |
| W. Bardsley (54), V.T. Trumper (214*) | Adelaide | 1910–11 | – | 118 | – | – | – | – | – |
| K.D. Walters (48), I.R. Redpath (77) | Bombay² | 1969–70 | – | – | – | – | 118 | – | – |
| G.S. Chappell (124), K.J. Hughes (130*) | Brisbane² | 1979–80 | – | – | 118 | – | – | – | – |
| A.R. Morris (157), A.L. Hassett (167) | Port Elizabeth | 1949–50 | – | 114 | – | – | – | – | – |
| G.S. Chappell (71), R. Edwards (53) | Brisbane² | 1974–75 | 114 | – | – | – | – | – | – |
| W.A. Brown (73), S.J. McCabe (88) | Nottingham | 1934 | 112 | – | – | – | – | – | – |
| A.F. Kippax (67), S.J. McCabe (71) | Melbourne | 1931–32 | – | 111 | – | – | – | – | – |
| G.S. Chappell (41), K.D. Walters (70) | Port-of-Spain | 1972–73 | – | – | 111 | – | – | – | – |
| A.M.J. Hilditch (113), A.R. Border (41) | Melbourne | 1984–85 | – | – | 111 | – | – | – | – |
| R.B. McCosker (109*), G.S. Chappell (54*) | Melbourne | 1975–76 | – | – | 110* | – | – | – | – |
| N.C. O'Neill (77), L.E. Favell (54) | Sydney | 1958–59 | 110 | – | – | – | – | – | – |
| C.G. Macartney (115), J.M. Taylor (50) | Leeds | 1921 | 109 | – | – | – | – | – | – |
| K.R. Miller (84), A.L. Hassett (53) | Johannesburg² | 1949–50 | – | 109 | – | – | – | – | – |
| A.L. Hassett (115), K.R. Miller (55) | Nottingham | 1953 | 109 | – | – | – | – | – | – |
| N.C. O'Neill (73), P.J.P. Burge (103) | Sydney | 1962–63 | 109 | – | – | – | – | – | – |
| G.S. Chappell (76), A.R. Border (124) | Melbourne | 1980–81 | – | – | – | – | 108 | – | – |
| K.J. Hughes (53), A.R. Border (118) | Brisbane² | 1983–84 | – | – | – | – | – | 108 | – |
| G.S. Chappell (73*), R. Edwards (52*) | Lord's | 1975 | 107* | – | – | – | – | – | – |
| K.J. Hughes (39*), D.W. Hookes (66*) | Brisbane² | 1982–83 | 107* | – | – | – | – | – | – |
| C. Hill (119), S.E. Gregory (29) | Sheffield | 1902 | 107 | – | – | – | – | – | – |
| M.A. Noble (133), W.W. Armstrong (48) | Sydney | 1903–04 | 106 | – | – | – | – | – | – |
| C.G. Macartney (116), J. Ryder (58) | Durban¹ | 1921–22 | – | 106 | – | – | – | – | – |
| A.L. Hassett (128), K.R. Miller (79) | Brisbane² | 1946–47 | 106 | – | – | – | – | – | – |
| W.M. Lawry (94), B.C. Booth (74) | Oval | 1964 | 106 | – | – | – | – | – | – |
| I.R. Redpath (58), I.C. Davis (50) | Christchurch | 1973–74 | – | – | – | 106 | – | – | – |
| G.S. Chappell (98*), K.J. Hughes (47) | Sydney | 1979–80 | 105 | – | – | – | – | – | – |
| G.N. Yallop (121), R.B. Simpson (100) | Adelaide | 1977–78 | – | – | – | – | 104 | – | – |
| C.S. Serjeant (81), K.D. Walters (53) | Lord's | 1977 | 103 | – | – | – | – | – | – |
| G.S. Chappell (70), K.D. Walters (51) | Adelaide | 1976–77 | – | – | – | – | – | 101 | – |
| G.N. Yallop (75), C.S. Serjeant (49) | Port-of-Spain | 1977–78 | – | – | 101 | – | – | – | – |
| G.S. Chappell (42), K.D. Walters (94) | Adelaide | 1973–74 | – | – | – | 100 | – | – | – |
| K.J. Hughes (48), D.W. Hookes (68) | Melbourne | 1982–83 | 100 | – | – | – | – | – | – |
| *Totals: (79)* | | | 38 | 10 | 12 | 2 | 10 | 7 | – |

**AUSTRALIA – 5th Wicket**

| | | | E | SA | WI | NZ | I | P | SL |
|---|---|---|---|---|---|---|---|---|---|
| S.G. Barnes (234), D.G. Bradman (234) | Sydney | 1946–47 | 405 | – | – | – | – | – | – |
| A.R. Morris (100*), D.G. Bradman (127*) | Melbourne | 1947–48 | – | – | – | – | 223* | – | – |
| K.R. Miller (109), R.G. Archer (128) | Kingston | 1954–55 | – | – | 220 | – | – | – | – |

**5th Wicket** *continued*

| | | | E | SA | WI | NZ | I | P | SL |
|---|---|---|---|---|---|---|---|---|---|---|
| R.B. Simpson (311), B.C. Booth (98) | Manchester | 1964 | 219 | – | – | – | – | – | – |
| A.R. Border (196), G.M. Ritchie (94) | Lord's | 1985 | 216 | – | – | – | – | – | – |
| P.J.P. Burge (120), K.D. Walters (115) | Melbourne | 1965–66 | 198 | – | – | – | – | – | – |
| W.M. Lawry (166), K.D. Walters (155) | Brisbane[2] | 1965–66 | 187 | – | – | – | – | – | – |
| P.J.P. Burge (181), B.C. Booth (71) | Oval | 1961 | 185 | – | – | – | – | – | – |
| D.G. Bradman (123), A.G. Fairfax (65) | Melbourne | 1928–29 | 183 | – | – | – | – | – | – |
| W.H. Ponsford (183), W.M. Woodfull (58) | Sydney | 1930–31 | – | – | 183 | – | – | – | – |
| G.S. Chappell (204), K.D. Walters (67) | Sydney | 1980–81 | – | – | – | 172 | – | – | – |
| G.S. Chappell (121), G.J. Cosier (168) | Melbourne | 1976–77 | – | – | – | – | – | 171 | – |
| A.R. Border (118), G.S. Chappell (150*) | Brisbane[2] | 1983–84 | – | – | – | – | 171 | – | – |
| R. Edwards (115), K.D. Walters (103) | Perth | 1974–75 | 170 | – | – | – | – | – | – |
| C.L. Badcock (118), R.G. Gregory (80) | Melbourne | 1936–37 | 161 | – | – | – | – | – | – |
| D.W. Hookes (143*), A.R. Border (47*) | Kandy | 1982–83 | – | – | – | – | – | – | 155* |
| G.S. Chappell (182), A.R. Border (64) | Sydney | 1983–84 | – | – | – | – | 153 | – | – |
| A.P. Sheahan (88), I.M. Chappell (73) | Manchester | 1968 | 152 | – | – | – | – | – | – |
| K.R. Miller (141*), I.W. Johnson (52) | Adelaide | 1946–47 | 150 | – | – | – | – | – | – |
| K.J. Hughes (137), A.R. Border (83) | Sydney | 1982–83 | 149 | – | – | – | – | – | – |
| G.S. Chappell (116*), R.W. Marsh (74) | Melbourne | 1972–73 | – | – | – | – | – | 146 | – |
| W.W. Armstrong (132), V.T. Trumper (87) | Melbourne | 1910–11 | – | 143 | – | – | – | – | – |
| S.E. Gregory (70), J. Darling (74) | Melbourne | 1894–95 | 142 | – | – | – | – | – | – |
| R.N. Harvey (178), S.J.E. Loxton (35) | Cape Town | 1949–50 | – | 140 | – | – | – | – | – |
| G. Giffen (161), S.E. Gregory (201) | Sydney | 1894–95 | 139 | – | – | – | – | – | – |
| D.G. Bradman (212), R.G. Gregory (50) | Adelaide | 1936–37 | 135 | – | – | – | – | – | – |
| R.N. Harvey (151*), S.J.E. Loxton (54) | Durban[2] | 1949–50 | – | 135 | – | – | – | – | – |
| I.R. Redpath (70), A.P. Sheahan (114) | Kanpur | 1969–70 | – | – | – | – | 131 | – | – |
| A.R. Border (124), K.D. Walters (78) | Melbourne | 1980–81 | – | – | – | – | 131 | – | – |
| G.S. Chappell (201), D.M. Wellham (36) | Brisbane[2] | 1981–82 | – | – | – | – | – | 131 | – |
| S.J. McCabe (187*), V.Y. Richardson (49) | Sydney | 1932–33 | 129 | – | – | – | – | – | – |
| A.R. Border (63), G.S. Chappell (114) | Melbourne | 1979–80 | 126 | – | – | – | – | – | – |
| F.A. Iredale (89), G.H.S. Trott (79) | Melbourne | 1897–98 | 124 | – | – | – | – | – | – |
| A.R. Border (98), D.W. Hookes (51) | St John's | 1983–84 | – | – | 124 | – | – | – | – |
| G.S. Chappell (123), R.W. Marsh (48) | Brisbane[2] | 1975–76 | – | – | 122 | – | – | – | – |
| D.G. Bradman (138), A.L. Hassett (137) | Nottingham | 1948 | 120 | – | – | – | – | – | – |
| W. Bardsley (136), V.T. Trumper (73) | Oval | 1909 | 118 | – | – | – | – | – | – |
| D.G. Bradman (299*), K.E. Rigg (35) | Adelaide | 1931–32 | – | 114 | – | – | – | – | – |
| G.S. Chappell (52), G.J. Cosier (109) | Melbourne | 1975–76 | – | – | 114 | – | – | – | – |
| K.D. Walters (71*), R.W. Marsh (55) | Adelaide | 1974–75 | 112 | – | – | – | – | – | – |
| K.J. Hughes (89), G.N. Yallop (58) | Leeds | 1981 | 112 | – | – | – | – | – | – |
| K.D. Walters (118), A.P. Sheahan (47) | Sydney | 1968–69 | – | – | 110 | – | – | – | – |
| V.T. Trumper (166), C. Hill (44) | Sydney | 1907–08 | 108 | – | – | – | – | – | – |
| T.P. Horan (124), G. Giffen (30) | Melbourne | 1881–82 | 107 | – | – | – | – | – | – |
| G.H.S. Trott (92), H. Graham (42) | Oval | 1893 | 106 | – | – | – | – | – | – |
| W.W. Armstrong (77), C.G. Macartney (54) | Melbourne | 1907–08 | 106 | – | – | – | – | – | – |
| G.S. Chappell (131), R. Edwards (28) | Lord's | 1972 | 106 | – | – | – | – | – | – |
| R.N. Harvey (112), S.J.E. Loxton (93) | Leeds | 1948 | 105 | – | – | – | – | – | – |
| G.S. Chappell (61), A.R. Border (78) | Adelaide | 1981–82 | – | – | 105 | – | – | – | – |
| N.C. O'Neill (181), K.D. Mackay (35) | Brisbane[2] | 1960–61 | – | – | 103 | – | – | – | – |
| B.C. Booth (169), R. Benaud (43) | Brisbane[2] | 1963–64 | – | 102 | – | – | – | – | – |
| K.D. Walters (102), I.R. Redpath (33) | Madras[1] | 1969–70 | – | – | – | – | 102 | – | – |
| J. Ryder (79), O.E. Nothling (44) | Sydney | 1928–29 | 101 | – | – | – | – | – | – |
| R.B. Simpson (176), S.J. Rixon (50) | Perth | 1977–78 | – | – | – | – | 101 | – | – |
| A.R. Border (84), D.M. Wellham (103) | Oval | 1981 | 101 | – | – | – | – | – | – |
| J. Darling (71), S.E. Gregory (117) | Oval | 1899 | 100 | – | – | – | – | – | – |
| P.M. Toohey (83), R.B. Simpson (39) | Perth | 1977–78 | – | – | – | – | 100 | – | – |
| | *Totals:* (57) | | 31 | 5 | 8 | – | 8 | 4 | 1 |

**AUSTRALIA – 6th Wicket**

| | | | E | SA | WI | NZ | I | P | SL |
|---|---|---|---|---|---|---|---|---|---|---|
| J.H.W. Fingleton (136), D.G. Bradman (270) | Melbourne | 1936–37 | 346 | – | – | – | – | – | – |
| I.R. Redpath (171), G.S. Chappell (108) | Perth | 1970–71 | 219 | – | – | – | – | – | – |
| K.R. Miller (137), R.G. Archer (98) | Bridgetown | 1954–55 | – | – | 206 | – | – | – | – |
| C. Kelleway (78), W.W. Armstrong (158) | Sydney | 1920–21 | 187 | – | – | – | – | – | – |
| G.M. Wood (172), G.M. Ritchie (146) | Nottingham | 1985 | 161 | – | – | – | – | – | – |
| T.R. Veivers (67), B.N. Jarman (78) | Bombay[2] | 1964–65 | – | – | – | – | 151 | – | – |
| J.M. Gregory (77), W.W. Armstrong (123*) | Melbourne | 1920–21 | 145 | – | – | – | – | – | – |
| S.E. Gregory (57), H. Graham (107) | Lord's | 1893 | 142 | – | – | – | – | – | – |

| 6th Wicket continued | | | E | SA | WI | NZ | I | P | SL |
|---|---|---|---|---|---|---|---|---|---|---|
| R.M. Cowper (83), T.R. Veivers (88) | Melbourne | 1964–65 | – | – | – | – | – | 139 | – |
| I.M. Chappell (151), B.N. Jarman (65) | Melbourne | 1967–68 | – | – | – | – | 134 | – | – |
| C.L. McCool (95), I.W. Johnson (47) | Brisbane[2] | 1946–47 | 131 | – | – | – | – | – | – |
| A.R. Border (146*), W.B. Phillips (39*) | Manchester | 1985 | 127* | – | – | – | – | – | – |
| G.N. Yallop (172), R.W. Marsh (71) | Faisalabad | 1979–80 | – | – | – | – | – | 127 | – |
| C. Kelleway (147), C.E. Pellew (104) | Adelaide | 1920–21 | 126 | – | – | – | – | – | – |
| A.R. Border (54), W.B. Phillips (76) | Georgetown | 1983–84 | – | – | 125 | – | – | – | – |
| V.Y. Richardson (138), C. Kelleway (32) | Melbourne | 1924–25 | 123 | – | – | – | – | – | – |
| K.D. Walters (155), T.R. Veivers (56*) | Brisbane[2] | 1965–66 | 119 | – | – | – | – | – | – |
| I.M. Chappell (138), H.B. Taber (46) | Delhi | 1969–70 | – | – | – | – | 118 | – | – |
| G.S. Chappell (182*), R.W. Marsh (38) | Sydney | 1975–76 | – | – | 117 | – | – | – | – |
| V.T. Trumper (113), R.B. Minnett (90) | Sydney | 1911–12 | 109 | – | – | – | – | – | – |
| C. Kelleway (59), V.S. Ransford (75) | Melbourne | 1910–11 | – | 107 | – | – | – | – | – |
| R.N. Harvey (151*), C.L. McCool (39*) | Durban[2] | 1949–50 | – | 106* | – | – | – | – | – |
| W.H. Ponsford (80), A.F. Kippax (42) | Sydney | 1924–25 | 105 | – | – | – | – | – | – |
| B.C. Booth (75), R. Benaud (43) | Sydney | 1963–64 | – | 100 | – | – | – | – | – |
| A.R. Border (98*), D.M. Jones (48) | Port-of-Spain | 1983–84 | – | – | 100 | – | – | – | – |
| | Totals: (25) | | 13 | 3 | 4 | – | 3 | 2 | – |

| AUSTRALIA – 7th Wicket | | | E | SA | WI | NZ | I | P | SL |
|---|---|---|---|---|---|---|---|---|---|---|
| K.D. Walters (250), G.J. Gilmour (101) | Christchurch | 1976–77 | – | – | – | 217 | – | – | – |
| G.N. Yallop (268), G.R.J. Matthews (75) | Melbourne | 1983–84 | – | – | – | – | – | 185 | – |
| R.W. Marsh (132), K.J. O'Keeffe (85) | Adelaide | 1973–74 | – | – | – | 168 | – | – | – |
| C. Hill (188), H. Trumble (46) | Melbourne | 1897–98 | 165 | – | – | – | – | – | – |
| R. Benaud (90), G.D. McKenzie (76) | Sydney | 1963–64 | – | 160 | – | – | – | – | – |
| K.R. Miller (145*), I.W. Johnson (77) | Sydney | 1950–51 | 150 | – | – | – | – | – | – |
| J. Ryder (201*), T.J.E. Andrews (72) | Adelaide | 1924–25 | 134 | – | – | – | – | – | – |
| A.K. Davidson (80), R. Benaud (52) | Brisbane[2] | 1960–61 | – | – | 134 | – | – | – | – |
| A.R. Border (153), G.R. Beard (49) | Lahore[2] | 1979–80 | – | – | – | – | – | 134 | – |
| K.R. Stackpole (134), G.D. Watson (50) | Cape Town | 1966–67 | – | 128 | – | – | – | – | – |
| R.W. Marsh (118), K.J. O'Keeffe (40) | Adelaide | 1972–73 | – | – | – | – | – | 120 | – |
| K.D. Mackay (31), R. Benaud (97) | Lord's | 1956 | 117 | – | – | – | – | – | – |
| K.D. Mackay (57), A.K. Davidson (71) | Sydney | 1958–59 | 115 | – | – | – | – | – | – |
| R. Benaud (64), A.T.W. Grout (74) | Melbourne | 1958–59 | 115 | – | – | – | – | – | – |
| H.L. Collins (61), J.M. Gregory (73) | Oval | 1926 | 107 | – | – | – | – | – | – |
| B.C. Booth (112), K.D. Mackay (86*) | Brisbane[2] | 1962–63 | 103 | – | – | – | – | – | – |
| G.S. Chappell (150*), G.F. Lawson (49) | Brisbane[2] | 1983–84 | – | – | – | – | – | 103 | – |
| K.C. Wessels (162), B. Yardley (53) | Brisbane[2] | 1982–83 | 100 | – | – | – | – | – | – |
| | Totals: (18) | | 9 | 2 | 1 | 2 | – | 4 | – |

| AUSTRALIA – 8th Wicket | | | E | SA | WI | NZ | I | P | SL |
|---|---|---|---|---|---|---|---|---|---|---|
| R.J. Hartigan (116), C. Hill (160) | Adelaide | 1907–08 | 243 | – | – | – | – | – | – |
| C.E. Pellew (116), J.M. Gregory (100) | Melbourne | 1920–21 | 173 | – | – | – | – | – | – |
| G.J. Bonnor (128), S.P. Jones (40) | Sydney | 1884–85 | 154 | – | – | – | – | – | – |
| D. Tallon (92), R.R. Lindwall (100) | Melbourne | 1946–47 | 154 | – | – | – | – | – | – |
| R. Benaud (128), I.W. Johnson (27*) | Kingston | 1954–55 | – | – | 137 | – | – | – | – |
| G.J. Cosier (168), K.J. O'Keeffe (28*) | Melbourne | 1976–77 | – | – | – | – | – | 117 | – |
| C. Kelleway (73), W.A.S. Oldfield (65*) | Sydney | 1924–25 | 116 | – | – | – | – | – | – |
| H. Graham (105), A.E. Trott (85*) | Sydney | 1894–95 | 112 | – | – | – | – | – | – |
| W.W. Armstrong (133*), H. Carter (66) | Melbourne | 1907–08 | 112 | – | – | – | – | – | – |
| A.R. Border (150*), R.J. Bright (26*) | Lahore[2] | 1979–80 | – | – | – | – | – | 109* | – |
| A.L. Hassett (137), R.R. Lindwall (42) | Nottingham | 1948 | 107 | – | – | – | – | – | – |
| P.J.P. Burge (160), N.J.N. Hawke (37) | Leeds | 1964 | 105 | – | – | – | – | – | – |
| | Totals: (12) | | 9 | – | 1 | – | – | 2 | – |

| AUSTRALIA – 9th Wicket | | | E | SA | WI | NZ | I | P | SL |
|---|---|---|---|---|---|---|---|---|---|---|
| S.E. Gregory (201), J.M. Blackham (74) | Sydney | 1894–95 | 154 | – | – | – | – | – | – |
| J. Ryder (201*), W.A.S. Oldfield (47) | Adelaide | 1924–25 | 108 | – | – | – | – | – | – |
| R.W. Marsh (91), J.W. Gleeson (30) | Manchester | 1972 | 104 | – | – | – | – | – | – |
| A.E.V. Hartkopf (80), W.A.S. Oldfield (39*) | Melbourne | 1924–25 | 100 | – | – | – | – | – | – |
| M.H.N. Walker (78*), M.F. Malone (46) | Oval | 1977 | 100 | – | – | – | – | – | – |
| | Totals: (5) | | 5 | – | – | – | – | – | – |

| AUSTRALIA – 10th Wicket | | | E | SA | WI | NZ | I | P | SL |
|---|---|---|---|---|---|---|---|---|---|
| J.M. Taylor (108), A.A. Mailey (46*) | Sydney | 1924–25 | 127 | – | – | – | – | – | – |
| R.A. Duff (104), W.W. Armstrong (45*) | Melbourne | 1901–02 | 120 | – | – | – | – | – | – |
| | *Totals: (2)* | | 2 | – | – | – | – | – | – |

| SOUTH AFRICA – (134) – 1st Wicket | | | E | A | NZ |
|---|---|---|---|---|---|
| B. Mitchell (123), I.J. Siedle (141) | Cape Town | 1930–31 | 260 | – | – |
| J.A.J. Christy (103), B. Mitchell (113) | Christchurch | 1931–32 | – | – | 196 |
| B. Mitchell (89), P.G.V. van der Bijl (97) | Durban[2] | 1938–39 | 191 | – | – |
| D.J. McGlew (133), T.L. Goddard (74) | Leeds | 1955 | 176 | – | – |
| D.J. McGlew (108), T.L. Goddard (90) | Johannesburg[3] | 1957–58 | – | 176 | – |
| B. Mitchell (61*), R.H. Catterall (98) | Birmingham | 1929 | 171 | – | – |
| B.A. Richards (81), E.J. Barlow (73) | Port Elizabeth | 1969–70 | – | 157 | – |
| H.W. Taylor (70), J.W. Zulch (82) | Johannesburg[1] | 1913–14 | 153 | – | – |
| D.J. McGlew (104*), T.L. Goddard (62) | Manchester | 1955 | 147 | – | – |
| D.J. McGlew (120), E.J. Barlow (67) | Johannesburg[3] | 1961–62 | – | – | 134 |
| T.L. Goddard (60), E.J. Barlow (96) | Johannesburg[3] | 1964–65 | 134 | – | – |
| A. Melville (78), P.G.V. van der Bijl (125) | Durban[2] | 1938–39 | 131 | – | – |
| H.W. Taylor (87), J.W. Zulch (60) | Port Elizabeth | 1913–14 | 129 | – | – |
| B. Mitchell (73), I.J. Siedle (57) | Durban[2] | 1930–31 | 127 | – | – |
| B. Mitchell (88), R.H. Catterall (67) | Birmingham | 1929 | 119 | – | – |
| T.L. Goddard (40), E.J. Barlow (92) | Wellington | 1963–64 | – | – | 117 |
| T.L. Goddard (63), E.J. Barlow (49) | Dunedin | 1963–64 | – | – | 117 |
| B. Mitchell (128), I.J. Siedle (35) | Oval | 1935 | 116 | – | – |
| H.W. Taylor (71), J.M.M. Commaille (47) | Cape Town | 1927–28 | 115 | – | – |
| T.L. Goddard (73), E.J. Barlow (61) | Auckland | 1963–64 | – | – | 115 |
| T.L. Goddard (61), E.J. Barlow (69) | Port Elizabeth | 1964–65 | 114 | – | – |
| D.J. McGlew (84), J.H.B. Waite (43) | Durban[2] | 1953–54 | – | – | 113 |
| T.L. Goddard (74), E.J. Barlow (46) | Port Elizabeth | 1966–67 | – | 112 | – |
| H.W. Taylor (91), R.H. Catterall (52) | Durban[2] | 1922–23 | 110 | – | – |
| A. Melville (67), P.G.V. van der Bijl (31) | Johannesburg[1] | 1938–39 | 108 | – | – |
| B. Mitchell (53), J.A.J. Christy (53) | Wellington | 1931–32 | – | – | 104 |
| D.J. McGlew (61), R.J. Westcott (43) | Johannesburg[2] | 1953–54 | – | – | 104 |
| B. Mitchell (56), E.A.B. Rowan (37) | Port Elizabeth | 1948–49 | 101 | – | – |
| | *Totals: (28)* | | 17 | 3 | 8 |

| SOUTH AFRICA – 2nd Wicket | | | E | A | NZ |
|---|---|---|---|---|---|
| E.A.B. Brown (236), C.B. van Ryneveld (83) | Leeds | 1951 | 198 | – | – |
| L.J. Tancred (97), C.B. Llewellyn (90) | Johannesburg[1] | 1902–03 | – | 173 | – |
| E.J. Barlow (138), A.J. Pithey (154) | Cape Town | 1964–65 | 172 | – | – |
| R.H. Catterall (76), H.W. Taylor (68) | Cape Town | 1922–23 | 155 | – | – |
| P.G.V. van der Bijl (87), E.A.B. Rowan (89*) | Cape Town | 1938–39 | 147 | – | – |
| A. Melville (104*), K.G. Viljoen (51*) | Nottingham | 1947 | 145* | – | – |
| P.W. Sherwell (115), C.M.H. Hathorn (30) | Lord's | 1907 | 139 | – | – |
| J.W. Zulch (105), G.A. Faulkner (56) | Adelaide | 1910–11 | – | 135 | – |
| B.A. Richards (126), A. Bacher (73) | Port Elizabeth | 1969–70 | – | 126 | – |
| T.L. Goddard (93), A.J. Pithey (49) | Sydney | 1963–64 | – | 124 | – |
| B. Mitchell (109), E.A.B. Rowan (67) | Durban[2] | 1938–39 | 119 | – | – |
| T.L. Goddard (112), A.J. Pithey (39) | Johannesburg[3] | 1964–65 | 115 | – | – |
| E.A.B. Rowan (86*), K.G. Viljoen (53) | Johannesburg[2] | 1948–49 | 113 | – | – |
| T.L. Goddard (67), J.H.B. Waite (61) | Johannesburg[3] | 1956–57 | 112 | – | – |
| J.H.B. Waite (62), W.R. Endean (162*) | Melbourne | 1952–53 | – | 111 | – |
| L.J. Tancred (73), G.C. White (147) | Johannesburg[1] | 1905–06 | 110 | – | – |
| J.W. Zulch (42), G.A. Faulkner (204) | Melbourne | 1910–11 | – | 107 | – |
| B. Mitchell (164*), E.A.B. Rowan (44) | Lord's | 1935 | 104 | – | – |
| B. Mitchell (46), J.A.J. Christy (63) | Melbourne | 1931–32 | – | 102 | – |
| | *Totals: (19)* | | 12 | 7 | – |

| SOUTH AFRICA – 3rd Wicket | | | E | A | NZ |
|---|---|---|---|---|---|
| E.J. Barlow (201), R.G. Pollock (175) | Adelaide | 1963–64 | – | 341 | – |
| A. Melville (189), A.D. Nourse (149) | Nottingham | 1947 | 319 | – | – |
| D.J. McGlew (105), J.H.B. Waite (134) | Durban[2] | 1957–58 | – | 231 | – |
| B. Mitchell (120), A.D. Nourse (112) | Cape Town | 1948–49 | 190 | – | – |
| B. Mitchell (189*), A.D. Nourse (97) | Oval | 1947 | 184 | – | – |
| E.A.B. Rowan (143), A.D. Nourse (66) | Durban[2] | 1949–50 | – | 167 | – |

**3rd Wicket** *continued*

| | | | E | A | NZ |
|---|---|---|---|---|---|
| E.A.B. Rowan (156*), A.D. Nourse (56*) | Johannesburg[2] | 1948–49 | 162* | – | – |
| J.W. Zulch (150), G.A. Faulkner (92) | Sydney | 1910–11 | – | 143 | – |
| E.J. Barlow (110), R.G. Pollock (87) | Johannesburg[3] | 1969–70 | – | 139 | – |
| H.W. Taylor (101), A.W. Nourse (63) | Johannesburg[1] | 1922–23 | 134 | – | – |
| A. Bacher (60*), R.G. Pollock (67*) | Durban[2] | 1966–67 | – | 127* | – |
| B. Mitchell (72), R.H. Catterall (54) | Johannesburg[1] | 1930–31 | 122 | – | – |
| B. Mitchell (95), H.W. Taylor (84) | Adelaide | 1931–32 | – | 121 | – |
| G.C. White (147), A.W. Nourse (55) | Johannesburg[1] | 1905–06 | 120 | – | – |
| B. Mitchell (75), H.W. Taylor (78) | Adelaide | 1931–32 | – | 120 | – |
| A. Melville (117), A.D. Nourse (61) | Lord's | 1947 | 118 | – | – |
| B. Mitchell (73), A.D. Nourse (73) | Johannesburg[1] | 1938–39 | 116 | – | – |
| E.A.B. Rowan (85), B. Mitchell (63) | Johannesburg[1] | 1938–39 | 116 | – | – |
| D.J. McGlew (120), R.A. McLean (78) | Johannesburg[3] | 1961–62 | – | – | 112 |
| G.A. Faulkner (204), A.W. Nourse (33) | Melbourne | 1910–11 | – | 110 | – |
| C.N. Frank (152), H.W. Taylor (80) | Johannesburg[1] | 1921–22 | – | 105 | – |
| D.J. McGlew (127), R.A. McLean (63) | Durban[2] | 1961–62 | – | – | 103 |
| B.A. Richards (140), R.G. Pollock (274) | Durban[2] | 1969–70 | – | 103 | – |
| B. Mitchell (99), A.D. Nourse (73) | Port Elizabeth | 1948–49 | 101 | – | – |
| G.A. Faulkner (78), A.W. Nourse (53) | Johannesburg[1] | 1909–10 | 100 | – | – |
| H.W. Taylor (91), A.W. Nourse (52) | Durban[2] | 1922–23 | 100 | – | – |
| | | *Totals: (26)* | *13* | *11* | *2* |

**SOUTH AFRICA – 4th Wicket**

| | | | E | A | NZ |
|---|---|---|---|---|---|
| H.W. Taylor (121), H.G. Deane (93) | Oval | 1929 | 214 | – | – |
| C.N. Frank (152), A.W. Nourse (111) | Johannesburg[1] | 1921–22 | – | 206 | – |
| B. Mitchell (99), W.W. Wade (125) | Port Elizabeth | 1948–49 | 150 | – | – |
| H.W. Taylor (117), R.H. Catterall (56) | Cape Town | 1930–31 | 148 | – | – |
| G.C. White (118), A.W. Nourse (69) | Durban[1] | 1909–10 | 143 | – | – |
| K.J. Funston (39), R.A. McLean (101) | Durban[2] | 1953–54 | – | – | 135 |
| B. Mitchell (45), A.D. Nourse (231) | Johannesburg[1] | 1935–36 | – | 129 | – |
| A.J. Pithey (76), J.H.B. Waite (77) | Melbourne | 1963–64 | – | 128 | – |
| A.D. Nourse (115), K.G. Viljoen (32) | Manchester | 1947 | 121 | – | – |
| S.J. Snooke (47), G.A. Faulkner (99) | Cape Town | 1909–10 | 120 | – | – |
| E.A.B. Rowan (49), A.D. Nourse (91) | Durban[2] | 1935–36 | – | 118 | – |
| A.J. Pithey (154), K.C. Bland (78) | Cape Town | 1964–65 | 117 | – | – |
| T.L. Goddard (99), J.H.B. Waite (77) | Oval | 1960 | 115 | – | – |
| G.C. White (72), G.A. Faulkner (76) | Johannesburg[1] | 1909–10 | 114 | – | – |
| M.J. Susskind (64), R.H. Catterall (120) | Lord's | 1924 | 112 | – | – |
| H.W. Taylor (176), W.V.S. Ling (38) | Johannesburg[1] | 1922–23 | 111 | – | – |
| J.H.B. Waite (44), K.J. Funston (92) | Adelaide | 1952–53 | – | 108 | – |
| J.F.W. Nicolson (78), R.H. Catterall (76) | Durban[2] | 1927–28 | 107 | – | – |
| W.R. Endean (87), J.C. Watkins (45) | Port Elizabeth | 1953–54 | – | – | 107 |
| A.D. Nourse (129*), W.W. Wade (54) | Johannesburg[2] | 1948–49 | 106 | – | – |
| J.H.B. Waite (115), W.R. Endean (50) | Johannesburg[3] | 1957–58 | – | 104 | – |
| D.J. McGlew (63), R.A. McLean (113) | Cape Town | 1961–62 | – | – | 101 |
| | | *Totals: (22)* | *13* | *6* | *3* |

**SOUTH AFRICA – 5th Wicket**

| | | | E | A | NZ |
|---|---|---|---|---|---|
| A.J. Pithey (95), J.H.B. Waite (64) | Johannesburg[3] | 1964–65 | 157 | – | – |
| R.H. Catterall (119), H.B. Cameron (53) | Durban[2] | 1927–28 | 135 | – | – |
| W.R. Endean (116), J.E. Cheetham (54) | Auckland | 1952–53 | – | – | 130 |
| J.H.B. Waite (59), W.R. Endean (77) | Johannesburg[3] | 1957–58 | – | 129 | – |
| A.D. Nourse (208), G.M. Fullerton (54) | Nottingham | 1951 | 121 | – | – |
| H.R. Lance (53), D.T. Lindsay (81) | Cape Town | 1966–67 | – | 119 | – |
| R.H. Catterall (120), J.M. Blanckenberg (56) | Birmingham | 1924 | 114 | – | – |
| G.A. Faulkner (115), C.B. Llewellyn (80) | Adelaide | 1910–11 | – | 109 | – |
| E.A.B. Rowan (236), R.A. McLean (67) | Leeds | 1951 | 108 | – | – |
| H.J. Keith (40*), R.A. McLean (76*) | Melbourne | 1952–53 | – | 106* | – |
| K.G. Viljoen (74), A. Melville (103) | Durban[2] | 1938–39 | 104 | – | – |
| | | *Totals: (11)* | *6* | *4* | *1* |

**SOUTH AFRICA – 6th Wicket**

| | | | E | A | NZ |
|---|---|---|---|---|---|
| R.G. Pollock (274), H.R. Lance (61) | Durban[2] | 1969–70 | – | 200 | – |
| J.H.B. Waite (113), P.L. Winslow (108) | Manchester | 1955 | 171 | – | – |
| K.C. Bland (144*), G.D. Varnals (23) | Johannesburg[3] | 1964–65 | 124 | – | – |

| **6th Wicket** *continued* | | | E | A | WI | NZ |
|---|---|---|---|---|---|---|
| K.C. Bland (126), D.T. Lindsay (65) | Sydney | 1963–64 | – | 118 | – | |
| R.G. Pollock (137), P.L. van der Merwe (66) | Port Elizabeth | 1964–65 | 113 | – | – | |
| R.G. Pollock (209), P.L. van der Merwe (50) | Cape Town | 1966–67 | – | 112 | – | |
| H.R. Lance (44), D.T. Lindsay (69) | Johannesburg³ | 1966–67 | – | 110 | – | |
| R.A. McLean (142), H.J. Keith (57) | Lord's | 1955 | 109 | – | – | |
| A.D. Nourse (231), F. Nicholson (29) | Johannesburg¹ | 1935–36 | – | 106 | – | |
| R.A. McLean (109), S. O'Linn (27) | Manchester | 1960 | 102 | – | – | |
| | *Totals: (10)* | | *5* | *5* | *–* | |

| **SOUTH AFRICA – 7th Wicket** | | | E | A | NZ |
|---|---|---|---|---|---|
| D.J. McGlew (255*), A.R.A. Murray (109) | Wellington | 1952–53 | – | – | 246 |
| D.T. Lindsay (182), P.L. van der Merwe (76) | Johannesburg³ | 1966–67 | – | 221 | – |
| H.G. Deane (73), E.P. Nupen (69) | Durban² | 1927–28 | 123 | – | – |
| G.C. White (81), A.W. Nourse (93*) | Johannesburg¹ | 1905–06 | 121 | – | – |
| J.E. Cheetham (66), P.N.F. Mansell (52) | Melbourne | 1952–53 | – | 111 | – |
| S. O'Linn (98), J.H.B. Waite (60) | Nottingham | 1960 | 109 | – | – |
| K.G. Viljoen (50), E.L. Dalton (102) | Johannesburg¹ | 1938–39 | 108 | – | – |
| A.D. Nourse (103), R.E. Grieveson (75) | Durban² | 1938–39 | 107 | – | – |
| X.C. Balaskas (122*), C.L. Vincent (33) | Wellington | 1931–32 | – | – | 105 |
| D.T. Lindsay (137), P.L. van der Merwe (42) | Durban² | 1966–67 | – | 103 | – |
| B. Mitchell (164*), A.B.C. Langton (44) | Lord's | 1935 | 101 | – | – |
| | *Totals: (11)* | | *6* | *3* | *2* |

| **SOUTH AFRICA – 8th Wicket** | | | E | A | NZ |
|---|---|---|---|---|---|
| A.W. Nourse (72), E.A. Halliwell (57) | Johannesburg¹ | 1902–03 | – | 124 | – |
| B. Mitchell (189*), L. Tuckett (40*) | Oval | 1947 | 109* | – | – |
| K.G. Viljoen (111), Q. McMillan (29) | Melbourne | 1931–32 | – | 104 | – |
| H.J. Tayfield (75), N.B.F. Mann (46) | Cape Town | 1949–50 | – | 102 | – |
| G.A. Faulkner (62), R.O. Schwarz (61) | Sydney | 1910–11 | – | 100 | – |
| | *Totals: (5)* | | *1* | *4* | *–* |

| **SOUTH AFRICA – 9th Wicket** | | | E | A | NZ |
|---|---|---|---|---|---|
| E.L. Dalton (117), A.B.C. Langton (73*) | Oval | 1935 | 137 | – | – |

| **SOUTH AFRICA – 10th Wicket** | | | E | A | NZ |
|---|---|---|---|---|---|
| H.G. Owen-Smith (129), A.J. Bell (26*) | Leeds | 1929 | 103 | – | – |

| **WEST INDIES – (277) – 1st Wicket** | | | E | A | NZ | I | P |
|---|---|---|---|---|---|---|---|
| C.G. Greenidge (154*), D.L. Haynes (136) | St John's | 1982–83 | – | – | – | 296 | – |
| C.G. Greenidge (120*), D.L. Haynes (103*) | Georgetown | 1983–84 | – | 250* | – | – | – |
| J.B. Stollmeyer (160), A.F. Rae (109) | Madras¹ | 1948–49 | – | – | – | 239 | – |
| C.G. Greenidge (97), D.L. Haynes (122) | Christchurch | 1979–80 | – | – | 225 | – | – |
| R.C. Fredericks (94), L.G. Rowe (120) | Kingston | 1973–74 | 206 | – | – | – | – |
| J.B. Stollmeyer (152), A.F. Rae (99) | Auckland | 1951–52 | – | – | 197 | – | – |
| R.C. Fredericks (109), C.G. Greenidge (115) | Leeds | 1976 | 192 | – | – | – | – |
| R.C. Fredericks (86*), C.G. Greenidge (85*) | Oval | 1976 | 182* | – | – | – | – |
| R.C. Fredericks (83), C.G. Greenidge (82) | Kingston | 1976–77 | – | – | – | – | 182 |
| G.M. Carew (107), A.G. Ganteaume (112) | Port-of-Spain | 1947–48 | 173 | – | – | – | – |
| C.G. Greenidge (84), D.L. Haynes (96) | Port-of-Spain | 1980–81 | 168 | – | – | – | – |
| C.G. Greenidge (127), D.L. Haynes (60) | Kingston | 1983–84 | – | 162 | – | – | – |
| C.C. Hunte (92), J.K. Holt (123) | Delhi | 1958–59 | – | – | – | 159 | – |
| R.C. Fredericks (52*), C.G. Greenidge (96) | Georgetown | 1976–77 | – | – | – | – | 154 |
| C.C. Hunte (81), B.A. Davis (68) | Bridgetown | 1964–65 | – | 145 | – | – | – |
| C.A. Roach (209), E.A.C. Hunte (53) | Georgetown | 1929–30 | 144 | – | – | – | – |
| J.B. Stollmeyer (76*), A.F. Rae (63*) | Port-of-Spain | 1952–53 | – | – | – | 142* | – |
| C.G. Greenidge (93), A.I. Kallicharran (124) | Bangalore | 1974–75 | – | – | – | 139† | – |
| J.B. Stollmeyer (66), A.F. Rae (104) | Bombay² | 1948–49 | – | – | – | 134 | – |
| C.G. Greenidge (64), D.L. Haynes (145) | Bridgetown | 1983–84 | – | 132 | – | – | – |
| C.G. Greenidge (80*), D.L. Haynes (55) | Bridgetown | 1977–78 | – | 131 | – | – | – |
| R.C. Fredericks (32), L.G. Rowe (302) | Bridgetown | 1973–74 | 126 | – | – | – | – |
| C.C. Hunte (114), R.B. Kanhai (62) | Georgetown | 1957–58 | – | – | – | – | 125 |
| C.C. Hunte (142), R.B. Kanhai (27) | Bridgetown | 1957–58 | – | – | – | – | 122 |
| G.S. Camacho (87), M.C. Carew (36) | Port-of-Spain | 1967–68 | 119 | – | – | – | – |

**1st Wicket** *continued*

| | | | E | A | NZ | I | P |
|---|---|---|---|---|---|---|---|
| C.C. Hunte (89), B.A. Davis (54) | Port-of-Spain | 1964–65 | – | 116 | – | – | – |
| R.C. Fredericks (50), C.G. Greenidge (101) | Manchester | 1976 | 116 | – | – | – | – |
| C.G. Greenidge (62), D.L. Haynes (84) | Kingston | 1980–81 | 116 | – | – | – | – |
| R.C. Fredericks (67), L.G. Rowe (123) | Port-of-Spain | 1973–74 | 110 | – | – | – | – |
| R.C. Fredericks (63), G.S. Camacho (67) | Lord's | 1969 | 106 | – | – | – | – |
| C.G. Greenidge (49), D.L. Haynes (43) | Leeds | 1984 | 106 | – | – | – | – |
| R.C. Fredericks (82), L.G. Rowe (47) | Kingston | 1975–76 | – | – | – | 105 | – |
| J.B. Stollmeyer (52*), A.F. Rae (46*) | Nottingham | 1950 | 103* | – | – | – | – |
| S.M. Nurse (73), G.S. Camacho (25) | Kingston | 1967–68 | 102 | – | – | – | – |
| R.C. Fredericks (39), M.C. Carew (64) | Sydney | 1968–69 | – | 100 | – | – | – |
| *Totals: (35)* | | | 15 | 7 | 2 | 7 | 4 |

† *177 runs were added for this wicket, R.C. Fredericks retired hurt and was succeeded by A.I. Kallicharran after 38 had been scored.*

**WEST INDIES – 2nd Wicket**

| | | | E | A | NZ | I | P |
|---|---|---|---|---|---|---|---|
| C.C. Hunte (260), G.St A. Sobers (365*) | Kingston | 1957–58 | – | – | – | – | 446 |
| C.G. Greenidge (214*), H.A. Gomes (92*) | Lord's | 1984 | 287* | – | – | – | – |
| G.St A. Sobers (125), C.L. Walcott (145) | Georgetown | 1957–58 | – | – | – | – | 269 |
| R.C. Fredericks (163), L.G. Rowe (214) | Kingston | 1971–72 | – | – | 269 | – | – |
| E.D.A.St J. McMorris (125), R.B. Kanhai (158) | Kingston | 1961–62 | – | – | – | 255 | – |
| L.G. Rowe (302), A.I. Kallicharran (119) | Bridgetown | 1973–74 | 249 | – | – | – | – |
| M.C. Carew (91), S.M. Nurse (258) | Christchurch | 1968–69 | – | – | 231 | – | – |
| R.K. Nunes (92), G.A. Headley (223) | Kingston | 1929–30 | 227 | – | – | – | – |
| D.L. Haynes (184), I.V.A. Richards (145) | Lord's | 1980 | 223 | – | – | – | – |
| J.K. Holt (166), F.M.M. Worrell (76*) | Bridgetown | 1953–54 | 222 | – | – | – | – |
| I. Barrow (105), G.A. Headley (169) | Manchester | 1933 | 200 | – | – | – | – |
| C.A. Roach (209), G.A. Headley (114) | Georgetown | 1929–30 | 192 | – | – | – | – |
| D.L. Haynes (90), R.B. Richardson (185) | Georgetown | 1984–85 | – | – | 191 | – | – |
| A.F. Rae (109), F.M.M. Worrell (138) | Oval | 1950 | 172 | – | – | – | – |
| M.C. Carew (109), S.M. Nurse (95) | Auckland | 1968–69 | – | – | 172 | – | – |
| D.M. Lewis (88), R.B. Kanhai (85) | Bridgetown | 1970–71 | – | – | – | 166 | – |
| M.C. Carew (83), R.B. Kanhai (94) | Brisbane[2] | 1968–69 | – | 165 | – | – | – |
| C.C. Hunte (79), R.B. Kanhai (115) | Adelaide | 1960–61 | – | 163 | – | – | – |
| C.A. Roach (77), G.A. Headley (176) | Bridgetown | 1929–30 | 156 | – | – | – | – |
| R.C. Fredericks (71), I.V.A. Richards (291) | Oval | 1976 | 154 | – | – | – | – |
| F.R. Martin (123), G.A. Headley (105) | Sydney | 1930–31 | – | 152 | – | – | – |
| C.C. Hunte (182), R.B. Kanhai (90) | Manchester | 1963 | 151 | – | – | – | – |
| D.L. Haynes (145), R.B. Richardson (131*) | Bridgetown | 1983–84 | – | 145 | – | – | – |
| C.G. Greenidge (76), I.V.A. Richards (74) | Adelaide | 1979–80 | – | 136 | – | – | – |
| C.C. Hunte (114), G.St A. Sobers (109*) | Georgetown | 1957–58 | – | – | – | – | 135 |
| J.B. Stollmeyer (60), J.K. Holt (94) | Kingston | 1953–54 | 134 | – | – | – | – |
| M.C. Carew (90), R.B. Kanhai (80) | Adelaide | 1968–69 | – | 132 | – | – | – |
| R.C. Fredericks (52), I.V.A. Richards (91) | Bridgetown | 1976–77 | – | – | – | – | 130 |
| D.L. Haynes (92), I.V.A. Richards (80) | Bridgetown | 1982–83 | – | – | 122 | – | – |
| C.G. Greenidge (63), I.V.A. Richards (114) | St John's | 1980–81 | 121 | – | – | – | – |
| E.D.A.St J. McMorris (50), R.B. Kanhai (139) | Port-of-Spain | 1961–62 | – | – | – | 119 | – |
| J.B. Stollmeyer (59), G.A. Headley (106) | Lord's | 1939 | 118 | – | – | – | – |
| D.L. Haynes (40), I.V.A. Richards (75) | Lahore[2] | 1980–81 | – | – | – | – | 117 |
| J.B. Stollmeyer (59), G.A. Headley (65) | Oval | 1939 | 113 | – | – | – | – |
| C.C. Hunte (108*), R.B. Kanhai (77) | Oval | 1963 | 113 | – | – | – | – |
| R.C. Fredericks (138), A.I. Kallicharran (34) | Lord's | 1976 | 113 | – | – | – | – |
| R.C. Fredericks (104), A.I. Kallicharran (98) | Bombay[3] | 1974–75 | – | – | – | 113 | – |
| C.G. Greenidge (48), I.V.A. Richards (96) | Melbourne | 1979–80 | – | 110 | – | – | – |
| C.G. Greenidge (101), I.V.A. Richards (135) | Manchester | 1976 | 108 | – | – | – | – |
| D.L. Haynes (28), I.V.A. Richards (76) | Adelaide | 1979–80 | – | 104 | – | – | – |
| R.C. Fredericks (43), R.B. Kanhai (69) | Sydney | 1968–69 | – | 103 | – | – | – |
| M.C. Carew (45), C.A. Davis (125*) | Georgetown | 1970–71 | – | – | – | 103 | – |
| J.K. Holt (60), O.G. Smith (104) | Kingston | 1954–55 | – | 102 | – | – | – |
| R.C. Fredericks (76), A.I. Kallicharran (91) | Port-of-Spain | 1972–73 | – | 102 | – | – | – |
| C.G. Greenidge (52), I.V.A. Richards (50) | Adelaide | 1981–82 | – | 100 | – | – | – |
| *Totals: (45)* | | | 18 | 12 | 4 | 6 | 5 |

**WEST INDIES – 3rd Wicket**

| | | | E | A | NZ | I | P |
|---|---|---|---|---|---|---|---|
| E. de C. Weekes (206), F.M.M. Worrell (167) | Port-of-Spain | 1953–54 | 338 | – | – | – | – |
| R.B. Richardson (154), I.V.A. Richards (178) | St. John's | 1983–84 | – | 308 | – | – | – |
| I.V.A. Richards (232), A.I. Kallicharran (97) | Nottingham | 1976 | 303 | – | – | – | – |
| S.M. Nurse (136), R.B. Kanhai (153) | Port-of-Spain | 1967–68 | 273 | – | – | – | – |
| C.L. Walcott (126), E. de C. Weekes (139) | Port-of-Spain | 1954–55 | – | 242 | – | – | – |
| I.V.A. Richards (142), A.I. Kallicharran (93) | Bridgetown | 1975–76 | – | – | – | 220 | – |
| H.A. Gomes (143), I.V.A. Richards (117) | Birmingham | 1984 | 206 | – | – | – | – |
| G.A. Headley (270*), J.E.D. Sealy (91) | Kingston | 1934–35 | 202 | – | – | – | – |
| R.B. Kanhai (129), S.M. Nurse (201) | Bridgetown | 1964–65 | – | 200 | – | – | – |
| F.M.M. Worrell (237), E. de C. Weekes (109) | Kingston | 1952–53 | – | – | – | 197 | – |
| I.V.A. Richards (291), L.G. Rowe (70) | Oval | 1976 | 191 | – | – | – | – |
| C.G. Greenidge (100), R.B. Richardson (78) | Port-of-Spain | 1984–85 | – | 185 | – | – | – |
| S.M. Nurse (168), B.F. Butcher (78*) | Auckland | 1968–69 | – | – | 174 | – | – |
| R.B. Kanhai (217), G.St A. Sobers (72) | Lahore[1] | 1958–59 | – | – | – | – | 162 |
| A.F. Rae (62), F.M.M. Worrell (261) | Nottingham | 1950 | 143 | – | – | – | – |
| G.A. Headley (176), F.I. de Caires (70) | Bridgetown | 1929–30 | 142 | – | – | – | – |
| R.B. Kanhai (157), C.H. Lloyd (63) | Lord's | 1973 | 138 | – | – | – | – |
| R.B. Kanhai (89), B.F. Butcher (49) | Georgetown | 1964–65 | – | 135 | – | – | – |
| E.D.A.St J. McMorris (73), G.St A. Sobers (147) | Kingston | 1959–60 | 133*† | – | – | – | – |
| I.V.A. Richards (135), C.H. Lloyd (43) | Manchester | 1976 | 132 | – | – | – | – |
| C.G. Greenidge (95), H.A. Gomes (60) | Adelaide | 1984–85 | – | 132 | – | – | – |
| S.F.A.F. Bacchus (250), R.R. Jumadeen (56) | Kanpur | 1978–79 | – | – | – | 129 | – |
| J.B. Stollmeyer (104*), E. de C. Weekes (55*) | Port-of-Spain | 1952–53 | – | – | – | 127* | – |
| C.L. Walcott (110), E. de C. Weekes (87*) | Port-of-Spain | 1954–55 | – | 127 | – | – | – |
| I.V.A. Richards (101), A.I. Kallicharran (67) | Adelaide | 1975–76 | – | 127 | – | – | – |
| R.C. Fredericks (169), A.I. Kallicharran (57) | Perth | 1975–76 | – | 124 | – | – | – |
| S.M. Nurse (70), R.B. Kanhai (84) | Melbourne | 1960–61 | – | 123 | – | – | – |
| R.B. Richardson (51), H.A. Gomes (68) | Melbourne | 1984–85 | – | 123 | – | – | – |
| I.V.A. Richards (98), A.I. Kallicharran (44) | Melbourne | 1975–76 | – | 117 | – | – | – |
| C.C. Hunte (81), B.F. Butcher (71) | Kingston | 1964–65 | – | 116 | – | – | – |
| L.G. Rowe (76), A.I. Kallicharran (50) | Kingston | 1972–73 | – | 116 | – | – | – |
| J.B. Stollmeyer (152), E. de C. Weekes (51) | Auckland | 1951–52 | – | – | 115 | – | – |
| R.B. Kanhai (55), G.St A. Sobers (145) | Georgetown | 1959–60 | 115 | – | – | – | – |
| R.B. Kanhai (158*), C.H. Lloyd (57) | Kingston | 1970–71 | – | – | – | 115 | – |
| D.L. Haynes (78), I.V.A. Richards (78) | Port-of-Spain | 1984–85 | – | – | 114 | – | – |
| A.I. Kallicharran (93), C.H. Lloyd (49) | Kingston | 1973–74 | 112 | – | – | – | – |
| G.A. Headley (105), G.C. Grant (62) | Sydney | 1930–31 | – | 110 | – | – | – |
| J.B. Stollmeyer (85), E. de C. Weekes (56) | Bombay[2] | 1948–49 | – | – | – | 110 | – |
| G.St A. Sobers (147), S.M. Nurse (70) | Kingston | 1959–60 | 110† | – | – | – | – |
| R.B. Kanhai (63), B.F. Butcher (209*) | Nottingham | 1966 | 110 | – | – | – | – |
| F.M.M. Worrell (191*), R.B. Kanhai (42) | Nottingham | 1957 | 109 | – | – | – | – |
| H.A. Gomes (63), A.I. Kallicharran (187) | Bombay[3] | 1978–79 | – | – | – | 109 | – |
| R.B. Kanhai (256), O.G. Smith (34) | Calcutta | 1958–59 | – | – | – | 108 | – |
| G.S. Camacho (71), B.F. Butcher (91) | Leeds | 1969 | 108 | – | – | – | – |
| I.V.A. Richards (114), E.H. Mattis (71) | St John's | 1980–81 | 108 | – | – | – | – |
| R.B. Richardson (185), H.A. Gomes (53) | Georgetown | 1984–85 | – | – | 106 | – | – |
| A.F. Rae (106), E. de C. Weekes (63) | Lord's | 1950 | 105 | – | – | – | – |
| I.V.A. Richards (140), A.I. Kallicharran (38) | Brisbane[2] | 1979–80 | – | 105 | – | – | – |
| J.B. Stollmeyer (78), G.E. Gomez (86) | Bridgetown | 1947–48 | 104 | – | – | – | – |
| A.I. Kallicharran (98), C.H. Lloyd (242*) | Bombay[3] | 1974–75 | – | – | – | 104 | – |
| C.G. Greenidge (69), R.B. Richardson (60) | Georgetown | 1984–85 | – | – | 104 | – | – |
| L.G. Rowe (123), C.H. Lloyd (52) | Port-of-Spain | 1973–74 | 102 | – | – | – | – |
| A.B. Williams (111), A.I. Kallicharran (55) | Calcutta | 1978–79 | – | – | – | 102 | – |
| A.I. Kallicharran (101), C.A. Davis (40) | Port-of-Spain | 1971–72 | – | – | 101 | – | – |
| | *Totals: (54)* | | *21* | *15* | *7* | *10* | *1* |

†*243 runs were added for this wicket, E.D.A.St J. McMorris retired hurt and was succeeded by S.M. Nurse after 133 had been scored.*

**WEST INDIES – 4th Wicket**

| | | | E | A | NZ | I | P |
|---|---|---|---|---|---|---|---|
| G.St A. Sobers (226), F.M.M. Worrell (197*) | Bridgetown | 1959–60 | 399 | – | – | – | – |
| F.M.M. Worrell (261), E. de C. Weekes (129) | Nottingham | 1950 | 283 | – | – | – | – |
| C.L. Walcott (152), G.E. Gomez (101) | Delhi | 1948–49 | – | – | – | 267 | – |
| R.B. Kanhai (150), G.St A. Sobers (152) | Georgetown | 1967–68 | 250 | – | – | – | – |
| H.A. Gomes (123), C.H. Lloyd (143) | Port-of-Spain | 1982–83 | – | – | – | 237 | – |

**4th Wicket** *continued*

| Partnership | Venue | Date | E | A | NZ | I | P |
|---|---|---|---|---|---|---|---|
| R.B. Kanhai (256), B.F. Butcher (103) | Calcutta | 1958–59 | – | – | – | 217 | – |
| F.M.M. Worrell (237), C.L. Walcott (118) | Kingston | 1952–53 | – | – | – | 213 | – |
| C.H. Lloyd (132), A.I. Kallicharran (80) | Oval | 1973 | 208 | – | – | – | – |
| C.G. Greenidge (107), C.H. Lloyd (163) | Bangalore | 1974–75 | – | – | – | 207 | – |
| L.G. Rowe (107), A.I. Kallicharran (101) | Brisbane[2] | 1975–76 | – | 198 | – | – | – |
| G.St A. Sobers (365*), C.L. Walcott (88*) | Kingston | 1957–58 | – | – | – | – | 188* |
| C.H. Lloyd (178), R.B. Kanhai (57) | Georgetown | 1972–73 | – | 187 | – | – | – |
| C.L. Walcott (110), G.St A. Sobers (64) | Kingston | 1954–55 | – | 179 | – | – | – |
| G.St A. Sobers (132), F.M.M. Worrell (65) | Brisbane[2] | 1960–61 | – | 174 | – | – | – |
| I.V.A. Richards (291), C.H. Lloyd (84) | Oval | 1976 | 174 | – | – | – | – |
| R.B. Kanhai (158*), G.St A. Sobers (93) | Kingston | 1970–71 | – | – | – | 173 | – |
| C.A. Davis (125*), G.St A. Sobers (108*) | Georgetown | 1970–71 | – | – | – | 170* | – |
| A.I. Kallicharran (127), C.H. Lloyd (86) | Port-of-Spain | 1977–78 | – | 170 | – | – | – |
| C.A. Davis (79), G.St A. Sobers (178*) | Bridgetown | 1970–71 | – | – | – | 167 | – |
| C.L. Walcott (220), B.H. Pairaudeau (71) | Bridgetown | 1953–54 | 165 | – | – | – | – |
| L. Baichan (105*), C.H. Lloyd (83) | Lahore[2] | 1974–75 | – | – | – | – | 164 |
| E. de C. Weekes (123), O.G. Smith (64) | Dunedin | 1955–56 | – | – | 162 | – | – |
| C.G. Greenidge (91), A.I. Kallicharran (75) | Christchurch | 1979–80 | – | – | 162 | – | – |
| B.F. Butcher (117), G.St A. Sobers (69) | Port-of-Spain | 1964–65 | – | 160 | – | – | – |
| S.M. Nurse (201), C.C. Hunte (75) | Bridgetown | 1964–65 | – | 146 | – | – | – |
| R.B. Kanhai (92), G.St A. Sobers (102) | Leeds | 1963 | 143 | – | – | – | – |
| A.I. Kallicharran (115), C.H. Lloyd (73) | Karachi | 1974–75 | – | – | – | – | 139 |
| E. de C. Weekes (86), C.L. Walcott (125) | Georgetown | 1952–53 | – | – | – | 130 | – |
| F.M.M. Worrell (71), C.L. Walcott (65) | Christchurch | 1951–52 | – | – | 129 | – | – |
| B.F. Butcher (71), O.G. Smith (100) | Delhi | 1958–59 | – | – | – | 127 | – |
| C.L. Walcott (73), F.M.M. Worrell (56) | Georgetown | 1954–55 | – | 125 | – | – | – |
| F.I. de Caires (80), J.E.D. Sealy (58) | Bridgetown | 1929–30 | 124 | – | – | – | – |
| I.V.A. Richards (177), C.H. Lloyd (68) | Port-of-Spain | 1975–76 | – | – | – | 124 | – |
| C.C. Hunte (182), G.St A. Sobers (64) | Manchester | 1963 | 120 | – | – | – | – |
| G.St A. Sobers (142*), O.G. Smith (58) | Bombay[2] | 1958–59 | – | – | – | 119 | – |
| I.V.A. Richards (140), L.G. Rowe (50) | Brisbane[2] | 1979–80 | – | 119 | – | – | – |
| R.B. Kanhai (85), C.H. Lloyd (118) | Port-of-Spain | 1967–68 | 116 | – | – | – | – |
| C.C. Hunte (101), C.H. Lloyd (82) | Bombay[2] | 1966–67 | – | – | – | 110 | – |
| C.L. Walcott (155), F.M.M. Worrell (61) | Kingston | 1954–55 | – | 109 | – | – | – |
| R.B. Kanhai (117), F.M.M. Worrell (71) | Adelaide | 1960–61 | – | 107 | – | – | – |
| B.F. Butcher (209*), S.M. Nurse (53) | Nottingham | 1966 | 107 | – | – | – | – |
| H.A. Gomes (38), C.H. Lloyd (68) | Ahmedabad | 1983–84 | – | – | – | 107 | – |
| I.V.A. Richards (72), C.H. Lloyd (39) | Lord's | 1984 | 103 | – | – | – | – |
| E. de C. Weekes (207), C.L. Walcott (47) | Port-of-Spain | 1952–53 | – | – | – | 101 | – |
| C.W. Smith (55), F.M.M. Worrell (82) | Sydney | 1960–61 | – | 101 | – | – | – |
| B.F. Butcher (60), C.H. Lloyd (113*) | Bridgetown | 1967–68 | 101 | – | – | – | – |
| *Totals: (46)* | | | **13** | **12** | **3** | **15** | **3** |

**WEST INDIES – 5th Wicket**

| Partnership | Venue | Date | E | A | NZ | I | P |
|---|---|---|---|---|---|---|---|
| S.M. Nurse (137), G.St A. Sobers (174) | Leeds | 1966 | 265 | – | – | – | – |
| E. de C. Weekes (207), B.H. Pairaudeau (115) | Port-of-Spain | 1952–53 | – | – | – | 219 | – |
| R.B. Kanhai (84), M.L.C. Foster (125) | Kingston | 1972–73 | – | 210 | – | – | – |
| C.G. Greenidge (223), P.J.L. Dujon (101) | Manchester | 1984 | 197 | – | – | – | – |
| F.M.M. Worrell (100), C.L. Walcott (115) | Auckland | 1951–52 | – | – | 189 | – | – |
| E. de C. Weekes (197), O.G. Smith (78) | Bridgetown | 1957–58 | – | – | – | – | 185 |
| C.A. Davis (105), G.St A. Sobers (132) | Port-of-Spain | 1970–71 | – | – | – | 177 | – |
| B.F. Butcher (209*), G.St A. Sobers (94) | Nottingham | 1966 | 173 | – | – | – | – |
| E. de C. Weekes (194), R.J. Christiani (74) | Bombay[2] | 1948–49 | – | – | – | 170 | – |
| L.G. Rowe (100), C.L. King (100*) | Christchurch | 1979–80 | – | – | 168 | – | – |
| A.I. Kallicharran (187), D.A. Murray (84) | Bombay[3] | 1978–79 | – | – | – | 167 | – |
| C.H. Lloyd (149), D.L. Murray (63) | Perth | 1975–76 | – | 164 | – | – | – |
| V.H. Stollmeyer (96), K.H. Weekes (137) | Oval | 1939 | 163 | – | – | – | – |
| S.F.A.F. Bacchus (250), D.A. Murray (44) | Kanpur | 1978–79 | – | – | – | 160 | – |
| C.H. Lloyd (100), H.A. Gomes (58) | Bridgetown | 1980–81 | 154 | – | – | – | – |
| G.St A. Sobers (142*), B.F. Butcher (64*) | Bombay[2] | 1958–59 | – | – | – | 134* | – |
| S.M. Nurse (74), G.St A. Sobers (67) | Melbourne | 1968–69 | – | 134 | – | – | – |
| A.L. Logie (130), C.H. Lloyd (50) | Bridgetown | 1982–83 | – | – | – | 133 | – |
| G.St A. Sobers (168), S.M. Nurse (43) | Sydney | 1960–61 | – | 128 | – | – | – |
| H.A. Gomes (143), C.H. Lloyd (71) | Birmingham | 1984 | 124 | – | – | – | – |
| R.B. Kanhai (104), G.St A. Sobers (81) | Oval | 1966 | 122 | – | – | – | – |
| I.V.A. Richards (130), D.L. Murray (46) | Port-of-Spain | 1975–76 | – | – | – | 122 | – |

**5th Wicket** *continued*

| | | | E | A | NZ | I | P |
|---|---|---|---|---|---|---|---|
| G.St A. Sobers (145), F.M.M. Worrell (38) | Georgetown | 1959–60 | 121 | – | – | – | – |
| E. de C. Weekes (156), D.St E. Atkinson (60) | Wellington | 1955–56 | – | – | 120 | – | – |
| I.V.A. Richards (192*), C.H. Lloyd (71) | Delhi | 1974–75 | – | – | – | 120 | – |
| C.H. Lloyd (95), H.A. Gomes (90*) | Kingston | 1980–81 | 118 | – | – | – | – |
| E. de C. Weekes (141), K.R. Rickards (67) | Kingston | 1947–48 | 116 | – | – | – | – |
| G.St A. Sobers (198), B.F. Butcher (60) | Kanpur | 1958–59 | – | – | – | 114 | – |
| L.G. Rowe (40), C.H. Lloyd (121) | Adelaide | 1979–80 | – | 113 | – | – | – |
| C.G. Greenidge (134), C.L. King (32) | Manchester | 1976 | 111 | – | – | – | – |
| R.B. Kanhai (90), S.M. Nurse (56) | Calcutta | 1966–67 | – | – | – | 105 | – |
| C.H. Lloyd (78*), G.St A. Sobers (53*) | Bombay² | 1966–67 | – | – | – | 102* | – |
| H.A. Gomes (124*), C.H. Lloyd (53) | Adelaide | 1981–82 | – | 102 | – | – | – |
| C.L. Walcott (51*), D.St E. Atkinson (53*) | Port-of-Spain | 1953–54 | 101* | – | – | – | – |
| F.C.M. Alexander (57), G.St A. Sobers (80) | Port-of-Spain | 1957–58 | – | – | – | – | 101 |
| G.St A. Sobers (66), E. de C. Weekes (90) | Lord's | 1957 | 100 | – | – | – | – |
| I.V.A. Richards (76), A.L. Logie (97) | Port-of-Spain | 1983–84 | – | 100 | – | – | – |
| *Totals: (37)* | | | *13* | *7* | *3* | *12* | *2* |

**WEST INDIES – 6th Wicket**

| | | | E | A | NZ | I | P |
|---|---|---|---|---|---|---|---|
| G.St A. Sobers (163*), D.A.J. Holford (105*) | Lord's | 1966 | 274* | – | – | – | – |
| C.A. Davis (183), G.St A. Sobers (142) | Bridgetown | 1971–72 | – | – | 254 | – | – |
| C.H. Lloyd (242*), D.L. Murray (91) | Bombay³ | 1974–75 | – | – | – | 250 | – |
| C.L. Walcott (168*), G.E. Gomez (70) | Lord's | 1950 | 211 | – | – | – | – |
| P.J.L. Dujon (110), C.H. Lloyd (106) | St John's | 1982–83 | – | – | – | 207 | – |
| F.M.M. Worrell (161), O.G. Smith (81) | Birmingham | 1957 | 190 | – | – | – | – |
| C.G. Greenidge (223), W.W. Davis (77) | Manchester | 1984 | 170 | – | – | – | – |
| R.B. Kanhai (105), D.L. Murray (90) | Bridgetown | 1972–73 | – | 165 | – | – | – |
| G.St A. Sobers (198), J.S. Solomon (86) | Kanpur | 1958–59 | – | – | – | 163 | – |
| G.St A. Sobers (106*), J.S. Solomon (69*) | Calcutta | 1958–59 | – | – | – | 160* | – |
| A.L. Logie (97), P.J.L. Dujon (130) | Port-of-Spain | 1983–84 | – | 158 | – | – | – |
| I.V.A. Richards (182*), C.H. Lloyd (66) | Bridgetown | 1980–81 | 153 | – | – | – | – |
| C.G. Greenidge (194), P.J.L. Dujon (81) | Kanpur | 1983–84 | – | – | – | 152 | – |
| R.B. Richardson (138), C.H. Lloyd (114) | Brisbane² | 1984–85 | – | 152 | – | – | – |
| C.H. Lloyd (157), D.L. Murray (52) | Bridgetown | 1976–77 | – | – | – | – | 151 |
| C.H. Lloyd (78), P.J.L. Dujon (77) | Adelaide | 1984–85 | – | 150 | – | – | – |
| C.L. Walcott (108), O.G. Smith (44) | Kingston | 1954–55 | – | 138 | – | – | – |
| C.H. Lloyd (103), A.L. Logie (63) | Delhi | 1983–84 | – | – | – | 131 | – |
| R.B. Richardson (131*), C.H. Lloyd (76) | Bridgetown | 1983–84 | – | 131 | – | – | – |
| G.St A. Sobers (161), D.A.J. Holford (32) | Manchester | 1966 | 127 | – | – | – | – |
| I.T. Shillingford (120), D.L. Murray (42) | Georgetown | 1976–77 | – | – | – | – | 123 |
| P.J.L. Dujon (84), C.H. Lloyd (67) | Bombay³ | 1983–84 | – | – | – | 119 | – |
| G.St A. Sobers (113), S.M. Nurse (137) | Sydney | 1968–69 | – | 118 | – | – | – |
| G.C. Grant (53*), E.L. Bartlett (84) | Adelaide | 1930–31 | – | 114 | – | – | – |
| R.C. Fredericks (150), D.L. Murray (25) | Birmingham | 1973 | 114 | – | – | – | – |
| F.M.M. Worrell (53), F.C.M. Alexander (87*) | Adelaide | 1960–61 | – | 113 | – | – | – |
| G.St A. Sobers (57), B.D. Julien (66) | Kingston | 1973–74 | 112 | – | – | – | – |
| G.St A. Sobers (153), F.M.M. Worrell (58) | Kingston | 1961–62 | – | – | – | 110 | – |
| B.F. Butcher (133), F.M.M. Worrell (33) | Lord's | 1963 | 110 | – | – | – | – |
| G. St A. Sobers (113*), D.A.J. Holford (35) | Kingston | 1967–68 | 110 | – | – | – | – |
| G.E. Gomez (74), J.D.C. Goddard (58*) | Oval | 1950 | 109 | – | – | – | – |
| G.St A. Sobers (178*), M.L.C. Foster (36*) | Bridgetown | 1970–71 | – | – | – | 107* | – |
| I.V.A. Richards (177), B.D. Julien (47) | Port-of-Spain | 1975–76 | – | – | – | 107 | – |
| D.L. Haynes (184), C.H. Lloyd (56) | Lord's | 1980 | 107 | – | – | – | – |
| E. de C. Weekes (156), A.P. Binns (27) | Wellington | 1955–56 | – | – | 106 | – | – |
| O.G. Smith (168), D.St E. Atkinson (46) | Nottingham | 1957 | 105 | – | – | – | – |
| A.L. Logie (52), P.J.L. Dujon (60*) | Georgetown | 1984–85 | – | 104 | – | – | – |
| J.D.C. Goddard (44), E. de C. Weekes (128) | Delhi | 1948–49 | – | – | – | 101 | – |
| B.F. Butcher (142), J.S. Solomon (43) | Madras² | 1958–59 | – | – | – | 101 | – |
| R.B. Kanhai (217), J.S. Solomon (56) | Lahore¹ | 1958–59 | – | – | – | – | 100 |
| *Totals: (40)* | | | *13* | *9* | *3* | *12* | *3* |

**WEST INDIES – 7th Wicket**

| | | | E | A | NZ | I | P |
|---|---|---|---|---|---|---|---|
| D.St E. Atkinson (219), C.C. Depeiza (122) | Bridgetown | 1954–55 | – | 347 | – | – | – |
| G.St A. Sobers (150*), B.D. Julien (121) | Lord's | 1973 | 155*† | – | – | – | – |
| O.G. Smith (168), J.D.C. Goddard (61) | Nottingham | 1957 | 154 | – | – | – | – |
| H.A. Gomes (127), P.J.L. Dujon (139) | Perth | 1984–85 | – | 149 | – | – | – |
| G.A. Headley (270*), R.S. Grant (77) | Kingston | 1934–35 | 147 | – | – | – | – |

**7th Wicket** *continued*

| | | | E | A | NZ | I | P |
|---|---|---|---|---|---|---|---|
| D.St E. Atkinson (85), J.D.C. Goddard (83*) | Christchurch | 1955–56 | – | – | 143 | – | – |
| I.V.A. Richards (208), M.D. Marshall (55) | Melbourne | 1984–85 | – | 139 | – | – | – |
| C.G. Greenidge (194), M.D. Marshall (92) | Kanpur | 1983–84 | – | – | – | 130 | – |
| G.St A. Sobers (153), I.L. Mendonça (78) | Kingston | 1961–62 | – | – | – | 127 | – |
| C.H. Lloyd (129), M.C. Carew (71*) | Brisbane[2] | 1968–69 | – | 120 | – | – | – |
| E. de C. Weekes (128), R.J. Christiani (107) | Delhi | 1948–49 | – | – | – | 118 | – |
| D.L. Murray (71), M.A. Holding (55) | Kingston | 1975–76 | – | – | – | 107 | – |
| J.S. Solomon (45), F.C.M. Alexander (70) | Kanpur | 1958–59 | – | – | – | 100 | – |
| A.I. Kallicharran (158), B.D. Julien (86*) | Port-of-Spain | 1973–74 | 100 | – | – | – | – |
| A.I. Kallicharran (98), D.R. Parry (12) | Madras[1] | 1978–79 | – | – | – | 100 | – |
| *Totals: (15)* | | | *4* | *4* | *1* | *6* | *–* |

†*231 runs were added for this wicket, G.St A. Sobers retired ill and was succeeded by K.D. Boyce after 155 had been scored.*

**WEST INDIES – 8th Wicket**

| | | | E | A | NZ | I | P |
|---|---|---|---|---|---|---|---|
| I.V.A. Richards (192*), K.D. Boyce (68) | Delhi | 1974–75 | – | – | – | 124 | – |

**WEST INDIES – 9th Wicket**

| | | | E | A | NZ | I | P |
|---|---|---|---|---|---|---|---|
| C.H. Lloyd (161*), A.M.E. Roberts (68) | Calcutta | 1983–84 | – | – | – | 161 | – |
| E.A.E. Baptiste (87*), M.A. Holding (69) | Birmingham | 1984 | 150 | – | – | – | – |
| D.A.J. Holford (80), J.L. Hendriks (37*) | Adelaide | 1968–69 | – | 122 | – | – | – |
| R.J. Christiani (107), D.St E. Atkinson (45) | Delhi | 1948–49 | – | – | – | 106 | – |
| *Totals: (4)* | | | *1* | *1* | *–* | *2* | *–* |

**WEST INDIES – 10th Wicket**
No instance – Highest Partnership

| | | | E | A | NZ | I | P |
|---|---|---|---|---|---|---|---|
| F.M.M. Worrell (73*), W.W. Hall (50*) | Port-of-Spain | 1961–62 | – | – | – | 98* | – |

**NEW ZEALAND – (94) – 1st Wicket**

| | | | E | A | SA | WI | I | P | SL |
|---|---|---|---|---|---|---|---|---|---|
| G.M. Turner (259), T.W. Jarvis (182) | Georgetown | 1971–72 | – | – | – | 387 | – | – | – |
| C.S. Dempster (136), J.E. Mills (117) | Wellington | 1929–30 | 276 | – | – | – | – | – | – |
| R.E. Redmond (107), G.M. Turner (58) | Auckland | 1972–73 | – | – | – | – | – | 159 | – |
| G.T. Dowling (83), T.W. Jarvis (55) | Lahore[2] | 1964–65 | – | – | – | – | – | 136 | – |
| B. Sutcliffe (58), W.A. Hadlee (116) | Christchurch | 1946–47 | 133 | – | – | – | – | – | – |
| G.O. Rabone (56), M.E. Chapple (76) | Cape Town | 1953–54 | – | – | 126 | – | – | – | – |
| B.A.G. Murray (74), G.T. Dowling (239) | Christchurch | 1967–68 | – | – | – | – | 126 | – | – |
| B. Sutcliffe (88), V.J. Scott (60) | Oval | 1949 | 121 | – | – | – | – | – | – |
| G.T. Dowling (76), G.M. Turner (38) | Christchurch | 1968–69 | – | – | – | 115 | – | – | – |
| B. Sutcliffe (82), V.J. Scott (43) | Leeds | 1949 | 112 | – | – | – | – | – | – |
| G.T. Dowling (71), G.M. Turner (40) | Auckland | 1968–69 | – | – | – | 112 | – | – | – |
| G.M. Turner (72), J.M. Parker (34) | Auckland | 1973–74 | – | 107 | – | – | – | – | – |
| G.T. Dowling (42), B.A.G. Murray (80) | Hyderabad | 1969–70 | – | – | – | – | 106 | – | – |
| S.N. McGregor (49), J.G. Leggat (50*) | Delhi | 1955–56 | – | – | – | – | 101 | – | – |
| *Totals: (14)* | | | *4* | *1* | *1* | *3* | *3* | *2* | *–* |

**NEW ZEALAND – 2nd Wicket**

| | | | E | A | SA | WI | I | P | SL |
|---|---|---|---|---|---|---|---|---|---|
| G.P. Howarth (84), J.J. Crowe (112) | Kingston | 1984–85 | – | – | – | 210 | – | – | – |
| J.G. Wright (88), G.P. Howarth (114) | Napier | 1978–79 | – | – | – | – | – | 195 | – |
| G.T. Dowling (143), B.E. Congdon (58) | Dunedin | 1967–68 | – | – | – | – | 155 | – | – |
| J.G. Wright (110), J.F. Reid (74) | Auckland | 1980–81 | – | – | – | – | 148 | – | – |
| G.M. Turner (95), B.E. Congdon (82) | Port-of-Spain | 1971–72 | – | – | – | 139 | – | – | – |
| B. Sutcliffe (116), J.R. Reid (50) | Christchurch | 1950–51 | 131 | – | – | – | – | – | – |
| B. Sutcliffe (230*), J.W. Guy (52) | Delhi | 1955–56 | – | – | – | – | 130 | – | – |
| B.A. Edgar (74), J.F. Reid (123*) | Christchurch | 1980–81 | – | – | – | – | 125 | – | – |
| J.G. Wright (62), G.P. Howarth (94) | Oval | 1978 | 123 | – | – | – | – | – | – |
| J.F.M. Morrison (58), J.M. Parker (121) | Auckland | 1974–75 | 116 | – | – | – | – | – | – |
| J.G. Wright (93), M.D. Crowe (37) | Leeds | 1983 | 116 | – | – | – | – | – | – |
| G.M. Turner (117), B.E. Congdon (58) | Christchurch | 1975–76 | – | – | – | – | 114 | – | – |
| J.G. Wright (40), J.J. Crowe (64) | Port-of-Spain | 1984–85 | – | – | – | 109 | – | – | – |
| G.M. Turner (79), J.F.M. Morrison (66) | Wellington | 1973–74 | – | 108 | – | – | – | – | – |
| G.M. Turner (65), J.M. Parker (104) | Bombay[3] | 1976–77 | – | – | – | – | 106 | – | – |
| *Totals: (15)* | | | *4* | *1* | *–* | *3* | *6* | *1* | *–* |

### NEW ZEALAND – 3rd Wicket

| | | | E | A | SA | WI | I | P | SL |
|---|---|---|---|---|---|---|---|---|---|
| B. Sutcliffe (230*), J.R. Reid (119*) | Delhi | 1955–56 | – | – | – | – | 222* | – | – |
| B.E. Congdon (175), B.F. Hastings (86) | Lord's | 1973 | 190 | – | – | – | – | – | – |
| J.W. Guy (91), J.R. Reid (120) | Calcutta | 1955–56 | – | – | – | – | 184 | – | – |
| B.W. Sinclair (130), J.R. Reid (88) | Lahore[2] | 1964–65 | – | – | – | – | – | 178 | – |
| B.E. Congdon (66), B.F. Hastings (83) | Nottingham | 1969 | 150 | – | – | – | – | – | – |
| J.F. Reid (158*), M.D. Crowe (84) | Auckland | 1984–85 | – | – | – | – | – | 137 | – |
| G.T. Dowling (129), R.W. Morgan (71) | Bombay[2] | 1964–65 | – | – | – | – | 134 | – | – |
| G.P. Howarth (65), J.M. Parker (56) | Melbourne | 1980–81 | – | 125 | – | – | – | – | – |
| B.E. Congdon (54), J.M. Parker (70) | Auckland | 1975–76 | – | – | – | – | 122 | – | – |
| J.G. Wright (88), G.P. Howarth (67) | Oval | 1983 | 120 | – | – | – | – | – | – |
| C.S. Dempster (120), M.L. Page (104) | Lord's | 1931 | 118 | – | – | – | – | – | – |
| B. Sutcliffe (137*), J.R. Reid (45*) | Hyderabad | 1955–56 | – | – | – | – | 108* | – | – |
| G.M. Turner (113), M.G. Burgess (54) | Kanpur | 1976–77 | – | – | – | – | 106 | – | – |
| G.T. Dowling (27), J.R. Reid (82) | Calcutta | 1964–65 | – | – | – | – | 101 | – | – |
| B.A.G. Murray (90), B.F. Hastings (80*) | Lahore[2] | 1969–70 | – | – | – | – | – | 101 | – |
| J.F. Reid (180), M.D. Crowe (45) | Colombo (CCC) | 1983–84 | – | – | – | – | – | – | 100 |
| Totals: (16) | | | 4 | 1 | – | – | 7 | 3 | 1 |

### NEW ZEALAND – 4th Wicket

| | | | E | A | SA | WI | I | P | SL |
|---|---|---|---|---|---|---|---|---|---|
| B.E. Congdon (132), B.F. Hastings (101) | Wellington | 1973–74 | – | 229 | – | – | – | – | – |
| B.E. Congdon (126), B.F. Hastings (105) | Bridgetown | 1971–72 | – | – | – | 175 | – | – | – |
| B.W. Sinclair (138), S.N. McGregor (62) | Auckland | 1963–64 | – | – | 171 | – | – | – | – |
| B.A. Edgar (161), J.V. Coney (73) | Auckland | 1981–82 | – | 154 | – | – | – | – | – |
| J.G. Wright (130), J.J. Crowe (128) | Auckland | 1983–84 | 154 | – | – | – | – | – | – |
| M.L. Page (104), R.C. Blunt (96) | Lord's | 1931 | 142 | – | – | – | – | – | – |
| G.P. Howarth (123), M.G. Burgess (68) | Lord's | 1978 | 130 | – | – | – | – | – | – |
| B.F. Hastings (72), M.G. Burgess (79) | Wellington | 1972–73 | – | – | – | – | – | 128 | – |
| G.T. Dowling (78), J.R. Reid (69) | Port Elizabeth | 1961–62 | – | – | 125 | – | – | – | – |
| J.F.M. Morrison (117), B.F. Hastings (83) | Sydney | 1973–74 | – | 124 | – | – | – | – | – |
| G.P. Howarth (147), J.M. Parker (42) | Christchurch | 1979–80 | – | – | – | 122 | – | – | – |
| G.P. Howarth (65), J.M. Parker (52) | Brisbane[2] | 1980–81 | – | 117 | – | – | – | – | – |
| G.M. Turner (110*), B.F. Hastings (46) | Christchurch | 1973–74 | – | 115 | – | – | – | – | – |
| G.M. Turner (98), J.M. Parker (41) | Christchurch | 1974–75 | 115 | – | – | – | – | – | – |
| B.E. Congdon (42), J.R. Reid (97) | Wellington | 1964–65 | – | – | – | – | – | 109 | – |
| G.T. Dowling (239), M.G. Burgess (26) | Christchurch | 1967–68 | – | – | – | – | 103 | – | – |
| Totals: (16) | | | 4 | 5 | 2 | 2 | 1 | 2 | – |

### NEW ZEALAND – 5th Wicket

| | | | E | A | SA | WI | I | P | SL |
|---|---|---|---|---|---|---|---|---|---|
| M.G. Burgess (111), R.W. Anderson (92) | Lahore[2] | 1976–77 | – | – | – | – | – | 183 | – |
| B.E. Congdon (176), V. Pollard (116) | Nottingham | 1973 | 177 | – | – | – | – | – | – |
| J.R. Reid (135), J.E.F. Beck (99) | Cape Town | 1953–54 | – | – | 174 | – | – | – | – |
| M.D. Crowe (84), J.V. Coney (111*) | Dunedin | 1984–85 | – | – | – | – | – | 157 | – |
| S.N. McGregor (111), N.S. Harford (93) | Lahore[1] | 1955–56 | – | – | – | – | – | 150 | – |
| P.G.Z. Harris (101), M.E. Chapple (69) | Cape Town | 1961–62 | – | – | 148 | – | – | – | – |
| M.D. Crowe (188), J.V. Coney (73) | Georgetown | 1984–85 | – | – | – | 142 | – | – | – |
| M.G. Burgess (104), M.J.F. Shrimpton (46) | Auckland | 1970–71 | 141 | – | – | – | – | – | – |
| M.P. Donnelly (64), F.B. Smith (96) | Leeds | 1949 | 120 | – | – | – | – | – | – |
| G.T. Dowling (239), K. Thomson (69) | Christchurch | 1967–68 | – | – | – | – | 119 | – | – |
| M.P. Donnelly (75), J.R. Reid (50) | Manchester | 1949 | 116 | – | – | – | – | – | – |
| M.D. Crowe (100), J.V. Coney (174*) | Wellington | 1983–84 | 114 | – | – | – | – | – | – |
| B.F. Hastings (117*), V. Pollard (44) | Christchurch | 1968–69 | – | – | – | 110 | – | – | – |
| M.G. Burgess (87), V. Pollard (62) | Leeds | 1973 | 106 | – | – | – | – | – | – |
| J.R. Reid (84), J.E.F. Beck (38) | Auckland | 1955–56 | – | – | – | 104 | – | – | – |
| T.W. Jarvis (77), B. Sutcliffe (54) | Delhi | 1964–65 | – | – | – | – | 104 | – | – |
| Totals: (16) | | | 6 | – | 2 | 3 | 2 | 3 | – |

### NEW ZEALAND – 6th Wicket

| | | | E | A | SA | WI | I | P | SL |
|---|---|---|---|---|---|---|---|---|---|
| G.M. Turner (223*), K.J. Wadsworth (78) | Kingston | 1971–72 | – | – | – | 220 | – | – | – |
| J.F. Reid (148), R.J. Hadlee (89) | Wellington | 1984–85 | – | – | – | – | – | 145 | – |
| J.F. Reid (180), J.V. Coney (92) | Colombo (CCC) | 1983–84 | – | – | – | – | – | – | 133 |
| M.G. Burgess (105), V. Pollard (105*) | Lord's | 1973 | 117 | – | – | – | – | – | – |
| J.M. Parker (121), K.J. Wadsworth (58) | Auckland | 1974–75 | 112 | – | – | – | – | – | – |
| M.G. Burgess (38), R.J. Hadlee (81) | Auckland | 1976–77 | – | 105 | – | – | – | – | – |
| H.G. Vivian (100), F.T. Badcock (53) | Wellington | 1931–32 | – | – | 100 | – | – | – | – |
| Totals: (7) | | | 2 | 1 | 1 | 1 | – | 1 | 1 |

**NEW ZEALAND – 7th Wicket**

| | | | E | A | SA | WI | I | P | SL |
|---|---|---|---|---|---|---|---|---|---|
| W.K. Lees (152), R.J. Hadlee (87) | Karachi | 1976–77 | – | – | – | – | – | 186 | – |
| B. Sutcliffe (151*), B.R. Taylor (105) | Calcutta | 1964–65 | – | – | – | – | 163 | – | – |
| M.D. Crowe (188), I.D.S. Smith (53) | Georgetown | 1984–85 | – | – | – | 143 | – | – | – |
| B. Sutcliffe (53), V. Pollard (81*) | Birmingham | 1965 | 104 | – | – | – | – | – | – |
| T.C. Lowry (80), H.M. McGirr (51) | Auckland | 1929–30 | 100 | – | – | – | – | – | – |
| Totals: (5) | | | 2 | – | – | 1 | 1 | 1 | – |

**NEW ZEALAND – 8th Wicket**

| | | | E | A | SA | WI | I | P | SL |
|---|---|---|---|---|---|---|---|---|---|
| B.E. Congdon (166*), R.S. Cunis (51) | Port-of-Spain | 1971–72 | – | – | – | 136 | – | – | – |
| D.A.R. Moloney (64), A.W. Roberts (66*) | Lord's | 1937 | 104 | – | – | – | – | – | – |
| B.W. Yuile (47*), D.R. Hadlee (56) | Karachi | 1969–70 | – | – | – | – | – | 100 | – |
| Totals: (3) | | | 1 | – | – | 1 | – | 1 | – |

**NEW ZEALAND – 9th Wicket**

| | | | E | A | SA | WI | I | P | SL |
|---|---|---|---|---|---|---|---|---|---|
| J.V. Coney (174*), B.L. Cairns (64) | Wellington | 1983–84 | 118 | – | – | – | – | – | – |

**NEW ZEALAND – 10th Wicket**

| | | | E | A | SA | WI | I | P | SL |
|---|---|---|---|---|---|---|---|---|---|
| B.F. Hastings (110), R.O. Collinge (68*) | Auckland | 1972–73 | – | – | – | – | – | 151 | – |

**INDIA – (200) – 1st Wicket**

| | | | E | A | WI | NZ | P | SL |
|---|---|---|---|---|---|---|---|---|
| M.H. Mankad (231), Pankaj Roy (173) | Madras[2] | 1955–56 | – | – | – | 413 | – | – |
| S.M. Gavaskar (221), C.P.S. Chauhan (80) | Oval | 1979 | 213 | – | – | – | – | – |
| V.M. Merchant (114), Mushtaq Ali (112) | Manchester | 1936 | 203 | – | – | – | – | – |
| S.M. Gavaskar (97), C.P.S. Chauhan (93) | Lahore[2] | 1978–79 | – | – | – | – | 192 | – |
| S.M. Gavaskar (123), C.P.S. Chauhan (73) | Bombay[3] | 1979–80 | – | 192 | – | – | – | – |
| S.M. Gavaskar (103*), A.D. Gaekwad (66*) | Bangalore | 1983–84 | – | – | – | – | 176* | – |
| S.M. Gavaskar (70), C.P.S. Chauhan (85) | Melbourne | 1980–81 | – | 165 | – | – | – | – |
| S.M. Gavaskar (155), Arun Lal (63) | Madras[1] | 1982–83 | – | – | – | – | – | 156 |
| S.M. Gavaskar (73), C.P.S. Chauhan (84) | Bombay[3] | 1978–79 | – | – | 153 | – | – | – |
| S.M. Gavaskar (66), A.D. Gaekwad (81*) | Kingston | 1975–76 | – | – | 136 | – | – | – |
| F.M. Engineer (66), S.M. Gavaskar (67) | Bombay[2] | 1972–73 | 135 | – | – | – | – | – |
| S.M. Gavaskar (49), F.M. Engineer (86) | Lord's | 1974 | 131 | – | – | – | – | – |
| D.N. Sardesai (28), F.M. Engineer (109) | Madras[1] | 1966–67 | – | – | 129 | – | – | – |
| S.M. Gavaskar (90), A.D. Gaekwad (39) | Ahmedabad | 1983–84 | – | – | 127 | – | – | – |
| S.M. Gavaskar (81), C.P.S. Chauhan (61) | Kanpur | 1979–80 | – | – | – | – | 125 | – |
| V.M. Merchant (78), Mushtaq Ali (46) | Manchester | 1946 | 124 | – | – | – | – | – |
| M.H. Mankad (116), C.T. Sarwate (36) | Melbourne | 1947–48 | – | 124 | – | – | – | – |
| S.M. Gavaskar (68), C.P.S. Chauhan (56) | Birmingham | 1979 | 124 | – | – | – | – | – |
| A.M. Mankad (53*), S.M. Gavaskar (64*) | Georgetown | 1970–71 | – | – | 123* | – | – | – |
| Pankaj Roy (99), N.J. Contractor (34) | Delhi | 1959–60 | – | 121 | – | – | – | – |
| M.L. Jaisimha (127), N.J. Contractor (39) | Delhi | 1961–62 | 121 | – | – | – | – | – |
| S.M. Gavaskar (119), A.D. Gaekwad (42) | Bombay[3] | 1976–77 | – | – | – | 120 | – | – |
| S.M. Gavaskar (120), C.P.S. Chauhan (60) | Delhi | 1978–79 | – | – | 119 | – | – | – |
| S.M. Gavaskar (76), C.P.S. Chauhan (58) | Kanpur | 1979–80 | – | 114 | – | – | – | – |
| S.M. Gavaskar (53), C.P.S. Chauhan (78) | Christchurch | 1980–81 | – | – | – | 114 | – | – |
| F.M. Engineer (77), A.M. Mankad (64) | Kanpur | 1969–70 | – | 111 | – | – | – | – |
| M.H. Mankad (72), Pankaj Roy (35) | Lord's | 1952 | 106 | – | – | – | – | – |
| S.M. Gavaskar (83), Arun Lal (51) | Lahore[2] | 1982–83 | – | – | – | – | 105 | – |
| Pankaj Roy (31*), M.H. Mankad (71*) | Calcutta | 1951–52 | 103* | – | – | – | – | – |
| S.M. Gavaskar (172), K. Srikkanth (65) | Bangalore | 1981–82 | 102 | – | – | – | – | – |
| Totals: (30) | | | 10 | 6 | 6 | 3 | 4 | 1 |

**INDIA – 2nd Wicket**

| | | | E | A | WI | NZ | P | SL |
|---|---|---|---|---|---|---|---|---|
| S.M. Gavaskar (182*), D.B. Vengsarkar (157*) | Calcutta | 1978–79 | – | – | 344* | – | – | – |
| Pankaj Roy (150), V.L. Manjrekar (118) | Kingston | 1952–53 | – | – | 237 | – | – | – |
| S.M. Gavaskar (116), S. Amarnath (124) | Auckland | 1975–76 | – | – | – | 204 | – | – |
| A.D. Gaekwad (72), M. Amarnath (116) | St John's | 1982–83 | – | – | 200 | – | – | – |
| S.M. Gavaskar (127), M. Amarnath (100) | Perth | 1977–78 | – | 193 | – | – | – | – |
| F.M. Engineer (121), A.L. Wadekar (87) | Bombay[2] | 1972–73 | 192 | – | – | – | – | – |
| S.M. Gavaskar (121), D.B. Vengsarkar (159) | Delhi | 1983–84 | – | – | 178 | – | – | – |
| S.M. Gavaskar (155), D.B. Vengsarkar (90) | Madras[1] | 1982–83 | – | – | – | – | – | 173 |
| A.D. Gaekwad (87), D.B. Vengsarkar (73) | Bangalore | 1978–79 | – | – | 170 | – | – | – |
| F.M. Engineer (87), A.L. Wadekar (91) | Leeds | 1967 | 168 | – | – | – | – | – |
| S.M. Gavaskar (86), E.D. Solkar (102) | Bombay[3] | 1974–75 | – | – | 168 | – | – | – |

**2nd Wicket** *continued*

| | | | E | A | WI | NZ | P | SL |
|---|---|---|---|---|---|---|---|---|
| S.M. Gavaskar (205), G.R. Viswanath (52) | Bombay[3] | 1978–79 | – | – | 155 | – | – | – |
| S.M. Gavaskar (221), D.B. Vengsarkar (52) | Oval | 1979 | 153 | – | – | – | – | – |
| S.M. Gavaskar (120), D.B. Vengsarkar (109) | Delhi | 1978–79 | – | – | 151 | – | – | – |
| K. Srikkanth (84), M. Azharuddin (122) | Kanpur | 1984–85 | 150 | – | – | – | – | – |
| C.P.S. Chauhan (88), M. Amarnath (90) | Perth | 1977–78 | – | 149 | – | – | – | – |
| S.M. Gavaskar (220), A.L. Wadekar (54) | Port-of-Spain | 1970–71 | – | – | 148 | – | – | – |
| V.L.Mehra (62), S.A. Durani (104) | Port-of-Spain | 1961–62 | – | – | 144 | – | – | – |
| B.K. Kunderan (192), D.N. Sardesai (65) | Madras[2] | 1963–64 | 143 | – | – | – | – | – |
| N.J. Contractor (92), P.R. Umrigar (76) | Delhi | 1958–59 | – | – | 137 | – | – | – |
| A.D. Gaekwad (48), D.B. Vengsarkar (100) | Bombay[3] | 1983–84 | – | – | 133 | – | – | – |
| M.L. Jaisimha (51), V.L. Manjrekar (84) | Bombay[2] | 1961–62 | 131 | – | – | – | – | – |
| S.M. Gavaskar (60), M. Amarnath (64) | Hyderabad | 1982–83 | – | – | – | – | 125 | – |
| M.H. Mankad (111), H.R. Adhikari (38) | Melbourne | 1947–48 | – | 124 | – | – | – | – |
| D.N. Sardesai (106), Hanumant Singh (82) | Delhi | 1964–65 | – | – | – | 123 | – | – |
| K.C. Ibrahim (85), R.S. Modi (63) | Delhi | 1948–49 | – | – | 121 | – | – | – |
| S.M. Gavaskar (137), M. Amarnath (53) | Karachi | 1978–79 | – | – | – | – | 117 | – |
| C.P.S. Chauhan (39), D.B. Vengsarkar (89) | Calcutta | 1979–80 | – | 117 | – | – | – | – |
| S.M. Gavaskar (66), M. Amarnath (70) | Kanpur | 1976–77 | – | – | – | 114 | – | – |
| R.J. Shastri (66), G.R. Viswanath (56) | Oval | 1982 | 113 | – | – | – | – | – |
| N.J. Contractor (56), A.A. Baig (112) | Manchester | 1959 | 109 | – | – | – | – | – |
| M.L. Jaisimha (70), V.L. Manjrekar (96) | Kanpur | 1961–62 | 109 | – | – | – | – | – |
| B.K. Kunderan (55), R.G. Nadkarni (122*) | Kanpur | 1963–64 | 109 | – | – | – | – | – |
| S.M. Gavaskar (102), M. Amarnath (85) | Port-of-Spain | 1975–76 | – | – | 108 | – | – | – |
| N.J. Contractor (92), R.F. Surti (64) | Delhi | 1960–61 | – | – | – | – | 107 | – |
| S.M. Gavaskar (67), M. Amarnath (103*) | Karachi | 1982–83 | – | – | – | – | 107 | – |
| S.M. Gavaskar (88), D.B. Vengsarkar (33) | Bangalore | 1979–80 | – | – | – | – | 105 | – |
| | *Totals: (37)* | | 10 | 4 | 14 | 3 | 5 | 1 |

**INDIA – 3rd Wicket**

| | | | E | A | WI | NZ | P | SL |
|---|---|---|---|---|---|---|---|---|
| G.R. Viswanath (222), Yashpal Sharma (140) | Madras[1] | 1981–82 | 316† | – | – | – | – | – |
| P.R. Umrigar (223), V.L. Manjrekar (118) | Hyderabad | 1955–56 | – | – | – | 238 | – | – |
| V.M. Merchant (154), V.S. Hazare (164*) | Delhi | 1951–52 | 211 | – | – | – | – | – |
| M.H. Mankad (184), V.S. Hazare (49) | Lord's | 1952 | 211 | – | – | – | – | – |
| D.B. Vengsarkar (103), G.R. Viswanath (113) | Lord's | 1979 | 210 | – | – | – | – | – |
| M. Amarnath (120), Yashpal Sharma (63*) | Lahore[2] | 1982–83 | – | – | – | – | 190 | – |
| Pankaj Roy (140), V.S. Hazare (155) | Bombay[2] | 1951–52 | 187 | – | – | – | – | – |
| L. Amarnath (118), C.K. Nayudu (67) | Bombay[1] | 1933–34 | 186 | – | – | – | – | – |
| A.D. Gaekwad (77*), G.R. Viswanath (103*) | Kanpur | 1976–77 | – | – | – | 163* | – | – |
| M. Amarnath (85), G.R. Viswanath (112) | Port-of-Spain | 1975–76 | – | – | 159 | – | – | – |
| S.M. Gavaskar (115), G.R. Viswanath (131) | Delhi | 1979–80 | – | 159 | – | – | – | – |
| R.M. Modi (112), V.S. Hazare (134*) | Bombay[2] | 1948–49 | – | – | 156 | – | – | – |
| R.G. Nadkarni (122*), D.N. Sardesai (87) | Kanpur | 1963–64 | 144 | – | – | – | – | – |
| C.P.S. Chauhan (79), G.R. Viswanath (179) | Kanpur | 1978–79 | – | – | 144 | – | – | – |
| Pankaj Roy (100), V.L. Manjrekar (90) | Calcutta | 1955–56 | – | – | – | 143 | – | – |
| N.J. Contractor (108), A.A. Baig (50) | Bombay[2] | 1959–60 | – | 133 | – | – | – | – |
| M. Amarnath (86), G.R. Viswanath (73) | Adelaide | 1977–78 | – | 131 | – | – | – | – |
| Pankaj Roy (67*), V.L. Manjrekar (74*) | Dacca | 1954–55 | – | – | – | – | 130* | – |
| R.S. Modi (80), V.S. Hazare (59) | Calcutta | 1948–49 | – | – | 129 | – | – | – |
| B.K. Kunderan (100), | | | | | | | | |
| Nawab of Pataudi, jr (203*) | Delhi | 1963–64 | 125 | – | – | – | – | – |
| Pankaj Roy (78), V.L. Manjrekar (59) | Bahawalpur | 1954–55 | – | – | – | – | 123 | – |
| S.M. Gavaskar (124), D.N. Sardesai (75) | Port-of-Spain | 1970–71 | – | – | 122 | – | – | – |
| S.M. Gavaskar (65), M. Amarnath (64) | Delhi | 1984–85 | 121 | – | – | – | – | – |
| A.L. Wadekar (99), R.F. Surti (43) | Melbourne | 1967–68 | – | 116 | – | – | – | – |
| C.P.S. Chauhan (84), G.R. Viswanath (52) | Kanpur | 1979–80 | – | 113 | – | – | – | – |
| M.L. Apte (64), V.S. Hazare (63) | Bridgetown | 1952–53 | – | – | 112 | – | – | – |
| M.L. Jaisimha (66), V.L. Manjrekar (59) | Bombay[2] | 1964–65 | – | 112 | – | – | – | – |
| S.M. Gavaskar (116), G.R. Viswanath (50) | Georgetown | 1970–71 | – | – | 112 | – | – | – |
| S.M. Gavaskar (147*), D.B. Vengsarkar (62) | Georgetown | 1982–83 | – | – | 112 | – | – | – |
| R.S. Modi (87), V.S. Hazare (58*) | Calcutta | 1948–49 | – | – | 108 | – | – | – |
| M. Amarnath (72), G.R. Viswanath (59) | Melbourne | 1977–78 | – | 105 | – | – | – | – |
| N.J. Contractor (86), Nawab of Pataudi, jr (103) | Madras[2] | 1961–62 | 104 | – | – | – | – | – |
| A.L. Wadekar (71), R.F. Surti (44) | Dunedin | 1967–68 | – | – | – | 103 | – | – |

| 3rd Wicket *continued* | | | E | A | WI | NZ | P | SL |
|---|---|---|---|---|---|---|---|---|
| A.L. Wadekar (55), G.R. Viswanath (59) | Madras¹ | 1969–70 | – | 102 | – | – | – | – |
| S.M. Gavaskar (89), G.R. Viswanath (145) | Faisalabad | 1978–79 | – | – | – | – | 101 | – |
| | *Totals: (35)* | | 10 | 8 | 9 | 4 | 4 | – |

†*415 runs were added for this wicket in two separate partnerships, D.B. Vengsarkar retiring hurt and being succeeded by Yashpal Sharma when 99 runs had been added.*
*Although the third wicket added 124 v Australia at Calcutta in 1979–80, this consisted of two partnerships: G.R. Viswanath added 37 with D.B. Vengsarkar (retired hurt) and a further 87 with Yashpal Sharma.*

| INDIA – 4th Wicket | | | E | A | WI | NZ | P | SL |
|---|---|---|---|---|---|---|---|---|
| V.S. Hazare (89), V.L. Manjrekar (133) | Leeds | 1952 | 222 | – | – | – | – | – |
| M. Amarnath (95), M. Azharuddin (105) | Madras¹ | 1984–85 | 190 | – | – | – | – | – |
| V.S. Hazare (146*), P.R. Umrigar (102) | Bombay² | 1952–53 | – | – | – | – | 183 | – |
| G.R. Viswanath (179), A.D. Gaekwad (102) | Kanpur | 1978–79 | – | – | 172 | – | – | – |
| P.R. Umrigar (223), A.G. Kripal Singh (100*) | Hyderabad | 1955–56 | – | – | – | 171 | – | – |
| M.H. Mankad (223), A.G. Kripal Singh (63) | Bombay² | 1955–56 | – | – | – | 167 | – | – |
| G.R. Viswanath (145), D.B. Vengsarkar (83) | Faisalabad | 1978–79 | – | – | – | – | 166 | – |
| D.B. Vengsarkar (112), G.R. Viswanath (161*) | Bangalore | 1979–80 | – | 159 | – | – | – | – |
| D.N. Sardesai (200*), C.G. Borde (109) | Bombay² | 1964–65 | – | – | – | 154 | – | – |
| Pankaj Roy (85), P.R. Umrigar (117) | Kingston | 1952–53 | – | – | 150 | – | – | – |
| A.V. Mankad (74), Nawab of Pataudi, jr (95) | Bombay² | 1969–70 | – | 146 | – | – | – | – |
| S.M. Gavaskar (127*), M. Amarnath (78) | Faisalabad | 1982–83 | – | – | – | – | 145 | – |
| D.B. Vengsarkar (159), R.J. Shastri (49) | Delhi | 1983–84 | – | – | 145 | – | – | – |
| V.S. Hazare (134*), L. Amarnath (58*) | Bombay² | 1948–49 | – | – | 144* | – | – | – |
| R.S. Modi (86), V.S. Hazare (122) | Bombay² | 1948–49 | – | – | 139 | – | – | – |
| S.M. Gavaskar (108), B.P. Patel (83) | Bombay³ | 1976–77 | 139 | – | – | – | – | – |
| C.G. Borde (87), Nawab of Pataudi, jr (113) | Delhi | 1964–65 | – | – | – | 138 | – | – |
| G.R. Viswanath (89), D.B. Vengsarkar (44) | Adelaide | 1977–78 | – | 136 | – | – | – | – |
| M.L. Apte (163*), P.R. Umrigar (67) | Port-of-Spain | 1952–53 | – | – | 135 | – | – | – |
| R.F. Surti (52), Nawab of Pataudi, jr (74) | Brisbane² | 1967–68 | – | 128 | – | – | – | – |
| G.R. Viswanath (79), D.B. Vengsarkar (48) | Sydney | 1977–78 | – | 125 | – | – | – | – |
| D.B. Vengsarkar (146*), Yashpal Sharma (60) | Delhi | 1979–80 | – | – | – | – | 122 | – |
| C.G. Borde (69), R.F. Surti (70) | Adelaide | 1967–68 | – | 121 | – | – | – | – |
| A.L. Wadekar (91*), G.R. Viswanath (44*) | Delhi | 1969–70 | – | 120* | – | – | – | – |
| S.M. Gavaskar (205), C.P.S. Chauhan (52) | Bombay³ | 1978–79 | – | – | 117 | – | – | – |
| M. Amarnath (78), M. Azharuddin (48) | Madras¹ | 1984–85 | 110 | – | – | – | – | – |
| C.G. Borde (96), H.R. Adhikari (40) | Delhi | 1958–59 | – | – | 108 | – | – | – |
| P.R. Umrigar (112), C.G. Borde (45) | Delhi | 1960–61 | – | – | – | – | 107† | – |
| M. Amarnath (117), Yashpal Sharma (50) | Port-of-Spain | 1982–83 | – | – | 106 | – | – | – |
| S.M. Gavaskar (147*), Yashpal Sharma (35*) | Georgetown | 1982–83 | – | – | 104* | – | – | – |
| R.F. Surti (67), Nawab of Pataudi, jr (52) | Christchurch | 1967–68 | – | – | – | 103 | – | – |
| G.R. Viswanath (73), Yashpal Sharma (62) | Bangalore | 1979–80 | – | – | – | – | 102 | – |
| F.M. Engineer (75), P. Sharma (49) | Delhi | 1974–75 | – | – | 101 | – | – | – |
| | *Totals: (33)* | | 4 | 7 | 11 | 5 | 6 | – |

† *123 runs were added for this wicket, N.J. Contractor retiring hurt and being succeeded by C.G. Borde after 16 had been scored.*
*Although the fourth wicket added 103 runs in the first innings v West Indies at Port-of-Spain in 1982–83, this consisted of two partnerships, M. Amarnath adding 16 with Yashpal Sharma (retired hurt) and a further 87 with R.J. Shastri.*

| INDIA – 5th Wicket | | | E | A | WI | NZ | P | SL |
|---|---|---|---|---|---|---|---|---|
| M. Azharuddin (110), R.J. Shastri (111) | Calcutta | 1984–85 | 214 | – | – | – | – | – |
| S.M. Gavaskar (156), B.P. Patel (115*) | Port-of-Spain | 1975–76 | – | – | 204 | – | – | – |
| S.M. Patil (127), R.J. Shastri (139) | Faisalabad | 1984–85 | – | – | – | – | 200 | – |
| Nawab of Pataudi, jr (203*), C.G. Borde (67*) | Delhi | 1963–64 | 190* | – | – | – | – | – |
| P.R. Umrigar (117), C.G. Borde (177*) | Madras² | 1960–61 | – | – | – | – | 177 | – |
| R.J. Shastri (102), Kapil Dev (98) | St John's | 1982–83 | – | – | 156 | – | – | – |
| S.A. Durani (73), G.R. Viswanath (113) | Bombay² | 1972–73 | 150 | – | – | – | – | – |
| C.G. Borde (69), S.A. Durani (71) | Bombay² | 1961–62 | 142 | – | – | – | – | – |
| D.B. Vengsarkar (157), Yashpal Sharma (37) | Lord's | 1982 | 142 | – | – | – | – | – |
| Hanumant Singh (73), Nawab of Pataudi, jr (148) | Leeds | 1967 | 134 | – | – | – | – | – |
| V.L. Manjrekar (189*), C.G. Borde (45) | Delhi | 1961–62 | 132 | – | – | – | – | – |
| P.R. Umrigar (69), D.G. Phadkar (65) | Port-of-Spain | 1952–53 | – | – | 131 | – | – | – |
| V.L. Manjrekar (177), G.S. Ramchand (72) | Delhi | 1955–56 | – | – | – | 127 | – | – |
| R.J. Shastri (77), R.M.H. Binny (65) | Bombay³ | 1983–84 | – | – | 127 | – | – | – |

**5th Wicket** *continued*

| | | | E | A | WI | NZ | P | SL |
|---|---|---|---|---|---|---|---|---|
| R.F. Surti (99), C.G. Borde (65*) | Auckland | 1967–68 | – | – | – | 126 | – | – |
| M. Amarnath (101*), R.J. Shastri (71) | Lahore² | 1984–85 | – | – | – | – | 126 | – |
| G.R. Viswanath (95), A.D. Gaekwad (51) | Bombay³ | 1974–75 | – | – | 121 | – | – | – |
| D.N. Sardesai (112), E.D. Solkar (55) | Port-of-Spain | 1970–71 | – | – | 114 | – | – | – |
| C.G. Borde (62), Nawab of Pataudi, jr (153) | Calcutta | 1964–65 | – | – | – | 110 | – | – |
| A.A. Baig (58), R.B. Kenny (55*) | Bombay² | 1959–60 | – | 109 | – | – | – | – |
| A.D. Gaekwad (102), M. Amarnath (101*) | Kanpur | 1978–79 | – | – | 109 | – | – | – |
| C.P.S. Chauhan (97), S.M. Patil (174) | Adelaide | 1980–81 | – | 108 | – | – | – | – |
| M. Amarnath (109*), S.M. Patil (68) | Lahore² | 1982–83 | – | – | – | – | 106 | – |
| S.M. Gavaskar (166), Yashpal Sharma (46) | Madras¹ | 1979–80 | – | – | – | – | 105 | – |
| | *Totals: (24)* | | 7 | 2 | 7 | 3 | 5 | – |

*Although the 5th wicket added 102 v Pakistan at Lahore in 1978–79, this consisted of two partnerships:
D.B. Vengsarkar added 57 with M. Amarnath (retired hurt) and a further 45 with S.M.H. Kirmani.*

**INDIA – 6th Wicket**

| | | | E | A | WI | NZ | P | SL |
|---|---|---|---|---|---|---|---|---|
| D.N. Sardesai (200*), Hanumant Singh (75*) | Bombay² | 1964–65 | – | – | – | 193* | – | – |
| V.S. Hazare (116), D.G. Phadkar (123) | Adelaide | 1947–48 | – | 188 | – | – | – | – |
| S.M. Gavaskar (236*), R.J. Shastri (72) | Madras¹ | 1983–84 | – | – | 170 | – | – | – |
| S.M. Patil (174), Yashpal Sharma (47) | Adelaide | 1980–81 | – | 147 | – | – | – | – |
| Nawab of Pataudi, jr (128*), C.G. Borde (49) | Madras² | 1964–65 | – | 142 | – | – | – | – |
| D.N. Sardesai (212), E.D. Solkar (61) | Kingston | 1970–71 | – | – | 137 | – | – | – |
| C.G. Borde (109), H.R. Adhikari (63) | Delhi | 1958–59 | – | – | 134 | – | – | – |
| S.M.H. Kirmani (43), Kapil Dev (97) | Oval | 1982 | 130 | – | – | – | – | – |
| V.L. Manjrekar (177), R.G. Nadkarni (68*) | Delhi | 1955–56 | – | – | – | 123 | – | – |
| A.D. Gaekwad (201), R.M.H. Binny (54) | Jullundur | 1983–84 | – | – | – | – | 121 | – |
| M.L. Jaisimha (101), C.G. Borde (63) | Brisbane² | 1967–68 | – | 119 | – | – | – | – |
| P.R. Umrigar (130), D.K. Gaekwad (43) | Port-of-Spain | 1952–53 | – | – | 118 | – | – | – |
| G.R. Viswanath (137), E.D. Solkar (35) | Kanpur | 1969–70 | – | 110 | – | – | – | – |
| V.S. Hazare (56), D.G. Phadkar (64) | Leeds | 1952 | 105 | – | – | – | – | – |
| D.G. Phadkar (61), P.R. Umrigar (130*) | Madras¹ | 1951–52 | 104 | – | – | – | – | – |
| E.D. Solkar (75), F.M. Engineer (63) | Delhi | 1972–73 | 103 | – | – | – | – | – |
| C.G. Borde (121), S.A. Durani (55) | Bombay² | 1966–67 | – | – | 102 | – | – | – |
| M. Amarnath (101*), Kapil Dev (62) | Kanpur | 1978–79 | – | – | 102 | – | – | – |
| | *Totals: (18)* | | 4 | 5 | 6 | 2 | 1 | – |

**INDIA – 7th Wicket**

| | | | E | A | WI | NZ | P | SL |
|---|---|---|---|---|---|---|---|---|
| R.J. Shastri (142), S.M.H. Kirmani (102) | Bombay³ | 1984–85 | 235 | – | – | – | – | – |
| D.N. Sardesai (150), E.D. Solkar (65) | Bridgetown | 1970–71 | – | – | 186 | – | – | – |
| Yashpal Sharma (55*), Kapil Dev (116) | Kanpur | 1981–82 | 169 | – | – | – | – | – |
| R.M.H. Binny (83*), Madan Lal (74) | Bangalore | 1983–84 | – | – | – | 155 | – | – |
| M.L. Apte (163*), M.H. Mankad (96) | Port-of-Spain | 1952–53 | – | – | 153 | – | – | – |
| C.G. Borde (84), S.A. Durani (90) | Bombay² | 1963–64 | 153 | – | – | – | – | – |
| Kapil Dev (100*), S.M.H. Kirmani (30) | Port-of-Spain | 1982–83 | – | – | 134 | – | – | – |
| V.S. Hazare (145), H.R. Adhikari (51) | Adelaide | 1947–48 | – | 132 | – | – | – | – |
| B.P. Patel (81), S.M.H. Kirmani (49) | Wellington | 1975–76 | – | – | – | 116 | – | – |
| | *Totals: (9)* | | 3 | 1 | 3 | 1 | 1 | – |

**INDIA – 8th Wicket**

| | | | E | A | WI | NZ | P | SL |
|---|---|---|---|---|---|---|---|---|
| R.G. Nadkarni (75), F.M. Engineer (90) | Madras² | 1964–65 | – | – | – | 143 | – | – |
| R.J. Shastri (93), S.M.H. Kirmani (67) | Delhi | 1981–82 | 128 | – | – | – | – | – |
| S.M.H. Kirmani (101*), K.D. Ghavri (86) | Bombay³ | 1979–80 | – | 127 | – | – | – | – |
| S.M.H. Kirmani (66), Madan Lal (54) | Faisalabad | 1982–83 | – | – | – | – | 122 | – |
| Yashpal Sharma (63), B.S. Sandhu (68) | Kingston | 1982–83 | – | – | 107 | – | – | – |
| R.G. Nadkarni (63), F.M. Engineer (65) | Madras² | 1961–62 | 101 | – | – | – | – | – |
| | *Totals: (6)* | | 2 | 1 | 1 | 1 | 1 | – |

**INDIA – 9th Wicket**

| | | | E | A | WI | NZ | P | SL |
|---|---|---|---|---|---|---|---|---|
| P.G. Joshi (52*), R.B. Desai (85) | Bombay² | 1960–61 | – | – | – | – | 149 | – |
| S.M. Gavaskar (236*), S.M.H. Kirmani (63*) | Madras¹ | 1983–84 | – | – | 143* | – | – | – |
| D.N. Sardesai (212), E.A.S. Prasanna (25) | Kingston | 1970–71 | – | – | 122 | – | – | – |
| R.M.H. Binny (39), Madan Lal (63*) | Kanpur | 1983–84 | – | – | 117 | – | – | – |
| S.M.H. Kirmani (88), B.S. Bedi (36) | Bombay³ | 1976–77 | – | – | – | 105 | – | – |
| S.M.H. Kirmani (78), N.S. Yadav (43) | Auckland | 1980–81 | – | – | – | 105 | – | – |
| R.J. Shastri (93), Madan Lal (44) | Delhi | 1981–82 | 104 | – | – | – | – | – |
| | *Totals: (7)* | | 1 | – | 3 | 2 | 1 | – |

| INDIA – 10th Wicket | | | E | A | WI | NZ | P | SL |
|---|---|---|---|---|---|---|---|---|
| H.R. Adhikari (81*), Ghulam Ahmed (50) | Delhi | 1952–53 | – | – | – | – | 109 | – |

| PAKISTAN – (130) – 1st Wicket | | | E | A | WI | NZ | I | SL |
|---|---|---|---|---|---|---|---|---|
| Khalid Ibadulla (166), Abdul Kadir (95) | Karachi | 1964–65 | – | 249 | – | – | – | – |
| Mohsin Khan (104), Shoaib Mohammad (80) | Lahore[2] | 1983–84 | 173 | – | – | – | – | – |
| Hanif Mohammad (62), Imtiaz Ahmed (135) | Madras[2] | 1960–61 | – | – | – | – | 162 | – |
| Majid Khan (167), Zaheer Abbas (80) | Georgetown | 1976–77 | – | – | 159† | – | – | – |
| Mohsin Khan (91), Mudassar Nazar (152) | Karachi | 1982–83 | – | – | – | – | 157 | – |
| Hanif Mohammad (337), Imtiaz Ahmed (91) | Bridgetown | 1957–58 | – | – | 152 | – | – | – |
| Sadiq Mohammad (34), Majid Khan (112) | Karachi | 1976–77 | – | – | – | 147 | – | – |
| Mohsin Khan (59), Mudassar Nazar (199) | Faisalabad | 1984–85 | – | – | – | – | 141 | – |
| Sadiq Mohammad (103*), Majid Khan (98) | Hyderabad | 1976–77 | – | – | – | 136*‡ | – | – |
| Hanif Mohammad (142), Alimuddin (64) | Bahawalpur | 1954–55 | – | – | – | – | 127 | – |
| Majid Khan (54), Sadiq Mohammad (81) | Port-of-Spain | 1976–77 | – | – | 123 | – | – | – |
| Mohsin Khan (76), Mudassar Nazar (79) | Faisalabad | 1982–83 | – | 123 | – | – | – | – |
| Hanif Mohammad (104), Alimuddin (50) | Dacca | 1961–62 | 122 | – | – | – | – | – |
| Mohammad Ilyas (126), Naushad Ali (39) | Karachi | 1964–65 | – | – | – | 121 | – | – |
| Majid Khan (76), Sadiq Mohammad (105) | Melbourne | 1976–77 | – | 113 | – | – | – | – |
| | Totals: (15) | | 2 | 3 | 3 | 3 | 4 | – |

†219 runs were added for this wicket, Sadiq Mohammad retired hurt and was succeeded by Zaheer Abbas after 60 had been scored.
‡164 runs were added for this wicket, Sadiq Mohammad retired hurt and was succeeded by Zaheer Abbas after 136 had been scored.
Although the 1st wicket added 128 v Australia at Melbourne in 1972–73, this consisted of two partnerships: Sadiq Mohammad added 31* with Saeed Ahmed (retired hurt) and a further 97 with Zaheer Abbas.

| PAKISTAN – 2nd Wicket | | | E | A | WI | NZ | I | SL |
|---|---|---|---|---|---|---|---|---|
| Zaheer Abbas (274), Mushtaq Mohammad (100) | Birmingham | 1971 | 291 | – | – | – | – | – |
| Mudassar Nazar (199), Qasim Omar (210) | Faisalabad | 1984–85 | – | – | – | – | 250 | – |
| Hanif Mohammad (160), Saeed Ahmed (121) | Bombay[2] | 1960–61 | – | – | – | – | 246 | – |
| Mohsin Khan (149), Qasim Omar (113) | Adelaide | 1983–84 | – | 233 | – | – | – | – |
| Sadiq Mohammad (137), Majid Khan (158) | Melbourne | 1972–73 | – | 195 | – | – | – | – |
| Hanif Mohammad (103), Saeed Ahmed (78) | Karachi | 1958–59 | – | – | 178 | – | – | – |
| Hanif Mohammad (96), Waqar Hassan (65) | Bombay[2] | 1952–53 | – | – | – | – | 165 | – |
| Mohsin Khan (129), Majid Khan (63) | Lahore[2] | 1981–82 | – | – | – | – | – | 151 |
| Mohsin Khan (200), Mansoor Akhtar (57) | Lord's | 1982 | 144 | – | – | – | – | – |
| Mudassar Nazar (95), Majid Khan (74) | Melbourne | 1981–82 | – | 141 | – | – | – | – |
| Imtiaz Ahmed (98), Mushtaq Mohammad (72) | Oval | 1962 | 137 | – | – | – | – | – |
| Majid Khan (108), Zaheer Abbas (59) | Melbourne | 1978–79 | – | 135 | – | – | – | – |
| Hanif Mohammad (81), Saeed Ahmed (64) | Port-of-Spain | 1957–58 | – | – | 130 | – | – | – |
| Sadiq Mohammad (105), Zaheer Abbas (90) | Melbourne | 1976–77 | – | 128 | – | – | – | – |
| Majid Khan (45), Wasim Bari (85) | Lahore[2] | 1978–79 | – | – | – | – | 125 | – |
| Mohsin Khan (58), Haroon Rashid (82) | Karachi | 1982–83 | – | 125 | – | – | – | – |
| Imtiaz Ahmed (122), Saeed Ahmed (52) | Kingston | 1957–58 | – | – | 118 | – | – | – |
| Mohammad Ilyas (56), Saeed Ahmed (68) | Rawalpindi | 1964–65 | – | – | – | 114 | – | – |
| Hanif Mohammad (111), Saeed Ahmed (69) | Dacca | 1961–62 | 113 | – | – | – | – | – |
| Hanif Mohammad (337), Alimuddin (37) | Bridgetown | 1957–58 | – | – | 112 | – | – | – |
| Mudassar Nazar (152), Javed Miandad (47) | Karachi | 1982–83 | – | – | – | – | 112 | – |
| Talat Ali (61), Javed Miandad (160*) | Christchurch | 1978–79 | – | – | – | 104 | – | – |
| Majid Khan (98), Zaheer Abbas (240) | Oval | 1974 | 100 | – | – | – | – | – |
| | Totals: (23) | | 5 | 6 | 4 | 2 | 5 | 1 |

| PAKISTAN – 3rd Wicket | | | E | A | WI | NZ | I | SL |
|---|---|---|---|---|---|---|---|---|
| Mudassar Nazar (231), Javed Miandad (280*) | Hyderabad | 1982–83 | – | – | – | – | 451 | – |
| Taslim Arif (210*), Javed Miandad (106*) | Faisalabad | 1979–80 | – | 223* | – | – | – | – |
| Mudassar Nazar (106), Javed Miandad (103) | Hyderabad | 1984–85 | – | – | – | 212 | – | – |
| Mudassar Nazar (114), Haroon Rashid (122) | Lahore[2] | 1977–78 | 180 | – | – | – | – | – |
| Zaheer Abbas (240), Mushtaq Mohammad (76) | Oval | 1974 | 172 | – | – | – | – | – |
| Sadiq Mohammad (166), Majid Khan (79) | Wellington | 1972–73 | – | – | – | 171 | – | – |
| Saeed Ahmed (97), Wazir Mohammad (189) | Port-of-Spain | 1957–58 | – | – | 169 | – | – | – |
| Saeed Ahmed (166), Shujauddin (45) | Lahore[2] | 1959–60 | – | 169 | – | – | – | – |
| Zaheer Abbas (96), Asif Iqbal (104) | Faisalabad | 1978–79 | – | – | – | – | 166 | – |

**3rd Wicket** *continued*

| | | | E | A | WI | NZ | I | SL |
|---|---|---|---|---|---|---|---|---|
| Hanif Mohammad (111), Javed Burki (140) | Dacca | 1961–62 | 156 | – | – | – | – | – |
| Hanif Mohammad (337), Saeed Ahmed (65) | Bridgetown | 1957–58 | – | – | 154 | – | – | – |
| Mudassar Nazar (152*), Javed Miandad (85) | Lahore[2] | 1982–83 | – | – | – | – | 148 | – |
| Qasim Omar (96), Javed Miandad (79) | Dunedin | 1984–85 | – | – | – | 141 | – | – |
| Saeed Ahmed (74), Javed Burki (138) | Lahore[2] | 1961–62 | 138 | – | – | – | – | – |
| Saeed Ahmed (150), Hanif Mohammad (79) | Georgetown | 1957–58 | – | – | 136 | – | – | – |
| Mudassar Nazar (126), Javed Miandad (76) | Bangalore | 1979–80 | – | – | – | – | 134 | – |
| Zaheer Abbas (72), Mushtaq Mohammad (57) | Leeds | 1971 | 129 | – | – | – | – | – |
| Qasim Omar (65), Javed Miandad (46) | Perth | 1983–84 | – | 125 | – | – | – | – |
| Majid Khan (99), Mushtaq Mohammad (99) | Karachi | 1972–73 | 121 | – | – | – | – | – |
| Saeed Ahmed (172), Javed Burki (29) | Karachi | 1964–65 | – | – | – | 114 | – | – |
| Majid Khan (110), Mushtaq Mohammad (61) | Auckland | 1972–73 | – | – | – | 104 | – | – |
| Qasim Omar (45), Javed Miandad (104) | Hyderabad | 1984–85 | – | – | – | 103 | – | |
| Imtiaz Ahmed (122), W. Mathias (77) | Kingston | 1957–58 | – | – | 101 | – | – | – |
| Majid Khan (41), Javed Miandad (57) | Multan | 1980–81 | – | – | 100 | – | – | – |
| Mudassar Nazar (65), Javed Miandad (54) | Leeds | 1982 | 100 | – | – | – | – | – |
| | | *Totals: (25)* | *7* | *3* | *5* | *6* | *4* | *–* |

**PAKISTAN – 4th Wicket**

| | | | E | A | WI | NZ | I | SL |
|---|---|---|---|---|---|---|---|---|
| Mushtaq Mohammad (201), Asif Iqbal (175) | Dunedin | 1972–73 | – | – | – | 350 | – | – |
| Javed Miandad (126), Zaheer Abbas (168) | Faisalabad | 1982–83 | – | – | – | – | 287 | – |
| Zaheer Abbas (176), Javed Miandad (154*) | Faisalabad | 1978–79 | – | – | – | – | 255 | – |
| Javed Miandad (206), Mushtaq Mohd (107) | Karachi | 1976–77 | – | – | – | 252 | – | – |
| Mushtaq Mohammad (101), Asif Iqbal (73) | Hyderabad | 1976–77 | – | – | – | 164 | – | – |
| Salim Malik (100*), Javed Miandad (92) | Karachi | 1981–82 | – | – | – | – | – | 162 |
| Mansoor Akhtar (111), Zaheer Abbas (126) | Faisalabad | 1982–83 | – | 155 | – | – | – | – |
| Wazir Mohd (189), Hanif Mohd (54) | Port-of-Spain | 1957–58 | – | – | 154 | – | – | – |
| Javed Burki (138), Mushtaq Mohammad (76) | Lahore[2] | 1961–62 | 153 | – | – | – | – | – |
| Mohsin Khan (200), Zaheer Abbas (75) | Lord's | 1982 | 153 | – | – | – | – | – |
| Mohsin Khan (135), Javed Miandad (138) | Lahore[2] | 1982–83 | – | 150 | – | – | – | – |
| Maqsood Ahmed (99), A.H. Kardar (44) | Lahore[1] | 1954–55 | – | – | – | – | 136 | – |
| Mohsin Khan (152), Zaheer Abbas (44) | Melbourne | 1983–84 | – | 132 | – | – | – | – |
| Salim Malik (116), Zaheer Abbas (68) | Faisalabad | 1983–84 | 130 | – | – | – | – | – |
| Javed Miandad (62), Zaheer Abbas (90) | Melbourne | 1981–82 | – | 128 | – | – | – | – |
| Hanif Mohammad (337), Wazir Mohd (35) | Bridgetown | 1957–58 | – | – | 121 | – | – | – |
| Mushtaq Mohammad (76), Wasim Raja (53) | Lord's | 1974 | 115 | – | – | – | – | – |
| Haroon Rashid (108), Javed Miandad (88*) | Hyderabad | 1977–78 | 112 | – | – | – | – | – |
| Mohsin Khan (94), Zaheer Abbas (215) | Lahore[2] | 1982–83 | – | – | – | – | 112 | – |
| Javed Miandad (39), Zaheer Abbas (186) | Karachi | 1982–83 | – | – | – | – | 110 | – |
| Majid Khan (92), Mushtaq Mohammad (121) | Port-of-Spain | 1976–77 | – | – | 108 | – | – | – |
| Mushtaq Mohammad (100*), Saeed Ahmed (64) | Nottingham | 1962 | 107 | – | – | – | – | – |
| Majid Khan (75), Zaheer Abbas (48) | Leeds | 1974 | 100 | – | – | – | – | – |
| Mudassar Nazar (114), Javed Miandad (71) | Lahore[2] | 1977–78 | 100 | – | – | – | – | – |
| | | *Totals: (24)* | *8* | *4* | *3* | *3* | *5* | *1* |

**PAKISTAN – 5th Wicket**

| | | | E | A | WI | NZ | I | SL |
|---|---|---|---|---|---|---|---|---|
| Javed Miandad (163), Asif Iqbal (166) | Lahore[2] | 1976–77 | – | – | – | 281 | – | – |
| Zaheer Abbas (186), Mudassar Nazar (119) | Karachi | 1982–83 | – | – | – | – | 213 | – |
| Javed Burki (101), Nasim-ul-Ghani (101) | Lord's | 1962 | 197 | – | – | – | – | – |
| Javed Miandad (131), Salim Malik (77) | Adelaide | 1983–84 | – | 186 | – | – | – | – |
| Alimuddin (103*), A.H. Kardar (93) | Karachi | 1954–55 | – | – | – | – | 155 | – |
| Mushtaq Mohammad (157), Asif Iqbal (68) | Hyderabad | 1972–73 | 153 | – | – | – | – | – |
| Zaheer Abbas (235*), Javed Miandad (35) | Lahore[2] | 1978–79 | – | – | – | – | 140 | – |
| Mushtaq Mohammad (121), Asif Iqbal (65) | Sydney | 1972–73 | – | 139 | – | – | – | – |
| Javed Miandad (85), Mushtaq Mohammad (67*) | Karachi | 1976–77 | – | – | – | 138 | – | – |
| Javed Burki (61), Mushtaq Mohammad (101) | Delhi | 1960–61 | – | – | – | – | 136 | – |
| Wasim Raja (97), Asif Iqbal (64) | Delhi | 1979–80 | – | – | – | – | 130 | – |
| Zaheer Abbas (80), Wasim Raja (43) | Brisbane[2] | 1981–82 | – | 125 | – | – | – | – |
| Javed Miandad (138), Zaheer Abbas (52) | Lahore[2] | 1982–83 | – | 123 | – | – | – | – |
| Salim Malik (116), Wasim Raja (112) | Faisalabad | 1983–84 | 123 | – | – | – | – | – |
| Qasim Omar (210), Salim Malik (102*) | Faisalabad | 1984–85 | – | – | – | – | 114 | – |
| Zaheer Abbas (85), Mudassar Nazar (78) | Nagpur | 1983–84 | – | – | – | – | 101 | – |
| | | *Totals: (16)* | *3* | *4* | *–* | *2* | *7* | *–* |

**PAKISTAN – 6th Wicket**

| | | | E | A | WI | NZ | I | SL |
|---|---|---|---|---|---|---|---|---|
| Hanif Mohammad (203*), Majid Khan (80) | Lahore² | 1964–65 | – | – | – | 217 | – | – |
| Salim Malik (107), Imran Khan (117) | Faisalabad | 1982–83 | – | – | – | – | 207 | – |
| Salim Malik (119*), Wasim Raja (60*) | Karachi | 1984–85 | – | – | – | 178* | – | – |
| Wazir Mohammad (106), A.H. Kardar (57) | Kingston | 1957–58 | – | – | 166 | – | – | – |
| Javed Miandad (100), Mushtaq Mohammad (78) | Karachi | 1978–79 | – | – | – | – | 154 | – |
| Zaheer Abbas (235*), Mushtaq Mohammad (67) | Lahore² | 1978–79 | – | – | – | – | 146 | – |
| Mushtaq Mohammad (157), Intikhab Alam (138) | Hyderabad | 1972–73 | 145 | – | – | – | – | – |
| Zaheer Abbas (215), Imran Khan (45) | Lahore² | 1982–83 | – | – | – | – | 117 | – |
| Mushtaq Mohammad (123), Aftab Baloch (60*) | Lahore² | 1974–75 | – | – | 116 | – | – | – |
| Mushtaq Mohammad (56), Wasim Raja (70) | Port-of-Spain | 1976–77 | – | – | 116 | – | – | – |
| Asif Iqbal (120), Javed Miandad (64) | Sydney | 1976–77 | – | 115 | – | – | – | – |
| Asif Iqbal (135), Wasim Raja (64) | Kingston | 1976–77 | – | – | 115 | – | – | – |
| Wazir Mohammad (67), A.H. Kardar (69) | Karachi | 1956–57 | – | 104 | – | – | – | – |
| Zaheer Abbas (134), Imran Khan (39) | Lahore² | 1981–82 | – | – | – | – | – | 100 |
| *Totals: (14)* | | | *1* | *2* | *4* | *2* | *4* | *1* |

**PAKISTAN – 7th Wicket**

| | | | E | A | WI | NZ | I | SL |
|---|---|---|---|---|---|---|---|---|
| Waqar Hassan (189), Imtiaz Ahmed (209) | Lahore¹ | 1955–56 | – | – | – | 308 | – | – |
| Zaheer Abbas (168*), Ashraf Ali (65) | Lahore² | 1984–85 | – | – | – | – | 142 | – |
| Wasim Raja (107*), Wasim Bari (58) | Karachi | 1974–75 | – | – | 128 | – | – | – |
| Intikhab Alam (64), Wasim Bari (72) | Adelaide | 1972–73 | – | 104 | – | – | – | – |
| Haroon Rashid (153), Tahir Naqqash (57) | Karachi | 1981–82 | – | – | – | – | – | 104 |
| *Totals: (5)* | | | *–* | *1* | *1* | *1* | *1* | *1* |

*Although the seventh wicket added 168 v West Indies in 1980–81, this consisted of two partnerships: Imran Khan added 72 with Abdul Qadir (retired hurt) and a further 96 with Sarfraz Nawaz.*

**PAKISTAN – 8th Wicket**

| | | | E | A | WI | NZ | I | SL |
|---|---|---|---|---|---|---|---|---|
| Hanif Mohammad (187*), Asif Iqbal (76) | Lord's | 1967 | 130 | – | – | – | – | – |
| Majid Khan (110*), Imran Khan (56) | Lahore² | 1979–80 | – | 111 | – | – | – | – |
| Imran Khan (83), Abdul Qadir (45) | Melbourne | 1983–84 | – | 108 | – | – | – | – |
| *Totals: (3)* | | | *1* | *2* | *–* | *–* | *–* | *–* |

**PAKISTAN – 9th Wicket**

| | | | E | A | WI | NZ | I | SL |
|---|---|---|---|---|---|---|---|---|
| Asif Iqbal (146), Intikhab Alam (51) | Oval | 1967 | 190 | – | – | – | – | – |
| Zaheer Abbas (82*), Sarfraz Nawaz (90) | Lahore² | 1983–84 | 161 | – | – | – | – | – |
| Haroon Rashid (153), Rashid Khan (59) | Karachi | 1981–82 | – | – | – | – | – | 127 |
| *Totals: (3)* | | | *2* | *–* | *–* | *–* | *–* | *1* |

**PAKISTAN – 10th Wicket**

| | | | E | A | WI | NZ | I | SL |
|---|---|---|---|---|---|---|---|---|
| Wasim Raja (71), Wasim Bari (60*) | Bridgetown | 1976–77 | – | – | 133 | – | – | – |
| Zulfiqar Ahmed (63*), Amir Elahi (47) | Madras¹ | 1952–53 | – | – | – | – | 104 | – |
| *Totals: (2)* | | | *–* | *–* | *1* | *–* | *1* | *–* |

**SRI LANKA – (10) – 1st Wicket**
No instance – highest partnership

| | | | E | A | NZ | I | P |
|---|---|---|---|---|---|---|---|
| S. Wettimuny (157), H.M. Goonatillake (27) | Faisalabad | 1981–82 | – | – | – | – | 77 |

**SRI LANKA – 2nd Wicket**

| | | | E | A | NZ | I | P |
|---|---|---|---|---|---|---|---|
| S. Wettimuny (157), R.L. Dias (98) | Faisalabad | 1981–82 | – | – | – | – | 217 |

**SRI LANKA – 3rd Wicket**

| | | | E | A | NZ | I | P |
|---|---|---|---|---|---|---|---|
| S. Wettimuny (65), R.L. Dias (108) | Colombo (SSC) | 1983–84 | – | – | 159*† | – | – |
| R.L. Dias (60), L.R.D. Mendis (105) | Madras¹ | 1982–83 | – | – | – | 153 | – |
| R.L. Dias (97), L.R.D. Mendis (105) | Madras¹ | 1982–83 | – | – | – | 110 | – |
| S. Wettimuny (190), R.L. Dias (32) | Lord's | 1984 | 101 | – | – | – | – |
| *Totals: (4)* | | | *1* | *–* | *1* | *2* | *–* |

*†163 runs were added for this wicket, S. Wettimuny retiring hurt and being succeeded by J.R. Ratnayeke after 159 had been added.*

**SRI LANKA – 4th Wicket**

| | | | E | A | NZ | I | P |
|---|---|---|---|---|---|---|---|
| S. Wettimuny (190), A. Ranatunga (84) | Lord's | 1984 | 148 | – | – | – | – |

**SRI LANKA – 5th Wicket**

| | | | E | A | NZ | I | P |
|---|---|---|---|---|---|---|---|
| S. Wettimuny (190), L.R.D. Mendis (111) | Lord's | 1984 | 150 | – | – | – | – |
| R.S. Madugalle (79), D.S. De Silva (61) | Wellington | 1982–83 | – | – | 130 | – | – |
| | Totals: (2) | | 1 | – | 1 | – | – |

**SRI LANKA – 6th Wicket**

| | | | E | A | NZ | I | P |
|---|---|---|---|---|---|---|---|
| S.A.R. Silva (102*), L.R.D. Mendis (94) | Lord's | 1984 | 138 | – | – | – | – |
| R.S. Madugalle (89*), A. Ranatunga (37) | Colombo (CCC) | 1983–84 | – | – | 109*† | – | – |
| | Totals: (2) | | 1 | – | 1 | – | – |

†119 runs were added for the sixth wicket, R.S. Madugalle retiring hurt and being succeeded by D.S. De Silva after 109 had been scored.

**SRI LANKA – 7th Wicket**
No instance – highest partnership

| | | | E | A | NZ | I | P |
|---|---|---|---|---|---|---|---|
| R.S. Madugalle (46), D.S. De Silva (49) | Madras[1] | 1982–83 | – | – | – | 77 | – |

**SRI LANKA – 8th Wicket**
No instance – highest partnership

| | | | E | A | NZ | I | P |
|---|---|---|---|---|---|---|---|
| R.S. Madugalle (91*), D.S. De Silva (25) | Faisalabad | 1981–82 | – | – | – | – | 61 |

**SRI LANKA – 9th Wicket**
No instance – highest partnership

| | | | E | A | NZ | I | P |
|---|---|---|---|---|---|---|---|
| J.R. Ratnayeke (23), A.L.F. De Mel (18) | Madras[1] | 1982–83 | – | – | – | 42 | – |

**SRI LANKA – 10th Wicket**
No instance – highest partnership

| | | | E | A | NZ | I | P |
|---|---|---|---|---|---|---|---|
| V.B. John (27*), M.J.G. Amerasinghe (34) | Kandy | 1983–84 | – | – | 60 | – | – |

# INDIVIDUAL RECORDS – BOWLING

## 100 WICKETS IN TESTS

| ENGLAND | Tests | Wkts | Avge | Opponents A | SA | WI | NZ | I | P | SL |
|---|---|---|---|---|---|---|---|---|---|---|
| I.T. Botham | 79 | 343 | 26.37 | 136 | — | 58 | 58 | 59 | 33 | 10 |
| R.G.D. Willis | 90 | 325 | 25.20 | 128 | — | 38 | 60 | 62 | 34 | 3 |
| F.S. Trueman | 67 | 307 | 21.57 | 79 | 27 | 86 | 40 | 53 | 22 | — |
| D.L. Underwood | 86 | 297 | 25.83 | 105 | — | 38 | 48 | 62 | 36 | 8 |
| J.B. Statham | 70 | 252 | 24.84 | 69 | 69 | 42 | 20 | 25 | 27 | — |
| A.V. Bedser | 51 | 236 | 24.89 | 104 | 54 | 11 | 13 | 44 | 10 | — |
| J.A. Snow | 49 | 202 | 26.66 | 83 | 4 | 72 | 20 | 16 | 7 | — |
| J.C. Laker | 46 | 193 | 21.24 | 79 | 32 | 51 | 21 | 8 | 2 | — |
| S.F. Barnes | 27 | 189 | 16.43 | 106 | 83 | — | — | — | — | — |
| G.A.R. Lock | 49 | 174 | 25.58 | 31 | 15 | 39 | 47 | 26 | 16 | — |
| M.W. Tate | 39 | 155 | 26.16 | 83 | 53 | 13 | 6 | — | — | — |
| F.J. Titmus | 53 | 153 | 32.22 | 47 | 27 | 15 | 28 | 27 | 9 | — |
| H. Verity | 40 | 144 | 24.37 | 59 | 31 | 9 | 7 | 38 | — | — |
| C.M. Old | 46 | 143 | 28.11 | 40 | — | 18 | 21 | 43 | 21 | — |
| A.W. Greig | 58 | 141 | 32.20 | 44 | — | 36 | 20 | 27 | 14 | — |
| T.E. Bailey | 61 | 132 | 29.21 | 42 | 28 | 29 | 32 | — | 1 | — |
| W. Rhodes | 58 | 127 | 26.96 | 109 | 8 | 10 | — | — | — | — |
| D.A. Allen | 39 | 122 | 30.97 | 28 | 21 | 15 | 13 | 21 | 24 | — |
| R. Illingworth | 61 | 122 | 31.20 | 34 | 6 | 19 | 22 | 31 | 10 | — |
| J. Briggs | 33 | 118 | 17.74 | 97 | 21 | — | — | — | — | — |
| G.G. Arnold | 34 | 115 | 28.29 | 30 | — | 17 | 20 | 27 | 21 | — |
| G.A. Lohmann | 18 | 112 | 10.75 | 77 | 35 | — | — | — | — | — |
| D.V.P. Wright | 34 | 108 | 39.11 | 48 | 37 | 11 | 8 | 4 | — | — |
| R. Peel | 20 | 102 | 16.81 | 102 | — | — | — | — | — | — |
| J.H. Wardle | 28 | 102 | 20.39 | 24 | 46 | 7 | 5 | — | 20 | — |
| C. Blythe | 19 | 100 | 18.63 | 41 | 59 | — | — | — | — | — |

| AUSTRALIA | Tests | Wkts | Avge | Opponents E | SA | WI | NZ | I | P | SL |
|---|---|---|---|---|---|---|---|---|---|---|
| D.K. Lillee | 70 | 355 | 23.92 | 167 | — | 55 | 38 | 21 | 71 | 3 |
| R. Benaud | 63 | 248 | 27.03 | 83 | 52 | 42 | — | 52 | 19 | — |
| G.D. McKenzie | 60 | 246 | 29.78 | 96 | 41 | 47 | — | 47 | 15 | — |
| R.R. Lindwall | 61 | 228 | 23.03 | 114 | 31 | 41 | 2 | 36 | 4 | — |
| C.V. Grimmett | 37 | 216 | 24.21 | 106 | 77 | 33 | — | — | — | — |
| J.R. Thomson | 51 | 200 | 28.00 | 100 | — | 62 | 6 | 22 | 10 | — |
| A.K. Davidson | 44 | 186 | 20.53 | 84 | 25 | 33 | — | 30 | 14 | — |
| K.R. Miller | 55 | 170 | 22.97 | 87 | 30 | 40 | 2 | 9 | 2 | — |
| W.A. Johnston | 40 | 160 | 23.91 | 75 | 44 | 25 | — | 16 | — | — |
| W.J. O'Reilly | 27 | 144 | 22.59 | 102 | 34 | — | 8 | — | — | — |
| H. Trumble | 32 | 141 | 21.78 | 141 | — | — | — | — | — | — |
| G.F. Lawson | 34 | 140 | 28.85 | 68 | — | 36 | 3 | — | 33 | — |
| M.H.N. Walker | 34 | 138 | 27.47 | 56 | — | 37 | 28 | — | 17 | — |
| A.A. Mallett | 38 | 132 | 29.84 | 50 | 6 | 16 | 19 | 28 | 13 | — |
| B. Yardley | 33 | 126 | 31.63 | 29 | — | 35 | 13 | 21 | 21 | 7 |
| R.M. Hogg | 38 | 123 | 28.44 | 56 | — | 22 | 10 | 15 | 19 | 1 |
| M.A. Noble | 42 | 121 | 25.00 | 115 | 6 | — | — | — | — | — |
| I.W. Johnson | 45 | 109 | 29.19 | 42 | 22 | 22 | — | 19 | 4 | — |
| G. Giffen | 31 | 103 | 27.09 | 103 | — | — | — | — | — | — |
| A.N. Connolly | 29 | 102 | 29.22 | 25 | 26 | 20 | — | 31 | — | — |
| C.T.B. Turner | 17 | 101 | 16.53 | 101 | — | — | — | — | — | — |

| SOUTH AFRICA | Tests | Wkts | Avge | Opponents E | A | NZ |
|---|---|---|---|---|---|---|
| H.J. Tayfield | 37 | 170 | 25.91 | 75 | 64 | 31 |
| T.L. Goddard | 41 | 123 | 26.22 | 63 | 53 | 7 |
| P.M. Pollock | 28 | 116 | 24.18 | 32 | 52 | 32 |
| N.A.T. Adcock | 26 | 104 | 21.10 | 57 | 14 | 33 |

### WEST INDIES

| | Tests | Wkts | Avge | Opponents E | A | NZ | I | P |
|---|---|---|---|---|---|---|---|---|
| L.R. Gibbs | 79 | **309** | 29.09 | 100 | 103 | 11 | 63 | 32 |
| G.St A. Sobers | 93 | **235** | 34.03 | 102 | 51 | 19 | 59 | 4 |
| M.A. Holding | 55 | **233** | 23.23 | 80 | 76 | 16 | 61 | — |
| J. Garner | 51 | **220** | 21.78 | 65 | 89 | 24 | 7 | 35 |
| A.M.E. Roberts | 47 | **202** | 25.61 | 50 | 51 | 3 | 67 | 31 |
| W.W. Hall | 48 | **192** | 26.38 | 65 | 45 | 1 | 65 | 16 |
| M.D. Marshall | 40 | **188** | 22.11 | 42 | 49 | 27 | 57 | 13 |
| S. Ramadhin | 43 | **158** | 28.98 | 80 | 22 | 32 | 15 | 9 |
| A.L. Valentine | 36 | **139** | 30.32 | 40 | 43 | 23 | 30 | 3 |
| C.E.H. Croft | 27 | **125** | 23.30 | 33 | 32 | 10 | — | 50 |
| V.A. Holder | 40 | **109** | 33.27 | 33 | 28 | 12 | 31 | 5 |

### NEW ZEALAND

| | Tests | Wkts | Avge | Opponents E | A | SA | WI | I | P | SL |
|---|---|---|---|---|---|---|---|---|---|---|
| R.J. Hadlee | 57 | **266** | 23.83 | 62 | 56 | — | 34 | 35 | 46 | 33 |
| B.L. Cairns | 42 | **130** | 32.07 | 32 | 23 | — | 17 | 22 | 21 | 15 |
| R.O. Collinge | 35 | **116** | 29.25 | 48 | 17 | — | — | 23 | 28 | — |
| B.R. Taylor | 30 | **111** | 26.60 | 28 | — | — | 32 | 29 | 22 | — |
| R.C. Motz | 32 | **100** | 31.48 | 28 | — | 21 | 17 | 22 | 12 | — |

### INDIA

| | Tests | Wkts | Avge | Opponents E | A | WI | NZ | P | SL |
|---|---|---|---|---|---|---|---|---|---|
| B.S. Bedi | 67 | **266** | 28.71 | 85 | 56 | 62 | 57 | 6 | — |
| Kapil Dev | 68 | **258** | 28.70 | 61 | 42 | 63 | 8 | 76 | 8 |
| B.S. Chandrasekhar | 58 | **242** | 29.74 | 95 | 38 | 65 | 36 | 8 | — |
| E.A.S. Prasanna | 49 | **189** | 30.38 | 41 | 57 | 34 | 55 | 2 | — |
| M.H. Mankad | 44 | **162** | 32.32 | 54 | 23 | 36 | 12 | 37 | — |
| S. Venkataraghavan | 57 | **156** | 36.11 | 23 | 20 | 68 | 44 | 1 | — |
| S.P. Gupte | 36 | **149** | 29.55 | 24 | 8 | 49 | 34 | 34 | — |
| D.R. Doshi | 33 | **114** | 30.71 | 36 | 38 | — | 5 | 27 | 8 |
| K.D. Ghavri | 39 | **109** | 33.54 | 19 | 32 | 36 | 5 | 17 | — |

### PAKISTAN

| | Tests | Wkts | Avge | Opponents E | A | WI | NZ | I | SL |
|---|---|---|---|---|---|---|---|---|---|
| Imran Khan | 51 | **232** | 22.91 | 26 | 60 | 35 | 24 | 73 | 14 |
| Sarfraz Nawaz | 55 | **177** | 32.75 | 37 | 52 | 26 | 26 | 36 | — |
| Fazal Mahmood | 34 | **139** | 24.70 | 25 | 24 | 41 | 5 | 44 | — |
| Iqbal Qasim | 41 | **137** | 29.16 | 14 | 45 | 19 | 22 | 22 | 15 |
| Intikhab Alam | 47 | **125** | 35.93 | 49 | 9 | 8 | 54 | 5 | — |
| Abdul Qadir | 33 | **114** | 35.11 | 41 | 34 | 8 | 14 | 17 | — |

## BEST BOWLING AVERAGES

*Qualification: 25 wickets*

| | | Tests | Balls | Runs | Wkts | Avge | 5wI | 10wM |
|---|---|---|---|---|---|---|---|---|
| G.A. Lohmann | E | 18 | 3821 | 1205 | 112 | **10.75** | 9 | 5 |
| J.J. Ferris | A/E | 9 | 2302 | 775 | 61 | **12.70** | 6 | 1 |
| A.E. Trott | A/E | 5 | 948 | 390 | 26 | **15.00** | 2 | – |
| M.J. Procter | SA | 7 | 1514 | 616 | 41 | **15.02** | 1 | – |
| W. Barnes | E | 21 | 2289 | 793 | 51 | **15.54** | 3 | – |
| W. Bates | E | 15 | 2364 | 821 | 50 | **16.42** | 4 | 1 |
| S.F. Barnes | E | 27 | 7873 | 3106 | 189 | **16.43** | 24 | 7 |
| C.T.B. Turner | A | 17 | 5179 | 1670 | 101 | **16.53** | 11 | 2 |
| R. Peel | E | 20 | 5216 | 1715 | 102 | **16.81** | 6 | 2 |
| J. Briggs | E | 33 | 5332 | 2094 | 118 | **17.74** | 9 | 4 |
| R. Appleyard | E | 9 | 1596 | 534 | 31 | **17.87** | 1 | – |
| W.S. Lees | E | 5 | 1256 | 467 | 26 | **17.96** | 2 | – |
| H. Ironmonger | A | 14 | 4695 | 1330 | 74 | **17.97** | 4 | 2 |
| G.B. Lawrence | SA | 5 | 1334 | 512 | 28 | **18.28** | 2 | – |

|  |  | Tests | Balls | Runs | Wkts | Avge | 5wI | 10wM |
|---|---|---|---|---|---|---|---|---|
| F.R. Spofforth | A | 18 | 4185 | 1731 | 94 | **18.41** | 7 | 4 |
| F.H. Tyson | E | 17 | 3452 | 1411 | 76 | **18.56** | 4 | 1 |
| C. Blythe | E | 19 | 4446 | 1863 | 100 | **18.63** | 9 | 4 |
| G.F. Bissett | SA | 4 | 989 | 469 | 25 | **18.76** | 2 | – |
| A.S. Kennedy | E | 5 | 1683 | 599 | 31 | **19.32** | 2 | – |

# MOST FREQUENT WICKET-TAKERS

*Qualification: 25 wickets*

|  |  | Balls/wkt | Tests | Balls | Runs | Wkts | Avge |
|---|---|---|---|---|---|---|---|
| G.A. Lohmann | E | **34.11** | 18 | 3821 | 1205 | 112 | 10.75 |
| A.E. Trott | A/E | **36.46** | 5 | 948 | 390 | 26 | 15.00 |
| M.J. Procter | SA | **36.92** | 7 | 1514 | 616 | 41 | 15.02 |
| J.J. Ferris | A/E | **37.73** | 9 | 2302 | 775 | 61 | 12.70 |
| B.J.T. Bosanquet | E | **38.80** | 7 | 970 | 604 | 25 | 24.16 |
| G.F. Bissett | SA | **39.56** | 4 | 989 | 469 | 25 | 18.76 |
| S.F. Barnes | E | **41.65** | 27 | 7873 | 3106 | 189 | 16.43 |

# MOST ECONOMICAL CAREER FIGURES

*Qualification: 2000 balls*

|  |  | Runs/100 balls | Tests | Balls | Runs | Wkts | Avge |
|---|---|---|---|---|---|---|---|
| W. Attewell | E | **21.96** | 10 | 2850 | 626 | 27 | 23.18 |
| C. Gladwin | E | **26.82** | 8 | 2129 | 571 | 15 | 38.06 |
| T.L. Goddard | SA | **27.48** | 41 | 11736 | 3226 | 123 | 26.22 |
| R.G. Nadkarni | I | **27.92** | 41 | 9165 | 2559 | 88 | 29.07 |
| H. Ironmonger | A | **28.32** | 14 | 4695 | 1330 | 74 | 17.97 |
| J.C. Watkins | SA | **29.09** | 15 | 2805 | 816 | 29 | 28.13 |
| K.D. Mackay | A | **29.71** | 37 | 5792 | 1721 | 50 | 34.42 |
| A.R.A. Murray | SA | **29.90** | 10 | 2374 | 710 | 18 | 39.44 |

# 25 WICKETS IN A SERIES

| ENGLAND |  | Venue | Tests | Opponents A | SA | WI | NZ | I | P |
|---|---|---|---|---|---|---|---|---|---|
| S.F. Barnes | 1913–14 | SA | 4 | — | **49** | — | — | — | — |
| J.C. Laker | 1956 | E | 5 | **46** | — | — | — | — | — |
| A.V. Bedser | 1953 | E | 5 | **39** | — | — | — | — | — |
| M.W. Tate | 1924–25 | A | 5 | **38** | — | — | — | — | — |
| G.A. Lohmann | 1895–96 | SA | 3 | — | **35** | — | — | — | — |
| S.F. Barnes | 1911–12 | A | 5 | **34** | — | — | — | — | — |
| S.F. Barnes | 1912 | E | 3 | — | **34** | — | — | — | — |
| G.A.R. Lock | 1958 | E | 5 | — | — | — | **34** | — | — |
| F.S. Trueman | 1963 | E | 5 | — | — | **34** | — | — | — |
| I.T. Botham | 1981 | E | 6 | **31** | — | — | — | — | — |
| H. Larwood | 1932–33 | A | 5 | **33** | — | — | — | — | — |
| T. Richardson | 1894–95 | A | 5 | **32** | — | — | — | — | — |
| F.R. Foster | 1911–12 | A | 5 | **32** | — | — | — | — | — |
| W. Rhodes | 1903–04 | A | 5 | **31** | — | — | — | — | — |
| A.S. Kennedy | 1922–23 | SA | 5 | — | **31** | — | — | — | — |
| J.A. Snow | 1970–71 | A | 6 | **31** | — | — | — | — | — |
| I.T. Botham | 1985 | E | 6 | **31** | — | — | — | — | — |
| J.N. Crawford | 1907–08 | A | 5 | **30** | — | — | — | — | — |
| A.V. Bedser | 1950–51 | A | 5 | **30** | — | — | — | — | — |
| A.V. Bedser | 1951 | E | 5 | — | **30** | — | — | — | — |
| F.S. Trueman | 1952 | E | 4 | — | — | — | — | **29** | — |
| D.L. Underwood | 1976–77 | I | 5 | — | — | — | — | **29** | — |
| R.G.D. Willis | 1981 | E | 6 | **29** | — | — | — | — | — |
| F.H. Tyson | 1954–55 | A | 5 | **28** | — | — | — | — | — |
| R. Peel | 1894–95 | A | 5 | **27** | — | — | — | — | — |
| M.W. Tate | 1924 | E | 5 | — | **27** | — | — | — | — |

| ENGLAND *continued* | | *Venue* | *Tests* | *Opponents* | | | | | |
|---|---|---|---|---|---|---|---|---|---|
| | | | | A | SA | WI | NZ | I | P |
| J.B. Statham | 1960 | E | 5 | — | 27 | — | — | — | — |
| F.J. Titmus | 1963–64 | I | 5 | — | — | — | — | 27 | — |
| J.A. Snow | 1967–68 | WI | 4 | — | — | 27 | — | — | — |
| R.G.D. Willis | 1977 | E | 5 | 27 | — | — | — | — | — |
| W.S. Lees | 1905–06 | SA | 5 | — | 26 | — | — | — | — |
| C. Blythe | 1907 | E | 3 | — | 26 | — | — | — | — |
| W. Voce | 1936–37 | A | 5 | 26 | — | — | — | — | — |
| J.H. Wardle | 1956–57 | SA | 4 | — | 26 | — | — | — | — |
| J.K. Lever | 1976–77 | I | 5 | — | — | — | — | 26 | — |
| A. Fielder | 1907–08 | A | 4 | 25 | — | — | — | — | — |
| J.C. White | 1928–29 | A | 5 | 25 | — | — | — | — | — |
| F.S. Trueman | 1960 | SA | 5 | — | 25 | — | — | — | — |

| AUSTRALIA | | *Venue* | *Tests* | E | SA | WI | NZ | I | P |
|---|---|---|---|---|---|---|---|---|---|
| C.V. Grimmett | 1935–36 | SA | 5 | — | 44 | — | — | — | — |
| T.M. Alderman | 1981 | E | 6 | 42 | — | — | — | — | — |
| R.M. Hogg | 1978–79 | A | 6 | 41 | — | — | — | — | — |
| D.K. Lillee | 1981 | E | 6 | 39 | — | — | — | — | — |
| W.J. Whitty | 1910–11 | A | 5 | — | 37 | — | — | — | — |
| A.A. Mailey | 1920–21 | A | 5 | 36 | — | — | — | — | — |
| G. Giffen | 1894–95 | A | 5 | 34 | — | — | — | — | — |
| G.F. Lawson | 1982–83 | A | 5 | 34 | — | — | — | — | — |
| C.V. Grimmett | 1930–31 | A | 5 | — | — | 33 | — | — | — |
| C.V. Grimmett | 1931–32 | A | 5 | — | 33 | — | — | — | — |
| A.K. Davidson | 1960–61 | A | 4 | — | — | 33 | — | — | — |
| J.R. Thomson | 1974–75 | A | 5 | 33 | — | — | — | — | — |
| M.A. Noble | 1901–02 | A | 5 | 32 | — | — | — | — | — |
| H.V. Hordern | 1911–12 | A | 5 | 32 | — | — | — | — | — |
| J.V. Saunders | 1907–08 | A | 5 | 31 | — | — | — | — | — |
| H. Ironmonger | 1931–32 | A | 4 | — | 31 | — | — | — | — |
| R. Benaud | 1958–59 | A | 5 | 31 | — | — | — | — | — |
| D.K. Lillee | 1972 | E | 5 | 31 | — | — | — | — | — |
| R. Benaud | 1957–58 | SA | 5 | — | 30 | — | — | — | — |
| G.D. McKenzie | 1968–69 | A | 5 | — | — | 30 | — | — | — |
| C.J. McDermott | 1985 | E | 6 | 30 | — | — | — | — | — |
| C.V. Grimmett | 1930 | E | 5 | 29 | — | — | — | — | — |
| A.K. Davidson | 1959–60 | I | 5 | — | — | — | — | 29 | — |
| R. Benaud | 1959–60 | I | 5 | — | — | — | — | 29 | — |
| G.D. McKenzie | 1964 | E | 5 | 29 | — | — | — | — | — |
| J.R. Thomson | 1975–76 | A | 6 | — | — | 29 | — | — | — |
| H. Trumble | 1901–02 | A | 5 | 28 | — | — | — | — | — |
| W.J. O'Reilly | 1934 | E | 5 | 28 | — | — | — | — | — |
| A.A. Mallett | 1969–70 | I | 5 | — | — | — | — | 28 | — |
| W.M. Clark | 1977–78 | A | 5 | — | — | — | — | 28 | — |
| E.A. McDonald | 1921 | E | 5 | 27 | — | — | — | — | — |
| W.J. O'Reilly | 1932–33 | A | 5 | 27 | — | — | — | — | — |
| W.J. O'Reilly | 1935–36 | SA | 5 | — | 27 | — | — | — | — |
| R.R. Lindwall | 1948 | E | 5 | 27 | — | — | — | — | — |
| W.A. Johnston | 1948 | E | 5 | 27 | — | — | — | — | — |
| D.K. Lillee | 1975–76 | A | 5 | — | — | 27 | — | — | — |
| E. Jones | 1899 | E | 5 | 26 | — | — | — | — | — |
| H. Trumble | 1902 | E | 3 | 26 | — | — | — | — | — |
| R.R. Lindwall | 1953 | E | 5 | 26 | — | — | — | — | — |
| J.W. Gleeson | 1968–69 | A | 5 | — | — | 26 | — | — | — |
| M.H.N. Walker | 1972–73 | WI | 5 | — | — | 26 | — | — | — |
| C.V. Grimmett | 1934 | E | 5 | 25 | — | — | — | — | — |
| W.J. O'Reilly | 1936–37 | A | 5 | 25 | — | — | — | — | — |
| A.K. Davidson | 1957–58 | SA | 5 | — | 25 | — | — | — | — |
| D.K. Lillee | 1974–75 | A | 6 | 25 | — | — | — | — | — |
| A.G. Hurst | 1978–79 | A | 6 | 25 | — | — | — | — | — |

| SOUTH AFRICA | | Venue | Tests | Opponents E | A | NZ |
|---|---|---|---|---|---|---|
| H.J. Tayfield | 1956–57 | SA | 5 | 37 | — | — |
| A.E.E. Vogler | 1909–10 | SA | 5 | 36 | — | — |
| H.J. Tayfield | 1952–53 | A | 5 | — | 30 | — |
| G.A. Faulkner | 1909–10 | SA | 5 | 29 | — | — |
| G.B. Lawrence | 1961–62 | SA | 5 | — | — | 28 |
| A.E. Hall | 1922–23 | SA | 4 | 27 | — | — |
| H.J. Tayfield | 1955 | E | 5 | 26 | — | — |
| N.A.T. Adcock | 1960 | E | 5 | 26 | — | — |
| T.L. Goddard | 1966–67 | SA | 5 | — | 26 | — |
| M.J. Procter | 1969–70 | SA | 4 | — | 26 | — |
| C.B. Llewellyn | 1902–03 | SA | 3 | — | 25 | — |
| R.O. Schwarz | 1910–11 | A | 5 | — | 25 | — |
| J.M. Blanckenberg | 1922–23 | SA | 5 | 25 | — | — |
| G.F. Bissett | 1927–28 | SA | 4 | 25 | — | — |
| T.L. Goddard | 1955 | E | 5 | 25 | — | — |
| P.M. Pollock | 1963–64 | A | 5 | — | 25 | — |
| J.T. Partridge | 1963–64 | A | 5 | — | 25 | — |

| WEST INDIES | | Venue | Tests | Opponents E | A | NZ | I | P |
|---|---|---|---|---|---|---|---|---|
| A.L. Valentine | 1950 | E | 4 | 33 | — | — | — | — |
| C.E.H. Croft | 1976–77 | WI | 5 | — | — | — | — | 33 |
| M.D. Marshall | 1983–84 | I | 6 | — | — | — | 33 | — |
| C.C. Griffith | 1963 | E | 5 | 32 | — | — | — | — |
| A.M.E. Roberts | 1974–75 | I | 5 | — | — | — | 32 | — |
| J. Garner | 1983–84 | WI | 5 | — | 31 | — | — | — |
| W.W. Hall | 1958–59 | I | 5 | — | — | — | 30 | — |
| M.A. Holding | 1983–84 | I | 6 | — | — | — | 30 | — |
| J. Garner | 1984 | E | 5 | 29 | — | — | — | — |
| A.L. Valentine | 1952–53 | WI | 5 | — | — | — | 28 | — |
| M.A. Holding | 1976 | E | 4 | 28 | — | — | — | — |
| A.M.E. Roberts | 1976 | E | 5 | 28 | — | — | — | — |
| M.D. Marshall | 1984–85 | A | 5 | — | 28 | — | — | — |
| W.W. Hall | 1961–62 | WI | 5 | — | — | — | 27 | — |
| M.D. Marshall | 1984–85 | WI | 4 | — | — | 27 | — | — |
| S. Ramadhin | 1950 | E | 4 | 26 | — | — | — | — |
| R. Gilchrist | 1958–59 | I | 4 | — | — | — | 26 | — |
| L.R. Gibbs | 1963 | E | 5 | 26 | — | — | — | — |
| L.R. Gibbs | 1972–73 | WI | 5 | — | 26 | — | — | — |
| J. Garner | 1980 | E | 5 | 26 | — | — | — | — |
| J. Garner | 1976–77 | WI | 5 | — | — | — | — | 25 |

| NEW ZEALAND | | Venue | Tests | Opponents E | A | SA | WI | I | P |
|---|---|---|---|---|---|---|---|---|---|
| B.R. Taylor | 1971–72 | WI | 4 | — | — | — | 27 | — | — |

| INDIA | | Venue | Tests | Opponents E | A | WI | NZ | P |
|---|---|---|---|---|---|---|---|---|
| B.S. Chandrasekhar | 1972–73 | I | 5 | 35 | — | — | — | — |
| M.H. Mankad | 1951–52 | I | 5 | 34 | — | — | — | — |
| S.P. Gupte | 1955–56 | I | 5 | — | — | — | 34 | — |
| Kapil Dev | 1979–80 | I | 6 | — | — | — | — | 32 |
| B.S. Bedi | 1977–78 | A | 5 | — | 31 | — | — | — |
| Kapil Dev | 1983–84 | I | 6 | — | — | 29 | — | — |
| B.S. Chandrasekhar | 1977–78 | A | 5 | — | 28 | — | — | — |
| Kapil Dev | 1979–80 | I | 6 | — | 28 | — | — | — |
| S.P. Gupte | 1952–53 | WI | 5 | — | — | 27 | — | — |
| K.D. Ghavri | 1978–79 | I | 6 | — | — | 27 | — | — |
| D.R. Doshi | 1979–80 | I | 6 | — | 27 | — | — | — |
| E.A.S. Prasanna | 1969–70 | I | 5 | — | 26 | — | — | — |
| M.H. Mankad | 1952–53 | I | 5 | — | — | — | — | 25 |

| INDIA continued | | Venue | Tests | Opponents | | | | |
|---|---|---|---|---|---|---|---|---|
| | | | | E | A | WI | NZ | P |
| E.A.S. Prasanna | 1967–68 | A | 4 | — | 25 | — | — | — |
| B.S. Bedi | 1972–73 | I | 5 | 25 | — | — | — | — |
| B.S. Bedi | 1976–77 | I | 5 | 25 | — | — | — | — |

| PAKISTAN | | Venue | Tests | Opponents | | | | |
|---|---|---|---|---|---|---|---|---|
| | | | | E | A | WI | NZ | I |
| Imran Khan | 1982–83 | P | 6 | — | — | — | — | 40 |
| Imran Khan | 1976–77 | WI | 5 | — | — | 25 | — | — |

# TEN WICKETS IN A MATCH
† On debut

| ENGLAND (86) | | | Opponents | | | | | |
|---|---|---|---|---|---|---|---|---|
| | | | A | SA | WI | NZ | I | P |
| J.C. Laker | 1956 | Manchester | 19-90 | — | — | — | — | — |
| S.F. Barnes | 1913–14 | Johannesburg[1] | — | 17-159 | — | — | — | — |
| J. Briggs | 1888–89 | Cape Town | — | 15-28 | — | — | — | — |
| G.A. Lohmann | 1895–96 | Port Elizabeth | — | 15-45 | — | — | — | — |
| C. Blythe | 1907 | Leeds | — | 15-99 | — | — | — | — |
| H. Verity | 1934 | Lord's | 15-104 | — | — | — | — | — |
| W. Rhodes | 1903–04 | Melbourne | 15-124 | — | — | — | — | — |
| A.V. Bedser | 1953 | Nottingham | 14-99 | — | — | — | — | — |
| W. Bates | 1882–83 | Melbourne | 14-102 | — | — | — | — | — |
| S.F. Barnes | 1913–14 | Durban[1] | — | 14-144 | — | — | — | — |
| S.F. Barnes | 1912 | Oval | — | 13-57 | — | — | — | — |
| D.L. Underwood | 1974 | Lord's | — | — | — | — | — | 13-71 |
| J.J. Ferris | 1891–92 | Cape Town | — | 13-91 | — | — | — | — |
| I.T. Botham | 1979–80 | Bombay[3] | — | — | — | — | 13-106 | — |
| A.W. Greig | 1973–74 | Port-of-Spain | — | — | 13-156 | — | — | — |
| S.F. Barnes | 1901–02 | Melbourne | 13-163 | — | — | — | — | — |
| T. Richardson | 1896 | Manchester | 13-244 | — | — | — | — | — |
| J.C. White | 1928–29 | Adelaide | 13-256 | — | — | — | — | — |
| G.A. Lohmann | 1895–96 | Johannesburg[1] | — | 12-71 | — | — | — | — |
| J.H. Wardle | 1956–57 | Cape Town | — | 12-89 | — | — | — | — |
| D.L. Underwood | 1970–71 | Christchurch | — | — | — | 12-97 | — | — |
| R. Tattersall | 1951 | Lord's | — | 12-101 | — | — | — | — |
| D.L. Underwood | 1969 | Oval | — | — | — | 12-101 | — | — |
| F. Martin† | 1890 | Oval | 12-102 | — | — | — | — | — |
| G.A. Lohmann | 1886 | Oval | 12-104 | — | — | — | — | — |
| A.V. Bedser | 1951 | Manchester | — | 12-112 | — | — | — | — |
| F.S. Trueman | 1963 | Birmingham | — | — | 12-119 | — | — | — |
| G. Geary | 1927–28 | Johannesburg[1] | — | 12-130 | — | — | — | — |
| J. Briggs | 1891–92 | Adelaide | 12-136 | — | — | — | — | — |
| A.P. Freeman | 1929 | Manchester | — | 12-171 | — | — | — | — |
| G.A.R. Lock | 1957 | Oval | — | — | 11-48 | — | — | — |
| G.A.R. Lock | 1958 | Leeds | — | — | — | 11-65 | — | — |
| R. Peel | 1888 | Manchester | 11-68 | — | — | — | — | — |
| D.L. Underwood | 1969 | Lord's | — | — | — | 11-70 | — | — |
| J. Briggs | 1886 | Lord's | 11-74 | — | — | — | — | — |
| W.H. Lockwood | 1902 | Manchester | 11-76 | — | — | — | — | — |
| N.G.B. Cook | 1983–84 | Karachi | — | — | — | — | — | 11-83 |
| G.A.R. Lock | 1958–59 | Christchurch | — | — | — | 11-84 | — | — |
| F.S. Trueman | 1961 | Leeds | 11-88 | — | — | — | — | — |
| A.E.R. Gilligan | 1924 | Birmingham | — | 11-90 | — | — | — | — |
| A.V. Bedser | 1946 | Manchester | — | — | — | — | 11-93 | — |
| C.S. Marriott† | 1933 | Oval | — | — | 11-96 | — | — | — |
| J.B. Statham | 1960 | Lord's | — | 11-97 | — | — | — | — |
| T.E. Bailey | 1957 | Lord's | — | — | — | 11-98 | — | — |
| C. Blythe | 1909 | Birmingham | 11-102 | — | — | — | — | — |
| S.F. Barnes | 1912 | Lord's | — | 11-110 | — | — | — | — |
| J.C. Laker | 1956 | Leeds | 11-113 | — | — | — | — | — |

|  |  |  | *Opponents* | | | | | |
| --- | --- | --- | --- | --- | --- | --- | --- | --- |
| **ENGLAND** *continued* |  |  | *A* | *SA* | *WI* | *NZ* | *I* | *P* |
| C. Blythe | 1905–06 | Cape Town | — | 11-118 | — | — | — | — |
| I.T. Botham | 1978 | Lord's | — | — | — | 11-140 | — | — |
| A.V. Bedser† | 1946 | Lord's | — | — | — | — | 11-145 | — |
| W. Voce | 1929–30 | Port-of-Spain | — | — | 11-149 | — | — | — |
| F.S. Trueman | 1963 | Lord's | — | — | 11-152 | — | — | — |
| H. Verity | 1933–34 | Madras¹ | — | — | — | — | 11-153 | — |
| N.A. Foster | 1984–85 | Madras¹ | — | — | — | — | 11-163 | — |
| T. Richardson | 1896 | Lord's | 11-173 | — | — | — | — | — |
| I.T. Botham | 1979–80 | Perth | 11-176 | — | — | — | — | — |
| D.L. Underwood | 1974–75 | Adelaide | 11-215 | — | — | — | — | — |
| M.W. Tate | 1924–25 | Sydney | 11-228 | — | — | — | — | — |
| F.E. Woolley | 1912 | Oval | 10-49 | — | — | — | — | — |
| W. Voce | 1936–37 | Brisbane² | 10-57 | — | — | — | — | — |
| R. Peel | 1887–88 | Sydney | 10-58 | — | — | — | — | — |
| J.T. Hearne | 1896 | Oval | 10-60 | — | — | — | — | — |
| J.K. Lever† | 1976–77 | Delhi | — | — | — | — | 10-70 | — |
| G.O.B. Allen | 1936 | Lord's | — | — | — | — | 10-78 | — |
| D.L. Underwood | 1972 | Leeds | 10-82 | — | — | — | — | — |
| G.A. Lohmann | 1886–87 | Sydney | 10-87 | — | — | — | — | — |
| A.P. Freeman | 1928 | Manchester | — | — | 10-93 | — | — | — |
| C. Blythe | 1909–10 | Cape Town | — | 10-104 | — | — | — | — |
| R.M. Ellison | 1985 | Birmingham | 10-104 | — | — | — | — | — |
| A.V. Bedser | 1950–51 | Melbourne | 10-105 | — | — | — | — | — |
| S.F. Barnes | 1913–14 | Durban¹ | — | 10-105 | — | — | — | — |
| S.F. Barnes | 1912 | Leeds | — | 10-115 | — | — | — | — |
| J.C. Laker | 1951 | Oval | — | 10-119 | — | — | — | — |
| H. Larwood | 1932–33 | Sydney | 10-124 | — | — | — | — | — |
| F.H. Tyson | 1954–55 | Sydney | 10-130 | — | — | — | — | — |
| G.A. Lohmann | 1891–92 | Sydney | 10-142 | — | — | — | — | — |
| J.A. Snow | 1967–68 | Georgetown | — | — | 10-142 | — | — | — |
| J. Briggs | 1893 | Oval | 10-148 | — | — | — | — | — |
| A.W. Greig | 1974–75 | Auckland | — | — | — | 10-149 | — | — |
| T. Richardson† | 1893 | Manchester | 10-156 | — | — | — | — | — |
| D.V.P. Wright | 1947 | Lord's | — | 10-175 | — | — | — | — |
| K. Farnes† | 1934 | Nottingham | 10-179 | — | — | — | — | — |
| G.T.S. Stevens | 1929–30 | Bridgetown | — | — | 10-195 | — | — | — |
| T. Richardson | 1897–98 | Sydney | 10-204 | — | — | — | — | — |
| A.P. Freeman | 1929 | Leeds | — | 10-207 | — | — | — | — |
| I.T. Botham | 1981 | Oval | 10-253 | — | — | — | — | — |
| **AUSTRALIA (60)** |  |  | *E* | *SA* | *WI* | *NZ* | *I* | *P* |
| R.A.L. Massie† | 1972 | Lord's | 16-137 | — | — | — | — | — |
| F.R. Spofforth | 1882 | Oval | 14-90 | — | — | — | — | — |
| C.V. Grimmett | 1931–32 | Adelaide | — | 14-199 | — | — | — | — |
| M.A. Noble | 1901–02 | Melbourne | 13-77 | — | — | — | — | — |
| F.R. Spofforth | 1878–79 | Melbourne | 13-110 | — | — | — | — | — |
| C.V. Grimmett | 1935–36 | Durban² | — | 13-173 | — | — | — | — |
| A.A. Mailey | 1920–21 | Melbourne | 13-236 | — | — | — | — | — |
| C.T.B. Turner | 1887–88 | Sydney | 12-87 | — | — | — | — | — |
| H. Trumble | 1896 | Oval | 12-89 | — | — | — | — | — |
| A.K. Davidson | 1959–60 | Kanpur | — | — | — | — | 12-124 | — |
| G. Dymock | 1979–80 | Kanpur | — | — | — | — | 12-166 | — |
| H. Trumble | 1902 | Oval | 12-173 | — | — | — | — | — |
| H.V. Hordern | 1911–12 | Sydney | 12-175 | — | — | — | — | — |
| H. Ironmonger | 1931–32 | Melbourne | — | 11-24 | — | — | — | — |
| E.R.H. Toshack | 1947–48 | Brisbane² | — | — | — | — | 11-31 | — |
| H. Ironmonger | 1930–31 | Melbourne | — | — | 11-79 | — | — | — |
| C.V. Grimmett† | 1924–25 | Sydney | 11-82 | — | — | — | — | — |
| C.G. Macartney | 1909 | Leeds | 11-85 | — | — | — | — | — |
| M.A. Noble | 1902 | Sheffield | 11-103 | — | — | — | — | — |
| R. Benaud | 1956–57 | Calcutta | — | — | — | — | 11-105 | — |
| F.R. Spofforth | 1882–83 | Sydney | 11-117 | — | — | — | — | — |
| C.G. Rackemann | 1983–84 | Perth | — | — | — | — | — | 11-118 |
| D.K. Lillee | 1976–77 | Auckland | — | — | — | 11-123 | — | — |
| W.J. O'Reilly | 1934 | Nottingham | 11-129 | — | — | — | — | — |

| AUSTRALIA continued | | | *Opponents* E | SA | WI | NZ | I | P |
|---|---|---|---|---|---|---|---|---|
| G.F. Lawson | 1982–83 | Brisbane[2] | 11-134 | — | — | — | — | — |
| D.K. Lillee | 1979–80 | Melbourne | 11-138 | — | — | — | — | — |
| D.K. Lillee | 1981 | Oval | 11-159 | — | — | — | — | — |
| G.E. Palmer | 1881–82 | Sydney | 11-165 | — | — | — | — | — |
| D.K. Lillee | 1976–77 | Melbourne | 11-165 | — | — | — | — | — |
| G.F. Lawson | 1984–85 | Adelaide | — | — | 11-181 | — | — | — |
| C.V. Grimmett | 1930–31 | Adelaide | — | — | 11-183 | — | — | — |
| A.K. Davidson | 1960–61 | Brisbane[2] | — | — | 11-222 | — | — | — |
| C.T.B. Turner | 1888 | Lord's | 10-63 | — | — | — | — | — |
| R.M. Hogg | 1978–79 | Melbourne | 10-66 | — | — | — | — | — |
| C.V. Grimmett | 1935–36 | Cape Town | — | 10-88 | — | — | — | — |
| G.D. McKenzie | 1964–65 | Madras[2] | — | — | — | — | 10-91 | — |
| C.V. Grimmett | 1935–36 | Johannesburg[1] | — | 10-110 | — | — | — | — |
| R.J. Bright | 1979–80 | Karachi | — | — | — | — | — | 10-111 |
| N.J.N. Hawke | 1964–65 | Georgetown | — | — | 10-115 | — | — | — |
| W.J. O'Reilly | 1938 | Leeds | 10-122 | — | — | — | — | — |
| R.M. Hogg | 1978–79 | Perth | 10-122 | — | — | — | — | — |
| G.E. Palmer | 1882–83 | Melbourne | 10-126 | — | — | — | — | — |
| D.K. Lillee | 1981–82 | Melbourne | — | — | 10-127 | — | — | — |
| H. Trumble | 1902 | Manchester | 10-128 | — | — | — | — | — |
| W.J. O'Reilly | 1932–33 | Melbourne | 10-129 | — | — | — | — | — |
| D.K. Lillee | 1976–77 | Melbourne | — | — | — | — | — | 10-135 |
| F.R. Spofforth | 1884–85 | Sydney | 10-144 | — | — | — | — | — |
| A.A. Mallett | 1969–70 | Madras[1] | — | — | — | — | 10-144 | — |
| R.G. Holland | 1984–85 | Sydney | — | — | 10-144 | — | — | — |
| G.D. McKenzie | 1967–68 | Melbourne | — | — | — | — | 10-151 | — |
| K.R. Miller | 1956 | Lord's | 10-152 | — | — | — | — | — |
| G.D. McKenzie | 1968–69 | Melbourne | — | — | 10-159 | — | — | — |
| G. Giffen | 1891–92 | Sydney | 10-160 | — | — | — | — | — |
| H.V. Hordern | 1911–12 | Sydney | 10-161 | — | — | — | — | — |
| E. Jones | 1899 | Lord's | 10-164 | — | — | — | — | — |
| D.K. Lillee | 1972 | Oval | 10-181 | — | — | — | — | — |
| B. Yardley | 1981–82 | Sydney | — | — | 10-185 | — | — | — |
| C.V. Grimmett | 1930 | Nottingham | 10-201 | — | — | — | — | — |
| L.O'B. Fleetwood-Smith | 1936–37 | Adelaide | 10-239 | — | — | — | — | — |
| A.A. Mailey | 1920–21 | Adelaide | 10-302 | — | — | — | — | — |

| SOUTH AFRICA (9) | | | E | A | NZ |
|---|---|---|---|---|---|
| H.J. Tayfield | 1952–53 | Melbourne | — | 13-165 | — |
| H.J. Tayfield | 1956–57 | Johannesburg[3] | 13-192 | — | — |
| S.J. Snooke | 1905–06 | Johannesburg[1] | 12-127 | — | — |
| A.E.E. Vogler | 1909–10 | Johannesburg[1] | 12-181 | — | — |
| A.E. Hall† | 1922–23 | Cape Town | 11-112 | — | — |
| E.P. Nupen | 1930–31 | Johannesburg[1] | 11-150 | — | — |
| S.F. Burke† | 1961–62 | Cape Town | — | — | 11-196 |
| P.M. Pollock | 1965 | Nottingham | 10-87 | — | — |
| C.B. Llewellyn | 1902–03 | Johannesburg[1] | — | 10-116 | — |

| WEST INDIES (16) | | | E | A | NZ | I | P |
|---|---|---|---|---|---|---|---|
| M.A. Holding | 1976 | Oval | 14-149 | — | — | — | — |
| A.M.E. Roberts | 1974–75 | Madras[1] | — | — | — | 12-121 | — |
| M.A. Holding | 1981–82 | Melbourne | — | 11-107 | — | — | — |
| M.D. Marshall | 1984–85 | Bridgetown | — | — | 11-120 | — | — |
| W.W. Hall | 1958–59 | Kanpur | — | — | — | 11-126 | — |
| K.D. Boyce | 1973 | Oval | 11-147 | — | — | — | — |
| S. Ramadhin | 1950 | Lord's | 11-152 | — | — | — | — |
| L.R. Gibbs | 1963 | Manchester | 11-157 | — | — | — | — |
| A.L. Valentine† | 1950 | Manchester | 11-204 | — | — | — | — |
| W. Ferguson | 1947–48 | Port-of-Spain | 11-229 | — | — | — | — |
| H.H.H. Johnson† | 1947–48 | Kingston | 10-96 | — | — | — | — |
| L.R. Gibbs | 1966 | Manchester | 10-106 | — | — | — | — |
| M.D. Marshall | 1984–85 | Adelaide | — | 10-107 | — | — | — |
| G.E. Gomez | 1951–52 | Sydney | — | 10-113 | — | — | — |
| A.M.E. Roberts | 1976 | Lord's | 10-123 | — | — | — | — |
| A.L. Valentine | 1950 | Oval | 10-160 | — | — | — | — |

| NEW ZEALAND (8) | | | E | A | WI | I | P | SL |
|---|---|---|---|---|---|---|---|---|
| R.J. Hadlee | 1975–76 | Wellington | — | — | — | 11-58 | — | — |
| R.J. Hadlee | 1979–80 | Dunedin | — | — | 11-102 | — | — | — |
| R.J. Hadlee | 1977–78 | Wellington | 10-100 | — | — | — | — | — |
| R.J. Hadlee | 1983–84 | Colombo (CCC) | — | — | — | — | — | 10-102 |
| E.J. Chatfield | 1984–85 | Port-of-Spain | — | — | 10-124 | — | — | — |
| J. Cowie | 1937 | Manchester | 10-140 | — | — | — | — | — |
| B.L. Cairns | 1983 | Leeds | 10-144 | — | — | — | — | — |
| G.B. Troup | 1979–80 | Auckland | — | — | 10-166 | — | — | — |

| INDIA (16) | | | E | A | WI | NZ | P |
|---|---|---|---|---|---|---|---|
| J.M. Patel | 1959–60 | Kanpur | — | 14-124 | — | — | — |
| M.H. Mankad | 1952–53 | Delhi | — | — | — | — | 13-131 |
| B.S. Chandrasekhar | 1977–78 | Melbourne | — | 12-104 | — | — | — |
| M.H. Mankad | 1951–52 | Madras[1] | 12-108 | — | — | — | — |
| S. Venkataraghavan | 1964–65 | Delhi | — | — | — | 12-152 | — |
| L. Sivaramakrishnan | 1984–85 | Bombay[3] | 12-181 | — | — | — | — |
| R.G. Nadkarni | 1964–65 | Madras[2] | — | 11-122 | — | — | — |
| E.A.S. Prasanna | 1975–76 | Auckland | — | — | — | 11-140 | — |
| Kapil Dev | 1979–80 | Madras[1] | — | — | — | — | 11-146 |
| B.S. Chandrasekhar | 1966–67 | Bombay[2] | — | — | 11-235 | — | — |
| Ghulam Ahmed | 1956–57 | Calcutta | — | 10-130 | — | — | — |
| Kapil Dev | 1983–84 | Ahmedabad | — | — | 10-135 | — | — |
| E.A.S. Prasanna | 1969–70 | Madras[1] | — | 10-174 | — | — | — |
| S.A. Durani | 1961–62 | Madras[2] | 10-177 | — | — | — | — |
| B.S. Bedi | 1977–78 | Perth | — | 10-194 | — | — | — |
| S.P. Gupte | 1958–59 | Kanpur | — | — | 10-223 | — | — |

| PAKISTAN (18) | | | E | A | WI | NZ | I | SL |
|---|---|---|---|---|---|---|---|---|
| Imran Khan | 1981–82 | Lahore[2] | — | — | — | — | — | 14-116 |
| Fazal Mahmood | 1956–57 | Karachi | — | 13-114 | — | — | — | — |
| Fazal Mahmood | 1952–53 | Lucknow | — | — | — | — | 12-94 | — |
| Fazal Mahmood | 1954 | Oval | 12-99 | — | — | — | — | — |
| Fazal Mahmood | 1958–59 | Dacca | — | — | 12-100 | — | — | — |
| Imran Khan | 1976–77 | Sydney | — | 12-165 | — | — | — | — |
| Zulfiqar Ahmed | 1955–56 | Karachi | — | — | — | 11-79 | — | — |
| Imran Khan | 1982–83 | Karachi | — | — | — | — | 11-79 | — |
| Iqbal Qasim | 1979–80 | Karachi | — | — | 11-118 | — | — | — |
| Sarfraz Nawaz | 1978–79 | Melbourne | — | — | 11-125 | — | — | — |
| Intikhab Alam | 1972–73 | Dunedin | — | — | — | 11-130 | — | — |
| Imran Khan | 1982–83 | Faisalabad | — | — | — | — | 11-180 | — |
| Sikander Bakht | 1979–80 | Delhi | — | — | — | — | 11-190 | — |
| Abdul Qadir | 1982–83 | Faisalabad | — | 11-218 | — | — | — | — |
| Wasim Raja | 1984–85 | Dunedin | — | — | — | 10-128 | — | — |
| Iqbal Qasim | 1979–80 | Bombay[3] | — | — | — | — | 10-175 | — |
| Intikhab Alam | 1969–70 | Dacca | — | — | — | 10-182 | — | — |
| Abdul Qadir | 1983–84 | Lahore[2] | 10-194 | — | — | — | — | — |

SRI LANKA
No instance of ten wickets in an innings.
Best analysis: D.S. De Silva 9-162 v Pakistan at Faisalabad in 1981–82.

# EIGHT WICKETS IN AN INNINGS
† On debut

| ENGLAND (23) | | | Opponents A | SA | WI | NZ | I | P |
|---|---|---|---|---|---|---|---|---|
| J.C. Laker | 1956 | Manchester | 10-53 | — | — | — | — | — |
| G.A. Lohmann | 1895–96 | Johannesburg[1] | — | 9-28 | — | — | — | — |
| J.C. Laker | 1956 | Manchester | 9-37 | — | — | — | — | — |
| S.F. Barnes | 1913–14 | Johannesburg[1] | — | 9-103 | — | — | — | — |
| G.A. Lohmann | 1895–96 | Port Elizabeth | — | 8-7 | — | — | — | — |
| J. Briggs | 1888–89 | Cape Town | — | 8-11 | — | — | — | — |
| S.F. Barnes | 1912 | Oval | — | 8-29 | — | — | — | — |

| ENGLAND continued | | | Opponents<br>A | SA | WI | NZ | I | P |
|---|---|---|---|---|---|---|---|---|
| F.S. Trueman | 1952 | Manchester | — | — | — | — | 8-31 | — |
| I.T. Botham | 1978 | Lord's | — | — | — | — | — | 8-34 |
| G.A. Lohmann | 1886–87 | Sydney | 8-35 | — | — | — | — | — |
| H. Verity | 1934 | Lord's | 8-43 | — | — | — | — | — |
| R.G.D. Willis | 1981 | Leeds | 8-43 | — | — | — | — | — |
| D.L. Underwood | 1974 | Lord's | — | — | — | — | — | 8-51 |
| S.F. Barnes | 1913–14 | Johannesburg[1] | — | 8-56 | — | — | — | — |
| G.A. Lohmann | 1891–92 | Sydney | 8-58 | — | — | — | — | — |
| C. Blythe | 1907 | Leeds | — | 8-59 | — | — | — | — |
| W. Rhodes | 1903–04 | Melbourne | 8-68 | — | — | — | — | — |
| L.C. Braund | 1903–04 | Melbourne | 8-81 | — | — | — | — | — |
| A.W. Greig | 1973–74 | Port-of-Spain | — | — | 8-86 | — | — | — |
| T. Richardson | 1897–98 | Sydney | 8-94 | — | — | — | — | — |
| I.T. Botham | 1984 | Lord's | — | — | 8-103 | — | — | — |
| B.J.T. Bosanquet | 1905 | Nottingham | 8-107 | — | — | — | — | — |
| J.C. White | 1928–29 | Adelaide | 8-126 | — | — | — | — | — |

| AUSTRALIA (11) | | | E | SA | WI | NZ | I | P |
|---|---|---|---|---|---|---|---|---|
| A.A. Mailey | 1920–21 | Melbourne | 9-121 | — | — | — | — | — |
| F. Laver | 1909 | Manchester | 8-31 | — | — | — | — | — |
| A.E. Trott† | 1894–95 | Adelaide | 8-43 | — | — | — | — | — |
| R.A.L. Massie† | 1972 | Lord's | 8-53 | — | — | — | — | — |
| A.A. Mallett | 1972–73 | Adelaide | — | — | — | — | — | 8-59 |
| H. Trumble | 1902 | Oval | 8-65 | — | — | — | — | — |
| G.D. McKenzie | 1968–69 | Melbourne | — | — | 8-71 | — | — | — |
| R.A.L. Massie† | 1972 | Lord's | 8-84 | — | — | — | — | — |
| G.F. Lawson | 1984–85 | Adelaide | — | — | 8-112 | — | — | — |
| C.J. McDermott | 1985 | Manchester | 8-141 | — | — | — | — | — |
| M.H.N. Walker | 1974–75 | Melbourne | 8-143 | — | — | — | — | — |

| SOUTH AFRICA (4) | | | E | A | NZ | | | |
|---|---|---|---|---|---|---|---|---|
| H.J. Tayfield | 1956–57 | Johannesburg[3] | 9-113 | — | — | | | |
| G.B. Lawrence | 1961–62 | Johannesburg[3] | — | — | 8-53 | | | |
| H.J. Tayfield | 1956–57 | Durban[2] | 8-69 | — | — | | | |
| S.J. Snooke | 1905–06 | Johannesburg[1] | 8-70 | — | — | | | |

| WEST INDIES (5) | | | E | A | NZ | I | P | |
|---|---|---|---|---|---|---|---|---|
| J.M. Noreiga | 1970–71 | Port-of-Spain | — | — | — | 9-95 | — | |
| C.E.H. Croft | 1976–77 | Port-of-Spain | — | — | — | — | 8-29 | |
| L.R. Gibbs | 1961–62 | Bridgetown | — | — | — | 8-38 | — | |
| M.A. Holding | 1976 | Oval | 8-92 | — | — | — | — | |
| A.L. Valentine† | 1950 | Manchester | 8-104 | — | — | — | — | |

**NEW ZEALAND**
No instance of eight wickets in an innings.
Best analysis: R.J. Hadlee 7-23 v India at Wellington in 1975–76.

| INDIA (9) | | | Opponents<br>E | A | WI | NZ | P | |
|---|---|---|---|---|---|---|---|---|
| J.M. Patel | 1959–60 | Kanpur | — | 9-69 | — | — | — | |
| Kapil Dev | 1983–84 | Ahmedabad | — | — | 9-83 | — | — | |
| S.P. Gupte | 1958–59 | Kanpur | — | — | 9-102 | — | — | |
| M.H. Mankad | 1952–53 | Delhi | — | — | — | — | 8-52 | |
| M.H. Mankad | 1951–52 | Madras[1] | 8-55 | — | — | — | — | |
| S. Venkataraghavan | 1964–65 | Delhi | — | — | — | 8-72 | — | |
| E.A.S. Prasanna | 1975–76 | Auckland | — | — | — | 8-76 | — | |
| B.S. Chandrasekhar | 1972–73 | Delhi | 8-79 | — | — | — | — | |
| Kapil Dev | 1982–83 | Lahore[2] | — | — | — | — | 8-85 | |

| PAKISTAN (4) | | | E | A | WI | NZ | I | SL |
|---|---|---|---|---|---|---|---|---|
| Sarfraz Nawaz | 1978–79 | Melbourne | — | 9-86 | — | — | — | — |
| Imran Khan | 1981–82 | Lahore[2] | — | — | — | — | — | 8-58 |
| Imran Khan | 1982–83 | Karachi | — | — | — | — | 8-60 | — |
| Sikander Bakht | 1979–80 | Delhi | — | — | — | — | 8-69 | — |

**SRI LANKA**
No instance of eight wickets in an innings.
Best analysis: J.R. Ratnayeke 5-42 v New Zealand at Colombo (SSC) 1983–84.

## OUTSTANDING INNINGS ANALYSES

| O | M | R | W | | | | |
|------|----|----|----|------------------|----------|--------------------------|---------|
| 51.2 | 23 | 53 | 10 | J.C. Laker | E v A | Manchester | 1956 |
| 14.2 | 6 | 28 | 9 | G.A. Lohmann | E v SA | Johannesburg[1] | 1895–96 |
| 16.4 | 4 | 37 | 9 | J.C. Laker | E v A | Manchester | 1956 |
| 9.4 | 5 | 7 | 8 | G.A. Lohmann | E v SA | Port Elizabeth | 1895–96 |
| 14.2 | 5 | 11 | 8 | J. Briggs | E v SA | Cape Town | 1888–89 |
| 19.1 | 11 | 17 | 7 | J. Briggs | E v SA | Cape Town | 1888–89 |
| 7.4 | 2 | 17 | 7 | M.A. Noble | A v E | Melbourne | 1901–02 |
| 11 | 3 | 17 | 7 | W. Rhodes | E v A | Birmingham | 1902 |
| 6.3 | 4 | 7 | 6 | A.E.R. Gilligan | E v SA | Birmingham | 1924 |
| 11.4 | 6 | 11 | 6 | S. Haigh | E v SA | Cape Town | 1898–99 |
| 11.6 | 7 | 12 | 6 | D.L. Underwood | E v NZ | Christchurch | 1970–71 |
| 14 | 7 | 13 | 6 | H.J. Tayfield | SA v NZ | Johannesburg[2] | 1953–54 |
| 18 | 11 | 15 | 6 | C.T.B. Turner | A v E | Sydney | 1886–87 |
| 16 | 8 | 15 | 6 | M.H.N. Walker | A v P | Sydney | 1972–73 |
| 2.3 | 1 | 2 | 5 | E.R.H. Toshack | A v I | Brisbane[2] | 1947–48 |
| 7.2 | 5 | 6 | 5 | H. Ironmonger | A v SA | Melbourne | 1931–32 |
| 12 | 8 | 5 | 4 | Pervez Sajjad | P v NZ | Rawalpindi | 1964–65 |
| 9 | 7 | 5 | 4 | K. Higgs | E v NZ | Christchurch | 1965–66 |
| 8 | 6 | 6 | 4 | P.H. Edmonds | E v P | Lord's | 1978 |
| 6.3 | 2 | 7 | 4 | J.C. White | E v A | Brisbane[1] | 1928–29 |
| 5 | 2 | 7 | 4 | J.H. Wardle | E v A | Manchester | 1953 |
| 6 | 3 | 7 | 4 | R. Appleyard | E v NZ | Auckland | 1954–55 |
| 3.4 | 3 | 0 | 3 | R. Benaud | A v I | Delhi | 1959–60 |

## HAT-TRICKS

| | | | |
|---------------------|----------------------------|------------------|---------|
| F.R. Spofforth | Australia v England | Melbourne | 1878–79 |
| W. Bates | England v Australia | Melbourne | 1882–83 |
| J. Briggs | England v Australia | Sydney | 1891–92 |
| G.A. Lohmann | England v South Africa | Port Elizabeth | 1895–96 |
| J.T. Hearne | England v Australia | Leeds | 1899 |
| H. Trumble | Australia v England | Melbourne | 1901–02 |
| H. Trumble‡ | Australia v England | Melbourne | 1903–04 |
| T.J. Matthews (2) | Australia v South Africa | Manchester | 1912 |
| M.J.C. Allom† | England v New Zealand | Christchurch | 1929–30 |
| T.W.J. Goddard | England v South Africa | Johannesburg[1] | 1938–39 |
| P.J. Loader | England v West Indies | Leeds | 1957 |
| L.F. Kline | Australia v South Africa | Cape Town | 1957–58 |
| W.W. Hall | West Indies v Pakistan | Lahore[1] | 1958–59 |
| G.M. Griffin‡ | South Africa v England | Lord's | 1960 |
| L.R. Gibbs | West Indies v Australia | Adelaide | 1960–61 |
| P.J. Petherick† | New Zealand v Pakistan | Lahore[2] | 1976–77 |

† *On debut*     ‡ *On final appearance*
*T.J. Matthews did the hat-trick in each innings on the second afternoon of the match and took all six wickets without assistance from fielders.*

## FOUR WICKETS IN FIVE BALLS

| | | | |
|-------------|----------------------------------------|----------------|---------|
| M.J.C. Allom | England v New Zealand | Christchurch | 1929–30 |
| | *On debut – in his eighth over – WOWWW* | | |
| C.M. Old | England v Pakistan | Birmingham | 1978 |
| | *In the same over – WWOWW – his third ball was a no-ball* | | |

# THREE WICKETS IN FOUR BALLS

| | | | |
|---|---|---|---|
| F.R. Spofforth (2) | Australia v England | Oval | 1882 |
| | Australia v England | Sydney | 1884–85 |
| J. Briggs | England v South Africa | Cape Town | 1888–89 |
| W.P. Howell | Australia v South Africa | Cape Town | 1902–03 |
| J.M. Gregory | Australia v England | Nottingham | 1921 |
| E.P. Nupen | South Africa v England | Johannesburg[1] | 1930–31 |
| W.J. O'Reilly | Australia v England | Manchester | 1934 |
| B. Mitchell | South Africa v England | Johannesburg[1] | 1935–36 |
| W. Voce | England v Australia | Sydney | 1936–37 |
| R.R. Lindwall | Australia v England | Adelaide | 1946–47 |
| K. Cranston | England v South Africa | Leeds | 1947 |
| R. Appleyard | England v New Zealand | Auckland | 1954–55 |
| R. Benaud | Australia v West Indies | Georgetown | 1954–55 |
| Fazal Mahmood | Pakistan v Australia | Karachi | 1956–57 |
| J.W. Martin | Australia v West Indies | Melbourne | 1960–61 |
| L.R. Gibbs | West Indies v Australia | Sydney | 1960–61 |
| K.D. Mackay | Australia v England | Birmingham | 1961 |
| W.W. Hall | West Indies v India | Port-of-Spain | 1961–62 |
| D. Shackleton | England v West Indies | Lord's | 1963 |
| G.D. McKenzie | Australia v West Indies | Port-of-Spain | 1964–65 |
| F.J. Titmus | England v New Zealand | Leeds | 1965 |
| P. Lever | England v Pakistan | Leeds | 1971 |
| D.K. Lillee (2) | Australia v England | Manchester | 1972 |
| | Australia v England | Oval | 1972 |
| C.M. Old | England v Pakistan | Birmingham | 1978 |
| S.T. Clarke | West Indies v Pakistan | Karachi | 1980–81 |
| R.J. Hadlee | New Zealand v Australia | Melbourne | 1980–81 |
| R.J. Shastri | India v New Zealand | Wellington | 1980–81 |
| I.T. Botham | England v Australia | Leeds | 1985 |

*K. Cranston, F.J. Titmus and C.M. Old each took four wickets in an over.*

# WICKET WITH FIRST BALL IN TEST CRICKET

| | Batsman dismissed | | | |
|---|---|---|---|---|
| A. Coningham | A.C. MacLaren | A v E | Melbourne | 1894–95 |
| W.M. Bradley | F. Laver | E v A | Manchester | 1899 |
| E.G. Arnold | V.T. Trumper | E v A | Sydney | 1903–04 |
| G.G. Macaulay | G.A.L. Hearne | E v SA | Cape Town | 1922–23 |
| M.W. Tate | M.J. Susskind | E v SA | Birmingham | 1924 |
| M. Henderson | E.W. Dawson | NZ v E | Christchurch | 1929–30 |
| H.D. Smith | E. Paynter | NZ v E | Christchurch | 1932–33 |
| T.F. Johnson | W.W. Keeton | WI v E | Oval | 1939 |
| R. Howorth | D.V. Dyer | E v SA | Oval | 1947 |
| Intikhab Alam | C.C. McDonald | P v A | Karachi | 1959–60 |

# MOST WICKETS BY A BOWLER IN ONE DAY

| | | | | | |
|---|---|---|---|---|---|
| 15 | J. Briggs | 15-28 | England v South Africa | Cape Town | 1888–89 |
| 14 | H. Verity | 14-80 | England v Australia | Lord's | 1934 |

# OVER 200 RUNS CONCEDED IN AN INNINGS

| O | M | R | W | | | | |
|---|---|---|---|---|---|---|---|
| 87 | 11 | 298 | 1 | L.O'B. Fleetwood-Smith | A v E | Oval | 1938 |
| 80.2 | 13 | 266 | 5 | O.C. Scott | WI v E | Kingston | 1929–30 |
| 54 | 5 | 259 | 0 | Khan Mohammad | P v WI | Kingston | 1957–58 |
| 85.2 | 20 | 247 | 2 | Fazal Mahmood | P v WI | Kingston | 1957–58 |
| 82 | 17 | 228 | 5 | M.H. Mankad | I v WI | Kingston | 1952–53 |
| 64.2 | 8 | 226 | 6 | B.S. Bedi | I v E | Lord's | 1974 |

| 38.4 | 3 | **220** | 7 | Kapil Dev | I v P | Faisalabad | 1982–83 |
| 71 | 8 | **204** | 6 | I.A.R. Peebles | E v A | Oval | 1930 |
| 75 | 16 | **202** | 3 | M.H. Mankad | I v WI | Bombay$^2$ | 1948–49 |
| 84 | 19 | **202** | 6 | Haseeb Ahsan | P v I | Madras$^2$ | 1960–61 |

## OVER 300 RUNS CONCEDED IN A MATCH

| *O* | *M* | **R** | *W* | | | | |
|---|---|---|---|---|---|---|---|
| 105.2 | 13 | **374** | 9 | O.C. Scott | WI v E | Kingston | 1929–30 |
| 63 | 3 | **308** | 7 | A.A. Mailey | A v E | Sydney | 1924–25 |
| 61.3 | 6 | **302** | 10 | A.A. Mailey | A v E | Adelaide | 1920–21 |

## BOWLERS UNCHANGED IN A COMPLETED INNINGS

| **ENGLAND** | | *Opponents* | | |
|---|---|---|---|---|
| F. Morley (2-34) | R.G. Barlow (7-40) | Australia (83) | Sydney | 1882–83 |
| G.A. Lohmann (7-36) | J. Briggs (3-28) | Australia (68) | Oval | 1886 |
| G.A. Lohmann (5-17) | R. Peel (5-18) | Australia (42) | Sydney | 1887–88 |
| J. Briggs (8-11) | A.J. Fothergill (1-30) | South Africa (43) | Cape Town | 1888–89 |
| J.J. Ferris (7-37) | F. Martin (2-39) | South Africa (83) | Cape Town | 1891–92 |
| J. Briggs (6-49) | G.A. Lohmann (3-46) | Australia (100) | Adelaide | 1891–92 |
| T. Richardson (6-39) | G.A. Lohmann (3-13) | Australia (53) | Lord's | 1896 |
| S. Haigh (6-11) | A.E. Trott (4-19) | South Africa (35) | Cape Town | 1898–99 |
| S.F. Barnes (6-42) | C. Blythe (4-64) | Australia (112) | Melbourne | 1901–02 |
| G.H. Hirst (4-28) | C. Blythe (6-44) | Australia (74) | Birmingham | 1909 |
| F.R. Foster (5-16) | S.F. Barnes (5-25) | South Africa (58) | Lord's | 1912 |
| A.E.R. Gilligan (6-7) | M.W. Tate (4-12) | South Africa (30) | Birmingham | 1924 |
| G.O.B. Allen (5-36) | W. Voce (4-16) | Australia (58) | Brisbane$^2$ | 1936–37 |

| **AUSTRALIA** | | *Opponents* | | |
|---|---|---|---|---|
| G.E. Palmer (7-68) | E. Evans (3-64) | England (133) | Sydney | 1881–82 |
| F.R. Spofforth (5-30) | G.E. Palmer (4-32) | England (77) | Sydney | 1884–85 |
| C.T.B. Turner (6-15) | J.J. Ferris (4-27) | England (45) | Sydney | 1886–87 |
| C.T.B. Turner (5-36) | J.J. Ferris (5-26) | England (62) | Lord's | 1888 |
| G. Giffen (5-26) | C.T.B. Turner (4-33) | England (72) | Sydney | 1894–95 |
| H. Trumble (3-38) | M.A. Noble (7-17) | England (61) | Melbourne | 1901–02 |
| M.A. Noble (5-54) | J.V. Saunders (5-43) | England (99) | Sydney | 1901–02 |

| **PAKISTAN** | | *Opponents* | | |
|---|---|---|---|---|
| Fazal Mahmood (6-34) | Khan Mohammad (4-43) | Australia (80) | Karachi | 1956–57 |

## 500 BALLS IN AN INNINGS

| **588** | S. Ramadhin | 98 | 35 | 179 | 2 | WI v E | Birmingham | 1957 |
|---|---|---|---|---|---|---|---|---|
| **571** | T.R. Veivers | 95.1 | 36 | 155 | 3 | A v E | Manchester | 1964 |
| **552** | A.L. Valentine | 92 | 49 | 140 | 3 | WI v E | Nottingham | 1950 |
| **522** | L.O'B. Fleetwood-Smith | 87 | 11 | 298 | 1 | A v E | Oval | 1938 |
| **512** | Fazal Mahmood | 85.2 | 20 | 247 | 2 | P v WI | Kingston | 1957–58 |
| **510** | W.J. O'Reilly | 85 | 26 | 178 | 3 | A v E | Oval | 1938 |
| **504** | Haseeb Ahsan | 84 | 19 | 202 | 6 | P v I | Madras$^2$ | 1960–61 |

## 700 BALLS IN A MATCH

| **774** | S. Ramadhin | 129 | 51 | 228 | 9 | WI v E | Birmingham | 1957 |
|---|---|---|---|---|---|---|---|---|
| **766** | H. Verity | 95.6 | 23 | 184 | 4 | E v SA | Durban$^2$ | 1938–39 |
| **749** | J.C. White | 124.5 | 37 | 256 | 13 | E v A | Adelaide | 1928–29 |
| **738** | N. Gordon | 92.2 | 17 | 256 | 1 | SA v E | Durban$^2$ | 1938–39 |
| **728** | A.B.C. Langton | 91 | 24 | 203 | 4 | SA v E | Durban$^2$ | 1938–39 |
| **712** | M.W. Tate | 89 | 19 | 228 | 11 | E v A | Sydney | 1924–25 |
| **708** | G. Giffen | 118 | 42 | 239 | 8 | A v E | Sydney | 1894–95 |

## DISMISSING ALL ELEVEN BATSMEN IN A MATCH

| | | | | |
|---|---|---|---|---|
| J.C. Laker | 19-90 | E v A | Manchester | 1956 |
| S. Venkataraghavan | 12-152 | I v NZ | Delhi | 1964–65 |
| G. Dymock | 12-166 | A v I | Kanpur | 1979–80 |

# INDIVIDUAL RECORDS – WICKET-KEEPING

## 100 DISMISSALS IN TESTS

| | | Tests | Dis | Ct | St | Opponents E | A | SA | WI | NZ | I | P | SL |
|---|---|---|---|---|---|---|---|---|---|---|---|---|---|
| R.W. Marsh | A | 96 | **355** | 343 | 12 | 148 | – | – | 65 | 58 | 16 | 68 | – |
| A.P.E. Knott | E | 95 | **269** | 250 | 19 | – | 105 | – | 43 | 26 | 54 | 41 | – |
| Wasim Bari | P | 81 | **228** | 201 | 27 | 54 | 66 | – | 21 | 32 | 55 | – | – |
| T.G. Evans | E | 91 | **219** | 173 | 46 | – | 76 | 59 | 37 | 28 | 12 | 7 | – |
| S.M.H. Kirmani | I | 85 | **193** | 157 | 36 | 42 | 36 | – | 36 | 28 | – | 50 | 1 |
| D.L. Murray | WI | 62 | **189** | 181 | 8 | 94 | 40 | 33 | – | 7 | 27 | 21 | – |
| A.T.W. Grout | A | 51 | **187** | 163 | 24 | 76 | – | – | 41 | – | 20 | 17 | – |
| R.W. Taylor | E | 57 | **174** | 167 | 7 | – | 57 | – | – | 45 | 40 | 29 | 3 |
| J.H.B. Waite | SA | 50 | **141** | 124 | 17 | 56 | 28 | 27 | – | 57 | – | – | – |
| W.A.S. Oldfield | A | 54 | **130** | 78 | 52 | 90 | – | 30 | 13 | – | – | – | – |
| J.M. Parks | E | 46 | **114** | 103† | 11 | – | 21 | – | 31 | 22 | 9 | 1 | – |
| P.J.L. Dujon | WI | 33 | **110** | 108‡ | 2 | 16 | 48 | – | – | 11 | 35 | – | – |

*Highest for other countries:*

| | | Tests | Dis | Ct | St | E | A | SA | WI | NZ | I | P | SL |
|---|---|---|---|---|---|---|---|---|---|---|---|---|---|
| K.J. Wadsworth | NZ | 33 | **96** | 92 | 4 | 28 | 19 | – | 12 | – | 22 | 15 | – |
| H.M. Goonatillake | SL | 5 | **13** | 10 | 3 | 2 | – | – | – | – | 3 | 8 | – |

† Including 2 catches in 3 Tests when not keeping wicket.
‡Including 2 catches in 2 Tests when not keeping wicket.

## 20 DISMISSALS IN A SERIES

| ENGLAND | | Venue | Tests | St | Opponents A | SA | WI | NZ | I | P |
|---|---|---|---|---|---|---|---|---|---|---|
| A.P.E. Knott | 1970–71 | A | 6 | 3 | 24 | – | – | – | – | – |
| A.P.E. Knott | 1974–75 | A | 6 | 1 | 23 | – | – | – | – | – |
| H. Strudwick | 1913–14 | SA | 5 | 6 | – | 21 | – | – | – | – |
| T.G. Evans | 1956–57 | SA | 5 | 2 | – | 20 | – | – | – | – |
| R.W. Taylor | 1978–79 | A | 6 | 2 | 20 | – | – | – | – | – |
| P.R. Downton | 1985 | E | 6 | 1 | 20 | – | – | – | – | – |

| AUSTRALIA | | Venue | Tests | St | E | SA | WI | NZ | I | P |
|---|---|---|---|---|---|---|---|---|---|---|
| R.W. Marsh | 1982–83 | A | 5 | – | 28 | – | – | – | – | – |
| R.W. Marsh | 1975–76 | A | 6 | – | – | – | 26 | – | – | – |
| A.T.W. Grout | 1960–61 | A | 5 | 3 | – | – | 23 | – | – | – |
| R.W. Marsh | 1972 | E | 5 | 2 | 23 | – | – | – | – | – |
| R.W. Marsh | 1981 | E | 6 | – | 23 | – | – | – | – | – |
| S.J. Rixon | 1977–78 | A | 5 | – | – | – | – | – | 22 | – |
| R.A. Saggers | 1949–50 | SA | 5 | 8 | – | 21 | – | – | – | – |
| G.R.A. Langley | 1951–52 | A | 5 | 5 | – | – | 21 | – | – | – |
| A.T.W. Grout | 1961 | E | 5 | 1 | 21 | – | – | – | – | – |
| R.W. Marsh | 1983–84 | A | 5 | – | – | – | – | – | – | 21 |
| D. Tallon | 1946–47 | A | 5 | 4 | 20 | – | – | – | – | – |
| G.R.A. Langley | 1954–55 | WI | 4 | 4 | – | – | 20 | – | – | – |
| A.T.W. Grout | 1958–59 | A | 5 | 3 | 20 | – | – | – | – | – |
| H.B. Taber | 1966–67 | SA | 5 | 1 | – | 20 | – | – | – | – |

| SOUTH AFRICA | | Venue | Tests | St | E | A | NZ |
|---|---|---|---|---|---|---|---|
| J.H.B. Waite | 1961–62 | SA | 5 | 3 | – | – | 26 |
| D.T. Lindsay | 1966–67 | SA | 5 | – | – | 24 | – |
| J.H.B. Waite | 1953–54 | SA | 5 | 7 | – | – | 23 |

| WEST INDIES | | Venue | Tests | St | E | A | NZ | I | P |
|---|---|---|---|---|---|---|---|---|---|
| D.L. Murray | 1963 | E | 5 | 2 | **24** | – | – | – | – |
| F.C.M. Alexander | 1959–60 | WI | 5 | 1 | **23** | – | – | – | – |
| P.J.L. Dujon | 1983–84 | WI | 5 | 1 | – | **20** | – | – | – |

| NEW ZEALAND | | Venue | Tests | St | E | A | SA | WI | I | P |
|---|---|---|---|---|---|---|---|---|---|---|
| A.E. Dick | 1961–62 | SA | | 2 | – | – | **23** | – | – | – |

*The most dismissals in a series for India is 19 by N.S. Tamhane (7 st) in 5 Tests v Pakistan in Pakistan 1954–55 and S.M.H. Kirmani (2 st) in 6 Tests v Pakistan in India 1979–80, for Pakistan 17 by Wasim Bari (2 st) in 6 Tests v India in Pakistan in 1982–83, and for Sri Lanka 9 by R.G. de Alwis (1st) in 3 Tests v New Zealand in Sri Lanka in 1983–84.*

# EIGHT DISMISSALS IN A MATCH
† *On debut*

| | | | St | Opponents | | | | | |
|---|---|---|---|---|---|---|---|---|---|
| **ENGLAND** | | | | A | SA | WI | NZ | I | P |
| R.W. Taylor | 1979–80 | Bombay[3] | – | – | – | – | – | 10 | – |
| L.E.G. Ames | 1933 | Oval | 2 | – | – | 8 | – | – | – |
| J.M. Parks | 1965–66 | Christchurch | – | – | – | – | 8 | – | – |

| **AUSTRALIA** | | | St | E | SA | WI | NZ | I | P |
|---|---|---|---|---|---|---|---|---|---|
| G.R.A. Langley | 1956 | Lord's | 1 | 9 | – | – | – | – | – |
| R.W. Marsh | 1982–83 | Brisbane[2] | – | 9 | – | – | – | – | – |
| J.J. Kelly | 1901–02 | Sydney | – | 8 | – | – | – | – | – |
| G.R.A. Langley | 1954–55 | Kingston | – | – | – | 8 | – | – | – |
| A.T.W. Grout | 1959–60 | Lahore[2] | 2 | – | – | – | – | – | 8 |
| A.T.W. Grout | 1961 | Lord's | – | 8 | – | – | – | – | – |
| H.B. Taber† | 1966–67 | Johannesburg[3] | 1 | – | 8 | – | – | – | – |
| R.W. Marsh | 1975–76 | Melbourne | – | – | – | 8 | – | – | – |
| R.W. Marsh | 1976–77 | Christchurch | – | – | – | – | 8 | – | – |
| R.W. Marsh | 1980–81 | Sydney | 1 | – | – | – | – | 8 | – |
| R.W. Marsh | 1982–83 | Adelaide | – | 8 | – | – | – | – | – |

| **SOUTH AFRICA** | | | St | E | A | NZ | | | |
|---|---|---|---|---|---|---|---|---|---|
| D.T. Lindsay | 1966–67 | Johannesburg[3] | – | – | 8 | – | | | |

| **WEST INDIES** | | | St | E | SA | WI | NZ | I | P |
|---|---|---|---|---|---|---|---|---|---|
| D.A. Murray | 1981–82 | Melbourne | – | – | 9 | – | – | – | – |

| **NEW ZEALAND** | | | St | E | A | SA | WI | I | P | SL |
|---|---|---|---|---|---|---|---|---|---|---|
| W.K. Lees | 1982–83 | Wellington | – | – | – | – | – | – | – | 8 |

| **PAKISTAN** | | | St | E | A | WI | NZ | I | |
|---|---|---|---|---|---|---|---|---|---|
| Wasim Bari | 1971 | Leeds | – | 8 | – | – | – | – | |

*The most dismissals in a match for India is 6 by S.M.H. Kirmani (four times), B.K. Kunderan, and N.S. Tamhane, and for Sri Lanka 6 by H.M. Goonatillake v Pakistan at Karachi in 1981–82.*

# FIVE DISMISSALS IN AN INNINGS
† *On debut*

| | | | St | Opponents | | | | | |
|---|---|---|---|---|---|---|---|---|---|
| **ENGLAND** | | | | A | SA | WI | NZ | I | P |
| R.W. Taylor | 1979–80 | Bombay[3] | – | – | – | – | – | 7 | – |
| J.T. Murray | 1967 | Lord's | – | – | – | – | – | 6 | – |
| J.G. Binks | 1963–64 | Calcutta | – | – | – | – | – | 5 | – |
| J.M. Parks | 1965–66 | Sydney | 2 | 5 | – | – | – | – | – |
| J.M. Parks | 1965–66 | Christchurch | – | – | – | – | 5 | – | – |
| A.P.E. Knott | 1974 | Manchester | 1 | – | – | – | – | 5 | – |
| R.W. Taylor | 1978 | Nottingham | – | – | – | – | 5 | – | – |
| R.W. Taylor | 1978–79 | Brisbane[2] | – | 5 | – | – | – | – | – |

| | | | *Opponents* | | | | | | |
|---|---|---|---|---|---|---|---|---|---|
| **AUSTRALIA** | | | St | E | SA | WI | NZ | I | P |
| A.T.W. Grout† | 1957–58 | Johannesburg³ | – | – | 6 | – | – | – | – |
| R.W. Marsh | 1982–83 | Brisbane² | – | 6 | – | – | – | – | – |
| W.A.S. Oldfield | 1924–25 | Melbourne | 4 | 5 | – | – | – | – | – |
| G.R.A. Langley | 1954–55 | Georgetown | 3 | – | – | 5 | – | – | – |
| G.R.A. Langley | 1954–55 | Kingston | – | – | – | 5 | – | – | – |
| G.R.A. Langley | 1956 | Lord's | – | 5 | – | – | – | – | – |
| A.T.W. Grout | 1957–58 | Durban² | 1 | – | 5 | – | – | – | – |
| A.T.W. Grout | 1959–60 | Lahore² | – | – | – | – | – | – | 5 |
| A.T.W. Grout | 1960–61 | Brisbane² | 1 | – | – | 5 | – | – | – |
| A.T.W. Grout | 1961 | Lord's | – | 5 | – | – | – | – | – |
| A.T.W. Grout | 1965–66 | Sydney | – | 5 | – | – | – | – | – |
| H.B. Taber† | 1966–67 | Johannesburg³ | – | – | 5 | – | – | – | – |
| H.B. Taber | 1968–69 | Sydney | – | – | – | 5 | – | – | – |
| H.B. Taber | 1969–70 | Port Elizabeth | – | – | 5 | – | – | – | – |
| R.W. Marsh | 1972 | Manchester | – | 5 | – | – | – | – | – |
| R.W. Marsh | 1972 | Nottingham | – | 5 | – | – | – | – | – |
| R.W. Marsh | 1973–74 | Sydney | – | – | – | – | 5 | – | – |
| R.W. Marsh | 1973–74 | Christchurch | – | – | – | – | 5 | – | – |
| R.W. Marsh | 1975–76 | Melbourne | – | – | – | 5 | – | – | – |
| R.W. Marsh | 1976–77 | Christchurch | – | – | – | – | 5 | – | – |
| J.A. Maclean† | 1978–79 | Brisbane² | – | 5 | – | – | – | – | – |
| K.J. Wright | 1978–79 | Melbourne | – | – | – | – | – | – | 5 |
| R.W. Marsh | 1979–80 | Brisbane² | – | – | – | 5 | – | – | – |
| R.W. Marsh | 1980–81 | Sydney | – | – | – | – | – | 5 | – |
| R.W. Marsh | 1981–82 | Perth | – | – | – | – | – | – | 5 |
| R.W. Marsh | 1983–84 | Perth | – | – | – | – | – | – | 5 |
| R.W. Marsh | 1983–84 | Sydney | – | – | – | – | – | – | 5 |
| W.B. Phillips | 1983–84 | Kingston | – | – | – | 5 | – | – | – |

| **SOUTH AFRICA** | | | St | E | A | NZ | | | |
|---|---|---|---|---|---|---|---|---|---|
| D.T. Lindsay | 1966–67 | Johannesburg³ | – | – | 6 | – | | | |

| **WEST INDIES** | | | St | E | A | NZ | I | P | |
|---|---|---|---|---|---|---|---|---|---|
| F.C.M. Alexander | 1959–60 | Bridgetown | – | 5 | – | – | – | – | |
| D.L. Murray | 1976 | Leeds | – | 5 | – | – | – | – | |
| D.L. Murray | 1976–77 | Georgetown | – | – | – | – | – | 5 | |
| D.A. Murray | 1978–79 | Delhi | – | – | – | – | 5 | – | |
| D.A. Murray | 1981–82 | Melbourne | – | – | 5 | – | – | – | |
| P.J.L. Dujon | 1982–83 | Kingston | – | – | – | – | 5 | – | |

| **NEW ZEALAND** | | | St | E | A | SA | WI | I | P | SL |
|---|---|---|---|---|---|---|---|---|---|---|
| R.I. Harford | 1967–68 | Wellington | – | – | – | – | – | 5 | – | – |
| K.J. Wadsworth | 1972–73 | Auckland | – | – | – | – | – | – | 5 | – |
| W.K. Lees | 1982–83 | Wellington | – | – | – | – | – | – | – | 5 |
| I.D.S. Smith | 1983–84 | Auckland | 1 | 5 | – | – | – | – | – | – |

| **INDIA** | | | St | E | A | WI | NZ | P | |
|---|---|---|---|---|---|---|---|---|---|
| S.M.H. Kirmani | 1975–76 | Christchurch | 1 | – | – | – | 6 | – | |
| B.K. Kunderan | 1961–62 | Bombay² | 2 | 5 | – | – | – | – | |
| S.M.H. Kirmani | 1982–83 | Faisalabad | – | – | – | – | – | 5 | |

| **PAKISTAN** | | | St | E | A | WI | NZ | I | |
|---|---|---|---|---|---|---|---|---|---|
| Wasim Bari | 1978–79 | Auckland | – | – | – | – | 7 | – | |
| Imtiaz Ahmed | 1959–60 | Lahore² | 1 | – | 5 | – | – | – | |
| Wasim Bari | 1971 | Leeds | – | 5 | – | – | – | – | |

# NO BYES CONCEDED IN TOTAL OF 500 RUNS

| 659-8d | T.G. Evans | E v A | Sydney | 1946–47 |
|---|---|---|---|---|
| 652 | S.M.H. Kirmani | I v P | Faisalabad | 1982–83 |
| 619 | J.L. Hendriks | WI v A | Sydney | 1968–69 |
| 559-9d | W.W. Wade | SA v E | Cape Town | 1938–39 |

| | | | | |
|---|---|---|---|---|
| 551 | J.J. Kelly | A v E | Sydney | 1897–98 |
| 551-9d | A.P.E. Knott | E v NZ | Lord's | 1973 |
| 544-5d | Imtiaz Ahmed | P v E | Birmingham | 1962 |
| 543-3d | T.M. Findlay | WI v NZ | Georgetown | 1971–72 |
| 532-9d | A.P.E. Knott | E v A | Oval | 1975 |
| 531 | D.T. Lindsay | SA v E | Johannesburg[3] | 1964–65 |
| 528 | S.M.H. Kirmani | I v A | Adelaide | 1980–81 |
| 526-7d | A.P.E. Knott | E v WI | Port-of-Spain | 1967–68 |
| 521 | W.A.S. Oldfield | A v E | Brisbane[1] | 1928–29 |
| 520 | J.H.B. Waite | SA v A | Melbourne | 1952–53 |
| 514-4d | R.G. de Alwis | SL v A | Kandy | 1982–83 |
| 510 | J.L. Hendriks | WI v A | Melbourne | 1968–69 |
| 509 | W.B. Phillips | A v WI | Bridgetown | 1983–84 |
| 507-6d | K.J. Wadsworth | NZ v P | Dunedin | 1972–73 |
| 503-8d | S.M.H. Kirmani | I v P | Faisalabad | 1978–79 |

## MOST BYES CONCEDED IN AN INNINGS

| | | | | |
|---|---|---|---|---|
| 37 | F.E. Woolley | E v A | Oval | 1934 |
| | *Deputised for L.E.G. Ames – injured – at age of 47* | | | |
| 33 | J.T. Murray | E v I | Bombay[2] | 1961–62 |
| 33 | J.M. Parks | E v WI | Kingston | 1967–68 |

# INDIVIDUAL RECORDS – FIELDING

## 100 CATCHES IN TESTS

| | | Tests | Ct | Opponents | | | | | | | |
|---|---|---|---|---|---|---|---|---|---|---|---|
| | | | | E | A | SA | WI | NZ | I | P | SL |
| G.S. Chappell | A | 87 | **122** | 61 | – | – | 16 | 18 | 5 | 22 | – |
| M.C. Cowdrey | E | 114 | **120** | – | 40 | 22 | 21 | 15 | 11 | 11 | – |
| R.B. Simpson · | A | 62 | **110** | 30 | – | 27 | 29 | – | 21 | 3 | – |
| W.R. Hammond | E | 85 | **110** | – | 43 | 30 | 22 | 9 | 6 | – | – |
| G.St A. Sobers | WI | 93 | **109** | 40 | 27 | – | – | 11 | 27 | 4 | – |
| I.M. Chappell | A | 75 | **105** | 31 | – | 11 | 24 | 16 | 17 | 6 | – |

*The records for South Africa, New Zealand, India, Pakistan and Sri Lanka are:*

| | | Tests | Ct | E | A | SA | WI | NZ | I | P | SL |
|---|---|---|---|---|---|---|---|---|---|---|---|
| B. Mitchell | SA | 42 | **56** | 43 | 10 | – | – | 3 | – | – | – |
| J.V. Coney | NZ | 40 | **46** | 10 | 13 | – | 3 | – | 1 | 10 | 9 |
| S.M. Gavaskar | I | 106 | **92** | 32 | 14 | – | 17 | 11 | – | 16 | 2 |
| Majid Khan | P | 63 | **70** | 14 | 13 | – | 14 | 19 | 9 | – | 1 |
| R.S. Madugalle | SL | 12 | **7** | 1 | – | – | – | 1 | – | 5 | – |

## 12 CATCHES IN A SERIES

| ENGLAND | | Venue | Tests | Opponents | | | | | | |
|---|---|---|---|---|---|---|---|---|---|---|
| | | | | A | SA | WI | NZ | I | P | SL |
| L.C. Braund | 1901–02 | A | 5 | **12** | – | – | – | – | – | – |
| W.R. Hammond | 1934 | E | 5 | **12** | – | – | – | – | – | – |
| J.T. Ikin | 1951 | E | 3 | – | **12** | – | – | – | – | – |
| A.W. Greig | 1974–75 | A | 6 | **12** | – | – | – | – | – | – |
| I.T. Botham | 1981 | E | 6 | **12** | – | – | – | – | – | – |

| AUSTRALIA | | Venue | Tests | E | SA | WI | NZ | I | P | SL |
|---|---|---|---|---|---|---|---|---|---|---|
| J.M. Gregory | 1920–21 | A | 5 | **15** | – | – | – | – | – | – |
| G.S. Chappell | 1974–75 | A | 6 | **14** | – | – | – | – | – | – |
| R.B. Simpson | 1957–58 | SA | 5 | – | **13** | – | – | – | – | – |
| R.B. Simpson | 1960–61 | A | 5 | – | – | **13** | – | – | – | – |
| D.F. Whatmore | 1979–80 | I | 5 | – | – | – | – | **12** | – | – |
| A.R. Border | 1981 | E | 6 | **12** | – | – | – | – | – | – |

| SOUTH AFRICA | | Venue | Tests | E | A | NZ |
|---|---|---|---|---|---|---|
| A.E.E. Vogler | 1909–10 | SA | 5 | **12** | – | – |
| B. Mitchell | 1930–31 | SA | 5 | **12** | – | – |
| T.L. Goddard | 1956–57 | SA | 5 | **12** | – | – |

| WEST INDIES | | Venue | Tests | E | A | NZ | I | P | SL |
|---|---|---|---|---|---|---|---|---|---|
| G.St A. Sobers | 1960–61 | A | 5 | – | **12** | – | – | – | – |

| INDIA | | Venue | Tests | E | A | WI | NZ | P | SL |
|---|---|---|---|---|---|---|---|---|---|
| E.D. Solkar | 1972–73 | I | 5 | **12** | – | – | – | – | – |

*The most catches by non-wicket-keepers in a series for New Zealand is 8 by B. Sutcliffe in 5 Tests v South Africa in South Africa 1953–54, by B.A.G. Murray in 4 Tests v India in New Zealand 1967–68, and by J.J. Crowe in 4 Tests v West Indies in West Indies 1984–85; and for Pakistan 9 by W. Mathias in 5 Tests v West Indies in West Indies 1957–58.*

# SIX CATCHES IN A MATCH
† On debut

| ENGLAND | | | Opponents A | SA | WI | NZ | I | P | SL |
|---|---|---|---|---|---|---|---|---|---|
| A. Shrewsbury | 1887–88 | Sydney | 6 | – | – | – | – | – | – |
| F.E. Woolley | 1911–12 | Sydney | 6 | – | – | – | – | – | – |
| M.C. Cowdrey | 1963 | Lord's | – | – | 6 | – | – | – | – |
| A.W. Greig | 1974 | Leeds | – | – | – | – | – | 6 | – |
| **A.J. Lamb** | **1983** | **Lord's** | – | – | – | 6 | – | – | – |

| AUSTRALIA | | | E | SA | WI | NZ | I | P | SL |
|---|---|---|---|---|---|---|---|---|---|
| G.S. Chappell | 1974–75 | Perth | 7 | – | – | – | – | – | – |
| J.M. Gregory | 1920–21 | Sydney | 6 | – | – | – | – | – | – |
| V.Y. Richardson | 1935–36 | Durban[2] | – | 6 | – | – | – | – | – |
| R.N. Harvey | 1962–63 | Sydney | 6 | – | – | – | – | – | – |
| I.M. Chappell | 1973–74 | Adelaide | – | – | – | 6 | – | – | – |
| D.F. Whatmore | 1979–80 | Kanpur | – | – | – | – | 6 | – | – |

| SOUTH AFRICA | | | E | A | NZ |
|---|---|---|---|---|---|
| A.E.E. Vogler | 1909–10 | Durban[1] | 6 | – | – |
| B. Mitchell | 1931–32 | Melbourne | – | 6 | – |

| WEST INDIES | | | E | A | NZ | I | P |
|---|---|---|---|---|---|---|---|
| G.St A. Sobers | 1973 | Lord's | 6 | – | – | – | – |

| INDIA | | | E | A | WI | NZ | P | SL |
|---|---|---|---|---|---|---|---|---|
| Yajurvindra Singh† | 1976–77 | Bangalore | 7 | – | – | – | – | – |
| E.D. Solkar | 1970–71 | Port-of-Spain | – | – | 6 | – | – | – |

# FIVE CATCHES IN AN INNINGS

| V.Y. Richardson | A v SA | Durban[2] | 1935–36 |
|---|---|---|---|
| Yajurvindra Singh | I v E | Bangalore | 1976–77 |

*Richardson was playing in his last Test and Yajurvindra in his first.*

# MOST SUBSTITUTE CATCHES BY ONE FIELDER IN A MATCH

FOUR
| Gursharan Singh | India v West Indies | Ahmedabad | 1983–84 |
|---|---|---|---|

THREE
| H. Strudwick | England v Australia | Melbourne | 1903–04 |
|---|---|---|---|
| W.V. Rodriguez | West Indies v India | Port-of-Spain | 1961–62 |
| Yajurvindra Singh | India v West Indies | Madras[1] | 1978–79 |
| Haroon Rashid | Pakistan v England | Leeds | 1982 |

# MOST SUBSTITUTE CATCHES BY ONE FIELDER IN AN INNINGS

THREE
| H. Strudwick | England v Australia | Melbourne | 1903–04 |
|---|---|---|---|
| Haroon Rashid | Pakistan v England | Leeds | 1982 |
| Gursharan Singh | India v West Indies | Ahmedabad | 1983–84 |

# INDIVIDUAL RECORDS –
# ALL-ROUND PERFORMANCES

## 1000 RUNS AND 100 WICKETS

| ENGLAND | Tests | Runs | Wkts | Tests for Double |
|---|---|---|---|---|
| T.E. Bailey | 61 | 2290 | 132 | 47 |
| I.T. Botham | 79 | 4409 | 343 | 21 |
| A.W. Greig | 58 | 3599 | 141 | 37 |
| R. Illingworth | 61 | 1836 | 122 | 47 |
| W. Rhodes | 58 | 2325 | 127 | 44 |
| M.W. Tate | 39 | 1198 | 155 | 33 |
| F.J. Titmus | 53 | 1449 | 153 | 40 |
| **AUSTRALIA** | | | | |
| R. Benaud | 63 | 2201 | 248 | 32 |
| A.K. Davidson | 44 | 1328 | 186 | 34 |
| G. Giffen | 31 | 1238 | 103 | 30 |
| I.W. Johnson | 45 | 1000 | 109 | 45 |
| R.R. Lindwall | 61 | 1502 | 228 | 38 |
| K.R. Miller | 55 | 2958 | 170 | 33 |
| M.A. Noble | 42 | 1997 | 121 | 27 |
| **SOUTH AFRICA** | | | | |
| T.L. Goddard | 41 | 2516 | 123 | 36 |
| **WEST INDIES** | | | | |
| G.St A. Sobers | 93 | 8032 | 235 | 48 |
| **NEW ZEALAND** | | | | |
| R.J. Hadlee | 57 | 2088 | 266 | 28 |
| **INDIA** | | | | |
| Kapil Dev | 68 | 2788 | 258 | 25 |
| M.H. Mankad | 44 | 2109 | 162 | 23 |
| **PAKISTAN** | | | | |
| Imran Khan | 51 | 2023 | 232 | 30 |
| Intikhab Alam | 47 | 1493 | 125 | 41 |
| Sarfraz Nawaz | 55 | 1045 | 177 | 55 |

## 1000 RUNS, 50 WICKETS AND 50 CATCHES

| ENGLAND | Tests | Runs | Wkts | Catches |
|---|---|---|---|---|
| I.T. Botham | 79 | 4409 | 343 | 92 |
| A.W. Greig | 58 | 3599 | 141 | 87 |
| W.R. Hammond | 85 | 7249 | 83 | 110 |
| W. Rhodes | 58 | 2325 | 127 | 60 |
| F.E. Woolley | 64 | 3283 | 83 | 64 |
| **AUSTRALIA** | | | | |
| R. Benaud | 63 | 2201 | 248 | 65 |
| R.B. Simpson | 62 | 4869 | 71 | 110 |
| **WEST INDIES** | | | | |
| G.St A. Sobers | 93 | 8032 | 235 | 109 |

# 1000 RUNS AND 100 WICKET-KEEPING DISMISSALS

| ENGLAND | Tests | Runs | Dismissals | Tests for Double |
|---|---|---|---|---|
| T.G. Evans | 91 | 2439 | 219 | 42 |
| A.P.E. Knott | 95 | 4389 | 269 | 30 |
| J.M. Parks | 46 | 1962 | 114 | 41 |
| R.W. Taylor | 57 | 1156 | 174 | 47 |
| | | | | |
| AUSTRALIA | | | | |
| R.W. Marsh | 96 | 3633 | 355 | 25 |
| W.A.S. Oldfield | 54 | 1427 | 130 | 41 |
| | | | | |
| SOUTH AFRICA | | | | |
| J.H.B. Waite | 50 | 2405 | 141 | 36 |
| | | | | |
| WEST INDIES | | | | |
| P.J.L. Dujon | 33 | 1764 | 110 | 30 |
| D.L. Murray | 62 | 1993 | 189 | 33 |
| | | | | |
| INDIA | | | | |
| S.M.H. Kirmani | 85 | 2717 | 193 | 42 |
| | | | | |
| PAKISTAN | | | | |
| Wasim Bari | 81 | 1366 | 228 | 53 |

# 250 RUNS AND 20 WICKETS IN A SERIES

| | Tests | Runs | Wkts | | |
|---|---|---|---|---|---|
| G. Giffen | 5 | 475 | 34 | Australia v England | 1894–95 |
| L.C. Braund | 5 | 256 | 21 | England v Australia | 1901–02 |
| G.A. Faulkner | 5 | 545 | 29 | South Africa v England | 1909–10 |
| G.J. Thompson | 5 | 267 | 23 | England v South Africa | 1909–10 |
| J.M. Gregory | 5 | 442 | 23 | Australia v England | 1920–21 |
| K.R. Miller | 5 | 362 | 20 | Australia v West Indies | 1951–52 |
| K.R. Miller | 5 | 439 | 20 | Australia v West Indies | 1954–55 |
| R. Benaud | 5 | 329 | 30 | Australia v South Africa | 1957–58 |
| G.St A. Sobers | 5 | 424 | 23 | West Indies v India | 1961–62 |
| G.St A. Sobers | 5 | 322 | 20 | West Indies v England | 1963 |
| G.St A. Sobers | 5 | 722 | 20 | West Indies v England | 1966 |
| T.L. Goddard | 5 | 294 | 26 | South Africa v Australia | 1966–67 |
| A.W. Greig | 5 | 430 | 24 | England v West Indies | 1973–74 |
| I.T. Botham | 6 | 291 | 23 | England v Australia | 1978–79 |
| Kapil Dev | 6 | 278 | 32 | India v Pakistan | 1979–80 |
| I.T. Botham | 6 | 399 | 34 | England v Australia | 1981 |
| Kapil Dev | 6 | 318 | 22 | India v England | 1981–82 |
| R.J. Hadlee | 4 | 301 | 21 | New Zealand v England | 1983 |
| I.T. Botham | 6 | 250 | 31 | England v Australia | 1985 |

# 250 RUNS AND 20 WICKET-KEEPING DISMISSALS IN A SERIES

| | Tests | Runs | Dis | | |
|---|---|---|---|---|---|
| J.H.B. Waite | 5 | 263 | 26 | South Africa v New Zealand | 1961–62 |
| D.T. Lindsay | 5 | 606 | 24 | South Africa v Australia | 1966–67 |
| A.P.E. Knott | 6 | 364 | 23 | England v Australia | 1974–75 |

# 500 RUNS IN A SERIES BY A WICKET-KEEPER

| | Tests | Runs | Avge | | |
|---|---|---|---|---|---|
| B.K. Kunderan | 5 | 525 | 52.50 | India v England | 1963–64 |
| D.T. Lindsay | 5 | 606 | 86.57 | South Africa v Australia | 1966–67 |

# MATCH DOUBLE – 100 RUNS AND 10 WICKETS

| A.K. Davidson | 44<br>80 | 5-135<br>6-87 | A v WI | Brisbane[2] | 1960–61 |
| I.T. Botham | 114 | 6-58<br>7-48 | E v I | Bombay[3] | 1979–80 |
| Imran Khan | 117 | 6-98<br>5-82 | P v I | Faisalabad | 1982–83 |

# A HUNDRED AND FIVE WICKETS IN AN INNINGS

† *On debut*

| ENGLAND | | | *Opponents* | | |
|---|---|---|---|---|---|
| A.W. Greig | 148 | 6-164 | West Indies | Bridgetown | 1973–74 |
| I.T. Botham | 103 | 5-73 | New Zealand | Christchurch | 1977–78 |
| I.T. Botham | 108 | 8-34 | Pakistan | Lord's | 1978 |
| I.T. Botham | 114 | 6-58<br>7-48 | India | Bombay[3] | 1979–80 |
| I.T. Botham | 149* | 6-95 | E v A | Leeds | 1981 |
| I.T. Botham | 138 | 5-59 | E v NZ | Wellington | 1983–84 |
| **AUSTRALIA** | | | | | |
| C. Kelleway | 114 | 5-33 | South Africa | Manchester | 1912 |
| J.M. Gregory | 100 | 7-69 | England | Melbourne | 1920–21 |
| K.R. Miller | 109 | 6-107 | West Indies | Kingston | 1954–55 |
| R. Benaud | 100 | 5-84 | South Africa | Johannesburg[3] | 1957–58 |
| **SOUTH AFRICA** | | | | | |
| J.H. Sinclair | 106 | 6-26 | England | Cape Town | 1898–99 |
| G.A. Faulkner | 123 | 5-120 | England | Johannesburg[1] | 1909–10 |
| **WEST INDIES** | | | | | |
| D.St E. Atkinson | 219 | 5-56 | Australia | Bridgetown | 1954–55 |
| O.G. Smith | 100 | 5-90 | India | Delhi | 1958–59 |
| G.St A. Sobers | 104 | 5-63 | India | Kingston | 1961–62 |
| G.St A. Sobers | 174 | 5-41 | England | Leeds | 1966 |
| **NEW ZEALAND** | | | | | |
| B.R. Taylor† | 105 | 5-86 | India | Calcutta | 1964–65 |
| **INDIA** | | | | | |
| M.H. Mankad | 184 | 5-196 | England | Lord's | 1952 |
| P.R. Umrigar | 172* | 5-107 | West Indies | Port-of-Spain | 1961–62 |
| **PAKISTAN** | | | | | |
| Mushtaq Mohammad | 201 | 5-49 | New Zealand | Dunedin | 1972–73 |
| Mushtaq Mohammad | 121 | 5-28 | West Indies | Port-of-Spain | 1976–77 |
| Imran Khan | 117 | 6-98<br>5-82 | P v I | Faisalabad | 1982–83 |

# A HUNDRED AND FIVE DISMISSALS IN AN INNINGS

| D.T. Lindsay | 182 | 6 ct | SA v A | Johannesburg[3] | 1966–67 |
| I.D.S. Smith | 113* | 4 ct, 1 st | NZ v E | Auckland | 1983–84 |

# INDIVIDUAL RECORDS – THE CAPTAINS

## RESULTS SUMMARY

| ENGLAND (64) | Tests as Captain | Opponents | | | | | | Results | | | Toss Won |
|---|---|---|---|---|---|---|---|---|---|---|---|
| | | A | SA | WI | NZ | I | P | W | L | D | |
| James Lillywhite | 2 | 2 | – | – | – | – | – | 1 | 1 | – | – |
| Lord Harris | 4 | 4 | – | – | – | – | – | 2 | 1 | 1 | 2 |
| A. Shaw | 4 | 4 | – | – | – | – | – | – | 2 | 2 | 4 |
| A.N. Hornby | 2 | 2 | – | – | – | – | – | – | 1 | 1 | 1 |
| Hon I.F.W. Bligh | 4 | 4 | – | – | – | – | – | 2 | 2 | – | 3 |
| A. Shrewsbury | 7 | 7 | – | – | – | – | – | 5 | 2 | – | 3 |
| A.G. Steel | 4 | 4 | – | – | – | – | – | 3 | 1 | – | 2 |
| W.W. Read | 2 | 1 | 1 | – | – | – | – | 2 | – | – | – |
| W.G. Grace | 13 | 13 | – | – | – | – | – | 8 | 3 | 2 | 4 |
| C.A. Smith | 1 | – | 1 | – | – | – | – | 1 | – | – | – |
| M.P. Bowden | 1 | – | 1 | – | – | – | – | 1 | – | – | 1 |
| A.E. Stoddart | 8 | 8 | – | – | – | – | – | 3 | 4 | 1 | 2 |
| T.C. O'Brien | 1 | – | 1 | – | – | – | – | 1 | – | – | – |
| Lord Hawke | 4 | – | 4 | – | – | – | – | 4 | – | – | 4 |
| A.C. MacLaren | 22 | 22 | – | – | – | – | – | 4 | 11 | 7 | 11 |
| P.F. Warner | 10 | 5 | 5 | – | – | – | – | 4 | 6 | – | 5 |
| Hon F.S. Jackson | 5 | 5 | – | – | – | – | – | 2 | – | 3 | 5 |
| R.E. Foster | 3 | – | 3 | – | – | – | – | 1 | – | 2 | 3 |
| F.L. Fane | 5 | 3 | 2 | – | – | – | – | 2 | 3 | – | 3 |
| A.O. Jones | 2 | 2 | – | – | – | – | – | – | 2 | – | 1 |
| H.D.G. Leveson Gower | 3 | – | 3 | – | – | – | – | 1 | 2 | – | – |
| J.W.H.T. Douglas | 18 | 12 | 6 | – | – | – | – | 8 | 8 | 2 | 7 |
| C.B. Fry | 6 | 3 | 3 | – | – | – | – | 4 | – | 2 | 4 |
| Hon L.H. Tennyson | 3 | 3 | – | – | – | – | – | – | 1 | 2 | 2 |
| F.T. Mann | 5 | – | 5 | – | – | – | – | 2 | 1 | 2 | 3 |
| A.E.R. Gilligan | 9 | 5 | 4 | – | – | – | – | 4 | 4 | 1 | 2 |
| A.W. Carr | 6 | 4 | 2 | – | – | – | – | 1 | – | 5 | 3 |
| A.P.F. Chapman | 17 | 9 | 5 | 3 | – | – | – | 9 | 2 | 6 | 9 |
| R.T. Stanyforth | 4 | – | 4 | – | – | – | – | 2 | 1 | 1 | – |
| G.T.S. Stevens | 1 | – | 1 | – | – | – | – | – | 1 | – | – |
| J.C. White | 4 | 1 | 3 | – | – | – | – | 1 | 1 | 2 | 3 |
| A.H.H. Gilligan | 4 | – | – | – | 4 | – | – | 1 | – | 3 | 1 |
| Hon F.S.G. Calthorpe | 4 | – | – | 4 | – | – | – | 1 | 1 | 2 | 2 |
| R.E.S. Wyatt | 16 | 5 | 5 | 5 | 1 | – | – | 3 | 5 | 8 | 12 |
| D.R. Jardine | 15 | 5 | – | 2 | 4 | 4 | – | 9 | 1 | 5 | 7 |
| C.F. Walters | 1 | 1 | – | – | – | – | – | – | 1 | – | – |
| G.O.B. Allen | 11 | 5 | – | 3 | – | 3 | – | 4 | 5 | 2 | 6 |
| R.W.V. Robins | 3 | – | – | – | 3 | – | – | 1 | – | 2 | 2 |
| W.R. Hammond | 20 | 8 | 5 | 3 | 1 | 3 | – | 4 | 3 | 13 | 12 |
| N.W.D. Yardley | 14 | 6 | 5 | 3 | – | – | – | 4 | 7 | 3 | 9 |
| K. Cranston | 1 | – | – | 1 | – | – | – | – | – | 1 | – |
| F.G. Mann | 7 | – | 5 | – | 2 | – | – | 2 | – | 5 | 5 |
| F.R. Brown | 15 | 5 | 5 | 1 | 4 | – | – | 5 | 6 | 4 | 3 |
| N.D. Howard | 4 | – | – | – | – | 4 | – | 1 | – | 3 | 2 |
| D.B. Carr | 1 | – | – | – | – | 1 | – | – | 1 | – | 1 |
| L. Hutton | 23 | 10 | – | 5 | 2 | 4 | 2 | 11 | 4 | 8 | 7 |
| Rev D.S. Sheppard | 2 | – | – | – | – | – | 2 | 1 | – | 1 | 1 |
| P.B.H. May | 41 | 13 | 10 | 8 | 7 | 3 | – | 20 | 10 | 11 | 26 |
| M.C. Cowdrey | 27 | 6 | 5 | 10 | – | 2 | 4 | 8 | 4 | 15 | 17 |
| E.R. Dexter | 30 | 10 | – | 5 | 3 | 5 | 7 | 9 | 7 | 14 | 13 |
| M.J.K. Smith | 25 | 5 | 8 | 1 | 6 | 5 | – | 5 | 3 | 17 | 10 |
| D.B. Close | 7 | – | – | 1 | – | 3 | 3 | 6 | – | 1 | 4 |
| T.W. Graveney | 1 | 1 | – | – | – | – | – | – | – | 1 | – |
| R. Illingworth | 31 | 11 | – | 6 | 8 | 3 | 3 | 12 | 5 | 14 | 15‡ |
| A.R. Lewis | 8 | – | – | – | – | 5 | 3 | 1 | 2 | 5 | 3 |

| | Tests as Captain | Opponents | | | | | | | Results | | | Toss Won |
|---|---|---|---|---|---|---|---|---|---|---|---|---|
| | | A | SA | WI | NZ | I | P | SL | W | L | D | |
| M.H. Denness | 19 | 6 | – | 5 | 2 | 3 | 3 | – | 6 | 5 | 8 | 9 |
| J.H. Edrich | 1 | 1 | – | – | – | – | – | – | – | 1 | – | – |
| A.W. Greig | 14 | 4 | – | 5 | – | 5 | – | – | 3 | 5 | 6 | 6 |
| J.M. Brearley | 31 | 18 | – | – | 3 | 5 | 5 | – | 18 | 4 | 9 | 13 |
| G. Boycott | 4 | – | – | – | 3 | – | 1 | – | 1 | 1 | 2 | 3 |
| I.T. Botham | 12 | 3 | – | 9 | – | – | – | – | – | 4 | 8 | 6 |
| K.W.R. Fletcher | 7 | – | – | – | – | 6 | – | 1 | 1 | 1 | 5 | 5 |
| R.G.D. Willis | 18 | 5 | – | – | 7 | 3 | 3 | – | 7 | 5 | 6 | 8 |
| D.I. Gower | 20 | 6 | – | 5 | – | 5 | 3 | 1 | 5 | 8 | 7 | 8 |
| | 617 | 257 | 102 | 85 | 60 | 72 | 39 | 2 | 227 | 159 | 231 | 303 |

‡ *Excluding toss won in abandoned Melbourne Test of 1970–71.*

| AUSTRALIA (38) | Tests as Captain | Opponents | | | | | | | Results | | | | Toss Won |
|---|---|---|---|---|---|---|---|---|---|---|---|---|---|
| | | E | SA | WI | NZ | I | P | SL | W | L | D | Tie | |
| D.W. Gregory | 3 | 3 | – | – | – | – | – | – | 2 | 1 | – | – | 2 |
| W.L. Murdoch | 16 | 16 | – | – | – | – | – | – | 5 | 7 | 4 | – | 7 |
| T.P. Horan | 2 | 2 | – | – | – | – | – | – | – | 2 | – | – | 1 |
| H.H. Massie | 1 | 1 | – | – | – | – | – | – | 1 | – | – | – | 1 |
| J.M. Blackham | 8 | 8 | – | – | – | – | – | – | 3 | 3 | 2 | – | 4 |
| H.J.H. Scott | 3 | 3 | – | – | – | – | – | – | – | 3 | – | – | 1 |
| P.S. McDonnell | 6 | 6 | – | – | – | – | – | – | 1 | 5 | – | – | 4 |
| G. Giffen | 4 | 4 | – | – | – | – | – | – | 2 | 2 | – | – | 3 |
| G.H.S. Trott | 8 | 8 | – | – | – | – | – | – | 5 | 3 | – | – | 5 |
| J. Darling | 21 | 18 | 3 | – | – | – | – | – | 7 | 4 | 10 | – | 7 |
| H. Trumble | 2 | 2 | – | – | – | – | – | – | 2 | – | – | – | 1 |
| M.A. Noble | 15 | 15 | – | – | – | – | – | – | 8 | 5 | 2 | – | 11 |
| C. Hill | 10 | 5 | 5 | – | – | – | – | – | 5 | 5 | – | – | – |
| S.E. Gregory | 6 | 3 | 3 | – | – | – | – | – | 2 | 1 | 3 | – | 1 |
| W.W. Armstrong | 10 | 10 | – | – | – | – | – | – | 8 | – | 2 | – | 4 |
| H.L. Collins | 11 | 8 | 3 | – | – | – | – | – | 5 | 2 | 4 | – | 7 |
| W. Bardsley | 2 | 2 | – | – | – | – | – | – | – | – | 2 | – | 1 |
| J. Ryder | 5 | 5 | – | – | – | – | – | – | 1 | 4 | – | – | 2 |
| W.M. Woodfull | 25 | 15 | 5 | 5 | – | – | – | – | 14 | 7 | 4 | – | 12 |
| V.Y. Richardson | 5 | – | 5 | – | – | – | – | – | 4 | – | 1 | – | 1 |
| D.G. Bradman | 24 | 19 | – | – | – | 5 | – | – | 15 | 3 | 6 | – | 10 |
| W.A. Brown | 1 | – | – | – | 1 | – | – | – | 1 | – | – | – | – |
| A.L. Hassett | 24 | 10 | 10 | – | – | – | – | – | 14 | 4 | 6 | – | 18 |
| A.R. Morris | 2 | 1 | – | 1 | – | – | – | – | – | 2 | – | – | 2 |
| I.W. Johnson | 17 | 9 | – | 5 | – | 2 | 1 | – | 7 | 5 | 5 | – | 6 |
| R.R. Lindwall | 1 | – | – | – | – | 1 | – | – | – | – | 1 | – | – |
| I.D. Craig | 5 | – | 5 | – | – | – | – | – | 3 | – | 2 | – | 3 |
| R. Benaud | 28 | 14 | 1 | 5 | – | 5 | 3 | – | 12 | 4 | 11 | 1 | 11 |
| R.N. Harvey | 1 | 1 | – | – | – | – | – | – | 1 | – | – | – | – |
| R.B. Simpson | 39 | 8 | 9 | 10 | – | 10 | 2 | – | 12 | 12 | 15 | – | 19 |
| B.C. Booth | 2 | 2 | – | – | – | – | – | – | – | 1 | 1 | – | 1 |
| W.M. Lawry | 25 | 9 | 4 | 5 | – | 7 | – | – | 9 | 8 | 8 | – | 8 |
| B.N. Jarman | 1 | 1 | – | – | – | – | – | – | – | – | 1 | – | 1 |
| I.M. Chappell | 30 | 16 | – | 5 | 6 | – | 3 | – | 15 | 5 | 10 | – | 17 |
| G.S. Chappell | 48 | 15 | – | 12 | 8 | 3 | 9 | 1 | 21 | 13 | 14 | – | 29 |
| G.N. Yallop | 7 | 6 | – | – | – | – | 1 | – | 1 | 6 | – | – | 6 |
| K.J. Hughes | 28 | 6 | – | 7 | – | 6 | 9 | – | 4 | 13 | 11 | – | 13 |
| A.R. Border | 9 | 6 | – | 3 | – | – | – | – | 2 | 4 | 3 | – | 4 |
| | 455 | 257 | 53 | 62 | 15 | 39 | 28 | 1 | 192 | 134 | 128 | 1 | 228 |

| SOUTH AFRICA (24) | Tests as Captain | Opponents E | A | NZ | Results W | L | D | Toss Won |
|---|---|---|---|---|---|---|---|---|
| O.R. Dunell | 1 | 1 | – | – | – | 1 | – | 1 |
| W.H. Milton | 2 | 2 | – | – | – | 2 | – | 1 |
| E.A. Halliwell | 3 | 2 | 1 | – | – | 3 | – | 1 |
| A.R. Richards | 1 | 1 | – | – | – | 1 | – | – |
| M. Bisset | 2 | 2 | – | – | – | 2 | – | – |
| H.M. Taberer | 1 | – | 1 | – | – | – | 1 | 1 |
| J.H. Anderson | 1 | – | 1 | – | – | 1 | – | – |
| P.W. Sherwell | 13 | 8 | 5 | – | 5 | 6 | 2 | 5 |
| S.J. Snooke | 5 | 5 | – | – | 3 | 2 | – | 3 |
| F. Mitchell | 3 | 1 | 2 | – | – | 3 | – | 2 |
| L.J. Tancred | 3 | 2 | 1 | – | – | 2 | 1 | 2 |
| H.W. Taylor | 18 | 15 | 3 | – | 1 | 10 | 7 | 11 |
| H.G. Deane | 12 | 12 | – | – | 2 | 4 | 6 | 9 |
| E.P. Nupen | 1 | 1 | – | – | 1 | – | – | – |
| H.B. Cameron | 9 | 2 | 5 | 2 | 2 | 5 | 2 | 3 |
| H.F. Wade | 10 | 5 | 5 | – | 1 | 4 | 5 | 5 |
| A. Melville | 10 | 10 | – | – | – | 4 | 6 | 4 |
| A.D. Nourse | 15 | 10 | 5 | – | 1 | 9 | 5 | 7 |
| J.E. Cheetham | 15 | 3 | 5 | 7 | 7 | 5 | 3 | 6 |
| D.J. McGlew | 14 | 8 | 1 | 5 | 4 | 6 | 4 | 4 |
| C.B. van Ryneveld | 8 | 4 | 4 | – | 2 | 4 | 2 | 3 |
| T.L. Goddard | 13 | 5 | 5 | 3 | 1 | 2 | 10 | 4 |
| P.L. van der Merwe | 8 | 3 | 5 | – | 4 | 1 | 3 | 4 |
| A. Bacher | 4 | – | 4 | – | 4 | – | – | 4 |
| | 172 | 102 | 53 | 17 | 38 | 77 | 57 | 80 |

| WEST INDIES (19) | Tests as Captain | Opponents E | A | NZ | I | P | Results W | L | D | Tie | Toss Won |
|---|---|---|---|---|---|---|---|---|---|---|---|
| R.K. Nunes | 4 | 4 | – | – | – | – | – | 3 | 1 | – | 2 |
| E.L.G. Hoad | 1 | 1 | – | – | – | – | – | – | 1 | – | 1 |
| N. Betancourt | 1 | 1 | – | – | – | – | – | 1 | – | – | – |
| M.P. Fernandes | 1 | 1 | – | – | – | – | 1 | – | – | – | 1 |
| G.C. Grant | 12 | 7 | 5 | – | – | – | 3 | 7 | 2 | – | 5 |
| R.S. Grant | 3 | 3 | – | – | – | – | – | 1 | 2 | – | 2 |
| G.A. Headley | 1 | 1 | – | – | – | – | – | – | 1 | – | 1 |
| G.E. Gomez | 1 | 1 | – | – | – | – | – | – | 1 | – | – |
| J.D.C. Goddard | 22 | 11 | 4 | 2 | 5 | – | 8 | 7 | 7 | – | 12 |
| J.B. Stollmeyer | 13 | 5 | 3 | – | 5 | – | 3 | 4 | 6 | – | 7 |
| D.St E. Atkinson | 7 | – | 3 | 4 | – | – | 3 | 3 | 1 | – | 3 |
| F.C.M. Alexander | 18 | 5 | – | – | 5 | 8 | 7 | 4 | 7 | – | 9 |
| F.M.M. Worrell | 15 | 5 | 5 | – | 5 | – | 9 | 3 | 2 | 1 | 9 |
| G.St A. Sobers | 39 | 13 | 10 | 8 | 8 | – | 9 | 10 | 20 | – | 27 |
| R.B. Kanhai | 13 | 8 | 5 | – | – | – | 3 | 3 | 7 | – | 6 |
| C.H. Lloyd | 74 | 18 | 22 | 3 | 20 | 11 | 36 | 12 | 26 | – | 35 |
| A.I. Kallicharran | 9 | – | 3 | – | 6 | – | 1 | 2 | 6 | – | 4 |
| D.L. Murray | 1 | – | 1 | – | – | – | – | – | 1 | – | 1 |
| I.V.A. Richards | 6 | 1 | 1 | 4 | – | – | 2 | – | 4 | – | 5 |
| | 241 | 85 | 62 | 21 | 54 | 19 | 85 | 60 | 95 | 1 | 130 |

| NEW ZEALAND (17) | Tests as Captain | Opponents E | A | SA | WI | I | P | SL | Results W | L | D | Toss Won |
|---|---|---|---|---|---|---|---|---|---|---|---|---|
| T.C. Lowry | 7 | 7 | – | – | – | – | – | – | – | 2 | 5 | 5 |
| M.L. Page | 7 | 5 | – | 2 | – | – | – | – | – | 3 | 4 | 4 |
| W.A. Hadlee | 8 | 7 | 1 | – | – | – | – | – | – | 2 | 6 | 4 |
| B. Sutcliffe | 4 | – | – | 2 | 2 | – | – | – | – | 3 | 1 | 4 |
| W.M. Wallace | 2 | – | – | 2 | – | – | – | – | – | 1 | 1 | – |

| | Tests as Captain | Opponents E | A | SA | WI | I | P | SL | Results W | L | D | Toss Won |
|---|---|---|---|---|---|---|---|---|---|---|---|---|
| G.O. Rabone | 5 | 2 | – | 3 | – | – | – | – | – | 4 | 1 | 2 |
| H.B. Cave | 9 | – | – | – | 1 | 5 | 3 | – | – | 5 | 4 | 5 |
| J.R. Reid | 34 | 13 | – | 8 | 3 | 4 | 6 | – | 3 | 18 | 13 | 17 |
| M.E. Chapple | 1 | 1 | – | – | – | – | – | – | – | – | 1 | – |
| B.W. Sinclair | 3 | 2 | – | – | – | 1 | – | – | – | 1 | 2 | 3 |
| G.T. Dowling | 19 | 5 | – | – | 5 | 6 | 3 | – | 4 | 7 | 8 | 10 |
| B.E. Congdon | 17 | 5 | 6 | – | 3 | – | 3 | – | 1 | 7 | 9 | 4 |
| G.M. Turner | 10 | – | 2 | – | – | 6 | 2 | – | 1 | 6 | 3 | 2 |
| J.M. Parker | 1 | – | – | – | – | – | 1 | – | – | – | 1 | – |
| M.G. Burgess | 10 | 6 | 1 | – | – | – | 3 | – | 1 | 6 | 3 | 4 |
| G.P. Howarth | 30 | 7 | 5 | – | 7 | 3 | 3 | 5 | 11 | 7 | 12 | 17 |
| J.V. Coney | 3 | – | – | – | – | – | 3 | – | – | 2 | 1 | 2 |
| | 170 | 60 | 15 | 17 | 21 | 25 | 27 | 5 | 21 | 74 | 75 | 83 |

| INDIA (21) | Tests as Captain | Opponents E | A | WI | NZ | P | SL | Results W | L | D | Toss Won |
|---|---|---|---|---|---|---|---|---|---|---|---|
| C.K. Nayudu | 4 | 4 | – | – | – | – | – | – | 3 | 1 | 1 |
| Maharajkumar of Vizianagram | 3 | 3 | – | – | – | – | – | – | 2 | 1 | 1 |
| Nawab of Pataudi, sr | 3 | 3 | – | – | – | – | – | – | 1 | 2 | 3 |
| L. Amarnath | 15 | – | 5 | 5 | – | 5 | – | 2 | 6 | 7 | 4 |
| V.S. Hazare | 14 | 9 | – | 5 | – | – | – | 1 | 5 | 8 | 8 |
| M.H. Mankad | 6 | – | – | 1 | – | 5 | – | – | 1 | 5 | 1 |
| Ghulam Ahmed | 3 | – | – | 2 | 1 | – | – | – | 2 | 1 | 1 |
| P.R. Umrigar | 8 | – | 3 | 1 | 4 | – | – | 2 | 2 | 4 | 6 |
| H.R. Adhikari | 1 | – | – | 1 | – | – | – | – | – | 1 | 1 |
| D.K. Gaekwad | 4 | 4 | – | – | – | – | – | – | 4 | – | 2 |
| P. Roy | 1 | 1 | – | – | – | – | – | – | 1 | – | 1 |
| G.S. Ramchand | 5 | – | 5 | – | – | – | – | 1 | 2 | 2 | 4 |
| N.J. Contractor | 12 | 5 | – | 2 | – | 5 | – | 2 | 2 | 8 | 7 |
| Nawab of Pataudi, jr | 40 | 8 | 11 | 10 | 11 | – | – | 9 | 19 | 12 | 20 |
| C.G. Borde | 1 | – | 1 | – | – | – | – | – | 1 | – | – |
| A.L. Wadekar | 16 | 11 | – | 5 | – | – | – | 4 | 4 | 8 | 7 |
| S. Venkataraghavan | 5 | 4 | – | 1 | – | – | – | – | 2 | 3 | 2 |
| S.M. Gavaskar | 47 | 14 | 9 | 6 | 4 | 13 | 1 | 9 | 8 | 30 | 22 |
| B.S. Bedi | 22 | 5 | 5 | 4 | 5 | 3 | – | 6 | 11 | 5 | 13 |
| G.R. Viswanath | 2 | 1 | – | – | – | 1 | – | – | 1 | 1 | 2 |
| Kapil Dev | 14 | – | – | 11 | – | 3 | – | – | 5 | 9 | 7 |
| | 126 | 72 | 39 | 54 | 25 | 35 | 1 | 36 | 82 | 108 | 113 |

| PAKISTAN (14) | Tests as Captain | Opponents E | A | WI | NZ | I | SL | Results W | L | D | Toss Won |
|---|---|---|---|---|---|---|---|---|---|---|---|
| A.H. Kardar | 23 | 4 | 1 | 5 | 3 | 10 | – | 6 | 6 | 11 | 10 |
| Fazal Mahmood | 10 | – | 2 | 3 | – | 5 | – | 2 | 2 | 6 | 6 |
| Imtiaz Ahmed | 4 | 3 | 1 | – | – | – | – | – | 2 | 2 | 4 |
| Javed Burki | 5 | 5 | – | – | – | – | – | – | 4 | 1 | 3 |
| Hanif Mohammad | 11 | 3 | 2 | – | 6 | – | – | 2 | 2 | 7 | 6 |
| Saeed Ahmed | 3 | 3 | – | – | – | – | – | – | – | 3 | 1 |
| Intikhab Alam | 17 | 6 | 3 | 2 | 6 | – | – | 1 | 5 | 11 | 12 |
| Majid Khan | 3 | 3 | – | – | – | – | – | – | – | 3 | 1 |
| Mushtaq Mohammad | 19 | – | 5 | 5 | 6 | 3 | – | 8 | 4 | 7 | 10 |
| Wasim Bari | 6 | 6 | – | – | – | – | – | – | 2 | 4 | 4 |
| Asif Iqbal | 6 | – | – | – | – | 6 | – | – | 2 | 4 | 3 |
| Javed Miandad | 16 | – | 6 | 4 | 3 | – | 3 | 4 | 5 | 7 | 6 |
| Imran Khan | 14 | 3 | 5 | – | – | 6 | – | 7 | 3 | 4 | 8 |
| Zaheer Abbas | 14 | 3 | 3 | – | 3 | 5 | – | 3 | 1 | 10 | 6 |
| | 151 | 39 | 28 | 19 | 27 | 35 | 3 | 33 | 38 | 80 | 80 |

| SRI LANKA (3) | Tests as Captain | Opponents E | A | NZ | I | P | Results W | L | D | Toss Won |
|---|---|---|---|---|---|---|---|---|---|---|
| B. Warnapura | 4 | 1 | – | – | 1 | 2 | – | 3 | 1 | 2 |
| L.R.D. Mendis | 6 | 1 | 1 | 3 | – | 1 | – | 3 | 3 | 2 |
| D.S. De Silva | 2 | – | – | 2 | – | – | – | 2 | – | 1 |
| | 12 | 2 | 1 | 5 | 1 | 3 | – | 8 | 4 | 5 |

# MOST CONSECUTIVE MATCHES AS CAPTAIN

| | | | | From | To |
|---|---|---|---|---|---|
| **England** | 35 | P.B.H. May | | 1955 | 1959 |
| **Australia** | 30 | I.M. Chappell | | 1970–71 | 1975 |
| **South Africa** | 18 | H.W. Taylor | | 1913–14 | 1924 |
| **West Indies** | 39 | G.St A. Sobers | | 1964–65 | 1971–72 |
| **New Zealand** | 34 | J.R. Reid | | 1955–56 | 1965 |
| **India** | 22 | B.S. Bedi | | 1975–76 | 1978–79 |
| | 22 | S.M. Gavaskar | | 1980–81 | 1982–83 |
| **Pakistan** | 23 | A.H. Kardar | | 1952–53 | 1957–58 |
| **Sri Lanka** | 5 | L.R.D. Mendis | | 1982–83 | 1984 |

*In addition to those listed above, the following had unbroken captaincy runs of 20 or more matches: 29 – C.H. Lloyd (WI); 25 – W.M. Woodfull (A), R. Illingworth (E); 21 – Nawab of Pataudi, jr (I); 20 – M.J.K. Smith (E), W.M. Lawry (A), J.M. Brearley (E).*

# WINNING ALL FIVE TOSSES IN A SERIES

| Captains | | Venue | |
|---|---|---|---|
| Hon F.S. Jackson | England v Australia | England | 1905 |
| M.A. Noble | Australia v England | England | 1909 |
| H.G. Deane | South Africa v England | South Africa | 1927–28 |
| J.D.C. Goddard | West Indies v India | India | 1948–49 |
| A.L. Hassett | Australia v England | England | 1953 |
| P.B.H. May (3) ⎱<br>M.C. Cowdrey (2) ⎰ | England v West Indies | West Indies | 1959–60 |
| M.C. Cowdrey | England v South Africa | England | 1960 |
| Nawab of Pataudi, jr | India v England | India | 1963–64 |
| G.St A. Sobers | West Indies v England | England | 1966 |
| G.St A. Sobers | West Indies v New Zealand | West Indies | 1971–72 |
| C.H. Lloyd | West Indies v India | West Indies | 1982–83 |

*The following Australian captains won five tosses during six-match series in Australia: I.M. Chappell v England 1974–75; G.S. Chappell v West Indies 1975–76; G.N. Yallop v England 1978–79. K.W.R. Fletcher (England) won five successive tosses during the six-match series in India in 1981–82. M.C. Cowdrey won the toss for England in nine consecutive Tests from 1959–60 to 1961.*

# CAPTAINS WHO ELECTED TO FIELD FIRST

† *In first match as captain*

| ENGLAND | Opponents | Result | | | |
|---|---|---|---|---|---|
| A.E. Stoddart | A | L | I + 147 runs | Sydney | 1894–95 |
| Lord Hawke | SA | W | I + 33 runs | Cape Town | 1895–96 |
| A.C. MacLaren | A | L | 229 runs | Melbourne | 1901–02 |
| A.O. Jones | A | L | 49 runs | Sydney | 1907–08 |
| J.W.H.T. Douglas | A | W | I + 225 runs | Melbourne | 1911–12 |
| A.W. Carr | A | D | | Leeds | 1926 |
| A.P.F. Chapman | SA | L | 28 runs | Johannesburg[1] | 1930–31 |
| A.P.F. Chapman | SA | D | | Durban[2] | 1930–31 |
| R.E.S. Wyatt | WI | W | 4 wkts | Bridgetown | 1934–35 |

| | Opponents | Result | | | |
|---|---|---|---|---|---|
| R.E.S. Wyatt | WI | L | 217 runs | Port-of-Spain | 1934–35 |
| R.E.S. Wyatt | SA | D | | Oval | 1935 |
| G.O.B. Allen† | I | W | 9 wkts | Lord's | 1936 |
| W.R. Hammond | NZ | D | | Christchurch | 1946–47 |
| F.R. Brown† | NZ | D | | Manchester | 1949 |
| L. Hutton | P | D | | Lord's | 1954 |
| L. Hutton | A | L | I + 154 runs | Brisbane[2] | 1954–55 |
| L. Hutton | NZ | W | 8 wkts | Dunedin | 1954–55 |
| P.B.H. May | A | L | 10 wkts | Adelaide | 1958–59 |
| E.R. Dexter | NZ | W | I + 47 runs | Wellington | 1962–63 |
| E.R. Dexter | A | D | | Lord's | 1964 |
| M.J.K. Smith | SA | D | | Johannesburg[3] | 1964–65 |
| M.J.K. Smith | SA | D | | Oval | 1965 |
| D.B. Close | P | W | 8 wkts | Oval | 1967 |
| R. Illingworth | A | D | | Nottingham | 1972 |
| M.H. Denness | A | L | 163 runs | Adelaide | 1974–75 |
| M.H. Denness | NZ | D | | Christchurch | 1974–75 |
| M.H. Denness | A | L | I + 85 runs | Birmingham | 1975 |
| A.W. Greig | A | L | 45 runs | Melbourne | 1976–77 |
| G. Boycott | NZ | L | 72 runs | Wellington | 1977–78 |
| J.M. Brearley | A | L | 138 runs | Perth | 1979–80 |
| I.T. Botham | WI | L | I + 79 runs | Port-of-Spain | 1980–81 |
| I.T. Botham | WI | L | 298 runs | Bridgetown | 1980–81 |
| J.M. Brearley | A | D | | Oval | 1981 |
| K.W.R. Fletcher | I | D | | Madras[1] | 1981–82 |
| R.G.D. Willis | A | L | 8 wkts | Adelaide | 1982–83 |
| D.I. Gower | SL | D | | Lord's | 1984 |
| D.I. Gower | A | D | | Manchester | 1985 |
| D.I. Gower | A | W | I + 118 runs | Birmingham | 1985 |

| **AUSTRALIA** | Opponents | Result | | | |
|---|---|---|---|---|---|
| P.S. McDonnell† | E | L | 13 runs | Sydney | 1886–87 |
| P.S. McDonnell | E | L | 126 runs | Sydney | 1887–88 |
| G. Giffen† | E | L | 94 runs | Melbourne | 1894–95 |
| M.A. Noble | E | W | 9 wkts | Lord's | 1909 |
| A.L. Hassett | WI | W | 7 wkts | Sydney | 1951–52 |
| A.L. Hassett | E | D | | Leeds | 1953 |
| A.R. Morris | E | L | 38 runs | Sydney | 1954–55 |
| I.W. Johnson | E | D | | Sydney | 1954–55 |
| R. Benaud | E | W | 9 wkts | Melbourne | 1958–59 |
| R. Benaud | P | W | 8 wkts | Dacca | 1959–60 |
| R. Benaud | WI | W | 2 wkts | Melbourne | 1960–61 |
| R.B. Simpson† | SA | W | 8 wkts | Melbourne | 1963–64 |
| R.B. Simpson | P | D | | Melbourne | 1964–65 |
| R.B. Simpson | WI | D | | Port-of-Spain | 1964–65 |
| R.B. Simpson | SA | L | 8 wkts | Durban[2] | 1966–67 |
| W.M. Lawry | WI | W | I + 30 runs | Melbourne | 1968–69 |
| W.M. Lawry | I | W | 10 wkts | Calcutta | 1969–70 |
| W.M. Lawry | E | D | | Perth | 1970–71 |
| I.M. Chappell† | E | L | 62 runs | Sydney | 1970–71 |
| I.M. Chappell | NZ | D | | Sydney | 1973–74 |
| I.M. Chappell | E | W | 9 wkts | Perth | 1974–75 |
| I.M. Chappell | E | D | | Melbourne | 1974–75 |
| G.S. Chappell | WI | W | 8 wkts | Melbourne | 1975–76 |
| G.S. Chappell | WI | W | 7 wkts | Sydney | 1975–76 |
| G.S. Chappell | NZ | W | 10 wkts | Auckland | 1976–77 |
| G.S. Chappell | E | D | | Oval | 1977 |
| R.B. Simpson | WI | L | 198 runs | Port-of-Spain | 1977–78 |
| G.N. Yallop | E | L | 166 runs | Perth | 1978–79 |
| G.N. Yallop | E | L | 205 runs | Adelaide | 1978–79 |
| G.N. Yallop | P | L | 71 runs | Melbourne | 1978–79 |
| K.J. Hughes† | P | W | 7 wkts | Perth | 1978–79 |
| G.S. Chappell | E | W | 6 wkts | Sydney | 1979–80 |
| G.S. Chappell | WI | L | 408 runs | Adelaide | 1979–80 |
| G.S. Chappell | NZ | W | 10 wkts | Brisbane[2] | 1980–81 |

|  | *Opponents* | *Result* | | | |
|---|---|---|---|---|---|
| G.S. Chappell | NZ | W | 8 wkts | Perth | 1980–81 |
| G.S. Chappell | I | L | 59 runs | Melbourne | 1980–81 |
| K.J. Hughes | E | W | 4 wkts | Nottingham | 1981 |
| K.J. Hughes | E | D | | Lord's | 1981 |
| G.S. Chappell | P | W | 10 wkts | Brisbane[2] | 1981–82 |
| G.S. Chappell | NZ | D | | Wellington | 1981–82 |
| G.S. Chappell | E | D | | Perth | 1982–83 |
| G.S. Chappell | E | W | 7 wkts | Brisbane[2] | 1982–83 |
| G.S. Chappell | E | L | 3 runs | Melbourne | 1982–83 |
| K.J. Hughes | P | W | 10 wkts | Sydney | 1983–84 |
| K.J. Hughes | WI | L | I + 112 runs | Perth | 1984–85 |
| A.R. Border | WI | D | | Melbourne | 1984–85 |
| A.R. Border | E | W | 4 wkts | Lord's | 1985 |

| **SOUTH AFRICA** | *Opponents* | *Result* | | | |
|---|---|---|---|---|---|
| E.A. Halliwell† | E | L | 288 runs | Port Elizabeth | 1895–96 |
| P.W. Sherwell | A | L | 530 runs | Melbourne | 1910–11 |
| P.W. Sherwell | A | L | 7 wkts | Sydney | 1910–11 |
| H.W. Taylor | E | L | I + 18 runs | Birmingham | 1924 |
| H.G. Deane | E | L | 87 runs | Cape Town | 1927–28 |
| H.G. Deane | E | W | 4 wkts | Johannesburg[1] | 1927–28 |
| H.G. Deane | E | W | 8 wkts | Durban[2] | 1927–28 |
| H.G. Deane | E | D | | Oval | 1929 |
| T.L. Goddard | A | D | | Sydney | 1963–64 |
| P.L. van der Merwe | A | W | 7 wkts | Port Elizabeth | 1966–67 |

| **WEST INDIES** | *Opponents* | *Result* | | | |
|---|---|---|---|---|---|
| R.S. Grant | E | D | | Manchester | 1939 |
| F.C.M. Alexander | P | L | 41 runs | Dacca | 1958–59 |
| F.M.M. Worrell | I | W | I + 30 runs | Bridgetown | 1961–62 |
| G.St A. Sobers | A | L | 382 runs | Sydney | 1968–69 |
| G.St A. Sobers | NZ | W | 5 wkts | Auckland | 1968–69 |
| G.St A. Sobers | I | D | | Kingston | 1970–71 |
| G.St A. Sobers | NZ | D | | Port-of-Spain | 1971–72 |
| R.B. Kanhai | E | W | 7 wkts | Port-of-Spain | 1973–74 |
| R.B. Kanhai | E | D | | Bridgetown | 1973–74 |
| C.H. Lloyd | P | D | | Lahore[2] | 1974–75 |
| C.H. Lloyd | I | W | 10 wkts | Kingston | 1975–76 |
| C.H. Lloyd | P | D | | Georgetown | 1976–77 |
| C.H. Lloyd | P | L | 266 runs | Port-of-Spain | 1976–77 |
| C.H. Lloyd | A | W | I + 106 runs | Port-of-Spain | 1977–78 |
| C.H. Lloyd | A | W | 9 wkts | Bridgetown | 1977–78 |
| A.I. Kallicharran | I | D | | Bombay[3] | 1978–79 |
| D.L. Murray† | A | D | | Brisbane[2] | 1979–80 |
| C.H. Lloyd | E | D | | Manchester | 1980 |
| I.V.A. Richards† | E | D | | Leeds | 1980 |
| C.H. Lloyd | E | D | | Kingston | 1980–81 |
| C.H. Lloyd | A | W | 5 wkts | Adelaide | 1981–82 |
| C.H. Lloyd | I | W | 4 wkts | Kingston | 1982–83 |
| C.H. Lloyd | I | D | | Port-of-Spain | 1982–83 |
| C.H. Lloyd | I | W | 10 wkts | Bridgetown | 1982–83 |
| C.H. Lloyd | I | D | | St John's | 1982–83 |
| I.V.A. Richards | A | D | | Port-of-Spain | 1983–84 |
| C.H. Lloyd | A | W | 10 wkts | Bridgetown | 1983–84 |
| C.H. Lloyd | A | W | 10 wkts | Kingston | 1983–84 |
| C.H. Lloyd | E | W | 9 wkts | Lord's | 1984 |
| C.H. Lloyd | A | W | 8 wkts | Brisbane[2] | 1984–85 |
| I.V.A. Richards | NZ | W | 10 wkts | Bridgetown | 1984–85 |

| **NEW ZEALAND** | *Opponents* | *Result* | | | |
|---|---|---|---|---|---|
| T.C. Lowry | E | D | | Auckland | 1929–30 |
| T.C. Lowry | E | D | | Manchester | 1931 |
| B. Sutcliffe | WI | D | | Auckland | 1951–52 |
| B. Sutcliffe | SA | L | 9 wkts | Johannesburg[2] | 1953–54 |
| J.R. Reid | SA | D | | Auckland | 1963–64 |
| J.R. Reid | P | D | | Lahore[2] | 1964–65 |

| | Opponents | Result | | | |
|---|---|---|---|---|---|
| G.T. Dowling | I | L | 272 runs | Auckland | 1967–68 |
| G.T. Dowling | WI | W | 6 wkts | Wellington | 1968–69 |
| G.T. Dowling | E | D | | Auckland | 1970–71 |
| B.E. Congdon | E | D | | Lord's | 1973 |
| B.E. Congdon | A | W | 5 wkts | Christchurch | 1973–74 |
| B.E. Congdon | A | L | 297 runs | Auckland | 1973–74 |
| G.M. Turner | A | D | | Christchurch | 1976–77 |
| M.G. Burgess | P | L | 128 runs | Christchurch | 1978–79 |
| G.P. Howarth | WI | D | | Christchurch | 1979–80 |
| G.P. Howarth | WI | D | | Auckland | 1979–80 |
| G.P. Howarth | A | D | | Melbourne | 1980–81 |
| G.P. Howarth | A | W | 5 wkts | Auckland | 1981–82 |
| G.P. Howarth | A | L | 8 wkts | Christchurch | 1981–82 |
| G.P. Howarth | SL | W | 6 wkts | Wellington | 1982–83 |
| G.P. Howarth | E | W | 5 wkts | Leeds | 1983 |
| G.P. Howarth | E | L | 127 runs | Lord's | 1983 |
| G.P. Howarth | SL | D | | Colombo (SSC) | 1983–84 |
| G.P. Howarth | P | W | I + 99 runs | Auckland | 1984–85 |
| G.P. Howarth | P | W | 2 wkts | Dunedin | 1984–85 |
| G.P. Howarth | WI | L | 10 wkts | Kingston | 1984–85 |

| **INDIA** | Opponents | Result | | | |
|---|---|---|---|---|---|
| Nawab of Pataudi, sr | E | D | | Manchester | 1946 |
| L. Amarnath | P | D | | Calcutta | 1952–53 |
| P.R. Umrigar | A | L | 94 runs | Calcutta | 1956–57 |
| Nawab of Pataudi, jr | E | D | | Kanpur | 1963–64 |
| Nawab of Pataudi, jr | A | D | | Calcutta | 1964–65 |
| Nawab of Pataudi, jr | A | L | 39 runs | Brisbane² | 1967–68 |
| Nawab of Pataudi, jr | A | L | 144 runs | Sydney | 1967–68 |
| Nawab of Pataudi, jr | NZ | L | 6 wkts | Christchurch | 1967–68 |
| A.L. Wadekar | WI | D | | Bridgetown | 1970–71 |
| Nawab of Pataudi, jr | WI | L | 267 runs | Bangalore | 1974–75 |
| B.S. Bedi | WI | D | | Port-of-Spain | 1975–76 |
| S.M. Gavaskar | A | D | | Adelaide | 1980–81 |
| S.M. Gavaskar | NZ | L | 62 runs | Wellington | 1980–81 |
| S.M. Gavaskar | P | D | | Lahore² (1st) | 1982–83 |
| S.M. Gavaskar | P | D | | Lahore² (5th) | 1982–83 |
| Kapil Dev | P | D | | Jullundur | 1983–84 |
| Kapil Dev | WI | L | 138 runs | Ahmedabad | 1983–84 |

| **PAKISTAN** | Opponents | Result | | | |
|---|---|---|---|---|---|
| Fazal Mahmood† | WI | W | 10 wkts | Karachi | 1958–59 |
| Javed Burki | E | L | I + 117 runs | Leeds | 1962 |
| Javed Burki | E | D | | Nottingham | 1962 |
| Hanif Mohammad | NZ | D | | Wellington | 1964–65 |
| Hanif Mohammad | NZ | W | I + 64 runs | Rawalpindi | 1964–65 |
| Intikhab Alam | A | L | 52 runs | Sydney | 1972–73 |
| Mushtaq Mohammad | I | W | 8 wkts | Lahore² | 1978–79 |
| Mushtaq Mohammad | NZ | D | | Auckland | 1978–79 |
| Javed Miandad | A | L | 286 runs | Perth | 1981–82 |
| Javed Miandad | SL | W | I + 102 runs | Lahore² | 1981–82 |
| Imran Khan | A | W | 9 wkts | Lahore² | 1982–83 |
| Imran Khan | I | W | I + 86 runs | Karachi | 1982–83 |
| Imran Khan | I | W | 10 wkts | Faisalabad | 1982–83 |
| Zaheer Abbas | A | L | I + 9 runs | Perth | 1983–84 |
| Zaheer Abbas | E | D | | Lahore² | 1983–84 |

| **SRI LANKA** | Opponents | Result | | | |
|---|---|---|---|---|---|
| D.S. De Silva | NZ | L | I + 25 runs | Christchurch | 1982–83 |

| SUMMARY | Captains | Instances | W | L | D |
|---|---|---|---|---|---|
| England | 25 | 38 | 8 | 15 | 15 |
| Australia | 14 | 47 | 21 | 14 | 12 |
| South Africa | 6 | 10 | 3 | 5 | 2 |
| West Indies | 9 | 31 | 14 | 3 | 14 |
| New Zealand | 8 | 26 | 7 | 7 | 12 |
| India | 8 | 17 | – | 7 | 10 |
| Pakistan | 8 | 15 | 7 | 4 | 4 |
| Sri Lanka | 1 | 1 | – | 1 | – |
| | 79 | 185 | 60 | 56 | 69 |

*Although R. Illingworth (England) elected to field on winning the toss in the Third Test against Australia at Melbourne in 1970–71, that instance is excluded from these tables because the match was abandoned without a ball being bowled.*

## YOUNGEST CAPTAINS

| Years | Days | | | | |
|---|---|---|---|---|---|
| 21 | 77 | Nawab of Pataudi, jr | I v WI | Bridgetown | 1961–62 |
| 22 | 194 | I.D. Craig | A v SA | Johannesburg[3] | 1957–58 |
| 22 | 260 | Javed Miandad | P v A | Karachi | 1979–80 |
| 22 | 306 | M. Bisset | SA v E | Johannesburg[1] | 1898–99 |
| 23 | 144 | M.P. Bowden | E v SA | Cape Town | 1888–89 |
| 23 | 217 | G.C. Grant | WI v A | Adelaide | 1930–31 |
| 23 | 292 | Hon I.F.W. Bligh | E v A | Melbourne | 1882–83 |

*The youngest New Zealand captain is J.M. Parker who was 25 years 251 days when he led his country against Pakistan at Karachi in 1976–77.*

## OLDEST CAPTAINS

| Years | Days | | | | |
|---|---|---|---|---|---|
| 50 | 320 | W.G. Grace | E v A | Nottingham | 1899 |
| 45 | 245 | G.O.B. Allen | E v WI | Kingston | 1947–48 |

# INDIVIDUAL RECORDS – GENERAL

## MOST TEST MATCH APPEARANCES

| For | Total | | Opponents E | A | SA | WI | NZ | I | P | SL |
|---|---|---|---|---|---|---|---|---|---|---|
| England | 114 | M.C. Cowdrey | – | 43 | 14 | 21 | 18 | 8 | 10 | – |
| Australia | 96 | R.W. Marsh | 42 | – | – | 17 | 14 | 3 | 20 | – |
| South Africa | 50 | J.H.B. Waite | 21 | 14 | – | – | 15 | – | – | – |
| West Indies | 110 | C.H. Lloyd | 34 | 29 | – | – | 8 | 28 | 11 | – |
| New Zealand | 61 | B.E. Congdon | 22 | 8 | – | 8 | – | 13 | 10 | – |
| India | 106 | S.M. Gavaskar | 35 | 14 | – | 27 | 9 | – | 20 | 1 |
| Pakistan | 76 | Zaheer Abbas | 14 | 20 | – | 8 | 14 | 19 | – | 1 |
| Sri Lanka | 12 | D.S. De Silva | 2 | 1 | – | – | 5 | 1 | 3 | – |
| | 12 | R.S. Madugalle | 2 | 1 | – | – | 5 | 1 | 3 | – |

## MOST CONSECUTIVE APPEARANCES

| | | | From | | | To | |
|---|---|---|---|---|---|---|---|
| 90‡ | S.M. Gavaskar | I | Bombay[3] | 1974–75 | Kanpur | 1984–85 |
| 87 | G.R. Viswanath | I | Georgetown | 1970–71 | Karachi | 1982–83 |
| 85 | G.St A. Sobers | WI | Port-of-Spain | 1954–55 | Port-of-Spain | 1971–72 |
| 71 | I.M. Chappell | A | Adelaide | 1965–66 | Melbourne | 1975–76 |
| 69‡ | A.R. Border | A | Melbourne | 1978–79 | Oval | 1985 |
| 66 | Kapil Dev | I | Faisalabad | 1978–79 | Delhi | 1984–85 |
| 65 | A.P.E. Knott | E | Auckland | 1970–71 | Oval | 1977 |
| 65 | I.T. Botham | E | Wellington | 1977–78 | Karachi | 1983–84 |
| 61 | R.B. Kanhai | WI | Birmingham | 1957 | Sydney | 1968–69 |
| 58† | J.R. Reid | NZ | Manchester | 1949 | Leeds | 1965 |
| 58† | A.W. Greig | E | Manchester | 1972 | Oval | 1977 |
| 56‡ | S.M.H. Kirmani | I | Madras[1] | 1979–80 | Kanpur | 1984–85 |
| 53 | K.J. Hughes | A | Brisbane[2] | 1978–79 | Sydney | 1982–83 |
| 53 | Javed Miandad | P | Lahore[2] | 1977–78 | Sydney | 1983–84 |
| 52 | F.E. Woolley | E | Oval | 1909 | Oval | 1926 |
| 52 | P.B.H. May | E | Oval | 1953 | Leeds | 1959 |
| 52 | R.W. Marsh | A | Brisbane[2] | 1970–71 | Oval | 1977 |
| 52‡ | D.L. Haynes | WI | Brisbane[2] | 1979–80 | Kingston | 1984–85 |
| 51 | G.S. Chappell | A | Perth | 1970–71 | Oval | 1977 |

*The most for South Africa is 45† by A.W. Nourse, and for Pakistan 45 by Asif Iqbal.*

*† His entire Test career.   ‡ To date*

## PLAYERS WHO REPRESENTED TWO COUNTRIES

| | | Total Tests |
|---|---|---|
| Amir Elahi | I (1) 1947–48 and P (5) 1952–53 | 6 |
| J.J. Ferris | A (8) 1886–87 to 1890 and E (1) 1891–92 | 9 |
| S.C. Guillen | WI (5) 1951–52 and NZ (3) 1955–56 | 8 |
| Gul Mahomed | I (8) 1946 to 1952–53 and P (1) 1956–57 | 9 |
| F. Hearne | E (2) 1888–89 and SA (4) 1891–92 to 1895–96 | 6 |
| A.H. Kardar | I (3) 1946† and P (23) 1952–53 to 1957–58 | 26 |
| W.E. Midwinter | A (8) 1876–77 to 1886–87 and E (4) 1881–82 | 12 |
| F. Mitchell | E (2) 1898–99 and SA (3) 1912 | 5 |
| W.L. Murdoch | A (18) 1876–77 to 1890 and E (1) 1891–92 | 19 |
| Nawab of Pataudi, sr | E (3) 1932–33 to 1934 and I (3) 1946 | 6 |
| A.E. Trott | A (3) 1894–95 and E (2) 1898–99 | 5 |
| S.M.J. Woods | A (3) 1888 and E (3) 1895–96 | 6 |

*† As 'Abdul Hafeez'*

# RELATED TEST PLAYERS

### FATHER AND TWO SONS
L. Amarnath and his sons M. and S. (India)
W.A. Hadlee and his sons D.R. and R.J. (New Zealand)

### FATHERS AND SONS
L. and M., S. Amarnath (India)
W.M. and R.W. Anderson (New Zealand)
M.C. and C.S. Cowdrey (England)
D.K. and A.D. Gaekwad (India)
E.J. and S.E. Gregory (Australia)
W.A. and D.R., R.J. Hadlee (New Zealand)
J. Hardstaff, sr and J. Hardstaff, jr (England)
G.A. and R.G.A. Headley (West Indies)
F. Hearne (England and South Africa) and G.A.L. Hearne (South Africa)
L. and R.A. Hutton (England)
Jahangir Khan (India) and Majid Khan (Pakistan)
J.D. and D.T. Lindsay (South Africa)
M.H. and A.V. Mankad (India)
F.T. and F.G. Mann (England)
Hanif Mohammad and Shoaib Mohammad (Pakistan)
Nazar Mohammad and Mudassar Nazar (Pakistan)
A.W. and A.D. Nourse (South Africa)
J.H. and J.M. Parks (England)
Nawab of Pataudi, sr (England and India) and Nawab of Pataudi, jr (India)
Pankaj and Pranab Roy (India)
O.C. and A.P.H. Scott (West Indies)
F.W. and M.W. Tate (England)
C.L. and D.C.H. Townsend (England)
L.R. and L. Tuckett (South Africa)
H.G. and G.E. Vivian (New Zealand)
S. Wazir Ali (India) and Khalid Wazir (Pakistan)

### FOUR BROTHERS
Hanif, Mushtaq, Sadiq and Wazir Mohammad (Pakistan)

*Hanif, Mushtaq and Sadiq all played against New Zealand at Karachi in 1969–70.*

### THREE BROTHERS
G.S., I.M. and T.M. Chappell
E.M., G.F. and W.G. Grace (England)
A., F. and G.G. Hearne (England) – F. Hearne also played for South Africa.
A.B., L.J. and V.M. Tancred (South Africa)

*All three Grace brothers played against Australia at The Oval in 1880.*
*A. and G.G. Hearne (E) and F. Hearne (SA) all played in the match between South Africa and England at Cape Town in 1891–92.*

### TWO BROTHERS
ENGLAND
A.E.R. and A.H.H. Gilligan
A.W. and I.A. Greig
G. and J.R. Gunn
D.W. and P.E. Richardson
C.T. and G.B. Studd
G.E. and J.T. Tyldesley
C.E.M. and E.R. Wilson

WEST INDIES
D.St E. and E.St E. Atkinson
F.J. and J.H. Cameron
C.M. and R.J. Christiani
B.A. and C.A. Davis
G.C. and R.S. Grant
N.E. and R.E. Marshall
E.L. and W.H. St Hill
J.B. and V.H. Stollmeyer

AUSTRALIA
K.A. and R.G. Archer
A.C. and C. Bannerman

NEW ZEALAND
B.P. and J.G. Bracewell
J.J. and M.D. Crowe

J. and R. Benaud
G. and W.F. Giffen
D.W. and E.J. Gregory
M.R. and R.N. Harvey
C.E. and R.W. McLeod
A.E. and G.H.S. Trott
H. and J.W. Trumble

SOUTH AFRICA
P.A.M. and R.H.M. Hands
A.J. and D.B. Pithey
P.M. and R.G. Pollock
A.R. and W.H.M. Richards
A.M.B. and E.A.B. Rowan
S.D. and S.J. Snooke
G.L. and L.E. Tapscott
D. and H.W. Taylor
H.F. and W.W. Wade

D.R. and R.J. Hadlee
G.P. and H.J. Howarth
J.M. and N.M. Parker

INDIA
M. and S. Amarnath
L. Amar Singh and L. Ramji
A.L. and M.L. Apte
B.P. and S.P. Gupte
A.G. Kripal Singh and A.G. Milkha Singh
C.K. and C.S. Nayudu
S. Nazir Ali and S. Wazir Ali

PAKISTAN
Ramiz Raja and Wasim Raja
Azmat Rana and Shafqat Rana
Pervez Sajjad and Waqar Hassan
Saeed Ahmed and Younis Ahmed

SRI LANKA
M. de S. and S. Wettimuny

# YOUNGEST TEST PLAYERS

| Years | Days | | | | |
|-------|------|--------------------------|----------|-----------------|---------|
| 15 | 124 | Mushtaq Mohammad | P v WI | Lahore[1] | 1958–59 |
| 16 | 191 | Aftab Baloch | P v NZ | Dacca | 1969–70 |
| 16 | 248 | Nasim-ul-Ghani | P v WI | Bridgetown | 1957–58 |
| 16 | 352 | Khalid Hassan | P v E | Nottingham | 1954 |
| 17 | 118 | L. Sivaramakrishnan | I v WI | St John's | 1982–83 |
| 17 | 122 | J.E.D. Sealy | WI v E | Bridgetown | 1929–30 |
| 17 | 193 | Maninder Singh | I v P | Karachi | 1982–83 |
| 17 | 239 | I.D. Craig | A v SA | Melbourne | 1952–53 |
| 17 | 245 | G.St A. Sobers | WI v E | Kingston | 1953–54 |
| 17 | 265 | V.L. Mehra | I v NZ | Bombay[2] | 1955–56 |
| 17 | 300 | Hanif Mohammad | P v I | Delhi | 1952–53 |
| 17 | 341 | Intikhab Alam | P v A | Karachi | 1959–60 |
| 18 | 13 | A.G. Milkha Singh | I v A | Madras[2] | 1959–60 |
| 18 | 26 | Majid Khan | P v A | Karachi | 1964–65 |
| 18 | 31 | M.R. Bynoe | WI v P | Lahore[1] | 1958–59 |
| 18 | 41 | Salahuddin | P v NZ | Rawalpindi | 1964–65 |
| 18 | 44 | Khalid Wazir | P v E | Lord's | 1954 |
| 18 | 78 | A. Ranatunga | SL v E | Colombo (SO) | 1981–82 |
| 18 | 105 | J.B. Stollmeyer | WI v E | Lord's | 1939 |
| 18 | 149 | D.B. Close | E v NZ | Manchester | 1949 |
| 18 | 173 | A.T. Roberts | WI v NZ | Auckland | 1955–56 |
| 18 | 186 | Haseeb Ahsan | P v WI | Bridgetown | 1957–58 |
| 18 | 190 | Imran Khan | P v E | Birmingham | 1971 |
| 18 | 197 | D.L. Freeman | NZ v E | Christchurch | 1932–33 |
| 18 | 232 | T.W. Garrett | A v E | Melbourne | 1876–77 |
| 18 | 242 | A.P.H. Scott | WI v I | Kingston | 1952–53 |
| 18 | 249 | B.S. Chandrasekhar | I v E | Bombay[2] | 1963–64 |
| 18 | 260 | Mohammad Ilyas | P v A | Melbourne | 1964–65 |
| 18 | 267 | H.G. Vivian | NZ v E | Oval | 1931 |
| 18 | 270 | R.J. Shastri | I v NZ | Wellington | 1980–81 |
| 18 | 295 | R.O. Collinge | NZ v P | Wellington | 1964–65 |
| 18 | 311 | P.A. De Silva | SL v E | Lord's | 1984 |
| 18 | 312 | S. Venkataraghavan | I v NZ | Madras[2] | 1964–65 |
| 18 | 316 | B.P. Bracewell | NZ v E | Oval | 1978 |
| 18 | 323 | Salim Malik | P v SL | Karachi | 1981–82 |

*The youngest player to represent South Africa was A.E. Ochse who was 19 years 1 day old when he appeared against England at Port Elizabeth in 1888–89.*

# OLDEST PLAYERS ON TEST DEBUT

| Years | Days | | | | |
|-------|------|-----------------|----------|--------------------------|---------|
| 49 | 119 | J. Southerton | E v A | Melbourne | 1876–77 |
| 47 | 284 | Miran Bux | P v I | Lahore[1] | 1954–55 |
| 46 | 253 | D.D. Blackie | A v E | Sydney | 1928–29 |
| 46 | 237 | H. Ironmonger | A v E | Brisbane[2] | 1928–29 |
| 42 | 242 | N. Betancourt | WI v E | Port-of-Spain | 1929–30 |
| 41 | 337 | E.R. Wilson | E v A | Sydney | 1920–21 |
| 41 | 27 | R.J.D. Jamshedji | I v E | Bombay[1] | 1933–34 |
| 40 | 345 | C.A. Wiles | WI v E | Manchester | 1933 |
| 40 | 216 | S. Kinneir | E v A | Sydney | 1911–12 |
| 40 | 110 | H.W. Lee | E v SA | Johannesburg[1] | 1930–31 |
| 40 | 56 | G.W.A. Chubb | SA v E | Nottingham | 1951 |
| 40 | 37 | C. Ramaswami | I v E | Manchester | 1936 |

*The oldest player to make his debut for New Zealand was H.M. McGirr who was 38 years 101 days old when he appeared against England at Auckland in 1929–30; and for Sri Lanka, D.S. De Silva who was 39 years 251 days old when he made his debut in his country's inaugural Test v England at Colombo (SO) in 1981–82.*

# OLDEST TEST PLAYERS

*Age on final day of their last Test match*

| Years | Days | | | | |
|-------|------|--------------------|----------|--------------------------|---------|
| 52 | 165 | W. Rhodes | E v WI | Kingston | 1929–30 |
| 50 | 327 | H. Ironmonger | A v E | Sydney | 1932–33 |
| 50 | 320 | W.G. Grace | E v A | Nottingham | 1899 |
| 50 | 303 | G. Gunn | E v WI | Kingston | 1929–30 |
| 49 | 139 | J. Southerton | E v A | Melbourne | 1876–77 |
| 47 | 302 | Miran Bux | P v I | Peshawar | 1954–55 |
| 47 | 249 | J.B. Hobbs | E v A | Oval | 1930 |
| 47 | 87 | F.E. Woolley | E v A | Oval | 1934 |
| 46 | 309 | D.D. Blackie | A v E | Adelaide | 1928–29 |
| 46 | 206 | A.W. Nourse | SA v E | Oval | 1924 |
| 46 | 202 | H. Strudwick | E v A | Oval | 1926 |
| 46 | 41 | E.H. Hendren | E v WI | Kingston | 1934–35 |
| 45 | 245 | G.O.B. Allen | E v WI | Kingston | 1947–48 |
| 45 | 215 | P. Holmes | E v I | Lord's | 1932 |
| 45 | 140 | D.B. Close | E v WI | Manchester | 1976 |
| 44 | 341 | E.G. Wynyard | E v SA | Johannesburg[1] | 1905–06 |
| 44 | 317 | J.M.M. Commaille | SA v E | Cape Town | 1927–28 |
| 44 | 238 | R. Abel | E v A | Manchester | 1902 |
| 44 | 236 | G.A. Headley | WI v E | Kingston | 1953–54 |
| 44 | 105 | Amir Elahi | P v I | Calcutta | 1952–53 |

*The ages of Indian and Pakistani players have not been confirmed.*

# LONGEST CAREERS
*From debut to final day of last match*

| Years | Days | | | From | | To | |
|-------|------|----------------|----|-------------|---------|------------|---------|
| 30 | 315 | W. Rhodes | E | Nottingham | 1899 | Kingston | 1929–30 |
| 26 | 355 | D.B. Close | E | Manchester | 1949 | Manchester | 1976 |
| 25 | 13 | F.E. Woolley | E | Oval | 1909 | Oval | 1934 |
| 24 | 10 | G.A. Headley | WI | Bridgetown | 1929–30 | Kingston | 1953–54 |
| 22 | 233 | J.B. Hobbs | E | Melbourne | 1907–08 | Oval | 1930 |
| 22 | 120 | G. Gunn | E | Sydney | 1907–08 | Kingston | 1929–30 |
| 22 | 18 | S.E. Gregory | A | Lord's | 1890 | Oval | 1912 |

# LONGEST INTERVALS BETWEEN APPEARANCES

| Years | Days | | | From | | To | |
|---|---|---|---|---|---|---|---|
| 17 | 316 | G. Gunn | E | Sydney | 1911–12 | Bridgetown | 1929–30 |
| 14 | 28 | D.C. Cleverley | NZ | Christchurch | 1931–32 | Wellington | 1945–46 |
| 13 | 53 | F. Mitchell | E/SA | Cape Town | 1898–99 | Manchester | 1912 |
| 13 | 32 | G.M. Carew | WI | Bridgetown | 1934–35 | Port-of-Spain | 1947–48 |
| 12 | 160 | L. Amarnath | I | Madras[1] | 1933–34 | Lord's | 1946 |
| 12 | 81 | W.E. Hollies | E | Kingston | 1934–35 | Nottingham | 1947 |
| 12 | 14 | Nawab of Pataudi, sr | E/I | Nottingham | 1934 | Lord's | 1946 |

# ON THE FIELD THROUGHOUT A MATCH

| | | | | Days |
|---|---|---|---|---|
| Nazar Mohammad | P v I | Lucknow | 1952–53 | 4 |
| D.J. McGlew | SA v NZ | Wellington | 1952–53 | 4 |
| C.A. Milton† | E v NZ | Leeds | 1958 | 3 |
| J.H. Edrich | E v NZ | Leeds | 1965 | 5 |
| D. Lloyd | E v I | Birmingham | 1974 | 3 |
| G. Boycott | E v A | Leeds | 1977 | 4 |
| Taslim Arif | P v A | Faisalabad | 1979–80 | 4 |
| S.M. Gavaskar | I v WI | Georgetown | 1982–83 | 5‡ |

† On debut
‡ Rain prevented play on two days

# INDIVIDUAL CAREER RECORDS

These career records for all players appearing in official Test matches are complete to the end of the 1985 English season.
Symbols: *not out; †left-handed batsman; ‡left-handed bowler.

## ENGLAND (513 players)

| | Tests | I | NO | BATTING AND FIELDING | | | | | | | BOWLING | | | | | | |
|---|---|---|---|---|---|---|---|---|---|---|---|---|---|---|---|---|---|
| | | | | HS | Runs | Avge | 100 | 50 | Ct | St | Balls | Runs | Wkts | Avge | BB | 5wI | 10wM |
| Abel, R. | 13 | 22 | 2 | 132* | 744 | 37.20 | 2 | 2 | 13 | — | — | | | | | | |
| Absolom, C.A. | 1 | 2 | 0 | 52 | 58 | 29.00 | — | 1 | - | — | — | | | | | | |
| Agnew, J.P. | 3 | 4 | 3 | 5 | 10 | 10.00 | — | — | — | — | 552 | 373 | 4 | 93.25 | 2-51 | — | — |
| Allen, D.A. | 39 | 51 | 15 | 88 | 918 | 25.50 | — | 5 | 10 | — | 11297 | 3779 | 122 | 30.97 | 5-30 | 4 | — |
| Allen, G.O.B. | 25 | 33 | 2 | 122 | 750 | 24.19 | 1 | 3 | 20 | — | 4386 | 2379 | 81 | 29.37 | 7-80 | 5 | 1 |
| Allom, M.J.C. | 5 | 3 | 2 | 8 | 14 | 14.00 | — | — | — | — | 817 | 265 | 14 | 18.92 | 5-38 | 1 | — |
| Allott, P.J.W. | 13 | 18 | 3 | 52* | 213 | 14.20 | — | 1 | 4 | — | 2225 | 1084 | 26 | 41.69 | 6-61 | 1 | — |
| Ames, L.E.G. | 47 | 72 | 12 | 149 | 2434 | 40.56 | 8 | 7 | 74 | 23 | — | | | | | | |
| Amiss, D.L. | 50 | 88 | 10 | 262* | 3612 | 46.30 | 11 | 11 | 24 | — | — | | | | | | |
| Andrew, K.V. | 2 | 4 | 1 | 15 | 29 | 9.66 | — | — | 1 | — | — | | | | | | |
| Appleyard, R. | 9 | 9 | 6 | 19* | 51 | 17.00 | — | — | 4 | — | 1596 | 554 | 31 | 17.87 | 5-51 | 1 | — |
| Archer, A.G. | 1 | 2 | 1 | 24* | 31 | 31.00 | — | — | 1 | — | — | | | | | | |
| Armitage, T. | 2 | 3 | 0 | 21 | 33 | 11.00 | — | — | — | — | 12 | 15 | 0 | — | — | — | — |
| Arnold, E.G. | 10 | 15 | 3 | 40 | 160 | 13.33 | — | 1 | — | — | 1683 | 788 | 31 | 25.41 | 5-37 | 1 | — |
| Arnold, G.G. | 34 | 46 | 11 | 59 | 421 | 12.02 | — | 1 | 8 | — | 7650 | 3254 | 115 | 28.29 | 6-45 | 6 | 1 |
| Arnold, J. | 1 | 2 | 0 | 34 | 34 | 17.00 | — | — | 9 | — | — | | | | | | |
| Astill, W.E. | 9 | 15 | 0 | 40 | 190 | 12.66 | — | — | 7 | — | 2182 | 856 | 25 | 34.24 | 4-58 | — | — |
| Athey, C.W.J. | 3 | 6 | 0 | 9 | 17 | 2.83 | — | — | 2 | — | — | | | | | | |
| Attewell, W. | 10 | 15 | 6 | 43* | 150 | 16.66 | — | — | 9 | — | 2850 | 626 | 27 | 23.18 | 4-42 | — | — |
| Bailey, T.E. | 61 | 91 | 14 | 134* | 2290 | 29.74 | 1 | 10 | 32 | — | 9712 | 3856 | 132 | 29.21 | 7-34 | 5 | 1 |
| Bairstow, D.L. | 4 | 7 | 1 | 59 | 125 | 20.83 | 1 | 1 | 12 | 1 | — | | | | | | |
| Bakewell, A.H. | 6 | 9 | 0 | 107 | 409 | 45.44 | 1 | 3 | 3 | — | 18 | 8 | 0 | — | — | — | — |
| Balderstone, J.C. | 2 | 4 | 0 | 35 | 39 | 9.75 | — | — | 3 | — | 96‡ | 80 | 1 | 80.00 | 1-80 | — | — |
| Barber, R.W. | 28 | 45† | 3 | 185 | 1495 | 35.59 | 1 | 9 | 21 | — | 3426 | 1806 | 42 | 43.00 | 4-132 | — | — |
| Barber, W. | 2 | 4 | 0 | 44 | 83 | 20.75 | — | — | 1 | — | 2 | 0 | 1 | 0.00 | 1-0 | — | — |
| Barlow, G.D. | 3 | 5† | 1 | 7* | 17 | 4.25 | — | — | — | — | — | | | | | | |
| Barlow, R.G. | 17 | 30 | 4 | 62 | 591 | 22.73 | — | 2 | 14 | — | 2456‡ | 767 | 34 | 22.55 | 7-40 | 3 | — |
| Barnes, S.F. | 27 | 39 | 9 | 38* | 242 | 8.06 | — | — | 12 | — | 7873 | 3106 | 189 | 16.43 | 9-103 | 24 | 7 |
| Barnes, W. | 21 | 33 | 2 | 134 | 725 | 23.38 | 1 | 5 | 19 | — | 2289 | 793 | 51 | 15.54 | 6-28 | 3 | — |
| Barnett, C.J. | 20 | 35 | 4 | 129 | 1098 | 35.41 | 2 | 5 | 14 | — | 256 | 93 | 0 | — | — | — | — |

INDIVIDUAL CAREER RECORDS—ENGLAND *continued*

| | Tests | I | NO | BATTING AND FIELDING | | | | | | | BOWLING | | | | | | |
|---|---|---|---|---|---|---|---|---|---|---|---|---|---|---|---|---|---|
| | | | | HS | Runs | Avge | 100 | 50 | Ct | St | Balls | Runs | Wkts | Avge | BB | 5wI | 10wM |
| Barratt, F. | 5 | 4 | 1 | 17 | 28 | 9.33 | — | — | 2 | — | 750 | 235 | 5 | 47.00 | 1-8 | — | — |
| Barrington, K.F. | 82 | 131 | 15 | 256 | 6806 | 58.67 | 20 | 35 | 58 | — | 2715 | 1300 | 29 | 44.82 | 3-4 | — | — |
| Barton, V.A. | 1 | 1 | 0 | 23 | 23 | 23.00 | — | — | — | — | | | | | | | |
| Bates, W. | 15 | 26 | 2 | 64 | 656 | 27.33 | — | 5 | 9 | — | 2364 | 821 | 50 | 16.42 | 7-28 | 4 | 1 |
| Bean, G. | 3 | 5 | 0 | 50 | 92 | 18.40 | — | 1 | 4 | — | | | | | | | |
| Bedser, A.V. | 51 | 71 | 15 | 79 | 714 | 12.75 | — | 1 | 26 | — | 15918 | 5876 | 236 | 24.89 | 7-44 | 15 | 5 |
| Berry, R. | 2 | 4† | 2 | 4* | 6 | 3.00 | — | — | 2 | — | 653‡ | 228 | 9 | 25.33 | 5-63 | 1 | — |
| Binks, J.G. | 2 | 4 | 0 | 55 | 91 | 22.75 | — | — | 8 | — | | | | | | | |
| Bird, M.C. | 10 | 16 | 1 | 61 | 280 | 18.66 | — | 1 | 5 | — | 264 | 120 | 8 | 15.00 | 3-11 | — | — |
| Birkenshaw, J. | 5 | 7† | 0 | 64 | 148 | 21.14 | — | 2 | 3 | — | 1017 | 469 | 13 | 36.07 | 5-57 | 1 | — |
| Bligh, *Hon* I.F.W. | 4 | 7 | 1 | 19 | 62 | 10.33 | — | 1 | 7 | — | | | | | | | |
| Blythe, C. | 19 | 31 | 12 | 27 | 183 | 9.63 | — | — | 6 | — | 4546‡ | 1863 | 100 | 18.63 | 8-59 | 9 | 4 |
| Board, J.H. | 6 | 12 | 2 | 29 | 108 | 10.80 | — | — | 8 | 3 | | | | | | | |
| Bolus, J.B. | 7 | 12 | 0 | 88 | 496 | 41.33 | — | 4 | 2 | — | 18‡ | 16 | 0 | — | — | — | — |
| Booth, M.W. | 2 | 2 | 0 | 32 | 46 | 23.00 | — | — | — | — | 312 | 130 | 7 | 18.57 | 4-49 | — | — |
| Bosanquet, B.J.T. | 7 | 14 | 3 | 27 | 147 | 13.36 | — | — | 9 | — | 970 | 604 | 25 | 24.16 | 8-107 | 2 | — |
| Botham, I.T. | 79 | 125 | 3 | 208 | 4409 | 36.13 | 13 | 20 | 92 | — | 18391 | 9046 | 343 | 26.37 | 8-34 | 25 | 4 |
| Bowden, M.P. | 2 | 2 | 0 | 25 | 25 | 12.50 | — | — | 1 | — | | | | | | | |
| Bowes, W.E. | 15 | 11 | 5 | 10* | 28 | 4.66 | — | — | 2 | — | 3655 | 1519 | 68 | 22.23 | 6-33 | 6 | — |
| Bowley, E.H. | 5 | 7 | 0 | 109 | 252 | 36.00 | 1 | — | 2 | — | 252 | 116 | 0 | — | — | — | — |
| Boycott, G. | 108 | 193 | 23 | 246* | 8114 | 47.72 | 22 | 42 | 33 | — | 944 | 382 | 7 | 54.57 | 3-47 | — | — |
| Bradley, W.M. | 2 | 2 | 1 | 23* | 23 | 23.00 | — | — | — | — | 625 | 233 | 6 | 38.83 | 5-67 | 1 | — |
| Braund, L.C. | 23 | 41 | 3 | 104 | 987 | 25.97 | 3 | 2 | 39 | — | 3803 | 1810 | 47 | 38.51 | 8-81 | 3 | — |
| Brearley, J.M. | 39 | 66 | 3 | 91 | 1442 | 22.88 | — | 9 | 52 | — | | | | | | | |
| Brearley, W. | 4 | 5 | 2 | 11* | 21 | 7.00 | — | — | — | — | 705 | 359 | 17 | 21.11 | 5-110 | 1 | — |
| Brennan, D.V. | 2 | 2 | 0 | 16 | 16 | 8.00 | — | — | — | 1 | | | | | | | |
| Briggs, J. | 33 | 50 | 5 | 121 | 815 | 18.11 | 1 | 2 | 12 | — | 5332‡ | 2094 | 118 | 17.74 | 8-11 | 9 | 4 |
| Broad, B.C. | 5 | 9† | 0 | 86 | 281 | 31.22 | 1 | 2 | 1 | — | | | | | | | |
| Brockwell, W. | 7 | 12 | 0 | 49 | 202 | 16.83 | — | 1 | 6 | — | 582 | 309 | 5 | 61.80 | 3-33 | — | — |
| Bromley-Davenport, H.R. | 4 | 6 | 0 | 84 | 128 | 21.33 | — | 1 | 1 | — | 155‡ | 98 | 4 | 24.50 | 2-46 | — | — |
| Brookes, D. | 1 | 2 | 0 | 10 | 17 | 8.50 | — | — | 1 | — | | | | | | | |
| Brown, A. | 2 | 1 | 1 | 3* | 3 | — | — | — | 1 | — | 323 | 150 | 3 | 50.00 | 3-27 | — | — |
| Brown, D.J. | 26 | 34 | 5 | 44* | 342 | 11.79 | — | — | 7 | — | 5098 | 2237 | 79 | 28.31 | 5-42 | 2 | — |
| Brown, F.R. | 22 | 30 | 1 | 79 | 734 | 25.31 | — | 5 | 22 | — | 3260 | 1398 | 45 | 31.06 | 5-49 | 1 | — |
| Brown, G. | 7 | 12† | 2 | 84 | 299 | 29.90 | — | 2 | 9 | 3 | | | | | | | |
| Brown, J.T. | 8 | 16 | 3 | 140 | 470 | 36.15 | 1 | 1 | 7 | — | 35 | 22 | 0 | — | — | — | — |

## INDIVIDUAL CAREER RECORDS—ENGLAND *continued*

| | | | | BATTING AND FIELDING | | | | | | | BOWLING | | | | | |
| | Tests | I | NO | HS | Runs | Avge | 100 | 50 | Ct | St | Balls | Runs | Wkts | Avge | BB | 5wI | 10wM |
|---|---|---|---|---|---|---|---|---|---|---|---|---|---|---|---|---|---|
| Buckenham, C.P. | 4 | 7 | 0 | 17 | 43 | 6.14 | – | – | 2 | – | 1182 | 593 | 21 | 28.23 | 5-115 | 1 | – |
| Butcher, A.R. | 1 | 2† | 0 | 20 | 34 | 17.00 | – | – | 1 | – | 12‡ | 9 | 0 | – | – | – | – |
| Butcher, R.O. | 3 | 5 | 0 | 32 | 71 | 14.20 | – | – | 3 | – | – | | | | | | |
| Butler, H.J. | 2 | 2 | 1 | 15* | 15 | 15.00 | – | – | 1 | – | 552 | 215 | 12 | 17.91 | 4-34 | – | – |
| Butt, H.R. | 3 | 4 | 1 | 13 | 22 | 7.33 | – | – | 1 | 1 | – | | | | | | |
| Calthorpe, *Hon.* F.S.G. | 4 | 7 | 0 | 49 | 129 | 18.42 | – | – | 3 | – | 204 | 91 | 1 | 91.00 | 1-38 | – | – |
| Carr, A.W. | 11 | 13 | 1 | 63 | 237 | 19.75 | – | 1 | 3 | – | – | | | | | | |
| Carr, D.B. | 2 | 4 | 0 | 76 | 135 | 33.75 | – | 1 | – | – | 210‡ | 140 | 2 | 70.00 | 2-84 | – | – |
| Carr, D.W. | 1 | 1 | 0 | 0 | 0 | 0.00 | – | – | – | – | 414 | 282 | 7 | 40.28 | 5-146 | 1 | – |
| Cartwright, T.W. | 5 | 7 | 2 | 9 | 26 | 5.20 | – | – | 2 | – | 1611 | 544 | 15 | 36.26 | 6-94 | 1 | – |
| Chapman, A.P.F. | 26 | 36† | 4 | 121 | 925 | 28.90 | 1 | 5 | 32 | – | 40‡ | 20 | 0 | – | – | – | – |
| Charlwood, H.R.J. | 2 | 4 | 0 | 36 | 63 | 15.75 | – | – | – | – | – | | | | | | |
| Chatterton, W. | 1 | 1 | 0 | 48 | 48 | 48.00 | – | – | – | – | – | | | | | | |
| Christopherson, S. | 1 | 1 | 0 | 17 | 17 | 17.00 | – | – | – | – | 136 | 69 | 1 | 69.00 | 1-52 | – | – |
| Clark, E.W. | 8 | 9† | 5 | 10 | 36 | 9.00 | – | – | 1 | – | 1931‡ | 899 | 32 | 28.09 | 5-98 | 1 | – |
| Clay, J.C. | 1 | – | – | – | – | – | – | – | – | – | 192 | 75 | 0 | – | – | – | – |
| Close, D.B. | 22 | 37† | 2 | 70 | 887 | 25.34 | – | 4 | 24 | – | 1212 | 532 | 18 | 29.55 | 4-35 | – | – |
| Coldwell, L.J. | 7 | 7 | 5 | 6* | 9 | 4.50 | – | – | 1 | – | 1668 | 610 | 22 | 27.72 | 6-85 | 1 | – |
| Compton, D.C.S. | 78 | 131 | 15 | 278 | 5807 | 50.06 | 17 | 28 | 49 | – | 2716‡ | 1410 | 25 | 56.40 | 5-70 | 1 | – |
| Cook, C. | 1 | 2 | 0 | 4 | 4 | 2.00 | – | – | – | – | 180‡ | 127 | 0 | – | – | – | – |
| Cook, G. | 7 | 13 | 0 | 66 | 203 | 15.61 | – | 2 | 9 | – | 42‡ | 27 | 0 | – | – | – | – |
| Cook, N.G.B. | 9 | 15 | 1 | 26 | 101 | 7.21 | – | – | 5 | – | 2990‡ | 1212 | 40 | 30.30 | 6-65 | 4 | 1 |
| Cope, G.A. | 3 | 3 | 0 | 22 | 40 | 13.33 | – | – | 1 | – | 864 | 277 | 8 | 34.62 | 3-102 | – | – |
| Copson, W.H. | 3 | 1 | 0 | 6 | 6 | 6.00 | – | – | – | – | 762 | 297 | 15 | 19.80 | 5-85 | 1 | – |
| Cornford, W.L. | 4 | 4 | 0 | 18 | 36 | 9.00 | – | – | 5 | 3 | – | | | | | | |
| Cottam, R.M.H. | 4 | 5 | 1 | 13 | 27 | 6.75 | – | – | 2 | – | 903 | 327 | 14 | 23.35 | 4-50 | – | – |
| Coventry, *Hon* C.J. | 2 | 2 | 1 | 12 | 13 | 13.00 | – | – | – | – | – | | | | | | |
| Cowans, N.G. | 19 | 29 | 7 | 36 | 175 | 7.95 | – | – | 9 | – | 3452 | 2003 | 51 | 39.27 | 6-77 | 2 | – |
| Cowdrey, C.S. | 5 | 6 | 1 | 38 | 96 | 19.20 | – | – | 5 | – | 366 | 288 | 4 | 72.00 | 2-65 | – | – |
| Cowdrey, M.C. | 114 | 188 | 15 | 182 | 7624 | 44.06 | 22 | 38 | 120 | – | 119 | 104 | 0 | – | – | – | – |
| Coxon, A. | 1 | 2† | 0 | 19 | 19 | 9.50 | – | – | 1 | – | 378 | 172 | 3 | 57.33 | 2-90 | – | – |
| Cranston, J. | 1 | 2† | 0 | 16 | 31 | 15.50 | – | – | 1 | – | – | | | | | | |
| Cranston, K. | 8 | 14 | 0 | 45 | 209 | 14.92 | – | 3 | 3 | – | 1010 | 461 | 18 | 25.61 | 4-12 | – | – |
| Crapp, J.F. | 7 | 13† | 2 | 56 | 319 | 29.00 | – | 7 | 7 | – | – | | | | | | |
| Crawford, J.N. | 12 | 23 | 2 | 74 | 469 | 22.33 | – | 2 | 13 | – | 2203 | 1150 | 39 | 29.48 | 5-48 | 3 | – |
| Cuttell, W.R. | 2 | 4 | 0 | 21 | 65 | 16.25 | – | – | 2 | – | 285 | 73 | 6 | 12.16 | 3-17 | – | – |

INDIVIDUAL CAREER RECORDS—ENGLAND *continued*

| | Tests | I | NO | BATTING AND FIELDING HS | Runs | Avge | 100 | 50 | Ct | St | BOWLING Balls | Runs | Wkts | Avge | BB | 5wI | 10wM |
|---|---|---|---|---|---|---|---|---|---|---|---|---|---|---|---|---|---|
| Dawson, E.W. | 5 | 9 | 0 | 55 | 175 | 19.44 | – | 1 | – | – | – | – | – | – | – | – | – |
| Dean, H. | 3 | 4† | 2 | 8 | 10 | 5.00 | – | – | 2 | – | 447‡ | 153 | 11 | 13.90 | 4-19 | – | – |
| Denness, M.H. | 28 | 45 | 3 | 188 | 1667 | 39.69 | 4 | 7 | 28 | – | – | – | – | – | – | – | – |
| Denton, D. | 11 | 22 | 1 | 104 | 424 | 20.19 | 1 | 1 | 8 | – | – | – | – | – | – | – | – |
| Dewes, J.G. | 5 | 10† | 0 | 67 | 121 | 12.10 | – | 1 | – | – | – | – | – | – | – | – | – |
| Dexter, E.R. | 62 | 102 | 8 | 205 | 4502 | 47.89 | 9 | 27 | 29 | – | 5317 | 2306 | 66 | 34.93 | 4-10 | – | – |
| Dilley, G.R. | 18 | 28† | 8 | 56 | 330 | 16.50 | – | 2 | 5 | – | 3130 | 1595 | 50 | 31.90 | 4-24 | – | – |
| Dipper, A.E. | 1 | 2 | 0 | 40 | 51 | 25.50 | – | – | – | – | – | – | – | – | – | – | – |
| Doggart, G.H.G. | 2 | 4 | 0 | 29 | 76 | 19.00 | – | – | 3 | – | – | – | – | – | – | – | – |
| D'Oliveira, B.L. | 44 | 70 | 8 | 158 | 2484 | 40.06 | 5 | 15 | 29 | – | 5706 | 1859 | 47 | 39.55 | 3-46 | – | – |
| Dollery, H.E. | 4 | 7 | 0 | 37 | 72 | 10.28 | – | – | 1 | – | – | – | – | – | – | – | – |
| Dolphin, A. | 1 | 2 | 0 | 1 | 1 | 0.50 | – | – | 1 | – | – | – | – | – | – | – | – |
| Douglas, J.W.H.T. | 23 | 35 | 2 | 119 | 962 | 29.15 | 1 | 6 | 9 | – | 2812 | 1486 | 45 | 33.02 | 5-46 | 1 | – |
| Downton, P.R. | 21 | 31 | 7 | 74 | 576 | 23.04 | – | 4 | 54 | 3 | – | – | – | – | – | – | – |
| Druce, N.F. | 5 | 9 | 0 | 64 | 252 | 28.00 | – | 1 | 5 | 3 | – | – | – | – | – | – | – |
| Ducat, A. | 1 | 2 | 0 | 3 | 5 | 2.50 | – | – | 1 | – | – | – | – | – | – | – | – |
| Duckworth, G. | 24 | 28 | 12 | 39* | 234 | 14.62 | – | – | 45 | 15 | – | – | – | – | – | – | – |
| Duleepsinhji, K.S. | 12 | 19 | 2 | 173 | 995 | 58.52 | 3 | 5 | 10 | – | 6 | 7 | 0 | – | – | – | – |
| Durston, F.J. | 1 | 2 | 1 | 6* | 8 | 8.00 | – | – | – | – | 202 | 136 | 5 | 27.20 | 4-102 | – | – |
| Edmonds, P.H. | 33 | 39 | 6 | 64 | 652 | 19.75 | – | 2 | 31 | – | 8232‡ | 2866 | 88 | 32.56 | 7-66 | 2 | – |
| Edrich, J.H. | 77 | 127† | 9 | 310* | 5138 | 43.54 | 12 | 24 | 43 | – | 30 | 23 | 0 | – | – | – | – |
| Edrich, W.J. | 39 | 63 | 2 | 219 | 2440 | 40.00 | 6 | 13 | 39 | – | 3234 | 1693 | 41 | 41.29 | 4-68 | – | – |
| Elliott, H. | 4 | 5 | 1 | 37* | 61 | 15.25 | – | – | 8 | 3 | – | – | – | – | – | – | – |
| Ellison, R.M. | 7 | 8† | 1 | 41 | 89 | 12.71 | – | – | 2 | – | 1559 | 674 | 27 | 24.96 | 6-77 | 2 | 1 |
| Emburey, J.E. | 28 | 39 | 8 | 57 | 456 | 14.70 | – | 1 | 18 | – | 6473 | 2240 | 75 | 29.86 | 6-33 | 3 | – |
| Emmett, G.M. | 1 | 2 | 0 | 10 | 10 | 5.00 | – | – | – | – | – | – | – | – | – | – | – |
| Emmett, T. | 7 | 13† | 1 | 48 | 160 | 13.33 | – | – | 9 | – | 728‡ | 284 | 9 | 31.55 | 7-68 | 1 | – |
| Evans, A.J. | 1 | 2 | 0 | 14 | 18 | 9.00 | – | – | – | – | – | – | – | – | – | – | – |
| Evans, T.G. | 91 | 133 | 14 | 104 | 2439 | 20.49 | 2 | 8 | 173 | 46 | – | – | – | – | – | – | – |
| Fagg, A.E. | 5 | 8 | 0 | 39 | 150 | 18.75 | – | – | 5 | – | – | – | – | – | – | – | – |
| Fane, F.L. | 14 | 27 | 1 | 143 | 682 | 26.23 | 1 | 3 | 6 | – | – | – | – | – | – | – | – |
| Farnes, K. | 15 | 17 | 5 | 20 | 58 | 4.83 | – | – | 1 | – | 3932 | 1719 | 60 | 28.65 | 6-96 | 3 | 1 |
| Farrimond, W. | 4 | 7 | 0 | 35 | 116 | 16.57 | – | – | 5 | 2 | – | – | – | – | – | – | – |
| Fender, P.G.H. | 13 | 21 | 1 | 60 | 380 | 19.00 | – | 2 | 14 | – | 2178 | 1185 | 29 | 40.86 | 5-90 | 2 | – |
| Ferris, J.J. | 1 | 1† | 0 | 16 | 16 | 16.00 | – | – | – | – | 272‡ | 91 | 13 | 7.00 | 7-37 | 2 | 1 |
| Fielder, A. | 6 | 12 | 5 | 20 | 78 | 11.14 | – | – | 4 | – | 1491 | 711 | 26 | 27.34 | 6-82 | 1 | – |

INDIVIDUAL CAREER RECORDS—ENGLAND *continued*

| | Tests | I | NO | HS | Runs | Avge | 100 | 50 | Ct | St | Balls | Runs | Wkts | Avge | BB | 5wI | 10wM |
|---|---|---|---|---|---|---|---|---|---|---|---|---|---|---|---|---|---|
| | | | | *BATTING AND FIELDING* | | | | | | | | | | *BOWLING* | | | |
| Fishlock, L.B. | 4 | 5† | 1 | 19* | 47 | 11.75 | – | – | 1 | – | – | – | – | – | – | – | – |
| Flavell, J.A. | 4 | 6† | 2 | 14 | 31 | 7.75 | – | – | – | – | 792 | 367 | 7 | 52.42 | 2-65 | – | – |
| Fletcher, K.W.R. | 59 | 96 | 14 | 216 | 3272 | 39.90 | 7 | 19 | 54 | – | 285 | 193 | 2 | 96.50 | 1-6 | – | – |
| Flowers, W. | 8 | 14 | 0 | 56 | 254 | 18.14 | – | 1 | 2 | – | 858 | 296 | 14 | 21.14 | 5-46 | 1 | – |
| Ford, F.G.J. | 5 | 9† | 0 | 48 | 168 | 18.66 | – | 1 | 5 | – | 210‡ | 129 | 1 | 129.00 | 1-47 | – | – |
| Foster, F.R. | 11 | 15 | 1 | 71 | 330 | 23.57 | – | 3 | 11 | – | 2447‡ | 926 | 45 | 20.57 | 6-91 | 4 | – |
| Foster, N.A. | 9 | 12 | 2 | 18* | 78 | 7.80 | – | – | 3 | – | 1974 | 985 | 27 | 36.48 | 6-104 | 3 | 1 |
| Foster, R.E. | 8 | 14 | 2 | 287 | 602 | 46.30 | 1 | 1 | 13 | – | – | – | – | – | – | – | – |
| Fothergill, A.J. | 2 | 2† | 0 | 32 | 33 | 16.50 | – | – | – | – | 321‡ | 90 | 8 | 11.25 | 4-19 | – | – |
| Fowler, G. | 21 | 37† | 0 | 201 | 1307 | 35.32 | 3 | 8 | 10 | – | 18 | 11 | 0 | – | – | – | – |
| Freeman, A.P. | 12 | 16 | 5 | 50* | 154 | 14.00 | – | 1 | 4 | – | 3732 | 1707 | 66 | 25.86 | 7-71 | 5 | 3 |
| Fry, C.B. | 26 | 41 | 3 | 144 | 1223 | 32.18 | 2 | 7 | 17 | – | 10 | 3 | 0 | – | – | – | – |
| Gatting, M.W. | 41 | 70 | 10 | 207 | 2246 | 37.43 | 4 | 13 | 35 | – | 332 | 167 | 2 | 83.50 | 1-14 | – | – |
| Gay, L.H. | 1 | 2 | 0 | 33 | 37 | 18.50 | – | – | 3 | 1 | – | – | – | – | – | – | – |
| Geary, G. | 14 | 20 | 4 | 66 | 249 | 15.56 | – | 2 | 13 | – | 3810 | 1353 | 46 | 29.41 | 7-70 | 4 | 1 |
| Gibb, P.A. | 8 | 13 | 0 | 120 | 581 | 44.69 | 2 | 3 | 3 | 1 | – | – | – | – | – | – | – |
| Gifford, N. | 15 | 20† | 9 | 25* | 179 | 16.27 | – | – | 8 | – | 3084‡ | 1026 | 33 | 31.09 | 5-55 | 1 | – |
| Gilligan, A.E.R. | 11 | 16 | 3 | 39* | 209 | 16.07 | – | 1 | 3 | – | 2404 | 1046 | 36 | 29.05 | 6-7 | 2 | 1 |
| Gilligan, A.H.H. | 4 | 4 | 0 | 32 | 71 | 17.75 | – | – | 1 | – | – | – | – | – | – | – | – |
| Gimblett, H. | 3 | 5 | 1 | 67* | 129 | 32.25 | – | 1 | 2 | – | – | – | – | – | – | – | – |
| Gladwin, C. | 8 | 11 | 5 | 51* | 170 | 28.33 | – | 1 | 3 | – | 2129 | 571 | 15 | 38.06 | 3-21 | – | – |
| Goddard, T.W.J. | 8 | 5 | 3 | 8 | 13 | 6.50 | – | – | 3 | – | 1563 | 588 | 22 | 26.72 | 6-29 | 1 | – |
| Gooch, G.A. | 48 | 84 | 4 | 196 | 3027 | 37.83 | 5 | 17 | 40 | – | 1185 | 450 | 10 | 45.00 | 2-12 | – | – |
| Gover, A.R. | 4 | 1 | 1 | 2* | 2 | – | – | – | 1 | – | 816 | 359 | 8 | 44.87 | 3-85 | – | – |
| Gower, D.I. | 76 | 129† | 11 | 215 | 5385 | 45.63 | 12 | 25 | 55 | – | 30 | 15 | 1 | 15.00 | 1-1 | – | – |
| Grace, E.M. | 1 | 2 | 0 | 36 | 36 | 18.00 | – | – | 1 | – | – | – | – | – | – | – | – |
| Grace, G.F. | 1 | 2 | 0 | 0 | 0 | 0.00 | – | – | 2 | – | – | – | – | – | – | – | – |
| Grace, W.G. | 22 | 36 | 2 | 170 | 1098 | 32.29 | 2 | 5 | 39 | – | 666 | 236 | 9 | 26.22 | 2-12 | – | – |
| Graveney, T.W. | 79 | 123 | 13 | 258 | 4882 | 44.38 | 11 | 20 | 80 | – | 260 | 167 | 1 | 167.00 | 1-34 | – | – |
| Greenhough, T. | 4 | 4 | 1 | 2 | 4 | 1.33 | – | – | 1 | – | 1129 | 357 | 16 | 22.31 | 5-35 | 1 | – |
| Greenwood, A. | 2 | 4 | 0 | 49 | 77 | 19.25 | – | – | 2 | – | – | – | – | – | – | – | – |
| Greig, A.W. | 58 | 93 | 4 | 148 | 3599 | 40.43 | 8 | 20 | 87 | – | 9802 | 4541 | 141 | 32.20 | 8-86 | 6 | 2 |
| Greig, I.A. | 2 | 4 | 0 | 14 | 26 | 6.50 | – | – | – | – | 188 | 114 | 4 | 28.50 | 4-53 | – | – |
| Grieve, B.A.F. | 2 | 3 | 2 | 14* | 40 | 40.00 | – | – | 5 | – | – | – | – | – | – | – | – |
| Griffith, S.C. | 3 | 5 | 0 | 140 | 157 | 31.40 | 1 | – | 5 | 1 | – | – | – | – | – | – | – |
| Gunn, G. | 15 | 29 | 1 | 122* | 1120 | 40.00 | 2 | 7 | 15 | – | 12 | 8 | 0 | – | – | – | – |
| Gunn, J.R. | 6 | 10† | 2 | 24 | 85 | 10.62 | – | – | 3 | – | 999‡ | 387 | 18 | 21.50 | 5-76 | 1 | – |

INDIVIDUAL CAREER RECORDS—ENGLAND *continued*

| | | | | BATTING AND FIELDING | | | | | | | | | | BOWLING | | | |
|---|---|---|---|---|---|---|---|---|---|---|---|---|---|---|---|---|---|
| | Tests | I | NO | HS | Runs | Avge | 100 | 50 | Ct | St | Balls | Runs | Wkts | Avge | BB | 5wI | 10wM |
| Gunn, W. | 11 | 20 | 2 | 102* | 392 | 21.77 | 1 | 1 | 5 | – | – | – | – | – | – | – | – |
| Haig, N.E. | 5 | 9 | 0 | 47 | 126 | 14.00 | – | – | 4 | – | 1026 | 448 | 13 | 34.46 | 3-73 | – | – |
| Haigh, S. | 11 | 18 | 3 | 25 | 113 | 7.53 | – | – | 8 | – | 1294 | 622 | 24 | 25.91 | 6-11 | 1 | – |
| Hallows, C. | 2 | 2† | 1 | 26 | 42 | 42.00 | – | – | – | – | – | – | – | – | – | – | – |
| Hammond, W.R. | 85 | 140 | 16 | 336* | 7249 | 58.45 | 22 | 24 | 110 | – | 7969 | 3138 | 83 | 37.80 | 5-36 | 2 | – |
| Hampshire, J.H. | 8 | 16 | 1 | 107 | 403 | 26.86 | 1 | 2 | 9 | – | – | – | – | – | – | – | – |
| Hardinge, H.T.W. | 1 | 2 | 0 | 25 | 30 | 15.00 | – | – | 1 | – | – | – | – | – | – | – | – |
| Hardstaff, J., sr | 5 | 10 | 0 | 72 | 311 | 31.10 | – | 3 | – | – | – | – | – | – | – | – | – |
| Hardstaff, J., jr | 23 | 38 | 3 | 205* | 1636 | 46.74 | 4 | 10 | 9 | – | – | – | – | – | – | – | – |
| Harris, *Lord* | 4 | 6 | 1 | 52 | 145 | 29.00 | – | 1 | 2 | – | 32 | 29 | 0 | – | – | – | – |
| Hartley, J.C. | 2 | 4 | 0 | 9 | 15 | 3.75 | – | – | 2 | – | 192 | 115 | 1 | 115.00 | 1-62 | – | – |
| Hawke, *Lord* | 5 | 8 | 1 | 30 | 55 | 7.85 | – | – | 3 | – | – | – | – | – | – | – | – |
| Hayes, E.G. | 5 | 9 | 1 | 35 | 86 | 10.75 | – | – | 2 | – | 90 | 52 | 1 | 52.00 | 1-28 | – | – |
| Hayes, F.C. | 9 | 17 | 1 | 106* | 244 | 15.25 | 1 | – | 7 | – | – | – | – | – | – | – | – |
| Hayward, T.W. | 35 | 60 | 2 | 137 | 1999 | 34.46 | 3 | 12 | 19 | – | 887 | 514 | 14 | 36.71 | 4-22 | – | – |
| Hearne, A. | 1 | 1 | 0 | 9 | 9 | 9.00 | – | – | 1 | – | – | – | – | – | – | – | – |
| Hearne, F. | 2 | 2 | 0 | 27 | 47 | 23.50 | – | – | – | – | – | – | – | – | – | – | – |
| Hearne, G.G. | 1 | 1† | 0 | 0 | 0 | 0.00 | – | – | 1 | – | – | – | – | – | – | – | – |
| Hearne, J.T. | 12 | 18 | 4 | 40 | 126 | 9.00 | – | – | 4 | – | 2976 | 1082 | 49 | 22.08 | 6-41 | 4 | 1 |
| Hearne, J.W. | 24 | 36 | 5 | 114 | 806 | 26.00 | 1 | 2 | 13 | – | 2926 | 1462 | 30 | 48.73 | 5-49 | 1 | – |
| Hemmings, E.E. | 5 | 10 | 1 | 95 | 198 | 22.00 | – | 1 | 4 | – | 1468 | 558 | 12 | 46.50 | 3-68 | – | – |
| Hendren, E.H. | 51 | 83 | 9 | 205* | 3525 | 47.63 | 7 | 21 | 33 | – | 47 | 31 | 1 | 31.00 | 1-27 | – | – |
| Hendrick, M. | 30 | 35 | 15 | 18 | 128 | 6.40 | – | – | 25 | – | 6208 | 2248 | 87 | 25.83 | 4-28 | 1 | – |
| Heseltine, C. | 2 | 2 | 0 | 18 | 18 | 9.00 | – | – | 3 | – | 157 | 84 | 5 | 16.80 | 5-38 | 2 | – |
| Higgs, K. | 15 | 19† | 3 | 63 | 185 | 11.56 | – | 1 | 4 | – | 4112 | 1473 | 71 | 20.74 | 6-91 | – | – |
| Hill, A. | 2 | 4 | 2 | 49 | 101 | 50.50 | – | 1 | 1 | – | 340 | 130 | 7 | 18.57 | 4-27 | – | – |
| Hill, A.J.L. | 3 | 4 | 0 | 124 | 251 | 62.75 | 1 | 1 | 1 | – | 40 | 8 | 4 | 2.00 | 4-8 | – | – |
| Hilton, M.J. | 4 | 6 | 1 | 15 | 37 | 7.40 | – | – | 1 | – | 1244‡ | 477 | 14 | 34.07 | 5-61 | 1 | – |
| Hirst, G.H. | 24 | 38 | 3 | 85 | 790 | 22.57 | – | 5 | 18 | – | 3967‡ | 1770 | 59 | 30.00 | 5-48 | 3 | – |
| Hitch, J.W. | 7 | 10 | 3 | 51* | 103 | 14.71 | – | 1 | 4 | – | 462 | 325 | 7 | 46.42 | 2-31 | – | – |
| Hobbs, J.B. | 61 | 102 | 7 | 211 | 5410 | 56.94 | 15 | 28 | 17 | – | 376 | 165 | 1 | 165.00 | 1-19 | – | – |
| Hobbs, R.N.S. | 7 | 8 | 3 | 15* | 34 | 6.80 | – | – | 8 | – | 1291 | 481 | 12 | 40.08 | 3-25 | – | – |
| Hollies, W.E. | 13 | 15 | 8 | 18* | 37 | 5.28 | – | – | 2 | – | 3554 | 1332 | 44 | 30.27 | 7-50 | 5 | – |
| Holmes, E.R.T. | 5 | 9 | 2 | 85* | 114 | 16.28 | – | 1 | 4 | – | 108 | 76 | 2 | 38.00 | 1-10 | – | – |
| Holmes, P. | 7 | 14 | 1 | 88 | 357 | 27.46 | – | 4 | 3 | – | – | – | – | – | – | – | – |
| Hone, L. | 1 | 2 | 0 | 7 | 13 | 6.50 | – | – | 2 | – | – | – | – | – | – | – | – |
| Hopwood, J.L. | 2 | 3 | 1 | 8 | 12 | 6.00 | – | – | – | – | 462‡ | 155 | 0 | – | – | – | – |

## INDIVIDUAL CAREER RECORDS—ENGLAND continued

| | Tests | I | NO | BATTING AND FIELDING HS | Runs | Avge | 100 | 50 | Ct | St | Balls | Runs | Wkts | BOWLING Avge | BB | 5wI | 10wM |
|---|---|---|---|---|---|---|---|---|---|---|---|---|---|---|---|---|---|
| Hornby, A.N. | 3 | 6 | 0 | 9 | 21 | 3.50 | – | – | – | – | 28 | 0 | 1 | 0.00 | 1-0 | – | – |
| Horton, M.J. | 2 | 2 | 0 | 58 | 60 | 30.00 | – | 1 | 2 | – | 238 | 59 | 2 | 29.50 | 2-24 | – | – |
| Howard, N.D. | 4 | 6 | 1 | 23 | 86 | 17.20 | – | – | 4 | – | – | – | | | | | |
| Howell, H. | 5 | 8 | 6 | 5 | 15 | 7.50 | – | – | – | – | 918 | 559 | 7 | 79.85 | 4-115 | – | – |
| Howorth, R. | 5 | 10† | 2 | 45* | 145 | 18.12 | – | – | 2 | – | 1536‡ | 635 | 19 | 33.42 | 6-124 | 1 | – |
| Humphries, J. | 3 | 6 | 1 | 16 | 44 | 8.80 | – | – | 7 | – | – | | | | | | |
| Hunter, J. | 5 | 7 | 2 | 39* | 93 | 18.60 | – | – | 8 | 3 | – | | | | | | |
| Hutchings, K.L. | 7 | 12 | 0 | 126 | 341 | 28.41 | 1 | 1 | 9 | – | 90 | 81 | 1 | 81.00 | 1-5 | – | – |
| Hutton, L. | 79 | 138 | 15 | 364 | 6971 | 56.67 | 19 | 33 | 57 | – | 260 | 232 | 3 | 77.33 | 1-2 | – | – |
| Hutton, R.A. | 5 | 8 | 2 | 81 | 219 | 36.50 | – | 2 | 9 | – | 738 | 257 | 9 | 28.55 | 3-72 | – | – |
| Iddon, J. | 5 | 7 | 1 | 73 | 170 | 28.33 | – | 2 | – | – | 66‡ | 27 | 0 | – | – | – | – |
| Ikin, J.T. | 18 | 31† | 2 | 60 | 606 | 20.89 | – | 3 | 31 | – | 572‡ | 354 | 3 | 118.00 | 1-38 | – | – |
| Illingworth, R. | 61 | 90 | 11 | 113 | 1836 | 23.24 | 2 | 5 | 45 | – | 11934 | 3807 | 122 | 31.20 | 6-29 | 3 | – |
| Insole, D.J. | 9 | 17 | 2 | 110* | 408 | 27.20 | 1 | 1 | 8 | – | – | | | | | | |
| Jackman, R.D. | 4 | 6 | 0 | 17 | 42 | 7.00 | – | – | – | – | 1070 | 445 | 14 | 31.78 | 4-110 | – | – |
| Jackson, Hon F.S. | 20 | 33 | 4 | 144* | 1415 | 48.79 | 5 | 6 | 10 | – | 1587 | 799 | 24 | 33.29 | 5-52 | 1 | – |
| Jackson, H.L. | 2 | 2 | 1 | 8 | 15 | 15.00 | – | – | 1 | – | 498 | 155 | 7 | 22.14 | 2-26 | – | – |
| Jameson, J.A. | 4 | 8 | 1 | 82 | 214 | 26.75 | – | 1 | – | – | 42 | 17 | 1 | 17.00 | 1-17 | – | – |
| Jardine, D.R. | 22 | 33 | 6 | 127 | 1296 | 48.00 | 1 | 10 | 26 | – | 6 | 10 | 0 | – | – | – | – |
| Jenkins, R.O. | 9 | 12 | 1 | 39 | 198 | 18.00 | – | – | 4 | – | 2118 | 1098 | 32 | 34.31 | 5-116 | 1 | – |
| Jessop, G.L. | 18 | 26 | 0 | 104 | 569 | 21.88 | 1 | 3 | 11 | – | 742 | 354 | 10 | 35.40 | 4-68 | – | – |
| Jones, A.O. | 12 | 21 | 0 | 34 | 291 | 13.85 | – | – | 15 | – | 228 | 133 | 3 | 44.33 | 3-73 | – | – |
| Jones, I.J. | 15 | 17 | 9 | 16 | 38 | 4.75 | – | – | 4 | – | 3546‡ | 1769 | 44 | 40.20 | 6-118 | 1 | – |
| Jupp, H. | 2 | 4 | 0 | 63 | 68 | 17.00 | – | 1 | 2 | – | – | | | | | | |
| Jupp, V.W.C. | 8 | 13 | 1 | 38 | 208 | 17.33 | – | 1 | 5 | – | 1301 | 616 | 28 | 22.00 | 4-37 | – | – |
| Keeton, W.W. | 2 | 4 | 0 | 25 | 57 | 14.25 | – | – | – | – | – | | | | | | |
| Kennedy, A.S. | 5 | 8 | 2 | 41* | 93 | 15.50 | – | – | 5 | – | 1683 | 599 | 31 | 19.32 | 5-76 | 2 | – |
| Kenyon, D. | 8 | 15 | 0 | 87 | 192 | 12.80 | – | 1 | 5 | – | – | | | | | | |
| Killick, E.T. | 2 | 4 | 0 | 31 | 81 | 20.25 | – | – | 2 | – | – | | | | | | |
| Kilner, R. | 9 | 8† | 1 | 74 | 233 | 33.28 | – | 2 | 6 | – | 2368‡ | 734 | 24 | 30.58 | 4-51 | – | – |
| King, J.H. | 1 | 2† | 0 | 60 | 64 | 32.00 | – | 1 | – | – | 162‡ | 99 | 1 | 99.00 | 1-99 | – | – |
| Kinneir, S.P. | 1 | 2† | 0 | 30 | 52 | 26.00 | – | – | – | – | – | | | | | | |
| Knight, A.E. | 3 | 6 | 1 | 70* | 81 | 16.20 | – | – | 1 | – | – | | | | | | |
| Knight, B.R. | 29 | 38 | 7 | 127 | 812 | 26.19 | 2 | – | 14 | – | 5377 | 2223 | 70 | 31.75 | 4-38 | – | – |
| Knight, D.J. | 2 | 4 | 0 | 38 | 54 | 13.50 | – | – | 1 | – | – | | | | | | |
| Knott, A.P.E. | 95 | 149 | 15 | 135 | 4389 | 32.75 | 5 | 30 | 250 | 19 | – | | | | | | |

## INDIVIDUAL CAREER RECORDS—ENGLAND continued

| | Tests | I | NO | HS | BATTING AND FIELDING Runs | Avge | 100 | 50 | Ct | St | Balls | Runs | Wkts | BOWLING Avge | BB | 5wI | 10wM |
|---|---|---|---|---|---|---|---|---|---|---|---|---|---|---|---|---|---|
| Knox, N.A. | 2 | 4 | 1 | 8* | 24 | 8.00 | – | – | – | – | 126 | 105 | 3 | 35.00 | 2-39 | – | – |
| Laker, J.C. | 46 | 63 | 15 | 63 | 676 | 14.08 | – | 2 | 12 | – | 12027 | 4101 | 193 | 21.24 | 10-53 | 9 | 3 |
| Lamb, A.J. | 38 | 64 | 6 | 137* | 2211 | 38.12 | 7 | 9 | 41 | – | 24 | 22 | 1 | 22.00 | 1-6 | – | – |
| Langridge, James | 8 | 9† | 0 | 70 | 242 | 26.88 | – | 1 | 6 | – | 1074‡ | 413 | 19 | 21.73 | 7-56 | 2 | – |
| Larkins, W. | 6 | 11 | 0 | 34 | 176 | 16.00 | – | – | 3 | – | | | | | | | |
| Larter, J.D.F. | 10 | 7 | 2 | 10 | 16 | 3.20 | – | – | 5 | – | 2172 | 941 | 37 | 25.43 | 5-57 | 2 | – |
| Larwood, H. | 21 | 28 | 3 | 98 | 485 | 19.40 | – | 2 | 15 | – | 4969 | 2212 | 78 | 28.35 | 6-32 | 4 | 1 |
| Leadbeater, E. | 2 | 2 | 0 | 38 | 40 | 20.00 | – | – | 3 | – | 289 | 218 | 2 | 109.00 | 1-38 | – | – |
| Lee, H.W. | 1 | 2 | 0 | 18 | 19 | 9.50 | – | – | – | – | | | | | | | |
| Lees, W.S. | 5 | 9 | 3 | 25* | 66 | 11.00 | – | – | 2 | – | 1256 | 467 | 26 | 17.96 | 6-78 | 2 | – |
| Legge, G.B. | 5 | 7 | 1 | 196 | 299 | 49.83 | 1 | 1 | 1 | – | 30 | 34 | 0 | – | – | – | – |
| Leslie, C.F.H. | 4 | 7 | 0 | 54 | 106 | 15.14 | – | 1 | – | – | 96 | 44 | 4 | 11.00 | 3-31 | – | – |
| Lever, J.K. | 20 | 29 | 4 | 53 | 306 | 12.24 | – | 1 | 11 | – | 4155‡ | 1785 | 67 | 26.64 | 7-46 | 3 | 1 |
| Lever, P. | 17 | 18 | 2 | 88* | 350 | 21.87 | – | 2 | 11 | – | 3571 | 1509 | 41 | 36.80 | 6-38 | 2 | – |
| Leveson Gower, H.D.G. | 3 | 6 | 1 | 31 | 95 | 23.75 | – | – | 1 | – | | | | | | | |
| Levett, W.H.V. | 1 | 2 | 1 | 5 | 7 | 7.00 | – | – | 3 | – | | | | | | | |
| Lewis, A.R. | 9 | 16 | 2 | 125 | 457 | 32.64 | 1 | 3 | 13 | – | | | | | | | |
| Leyland, M. | 41 | 65† | 5 | 187 | 2764 | 46.06 | 9 | 10 | 70 | – | 1103‡ | 585 | 6 | 97.50 | 3-91 | – | – |
| Lilley, A.F.A. | 35 | 52 | 8 | 84 | 903 | 20.52 | – | 4 | 70 | 22 | 25 | 23 | 1 | 23.00 | 1-23 | – | – |
| Lillywhite, James | 2 | 3† | 1 | 10 | 16 | 8.00 | – | – | 1 | – | 340‡ | 126 | 8 | 15.75 | 4-70 | – | – |
| Lloyd, D. | 9 | 15‡ | 2 | 214* | 552 | 42.46 | 1 | – | 11 | – | 24‡ | 17 | 0 | – | – | – | – |
| Lloyd, T.A. | 1 | 1‡ | 1 | 10* | 10 | – | – | – | – | – | | | | | | | |
| Loader, P.J. | 13 | 19 | 6 | 17 | 76 | 5.84 | – | – | 2 | – | 2662 | 878 | 39 | 22.51 | 6-36 | 1 | – |
| Lock, G.A.R. | 49 | 63 | 9 | 89 | 742 | 13.74 | – | 3 | 59 | – | 13147‡ | 4451 | 174 | 25.58 | 7-35 | 9 | 3 |
| Lockwood, W.H. | 12 | 16 | 3 | 52* | 231 | 17.76 | – | 1 | 4 | – | 1970 | 884 | 43 | 20.55 | 7-71 | 5 | 1 |
| Lohmann, G.A. | 18 | 26 | 2 | 62* | 213 | 8.87 | – | – | 28 | – | 3821 | 1205 | 112 | 10.75 | 9-28 | 9 | 5 |
| Lowson, F.A. | 7 | 13 | 0 | 68 | 245 | 18.84 | – | 2 | 5 | – | | | | | | | |
| Lucas, A.P. | 5 | 9 | 1 | 55 | 157 | 19.62 | – | 1 | 1 | – | 120 | 54 | 0 | – | – | – | – |
| Luckhurst, B.W. | 21 | 41 | 5 | 131 | 1298 | 36.05 | 4 | 5 | 14 | – | 57‡ | 32 | 1 | 32.00 | 1-9 | – | – |
| Lyttelton, Hon A. | 4 | 7 | 1 | 31 | 94 | 15.66 | – | – | 2 | – | 48 | 19 | 4 | 4.75 | 4-19 | – | – |
| Macaulay, G.G. | 8 | 10 | 4 | 76 | 112 | 18.66 | – | 1 | 5 | – | 1701 | 662 | 24 | 27.58 | 5-64 | 1 | – |
| MacBryan, J.C.W. | 1 | – | – | – | – | – | – | – | 4 | – | | | | | | | |
| McConnon, J.E. | 2 | 3 | 1 | 11 | 18 | 9.00 | – | – | 4 | – | 216 | 74 | 4 | 18.50 | 3-19 | – | – |
| McGahey, C.P. | 2 | 4 | 0 | 18 | 38 | 9.50 | – | – | 1 | – | | | | | | | |
| MacGregor, G. | 8 | 11 | 3 | 31 | 96 | 12.00 | – | – | 14 | 3 | | | | | | | |
| McIntyre, A.J.W. | 3 | 6 | 0 | 7 | 19 | 3.16 | – | – | 8 | 1 | | | | | | | |

INDIVIDUAL CAREER RECORDS—ENGLAND *continued*

| | | | | BATTING AND FIELDING | | | | | | | | | BOWLING | | | |
|---|---|---|---|---|---|---|---|---|---|---|---|---|---|---|---|---|
| | Tests | I | NO | HS | Runs | Avge | 100 | 50 | Ct | St | Balls | Runs | Wkts | Avge | BB | 5wI | 10wM |
| MacKinnon, F.A. | 1 | 2 | 0 | 5 | 5 | 2.50 | – | – | – | – | – | | – | – | – | – | – |
| MacLaren, A.C. | 35 | 61 | 4 | 140 | 1931 | 33.87 | 5 | 8 | 29 | – | – | | – | – | – | – | – |
| McMaster, J.E.P. | 1 | 1 | 0 | 0 | 0 | 0.00 | – | – | – | – | – | | – | – | – | – | – |
| Makepeace, J.W.H. | 4 | 8 | 0 | 117 | 279 | 34.87 | 1 | 2 | – | – | – | | – | – | – | – | – |
| Mann, F.G. | 7 | 12 | 2 | 136* | 376 | 37.60 | 1 | 2 | 3 | – | – | | – | – | – | – | – |
| Mann, F.T. | 5 | 9 | 1 | 84 | 281 | 35.12 | – | 2 | 4 | – | – | | – | – | – | – | – |
| Marks, V.J. | 6 | 10 | 1 | 83 | 249 | 27.66 | – | 3 | – | – | 1082 | 484 | 11 | 44.00 | 3-78 | – | – |
| Marriott, C.S. | 1 | 1 | 1 | 0 | 0 | 0.00 | – | – | – | – | 247 | 96 | 11 | 8.72 | 6-59 | 2 | 1 |
| Martin, F. | 2 | 2† | 0 | 13 | 14 | 7.00 | – | – | 1 | – | 410‡ | 141 | 14 | 10.07 | 6-50 | 2 | 1 |
| Martin, J.W. | 1 | 2 | 0 | 26 | 26 | 13.00 | – | – | 2 | – | 270 | 129 | 1 | 129.00 | 1-111 | – | – |
| Mason, J.R. | 5 | 10 | 0 | 32 | 129 | 12.90 | – | – | 3 | – | 324 | 149 | 2 | 74.50 | 1-8 | – | – |
| Matthews, A.D.G. | 1 | 1 | 1 | 2* | 2 | – | – | – | 1 | – | 180 | 65 | 2 | 32.50 | 1-13 | – | – |
| May, P.B.H. | 66 | 106 | 9 | 285* | 4537 | 46.77 | 13 | 22 | 42 | – | – | | – | – | – | – | – |
| Mead, C.P. | 17 | 26† | 2 | 182* | 1185 | 49.37 | 4 | 3 | 4 | – | – | | – | – | – | – | – |
| Mead, W. | 4 | 7 | 2 | 7 | 7 | 3.50 | – | – | 1 | – | 265 | 91 | 1 | 91.00 | 1-91 | – | – |
| Midwinter, W.E. | 4 | 7 | 0 | 36 | 95 | 13.57 | – | – | 5 | – | 776 | 272 | 10 | 27.20 | 4-81 | – | – |
| Milburn, C. | 9 | 16 | 2 | 139 | 654 | 46.71 | 2 | 2 | 7 | – | – | | – | – | – | – | – |
| Miller, A.M. | 1 | 2 | 2 | 20* | 24 | – | – | – | – | – | – | | – | – | – | – | – |
| Miller, G. | 34 | 51 | 4 | 98* | 1213 | 25.80 | – | 7 | 17 | – | 5149 | 1859 | 60 | 30.98 | 5-44 | 1 | – |
| Milligan, F.W. | 2 | 4 | 0 | 38 | 58 | 14.50 | – | – | 1 | – | 45 | 29 | 9 | – | – | – | – |
| Millman, G. | 6 | 7 | 2 | 32* | 60 | 12.00 | – | – | 13 | 2 | – | | – | – | – | – | – |
| Milton, C.A. | 6 | 9 | 1 | 104* | 204 | 25.50 | 1 | – | 5 | – | 24 | 12 | 0 | – | – | – | – |
| Mitchell, A. | 6 | 10 | 1 | 72 | 298 | 29.80 | – | 2 | 9 | – | 6 | 4 | 0 | – | – | – | – |
| Mitchell, F. | 2 | 4 | 0 | 41 | 88 | 22.00 | – | – | 2 | – | – | | – | – | – | – | – |
| Mitchell, T.B. | 5 | 6 | 2 | 9 | 20 | 5.00 | – | – | 1 | – | 894 | 498 | 8 | 62.25 | 2-49 | – | – |
| Mitchell-Innes, N.S. | 1 | 1 | 0 | 5 | 5 | 5.00 | – | – | – | – | – | | – | – | – | – | – |
| Mold, A.W. | 3 | 3 | 0 | 0* | 0 | 0.00 | – | – | 1 | – | 491 | 234 | 7 | 33.42 | 3-44 | – | – |
| Moon, L.J. | 4 | 8 | 0 | 36 | 182 | 22.75 | – | – | 4 | – | – | | – | – | – | – | – |
| Morley, F. | 4 | 6† | 2 | 2* | 6 | 1.50 | – | – | 4 | – | 972‡ | 296 | 16 | 18.50 | 5-56 | 1 | – |
| Mortimore, J.B. | 9 | 12 | 2 | 73* | 243 | 24.30 | – | 1 | 3 | – | 2162 | 733 | 13 | 56.38 | 3-36 | – | – |
| Moss, A.E. | 9 | 7 | 1 | 26 | 61 | 10.16 | – | – | 1 | – | 1657 | 626 | 21 | 29.80 | 4-35 | – | – |
| Murdoch, W.L. | 1 | 1 | 1 | 12 | 12 | 12.00 | – | – | – | 1 | – | | – | – | – | – | – |
| Murray, J.T. | 21 | 28 | 5 | 112 | 506 | 22.00 | 1 | 2 | 52 | 3 | – | | – | – | – | – | – |
| Newham, W. | 1 | 2 | 0 | 17 | 26 | 13.00 | – | – | – | – | – | | – | – | – | – | – |
| Nichols, M.S. | 14 | 19† | 7 | 78* | 355 | 29.58 | – | 2 | 11 | – | 2565 | 1152 | 41 | 28.09 | 6-35 | 2 | – |
| Oakman, A.S.M. | 2 | 2 | 0 | 10 | 14 | 7.00 | – | – | 7 | – | 48 | 21 | 0 | – | – | – | – |

INDIVIDUAL CAREER RECORDS—ENGLAND *continued*

| | | | | BATTING AND FIELDING | | | | | | | BOWLING | | | | | | |
|---|---|---|---|---|---|---|---|---|---|---|---|---|---|---|---|---|---|
| | Tests | I | NO | HS | Runs | Avge | 100 | 50 | Ct | St | Balls | Runs | Wkts | Avge | BB | 5wI | 10wM |
| O'Brien, T.C. | 5 | 8 | 0 | 20 | 59 | 7.37 | – | – | 4 | – | 162 | 72 | 1 | 72.00 | 1-31 | – | – |
| O'Connor, J. | 4 | 7 | 0 | 51 | 153 | 21.85 | – | 1 | 2 | – | 12 | 8 | 0 | – | – | – | – |
| Old, C.M. | 46 | 66† | 9 | 65 | 845 | 14.82 | – | 2 | 22 | – | 8858 | 4020 | 143 | 28.11 | 7-50 | 4 | – |
| Oldfield, N. | 1 | 2 | 0 | 80 | 99 | 49.50 | – | 1 | – | – | | | | | | | |
| Padgett, D.E.V. | 2 | 4 | 0 | 31 | 51 | 12.75 | – | – | – | – | | | | | | | |
| Paine, G.A.E. | 4 | 7 | 1 | 49 | 97 | 16.16 | – | – | 5 | – | 1044‡ | 467 | 17 | 27.47 | 5-168 | 1 | – |
| Palairet, L.C.H. | 2 | 4 | 0 | 20 | 49 | 12.25 | – | – | 2 | – | | | | | | | |
| Palmer, C.H. | 1 | 2 | 0 | 22 | 22 | 11.00 | – | – | – | – | 30 | 15 | 0 | – | – | – | – |
| Palmer, K.E. | 1 | 1 | 0 | 10 | 10 | 10.00 | – | – | – | – | 378 | 189 | 1 | 189.00 | 1-113 | – | – |
| Parfitt, P.H. | 37 | 52† | 6 | 131* | 1882 | 40.91 | 7 | 6 | 42 | – | 1326 | 574 | 12 | 47.83 | 2-5 | – | – |
| Parker, C.W.L. | 1 | 1 | 1 | 3* | 3 | – | – | – | – | – | 168‡ | 32 | 2 | 16.00 | 2-32 | – | – |
| Parker, P.W.G. | 1 | 2 | 0 | 13 | 13 | 6.50 | – | – | – | – | | | | | | | |
| Parkhouse, W.G.A. | 7 | 13 | 0 | 78 | 373 | 28.69 | – | 2 | 3 | – | | | | | | | |
| Parkin, C.H. | 10 | 16 | 3 | 36 | 160 | 12.30 | – | – | 3 | – | 2095 | 1128 | 32 | 35.25 | 5-38 | 2 | – |
| Parks, J.H. | 1 | 2 | 0 | 22 | 29 | 14.50 | – | – | – | – | 126 | 36 | 3 | 12.00 | 2-26 | – | – |
| Parks, J.M. | 46 | 68 | 7 | 108* | 1962 | 32.16 | 2 | 9 | 103 | 11 | 54 | 51 | 1 | 51.00 | 1-43 | – | – |
| Pataudi, Nawab of, sr | 3 | 5 | 0 | 102 | 144 | 28.80 | 1 | – | – | – | | | | | | | |
| Paynter, E. | 20 | 31† | 5 | 243 | 1540 | 59.23 | 4 | 7 | 7 | – | | | | | | | |
| Peate, E. | 9 | 14† | 8 | 13 | 70 | 11.66 | – | – | 2 | – | 2096‡ | 682 | 31 | 22.00 | 6-85 | 2 | – |
| Peebles, I.A.R. | 13 | 17 | 8 | 26 | 98 | 10.88 | – | – | 5 | – | 2882 | 1391 | 45 | 30.91 | 6-63 | 3 | – |
| Peel, R. | 20 | 33† | 4 | 83 | 427 | 14.72 | – | 3 | 17 | – | 5216‡ | 1715 | 102 | 16.81 | 7-31 | 6 | 2 |
| Penn, F. | 1 | 2 | 1 | 27* | 50 | 50.00 | – | – | – | – | 12 | 2 | 0 | – | – | – | – |
| Perks, R.T.D. | 2 | 2† | 2 | 2* | 3 | – | – | – | 1 | – | 829 | 355 | 11 | 32.27 | 5-100 | 2 | – |
| Philipson, H. | 5 | 8 | 1 | 30 | 63 | 9.00 | – | – | 8 | 3 | | | | | | | |
| Pigott, A.C.S. | 1 | 2 | 1 | 8* | 12 | 12.00 | – | – | – | – | 102 | 75 | 2 | 37.50 | 2-75 | – | – |
| Pilling, R. | 8 | 13 | 1 | 23 | 91 | 7.58 | – | – | 10 | 4 | | | | | | | |
| Place, W. | 3 | 6 | 1 | 107 | 144 | 28.80 | 1 | – | – | – | | | | | | | |
| Pocock, P.I. | 25 | 37 | 4 | 33 | 206 | 6.24 | – | – | 15 | – | 6650 | 2976 | 67 | 44.41 | 6-79 | 3 | – |
| Pollard, R. | 4 | 3 | 2 | 10* | 13 | 13.00 | – | – | 3 | – | 1102 | 378 | 15 | 25.20 | 5-24 | 1 | – |
| Poole, C.J. | 3 | 5† | 1 | 69 | 161 | 40.25 | – | 2 | 1‡ | – | 30 | 9 | 0 | – | – | – | – |
| Pope, G.H. | 1 | 1 | 1 | 8* | 8 | – | – | – | – | – | 218 | 85 | 1 | 85.00 | 1-49 | – | – |
| Pougher, A.D. | 1 | 1 | 0 | 17 | 17 | 17.00 | – | – | – | – | 105 | 26 | 3 | 8.66 | 3-26 | – | – |
| Price, J.S.E. | 15 | 15† | 6 | 32 | 66 | 7.33 | – | – | 2 | – | 2724 | 1401 | 40 | 35.02 | 5-73 | 1 | – |
| Price, W.F.F. | 1 | 2 | 0 | 6 | 6 | 3.00 | – | – | 7 | – | | | | | | | |
| Prideaux, R.M. | 3 | 6 | 1 | 64 | 102 | 20.40 | – | 1 | – | – | 12 | 0 | 0 | – | – | – | – |
| Pringle, D.R. | 10 | 17 | 3 | 47* | 247 | 17.64 | – | – | 3 | – | 1520 | 752 | 16 | 47.00 | 5-108 | 1 | – |
| Pullar, G. | 28 | 49† | 4 | 175 | 1974 | 43.86 | 4 | 12 | 2 | – | 66 | 37 | 1 | 37.00 | 1-1 | – | – |

## INDIVIDUAL CAREER RECORDS—ENGLAND continued

| | | | | BATTING AND FIELDING | | | | | | | BOWLING | | | | | | |
|---|---|---|---|---|---|---|---|---|---|---|---|---|---|---|---|---|---|
| | Tests | I | NO | HS | Runs | Avge | 100 | 50 | Ct | St | Balls | Runs | Wkts | Avge | BB | 5wI | 10wM |
| Quaife, W.G. | 7 | 13 | 1 | 68 | 228 | 19.00 | – | 1 | 4 | – | 15 | 6 | 0 | – | – | – | – |
| Radley, C.T. | 8 | 10 | 0 | 158 | 481 | 48.10 | 2 | 2 | 4 | – | – | – | – | – | – | – | – |
| Randall, D.W. | 47 | 79 | 5 | 174 | 2470 | 33.37 | 7 | 12 | 31 | – | 16 | 3 | 0 | – | – | – | – |
| Ranjitsinhji, K.S. | 15 | 26 | 4 | 175 | 989 | 44.95 | 2 | 6 | 13 | – | 97 | 39 | 1 | 39.00 | 1-23 | – | – |
| Read, H.D. | 1 | – | – | – | – | – | – | – | – | – | 270 | 200 | 6 | 33.33 | 4-136 | – | – |
| Read, J.M. | 17 | 29 | 2 | 57 | 463 | 17.14 | – | 2 | 8 | – | – | – | – | – | – | – | – |
| Read, W.W. | 18 | 27 | 1 | 117 | 720 | 27.69 | 1 | 5 | 16 | – | 60 | 63 | 0 | – | – | – | – |
| Relf, A.E. | 13 | 21 | 3 | 63 | 416 | 23.11 | – | 1 | 14 | – | 1764 | 624 | 25 | 24.96 | 5-85 | 1 | – |
| Rhodes, H.J. | 2 | 1 | 1 | 0* | 0 | – | – | – | – | – | 449 | 244 | 9 | 27.11 | 4-50 | – | – |
| Rhodes, W. | 58 | 98 | 21 | 179 | 2325 | 30.19 | 2 | 11 | 60 | – | 8231‡ | 3425 | 127 | 26.96 | 8-68 | 6 | 1 |
| Richardson, D.W. | 1 | 1† | 0 | 33 | 33 | 33.00 | – | – | 1 | – | – | – | – | – | – | – | – |
| Richardson, P.E. | 34 | 56† | 1 | 126 | 2061 | 37.47 | 5 | 9 | 6 | – | 120 | 48 | 3 | 16.00 | 2-10 | – | – |
| Richardson, T. | 14 | 24 | 8 | 25* | 177 | 11.06 | – | – | 5 | – | 4497 | 2220 | 88 | 25.22 | 8-94 | 11 | 4 |
| Richmond, T.L. | 1 | 2 | 0 | 4 | 6 | 3.00 | – | – | – | – | 114 | 86 | 2 | 43.00 | 2-69 | – | – |
| Ridgway, F. | 5 | 6 | 0 | 24 | 49 | 8.16 | – | – | 3 | – | 793 | 379 | 7 | 54.14 | 4-83 | – | – |
| Robertson, J.D.B. | 11 | 21 | 2 | 133 | 881 | 46.36 | 2 | 6 | 6 | – | 138 | 58 | 2 | 29.00 | 2-17 | – | – |
| Robins, R.W.V. | 19 | 27 | 4 | 108 | 612 | 26.60 | 1 | 4 | 12 | – | 3318 | 1758 | 64 | 27.46 | 6-32 | 1 | – |
| Robinson, R.T. | 11 | 18 | 3 | 175 | 934 | 62.26 | 3 | 3 | 5 | – | 6 | 0 | 0 | – | – | – | – |
| Roope, G.R.J. | 21 | 32 | 4 | 77 | 860 | 30.71 | – | 7 | 35 | – | 172 | 76 | 0 | – | – | – | – |
| Root, C.F. | 3 | – | – | – | – | – | – | – | 1 | – | 642 | 194 | 8 | 24.25 | 4-84 | – | – |
| Rose, B.C. | 9 | 16† | 2 | 70 | 358 | 25.57 | – | 2 | 4 | – | – | – | – | – | – | – | – |
| Royle, V.P.F.A. | 1 | 2 | 0 | 18 | 21 | 10.50 | – | – | 2 | – | 16 | 6 | 0 | – | – | – | – |
| Rumsey, F.E. | 5 | 5 | 3 | 21* | 30 | 15.00 | – | – | – | – | 1145‡ | 461 | 17 | 27.11 | 4-25 | – | – |
| Russell, C.A.G. | 10 | 18 | 2 | 140 | 910 | 56.87 | 5 | 2 | 8 | – | 144 | 44 | 0 | – | – | – | – |
| Russell, W.E. | 10 | 18 | 1 | 70 | 362 | 21.29 | – | 2 | 4 | – | – | – | – | – | – | – | – |
| Sandham, A. | 14 | 23 | 0 | 325 | 879 | 38.21 | 2 | 3 | 4 | – | 35 | 20 | 0 | – | – | – | – |
| Schultz, S.S. | 1 | 2 | 1 | 20 | 20 | 20.00 | – | – | – | – | 20‡ | 26 | 1 | 26.00 | 1-16 | – | – |
| Scotton, W.H. | 15 | 25† | 2 | 90 | 510 | 22.17 | – | 3 | 4 | – | – | – | – | – | – | – | – |
| Selby, J. | 6 | 12 | 1 | 70 | 256 | 23.27 | – | 2 | 1 | – | – | – | – | – | – | – | – |
| Selvey, M.W.W. | 3 | 5 | 3 | 5* | 15 | 7.50 | – | – | 1 | – | 492 | 343 | 6 | 57.16 | 4-41 | – | – |
| Shackleton, D. | 7 | 13 | 7 | 42 | 113 | 18.83 | – | – | 1 | – | 2078 | 768 | 18 | 42.66 | 4-72 | – | – |
| Sharp, J. | 3 | 6 | 2 | 105 | 188 | 47.00 | 1 | 1 | 1 | – | 183 | 111 | 3 | 37.00 | 3-67 | – | – |
| Sharpe, J.W. | 3 | 6 | 4 | 26 | 44 | 22.00 | – | – | 2 | – | 975 | 305 | 11 | 27.72 | 6-84 | 1 | – |
| Sharpe, P.J. | 12 | 21 | 4 | 111 | 786 | 46.23 | 1 | 4 | 17 | – | – | – | – | – | – | – | – |
| Shaw, A. | 7 | 12 | 1 | 40 | 111 | 10.09 | – | – | 4 | – | 1099 | 285 | 12 | 23.75 | 5-38 | 1 | 1 |
| Sheppard, Rev D.S. | 22 | 33 | 2 | 119 | 1172 | 37.80 | 3 | 6 | 12 | – | – | – | – | – | – | – | – |
| Sherwin, M. | 3 | 6 | 4 | 21* | 30 | 15.00 | – | – | 5 | 2 | – | – | – | – | – | – | – |

**INDIVIDUAL CAREER RECORDS—ENGLAND** *continued*

| | Tests | I | NO | HS | Runs | Avge | 100 | 50 | Ct | St | Balls | Runs | Wkts | Avge | BB | 5wI | 10wM |
|---|---|---|---|---|---|---|---|---|---|---|---|---|---|---|---|---|---|
| | | | | | | BATTING AND FIELDING | | | | | | | | BOWLING | | | |
| Shrewsbury, A. | 23 | 40 | 4 | 164 | 1277 | 35.47 | 3 | 4 | 29 | – | 12 | 2 | 0 | – | – | – | – |
| Shuter, J. | 1 | 1 | 0 | 28 | 28 | 28.00 | – | – | 1 | – | – | – | – | – | – | – | – |
| Shuttleworth, K. | 5 | 6 | 0 | 21 | 46 | 7.66 | – | – | 1 | – | 1071 | 427 | 12 | 35.58 | 5-47 | 1 | – |
| Sidebottom, A. | 1 | 1 | 0 | 2 | 2 | 2.00 | – | – | – | – | 112 | 65 | 1 | 65.00 | 1-65 | – | – |
| Simpson, R.T. | 27 | 45 | 3 | 156* | 1401 | 33.35 | 4 | 6 | 5 | – | 45 | 22 | 2 | 11.00 | 2-4 | – | – |
| Simpson-Hayward, G.H.T. | 5 | 8 | 1 | 29* | 105 | 15.00 | – | – | 1 | – | 898 | 420 | 23 | 18.26 | 6-43 | 2 | – |
| Sims, J.M. | 4 | 4 | 0 | 12 | 16 | 4.00 | – | – | 6 | – | 887 | 480 | 11 | 43.63 | 5-73 | 1 | – |
| Sinfield, R.A. | 1 | 1 | 0 | 6 | 6 | 6.00 | – | – | – | – | 378 | 123 | 2 | 61.50 | 1-51 | – | – |
| Smailes, T.F. | 1 | 1† | 0 | 25 | 25 | 25.00 | – | – | – | – | 120 | 62 | 3 | 20.66 | 3-44 | – | – |
| Smith, A.C. | 6 | 7 | 3 | 69* | 118 | 29.50 | – | 1 | 20 | – | – | – | – | – | – | – | – |
| Smith, C.A. | 1 | 1 | 0 | 3 | 3 | 3.00 | – | – | – | – | 154 | 61 | 7 | 8.71 | 5-19 | 1 | – |
| Smith, C.I.J. | 5 | 10 | 0 | 27 | 102 | 10.20 | – | – | 1 | – | 930 | 393 | 15 | 26.20 | 5-16 | 1 | – |
| Smith, C.L. | 7 | 12 | 0 | 91 | 358 | 32.54 | – | 2 | 5 | – | 102 | 39 | 3 | 13.00 | 2-31 | – | – |
| Smith, D. | 2 | 4† | 0 | 57 | 128 | 32.00 | – | 1 | 1 | – | – | – | – | – | – | – | – |
| Smith, D.R. | 5 | 5 | 1 | 34 | 38 | 9.50 | – | – | 2 | – | 972 | 359 | 6 | 59.83 | 2-60 | – | – |
| Smith, D.V. | 3 | 4† | 1 | 16* | 25 | 8.33 | – | – | – | – | 270‡ | 97 | 1 | 97.00 | 1-12 | – | – |
| Smith, E.J. | 11 | 14 | 1 | 22 | 113 | 8.69 | – | – | 17 | 3 | – | – | – | – | – | – | – |
| Smith, H. | 1 | 1 | 0 | 7 | 7 | 7.00 | – | – | 1 | – | – | – | – | – | – | – | – |
| Smith, M.J.K. | 50 | 78 | 6 | 121 | 2278 | 31.63 | 3 | 11 | 53 | – | 214 | 128 | 1 | 128.00 | 1-10 | – | – |
| Smith, T.P.B. | 4 | 5 | 0 | 24 | 33 | 6.60 | – | – | 1 | – | 538 | 319 | 3 | 106.33 | 2-172 | – | – |
| Smithson, G.A. | 2 | 3† | 0 | 35 | 70 | 23.33 | – | – | – | – | – | – | – | – | – | – | – |
| Snow, J.A. | 49 | 71 | 14 | 73 | 772 | 13.54 | – | 2 | 16 | – | 12021 | 5387 | 202 | 26.66 | 7-40 | 8 | 1 |
| Southerton, J. | 2 | 3 | 1 | 6 | 7 | 3.50 | – | – | 2 | – | 263 | 107 | 7 | 15.28 | 4-46 | – | – |
| Spooner, R.H. | 10 | 15 | 0 | 119 | 481 | 32.06 | 1 | 4 | 4 | – | – | – | – | – | – | – | – |
| Spooner, R.T. | 7 | 14† | 1 | 92 | 354 | 27.23 | – | 3 | 10 | 2 | – | – | – | – | – | – | – |
| Stanyforth, R.T. | 4 | 6 | 1 | 6* | 13 | 2.60 | – | – | 7 | 2 | – | – | – | – | – | – | – |
| Staples, S.J. | 3 | 5 | 0 | 39 | 65 | 13.00 | – | – | – | – | 1149 | 435 | 15 | 29.00 | 3-50 | – | – |
| Statham, J.B. | 70 | 87† | 28 | 38 | 675 | 11.44 | – | – | 28 | – | 16056 | 6261 | 252 | 24.84 | 7-39 | 9 | 1 |
| Steel, A.G. | 13 | 20 | 3 | 148 | 600 | 35.29 | 2 | 1 | 5 | – | 1364 | 605 | 29 | 20.86 | 3-27 | 1 | – |
| Steele, D.S. | 8 | 16 | 0 | 106 | 673 | 42.06 | 1 | 5 | 7 | – | 88‡ | 39 | 2 | 19.50 | 1-1 | – | – |
| Stevens, G.T.S. | 10 | 17 | 1 | 69 | 263 | 15.47 | – | 1 | 9 | – | 1186 | 648 | 20 | 32.40 | 5-90 | 2 | – |
| Stevenson, G.B. | 2 | 2 | 1 | 27* | 28 | 28.00 | – | – | – | – | 312 | 183 | 5 | 36.60 | 3-111 | – | – |
| Stewart, M.J. | 8 | 12 | 0 | 87 | 385 | 35.00 | – | 2 | 6 | – | – | – | – | – | – | – | – |
| Stoddart, A.E. | 16 | 30 | 2 | 173 | 996 | 35.57 | 2 | 3 | 6 | – | 162 | 94 | 2 | 47.00 | 1-10 | – | – |
| Storer, W. | 6 | 11 | 0 | 51 | 215 | 19.54 | – | 1 | 11 | 1 | 168 | 108 | 2 | 54.00 | 1-24 | – | – |
| Street, G.B. | 1 | 2 | 1 | 7* | 11 | 11.00 | – | – | – | 1 | – | – | – | – | – | – | – |
| Strudwick, H. | 28 | 42 | 13 | 24 | 230 | 7.93 | – | – | 60 | 12 | – | – | – | – | – | – | – |
| Studd, C.T. | 5 | 9 | 1 | 48 | 160 | 20.00 | – | – | 5 | – | 384 | 98 | 3 | 32.66 | 2-35 | – | – |

INDIVIDUAL CAREER RECORDS—ENGLAND *continued*

| | | | | BATTING AND FIELDING | | | | | | | BOWLING | | | | | | |
|---|---|---|---|---|---|---|---|---|---|---|---|---|---|---|---|---|---|
| | Tests | I | NO | HS | Runs | Avge | 100 | 50 | Ct | St | Balls | Runs | Wkts | Avge | BB | 5wI | 10wM |
| Studd, G.B. | 4 | 7 | 0 | 9 | 31 | 4.42 | – | – | 8 | – | 6 | 2 | 0 | – | – | – | – |
| Subba Row, R. | 13 | 22† | 1 | 137 | 984 | 46.85 | 3 | 4 | 5 | – | – | | | | | | |
| Sugg, F.H. | 2 | 2 | 0 | 31 | 55 | 27.50 | – | – | – | – | – | | | | | | |
| Sutcliffe, H. | 54 | 84 | 9 | 194 | 4555 | 60.73 | 16 | 23 | 23 | – | – | | | | | | |
| Swetman, R. | 11 | 17 | 2 | 65 | 254 | 16.93 | – | 1 | 24 | 2 | – | | | | | | |
| Tate, F.W. | 1 | 2 | 1 | 5* | 9 | 9.00 | – | – | 2 | – | 96 | 51 | 2 | 25.50 | 2-7 | – | – |
| Tate, M.W. | 39 | 52 | 5 | 100* | 1198 | 25.48 | 1 | 5 | 11 | – | 12523 | 4055 | 155 | 26.16 | 6-42 | 7 | 1 |
| Tattersall, R. | 16 | 17† | 7 | 10* | 50 | 5.00 | – | – | 8 | – | 4228 | 1513 | 58 | 26.08 | 7-52 | 4 | 1 |
| Tavaré, C.J. | 30 | 55 | 2 | 149 | 1753 | 33.07 | 2 | 12 | 20 | – | 30 | 11 | 0 | – | – | – | – |
| Taylor, K. | 3 | 5 | 0 | 24 | 57 | 11.40 | – | – | 1 | – | 12 | 6 | 0 | – | – | – | – |
| Taylor, L.B. | 2 | 1 | 1 | 1* | 1 | – | – | – | – | – | 381 | 178 | 4 | 44.50 | 2-34 | – | – |
| Taylor, R.W. | 57 | 83 | 12 | 97 | 1156 | 16.28 | – | 3 | 167 | 7 | 12 | 6 | 0 | – | – | – | – |
| Tennyson, *Hon* L.H. | 9 | 12 | 1 | 74* | 345 | 31.36 | – | 4 | 6 | – | 6 | 1 | 0 | – | – | – | – |
| Terry, V.P. | 2 | 3 | 0 | 8 | 16 | 5.33 | – | – | 2 | – | – | | | | | | |
| Thompson, G.J. | 6 | 10 | 1 | 63 | 273 | 30.33 | – | 2 | 5 | – | 1367 | 638 | 23 | 27.73 | 4-50 | – | – |
| Thomson, N.I. | 5 | 4 | 1 | 39 | 69 | 23.00 | – | – | 3 | – | 1488 | 568 | 9 | 63.11 | 2-55 | – | – |
| Titmus, F.J. | 53 | 76 | 11 | 84* | 1449 | 22.29 | – | 10 | 35 | – | 15118 | 4931 | 153 | 32.22 | 7-79 | 7 | – |
| Tolchard, R.W. | 4 | 7 | 2 | 67 | 129 | 25.80 | – | 1 | 5 | – | – | | | | | | |
| Townsend, C.L. | 2 | 3† | 0 | 38 | 51 | 17.00 | – | – | – | – | 140 | 75 | 3 | 25.00 | 3-50 | – | – |
| Townsend, D.C.H. | 3 | 6 | 0 | 36 | 77 | 12.83 | – | – | 1 | – | 6 | 9 | 0 | – | – | – | – |
| Townsend, L.F. | 4 | 6 | 0 | 40 | 97 | 16.16 | – | – | 2 | – | 399 | 205 | 6 | 34.16 | 2-22 | – | – |
| Tremlett, M.F. | 3 | 5 | 2 | 18* | 20 | 6.66 | – | – | – | – | 492 | 226 | 4 | 56.50 | 2-98 | – | – |
| Trott, A.E. | 3 | 4 | 0 | 16 | 23 | 5.75 | – | – | – | – | 474 | 198 | 17 | 11.64 | 5-49 | 1 | – |
| Trueman, F.S. | 67 | 85 | 14 | 39* | 981 | 13.81 | – | – | 64 | – | 15178 | 6625 | 307 | 21.57 | 8-31 | 17 | 3 |
| Tufnell, N.C. | 1 | 1 | 0 | 14 | 14 | 14.00 | – | – | 1 | 1 | – | | | | | | |
| Turnbull, M.J.L. | 9 | 13 | 2 | 61 | 224 | 20.36 | – | 1 | 1 | – | – | | | | | | |
| Tyldesley, G.E. | 14 | 20 | 2 | 122 | 990 | 55.00 | 3 | 6 | 2 | – | 3 | 2 | 0 | – | – | – | – |
| Tyldesley, J.T. | 31 | 55 | 1 | 138 | 1661 | 30.75 | 4 | 9 | 16 | – | – | | | | | | |
| Tyldesley, R.K. | 7 | 7 | 1 | 29 | 47 | 7.83 | – | 1 | 1 | – | 1615 | 619 | 19 | 32.57 | 3-50 | – | – |
| Tylecote, E.F.S. | 6 | 9 | 1 | 66 | 152 | 19.00 | – | 1 | 5 | 5 | – | | | | | | |
| Tyler, E.J. | 1 | 1† | 0 | 0 | 0 | 0.00 | – | – | – | – | 145‡ | 65 | 4 | 16.25 | 3-49 | – | – |
| Tyson, F.H. | 17 | 24 | 3 | 37* | 230 | 10.95 | – | – | 4 | – | 3452 | 1411 | 76 | 18.56 | 7-27 | 4 | 1 |
| Ulyett, G. | 25 | 39 | 0 | 149 | 949 | 24.33 | 1 | 7 | 19 | – | 2627 | 1020 | 50 | 20.40 | 7-36 | 1 | – |
| Underwood, D.L. | 86 | 116 | 35 | 45* | 937 | 11.56 | – | – | 44 | – | 21862‡ | 7674 | 297 | 25.83 | 8-51 | 17 | 6 |
| Valentine, B.H. | 7 | 9 | 2 | 136 | 454 | 64.85 | 2 | 1 | 2 | – | – | | | | | | |
| Verity, H. | 40 | 44 | 12 | 66* | 669 | 20.90 | – | 3 | 30 | – | 11173‡ | 3510 | 144 | 24.37 | 8-43 | 5 | 2 |

## INDIVIDUAL CAREER RECORDS—ENGLAND *continued*

| | Tests | I | NO | BATTING AND FIELDING | | | | | | | BOWLING | | | | | | |
|---|---|---|---|---|---|---|---|---|---|---|---|---|---|---|---|---|---|
| | | | | HS | Runs | Avge | 100 | 50 | Ct | St | Balls | Runs | Wkts | Avge | BB | 5wI | 10wM |
| Vernon, G.F. | 1 | 2 | 1 | 11* | 14 | 14.00 | – | – | – | – | – | – | – | – | – | – | – |
| Vine, J. | 2 | 3 | 2 | 36 | 46 | 46.00 | – | – | – | – | – | – | – | – | – | – | – |
| Voce, W. | 27 | 38 | 15 | 66 | 308 | 13.39 | – | 1 | 15 | – | 6360‡ | 2733 | 98 | 27.88 | 7-70 | 3 | 2 |
| Waddington, A. | 2 | 4 | 0 | 7 | 16 | 4.00 | – | – | 1 | – | 276‡ | 119 | 1 | 119.00 | 1-35 | – | – |
| Wainwright, E. | 5 | 9 | 0 | 49 | 132 | 14.66 | – | – | 2 | – | 127 | 73 | 0 | – | – | – | – |
| Walker, P.M. | 3 | 4 | 0 | 52 | 128 | 32.00 | – | 1 | 5 | – | 78‡ | 34 | 0 | – | – | – | – |
| Walters, C.F. | 11 | 18 | 3 | 102 | 784 | 52.26 | 1 | 7 | 6 | – | – | – | – | – | – | – | – |
| Ward, Alan | 5 | 6 | 1 | 21 | 40 | 8.00 | – | – | 3 | – | 761 | 453 | 14 | 32.35 | 4-61 | – | – |
| Ward, Albert | 7 | 13 | 0 | 117 | 487 | 37.46 | 1 | 3 | 1 | – | – | – | – | – | – | – | – |
| Wardle, J.H. | 28 | 41† | 8 | 66 | 653 | 19.78 | – | 2 | 12 | – | 6597‡ | 2080 | 102 | 20.39 | 7-36 | 5 | 1 |
| Warner, P.F. | 15 | 28 | 2 | 132* | 622 | 23.92 | 1 | 3 | 3 | – | – | – | – | – | – | – | – |
| Warr, J.J. | 2 | 4 | 0 | 4 | 4 | 1.00 | – | – | 1 | – | 584 | 281 | 1 | 281.00 | 1-76 | – | – |
| Warren, A. | 1 | 1 | 0 | 7 | 7 | 7.00 | – | – | – | – | 236 | 113 | 6 | 18.83 | 5-57 | 1 | – |
| Washbrook, C. | 37 | 66 | 6 | 195 | 2569 | 42.81 | 6 | 12 | 12 | – | 36 | 33 | 1 | 33.00 | 1-25 | – | – |
| Watkins, A.J. | 15 | 24† | 4 | 137* | 810 | 40.50 | 2 | 4 | 17 | – | 1364‡ | 554 | 11 | 50.36 | 3-20 | – | – |
| Watson, W. | 23 | 37† | 3 | 116 | 879 | 25.85 | 2 | 3 | 8 | – | – | – | – | – | – | – | – |
| Webbe, A.J. | 1 | 2 | 0 | 4 | 4 | 2.00 | – | – | 2 | – | – | – | – | – | – | – | – |
| Wellard, A.W. | 2 | 4 | 0 | 38 | 47 | 11.75 | – | – | 2 | – | 456 | 237 | 7 | 33.85 | 4-81 | – | – |
| Wharton, A. | 1 | 2† | 0 | 13 | 20 | 10.00 | – | – | – | – | – | – | – | – | – | – | – |
| White, D.W. | 2 | 2† | 0 | 0 | 0 | 0.00 | – | – | – | – | 220 | 119 | 4 | 29.75 | 3-65 | – | 1 |
| White, J.C. | 15 | 22 | 9 | 29 | 239 | 18.38 | – | – | 6 | – | 4801‡ | 1581 | 49 | 32.26 | 8-126 | 3 | 1 |
| Whysall, W.W. | 4 | 7 | 0 | 76 | 209 | 29.85 | – | 2 | 7 | – | 16 | 9 | 0 | – | – | – | – |
| Wilkinson, L.L. | 3 | 2 | 1 | 2 | 3 | 3.00 | – | – | – | – | 573 | 271 | 7 | 38.71 | 2-12 | – | – |
| Willey, P. | 21 | 40 | 6 | 102* | 962 | 28.29 | 2 | 4 | 3 | – | 1067 | 441 | 6 | 73.50 | 2-73 | – | – |
| Willis, R.G.D. | 90 | 128 | 55 | 28* | 840 | 11.50 | – | – | 39 | – | 17357 | 8190 | 325 | 25.20 | 8-43 | 16 | – |
| Wilson, C.E.M. | 2 | 4 | 1 | 18 | 42 | 14.00 | – | – | 1 | – | – | – | – | – | – | – | – |
| Wilson, D. | 6 | 7† | 1 | 42 | 75 | 12.50 | – | – | 1 | – | 1472‡ | 466 | 11 | 42.36 | 2-17 | – | – |
| Wilson, E.R. | 1 | 2 | 0 | 5 | 10 | 5.00 | – | – | – | – | 123 | 36 | 3 | 12.00 | 2-28 | – | – |
| Wood, A. | 4 | 5 | 1 | 53 | 80 | 20.00 | – | – | 10 | 1 | – | – | 0 | – | – | – | – |
| Wood, B. | 12 | 21 | 0 | 90 | 454 | 21.61 | – | 1 | 6 | – | 98 | 50 | 0 | – | – | – | – |
| Wood, G.E.C. | 3 | 2 | 0 | 6 | 7 | 3.50 | – | – | 5 | 1 | – | – | – | – | – | – | – |
| Wood, H. | 4 | 4 | 1 | 134* | 204 | 68.00 | 1 | – | 2 | 1 | – | – | – | – | – | – | – |
| Wood, R. | 1 | 2† | 0 | 6 | 6 | 3.00 | – | – | – | 1 | – | – | – | – | – | – | – |
| Woods, S.M.J. | 3 | 4 | 0 | 53 | 122 | 30.50 | – | 1 | 4 | – | 195 | 129 | 5 | 25.80 | 3-28 | – | – |
| Woolley, F.E. | 64 | 98† | 7 | 154 | 3283 | 36.07 | 5 | 23 | 64 | – | 6495‡ | 2815 | 83 | 33.91 | 7-76 | 4 | 1 |
| Woolmer, R.A. | 19 | 34 | 2 | 149 | 1059 | 33.09 | 3 | 2 | 10 | – | 546 | 299 | 4 | 74.75 | 1-8 | – | – |
| Worthington, T.S. | 9 | 11 | 0 | 128 | 321 | 29.18 | 1 | 1 | 8 | – | 633 | 316 | 8 | 39.50 | 2-19 | – | – |

## INDIVIDUAL CAREER RECORDS—ENGLAND continued

| | Tests | I | NO | HS | Runs | Avge | 100 | 50 | Ct | St | Balls | Runs | Wkts | Avge | BB | 5wI | 10wM |
|---|---|---|---|---|---|---|---|---|---|---|---|---|---|---|---|---|---|
| | | | | | *BATTING AND FIELDING* | | | | | | | | | *BOWLING* | | | |
| Wright, C.W. | 3 | 4 | 0 | 71 | 125 | 31.25 | – | 1 | – | – | 8135 | 4224 | 108 | 39.11 | 7-105 | 6 | 1 |
| Wright, D.V.P. | 34 | 39 | 13 | 45 | 289 | 11.11 | – | – | 10 | – | 1395 | 642 | 18 | 35.66 | 3-4 | – | – |
| Wyatt, R.E.S. | 40 | 64 | 6 | 149 | 1839 | 31.70 | 2 | 12 | 16 | – | 24 | 17 | 0 | – | – | – | – |
| Wynyard, E.G. | 3 | 6 | 0 | 30 | 72 | 12.00 | – | – | – | – | | | | | | | |
| Yardley, N.W.D. | 20 | 34 | 2 | 99 | 812 | 25.37 | – | 4 | 14 | – | 1662 | 707 | 21 | 33.66 | 3-67 | – | – |
| Young, H.I. | 2 | 2 | 0 | 43 | 43 | 21.50 | – | – | 1 | – | 556‡ | 262 | 12 | 21.83 | 4-30 | – | – |
| Young, J.A. | 8 | 10 | 5 | 10* | 28 | 5.60 | – | – | 5 | – | 2368‡ | 757 | 17 | 44.52 | 3-65 | – | – |
| Young, R.A. | 2 | 4 | 0 | 13 | 27 | 6.75 | – | – | 6 | – | | | | | | | |

## AUSTRALIA (330 players)

| | Tests | I | NO | HS | Runs | Avge | 100 | 50 | Ct | St | Balls | Runs | Wkts | Avge | BB | 5wI | 10wM |
|---|---|---|---|---|---|---|---|---|---|---|---|---|---|---|---|---|---|
| | | | | | *BATTING AND FIELDING* | | | | | | | | | *BOWLING* | | | |
| A'Beckett, E.L. | 4 | 7 | 0 | 41 | 143 | 20.42 | – | – | 4 | – | 1062 | 317 | 3 | 105.66 | 1-41 | – | – |
| Alderman, T.M. | 22 | 33 | 15 | 23 | 113 | 6.27 | – | – | 17 | – | 5373 | 2597 | 79 | 32.87 | 6-128 | 5 | – |
| Alexander, G. | 2 | 4 | 0 | 33 | 52 | 13.00 | – | – | 2 | – | 168 | 93 | 2 | 46.50 | 2-69 | – | – |
| Alexander, H.H. | 1 | 2 | 1 | 17* | 17 | 17.00 | – | – | – | – | 276 | 154 | 1 | 154.00 | 1-129 | – | – |
| Allan, F.E. | 1 | 1† | 0 | 5 | 5 | 5.00 | – | – | – | – | 180‡ | 80 | 4 | 20.00 | 2-30 | – | – |
| Allan, P.J. | 1 | – | – | – | – | – | – | – | – | – | 192 | 83 | 2 | 41.50 | 2-58 | – | – |
| Allen, R.C. | 1 | 2 | 0 | 30 | 44 | 22.00 | – | – | – | – | | | | | | | |
| Andrews, T.J.E. | 16 | 23 | 1 | 94 | 592 | 26.90 | – | 4 | 12 | – | 156 | 116 | 1 | 116.00 | 1-23 | – | – |
| Archer, K.A. | 5 | 9 | 0 | 48 | 234 | 26.00 | – | 2 | – | – | | | | | | | |
| Archer, R.G. | 19 | 30 | 1 | 128 | 713 | 24.58 | 1 | 2 | 20 | – | 3576 | 1318 | 48 | 27.45 | 5-53 | 1 | – |
| Armstrong, W.W. | 50 | 84 | 10 | 159* | 2863 | 38.68 | 6 | 8 | 44 | – | 8022 | 2923 | 87 | 33.59 | 6-35 | 3 | – |
| Badcock, C.L. | 7 | 12 | 1 | 118 | 160 | 14.54 | 1 | – | 3 | – | | | | | | | |
| Bannerman, A.C. | 28 | 50 | 2 | 94 | 1108 | 23.08 | – | 8 | 21 | – | 292 | 163 | 4 | 40.75 | 3-111 | – | – |
| Bannerman, C. | 3 | 6 | 2 | 165* | 239 | 59.75 | 1 | – | – | – | | | | | | | |
| Bardsley, W. | 41 | 66† | 5 | 193* | 2469 | 40.47 | 6 | 14 | 12 | – | | | | | | | |
| Barnes, S.G. | 13 | 19 | 2 | 234 | 1072 | 63.05 | 3 | 5 | 14 | – | 594 | 218 | 5 | 54.50 | 2-25 | – | – |
| Barnett, B.A. | 4 | 8† | 1 | 57 | 195 | 27.85 | – | 1 | 3 | 2 | | | | | | | |
| Barrett, J.E. | 2 | 4† | 1 | 67* | 80 | 26.66 | – | 1 | 1 | – | | | | | | | |
| Beard, G.R. | 3 | 5 | 0 | 49 | 114 | 22.80 | – | – | – | – | 259 | 109 | 1 | 109.00 | 1-26 | – | – |
| Benaud, J. | 3 | 5 | 0 | 142 | 223 | 44.60 | 1 | – | – | – | 24 | 12 | 2 | 6.00 | 2-12 | – | – |
| Benaud, R. | 63 | 97 | 7 | 122 | 2201 | 24.45 | 3 | 9 | 65 | – | 19108 | 6704 | 248 | 27.03 | 7-72 | 16 | 1 |
| Bennett, M.J. | 3 | 5 | 2 | 23 | 71 | 23.66 | – | – | 5 | – | 665‡ | 325 | 6 | 54.16 | 3-79 | – | – |
| Blackham, J.M. | 35 | 62 | 11 | 74 | 800 | 15.68 | – | 4 | 37 | 24 | | | | | | | |
| Blackie, D.D. | 3 | 6† | 3 | 11* | 24 | 8.00 | – | – | 2 | – | 1260 | 444 | 14 | 31.71 | 6-94 | 1 | – |

## INDIVIDUAL CAREER RECORDS—AUSTRALIA *continued*

| | | | | BATTING AND FIELDING | | | | | | | BOWLING | | | | | | |
|---|---|---|---|---|---|---|---|---|---|---|---|---|---|---|---|---|---|
| | Tests | I | NO | HS | Runs | Avge | 100 | 50 | Ct | St | Balls | Runs | Wkts | Avge | BB | 5wI | 10wM |
| Bonnor, G.J. | 17 | 30 | 0 | 128 | 512 | 17.06 | 1 | 2 | 16 | — | 164 | 84 | 2 | 42.00 | 1-5 | — | — |
| Boon, D.C. | 7 | 12 | 0 | 61 | 256 | 21.33 | — | 2 | 6 | — | — | — | — | — | — | — | — |
| Booth, B.C. | 29 | 48 | 6 | 169 | 1773 | 42.21 | 5 | 10 | 17 | — | 436 | 146 | 3 | 48.66 | 2-33 | — | — |
| Border, A.R. | 72 | 127† | 22 | 196 | 5332 | 50.78 | 14 | 29 | 81 | — | 1582‡ | 625 | 15 | 41.66 | 3-20 | — | — |
| Boyle, H.F. | 12 | 16 | 4 | 36* | 153 | 12.75 | — | — | 10 | — | 1744 | 641 | 32 | 20.03 | 6-42 | 1 | — |
| Bradman, D.G. | 52 | 80 | 10 | 334 | 6996 | 99.94 | 29 | 13 | 32 | — | 160 | 72 | 2 | 36.00 | 1-8 | — | — |
| Bright, R.J. | 16 | 27 | 5 | 33 | 303 | 13.77 | — | — | 8 | — | 3598‡ | 1343 | 37 | 36.29 | 7-87 | 3 | 1 |
| Bromley, E.H. | 2 | 4† | 0 | 26 | 38 | 9.50 | — | — | 2 | — | 60‡ | 19 | 0 | — | — | — | — |
| Brown, W.A. | 22 | 35 | 1 | 206* | 1592 | 46.82 | 4 | 9 | 14 | — | — | — | — | — | — | — | — |
| Bruce, W. | 14 | 26† | 2 | 80 | 702 | 29.25 | — | 5 | 12 | — | 988‡ | 440 | 12 | 36.66 | 3-88 | — | — |
| Burge, P.J.P. | 42 | 68 | 8 | 181 | 2290 | 38.16 | 4 | 12 | 23 | — | — | — | — | — | — | — | — |
| Burke, J.W. | 24 | 44 | 7 | 189 | 1280 | 34.59 | 3 | 5 | 18 | — | 814 | 230 | 8 | 28.75 | 4-37 | — | — |
| Burn, E.J.K. | 2 | 4 | 0 | 19 | 41 | 10.25 | — | — | — | — | — | — | — | — | — | — | — |
| Burton, F.J. | 2 | 4 | 2 | 2* | 4 | 2.00 | — | — | 1 | 1 | — | — | — | — | — | — | — |
| Callaway, S.T. | 3 | 6 | 1 | 41 | 87 | 17.40 | — | — | — | — | 471 | 142 | 6 | 23.66 | 5-37 | 1 | — |
| Callen, I.W. | 1 | 2† | 2 | 22* | 26 | — | — | — | 1 | — | 440 | 191 | 6 | 31.83 | 3-83 | — | — |
| Carkeek, W. | 6 | 5† | 2 | 6* | 16 | 5.33 | — | — | 6 | — | — | — | — | — | — | — | — |
| Carlson, P.H. | 2 | 4 | 0 | 21 | 23 | 5.75 | — | — | 2 | — | 368 | 99 | 2 | 49.50 | 2-41 | — | — |
| Carter, H. | 28 | 47 | 9 | 72 | 873 | 22.97 | — | 4 | 44 | 21 | — | — | — | — | — | — | — |
| Chappell, G.S. | 87 | 151 | 19 | 247* | 7110 | 53.86 | 24 | 31 | 122 | — | 5227 | 1913 | 47 | 40.70 | 5-61 | 1 | — |
| Chappell, I.M. | 75 | 136 | 10 | 196 | 5345 | 42.42 | 14 | 26 | 105 | — | 2873 | 1316 | 20 | 65.80 | 2-21 | — | — |
| Chappell, T.M. | 3 | 6 | 1 | 27 | 79 | 15.80 | — | — | 2 | — | 45 | 24 | 3 | 8.00 | 3-18 | — | — |
| Charlton, P.C. | 2 | 4 | 0 | 11 | 29 | 7.25 | — | — | — | — | — | — | — | — | — | — | — |
| Chipperfield, A.G. | 14 | 20 | 3 | 109 | 552 | 32.47 | 1 | 2 | 15 | — | 924 | 437 | 5 | 87.40 | 3-91 | — | — |
| Clark, W.M. | 10 | 19 | 2 | 33 | 98 | 5.76 | — | — | 6 | — | 2793 | 1265 | 44 | 28.75 | 4-46 | — | — |
| Colley, D.J. | 3 | 4 | 0 | 54 | 84 | 21.00 | — | 1 | 1 | — | 729 | 312 | 6 | 52.00 | 3-83 | — | — |
| Collins, H.J. | 19 | 31 | 1 | 203 | 1352 | 45.06 | 4 | 6 | 13 | — | 654‡ | 252 | 4 | 63.00 | 2-47 | — | — |
| Coningham, A. | 1 | 2† | 0 | 10 | 13 | 6.50 | — | — | — | — | 186‡ | 76 | 2 | 38.00 | 2-17 | — | — |
| Connolly, A.N. | 29 | 45 | 20 | 37 | 260 | 10.40 | — | — | 17 | — | 7818 | 2981 | 102 | 29.22 | 6-47 | 4 | — |
| Cooper, B.B. | 1 | 2 | 0 | 15 | 18 | 9.00 | — | — | 2 | — | — | — | — | — | — | — | — |
| Cooper, W.H. | 2 | 3 | 1 | 7 | 13 | 6.50 | — | — | 1 | — | 466 | 226 | 9 | 25.11 | 6-120 | 1 | — |
| Corling, G.E. | 5 | 4 | 1 | 3 | 5 | 1.66 | — | — | — | — | 1159 | 447 | 12 | 37.25 | 4-60 | — | — |
| Cosier, G.J. | 18 | 32 | 1 | 168 | 897 | 28.93 | 2 | 3 | 14 | — | 899 | 341 | 5 | 68.20 | 2-26 | — | — |
| Cottam, J.T. | 1 | 2 | 0 | 3 | 4 | 2.00 | — | — | — | — | — | — | — | — | — | — | — |
| Cotter, A. | 21 | 37 | 2 | 45 | 457 | 13.05 | — | — | 8 | — | 4633 | 2549 | 89 | 28.64 | 7-148 | 7 | — |
| Coulthard, G. | 1 | 1 | 1 | 6* | 6 | — | — | — | — | — | — | — | — | — | — | — | — |
| Cowper, R.M. | 27 | 46† | 2 | 307 | 2061 | 46.84 | 5 | 10 | 21 | — | 3005 | 1139 | 36 | 31.63 | 4-48 | — | — |

INDIVIDUAL CAREER RECORDS—AUSTRALIA *continued*

| | | | | BATTING AND FIELDING | | | | | | | BOWLING | | | | | | |
| --- | --- | --- | --- | --- | --- | --- | --- | --- | --- | --- | --- | --- | --- | --- | --- | --- | --- |
| | Tests | I | NO | HS | Runs | Avge | 100 | 50 | Ct | St | Balls | Runs | Wkts | Avge | BB | 5wI | 10wM |
| Craig, I.D. | 11 | 18 | 0 | 53 | 358 | 19.88 | — | 2 | 2 | — | — | — | — | — | — | — | — |
| Crawford, W.P.A. | 4 | 5 | 2 | 34 | 53 | 17.66 | — | — | 1 | — | 437 | 107 | 7 | 15.28 | 3-28 | — | — |
| Darling, J. | 34 | 60† | 2 | 178 | 1657 | 28.56 | 3 | 8 | 27 | — | — | — | — | — | — | — | — |
| Darling, L.S. | 12 | 18† | 1 | 85 | 474 | 27.88 | — | 3 | 8 | — | 162 | 65 | 0 | — | — | — | — |
| Darling, W.M. | 14 | 27 | 1 | 91 | 697 | 26.80 | — | 6 | 5 | — | — | — | — | — | — | — | — |
| Davidson, A.K. | 44 | 61† | 7 | 80 | 1328 | 24.59 | 1 | 5 | 42 | — | 11587‡ | 3819 | 186 | 20.53 | 7-93 | 14 | 2 |
| Davis, I.C. | 15 | 27 | 1 | 105 | 692 | 26.61 | — | 4 | 9 | — | — | — | — | — | — | — | — |
| De Courcy, J.H. | 3 | 6 | 1 | 41 | 81 | 16.20 | — | — | 3 | — | — | — | — | — | — | — | — |
| Dell, A.R. | 2 | 2 | 2 | 3* | 6 | — | — | — | — | — | 559‡ | 160 | 6 | 26.66 | 3-65 | — | — |
| Donnan, H. | 5 | 10 | 1 | 15 | 75 | 8.33 | — | — | 1 | — | 54 | 22 | 0 | — | — | — | — |
| Dooland, B. | 3 | 5 | 1 | 29 | 76 | 19.00 | — | — | 3 | — | 880 | 419 | 9 | 46.55 | 4-69 | — | — |
| Duff, R.A. | 22 | 40 | 3 | 146 | 1317 | 35.59 | 2 | 6 | 14 | — | 180 | 85 | 4 | 21.25 | 2-43 | — | — |
| Duncan, J.R.F. | 1 | 1 | — | 3 | 3 | 3.00 | — | — | — | — | 112 | 30 | 0 | — | — | — | — |
| Dymock, G. | 21 | 32† | 7 | 31* | 236 | 9.44 | — | — | 1 | — | 5545‡ | 2216 | 78 | 27.12 | 7-67 | 5 | 1 |
| Dyson, J. | 30 | 58 | 7 | 127* | 1359 | 26.64 | 2 | 5 | 10 | — | — | — | — | — | — | — | — |
| Eady, C.J. | 2 | 4 | 1 | 10* | 20 | 6.66 | — | — | 2 | — | 223 | 112 | 7 | 16.00 | 3-30 | — | — |
| Eastwood, K.H. | 1 | 2† | 0 | 5 | 5 | 2.50 | — | — | — | — | 40‡ | 21 | 1 | 21.00 | 1-21 | — | — |
| Ebeling, H.I. | 3 | 2 | 0 | 41 | 43 | 21.50 | — | — | — | — | 186 | 89 | 3 | 29.66 | 3-74 | — | — |
| Edwards, J.D. | 3 | 6 | 3 | 26 | 48 | 9.60 | — | — | 1 | — | — | — | — | — | — | — | — |
| Edwards, R. | 20 | 32 | 3 | 170* | 1171 | 40.37 | 2 | 9 | 7 | — | 12 | 20 | 0 | — | — | — | — |
| Edwards, W.J. | 3 | 6† | 0 | 30 | 68 | 11.33 | — | — | — | — | — | — | — | — | — | — | — |
| Emery, S.H. | 4 | 2 | 0 | 5 | 6 | 3.00 | — | — | 2 | — | 462 | 249 | 5 | 49.80 | 2-46 | — | — |
| Evans, E. | 6 | 10 | 2 | 33 | 82 | 10.25 | — | — | 5 | — | 1247 | 332 | 7 | 47.42 | 3-64 | — | — |
| Fairfax, A.G. | 10 | 12 | 4 | 65 | 410 | 51.25 | — | 4 | 15 | — | 1520 | 645 | 21 | 30.71 | 4-31 | — | — |
| Favell, L.E. | 19 | 31 | 3 | 101 | 757 | 27.03 | 1 | 5 | 9 | — | — | — | — | — | — | — | — |
| Ferris, J.J. | 8 | 16† | 4 | 20* | 98 | 8.16 | — | — | 4 | — | 2030‡ | 684 | 48 | 14.25 | 5-26 | 4 | — |
| Fingleton, J.H.W. | 18 | 29 | 1 | 136 | 1189 | 42.46 | 5 | 3 | 13 | — | — | — | — | — | — | — | — |
| Fleetwood-Smith, L.O'B. | 10 | 11 | 5 | 16* | 54 | 9.00 | — | — | — | — | 3093‡ | 1570 | 42 | 37.38 | 6-110 | 2 | 1 |
| Francis, B.C. | 3 | 5 | 0 | 27 | 52 | 10.40 | — | — | 1 | — | — | — | — | — | — | — | — |
| Freeman, E.W. | 11 | 18 | 1 | 76 | 345 | 19.16 | — | 2 | 5 | — | 2183 | 1128 | 34 | 33.17 | 4-52 | — | — |
| Freer, F.W. | 1 | 1 | 1 | 28* | 28 | — | — | — | — | — | 160 | 74 | 3 | 24.66 | 2-49 | — | — |
| Gannon, J.B. | 3 | 5 | 4 | 3* | 3 | 3.00 | — | — | 3 | — | 726‡ | 361 | 11 | 32.81 | 4-77 | — | — |
| Garrett, T.W. | 19 | 33 | 6 | 51* | 339 | 12.55 | — | 1 | 7 | — | 2708 | 970 | 36 | 26.94 | 6-78 | 2 | — |
| Gaunt, R.A. | 3 | 4† | 2 | 3 | 6 | 3.00 | — | — | 1 | — | 716 | 310 | 7 | 44.28 | 3-53 | — | — |
| Gehrs, D.R.A. | 6 | 11 | 1 | 67 | 221 | 20.09 | — | 2 | 6 | — | 6 | 4 | 0 | — | — | — | — |
| Giffen, G. | 31 | 53 | 0 | 161 | 1238 | 23.35 | 1 | 6 | 24 | — | 6391 | 2791 | 103 | 27.09 | 7-117 | 7 | 1 |

## INDIVIDUAL CAREER RECORDS—AUSTRALIA *continued*

| | Tests | I | NO | HS | Runs | Avge | 100 | 50 | Ct | St | Balls | Runs | Wkts | Avge | BB | 5wI | 10wM |
|---|---|---|---|---|---|---|---|---|---|---|---|---|---|---|---|---|---|
| | | | | | BATTING AND FIELDING | | | | | | | | | BOWLING | | | |
| Giffen, W.F. | 3 | 6 | 0 | 3 | 11 | 1.83 | – | – | 1 | – | – | – | – | – | – | – | – |
| Gilbert, D.R. | 1 | 2 | 1 | 1 | 1 | 1.00 | – | – | – | – | 126 | 96 | 1 | 96.00 | 1-96 | – | – |
| Gilmour, G.J. | 15 | 22† | 1 | 101 | 483 | 23.00 | 1 | 3 | 8 | – | 2661‡ | 1406 | 54 | 26.03 | 6-85 | 3 | – |
| Gleeson, J.W. | 29 | 46 | 8 | 45 | 395 | 10.39 | – | – | 17 | – | 8857 | 3367 | 93 | 36.20 | 5-61 | 3 | – |
| Graham, H. | 6 | 10 | 0 | 107 | 301 | 30.10 | 2 | – | 3 | – | – | – | – | – | – | – | – |
| Gregory, D.W. | 3 | 5 | 2 | 43 | 60 | 20.00 | – | – | – | – | 20 | 9 | 0 | – | – | – | – |
| Gregory, E.J. | 1 | 2 | 0 | 11 | 11 | 5.50 | – | – | 1 | – | – | – | – | – | – | – | – |
| Gregory, J.M. | 24 | 34† | 3 | 119 | 1146 | 36.96 | 2 | 7 | 37 | – | 5582 | 2648 | 85 | 31.15 | 7-69 | 4 | – |
| Gregory, R.G. | 2 | 3 | 0 | 80 | 153 | 51.00 | – | 2 | 1 | – | 24 | 14 | 0 | – | – | – | – |
| Gregory, S.E. | 58 | 100 | 7 | 201 | 2282 | 24.53 | 4 | 8 | 25 | – | 30 | 33 | 0 | – | – | – | – |
| Grimmett, C.V. | 37 | 50 | 10 | 50 | 557 | 13.92 | – | 1 | 17 | – | 14513 | 5231 | 216 | 24.21 | 7-40 | 21 | 7 |
| Groube, T.U. | 1 | 2 | 0 | 11 | 11 | 5.50 | – | – | – | – | – | – | – | – | – | – | – |
| Grout, A.T.W. | 51 | 67 | 8 | 74 | 890 | 15.08 | – | 3 | 163 | 24 | – | – | – | – | – | – | – |
| Guest, C.E.J. | 1 | 1 | 0 | 11 | 11 | 11.00 | – | – | – | – | 144 | 59 | 0 | – | – | – | – |
| Hamence, R.A. | 3 | 4 | 1 | 30* | 81 | 27.00 | – | – | 1 | – | – | – | – | – | – | – | – |
| Hammond, J.R. | 5 | 5 | 2 | 19 | 28 | 9.33 | – | – | 2 | – | 1031 | 488 | 15 | 32.53 | 4-38 | – | – |
| Harry, J. | 1 | 2 | 0 | 6 | 8 | 4.00 | – | – | 1 | – | – | – | – | – | – | – | – |
| Hartigan, R.J. | 2 | 4 | 0 | 116 | 170 | 42.50 | 1 | – | 1 | – | 12 | 7 | 0 | – | – | – | – |
| Hartkopf, A.E.V. | 1 | 2 | 0 | 80 | 80 | 40.00 | – | 1 | – | – | 240 | 134 | 1 | 134.00 | 1-120 | – | – |
| Harvey, M.R. | 1 | 2 | 0 | 31 | 43 | 21.50 | – | – | – | – | – | – | – | – | – | – | – |
| Harvey, R.N. | 79 | 137† | 10 | 205 | 6149 | 48.41 | 21 | 24 | 64 | – | 414 | 120 | 3 | 40.00 | 1-8 | – | – |
| Hassett, A.L. | 43 | 69 | 3 | 198* | 3073 | 46.56 | 10 | 11 | 30 | – | 111 | 78 | 0 | – | – | – | – |
| Hawke, N.J.N. | 27 | 37 | 15 | 45* | 365 | 16.59 | – | – | 9 | – | 6974 | 2677 | 91 | 29.41 | 7-105 | 6 | 1 |
| Hazlitt, G.R. | 9 | 12 | 4 | 34* | 89 | 11.12 | – | – | 4 | – | 1563 | 623 | 23 | 27.08 | 7-25 | 1 | – |
| Hendry, H.S.T.L. | 11 | 18 | 2 | 112 | 335 | 20.93 | 1 | – | 10 | – | 1706 | 640 | 16 | 40.00 | 3-36 | – | – |
| Hibbert, P.A. | 1 | 2† | 0 | 13 | 15 | 7.50 | – | – | 1 | – | – | – | – | – | – | – | – |
| Higgs, J.D. | 22 | 36 | 16 | 16 | 111 | 5.55 | – | – | 3 | – | 4752 | 2057 | 66 | 31.16 | 7-143 | 2 | – |
| Hilditch, A.M.J. | 17 | 32 | 0 | 119 | 1061 | 33.15 | 2 | 6 | 13 | – | – | – | – | – | – | – | – |
| Hill, C. | 49 | 89† | 2 | 191 | 3412 | 39.21 | 7 | 19 | 33 | – | – | – | – | – | – | – | – |
| Hill, J.C. | 3 | 6 | 3 | 8* | 12 | 7.00 | – | – | 2 | – | 606 | 273 | 8 | 34.12 | 3-35 | – | – |
| Hoare, D.E. | 1 | 2 | 0 | 35 | 35 | 17.50 | – | – | 2 | – | 232 | 156 | 2 | 78.00 | 2-68 | – | – |
| Hodges, J.H. | 2 | 4† | 1 | 8 | 10 | 3.33 | – | – | – | – | 136‡ | 84 | 6 | 14.00 | 2-7 | – | – |
| Hogan, T.G. | 7 | 12 | 2 | 42* | 205 | 18.63 | – | 1 | 7 | – | 1436‡ | 706 | 15 | 47.06 | 5-66 | 1 | – |
| Hogg, R.M. | 38 | 58 | 13 | 52 | 439 | 9.75 | – | 1 | 6 | – | 7633 | 3503 | 123 | 28.47 | 6-74 | 6 | 2 |
| Hole, G.B. | 18 | 33 | 2 | 66 | 789 | 25.45 | – | 6 | 21 | – | 398 | 126 | 3 | 42.00 | 1-9 | – | – |
| Holland, R.G. | 7 | 9 | 2 | 10 | 30 | 4.28 | – | – | 2 | – | 1815 | 869 | 20 | 43.45 | 6-54 | 2 | 1 |
| Hookes, D.W. | 19 | 34† | 2 | 143* | 1171 | 36.59 | 1 | 8 | 8 | – | 78‡ | 35 | 0 | – | – | – | – |

## INDIVIDUAL CAREER RECORDS—AUSTRALIA continued

| | Tests | I | NO | HS | Runs | Avge | 100 | 50 | Ct | St | Balls | Runs | Wkts | Avge | BB | 5wI | 10wM |
|---|---|---|---|---|---|---|---|---|---|---|---|---|---|---|---|---|---|
| | | | | | | BATTING AND FIELDING | | | | | | | | BOWLING | | | |
| Hopkins, A.J.Y. | 20 | 33 | 2 | 43 | 509 | 16.42 | — | 1 | 11 | — | 1327 | 696 | 26 | 26.76 | 4-81 | 1 | — |
| Horan, T.P. | 15 | 27 | 2 | 124 | 471 | 18.84 | 1 | 1 | 6 | — | 373 | 143 | 11 | 13.00 | 6-40 | 1 | 2 |
| Hordern, H.V. | 7 | 13 | 2 | 50 | 254 | 23.09 | — | — | 6 | — | 2148 | 1075 | 46 | 23.36 | 7-90 | 5 | 2 |
| Hornibrook, P.M. | 6 | 7† | 1 | 26 | 60 | 10.00 | — | — | 7 | — | 1579‡ | 664 | 17 | 39.05 | 7-92 | 1 | — |
| Howell, W.P. | 18 | 27† | 6 | 35 | 158 | 7.52 | — | — | 12 | — | 3892 | 1407 | 49 | 28.71 | 5-81 | 1 | — |
| Hughes, K.J. | 70 | 124 | 6 | 213 | 4415 | 37.41 | 9 | 22 | 50 | — | 85 | 28 | 0 | — | — | — | — |
| Hunt, W.A. | 1 | 1† | 0 | 0 | 0 | 0.00 | — | — | 1 | — | 96‡ | 39 | 0 | — | — | — | — |
| Hurst, A.G. | 12 | 20 | 3 | 26 | 102 | 6.00 | — | — | 3 | — | 3054 | 1200 | 43 | 27.90 | 5-28 | 2 | — |
| Hurwood, A. | 2 | 2 | 0 | 5 | 5 | 2.50 | — | — | 2 | — | 517 | 170 | 11 | 15.45 | 4-22 | — | — |
| Inverarity, R.J. | 6 | 11 | 1 | 56 | 174 | 17.40 | — | 1 | 4 | — | 372‡ | 93 | 4 | 23.25 | 3-26 | — | — |
| Iredale, F.A. | 14 | 23 | 1 | 140 | 807 | 36.68 | 2 | 4 | 16 | — | 12 | 3 | 0 | — | — | — | — |
| Ironmonger, H. | 14 | 21† | 5 | 12 | 42 | 2.62 | — | — | 3 | — | 4695‡ | 1330 | 74 | 17.97 | 7-23 | 4 | 2 |
| Iverson, J.B. | 5 | 7 | 3 | 1* | 3 | 0.75 | — | — | 2 | — | 1108 | 320 | 21 | 15.23 | 6-27 | 1 | — |
| Jackson, A.A. | 8 | 11 | 1 | 164 | 474 | 47.40 | 1 | 2 | 7 | — | — | — | — | — | — | — | — |
| Jarman, B.N. | 19 | 30 | 3 | 78 | 400 | 14.81 | — | 2 | 50 | 4 | — | — | — | — | — | — | — |
| Jarvis, A.H. | 11 | 21 | 3 | 82 | 303 | 16.83 | — | 1 | 9 | 9 | — | — | — | — | — | — | — |
| Jenner, T.J. | 9 | 14 | 5 | 74 | 208 | 23.11 | — | — | 5 | 1 | 1881 | 749 | 24 | 31.20 | 5-90 | 1 | — |
| Jennings, C.B. | 6 | 8 | 2 | 32 | 107 | 17.83 | — | — | 5 | — | — | — | — | — | — | — | — |
| Johnson, I.W. | 45 | 66 | 12 | 77 | 1000 | 18.51 | — | 6 | 30 | — | 8780 | 3182 | 109 | 29.19 | 7-44 | 3 | — |
| Johnson, L.J. | 1 | 1 | 1 | 25* | 25 | — | — | — | 2 | — | 282 | 74 | 6 | 12.33 | 3-8 | — | — |
| Johnston, W.A. | 40 | 49† | 25 | 29 | 273 | 11.37 | — | — | 16 | — | 11048‡ | 3826 | 160 | 23.91 | 6-44 | 7 | — |
| Jones, D.M. | 2 | 4 | 0 | 48 | 65 | 16.25 | — | — | 1 | — | — | — | — | — | — | — | — |
| Jones, E. | 19 | 26 | 4 | 20 | 126 | 5.04 | — | 1 | 21 | — | 3748 | 1857 | 64 | 29.01 | 7-88 | 3 | 1 |
| Jones, S.P. | 12 | 24 | 4 | 87 | 432 | 21.60 | — | 1 | 12 | — | 262 | 112 | 6 | 18.66 | 4-47 | — | — |
| Joslin, L.R. | 1 | 2† | 0 | 7 | 9 | 4.50 | — | — | — | — | — | — | — | — | — | — | — |
| Kelleway, C. | 26 | 42 | 4 | 147 | 1422 | 37.42 | 3 | 6 | 24 | — | 4363 | 1683 | 52 | 32.36 | 5-33 | 1 | — |
| Kelly, J.J. | 36 | 56 | 17 | 46* | 664 | 17.02 | — | — | 43 | 20 | — | — | — | — | — | — | — |
| Kelly, T.J.D. | 2 | 3 | 0 | 35 | 64 | 21.33 | — | — | 1 | — | — | — | — | — | — | — | — |
| Kendall, T. | 2 | 4† | 1 | 17* | 39 | 13.00 | — | — | 2 | — | 563‡ | 215 | 14 | 15.35 | 7-55 | 1 | — |
| Kent, M.F. | 3 | 6 | 0 | 54 | 171 | 28.50 | — | 2 | 6 | — | — | — | — | — | — | — | — |
| Kippax, A.F. | 22 | 34 | 1 | 146 | 1192 | 36.12 | 2 | 8 | 13 | — | 72 | 19 | 0 | — | — | — | — |
| Kline, L.F. | 13 | 16† | 9 | 15* | 58 | 8.28 | — | — | 9 | — | 2373‡ | 776 | 34 | 22.82 | 7-75 | 1 | — |
| Laird, B.M. | 21 | 40 | 2 | 92 | 1341 | 35.28 | — | 11 | 16 | — | 18 | 12 | 0 | — | — | — | — |
| Langley, G.R.A. | 26 | 37 | 12 | 53 | 374 | 14.96 | — | 1 | 83 | 15 | — | — | — | — | — | — | — |
| Laughlin, T.J. | 3 | 5† | 0 | 35 | 87 | 17.40 | — | — | 3 | — | 516 | 262 | 6 | 43.66 | 5-101 | 1 | — |

INDIVIDUAL CAREER RECORDS—AUSTRALIA *continued*

| | | | | BATTING AND FIELDING | | | | | | | BOWLING | | | | | | |
|---|---|---|---|---|---|---|---|---|---|---|---|---|---|---|---|---|---|
| | Tests | I | NO | HS | Runs | Avge | 100 | 50 | Ct | St | Balls | Runs | Wkts | Avge | BB | 5wI | 10wM |
| Laver, F. | 15 | 23 | 6 | 45 | 196 | 11.52 | – | – | 8 | – | 2361 | 964 | 37 | 26.05 | 8-31 | 2 | – |
| Lawry, W.M. | 67 | 123† | 12 | 210 | 5234 | 47.15 | 13 | 27 | 30 | – | 14‡ | 6 | 0 | – | – | – | – |
| Lawson, G.F. | 34 | 55 | 10 | 57* | 696 | 15.46 | – | 3 | 7 | – | 7776 | 4040 | 140 | 28.85 | 8-112 | 10 | 2 |
| Lee, P.K. | 2 | 3 | 0 | 42 | 57 | 19.00 | – | – | 1 | – | 436 | 212 | 5 | 42.40 | 4-111 | – | – |
| Lillee, D.K. | 70 | 90 | 24 | 73* | 905 | 13.71 | – | 1 | 23 | – | 18467 | 8493 | 355 | 23.92 | 7-83 | 23 | 7 |
| Lindwall, R.R. | 61 | 84 | 13 | 118 | 1502 | 21.15 | 2 | 5 | 26 | – | 13650 | 5251 | 228 | 23.03 | 7-38 | 12 | – |
| Love, H.S.B. | 1 | 2 | 0 | 5 | 8 | 4.00 | – | – | 3 | – | | | | | | | |
| Loxton, S.J.E. | 12 | 15 | 0 | 101 | 554 | 36.93 | 1 | 3 | 7 | – | 906 | 349 | 8 | 43.62 | 3-55 | – | – |
| Lyons, J.J. | 14 | 27 | 0 | 134 | 731 | 27.07 | 1 | 3 | 3 | – | 316 | 149 | 6 | 24.83 | 5-30 | 1 | – |
| McAlister, P.A. | 8 | 16 | 1 | 41 | 252 | 16.80 | – | – | 10 | – | | | | | | | |
| Macartney, C.G. | 35 | 55 | 4 | 170 | 2131 | 41.78 | 7 | 9 | 17 | – | 3561‡ | 1240 | 45 | 27.55 | 7-58 | 2 | 1 |
| McCabe, S.J. | 39 | 62 | 5 | 232 | 2748 | 48.21 | 6 | 13 | 41 | – | 3746 | 1543 | 36 | 42.86 | 4-13 | – | – |
| McCool, C.L. | 14 | 17 | 4 | 104* | 459 | 35.30 | – | 1 | 14 | – | 2504 | 958 | 36 | 26.61 | 5-41 | 3 | – |
| McCormick, E.L. | 12 | 14† | 5 | 17* | 54 | 6.00 | – | – | 8 | – | 2107 | 1079 | 36 | 29.97 | 4-101 | – | – |
| McCosker, R.B. | 25 | 46 | 5 | 127 | 1622 | 39.56 | 4 | 9 | 21 | – | | | | | | | |
| McDermott, C.J. | 8 | 11 | 1 | 35 | 107 | 10.70 | – | – | 3 | – | 1820 | 1174 | 40 | 29.35 | 8-141 | 2 | – |
| McDonald, C.C. | 47 | 83 | 4 | 170 | 3107 | 39.32 | 5 | 17 | 14 | – | 8 | 3 | 0 | – | – | – | – |
| McDonald, E.A. | 11 | 12 | 5 | 36 | 116 | 16.57 | – | – | 3 | – | 2885 | 1431 | 43 | 33.27 | 5-32 | 2 | – |
| McDonnell, P.S. | 19 | 34 | 1 | 147 | 950 | 28.78 | 3 | 2 | 6 | – | 52 | 53 | 0 | – | – | – | – |
| McIlwraith, J. | 1 | 2 | 0 | 7 | 9 | 4.50 | – | – | 1 | – | | | | | | | |
| Mackay, K.D. | 37 | 52† | 7 | 89 | 1507 | 33.48 | – | 13 | 16 | – | 5792 | 1721 | 50 | 34.42 | 6-42 | 2 | – |
| McKenzie, G.D. | 60 | 89 | 12 | 76 | 945 | 12.27 | – | 2 | 34 | – | 17681 | 7328 | 246 | 29.78 | 8-71 | 16 | 3 |
| McKibbin, T.R. | 5 | 8† | 2 | 28 | 88 | 14.66 | – | – | 4 | – | 1032 | 496 | 17 | 29.17 | 3-35 | – | – |
| McLaren, J.W. | 1 | 2 | 2 | 0* | 0 | – | – | – | – | – | 144 | 70 | 1 | 70.00 | 1-23 | – | – |
| Maclean, J.A. | 4 | 8 | 1 | 33* | 79 | 11.28 | – | – | 18 | 1 | | | | | | | |
| McLeod, C.E. | 17 | 29 | 5 | 112 | 573 | 23.87 | 1 | 4 | 9 | – | 3374 | 1325 | 33 | 40.15 | 5-65 | 2 | – |
| McLeod, R.W. | 6 | 11† | 0 | 31 | 146 | 13.27 | – | – | 3 | – | 1089 | 384 | 12 | 32.00 | 5-55 | 1 | – |
| McShane, P.G. | 3 | 6† | 1 | 12* | 26 | 5.20 | – | – | 2 | – | 108‡ | 48 | 1 | 48.00 | 1-39 | – | – |
| Maddocks, L.V. | 7 | 12 | 2 | 69 | 117 | 17.70 | – | 1 | 18 | 1 | | | | | | | |
| Maguire, J.N. | 3 | 5 | 2 | 15* | 28 | 7.00 | – | – | 2 | – | 616 | 324 | 10 | 32.40 | 4-57 | – | – |
| Mailey, A.A. | 21 | 29 | 9 | 46* | 222 | 11.10 | – | – | 14 | – | 6119 | 3358 | 99 | 33.91 | 9-121 | 6 | 2 |
| Mallett, A.A. | 38 | 50 | 13 | 43* | 430 | 11.62 | – | – | 30 | – | 9990 | 3940 | 132 | 29.84 | 8-59 | 6 | 1 |
| Malone, M.F. | 1 | 1 | 0 | 46 | 46 | 46.00 | – | – | – | – | 342 | 77 | 6 | 12.83 | 5-63 | 1 | – |
| Mann, A.L. | 4 | 8† | 0 | 105 | 189 | 23.62 | 1 | – | 2 | – | 552 | 316 | 4 | 79.00 | 3-12 | – | – |
| Marr, A.P. | 1 | 2 | 0 | 5 | 5 | 2.50 | – | – | – | – | 48 | 14 | 0 | – | – | – | – |
| Marsh, R.W. | 96 | 150† | 13 | 132 | 3633 | 26.51 | 3 | 16 | 343 | 12 | 72 | 54 | 0 | – | – | – | – |
| Martin, J.W. | 8 | 13† | 1 | 55 | 214 | 17.83 | – | 1 | 5 | – | 1846‡ | 832 | 17 | 48.94 | 3-56 | – | – |

INDIVIDUAL CAREER RECORDS—AUSTRALIA *continued*

| | Tests | I | NO | HS | Runs | Avge | 100 | 50 | Ct | St | Balls | Runs | Wkts | Avge | BB | 5wI | 10wM |
|---|---|---|---|---|---|---|---|---|---|---|---|---|---|---|---|---|---|
| Massie, H.H. | 9 | 16 | 0 | 55 | 249 | 15.56 | – | 1 | 5 | – | – | – | – | – | – | – | – |
| Massie, R.A.L. | 6 | 8† | 1 | 42 | 78 | 11.14 | – | – | 1 | – | 1739 | 647 | 31 | 20.87 | 8-53 | 2 | 1 |
| Matthews, G.R.J. | 5 | 8† | 1 | 75 | 139 | 19.85 | – | 1 | 1 | – | 601 | 317 | 7 | 45.28 | 2-48 | – | – |
| Matthews, T.J. | 8 | 10 | 1 | 53 | 153 | 17.00 | – | 1 | 7 | – | 1081 | 419 | 16 | 26.18 | 4-29 | – | – |
| Mayne, E.R. | 4 | 4 | 1 | 25* | 64 | 21.33 | – | – | 2 | – | 6 | 1 | 0 | – | – | – | – |
| Mayne, L.C. | 6 | 11† | 3 | 13 | 76 | 9.50 | – | – | 3 | – | 1251 | 628 | 19 | 33.05 | 4-43 | – | – |
| Meckiff, I. | 18 | 20 | 7 | 45 | 154 | 11.84 | – | – | 9 | – | 3734‡ | 1423 | 45 | 31.62 | 6-38 | 2 | – |
| Meuleman, K.D. | 1 | 1 | 0 | 0 | 0 | 0.00 | – | – | 1 | – | – | – | – | – | – | – | – |
| Midwinter, W.E. | 8 | 14 | 1 | 37 | 174 | 13.38 | – | 1 | 5 | – | 949 | 333 | 14 | 23.78 | 5-78 | 1 | 1 |
| Miller, K.R. | 55 | 87 | 7 | 147 | 2958 | 36.97 | 7 | 13 | 38 | – | 10461 | 3906 | 170 | 22.97 | 7-60 | 7 | 1 |
| Minnett, R.B. | 9 | 15 | 0 | 90 | 391 | 26.06 | – | 13 | – | – | 589 | 290 | 11 | 26.36 | 4-34 | – | – |
| Misson, F.M. | 5 | 5 | 3 | 25* | 38 | 19.00 | – | – | 6 | – | 1197 | 616 | 16 | 38.50 | 4-58 | – | – |
| Moroney, J. | 7 | 12 | 1 | 118 | 383 | 34.81 | 2 | 1 | – | – | – | – | – | – | – | – | – |
| Morris, A.R. | 46 | 79† | 3 | 206 | 3533 | 46.48 | 12 | 12 | 15 | – | 111‡ | 50 | 2 | 25.00 | 1-5 | – | – |
| Morris, S. | 1 | 2 | 1 | 10* | 14 | 14.00 | – | – | – | – | 136 | 73 | 2 | 36.50 | 2-73 | – | – |
| Moses, H. | 6 | 10† | 0 | 33 | 198 | 19.80 | – | 1 | 1 | – | – | – | – | – | – | – | – |
| Moss, J.K. | 1 | 2† | 1 | 38* | 60 | 60.00 | – | – | – | – | – | – | – | – | – | – | – |
| Moule, W.H. | 1 | 2 | 0 | 34 | 40 | 20.00 | – | – | 1 | – | 51 | 23 | 3 | 7.66 | 3-23 | – | – |
| Murdoch, W.L. | 18 | 33 | 5 | 211 | 896 | 32.00 | 2 | 1 | 13 | 1 | – | – | – | – | – | – | – |
| Musgrove, H. | 1 | 2 | 0 | 9 | 13 | 6.50 | – | – | – | – | – | – | – | – | – | – | – |
| Nagel, L.E. | 1 | 2 | 1 | 21* | 21 | 21.00 | – | – | – | – | 262 | 110 | 2 | 55.00 | 2-110 | – | – |
| Nash, L.J. | 2 | 2 | 0 | 17 | 30 | 15.00 | – | – | 6 | – | 311 | 126 | 10 | 12.60 | 4-18 | – | – |
| Nitschke, H.C. | 2 | 2† | 0 | 47 | 53 | 26.50 | – | – | 3 | – | – | – | – | – | – | – | – |
| Noble, M.A. | 42 | 73 | 7 | 133 | 1997 | 30.25 | 1 | 16 | 26 | – | 7159 | 3025 | 121 | 25.00 | 7-17 | 9 | 2 |
| Noblet, G. | 3 | 4 | 1 | 13* | 22 | 7.33 | – | – | 1 | – | 774 | 183 | 7 | 26.14 | 3-21 | – | – |
| Nothling, O.E. | 1 | 2 | 0 | 44 | 52 | 26.00 | – | – | 1 | – | 276 | 72 | 0 | – | – | – | – |
| O'Brien, L.P.J. | 5 | 8† | 0 | 61 | 211 | 26.37 | – | 2 | 3 | – | – | – | – | – | – | – | – |
| O'Connor, J.D.A. | 4 | 8† | 1 | 20 | 86 | 12.28 | – | – | 3 | – | 692 | 340 | 13 | 26.15 | 5-40 | 1 | – |
| O'Donnell, S.P. | 5 | 8 | 0 | 48 | 184 | 26.28 | – | – | 3 | – | 874 | 487 | 6 | 81.16 | 3-37 | – | – |
| Ogilvie, A.D. | 5 | 10 | 0 | 47 | 178 | 17.80 | – | – | 5 | – | – | – | – | – | – | – | – |
| O'Keeffe, K.J. | 24 | 34 | 9 | 85 | 644 | 25.76 | – | 1 | 15 | – | 5384 | 2018 | 53 | 38.07 | 5-101 | 1 | – |
| Oldfield, W.A.S. | 54 | 80 | 17 | 65* | 1427 | 22.65 | – | 4 | 78 | 52 | – | – | – | – | – | – | – |
| O'Neill, N.C. | 42 | 69 | 8 | 181 | 2779 | 45.55 | 6 | 15 | 21 | – | 1392 | 667 | 17 | 39.23 | 4-41 | – | – |
| O'Reilly, W.J. | 27 | 39† | 7 | 56* | 410 | 12.81 | – | 1 | 7 | – | 10024 | 3254 | 144 | 22.59 | 7-54 | 11 | 3 |
| Oxenham, R.K. | 7 | 10 | 0 | 48 | 151 | 15.10 | – | – | 4 | – | 1802 | 522 | 14 | 37.28 | 4-39 | – | – |
| Palmer, G.E. | 17 | 25 | 4 | 48 | 296 | 14.09 | – | – | 13 | – | 4517 | 1678 | 78 | 21.51 | 7-65 | 6 | 2 |

INDIVIDUAL CAREER RECORDS—AUSTRALIA *continued*

| | | | | *BATTING AND FIELDING* | | | | | | | *BOWLING* | | | | | | |
|---|---|---|---|---|---|---|---|---|---|---|---|---|---|---|---|---|---|
| | Tests | I | NO | HS | Runs | Avge | 100 | 50 | Ct | St | Balls | Runs | Wkts | Avge | BB | 5wI | 10wM |
| Park, R.L. | 1 | 1 | 0 | 0 | 0 | 0.00 | – | – | – | – | 6 | 9 | 0 | – | – | – | – |
| Pascoe, L.S. | 14 | 19 | 9 | 30* | 106 | 10.60 | – | – | 2 | – | 3403 | 1668 | 64 | 26.06 | 5-59 | 1 | – |
| Pellew, C.E. | 10 | 14 | 1 | 116 | 484 | 37.23 | 2 | 1 | 4 | – | 78 | 34 | 0 | – | – | – | – |
| Phillips, W.B. | 18 | 32† | 2 | 159 | 1106 | 38.86 | 2 | 5 | 35 | – | – | – | – | – | – | – | – |
| Philpott, P.I. | 8 | 10 | 1 | 22 | 93 | 10.33 | – | – | 5 | – | 2262 | 1000 | 26 | 38.46 | 5-90 | 1 | – |
| Ponsford, W.H. | 29 | 48 | 4 | 266 | 2122 | 48.22 | 7 | 6 | 21 | – | – | – | – | – | – | – | – |
| Pope, R.J. | 1 | 2 | 0 | 3 | 3 | 1.50 | – | – | – | – | – | – | – | – | – | – | – |
| Rackemann, C.G. | 5 | 5 | 0 | 12 | 16 | 3.20 | – | – | 2 | – | 936 | 540 | 23 | 23.47 | 6-86 | 3 | 1 |
| Ransford, V.S. | 20 | 39† | 6 | 143* | 1211 | 37.84 | 1 | 7 | 10 | – | 43‡ | 28 | 1 | 28.00 | 1-9 | – | – |
| Redpath, I.R. | 66 | 120 | 11 | 171 | 4737 | 43.45 | 8 | 31 | 83 | – | 64 | 41 | 0 | – | – | – | – |
| Reedman, J.C. | 1 | 2 | 0 | 17 | 21 | 10.50 | – | – | 1 | – | 57 | 24 | 1 | 24.00 | 1-12 | – | – |
| Renneberg, D.A. | 8 | 13 | 7 | 9 | 22 | 3.66 | – | – | 2 | – | 1598 | 830 | 23 | 36.08 | 5-39 | 2 | – |
| Richardson, A.J. | 9 | 13 | 0 | 100 | 403 | 31.00 | 1 | 2 | 1 | – | 1812 | 521 | 12 | 43.41 | 2-20 | – | – |
| Richardson, V.Y. | 19 | 30 | 0 | 138 | 706 | 23.53 | 1 | 1 | 24 | – | – | – | – | – | – | – | – |
| Rigg, K.E. | 8 | 12 | 0 | 127 | 401 | 33.41 | 1 | 4 | 5 | – | – | – | – | – | – | – | – |
| Ring, D.T. | 13 | 21 | 2 | 67 | 426 | 22.42 | – | 4 | 5 | – | 3024 | 1305 | 35 | 37.28 | 6-72 | 2 | – |
| Ritchie, G.M. | 15 | 28 | 2 | 146 | 871 | 33.50 | 2 | 4 | 8 | – | 6 | 10 | 0 | – | – | – | – |
| Rixon, S.J. | 13 | 24 | 3 | 54 | 394 | 18.76 | – | 2 | 42 | 5 | – | – | – | – | – | – | – |
| Robertson, W.R. | 1 | 2 | 0 | 2 | 2 | 1.00 | – | – | – | – | 44 | 24 | 0 | – | – | – | – |
| Robinson, R.D. | 3 | 6 | 0 | 34 | 100 | 16.66 | – | – | 4 | – | – | – | – | – | – | – | – |
| Robinson, R.H. | 1 | 2 | 0 | 3 | 5 | 2.50 | – | – | 1 | – | – | – | – | – | – | – | – |
| Rorke, G.F. | 4 | 4† | 2 | 7 | 9 | 4.50 | – | – | 1 | – | 703 | 203 | 10 | 20.30 | 3-23 | – | – |
| Rutherford, J.W. | 1 | 1 | 0 | 30 | 30 | 30.00 | – | – | – | – | 36 | 15 | 1 | 15.00 | 1-11 | – | – |
| Ryder, J. | 20 | 32 | 5 | 201* | 1394 | 51.62 | 3 | 9 | 17 | – | 1897 | 743 | 17 | 43.70 | 2-20 | – | – |
| Saggers, R.A. | 6 | 5 | 2 | 14 | 30 | 10.00 | – | – | 16 | 8 | – | – | – | – | – | – | – |
| Saunders, J.V. | 14 | 23† | 6 | 11* | 39 | 2.29 | – | – | 5 | – | 3565‡ | 1796 | 79 | 22.73 | 7-34 | 6 | – |
| Scott, H.J.H. | 8 | 14 | 1 | 102 | 359 | 27.61 | 1 | 1 | 8 | – | 28 | 26 | 0 | – | – | – | – |
| Sellers, R.H.D. | 1 | 1 | 0 | 0 | 0 | 0.00 | – | – | 1 | – | 30 | 17 | 0 | – | – | – | – |
| Serjeant, C.S. | 12 | 23 | 1 | 124 | 522 | 23.72 | 1 | 2 | 13 | – | – | – | – | – | – | – | – |
| Sheahan, A.P. | 31 | 53 | 6 | 127 | 1594 | 33.91 | 2 | 7 | 17 | – | – | – | – | – | – | – | – |
| Shepherd, B.K. | 9 | 14† | 2 | 96 | 502 | 41.83 | – | 5 | 2 | – | – | – | – | – | – | – | – |
| Sievers, M.W. | 3 | 6 | 1 | 25* | 67 | 13.40 | – | – | 4 | – | 602 | 161 | 9 | 17.88 | 5-21 | 1 | – |
| Simpson, R.B. | 62 | 111 | 7 | 311 | 4869 | 46.81 | 10 | 27 | 110 | – | 6881 | 3001 | 71 | 42.26 | 5-57 | 2 | – |
| Sincock, D.J. | 3 | 4 | 1 | 29 | 80 | 26.66 | – | – | 2 | – | 724‡ | 410 | 8 | 51.25 | 3-67 | – | – |
| Slater, K.N. | 1 | 1 | 1 | 1* | 1 | – | – | – | – | – | 256 | 101 | 2 | 50.50 | 2-40 | – | – |
| Sleep, P.R. | 4 | 8 | 0 | 64 | 114 | 14.25 | – | 1 | – | – | 589 | 381 | 3 | 127.00 | 1-16 | – | – |
| Slight, J. | 1 | 2 | 0 | 11 | 11 | 5.50 | – | – | – | – | – | – | – | – | – | – | – |

## INDIVIDUAL CAREER RECORDS—AUSTRALIA *continued*

|  | Tests | I | NO | HS | Runs | Avge | 100 | 50 | Ct | St | Balls | Runs | Wkts | Avge | BB | 5wI | 10wM |
|---|---|---|---|---|---|---|---|---|---|---|---|---|---|---|---|---|---|
| Smith, D.B.M. | 2 | 3 | 1 | 24* | 30 | 15.00 | – | – | – | – | – | – | – | – | – | – | – |
| Smith, S.B. | 3 | 5 | 0 | 12 | 41 | 8.20 | – | – | – | – | – | – | – | – | – | – | – |
| Spofforth, F.R. | 18 | 29 | 6 | 50 | 217 | 9.43 | – | – | 11 | – | 4185 | 1731 | 94 | 18.41 | 7-44 | 7 | 4 |
| Stackpole, K.R. | 43 | 80 | 5 | 207 | 2807 | 37.42 | 7 | 14 | 47 | – | 2321 | 1001 | 15 | 66.73 | 2-33 | – | – |
| Stevens, G.B. | 4 | 7 | 0 | 28 | 112 | 16.00 | – | – | 2 | – | – | – | – | – | – | – | – |
| Taber, H.B. | 16 | 27 | 5 | 48 | 353 | 16.04 | – | – | 56 | 4 | – | – | – | – | – | – | – |
| Tallon, D. | 21 | 26 | 3 | 92 | 394 | 17.13 | – | 2 | 50 | 8 | – | – | – | – | – | – | – |
| Taylor, J.M. | 20 | 28 | 0 | 108 | 997 | 35.60 | 1 | 8 | 11 | – | 114 | 45 | 1 | 45.00 | 1-25 | – | – |
| Thompson, N. | 2 | 4 | 0 | 41 | 67 | 16.75 | – | – | 3 | – | 112 | 31 | 1 | 31.00 | 1-14 | – | – |
| Thoms, G.R. | 1 | 2 | 0 | 28 | 44 | 22.00 | – | – | 3 | – | – | – | – | – | – | – | – |
| Thomson, A.L. | 4 | 5 | 4 | 12* | 22 | 22.00 | – | – | – | – | 1519 | 654 | 12 | 54.50 | 3-79 | – | – |
| Thomson, J.R. | 51 | 73 | 20 | 49 | 679 | 12.81 | – | – | 20 | – | 10535 | 5601 | 200 | 28.00 | 6-46 | 8 | – |
| Thurlow, H.M. | 1 | 1 | 0 | 0 | 0 | 0.00 | – | – | – | – | 234 | 86 | 0 | – | – | – | – |
| Toohey, P.M. | 15 | 29 | 1 | 122 | 893 | 31.89 | 1 | 7 | 9 | – | – | 4 | 0 | – | – | – | – |
| Toshack, E.R.H. | 12 | 11 | 6 | 20* | 73 | 14.60 | – | – | 4 | – | 3140‡ | 989 | 47 | 21.04 | 6-29 | 4 | – |
| Travers, J.P.F. | 3 | 2† | 0 | 9 | 10 | 5.00 | – | – | 1 | – | 48‡ | 14 | 1 | 14.00 | 1-14 | – | – |
| Tribe, G.E. | 3 | 3† | 1 | 25* | 35 | 17.50 | – | – | – | – | 760‡ | 330 | 2 | 165.00 | 2-48 | – | – |
| Trott, A.E. | 3 | 5 | 3 | 85* | 205 | 102.50 | – | 2 | 4 | – | 474 | 192 | 9 | 21.33 | 8-43 | 1 | – |
| Trott, G.H.S. | 24 | 42 | 0 | 143 | 921 | 21.92 | 1 | 4 | 21 | – | 1890 | 1019 | 29 | 35.13 | 4-71 | – | – |
| Trumble, H. | 32 | 57 | 14 | 70 | 851 | 19.79 | – | 4 | 45 | – | 8099 | 3072 | 141 | 21.78 | 8-65 | 9 | 3 |
| Trumble, J.W. | 7 | 13 | 1 | 59 | 243 | 20.25 | – | 1 | 3 | – | 600 | 222 | 10 | 22.20 | 3-29 | – | – |
| Trumper, V.T. | 48 | 89 | 8 | 214* | 3163 | 39.04 | 8 | 13 | 31 | – | 546 | 317 | 8 | 39.62 | 3-60 | – | – |
| Turner, A. | 14 | 27† | 1 | 136 | 768 | 29.53 | 1 | 3 | 15 | – | – | – | – | – | – | – | – |
| Turner, C.T.B. | 17 | 32 | 4 | 29 | 323 | 11.53 | – | – | 8 | – | 5179 | 1670 | 101 | 16.53 | 7-43 | 11 | 2 |
| Veivers, T.R. | 21 | 30† | 4 | 88 | 813 | 31.26 | – | 7 | 7 | – | 4191 | 1375 | 33 | 41.66 | 4-68 | – | – |
| Waite, M.G. | 2 | 3 | 0 | 8 | 11 | 3.66 | – | – | 1 | – | 552 | 190 | 1 | 190.00 | 1-150 | – | – |
| Walker, M.H.N. | 34 | 43 | 13 | 78* | 586 | 19.53 | – | 1 | 12 | – | 10094 | 3792 | 138 | 27.47 | 8-143 | 6 | – |
| Wall, T.W. | 18 | 24 | 5 | 20 | 121 | 6.36 | – | – | 11 | – | 4812 | 2010 | 56 | 35.89 | 5-14 | 3 | – |
| Walters, F.H. | 1 | 2 | 0 | 7 | 12 | 6.00 | – | – | 2 | – | – | – | – | – | – | – | – |
| Walters, K.D. | 74 | 125 | 14 | 250 | 5357 | 48.26 | 15 | 33 | 43 | – | 3295 | 1425 | 49 | 29.08 | 5-66 | 1 | – |
| Ward, F.A. | 4 | 8 | 2 | 18 | 36 | 6.00 | – | – | 1 | – | 1268 | 574 | 11 | 52.18 | 6-102 | 1 | – |
| Watkins, J.R. | 1 | 2 | 1 | 36 | 39 | 39.00 | – | – | 1 | – | 48 | 21 | 0 | – | – | – | – |
| Watson, G.D. | 5 | 9 | 0 | 50 | 97 | 10.77 | – | 1 | 2 | – | 552 | 254 | 6 | 42.33 | 2-67 | – | – |
| Watson, W.J. | 4 | 7 | 1 | 30 | 106 | 17.66 | – | – | 2 | – | 6 | 5 | 0 | – | – | – | – |

## INDIVIDUAL CAREER RECORDS—AUSTRALIA *continued*

| | Tests | I | NO | HS | Runs | Avge | 100 | 50 | Ct | St | Balls | Runs | Wkts | Avge | BB | 5wI | 10wM |
|---|---|---|---|---|---|---|---|---|---|---|---|---|---|---|---|---|---|
| | | | | *BATTING AND FIELDING* | | | | | | | | | | *BOWLING* | | | |
| Wellham, D.M. | 5 | 9 | 0 | 103 | 239 | 26.55 | 1 | – | 2 | – | – | 35 | 0 | – | – | – | – |
| Wessels, K.C. | 23 | 40† | 1 | 179 | 1688 | 43.28 | 4 | 8 | 18 | – | 84 | 35 | 0 | – | – | – | – |
| Whatmore, D.F. | 7 | 13 | 0 | 77 | 293 | 22.53 | – | 2 | 13 | – | 30 | 11 | 0 | – | – | – | – |
| Whitney, M.R. | 2 | 4 | 0 | 4 | 4 | 1.00 | – | – | – | – | 468‡ | 246 | 5 | 49.20 | 2-50 | – | – |
| Whitty, W.J. | 14 | 19 | 7 | 39* | 161 | 13.41 | – | – | 4 | – | 3357‡ | 1373 | 65 | 21.12 | 6-17 | 3 | – |
| Wiener, J.M. | 6 | 11 | 0 | 93 | 281 | 25.54 | – | 2 | 4 | – | 78 | 41 | 0 | – | – | – | – |
| Wilson, J.W. | 1 | – | – | – | – | – | – | – | – | – | 216‡ | 64 | 1 | 64.00 | 1-25 | – | – |
| Wood, G.M. | 53 | 101† | 5 | 172 | 3109 | 32.38 | 8 | 13 | 38 | – | – | – | – | – | – | – | – |
| Woodcock, A.J. | 1 | 1 | 0 | 27 | 27 | 27.00 | – | – | 1 | – | – | – | – | – | – | – | – |
| Woodfull, W.M. | 35 | 54 | 4 | 161 | 2300 | 46.00 | 7 | 13 | 7 | – | – | – | – | – | – | – | – |
| Woods, S.M.J. | 3 | 6 | 0 | 18 | 32 | 5.33 | – | – | 1 | – | 217 | 121 | 5 | 24.20 | 2-35 | – | – |
| Woolley, R.D. | 2 | 2 | 0 | 13 | 21 | 10.50 | – | – | 7 | – | – | – | – | – | – | – | – |
| Worrall, J. | 11 | 22 | 3 | 76 | 478 | 25.15 | – | 5 | 13 | – | 255 | 127 | 1 | 127.00 | 1-97 | – | – |
| Wright, K.J. | 10 | 18 | 5 | 55* | 219 | 16.84 | – | 1 | 31 | 4 | – | – | – | – | – | – | – |
| Yallop, G.N. | 39 | 70† | 3 | 268 | 2756 | 41.13 | 8 | 9 | 23 | – | 192‡ | 116 | 1 | 116.00 | 1-21 | – | – |
| Yardley, B. | 33 | 54 | 4 | 74 | 978 | 19.56 | – | 4 | 31 | – | 8909 | 3986 | 126 | 31.63 | 7-98 | 6 | 1 |

### SOUTH AFRICA (235 players)

| | Tests | I | NO | HS | Runs | Avge | 100 | 50 | Ct | St | Balls | Runs | Wkts | Avge | BB | 5wI | 10wM |
|---|---|---|---|---|---|---|---|---|---|---|---|---|---|---|---|---|---|
| | | | | *BATTING AND FIELDING* | | | | | | | | | | *BOWLING* | | | |
| Adcock, N.A.T. | 26 | 39 | 12 | 24 | 146 | 5.40 | – | – | 4 | – | 6391 | 2195 | 104 | 21.10 | 6-43 | 5 | – |
| Anderson, J.H. | 1 | 2 | 0 | 32 | 43 | 21.50 | – | – | 1 | – | – | – | – | – | – | – | – |
| Ashley, W.H. | 1 | 2 | 0 | 1 | 1 | 0.50 | – | – | – | – | 173‡ | 95 | 7 | 13.57 | 7-95 | 1 | – |
| Bacher, A. | 12 | 22 | 1 | 73 | 679 | 32.33 | – | 6 | 10 | – | – | – | – | – | – | – | – |
| Balaskas, X.C. | 9 | 13 | 1 | 122* | 174 | 14.50 | – | – | 5 | – | 1572 | 806 | 22 | 36.63 | 5-49 | 1 | – |
| Barlow, E.J. | 30 | 57 | 2 | 201 | 2516 | 45.74 | 6 | 15 | 35 | – | 3021 | 1362 | 40 | 34.05 | 5-85 | 1 | – |
| Baumgartner, H.V. | 1 | 2 | 0 | 16 | 19 | 9.50 | – | – | 1 | – | 166‡ | 99 | 2 | 49.50 | 2-99 | – | – |
| Beaumont, R. | 5 | 9 | 0 | 31 | 70 | 7.77 | – | – | 2 | – | 6 | 0 | 0 | – | – | – | – |
| Begbie, D.W. | 5 | 7 | 0 | 48 | 138 | 19.71 | – | – | 2 | – | 160 | 130 | 1 | 130.00 | 1-38 | – | – |
| Bell, A.J. | 16 | 23 | 12 | 26* | 69 | 6.27 | – | – | 6 | 1 | 3342 | 1567 | 48 | 32.64 | 6-99 | 4 | – |
| Bisset, M. | 3 | 6 | 2 | 35 | 103 | 25.75 | – | – | 2 | – | – | – | – | – | – | – | – |
| Bissett, G.F. | 4 | 4 | 2 | 23 | 38 | 19.00 | – | – | – | – | 989 | 469 | 25 | 18.76 | 7-29 | 2 | – |
| Blanckenberg, J.M. | 18 | 30 | 7 | 59 | 455 | 19.78 | – | 2 | 9 | – | 3888 | 1817 | 60 | 30.28 | 6-76 | 4 | – |
| Bland, K.C. | 21 | 39 | 5 | 144* | 1669 | 49.08 | 3 | 9 | 10 | – | 394 | 125 | 2 | 62.50 | 2-16 | – | – |
| Bock, E.G. | 1 | 2 | 2 | 9* | 11 | – | – | – | – | – | 138 | 91 | 0 | – | – | – | – |
| Bond, G.E. | 1 | 1 | 0 | 0 | 0 | 0.00 | – | – | – | – | 16 | 16 | 0 | – | – | – | – |
| Botten, J.T. | 3 | 6 | 0 | 33 | 65 | 10.83 | – | – | 1 | – | 828 | 337 | 8 | 42.12 | 2-56 | – | – |

INDIVIDUAL CAREER RECORDS—SOUTH AFRICA *continued*

| | BATTING AND FIELDING | | | | | | | | | | BOWLING | | | | | | |
|---|---|---|---|---|---|---|---|---|---|---|---|---|---|---|---|---|---|
| | Tests | I | NO | HS | Runs | Avge | 100 | 50 | Ct | St | Balls | Runs | Wkts | Avge | BB | 5wI | 10wM |
| Brann, W.H. | 3 | 5 | 0 | 50 | 71 | 14.20 | – | 1 | 2 | – | – | – | – | – | – | – | – |
| Briscoe, A.W. | 5 | 3 | 0 | 16 | 33 | 11.00 | – | – | 1 | – | – | – | – | – | – | – | – |
| Bromfield, H.D. | 9 | 12 | 7 | 21 | 59 | 11.80 | – | – | 13 | – | 1810 | 599 | 17 | 35.23 | 5-88 | 1 | – |
| Brown, L.S. | 2 | 3 | 0 | 8 | 17 | 5.66 | – | – | – | – | 318 | 189 | 3 | 63.00 | 1-30 | – | – |
| Burger, C.G. de V. | 2 | 4 | 1 | 37* | 62 | 20.66 | – | – | 1 | – | – | – | – | – | – | – | – |
| Burke, S.F. | 2 | 4 | 1 | 20 | 42 | 14.00 | – | – | – | – | 660 | 257 | 11 | 23.36 | 6-128 | 2 | 1 |
| Buys, I.D. | 1 | 2 | 1 | 4* | 4 | 4.00 | – | – | – | – | 144 | 52 | 0 | – | – | – | – |
| Cameron, H.B. | 26 | 45 | 4 | 90 | 1239 | 30.21 | – | 10 | 39 | 12 | – | – | – | – | – | – | – |
| Campbell, T. | 5 | 9 | 3 | 48 | 90 | 15.00 | – | – | 7 | 1 | – | – | – | – | – | – | – |
| Carlstein, P.R. | 8 | 14 | 1 | 42 | 190 | 14.61 | – | – | 3 | – | – | – | – | – | – | – | – |
| Carter, C.P. | 10 | 15 | 5 | 45 | 181 | 18.10 | – | – | 2 | – | 1475‡ | 694 | 28 | 24.78 | 6-50 | 2 | – |
| Catterall, R.H. | 24 | 43 | 2 | 120 | 1555 | 37.92 | 3 | 11 | 12 | – | 342 | 162 | 7 | 23.14 | 3-15 | – | – |
| Chapman, H.W. | 2 | 4 | 1 | 17 | 39 | 13.00 | – | – | – | – | 126 | 104 | 1 | 104.00 | 1-51 | – | – |
| Cheetham, J.E. | 24 | 43 | 6 | 89 | 883 | 23.86 | – | 5 | 13 | – | 6 | 2 | 0 | – | – | – | – |
| Chevalier, G.A. | 1 | 2 | 1 | 0* | 0 | 0.00 | – | – | – | – | 253‡ | 100 | 5 | 20.00 | 3-68 | – | – |
| Christy, J.A.J. | 10 | 18 | 0 | 103 | 618 | 34.33 | 1 | 5 | 3 | – | 138 | 92 | 2 | 46.00 | 1-15 | – | – |
| Chubb, G.W.A. | 5 | 9 | 3 | 15* | 63 | 10.50 | – | – | – | – | 1425 | 577 | 21 | 27.47 | 6-51 | 2 | – |
| Cochran, J.A.K. | 1 | 1 | 0 | 4 | 4 | 4.00 | – | – | – | – | 138 | 47 | 0 | – | – | – | – |
| Coen, S.K. | 2 | 4 | 2 | 41* | 101 | 50.50 | – | – | 1 | – | 12 | 7 | 0 | – | – | – | – |
| Commaille, J.M.M. | 12 | 22 | 1 | 47 | 355 | 16.90 | – | – | 1 | – | – | – | – | – | – | – | – |
| Conyngham, D.P. | 1 | 2 | 2 | 3* | 6 | – | – | – | 1 | – | 366 | 103 | 2 | 51.50 | 1-40 | – | – |
| Cook, F.J. | 1 | 2 | 0 | 7 | 7 | 3.50 | – | – | – | – | – | – | – | – | – | – | – |
| Cooper, A.H.C. | 1 | 2 | 0 | 6 | 6 | 3.00 | – | – | 1 | – | – | – | – | – | – | – | – |
| Cox, J.L. | 3 | 6 | 1 | 12* | 17 | 3.40 | – | – | 1 | – | 576 | 245 | 4 | 61.25 | 2-74 | – | – |
| Cripps, G. | 1 | 2 | 0 | 18 | 21 | 10.50 | – | – | – | – | 15 | 23 | 0 | – | – | – | – |
| Crisp, R.J. | 9 | 13 | 1 | 35 | 123 | 10.25 | – | – | 3 | – | 1428 | 747 | 20 | 37.35 | 5-99 | 1 | – |
| Curnow, S.H. | 7 | 14 | 0 | 47 | 168 | 12.00 | – | – | 5 | – | – | – | – | – | – | – | – |
| Dalton, E.L. | 15 | 24 | 2 | 117 | 698 | 31.72 | 2 | 3 | 5 | – | 864 | 490 | 12 | 40.83 | 4-59 | – | – |
| Davies, E.Q. | 5 | 8 | 3 | 3 | 9 | 1.80 | – | – | – | – | 768 | 481 | 7 | 68.71 | 4-75 | – | – |
| Dawson, O.C. | 9 | 15 | 1 | 55 | 293 | 20.92 | – | 1 | 10 | – | 1294 | 578 | 10 | 57.80 | 2-57 | – | – |
| Deane, H.G. | 17 | 27 | 2 | 93 | 628 | 25.12 | – | 3 | 8 | – | – | – | – | – | – | – | – |
| Dixon, C.D. | 1 | 2 | 0 | 0 | 0 | 0.00 | – | – | 1 | – | 240 | 118 | 3 | 39.33 | 2-62 | – | – |
| Dower, R.R. | 1 | 2 | 0 | 9 | 9 | 4.50 | – | – | 2 | – | – | – | – | – | – | – | – |
| Draper, R.G. | 2 | 3 | 0 | 15 | 25 | 8.33 | – | – | – | – | – | – | – | – | – | – | – |
| Duckworth, C.A.R. | 2 | 4 | 0 | 13 | 28 | 7.00 | – | – | 3 | – | – | – | – | – | – | – | – |
| Dumbrill, R. | 5 | 10 | 0 | 36 | 153 | 15.30 | – | – | 3 | – | 816 | 336 | 9 | 37.33 | 4-30 | – | – |
| Duminy, J.P. | 3 | 6† | 0 | 12 | 30 | 5.00 | – | – | 2 | – | 60‡ | 39 | 1 | 39.00 | 1-17 | – | – |

## INDIVIDUAL CAREER RECORDS—SOUTH AFRICA *continued*

| | BATTING AND FIELDING | | | | | | | | | BOWLING | | | | | | |
|---|---|---|---|---|---|---|---|---|---|---|---|---|---|---|---|---|
| | Tests | I | NO | HS | Runs | Avge | 100 | 50 | Ct | St | Balls | Runs | Wkts | Avge | BB | 5wI | 10wM |
| Dunell, O.R. | 2 | 4 | 1 | 26* | 42 | 14.00 | – | – | 1 | – | 144 | 51 | 3 | 17.00 | 2-22 | – | – |
| Du Preez, J.H. | 2 | 2 | 0 | 0 | 0 | 0.00 | – | – | 2 | – | 85 | 47 | 1 | 47.00 | 1-47 | – | – |
| Du Toit, J.F. | 1 | 2 | 2 | 2* | 2 | – | – | – | 1 | – | 66‡ | 46 | 0 | – | – | – | – |
| Dyer, D.V. | 3 | 6 | 0 | 62 | 96 | 16.00 | – | 1 | – | – | – | | | | | | |
| Elgie, M.K. | 3 | 6 | 0 | 56 | 75 | 12.50 | – | 1 | 4 | – | – | | | | | | |
| Endean, W.R. | 28 | 52 | 4 | 162* | 1630 | 33.95 | 3 | 8 | 41 | – | | | | | | | |
| Farrer, W.S. | 6 | 10 | 2 | 40 | 221 | 27.62 | – | – | 2 | – | | | | | | | |
| Faulkner, G.A. | 25 | 47 | 4 | 204 | 1754 | 40.79 | 4 | 8 | 20 | – | 4227 | 2180 | 82 | 26.58 | 7-84 | 4 | – |
| Fellows-Smith, J.P. | 4 | 8 | 2 | 35 | 166 | 27.66 | – | – | 2 | – | 114 | 61 | 0 | – | – | – | – |
| Fichardt, C.G. | 2 | 4 | 0 | 10 | 15 | 3.75 | – | – | 2 | – | | | | | | | |
| Finlason, C.E. | 1 | 2 | 0 | 6 | 6 | 3.00 | – | – | – | – | 12 | 7 | 0 | – | – | – | – |
| Floquet, C.E. | 1 | 2 | 1 | 11* | 12 | 12.00 | – | – | – | – | 48 | 24 | 0 | – | – | – | – |
| Francis, H.H. | 2 | 4 | 0 | 29 | 39 | 9.75 | – | – | 1 | – | | | | | | | |
| Francois, C.M. | 5 | 9 | 1 | 72 | 252 | 31.50 | – | 1 | 5 | – | 684 | 225 | 6 | 37.50 | 3-23 | – | – |
| Frank, C.N. | 3 | 6 | 0 | 152 | 236 | 39.33 | 1 | 1 | – | – | | | | | | | |
| Frank, W.H.B. | 1 | 2 | 0 | 5 | 7 | 3.50 | – | – | – | – | 58 | 52 | 1 | 52.00 | 1-52 | – | – |
| Fuller, E.R.H. | 7 | 9 | 1 | 17 | 64 | 8.00 | – | – | 3 | – | 1898 | 668 | 22 | 30.36 | 5-66 | 1 | – |
| Fullerton, G.M. | 7 | 13 | 0 | 88 | 325 | 25.00 | – | 3 | 10 | 2 | | | | | | | |
| Funston, K.J. | 18 | 33 | 1 | 92 | 824 | 25.75 | – | 5 | 7 | – | | | | | | | |
| Gamsy, D. | 2 | 3 | 1 | 30* | 39 | 19.50 | – | – | 5 | 2 | | | | | | | |
| Gleeson, R.A. | 1 | 2 | 1 | 3 | 4 | 4.00 | – | – | 2 | – | | | | | | | |
| Glover, G.K. | 1 | 2 | 1 | 18* | 21 | 21.00 | – | – | – | – | 65 | 28 | 1 | 28.00 | 1-28 | – | – |
| Goddard, T.L. | 41 | 78† | 5 | 112 | 2516 | 34.46 | 1 | 18 | 48 | – | 11736‡ | 3226 | 123 | 26.22 | 6-53 | 5 | – |
| Gordon, N. | 5 | 6 | 2 | 7* | 8 | 2.00 | – | – | 1 | – | 1966 | 807 | 20 | 40.35 | 5-103 | 2 | – |
| Graham, R. | 2 | 4 | 0 | 4 | 6 | 1.50 | – | – | 2 | – | 240 | 127 | 3 | 42.33 | 2-22 | – | – |
| Grieveson, R.E. | 2 | 2 | 0 | 75 | 114 | 57.00 | – | 1 | 7 | 3 | | | | | | | |
| Griffin, G.M. | 2 | 4 | 0 | 14 | 25 | 6.25 | – | – | – | – | 432 | 192 | 8 | 24.00 | 4-87 | – | – |
| Hall, A.E. | 7 | 8 | 2 | 5 | 11 | 1.83 | – | – | 4 | – | 2361‡ | 886 | 40 | 22.15 | 7-63 | 3 | 1 |
| Hall, G.G. | 1 | 1 | 0 | 0 | 0 | 0.00 | – | – | – | – | 186 | 94 | 1 | 94.00 | 1-94 | – | – |
| Halliwell, E.A. | 8 | 15 | 0 | 57 | 188 | 12.53 | – | 1 | 9 | 2 | | | | | | | |
| Halse, C.G. | 3 | 3 | 3 | 19* | 30 | – | – | – | 1 | – | 587 | 260 | 6 | 43.33 | 3-50 | – | – |
| Hands, P.A.M. | 7 | 12 | 0 | 83 | 300 | 25.00 | – | 2 | 3 | – | 37 | 18 | 0 | – | – | – | – |
| Hands, R.H.M. | 1 | 2 | 0 | 7 | 7 | 3.50 | – | – | – | – | | | | | | | |
| Hanley, M.A. | 1 | 1 | 0 | 0 | 0 | 0.00 | – | – | 1 | – | 232 | 88 | 1 | 88.00 | 1-57 | – | – |
| Harris, T.A. | 3 | 5 | 1 | 60 | 100 | 25.00 | – | 1 | 1 | – | | | | | | | |

## INDIVIDUAL CAREER RECORDS—SOUTH AFRICA *continued*

| | | | | BATTING AND FIELDING | | | | | | | | BOWLING | | | | | |
| --- | --- | --- | --- | --- | --- | --- | --- | --- | --- | --- | --- | --- | --- | --- | --- | --- | --- |
| | Tests | I | NO | HS | Runs | Avge | 100 | 50 | Ct | St | Balls | Runs | Wkts | Avge | BB | 5wI | 10wM |
| Hartigan, G.P.D. | 5 | 10 | 0 | 51 | 114 | 11.40 | – | 1 | – | – | 252 | 141 | 1 | 141.00 | 1-72 | – | – |
| Harvey, R.L. | 2 | 4 | 0 | 28 | 51 | 12.75 | – | – | 5 | – | – | | | | | | |
| Hathorn, C.M.H. | 12 | 20 | 1 | 102 | 325 | 17.10 | 1 | – | 2 | – | – | | | | | | |
| Hearne, F. | 4 | 8 | 0 | 30 | 121 | 15.12 | – | – | 3 | – | 62 | 40 | 2 | 20.00 | 2-40 | – | – |
| Hearne, G.A.L. | 3 | 5 | 0 | 28 | 59 | 11.80 | – | – | 8 | – | | | | | | | |
| Heine, P.S. | 14 | 24 | 3 | 31 | 209 | 9.95 | – | – | – | – | 3890 | 1455 | 58 | 25.08 | 6-58 | 4 | – |
| Hime, C.F.W. | 1 | 2 | 0 | 8 | 8 | 4.00 | – | – | – | – | 55 | 31 | 1 | 31.00 | 1-20 | – | – |
| Hutchinson, P. | 2 | 4 | 0 | 11 | 14 | 3.50 | – | – | 3 | – | – | | | | | | |
| Ironside, D.E.J. | 3 | 4 | 2 | 13 | 37 | 18.50 | – | – | 1 | – | 985 | 275 | 15 | 18.33 | 5-51 | 1 | – |
| Irvine, B.L. | 4 | 7† | 0 | 102 | 353 | 50.42 | 1 | 2 | 2 | – | – | | | | | | |
| Johnson, C.L. | 1 | 2 | 0 | 7 | 10 | 5.00 | – | – | 1 | – | 140 | 57 | 0 | – | – | – | – |
| Keith, H.J. | 8 | 16† | 1 | 73 | 318 | 21.20 | – | 2 | 9 | – | 108‡ | 63 | 0 | – | – | – | – |
| Kempis, G.A. | 1 | 2 | 1 | 0* | 0 | 0.00 | – | – | – | – | 168‡ | 76 | 4 | 19.00 | 3-53 | – | – |
| Kotze, J.J. | 3 | 5 | 0 | 2 | 2 | 0.40 | – | – | 3 | – | 413 | 243 | 6 | 40.50 | 3-64 | – | – |
| Kuys, F. | 1 | 2 | 0 | 26 | 26 | 13.00 | – | – | – | – | 60 | 31 | 2 | 15.50 | 2-31 | – | – |
| Lance, H.R. | 13 | 22 | 1 | 70 | 591 | 28.14 | – | 5 | 7 | – | 948 | 479 | 12 | 39.91 | 3-30 | – | – |
| Langton, A.B.C. | 15 | 23 | 4 | 73* | 298 | 15.68 | – | 2 | 8 | – | 4199 | 1827 | 40 | 45.67 | 5-58 | 1 | – |
| Lawrence, G.B. | 5 | 8 | 0 | 43 | 141 | 17.62 | – | – | 2 | – | 1334 | 512 | 28 | 18.28 | 8-53 | 2 | – |
| Le Roux, F.L. | 1 | 2 | 0 | 1 | 1 | 0.50 | – | – | – | – | 54 | 24 | 0 | – | | | |
| Lewis, P.T. | 1 | 2 | 0 | 0 | 0 | 0.00 | – | – | – | – | | | | | | | |
| Lindsay, D.T. | 19 | 31 | 1 | 182 | 1130 | 37.66 | 3 | 5 | 57 | 2 | – | | | | | | |
| Lindsay, J.D. | 3 | 5 | 2 | 9* | 21 | 7.00 | – | – | 4 | 1 | – | | | | | | |
| Lindsay, N.V. | 1 | 2 | 0 | 29 | 35 | 17.50 | – | – | 1 | – | – | | | | | | |
| Ling, W.V.S. | 6 | 10 | 0 | 38 | 168 | 16.80 | – | – | 1 | – | 18 | 20 | 0 | – | – | – | – |
| Llewellyn, C.B. | 15 | 28† | 1 | 90 | 544 | 20.14 | – | 4 | 7 | – | 2292‡ | 1421 | 48 | 29.60 | 6-92 | 4 | 1 |
| Lundie, E.B. | 1 | 2 | 1 | 1 | 1 | 1.00 | – | – | – | – | 286 | 107 | 4 | 26.75 | 4-101 | – | – |
| Macaulay, M.J. | 1 | 2 | 0 | 21 | 33 | 16.50 | – | – | – | – | 276‡ | 73 | 2 | 36.50 | 1-10 | – | – |
| McCarthy, C.N. | 15 | 24 | 15 | 5 | 28 | 3.11 | – | – | 6 | – | 3499 | 1510 | 36 | 41.94 | 6-43 | 2 | – |
| McGlew, D.J. | 34 | 64 | 6 | 255* | 2440 | 42.06 | 7 | 10 | 18 | – | 32 | 23 | 0 | – | | | |
| McKinnon, A.H. | 8 | 13 | 7 | 27 | 107 | 17.83 | – | – | 1 | – | 2546‡ | 925 | 26 | 35.57 | 4-128 | – | – |
| McLean, R.A. | 40 | 73 | 3 | 142 | 2120 | 30.28 | 5 | 10 | 23 | – | 4 | 1 | 0 | – | | | |
| McMillan, Q. | 13 | 21 | 4 | 50* | 306 | 18.00 | – | 1 | 8 | – | 2021 | 1243 | 36 | 34.52 | 5-66 | 2 | – |
| Mann, N.B.F. | 19 | 31 | 1 | 52 | 400 | 13.33 | – | 1 | 3 | – | 5796‡ | 1920 | 58 | 33.10 | 6-59 | 1 | – |
| Mansell, P.N.F. | 13 | 22 | 2 | 90 | 355 | 17.75 | – | 2 | 15 | – | 1506 | 736 | 11 | 66.90 | 3-58 | – | – |
| Markham, L.A. | 1 | 1 | 0 | 20 | 20 | 20.00 | – | – | – | – | 104 | 72 | 1 | 72.00 | 1-34 | – | – |

## INDIVIDUAL CAREER RECORDS—SOUTH AFRICA continued

| | Tests | I | NO | HS | Runs | Avge | 100 | 50 | Ct | St | Balls | Runs | Wkts | Avge | BB | 5wI | 10wM |
|---|---|---|---|---|---|---|---|---|---|---|---|---|---|---|---|---|---|
| | | | | | BATTING AND FIELDING | | | | | | | BOWLING | | | | | |
| Marx, W.F.E. | 3 | 6† | 0 | 36 | 125 | 20.83 | – | – | – | – | 228‡ | 144 | 4 | 36.00 | 3-85 | – | – |
| Meintjes, D.J. | 2 | 3 | 0 | 21 | 43 | 14.33 | – | – | 3 | – | 246 | 115 | 6 | 19.16 | 3-38 | 2 | – |
| Melle, M.G. | 7 | 12 | 4 | 17 | 68 | 8.50 | – | – | 4 | – | 1667 | 851 | 26 | 32.73 | 6-71 | 2 | – |
| Melville, A. | 11 | 19 | 2 | 189 | 894 | 52.58 | 4 | 3 | 8 | – | | | | | | | |
| Middleton, J. | 6 | 12 | 5 | 22 | 52 | 7.42 | – | – | 1 | – | 1064‡ | 442 | 24 | 18.41 | 5-51 | 2 | – |
| Mills, C. | 1 | 2 | 0 | 21 | 25 | 12.50 | – | – | 2 | – | 140 | 83 | 2 | 41.50 | 2-83 | – | – |
| Milton, W.H. | 3 | 6 | 0 | 21 | 68 | 11.33 | – | – | 1 | – | 79 | 48 | 2 | 24.00 | 1-5 | – | – |
| Mitchell, B. | 42 | 80 | 9 | 189* | 3471 | 48.88 | 8 | 21 | 56 | – | 2519 | 1380 | 27 | 51.11 | 5-87 | 1 | – |
| Mitchell, F. | 3 | 6 | 0 | 12 | 28 | 4.66 | – | – | – | – | | | | | | | |
| Morkel, D.P.B. | 16 | 28 | 1 | 88 | 663 | 24.55 | – | 4 | 13 | – | 1704 | 821 | 18 | 45.61 | 4-93 | – | – |
| Murray, A.R.A. | 10 | 14 | 1 | 109 | 289 | 22.23 | 1 | 1 | 3 | – | 2374 | 710 | 18 | 39.44 | 4-169 | – | – |
| Nel, J.D. | 6 | 11 | 0 | 38 | 150 | 13.63 | – | – | 1 | – | | | | | | | |
| Newberry, C. | 4 | 8 | 0 | 16 | 62 | 7.75 | – | – | 3 | – | 558 | 268 | 11 | 24.36 | 4-72 | – | – |
| Newson, E.S. | 3 | 5 | 1 | 16 | 30 | 7.50 | – | – | 3 | – | 874 | 265 | 4 | 66.25 | 2-58 | – | – |
| Nicholson, F. | 4 | 8 | 0 | 29 | 76 | 10.85 | – | – | 3 | – | | | | | | | |
| Nicolson, J.F.W. | 3 | 5† | 0 | 78 | 179 | 35.80 | – | 1 | – | – | 24 | 17 | 0 | – | – | – | – |
| Norton, N.O. | 1 | 2 | 0 | 7 | 9 | 4.50 | – | – | 1 | – | 90 | 47 | 4 | 11.75 | 4-47 | – | – |
| Nourse, A.D. | 34 | 62 | 7 | 231 | 2960 | 53.81 | 9 | 14 | 12 | – | 20 | 9 | 0 | – | – | – | – |
| Nourse, A.W. | 45 | 83† | 8 | 111 | 2234 | 29.78 | 1 | 15 | 43 | – | 3234 | 1553 | 41 | 37.87 | 4-25 | – | – |
| Nupen, E.P. | 17 | 31 | 7 | 69 | 348 | 14.50 | – | 2 | 9 | – | 4159 | 1788 | 50 | 35.76 | 6-46 | 5 | 1 |
| Ochse, A.E. | 2 | 4 | 1 | 8 | 16 | 4.00 | – | – | 1 | – | | | | | | | |
| Ochse, A.L. | 3 | 4 | 1 | 4* | 11 | 3.66 | – | – | 1 | – | 649 | 362 | 10 | 36.20 | 4-79 | – | – |
| O'Linn, S. | 7 | 12† | 1 | 98 | 297 | 27.00 | – | 2 | 4 | – | | | | | | | |
| Owen-Smith, H.G. | 5 | 8 | 2 | 129 | 252 | 42.00 | 1 | 1 | 4 | – | 156 | 113 | 0 | – | – | – | – |
| Palm, A.W. | 1 | 2 | 0 | 13 | 15 | 7.50 | – | – | 1 | – | | | | | | | |
| Parker, G.M. | 2 | 4 | 3 | 2* | 3 | 1.50 | – | – | – | – | 366 | 273 | 8 | 34.12 | 6-152 | 1 | – |
| Parkin, D.C. | 1 | 2 | 0 | 6 | 6 | 3.00 | – | – | 1 | – | 130 | 82 | 3 | 27.33 | 3-82 | – | – |
| Partridge, J.T. | 11 | 12 | 5 | 13* | 73 | 10.42 | – | – | 6 | – | 3684 | 1373 | 44 | 31.20 | 7-91 | 3 | – |
| Pearse, C.O.C. | 3 | 6 | 0 | 31 | 55 | 9.16 | – | – | 1 | – | 144 | 106 | 3 | 35.33 | 3-56 | – | – |
| Pegler, S.J. | 16 | 28 | 5 | 35* | 356 | 15.47 | – | 4 | 5 | – | 2989 | 1572 | 47 | 33.44 | 7-65 | 2 | – |
| Pithey, A.J. | 17 | 27 | 1 | 154 | 819 | 31.50 | 1 | 4 | 5 | – | 12 | 5 | 0 | – | – | – | – |
| Pithey, D.B. | 8 | 12 | 1 | 55 | 138 | 12.54 | – | 1 | 6 | – | 1424 | 577 | 12 | 48.08 | 6-58 | 1 | – |
| Plimsoll, J.B. | 1 | 2 | 1 | 8* | 16 | 16.00 | – | – | – | – | 237‡ | 143 | 3 | 47.66 | 3-128 | – | – |
| Pollock, P.M. | 28 | 41 | 13 | 75* | 607 | 21.67 | – | 2 | 9 | – | 6522 | 2806 | 116 | 24.18 | 6-38 | 9 | 1 |
| Pollock, R.G. | 23 | 41† | 4 | 274 | 2256 | 60.97 | 7 | 11 | 17 | – | 414 | 204 | 4 | 51.00 | 2-50 | – | – |
| Poore, R.M. | 3 | 6 | 0 | 20 | 76 | 12.66 | – | – | 3 | – | 9 | 4 | 1 | 4.00 | 1-4 | – | – |

## INDIVIDUAL CAREER RECORDS—SOUTH AFRICA *continued*

| | Tests | I | NO | HS | Runs | Avge | 100 | 50 | Ct | St | Balls | Runs | Wkts | Avge | BB | 5wI | 10wM |
|---|---|---|---|---|---|---|---|---|---|---|---|---|---|---|---|---|---|
| Pothecary, J.E. | 3 | 4 | 0 | 12 | 26 | 6.50 | — | — | 2 | — | 828 | 354 | 9 | 39.33 | 4-58 | — | — |
| Powell, A.W. | 1 | 2 | 0 | 11 | 16 | 8.00 | — | — | 2 | — | 20 | 10 | 1 | 10.00 | 1-10 | — | — |
| Prince, C.F.H. | 1 | 2 | 0 | 5 | 6 | 3.00 | — | — | — | — | | | | | | 1 | — |
| Procter, M.J. | 7 | 10 | 1 | 48 | 226 | 25.11 | — | — | 4 | — | 1514 | 616 | 41 | 15.02 | 6-73 | 1 | — |
| Promnitz, H.L.E. | 2 | 4 | 0 | 5 | 14 | 3.50 | — | — | 2 | — | 528 | 161 | 8 | 20.12 | 5-58 | 1 | — |
| Quinn, N.A. | 12 | 18 | 3 | 28 | 90 | 6.00 | — | — | 1 | — | 2922‡ | 1145 | 35 | 32.71 | 6-92 | 1 | — |
| Reid, N. | 1 | 2 | 0 | 11 | 17 | 8.50 | — | — | — | — | 126 | 63 | 2 | 31.50 | 2-63 | — | — |
| Richards, A.R. | 1 | 2 | 0 | 6 | 6 | 3.00 | — | — | — | — | | | | | | — | — |
| Richards, B.A. | 4 | 7 | 0 | 140 | 508 | 72.57 | 2 | 2 | 3 | — | 72 | 26 | 1 | 26.00 | 1-12 | — | — |
| Richards, W.H.M. | 1 | 2 | 0 | 4 | 4 | 2.00 | — | — | — | — | | | | | | — | — |
| Robertson, J.B. | 3 | 6 | 1 | 17 | 51 | 10.20 | — | — | 2 | — | 738 | 321 | 6 | 53.50 | 3-143 | — | — |
| Rose-Innes, A. | 2 | 4 | 0 | 13 | 14 | 3.50 | — | — | 2 | — | 128† | 89 | 5 | 17.80 | 5-43 | 1 | — |
| Routledge, T.W. | 4 | 8 | 0 | 24 | 72 | 9.00 | — | — | 2 | — | | | | | | — | — |
| Rowan, A.M.B. | 15 | 23 | 6 | 41 | 290 | 17.05 | — | — | 7 | — | 5193 | 2084 | 54 | 38.59 | 5-68 | 4 | — |
| Rowan, E.A.B. | 26 | 50 | 5 | 236 | 1965 | 43.66 | 3 | 12 | 14 | — | 19 | 7 | 0 | — | — | — | — |
| Rowe, G.A. | 5 | 9 | 3 | 13* | 26 | 4.33 | — | — | 4 | — | 998‡ | 456 | 15 | 30.40 | 5-115 | 1 | — |
| Samuelson, S.V. | 1 | 2 | 0 | 15 | 22 | 11.00 | — | — | 1 | — | 108 | 64 | 0 | — | — | — | — |
| Schwarz, R.O. | 20 | 35 | 8 | 61 | 374 | 13.85 | — | 1 | 18 | — | 2639 | 1417 | 55 | 25.76 | 6-47 | 2 | — |
| Seccull, A.W. | 1 | 2 | 1 | 17* | 23 | 23.00 | — | — | 1 | — | 60 | 37 | 2 | 18.50 | 2-37 | — | — |
| Seymour, M.A. | 7 | 10 | 3 | 36 | 84 | 12.00 | — | — | 2 | — | 1458 | 588 | 9 | 65.33 | 3-80 | — | — |
| Shalders, W.A. | 12 | 23 | 1 | 42 | 355 | 16.13 | — | — | 3 | — | 48 | 6 | 1 | 6.00 | 1-6 | — | — |
| Shepstone, G.H. | 2 | 4 | 1 | 21 | 38 | 9.50 | — | — | 2 | — | 115 | 47 | 0 | — | — | — | — |
| Sherwell, P.W. | 13 | 22 | 4 | 115 | 427 | 23.72 | 1 | 1 | 20 | 16 | | | | | | — | — |
| Siedle, I.J. | 18 | 34 | 0 | 141 | 977 | 28.73 | 1 | 5 | 7 | — | 19 | 7 | 1 | 7.00 | 1-7 | — | — |
| Sinclair, J.H. | 25 | 47 | 1 | 106 | 1069 | 23.23 | 3 | 3 | 9 | — | 3598 | 1996 | 63 | 31.68 | 6-26 | 1 | — |
| Smith, C.J.E. | 3 | 6 | 1 | 45 | 106 | 21.20 | — | — | 2 | — | | | | | | — | — |
| Smith, F.W. | 3 | 6 | 1 | 12 | 45 | 9.00 | — | — | 2 | — | | | | | | — | — |
| Smith, V.I. | 9 | 16 | 6 | 11* | 39 | 3.90 | — | — | 3 | — | 1655 | 769 | 12 | 64.08 | 4-143 | — | — |
| Snooke, S.D. | 1 | 1 | 0 | 0 | 0 | 0.00 | — | — | 2 | — | | | | | | — | — |
| Snooke, S.J. | 26 | 46 | 1 | 103 | 1008 | 22.40 | 1 | 5 | 24 | — | 1620 | 702 | 35 | 20.05 | 8-70 | 1 | 1 |
| Solomon, W.R.T. | 1 | 2 | 1 | 2 | 4 | 2.00 | — | — | 1 | — | | | | | | — | — |
| Stewart, R.B. | 1 | 2 | 0 | 9 | 13 | 6.50 | — | — | 2 | — | | | | | | — | — |
| Stricker, L.A. | 13 | 24 | 0 | 48 | 342 | 14.25 | — | — | 3 | — | 174 | 105 | 1 | 105.00 | 1-36 | — | — |
| Susskind, M.J. | 5 | 8 | 0 | 65 | 268 | 33.50 | — | 4 | 1 | — | | | | | | — | — |
| Taberer, H.M. | 1 | 1 | 0 | 2 | 2 | 2.00 | — | — | — | — | 60 | 48 | 1 | 48.00 | 1-25 | — | — |

## INDIVIDUAL CAREER RECORDS—SOUTH AFRICA continued

| | Tests | I | NO | HS | Runs | Avge | 100 | 50 | Ct | St | Balls | Runs | Wkts | Avge | BB | 5wI | 10wM |
|---|---|---|---|---|---|---|---|---|---|---|---|---|---|---|---|---|---|
| | | | | | | *BATTING AND FIELDING* | | | | | | | | *BOWLING* | | | |
| Tancred, A.B. | 2 | 4 | 1 | 29 | 87 | 29.00 | – | – | 2 | – | – | – | – | – | – | – | – |
| Tancred, L.J. | 14 | 26 | 1 | 97 | 530 | 21.20 | – | 2 | 3 | – | – | – | – | – | – | – | – |
| Tancred, V.M. | 1 | 2 | 0 | 18 | 25 | 12.50 | – | – | 1 | – | – | – | – | – | – | – | – |
| Tapscott, G.L. | 1 | 2 | 0 | 4 | 5 | 2.50 | – | – | – | – | – | – | – | – | – | – | – |
| Tapscott, L.E. | 2 | 3 | 1 | 50* | 58 | 29.00 | – | 1 | 1 | – | 12 | 2 | 0 | – | – | – | – |
| Tayfield, H.J. | 37 | 60 | 9 | 75 | 862 | 16.90 | – | 2 | 26 | – | 13568 | 4405 | 170 | 25.91 | 9-113 | 14 | 2 |
| Taylor, A.I. | 1 | 2 | 0 | 12 | 18 | 9.00 | – | – | – | – | – | – | – | – | – | – | – |
| Taylor, D. | 2 | 4 | 0 | 36 | 85 | 21.25 | – | – | – | – | – | – | – | – | – | – | – |
| Taylor, H.W. | 42 | 76 | 4 | 176 | 2936 | 40.77 | 7 | 17 | 19 | – | 342 | 156 | 5 | 31.20 | 3-15 | – | – |
| Theunissen, N.H. | 1 | 2 | 1 | 2* | 2 | 2.00 | – | – | 1 | – | 80 | 51 | 0 | – | – | – | – |
| Thornton, P.G. | 1 | 1† | 1 | 1* | 1 | – | – | – | 1 | – | 24‡ | 20 | 1 | 20.00 | 1-20 | – | – |
| Tomlinson, D.S. | 1 | 1 | 0 | 9 | 9 | 9.00 | – | – | – | – | 60 | 38 | 0 | – | – | – | – |
| Traicos, A.J. | 3 | 4 | 2 | 5* | 8 | 4.00 | – | – | 4 | – | 470 | 207 | 4 | 51.75 | 2-70 | – | – |
| Trimborn, P.H.J. | 4 | 4 | 2 | 11* | 13 | 6.50 | – | – | 7 | – | 747 | 257 | 11 | 23.36 | 3-12 | – | – |
| Tuckett, L. | 9 | 14 | 3 | 40* | 131 | 11.90 | – | – | 9 | – | 2104 | 980 | 19 | 51.57 | 5-68 | 2 | – |
| Tuckett, L.R. | 1 | 2 | 1 | 0* | 0 | 0.00 | – | – | 2 | – | 120 | 69 | 0 | – | – | – | – |
| Twentyman-Jones, P.S. | 1 | 2 | 0 | 0 | 0 | 0.00 | – | – | – | – | – | – | – | – | – | – | – |
| Van der Bijl, P.G.V. | 5 | 9 | 0 | 125 | 460 | 51.11 | 1 | 2 | 1 | – | – | – | – | – | – | – | – |
| Van der Merwe, E.A. | 2 | 4 | 1 | 19 | 27 | 9.00 | – | – | 3 | 1 | – | – | – | – | – | – | – |
| Van der Merwe, P.L. | 15 | 23 | 2 | 76 | 533 | 25.38 | – | 3 | 11 | 2 | 79‡ | 22 | 1 | 22.00 | 1-6 | – | – |
| Van Ryneveld, C.B. | 19 | 33 | 2 | 83 | 724 | 26.81 | – | 3 | 14 | 17 | 1554 | 671 | 17 | 39.47 | 4-67 | – | – |
| Varnals, G.D. | 3 | 6 | 0 | 23 | 97 | 16.16 | – | – | – | – | 12 | 2 | 0 | – | – | – | – |
| Viljoen, K.G. | 27 | 50 | 2 | 124 | 1365 | 28.43 | 2 | 9 | 5 | – | 48 | 23 | 0 | – | – | – | – |
| Vincent, C.L. | 25 | 38 | 12 | 60 | 526 | 20.23 | – | 2 | 27 | – | 5851‡ | 2631 | 84 | 31.32 | 6-51 | 3 | – |
| Vincent, C.H. | 3 | 6† | 0 | 9 | 26 | 4.33 | – | – | 1 | – | 369‡ | 193 | 4 | 48.25 | 3-88 | – | – |
| Vogler, A.E.E. | 15 | 26 | 6 | 65 | 340 | 17.00 | – | 2 | 20 | – | 2764 | 1455 | 64 | 22.73 | 7-94 | 5 | 1 |
| Wade, H.F. | 10 | 18 | 2 | 40* | 327 | 20.43 | – | – | 4 | – | – | – | – | – | – | – | – |
| Wade, W.W. | 11 | 19 | 1 | 125 | 511 | 28.38 | 1 | 3 | 15 | 2 | – | – | – | – | – | – | – |
| Waite, J.H.B. | 50 | 86 | 7 | 134 | 2405 | 30.44 | 4 | 16 | 124 | 17 | – | – | – | – | – | – | – |
| Walter, K.A. | 2 | 3 | 0 | 10 | 11 | 3.66 | – | – | 3 | – | 495 | 197 | 6 | 32.83 | 4-63 | – | – |
| Ward, T.A. | 23 | 42 | 9 | 64 | 459 | 13.90 | – | 2 | 19 | 13 | – | – | – | – | – | – | – |
| Watkins, J.C. | 15 | 27 | 1 | 92 | 612 | 23.53 | – | 3 | 12 | – | 2805 | 816 | 29 | 28.13 | 4-22 | – | – |
| Wesley, C. | 3 | 5† | 0 | 35 | 49 | 9.80 | – | – | 1 | – | – | – | – | – | – | – | – |
| Westcott, R.J. | 5 | 9 | 0 | 62 | 166 | 18.44 | – | 1 | – | – | 32 | 22 | 0 | – | – | – | – |
| White, G.C. | 17 | 31 | 2 | 147 | 872 | 30.06 | 2 | 4 | 10 | – | 498 | 301 | 9 | 33.44 | 4-47 | – | – |
| Willoughby, J.T. | 2 | 4 | 0 | 5 | 8 | 2.00 | – | – | – | – | 275 | 159 | 6 | 26.50 | 2-37 | – | – |

INDIVIDUAL CAREER RECORDS—SOUTH AFRICA *continued*

| | Tests | I | NO | HS | Runs | Avge | 100 | 50 | Ct | St | Balls | Runs | Wkts | Avge | BB | 5wI | 10wM |
|---|---|---|---|---|---|---|---|---|---|---|---|---|---|---|---|---|---|
| Wimble, C.S. | 1 | 2 | 0 | 0 | 0 | 0.00 | – | – | – | – | – | – | – | – | – | – | – |
| Winslow, P.L. | 5 | 9 | 0 | 108 | 186 | 20.66 | 1 | – | 1 | – | – | – | – | – | – | – | – |
| Wynne, O.E. | 6 | 12 | 0 | 50 | 219 | 18.25 | – | 1 | 3 | – | – | – | – | – | – | – | – |
| Zulch, J.W. | 16 | 32 | 2 | 150 | 985 | 32.83 | 2 | 4 | 4 | – | 24 | 28 | 0 | – | – | – | – |

**WEST INDIES (184 players)**

| | Tests | I | NO | HS | Runs | Avge | 100 | 50 | Ct | St | Balls | Runs | Wkts | Avge | BB | 5wI | 10wM |
|---|---|---|---|---|---|---|---|---|---|---|---|---|---|---|---|---|---|
| Achong, E.E. | 6 | 11† | 1 | 22 | 81 | 8.10 | – | – | 6 | – | 918‡ | 378 | 8 | 47.25 | 2-64 | – | – |
| Alexander, F.C.M. | 25 | 38 | 6 | 108 | 961 | 30.03 | 1 | 7 | 85 | 5 | – | – | – | – | – | – | – |
| Ali, Imtiaz | 1 | 1 | 1 | 1* | – | – | – | – | – | – | 204 | 89 | 2 | 44.50 | 2-37 | – | – |
| Ali, Inshan | 12 | 18† | 2 | 25 | 172 | 10.75 | – | – | 7 | – | 3718‡ | 1621 | 34 | 47.67 | 5-59 | 1 | – |
| Allan, D.W. | 5 | 7 | 1 | 40* | 75 | 12.50 | – | – | 15 | 3 | – | – | – | – | – | – | – |
| Asgarali, N.R. | 2 | 4 | 0 | 29 | 62 | 15.50 | – | – | – | – | – | – | – | – | – | – | – |
| Atkinson, D.St E. | 22 | 35 | 6 | 219 | 922 | 31.79 | 1 | 5 | 11 | – | 5201 | 1647 | 47 | 35.04 | 7-53 | 3 | – |
| Atkinson, E.St E. | 8 | 9 | 1 | 37 | 126 | 15.75 | – | – | 2 | – | 1634 | 589 | 25 | 23.56 | 5-42 | 1 | – |
| Austin, R.A. | 2 | 2 | 0 | 20 | 22 | 11.00 | – | – | 2 | – | 6 | 5 | 0 | – | – | – | – |
| Bacchus, S.F.A.F. | 19 | 30 | 0 | 250 | 782 | 26.06 | 1 | 3 | 17 | – | 6 | 3 | 0 | – | – | – | – |
| Baichan, L. | 3 | 6† | 2 | 105* | 184 | 46.00 | 1 | 1 | 2 | – | – | – | – | – | – | – | – |
| Baptiste, E.A.E. | 9 | 10 | 1 | 7* | 224 | 24.88 | – | 1 | 2 | – | 1224 | 486 | 15 | 32.40 | 3-31 | – | – |
| Barrett, A.G. | 6 | 7 | 1 | 19 | 40 | 6.66 | – | – | – | – | 1612 | 603 | 13 | 46.38 | 3-43 | – | – |
| Barrow, I. | 11 | 19 | 2 | 105 | 276 | 16.23 | 1 | 1 | 17 | 5 | – | – | – | – | – | – | – |
| Bartlett, E.L. | 5 | 8 | 1 | 84 | 131 | 18.71 | – | – | 2 | – | – | – | – | – | – | – | – |
| Betancourt, N. | 1 | 2 | 0 | 39 | 52 | 26.00 | – | – | – | 3 | – | – | – | – | – | – | – |
| Binns, A.P. | 5 | 8 | 1 | 27 | 64 | 9.14 | – | – | 14 | 3 | – | – | – | – | – | – | – |
| Birkett, L.S. | 4 | 8 | 0 | 64 | 136 | 17.00 | – | 1 | 4 | – | 126 | 71 | 1 | 71.00 | 1-16 | – | – |
| Boyce, K.D. | 21 | 30 | 3 | 95* | 657 | 24.33 | – | 4 | 5 | – | 3501 | 1801 | 60 | 30.01 | 6-77 | 2 | 1 |
| Browne, C.R. | 4 | 8 | 1 | 70* | 176 | 25.14 | – | 1 | 1 | – | 840 | 288 | 6 | 48.00 | 2-72 | – | – |
| Butcher, B.F. | 44 | 78 | 6 | 209* | 3104 | 43.11 | 7 | 16 | 15 | – | 256 | 90 | 5 | 18.00 | 5-34 | 1 | – |
| Butler, L.S. | 1 | 1 | 0 | 16 | 16 | 16.00 | – | – | – | – | 240 | 151 | 2 | 75.50 | 2-151 | – | – |
| Butts, C.G. | 1 | 1 | 0 | 9 | 9 | 9.00 | – | – | – | – | 282 | 113 | 0 | – | – | – | – |
| Bynoe, M.R. | 4 | 6 | 0 | 48 | 111 | 18.50 | – | – | 4 | – | 30‡ | 5 | 1 | 5.00 | 1-5 | – | – |
| Camacho, G.S. | 11 | 22 | 0 | 87 | 640 | 29.09 | – | 4 | 4 | – | 18 | 12 | 0 | – | – | – | – |
| Cameron, F.J. | 5 | 7 | 1 | 75* | 151 | 25.16 | – | 1 | – | – | 786 | 278 | 3 | 92.66 | 2-74 | – | – |
| Cameron, J.H. | 2 | 3 | 0 | 5 | 6 | 2.00 | – | – | – | – | 232 | 88 | 3 | 29.33 | 3-66 | – | – |

## INDIVIDUAL CAREER RECORDS—WEST INDIES *continued*

| | | | | BATTING AND FIELDING | | | | | | | BOWLING | | | | | | |
|---|---|---|---|---|---|---|---|---|---|---|---|---|---|---|---|---|---|
| | Tests | I | NO | HS | Runs | Avge | 100 | 50 | Ct | St | Balls | Runs | Wkts | Avge | BB | 5wI | 10wM |
| Carew, G.M. | 4 | 7 | 1 | 107 | 170 | 28.33 | 1 | 1 | 1 | – | 18‡ | 2 | 0 | – | – | – | – |
| Carew, M.C. | 19 | 36† | 3 | 109 | 1127 | 34.15 | 1 | 5 | 13 | – | 1174 | 437 | 8 | 54.62 | 1-11 | – | – |
| Challenor, G. | 3 | 6 | 0 | 46 | 101 | 16.83 | – | – | – | – | – | – | – | – | – | – | – |
| Chang, H.S. | 1 | 2† | 0 | 8 | 8 | 4.00 | – | – | – | – | – | – | – | – | – | – | – |
| Christiani, C.M. | 4 | 7 | 2 | 32* | 98 | 19.60 | – | – | 6 | 1 | – | – | – | – | – | – | – |
| Christiani, R.J. | 22 | 37 | 3 | 107 | 896 | 26.35 | 1 | 4 | 19 | 2 | 234 | 108 | 3 | 36.00 | 3-52 | – | – |
| Clarke, C.B. | 3 | 4 | 1 | 2 | 3 | 1.00 | – | – | – | – | 456 | 261 | 6 | 43.50 | 3-59 | – | – |
| Clarke, S.T. | 11 | 16 | 5 | 35* | 172 | 15.63 | – | – | 2 | – | 2477 | 1171 | 42 | 27.88 | 5-126 | 1 | – |
| Constantine, L.N. | 18 | 33 | 0 | 90 | 635 | 19.24 | – | 4 | 28 | – | 3583 | 1746 | 58 | 30.10 | 5-75 | 2 | – |
| Croft, C.E.H. | 27 | 37 | 22 | 33 | 158 | 10.53 | – | – | 8 | – | 6165 | 2913 | 125 | 23.30 | 8-29 | 3 | – |
| Da Costa, O.C. | 5 | 9 | 1 | 39 | 153 | 19.12 | – | – | 5 | – | 372 | 175 | 3 | 58.33 | 1-14 | – | – |
| Daniel, W.W. | 10 | 11 | 4 | 11 | 46 | 6.57 | – | – | 4 | – | 1754 | 910 | 36 | 25.27 | 5-39 | 1 | 1 |
| Davis, B.A. | 4 | 8 | 0 | 68 | 245 | 30.62 | – | 3 | 1 | – | – | – | – | – | – | – | – |
| Davis, C.A. | 15 | 29 | 5 | 183 | 1301 | 54.20 | 4 | 4 | 4 | – | 894 | 330 | 2 | 165.00 | 1-27 | – | – |
| Davis, W.W. | 11 | 12 | 4 | 77 | 157 | 19.62 | – | 1 | 7 | – | 2100 | 1082 | 32 | 33.81 | 4-19 | – | – |
| De Caires, F.I. | 3 | 6 | 0 | 80 | 232 | 38.66 | – | 2 | 1 | – | 12 | 9 | 0 | – | – | – | – |
| Depeiza, C.C. | 5 | 8 | 2 | 122 | 187 | 31.16 | 1 | – | 7 | 4 | 30 | 15 | 0 | – | – | – | – |
| Dewdney, D.T. | 9 | 12 | 5 | 5* | 17 | 2.42 | – | – | 3 | – | 1641 | 807 | 21 | 38.42 | 5-21 | 1 | – |
| Dowe, U.G. | 4 | 3 | 2 | 5* | 8 | 8.00 | – | – | – | – | 1014 | 534 | 12 | 44.50 | 4-69 | – | – |
| Dujon, P.J.L. | 33 | 44 | 4 | 139 | 1764 | 44.10 | 4 | 9 | 108 | 2 | – | – | – | – | – | – | – |
| Edwards, R.M. | 5 | 8 | 1 | 22 | 65 | 9.28 | – | – | – | – | 1311 | 626 | 18 | 34.77 | 5-84 | 1 | – |
| Ferguson, W. | 8 | 10 | 3 | 75 | 200 | 28.57 | – | 2 | 11 | – | 2568 | 1165 | 34 | 34.26 | 6-92 | 3 | 1 |
| Fernandes, M.P. | 2 | 4 | 0 | 22 | 49 | 12.25 | – | – | – | – | – | – | – | – | – | – | – |
| Findlay, T.M. | 10 | 16 | 3 | 44* | 212 | 16.30 | – | – | 19 | 2 | – | – | – | – | – | – | – |
| Foster, M.L.C. | 14 | 24 | 5 | 125 | 580 | 30.52 | 1 | 1 | 3 | – | 1776 | 600 | 9 | 66.66 | 2-41 | – | – |
| Francis, G.N. | 10 | 18 | 4 | 19* | 81 | 5.78 | – | – | 7 | – | 1619 | 763 | 23 | 33.17 | 4-40 | – | – |
| Frederick, M. | 1 | 2 | 0 | 30 | 30 | 15.00 | – | – | – | – | – | – | – | – | – | – | – |
| Fredericks, R.C. | 59 | 109† | 7 | 169 | 4334 | 42.49 | 8 | 26 | 62 | – | 1187‡ | 548 | 7 | 78.28 | 1-12 | – | – |
| Fuller, R.L. | 1 | 1 | 0 | 1 | 1 | 1.00 | – | – | – | – | 48 | 12 | 0 | – | – | – | – |
| Furlonge, H.A. | 3 | 5 | 0 | 64 | 99 | 19.80 | – | 1 | – | – | – | – | – | – | – | – | – |
| Ganteaume, A.G. | 1 | 1 | 0 | 112 | 112 | 112.00 | 1 | – | – | – | – | – | – | – | – | – | – |
| Garner, J. | 51 | 60 | 13 | 60 | 609 | 12.95 | – | 1 | 37 | – | 11770 | 4792 | 220 | 21.78 | 6-56 | 6 | – |
| Gaskin, B.B.M. | 2 | 3 | 0 | 10 | 17 | 5.66 | – | – | 1 | – | 474 | 158 | 2 | 79.00 | 1-15 | – | – |
| Gibbs, G.L. | 1 | 2† | 0 | 12 | 12 | 6.00 | – | – | 1 | – | 24‡ | 7 | 0 | – | – | – | – |
| Gibbs, L.R. | 79 | 109 | 39 | 25 | 488 | 6.97 | – | – | 52 | – | 27115 | 8989 | 309 | 29.09 | 8-38 | 18 | 2 |
| Gilchrist, R. | 13 | 14 | 3 | 12 | 60 | 5.45 | – | – | 4 | – | 3227 | 1521 | 57 | 26.68 | 6-55 | 1 | – |

## INDIVIDUAL CAREER RECORDS—WEST INDIES *continued*

| | Tests | I | NO | HS | Runs | Avge | 100 | 50 | Ct | St | Balls | Runs | Wkts | Avge | BB | 5wI | 10wM |
|---|---|---|---|---|---|---|---|---|---|---|---|---|---|---|---|---|---|
| Gladstone, G. | 1 | 1† | 1 | 12* | 12 | – | – | – | – | – | 300‡ | 189 | 1 | 189.00 | 1-139 | – | – |
| Goddard, J.D.C. | 27 | 39† | 11 | 83* | 859 | 30.67 | – | 4 | 22 | – | 2931 | 1050 | 33 | 31.81 | 5-31 | 1 | – |
| Gomes, H.A. | 49 | 75† | 10 | 143 | 2841 | 43.70 | 9 | 12 | 15 | – | 2215 | 867 | 13 | 66.69 | 2-20 | – | – |
| Gomez, G.E. | 29 | 46 | 5 | 101 | 1243 | 30.31 | 1 | 8 | 18 | – | 5236 | 1590 | 58 | 27.41 | 7-55 | 1 | – |
| Grant, G.C. | 12 | 21 | 5 | 71* | 413 | 25.81 | – | 3 | 10 | – | 24 | 18 | 0 | – | – | – | – |
| Grant, R.S. | 7 | 11 | 1 | 77 | 220 | 22.00 | – | 1 | 13 | – | 986 | 353 | 11 | 32.09 | 3-68 | – | – |
| Greenidge, A.E. | 6 | 10 | 0 | 69 | 222 | 22.20 | – | 2 | 5 | – | – | – | – | – | – | – | – |
| Greenidge, C.G. | 66 | 111 | 13 | 223 | 4816 | 49.14 | 12 | 26 | 62 | – | 26 | 4 | 0 | – | – | – | – |
| Greenidge, G.A. | 5 | 9 | 2 | 50 | 209 | 29.85 | – | 1 | 3 | – | 156 | 75 | 0 | – | – | – | – |
| Grell, M.G. | 1 | 2 | 0 | 21 | 34 | 17.00 | – | – | 1 | – | 30 | 17 | 0 | – | – | – | – |
| Griffith, C.C. | 28 | 42 | 10 | 54 | 530 | 16.56 | – | 1 | 16 | – | 5631 | 2683 | 94 | 28.54 | 6-36 | 5 | – |
| Griffith, H.C. | 13 | 23 | 5 | 18 | 91 | 5.05 | – | – | 4 | – | 2663 | 1243 | 44 | 28.25 | 6-103 | 2 | – |
| Guillen, S.C. | 5 | 6 | 2 | 54 | 104 | 26.00 | – | 1 | 9 | 2 | – | – | – | – | – | – | – |
| Hall, W.W. | 48 | 66 | 14 | 50* | 818 | 15.73 | – | 2 | 11 | – | 10421 | 5066 | 192 | 26.38 | 7-69 | 9 | 1 |
| Harper, R.A. | 14 | 17 | 2 | 39* | 203 | 13.53 | – | – | 19 | – | 2548 | 966 | 34 | 28.41 | 6-57 | 1 | – |
| Haynes, D.L. | 54 | 88 | 7 | 184 | 3234 | 39.92 | 7 | 20 | 33 | – | 18 | 8 | 1 | 8.00 | 1-2 | – | – |
| Headley, G.A. | 22 | 40 | 4 | 270* | 2190 | 60.83 | 10 | 5 | 14 | – | 398 | 230 | 0 | – | – | – | – |
| Headley, R.G.A. | 2 | 4† | 0 | 42 | 62 | 15.50 | – | – | 2 | – | – | – | – | – | – | – | – |
| Hendriks, J.L. | 20 | 32 | 8 | 64 | 447 | 18.62 | – | 2 | 42 | 5 | – | – | – | – | – | – | – |
| Hoad, E.L.G. | 4 | 8 | 0 | 36 | 98 | 12.25 | – | – | 1 | – | – | – | – | – | – | – | – |
| Holder, V.A. | 40 | 59 | 11 | 42 | 682 | 14.20 | – | – | 16 | – | 9095 | 3627 | 109 | 33.27 | 6-28 | 3 | – |
| Holding, M.A. | 55 | 71 | 10 | 69 | 786 | 12.88 | – | 5 | 18 | – | 11842 | 5414 | 233 | 23.23 | 8-92 | 13 | 2 |
| Holford, D.A.J. | 24 | 39 | 5 | 105* | 768 | 22.58 | 1 | 3 | 18 | – | 4816 | 2009 | 51 | 39.39 | 5-23 | 1 | – |
| Holt, J.K. | 17 | 31 | 2 | 166 | 1066 | 36.75 | 2 | 5 | 8 | – | 30 | 20 | 0 | – | – | – | – |
| Howard, A.B. | 1 | – | – | – | – | – | – | – | – | – | 372 | 140 | 2 | 70.00 | 2-140 | – | – |
| Hunte, C.C. | 44 | 78 | 6 | 260 | 3245 | 45.06 | 8 | 13 | 16 | – | 270 | 110 | 2 | 55.00 | 1-17 | – | – |
| Hunte, E.A.C. | 3 | 6 | 1 | 58 | 166 | 33.20 | – | 2 | 5 | 1 | – | – | – | – | – | – | – |
| Hylton, L.G. | 6 | 8 | 2 | 19 | 70 | 11.66 | – | – | 1 | – | 965 | 418 | 16 | 26.12 | 4-27 | – | – |
| Johnson, H.H.H. | 3 | 4 | 0 | 22 | 38 | 9.50 | – | – | – | – | 789 | 238 | 13 | 18.30 | 5-41 | 2 | 1 |
| Johnson, T.F. | 1 | 1† | 1 | 9* | 9 | – | – | – | 1 | – | 240‡ | 129 | 3 | 43.00 | 2-53 | – | – |
| Jones, C.M. | 4 | 7† | 0 | 19 | 63 | 9.00 | – | – | 3 | – | 102‡ | 11 | 0 | – | – | – | – |
| Jones, P.E. | 9 | 11 | 2 | 10* | 47 | 5.22 | – | – | 4 | – | 1842 | 751 | 25 | 30.04 | 5-85 | 1 | – |
| Julien, B.D. | 24 | 34 | 6 | 121 | 866 | 30.92 | 2 | 3 | 14 | – | 4542‡ | 1868 | 50 | 37.36 | 5-57 | 1 | – |
| Jumadeen, R.R. | 12 | 14 | 10 | 56 | 84 | 21.00 | – | 1 | 4 | – | 3140‡ | 1141 | 29 | 39.34 | 4-72 | – | – |
| Kallicharran, A.I. | 66 | 109† | 10 | 187 | 4399 | 44.43 | 12 | 21 | 51 | – | 406 | 158 | 4 | 39.50 | 2-16 | – | – |
| Kanhai, R.B. | 79 | 137 | 6 | 256 | 6227 | 47.53 | 15 | 28 | 50 | – | 183 | 85 | 0 | – | – | – | – |

## INDIVIDUAL CAREER RECORDS—WEST INDIES *continued*

| | Tests | I | NO | BATTING AND FIELDING HS | Runs | Avge | 100 | 50 | Ct | St | BOWLING Balls | Runs | Wkts | Avge | BB | 5wI | 10wM |
|---|---|---|---|---|---|---|---|---|---|---|---|---|---|---|---|---|---|
| Kentish, E.S.M. | 2 | 2 | 1 | 1* | 1 | 1.00 | – | – | 1 | – | 540 | 178 | 8 | 22.25 | 5-49 | 1 | – |
| King, C.L. | 9 | 16 | 3 | 100* | 418 | 32.15 | 1 | 2 | 5 | – | 582 | 282 | 3 | 94.00 | 1-30 | – | – |
| King, F.M. | 14 | 17 | 3 | 21 | 116 | 8.28 | – | – | 5 | – | 2869 | 1159 | 29 | 39.96 | 5-74 | 1 | – |
| King, L.A. | 2 | 4 | 0 | 20 | 41 | 10.25 | – | – | 2 | – | 476 | 154 | 9 | 17.11 | 5-46 | 1 | – |
| Lashley, P.D. | 4 | 7† | 0 | 49 | 159 | 22.71 | – | – | 4 | – | 18 | 1 | 1 | 1.00 | 1-1 | – | – |
| Legall, R.A. | 4 | 5 | 0 | 23 | 50 | 10.00 | – | – | 8 | 1 | – | | | | | | |
| Lewis, D.M. | 3 | 5 | 2 | 88 | 259 | 86.33 | – | 3 | 8 | – | – | | | | | | |
| Lloyd, C.H. | 110 | 175† | 14 | 242* | 7515 | 46.67 | 19 | 39 | 90 | – | 1716 | 622 | 10 | 62.20 | 2-13 | – | – |
| Logie, A.L. | 13 | 17 | 1 | 130 | 493 | 30.81 | 1 | 3 | 7 | – | 7 | 4 | 0 | – | – | – | – |
| McMorris, E.D.A.St J. | 13 | 21 | 0 | 125 | 564 | 26.85 | 1 | 3 | 5 | – | – | | | | | | |
| McWatt, C.A. | 6 | 9† | 2 | 54 | 202 | 28.85 | – | 2 | 9 | 1 | 24 | 16 | 1 | 16.00 | 1-16 | – | – |
| Madray, I.S. | 2 | 3 | 0 | 2 | 3 | 1.00 | – | – | 2 | – | 210 | 108 | 0 | – | – | – | – |
| Marshall, M.D. | 40 | 48 | 3 | 92 | 800 | 17.77 | – | 5 | 19 | – | 8863 | 4157 | 188 | 22.11 | 7-53 | 13 | 2 |
| Marshall, N.E. | 1 | 2 | 0 | 8 | 8 | 4.00 | – | – | – | – | 279 | 62 | 2 | 31.00 | 1-22 | – | – |
| Marshall, R.E. | 4 | 7 | 0 | 30 | 143 | 20.42 | – | – | 1 | – | 52 | 15 | 0 | – | – | – | – |
| Martin, F.R. | 9 | 18† | 1 | 123* | 486 | 28.58 | 1 | – | 2 | – | 1346‡ | 619 | 8 | 77.37 | 3-91 | – | – |
| Martindale, E.A. | 10 | 14 | 3 | 22 | 58 | 5.27 | – | – | 5 | – | 1605 | 804 | 37 | 21.72 | 5-22 | 3 | – |
| Mattis, E.H. | 4 | 5 | 0 | 71 | 145 | 29.00 | – | 1 | 8 | – | 36 | 14 | 0 | – | – | – | – |
| Mendonça, I.L. | 2 | 2 | 0 | 78 | 81 | 40.50 | – | 1 | 8 | 2 | – | | | | | | |
| Merry, C.A. | 2 | 4 | 0 | 13 | 34 | 8.50 | – | – | 1 | – | – | | | | | | |
| Miller, R. | 1 | 1† | 0 | 23 | 23 | 23.00 | – | – | – | – | 96 | 28 | 0 | – | – | – | – |
| Mudie, G.H. | 1 | 1† | 0 | 5 | 5 | 5.00 | – | – | – | – | 174‡ | 40 | 3 | 13.33 | 2-23 | – | – |
| Murray, D.A. | 19 | 31 | 3 | 84 | 601 | 21.46 | – | 3 | 57 | 5 | – | | | | | | |
| Murray, D.L. | 62 | 96 | 9 | 91 | 1993 | 22.90 | – | 11 | 181 | 8 | – | | | | | | |
| Nanan, R. | 1 | 2 | 0 | 8 | 16 | 8.00 | – | – | 2 | – | 216 | 91 | 4 | 22.75 | 2-37 | – | – |
| Neblett, J.M. | 1 | 2† | 1 | 11* | 16 | 16.00 | – | – | – | – | 216‡ | 75 | 1 | 75.00 | 1-44 | – | – |
| Noreiga, J.M. | 4 | 5 | 2 | 9 | 11 | 3.66 | – | – | 2 | – | 1322 | 493 | 17 | 29.00 | 9-95 | 2 | – |
| Nunes, R.K. | 4 | 8† | 0 | 92 | 245 | 30.62 | – | 2 | 2 | – | – | | | | | | |
| Nurse, S.M. | 29 | 54 | 1 | 258 | 2523 | 47.60 | 6 | 10 | 21 | – | 42 | 7 | 0 | – | – | – | – |
| Padmore, A.L. | 2 | 2 | 1 | 8* | 8 | 8.00 | – | – | – | – | 474 | 135 | 1 | 135.00 | 1-36 | – | – |
| Pairaudeau, B.H. | 13 | 21 | 0 | 115 | 454 | 21.61 | 1 | 3 | 6 | – | 6 | 3 | 0 | – | – | – | – |
| Parry, D.R. | 12 | 20 | 3 | 65 | 381 | 22.41 | – | 3 | 4 | – | 1909 | 936 | 23 | 40.69 | 5-15 | 1 | – |
| Passailaigue, C.C. | 1 | 2 | 1 | 44 | 46 | 46.00 | – | – | 3 | – | 12 | 15 | 0 | – | – | – | – |
| Philip, N. | 9 | 15 | 5 | 47 | 297 | 29.70 | – | 1 | 5 | – | 1820 | 1041 | 28 | 37.17 | 4-48 | – | – |
| Pierre, L.R. | 1 | – | – | – | – | – | – | – | – | – | 42 | 28 | 0 | – | – | – | – |
| Rae, A.F. | 15 | 24† | 2 | 109 | 1016 | 46.18 | 4 | 4 | 10 | – | – | | | | | | |

INDIVIDUAL CAREER RECORDS—WEST INDIES *continued*

| | Tests | I | NO | BATTING AND FIELDING HS | Runs | Avge | 100 | 50 | Ct | St | BOWLING Balls | Runs | Wkts | Avge | BB | 5wI | 10wM |
|---|---|---|---|---|---|---|---|---|---|---|---|---|---|---|---|---|---|
| Ramadhin, S. | 43 | 58 | 14 | 44 | 361 | 8.20 | – | – | 9 | – | 13939 | 4579 | 158 | 28.98 | 7-49 | 10 | 1 |
| Richards, I.V.A. | 77 | 116 | 7 | 291 | 5889 | 54.02 | 19 | 25 | 77 | – | 2812 | 1023 | 19 | 53.84 | 2-20 | – | – |
| Richardson, R.B. | 15 | 22 | 1 | 185 | 967 | 46.04 | 4 | 3 | 19 | – | 12 | 0 | 0 | – | – | – | – |
| Rickards, K.R. | 2 | 3 | – | 67 | 104 | 34.66 | – | 1 | – | – | | | | | | | |
| Roach, C.A. | 16 | 32 | 0 | 209 | 952 | 30.70 | 2 | 6 | 5 | – | 222 | 103 | 2 | 51.50 | 1-18 | – | – |
| Roberts, A.M.E. | 47 | 62 | 11 | 68 | 762 | 14.94 | – | 3 | 9 | – | 11136 | 5174 | 202 | 25.61 | 7-54 | 11 | 2 |
| Roberts, A.T. | 1 | 2 | 0 | 28 | 28 | 14.00 | – | – | – | – | | | | | | | |
| Rodriguez, W.V. | 5 | 7 | 0 | 50 | 96 | 13.71 | – | – | 3 | – | 573 | 374 | 7 | 53.42 | 3-51 | – | – |
| Rowe, L.G. | 30 | 49 | 2 | 302 | 2047 | 43.55 | 7 | 7 | 17 | – | 86 | 44 | 0 | – | – | – | – |
| St Hill, E.L. | 2 | 4 | 0 | 12 | 18 | 4.50 | – | – | 1 | – | 558 | 221 | 3 | 73.66 | 2-110 | – | – |
| St Hill, W.H. | 3 | 6 | 0 | 38 | 117 | 19.50 | – | – | – | – | 12 | 9 | 0 | – | – | – | – |
| Scarlett, R.O. | 3 | 4 | 1 | 29* | 54 | 18.00 | – | – | 2 | – | 804 | 209 | 2 | 104.50 | 1-46 | – | – |
| Scott, A.P.H. | 1 | 1 | 0 | 5 | 5 | 5.00 | – | – | – | – | 264 | 140 | 0 | – | – | – | – |
| Scott, O.C. | 8 | 13 | 3 | 35 | 171 | 17.10 | – | – | 1 | – | 1405 | 925 | 22 | 42.04 | 5-266 | 1 | – |
| Sealey, B.J. | 1 | 2 | 0 | 29 | 41 | 20.50 | – | – | – | – | 30 | 10 | 1 | 10.00 | 1-10 | – | – |
| Sealy, J.E.D. | 11 | 19 | 2 | 92 | 478 | 28.11 | – | 3 | 6 | 1 | 156 | 94 | 3 | 31.33 | 2-7 | – | – |
| Shepherd, J.N. | 5 | 8 | 0 | 32 | 77 | 9.62 | – | – | 4 | – | 1445 | 479 | 19 | 25.21 | 5-104 | 1 | – |
| Shillingford, G.C. | 7 | 8† | 1 | 25 | 57 | 8.14 | – | – | 2 | – | 1181 | 537 | 15 | 35.80 | 3-63 | – | – |
| Shillingford, I.T. | 4 | 7 | 0 | 120 | 218 | 31.14 | 1 | – | 1 | – | | | | | | | |
| Shivnarine, S. | 8 | 14 | 1 | 63 | 379 | 29.15 | – | 4 | 6 | – | 336‡ | 167 | 1 | 167.00 | 1-13 | – | – |
| Singh, C.K. | 2 | 3† | 1 | 11 | 11 | 3.66 | – | – | 2 | – | 506‡ | 166 | 5 | 33.20 | 2-28 | – | – |
| Small, J.A. | 3 | 6 | 0 | 52 | 79 | 13.16 | – | 1 | 3 | – | 366 | 184 | 3 | 61.33 | 2-67 | – | – |
| Small, M.A. | 2 | 1 | 1 | 3* | 3 | – | – | – | – | – | 270 | 153 | 4 | 38.25 | 3-40 | – | – |
| Smith, C.W. | 5 | 10 | 0 | 55 | 222 | 24.66 | – | 1 | 4 | 1 | | | | | | | |
| Smith, O.G. | 26 | 42 | 0 | 168 | 1331 | 31.69 | 4 | 6 | 9 | – | 4431 | 1625 | 48 | 33.85 | 5-90 | 1 | – |
| Sobers, G.St A. | 93† | 160 | 21 | 365* | 8032 | 57.78 | 26 | 30 | 109 | – | 21599‡ | 7999 | 235 | 34.03 | 6-73 | 6 | – |
| Solomon, J.S. | 27 | 46 | 7 | 100* | 1326 | 34.00 | 1 | 9 | 13 | – | 702 | 268 | 4 | 67.00 | 1-20 | – | – |
| Stayers, S.C. | 4 | 4 | 1 | 35* | 58 | 19.33 | – | – | – | – | 636 | 364 | 9 | 40.44 | 3-65 | – | – |
| Stollmeyer, J.B. | 32 | 56 | 5 | 160 | 2159 | 42.33 | 4 | 12 | 20 | – | 990 | 507 | 13 | 39.00 | 3-32 | – | – |
| Stollmeyer, V.H. | 1 | 1 | 0 | 96 | 96 | 96.00 | – | 1 | – | – | | | | | | | |
| Taylor, J.O. | 3 | 5 | 3 | 4* | 4 | 2.00 | – | – | – | – | 672 | 273 | 10 | 27.30 | 5-109 | 1 | – |
| Trim, J. | 4 | 5 | 1 | 12 | 21 | 5.25 | – | – | 2 | – | 794 | 291 | 18 | 16.16 | 5-34 | 1 | – |
| Valentine, A.L. | 36 | 51 | 21 | 14 | 141 | 4.70 | – | – | 13 | – | 12953‡ | 4215 | 139 | 30.32 | 8-104 | 8 | 2 |
| Valentine, V.A. | 2 | 4 | 1 | 19* | 35 | 11.66 | – | – | – | – | 288 | 104 | 1 | 104.00 | 1-55 | – | – |
| Walcott, C.L. | 44 | 74 | 7 | 220 | 3798 | 56.68 | 15 | 14 | 53 | 11 | 1194 | 408 | 11 | 37.09 | 3-50 | – | – |
| Walcott, L.A. | 1 | 2 | 1 | 24 | 40 | 40.00 | – | – | – | – | 48 | 32 | 1 | 32.00 | 1-17 | – | – |

## INDIVIDUAL CAREER RECORDS—WEST INDIES *continued*

| | Tests | I | NO | HS | Runs | Avge | 100 | 50 | Ct | St | Balls | Runs | Wkts | Avge | BB | 5wI | 10wM |
|---|---|---|---|---|---|---|---|---|---|---|---|---|---|---|---|---|---|
| | | | | *BATTING AND FIELDING* | | | | | | | *BOWLING* | | | | | | |
| Walsh, C.A. | 6 | 7 | 4 | 18* | 44 | 14.66 | – | – | 2 | – | 1028 | 507 | 16 | 31.68 | 3-55 | – | – |
| Watson, C.D. | 7 | 6 | 1 | 5 | 12 | 2.40 | – | – | 1 | – | 1458 | 724 | 19 | 38.10 | 4-62 | – | – |
| Weekes, E. de C. | 48 | 81 | 5 | 207 | 4455 | 58.61 | 15 | 19 | 49 | – | 122 | 77 | 1 | 77.00 | 1-8 | – | – |
| Weekes, K.H. | 2 | 3† | 0 | 137* | 173 | 57.66 | 1 | 1 | 1 | – | | | | | | – | – |
| White, A.W. | 2 | 4 | 1 | 57* | 71 | 23.66 | – | 1 | 1 | – | 491 | 152 | 3 | 50.66 | 2-34 | – | – |
| Wight, C.V. | 2 | 3 | 0 | 23 | 67 | 22.33 | – | – | – | – | 30 | 6 | 0 | – | – | – | – |
| Wight, G.L. | 1 | 1 | 0 | 21 | 21 | 21.00 | – | – | – | – | | | | | | – | – |
| Wiles, C.A. | 1 | 2 | 0 | 2 | 2 | 1.00 | – | – | – | – | | | | | | – | – |
| Willett, E.T. | 5 | 8† | 3 | 26 | 74 | 14.80 | – | – | – | – | 1326‡ | 482 | 11 | 43.81 | 3-33 | – | – |
| Williams, A.B. | 7 | 12 | 0 | 111 | 469 | 39.08 | 2 | 1 | 5 | – | | | | | | – | – |
| Williams, E.A.V. | 4 | 6 | 0 | 72 | 113 | 18.83 | – | 1 | 2 | – | 796 | 241 | 9 | 26.77 | 3-51 | – | – |
| Wishart, K.L. | 1 | 2† | 0 | 52 | 52 | 26.00 | – | – | – | – | | | | | | – | – |
| Worrell, F.M.M. | 51 | 87 | 9 | 261 | 3860 | 49.48 | 9 | 22 | 43 | – | 7141‡ | 2672 | 69 | 38.72 | 7-70 | 2 | – |

## NEW ZEALAND (155 players)

| | Tests | I | NO | HS | Runs | Avge | 100 | 50 | Ct | St | Balls | Runs | Wkts | Avge | BB | 5wI | 10wM |
|---|---|---|---|---|---|---|---|---|---|---|---|---|---|---|---|---|---|
| | | | | *BATTING AND FIELDING* | | | | | | | *BOWLING* | | | | | | |
| Alabaster, J.C. | 21 | 34 | 6 | 34 | 272 | 9.71 | – | – | 7 | – | 3992 | 1863 | 49 | 38.02 | 4-46 | – | – |
| Allcott, C.F.W. | 6 | 7† | 2 | 33 | 113 | 22.60 | – | – | 3 | – | 1206‡ | 541 | 6 | 90.16 | 2-102 | – | – |
| Anderson, R.W. | 9 | 18 | 0 | 92 | 423 | 23.50 | – | 3 | 1 | – | | | | | | – | – |
| Anderson, W.M. | 1 | 2† | 0 | 4 | 5 | 2.50 | – | – | – | – | | | | | | – | – |
| Andrews, B. | 2 | 3 | 2 | 17 | 22 | 22.00 | – | – | 1 | – | 256 | 154 | 2 | 77.00 | 2-40 | – | – |
| Badcock, F.T. | 7 | 9 | 2 | 64 | 137 | 19.57 | – | 2 | 1 | – | 1608 | 610 | 16 | 38.12 | 4-80 | – | – |
| Barber, R.T. | 1 | 2 | 0 | 12 | 17 | 8.50 | – | – | 1 | – | | | | | | – | – |
| Bartlett, G.A. | 10 | 18 | 1 | 40 | 263 | 15.47 | – | – | 8 | – | 1768 | 792 | 24 | 33.00 | 6-38 | 1 | – |
| Barton, P.T. | 7 | 14 | 0 | 109 | 285 | 20.35 | 1 | 1 | 4 | – | | | | | | – | – |
| Beard, D.D. | 4 | 7 | 2 | 31 | 101 | 20.20 | – | – | 2 | – | 806 | 302 | 9 | 33.55 | 3-22 | – | – |
| Beck, J.E.F. | 8 | 15† | 0 | 99 | 394 | 26.26 | – | 3 | 1 | – | | | | | | – | – |
| Bell, W. | 2 | 3 | 3 | 21* | 21 | – | – | – | – | – | 491 | 235 | 2 | 117.50 | 1-54 | – | – |
| Bilby, G.P. | 2 | 4 | 0 | 28 | 55 | 13.75 | – | – | 3 | – | | | | | | – | – |
| Blair, R.W. | 19 | 34 | 6 | 64* | 189 | 6.75 | – | 1 | 5 | – | 3525 | 1515 | 43 | 35.23 | 4-85 | – | – |
| Blunt, R.C. | 9 | 13 | 1 | 96 | 330 | 27.50 | – | 1 | 5 | – | 936 | 472 | 12 | 39.33 | 3-17 | – | – |
| Bolton, B.A. | 2 | 3 | 0 | 33 | 59 | 19.66 | – | – | 1 | – | | | | | | – | – |
| Boock, S.L. | 25 | 35 | 8 | 35 | 152 | 5.62 | – | – | 13 | – | 5309‡ | 2000 | 62 | 32.25 | 7-87 | 4 | – |
| Bracewell, B.P. | 6 | 12 | 2 | 8 | 24 | 2.40 | – | – | – | – | 1036 | 585 | 14 | 41.78 | 3-110 | 1 | – |
| Bracewell, J.G. | 13 | 21 | 3 | 30 | 190 | 10.55 | – | – | 12 | – | 2476 | 1095 | 30 | 36.50 | 5-75 | 1 | – |
| Bradburn, W.P. | 2 | 4 | 0 | 32 | 62 | 15.50 | – | – | 2 | – | | | | | | – | – |

## INDIVIDUAL CAREER RECORDS—NEW ZEALAND continued

| | Tests | I | NO | BATTING AND FIELDING HS | Runs | Avge | 100 | 50 | Ct | St | BOWLING Balls | Runs | Wkts | Avge | BB | 5wI | 10wM |
|---|---|---|---|---|---|---|---|---|---|---|---|---|---|---|---|---|---|
| Burgess, M.G. | 50 | 92 | 6 | 119* | 2684 | 31.20 | 5 | 14 | 34 | — | 498 | 212 | 6 | 35.33 | 3-23 | — | — |
| Burke, C. | 1 | 2 | 0 | 3 | 4 | 2.00 | — | — | — | — | 66 | 30 | 2 | 15.00 | 2-30 | — | — |
| Burtt, T.B. | 10 | 15 | 3 | 42 | 252 | 21.00 | — | — | 2 | — | 2593‡ | 1170 | 33 | 35.45 | 6-162 | 3 | — |
| Butterfield, L.A. | 1 | 2 | 0 | 0 | 0 | 0.00 | — | — | — | — | 78 | 24 | 0 | — | — | — | — |
| Cairns, B.L. | 42 | 64 | 8 | 64 | 928 | 16.57 | — | 2 | 30 | — | 10388 | 4171 | 130 | 32.08 | 7-74 | 6 | 1 |
| Cameron, F.J. | 19 | 30 | 20 | 27* | 116 | 11.60 | — | — | 2 | — | 4570 | 1849 | 62 | 29.82 | 5-34 | 3 | — |
| Cave, H.B. | 19 | 31 | 5 | 22* | 229 | 8.80 | — | — | 8 | — | 4074 | 1467 | 34 | 43.14 | 4-21 | — | — |
| Chapple, M.E. | 14 | 27 | 1 | 76 | 497 | 19.11 | — | 3 | 10 | — | 248‡ | 84 | 1 | 84.00 | 1-24 | — | — |
| Chatfield, E.J. | 23 | 32 | 21 | 21* | 126 | 11.45 | — | — | 3 | — | 5316 | 2208 | 70 | 31.54 | 6-73 | 3 | 1 |
| Cleverley, D.C. | 2 | 4† | 3 | 10* | 19 | 19.00 | — | — | — | — | 222 | 130 | 0 | — | — | — | — |
| Collinge, R.O. | 35 | 50 | 13 | 68* | 533 | 14.40 | — | 2 | 10 | — | 7689‡ | 3392 | 116 | 29.24 | 6-63 | 3 | — |
| Colquhoun, I.A. | 2 | 4 | 2 | 1* | 1 | 0.50 | — | — | 4 | — | | | | | | | |
| Coney, J.V. | 40 | 67 | 12 | 174* | 2094 | 38.07 | 2 | 13 | 46 | — | 2151 | 706 | 21 | 33.61 | 3-28 | — | — |
| Congdon, B.E. | 61 | 114 | 7 | 176 | 3448 | 32.22 | 7 | 19 | 44 | — | 5620 | 2154 | 59 | 36.50 | 5-65 | 1 | — |
| Cowie, J. | 9 | 13 | 4 | 45 | 90 | 10.00 | — | — | 3 | — | 2028 | 969 | 45 | 21.53 | 6-40 | 4 | 1 |
| Cresswell, G.F. | 3 | 5† | 3 | 12* | 14 | 7.00 | — | — | 1 | — | 650 | 292 | 13 | 22.46 | 6-168 | 1 | — |
| Cromb, I.B. | 5 | 8 | 2 | 51* | 123 | 20.50 | — | 1 | 1 | — | 960 | 442 | 8 | 55.25 | 3-113 | — | — |
| Crowe, J.J. | 20 | 33 | 1 | 128 | 936 | 29.25 | 2 | 5 | 27 | — | 18 | 9 | 0 | — | — | — | — |
| Crowe, M.D. | 23 | 38 | 1 | 188 | 1113 | 30.08 | 2 | 4 | 27 | — | 885 | 445 | 12 | 37.08 | 2-25 | — | — |
| Cunis, R.S. | 20 | 31 | 8 | 51 | 295 | 12.82 | — | 1 | 1 | — | 4250 | 1887 | 51 | 37.00 | 6-76 | 1 | — |
| D'Arcy, J.W. | 5 | 10 | 0 | 33 | 136 | 13.60 | — | — | — | — | | | | | | | |
| Dempster, C.S. | 10 | 15 | 4 | 136 | 723 | 65.72 | 2 | 5 | 2 | — | 5 | 10 | 0 | — | — | — | — |
| Dempster, E.W. | 5 | 8† | 2 | 47 | 106 | 17.66 | — | 1 | 1 | — | 544‡ | 219 | 2 | 109.50 | 1-24 | — | — |
| Dick, A.E. | 17 | 30 | 4 | 50* | 370 | 14.23 | — | 1 | 47 | 4 | | | | | | | |
| Dickinson, G.R. | 3 | 5 | 0 | 11 | 31 | 6.20 | — | — | 3 | — | 451 | 245 | 8 | 30.62 | 3-66 | — | — |
| Donnelly, M.P. | 7 | 12† | 1 | 206 | 582 | 52.90 | 1 | 4 | 7 | — | 30‡ | 20 | 0 | — | — | — | — |
| Dowling, G.T. | 39 | 77 | 3 | 239 | 2306 | 31.16 | 3 | 11 | 23 | — | 36 | 19 | 1 | 19.00 | 1-19 | — | — |
| Dunning, J.A. | 4 | 6 | 1 | 19 | 38 | 7.60 | — | — | 2 | — | 830 | 493 | 5 | 98.60 | 2-35 | — | — |
| Edgar, B.A. | 30 | 53† | 3 | 161 | 1577 | 31.54 | 3 | 8 | 13 | — | 18 | 3 | 0 | — | — | — | — |
| Edwards, G.N. | 8 | 15 | 0 | 55 | 377 | 25.13 | — | 3 | 7 | — | | | | | | | |
| Emery, R.W.G. | 2 | 4 | 0 | 28 | 46 | 11.50 | — | — | — | — | 46 | 52 | 2 | 26.00 | 2-52 | — | — |
| Fisher, F.E. | 1 | 2 | 0 | 14 | 23 | 11.50 | — | — | — | — | 204‡ | 78 | 1 | 78.00 | 1-78 | — | — |
| Foley, H. | 1 | 2† | 0 | 2 | 4 | 2.00 | — | — | — | — | | | | | | | |
| Franklin, T.J. | 1 | 2 | 0 | 7 | 9 | 4.50 | — | — | — | — | | | | | | | |
| Freeman, D.L. | 2 | 2 | 0 | 1 | 2 | 1.00 | — | — | — | — | 240 | 169 | 1 | 169.00 | 1-91 | — | — |

## INDIVIDUAL CAREER RECORDS—NEW ZEALAND *continued*

| | Tests | I | NO | HS | BATTING AND FIELDING | | | | | | Balls | Runs | Wkts | BOWLING | | | |
|---|---|---|---|---|---|---|---|---|---|---|---|---|---|---|---|---|---|
| | | | | | Runs | Avge | 100 | 50 | Ct | St | | | | Avge | BB | 5wI | 10wM |
| Gallichan, N. | 1 | 2 | 0 | 30 | 32 | 16.00 | – | – | – | – | 264‡ | 113 | 3 | 37.66 | 3-99 | – | – |
| Gedye, S.G. | 4 | 8 | 0 | 55 | 193 | 24.12 | – | 2 | – | – | – | – | – | – | – | – | – |
| Gray, E.J. | 4 | 8 | 0 | 25 | 86 | 10.75 | – | – | 2 | – | 642‡ | 311 | 8 | 38.87 | 3-73 | – | – |
| Guillen, S.C. | 3 | 6 | 0 | 41 | 98 | 16.33 | – | – | 4 | 1 | – | – | – | – | – | – | – |
| Guy, J.W. | 12 | 23† | 2 | 102 | 440 | 20.95 | 1 | 3 | 2 | – | – | – | – | – | – | – | – |
| Hadlee, D.R. | 26 | 42 | 5 | 56 | 530 | 14.32 | – | 1 | 8 | – | 4883 | 2389 | 71 | 33.64 | 4-30 | – | – |
| Hadlee, R.J. | 57 | 96† | 12 | 103 | 2088 | 24.85 | 1 | 10 | 29 | – | 14292 | 6342 | 266 | 23.84 | 7-23 | 19 | 4 |
| Hadlee, W.A. | 11 | 19 | 1 | 116 | 543 | 30.16 | – | 2 | 6 | – | – | – | – | – | – | – | – |
| Harford, N.S. | 8 | 15 | 0 | 93 | 229 | 15.26 | – | 2 | 11 | – | – | – | – | – | – | – | – |
| Harford, R.I. | 3 | 5† | 2 | 6 | 7 | 2.33 | – | – | 6 | – | – | – | – | – | – | – | – |
| Harris, P.G.Z. | 9 | 18 | 1 | 101 | 378 | 22.23 | 1 | 1 | – | – | 42 | 14 | 0 | – | – | – | – |
| Harris, R.M. | 2 | 3 | 0 | 13 | 31 | 10.33 | – | – | – | – | – | – | – | – | – | – | – |
| Hastings, B.F. | 31 | 56 | 6 | 117* | 1510 | 30.20 | 4 | 7 | 23 | – | 22 | 9 | 0 | – | – | – | – |
| Hayes, J.A. | 15 | 22 | 7 | 19 | 73 | 4.86 | – | – | 3 | – | 2675 | 1217 | 30 | 40.56 | 4-36 | – | – |
| Henderson, M. | 1 | 2† | 1 | 6 | 8 | 8.00 | – | – | 1 | – | 90‡ | 64 | 2 | 32.00 | 2-38 | – | – |
| Hough, K.W. | 2 | 3 | 2 | 31* | 62 | 62.00 | – | – | 1 | – | 462 | 175 | 6 | 29.16 | 3-79 | – | – |
| Howarth, G.P. | 47 | 83 | 5 | 147 | 2531 | 32.44 | 6 | 11 | 29 | – | 614 | 271 | 3 | 90.33 | 1-13 | – | – |
| Howarth, H.J. | 30 | 42† | 18 | 61 | 291 | 12.12 | – | 1 | 33 | – | 8833‡ | 3178 | 86 | 36.95 | 5-34 | 2 | – |
| James, K.C. | 11 | 13 | 2 | 14 | 52 | 4.72 | – | – | 11 | 5 | – | – | – | – | – | – | – |
| Jarvis, T.W. | 13 | 22 | 1 | 182 | 625 | 29.76 | 1 | 2 | 3 | – | 12 | 3 | 0 | – | – | – | – |
| Kerr, J.L. | 7 | 12 | 1 | 59 | 212 | 19.27 | – | 1 | 4 | – | – | – | – | – | – | – | – |
| Lees, W.K. | 21 | 37 | 4 | 152 | 778 | 23.57 | 1 | 1 | 52 | 7 | 5 | 4 | 0 | – | – | – | – |
| Leggat, I.B. | 1 | 1 | 0 | 0 | 0 | 0.00 | – | – | 2 | – | 24 | 6 | 0 | – | – | – | – |
| Leggat, J.G. | 9 | 18 | 2 | 61 | 351 | 21.93 | – | 2 | – | – | – | – | – | – | – | – | – |
| Lissette, A.F. | 2 | 4 | 2 | 1* | 2 | 1.00 | – | – | 1 | – | 288‡ | 124 | 3 | 41.33 | 2-73 | – | – |
| Lowry, T.C. | 7 | 8 | 0 | 80 | 223 | 27.87 | – | 2 | 8 | – | 12 | 5 | 0 | – | – | – | – |
| McEwan, P.E. | 4 | 7 | 1 | 40* | 96 | 16.00 | – | – | 5 | – | 36 | 13 | 0 | – | – | – | – |
| MacGibbon, A.R. | 26 | 46 | 5 | 66 | 814 | 19.85 | – | 3 | 13 | – | 5659 | 2160 | 70 | 30.85 | 5-64 | 1 | – |
| McGirr, H.M. | 2 | 1 | 0 | 51 | 51 | 51.00 | – | 1 | – | – | 180 | 115 | 1 | 115.00 | 1-65 | – | – |
| McGregor, S.N. | 25 | 47 | 2 | 111 | 892 | 19.82 | 1 | 3 | 9 | – | – | – | – | – | – | – | – |
| McLeod, E.G. | 1 | 2† | 1 | 16 | 18 | 18.00 | – | – | – | – | 12 | 5 | 0 | – | – | – | – |
| McMahon, T.G. | 5 | 7 | 4 | 4* | 7 | 2.33 | – | – | 7 | 1 | – | – | – | – | – | – | – |
| McRae, D.A.N. | 1 | 2† | 0 | 8 | 8 | 4.00 | – | – | – | – | 84‡ | 44 | 0 | – | – | – | – |
| Matheson, A.M. | 2 | 1 | 0 | 7 | 7 | 7.00 | – | – | 2 | – | 282 | 136 | 2 | 68.00 | 2-7 | – | – |
| Meale, T. | 2 | 4† | 0 | 10 | 21 | 5.25 | – | – | – | – | – | – | – | – | – | – | – |

## INDIVIDUAL CAREER RECORDS—NEW ZEALAND *continued*

| | | | | BATTING AND FIELDING | | | | | | BOWLING | | | | | | |
|---|---|---|---|---|---|---|---|---|---|---|---|---|---|---|---|---|
| | Tests | I | NO | HS | Runs | Avge | 100 | 50 | Ct | St | Balls | Runs | Wkts | Avge | BB | 5wI | 10wM |
| Merritt, W.E. | 6 | 8 | 1 | 19 | 73 | 10.42 | – | – | 2 | – | 936 | 617 | 12 | 51.41 | 4-104 | – | – |
| Meuli, E.M. | 1 | 2 | 0 | 23 | 38 | 19.00 | – | – | – | – | – | | | | | | |
| Milburn, B.D. | 3 | 3 | 2 | 4* | 8 | 8.00 | – | – | 6 | 2 | – | | | | | | |
| Miller, L.S.M. | 13 | 25† | 0 | 47 | 346 | 13.84 | – | – | 1 | – | 2 | 1 | 0 | – | – | – | – |
| Mills, J.E. | 7 | 10† | 1 | 117 | 241 | 26.77 | 1 | – | 1 | – | 2 | 1 | 0 | – | – | – | – |
| Moir, A.M. | 17 | 30 | 8 | 41* | 327 | 14.86 | – | 1 | 2 | – | 2650 | 1418 | 28 | 50.64 | 6-155 | 2 | – |
| Moloney, D.A.R. | 3 | 6 | 0 | 64 | 156 | 26.00 | – | 1 | 3 | – | 12 | 9 | 0 | – | – | – | – |
| Mooney, F.L.H. | 14 | 22 | 2 | 46 | 343 | 17.15 | – | – | 22 | 8 | 8 | 0 | 0 | – | – | – | – |
| Morgan, R.W. | 20 | 34 | 1 | 97 | 734 | 22.24 | – | 5 | 12 | – | 1114 | 609 | 5 | 121.80 | 1-16 | – | – |
| Morrison, B.D. | 1 | 2† | 0 | 10 | 10 | 5.00 | – | – | – | – | 186 | 129 | 2 | 64.50 | 2-129 | – | – |
| Morrison, J.F.M. | 17 | 29 | 0 | 117 | 656 | 22.62 | 1 | 3 | 9 | – | 264‡ | 71 | 2 | 35.50 | 2-52 | – | – |
| Motz, R.C. | 32 | 56 | 3 | 60 | 612 | 11.54 | – | 3 | 9 | – | 7034 | 3148 | 100 | 31.48 | 6-63 | 5 | – |
| Murray, B.A.G. | 13 | 26 | 1 | 90 | 598 | 23.92 | – | 5 | 21 | – | 6 | 0 | 1 | 0.00 | 1-0 | – | – |
| Newman, J. | 3 | 4 | 0 | 19 | 33 | 8.25 | – | – | – | – | 425‡ | 254 | 2 | 127.00 | 2-76 | – | – |
| O'Sullivan, D.R. | 11 | 21 | 4 | 23* | 158 | 9.29 | – | – | 2 | – | 2744‡ | 1224 | 18 | 68.00 | 5-148 | 1 | – |
| Overton, G.W.F. | 3 | 6† | 1 | 3* | 8 | 1.60 | – | – | 1 | – | 729 | 258 | 9 | 28.66 | 3-65 | – | – |
| Page, M.L. | 14 | 20 | 0 | 104 | 492 | 24.60 | 1 | 2 | 6 | – | 379 | 231 | 5 | 46.20 | 2-21 | – | – |
| Parker, J.M. | 36 | 63 | 2 | 121 | 1498 | 24.55 | 3 | 5 | 30 | – | 40 | 24 | 1 | 24.00 | 1-24 | – | – |
| Parker, N.M. | 3 | 6 | 0 | 40 | 89 | 14.83 | – | – | 2 | – | – | | | | | | |
| Petherick, P.J. | 6 | 11 | 4 | 13 | 34 | 4.85 | – | – | 4 | – | 1305 | 681 | 16 | 42.56 | 3-90 | – | – |
| Petrie, E.C. | 14 | 25 | 5 | 55 | 258 | 12.90 | – | 1 | 25 | – | | | | | | | |
| Playle, W.R. | 8 | 15 | 0 | 65 | 151 | 10.06 | – | 1 | 4 | – | | | | | | | |
| Pollard, V. | 32 | 59 | 7 | 116 | 1266 | 24.34 | 2 | 7 | 19 | – | 4421 | 1853 | 40 | 46.32 | 3-3 | – | – |
| Poore, M.B. | 14 | 24 | 1 | 45 | 355 | 15.43 | – | – | 1 | – | 788 | 367 | 9 | 40.77 | 2-28 | – | – |
| Puna, N. | 3 | 5 | 3 | 18* | 31 | 15.50 | – | – | 1 | – | 480 | 240 | 4 | 60.00 | 2-40 | – | – |
| Rabone, G.O. | 12 | 20 | 2 | 107 | 562 | 31.22 | 1 | 2 | 5 | – | 1385 | 635 | 16 | 39.68 | 6-68 | 1 | – |
| Redmond, R.E. | 1 | 2† | 0 | 107 | 163 | 81.50 | 1 | 1 | – | – | | | | | | | |
| Reid, J.F. | 13 | 22† | 2 | 180 | 1077 | 53.85 | 5 | 2 | 7 | – | | | | | | | |
| Reid, J.R. | 58 | 108 | 5 | 142 | 3428 | 33.28 | 6 | 22 | 43 | 1 | 7725 | 2835 | 85 | 33.35 | 6-60 | 1 | – |
| Roberts, A.D.G. | 7 | 12 | 1 | 84* | 254 | 23.09 | – | 1 | 4 | – | 440 | 182 | 4 | 45.50 | 1-12 | – | – |
| Roberts, A.W. | 5 | 10 | 1 | 66* | 248 | 27.55 | – | 3 | 4 | – | 459 | 209 | 7 | 29.85 | 4-101 | – | – |
| Rowe, C.G. | 1 | 2 | 0 | 0 | 0 | 0.00 | – | – | 1 | – | | | | | | | |
| Rutherford, K.R. | 4 | 7 | 0 | 5 | 12 | 1.71 | – | – | 1 | – | 58 | 48 | 1 | 48.00 | 1-38 | – | – |
| Scott, R.H. | 1 | 1 | 0 | 18 | 18 | 18.00 | – | – | – | – | 138 | 74 | 1 | 74.00 | 1-74 | – | – |
| Scott, V.J. | 10 | 17 | 1 | 84 | 458 | 28.62 | – | 3 | 7 | – | 18 | 14 | 0 | – | – | – | – |

INDIVIDUAL CAREER RECORDS—NEW ZEALAND *continued*

| | | BATTING AND FIELDING | | | | | | | | | BOWLING | | | | | | |
|---|---|---|---|---|---|---|---|---|---|---|---|---|---|---|---|---|---|
| | Tests | I | NO | HS | Runs | Avge | 100 | 50 | Ct | St | Balls | Runs | Wkts | Avge | BB | 5wI | 10wM |
| Shrimpton, M.J.F. | 10 | 19 | 0 | 46 | 265 | 13.94 | – | 3 | 2 | – | 257 | 158 | 5 | 31.60 | 3-35 | – | – |
| Sinclair, B.W. | 21 | 40 | 1 | 138 | 1148 | 29.43 | 3 | 3 | 8 | – | 60 | 32 | 2 | 16.00 | 2-32 | – | – |
| Sinclair, I.M. | 2 | 4† | 1 | 18* | 25 | 8.33 | – | – | 1 | – | 233 | 120 | 1 | 120.00 | 1-79 | – | – |
| Smith, F.B. | 4 | 6 | 0 | 96 | 237 | 47.40 | – | 2 | 1 | – | – | – | – | – | – | – | – |
| Smith, H.D. | 1 | 1 | 1 | 4 | 4 | 4.00 | – | – | – | – | 120 | 113 | 1 | 113.00 | 1-113 | – | – |
| Smith, I.D.S. | 25 | 37 | 8 | 113* | 709 | 24.44 | 1 | 2 | 67 | 3 | 18 | 5 | 0 | – | – | – | – |
| Snedden, C.A. | 1 | – | – | – | – | – | – | – | – | – | 96 | 46 | 0 | – | – | – | – |
| Snedden, M.C. | 10 | 12† | 2 | 32 | 147 | 14.70 | – | – | 2 | – | 1698 | 819 | 23 | 35.60 | 3-21 | – | – |
| Sparling, J.T. | 11 | 20 | 2 | 50 | 229 | 12.72 | – | 1 | 3 | – | 708 | 327 | 5 | 65.40 | 1-9 | – | – |
| Stirling, D.A. | 4 | 7 | 1 | 16 | 64 | 10.66 | – | – | – | – | 638 | 420 | 10 | 42.00 | 4-88 | – | – |
| Sutcliffe, B. | 42 | 76† | 8 | 230* | 2727 | 40.10 | 5 | 15 | 20 | – | 538‡ | 344 | 4 | 86.00 | 2-38 | – | – |
| Taylor, B.R. | 30 | 50† | 6 | 124 | 898 | 20.40 | 2 | 2 | 10 | – | 6334 | 2953 | 111 | 26.60 | 7-74 | 4 | – |
| Taylor, D.D. | 3 | 5 | 0 | 77 | 159 | 31.80 | – | 1 | 2 | – | – | – | – | – | – | – | – |
| Thomson, K. | 2 | 4 | 1 | 69 | 94 | 31.33 | – | 1 | – | – | 21 | 9 | 1 | 9.00 | 1-9 | – | – |
| Tindill, E.W.T. | 5 | 9† | 1 | 37* | 73 | 9.12 | – | – | 6 | 1 | – | – | – | – | – | – | – |
| Troup, G.B. | 13 | 17 | 6 | 13* | 45 | 4.09 | – | – | 2 | – | 2721‡ | 1214 | 36 | 33.72 | 6-95 | 1 | 1 |
| Truscott, P.B. | 1 | 2 | 0 | 26 | 29 | 14.50 | – | – | 1 | – | 12 | 5 | 0 | – | – | – | – |
| Turner, G.M. | 41 | 73 | 6 | 259 | 2991 | 44.64 | 7 | 14 | 42 | – | – | – | – | – | – | – | – |
| Vivian, G.E. | 5 | 6† | 0 | 43 | 110 | 18.33 | – | – | 3 | – | 198 | 107 | 1 | 107.00 | 1-14 | – | – |
| Vivian, H.G. | 7 | 10† | 0 | 100 | 421 | 42.10 | 1 | 5 | 4 | – | 1311‡ | 633 | 17 | 37.23 | 4-58 | – | – |
| Wadsworth, K.J. | 33 | 51 | 4 | 80 | 1010 | 21.48 | – | 5 | 92 | 4 | – | – | – | – | – | – | – |
| Wallace, W.M. | 13 | 21 | 0 | 66 | 439 | 20.90 | – | 5 | 5 | – | 6 | 5 | 0 | – | – | – | – |
| Ward, J.T. | 8 | 12 | 6 | 35* | 75 | 12.50 | – | – | 16 | 1 | – | – | – | – | – | – | – |
| Watt, L. | 1 | 2 | 0 | 2 | 2 | 1.00 | – | – | – | – | – | – | – | – | – | – | – |
| Webb, M.G. | 3 | 2 | 0 | 12 | 12 | 6.00 | – | – | – | – | 732 | 471 | 4 | 117.75 | 2-114 | – | – |
| Webb, P.N. | 2 | 3 | 0 | 5 | 11 | 3.66 | – | – | 2 | – | – | – | – | – | – | – | – |
| Weir, G.L. | 11 | 16 | 2 | 74* | 416 | 29.71 | – | 3 | 3 | – | 342 | 209 | 7 | 29.85 | 3-38 | – | – |
| Whitelaw, P.E. | 2 | 4 | 2 | 30 | 64 | 32.00 | – | – | – | – | – | – | – | – | – | – | – |
| Wright, J.G. | 41 | 71† | 2 | 141 | 2133 | 30.91 | 4 | 9 | 22 | – | 30 | 5 | 0 | – | – | – | – |
| Yuile, B.W. | 17 | 33 | 6 | 64 | 481 | 17.81 | – | 1 | 12 | – | 2897‡ | 1213 | 34 | 35.67 | 4-43 | – | – |

## INDIVIDUAL CAREER RECORDS—INDIA

| INDIA (170 players) | Tests | I | NO | HS | Runs | Avge | 100 | 50 | Ct | St | Balls | Runs | Wkts | Avge | BB | 5wI | 10wM |
|---|---|---|---|---|---|---|---|---|---|---|---|---|---|---|---|---|---|
| Abdul Hafeez – see Kardar, A.H. | | | | | | | | | | | | | | | | | |
| Abid Ali, S. | 29 | 53 | 3 | 81 | 1018 | 20.36 | – | 6 | 32 | – | 4164 | 1980 | 47 | 42.12 | 6-55 | 1 | – |
| Adhikari, H.R. | 21 | 36 | 8 | 114* | 872 | 31.14 | 1 | 4 | 8 | – | 170 | 82 | 3 | 27.33 | 3-68 | – | – |
| Amarnath, L. | 24 | 40 | 4 | 118 | 878 | 24.38 | – | 4 | 13 | – | 4241 | 1481 | 45 | 32.91 | 5-96 | 2 | – |
| Amarnath, M. | 49 | 83 | 7 | 120 | 3241 | 42.64 | 8 | 19 | 37 | – | 3275 | 1629 | 29 | 56.17 | 4-63 | – | – |
| Amarnath, S. | 10 | 18† | 0 | 124 | 550 | 30.55 | 1 | 3 | 4 | – | 11 | 5 | 1 | 5.00 | 1-5 | – | – |
| Amar Singh, L. | 7 | 14 | 1 | 51 | 292 | 22.46 | – | 1 | 3 | – | 2182 | 858 | 28 | 30.64 | 7-86 | 2 | – |
| Amir Elahi | 1 | 2 | 0 | 13 | 17 | 8.50 | – | – | – | – | – | | | | | | |
| Apte, A.L. | 1 | 2 | 0 | 8 | 15 | 7.50 | – | – | – | – | – | | | | | | |
| Apte, M.L. | 7 | 13 | 2 | 163* | 542 | 49.27 | 1 | 3 | 2 | – | 6 | 3 | 0 | – | – | – | – |
| Arun Lal | 4 | 7 | 0 | 63 | 164 | 23.42 | – | 2 | 5 | – | 7 | 6 | 0 | – | – | – | – |
| Azad, K | 7 | 12 | 0 | 24 | 135 | 11.25 | – | 1 | 3 | – | 750 | 373 | 4 | 124.33 | 2-84 | – | – |
| Azharuddin, M. | 3 | 5 | 1 | 122 | 439 | 109.75 | 3 | – | 1 | – | 6 | 8 | 0 | – | – | – | – |
| Baig, A.A. | 10 | 18 | 0 | 112 | 428 | 23.77 | 1 | 2 | 6 | – | 18 | 15 | 0 | – | – | – | – |
| Banerjee, S.A. | 1 | 1 | 0 | 0 | 0 | 0.00 | – | – | 3 | – | 306 | 181 | 5 | 36.20 | 4-120 | – | – |
| Banerjee, S.N. | 1 | 2 | 0 | 8 | 13 | 6.50 | – | – | – | – | 273 | 127 | 5 | 25.40 | 4-54 | – | – |
| Baqa Jilani, M. | 1 | 2 | 1 | 12 | 16 | 16.00 | – | – | – | – | 90 | 55 | 0 | – | – | – | – |
| Bedi, B.S. | 67 | 101 | 28 | 50* | 656 | 8.98 | – | 1 | 26 | – | 21364‡ | 7637 | 266 | 28.71 | 7-98 | 14 | 1 |
| Bhandari, P. | 3 | 4 | 0 | 39 | 77 | 19.25 | – | – | 1 | – | 78 | 39 | 0 | – | – | – | – |
| Bhat, A.R. | 3 | 3† | 1 | 6 | 6 | 3.00 | – | – | – | – | 438‡ | 151 | 4 | 37.75 | 2-65 | – | – |
| Binny, R.M.H. | 18 | 30 | 3 | 83* | 618 | 22.88 | – | 4 | 7 | – | 1817 | 1041 | 24 | 43.37 | 3-18 | – | – |
| Borde, C.G. | 55 | 97 | 11 | 177* | 3061 | 35.59 | 5 | 18 | 37 | – | 5695 | 2417 | 52 | 46.48 | 5-88 | 1 | – |
| Chandrasekhar, B.S. | 58 | 80 | 39 | 22 | 167 | 4.07 | – | – | 25 | – | 15963 | 7199 | 242 | 29.74 | 8-79 | 16 | 2 |
| Chauhan, C.P.S. | 40 | 68 | 2 | 97 | 2084 | 31.57 | – | 16 | 38 | – | 174 | 106 | 2 | 53.00 | 1-4 | – | – |
| Chowdhury, N.R. | 2 | 2 | 1 | 3* | 3 | 3.00 | – | – | – | – | 516 | 205 | 1 | 205.00 | 1-130 | – | – |
| Colah, S.H.M. | 2 | 4 | 0 | 31 | 69 | 17.25 | – | – | 2 | – | – | | | | | | |
| Contractor, N.J. | 31 | 52† | 1 | 108 | 1611 | 31.58 | 1 | 11 | 18 | – | 186 | 80 | 1 | 80.00 | 1-9 | – | – |
| Dani, H.T. | 1 | – | – | – | – | – | – | – | 1 | – | 60 | 19 | 1 | 19.00 | 1-9 | – | – |
| Desai, R.B. | 28 | 44 | 13 | 85 | 418 | 13.48 | – | 1 | 9 | – | 5597 | 2761 | 74 | 37.31 | 6-56 | 2 | – |
| Dilawar Hussain | 3 | 6 | 0 | 59 | 254 | 42.33 | – | 3 | 6 | 1 | – | | | | | | |
| Divecha, R.V. | 5 | 5 | 0 | 26 | 60 | 12.00 | – | – | 5 | – | 1044 | 361 | 11 | 32.81 | 3-102 | – | – |
| Doshi, D.R. | 33 | 38† | 10 | 20 | 129 | 4.60 | – | – | 10 | – | 9322‡ | 3502 | 114 | 30.71 | 6-102 | 6 | – |
| Durani, S.A. | 29 | 50† | 2 | 104 | 1202 | 25.04 | 1 | 7 | 14 | – | 6446‡ | 2657 | 75 | 35.42 | 6-73 | 3 | 1 |
| Engineer, F.M. | 46 | 87 | 3 | 121 | 2611 | 31.08 | 2 | 16 | 66 | 16 | – | | | | | | |
| Gadkari, C.V. | 6 | 10 | 4 | 50* | 129 | 21.50 | – | 1 | 6 | – | 102 | 45 | 0 | – | – | – | – |

## INDIVIDUAL CAREER RECORDS—INDIA *continued*

| | | | | BATTING AND FIELDING | | | | | | | BOWLING | | | | | | |
|---|---|---|---|---|---|---|---|---|---|---|---|---|---|---|---|---|---|
| | Tests | I | NO | HS | Runs | Avge | 100 | 50 | Ct | St | Balls | Runs | Wkts | Avge | BB | 5wI | 10wM |
| Gaekwad, A.D. | 40 | 70 | 4 | 201 | 1985 | 30.07 | 2 | 10 | 15 | — | 334 | 187 | 2 | 93.50 | 1-4 | — | — |
| Gaekwad, D.K. | 11 | 20 | 1 | 52 | 350 | 18.42 | — | 1 | 5 | — | 12 | 12 | 0 | — | — | — | — |
| Gaekwad, H.G. | 1 | 2† | 0 | 14 | 22 | 11.00 | — | — | — | — | 222‡ | 47 | 0 | — | — | — | — |
| Gandotra, A. | 2 | 4† | 0 | 18 | 54 | 13.50 | — | — | 1 | — | 6‡ | 5 | 0 | — | — | — | — |
| Gavaskar, S.M. | 106 | 185 | 14 | 236* | 8654 | 50.60 | 30 | 37 | 92 | — | 350 | 187 | 1 | 187.00 | 1-34 | — | — |
| Ghavri, K.D. | 39 | 57† | 14 | 86 | 913 | 21.23 | — | 2 | 16 | — | 7042‡ | 3656 | 109 | 33.54 | 5-33 | 4 | — |
| Ghorpade, J.M. | 8 | 15 | 0 | 41 | 229 | 15.26 | — | 1 | 4 | — | 150 | 131 | 0 | — | — | — | — |
| Ghulam Ahmed | 22 | 31 | 9 | 50 | 192 | 8.72 | — | 1 | 11 | — | 5650 | 2052 | 68 | 30.17 | 7-49 | 4 | 1 |
| Gopalan, M.J. | 1 | 2 | 1 | 11* | 18 | 18.00 | — | — | 3 | — | 114 | 39 | 1 | 39.00 | 1-39 | — | — |
| Gopinath, C.D. | 8 | 12 | 1 | 50* | 242 | 22.00 | — | 1 | 2 | — | 48 | 11 | 1 | 11.00 | 1-11 | — | — |
| Guard, G.M. | 2 | 2† | 0 | 7 | 11 | 5.50 | — | — | 2 | — | 396‡ | 182 | 3 | 60.66 | 2-69 | — | — |
| Guha, S. | 4 | 7 | 2 | 6 | 17 | 3.40 | — | — | 2 | — | 674 | 311 | 3 | 103.66 | 2-55 | — | — |
| Gul Mahomed | 8 | 15† | 0 | 34 | 166 | 11.06 | — | — | 3 | — | 77‡ | 24 | 2 | 12.00 | 2-21 | — | — |
| Gupte, B.P. | 3 | 3 | 2 | 17* | 28 | 28.00 | — | — | — | — | 678 | 349 | 3 | 116.33 | 1-54 | — | — |
| Gupte, S.P. | 36 | 42 | 13 | 21 | 183 | 6.31 | — | — | 14 | — | 11284 | 4403 | 149 | 29.55 | 9-102 | 12 | 1 |
| Hanumant Singh | 14 | 24 | 2 | 105 | 686 | 31.18 | 1 | 5 | 11 | — | 66 | 51 | 0 | — | — | — | — |
| Hardikar, M.S. | 2 | 4 | 1 | 32* | 56 | 18.66 | — | — | 3 | — | 108 | 55 | 1 | 55.00 | 1-9 | — | — |
| Hazare, V.S. | 30 | 52 | 6 | 164* | 2192 | 47.65 | 7 | 9 | 11 | — | 2840 | 1220 | 20 | 61.00 | 4-29 | — | — |
| Hindlekar, D.D. | 4 | 7 | 2 | 26 | 71 | 14.20 | — | — | 3 | — | — | — | — | — | — | — | — |
| Ibrahim, K.C. | 4 | 8 | 0 | 85 | 169 | 21.12 | — | 1 | — | — | — | — | — | — | — | — | — |
| Indrajitsinhji, K.S. | 4 | 7 | 1 | 23 | 51 | 8.50 | — | — | 6 | 3 | — | — | — | — | — | — | — |
| Irani, J.K. | 2 | 3 | 2 | 2* | 3 | 3.00 | — | — | 2 | 1 | — | — | — | — | — | — | — |
| Jahangir Khan, M. | 4 | 7 | 0 | 13 | 39 | 5.57 | — | — | 4 | — | 606 | 255 | 4 | 63.75 | 4-60 | — | — |
| Jai, L.P. | 1 | 2 | 0 | 19 | 19 | 9.50 | — | — | — | — | — | — | — | — | — | — | — |
| Jaisimha, M.L. | 39 | 71 | 4 | 129 | 2056 | 30.68 | 3 | 12 | 17 | — | 2097 | 829 | 9 | 92.11 | 2-54 | — | — |
| Jamshedji, R.J.D. | 1 | 2 | 2 | 4* | 5 | — | — | — | 2 | — | 210‡ | 137 | 3 | 45.66 | 3-137 | — | — |
| Jayantilal, K. | 1 | 1 | 0 | 5 | 5 | 5.00 | — | — | — | — | — | — | — | — | — | — | — |
| Joshi, P.G. | 12 | 20 | 1 | 52* | 207 | 10.89 | — | 1 | 18 | 9 | — | — | — | — | — | — | — |
| Kanitkar, H.S. | 2 | 4 | 0 | 65 | 111 | 27.75 | — | 1 | — | — | — | — | — | — | — | — | — |
| Kapil Dev | 68 | 101 | 9 | 126* | 2788 | 30.30 | 3 | 15 | 26 | — | 14522 | 7406 | 258 | 28.70 | 9-83 | 18 | 2 |
| Kardar, A.H. | 3 | 5† | 0 | 43 | 80 | 16.00 | — | — | 1 | — | — | — | — | — | — | — | — |
| Kenny, R.B. | 5 | 10 | 1 | 62 | 245 | 27.22 | — | 3 | 1 | — | — | — | — | — | — | — | — |
| Kirmani, S.M.H. | 85 | 122 | 22 | 102 | 2717 | 27.17 | 2 | 12 | 157 | 36 | 19 | 13 | 1 | 13.00 | 1-9 | — | — |
| Kishenchand, G. | 5 | 10 | 0 | 44 | 89 | 8.90 | — | 1 | 1 | — | — | — | — | — | — | — | — |
| Kripal Singh, A.G. | 14 | 20 | 5 | 100* | 422 | 28.13 | 1 | 2 | 4 | — | 1518 | 584 | 10 | 58.40 | 3-43 | — | — |
| Krishnamurthy, P. | 5 | 6 | 0 | 20 | 33 | 5.50 | — | — | 7 | 1 | — | — | — | — | — | — | — |

## INDIVIDUAL CAREER RECORDS—INDIA *continued*

| | | | | | BATTING AND FIELDING | | | | | | BOWLING | | | | | | |
|---|---|---|---|---|---|---|---|---|---|---|---|---|---|---|---|---|---|
| | Tests | I | NO | HS | Runs | Avge | 100 | 50 | Ct | St | Balls | Runs | Wkts | Avge | BB | 5wI | 10wM |
| Kulkarni, U.N. | 4 | 8† | 5 | 7 | 13 | 4.33 | — | — | — | — | 448‡ | 238 | 5 | 47.60 | 2-37 | — | — |
| Kumar, V.V. | 2 | 2 | 0 | 6 | 6 | 3.00 | — | — | 2 | — | 605 | 202 | 7 | 28.85 | 5-64 | 1 | — |
| Kunderan, B.K. | 18 | 34 | 4 | 192 | 981 | 32.70 | 2 | 3 | 23 | 7 | 24 | 13 | 0 | — | — | — | — |
| Lall Singh | 1 | 2 | 0 | 29 | 44 | 22.00 | — | — | 1 | — | — | | | | | | |
| Madan Lal | 38 | 60 | 16 | 74 | 1000 | 22.72 | — | 5 | 15 | 1 | 5872 | 2798 | 68 | 41.14 | 5-23 | 4 | — |
| Maka, E.S. | 2 | 1 | 1 | 2* | 2 | — | — | — | 2 | 1 | | | | | | | |
| Malhotra, A. | 7 | 10 | 1 | 72* | 226 | 25.11 | — | 1 | 2 | — | 18 | 3 | 0 | — | — | — | — |
| Maninder Singh | 13 | 15 | 5 | 15 | 58 | 5.80 | — | — | 3 | — | 2568‡ | 1060 | 16 | 66.25 | 4-85 | — | — |
| Manjrekar, V.L. | 55 | 92 | 10 | 189* | 3208 | 39.12 | 7 | 15 | 19 | 2 | 204 | 44 | 1 | 44.00 | 1-16 | — | — |
| Mankad, A.M. | 22 | 42 | 3 | 97 | 991 | 25.41 | — | 6 | 12 | — | 41 | 43 | 0 | — | — | — | — |
| Mankad, M.V. | 44 | 72 | 5 | 231 | 2109 | 31.47 | 5 | 6 | 33 | 1 | 14686‡ | 5236 | 162 | 32.32 | 8-52 | 8 | 2 |
| Mantri, M.K. | 4 | 8 | 1 | 39 | 67 | 9.57 | — | — | 8 | 1 | | | | | | | |
| Meherhomji, K.R. | 1 | 1 | 1 | 0* | 0 | — | — | — | 1 | — | | | | | | | |
| Mehra, V.L. | 8 | 14 | 1 | 62 | 329 | 25.30 | — | 2 | 1 | — | 36 | 6 | 0 | — | — | — | — |
| Merchant, V.M. | 10 | 18 | 0 | 154 | 859 | 47.72 | 3 | 3 | 7 | — | 54 | 40 | 0 | — | — | — | — |
| Milkha Singh, A.G. | 4 | 6† | 0 | 35 | 92 | 15.33 | — | — | 2 | — | 6 | 2 | 0 | — | — | — | — |
| Modi, R.S. | 10 | 17 | 1 | 112 | 736 | 46.00 | 1 | 6 | 3 | — | 30 | 14 | 0 | — | — | — | — |
| Muddiah, V.M. | 2 | 3 | 1 | 11 | 11 | 5.50 | — | — | — | — | 318 | 134 | 3 | 44.66 | 2-40 | — | — |
| Mushtaq Ali | 11 | 20 | 1 | 112 | 612 | 32.21 | 2 | 3 | 7 | — | 378‡ | 202 | 3 | 67.33 | 1-45 | — | — |
| Nadkarni, R.G. | 41 | 67† | 12 | 122* | 1414 | 25.70 | 1 | 7 | 22 | — | 9165‡ | 2559 | 88 | 29.07 | 6-43 | 4 | 1 |
| Naik, S.S. | 3 | 6 | 0 | 77 | 141 | 23.50 | — | 1 | — | — | | | | | | | |
| Naoomal Jèoomal | 3 | 5 | 1 | 43 | 108 | 27.00 | — | — | — | — | 108‡ | 68 | 2 | 34.00 | 1-4 | — | — |
| Narasimha Rao, M.V. | 4 | 6 | 1 | 20* | 46 | 9.20 | — | — | 8 | — | 463 | 227 | 3 | 75.66 | 2-46 | — | — |
| Navle, J.G. | 2 | 4 | 0 | 13 | 42 | 10.50 | — | — | 1 | — | | | | | | | |
| Nayak, S.V. | 2 | 3† | 1 | 11 | 19 | 9.50 | — | — | — | — | 231 | 132 | 1 | 132.00 | 1-16 | — | — |
| Nayudu, C.K. | 7 | 14 | 0 | 81 | 350 | 25.00 | — | 2 | 4 | — | 858 | 386 | 9 | 42.88 | 3-40 | — | — |
| Nayudu, C.S. | 11 | 19 | 3 | 36 | 147 | 9.18 | — | — | 3 | — | 522 | 359 | 2 | 179.50 | 1-19 | — | — |
| Nazir Ali, S. | 2 | 4 | 0 | 13 | 30 | 7.50 | — | — | — | — | 138 | 83 | 4 | 20.75 | 4-83 | — | — |
| Nissar, Mahomed | 6 | 11 | 3 | 14 | 55 | 6.87 | — | — | 2 | — | 1211 | 707 | 25 | 28.28 | 5-90 | 3 | — |
| Nyalchand, S. | 1 | 2† | 1 | 6* | 7 | 7.00 | — | — | — | — | 384‡ | 97 | 3 | 32.33 | 3-97 | — | — |
| Pai, A.M. | 1 | 2† | 0 | 9 | 10 | 5.00 | — | — | — | — | 114 | 31 | 2 | 15.50 | 2-29 | — | — |
| Palia, P.E. | 2 | 4† | 1 | 16 | 29 | 9.66 | — | — | — | — | 42‡ | 13 | 0 | — | — | — | — |
| Parkar, G.A. | 1 | 2 | 0 | 6 | 7 | 3.50 | — | — | 1 | — | — | | | | | | |
| Parkar, R.D. | 2 | 4 | 0 | 35 | 80 | 20.00 | — | — | — | — | | | | | | | |
| Parsana, D.D. | 2 | 2† | 1 | 1 | 1 | 0.50 | — | — | — | — | 120‡ | 50 | 1 | 50.00 | 1-32 | — | — |
| Patankar, C.T. | 1 | 2 | 1 | 13 | 14 | 14.00 | — | — | 3 | 1 | | | | | | | |

## INDIVIDUAL CAREER RECORDS—INDIA *continued*

Columns under *BATTING AND FIELDING*: HS, Runs, Avge, 100, 50, Ct, St. Columns under *BOWLING*: Balls, Runs, Wkts, Avge, BB, 5wI, 10wM.

| | Tests | I | NO | HS | Runs | Avge | 100 | 50 | Ct | St | Balls | Runs | Wkts | Avge | BB | 5wI | 10wM |
|---|---|---|---|---|---|---|---|---|---|---|---|---|---|---|---|---|---|
| Pataudi, *Nawab of, sr* | 3 | 5 | 0 | 22 | 55 | 11.00 | — | — | — | — | 132 | 88 | 1 | 88.00 | 1-10 | — | — |
| Pataudi, *Nawab of, jr* | 46 | 83 | 3 | 203* | 2793 | 34.91 | 6 | 16 | 27 | — | — | — | — | — | — | — | — |
| Patel, B.P. | 21 | 38 | 5 | 115* | 972 | 29.45 | 1 | 5 | 17 | — | — | — | — | — | — | — | — |
| Patel, J.M. | 7 | 10 | 1 | 12 | 25 | 2.77 | — | — | 2 | — | 1725 | 637 | 29 | 21.96 | 9-69 | 2 | 1 |
| Patiala, *Yuvraj of* | 1 | 2 | 0 | 60 | 84 | 42.00 | — | 1 | 2 | — | — | — | — | — | — | — | — |
| Patil, S.M. | 29 | 47 | 4 | 174 | 1588 | 36.93 | 4 | 7 | 12 | — | 645 | 240 | 9 | 26.66 | 2-28 | — | — |
| Patil, S.R. | 1 | 1 | 1 | 14* | 14 | — | — | — | 1 | — | 138 | 51 | 2 | 25.50 | 1-15 | — | — |
| Phadkar, D.G. | 31 | 45 | 7 | 123 | 1229 | 32.34 | 2 | 8 | 21 | — | 5994 | 2285 | 62 | 36.85 | 7-159 | 3 | — |
| Prabhakar, M. | 2 | 4 | 1 | 35* | 86 | 28.66 | — | — | — | — | 174 | 102 | 1 | 102.00 | 1-68 | — | — |
| Prasanna, E.A.S. | 49 | 84 | 20 | 37 | 735 | 11.48 | — | — | 18 | — | 14353 | 5742 | 189 | 30.38 | 8-76 | 10 | 2 |
| Punjabi, P.H. | 5 | 10 | 0 | 33 | 164 | 16.40 | — | — | 5 | — | — | — | — | — | — | — | — |
| Rai Singh, K. | 1 | 2 | 0 | 24 | 26 | 13.00 | — | — | — | — | — | — | — | — | — | — | — |
| Rajindernath, V. | 1 | — | — | — | — | — | — | — | — | 4 | — | — | — | — | — | — | — |
| Rajinder Pal | 2 | 2 | 1 | 3* | 6 | 6.00 | — | — | — | — | 78 | 22 | 0 | — | — | — | — |
| Ramaswami, C. | 2 | 4† | 1 | 60 | 170 | 56.66 | — | 1 | — | — | — | — | — | — | — | — | — |
| Ramchand, G.S. | 33 | 53 | 5 | 109 | 1180 | 24.58 | 2 | 5 | 20 | — | 4976 | 1899 | 41 | 46.31 | 6-49 | 1 | — |
| Ramji, L. | 1 | 2 | 0 | 1 | 1 | 0.50 | — | — | 1 | — | 138 | 64 | 0 | — | — | — | — |
| Rangachari, C.R. | 4 | 6 | 3 | 8* | 8 | 2.66 | — | — | — | — | 846 | 493 | 9 | 54.77 | 5-107 | 1 | — |
| Rangnekar, K.M. | 3 | 6† | 0 | 18 | 33 | 5.50 | — | — | 1 | — | — | — | — | — | — | — | — |
| Ranjane, V.B. | 7 | 9 | 3 | 16 | 40 | 6.66 | — | — | 1 | — | 1265 | 649 | 19 | 34.15 | 4-72 | — | — |
| Reddy, B. | 4 | 5 | 1 | 21 | 38 | 9.50 | — | — | 9 | 2 | — | — | — | — | — | — | — |
| Rege, M.R. | 1 | 2 | 0 | 15 | 15 | 7.50 | — | — | 1 | — | — | — | — | — | — | — | — |
| Roy, A. | 4 | 7† | 0 | 48 | 91 | 13.00 | — | — | — | — | — | — | — | — | — | — | — |
| Roy, Pankaj | 43 | 79 | 4 | 173 | 2442 | 32.56 | 5 | 9 | 16 | — | 104 | 66 | 1 | 66.00 | 1-6 | — | — |
| Roy, Pranab | 2 | 3 | 1 | 60* | 71 | 35.50 | — | 1 | 1 | — | — | — | — | — | — | — | — |
| Sandhu, B.S. | 8 | 11 | 4 | 71 | 214 | 30.57 | — | 2 | 1 | — | 1020 | 557 | 10 | 55.70 | 3-87 | — | — |
| Sardesai, D.N. | 30 | 55 | 4 | 212 | 2001 | 39.23 | 5 | 9 | 4 | — | 59 | 45 | 0 | — | — | — | — |
| Sarwate, C.T. | 9 | 17 | 1 | 37 | 208 | 13.00 | — | — | — | — | 658 | 374 | 3 | 124.66 | 1-16 | — | — |
| Saxena, R.C. | 1 | 2 | 0 | 16 | 25 | 12.50 | — | — | — | — | 12 | 11 | 0 | — | — | — | — |
| Sekar, T.A.P. | 2 | 1 | 1 | 0* | 0 | — | — | — | — | — | 204 | 129 | 0 | — | — | — | — |
| Sen, P. | 14 | 18 | 4 | 25 | 165 | 11.78 | — | — | 20 | 11 | — | — | — | — | — | — | — |
| Sengupta, A.K. | 1 | 2 | 0 | 8 | 9 | 4.50 | — | — | 1 | — | — | — | — | — | — | — | — |
| Sharma, C. | 5 | 6 | 4 | 18* | 62 | 31.00 | — | — | 1 | — | 669 | 433 | 8 | 54.12 | 4-38 | — | — |
| Sharma, G. | 5 | — | — | — | — | — | — | — | 1 | — | 426 | 132 | 3 | 44.00 | 3-115 | — | — |
| Sharma, P. | 5 | 10 | 0 | 54 | 187 | 18.70 | — | 1 | 1 | — | 24 | 8 | 0 | — | — | — | — |
| Shastri, R.J. | 34 | 53 | 8 | 142 | 1676 | 37.24 | 5 | 7 | 15 | — | 7684‡ | 2947 | 73 | 40.36 | 5-75 | 2 | — |
| Shinde, S.G. | 7 | 11 | 5 | 14 | 85 | 14.16 | — | — | — | — | 1515 | 717 | 12 | 59.75 | 6-91 | 1 | — |

## INDIVIDUAL CAREER RECORDS—INDIA continued

| | | | | BATTING AND FIELDING | | | | | | | BOWLING | | | | | | |
|---|---|---|---|---|---|---|---|---|---|---|---|---|---|---|---|---|---|
| | Tests | I | NO | HS | Runs | Avge | 100 | 50 | Ct | St | Balls | Runs | Wkts | Avge | BB | 5wI | 10wM |
| Shodhan, R.H. | 3 | 4† | 1 | 110 | 181 | 60.33 | 1 | — | 1 | — | 60‡ | 26 | 0 | — | — | — | — |
| Shukla, R.S. | 1 | — | 0 | — | — | — | — | — | — | — | 294 | 152 | 2 | 76.00 | 2-82 | — | — |
| Sidhu, N.S. | 2 | 3 | 0 | 20 | 39 | 13.00 | — | — | 1 | — | 6 | 9 | 0 | — | — | — | — |
| Sivaramakrishnan, L. | 6 | 6 | 1 | 25 | 76 | 15.20 | — | — | 2 | — | 1797 | 818 | 23 | 35.56 | 6-64 | 3 | 1 |
| Sohoni, S.W. | 4 | 7 | 2 | 29* | 83 | 16.60 | — | — | 2 | — | 532 | 202 | 2 | 101.00 | 1-16 | — | — |
| Solkar, E.D. | 27 | 48† | 6 | 102 | 1068 | 25.42 | 1 | 6 | 53 | — | 2265‡ | 1070 | 18 | 59.44 | 3-28 | — | — |
| Sood, M.M. | 1 | 2 | 0 | 3 | 3 | 1.50 | — | — | — | — | 48 | 21 | 0 | — | — | — | — |
| Srikkanth, K. | 8 | 13 | 1 | 84 | 288 | 24.00 | — | 2 | 3 | — | — | — | — | — | — | — | — |
| Srinivasan, T.E. | 1 | 2 | 0 | 29 | 48 | 24.00 | — | — | — | — | — | — | — | — | — | — | — |
| Subramanya, V. | 9 | 15 | 1 | 75 | 263 | 18.78 | — | 2 | 9 | — | 444 | 201 | 3 | 67.00 | 2-32 | — | — |
| Sunderam, G.R. | 2 | 1 | 1 | 3* | 3 | — | — | — | — | — | 396 | 166 | 3 | 55.33 | 2-46 | — | — |
| Surendranath | 11 | 20 | 7 | 27 | 136 | 10.46 | — | — | 4 | — | 2602 | 1053 | 26 | 40.50 | 5-75 | 2 | — |
| Surti, R.F. | 26 | 48† | 4 | 99 | 1263 | 28.70 | — | 9 | 26 | — | 3870‡ | 1962 | 42 | 46.71 | 5-74 | 1 | — |
| Swamy, V.N. | 1 | — | — | — | — | — | — | — | — | — | 108 | 45 | 0 | — | — | — | — |
| Tamhane, N.S. | 21 | 27 | 5 | 54* | 225 | 10.22 | — | 1 | 35 | 16 | — | — | — | — | — | — | — |
| Tarapore, K.K. | 1 | 1 | 0 | 2 | 2 | 2.00 | — | — | — | — | 114‡ | 72 | 0 | — | — | — | — |
| Umrigar, P.R. | 59 | 94 | 8 | 223 | 3631 | 42.22 | 12 | 14 | 33 | — | 4725 | 1473 | 35 | 42.08 | 6-74 | 2 | — |
| Vengsarkar, D.B. | 76 | 124 | 11 | 159* | 4328 | 38.30 | 9 | 22 | 52 | — | 47 | 36 | 0 | — | — | — | — |
| Venkataraghavan, S. | 57 | 76 | 12 | 64 | 748 | 11.68 | — | 2 | 44 | — | 14877 | 5634 | 156 | 36.11 | 8-72 | 3 | 1 |
| Viswanath, G.R. | 91 | 155 | 10 | 222 | 6080 | 41.93 | 14 | 35 | 63 | — | 70 | 46 | 1 | 46.00 | 1-11 | — | — |
| Vizianagram, Maharajkumar of | 3 | 6 | 2 | 19* | 33 | 8.25 | — | — | 1 | — | — | — | — | — | — | — | — |
| Wadekar, A.L. | 37 | 71† | 3 | 143 | 2113 | 31.07 | 1 | 14 | 46 | — | 61‡ | 55 | 0 | — | — | — | — |
| Wazir Ali, S. | 7 | 14 | 0 | 42 | 237 | 16.92 | — | — | 1 | — | 30 | 25 | 0 | — | — | — | — |
| Yadav, N.S. | 23 | 30 | 9 | 43* | 308 | 14.66 | — | — | 7 | — | 5047 | 2336 | 60 | 38.93 | 5-131 | 1 | — |
| Yajurvindra Singh | 4 | 7 | 1 | 43* | 109 | 18.16 | — | — | 11 | — | 120 | 50 | 0 | — | — | — | — |
| Yashpal Sharma | 37 | 59 | 11 | 140 | 1606 | 33.45 | 2 | 9 | 16 | — | 30 | 17 | 1 | 17.00 | 1-6 | — | — |
| Yograj Singh | 1 | 2 | 0 | 6 | 10 | 5.00 | — | — | — | — | 90 | 63 | 1 | 63.00 | 1-63 | — | — |

INDIVIDUAL CAREER RECORDS—PAKISTAN

| PAKISTAN (102 players) | Tests | I | NO | HS | Runs | Avge | 100 | 50 | Ct | St | Balls | Runs | Wkts | Avge | BB | 5wI | 10wM |
|---|---|---|---|---|---|---|---|---|---|---|---|---|---|---|---|---|---|
| | | | | | | BATTING AND FIELDING | | | | | | BOWLING | | | | | |
| Abdul Kadir | 4 | 8 | 0 | 95 | 272 | 34.00 | – | 2 | 10 | 1 | – | – | – | – | – | – | – |
| Abdul Qadir | 33 | 40 | 4 | 54 | 550 | 15.27 | – | 2 | – | – | 8778 | 4002 | 114 | 35.10 | 7-142 | 8 | 2 |
| Afaq Hussain | 2 | 4 | 4 | 35* | 66 | – | – | – | 2 | – | 240 | 106 | 1 | 106.00 | 1-40 | – | – |
| Aftab Baloch | 2 | 3 | 1 | 60* | 97 | 48.50 | – | 1 | – | – | 44 | 17 | 0 | – | – | – | – |
| Aftab Gul | 6 | 8 | 0 | 33 | 182 | 22.75 | – | 1 | 3 | – | 6 | 4 | 0 | – | – | – | – |
| Agha Saadat Ali | 1 | 1 | 1 | 8* | 8 | – | – | – | 3 | – | – | – | – | – | – | – | – |
| Agha Zahid | 1 | 2 | 0 | 14 | 15 | 7.50 | – | – | 3 | – | – | – | – | – | – | – | – |
| Alimuddin | 25 | 45 | 2 | 109 | 1091 | 25.37 | 2 | 7 | 8 | – | 84 | 75 | 1 | 75.00 | 1-17 | – | – |
| Amir Elahi | 5 | 7 | 1 | 47 | 65 | 10.83 | – | – | – | – | 400 | 248 | 7 | 35.42 | 4-134 | – | – |
| Anil Dalpat | 9 | 12 | 1 | 52 | 167 | 15.18 | – | 1 | 22 | 3 | – | – | – | – | – | – | – |
| Anwar Hussain | 4 | 6 | 0 | 17 | 42 | 7.00 | – | – | – | – | 36 | 29 | 1 | 29.00 | 1-25 | – | – |
| Anwar Khan | 1 | 2 | 1 | 12 | 15 | 15.00 | – | – | – | – | 32 | 12 | 0 | – | – | – | – |
| Arif Butt | 3 | 5 | 0 | 20 | 59 | 11.80 | – | – | – | – | 666 | 288 | 14 | 20.57 | 6-89 | 1 | – |
| Ashraf Ali | 4 | 5 | 3 | 65 | 206 | 103.00 | – | 2 | 6 | 2 | – | – | – | – | – | – | – |
| Asif Iqbal | 58 | 99 | 7 | 175 | 3575 | 38.85 | 11 | 12 | 36 | – | 3864 | 1502 | 53 | 28.33 | 5-48 | 2 | – |
| Asif Masood | 16 | 19 | 10 | 30* | 93 | 10.33 | – | – | 5 | – | 3038 | 1568 | 38 | 41.26 | 5-111 | 1 | – |
| Azeem Hafeez | 18 | 21‡ | 5 | 24 | 134 | 8.37 | – | – | 1 | – | 4351‡ | 2204 | 63 | 34.98 | 6-46 | 4 | – |
| Azhar Khan | 1 | 1 | 0 | 14 | 14 | 14.00 | – | – | – | – | 18 | 2 | 1 | 2.00 | 1-1 | – | – |
| Azmat Rana | 1 | 1‡ | 0 | 49 | 49 | 49.00 | – | – | – | – | – | – | – | – | – | – | – |
| D'Souza, A. | 6 | 10 | 8 | 23* | 76 | 38.00 | – | – | 3 | – | 1587 | 745 | 17 | 43.82 | 5-112 | 1 | – |
| Ehteshamuddin | 5 | 3 | 1 | 2 | 2 | 1.00 | – | – | 2 | – | 940 | 375 | 16 | 23.43 | 5-47 | 1 | – |
| Farooq Hamid | 1 | 2 | 0 | 3 | 3 | 1.50 | – | – | – | – | 184 | 107 | 1 | 107.00 | 1-82 | – | – |
| Farrukh Zaman | 1 | 1 | – | – | – | – | – | – | – | – | 80‡ | 15 | 0 | – | – | – | – |
| Fazal Mahmood | 34 | 50 | 6 | 60 | 620 | 14.09 | – | 1 | 11 | – | 9834 | 3434 | 139 | 24.70 | 7-42 | 13 | 4 |
| Ghazali, M.E.Z. | 2 | 4 | 0 | 18 | 32 | 8.00 | – | – | – | – | 48 | 18 | 0 | – | – | – | – |
| Ghulam Abbas | 1 | 2† | 0 | 12 | 12 | 6.00 | – | – | – | – | – | – | – | – | – | – | – |
| Gul Mahomed | 1 | 2† | 1 | 27* | 39 | 39.00 | – | – | – | – | – | – | – | – | – | – | – |
| Hanif Mohammad | 55 | 97 | 8 | 337 | 3915 | 43.98 | 12 | 15 | 40 | – | 206 | 95 | 1 | 95.00 | 1-1 | – | – |
| Haroon Rashid | 23 | 36 | 1 | 153 | 1217 | 34.77 | 3 | 5 | 16 | – | 8 | 3 | 0 | – | – | – | – |
| Haseeb Ahsan | 12 | 16 | 7 | 14 | 61 | 6.77 | – | – | 1 | – | 2835 | 1330 | 27 | 49.25 | 6-202 | 2 | – |
| Ibadulla, K. – see Khalid Ibadulla | | | | | | | | | | | | | | | | | |
| Ijaz Butt | 8 | 16 | 2 | 58 | 279 | 19.92 | – | 1 | 5 | – | – | – | – | – | – | – | – |
| Ijaz Faqih | 2 | 4 | 0 | 34 | 63 | 15.75 | – | – | – | – | 156 | 85 | 1 | 85.00 | 1-76 | – | – |
| Imran Khan | 51 | 77 | 12 | 123 | 2023 | 31.12 | 2 | 7 | 16 | – | 12551 | 5316 | 232 | 22.91 | 8-58 | 16 | 4 |
| Imtiaz Ahmed | 41 | 72 | 1 | 209 | 2079 | 29.28 | 3 | 11 | 77 | 16 | 6 | 0 | 0 | – | – | – | – |

## INDIVIDUAL CAREER RECORDS—PAKISTAN *continued*

| | | | | BATTING AND FIELDING | | | | | | | BOWLING | | | | | | |
| --- | --- | --- | --- | --- | --- | --- | --- | --- | --- | --- | --- | --- | --- | --- | --- | --- | --- |
| | Tests | I | NO | HS | Runs | Avge | 100 | 50 | Ct | St | Balls | Runs | Wkts | Avge | BB | 5wI | 10wM |
| Intikhab Alam | 47 | 77 | 10 | 138 | 1493 | 22.28 | 1 | 8 | 20 | — | 10474 | 4494 | 125 | 35.95 | 7-52 | 5 | 2 |
| Iqbal Qasim | 41 | 46† | 14 | 56 | 380 | 11.87 | — | 1 | 32 | — | 10786‡ | 3994 | 137 | 29.15 | 7-49 | 5 | 2 |
| Israr Ali | 4 | 8† | 1 | 10 | 33 | 4.71 | — | — | 1 | — | 318‡ | 165 | 6 | 27.50 | 2-29 | — | — |
| Jalaluddin | 5 | 3 | 2 | 2 | 4 | 3.00 | — | — | — | — | 963 | 448 | 10 | 44.80 | 3-77 | — | — |
| Javed Akhtar | 1 | 2 | 1 | 2* | 4 | 4.00 | — | — | — | — | 96 | 52 | 0 | — | — | — | — |
| Javed Burki | 25 | 48 | 4 | 140 | 1341 | 30.47 | 3 | 4 | 7 | — | 42 | 23 | 0 | — | — | — | — |
| Javed Miandad | 68 | 108 | 16 | 280* | 5044 | 54.82 | 13 | 27 | 59 | 1 | 1446 | 672 | 17 | 39.52 | 3-74 | — | — |
| Kardar, A.H. | 23 | 37† | 3 | 93 | 847 | 24.91 | — | 5 | 15 | — | 2712‡ | 954 | 21 | 45.42 | 3-35 | — | — |
| Khalid Hassan | 1 | 2 | 1 | 10 | 17 | 17.00 | — | — | — | — | 126 | 116 | 2 | 58.00 | 2-116 | — | — |
| Khalid Ibadulla | 4 | 8 | 0 | 166 | 253 | 31.62 | 1 | — | 3 | — | 336 | 99 | 1 | 99.00 | 1-42 | — | — |
| Khalid Wazir | 2 | 3 | 1 | 9* | 14 | 7.00 | — | — | — | — | — | — | — | — | — | — | — |
| Khan Mohammad | 13 | 17 | 7 | 26* | 100 | 10.00 | — | — | 4 | — | 3157 | 1292 | 54 | 23.92 | 6-21 | 4 | — |
| Liaquat Ali | 5 | 7 | 3 | 12 | 28 | 7.00 | — | — | 1 | — | 808‡ | 359 | 6 | 59.83 | 3-80 | — | — |
| Mahmood Hussain | 27 | 39 | 6 | 35 | 336 | 10.18 | — | — | 5 | — | 5910 | 2628 | 68 | 38.64 | 6-67 | 2 | — |
| Majid Khan | 63 | 106 | 5 | 167 | 3931 | 38.92 | 8 | 19 | 70 | — | 3584 | 1456 | 27 | 53.92 | 4-45 | — | — |
| Mansoor Akhtar | 13 | 22 | 3 | 111 | 484 | 25.47 | 1 | 2 | 7 | — | 138 | 76 | 1 | 76.00 | 1-74 | — | — |
| Manzoor Elahi | 2 | 3 | 1 | 26 | 49 | 24.50 | — | — | 3 | — | 462 | 191 | 3 | 63.66 | 2-12 | — | — |
| Maqsood Ahmed | 16 | 27 | 1 | 99 | 507 | 19.50 | — | 2 | 13 | — | 76 | 20 | 0 | — | — | — | — |
| Mathias, W. | 21 | 36 | 3 | 77 | 783 | 23.72 | — | 3 | 22 | — | 24 | — | — | — | — | — | — |
| Miran Bux | 2 | 3 | 2 | 1* | 1 | 1.00 | — | — | — | — | 348 | 115 | 2 | 57.50 | 2-82 | — | — |
| Mohammad Aslam | 1 | 2 | 0 | 18 | 34 | 17.00 | — | — | — | — | — | — | — | — | — | — | — |
| Mohammad Farooq | 7 | 9 | 4 | 47 | 85 | 17.00 | — | — | 1 | — | 1422 | 682 | 21 | 32.47 | 4-70 | — | — |
| Mohammad Ilyas | 10 | 19 | 0 | 126 | 441 | 23.21 | 1 | 2 | 6 | — | 84 | 63 | 0 | — | — | — | — |
| Mohammad Munaf | 4 | 7 | 2 | 19 | 63 | 12.60 | — | — | — | — | 769 | 341 | 11 | 31.00 | 4-42 | 3 | — |
| Mohammad Nazir | 14 | 18 | 10 | 29* | 144 | 18.00 | — | — | 4 | — | 3262 | 1123 | 34 | 33.02 | 7-99 | — | — |
| Mohsin Kamal | 1 | 1 | 0 | 0 | 0 | 0.00 | — | — | — | — | 192 | 125 | 2 | 62.50 | 1-59 | — | — |
| Mohsin Khan | 40 | 65 | 5 | 200 | 2468 | 41.13 | 7 | 8 | 31 | — | 86 | 30 | 0 | — | — | — | — |
| Mudassar Nazar | 52 | 81 | 5 | 231 | 3099 | 40.77 | 8 | 12 | 37 | — | 4141 | 1795 | 45 | 39.88 | 6-32 | 1 | — |
| Mufasir-ul-Haq | 1 | 1 | 1 | 8* | 8 | — | — | — | — | — | 222‡ | 84 | 3 | 28.00 | 2-50 | — | — |
| Munir Malik | 3 | 4 | 1 | 4 | 7 | 2.33 | — | — | 1 | — | 684 | 358 | 9 | 39.77 | 5-128 | 1 | — |
| Mushtaq Mohammad | 57 | 100 | 7 | 201 | 3643 | 39.17 | 10 | 19 | 42 | — | 5260 | 2309 | 79 | 29.22 | 5-28 | 3 | — |
| Nasim-ul-Ghani | 29 | 50† | 5 | 101 | 747 | 16.60 | 1 | 2 | 11 | — | 4406‡ | 1959 | 52 | 37.67 | 6-67 | 2 | — |
| Naushad Ali | 6 | 11 | 0 | 39 | 156 | 14.18 | — | — | 9 | — | — | — | — | — | — | — | — |
| Nazar Mohammad | 5 | 8 | 1 | 124* | 277 | 39.57 | 1 | 1 | 7 | — | 12 | 4 | 0 | — | — | — | — |
| Niaz Ahmed | 2 | 3 | 3 | 16* | 17 | — | — | — | 1 | — | 294 | 94 | 3 | 31.33 | 2-72 | — | — |

**INDIVIDUAL CAREER RECORDS—PAKISTAN** *continued*

| | Tests | I | NO | HS | Runs | Avge | 100 | 50 | Ct | St | Balls | Runs | Wkts | Avge | BB | 5wI | 10wM |
|---|---|---|---|---|---|---|---|---|---|---|---|---|---|---|---|---|---|
| Pervez Sajjad | 19 | 20 | 11 | 24 | 123 | 13.66 | – | – | 9 | – | 4145‡ | 1410 | 59 | 23.89 | 7-74 | 3 | – |
| Qasim Omar | 17 | 29 | 1 | 210 | 1128 | 40.28 | 2 | 4 | 11 | – | 6 | 0 | 0 | – | – | – | – |
| Ramiz Raja | 2 | 4 | 1 | 26 | 34 | 11.33 | – | – | 4 | – | – | | | | | – | – |
| Rashid Khan | 4 | 6 | 3 | 59 | 155 | 51.66 | – | 1 | 2 | – | 738 | 360 | 8 | 45.00 | 3-129 | – | – |
| Rehman, S.F. | 1 | 2 | 0 | 8 | 10 | 5.00 | – | – | 1 | – | 204 | 99 | 1 | 99.00 | 1-43 | – | – |
| Rizwan-un-Zaman | 3 | 6 | 0 | 42 | 112 | 18.66 | – | – | 1 | – | 102 | 39 | 3 | 13.00 | 3-26 | – | – |
| Sadiq Mohammad | 41 | 74† | 2 | 166 | 2579 | 35.81 | 5 | 10 | 28 | – | 199 | 98 | 0 | – | – | – | – |
| Saeed Ahmed | 41 | 78 | 4 | 172 | 2991 | 40.41 | 5 | 16 | 13 | – | 1980 | 802 | 22 | 36.45 | 4-64 | 1 | – |
| Salahuddin | 5 | 8 | 2 | 34* | 117 | 19.50 | – | – | 3 | – | 546 | 187 | 7 | 26.71 | 2-36 | – | – |
| Salim Altaf | 21 | 31 | 12 | 53* | 276 | 14.52 | – | 1 | 3 | – | 4001 | 1710 | 46 | 37.17 | 4-11 | – | – |
| Salim Malik | 24 | 34 | 6 | 119* | 1242 | 44.35 | 5 | 6 | 27 | – | 122 | 61 | 3 | 20.33 | 1-3 | – | – |
| Salim Yousuf | 1 | 1 | 0 | 4 | 4 | 4.00 | – | – | 5 | 2 | – | | | | | – | – |
| Sarfraz Nawaz | 55 | 72 | 13 | 90 | 1045 | 17.71 | – | 4 | 26 | – | 13927 | 5798 | 177 | 32.75 | 9-86 | 4 | 1 |
| Shafiq Ahmed | 6 | 10 | 1 | 27* | 99 | 11.00 | – | – | – | – | 8 | 1 | 0 | – | – | – | – |
| Shafqat Rana | 5 | 7 | 0 | 95 | 221 | 31.57 | – | 2 | 5 | – | 36 | 9 | 1 | 9.00 | 1-2 | – | – |
| Shahid Israr | 1 | 1 | 1 | 7* | 7 | – | – | – | 2 | 1 | – | | | | | – | – |
| Shahid Mahmood | 1 | 2† | 0 | 16 | 25 | 12.50 | – | – | 2 | – | 36‡ | 23 | 0 | – | – | – | – |
| Sharpe, D. | 3 | 6 | 0 | 56 | 134 | 22.33 | – | 1 | 2 | – | – | | | | | – | – |
| Shoaib Mohammad | 5 | 8 | 1 | 80 | 180 | 25.71 | – | 1 | 8 | – | 6 | 4 | 0 | – | – | – | – |
| Shujauddin | 19 | 32 | 6 | 47 | 395 | 15.19 | – | – | 8 | – | 2313‡ | 801 | 20 | 40.05 | 3-18 | – | – |
| Sikander Bakht | 26 | 35 | 12 | 22* | 146 | 6.34 | – | – | 7 | – | 4870 | 2411 | 67 | 35.98 | 8-69 | 3 | 1 |
| Tahir Naqqash | 15 | 19 | 5 | 57 | 300 | 21.42 | – | 1 | 3 | – | 2800 | 1398 | 34 | 41.11 | 5-40 | 2 | – |
| Talat Ali | 10 | 18 | 2 | 61 | 370 | 23.12 | – | 2 | 4 | – | 20 | 7 | 0 | – | – | – | – |
| Taslim Arif | 6 | 10 | 2 | 210* | 501 | 62.62 | 1 | 2 | 6 | 3 | 30 | 28 | 1 | 28.00 | 1-28 | – | – |
| Tausif Ahmed | 10 | 7 | 4 | 18 | 51 | 17.00 | – | – | 4 | – | 2310 | 924 | 29 | 31.86 | 4-58 | – | – |
| Waqar Hassan | 21 | 35 | 1 | 189 | 1071 | 31.50 | 1 | 6 | 10 | – | 6 | 10 | 0 | – | – | – | – |
| Wasim Akram | 2 | 4 | 3 | 8* | 9 | 9.00 | – | – | – | – | 562‡ | 233 | 12 | 19.41 | 5-56 | 2 | 1 |
| Wasim Bari | 81 | 112 | 26 | 85 | 1366 | 15.88 | – | 6 | 201 | 27 | 8 | 2 | 0 | – | – | – | – |
| Wasim Raja | 57 | 92† | 14 | 125 | 2821 | 36.16 | 4 | 18 | 20 | – | 4082 | 1826 | 51 | 35.80 | 4-50 | – | – |
| Wazir Mohammad | 20 | 33 | 4 | 189 | 801 | 27.62 | 2 | 3 | 5 | – | 24 | 15 | 0 | – | – | – | – |
| Younis Ahmed | 2 | 4† | 0 | 62 | 89 | 22.25 | – | 1 | – | – | – | | | | | – | – |
| Zaheer Abbas | 76 | 123 | 11 | 274 | 5058 | 45.16 | 12 | 20 | 34 | – | 370 | 132 | 3 | 44.00 | 2-21 | – | – |
| Zulfiqar Ahmed | 9 | 10 | 4 | 63* | 200 | 33.33 | – | 1 | 5 | – | 1285 | 366 | 20 | 18.30 | 6-42 | 2 | 1 |

## INDIVIDUAL CAREER RECORDS—SRI LANKA

| SRI LANKA (27 players) | Tests | I | NO | BATTING AND FIELDING HS | Runs | Avge | 100 | 50 | Ct | St | BOWLING Balls | Runs | Wkts | Avge | BB | 5wI | 10wM |
|---|---|---|---|---|---|---|---|---|---|---|---|---|---|---|---|---|---|
| Amerasinghe, M.J.G. | 2 | 4 | 1 | 34 | 54 | 18.00 | – | – | 3 | – | 300‡ | 150 | 3 | 50.00 | 2-73 | – | – |
| De Alwis, R.G. | 5 | 10 | 0 | 28 | 102 | 10.20 | – | – | 9 | 1 | – | | | | | | |
| De Mel, A.L.F. | 7 | 14 | 3 | 34 | 188 | 17.09 | – | – | 5 | – | 1515 | 1015 | 29 | 35.00 | 5-68 | 1 | – |
| De Silva, D.S. | 12 | 22 | 3 | 61 | 406 | 21.36 | – | 2 | 5 | – | 3031 | 1347 | 37 | 36.40 | 5-59 | 1 | – |
| De Silva, G.R.A. | 4 | 7 | 2 | 41 | 14 | 8.20 | – | – | – | – | 962‡ | 385 | 7 | 55.00 | 2-38 | – | – |
| De Silva, P.A. | 1 | 2 | 0 | 16 | 19 | 9.50 | – | – | – | – | – | | | | | | |
| Dias, R.L. | 9 | 17 | 0 | 109 | 747 | 43.94 | 2 | 5 | 6 | – | – | | | | | | |
| Fernando, E.R.N.S. | 5 | 10 | 0 | 46 | 112 | 11.20 | – | – | – | – | – | | | | | | |
| Goonasekera, Y. | 2 | 4† | 0 | 23 | 48 | 12.00 | – | – | 6 | – | – | | | | | | |
| Goonatillake, H.M. | 5 | 10 | 2 | 56 | 177 | 22.12 | – | 1 | 10 | 3 | – | | | | | | |
| Guneratne, R.P.W. | 1 | 2 | 2 | 0* | 0 | – | – | – | – | – | 102 | 84 | 0 | – | – | – | – |
| Jayasekera, R.S.A. | 2 | 2 | 0 | 2 | 2 | 1.00 | – | – | – | – | – | | | | | | |
| Jeganathan, S. | 2 | 4 | 0 | 8 | 19 | 4.75 | – | – | 2 | – | 30‡ | 12 | 0 | – | – | – | – |
| John V.B. | 6 | 10 | 5 | 27* | 53 | 10.60 | – | – | 2 | – | 1281 | 614 | 28 | 21.92 | 5-60 | 2 | – |
| Kaluperuma, L.W. | 2 | 4 | 1 | 11* | 12 | 4.00 | – | – | 2 | – | 162 | 93 | 0 | – | – | – | – |
| Kaluperuma, S.M.S. | 3 | 6 | 0 | 23 | 82 | 13.66 | – | – | 6 | – | 162 | 62 | 2 | 31.00 | 2-17 | – | – |
| Madugalle, R.S. | 12 | 24 | 3 | 91* | 681 | 32.42 | – | 4 | 7 | – | 24 | 4 | 0 | – | – | – | – |
| Mendis, L.R.D. | 10 | 20 | 0 | 111 | 726 | 36.30 | 3 | 3 | 4 | – | – | | | | | | |
| Ranasinghe, A.N. | 2 | 4 | 0 | 77 | 88 | 22.00 | – | 1 | – | – | 114‡ | 69 | 1 | 69.00 | 1-23 | – | – |
| Ranatunga, A. | 9 | 18† | 0 | 90 | 521 | 28.94 | – | 5 | 3 | – | 432 | 173 | 5 | 34.60 | 2-17 | – | – |
| Ratnayake, R.J. | 4 | 8 | 0 | 30 | 76 | 9.50 | – | – | 3 | – | 678 | 405 | 8 | 50.62 | 4-81 | – | – |
| Ratnayeke, J.R. | 8 | 16† | 4 | 29* | 150 | 12.50 | – | – | 1 | – | 1385 | 687 | 17 | 40.41 | 5-42 | 1 | – |
| Silva, S.A.R. | 2 | 4† | 1 | 102* | 118 | 39.33 | 1 | – | 5 | – | – | | | | | | |
| Warnapura, B. | 4 | 8 | 0 | 38 | 96 | 12.00 | – | – | 2 | – | 90 | 46 | 0 | – | – | – | – |
| Wettimuny, M. de S. | 2 | 4 | 0 | 17 | 38 | 7.00 | – | – | 2 | – | – | | | | | | |
| Wettimuny, S. | 11 | 22 | 1 | 190 | 189 | 39.00 | 2 | 4 | 4 | – | 12 | 21 | 0 | – | – | – | – |
| Wijesuriya, R.G.C.E. | 1 | 2 | 0 | 3 | 3 | 1.50 | – | – | – | – | 144‡ | 105 | 0 | – | – | – | – |

# COMPLETE TEST RECORD FOR PLAYERS REPRESENTING TWO COUNTRIES

| | | | | | BATTING AND FIELDING | | | | | | | BOWLING | | | | | |
| | Teams | Tests | I | NO | HS | Runs | Avge | 100 | 50 | Ct | St | Balls | Runs | Wkts | Avge | BB | 5wI | 10wM |
|---|---|---|---|---|---|---|---|---|---|---|---|---|---|---|---|---|---|---|
| Amir Elahi | I/P | 6 | 9 | 1 | 47 | 82 | 10.25 | – | – | – | – | 400 | 248 | 7 | 35.42 | 4-134 | – | 1 |
| Ferris, J.J. | A/E | 9 | 17† | 4 | 20* | 114 | 8.76 | – | 1 | 4 | – | 2302‡ | 775 | 61 | 12.70 | 7-37 | 6 | 1 |
| Guillen, S.C. | WI/NZ | 8 | 12 | 2 | 54 | 202 | 20.20 | – | – | 13 | 3 | – | | | | | – | – |
| Gul Mahomed | I/P | 9 | 17† | 1 | 34 | 205 | 12.81 | – | – | 3 | – | 77‡ | 24 | 2 | 12.00 | 2-21 | – | – |
| Hearne, F. | E/SA | 6 | 10 | 0 | 30 | 168 | 16.80 | – | – | 3 | – | 62 | 40 | 2 | 20.00 | 2-40 | – | – |
| Kardar, A.H. | I/P | 26 | 42† | 3 | 93 | 927 | 23.76 | – | 5 | 16 | – | 2712‡ | 954 | 21 | 45.42 | 3-35 | 1 | – |
| Midwinter, W.E. | E/A | 12 | 21 | 1 | 37 | 269 | 13.45 | – | – | 10 | – | 1725 | 605 | 24 | 25.20 | 5-78 | 1 | – |
| Mitchell, F. | E/SA | 5 | 10 | 0 | 41 | 116 | 11.60 | – | – | 2 | – | – | | | | | | |
| Murdoch, W.L. | A/E | 19 | 34 | 5 | 211 | 908 | 31.31 | 2 | 1 | 13 | 2 | – | | | | | | |
| Pataudi, Nawab of, sr | E/I | 6 | 10 | 0 | 102 | 199 | 19.90 | 1 | – | 4 | – | – | | | | | | |
| Trott, A.E. | A/E | 5 | 9 | 3 | 85* | 228 | 38.00 | – | 2 | 4 | – | 948 | 390 | 26 | 15.00 | 8-43 | 2 | – |
| Woods, S.M.J. | A/E | 6 | 10 | 0 | 53 | 154 | 15.40 | – | 1 | 5 | – | 412 | 250 | 10 | 25.00 | 3-28 | – | – |

# UMPIRES' RECORDS

## MOST TEST MATCHES

| Tests | | Venue | From | To |
|---|---|---|---|---|
| 48 | F. Chester | England | 1924 | 1955 |
| 42 | C.S. Elliott | England (41) | 1957 | 1974 |
| | | New Zealand (1) | 1970–71 | |
| 33 | J.S. Buller | England | 1956 | 1969 |
| 32 | R.W. Crockett | Australia | 1901–02 | 1924–25 |
| 32 | H.D. Bird | England | 1973 | 1985 |
| 31 | D. Sang Hue | West Indies | 1961–62 | 1980–81 |
| 30 | D.J. Constant | England | 1971 | 1985 |
| 29 | J. Phillips | England (11) | 1893 | 1905 |
| | | Australia (13) | 1884–85 | 1897–98 |
| | | South Africa (5) | 1905–06 | |
| 29 | F.S. Lee | England | 1949 | 1962 |
| 29 | C.J. Egar | Australia | 1960–61 | 1968–69 |
| 25 | R. Gosein | West Indies | 1964–65 | 1977–78 |
| 25 | L.P. Rowan | Australia | 1962–63 | 1970–71 |

*Most in other countries:*

| | | | | |
|---|---|---|---|---|
| 24 | Shujauddin | Pakistan | 1954–55 | 1978–79 |
| 20 | F.R. Goodall | New Zealand | 1964–65 | 1983–84 |
| 17 | B.Satyaji Rao | India | 1960–61 | 1978–79 |
| 17 | Swaroop Kishen | India | 1978–79 | 1984–85 |
| 14 | R.G.A. Ashman | South Africa | 1935–36 | 1949–50 |
| 4 | H.C. Felsinger | Sri Lanka | 1981–82 | 1983–84 |

*C.J. Egar and L.P. Rowan stood together in 19 Test matches, four more than the partnership of R. Gosein and D. Sang Hue.*

# WISDEN
## Cricket Library

### THE
# WISDEN
## BOOK OF
# TEST CRICKET

## Compiled and edited by Bill Frindall
### *With a foreword by*
### *Sir Donald Bradman A.C.*

The completely revised, corrected and updated version of
this classic Wisden Library title.
A complete record of nearly 1,000 Test Matches
played from 1877 to 1984, it now includes a host of new
features which make it even more valuable than before
to cricket lovers everywhere.

1088pp   £29.50

Macdonald Queen Anne Press